THE HODDER AND STOUGHTON
ILLUSTRATED
BIBLE
DICTIONARY

A spectacular view of the Dead Sea, situated at the lowest point on
earth in the hot, desolate wilderness of southern Palestine (see

THE HODDER AND STOUGHTON
ILLUSTRATED
BIBLE
DICTIONARY

An authoritative one-volume reference work on the Bible,
with full colour illustrations

General Editor: Herbert Lockyer, Sr.

Consulting Editors
F. F. Bruce
R. K. Harrison
Ronald Youngblood
Kermit Ecklebarger

Hodder & Stoughton
LONDON SYDNEY AUCKLAND TORONTO

British Library Cataloguing in Publication Data.

Hodder & Stoughton illustrated Bible dictionary; authoritative one-volume—reference work on the Bible with full colour illustrations
  1. Bible——Dictionaries
  I. Lockyer, Herbert
  II. Bruce, F. F.
  220.3'21   BF440

  ISBN 0 340 41943 1

Hodder & Stoughton Editorial Office: 47 Bedford Square, London WC1B 3DP.

A Dictionary for General Bible Readers

Most one-volume Bible dictionaries are aimed at scholars and specialists—people who already have a thorough understanding of the Bible. But this dictionary has been designed, written, and edited with the needs of general readers in mind. Persons with no formal training in biblical history or languages should find *Nelson's Illustrated Bible Dictionary* a helpful resource for understanding the Word of God and its timeless message.

Scores of leading evangelical scholars contributed articles for this project. All these articles were then subjected to a rigorous editorial process—including revising and rewriting—to sharpen their focus for the intended audience and to make sure all essential facts on these biblical subjects were covered.

This editing procedure was a long, laborious task which took several years. But the results were worth the effort. *Nelson's Illustrated Bible Dictionary* is a one-volume sourcebook of biblical information that is accurate, thorough, up-to-date, and easy to understand. More than 5,500 individual articles on the people, places, things, and doctrines of the Bible appear in the book, making it one of the most comprehensive Bible dictionaries ever published.

Hundreds of full-color photographs of significant biblical subjects appear in large format throughout the book. The editors reviewed thousands of slides—many from private collections never before published—to select only the best for illustrating and clarifying important articles in the book.

Readers of *Nelson's Illustrated Bible Dictionary* will also appreciate the detailed outlines of books of the Bible which appear with the general articles about these books. These should be especially helpful to Sunday school leaders and Bible teachers.

Another helpful feature is the book's extensive cross-reference system, which makes it easy to use with most of the popular English translations of the Bible in circulation today. The key words in each article in the book are based on the New King James Version of the Bible (NKJV), but variant names from five additional translations—KJV, NASB, NEB, NIV, and RSV—are cross-referenced to this list.

Throughout the book, readers are also referred to related articles in the dictionary for further information. An article on the Levites, for example, might contain a reference to priests (appearing like this in large capital letters and small capital letters: PRIESTS). This code tells the reader to turn to the article on priests in the dictionary for related information that should contribute to a better understanding of the Levites.

Finally, nine full-color maps from major periods of biblical history appear at the back of the book. A handy index preceding these maps helps the reader locate sites of specific cities, rivers, mountains, and nations in biblical times. General articles about selected sites in the dictionary also refer the reader to these end maps and their grid coordinates for these respective places.

The creation of a book this large is a complex task that requires the skills of many specialists—Bible scholars, proofreaders, copyeditors, writers, editors, word processing specialists, typesetters, photo selectors, artists, and photographers. A list of many of those who contributed their talents to this book appears on the following pages. Our thanks to all the members of this loyal and committed team who helped make *Nelson's Illustrated Bible Dictionary* a reality.

—The Publishers

Contributors

Robert L. Alden
Conservative Baptist Seminary
Denver, Colorado

Leslie C. Allen
Fuller Theological Seminary
Pasadena, California

Ronald B. Allen
Western Conservative Baptist Seminary
Portland, Oregon

Timothy R. Ashley
Acadia Divinity College
Wolfville, Nova Scotia, Canada

David W. Baker
Regent College
Vancouver, Canada

John J. Bimson
Trinity College
Bristol, England

E. M. Blaiklock
Auckland, New Zealand

Gerald Borchert
Southern Baptist Theological Seminary
Louisville, Kentucky

Stephen G. Brown
Los Angeles Baptist College
Newhall, California

F. F. Bruce
University of Manchester
Manchester, England

John A. Burns
Criswell Center for Biblical Studies
Dallas, Texas

Newton L. Bush
Lima, Ohio

G. Lloyd Carr
Gordon College
Wenham, Massachusetts

E. Clark Copeland
Reformed Presbyterian Theological
   Seminary
Pittsburgh, Pennsylvania

Leonard J. Coppes
Denver, Colorado

Walter M. Dunnett
Northwestern College
Roseville, Minnesota

Kendell H. Easley
Toccoa Falls College
Toccoa Falls, Georgia

Kermit A. Ecklebarger
Conservative Baptist Seminary
Denver, Colorado

James R. Edwards
Jamestown College
Jamestown, North Dakota

John M. Elliott
Aurora, Illinois

Millard J. Erickson
Bethel Theological Seminary
St. Paul, Minnesota

Harvey E. Finley
Nazarene Theological Seminary
Kansas City, Missouri

Royce G. Gruenler
Gordon-Conwell Theological Seminary
South Hamilton, Massachusetts

Timothy Hadley
Ohio Valley College
Parkersburg, West Virginia

Donald A. Hagner
Fuller Theological Seminary
Pasadena, California

R. K. Harrison
Wycliffe College
Toronto, Canada

Harvey Hartman
Liberty Baptist College
Lynchburg, Virginia

Robert Hendren
Donelson, Tennessee

Herschel H. Hobbs
Oklahoma City, Oklahoma

Harold W. Hoehner
Dallas Theological Seminary
Dallas, Texas

John J. Hughes
Whitefish, Montana

Robert Hughes
Miami Christian College
Miami, Florida

Harry B. Hunt, Jr.
Southwestern Baptist Theological
   Seminary
Fort Worth, Texas

W. Bingham Hunter
Talbot Theological Seminary
La Mirada, California

David K. Huttar
Nyack College
Nyack, New York

William W. Klein
Conservative Baptist Seminary
Denver, Colorado

Woodrow M. Kroll
Practical Bible Training School
Bible School Park, New York

Alvin S. Lawhead
Nazarene Theological Seminary
Kansas City, Missouri

Gordon Lewis
Conservative Baptist Seminary
Denver, Colorado

Jack P. Lewis
Harding Graduate School of Religion
Memphis, Tennessee

Walter L. Liefeld
Trinity Evangelical Divinity School
Deerfield, Illinois

G. Herbert Livingston
Asbury Theological Seminary
Wilmore, Kentucky

Tremper Longman, III
Westminster Theological Seminary
Philadelphia, Pennsylvania

Robert S. MacLennan
Edina, Minnesota

W. Harold Mare
Covenant Theological Seminary
St. Louis, Missouri

Elmer A. Martens
Mennonite Brethren Biblical Seminary
Fresno, California

Wayne O. McCready
University of Calgary
Alberta, Canada

Robert R. Moore
Asbury College
Wilmore, Kentucky

Scot McKnight
Trinity Evangelical Divinity School
Deerfield, Illinois

Janet McNish
Nashville, Tennessee

William Mounce
Azusa Pacific College
Azusa, California

John Nolland
Regent College
Vancouver, Canada

Dave O'Brien
St. Paul Bible College
Bible College, Minnesota

Vernon S. Olson
St. Bonifacius, Minnesota

Grant R. Osborne
Trinity Evangelical Divinity School
Deerfield, Illinois

Mildred Ottinger
Nashville, Tennessee

Arthur G. Patzia
Bethel Theological Seminary
St. Paul, Minnesota

Gary Pratico
Gordon-Conwell Divinity School
South Hamilton, Massachusetts

Richard A. Purdy
West Norwalk, Connecticut

Robert V. Rakestraw
The Criswell College
Dallas, Texas

John Rasko
Alaska Bible College
Glennallen, Alaska

Richard O. Rigsby
Talbot Theological Seminary
La Mirada, California

Allen P. Ross
Dallas Theological Seminary
Dallas, Texas

Glenn E. Schaefer
Simpson College
San Francisco, California

Stephen R. Schrader
Liberty Baptist Seminary
Lynchburg, Virginia

Jack B. Scott
Decatur, Georgia

Martin J. Selman
Spurgeon's College
London, England

Norman Shepherd
Minneapolis, Minnesota

Gary V. Smith
Bethel Theological Seminary
St. Paul, Minnesota

Douglas K. Stuart
Gordon-Conwell Theological Seminary
South Hamilton, Massachusetts

Robert L. Thomas
Talbot Theological Seminary
La Mirada, California

Willem A. VanGemeren
Reformed Theological Seminary
Jackson, Mississippi

Dolores Walker
Walla Walla, Washington

Larry L. Walker
Mid-America Baptist Seminary
Memphis, Tennessee

Daniel B. Wallace
Mukilteo, Washington

Forest Weddle
Fort Wayne Bible College
Fort Wayne, Indiana

Tom Wells
Cincinnati, Ohio

Stephen Westerholm
Toronto, Canada

Frederick E. Young
Central Baptist Seminary
Kansas City, Kansas

Ronald Youngblood
Bethel Theological Seminary, West
San Diego, California

Editorial Staff

General Editor
Herbert Lockyer, Sr.

Consulting Editors
F. F. Bruce
R. K. Harrison
Ronald Youngblood
Kermit Ecklebarger

Project Coordinator
George W. Knight

Production Specialist
Garry Smith

Art and Layout Design
Will Graphics

Photo Consultant
Ralph White

Editorial Advisors
Joe Allison
Paul Franklyn
Gary Luttrell
Bruce Nygren
Roy Perry
Ron Pitkin
Larry Stone

Articles and Teaching Outlines on Books of the Bible

Old Testament

New Testament

Charts, Tables, and Maps

Traditional tomb of Barnabas, on the island of Cyprus in the Mediterranean Sea (see page 134).

A

AARON [EHR un] (meaning unknown) — brother of Moses and first high priest of the Hebrew nation. Very little is known about Aaron's early life, other than his marriage to Elisheba, daughter of Amminadab (Ex. 6:23).

When God called Moses to lead the Hebrew people out of slavery in Egypt, Moses protested that he would not be able to speak convincingly to the Pharaoh. So Aaron was designated by God as Moses' official spokesman (Ex. 4:14–16). At Moses' instruction, Aaron also performed miracles as signs for the release of the Hebrews. Aaron's rod turned into a serpent that swallowed the rods of the Egyptian magicians (Ex. 7:8–20). Aaron also caused frogs to cover the land by stretching his rod over the lakes and streams of Egypt (Ex. 8:6).

Aaron held an important place of leadership because of his work with his brother Moses. A central figure in the EXODUS from Egypt, he also received instructions from God for observing the first PASSOVER (Ex. 12:1). In the wilderness he assisted Moses in keeping order and rendering judgments over the people (Num. 15:33). Both he and Moses were singled out when the people complained about the harsh conditions of these wilderness years (Num. 14:2).

When the priesthood was instituted in the wilderness, Moses consecrated Aaron as the first high priest of Israel (Exodus 28—29; Leviticus 8—9). The priesthood was set within the tribe of Levi, from which Aaron was descended. Aaron's sons (Nadab, Abihu, Eleazar, and Ithamar) inherited the position of high priest from their father (Num. 3:2–3). Aaron was given special robes to wear, signifying his status within the priesthood (Lev. 8:7–9). At his death the robes were transferred to his oldest living son, Eleazar (Num. 20:25–28). The TABERNACLE, the main sanctuary of worship, was placed under Aaron's supervision (Numbers 4). He received instructions from God on the functions of the priesthood and the tabernacle (Numbers 18). He alone, serving in the capacity of high priest, went into the Holy of Holies once a year to represent the people on the DAY OF ATONEMENT.

In spite of his responsibility for the spiritual leadership of the nation, Aaron committed a serious sin in the wilderness surrounding Mount Sinai. While Moses was on the mountain praying to God and receiving His commandments, the people began to build a golden calf to worship. Aaron made no attempt to stop the people and even issued instructions on how to build the image (Ex. 32:1–10). Aaron was saved from God's wrath only because Moses interceded on his behalf (Deut. 9:20).

After all their years of leading the people, neither Moses nor Aaron was permitted to enter the Prom-

A model of Aaron in the distinctive dress of the high priest, including the ephod with 12 precious stones representing the tribes of Israel (Numbers 17).
Photo: Amsterdam Bible Museum

ised Land. Apparently this was because they did not make it clear that God would provide for the Hebrews' needs when they believed they would die for lack of water in the wilderness (Num. 20:12). Aaron died first at Mount Hor, and Moses died later in Moab.

Upon arriving at Mount Hor from the wilderness of Kadesh, Aaron was accompanied by Moses and his son Eleazar to the top of the mountain. Here he was stripped of his high priestly garments, which were transferred to Eleazar. After Aaron's death, the community mourned for 30 days (Num. 20: 22–29).

The Book of Hebrews contrasts the imperfect priesthood of Aaron with the perfect priesthood of Christ (Heb. 5:2–5; 7:11–12). Christ's priesthood is compared to the order of MELCHIZEDEK because it is an eternal office with no beginning and no end. Thus, it replaces the priesthood of Aaron.

AARON'S ROD — a rod mentioned on two dramatic occasions in the Old Testament. When Moses and Aaron appeared before Pharaoh, Aaron cast down his rod and it became a serpent. When the magicians of Egypt did the same thing, "Aaron's rod swallowed up their rods" (Ex. 7:12). Later, Aaron struck the waters of Egypt with his rod and they turned to blood (7:15–20).

During the wilderness wandering, Aaron's rod was the only staff that produced buds, blossoms, and almonds, indicating God's choice of Aaron and his descendants as priests (Num. 17:1–10).

AARONITES [EHR un ites] — the descendants of Aaron and therefore a part of the priestly tribe of Levi. Led by Jehoiada, 3,700 Aaronites fought with David against Saul after David was made king (1 Chr. 12:27).

AB (see CALENDAR).

ABADDON [ah BAD un] (destruction) — a term found only once in most English translations of the Bible (Rev. 9:11). Abaddon is a transliteration of a Hebrew word which occurs six other times in the Bible, usually translated "destruction" (Job 26:6; 28:22; 31:12; Ps. 88:11; Prov. 15:11; 27:20). In three of these places, it occurs in the phrase "Hell and Destruction" (Job 26:6; Prov. 15:11; 27:20). The Hebrew nouns translated "Hell" and "Destruction" are Sheol and Abaddon respectively. They appear to be synonymous terms for the abode of the dead or the grave.

In the Book of Revelation, Abaddon is not a place—the realm of the dead—but a person—the angel who reigns over the abyss.

Also see HADES; HELL; SHEOL.

ABAGTHA [uh BAG thuh] (happy, prosperous) — one of the seven chamberlains, or eunuchs, chosen by the Persian king Ahasuerus (Xerxes) to bring his queen, Vashti, to the royal banquet (Esth. 1:10).

ABANA [AB ah nah] — a form of ABANAH.

ABANAH [AB ah nah] (story) — the chief river of

Damascus. The Abanah flowed through the center of this great city. With the Pharpar, it supplied an abundance of water, making the country around it one of the most beautiful and fertile spots in the world. When Naaman the leper was asked to bathe in the Jordan River seven times, he complained that he would rather bathe in the Abanah or the Pharpar (2 Kin. 5:12; Abana, KJV, NIV, RSV).

ABARIM [AB ah rim] (the regions beyond) — a range of mountains east of the Dead Sea and the Jordan River valley. Mount Nebo was part of this mountain range. These mountains gave a panoramic view of the surrounding country. From Mount Nebo Moses surveyed the Promised Land before he died (Deut. 32:49; Num. 27:12).

ABBA [AB ah] (father) — an Aramaic word which corresponds to our "Daddy" or "Papa." It is found three times in the New Testament: in the Garden of Gethsemane, Jesus prayed, "Abba, Father" (Mark 14:36); the apostle Paul linked the Christian's cry of "Abba, Father" with the "Spirit of adoption" (Rom. 8:15); and, again, Paul writes, "Because you are sons, God has sent forth the Spirit of His son into your hearts, crying out, 'Abba, Father!'" (Gal. 4:6). What a blessed privilege it is to be given the right to call the great Creator, "Our Father"!

ABDA [AB dah] (servant or worshiper) — the name of two men in the Old Testament:

1. The father of Adoniram, Solomon's officer in charge of the labor force (l Kin. 4:6).

2. A chief Levite, the son of Shammua, who lived in Jerusalem after the Captivity (Neh. 11:17). He is also called Obadiah (1 Chr. 9:16).

ABDEEL [AB dih ell] (servant of God) — the father of Shelemiah, who was commanded by Jehoiakim, king of Judah, to arrest Jeremiah the prophet and Baruch the scribe (Jer. 36:26).

ABDI [AB dih] (servant of Jehovah) — the name of two or three men in the Old Testament:

1. A Levite of the family of Merari; he was the son of Malluch and the father of Kishi (1 Chr. 6:44).

2. A Levite contemporary with Hezekiah king of Judah (2 Chr. 29:12). This person may be the same as Abdi No. 1.

3. One of Elam's sons who divorced his pagan wife after the Captivity (Ezra 10:26).

ABDIEL [AB dih ell] (servant of God) — a man of the tribe of Gad who lived "in Gilead, in Bashan" (1 Chr. 5:15).

ABDON [AB done] (service) — a name given to one city and four men:

1. A Levitical city in Asher (Josh. 21:30; 1 Chr. 6:74), also called Ebron (Josh. 19:28).

2. A son of Hillel, a native of Pirathon in the tribe of Ephraim. He judged Israel eight years (Judg. 12:13–15).

3. A Benjamite who lived in Jerusalem (1 Chr. 8:23).

righteous Abel" (Matt. 23:35; Luke 11:51) and implied that Abel, the first righteous martyr, anticipated in symbol His own death on Calvary at the hands of evil men. The blood of the new covenant, however, "speaks better things than that of Abel" (Heb. 12:24). The blood of Abel cried out for vengeance; the blood of Christ speaks of salvation.

2. A large stone in the field of Joshua of Beth Shemesh on which the ARK OF THE COVENANT was set by the Philistines (1 Sam. 6:18).

3. A fortified city in northern Israel, which Joab besieged after the rebellion of Sheba (2 Sam. 20:14–15, 18). This city, called Abel of Beth Maachah, is probably the same place as ABEL BETH MAACHAH.

ABEL ACACIA GROVE [A bell a KAY shuh grove] — a site northeast of the Dead Sea in the plains of Moab, also called Acacia Grove. It was here that the Israelites camped just before crossing the Jordan and entering the Promised Land (Num. 25:1; Josh. 2:1; 3:1; Mic. 6:5; Shittim, KJV). It was probably the same place as Abel–shittim (Num. 33:49, KJV).

Its exact location is uncertain. Most scholars identify Acacia Grove with Tell el–Hamman, although some think it was at nearby Tell el–Kefrein. Many notable events occurred while the Israelites were camped here. Here many Israelites took Moabite women for their wives and worshiped Moabite gods. As punishment, God allowed a plague to kill 24,000 Israelites (Num. 25:9).

At this campsite Moses also took a military census of the Israelite tribes, establishing the number of those 20 years old and above who were able to go to war (Num. 26:2). At Acacia Grove God also revealed to Moses that he would not be allowed to cross the Jordan River and that Joshua would be his successor as leader of the people (Num. 27:12–23).

After Moses ascended Mount Nebo and died (Deuteronomy 34), Joshua sent out two spies from Acacia Grove to examine the defense of Jericho (Josh. 2:1). Upon their return, the Israelites broke camp and crossed the Jordan River, finally entering the land which God had promised to Abraham and his descendants hundreds of years earlier (Josh. 3:1).

ABEL BETH MAACAH [A bell beth MAY uh kah] (*meadow of the house of Maacah*) — a fortified town near the town of Dan in the area of the tribe of Naphtali. It was attacked by Joab (2 Sam. 20:14), Ben-Hadad (1 Kin. 15:20), and Tiglath-Pileser (2 Kin. 15:29). The name of the town is also given as Abel Maim, meaning "Abel on the waters" (2 Chr. 16:4). It is described as a "mother in Israel"—meaning a place of great importance, having many "daughters," or inhabitants.

ABEL CHERAMIM [A bell CARE uh meem] — a form of ABEL KERAMIM.

ABEL KERAMIM [A bell CARE uh meem] (*meadow of vineyards*) — a city east of the Jordan River and northeast of the Dead Sea. Abel

Photo by Willem A. VanGemeren

The mound of Abel Beth Maacah in the northern part of Naphtali.

4. The firstborn son of Jeiel from Maacah and an ancestor of King Saul (1 Chr. 8:30; 9:35–36).

5. A son of Micah who was sent by King Josiah to inquire of God about the Book of the Law found in the Temple (2 Chr. 34:20). Abdon is also called Achbor (2 Kin. 22:12).

ABED–NEGO [uh BED knee goe] (*servant of Nego*) — the Chaldean name given to Azariah in King Nebuchadnezzar's court when he was chosen as one of the king's servants (Dan. 1:7; 2:49). With Shadrach and Meshach, Abed-Nego was thrown into the fiery furnace for refusing to bow down and worship a golden image. The three men were miraculously protected from the fire (Dan. 3:12–30). Like the three Hebrew children in the fiery furnace, the nation of Israel endured the Captivity and were miraculously protected by God.

ABEL [A buhl] (*breath, vapor*) — the name of a person and two places in the Old Testament:

1. The second son of Adam and Eve (Gen. 4:2). His brother Cain, who was a farmer, brought an offering of his produce to the Lord. Abel, a shepherd, brought to the Lord an offering "of the firstlings [the best quality] of his flock." Genesis records: "And the Lord respected Abel and his offering, but he did not respect Cain and his offering" (Gen. 4:4–5). Envious of Abel, Cain killed his brother and was cursed by God for the murder.

In the New Testament, Abel is described as a man of faith, who "offered a more excellent sacrifice than Cain" (Heb. 11:4). Cain murdered his brother Abel, writes John, "because his [Cain's] works were evil and his brother's [Abel's] righteous" (1 John 3:12). Jesus spoke of "the blood of

Keramim was the farthest extent of Jephthah's military campaign against the Ammonites (Judg. 11:33; Abel Cheramim, KJV).

ABEL MAIM [A bell may im] — a city in northern Palestine (2 Chr. 16:4; Abel-mayim, NEB), usually called ABEL BETH MAACHAH.

ABEL MAYIM — a form of ABEL MAIM.

ABEL MEHOLAH [A bell me HOE lah] (*meadow of dancing*) — a town east of the Jordan River in the hill country of Gilead. It was the residence (and perhaps also the birthplace) of Elisha the prophet (1 Kin. 4:12; 19:16). In 1943, archaeologist Nelson Glueck identified Abel Meholah with Tell el-Maqlub, by the Wadi el-Yabis.

ABEL MIZRAIM [A bell MIZ rah ihm] (see ATAD).

ABEL SHITTIM [A bell SHIT tihm] — a form of ABEL ACACIA GROVE.

ABEZ [A bez] (meaning unknown) — a town in northern Palestine allotted to the tribe of Issachar (Josh. 19:20; Ebez, NASB, NEB, NIV, RSV).

ABI [a BEE] (*my father*) — a daughter of Zechariah, wife of Ahaz, and mother of King Hezekiah of Judah (2 Kin. 18:2). Abi is also called Abijah (2 Chr. 29:1).

ABIA [ah BEE uh] — a form of ABIJAM.

ABI ALBON [A bih AL bonn] — a form of ABIEL.

ABIASAPH [a BY uh saf] (*father has gathered*) — a son or descendant of Korah the Levite (Ex. 6:24). It is unclear whether he was the same person as Ebiasaph (1 Chr. 6:23, 37; 9:19).

ABIATHAR [a BY uh thar] (*father of abundance*) — one of two chief priests in the court of David. Abiathar was the son of Ahimelech of the priestly clan of Eli from Shiloh (1 Sam. 22:20). When the residents of the priestly village of Nob were massacred by Saul for helping David, Abiathar was the only one to escape (1 Sam. 22:6–23). When David eventually became king, he appointed Abiathar, along with Zadok, as priests in the royal court (2 Sam. 8:17; 1 Chr. 18:16).

When David's son Absalom tried to take his throne by force, David was forced to leave Jerusalem. Zadok and Abiathar carried the ARK OF THE COVENANT out of the capital city but later returned it at the command of David (2 Sam. 15:29). Both priests remained in Jerusalem to inform David of Absalom's plans (2 Sam. 15:34). After Absalom's death, Abiathar and Zadok carried the message of reconciliation to Amasa and the elders of Judah (2 Sam. 19:11–14).

During the struggle over who would succeed as king, Abiathar supported Adonijah. When Solomon emerged as the new ruler, Zadok was appointed priest of the royal court, while Abiathar escaped execution only because of his earlier loyalty to David. He and his family were banished to Anathoth, and his rights and privileges as a Jerusalem priest were taken away (1 Kin. 1:7–25; 2:22–35).

Some scholars believe Abiathar may have written portions of 1 and 2 Samuel, especially the sections describing the royal court life under David. But there is no strong evidence to support this theory.

ABIB [A bibb] (*sprouting* or *budding*) — the first month of the Hebrew calendar (corresponding to our March–April). On the 15th of this month, the people of Israel left Egypt. Abib was made the first month of the year in commemoration of the Exodus (Ex. 23:15; Deut. 16:1;). The Passover and the Feast of Unleavened Bread were celebrated during the month of Abib. After the Captivity, the month was called Nisan (Neh. 2:1; Esth. 3:7). Also see CALENDAR.

ABIDA, ABIDAH [uh BY duh] (*father of knowledge*) — the fourth son of Midian, who was the fourth son of Abraham and Keturah (Gen. 25:4; 1 Chr. 1:33).

ABIDAN [uh BY duhn] (*my father is judge*) — a son of Gideoni and the leader of the Benjamites who represented his tribe when the census was taken during the wilderness wandering (Num. 2:22; 7:60, 65).

ABIEL [A bih ell] (*my God is father*) — the name of two Old Testament men:
1. An ancestor of Saul, the first king of Israel (1 Sam. 9:1; 14:51).
2. An Arbathite, one of David's mighty men (1 Chr. 11:32), also called Abi Albon (2 Sam. 23:31).

ABIEZER [a bih EE zur] (*father of help*) — two Old Testament men bear this consoling name:
1. The son of Hammoleketh (Josh. 17:2; 1 Chr. 7:18). The renowned Gideon belonged to this family. Possibly this Abiezer is the same person as Jeezer (Num. 26:30).
2. One of David's mighty men. He was from the town of Anathoth—which later became the birthplace of the prophet Jeremiah (1 Chr. 27:12).

ABIEZRITE [a bih EZ rite] (*belonging to Abiezer*) — a person who belonged to the family of ABIEZER (Judg. 6:11, 24; 8:32).

ABIGAIL [AB ih gale] (*father of joy*) — two Old Testament women had this delightful name:
1. Wife of Nabal the Carmelite and, after his death, of David (1 Sam. 25:3, 14–42; 2 Sam. 2:2; 1 Chr. 3:1). Abigail's husband, Nabal, was an ill-tempered, drunken man. When David was hiding from the jealous King Saul, he asked Nabal for food for himself and his men. Nabal blatantly refused. Angered, David threatened to plunder Nabal's possessions and kill Nabal himself. Abigail, in her wisdom, gathered enough food for David's men, rode out to meet David, and bowed before him to show her respect. By agreeing with David

that Nabal had acted with great disrespect, she stemmed David's anger. To Abigail's credit, she did not leave her godless husband. When Nabal died, apparently from shock at discovering his near brush with death, David married Abigail and she later bore him a son, Chileab.

2. A sister or half-sister of David and mother of Amasa, whom Absalom made captain of the army instead of Joab (2 Sam. 17:25; Abigal, RSV, NEB; 1 Chr. 2:16-17). The exact identification of Nahash, parent of Abigail (2 Sam. 17:25), is uncertain.

ABIGAL — a form of ABIGAIL.

ABIHAIL [AB ih hal] (*father of strength*) — a name used to denote both men and women of the Old Testament:

1. A Levite and the father of Zuriel in the time of Moses (Num. 3:35).

2. The wife of Abishur, a descendant of Hezron of the tribe of Judah (1 Chr. 2:29).

3. The head of a family in the tribe of Gad who lived in Gilead of Bashan (1 Chr. 5:14).

4. A daughter of Eliab (David's brother) and the wife of King Rehoboam (2 Chr. 11:18).

5. The father of Queen Esther, who became the wife of Ahasuerus (Xerxes I, 485-464 B.C.), king of Persia, in the place of Vashti. Abihail was therefore also an uncle of Mordecai (Esth. 2:15; 9:29).

ABIHU [a BIH hoo] (*he is my father*) — second son of Aaron and Elisheba (Ex. 6:23). Abihu was destroyed, along with his brother NADAB, in the Wilderness of Sinai for offering "profane fire" (Lev. 10:1) before the Lord. Exactly why the fire was "profane" is not certain; perhaps Abihu and Nadab rebelled against the authority of Moses and Aaron by presuming to bring an unauthorized offering before the Lord. If so, their action implies a pride and arrogance which the Lord despises.

ABIHUD [a BIH hud] (*father of honor*) — a son of Bela, who was the oldest son of Benjamin (1 Chr. 8:3).

ABIJAH [a BUY jah] (*the Lord is my Father*) — the name of eight people in the Old Testament:

1. A son of Jeroboam who died in youth, in fulfillment of the prophesy of Abijah (1 Kin. 14:1-18).

2. The wife of Hezron, a man of the tribe of Judah (1 Chr. 2:24).

3. A descendant of Benjamin (or perhaps of Zebulun) through Becher (1 Chr. 7:8).

4. A descendant of Aaron, who was a priest in the time of David (1 Chr. 24:10).

5. A son of Rehoboam and Maacah the granddaughter of Absalom (2 Chr. 11:20, 22). Also see ABIJAM.

6. The mother of Hezekiah, king of Judah (2 Chr. 29:1). Abijah is also called Abi (2 Kin. 18:2).

7. A priest who signed Nehemiah's covenant (Neh. 10:7).

8. A priest who returned to Jerusalem from Babylon with Zerubbabel (Neh. 12:1-4, 12-17).

ABIJAM [a BUY jam] (*father of the sea*) — a king of Judah and son of Rehoboam and Maacah the daughter of Absolom. When King Rehoboam died, Abijam succeeded to Judah's throne. He had 14 wives, 22 sons, and 16 daughters. When he died, after reigning for three years, his son ASA became king (1 Kin. 14:31.) He is also called Abijah (2 Chr. 11:20, 22). The KJV has Abia (Matt. 1:7), listing him as an ancestor of Jesus.

ABILENE [ab uh LEE knee] (*region of Abila*) — a district near the Anti-Lebanon Mountains. It derived its name from Abila, its capital, which was located on the Abana (modern Barada) River some 29 to 32 kilometers (18 or 20 miles) northwest of Damascus. Originally a part of the Iturean kingdom of Ptolemy Mennaeus (about 85-40 B.C.), Abilene was broken up when King Lysanias I (40-36 B.C.) was put to death by Mark Antony. It became the tetrarchy of a younger Lysanias "in the fifteenth year of the reign of Tiberias Caesar" (Luke 3:1), when John the Baptist began his ministry.

ABIMAEL [ah BIM uh ell] (*my Father is God*) — the ninth of the 13 sons of Joktan, a descendant of Shem (Gen. 10:28; 1 Chr. 1:22).

ABIMELECH [uh BIM eh leck] (*my father is king*) — the name of five men in the Old Testament:

1. The king of Gerar in the time of Abraham (Gen. 20:1-18; 21:22-34). Fearing for his own safety, Abraham introduced Sarah, his wife, as his sister when he entered Abimelech's territory. Abimelech claimed Sarah for his harem, only to be warned in a dream that he had taken the wife of another man. Then Abimelech returned Sarah to Abraham. The two men made a covenant with each other, and Abraham asked God to reward the king by giving him many children. Many scholars believe that the word Abimelech is not a proper name but a royal title of the Philistine kings, just as Pharaoh was a title for Egyptian kings.

2. The king of Gerar in the time of Isaac (Gen. 26:1-31).

3. The ruler of the city of Shechem during the period of the judges (Judg. 8:30—10:1; 2 Sam. 11:21). Abimelech was a son of Gideon by a concubine from Shechem. Abimelech tried to become king, and he did reign over Israel for three years (Judg. 9:22). In order to eliminate all who might challenge his authority, he killed all the other sons of Gideon—his brothers and half-brothers—who were potential successors of his father (Judg. 9:5).

Abimelech was killed in a battle at Thebez, a city northeast of Shechem which he surrounded with his army. When Abimelech ventured too close to the city's walls, a woman dropped a millstone on his head, crushing his skull. Abimelech commanded his armorbearer to kill him so it could not be said that he died at the hands of a woman (Judg. 9:50-54; 2 Sam. 11:21).

4. A priest in the time of David (1 Chr. 18:16).

5. A Philistine king whom David met while fleeing from King Saul (Psalm 34, title). Abimelech is

apparently the royal title of ACHISH the king of Gath (1 Sam. 21:10–15).

ABINADAB [uh BEN a dab] (*father of liberality*) — the name of four Old Testament men:

1. An Israelite of the tribe of Judah in whose house the ARK OF THE COVENANT was placed after being returned by the Philistines (1 Sam. 7:1; 1 Chr. 13:7).

2. The second son of Jesse; a brother of David (1 Sam. 17:13; 1 Chr. 2:13).

3. A son of King Saul slain at Mount Gilboa by the Philistines (1 Sam. 31:2; 1 Chr. 10:2).

4. The father of one of Solomon's officers, who was set over Dor in the territory of Issachar (1 Kin. 4:11).

ABINOAM [ah BEN oh am] (*father of pleasantness*) — the father of Barak of the tribe of Naphtali (Judg. 4:6; 5:1).

ABIRAM [ah BY ram] (*my father is exalted*) — the name of two people in the Old Testament:

1. A son of Eliab, a Reubenite, who joined in the rebellion of KORAH and conspired against Moses and Aaron in the wilderness. He died in an earthquake, which served as a fitting judgment for his sin (Num. 16:1–33).

2. The firstborn of Hiel of Bethel who rebuilt the city of Jericho (1 Kin. 16:34).

ABISHAG [AB ih shag] (*cause of wandering*) — a young woman from Shunem employed by David's physicians to care for him in his old age (1 Kin. 1:1–4, 15). The treatment implies that through physical contact Abishag's youth could revive a dying David. The treatment failed. After David's death, one of his sons, Adonijah, asked permission to marry Abishag (1 Kin. 2:17). Solomon saw Adonijah's request as an attempt to seize the throne. He had Adonijah killed (1 Kin. 2:13–25).

ABISHAI [ah BISH a eye] (*source of wealth*) — the oldest son of Zeruiah, David's half-sister, and brother of Joab and Asahel (2 Sam. 2:18). He was one of David's mighty men (2 Sam. 23:18; 1 Chr. 11:20). He helped David in the fight with Ishbi-Benob the giant (2 Sam. 21:16–17). A headstrong and impulsive man, he nevertheless maintained an unswerving loyalty to David through such crises as the rebellions of Absalom and Sheba (2 Sam. 16:9, 18—20).

ABISHALOM [ah BISH ah lom]—a form of ABSALOM.

ABISHUA [ah BISH you ah] (*father of salvation*) — the name of two men in the Old Testament:

1. The son of Phinehas and the fourth high priest of Israel (1 Chr. 6:4–5).

2. The fourth son of Bela, who was a son of Benjamin (1 Chr. 8:4).

ABISHUR [ah BY shur] (*my father is a wall*) — the second son of Shammai, of the tribe of Judah (1 Chr. 2:28–29).

ABITAL [ah BY tuhl] (*father of dew*) — a wife of King David and the mother of Shephatiah, the fifth son born to David while he was at Hebron (2 Sam. 3:4; 1 Chr. 3:3).

ABITUB [ah BY tub] (*my father is good*) — a descendant of Benjamin listed in the family tree of King Saul (1 Chr. 8:11).

ABIUD [ah BY ud] (*my father is majesty*) — an ancestor of Jesus, listed in the Gospel of Matthew (Matt. 1:13).

ABLUTION — the ceremonial washing of one's body, vessels, and clothing for the purpose of religious purification. This word is not found in the NKJV, but it occurs in Hebrew 6:2 and 9:10 in the RSV. In both places the Greek word is *baptismos* (literally, "dipping"), which can be translated "washings" (Heb. 9:10).

Ablutions have nothing to do with washing one's body for sanitary or hygienic purposes. Rather, these were performed in order to remove ritual defilement. Some of the causes of ritual uncleanness in Bible times were bloodshed (Lev. 17), childbirth (Lev. 12), sexual intercourse (Lev. 18), leprosy (Lev. 12), menstruation (Lev. 15), and contact with dead bodies (Numb. 19).

At Mount Sinai, the Israelites were told to wash (literally, "trample") their clothes in preparation for worship (Ex. 19:10, 14). Similarly, the Levites as well as Aaron and his sons were prepared for service by washing their clothes and their bodies (Ex. 40:12–13).

By New Testament times, ceremonial washings became almost an end in themselves. The Pharisees were preoccupied with ritual purifications (Matt. 15:2; Mark 7:4). Jesus exhorted the scribes and Pharisees to "cleanse the inside of the cup and dish"—that is, cleanse their hearts and spirits—and not just wash the outside by religious rituals. Moral filth cannot be washed away with physical cleansing agents (Jer. 2:22; Is. 1:16). Jesus Christ is to be praised, for He "loved us and washed us from our sins in His own blood" (Rev. 1:5; Rev. 7:14).

ABNER [AB nar] (*the father is a lamp*) — the commander in chief of the army of Saul, first king of the nation of Israel (1 Sam. 14:50–51; 17:55).

As Saul's highest military official, Abner occupied a seat of honor in the king's court (1 Sam. 20:25). He was the person who inquired about David after his battle with the giant, Goliath, and who introduced David to King Saul (1 Sam. 17:55–58). Abner also was the commander of the guard that was supposedly protecting Saul when David entered the camp of the king while everyone was asleep (1 Sam. 26:5–7).

After the death of Saul and his three sons in a battle with the Philistines (1 Sam. 31:1–6), Abner established Saul's son Ishbosheth as king. His capital was at Mahanaim on the east side of the Jordan River. Only the tribe of Judah, of the 12 tribes of the nation, followed the leadership of David (2 Sam. 2:8–11). In the warfare that broke out between the forces of David and Ishbosheth, Abner killed a brother of Joab—one of David's military officers—in self-defense (2 Sam. 2:12—3:1).

Still later, a crisis developed between Abner and Ishbosheth when Abner took one of Saul's concubines. Ishbosheth accused Abner of plotting to take over the kingship. The rift between them became so pronounced that Abner eventually shifted his loyalties to David. This move by Abner was significant, because Abner was able to persuade the elders of all the tribes of Israel to follow David's leadership (2 Sam. 3:6–21).

Soon after this turning point in David's political career, Abner was killed by David's commander Joab in an act of vengeance over the death of his brother (2 Sam. 3:22–30). This presented David with a troublesome situation. Abner's death looked like the execution of an opponent who had delivered the tribal loyalties which the king needed to establish control over the entire nation. To counter any backlash, David reprimanded Joab publicly and had Abner buried with full honors (2 Sam. 3:27–39).

ABOMINATION — anything that offends the spiritual, religious, or moral sense of a person and causes extreme disgust, hatred, or loathing. Among the objects described as an "abomination" were the carved images of pagan gods (Deut. 7:25–26), the sacrifice to God of inferior, blemished animals (Deut. 17:1), the practice of idolatry (Deut. 17:2–5), and the fashioning of a "carved or molded image" of a false god (Deut. 27:15; Is. 44:19).

Other abominations were sexual transgressions (Leviticus 18), the adoption of the dress of the opposite sex (Deut. 22:5), and the practice of magic, witchcraft, and "spiritism" (Deut. 18:9–12). Most of the Hebrew words translated "abomination" have the meaning of "impure," "filthy," and "unclean"—that which is foul-smelling and objectionable to a holy God.

ABOMINATION OF DESOLATION — a despicable misuse of the Temple of the Lord during a time of great trouble—an event foretold by the prophet Daniel.

The phrase is found in Matthew 24:15 and Mark 13:14 as a quotation from Daniel 11:31 and 12:11. In Daniel, the words mean "the abomination that makes desolate." In other words, Daniel prophesied that the Temple would be used for an "abominable" purpose at some time in the future. As a result, God's faithful people would no longer worship there—so great would be their moral revulsion, contempt, and abhorrence at the sacrilege—and the Temple would become "desolate."

According to the verses in the gospels, a similar misuse of the Temple would take place in the future. This would show that a time of great trouble was coming on Judea. People should take warning and flee to the mountains (Matt. 24:16; Mark 13:14).

Some believe Daniel's prophecy was fulfilled about 165 B.C. when Antiochus IV (Epiphanes),

Greek ruler of Syria, polluted the Jewish Temple in Jerusalem by sacrificing a pig on the holy altar. This sacrificing of an UNCLEAN pig was the worst kind of abomination that could have taken place. These people also believe the prophecy in the Gospels of Matthew and Mark was fulfilled when the Romans sacked the Jewish Temple about A.D. 70. But others believe just as strongly that neither of these prophecies has yet been completely fulfilled. They insist that the abomination of desolation refers to the idolatrous image or the "man of sin" who will take over God's place in the Temple and make people bow down and worship him (2 Thess. 2:3–4). According to this interpretation, this will be the final act of sacrilege that marks the beginning of the end time.

ABRAHAM [AY bruh ham] (*father of a multitude*); originally Abram (*exalted father*) — the first great PATRIARCH of ancient Israel and a primary model of faithfulness for Christianity. The accounts about Abraham are found in Genesis 11:26—25:11, with the biblical writer focusing on four important aspects of his life.

The Migration. Abraham's story begins with his migration with the rest of his family from UR of the Chaldeans in ancient southern Babylonia (Gen. 11:31). He and his family moved north along the trade routes of the ancient world and settled in the flourishing trade center of HARAN, several hundred miles to the northwest.

While living in Haran, at the age of 75 Abraham received a call from God to go to a strange, unknown land that God would show him. The Lord promised Abraham that He would make him and his descendants a great nation (Gen. 12:1-3). The promise must have seemed unbelievable to Abraham because his wife Sarah (called Sarai in the early part of the story) was childless (Gen. 11:30-31; 17:15). But Abraham obeyed God with no hint of doubt or disbelief. He took his wife and his nephew, Lot, and went to the land that God would show him.

Abraham moved south along the trade routes from Haran, through Shechem and Bethel to the land of Canaan. Canaan was a populated area at the time, inhabited by the war-like Canaanites; so Abraham's belief that God would ultimately give this land to him and his descendants was an act of faith. The circumstances seemed quite difficult, but Abraham's faith in God's promises allowed him to trust in the Lord.

The Famine and the Separation from Lot. Because of a severe famine in the land of Canaan, Abraham moved to Egypt for a short time (Gen. 12:10-20). During this trip, Abraham introduced Sarah to the Egyptians as his sister rather than as his wife in order to avoid trouble. Pharaoh, the Egyptian ruler, then took Sarah as his wife. It was only because "the Lord plagued Pharaoh and his house with great plagues because of Sarai, Abram's wife" (Gen. 12:17), that Sarah was returned to Abraham.

Upon his return from Egypt, Abraham and his

Traditional well of Abraham in the plains of Mamre (Gen. 21:22-32).

Photo by Howard Vos

nephew, Lot, quarreled over pasturelands and went separate ways (Gen. 13:8–9). Lot settled in the Jordan River Valley, while Abraham moved into Canaan. After this split, God reaffirmed His promise to Abraham: "And I will make your descendants as the dust of the earth; so that if a man could number the dust of the earth, then your descendants also could be numbered" (Gen. 13:16).

Apparently Abraham headed a strong military force by this time as he is called "Abram the Hebrew" (Gen. 14:13). He succeeded in rescuing his nephew Lot from the tribal chieftains who had captured him while raiding the cities of Sodom and Gomorrah (Gen. 14:14–17).

The Promise Reaffirmed. In Genesis 15 the Lord reaffirmed His promise to Abraham. The relationship between God and Abraham should be understood as a COVENANT relationship—the most common form of arrangement between individuals in the ancient world. According to such an arrangement, individuals or groups agreed to abide by certain conditions that governed their relationship to each other. In this case Abraham agreed to go to the land that God would show him (an act of faith on his part), and God agreed to make Abraham a great nation (Gen. 12:1–3). However, in Genesis 15 Abraham became anxious about the promise of a nation being found in his descendants because of his advanced age. The Lord thus reaffirmed the earlier covenant.

As we know from recent archaeological discoveries, a common practice of that time among heirless families was to adopt a slave who would inherit the master's goods. Therefore, because Abraham was childless, he proposed to make a slave, ELIEZER of Damascus, his heir (Gen. 15:2). But God rejected this action and challenged Abraham's faith: "Then He [God] brought him [Abraham] outside and said, 'Look now toward heaven, and count the stars if you are able to number them.' And He said to him, 'So shall your descendants be' " (Gen. 15:5). Abraham's response is the model of believing faith. "And he [Abraham] believed in the Lord, and He [God] accounted it to him for righteousness" (Gen. 15:6).

The rest of chapter 15 consists of a ceremony between Abraham and God that was commonly used in the ancient world to formalize a covenant (Gen. 15:7–21).

According to Genesis 16, Sarah, because she had not borne a child, provided Abraham with a handmaiden. This also appears to be a familiar custom of the ancient world. According to this custom, if the wife had not had a child (preferably a male) by a certain time in the marriage, she was obligated to provide a substitute (usually a slavewoman) to bear a child to her husband and thereby insure the leadership of the clan. Thus, Hagar, the Egyptian maidservant, had a son by Abraham and named him ISHMAEL. Although Ishmael was not understood to be the child that would carry on the line promised to Abraham, he was given a favorable blessing (Gen. 16:10–13; 17:20).

The most substantial account of the covenant between Abraham and God is given in Genesis 17—a covenant that extended the promise of the land and descendants to further generations. This covenant required Abraham and the male members of his household to be circumcised as the sign of the agreement (Gen. 17:10–14). In this chapter Abraham and Sarah receive their new names. (Their old names were Abram and Sarai.) The name of the son whom God promises that Sarah will bear is designated as Isaac (Gen. 17:19–21). The practice of CIRCUMCISION instituted at this time is not unique to the ancient Hebrews, but its emphasis as a religious requirement is a unique feature of God's Covenant People. It became a visible symbol of the covenant between Abraham and his descendants and their redeemer God.

After Isaac was born to Sarah (Gen. 21:1–7), Sarah was unhappy with the presence of Hagar and Ishmael. She asked Abraham to cast them out of his family, which he did after the Lord told him they would have His protection. Ishmael does not play an important role in the rest of Abraham's story; he does reenter the picture in Genesis 25:9, accompanying Isaac at Abraham's death.

The Supreme Test. God's command for Abraham to sacrifice his beloved son Isaac was the crucial test of his faith. He was willing to give up his son in obedience to God, although at the last moment the Lord intervened to save Isaac (Gen. 22:1–13). The Lord's promise of descendants as numerous as the stars of the heavens was once again reaffirmed as a result of Abraham's unquestioning obedience (Gen. 22:16–18).

Abraham did not want Isaac to marry a woman from one of the local tribes. Possibly he feared this would introduce Canaanite religious practices into the Hebrew clan. Thus, Abraham sent a senior servant to Haran, the city from which he had migrated, to find a wife for Isaac. This mission was successful, and Isaac eventually married REBEKAH, the daughter of Abraham's brother Laban (Gen. 24:1–67). Sarah had died some time earlier (Gen. 23:1–20); Abraham eventually remarried and fathered several children by Keturah (Gen. 25:1–6). Abraham died at the age of 175 and was buried alongside Sarah in the cave of Machpelah, near Hebron (Gen. 25:7–11).

Summary. Abraham was the father of the Hebrews and the prime example of a righteous man. In spite of impossible odds, Abraham had faith in the promises of God. Therefore, he is presented as a model for human behavior. Hospitable to strangers (Gen. 18:1–8), he was a God-fearing man (Gen. 22:1–18) who was obedient to God's laws (Gen. 26:5). The promises originally given to Abraham were passed on to his son Isaac (Gen. 26:3), and to his grandson Jacob (Gen. 28:13; 35:11–12). In later biblical references, the God of Israel is frequently identified as the God of Abraham (Gen. 26:24), and Israel is often called the people "of the God of Abraham" (Ps. 47:9; 105:6; Is. 41:8). Abraham was such an important figure in the history of God's people that when they were in trouble, Israel appealed to God to remember the covenant made with Abraham (Ex. 32:13; Deut. 9:27; Ps. 105:9).

In the New Testament, Abraham is presented as the supreme model of vital faith and as the prime example of the faith required for the Christian believer (Gal. 3:6–9; 4:28). He is viewed as the spiritual father for all who share a similar faith in Christ (Matt. 3:9; Luke 13:16; Rom. 11:1).

ABRAHAM'S BOSOM — a synonym for the life hereafter. According to the Old Testament, when a person died he went to "be with his fathers" (Gen. 15:15; 47:30; Deut. 31:16; Judg. 2:10). The patri-

The site of ancient Shechem—on the fertile valley between Mt. Gerizim (left) and Mt. Ebal (right)—where Abraham built an altar to the Lord (Gen. 12:6-7).

arch Abraham was regarded as the "father" of the Jews (Luke 3:8; John 8:37–40). At death, therefore, the Jew went to his forefathers or, more specifically, to join "father Abraham."

The only use in the Bible of "Abraham's bosom" occurs in Jesus' parable of the rich man and Lazarus (Luke 16:19–31), in which the beggar is described as being "carried by the angels to Abraham's bosom" (v. 22). A great gulf or chasm separated him from the rich man, who was being tormented in the flames of Hades.

ABRAM [A bruhm] (*high father*) — the original name of ABRAHAM, the great patriarch of Israel (Gen. 17:5).

ABRONAH [a BROH nah] (*coast*) — one of the encampments of the Israelites in the wilderness (Num. 33:34; Ebronah, KJV).

ABSALOM [AB suh lum] (*father of peace*) — the arrogant and vain son of David who tried to take the kingship from his father by force.

Absalom was David's third son by Maacah, the daughter of the king of GESHUR (2 Sam. 3:3; 1 Chr. 3:2). Of royal descent on both sides, Absalom was a potential heir to the throne. Attractive in appearance and charming in manners, Absalom was also a popular prince with the people and a favorite of his father. He was especially noted for his beautiful long hair, in which he took great pride (2 Sam. 14:25–26).

During the height of Israel's prosperity under David's rule, another of David's sons, Amnon, raped his half-sister Tamar—Absalom's sister (2 Sam. 13:1–22). Absalom took it upon himself to avenge this dishonor, eventually succeeding after two years in having Amnon murdered by his servants (2 Sam. 13:23–29). Fearing his father's wrath, Absalom fled into exile. He stayed with his grandfather Talmai in Geshur for three years (2 Sam. 13:37–38).

Since Absalom was one of David's favorite sons, the king longed for his return (2 Sam. 13:39) in spite of his crime. Joab, one of David's advisors, urged that Absalom be allowed to return to Jerusalem on probation but that he not be allowed to appear before David.

Absalom did return to Jerusalem, but this turned out to be an ill-advised move on David's part. Absalom secretly plotted a revolt against the throne. Taking advantage of his natural appeal and his handsome appearance to win the favor of the people, he also aroused discontent by implying that he could rule more justly than his father.

When the plot was ready, Absalom obtained permission to go to Hebron to worship. Meanwhile, he had sent spies throughout the tribes, inviting those favorable to him to meet at Hebron (2 Sam. 15:7–11). After gathering these warriors, he then enlisted Ahithophel, a disloyal official of David, as his aide and advisor (2 Sam. 15:12).

When David learned of these rebellious acts, he fled to Mahanaim, beyond the Jordan River (2

Photo by E. B. Trovillion

This tomb in the Kidron Valley is called Absalom's Tomb, but it was probably built several centuries after Absalom's time.

Sam. 17:24). Under Ahithophel's advice, Absalom entered Jerusalem and publicly took possession of the wives in his father's harem who had been left in the city. By this act Absalom demonstrated that he would never be reconciled with his father, and even more of the people rallied to his cause.

Absalom then called a council to determine what action to take against David. Present at this meeting was Hushai, a loyal advisor to David who pretended to follow Absalom in order to spy on the proceedings. Ahithophel advised that Absalom move against the retreating king as quickly as possible, but Hushai countered by pointing out that if the attack failed, his revolt would fail. He advised instead that Absalom gather all his forces for one full-scale attack. Absalom heeded Hushai's counsel, giving David time to assemble an army.

Absalom was formally anointed king after taking Jerusalem (2 Sam. 19:10). He appointed Amasa as captain of his army, then crossed the Jordan to meet his father's forces. The battle took place in the woods of Ephraim, where Absalom's recruits were no match for David's veterans. Absalom's army was defeated, and 20,000 of his men were killed (2 Sam. 18:6–7).

Absalom tried to flee from the forest on a mule, but his head caught in the thick boughs of a terebinth tree. Joab, the captain of David's army, then killed Absalom in spite of David's request that he not be harmed. Upon hearing the news of his death, David moaned, "O my son Absalom—my son, my son Absalom—if only I had died in your place! O Absalom my son, my son!" (2 Sam. 18:33). These are some of the saddest words in the Bible.

Absalom had many talents and abilities. But he was also spoiled, impatient, and overly ambitious. These, along with his vanity and pride, led to his tragic death. His body was cast into a pit, over which a great heap of stones was piled as a sign of contempt (2 Sam. 18:17). A large mausoleum called Absalom's Monument, located in the Kidron Valley east of Jerusalem, was built centuries after Absalom's death. It does not mark the site of his burial place.

ABSALOM'S MONUMENT — a pillar or monument which Absalom set up for himself in the King's Valley (2 Sam. 18:18; Absalom's place; KJV). What a contrast to his dishonored grave (2 Sam. 18:17)!

ABSOLUTION — a release from sins pronounced by a priest as, for example, in the sacrament of penance (Roman Catholic Church). Absolution is an ecclesiastical term, not found in the Bible, which proclaims the atoning work of Christ as the only way a sinner may receive "absolution" or forgiveness (Luke 7:36–50; Col. 1:13–14).

ABSTINENCE — the voluntary, self–imposed, and deliberate denial of certain pleasures, such as food, drink, and sex. The noun abstinence is found only once in the KJV (Acts 27:21), where the apostle Paul is described as having experienced "long abstinence." The verb abstain is found six times in the KJV (Acts 15:20, 29; 1 Thess. 4:3; 5:22; 1 Tim. 4:3; 1 Pet. 1:11).

Abstinence is basically of two kinds: (1) a total abstinence involving an absolute renunciation of a forbidden thing, such as in a NAZIRITE vow; and (2) a temporary abstinence as, for example, the mutual consent of husband and wife to give up sexual relations for a time, in order to give themselves "to fasting and prayer" (1 Cor. 7:5).

The Israelites were commanded to abstain from eating flesh that contained blood (Gen. 9:4). They were to refrain from eating certain animals (Leviticus 11). Priests could not drink wine while exercising their holy ministries (Lev. 10:9). Others abstained from drinking wine (Jer. 35:6).

The apostle Paul taught that the Christian lives by the laws of love and freedom—and that he should voluntarily abstain from food sacrificed to idols, lest it cause a weaker brother or sister in Christ to stumble (Rom. 14:1–23; 1 Cor. 8:1–13). The believer's body, said Paul, is the "temple of the Holy Spirit" (1 Cor. 6:19) and should not be polluted by unclean things.

Paul also exhorted the church of the Thessalonians to "abstain from sexual immorality" (1 Thess. 4:3); indeed, they were to "abstain from every form of evil" (1 Thess. 5:22).

The Christian is called to live a life of unselfish and sacrificial love. Abstinence should always seek to glorify God and to build up fellow believers in the faith.

ABYSS [ah BISS] — the bottomless pit or the chaotic deep. Originally, this term represented a deep mass of waters, and was associated with the water which God created with the earth. Darkness is said to have been on the face of the deep or abyss (Gen. 1:2).

The term is used in several other ways in the Bible. It describes the prison of disobedient spirits, or the world of the dead (Luke 8:31; Rom. 10:7). Terms like "the pit" and "bottomless pit" represent the abode of all the wicked dead.

ABYSSINIA [AB ih sin ee uh] — another word for ETHIOPIA.

ACACIA [ah KAY shuh] (see PLANTS OF THE BIBLE).

ACACIA GROVE [uh KAY shuh] — a form of ABEL ACACIA GROVE.

ACACIAS, VALLEY OF [uh KAY shuhs] — a dry valley where only the acacia tree grows (Joel 3:18). According to Joel's prophecy, in the end time a fountain of refreshing water will flow from the Temple ("the house of the Lord") and give new life to the parched and barren valley.

ACCAD [ACK add] (*fortress*) — one of four cities built by Nimrod in the land of Shinar—which were "the beginning of his kingdom" (Gen. 10:10; Akkad, NIV). The name was extended to describe the land of Accad, which was the northern division of ancient BABYLONIA. Accad was the region between the Tigris and Euphrates Rivers—where the two rivers are close together and flow in roughly parallel courses.

The dynasty of Accad was founded by Sargon the Great sometime between the 23rd and 21st centuries B.C. The name Accad survives in references to one of the earliest recorded Semitic languages, Accadian or Akkadian, which had two major dialects, Assyrian and Babylonian. It was written in the wedge–shaped characters (CUNEIFORM) developed by the Sumerians.

The location of Accad is not positively identified, but it is thought by some to be about 15 kilometers (9 miles) from modern Baghdad.

ACCEPT, ACCEPTANCE — to receive or treat with favor. In the Bible, a person is accepted by the grace, mercy, or covenant-love of God through faith and repentance.

When the Bible mentions individuals being accepted by God, offerings frequently are mentioned (Gen. 4:3–7; Job 42:8–9). In the Old Testament, offerings were acceptable to God when made as prescribed (Lev. 1:4; 22:27), but they were unacceptable when God's instructions were ignored (Lev. 7:18; 19:7; 22:23–25). However, they were flatly rejected when the attitude of one's heart was wayward or irreverent (Amos 5:22; Jer. 14:10; Mal. 1:8, 10).

In the primary New Testament passage on acceptance, the apostle Paul explains that God has fully accepted believers through the merits of Christ (Eph. 1:6). God will not reject them; He opens Himself to His own by welcoming them.

The apostle speaks also of a teaching "worthy of all acceptance," or deserving of universal, wholehearted welcome by Christians (1 Tim. 1:15; 4:9). Worship, prayers, the work of one's hands, spiritual sacrifices, and life's service can be favorably received by God (Ps. 19:14; 2 Cor. 5:9). God accepts us fully in Jesus Christ because of His offering and receives what we return to Him.

ACCESS — the privilege of being introduced to God. Access to God is that positive, friendly relationship with the Father in which we have confidence that we are pleasing and acceptable to Him. Jesus is the "new and living way" (Heb. 10:20) who gives us access to God.

ACCHO [ACK coe] — a form of ACCO.

ACCO [ACK coe] (*hot sand*) — a city of Palestine on the Mediterranean coast about 40 kilometers (25 miles) south of Tyre and about 15 kilometers (9 miles) north of Mount Carmel (see Map 3, B–2). Situated on the north shore of a broad bay, Acco was at the entrance to the rich, fertile plain of Esdraelon. Although Acco was located in the portion of land assigned to the tribe of Asher, the Hebrews were never able to drive out the original Canaanite inhabitants (Judg. 1:31; Accho, KJV).

Acco was mentioned in the AMARNA letters of the 14th century B.C. In the Hellenistic period the name was changed to Ptolemais. It came under Roman domination in 65 B.C.

Acco is mentioned only once in the New Testament and then as Ptolemais (Acts 21:7), the name coming from Ptolemy, the king of Egypt who re-built the city around 100 B.C. Sailing from Tyre to Caesarea at the end of the third missionary journey, the apostle Paul docked at Ptolemais and spent the day with his fellow Christians while his ship was anchored in the harbor.

During the Crusades, Ptolemais recaptured some of its former prominence under the name Acre, by which name it is still known today. Its importance has once again waned, being overshadowed by the city of Haifa, which lies directly across the bay.

ACCOMMODATION — the process by which God adapts His revelation of Himself to the thought systems of the human mind so we can understand something of who He is and how He does His work.

God made the world a fit place for the revelation of Himself. He also made man capable of understanding that revelation. The images God takes from the world to describe Himself are appropriate and true because the creation reflects its Creator. "The heavens declare the glory of God; and the firmament shows His handiwork," the psalmist affirmed (Ps. 19:1). Man, the crowning achievement of God's creation—made in His very image and likeness (Gen. 1:26)—was made to fellowship and communicate with his Creator.

Because of the difference between God's supreme nature as Creator and man's weak nature as His creature, all revelation on God's part involves accommodation to man's level of understanding. Thus in the Bible God is described in human terms (the technical word for this is ANTHROPOMORPHISM). Scripture speaks of God's eyes, fingers, and hands; He is a God who sees and touches His creation. He is also portrayed with such emotions as jealousy and anger. This is the Bible's way of declaring that He is a God who feels and responds to His creatures.

The apostle Paul visited Acco after he returned from his third missionary journey (Acts 21:7).

God's greatest act of accommodation occurred when Jesus, God's Son, took on the form of a human being. The Gospel of John declares, "The Word became flesh and dwelt among us, and we beheld His glory, the glory as of the only begotten of the Father, full of grace and truth" (John 1:14). Jesus, the only begotten God (John 1:18, NASB), accommodated Himself to the limitations of human nature in order to declare the Father to us, showing how far He was willing to go to set us free from our sin.

ACCOUNTABILITY — the biblical principle that man is answerable to his Maker for his thoughts, words, and deeds. The Bible plainly teaches that "the whole world [is] accountable to God" (Rom. 3:19, NASB) and that "all have sinned and fall short of the glory of God" (Rom. 3:23). This means we cannot experience God's GRACE until we first see ourselves as sinners who are without excuse. Christians are accountable to God individually (Rom. 14:12), and corporately as well, "for we are members of one another" (Eph. 4:25).

All who trust Jesus Christ as their Savior are forgiven for the penalty of their sins. They also receive the strength to fight the presence of sin in their lives (Gal. 5:16-25). Thus, our accountability is matched by God's grace and FORGIVENESS.

ACCURSED — under a curse, doomed; anything on which a curse has been pronounced, such as the city of Jericho (Josh. 6:17-18). The apostle Paul pronounced a curse on anyone who preaches a false gospel (Gal. 1:8-9). Also see ANATHEMA.

ACCUSER (see SATAN).

ACELDAMA [ah kell DA mah] — a form of AKELDAMA.

ACHAIA [ah KAY yah] — in Roman times, the name for the whole of Greece, except Thessaly (see Map 7, B-2). The Romans gave the region this name when they captured Corinth and destroyed the Achaian League in 146 B.C. Later it comprised several Grecian cities, including Athens.

The apostle Paul passed through Achaia on his way to Jerusalem (Acts 19:21). He also appeared before Gallio, the proconsul of Achaia, when the Jewish leaders tried to convince him to prosecute Paul for worship contrary to Jewish law (Acts 18:13). Gallio refused to accept the case and Paul was set free (Acts 18:12-17).

ACHAICUS [uh KAY ih cus] (*belonging to Achaia*) — a Christian of Corinth who, along with Stephanas and Fortunatus, visited the apostle Paul at Ephesus and refreshed his spirit (1 Cor. 16:17).

ACHAN [A kinn] (*trouble*) — son of Carmi of the tribe of Judah who unintentionally brought about the Israelites' defeat at Ai (Josh. 7:1, 18-24). He is called *Achar* in 1 Chronicles 2:7, and described as the "troubler of Israel, who transgressed in the accursed thing."

During the Israelites' destruction of Jericho,

Achan took a Babylonian garment, 200 shekels of silver, and a wedge of gold and hid them in his tent. Before the battle, the Lord had designated everything in Jericho an "accursed thing" and commanded that everything be destroyed, lest Israel also become cursed because their camp contained Canaanite spoils. The Israelites were defeated near the city of Ai because Achan had brought the "accursed thing" into their camp.

Also see ACHOR.

ACHAR [a CARR] — a form of ACHAN.

ACHAZ [a KAZZ] — a form of AHAZ.

ACHBOR [ACK bar] (*a mouse*) — the name of two or three men in the Old Testament:

1. The father of Baal-Hanan (Gen. 36:31, 38-39).

2. One of five men sent by King Josiah to ask Huldah the prophetess about the Book of the Law discovered in the Temple (2 Kin. 22:12, 14).

3. A Jew who lived during the reign of King Jehoiakim of Judah (Jer. 26:20-23). He may be the same person as Achbor No. 2.

ACHIM [A kem] (*troubles*) — an ancestor of Joseph the husband of Mary (Matt. 1:14), listed in the genealogy of Jesus (Matt. 1:17) as the son of Zadok and the father of Eliud.

ACHISH [A kish] (meaning unknown) — a king of the Philistine city of Gath, to whom David fled for refuge when King Saul sought his life (1 Sam. 21:10-14; 27:2-12). David formed an alliance with Achish, who always treated him with great kindness (1 Sam. 28:1-2).

Because the Philistine lords resisted the league between Achish and David, Achish was forced to send David away (1 Sam. 29:2-9). Achish is called ABIMELECH in the title of Psalm 34.

ACHMETHA [AK mee thah] (*a fortress*) — the capital of the empire of the Medes. Later it became one of the capitals of the Persian and Parthian Empires. Achmetha was surrounded by seven concentric walls; since the city was built on a hill, the inner walls thus rose above the outer ones. Each wall was painted a different color.

Achmetha was also a treasure city, known for its luxury and splendor. When Cyrus the Great of Persia captured Achmetha in 550 B.C., he made it his summer residence, seeking escape from the terrible heat of Persia. At the time of Cyrus the imperial records were kept here, according to Ezra 6:2. When Darius I ordered a search of the palace library in Achmetha, a scroll was discovered upon which was written the decree of Cyrus permitting the Jews to return to Jerusalem and authorizing them to rebuild the Temple.

In 330 B.C. Alexander the Great conquered Achmetha, destroying its walls and looting its palaces. Hamadan, Iran, occupies the site today, about 280 kilometers (175 miles) southwest of Teheran. Most modern versions (such as NIV, NAS, NEB, and RSV) translate Ecbatana.

The acropolis at Athens, site of the beautiful Parthenon and other buildings of the ancient Greeks.

ACHOR [A kore] (*trouble*) — a valley near Jericho where Achan was stoned to death during the time of Joshua (Josh. 7:24, 26). The prophets used the phrase "the Valley of Achor" (Is. 65:10) to symbolize the idyllic state of contentment and peace of the Messianic age (Hos. 2:15).

ACHSA [ACK sah] — a form of ACHSAH.

ACHSAH [ACK sah] (*ankle ornament*) — the only daughter of Caleb (1 Chr. 2:49; Achsa, KJV). Caleb promised Achsah in marriage to anyone who would capture the city of Debir (formerly known as Kirjath Sepher). When Othniel, Caleb's nephew, took the town, Caleb gave his daughter a portion of the Negev (land in the South), as a dowry. Achsah also wanted springs to water her land and thus Caleb gave her "the upper springs and the lower springs" (Josh. 15:16–19; Judg. 1:12–15). The NIV translates Acsah.

ACHSHAPH [ACK shaf] (meaning unknown) — a Canaanite city situated in the northern part of the territory conquered by Joshua (Josh. 11:1; 12:7, 20; 19:24–25). It was in the territory allotted to the tribe of Asher. Modern scholarship identifies Achshaph as Tell Kisan, about ten kilometers (six miles) southeast of Acre.

ACHZIB [ACK zib] (*falsehood*) — the name of two towns in Israel:
1. A town in the Shephelah, the lowland of western Judah (Josh. 15:44), probably the same town as CHEZIB (Gen. 38:5) and CHOZEBA (1 Chr. 4:22).
2. A town in western Galilee, on the Mediterranean Sea near the border of ancient Phoenicia (Josh. 19:29; Judg. 1:31). Identified as modern ez-Zib, Achzib was located about 15 kilometers (9 miles) north of Acre.

ACRE [ah CREE] — a form of ACCO.

ACRE (see WEIGHTS AND MEASURES).

ACROPOLIS [uh CROP oh lis] (*topmost city*) — an elevated, fortified part of an ancient Greek city, such as Athens, Philippi, and Corinth. The Acropolis of Athens, the most famous acropolis of all ancient cities, was located on a hill about 500 feet high. It was adorned with stunning architectural works. Among these works was the Parthenon, a magnificent temple with 8 Doric columns in front and rear and 17 along each side.

ACROSTIC — a literary device by which sets of letters (such as the first or last letters of a line) are taken in order to form a word, phrase, or a regular sequence of letters of the alphabet.

The ancient Hebrews realized the importance of words and various literary devices such as puns, allusions, and acrostics. The best example of an acrostic in the Bible is Psalm 119 and Psalm 34, both based on the Hebrew alphabet of 22 letters, from Aleph to Tau ("A" to "Z"). This Psalm has 176 verses — eight verses for each of the 22 Hebrew letters.

In the original Hebrew of Psalm 119, verses 1–8 begin with ALEPH; verses 9–16 begin with BETH; verses 17–14 begin with GIMEL; and so forth. Parts of Psalms 9, 10, 25, 37, 111, 112, and 145 and Lamentations 1—4 are also acrostic — as are the last 22 verses of the book of Proverbs, which contain a description of a virtuous wife (Prov. 31:10–21).

ACSAH [ack SAH] — a form of ACHSAH.

ACTS, APOCRYPHAL (see APOCRYPHA).

ACTS OF THE APOSTLES — the one historical book of the New Testament which traces the development of the early church after the Ascension of Jesus. Standing between the Gospels and the Epistles, the Book of Acts is a bridge between the life of Jesus and the ministry of the apostle Paul. As such, it offers invaluable information about the development of the early church.

The title of Acts is somewhat misleading, for only a few of the apostles of Jesus are mentioned in the book. In reality, Acts relates some acts of some of the apostles, primarily Peter and Paul, and involves a time–span of about 32 years—from the Ascension of Jesus (about A.D. 30) to Paul's imprisonment in Rome (about A.D. 62).

Structure of the Book. The Acts of the Apostles is like a drama with two main characters, Peter and Paul. This drama portrays the spread of the gospel from Jerusalem—the city where Jesus was crucified—to Rome, the capital of the Roman Empire.

Authorship and Date. There can be little doubt that the Book of Acts and the Gospel of Luke come from the same author. Each book is the length of a scroll (about 35 feet), and each is addressed to the same individual, Theophilus. The similarities between the Gospel of Luke and the Book of Acts in literary style, vocabulary, and theological ideas are unmistakable. Although the author does not identify himself by name, scholars have ascribed the authorship of both books to Luke, the companion of Paul (see LUKE, GOSPEL OF).

It is difficult to say when Acts was written. We know only that it follows the Gospel: "The former account [Gospel of Luke] I made, O Theophilus" (Acts 1:1). If the Gospel were written in the early 70's, Acts would have been composed shortly thereafter. Many scholars date Acts as early as A.D. 62 because it ends abruptly with Paul's imprisonment in Rome.

Luke is a reliable historian, in part because of the sources he used. He was closely associated with many events of Paul's mission, and this results in greater vividness in the latter half of Acts. At three places in Acts (16:10–17, 20:5—21:18, and 27:1—28:16) the narrative changes to the first person ("we"), indicating that LUKE was personally present. Luke also may have had access to written documents (for example, the decree of the Council of Jerusalem, Acts 15:23; or letters from early Christian leaders).

Above all, Luke had the benefit of a wide circle of contacts. In the Book of Acts he mentions 95 different persons from 32 countries, 54 cities, and 9 Mediterranean islands. From these he gathered information for the first part of Acts (especially chaps. 1—12) and for the gospel. Luke, however, writes selective history, focusing only on the course of the gospel from Jerusalem to Rome.

Historical Setting. As in the Gospel of Luke, Luke writes to Gentiles. He wants his audience to know the truthful and triumphant course of the gospel, beginning in Jesus and continuing in the church (Acts 1:1).

This is his primary motive for writing the Book of Acts. In addition, however, Luke defends, where

This Greek inscription at Athens contains the text of Paul's speech which he delivered at the Areopagus (Acts 17:22-31).

Photo by Gustav Jeeninga

possible, the Christian faith from suspicion of sedition or superstition. The "Way" (9:2) is not a secret, subversive cult (26:26). On the contrary, it is proclaimed in the city squares for all to hear and judge. This is one reason the many public speeches were included in Acts. Neither is Christianity politically dangerous. If Christians are suspected of sedition against Rome, Luke shows that in each instance where they are brought before Roman authorities they are acquitted (Acts 16:39; 17:6; 18:12; 19:37; 23:29; 25:25; 26:31). Luke devotes nearly one third

of Acts (chaps. 21—28) to Paul's imprisonment. He does this not only to show that the gospel reaches its destination in spite of insurmountable obstacles, but also to show that Paul and his message are not politically subversive.

Theological Contribution. The Acts of the Apostles could justly be entitled, "The Acts of the Holy Spirit," for the Spirit is mentioned nearly 60 times in the book. In His parting words, Jesus reminds the disciples of the promise of the Father (1:4–8); ten days later the power of the Spirit descends at

ACTS: A Teaching Outline

Part One: The Witness in Jerusalem (1:1—8:3)

Pentecost (2:1–4). Persons "from every nation under heaven" (2:5) are enabled by the Holy Spirit to hear "the wonderful works of God" (2:11), and so the Christian church was born.

Pentecost was a reversal of the Tower of Babel, where language became confused and nations were separated by misunderstanding (Gen. 11:1–9). At Pentecost, the Holy Spirit gathered persons from every nation into one united fellowship. From Pentecost onward, the Holy Spirit directs the unfolding drama of the growth of the church.

Acts contains portraits of many outstanding Christians of the early church. Barnabas exemplifies generosity (4:36–37), Stephen forgiveness (7:60), Philip and Paul obedience (8:26; 26:19), Cornelius piety (10:2), and the witness of the early church vibrates with boldness (2:29; 4:13, 29, 31; 28:31). Ordinary people are empowered to perform extraordinary feats. A faltering apostle is empowered to address multitudes (2:14) or make a defense before rulers (4:8). A prayer fellowship is shaken (4:31); a deacon defends his faith by martyrdom

(7:58). The despised Samaritans receive the Spirit (8:4–8), as does a Gentile soldier (10:1–48). A staunch persecutor of the gospel is converted (9:1–19), and through him the gospel reaches the capital of the world!

Paul reaches Rome in chains. Circumstances, too, may be adverse: persecutions (8:3–4; 11:19), famines (11:27–30), opposition (13:45), or violent storms (27:1–44). Through it all, however, the Holy Spirit directs the drama so that "all things work together for good" (Rom. 8:28) to further the cause of Christ.

Special Considerations. Nearly one fifth of Acts consists of speeches, primarily from Peter, Stephen, and Paul. Common to each of the speeches is a basic framework of gospel proclamation. This proclamation can be outlined as follows:

1. The promises of God in the Old Testament are now fulfilled.

2. The Messiah has come in Jesus of Nazareth.

a. He did good and mighty works by the power of God.

b. He was crucified according to the purpose of God.

c. He was raised from the dead by the power of God.

d. He now reigns by the power of God.

e. He will come again to judge and restore all things for the purpose of God.

3. All who hear should repent and be baptized.

This outline is our earliest example of the gospel proclaimed by the early church. It is the "foundation of the apostles and prophets, Jesus Christ Himself being the chief cornerstone" (Eph. 2:20), upon which the church is built. In this sense, the Book of Acts is not yet completed, for each generation is enabled by the Holy Spirit to add its chapters by proclaiming the "wonderful works of God" (2:11).

ADADAH [ADD a dah] (*bordering*) — a city in southern Judah (Josh. 15:22) "toward the border of Edom" (v. 21; Ararah, NEB).

ADAH [A duh] (*adornment*) — the name of two women of the Old Testament:

1. One of the two wives of Lamech and the mother of JABAL and JUBAL (Gen. 4:19–21, 23).

2. One of Esau's wives and the daughter of Elon the Hittite (Gen. 36:1–4). She was the mother of Esau's firstborn, Eliphaz, and the ancestress of the Edomites.

ADAIAH [a DYE yuh] (*Jehovah has adorned*) — the name of eight or nine men in the Old Testament:

1. A man of Bozcath whose daughter Jedidah was the mother of King Josiah of Israel (2 Kin. 22:1).

2. An ancestor of Asaph (1 Chr. 6:41–43).

3. A son of Shimei of the tribe of Benjamin (1 Chr. 8:1, 21).

4. A descendant of Aaron who returned to Jerusalem following the Captivity (1 Chr. 9:10–12).

5. The father of Masseiah (2 Chr. 23:1).

6, 7. Two different men, one of the family of Bani

and one of the family of Binnui (RSV), who divorced their pagan wives after the Captivity (Ezra 10:29, 39).

8. A son of Joiarib and a descendant of Judah by Perez —and thus a member of the royal line of David (Neh. 11:5).

9. A Levite of the family of Aaron, probably the same as Adaiah No. 4. (Neh. 11:12).

ADALIA [uh DAY lyuh] (meaning unknown) — one of the ten sons of Haman who were hanged like their father (Esth. 9:8–10).

ADAM [ADD um] (*red, ground*) — the name of a man and a city in the Old Testament:

1. The first man, created by God on the sixth day of creation, and placed in the Garden of Eden (Gen. 2:19–23; 3:8–9, 17, 20–21; 4:1, 25; 5:1–5). He and his wife EVE, created by God from one of Adam's ribs (Gen. 2:21–22), became the ancestors of all people now living on the earth. Adam was unique and distinct from the animals in several ways. His creation is described separately from that of the animals and the rest of God's creative acts (Gen. 1:3–25; 1:26–27; 2:7).

God breathed into Adam's body of "dust" the divine "breath of life; and man became a living being" (Gen. 2:7). God also made man in his own image and likeness. The exact words are, "Let Us make man in Our image, according to Our likeness" (Gen. 1:26). The apostle Paul interprets this to mean that God created man with spiritual, rational, emotional, and moral qualities (Eph. 4:24–32; Col. 3:8–10).

God placed Adam in the Garden of Eden where he was to work the ground (Gen. 2:5, 15) and take care of the animals (Gen. 1:26–28; 2:19–20). God made Eve as a "helper comparable to" Adam (Gen. 2:20), creating her out of one of Adam's ribs so they were "one flesh" (Gen. 2:24).

God told the human pair, "Be fruitful and multiply; fill the earth" (Gen. 1:28). As a consequence, they had a number of children: Cain, Abel, Seth, and a number of other sons and daughters (Gen. 4:1–2; 5:3–4). Created in innocence, they did not know sin (Gen. 2:25).

Genesis 3 tells how Adam failed to keep God's command not to eat of the tree of the knowledge of good and evil. The consequence of this disobedience was death (Gen. 2:17), both physical (Gen. 5:5) and spiritual (Eph. 2:1). Eve disobeyed first, lured by pride and the desire for pleasure (Gen. 3:5–6; 1 Tim. 2:14). Then Adam, with full knowledge of the consequences, joined Eve in rebellion against God (Gen. 3:6).

The consequences of disobedience were: (1) loss of innocence (Gen. 3:7); (2) continued enmity between the seed of the woman [Christ] (Gen. 3:15; Gal. 3:16) and the seed of the serpent [SATAN and his followers] (John 8:44); (3) the cursing of the ground and the resultant hard labor for man (Gen. 3:17–19); (4) the hard labor of childbirth (Gen. 3:16); (5) the submission of woman to her husband (Gen. 3:16; Eph. 5:22–23); and (6) separation from

God (Gen. 3:23–24; 2 Thess. 1:9). Adam lived 930 years (Gen. 5:5).

The New Testament emphasizes the oneness of Adam and Eve (Matt. 19:3–9) showing that Adam represented man in bringing the human race into sin and death (Rom. 5:12–19; 1 Cor. 15:22). In contrast, Christ, the "last Adam," represented His redeemed people in bringing justification and eternal life to them (Rom. 5:15–21).

2. A city located "beside Zaretan" (Josh. 3:16), near the junction of the Jabbok River and the Jordan River, about 30 kilometers (18 miles) north of Jericho.

ADAM, BOOKS OF (see PSEUDEPIGRAPHA).

ADAMAH [AD uh mah] (*earth*) — a fortified city in the territory of Naphtali. Its exact location is uncertain, but it was near Chinnereth and Ramah (Josh. 19:35–36) northwest of the Sea of Galilee.

ADAMANT (see JEWELS AND PRECIOUS STONES).

ADAMI NEKEB [AD ah me NEH keb] (*Adam of the pass*) — a place in lower Galilee on the border of Naphtali (Josh. 19:33).

ADAR [a DARR] (*cloudy*) — the name of a city and a month:

1. A town in southern Judah (Josh. 15:3), also called HAZAR ADDAR (Num. 34:4).

2. The Babylonian name of the 12th month of the Jewish year (Ezra 6:15; Esth. 3:7, 13; 8:12; 9:1, 15–21). It began with the new moon in February and ended at the new moon in March.

ADBEEL [AD bee el] (*God has disciplined*) — the third of the 12 sons of Ishmael (Gen. 25:13). Adbeel is also believed by scholars to be the name of an Arabian tribe located in northwest Arabia.

ADDAN [ADD un] (*strong*) — an unidentified place in Babylon from which returning captives came with Zerubbabel to Jerusalem (Ezra 2:59; Addon, Neh. 7:61). Some scholars believe Addan was the name of a man who was unable to produce his genealogy to prove he was an Israelite.

ADDAR [ad DAR] (*cloudy*) — a son of Bela and the grandson of Benjamin (1 Chr. 8:3), also called ARD (Num. 26:40).

ADDAX, ADDER (see ANIMALS OF THE BIBLE).

ADDI [AD ee] — an ancestor of Joseph listed in the genealogy of Jesus Christ (Luke 3:28). Addi is the Greek form of IDDO.

ADDON [AD un] — a form of ADDAN.

ADER [A duhr] — a form of EDER.

ADIEL [A dih el] (*ornament of God*) — the name of three men in the Old Testament:

1. One of the family heads of the tribe of Simeon in the time of Hezekiah (1 Chr. 4:36).

2. The father of Maasai, who helped rebuild the Temple after the Captivity (1 Chr. 9:12).

3. The father of Azmaveth (1 Chr. 27:25).

ADIN [A dun] (*voluptuous*) — the father and ancestor of a family known as "the people of Adin" (Ezra 2:15), "the sons of Adin" (Ezra 8:6), or "the children of Adin" (Neh. 7:20). This family returned from captivity in Babylonia to Jerusalem with Zerubbabel and Ezra (Neh. 10:16).

ADINA [AD uh nah] (*ornament*) — the son of Shiza the Reubenite and one of David's mighty men (1 Chr. 11:42).

ADINO [AD ih noe] (*he wielded his spear*) — the name given to JOSHEB-BASSHEBETH the Tachmonite, chief captain of David's mighty men. He was given the name Adino the Eznite "because he had killed 800 men at one time" (2 Sam. 23:8).

ADITHAIM [ad ih THAH em] (*two ways*) — a city in the Shephelah, or lowland, of Judah (Josh. 15:33, 36). Its exact location is unknown.

ADJURATION — an earnest urging or advising; the action by which a person in authority imposes the obligations of an OATH upon another. Some of those who adjured others were King Saul, King Ahab, and some itinerant Jewish exorcists (1 Sam. 14:24; 1 Kin. 22:16; Mark 5:7; Acts 19:13).

Perhaps the most famous example of adjuration in the Bible is found in Matthew 26:63. The high priest said to Jesus, "I adjure You by the living God that You tell us if You are the Christ, the Son of God." The words "I adjure You" in this case mean, "I solemnly command that you testify on oath and tell the truth, the whole truth, and nothing but the truth."

ADLAI [AD lah eye] (*Jehovah is just*) — the father of Shaphat, a chief herdsman (1 Chr. 27:29) in the time of David.

ADMAH [AD muh] (*red earth*) — one of the CITIES OF THE PLAIN, destroyed with Sodom, Gomorrah, and the other cities (Deut. 29:23). Some scholars identify Admah with the city of ADAM (Josh. 3:16).

ADMATHA [AD mah thah] (*unconquered*) — a high Persian official at Shushan (SUSA), one of seven princes "who had access to the king's presence" (Esth. 1:14).

ADNA [AD nuh] (*pleasure*) — the name of two men in the Old Testament:

1. A son of Pahath–Moab who divorced his pagan wife (Ezra 10:30).

2. A priest who returned from the Captivity in the time of the high priest Joiakim (Neh. 12:12, 15).

ADNAH [AD nuh] (*pleasure*) — the name of two men in the Old Testament:

1. A warrior of the tribe of Manasseh who joined David's army at Ziklag (1 Chr. 12:20).

2. A man of high military rank in King Jehoshaphat's army (2 Chr. 17:14).

ADONI–BEZEK [a DAWN ih BEE zek] (*lord of Bezek*) — a king of Bezek, which was located in the territory allotted to Judah. After he was captured by the men of Judah and Simeon, his thumbs and big toes were cut off (Judg. 1:5-7). Adoni-Bezek reaped what he had sowed, for he himself had previously cut off the thumbs and big toes of 70 kings (Judg. 1:7).

ADONI–ZEDEK [ad DAWN ih ZEH deck] (*my lord is justice*) — one of the five kings of the Amorites who fought against Joshua at Gibeon (Josh. 10:1-27). When Adoni-Zedek and his four allies took refuge in a cave near MAKKEDAH, Joshua had them sealed inside while he pursued their armies. Later, the Israelites returned to the cave, removed the five kings, and "put their feet on their necks" (Josh. 10:24) as a sign of triumph. After they were killed, their bodies were hung on five trees for public display. Then they were taken down and cast into the cave, which was sealed with stones.

ADONIJAH [add oh NYE juh] (*Jehovah is my Lord*) — the name of three men in the Old Testament:

1. The fourth of the six sons born to David while he was at Hebron (2 Sam. 3:4). Adonijah's mother was Haggith. With the exception of Absalom, David apparently favored Adonijah over his other five sons. When David was old, Adonijah attempted to seize the throne, although he probably knew that his father intended Solomon to succeed him (1 Kin. 1:13).

Adonijah won two important people to his cause—Joab, the captain of the army, and Abiathar, the priest. At an open-air feast at the stone of Zoheleth beside En Rogel, he had himself proclaimed king.

But Adonijah had not won over Zadok the priest, Benaiah the commander of the royal bodyguard, or Nathan the prophet. Bathsheba, Solomon's mother, and Nathan told David of Adonijah's activities; David imediately ordered Solomon, who had been divinely chosen as David's successor, to be proclaimed king. When Adonijah sought sanctuary at the altar (1 Kin. 1:5-50), Solomon forgave him.

Adonijah, however, foolishly made another attempt to become king—this time after David's death. He asked that David's widow, the beautiful Abishag, be given to him in marriage. According to the custom of the day, claiming a king's wife or concubine amounted to the same thing as claiming his throne. This time Solomon ordered that Adonijah be killed (1 Kin. 2:13, 25).

2. One of the Levites sent by Jehoshaphat to instruct the people of Judah in the law (2 Chr. 17:8).

3. A chieftain who, with Nehemiah, sealed the covenant (Neh. 10:14-16); he is also called ADONIKAM (Ezra 2:13).

ADONIKAM [ad oh NYE kum] (*my lord has risen*) — an Israelite whose descendants returned to Palestine from Babylon after the Captivity (Ezra 2:13;

8:13; Neh. 7:18). Apparently he is the ADONIJAH of Nehemiah 10:16.

ADONIRAM [ad oh NYE rum] (*my Lord is exalted*) — the son of Abda and an officer under kings David, Solomon, and Rehoboam. David placed Adoniram "in charge of revenue" (2 Sam. 20:24), and Solomon appointed him "over the labor force" (1 Kin. 4:6; 5:14)—a group sent to work in his enforced labor crews in Lebanon.

When the northern tribes rebelled against Rehoboam, Rehoboam sent Adoniram to force the rebels to obey the king, but "all Israel stoned him...and he died" (1 Kin. 12:18; 2 Chr. 10:18). Adoniram also was called Adoram (2 Sam. 20:24; 1 Kin. 12:18) and Hadoram (2 Chr. 10:18).

ADOPTION — the act of taking voluntarily a child of other parents as one's child; in a theological sense, the act of God's grace by which sinful people are brought into his redeemed family.

In the New Testament, the Greek word translated adoption literally means "placing as a son." It is a legal term that expresses the process by which a man brings another person into his family, endowing him with the status and privileges of a biological son or daughter.

In the Old Testament, adoption was never common among the Israelites. Adoption in the Old Testament was done by foreigners or by Jews influenced by foreign customs. Pharaoh's daughter adopted Moses (Ex. 2:10) and another pharaoh adopted Genubath (1 Kin. 11:20). Furthermore, there is no Hebrew word to describe the process of adoption. When the Pharaoh's daughter adopted Moses, the text says, "And he became her son" (Ex. 2:10).

By New Testament times, Roman customs exercised a great deal of influence on Jewish family life. One custom is particularly significant in relation to adoption. Roman law required that the adopter be a male and childless; the one to be adopted had to be an independent adult, able to agree to be adopted. In the eyes of the law, the adopted one became a new creature; he was regarded as being born again into the new family—an illustration of what happens to the believer at conversion.

The apostle Paul used this legal concept of adoption as an analogy to show the believer's relationship to God. Although similar ideas are found throughout the New Testament, the word adoption, used in a theological sense, is found only in the writings of Paul (Rom. 8:15, 23; 9:4).

In Ephesians, Paul's emphasis is that our adoption rests with God, who "predestined us to adoption as sons" (Eph. 1:5). In his letter to the Romans, Paul used the term to describe Israel's place of honor in God's plan (Rom. 9:4). However, Gentile believers have also been given the "Spirit of adoption," which allows them to cry, "Abba, Father" (Gal. 4:6).

God's adoption of the believer also has a future dimension, the assurance that the believer's body will be resurrected (Rom. 8:23).

Photo: Egyptian National Museum

In this scene from an Egyptian tomb, a princess is adorned with a hairdressing by her servant.

ADORAIM [ad oh RAY em] (meaning unknown) — a city in southwest Judah rebuilt and fortified by Rehoboam, son of Solomon (2 Chr. 11:5, 9). It is now known as Dura, located about eight kilometers (five miles) southwest of Hebron.

ADORAM [a DOH rum] — a form of ADONIRAM.

ADORATION — the act of worship, of paying honor, reverence, and obedience to God. The word adoration does not occur in most English versions of the Bible (such as the KJV, NKJV, and RSV), but the concept of adoration as worship is implied in many places in the Bible. Also see WORSHIP.

ADORN — to decorate or beautify. In the New Testament, the Temple (Luke 21:5), the monuments of the righteous (Matt. 23:29), and an empty house (Matt. 12:44; Luke 11:25) are all adorned.

ADRAMMELECH [a DRAM uh leck] (*Adar is king*) — the name of a pagan god and a man in the Old Testament:
1. A pagan god to whom the colonists of Samaria sacrificed their children (2 Kin. 17:31). Also see GODS, PAGAN.
2. A son of the Assyrian king Sennacherib. He and his brother, Sharezer, killed their father (2 Kin. 19:37; Is. 37:38).

ADRAMYTTIUM [add rah MITT ee um] (meaning unknown) — an important seaport of the Roman province of Asia, situated in northwestern Asia Minor, in what is modern Turkey. As a prisoner, the apostle Paul boarded "a ship of Adramyttium" (Acts 27:2) on his way to Rome. The site is now called Karatash, but a nearby town, EDREMIT, preserves the name.

ADRIA [A drih uh] — a form of ADRIATIC.

ADRIATIC [a drih AT ick] — a name for the central part of the Mediterranean Sea south of Italy (see Map 7, B–1). It is mentioned in Luke's account of Paul's voyage to Rome (Acts 27:27). Paul's courage in the midst of this terrible storm is an inspiration: "Do not be afraid...for I believe God" (Acts 27:24–25). The Greek geographer Strabo (63 B.C.?—A.D. 24?) identified the Adriatic as the Gulf of Adria, pointing out that the name comes from the old Etruscan city of Atria. The KJV translates as Adria.

ADRIEL [A drih el] (*God is my help*) — a son of Barzillai the Meholathite, of the tribe of Issachar. Adriel was also the husband of Merab, the daughter of King Saul, who was given to Adriel in marriage (1 Sam. 18:19; 2 Sam. 21:8).

ADULLAM [a DULL um] (*refuge*) — the name of a city (see Map 3, A–4) and a cave:
1. A city in the Shephelah, or lowland, of Judah, situated southwest of Jerusalem (Josh. 12:15; 15:35). It first appears as a Canaanite city (2 Chr. 11:5, 7; Mic. 1:15).
2. A large cave near the city of Adullam (1 Sam. 22:1; 1 Chr. 11:15), where David hid when he was a fugitive from King Saul.

ADULLAMITE [a DULL uh mite] (*belonging to Adullam*) — a person from ADULLAM. The only Adullamite mentioned in the Bible is Hirah, a friend of Judah (Gen. 38:1, 12, 20).

ADULTERY — willful sexual intercourse with someone other than one's husband or wife. Jesus expanded the meaning of adultery to include the cultivation of lust: "Whoever looks at a woman to lust for her has already committed adultery with her in his heart" (Matt. 5:28).

In the Ten Commandments God emphatically prohibited adultery when He said, "You shall not commit adultery" (Ex. 20:14). Under Mosaic Law, when a couple was caught in the act of adultery, both parties were to be killed (Deut. 22:22).

Adultery plays havoc with personal, domestic, and national happiness. A case in point is David's affair with Bathsheba. Their adultery led to a cover-up, which was followed by the murder of Bathsheba's husband (2 Samuel 11). Nathan the prophet later came to David, accusing him of his sin and declaring that because of it, violence would become commonplace in David's household (2 Sam. 12:10). One disaster after another struck his family, including rape, murder, and revolt (2 Samuel 13—15).

Adultery reached epidemic proportions in Jeremiah's time. The prophet repeatedly spoke out against this and other sins (Jer. 7:9; 23:10). The problem was so rampant that even the other prophets of Jerusalem were guilty of it (Jer. 23:14), and Jeremiah predicted God's judgment on them (Jer. 23:15).

Occasionally, the marriage covenant was used as an analogy to describe God's relationship to His people. When the people of Israel and Judah refused to obey Him, or when they practiced idolatry, the prophets accused them of spiritual adultery (Jer. 3:6–10).

The record of the woman taken in adultery—who, according to the law of Moses, should have been stoned to death—reveals the wisdom and grace of Jesus (John 8:3–9). He knew that her accusers were not without sin; and, therefore, they were being self-righteous when they condemned her. When Jesus said to her, "Go and sin no more" (John 8:11), He did not excuse her sin; he forgave her of it and warned against continuing in adultery.

The apostle Paul catalogued a series of sins that exclude a person from the kingdom of God. The sin of adultery was included in these lists (1 Cor. 6:9).

ADUMMIM [a DUM em] (*bloody*) — a pass leading down from the hill country surrounding Jerusalem to the lowlands of Jericho and the Jordan River valley near the boundary between Benjamin and Judah. Jesus' parable of the Good Samaritan refers to this area (Luke 10:30). Known in the Bible as the "Ascent of Adummim" (Josh. 15:7; 18:17), its modern name is Tal at ed-Damm. Modern tourists are shown the "Inn of the Good Samaritan," at a place where the Jericho Road enters a narrow gorge that leads into the pass.

ADVENT, SECOND (see ESCHATOLOGY; SECOND COMING).

ADVERSARY — one who opposes or hinders another. In the Bible, this word is often used of SATAN, the adversary of God and His plan of righteousness and redemption in the world. Since his fall, Satan has opposed God's plan to establish His kingdom on earth. He tricked Eve (Gen. 3:1–5) in order to use man to establish his kingdom rather than God's. Satan later opposed Jesus by questioning His identity as the Messiah and by tempting Him to misuse His powers as God's Son (Matt. 4:1–11).

Satan is still the Christian's adversary (1 Pet. 5:8), but we have an ADVOCATE, Jesus Christ (1 John 2:1), who enables us to overcome his temptation.

ADVOCATE — one who pleads another's cause before a tribunal or judicial court. The word advocate is found only once in the NKJV: "If anyone sins, we have an Advocate with the Father, Jesus Christ the righteous" (1 John 2:1). The Greek word translated as advocate here is also found four times in the Gospel of John, all referring to the Holy Spirit (John 14:16, 26; 15:26; 16:7; helper, NKJV).

Christians need an Advocate because of the ADVERSARY, the devil or Satan, who accuses us before God (1 Pet. 5:8; Rev. 12:10). If Satan is the "prosecuting attorney," Christ and the Holy Spirit are the legal advocates, the "defense attorneys," who help, defend, counsel, and comfort us; they plead the Christian's case before God day and night, providing a continuing remedy for sin.

AENEAS [ee NEE us] (*a Trojan hero*) — a paralyzed man at Lydda healed by Peter (Acts 9:34–35).

AENON [EE none] (*springs*) — a place in Palestine near Salim, where John the Baptist was baptizing at the time of Jesus' ministry in Judea (John 3:22–23). Scholars are uncertain of the location of Aenon. Most likely, Aenon was close to the Jordan River, "because there was much water there" (John 3:23). If its name came from its surroundings, however, Aenon may have been a place where natural springs supplied water.

AEON (see AGE; TIME).

AFFLICTION — any condition or problem that produces suffering or pain. The Bible speaks of two types of affliction—suffering that represents God's judgment on sin (Is. 53:4; Matt. 24:29; Rom. 2:9), and suffering that brings about the purifying of the believer as he identifies with Christ (Rom. 5:3–5; 2 Thess. 1:4–7).

God's judgment on the sin of unbelievers is designed to punish them, while the second type of affliction is designed to perfect Christians and prepare them for greater service in God's kingdom. The believer's attitude through all affliction should be the declaration of the apostle Paul, "For I consider that the sufferings of this present time are not worthy to be compared with the glory which shall be revealed in us" (Rom. 8:18).

AFTERNOON — literally, the declining of the day (Judg. 19:8), beginning about 4:00 P.M. Also see CALENDAR; TIME.

AGABUS [AG uh bus] (*desire*) — a Christian prophet of Jerusalem who went to Antioch of Syria while Paul and Barnabas were there, and "showed by the Spirit that there was going to be a great famine throughout all the world" (Acts 11:28). Later, when Paul and his companions were at Caesarea, Agabus the prophet gave a symbolic demonstration of Paul's impending arrest. Agabus bound his own hands and feet with Paul's belt. Then he predicted that the owner of the belt would be bound like this by the Jews and delivered into the hands of the Gentiles (Acts 21:10–11).

AGAG [A gag] (meaning unknown) — the name of two kings in the Old Testament:
1. The king of the Amalekites mentioned by Balaam (Num. 24:7).
2. A king of the Amalekites whose army was defeated by the forces of Saul. Instead of slaying Agag as God told him to do, Saul spared his life. Because of his disobedience, Saul was rebuked by the prophet Samuel and rejected by the Lord. David was then anointed king in Saul's place (1 Sam. 15:33).

AGAGITE [A gah gite] (*belonging to Agag*) — a term of contempt for Haman, the enemy of the Jews (Esth. 3:1; 9:24). The term is probably synonymous with AMALEKITE (Ex. 17:8–16).

AGAPE [ah GAH pay] — a Greek word for love used often in the New Testament (John 13:35; 1 Cor. 13; 1 John 4:7–18). Contrary to popular understanding, the significance of *agape* is not that it is an unconditional love, but that it is primarily a love of the will rather than the emotions. The New Testament never speaks of God loving unbelieving human beings with emotional love or a love which expects something in return. But He loves with His will—with *agapao* (John 3:16; Rom. 5:8). The reason for this is that God can find nothing enjoyable about a sinner on whom His wrath still abides. So He loves by His will; it is His nature to love. Also see LOVE, LOVE FEAST.

AGAR [A gahr] — Greek form of HAGAR.

AGATE (see JEWELS AND PRECIOUS STONES).

AGE — an era or specified period of time during which certain related events come to pass. As used in the New Testament, age generally refers to the present era, as opposed to the future age. According to the apostle Paul, Satan is "the god of this age" (2 Cor. 4:4). But the age to come will belong to Jesus Christ and His rule of justice and righteousness (Heb. 6:5). Also see TIME.

AGEE [A ghee] (*fugitive*) — a Hararite, the father of one of David's mighty men (2 Sam. 23:11).

AGORA [ah GOE ruh] — the Greek word for MARKETPLACE (Acts 16:19). The agora was a large open space, often found near the gates of cities in

The Agora, or marketplace, at Ephesus with the remains of shops and government buildings.

Photo by Gustav Jeeninga

New Testament times, where goods were bought and sold. The agora was also the site for public assemblies. While in Athens, the apostle Paul shared his faith with people in the agora (Acts 17:17).

AGRAPHA [AG rah fuh] (*unwritten things*) — statements supposedly made by Jesus which are not included in the Gospels of Matthew, Mark, Luke, or John or referred to anywhere else in the New Testament.

Jesus must have made many statements that were not recorded by any of the writers of the four gospels. For example, the Book of Acts records that Jesus taught, "It is more blessed to give than to receive" (Acts 20:35); but none of the gospels record this saying. But beyond the Bible, many other books were written that also claim to contain statements made by Jesus. Although Jesus may have made a few of these statements, the vast majority were not spoken by Him.

Many of these sayings were created because people were curious about matters the four gospels did not discuss, such as what Jesus was like when he was a boy. Others were created because the writer wanted to prove that a certain belief came from Jesus, when in fact it did not. Some writers may actually have thought the sayings they were recording did come from Jesus, and they wanted to write them down so they would not be forgotten.

A book known as the Gospel of Thomas records an incident when a child threw a stone at the boy Jesus. Jesus said, "Thou shalt not finish thy course," and the child fell down dead. This account does not match what we know about Jesus from the four gospels; so the Gospel of Thomas was rejected as a false book by the early church.

Because most of the agrapha are not based on actual events in Jesus' life, they are of little value in determining what Jesus actually said and did. But the Gospels of Matthew, Mark, Luke, and John can be trusted as authentic accounts of the life and ministry of our Lord.

AGRICULTURE — the science, art, and business of cultivating the soil, producing crops, and raising livestock; farming. Israel's society remained basically agricultural throughout biblical times. Although cities and towns developed in Israel as early as the time of David and Solomon, both Old and New Testaments contain many references to agricultural customs and practices.

The Bible indicates that one of man's basic tasks was to "till and keep" the land (Gen. 2:15, RSV), so that man is seen as a being with divinely given ability to be a gardener or farmer. Man's close relationship with the soil is also indicated by the similarity between two Hebrew words for man (*adam*) and earth (*adamah*).

Although Abraham, Isaac, and Jacob moved about within Palestine and were concerned primarily with looking after their flocks, they were also involved in farming. Isaac, for example, was instantly aware of the "smell of a field" on Esau's clothes. He prayed that Jacob might be blessed with "plenty of grain and wine" (Gen. 27:27–28).

When the Israelites settled in the land of Canaan, they were largely confined to the heavily wooded hill country, while the Canaanites continued in the valleys and along the coast (Judg. 1:27–33). The Israelites, therefore, began the long process of clear-

Productive farmland near Jabesh Gilead, demonstrating progressive agricultural methods in use in the Holy Land today.
Photo by Gustav Jeeninga

Photo by Gustav Jeeninga

Lemon trees at Tel Aviv, Israel, in a modern citrus-farming operation.

ing the forests. The uplands of Ephraim and Judah as well as the land east of the Jordan River were gradually made suitable for cultivation.

With the expansion of Israel during the time of the United Kingdom under David and Solomon, agricultural activity prospered (1 Kin. 4:25). Some agricultural products, such as wheat, olive oil, and honey, were even exported (Ezek. 27:17). Certain kings, such as David (1 Chr. 27:26–31) and Hezekiah (2 Chr. 32:28), took a special interest in agricultural production, and none more so than Uzziah, who is described as one who "loved the soil" (2 Chr. 26:10). This prosperity, however, was not enjoyed by everyone. Ahab's attempt to take over Naboth's vineyard (1 Kings 21) is only one example of how the poor were exploited. The prophet Isaiah condemned those who "add field to field" (Is. 5:8).

The years of Israel's CAPTIVITY in Babylon brought a considerable decline in agricultural activity. Much of the land was neglected, desolation was increased by the ravages of wild animals (2 Kin. 17:25–27), and only the poor were left to till the land "as vinedressers and farmers" (2 Kin. 25:12).

Some restoration of agriculture took place after the return from captivity, but some of the earlier problems persisted. In the prophet Haggai's time, God's corrective judgment had a noticeable effect on food production (Hag. 1:11). And Nehemiah received complaints from the poor concerning the financial difficulties they were experiencing in keeping their farms going (Neh. 5:11).

Agriculture was also important in New Testa-

ment times. Jesus made frequent reference to the land and its products in His teaching, indicating that He and His hearers were quite familiar with such matters. Matthew 13, for example, contains four agricultural parables—the sower (vv. 1–23), the wheat and the tares (vv. 24–30, 36–43), the mustard seed (vv. 31–32), and the treasure hidden in the field (v. 44). Other New Testament writers also refer to agricultural matters. The apostle Paul, for example, spoke of reaping and sowing (Gal. 6:7–10) and the cultivation of olive trees (Rom. 11:17–24); and James referred to the farmer patiently waiting for the rain (James 5:7).

The Bible supplies two striking agricultural metaphors concerning the purposes of God. God Himself is twice described as a farmer. He is the "vinedresser" who tends the vine, which is both Christ and those who abide in Him (John 15:1–8); and He farms the field of His church, where He is working to produce a perfect harvest (1 Cor. 2:7, 9). The second picture is slightly different. It illustrates God's constant supply of rich and varied food for His people, especially in heaven. This idea is found both in the Old Testament prophets (Amos 9:13–15; Joel 2:18–19) and in John's vision of the New Jerusalem, where the tree of life produces 12 different monthly crops of fruit (Rev. 22:2).

The traditional picture of Palestine is that of "a land flowing with milk and honey" (Ex. 3:8, 17). This view is supported elsewhere in the Bible, as in Deuteronomy 8:8: "A land of wheat and barley, of vines and fig trees and pomegranates, a land of olive oil and honey." But the fertility of the land was neither automatic nor uniform. The Old Testament in particular continually stresses that success and prosperity in agriculture came from God and that His blessing was closely associated with the people's trust in God and their obedience to His word (Deuteronomy 28).

Thus, agricultural labor was tied up with spiritual and moral attitudes. Bumper crops could not be guaranteed through the correct observance of ritual, as the idol worshipers of Canaan imagined. Many Israelites, however, were seduced by Canaanite ways, influenced by the unpredictability of Palestine's climate and the undemanding morality of Canaanite religion, as well as by their desire for a good harvest.

One reminder that thanksgiving and worship were due to the Lord for multiplying their crops and flocks came through Israel's festivals, which were closely associated with the agricultural year. Passover with unleavened bread was celebrated at the beginning of the barley harvest. This was followed 50 days later by the Feast of Weeks or Pentecost with the offering of the firstfruits of the wheat harvest.

The Feast of Tabernacles, or Ingathering, took place when the harvest was complete. Because these festivals sometimes degenerated into the mere performance of ritualism, the prophets brought a further reminder that Jehovah, and not Baal, was the true Lord of the harvest. The prophet Hosea ac-

Photo by Gustav Jeeninga

Hillside terracing—a technique for preventing soil erosion—in the farmlands surrounding Bethlehem.

tually said of Israel, "For she did not know that I [the Lord] gave her grain, new wine, and oil" (Hos. 2:8), so steeped had they become in paganism. When the people failed to respond even to this clear message, the prophets announced God's judgment on the land as well as the people (Jer. 12:7–13; Amos 4:6–10), although they still gave hope for the future (Ezek. 36:30; Hos. 2:21–23).

Israelite agriculture included the farming of the land and the rearing of animals. In the days of the patriarchs, livestock farming was the major activity; but as the Israelites settled in the land, the role of animals became less important. Herds and flocks were kept basically for their wealth and for food, although meat was much less important than it is in modern Western society. Most families also owned work animals, the ox being the most valuable and the donkey the most common. Neither horses nor camels were used much in agriculture. Horses were kept mostly for military use and camels for trading purposes.

The growing of crops in ancient Israel was no easy matter. Palestine's location between the Mediterranean Sea and the desert produced unpredictable rainfall. The growth of vegetation in some lowland areas, such as the Jordan River Valley and parts of the Plain of Sharon along the coast were so luxuriant that they contained mostly dense forests. Other areas, mainly in the east, were dry and barren, with stony terrain and only occasional rain. These were impossible to farm and unable to support a settled population. Even the areas that could be cultivated had their continual hazards, such as locusts, hail, desert storms, and invading armies. The Israelite farmer well understood the truth of Genesis 3:19: "In the sweat of your face you shall eat bread."

The pattern of the agricultural year in the land of Palestine can be reconstructed only with difficulty. Many details remain unknown, and there must have been considerable variation from place to place. The period of sowing and plowing began around the middle of October at the time of the early rains. This was followed by harrowing and weeding. The latter rains were vital for ripening the crops, and the rainy season usually ended around early April. Harvesting began with the barley harvest, around the middle of April. The gathering of the grain harvest, the summer fruits, and the grapes lasted until August and September, although the last olives were finally picked in November.

An early Hebrew inscription from the 10th century B.C., found at Gezer and known as the "Gezer Calendar," lists various agricultural activities through the months of the year. Its purpose is unknown, although it is often thought to have been a child's exercise tablet. The approximate translation is as follows: "Two months of harvest. Two months of sowing. Two months of late planting. Month of reaping flax. Month of reaping barley. Month of reaping and measuring. Two months of vine tending. Month of summer fruit."

The Old Testament consistently refers to the three basic Israelite crops: grain, grapes, and olives. Psalm 104:15, for example, speaks of God providing "wine that makes glad the heart of man, oil to make his face shine, and bread which sustains man's heart" (Deut. 7:13; 2 Kin. 18:32; Neh. 5:11). Of the grain crops, wheat was grown mainly in the central area of the western highlands (Manasseh) and in Gilead and Bashan, east of the Jordan River. Barley was grown in the drier south and east, especially in Philistia. Barley is able to grow in poorer soils than wheat, and it has a shorter ripening period.

Seed was usually broadcast and then plowed or

raked into the soil, although occasionally plowing was done before sowing. A single wooden plow with a metal tip was normally used; it was pulled by a pair of oxen or donkeys. The animals were yoked together with either a single yoke or a double yoke with bars over and under the neck. An ox goad, a long staff with a nail or metal tip, was used to control the animals (Judg. 3:31).

Harvest was an important time, and workers were hired especially for the occasion. The standing grain was cut with a scythe or sickle, then brought in bundles to the threshing floor where it was threshed and separated from the chaff. Finally it was stored, either in earthenware jars or in underground silos. The prophet Isaiah referred to the various processes involved in growing grain, observing that it was an occasion for wonder and praise of God (Is. 28:23–29).

Vineyards were concentrated on the terraces of the Judean hills, although they were also found in the Carmel area and in parts of the region east of the Jordan River. Isaiah 5:1-7 gives some idea of the hard labor involved in preparing and cultivating vineyards. Vines were often left to trail on the ground. As the fruit began to ripen from July onwards, people built watchtowers, or temporary booths, to keep watch for both human and animal intruders. Harvesting the grapes and making wine were great social occasions. The Old Testament law allowed a person to eat grapes while collecting them, but not to put them in his own basket while in someone else's field (Deut. 23:24). The grapes were mainly used for wine, but some were dried as raisins.

Olive trees need little cultivation, as they can grow in shallow soils and survive long periods of drought. They were grown in the central uplands of Ephraim and Carmel and parts of Gilead. Olives were the last crop to be picked—as late as October and November—and they were used mainly for their oil.

In addition to the three main crops, a variety of fruit and vegetables was also grown in Bible times. The importance of vegetables is indicated by Ahab's desire to turn Naboth's vineyard into a vegetable garden. Melons, cucumbers, leeks, herbs, and spices were probably grown in the kitchen gardens of the nobility, while the poor had to be content with beans and lentils, which were often grown between the vines of other crops (2 Sam. 17:28).

Summer fruits were eagerly awaited in the heat as a tasty and refreshing supplement to the regular diet. Figs and pomegranates seem to have been particularly popular (Hos. 9:10; Hag. 2:19), and the prophet Amos was involved in the production of sycamore figs (Amos 7:14). Dates were cultivated in the Jericho region, and nuts such as almond and pistachio were also enjoyed (Gen. 43:11; Song 6:11).

Also see FOOD, HARVEST.

AGRIPPA I [a GRIP uh] — Roman ruler of Galilee and eventual ruler of the territory previously governed by his grandfather, Herod the Great. Agrippa persecuted the Christians in Jerusalem (Acts 12:1-23) during his reign in Judea from A.D. 41 until his death in A.D. 44. Also see HEROD.

AGRIPPA II [a GRIP uh] — son of Herod Agrippa I and great–grandson of Herod the Great. He was appointed by the Roman Emperor Claudius as ruler of Abilene, part of Galilee, Iturea, and Trachonitis. Shortly before the apostle Paul was taken prisoner to Rome, he appeared before Herod Agrippa II (Acts 25:13—26:32). Also see HEROD.

AGUE (see DISEASES OF THE BIBLE).

AGUR [A ghur] (*he who gathers*) — a son of Jakeh and one of the contributors to the book of Proverbs (Prov. 30:1). His celebrated prayer (Prov. 30:8-9) asks for deliverance from economic extremes.

AHAB [A hab] (*father is brother*) — the name of two men in the Old Testament:

1. The son of Omri and the seventh king of Israel (1 Kin. 16:30). Under the influence of Jezebel his wife, Ahab gave Baal equal place with God. Ahab also built a temple to Baal in which he erected a "wooden image" of the Canaanite goddess Asherah (1 Kin. 16:33). At Jezebel's urging, Ahab opposed the worship of Jehovah, destroyed His altars, and killed His prophets. He reigned over Israel in Samaria for 22 years (873–853 B.C.) (1 Kin. 16:29).

Ahab strengthened the friendly relations with Phoenicia that David had begun when he was king of the United Kingdom. He sealed the friendship between the two nations with a political marriage to Jezebel, the notoriously wicked daughter of Ethbaal, king of the Sidonians (1 Kin. 16:31). Ahab was the first king of Israel to establish peaceful relations with Judah.

False religion soon led to immoral civil acts. Because Jezebel had neither religious scruples nor regard for Hebrew civil laws (Lev. 25:23-34), she had Naboth tried unjustly and killed so that Ahab could take over his property (1 Kin. 21:1-16).

Throughout Ahab's reign, the prophet ELIJAH stood in open opposition to Ahab and the worship of Baal. Ahab also had frequent conflicts with Ben–Hadad, King of Syria, who once besieged Ahab's capital city, Samaria, but was driven off (1 Kin. 20:1-21).

Later, Ahab defeated Ben–Hadad in a battle at Aphek (1 Kin. 20:22-34); but Ahab was lenient with him, perhaps in view of a greater threat, Shalmaneser III of Assyria. In 853 B.C., Ahab and Ben–Hadad joined in a coalition to stop Shalmaneser's army at Qarqar on the Orontes River in Syria. Ahab contributed 2,000 chariots and 10,000 soldiers to this coalition. Still later, Ahab fought Ben–Hadad again. In spite of his precautions, Ahab was killed at Ramoth Gilead (1 Kin. 22:1-38).

Ahab was a capable leader and an avid builder. He completed and adorned the capital city of Samaria, which his father Omri had begun. Archaeological discoveries show that Ahab's "ivory house"

Photo by Howard Vos

Remains of a palace from Ahab's time, uncovered in an excavation at the site of ancient Samaria.

(1 Kin. 22:39; Amos 3:15) was faced with white stone, which gave it the appearance of ivory. It also was decorated with ivory inlays. The ivory fragments that have been found show similarities with Phoenician ivories of the period. These findings illustrate the close political and social ties that existed between Israel and Phoenicia. Archaeology has also shown that Ahab refortified the cities of Megiddo and Hazor, probably in defense against growing threats from Syria and Assyria.

Ahab's story is particularly sad because of his great potential. His tragedy was forming an alliance with Jezebel and turning from God to serve idols.

2. The son of Kolaiah and one of two false prophets denounced by Jeremiah (Jer. 29:21–23). Because Ahab prophesied falsely in God's name, Jeremiah declared that he would die at the hand of Nebuchadnezzar, king of Babylon, and would be cursed by all Babylonian captives from Judah.

AHARAH [a HAR uh] (perhaps *brother of Rah*) — Benjamin's third son (1 Chr. 8:1). He is also called Ehi (Gen. 46:21) and Ahiram (Num. 26:38).

AHARHEL [a HAR hell] (*brother of Rachel*) — a son of Harum and the founder of a family included in the tribe of Judah (1 Chr. 4:8).

AHASAI [a HAH sigh] — a form of AHZAI.

AHASBAI [a HAS bih] (*blooming*) — the father of one of David's mighty men (2 Sam. 23:34).

AHASUERUS [ah has you EH rus] (*mighty man*) — the name of two kings in the Old Testament:

1. A king of Persia and the husband of the Jewess ESTHER. Scholars generally agree that Ahasuerus is the same person as Xerxes I (485–464 B.C.).

The picture of Ahasuerus presented in the Book of Esther—the vastness of his empire (1:1), his riches (1:4), his sensuality and feasting (1:13–22), and his cruelty and lack of foresight (1:13–22)—is consistent with the description of Xerxes provided by the Greek historian Herodotus. Ahasuerus succeeded his father, Darius Hystaspis, in 485 B.C.

The Book of Esther tells the story of how Ahasuerus banished his queen, Vashti, because of her refusal to parade herself before the drunken merrymakers at one of his feasts. Following a two–year search for Vashti's replacement, Ahasuerus chose Esther as his queen. Esther and her people, the Jews, were in Persia as a consequence of the fall of Jerusalem (in 586 B.C.) and the scattering of the Jews into captivity in foreign lands.

Ahasuerus' advisor, Haman, hated the Jews; he prevailed upon Ahasuerus to order them to be wiped out—an order which the king gave with little concern for its consequences. During a sleepless night, Ahasuerus sent for his royal records and read of how the Jew Mordecai, Esther's guardian, had uncovered a plot to kill the king and thus had saved his life. Ahasuerus' discovery led to Mordecai's being raised to a position of honor in the kingdom. Haman's treachery soon led to his own fall, and he and his ten sons were hanged on the gallows he had previously prepared for Mordecai.

In 464 B.C. a courtier murdered Ahasuerus, and his son, Artaxerxes Longimanus, succeeded him. In Ezra 4:6, the reign of Ahasuerus is mentioned chronologically between Cyrus (v. 5) and Arta-xerxes (v. 7).

2. A king of the Medes and the father of Darius (Dan. 9:1).

AHAVA [a HAH vuh] *(stream)* — a town in Babylon situated near a small river or canal of the same name. Ezra and his companions camped for three days on the banks of this stream as they prepared for the long journey to Jerusalem (Ezra 8:15, 21, 31). The exact location of Ahava has not been identified.

AHAZ [A has] *(he has grasped)* — the name of two men in the Old Testament:

1. A son of Jotham and the 11th king of Judah (2 Kin. 15:38; 16:1–20). He was an ungodly king who promoted the worship of Molech, with its pagan rites of human sacrifice (2 Chr. 28:1–4).

The reign of Ahaz probably overlapped the reign of his father Jotham and possibly the reign of his own son Hezekiah. His age when he became king was 20 and he reigned for 16 years, beginning about 735 B.C.

Early in his reign Ahaz adopted policies that favored Assyria. When he refused to join the anti-Assyrian alliance of Pekah of Israel and Rezin of Syria, they invaded Judah and besieged Jerusalem, threatening to dethrone Ahaz and replace him with a puppet king (Is. 7:1–6). Pekah and Rezin killed 120,000 people and took 200,000 captives. However, through the intervention of Oded the prophet, the captives were released immediately (2 Chr. 28:5–15).

In view of his precarious circumstances, Ahaz requested help from Tiglath-Pileser III, king of Assyria, offering him silver and gold. At first the plan worked, and Assyria invaded Israel and Syria (2 Kin. 15:29). Ultimately, however, Assyria "distressed" Ahaz, demanding excessive tribute (2 Chr. 28:20–21).

Spiritually, Ahaz stopped following in the ways of the four relatively good kings who had preceded him (Joash, Amaziah, Azariah, and Jotham). He made images of Baal, offered infant sacrifices in the Valley of Hinnom, and sacrificed in the high places (2 Chr. 28:1–4). He came under further pagan influence at Damascus where he had gone to meet Tiglath-Pileser III. Seeing a pagan altar there, he commanded Uriah the priest at Jerusalem to build a copy of it. He then established it as the official place of the bronze altar.

It was to King Ahaz that Isaiah's evangelistic announcement of the promised Immanuel was made (Is. 7:10–17). The prophet Isaiah sent a message to the terrified Ahaz, but Ahaz would not turn to God and trust Him for deliverance. Instead, he plunged deeper into idolatry and self-destruction. Ahaz's conduct brought divine judgment to Judah in the form of military defeats. Edom revolted and took captives from Judah. The Philistines invaded Judah, capturing several cities. Rezin of Damascus seized control of Elath, Judah's port on the Gulf of Aqaba (2 Kin. 16:5–6).

At his death, Ahaz was buried without honor in Jerusalem. He was not deemed worthy of a burial in the royal tombs (2 Chr. 28:27). He is also called Achaz (Matt. 1:9, KJV).

2. A Benjamite and descendant of King Saul. Ahaz was a son of Micah and the father of Jehoaddah (1 Chr. 8:35–36; 9:42).

AHAZ, DIAL OF (see SUN DIAL OF AHAZ).

AHAZIAH [a huh ZIE uh] *(Jehovah sustains)* — the name of two kings in the Old Testament:

1. The son and successor of Ahab and the ninth king of Israel (1 Kin. 22:40, 49, 51). Ahaziah reigned from 853 to 852 B.C.

The son of JEZEBEL, Ahaziah followed policies which showed evidence of his mother's pagan influence. After reigning only two years, he "fell through the lattice of his upper room in Samaria" (2 Kin. 1:2) and was seriously injured. Sending his messengers to ask Baal-Zebub, the god of Ekron, about his recovery, Ahaziah was frustrated when the prophet Elijah interrupted their mission and prophesied Ahaziah's death. Enraged by Elijah's predictions, Ahaziah tried to seize him, but the men sent to capture the prophet were destroyed by fire from heaven and Elijah's prophecy was quickly fulfilled (2 Kin. 1:9–17).

At the time of Ahaziah's ascent to the throne, Mesha, the king of Moab, rebelled because of the tribute imposed on him by Omri, Ahaziah's grandfather (2 Kin. 1:1; 3:4–5). Ahaziah formed an alliance with Jehoshaphat, king of Judah, to build ships and trade with other nations. God judged this effort and it failed (1 Kin. 22:49).

2. The son and successor of Joram and the nephew of Ahaziah No. 1 (2 Kin. 8:24–26). Ahaziah is also called Jehoahaz (2 Chr. 21:17; 25:23) and Azariah (2 Chr. 22:6). The sixth king of Judah, Ahaziah reigned for only one year (841 B.C.).

Ahaziah became king at age 22 (2 Kin. 8:26; 2 Chr. 22:1). His wicked reign was heavily influenced by his mother Athaliah, who was the evil power behind his throne: "He walked in the way of the house of Ahab" (2 Kin. 8:27).

Ahaziah cultivated relations with Israel and joined with his uncle, King Jehoram (2 Kin. 1:17; 9:24; 2 Chr. 22:5–7) in a military expedition at Ramoth Gilead against Hazael, king of Syria. Jehoram was wounded and returned to Jezreel, near Mount Gilboa, to convalesce. While visiting his uncle Jehoram, Ahaziah was killed by Jehu, Israel's captain, who had been ordered by God to exterminate the house of Ahab (2 Kin. 9:4–10).

AHBAN [AH bun] *(brother of an intelligent one)* — a son of Abishur and Abihail, in the genealogy of Jerahmeel (1 Chr. 2:29).

AHER [A hehr] *(one that is behind)* — a descendant of Benjamin (1 Chr. 7:12). His name may be a contraction of Ahiram (Num. 26:38) or Aharah (1 Chr. 8:1).

AHI [A high] *(my brother)* — the name of two men in the Old Testament:

Hiram, king of Tyre (also known as Ahiram), seated on a throne, in this stone carving from his tomb.

1. A son of Abdiel, of the tribe of Gad (1 Chr. 5:15).

2. A son of Shemer, of the tribe of Asher (1 Chr. 7:34).

AHIAH [a HIGH uh] — a form of AHIJAH.

AHIAM [a HIGH um] (*uncle*) — one of David's mighty men, a son of Sharar (2 Sam. 23:33) the Hararite.

AHIAN [A HIGH un] (*little brother*) — a son of Shemida, of the tribe of Manasseh (1 Chr. 7:19).

AHIEZER [ah hih EE zur] (*brother of help*) — the name of two men in the Old Testament:

1. A son of Ammishaddai and head of the tribe of Dan at the time of Israel's wandering in the wilderness (Num. 1:12).

2. A chief of the tribe of Dan (1 Chr. 12:3).

AHIHUD [a HIGH hud] (*brother of honor*) — the name of two men in the Old Testament:

1. A prince from the tribe of Asher who helped divide the land of Canaan (Num. 34:27).

2. A son of Ehud, of the tribe of Benjamin (1 Chr. 8:7).

AHIJAH [a HIGH juh] (*my Brother is Jehovah*) — the name of nine men in the Old Testament:

1. The performer of high–priestly functions at Gibeah during part of Saul's reign (1 Sam. 14:3, 18). Many scholars identify him with Ahimelech, the priest at Nob who is also identified as a son of Ahitub (1 Sam. 22:9). Ahijah's name is usually spelled Ahiah, a variant of Ahijah.

2. A secretary or scribe in Solomon's reign and a son of Shisha (1 Kin. 4:3); also spelled Ahiah.

3. The prophet from Shiloh who prophesied Israel's division into two kingdoms because of its idolatries (1 Kin. 11:29–39). While Solomon was king, Jeroboam rebelled against him. Ahijah tore his own garment into 12 pieces and instructed Jeroboam to take ten of them. This symbolic action indicated that Jeroboam would be king over the ten tribes which would be known as the northern kingdom of Israel. Ahijah stood up for the people in the face of their oppression under Solomon and Rehoboam.

Later, King Jeroboam disguised his queen and sent her to the aging and nearly blind prophet to ask whether their sick child would recover. Ahijah prophesied that because of Jeroboam's wickedness the child would die (1 Kin. 14:1–18). His prophecies were also put into writing (2 Chr. 9:29).

4. The father of Baasha, who killed Jeroboam's son Nadab. He then reigned over Israel in his stead (1 Kin. 15:27).

5. A man of the tribe of Judah and a son of Jerahmeel (1 Chr. 2:25).

6. A Benjamite who helped carry off the inhabitants of Geba (1 Chr. 8:7).

7. One of David's mighty men (1 Chr. 11:36).

8. A Levite during David's reign (1 Chr. 26:20) who kept the Temple treasury.

9. One of the priests who, with Nehemiah, sealed the covenant (Neh. 10:26).

AHIKAM [a HIGH kumm] (*my brother has risen*) — a son of Shaphan and an officer in King Josiah's court. He was a member of the delegation sent by Josiah to the prophetess Huldah (2 Kin. 22:12–14). He helped protect the prophet Jeremiah from the persecutions of King Jehoiakim (Jer. 26:24).

AHILUD [a HIGH lud] (*a brother is born*) — the father of Jehoshaphat, "secretary of state" (NEB) or "recorder" for David and Solomon (2 Sam. 8:16).

AHIMAAZ [a HEM a az] (*powerful brother*) — the name of two or three men in the Old Testament:
1. The father of Saul's wife, Ahinoam (1 Sam. 14:50).
2. A son of Zadok the high priest. Ahimaaz kept David informed of Absalom's revolt after the king was forced to flee Jerusalem (2 Sam. 15:27). This "spy" system worked well at first, but it was later discovered, and Ahimaaz and Jonathan fled for their lives (2 Sam. 17:18).
3. Solomon's son-in-law and governor in Naphtali (1 Kin. 4:15). Ahimaaz married Basemath, the daughter of King Solomon. He may be the same person as Ahimaaz No. 2.

AHIMAN [a HIGH mun] (meaning unknown) — the name of two men in the Old Testament:
1. One of the three descendants of Anak, or Anakim (Num. 13:22; Judg. 1:10), a famous race of giants who lived at Hebron when the Hebrew spies surveyed the land.
2. A Levite gatekeeper in the Temple (1 Chr. 9:17).

AHIMELECH [a HEM eh leck] (*my brother is king*) — the name of two men in the Old Testament:
1. A high priest at Nob who helped David when he fled from King Saul (1 Sam. 22:18).
2. A Hittite who befriended David when he hid in the wilderness from King Saul (1 Sam. 26:6).

AHIMOTH [a HIGH moth] (*brother of death*) — a son of the Levite Elkanah (1 Chr. 6:25).

AHINADAB [a HEN uh dab] (*brother of liberality*) — a son of Iddo and one of Solomon's 12 supply officers (1 Kin. 4:14).

AHINOAM [a HEN oh am] (*my brother is joy*) — the name of two women in the Old Testament:
1. A daughter of Ahimaaz and a wife of King Saul (1 Sam. 14:49–50).
2. One of David's wives, the mother of Amnon (1 Sam. 25:43; 2 Sam. 3:2).

AHIO [a HIGH oh] (*his brother*) — the name of three men in the Old Testament:
1. Abinadab's son and Uzzah's brother (2 Sam. 6:3–4; 1 Chr. 13:7). When the ARK OF THE COVENANT was being transported to Jerusalem, Ahio and Uzzah drove the cart (2 Sam. 6:6–7).
2. A son of Elpaal the Benjamite (1 Chr. 8:14).
3. A son of Jeiel the Benjamite by his wife Maacah (1 Chr. 8:31; 9:37) and an ancestor of King Saul.

AHIRA [a HIGH ruh] (meaning unknown) — a son of Enan and leader of the tribe of Naphtali in

the wilderness. Ahiram was one of the heads of the 12 tribes who helped Moses take a census shortly after the Exodus (Num. 1:15; 10:27).

AHIRAM [a HIGH rum] (*my brother is exalted*) — the third son of Benjamin and the founder of a family called the AHIRAMITES (Num. 26:38). Ahiram was probably the same man as Aharah (1 Chr. 8:1), also called Ehi (Gen. 46:21) and Aher (1 Chr. 7:12).

AHIRAMITES [a HIGH rum ites] — descendants of AHIRAM.

AHISAMACH [a HIS ah mack] (*my brother sustains*) — a man of the tribe of Dan and a craftsman who worked on the tabernacle in the wilderness (Ex. 31:6).

AHISHAHAR [a HISH ah har] (*brother of the dawn*) — according to 1 Chronicles 7:10, a son of Bilhan, a grandson of Jediael, and a great-grandson of Benjamin.

AHISHAR [a HIGH shar] (*brother of song*) — an official or servant of King Solomon (1 Kin. 4:6).

AHITHOPHEL [a HITH oh fell] (*brother of folly*) — one of David's counselors who assisted Absalom in his revolt. When Absalom rebelled against David, Ahithophel apparently believed his own popularity would bring success to Absalom's revolt. Possibly sensing a chance to rise to power himself, Ahithophel advised Absalom to take David's harem (2 Sam. 15:12; 16:21)—an act equivalent to claiming the throne.

Ahithophel also advised Absalom to pursue David, who had fled Jerusalem. But Absalom chose to listen to Hushai, who advised the prince not to pursue his father. Sensing that Absalom's rebellion was doomed, Ahithophel put his household in order and hanged himself (2 Sam. 17:23)—one of the few cases of suicide in the Bible.

AHITUB [a HIGH tuhb] (*my brother is goodness*) — the name of three men in the Old Testament:
1. A son of Phinehas and grandson of Eli. Ahitub probably became high priest upon his grandfather's death (1 Sam. 4:11).
2. A son of Amariah and father of Zadok, who later was made high priest by King Saul after Ahimelech's death (2 Sam. 8:17; 1 Chr. 6:7–8, 52; 18:16; Ezra 7:2). The Ahitub of 1 Chronicles 6:8, 11–12 is probably the Azariah of 2 Chronicles 31:10.
3. The father of Meraioth and "officer over the house of God" (1 Chr. 9:11).

AHLAB [A lub] (*fertile, fruitful*) — a town of Asher. The Israelites failed to dislodge Asher's Canaanite inhabitants (Judg. 1:31). Its location is uncertain.

AHLAI [A lih] (meaning unknown) — the name of two people in the Old Testament:
1. One of several daughters of Sheshan (1 Chr. 2:31) and a descendant of Perez, Judah's older son by TAMAR (Matt. 1:3).

2. The father of one of David's mighty men (1 Chr. 11:41).

AHOAH [a HOE uh] (*Jehovah is brother*) — a son of Bela in the genealogy of Benjamin (1 Chr. 8:4). Ahoah is called Ahijah in 1 Chronicles 8:7.

AHOHI [a HOE high] — a form of AHOHITE.

AHOHITE [a HOE hite] (*belonging to Ahoah*) — a term for the descendants of Ahoah (1 Chr. 8:4). This tribe had a flair for military affairs (2 Sam. 23:9,28; 1 Chr. 11:12, 29). The RSV translates "son of Ahohi" (2 Sam. 23:9) instead of "the Ahohite."

AHOLAH [a HOE la] — a form of OHOLAH.

AHOLIAB [a HOE lih ab] (*tent of the father*) — a son of Ahisamach of the tribe of Dan. During the time of Moses, he was chosen to work with Bezaleel and other craftsmen in preparing the furniture of the tabernacle (Ex. 31:6; 35:34; 36:1-2; 38:23; Oholiab, RSV, NIV).

AHOLIBAH [a HOE lih bah]—a form of OHOLIBAH.

AHOLIBAMAH [a HOE lih BAH muh] (*tent of the high place*) — the name of one man and one woman in the Old Testament:

1. A wife of Esau (Gen. 36:5, 14). In Genesis 26:34 she is called "Judith the daughter of Beeri the Hittite."

2. The chief of an Edomite clan (Gen. 36:4l; 1 Chr. 1:52; Oholibamah, RSV, NIV).

AHUMAI [A HUE mih] (meaning unknown) — a son of Jahath and a descendant of Judah (1 Chr. 4:2).

AHUZAM [a HUE zem] — a form of AHUZZAM.

AHUZZAM [a HUZ um] (*possessing*) — a son of Ashhur and Naarah in the genealogy of Judah (1 Chr. 4:6; Ahuzam, KJV).

AHUZZATH [a HUZZ ath] (meaning unknown) — a friend of Abimelech who was "King of Gerar" (Gen. 20:2) or "King of the Philistines" (Gen. 26:1). Ahuzzath accompanied King Abimelech on a journey from Gerar to BEERSHEBA in an effort to make a covenant with Isaac (Gen. 26:26).

AHZAI [A zih] (*Jehovah has seized*) — a priest who lived in Jerusalem in Ezra's time (Neh. 11:13; Ahasai, KJV).

AI [A eye] (*the ruin*) — the name of two cities in the Old Testament:

1. A Canaanite city (see Map 3, B-4) of Palestine (Gen. 12:8; Josh. 10:1), east of Bethel (Gen. 12:8), "beside Beth Aven" (Josh. 7:2), and north of Michmash (Is. 10:28). Many years before Joshua's time, Abraham pitched his tent at Ai before journeying to Egypt (Gen. 12:8).

Ai figures prominently in the story of Israel's conquest of Palestine. After Joshua conquered Jericho, he sent men from Jericho to spy out Ai and the surrounding countryside. Because Ai was small, the spies assured Joshua that he could take Ai with only a handful of soldiers.

Joshua dispatched about 3,000 soldiers to attack Ai. This army was soundly defeated, due to Achan's sin of taking spoils from Jericho contrary to God's commandment. When God singled out Achan and his family, the people stoned them to death. Joshua then sent 30,000 soldiers against Ai and captured the city by a clever military tactic— an ambush (Joshua 7—8).

Although Ai has been identified with modern et-Tell, situated southeast of Bethel, recent archaeological discoveries conflict with this placement and make this identification uncertain. Ai is also called Aiath (Is. 10:28, KJV), Aija (Neh. 11:31, KJV), and Hai (Gen. 12:8, 13:3, KJV).

2. An Ammonite city in Moab (Jer. 49:3).

AIAH [a EYE ah] (*falcon*) — the father of Rizpah, a concubine of King Saul (2 Sam. 3:7). Two of his grandsons were hanged by King David to appease the Gibeonites (2 Sam. 21:8, 10–11).

AIATH [a EYE ath] — a form of AI.

AIJA [a EYE juh] — a form of AI.

AIJALON [A juh lon] (*place of deer*) — the name of two cities in Israel:

1. A city in the Shephelah, the lowlands west of Jerusalem (see Map 3, A-4). It was one of the CITIES OF REFUGE (Josh. 19:42; 1 Sam. 14:31). It belonged to the tribe of Dan and was assigned to the Kohathite Levites. The area surrounding Aijalon was the scene of the famous battle between Joshua and the five Amorite kings. This was the battle where Joshua made the sun stand still, while the Israelites destroyed their enemies (Josh. 10:12–14). After the ten tribes seceded to form the northern kingdom of Israel, Aijalon was fortified by Rehoboam (1 Chr. 8:13; 2 Chr. 11:10). In the days of King Ahaz, the city was captured by the Philistines (2 Chr. 28:18).

Aijalon is identified with Yalo, a village situated about 23 kilometers (14 miles) northwest of Jerusalem (Josh. 10:12; 19:42; 2 Chr. 28:18; Ajalon, KJV).

2. A site "in the country of Zebulun" where Elon the judge was buried (Judg. 12:12).

AIJELETH SHAHAR [A juh leth SHAY har] (*deer of the dawn*) — probably the name of a specific tune used with Psalm 22. The words appear as part of the title of this psalm in the KJV.

AIN (ane) (*fountain*) — the name of two cities in the Old Testament:

1. An unidentified place in northwest Canaan (Num. 34:11).

2. A city originally given to Judah but later transferred to Simeon. It was assigned to the Levites (Josh. 21:16). In three places in the Bible, Ain is mentioned with another city, Rimmon (Josh. 15:32; 19:7; 1 Chr. 4:32), and perhaps should be read as Ain-Rimmon. It occurs as Rimmon in Nehemiah 11:19.

AIR — the atmosphere or the region through which the birds fly. "Speaking into the air" (1 Cor. 14:9) means to waste one's breath, to speak in a way that cannot be understand.

The apostle Paul used this word of the region where man exists. "The prince of the power of the air" (Eph. 2:2), the devil or Satan, is busy at work in the same region. At the coming of the Lord, however, believers will rise to meet Christ in the air (1 Thess. 4:17), which the devil has unlawfully claimed as his own.

AJAH [A yah] (*hawk*) — a son of Zibeon (Gen. 36:24; 1 Chr. 1:40).

AJALON [AJ uh lun] — a form of AIJALON.

AKAN [A ken] (*twisted*) — a son of Ezer and grandson of Seir the Horite (Gen. 36:27). Akan is also called JAAKAN (1 Chr. 1:42).

AKELDAMA [ah kell DA mah] (*field of blood*) — a field located outside the walls of Jerusalem. According to Matthew, this field was purchased by the chief priests with the 30 pieces of silver which they paid to Judas for betraying Jesus. Remorseful at having betrayed innocent blood, Judas flung the 30 pieces of silver on the floor of the Temple and went out and hanged himself. The priests would not put the coins in the Temple treasury, for they were tainted with "the price of blood." So they took the money and bought the potter's field, in which to bury strangers (Matt. 27:3–10).

According to Luke, however, the field was purchased by Judas himself with the 30 pieces of silver. Apparently it was this field that became known as "Akel Dama, or Field of Blood" (Acts 1:18–19; Aceldama, KJV)—the place where Judas died. Apparently, Judas did not personally buy the field; he "bought" it only in the sense that his own money, thrown down on the Temple floor, was used by the chief priests to purchase the field.

A tradition from the fourth century places this plot of ground on the Hill of Evil Counsel, a level plot overlooking the Valley of Hinnom.

AKKAD [ACK kad] — a form of ACCAD.

AKKUB [ACK kub] (meaning unknown) — the name of four men in the Old Testament:

1. A son of Elioenai, a descendant of Zerubbabel and of King David (1 Chr. 3:24).

2. The head of a family of Levite gatekeepers in the Temple after the Captivity (Ezra 2:42; Neh. 7:45).

3. The head of a family of Temple servants (NETHINIM) who returned to Jerusalem after the Captivity (Ezra 2:45).

4. A Levite who helped Ezra read and interpret the law (Neh. 8:7).

AKRABBIM, ASCENT OF [ack RAB im] (*scorpions*) — an ascending slope and mountain pass located on the southeast border of Judah near the Dead Sea and the Wilderness of Zin (Num. 34:4). As its name implies, this area abounded in scorpi-

Photo by Howard Vos

The Valley of Hinnom near Jerusalem, with the traditional site of Akeldama in the fenced area (Matt. 27:3-10).

ons. Its Greek name was *Akrabattene*.

ALABASTER (see MINERALS OF THE BIBLE).

ALAMETH [AL ah meth] — a form of ALEMETH.

ALAMMELECH [al LAM eh leck] (*oak of a king*) — a town of the tribe of Asher (Josh. 19:26), location unknown.

ALAMOTH [AL ah mohth] (probably *soprano*) — a musical term of uncertain meaning. (1 Chr. 15:20; Ps. 46 title). It may have meant to sing in a high-pitched, or soprano, voice.

ALARM — a warning signal, usually sounded among the Israelites by the blowing of two silver trumpets. The trumpets were sounded when the people were to assemble, disperse, march into battle, or gather for feasts and festivals (Num. 10:1–10; Jer. 4:19).

ALEMETH [AL eh meth] (*hiding place*) — the name of one town and two men:

1. A priestly town of the tribe of Benjamin near Geba and Anathoth (1 Chr. 6:60). It is also called ALMON (Josh. 21:18).

2. A son of Becher and the grandson of Benjamin (1 Chr. 7:8; Alameth, KJV).

3. A son of Jehoaddah (1 Chr. 8:36). Alemeth also was a descendant of Jonathan and King Saul.

ALEPH [AH lef] — the first letter of the Hebrew alphabet, used as a heading over Psalm 119:1-8. In the original Hebrew language, each line of these eight verses began with the letter aleph. Also see ACROSTIC.

ALEXANDER [EH leg zan dur] (*defender of men*) — the name of five or six men in the Bible:

1. Alexander III (the Great), son of Philip II (King of Macedon) and founder of the Hellenistic (Greek) Empire. He was born in 356 B.C. and ascended the Macedonian throne in 336 B.C. Advised by his teacher Aristotle that he could rule the world if he could make people adopt the Greek culture, Alexander extended his empire east from Greece, around the Mediterranean Sea to Egypt, and then to the borders of India. He died in Babylon in 323 B.C. at the age of 33. Because he did not leave an heir who could continue his reign, Alexander's three generals divided his kingdom, with Ptolemy taking Egypt, Seleucus the East, and Cassander Macedonia.

Although Alexander the Great is not mentioned directly in the Old or New Testament, many scholars think that "the large horn that is between [the] eyes...of the male goat" (Dan. 8:21) and the "mighty king" in the vision of Daniel 11:3-4 may refer to him.

Alexander encouraged the Jews to settle in Alexandria, the city he founded after conquering Egypt. It was at Alexandria that a Greek translation of the Old Testament, known as the SEPTUAGINT, was developed.

2. A son of Simon, a Cyrenian who carried the cross for Jesus (Mark 15:21), and a brother of Rufus.

3. A member of the family of Annas, the Jewish high priest (Acts 4:6). Both Annas and Alexander were in Jerusalem during the trial of Peter and John.

4. A Jew who lived at Ephesus during the riot started by Demetrius and the silversmiths who opposed Paul's preaching (Acts 19:21-41). The Jews sought to use Alexander to convince the Ephesians that they had nothing to do with Paul and the Christians (Acts 19:33).

5. One of two heretical teachers at Ephesus mentioned by the apostle Paul. With Hymenaeus, he is said to have "suffered shipwreck" of the faith. He was "delivered to Satan" (1 Tim. 1:19-20) by Paul. Perhaps this was some form of excommunication from the church.

6. The coppersmith who did Paul "much harm" (2 Tim. 4:14). Some scholars identify him with Alexander No. 4 and suggest that he may have been a silversmith engaged in activity that was unlawful for a Jew. Other scholars suggest he might be Alexander No. 5 — one who was associated with Christianity and then became hostile to Paul and the church after being "delivered to Satan."

ALEXANDRIA [eh leg ZAN drih uh] — the capital of Egypt during the Greek and Roman periods. Situated on the Mediterranean Sea at the western edge of the Nile delta, the city was established by Alexander the Great when he conquered Egypt in 331 B.C. After Alexander's death, the capital of Egypt was moved from Memphis to Alexandria; and it became one of the most significant cities of the Greek Empire. The population of Alexandria included native Egyptians, learned Greeks, and many Jews. The commercial strength of the city was aided by the famous towering lighthouse that guided ships into port. Paul himself sailed in an Alexandrian ship on his way to Rome (Acts 27:6; 28:11).

As a cultural center, Alexandria had a large museum and a library that attracted many scholars and writers. These learned people carried out research to establish accurate versions of the important Greek myths and epics as well as scientific investigations in astronomy, botany, and mathematics. One of the results of these interests was the commissioning of 70 Jewish scholars to translate the Old Testament from Hebrew to Greek. The translation which they produced is known as the SEPTUAGINT.

Philo and other learned Jews in Alexandria wrote many books in defense of the Jewish faith to show that their beliefs were consistent with Greek philosophical thinking. This sometimes resulted in unusual methods of interpretation because the literal understanding of Scripture often was mixed with fanciful explanations — a type of interpretation known as ALLEGORY. A Christian school of thought that used the allegorical method grew up in Alexandria, led by such great church fathers as Clement and Origen.

Bust of Alexander the Great, Greek military conqueror.
Photo by Howard Vos

Aerial photograph of the coastal site of Alexandria, Egypt. The location of the ancient city is shown within the white lines.

Apollos, a believer from Alexandria, who worked with the church at Corinth after it was founded by the apostle Paul, may have attended one of these early schools. The Book of Acts describes Apollos as one who was well versed in the Scripture (Acts 18:24). Because the Book of Hebrews reflects thinking that is similar to writings from Alexandria, some scholars believe Apollos may have written the book.

The early church father Eusebius recorded the tradition that John Mark was one of the first missionaries who brought the message of Christ to the people of Alexandria. Years earlier, prominent Jews from Alexandria who gathered in Jerusalem strongly opposed Stephen's preaching about Christ (Acts 6:9).

ALEXANDRIANS [eh leg ZAN drih un] — residents of the city of ALEXANDRIA (in Egypt). Certain Alexandrians at Jerusalem, who belonged to the "Synagogue of the Freedmen" (Acts 6:9) disputed with Stephen and stirred up opposition to him.

ALGUM (see PLANTS OF THE BIBLE).

ALIAH [a LIE ah] — a form of ALVAH.

ALIAN [AL ih un] — a form of ALVAN.

ALIEN — a foreigner, sojourner, or stranger from a country other than Israel. Aliens did not enjoy the rights of the citizens of Israel (Deut. 14:21; Job 19:15; Ps. 69:8). To the Jews an alien was a Gentile or non-Israelite. Also see FOREIGNER.

ALLEGORY — a symbolic representation of a truth about human conduct or experience. The word allegory is found only once in the King James Version. In Galatians 4:24 it translates the Greek verb *allegoreo*, which means to say something different from what the words normally imply. The NKJV translates it by the word symbolic.

As a literary device, an allegory may consist of only a few lines or it may be sustained through an entire book. According to traditional Jewish and Christian interpretation, the entire book of the Song of Solomon is an allegory: of God and his wife, Israel (Jewish) or of Christ and his bride, the church (Christian). Other examples of allegory in the Old Testament are Psalm 80:8–19 and Ecclesiastes 12:3–7. In Psalm 80 the pronouns we and us identify the vine as Israel (vv. 18–19).

In the New Testament, Jesus' parable of the wheat and the tares (Matt. 13:24–30, 36–43) is a good example of allegory. The apostle Paul also used allegories when writing. In Ephesians 6:11–17 he urges his readers to "put on the whole armor of God" and then gives the symbolic spiritual designation for each article worn by the Christian soldier. And in 1 Corinthians 10:1–4, Paul gives an allegory which compares the experience of Moses and the Israelites to Christian baptism and the Lord's Supper.

Perhaps the most memorable of Paul's allegories, however, is found in Galatians 4:21–31: Hagar and Sarah, Ishmael and Isaac. One of them (Ishmael) was born to the bondwoman Hagar; the other (Isaac) was born to a freewoman, Sarah. Hagar and Ishmael are symbolic of the Old Covenant: the law from Mount Sinai that brings all flesh into bondage. Sarah and Isaac are symbolic of the New Covenant: the gospel of grace from Mount Calvary that gives spiritual freedom. When Paul concluded by saying, "So then, brethren, we are not children of the bondwoman but of the free [woman]," he was urging his readers to reject the bondage of legalism—salvation by keeping the law—and to live by faith in Christ.

ALLELUIA [al e LOO yuh] (*praise the Lord*) — a Greek form of the Hebrew word *Hallelujah*, used to express joy, praise, and thanksgiving.

The words, "Praise the Lord," found often in the Psalms, are a translation of the Hebrew *Hallelujah* (Ps. 104:35; 116:19; 147:1). The word was probably a standardized call to worship in the Temple, since it usually appears at the beginning or end of a psalm.

ALLIANCE — an agreement or treaty among two or more nations for the purpose of providing mutual trading privileges or military protection. Alliances between the PATRIARCHS and foreigners were common—for example, Abraham with Abimelech of Gerar (Gen. 21:22–34) and Jacob with Laban (Gen. 31:43–55). At Sinai Israel was forbidden to make alliances with the Canaanites (Ex. 23:32). This was to keep Israel's loyalties from being divided between God and pagan powers.

During the conquest of the land of Canaan, the Israelites were tricked into an alliance with the Gibeonites (Joshua 9). Later, during the period of the judges, the individual Hebrew tribes apparently made alliances with one another for their common defense (Judg. 4:10; 6:35).

King David entered into several foreign treaties— for example, with Achish of Gath (1 Sam. 27:1–12) and Hiram of Tyre (1 Kin. 5:1–12). Solomon's many marriages probably included alliances with other nations (1 Kin. 3:1; 9:16; 11:1–3). Other Hebrew kings formed many alliances, such as Asa with Ben–Hadad of Syria (1 Kin. 15:18–20; 2 Chr. 16:1–6). Judah's attempts to make alliances with Egypt were responsible for the attacks of Nebuchadnezzar of Babylon on Jerusalem in 597 B.C. and 587 B.C. (2 Kin. 24:1, 20; also Ezek. 17:12–21).

The prophets warned the nation of Israel against forming alliances that sought to replace dependence on God with reliance on a foreign power (Jer. 2:18, 36; Ezek. 23:11–21).

ALLON [AL lun] (*oak* or *terebinth*) — a son of Jedaiah and the father of Shiphi, of the tribe of Simeon (1 Chr. 4:37). The word is also found in Joshua 19:33 (KJV), as a town of Naphtali, but the NKJV translates "the terebinth tree"; the RSV has "the oak"; and the NIV has "the large tree."

ALLON BACHUTH [AL lun BACK uth] (*oak of weeping*) — a place "below Bethel", the name of the burial place of Deborah, the nurse of Rebekah (Isaac's wife).

ALLOTMENT — in the Old Testament a system of land tenure used in Israel to distribute the land to the tribes, clans and families. Joshua 13—19 describes the division of the land on both sides of the Jordan River among the tribes of Israel, with each tribe except the Levites receiving a specific territory.

How the allotment was determined is not explained, but many scholars believe the 'lot' involved the use of the URIM AND THUMMIM (Ex. 28:30; Lev. 8:8; Deut. 33:8; Ezra 2:63; Neh. 7:65), which were two stones kept in the breastplate (or pouch) on the high priest's ephod and used in determining God's will.

Over a period of time, a reallotment, or redistribution of the land was necessary. This explains the provision for a "Year of Jubilee" (Lev. 25:8–55; 27:17–24; Num. 36:4). Every 50th year, the allotments were to be restored to their original owners— a practice which helped prevent drastic inequalities of wealth and poverty.

Because the Lord himself was the "lot" (allotment, portion, or inheritance) of the Levites (or priests), the tribe of Levi received no allotment of land (Num. 18:20; Deut. 10:9; Josh. 13:14). They were allowed, however, to live among all the tribes.

ALMIGHTY (see GOD, NAMES OF).

ALMODAD [al MOE dad] (*God is a friend*) — a son of Joktan (1 Chr. 1:19–23).

ALMON [AL mon] (*hiding place*) — a priestly town in the tribe of Benjamin (Josh 21:18), also called Alemeth (1 Chr. 6:60). It probably is to be identified with Khirbet Almit, a mound northeast of Jerusalem.

ALMON DIBLATHAIM [AL mon dibb lah THAY em] (meaning unknown) — a stopping place during the wilderness journey of the Israelites (situated in Moab), between Dibon Gad and the mountains of Abarim. (Num. 33:46–47). It may be the same place as Beth Diblathaim.

ALMOND, ALMUG, ALOES (see PLANTS OF THE BIBLE).

ALMS — money given out of mercy for the poor. The Israelite was commanded to be generous in opening his hand wide to the poor and needy (Deut. 15:11). Gleanings from vineyards, orchards, olive groves, and fields should be made available to the poor (Lev. 19:9–10; Ruth 2:2, 7–8). Blessings were promised to those who were generous in aiding the poor (Prov. 14:21; 19:17). Eventually, the notion developed that almsgiving had power to atone for the giver's sins.

By Jesus' time, the word righteousness was tied closely to the word alms. Thus, when Jesus taught about "charitable deeds" (or almsgiving; Matt. 6:2–4), prayer (Matt. 6:5–15), and fasting (Matt. 6:16–18), he prefaced his teachings by saying, "Beware of practicing your piety [literally, righteousness] before men in order to be seen by them" (Matt. 6:1). In this way he taught that the giving of alms to the poor must not become a theatrical display to win people's applause; the praise that comes from God is more important.

The Book of Acts comments favorably on several instances of almsgiving. A certain disciple at Joppa—a woman named Tabitha, or Dorcas—was full of good works and charitable deeds (Acts 9:36). A God-fearing man named Cornelius "gave alms generously to the people, and prayed to God always" (Acts 10:2). Then, as now, God acknowledges those who give gifts of bread to the hungry and in other ways show compassion to the needy (Is. 58:6–8; 1 John 3:17).

ALOTH [A lohth] (*ascents*) — a place in Northern Palestine put under the charge of Baanah, one of Solomon's officials (1 Kin. 4:16). Aloth is possibly the same place as BEALOTH (Josh. 15:24).

ALPHA AND OMEGA [AL fuh, oh MAY guh] — the first and last letters of the Greek alphabet. This title is given to God the Father and God the Son (Rev. 1:8, 21:6). The risen Christ says, "I am the Alpha and the Omega, the Beginning and the End, the First and the Last" (Rev. 22:13). By calling Jesus Christ the Alpha and the Omega, the writer of the book of Revelation acknowledged that He is both the Creator and the Redeemer and the Final Judge of all things.

ALPHABET (see WRITING).

ALPHAEUS [al FEE us] (*leader* or *chief*) — the name of two men in the New Testament:
1. The father of James the Less, the apostle and writer of the epistle which bears his name (Matt. 10:3; Acts 1:13).
2. The father of Levi (or Matthew), the apostle and writer of the first gospel (Mark 2:14).

ALTAR — a table, platform, or elevated place on which a priest placed a sacrifice as an offering to God. The nature of altars changed considerably during the several centuries from Old Testament times to New Testament days. In addition to describing altars dedicated to God, the Bible speaks frequently also of pagan altars, particularly those associated with the false worship of the Canaanites.

Altars in the Old Testament. The first altar in the Bible was the one built by Noah after the Flood (Gen. 8:20). The next several altars mentioned appear in connection with the patriarch Abraham and his wanderings. His first altar, at Shechem, seemed to serve as a symbol of his possession of the land (Gen. 12:7). At his altars between Bethel and Ai (Gen. 12:8) and at Hebron (Gen. 13:18), he sacrificed animals and called upon the name of the Lord. Abraham built his last altar on top of a mountain in the land of Moriah (Gen. 22:9). To these altars, his son Isaac added one at Beersheba (Gen. 26:25). Isaac's son Jacob built no new altars; but he restored those which Abraham had built at Shechem (Gen. 33:20) and Bethel (Gen. 35:1, 3).

The Hebrew word for altar means "a place of slaughter or sacrifice." But the altars of the Old Testament were not restricted to offerings of animals as sacrifices. Joshua 22:26–29 indicates that altars were occasionally used to remind the Israelites of their heritage or to call attention to a major event. Sometimes an altar might even be used as a place for refuge (1 Kin. 1:50–51; 2:28).

During the days of Moses, two priestly altars assumed important roles in the ritual of the TABERNACLE in the wilderness. These were the altar of burnt offering and the altar of incense.

The altar of burnt offering (Ex. 27:1–8) was placed in front of the entrance to the tabernacle (Ex. 40:6), where it was used for the daily burnt offering and meal offering. This altar declared that entry into the presence of God must be preceded by sacrificial ATONEMENT for sin. The altar of burnt

Excavations at ancient Megiddo, showing the oval altar used for pagan sacrifices in the foreground.
Photo by Gustav Jeeninga

offering was made of acacia wood, overlaid with bronze. The corners of the altar extended at the top into projections that looked like horns.

The altar of incense (Ex. 30:1-10) stood just before the veil inside the tabernacle that separated the most holy place from the rest of the worship area (Ex. 40:26-27). Priests burned incense on this altar every day so its fragrance would fill the tabernacle when the sacrificial blood was sprinkled on the altar of burnt offering.

As the first king of Israel, Saul built an altar during his conquest of the Philistines for the sacrifice of sheep, oxen, and calves (1 Sam. 14:35). Later David erected an altar on a threshing floor of natural stone that he bought from Araunah the Jebusite (2 Sam. 24:15-25). This site became the central place of sacrifice in the TEMPLE after it was constructed by Solomon, David's son and successor. Some have identified this site with the large rock structure in the city of Jerusalem now seen under the famous mosque known as the Dome of the Rock.

After building the Temple in Jerusalem, Solomon constructed an altar (2 Chr. 4:1) larger than the one Moses had built, probably adapting it to the size of the Temple. This was the altar restored later by King Asa (2 Chr. 15:8). Still later, King Ahaz had Solomon's altar moved to the northern part of the Temple courtyard (2 Kin. 16:14-15). This was also the same altar cleansed by Hezekiah (2 Chr. 29:18) and rebuilt by Manasseh (2 Chr. 33:16) at later times in Old Testament history.

The incense altar of the tabernacle was also replaced by Solomon's altar made of cedar and overlaid with gold (1 Kin. 6:20, 22; 7:48). Incense was burned every morning and evening on this altar. The priest also sprinkled the blood of a sacrificial animal on the incense altar to make atonement for his sins and the sins of the people. The incense altar was also symbolic of prayer. It is the only altar that appears in the heavenly temple (Is. 6:6; Rev. 8:3).

When the captives returned to Jerusalem following their years of captivity in Babylon, one of their first acts was to build an altar (Ezra 3:3).

Altars in the New Testament. In addition to the Temple of the Jewish people with its altars, the New Testament refers to the altar in Athens that was dedicated "TO THE UNKNOWN GOD" (Acts 17:23). No physical Christian altar appears in the New Testament. The statement "we have an altar" (Heb. 13:10) refers to the sacrifice of Christ. The altar of incense mentioned in Revelation 8:3 belongs to the heavenly temple. In this heavenly temple there is no need for an altar of burnt offering since atonement for our sins is now complete through the death of Jesus Christ.

Canaanite Altars. Archaeology has turned up many Canaanite altars from all periods of Old Testament history. A kind of table or altar built into the rear wall of a temple in ancient Megiddo has been dated at about 3000 B.C. Also uncovered at Megiddo was a large stone altar from about that same period.

Canaanite altars were constructed of earth, stone, or metal. Stone altars have been preserved in Israel. Their form ranges from unworked, detached rocks to carefully cut natural stone. Altars of earth are mentioned in the ancient records, but none have been preserved, with the possible exception of an Israelite altar at Arad. These were the simplest altars, probably built by the common people.

References to altars dedicated to pagan gods other than the one true God appear throughout the Old Testament. They were devoted to the Baals (2 Chr. 33:3) and various other Canaanite gods and goddesses (Deut. 12:3)—Chemosh the god of Moab, Ashtoreth of the Sidonians, and Molech of the Ammonites (1 Kin. 11:5-7). The Lord gave specific instructions that these pagan altars should be torn down and destroyed before altars dedicated to His worship were built (Deut. 12:2-3).

AL TASHCHETH [al TAS keth] (meaning unknown) — a word or phrase found in the titles of Psalms 57, 58, 59, and 75. Its meaning is uncertain.

ALUSH [A luhsh] (*wild place*) — a desert camp of the Israelites (Num. 33:13-14).

ALVAH (AL vuh) (*sublimity*) — a chief of Edom descended from Esau (Gen 36:40), also spelled Aliah (1 Chr. 1:51).

ALVAN [AL vann] (*sublime*) — the oldest son of Shobal and a descendant of Seir the Horite (Gen. 36:23). His name is also spelled Alian (1 Chr. 1:40).

AMAD [A madd] (*a station*) — a town in Northern Palestine, assigned to the tribe of Asher (Josh. 19:26).

AMAL [A mal] (*sorrow*) — a son of Helem in the genealogy of Asher (1 Chr. 7:35).

AMALEK [AM uh leck] (*warlike*) — a grandson of Esau and son of Eliphaz by Timnah, his concubine (Gen. 36:12; 1 Chr. 1:36). A chieftain of an Edomite tribe (Gen. 36:16), Amalek gave his name to the AMALEKITES.

AMALEKITES [AM uh leck ites] — an ancient wandering tribe descended from Esau's grandson Amalek (Gen. 36:12, 16; 1 Chr. 1:36). The main territory of the Amalekites was in the Sinai peninsula and in the Negev, the southern part of present-day Israel. But they roamed widely throughout the territory later settled by the people of Israel. Throughout the Old Testament the Amalekites were bitter foes of the Israelites.

The Amalekites are first mentioned in the time of Abraham, when a group of kings under the leadership of CHEDORLAOMER defeated Amalek (Gen. 14:7). At the time of Israel's journey through the wilderness, the Amalekites lived in the southern part of the land promised to Israel. The Amalekites attacked the Israelites, but Joshua later defeated them in a battle at Rephidim (Ex. 17:8-16). Because of their treacherous attacks, Moses declared that God would continually wage war against them (Ex. 17:14-16).

During the period of the judges, the Amalekites joined forces with the Ammonites and Eglon, king of Moab, to attack and capture Jericho, the city of palms (Judg. 3:13). Along with the Midianites and the people of the East, they were defeated in the Valley of Jezreel by Gideon's army (Judg. 6:3, 33; 7:12–22).

Eventually the Amalekites gained a mountain in the land of Ephraim. King Saul of Israel won this area back and then chased the Amalekites from the land (1 Sam. 14:48; 15:1–9). But Saul did not destroy the rich booty of livestock as God commanded and was rebuked by the prophet Samuel (1 Sam. 15:10–33).

The Amalekites continued to raid Israel. David attacked and defeated them (1 Sam. 27:8–10), but they countered by raiding Ziklag and carrying off two of David's wives. He pursued and defeated them (1 Sam. 30:1–31), executing one of them for killing Saul in an earlier battle (2 Sam. 1:1–16).

In the days of Hezekiah, 500 men of the tribe of Simeon defeated the Amalekites. Consequently, the Simeonites took their land and the Amalekites became a dispossessed people (1 Chr. 4:39–43).

AMAM [A mam] (*gathering place*) — an unidentified town in Southern Palestine assigned to Judah in the ALLOTMENT of the land (Josh. 15:26).

AMANA [a MAH nuh] (*constant*) — a mountain mentioned in the Song of Solomon (4:8), along with Lebanon, Senir, and Hermon. It may refer to Mount Amanus, part of the Anti-Lebanon range.

AMARANTH [am uh RANTH] (see PLANTS OF THE BIBLE).

AMARIAH [am ah RYE uh] (*Jehovah has said*) — the name of nine Old Testament men:

1. A son of the priest Meraioth, who was descended from Phinehas, a grandson of Aaron (1 Chr. 6:7, 52; Ezra 7:3).

2. A son of Azariah, who was a high priest during Solomon's reign (1 Chr. 6:11).

3. A Levite descended from Kohath (1 Chr. 23:19; 24:23).

4. A chief priest during Jehoshaphat's reign (2 Chr. 19:11).

5. A priest appointed by King Hezekiah to help distribute "the freewill offerings to God" (2 Chr. 31:14–15).

6. A man of the family of Bani who divorced his foreign wife after the Captivity (Ezra 10:42).

7. One of the priests who, along with Nehemiah, sealed the covenant (Neh. 10:3).

8. A descendant of Judah through Perez (Neh. 11:4).

9. An ancestor of the prophet Zephaniah, who lived during King Josiah's reign. (Zeph. 1:1).

AMARNA, TELL EL [a MAR nuh] — the modern name of the site of Akhenaten, capital of Egypt during the reign of Amunhotep IV (about 1375–1358 B.C.), and the site of an important archaeological find.

Amunhotep IV, who changed his name to Akhenaten, rejected the predominant gods of Egypt that were worshiped at Thebes in order to further the worship of Aten, the sun god. In the process of rejecting the old religion and setting up worship of Aten, Akhenaten almost created a monotheistic (one-god) religion. After Akhenaten died, his capital at Tell el-Amarna was destroyed and the worship of Aten was rejected for the more traditional gods at Thebes.

In 1887 a peasant woman discovered some tablets in the ruins of this ancient capital. Archaeologists carefully examined the area and found fragments of about 350 documents in a wedge-shaped CUNEIFORM script that was popular in ancient Mesopotamia. Many of these clay tablets were written on both sides with messages from various small city–state kings in Palestine. Others contained treaties between countries, such as Egypt and the Hittites.

The tablets from Palestine describe the internal strife in Palestine and the weakened Egyptian control over the country shortly after the period when the Israelites invaded the land under Joshua. The king of Byblos wrote almost 60 letters protesting the lack of military support given to him by the Egyptian king. Letters from the kings of Shechem, Megiddo, Hebron, Tyre, Hazor, and even Jerusalem were found in these royal archives. They provide firsthand geographical and historical information about political events and important people during this period.

The advanced state of writing, references to irrigation, olives, corn, ships, chariots, silver, gold, and copper, and even the price of a bride have provided many new insights into the culture of Palestine. They show clearly that Palestine was far from being an uncultured land. The language of the tablets themselves is primarily the Babylonian language, but various Canaanite words and grammatical forms appear. These give a firsthand knowledge of the language spoken by the Canaanites.

Tell el-Amarna is situated about 320 kilometers (200 miles) south of Cairo on the east bank of the Nile River.

AMASA [AM ah sah] (*burden-bearer*) — the name of two men in the Old Testament:

1. David's nephew, the son of Jether and Abigail (1 Chr. 2:17). Amasa was also the cousin of Joab, a captain in David's army (2 Sam. 17:25). When Absalom rebelled against his father David, he appointed Amasa commander of the rebel army. After Absalom was defeated and killed by Joab (2 Sam. 18:14), David forgave Amasa and appointed him commander of the royal army in place of Joab (2 Sam. 19:13).

2. A leader of the Ephraimites and a son of Hadlai (2 Chr. 28:12). Amasa followed the lead of the prophet Oded. He advised that the prisoners from Judah (captured by King Pekah of Israel in his campaign against King Ahaz of Judah) be fed, clothed,

and transported back to their homes in Jericho.

AMASAI [a MASS a eye] (*Jehovah has borne*) — the name of three men in the Old Testament:

1. A son of Elkanah and a descendant of Kohath (1 Chr. 6:25, 2 Chr. 29:12).

2. A chieftain who joined David at Ziklag. Amasai became one of David's captains (1 Chr. 12:18).

3. A Levite who helped move the ARK OF THE COVENANT to Jerusalem (1 Chr. 15:24).

AMASHAI [a MASH eye] (*carrying spoil*) — a priest who lived in Jerusalem in the time of Nehemiah (Neh. 11:13; Amashsai, RSV).

AMASHSAI [a MASH sigh] — a form of AMASHAI.

AMASIAH [am ah SIGH ah] (*burden of Jehovah*) — a son of Zichri and a commander in the army of King Jehoshaphat of Judah (2 Chr.17:16).

AMAU [A moe] (meaning unknown) — the land from which Balak, king of Moab, summoned Balaam the soothsayer (Num. 22:5; Amaw, RSV).

AMAW [A moe] — a form of AMAU.

AMAZIAH [am ah ZIE uh] (*Jehovah is mighty*) — the name of four men in the Old Testament:

1. The son of King Joash (2 Kin. 14:1–20; 2 Chr. 25:1). Amaziah was 25 years old when he began his reign as the ninth king of Judah. He followed in the steps of his father, doing "what was right in the sight of the Lord" (2 Kin. 14:3). However, he permitted the high places of false worship to stand (2 Kin. 14:4). After becoming king, Amaziah built up an army in Judah, adding to these ranks 100,000 mercenaries, or paid troops, from Israel to war against Edom (2 Chr. 25:6). Warned by a "man of God" that if he used the mercenaries he was inviting certain defeat (2 Chr. 25:7), he sent them home. He incurred their wrath for this action (2 Chr. 25:10).

Following a stunning victory over the Edomites, Amaziah embraced the gods of Edom (2 Chr. 25:14). The folly of his action was exposed by the ironic question of a godly priest, "Why have you sought the gods of the people, which could not rescue their own people from your hand?" (2 Chr. 25:15). Meanwhile the mercenaries he had dismissed attacked several towns in Judah, killing 3,000 and taking much spoil (2 Chr. 25:13).

Apparently filled with pride over his victory, Amaziah challenged the king of Israel, Joash (or Jehoash) to war and suffered defeat at Beth Shemesh. The Bible notes that this was God's punishment for Amaziah's sin of idolatry (2 Chr. 25:20). King Joash destroyed a large section of the wall of Jerusalem, and claimed spoil from the Temple and the king's treasury. He also took hostages back to Samaria, possibly even King Amaziah (2 Chr. 25:23–24). Amaziah outlived Joash by 15 years. Learning of a conspiracy against him in Jerusalem, he fled to Lachish. However, his enemies followed and assassinated him there, ending a reign of 29 years (2 Chr. 25:25–28).

2. The father of Joshah (1 Chr. 4:34–43).

3. A Levite of the family of Merari and the son of Hilkiah (1 Chr. 6:45).

4. A priest at Bethel who sought to silence the prophet Amos (Amos 7:10–17).

AMBASSADOR (see OCCUPATIONS AND TRADES).

AMBER (see JEWELS AND PRECIOUS STONES).

AMBITION, SELFISH — a spirit of strife and selfishness condemned by the apostle Paul (2 Cor. 12:20; Gal. 5:20). This type of behavior is alien to the spirit of Christ and inappropriate for Christian believers.

AMEN [A min] (*so be it*) — a solemn word by which a person confirms a statement, an oath, or a covenant (Num. 5:22; Neh. 5:13). It is also used in worship to affirm an address, psalm, or prayer.

In Isaiah 65:16 the Lord is called "the God of truth"; the original Hebrew means, "the God of Amen." This is Isaiah's way of saying that the Lord is the One who remains eternally true, the One who can always be relied on. In the New Testament, our Lord Jesus Christ is given the same title: "the Amen, the Faithful and True Witness" (Rev. 3:14). He, too, is eternally true and reliable.

AMERICAN STANDARD VERSION (see BIBLE VERSIONS AND TRANSLATIONS).

AMETHYST (see JEWELS AND PRECIOUS STONES).

AMI [A mih] — a form of AMON.

AMINADAB [a MEN uh dab] — Greek form of AMMINADAB.

AMITTAI [a MIT ih] (*faithful*) — the father of the prophet Jonah (2 Kin. 14:25; Jon. 1:1).

AMMAH [AM muh] (*mother* or *beginning*) — a hill in the country of Benjamin (2 Sam. 2:24). Joab and Abishai stopped here after their victory over Abner in the battle of Gibeon before traveling on to Hebron.

AMMI [AM mih] (*my people*) — the symbolic name which God told the prophet Hosea to give to the people of Israel. This name was a sign of God's forgiveness and acceptance of those who had wandered away from him (Hos. 2:1, 23).

AMMIEL [AM ih ell] (*kinsman of God*) — the name of four Old Testament men:

1. A son of Gemalli and one of those sent by Moses to spy out the land of Canaan (Num. 13:12).

2. The father of Machir, an inhabitant of Lo Debar (2 Sam. 9:4–5; 17:27).

3. The father of Bathsheba (Bathshua), one of David's wives (1 Chr. 3:5). He is called Eliam in 2 Samuel 11:3.

4. A son of Obed–Edom, whose family served as gatekeepers for the tabernacle (1 Chr. 26:5).

AMMIHUD [a MIH hud] (*man of praiseworthiness*) — the name of five Old Testament men:

1. The father of Elishama, chief of the tribe of Ephraim during Israel's 40 years in the wilderness (Num. 1:10; 10:22). Ammihud was Joshua's great-grandfather (1 Chr. 7:26).

2. A man of the tribe of Simeon in the time of Moses (Num. 34:20).

3. A man of the tribe of Naphtali in Moses' time (Num. 34:28).

4. The father of Talmai, king of Geshur (2 Sam. 13:37).

5. A descendant of Judah through Perez and a son of Omri (1 Chr. 9:4). He returned to Jerusalem after the Captivity.

AMMINADAB [ah MEN ah dab] (*my people is noble*) — the name of three men in the Old Testament:

1. The father of Elisheba, Aaron's wife (Ex. 6:23). Amminadab's name appears as an ancestor of David (Ruth 4:19–22) and, thus, as an ancestor of Jesus (Matt. 1:4; Luke 3:33).

2. A chief of a Levitical group, and one of the sons of Kohath, during David's reign (1 Chr. 6:22). He is also called Izhar (1 Chr. 6:37–38).

3. One of the Levites who helped bring the ARK OF THE COVENANT to Jerusalem (1 Chr. 15:10–11).

AMMINADIB [am MEN ah dib] (*my noble people*) — a chariot driver mentioned in the Song of Solomon (6:12) in the KJV. Other translations render the word Amminadib as "my noble people."

AMMISHADDAI [AM ih shad eye] (*the Almighty is my kinsman*) — the father of Ahiezer (Num. 1:12;

7:66–71; 10:25). Ahiezer was a captain of the tribe of Dan during the wilderness journey.

AMMIZABAD [ah MIZ ah bad] (*the kinsman has endowed*) — the son of Benaiah, one of David's captains (1 Chr. 27:6).

AMMON [AM muhn] (*kinsman* or *people*) — the name of a man and an ancient kingdom in the Old Testament:

1. The son of LOT by his younger daughter. He is the same person as BEN–AMMI and is described as "the father [ancestor] of the people of Ammon" (Gen. 19:38).

2. The land of Ammon, settled by those who were descended from Ammon (or Ben–Ammi), Lot's son. Ammon was born in a cave near Zoar (Gen. 19:30–38), a city near the southern end of the Dead Sea (see Map 2, D–1). The land of the AMMONITES generally was located in the area north and east of Moab, a region between the River Arnon and the River Jabbok. Its capital city was Rabbah (Deut. 3:11; 2 Sam. 11:1). Amman, the name of the capital of the modern kingdom of Jordan, is a continuing use of this ancient name.

AMMONITES [AM muhn ites] — a nomadic race descended from AMMON, Lot's son, who became enemies of the people of Israel during their later history. During the days of the Exodus, the Israelites were instructed by God not to associate with the Ammonites (Deut. 23:3). No reason is given in the Bible for such hostility, but the rift between the two peoples continued across several centuries.

In the days of the judges, Eglon, king of Moab, enlisted the aid of the Ammonites in taking Jericho

Ruins of a pagan temple of the Amorites, at Shechem.
Photo by Howard Vos

from the Hebrew people (Judg. 3:13). In Saul's time, Nahash, the Ammonite king, attacked Jabesh Gilead. Saul responded to the call for help and saved the people of Jabesh Gilead from being captured by Nahash (1 Sam. 11:1–11).

Later in the history of the Israelites, Ammonites were among the armies allied against King Jehoshaphat; God caused confusion among them, and they destroyed themselves (2 Chr. 20:1–23). The prophets of the Old Testament often pronounced God's judgment against the Ammonites (Jer. 9:26; Amos 1:13–15). Archaeological evidence suggests that Ammonite civilization continued from about 1200 B.C. to 600 B.C.

AMMONITESS [AM muhn ite ess] (*woman of the Ammonites*) — a word used to describe NAAMAH, mother of Rehoboam (1 Kin. 14:21), and SHIMEATH, mother of Zabad (2 Chr. 24:26).

AMNON [AM nun] (*faithful*) — the name of two men in the Old Testament:

1. The oldest son of David, born at Hebron while that city was still capital of the nation of Israel (2 Sam. 3:2; 1 Chr. 3:1). Amnon raped Tamar, his half–sister, incurring the wrath of Absalom, Tamar's full brother. After two years, Absalom had Amnon murdered.

2. A son of Shimon (or Shammai), a descendant of Judah (1 Chr. 4:20).

AMOK [A mock] (*unsearchable*) — a priest who returned to Jerusalem with Zerubbabel after the Captivity (Neh. 12:7). Amok was the ancestor of a priestly family (Neh. 12:20).

AMON [A mun] (*faithful*) — the name of three men in the Old Testament:

1. A governor of Samaria (1 Kin. 22:26; 2 Chr. 18:25). When the prophet Micaiah prophesied that Ahab, king of Israel, would be killed in battle, he was sent to Amon as a prisoner.

2. A son of Manasseh and a king of Judah (2 Kin. 21:18–26; 2 Chr. 33:20–25). Amon became king at the age of 22 and reigned for only two years. His reign was characterized by idolatry, and he turned his back on the God of Israel.

Finally, Amon's own servants conspired to kill him, possibly because his corruption and idolatry had made him a weak king and they hoped to claim the throne for themselves. However, after Amon was assassinated, the people of Judah killed the conspirators and set Amon's eight–year–old son, Josiah, on the throne. Amon is mentioned in the New Testament as an ancestor of Jesus (Matt. 1:10).

3. The head of a captive family that returned to Israel from Babylon (Neh. 7:59). He was a descendant of one of Solomon's servants. He is also called Ami (Ezra 2:57).

AMORITES [AM oh rites] (*Westerners*) — the inhabitants of the land west of the Euphrates River, which included Palestine, Lebanon, and Syria (see Map 1, C–2). The Amorites were one of the major tribes, or national groups, living in Canaan. The Old Testament frequently uses "Amorites" as a synonym for Canaanites in general. The Book of Genesis cites Canaan as the ancestor of the Amorites (Gen. 10:16).

Shortly before 2000 B.C., the Amorites lived in the wilderness regions of what today is western Saudi Arabia and southern Syria. In the court records of ACCAD and SUMER they were known as barbarians, or uncivilized people. Beginning about 2000 B.C., Amorites migrated eastward to Babylon in large numbers. There they captured major cities and regions from the native Mesopotamians.

Throughout Old Testament times, other Amorites remained in Syria, Phoenicia, and the desert regions to the south (Josh. 13:4). A significant number, however, settled in the land of Palestine itself, eventually occupying large areas both east and west of the Jordan River (Judg. 11:19–22). These Amorites spoke a dialect which was closely related to Canaanite and Hebrew. Occasionally, the Amorites were identified as a Canaanite tribe (Gen. 10:16). At other times they were called the people of Canaan (Deut. 1:27).

When Israel invaded Canaan under Joshua, the first Israelite victories came against the Amorite kings Sihon and Og, who ruled much of the Promised Land east of the Jordan River (Josh. 12:1–6). Various cities west of the Jordan—Jerusalem, Hebron, Jarmuth, Lachish, and Eglon—also were called "Amorite" cities (Josh. 10:5), even though Jerusalem was also known as a Jebusite city.

While conquering Canaan, the Israelites frequently fought with the Amorites. After the Israelites prevailed, the Amorites who had not been killed remained in Canaan and became servants to the Israelites (1 Kin. 9:20–21).

Much of our knowledge about the Amorites and their culture comes from clay tablets discovered at MARI, a major Amorite city situated on the Euphrates River in western Mesopotamia.

AMOS [AIM us] (*burden bearer*) — the famous shepherd–prophet of the Old Testament who denounced the people of the northern kingdom of Israel for their idol worship, graft and corruption, and oppression of the poor. His prophecies and the few facts known about his life are found in the Book of Amos.

Although he prophesied to the Northern Kingdom, Amos was a native of Judah, Israel's sister nation to the south. He came from the village of Tekoa (Amos 1:1), situated about 16 kilometers (10 miles) south of Jerusalem.

On one occasion, Amos' authority in Israel was questioned by a priest who served in the court of King Jeroboam II, and Amos admitted he was not descended from a line of prophets or other religious officials. By vocation, he claimed to be nothing but "a herdsman and a tender of sycamore fruit" (Amos 7:14), but he pointed out that his right to speak came from the highest authority of all: "The Lord took me as I followed the flock, and the Lord said to me, 'Go, prophesy to My people Israel' " (Amos 7:15).

Amos spoke because the Lord had called him to deliver His message of judgment. This is one of the clearest statements of the compulsion of the divine call to be found in the Bible.

The theme of Amos' message was that Israel had rejected the one true God in order to worship false gods. He also condemned the wealthy class of the nation for cheating the poor through oppressive taxes (Amos 5:11) and the use of false weights and measures (Amos 8:5). He urged the people to turn from their sinful ways, to acknowledge God as their Maker and Redeemer, and to restore justice and righteousness in their dealings with others.

Amaziah the priest, who served in the court of King Jeroboam, made a report to the king about Amos and his message (Amos 7:10–13). This probably indicates that the prophet's stern warning created quite a stir throughout the land. But there is no record that the nation changed its ways as a result of Amos' message. About 40 years after his prophecies, Israel collapsed when the Assyrians overran their capital city, Samaria, and carried away the leading citizens as captives.

After preaching in Israel, Amos probably returned to his home in Tekoa. No facts are known about his later life or death. He will always serve as an example of courage and faithfulness.

AMOS, BOOK OF — a prophetic book of the Old Testament noted for its fiery denunciation of the northern kingdom of Israel during a time of widespread idol worship and indulgent living. The book is named for its author, the prophet AMOS, whose name means "burden bearer." Amos lived up to his name as he declared God's message of judgment in dramatic fashion to a sinful and disobedient people.

Structure of the Book. The nine chapters of the Book of Amos emphasize one central theme: The

AMOS: A Teaching Outline

people of the nation of Israel have broken their COVENANT with God, and His judgment against their sin will be severe. After a brief introduction of Amos as the prophet (1:1–2), the book falls naturally into three major sections: (1) judgment against the nations, including Judah and Israel (1:3—2:16); (2) sermons of judgment against Israel (3:1—6:14); and (3) visions of God's judgment (7:1—9:10). The book concludes with a promise of Israel's restoration (9:11–15).

In the first major section of the book Amos begins with biting words of judgment against the six nations surrounding the lands of Judah and Israel. These nations are Damascus (1:3–5), Gaza (1:6–8), Tyre (1:9–10), Edom (1:11–12), Ammon (1:13–15), and Moab (2:1–3). Next he announces God's judgment against Judah, Israel's sister nation to the south (2:4–5). Because of Israel's bitterness toward Judah, Amos' listeners must have greeted this cry of doom with pleasant agreement.

But Amos was only warming up to the main part of his sermon. Suddenly he launched into a vivid description of God's judgment against the nation of Israel. With biting sarcasm, Amos condemned the citizens of Israel for their oppression of the poor (2:7), worship of idols (2:8), rejection of God's salvation (2:9, 12), and defilement of the Lord's holy name (2:7). Hypocrisy, greed, and injustice prevailed throughout the land. True worship had been replaced by empty ritualism and dependence on pagan gods. And Amos made it plain that Israel would be judged severely unless the people turned from their sin and looked to the one true God for strength and guidance.

In the second major section of his book (3:1—6:14), Amos preached three biting sermons of judgment against the nation of Israel. He referred to the wealthy, luxury–seeking women of Samaria—the capital city of Israel—as "cows of Bashan" (4:1). He also attacked the system of idol worship which King Jeroboam had established in the cities of Bethel and Gilgal (4:4; 5:5).

Following these sermons of judgment, Amos moved on in the third major section of his book (7:1—9:10) to present five visions of God's approaching judgment. The prophet's vision of a basket of fruit is particularly graphic. He described the nation of Israel as a basket of summer fruit, implying that it would soon spoil and rot in the blistering sun of God's judgment (8:1–14).

Following these messages of judgment, the Book of Amos ends on a positive, optimistic note. Amos predicted that the people of Israel would be restored to their special place in God's service after their season of judgment had come to an end (9:11–15). This note of hope is characteristic of the Hebrew prophets. They pointed to a glorious future for God's people, even in the midst of dark times. This positive spirit, which issued from Amos' deep faith in God, sustained the prophet and gave him hope for the future.

Authorship and Date. The author of this book was the prophet Amos, since it is clearly identified in the introduction as "the words of Amos" (1:1). Amos was a humble herdsman, or shepherd, of Tekoa (1:1), a village near Jerusalem in the southern kingdom of Judah. But God called him to deliver His message of judgment to the people who lived in Israel, Judah's sister nation to the north. Amos indicated in his book that he prophesied during the reigns of King Uzziah (Azariah) in Judah and King Jeroboam II in Israel (1:1). This places his prophecy at about 760 B.C. He must have written the book some time after this date, perhaps after returning to his home in Tekoa.

In one revealing passage in his book, Amos indicates that he was "no prophet, nor was I a son of a prophet, but I was a herdsman and a tender of sycamore fruit" (7:14). In spite of this humble background, he was called by God to preach His message of repentance and judgment to a rebellious nation (7:15–16). His unquestioning obedience and his clear proclamation of God's message show that he was committed to the Lord and His principles of holiness and righteousness. Amos' keen sense of justice and fairness also comes through clearly in the book.

Historical Setting. Amos prophesied during the reign of Jeroboam II of Israel (793–753 B.C.), a time of peace and prosperity. The prophet speaks of the excessive luxury of the wealthy (6:3–7), who had no concern for the needs of the poor. Religiously, the nation had departed from the worship of the one true God. Jeroboam encouraged the practice of fertility cults, mixing an element of BAAL worship with Israel's faith in their Lord of the Covenant. The situation clearly called for a courageous prophet who could call the nation back to authentic faith as well as a policy of fairness and justice in their dealings with their fellow citizens.

Theological Contribution. Amos is known as the great "prophet of righteousness" of the Old Testament. His book underlines the principle that religion demands righteous behavior. True religion is not a matter of observing all the right feast days, offering burnt offerings, and worshiping at the sanctuary. Authentic worship results in changed behavior—seeking God's will, treating others with justice, and following God's commands. This great insight is summarized by these famous words from the prophet: "Let justice run down like water, and righteousness like a mighty stream" (5:24).

Special Considerations. Although Amos was a shepherd by occupation, his book gives evidence of careful literary craftsmanship. One technique which he used was puns or plays on words to drive home his message. Unfortunately, they do not translate easily into English. In his vision of the summer fruit, for example, Amos spoke of the coming of God's judgment with a word that sounds very similar to the Hebrew word for fruit (8:1–2). The summer fruit (*qayits*) suggested the end (*qets*) of the kingdom of Israel (RSV). Like ripe summer fruit, Israel was ripe for God's judgment.

Another literary device which Amos used in his sermons of judgment against the nations is known as numerical parallelism: "For three transgressions...and for four..." (1:3). He repeated this phrase seven times as he covered the sins of the various nations around Israel (1:3, 6, 9, 11, 13; 2:1, 4). The reader can almost feel the suspense building until the prophet reaches the dramatic climax of his sermon: "For three transgressions of Israel, and for four, I will not turn away its punishment, because they sell the righteous for silver, and the poor for a pair of sandals" (2:6).

The Book of Amos is one of the most eloquent cries for justice and righteousness to be found in the Bible. And it came through a humble shepherd who dared to deliver God's message to the wealthy and influential people of his day. His message is just as timely for our world, since God still places a higher value on justice and righteousness than on silver and gold and the things that money will buy.

AMOZ [A mozz] (*strong*) — the father of the prophet Isaiah (Is. 1:1; 13:1; 38:1). According to a tradition of the rabbis, Amoz was a brother of King Amaziah of Judah (reigned about 796–767 B.C.) and, like his son Isaiah, also a prophet.

AMPHIPOLIS [am FIP oh liss] (*surrounded city*) — a city of Macedonia (see Map 7, B-1) through which the apostle Paul passed on his second missionary journey (Acts 17:1). Amphipolis was situated about 50 kilometers (30 miles) southwest of Philippi. It was almost completely surrounded by a bend in the River Strymon.

Situated on a terraced hill, the city was highly visible from land and sea. A large monument, the Lion of Amphipolis, commemorating a military victory, stands guard today at the ancient site, as it did in Paul's time.

AMPLIAS [AM plih ahs] (*large, enlarged*) — a Christian in Rome greeted by the apostle Paul as "my beloved in the Lord" (Rom. 16:8; Ampliatus, NASB, NEB, NIV, RSV).

AMPLIATUS [am plih AH tus] — a form of AMPLIAS.

AMRAM [AM ram] (*exalted people*) — the name of three men in the Old Testament:

1. A son of Kohath and the father of Moses, Aaron, and Miriam by Jochebed, Kohath's sister (Ex. 6:18, 20). Amram was the father of the AMRAMITES, the Levitical family that served in the wilderness tabernacle and perhaps in the Temple in Jerusalem (Num. 3:27; 1 Chr. 26:23).

2. The KJV spelling of Hamran (1 Chr. 1:41). The name should probably be HEMDAN, as recorded in the Septuagint (Greek) version (Gen. 36:26).

3. A son of Bani who divorced his foreign wife after the Captivity (Ezra 10:34).

AMRAMITES [AM ram ites] — descendants of AMRAM (Num. 3:27; 1 Chr. 26:23). The Amramites were a branch of the priestly family of KOHATHITES.

Photo by Howard Vos

A statue of a lion still stands today at the site of ancient Amphipolis, as it did in Paul's time.

AMRAPHEL [Am rah fell] (meaning unknown) — a king of Shinar who invaded Canaan during Abraham's time (Gen. 14:1,9). While some have tried to identify Amraphel with Hammurabi, founder of the first Babylonian dynasty, all efforts to identify him or pinpoint the location of Shinar have failed.

AMULET — a charm or ornament usually assumed to have supernatural powers. Often inscribed with magic incantations, amulets supposedly protected the wearer from evil—such as sickness, disease, accidents, witchcraft, evil spirits, and demons. They also were thought to serve as aids to success.

Although the word amulet does not occur in the KJV or the NKJV, several modern versions do use it. For instance amulets are included in a list of garments and accessories worn by the women of Jerusalem (Is. 3:20, RSV). In this instance the word does not have any religious significance.

AMZI [Am zih] (*my strength*) — the name of two men in the Old Testament:

1. A descendant of Merari, of the tribe of Levi (1 Chr. 6:46).

2. An ancestor of Adaiah (Neh. 11:12).

ANAB [A nab] (*grapes*) — a town in the mountains of Judah captured by Joshua (Josh. 11:21; 15:50). The present–day Khirbet Anab is situated about 21 kilometers (13 miles) southwest of Hebron.

ANAH [A nah] (*answering* or *speech*) — the name of one woman and two men in the Old Testament:

1. Zibeon's daughter and the mother of one of Esau's wives, Aholibamah (Gen. 36:2, 14, 18, 25).

2. A son of Seir and brother of the HORITE chief Zibeon (Gen. 36:20, 29; 1 Chr. 1:38). This Anah may be a tribal name rather than a personal name.

3. A son of Zibeon who discovered hot springs in the wilderness (Gen. 36:24; 1 Chr. 1:40–41).

ANAHARATH [uh NAY ha rath] (*narrow way*) — a town in the Valley of Jezreel allotted to the tribe of Issachar (Josh. 19:19).

ANAIAH [a NIGH uh] (*Jehovah has answered*) — the name of one or two men in the Old Testament:

1. A leader who helped Ezra read the law (Neh. 8:4).

2. An Israelite who sealed the covenant under Nehemiah (Neh. 10:22). He may be the same person as Anaiah No. 1.

ANAK [A knack] (*giant*) — a son of Arba, who gave his name to Kirjath Arba, or Hebron (Josh. 15:13–14). Anak had three sons, whose descendants were giants, the ANAKIM.

ANAKIM [AN uh kim] (*giants*) — a race of fierce giants (Deut. 1:28; 2:10–11; Josh. 14:12, 15) descended from ANAK. So gigantic were they that the spies sent out by Moses considered themselves as mere grasshoppers compared to the Anakim (Num. 13:33). Under Joshua, however, the Israelites destroyed many of the Anakim. A remnant of these giants took refuge among the Philistines.

ANAMIM [AN uh mem] (*rockmen*) — descendants of Mizraim, the second son of Ham (Gen. 10:13; 1 Chr. 1:11).

ANAMMELECH [ah NAM uh leck] (see GODS, PAGAN).

ANAN [A nan] (*a cloud*) — a leader of the Israelites who sealed the covenant after returning from the Captivity (Neh. 10:26).

ANANI [a NAH nih] (*God has appeared*) — a son of Elioenai, a descendant of Zerubbabel and King David (1 Chr. 3:24).

ANANIAH [an uh NYE uh] (*Jehovah is a protector*) — the name of a person and a place:

1. An ancestor of Azariah (Neh. 3:23).

2. A town in Benjamin (Neh. 11:32).

ANANIAS [an uh NYE us] (*God is gracious*) — the name of three New Testament men:

1. A Christian in the early church at Jerusalem (Acts 5:1–11). With the knowledge of his wife, SAPPHIRA, Ananias sold a piece of property and brought only a portion of the proceeds from its sale to Peter, claiming this represented the total amount realized from the sale. When Peter rebuked him for lying about the amount, Ananias immediately fell down and died. Sapphira later repeated the same falsehood, and she also fell down and died. Apparently, their pretense to be something they were

not caused God to strike Ananias and Sapphira dead.

2. A Christian disciple living in Damascus at the time of Paul's conversion (Acts 9:10–18; 22:12–16). In a vision the Lord told Ananias of Paul's conversion and directed him to go to Paul and welcome him into the church. Aware of Paul's reputation as a persecutor of Christians, Ananias reacted with alarm. When the Lord informed him that Paul was "a chosen vessel of Mine" (Acts 9:15), Ananias went to Paul and laid his hands upon him. Paul's sight was restored immediately, and he received the Holy Spirit. Immediately, Paul received his sight and was baptized (Acts 9:18).

3. The Jewish high priest before whom Paul appeared after his arrest in Jerusalem following his third missionary journey, about A.D. 58 (Acts 23:2). Ananias was also one of those who spoke against Paul before the Roman governor Felix (Acts 24:1). Ananias was appointed high priest about A.D. 48 by Herod. In A.D. 52 the governor of Syria sent Ananias to Rome to be tried for the Jews' violent treatment of the Samaritans. Ananias was acquitted of the charges through Agrippa's influence, and he was returned to his office in Jerusalem. About A.D. 59 Ananias was deposed by Agrippa. Known to the Jews as a Roman collaborator, Ananias was murdered by a Jewish mob at the beginning of the Jewish–Roman War of A.D. 66–70.

ANATH [A nath] (meaning unknown) — the father of SHAMGAR (Judg. 3:31; 5:6), the third judge of Israel. Some scholars believe Anath is a contraction of BETH ANATH, an ancient fortified city of the Canaanites near the border of Naphtali and Asher. If this is correct, then Anath was the place from which Shamgar came, not his father.

ANATHEMA [ah NATH a mah] (*accursed*) — the transliteration of a Greek word which means "accursed" or "separated" (Luke 21:5; Rom. 9:3; Gal. 1:8–9). In the Old Testament, the word is applied to the images, altars, and sacred objects of the Canaanites (Deut. 7:23–26). The gold and silver images of their gods were "accursed" (Deut. 7:26); they were not to be kept by the Israelites but were to be destroyed with fire.

To act greedily and take what was "devoted to destruction" brought the curse on the taker as well as the entire congregation of Israel, as in the case of Achan (Josh. 7:1, 11–12, 20–26).

With a self–condemning oath (Mark 14:71), Peter denied that he knew Jesus. Paul pronounced a curse on preachers of a false gospel (Gal. 1:8–9). In Romans 9:3–4 Paul said, "I could wish that I myself were accursed from Christ for my brethren, my kinsmen according to the flesh, who are Israelites." The phrase "accursed from Christ" means to be separated from all benefits of Jesus' life, death, and resurrection.

Early in church history, the term anathema took on an ecclesiastical meaning and was applied to a person expelled from the church because of moral offenses or persistence in heresy. The person who continued in stubborn rebellion against the church was considered "devoted to destruction." Today the Roman Catholic Church often uses the term anathema in declarations against what it considers false beliefs.

ANATHOTH [AN uh tahth] (*answered prayers*) — the name of two men and one city in the Old Testament:

1. A city in the tribe of Benjamin given to the Levites (1 Kin. 2:26). Anathoth was the birthplace of the prophet Jeremiah (Jer. 1:1; 29:27). During a time of siege, the Lord instructed Jeremiah to purchase a field in Anathoth. This was to serve as a sign of God's promised redemption of Israel (Jer. 32:7–9). Anathoth was located about five kilometers (three miles) northeast of Jerusalem.

2. A son of Becher (1 Chr. 7:8).

3. A leader of the people who placed his seal on the covenant, along with Nehemiah (Neh. 10:19).

ANATHOTHITE [AN uh tahth ight] — a native or resident of the city of Anathoth (2 Sam. 23:27; Anethothite, KJV; 1 Chr. 27:12; Anetothite, KJV).

ANCESTOR WORSHIP — a form of superstitious religion in which the living seek to deify the spirits of their departed relatives. It is likely that ancestor worship occurred among the Canaanites and other pagan neighbors of Israel, particularly the Syrians. No conclusive evidence exists, however, to indicate that ancestor worship or a cult of the dead was ever a part of the religion of Israel. Although prohibitions against such practices were given (Lev. 19:28; Deut. 14:1; 26:14), these commands were probably given to warn Israel not to begin ancestor worship rather than to command that it be stopped.

ANCHOR — a heavy object on a ship cast overboard to hold the vessel in a particular place (Mark 6:53; Acts 27:29–30, 40). The writer of the Book of Hebrews had the holding power of an anchor in mind when he wrote, "This hope we have as an anchor of the soul, both sure and steadfast" (Heb. 6:19). The strong and trustworthy promises of God serve as an anchor to calm our fears in the storms of life.

ANCIENT OF DAYS — a name for God used by the prophet Daniel, who portrayed God on His throne, judging the great world empires of his day (Dan. 7:9, 13, 22). Also see GOD, NAMES OF.

ANCIENTS (see ELDERS).

ANCIENT VERSIONS (see BIBLE VERSIONS AND TRANSLATIONS).

ANDREW [AN droo] (*manly*) — brother of Simon Peter and one of Jesus' first disciples. Both Andrew and Peter were fishermen (Matt. 4:18; Mark 1:16–18) from Bethsaida (John 1:44), on the northwest coast of the Sea of Galilee. They also had a house at Capernaum in this vicinity (Mark 1:29).

According to the Gospel of John, Andrew and an unnamed friend were among the followers of John the Baptist (John 1:35–40). When John the Baptist identified Jesus as the Lamb of God, both he and Andrew followed Jesus (John 1:41). Andrew then brought his brother Simon to meet the Messiah (John 1:43–51)—an action that continues to be a model for all who bring others to Christ.

At the feeding of the 5,000, Andrew called Jesus' attention to the boy with five barley loaves and two fish (John 6:5–9). Later Philip and Andrew decided to bring to Jesus the request of certain Greeks for an audience with Him (John 12:20–22). Andrew is mentioned a final time in the gospels, when he asked Jesus a question concerning last things in the company of Peter, James, and John (Mark 13:3–4).

All lists of the disciples name Andrew among the first four (Matt. 10:2–4; Mark 3:16–19; Luke 6:14–16; Acts 1:13). According to tradition, Andrew was martyred at Patrae in Achaia by crucifixion on an X-shaped cross. According to Eusebius, Andrew's field of labor was Scythia, the region north of the Black Sea. For this reason he became the patron saint of Russia. He is also considered the patron saint of Scotland.

ANDRONICUS [an droe NYE kus] (*conquer*) — a Christian in Rome to whom the apostle Paul sent greetings (Rom. 16:7). Andronicus had become a Christian before Paul. He may have been well known as a traveling evangelist or preacher.

ANEM [A nem] (*double fountain*) — a place listed among the cities of Issachar and assigned to the priests (1 Chr. 6:73). Located about 11 kilometers (7 miles) southwest of Mount Gilboa, Anem's modern name is Jenin.

ANER [A nare] (*waterfall*) — the name of an Old Testament man and a city:

1. An Amorite chief who joined forces with Abraham in his battle with Chedorlaomer (Gen. 14:13, 24).

2. A city assigned to the Kohathites (1 Chr. 6:70) and located west of the Jordan River in the area belonging to Manasseh. It is probably the same place as Taanach (Judg. 1:27).

ANETHOTHITE, ANETOTHITE [AN uh thow thight, AN uh TOE thight] — a form of ANATHOTHITE.

ANGEL — a member of an order of heavenly beings who are superior to man in power and intelligence. By nature angels are spiritual beings (Heb. 1:14). Their nature is superior to human nature (Heb. 2:7), and they have superhuman power and knowledge (2 Sam. 14:17, 20; 2 Pet. 2:11). They are not, however, all-powerful and all-knowing (Ps. 103:20; 2 Thess. 1:7).

Artistic portrayals of angels as winged beings are generally without basis in the Bible. Rarely is an angel so described. (For exceptions, compare the CHERUBIM and SERAPHIM and the living creatures—Ex. 25:20; Ezek. 1:6; Rev. 4:8.)

The Relation of Angels. Angels were created by God (Ps. 148:2, 5) and were present to rejoice when He created the world (Job 38:4–7). In their original state they were holy, but before the creation of the world some of them rebelled against God and lost this exalted position. The leading angel in this revolt became the devil, also known as SATAN (Gen. 3:4, 14; Ezek. 28:12–16; Rev. 12:4, 7–9). Another of the fallen angels is named Abaddon or Apollyon (Rev. 9:11), "the angel of the bottomless pit" [abyss], NASB, NIV, RSV.

Two of the vast company of unfallen angels are named in the Bible. They are the archangels Michael (Dan. 10:13, 21; 12:1; Jude 9; Rev. 12:7) and Gabriel (Dan. 8:16; 9:21; Luke 1:19, 26). Michael has the special task of caring for Israel, and Gabriel communicates special messages to God's servants.

The vast army of unfallen angels delight in praising the name of the Lord continually (Ps. 103:21; 148:1–2). Large numbers of them remain at God's side, ready to do His every command (1 Kin. 22:19). Angels in God's presence include the cherubim, seraphim, and living creatures (or living beings) (Ex. 25:20; Is. 6:2; Ezek. 1:5–6; Rev. 4:6).

Unfallen angels are known for their reverence for God and their obedience to His will. Angels represent God in making significant announcements of good news (Gen. 18:9–10; Luke 1:13, 30; 2:8–15). On His behalf they also warn of coming dangers (Gen. 18:16—19:29; Matt. 2:13). In some cases they are God's agents in the destruction and judgment of evil (Gen. 19:13; 2 Sam. 24:16).

Of special importance in the Old Testament is the ANGEL OF THE LORD (Gen. 16:7; 22:11; 31:11). This angel is depicted as a visible manifestation of God Himself. He has powers and characteristics that belong only to God, such as the power to forgive sins (Ex. 23:20–21). His similarities to Jesus lead most scholars to conclude that He is the pre-incarnate Word present with God at the creation of the world (John 1:1, 14).

The Relation of Angels to Man. When visible to human beings, angels consistently appear in human form (Gen. 18:2; Dan. 10:18; Zech. 2:1). Sometimes, however, their appearance inspires awe (Judg. 13:6; Matt. 28:3–4; Luke 24:4).

Angels are never known to appear to wicked people—only to those whom the Bible views as good, such as Abraham, Moses, David, Daniel, Jesus, Peter, and Paul. They are charged with caring for such people and serving them in times of need (Ps. 91:11–12; Heb. 1:14). They also guide and instruct good people (Gen. 24:7, 40; Ex. 14:19). This task is illustrated by the role the angels played in God's giving of the Law to Moses (Acts 7:38, 53; Heb. 2:2). Sometimes their guidance comes through human dreams (Gen. 28:12; 31:11).

Angels also protect the people of God (Ex. 14:19–20; Dan. 3:28; Matt. 26:53). They meet a wide variety of human needs, including relieving hunger and thirst (Gen. 21:17–19; Mark 1:13) and overcoming loneliness and dread (Luke 22:43). They sometimes deliver the people of God from danger (Acts 5:19; 12:6–11).

Although they are not the objects of salvation, angels are interested in the salvation of human beings (Luke 15:10; 1 Cor. 4:9). They also were particularly active in the events surrounding the birth and resurrection of Jesus (Matt. 1:20; 2:13, 19; 28:2; Luke 1:11–38; 2:9–15; 22:43; 24:23; John 20:12). The frequency with which angels participate in human affairs has diminished since Pentecost, probably because of the larger role played by the Holy Spirit in the lives of Christians since then.

Jesus spoke frequently of angels, both good and bad (Matt. 13:41; 26:53; Mark 8:38; Luke 12:8–9). Angels are quite real, and they play a vital part in God's plan for the world.

ANGEL OF THE LORD — a mysterious messenger of God, sometimes described as the Lord Himself (Gen. 16:10–13; Ex. 3:2–6; 23:20; Judg. 6:11–18), but at other times as one sent by God. The Lord used this messenger to appear to human beings who otherwise would not be able to see Him and live (Ex. 33:20).

The Angel of the Lord performed actions associated with God, such as revelation, deliverance, and destruction; but he can be spoken of as distinct from God (2 Sam. 24:16; Zech. 1:12). This special relationship is a mystery similar to that between Jesus and God in the New Testament.

ANGELS, FALLEN — heavenly beings or divine messengers created by God who rebelled against Him and were cast out of heaven. The lord or prince of these fallen angels is Satan (Rev. 12:7–9). Fallen angels, or messengers, continue to serve Satan; but their power is limited. Judgment awaits them in the future (Matt. 25:41; Rev. 12:9). The fallen angels referred to in 2 Peter 2:4 and Jude 6 are possibly the beings referred to as "sons of God" in Genesis 6:1–4. There is no real distinction between fallen angels and DEMONS.

ANGER (see WRATH).

ANGLE — an old English word in the KJV which means "hook" (Is. 19:8; Hab. 1:15).

ANIAM [a NIGH am] *(lamentation)* — a son of Shemida of the tribe of Manasseh (1 Chr. 7:19).

ANIM [A nem] *(fountains)* — a town in the hill country of Judah (Josh. 15:50), located about 16 kilometers (10 miles) south of Hebron.

ANIMALS OF THE BIBLE — The Bible shows a vital interest in every aspect of nature. However, it tends to look upon nature more in terms of how mankind experiences it than in terms of scientific interest. Furthermore, the Bible frequently draws spiritual lessons from its observations. God created all things; He is also concerned for His creation. Not even a common sparrow falls to the ground without His notice (Matt. 10:29).

Scores of specific animals are named in the Bible. But many of these names are simply the educated guesses of translators. In some cases, the meaning is obvious to translators, and in others the passage gives helpful clues. But other passages offer no clue at all to which specific animals are intended. In those cases, the meaning of animal names has been lost.

This problem is complicated by the fact that the animal life of Palestine has changed over the centuries. One naturalist claimed that it was impossible that certain passages of Scripture could really mean lion; no lions lived in the Holy Land with which he was familiar. But, as is true in many areas of the world, some animals of the biblical world have since become extinct. To make matters even more complicated, over the centuries the words used to describe certain animals have changed. Scholars who have done much work in the language of the Bible and have studied the evidence from archaeology are not always clear or final in their conclusions. When a single term has as many as ten possible meanings, it is no wonder that different names are given for the same animals in different translations of the Bible.

The Bible classifies animals quite broadly. Sometimes its terms are unfamiliar to modern ears. For instance, Genesis 1:28 divides animal life into fish, fowl, and living things. The words flesh and beast often imply animal life in general. Beast also refers to wildlife, in contrast to cattle, which means the domesticated animals (sheep, goats, asses, and pigs, as well as cows and oxen). Fowl means all bird life, not just domesticated fowl. Since Genesis 1:20 obviously refers to fish, whales probably indicates larger sea creatures. Creeping things (swarming things) includes reptiles, amphibians, insects, and small animals that scamper around, such as mice.

The most basic division of animal life — clean and unclean — was in effect very early in Israel's history. Clean animals, the Jews believed, were acceptable to God for sacrifices and were thus permitted as food. All others were considered unclean, or unacceptable for sacrificing or eating.

Distinguishing between clean and unclean animals was the responsibility of the priest (Lev. 11:47). Guidelines for this procedure were given in detail in Leviticus 11. Of the larger mammals, God said, "Whatever divides the hoof, having cloven hooves and chewing the cud—that you may eat" (Lev. 11:3). Birds were an important source of food; so the few unclean ones were listed. These were mostly scavenger birds that ate flesh. Though neighboring peoples ate lizards, snakes, and turtles, Jews considered all reptiles unclean. Fish with scales and fins were clean; but shellfish, eels, and sharks were unclean. Most insects were unclean, with the exception of locusts, grasshoppers, and some beetles, which could be eaten.

Early Christians inherited this historic concern of the Hebrew people with clean and unclean animals. The Christians' concern was whether meat bought in the marketplace might have come from Roman sacrifices. Paul counseled them that nothing was

How Versions of the Bible Sometimes Differ in Translation of Animal Names

This chart shows clearly that six popular translations of the Bible—the New King James Version, King James Version, Revised Standard Version, New International Version, New English Bible, and the New American Standard Bible—sometimes disagree in their translations of the names of animals in the Bible. These differences exist because scholars disagree on the precise meaning of these words in the original language in which the Bible was written.

REFERENCE	NKJV	KJV	RSV	NIV	NEB	NASB
Ex. 8:17	lice	lice	gnats	gnats	maggots	gnats
Ex. 36:19	badger skins	badger skins	goatskins	hides of sea cows	porpoise hides	porpoise skins
Lev. 11:18	jackdaw	pelican	pelican	desert owl	horned owl	pelican
Num. 23:22	wild ox	unicorn	wild ox	wild ox	wild ox	wild ox
2 Sam. 6:13	fatted sheep	fatlings	fatling	fattened calf	buffalo	fatling
1 Kin. 10:22	monkeys	peacocks	peacocks	baboons	monkeys	peacocks
Ps. 104:18	rock badgers	coneys	badgers	coneys	rock badgers	rock badgers
Is. 11:8	viper	cockatrice	adder	viper	viper	viper
Is. 14:23	porcupine	bittern	hedgehog	owl	bustard	hedgehog
Is. 34:11	pelican	cormorant	hawk	desert owl	horned owl	pelican
Jer. 8:7	swallow	swallow	swallow	thrush	wryneck	thrush
Lam. 5:18	foxes	foxes	jackals	jackals	jackals	foxes
Amos 4:9	locust	palmerworm	locust	locust	locust	caterpillar
Zeph. 2:14	pelican	cormorant	vulture	desert owl	horned owl	pelican

"unclean of itself" (Rom. 14:14). Peter, a devout Jew who would not think of eating an unclean animal, was instructed to do so in a vision (Acts 10). He interpreted the angel's message, "What God has cleansed you must not call common," as a call to carry the message of the gospel to nonjewish nations.

Almost since the Fall of man, people sacrificed animals to God. The first biblical mention of this practice is Abel's offering of a lamb (Gen. 4:4). Animal sacrifice was an essential part of Jewish worship until the Temple in Jerusalem was destroyed in A.D. 70. Forced to abandon the practice, Jews replaced it with the study of the Law and fellowship and worship in synagogues.

Moses spelled out strict rules for animal sacrifice. Many of these guidelines are found in the Book of Leviticus in the Old Testament. Only clean animals were acceptable, and they had to be at least eight days old, with no blemishes or flaws. A bullock, kid, or lamb was the usual offering. In some cases, older animals, doves, or pigeons were brought. A very poor man, who could not afford even a bird, might offer a measure of fine flour in its place.

Although they practiced animal sacrifice, the Jewish people believed in humane treatment of their animals. The Old Testament contains many warnings against mistreating livestock. The Law itself provided that animals should receive a day of rest during the week, along with their masters. Israel also had a distinctive attitude toward animals. Unlike their neighbors, they did not worship animals. Egypt, for instance, considered the bull and cat sacred, and Greece worshiped the serpent. It was common for a nation of the ancient world to be represented by an animal on its coins. But the prohibition against making graven images prevented this practice in the nation of Israel.

Many Old Testament writers were students of nature, quick to draw parallels between animal and human behavior. In the creation and the creatures that filled it, they saw evidence of the power of God Almighty, Maker of heaven and earth.

The following animals are mentioned or implied in the Bible. This list is keyed to the New King James Version, with cross references from five additional popular translations — KJV, NASB, NEB, NIV, and RSV. Animals in this listing include mammals, insects, and reptiles.

Addax (see *Antelope*).

Adder (see *Snake*).

Ant. Approximately 100 species of ants live in the Holy Land. Harvester ants are the ones meant in Proverbs 6:6-8 and 30:25. These tiny insects settle near grain fields, carrying seed after seed into their private storehouses. In cold weather these ants cluster together and hibernate. When winter comes, they have food stored up until the next harvest.

God has provided ants with such amazing instincts that they appear to reason and plan ahead. If stored grain gets wet, they haul it out into the sun to dry. Their hard work was considered a worthy example for human beings by the writer of Proverbs (Prov. 6:6-8; 30:25).

Antelope. Antelope are cud-chewing, hollow-horned animals related to goats. Early European Bible translators were not acquainted with antelope, which roam the grassy plains and forests of Asia and Africa; so they called the antelope deer instead. Antelope are listed among clean wild game (Deut. 14:5), and among King Solomon's table provisions (1 Kin. 4:23).

When threatened, antelope flee in breathtaking leaps. So speedy were they that hunters in Bible times sometimes needed nets to catch them (Is. 51:20). Sometimes a grazing herd of antelope is joined by other animals that profit from their ability to spot an enemy or smell water at a great distance.

Various Bible translations mention three types of antelopes. The addax is a large, light–colored antelope with spiral horns. The oryx is a large African antelope, whose long horns are nearly straight. Most familiar to Bible writers was the gazelle, which stands less than a yard (approximately one meter) high at the shoulders.

The word gazelle is Arabic for "affectionate." Young gazelles were taken as pets. Poets made much of their dark, liquid eyes and delicate beauty. King David's soldier, Asahel, gifted with both speed and endurance, was "as fleet of foot as a wild gazelle" (2 Sam. 2:18). The woman of good works whom Peter raised to life was called Tabitha (Hebrew for gazelle), or Dorcas (Acts 9:36). The dorcas gazelle, once common, almost became extinct. Protected by the modern nation of Israel, it is now an agricultural nuisance.

Ape. King Solomon brought apes from tropical and semi–tropical regions of the ancient world to Israel. Solomon's zoo probably contained a variety of apes, monkeys, and baboons (1 Kin. 10:22; 2 Chr. 9:21). Some commentators suggest that Isaiah's reference to the "satyrs" who "dance" and "cry to [their] fellow[s]" (Is. 13:21; 34:14, KJV) would fit the dogfaced baboon honored by the Egyptians. Also see *Monkey*.

Asp (see *Snake*).

Ass (see *Donkey*).

Baboon (see *Ape*).

Badger. Only the skin of badgers is mentioned in the Bible and even this is questionable. Exodus 26:14 and Numbers 4:6-25 speak of the coverings for the tent of the tabernacle. The Hebrew word *tachash* is translated "badger skins." However, no one really knows what the Hebrews meant by this word. Other translators render it as "goatskins" (RSV), "porpoise-hides" (NEB), or "hides of sea cows" (NIV).

Possibly this word did mean badgers. Coarse badger hair would certainly be a protective cushion between the fine fabrics in which the articles of worship were wrapped for travel. The KJV translates the word as "badgers' skins" in Ezekiel 16:10, which refers to a foot covering. The RSV translates "leather."

Bat. Bats are flying mammals. They are included

on the list of unclean fowl (Lev. 11:19). About 15 species of bats live in the Holy Land. Most feed on insects or fruit.

Bats hunt their food at night. An amazing built-in sonar system enables them to fly safely in total darkness. They sleep hanging upside down, often with their wings wrapped around them. Some species gather in caves. Isaiah 2:20 pictures discarded idols being cast "to the moles and bats," as if to say that is where such abominations belong.

Bear. In Old Testament times, bears were a threat to man and beast. They ate honey, fruit, and livestock; so they harmed both crops and herds. Bears are easily angered, and the Asian black bear is exceptionally fierce. This bear is prone to attack man, with or without provocation, as did the two female bears that mauled the boys who taunted the prophet Elisha (2 Kin. 2:24). It was a mark of David's courage that he killed a bear that stole from his flock (1 Sam. 17:34–37).

A bear "robbed of her cubs" (2 Sam. 17:8) was legendary because of her fierceness. Since bears are rather clumsy, they sometimes lie in ambush, waiting for prey to come to them (Lam. 3:10). The era of peace shall arrive when, as Isaiah 11:7 predicts, "the cow and the bear shall graze" side by side.

Bee. Bees are not mentioned often in the Bible, but honey is. Honey was the major sweetening substance for primitive peoples. Beekeeping was practiced in Canaan. Indeed, the Jews spoke of the Promised Land as a region flowing with milk and honey. Honey was among the gifts Jacob sent to Joseph in Egypt (Gen. 43:11). Ezekiel 27:17 notes that Israel marketed honey in Tyre.

Bees may remind us of honey, but biblical writers saw angry bees as a picture of God's wrath (Ps. 118:12). These insects can be ferocious when disturbed or threatened. Wild bees of Palestine often choose strange hives. They may hide their honeycombs in the crannies of high rocks (Deut. 32:13). One swarm even settled in the carcass of a lion (Judg. 14:8).

Beetle. Beetles fly, but they do not leap (Lev. 11:21). Crickets, which are related to locusts, both fly and leap. Some scholars contend that katydid, or locusts, are more likely the correct translations of this one biblical reference to beetles or crickets.

Behemoth. Behemoth could mean elephant, crocodile, hippopotamus, water buffalo, or mythological monster. The word appears in Job 40:15, where God humbles Job by praising two of His creations, behemoth and Leviathan. Hippopotamus is the best choice for the precise meaning of behemoth. Hippos submerge themselves in rivers and bask in cool marshes. Yet they can climb up riverbanks and hillsides, devouring vegetation. An angered hippo can bite a man in half or crush a canoe with his enormous jaws.

Bittern. This bird is similar to the heron. The KJV uses "bittern" in Isaiah 14:23; 34:11; and Zephaniah 2:14, referring to a creature that dwells in ruined places—a symbol of abandonment. The bittern can be found in marshes all over the world. His loud cry, hollow and drumlike, booms through the darkness while he hunts his prey. The bittern was considered an omen of desolation and a prophecy of evil. Bitterns are large birds, about two feet long, with a gift of camouflage. A bittern may freeze with his long beak tilted skyward and be overlooked among reeds swaying gently in the wind. Bitterns eat frogs, snails, worms, and small fish.

Other translations of the Hebrew word for bittern are hedgehog (Is. 14:23; Zeph. 2:14, RSV) and porcupine (Is. 14:23, NKJV; Is. 34:11, RSV, NKJV).

Black Vulture (see *Osprey*).

Boar (see *Swine*).

Buck (see *Deer*).

Buffalo (see *Cattle*).

Bull, Bullock (see *Cattle*).

Bustard (see *Porcupine*).

Buzzard (see *Vulture*).

Calf (see *Cattle*).

Camel. Although it is an ugly beast, the camel is prized in desert countries. From the time of Abraham, the Bible mentions camels frequently, mostly in lists of possessions. Large herds of camels were a sign of wealth.

Jeremiah spoke of the "swift dromedary" (Jer. 2:23), a camel raised for riding and racing. Jesus talked of "blind guides, who strain out a gnat and swallow a camel!" (Matt. 23:24), and predicted, "It is easier for a camel to go through the eye of a needle than for a rich man to enter the kingdom of God" (Matt. 19:24).

Camels are bad-tempered, prone to spit and grumble when they take on a load. But they are well suited for harsh desert life. With a heavy coat as insulation, this animal perspires little; and his well-balanced system does not require much liquid. He can go for weeks or even months without water. When he does drink, he takes only enough to replace lost moisture. Each one of his three stomachs can hold 23 liters (5 gallons) of water. In the hump on his back the camel stores fat for times when food is scarce. Then the hump shrinks when his body draws on that reserve.

The camel stands 20 meters (6 feet) or higher at the shoulder. He is trained to kneel on his leathery knees to take on a load. He holds his head high with what seems to be a haughty air, but he is merely peering out from under bushy eyebrows. Like his tightly closing lips and nostrils, his eyebrows protect him against desert sandstorms. His tough feet are ideal for walking through sharp rocks and hot sands.

The Hebrew people used camels primarily as pack animals. They were indispensable for traveling the desert routes, carrying several hundred pounds on their backs. The Jews also rode camels and milked them, although they considered camels unclean and did not eat them (Lev. 11:4).

The Arabs, however, let no part of a camel go to waste. They ate camel meat and wove the soft fur into warm, durable cloth. John the Baptist was

Photo by Gustav Jeeninga

In addition to serving as a beast of burden, the camel provided milk and leather for the ancient Hebrew people.

clothed in a garment of camel's hair (Matt. 3:4). The tough hide made good leather for sandals and water bags, and camel-dung chips served as fuel. Even the dried bones of camels were carved like ivory.

Desert tribes rode camels to war (Judg. 7:12), and camels were seized as spoils of war.

Cankerworm (see *Worm*).

Cat. Cats were common throughout the ancient world, but they are mentioned only in the APOCRYPHA (Epistle of Jeremiah 21). The Hebrews may have avoided cats since the Egyptians worshiped them. The Romans made cats a symbol of liberty. Cats and mongooses were probably used to control rats and mice in places where grain was stored.

Caterpillar (see *Moth, Worm*).

Cattle. If we think of cattle as a group of cows, we must adjust our thinking when we read the Bible. The word cattle is usually a general reference to livestock (Gen. 30:32; 31:10). What we think of as cattle, the Bible calls oxen. A wild ox—a massive, untameable beast—is also mentioned (Job 39:9–10). The KJV calls it a unicorn.

The Bible also uses many specific terms to refer to cattle: kine, for instance, the plural of cow, and beeves, the plural of beef. But then as now, a male was a bull, a female was a cow, and their offspring was a calf. Until she bore a calf, a young female was known as a heifer; the young male was a bullock.

Some oxen were raised for sacrifice or prime quality meat. Rather than running with the herd, they were fed in a small enclosure. Fatling, fatted calf, fed beasts, stalled ox, fattened cattle and yearling described such well-cared-for animals. One translation even refers to buffalo (2 Sam. 6:13, NEB), when fatling seems to be the obvious reference. A similar term, firstling, refers to the first offspring of any livestock. All firstborn males belonged to the Lord (Gen. 4:4; Ex. 13:12).

Oxen were hollow-horned, divided-hoof, cud-chewing animals considered "clean" by the Jews. They needed considerable food and space because of their large size, so a person who kept many cattle was rich indeed. The pastures and grain country of Bashan, located east of the Jordan River and south of Damascus, were ideal places to raise oxen.

Scripture speaks of oxen as a measure of wealth (Job 42:12), beasts of burden (1 Chr. 12:40), draft animals (Deut. 22:10), meat (Gen. 18:7), and sacrificial offerings (2 Sam. 6:13).

Bulls (as opposed to work oxen) were allowed a large measure of freedom. Strong, fearsome beasts, they were often used as symbols. The BRONZE SEA in the Temple rested on the backs of 12 brass oxen—perhaps to show that Israel's strength was dedicated to the Lord (1 Kin. 7:23). Anyone who has trembled at a bully can identify with King David's frustration with his enemies, whom he compared to the "strong bulls of Bashan" (Ps. 22:12).

The Old Testament showed concern for the humane treatment of oxen (Deut. 22:4) and provided legal recourse for a person wounded by an ox (Ex. 21:28–36).

While in Egypt, the Hebrews were surrounded by bull worshipers. After the Exodus, they began to despair of Moses and his invisible God. So Aaron melted down their jewelry to make a visible idol, a golden calf. The people were punished severely for this idolatry, but some of their descendants fell into the same sin (Exodus 32; 1 Kin. 12:18).

Chameleon (see *Lizard*).

Chamois. The KJV has "chamois" for the goat or antelope of Deuteronomy 14:5. The chamois ("goat antelope") of Europe never lived in Palestine. Since the Hebrews were allowed to eat this animal, it must have been very familiar in their country. It may have been a wild goat (ibex?) or a type of wild mountain sheep. Also see *Sheep*.

Chicken (see *Fowl*).

Cobra (see *Snake*).

Cock (see *Fowl*).

Cockatrice (see *Snake*).

Colt (see *Donkey; Horse*).

Coney (see *Rock Badger*).

Cormorant. Both the prophets Isaiah and Zephaniah linked the cormorant or "the pelican" (NKJV) with the bittern to describe the ruin God brings in judgment upon man's proud cities (Is. 34:11; Zeph. 2:14). The cormorant (or "the fisher owl," NKJV) was listed among the few birds the Israelites were not to eat (Lev. 11:17; Deut. 14:17).

Cormorants are large fish-eating birds, related to pelicans, with hooked beaks and webbed feet. They dive into the water to catch fish; they swim well; and they can stay under water for a long time.

The cormorant found in Israel has a black head, yellow-circled eyes, and green highlights in its black plumage. As the prophets suggested (Is. 34:11; Zeph. 2:14), the cormorant would be an unsettling sight in the swampy pools of a ruined city.

Cow (see *Cattle*).

Crane. Cranes are the largest of several migratory birds that fly over Palestine (Jer. 8:7) in noisy flocks of thousands.

Hezekiah, king of Judah, thinking he was dying, chattered and clamored "like a crane" (Is. 38:14; swift, NIV). This must have been quite a noise. With a windpipe coiled like a french horn, cranes produce one of the loudest bird calls in the world.

Cricket (see *Beetle*).

Crocodile. The land crocodile appears as an unclean beast in the RSV rendering of Leviticus 11:30. Many scholars assume that the crocodile is the mysterious "Leviathan" (whale, NEB) praised by Job (Job 41:1–34) and mentioned in Psalm 74:14; 104:26; and Isaiah 27:1.

Crocodiles used to live in rivers in the Holy Land, including the Jordan, but they have now disappeared from this region. A long, heavy animal, the crocodile has a tough hide covered with overlapping scales. His eyes and nostrils are high on his head; so he can float almost totally submerged. Crocodiles are extremely dangerous, with strong jaws and sharp teeth. They ordinarily eat small animals, birds, and fish, but occasionally will attack larger animals or man.

Crow (see *Raven*).

Cuckoo. Cuckoos are insect-eating migratory birds that appear in Israel during the summer. Scholars feel that the Hebrew word was incorrectly rendered cuckow in the KJV. There is no obvious reason why the cuckoo would be considered an unclean bird (Lev. 11:16; Deut. 14:15). The NKJV translates "seagull."

Cuckow (see *Cuckoo*).

Deer. From early times, deer were game animals. Isaac's son Esau was "a skillful hunter" (Gen. 25:27). And it was Isaac's craving for deer meat that enabled Jacob to steal his dying father's blessing (Gen. 27). Deer were still plentiful in Palestine in Solomon's day and were served at his table (1 Kin. 4:23). Jews could eat deer because this animal "chews the cud" and "divides the hoof." (A deer track perfectly illustrates a "divided hoof.")

The Bible contains many references to deer. The animal was admired for its agility and grace, its ability to sense danger quickly, and its swiftness. Biblical writers also noted the doe's gentle care of her young. A young deer is called a fawn (Song 4:5; 7:3). The psalmist thought of the long journey for water that a deer faces in dry seasons and exclaimed: "As the deer pants for the water brooks, so pants my soul for You, O God" (Ps. 42:1). Isaiah wrote of the feelings of joy and elation when he wrote, "the lame shall leap like a deer" (35:6).

Scholars are not sure of the precise species or kind of deer Esau hunted or Solomon served. The terms stag or buck (male), hart (male), and hind (female) are used of the red deer common in Europe, which has never lived in Palestine. Likely candidates are the fallow deer (Deut. 14:5, KJV), which was common in Mesopotamia, and the roe deer, often called by its male name, roe buck (Deut. 14:5, RSV). Bible translators often interchanged terms for various kinds of deer, and for gazelle as well; so readers must settle for informed guesses about the exact species intended. Also see *Antelope*, *Gazelle*.

Dog. In ancient Israel, the dog was not "man's best friend." In fact, calling someone a dog was one of the most offensive ways of insulting that person. The Bible mentions dogs frequently; most of the references are derogatory. Even in New Testament times, Jews called Gentiles "dogs" (Matt. 15:26). The term "dog" also referred to a male prostitute (Deut. 23:18). Unbelievers who were shut out of the New Jerusalem were also termed "dogs" (Rev. 22:15)—probably a reference to their sexual immorality. Moslems later applied the insult to Christians.

The dog may have been the first animal in the ancient world to be tamed. Ancient Egyptians raced greyhounds, mentioned by Solomon in his Proverbs (Prov. 30:31, NKJV), and the Greeks raised mastiffs. But dogs in Palestine were more wild than tame. They often banded together in packs and lived off the refuse and food supplies of a village. Some dogs were useful as watchdogs or guardians of sheep, but even they were not altogether reliable (Is. 56:10).

Donkey. One of the first animals tamed by man, the donkey was a necessity in Bible times. It is mentioned frequently in the Bible. Wild donkeys (referred to as the onager in Job 39:5, NKJV) also

Although small in size, donkeys were strong enough to carry travelers and transport heavy loads in Bible times.

roamed the land. "Like a wild donkey" (Hos. 8:9) described a headstrong, untamed nature. But the domesticated donkey was an obedient servant.

Donkeys stand about 1.3 meters (4 feet) high. They are usually gray, reddish-brown, or white. The long-suffering donkey often won the affection of the household and was decorated with beads and bright ribbons. But his true role was to serve as a work animal. He trampled seed, turned the millstone to grind grain, and pulled the plow.

Donkey caravans were the freight trains and transport trucks of ancient times. These animals could carry great weight in spite of their small size. Since they required only a fraction as much fodder as a horse, they were more economical to own. The donkey was also a safe and comfortable animal to ride. They were ridden by rich and poor alike. When Jesus entered Jerusalem, he signaled his peaceful intentions by riding a young donkey rather than a prancing war-horse.

The offspring of a male donkey (jack) and female horse (mare) was a mule. The mule had the sure-footedness and endurance of the donkey, coupled with the greater size and strength of the horse. Crossbreeding like this was outlawed among the Jewish people (Lev. 19:19), but from David's time mules were imported and increasingly used by the Israelites (2 Sam. 18:9; 1 Kin. 1:33; 18:5). Ezra 2:66 records that the Israelites brought 245 mules with them when they returned from captivity in Babylon.

Dove. Doves and pigeons belong to the same family. They are often mentioned in the Bible as if they are the same animal. The rock dove found in Palestine is the wild ancestor of our common street pigeon. Turtledoves are migrants. They spend the months of April to October in the Holy Land, filling the air with soft cooing when they arrive each Spring (Song 2:11–12).

Doves come in several colors, from pure white to the chestnut-colored palm turtledove. Even the plain gray pigeon has a silver sheen. Solomon waxed poetic over doves' eyes. David longed for "wings like a dove" (Ps. 55:6), so he could fly away from his enemies.

Pigeons were probably the first domesticated bird. When people realized doves could travel long distances and always find their way home, they used them to carry messages. Homing pigeons have keen eyes with which they spot landmarks to help them stay on the right route.

Hebrews ate pigeons and, from Abraham's time, used them in sacrifice. Even a poor man could provide a pigeon or two for worship, as Joseph and Mary did at Jesus' circumcision (Luke 2:21–24; Lev. 12:8).

Doves appear to express affection, stroking each other, and "billing and cooing." They mate for life, sharing nesting and parenting duties. They are gentle birds that never resist attack or retaliate against their enemies. Even when her young are attacked, a dove will give only a pitiful call of distress.

Because of its innocence and gentle nature, the dove is a common religious symbol. The Holy Spirit took the form of a dove at Jesus' baptism (Matt. 3:16; Mark 1:10; Luke 3:22). The dove also symbolizes peace, love, forgiveness, and the church.

Dragon. Dragons are imaginary beasts with a long history in the folklore of many cultures. Usually the dragon is a crafty creature that represents evil. The word dragon, as used in some translations of the Bible, is often confusing. Occasionally this word is used when the intended meaning was probably jackal (Lam. 4:3, RSV), sea serpent or serpent (Ps. 91:13, RSV), or even crocodile (Ezek. 29:3–4).

This huge, fire-breathing monster with terrifying wings and claws is a symbol of Satan (Rev. 12:3–17; 16:13; 20:2). In the church of early Christian history, dragons represented sin. Christian art often depicts a dragon at the feet of Jesus—to show His triumph over sin.

Dromedary (see *Camel*).

Eagle. Eagles are included among the unclean birds mentioned in the Bible (Lev. 11:13, NKJV), but they were admired as majestic birds. The golden eagle, which is really dark brown with sprinkles of gold, has a 26-meter (8-feet) wing-spread. It nests in high places that are inaccessible (Jer. 49:16). There, in a nest which the eagle makes larger each year, the eagle hatches two eggs. Usually only one eaglet survives to adulthood.

An eagle has keen eyesight. He can spot his prey while soaring hundreds of feet in the air. Like a lightning bolt, he drops to sieze it, killing it quickly with his powerful claws. Then he swoops back to his nest to rip the meat apart and share it with his young.

A mother eagle carries her eaglet on her back until it masters the art of flying. Moses used this familiar picture from nature to describe God's care for His people. God stirred up Jacob (the nation of Israel), and carried His people on His wings (Deut. 32:11–12) as He delivered them from slavery in Egypt.

Solomon marveled at "the way of an eagle in the air" (Prov. 30:19). An eagle can stay aloft for hours, rarely moving his wings and riding wind currents. But many passages in the Bible also speak of the swiftness of the eagle's flight (Deut. 28:49).

The belief that an eagle renews its strength and youthful appearance after shedding its feathers gave rise to Psalm 103:5 and Isaiah 40:31. Eagles do have a long lifespan, living 20 to 30 years in the wild, and longer in captivity.

In the Old Testament, prophets spoke of the eagle as a symbol of God's judgment (Jer. 48:40; Ezek. 17:3, 7). In Revelation 12:14, "two wings of a great eagle" portray God's intervention to deliver His people from persecution.

Eagle Owl (see *Owl*).

Elephant. No elephants lived in Palestine. But they were native to the neighboring continents of Africa and Asia. Wealthy Jews sometimes imported the ivory which came from their great tusks. King Solomon "made a great throne of ivory, and overlaid it with pure gold" (1 Kin. 10:18). And King Ahab built an "ivory house" (1 Kin. 22:39).

Ewe (see *Sheep*).

Falcon. In some translations of the Bible the falcon appears in the lists of unclean birds (Lev. 11:14; Deut. 14:13, NKJV). As a bird of prey, it is often grouped with hawks. But a falcon is not a true hawk. The sport of hunting with trained falcons originated in ancient Persia. Great numbers of falcons are still seen in Palestine, as they surely were in Bible times (Job 28:7).

Fallow Deer (see *Deer*).

Fawn (see *Deer*).

Ferret (see *Lizard*).

Fish. According to one authority, 45 species of fish are found in the inland waters of Palestine. Many more live in the Mediterranean Sea. But the Bible gives no details on any specific species of fish.

Fish, just like other animals, were divided into clean and unclean categories. Fish with fins and scales were considered clean, and they made a popular Sabbath meal. Unclean fish included catfish, eels, and probably sharks and lampreys, as well as shellfish. The Hebrews also considered whales and porpoises as fish, since they lived in the sea.

Fishing was a major industry among the Jewish people. Jerusalem had a Fish Gate, and presumably a fish market. Fish were caught with nets (Hab. 1:15), hooks (Is. 19:8; Matt. 17:27), and harpoons and spears (Job 41:7). The catch was preserved by salting and drying or storing in salt water.

The Bible contains many references to fish and fishing. Habbakuk 1:14–17 compares captive Israel to helpless fish gathered into a dragnet by her enemies. Jesus, on the other hand, called his disciples to become "fishers of men" (Matt. 4:19; Mark 1:17). Since the time of the early church, the fish has been a symbol of Christianity. The Greek word for fish—*ichthus*—is an acrostic for "Jesus Christ, Son of God, Savior."

Fisher Owl (see *Cormorant*).

Flea. Fleas flourished in the sand and dust of the Holy Land. Classified as parasites, these tiny insects attach themselves to a body and suck blood from their host. Fleas have no wings, but they do have strong legs and can jump several inches at one leap. The flea that lives on man is tiny, but it can be very irritating. David described himself as a mere flea being pursued by a king (1 Sam. 24:14; 26:20). He may have seemed insignificant, but he irritated King Saul.

Fly. The "flies" of the Bible included the common housefly, as well as other two-winged insects. Many of these were biting insects. This explains the "devouring" flies of Psalm 78:45. The flies visited as a plague upon the Egyptians probably included the housefly and the stinging sand fly, as well as gnats and mosquitoes.

The prophet Isaiah's reference to the "fly that is in the farthest part of the rivers of Egypt" (7:18) may have been a symbol of swarms of Egyptian soldiers. Or, he could have had in mind the dreaded tsetse fly of Africa, which spreads sleeping sickness. Still another possibility is the olive fly, which could ruin a crop of ripe olives.

Solomon's "fly in the ointment" (Eccl. 10:1) has become a proverb. So also has Jesus' "straining out a gnat"—which referred to the custom of straining wine to take out the impurities before it was served (Matt. 23:24).

Fowl. Most people assume that hens and roosters (cocks) were common in Palestine, but they are rarely mentioned in the Bible. Domestic chickens probably descended from the red jungle fowl of Asia. Cocks were bred for the ancient sport of cockfighting before hens were raised for meat and eggs.

The crowing of cocks served the ancient world as an alarm clock. Cocks crowed about midnight and again about 3 A.M. Soldiers often rotated their guard duty at this regular signal. Jesus predicted that Peter would deny Him three times before the cock crowed (Matt. 26:34; Mark 14:30; Luke 22:34; John 13:38).

Wild or tame, chickens gather in flocks. Jesus must have been familiar with this flocking instinct. He spoke of a mother hen that tucks a whole brood of chicks under her wings for safety (Matt. 23:37; Luke 13:34).

The "fatted fowl" provided for King Solomon (1 Kin. 4:23) may have been geese. Ancient carvings from Megiddo show peasant women carrying fat geese. Geese also appear in Egyptian tomb paintings.

Fox. Foxes were common predators in Bible times. Since they fed on small rodents like rats and mice, they helped to protect the grain crops. But their fondness for grapes caused farmers much grief. Sometimes they even tunneled under protective walls to feast on grapevines (Song 2:15). Foxes also settle in holes and burrows, often those abandoned by other animals. Jesus pointed out that foxes have holes, but the Son of Man had nowhere to lay His head (Matt. 8:20).

Foxes have a keen sense of sight, smell, and hearing. They are also clever enough to lie in wait for prey. They may even play dead to attract a bird within striking range. When hunted, they are cunning and devious, misleading their pursuers. Jesus compared Herod, the Roman tetrarch of Galilee and Perea, to a fox, because of his crafty, devious nature (Luke 13:32).

"The land of Shual" (1 Sam. 13:17) may have been fox country, for *shual* means "fox" or "jackal." Also see *Jackal*.

Frog. Frogs are mentioned several times in the Bible (Ex. 8:2–13; Ps. 105:30; Rev. 16:13). All but the passage in Revelation refer to the plague of frogs in Egypt. The ancient Egyptians connected frogs with fertility and the life cycle, so they considered frogs sacred. What dismay it must have caused when the frogs multiplied uncontrollably and then died and the Egyptians had to gather these sacred animals into stinking heaps. Revelation 16:13 speaks of frogs as the symbol of unclean spirits.

Gazelle (see *Antelope*).

Gecko (see *Lizard*).

Gier Eagle (see *Vulture*).

Glede (see *Hawk*).

Gnat (see *Fly*).

Goat. In Bible times, Hebrew shepherds treasured the goat because it was such a useful animal. They wove its hair into a type of rough cloth. They drank the goat's milk which is sweet and more nutritious than cow's milk—ideal for making cheese. They even used goatskin bottles to transport water and wine. When the hide of these containers wore thin, they leaked and had to be patched (Josh. 9:4; Matt. 9:17).

Goats often grazed with sheep in mixed flocks. Unlike their gentle and helpless cousins, goats were independent, willful, and curious. Bible writers sometimes used goats to symbolize irresponsible leadership (Jer. 50:8; Zech. 10:3). In Jesus' parable of the Great Judgment (Matt. 25:32–33), the goats represented the unrighteous who could not enter His kingdom.

Goats were often sacrificed in the worship system of ancient Israel. In an early ritual, the Hebrews used two goats. They sacrificed one, sprinkling its blood upon the back of the other. This scapegoat was then sent into the wilderness, symbolically bearing the sins of the people (Lev. 16:10).

Young goats are referred to as kids in the Bible (Gen. 27:9, 16; Num. 7:87). The wild goat of Palestine is known as the ibex (Deut. 14:5, RSV, NIV; mountain goat, NKJV; pygarg, KJV; satyr, KJV, RSV).

Goose (see *Fowl*).

Grasshopper. Numerous references to grasshoppers and locusts in the Bible show what an impact these insects had in the hot, dry lands of the ancient world. Some of these references are literal (Ex. 10:4–19) while others are symbolic (Num. 13:33).

The terms grasshopper and locust are often used interchangeably. A locust is one kind of grasshopper. Another term used rarely for these insects is katydid (Lev. 11:22, NIV). It has a brown–colored body two to three inches long. Airborne, with two sets of wings, the locust was dreaded because of its destructive power as a foliage–eating insect in the ancient world.

The eighth plague that God sent upon the Egyptians was an invasion of locusts. Millions of these insects may be included in one of these swarms, which usually occur in the spring. Locusts in such numbers speedily eat every plant in sight, totally destroying the crops. A locust plague is practically unstoppable. Water does not work; for when enough locusts drown, the survivors use their bodies as a bridge. They have also been known to smother fires that had been set to destroy them. Even modern farmers wrestle with this problem, often resorting to poisoning the adults and harrowing fields in the fall to destroy the eggs before they can hatch in the spring.

Chapter 9 of the Book of Revelation presents a

Photo by Bernice Johnson

The pagan god Horus of the ancient Egyptians was represented as a hawk—a common bird throughout the ancient Near East.

nightmarish prospect: locusts with special powers will be unleashed upon mankind for five months.

Locusts do not always appear in swarms. Hot weather normally brings a few solitary grasshoppers and locusts to the Holy Land. But scientists have learned that under certain conditions of climate and food scarcity, chemical changes take place in the female locust. These cause more eggs to hatch, sending millions of locusts into the air at the same time in search of food.

Many people, including the Jews, eat locusts (Lev. 11:22). These insects may be boiled, fried, or dried. Locusts were part of the wilderness diet of John the Baptist (Matt. 3:4).

Great Lizard (see *Lizard*).

Great Owl (see *Owl*).

Greyhound (see *Dog*).

Griffon (see *Vulture*).

Grub (see *Worm*).

Hare. Hares were plentiful in Palestine, but they are mentioned in the Bible only as forbidden food (Lev. 11:6; rabbit, NIV, NASB). They look like large rabbits with longer ears and legs. The common jackrabbit is actually a hare. Unlike rabbits, hares are born furry and able to see. Hares were mistakenly thought to chew the cud, but they were considered unclean because they did not have divided hoofs (Lev. 11:6; Deut. 14:7). Perhaps they were forbidden because they are rodents, but the Hebrews' Arab neighbors did not hesitate to hunt them for food.

Hart (see *Deer*).

Hawk. Hawks are the fierce little brothers in the eagle and vulture family. Adult hawks vary from one to two feet in length. They are known for their exceptional eyesight, which is about eight times as keen as man's. Solomon remarked, "Surely, in vain the net is spread in the sight of any bird" (Prov. 1:17).

The farsighted hawk not only detects nets from a distance, but he can also see mice, insects, and birds. He strikes with devastating swiftness, his powerful claws crushing his prey, which he eats whole.

Some 18 species of hawk exist in Palestine, among them the small sparrow hawk. This hawk, which Egyptians considered sacred, nests in a hollow tree, amid old ruins, or upon a rock. As winter approaches, it migrates to a warmer climate.

Harrier hawks are found in the valleys and low-lying plains. They glide nearer the ground and "harry" other birds by forcing them to land.

Kites (gledes) are a larger breed of hawk, with long narrow wings (Deut. 14:13). Red kites, black kites, and Egyptian kites are found in Palestine. Kites in Syria hide their nests by draping them with cloth scraps or animal skins. Just as they abstained from eating other birds of prey, Israelites did not eat hawks (Lev. 11:16; Deut. 14:15).

Hedgehog (see *Porcupine*).

Heifer (see *Cattle*).

Hen (see *Fowl*).

Heron. The Bible mentions herons only in the lists of unclean birds (Lev. 11:19; Deut. 14:18). Several species of herons and egrets made their home in Palestine. Egyptian carvings picture herons and their nests among the reeds of marshes and lakes.

A tall, graceful bird, the heron flies with its neck curled and its long legs stretched out behind. The heron eats fish, frogs, and small reptiles, which it spears swiftly with a long, sharp beak.

Hind (see *Deer*).

Hippopotamus (see *Behemoth*).

Hoopoe. The hoopoe is a beautiful bird with a disgusting habit: it probes foul places for insects with its sharp, slender beak. Its wing feathers bear a zebra stripe, and its head sports a lovely crown of feathers. When frightened, the hoopoe may flutter his crest or drop to the ground and play dead. The offensive odor picked up from its feeding grounds is enough to drive away most of its enemies.

Called lapwing in the KJV, the hoopoe is on the list of unclean birds (Lev. 11:19; Deut. 14:18). It is frequently seen throughout the Holy Land today.

Horned Owl (see *Owl*).

Hornet (see *Wasp*).

Horse. Horses are mentioned often in the Bible. But they were of little importance to the average Hebrew, who found it more practical to keep a donkey to ride or an ox to pull the plow. Horses were traded for food when money failed during a famine in Egypt (Gen. 47:17). Some kings used swift horses rather than camels to carry messages (Esth. 8:10, 14). But for the most part, Hebrews thought of horses in terms of war.

Pharaoh's horses and chariots pursued when Moses led the Israelites out of Egypt (Ex. 14:9). Their Canaanite enemies met them with many horses and chariots, but they still fell before the Israelites (Josh. 11:4–9). Repeatedly God warned the Hebrews not to place their faith in the strength and speed of horses (Ps. 20:7) or to "multiply" horses (Deut. 17:16).

In spite of these warnings, David and Solomon did multiply horses, even importing them from other countries. Solomon had a sizeable cavalry as well as horses to draw war chariots.

The prophet Jeremiah used the word stallion in speaking of horses (Jer. 8:16; 47:3; 50:11, RSV). He

The hyena, considered unclean and forbidden as food by the Hebrews because it was a scavenger that ate dead animals.

Photo by Amikam Shoob

warned the nation of Judah that it would fall to a conquering army that would be riding prancing stallions. He also used the symbol of a "well-fed, lusty stallion" (Jer. 5:8, NKJV) to describe the idolatry and unfaithfulness of God's people.

The New Testament tells of the "Four Horsemen of the Apocalypse," who ride out to ravage the earth in the end times (Rev. 6:1-8). But even more dramatic than this is the entrance of a white horse bearing the "King of kings and Lord of lords" (Rev. 19:11-16).

Horseleach (see *Leech*).

Hound (see *Dog*).

Hyena. Hyenas were plentiful in Bible times. "Doleful creatures" (KJV) and "beasts of the field" (Is. 13:21; Jer. 12:9) may refer to hyenas. The place name Zeboim (1 Sam. 13:18; Neh. 11:34) means "hyena." A member of the dog family, hyenas have square snouts and powerful jaws. They run down prey and may even attack human beings. The Israelites hated hyenas and considered them unclean because they are scavengers. Sometimes they would even dig up and devour dead bodies. Hyenas hunt at night. Their eerie howls sound like demented laughter. A reference by the prophet Isaiah to the hyena is also translated as jackal (Is. 13:22, RSV). Also see *Jackal*.

Ibex (see *Goat*).

Jackal. The prophet Isaiah spoke of jackals—wild dogs that make their dens in desolate places (Is. 34:13). As scavengers, jackals also fed on garbage in towns and villages in Bible times.

Jackals have an unpleasant smell, and they make a yapping and howling noise at night. They are also agricultural pests. Palestinian farmers put up shelters for watchmen, who guarded their cucumber fields against jackals. Some farmers heaped up whitewashed stones to frighten the jackals, just as scarecrows are used in other places.

Bible references to jackals are confusing, since jackal, fox, dragon, and wolf may be used interchangeably, depending on the translation. The "foxes" to whose tails Samson tied torches were probably jackals which, unlike foxes, travel in packs (Judg. 15:4). Also see *Fox*.

Jackdaw (see *Pelican*).

Jerboa (see *Mouse*).

Katydid (see *Grasshopper*).

Kid (see *Goat*).

Kine (see *Cattle*).

Kite (see *Hawk*).

Lamb (see *Sheep*).

Lapwing (see *Hoopoe*).

Leech. A leech may be described as a type of worm with suckers at each end of its body. One end also contains a mouth. Some species of this animal even have tiny teeth. Parasitic leeches attach themselves to a person or an animal, from which it sucks blood for nourishment. A leech of this type secretes chemicals which keep the blood flowing freely.

In primitive times, physicians used leeches to "bleed" a patient and purge his body of what was thought to be contaminated blood. But an untended leech could cause pain and damage. In his Proverbs, Solomon may have had the blood-sucking nature of this animal in mind when he spoke of the leech's "two daughters" who cry "Give! Give!" (Prov. 30:15).

Leopard. The huge cats known as leopards were familiar in Palestine, and the Hebrews had good reason to fear them. Smaller and lighter than lions, leopards are better hunters. They are swift, wary, and intelligent; and they can climb trees as easily as a domestic cat. A leopard is also strong enough to

The ibex, also referred to in the Bible as the wild goat (Deut. 14:5, NKJV).

Photo by Amikam Shoob

drag his prey to a tree branch, where he can devour it out of reach of lions or hyenas. Although leopards do not usually attack human beings, Jeremiah portrayed them symbolically as an instrument of God's judgment: "A leopard will watch over their cities. Everyone who goes out from there shall be torn in pieces" (Jer. 5:6).

The books of Daniel and Revelation use the leopard as a symbol of swiftness in cruelty (Dan. 7:6; Rev. 13:2). Isaiah suggested that a day of peace would come when the savage leopard would not harm a young goat (11:6).

Leviathan (see *Crocodile*).

Lice. Lice thrive in dry, dusty climates where sanitation is poor. These tiny insects are parasites with flat, colorless bodies. They cling to animals, humans, or plants, sucking blood or sap. The Egyptian nobles and priests shaved their heads and beards so lice could find no hiding place on their bodies. An infestation of lice, the third plague of the Exodus, must have been particularly bothersome to them (Ex. 8:16–18; gnats, RSV, NIV, NASB; maggots, NEB).

Lion. The lion was the most awesome and dangerous wild beast in Palestine. His tawny hide blended into the golden fields and sandy wastes. Lions hid in forests and sometimes pounced from the thickets near the Jordan River (Jer. 49:19).

The Bible contains many references to lions. Daniel miraculously survived a night in a lions' den (Daniel 6). Samson and David killed lions singlehandedly (Judg. 14:5–6; 1 Sam. 17:34–37). Kings hunted lions for sport. According to Ezekiel 19:1–9, lions were also captured with pits and nets.

The lion's majestic appearance and fearsome roar prompted many comparisons. The prophet Joel declared, "The Lord also will roar from Zion" (Joel 3:16). The apostle Peter wrote: "Be sober, be vigilant; because your adversary the devil walks about like a roaring lion." The prophet Hosea foretold that God would be like a protective lion for the nation of Israel (Hos. 5:14; panther, NEB).

Largest and grandest of cats, the lion is filled with power. A swat of his paw can kill. His massive body forces him to rely on strength instead of speed in his hunting.

A lion looks and sounds so imposing that he symbolizes royalty and courage. The highest compliment which biblical writers could give was to indicate that a person had the face or heart of a lion. *Ari,* the most common term for lion, means "the strong one." In Isaiah 29:1 Jerusalem is called "Ariel," implying that the capital of the Jewish nation is "the strong [lion-like] city of God." In some translations of the Bible, a young lion is called a cub (Gen. 49:9, NIV), while other translations use the word whelp (Gen. 49:9).

The Israelite tribes of Judah, Dan, and Gad—and also the nation of Babylon—adopted the lion as their symbol. Jesus is called "the lion of Judah" (Rev. 5:5). Isaiah the prophet foretold that at the end of time, the Prince of Peace would tame even the fierce heart of the lion (Is. 9:6–7; 11:1–9).

Little Owl (see *Owl*).

Lizard. Lizards receive little attention in the Bible, although they are common in Palestine. They appeared on the list of unclean animals (Lev. 11:30) and were thus forbidden as food to the Israelites.

The lizard comes in many species. Some of the small lizards often pass for snakes, while larger versions of this animal resemble the crocodile. All lizards are cold-blooded reptiles. Since their body temperature depends on their surroundings, they thrive in the tropics and in deserts. But when the sun gets too hot even for them, they lie in the shade or burrow into the sand. One species is even called a sand lizard (Lev. 11:30; skink, NIV).

Lizards are ingenious in the different ways they move. Some unfurl skin-like sails and soar from tree to tree. Monitor lizards (probably the Bible's great lizard, Lev. 11:29, RSV, NIV) swim well. They can also climb trees. Many lizards scamper rapidly across the ground. Others have poorly developed legs or no legs at all. But the little gecko (translated ferret in KJV, Lev. 11:30) can walk across a plaster ceiling upside down or cling to a pane of glass. His toes end in a pad made of hundreds of tiny hooks, capped with a hidden claw. This enables him to get a foothold on smooth surfaces. Geckos are abundant in Palestine.

Most lizards eat insects. Larger species of this reptile also eat small animals or plants. The chameleon's sticky tongue, nearly as long as his body, whips out to catch insects. Chameleons are also common in Palestine. They are so narrow they look as if they have been squashed, and their bulging eyes can see in opposite directions. They have a long tail that can grasp a branch or coil into a spiral when at rest. Chameleons move at a slow, deliberate pace.

The chameleon is known for its ability to change its color to match its surroundings. Actually, this is a common protective trait for most species of lizards. Another defensive tactic is the use of tricks or bluffs. The glass snake, a type of lizard, escapes capture by shedding its wiggling tail. Other lizards hiss, puff up, or use their tails as whips.

Locust (see *Grasshopper*).

Maggot (see *Lice*; *Worm*).

Mare (see *Horse*).

Mole. Palestine has no true moles. The few Bible references to moles probably mean a burrowing rat that resembles a mole. "Mole rats" live underground and feed on roots and bulbs, to the distress of farmers. Their tiny ears and eyes are nearly hidden in their thick coats of fur. Because these mole rats live in darkness, the prophet Isaiah referred to them as symbols of the spiritually blind. The NEB translates "dung-beetles" (Is. 2:20). Also see *Weasel*.

Mole Rat (see *Weasel*).

Monitor Lizard (see *Lizard*).

Monkey. Monkeys are not native to Palestine. So King Solomon apparently had them imported from other nations, along with apes and other exotic goods such as ivory, silver, and gold. They may have come from India, Africa, or even parts of Lower Egypt. The NKJV has "monkeys" in 1 Kings 10:22 and 2 Chronicles 9:21. Other versions translate as "peacocks." Also see *Ape*.

Moth. Moths are mentioned several times in the Bible as a symbol of destructiveness and the perishable nature of all earthly goods. In Hosea 5:12, God says, "I will be to Ephraim like a moth." Just as the damage caused by moths takes place slowly and undetected, so God would quietly, but inevitably, bring judgment upon His backsliding people.

The female moth lays her eggs upon garments. When the eggs hatch into caterpillars, they feed on the fibers, eventually leaving the garment full of holes. Jesus warned against placing too much confidence and hope in worldly possessions that could be wiped out so easily by moths (Matt. 6:19; Luke 12:33).

Mountain Sheep (see *Sheep*).

Mouse. About 40 kinds of mice are found in the Holy Land. These include house and field mice, moles, small rats, jerboas, and even hamsters. Arabs ate hamsters, but the Hebrew people considered all rodents unclean (Lev. 11:29; Is. 66:17).

In spite of its small size, the mouse is one of the most destructive animals in the world. Swarms of mice threatened grain crops in ancient times. When the Philistines stole the ARK OF THE COVENANT, God punished them by sending a swarm of mice which infected them with a disease (1 Sam. 6:4–5, 11, 18; rats, NKJV).

Mule (see *Donkey*).

Night Creature (see *Owl*).

Nighthawk. This is another bird mentioned in the Bible only on the list of unclean birds (Lev. 11:16; Deut. 14:15). No specific characteristics are given which might help to identify the bird. Nighthawks, also called nightjars, are found in the Holy Land, but they are not predators. There is no obvious reason why nighthawks would be considered unclean by the Israelites. Other translations render the Hebrew word for nighthawk as owl (NASB) or screech owl (NIV). After sunset, nighthawks fly high into the air to hunt for insects. They build nests near the ground in thickets or hedges.

Onager (see *Donkey*).

Oryx (see *Antelope*).

Osprey. Sometimes called fish hawk or fishing eagle, the osprey is a member of the hawk family. With a six–foot wingspan, it is one of the larger birds of prey. The osprey appears on the list of "unclean birds" (Lev. 11:13; Deut. 14:12). Some scholars think the term refers to the black vulture. Also see *Vulture*.

Ossifrage (see *Vulture*).

Ostrich. Several Scripture passages that refer to owls in the KJV are rendered ostrich in the RSV. This strange bird was a common sight in the deserts of Israel and Sinai in Bible times. Earth's largest living bird, the ostrich may stand about 2.5 meters (eight feet) tall. While it cannot fly, this unusual animal with its long steps, which can cover 15 feet per stride at top speed, can outrun a horse. Sometimes an ostrich will use its wings as a sail to achieve even greater speed. An adult ostrich fears only man and lions, and it may live as long as 70 years.

The popular belief that ostriches hide their heads in the sand is not true. However, when a young ostrich senses danger, it will crouch near the ground and stretch out its long neck to lessen the possibility of being seen.

This enormous bird has only a walnut–sized brain. But God has given it certain helpful instincts, along with its great physical stamina. Like a camel, the ostrich is fitted for desert life. It eats coarse food and can go for a long time without water. Its head, neck, and powerful legs have no feathers. This helps to keep the bird cool in the hot desert climate. Its huge eyes enable it to spot danger from a great distance, and its long eyelashes protect its eyes from dust and sand. The male ostrich has a cry that is similar to a lion's roar.

Unlike most other birds, the ostrich does not build a nest to protect its young. The female ostrich deposits her eggs on the desert floor and covers them with sand. These eggs are generally left unattended during the day, since the desert sun serves as a natural incubator. Job compared these habits unfavorably with the more traditional nesting instincts of the stork (Job 39:13–18).

Owl. The owl is mentioned several times in the Bible (Lev. 11:16–17; Ps. 102:6; Jer. 50:39; Mic. 1:8). The largest species native to Palestine is the great owl, sometimes called an eagle owl. Several varieties of smaller owls are also common. Among them are screech owls, whose calls and whistles bring an eerie feeling in the night.

Other varieties of owls mentioned by different translations of the Bible include the short–eared owl (Lev. 11:16, NKJV, NEB); long–eared owl (Lev. 11:16, NEB); horned owl (Lev. 11:16, NIV); little owl (Lev. 11:17, KJV, NIV, NASB); tawny owl (Lev. 11:17, NEB); fisher owl (Lev. 11:17, NKJV); desert owl (Lev. 11:18, NIV); and white owl (Lev. 11:18, NKJV, NIV, NASB).

The owl is no wiser than any other bird, but his facial features give him a thoughtful and solemn look. Owls have round faces with a circle of feathers around their heads, framing and highlighting their large eyes. These feathers also serve as a sound collector for the ears. An owl's fluffy feathers make him appear larger than he actually is. They also enable him to fly silently, since the edges of the feathers pierce the air with little wind resistance.

Owls have good night vision, which enables them to stalk their prey at night. Unlike other birds, whose eyes are set on opposite sides of their head, the owl looks directly ahead. He navigates in the dark mostly by sound. Alerted by a noise, he plunges in toward his prey with his claws spread for the kill.

Owls serve a useful agricultural purpose, since they feed on rats, mice, and other rodents. But the Hebrew people considered the owl an unclean bird

Photo by Amikam Shoob

The porcupine is the largest rodent found in Israel.

and often associated it with scenes of desolation. The scops owl may be the satyr of such verses as Isaiah 13:21 and 34:14 (night creature, NKJV). It has a horned look and does a hop–like dance much like a goat.

Ox, Oxen (see *Cattle*).

Palmerworm (see *Worm*).

Panther (see *Lion*).

Partridge. From early times, the partridge has been a game bird. They were among the birds which could be eaten as clean food by the Jewish people. Two species, the sand partridge (Is. 34:15, NEB) and the chukar, are common in Palestine.

Partridges live in fields, feeding on grain and insects. They usually travel in coveys of 12 to 30 birds. Their meat is tasty, and the bird is clever enough to give the hunter a fine chase. It takes sharp eyes to spot the mottled feathers of a partridge. When alarmed, the bird will hide in a hole, crouch among loose stones, or fly from tree to tree with loudly whirring wings. David compared himself to a partridge when he was fleeing from Saul (1 Sam. 26:20).

The prophet Jeremiah compared the person who gathered riches by unrighteous means to a partridge that gathers a brood of young birds which she has not hatched (Jer. 17:11).

Peacock. According to the KJV, Solomon imported peacocks from other nations for his royal courts in Israel (1 Kin. 10:22; 2 Chr. 9:21). A peacock, the male of the species, is about the size of a turkey, with feathers of brilliant blue, green, and purple. He parades in front of the female, spreading his train of gorgeous long plumes behind him like a huge fan. Some versions of the Bible translate this term as monkeys, peacocks, or baboons.

Pelican. The pelican is one of the largest web–footed birds, often reaching 2 meters (6 feet) in length with a 3 meter (10-foot) wingspread. But in spite of its great size, the pelican swims and flies well.

Pelicans live in colonies, and they are known as experts at catching fish for food. Their long bills

have an elastic pouch on the bottom half. With this pouch a pelican scoops up several quarts of water along with his prey. The pouch serves also as a dinner bowl for baby pelicans, who dip into it for a partially digested treat.

Beautiful in flight, the pelican is a haunting, solitary figure when at rest. Perhaps this was the image in David's mind when he declared, "I am like a pelican of the wilderness" (Ps. 102:6). Other translations render the word as vulture, desert–owl, or jackdaw.

Pig (see *Swine*).

Pigeon (see *Dove*).

Porcupine. The prophets Isaiah and Zephaniah mention a wild creature that lived in desolate ruined places (Is. 14:23; 34:11; Zeph. 2:14). The KJV calls it a bittern, but the RSV translates the animal as hedgehog or porcupine (bustard, NEB). Palestine does have porcupines, even today. They are small animals with sharp needles all over their backs. When in danger, the porcupine rolls up into a prickly ball.

Porpoise (see *Badger*).

Pygarg. The Hebrew term translated pygarg in Deuteronomy 14:5 means "leaper." The RSV translates ibex and the NKJV has mountain goat or addax (margin). This animal probably was the white–rumped antelope. Also see *Antelope, Goat*.

Quail. In Palestine, the quail is a migrating bird that arrives in droves along the shores of the Mediterranean Sea. With their strong flying muscles, these birds can fly rapidly for a short time. When migrating, however, they stretch their wings and allow the wind to bear them along. Sometimes they reach land so exhausted after their long flight that they can be caught by hand.

Most of the time quail remain on the ground, scratching for food and helping farmers by eating insects. Their brown–speckled bodies are inconspicuous, but they often give away their presence by a shrill whistle.

The Hebrew people probably ate dried, salted quail while they were enslaved by the Egyptians. When they longed for meat in the Sinai desert, God promised He would provide enough meat for a month. Then He directed thousands of quail to their camp, where the birds dropped in exhaustion (Num. 11:31–34; Ex. 16:13; Ps. 105:40).

Rabbit (see *Hare*).

Ram (see *Sheep*).

Rat (see *Mouse*).

Raven. In the Bible, raven is a catch–all term for crows, ravens, rooks, jackdaws, magpies, and jays. All were considered unclean by the Jewish people (Lev. 11:15). With a wingspread of about 1 meter (three feet), the raven is the largest member of this family.

Ravens are scavenger birds that will eat almost anything. Their harsh cry has probably contributed to their reputation as birds of ill omen. Since they have keen eyes and strong wings, this may explain why the first bird Noah sent from the ark was a raven (Gen. 8:7). These birds were also known for their practice of pecking out the eyes of a body—a quick way to determine whether their meal was actually dead! (Prov. 30:17).

The Bible indicates that God feeds even young ravens (Job 38:41). Jesus used a similar example to illustrate God's care (Luke 12:24). Because God sent ravens to feed the prophet Elijah, ravens are also associated with God's protective care (1 Kin. 17:4, 6). Solomon brought the expression, "black as a raven," into common use (Song 5:11).

Rock Badger. The rock badger or rock hyrax is a rabbit-sized furry animal. With short ears, sharp teeth, and black-button eyes, it resembles an overgrown guinea pig (Lev. 11:5; coney, KJV, NIV).

"The rock badgers are a feeble folk, yet they make their homes in the crags," says Proverbs 30:26, holding them up as little things that are "exceedingly wise." Feeble, or defenseless they may be, but they find safety in steep, rocky terrain. Their feet have a suction-like grip that enables them to scamper among rocky outcroppings. Their enemies easily overlook a rock badger stretched out motionless on a sun-warmed rock.

Rock Goat (see *Sheep*).
Rock Hyrax (see *Rock Badger*).
Roe Buck (see *Deer*).
Sand Fly (see *Fly*).
Sand Lizard (see *Lizard*).
Sand Partridge (see *Partridge*).
Sand Viper (see *Snake*).
Satyr (see *Goat; Owl*).
Scorpion. The scorpion is a small crawling animal that looks like a flat lobster. A member of the spider family, it has eight legs, two sets of pincers, and a tail with a poisonous stinger. A scorpion feeds on spiders and insects, which it rips apart with its claws. It uses its poisonous sting only when threatened or when it attacks large prey. This sting is seldom fatal, but it can be very painful (Rev. 9:5).

Several species of the scorpion are found in Palestine. Their bite is poisonous but generally not fatal to human beings (Deut. 8:14-15).

Photo by Gustav Jeeninga

During the day, scorpions escape the desert heat by hiding under rocks. They come out at night to hunt and eat. Inhabitants of Bible lands feared scorpions. These animals were an ever-present danger when Moses led the children of Israel through the hot, rocky wilderness (Deut. 8:15).

Jesus' words in Luke 11:12 about giving a person a scorpion instead of an egg may refer to a light-colored scorpion, which could be mistaken for an egg when in a coiled position. The prophet Ezekiel was told by God not to be afraid of his enemies, who were referred to symbolically as scorpions (Ezek. 2:6). King Rehoboam's threat did not mean he would use scorpions as whips (1 Kin. 12:14). In those days a barbed whip or scourge was called a "scorpion."

Screech Owl (see *Owl*).
Sea Cow (see *Badger*).
Sea Gull. Sea gulls are birds about the size of pigeons. They have long wings, which they use to swoop and soar gracefully on air currents. Gulls gather in flocks near bodies of water. They are scavengers who eat garbage as well as fish and insects. Sea gulls are mentioned only in some translations of the Bible. Others translate the Hebrew term as cuckoo, sea mew, or owl (Lev. 11:16; Deut. 14:15).

Sea Mew (see *Sea Gull*).
Sea Monster. Several terms are used in the Bible to describe large sea creatures: sea monsters or serpents, dragons, great fish, whales, and Leviathan. All of these do not refer to one animal, but it is impossible to match the terms with specific marine life. For instance, many animals have been mistaken for sea serpents—large eels, sharks, and giant squid. The Mediterranean and Red Seas contain whales and enough other such "monsters" to provide plenty of material for sea-related scare tales.

Dragons are mythical creatures that appear in many ancient cultures. The prophet Ezekiel saw images of dragons on the city gates when he was exiled in Babylon. The book of Revelation refers to Satan as "a great, fiery red dragon" (12:3). However, Ezekiel and the writer of the Psalms also used the word dragon as a synonym for whale.

Whales, of course, were real creatures that may have been a common sight in the Mediterranean Sea during Bible times. The NEB refers to them in Psalm 148:7 as water-spouts, a possible reference to the sperm whale.

Serpent (see *Snake*).

Sheep. Sheep are mentioned more frequently than any other animal in the Bible—about 750 times. This is only natural since the Hebrew people were known early in their history as a race of wandering herdsmen. Even in the days of the kings, the simple shepherd's life seemed the ideal calling. The Bible makes many comparisons between the ways of sheep and human beings. In the New Testament the church is often compared to a sheepfold.

Well-suited for Palestine's dry plains, sheep fed on grass, woods, and shrubs. They could get along

Photo by Amikam Shoob

The skink, also called the sand lizard (Lev. 11:30, NKJV), is a common reptile in the desert places of the Holy Land.

for long periods without water. Sheep in clusters are easily led, so a single shepherd could watch over a large flock.

Sheep today are bred for white wool. But the sheep of Bible times were probably brown or a mixture of black and white. Modern farmers clip off the tails of sheep for sanitary reasons, but fat tails were prized on biblical sheep. The Hebrews called this "the whole fat tail." When they offered this prized part of the sheep as a burnt offering to God, they burned the "entire fat-tail cut off close by the spine" (Lev. 3:9, NEB).

Sheep were also valuable because they provided meat for the Hebrew diet. Mutton was a nutritious food, and it could be packed away and preserved for winter. And before man learned to spin and weave wool, shepherds wore warm sheepskin jackets.

By nature, sheep are helpless creatures. They depend on shepherds to lead them to water and pasture, to fight off wild beasts, and to anoint their faces with oil when a snake nips them from the grass. Sheep are social animals that gather in flocks, but they tend to wander off and fall into a crevice or get caught in a thorn bush. Then the shepherd must leave the rest of his flock to search for the stray. Jesus used this familiar picture when He described a shepherd who left 99 sheep in the fold to search for one that had wandered off. The God of the Hebrews revealed His nurturing nature by speaking of himself as a shepherd (Psalm 23). Jesus also described Himself as the Good Shepherd who takes care of His sheep (John 10:1–18).

A unique relationship existed between shepherd and sheep. He knew them by name, and they in turn recognized his voice. Sheep were models of submissiveness. Because he demonstrated purity and trustful obedience to the Father, Jesus was also called "the Lamb of God" (John 1:29, 36).

Wild sheep, high-spirited and independent, lived among the tall peaks of Palestine's mountains. Like their domesticated cousins, they flocked together, but their disposition more nearly resembled goats. They are referred to as mountain sheep (Deut. 14:5,

NKJV, RSV, NIV, NASB), chamois (KJV), and rock goat (NEB).

Wild or domestic, the male sheep is called a ram; the female is called a ewe.

Skink (See Lizard).

Snail. Snails are small, slow-crawling animals with a soft body protected by a coiled shell. They move with wave-like motions of their single foot, secreting a slime as they go to make their travel easier. The psalmist may have had this peculiar motion in mind when he spoke of the snail "which melts away as it goes" (Ps. 58:8).

The snail in Leviticus 11:30 (KJV) is probably a skink, a type of sand lizard.

Snake. A snake is the Bible's first—and final—animal villain (Genesis 3; Rev. 20:2). Throughout the Old and New Testaments, several different words for snake or serpent appear some 20 times. Scholars can only make educated guesses as to which of Palestine's many species of snakes are meant in most verses.

The asp and adder are both common in the Holy Land. The asp is a type of cobra with its familiar hood, although its hood is not as pronounced as the Indian cobra's. There is also a desert cobra, which has no hood at all. Adder and viper are two different words for the same deadly snake. A horned viper and sawscale, or carpet viper, are native to Israel. Another species mentioned in the Bible is the sand viper (Is. 30:6, NEB).

In the wilderness, the Israelites were plagued by fiery serpents (Num. 21:6). "Fiery" may indicate the burning fever caused by their bite. Or it may refer to the puff adder, which has yellow, flame-like markings. The cockatrice of the KJV was a mythological monster. It had the wings and head of a cock and the tail of a dragon. According to the superstitious legend about this animal, its look could kill.

Most snakes in Palestine were non-poisonous, but the Jewish people feared and hated all snakes. In the Bible the serpent is often referred to as the symbol of evil and wrongdoing (Ps. 140:3; Jer. 8:17).

A flock of storks in the Huleh Nature Reserve in Israel.

Photo by Willem A. VanGemeren

In spite of this attitude among the Jews, some of Israel's neighbors associated serpents with health, life, and immortality. The kingdom of Lower Egypt took the cobra as its official symbol. Even Moses once lifted up a BRONZE SERPENT before the Israelites at God's command to save the people from the fiery serpents in the wilderness (Num. 21:9). Some continued to worship that bronze serpent until King Hezekiah destroyed it generations later (2 Kin. 18:4).

Snakes are fascinating creatures. Scales on their undersides provide traction. Their forked tongues flick rapidly in and out to collect sensations of touch and smell. Psalm 58:4 is correct in speaking of the "deaf cobra," since snakes have no ears to receive sound waves. Like deaf persons, they rely on physical vibrations to pick up sounds. Thus cobras are not charmed by music, but by movement.

A snake's spine may contain as many as 300 tiny vertebrae. This gives them their amazing flexibility to coil and curve. Their mouths are hinged to permit them to swallow and eat creatures much larger than themselves. Their eyes are protected by transparent lids which are always open, causing scientists to wonder if snakes ever sleep.

Sow (see *Swine*).

Sparrow. Sparrow is the name given to several different species of birds in the Bible. They ate grain and insects and gathered in noisy flocks. The psalmist wrote, "I...am like a sparrow alone on the housetop" (Ps. 102:7). These tiny birds were such social creatures that a lone sparrow was the symbol of deep loneliness.

Sparrows build their untidy nests in the eaves of houses. Sparrows were not driven away when they built their nests in the Temple (Ps. 84:3).

In Jesus' time sparrows sold for a very low price—two for a copper coin, five for two copper coins (Matt. 10:29; Luke 12:6). Perhaps this was the Temple price, for they were considered a poor man's sacrifice. Those who could not afford to sacrifice a sheep or a goat might bring a sparrow. Moses once directed healed lepers to bring two sparrows to the Temple for a cleansing ceremony (Lev. 14:1-7).

Sometimes it seems that only God cares for sparrows. Cats, hawks, and naughty boys prey upon them. People complain about how they multiply, considering them pests. Yet, Jesus declared, "Not one of them falls to the ground apart from your Father's will" (Matt. 10:29). We may not esteem the little sparrow, but the Son of God used it to illustrate our Heavenly Father's watchful care: "You are of more value than many sparrows" (Matt. 10:31; Luke 12:7).

Spider. Hundreds of different species of spiders are found in the Holy Land. A spider's skill at spinning threads into a web is one of nature's miracles. The fragile web of a spider is used to demonstrate the folly of placing confidence in something other than the stable, dependable God (Job 8:14).

Spiders trap their victims in their webs and dissolve them with pre-digestive juices so they can be eaten. Oil on the spider's body keeps it from being entangled in its own web.

Sponge. The sponge is a plant-like animal that lives on the ocean floor. It absorbs nourishment from water passing through its body. When a sponge is removed from water, the cells die, leaving a skeleton. The skeletons of some sponges are flexible and porous. These have been used for centuries as cleaning and water-absorbing tools. Such a sponge, dipped in sour wine, was offered to Christ on the cross (Matt. 27:48; Mark 15:36; John 19:29).

Stag (see *Deer*).

Stork. This goose-sized bird looks ungainly in flight, with its legs dangling and its wings slowly flapping. But people in Palestine were always glad to see the storks on their yearly migration from Europe to Africa. Storks had the reputation of bringing good luck. If they were numerous, surely crops would be good. Farmers welcomed storks because they helped their crops by eating insects.

Both black and white storks were often seen in Palestine. White storks nest as high as possible—often on chimneys. But since houses in the Holy Land had low, flat roofs, they nested instead in the fir trees (Ps. 104:17). In spite of their commendable features, storks were considered unclean (Lev. 11:19; Deut. 14:18).

Swallow. The swallow is a migratory bird quite familiar to residents of the Holy Land. Frequently on the move to warmer climates, swallows gather in huge flocks to travel thousands of miles. A chattering flock can make quite a racket (Is. 38:14). The psalmist makes an interesting distinction between the sparrow, who finds a home, and the swallow, who gets a nest (Ps. 84:3). Only a permanent resident needs a home. Some translations render the Hebrew word for swallow as thrush (Jer. 8:7, NIV, NASB) or wryneck (Jer. 8:7, NEB).

Swallows spend most of their time in the air, catching insects on the wing. They are beautiful birds, brightly colored, with forked tails.

Swan. Swans are seen occasionally in Palestine. As vegetarians, they are related to ducks and geese. Alternate translations of the Hebrew term for swan include ibis, stork, white owl, and water hen. These are better translations, since there seems to be no reason why swans would have been considered unclean (Lev. 11:18, KJV).

Swift. The swift is a small migratory bird often confused with the swallow. Although they are similar, the two birds come from different families. Swifts are strong fliers that can travel short distances at over 100 m.p.h. They spend much of their time feeding on airborne insects.

The prophet Jeremiah must have known the migrating habits of the swift. He spoke of this bird and others that "observe the time of their coming." Unlike these birds, he observed, the rebellious people of the nation of Judah "do not know the judgment of the Lord" (Jer. 8:7).

Swine. The Jewish people had nothing to do with pigs, but these animals still received much attention in the Bible. In Psalm 80:13, Israel's enemies were likened to a "boar out of the woods." Vicious wild pigs (boars) ranged throughout Palestine. Owners of vineyards hated them, because they devoured grapes and trampled their vines. Dogs and men alike feared their razor-sharp tusks. In modern times, the boar is the largest game animal in Israel.

Domesticated pigs (swine) were also raised in Palestine—by Gentiles or unorthodox Jews. Pigs were ceremonially unclean, supposedly because

they did not "chew the cud." The symbol of greed and filth, pigs symbolized a person's unredeemed nature (2 Pet. 2:22). Jesus told a story of a prodigal son who really hit bottom when he had to take care of hogs and even eat food intended for them (Luke 15:15–16).

Tawny Owl (see *Owl*).

Thrush (see *Swift*).

Tortoise (see *Turtle*).

Turtle. Both turtles and tortoises (a type often found in Palestine) and their eggs and meat were eaten. In Numbers 6:10 and Jeremiah 8:7 (KJV), turtle is simply an abbreviation of turtledove. The context clearly indicates that a bird is meant, not the silent, slow-moving turtle.

Turtledove (see *Dove*).

Unicorn. A unicorn is a mythical creature, similar to a horse, with a single spiral horn growing out of its forehead. In the Middle Ages, the unicorn appeared in paintings as a symbol of purity. Many people believed an animal like this really lived. In the Bible, most verses that refer to the unicorn emphasize its great strength (Num. 23:22; 24:8; Deut. 33:17). The biblical writer may have had the aurochs in mind. This horned wild ox was so large and powerful that no one could control or tame it (Job 39:9–10; Ps. 22:21; 92:10; Is. 34:7).

Viper (see *Snake*).

Vulture. Vultures are large, loathsome members of the hawk family. The largest species have a wing-spread of about 32 meters (9 to 10 feet). Most vultures have bare heads and necks. However, the lammergeier (bearded vulture) has dirty-white neck feathers and a tassel of dark feathers hanging from its beak. The Egyptian vulture likewise has neck feathers. A griffon's long neck is covered with fine white down.

The lammergeier is also called the ossifrage (see Lev. 11:13; Deut. 14:12) or the gier eagle (Lev. 11:18; Deut. 14:17).

Vultures feed on dead bodies. For this reason they were considered UNCLEAN animals by the Jewish people (Lev. 11:13; Deut. 14:12–13). Other versions of the Bible translate the word as buzzard, falcon, and bustard.

Wasp. These overgrown relatives of bees are known for their painful sting. Wasps are common throughout the Holy Land. Hornets are a large species of wasp. So savage were these insects when disturbed that Egyptian soldiers used hornets as a symbol of their military might. When the people of Israel were marching toward the Promised Land, God promised He would send hornets before them to drive the Canaanites out of the land (Ex. 23:28). Ancient writers claim that entire tribes were sometimes driven out of a country by wasps or hornets.

Weasel. These animals live in almost every country, including Palestine. They are small and furry, with thin, long bodies and short legs. Weasels eat small animals and have a reputation for stealing eggs. The Bible mentions them only in Leviticus 11:29, in the list of unclean animals. Some modern sources believe the mole (NASB) or mole–rat (NEB) was meant in this verse.

Whale (see *Crocodile; Sea Monster*).

Wild Boar (see *Swine*).

Wild Donkey (see *Donkey*).

Wild Goat (see *Goat*).

Wild Ox (see *Cattle; Unicorn*).

Wolf. Wolves were a menace to the sheep farmers of Palestine. Man's first dogs were probably tamed wolf pups. Perhaps this kinship enabled wolves to lurk near sheepfolds and gain their reputation for treachery.

Of his youngest son, the patriarch Jacob said: "Benjamin is a ravenous wolf" (Gen. 49:27). The Hebrew word translated ravenous means "to rip and tear," indicating the bloodthirsty nature of the wolf. Wolves seem particularly cruel because they seek out the weak, old, and defenseless as victims. The flow of blood incites them to rip and tear even more with their powerful jaws.

In many Bible references, wolves represent ruthless enemies. Jesus warned of false prophets "who come...in sheep's clothing, but inwardly...are ravenous wolves" (Matt. 7:15).

Worm. Worms have no backbone, legs, or eyes, although their bodies are sensitive to light and temperature. But they do play a useful role. They improve the soil by working decaying vegetation into the earth and aerating it with their tunnels.

The Bible speaks both literally and figuratively of worms. The word worm also refers to a worm–like creature, such as insect larva. For instance, the palmerworm, cankerworm, and caterpillar of Joel 1:4 are all caterpillars, which is the larval stage of various moths. (The NKJV, however, translates these as various kinds of locusts.) Grub is another word used for worm in various translations (Is. 51:8, NEB, NASB). Job 7:5 and other passages, which refer to infestation of worms, probably mean maggots, the larvae of flies. Decaying matter often teems with tiny wormlike maggots.

Some worms, such as tapeworms and pinworms, are parasites which invade the human body. Thus Herod could be described as "eaten by worms" (Acts 12:23).

The common earthworm also appears in the Bible. Micah 7:17 refers to worms (snakes, NKJV) coming out of their holes. Perhaps it was an earthworm also that God appointed to strike at the root of Jonah's shade (Jon. 4:7). The psalmist lamented: "I am a worm...and despised" (Ps. 22:6). Job claimed kinship with the lowly worm (Job 17:14). Isaiah 41:14 uses "you worm Jacob" as a metaphor of weakness. The Jews associated worms and fire with the place reserved for the ungodly dead (Is. 66:24; Mark 9:44, 48).

Wryneck (see *Swallow*).

ANIMALS, UNCLEAN (see UNCLEAN).

ANIMALS, WORSHIP OF — a form of pagan worship practiced in the ancient world, especially by the Egyptians, who held certain animals sacred. Some scholars believe that Israel's fashioning of the golden calf during the time of Moses was an imitation of Egyptian animal worship. Both the Old and New Testaments forbid such worship (Ex. 20:2–5; Deut. 5:6–9; Rom. 1:22–25). Also see GODS, PAGAN.

ANISE (see PLANTS OF THE BIBLE).

ANKLE CHAIN — a chain of precious metal that linked a pair of ANKLETS, decorative rings around a person's ankles, in Bible times. Ankle chains forced the wearer to take small steps in rapid fashion. Also see DRESS OF THE BIBLE.

ANKLETS — rings of precious metals around the ankle. Anklets were popular in the ancient world, and archaeologists have unearthed many different types. They varied greatly in size and design. Apparently, some people who wore them even attached small bells to the anklets to make them jingle (Is. 3:16, 18). Some anklets were hollow. This design increased the sound when they were struck together. Some scholars think the sound of anklets joined with an ANKLE CHAIN may have announced the approach of Jeroboam's wife (1 Kin. 14:6).

ANNA [AN ah] *(favor)* — a widow, daughter of Phanuel of the tribe of Asher (Luke 2:36). She was at the Temple in Jerusalem when Mary and Joseph brought Jesus to be dedicated (Luke 2:27). Anna recognized Jesus as the long–awaited Messiah (Luke 2:37–38).

ANNAS [AN us] *(grace of Jehovah)* — one of the high priests at Jerusalem, along with CAIAPHAS, when John the Baptist began his ministry, about A.D. 26 (Luke 3:2). Quirinius, governor of Syria, appointed Annas as high priest about A.D. 6 or 7. Although Annas was deposed by Valerius Gratus, the PROCURATOR of Judea, about A.D. 15, he was still the most influential of the priests and continued to carry the title of high priest (Luke 3:2; Acts 4:6).

After his removal, Annas was officially succeeded by each of his five sons, one grandson, and his son–in–law CAIAPHAS, the high priest who presided at the trial of Jesus (Matt. 26:3, 57; John 18:13–14). During His trial, Jesus was first taken to Annas, who then sent Jesus to Caiaphas (John 18:13, 24). Both Annas and Caiaphas were among the principal examiners when Peter and John were arrested (Acts 4:6).

ANNUNCIATION — the announcement by the angel Gabriel (Luke 1:26–38) to the Virgin Mary of the forthcoming birth of Jesus. The angel told Mary that the Holy Spirit would cause her to conceive a child, and "that Holy One who is to be born will be called the Son of God" (Luke 1:35). Also see VIRGIN BIRTH.

ANOINT, ANOINTING — to authorize, or set apart, a person for a particular work or service (Is. 61:1). The anointed person belonged to God in a special sense. The phrases, "the Lord's anointed," "God's anointed," "My anointed," "Your anointed," or "His anointed" are used of Saul (1 Sam. 26:9, 11), David (2 Sam. 22:51), and Solomon (2 Chr. 6:42). In the New Testament, all who are Christ's disciples are said to be anointed; they are God's very own, set apart and commissioned for service (2 Cor. 1:21).

Priests, kings, and prophets were anointed. Oil was poured on the head of the person being anointed (Ex. 29:7). Kings were set apart through the ritual of anointing, which was performed by a prophet who acted in God's power and authority (1 Sam. 15:1). The Old Testament also records two instances of the anointing of a prophet (1 Kin. 19:16; Is. 61:1).

Jesus the Messiah is described as "anointed." This description is found in the psalms of the Old Testament which prophesy the coming of Christ and in the preaching of the apostle Peter in the Book of Acts.

In the New Testament, anointing was frequently used in connection with healing. The Holy Spirit's activities in a believer's life are pictured in terms associated with anointing. Jesus' disciples anointed the sick (Mark 6:13), and James instructed the elders of the church to anoint the sick with oil (James 5:14). This anointing was for the purpose of healing.

Anointing in the New Testament also refers to the anointing of the Holy Spirit, which brings understanding (1 John 2:20, 27). This anointing is not only for kings, priests, and prophets; it is for everyone who believes in the Lord Jesus Christ. The anointing occurs physically with a substance such as oil, myrrh, or balsam. But this is also a spiritual

King Ashurnasirpal of Assyria being anointed by a winged deity, in a carving from his excavated palace.
Photo by Howard Vos

anointing, as the Holy Spirit anoints a person's heart and mind with the love and truth of God.

ANSWER (see WITNESS).

ANT (see ANIMALS OF THE BIBLE).

ANTEDILUVIANS — the people who lived before the FLOOD. They possessed some skills that compare with modern technology. For example, Cain built cities (Gen. 4:17), Jubal was a musician (Gen. 4:21), and Tubal–Cain was an "instructor of every craftsman in bronze and iron" (Gen. 4:22). Such crafts imply the skills to mine, smelt, and purify brass and iron. That Noah could construct his huge ark is witness to the engineering skills and tools that were available. The antediluvians also lived long lives. Adam lived 930 years; Seth 912 years; Mahalaleel 895 years; Jared 962 years; Methuselah 969 years; Lamech 777 years (Gen. 5:5–31).

Before the Flood, sin was rampant. Life was marked by disobedience, murder, and immorality: "The earth also was corrupt before God, and the earth was filled with violence" (Gen. 6:11). Man's spiritual condition was appalling.

Both Noah and Enoch preached to the antediluvians (2 Pet. 2:5; Jude 14–15). Their preaching, however, was not heeded; and the sinful world was destroyed by the Flood. Noah was the only righteous man whom God could find on the entire earth at the time: "Noah was a just man, perfect in his generations. Noah walked with God" (Gen. 6:9).

In the New Testament, Jesus compared the antediluvians—who were "eating and drinking, marrying and giving in marriage"—to the people who will be living in the end times (Matt. 24:37–41). His words point to the need for watchfulness, for "as it was in the days of Noah, so it will be in the days of the Son of Man" (Luke 17:26).

ANTELOPE (see ANIMALS OF THE BIBLE).

ANTHOTHIJAH [an thoe THIGH juh] — a form of ANTOTHIJAH.

ANTHROPOMORPHISM — the practice of describing God in human terms, as if He has feet (Ex. 24:10), hands (John 10:29), a face (Matt. 18:10), a heart (Hos. 11:8), and so forth. Although the Old and New Testaments deny any literal similarity of form between God and His creatures (Job 9:32; John 4:24), the Bible frequently uses such human language to affirm that God is personal and active in His creation.

The appearance of Jesus, God's Son, in a human body is a literal revelation of God in the form of man. Jesus was "in the form of God," but He took "the form of a servant," the "likeness" and "appearance" of man (Phil. 2:6–8), to save us and reveal the depth of God's love (John 14:9; 1 John 1:1–2). Therefore, with respect to Jesus, we can literally speak of God in human form. Also see GOD.

ANTHROPOPATHISM — the practice of describing God as if He displays human emotions, such as jealousy (Ex. 20:5), anger (Ps. 77:9), love (Jon. 4:2), and mercy (Ps. 103:8). Although the Old and New Testaments plainly show that God is beyond our human experiences (Is. 40:18; 1 Cor. 2:14; 1 Tim. 6:16), the Bible frequently uses such language to declare that God is personal and that He responds to the actions of His creatures. Also see GOD.

ANTICHRIST, THE — a false prophet and evil being who will set himself up against Christ and the people of God in the last days before the SECOND COMING. The term is used only in the writings of John in the New Testament. It refers to one who stands in opposition to all that Jesus Christ represents (1 John 2:18, 22; 4:3; 2 John 7). John wrote that several antichrists existed already in his day—false teachers who denied the deity and the incarnation of Christ—but that the supreme Antichrist of history would appear at some future time.

The Antichrist's primary work is deception, which also characterizes SATAN in his attempts to undermine the work of God in the world. Satan's deception began in the Garden of Eden (Genesis 3) and will continue until the end of time. The DRAGON (or serpent) of Revelation 12 is Satan, the Serpent mentioned in Genesis 3. Thus the thread of Satan's deceptive work may be traced from Genesis through Revelation. That work reaches its climax in the Antichrist, who receives his authority and power from the dragon, Satan (Rev. 13:4).

The work of Satan through the Antichrist is clearly rooted in the prophecies of Daniel. Daniel spoke of a dreadful beast with ten horns and one little horn (Dan. 7:7–8). The Ancient of Days will kill the beast and throw it in the fire (Dan. 7:11). Then, according to Daniel, one like the Son of Man will receive the everlasting kingdom (Dan. 7:13–14).

The Antichrist will be the sum total of the beasts referred to in Daniel 7 (Rev. 13:1–4). He will speak arrogant, boastful words; and he will be aided by a FALSE PROPHET, who will make the entire earth worship him (Rev. 13:11–12) and receive his mark (Rev. 13:16–17). The number of the beast, says John, is 666—a mysterious code name.

Those who worship the Antichrist will experience certain doom through the wrath of God (Rev. 14:9–11). The Antichrist makes war against Christ and His army, but he is captured and is "cast alive into the lake of fire burning with brimstone" (Rev. 19:20). He is later joined by the DEVIL; together they "will be tormented day and night forever and ever" (Rev. 20:10). The devil, the BEAST (or Antichrist), and the false prophet form a kind of unholy trinity, counterfeiting Father, Son, and Holy Spirit. After much wickedness and suffering has been loosed against Christ and His people, the satanic rebellion will be crushed by the power of God.

Although the apostle Paul does not use the term Antichrist, he surely had the Antichrist in mind when he wrote of the great apostasy, or falling away, that would occur before the return of Christ (2 Thess. 2:1–12). The Antichrist is also called the lawless one (v. 9) who, empowered and inspired by Satan, will lead the final rebellion against God (v. 3, NEB), but will be destroyed at the coming of the Lord. Paul urges believers to stand firm in the faith and not be deceived by the Antichrist who will display "all kinds of counterfeit miracles, signs and wonders" (2 Thess. 2:9, NIV).

The main reason the Bible discusses the Antichrist is not to encourage idle speculation, but to warn believers not to be misled by his deceit (Matt. 24:4–5, 23–24). The times when the Antichrist will appear will be very hard for the faithful. They need to be prepared with special instructions on how to deal with this unsettling event.

ANTIMONY (see MINERALS OF THE BIBLE).

ANTIOCH OF PISIDIA [AN tih ock, pih SID ih uh] — a city of southern Asia Minor in Phrygia, situated just north of the territory of Pisidia (see Map 7, D–2). Antioch was an important first–century commercial center and an important center for the spread of the gospel. Founded by Seleucus Nicator (about 300 B.C.), it became a great center for commerce and was inhabited by many Jews.

The apostle Paul preached in this city's synagogue and founded a church there during his first missionary journey (Acts 13:14–49). Just as Antioch exerted great cultural and political influence over the surrounding area, so also it became a strong base from which to launch the church's evangelistic outreach (Acts 13:42–49). In reaction to Paul's success, the Jews at Antioch caused some influential women to turn against the gospel and had Paul driven out of the city (Acts 13:50).

ANTIOCH OF SYRIA [AN tih ock, SIHR ih uh] — the capital of the Roman province of Syria which played an important part in the first–century expansion of the church. Antioch was situated on the east bank of the Orontes River, about 27 kilometers (16.5 miles) from the Mediterranean Sea and 485 kilometers (300 miles) north of Jerusalem (see Map 6, D–2). The city was founded about 300 B.C. by Seleucus I Nicator, one of the three successors to ALEXANDER the Great, and named for his father Antiochus.

The early history of the church is closely connected with Antioch of Syria. One of the first seven "deacons," Nicolas, was a "proselyte from Antioch" (Acts 6:5). After the stoning of Stephen (Acts 7:54–60), great persecution caused certain disciples to flee from Jerusalem to Antioch where they preached the Gospel to the Jews (Acts 8:1; 11:19). Others arrived later and had success preaching to the Gentiles (Acts 11:20–21).

When the church leaders at Jerusalem heard of this success in Antioch, they sent Barnabas to visit the church there (Acts 11:25–26).

Apparently, Paul and Barnabas used Antioch as the base for their missionary journeys into Asia Mi-

Photo by Howard Vos

Tyche, the goddess of good fortune, connected with the pagan worship of the residents of Antioch of Syria.

nor (Acts 13:1–3; 15:36–41; 18:22–23). Following the first missionary journey, Antioch became the scene of an important dispute. Certain men from Judea taught that Gentile converts must be circumcised and follow other rules for converts to Judaism before becoming Christians (Acts 15:1–2). This theological disagreement led to a church council at Jerusalem. Paul and Barnabas were sent here to report how God had given them success in bringing the gospel to the Gentiles. The council decided that Gentile converts did not have to be circumcised. Antioch is now known as Antakya, in modern–day Turkey.

ANTIOCHUS [an TIE oh kus] (*withstander*) — the name of 13 members of the Seleucid dynasty of Syria. The SELEUCIDS governed Palestine from 280 B.C., following the division of ALEXANDER the Great's empire, until the Roman commander Pompey made Syria a Roman province in 63 B.C. The Book of Daniel prophesies about the following three of these rulers, although it mentions none of them by name:

1. Antiochus II (261–246 B.C.), surnamed Theos ("god"). He was a drunken, immoral ruler easily swayed by favorites. The prophecy in Daniel 11:6 probably refers to him; for he divorced his wife Laodice, who was his half sister, to marry Berneice, the daughter of Ptolemy, the ruler of Egypt.

2. Antiochus III (223–187 B.C.), surnamed Megas ("the Great"). He was the second son of Seleucus II Callinicus and the successor of his older brother, Seleucus III Soter. The Seleucids of Syria

and the Ptolemies of Egypt waged a continual struggle for control in Palestine. Antiochus III finally defeated the Egyptian general Scopas at Pani, or Panias (the New Testament CAESAREA PHILIPPI), in 198 B.C., giving the Seleucids complete control of Palestine. This victory eventually led to the worst persecution the Jews had yet endured. Some scholars see Daniel 11:10–19 as a reference to Antiochus III, but the allusion is vague.

3. Antiochus IV (175–164 B.C.), surnamed Epiphanes (God manifest) but called by his enemies Epimanes (madman). Antiochus IV was one of the cruelest rulers of all time. Like his father, Antiochus III the Great, he was enterprising and ambitious; however, he had a tendency to cruelty that bordered on madness. His primary aim—to unify his empire by spreading Greek civilization and culture—brought him into direct conflict with the Jews. This conflict broke into open rebellion in 167 B.C. Accounts of these conflicts are found in the apocryphal book of 2 Maccabees.

The revolt began with Antiochus' edict that sought to unite all the peoples of his kingdom in religion, law, and custom. The Jews were the only people who would not adhere to this edict. Antiochus issued regulations against observing the Sabbath, practicing circumcision, and keeping all food laws. These regulations were followed by the "ABOMINATION OF DESOLATION" (Dan. 11:31)—the erection of the altar of the Greek god Zeus over the altar of the burnt offering in the Temple. Jews were forced to participate in heathen festivities and were put to death if they were caught with the Book of the Law in their possession.

As the revolt, led by Judas Maccabeus, gained momentum, the people of Israel united to overthrow Seleucid domination of their land. The Syrians were routed and the Temple was cleansed on the 25th of Chislev, 165 B.C. This cleansing is now observed by the Jews as the Feast of Lights (Hanukkah), around December 25. According to ancient writers, Antiochus IV withdrew into the East following his defeat. He died in Persia a madman. Some scholars see the "little horn" of Daniel 8:9 as a reference to Antiochus IV Epiphanes.

Coin issued by Antiochus IV Epiphanes, Syrian ruler whose desecration of the Jewish temple triggered the revolt of the Maccabees.

ANTIPAS [AN tih pas] (*against all*) — the name of two New Testament men:

1. A son of Herod the Great. (See HEROD ANTIPAS.)

2. A Christian martyr of the church of Pergamos (Rev. 2:13). According to tradition, he became bishop of Pergamos.

ANTIPATRIS [an TIP uh tris] (*belonging to Antipater*) — a city built on the Plain of Sharon by Herod the Great and named in honor of his father, Antipater (see Map 6, A–3). Located on the Roman military road between Jerusalem and Caesarea, Antipatris was the lodging–place for the apostle Paul and the Roman soldiers who were transporting him as a prisoner to Felix, the governor of Judea (Acts 23:31). The city was the site of the Old Testament APHEK (Josh. 12:18; 1 Sam. 4:1; 29:1).

ANTITYPE [AN tih type] — a fulfillment or completion of an earlier truth revealed in the Bible. Baptism in the New Testament, for example, as an expression of one's salvation, fulfills the function served by Noah's ark in the Old Testament. Thus, Noah's ark was a type, and baptism was an antitype (1 Pet. 3:21).

ANTONIA, TOWER OF [an TONE ih ah] — a fortress–palace rebuilt by Herod the Great and situated at the northwest corner of the Temple area. An earlier tower constructed on this site may possibly go back to the time of King Solomon. Herod named the rebuilt tower after his friend, Mark Antony.

The fortress was rectangular in shape, measuring about 165 meters (490 feet) by 87 meters (260 feet), with walls about 19 meters (60 feet) high. Each corner had a high tower, three of which were 24 meters (75 feet) high. The tower in the northwest corner, which overlooked the Temple area, however, was about 32 meters (100 feet) high. Stairs connected the Antonia with the Temple area (see Acts 21:35, 40).

Soldiers from the Antonia ("the barracks") rescued the apostle Paul from enraged crowds on several occasions (Acts 21:27–36; 22:24; 23:10). Paul was held in the fortress in protective custody until a military escort took him to Caesarea (Acts 23:12–24; 23:31–35).

ANTOTHIJAH [an toe THIE jah] (*belonging to Anathoth*) — a descendant of Shashak (1 Chr. 8:24; Anthothijah, NASB, NIV, RSV).

ANTOTHITE [AN tahth ight] — a form of ANATHOTHITE.

ANUB [A nubb] (meaning unknown) — a son of Koz in the genealogy of Judah (1 Chr. 4:8).

ANVIL (see TOOLS OF THE BIBLE).

APE (see ANIMALS OF THE BIBLE).

APELLES [a PELL ez] — a Christian at Rome to whom the apostle Paul sent greetings, describing Apelles as "approved in Christ" (Rom. 16:10).

APHARSACHITES [a FAR sack ites] — KJV word for an eastern tribe from beyond the Euphrates River settled in Samaria by the king of Assyria (Ezra 5:6; 6:6).

APHARSATHCHITES [a FAR sath kites] (meaning unknown) — KJV word for an unknown people of the Assyrian Empire. Apparently they were Assyrian or Persian colonists (Ezra 4:9) settled in Samaria by Ashurbanipal, king of Assyria (Ezra 4:10). They are probably the same people as the APHARSACHITES of Ezra 5:6; 6:6.

Site of ancient Aphek, a Philistine city conquered by Joshua (Josh. 12:7, 18).
Photo by Willem A. VanGemeren

APHEK [A fek] (*fortress*) — the name of several ancient Palestinian towns:

1. A city of the plain of Sharon. Joshua conquered the king of Aphek while taking the Promised Land (Josh. 12:18).

2. A town mentioned in Joshua 13:4 as located in the northern edge of Canaanite territory.

3. A town in the territory alloted to the tribe of Asher (Josh 19:30; Aphik, Judg. 1:31). The Asherites were unable to expel the Canaanites from this city.

4. A town east of the Sea of Galilee (see Map 3, A–3) where God gave Ahab victory over Ben–Hadad and the Syrian army (1 Kin. 20:26–30). Later the prophet Elisha, while on his deathbed, prophesied Israel's victory at Aphek over the Syrian army (2 Kin. 13:17).

APHEKAH [a FEE kuh] (*fortress*) — a village in the hill country of Judah (Josh. 15:53).

APHIAH [a FIE ah] (meaning unknown) — a Benjamite who was an ancestor of King Saul (1 Sam. 9:1).

APHIK [A fick] — a form of APHEK No. 3.

APHRAH [AF ruh] — a form of BETH APHRAH.

APHSES [AF sez] — a form of HAPPIZZEZ.

APIS [A pis] — the sacred bull–god of Memphis (the biblical NOPH) worshiped by the ancient Egyptians (Jer. 46:15; NEB, RSV). Apis was thought to be the reincarnation of Ptah, a creator god. Some scholars believe the Apis bull inspired the Israelites to make the golden calf at Mount Sinai (Exodus 32).

APOCALYPSE [a POCK ah lips] (see REVELATION OF JOHN).

APOCALYPTIC LITERATURE [a pock uh LIP tik] — a certain type of Jewish and Christian literature written in Egypt and Palestine during the period from 200 B.C. to A.D 200. The word *apocalypse* is a Greek word meaning "revelation." Therefore, apocalyptic literature is a special kind of writing that arose among the Jews and Christians to reveal certain mysteries about heaven and earth, humankind and God, angels and demons, the life of the world today, and the world to come.

Apocalyptic literature probably arose in the tradition of the PROPHETS of Israel, but it came several centuries after their time. The last prophet of Israel, Malachi, wrote about 450 B.C. Two books in the Bible—the Book of Daniel in the Old Testament and the New Testament Book of Revelation—are good examples of the apocalyptic literary form.

The following additional Jewish and Christian books are also classified as apocalyptic by most Bible scholars: Apocalypse of Abraham, Apocalypse of Baruch, Ascension of Isaiah, Assumption of Moses, 2 Baruch, Book of Jubilees, 1 and 2 Enoch, Life of Adam and Eve, the Sybilline Oracles, Testament of Abraham, and the Testaments of the 12 Patriarchs. Most of these books are found in the PSEUDEPIGRAPHA of the Old Testament.

In 1974 several apocalyptic books and fragments were found among the Dead Sea Scrolls, including the War Scroll and Book of Mysteries. In the second and third century A.D., Christian writers produced a number of apocalypses, including The Revelation of Peter, The Revelation of Paul, and The Revelation of Thomas. All these writings are included in a collection known as the New Testament Apocrypha.

Most of the apocalyptic books were written by Jews in reaction to the oppression of their people by foreign powers. Often they wrote to explain why evil seemed to prosper while the righteous suffered. The Christian apocalyptic writings were influenced by these earlier Jewish works. The Book of Revelation in the New Testament uses symbols and images that occur in the Book of Enoch, and the book known as 4 Ezra, written about A.D. 100, seems to parallel the New Testament book of Revelation in several ways. The close similarities between Jewish and Christian apocalyptic literature explains why scholars group them into one category and study both Jewish and Christian apocalyptic literature together.

Characteristics. Apocalyptic literature has certain literary devices or styles that set it apart from other literature.

Visions—Although other types of literature use visions to communicate (see Isaiah 6), apocalyptic literature uses visions as a way of revealing secrets from heaven about the present and the future of humankind. Often these visions are caused by some trauma or major personal or social event that created a crisis in the writer's experience (compare Rev. 1:10 with 4 Ezra 3:1). These visions lead in turn to further explanations about coming events or other visions and dreams.

Ethics—As a result of these visionary experiences, the writer draws ethical conclusions. In Revelation 2—3, John writes seven letters to seven churches in western Asia Minor. Each letter is addressed to specific issues facing the church. These letters were written after John saw a vision and was commissioned by God to write (Rev. 1:19). They call the churches to specific ethical or moral decisions.

Anonymous authorship—The Book of Revelation in the New Testament is the only book of apocalyptic literature that gives the name of the author. All other apocalyptic books are attributed to famous prophets of the past, such as Ezra, Enoch, Baruch, Jeremiah, Abraham, Moses, and Adam. The reason why these authors identified their writings with great persons in Israel's history probably was to add credibility to their work. A vision from Enoch, for example, would carry more weight than if it were from some contemporary writer.

Powerful symbolism — Each of the apocalyptic books is rich in symbolism. The reader's imagination is stretched. Those who read the apocalyptic books just after they had been written knew the meaning of the symbols used by the author. The

Photo by Amikam Shoob

Scorpions were sometimes mentioned in prophetic and apocalyptic writings as graphic symbols of divine judgment (Rev. 9:3, 10).

events of the time, evil rulers, and pagan nations are symbolized by distorted animals and beasts, horrible signs from heaven, or a chaotic flowing of waters. But the people who are faithful to God are portrayed as majestic animals, like a lion, or a well kept plant. The purpose of this symbolism was to make the contrast between good and evil obvious to the reader.

Messages. Through the apocalyptic books, the authors communicated several important messages to their readers. The following themes occur in all the apocalyptic writings.

The end is coming soon—Throughout these books the authors write about the arrival of the end times within the near future: "For the youth of this world is past, and the strength of the creation already exhausted and the advent of the times is very short, yea, they have passed by: and the pitcher is near to the cistern, and the ship to the port, and the course of the journey to the city, and life to its consummation" (2 Baruch 85:10).

In the other books various images are used to spell out the coming end. This apocalyptic view of the last days gives a certain urgency to these writings.

The whole universe involved—The end of the world is not a solitary event for the earth alone; it extends to the whole universe. This planet is only a part of a greater tragedy. An awful time is in store, for all nations of the earth will "be seized with great panic" (4 Ezra 5:1).

History divided into fixed segments—Along with a pessimistic view of history, the apocalyptic books declare that history has been determined by God before creation. World history is divided into fixed

time periods. These fixed segments have been established, and mankind simply lives out the already established drama.

History may be divided into two periods—this world, which is ruled by Satan and his legions, and the next world, in which wickedness will be abolished and God will rule supreme.

Angels and demons—Apocalyptic literature is filled with angels and demons who are actively involved in the drama of events. The problem of evil is explained by pointing to the demons and Satan himself as the forces that cause evil. Angels who have not fallen (1 Enoch 6—36) are used by God to protect and serve his faithful people. The Books of Enoch, Testament of the Twelve Patriarchs, and Jubilees give detailed descriptions of the task of angels and demons. These truths are also echoed by the Book of Revelation in the New Testament.

The New Heaven and the New Earth. The end times as portrayed in the apocalyptic writings return to the beginning of creation. Out of heaven will come a new heaven and a new earth. The old will be destroyed, replaced by a new creation where God will rule (Revelation 20—22; 2 Enoch 65:7-10; 2 Baruch 48). Only those who have been faithful to God's law will be saved.

The Kingdom of God. Enoch 41 describes the place from which all the world will be judged. Other apocalyptic books describe the Kingdom of God as the ultimate rule in the new creation (Enoch 84:3; Rev. 11:15; Dan. 4:17). All through the apocalyptic literature the image of the Kingdom or rule of God is central. All events are determined from God's throne.

A Messiah. A Messiah or mediator between God

and man appears in most of the apocalyptic writings as one who accomplishes the final salvation of the world. This figure appears either as a Messiah, a son of man, or chosen one, or as a mediator between God and man.

Glory. The righteous have suffered in this world because it has been ruled by Satan. But this situation will change in the future. This vision of glory appears as a word of hope or encouragement to the faithful—those who trust in God. Glory will come to God's people. They have the power necessary to live full and meaningful lives in this world now.

APOCRYPHA, THE [a POCK rih fuh] — a group of books written during a time of turmoil in the history of the Jewish people, from about 200 B.C. to about A.D. 100. These books fall into two main divisions, Old Testament apocryphal books and New Testament apocryphal books.

The Old Testament books, 15 in number, were written during the period from about 150 B.C. to about A.D. 70, when the Jewish people were in rebellion against the repression of foreign military rulers. These books were excluded from some early versions of the Old Testament but included in others. This explains why Bibles used by Roman Catholics contain the Old Testament Apocrypha, while they are not included in most Protestant editions of the Bible.

The books known as the New Testament Apocrypha were written during the second and third centuries A.D., long after the death of the apostles and other eyewitnesses to the life and ministry of Jesus. None of these books were included in the New Testament because they were judged as unworthy and not authoritative by officials of the early church.

The Old Testament Apocrypha. The series of events that led to the writing of the Old Testament apocryphal books began in 167 B.C., when the Jews revolted against the king of Syria, Antiochus IV Epiphanes. A pious Jewish priest, Mattathias, and his sons led the rebellion. Mattathias refused to obey Antiochus' command that the Jews worship his gods and offer a pagan sacrifice. Mattathias killed the Syrian official as well as a fellow Jew who was offering the sacrifice and declared: "Follow me, every one of you who is zealous for the law and strives to maintain the covenant. He and his sons took to the hills, leaving all their belongings behind in the town" (1 Macc. 2:27-28, NEB).

Guerrilla warfare against the Syrians followed, until the Jews established control of Palestine. Early in the revolt one of the sons of Mattathias, Judas Maccabeus (Maccabeus means "hammer"), cleansed the Temple in Jerusalem from the pollution of the Syrian sacrifices. This day has been celebrated annually by the Jews since that time in the festival known as Chanukah (or Hanukkah), the Feast of Dedication (John 10:22).

These events helped stir the Jewish people to rededicate themselves to the law of Moses. In the fight to establish their independence and uphold their traditions, some Jewish authors wrote to encourage their own people. The apocryphal books show clearly that the authors were enthusiastic for faith in God and the study of His Word.

From 142 to 63 B.C. the Jews were led in their rebellion against foreign oppression by the family of Mattathias, known as the Hasmoneans. Simon Asamonaios was the grandfather of Mattathias, and his name was applied to all the members of this great family. In spite of the respect given to the Hasmoneans in the early years of their influence, civil strife again plagued the Jews. The Syrians continued to fight for power over the land of Israel. Judas Maccabeus finally made an agreement with Rome that the Romans would come to the aid of the Jews if they should need assistance in their struggle. About a century later some of the Jews did appeal to Rome for help. Pompey, a powerful Roman general, brought order to Jerusalem and made Judea part of a Roman province.

In 37 B.C. the land of Israel, called Palestine, was placed under the rule of a Roman official, Herod the Great (37-4 B.C.). Herod was actually a Roman vassal and was hated by most of the Jews. In spite of this hostility, Herod managed to launch an ambitious building program in Palestine. He created the magnificent port city of CAESAREA on the Mediterranean Sea and improved the Temple in Jerusalem. The western wall still stands today in Jerusalem as evidence of Herod's skill as a builder.

After Herod's death (4 B.C.), his sons divided Palestine into four regions, ruling the land with varying degrees of success. In A.D. 66 the Jews again grew angry over the foreign domination of their land. Under the encouragement of radical freedom fighters known as ZEALOTS, the Jews started a disastrous war with the Romans. This led to the destruction of Jerusalem and the Temple in A.D. 70 and the end of the Jewish nation.

This brief historical sketch provides the background for the Old Testament apocryphal writings. The Jewish people were continually wondering what God was saying to them through their struggles. Out of their experiences arose the books of the Apocrypha. Following are brief descriptions of the books in this Old Testament collection.

Baruch—This book is a collection of materials written during the period from 150 B.C. to 60 B.C. Set in the period of the prophet Jeremiah and his secretary Baruch around 585 B.C., it actually speaks to Jews who were living during the period of the Hasmoneans (142-63 B.C.). It was written originally in Hebrew and later was translated into Greek.

Baruch contains a letter (1:1-14), a prayer-sermon (1:15—3:8), a hymn (3:9—4:4), and a lament (4:5—5:9). Jerusalem had fallen into the hands of the enemy, but this book declared that God will not forget His people. The refrain, "Take heart, my children! Cry out to God, and he will rescue you from tyranny and from the power of your enemies" (4:21, NEB), echoes throughout Baruch. Some scholars believe Baruch was reworked many times and then was put into its final form by a rabbi in Palestine after the destruction of the Temple in A.D. 70.

Bel and the Dragon—This book is an addition to the Old Testament's Book of Daniel and was written by a Jew in Palestine around 50 B.C. The author used Babylonian mythology to declare that the God of the Hebrews can outwit the tricks of the priests of Babylon through the faith of the prophet Daniel. Daniel demonstrated that there is no God other than the Lord God of the Hebrews and that Bel, the supposed God of Babylon, does not exist. In this book Daniel also killed a dragon in a clever way. This was the author's way of showing that pagan gods are worshiped because the priests deceive the people. Only God is worthy of our praise, because He is a living God.

Ecclesiasticus, or the Wisdom of Jesus, Son of Sirach—This is a book of wisdom teachings in the Apocrypha. It should not be confused with the Book of Ecclesiastes in the Old Testament. The word Ecclesiasticus means "The Church Book" in Latin. But the title of the Book of Ecclesiastes comes from a Greek word which means "assembly" or "gathering."

Ecclesiasticus is a masterpiece of wisdom literature, organized into teachable units. Many subjects are contained in this work, including faith in God as Creator and Sustainer of life, love of wisdom and ethical conduct, virtue and good deeds, the value of the tradition of the past, proper behavior in eating and drinking, work and commerce, study and teaching, poverty and wealth, and health and sickness. It was written by Jesus ben Eleazar ben Sira, a Jew living in Jerusalem around 190 B.C.

The author of Ecclesiasticus upholds Israel's traditions as a channel through which God's Word is communicated. His essay on the great people in Israel's history gives the reader an appreciation for the kind of people who make our world pleasant and worthwhile. The righteous person receives a reward from God, while the sinner and unbeliever will be punished. The final chapter, 51, contains a beautiful prayer.

Esdras, Books of—The First Book of Esdras is a historical narrative taken from 2 Chronicles 35:1; 36:23; Ezra 1:1–11; 2:1—3:13; 4:1—10:44; and Nehemiah 7:73—8:12 of the Old Testament. It begins with the Passover celebrated by Josiah, the king of Judah (640–609 B.C.). Then the book discusses Josiah's death in the battle of Megiddo and continues with the story of the events leading up to the fall of Jerusalem and the deportation of the Jews to Babylon (587 B.C.). Cyrus, the great king of the Medes who freed the Jews from bondage in Babylon in 539 B.C., is also described.

Included in the Book of 1 Esdras is a description of the building of the Temple by the returned exiles in Jerusalem and the problems encountered in its reconstruction. An interesting part of the story is the trouble that the Jews had with the Samaritans. Thus, 1 Esdras provides an excellent background for a better understanding of the conflict between the Jews and Samaritans—a problem mentioned throughout the four gospels in the New Testament.

The story of the three young men (1 Esdras 3:1—5:6) who guarded the Persian King Darius I (522–486 B.C.) is an interesting drama. The guards were instructed to write down what they considered to be the most powerful thing on earth. Their answers and the surprise fourth answer (trust) make this book a delightful contribution to the wisdom writings of the Jewish people.

The purpose of the book of 1 Esdras was to promote the value of worship of the Lord among Jews. It was probably written during the time of the Hasmoneans, about 150 B.C., by a zealous Jew who held to this worship tradition and encouraged others to do the same.

The Second Book of Esdras was probably written during the same time period as the Book of Revelation in the New Testament, around A.D. 96, by a Palestinian Jew who was disillusioned over the destruction of the Temple of Jerusalem in A.D. 70. He was puzzled by the apparent evil in a world where God was supposed to be in control.

The word Babylon in 2 Esdras is a code name for Rome. According to the writer, Rome had become

The Order of the Apocrypha

The individual books of the Old Testament Apocrypha are arranged in alphabetical order in the accompanying article. But here is the order in which these 15 books are generally arranged in Bibles that contain the Apocrypha:

1. First Esdras
2. Second Esdras
3. Tobit
4. Judith
5. The Additions to Esther
6. The Wisdom of Solomon
7. Ecclesiasticus, or the Wisdom of Jesus, the Son of Sirach
8. Baruch
9. The Letter of Jeremiah
10. The Prayer of Azariah and the Song of the Three Young Men
11. Susanna
12. Bel and the Dragon
13. The Prayer of Manasseh
14. First Maccabees
15. Second Maccabees

Remains of Antioch of Syria, capital of the dynasty which ruled Palestine during the era of the Maccabees and the writing of much of the Old Testament Apocrypha.

evil in A.D. 96–100. The book is a good example of Jewish APOCALYPTIC LITERATURE. In many ways it is like the Book of Revelation in the New Testament. The revelations in the book lament the destruction of Jerusalem and deal with the questions of the reward of the righteous, the punishment of the wicked, and the end of the age.

This gloomy book is tied together with a thread of hope. Deliverance for God's people is assured. God is ultimately in control of history, and His Word (in written form) will never disappear.

Esther, Additions to the Book of—The Old Testament Book of Esther does not mention the name of God or any worship rituals. Most scholars agree that these apocryphal additions to the Book of Esther were written to connect Esther to the traditions of Israel's faith in a more explicit way.

Jeremiah, Epistle of—This letter is a sermon against idolatry. It asks the readers to beware of false gods. The date of its writing is unknown, although some scholars have suggested a date as early as 541 B.C. Others believe it was written during the time of the invasion of Palestine by the Romans in 63 B.C. Some fragments of the letter were discovered among the DEAD SEA SCROLLS in the caves of Qumran.

Judith—This book contains one of the most delightful stories in the Apocrypha. A wise and intelligent Jewish woman, Judith was devoted to observing the law of Moses. The story takes place during the reign of a king of Assyria named Nebuchadnezzar. His general, Holophernes, was about to destroy the Jewish inhabitants of the city of Be-

thulia when Judith came to the aid of her fellow Jews. The people prayed to God for help, allowing Him five days in which to help them, or they would surrender (1:1—7:32). Judith went to the enemy camp and beheaded Holophernes, bringing his head back to the Jews of the city. Terrified, the Assyrians fled (8:1—16:29), and the Jews were saved.

Judith appealed to Jews living during a time of discouragement and defeat. It was probably written during the Hasmonean period (142–63 B.C.). Judith emphasized the importance of faithfulness to the law of Moses and the power of God in the lives of His people.

Maccabees, Books of—The First Book of Maccabees is a history of the struggle of the Jews in Judea under the leadership of one family, the Hasmoneans, from about 175 to 135 B.C. Judas Maccabeus was the family's most famous leader. Most of the action took place in and around Jerusalem. The book includes speeches, prayers, laments, and psalms of victory, all woven into a beautiful history of the Jews of that period. The author was probably a Jew living in Jerusalem who supported the Maccabean revolt and the importance of the law of Moses. Some scholars suggest that one of the members of the family of the Maccabees wrote the book, some time during the period from 103 to 63 B.C. The theme of the book is that faithful obedience to the law brings success by God's standards.

The Second Book of Maccabees is a two–part work that describes the events that occurred in Judea from 191 to 162 B.C. In a sense, it serves as a prelude to the Book of 1 Maccabees. The first part of the book (1:1—2:18) consists of two letters. One of the letters (1:1-10) was from Jews in Jerusalem to Jews in Egypt, telling them how to observe the Jewish holiday of Chanukah (or Hanukkah) which celebrates the cleansing of the Temple under Judas Maccabeus in 164 B.C. The other letter (1:10—2:18) was sent by the same group of Jews in Jerusalem to Aristobulus, a Jewish teacher in Egypt, encouraging him to celebrate the Temple festival.

The second section of the Second Book of Maccabees (2:19—15:40) describes events in Judea from 191 to 162 B.C. A good description of the celebration of Chanukah (Hanukkah) appears in 10:1-9. The entire book is important because of its teaching that the world was created "out of nothing" (7:28), and its clear statement of belief in the resurrection of the dead (7:9, 14, 23, 29).

Prayer of Azariah and the Song of the Three Young Men—This brief book is included in the Apocrypha because it represents an addition to the Old Testament Book of Daniel. It probably was written about 150 B.C. by a pious Jew who expanded the famous story in Daniel 3 about Shadrach, Meshach, and Abed-Nego—the three young Hebrews who were thrown into the fiery furnace by the king of Babylon.

According to this addition to the biblical account, Azariah (Abed-Nego) began to pray while they were in the fire (vv. 1–22). After the prayer, all three began to sing as they stood in the flames (vv. 28–68). Their songs came from various psalms of the Jewish people.

Prayer of Manasseh—This book is an addition to the Old Testament Book of 2 Chronicles. Manasseh was one of the most wicked kings in Israel's history. He burned his sons as offerings (2 Chr. 33:6) and practiced magic. After a humiliating defeat in battle, Manasseh repented of his sin, and God forgave him (2 Chr. 33:10-13). The Prayer of Manasseh was probably written later by a pious Jew who blended various psalms and prayers into this beautiful prayer of repentance.

The outline of the prayer follows a typical outline for a worship service: invocation and praise to God (vv. 1-7), confession of sins (vv. 8-12), a request for forgiveness (v. 13), and a concluding thanksgiving (vv. 14-15).

Song of the Three Young Men (see *Prayer of Azariah*).

Susanna—This book is an addition to the Old Testament Book of Daniel. It is full of suspenseful tragedy and wisdom. Written around 110-60 B.C. by a Jew in Palestine, the story is about a woman named Susanna, who was nearly sexually abused by two respected elders of the community. Susanna was brought to court by the elders on a charge of adultery. She stood condemned and sentenced to death until Daniel raised an objection and proved that the two elders had lied.

This is a powerful story that challenges the normal method of taking evidence in Jewish courts during the first century B.C. Susanna is important because it gives insights into the Jewish legal process during that time and because it supports another view of how evidence can be taken from a witness.

Tobit—This book is a narrative about Tobit, a Jew who was taken into captivity to Nineveh, the capital of Assyria, after the defeat of Israel in 722 B.C. Tobit was a strict observer of the law of Moses who met with unfortunate circumstances. One night he was blinded by droppings from a swallow that fell into his eyes. God heard the prayers of Tobit and another Jew, Sarah, who was living to the east in Babylon or Media. God sent his angel, Raphael, to save them both. Through Tobit's son Tobias and the angel Raphael, God was able to help Tobit and Sarah. The story ends happily as Tobias marries Sarah and defeats a demon named Asmodeus and the two reestablish order in their lives. Tobit was written to show the place of fasting and prayer in the lives of the faithful. It teaches that God breaks into human history, using His angels to rescue people.

Wisdom of Solomon—This book, along with the Book of Ecclesiaticus in the Apocrypha, is similar to the Book of Proverbs in the Old Testament. Classified as wisdom books, all these works are profound in their understanding and insight into practical matters of daily life. The Wisdom of Solomon was named after the great wise man of Israel, King Solomon, who reigned from 970 to 931 B.C. Solomon was the model for all wise people who followed him. Many proverbs or wise sayings written many centuries after Solomon, such as this book, were attributed to him. It was composed some time around 100 to 50 B.C.

The Wisdom of Solomon is organized into various topics for convenient use by those who study the book. The first section (1:1—5:23) declares that wisdom is given only to a righteous person. The second section (6:1—9:19) deals with political issues, such as God's part in judging the wicked rulers. The third section (10:1—19:21) deals with the actions of God among His people, His protection of Israel, and His punishment of their enemies.

The whole book assumes that as Creator, God is actively involved in human affairs. Wisdom comes from God and is necessary for preservation and creativity in this world. Immortality awaits those who live by this wisdom.

The New Testament Apocrypha. The New Testament Apocrypha contains several writings that were similar to New Testament books but which were not included as a part of the New Testament. These writings were greatly influenced by the philosophies and religions of the cities or nations out of which they came. Some of the apocryphal gospels were written to replace the gospels of the New Testament but were declared false writings by officials of the early church.

Often the apocryphal books from the early history of the church present stories and legends meant to fill in information about the apostles and Jesus that is lacking in the New Testament. For example, some New Testament apocryphal works

Tomb complex of the Bene Hezir (center) near Jerusalem—burial site of a priestly family of the Maccabean period.

claim to give details on the childhood of Jesus (Pro-tevangelium of James, The Gospel of Thomas) as well as a description of how Jesus was raised from the dead (The Gospel of Peter). These writings expand on the accounts found in the New Testament.

Other apocryphal writings that expand or explain the gospel stories include The Gospel of the Egyptians, The Gospel of Truth, The Gospel of the Twelve, The Gospel of Philip, The Gospel of Judas, The Gospel of Bartholomew, The Gospel According to Mary, The Gospel of Nicodemus, and The Questions of Bartholomew. These are only a few of the 59 fragments and gospel–related writings in the New Testament Apocrypha.

The Acts of the Apostles in the New Testament is also paralleled by several apocryphal books. These include stories about the apostles themselves written in the second and third century. Titles of some of these books are The Acts of John, The Acts of Peter, The Acts of Paul, The Acts of Andrew and The Acts of Thomas.

The Acts of John, for example, tells the story of the disciple, John, his journey from Jerusalem to Rome, and his imprisonment on an island off the coast of modern–day Turkey called Patmos (see Rev. 1:9). Other travels of this apostle appear in the book, and he finally dies in Ephesus. Some scholars believe these second–century books may be based on some historical facts. They do give Bible researchers a better understanding of the origin of the early church.

The last group of New Testament apocryphal writings consists of APOCALYPTIC books. The New Testament Book of Revelation inspired the early Christians to write their own books that were similar in content and style. Probably the most popular of the apocryphal apocalypses are the Apocalypse of Peter, the Apocalypse of Paul, and the Apocalypse of Thomas. These apocalypses give Bible scholars a clear picture of the early Christian's view of heaven and hell, since they emphasize the state of sinners after death.

While these apocryphal New Testament books are interesting and informative, none are considered authoritative like the books of the New Testament. For various reasons, these books were judged unworthy and were not accepted as authoritative when the New Testament took its final form in the third century A.D. Thus, God has worked throughout history not only to inspire the Bible but also to preserve its authenticity and integrity so it can serve as a standard and guide for all believers.

APOLLONIA [ap oh LONE ih ah] (*place of Apollo*) — a Greek city (see Map 7, B–1) on the Egnatian Way of Macedonia about 45 kilometers (28 miles) west of Amphipolis. Paul and Silas passed through Apollonia on their way from Philippi to Thessalonica (Acts 17:1).

APOLLOS [a POL lus] (*destroyer*) — a learned and eloquent Jew from Alexandria in Egypt and an influential leader in the early church. Well–versed in the Old Testament, Apollos was a disciple of John the Baptist and "taught accurately the things of the Lord" (Acts 18:25). However, while Apollos knew some of Jesus' teaching, "he knew only the baptism of John" (Acts 18:25). When Aquila and Priscilla, two other leaders in the early church, arrived in Ephesus, they instructed Apollos more accurately in the way of God (Acts 18:26).

In Corinth, Apollos publicly contended with the Jewish leaders and refuted their objections to Christian teaching. He was apparently quite popular in Corinth, for in 1 Corinthians 1:12 Paul wrote of four parties into which the church at Corinth had become divided: one "following" Apollos, one Paul, one Cephas [Peter], and one Christ. In dealing with this division, Paul compared himself to the one who planted and Apollos to the one who watered what was already planted (1 Cor. 3:6).

APOSTASY — a falling away from the faith. The nation of Israel fell into repeated backslidings (Jer. 5:6, RSV). The prophet Jeremiah predicted the judgment of God upon such disloyalty: "Your wickedness will chasten you, and your apostasy will reprove you" (Jer. 2:19, RSV).

Some of the noted apostates in the Bible are: King Saul, who turned back from following the Lord (1 Sam. 15:11); Hymenaeus and Alexander, who "suffered shipwreck" of their faith (1 Tim. 1:19–20); and Demas, who forsook the apostle Paul because he loved this present world (2 Tim. 4:10).

In Acts 21:21 the apostle Paul was described falsely as one who taught the Jews living among the Gentiles to commit apostasy (forsake, NKJV). Second Thessalonians 2:3 declares that the Day of Christ "will not come unless the apostasy comes first" (NASB). This great apostasy will be the time of "the final rebellion against God, when wickedness will be revealed in human form" (2 Thess. 2:3, NEB).

Apostasy is generally defined as the determined, willful rejection of Christ and His teachings by a Christian believer (Heb. 10:26–29; John 15:22). This is different from false belief, or error, which is the result of ignorance. Some Christian groups teach that apostasy is impossible for those persons who have truly accepted Jesus as Savior and Lord.

APOSTLE — a special messenger of Jesus Christ; a person to whom Jesus delegated authority for certain tasks. The word apostle is used of those twelve disciples whom Jesus sent out, two by two, during His ministry in Galilee to expand His own ministry of preaching and healing. It was on that occasion, evidently, that they were first called "apostles" (Mark 3:14; 6:30).

These same disciples, with the exception of Judas Iscariot, were recommissioned by Jesus after His resurrection to be His witnesses throughout the world (Luke 24:46–49; Acts 1:8). After Jesus' ASCENSION, the apostles brought their number to twelve by choosing Matthias (Acts 1:23–26).

The word apostle is sometimes used in the New Testament in a general sense of "messenger." For instance, when delegates of Christian communities were charged with conveying those churches' contributions to a charitable fund, they were described by Paul as "messengers [apostles] of the churches" (2 Cor. 8:23). Jesus also used the word this way when He quoted the proverb, "A servant is not greater than his master, nor he who is sent [literally, "an apostle"] greater than he who sent him" (John 13:16). Jesus Himself is called "the Apostle...of our confession" (Heb. 3:1), a reference to His function as God's special Messenger to the world.

The word apostle has a wider meaning in the letters of the apostle Paul. It includes people who, like himself, were not included in the Twelve, but who saw the risen Christ and were specially commissioned by Him. Paul's claim to be an apostle was questioned by others. He based his apostleship, however on the direct call of the exalted Lord who appeared to him on the Damascus Road and on the Lord's blessing of his ministry in winning converts and establishing churches (1 Cor. 15:10).

Apparently, Paul also counted James, the Lord's brother, as an apostle (Gal. 1:19). This James was not one of the Twelve; in fact, he was not a believer in Jesus before the Crucifixion (John 7:5). It was the resurrected Lord who 'appeared to James" (1 Cor. 15:7) and presumably commissioned him for his ministry. When Paul says Jesus was seen not only by James but also by "all the apostles" (1 Cor. 15:7), he seems to be describing a wider group than "the Twelve" to whom Jesus appeared earlier (1 Cor. 15:5).

In 1 Corinthians 12:28 and Ephesians 4:11, apostles are listed along with prophets and other saints as part of the foundation of the household of God. In this strictly New Testament sense, apostles are confined to the first generation of Christians.

At an early stage in the church's history it was agreed that apostles to the Jews and Gentiles should be divided into separate camps. Paul and Barnabas were to concentrate on the evangelization of Gentiles; Peter, John, and James (the Lord's brother) were to continue evangelizing Jews (Gal. 2:7–9).

As pioneers in the work of making converts and planting churches, apostles were exposed to special dangers. When persecution erupted, they were the primary targets for attack (1 Cor. 4:9–13). Paul, in particular, welcomed the suffering which he endured as an apostle because it was his way of participating in the suffering of Christ (Rom. 8:17; 2 Cor. 1:5–7).

The authority committed to the apostles by Christ was unique. It could not be transmitted to others. The apostles could install elders or other leaders and teachers in the churches, and they could authorize them to assume special responsibilities; but apostolic authority could not be transferred. Their authority has not come to us through their successors; it has come through their writings, which are contained in the New Testament.

APOSTLE'S CREED (see CREEDS).

APOSTOLIC, APOSTOLICAL — of or pertaining to the twelve apostles or the faith, teaching, and practice of these apostles. While the word "apostolic" does not appear in the New Testament, the period in early church history when the Apostles were alive is commonly called the APOSTOLIC AGE.

APOSTOLIC AGE — that period of church history when the apostles were alive, beginning with the Day of Pentecost (about A.D. 30) and ending near the conclusion of the first century (about A.D. 100) with the death of the apostle John. During the apostolic age, all the books of the New Testament were written, including the four gospels, the Book of Acts, the letters of Paul, the general letters, and the Book of Revelation.

APOSTOLIC COUNCIL — the assembly of apostles and elders of the New Testament church in Jerusalem (A.D. 50). This council considered the question of whether Gentiles had to be circumcised and keep certain other laws of the Jewish faith in order to be members of the church (Acts 15). This assembly decided that a Gentile does not first have to become a Jew in order to be a Christian.

APOTHECARY (see OCCUPATIONS AND TRADES).

APPAIM [AP a em] (*nostrils*) — a son of Nadab and the father of Ishi (1 Chr. 2:30–31).

APPAREL (see DRESS OF THE BIBLE).

APPEAL — a strong or urgent request. Such an appeal is appropriate in a court of law. In Old Testament times, Moses set up an arrangement similiar to an appeals court (Ex. 18:26). Job, while suffering, pressed his case beyond his "comforters" to God Himself as the last court of appeal (Job 31:35).

In the New Testament, the apostle Paul requested that his trial come before the highest Roman authority: "I appeal to Caesar" (Acts 25:11). In situations of spiritual watchcare, leaders frequently appealed to those who were in their charge. Paul appealed to Philemon in behalf of Onesimus "for love's sake" (Philem. 9).

The Bible is a book of appeals—from God to man, from man to God, and from man to man.

APPHIA [AF ih uh] (*endearment*) — a Christian woman of Colossae (Philem. 2). Since she is mentioned in a domestic matter, she may have been Philemon's wife, or possibly the mother or sister of Archippus.

APPIAN WAY [AP pih un] — an ancient Roman road built by Appius Claudius. It ran from Rome to Brundisium on the Adriatic Sea. Paul traveled this road from near the city of Puteoli to Rome, where he was imprisoned (Acts 28:13–16).

APPII FORUM [AP ih eye] (*marketplace of Appius*) — a town in Italy located about 64 kilometers (40 miles) southeast of Rome on the Appian Way (see Map 8, A–1) where the apostle Paul was welcomed by Christians from Rome (Acts 28:15).

APPLE (see PLANTS OF THE BIBLE).

APPLE OF THE EYE — an old English expression referring to the pupil of the eye. This phrase is used symbolically of something cherished, precious, and protected (Deut. 32:10; Zech. 2:8).

APRON — a loincloth or girdle which apparently covered only the loins, or the front of one's body (Gen. 3:7; KVJ, RSV).

AQABAH, GULF OF [ACK ah bah] (see RED SEA).

A section of the Appian Way, a road built by the Romans, south of the city of Rome.

Photo by Howard Vos

Photo by Gustav Jeeninga
Roman aqueduct at Caesarea Maritima, showing the Romans' expertise at building such water transport systems.

AQUEDUCT — a channel for transporting water from a remote source to a city. Israel's climate provides abundant rainfall in the winter months, but there is seldom any rain from May to October. This, along with the scarcity of good water supplies, made it necessary to build artificial storage areas to catch the winter rains. Elaborate systems of stone and masonry aqueducts and storage pools were sometimes constructed to bring water from the hill country to the cities and larger towns.

The best-known biblical accounts of the building of an aqueduct occur in 2 Kings 20:20 and 2 Chronicles 32:30. King Hezekiah of Judah had a tunnel dug under the city of Jerusalem to bring water from the spring outside the city to the Siloam reservoir inside the city wall. Across part of the course the workmen cut a tunnel through solid rock to complete the aqueduct. "Hezekiah's Tunnel" is still a major tourist attraction in Jerusalem.

"Solomon's Pools" near Bethlehem are part of an ancient aqueduct system that brought water from the hills south of Jerusalem into the Temple area. During his administration, Pontius Pilate, Roman governor of Judea, built an aqueduct to bring water to Jerusalem. Some scholars suggest that the Tower of Siloam (Luke 13:4) that fell and killed 18 people may have been part of that building project.

AQUILA [A kwil uh] (*eagle*) — a Jewish Christian living in Corinth with his wife PRISCILLA at the time of Paul's arrival from Athens (Acts. 18:2). Aquila was born in PONTUS (located in Asia Minor) but lived in Rome until the emperor Claudius commanded that all Jews leave the city. He and Priscilla moved to Corinth, where Aquila took up his trade, tentmaking.

When Paul left Corinth, Aquila and Priscilla traveled with him as far as Ephesus (1 Cor. 16:19), where they met Apollos and instructed him more thoroughly in the Christian faith (Acts 18:24–26). Apparently, they returned to Rome, because Paul sent them greetings in his letter to the Romans (Rom. 16:3).

AR [ar] (*city*) — one of the chief cities of Moab, situated about 32 kilometers (20 miles) east of the Dead Sea on the southern bank of the Arnon River (Num. 21:15; Is. 15:1). It is probably the same place as "the city of Moab" (Num. 22:36).

ARA [A ruh] (*strong*) — a son of Jether, of the tribe of Asher (1 Chr. 7:38).

ARAB [A rab] (*ambush*) — a village in the hill country of Hebron allotted to the tribe of Judah after the conquest of Canaan by Joshua (Josh. 15:52).

ARABAH [AIR ah bah] (*plain, desert*) — a major region of the land of Israel (see Map 2, C-1), referring usually to the entire valley region between Mount Hermon in the north to the Red Sea in the south (Num. 22:1; Deut. 1:7). The Arabah is more than 390 kilometers (240 miles) long, varying in width from 10 to 40 kilometers (6 to 25 miles).

The Arabah includes the Sea of Galilee, the Jordan River valley, the Dead Sea, and the area between the Dead Sea and the Red Sea. Much of this region lies below sea level, and the Dead Sea, which lies at approximately 394 meters (1,292 feet) below sea level, is the lowest spot on the earth's surface. The NKJV refers several times to the "Sea of the Arabah," meaning the Salt Sea or the Dead Sea (Deut. 3:17; Josh. 3:16; 2 Kin. 14:25).

Before their entry into the Promised Land, the people of Israel camped in the Arabah, in an area called "the plains of Moab" (Num. 22:1), just north of the Dead Sea. While the Israelites were camped there, God turned Balaam's curses to blessings (Num. 22:1—24:25), Israel committed idolatry and immorality (Num. 25), Moses renewed the covenant, and Joshua sent out spies to prepare for the invasion of Canaan (Josh.1:1—3:17).

ARABIA [uh RAY bih uh] (*wilderness*) — the large peninsula east of Egypt, between the Red Sea and the Persian Gulf (see Map 1, C–3). About 1,300 kilometers (800 miles) wide and 2,300 kilometers (1,400 miles) long, Arabia is nearly one-third the size of the United States. It has almost no rainfall except along the coast, where it measures about 51 centimeters (20 inches) per year. There is only one river and one lake in the entire peninsula. Although a sudden shower may create a short–lived stream, most of the water in Arabia comes from deep wells or desert oases. Consequently, there is little agricultural activity on the peninsula.

The Arabian peninsula is a sandy, rocky desert with high mountain ranges on the western and southern coasts. The western mountains reach a height of 3,660 meters (12,000 feet) and show some evidence of past volcanic activity. Because of this volcanic activity, a few scholars have suggested that

Mount Sinai was located in the western region of this mountain range. However, the traditional site at the southern end of the Sinai Peninsula is much more likely. Much of the sandy interior of Arabia is uninhabited, although there is barely enough grass on the lower mountain slopes to support its nomadic population. In addition to its lack of water, the desert was known for its sandstorms driven by violent winds (Job 1:19; 27:20–21).

The queen of Sheba came from Arabia, bringing gold, spices, and precious stones to Solomon (1 Kin. 10:2, 10, 14; 2 Chr. 9:1, 9, 14). Solomon and other kings sent their ships to Ophir in Arabia to bring back gold (1 Kin. 9:28; 2 Chr. 9:10). Ophir, Raamah, and Sheba were famous for their gold, silver, and precious stones (Job 22:24; Is. 13:12; Ezek. 27:22).

The people who lived in Arabia included the children of Joktan (Gen. 10:26–30), Cush (Gen. 10:7), the sons of Abraham and Keturah (Gen. 25:1–6), and Esau (Gen.36). The "country of the east" (Gen. 25:6) is probably a reference to Arabia. The early history of many of these peoples is unknown. Israel's earliest contacts with the inhabitants of Arabia probably came through their camel caravans. Some of them oppressed the Israelites during the time of the judges, but God delivered Israel from them by raising up the judge Gideon (Judg. 6:11).

David subdued some of the Arabian tribes that were close to Israel (2 Sam. 8:3–14), and Solomon established extensive trade relations with more distant tribes in Arabia to obtain their gold for his building projects (1 Kin. 9:28; 10:2, 11). Jehoshaphat, king of Judah, received rams and goats from the Arabians as tribute (2 Chr. 17:10–12), but after his death they revolted and refused to pay tribute to his son Jehoram. Instead, they invaded Je-

The hot, barren deserts of the Arabah in southern Palestine.

rusalem and carried away Jehoram's wealth, his wives, and all but his youngest son (2 Chr. 21:16–17).

Most of the tribes of southern and eastern Arabia were not well-known to Israel. Joel referred to the slave-trading Sabeans [Shebaites] as a people who lived far away (Joel 3:8). Isaiah pictured the Arabians wandering as far east as Babylon (Is. 13:19, 20). Tribes which lived closer—those at Tema, Dedan, and Kedar—were included in Isaiah's prophecies of judgment against the foreign nations (Is. 21:13–17). Jeremiah also announced God's judgment upon Dedan, Tema, Buz, Kedar, Hazor, and all the kings of Arabia (Jer. 25:23–24; 49:28–33).

Although most of Israel's knowledge of the Arabians and their habits (Jer. 3:2) was due to a passing association with their caravan traders (Ezek. 27:21), some Arabians eventually settled in Palestine. While attempting to rebuild the walls of Jerusalem, Nehemiah struggled against Geshem the Arab, who scorned and despised the Jews (Neh. 2:19). When this tactic failed to discourage the work on Jerusalem's walls, the Arabs, Ammonites, Ashdodites, and others planned to attack the city by force (Neh. 4:7–13). When this strategy also failed, Sanballat, Tobiah, and Geshem the Arab set a trap to lure Nehemiah out of the city and kill him (Neh. 6:1–7). Nehemiah prayed for guidance, and God delivered him from this plot.

It is likely that Job was from Arabia. Uz, the home of Job (Job 1:1), appears to be named after a descendant of Esau and the Edomites (Gen. 36:28; Lam. 4:21). Eliphaz, one of Job's comforters, was from Teman, a city in Arabia (Job 2:11). Bands of Sabeans [Shebaites] and Chaldeans were close enough to attack Job's cattle (Job 1:15, 17). A great desert wind destroyed the house of Job's children (Job 1:19). The dialogue between Job and his comforters is filled with desert imagery and animals (Job 39).

ARABIC VERSIONS (see Bible Versions and Translations).

ARAD [A rad] (*fugitive*) — the name of a city (see Map 2, C–1) and a man in the Old Testament:

1. A Canaanite city in the southern wilderness of Judah whose inhabitants fought against the Israelites at Mount Hor but were defeated by Joshua (Josh. 12:14). It was situated about 32 kilometers (20 miles) south of Hebron. The site today is marked by Tell Arad.

2. A descendant of Beriah and one of the principal men of Aijalon (1 Chr. 8:15).

ARAH [A rah] (*wayfarer*) — the name of two Old Testament men:

1. A son of Ulla, of the tribe of Asher (1 Chr. 7:39).

2. The father of a family that returned from the Captivity with Zerubbabel (Ezra 2:5; Neh. 7:10).

ARAM [A ram] (*exalted*) — the name of four men and one region (see Map 1, C–2) in the Bible:

1. A descendant of Shem. This Aram was the ancestor of the Arameans (Gen. 10:22–23).

2. A son of Abraham's nephew, Kemuel (Gen. 22:21).

3. An area that may be translated generally as Syria or Mesopotamia (1 Chr. 2:23). The Arameans occupied a large plain that reached from the Taurus Mountains (on the north) to Damascus and beyond (on the south), and from the Euphrates River (on the east) to the Lebanon Mountains (on the west). Also see Arameans.

4. A son of Shemer, of the tribe of Asher (1 Chr. 7:34).

5. A Greek form of Ram, the father of Amminadab (Matt. 1:3, KJV; Luke 3:33, KJV).

ARAM DAMMESEK [AIR um DAM mah seck] — an ancient name for Syria of Damascus, conquered by David (2 Sam. 8:5–6, KJV).

Arabian desert-dwellers with their flocks at a watering place in the Arabah.

ARAM–NAHARAIM [A ram nuh ha RAY im] (*Aram of the two rivers*) — the northern section of the land between the Tigris and the Euphrates Rivers. Psalm 60 refers to David's war with two districts of Syria: Aram–naharaim and Aram–zobah (Psalm 60, title, KJV).

ARAMAIC LANGUAGE (see LANGUAGES OF THE BIBLE).

ARAMAIC VERSION (see BIBLE VERSIONS AND TRANSLATIONS; TARGUM).

ARAMEANS [AIR ah mee unz] — an ancient desert people who flourished along with the Israelites during much of their history, sometimes as enemies and sometimes as friends.

The region of the Arameans, the land of ARAM, extended from the Lebanon Mountains on the west eastward to the Euphrates River and from the Taurus Mountains on the north southward to Damascus. Arameans were among the ancient peoples who settled the Near East as early as 2250 B.C. They were fully established as a separate kingdom by the 12th century B.C., which made their history parallel with Israel's.

The Arameans made their presence felt internationally during the time of the judges, when they existed in large numbers in the region east of the Jordan River. An Aramean ruler, Cushan–Rishathaim, overran the land of Israel and oppressed it for eight years (Judg. 3:8–10).

In later years, David extended the boundary of Israel to the Euphrates River by subduing the Aramean rulers Hadadezer of Zobah and Toi of Hamath (2 Sam. 8:1–13). But a third Aramean official, Rezon, fled to Damascus and founded a strong Aramean city–state there (1 Kin. 11:23–24). This city–state was Israel's bitter foe for many generations.

Between quarrels and hostilities, there were times when either the nation of Judah or the nation of Israel was allied with Aram against a common foe. Judah and Aram were allied with each other against Israel (1 Kin. 15:18–20); Israel and Aram were allies against Judah (2 Kin. 16:5). Judah also joined with Assyria against Israel and Aram.

The result of this strong alliance was the downfall of Damascus and the end of the Aramean power, about 732 B.C. (2 Kin. 16:7–18). Many Arameans were taken as hostages to other lands, in keeping with the foreign policy of the conquering Assyrians.

ARAMITESS [AIR ah MIGHT ess] — a woman of ARAM (1 Chr. 7:14, KJV); she was the concubine of Manasseh and the mother of Machir.

ARAN [A ran] — a son of Dishan and a descendant of Seir the Horite (Gen. 36:28; 1 Chr. 1:42).

ARARAH [AIR ah rah] — a form of ADADAH.

ARARAT [AIR uh rat] — the mountainous region between the Black Sea and the Caspian Sea where Noah's ark rested when the Flood subsided (Gen.

8:4). From this region streams converge to form the Tigris and the Euphrates Rivers. Originally, Ararat referred to the whole mountainous area; its use, however has gradually come to be restricted to the huge volcanic mountain at the borders of Turkey, Iran, and the Soviet Union.

This volcanic mountain includes two peaks, 5,600 meters (17,000 feet) and 4,200 meters (13,000 feet) above sea level. The taller peak rises 920 meters (3,000 feet) above the line of perpetual snow. Some people believe that Noah's ark still rests on Mount Ararat, and occasional expeditions have been launched to find it. However, shifting glaciers, avalanches, hidden crevices, and sudden storms make the mountain so difficult to climb that it is referred to by the native inhabitants of that region as "the Painful Mountain."

ARAUNAH [a ROW nah] (*aristocrat*) — a JEBUSITE who owned a threshing floor on Mount Moriah in Jerusalem. King David purchased the threshing floor on which to build an altar to the Lord (2 Sam. 24:16–24). Later, this land was the site on which Solomon's Temple was built (2 Chr. 3:1).

ARBA [AR bah] (*four*) — the ancestor of ANAK the giant. The city of Hebron, in the mountains of Judah, got its early name, Kirjath Arba, from him (Josh. 21:11).

ARBATHITE [AR bah thight] — one who lived in the ARABAH, a barren wilderness in the Jordan River valley (2 Sam. 23:31).

ARBITE [AR bight] — a native of ARAB, a village in the hill country of Judah (Josh. 15:52).

ARCH (see ARCHITECTURE).

ARCHAEOLOGY OF THE BIBLE — The word archaeology comes from two Greek words meaning "a study of ancient things." But the term usually applies today to a study of excavated materials belonging to a former era. Biblical archaeology is the scientific study, by excavation, examination, and publication, of the evidences of cultures and civilizations from the biblical period. Archaeological findings help scholars, as well as Bible students, in understanding the Bible better. They reveal what life was like in biblical times, throw light on obscure passages of Scripture, and help us appreciate the historical context of the Bible.

Archaeology is a complex science, calling on the assistance of other sciences, such as chemistry, anthropology, and zoology. Many talented professionals—including engineers, historians, chemists, paleontologists, photographers, artists, and surveyors—are involved in the discovery, interpretation, and publication of archaeological knowledge.

Every object an archaeologist discovers—whether a piece of bone, pottery, metal, stone, or wood—is studied in detail. The archaeologist's work often requires translating ancient writings and studying an ancient city's art and architecture. These detailed studies are carried out in museums and laboratories, but the archaeologist must first recover the material by carefully excavating an ancient city.

For the New Testament period, biblical archaeology has concentrated upon a geographical area that parallels the reaches of the old Roman Empire. The area is somewhat smaller for Old Testament times; and the focus shifts eastward to include the Mesopotamian Valley and Persia (modern Iran).

The hub for Old Testament research is Palestine, or Israel (ancient Canaan), but it fans out to include the great empires in the Nile and Mesopotamian valleys. The culture of Phoenicia (modern Lebanon) was very similar to that of Canaan to the south. Syria to the east is also studied because its history often was tied to Israel's. Still farther north, Asia Minor was the homeland of the Hittites and several Greek cultures.

Until the early 1800s, little was known of biblical times and customs, except what was written in the Old Testament. Although the Greek historians preserved considerable background material on New Testament times, little documentation was found for the Old Testament period. The reason for this is that Alexander the Great forced the Greek language and customs upon all the lands his armies conquered. This policy almost destroyed the languages and culture of Egypt, Persia, Canaan, and Babylon. Before the rise of modern archaeology, scarcely any historical evidence was available to illustrate or confirm the history and literature of the Old Testament.

Modern Near Eastern archaeology began during the 18th century. Before that, some research had been done by collectors of antiquities, usually museums or wealthy individuals. Biblical archaeology probably began with the discovery of the ROSETTA STONE during Napoleon's invasion of Egypt in 1799. Discovered by an officer in the expedition, the stone was inscribed in three columns consisting of Greek, Egyptian hieroglyphics, and later Egyptian script. With Napoleon's encouragement, the stone was studied and recorded with scientific accuracy, then displayed in the British Museum. This discovery opened the door to the study of the remains of ancient Egypt, a rich resource for biblical researchers.

How Ancient Ruins (Tells) Were Formed. In ancient times, cities were usually built on sites that were easy to defend and were located near a source of water and on a good trade route. The homes were constructed primarily of sun-baked bricks, which could be destroyed quite easily by flood, earthquakes, or enemy attack. In rebuilding the town, the inhabitants would usually level the rubble and debris and build new buildings on the same location. Cities continued to be destroyed by windstorm, enemy attack, or other catastrophes until gradually a mound of earth containing remnants of buildings, tools, vases, and pottery rose on the site. Eventually many layers of habitation lay upon one another.

The sites of these mounds in the ancient Near East are called *tells*, the Arabic word for mounds.

These mounds do not look like natural hills, appearing instead as unnatural rounded humps on the landscape. They often rise from their surroundings by as much as 15 to 23 meters (50 to 75 feet).

If a city was destroyed by famine, disease, earthquake, or some other natural catastrophe, the townspeople might conclude that the gods had cursed their city and that it would be unwise to rebuild on the same site. The area might lie unused for hundreds of years until a new group decided to build again on this strategically located site.

When a site is occupied continuously by the same group of people, one layer or stratum of the mound is very similar to the next. Some slight changes in artifacts and ways of doing things, such as the method of baking pottery or the shape of certain tools, will occur in an orderly fashion from generation to generation. If a long period with no habitation has taken place between layers, the new people who inhabit the mound may have discovered new techniques. Also peoples with new skills—perhaps the conquerors of the former dwellers—may inhabit the site. A sharp change in the pattern of living or in types of artifacts discovered may indicate a gap in habitation of the site.

As he excavates these ancient sites, an archaeologist will first find large stationary objects such as houses, monuments, tombs, and fortresses. Also there will be smaller artifacts such as jewelry, tools, weapons, and cooking utensils. Archaeology provides the Bible researcher with the rich remains of material culture over the course of centuries to supplement what is recorded in the Bible, as well as in art and literature.

How the Archaeologist Does His Work. In organizing his work (called a dig), the archaeologist first will divide the site, or area, by a "grid system," using lines parallel to the longitude and latitude of the area. A "field," 5.8 meters (19 feet) square, is then divided into four squares or quadrants, leaving room for a catwalk among them to observe the work. Each area has an area supervisor, who in turn works under the supervision of the excavation director. The area supervisor is responsible for directing the actual digging in his area and recording everything as it comes from the ground. It is more important to excavate small areas in detail than to excavate a large area carelessly.

Those who actually work the site are of three categories: Pickmen carefully break up the soil, noticing every difference in the hardness of the earth and how it is compacted. It takes skill to distinguish a clay wall from ordinary packed clay or to develop the delicate touch that can bring forth a vase or a human bone unharmed. Hoemen work over the loosened soil, saving anything of potential interest. Basketmen carry off the excavated dirt, perhaps using a sieve to sift the soil—to be sure nothing of value is discarded. Often archaeology students serve as laborers on expeditions.

Everything found in a quadrant of the site is collected in an individual basket and tagged with all pertinent information, including the date and loca-

Photo by Gustav Jeeninga

An archaeologist carefully uncovers a skeleton at an excavation near Caesarea Maritima.

tion of discovery. The baskets are then photographed and evaluated by experts who record all the data. The materials and information then go to laboratories and museums where they are studied in detail. Conclusions are then published by the excavation director and are circulated to other archaeologists and scholars.

In 1832, while a Danish archaeologist, C. J. Thomsen, was classifying some implements for display in a Copenhagen museum, he wondered about the age of the various tools made of iron, bronze, and stone. Returning to the peat bog where the implements had been found, he discovered that artifacts made of stone were found in the bottom layer. Higher levels contained many tools made of copper and bronze. At the top of the bog were instruments of iron, indicating they were made last. (We now speak of the Stone Age, the Bronze Age, and the Iron Age.)

Thomsen had made a very simple application of the principle of stratigraphy, or keeping track of the layers of soil in which artifacts were found to establish a sequence of events. The archaeologist bases many of his conclusions on his study and evaluation of the various strata of the mound.

An archaeologist can determine how many times a town has been destroyed and rebuilt, but he will want to know the date of each occupation, how long it lasted, and why it was destroyed. Each level of occupation will contain the foundations of walls and buildings and often a layer of debris from the destruction. Also the articles of everyday living such as weapons, tools, pottery, and ornaments will be revealed. Sometimes the different strata are separated by thick layers of ash from a great fire. At other times, only a difference in soil color or compactness distinguishes the levels.

Furthermore, during centuries when the mound was not inhabited, erosion and random digging at the site can disrupt a stratum. A new group of settlers may have dug foundations, garbage pits, or trenches deep into an earlier layer, making the job of the archaeologist more difficult.

POTTERY is one of the most important keys to dating the strata of a tell. Pottery typology, or the study of various types of pottery, is now refined to almost an exact science. The scientist can call upon the detailed knowledge of the characteristics of pottery of each period to identify and date the pottery, usually within a half century of the exact time when it was made. The scientific method of carbon-14 dating is also used to establish the age of some archaeological materials.

Earlier pottery designs were simple and functional; later vessels became more delicate and elaborate, often showing Persian and Greek influences. The method of baking the clay can also indicate the approximate time when it was made. Changes in everyday objects such as lamps, tools, weapons, and jewelry help scientists identify broader periods of history. Coin collectors, then as now, might possess very old coins so these are not as reliable a method of identifying a period.

How Archaeology Helps Us Understand the Bible. During the early years of exploring Bible lands, archaeologists hoped to make discoveries that would confirm the main events of Bible history. Today's archaeologists realize that many things about the Bible cannot be proved in a direct way. Instead of providing proof of specific events, archaeology is used to increase our knowledge of the everyday life, the history, and the customs of the people who appear in the Bible's long story—the Egyptians, Phoenicians, Philistines, Moabites, Assyrians, Babylonians, and others, as well as the Hebrews. For example, discoveries of ancient texts on clay tablets—in many languages—show us what the various peoples of the ancient Near East thought about the gods they worshiped, as well as the types of laws by which they lived. Ancient texts also tell us of alliances, trade agreements, and wars between the great cities and nations of the past.

Archaeological discoveries paint in the background of the Bible, helping to explain many of its events. Thanks to archaeology, we now know that in the time of Abraham (about 2000 B.C.) many thriving cities existed in the ancient Near East. Civilization was already over a thousand years old in Egypt and in the region of the Tigris and Euphrates Rivers. It was from a city on the Euphrates River, called Ur, that Abraham (then called Abram) began the journey that eventually brought him to the land of Canaan (Gen. 11:31). The excavation of Ur early in this century (1922–1934) by Sir Charles Leonard Woolley revealed that Abraham was surrounded by idolatry on all sides when God called him to begin a new people through which God could do His redemptive work.

The discovery of large bodies of CUNEIFORM literature in Babylon and other places also has proved most revealing. For example, the AMARNA Letters

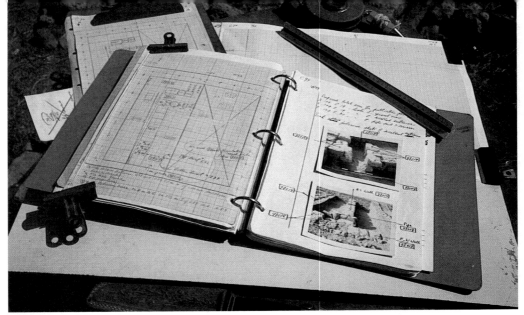

An archaeologist's notebook, containing detailed records of everything uncovered in an excavation.

from Egypt give an inside glance into conditions in Palestine just before the conquest by Joshua and the Israelites.

In 1890 the famed archaeologist Flinders Petrie began an exploration at Tell el–Hesi in southwestern Palestine. He carefully recorded the pieces and types of broken pottery found at each level of occupation. This exploration helped refine the method known as "ceramic chronology," which is one of the methods still used to date ancient finds.

Inscriptions and ancient manuscripts also have made an important contribution to biblical study. In fact, today's archaeological work is increasingly concerned with the text of the Bible. Intensive study of more than 3,000 New Testament Greek manuscripts dating from the second century A.D. and subsequent years has shown that the New Testament text has been preserved remarkably from that time. Not one doctrine has been perverted due to major errors in transmission.

The science of papyrology developed after large quantities of PAPYRI, or ancient writing materials, were discovered in Egypt around the turn of the century. The papyri, written on paper made from the papyrus reed of Egypt, included a wide variety of topics presented in several languages. More than 70 papyri containing portions of the New Testament have been found. These fragments help to confirm the texts of the longer manuscripts dating to the fourth century A.D. and following. Since many of the papyri date to the first three centuries after Christ, the impact of papyrology upon biblical studies has been significant. These discoveries make it possible to establish the grammar of the period and, thus, to date the composition of New Testament books to the first century A.D.

The mass of papyri also demonstrated that New Testament Greek was not invented by New Testament writers. Instead, it was the common language generally used during the first century of the Christian era. Moreover, the papyri have shown that the New Testament contained good grammar, judged by first–century standards.

The search for buildings and places associated with the ministry of Jesus has taken place for centuries. A synagogue was unearthed in Capernaum, although it hardly can be the one in which Jesus taught (Mark 1:21). It may well be the successor of the synagogue Jesus knew, however. Archaeologists think they may have discovered Peter's house at the same site (Matt. 8:14). Graffiti on the plastered wall of this second–century house clearly links it with Peter. Atop Mount Gerizim, excavations have uncovered the foundations of the Samaritan Temple. Although tradition has assigned sites for the birth and the crucifixion of Jesus, archaeologists disagree on the authenticity of these locations.

Significant Archaeological Digs and Their Contributions. Many important archaeological discoveries of this century have contributed to Bible knowledge. Following are descriptions of five of these projects, with an analysis of their contribution.

The Law Code of Hammurabi—In 1901 a slab of black marble over seven feet tall and six feet wide, containing over 300 paragraphs of legal inscriptions, was discovered at Susa (Shushan) in ancient Elam. Engraved on the large rock were legal provisions dealing with the social, domestic, and moral life of the ancient Babylonian people of King Hammurabi's time (about 1792–1750 B.C.). The Code furnishes important background material for comparison with other ancient bodies of law, particu-

Photo by Gustav Jeeninga

A coin specialist cleans and sorts ancient coins at the site of an archaeological dig.

larly the law of the Pentateuch.

The fact that Hammurabi's Code is older by three centuries than the laws of Moses has ruined some of the theories of critics and has given rise to others. A discovery of this sort illustrates how archaeology roots out views that earlier placed the origin of many of the laws attributed to Moses at a much later time. The discovery of Hammurabi's laws indicate that the Law of Moses is neither borrowed from, nor dependent upon, the Babylonian, but that it is divinely given as it claims to be.

The resemblances between the Mosaic laws and the Code of Hammurabi are clearly due to the similarity of the general intellectual and cultural heritage of the Hebrews and the Babylonians at that ancient time. The striking differences, however, demonstrate that there is no direct borrowing and that the Mosaic law—although later by three centuries—is in no way dependent upon the Babylonian.

The two laws are radically different in their origins and morality. The Babylonian laws are alleged to have been received by Hammurabi from the sun god, Shamash. Moses received his laws directly from the Lord. Hammurabi's laws list at least ten varieties of bodily mutilation prescribed for various offenses. For example, if a physician performed an operation that was unsuccessful, his hand was to be cut off.

By contrast, in the Mosaic legislation, only one instance of mutilation occurs, where a wife's hand is to be severed (Deut. 25:11–12). Also in the Hebrew laws a greater value is placed upon human life. A stricter regard for the honor of womanhood is evident and masters are ordered to treat their slaves more humanely.

The City of Ur—Ur was an important city of an-

cient Babylonia situated on the Euphrates River in lower Mesopotamia, or present–day Iraq. But the glory of the city was suddenly destroyed about 1960 B.C. Foreigners stormed down from the surrounding hills, captured the reigning king, Ibbi–Sin, and reduced the city to ruins. So complete was its destruction that the city lay buried in oblivion until it was excavated in modern times by archaeologists.

Abraham lived in the city of Ur at the height of its splendor. The city was a center of religion and industry. The Babylonians worshiped many gods, but the moon god Sin was supreme. Accordingly, Ur was a theocracy centered in worship of the moon deity. Abraham's father, Terah, probably worshiped at the altar of Sin.

God's sovereign grace called Abraham out of this polluted atmosphere to begin a new line of people, the Hebrews, who were to be separated from idolatry and to become a blessing to all mankind. The archaeological findings of ancient Ur have greatly illuminated the biblical references to the patriarch Abraham and have given a much wider view of the ancient world around 2000 B.C.

The Ras Shamra Tablets—Recovered in another significant excavation were hundreds of clay tablets that had been housed in a library located between two pagan temples in Ugarit, modern Ras Shamra in Syria. These tablets date from about the 15th century B.C. They were inscribed in the earliest known alphabet written in wedge–shaped signs. The strange writing was recognized as ancient Canaanite in origin, and it turned out to be religious and cultic (related to worship) in nature. The tablets were inscribed in a dialect closely akin to biblical Hebrew and Phoenician.

So important were the initial discoveries that archaeologist Claude F. Schaeffer continued excavations in the area from 1929 to 1937. Aside from the knowledge gained about the ancient city of Ugarit, the Ras Shamra texts have great literary importance. The translation of the texts showed the important parallels between the Ugaritic and Hebrew literary style and vocabulary. These texts have been invaluable to scholars studying Hebrew poetry and the general literary style and vocabulary of Old Testament Hebrew.

The most important contribution of the religious texts from Ras Shamra consists of the background material they provide for careful study of the pagan religions mentioned repeatedly in the Old Testament. As a result of archaeological work, an independent witness to the degenerate nature of Canaanite cults is now available. No longer can critics accuse the Old Testament of projecting a bloodthirsty mentality because Joshua ordered that all Canaanites be destroyed. This order was given to purge the immoral worship of the Canaanites from the land.

The Lachish Letters—In the excavations of Lachish, a city in southwestern Palestine, the most astonishing finds consisted of letters imbedded in a layer of burned charcoal and ashes. Written in Hebrew of the ancient Phoenician script, the documents throw additional light on the life and times of the prophet Jeremiah. The letters, called ostraca, were inscribed on pieces of broken pottery. Most of the letters were written by a citizen named Hoshayahu, who was stationed at a military outpost. He sent these letters to Yaosh, evidently a high-ranking officer in the garrison at Lachish.

The Babylonians had attacked and partly burned Lachish some ten years earlier during the reign of King Jehoiakim of Judah. These letters were found in the layers of ashes that represent the final destruction of the city. This dates them from 588–587 B.C., when Nebuchadnezzar of Babylon made his final siege of the Hebrew cities of Jerusalem, Lachish, and Azekah.

One letter lists names, the majority of which are found in the Old Testament; two letters consist largely of greetings; another letter describes movements of troops and makes an interesting reference to an unnamed prophet and his word of warning. The Lachish Letters give an independent view of conditions in Judah during the last days before the fall of Jerusalem.

The prophet Jeremiah conducted his ministry in these times. His reference to Azekah and Lachish says, "When the king of Babylon's army fought against Jerusalem and all the cities of Judah that were left, against Lachish, and Azekah: for only these fortified cities remained of the cities of Judah" (Jer. 34:7).

Tell ez–Zakariyeh has been identified as the ancient city of Azekah. It had a strong inner fortress buttressed with eight large towers. The Lachish Letters concern the time just prior to the fall of the city and present the same conditions of turmoil and confusion that are revealed in the Book of Jeremiah. This information is of immense value in explaining historical backgrounds and illuminating Old Testament Scripture.

The Dead Sea Scrolls—The greatest manuscript discovery of modern times began with the uncovering of the Dead Sea Scrolls in 1947. A young shep-

Even minute particles, such as these microflints and bones, must be carefully sorted and analyzed after they are uncovered by archaeologists.

Photo by Gustav Jeeninga

herd boy stumbled upon a cave south of Jericho containing numerous leather scrolls of Hebrew and Aramaic writing and some 600 fragmentary inscriptions. Great excitement quickly spread throughout the archaeological world. In 1952, new caves containing fragments of later scrolls in Hebrew, Greek, and Aramaic were found enclosed in jars. These startling discoveries have been followed by the uncovering of other manuscripts around the Dead Sea area, particularly at QUMRAN.

After intensive study, scholars dated the manuscripts from as early as 250 B.C. to as late as A.D. 68. Although attacks have been made against the age and authenticity of the manuscripts, two lines of evidence establish their integrity. Radiocarbon count, a scientific method of dating, places the linen in which the scrolls were wrapped in the general period of 175 B.C. to A.D. 225. Scholars of ancient writing (paleographers) date documents by the form of the letters and the method of writing. This line of evidence also places the Dead Sea Scrolls during the period of time about three centuries before A.D. 70.

The scrolls contain ancient texts of parts of the Old Testament, as well as writing that originated between the Old and New Testament periods. The biblical section contains two scrolls of Isaiah, one complete, and fragments of several Old Testament books. Coins found at the site at Qumran reveal that the settlement was founded about 135 B.C. It was abandoned during the Jewish war with the Romans in A.D. 66–73.

The scrolls discovered along the Dead Sea were part of the library of the people who lived at Qumran, possibly the ESSENES, a religious group mentioned by ancient writers. The sect was even stricter in its interpretation of the religious laws than the PHARISEES of the New Testament. Some scholars believe that John the Baptist may have lived among these people before beginning his work of announcing the ministry of Jesus.

The Essenes expected the coming of a new age, ushered in by a ruler who would serve as a prophet and a priest. Although the finds at Qumran do not relate directly to any events described in the Bible, they throw useful light on the way certain people thought during the period between the Old and New Testaments.

A full text of the Book of Isaiah is the best known of the discoveries at Qumran, although other texts discovered are also significant. As a group, the documents make up the oldest existing manuscripts of the Bible in any language. One of the caves yielded 18 scraps of papyri written entirely in Greek. Some have identified them as fragments of the earliest New Testament version yet discovered, claiming that one of them, a fragment of Mark's Gospel, dates from about 15 years after the events recorded. Although this dating is disputed by many, the Dead Sea material in general has had a stabilizing effect upon New Testament criticism.

The thrilling story of biblical archaeology is not completed. Scholars are now studying thousands of clay tablets found at Ebla in northern Syria—a task that will require a generation of careful study and analysis. Dialogue between the biblical text and archaeological finds must continue because each can help us understand and interpret the other. The Bible helps us appreciate the archaeologist's discoveries, while biblical archaeology helps us understand and interpret the message of God's inspired Word.

In spite of its great contribution to biblical studies, there are certain things that archaeology cannot do. In general, it cannot prove that a particular Bible event happened or that a specific person mentioned in the Bible actually existed. This is true because of the small amount of evidence archaeology can really recover. Many objects do not survive long enough for a modern archaeologist to discover.

Paper, wood, and clothing will rot away quickly unless they are buried in extremely dry conditions. Also, archaeology discovers only a small portion of the things that do survive. For example, the careful and detailed exploration at Hazor, an ancient city in Israel, between 1956 and 1970 uncovered only a small fraction of the whole mound. It has been estimated that to excavate every area of Hazor's 21 strata would take 800 years.

The truth of the Bible is not only a matter of facts, but of their interpretation. Even if we could prove the accuracy of the entire Bible, its redemptive significance would not be proven. Because the Christian faith is based on historical events, Christians should welcome any supportive evidence that archaeology can provide—but they do not anchor their faith to it.

Neither lack of evidence nor critical skepticism can disprove God's Word. It is better to emphasize how archaeology helps us understand the Bible than to believe that it proves the Bible true. It is heartening, however, to note that so far there has been no instance of an archaeological discovery conclusively proving the Bible to be in error.

ARCHANGEL — in the celestial hierarchy, a spiritual being next in rank above an angel. The word archangel occurs several times in the Bible. In the New Testament the voice of an archangel and the sounding of the trumpet of God will signal the coming of Christ for His people (1 Thess. 4:16) and Michael the archangel disputed with the devil about the body of Moses (Jude 9). In the Old Testament, Michael is described as having a great power and authority (Dan. 10:13) and is the guardian of Israel (Dan. 10:21), especially in the "time of trouble" in the last days (Dan. 12:1).

ARCHELAUS [ar key LAY us] (*people's chief*) — the elder son of King Herod the Great by Malthace (Matt. 2:22). When Herod died in 4 B.C., his kingdom was divided among his sons. Archelaus was made ethnarch, inheriting the largest portion, Judea and Samaria. Because the Jews resented the Herod family so strongly, Archelaus wisely waited to assume the throne and petitioned the emperor

Augustus in Rome before taking it for himself. However, a riot broke out during the Passover celebration, and a large contingent of Jews petitioned him to intervene and stop the conflict. In the battle that followed, nearly 3,000 people were killed. Because of this, the Jews sent a delegation to Rome to demand that Archelaus not be permitted to inherit the kingdom. However, Augustus gave the largest portion of the kingdom of Judea to Archelaus, but only as ETHNARCH (governor), a position inferior to king.

The Jewish historian Josephus records that because of his disappointment at being made ethnarch only, Archelaus treated both the Jews and Samaritans cruelly. In A.D. 6, the ninth year of his reign, he was removed from office following the complaints of a delegation of Jews and Samaritans. He was banished to Vienne in southern France, and his wealth was confiscated by Rome.

ARCHER (see OCCUPATIONS AND TRADES).

ARCHEVITES [AR keh vites] — KJV translation for "people of Erech" (Ezra 4:9). The Archevites probably were Babylonian colonists sent by Ashurbanipal (Osnapper), king of Assyria, to settle in Samaria after the fall of Israel.

ARCHIPPUS [ar KIP pus] (*chief groom*) — a Christian at Colosse who held an official position in the church. The apostle Paul called him "our fellow soldier" (Philem. 2) and exhorted him to fulfill his ministry in the Lord (Col. 4:17).

ARCHITECTURE — the art and science of designing and building structures, especially ones in which people live and work. The words architecture and architect do not occur in the Bible except in Hebrews 11:10 (NIV, NEB, NASB). The focus of the Bible is on man's relationship to God and not on the physical aspects of man's culture. But a study of the architecture of the Bible is important because of the insights it can give on how people lived during these ancient times.

What Bible students know about architecture comes almost entirely from the numerous excavations that have taken place in the Near East during the past 150 years. Today that knowledge is considerable. As archaeology has matured and its techniques have improved, scholars are in the position to learn a great deal about life during biblical times. But our understanding is still very incomplete.

Bible students are limited because the vast majority of the available information still lies buried under the earth. Of the scores of known cities and villages in the Near East, only a fraction have been touched by trained archaeologists. Virtually all of those that have been excavated have been only partially done. Archaeologists project that it would take 800 years to excavate Hazor, the largest ancient ruined city known, at the current rate of excavation.

Scholars are also limited in their understanding of the architecture of the ancient Near East because destruction and the passing of time leave very little to uncover and study. Usually little more than the foundations of an ancient structure remain. This offers limited opportunity to learn about such things as doors, windows, walls, and the roof or how the entire structure was built.

In spite of its difficulties, studying the architecture of Bible times is a worthwhile undertaking. Its greatest value consists of the light it throws on difficult biblical passages. For example, Rahab's house in Jericho was described as if it were a part of the city wall. She lowered the Israelite spies down from a window and let them escape (Josh. 2:1–15). Archaeologists have discovered that some cities of that time had casemate walls—a type of construction in which two parallel walls about five or more feet apart were tied together with short walls at regular intervals. This created a cavity with a series of rooms. Sometimes these rooms were used as houses built inside the wall. Apparently such an arrangement was in use at Jericho at the time when Joshua and the Israelites captured the city.

The architecture of a people at any one time represents a blend of many different factors. One factor was the available building materials. Stone and mud were common in Bible times, so these are what the builders used. Climate also plays a major role. The mild climate of Palestine allowed many activities to take place in the open air; so a courtyard served as an essential part of most houses. The lack of rain during half the year, and no significant snowfall, made a flat roof a practical architectural feature in the land of Palestine.

Massive stones, carefully cut and fitted into place, were used extensively in the architecture of the ancient world.

Tradition is another major consideration. Change did not take place rapidly in ancient times. The housing of one period is generally about the same as that from several centuries earlier. Often changes in architecture came as a result of contact with the outside world. Contact through trade, conquest, or political alliances could bring major changes. The widespread use of cut stones in public buildings during the early part of the United Kingdom under David and Solomon can be traced to Israel's close contacts with the Phoenicians, who were expert stoneworkers.

Although architects of the ancient world designed and guided the construction of public buildings, the ordinary person usually built his own home with the help of friends. He was more interested in whether the house would be safe and comfortable for his family than he was in its appearance. Only the wealthy could afford to beautify their homes and hire craftsmen to include some of the features found in royal palaces.

Building Materials. Palestine is a rugged, rocky land with many mountains. Because of the scarcity of forests, wood was not plentiful enough to be used as the major building material. The Israelites used two materials that were more common—clay and rock. The typical building had walls made of limestone rocks, piled on top of one another. Holes between the rocks were filled with smaller rocks. Then the entire wall was covered with a layer of mud or plaster. Only rarely were the stones cut or shaped in any way.

The neighbors of the Israelites, the Phoenicians and the Canaanites, were experts at stone working. Unlike the Israelites, they used cut stone in their public buildings and palaces. Limestone is an excellent stone for such purposes, because it is soft enough to be chiseled easily. Often the stones were squared on the sides that touched other stones in the wall while the two faces were left rough.

Walls in Old Testament times were sometimes made of rectangular blocks in what is called the header–stretcher method. Two blocks set perpendicular to the wall were placed between three blocks placed parallel to the wall, with the next course staggered a bit so that the joints did not align. Because earthquakes were common in the area, occasionally wood beams were used to tie the whole wall together. At times squared stones were used at the corners of buildings, and the section of wall between the corners was made of rubble or odd–shaped stones.

Squared stone was used in Israel during periods of the nation's close contact with Phoenicia. Solomon, for instance, employed large crews of Phoenicians in his building projects, which made extensive use of such stone. The same practice was followed during the reign of Ahab, whose wife Jezebel was a Phoenician princess. But during most other periods of their history, the Israelites used uncut stones in their buildings.

The most prolific builder in Palestine was Herod the Great, king of Judea from about 37 B.C. to 4 B.C. A Bible student can visit few places in Palestine without being near the ruins of something he built. The stoneworkers he employed were true craftsmen. Without modern equipment or power tools, these men cut and moved large rectangular stones weighing several tons and placed them together without mortar. The joints of those ruins are so tight even today that it is difficult to slip a knife blade between the layers of stone.

In areas of Palestine where stone was lacking or unsuitable, mud bricks were the dominant building material. Mud bricks were familiar to the Hebrew people, because their ancestors had spent many years constructing large buildings for the king of Egypt. Bricks were made by preparing a suitable clay, adding water, and mixing them to the right consistency. Straw was sometimes added as a bonding agent. The bricks were formed in square or rectangular molds and then placed in the sun to dry.

In the civilizations that flourished between the Tigris and Euphrates Rivers, such as ancient Babylon, bricks were often stamped with the name of the reigning king. When the bricks were to be subjected to the weather or heavy use, they were baked. Mud bricks usually were joined with mud for mortar, although occasionally bitumen was used. Bitumen was a natural tar–like substance.

The problem with mud bricks is that they tend to dissolve when subjected to water over a period of time. Walls were sometimes sealed with a layer of waterproof plaster to prevent this. Otherwise, the homeowner had to repair the lower part of the wall periodically because of water erosion. When archaeologists excavate a site, they must take great care not to dig through mud–brick walls, since these are very similar to the ground around them.

City walls were sometimes built from both mud bricks and stone. The foundation and lower courses would be made of stone, with the upper part formed of mud bricks. It is hard to know how common this building method was in Israel, since archaeologists rarely find walls still standing that are more than a few feet high.

Roofs in buildings of all periods in Palestine were usually flat. They were constructed by placing logs or squared beams on top of walls. Next came a layer of branches, thatch, or reeds, and finally a layer of packed clay or plaster. If clay was used as the final layer, it had to be repaired frequently. Large stone rollers that were used to pack the clay have been found by archaeologists.

Arched roofs first appeared in Palestine around the fifth century B.C. during the time of Persian domination. By the time of Christ they were common in the homes of the wealthy. Sometimes these roofs were constructed from mud bricks or stone, and sometimes from beams, thatch, and mud, like the typical flat roof.

Pillars were used when the room was too wide to be spanned easily with the shorter beams available. This construction technique was first used long before the time of Abraham. Pillars were made of a variety of materials, including squared slabs of

Photo by Gustav Jeeninga

Ancient Baalbek, the site of a temple dedicated to Jupiter, contains excellent examples of classical Roman architecture.

limestone, mud bricks, and stone bases topped by wooden posts.

Construction of Fortifications. During Old Testament times, most cities were surrounded by two walls, the outer being the thicker. Sometimes the two walls were tied together at regular intervals by short connecting walls, forming what archaeologists call a casemate wall. A typical casemate wall might have an outer wall five feet thick, an inner wall four feet thick, and connecting joints between them about every five feet. Such a wall had greater strength than just the outer wall by itself. Walls of this type have been uncovered at Megiddo, Hazor, and other cities from the period of the United Kingdom in Israel's history.

But casemate walls were generally abandoned in favor of a single, more massive wall. The Assyrians introduced an improved battering ram that enabled them to break down ordinary casemate walls in a matter of days. Casemate walls continued in use in some places, such as at Masada. Sometimes an existing casemate wall was used, but the gaps within the casemate were filled with rubble.

The wall that replaced the casemate wall is called the offset–inset wall. This wall was considerably thicker and had a series of offsets, or projecting towers, that added strength and allowed a city's defenders, in many places, to fire on the attackers from three sides.

City walls were usually built of massive boulders piled on top of one another. Smaller stones were used at the top of the wall and to fill in the gaps between the larger rocks at the bottom. The whole wall, from top to bottom, was generally plastered with a limestone and mud mixture. King Solomon used squared stones in the walls of Megiddo, Gezer, and other fortified cities, but this was the exception rather than the rule until some time after the fall of Jerusalem in 586 B.C. Occasionally mud bricks were used in a wall's construction. The city wall at Dan during the time of Abraham and his immediate descendants is a good example of this type.

Builders of city walls made the approaches to the city as difficult as possible for the attackers. Most cities were located on high ground as a defensive measure. As cities were destroyed, leveled, and rebuilt, the ground upon which they were situated rose higher. During the period after 1000 B.C., many old cities, such as Beth Shan and Hazor, sat on more than nine meters (30 feet) of ruins from previous occupations. These steep slopes were often plastered to make them smooth and then covered by the defenders with oil to make them difficult to climb.

If the wall was not protected by a natural slope, the defenders sometimes dug a wide, dry moat around the wall as an additional defensive measure. This was very common in Palestine at the time of the patriarchs when some cities expanded greatly in size. At Hazor, a huge, dry moat was dug on the western side of the lower city. The dirt from this moat was heaped up around the wall to continue the slope and to create an artificial ridge. A defensive wall was then built on top of this ridge.

The city gate was a favorite target for an attacking army. To prevent direct attack on the gate, the defenders often placed the road leading up to the gate parallel to the wall. The road was then arranged so it made a turn just in front of the gate. This allowed the defenders to get a good shot at the attackers just before they reached the gate.

Often a series of two or three gates were built through the walls. After the attackers had battered down the first gate and were working on the second, they could be hit from all sides by the defenders. The attackers were also greatly limited by this arrangement because only a few at a time could work in the cramped space to break down the second gate. Virtually identical quadruple gateways have been discovered at Megiddo, Hazor, and Gezer.

Another element of a city's defense system was the citadel, or upper city, which had its own walls and gates. It was a smaller city within the larger city. Often this upper section was the original city, and the lower part represented an expansion as the population had increased. The palace, or the residence of the king or other ruling officials, and related buildings frequently were located in this area. If the outer walls were broken, the defenders would fall back to the citadel and use it as their new line of defense.

Construction of Palaces. Little is known about the royal palaces of Samaria and Jerusalem besides the few facts gleaned from the Bible itself. While the remains of Solomon's palace in Jerusalem have been destroyed, King Saul's palace-fortress at Gibeah, 4.5 kilometers (three miles) north of Jerusalem, has been uncovered by archaeologists. It consisted of a large rectangular courtyard surrounded by a casemate wall, with a large square tower in each corner.

The excavators found only one corner of the palace intact. Only the first floor storage area was found. Much of the rest had eroded. The second floor, where the living quarters of Saul would have been located, was gone. What remained spoke of a rustic, simple existence—nothing like the lavish palace of Solomon. Saul's royal palace was probably much like the palace of Jebusite Jerusalem from which David reigned after he captured the city.

Because of the clear Phoenician influence during Solomon's reign, Syrian palaces from Solomon's time should provide a glimpse of what Solomon's palace might have looked like. The typical layout for palaces in northern Syria at that time is called the bit–hilani palace. A number of these palaces have been excavated, and all have basically the same plan.

The approach to the palace was by means of a short flight of stairs that led to a recessed porch enclosed by the building on three sides. The porch was supported by one to three pillars. To the side of this porch was a flight of stairs that led to the royal apartments upstairs. Straight ahead was the entrance to the throne room, which was situated at right angles to the entrance. This meant that a person entering the building had to turn to face the throne. Around the throne room were a number of administrative and storage rooms, as well as the royal quarters. The servants' quarters were located at one end of the palace, out of sight.

The lower part of the walls in public areas of the royal palace were frequently covered with large slabs of carved, decorated stone. The walls had foundations and lower courses of stone, but the upper walls were constructed of a pattern of mud bricks and squared wooden beams. The wood did not show because the whole wall was covered with plaster and usually painted. Some scholars believe wood may have been included to make the palace earthquake–proof.

Solomon built an elaborate royal palace for himself in Jerusalem after he constructed the Temple. Jerusalem was built on the southern end of a long ridge that ran from north to south. The Temple was located on a higher area to the north of the old, original city. Solomon built his palace between the city and the Temple in an area where the ridge narrowed. He widened the ridge by building a sloping stone wall that ran down into the Kidron Valley.

Most of this sloping wall has been uncovered by archaeologists. Unfortunately, the top of the ridge had been stripped to bedrock and quarried extensively at some time in the past, so nothing remains of Solomon's palace and most of the original city of Jerusalem.

The columns of the temple to Jupiter at Baalbek were capped by this elaborate carving. The lion's head served as a downspout for the gutters.
Photo by Gustav Jeeninga

The palace of King Darius I at Persepolis, showing the distinctive Persian style of architecture.

Judging from the biblical description of Solomon's palace in 1 Kings 7, archaeologists know it consisted of a series of public and private rooms built around several courtyards. There was an official throne room, a hall of pillars, and a house of the forest of Lebanon, as well as the royal private quarters for Solomon himself and separate quarters for his many wives. First Kings 7:1–12 specifically names a complex for the Egyptian princess whom he married. A large section of housing must have been provided also for Solomon's many servants and craftsmen who kept the royal household running. Administrative and storage sections were probably also a part of the palace complex.

After the northern tribes split from Judah to form their own nation of Israel, they eventually chose Samaria as their capital. Samaria was partially excavated in the 1930s. Unlike Jerusalem, the city was almost entirely taken up with official buildings. Portions of the royal palaces of Omri and his son Ahab came to light.

Architecture of Temples. The site of the Temple in Jerusalem is covered today by the Dome of the Rock, a Muslim holy place, making excavation impossible. But judging from the description of the Temple in 1 Kings 6, this structure consisted of two parts—the Holy Place and the Holy of Holies. In front of the Temple stood a porch with two pillars known as Jachin and Boaz (1 Kin. 7:21). But the description from the Bible is not complete enough to help scholars make an accurate reconstruction, although several attempts have been made.

With the discovery of a Syrian temple that had a plan very similar to the Jerusalem Temple, most scholars today look to palaces of the same time for help in understanding the appearance of Solomon's Temple. This is a sensible approach, because Solomon employed a number of Phoenician craftsmen from the territory of the Syrians to help build the Temple. The man responsible for all the bronze objects in the structure was a half–Israelite from Tyre named Hiram.

In the temple from Syria discovered at Tell Tainat, the porch was enclosed on three sides, like the porch of a bit–hilani palace. The two columns in front supported the roof of this porch and were not free–standing. A Canaanite shrine from Hazor that dates to about the time of Moses followed a similar plan. The walls of this shrine had timbers placed between courses of stone, just like the design of Solomon's palace (1 Kings 12).

An Israelite temple has been discovered at Arad, a town in the southern part of Judah. The overall plan was similar to that of the tabernacle and the Temple. It had an outer courtyard with an altar, an inner courtyard, two bases for pillars to flank the entrance to the Temple, a Holy Place, and a Holy of Holies. The Holy of Holies contained two incense altars, a small raised area, and a stone pillar. This temple was built when the Israelites occupied the site around 1000 B.C. It apparently continued in use until the time of Hezekiah and Josiah of Judah about 700 B.C. These two kings sought to eliminate the numerous regional worship places scattered throughout the country in order to concentrate worship of God in the Temple at Jerusalem and prevent idolatry in the land.

The Temple of Solomon in Jerusalem was renovated several times before its destruction by the invading Babylonians in 586 B.C. When the Jews rebuilt it upon their return to Jerusalem about 50 years later, it was a much more modest structure (Hag. 2:3). Nothing is known about the appearance of the second Temple. Herod the Great, king of Judea from 37 B.C. to 4 B.C., started a total rebuilding of the Temple, enlarging the outer court considerably. Work on this Temple was still being done under other Roman officials when Jesus was crucified in Jerusalem. The structure was not completed until A.D. 64, just six years before it was destroyed by the Romans when they put down a revolt by the Jews.

Bits and pieces of this Temple have been found in excavations that have taken place outside the walls of the Temple enclosure. The only known description of "Herod's Temple" comes from the Jewish historian Josephus. Impressive because of its extensive use of gold and other expensive materials, it was considered one of the wonders of the ancient world at that time.

Houses. During the 2,000 years from Abraham's time until Jesus' earthly ministry, the home of the common people in Palestine did not change a great deal. They sometimes contained two stories and consisted of several rooms arranged around a courtyard. The walls were made of stone rubble and covered with plaster or mud, although in some areas of the nation the walls were constructed of mud bricks.

The floors of these houses were generally made of packed clay. The flat roof was formed by placing logs across the tops of the walls, which were covered first by boards or branches, then thatch or reeds, and finally a layer of clay. Most homes were owner-built.

In the mild climate of Palestine, many family activities took place outside the house in the courtyard. Here food was prepared and the children played. The flat roof provided another place for outside activities. As a safety measure, it was surrounded by a low wall, in keeping with the Jewish law, to prevent people from falling off the roof. In the crowded cities, families slept on the roofs during hot summer nights. A food storage room or extra bedroom might also be located on the roof. If the house had two stories, the family generally lived upstairs. Downstairs was reserved for storage and the family's domestic animals. By modern standards, these houses were plain and unimpressive. Walls might be plastered and whitewashed to make the interior brighter, but ornate trim and other frills were reserved for the wealthy.

The homes of wealthy families had more variety. The largest houses in Palestinian cities at the time of Abraham were similar to homes in Mesopotamia. At the time of Christ, they resembled those found throughout the Roman Empire, with arched roofs, tiled floors, and porches surrounding the courtyards.

The only authentically Israelite house was the four-room house. This type of structure first appeared in Israelite towns about 1000 B.C. and continued essentially unchanged for several centuries.

A four-room house consisted of a long, rectangular courtyard with a row of rooms on each side. The house was entered through a door in one of the narrow walls of the courtyard. At the other end of the courtyard was another row of rooms. The resulting house was U-shaped, with the courtyard in the middle. Sometimes the rooms along one side were left open on the courtyard side. These were probably used as a stable area for the livestock. Many of these four-room houses had a second story with the bedrooms located upstairs.

The typical house of this style had about 900 to 1,500 square feet, depending on whether it was one or two stories. But this area included the courtyard, the stables, and a large food storage area as well as living space. And if the family practiced a trade, this was also carried out in a room at home.

ARCHITES [AR kites] — members of the clan of Ataroth in Ephraim (Josh. 16:2). Hushai the Archite was King David's "secret agent" in Absalom's rebellion. Ahithophel advised Absalom to pursue and destroy David's army, but Hushai encouraged Absalom to wait (2 Sam. 15:32; 1 Chr. 27:33). Absalom waited and was defeated (2 Sam. 18:1–18).

ARCHWAY — a roofed and partially enclosed section in the Temple in Jerusalem which was described by the prophet Ezekiel in his vision (Ezek. 40:16–36). Other words used to describe this part of the Temple are arch (1 Kin. 6:3, KJV) and vestibule (1 Chr. 28:11, NKJV). Also see ARCHITECTURE.

ARCTURUS [ark TOO rus] (*the bear keeper*) — KJV translation of a Hebrew word meaning "crowd," and referring to a constellation of stars. The NKJV translates the word as "the Bear" (Job 9:9) and "the Great Bear with its cubs" (Job 38:32)—the "cubs" being a reference to the seven main stars of this constellation.

ARD [ard] (*descent*) — the name of two men in the Old Testament.

1. A son of Benjamin (Gen. 46:21).

2. A son of Bela and a grandson of Benjamin (Num. 26:40), also called Addar (1 Chr. 8:3).

ARDITE [ARD ite] — a descendant of ARD (Num. 26:40).

ARDON [AR dun] (*descendant*) — a son of Caleb (1 Chr. 2:18).

ARELI [a REE lih] (*heroic*) — a son of Gad (Gen. 46:16) and founder of the tribal family known as the ARELITES (Num. 26:17).

ARELITES [a REE lites] — descendants of ARELI (Num. 26:17).

AREOPAGITE [air ee OP ah gyte] — a member of

the court, or council, of the AREOPAGUS (Acts 17:34). Also see DIONYSIUS.

AREOPAGUS [air ee OP ah gus] (*hill of Ares*) — a limestone hill in Athens situated between the ACROPOLIS and the AGORA; by association, also the council which often met on the hill. The apostle Paul addressed the Areopagus in his "philosophical sermon" which attempted to meet the objections of the Epicurean and Stoic philosophers to the gospel (Acts 17:16–34).

Paul's speech before the Areopagus (Acts 17:22–31) is a good example of the council meeting to discuss and evaluate a philosophical issue. Paul argued about the nature of God and the way God relates to human beings, especially through Jesus Christ. Paul's argument must have made an impact in the council. "Dionysius the Areopagite" was among those who joined Paul and believed in Christ (Acts 17:34).

Paul's argument on the Areopagus is extremely important. It identifies the decisive difference between Greek philosophy and the Christian faith. Apparently the philosophers were not greatly troubled by Paul's talking about God or God's relationship to people. But when he spoke of the resurrection of Jesus, they mocked him, although some apparently gave his words careful thought (Acts 17:32). The resurrection of Jesus was, and continues to be, a decisive element in Christian theology. It always provokes controversy among unbelievers.

Today Paul's speech is affixed in Greek on a tablet at the entrance to the Areopagus. With the benches carved into the rock and the worn steps to the summit, it stands as a monument to a time when the Athenians deliberated before the gods and missed the significance of the One whom Paul identified with the "unknown God" (Acts 17:23).

ARETAS [AIR ee tus] (*one who pleases*) — a name borne by Arabian kings at Damascus and Petra. The Aretas mentioned in 2 Corinthians 11:32–33 was Aretas IV (9 B.C.—A.D. 40).

ARGOB [AR gob] (*stony*) — the name of a place and a man in the Old Testament:

1. A district in the kingdom of Og, in northern TRANSJORDAN. It was either a part of Bashan or was a word for the region of Bashan itself.

2. A man mentioned in connection with the murder of Pekahiah (2 Kin. 15:25).

ARIDAI [a RID a eye] (*delight of Hari*) — a son of Haman who was hanged like his father (Esth. 9:9).

ARIDATHA [a RID ah thah] (*given by Hari*) — a son of Haman who was hanged like his father (Esth. 9:8).

ARIEH [a RIE ee] (*lion of Jehovah*) — a man mentioned in connection with the murder of Pekahiah (2 Kin. 15:25).

ARIEL [AIR ih el] (*lion of God*) — the name of a city and three men in the Bible:

1, 2. Two men of Moab killed by Benaiah. They are called "lion-like heroes" (2 Sam. 23:20; 1 Chr. 11:22). Because of uncertainty about the exact meaning of the phrase, it is translated as "sons of Ariel" (NASB), "two Ariels" (RSV), and "best men" (NIV).

The Areopagus (Mars' Hill) is a little hill near the acropolis in Athens where Paul may have been brought before the philosophers of this city (Acts 17:16-34).

Photo by Gustav Jeeninga

A stone carving of the Ark of the Covenant, discovered at the excavation of a synagogue in Capernaum.

3. The man whom Ezra sent to Iddo at Casiphia (Ezra 8:16).

4. The symbolic name of Jerusalem (Is. 29:1–2, 7), perhaps applied to the city because the lion was the emblem of the tribe of Judah (Gen. 49:9).

ARIMATHEA [air ih mah THEE ah] (*a height*) — a city in the Judean hills northwest of Jerusalem (see Map 6, A–4). It was the home of Joseph, a member of the Jewish Sanhedrin in Jerusalem, who placed the body of Jesus in his new tomb (Luke 23:50).

ARIOCH [AIR ih ock] (meaning unknown) — the name of two men in the Old Testament:

1. The king of Ellasar, a city probably located in Southern Babylonia. Arioch was an ally of CHE-DORLAOMER in his fight to regain control over the rebellious kings of Sodom, Gomorrah, Admah, Zeboiim, and Belah (Gen. 14:1–9).

2. The captain of Nebuchadnezzar's bodyguard (Dan. 2:14–15, 24–25).

ARISAI [a RIS ah eye] (meaning unknown) — a son of Haman who was hanged like his father (Esth. 9:9).

ARISTARCHUS [air ihs TAR kus] (*the best ruler*) — a Macedonian of Thessalonica who traveled with the apostle Paul on his third missionary journey through Asia Minor (Acts 19:29; 20:4; 27:2). He was with Paul during the riot at Ephesus (Acts 19:29); later, he preceded Paul to Troas (Acts 20:4–6). A faithful companion and friend, Aristarchus accompanied Paul to Rome (Acts 27:2), where he attended the apostle and shared his imprisonment.

ARISTOBULUS [a ris tow BUE lus] (*best adviser*) — a Roman to whose household the apostle Paul sent greetings (Rom. 16:10). According to an old tradition, Aristobulus was a brother of Barnabas and he was ordained a bishop by Paul and Barnabas. There is no historical evidence, however, for this tradition.

ARK OF THE COVENANT — a sacred portable chest which—along with its two related items, the MERCY SEAT and CHERUBIM—was the most important sacred object of the Israelites during the wilderness period. It was also known as the ark of the Lord (Josh. 6:11), the ark of God (1 Sam. 3:3), and the ark of the Testimony (Ex. 25:22).

The ark of the covenant was the only article of furniture in the innermost room, or Holy of Holies, of Moses' tabernacle and of Solomon's Temple. From between the two cherubim that were on the ark of the Testimony, God spoke to Moses. Once a year the high priest could enter the Holy of Holies, but only with sacrificial blood that he sprinkled on the mercy seat for the atonement of sin.

Description. The Hebrew word translated as ark is also translated as coffin. In the last verse of the book of Genesis, this word is used of the coffin in which Joseph's embalmed body was placed after he died in Egypt (Gen. 50:26). The ark of the covenant was also a "coffin," or chest 2½ cubits long, 1½ cu-

cubits wide, and 1 ½ cubits deep (or, in inches, about 45 by 27 by 27). The builder of the ark was a man named Bezaleel (Ex. 37:1).

The ark was made of acacia wood (shittim wood, KJV) overlaid with gold. It had four rings of gold through which carrying poles were inserted (Ex. 37:1-9). These poles were never removed from the rings, apparently to show that the ark was a portable sanctuary. Even when the ark was placed in Solomon's Temple, the poles stayed in place, and they could be seen from a certain point outside the inner sanctuary (1 Kin. 8:8).

The ark had a gold cover known as the "mercy seat" (Ex. 25:17-22) because the Israelites believed the ark was God's throne. The ark had a gold molding or "crown" surrounding the top edge. The mercy seat was a slab of pure gold which fit exactly within the crown of the ark, so the mercy seat could not slide around during transportation.

Of one piece with the mercy seat were two angelic statues called cherubim. They stood at opposite ends of the mercy seat, facing each other with wings outstretched above and their faces bowed toward the mercy seat. They marked the place where the Lord dwelled as well as the place where the Lord communicated with Moses.

Contents. Within the ark were the two stone tablets containing the Ten Commandments (Ex. 25:16, 21), considered to be the basis of the covenant between God and His people Israel. Thus the ark was often called the ark of the Testimony. The golden pot of MANNA, which God miraculously preserved as a testimony to future generations (Ex. 16:32-34), was also deposited in the ark. The third item in the ark was AARON'S ROD that budded to prove that Aaron was God's chosen (Num. 17:1-11).

While the New Testament states that the ark contained these three items (Heb. 9:4), the ark must have lost two of them through the years. At the dedication of Solomon's Temple, Aaron's rod and the golden pot of manna were gone: "There was nothing in the ark except the two tablets of stone which Moses put there at Horeb" (1 Kin. 8:9).

History. The ark was carried by the sons of Levi during the wilderness wanderings (Deut. 31:9). Carried into the Jordan River by the priests, the ark caused the waters to part so Israel could cross on dry ground (Josh. 3:6—4:18). During the conquest of the land of Canaan, the ark was carried at the fall of Jericho (Josh. 6:4-11); later it was deposited at Shiloh, which had become the home of the tabernacle (Josh. 18:1).

Trusting the "magic power" of the ark rather than God, the Israelites took the ark into battle against the Philistines and suffered a crushing defeat (1 Sam. 4:1-11). The Philistines captured the ark, only to send it back when disaster struck their camp (1 Samuel 5—6). It remained at Kirjath Jearim until David brought it to Jerusalem (1 Chr. 13:3-14; 15:1-28). Solomon established it in the Holy of Holies of the Temple which he built.

Nothing is known of what became of the ark. It disappeared when Nebuchadnezzar's armies destroyed Jerusalem in 586 B.C., and was not available when the second and third temples were built. In the many synagogues that arose after the Captivity, a chest or ark containing the Torah (scrolls of the Law) and other sacred books was placed in an area shut off from the rest of the building, just as the original ark was placed in the Holy of Holies of the Temple.

ARK OF MOSES — a small basket-like container in which Moses was hidden by his mother to save him from the slaughter of Hebrew children by the Egyptian Pharaoh (Ex. 2:3-6). The basket was made of woven PAPYRUS reeds and sealed with a tar-like pitch. The lid on the basket kept insects and the sun off the child so he could sleep. The ark was discovered by the daughter of Pharaoh when she came to bathe at the river.

ARK, NOAH'S — a vessel built by Noah to save him, his family, and animals from the Flood (Gen. 6:14—9:18). God commanded Noah to make the ark of gopherwood (Gen. 6:14). Many scholars believe gopherwood is cypress, which was noted for its lightness and durability and therefore was used extensively in shipbuilding by the Phoenicians.

Noah's ark was 300 cubits long, 50 cubits wide, and 30 cubits high (Gen. 6:15)—about 450 feet long, 75 feet wide, and 45 feet high. The ark was constructed with three "decks," or stories (Gen. 6:16). When Noah and his family and all the animals entered the ark, God himself shut its door to insure their safety against the raging flood (Gen. 7:16). In this way God sealed the judgment against the ungodly who had refused to heed Noah's warnings. When the waters subsided after the Flood, the ark rested on the mountains of ARARAT (Gen. 8:4).

In the New Testament, Jesus spoke of the Flood and of Noah and the ark, comparing "the days of Noah" with the time of "the coming of the Son of Man" (Matt. 24:37-38; Luke 17:26-27). The ark is a striking illustration of Christ, who preserves us from the flood of divine judgment.

ARK, TESTIMONY (see ARK OF THE COVENANT).

ARKITES [AR kights] — a tribe descended from Canaan (1 Chr. 1:15). They lived at Arka, in PHOENICIA. The modern site is Tell 'Arka, located about 19 kilometers (12 miles) north of Tripolis, in Syria.

ARM — a word frequently used by the Bible as a symbol of God's power, strength, or might (Ps. 89:13; Is. 53:1). The most common reference is to His deliverance during the Exodus, when He redeemed Israel from bondage in Egypt (Ps. 77:15; Is. 63:12).

ARMAGEDDON [ar mah GED un] (*mountain of Megiddo*) — the site of the final battle of this age in which God intervenes to destroy the armies of Satan and to cast Satan into the bottomless pit (Rev. 16:16; 20:1-3, 7-10). Scholars disagree about the exact location of this place, but the most likely pos-

An artist's conception of Noah's ark, based on information from an explorer who claimed he saw the ark on Mt. Ararat in 1908.

sibility is the valley between Mount Carmel and the city of Jezreel. This valley (known as the Valley of Jezreel and sometimes referred to as the Plain of Esdraelon) was the crossroads of two ancient trade routes and thus was a strategic military site. Armageddon is the Greek word for this area, which was the scene of many ancient battles.

Because of this history, Megiddo became a symbol of the final conflict between God and the forces of evil. According to the Book of Revelation, at Armageddon "the cup of the wine of the fierceness of His [God's] wrath" (Rev. 16:19) will be poured out, and the forces of evil will be overthrown and destroyed.

ARMENIAN VERSIONS (see BIBLE VERSIONS AND TRANSLATIONS).

ARMONI [ar MOE nih] (*of the palace*) — a son of King Saul by his concubine Rizpah, daughter of Aiah (2 Sam. 21:1, 8–9).

ARMOR (see ARMS, ARMOR OF THE BIBLE).

ARMOR BEARER (see OCCUPATIONS AND TRADES).

ARMOR OF GOD — an expression that symbolizes the combat equipment of a Christian soldier who fights against spiritual wickedness; the full resources of God which are available to all who take up the cross and follow Christ. Because our spiritual enemy is stronger than we are, we must "put on the whole armor of God" (Eph. 6:11, 13).

ARMORER (see OCCUPATIONS AND TRADES).

ARMORY — an official storehouse, or treasury, for military weapons (2 Kin. 20:13; Is. 39:2). In Jeremiah 50:25, the word armory and the term "weapons of His indignation" are used as a symbol of God's wrath and judgment over Israel's sin.

ARMS, ARMOR OF THE BIBLE — weapons of war used for offense and defense. Since warfare is mentioned so frequently in the Bible, arms and armor are also frequently mentioned.

Knowledge about arms and armor in Palestine and surrounding nations comes from archeological discoveries, ancient engravings showing battle scenes, and references and descriptions in the Bible and other documents from the ancient world.

The forms and uses of weapons and armor changed from the beginning of the Old Testament period until the end of the New Testament period. Certain weapons that were very important in one period became outdated and fell from use in a later time. This occurred because nations competed with one another in developing more effective weapons. When one nation developed a shield that could not be penetrated effectively by the arrows of an enemy, then the enemy set out to develop a more powerful bow and better arrows. The weapons race is nothing new. It has been with men and nations since earliest history.

The following offensive and defensive weapons and armor are mentioned in the Bible. This list is keyed to the New King James Version, with cross references from five additional popular translations—KJV, NASB, NEB, NIV, and RSV.

Arrow (see *Bow*).

Ax/Mace. Battle ax (Jer. 51:20, NKJV, KJV, NEB) and war club (Jer. 51:20, NIV, NASB) are names used by various translations of the Bible for the ancient ax, also known as the mace. Maces and axes are simple extensions of the club. A mace is a club with a metal head for greater efficiency in hand-to-hand combat. A mace was used frequently in the period before Abraham. But with the development of helmets, the mace was less effective. Maces continued to serve a symbolic function.

Photo by Howard Vos

A Roman soldier in battle gear, demonstrating some of the pieces of "spiritual armor" mentioned by the apostle Paul (Eph. 6:10-18).

For instance, the scepter, a symbol of authority used by ancient kings, probably had its origin in the war mace.

Axes remained important military weapons throughout the Old Testament period. An ax also served as a domestic tool (1 Chr. 20:3). One major problem in making axes was the fastening of ax heads to the handles. A fascinating miracle recorded in the Old Testament concerns a poorly fastened ax head that flew off its handle into the Jordan River. The prophet Elisha recovered the ax head by causing it to float (2 Kin. 6:5-7).

The ax remained an important military weapon because of its ability to pierce armor. The Old Testament describes the Egyptian (Jer. 46:22) and Babylonian armies (Ezek. 26:9) as attacking with axes. During Israel's early history, few axes existed in Palestine because the Philistines had a monopoly on metalwork (1 Sam. 13:19-23).

Battering Ram. The battering ram was a war machine used to destroy a city's walls (Ezek. 26:9; engine of war, KJV). Although the battering ram was made in many shapes and sizes, a typical one featured a long, pointed pole that was driven with great force against a fortified city's massive stone walls. It took a crew of several men to operate the battering ram. Many models provided extensive protection for the crew, since the city's defenders usually fired upon them as they worked. The whole machine was mounted on wheels for easy movement. The prophet Ezekiel showed a knowledge of the use of battering rams (Ezek. 4:2; 21:22).

Battle Ax (see *Axe/Mace*).
Battle Bow (see *Bow*).
Belt (see *Body Armor*).

Body Armor. By about 3000 B.C., primitive body armor was worn by soldiers in many nations of the ancient world. The term armor may describe anything from thick leather clothing to metal mail. General terms for body armor used in different translations of the Bible include coat of mail (Ex. 28:32, NKJV, NASB); habergeon (Ex. 28:32, KJV); and brigandine (Jer. 46:4, KJV).

Specific pieces of armor for the body mentioned in the Bible include: breastplate (Neh. 4:16, NASB); belt, a wide piece of metal that protected a warrior's lower trunk and stomach (1 Sam. 18:4; girdle, RSV); and greaves, protective devices for the legs (1 Sam. 16:5).

Bow. Bows were the most characteristic weapons of warfare in the Old Testament period, serving often as the decisive element in a battle. Simple bows were used in the prehistoric period, mostly for hunting.

Simple bows, composed of a piece of wood and string, were easy to make. Bows like this did not have much power or range; so the composite bow was developed early in the history of the Near East. The composite bow was a combination of wood and animal horn. This combination of materials provided the bow with the flexibility and strength needed for effective combat. But a composite bow was difficult to use. Thus certain units within an army were specially trained to shoot the bow.

The bow was usually the first weapon fired in an open-field battle, because the archers of the hostile armies could send arrows from long distances. Chariot troops often were equipped with bows. This combination of mobility and fire power made the army a potent war machine. When attacking a city, the archers of the attacking army would try to pick city defenders off the walls. Archers of the defending city would use their bows to try to keep the army from getting close enough to break down the city's defenses.

The destructive agent of a bow was the arrow, a long, slender shaft of wood with a tip of sharp stone or metal. The archer was also equipped with a quiver, a deep, narrow basket constructed especially for arrows.

Bows, arrows, and archers are mentioned often in the Old Testament, beginning with the boy Ishmael, who "became an archer" (Gen. 21:20; expert with the bow, RSV). Another term for bow used by some translations is battle bow (Zech. 9:10, NKJV, RSV, NIV).

Breast Plate (see *Body Armor*).
Brigandine (see *Body Armor*).
Buckler (see *Shield*).

Chariot. The chariot rivalled the composite bow in its effectiveness as a weapon. But only wealthier nations could establish and maintain a chariot force.

Chariots were introduced in MESOPOTAMIA (the land between the Tigris and Euphrates Rivers) about 2800 B.C. These machines of war served as mobile firing platforms. The advantage of the chariot is that it can bring great firepower quickly to the key point of the battle. Chariots came in many different forms. They could be two-wheeled or four-wheeled, drawn by two to four houses. Some chariots would carry as many as four warriors.

In combat a chariot usually carried two soldiers—a driver who controlled the reins and a warrior who needed both arms free to fire his bow. In some cases, depending on the nation and the period of history, a third person might serve as a shield-bearer to protect both the warrior and the driver. The warrior was usually equipped with a bow, as well as a medium-range weapon, such as the javelin or spear.

The first chariots mentioned in the Bible belonged to Egypt. Joseph rode in a chariot behind the Pharaoh (Gen. 41:43). A later Pharaoh pursued Moses and the Israelites with his chariot corps (Ex. 14:6-9).

At first, the nation of Israel rejected chariots as tools of warfare (Josh. 11:4-9). Most of Palestine was not suitable for chariot warfare because of its high hills and deep ravines. Also, the spirit of conquest under Joshua was such that the use of a powerful weapon like the chariot might have led Israel to boast in their own power rather than God's. Solomon, however, developed a chariot corps in his army (1 Kin. 4:26; 9:19). But the chariots in the Israelite and Judean armies had radically diminished by a later time in the history of the Jewish people (2 Kin. 13:7).

Club. The most primitive weapon of all was the club, consisting in its early development of little more than a piece of wood especially shaped for hand-to-hand combat. In later years metal was

A reconstructed Roman catapult. While catapults are not mentioned in the Bible, these war machines were used in ancient times to hurl huge stones at the enemy.
Photo by Gustav Jeeninga

added to these primitive weapons, and they evolved into a type of war club (Prov. 25:15, RSV) or mace. Another variation on the club was the staff, generally used by shepherds to care for their flocks but also mentioned in the Bible as a weapon of war (2 Sam. 23:21; 1 Chr. 11:23). Other words for club used by different translations of the Bible include maul (Prov. 25:18, KJV) and cudgel (Matt. 26:47, NEB).

Coat of Mail (see *Body Armor*).

Cudgel (see *Club*).

Dagger/Sword. Different translations of the Bible speak of the dagger and the sword as if these two weapons were basically the same. A sword was a piercing or cutting weapon, with which a warrior might stab or slash an enemy. Some swords were designed to pierce, others to slash. All swords had two parts, a handle or hilt and a blade. The blade was usually straight, but one unusual variation was the sickle sword. This weapon featured a curved blade with the sharp edge on the outside. Swords were the basic weapon of a Hebrew soldier. The Biblical phrase that identified a man as a soldier was that he "drew the sword" (2 Kin. 3:26).

Daggers were similar to swords in that they were composed of a hilt and a blade and were used to stab. Their advantage over swords was their ability to be hidden. EHUD, the judge, exploited this advantage by hiding a dagger and stabbing the oppressor Eglon (Judg. 3:16-22).

Dart (see *Javelin/Spear*).

Engine of War (see *Battering Ram*).

Girdle (see *Body Armor*).

Greaves (see *Body Armor*).

Handpike (see *Javelin/Spear*).

Handstaff (see *Javelin/Spear*).

Helmet. The helmet was a type of hat worn by warriors to protect their heads from physical blows in a military battle (1 Sam. 17:5; Jer. 46:4). Helmets came in all shapes and sizes and were made from many different materials, although metal was the most effective. Since the head is the most vulnerable part of the body, it was the first area covered by armor.

Javelin/Spear. In various translations of the Bible, these two terms are used interchangeably to refer to the same basic weapon—a long, slender shaft with a metal point. The only difference between them is that a spear was heavier and larger than a javelin. Therefore, a spear was used as a thrusting weapon as well as a throwing weapon.

Spears and javelins are mentioned often in the Old Testament. At God's command, Joshua stretched out his spear toward Ai to show that the city would fall to the Israelites (Josh. 8:18, 19). In a fit of jealousy, Saul tried to kill David with a spear (1 Sam. 18:10, 11).

Other words for spear or javelin used in various translations of the Bible are dart (2 Sam. 18:14, KJV, RSV); handpike (Ezek. 39:9, RSV); handstaff (Ezek. 39:9, KJV); lance or lancet (Judg. 5:8, NEB; 1 Kin. 18:28, NKJV); and throwing stick (Ezek. 39:9, NEB).

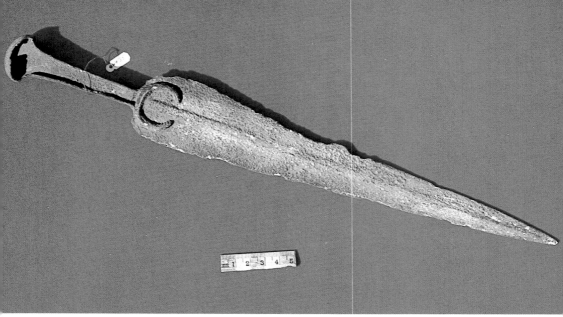

A bronze dagger. Daggers and swords were common weapons of Bible times.

Lance, Lancet (see *Javelin/Spear*).
Mace (see *Ax/Mace*).
Maul (see *Club*).
Quiver (see *Bow*).
Shield. The shield was a hard object, generally made of metal, with which a warrior protected his body from the weapons of the enemy. In the biblical period, shields came in all sizes and shapes. Some shields were made of leather or wood. Another word for shield is buckler (1 Chr. 5:18, KJV; 1 Kin. 10:6, NEB).
Sling. The sling was first developed and used by shepherds for protecting their livestock against wild animals. This was a simple weapon, composed generally of a small piece of leather or animal hide. Small stones or pebbles were generally used as ammunition in a sling. While the sling is a simple weapon in terms of construction, it is difficult to fire with accuracy. Only trained and experienced soldiers were equipped with slings.

Next to archers, the slingmen were the most effective long–range warriors in Old Testament times. The advantage of such a long–range weapon is illustrated by the most famous sling story of all—David's victory over Goliath. The young, inexperienced David killed the giant because of his trust in God. David also had a decided advantage in the contest because Goliath was armed with a spear and a sword, both of which were short–range weapons.

Slingers were important elements in the Israelite army. The Benjamites also had a unit of 700 left–handed slingers who could "sling a stone at a hair's breadth and not miss" (Judg. 20:16).
Spear (see *Javelin/Spear*).
Staff (see *Club*).
Sword (see *Dagger/Sword*).

Throwing Stick (see *Javelin/Spear*).
War Club (see *Club*).
In addition to their military application, arms and armor are also spoken of in a figurative or symbolic way in the Bible. For example, the Bible itself is often called a sword (Eph. 6:17). God's Word, like a sword, is able to slash to the very heart of man (Heb. 4:12). Jesus Christ is portrayed as bearing a sword in His mouth (Rev. 1:16; 19:15). The sword also is an image for God's Word. The Psalms often refer to God as a shield because He protects His people (3:3; 28:7; 33:20).

The fullest development of armor imagery occurs in the Epistle to the Ephesians in the New Testament. The apostle Paul compared the Christian's struggles with evil to a battle in which God provides the believer with the armor and weapons needed to protect oneself against the enemy, Satan: "Put on the whole armor of God, that you may be able to stand against the wiles of the devil" (Eph. 6:10).

ARMY — a large body of warriors organized and trained for warfare. The nation of Israel developed a regular standing army at a relatively late time in its history. One reason for this is that the nation lacked political unity until the time of the United Kingdom under David and Solomon. The sense that God was the Divine Warrior and would protect His people regardless of their military strength may have been another reason why they were slow to develop an army.

Thus, from the time of Abraham to the beginning of Saul's reign there was no regular army, continually prepared to respond to foreign attacks. Instead, the call would go out at the moment of crisis; and able–bodied, non–exempt males would gather in response. The first example comes from

Genesis 14, when Abraham's nephew Lot was kidnapped by Chedorlaomer, king of Elam, and his allies. Abraham rallied to Lot's aid by gathering 318 trained men of his household and defeating the foreign forces.

During the years of the Exodus, wilderness wanderings, and conquest of the land of Canaan, the whole nation was temporarily changed into an army. All the men from every tribe participated in the warfare. Numbers 2 pictures the nation of Israel camped as an army in battle, with their Heavenly Commander in the center and the various divisions (individual tribes) dwelling under their battle banners. The same chapter describes the position of each tribe marching behind the ARK of the COVENANT as they traveled toward Palestine and holy war. At this time the army was under the command of Moses, and later of Joshua; but each tribal division had its own leader as well.

The period of the judges that followed was characterized by lack of unity and purpose. This was true militarily as well as politically and religiously. At times of military crisis, God would raise up a military leader, called a JUDGE, who would then seek the aid of the tribes in order to gather an army. Judges 5 (particularly vv. 15–18) shows that Deborah, one of these judges, met with reluctance or indifference from some of the tribes.

The development of a regular standing army in Israel came only after a strong, centralized political system had developed. This came with kings Saul, David, and Solomon. Although Saul began his reign as a type of gifted leader, as were the earlier judges, he soon began to form a permanent army (1 Sam. 13:2; 24:2; 26:2). Nevertheless, the army had

to be supported by food and other supplies from the homes of individual soldiers (1 Sam. 17:17–19).

What Saul began, David continued. He increased the army, brought in hired troops from other regions who were loyal to him alone (2 Sam. 15:19–22), and turned over the direct leadership of his armies to a commander in chief (Joab). Under David Israel also became more aggressive in its offensive military policies, absorbing neighboring states like Ammon (2 Sam. 11:1; 1 Chr. 20:1–3). David established a system of rotating troops with 12 groups of 24,000 men serving one month of the year (1 Chronicles 27). Although Solomon's reign was peaceful, he further expanded the army, adding chariots and horsemen (1 Kin. 10:26).

The standing army came into existence with these three kings. It continued (though divided along with the kingdom after the death of Solomon) until 586 B.C., when Israel ceased to exist as a political entity.

The most important army to the faithful Israelite was not a human army; it was God's holy army. The human army could not succeed unless the Lord of hosts led his troops into battle. Thus Joshua conferred with the "commander of the army of the Lord" before the battle of Jericho (Josh. 5:13). David awaited the movement of God's army in the balsam trees before attacking the Philistines (2 Sam. 5:24). The prophet Elisha prayed that God would open the eyes of Gehazi so he might be comforted by seeing the power of God's army (2 Kin. 6:8–23).

ARNAN [AR nan] (*strong, quick*) — a descendant of David through Zerubbabel and founder of a tribal family (1 Chr. 3:21).

King Sennacherib of Assyria under escort of his royal guard, in a carving from Sennacherib's palace in Nineveh.

Photo by Howard Vos

A fine example of mosaic art, this map shows Palestine in the sixth century A.D. Note the city of Jericho in the lower part of the mosaic.

ARNON [AR none] (*roaring stream*) — a swift river that runs through the mountains of TRANSJORDAN and empties into the Dead Sea (see Map 2, C–1). It served as the boundary between Moab and the Amorites (Num. 21:13), the tribes of Israel (Num. 21:24; Deut. 2:24, 36) and the tribe of Reuben (Josh. 13:16). Now known as the Wadi el-Mojib, it flows through the rugged sandstone ravine that rises more than 503 meters (1,650 feet) above the river.

AROD [AY rod] (*hunchbacked*) — a son of Gad (Num. 26:17) and founder of the Arodites (Num. 26:17). He is also called Arodi (Gen. 46:16).

ARODI [AR oh dih] — a form of AROD.

AROER [ah ROW er] (*ruins*) — the name of three towns in the Old Testament:

1. A town on the northern bank of the Arnon River (see Map 3, C–5) taken from Sihon, king of the Amorites, and assigned to the tribes of Reuben and Gad (Deut. 2:36; 3:12). Because Aroer was the southernmost town of the northern kingdom of Israel and on the east side of the Jordan River, it was known as "the Beersheba of the East."

2. A town of Gilead situated east of Rabbah. Following Israel's conquest of the Promised Land, it was restored and enlarged by the descendants of Gad (Num. 32:34). Its exact location is not known.

3. A town in southern Judah about 19 kilometers (12 miles) southeast of Beersheba (1 Sam. 30:28).

AROERITE [ah ROW er ite] — a native or inhabitant of Aroer. Hotham is referred to as "the Aroerite" (1 Chr. 11:44).

ARPAD [AR pad] (*resting place*) — a fortified city in northern Syria, identified as modern Tell Erfad, situated about 40 kilometers (25 miles) north of Aleppo. Arpad was captured in 740 B.C., following a three-year siege by Tiglath-Pileser III of Assyria (Is. 36:19; Arphad, KJV).

ARPHAD [AR fad] — a form of ARPAD.

ARPHAXAD [ar FAK sad] (*one who heals*) — a son of Shem (Gen. 10:22) and the father of Salah. Arphaxad was the first patriarch born after the Flood, and he lived for 438 years. He was an ancestor of Jesus (Luke 3:36).

ARROWS (see ARMS, ARMOR OF THE BIBLE).

ART — the conscious use of skill and creative imagination, especially in the creation of beautiful objects. Bible students find it difficult to gain a clear picture of the art of the Hebrew people. Except for the descriptions of the tabernacle and the Temple in the Bible, art is really not discussed at all in the Scriptures. Most of what is known on this subject has been gathered from the work of archaeologists.

Even archaeology has uncovered very few samples of the artistic skills of the Israelites. By the time a site is excavated, most writings, paintings, and drawings—even works of art that might have been plastered on walls—have long since disappeared.

Another factor that makes this subject a difficult study is the commandment from the Old Testament Law that directed the Hebrew people not to make any graven image (Ex. 20:4). This commandment caused the Israelites to shun certain forms of art, such as painting and sculpture. They expressed their artistic talents and skills through such pursuits as architecture, pottery, metal-working, and bone and ivory carving.

Architecture. The most significant building project for Israel was the Temple. Solomon spent seven years and huge sums of money in building God's house in Jerusalem. God felt it important that a lengthy description of both the Temple and its predecessor, the tabernacle, be included in the Bible (Exodus 35—38).

Unfortunately, these descriptions, while giving the dimensions and a number of details, do not reveal very much about the artistic abilities of the Israelites. Native craftsmen did fashion the furnishings used in the tabernacle. But King Solomon hired thousands of craftsmen to assist in building the Temple. He sent to Phoenicia and summoned Hiram of Tyre, a master craftsman who cast the bronze objects and fashioned the latticework that served as furnishings for the Temple (1 Kin. 7:13-45). Also see ARCHITECTURE.

Pottery. Pottery was a common art form in Palestine. Because pottery does not decay like wood, it has become a major focus of archaeologists in the Near East. It is used to establish the age of a site and to trace cultural influences. Much of the pottery used by the Israelites was drab and unimaginative, indicating it was viewed in practical instead of artistic terms.

The most common forms of Israelite pottery were open bowls, cooking pots of various sizes,

Artistic craftsmanship from the ancient world is evident in this golden bull's head on a lyre, discovered at ancient Ur.

Photo by Gustav Jeeninga

Photo by Howard Vos

A colorful dolphin fresco from the queen's chamber of the Minoan palace at Knossos, Crete, 15th century B.C.

jugs for holding liquids, and chalices or goblets for drinking vessels. Some types of pottery were burnished so they had a glossy finish, usually red in color. Some were painted with geometric patterns, while others had pictures of human-headed lions, palm trees, bulls, or fish.

The pottery of New Testament times showed a sharp improvement in quality. The vessels were made of finer clays and gave evidence of better firing techniques.

Metal-working. Although the Israelites were experts in the working of metal, few examples of their craftsmanship have survived to the present day. Since metal can be easily melted down and recast, this was the probable fate of most metal works of art.

Probably the biggest metal-working project the Israelites undertook was the casting of the BRONZE SEA for the Temple in Jerusalem after it was constructed by Solomon (1 Kin. 7:23-26; 2 Chr. 4:2-5). This massive bowl, about 4.5 meters (14 feet) in diameter, rested on the backs of 12 oxen, also cast from bronze. The pillars of JACHIN and BOAZ, which flanked the entrance to the Temple, were also cast from this metal (1 Kin. 7:21; 2 Chr. 3:17). Gold and silver were used for smaller objects and as decorative trim on other objects in the Temple. Gold leaf was used to cover the doors of the Temple and the cherubim (1 Kin. 6:23-35).

Since iron was a difficult metal to work with, the Israelites usually used it for objects that required great strength, such as plow points and ax heads. They apparently learned the art of iron-working from the Philistines.

Bone and Ivory Carving. The carving of bone and ivory was an art practiced in Palestine as early as about 4000 B.C. The ivory came from Syria to the north, where elephants were common. The Canaanites and Phoenicians were masters of this craft.

Photo by Howard Vos

The tomb of Artaxerxes, cut into the cliffs above the ruins of Persepolis, Persia's ancient capital.

A number of ivory pieces were discovered by archaeologists at Samaria, the capital of Israel, from the time of Ahab.

Ivory was sometimes carved into small objects, such as an ointment jar with a hand-shaped stopper found at the ancient city of Lachish. More common was the use of ivory inlays in furniture and wall panels. The prophet Amos condemned the excessive wealth and materialism of Israel. One of the examples he pointed to were the beds and houses of ivory (Amos 3:15; 6:4). He was probably referring to the use of such ivory inlays among the wealthy citizens of Samaria, Israel's capital city.

ARTAXERXES [ar tuh ZERK sees] (*possessor of an exalted kingdom*) — a king of Persia in whose court Ezra and Nehemiah were officials (Ezra 7:1, 7). Known as Artaxerxes I Longimanus (long-handed), he temporarily halted the rebuilding program at Jerusalem that Cyrus, his predecessor, had encouraged (Ezra 4:7-23), but later allowed it to continue (Ezra 6:14). In the seventh year of his reign (about 458 B.C.), he authorized the mission of Ezra to lead a large number of Israelites back from the Captivity to Jerusalem (Ezra 7:1-28).

In the 20th year of the reign of Artaxerxes (about 445 B.C.), he allowed Nehemiah to return to Jerusalem and to begin rebuilding the walls of that city (Neh. 2:1-10; 13:6). The Septuagint consistently has Artaxerxes instead of Ahasuerus (KJV) throughout the Book of Esther. Most scholars today believe the reference in Esther is to Xerxes I, the father of Artaxerxes I Longimanus.

ARTEMAS, ARTEMIS [AR teh mas, AR teh mis] (see Gods, Pagan).

ARTIFICER, ARTISAN (see Occupations and Trades).

ARUBBOTH [ah RUB ohth] (*lattices*) — one of the many districts from which Solomon secured food for his large household (1 Kin. 4:10; Aruboth, NEB). Arubboth probably is to be identified with Arrabeh, situated between Megiddo and Samaria.

ARUMAH [a ROO mah] (*lofty*) — a town to which Abimelech was driven when he was expelled from Shechem (Judg. 9:41). Its exact location is unknown.

ARVAD [AR vad] (*refuge*) — a Phoenician city on a small island 3 kilometers (2 miles) off the Syrian coast and about 200 kilometers (125 miles) north of Tyre (Ezek. 27:8, 11). Arvad was renowned for its magnificent buildings. Its people, called Arvadites, were known for their artistic abilities and their success as warriors and sailors. The modern city of Ruwad is located on this island.

ARVADITES [AR va dites] — a Canaanite tribe named after the city of Arvad (Gen. 10:18).

ARZA [AR zah] (*delight*) — the steward of the house of Elah, king of Israel, in the city of Tirzah (1 Kin. 16:9).

ASA [AY sah] (*healer*) — the name of two men in the Old Testament:

1. The third king of Judah (911–870 B.C.) and the son of Abijam, king of Judah. Asa was the grandson of King Rehoboam and Maachah (1 Kin. 15:8–24). The first ten years of Asa's reign were peaceful and prosperous. He led many religious reforms, "banished the perverted persons from the land" (1

Kin. 15:12), and broke down pagan images and idols.

When he received further direction and encouragement from the prophet Azariah, Asa became more zealous in his call for revival. He restored the altar and called upon the tribes of Judah and Benjamin to renew their COVENANT with God at Jerusalem. When Israelites from the tribes of Ephraim, Manasseh, and Simeon saw how God had blessed Asa, they joined him in renewing their loyalty to the covenant.

Asa had two major confrontations with foreign nations. When the Ethiopian king Zerah attacked Asa with superior forces, Asa put his trust in God and dealt the Ethiopians a humiliating blow (1 Chr. 14:11–12). But his second confrontation did not yield such glorious results. When Baasha, king of Israel, fortified Ramah in an attempt to blockade Asa and prevent anyone from traveling to or from Jerusalem, Asa hired Ben-Hadad, king of Syria, to thwart Baasha's plans (2 Chr. 16:1–6). Ben-Hadad invaded northern Israel and forced Baasha to withdraw from Ramah. When the prophet ("seer") Hanani rebuked him for relying on Ben-Hadad instead of the Lord, Asa was enraged and put Hanani into prison (2 Chr. 16:7–10).

When Asa contracted a disease in his feet in the 39th year of his reign, he did not seek the Lord, but he consulted physicians instead (2 Chr. 16:12). Shortly thereafter, he died and was buried in Jerusalem.

2. A son of Elkanah and a Levite who lived in one of the villages of the Netophathites (1 Chr. 9:16).

ASAHEL [AS ah hell] (*God is doer*) — the name of four men in the Old Testament:

1. A son of Zeruiah, David's half-sister, and the brother of Joab and Abishai. Asahel was "as fleet of foot as a wild gazelle" (2 Sam. 2:18), but his ability to run swiftly was his downfall. When Asahel pursued Abner in battle, Abner killed him with his spear (2 Sam. 2:23).

2. One of the Levites sent by King Jehoshaphat to teach the Law to the people (2 Chr. 17:8).

3. A Levite appointed by King Hezekiah as an overseer of the Temple offerings (2 Chr. 31:13).

4. The father of Jonathan. Jonathan helped Ezra deal with those who had married pagan women during the Captivity (Ezra 10:15).

ASAHIAH [as ah HIGH ah] — a form of ASAIAH.

ASAIAH [as EYE ah] (*Jehovah has made*) — the name of four men in the Old Testament:

1. An officer of King Josiah. Asaiah inquired of HULDAH the prophetess about the Book of the Law discovered in the Temple (2 Kin. 22:12, 14; Asahiah, KJV, RSV).

2. A descendant of Simeon (1 Chr. 4:36).

3. A descendant of Merari. Asaiah helped move the ARK OF THE COVENANT from the house of Obed-Edom to Jerusalem (1 Chr. 15:6, 11–12).

4. A Shilonite who lived in Jerusalem after the

Captivity (1 Chr. 9:5). He was also called Maaseiah (Neh. 11:5).

ASAPH [AY saf] (*Jehovah has gathered*) — the name of several Old Testament men:

1. The father of Joah (2 Kin. 18:18, 37).

2. A Levite and the son of Berachiah the Gershonite (2 Chr. 20:14). Asaph sounded cymbals before the ARK OF THE COVENANT when it was moved from the house of Obed-Edom to Jerusalem (1 Chr. 15:16–19). Asaph's family became one of the three families given responsibility for music and song in the Temple (1 Chr. 25:1–9). Following the Captivity, 128 singers from this family returned from Babylon and conducted the singing when the foundations of Zerubbabel's temple were laid (Ezra 2:41; 3:10). Twelve psalms (Psalms 50; 73–83) are attributed to the family of Asaph.

3. A Levite whose descendants lived in Jerusalem after the Captivity (1 Chr. 9:15). This Asaph may be the name of a guild of musicians among the descendants of Asaph No. 2.

4. A Levite descendant of Kohath (1 Chr. 26:1).

5. The keeper of the king's forest under the Persian king ARTAXERXES I Longimanus (Neh. 2:8).

ASAREEL [ah SAY reh el] — a form of ASAREL.

ASAREL [AS ah rel] (*God is joined*) — a son of Jehaleleel in the genealogy of Judah (1 Chr. 4:16, Asareel, NEB, KJV).

ASARELAH [as ah RAY lah] — a form of ASHARELAH.

ASCENSION OF CHRIST — the dramatic departure of the risen Christ from His earthly, bodily ministry among His followers. Since His birth in Bethlehem by the miracle of the INCARNATION, Christ had lived physically on earth. But 40 days after the resurrection, His earthly ministry ceased with His ascension into heaven (Mark 16:19; Luke 24:50–51; Acts 1:9–11). To a large extent the ascension was for the benefit of Jesus' followers. They could no longer expect His physical presence. They must now wait for the promised Holy Spirit through whom the work of Jesus would continue.

Jesus' departure into heaven was a bodily ascension in His resurrection body. Stephen and Paul both reported seeing Jesus in bodily form after His ascension (Acts 7:56; 9:27; 1 Cor. 15:8).

The ascension marked the beginning of Christ's intercession for His followers at the right hand of God. There He makes continual intercession for all believers (Rom. 8:34; Heb. 4:14; 6:20; 7:25). Although Christ is not physically present with His people today, He is no less concerned for them or less active on their behalf. Christians enjoy peace, hope, and security because Christ is their advocate with the Father (1 John 2:1).

The ascension set in motion the coming of the Holy Spirit with His gifts for believers (John 14:16–18, 26; 16:7–15; Acts 2:23; Eph. 4:11–12). God determined that the presence of Jesus would be replaced by the presence of the Holy Spirit, who could be everywhere at the same time. Jesus' followers now enjoy the presence of the Spirit and the operation of the Spirit's gifts through them.

One additional result of the ascension is that Jesus began His heavenly reign at the right hand of the Father (1 Cor. 15:20–28). This reign will last until His SECOND COMING, when He will return to the earth as the reigning Messiah (Acts 3:20–21).

Finally, the ascension of Christ is the pledge of His second coming: "This same Jesus, who was taken up from you into heaven, will so come in like manner as you saw Him go into heaven" (Acts 1:11). Jesus will return to earth in bodily form just as He ascended into heaven.

Also see RESURRECTION; SECOND COMING.

ASCENSION OF ISAIAH (see APOCALYPTIC LITERATURE).

ASCENT OF AKRABBIM [ACK rah bim] (see AKRABBIM, ASCENT OF).

ASCENTS, SONG OF — a phrase that occurs in the titles of 15 psalms (Psalms 120—134). "Ascents" translates the Hebrew word *ma'aloth*, which means "goings up." These songs may have been "Pilgrim Psalms" sung by those who were "going up" to Jerusalem and "ascending" to the Temple (1 Sam. 1:3; Is. 30:29).

ASENATH [AS ih nath] (meaning unknown) — the Egyptian wife of Joseph and the mother of Manasseh and Ephraim (Gen. 41:45, 50–52; 46:20). Asenath was the daughter of Poti–Pherah, priest of On. Pharaoh himself may have arranged the marriage between Joseph and Asenath to help Joseph adjust to life in Egypt.

ASER [AY zer] — Greek form of ASHER.

ASH (see PLANTS OF THE BIBLE).

ASHAN [AY shan] (*smoke*) — a city of the Levites in the SHEPHELAH, or low country, of Judah (Josh. 15:42). Ashan was first allotted to the tribe of Judah, but later it was assigned to the tribe of Simeon (Josh. 19:7). It is also called Ain (Josh. 21:16) and is probably the same city as Chorashan (1 Sam. 30:30). The site is identified with Khirbet Asan, situated about eight kilometers (five miles) northwest of Beersheba.

ASHARELAH [ash ah RAY la] (*God has fulfilled with joy*) — a son of Asaph appointed by King David to be in charge of the Temple music (1 Chr. 25:2, 14; Jesharelah, Asarelah, KJV; Jesarelah, NIV).

ASHBEA [ASH bih ah] (meaning unknown) — the name given to a family of "linen workers" of the house of Ashbea (1 Chr. 4:21). It probably refers to the place where they lived.

ASHBEL [ASH bell] (*man of Baal*) — a son of Benjamin (1 Chr. 8:1) and the ancestor of a tribal family known as the ASHBELITES (Num. 26:38). Apparently Ashbel was also called Jediael (1 Chr. 7:6).

ASHBELITES [ASH bell ites] — descendants of ASHBEL.

ASHCHENAZ [ASH keh nazz] — a form of ASHKENAZ.

ASHDOD [ASH dahd] (*fortress*) — one of the five principal Philistine cities (1 Sam. 6:17), situated 5 kilometers (3 miles) from the Mediterranean coast and 32 kilometers (20 miles) north of Gaza (see Map 3, A–4). The city's military and economic significance was enhanced by its location on the main highway between Egypt and Syria.

Joshua and the Israelites drove the Canaanites out of the hill country of Judah, but the ANAKIM—a group of Canaanites—remained in Ashdod, Gaza, and Gath (Josh. 11:22). During the time of Eli and Samuel, the ARK OF THE COVENANT accompanied Israel's army (1 Sam. 4:3). When the Philistines defeated Israel, they took the ark to the temple of DAGON in Ashdod (1 Sam. 5:1–7).

Uzziah, the powerful king of Judah, captured Ashdod (2 Chr. 26:6). The prophet Amos predicted the destruction of the city because of its inhumane treatment of Israelites (Amos 1:8; 3:9). When Sargon, king of Assyria, destroyed Ashdod in 711 B.C., he fulfilled this prophecy (Is. 20:1).

In New Testament times, Ashdod was renamed AZOTUS. Philip the evangelist preached in all the cities from Azotus to Caesarea (Acts 8:40).

ASHDODITES [ASH dodd ites] — natives or inhabitants of ASHDOD (Josh. 13:3; Ashdothites, KJV; Neh. 4:7).

ASHDOTH–PISGAH [ASH dahth PIZ gah] (*springs of Pisgah*) — the slopes of a mountain at PISGAH, near the northeastern shore of the Dead Sea (Josh. 12:3; 13:20).

ASHER [ASH err] (*happy*) — the name of a man and a city in the Bible:

1. The eighth son of Jacob, the second by Leah's maidservant, Zilpah (Gen. 30:13). On his deathbed Jacob blessed Asher: "Bread from Asher shall be rich, and he shall yield royal dainties" (Gen. 49:20).

2. A city situated east of Shechem on the road to Beth Shean, in the half-tribe of Manasseh west of the Jordan River (Josh. 17:7).

ASHER, TRIBE OF — a tribe descended from Asher and that part of Canaan where the tribe of Asher lived (Josh. 19:24, 31–34). The territory of Asher extended to the northern boundary of Palestine; its southern border was the tribe of Manasseh and the mountains of Mount Carmel. Asher was bounded on the west by the Mediterranean Sea and on the east by the tribe of Naphtali. The Asherites never succeeded in expelling the inhabitants of the Phoenician strongholds—such as Tyre, Sidon, and Acco (Judg. 1:31–32)—which were in their territory.

ASHERAH, ASHERIM, ASHEROTH [ash EH rah, ash EH rim, ash EH rahth] (see GODS, PAGAN).

ASHERITES [ASH err ites] — descendants of ASHER and members of his tribe (Judg. 1:32).

ASHES — the powdery residue of burned material; the ashes that remained after the sacrifice of animals as burnt offerings were carried away and disposed of by a priest.

The word ashes is also used figuratively in the Bible. Ashes were a sign of mourning, as when Mordecai tore his clothes, put on sackcloth and ashes, and cried out with a loud and bitter cry (Esth. 4:1). In the Book of Job, ashes are symbolic of dejection (2:8) as well as repentance (42:6).

The prophet Isaiah spoke of the idolater as a person who "feeds on ashes" (Is. 44:20)—a figure of vanity and deceit. He also uses the word positively of the Messiah, who would give "beauty for ashes" (Is. 61:3)—a symbol of the change God brought through Jesus.

ASHHUR [ASH shure] (meaning unknown) — a son of Hezron and Abiah and the father of TEKOA (1 Chr. 2:24; 4:5; Ashur, KJV). Ashhur probably was the "father" of Tekoa, a city in Judah situated between Bethlehem and Hebron, in the sense of being its settler or founder.

ASHIMA, ASHIMAH [a SHIH mah] (see GODS, PAGAN).

ASHKALONITE [ASH kuh lon ite] — a form of ASHKELONITE.

ASHKELON [ASH kuh lon] (*migration*) — one of the five principal cities of the Philistines (Josh. 13:3). Situated on the seacoast (see Map 3, A–4) 19 kilometers (12 miles) north of Gaza, Ashkelon and her sister cities (Ashdod, Gath, Gaza, and Ekron) posed a serious threat to the Israelites during the period of the JUDGES. Shortly after Joshua's death, Ashkelon was captured and was briefly controlled by the tribe of Judah (Judg. 1:18). A few years later Samson killed 30 men from this city (Judg. 14:19). During most of the Old Testament era, however, Ashkelon remained politically and militarily independent of Israel.

In the eighth century B.C. Ashkelon was denounced by the prophet Amos (Amos 1:8). Shortly before the Babylonian Captivity, Zephaniah prophesied that the Jews would return from Babylon and occupy the ruins of Ashkelon (Zeph. 2:4, 7). Zechariah also prophesied the destruction of Ashkelon (Zech. 9:5). Ashkelon is not mentioned in the New Testament.

ASHKELONITES [ASH kuh lon ites] — natives or inhabitants of ASHKELON (Josh. 13:3; Ashkalonites, KJV).

ASHKENAZ [ASH keh nazz] (*a fire that spreads*) — the oldest son of Gomer and a grandson of Japheth. Ashkenaz also became the name of a people that settled in the vicinity of Armenia. It is also spelled Ashchenaz (1 Chr. 1:6, KJV; Jer. 51:27, KJV, NKJV).

ASHNAH [ASH nah] (*firm*) — the name of two cities in the Book of Joshua:

1. A village in the SHEPHELAH, or lowland plain, of Judah (Josh. 15:33).

2. A village situated farther south in the Shephelah (Josh. 15:43).

The exact location of these cities has not been established.

ASHPENAZ [ASH peh nazz] (meaning unknown) — the master of the eunuchs at Babylon during the reign of King Nebuchadnezzar. The king entrusted the people of Israel who had been taken captive to his care (Dan. 1:3).

ASHRIEL [ASH rih ell] — a form of ASRIEL.

ASHTAROTH [ASH tah rahth] (*wives*) — the plural form of Ashtoreth, a pagan goddess. First Samuel 31:10 connects her with the Philistines, and 1 Kings 11:5 connects her with the Sidonians. She was often considered the companion or partner of the male god BAAL (Judg. 2:13).

Apparently the worship of these goddesses was practiced by the Israelites from time to time. Solomon compromised his faith by worshiping at the altar of Ashtaroth (1 Kin. 11:5, 33). Along with the Baalim (the plural of Baal), the Ashtaroth were thought by the Philistines to be responsible for fertility and the growth of crops and herds.

The Ashtaroth were worshiped by other peoples under such names as Astarte (Phoenicians and Canaanites), Inanna (Sumerians), Ishtar (Babylonians), Aphrodite (Greeks), and Venus (Romans). All these were goddesses of sensual love and fertility. Also see GODS, PAGAN; IDOLATRY.

ASHTAROTH, CITY OF [ASH tah rahth] (meaning unknown) — a city in the northern TRANSJORDAN area of Israel which served as one of the CITIES OF REFUGE. In Joshua's time, Ashtaroth was the home of OG, king of Bashan (Josh. 9:10).

ASHTERATHITE [ASH teh rah thite] — a native or inhabitant of ASHTAROTH, an ancient city of BASHAN situated northeast of the Sea of Galilee. Uzzia, one of David's mighty men, was an Ashterathite (1 Chr. 11:44).

ASHTEROTH KARNAIM [ASH tah rahth kar NAY em] (*Ashtaroth of the two horns*) — a city in which the REPHAIM lived during the invasion of Chedorlaomer (Gen. 14:5). It probably was located in Bashan, east of the Jordan River. It may also have been the same place as Astaroth (Deut. 1:4) or Ashtaroth (Josh. 9:10).

ASHTORETH [ASH toh rehth] — a form of ASHTAROTH.

ASHUR [ASH shure] — a form of ASHHUR.

ASHURBANIPAL [a SHOOR ban ih pal] (*Ashur is creating an heir*) — the last of the great kings of Assyria, from about 668 to about 626 B.C. He was the son and successor of the Assyrian king Esarhaddon. Most scholars now identify him with the

Photo by Gustav Jeeninga

Photo by Gustav Jeeninga

King Ashurbanipal of Assyria is anointed by divine creatures, in this carving from his era.

"great and noble" OSNAPPER of Ezra 4:10. Apparently, Ashurbanipal was the monarch who made King Manasseh of Judah, along with 21 other kings, pay tribute to him and kiss his feet.

A large part of Ashurbanipal's reign was spent in a tug-of-war with his own brother, Shamash-shum-ukin, who was viceroy of Babylon. Outright rebellion against Ashurbanipal broke out in 652 B.C. and ended in 648 B.C. following a two-year siege of Babylon by the Assyrians that resulted in famine.

The mighty Assyrian Empire disintegrated under Ashurbanipal's son, Sinsharishkun (627 [?]–612 B.C.). Upon his death Babylon fell immediately to Nabopolassar, founder of a new Babylonian Empire; and the Medes and Babylonians destroyed NINEVEH, the capital city of Assyria.

ASHURITES [ASH err ites] — one of the peoples over whom Saul's son Ishbosheth was made king (2 Sam. 2:9). They lived in northern Israel and may be the same as the Asherites (Judg. 1:32) or the Asshurim (Gen. 25:3).

ASHURNASIRPAL [ash or NAS ir pal] (meaning unknown) — a king of Assyria who reigned early in the ninth century B.C., when Assyria was at the height of its power (about 884–860 B.C.). King Jehoshaphat of Judah (873–848 B.C.) and King Ahab of Israel (874–853 B.C.) were his contemporaries.

ASHVATH [ASH vath] (*wrought*) — a son of Japhlet, of the tribe of Asher (1 Chr. 7:33).

ASIA [AY zyuh] (*eastern*) — a Roman province in western ASIA MINOR which included Mysia, Lydia, Caria, and the coastal islands as well as western Phrygia. The borders of this province were, for the most part, those of the earlier kingdom of Pergamos.

The kingdom of Pergamos gained its independence from the SELEUCIDS with help from the Romans. By the time of AUGUSTUS, the first Roman emperor (27 B.C.—A.D. 14), Asia had become a senatorial province (a Roman political division governed by a proconsul), with Pergamos as its capital.

Three cities continued to compete for the role of principal city: Ephesus, Smyrna, and Pergamos—the first three cities mentioned in the Book of Revelation (see Rev. 1:11; 2:1–17). Eventually, Ephesus became the chief commercial center and was known as the most prominent city of the province. The Roman Senate granted both Ephesus and Pergamos the right to have three imperial temples for the worship of the emperors.

Although scholars disagree on the time when Ephesus became the capital, it probably occurred after the death of the apostle Paul and perhaps as late as the time of the emperor Hadrian (about A.D. 129). The fact that the martyr Antipas is mentioned in connection with Pergamos (Rev. 2:13) argues for the capital's being at Pergamos during the time the Book of Revelation was written.

The governor of a senatorial province was called a PROCONSUL, and the proconsulship of Asia became one of the most prized among all in the Roman Empire. The wealth and culture of Asia was legendary. When the New Testament mentions the officers of Ephesus, the term used is Asiarchs (local elected authorities), or "officials of Asia" (Acts 19:31).

The seven cities mentioned in the Book of Revelation follow two principal north–south roads of

Asia, beginning with Ephesus, the largest city, and ending inland with Laodicea. John must have known these cities of Asia fairly well, because each of the letters (Revelation 2—3) alludes to some important fact about that city.

At the beginning of his second missionary journey, the apostle Paul was "forbidden by the Holy Spirit to preach the word in Asia" (Acts 16:6). Thus, he made his way to Troas, the northwestern seaport of Asia, and entered Europe (Acts 16:6–10). On his return trip, however, he visited Ephesus (Acts 18:9). On his third missionary journey, he spent more than two years in ministry in this region. During this time, "all who dwelt in Asia heard the word of the Lord Jesus, both Jews and Greeks" (Acts 19:10).

ASIA MINOR — a peninsula, also called Anatolia, situated in the extreme western part of the continent of Asia. Asia Minor was bounded on the north by the Black Sea, the Sea of Marmara, and the Dardanelles; the Aegean Sea on the west; and Syria and the Mediterranean Sea on the south.

Roughly identical with the modern nation of Turkey, Asia Minor was a high plateau crossed by mountains, especially the Taurus Mountains near the southern coast. In the New Testament, the term Asia is ambiguous, sometimes referring to the peninsula of Asia Minor as a whole (Acts 19:26–27), but more often referring to proconsular Asia, situated in the western part of the peninsula (Acts 2:9; 6:9). The writer of Acts appears to use the term Asia to describe the region of the province of Asia around Ephesus. He refers to other regions of the province as Phrygia and Mysia (Acts 2:9–10; 16:6–7). Also see SEVEN CHURCHES OF ASIA.

ASIARCHS [AY zih arks] (*rulers of Asia*) — city officials in the Roman province of Asia; (Acts 19:31; officials of Asia NKJV; officials of the prov-

ince, NIV; dignitaries of the province, NEB) who befriended the apostle Paul at Ephesus.

ASIEL [AY zih el] (*God is maker*) — a descendant of Simeon and an ancestor of Jehu (1 Chr. 4:35).

ASNAH [AS nah] (*thornbush*) — one of the NETHINIM (Temple servants) whose descendants returned to Jerusalem after the Captivity in Babylon (Ezra 2:50).

ASNAPPER [as NAP per] — a form of OSNAPPER, the biblical name for ASHURBANIPAL.

ASP (see ANIMALS OF THE BIBLE).

ASPATHA [as PAY thah] (meaning unknown) — a son of Haman who was hanged like his father (Esth. 9:7).

ASPEN (see PLANTS OF THE BIBLE).

ASPHALT (see MINERALS OF THE BIBLE).

ASPHODEL (see PLANTS OF THE BIBLE).

ASRIEL [AS rih ell] (*God has filled with joy*) — a man of the tribe of Manasseh, of the house of Gilead, who was listed in the second census in the wilderness (Josh. 17:2; Ashriel, 1 Chr. 7:14, KJV).

ASRIELITES [AS rih ell ites] — the family name of the descendants of ASRIEL (Num. 26:31).

ASS (see ANIMALS OF THE BIBLE).

ASSASSINS — a fanatical group of Jewish nationalists in the first century A.D. Four thousand of them followed an Egyptian who promised to lead them in a rebellion against the Romans (Acts 21:38). The Roman commander at Jerusalem wondered if the apostle Paul were a member of this group (Acts 21:38).

ASSEMBLY (see CONGREGATION).

The Taurus Mountains north of Tarsus in Cilicia, in the Roman province of Asia.
Photo by Howard Vos

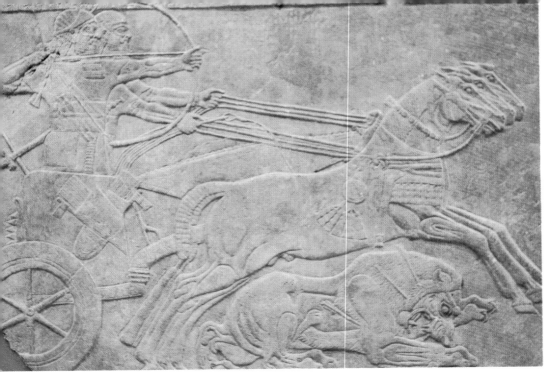

King Ashurnasirpal of Assyria pursues the royal sport of lion hunting, in this carving from his palace at Nimrud.

ASSHUR [AS shoor] (*level plain*) — the name of a people, a man, and a foreign god:

1. A word denoting ASSYRIA, a city of Assyria, or the Assyrians as a people (Gen. 10:11; Num. 24:22, 24; Ezra 4:2; Assur, KJV).

2. A son of Shem (1 Chr. 1:17). He is regarded as the ancestor of the Assyrians.

3. The chief god of the Assyrians. Asshur was a god of war, conquest, and military strength.

Also see GODS, PAGAN.

ASSHURIM [a SHOO rim] (*mighty ones*) — a son of Dedan or an obscure tribe that traced its family tree to him (Gen. 25:3).

ASSIR [AS err] (*prisoner*) — the name of three Old Testament men:

1. A son of Korah (Ex. 6:24; 1 Chr. 6:22).

2. A son of Jehoiachin, king of Judah (1 Chr. 3:17).

3. A son of Ebiasaph (1 Chr. 6:23, 37).

ASSOS [AS ohs] (*approaching*) — a seaport of the Roman province of MYSIA in Asia Minor, not far from Troas (see Map 8, C–2). While on his third missionary journey, the apostle Paul walked overland from Troas to Assos while Luke and the others took the longer trip around the cape (Acts 20:13–14).

ASSUMPTION OF MOSES (see PSEUDEPI-GRAPHA).

ASSUR [AS err] — a form of ASSHUR.

ASSURANCE — the state of being assured; freedom from doubt and uncertainty. As a theological concept, assurance is one of the richest doctrines of the Bible. It refers to the believer's full confidence and conviction that the penalty of his sins has been paid and that heaven has been secured as his eternal destiny by Christ's death and resurrection.

Assurance means that the Christian not only possesses salvation, but that he also knows what he possesses—he is *assured* of this salvation. First John 5:12 speaks of security ("He who has the Son has life") and the following verse speaks of assurance ("you may know that you have eternal life").

The basis of assurance must never be our own subjective experience, which can waver with fear, doubt, and uncertainty. True assurance is founded on the Word of God alone—the Holy Spirit bearing witness to our spirits that the Word of God is true and reliable. When the believer, by faith, stands upon the Word of God (such passages as John 10:27–29 and Romans 8:35–39 speak clearly of the assurance of our faith), he gains a joyous freedom to live the Christian life. He has been forgiven by God in Christ and is now free to forgive others, to love as he has first been loved by God.

Assurance, then, is not just a "theological" concept but a practical matter. As long as a person is uncertain about his own standing before God, he is defensive and self-centered. But fully assured of God's salvation, the believer can begin to walk in the footsteps of Christ (1 John 4:17–19).

Assyrian warriors in battle with an enemy force aboard a papyrus boat, in this carving from Sennacherib's palace at Nineveh.

ASSYRIA [as SIHR ih ah] — a kingdom between the Tigris and Euphrates Rivers that dominated the ancient world from the ninth century to the seventh century B.C. (see Map 1, D–1). After defeating the northern kingdom of Israel in 722 B.C., the Assyrians carried away thousands of Israelites and resettled them in other parts of the Assyrian Empire. This was a blow from which the nation of Israel never recovered.

The early inhabitants of Assyria were ancient tribesmen (Gen. 10:22) who probably migrated from Babylonia. They grew powerful enough around 1300 B.C. to conquer Babylonia. For the next 700 years they were the leading power in the ancient world, with their leading rival nation, Babylon, constantly challenging them for this position.

Tiglath–Pileser I (1120–1100 B.C.) built the Assyrian kingdom to the most extensive empire of the age. But under his successors, it declined in power and influence. This decline offered the united kingdom of Judah, under the leadership of David and Solomon, the opportunity to reach its greatest limits. If the Assyrians had been more powerful at that time, they probably would have interfered with the internal affairs of the Hebrew people, even at that early date.

After the Assyrians had languished in weakness for an extended period, Ashurnasirpal (884–860 B.C.) restored much of the prestige of the empire. His son, Shalmaneser III, succeeded him, and reigned from about 860 to 825 B.C. Shalmaneser

was the first Assyrian king to come into conflict with the northern kingdom of Israel.

In an effort to halt the Assyrian expansion, a group of surrounding nations formed a coalition, of which Israel was a part. Ahab was king of Israel during this time. But the coalition eventually split up, allowing the Assyrians to continue their relentless conquest of surrounding territories.

During the period from 833 to 745 B.C., Assyria was engaged in internal struggles as well as war with Syria. This allowed Israel to operate without threat from the Assyrian army. During this time, Jeroboam II, king of Israel, was able to raise the Northern Kingdom to the status of a major nation among the countries of the ancient Near East.

The rise of Tiglath–Pileser III (745–727 B.C.) marked the beginning of a renewed period of Assyrian oppression for the nation of Israel. Tiglath–Pileser, known also in the Bible as PUL (2 Kin. 15:19), set out to regain territories previously occupied by the Assyrians. He was resisted by a coalition led by Rezin of Damascus and Pekah of Israel. These rulers tried to force Ahaz, king of Judah, to join them. When Ahaz refused, Rezin and Pekah marched on Jerusalem, intent on destroying the city. Against the counsel of the prophet Isaiah, Ahaz enlisted the aid of Tiglath–Pileser for protection. This protection cost dearly. From that day forth, Israel was required to pay tribute to Assyria. Israel also was forced to adopt some of the religious practices of the Assyrians (2 Kings 16).

A gigantic winged bull, symbol of the Assyrian Empire.

Tiglath-Pileser was succeeded by his son, Shalmaneser V (727-722 B.C.). When Hoshea, king of Israel, who had been placed on the throne by Tiglath-Pileser, refused to pay the required tribute, Shalmaneser attacked Samaria, the capital of Israel. After a long siege, Israel fell to Assyria in 722 B.C., perhaps to Sargon II; and 27,000 inhabitants of Israel were deported to Assyrian territories. This event marked the end of the northern kingdom of Israel. Most of the deported Hebrews never returned to their homeland.

Israel's sister nation, the southern kingdom of Judah, also felt the power of the Assyrian Empire. In 701 B.C., Sennacherib, king of Assyria (705-681 B.C.), planned an attack on Jerusalem. However, the Assyrian army was struck by a plague, which the Bible referred to as "the angel of the Lord" (2 Kin. 19:35). Thousands of Assyrian soldiers died, and Sennacherib was forced to retreat from his invasion. Thus, Jerusalem was saved from Assyrian oppression by divine intervention.

The religion of the Assyrians, much like that of the Babylonians, emphasized worship of nature. They believed every object of nature was possessed by a spirit. The chief god was Asshur. All other primary gods whom they worshiped were related to the objects of nature. These included Anu, god of the heavens; Bel, god of the region inhabited by man, beasts, and birds; Ea, god of the waters; Sin, the moon-god; Shamash, the sun-god; and Ramman, god of the storms. These gods were followed by five gods of the planets. In addition to these primary gods, lesser gods also were worshiped. In some cases, various cities had their own patron gods. The pagan worship of the Assyrians was

soundly condemned by several prophets of the Old Testament (Is. 10:5; Ezek. 16:28; Hos. 8:9).

The favorite pursuits of the Assyrian kings were war and hunting. Archaeologists have discovered that the Assyrians were merciless and savage people. The Assyrian army was ruthless and effective. Its cruelty included burning cities, burning children, impaling victims on stakes, beheading, and chopping off hands. But, like Babylon, whom God used as an instrument of judgment against Judah, Assyria became God's channel of punishment and judgment against Israel because of their sin and idolatry.

Because of the cruelty and paganism of the Assyrians, the Hebrew people harbored deep-seated hostility against this nation. This attitude is revealed clearly in the Book of Jonah. When God instructed Jonah to preach to Nineveh, the capital of Assyria, Jonah refused and went in the opposite direction. After he finally went to Nineveh, the prophet was disappointed with God because He spared the city.

ASTARTE [as TAR teh] (see GODS, PAGAN).

ASTROLOGER (see ASTROLOGY; OCCUPATIONS AND TRADES).

ASTROLOGY — the study of the sun, moon, planets, and stars in the belief that they influence individuals and the course of human events. Astrology attempts to predict the future by analyzing the movements of these heavenly bodies.

Although the word astrology does not appear in the Bible, the word astrologers does. The prophet Isaiah taunted the Babylonians to go to the powerless "astrologers, the stargazers, and the monthly prognosticators" (Is. 47:13) for their salvation. The word is found eight times in the book of Daniel, in association with "magicians," "sorcerers," "Chaldeans," "wise men," and "soothsayers" (Dan. 1:20; 2:2, 10, 27; 4:7; 5:7, 11, 15). Some Bible scholars believe the "wise men" or Magi who saw the star of the infant Jesus (Matt. 2:1-12) were astrologers. We do know that the earliest records of astrology have come from Mesopotamia—the land between the Tigris and Euphrates rivers where the ancient Babylonians flourished.

The attempt to forecast the future from the stars probably arose very naturally in the ancient world. These beliefs would have come from observing that the signs in the heavens and events on earth are sometimes related. For instance, it is evident that the winter season begins at the same time when the sun begins to set low in the sky. It takes only one step of logic to conclude that when the sun begins to dip low in the sky, it causes winter to come. Given the lack of scientific thought in the ancient Near East, it required only one further step of logic to conclude that other movements of the sun, moon, or stars affect historical events. An example of this kind of reasoning is found in a letter addressed to the Assyrian king ESARHADDON. "If the planet Jupiter is present during an eclipse," the letter

Photo by Howard Vos

Egyptian signs of the zodiac, from the tomb of the Pharaoh Seti I at Thebes.

stated, "it is good for the king because an important person in court will die in his stead."

The close association in Babylonian thought between the stars and the gods led ancient sky-watchers to stress their impact on human affairs. This association may be seen clearly in the unique script used to write their language. The sign used to distinguish a god's name was the sign of the star.

The Bible classes astrology with other techniques for predicting the future. Going to the stars for guidance was the same as idolatry to biblical writers. Samuel equated the two in his denunciation of Saul (1 Sam. 15:23).

The Bible's contempt for astrology is most clearly seen in its prohibition of any technique to aid in predicting the future. Astrology assumes that God does not control history. It assumes that history is governed by the affairs of the pagan gods as revealed in the movement of the planets. The believer knows that a sovereign God rules this world. He also knows that resorting to astrology is a denial of the life of faith by which one trusts God and not his lucky stars for the future.

Also see ASTRONOMY; GODS, PAGAN; MAGIC, SORCERY, AND DIVINATION.

ASTRONOMY — the scientific study of the solar system and the systematic arrangement of information about the nature, size, and movements of the earth, moon, sun, and stars.

Origins. Modern astronomy began with the work of Nicolaus Copernicus (1473–1543), a Polish scientist whose discoveries revolutionized science's view of the universe. Prior to Copernicus, Ptolemy, a Greco–Egyptian astronomer of the second century A.D., had proposed that the Earth was stationary at the center of the universe, and that the

planets moved around it. Ptolemy compiled a series of more than 80 observations of the positions of planets and solar and lunar eclipses in a 13–volume work called the *Almagest.* The details that Ptolemy provided made it possible for modern historians to establish reliable dates for many events of ancient history.

Ptolemy's view of our solar system was accepted for over 1,000 years by both scientists and the church until it was overturned by Copernicus' famous proof that the Earth revolves around the sun. This event marked the beginning of astronomy as a modern science.

Early Astronomers. Although the model of the universe accepted by ancient peoples was inaccurate, their attempts to explain how the universe works can be traced back thousands of years. In ancient times, the positions of the planets in relation to one another was thought to have an impact on the course of history. This accounts for astronomy's origins in ASTROLOGY and similar mystical practices.

The earliest recorded observations of the heavens relate to the rising and setting of Venus. These date from around 1650 B.C., and they were probably conducted in an attempt to predict the future. But these observations were also useful in establishing an ancient calendar based on the movement of the sun and stars. Lacking technical devices and a system of mathematics, these ancient astronomers relied solely upon the naked eye for their observations. This meant that only about 2,000 stars were visible to them.

Importance in Bible Study. The value of astronomy for the study of Scripture lies in astronomy's ability to fix absolute dates for some biblical events.

ASUPPIM, HOUSE OF _____

Ancient chronologies of major world events were kept carefully. But they usually dated from the year a king was crowned or the year he died; in some cases they date from a great natural disaster. Since those fixed times are no longer precisely known, it is difficult to assign accurate dates for them, although they are well-documented.

The process by which scholars determine the date of biblical events using astronomical data from the past is very technical. It is probably sufficient to point out that by comparing Ptolemy's observations with certain biblical passages, scholars have determined that the last year of the reign of King Ahab of Israel was 853 B.C. The first year of Jehu, who took the throne by force from the family of Ahab, was 841 B.C. Based on these dates, the chronology of Scripture dates back to 931 B.C. as the year in which Jeroboam I led the northern tribes in a revolt from Rehoboam, Solomon's son.

Biblical References. The basic orientation of the Bible to astronomy is clearly illustrated in the book of Genesis, which explains why God created the heavenly bodies (Genesis 1—2). The Bible makes only scattered references to them, and none are scientific in the modern sense. Many of these passages refer to the regular movements of the sun and moon to indicate the passage of time. Ancient Israel had a lunar calendar that tied religious events to certain seasons of the year. The times for their annual FEASTS and FESTIVALS depended on the new moon, the full moon, and the position of the sun in both spring and autumn. The planets, by contrast, are referred to by the Bible as objects of idolatry (2 Kin. 23:5), probably because the ancient Babylonians were known to practice such forms of idolatry.

Astronomical references in the Bible are often poetic (Amos 5:8). Their purpose is to show God's glory, not to provide scientific details about the universe. The important truth for the Hebrews as they observed the stars was that "the heavens declare the glory of God; and the firmament shows His handiwork" (Ps. 19:1). Through the beauty of the heavens and the regular movement of the sun and stars, they could see God at work in His world.

The prophet Joel may have referred to total eclipses of the sun and moon (Joel 2:31). Falling stars are mentioned in both the Old and New Testaments (Is. 34:4; Rev. 6:13). Many scholars believe the star that marked the place where Jesus was born was an astronomical event, perhaps occurring when Saturn and Jupiter lined up along their orbits in the sky. Scientists have documented that such a phenomenon did occur at about the time of Jesus' birth in Bethlehem.

ASUPPIM, HOUSE OF [a SUP im] (*storehouses*)— buildings for storing Temple goods, located near the southern door of the Temple in the outer court (1 Chr. 26:15, 17, KJV). Asuppim is the transliteration of a Hebrew word which most modern versions translate as "STOREHOUSE" or "storehouses."

ASYLUM (see REFUGE, CITIES OF).

Photo by Gustav Jeeninga

The Porch of the Maidens, connected to the temple known as the Erechtheum in Athens.

ASYNCRITUS [a SIN cry tus] (*incomparable*) — a Christian in Rome to whom the apostle Paul sent greetings (Rom. 16:14).

ATAD [A tad] (*thornbush*) — either a person or a place referred to in Genesis 50:10–11. The 'threshing floor of Atad,' apparently situated east of the Jordan River, was used as a campsite by Joseph and his brothers as they prepared to take Jacob's body back to Canaan. The place was renamed Abel Mizraim, meaning "mourning of the Egyptians."

ATARAH [AT a rah] (*crown*) — the second wife of Jerahmeel and mother of Onam (1 Chr. 2:26–28).

ATAROTH [AT ah rahth] (*crowns, diadems*) — the name of three or four places and possibly one person in the Old Testament:

1. A town east of the Jordan River in the territory of Reuben. Ataroth was rebuilt and fortified by the tribe of Gad (Num. 32:3, 34). It has been identified as the modern Khirbet Attarus.

2. A place on the border between Ephraim and Benjamin (Josh. 16:2). It is probably the same place as Ataroth Addar (Josh. 16:5) and Ataroth Adar (Josh. 18:13).

3. A place in northeast Ephraim near Jericho (Josh. 16:7).

4. A person or a place connected with the descendants of Caleb (1 Chr. 2:54, KJV).

ATAROTH ADAR [AT ah rahth AY dar] — a place along the border of Ephraim and Benjamin (Josh. 18:3).

ATER [AY tehr] (*crippled*) — the ancestor of a family that returned from Babylon after the Captivity (Neh. 7:21).

ATHACH [AY thak] (*lodging*) — a village of Judah befriended by David (1 Sam. 30:30). Some scholars identify the city with Ether (Josh. 15:42; 19:7), but this is uncertain.

ATHAIAH [a THAY yah] (*Jehovah is helper*) — a son of Uzziah and a member of the tribe of Judah in Nehemiah's time (Neh. 11:4). He may be the same person as Uthai (1 Chr. 9:4).

ATHALIAH [ath ah LIE ah] (*Jehovah is strong*) — the name of one woman and two men in the Old Testament:

1. The queen of Judah for six years (2 Kin. 11:1–3). Athaliah was the daughter of King Ahab of Israel. Presumably, Jezebel was her mother.

Athaliah married Jehoram (or Joram), son of Jehoshaphat, king of Judah. Jehoram reigned only eight years and was succeeded by his son Ahaziah, who died after reigning only one year. Desiring the throne for herself, Athaliah ruthlessly killed all her grandsons—except the infant Joash, who was hidden by his aunt (2 Kin. 11:2).

Athaliah apparently inherited Jezebel's ruthlessness. She was a tyrant whose every whim had to be obeyed. As her mother had done in Israel, Athaliah introduced Baal worship in Judah and in so doing destroyed part of the Temple.

Joash was hidden in the house of the Lord for six years (2 Kin. 11:3), while Athaliah reigned over the land (841–835 B.C). In the seventh year, the high priest Jehoiada declared Joash the lawful king of Ju-

dah. Guards removed Athaliah from the Temple before killing her, to avoid defiling the Temple with her blood (2 Kin. 11:13–16; 2 Chr. 23:12–15).

Athaliah reaped what she sowed. She gained the throne through murder and lost her life in the same way. She also failed to thwart God's promise, because she did not destroy the Davidic line, through which the Messiah was to be born.

2. A son of Jeroham, a Benjamite (1 Chr. 8:26).
3. The father of Jeshaiah (Ezra 8:7).

ATHARIM [ATH ah rim] (*spies*) — a place mentioned in connection with the Exodus. Moses led the Israelites from Kadesh by way of Mount Hor on their way to Canaan by "the road to Atharim" (Num. 21:1). The king of Arad attacked the Israelites while they journeyed on that road. The location of Atharim is unknown.

ATHEIST — one who denies the existence of God. The only occurrence in the New Testament of the Greek word *atheoi*—"atheists" or "godless ones"—is in Ephesians 2:12, where those who are separated from Christ are described as "having no hope and without God." The early Christians were often called "atheists" because they refused to worship the pagan gods of their neighbors.

ATHENIANS [uh THEE knee uns] — natives or inhabitants of ATHENS (Acts 17:21).

ATHENS [ATH ins] — the capital city of the ancient Greek state of Attica and the modern capital of Greece (see Map 7, B–2). It was the center of Greek art, architecture, literature, and politics during the golden age of Grecian history (the fifth century B.C.) and was visited by the apostle Paul on his second missionary journey (Acts 17:15—18:1).

Even today the visitor to Athens is impressed by the city's ancient glory. The ACROPOLIS (the great

The beautiful Parthenon in Athens, dedicated to the Greek goddess Athena.
Photo by Howard Vos

central hill)—with its Parthenon (the temple dedicated to the virgin Athena, the goddess of wisdom and the arts), its Erechtheion (the unique double sanctuary dedicated to Athena and Neptune), its Propylaea (the magnificent entrance), and its small temple to Wingless Victory (symbolizing the Athenian hope that victory would never leave them)—stand as monuments to the city's glorious past.

The history of Athens goes back before 3000 B.C., when a small village grew up on the slopes of the Acropolis. As it developed, Athens became a sea power with its port at Piraeus about eight kilometers (five miles) distant and its navy stationed at Phaleron. Its government developed in stages and in about 509 B.C. Cleisthenes provided a new constitution which became the basis of Athenian democracy.

Athens' history involved a number of battles with other city-states, such as Sparta, and with the Persians, who were led by Darius and Xerxes. In the sea battle with the Persians at Salamis (480 B.C.), the Athenians won decisively, but the retreating Persians burned Athens.

The rebuilding of Athens began under Themistocles and Athens started its golden age under Pericles (about 495–429 B.C.). Learning was stimulated and philosophers found Athens a congenial home (with the exception of Socrates, whom the Athenians put to death in 399 B.C.). Plato founded his famous school, the Academy, in 388 B.C.

As one visits the museum in Athens filled with statues and the theater of Dionysus with the heads of the gods removed, one recalls Paul's assessment of Athens as a city "given over to idols" (Acts 17:16). As one walks through the Agora (marketplace) and visits the reconstructed porch of Attalus, one remembers that in porches like these the ancient Greek philosophers used to debate. Acts 17:18, for instance, describes Paul's encounter with "certain Epicurean and Stoic philosophers." In fact, the Stoics, the followers of Zeno (342?–270? B.C.), took their name from these porches. In this area, between the Acropolis and the Agora, lies the hill known as the AREOPAGUS (Mars' Hill), where Paul may have made his defense before the council of Athens (Acts 17:22–31).

ATHLAI [ATH lay eye] (*Jehovah is strong*) — a son of Bebai who divorced his pagan wife (Ezra 10:28).

ATONEMENT — the act by which God restores a relationship of harmony and unity between Himself and human beings. The word can be broken into three parts which express this great truth in simple but profound terms: "at-one-ment." Through God's atoning grace and forgiveness, we are reinstated to a relationship of at-one-ment with God, in spite of our sin.

Human Need. Because of Adam's sin (Rom. 5:18; 1 Cor. 15:22) and our own personal sins (Col. 1:21), no person is worthy of relationship with a Holy God (Eccl. 7:20; Rom. 3:23). Since we are helpless to correct this situation (Prov. 20:9) and can do nothing to hide our sin from God (Heb.

4:13), we all stand condemned by sin (Rom. 3:19). It is human nature (our sinfulness) and God's nature (His holy wrath against sin) which makes us "enemies" (Rom. 5:10).

God's Gift: Atonement. God's gracious response to the helplessness of His chosen people, the nation of Israel, was to give them a means of RECONCILIATION through Old Testament covenant Law. This came in the sacrificial system where the death, or "blood" of the animal was accepted by God as a substitute for the death (Ezek. 18:20) which the sinner deserved: "For the life of the flesh is in the blood, and I have given it to you upon the altar to make atonement for your souls" (Lev. 17:11).

The Law required that the sacrificial victims must be free from defect, and buying them always involved some cost to the sinner. But an animal's death did not automatically make people right with God in some simple, mechanical way. The hostility between God and man because of sin is a personal matter. God for His part personally gave the means of atonement in the sacrificial system; men and women for their part personally are expected to recognize the seriousness of their sin (Lev. 16:29–30; Mic. 6:6–8). They must also identify themselves personally with the victim that dies: "Then he shall put his hand on the head of the burnt offering, and it will be accepted on his behalf to make atonement for him" (Lev. 1:4).

In the Old Testament, God Himself brought about atonement by graciously providing the appointed sacrifices. The priests represented Him in the atonement ritual, and the sinner received the benefits of being reconciled to God in forgiveness and harmony.

Although Old Testament believers were truly forgiven and received genuine atonement through animal sacrifice, the New Testament clearly states that during the Old Testament period God's justice was not served: "For it is not possible that the blood of bulls and goats could take away sins" (Heb. 10:4). Atonement was possible "because in His forbearance God had passed over the sins that were previously committed" (Rom. 3:25). However, God's justice was served in the death of Jesus Christ as a substitute who "not with the blood of goats and calves, but with His own blood He entered the Most Holy Place once for all, having obtained eternal redemption" (Heb. 9:12). "And for this reason He is the Mediator of the new covenant" (Heb. 9:15).

Our Response. The Lord Jesus came according to God's will (Acts 2:23; 1 Pet. 1:20) "to give His life a ransom for many" (Mark 10:45), or "for all" (1 Tim. 2:6). Though God "laid on Him the iniquity of us all" (Is. 53:6; also 2 Cor. 5:21; Gal. 3:13), yet Christ "has loved us and given Himself for us, an offering and a sacrifice to God" (Eph. 5:2), so that those who believe in Him (Rom. 3:22) might receive atonement and "be saved from [God's] wrath" (Rom. 5:9) through "the precious blood of Christ" (1 Pet. 1:19).

No believer who truly understands the awesome

holiness of God's wrath and the terrible hopelessness that comes from personal sin can fail to be overwhelmed by the deep love of Jesus for each of us, and the wonder of God's gracious gift of eternal atonement through Christ. Through Jesus, God will present us "faultless before the presence of His glory with exceeding joy" (Jude 24).

ATONEMENT, DAY OF (see FEASTS AND FESTIVALS).

ATROTH BETH JOAB [AT rawth beth JOE ab] (*the crowns of the house of Joab*) — a town of Judah, apparently near Bethlehem (1 Chr. 2:54).

ATTAI [AT ay eye] (*timely*) — the name of three Old Testament men:
1. A grandson of Sheshan the Jerahmeelite through Sheshan's daughter Ahlai and her husband Jarha (1 Chr. 2:35–36).
2. A Gadite soldier who joined David at Ziklag (1 Chr. 12:8).
3. The second son of King Rehoboam by his second wife, Maacah (2 Chr. 11:20).

ATTALIA [at ah LIE ah] — a city on the seacoast of Pamphylia in modern Turkey. Attalia derived its name from Attalus Philadelphus, the king of Pergamos (159–138 B.C.). At the end of Paul's first missionary journey, he preached in Attalia (Acts 14:25). From there he sailed to Antioch, where the journey had begun (Acts 14:26). Known today by the name Adalia, Attalia is the main seaport on the Gulf of Adalia.

ATTENDANT (see OCCUPATIONS AND TRADES).

ATTIRE (see DRESS OF THE BIBLE).

AUGURY (see MAGIC, SORCERY, AND DIVINATION).

Bust of Augustus Caesar, first emperor of the Roman Empire.

AUGUSTAN REGIMENT — one of five cohorts, or regiments, of the Roman army stationed at or near CAESAREA. While the apostle Paul was being transported to Rome as a prisoner, he was put in the charge of "one named Julius, a centurion of the Augustan Regiment" (Acts 27:1). A regiment, or cohort, was made up of about 600 infantrymen.

AUGUSTUS [aw GUS tus] (*consecrated, holy, sacred*) — a title of honor bestowed upon Octavian, the first Roman emperor. Luke refers to him as "Caesar Augustus" (Luke 2:1). A nephew of Julius Caesar, Octavian was born in 63 B.C. In 43 B.C., Octavian, Lepidus, and Mark Antony were named as the Second Triumvirate, the three rulers who shared the office of emperor. When Mark Antony was defeated by Octavian at the Battle of Actium (in Greece; 31 B.C.), Octavian became the sole ruler of Rome and reigned as emperor for more than 44 years, until his death in A.D. 14. It was during his reign that Jesus was born (Luke 2:1).

Augustus reigned during a time of peace and extensive architectural achievements. After his death, the title "Augustus" was given to all Roman emperors. The "Augustus Caesar" mentioned in Acts 25:21, 25, for instance, is not Octavian but Nero.

Also see CAESAR.

AUNT — an uncle's wife (Lev. 18:14; 20:20) or a father's sister (Ex. 6:20). Amram married his aunt, Jochebed, and she bore Aaron and Moses (Ex. 6:20). Also see FAMILY.

AUTHORITY — the power or right to do something, particularly to give orders and see that they are followed. The word authority as used in the Bible usually means a person's right to do certain things because of the position or office he holds. This word emphasizes the legality and right, more than the physical strength, needed to do something.

The two basic forms of authority are intrinsic authority (belonging to one's essential nature) and derived authority (given to one from another source). Since "there is no authority except from God" (Rom. 13:1), every kind of authority other than that of God Himself is derived and therefore secondary to God's power (John 19:11).

God's authority is absolute and unconditional (Ps. 29:10; Isaiah 40). He has authority over nature (Job 38), governments (Dan. 4:17, 34–35), and history (Acts 1:7; 17:24–31); and He has the power to send people to hell (Luke 12:5). Jesus Christ has the same intrinsic authority as the Father (John 10:25–30), although this authority is said to be given to Christ from His Father, just as the authority of the Holy Spirit is given to Him from the Father and the Son (John 14:26; 15:26; 16:13–15). Christ has the authority to forgive sins (John 5:26–27), to lay down His life and take it up again (John 10:17–18), and to give eternal life (John 17:2). The people were astonished at this authority which Jesus revealed when He taught and performed miracles (Matt. 7:28–29; 8:27; Luke 4:36).

In addition to the intrinsic authority of God, the

Bible speaks of many kinds of derived power. Some of the most important of these are the authority of civil governments (Rom. 13:1-7), parents (Eph. 6:1-4), employers (Eph. 6:5-9), church leaders (Heb. 13:7, 17), angels (Luke 1:19-20), Satan (Luke 4:6), and evil spirits other than Satan (Eph. 6:11-12). There are vast differences among these kinds of authority. Some are permitted by God only for a time.

One derived authority is above every other kind of derived authority, and that is the Bible. Because the Bible is inspired by God (2 Tim. 3:16; 2 Pet. 1:20-21), it has divine power and authority. God did not give the Scriptures to be read only, but to be believed and obeyed.

Christians are often given certain authority to exercise. This includes the authority of a parent or a church leader. The most noble use of authority is for serving others. "Let...he who governs," Jesus said, be "as he who serves.... I am among you as the One who serves" (Luke 22:26-27). The Christian who seeks to follow Christ's example will learn to use authority with others more than over others. The wise Christian remembers that all derived authority will one day be returned to the God who gave it (1 Cor. 15:24-28). But the rewards of faithful service will endure throughout eternity (1 John 2:17).

AUTHORIZED VERSION (see BIBLE VERSIONS AND TRANSLATIONS).

AVA [AY vah] (*region*) — a city (or perhaps a district or province) of the Assyrian Empire. Sargon, king of Assyria, brought settlers from Ava to colonize Samaria after the nation of Israel fell to his forces (2 Kin. 17:24). The province is also identified as Ivah (2 Kin. 18:34). Ava is spelled Avva in some translations.

AVEN [AY ven] (*wickedness*) — the name of two cities and one valley in the Old Testament:

1. The ancient Egyptian city of ON, called Heliopolis (city of the sun) by the Greeks. It was one of the principal centers of Egyptian sun-worship (Ezek. 30:17). Aven is thought to be a deliberate misvocalization for the word On, which means "strength." If so, Ezekiel was using a pun that expressed his contempt for the city of strength that had become a city of idolatry. On was located just north of Memphis at the southern edge of the Nile Delta.

2. A shortened form of BETH AVEN (Hos. 10:8). Hosea used this name contemptuously of Bethel ("house of God") to declare that it had become a house of idolatry.

3. A town after which a valley near Damascus was named (Amos 1:5).

AVENGER OF BLOOD — a relative responsible for avenging an injury to a member of his family or clan—especially murder (Deut. 19:6, 12; 2 Sam. 14:11).

A kind of primitive justice existed among the various families, clans, and tribes of the ancient Hebrews in the Old Testament. Being related by blood, each of these groups was responsible for the care and protection of its own members, even to the point of avenging wrongs inflicted upon the clan. This responsibility fell to the victim's closest relative, who would seek to find and kill the murderer (Judg. 8:18-21). The trouble with this primitive system of justice is that the avenger of blood, having killed the murderer of his kinsman, might himself be killed by a member of the opposing clan, thus setting in motion a vicious blood feud.

Plainly, vengeance could not be allowed to flourish, or it would lead to chaos. The Law of Moses established certain guidelines or limits concerning the avenger of blood. Six cities of refuge were established to which the slayer could flee for protection: Kedesh, Shechem, Kirjath Arba (also called Hebron), Bezer, Ramoth in Gilead, and Golan (Josh. 20:1-9). If someone killed another by accident, he was not necessarily liable to punishment (Deut. 19:4-6). The community would decide if the crime was murder or manslaughter (Num. 35:24). If it was manslaughter, the slayer could stay safely in one of these cities of refuge, where the avenger of blood could not hurt him (Deut. 4:41-43; Josh. 20:1-9).

But if a person was guilty of murder, he could not be saved by fleeing to a city of refuge (Ex. 21:14). Even if he were to flee to the tabernacle (or Temple) and take "hold of the horns of the altar" (1 Kin. 1:50-51; 2:28)—both an appeal for mercy and a claim to the protection of the sanctuary—he could be put to death by the avenger (1 Kin. 2:25, 34).

In contrast to these provisions of the Old Testament law, Jesus taught us to love our enemies (Matt. 5:44). One must forgive his brother, not merely "up to seven times, but up to seventy times seven" (Matt. 18:22). Only by love, forgiveness, and mercy can the vicious cycle of hatred and revenge be broken.

Also see CITIES OF REFUGE; KINSMAN.

AVIM [AV em] (*villagers*) — the name of a tribe and a town in the Old Testament:

1. A native tribe of the Canaanites who lived on the Philistine plain "as far as Gaza" (Deut. 2:23). Most of the Avim were destroyed or driven off by the Philistines. The reference to the Avites (Josh. 13:3; Avvim, NEB, RSV) is to these same Avim.

2. A town of the territory of Benjamin, probably situated near Bethel (Josh. 18:23; Avvim, NEB, RSV).

AVITES [AV ites] (*villagers*) — the name of two tribes in the Old Testament:

1. A native tribe of the Canaanites who lived on the Philistine plain (Josh. 13:3). The NKJV also translates this tribe as AVIM (Deut. 2:23; Avvim, RSV, NEB).

2. The people of AVA, a city of the Assyrian Empire from which people were brought to help colonize Samaria (2 Kin. 17:31; Avvites, RSV, NEB).

AVITH [AY vihth] (*ruins*) — the capital city of Hadad, king of Edom (1 Chr. 1:46).

AVVA [AV vah] — a form of AVA.

AVVIM [AV vem] — a form of AVIM (Deut. 2:23; Josh. 18:23) and AVITES (Josh. 13:3).

AVVITES [AV vites] — a form of AVITES.

AWL (see TOOLS OF THE BIBLE).

AX (see ARMS, ARMOR OF THE BIBLE; TOOLS OF THE BIBLE).

AXLE — a supporting shaft upon which wheels revolve. Solomon's Temple had ten bronze carts, each with four bronze wheels and axles of bronze (1 Kin. 7:30, 32; axletrees, KJV).

AYIN [EYE yin] — the 16th letter of the Hebrew alphabet, used as a heading over Psalm 119:121-128 (Ain, KJV). In the original Hebrew language, each line of these eight verses began with the letter ayin.
Also see ACROSTIC.

AYYAH [EYE yah] (*heap, ruin*) — one of the towns settled by the tribe of Ephraim (1 Chr. 7:28; Gaza, KJV, NEB). Some scholars suggest that Ayyah may be the same place as Aija (Neh. 11:31), another spelling of AI, a city near Jericho.

AZAL [AY zal] (*slope*) — a place near Jerusalem (Zech. 14:5), location unknown.

AZALIAH [az ah LIE ah] (*Jehovah is noble*) — a son of Meshullam and the father of Shaphan the scribe (2 Kin. 22:3).

AZANIAH [AZ ah NIE ah] (*the Lord has heard*) — a Levite who sealed the covenant under Nehemiah (Neh. 10:9).

AZARAEL [AZ ar ay el] — a form of AZAREL.

AZAREEL [a ZAY reh el] (*God is helper*) — the name of three men in the Old Testament:
1. A Levite of the family of Korah (1 Chr. 12:6; Azarel, RSV).
2. A son of Bani. Azareel divorced his pagan wife after the Captivity (Ezra 10:41; Azarel, RSV).
3. A priest of the family of Immer (Neh. 11:13; Azarel, RSV).

AZAREL [AZ ah rel] (*God is helper*) — the name of three men in the Old Testament:
1. A priest responsible for the song service of the Temple (1 Chr. 25:18; Azareel, KJV, NEB). He is also called Uzziel (1 Chr. 25:4) and may be the same person as Asharelah (1 Chr. 25:2).
2. A son of Jehoram, who was the chief of the tribe of Dan (1 Chr. 27:22; Azareel, KJV, NEB).
3. A musician who played the trumpet at the dedication of the new Temple (Neh. 12:36; Azareel, KJV).

AZARIAH [az ah RYE ah] (*Jehovah has helped*) — the name of 28 men in the Old Testament:
1. One of Solomon's officials (1 Kin. 4:2).
2. A son of Nathan (1 Kin. 4:5). Azariah was in

charge of the officers who oversaw Solomon's 12 districts (1 Kin. 4:5).
3. An alternate name for UZZIAH, king of Judah (2 Kin. 14:21; 1 Chr. 3:12).
4. A son of Ethan of the tribe of Judah (1 Chr. 2:8).
5. A descendant of Jerahmeel (1 Chr. 2:38–39).
6. A son of Ahimaaz and grandson of Zadok (1 Chr. 6:9).
7. A son of Johanan and grandson of Azariah (1 Chr. 6:10–11).
8. A son of Hilkiah and high priest under King Josiah (1 Chr. 6:13–14; 9:11; Ezra 7:1).
9. A Levite and an ancestor of Heman the musician (1 Chr. 6:36).
10. The son of Oded (2 Chr. 15:1). Azariah was the prophet who encouraged King Asa of Judah to continue his religious reform.
11. A son of King Jehoshaphat of Judah who was killed when his brother, Jehoram, succeeded to the throne (2 Chr. 21:2).
12. Another son of King Jehoshaphat (2 Chr. 21:2, Azaryahu, NKJV, NASB; Azariahu, NIV).
13. A son of Jehoram (2 Chr. 22:6). In this verse, Azariah appears to be a copyist's error for Ahaziah.
14. A son of Obed (2 Chr. 23:1). Azariah was an army officer who helped overthrow Queen Athaliah and make Joash king of Judah.
15. A son of Jehoram who assisted in the conspiracy mentioned in Azariah No. 14 (2 Chr. 23:1).
16. A chief priest under King Uzziah (2 Chr. 26:17, 20).
17. A son of Johanan (2 Chr. 28:12). Azariah was an Ephraimite chief.
18. The father of Joel (2 Chr. 29:12).
19. A son of Jehalelel (2 Chr. 29:12). Azariah was a Levite who assisted in Temple reform under Hezekiah.
20. The "chief priest" and "ruler of the house of God" (2 Chr. 31:10, 13) during the reign of Hezekiah, king of Judah.
21. A son of Meraioth (Ezra 7:3), an ancestor of Ezra.
22. A son of Maaseiah (Neh. 3:23–24).
23. An Israelite who returned to Jerusalem with Zerubbabel after the Captivity (Neh. 7:7).
24. A priest who explained the Law as Ezra read it to the people (Neh. 8:7).
25. A priest who sealed the covenant under Nehemiah (Neh. 10:2).
26. A prince of Judah who assisted in the dedication of Jerusalem's rebuilt walls (Neh. 12:33).
27. A son of Hoshaiah (Jer. 43:2) and a person who opposed the prophet Jeremiah.
28. The Hebrew name of ABED–NEGO, whom Nebuchadnezzar placed in the fiery furnace (Dan. 1:6–7, 11, 19; 2:17).

AZARIAH, PRAYER OF (see APOCRYPHA).

AZARIAHU [az uh RYE uh hoo] (see AZARYAHU).

AZARYAHU [AHZ ar yuh hoo] (*Jehovah is help*) — a son of King Jehoshaphat of Judah (2 Chr. 21:2;

Azariah, KJV, RSV, NEB; Azariahu, NIV). Azaryahu was killed by his brother Jehoram, who
siezed the throne at Jehoshaphat's death.

AZAZ [AY zaz] (*Jehovah is strong*) — a son of
Shema in the genealogy of Reuben (1 Chr. 5:8).

AZAZEL [az ah ZEL] — RSV, KJV word for
SCAPEGOAT.

AZAZIAH [az ah ZIE ah] (*Jehovah is strong*) — the
name of three men in the books of Chronicles:
1. A Levite in the musical services of the tabernacle when David moved the ARK OF THE COVENANT
to Jerusalem (1 Chr. 15:21).
2. The father of Hoshea (1 Chr. 27:20).
3. A Levite in charge of the Temple offerings during the reign of King Hezekiah (2 Chr. 31:13).

AZBUK [AZ buck] (*pardon*) — the father of Nehemiah (Neh. 3:16).

AZEKAH [a ZEE kah] (*a place tilled*) — a fortified
city of Judah near Socoh, situated in the lowland
country between Lachish and Jerusalem (see Map
3, A–4). Azekah is mentioned in connection with
Joshua's pursuit of the Canaanites (Josh. 10:10–11),
with Goliath's death (1 Sam. 17:1), with Rehoboam, who fortified it (2 Chr. 11:9), and with Nebuchadnezzar king of Babylon, who beseiged the
city (Jer. 34:7; Josh. 15:35; Neh. 11:30).

AZEL [AY zel] (*well-rooted, noble*) — a son of
Eleasah and a descendant of King Saul through Jonathan. Azel was the father of six sons (1 Chr. 8:37–
38).

AZEM [AY zem] — a form of EZEM.

AZGAD [AZ gad] (*Gad is strong*) — the name of
three men who lived in the time of Ezra and Nehemiah:
1. A man whose descendants returned from the
Captivity with Zerubbabel (Ezra 2:12; Neh. 7:17).
2. An ancestor of Johanan, who accompanied
Ezra back to Jerusalem (Ezra 8:12).
3. A man who sealed the covenant after the Captivity (Neh. 10:15).

AZIEL [AY zi el] (*God has nourished*) — a Levite
musician who helped transport the ARK OF THE
COVENANT to Jerusalem (1 Chr. 15:20). His full
name was Jaaziel (1 Chr. 15:18).

AZIZA [a ZIE zah] (*powerful*) — a son of Zattu
who divorced his pagan wife after the Captivity
(Ezra 10:27).

AZMAVETH [az MAH veth] (*strong as death*) —
the name of several men and one village in the Old
Testament:
1. One of David's mighty men. He was from Bahurim, a small village near Jerusalem (2 Sam.
23:31; 1 Chr. 11:33).
2. A son of Jehoaddah (1 Chr. 8:36), or Jarah (1
Chr. 9:42). Azmaveth was a descendant of King
Saul.

3. The father of Pelet and Jeziel (1 Chr. 12:1–3).
He may be the same person as Azmaveth No. 1.
4. A treasury official during David's reign (1 Chr.
27:25).
5. A village near the border of Judah and Benjamin, about eight kilometers (five miles) northeast
of Jerusalem. Forty-two men of Azmaveth returned
from the Captivity with Zerubbabel (Ezra 2:24).
Musicians and singers from this village helped dedicate the rebuilt wall of Jerusalem (Neh. 12:29). This
village was also called Beth Azmaveth (Neh. 7:28).

AZMON [AZ mun] (*fortress*) — a place on the
southwest border of Judah, between Hazar Addar
and the "Brook of Egypt" (Num. 34:4–5; Josh.
15:4).

AZNOTH TABOR [AZ nohth TAY bor] (*peaks of
Tabor*) — a place near the southern boundary of
Naphtali (Josh. 19:34). It may be Umm Jebeil, near
Mount Tabor.

AZOR [AY zor] (*helper*) — an ancestor of Jesus
(Matt. 1:13–14).

AZOTUS [a ZOH tus] (*fortress*) — the Greek name
of ASHDOD (Acts 8:40).

AZRIEL [AZ rih el] (*God is helper*) — the name of
three Old Testament men:
1. A chief of the tribe of Manasseh (1 Chr. 5:24).
2. An ancestor of Jerimoth (1 Chr. 27:19).
3. The father of Seraiah (Jer. 36:26).

AZRIKAM [AZ rih kam] (*my help has risen*) — the
name of four men in the Old Testament:
1. A descendant of King David through Zerubbabel (1 Chr. 3:23).
2. The oldest son of Azel and a descendant of
King Saul (1 Chr. 8:38; 9:44).
3. A Levite who lived in Jerusalem after the Captivity (1 Chr. 9:14; Neh. 11:15).
4. Governor of the house of Ahaz (2 Chr. 28:7).

AZUBAH [a ZOO buh] (*forsaken*) — the name of
two women in the Old Testament:
1. The mother of Jehoshaphat, a king of Judah (1
Kin. 22:42).
2. Caleb's first wife and the mother of his three
sons, Jesher, Shobab, and Ardon (1 Chr. 2:18–19).

AZUR [AY zer] (*helper*) — the father of Hananiah
the false prophet (Jer. 28:1; AZZUR, RSV, NIV,
NEB).

AZZAN [AZ an] (*sharp*) — the father of Paltiel, of
the tribe of Issachar. Paltiel helped Eleazar and
Joshua divide the land among the tribes (Num.
34:26).

AZZUR [AZ err] (*helper*) — the name of two men
in the Old Testament:
1. An Israelite who sealed the covenant under Nehemiah (Neh. 10:17).
2. The father of Jaazaniah, a prince whom Ezekiel saw in a vision (Ezek. 11:1; Azur, KJV).

B

BAAL [BAY uhl] (*lord, master*) — the name of one of more false gods, a place, and two people in the Old Testament:

1. A fertility and nature god of the Canaanites and Phoenicians. Also see GODS, PAGAN.
2. A city in the tribe of Simeon (1 Chr. 4:33), the same place as Baalath Beer (Josh. 19:8).
3. A descendant of Reuben (1 Chr. 5:5–6).
4. A descendant of Benjamin listed in the family tree of King Saul (1 Chr. 8:30; 9:36).

BAAL–BERITH [BAY uhl BEE rith] (see GODS, PAGAN).

BAAL GAD [BAY uhl gad] (*lord of Gad*) — a town "in the Valley of Lebanon below Mount Hermon" (Josh. 11:17). Joshua marched as far north as this city in his conquest of Canaan (Josh. 12:7; 13:5).

BAAL HAMON [BAY uhl HAY mahn] (*lord of the abundance*) — an unknown place where Solomon had a fertile vineyard (Song 8:11).

BAAL–HANAN [BAY uhl HAY nun] (*Baal is gracious*) — the name of two men in the Old Testament:

1. A king of Edom (Gen. 36:38–39; 1 Chr. 1:49–50).
2. A man appointed custodian of olive and sycamore trees by David (1 Chr. 27:28).

BAAL HAZOR [BAY uhl HAY zor] (*lord of Hazor*) — a place (2 Sam. 13:23) where Amnon was murdered by Absalom's servants in revenge for Amnon's rape of Abasalom's sister, Tamar (1 Sam. 13:14, 29).

BAAL HERMON [BAY uhl HUR mon] (*lord of Hermon*) — the name of a mountain and a city in the Old Testament:

1. A mountain east of Lebanon (Judg. 3:3).
2. A city near Mount Hermon (1 Chr. 5:23).

BAAL MEON [BAY uhl ME own] (*lord of Meon*) — an ancient Amorite city on the northern border of Moab assigned to the tribe of Reuben (Num. 32:38). Baal Meon is also called Beon (Num. 32:3), Beth Baal Meon (Josh. 13:17), and Beth Meon (Jer. 48:23).

BAAL OF PEOR [BAY uhl PEA ore] (see GODS, PAGAN).

BAAL PERAZIM [BAY uhl PER uh zem] (*lord of breaches*) — a place near the valley of Rephaim where King David won a great victory over the Philistines (2 Sam. 5:20; 1 Chr. 14:11).

BAAL SHALISHA [BAY uhl SHALL ih shah] (*lord of Shalisha*) — a village of Ephraim, near Gilgal. A man from this place brought the prophet Elisha "bread of the firstfruits" to eat (2 Kin. 4:42).

BAAL TAMAR [BAY uhl TAY mar] (*lord of the palm tree*) — a place in Benjamin, between Bethel and Gibeah, where the Israelites prepared for battle (Judg. 20:33) before attacking the city of GIBEAH.

BAAL–ZEBUB [BAY uhl ZEE bub] (see GODS, PAGAN).

BAAL ZEPHON [BAY uhl ZEE fon] (*Baal of winter*) — a place in Egypt that was "opposite," or in front of, the Israelites while they were camped "before Pi Hahiroth, between Migdol and the sea" (Ex. 14:2, 9), just before they crossed the Red Sea (see Map 2, B–1).

BAALAH [BAY uh lah] (*mistress*) — a feminine form of Baal that refers to three different places in Palestine:

1. Another name for the town KIRJATH JEARIM (Josh. 15:9–10).
2. A hill in southern Judah, between Ekron and Jabneel (Josh. 15:11).
3. A town in southern Judah, near the border of Edom (Josh. 15:29).

BAALATH [BAY uh lath] (*mistress*) — a town near Gezer (Josh. 19:44) which became one of Solomon's storage cities (1 Kin. 9:18; 2 Chr. 8:6).

BAALATH BEER [BAY uh lath BEH ear] (*mistress of a well*) — a border town of the tribe of Simeon, sometimes called "Ramah of the South" (1 Sam. 30:27). It is identical with the city of Baal (1 Chr. 4:33). Also see BEALOTH.

BAALBEK [BAY uhl beck] (*city of Baal*) — an ancient city of Lebanon, situated north of Damascus. The city is not mentioned in the Bible, but it was notable in Roman days.

BAALE JUDAH [BAY uh leh Joo duh] (*Baalah of Judah*) — a town from which David brought the ARK OF THE COVENANT to Jerusalem (2 Sam. 6:2).

BAALI [BAY uh lih] (*my lord, my master*) — a term used in the KJV that refers to a subservient relationship either to a ruler or master or to BAAL. Because of Israel's idolatry, the prophet Hosea used the term to explain God's relationship to the nation as one of a master over a servant, rather than one of a loving husband (Hos. 2:16).

BAALIM [BAY uh lem] (see GODS, PAGAN).

BAALIS [BAY uh lis] (*lord of joy*) — a king of the Ammonites at the time when Jerusalem was destroyed by Nebuchadnezzar of Babylon (Jer. 40:14).

BAANA [BAY uh nah] (*son of grief*) — the name of two men in the Old Testament:
1. Solomon's supply officer, in the area of the plain of Esdraelon (1 Kin. 4:12).
2. The father of Zadok (Neh. 3:4).

BAANAH [BAY UH nah] (*son of grief*) — the name of four men in the Old Testament:
1. A captain in the army of ISHBOSHETH, the son of King Saul. Baanah was one of the murderers of Ishbosheth; David had him put to death for his crime (2 Sam. 4:1–12).
2. One of David's mighty men (2 Sam. 23:29).
3. Solomon's supply officer in Asher (1 Kin. 4:16).
4. A captive who returned to Jerusalem with Zerubbabel (Ezra 2:2; Neh. 7:7; 10:27).

BAARA [BAY uh rah] (*the burning one*) — a Moabite wife of Shaharaim, a Benjamite (1 Chr. 8:8).

BAASEIAH [BAY ah SIGH yah] (*Jehovah is bold*) — a descendant of Gershon (1 Chr. 6:43) and an ancestor of Asaph the musician (1 Chr. 6:40).

BAASHA [BAY uh shah] (*Baal hears*) — the son of Ahijah, of the tribe of Issachar, and the third king of the northern kingdom of Israel. Baasha succeeded Nadab, the son of Jeroboam I, as king by assassinating him. Then he murdered every member of the royal house, removing all who might claim his throne (1 Kin. 15:27–29).

Baasha's 24–year reign (909–885 B.C.) was characterized by war with Asa, king of Judah (1 Kin. 15:32; Jer. 41:9). He fortified RAMAH (2 Chr. 16:1), six kilometers (four miles) north of Jerusalem, to control traffic from the north to Jerusalem during a time of spiritual awakening under Asa (2 Chr. 15:1–10). When the Syrian king, Ben–Hadad, invaded Israel, Baasha withdrew to defend his cities (1 Kin. 15:16–21).

Baasha's dynasty ended as it began; his son Elah was murdered by a servant, and the royal household of Baasha came to an end (1 Kin. 16:8–11).

BABBLER — a term of ridicule and contempt hurled at the apostle Paul by the Stoic and Epicurean philosophers at Athens (Acts 17:18). The Greek word for this term means "seed–picker." The philosophers were calling Paul an ignorant parasite who peddles scraps of information which he does not understand.

BABEL, TOWER OF [BAY buhl] — an ancient tower symbolizing man's pride and rebellion that was built during the period after the FLOOD.

The narrative of the Tower of Babel appears in Genesis 11:1–9 as the climax to the account of early mankind found in Genesis 1—11. The geographical setting is a plain in the land of Shinar (Gen. 11:2). In the light of information contained in Genesis 10:10, Shinar probably refers to Babylonia.

The tower was constructed of brick, because there was no stone in southern Mesopotamia. It corresponds in general to a notable feature of Babylonian religion, the ZIGGURAT or temple tower. The one built at Ur in southern Mesopotamia about 2100 B.C. was a pyramid consisting of three terraces of diminishing size as the building ascended, topped by a temple. Converging stairways on one side led up to the temple. Its surviving lower two terraces were about 21 meters (70 feet) high. The outside of the structure was built of fired bricks and bituminous mortar, just like the tower described in Genesis 11:3.

The narrative in Genesis 11 is told with irony and with a negative attitude toward the people involved. Men delight in bricks, but the narrator and readers know that these are an inferior substitute for stone (Is. 9:10). To men the tower is a sky–scraper (Deut. 1:28), but to God it is so small that He must come down from heaven to catch a glimpse of this tiny effort. The construction of the tower and city is described as an act of self–glorification by the builders. Men seek for their own security in community life and culture, independent of God. This is human initiative apart from God (Ps. 127:1). As such, the activity is evil and sinful.

The account moves from a description of the sin to a narration of the punishment. God has to step in to prevent men from seizing yet more power for themselves and going beyond the limits of their creaturehood (Gen. 3:22). Their communication with each other to advance their efforts is frustrated because they begin to speak different languages. Finally, they abandon the building of the city and go their own way, becoming scattered over the earth.

The climax of the story occurs when the city is identified with *Babel*, the Hebrew name for Babylon. This nation's sophisticated culture and power deliberately excluded God. Just as the Old Testament prophets foresaw the future downfall of Babylon in spite of its glory (Is. 13:19; Rev. 18), this downfall is anticipated in Genesis 11: the end corresponds to the beginning.

God's rejection of the nations symbolized by the Tower of Babel is reversed in Genesis 12:1–3 by the call of Abraham, through whom all nations would be blessed. Ultimately the sinful and rejected condition of mankind, which is clearly shown by the diversity of human language and territory described in this account, needed PENTECOST as its answer. On this day the Holy Spirit was poured out on all

A glazed relief of a bull, discovered in the excavation of ancient Babylon.

people so they understood one another, although they spoke different languages (Acts 2:1–11; Eph. 2:14–18). The barriers that divide men and nations were thus removed.

BABOON (see ANIMALS OF THE BIBLE).

BABYLON, CITY OF [BAB uh lon] — ancient walled city between the Tigris and Euphrates Rivers and capital of the Babylonian Empire. The leading citizens of the nation of Judah were carried to this city as captives about 587 B.C. after Jerusalem fell to the invading Babylonians. Biblical writers often portrayed this ancient capital of the Babylonian people as the model of paganism and idolatry (Jer. 51:44; Dan. 4:30).

Babylon was situated along the Euphrates River about 485 kilometers (300 miles) northwest of the Persian Gulf and about 49 kilometers (30 miles) southwest of modern Baghdad in Iraq. Its origins are unknown. According to Babylonian tradition, it was built by the god Marduk. The city must have been built some time before 2300 B.C., because it was destroyed about that time by an invading enemy king. This makes Babylon one of the oldest cities of the ancient world. Genesis 10:10 mentions Babel as part of the empire of Nimrod.

Some time during its early history, the city of Babylon became a small independent kingdom. Its most famous king was HAMMURABI (about 1728–1686 B.C.), who conquered southern Mesopotamia and territory to the north as far as Mari. He was known for his revision of a code of law that showed concern for the welfare of the people under his rule. But the dynasty which he established declined under his successors. It came to an end with the conquest of Babylon by the Hittite king Murshilish I about 1595 B.C. Then the Kassites took over for a

period, ruling southern Mesopotamia from the city of Babylon as their capital. The Assyrians attacked and plundered Babylon about 1250 B.C., but it recovered and flourished for another century until the Assyrians succeeded in taking over the city with their superior forces about 1100 B.C.

After Tiglath-Pileser I of Assyria arrived on the scene, the city of Babylon became subject to Assyria by treaty or conquest. Tiglath-Pileser III (745–727 B.C.) declared himself king of Babylon with the name Pulu (Pul, 2 Kin. 15:19), deporting a number of its citizens to the subdued territory of the northern kingdom of Israel (2 Kin. 17:24).

In 721 B.C. a Chaldean prince, Marduk-apal-iddin, seized control of Babylon and became a thorn in Assyria's side for a number of years. He apparently planned a large-scale rebellion of eastern and western parts of the Assyrian Empire (2 Kin. 20:12). In retaliation against this rebellion, Sennacherib of Assyria (704–681 B.C.) attacked Babylon in 689 B.C., totally destroying it, although it was rebuilt by his successor Esarhaddon (680–669 B.C.). After this, Assyrian power gradually weakened, so the city and kingdom of Babylon grew stronger once again.

In 625 B.C. Nabopolassar seized the throne of Babylon. He was succeeded by Nebuchadnezzar II (605–562 B.C.), the greatest king of Babylon, who enlarged the capital city to an area of six square miles and beautified it with magnificent buildings. This period of the city's development has been the focal point of all archaeological research done in ancient Babylon. The city's massive double walls spanned both sides of the Euphrates River. Set into these walls were eight major gates. One of the numerous pagan temples in the city was that of the patron god Marduk, flanked by a ZIGGURAT or temple–tower. To this temple a sacred processional way led from the main gate, the Ishtar Gate. Both the gate and the walls facing the way were decorated with colored enameled bricks which were decorated with lions, dragons, and bulls.

The city of Babylon also contained a palace complex, or residence for the king. On the northwest side of this palace area, the famous terraced "hanging gardens" may have been situated. According to tradition, Nebuchadnezzar built these gardens for one of his foreign wives to remind her of the scenery of her homeland.

Babylon's glory reflected the king's imperial power. Captured kings were brought to his court at Babylon. These included the Judean kings Jehoiachin (2 Kin. 24:15) and Zedekiah (2 Kin. 25:7). During the reign of Nabonidus (555–539 B.C.), while Belshazzar was co–regent (Daniel 5), the city surrendered to the Persians without opposition.

Eventually the balance of power passed from the Persians to Alexander the Great of Greece, to whom Babylon willingly submitted in 331 B.C. Alexander planned to refurbish and expand the city and make it his capital, but he died before accomplishing these plans. The city later fell into insignificance because one of Alexander's successors founded a new capital at Seleucia, a short distance away.

In the Old Testament the prophetic books of Isaiah and Jeremiah predicted the downfall of the city of Babylon. This would happen as God's punishment of the Babylonians because of their destruction of Jerusalem and their deportation of the citizens of Judah (Is. 14:22; 21:9; 43:14; Jer. 50:9; 51:37). Today, the ruins of this ancient city stand as an eloquent testimony to the passing of proud empires and to the providential hand of God in history.

This drawing of Babylon shows the main avenue of the city, passing through the Gate of Ishtar in the city wall.

BABYLON IN THE NEW TESTAMENT — In the Book of Revelation the world in rebellion against God is called "Babylon." The Old Testament prophets often prophesied the fall of Babylon, the capital of an empire that destroyed God's city, Jerusalem, and carried His people away as captives. So in Revelation Babylon is a word–picture for a society which persecuted God's people but which God will eventually destroy.

When the Book of Revelation was written, Babylon may have been a kind of code name for pre–Christian Rome that was built on seven hills (Rev. 17:9) and which was already persecuting the church. Since that time, generations of Christians have been able to identify their own Babylons and have found reassurance in Revelation's message.

In Revelation 14:8 Babylon's power to make people resist God's claims in the gospel is admitted, but its doom is certain. In Revelation 16:19 Babylon is a "great city" that falls because God remembers its sin and brings His punishment. Throughout chapters 17—18 Babylon is prominent, pictured as a prostitute because it seduces people away from God with its glamor. But it is a false union which cannot satisfy.

"Babylon" stands over against the church, the "New Jerusalem" (Rev. 21:2), which is "the bride, the Lamb's wife" (Rev. 21:9). God reveals the "mystery" or divine truth (Rev. 17:5) about it and all such manmade societies that are organized independently of God. Its fall is celebrated by God's people (Rev. 18:20; 19:1–5).

In Matthew 1:11–12, 17, Judah's captivity in Babylon is mentioned in Jesus' genealogy. In Acts 7:43 Babylon appears in Stephen's famous speech about the history of the Jewish people. In 1 Peter 5:13 "Babylon" probably refers to the city of Rome.

BABYLONIA [bab i LAWN ih uh] — ancient pagan empire between the Tigris and Euphrates Rivers in southern Mesopotamia. The Babylonians struggled with the neighboring Assyrians for domination of the ancient world during much of their history. At the height of their power, the Babylonians overpowered the nation of Judah, destroyed Jerusalem, and carried God's Covenant People into captivity about 587 B.C.

The fortunes of the Babylonians rose and fell during the long sweep of Old Testament history— from about 2000 B.C. to about 500 B.C. References to these ancient people—their culture, religion, and military power—occur throughout the Old Testament.

Babylonia was a long, narrow country about 65 kilometers (40 miles) wide at its widest point and having an area of about 8,000 square miles. It was bordered on the north by Assyria, on the east by Elam, on the south and west by the Arabian desert, and on the southeast by the Persian Gulf.

Among the earliest inhabitants of this region were the Sumerians, whom the Bible refers to as the people of the "land of Shinar" (Gen. 10:10). Sargon, from one of the Sumerian cities, united the

Photo: Matson Photo Collection

The ruins of Babylon, once the proud capital city of a mighty empire.

people of Babylonia under his rule about 2300 B.C. Many scholars believe Sargon was the same person as Nimrod (Gen. 10:8).

Around 2000 B.C. HAMMURABI emerged as the ruler of Babylonia. He expanded the borders of the Empire and organized its laws into a written system, referred to by scholars as the Code of Hammurabi. About this time Abraham left UR, one of the ancient cities in lower Babylon, and moved to Haran, a city in the north. Still later, Abraham left Haran and migrated into the land of Canaan under God's promise that he would become the father of a great nation (Gen. 12:1–20).

Any account of Babylonia must also mention Assyria, which bordered Babylonia on the north. Assyria's development was often intertwined with the course of Babylonian history. About 1270 B.C., the Assyrians overpowered Babylonia. For the next 700 years, Babylonia was a second-rate power as the Assyrians dominated the ancient world.

Around 626 B.C., Babylonian independence was finally won from Assyria by a leader named Nabopolassar. Under his leadership, Babylonia again became a great empire. In 605 B.C., Nebuchadnezzar, the son of Nabopolassar, became ruler and reigned for 44 years. Under him the Babylonian Empire reached its greatest strength. Using the treasures which he took from other nations, Nebuchadnezzar built BABYLON, the capital city of Babylonia, into one of the leading cities of the world. The famous hanging gardens of Babylon were known as one of the seven wonders of the ancient world.

In 587 B.C., the Babylonians destroyed Jerusalem and carried the leading citizens of the nation of Judah as captives to Babylon. During this period of captivity, the Persians conquered Babylonia, and the Babylonians passed from the scene as a world power.

During its long history, Babylonia attained a high level of civilization that was influential beyond its borders. Sumerian culture was its basis, which later Babylonians regarded as traditional. In the realm of religion, the Sumerians already had a system of gods, each with a main temple in a particular city. The chief gods were Anu, god of heaven; Enlil, god of the air; and Enki or Ea, god of the subterranean ocean. Others were Shamash, the sun-god; Sin, the moon-god; Ishtar, goddess of love and war; and Adad, the storm-god. The Amorites

This reconstruction of Babylon from the time of King Nebuchadnezzar II shows the huge ziggurat on the left and the temple of the pagan god Marduk on the right.

promoted the god Marduk at the city of Babylon, so that he became the chief god of the Babylonian religion, beginning about 1100 B.C.

Babylonian religion was temple-centered, with elaborate festivals and many different types of priests, especially the exorcist and the diviner, whose function was to drive away evil spirits.

Babylonian literature was dominated by mythology and legends. Among these was a creation myth written to glorify a god known as Marduk. According to this myth, Marduk created heaven and earth from the corpse of the goddess Tiamat. Another work was the Gilgamish Epic, a flood story written about 2000 B.C. Scientific literature of the Babylonians included treatises on astronomy, mathematics, medicine, chemistry, botany, and zoology.

An important aspect of Babylonian culture was a codified system of law. Hammurabi's famous code was the successor of earlier collections of laws going back to about 2050 B.C. The Babylonians used art for the national celebration of great events and glorification of the gods. It was marked by stylized and symbolic representations, but it expressed realism and spontaneity in the depiction of animals.

The Old Testament contains many references to Babylonia. Genesis 10:10 mentions four Babylonian cities, Babel (Babylon), Erech (Uruk), Accad (Agade) and Calneh. These, along with Assyria, were ruled by Nimrod.

BACA, VALLEY OF [BAH kah] (meaning unknown) — a valley in Palestine, thought by some scholars to be the same place as the Valley of Rephaim (2 Sam. 5:22–24; Ps. 84:6).

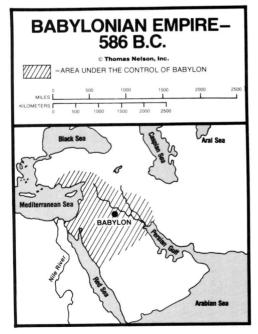

BABYLONIAN EMPIRE– 586 B.C.

© Thomas Nelson, Inc.

▨ =AREA UNDER THE CONTROL OF BABYLON

BACCHUS [BAHK us] (see GODS, PAGAN).

BACHRITES [BACK rites] — descendants of BECHER, a son of Benjamin (Num.26:35).

BACKBITE — to speak slanderously or spitefully about a person (Ps. 15:3; Rom. 1:30). Backbiting involves an element of deceit and cowardice. It should be avoided by Christians.

BACKSLIDE — to revert to sin or wrongdoing; to lapse morally or in the practice of religion. "Backsliding" is a term found mainly in the Book of Jeremiah (2:19; 31:22; 49:4). It refers to the lapse of the nation of Israel into paganism and idolatry.

BADGER (see ANIMALS OF THE BIBLE).

BAG — a small satchel or sack in which food, clothes, and other provisions for a journey were carried. Usually made of leather, it was slung over the shoulder or fastened to a belt. When he was a shepherd, David carried such a bag (1 Sam. 17:40).

Jesus prohibited His disciples from taking with them such traveling bags (Matt. 10:10; Mark 6:8; Luke 9:3). He asked them if their needs had been met. In spite of the absence of their provision bag, they affirmed they had lacked for nothing.

Also see PURSE, BAG.

BAGPIPE (see MUSICAL INSTRUMENTS).

BAHARUM [bah HAH rum] — a form of BAHURIM.

BAHARUMITE [bah HAH rum ite] — a person who lived in BAHURIM (2 Sam. 23:31; 1 Chr. 11:33).

BAHURIM [bah HOO rim] (*young men*) — a village near the Mount of Olives, located east of Jerusalem in the territory of Benjamin (2 Sam. 3:16). During Absalom's rebellion, King David fled along the old Jerusalem-to-Jericho road and passed through Bahurim. Later Jonathan and Ahimaaz hid themselves in a well at Bahurim when they were fleeing the forces of Absalom (2 Sam. 17:18–21).

BAJITH [BAY jith] (*house*) — the KJV spelling of a place in Moab. The NKJV has "the temple [house] of Dibon" (Is. 15:2).

BAKBAKKAR [back BACK ur] (*diligent seacher*) — a Levite who returned from the Captivity (1 Chr. 9:15).

BAKBUK [BACK buk] (*flask*) — one of the NETHINIM (Temple servants) whose descendants returned from the Captivity (Ezra 2:51; Neh. 7:53).

BAKBUKIAH [back bue KIE uh] (*Jehovah's pitcher*) — the name of one or more men in the Old Testament:

1. A Levite who lived in Jerusalem after the Captivity (Neh. 11:17), possibly the same person as Bakbakkar (1 Chr. 9:15).

2. A Levite who returned from the Captivity with Zerubbabel (Neh. 12:9).

3. A Levite who watched over the Temple storerooms (Neh. 12:25).

Any two, or all three, of these men may be the same person.

BAKER (see OCCUPATIONS AND TRADES; BREAD).

BALAAM [BAY lum] (*lord of the people*) — a magician or soothsayer (Josh. 13:22) who was summoned by the Moabite king BALAK to curse the Israelites before they entered Canaan (Num. 22:5—24:25; Deut. 23:4–5).

Balaam lived in ARAM in the town of Pethor on the Euphrates River. A curious mixture of good and evil, Balaam wavered when he was asked by Balak to curse the Israelites. But he finally agreed to go when the Lord specifically instructed him to go to Balak (Num. 22:20).

The exact meaning of the account of Balaam's "stubborn" donkey is not clear. After telling Balaam it was all right to go, God either tried to forbid him from going or wanted to impress upon him that he should speak only what he was told to say. When the angel of the Lord blocked their way, the donkey balked three times and was beaten by Balaam, who had not seen the angel. Finally, after the third beating, the donkey spoke, reproving Balaam.

When the angel told Balaam, "Your way is perverse before Me" (Num. 22:32), Balaam offered to return home. The angel told him to go on, however, and reminded him to speak only the words which God gave him to speak.

Balaam and Balak met at the River Arnon and traveled to "the high places of Baal" (Num. 22:41). From there they could see part of the Israelite encampment at Acacia Grove (Num. 25:1). After sacrificing on seven altars, Balaam went off alone. When he heard the word of God, he returned to Balak and blessed the people whom Balak wanted him to curse.

The New Testament mentions Balaam in three passages. Peter speaks of false teachers who "have forsaken the right way and gone astray, following the way of Balaam" (2 Pet. 2:15). Jude speaks of backsliders who "have run greedily in the error of Balaam for profit" (Jude 11). Balaam's error was greed or covetousness; he was well paid to bring a curse upon the people of Israel.

The nature of Balaam's curse is made clear by John in the Book of Revelation. It refers to some members of the church in Pergamos who held "the doctrine of Balaam, who taught Balak to put a stumbling block before the children of Israel, to eat things sacrificed to idols and to commit sexual immorality" (Rev. 2:14).

Before leaving Balak, Balaam apparently told the Moabite leader that Israel could be defeated if its people were seduced to worship Baal, "to eat things sacrificed to idols and to commit sexual immorality" (Rev. 2:14). Indeed, this was exactly what happened: "The people [of Israel] began to commit harlotry with the women of Moab. They invited the people to the sacrifice of their gods, and the

people ate and bowed down to their gods. So Israel was joined to Baal of Peor, and the anger of the Lord was aroused against Israel" (Num. 25:1-3).

In condemning "the way of Balaam," the New Testament condemns the greed of all who are well paid to tempt God's people to compromise their moral standards.

BALADAN [BAL uh dan] — the father of MERODACH–BALADAN (Is. 39:1), king of Babylon during the reign of Hezekiah, king of Judah.

BALAH [BAY luh] (*withered*) — an unidentified town in southern Judah (Josh. 19:3), also called Bilhah (1 Chr. 4:29) and Baalah (Josh. 15:29).

BALAK [BAY lack] (*destroyer*) — the king of Moab near the end of the wilderness wanderings of the Israelites. Because Balak feared the Israelites, he hired BALAAM the soothsayer to curse Israel (Num. 22—24; Josh. 24:9). But Balaam blessed Israel instead.

BALANCES — devices to measure weight. At the time of the Exodus and following, the Israelites probably used the common balances of Egypt. These balances consisted of a vertical beam and a horizontal crossbeam which was loosely attached to it at its center. A pan was suspended from each end of the crossbeam.

In the Bible, "balances" are often used in a figurative way. The Lord told the Israelites, "You shall have just balances, just weights" (Lev. 19:36; Ezek. 45:10). The "just balances" in these passages symbolize honesty, righteousness, justice, and fair dealing (Job 31:6; Ps. 62:9; Prov. 16:11). "False balances" symbolize evil and bring the displeasure and judgment of God (Prov. 11:1; Mic. 6:11). "A pair of scales" (Rev. 6:5), used in connection with the sale of wheat and barley (v. 6), symbolize famine.

BALDNESS — the condition of having no hair on one's head. Because the Israelites regarded the hair as a special ornament and glory, the condition of baldness carried a stigma of shame. This way of thinking probably expressed Israel's disgust for the practices of certain pagans, who customarily shaved their heads. To shave one's head was to behave like a Canaanite—a person associated with idolatrous and immoral practices.

One of the duties of a priest was to distinguish between natural baldness and baldness caused by leprosy (Lev. 13:40-44). "Baldhead" was a term of contempt and derision hurled by some youths at the prophet Elisha (2 Kin. 2:23). The prophets mention baldness as a sign of mourning (Is. 15:2; Jer. 7:29). Baldness is also used symbolically to indicate the barrenness of Philistia after the judgment of God (Jer. 47:5).

BALM (see PLANTS OF THE BIBLE).

BALM OF GILEAD — a vegetable product of GILEAD exported to such nations as Egypt and Phoenicia. After Joseph's brothers cast him into a pit, they saw an Ishmaelite caravan "coming from Gilead with their camels, bearing spices, balm, and myrrh on their way to carry them down to Egypt" (Gen. 37:25).

Apparently, the balm of Gilead was an aromatic resin used as an incense and a medical ointment used for the healing of wounds. Its identity, however, has not been clearly established. The prophet Jeremiah asked, "Is there no balm in Gilead,/Is there no physician there?" (Jer. 8:22). The New Testament declares that there is a Balm in Gilead: Jesus Christ, the Great Physician.

BALSAM (see PLANTS OF THE BIBLE).

BAMAH [BAY muh] (*high place*) — a "hill-shrine" (Ezek. 20:29, NEB), or place of idolatrous worship. Ezekiel used the word as a term of contempt. Compare the great "high place" at Gibeon (1 Kin. 3:4; 2 Chr. 1:3). Also see HIGH PLACES.

BAMOTH [BAY moth] (*high places*) — a city of Moab, situated east of the Jordan River near Mount Nebo. Bamoth was the site of an encampment during the wilderness journey of the Hebrew people (Num. 21:19-20). The city probably is identical with Bamoth Baal, "the high places of Baal" (Num. 22:41; Josh. 13:17).

BAMOTH BAAL [BAY moth BAY uhl] (see BAMOTH).

BAN — a vow or pledge under which property or persons devoted to pagan worship were destroyed. The Levitical law stated, "No person under the ban [devoted to destruction, NIV] shall be redeemed, but shall surely be put to death" (Lev. 27:29). This was probably the authority under which Joshua destroyed many of the settlements throughout Palestine as the Hebrew people conquered the land (Josh. 6:17-21). Also see ANATHEMA.

BANI [BUH nee] (*built*) — the name of several Old Testament men:

1. A Gadite who was one of David's mighty men (2 Sam. 23:36).

2. A Levite of the Merari family and a son of Shamer (1 Chr. 6:46).

3. A descendant of Judah through Peres (1 Chr. 9:4).

4. Founder of a family that returned with Zerubbabel from Captivity in Babylon (Ezra 2:10). Some members of his family had taken foreign wives (Ezra 10:29). A representative of this family sealed the covenant (Neh. 10:14). The family is also called BINNUI (Neh. 7:15).

5. A descendant of Bani No. 4 who married a foreign wife while in Captivity (Ezra 10:34, 38).

6. The father of Rehum, who was one of the Levites who helped repair part of Jerusalem's walls (Neh. 3:17; 8:7).

7. A Levite who sealed the covenant and regulated the people's devotions after Ezra explained the Law (Neh. 10:13). He may be the same person as Bani No. 6.

8. A Levite of the sons of Asaph (Neh. 11:22). He may be the same person as Bani No. 6 or Bani No. 7.

BANISH — to condemn to exile. Unlike the law codes of the Greeks and Romans, the Mosaic Law made no provision for legal banishment. In effect, however, those who were driven off the land by war were "banished" (Is. 16:3-4), as were those who became self-exiled in fleeing from their crimes (2 Sam. 13:37-38; 14:13-14). According to a strong tradition in the early church, the apostle John was exiled, or banished, to the island of Patmos, where he wrote the Book of Revelation (Rev. 1:9).

BANKER (see OCCUPATIONS AND TRADES).

BANKING — the business of a bank; the occupation of a banker. Institutional banking was not known in ancient Israel until the time of the Captivity (586 B.C.), because money as such did not exist in the ancient world at this time. The lending of money at interest, a traditional function of banks, was forbidden in Old Testament law, at least among native Israelites (Ex. 22:25; Deut. 23:19-20). People protected their valuable possessions by burying them (Matt. 13:44; Luke 19:20) or depositing them in temples or palaces.

During the Captivity the Israelites became familiar with Babylonian banking institutions. Some Jews even joined the banking industry and became prominent officers. By New Testament times banking was an established institution. Although Jesus' parable of the talents (or minas) shows that bankers received money for safekeeping and also paid interest (Matt. 25:27; Luke 19:23), the most common reference to first-century banking in the New Testament is to moneychanging (Matt. 21:12).

BANNER — a flag, ensign, streamer, or emblem attached to the end of a standard. Banners served as rallying points for military, national, or religious purposes. Four large banner-bearing standards (one on each of the four sides of the tabernacle of meeting) were used by the twelve tribes of Israel during their wilderness journeys (Num. 1:52; 2:2-3). A smaller standard, or banner, was used by each separate tribe (Num. 2:2, 34).

The most common use of banners was for military campaigns. A large signal-flag usually was erected on a hill or other high place; it served as a signal for the war-trumpets to be blown (Is. 5:26; 18:3; Jer. 4:6). When the Israelites fought the Amalekites at REPHIDIM, Moses held up his hand, thus becoming a living banner symbolizing God's presence to help His people win the victory (Ex. 17:8-16). After the battle, Moses built an altar and called it "Jehovah-nissi" (Ex. 17:15, KJV; The Lord Is My Banner; NKJV).

BANQUET — an elaborate meal, frequently given in honor of an individual or for some other special occasion.

Notable Old Testament banquets include that of AHASUERUS (Xerxes I), at which Vashti refused to

Photo by Gustav Jeeninga

A baptistry, or bath, used for purification ceremonies in the Essene community at Qumran.

allow herself to be displayed (Esth. 1); the two banquets of ESTHER, at which she exposed the plot of Haman to destroy the Jews (Esth. 5:4; 7:2); and that of Belshazzar, at which the gold and silver vessels stolen from the Temple by Nebuchadnezzar were used and at which the handwriting appeared on the wall (Dan. 5).

The New Testament speaks of the messianic banquet—a banquet at the end of this age—at which the patriarchs and all the righteous will be guests, but from which the wicked will be excluded (Matt. 8:11; Luke 13:29). The Book of Revelation concludes with all people invited to one or the other of the two banquets. At "the supper of the great God" (Rev. 19:17), the scavenger birds are invited to devour the defeated kings of the earth and their armies; at "the marriage supper of the Lamb" (Rev. 19:9), Christ will have fellowship with the faithful.

BAPTISM — a ritual practiced in the New Testament church that is still used in various forms by different denominations and branches of the Christian church. Baptism involves the application of water to the body of a person. It is frequently thought of as an act by which the believer enters the fellowship of the church. Widely differing interpretations of the act exist among Christian groups. They have different views on the nature of baptism, who should be baptized, and the appropriate method by which baptism should be administered.

The Nature of Baptism. Three major positions on the nature of baptism exist among Christian groups.

The sacramental view—According to this belief, baptism is a means by which God conveys grace. By undergoing this rite, the person baptized receives REMISSION of sins, and is regenerated or given a new nature and an awakened or strengthened faith. Both Roman Catholics and Lutherans have this view of the nature of baptism.

The traditional Roman Catholic belief emphasizes the rite itself—that the power to convey grace is contained within the sacrament of baptism. It is not the water but the sacrament as established by God and administered by the church that produces this change.

The Lutherans, on the other hand, concentrate on the faith that is present in the person being baptized. They also emphasize the value of the preaching of the word. Preaching awakens faith in a believer by entering the ear to strike the heart. Baptism enters the eye to reach and move the heart.

One Scripture especially important to the advocates of the sacramental view of baptism is John 3:5: "Unless one is born of water and the Spirit, he cannot enter the kingdom of God." They also believe that the act of baptism itself produces a change in the life of the believer.

The covenantal view—Other Christian groups think of baptism not as a means by which salvation is brought about, but as a sign and seal of the COVENANT. The covenant is God's pledge to save man. Because of what He has done and what He has promised, God forgives and regenerates. On the one hand, baptism is a sign of the covenant. On the other, it is the means by which people enter into that covenant.

The benefits of God's covenant are granted to all adults who receive baptism and to all infants who, upon reaching maturity, remain faithful to the vows made on their behalf at baptism. The covenant, rather than the sacrament or another person's faith, is seen as the means of salvation; and baptism is a vital part of this covenant relationship.

In the covenantal view, baptism serves the same purpose for New Testament believers that circumcision did for Old Testament believers. For the Jews, circumcision was the external and visible sign that they were within the covenant that God had established with Abraham. Converts to Judaism (or proselytes) also had to undergo this rite. But now under the new covenant, baptism instead of circumcision is required.

Circumcision refers to a cutting away of sin and a change of heart (Deut. 10:16; Ezek. 44:7, 9). Similarly, baptism also depicts a washing away of sin (Acts 2:38; Titus 3:5) and a spiritual renewal (Rom. 6:4; Col. 2:11–12). In fact, these two procedures are clearly linked in Colossians 2:11–12: "In Him you were also circumcised with the circumcision made without hands, by putting off the body of the sins of the flesh, by the circumcision of Christ, buried with Him in baptism, in which you also were raised with Him through faith in the working of God, who raised Him from the dead."

The symbolical view—This view stresses the symbolic nature of baptism by emphasizing that baptism does not cause an inward change or alter a person's relationship to God in any way. Baptism is a token, or an outward indication, of the inner change which has already occurred in the believer's life. It serves as a public identification of the person with Jesus Christ, and thus also as a public testimony of the change that has occurred. It is an act of initiation. It is baptism into the name of Jesus.

According to the symbolic view, baptism is not so much an initiation into the Christian life as into the Christian church. A distinction is drawn between the invisible or universal church, which consists of all believers in Christ, and the visible or local church, a gathering of believers in a specific place.

This position explains that the church practices baptism and the believer submits to it because Jesus commanded that this be done and He gave us the example by being baptized Himself. Thus, baptism is an act of obedience, commitment, and proclamation.

According to this understanding of baptism, no spiritual benefit occurs because of baptism. Rather than producing REGENERATION of faith, baptism always comes after faith and the salvation that faith produces. The only spiritual value of baptism is that it establishes membership in the church and exposes the believer to the values of this type of fellowship.

The Subjects of Baptism. Another issue over which Christian groups disagree is the question of who should be baptized. Should only those who have come to a personal, conscious decision of faith be baptized? Or, should children be included in this rite? And if children are proper subjects, should all children, or only the children of believing parents, be baptized?

Infant baptism—Groups that practice baptism of infants baptize not only infants but also adults who have come to faith in Christ. One of the arguments proposed in favor of baptizing infants is that entire households were baptized in New Testament times (Acts 16:15, 33). Certainly such households or families must have included children. Consequently, groups who hold this position believe this practice should be extended to the present day.

A second argument cited is Jesus' treatment of children. Jesus commanded the disciples to bring the children to Him. When they did so, He blessed them (Mark 10:13–16). Because of this example from Jesus, it would seem inconsistent to deny baptism to children today.

A third argument put forth by covenant theologians is that children were participants in the Old Testament covenant: "And I will establish My covenant between Me and you and your descendants after you in their generations, for an everlasting covenant, to be God to you and your descendants after you" (Gen. 17:7). They were present when the covenant was renewed (Deut. 29:10–13; Josh. 8:35). They had a standing in the congregation of Israel and were present in their religious assemblies (Joel 2:16). The promises of God were given to the children as well as adults (Is. 54:13; Jer. 31:34). Circumcision was administered to infants in the Old Testament. Since baptism has now replaced circumcision, it is natural that it should be administered to children, according to those who practice infant baptism.

Those who believe in baptismal regeneration (Catholics especially) argue that baptism of infants is necessary. In traditional Roman Catholic teaching, unbaptized infants who die cannot enter heaven in this state, but are instead consigned to a state of limbo. If this fate is to be avoided, they must be baptized in order to remove the guilt of their sins and receive new life.

Although Lutherans also believe in baptismal regeneration, they are not as certain that God's grace is communicated through this sacrament. They believe that God may have some method, perhaps as yet unrevealed to us, of producing faith in the unbaptized. But this, if it is true, would apply only to children of believers. Lutherans are careful to affirm that this whole area of belief is a mystery, known only to God.

A final argument presented in support of infant baptism is the historical evidence. Infant baptism has been practiced in the church from early times, certainly as early as the second century, according to those groups that baptize infants.

An issue which divides those groups that practice infant baptism is the question of which infants should be baptized. In general, the covenant theologians (Presbyterians, Lutherans, and the various Reformed groups) insist that only the children of believing parents (hence, members of the covenant) should be included. Roman Catholics, however, tend to baptize even infants and children whose parents have not made such a commitment. These different positions on this question show how these groups feel about the role of personal faith in one's salvation.

For Roman Catholics, this question presents no real difficulty, since they believe the sacrament of baptism has power in itself to bring about salvation. The only faith necessary is that someone has enough faith to bring and present the child. Faith is also necessary for the person administering baptism. He must believe that the sacrament has saving power.

Lutherans, however, with their strong emphasis on faith as the means of salvation, face a more difficult problem. It is obvious that an infant does not have faith. One way of handling this problem is to resort to the concept of unconscious faith. Reasoning power and self–consciousness, they point out, must not be thought of as faith. Luther observed that a person does not cease to have faith when he is asleep or when he is preoccupied or working strenuously. Thus Lutherans believe the Bible teaches the implicit faith of infants (Matt. 18:6; Luke 1:15; 1 John 2:13). If Jesus could speak of "these little ones who believe in Me," (Matt. 18:6), and if John the Baptist was filled with the Holy Spirit even from his mother's womb, then little chil-

A baptistry in the form of a cross in the Church of St. John at Ephesus.

Photo by Howard Vos

dren can have implicit faith. Lutherans also believe that the faith necessary for the salvation of children can be communicated through their parents.

For the covenant theologians, the problem of the faith of children is not a difficult issue. It is a potential faith. So also is the salvation. God promises to give the benefits signified in baptism to all adults who receive it by faith. This same promise is extended to all infants who, when they grow to maturity, remain faithful to the vows that were made on their behalf at the time of their baptism. In this view, baptism's saving work depends on the faith that will be, rather than upon the faith that is.

Believer's baptism—Those who hold to this view believe that baptism should be restricted to those who actually exercise faith. This approach excludes infants, who could not possibly have such faith. The proper candidates for baptism are those who already have experienced the new birth on the basis of their personal faith and who give evidence of this salvation in their lives.

Both positive and negative arguments are advanced in support of this view. The positive approach argues from evidence in the New Testament. In every instance of New Testament baptism in which the specific identity of the persons was known, the persons being baptized were adults. Further, the condition required for baptism was personal, conscious faith. Without this, adherents of believer's baptism point out, baptism was not administered. This is especially evident in the Book of Acts (2:37–41; 8:12; 10:47; 18:8; 19:4–5), as well as Matthew 3:2–6 and 28:19. In the New Testament church repentance and faith came first, followed by baptism.

The negative arguments given to support believer's baptism are generally responses to the arguments for infant baptism. One of these revolves around the household baptism issue. Paul spoke the word to the Philippian jailer and all the people in his house. And the jailer "rejoiced, having believed in God with all his household" (Acts 16:34). Crispus, the synagogue ruler, also "believed on the Lord with all his household" (Acts 18:8). Those who hold to believer's baptism only point out that these passages do not state specifically that infants were included among those baptized. All the people in these households could have been adults.

The other argument concerns Jesus' blessing of the children. The believer's baptism position on this incident from Jesus' life is that baptism is not mentioned or even implied. These children illustrate simplicity and trust, like that which all believers should display. Jesus blessed the children, these groups agree, but this was not baptism. Many believer's baptism groups do practice a ritual known as child dedication, which is more nearly a dedication of the parents than of the child.

The Form of Baptism. The final major issue is the method or form of baptism—whether by immersion, pouring, or sprinkling. On this issue, Christian groups organize into two major camps—those which insist upon the exclusive use of immersion, and those which permit and practice other forms.

The immersionist position—This group insists that immersion is the only valid form of baptism. One of their strongest arguments revolves around the Greek word for baptism in the New Testament. Its predominant meaning is "to immerse" or "to dip," implying that the candidate was plunged beneath the water. But there are also other arguments that strongly suggest that immersion was the form of baptism used in the early church.

The *Didache,* a manual of Christian instruction written in A.D. 110–120, stated that immersion should be used generally and that other forms of baptism should be used only when immersion was not possible.

In addition, the circumstances involved in some of the biblical descriptions of baptism imply immersion. Thus, John the Baptist was baptizing in Aenon near Salim, "because there was much water there" (John 3:23). Jesus apparently went down into the water to be baptized by John (Matt. 3:16). The Ethiopian said, "See, here is water. What hinders me from being baptized?" (Acts 8:36).

The symbolism involved in baptism also seems to argue that immersion was the biblical mode, according to those groups that practice immersion exclusively. Romans 6:4–6 identifies baptism with the believer's death (and burial) to sin and resurrection to new life, as well as the death and resurrection of Christ. Only immersion adequately depicts this meaning, according to the immersionist position.

The pluralistic position—Holders of this view believe that immersion, pouring, and sprinkling are all appropriate forms of baptism. They point out that the Greek word for baptism in the New Testament is sometimes ambiguous in its usage. While its most common meaning in classical Greek was to dip, to plunge, or to immerse, it also carried other meanings as well. Thus, the question cannot be resolved upon linguistic grounds.

These groups also argue from inference that immersion must not have been the exclusive method used in New Testament times. For example, could John have been physically capable of immersing all the persons who came to him for baptism? Did the Philippian jailer leave his jail to be baptized? If not, how would he have been immersed? Was enough water for immersion brought to Cornelius' house? Or, did the apostle Paul leave the place where Ananias found him in order to be immersed?

Those groups that use sprinkling or pouring also point out that immersion may not be the best form for showing what baptism really means. They see the major meaning of baptism as purification. They point out that the various cleansing ceremonies in the Old Testament were performed by a variety of means—immersion, pouring, and sprinkling (Mark 7:4; Heb. 9:10). Others note the close association between baptism and the outpouring of the Holy Spirit, which was from above. Thus, in their view, true baptism requires the symbolism of pouring rather than immersion.

BAPTISM OF FIRE — a concept used by John the Baptist to describe the work of Christ: "He [Christ] will baptize you with the Holy Spirit and fire" (Matt. 3:11; Luke 3:16). Some scholars believe that two different baptisms are mentioned here: "the baptism of the Holy Spirit" (the baptism that brings mercy, forgiveness, and life) and "the baptism of fire" (the baptism that brings judgment, condemna-

Photo by Gustav Jeeninga

The tomb of Barnabas on the island of Cyprus in the Mediterranean Sea.

tion, and death). When this interpretation is followed, the baptism of the Holy Spirit belongs to the present age of grace and the baptism of fire belongs to a future age of judgment.

Other scholars believe that only one baptism is meant: Christ baptizes "with the Holy Spirit and fire." They point to the experience of the Day of Pentecost when "there appeared to them divided tongues, as of fire, and one sat upon each of them. And they were all filled with the Holy Spirit" (Acts. 2:3–4). These scholars see this as a reference to the work of the Holy Spirit in purifying God's people.

BAPTISM FOR THE DEAD. A practice mentioned by the apostle Paul (1 Cor. 15:2). The exact meaning of this passage is uncertain. Some scholars believe it refers to a re-baptism of Christians for the benefit of people who had died unbaptized but already believing. But other scholars insist it refers to a baptismal formula in the Corinthian church which promised that believers would rise from the dead at the end of time to reign with Christ.

BAR- [bahr] — the Aramaic equivalent of the Hebrew *ben*, which also means "son." In the New Testament, Bar frequently occurs as the prefix to names of persons, such as Barabbas and Bar-Jonah. The meaning of these names is "son of Abbas," and "son of Jonah."

BARABBAS [buh RAB bas] (*son of Abbas*) — a "robber" (John 18:40) and "notorious prisoner" (Matt. 27:16) who was chosen by the mob in Jerusalem to be released instead of Jesus. Barabbas had been imprisoned for insurrection and murder (Luke 23:19, 25; Mark 15:7). Pilate offered to give the crowd either Jesus or Barabbas. The mob demanded that he release Barabbas and crucify Jesus. There is no further mention of Barabbas after he was released.

BARACHEL [BAR ah kell] (*God has blessed*) — the father of Elihu, who was one of Job's "friends" (Job 32:2, 6).

BARACHIAH [bar ah KIE uh] — a form of BERECHIAH.

BARACHIAS [bar ah KIE us] — a form of BERECHIAH.

BARAK [BAR ack] (*lightning*) — a son of Abinoam of the city of KEDESH. Barak was summoned by DEBORAH, a PROPHETESS who was judging Israel at that time. Deborah told Barak to raise a militia of 10,000 men to fight JABIN, king of Canaan, who had oppressed Israel for 20 years. The commander-in-chief of Jabin's army was SISERA.

Apparently during the battle, the Lord sent a great thunderstorm. The rain swelled the Kishon River and the plain surrounding the battle area, making Sisera's 900 iron chariots useless (Judg. 5:21). The Israelites routed the Canaanites. The victory is described twice: in prose (Judges 4) and in poetry, by the beautiful "Song of Deborah" (Judges 5). Barak is listed in the New Testament among the heroes of faith (Heb. 11:32).

BARBARIAN — A person who is different from the dominant class or group. Originally, this term (*barbaros*) had no negative connotation. The Greeks used it to describe anyone who did not speak the Greek language. Later, when Rome conquered Greece and absorbed its culture, the word *barbarian* signified those whose lives were not ordered by Greco-Roman culture.

When the apostle Paul used the phrase "Greeks and barbarians" (Rom. 1:14), he was speaking of all mankind. The "barbarians" (Acts 28:4, KJV) who aided the apostle Paul on the island of Melita do not appear to have been uncivilized. In this instance the word meant something very similar to the word foreigner. It is good to remember the apostle Paul's declaration that in Christ all human distinctions disappear (Gal. 3:26–29).

BARBER (see OCCUPATIONS AND TRADES).

BAREFOOT — wearing nothing on one's feet. To go barefoot outside was a sign of great distress. The prophet Isaiah "walked naked and barefoot three years" (Is. 20:2–4) to portray the distress and embarrassment that would fall on Egypt and Ethiopia. Going barefoot also was a sign of mourning (2 Sam. 15:30; Ezek. 24:17, 23) and poverty (Luke 15:22).

BARHUMITE [bar HOO mite] — an inhabitant of BAHURIM, a city in the territory of Benjamin (2 Sam. 23:31).

BARIAH [buh RIE ah] (*fleeing*) — a son of Shemaiah, of the tribe of Judah (1 Chr. 3:22).

BAR-JESUS [bar GEE zus] (*son of Jesus*) — a false prophet who opposed Barnabas and Paul at Paphos, a town on the island of Cyprus (Acts 13:4–12). He is also called Elymas, which means a "magician" or "sorcerer." Bar-Jesus was temporarily struck blind because of his opposition to the gospel.

BAR-JONAH [bar JO nuh] (*son of Jonah*) — the family name of the apostle PETER (Matt. 16:17; John 1:42; 21:15–17).

BARKOS [bar KOS] (meaning unknown) — an ancestor of a family of servants in the Temple who returned from the Captivity with Zerubbabel (Ezra 2:53; Neh. 7:55).

BARLEY (see PLANTS OF THE BIBLE).

BARN — a storehouse for seed or grain (Luke 3:17). In biblical times, such granaries or storerooms were usually underground. Also see STOREHOUSE, STORAGE CITY.

BARNABAS [BAR nuh bus] (*son of encouragement*) — an apostle in the early church (Acts 4:36–37; 11:19–26) and Paul's companion on his first missionary journey (Acts 13:1—15:41). A LEVITE from the island of Cyprus, Barnabas' given name was Joseph, or Joses (Acts 4:36). When he became a Christian, he sold his land and gave the money to the Jerusalem apostles (Acts 4:36–37).

Early in the history of the church, Barnabas went to Antioch to check on the growth of this early group of Christians. Then he journeyed to Tarsus and brought Saul (as PAUL was still called) back to minister with him to the Christians in Antioch (Acts 11:25). At this point Barnabas apparently was the leader of the church at Antioch, because his name is repeatedly mentioned before Paul's in the Book of Acts. But after Saul's name was changed to Paul, his name is always mentioned after Paul's (Acts 13:43).

Because of his good reputation, Barnabas was able to calm the fear of Saul among the Christians in Jerusalem (Acts 9:27). He and Saul also brought money from Antioch to the Jerusalem church when it was suffering a great famine (Acts 11:27-30). Shortly thereafter, the Holy Spirit led the Antioch church to commission Barnabas and Paul, along with John Mark, Barnabas' cousin, to make a missionary journey (Acts 13:1-3) to Cyprus and the provinces of Asia Minor.

A rift eventually developed between Barnabas and Paul over John Mark (Col. 4:10). Barnabas wanted to take John Mark on their second missionary journey. Paul, however, felt John Mark should stay behind because he had left the first mission at Cyprus (Acts 13:13). Paul and Barnabas went their separate ways, and Barnabas took John Mark with him on a second mission to Cyprus. Paul and Silas traveled through Syria and Cilicia (Acts 15:36-41).

BARRACKS — a building or group of buildings used for lodging soldiers. The word appears in Book of Acts, where it refers to the Fortress of AN-TONIA in Jerusalem (Acts 21:34; 22:24; 23:10; castle, KJV). The Antonia overlooked the Temple area; it contained the Roman troops that were stationed in Jerusalem to curb any outbreak of violence in the city. When the apostle Paul was threatened by a mob of Jews, soldiers from Antonia rescued him and took him into the barracks for protection. Also see CASTLE.

BARREL — the KJV translation of the Hebrew word *kad,* which means "an earthen jar." The NKJV has bin (1 Kin. 17:12, 14, 16) and WATERPOTS (1 Kin. 18:33).

BARREN — the condition of being unable to bear children. In the Bible, the term is also applied figuratively to anything that is unproductive, such as land (2 Kin. 2:19) or a nation (Is. 54:1). In the Old Testament, barrenness was looked on as a curse or punishment from God (Gen. 16:2; 20:18; 1 Sam. 1:5-7). Old Testament women who are described as barren include Sarah, Rebekah, Rachel, and Hannah (Gen. 11:30; 25:21; 29:31: Judg. 13:2-3; 1 Sam. 2:5).

BARSABAS [BAR sah bus] (son of the sabbath) — the name of two men in the New Testament:

1. Joseph, surnamed Justus, one of the two disciples nominated to replace Judas Iscariot as an apostle (Acts 1:23; Barsabbas, NASB, NEB).

2. A disciple who, along with Silas, was sent as a

Inscribed pottery from Samaria from the eighth century B.C. Two lines of the inscription begin with the name Baruch.

delegate to accompany Paul and Barnabas to Antioch of Syria (Acts 15:22, 27). These delegates carried a letter from the JERUSALEM COUNCIL to the Gentile Christians in Antioch, Syria, and Cilicia, informing them of the council's action (Acts 15:23).

BARSABBAS [BAR sah bus] — a form of BARSABAS.

BARTHOLOMEW [bar THOL oh mew] (*son of Tolmai*) — one of the twelve apostles of Jesus, according to the four lists given in the New Testament (Matt. 10:3; Mark 3:18; Luke 6:14; Acts 1:13). Many scholars equate Bartholomew with NATHANAEL (John 1:45-49), but no proof of this identification exists, except by inference. According to church tradition, Bartholomew was a missionary to various countries, such as Armenia and India. He is reported to have preached the gospel along with Philip and Thomas. According to another tradition, he was crucified upside down after being flayed alive.

BARTHOLOMEW, GOSPEL OF (see APOCRYPHA).

BARTIMAEUS [bar tih MEE us] (*son of Timaeus*) — a blind man of Jericho healed by Jesus (Mark 10:46-52). As he sat by the road begging, Bartimaeus cried out, "Jesus, Son of David, have mercy on me!" (v.47). Jesus replied, "Go your way; your faith has made you well" (v. 52).

BARTIMEUS [bar tih MEE us] — a form of BARTIMAEUS.

BARUCH [BAY rook] (*blessed*) — the name of three or four men in the Old Testament:

1. A son of Zabbai. Baruch helped Nehemiah repair the walls of Jerusalem (Neh. 3:20).

2. A man who sealed the covenant with Nehemiah (Neh. 10:6). He may be the same person as Baruch No. 1.

3. A son of Col–Hozeh and a returned captive of the tribe of Judah (Neh. 11:5).

4. The scribe or secretary of Jeremiah the prophet (Jer. 32:12–16; 36:1–32). A son of Neriah, Baruch was a member of a prominent Judean family. In the fourth year of the reign of Jehoiakim, king of Judah (about 605 B.C.), Baruch wrote Jeremiah's prophecies of destruction from the prophet's dictation (Jer. 36:1–8). Baruch read Jeremiah's words publicly on a day of fasting, then read them to the officials of the king's court.

BARUCH, APOCALYPSE OF (see Apocalyptic Literature).

BARUCH, BOOK OF [BAY rook] (see Apocrypha).

BARZILLAI [bar ZILL ay eye] (*made of iron*) — the name of three men in the Old Testament:

1. A Meholathite whose son was married to one of King Saul's daughters (1 Sam. 18:19; 2 Sam. 21:8).

2. A member of the tribe of Gilead from Rogelim who brought provisions to David and his army at Mahanaim, where they had fled from Absalom (2 Sam. 17:27–29). On his deathbed, David remembered Barzillai's kindness and reminded Solomon to care for his children (1 Kin. 2:7).

3. A priest whose genealogy was lost during the Captivity (Ezra 2:61; Neh. 7:63). Apparently he married a daughter of Barzillai No. 2 and adopted his wife's family name.

BASEMATH [BAHS ih math] (*sweet–smelling perfume*) — the name of two or three women in the Old Testament:

1. One of Esau's wives and the daughter of Elon the Hittite (Gen. 26:34; Bashemath, KJV). She is also called Adah (Gen. 36:2). Esau married her out of spite because Isaac, Esau's father, was displeased with Esau's other wives, who were Canaanites.

2. One of Esau's wives and the daughter of Ishmael (Gen. 36:3–4, 10, 13, 17; Bashemath, KJV). She is also called Mahalath (Gen. 28:9). Some scholars believe she is the same person as Basemath No. 1.

3. A daughter of Solomon and wife of Ahimaaz (1 Kin. 4:15; Basmath, KJV).

BASHAN [BAY shan] (*fertile plain*) — the territory east of the Jordan River and the Sea of Galilee (see Map 3, C–2).

At the time of the Exodus, King Og ruled Bashan. His kingdom included 60 cities (Num. 21:33; Deut. 3:4; 29:7). His capital was at Ashtaroth. When Og was defeated at Edrei (Deut. 3:1–3), the territory was given to the half–tribe of Manasseh (Deut. 3:13), except for the cities of Golan and Be Eshterah, which were give to the Levites (Josh. 21:27). In the days of Jehu, the region was captured by the Aramean king, Hazael (2 Kin. 10:32–33).

A rich, fertile tableland about 490 to 700 meters (1600 to 2300 feet) above sea level, with abundant rainfall and volcanic soil, Bashan became the "breadbasket" of the region. Wheat fields and livestock were abundant. But in the Old Testament, the prosperity of Bashan became a symbol of selfish indulgence and arrogant pride. Evil persons who attacked the righteous were compared to "strong bulls of Bashan" (Ps. 22:12). The pampered, pleasure–seeking women of Samaria were called "cows of Bashan" (Amos 4:1).

BASHAN, MOUNTAIN OF — probably another name for Mount Hermon, situated along the northern border of Bashan (Ps. 68:15).

BASIN — a round, shallow container, such as a cup or bowl, used primarily for holding liquids. Basins were used for washing (John 13:5), for holding wine and other liquids (Ex. 24:6), and for receiving the blood of sacrifices (Zech. 9:15). Usually basins were fashioned out of bronze, brass, or earthenware, although the priests used vessels of bronze or silver (Num. 7:13). The vessels for Solomon's Temple were of gold (1 Chr. 28:17).

The Gospel of John tells how Jesus "poured water into a basin and began to wash his disciples' feet" (John 13:5), teaching them the importance of humility and loving service. When Jesus was eating with His disciples, while dipping His hand in a dish that most likely was a basin, He predicted His betrayal and death (Matt. 26:21–25).

BASKET — a container made of woven cane or other fibers. The Bible provides sparse information about the size and shape of baskets. They were fashioned out of various materials: willow, rush, palm–leaf twigs, and even a mixture of straw and clay. Some had handles and lids. These baskets served various purposes and were known by different names.

Baskets were used for carrying bread (Gen. 40:17), for grape–gathering (Jer. 6:9), for holding the offered first–fruits (Deut. 26:2), for carrying various fruits (Jer. 24:1), for carrying clay to the brickyard (Ps. 81:6), or for holding bulky articles (2 Kin. 10:7). The most ingenious use of these containers was when Paul was lowered in a basket over a wall to escape his foes (Acts 9:25; 2 Cor. 11:33).

When God said to Moses, "Blessed shall be your basket and your kneading bowl" (Deut. 28:5), He emphasized that abundance is the reward of obedient service. But the reverse is indicated in the warning, "Cursed shall be your basket and your kneading bowl" (Deut. 28:17); disobedience leaves empty hands and desolate hearts.

BASKET MAKER (see Occupations and Trades).

Photo by Howard Vos

Part of the elaborate bath complex of the Roman ruler, Herod the Great, discovered at New Testament Jericho.

BASMATH [BAHS math] — a form of BASEMATH.

BASTARD — a person of illegitimate birth. The term may refer to the offspring of incest. Such a person was not allowed to enter the Lord's assembly: "A bastard shall not enter into the congregation of the Lord" (Deut. 23:2, KJV). "A bastard shall dwell in ASHDOD" (Zech. 9:6, KJV) refers to the "mixed race" (other translations are "mongrel people" and "half-breeds") who would settle in the Philistine city.

In the New Testament, the word bastards (Heb. 12:8, KJV) translates the Greek noun *nothoi*, which means "sons born out of wedlock." The "illegitimate children" (NIV) mentioned in this verse are those who do not experience the chastening or discipline of the Lord—those who do not share the privileges of God's children.

BAT (see ANIMALS OF THE BIBLE).

BATH (see WEIGHTS AND MEASURES).

BATHING — a washing or soaking of the body in water for cleansing. Water was scarce in Bible times, but laws of ritual demanded much washing. The Israelites washed their hands after returning from the market, before meals, and at many other times; and they immersed their bodies before entering the synagogue or Temple courts. Archaeologists have discovered such ritual baths close to the broad steps leading up to Herod's Temple, as well as many other archaeological sites.

Bathing for the purpose of physical cleansing or hygiene is seldom mentioned in the Bible. Bathsheba was bathing when David spied her from his rooftop (2 Sam. 11:2). Pharaoh's daughter was on her way to the river to bathe when she found the baby Moses (Ex. 2:5, RSV). At Masada, Herod had splendid Greco-Roman baths with hot and cold water rooms. Archaeologists have discovered a swimming pool at Herod's palace at Jericho which, according to the Jewish historian Josephus, was the scene of Herod's murder of a young priest by drowning.

Even before Abraham's time, the homes of Ur in ancient Mesopotamia had a tile drain in the entryway. A servant met visitors, removed their sandals, and washed their feet. Jesus taught the lesson of becoming a servant by washing the disciples' feet (John 13:3–17). If the home had no servant, it was the wife's duty to perform this task. Therefore, Paul describes the faithful widow as one who has "brought up children...lodged strangers...washed the saints' feet" (1 Tim. 5:10).

BATH RABBIM [bath RAB beam] (*daughter of multitudes*) — a gate in the ancient city of Heshbon. Near this gate were the pools to which the "beloved" compared the beautiful eyes of the SHULAMITE woman (Song 7:4).

BATHSHEBA [bath SHE buh] (meaning unknown) — a wife of Uriah the Hittite and of King David (2 Sam. 11; 12:24). Standing on the flat roof of his palace in Jerusalem one evening, David saw the beautiful Bathsheba bathing on the roof of a nearby house. With his passion aroused, David committed adultery with Bathsheba. Out of that union Bathsheba conceived a child.

When David discovered her pregnancy, he hurriedly sent for Uriah, who was in battle with the Ammonites. But Uriah refused to engage in marital relations with his wife while his companions were involved in battle. When David's attempt to trick Uriah failed, he sent him back into battle. This time, David ordered that Uriah be placed at the front of the battle and that his fellow soldiers retreat from him, so that he might be killed. After a period of mourning, Bathsheba became David's wife (2 Sam. 11:27). But the child conceived in adultery died.

When Nathan the prophet confronted David with the enormity of his sin, David repented (2 Sam. 12:13). God blessed them with four more children—Shammua (or Shimea), Shobab, Nathan, and Solomon (1 Chr. 3:5). The New Testament mentions Bathsheba indirectly in the genealogy of Jesus (Matt. 1:6). Bathsheba is also called Bathshua (1 Chr. 3:5).

BATHSHUA [BATH shoo uh] (*daughter of Shua*) — the name of two women in the Old Testament:

1. A variant form of BATHSHEBA, third wife of King David (1 Chr. 3:5).

2. A wife of Judah (1 Chr. 2:3, RSV).

BATTERING RAM (see ARMS, ARMOR OF THE BIBLE).

BATTLE — armed combat between two enemy forces. Palestine has been the scene of numerous battles. Conflict was so frequent in Old Testament times that the spring of the year was known as "the time when kings go out to battle" (2 Sam. 11:1; 1 Chr. 20:1). The first battle mentioned in the Bible is the one in which CHEDORLAOMER and three other kings attacked the five kings who ruled over the cities of the plain (Gen. 14:8). The last mentioned is the battle of ARMAGEDDON, also called "the battle of that great day of God Almighty" (Rev. 16:14;

Photo by Howard Vos

Assyrian archers and slingers in a battle scene from the palace of King Sennacherib at Nineveh.

also Rev. 20:8). Also see ARMS; WAR.

BATTLE AX, BATTLE BOW (see ARMS, ARMOR OF THE BIBLE).

BATTLEMENT — a protective wall surrounding the flat roofs of houses in Bible times. This wall was required by law (Deut. 22:8, KJV) to prevent accidental injuries by falling. "Battlements" (Jer. 5:10, KJV) on a city wall also served to protect soldiers from enemy attack (Song 8:9, NKJV, RSV; Zeph. 1:16, RSV).

BAVAI [BAHV ay eye] (*wisher*) — an Israelite who helped rebuild the wall of Jerusalem (Neh. 3:18; Bavvai, NASB, RSV).

BAVVAI [BAHV ay eye] — a form of BAVAI.

BAY TREE (see PLANTS OF THE BIBLE).

BAZLITH [BAZ lihth] (*asking*) — one of the NETHINIM (Temple servants) whose descendants returned from the Captivity (Ezra 2:52; Neh. 7:54).

These six-inch high wooden models of an Egyptian infantry unit were discovered in an Egyptian tomb which dated to about 1800 B.C.

BDELLIUM (see JEWELS AND PRECIOUS STONES).

BEALIAH [bee ah LIE uh] (*Jehovah is Lord*) — a Benjamite warrior who joined David at Ziklag (1 Chr. 12:5).

BEALOTH [BEE uh loth] (*possessors*) — the name of two towns in the Old Testament:
1. A town in southern Judah (Josh. 15:24). It may be identical with Baalath Beer (Josh. 19:8).
2. A town associated with the territory of Asher (1 Kin. 4:16, RSV). Baanah was in charge of this administrative district under Solomon.

BEAM — a huge timber that supports the roof and floor of a large building. Heavy wooden beams, cut from the famed cedars of Lebanon, were used in the construction of the Temple in Solomon's time (1 Kin. 6:36). Also see ARCHITECTURE.

BEAN (see PLANTS OF THE BIBLE).

BEAR (see ANIMALS OF THE BIBLE).

BEARD — the hair on a man's face. In biblical times most adult males of Israel wore full beards. An oiled and well-kept beard was a mark of pride (Ps. 133:2). The Law of Moses required Israelite men not to "disfigure the edges" of their beards (Lev. 19:27), a common practice of Israel's pagan neighbors.
To shave or pull out part of the beard was a sign of grief (Jer. 48:37–38), and to cut off someone's beard was to insult him (2 Sam. 10:4–5). Isaiah 7:20 pictures God's judgment on Israel as a shaving of the nation's beard, an intentional disgrace. The word beard does not appear in the New Testament.

BEAST — literally, an animal; figuratively, a symbol, often prophetic. The word beast is used literally in three ways in the Bible: (1) any animal, both CLEAN and UNCLEAN (Gen. 6:7; 7:2; Lev. 11:1–8); (2) a wild animal, as distinguished from domesticated animals (Gen. 1:24; 7:21; 37:20; Ex. 23:11); and (3) a domesticated animal (Gen. 1:24; 2:20; Ex. 19:13).
As a prophetic symbol, the word beast is used especially in the Book of Daniel and the Book of Revelation. The four beasts of Daniel symbolize four cruel, tyrannical governments: (1) a lion (Babylon); (2) a bear (Media); (3) a leopard (Persia); and (4) a dreadful and terrible beast (Greece). See Daniel 7:3–7. In the Book of Revelation, two beasts are described in detail: the beast from the sea, a composite of the four beasts of Daniel (Rev. 13:1–10), and the beast from the land (Rev. 13:11–18). Apparently, these two beasts symbolize political and religious power respectively.
In John's day, at the time when he wrote the Book of Revelation, the two "beasts" which opposed and persecuted the church were the Roman Empire (the political "beast from the sea") and the cult of emperor worship (the religious "beast from the land"). Together with the Dragon (Satan), they formed an unholy trinity that tried to destroy God's people.

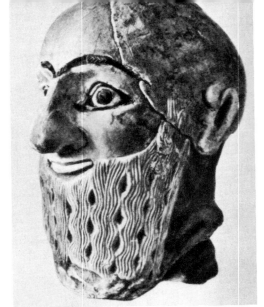

Plaster head discovered in the excavation of Mari in Mesopotamia, showing the full beard worn by ancient Sumerian and Hebrew men.

The Bible often uses the word beast in other symbolical or figurative ways. For instance, the psalmist wrote, "I was like a beast before You" (Ps. 73:22), referring to his foolish, ignorant, and brutish behavior. The apostle Paul wrote, "I have fought with beasts at Ephesus" (1 Cor. 15:32)—a metaphor for the enemies who fought ferociously against him and the gospel of Christ which he preached.
Also see ANIMALS OF THE BIBLE.

BEATING — a form of physical punishment commonly used throughout the ancient world. Beating was administered with a rod, as distinguished from scourging, which was administered with a whip. The Law of Moses recognized beating as a legal punishment. The offender was forced to lie down, then was beaten with 40 blows (Deut. 25:2–3). Later Jewish practice reduced such beatings to 39 blows—"forty stripes minus one," lest the Law of Moses be broken through an oversight. Thus the apostle Paul was beaten "forty stripes minus one" on five occasions (2 Cor. 11:24). Also see SCOURGE.

BEATITUDES, THE — the eight declarations of blessedness made by Jesus at the beginning of the Sermon on the Mount (Matt. 5:3–12), each beginning with "Blessed are..." Some scholars speak of seven, nine, or ten beatitudes, but the number appears to be eight (verses 10–12 of Matthew 5 being one beatitude).
The Greek word translated blessed means "spiritual well-being and prosperity," the deep joy of the soul. The blessed have a share in salvation, and have entered the kingdom of God, experiencing a

foretaste of heaven. Some scholars render each beatitude as an exclamation: "O the bliss [or blessedness] of..."

The Beatitudes describe the ideal disciple, and his rewards, both present and future. The person whom Jesus describes in this passage has a different quality of character and lifestyle than those still "outside the kingdom."

As a literary form, the beatitude is also found often in the Old Testament, especially in the Psalms (1:1; 34:8; 65:4; 128:1), and often in the New Testament also (John 20:29; 14:22; James 1:12; Rev. 14:13). Also see SERMON ON THE MOUNT.

BEAUTIFUL GATE (see GATES OF JERUSALEM AND THE TEMPLE).

BEBAI [BEE buh eye] (*fatherly*) — the name of two or three men in the Old Testament:

1. An ancestor of Israelites who returned from the Captivity. The people of Bebai numbered 623 (Ezra 2:11) or 628 (Neh. 7:16).

2. An ancestor of other Israelites who returned from the Captivity (Ezra 8:11; 10:28). This Bebai may be the same person as Bebai No. 1.

3. One who sealed the covenant after the Captivity (Neh. 10:15).

BECHER [BECK ur] (*youth*) — the name of one or two men in the Old Testament:

1. The second son of Benjamin (Gen. 46:21; 1 Chr. 7:6, 8). Becher went to Egypt with Jacob. Some scholars believe he married an Ephraimite heiress, whose family had been decimated by the Philistines, in order to raise up children to her clan.

2. A son of Ephraim and head of the family of the Bachrites (Num. 26:35). He is also called Bered (1 Chr. 7:20). He may be the same person as Becher No. 1.

BECHERITES [BECK ur ites] — a form of BACHRITES.

BECHORATH [beh KOE rath] (*firstborn*) — an ancestor of Saul, the first king of Israel (1 Sam. 9:1; Becorath, NAS, RSV).

BECORATH [beh KOE rath] — a form of BECHORATH.

BED, BEDROOM — a place for reclining and sleeping. Even the best beds in Bible times would be considered uncomfortable by modern standards. Most people slept on a mat spread on the floor. During the day, the mats were rolled up and stored. Sometimes the mats were placed on a raised platform, above cold drafts during the winter time.

The wealthier classes often had an actual bed to sleep on. The simplest bed was a rectangular wooden frame on legs. Ropes or webs of cloth were stretched across the frame, on which a mat was placed. Some of the wealthy had very elaborate bed frames with gold and silver trim and ivory inlay. Amos, in speaking of beds of ivory (Amos 6:4), probably referred to the ivory trim that decorated their beds.

Poor people usually slept in their clothes with a cloak or cover to ward off the cold. Most people of this class had a single cloak that served as both their coat and also as their cover at night. The Mosaic law forbade the Israelites from keeping a cloak, taken to secure a debt, beyond sunset to make sure the person had a cover to sleep under (Ex. 22:26–27, Deut. 24:13).

In the summer, it was common for people to move onto the roof and sleep in the open. Roofs were usually flat, serving as living quarters when the weather allowed. The houses of the wealthy would frequently have separate sleeping quarters. If the house had two floors, the second story was the preferred location for a bedroom. A Shunammite woman provided Elisha with his own separate room on the roof because he frequently stayed with the woman and her elderly husband. The room was furnished with a bed, a table, a chair, and a lampstand (2 Kin. 4:10). This represented well-equipped sleeping quarters in that day. This is in keeping with the description of the lady as "a notable woman" (v. 8), one of social prominence and wealth.

In the Bible the bed is seen not only as a place to sleep, but also as a place of meditation and prayer. For instance, David meditated on his bed late at night (Ps. 63:6); and the prophets received revelations from God while lying on their beds (1 Sam. 3:3). A bed was also a place of ease and luxury (Amos 6:4), laziness (Prov. 26:14), and scheming (Ps. 36:4).

BEDAD [BEE dad] (*separation*) — the father of Hadad, king of Edom (Gen. 36:35; 1 Chr. 1:46).

BEDAN [BEE dan] (*son of judgment*) — the name of two men in the Old Testament:

1. A judge of Israel (1 Sam. 12:11). He is not mentioned in the Book of Judges, however.

2. A son of Ulam of the tribe of Manasseh (1 Chr. 7:17).

BEDEIAH [bee DIE yuh] (*servant of Jehovah*) — a son of Bani who divorced his pagan wife after the Captivity (Ezra 10:35).

BEE (see ANIMALS OF THE BIBLE).

BEELIADA [bee uh LIE ah duh] (*Baal knows*) — a son of David (1 Chr. 14:7). He is also called Eliada (2 Sam. 5:16; 1 Chr. 3:8).

BEELZEBUB [bee EL zih bub] — New Testament form of Baal Zebub (see GODS, PAGAN).

BEELZEBUL [bee EL zih buhl] — a form of Baal Zebub (see GODS, PAGAN).

BEER [BEE ear] (*a well*) — the name of two places in the Old Testament:

1. A place in the land of Moab where the Israelites camped during their wanderings (Num. 21:16–18). Beer is possibly the same place as Beer Elim (Is. 15:8).

2. A town in the tribe of Judah to which Jotham fled from his brother Abimelech (Judg. 9:21). This Beer is possibly the same place as BEEROTH.

BEER ELIM [BEE ear EH leum] (*well of heroes*) — a village of Southern Moab (Is. 15:8), possibly the same place where the Israelites rested during their wilderness journey (Num. 21:16). See BEER No. 1.

BEER LAHAI ROI [BEE ear lah HIGH roy] (*the well of the Living One*) — a well in the wilderness between Kadesh Barnea and Bered in the Desert of Shur (Gen. 16:14). It received its name when an angel appeared to Hagar in this place. Hagar's son Ishmael lived here both before and after the death of Abraham his father (Gen. 24:62; 25:11).

BEERA [bee EAR ah] (*expounder*) — a descendant of Asher (1 Chr. 7:37).

BEERAH [bee EAR ah] (*expounder*) — a chieftain of the Reubenites who was deported to Assyria by TIGLATH-PILESER (1 Chr. 5:6).

BEERI [bee EAR ih] (*man of a fountain*) — the name of two men in the Old Testament:
1. A Hittite, the father of Judith (Gen. 26:34).
2. The father of HOSEA the prophet (Hos. 1:1).

BEEROTH [bee uh ROTH] (*wells*) — the name of two places in the Old Testament:
1. A place on the border of Edom where Israel camped during its wilderness wandering (Deut. 10:6). This place is variously translated as "Beeroth of the children of Jaakan" (KJV); "the wells of Bene Jaakan" (NKJV); and "Beeroth-bene-jaakan" (NEB). Beeroth may possibly be the modern Birein, located north of Kadesh Barnea.
2. A city of Gibeon assigned to the tribe of Benjamin. It was one of four cities of the Hivites that deceived Joshua into making a treaty of peace (Josh. 9:17; 18:25; 2 Sam. 4:2).

BEEROTH BENE JAAKAN [bee uh ROTH BEN e JAY uh can] — a form of BEEROTH.

BEEROTHITE [bee uh ROTH ite] — a native or inhabitant of BEEROTH (2 Sam. 4:2-3), also spelled Berothite (1 Chr. 11:39).

BEERSHEBA [BEE ur SHE buh] (*well of the seven*) — the chief city of the NEGEV (see Map 2, C-1). Beersheba was situated in the territory of Simeon (Josh. 19:1-2) and was "at the limits of the tribe of the children of Judah, toward the border of Edom in the South" (Josh. 15:21). Midway between the Mediterranean Sea and the southern end of the Dead Sea, Beersheba was considered the southern extremity of the Promised Land, giving rise to the often-used expression, "from Dan [in the north] to Beersheba" (Judg. 20:1) or "from Beersheba to Dan" (1 Chr. 21:2).

In Beersheba Abraham and Abimelech, king of GERAR (in Philistia), made a covenant and swore an oath of mutual assistance (Gen. 21:31). Abraham pledged to Abimelech seven ewe lambs to bear witness to the sincerity of his oath; from this transaction came the name Beersheba. It was in the Wilderness of Beersheba that Hagar wandered as she fled from Sarah (Gen. 21:33). Abraham dug a well and also planted a tamarisk tree here (Gen.

21:33), and he returned to Beersheba after God prevented him from offering Isaac as a sacrifice on Mount Moriah (Gen. 22:19).

At Beersheba a number of important encounters took place between God and man. Here God appeared to Hagar (Gen. 21:17), Isaac (Gen. 26:23-33), and Jacob (Gen. 46:1-5). Ancient Beersheba has been identified with a large tract known as Tell es-Saba, situated about three kilometers (two miles) east of the modern city.

BEETLE (see ANIMALS OF THE BIBLE).

BEGGAR (see OCCUPATIONS AND TRADES).

BEGINNING — a title for Christ which describes His existence before time began. The Gospel of John declares that Jesus was present with the Father in the "beginning," and, therefore, the Creator of all things (John 1:2). Christ is called "the Beginning" (Col. 1:18), "the Beginning of the creation of God" (Rev. 3:14), and "the Beginning and the End" (Rev. 1:8; 21:6; 22:13).

BEGOTTEN — a New Testament word that describes Christ as the only, or unique, Son of His heavenly Father (John 3:16-18; Heb. 11:17; 1 John 4:9). The Greek word expresses the idea of distinctiveness—"one of a kind." As the unique, sinless Son, Jesus accomplished our salvation through His death on the cross.

BEHEMOTH [bee uh MOTH] (see ANIMALS OF THE BIBLE).

BEKAH [beh KAH] (see MONEY OF THE BIBLE; WEIGHTS AND MEASURES).

BEL [bell] (see GODS, PAGAN).

BEL AND THE DRAGON (see APOCRYPHA).

BELA [BEE lah] (*consuming* or *devouring*) — the name of three men and one place in the Old Testament:
1. One of the cities of the plain near the Dead Sea; it is identified as Zoar (Gen. 14:2).
2. A king of Edom (Gen. 36:32-33; 1 Chr. 1:43-44) who reigned in the city of Dinhabah, possibly situated just south of the River Arnon.
3. The oldest son of Benjamin and the head of the family of Belaites (Gen. 46:21; Num. 26:38, 40). The name is also spelled Belah (Gen. 46:21).
4. A son of Ahaz, of the tribe of Reuben (1 Chr. 5:8).

BELAH [BEE lah] — a form of BELA.

BELAITES [BEE luh ites] — descendants of BELA (Num. 26:38).

BELIAL [BEE lih uhl] (*worthlessness*) — an Old Testament term designating a person as godless or lawless. The NKJV translates corrupt (1 Sam. 2:12), perverted (Judg. 19:22), rebel (2 Sam. 20:1), scoundrel (1 Kin. 21:10, 13), worthless men (1 Sam. 30:22), and worthless rogues (2 Sam. 16:7). A "daughter of Belial" (1 Sam. 1:16, KJV) means a wicked woman (NKJV, NIV), one who is base (RSV) and worthless (NASB).

Belial sometimes takes the form of a proper name (or a personification), applied to a demon or to Satan (Nah. 1:15). Many scholars believe that Belial is another name for SATAN.

BELIEVE, BELIEVERS — to place one's trust in God's truth; one who takes God at His word and trusts in Him for salvation.

Mere assent to God's truth is not saving faith, according to the Bible (John 8:31–46; Acts 8:13–24; James 2:14–26). Neither is total commitment of oneself to Jesus as Lord a form of saving faith. Such a view places too much emphasis on the act of belief, as opposed to the object of belief—Jesus Christ. This view also goes beyond the biblical evidence of faith as reception of a gift (John 4:1–42; Eph. 2:8–10).

A belief that saves is one that rests in the finished work of Christ; it trusts God alone for salvation (John 3:16). Believers are those who have trusted God with their will as well as their mind (Rom. 1:16; 3:22; 1 Thess. 1:7). Some of the classic New Testament references dealing with belief, or faith, are John 3:16, 36; Acts 16:31; Rom. 3:21—5:1; Gal. 2:16; Eph. 2:8–10; and 1 John 5:1.

BELL (see MUSICAL INSTRUMENTS).

BELLOWS (see TOOLS OF THE BIBLE).

BELLY — the stomach or abdominal region of the human body (Judg. 3:21–22; Ps. 17:14). The word rendered as "belly" in some translations is translated as "heart" in others. In the New Testament, John used belly (KJV; heart, NKJV) as a figure of a person's true inner self—his intellectual and emotional life (John 7:38). The apostle Paul thought of the belly, or the heart, as the seat of one's physical appetites, sensual pleasures, and worldly satisfactions (Rom. 16:18; Phil. 3:19).

BELOVED DISCIPLE — a title for one of the 12 disciples of Jesus (John 13:23; 19:26; 20:2; 21:7, 20). Many scholars believe it refers to the apostle JOHN.

BELSHAZZAR [bell SHAZ zur] (*Bel, protect the king*) — the oldest son of Nabonidus and the last king of the Neo–Babylonian Empire (Dan. 5:1–2; 7:1; 8:1). According to Daniel 5, Belshazzar was a king given to sensual pleasure. He held a drunken banquet involving his wives, concubines, and a thousand of his lords, or 'nobles' (Dan. 5:1, NAS, NIV, NEB). At the banquet Belshazzar and his guests drank from the sacred vessels which his "father" (Dan. 5:2)—or grandfather—Nebuchadnezzar had brought from the Temple in Jerusalem, thus insulting the captive Jews and their God.

In the midst of the revelry, the fingers of a hand began writing these words on the wall: "MENE, MENE, TEKEL, UPHARSIN" (Dan. 5:25). Daniel tells us that upon seeing these words Belshazzar became troubled "so that the joints of his hips loosened and his knees knocked against each other" (Dan. 5:6).

At the queen's advice, Belshazzar sent for Daniel, who interpreted the writing as a signal of doom for the Babylonian Empire: "MENE: God has numbered your kingdom, and finished it; TEKEL: You have been weighed in the balances, and found wanting; PERES: Your kingdom has been divided, and given to the Medes and Persians" (Dan. 5:26–28). That very night, the soldiers of DARIUS the

Excavations at ancient Beersheba near Jerusalem in southern Palestine.
Photo: Levant Photo Service

Mede—possibly another name for Cyrus the Persian—captured Babylon and Belshazzar was killed.

BELT (see Arms, Armor of the Bible; Dress of the Bible).

BELTESHAZZAR [bell tuh SHAZ zur] (*may Bel protect his life*) — the Hebrew form of the Babylonian name given to Daniel by the chief of Nebuchadnezzar's eunuchs (Dan. 1:7; 5:12). This name should not be confused with Belshazzar.

BEN [bin] (*son*) — the name of a man and a Hebrew word used as a prefix in the Old Testament:
1. A Levite at the time when the Ark of the Covenant was brought to Jerusalem (1 Chr. 15:18).
2. The Hebrew prefix which means "son." Usually it referred to a male descendant, as a prefix in proper names, such as Ben-Ammi, "son of my people" (Gen. 19:38); and Ben-Oni, "son of my sorrow" (Gen. 35:18). Occasionally, however, the word is used as a term of endearment, as when Eli called Samuel "my son" (1 Sam. 3:6, 16). When preceding a word that defines some quality, ability, or characteristic, ben can be used descriptively. For example, "sons of Belial" (Judg. 19:22, KJV) means "perverted men."

BEN-ABINADAB [BEN ah BIN uh dab] (*son of Abinadab*) — a son-in-law of King Solomon and one of the 12 officers who provided food for the king and his household (1 Kin. 4:11).

BEN-AMMI [ben AHM ih] (*son of my people*) — a son of Lot and founder of the Ammonites (Gen. 19:32–38).

BEN-DEKAR [ben dih CAR] — a form of Ben-Deker.

BEN-DEKER [ben DECK ur] (*son of Deker*) — one of the 12 officers who provided food for King Solomon and his household (1 Kin. 4:9; Ben-dekar, NEB).

BEN-GEBER [ben GHE bur] (*son of a strong man*) — one of Solomon's supply officers who provided food for the royal household (1 Kin. 4:13).

BEN-HADAD [ben HAY dad] (*son of* [the god] *Hadad*) — the name of two or three kings of Damascus in Syria during the ninth and eighth centuries B.C. Because more than one king had this name, it is not always possible to be certain which king is indicated by a given reference in the Old Testament.
1. Ben-Hadad I (900—860? B.C.), "the son of Tabrimmon, the son of Hezion, king of Syria" (1 Kin. 15:18). Ben-Hadad I was king of Damascus during the reign of Israel's King Baasha (909–886 B.C.). These two kings joined in an alliance to invade Judah, but King Asa of Judah persuaded Ben-Hadad to change sides by paying him to invade Israel instead (1 Kin. 15:19–20; 2 Chr. 16:1–4). This forced Baasha to withdraw from Judah to protect his own interests. This Ben-Hadad is also known from the famous stone monument which he erected

after making a treaty with King Pygmalion of Tyre about 860 B.C.
2. Ben-Hadad II (860–843? B.C.), the son of Ben-Hadad I. Ben-Hadad I may have reigned as long as 57 years (900–843 B.C.). If so, the information given here about Ben-Hadad II would properly refer to Ben-Hadad I. However, it is likely that Ben-Hadad I died sometime during the reign of King Ahab of Israel (874–852 B.C.) and was succeeded by a son, Ben-Hadad II. The Bible does not mention this transition, but Assyrian records from 853 B.C. do mention Hadadezer as king of Damascus. This was probably the throne name used by a new king, Ben-Hadad II.

This Ben-Hadad also continued to invade and oppress the northern kingdom of Israel each year during the reign of King Ahab. Finally, Ahab defeated the Syrians in two successive years and captured Ben-Hadad (1 Kin. 20:1–33). As a price for releasing Ben-Hadad, Ahab received the right for Israelite merchants to trade in the marketplaces of Damascus (1 Kin. 20:34).

In 853 B.C. Ben-Hadad II led a coalition of neighboring nations, including Israel, in a major battle in Qarqar in Syria against the forces of Shalmaneser III, king of Assyria. Shalmaneser, who had been exacting tribute from Syria and Palestine under the threat of military destruction, was driven out of Palestine. Some time later, Ahab of Israel and King Jehoshaphat of Judah joined forces to attack Ben-Hadad II. Their object was to regain Ramoth Gilead, originally part of Israel. Ahab and Jehoshaphat ignored the unpleasant warning of defeat spoken by Micaiah, a true prophet of the Lord, and were defeated by Ben-Hadad II. Ahab also lost his life in the battle (1 Kin. 22:1–38).

Ben-Hadad II is probably the unnamed "king of Syria" whose officer Naaman was healed of leprosy by the prophet Elisha (2 Kin. 5:1–19). Ben-Hadad himself also sent a servant, Hazael, to inquire of Elisha concerning his own illness (2 Kin. 8:7–10). Hazael later murdered Ben-Hadad and became King of Damascus (Syria), just as Elisha had prophesied (2 Kin. 8:12–15). Hazael also oppressed Israel during his reign (2 Kin. 10:32; 13:22). Hazael reigned as king of Syria from about 843 B.C. to about 798 B.C.

3. Ben-Hadad III, the son of Hazael. He succeeded his father as king of Damascus about 798 B.C. and reigned until about 722 B.C. When the Israelite king Joash (798–782 B.C.) came to power, he won back Israelite territory from Ben-Hadad III, defeating him in battle three times (2 Kin. 13:25). Joash's son, King Jeroboam II, also was successful in battle against Ben-Hadad III and expanded Israel to its full borders (2 Kin. 14:13–28).

Having failed in his battles against Israel, Ben-Hadad III led a coalition of Syrian kings against Zakir, the king of Hamath, who had attempted to expand his kingdom at the expense of the other kings. Ben-Hadad lost this war also. An Aramaic stone monument mentions Ben–Hadad III by name. Eventually, "the palaces of Ben–hadad" (Amos 1:4) in Damascus were destroyed by invading Assyrian armies, just as the prophet Amos had predicted.

BEN–HAIL [ben HAY ill] (*son of strength*) — a prince and teacher during the reign of King Jehoshaphat of Judah (2 Chr. 17:7; Ben–hayil, NEB).

BEN–HANAN [ben HAY nan] (*son of grace*) — a son of Shimon, of the tribe of Judah (1 Chr. 4:20).

BEN–HAYIL [ben HAY ill] — a form of BEN–HAIL.

BEN–HESED [ben HEE sid] (*faithfulness*) — one of Solomon's 12 supply officers, in charge of three cities in the Plain of Sharon: Arubboth, Sochoh, and Hepher (1 Kin. 4:10).

BEN–HUR [ben HER] (*son of Hur*) — one of Solomon's 12 supply officers responsible for providing food for the royal household (1 Kin. 4:8).

BEN–JAHAZIEL [ben JAY zih el] (*son of Jahaziel*) — a chief of the people who returned from the Captivity in Babylon (Ezra 8:5).

BEN JOSIPHIAH [ben joe zy FIE uh] (*son of Josiphiah*) — one of the sons of Bani who returned from the Captivity with Ezra (Ezra 8:10).

BEN–ONI [ben OWN ih] (*son of my pain*) — the name given by the dying Rachel to her newborn son (Gen. 35:18). Jacob later changed the name to BENJAMIN.

BEN–ZOHETH [ben ZOE heth] (*son of Zoheth*) — a son of Ishi, of the tribe of Judah (1 Chr. 4:20).

BENAIAH [beh NIE yuh] (*Jehovah has built*) — the name of 11 or 12 men in the Old Testament:
 1. One of David's mighty men (2 Sam. 23:30; 1 Chr. 27:14).
 2. A loyal supporter of David and Solomon (1 Kin. 1:8; 4:4; 1 Chr. 27:5). Benaiah commanded the CHERETHITES and the PELETHITES, David's bodyguard (2 Sam. 8:18; 20:23; 1 Chr. 18:17). A Levite, Benaiah remained loyal to David when David's son Absalom rebelled. When another of David's sons, Adonijah, tried to seize the king's throne and prevent Solomon from becoming king, Benaiah escorted Solomon to Gihon, where he was anointed king (1 Kin. 1:32–45). Benaiah carried out Solomon's orders to execute Adonijah (1 Kin. 2:25) and Joab (1 Kin. 2:34). Solomon then made Benaiah commander in chief over the army (1 Kin. 2:35). Benaiah was famous for three courageous deeds: (1) climbing down into a pit and killing a lion; (2) killing two lion-like warriors of Moab; and (3) killing an Egyptian giant with the giant's own weapon (2 Sam. 23:20–22; 1 Chr. 11:22–24).
 3. The head of a family of the tribe of Simeon during Hezekiah's reign (1 Chr. 4:36).
 4. A priest who played the harp before the ARK OF THE COVENANT when it was being brought by David to Jerusalem (1 Chr. 15:18, 20, 24; 16:5–6).
 5. The father of one of David's counselors (1 Chr. 27:34).

 6. The grandfather of JAHAZIEL (2 Chr. 20:14).
 7. A Levite overseer of offerings in the Temple during Hezekiah's reign (2 Chr. 31:13).
 8, 9, 10, 11. Four men who had married pagan wives during the Captivity and who heeded Ezra's call to divorce them. They were sons of Parosh, Pahath-Moab, Bani, and Nebo respectively (Ezra 10:25, 30, 35, 43).
 12. The father of PELATIAH (Ezek. 11:1, 13).

BENCH — the rowing bench of a ship (Ezek. 27:6, KJV). The same Hebrew word is used for the "boards" of acacia wood in the tabernacle (Ex. 26:15).

BENE BERAK [ben in BEH rack] (*sons of lightning*) — a town allotted to the tribe of Dan (Josh. 19:45). It is now identified with Ibn Ibrak, situated about six kilometers (four miles) east of modern Jaffa (Joppa).

BENE JAAKAN [ben eh JAY ah can] (*sons of intelligence*) — a place on the border of Edom where the wandering Israelites camped (Num. 33:31–32). JAAKAN, one of the sons of Ezer, apparently gave his name to this place (1 Chr. 1:42); he is called Akan in Genesis 36:27. Also see BEEROTH.

BENE–KEDEM [ben eh KED um] (*sons of the East*) — a people or peoples, often mentioned together with the Midianites and the Amalekites, who lived east of the Jordan River (Judg. 6:3).

BENEDICTION — a prayer that God may bestow certain blessings on His people. In Old Testament times, a regular part of the Temple service was pronouncing the benediction. The form of the priestly benediction was prescribed in the law: "The Lord bless you and keep you;/The Lord make His face shine upon you,/And be gracious to you;/And give you peace" (Num. 6:24–26).
 The so-called Apostolic benediction is often used at the conclusion of a Christian worship service: "The grace of the Lord Jesus Christ, and the love of God, and the communion of the Holy Spirit be with you all. Amen" (2 Cor. 13:14).

BENEFACTOR — a title bestowed upon gods, kings, and people of outstanding achievement. Jesus spoke of Gentile kings who exercise power and authority over their subjects as "benefactors" (Luke 22:25). He contrasted this earthly system with the kingdom of God. His disciples should not seek to be served but to serve others.

BENINU [beh NIE noo] (*our son*) — a Levite who sealed the covenant after returning from the Captivity (Neh. 10:13).

BENJAMIN [BEN juh mun] (*son of the right hand*) — the name of three or four men in the Old Testament:
 1. Jacob's youngest son, born to his favorite wife, RACHEL (Gen. 35:18, 24). After giving birth to Benjamin, the dying Rachel named him Ben-Oni (Gen. 35:18), which means "son of my pain." But Jacob

renamed him Benjamin. When Jacob lost his beloved son JOSEPH, he became very attached to Benjamin because Benjamin was the only surviving son of Rachel. When his sons went to Egypt in search of food to relieve a famine, Jacob was reluctant to let Benjamin go with them (Gen. 43:1–17).

It is apparent that Joseph also loved Benjamin, his only full brother (Gen. 43:29–34). During this trip Joseph ordered that his silver cup be planted in Benjamin's sack. The reaction of Jacob and Benjamin's brothers shows the great love they had for Benjamin (Gen. 44). Benjamin had five sons and two grandsons, and he became the founder of the tribe that carried his name (Gen. 46:21; Num. 26:38–41; 1 Chr. 7:6–12; 8:1–40).

2. A son of Bilhan, a Benjamite (1 Chr. 7:10).

3. A son of Harim who lived in Jerusalem following the return from the Captivity. Benjamin divorced his pagan wife at Ezra's urging (Ezra 10:31–32).

4. A priest during the time of Nehemiah (Neh. 12:34) who helped repair and dedicate the wall of Jerusalem (Neh. 3:23). He may be the same person as Benjamin No. 3.

BENJAMIN, TRIBE OF — the tribe descended from Benjamin (Num. 1:36–37; Judg. 1:21). Its northern boundary ran westward from the Jordan River through Bethel and just south of Lower Beth Horon; its western boundary picked up at this point to Kirjath Jearim; its southern border ran eastward to the northern point of the Dead Sea; and its easternmost limit was the Jordan River (Josh. 18:11–20). The chief towns in this hilly, fertile region were Jerusalem, Jericho, Bethel, Gibeon, Gibeath, and Mizpah (Josh. 18:21–28).

Saul, Israel's first king, was a Benjamite, and the Benjamites supported Saul over David (2 Sam. 2:9, 15; 1 Chr. 12:29). Although the Benjamites continued to show some unrest throughout David's reign (2 Sam. 20:1; Ps. 7), most of the tribe remained loyal to the house of David and became part of the southern kingdom of Judah when Israel divided into two nations (1 Kin. 12:21; Ezra 4:1). Saul of Tarsus, who later became known as the apostle Paul, was a Benjamite (Phil. 3:5).

BENJAMIN'S GATE (see GATES OF JERUSALEM AND THE TEMPLE).

BENJAMITE [BEN juh mite] — any person who belonged to the tribe of BENJAMIN (Judg. 3:15; 19:16; Benjaminite, RSV).

BENO [BEE noe] (*his son*) — a descendant of the tribe of Levi through MERARI (1 Chr. 24:26–27).

BEON [BEE ahn] (*lord* or *house of On*) — an ancient Amorite city situated east of the Jordan River on the frontier of Moab (Num. 32:3). It was also known as BAAL MEON (Num. 32:38; 1 Chr. 5:8; Ezek. 25:9), and Beth Baal Meon (Josh. 13:17).

BEOR [BEE or] (*a torch*) — the name of two men in the Old Testament:

1. The father of Bela, king of Edom (Gen. 36:32; 1 Chr. 1:43).

2. The father of Balaam, the seer hired by Balaak to curse the Israelites (Deut. 23:4; Josh. 24:9). Beor is also called Bosor (2 Pet. 2:15; KJV).

BERA [BEE rah] (meaning unknown) — a king of Sodom (Gen. 14:2). During the time of Abraham he was defeated by Chedorlaomer in the Valley of Siddim.

BERACAH [BEHR uh kah] — a form of BERACHAH.

BERACHAH [BEHR ah kah] (*blessing*) — the name of a man and a place in the Old Testament:

1. A Benjamite who joined David's army at Ziklag (1 Chr. 12:3; Beracah, NASB, NIV, RSV).

2. A valley in Judah near Tekoa (2 Chr. 20:26). King Jehoshaphat named this place when his people assembled here to bless the Lord after the defeat of their enemies.

BERAIAH [beh RIE uh] (*Jehovah has created*) — a chief of the tribe of Benjamin (1 Chr. 8:21).

BEREA [beh REE ah] — a city of Macedonia (see Map 7, B–1) about 73 kilometers (45 miles) west of Thessalonica (modern Salonika). On his first missionary journey, the apostle Paul preached at Berea (Acts 17:10) with much success. The Bereans were "more fair-minded than those in Thessalonica," because they "searched the Scriptures daily to find out whether these things were so" (Acts 17:11).

BERECHIAH [behr ah KIE uh] (*Jehovah has blessed*) — the name of seven men in the Old Testament:

1. A son of Zerubbabel and a descendant of David (1 Chr. 3:20).

2. A Levite who lived in Jerusalem after the Captivity (1 Chr. 9:16).

3. A Levite, the father of Asaph the singer (1 Chr. 15:17), also called Berachiah (1 Chr. 6:39).

4. One of the "doorkeepers for the ark" (1 Chr. 15:23) in David's time.

5. A chief of the tribe of Ephraim (2 Chr. 28:12).

6. The father of Meshullam (Neh. 3:4, 30; 6:18).

7. A son of Iddo the prophet and the father of Zechariah the prophet (Zech. 1:1, 7; Matt. 23:35; Barachias, KJV; Barachiah, RSV; also see JEBERECHIAH, Is. 8:2).

BERED [BEH rid] (*hail*) — the name of a place and a person in the Old Testament:

1. A place (perhaps a town) in the Wilderness of Shur or the southern desert of Palestine. Between Bered and Kadesh Barnea lay the well called BEER LAHAI ROI (Gen. 16:14).

2. A descendant of Ephraim (1 Chr. 7:20). Some think he is the same person as BECHER (Num. 26:35).

BERI [BEH rih] (*expounder*) — a son of Zophah, of the tribe of Asher (1 Chr. 7:36).

BERIAH [beh RYE uh] (*tragedy, misfortune*) — the name of four men in the Old Testament:

1. A descendant of Asher and the father of Heber and Malchiel (Gen. 46:17; Num. 26:44-45; 1 Chr. 7:30-31). Beriah was the head of the family of Beriites (Num. 26:44).

2. A descendant of Ephraim (1 Chr. 7:23), born after his brothers were killed by the Philistines.

3. A descendant of Benjamin (1 Chr. 8:13, 16).

4. A Levite, a son of Shimei the Gershonite (1 Chr. 23:10-11).

BERIITES [BEH rih ites] (*unfortunate*) — the family name of Beriah, the son of Asher (Num. 26:44).

BERITES [BEH rites] (*belonging to Beri*) — the descendants of BICHRI. The only mention of this clan is when Joab visited them in his pursuit of Sheba, the son of Bichri (2 Sam. 20:14; Bichrites, RSV, NEB).

BERITH [BEH rith] (see GODS, PAGAN).

BERNICE [ber NIH see] (*victorious*) — the oldest daughter of Herod Agrippa I, who ruled Palestine A.D. 37-44 (Acts 25:13). According to the historian Josephus, she was first married to a man named Marcus and later to her uncle Herod, king of Chalcis, who soon afterward died. She later married Polemo, king of Cilicia, but deserted him shortly after their wedding. Then she made her way to Jerusalem, where she lived with Agrippa II. She was with Agrippa II when the apostle Paul made his defense before him (Acts 25:13, 23; 26:30).

Bernice eventually became a mistress to a Roman emperor Vespasian, then of his son Titus. Bernice and her sister Drusilla (Acts 24:24) were two of the most corrupt and shameless women of their time.

BERODACH-BALADAN [bih ROE dak BAL uh dan] — a form of MERODACH-BALADAN.

BEROTHAH [beh ROW thah] (*wells*) — a town in northern Palestine between Damascus and Hamath. The prophet Ezekiel saw it as the northernmost area of the restored promised land (Ezek. 47:16; Berutha, NEB). It is also called Berothai (2 Sam. 8:8), or Cun (1 Chr. 18:8).

BEROTHAI [beh ROW thigh] — a form of BEROTHAH.

BEROTHITE [beh ROW thite] — a native or inhabitant of BEEROTH. A man referred to as Naharai the Berothite was Joab's armorbearer (1 Chr. 11:39; also spelled Beerothite, 2 Sam. 23:37).

BERUTHA [beh ROO thuh] — a form of BEROTHAH.

BERYL [BEHR ul] (see JEWELS AND PRECIOUS STONES).

BESAI [BEE sigh] (meaning unknown) — a man whose descendants returned to Jerusalem with Zerubbabel after the Captivity (Ezra 2:49; Neh. 7:52).

BESODEIAH [bes oh DEE yuh] (*in the intimate counsel of Jehovah*) — the father of Meshullam, who helped repair the Old Gate of Jerusalem (Neh. 3:6).

BESOM [BEE some] — KJV, NEB rendering of "broom" (Is. 14:23). Isaiah predicted that "the besom [broom] of destruction" would sweep Babylon away as so much rubbish before the Lord's purifying anger.

BESOR, THE BROOK [BEE sawr] (*cold*) — a wadi, or dry riverbed, south of Ziklag where David and 600 of his men battled the Amalekites.

BESTIALITY — sexual intercourse between a human being and an animal. According to the Mosaic Law, both the beast and the guilty person were to be put to death for this abomination (Ex. 22:19; Lev. 18:23; Deut. 27:21).

BETAH [BEE tah] (*trust, confidence*) — a city of Zobah which David captured from HADADEZER (2 Sam. 8:8). It is identical with Tibhath (1 Chr. 18:8).

BETEN [BEE tehn] (*abdomen*) — a village of the tribe of Asher (Josh. 19:25). Beten may be the present-day Abtun, about 18 kilometers (11 miles) south of Akko (Acre), not far from Mount Carmel.

BETH [beth] (*house*) — the name of a Hebrew letter and a prefix used in Hebrew names:

1. The name of the second letter of the Hebrew alphabet. Its name, "house," comes from the fact that an early form of the letter was a primitive representation of a dwelling.

2. A prefix used in many compound words, such as Beth Anath (house of Anath) or Beth Arabah (house of the desert).

Also see ACROSTIC.

BETH ACACIA [beth ah KAY shuh] (*house of acacia*) — a town of the Jordan Valley between Zerarah and Jezreel, noted for its acacia trees (Judg. 7:22; Beth-shittah, NAS, NEB, NIV, KJV, RSV). The MIDIANITES fled to this town to escape Gideon.

BETH ANATH [beth AY nath] — a fortified city in the territory of Naphtali, situated between Horem and Beth Shemesh (Josh. 19:38). The Canaanites were not expelled from this city during Israel's conquest of the land.

BETH ANOTH [beth AY noth] (*house of Anoth*) — a town in the hill country of Judah, near Hebron (Josh. 15:59).

BETH APHRAH [beth AF ruh] (*house of dust*) — a Philistine city (Mic. 1:10; Beth-le-aphrah, NASB, RSV; Aphrah, KJV). Some scholars, however, believe an allusion to Bethel or Ophrah may be intended.

BETH ARABAH [beth AIR uh bah] (*house of the desert*) — a city in the wilderness of Judah (Josh. 15: 61-62). Since Beth Arabah is also named as a city of Benjamin (Josh. 18:18), it must have been on or near the boundary between the territories of Judah and Benjamin, at the north end of the DEAD SEA. It may be identified with Ain el-Gharabah, southeast of Jericho.

BETH ARAM [beth A ram] — a form of BETH HARAM and BETH HARAN.

BETH ARBEL [beth ARR bell] (*house of ambush*) — a town plundered by Shalman (Hos. 10:14). Some scholars believe this Shalman was a king of Moab and that the town was Arbela in the region of Pella in TRANSJORDAN. Others argue that Shalman was Shalmaneser V of Assyria and that Beth Arbel was Arbela of Galilee.

BETH AVEN [beth A van] (*house of idols*) — a town in the hill country of Benjamin east of Bethel and west of Michmash (Josh. 7:2). Some scholars believe Beth Aven was an older name for Ai. The prophet Hosea used the name symbolically to say that Bethel ("the house of God") had become Beth Aven ("the house of idols") because of the golden calf set up at Bethel by Jeroboam, the first king of the northern kingdom of Israel (1 Kin. 12:28–29).

BETH AZMAVETH [beth az MAY veth] (*house of Azmaveth*) — a town near Jerusalem between Anathoth and Geba (Neh. 7:28), also called Azmaveth (Ezra 2:24; Beth–azmoth, NEB).

BETH–AZMOTH [beth AZ moth] — a form of BETH AZMAVETH.

BETH BAAL MEON [beth BAY uhl ME ahn] (*Baal's dwelling place*) — an Amorite city east of the Jordan River on the northern border of Moab allotted to the Reubenites (Josh. 13:17). It also was called Beon (Num. 32:3), Baal Meon (Num. 32:38), and Beth Meon (Jer. 48:23).

BETH BARAH [beth BAH rah] (*house of crossing*) — a place in the Jordan River Valley near the site of Gideon's victory over the Midianites (Judg. 7:24). Beth Barah may have been a ford or crossing near the place where the brook of Far'ah ran into the JORDAN RIVER. Beth Barah should not be confused with "Bethabara (Bethany, NASB, NEB, NIV, RSV) beyond the Jordan" (John 1:28), a place east of the Jordan River.

BETH BIREI [beth BEER ih eye] — a form of BETH BIRI.

BETH BIRI [beth BIH rih] (*house of my creation*) — a town of southern Judah assigned to the tribe of Simeon (1 Chr. 4:31; Beth–birei, NEB, KJV). It is perhaps the same as Beth Lebaoth (Josh. 19:6) or Lebaoth (Josh. 15:32).

BETH CAR [beth karr] (*house of a lamb*) — a place near MIZPAH where Israel pursued the Philistines during the battle of EBENEZER (1 Sam. 7:11–12). The exact site is unknown.

BETH DAGON [beth DAY gun] (meaning unknown) — the name of two towns in the Old Testament:

1. A town in the lowland of Judah near Philistine territory (Josh. 15:41). It may be modern Khirbet Dajun.

2. A town on the border between Asher and Zebulun (Josh. 19:27). It probably is modern Jelamet el–Atika at the foot of Mount Carmel.

BETH DIBLATHAIM [beth dib lah THAY em] (*house of two fig cakes*) — a Moabite town associated with Dibon and Nebo (Jer. 48:22), perhaps the same place as Almon Diblathaim (Num. 33:46–47).

BETH EDEN [beth EE dun] (*house of delight*) — a city–state in Mesopotamia (Amos 1:5). This city–state is mentioned in Assyrian records by the name Bit–Adini, situated on both sides of the Euphrates River north of the Balikh River. According to the prophet Amos, the people of the Aramean city would be taken captive and exiled to Kir by the Assyrians under Tiglath–Pileser (Amos 1:5).

BETH EKED OF THE SHEPHERDS [beth EE ked] (*house of shearing*) — a place on the road from Jezreel to Samaria where Jehu met and killed 42 relatives of King Ahaziah of Judah (2 Kin. 10:12–14; the shearing house, KJV; a shepherds' shelter, NEB). Jehu killed them at the well of Beth Eked, leaving no survivors. Some scholars identify this site with Beit–Qad, about 26 kilometers (16 miles) northeast of Samaria.

BETH EMEK [beth EE meck] (*house of the valley*) — a town of Asher near the border of Zebulun, in the Valley of Jipthah El (Josh. 19:27). It may be the modern Tell Mimas, located about 10.5 kilometers (6.5 miles) northeast of Acre (modern Akko).

BETH EZEL [beth EE zul] (*adjoining house*) — a town of southern Judah mentioned with other towns in the SHEPHELAH and Philistine plain (Mic. 1:11).

BETH GADER [beth GAY dur] (*house of walls*) — a town of Judah (1 Chr. 2:51), perhaps the same place as Geder (Josh. 12:13).

BETH GAMUL [beth GAY mull] (*place of recompense*) — an unwalled city on the plain of Moab about 11 kilometers (7 miles) east of Dibon (Jer. 48:23).

BETH HACCEREM [beth HACK uh rim] — a form of BETH HACCHEREM.

BETH HACCHEREM [beth HACK uh rim] (*house of the vineyard*) — a village near Jerusalem where signal–fires were sent up to warn of an invasion (Jer. 6:1; Neh. 3:14; Beth Haccherem, RSV). Some scholars identify Beth Haccherem as present–day Ramet Rahel, situated about three kilometers (two miles) south of Jerusalem.

BETH HAGGAN [beth HAG un] (*garden house*) — a town toward which King AHAZIAH fled as he escaped from Jehu (2 Kin. 9:27).

BETH HARAM [beth HAR em] — a town of Canaan allotted to the tribe of Gad in Joshua's time (Josh. 13:27), probably the same place as BETH HARAN (Num. 32:36).

BETH HARAN [beth HAY ran] (*house of the heights*) — an Amorite city captured and fortified by the tribe of Gad (Num. 32:36; Josh. 13:27; Beth–aram, KJV).

BETH HOGLAH [beth HOG luh] (*house of the partridge*) — a city of the tribe of Benjamin about six kilometers (four miles) southeast of Jericho near the border of Judah (Josh. 15:6; Beth–hogla, KJV).

BETH HORON [beth HOE run] (*house of hollowness*) — twin towns named after Horon, the Canaanite god of the underworld. The two towns, Upper and Lower Beth Horon (Josh. 16:3, 5), were separated by only a few miles. The towns were situated at the west end of the Ephraimite mountains on the boundary line between the territories of Benjamin and Ephraim. They were assigned to Ephraim and given to the KOHATHITES (Josh. 21:20–22).

These twin towns were called Upper and Lower because of the great difference in elevation between them. Upper Beth Horon was approximately 615 meters (2,000 feet) above sea level, while Lower Beth Horon was only 369 meters (1,200 feet) above sea level. The steep descent between them provided the best pass through the mountains from Jerusalem to Joppa (modern Jaffa) and the Mediterranean Sea. For this reason both towns became heavily fortified at various periods in history as a means of defense for Jerusalem.

The historical record of these cities reads like a page out of a war manual. When Joshua overcame the Amorites, in the battle where the sun stood still, "the Lord routed them before Israel, killed them with a great slaughter at Gibeon, [and] chased them along the road that goes to Beth Horon" (Josh. 10:10). When the Philistines fought against King Saul at Michmash, they sent a company of soldiers along the "road to Beth Horon" (1 Sam. 13:18).

BETH JESHIMOTH [beth JEHSH ih moth] (*house of the wastes*) — a town situated in the ABARIM mountain range east of the place where the Jordan River flows into the Dead Sea, also called Beth Jesimoth (Num. 33:49). It was one of the limits of Israel's encampment before the people crossed the Jordan.

BETH JESIMOTH [beth JESS ih moth] — a form of BETH JESHIMOTH.

BETH–LE–APHRAH [beth leh AF ruh] — a form of BETH APHRAH.

BETH LEBAOTH [beth leh BAY oth] (*house of lionesses*) — a town of southern Judah assigned to the tribe of Simeon (Josh. 19:6). The city is also known as Lebaoth (Josh. 15:32). Located near Sharuhen, it may be identical with Beth Biri (1 Chr. 4:31).

BETH MARCABOTH [beth MAR kuh both] (*house of chariots*) — a town of the Simeonites in southern Judah mentioned along with Hazar Susah as a city in the NEGEB near Ziklag (Josh. 19:5).

BETH MEON [beth ME ahn] (*place of habitation*) — a city of Moab (Jer. 48:23). Also see BEON; BAAL MEON; and BETH BAAL MEON.

BETH MILLO [beth MILL oh] (*place of a mound*) — an ancient fortification in or near Shechem, a city in central Palestine, in the hill country of Ephraim (Judg. 9:6). The reference may be to the fortified citadel of Shechem, whose inhabitants were among those who proclaimed Abimelech king. Also see MILLO.

BETH NIMRAH [beth NIM rah] (*house of the leopard*) — a fortified city built by the Gadites in Gilead, east of the Jordan River (Num. 32:36). It is also called Nimrah (Num. 32:3).

BETH PAZZEZ [beth PAZ ez] (*house of destruction*) — a border town in Issachar (Josh. 19:21), near En Haddah and Mount Tabor. It may be modern Kerm el–Haditheh.

BETH PELET [beth PUH let] (*house of escape*) — a town in the NEGEB of Judah, toward the border of Edom (Josh. 15:27; Neh. 11:26; Beth–phelet, KJV).

BETH PEOR [beth PEA oar] (*house of the opening*) — a town of Moab near Pisgah that was allotted to the tribe of Reuben. The Israelites maintained their main encampment near this site while warring against Sihon and Og (Deut. 4:46). It was "in a valley in the land of Moab, opposite Beth Peor" (Deut. 34:6) that Moses was buried.

BETH–PHELET [beth FUH let] — a form of BETH PELET.

BETH–RAPHA [beth RAY fuh] (*house of healing*) — a man listed in the genealogy of Judah. He was a son of Eshton (1 Chr. 4:12).

BETH REHOB [beth REH hob] (*place of a street*) — a town of the Jordan River Valley north of the Sea of Galilee near Dan (Judg. 18:28). It was also called REHOB (Num. 13:21). Apparently, Beth Rehob was one of the small kingdoms of Aram or Syria, located east of Gilead (2 Sam. 10:6).

BETH SHAN [BETH shan] (*place of security*) — a city at the junction of the Jezreel and Jordan valleys. Beth Shan shows evidence of occupation from prehistoric times throughout the biblical period. Archaeologists unearthed 18 separate levels of occupation. This continuous occupation probably was due to natural and geographic factors. The many springs in the area, combined with the intense heat that is characteristic of the Jordan Valley, made Beth Shan a garden paradise.

Beth Shan's location at the crossroads of Palestine's two great valleys meant that all traffic through Palestine—from Egypt to Damascus and from the Mediterranean coast to the East—had to pass by the city.

After the Egyptian pharaoh Thutmose III's victory at MEGIDDO (about 1482 B.C.), the fortress at Beth Shan passed into Egyptian hands for three centuries. Joshua was unable to capture Beth Shan; his infantry could not cope with its iron chariots (Josh. 17:16). Later, the Philistines occupied the city; and after Saul's tragic last battle near Mount Gilboa, the Philistines "put his armor in the temple

Photo by Willem A. VanGemeren

A theater from the Roman period, with the mound of ancient Beth Shan (1 Sam. 31:8-10) in the background.

of ASHTAROTH as an offering and 'fastened his body to the wall of Beth Shan' " (1 Sam. 31:10). That Israel eventually gained control of the city is evidenced by the garrison which Solomon kept here (1 Kin. 4:12). In some places the name occurs as Beth Shean (Josh. 17:11, 16; Judg. 1:27).

During the intertestamental period, the name of Beth Shan was changed to Scythopolis (city of Scythians), which Josephus called the largest of the DECAPOLIS, perhaps meaning it was the capital. In spite of its importance, this city is not mentioned in the New Testament.

BETH SHEAN [beth SHEEN] — a form of BETH SHAN.

BETH SHEMESH [beth SHEH mesh] (*house of the sun*) — a name for three or four cities in the Old Testament:

1. A town in the Valley of Sorek, 24 kilometers (15 miles) west of Jerusalem (see Map 3, A-4). It was situated northwest of Judah's territory near the Philistine border (Josh. 15:10). It was probably the same city as Ir Shemesh (Josh. 19:41), which was allotted to the tribe of Dan. Later, Judah gave Beth Shemesh to the Levites (Josh. 21:16).

After their victory at APHEK (1 Sam. 4), the Philistines took the ARK OF THE COVENANT to Ashdod and Ekron, cities upon which God's judgment quickly fell (1 Sam. 5). The ark was removed then to Beth Shemesh (1 Sam. 6:10—7:2), where it remained until it was taken to KIRJATH JEARIM. Later, Beth Shemesh was in the second administrative dis-

trict of Solomon (1 Kin. 4:9). At Beth Shemesh Israel's king, JEHOASH, and Judah's king, AMAZIAH, met in battle (2 Kin. 14:11–14).

2. A city in Issachar located between MOUNT TABOR and the Jordan River (Josh. 19:22). The Canaanites were not driven out of this city but they paid tribute to the Israelites (Judg. 1:33).

3. A Canaanite city in Naphtali whose inhabitants were not driven out of the land (Josh. 19:38). Some scholars identify this city with Beth Shemesh No. 2.

4. The Hebrew rendering of the Egyptian city of On, called Heliopolis in Greek, at which the temple of the sun-god Ra was situated. Jeremiah prophesied that the Lord would break the images of this Beth Shemesh and burn the houses of Egypt's gods (Jer. 43:13).

BETH–SHITTAH [beth SHIT tah] — a form of BETH ACACIA.

BETH TAPPUAH [beth TAP you ah] (*house of apricots*) — a town in the hill country of Judah about six kilometers (four miles) northwest of Hebron (Josh. 15:53).

BETH ZUR [beth ZOOR] (*house of rock*) — the name of a person and a place in the Old Testament:

1. A city in the mountains of Judah. Beth Zur commanded the road from Beersheba to Jerusalem. King Rehoboam strengthened its fortifications (Neh. 3:16).

2. A son of Maon (1 Chr. 2:45).

BETHABARA [beth AB ah ruh] (*house of the ford*) — an unidentified place on the eastern bank of the Jordan River where John the Baptist baptized (John 1:28).

BETHANY [BETH ah nih] (*house of unripe figs*) — the name of two villages in the New Testament:

1. A village on the southeastern slopes of the MOUNT OF OLIVES (see Map 6, B–4) about three kilometers (two miles) east of Jerusalem near the road to Jericho (Mark 11:1). Bethany was the scene of some of the most important events of Jesus' life. It was the home of Martha, Mary, and Lazarus and the place where Jesus raised Lazarus from the dead (John 11). During Jesus' final week, He spent at least one night in Bethany (Matt. 21:17). At Bethany Jesus was anointed by Mary in the home of Simon the leper (Matt. 26:6–13).

2. A village in TRANSJORDAN where John the Baptist was baptizing. Its exact location is not known.

BETHEL [BETH uhl] (*house of God*) — the name of two cities in the Old Testament:

1. A city of Palestine about 19 kilometers (12 miles) north of Jerusalem (see Map 3, B–4). Bethel is first mentioned in the Bible in connection with the patriarch Abraham, who "pitched his tent with Bethel on the west and...built an altar to the Lord" (Gen. 12:8; 13:3). The region around Bethel is still suitable for grazing by livestock.

Jacob, Abraham's grandson, had a life–changing experience at this site. He had a vision of a staircase reaching into the heavens with the angels of God "ascending and descending on it" (Gen. 28:12). Jacob called the name of that place Bethel, "the house of God" (Gen. 28:19). He erected a pillar at Bethel to mark the spot of his vision (Gen. 28:22; 31:13). Jacob later built an altar at Bethel, where he worshiped the Lord (Gen. 35:1–16).

During Israel's war with the Benjamites in later years (Judg. 20), the children of Israel suffered two disastrous defeats (Judg. 20:21, 25). They went to Bethel (the house of God, NKJV) to inquire of the Lord, for the ARK OF THE COVENANT was located there (Judg. 20:26–27). At Bethel they built an altar and offered burnt offerings and peace offerings before the Lord. The third battle ended in disaster for the Benjamites. At the end of the war the Israelites returned to Bethel (the house of God, NKJV), built an altar, and again offered burnt offerings and peace offerings (Judg. 21:1–4).

After the death of Solomon and the division of his kingdom, Jeroboam, the king of Israel (the Northern Kingdom), set up two calves of gold, one in Bethel and one in Dan (1 Kin. 12:29, 32–33). Thus, Bethel became a great center of idolatry (1 Kin. 13:1–32; 2 Kin. 10:29) and the chief sanctuary of Israel, rivaling the Temple in Jerusalem.

The prophets Jeremiah and Amos denounced Bethel for its idolatries (Jer. 48:13; Amos 5:5–6). Hosea, deploring its great wickedness (Hos. 10:5, 15), called it BETH AVEN ('house of harlotry'), because of the golden calf set up there. Bethel, the house of God, had deteriorated into Beth Aven, the house of idolatry.

In a religious reformation that sought to restore the true worship of God, King Josiah broke down the altar at Bethel (2 Kin. 23:15). Still later in Israel's history, Bethel was occupied by Jewish people who returned from the Captivity in Babylon with Zerubbabel (Ezra 2:28; Neh. 7:32). The place again reverted to the Benjamites (Neh. 11:31). The city was destroyed about 540 B.C. by a great fire. This destruction may have been the work of Nabonidus of Babylon or of the Persians in the period just before Darius. Today the site of Bethel is occupied by a small village called Beitin.

The New Testament does not refer to Bethel, but Jesus must have gone through this area on His trips. The city was situated on the main road from Shechem to Jerusalem.

2. A city in the territory of Simeon (1 Sam. 30:27). Scholars believe this Bethel is a variant reading for Bethul (Josh. 19:4) or Bethuel (1 Chr. 4:30). See BETHUEL No. 2.

BETHER [BEE thur] (*division, split*) — a small range of hills between Bethlehem and Jerusalem (Song 2:17).

BETHESDA [buh THEZ duh] (*house of grace*) — a pool in the northeastern part of Jerusalem, near the Sheep Gate. At this pool Jesus healed the man "who had an infirmity thirty–eight years" (John 5:5). Archaeologists have discovered two pools in this vicinity, 16 1/2 and 19 1/2 meters (55 and 65 feet) long respectively. The shorter pool had five arches over it with a porch beneath each arch, corresponding to the description given in John 5:2.

Archaeologists excavate the ancient Canaanite sacrificial center at Bethel.
Photo by Howard Vos

The Crusaders later built a church on this site to commemorate the healing miracle that took place.

The man who had been lame for 38 years came to the pool hoping to be cured by its miraculous waters; instead he was healed by the word of Jesus (John 5:1–15).

BETHLEHEM [BETH luh him] (*house of bread*) — the name of two cities and possibly one man in the Bible:

1. The birthplace of Jesus Christ (see Map 3, B–4). Bethlehem was situated about eight kilometers (five miles) south of Jerusalem in the district known as Ephrathah (Mic. 5:2), a region known for its fertile hills and valleys.

Bethlehem was the burial place of Rachel, the wife of Jacob (Gen. 35:19). The original home of Naomi and her family, it was also the setting for much of the Book of Ruth. Bethlehem also was the ancestral home of David (1 Sam. 17:12) and was rebuilt and fortified by King Rehoboam (2 Chr. 11:6).

The most important Old Testament figure associated with Bethlehem was David, Israel's great king. At Bethlehem Samuel anointed David as Saul's successor. Although David made Jerusalem his capital city, he never lost his love for Bethlehem. Second Samuel 23:14–17 is a warm story about David's longing for a drink of water from the well of Bethlehem, which was a Philistine garrison at the time. But when three of David's mighty men broke through the Philistine lines to draw a drink of water, David refused to drink it because of the blood that had been shed for it.

The prophet Micah predicted that Bethlehem would be the birthplace of the Messiah (Mic. 5:2), a prophecy quoted in Matthew 2:6. It is significant that the King of kings, who was of the house of David, was born in David's ancestral home. According to Luke 2:11, Jesus was born in "the city of David," Bethlehem. Christ, who is the Bread of Life, was cradled in a town whose name means "house of bread."

The Church of the Nativity, which marks the birthplace of the Savior, is one of the best authenticated sites in the Holy Land. The present structure, built over the cave area which served as a stable for the inn, goes back to the time of the Roman emperor Justinian (sixth century A.D.). This church replaces an earlier building, built in A.D. 330 by Helena, the mother of the Roman emperor Constantine.

2. A town in the land of Zebulun (Josh. 19:15).

3. A son of Salma, a descendant of Caleb (1 Chr. 2:51). As the "father" of Bethlehem, Salma may have been the founder of Bethlehem rather than being the father of a son named "Bethlehem."

BETHLEHEMITE [BETH luh him ite] — a native or inhabitant of BETHLEHEM (1 Sam. 16:1).

BETHPHAGE [beth FAY jeh] (*house of unripe figs*) — a village near Bethany, on or near the road from Jerusalem to Jericho. It has been described as a "suburb" of Jerusalem. The site is mentioned only in connection with Jesus' triumphal entry (Matt. 21:1). From Bethphage Jesus sent two of His disciples into the next village to obtain a colt for Him to ride on the Sunday before His crucifixion.

BETHSAIDA [beth SAY ih duh] (*house of fishing*) — the name of one or possibly two cities in the New Testament:

1. Bethsaida, which was later called Julias, was situated three kilometers (two miles) north of the Sea of Galilee and east of the Jordan River (see Map 6, C–2). The name Julias was given to it by the tetrarch Philip (Luke 3:1), after Julia, the daughter of Caesar Augustus. In the wilderness near Bethsaida, Jesus fed the 5,000 and healed the multitudes (Luke 9:10–17). It was also in Bethsaida that He restored sight to a blind man (Mark 8:22).

Bethlehem, in the hill country of Judah—the home of David and the birthplace of Jesus (1 Sam. 16:1, 4; Luke 2:11).

Photo by Gustav Jeeninga

2. The gospels of Mark, Luke, and John seem to speak of another Bethsaida which was the home of Philip, Andrew, and Peter (John 1:44) and perhaps of James and John (Luke 5:10). This city was situated northwest of the Sea of Galilee in the fertile plain of Gennesaret (Mark 6:45, 53) near Capernaum (John 6:17) in the province of Galilee (John 12:21).

Some scholars argue that there was only one city called Bethsaida. The Jewish historian Josephus identified the Bethsaida developed by Philip as being near the Jordan in "Lower Gaulanitis." Yet, the gospels seem to indicate that there was another Bethsaida west of the Jordan River (for example, see Mark 6:45, 53). Philip, Peter, and Andrew were from "Bethsaida of Galilee" (John 12:21). Bethsaida–Julias could not be considered to be "of Galilee." The close connection of Bethsaida with CHORAZIN (Matt. 11:21) and CAPERNAUM (Matt. 11:23) as the center of Jesus' ministry in Galilee is strong evidence for another Bethsaida situated closer to them.

BETHUEL [beh THUE el] (*abode of God*) — the name of a person and a place in the Old Testament:
1. A son of Nahor and Milcah. Bethuel also was Abraham's nephew and the father of Laban and Rebekah (Gen. 22:22–23).
2. A city in the territory of Simeon near Hormah and Ziklag (1 Chr. 4:30; Josh. 19:4, Bethul, KJV).

BETHUL [beh THOOL] — a form of BETHUEL.

BETONIM [BET oh nim] (*pistachio nuts*) — a town east of the Jordan River in northern Gad (Josh. 13:26), probably the same place as Khirbet Batneh or Batana.

BETROTHAL — a mutual promise or contract for a future marriage (Deut. 20:7; Jer. 2:2; Luke 1:27).

The selection of the bride was followed by the betrothal, not to be entirely equated with the modern concept of engagement. A betrothal was undertaken by a friend or agent representing the bridegroom and by the parents representing the bride. It was confirmed by oaths and was accompanied with presents to the bride and often to the bride's parents.

The betrothal was celebrated by a feast. In some instances, it was customary for the bridegroom to place a ring, a token of love and fidelity, on the bride's finger. In Hebrew custom, betrothal was actually part of the marriage process. A change of intention by one of the partners after he or she was betrothed was a serious matter, subject in some instances to penalty by fine.

The most important instance of betrothal in the Bible is the one between Joseph and Mary (Matt. 1:18–19). A Jewish betrothal could be dissolved only by the man's giving the woman a certificate of divorce. A betrothal usually lasted for one year. During that year the couple were known as husband and wife, although they did not have the right to be united sexually.

Betrothal was much more closely linked with

marriage than our modern engagement. But the actual marriage took place only when the bridegroom took the bride to his home and the marriage was consummated in the sexual union.

Also see MARRIAGE; WEDDINGS.

BEULAH [BUE luh] (*married*) — Isaiah's name for the Promised Land after the Captivity — a symbol of Israel's future blessedness and prosperity (Is. 62:4).

BEWITCH — to hypnotize, charm, or cast an evil spell. The "foolish Galatians" (Gal. 3:1) had been bewitched, or led into theological and moral error, by the false teachings of the JUDAIZERS.

BEZAANANNIM [bee za ah NAN em] — a form of ZAANANNIM.

BEZAI [BEE zay eye] (meaning unknown) — the founder of a family of Israelites who returned from the Captivity (Ezra 2:17; Neh. 7:23).

BEZALEEL [BEZ ah leel] (*in the shadow of God*) — the name of two Old Testament men:
1. The chief architect and designer of the tabernacle (Ex. 36:1–2; Bezalel, NASB, NEB, NIV, RSV). Along with Aholiab of the tribe of Dan, Bezaleel supervised the tabernacle's construction and the manufacture of its furniture.
2. One who divorced his pagan wife after the Captivity (Ezra 10:30).

BEZALEL [bez uh LEL] — a form of BEZALEEL.

BEZEK [BEE zeck] (*lightning*) — the name of a town and a place in the Old Testament:
1. A town in the territory allotted to the tribe of Judah (Judg. 1:4–5).
2. The place where Saul assembled his army on the eve of a great victory over Nahash the Ammonite. At this battle JABESH GILEAD was saved from the Ammonites (1 Sam. 11:8). The exact location of this place is unknown.

BEZER [BEE zur] (*strong*) — the name of a man and a city in the Old Testament:
1. A fortified city within the territory of Reuben (see Map 3, C–4), set apart by Moses as one of three cities of refuge east of the Jordan River (Deut. 4:40–43).
2. A son of Zophah, one of the chiefs of Asher (1 Chr. 7:37).

BIBLE, THE — the sacred Book, or collection of books, accepted by the Christian church as uniquely inspired by God, and thus authoritative, providing guidelines for belief and behavior.

Major Divisions. The Bible contains two major sections known as the Old Testament and the New Testament. The books of the Old Testament were written over a period of about 1,000 years in the Hebrew language, except for a few selected passages, which were written in Aramaic. The Old Testament tells of the preparation that was made for Christ's coming.

The New Testament was written over a period of about 100 years. The original language in which it

A Glance at the Major Divisions and Individual Books of the Bible

OLD TESTAMENT

Books of the Pentateuch, or the Law

Book	Summary
Genesis	Creation and the establishment of the covenant relationship
Exodus	Deliverance of the people of Israel from slavery in Egypt
Leviticus	The ceremonial law
Numbers	Wandering of God's people in the wilderness
Deuteronomy	The second giving of the law by Moses before the people occupy the Promised Land

Books about the History of Israel

Book	Summary
Joshua	The capture and settlement of the Promised Land
Judges	The nation of Israel is rescued by a series of judges, or military leaders
Ruth	A beautiful story of God's love and care
1 and 2 Samuel	The early history of Israel, including the reigns of Saul and David
1 and 2 Kings	A political history of Israel, focusing on the reigns of selected kings from the time of Solomon to the captivity of the Jewish people by Babylon
1 and 2 Chronicles	A religious history of Israel, covering the same period of time as 2 Samuel and 1 and 2 Kings
Ezra	The return of the Jewish people from captivity in Babylon
Nehemiah	The rebuilding of the walls of Jerusalem after the exiles returned from Babylon
Esther	God's care for His people under Gentile rule

Books of Wisdom Writings

Book	Summary
Job	An examination of the problems of evil and human suffering
Psalms	The song book or hymnal of ancient Israel
Proverbs	Wise sayings and observations designed to develop proper attitudes and behavior
Ecclesiastes	A philosophical description of the emptiness of life without God
Song of Solomon	A love song portraying the beauty of a human love relationship as a symbol of divine love

Books of the Major Prophets

Book	Summary
Isaiah	The outstanding prophet of condemnation and Messianic consolation
Jeremiah	A message of judgment against Judah's moral and spiritual decay
Lamentations	Jeremiah's five poems of lament over fallen Jerusalem
Ezekiel	A prophecy of judgment during the Babylonian Captivity
Daniel	A book of prophecy about the end time

Books of the Minor Prophets

Book	Summary
Hosea	A message of Israel's condemnation followed by God's forgiveness
Joel	A prediction of foreign invasion as a form of judgment by God
Amos	A prophecy of eight pronouncements of judgment against Israel
Obadiah	A book prophesying the total destruction of Edom
Jonah	A reluctant prophet who led Nineveh to repentance
Micah	A prediction of judgment and a promise of Messianic restoration
Nahum	A prophecy of the destruction of Nineveh
Habakkuk	A prophet who questioned God and praised His approaching judgment against Judah
Zephaniah	A prediction of destructive judgment followed by tremendous blessing
Haggai	After the return from Babylon, a call to rebuild the Temple
Zechariah	A Messianic prophecy calling for the completion of construction on the Temple
Malachi	A prophecy of destruction followed by Messianic blessing

NEW TESTAMENT

The Gospels

Book	Summary
Matthew	Christ presented as the fulfillment of Old Testament Messianic prophecy
Mark	Probably the earliest of the gospels, focusing on Christ's ministry
Luke	Fullest biography of Christ, focusing on His perfection and ministry of salvation
John	The most symbolic gospel which presents Christ as the divine Son of God

History of the Early Church

Book	Summary
Acts	A history of the expansion of the early church

Epistles (Letters) of the Apostle Paul

Book	Summary
Romans	An explanation of the Christian faith for both Jews and Gentiles, addressed to the church at Rome
1 Corinthians	Instructions to the church at Corinth dealing with problems among Christians
2 Corinthians	Paul's defense and explanation of his apostleship
Galatians	An account of the necessity of salvation by divine grace rather than the law
Ephesians	A letter to the church at Ephesus explaining the believer's position in Christ
Philippians	A joyful letter to the church at Philippi, telling of Paul's conquering faith during imprisonment
Colossians	An account of the supremacy of Christ, written to the church of Colossae
1 and 2 Thessalonians	Instructions to the church at Thessalonica about the coming of the Lord
1 and 2 Timothy	Manuals of leadership for the young pastor at Ephesus
Titus	A manual of Christian conduct for church leaders, written to a young pastor at Crete
Philemon	An appeal for Christian unity and forgiveness for a runaway slave

General Epistles (Letters)

Book	Summary
Hebrews	A presentation of Jesus Christ as High Priest, addressed to Jewish believers
James	Practical instructions for applied Christianity
1 Peter	Encouragement and comfort from Peter to suffering Christians
2 Peter	Peter's warning against false teachers
1 John	John's reminder of the full humanity of Christ
2 John	John's letter of encouragement and approval
3 John	John's personal note of appreciation to Gaius
Jude	A strong warning against false teachers
Revelation	An encouraging prophecy of the final days and God's ultimate triumph

was written was Greek. This portion of the Bible tells of Christ's coming, His life and ministry, and the growth of the early church.

The English word testament normally refers to a person's will, the document which bequeaths property to those who will inherit it after the owner's death. But the meaning of testament from both the Hebrew and the Greek languages is "settlement," "treaty," or "covenant." Of these three English words, "COVENANT" best captures the meaning of the word testament. Thus, the two collections that make up the Bible can best be described as the books of the old covenant and the books of the new covenant.

The old covenant is the covenant sealed at Mount Sinai in the days of Moses. By this covenant, the living and true God, who had delivered the Israelites from slavery in Egypt, promised to bless them as His special people. They were also to worship Him alone as their God and to accept His law as their rule for life (Ex. 19:3-6; 24:3-8).

The new covenant was announced by Jesus as he spoke to His disciples in the upper room in Jerusalem the night before His death. When He gave them a cup of wine to drink, Jesus declared that this symbolized "the new covenant in My blood" (Luke 22:20; 1 Cor. 11:25).

Between the times of Moses and Jesus, the prophet Jeremiah foresaw a day when God would make a new covenant with His people. Under this new covenant, God would inscribe His laws on the hearts of people rather than on tablets of stone (Jer. 31:31-34). In the New Testament, this new covenant of which Jeremiah spoke is identifed with the covenant inaugurated by Jesus (Heb. 8:6-13).

While these two covenants, the old and the new, launched great spiritual movements, Christians believe these movements are actually two phases of one great act through which God has revealed His will to His people and called for their positive response. The second covenant is the fulfillment of what was promised in the first.

In the form in which it has been handed down among the Jewish people, the Old Testament, or Hebrew Bible, contains three divisions: the Law, the Prophets, and the Writings. The Law consists of Genesis, Exodus, Leviticus, Numbers, and Deuteronomy; this section of the Old Testament is also known as the PENTATEUCH. The Prophets fall into two subdivisions: the former prophets (Joshua, Judges, First and Second Samuel, and First and Second Kings) and the latter prophets (Isaiah, Jeremiah, Ezekiel, and the Book of the Twelve Prophets—Hosea through Malachi). The rest of the books are gathered together in the Writings: Psalms, Proverbs, Job, Song of Solomon, Ruth, Lamentations, Ecclesiastes, Esther, Daniel, Ezra-Nehemiah (counted as one book), and First and Second Chronicles.

The arrangement of the Old Testament with which readers today are most familiar has been inherited from the pre-Christian Greek translation of the Old Testament (the SEPTUAGINT)—an arrangement which was also followed by the later Latin Bible (the Vulgate). This arrangement has four divisions: the Pentateuch, the historical books, poetry, and prophecy.

The New Testament opens with five narrative books—the four gospels and the Acts of the Apostles. The gospels deal with the ministry, death, and resurrection of Jesus. The Book of Acts continues the story of the development of the early church across the next 30 years. Acts serves as a sequel to the gospels in general; originally it was written as a sequel to the Gospel of Luke in particular.

Twenty-one letters, or epistles, follow the historical narratives. Thirteen of these letters bear the name of the apostle Paul as writer, while the remaining eight are the work of other apostles or of authors associated with apostles. The last book in the New Testament, the Revelation of John, portrays through visions and symbolic language the accomplishment of God's purpose in the world and the ultimate triumph of Christ.

Authority of the Bible. The authority of the Bible is implied by its title, "the Word of God." It is the written record of the Word of God which came to prophets, apostles, and other spokesmen, and which "became flesh" in Jesus Christ. Christians believe Jesus Christ was the Word of God in a unique sense. Through Jesus, God communicated the perfect revelation of Himself to mankind. For Christians the authority of the Bible is related to the authority of Christ. The Old Testament was the Bible that Jesus used—the authority to which He made constant appeal and whose teachings He accepted and followed. When Jesus was arrested in the Garden of Gethsemane and led away to His execution, He submitted with the words, "The Scriptures must be fulfilled" (Mark 14:49). He saw His mission in the world as a fulfillment of the predictions of the Old Testament.

The New Testament presents the record of Jesus' life, teachings, death, and resurrection; a narrative of the beginning of the Christian church with the coming of the Holy Spirit; and the story of the extension of the gospel and the planting of the church during the following generation. It also contains the written teachings of Jesus' apostles and other early Christians who applied the principles of His teaching and redemptive work to their lives.

Revelation and Response. According to the Bible, God has made Himself known in a variety of ways. "The heavens declare the glory of God" (Ps. 19:1). "For since the creation of the world His invisible attributes are clearly seen, being understood by the things that are made, even His eternal power and Godhead" (Rom. 1:20). But while God is revealed in His creation and through the inner voice of man's conscience, the primary means by which He has made Himself known is through the Bible.

God has revealed Himself through His mighty acts and in the words of His messengers, or spokesmen. Either of these ways is incomplete without the other. In the Old Testament record, none of the

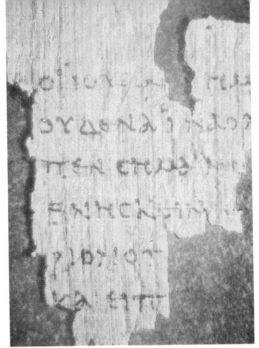

Papyrus fragments of portions of John 18 which date from about A.D. 125-150.

mighty acts of God is emphasized more than the EXODUS—God's deliverance of the Israelites from Egyptian bondage. As He delivered His people, God repeatedly identified Himself as their redeemer God: "I am the Lord your God, who brought you out of the land of Egypt, out of the house of bondage. You shall have no other gods before Me" (Ex. 20:2-3).

If they had been delivered with no explanation, the nation of Israel would have learned little about the God who redeemed His people. The Israelites might have guessed that in such events as the plagues of Egypt and the parting of the waters of the Red Sea, some supernatural power was at work on their behalf. But they would not have known the nature of this power or God's purpose for them as a people.

God also communicated with His people, the nation of Israel, through Moses, to whom He had already made Himself known in the vision of the burning bush. God instructed Moses to tell his fellow Israelites what had been revealed to him. This was no impersonal force at work, but the God of their ancestors, Abraham, Isaac, and Jacob. In fulfillment of His promises to them, God was acting now on behalf of their descendants.

In communicating with His people, God revealed both His identity and His purpose. His purpose was to make the Israelites a nation dedicated to His service alone. This message, conveyed to the Israelites through Moses, would have been ineffective if God had not delivered them personally. On the other hand, His deliverance would have been meaningless without the message. Together both constituted the Word of God to the Israelites—the saving message of the God who both speaks and acts.

This pattern of God's mighty acts and the prophetic word interacting with each other continues throughout the course of biblical history. The Babylonian CAPTIVITY is a good example of this process. A succession of prophets warned the people that if they did not mend their ways, Captivity would come on them as judgment. But even during the years of the Captivity the prophets continued to speak, encouraging the captives and promising that God would deliver them from their plight.

The prophets were God's primary spokesmen to the people of Israel in Old Testament times. But they were not His only messengers. Priests and sages, or wise men, were other agents through whom God's will was made known. The teachings of many of these messengers are preserved in the Bible.

In addition to God's revelation of Himself through the Bible, God's Word also records the response of those to whom the revelation was given. Too often the response was unbelief and disobedience. But at other times, people responded in faith and obedience. The Psalms, especially, proclaim the grateful response of men and women who experienced the grace and righteousness of God. These faithful people sometimes voiced their appreciation in words addressed directly to God. At other times they reported to others what God had come to mean to them.

In the New Testament writings, revelation and response came together in the person of Jesus Christ. On the one hand, Jesus was God's perfect revelation of Himself—He was the divine Word in human form. His works of mercy and power portrayed God in action, especially His supreme act of sacrifice to bring about "the redemption that is in Christ Jesus" (Rom. 3:24). His teaching expressed the mind of God.

The words and acts of Jesus also proclaimed the meaning and purpose of His works. For example, His act of casting out demons "with the finger of God" (Luke 11:20) was a token that the kingdom of God had come upon them. He also declared that His death, which he interpreted as the fulfillment of prophetic Scripture (Mark 14:49), was "a ransom for many" (Mark 10:45).

In his life and ministry, Jesus also illustrated the perfect human response of faith and obedience to God. Jesus was "the Apostle [God's Messenger to us] and High Priest [our Representative with God] of our confession" (Heb. 3:1). Thus, Jesus performed the mighty acts of God and He spoke authoritatively as God's Messenger and Prophet.

Preservation of the Bible. The Bible is a written, authoritative record by which any teaching or theory may be judged. But behind the writing lay periods of time when these messages were circulated in spoken form. The stories of the patriarchs were passed from generation to generation by word of mouth before they were written. The messages of the prophets were delivered orally before they were fixed in writing. Narratives of the life and ministry of Christ were repeated orally for two or three decades before they were given literary form. But the Bible owes its preservation to the fact that all these oral narratives were eventually reduced to writing. Just as God originally inspired the Bible, He has used this means to preserve His Word for future generations.

The first person in the Bible to write anything down was Moses. God instructed Moses to write as a permanent memorial the divine vow that the name of Amalek would be blotted out (Ex. 17:14). From that time until the end of the New Testament age, the writing of the many books and parts of the Bible continued.

None of the original biblical documents—referred to by scholars as the "original autographs"—has survived. No scrap of parchment or papyrus bearing the handwriting of any of the biblical authors has been discovered. But before the original documents disappeared, they were copied. These copies of the original writings are the texts on which current translations of the Bible are based.

The process of copying and recopying the Bible has continued to our time. Until the middle of the 15th century A.D., all the copying was done by hand. Then, with the invention of printing in Europe, copies could be made in greater quantities by using this new process. Each copy of the Bible had to be produced slowly by hand with the old system, but now the printing press could produce thousands of copies in a short time. This made the Scriptures available to many people, rather than just the few who could afford handmade copies.

The older handwritten copies of Bible texts are called manuscripts. Early manuscripts for the books of the Bible were written on papyrus or skin. Papyrus was a type of ancient paper manufactured from a reed plant that grew in the Nile Valley and similar environments. Papyrus was inexpensive,

but it was not very durable. It rotted quickly when exposed to dampness.

The ancient papyrus manuscripts which have been discovered were found in the dry sands of Egypt and other arid places. Great quantities of inscribed papyri have been recovered from the Egyptian sands during the last hundred years dating from the period shortly before and after the beginning of the Christian era, about A.D. 30. A few scraps of papyri containing ancient texts of the Bible have been among the recovered manuscripts.

The skins of animals proved to be a much more durable writing material than papyrus. Many different writing materials were manufactured from such skins. Some were a coarse form of leather. Others were subjected to a special refining process, emerging as a writing material known as parchment. Vellum, another valued writing material, was made from calfskin. Some of the most important manuscripts of the Bible were written on vellum.

The Canon of the Bible. The word canon means a "rod"—specifically, a rod with graduated marks used for measuring length. This word refers to the list of individual books that were eventually judged as authoritative and included as a part of the Old Testament and the New Testament.

The early formation of the canon of the Old Testament is not easy to trace. Its threefold division in its early history—the Law, the Prophets, and the Writings—may reflect the three stages of its formation. From the beginning, the Law was accepted, even if it was not always obeyed. Evidence of its acceptance would include Moses' reading of "the Book of the Covenant" to the people at Mount Sinai and the people's response, "All that the Lord has said we will do, and be obedient" (Ex. 24:7).

Further evidence of acceptance of the Law includes the discovery of the "Book of the Law," probably the Book of Deuteronomy, in the Temple of Jerusalem during King Josiah's reign and the religious reform which followed (2 Kin. 22:8—23:25).

Hills near the village of Anathoth, home of the prophet Jeremiah (Jer. 1:1).
Photo: Levant Photo Service

Also, following the return of the Jewish people from the Babylonian Captivity, "the Book of the Law of Moses" was read to the people of Jerusalem under Ezra's direction. This book became the constitution of their new nation (Neh. 8:1-18).

The second division of the Old Testament accepted by the Jewish people was the Prophets. The prophets' words were preserved from the beginning by their disciples, or by others who recognized the prophets as messengers of God. In general, their words were probably written shortly after they were spoken, for their authority as God's messengers came before their widespread acceptance by the Jewish people. The words of the prophets were not regarded as authoritative because they were included in the Old Testament; they were included because they were considered to be authoritative.

The third division of the Hebrew Old Testament, the Writings, may have remained "open" longer than the first two. Scholars know less about the formation of this division than the first two.

The "Bible" which Jesus used was the Hebrew Old Testament. He left no instructions about forming a new collection of authoritative writings to stand beside the books which He and His disciples accepted as God's Word. The Old Testament was also the Bible of the early church, but it was the Old Testament as fulfilled by Jesus. Early Christians interpreted the Old Testament in the light of His person and work. This new perspective controlled the early church's interpretation to such a degree that, while Jews and Christians shared the same Bible, they understood it so differently that they might almost have been using two different Bibles.

The works and words of Jesus were first communicated in spoken form. The apostles and their associates proclaimed the gospel by word of mouth. Paul taught the believers orally in the churches which he founded when he was present. But when he was absent, he communicated through his letters.

Quite early in its history, the church felt a need for a written account of the teachings of Jesus. His teachings did provide the basis for the new Christian way of life. But the church grew so large that many converts were unable to rely on the instructions of those who had heard and memorized the teachings of Jesus. From about A.D. 50 onward, probably more than one written collection of sayings of Jesus circulated in the churches. The earliest written gospel appears to have been the Gospel of Mark, written about A.D. 64.

An individual gospel, a letter from an apostle, or even several works circulating independently, would not amount to a canon, or an authoritative list of books. A canon implies a collection of writings. There is evidence that two collections of Christian writings circulated among the churches at the beginning of the second century. One of these was the gospel collection—the four writings which are commonly called the four gospels. The other collection was the Pauline collection, or the letters

of the apostle Paul. The anonymous letter to the Hebrews was added to this second collection at an early date.

Early Christians continued to accept the Old Testament as authoritative. But they could interpret the Old Testament in the light of Jesus' deeds and words only if they had a reliable record of them. So, alongside Moses and the prophets, they had these early writings about Jesus and letters from the apostles, who had known Jesus in the flesh.

When officials of the early church sought to make a list of books about Jesus and the early church which they considered authoritative, they retained the Old Testament, on the authority of Jesus and His apostles. Along with these books they recognized as authoritative the writings of the new age—four gospels, or biographies on the life and ministry of Jesus; the 13 letters of Paul; and letters of other apostles and their companions. The gospel collection and the apostolic collection were joined together by the Book of Acts, which served as a sequel to the gospel story, as well as a narrative background for the earlier epistles.

The primary standard applied to a book was that it must be written either by an apostle or by someone close to the apostles. This guaranteed that their writing about Jesus and the early church would have the authenticity of an eyewitness account. As in the earliest phase of the church's existence, "the apostles' doctrine" (Acts 2:42) was the basis of its life and thought. The apostolic writings formed the charter, or foundation documents, of the church.

None of the books written after the death of the apostles were included in the New Testament, although early church officials recognized they did have some value as inspirational documents. The fact that they were written later ruled them out for consideration among the church's foundation documents. These other writings might be suitable for reading aloud in church because of their edifying character, but only the apostolic writings carried ultimate authority. They alone could be used as the basis of the church's belief and practice.

Behind the Bible is a thrilling story of how God revealed Himself and His will to human spokesmen and then acted throughout history to preserve His Word and pass it along to future generations. In the words of the prophet Isaiah, "The grass withers, the flower fades, but the word of our God stands forever" (Is. 40:8).

BIBLE, INTERPRETATION OF, OR HERMENEUTICS — the science and art of biblical interpretation. Correct Bible interpretation should answer the question, "How do I understand what this particular passage means?" Because there are rules which govern its use, it is a science. Because knowing the rules is not enough, it also is an art. Practice to learn how to use the rules is also required.

The question of how to interpret the Bible is not a minor issue. It is, in a sense, one of the battlegrounds for our souls. If Satan had a list of what he

Portions of a commentary on the Book of Habakkuk—one of the ancient documents included among the Dead Sea Scrolls.

does not want us to do, Bible study would be at the top, along with prayer and worship. Through study of Scripture we learn who Jesus is and are enabled to become like Him. How can we become like Him, if we do not know what He is like? Devotional studies are important, but they must result from a serious study of Scripture. The apostle Paul prayed that the Colossians might be "filled with the knowledge of His will in all wisdom and spiritual understanding" (Col. 1:9).

Knowing Scripture as well as obeying it are the twin foundations of a godly life. A godly life produces the further desire to study God's Word. Bible interpretation done properly, therefore, takes the student from study to application back to study and on to further application in a mounting spiral toward God. Satan's attempt to take away our desire to study Scripture is nothing less than an attempt to remove the basis of our spiritual growth and stability.

The Basic Principles of Bible Study. Six basic principles are at the heart of a sound method of biblical interpretation.

1. Because Scripture is a divine Book, and because of our limitation as humans, prayer is an absolute necessity as we study the Bible. Paul teaches that the non-Christian and the spiritually immature Christian are limited in their ability to know Christian things (1 Cor. 2:14—3:3). Therefore, we must pray that God will bridge the gap that separates us from understanding spiritual things, by having the Holy Spirit teach us (John 14:26; 16:13). Without this illumination or insight from God's

Spirit, we cannot learn. This need for insight was the concept Paul referred to when he told Timothy to "reflect on what I am saying, for the Lord will give you insight into all this" (2 Tim. 2:7, NIV).

2. The Bible is also a human book and, to a degree, must be interpreted like any other book. This brings us to the principle of common sense. For example, the grammatical–historical method of studying the Bible instructs us to look at the passage carefully to see what it says literally, and to understand a biblical statement in light of its historical background. We understand a historical statement as a straightforward statement and do not change its literal, grammatical sense. This is "common sense."

Another example of the common sense principle is illustrated when Jesus says Christians can have anything for which they ask (John 15:7). Common sense tells us that there must be some limitation on this statement because we realize that Christians in fact do not have whatever they would like. (First John 5:14 confirms that the limitation is God's will.) Using the common sense principle in this way can be dangerous because it could become an excuse for cutting out any portion of Scripture we do not happen to like. But if our common sense is controlled by God, it is a valid principle of interpreting the Bible.

3. We interpret the Bible properly when we learn to ask the right questions of the text. The problem here is that many people do not know what the right questions are, or they are too lazy to learn. Biblical interpretation is a science, and the rules it

uses take time, energy, and a serious commitment to learn. But when learned, there is much more satisfaction in asking the right questions than in merely guessing.

4. The primary rule of biblical interpretation is "context." This cannot be emphasized too strongly. If the Bible student would merely let a passage speak for itself within the context of the paragraph, chapter, or book, the majority of all errors in interpretation would be avoided.

The problem is our bias, or our subjectivity. Many times we approach a passage thinking we already understand it. In the process we read our own meaning into the passage. This is called eisegesis. (*Eis* is a Greek preposition meaning "into.") But interpreting the Bible correctly demands that we listen to what the text itself is saying, and then draw the meaning out of the passage. This is called exegesis. (*Ex* is a Greek preposition meaning "out of.") If we let a passage be defined by what it and the surrounding verses say, then we have taken a large step toward interpreting the Bible properly. Only by watching the context carefully and by letting the passage speak for itself do we give Scripture the respect it deserves.

Of course, it is impossible to dismiss totally our own bias and subjectivity. Our interpretation will always be colored by our culture and our opinions about the passage, or perhaps by our theological beliefs, which are partially based on the passage. But this should not discourage our attempt to let the passage speak for itself as freely as possible, without being weighed down with our personal opinions and views.

5. These four key words—*observation, interpretation, evaluation,* and *application*—are the heart of all approaches to finding out what the Bible means. They provide the structure of what questions you ask of the text, and when.

Observation: Do I understand the basic facts of the passage such as the meaning of all the words? *Interpretation:* What did the author mean in his own historical setting? *Evaluation:* What does this passage mean in today's culture? *Application:* How can I apply what I have learned to how I live my life?

6. Interpreting the Bible correctly is a two-step process. We must first discover what the passage meant in the day and age of the author. Then we must discover its message for us in today's culture. *Observation* and *interpretation* apply to the first step; *evaluation* and *application* apply to the second.

Why are these two steps important? First, the Bible was not actually written directly to us, and it makes sense to put ourselves in the shoes of the original audience if we are to understand its message properly. Second, these steps force us to *understand* the meaning of the passage before we *apply* it to our lives. Surprisingly, this step is often overlooked. Third, the two steps separate us from the text, thereby helping to prevent eisegesis, since it separates what the text says from how it affects us today.

Photo by Howard Vos

Starting blocks for runners at a stadium in the Greek city of Delphi. The apostle Paul used imagery from these races in his writings (2 Tim. 4:7).

The Four Stages of Biblical Interpretation. Using the four key words in their proper sequence, we are ready to interpret the Bible correctly.

1. *Stage one: observation*—The question asked in this stage is, Do I understand all the facts in this passage? Do I know the context before and after this passage? Do I know the meanings of all the words? Do I understand the general flow of the discussion? Do I understand the cultural background? It is necessary to clear up all the factual problems before moving into the theological meaning of the passage.

For example, in 1 Corinthians 8 the apostle Paul discusses eating meat that had been offered to idols. What is the background? When meat was sacrificed to an idol, that which was not eaten by the priests was sold at the market. Some Corinthian Christians said it was permissible to eat the meat since idols are nothing but wood and stone. Others thought it was not permissible because it might appear they were still involved in pagan worship. Only after we understand these facts may we go on to the next stage of interpretation.

2. *Stage two: interpretation*—The basic question asked in this stage is, What did the author mean in his own historical setting? We must put ourselves in the shoes of Scripture's original audience. To answer this question, there are two further questions we may ask. The first is, What does the passage actually say? Many times we forget to look carefully at what a passage says. Some cite Matthew 5:21–22 as proof that to think bad is just as wrong as doing it. Is anger as bad as murder? Of course not. (Common sense tells us that, if nothing else.) But the text

does not actually say they are the same. It says the law against murder is not fully obeyed by mere outward obedience, but by maintaining the proper attitude of not being angry, which in turn prohibits the outward act of murder.

The second question is, Does the context help define the meaning of the passage? For example, what does Scripture mean when it says, "There is no God" (Ps. 53:1)? Context shows this is a statement made by a fool. What does Paul mean when he says Jesus will return like "a thief in the night" (1 Thess. 5:2)? Context shows it means His coming will be sudden (v. 3). Should women remain totally silent in the church (1 Cor. 14:34)? No, since the context of 1 Corinthians 11:5 shows that women may pray or prophesy.

Does Jesus' statement, "When you fast, do not be like the hypocrites" (Matt. 6:16) demand that His disciples fast? No, because Matthew 9:14 shows that Jesus' disciples did not fast while He was alive. (The beauty of using Scripture to interpret Scripture is that when the Bible answers its own questions, then we know the answer is correct.) The twin matters of what the text actually says and the passage's context help complete the second stage of interpretation.

There are times when even these two questions will not help us understand the meaning of a passage. Sometimes we have to read between the lines and make an educated guess as to what the passage means. This is fine when necessary. But we must remember that we are guessing, and we must keep an open mind to other possible interpretations.

Integrity is also a necessary element in all biblical interpretation. If we tell someone about what a friend said, we should try to be as accurate as possible. If we are not sure about a certain point, we should say, "I think this is what he said." We all do this with our friends. So why then, when we interpret Scripture, do many of us lose that integrity?

Why do we not read the text carefully? Why do we read between the lines, make fanciful interpretations that are more a product of our imagination than reverent study, and then insist that this is what the text actually says?

In interpreting the Bible, we must never forget whose letters we are reading. They have come from the mouth of God Himself, and they demand respect. They demand to speak for themselves. They demand that we be honest and have integrity. We must not put our guesswork on the same level as the words of God.

How do we interpret 1 Corinthians 8? Once we understand the facts and background of the passage, once we have asked what the passage actually is saying and what is its context, then we see that Paul is teaching the principle of voluntarily refraining from a practice which, although not wrong in and of itself, might be harmful to a fellow Christian. We have completed the first step of interpretation. We have seen what the passage meant in the day and age of the author.

3. *Stage three: evaluation*—The stage of evaluation asks, What does the passage mean in today's culture? It is the issue of whether a passage of Scripture applies to us today, or whether it is limited to the culture in which it was originally written.

The question raised by the evaluation process is answered one of two ways. Either the passage is applied directly to our culture, or it must be reapplied because of cultural differences. The vast majority of New Testament teaching can be applied directly to 20th century culture. If we love God, regardless of when or where we live, then we must obey His commandments (John 14:15). This teaching is true in any culture for all times.

But sometimes a Biblical teaching is directed so specifically to the culture of the ancient world that another culture cannot understand it. For example,

The mound, or tell, of Mizpah—an ancient fortified city in the Kingdom of Judah during King Asa's time (1 Kin. 15:22).

Photo: Levant Photo Service

Photo: Levant Photo Service

Arch over a Roman road near the New Testament city of Thessalonica, now known as Salonika.

Western culture today generally does not sacrifice meat to idols, and therefore the meaning of 1 Corinthians 8 may be lost. How then do we evaluate its meaning for us?

It is helpful at this point to define two terms. A "cultural expression" is a statement that can be understood only within a certain cultural context. An "eternal principle" is a principle that God uses to govern the world regardless of culture. "I will never again eat meat, lest it make my brother stumble" (1 Cor. 8:13), is a cultural expression because it is understandable only within those cultures that offer meat to idols. "God is love" (1 John 4:8) is an eternal principle because it is understandable in all cultures.

But we should clearly understand that every cultural expression in the Bible is the result of some eternal principle. And even though a cultural expression cannot be carried over directly to another culture, the eternal principle behind it can. Just because it is cultural does not mean it can be ignored.

A good example of this important principle might be the teaching that we should always be polite when we are guests for dinner. In America, this principle could express itself as "Eat all the food on the table lest you insult your host's cooking." But in Uganda it is important that food be left on the serving plates lest it appear your host has not sufficiently provided for you.

Therefore, whereas the principle shows itself in America as "Eat all the food," the same principle shows itself in Uganda as "Leave some of the food on the serving plates." *The task of the Biblical interpreter is to look through any cultural expression to the eternal principle that gave rise to it, and to reapply the principle in his own culture.* This is the process of evaluation. Is it cultural? If it is, how does the eternal principle which gave rise to the cultural expression reapply in the new culture?

Two implications can be drawn from this. First, if a statement is cultural, then there must be a principle that gave rise to the cultural statement. But if no principle can be found, then what was thought to be cultural must in fact be an eternal principle. Second, if the interpreter is not sure whether a statement is cultural, would it not be better to be safe and view the statement as eternal, lest a command of God be ignored?

We should also remember that just as a biblical passage can be set in its culture, so the interpreter is likewise controlled to some extent by his own culture. Many people today do not believe that the biblical accounts of miracles are true. For example, some scholars argue that miracles were a part of first century culture and were believed by the people in Jesus' day. But this is the 20th century and people do not believe in miracles in this culture. But these scholars' views on the impossibility of the supernatural are likewise influenced by the materialistic, science-oriented culture in which they live. We must be careful about allowing our own culture to influence our view of Scripture.

4. *Stage four: application*—Up to this point, the process of interpreting the Bible has been academic. But it is absolutely essential to recognize that the purpose and goal of Bible study is a godly life. Study is not complete until we put into practice what we have learned.

The question to ask at this stage of interpretation is, "How can I apply what I have learned to how I live my life?" The academic and the practical are thus fused into a meaningful approach to the Bible's message. Some people dismiss the academic as boring and trivial. Others reject the application as unnecessary. Both extremes are equally wrong. The Bible interpreter must walk the tightrope between these approaches. A three-act play is unsatisfying without the final act. The last act, without the first two, does not make sense. Sometimes in Bible study it is necessary to emphasize the academic when the passage is difficult to understand, or to emphasize the application when the passage's practical relevance is confusing. But one of these approaches should never be used to the exclusion of the other.

Special Problems in Interpreting the Bible. Scripture, like any other book, uses figures of speech and different types of literature that can be difficult to understand. These call for special rules for the Bible interpreter.

1. *Hyperbole*—A hyperbole is an exaggeration used for effect—an overstatement. "I'm so hungry I could eat a horse" obviously is not literally true. It is an exaggeration used to convey the idea of extreme hunger. Most hyperboles are easily recognized because we use them all the time. But sometimes they are not. For example, the apostle John made a statement something like this in his gospel: If everything Jesus ever did were written down, the world could not hold all the books (John 21:25). Surely John expected us to see that he was overstating his point. It is a graphic picture of how much Jesus did, but one painted in hyperbolic fashion.

2. *Metaphor*—A simile makes a comparison by using a word such as "like": "Life is like a circus." A metaphor is a similar comparison, except that it omits the word "like": "The world is a stage." Metaphors such as "I am the door" (John 10:9) are easily recognized. But what about Jesus' words at the Last Supper: "This is My body" (Luke 22:19)? Jesus probably intended this statement to be understood metaphorically rather than literally or physically.

3. *Anthropomorphism*—Do rivers have hands to clap (Ps. 98:8)? Does God have eyes (Ps. 33:18), although He is spirit (John 4:24)? Anthropomorphisms in the Bible describe non-human objects as though they have human characteristics. But how do we understand those verses that say God "repents" (Ex. 32:12; Jer. 18:8; relents, regrets, NKJV)? Does God change His mind? Or do these verses describe God from a human point of view?

4. *Parable*—"Once upon a time in a far-away land there lived a fairy princess." We do not understand this sentence in a scientific or literal sense. We recognize that it comes from a certain type of literature, and thus we do not interpret it historically. Different types of literature fall into different categories, each of which has its own rules of interpretation.

Parables are one type of literature in the Bible.

We interpret them properly by picturing the story in our minds as if we lived in Jesus' day, finding the one main point, and not giving meaning to all the details. The difference between allegory and parable is important to understand. An allegory is a totally made-up story. Even the details of an allegory may be significant. *Pilgrims Progress* is the classic example of allegory in which even minute details refer to other things. But a parable is a story taken from everyday life. In a parable the speaker may not treat the details as important. They may be given to help the reader picture the situation more clearly.

Although a few parables have allegorical elements, most parables teach only one main point. The parable of the sower (Matt. 13:3–23) is part allegory because the sower, seed, ground, birds, sun, and weeds all stand for something else: Jesus, Word, Jesus' audience, Satan, persecution, and the cares of the world. But what about the parable of the judge (Luke 18:1–14)?

If the woman represents the disciple, is God the unjust judge? Is the purpose of the parable of the rich man and Lazarus (Luke 16:19–31) to teach that you cannot travel between heaven and hell? The standard procedure for interpreting parables is to find the one main point and to view the details of the story simply as illustrations, but not as the direct teaching of the parable.

5. *Prophecy*—There are two points to remember when interpreting prophecy. The first is that what the prophet foresaw as one event may actually be two or more. The Old Testament thought of the "Day of the Lord" (Is. 2:12) as one event. But the last days actually began at Pentecost (Acts 2:20) and will conclude at Christ's return (2 Thess. 2:2).

The second point to remember is that although much Old Testament prophecy is fulfilled in the New Testament, much was fulfilled in the Old Testament and then again in the New. Isaiah's prophecy in 7:14 was fulfilled in Isaiah's day, and again by Jesus' birth (Matt. 1:23). Isaiah's prophecy had a more complete meaning in that it was to be fulfilled again at a more distant time in the future.

6. *Poetry*—Hebrew poetry does not concentrate on rhythm or rhyme. It expresses itself by parallelism. Two phrases are joined so that the second repeats the first with different words (Ps. 95:2), or the second states the opposite of the first (Prov. 15:5), or the second adds a new thought to the first (Prov. 15:3). Sometimes the couplet will be arranged with the second phrase reversing the order of the first (Prov. 15:21). Therefore, when interpreting poetry, the Bible student must recognize the type of parallelism being used, since the phrases interpret each other.

7. *Apocalyptic*—This type of literature in the Bible is the most misunderstood by interpreters today because it is no longer used. It has specific rules of interpretation. Its most noticeable characteristic is its use of strange, symbolic figures, such as those in the Book of Revelation.

The key to interpreting these figures lies in the

Book of Revelation itself. In 1:20 the seven stars are interpreted as representing the seven angels, and the seven lampstands stand for the seven churches. In 17:9-10 the seven-headed beast stands for the seven hills, and in 17:18 the woman is identified as the city which rules the earth. Therefore, to understand APOCALYPTIC LITERATURE, and Revelation in particular, we must interpret the imagery as very figurative. The images are describing things and spiritual realities in figurative language.

Some might object that this is not understanding the Bible literally. But since the Book of Revelation interprets its own images in figurative terms, the images must serve as figurative descriptions of real things. Therefore, to understand the book literally, we must understand it figuratively.

In interpreting the Bible, we must remember from Whom it comes. We are handling the Lord's message. This demands an attitude of respect and our willingness to subject ourselves to its authority.

BIBLE VERSIONS AND TRANSLATIONS —
The Bible was written across a period of several centuries in the languages of Hebrew and Aramaic (Old Testament) and Greek (New Testament). With the changing of nations and cultures across the centuries, these original writings have been translated many times to make the Bible available in different languages. Following are the major versions and translations of the Bible that have been issued during the past 2,200 years. Just as God inspired people to write His Word, He also has preserved the Bible by using human instruments to pass it on to succeeding generations.

Ancient Versions. Ancient versions of the Bible are those that were produced in classical languages such as Greek, Syriac, and Latin. The following an-cient versions were issued during a 600-year period from about 200 B.C. to A.D. 400.

Greek—The oldest Bible translation in the world was made in Alexandria, Egypt, where the Old Testament was translated from Hebrew into Greek for the benefit of the Greek-speaking Jews of that city. A Jewish community had existed in Alexandria almost from its foundation by ALEXANDER the Great in 331 B.C. In two or three generations this community had forgotten its native Palestinian language. These Jews realized they needed the Hebrew Scriptures rendered into the only language they knew—Greek. The first section of the Hebrew Bible to be translated into Greek was the PENTATEUCH, or the first five books of the Old Testament, some time before 200 B.C. Other parts were translated during the next century.

This version is commonly called the SEPTUAGINT, from *septuaginta*, the Latin word for 70 (LXX). This name was selected because of a tradition that the Pentateuch was translated into Greek by about 70 elders of Israel who were brought to Alexandria especially for this purpose.

Only a few fragments of this version survive from the period before Christ. Most copies of the Greek Old Testament belong to the Christian era and were made by Christians. The John Rylands University Library, Manchester, England, owns a fragment of Deuteronomy in Greek from the second century B.C. Another fragment of the same book in Greek dating from about the same time exists in Cairo. Other fragments of the Septuagint have been identified among the texts known as the DEAD SEA SCROLLS, discovered in 1947.

When Christianity penetrated the world of the Greek-speaking Jews, and then the Gentiles, the Septuagint was the Bible used for preaching the

The Jordan River valley south of Jericho near the Dead Sea.

gospel. Most of the Old Testament quotations in the New Testament are taken from this Greek Bible. In fact, the Christians adopted the Septuagint so wholeheartedly that the Jewish people lost interest in it. They produced other Greek versions that did not lend themselves so easily to Christian interpretation.

The Septuagint thus became the "authorized version" of the early Gentile churches. To this day it is the official version of the Old Testament used in the Greek Orthodox Church. After the books of the New Testament were written and accepted by the early church, they were added to the Old Testament Septuagint to form the complete Greek version of the Bible.

The Septuagint was based on a Hebrew text much older than most surviving Hebrew manuscripts of the Old Testament. Occasionally, this Greek Old Testament helps scholars to reconstruct the wording of a passage where it has been lost or miscopied by scribes as the text was passed down across the centuries. An early instance of this occurs in Genesis 4:8, where Cain's words to Abel, "Let us go out to the field," are reproduced from the Septuagint in the RSV and other modern versions. These words had been lost from the standard Hebrew text, but they were necessary to complete the sense of the English translation.

Aramaic targums—The word targum means "translation." After their return from CAPTIVITY in Babylon, many Jews spoke Aramaic, a sister-language, instead of the pure Hebrew of their ancestors. They found it difficult to follow the reading of the Hebrew Scriptures at worship. So they adopted the practice of providing an oral paraphrase into Aramaic when the Scriptures were read in Hebrew. The person who provided this paraphrase, the Turgeman, was an official in the synagogue.

One of the earliest examples of such a paraphrase occurs in Nehemiah 8:8. Because of the work of Ezra, the Pentateuch, or the first five books of the Old Testament, was officially recognized as the constitution of the Jewish state during the days of the Persian Empire. This constitution was read publicly to the whole community after their return to Jerusalem. The appointed readers "read distinctly [or, *with interpretation*] from the book, in the Law of God; and they gave the sense, and helped them understand the reading."

The phrase "with interpretation" appears as a marginal reading in several modern versions (for example, the RSV), but it probably indicates exactly what happened. The Hebrew text was read, followed by an oral paraphrase in Aramaic so everyone would be sure to understand.

This practice continued as standard in the Jewish synagogue for a long time. The targum, or paraphrase of the Hebrew, was not read from a written document, lest some in the congregation might think the authoritative law was being read. Some religious leaders apparently held that the targum should not be written down, even for use outside the synagogue.

In time, all objections to a written targum disappeared. A number of such paraphrases began to be used. Official Jewish recognition was given to two in particular—the Targum of Onkelos on the Pentateuch and the Targum of Jonathan on the Prophets. Some were far from being word-for-word translations. As expanded paraphrases, they included interpretations and comments on the biblical text.

Some New Testament writers indicate knowledge of targumic interpretations in their quotations from the Old Testament. For example, "Vengeance is Mine, I will repay" (Rom. 12:19; Heb. 10:30) is a quotation from Deuteronomy 32:35; but it conforms neither to the Hebrew text nor to the Greek text of the Septuagint. This particular phrase comes from the Targum. Again, the words of Ephesians 4:8, "When He ascended on high, He led captivity captive, and gave gifts to men," are taken from Psalm 68:18. But the Hebrew and Septuagint texts speak of the *receiving* of gifts. Only the Targum on this text mentions the giving of gifts.

Syriac—The term Syriac describes the Eastern Aramaic language spoken in Northern Mesopotamia, the land between the Tigris and Euphrates Rivers northeast of the land of Palestine. Large Jewish settlements were located there. At some point, the Old Testament must have been translated into Syriac for their benefit.

As Christianity expanded, this area became an important center of Christian life and action. The Christians in northern Mesopotamia inherited the Syriac Old Testament and added a Syriac translation of the New Testament to it. This "authorized version" of the Syriac Bible is called the Peshitta (the "common" or "simple" version). In its present

Title page from an early copy of the King James Version of the Bible, published originally in 1611.

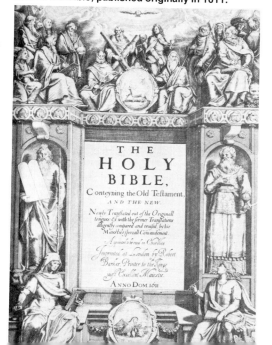

form, it goes back to the beginning of the fifth century A.D. But there were earlier Syriac translations of parts of the New Testament. Two important manuscripts of the Gospels exist in an Old Syriac version, which probably goes back to about the second century A.D.

The Syriac-speaking church was very missionary-minded. It carried the gospel into Central Asia, evangelizing India and parts of China. It translated portions of the Bible from Syriac into the local languages of these areas which it evangelized. The earliest forms of the Bible in the languages of Armenia and Georgia (north of Armenia) were based on the Syriac version.

Coptic—Coptic was a highly developed form of the native language of the ancient Egyptians. Christianity was planted in Egypt while some of the twelve apostles were still alive, although there is no record of how it was carried there. With the development of a Christian community in Egypt, the need arose for a Bible in the Coptic tongue. To this day the Coptic Church of Egypt uses the Bohairic version of the Coptic Bible, translated in the early centuries from the Septuagint and the Greek New Testament into the dialect of Lower Egypt. Earlier still is the Sahidic version, in the dialect of Upper Egypt.

Gothic—Across the Rhine and Danube frontiers of the Roman Empire lived a race of people known as the Goths. The evangelization of the Ostrogoths, those who lived north of the Danube River, began in the third century. About A.D. 360 Bishop Ulfilas, "the apostle of the Goths," led his converts south of the Danube to settle in what is now Bulgaria. There he translated the Bible into their language. The Gothic version was the first translation of the Bible into a language of the Germanic family. English, German, Dutch, and Scandinavian belong to this language group.

Latin—The need for a Latin Bible first arose during the second century A.D., when Latin began to replace Greek as the dominant language of the Roman Empire. The first Old Testament sections of the Latin Bible were considered unreliable, since they were actually a translation of a translation. They were based on the Septuagint, which, in turn, was a translation of the Hebrew Bible into Greek. Since the New Testament was written originally in Greek, it was translated directly into the Latin language. Several competing New Testament translations were in use throughout the Latin-speaking world as early as about A.D. 250.

The task of producing one standard Latin Bible to replace these competing translations was entrusted by Damasus, bishop of Rome (366–384), to his secretary Jerome. Jerome undertook the task unwillingly, knowing that replacing an old version with a new is bound to cause offense, even if the new is better. He began with a revision of the gospels, followed by the Psalms. After completing the New Testament, Jerome mastered the Hebrew language in order to translate the Old Testament into Latin. He completed this work in A.D. 405.

William Tyndale, shown seated in this painting, translates the New Testament into English—one of the first versions to be published in the language of the common people.

Jerome's translation of the Bible is known as the Latin Vulgate. It did not win instant acceptance. Many were suspicious of it because it varied so much from the version with which they were familiar. But in time its superior merits caused it to gain popularity.

The best surviving manuscript of the Latin Vulgate, the Codex Amiatinus, is now in the Laurentian Library of Florence, Italy. Written in a monastery in Northumbria, England, it was presented to Pope Gregory II in 716.

The Latin Vulgate is especially important because it was the medium through which the gospel arrived in Western Europe. It remained the standard version in this part of the world for centuries. In 1546 the Council of Trent directed that only "this same ancient and vulgate edition...be held as authentic in public lecture, disputations, sermons and expository discourses, and that no one make bold or presume to reject it on any pretext." Until the 20th century no translations of the Bible except those based on the Vulgate were recognized as authoritative by the Roman Catholic Church.

The Old English Versions. Until the beginning of the 16th century, all Bible versions in the languages of the masses of Western Europe were based on the Latin Vulgate. Among these, the Old English versions are of special interest. Most of these versions consisted of only parts of the Bible, and even these had limited circulation. In this period few of the people of ancient England could read. Many of the familiar stories of the Bible were turned into verse and set to music so they could be sung and memorized.

Caedmon, the unlettered poet of Whitby, is said to have turned the whole history of salvation into song in the seventh century. Bede, the monk of Jarrow, the most learned man of his day in Western Europe, devoted the last ten days of his life to turning the gospels into English so they could be read by the common man.

Alfred the Great, king of a large part of southern and western England, defeated the Danish invaders in 878. He published a code of laws that was introduced by an Old English translation of the Ten Commandments and other brief passages from the Bible.

The parts of the Bible most favored for translating during this period were those often read or recited during worship services, especially the Psalms and the gospels. An Old English version of the Psalms by Bishop Aldhelm dates from soon after 700. A manuscript called the Wessex Gospels dates from the middle of the tenth century.

Some of the earliest Old English versions of Scripture were written between the lines of Latin-language manuscripts. The manuscript known as the Lindisfarne Gospels (now in the British Museum, London) was produced originally in Latin shortly before 700. Two and a half centuries later a priest named Aldred wrote between the lines of the text a literal translation in the Northumbrian dialect of Old English. Bible texts of this type, with some letters decorated in gold and silver, are known as illustrated manuscripts.

Wycliffe's Versions. In the early Middle Ages, parts of the Bible were translated from Latin into several of the dialects of Western Europe. These included versions in the Bohemian, Czech, and Italian languages, as well as the Provencial dialect of southeastern France. But none of these compare in importance with the work of John Wycliffe, pioneering reformer who translated the entire Bible from Latin into the English language.

Wycliffe (c. 1330–1384), master of Balliol College, Oxford, was a distinguished scholar and preacher. But he was also a social reformer who wanted to replace the feudal organization of state and church with a system that emphasized man's direct responsibility to God. The constitution of this new order would be the law of God, which Wycliffe equated with the Bible. Before this could happen, the law of God had to be accessible to the laity as well as the clergy, the unlearned as well as the learned. This called for a Bible in English as well as Latin so Wycliffe and his associates undertook the task of translating the entire Bible from the Latin Vulgate into contemporary English.

There were actually two Wycliffe versions of the Bible—an earlier one, produced between 1380 and 1384 during Wycliffe's lifetime, and a later version completed in 1395, 11 years after his death.

The earlier version is a thoroughly literal translation. Wycliffe followed the Latin construction without attempting to render the meaning into good English idiom. The translators produced a literal version because it was intended to serve as the lawbook of the new order. The Latin text of the lawbook was already established, and the English text had to follow it word for word. About two thirds of this version was produced by one of Wycliffe's supporters, Nicholas of Hereford. Wycliffe himself may have done some of the translation work on the remaining portion. By the time this first translation was completed, the movement with

A scroll of the Pentateuch in the Hebrew language, used for liturgical purposes in a Jewish synagogue.
Photo by Gustav Jeeninga

Photo by Gustav Jeeninga

An archaeological excavation underway at the site of ancient Zaretan (Josh. 3:16) in southern Palestine.

which this English social reformer was associated was condemned by the authorities.

The second Wycliffe version was the work of his secretary, John Purvey. It was based on the earlier version, but it rendered the text into idiomatic English. Purvey's version became very popular, although its circulation was restricted by church officials. It was suppressed in 1408 by a document known as the "Constitutions of Oxford," which forbade anyone to translate or even to read any part of the Bible in English without the permission of a bishop or a local church council. These constitutions remained in force for more than a century.

From Wycliffe to King James. More than 200 years passed from the time that Wycliffe's second English version was issued (1395) until the historic King James Version was published in 1611. These were fruitful years for new versions of the Bible. The stage was set for the monumental King James Bible by five different English translations that were issued during these years.

Tyndale—The years from about 1450 onward brought exciting cultural changes in Western Europe. The revival of interest in classical and biblical learning was already under way when it received a stimulus from the migration of Greek scholars to the West after the fall of Constantinople to the Turks in 1453. With the invention of printing in Germany, the promoters of the new learning found a new technology at their disposal.

Among the first products of the printing press were editions of the Bible. The first major work to be printed was the famous Gutenberg edition of the Latin Bible, in 1456. The following decades brought printed editions of the Hebrew Bible, the Greek New Testament, and the Septuagint. The leaders of the Protestant Reformation were quick to take advantage of this new invention to help advance their efforts in church reform.

Making the Bible available in the tongue of the common people was a major strategy in the Reformers' policy. Martin Luther, leader of the Reformation, translated the New Testament from Greek into German in 1522 and the Old Testament from Hebrew into German in the following years. What Luther did for the Germans, William Tyndale did for the people of England.

After completing his studies at the Universities of Oxford and Cambridge, William Tyndale (c. 1495–1536) devoted his time and talents to providing his fellow Englishmen with the Scriptures in their own language. He hoped that Bishop Tunstall of London would sponsor his project of translating the Bible, but the bishop refused to do so. Tyndale then went to Germany in 1524 to undertake his project. By August of 1525 his English New Testament was complete.

Tyndale began printing his new version at Cologne, but this was interrupted by the city authorities. The printing work was then carried through by Peter Schoeffer in Worms, who produced an edition of 6,000 copies. Soon this new Bible was selling in England, although it had been officially banned by the church.

Tyndale's translation differed in two important respects from the versions of Wycliffe. It was ren-

The mound of Ziklag, a base of operation for David's army during the early years of his reign (1 Sam. 27:6).

dered not from the Latin language but from the Greek original, and it circulated in printed form, not as a handcopied manuscript. From the New Testament, Tyndale moved to the Old, issuing an edition of the Pentateuch, then the Book of Jonah, and a revision of Genesis. Later, in 1534, Tyndale issued a revision of his New Testament, justly described as "altogether Tyndale's noblest monument."

A further revision of the New Testament appeared in 1535. In May of that year Tyndale was arrested. After an imprisonment of 17 months, he was sentenced to death as a heretic; he was strangled and burned at the stake at Vilvorde, near Brussels, on October 6, 1536.

Tyndale started a tradition in the history of the English Bible that has endured to this day. What is commonly called "Bible English" is really Tyndale's English. His wording in those portions of the Bible which he translated was retained in the King James Version to a great degree. The latest in the succession of revisions which stand in the Tyndale tradition is the New King James Version. But even those versions that did not set out to adhere to his tradition, such as the New International Version, show his influence.

Coverdale and Matthew—At the time of Tyndale's death, a printed edition of the English Bible, bearing a dedication to King Henry VIII, had been circulating in England for nearly a year. This was the first edition of the Bible issued by Miles Coverdale (1488–1568), one of Tyndale's friends and associates. This English version reproduced Tyndale's

translation of the Pentateuch and the New Testament; the rest of the Old Testament was translated into English from Latin and German versions.

Coverdale's Bible of 1535 was the first complete English Bible in print. A second and third edition appeared in 1537. The title page bore the words: "Set forth with the King's most gracious licence." But this was not the only English Bible to appear in 1537 with these words on the title page. Another of Tyndale's associates, John Rogers, published an edition of the Bible that year under the name, "Thomas Matthew." "Matthew's Bible" was similar to Coverdale's with one exception: its translation of the historical books from Joshua to 2 Chronicles was one that Tyndale had finished without publishing before his death.

The Great Bible—Official policy toward the translation and circulation of the Bible in England changed quickly. King Henry's break with the Roman Catholic pope in Rome in 1534 had something to do with it, but deeper factors were also involved. A landmark in the history of the English Bible was the royal injunction of September 1538, directing that "one book of the whole Bible of the largest volume in English" should be placed in every parish church in England where the people could have access to it. When this decree was issued, another version of the Bible—the "Great Bible"—was being prepared so this commandment could be followed.

Publication of the Great Bible was delayed because French officials halted its production in Paris, where it was being printed. The printing was then transferred to London, where the Great Bible appeared in 1539. The Great Bible was Coverdale's revision of Matthew's Bible, which means that it was essentially a copy of Tyndale's translation. It quickly became the "authorized version" of the English Bible.

One part of the Great Bible remained in use long after the version as a whole had been replaced by later and better versions. To this day the Psalter in the Book of Common Prayer that is sung in the services of the Church of England is the Psalms contained in the Great Bible.

The Geneva Bible—During the reign of Mary Tudor of England (1553–1558), many English Reformers sought refuge in other parts of Europe because of her policy of persecution. One community of English refugees settled in Geneva, Switzerland, where John Knox was pastor of the English congregation and where John Calvin dominated theological study. Many of these English refugees were fine scholars, and they began work on a new English version of the Bible. A preliminary edition of the New Testament (Whittingham's New Testament) was published in 1557. This was the first edition of any part of the English Bible to have the text divided into verses. The whole Bible appeared in 1560.

This "Geneva Bible" was the first English Bible to be translated in its entirety from the original biblical languages. Widely recognized as the best English version of the Bible that had yet appeared, it quickly became the accepted version in Scotland. In England it also attained instant popularity among the people, although it was not accepted by church officials. After the publication of the King James Version in 1611, the Geneva Bible remained popular. This was the Bible which the Pilgrims took with them to the new world in 1620; to them the King James Version was a compromise and an inferior production. The Geneva Bible was printed until 1644 and was still found in use 30 years later.

The Bishops' Bible—The rival version to the Geneva Bible sponsored by church leaders in England was published in 1568. It was called the Bishops' Bible because all the translators were either bishops at the time or became bishops later. It was a good translation, based throughout on the original languages; but it was not as sound in scholarship as the Geneva Bible.

The King James Version—Shortly after James VI of Scotland ascended the throne of England as James I (1603), he convened a conference to settle matters under dispute in the Church of England. The only important result of this conference was an approval to begin work on the King James Version of the English Bible (KJV).

A group of 47 scholars, divided into six teams, was appointed to undertake the work of preparing the new version. Three teams worked on the Old Testament; two were responsible for the New Testament; and one worked on the Apocrypha. They used the 1602 edition of the Bishops' Bible as the basis of their revision, but they had access to many other versions and helps, as well as the texts in the original biblical languages. When the six groups had completed their task, the final draft was reviewed by a committee of 12. The King James Version was published in 1611.

The new version won wide acceptance among the people of the English–speaking world. Nonsectarian in tone and approach, it did not favor one shade of theological or ecclesiastical opinion over another. The translators had an almost instinctive sense of good English style; the prose rhythms of the version gave it a secure place in the popular memory. Never was a version of the Bible more admirably suited for reading aloud in public.

Although there was some resistance to the King James Version at first, it quickly made a place for itself. For more than three centuries, it has remained "The Bible" throughout the English–speaking world.

Catholic Versions. A generation before the appearance of the King James Bible, an English version of the Bible for Roman Catholics was undertaken by the faculty of the English College at Douai, France. Unlike the Geneva Bible, which was translated from the original languages, the Douai (or Douay) Bible was translated from the Latin Vulgate. The translator of the Douai Bible was Gregory Martin, formerly an Oxford scholar, who translated two chapters a day until the project was finished. Each section was then revised by two of his colleagues. The New Testament portion of this version was issued in 1582 and the Old Testament in 1609–10.

The Douai Bible was scholarly and accurate, but the English style and vocabulary were modeled on Latin usage. It would not have become popular among the Catholic laity if it had not been for the work of Richard Challoner (1691–1781), who revised it thoroughly between 1749 and 1772. What has generally been called the Douai Bible since Challoner's day is in fact the Douai Bible as revised by Challoner. In several respects it was a new version. Until 1945 this Douai revision by Challoner remained the only version of the Bible officially sanctioned for English–speaking Catholics.

Nineteenth Century Revisions. During the 18th century and the earlier part of the 19th century, several private attempts were made at revising the King James Version. The reasons for revision included the outdated English of the KJV, the progress made by scholars in understanding the original languages of the Bible, and the availability of better texts in the original biblical languages, especially the Greek text of the New Testament.

One of the most influential private revisions was Henry Alford's *New Testament* (1869). In the preface to this translation, Alford expressed the hope that his work would be replaced soon by an official revision of the KJV.

This hope was fulfilled in 1870 when the Church of England initiated plans for a revision. Two groups of revisers were appointed, one for the Old Testament and one for the New. Representatives of

British churches other than the Church of England were included on these committees. Before long, parallel companies of revisers were set up in the United States. At first these groups worked under the hope that one version might be produced for both England and the United States. But this was not to be. The American scholars, conservative as they were in their procedure, could not be bound by the stricter conservatism of their British counterparts. The three installments of the British revision (RV) appeared in 1881, in 1885, and in 1894. The American revision, or American Standard Version (ASV), was released in 1901, but did not include the Apocrypha.

The RV and ASV were solid works of scholarship. The Old Testament revisers had a much better grasp of Hebrew than the original translators of the King James Bible. The New Testament revision was based on a much more accurate Greek text than had been available in 1611. Although the RV and ASV were suitable for Bible study, they did not gain popular acceptance, mainly because their translators paid little attention to style and rhythm as they rendered the biblical languages into English.

Twentieth Century Enterprises. The first half of the 20th century was marked by a succession of brilliant private enterprises in translation—both for the New Testament alone and for the whole Bible.

Twentieth Century New Testament—The earliest of these was the Twentieth Century New Testament, a project conducted by a group of intelligent laypersons who used Westcott and Hort's edition of the Greek New Testament (1881) as their basic text. They were concerned that no existing version (not even the RV) made the Bible plain to young people, and they set out to supply this need. They completed their work in 1901; a revised edition appeared in 1904.

Weymouth—Richard Francis Weymouth, a Greek scholar, published an edition of the Greek New Tes-

tament called *The Resultant Greek Testament* in 1886. Later he issued a translation of this text, *The New Testament in Modern Speech*, which appeared in 1903, shortly after his death. The "modern speech" into which this translation was rendered was dignified contemporary usage and it paid special attention to accuracy in the translation of details such as the definite article and tenses.

Moffatt—Much more colloquial than Weymouth's version was *The New Testament: A New Translation* (1913) by James Moffatt. Moffatt was a Scot, and his translation bore traces of the idiom of his native land. While his unique expressions shocked some readers accustomed to more dignified Bible English, they brought home the meaning of the text with greater clarity than ever before.

In 1924 Moffatt added *The Old Testament: A New Translation*; in 1928 the whole work appeared in one volume, entitled *A New Translation of the Bible*. In both Testaments Moffatt occasionally took greater liberties with the wording and order than was proper for a translator; yet to this day one of the best ways to get a quick grasp of the general sense of a book of the Bible is to read it through in Moffatt's translation.

Goodspeed—Edgar J. Goodspeed of the University of Chicago produced *The New Testament: An American Translation* in 1923. He was convinced that most Bible versions were translated into "British English"; so he tried to provide a version free from expressions that might be strange to Americans. A companion work, *The Old Testament: An American Translation*, edited by J. M. Powis Smith and three other scholars, was issued in 1927. In 1938 Goodspeed's translation of the Apocrypha appeared. This was the final contribution to *The Complete Bible: An American Translation*.

The Revised Standard Version. The Revised Standard Version (RSV) is one of the last versions in the long line of English Bible translations that stem

Roman ruins at Hierapolis, a city in the province of Asia mentioned by the apostle Paul (Col. 4:13).
Photo: Levant Photo Service

from William Tyndale. Although it is a North American production, it has been widely accepted in the whole English–speaking world.

The RSV was launched as a revision of the KJV (1611), RV (1885), and ASV (1901). Authorized by the International Council of Religious Education, it is copyrighted by the Division of Christian Education of the National Council of Churches in the USA. The New Testament first appeared in 1946, the two Testaments in 1952, and the Apocrypha in 1957. A new edition in 1962 incorporated 85 minor changes in wording.

A Catholic edition of the RSV New Testament appeared in 1964, followed by the whole Bible in 1966. In 1973 a further edition of the RSV appeared (including revisions made in the 1971 edition of the New Testament). This version of the Bible was approved for use by Protestants, Roman Catholics, and the Greek Orthodox Church, making it an English Bible for all faiths.

New Catholic Versions. Several new versions of the English Bible designed especially for Catholic readers have appeared during the 20th century.

Knox—In 1940 Ronald Knox, an English priest with exceptional literary gifts, was commissioned by his superiors to undertake a new Bible translation. At that time it was out of the question for a translation for Catholic readers to be based on anything other than the Latin Vulgate. The Vulgate served as the base of Knox's version, but he paid attention to the original Greek and Hebrew texts. His New Testament appeared in 1945, followed by the Old Testament in 1949.

Knox had a flair for adapting his English expressions to the rigid restrictions of the Latin Vulgate style. But the progress of the biblical movement in the Catholic Church in recent years has made his translation outdated. No longer must all Catholic versions of the Bible be based on the Latin Vulgate.

The Jerusalem Bible—The Jerusalem Bible was originally a French translation of the Bible, sponsored by the Dominican faculty of the Ecole Biblique et Archeologique in Jerusalem. A one–volume edition of the work, with fewer technical notes, was issued in 1956. The English counterpart to this volume, prepared under the editorship of Alexander Jones, was published in 1966. The biblical text was translated from the Hebrew and Greek languages, although the French version was consulted throughout for guidance where variant readings or interpretations were involved.

The Jerusalem Bible is a scholarly production with a high degree of literary skill. While it is the work of Catholic translators, it is nonsectarian. Readers of many religious traditions use the Jerusalem Bible.

The New American Bible—The New American Bible (NAB) was launched as a revision of the Douai (or Douay) Bible for American readers. In the beginning the revision was sponsored by the Episcopal Confraternity of Christian Doctrine, and the resulting work was called the Confraternity Version. The translators were scholars who belonged to the Catholic Biblical Association of America.

The New Testament of this translation first appeared in 1941. While it was a revision of the Douai text, which was based in turn on the Latin Vulgate, the translators at times went back to the Greek text behind the Latin. They drew attention in their notes to places where the Greek and Latin texts differed.

As the project progressed, the translators moved away from the Latin Vulgate as their text, basing it instead on the Greek and Hebrew text. So radical was this fresh approach that a new name seemed appropriate for the version when the entire Bible was completed in 1970. It was no longer called the Confraternity Version but the New American Bible. This new name may have been influenced also by the title of the New English Bible, which had appeared earlier in the same year.

The New English Bible. When the copyright of the British Revised Version was about to expire (1935), the owners of the copyright, the Oxford and Cambridge University Presses, consulted scholars about the possibility of a revision to bring this translation up to date. Later the scope of the project changed so that an entirely new translation, rather than a revision of an old translation, was commissioned.

The initiative in this enterprise was taken by the Church of Scotland in 1946. It approached other British churches, and a joint committee was set up in 1947 to make plans for a new translation of the Bible into modern English. The joint committee included representatives of the principal non–Roman churches of Great Britain and Ireland, agents of Bible societies, and officials of Oxford and Cambridge University Presses. The translators' goal was to issue a version "genuinely English in idiom...a 'timeless' English, avoiding equally both archaisms and transient modernisms."

The New Testament of the New English Bible (NEB) was published in March 1961; the whole Bible, together with the Apocrypha, appeared in March 1970. Between 1961 and 1970 the New Testament received some further revision.

In one respect the New English Bible reverted to the policy of the translators of the King James Version; sometimes they rendered the same Hebrew or Greek word with different English words. This means the student who cannot use the Hebrew or Greek texts will be unable to use this version for detailed word study. Sometimes the NEB makes a useful distinction in its selection of words, as when "church" is reserved for the universal company of Christian believers and "congregation" is used for a local group of believers. But a useful distinction made by the RV, ASV, and RSV is sometimes obscured by the NEB. A good example is when the same word, "devil or devils," is used by the NEB for Satan as well as the beings which should more correctly be called "demons." Two different Greek words for these beings are used in the original texts, and there is no good reason why they should be called the same thing by the NEB.

Paraphrases and Simplified Versions. Some translators have attempted to bring out the meaning of the biblical text by using either simplified or amplified vocabularies. Other translations that fall into this category are those that use lists of words considered basic to the English language.

Williams—Charles B. Williams, in *The New Testament in the Language of the People* (1937), tried to express the more delicate shades of meaning in Greek tenses by using a fuller wording. Thus, the command of Ephesians 4:25, "Let every one speak the truth with his neighbor" (RSV), is expressed, "You must...each of you practice telling the truth to his neighbor."

Wuest—What Williams did for Greek tenses, Kenneth S. Wuest did for all parts of speech in his *Expanded Translation of the New Testament* (1956–59). In this translation, the familiar Bible phrase, "Husbands, love your wives" (Eph. 5:25) appears as, "The husbands, be loving your wives with a love self-sacrificial in its nature."

Amplified Bible—In *The Amplified Bible* (1958–65), a committee of 12 editors working for the Lockman Foundation of La Habra, California, incorporated alternative translations or additional words that would normally appear in margins or footnotes into their translation of the text. One fault of this translation is that it gives the reader no guidance to aid in choosing the proper alternative reading for specific passages.

New Testament in Basic English—Basic English is a simplified form of the language, created by C. K. Ogden, which attempts to communicate ideas with a simplified vocabulary of 850 words. In the 1930s Ogden's foundation, the Orthological Institute, commissioned an English biblical scholar, S. H. Hooke, to produce a Basic English version of the Bible. For this purpose the basic vocabulary of 850 words was expanded to 1,000 by adding special Bible words and others helpful in the reading and understanding of poetry. *The New Testament in Basic English* appeared in 1940; the complete Bible was published in 1949.

Williams—Charles Kingsley Williams, who had experience in teaching students whose native tongue was not English, produced *The New Testament: A New Translation in Plain English* in 1952. He used a "plain English" list of less than 1,700 words in this translation.

Phillips—J. B. Phillips, an Anglican clergyman, relieved the tedium of fire-watching and similar night-time duties during World War II by turning Paul's letters into English. This work was not a strict translation but a paraphrase that made the apostle's arguments meaningful for younger readers. He published *Letters to Young Churches* in 1947, and it became an instant success. The style was lively and forceful; the apostle Paul came across as a real man who had something important to say.

Phillips followed up on his initial success by releasing other parts of the New Testament. *The Gospels in Modern English* followed in 1952; *The Young Church in Action* (the Book of of Acts) appeared in 1955; and *The Book of Revelation* was published in 1957. In 1958 the whole work appeared in one volume, *The New Testament in Modern English*. A completely revised edition of this paraphrase was issued in 1972, but many readers prefer the earlier edition.

The Living Bible—Like J. B. Phillips' work, *The Living Bible* is a paraphrase that began with a rendering of the New Testament letters—*Living Letters* (1962). The translator, Kenneth N. Taylor, prepared this paraphrase initially for his own children, who found it difficult to follow the apostle Paul's thought when his letters were read in family worship. Taylor went on to paraphrase the rest of the New Testament, then the Old Testament, until *The Living Bible* was published complete in 1971. This paraphrase is especially popular with young people. Many adults have also found that it brings the message of the Bible home to them in language they can understand.

The Good News Bible—In 1966 the American Bible Society issued *Today's English Version* (also entitled *Good News for Modern Man*), a translation of the New Testament, in simple, contemporary English. The aim of this version was similar to the preceding basic English and plain English versions, but *The Good News Bible* used no limited vocabulary list. In 1976 the entire *Bible in Today's English Version* was published.

The translators of *The Good News Bible* worked to achieve "dynamic equivalence." They wanted this translation to have the same effect on modern readers that the original text produced on those who first read it. The *Good News Bible* has gained wide acceptance, and similar translations have been produced in a number of other languages.

Miscellaneous Simplified Versions—Other simplified translations of the Bible include Clarence Jordan's *Cotton Patch Version* (1968–70), which renders portions of the New Testament into the unique idiom of the American South. Also included in this category is Carl Burke's *God Is For Real, Man* (1967) and *Treat Me Cool, Lord* (1969). These were written in the unique language of prison inmates while Burke was serving as a jail chaplain.

New American Standard Bible. An editorial board of 54 scholars began work on this translation in the 1960s. They were determined to issue a new and revised translation based on the American Standard Version of 1901 in order to keep that version alive and usable among the Bible-reading public. Sponsored by the Lockman Foundation, the complete Bible of the NASB was published in 1971 after 11 years of careful, scholarly work. The translators used the most dependable Hebrew and Greek texts available. The editorial board has continued to function since publication of the Bible, making minor revisions and refinements in the translation as better texts of the original languages of the Bible became available.

New International Version. The New International Version (NIV) is a completely new translation of

Photo: Levant Photo Service

Abraham's Well at the ancient city of Beersheba.

the Bible, sponsored by the New York International Bible Society. It is the work of an international and transdenominational team of scholars, drawn mainly from the United States but also including scholars from Canada, Britain, Australia, and New Zealand. The sponsors of the NIV claim it is "written in the language of the common man," but its language is more literary than the "common English" of the Good News Bible.

The translators of the NIV were familiar with traditional Bible English. They used the language of the King James Version where it was "accurate, clear, and readable." But they made many significant changes. Unlike the RSV and NEB (which retained "thee," "thou," and "thy" when God was being addressed), the NIV uses "you" and "your." The New Testament of this version was published in 1973; the whole Bible appeared in 1978.

New King James Version. The original King James Version, first published in 1611, has been the favorite translation among English-speaking peoples for more than three centuries. During its long history, the King James Bible has been updated and revised several times to reflect changes in speech as well as growing knowledge of the original text of the Scriptures. Previous major revisions of this translation were issued in 1629, 1638, 1762, and 1769.

During the 1970s, Thomas Nelson Publishers of Nashville, Tennessee, sensed the need for a fifth major revision. Over 130 Bible scholars were selected to work on the New King James Version. The translators worked from the earliest and most trustworthy Hebrew and Greek texts available and also used the 1769 King James revision as a general guide to make sure the new edition preserved the majestic style and devotional quality of the original King James.

The most noticeable change in the New King James is replacement of the "thee's" and "thou's" and other archaic pronouns with their modern English equivalent. The "-est" and "-eth" verb endings also were eliminated in favor of more contemporary English idioms. The New Testament with Psalms was released in 1980, followed by the Old Testament in 1982.

Miscellaneous Translations. Many English translations have not been mentioned in this article. Among Jewish translations of the Hebrew Bible, special reference should be made to *A New Translation of the Holy Scriptures according to the Masoretic Text*, produced in installments since 1963 by a committee working under the chairmanship of H. M. Orlinsky. *The Authentic New Testament* (1955) is a translation by a well-known Jewish scholar, Hugh J. Schonfield.

Brief mention should be made of the following translations: The Penguin Classics edition of *The Four Gospels*, by E. V. Rieu (1952) and *The Acts of the Apostles*, by C. H. Rieu (1957); the *Berkeley Version* (New Testament, 1945; Bible, 1959), revised as *The Modern Language Bible* (1969); the *New World Translation* of Jehovah's Witnesses (1961); *The New Testament in the Language of Today*, by William F. Beck, a Lutheran scholar (1963); and *The New Testament* in the translation of William Barclay (1968–69).

BIBLICAL CRITICISM — the application of one or more techniques in the scientific study of the Bible. These techniques are not peculiar to Bible study; they would be equally helpful in the study of the writings of Homer or Shakespeare. Their primary intention is to help the reader of the Bible understand it better; for that reason biblical criticism examines the Greek and Hebrew texts (textual criticism), the historical setting of the various parts of the Bible (historical criticism), and various literary questions regarding how, when, where and why the books of the Bible were first written (literary criticism). These methods of study, when done with reverence for Scripture, should assist a student's appreciation for the INSPIRATION of the Bible.

Textual Criticism. This is the attempt to determine, as accurately as possible, the wording of the text of the Bible as first written down under the inspiration of the Holy Spirit. Since none of the original documents has survived and the text is available only in copies, it is necessary to compare the early copies with each other. This allows the textual critic to classify these early copies into groups exhibiting certain common features and to decide why their differences occurred and what the original wording most likely was.

The early copies on which textual critics work consist mainly of manuscripts in the original languages, translations into other languages, and biblical quotations made by Jewish and Christian writers. (Also see BIBLE, BIBLE VERSIONS AND TRANSLATIONS.)

Historical Criticism. The examination of the Bible in light of its historical setting. This is particularly important because the Bible was written over a period of more than one thousand years. The story the Bible records extends from the beginning of civilization in the ancient world to the Roman Empire of the first century A.D.

Historical criticism is helpful in determining when the books of the Bible were written. It is also helpful in determining a book's "dramatic date"—that is, when the people it describes lived and its events happened. The dramatic date of Genesis, for instance, is much earlier than the date when it was written. Historical criticism asks if the stories of the patriarchs—Abraham, Isaac, Jacob and Joseph—reflect the conditions of the times in which they lived.

The consensus is that these stories better reflect their dramatic date than the dates of their writing, just as the picture presented in the New Testament best reflects what is known about the early part of the first century A.D.

Literary Criticism. The study of how, when, where, and why the books of the Bible were written. Literary criticism may be divided into questions concerning sources, tradition, redaction, and authorship.

1. *Source criticism* attempts to determine whether the writers of the books of the Bible used earlier sources of information and, if so, whether those sources were oral or written. Some biblical books clearly indicate their dependence on earlier sources: 1 and 2 Chronicles, Luke and Acts. Some of the sources for the Chronicles are still available to us in 1 and 2 Samuel and 1 and 2 Kings, which were written earlier. The author of Luke and Acts says that much of his information was handed on by

The Wilderness of Sin, an uninhabited region through which the Israelites passed between Elim and Mt. Sinai (Ex. 16:1).
Photo by Howard Vos

"those who from the beginning were eyewitnesses and ministers of the word" (Luke 1:2).

However, these sources usually have not survived independently and their identification and reconstruction cannot be certain. It is fairly clear, however, that the Gospels of Matthew, Mark, and Luke draw on common sources; their two most widely agreed sources are one that related the story of Jesus and one that contained a collection of His teachings.

2. *Tradition criticism* (including form criticism) studies how information was passed from one generation to another before it was put in its present form. Tradition is simply that which is handed down; it may be divinely authoritative, or it may be merely "the tradition of men" (Mark 7:8; Col. 2:8). Sometimes a tradition was handed on by word of mouth for several generations before it was written down, as in the record of the patriarchs in Genesis. Sometimes a tradition was handed on by word of mouth for only 20 or 30 years, as in the records of the works and words of Jesus before the gospels were written.

Tradition criticism attempts to trace the stages by which these traditions were handed down, the forms which they took at those various stages, and the forms in which they reached the people who committed them to writing.

Form criticism is the branch of tradition criticism that examines the various "forms"—e.g. parables, miracles, discourses—by which the traditions took shape. Form criticism has been applied to many areas of the biblical literature, such as the composition of the Psalms, the prophet's calls to their ministries, and the contents of the gospels. Some scholars have, for instance, classified various psalms as "Royal" psalms, "Lament" psalms, "Torah" (Law) psalms, "Praise" psalms, etc.

Classifying sections of the Bible according to the form they take can provide an additional perspective from which one can better understand the text of Scripture. However, this method must be used with great caution and restraint to avoid imposing the interpreter's own assumptions on the Bible.

3. *Redaction criticism* attempts to understand the contribution to the finished manuscript made by the person who finally committed the oral or written traditions to writing. This may be illustrated from the Gospel of Luke. Luke makes no claim to have been an eyewitness of the events of Jesus' ministry; everything he records in the Gospel was received from others. Tradition criticism studies what Luke received and the state in which he received it. Redaction criticism studies what he did with what he received. Luke (and the same can be said of the other evangelists) was a responsible author who set the stamp of his own personality on what he wrote.

It is important to remember that an author's personal contribution to the finished book was no less reliable (and, hence, no less authoritative) than the tradition which he received. Unfortunately, some redaction critics make the error of assuming that the author's work is inauthentic, ignoring the work of the Holy Spirit in inspiring the writers of the Bible.

4. *Authorship and destination criticism* involve the attempt to determine the authorship of a work, as well as the person, group, or wider public for whom it was written. Sometimes there is no need for inquiry into these matters; Paul's letter to the Romans, for example, is clearly the work of the apostle Paul and was sent by him to the Christians in Rome. But the judicious use of literary criticism will throw further light on the circumstances which led to the writing of the book and the purpose for which Romans was sent. When, however, a work is

Remains of a Roman warehouse at Ostia, Italy, a city situated at the mouth of the Tiber River.
Photo by Howard Vos

anonymous, critical inquiry may help us to discover what sort of person the author was. For example, we do not know for certain who wrote the letter to the Hebrews. However, by looking critically at Hebrews we can learn much about the character of the author and a little about the character and situation of the people to whom the letter was written.

BIBLICAL ETHICS — living righteously—doing what is good and refraining from what is evil—in accordance with the will of God. The term refers not to human theories or opinions about what is right and wrong but to God's revealed truth about these matters. Questions of human conduct prevail throughout the Bible. God's revelation through His written Word narrates the story of man's ethical failure, God's redeeming grace, and the ethical renewal of His people.

God's people are called to holiness because they are God's people: "You shall therefore be holy, for I am holy" (Lev. 11:45). The New Testament counterpart to this principle is found in Matthew 5:48: "Therefore you shall be perfect, just as your Father in heaven is perfect."

God gave the Law to the nation of Israel as a standard of righteousness. This was the revealed will of God for His people. But His commandments were given in a context of GRACE. When the TEN COMMANDMENTS were given through Moses, they were introduced with a statement supporting the relationship that had already been established between God and His people whom He delivered from Egypt (Ex. 20:2; Deut. 5:6). God's commandments are always given to those who are already His people by grace.

This truth carries through to the New Testament. Jesus' ethical teaching in the Sermon on the Mount was preceded by the BEATITUDES, which reminded Jesus' disciples that God's grace comes before His commands (Matt. 5:3–12).

This connection between God's demands and His grace means that biblical ethics must always be understood in terms of what God has already done for His people. Grace precedes Law, just as doctrine always precedes ethics in the letters of the New Testament. So ethics should not be regarded as the center of the Christian faith. Correct behavior is the outflow or product of grace—the proper response in those who have experienced God's grace.

For the Christian the ultimate standard of ethics is Jesus Christ and His teachings. The Christian is not under the Law of the Old Testament (Eph. 2:14–16). But since the ethical teachings of Jesus sum up the true meaning of the Old Testament Law, following His teachings fulfills the Law. So there is a direct relationship between the concept of righteousness as revealed in the Old Testament and later in the New.

The Ten Commandments, for example, are referred to as positive ethical instruction in the New Testament (Rom. 13:9). Yet the commandment concerning the SABBATH is no longer in force (Col.

Photo by Gustav Jeeninga

Secluded site of the monastery of Koziba on the old road from Jerusalem to Jericho in southern Palestine.

2:15–16). And the ceremonial law, involving sacrificial rituals in the Temple, no longer is in effect because of the ultimate sacrifice of Christ (Heb. 10:12–18).

Jesus' commandment to love is the essence of Christian ethics. When a Pharisee asked Jesus to identify "the great commandment in the law," Jesus answered, " 'You shall love the Lord your God with all your heart, with all your soul, and with all your mind.' This is the first and great commandment. And the second is like it: 'You shall love your neighbor as yourself.' On these two commandments hang all the Law and the prophets" (Matt. 22:37–40). The apostle Paul also declared that all the commandments are "summed up in this saying, namely, 'You shall love your neighbor as yourself.' Love does no harm to a neighbor; therefore love is the fulfillment of the Law" (Rom. 13:9–10). This great love commandment summarizes and fulfills the intention of the Old Testament Law.

While love is the summary of Christian ethics, the New Testament contains many specific ethical instructions. A basic pattern for this ethical teaching is the contrast between our old existence before faith in Christ and our new existence in Him. Christians are called to leave behind their old conduct and to put on the new (Eph. 4:22–24), to walk in newness of life (Rom. 6:4), and to exhibit the fruit of the Spirit (Gal. 5:22–23).

Although as Christians we are free from the Law, we are not to use that liberty "as an opportunity for the flesh, but through love" to "serve one another" (Gal. 5:13). Love is best expressed through service and self-giving (Matt. 20:26–27). These points lead

The great theater at Ephesus, where Paul was almost mobbed by the worshipers of the pagan goddess Diana (Acts 19:21-41).

naturally to the observation that Jesus Himself is the supreme example of righteousness. Christian ethics are summed up not only in His teaching, but in His life as well. So true discipleship consists of following Jesus (Eph. 5:2) and being conformed to His image (Rom. 8:29).

The call for righteousness is directed to the individual, but ethics also has an important social dimension. The centrality of love indicates this very clearly. The prophets of the Old Testament emphasized the connection between righteousness and social justice. The ethical teaching of the Bible as followed by Christians will have an impact on the world (Matt. 5:13-16). But in spite of all these truths, the Bible does not call for a social program to be imposed upon the world. The ethics of the Bible are for the people of God. The Sermon on the Mount is for disciples of Christ. As Christians follow biblical ethics, the world will be affected for good by them.

Also see HOLY, HOLINESS; RIGHTEOUSNESS; SERMON ON THE MOUNT.

BIBLICAL THEOLOGY — theology as it is understood from the perspective of the biblical writers themselves. This category of theology must be carefully distinguished from systematic theology, which systematizes and re-expresses the teachings of the Bible through the use of modern concepts and categories. Biblical theology is *biblical* because it states the theology of the Bible by limiting itself to the language, categories, and perspectives of the biblical writers. It attempts to arrive at this understanding without modern theological biases or assumptions.

Biblical theology is historical in its orientation. It attempts to get into the minds of the authors of Scripture in order to arrive at the meanings they intended for their original readers. This means that biblical theology is dependent upon careful interpretation of the biblical texts in their original languages. But biblical theology is much more complex than merely compiling Bible verses on various themes or subjects in the Bible, followed by a summary of this material. This approach would not be sensitive to the various historical contexts and specific emphases of the biblical writers.

Biblical theology does attempt to systematize, but only to the extent that this can be done without imposing an artificial structure upon the biblical writers. The biblical theologian will go no further than these writers went in systematizing their material. His concern is to represent their perspectives as clearly and as faithfully as possible.

Unity and Diversity. Biblical theology is divided into Old Testament theology and New Testament theology, although the relation between the two also concerns biblical theologians. Further specialization also occurs within both Old Testament and New Testament theologies. Biblical theologians often speak of the theologies of Deuteronomy, Isaiah, Paul, or Matthew. This is in keeping with the emphasis of biblical theology upon the distinctives of the individual biblical writers.

But a big part of the task of biblical theology is to pull together the common emphases of the biblical writers and to seek the unity of their writings. Although these inspired writers have different contributions to make to the subject of God and His revelation, their writings are compatible with each other. Thus biblical theology focuses on the diversity that exists within the larger unity of Scripture, and tries to set forth that which unifies, without ignoring the diversity.

Method. As long as the interpreter gives sufficient attention to the distinctives of the various writers, biblical theology can organize its work topically, according to main subjects. But because biblical theology is primarily interested in historical understanding, it is better to proceed chronologically. Thus, the biblical theologian works his way progressively through the Bible, tracing the progress of revelation and the development of theological thought, from the earliest writers to the latest. The focus is not on the religious experience of the people, but on the revelation of God and His people's understanding of His acts.

History of Salvation. Biblical theologians seek to find the best organizing principle or idea that serves as the center of a biblical theology. Old Testament theologians have suggested such ideas as the covenant, the Lordship of God, the presence of God, and the people of God. New Testament theologians have mentioned the kingdom of God, grace, salvation, resurrection, and kerygma (a summary of the main points in the preaching of the earliest Christians in the Book of Acts).

Any of these concepts can be used as an organizing principle, for all the central concepts of the Bible are related. But certainly one of the most helpful suggestions to come from biblical theologians is the idea of "salvation history." This refers to the saving acts of God in history. It is an ideal organizing principle for both Old and New Testaments.

Many biblical theologians believe the most effective way to look at the Bible is in terms of God's special acts of salvation on behalf of His people Israel and the church. But they see these various individual events as a unity, moving from promise to completion. Thus, "salvation history" is a single great plan of salvation that finds its ultimate fulfillment in the work of Christ. Following is a broad overview of the events in this salvation history.

The Old Testament as Promise. Two basic theological truths of the Old Testament are God as Creator and God as Redeemer. The created order is God's not only because He created it, but also because He is in the process of redeeming it from its rebellion and sin. The Bible is the story of God setting right what went wrong with His creation because of the fall of Adam.

The history of salvation begins with the call of Abraham and the covenant between Abraham and God (Gen. 12:1–3). This story reaches its conclusion in the coming of Jesus Christ. The election of the nation of Israel as God's special people is not for their sake alone, but for the sake of all the peoples of the world ("in you all the families of the earth shall be blessed," Gen. 12:3). This blessing is ultimately experienced by the church through faith in Jesus Christ.

The great redemptive act of the Old Testament is the Exodus, the deliverance of God's people from bondage in Egypt. This is the Old Testament counterpart to the deliverance brought about by Christ through His death on the cross. Through the Exodus, God revealed not only His sovereign power, but also his faithfulness and the depth of His covenant love for Israel. This was followed immediately by the covenant between God and His people renewed at Mount Sinai and the giving of the Law. God had already entered into covenant relationship

Typical desert scene in the land of the ancient Edomites in the region south of the Dead Sea.
Photo: Levant Photo Service

with His people and had miraculously delivered them. This means that obedience to the Law cannot be understood as a requirement for becoming the people of God and enjoying His favor. The Law was given in the context of God's grace.

From the perspective of the New Testament, the Law may be interpreted as having several purposes. It was given to instruct the people about the absolute holiness of God and the sinfulness of humanity. The Law also set Israel apart from the surrounding nations in order that the Hebrews might be the pure channel by which the Messiah could come and accomplish His saving work for all humanity.

Through the prophets of the Old Testament the work of Christ was anticipated most clearly. They cautioned the people against presuming upon their relationship with God, as though being a member of the Jewish race were a virtue in itself. And they tried to lift the people's eyes from their national and political concerns to God's love for all nations. God's intent was to transform the entire fallen creation; He was not concerned only with the political sovereignty of the nation of Israel.

All along God was up to something far greater than Israel realized. He was planning to do a new thing (Is. 42:10; 65:17). The prophet Jeremiah expressed this truth by referring to a "new covenant" which God would establish in the future (Jer. 31:31–34). The old covenant, particularly the Law, could not accomplish the goal which God had for His people and His creation. In the new covenant His Law would be written on the hearts of His people, and they would enjoy the lasting forgiveness of their sins.

God preserved His people through the experiences of the division of the kingdom, the destruction of the nations of Israel and Judah, the CAPTIVITY, and the resettlement of His people in Jerusalem. He continued to reveal Himself and His purposes through the prophets, who increasingly spoke of what God would do in the near future. In this spirit of anticipation His people entered the New Testament era with its great announcement of fulfillment and hope in Jesus Christ.

The New Testament as Fulfillment: the Church. The New Testament announced the ministry of Jesus as the turning point of the ages, the beginning of the great fulfillment proclaimed by the prophets. It is impossible to exaggerate the centrality of this theme of fulfillment in the New Testament. The constant use of quotations from the Old Testament in the New Testament clearly demonstrates this point.

According to the first three gospels, the message of Jesus was that the kingdom of God had arrived. The kingdom was expressed in both the words and deeds of Jesus. The presence of the kingdom depends directly on the presence of the Messianic King. With His arrival, the fulfillment of the end time has already begun, although it is clear that the final realization of God's purpose remains yet in the future.

The death of Jesus was important as the basis of the kingdom. The rule of God cannot be experienced in any age, present or future, without the atoning sacrifice that reconciles sinners with a holy God. Thus the death of Jesus became central for the theology of the New Testament. But the resurrection was equally important. In this event, the new order of the new creation broke directly into the present age. The resurrection of Christ was assurance of the truths which He had proclaimed, as well as the resurrection of the dead at the end of time.

The pouring out of the Holy Spirit at PENTECOST depended on the finished work of Christ in His death and resurrection. This was a certain sign of the new age brought by Christ and the mark of the new people of God, the church. The ministry of the Spirit guarantees that the results of Christ's work are experienced in the believer's life until Jesus returns to earth.

In the sermons preached by the first Christians (in the first half of the Book of Acts), we see the main points of the faith of the early church. In fulfillment of prophecy, Jesus was born of the line of David, was crucified, died, and was buried. But He arose from the dead and will return some day as Judge. The possibility of repentance and salvation is thus founded directly on these saving acts of God in His Son.

The letters of the New Testament contain interpretation and application of these events. The letters, or epistles, are divided into two main sections—doctrine and ethics. In the doctrinal sections of these letters, the meaning of Christ's work is described. The ethical sections always build on the doctrinal foundations, instructing Christians on how to live the Christian life.

In both the doctrinal and the ethical sections of the epistles, the excitement of the fulfillment experienced through Jesus Christ always is foremost. The work of Christ, particularly in the Cross and the Resurrection, is considered the saving act of God. These are compared to the saving acts of God in the Old Testament. Thus, in biblical theology, the promises of God in the Old Testament are fulfilled in God's great act of redemption through His Son in the New.

BICHRI [BICK rih] (*firstborn*) — a Benjamite, the father of Sheba who rebelled against King David following Absalom's death (2 Sam. 20:1–22).

BICHRITES [BICK rites] — a form of BERITES.

BIDKAR [BID car] (meaning unknown) — one of Jehu's captains. Bidkar threw the body of King JORAM (Jehoram) into the field of Naboth the Jezreelite after Jehu killed him (2 Kin. 9:25).

BIER [beer] — a stand on which a corpse or a coffin containing a corpse is placed before burial; a coffin together with its stand (2 Sam. 3:31; Luke 7:14, KJV).

BIGTHA [BIG thuh] (*gift of God*) — one of the

seven eunuchs, or chamberlains, who had charge of the harem of King Ahasuerus (Xerxes) of Persia (Esth. 1:10). He may be the same person as BIGTHAN.

BIGTHAN [BIG than] (*gift of god*) — one of the two eunuchs or chamberlains who conspired to take the life of King Ahasuerus (Xerxes) of Persia. They were hanged for their treachery when Mordecai discovered their conspiracy (Esth. 2:21). Bigthan may be the same person as BIGTHA.

BIGVAI [BIG vah eye] (*fortunate*) — the head of one of the families who returned from Babylon with Zerubbabel (Ezra 2:2).

BILDAD [BILL dad] (meaning unknown) — the second of the "friends" or "comforters" of Job. In his three speeches to Job (Job 8:1–22; 18:1–21; 25:1–6), Bildad expressed the belief that all suffering is the direct result of one's sin. He had little patience with the questionings and searchings of Job. He is called "Bildad the Shuhite" (Job. 2:11), which means he belonged to an Aramean nomadic tribe that lived in the TRANSJORDAN area southeast of Palestine. Also see ELIHU, ELIPHAZ, ZOPHAR.

BILEAM [BILL ee ahm] (*place of conquest*) — a city in the western half of the tribe of Manasseh. West of the Jordan River, Bileam was assigned to the Kohathite Levites (1 Chr. 6:70). It probably is the same place as IBLEAM (Josh. 17:11).

BILGAH [BILL guh] (*brightness*) — the name of two men in the Old Testament:
1. Chief of the 15th band of priests officiating in Temple service in King David's time (1 Chr. 24:14).
2. A chief of the priests who returned from the Captivity with Zerubbabel (Neh. 12:5, 18). He may be the same person as BILGAI (Neh. 10:8).

BILGAI [BILL gay eye] (*cheerfulness*) — one who sealed the covenant after the Captivity (Neh. 10:8)—perhaps the same person as Bilgah (Neh. 12:5, 18).

BILHAH [BILL hah] (*unconcerned*) — the name of a woman and a town in the Old Testament:

A woman giving birth with the assistance of a midwife, in this eighth century B.C. clay statue from Cyprus.

Photo: Cyprus Dept. of Antiquities

1. A slave girl, or CONCUBINE (Gen. 30:3–5, 7), who bore two of Jacob's sons, DAN and NAPHTALI (Gen. 35:25).
2. A town inhabited by the family of Simeon (1 Chr. 4:29), apparently the same as Baalah (Josh. 15:29) and Balah (Josh. 19:3).

BILHAN [BILL han] (*foolish*) — the name of two men in the Old Testament:
1. A son of Ezer, a descendant of Seir the Horite (1 Chr. 1:42).
2. A son of Jediael, of the tribe of Benjamin (1 Chr. 7:10).

BILSHAN [BILL shan] (*their lord*) — an Israelite leader who returned from captivity in Babylon to Jerusalem with Zerubbabel (Ezra 2:2).

BIMHAL [BIM hal] (*son of circumcision*) — a son of Japhlet, an Asherite (1 Chr. 7:33).

BINDING AND LOOSING — a phrase describing the authority and power that Jesus assigned to His disciples, allowing them to forbid or allow certain kinds of conduct.

This phrase occurs only twice in the New Testament. In the first instance (Matt. 16:19), Jesus gave Peter "the keys of the kingdom of heaven" and told him "whatever you bind on earth will be bound [literally, "shall have been bound"] in heaven, and whatever you loose on earth will be loosed ["shall have been loosed"] in heaven." This means that Peter was granted the authority to pronounce the freedom or condemnation of a person, based on that person's response to the gospel. The tense of the verbs "shall have been" indicates that this fact was already established in the will of the Father.

In Matthew 18:18 the same words were spoken by Jesus to all the disciples, granting them authority in matters of church discipline.

BINEA [BIN ee ah] (*a wanderer*) — a descendant of Jonathan, Saul's son, in the genealogy of Benjamin (1 Chr. 8:37).

BINNUI [BIN you eye] (*a building up*) — the name of five men in the Old Testament:
1. A Levite whose son was among those who weighed the gold and silver vessels brought from Babylon by Ezra (Ezra 8:33).
2. A son of Pahath–Moab who divorced his pagan wife after the Captivity (Ezra 10:30).
3. A son of Bani who divorced his pagan wife after the Captivity (Ezra 10:38).
4. One of the family of Henadad who returned from Babylon with Zerubbabel (Neh. 12:8).
5. One whose descendants returned from Babylon to Jerusalem with Zerubbabel (Neh. 7:15). He is also called Bani (Ezra 2:10).

BIRDS (see ANIMALS OF THE BIBLE).

BIRSHA [BURR shah] (*strong*) — a king of Gomorrah who fought against Chedorlaomer, king of Elam (Gen. 14:2).

BIRTH — the act of bringing forth young from the womb. Although birth can be quick (Ex. 1:19), in the Bible a woman's period of labor is characteristically described as a time of pain and anguish (Gen. 3:16) and birth is often used as a symbol of pain and suffering (Ps. 48:6). It also can be a time of joy and celebration because "a human being has been born into the world" (John 16:21).

One also enters a new life with Jesus Christ by the process of the NEW BIRTH, a birth by the Holy Spirit rather than by one's parents (John 3:1–21). Also see REGENERATION; VIRGIN BIRTH.

BIRTH, NEW (see NEW BIRTH).

BIRTH, VIRGIN (see VIRGIN BIRTH).

BIRTHDAY — the day or anniversary of one's birth. The word birthday is used three times in the Bible: once of Pharaoh (Gen. 40) and twice of Herod Antipas (Matt. 14:6; Mark 6:21). The birthdays of kings and other high officials were regularly celebrated, especially in Egypt and Persia. But the anniversary of a common person's birth apparently was not celebrated as much as it is today.

BIRTHRIGHT — a right, privilege, or possession to which a person, especially the firstborn son, was entitled by birth in Bible times. In Israel, as in the rest of the ancient world, the firstborn son enjoyed a favored position. His birthright included a double portion of his father's assets upon his death (Deut. 21:17). Part of the firstborn's benefits also were a special blessing from the father and the privilege of leadership of the family (Gen. 43:33).

The inheritance rights of the firstborn were protected by law, so the father could not give his benefits to a younger son (Deut. 21:15–17). The firstborn himself, however, could lose the birthright. Because he committed incest with his father's concubine (Gen. 35:22), Reuben lost his favored position (Chr. 5:1–2), while Esau sold his birthright to his younger brother Jacob for a stew of lentils (Gen. 25:29–34), or for "one morsel of food" (Heb. 12:16).

Jesus was both the firstborn of his heavenly Father (John 3:16), and his earthly mother, Mary (Luke 2:7); so he enjoyed the rights and privileges of the Jewish birthright. All Christians are His brothers, sharing in His spiritual inheritance (Rom. 8:17). They are counted as "firstborn" by God's grace (Heb. 12:23).

BIRTHSTOOL — an object, probably a chair of a special type, upon which a woman sat during childbirth (Ex. 1:16). It may have been of Egyptian origin. The same Hebrew word is also found in Jeremiah 18:3, where it refers to a potter's wheel.

BIRZAITH [burr ZAY ihth] (*well of the olive tree*) — a man listed in the genealogy of the tribe of Asher. Birzaith was a son of Malchiel, a grandson of Beriah, and a great–grandson of Asher (1 Chr. 7:31).

BISHLAM [BISH lum] (*son of peace*) — a resident of Palestine at the time when Zerubbabel returned from captivity. Bishlam wrote a letter of protest to Artaxerxes, king of Persia, because the Jews were rebuilding the walls of Jerusalem (Ezra 4:7).

BISHOP — an overseer, elder, or pastor charged with the responsibility of spiritual leadership in a local church in New Testament times.

Before the church was founded, the Greek word for bishop was used in a general sense to refer to local gods as those who watched over people or countries. The word was later applied to men, including those who held positions as magistrates or other government offices. And eventually the term was extended to refer to officials in religious communities with various functions, including those who supervised the revenues of pagan temples.

The SEPTUAGINT (Greek translation of the Old Testament) uses bishop to refer to those who exercise power; sometimes it indicates those who hold positions of authority. It represents a Hebrew term that refers to those who are overseers or officers (Num. 4:16; Neh. 9:9).

In the New Testament, Jesus is called the "Overseer of your souls" (1 Pet. 2:25). In this passage the word is associated with the term shepherd. It is also used to identify the leader of a Christian community or the one who filled the office of overseer. In Acts 20:28 the elders of the church at Ephesus summoned to meet Paul are identified as overseers. Their responsibility, given by the Holy Spirit, was "to shepherd the church of God." In Philippians 1 bishops are associated with deacons, and the qualifications are outlined in 1 Timothy 3:2–7 and Titus 1:7–9. Included are standards for his personal and home life, as well as the bishop's relationships with non-believers.

In Acts 20:17, 28 and Titus 1:5, 7, the terms bishop and elder are used synonymously. Also the word bishop, or its related words, appears to be synonymous with the word shepherd, or its equivalents (Acts 20:28; 1 Pet. 2:25; 5:2).

In his work, the bishop was to oversee the flock of God, to shepherd his people, to protect them from enemies, and to teach, exhort, and encourage. He was to accomplish this primarily by being an example to his people. He was to do this willingly and with an eager spirit, not by coercion or for financial gain. To desire a position as bishop, the apostle Paul declared, was to desire a good work (1 Tim. 3:1). Also see ELDER.

BISHOP'S BIBLE (see BIBLE VERSIONS AND TRANSLATIONS).

BIT AND BRIDLE — The bridle refers to the headgear of a harness; the bit is the metal mouthpiece by which the bridle works to control an animal. These two words appear together in Psalm 32:9. James applied the terms "bit" and "bridle" as symbols of the believer's submission to God's control: "If anyone...thinks he is religious, and does not bridle his tongue...this one's religion is useless" (James 1:26).

BITHIAH [bih THIH uh] (*daughter of Jehovah*) — a daughter of Pharaoh who was married to Mered, a descendant of Judah (1 Chr. 4:18). Some scholars feel that "daughter of Pharaoh" is a euphemism for "Egyptian woman" and does not necessarily imply that she was a member of the royal family.

BITHRON [BIHTH run] — a gorge or grove by which Abner and his men approached Mahanaim following Asahel's death (2 Sam. 2:29). Bithron was probably in the ARABAH (southern wilderness) on the east side of the Jordan River, in the territory of Gad.

BITHYNIA [bih THIN ih uh] (meaning unknown) — a coastal province in northwestern ASIA MINOR (see Map 7, C–1). Bithynia was bounded on the north by the Black Sea, on the south and east by Phrygia and Galatia, and on the west by Mysia. While at Mysia, Paul and Silas decided to go into Bithynia "but the Spirit did not permit them" (Acts 16:7). Later, however, the gospel reached the province; and many of the citizens of Bithynia became Christians (1 Pet. 1:1–2). The experience of Paul and Silas illustrates that God's delays are not always denials.

BITTER HERBS — herbs eaten by the Hebrew people during their celebration of the PASSOVER. Those herbs helped them remember their bitter experience as an enslaved people in Egypt (Ex. 1:14; 12:8; Num. 9:11). These herbs may have included such plants as sorrell, dandelions, and horseradish.

BITTERN (see ANIMALS OF THE BIBLE).

BITTERNESS — in the Old Testament, a symbol of hard bondage, misery, and the ruin that follows immorality (Ex. 1:14). The Passover was to be eaten with "bitter herbs" (Num. 9:11), representing the affliction of Egyptian bondage. The waters of Marah were "bitter," probably meaning salty, briny, brackish (Ex. 15:23). A "bitter day" (Amos 8:10) was a time of lamentation and mourning. "A bitter…nation" (Hab. 1:6) described the Chaldeans as a fierce, warlike people who brought misery and destruction wherever they went.

In the New Testament, the "gall of bitterness" (Acts 8:23, KJV) describes a spiritual poisoning—a heart of great wickedness—in Simon the sorcerer. A "root of bitterness" (Heb. 12:15) is a wicked person or a sin that leads to denial of the faith.

BITTERWEED (see PLANTS OF THE BIBLE).

BITUMEN (see MINERALS OF THE BIBLE).

BIZIOTHIAH [BIHZ ih oh thigh ah] — a form of BIZJOTHJAH.

BIZJOTHJAH [bihz JOTH jah] (meaning unknown) — a town in southern Judah near Beersheba (Josh. 15:28; Biziothiah, NAS, NIV, RSV).

BIZTHA [BIHZ thah] (bound) — one of the seven eunuchs, or chamberlains, who had charge of the harem of King Ahasuerus (Xerxes) of Persia (Esth. 1:10).

BLACK (see COLORS OF THE BIBLE).

BLACK VULTURE (see ANIMALS OF THE BIBLE).

BLACKSMITH (see OCCUPATIONS AND TRADES).

BLAINS (see DISEASES OF THE BIBLE).

BLASPHEMY — the act of cursing, slandering, reviling or showing contempt or lack of reverence for God. In the Old Testament, blaspheming God was a serious crime punishable by death (Lev. 24:15–16). It was a violation of the Third Commandment, which required that the name and reputation of the Lord be upheld (Ex. 20:7)

The unbelieving Jews of Jesus' day charged Him with blasphemy because they thought of Him only as a man while He claimed to be God's Son (Matt. 9:3). Actually, the lawlessness of the Jews themselves was causing God's name to be blasphemed among the Gentiles (Rom. 2:24). By their bitter opposition to Jesus and His gospel, they themselves were guilty of blasphemy (Acts 18:6). Jesus condemned as blasphemy their attributing the work of the Holy Spirit to Satan (Matt. 12:31–32).

Christians are commanded to avoid behavior that blasphemes the Lord's name and teaching (1 Tim. 6:1).

BLAST, BLASTING — the withering of plant life caused by a hot, dry wind from the desert (Amos 4:9). In his dream in Egypt, the Pharaoh saw seven heads of grain "blighted [blasted, KJV] by the east wind" (Gen. 41:6). Joseph interpreted this to mean seven years of famine.

BLASTUS [BLAS tus] (a bud) — the servant—literally "the one over the bed–chamber"—of Herod Agrippa I (Acts 12:20).

BLEACHER (see OCCUPATIONS AND TRADES).

BLEMISH (see DISABILITIES AND DEFORMITIES).

BLESS, BLESSING — the act of declaring, or wishing, God's favor and goodness upon others. The blessing is not only the good effect of words; it also has the power to bring them to pass. In the Bible, important persons blessed those with less power or influence. The patriarchs pronounced benefits upon their children, often near their own deaths (Gen. 49:1–28). Even if spoken by mistake, once a blessing was given it could not be taken back (Genesis 27).

Leaders often blessed people, especially when getting ready to leave them. These included Moses (Deuteronomy 33), Joshua (22:6–7), and Jesus (Luke 24:50). Equals could bless each other by being friendly (Gen. 12:3). One can also bless God, showing gratitude to Him (Deut. 8:10) in songs of praise (Ps. 103:1–2).

God also blesses people by giving life, riches, fruitfulness, or plenty (Gen. 1:22, 28). His greatest blessing is turning us from evil (Acts 3:25–26) and forgiving our sins (Rom. 4:7–8).

Cases of the opposite of blessing, or cursing, are often cited in the Bible (Deut. 27:11–26). Although the natural reaction to a curse is to curse back, Christians are called to bless—to ask for the person's benefit (Matt. 5:44).

BLESSING, CUP OF — a technical term for the third of the cups drunk at the Jewish PASSOVER. It was used by the apostle Paul in his description of the LORD's SUPPER (1 Cor. 10:16).

BLIGHT — a reference to two kinds of diseases which attack grain. The phrase "blighted by the east wind" (Gen. 41:6, 23, 27) indicates the withering or burning of ears of grain caused by a scorching, destructive wind. Blight also refers to a pestilence similar to mildew which turns the grain yellow and causes it to stop growing (Amos 4:9).

BLINDNESS (see DISEASES OF THE BIBLE).

BLOOD — the red fluid circulating in the body that takes nourishment to the body parts and carries away waste. The word blood is often used literally in Scripture. Sometimes the word refers to the blood of animals (Gen. 37:31); at other times it refers to human blood (1 Kin. 22:35). The word is also used figuratively in the Bible. It may mean "blood red" (Joel 2:31) or "murder" (Matt. 27:24). The phrase "flesh and blood" means humanity (Heb. 2:14).

But the most important biblical concept in regard to blood is the spiritual significance of the blood of sacrificial animals. Although some scholars believe

the blood primarily means the animal's *life*, most agree that blood refers to the animal's *death*. Most of the Old Testament passages that discuss sacrifices mention the death of the animal, not its life (Lev. 4:4–5). The Bible makes it clear that the satisfaction or payment for human sins was made by the death of a specified animal substitute: "For the life of the flesh is in the blood, and I have given it to you upon the altar to make atonement for your souls; for it is the blood that makes atonement for the soul" (Lev. 17:11).

In the New Testament, this Old Testament idea of sacrifice is applied to Christ's blood. References to the "blood of Christ" always mean the sacrificial death of Jesus on the cross. References to the blood of Christ were made by Paul (Rom. 3:25); Peter (1 Pet. 1:19); John (Rev. 1:5) and the author of Hebrews (Heb. 9:14). Although all have sinned, "we have redemption through His blood, the forgiveness of sins" (Eph. 1:7).

BLOOD, AVENGER (see AVENGER OF BLOOD).

BLOOD, FLOW OF, BLOODY FLUX (see DISEASES OF THE BIBLE).

BLOODY SWEAT — Jesus' heavy drops of perspiration as He agonized in prayer over His approaching death (Luke 22:44). Luke did not mean to imply that Jesus literally sweat blood. Rather, His distress was so great that drops of sweat fell from His brow like blood runs from a deep wound. This shows

Ancient altar from Phoenicia, showing a water jar at one end and a receptacle for catching blood from the animal sacrifices at the other.

Photo by Howard Vos

clearly that doing the will of God is not always easy or enjoyable. But in spite of His distress, Jesus refused to reject His mission. He desired above all else to fulfill God's plan.

BLUE (see COLORS OF THE BIBLE).

BOANERGES [boh uh NUR jeez] (*sons of thunder*) — the name given by Christ to the sons of Zebedee—James and John (Mark 3:17)—referring to their fervent spirit and boldness (Matt. 20:20–24; Mark 9:38; Luke 9:54).

BOAR (see ANIMALS OF THE BIBLE).

BOAT — a small vessel propelled by oars or a sail; a fishing boat. In the NKJV the word boat is found only in the New Testament, in the four gospels. The boats mentioned are usually associated with the ministry of Jesus and His disciples in the area around the Sea of Galilee. At least four of Jesus' disciples were fisherman—Simon Peter, Andrew, James, and John (Matt. 4:18–22; Mark 1:16–20). On one occasion, when the multitude pressed too closely to Him, Jesus got into a boat and taught the people (Matt. 13:2; Mark 4:1). Also see SHIP.

BOAZ [BOE az] (*strength*) — the name of a prominent man and an object in the Temple:

1. A wealthy and honorable man of Bethlehem from the tribe of Judah. He was a kinsman of Elimelech, Naomi's husband, and he became the husband of RUTH, Naomi's widowed daughter-in-law (Ruth 2—4). Through their son Obed, Boaz and Ruth became ancestors of King David and of the Lord Jesus Christ (Matt. 1:5).

2. One of the two bronze pillars of King Solomon's magnificent Temple (2 Chr. 3:17). The name of the other was JACHIN.

BOCHERU [BAHK ih roo] (*youth*) — one of the six sons of Azel, a Benjamite of the family of King Saul (1 Chr. 8:38).

BOCHIM [BOE kem] (*weepers*) — a place on the mountain near Bethel where the Angel of the Lord rebuked the nation of Israel and the people repented and wept (Judg. 2:1, 5; Bokim, NEB, NIV).

BODY — the material or physical part of man, whether alive or dead. Some religions consider the body evil or inferior to the soul, but the Bible teaches that the body is God's good gift to man (Gen. 2:7). It is a necessary ingredient for a fully human existence. In the Old Testament the word body sometimes means "corpse" (Num. 6:6). Occasionally the reference is to the body as that part of man that is involved in reproduction (Deut. 28:4).

In the New Testament these Old Testament meanings are carried forward, but new insights appear. Paul teaches that the body is often the instrument of sin (1 Cor. 6:18); that the body must die as a penalty for sin (Rom. 7:24); and that sin dishonors a person's body (Rom. 1:24). On the other hand, believers in Christ may "put to death the

The fields of Boaz, near the city of Bethlehem (Ruth 2:1-4).

Photo by Howard Vos

deeds of the body" (Rom. 8:13) and present their bodies as holy sacrifices which please God (Rom. 12:1).

Since human life requires a body, sometimes the term body symbolizes the whole person. Both Jesus and Paul used the word in this way (Matt. 6:22–23; Phil 1:20). The Bible reveals little about existence after the death of the body. But complete salvation and full humanity begin not at death but at the return of Christ. Only then do believers receive their eternal resurrection bodies (1 Cor. 15:35–49).

Also see BODY, SPIRITUAL; BODY OF CHRIST.

BODY ARMOR (see ARMS, ARMOR OF THE BIBLE).

BODY OF CHRIST — a phrase used in three senses in the Bible:

1. The phrase refers to the physical body of Jesus. Not to believe He has had such a human body is heresy (1 John 4:3). His glorified body is the model for the resurrection bodies of Christians (Phil. 3:31).

2. "Body of Christ" is used of the bread of the Lord's Supper (1 Cor. 10:16).

3. The apostle Paul uses the phrase as a symbol of the church. In Romans 12:14–15 and 1 Corinthians 12:12–27, he emphasizes the church's unity, even though there are varied gifts, ministries, and personalities. In Ephesians 4:4–12 and Colossians 1:18–24 Christ as the head of the church is the focus of Paul's ministry.

BODY, SPIRITUAL — the body of a person after its resurrection and glorification, no longer subject to sin, disease, and death. After His resurrection, Jesus was not a ghost or a spirit; he was able to eat "a piece of a broiled fish and some honeycomb" (Luke 24:42). And yet Jesus' body already had certain spiritual qualities. Even before His ascension He was able to enter a room where His disciples were assembled, although the doors were shut (John 20:19).

The apostle Paul specifically mentions the "spiritual body" in his first epistle to the Corinthians (1 Cor. 15:42–44). Paul made it clear that the spiritual body is not subject to sin or death. Paul encouraged believers to hold fast to their faith in Christ, who will give them their spiritual body in the life to come.

BOHAN [BOE han] (thumb) — a son or descendant of Reuben for whom a boundary stone—apparently marking the boundary between the territories of Judah and Benjamin—was named (Josh. 18:17).

BOILS (see DISEASES OF THE BIBLE).

BOKIM [BOE kem] — a form of BOCHIM.

BOLT (see LOCK).

BOND — an obligation or restraint of any kind. In the Bible, the word is used literally, of the fetters and chains of prisoners (Judg. 15:14). In a figurative sense, it refers to the bonds of sin and wicked-

ness (Is. 58:6), covenant obligation (Ezek. 20:37), and peace and love (Eph. 4:3).

BONDAGE (see SLAVE, SLAVERY).

BONDMAN, BOND SERVANT (see SLAVERY).

BONE, BONES — the skeletal framework of the human body. The bones of Joseph were revered by the Israelites (Ex. 13:19). In the prophet Ezekiel's vision of the valley of dry bones (Ezek. 37:1–14), the dead bones came to life, showing the nation of Israel would be restored after their years of CAPTIVITY in Babylon.

BONNET — KJV word for TURBAN, a distinctive type of headdress worn by men in Bible times. Also see DRESS OF THE BIBLE.

BOOK — a collection of written sheets, bound together along one edge and protected by a cover. In Bible times a book was almost anything in written form, usually preserved on a scroll, a roll of papyrus, leather, or parchment.

Old Testament references to a book were more comprehensive than our modern usage of the word. For example, the Bible uses scroll and book almost interchangeably to specify a certificate or a bill— any written notice certifying a contract or a decision (Ex. 17:14). By these standards, a simple sales receipt could be called a book.

Book and scroll were used interchangeably until the second century A.D. when the CODEX was introduced. The codex was man's first attempt to stack sheets, fasten them together, and bind them on one edge. This forerunner of today's book eliminated the problem of rolling and unrolling several bulky scrolls in order to read a written document.

The Bible sometimes uses the idea of book in a figurative manner. To "eat a book" (Ezek. 2:8—3:3) refers to the need to absorb the Word of God into one's system, just as the body digests food. The Hebrew nation understood exactly what this meant; on their first day of school six–year–old boys were given small cakes with Old Testament verses written on them to eat. They also licked honey off their slates and were admonished to absorb the teachings of the Old Testament just as they had eaten these cakes and honey.

Some references to symbolic language also appear in Bible passages that mention the "Book of Life" (Phil. 4:3). All Jewish people were registered in the citizenship book (Jer. 22:30). Heaven is the city whose citizens are recorded in the "Book of Life," including the ones already there and those on the way.

The Bible also speaks of a "sealed book"—one with its contents unrevealed (Dan. 12:4). However, these unsealed books can be understood with the right key. In Revelation 5:5 and 22:10, only the Son of God was worthy to open the seals of the book of the future.

The "book of the genealogy" was a book containing a family's genealogical record. It could even be the record of a nation, such as a history book (Matt. 1:1).

A "book of remembrance" refers to a book with the names and deeds of people who had done special favors for the king. This custom originated in ancient Persia. The name of MORDECAI was written in King Ahasuerus' book when he saved the king's life by reporting a plot to kill him (Esth. 6:1-2). Malachi 3:16 refers to such a "book of remembrance" in which the names of those who fear the Lord and meditate on His name are recorded.

Luke 1:1 refers to a "narrative" of the account of the life of Christ. John 21:25 indicates that such an account would be so long that "even the world itself could not contain the books that would be written."

Also see LIBRARY; WRITING.

BOOK OF THE COVENANT (see COVENANT, BOOK OF).

BOOK OF LIFE — a heavenly book in which the names of the righteous (the redeemed or saved) are written. The concept of God's having a "book of life" was probably first enunciated by Moses, who prayed that God would blot him out of God's book rather than dooming his fellow Israelites (Ex. 32:32–33). This concept likely arose from the practice of registering people by genealogy (Neh. 7:5, 64) and keeping a record of priests and Levites (Neh. 12:22–23).

At the end of time (Rev. 20:11–15), those whose names are not written in the Book of Life will be "cast into the lake of fire" (Rev. 20:15). But those whose names appear here (Rev. 21:27) will be allowed to enter the New Jerusalem.

BOOTH — a temporary shelter made of shrubs and tree branches, which protected cattle against the weather (Gen. 33:17). Booths were used also by keepers of vineyards (Is. 1:8) and soldiers on the battlefield.

During the Feast of Tabernacles (or Feast of Booths), the Israelites made booths and lived in them for seven days. This was to remind them of their temporary dwellings in the wilderness, when God delivered them from Egyptian bondage (Neh. 8:13–18). The Book of Job uses "booth" as a symbol of the transitory, impermanent security of the wicked (Job 27:18).

Also see FEASTS AND FESTIVALS.

BOOTHS, FEAST OF (see FEASTS AND FESTIVALS).

BOOTY — plunder and spoils of war. Booty consisted of everything of value taken in battle—gold and silver, clothing, food, household items, weapons, implements of agriculture, camels, sheep, cattle, and men, women, and children to be used as slaves (Gen. 14:11–12; Jer. 49:32).

BOOZ [BOE ahz] — Greek form of BOAZ.

BORDER — a word referring to an enclosed place (Gen. 10:19), a boundary line (Num. 34:3–12), a

landmark (Hos. 5:10), or the fringe of a garment (Luke 8:44). In the ancient world, boundary stones were often used to mark property lines (Deut. 19:14).

BORN AGAIN (see NEW BIRTH).

BORROW, BORROWING — to receive something with the intention of returning it. In ancient Israel borrowing was not done to set up or expand a business; instead, it was to allow peasant farmers to survive through periods of poverty. Therefore, biblical regulations emphasize neighborliness and helpfulness (Deut. 15:1–11). When loans were made, the borrowers gave the creditors a pledge to guarantee the loan would be repaid (Ex. 22:26–27). This pledge was returned once the loan was repaid.

By New Testament times, the economy had changed drastically and commercial loans were common (Luke 16:1–8). Jesus did not condemn charging interest (Luke 19:23). However, he did admonish lenders to be fair with creditors and to show them the love and respect they expected themselves (Luke 6:31).

BOSCATH [BAHS kath] — a form of BOZKATH.

BOSOM — another word for the chest of the human body, usually used symbolically in the Bible to suggest closeness or intimacy. Receiving something into the bosom means accepting it completely (Is. 40:11). The word bosom may also imply a person's inner thoughts (Ps. 35:13, KJV; heart, NKJV). "Abraham's bosom" symbolizes a place of honor (Luke 16:22–23). Bosom also suggests the intimacy between Jesus and His heavenly Father (John 1:18).

BOSOM, ABRAHAM (see ABRAHAM'S BOSOM).

BOTCH (see DISEASES OF THE BIBLE).

BOTTLE — a container for carrying liquids (Jer. 13:12). Bottle is actually a mistranslation, since glass bottles as we know them were not in use in Old Testament times. Liquid–carrying containers were made of pottery or leather.

Large pottery jugs were used to carry water from the village well and to store it in the house. Job 38:37 describes the storm clouds as the "bottles of heaven."

As pottery was breakable and unsuitable for many uses, some "bottles" were animal skins (usually goatskin) sewn together and sealed to make them watertight. The Bible contains many references to these skins containing wine (Josh 9:4), water (Ps. 33:7), or milk (Judg. 4:19).

Jesus recognized that wineskins, once they had been used, tend to become brittle. When subjected to the increasing pressure caused by the fermenting process of wine-making, they would burst, causing the loss of the wine (Luke 5:37–38). New skins were more resilient and flexible, able to take the pressure of such fermentation.

Small pottery flasks were used for oil (1 Kin. 17:12) or honey (1 Kin. 14:3). The prophet Jeremiah spoke of one of these honey jars in his object lesson about God's certain destruction of the nation of Judah (Jer. 19:1, 10).

Also see POTTERY; WINESKIN.

BOTTOMLESS PIT (see ABYSS).

BOUNDARY STONES — landmarks that mark the boundary lines between fields, districts, and nations (Gen. 31:51-52). In Bible times, removing boundary stones was prohibited by the Mosaic Law (Deut. 19:14; Prov. 23:10). Also see BORDER; LANDMARK.

BOW (see ARMS, ARMOR OF THE BIBLE).

BOWELS — the internal parts of a person's body. Symbolically, the bowels were considered the seat of emotions and feelings, much like the use of the word "heart." Hence "bowels" means pity, compassion, and tenderness.

BOWING — the practice of bowing down or bending the knee. In a more pronounced form, it involved prostration, the practice of falling upon the knees, gradually inclining the body, and touching the forehead to the ground. In Bible times such practices were intended to convey an attitude of reverence, respect, humility, and homage toward others. When he met Esau, Jacob "bowed himself to the ground seven times" (Gen. 33:3).

BOWL — a shallow container for holding food or fluids. In the Old Testament, bowls are often spoken of in connection with the sanctuary and its services. Vessels holding the olive oil for the seven-branched lampstand in the Holy Place were called bowls (Ex. 25:29-34), and the sacrifices offered by the leaders of Israel at the dedication of the tabernacle were made in silver bowls (Num. 7:13-85).

The word bowl sometimes designates a kneading trough or bread bowl (Ex. 12:34) or a large banquet bowl (Judg. 5:25). Also see BASIN; CUP; VESSEL.

BOWSHOT — the distance an arrow can be shot (Gen. 21:16).

BOX — a container for holding oil, perfume, or a similar substance. Elisha the prophet sent an apprentice prophet with a box (2 Kin. 9:1, 3, KJV) of oil to anoint Jehu as king of Israel. Other translations are flask (NKJV), jar (RSV), and bottle (NEB). Also see FLASK.

BOX TREE (see PLANTS OF THE BIBLE).

BOZEZ [BOE zez] (*shining*) — one of two sharp rocks in the mountain pass between Michmash and Gibeah which Jonathan, the son of Saul, climbed in his attack upon the Philistines (1 Sam. 14:4-5).

BOZKATH [BAHZ kath] (*height*) — a town between Eglon and Lachish (Josh. 15:39) and the birthplace of Adaiah, the mother of King Josiah (2 Kin. 22:1; Boscath, KJV).

BOZRAH [BAHZ ruh] (*shepherd*) — the name of two cities in the Old Testament:

1. The royal city of Edom (see Map 4, B-5), on which several of the prophets pronounced divine

judgment (Jer. 49:13, 22). The Lord is represented as coming from Bozrah, wearing blood-sprinkled garments, having trodden the winepress of His wrath upon the Gentile nations (Is. 63:1-6).

2. A city in the tableland of Moab, which also received prophecy of coming divine judgment (Jer. 48:24).

BRACELET — a piece of jewelry, usually of gold or silver, worn on the wrist of women in Bible times (Gen. 24:22; Is. 3:19). King Saul is also described as wearing a bracelet (2 Sam. 1:10), but this was probably an arm band worn by the Hebrew warriors of his day. Also see JEWELRY.

BRANCH — a secondary stem or limb growing from the trunk of a tree. The arms of the golden lampstand made for the tabernacle are also described as branches (Ex. 37:17-22). But the most significant use of this word in the Bible is a symbolic title for the MESSIAH.

This messianic usage apparently originated with the prophet Isaiah (4:2; 11:1). It reappeared in the prophecies of Jeremiah, where it referred to a future king in the line of David, whose coming would bring judgment and righteousness (Jer. 23:5-6). After the Captivity, the term was a recognized title of the Messiah (Zech. 3:8). By this time it had taken on a priestly, as well as a kingly, meaning. Both parts of this expectation are fulfilled by Christ, the Son of David, who is also our great High Priest.

BRASS (see METALS OF THE BIBLE.)

BRAY — to utter the loud, harsh cry of a donkey (Job 6:5). The same word is used to describe the empty words of those who mocked and ridiculed Job (Job 30:7).

BRAZEN SEA (see BRONZE SEA).

BRAZEN SERPENT (see BRONZE SERPENT).

BREAD — a staple food made from flour or meal and mixed with a liquid, usually combined with leaven and kneaded, then shaped into loaves and baked.

Bread played an important role in Israel's worship. During the celebration of PENTECOST, "two wave loaves of two-tenths of an ephah...of fine flour...baked with leaven" were offered with the animal sacrifices (Lev. 23:17). A type of ritualistic bread known as SHOWBREAD consisted of 12 loaves baked without leaven by the Levites and placed weekly in the tabernacle, and later in the Temple (Ex. 25:30). When removed at the end of the week, the loaves were eaten by the priests. The purpose of the showbread was to symbolize God's presence with His people.

When fleeing from bondage in Egypt, the Israelites made unleavened bread, or bread without yeast (Ex. 12:8; 13:6-7). For that reason, the EXODUS was remembered annually by eating unleavened bread for a period of seven days (Lev. 23:6). This celebration was called "the Days of Unleavened Bread" (Acts 12:3).

Photo by Howard Vos

Mills for grinding wheat at an ancient bakery in Ostia, Italy.

In the New Testament, Satan tempted Jesus by saying, "If You are the Son of God, command that these stones become bread." But Jesus answered, "It is written, 'Man shall not live by bread alone, but by every word that proceeds from the mouth of God'" (Matt. 4:3–4).

In the Lord's Prayer, Jesus taught his disciples to pray, "Give us this day our daily bread" (Matt. 6:11). In the Gospel of John, Jesus called Himself "the true bread from heaven" (6:32), "the bread of God" (6:33), "the bread of life" (6:35), and "the bread which came down from heaven" (6:41). The Old Testament background for these references is the MANNA that fell miraculously from heaven to sustain God's people during the Exodus (Exodus 16). Symbolically, Jesus is the heavenly manna, the spiritual or supernatural food given by the heavenly Father to those who ask, seek, and knock (Rev. 2:17).

On the night before His crucifixion, Jesus instituted the Lord's Supper: "And as they were eating, Jesus took bread, blessed it and broke it, and gave to the disciples and said, 'Take, eat; this is My body'" (Matt. 26:26). By His sacrifice, Christ became the Bread of Life for His people, that they may eat of Him and find forgiveness of sin and eternal life.

Bread is also spoken of often in figurative language in the Bible. "The bread of tears" (Ps. 80:5) and "the bread of sorrows" (Ps. 127:2) refer to food eaten in grief and distress. The "bread of mourners" (Hos. 9:4) is bread eaten at the time of death. The "bread of adversity" symbolizes hardship (Is. 30:20). The virtuous woman does not eat "the bread of idleness" (Prov. 31:27); she is diligent, hard–working, and productive.

Securing bread "without money and without price" (Is. 55:1) is finding that free gift of God that not only satisfies spiritual needs, but also bestows abundant life.

BREAD, FEAST OF UNLEAVENED (see FEASTS AND FESTIVALS).

BREAST — a word for the chest of the human body. The word is usually used literally in the Bible. Beating one's breast was a sign of intense sorrow (Luke 23:48). The disciple whom Jesus loved leaned on Jesus' breast (John 13:23, 25), indicating a feeling of love and close comradeship.

BREASTPLATE (see ARMS, ARMOR OF THE BIBLE).

BREASTPLATE, HIGH PRIEST (see PRIEST, HIGH).

BREATH — air drawn into the body to sustain life. Since breathing is the most obvious sign of life, the phrase breath of life is used frequently in the Bible to mean "alive" or "living" (Gen. 2:7; 6:17). Breath is recognized as the gift of God to His creatures (Job 12:10). But since breath is usually invisible, it also may symbolize something without substance or a temporary state of existence (Ps. 144:4).

In a different sense, the "breath of God" (Job 37:10) signifies God's power. This stands in striking contrast to heathen gods, which have neither power nor life. The word breath may be used figuratively, as when Jesus "breathed" the Holy Spirit upon His disciples (John 20:22).

BREECHES — KJV word for TROUSERS. Also see DRESS OF THE BIBLE.

BRETHREN (see BROTHER).

BREWER (see OCCUPATIONS AND TRADES).

BRIBE — a payment—such as money or a favor—given to someone to induce him to act dishonestly. The Bible frequently condemns the giving and receiving of bribes (Amos 5:12). The psalmist spoke of sinners and bloodthirsty men "whose right hand is full of bribes" (Ps. 26:10).

BRICK — a common building material in the ancient world, usually rectangular in shape and composed of clay or mud, along with other ingredients such as straw or sand. Bricks were usually baked by the sun; but they could also be fired in a kiln, or oven, to produce greater strength and hardness. Fired bricks were most common in Roman times, although they were made earlier, especially in Mesopotamia. An allusion to the process of firing bricks is found in the story of the Tower of Babel (Gen. 11:3).

The earliest bricks were shaped by hand; later, they were formed with wooden molds. Brickmaking involved several stages. A good clay source was absolutely necessary; then the clay was sifted and mixed to the desired consistency by adding water. Generally, a temper, often straw, was added; this temper acted as a binder for poor clays and prevented warping and cracking during the drying process. Following this, the bricks were shaped and then dried. Bricks were often inscribed with an official's name, the name of a building, or a dedicatory inscription.

The Bible contains a few references to brickmaking. David forced the defeated Ammonites to labor at the brick works (2 Sam. 12:31). The Pharaoh in Egypt withheld straw from the Israelite brickmakers while demanding that they maintain the daily quota of brick production (Ex. 5:7-9).

BRICKMAKER, **BRICKWORKER** (see OCCUPATIONS AND TRADES).

BRIDE — a woman who has recently been married or is about to be married. In biblical times, it was customary for fathers to select wives for their sons (Gen. 38:6). Occasionally, a son might express his preference for a bride to his father, and his father would negotiate with the parents or guardians of the young woman in question (Gen. 34:4, 8). The father of the young woman also might initiate wedding proposals (Ex. 2:21).

On her wedding day, the bride bathed and put on white robes, often richly embroidered. She put her bridal girdle around her waist, covered her face with a veil, and adorned her head with a garland.

The bridegroom, attended by his friends, set out from his house to the house of his bride's parents. The procession was a happy occasion, and was often accompanied by singers and musicians. He took his bride back to his own (or his parents') house accompanied by singing, the playing of musical instruments, and dancing. The wedding festivities continued for one or two weeks (Judg. 14:12).

In the Old Testament, the word marriage is used to describe God's spiritual relationship with his chosen people, Israel (Ps. 45; Is. 54:6). When God's people fell into sin, especially idolatry, the sin was likened to adultery on the part of a wife (Jer. 3:1–20).

In the New Testament, the analogy is continued: Christ is the Bridegroom (John 3:29), and the church is His bride (Eph. 5:25-33). The apostle Paul counsels husbands and wives to imitate the

A brick from ancient Babylon impressed with the name of King Nebuchadnezzar.
Photo by Gustav Jeeninga

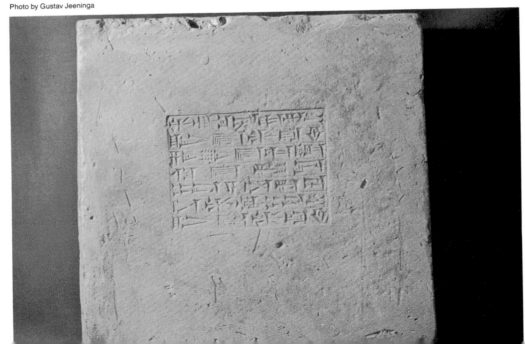

spiritual closeness and love which Christ has for His bride, the church (Eph. 5:22-33).

BRIDEGROOM — a man who has recently been married or is about to be married. The term is applied symbolically to the MESSIAH. John the Baptist called Jesus the "bridegroom" (John 3:29). Jesus referred to Himself as the "bridegroom" (Matt. 9:15). Jesus' bride, of course, is the church—those who are spiritually united with Him by faith.

BRIDEGROOM, FRIEND OF THE — the "best man" in the wedding ceremony of the ancient world. He was the one who assisted in planning and arranging the marriage. In John 3:29, the reference is to John the Baptist (the "bridegroom" being Jesus).

BRIDLE (see BIT AND BRIDLE).

BRIER (see PLANTS OF THE BIBLE).

BRIGANDINE (see ARMS, ARMOR OF THE BIBLE).

BRIMSTONE (see MINERALS OF THE BIBLE).

BROIDERED (see NEEDLEWORK; EMBROIDERY).

BROKEN–FOOTED, BROKEN–HANDED (see DISABILITIES AND DEFORMITIES).

BRONZE (see MINERALS OF THE BIBLE).

BRONZE SEA — a huge basin made of cast bronze near the entrance of the Temple and in front of the altar (1 Kin. 7:23-26). The bronze sea was cast by Hiram, a bronze worker employed by Solomon (1 Kin. 7:13-14). The bronze sea was supported by 12 oxen—or bulls—a group of three animals pointing toward each of the four points of the compass. According to 2 Chronicles 4:6, the purpose of the sea was "for the priests to wash in." The Babylonians broke the bronze sea and carried the pieces to Babylon (2 Kin. 25:13).

BRONZE SERPENT — a metal image that Moses raised on a pole in the wilderness at God's command to save the Israelites from death and destruction (Num. 21:4-9).

Israel's unbelief and rebellion during the Exodus from Egypt resulted in God's judgment. God sent "fiery serpents" (Num. 21:6; poisonous or venomous snakes, NEB, NIV), and many Israelites were bitten. Because they repented and begged for deliverance, God instructed Moses to make a bronze serpent (serpent of brass, KJV) and place it on a pole. All who looked at the bronze serpent were saved from death.

When the Israelites entered the land of Canaan, they carried the bronze serpent with them and preserved it until the time of Hezekiah, king of Judah (715–686 B.C.). During his religious reform, Hezekiah destroyed the image because it had been turned into an idol which the people regarded with superstitious reverence (2 Kin. 18:4).

Jesus compared His coming crucifixion to this saving event in the wilderness: "As Moses lifted up the serpent in the wilderness, even so must the Son of man be lifted up, that whoever believes in Him should not perish but have eternal life" (John 3:14–15). Just as the bronze serpent brought deliverance from poisonous snakes, so the Son of Man would be raised to deliver His people from sin. Just as the Israelites had to look in faith at the bronze serpent to be saved from death, so we must look in faith at the crucified Christ to have eternal life.

BRONZE WORKER (see OCCUPATIONS AND TRADES.)

An Egyptian brickmaker using the ancient method of drying bricks in the sun.

Photo by Willem A. VanGemeren

A flock of goats drinking from the Brook Kidron, which begins northeast of Jerusalem and empties eventually into the Dead Sea.

BROOK — a small stream, running through a deep valley, such as the Arnon (Num. 21:13), Jabbok (Num. 21:24), and Kidron (2 Sam. 15:23). The word brook can also refer to the bed of such a stream, called a *wadi* in Arabic—a stream that is usually dry except during the rainy season.

BROOM (see PLANTS OF THE BIBLE).

BROTHER — a male offspring of one's parents or of one's father or mother. Famous brothers of the Bible include Moses and Aaron (Ex. 6:20), and Peter and Andrew (Matt. 4:18). The term brother was also used in the early church to refer to the love of Christian believers for one another (Acts 9:17). Also see FAMILY.

BROTHERLY LOVE — the love of brothers (or sisters) for each other; the love of fellow Christians for one another, all being children of the same Father in a special sense. Occasionally the New Testament uses the word brother to refer simply to another human being, whether a Christian or not (Matt. 25:40), or to one's fellow countryman (Rom. 9:3). Usually, however, it is used of a fellow believer in Christ. This is true of all places where the concept of brotherly love, or brotherly kindness, appears.

In the Old Testament, Israelites were taught not to hate their brothers: "You shall not hate your brother in your heart...but you shall love your neighbor as yourself" (Lev. 19:17–18). This emphasis is continued and is made even more positive in the New Testament. Believers are exhorted to "be kindly affectionate to one another with brotherly love" (Rom. 12:10), to "let brotherly love continue" (Heb. 13:1), to "love the brotherhood" (1 Pet. 2:17), and to "love as brothers" (1 Pet. 3:8).

Brotherly love is to be the badge, or hallmark, of a Christian (John 13:35). The Greek word for brotherly love (*Philadelphia*) appears as the name of a city in the province of Asia mentioned in the Book of Revelation (Rev. 1:11).

BROTHERS, LORD'S — Jesus' half-brothers, sons of Mary and Joseph. In 1 Corinthians 9:5 Paul mentions in passing the ministry of "the brothers of the Lord." Also, in Galatians 1:19 Paul calls James "the Lord's brother." The gospels list four brothers in all—"James, Joses (or Joseph, NASB, NEB, NIV, RSV), Simon, and Judas" (Matt. 13:55), in addition to unnamed sisters.

Some have questioned whether "brothers" should be understood in a literal sense. Those who argue that Mary remained a virgin throughout her life take the word brothers to refer either to sons of Joseph by a prior marriage or to cousins of Jesus. But both these possibilities are unlikely.

The gospels do not suggest that Mary was a perpetual virgin. The designation of Jesus as Mary's "firstborn Son" implies that she had other sons as well (Matt. 1:25). No New Testament evidence can be cited in support of the "sons of Joseph" theory. Likewise, the possibility that they were the cousins of Jesus finds no New Testament confirmation.

Other words in the Greek language are generally used to indicate "cousin" (Col. 4:10), "sister's son" (Acts 23:16), or the more general "relatives" (Mark 6:4). The gospels probably would not have called these four the "Lord's brothers" if, in fact, they were really cousins.

Finally, the incident recorded in Matthew 12:46–50 is decisive. Here, as elsewhere (Mark 3:31–35; Luke 8:19–21; John 2:12; Acts 1:14), Jesus' mother is mentioned along with his brothers as if they were all in one family. Jesus grew up in a typical family of the time. This formed part of His training as one who was fully human as well as fully divine.

BROTHER'S WIFE — a biblical term for "sister-in-law" (Deut. 25:7). During Old Testament days, if a man died with no male heir, his brother was obligated to marry his widow and produce a son. This son would continue the family's name and would honor the dead brother. This custom was known as LEVIRATE MARRIAGE. The marriage of Boaz to Ruth is a good example of this practice (Ruth 4:1–10). Also see FAMILY.

BROWN (see COLORS OF THE BIBLE).

BRUISE — a surface wound. In Bible times, animals with bruises were unacceptable sacrifices (Lev. 22:24). But the sacrificial death of Jesus required him to be "bruised for our iniquities" (Is. 53:5), a fulfillment of Genesis 3:15 (also see Is. 53:10). The prophet Isaiah also spoke of the bruised body of the nation of Judah to indicate its sin and moral decay (Is. 1:6).

BUCK (see ANIMALS OF THE BIBLE).

BUCKET — a container made of animal skin and used for drawing water from a well or cistern (Num. 24:7; Is. 40:15). The mouth of the leather bucket was kept open by two sticks or crosspieces. A similar kind of container is still used in some parts of Palestine.

BUCKLER (see ARMS, ARMOR OF THE BIBLE).

BUFFALO (see ANIMALS OF THE BIBLE).

BUGLE (see MUSICAL INSTRUMENTS).

BUILDER (see OCCUPATIONS AND TRADES).

BUKKI [BUHK eye] (*proved of God*) — the name of two men in the Old Testament:
1. A chief of the tribe of Dan appointed by Moses to help divide the inheritance among the tribes (Num. 34:22).
2. A son of Abishua (1 Chr. 6:5, 51).

BUKKIAH [Buh KIE ah] (perhaps *proved of God*) — a son of Heman and a musician in the Temple (1 Chr. 25:4, 13).

BUL [bool] (meaning unknown) — the Canaanite and Phoenician name of the eighth month of the Jewish year (1 Kin. 6:38). Also see CALENDAR.

BULL, BULLOCK (see ANIMALS OF THE BIBLE).

BULRUSH (see PLANTS OF THE BIBLE).

BULRUSHES, ARK OF (see ARK OF MOSES).

BULWARKS — towers built along city walls from which defenders shot arrows and hurled large stones at the enemy (Ps. 48:13; Is. 26:1).

BUNAH [BYOO nuh] (*understanding*) — the head of a family of the tribe of Judah (1 Chr. 2:25).

BUNNI [BUHN eye] (*my understanding*) — the name of two or three men in the Old Testament:
1. A contemporary of Ezra who was present when the Book of the Law was read (Neh. 9:4).
2. A leader of the people who sealed the covenant with Nehemiah (Neh. 10:15).
3. The father of Hashabiah and a Temple official (Neh. 11:15), perhaps the same person as Bunni No. 1.

BURDEN — a heavy load or weight. This weight can be a literal burden (Ex. 23:5) or a figurative burden (Num. 11:11, 17). The prophets frequently spoke of their messages as burdens. A prophetic utterance or oracle usually was ominous and foreboding, a denouncing of evil and a pronouncing of judgment against a place or a people (Is. 13:1; Ezek. 12:10; Hos. 8:10).

BURGLARY (see CRIME).

BURIAL — the interment of the dead. Due to the hot climate of Palestine, dead bodies decayed rapidly, so burial usually took place within a few hours after death. If someone died late in the day, burial took place the next day, but always within 24 hours after death.

When death occurred, the oldest son or nearest of kin closed the eyes of the dead (Gen. 46:4), and the mouth was closed and the jaws bound up (John 11:44). After the body was washed (Acts 9:37), it was usually wrapped in cloth. The wealthy used linen with spices placed between the folds (John 19:40).

The Hebrews did not follow the Greek custom of cremation, except in an emergency, such as in the case of Saul and his sons, who were slain by the Philistines (1 Sam. 31:12). After the valiant men had burned the bodies of Saul and his sons, however, they buried their bones (1 Sam. 31:13).

Neither did the Israelites generally use coffins or embalm their dead. The only biblical mention of a COFFIN (KJV) is in Genesis 50:26, where it may refer to a sarcophagus made of limestone. After it was wrapped, the body was placed on a BIER and taken to the burial place.

Depending upon economic and social status, burial was either in a shallow grave covered with stones or in a cave or tomb hewn out of stone. Tombs were made secure by rolling a circular stone over the entrance and sealing the tomb (Mark 16:3–4). This was done to secure the body from animals. Graves were often marked with a large, upright stone.

For a body not to be buried was considered a great shame and a sign of God's judgment (1 Kin. 14:11; 2 Kin. 9:36–37). Unburied bodies polluted the land (Ezek. 39:11–16).

The Egyptians and the Babylonians took great pains to prepare their dead for the afterlife. Personal belongings, as well as food and drink, were often placed in the graves. The Egyptians perfected the intricate process of mummification, which included EMBALMING. In the intricate interiors of the pyramids, the mummified bodies of Egyptian royalty were buried. Babylonians, Greeks, and Romans often cremated their dead and deposited their ashes in ornate funeral urns.

BURN, BURNING — to consume with fire. The words are used often in a literal way, as the burning bush (Ex. 3:2) and the fiery furnace (Dan. 20–25). They are also used figuratively, of anger (Ex. 32:10–11), jealousy (Ps. 79:5), and strong emotion (Luke 24:32).

BURNING BUSH — the flaming shrub at Mount Horeb through which Moses became aware of the presence of God (Ex. 3:2–4). Attracted by the phenomenon, Moses turned aside to see why the bush did not burn. Some scholars believe the burning bush symbolized Israel, which had endured and survived the "fiery trial" of Egyptian bondage. The bush may have been a thorn bush. Also see PLANTS OF THE BIBLE.

BURNT OFFERING (see SACRIFICIAL OFFERINGS).

BUSHEL (see WEIGHTS AND MEASURES).

BUSTARD (see ANIMALS OF THE BIBLE).

BUSYBODY — a gossipy, meddlesome person; one who pries into the affairs of others (II Thess. 3:11). This type of behavior is not appropriate for Christians.

BUTLER (see OCCUPATIONS AND TRADES).

BUTTER — a food made by churning milk. Abraham offered butter and milk and freshly cooked veal to his three heavenly guests (Gen. 18:8). Some references to "butter" in the KJV are translated by the NKJV as "curds" (Deut. 32:14) and "cream" (Judg. 5:25). In making butter, milk was taken from a camel, cow, goat, or sheep and poured into an animal skin. The skin was then suspended between two poles and pushed back and forth until the butter was ready.

BUYING — the act of taking possession of goods or property in exchange for money. The Bible contains many references to the practices of buying and selling. Abraham bought the cave of Machpelah, near Hebron (Gen. 23), and David bought the threshing floor of Araunah the Jebusite (2 Sam. 24:18–25). The prophet Amos denounced those who cheated the poor in their acts of buying and selling (Amos 8:5–6).

The world of commerce provides one of the most beautiful descriptions of the sacrifice of Christ to be found in the Bible. The church founded by Jesus, according to the apostle Paul, was "purchased with His own blood" (Acts 20:28). This purchase price is a measure of the importance which God places on His people.

BUZ [buhz] (*contempt*) — the name of two men and one place in the Old Testament:

1. The second son of Milcah and Nahor (Gen. 22:21).

2. A son of Abihail in the genealogy of the tribe of Gad (1 Chr. 5:14).

3. A place mentioned in Jeremiah 25:23 from which Elihu's father, "the Buzite," came (Job 32:2, 6). Buz probably was in northern Arabia, although the exact location is uncertain.

BUZI [BYOO zie] (meaning unknown) — the father of the prophet Ezekiel (Ezek. 1:3).

BUZITE [BYOO zite] — one who belonged to the Aramean tribe of BUZ (Job 32:2, 6; Jer. 25:23).

BUZZARD (see ANIMALS OF THE BIBLE).

BYBLOS [BIB lahs] — a form of GEBAL.

C

CABBON [KAB on] (*surround*) — a town in the Shephelah, or lowland plain, of Judah near Eglon and Lachish (Josh. 15:40).

CABUL [ka BUL] (*sterile, unproductive*) — the name of a town and a district in the Old Testament:

1. A border town in the territory of Asher (Josh. 19:27), still known as Kabul, a village located about 14 kilometers (9 miles) southeast of Acre.

2. A district in Galilee (or Naphtali) made up of 30 cities. After Hiram, king of Tyre, received these cities as a gift from King Solomon, he gave the name Cabul to this region (1 Kin. 9:13; 2 Chr. 8:2).

CAESAR [SEE zur] — a title applied to several emperors of the Roman Empire, beginning with Augustus. Several of these emperors are mentioned in the New Testament:

1. Augustus (27 B.C.—A.D. 14), who issued a decree for the registration of all persons within the bounds of the Roman Empire (Luke 2:1). This involved the province of Judea in Palestine, thus affecting the lives of Joseph and Mary, who traveled to Bethlehem to register. During this trip Jesus was born.

2. Tiberius (A.D. 14–37), the stepson of Augustus, is the "Caesar" mentioned in the Gospels (except for Luke 2:1). He was suspicious of rivals and severe in discipline of offenders (Matt. 22:17; Luke 3:1; 20:22; 23:2; John 19:12).

3. Claudius (A.D. 41–54), who attempted to reduce strife within the empire, as shown by his decree mentioned in Acts 18:2. He is also mentioned in Acts 11:28.

4. Nero (A.D. 54–68), known more for his various artistic pursuits than for his role as emperor. In the final years of his reign, his mind deteriorated and he ended his life by suicide. He was the first Roman emperor to persecute Christians (in Rome, A.D. 64). The apostle Paul appealed to Nero for Roman justice (Acts 25:11), probably about A.D.

Ruins of the palaces of the Caesars, emperors of the Roman Empire, in the capital city of Rome.
Photo by Howard Vos

60. Also see Acts 17:7; 25:8, 12, 21; 26:32; 27:24; 28:19.

Also see AUGUSTUS; CLAUDIUS; NERO; TIBERIUS.

CAESAREA [sess uh REE uh] (*pertaining to Caesar*) — an important biblical seaport located between modern Haifa and Jerusalem (see Map 6, A–3). Built at enormous expense by HEROD the Great between 25 and 13 B.C., and named in honor of Caesar Augustus, the city was sometimes called Caesarea of Palestine to distinguish it from Caesarea Philippi.

Herod spent 12 years building his seaport jewel on the site of an ancient Phoenician city named Strato's Tower. He constructed a huge breakwater. The enormous stones he used in this project were 15.25 meters (50 feet) long, 5.5 meters (18 feet) wide and 2.75 meters (nine feet) deep. Some of them still can be seen extending 45.75 meters (150 feet) from the shore.

Caesarea frequently was the scene of disturbances as cities of mixed Jewish–Gentile population tended to be. When Pilate was procurator of Judea, he lived in the govenor's residence at Caesarea. Philip the evangelist preached there (Acts 8:40), and Peter was sent there to minister to the Roman centurion CORNELIUS (Acts 10:1, 24; 11:11). Herod Agrippa I died at Caesarea, being "eaten of worms" (Acts 12:19–23).

Caesarea was prominent in the ministry of the apostle Paul as well. After Paul's conversion, some brethren brought him to the port at Caesarea to escape the Hellenists and sail to his hometown of Tarsus (Acts 9:30). Paul made Caesarea his port of call after both his second and third missionary journeys (Acts 18:22, 21:8). Felix sent Paul to Caesarea for trial (Acts 23:23, 33) and the apostle spent two years in prison before making his celebrated defense before Festus and Agrippa (Acts 26). Paul sailed from the harbor in chains to appeal his case before the emperor in Rome (Acts 25:11; 26:1–13).

CAESAREA PHILIPPI [sess uh REE uh fill uh PIE] (*Caesar's city of Philippi*) — a city on the southwestern slope of Mount Hermon (see Map 6, C–1) and the northernmost extent of Jesus' ministry (Matt. 16:13; Mark 8:27). In New Testament times the city was known as Paneas, although Philip the tetrarch renamed the city Caesarea Philippi, in honor of the Roman emperor Augustus Caesar. Agrippa II later changed its name to Neronias, in honor of Nero. The present-day village of Baniyas is built on the same site. It was near Caesarea Philippi that Jesus asked His disciples who He was and received the inspired answer from Simon Peter: "You are the Christ, the Son of the living God" (Matt. 16:16).

CAESAR'S HOUSEHOLD — all the slaves and freemen in the emperor's palace on the Palatine Hill at Rome. Paul sent his greeting to them at the close of his letter to the Philippians (Phil. 4:22; imperial establishment, NEB). Some scholars believe the term also referred to the imperial servants who lived in the rest of Italy and the provinces.

CAGE — an enclosure for confining birds (Jer. 5:27) and other animals. Ezekiel's poetic description of a "young lion" that is captured and put in a cage (Ezek. 19:2–9) is a reference to King Jehoiachin of Judah, who was taken captive by Nebuchadnezzar, king of Babylon. The Hebrew word frequently rendered "cage" is translated as "basket" in Amos 8:1–2.

CAIAPHAS [KY uh fuhs] (*a searcher*) — the high priest of Israel appointed about A.D. 18 by the Roman procurator, Valerius Gratus. Caiaphas and his father-in-law, Annas, were high priests when John the Baptist began his preaching (Matt. 26:3, 57; Luke 3:2). Caiaphas also was a member of the Sadducees.

After Jesus raised LAZARUS from the dead, Jewish leaders became alarmed at Jesus' increasing popularity. The SANHEDRIN quickly called a meeting, during which Caiaphas called for Jesus' death. As High Priest, Caiaphas' words carried great authority, and his counsel was followed (John 11:49–53). Subsequently, Caiaphas plotted the arrest of Jesus (Matt. 26:3–4) and was a participant in the illegal trial of Jesus (Matt. 26:57–68).

The final appearance of Caiaphas in the New Testament was at the trial of Peter and John. He was one of the leaders who questioned the two disciples about the miraculous healing of the lame man "at the gate of the temple which is called Beautiful" (Acts 3:2; Acts 4:6).

CAIN [kane] (*possessed*) — the name of a person and a city in the Old Testament:
1. The eldest son of Adam and Eve and the brother of Abel (Gen. 4:1–25). Cain was the first murderer. A farmer by occupation, Cain brought fruits of the ground as a sacrifice to God. His brother Abel, a shepherd, sacrificed a lamb from his flock. The Lord accepted Abel's offering but rejected Cain's (Gen. 4:7). The proof of Cain's wrong standing before God is seen in his impulse to kill his own brother Abel when his own offering was rejected (Gen. 4:8).

The New Testament refers to Cain in three places. Abel's offering to God was "a more excellent sacrifice" than Cain's because Abel was "righteous." His heart was right with God, and Cain's was not (Heb. 11:4). John calls Cain "the wicked one" and asks why he murdered his brother; the answer was, "Because his works were evil, and his brother's righteous" (1 John 3:12). Jude warns his readers to beware of those who have "gone in the way of Cain" (Jude 11).

2. A town in the mountains of Southern Judah, also spelled KAIN (Josh. 15:57).

CAINAN [kay EYE nuhn] (meaning unknown) — the name of two men in the Bible:
1. A son of Enosh and an ancestor of Jesus (Gen. 5:9–14; Luke 3:38), also spelled Kenan (1 Chr. 1:2, KJV).
2. A son of Arphaxad and an ancestor of Jesus (Luke 3:36).

These man-made stone breakwaters built by the Romans turned Caesarea into a major Mediterranean port city.

CAKE — a small, round piece of BREAD, baked in a pan or on a griddle (Lev. 24:5).

CALAH [KAY luh] (*holy gate*) — a city of Assyria which, according to Genesis 10:8–12, was built by Nimrod. Located where the Tigris and Zab rivers come together, Calah was rebuilt and fortified by SHALMANESER I (about 1274–1245 B.C.) and was made the place where the Assyrian king lived by ASHURNASIRPAL (about 884–859 B.C.). The ruins of this city, now called Nimrud, are situated approximately 29 kilometers (18 miles) south of Nineveh.

CALAMUS (see PLANTS OF THE BIBLE).

CALCOL [KAL kahl] (*sustaining* or *nourishing*) — a descendant of Judah (1 Chr. 2:6), also spelled Chalcol (1 Kin. 4:31).

CALDRON — a ceramic or metal container for boiling flesh, either for ceremonial or domestic purposes (2 Chr. 35:13; Mic. 3:3). Metallic pots for cooking have been found in Babylon, Egypt, and Mesopotamia.

CALEB [KAY lubb] (*dog*) — the name of three men in the Old Testament:

1. One of the 12 spies sent by Moses to investigate the land of Canaan (Num. 13:6, 30; 14:6, 24, 30, 38). Ten of the 12 spies frightened the Israelites with reports of fortified cities and gigantic peoples. Compared to the giants in the land, they saw themselves as "grasshoppers" (Num. 13:33).

Joshua and Caleb also saw the fortified cities in the land, but they reacted in faith rather than fear. They advised Moses and Aaron and the Israelites to attack Canaan immediately (Num. 13:30). The Israelites listened to the spies rather than the two, and the Lord viewed their fear as a lack of faith, and judged them for their spiritual timidity. Of all the adults alive at that time, only Caleb and Joshua would live to possess the land (Josh. 14:6–15).

Caleb was also part of the group selected by Moses to help divide the land among the tribes. He was 85 years old when Canaan was finally conquered. Hebron was given to Caleb as a divine inheritance.

2. A son of Hezron of the family of Perez of the tribe of Judah (1 Chr. 2:9, 18–19, 42). Descended from this Caleb were Aaron's associate Hur and Hur's grandson Bezaleel, a skilled craftsman. An alternate spelling of the name is Chelubai (1 Chr. 2:9).

3. A son of Hur (1 Chr. 24). Some translations, however, treat this name as a place. Also see CALEB EPHRATHAH.

CALEB EPHRATHAH [KAY lubb EF ray thuh] — according to the NKJV, the place where HEZRON died (1 Chr. 2:24; Caleb–Ephrath, KJV). The RSV and the NEB, however, follow the Septuagint and translate the Hebrew phrase to refer to Caleb's relation with the wife of Hezron: "After the death of Hezron, Caleb went in to [had intercourse with] Ephrathah, the wife of Hezron his father, and she bore him Ashur, the father [founder] of Tekoa" (1 Chr. 2:24).

CALENDAR — a system of reckoning time, usually based on a recurrent natural cycle (such as the sun through the seasons or the moon through its phases); a table, or tabular register, of days according to a system usually covering one year and referring the days of each month to the days of the week.

From the beginning of recorded history, the calendar has been used to keep records and predict the time for the changing of the seasons. The calendar provided a framework in which man could plan his work. It was an effective timetable for marking various religious festivals that were to be celebrated at regular intervals.

Calendar Units

The day—In calendar terms, the day is the smallest and most consistent unit of time. In the ancient world, the term day was used in two senses. It described a 24–hour period, as well as daylight in contrast to the night (Gen. 1:5). The beginning point of the 24–hour day varied. The Bible contains references to the day beginning in the morning (Gen. 19:34; Acts 23:32) as well as in the evening (Neh. 13:19). In the time of the Roman Empire, the day may have begun at midnight, as indicated by the Gospel of John (4:6; 19:14).

The dawn was the twilight before sunrise (1 Sam. 30:17; Matt. 28:1). The evening was the late afternoon (Deut. 16:6) between the day and the night (Jer. 6:4; Prov. 7:9), or it could mean literally "late" in the day (Mark 11:19) just before the stars came out (Neh. 4:21). Noon was the end of the morning (1 Kin. 18:26) which marked mealtime (Gen. 43:16). Noon was also referred to as "midday" (Neh. 8:3), "broad daylight" (Amos 8:9), and "heat of the day" (2 Sam. 4:5).

The day was divided into three parts: evening, morning, and noon (Ps. 55:17). Midnight was the midpoint of the night (Matt. 25:6; Acts 20:7). In the Old Testament the night was divided into three watches (Judg. 7:19; Ex. 14:24), while it was divided into four watches in the New Testament (Matt. 14:25; Mark 13:35). The term hour was used to mean "immediately" (Dan 3:6, 15), or it could express the idea of one–twelfth of daylight (John 11:9).

The week—The week was a seven–day unit begun at the time of creation (Gen. 1:31—2:2). The word week means "seven" (Gen. 29:27; Luke 18:12), in the Bible the days of the week were called the "first day," "third day," and so forth (Gen. 1:8–31; Matt. 28:1), although the seventh day was known as "sabbath" (Ex. 16:23; Matt. 12:1). The day before the Sabbath was called "the Preparation Day" (Mark 15:42), and Christians referred to the first day of the week as 'the Lord's Day" (Rev. 1:10).

The month—The month was a unit of time closely tied to the moon. The Hebrew word for "month" also meant "moon" (Deut. 33:14, NIV, NASB). The reason for the connection between the month and the moon is that the beginning of a month was marked by a new moon. The moon was carefully observed by the people of Bible times.

When it appeared as a thin crescent, it marked the beginning of a new month.

The lunar month was about 29 days long. Therefore, the first crescent of the new moon would appear 29 or 30 days after the previous new moon. At times the crescent was not visible because of clouds. But this was allowed for with a rule that the new moon would never be reckoned as more than 30 days after the last new moon. This prevented too much variation in the calendar.

The year—The Hebrew word for year comes from the idea of change or repeated action. Thus the year expresses the concept of "a complete cycle of change." Due to the repeated seasons, man set up a calendar to account for yearly events and to alert him of the coming seasons. The calendar revolved around the agricultural cycles. Man observed the climatic changes and the length of days in his planting and harvesting. Religious festivals were also established to parallel the agricultural year. No major religious festival, for example, was celebrated during the busy harvest season. Man observed that there were four seasons and that the year was about 365 days long. Although the calendars were not always precise, adjustments were made periodically to account for the lack of precision.

Calendar Systems

In the Old Testament—The marking of time in Old Testament days revolved primarily around the months, seasonal religious festivals, and the year. The month was marked by the first appearance of the crescent of the new moon at sunset. The first day of each month was considered a holy day marked by special sacrifices (Num. 28:11–15), and it was to be announced with the blowing of trumpets (Num. 10:10; Ps. 81:3).

Normally the months were designated numerically: first (Ex. 12:2), second (Ex. 16:1), third (Ex. 19:1), fourth (2 Kin. 25:3), fifth (Jer. 28:1), sixth (1 Chr. 27:9), seventh (Gen. 8:4), eighth (Zech. 1:1), ninth (Ezra 10:9), tenth (Gen. 8:5), eleventh (Deut. 1:3) and twelfth (Esth. 3:7).

The first month of the Hebrew calendar was in the spring, around March/April. In their early history the Israelites adopted Canaanite names for the months which were connected with agriculture and climate. Only four of these names are mentioned in the Old Testament. The month Abib (Ex. 13:4; 23:15) was the first month (around March/April), which was at the time of barley harvest. The word Abib means "ripening of grain" (Lev. 2:14). The month Ziv (1 Kin. 6:1, 37; Zif, KJV) was the second month (April/May). This word means "splendor," and it refers to the beauty of flowers blooming at that time. Ethanim (1 Kin. 8:2) was the seventh month (September/October), which occurred during the rainy season. Bul (2 Kin. 6:38) was the eighth month (October/November). Its name may have reference to "rain," since the eighth month was between the early and latter rains. These four names for the months were associated with the most important agricultural times of the year.

In its later history the nation of Israel adopted all

12 months of the Babylonian calendar as their civil calendar. But not all of the 12 months are listed in the Bible. The seven that occur are: Nisan, the first month (Neh. 2:1); Sivan, the third month (Esth. 8:9); Elul, the sixth month (Neh. 6:15); Chislev, the ninth month (Zech. 7:1); Tebeth, the tenth month (Esth. 2:16); Shebat, the eleventh month (Zech. 1:7); and Adar, the twelfth month (Ezra 6:15). The first month of this calendar also fell during the springtime.

Since Israel was an agricultural society, its calendar worked well for the people and their religious festivals. In the first month (coinciding with our March/April), the fourteenth day was Passover (Ex. 12:18); the fifteenth day through the twenty-first day was Unleavened Bread (Lev. 23:6); the sixteenth day was Firstfruits (Lev. 23:10–14), dedicating the first-ripe barley sprigs. The second month (April/May) marked the celebration of a later Passover, in case some had missed the first celebration (Num. 9:10–11).

On the sixth day of the third month (May/June), the people celebrated Pentecost, which was also called the Feast of Weeks (Lev. 23:15–22), in commemoration of the completion of the barley and wheat harvests. In the seventh month (September/October), the first day was the Feast of Trumpets (Lev. 23:23–25; Num. 29:1), celebrating the New Year; the tenth day was the Day of Atonement (Lev. 16:29–34; 23:26–32); the fifteenth to the twenty-second days were the Feast of Tabernacles or Ingathering (Lev. 23:33–43) in commemoration of all the harvests of the year. Thus, the feasts revolved around the harvests.

With regard to the year, the Jewish historian Josephus stated that Israel had two New Years—the commercial New Year, which began in the fall (seventh month), and the religious New Year, which began in the spring (first month). Since the months were based on the lunar system and since each month averaged 29 1/2 days, the year would be 354 days, or 11 days short of the solar year. In just three years the calendar would be off more than a month.

To reconcile the lunar month with the solar year, Babylon had a sophisticated system where seven months would be added to the calendar over a 19-year cycle, resulting in an error of only two hours and four minutes by the end of the cycle. This is remarkable accuracy for that day. Israel must have adjusted her calendar in a similar fashion by adding a "Second Adar" month whenever necessary.

Between the Testaments—During the period when the Greeks ruled the ancient world, the Seleucid calendar system was most widely used. Two basic systems were used for reckoning time in the Seleucid era—the Macedonian calendar and the Babylonian calendar. It is difficult to be dogmatic as to which system was used, but the Jewish people seem to have used the Macedonian calendar. This means the Seleucid era in Jewish history began on the first day of their seventh month, Tishri, about 312/311 B.C.

In the New Testament—The New Testament contains no references to the Roman or Gentile calendar or to the Jewish calendar, except in speaking of the days of the week. There is also one reference to the "new moon" (Col. 2:16). The Sabbath, Saturday, is mentioned about 60 times (for instance, Matt. 12:1–12). The New Testament also mentions the "first day," Sunday (Mark 16:2; Luke 24:1; Acts 20:7; 1 Cor. 16:2), "the Lord's Day," Sunday (Rev. 1:10), and the "Day of Preparation," or "Preparation Day," Friday (Matt. 27:62; Mark 15:42; Luke 23:54; John 19:14, 31, 42). However, these are references to the cultic aspects of the Jewish calendar. Frequent mention is made, especially in the Gospel of John, of the Passover (John 2:13, 23; 6:4; 11:55; 12:1; 13:1; 18:39). Other festivals mentioned in the New Testament are Unleavened Bread (Matt. 26:17; Mark 14:1, 12), Pentecost (Acts 2:1; 20:16; 1 Cor. 16:8), Feast of Tabernacles (John 7:2), and the Feast of Dedication (John 10:22).

Although the New Testament makes no references to the Roman or Gentile calendar, it does refer to the reigns of rulers. The most specific example is Luke 3:1, which speaks of "the fifteenth year of the reign of Tiberius Caesar." This refers to the time of the rulers then in office in Judea and the surrounding territories and to the beginning of the ministry of John the Baptist. This must have been in A.D. 28–29, assuming that Luke used either the Julian calendar, which began in January, or the regnal calendar, which began in August. The most general references speak not of the year but of the reigns of emperors Caesar Augustus (Luke 2:1) and Claudius Caesar (Acts 11:28), of provincial governors Quirinius (Luke 2:2) and Gallio (Acts 18:12), of King Herod (Matt. 2:1; Luke 1:5), and of the ethnarch Aretas (2 Cor. 11:32).

One New Testament calendar problem is that the Gospels of Matthew, Mark, and Luke portray Jesus as having celebrated the Passover with His disciples on the eve of His betrayal (Matt. 26:19–20; Mark 24:16–17; Luke 22:13–15), whereas the Gospel of John pictures the Jews as not having celebrated the Passover at this time (John 18:28). Many attempts have been made to reconcile this problem.

Possibly, the solution is that the first three gospels reckoned their timetable of the crucifixion events according to the Galilean method (beginning the day at sunrise) which was used by Jesus, the disciples, and the Pharisees. But John may have reckoned according to the Judean method (beginning the day at sunset), a system used by the Sadducees. If this is true, different calendar systems may have been in use at the same time within the nation of Israel.

CALF (see ANIMALS OF THE BIBLE).

CALF WORSHIP (see GODS, PAGAN; GOLDEN CALF).

CALL, CALLING — an important theological idea with several different meanings in the Bible:

1. God's call of individuals to SALVATION, made

possible by the sacrifice of Jesus Christ on the cross (Rom. 8:28–30; 1 Thess. 2:12). God's call to salvation also involves the believer in the high calling of living his life in service to others (1 Cor. 7:20).

2. To call on God for help, or to pray. The Bible contains numerous examples of people who, in their distress, called upon the name of the Lord (Gen. 4:26). God is portrayed as a compassionate, concerned, and personal Deliverer who hears the prayers of His people.

3. To name or to call by name (Gen. 17:5; Luke 1:13). Man has been given the right to name because he is created in the image of God. His role as namer is one of the ways in which He exercises His dominion over the world (Gen. 1:26; 2:19, 23).

Also see ELECTION.

CALNEH [KAL neh] (*fortress*) — a city in Mesopotamia whose exact location is unknown. In Genesis 10:10 it is included among the cities of the kingdom of NIMROD, the mighty hunter. This suggests a location in southern Mesopotamia. However, Amos 6:1–2 includes Calneh in a list of cities in Northern Mesopotamia. There may have been two places with this name, or perhaps the northern town was later named after the earlier settlement. Calno (Is. 10:9) may be identical with Calneh.

CALNO [KAL no] (*futility*) — a city conquered by the Assyrians (Is. 10:9). Isaiah the prophet reported the arrogant boast of the Assyrians, who said that just as Calno had fallen, so would Jerusalem. Calno is probably the same place as Calneh (Gen 10:10; Amos 6:2). The site has not yet been identified.

CALVARY [KAL vuh rih] (from the Latin word *calvaria*, "the skull") — the name used in the KJV and NKJV for the place outside Jerusalem where the Lord Jesus was crucified (Luke 23:33). No one knows for sure why this place was called "the skull." The most likely reason is that the site was a place of execution; the skull is a widely recognized symbol for death. The site may have been associated with a cemetery, although its location near Jerusalem makes it improbable that skulls could be viewed there. Perhaps the area was an outcropping of rock that in some way resembled a skull.

Mark 15:40 and Luke 23:49 indicate that some people viewed Jesus' crucifixion from a distance. John 19:20 says the place was "near the city" of Jerusalem; and Hebrews 13:12 reports that our Lord "suffered outside the gate," which means outside the city walls. From Matthew's reference to "those who passed by" (27:39), it seems the site was close to a well-traveled road. It also is reasonable to think that Joseph's tomb (John 19:41) was quite close. But these geographical hints are very general. The Bible does not clearly indicate exactly where Jesus died.

Sites of the crucifixion have been proposed on every side of Jerusalem. One factor that makes it difficult to pinpoint the site is that Jerusalem was destroyed in A.D. 70 by the Romans, and another Jewish revolt was crushed in a similar manner in A.D. 135. Many geographical features and the location of the city walls were greatly changed because of these and a series of conflicts that continued for centuries.

Except in areas that have been excavated, Jerusalem's present walls date from more recent times. The presence of modern buildings prevents digging to find where the walls were located during New Testament times. Some groups claim to have found the very place where Jesus died, but these complicating factors make it unlikely.

At present, Christian opinion is divided over two possible sites for Calvary. One is on the grounds of the Church of the Holy Sepulcher. The other, called

Cana of Galilee, the village where Jesus performed His first miracle.

Photo by Gustav Jeeninga

"Gordon's Calvary," is about 229 meters (250 yards) northeast of the Damascus Gate in the old city wall.

A tradition going back to the fourth century says that a search was initiated by the Christian historian Eusebius and that the site was found by Bishop Marcarius. Later the Roman Emperor Constantine built a church on the site. Previously the place was the location of a temple to Aphrodite. Tradition also has it that while looking for Jesus' tomb, Constantine's mother Helena found part of "the true cross" on which Jesus died. These traditions are very old, but their historical value is uncertain. The Church of the Holy Sepulcher is now inside what is called "the old city," but supporters claim the location was outside the walls of the city in New Testament times.

Following an earlier lead, a British general, Charles Gordon, in 1885 strongly advocated the other major site, which is clearly outside the existing city walls. The place is a grass–covered rocky knoll which, due to excavations (perhaps mining) some time during the past three centuries, now looks something like a skull when viewed from one direction. Beside the hill is what has been called "Jeremiah's Grotto," where a first–century tomb has been recently landscaped to produce a garden setting. This area is sometimes called the "Garden Tomb."

The site known as "Gordon's Calvary" has commended itself especially to Protestants, while the location supported by the Church of the Holy Sepulcher is highly regarded by the Roman Catholic and Orthodox churches.

For Christians, it is the fact of our Lord's self–sacrifice—"that Christ died for our sins according to the Scriptures, and that He was buried, and that He rose again" (1 Cor. 15:3–4)—not the location which should concern us. At "Calvary," Golgotha's cross—"the emblem of suffering and shame"—became the symbol of love, blessing, and hope.

The Hebrew name for the place where Jesus was crucified is Golgotha (Matt. 27:33; Mark 15:22; John 19:17).

CAMEL (see ANIMALS OF THE BIBLE).

CAMEL DRIVER (see OCCUPATIONS AND TRADES).

CAMEL'S HAIR — hair taken from the back, hump, and underside of a camel. It was woven into a coarse cloth used for tent covers and coats for camel drivers and shepherds. A "robe of coarse hair" (Zech. 13:4) was an appropriate article of clothing for a prophet. John the Baptist wore a garment of camel's hair in the wilderness (Matt. 3:4; Mark 1:6). Jesus contrasted John's dress with the "soft garments" of those who live in king's houses (Matt. 11:8; Luke 7:25).

CAMEL–THORN (see PLANTS OF THE BIBLE).

CAMON [KAY mun] (*standing place*) — the burial place of Jair the Gileadite, who judged Israel for 22 years (Judg. 10:5; Kamon, NASB, NEB, NIV, RSV). The site is unknown.

CAMP, ENCAMPMENT — a temporary dwelling place. The sites where the Hebrew people stopped during their escape from Egypt and the period of the wilderness wandering are called camps.

As the 12 tribes journeyed toward the land of Canaan, their temporary camps were to be set up in a specific manner. The tabernacle of meeting was erected in the center, surrounded by the Levites in their own encampment. The next circle consisted of the 12 tribes themselves, three tribes on each side of the tabernacle (Num. 1:50—2:34). The Book of Numbers also contains specific instructions for breaking camp and the order of their march (Num. 2:1—3:51; 10:21–28). In later times some of the language from the Book of Numbers was used to describe the service of the Levites at the Temple (1 Chr. 9:18–19).

Acts 21:34 uses the common Greek word for camp, although most modern English versions translate the word as barracks (NIV, NKJV, RSV, NASB). Hebrews 13:11–13 uses the figure of the Hebrew camp to compare the death of Jesus "outside the gate" with the burning of the carcasses of sacrificial animals "outside the camp" in Old Testament times (Ex. 29:14; Num. 19:3, 7). In Revelation 20:9 the reference to "the camp of the saints" symbolizes the triumphant church at the end of time.

CANA [KANE nuh] (*place of reeds*) — a village of Galilee (see Map 6, B–2) where Jesus performed his first miracle—turning water into wine (John 2:1, 11). Cana was the home of Nathanael, one of the Twelve (John 21:2). Its probable location is about 13 kilometers (8 miles) northeast of Nazareth.

CANAAN [KANE un] (*merchant* or *trader*) — the name of a man and a land or region in the Old Testament:

1. The fourth son of Ham and the grandson of Noah (Gen. 9:18–27; 10:6, 15). Ham's descendants were dispersed into several distinctive tribes, such as the Jebusites and the Zemarites. These people became known collectively in later years as the CANAANITES, pagan inhabitants of the land that God promised to Abraham and his descendants. Under the leadership of Joshua, the Jewish people occupied the land of Canaan and divided it among the twelve tribes of the nation of Israel.

2. The region along the Mediterranean Sea (see Map 1, C–2) occupied by the Canaanites before it was taken and settled by the Jewish people (Gen. 11:31; Josh. 5:12). The land of Canaan stretched from the Jordan River on the east to the Mediterranean Sea on the west. From south to north, it covered the territory between the Sinai Peninsula and the ancient coastal nation of Phoenicia. Much of this territory was dry, mountainous, and rocky, unfit for cultivation. But it also contained many fertile farmlands, particularly in the river valleys and the coastal plains along the sea. While leading the peo-

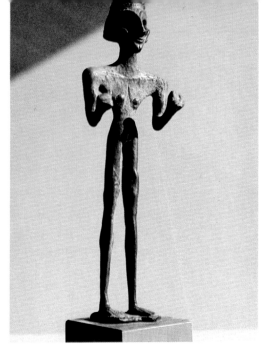

Photo by Gustav Jeeninga

A statue of Baal, a prominent pagan god of the ancient Canaanites.

ple of Israel toward the land of Canaan, Moses sent scouts, or spies, into the territory on a fact-finding mission. They returned with grapes, pomegranates, and figs to verify the fertility of the land (Num. 13:2, 17, 23).

The land of Canaan was ideally situated on the trade routes that stretched from Egypt in the south to Syria and Phoenicia in the north and the ancient Babylonian Empire to the east. This location gave the small region a strategic position in the ancient world. After the Israelites captured the land of Canaan, they developed a thriving commercial system by trading goods with other nations along these routes.

CANAANITES [KANE un ites] — an ancient tribe that lived in the land of Palestine before they were displaced by the nation of Israel. The Canaanites, along with the Amorites, settled the land well before 2000 B.C. Archaeological exploration of their native land and adjacent territories has provided information on many aspects of their culture. Among the numerous sites excavated in ancient Canaan, or the present-day Holy Land, are Hazor, Megiddo, Beth Shan, Jericho, Jebus (Jerusalem), Debir, Lachish, and Arad. Sites in the northern part of ancient Canaan include Byblos and Ras Shamra (Ugarit) along the coast of the Mediterranean Sea and Hamath on the Orontes River.

Although both Canaanites and Amorites were established in Canaan before 2000 B.C., the Canaanites established their civilization as dominant from 2100 to 1550 B.C. Their society had several classes, ranging from the ruling nobility to the peasants. The Canaanites used a particular CUNEIFORM language, featuring a wedge-shaped alphabet. Their land was also dotted with walled cities. Several of these served as the centers of city-states, each having its own king, or mayor, and army.

The Canaanites, therefore, were a highly civilized people in many ways when Joshua led the Israelites across the Jordan River to conquer the people and settle the land. Canaanite history ended with the Israelite conquest. But certain segments of Canaanite culture remained to make both positive and negative impacts on the life of God's Covenant People.

Canaanite Language and Literature. Knowledge of Canaanite language and literature was enhanced by the discovery of the Ugaritic Texts at Ras Shamra, an ancient site along the Mediterranean coast in modern Syria. Accidental discovery of a vaulted room by a farmer while plowing his field on the top of Ras Shamra led to several full-scale excavations by Claude F. A. Schaeffer, the first in 1929. These excavations resulted in the recovery of a store of religious texts and other documents on clay tablets. These writings have yielded a great deal of knowledge about Canaanite life, particularly their form of religion.

The Canaanite language in written form, as revealed by the Ugaritic Texts of Ras Shamra, is an alphabetic cuneiform (wedge-shaped) type of writing. This form contrasts markedly with the syllabic cuneiform of the ancient Babylonian and Assyrian languages. It does have many similarities to other ancient languages of the Middle Eastern world during this period, but it also has many significant differences. These differences are so significant that archaeologists can say with certainty that the Canaanites developed a language all their own.

The Ugaritic Texts from Ras Shamra are by far the most significant literary sources of the Canaanite language in the alphabetic cuneiform script. These texts go back to the 14th century B.C. or earlier. Most of them are of a religious nature, providing valuable details on both the literature and the religion of the Canaanites. These texts have also given Bible scholars a better understanding of Old Testament writings and background.

The texts of greatest importance for giving details on Canaanite religion are three mythologies: (1) The Baal Epic, an account of the activities of Baal, including his building of a temple; (2) the Legend of Aqhat, the only son of an ancient Canaanite king; and (3) the Legend of King Keret of Hubur, who suffered the loss of his family and who later obtained another wife by conquest. In doing so, however, he displeased the gods.

Comparative studies between these texts and Old Testament writings, particularly early Hebrew poems and the Psalms, show how the Old Testament has been influenced by its ancient setting. But they also show that the Hebrews' faith in their one Redeemer God was a dramatic contrast to the pagan religion of the Canaanites.

Canaanite Religion. The Canaanite religion featured many gods. These gods were worshiped with elaborate ritual. Various kinds of cultic personnel, or priests, officiated at these pagan ceremonies. Their religious system also featured many different places of worship, varying from simple outdoor altars to massive stone temples.

The Old Testament refers frequently to Baal (Num. 22:41), Baals (Hos. 2:13, 17), or a Baal of a particular place, such as Baal of Peor (Num. 25:3, 5). The Old Testament also refers to Asherah (1 Kin. 18:19), Ashtoreth (1 Kin. 11:5, 33), and the Ashtoreths (Judg. 2:13). References to these Canaanite gods always carry strong denunciations by the biblical writers. But these names mentioned in the Old Testament are only a few of the many additional names for Canaanite gods that appear in the Ugaritic Texts.

The highest of all the Canaanite gods was El, as shown clearly by the Ugaritic Texts. But El chose to remain in the background, conferring power and authority upon his brood of gods and goddesses. The main goddess by whom El fathered children was Asherah. She and El were the parents of more than 70 other deities. The Baal mentioned frequently in the Old Testament was lord among the gods because of authority granted by El. Baal was known chiefly as the god of fertility and as god of the storm. Temples were built in his name at a number of sites in the Palestine region, including one at Ugarit.

Three Canaanite goddesses mentioned frequently in the Ugaritic Texts are Anath (Judg 3:31), Asherah, and Astarte (Ashtoreth of the Old Testament). Among the many other deities of the Canaanites were Resheph, god of pestilence, and Mot, god of drought and death.

Excavation of a temple of the Canaanites at Beth Shan from the 14th century B.C.

Canaanite religion had a number of features that were similar to certain practices of the religious system of the Israelites. Like the Hebrews, the Canaanites offered various kinds of offerings to their gods. Animals offered included sheep, cattle, and certain wild animals. A high priest among the Canaanites served as the head of 12 priestly families. Other important worship leaders who served in the Canaanite temples included singers, who used liturgy or a form of psalmody; consecrated persons—in effect, male and female prostitutes; vestment makers and sculptors; and priest–scribes, who were responsible for preserving important literary traditions. Like the Hebrew feasts and festivals, the celebrations of the Canaanites also paralleled the seasons or cycles of the agricultural year.

But in other important ways, Canaanite and Hebrew religion were poles apart. The religion of these pagan people was basically a fertility cult. At temples scattered throughout their land, Canaanite worshipers actually participated in lewd, immoral acts with "sacred" prostitutes. Theirs was a depraved form of worship that appealed to the base instincts of man's animal nature. In contrast, the Hebrews worshiped a holy God who insisted on purity and righteousness among His people.

Although the Hebrews were called to a high ethical plane in their worship, at times the sensual appeal of the Canaanite cults enticed them into sin and idolatry. This explains the strong appeal which Joshua made to the people of Israel in his farewell speech. Joshua had led the Hebrews to take the land, but many of the Canaanites still remained. The aging warrior knew their form of pagan worship would be a strong temptation to the people. Thus he declared, "Put away the foreign gods which are among you, and incline your heart to the Lord God of Israel" (Josh. 24:23).

CANAANITESS [CANE un ight ess] — a woman of CANAAN (1 Chr. 2:3; a Canaanite woman, NEB, NIV). Shua (Bathshua, RSV) the Canaanitess, was the wife of Judah.

CANAANITE, SIMON [KANE un ite] (see SIMON CANAANITE).

CANALS — the RSV translation of a Hebrew word referring to the branches, or delta arms, of the Nile River (Ex. 7:19; 8:5). The word refers especially to the lesser, slower–moving channels which form a connecting network of waterways in the Egyptian delta.

CANANAEAN [kane uh NEE uhn] (see CANAANITE).

CANCER — a malignant growth, or tumor, that invades healthy body tissue or cells. The apostle Paul described the "godless chatter" (2 Tim. 2:16; NIV, RSV) of worldly people, and the false message they proclaim, as a "cancer" (2 Tim. 2:17; gangrene, NASB, NEB, NIV, RSV) that threatened the health and vitality of the church.

CANDACE [KAN duh see] (*queen* or *ruler of chil-*

dren) — a queen of Ethiopia (Acts 8:27). Candace, a title, did not refer to a particular queen but to a line of queens. The eunuch of the Candace in Acts was converted to Christianity by Philip the evangelist (Acts 8:26–39).

CANDLE — a mass of tallow or wax containing a linen or cotton wick that is burned to give light. The people of biblical times did not use candles as such. The NKJV translates as lamp (Job 18:6; Prov. 20:27; Luke 8:16).

The lamps of the ancient world were shallow bowls with a pinched rim. A wick was laid in these grooves, with one end extending above the lip of the lamp while the other end rested in the olive oil, which provided fuel. Also see LAMP, LAMPSTAND.

CANDLESTICK (see TABERNACLE).

CANE (see PLANTS OF THE BIBLE).

CANKER (see DISEASES OF THE BIBLE).

CANKERWORM (see ANIMALS OF THE BIBLE).

CANNEH [KAN eh] (*distinguished*) — a place mentioned in Ezekiel 27:23 along with Eden and Haran, which suggests a location in Mesopotamia.

CANON (see BIBLE).

CANOPY — any high, overarching covering. A canopy covered the vestibule on Solomon's Hall of Pillars (1 Kin. 7:6). A wooden canopy was on the front of the vestibule outside Ezekiel's temple (Ezek. 41:25). The word is used figuratively twice.

Elihu proclaimed God's majesty by referring to "the thunder from his canopy" (Job 36:29). The psalmist, in speaking of God the sovereign Creator, declared, "His canopy around him was dark waters" (Ps. 18:11).

CANTICLES (see SONG OF SOLOMON).

CAPERBERRY (see PLANTS OF THE BIBLE).

CAPERNAUM [kuh PURR nay uhm] (*village of Nahum*) — the most important city on the northern shore of the Sea of Galilee (see Map 6, C–2) in New Testament times and the center of much of Jesus' ministry. Capernaum is not mentioned in the Old Testament; in all likelihood, it was founded sometime after the Jews returned from captivity.

By the New Testament era, Capernaum was large enough that it always was called a "city" (Matt. 9:1; Mark 1:33). It had its own synagogue, in which Jesus frequently taught (Mark 1:21; Luke 4:31–38; John 6:59). Apparently the synagogue was built by the Roman soldiers garrisoned in Capernaum (Matt. 8:8; Luke 7:1–10). The synagogue was a center for the Roman system of taxation; for it had a permanent office of taxation (Matt. 9:9; Mark 2:14; Luke 5:27), and itinerant tax collectors operated in the city (Matt. 17:24).

After being rejected in His hometown, Nazareth, Jesus made Capernaum the center of His ministry in Galilee. He performed many miracles here, including the healing of the centurion's paralyzed servant (Matt. 8:5–13), a paralytic carried by four

Aerial view of the synagogue at Capernaum, a city on the shore of the Sea of Galilee.

Photo by Werner Braun

Photo by Howard Vos

Reconstruction of the royal palace on the island of Crete, or Caphtor, showing stairs leading to the throne room.

friends (Mark 2:1–12), Peter's mother–in–law (Matt. 8:14–15; Mark 1:29–31), and the nobleman's son (John 4:46–54).

As Jesus walked by the Sea of Galilee near Capernaum, He called the fishermen Simon, Andrew, James, and John to be his disciples (Mark 1:16–21, 29). It was also in "His own city" (Capernaum) that Jesus called the tax collector Matthew (Matt. 9:1, 9; Mark 2:13:14). Immediately following the feeding of the five thousand, Jesus delivered His discourse on the Bread of Life near this city (John 6:32).

Although Jesus centered His ministry in Capernaum, the people of that city did not follow him. Jesus pronounced a curse on the city for its unbelief (Matt. 11:23–24), predicting its ruin (Luke 10:15). So strikingly did this prophecy come true that only recently has Tell Hum been identified confidently as ancient Capernaum.

CAPH [kaf] (see KAPH).

CAPHTOR [KAF tawr] (meaning unknown) — the island or maritime area from which the Philistines originally came (Deut. 2:23; Jer. 47:4; Amos 9:7). Scholars are divided concerning the location of Caphtor. The most probable location is the island of CRETE, together with the nearby Aegean isles. The SEPTUAGINT, however, has Cappadocia, a province in eastern Asia Minor, instead of Caphtor (Deut. 2:23; Amos 9:7). The Caphtorim (Gen. 10:14; Deut. 2:23; 1 Chr. 1:12) were people who came from Caphtor.

CAPITAL — the decorative crown at the top of a supporting pillar in a large building. The huge pillars known as JACHIN AND BOAZ in Solomon's Temple in Jerusalem featured such ornamental capitals, cast from bronze (1 Kin. 7:16). Also see ARCHITECTURE.

CAPPADOCIA [kap uh DOH shih uh] (meaning unknown) — a large Roman province in eastern Asia Minor (see Map 7, D–2). It was bounded on the north by Pontus and the mountains along the Halys River, on the east by Armenia and the Euphrates River, on the south by Cilicia and the Taurus Mountains, and on the west by Lycaonia and Galatia. Visitors from Cappadocia were at Jerusalem on the Day of PENTECOST (Acts 2:1, 9), and the apostle Peter included this province in his first letter to the converts of the DISPERSION (1 Pet. 1:1). Christianity apparently spread northward into Cappadocia from Tarsus of Cilicia, through the Cilician Gates (a gap in the Tarsus Mountains), and then on to Pontus and Galatia.

CAPSTONE — the uppermost stone in a building project, sometimes used to tie two intersecting walls together (Zech. 4:7). As the top stone of a structure or wall, the capstone was the crowning point.

CAPTIVE — a person taken and held as a prisoner, especially by an enemy in war (2 Sam. 8:2; 1 Kin. 20:32; 2 Kin. 25:7). The word is used of the MESSIAH in Psalm 68:18: "You have led captivity captive," speaking of the freedom Jesus would bring (Eph. 4:8).

CAPTIVITY — the state or condition of being in bondage to one's enemies, especially if this involves deportation to a foreign land. The term captivity is commonly used to describe two periods when the nations of Israel (722–721 B.C.) and Judah (597 B.C. and later) were taken away from their native lands and into Exile.

The Captivity of Israel, the Ten Northern Tribes. The first captivity was partly the result of Assyria's march toward Palestine in an attempt to reduce the power of the Syrian Empire. Since about 950 B.C., the Syrians had extended their borders eastward to Assyria. On the south and west they had attacked the kingdom of Israel.

Syria and Israel quickly forgot their quarrel in the face of Assyria's threat. They formed an alliance and fought a great battle against the Assyrians in 853 B.C. at Qarqar in Syria. The Assyrians were severely defeated, effectively checking their threat for several years. Soon the old hostility between Syria and Israel flared anew.

In 841 B.C. the Assyrians began another campaign. This time King Jehu of Israel (about 841–814 B.C.) chose to pay tribute to Assyria and not join with Syria. For four years the Assyrians attacked the Syrians without success. For a short period Syria was dominant in the Near East, but its power ended when a new Assyrian King, Tiglath–Pileser III, ascended to the throne.

The new king was determined to crush the power of Syria and its allies. Accordingly, he attacked King Menahem of Israel (who reigned from about 752–742 B.C.), who quickly paid tribute to Assyria. The Syrians tried to persuade Judah to ally with them against Assyria; they even marched through Judah and occupied the port of Elath on the Gulf of Aqabah to show their strength. Instead, King Ahaz of Judah (who ruled from about 732–716 B.C.) urgently appealed to the Assyrians for help. Tiglath–Pileser responded by attacking the Syrians and besieging their capital, Damascus.

When Damascus fell in 732 B.C., Tiglath–Pileser then attacked Israel, preventing it from further aiding the Syrians. He took the tribes of Gad and Reuben and the half-tribe of Manasseh to Mesopotamia as captives (2 Kin. 15:29). He also made the remaining tribes pay tribute. However, when Tiglath–Pileser died (about 727 B.C.), the Israelites stopped sending tribute to Assyria. Instead, they allied themselves secretly with Egypt. Assyria reacted quickly and attacked Samaria; three years later, in 722 B.C., the city finally fell. The rest of the Israelite tribes were taken captive to Assyria, and the Northern Kingdom came to an end. The Hebrew prophets interpreted this event as God's punishment for Israel's idolatry and rejection of covenant spirituality (Amos 5:1–15). There is no record of the tribes of the nation of Israel ever returning to the land.

The Captivity of Judah, the Southern Kingdom. Israel's collapse ought to have served as a warning to rebellious Judah, which now had no protection against attack by the Assyrians. Assyria was determined to reduce Egypt's influence in Palestine and Syria. Since Judah already had political contact with Egypt, the slightest move toward Egypt would bring the wrath of the Assyrians. In an astute move, King Hezekiah of Judah (about 716–686 B.C.) took advantage of the tension between Egypt and Syria and made Judah independent of both. He also regained control of the Philistine cities in the land.

When Sennacherib succeeded Sargon II in 705 B.C. as king of Assyria, he continued Assyria's westward expansion. Assyria, however, was under increasing pressure from the east. The Babylonian Empire was reviving, and its king sought to draw Judah and Egypt into an alliance against Assyria. In 701 B.C. the Assyrian armies got as far as the Mediterranean, but failed to conquer Jerusalem. About 650 B.C. Palestine and Egypt revolted against Assyrian domination, but Assyria quickly crushed them. Assyria's power, however, was on the decline; and its end occurred when Babylon gained its independence about 626 B.C. The battles of the next 16 years resulted in the complete collapse of the Assyrian Empire.

Pharaoh Necho of Egypt allied with the faltering

Scene from a tomb depicting brickmaking in ancient Egypt. During their years of enslavement in Egypt, the Hebrew people performed these brickmaking chores.

Assyrian armies in order to protect his own interests, but his action could not prevent disaster. Instead, he attracted the attention of the Babylonians, who defeated the Egyptian armies at Carchemish in 605 B.C. and placed Judah under tribute. Three years later King Jehoiakim of Judah rebelled, and in 597 B.C. powerful Babylonian and Chaldean armies conquered Jerusalem and took "three thousand and twenty-three Jews" captive to Mesopotamia (Jer. 52:28). This was the first of three such deportations; the second (587 B.C.) and third (581 B.C.) involved 832 and 745 captives, respectively (Jer. 52:29–30) and ended the kingdom of Judah.

Little is known about Israel and Judah's life during the captivity. Captivity meant a shameful and humiliating punishment for this disobedient, idolatrous people. The royal court of Judah was taken into captivity, along with the priests, skilled workers, and anyone else who might ever lead a revolt against Babylon. The captives realized that God had finally brought the long-standing covenant curses (Deut. 28:15–68) to bear upon them. Torn from their homes and familiar surroundings, they were forced to travel across a hot desert to a strange land to work as slaves for their conquerors.

The punishment of captivity lasted 70 years for Judah; then the penitent were allowed to return to Palestine under the leadership of Ezra and Nehemiah. Israel's tribes, however, never returned and became lost to history.

Also see DISPERSION.

CARAVAN — a company of people, often merchants with pack animals such as donkeys and camels, traveling together, especially through desert or hostile regions (Job 6:19). Genesis 37:25 mentions "a company of Ishmaelites, coming from Gilead with their camels, bearing spices, balm, and myrrh, on their way to carry them down to Egypt."

The main trade routes connecting Egypt and Arabia with Syria and Babylonia passed through Canaan. Arab caravans carrying all sorts of spices and incense regularly traveled through Canaan on these routes; their presence was a natural part of life in Israel.

CARBUNCLE (see JEWELS AND PRECIOUS STONES).

CARCAS [KAHR cuss] (*vulture*) — one of the seven eunuchs, or chamberlains, who had charge of the harem of King Ahasuerus (Xerxes) of Persia. (Esth. 1:10; CARKAS, RSV).

CARCASS — the dead body of a beast or a human being (Gen. 15:11; 1 Kin. 13:22). The NKJV often translates corpse. The Book of Leviticus lists those animals which are forbidden as food and whose carcasses one must not touch, lest one become unclean (Lev. 11:8–40). A person was also rendered unclean if he touched a bone of a dead man, or a grave.

CARCHEMISH [KAHR kem ish] (*city of Chemosh*) — a city west of the Euphrates River in Mesopotamia (2 Chr. 35:20; Is. 10:9; Jer. 46:2). Carchemish was the ancient capital of the HITTITES; later it became a fortified city of the Assyrians. It was the site of one of the important battles of ancient history.

In 605 B.C., the army of Pharaoh Necho of Egypt and the army of Nebuchadnezzar II of Babylon collided at Carchemish, and the Egyptians suffered a crushing defeat. This victory allowed the Babylonians to assume control of the Syrian–Palestinian region. Before the battle of Carchemish, King Josiah of Judah tried to block the advance of Pharaoh Necho in his march northward. He was fatally wounded in the Valley of Megiddo (2 Chr. 35:20–24).

CARE — a burden, worry, or anxiety. Care is the English translation of the Greek noun *merimna*, which means "drawn in different directions," therefore, division, distraction, worry, anxiety. The gospels use this word in Jesus' parable of the sower; Jesus speaks of the cares of the world that choke the word of the kingdom of God (Matt. 13:22; Mark 4:19; Luke 8:14). God cares for His people and asks them to cast all their cares on Him.

CAREAH [keh REE ah] — a form of KAREAH.

CARGO — the goods carried in a merchant ship or

A camel caravan moves slowly across the Arabian desert on the trade routes between Egypt and Mesopotamia.

Photo by Willem A. VanGemeren

A modern highway on a pass through Mount Carmel, near Megiddo.

other vehicle. When a storm battered the ship on which Jonah traveled, the sailors were afraid "and threw the cargo [wares, KJV] that was in the ship into the sea, to lighten the load" (Jon. 1:4–5).

CARKAS [KAHR cuss] — a form of CARCAS.

CARMEL [KAHR muhl] (*fruit garden, orchard*) — the name of a mountain range and a town in the Old Testament:

1. A town in the hill country of Judah (Josh. 15:55; 1 Sam. 25:2, 5, 7, 40). It has been identified as present–day Khirbet el–Kermel, about 13 kilometers (8 miles) southeast of Hebron. Carmel, near Maon, was the home of a very rich and very foolish man named Nabal. This man was a stubborn, churlish fellow who insulted David by refusing to show hospitality to David's servants. The Lord struck Nabal so that "his heart died within him, and he became like a stone" (1 Sam. 25:37). After Nabal's death, David sent for Abigail the Carmelitess, widow of Nabal, to take her as his wife. Abigail, "a woman of good understanding and beautiful appearance" (1 Sam. 25:3), became one of David's wives. Hezrai (2 Sam. 23:35), or Hezro (1 Chr. 11:37), one of David's mighty men, also came from Carmel.

2. A mountain range stretching about 21 kilometers (13 miles) from the Mediterranean coast southeast to the Plain of Dothan (see Map 3, B–2). At the Bay of Accho (Acre), near the modern city of Haifa, this mountain range juts out into the Mediterranean Sea in a promontory named Mount Carmel. It rises sharply from the seacoast to a height of 143 meters (470 feet) near Haifa. The mountain range as a whole averages over 1,000 feet above sea level, with 530 meters (1,742 feet) being the summit.

The Canaanites built sanctuaries to pagan weather deities on this mountain. Thus, Carmel was an appropriate site for a confrontation between Elijah, the prophet of Jehovah, and the "prophets of Baal" (1 Kin. 18:19–20), the idolatrous Canaanite priests. It was also from the top of Mount Carmel that Elijah saw a sign of the coming storm: "a cloud, as small as a man's hand, rising out of the sea" (1 Kin. 18:44), a cloud which signaled the end of a prolonged drought. The prophet Elisha also visited Mount Carmel (2 Kin. 2:25; 4:25).

CARMELITE [KAHR muhl ite] — a native or inhabitant of the town of Carmel in Judah. NABAL, the husband of Abigail (1 Sam. 30:5; 2 Sam. 2:2; 3:3), and HEZRAI (2 Sam. 23:35), or HEZRO (1 Chr. 11:37), one of David's mighty men, were both Carmelites.

CARMELITESS [KAHR muhl ite ess] — a female inhabitant or native of the town in Carmel in Judah. Abigail, the widow of Nabal, is the only person in Scripture to have this description (1 Sam. 27:3; 1 Chr. 3:1).

CARMI [KAHR mye] (*vineyard owner, vinedresser*) — the name of two or three men in the Old Testament:

1. A son of Reuben who went to Egypt with Jacob (Gen. 46:1–9).

2. A descendant of Judah and the father of Achan (Josh. 7:1, 18), or Achar (1 Chr. 2:7).

3. A son of Judah (1 Chr. 4:1). He may be the same person as Carmi No. 2, although some scholars see this Carmi as an alternative form of Caleb.

CARNAL — sensual, worldly, non–spiritual; relating to or given to the crude desires and appetites of the FLESH or body. The apostle Paul contrasts "spiritual people"—that is, those who are under the control of the Holy Spirit—with those who are "carnal"—those under the control of the flesh (1 Cor. 3:1–4; Rom. 8:5–7). The word carnal is usually reserved in the New Testament to describe worldly Christians.

CARPENTER (see OCCUPATIONS AND TRADES).

CARPUS [KAHR puhs] (*fruit*) — a resident of TROAS with whom the apostle Paul left his cloak. Paul later sent for the cloak (2 Tim. 4:13).

CARRIAGE — KJV word for baggage that is packed, assembled, and carried on a journey. NKJV translations of this word include "supplies" (1 Sam. 17:22), "equipment" (Is. 10:28), "goods" (Judg. 18:21), and "carriages" (Is. 46:1).

CARRION VULTURE (see ANIMALS OF THE BIBLE).

CARSHENA [kahr SHE nuh] (*plowman*) — a high Persian official at Shushan (Susa). He was one of seven princes "who had access to the king's presence" (Esth. 1:14). The "king" was Ahasuerus, generally identified as Xerxes I (485–464 B.C.).

Photo by Gustav Jeeninga

Several passengers in a cart cross the river at Philippi near the site of the ancient New Testament city.

CART — a two-wheeled vehicle used for transporting goods in Bible times (Num. 7:3, 6–8). The first mention of a cart in the Bible is the reference to the carts that Joseph gave to the "sons of Israel" to bring his father Jacob and their wives and children to Egypt (Gen. 45:19; 21, 27; 46:5).

Normally made of wood (1 Sam. 6:14), carts had either two or four wheels. If they were used to carry passengers, they might have a canopy to protect the riders from the weather (Num. 7:3). But they were generally used to carry the crops from the fields (Amos 2:13) or to transport heavy objects for some distance (1 Sam. 6:6–16). Oxen were usually used to pull a cart.

The reference in Isaiah 5:18 to sinning "as if with a cart rope" may mean "big sins," since heavy rope was needed to hitch the cart to an animal.

Also see WAGON.

CARVER (see OCCUPATIONS AND TRADES).

CASEMENT — KJV term for the small opening in a wall that allowed an outside view and provided for ventilation (Prov. 7:6; lattice, NKJV). Also see HOUSE.

CASIPHIA [kuh SIF ih uh] (perhaps *place of silversmiths*) — an unidentified place (perhaps a city or a district) in Babylonia, "by the river that flows to Ahava" (Ezra 8:15). Ezra sent for priests from this place, with a view toward their accompanying him to Jerusalem and serving in the Temple (Ezra 8:17). Apparently, Casiphia was on or near the road between Babylon and Jerusalem.

CASLUHIM [KASS lyoo him] (*people of Kasluh*) — a tribe descended from MIZRAIM (the regular Hebrew word for Egypt), son of Ham. The Bible speaks of the "Casluhim (from whom came the Philistines and [the] Caphtorim" (Gen. 10:14; 1 Chr. 1:12). The Casluhim may have lived in Upper Egypt.

CASPERBERRY (see PLANTS OF THE BIBLE).

CASSIA (see PLANTS OF THE BIBLE).

CASTAWAY — KJV word for DISQUALIFIED (1 Cor. 9:27).

CASTLE — a large fortified building. Fortified towers were often situated on a country's borders,

Excavations of the castle, or fortress-palace, of Herod the Great, showing the site of the royal gardens in the foreground.

Photo by Howard Vos

In prehistoric times, families lived in some of these caves in the vicinity of Mount Carmel.

or in other strategic places such as mountain passes, to guard against invading armies (2 Chr. 27:4). They served as the first line of Israel's defense. First Chronicles 11:5, 7 refers to the castle, or stronghold, of Jerusalem. Larger cities in biblical times often had an upper and a lower city. The upper city was usually on an elevated site where the earlier town had been situated; it was called the castle or fortress. With its own wall system, the upper city served as a second line of defense if the outer wall protecting the lower city was broken or scaled.

The word castle also appears in the Book of Acts, referring to the Fortress of ANTONIA in Jerusalem. This fortress overlooked the Temple area. Roman troops were stationed here to curb any outbreaks of violence. When the apostle Paul was threatened by a mob in Jerusalem, soldiers from Antonia rescued him and took him into the fortress, or CASTLE, for protection (Acts 21:34; 22:24; 23:10, KJV; barracks, NKJV).

Also see BARRACKS.

CASTOR AND POLLUX [KASS tur, POL uks] (see GODS, PAGAN).

CAT (see ANIMALS OF THE BIBLE).

CATACOMBS — deep, underground tunnels and vaults intended, for the most part, for the burial of the dead. The famous catacombs of Rome were used as places of refuge by the early Christians, who sought to escape persecution from the Roman Empire. They also conducted religious services there. These catacombs are situated outside the city gates, about 7.6 to 20 meters (25 to 65 feet) below the ground. The catacombs are not mentioned in the Bible.

CATERPILLAR (see ANIMALS OF THE BIBLE).

CATHOLIC EPISTLES — the traditional designation of seven letters in the New Testament: James; 1 and 2 Peter; 1, 2, and 3 John; and Jude. The word catholic means "general, worldwide, universal." When applied to these non–Pauline epistles, it means they were circulated generally throughout the whole of Christendom and not just sent to a specific local church. Also see EPISTLE.

CATTLE (see ANIMALS OF THE BIBLE).

CAUDA [KAW duh] — a form of CLAUDA.

CAUL — KJV word which refers to the fatty lobe attached to the liver (Ex. 29:13, 22) and the fleshy sack surrounding the heart (Hos. 13:8).

CAUSEWAY — a raised road. The only causeway in the Bible was one that ascended from the lower city of Jerusalem to the Temple (1 Chr. 26:16, 18). The NKJV translation is highway. It is also called entryway (2 Chr. 9:4) and walkway (2 Chr. 9:11).

CAVALRY — warriors or soldiers on horseback, assigned to battles that require great mobility. The Bible mentions the cavalry units of Solomon (1 Kin. 9:19, 22; 2 Chr. 8:6, 9), Ben–Hadad the king of Syria (1 Kin. 20:20), and the Chaldeans (Hab. 1:8; horsemen, KJV, RSV). Both the Egyptians and the Canaanites had cavalries that threatened the Israelites at various times (Ex. 14:9; 15:19; Judg. 4:15).

CAVE — a natural underground chamber open to the surface; a cavern or hollow place in the side of a hill or cliff. Because of the abundance of limestone in which caves easily form, the land of Israel has

Photo by Howard Vos

The Saronic Gulf at Cenchrea, which served as the port for the city of Corinth.

many caves.

The principle caves mentioned in the Bible are: Machpelah, the burial place of Abraham and Sarah, Isaac and Rebekah, Jacob and Leah (Gen. 23:9–20; 49:30; 50:13); Makkedah, where five Amorite kings hid from Joshua (Josh. 10:16–27); and Adullam, where David hid from King Saul (1 Sam. 22:1).

After the destruction of Sodom, Lot and his two daughters lived in a cave (Gen. 19:30). When Elijah the prophet was threatened by Jezebel, he fled to a cave in Mount Horeb (1 Kin. 19:9, 13). The tomb of Lazarus was a cave at Bethany (John 11:38).

CEDAR (see PLANTS OF THE BIBLE).

Huge storage jars discovered in the storage area of a royal palace on the Island of Crete.

Photo by Howard Vos

CEILING — the covering or lining of the interior upper surface of a room. This word is used to describe the construction of Solomon's TEMPLE in Jerusalem. He paneled the walls with cedar wood "from the floor...to the ceiling" (1 Kin. 6:15). Also see ARCHITECTURE.

CELEBRATE (see WORSHIP).

CELLAR — KJV word for an underground storage area for oil or wine (1 Chr. 27:27, 28; supply store, NKJV). Also see HOUSE.

CENCHREA [SEN krih uh] — a seaport town in Greece about 11 kilometers (7 miles) east of Corinth. During his second missionary journey, the apostle Paul sailed from Cenchrea on his return to Syria (Acts 18:18; Cenchreae, RSV). Phoebe was a servant of the church in this town (Rom. 16:1).

CENCHREAE [SEN krih uh] — a form of CENCHREA.

CENSER — a container, probably a ladle or shovel-like device, used for carrying live coals of fire, on which incense were burned (Num. 16:6, 17–18, 37–39, 46). The censers of the tabernacle were of bronze (Ex. 27:3; Lev. 16:12); those of the Temple were "of pure gold" (1 Kin. 7:50; 2 Chr. 4:22).

In the Temple worship, the use of the censer and the right to burn incense were jealously guarded prerogatives of the priests, the sons of Aaron. When UZZIAH (or Azariah), king of Judah; unlawfully entered the Temple of the Lord and presumed to take a censer in his hand and burn incense on the altar, he was stricken with leprosy as punishment (2 Chr. 26:16–23). The censer was used in the purification ritual on the Day of Atonement (Lev. 16:12–14).

CENSUS — an official counting and registration of citizens; a property evaluation for tax purposes in early Rome.

The first numbering of the people in the Old Testament occurred at the time of the EXODUS. All men 20 years or older who were able to go to war were counted (Num. 1:2–46). One purpose of this census was to help in the distribution of the land (Num. 26:52–56). After the CAPTIVITY, there was another census (Ezra 2) of men to show how many had returned from Babylonian captivity and also as an aid for the distribution of the land.

In New Testament times the Roman government conducted periodic countings of the people to assess the amount of tax their country should pay to the treasury of the Roman Empire. The New Testament mentions two censuses. At the time of Jesus' birth, Joseph and Mary went to Bethlehem to be registered (Luke 2:1–5). This was probably a census required of all nations under the rule of Rome. All citizens were required to return to their places of birth for an official registration of their property for tax purposes.

The second Roman census was conducted to make an assessment of the property of Judea in A.D. 6. At this time Judea came under direct Roman rule. Because of this, Judas of Galilee incited a revolt, stating that the Jews should be ruled by God rather than by a foreign power (Acts 5:37).

The Roman system of taking census began in 10–9 B.C. Such a registration took place every 14 years.

CENTURION (see OCCUPATIONS AND TRADES).

CEPHAS [SEE fuhs] (*rock*) — the Aramaic name of Simon the son of Jonah (John 1:42), given to him by Christ.

CHAFF — the fine, dry material, such as husks (seed coverings) and other debris, which is separated from the seed in the process of threshing grain. In the Bible, chaff symbolizes worthless, evil, or wicked persons (or things) that are about to be destroyed (Ps. 1:4; Matt. 3:12; Luke 3:17). It is a fitting figure of speech to describe complete destruction by judgment. "The ungodly," said the psalmist, "are like the chaff which the wind drives away" (Ps. 1:4). Also see WINNOWING.

CHAINS — a word with several different meanings in the Bible:

1. An insignia of office. Pharaoh put a chain of gold around Joseph's neck—a sign of royal favor (Gen. 41:42). Belshazzar did the same for Daniel (Dan. 5:7, 16, 29). Ezekiel used the word to symbolize God's sovereign love for Jerusalem (Ezek. 16:11).

2. An ornament (Prov. 1:9; Song 1:10). Two braided chains of pure gold fastened the BREASTPLATE of the high priest to the EPHOD (Ex. 28:14, 22; 39:17). Seven ornamental chains were used to deco-

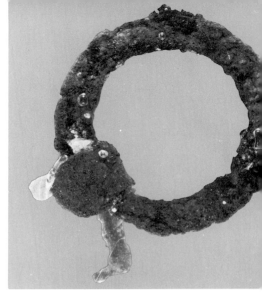

Photo: Haifa Maritime Museum

These slave chains from the Roman era were found underwater off the coast of Israel.

rate each of the two capitals atop the bronze pillars of the Temple (1 Kin. 7:17; 2 Chr. 3:5, 16). Idols were often decorated with silver chains (Is. 40:19).

3. Fetters to bind prisoners. The apostle Paul was bound to a Roman soldier by a chain (Acts 28:20; 2 Tim. 1:16). Describing himself as "an ambassador in chains" (Eph. 6:20), Paul wished that King Agrippa could be altogether as he was, "except for these chains" (Acts 26:29). The apostle Peter was bound between two Roman soldiers by two chains (Acts 12:6–7).

CHALCEDONY [kal SED neh] (see JEWELS AND PRECIOUS STONES).

CHALCOL [KAL kahl] — a form of CALCOL.

CHALDEA [kal DEE uh] — originally, a small territory bordering the head of the Persian Gulf between the Arabian desert and the Euphrates delta—the lower Tigris and Euphrates valley, or the southern portion of Babylonia. Later, after the reign of Nebuchadnezzar II (king of Babylon from 605 to 562 B.C.), the term Chaldea came to include practically all of Babylon.

In the NKJV the term Chaldea is found only in the books of Jeremiah and Ezekiel. Jeremiah prophesied the fall of Babylon by saying, "Chaldea shall become plunder" (Jer. 50:10) and "I will repay Babylon, and all the inhabitants of Chaldea for all the evil they have done" (Jer. 51:24). In a vision, the Spirit of God took Ezekiel into Chaldea to his fellow Jews in captivity (Ezek. 11:24). Ezekiel later referred to "the Babylonians of Chaldea" (Ezek. 16:29; 23:15–16).

Also see BABYLONIA; CHALDEANS.

CHALDEAN ASTROLOGERS [kal DEE uhn] (see ASTROLOGY).

CHALDEANS [kal DEE unz] — one of the ancient peoples that formed the dominant population in Babylonia, especially after the empire of Nebuchadnezzar II (king of Babylon from 605 to 562 B.C.).

The Chaldeans are first mentioned in secular literature in the annals of the Assyrian King Ashurnasirpal II (who reigned from 884-883 to 859 B.C.). Earlier documents refer to the same area as the "sea lands." In 850 B.C. Shalmaneser III, king of Assyria (reigned from 859 to 824 B.C.), raided Chaldea and reached the Persian Gulf, which he called the "Sea of Kaldu." On the accession of Sargon II (reigned from 722-721 to 705 B.C.) to the Assyrian throne, the Chaldean Marduk–apla–iddina II—in the Bible called Merodach–Baladan (Is. 39:1) or Berodach–Baladan (2 Kin. 20:12)—a ruler of Bit-Yakin (a district of Chaldea), rebelled against the Assyrians and became king of Babylon.

In spite of Assyrian opposition, Merodach-Baladan held power from 722-721 to 710 B.C. In 712 B.C. (2 Kin. 20:12-19; Is. 39:1-8) he sent an embassy to Hezekiah, king of Judah, inviting him to join a confederacy with Babylon, Phoenicia, Moab, Edom, Philistia, and Egypt against Assyria. After Merodach–Baladan seized power, the Chaldeans became the dominant race in Babylon (Is. 13:19; 47:1, 5; 48:14, 20). He finally fled, however, and Bit-Yakin was placed under Assyrian control.

When Assyrian power declined, a Chaldean governor, Nabopolassar (the father of Nebuchadnezzar) led a revolt. In 625 B.C., he became king of Babylon and founded a Chaldean dynasty that lasted until the Persian invasion of 539 B.C., led by Cyrus the Great (king of Persia from 550 to 529 B.C.). The prestige of Nabopolassar's successors, Nabu–kudurri–usur (Nebuchadnezzar; king of Babylon from 605 to 562 B.C.) and Nabonidus (king of Babylon from 556 to 539 B.C.), was such that the term Chaldean became synonymous with the term Babylonian.

Nebuchadnezzar was the king involved in the capture of Jerusalem and the deportation of its inhabitants into Babylonian captivity (2 Kin. 24:1-2; Jer. 25:1; 26:9-11; 52:30). The son of Nebuchadnezzar, Awel-Marduk (called Evil-Merodach in 2 Kin. 25:27 and Jer. 52:31), freed Jehoiachin, king of Judah, from prison after he had been there for 37 years. He gave Jehoiachin a position of prominence among the captive kings and a daily allowance of food for the rest of his life.

In the Bible the term Chaldeans is first mentioned in connection with Haran—the son of Terah and brother of Abram—who "died before his father Terah in his native land, in Ur of the Chaldeans" (Gen. 11:28). The Book of Genesis tells us that "Terah took his son Abram [Abraham] and his grandson Lot, the son of Haran, and his daughter-in-law Sarai [Sarah], his son Abram's wife, and they went out...from Ur of the Chaldeans to go to the land of Canaan" (Gen. 11:31). Abraham lived in Ur of the Chaldeans before the Chaldeans dominated Babylon.

The term Chaldean also was used by several ancient authors to denote the priests and other persons educated in the classical Babylonian literature, especially in traditions of astronomy and astrology. Some scholars believe the "wise men [magoi] from the East" (Matt. 2:1) who came to Jerusalem at the time of Jesus' birth may have been Chaldean astrologers.

In the Bible most of the references to Chaldeans appear in the Book of Jeremiah (21:4, 9; 35:11; 51:4, 54). Jeremiah identified the Chaldeans with the Babylonians, who besieged the city of Jerusalem during the reign of Nebuchadnezzar, looted the Temple, and carried the Israelites into captivity.

CHALDEANS, UR OF THE [kal DEE uhns] (see UR OF THE CHALDEANS).

CHALKSTONE (see MINERALS OF THE BIBLE).

CHAMBER — a ROOM in a house or a public building (Gen. 43:30). The upper chamber was a room on the roof, often favored because of its cool location (2 Kin. 23:12). Chamber is also used symbolically in the Bible; the psalmist praised God for sending rain on the earth from "His upper chambers" (Ps. 104:13). Also see HOUSE.

CHAMBERLAIN (see OCCUPATIONS AND TRADES).

CHAMELEON, CHAMOIS (see ANIMALS OF THE BIBLE).

CHAMPION (go-between) — a word used to describe the Philistine giant Goliath (1 Sam. 17:4, 23, 51).

CHANCELLOR (see OCCUPATIONS AND TRADES).

CHANGERS, MONEY (see MONEY CHANGERS).

CHANT (see MUSIC IN THE BIBLE).

CHAPITER (see ARCHITECTURE).

CHARCOAL — a dark carbon substance usually prepared from wood by charring in a kiln (Prov. 26:21; coals, KJV; bellows, NEB). Charcoal was used for heating (Is. 47:14; John 18:18) and cooking (Is. 44:19; John 21:9) and by blacksmiths (Is. 44:12; 54:16).

CHARGER — KJV word for PLATTER.

CHARIOT (see ARMS, ARMOR OF THE BIBLE).

CHARIOTEER (see OCCUPATIONS AND TRADES).

CHARIOTS OF THE SUN — articles removed from the entrance to the Temple by Josiah, king of Judah, and burned. These articles may have been idolatrous golden images of some king (2 Kin. 23:11). Both the Mesopotamian and the Greek cultures believed in a sun-god who drove his chariot across the sky. Apparently a cult of sun worshipers also thrived in Israel at times (Deut. 17:3; Ezek. 8:16).

CHARITY — KJV Word for LOVE.

CHARM (see MAGIC, SORCERY AND DIVINATION).

CHARRAN [KAR uhn] — a form of HARAN.

CHASTE — inwardly pure. While this purity is inward in nature, it also affects a person's conduct (1 Pet. 3:2). As commonly understood, the word chaste is applied to sexuality; the chaste person is innocent of sexual impurity, in desire, imagination, and action (2 Cor. 11:2; Titus 2:5). Some modern translations use the word pure where the KJV uses chaste.

CHASTEN (see CHASTISEMENT).

CHASTISEMENT — an infliction of punishment (as by whipping or beating). In the Bible the term chastisement usually refers to punishment or discipline inflicted by God for the purpose of (1) education, instruction, and training (Job 4:3; Ps. 6:7); (2) corrective guidance (2 Tim. 2:25); and (3) discipline, in the sense of corrective physical punishment (Prov. 22:15; Heb. 12:5–11; Rev. 3:19).

One marvelous passage that does not fit into any of these three categories is Isaiah's portrait of the Suffering Servant: "He was wounded for our transgressions, He was bruised for our iniquities; the chastisement for our peace was upon Him, and by His stripes we are healed" (Is. 53:5). Christians believe that Isaiah was speaking of Jesus Christ, who died in our place, and for us.

CHEBAR [KEE bahr] (*joining*) — a "river" of Chaldea. The Jewish captives, including the prophet Ezekiel, lived along the banks of this river at the village of Tel Abib (Ezek. 1:1, 3; 3:15, 23). It was here that Ezekiel saw several of his remarkable visions (Ezek. 10:15, 20, 22; 43:3). Actually, the Chebar was most likely not a river at all, but the famous Royal Canal of Nebuchadnezzar that connected the Tigris and Euphrates Rivers.

CHECKER WORK — KJV words for LATTICE NETWORK.

CHEDORLAOMER [ked awr LAY oh muhr] (*servant of* [the Canaanite God] *Lagamar*) — a king of ELAM, a country east of Babylonia, in Abraham's day (Gen. 14:1, 4–5, 9, 17). Allied with three other Mesopotamian kings—Amraphel of Shinar, Arioch of Ellasar, and Tidal of "nations"—Chedorlaomer led a campaign against southern Palestine and defeated the inhabitants in the Valley of SIDDIM near the Dead Sea. The conquered people served Chedorlaomer for 12 years, but in the 13th year they rebelled (Gen. 14:4).

Chedorlaomer came again with his allies and conquered the region east of the Jordan River from Bashan southward to the Red Sea as well as the plain around the Dead Sea, thus gaining control of the lucrative caravan routes from Arabia and Egypt through Canaan. In making this conquest, Chedorlaomer captured Lot, Abraham's nephew. Aided by his allies and numerous servants, Abraham launched a night attack on Chedorlaomer at Dan, defeating him and recovering Lot and the spoils.

CHEEK — either side of the face between the eye, mouth, and ear. To smite someone on the cheek was a serious insult (Job 16:10; Mic. 5:1). Jesus' command to turn the other cheek when struck (Matt. 5:39) is an important statement of how those who follow him are to respond to insult.

CHEESE — a food produced from curdled milk. In the desert climate of Palestine, cheesemaking preserved surplus milk for future use without refrigeration. Although the word occurs only three times in the Bible, cheese was probably more common in ancient Israel than this might indicate. The Tyropoeon [literally, cheesemakers] Valley of Jerusalem apparently was the center of the cheesemaking industry.

Jewish tradition prohibited the eating of cheese made by a Gentile because it may have been made from the milk of an animal offered to idols. Modern orthodox Jews still require rigid controls over cheesemaking.

CHELAL [KEE lal] (*completeness*) — an Israelite who divorced his pagan wife after the Captivity (Ezra 10:30).

CHELLUH [KEL oo] — a form of CHELUH.

CHELUB [KEE luhb] (*bird's cage*) — the name of two men in the Old Testament:
1. A brother of Shuhah, a Judahite (1 Chr. 4:11).
2. The father of Ezri, a supervisor of those who tilled the soil during David's reign (1 Chr. 27:26).

CHELUBAI [kih LOO bye] (*bold*) — a son of Hezron and grandfather of Caleb (1 Chr. 2:9, 18, 42).

CHELUH [KEL oo] ([Jehovah is] *perfect*) — a Levite who divorced his pagan wife after the Captivity (Ezra 10:35; Chelluh, KJV; Cheluhi, RSV, NASB; Keluhi, NIV, NEB).

CHELUHI [keh LOU high] — a form of CHELUH.

CHEMARIM [KEM uh rim] (meaning unknown) — the KJV transliteration of the Hebrew word *kemarim* (Zeph. 1:4; idolatrous priests, RSV, NKJV, NIV, NASB; heathen priest, NEB). The word also refers to the idolatrous priests (2 Kin. 23:5, NKJV) appointed by the kings of Judah for the worship of the high places, and to the priests (Hos. 10:5, NKJV) of the calf–idols at Bethel.

CHEMOSH [KEE mahsh] (see GODS, PAGAN).

CHENAANAH [kih NAY uh nuh] (meaning unknown) — the name of two men in the Old Testament:
1. The father or ancestor of Zedekiah (1 Kin. 22:11, 24; 2 Chr. 18:10, 23).
2. A son of Bilhan, listed in the family of Benjamin (1 Chr. 7:10).

CHENANI [Kih NAY eye] (*Jehovah has established*) — a Levite who assisted at Ezra's public reading of the Book of the Law (Neh. 9:4).

CHENANIAH [ken uh NYE uh] (*Jehovah has established*) — a chief Levite during the days when David brought the ARK OF THE COVENANT to the Temple (1 Chr. 15:22, 27).

CHEPHAR HAAMMONI [KEE fur AM uh nye] (*village of the Ammonites*) — a town assigned to the tribe of Benjamin (Josh. 18:24).

CHEPHIRAH [kih FYE ruh] (*village, town*) — a city of Gibeon given to the tribe of Benjamin (Josh. 9:17; 18:26; Ezra 2:25; Neh. 7:29). It is identified as modern Khirbet Kefireh, about eight kilometers (five miles) southwest of el-Jib (ancient Gibeon).

CHERAN [KEE ruhn] (*lyre*) — a son of Dishon (Gen. 36:26; 1 Chr. 1:41).

CHERETHITES [KER ih thites] — a tribe inhabiting the NEGEB (or southern area) of Philistia (1 Sam. 30:14; Ezek. 25:16; Zeph. 2:5). The tribe probably emigrated from the island of Crete. Along with the PELETHITES, the Cherethites formed David's personal army (2 Sam. 8:18; 15:18; 20:7).

CHERITH [KEE rith] (*gorge, trench*) — a wadi (a dry riverbed) of Gilead, east of the Jordan River, where the prophet ELIJAH hid from King Ahab and was fed by ravens (1 Kin. 17:3, 5). It is probably the same as Wadi Yabis, near Beth Shean.

CHERUB [CARE ub] (*held fast*) — a place in Babylonia where some Jewish citizens lived during the Captivity. The persons who returned to Palestine from this place could not prove their Israelite descent (Ezra 2:59; Neh. 7:61). The exact location of Cherub is unknown.

CHERUBIM [CHEER oo beam] (meaning unknown) — winged angelic beings, often associated with worship and praise of God. The cherubim are first mentioned in the Bible in Genesis 3:24. When God drove Adam and Eve from the Garden of Eden, He placed cherubim at the east of the garden, "and a flaming sword which turned every way, to guard the way to the tree of life."

According to the prophets, cherubim belong to the category of unfallen angels; at one time, however, Satan or Lucifer was a cherub (Ezek. 28:14, 16), until he rebelled against God (Is. 14:12–14; Ezek. 28:12–19).

Symbolic representations of cherubim were used in the TABERNACLE in the wilderness. Two cherubim made of gold were stationed at the two ends of the MERCY SEAT, above the ARK OF THE COVENANT in the HOLY OF HOLIES (Ex. 25:17–22; 1 Chr. 28:18; Heb. 9:5). Artistic designs of cherubim decorated the ten curtains (Ex. 26:1; 36:8) and the veil (Ex. 26:31; 2 Chr. 3:14) of the tabernacle.

When Solomon built the Temple, he ordered that two cherubim be made of olive wood and overlaid with gold. Each measured ten cubits (4.6 meters or 15 feet) high with a wingspread of ten cubits (4.6 meters or 15 feet) (1 Kin. 6:23–28; 8:6–7; 2 Chr. 3:10–13; 5:7–8). These gigantic cherubim were placed inside the inner sanctuary, or in the Most Holy Place in the Temple. Their wings were spread over the ark of the covenant. The woodwork throughout the Temple was decorated with engraved figures of cherubim, trees, and flowers (1 Kin. 6:29–35; 7:29, 36; 2 Chr. 3:7).

A careful comparison of the first and tenth chapters of the book of Ezekiel shows clearly that the "four living creatures" (Ezek. 1:5) were the same beings as the cherubim (Ezekiel 10). Each had four faces—that of a man, a lion, an ox, and an eagle (Ezek. 1:10; also 10:14)—and each had four wings. In their appearance, the cherubim "had the likeness of a man" (Ezek. 1:5). These cherubim used two of their wings for flying and the other two for covering their bodies (Ezek. 1:6, 11, 23). Under their wings the cherubim appeared to have the form, or likeness, of a man's hand (Ezek. 1:8; 10:7–8, 21).

The imagery of Revelation 4:6–9 seems to be inspired, at least in part, by the prophecies of Ezekiel. The "four living creatures" described here, as well as the cherubim of Ezekiel, served the purpose of magnifying the holiness and power of God. This is one of their main responsibilities throughout the Bible. In addition to singing God's praises, they also served as a visible reminder of the majesty and glory of God and His abiding presence with His people.

In some ways, the cherubim were similar to the SERAPHIM, another form of angelic being mentioned in the Bible. Both were winged beings, and both surrounded God on His throne (Is. 6:2–3). But the seraphim of the prophet Isaiah's vision were vocal in their praise of God, singing "Holy, holy is the Lord of hosts" (Is. 6:3). Nowhere else in the Bible do the cherubim break forth in such exuberant praise. They apparently played a quieter, more restrained role in worship.

CHESALON [KESS uh lahn] (*slope*) — a town near Mount Jearim on the northern boundary of Judah (Josh. 15:10). It is identified with modern Kesla, about 15 kilometers (nine miles) west of Jerusalem.

CHESED [KEE sed] (*gain*) — the fourth son of Nahor and a nephew of Abraham (Gen. 22:22).

CHESIL [KEE sil] (*a fool*) — a village in southern Judah, named with Eltolad, Hormah, and Ziklag (Josh. 15:30).

CHEST — a word with two distinct meanings in the Bible:

1. The trunk, or rib cage, of the human body (Dan. 2:32).

2. A wooden box, or container (2 Chr. 24:3–11).

CHESTNUT (see PLANTS OF THE BIBLE).

CHESULLOTH [kih SUHL ahth] (*loins*) — a town between Jezreel and Shunem in the territory assigned to Issachar (Josh. 19:18). This site is identified as modern Iksal, about five kilometers (three miles) southeast of Nazareth.

CHETH [hayth] — a form of HETH.

CHEZIB [KEE zib] — a form of ACHZIB.

Photo by Gustav Jeeninga

Ruins of Chorazin, a town condemned by Jesus because of its unbelief (Matt. 11:21).

CHICKEN (see ANIMALS OF THE BIBLE).

CHIDON [KYE dun] (*a javelin*) — the name of the threshing floor where Uzza (or Uzzah) was struck dead for touching the ARK OF THE COVENANT (1 Chr. 13:9). In a parallel account the name is given as Nachon (2 Sam. 6:6).

CHIEF — the leader of a family, clan, or tribe (Gen. 36:15–43); a chieftain, ruler, or prince of a people. The word is also used in various administrative titles, such as chief butler and chief baker (Gen. 40:2—41:10).

CHILD, CHILDREN — offspring born to a husband and wife in the marriage relationship. To the Hebrews, children were considered gifts from God, and to be childless was considered a reproach (Gen. 16:4; Luke 1:25). Jesus clearly expressed his love and respect for children (Mark 9:36–37). He used the innocence and openness of children to illustrate the attitude necessary for entering the KINGDOM OF GOD (Matt. 18:2–3). Also see FAMILY.

CHILDREN OF GOD (see SONS OF GOD).

CHILDBEARING — the act of giving birth to offspring (Gen. 18:11; 1 Tim. 2:15). A birth is a joyful occasion (John 16:21). But it is also a painful event, characterized by agony and travail, following God's curse on Eve (Gen. 3:16). This agony is so well-known that childbearing became symbolic of any time of sorrow and suffering (Ps. 48:6; Is. 13:8). The prophet Jeremiah was especially fond of this analogy (Jer. 4:31; 13:21; 49:24; 50:43). In His Olivet Discourse, Jesus applied this image to the sorrows that start the Messianic age (Matt. 24:8). The apostle Paul twice used this figure of speech (Rom. 8:22; Gal. 4:19).

Midwives were generally present to assist mothers at the time of birth (Gen. 35:17; 38:28). When Israel suffered in Egypt, God blessed two midwives and removed some of the effects of Eve's curse by giving Israelite women easier childbirth (Ex. 1:19).

Also see BIRTH; TRAVAIL.

CHILEAB [KIL ih ab] (*restraint of father*) — a son of David and Abigail (2 Sam. 3:3); he also was called Daniel (1 Chr. 3:1).

CHILION [KIL ih ahn] (*wasting away*) — the younger son of Elimelech and Naomi and the husband of Orpah, Ruth's sister-in-law (Ruth 1:2, 5; 4:9).

CHILMAD [KIL mad] (*closed*) — a place, apparently in Mesopotamia, that traded with Tyre (Ezek. 27:23). It is mentioned in connection with Eden, Haran, and Assyria. The exact location is unknown.

CHIMHAM [KIM ham] (*of a pallid face*) — a friend and political supporter of David. After Absalom's defeat, he returned from beyond the Jordan River with David to Jerusalem (2 Sam. 19:37-40). The "habitation [or lodging place] of Chimham" (Jer. 41:17) may have been an inn given to Chimham by David as a reward for his loyalty.

CHIMNEY — an opening in an outside wall of a house through which smoke from a fire could escape (Hos. 13:3). An opening like this was generally a feature in poorer households, which used wood as a fuel. The wealthy classes often lit a fire in the outside court for warmth at night (Mark 14:54; Luke 22:55). Also see HOUSE.

CHINNERETH, CHINNEROTH, CINNEROTH
[SIN uh roth] (*lute, harp*) — the name of a sea (see Map 3, C–2), a region, and a city in the Bible:

1. The early name of the SEA OF GALILEE (Num. 34:11; Josh. 12:3; 13:27). It was also called the "Lake of Gennesaret" (Luke 5:1) and the "Sea of Tiberias" (John 6:1; 21:1).

2. A fortified city of Naphtali on the northwest shore of the Sea of Galilee surrounding the city of Chinnereth (Deut. 3:17; Josh. 19:35).

3. A region in the territory of Naphtali commonly identified with the Plain of Gennesaret (1 Kin. 15:20).

CHIOS [KYE ahs] (*open*) — an island in the Aegean Sea—between Greece and Asia Minor (see Map 8, C–2)—at the entrance to the Gulf of Smyrna (modern Izmir). On his return to Jerusalem during his third missionary journey, the apostle Paul "sailed...opposite Chios" (Acts 20:15). Situated between the islands of Lesbon and Samos, Chios rests about eight kilometers (five miles) from the mainland of Asia Minor. The island was famous for its wine, wheat, figs, and gum mastic.

CHISEL (see TOOLS OF THE BIBLE).

CHISLEV [KIZZ lehv] (*hunter*) — the ninth month in the Hebrew calendar (Neh. 1:1; Zech. 7:1; Chisleu, KJV). Also see CALENDAR.

CHISLON [KIZ lahn] (*strength*) — the father of ELIDAD (Num. 34:21).

CHISLOTH TABOR [KISS lahth TAY bawr] (*the loins of Tabor*) — a place on the border of Zebulun at the foot of Mount Tabor (Josh. 19:12). Also see CHESULLOTH.

CHITLISH [KIT lish] — a form of KITHLISH.

CHITTIM [KIT im] — a form of KITTIM.

CHIUN [KYE uhn] (see GODS, PAGAN).

CHLOE [KLOH ee] (*tender sprout*) — a woman, presumably a Christian, possibly from Corinth or Ephesus, who knew of the divisions and dissensions within the church at Corinth (1 Cor. 1:11).

CHOINIX, MEASURE (see WEIGHTS AND MEASURES).

CHORASHAN [kawr ASH uhn] — a form of ASHAN and BORASHAN.

CHORAZIN [koh RAY zin] (*secret*) — a city north of the Sea of Galilee (see Map 6, C–2) where Jesus performed many "mighty works" (Matt. 11:21; Luke 10:13). It has been identified as present–day Khirbet Kerazeh, about three kilometers (two miles) north of Capernaum (present–day Tell Hum). Jesus pronounced judgment upon Chorazin because it did not repent and believe.

CHOSEN (see ELECTION).

CHOSEN PEOPLE — a name for the Hebrew people, whom God chose as His special instruments. As a holy people set apart to worship God, they were to make His name known throughout the earth (Deut. 7:6, 7; Ps. 105:43). In the New Testament, Peter describes Christians as members of a "chosen generation" (1 Pet. 2:9).

CHOZEBA [koh ZEE buh] (*deceitful*) — a village of Judah (1 Chr. 4:22), probably the same as Achzib (Josh. 15:44; Mic. 1:14) and Chezib (Gen. 38:5). Another spelling is Cozeba (RSV).

CHRIST (*anointed one*) — a name for Jesus which showed that He was the long–awaited king and deliverer. For centuries the Jewish people had looked for a prophesied Messiah, a deliverer who would usher in a kingdom of peace and prosperity (Ps. 110; Is. 32:1–8; Amos 9:13). Jesus was clearly identified as this Messiah in Peter's great confession, "You are the Christ, the Son of the living God" (Matt. 16:16). Also see JESUS CHRIST; MESSIAH.

CHRIST, ASCENSION OF (see ASCENSION OF CHRIST).

CHRIST, CRUCIFIXION OF (see CRUCIFIXION OF CHRIST).

CHRIST, DEATH OF (see ATONEMENT; CRUCIFIXION OF CHRIST).

CHRIST, DIVINITY OF (see INCARNATION).

CHRIST, HUMANITY OF (see JESUS CHRIST).

CHRIST, PERSON OF (see INCARNATION; JESUS CHRIST).

CHRIST, TEMPTATION OF (see TEMPTATION OF CHRIST).

CHRISTIAN — an adherent or follower of Christ. The word occurs three times in the New Testament: "The disciples were first called Christians in Antioch" (Acts 11:26); Agrippa said to Paul, "You almost persuade me to be a Christian" (Acts 26:28); Peter exhorted, "If anyone suffers as a Christian, let him not be ashamed" (1 Pet. 4:16). In each instance, the word Christian assumes that the person called by the name was a follower of Christ. Christians were loyal to Christ, just as the Herodians were loyal to Herod (Matt. 22:16; Mark 3:6; 12:13).

The designation of the early followers of Christ as Christians was initiated by the non–Christian population of Antioch. Originally it may have been a term of derision. Eventually, however, Christians used it of themselves as a name of honor, not of shame. Prior to their adoption of the name, the Christians called themselves believers (Acts 5:14), brothers (Acts 6:3), or saints (Acts 9:13), names which also continued to be used.

In modern times the name Christian has been somewhat emptied of its true meaning as a follower of Christ. To some today, Christian means little more than a European or American who is not Jewish, while others have sought to make its proper use the name of a particular denomination. However, its original meaning is a noble one, of which any follower of Christ can rightly be proud.

Photo by Gustav Jeeninga

Early Christians were forced to fight in gladiatorial contests in the Colosseum, an amphitheater in the city of Rome.

CHRISTIANITY — the Christian religion, based on Jesus Christ, the only Savior and Mediator between God the Father and sinful man.

Christianity is unique among all the religions of the world. Most of them emphasize the life of the founder, but Christianity is based on the death of Jesus Christ. The death of Jesus is unique for it was prophesied in the opening pages of the Bible (Gen. 3:15) and came to pass in the New Testament age thousands of years later.

Not only is the death of Christ absolutely essential to Christianity. So is His resurrection. His death and resurrection are so important that all four gospels—Matthew, Mark, Luke, and John—devote one-fifth of their teachings to this combined subject. Mark 10:45 summarizes this unique mission of Christ's: "For even the Son of Man did not come to be served, but to serve, and to give His life a ransom for many."

The world already had plenty of religions and gods at the time of Jesus' birth. The Romans had combined their gods with those of the Greeks, and thousands of deities were worshiped. None of these gods had ever lived; most were based on imagination or heroic stories. But Jesus had actually lived in Palestine, had been crucified under Pontius Pilate (the Roman governor of Judea), and had been raised from the dead by the power of God the Father.

People who worshiped the mythical gods actually chose to ignore the visible signs of truth that pointed them toward God and eventually to salvation through grace (Rom. 1:20–21). This plan of salvation came to full maturity on the Cross.

In the apostle Paul's time there was a grave danger that Jewish converts to Christianity would make the new religion nothing more than an extension of Judaism. Paul fought to keep salvation–by–grace–plus–nothing the essence of Christianity (Eph. 2:8–9).

Paul's conflict was with a group of converts called JUDAIZERS (Acts 15; Galatians 2), who thought a Gentile convert had to be circumcised before he could become a Christian. Paul, Barnabas, and others traveled to Jerusalem, the center of Judaism, to settle the issue with the church leaders. In effect, Christianity was declared to be a full-grown, independent religion, not simply an extension of the Jewish faith.

Today, Paul's battle cry still rings forth as the banner of the Christian faith: "A man is not justified by the works of the law but by faith in Jesus Christ" (Gal. 2:16). Salvation is available only through Christ (Acts 4:12), made possible by His death, burial, and resurrection. Christianity is more than a creed, more than a religion; it is a way of life for all who accept Jesus Christ as Lord and Savior.

CHRONICLES, BOOKS OF FIRST AND SECOND — two historical books of the Old Testament which may be characterized as "books of hope." In broad, selective strokes, these books trace the history of the nation of Israel from Adam to the CAP-

Interior view of the massive Colosseum, which covered about six acres and reflected the splendor of ancient Rome.

TIVITY and Restoration. Much of this material is a repetition of that found in the books of 1 and 2 Samuel and 1 and 2 Kings. But the writer of Chronicles apparently wrote his history to encourage the exiles who had returned to Jerusalem after more than 50 years of captivity in Babylon. This selective history reminded them of Israel's glorious days from the past and gave them hope for the future as they pondered God's promises to His Covenant People.

Structure of the Book. The books of 1 and 2 Chronicles were written originally as one unbroken book. In later translations of the Bible, however, this long narrative was divided into two shorter books. Each of these books falls naturally into two major divisions.

The first nine chapters of 1 Chronicles contain long genealogies, or family histories, that are composed of information from the earliest historical books of the Bible. These genealogies take the reader from the descendants of Adam up through the ancestors of King DAVID. Special attention is given to the families of priests and Levites (6:1–81; 9:1–34), Saul's family, and particularly to the family of David (chaps. 2—3). The second major section of the book (chaps. 10-29) focuses on the reign of King David. This long account begins with the death of Saul (chap. 10), omitting the historical facts that preceded this event. Saul's death is reported to establish the fact that he was unqualified for office and that David was God's choice for this responsibility (10:14).

The account of David's reign is presented in a positive light, with all the details about David's great sin omitted. First Chronicles also lists the names of all those associated with him as mighty men (chaps. 11—12), and records his great victories (chaps. 14, 18—20). This section of the book also lists the names of the Levites, priests, and musicians in David's administration (chaps. 23—26), as well as other state officials (chap. 27). Also included is David's work in establishing Jerusalem as his capital city (11:4-9), and as the center of worship (chaps. 13, 15—16, 22, 28—29).

The Book of 2 Chronicles also contains two major sections. Chapters 1—9 focus on the rule of King SOLOMON, whose greatest accomplishment was the building of the TEMPLE in Jerusalem. Included is correspondence between Solomon and Hiram, king of Tyre, about building materials (chap. 2), as well as a full account of the dedication service when the Temple was completed (chaps. 5—7). The second major section (chaps. 10—36) is a highly selective account of the kings of Judah—from Rehoboam (chaps. 10—12) until the time of the Captivity (chap. 36). Kings given prominence in this narrative include Abijah (chap. 13), Asa (chaps. 14—16), Jehoshaphat (chaps. 17—20), Joash (chaps. 23—24), Amaziah (chap. 25), Uzziah or Azariah (chap. 26), Hezekiah (chaps. 29—32), and Josiah (chaps. 34—35). The book ends with the proclamation of King Cyrus of Persia allowing the return of the Jews to rebuild their Temple in Jerusalem (36:22-23).

One particularly interesting fact about the Book of 2 Chronicles is that it includes little information about the kings of the northern kingdom, Israel. And the facts which it gives about the kings of Judah are mostly positive. This indicates the author was interested in tracing the line of David and showing that Judah was the nation which remained faithful to the covenant between God and His people. This fact would have been encouraging to the exiles who returned to Jerusalem to rebuild the Temple. They felt they were continuing the forms and traditions which set them apart as the true worshipers of God and gave them a sense of identity as God's Covenant People.

Authorship and Date. The author of the Books of 1 and 2 Chronicles is unknown, although Ezra the priest and scribe seems the most likely possibility. As in 1 and 2 Chronicles, the Books of Ezra and Nehemiah were written originally as one unbroken book in the Hebrew language. And the last two verses of 2 Chronicles are repeated in the first three verses of the Book of Ezra, probably indicating they went together in the original version. Most scholars agree that these four books were written and compiled by the same person, but not all accept the theory of Ezra's authorship.

Ezra, however, remains the best candidate for this honor because of his important role among the community of exiles in Jerusalem. After leading a group to return to their homeland, he worked with another Jewish leader, Nehemiah, to strengthen the people's commitment to God's law (Ezra 10:17–19; Neh. 8:1–8; 9:1–3). He must have written all four of these books—1 and 2 Chronicles, Ezra and Nehemiah—after he arrived in Jerusalem about 457 B.C. and led the reforms among the people.

FIRST CHRONICLES: A Teaching Outline

Part One: The Royal Line of David (1:1—9:44)

The Chronicler used many sources in writing his book, including the Books of Samuel and Kings. He also used court histories, as did earlier writers, and prophetic narratives. One illustration of this procedure can be observed in 2 Chronicles 9:29, at the end of the story of Solomon.

Historical Setting. The Books of 1 and 2 Chronicles cover several centuries of the history of God's Covenant People—from the founders of the nation until the end of their captivity in Babylon and Persia about 538 B.C. But the books were written with a specific purpose in mind—to give comfort and hope to those who returned to Jerusalem.

The stage was set for the return of the Jewish people to Jerusalem after the Persians defeated Babylon and became the dominant power of the ancient world. The Babylonians had held the Jewish people captive for more than 50 years, but the Persians had a different foreign policy. They believed in letting their subject nations live in their own native regions under the authority of a ruling governor. They allowed the Jewish people to return to Jerusalem in several different stages, beginning with the first wave under ZERUBBABEL in 538 B.C. (2 Chr. 36:22–23).

After they returned to Jerusalem and rebuilt the Temple, the remnant of God's Covenant People needed constant encouragement. Keeping their faith and traditions alive required continual struggle. The situation called for determination and a strong sense of hope—hope that the promises of God to David would not be forgotten, and that a king from this royal line would rule again one day among God's people. This was the unique situation to which the Books of 1 and 2 Chronicles were addressed.

Theological Contribution. The Books of 1 and 2 Chronicles tie the entire sweep of the Old Testament together into one great affirmation of hope. These books should not only be read as histories, but for their insights into how God has kept faith with His Covenant People across the centuries. By

SECOND CHRONICLES: A Teaching Outline

selecting events that show how God has kept His promises, the author presents a beautiful doctrine of hope that begins with Adam (1 Chr. 1:1) and stretches to the end of the Captivity of God's people thousands of years later (2 Chr. 36:22–23). The clear implication for Christians today is that He is still a God of hope whose ultimate purpose will prevail in the world and in the lives of His people.

CHRONOLOGY, NEW TESTAMENT

CHRONOLOGY, NEW TESTAMENT — the chronology of the New Testament has been debated over the centuries. This is due partly to the limited data given in the biblical record. The biblical writers were more interested in the events that occurred than in the exact dates when they took place. Many times specific chronological facts are given as incidental remarks in the Bible. From these facts scholars attempt to reconstruct a chronological framework.

The Chronology of the Life of Jesus. The first task which the student of the New Testament faces is to construct a chronology of the life of Jesus. The following high points in His life and ministry, with approximate dates, are accepted by most New Testament scholars.

His birth—According to Matthew 2:1 and Luke 1:5, Jesus' birth happened before Herod the Great's death, which was no later than March or April in 4 B.C. Luke 2:1–5 states that just before Jesus' birth, Quirinius took a census of Israel while he was governor of Syria. The date of Quirinius' governorship is debated. Some scholars believe Quirinius was governor of Syria twice: once around the time of Herod's death and then a decade later in A.D. 6–7.

Another chronological note is that when Herod was tricked by the Wise Men who visited the baby Jesus, he ordered all children two years and younger to be killed. Some think this would indicate that Jesus was born two years before Herod's order. This is not necessarily true, for Herod was more likely just making sure that he would not miss Jesus in this senseless slaughter. Furthermore, some try to make the star in the East a conjunction of several stars. Again, the text talks about one star that seemed special to the wise men. A conjunction of stars would not have signified the birth of a king, according to the astrology of that day.

In conclusion, it seems that Jesus was born some time around 6 to 4 B.C., with the probability that it was the winter of 5/4 B.C. just before Herod's death.

The beginning of His ministry—Luke 3:1–3 states that John the Baptist's ministry began in the 15th year of Tiberius Caesar. Tiberius began reigning in August in A.D. 14. So this would mean that John the Baptist's ministry began some time in A.D. 29. From the gospel narratives about Jesus, it seems that He was baptized and began His ministry shortly after John began preaching. Luke 3:23 states that Jesus was "about" 30 years of age when He began His ministry. If Jesus was born in the winter of 5/4 B.C. and began His ministry in the summer or fall of A.D. 29, He would have been 32.

The duration of His ministry—Although a few scholars hold to a one- or two-year ministry of Jesus, most think He had at least a three-year ministry. The Gospel of John records three specific Passover celebrations during Jesus' ministry (John 2:13; 6:4; 11:55), which would account for at least two years of His ministry. However, it is thought that an additional year must be added between the Passovers of John 2:13 and 6:4. The reasons for this additional year come from two notes about time in John.

In John 4:35 Jesus speaks of four months before harvest, which would mean that He was in Samaria around January or February after the Passover celebration of John 2:13. John 5:1 also mentions a "feast." Although scholars disagree on the identification of this feast, it probably refers to Passover or the Feast of Tabernacles.

Thus, after the Passover of John 2:13 there is the reference to January or February of John 4:35 and a "feast" of John 5:1. This most likely refers to the Passover or Feast of Tabernacles before the Passover of John 6:4. Thus, there is a two-year interval between the Passovers of John 2:13 and 6:4 and a one-year interval between the Passovers of John 6:4 and 11:55. Therefore, if Jesus began His ministry in the summer or autumn of A.D. 29 and His first Passover is to be identified as the one mentioned in A.D. 30 and the last one is in A.D. 33, the duration of His ministry would be about three and a half years.

Jesus' ministry before the first Passover in A.D.

Ephesus was a prominent city of the New Testament era. Still visible today is this beautiful marble street which led to the nearby harbor.
Photo by Howard Vos

30 would include the temptation (Matt. 4:1–11; Mark 1:12–13; Luke 4:1–13), the call of His first disciples (Matt. 4:18–22; Mark 1:16–20; John 1:35–51), the wedding at Cana (John 2:1–11), and His journey to Capernaum (John 2:12) just before He went to Jerusalem for His first Passover (John 2:13).

After this Passover Jesus' ministry was primarily in Jerusalem and Judea (John 3:1–26). Following John the Baptist's imprisonment, Jesus moved to Galilee (Matt. 4:12–17; Mark 1:14–15; Luke 4:14–15; John 4:3–36). He continued His ministry in Galilee until John the Baptist was executed. Although the date of the beheading is not specified, it occurred at about the same time as the feeding of the 5,000 (Matt. 14:13–21; Mark 6:30–44; Luke 9:10–17), which happened some time around the Passover of A.D. 32 (John 6:4).

After this Passover Jesus withdrew from public ministry to be with His disciples. Other events during the final year of His ministry included His journey to Phoenicia (Matt. 15:21–28; Mark 7:24–30), the feeding of the 4,000 (Matt. 15:32–39; Mark 8:1–10), Peter's confession at Caesarea Philippi (Matt. 16:13–23; Mark 8:27–33; Luke 9:18–22), and the Transfiguration (Matt. 17:1–8; Mark 9:2–8; Luke 9:28–36). Finally, Jesus went to Jerusalem to be crucified during the Passover celebration of A.D. 33 (John 11:55).

The date of His death—Since Jesus was tried by Pilate, His death occurred during Pilate's governorship, which lasted from A.D. 26 to A.D. 36. Astronomically, Jesus' death fits best with either A.D. 30 or 33. Because of the political situation and other facts surrounding Jesus' life, it seems that A.D. 33 is the best date for the crucifixion. The day of the week of His crucifixion has been debated. But it seems best to consider it as Friday, since His body was laid in the tomb on the evening of the "Day of Preparation" (technical term for Friday), the day before the Sabbath (Matt. 27:62; 28:1; Mark 15:42; Luke 23:54, 56; John 19:31, 42). Thus Jesus was crucified on Friday, April 3, in A.D. 33.

The Chronology of the Apostolic Age. Another important task in New Testament studies is to construct a chronology of the important events that occurred during the lives of the apostles and the early years of the Christian church.

The Book of Acts and the New Testament epistles serve as the basis of the chronology of the age of the apostles. References to the political leaders during this time help pinpoint the dates.

From Pentecost to Paul's second Jerusalem visit—Pentecost, which would have occurred on May 24, A.D. 33, is the starting point of the apostolic age. To establish the date of Paul's conversion, scholars have determined the time of Paul's first two visits to Jerusalem. The first visit occurred three years after his conversion (Acts 9:26–29; Gal. 1:18) when he escaped from Damascus while it was under Aretas' control (2 Cor. 11:32–33). The Romans let Aretas control Damascus from A.D. 37 until his death in A.D. 39. Thus Paul's conversion would have occurred some time between A.D. 33 and A.D. 36.

Paul's second visit to Jerusalem was 14 years after his conversion (Gal. 2:1–10) when he brought relief to the Christians suffering a famine (Acts. 11:28–30; 12:25). According to the Jewish historian Josephus, Helena, queen of Adiabne, shipped figs from Cyprus and grain from Egypt, probably at the height of the famine (A.D. 47–48), or shortly there-

Ruins of the great outdoor theater at Ephesus (bottom and lower right of photo), where Paul was almost mobbed by pagan worshipers because he proclaimed allegiance to the one true God (Acts 19:21-41).

Photo by Howard Vos

after. Paul brought contributions after the provision from Helena and would have come to Jerusalem a second time around A.D. 47-48. Counting 14 years between his conversion and this visit would mean that Paul's conversion occurred in A.D. 33 or 34, although it could have been later, since the ancients counted parts of years as whole years. Most likely Paul's conversion was some time in A.D. 35, probably in the summer of that year.

The events in the first part of Acts may be summarized as follows: Peter's ministry in Jerusalem, A.D. 33-35 (Acts 2—5); Stephen's martyrdom in the spring of A.D. 35 (Acts 6—7); Paul's conversion in the summer of A.D. 35 (Acts 9:1-7); Paul in Damascus and Arabia, A.D. 35-37 (Acts 9:8-25; Gal. l:16-17); Paul's first visit to Jerusalem and ministry in Tarsus and Syria-Cilicia, A.D. 37 (Acts 9:26-30; Gal. 1:18-21); Peter's ministry to the Gentiles, A.D. 40-41 (Acts 10:1—11:18); Barnabas' and Paul's journey to Antioch, A.D. 41-43 (Acts 19:19-26); Agabus' prediction of famine, A.D. 44 (Acts 11:27-28); James' martyrdom during Agrippa I's persecution, A.D. 44 (Acts 12); and Paul's second visit to Jerusalem and his return to Antioch, A.D. 47-48 (Acts 11:30; 12:25; Gal. 2:1-10).

Paul's first missionary journey—On his first missionary journey (Acts 13—14), Paul went from Antioch to Cyprus when Sergius Paulus ruled as proconsul before A.D. 51 and most likely in A.D. 46-48. Paul next went to the Galatian churches in Asia Minor and then returned to Antioch. This journey lasted from the spring of A.D. 48 to the fall of A.D. 49. Upon his return to Antioch, he saw Peter (Gal. 2:11-16) and wrote the Book of Galatians. Paul's third visit to Jerusalem in the autumn of A.D. 49 was to attend the Jerusalem Council (Acts 15), after which he returned and wintered at Antioch in A.D. 49/50.

Paul's second missionary journey—Paul's second missionary journey began in the spring of A.D. 50 and ended in the fall of A.D. 52 (Acts 15:36—18:22). He revisited the Galatian churches and went on to Troas. Crossing over into Europe, he founded churches at Philippi, Thessalonica, and Berea. He waited in Athens for Silas and Timothy and then went to Corinth and stayed there a year and a half (Acts 18:11), from the spring of A.D. 51 to the fall of A.D. 52. Paul wrote 1 and 2 Thessalonians in A.D. 51 while he was in Corinth. Two chronological notes need to be considered.

First, while at Corinth he met Priscilla and Aquila, who had fled Italy because of the persecution of the Jews in A.D. 49 (Acts 18:2). Hence, Paul could not have come to Corinth before A.D. 49. Second, Paul was tried before Gallio (Acts 18:12-16), who was the proconsul of Achaia from the summer of A.D. 51 to the summer of A.D. 52. Thus, Paul must have been in Corinth some time during Gallio's rule. After his long stay in Corinth, Paul brought Priscilla and Aquila to Ephesus and then moved on to Jerusalem (fourth visit) and returned to Antioch for the winter in A.D. 52/53.

Paul's third missionary journey—Paul's third missionary journey was from the spring of A.D. 53 to the spring of A.D. 57 (Acts 18:23—21:16). Leaving Antioch, he revisited the Galatian churches, arriving in Ephesus around the fall of A.D. 53 and staying there until the spring of A.D. 56. Just before his departure from Ephesus, he wrote 1 Corinthians. Because of the riot at Ephesus, he left for Macedonia. From Macedonia he wrote 2 Corinthians (fall of A.D. 56). He traveled to Corinth, wintered there in A.D. 56/57, and wrote Romans. In the spring of A.D. 57 he revisited the churches in Macedonia, went to Miletus to meet the Ephesian elders, and then went on to Jerusalem (fifth visit) for the Feast of Pentecost in A.D. 57.

Paul's imprisonments—While in Jerusalem, Paul was arrested and taken to Caesarea, where he was tried by Felix and imprisoned for two years in A.D. 57-59 (Acts 21:26-27). Although there is debate concerning the time that Festus succeeded Felix, it is likely that this succession occurred in the summer of A.D. 59. Paul was heard first by Festus (Acts 25:7-12) and shortly afterwards by Agrippa II (Acts 26). Then he appealed to Caesar.

Paul went to Rome on a hazardous journey from August of A.D. 59 to February of A.D. 60 and was imprisoned from the spring of A.D. 60 to the spring of A.D. 62 (Acts 27—28). While in prison Paul wrote Ephesians, Colossians, Philemon, and Philippians.

Chronology from this point on is drawn from inferences in the epistles in the New Testament and other evidence from the early church. It seems likely that Paul was released after a two-year imprisonment in Rome and went to Ephesus and Colosse and then left for Macedonia. In the fall of A.D. 62 Paul wrote to Timothy at Ephesus. Also in A.D. 62, James, the brother of Jesus, was martyred during the time of anarchy between the death of Festus and Albinus' arrival. Peter probably went to Rome that year and remained there until his martyrdom in the persecution of the Roman emperor Nero in A.D. 64. While Peter was in Rome, the Gospel of Mark may have been written under Peter's guidance. Also, Peter would have written his two epistles.

Paul moved to Asia Minor in the spring of A.D. 63 and remained there until the spring of A.D. 64. He then went to Spain from the spring of A.D. 64 to the spring of A.D. 66. Leaving Spain, he went to Crete with Titus and left Titus there while he went on to Asia Minor in the summer/autumn of A.D. 66. While here he wrote the Epistle to Titus. Paul spent the winter of A.D. 66/67 at Nicopolis (Titus 3:12), after which he went to Macedonia and Greece. But he was arrested and brought to Rome in the fall of A.D. 67 for his second Roman imprisonment. While there he wrote 2 Timothy. Paul was executed around the spring of A.D. 68.

About two years after Paul's death, Jerusalem was destroyed. At that time only a few remaining books of the New Testament had not been written. It is possible that the Gospel of John was written around A.D. 70. Jude may have been written about

A.D. 75, the three epistles of John about A.D. 85–95, and the Book of Revelation about A.D. 95–96. This marked the end of the age of the apostles.

CHRONOLOGY, OLD TESTAMENT — the scientific identification of the time when the events recorded in the Old Testament took place. With all the information the Old Testament contains, some of it detailed and lengthy, drawing up a settled list of dates for the events it reports might appear to be a simple task. Actually it is very difficult. Not only do we not have a sufficiently continuous record of events; much of the information we do have can be interpreted in different ways.

It is hard to relate specific events in Hebrew history to what was taking place in neighboring nations until about the eighth century B.C. In turn, dating the events of each of these nations presents its own problems. Finally, the systems by which Israel and its neighbors kept track of time and events are not clear.

Problems in Establishing a Chronology. The first of these obstacles can be illustrated from the work of the seventeenth–century Archbishop James Ussher, who treated the biblical genealogies as though they were modern records of generation-by-generation descent. Basing his work on that assumption, he calculated back to the time of CREATION, which he set at 4004 B.C. More recent information about ancient lists of descendants, however, indicates that unimportant family members often were omitted. This led to compressed lists that did not precisely conform to the period of time that they were supposed to cover.

Ussher also took the ages of the people who lived before the Flood at face value. Later research has shown that they appear to be based upon an ancient Sumerian system of reckoning—such as that used for the Sumerian king lists—which we do not yet understand. As a result, Ussher's chronology is totally inaccurate until the time of Moses—a period which itself is also a matter of considerable debate among scholars.

If it were possible to link the period of the biblical Flood with what was happening in the rest of the world, as described in Sumerian or Babylonian literature, Old Testament chronology would be a simple matter. But there are a number of reasons why this is impossible.

The first problem is that there was no uniform basis in the ancient world on which dates were reckoned. When attempts at dating were made, they were often expressed in phrases such as "after the earthquake," or "in the fourth year of the king." While these statements were perfectly clear to everyone who read them at the time of their writing, they are completely meaningless for comparing the events that took place in that culture with events that happened at the same time somewhere else. Consequently, the problems involved in trying to establish dates from the Ancient Near East in general also apply to the attempt to establish dates for Old Testament events.

Photo by Howard Vos

Statue of Amenhotep II of Egypt. Many scholars believe he was the ruling Pharaoh when the Hebrew people were delivered from slavery under the leadership of Moses.

Scholars who have tried to establish dating sequences for Babylonian history have found themselves embarrassed by two dating sequences for one of the earlier periods. There is a "high" chronology for the First Babylonian Dynasty; it is arrived at by connecting Amraphel, king of Shinar (Gen. 14:1), with HAMMURABI of Babylon and giving him a date of about 2123–2031 B.C. By contrast, the "low" chronology places Hammurabi between about 1728 and 1686 B.C. Even this late date, however, is regarded as too high by some scholars, who interpret the data quite differently.

A similar situation is true for Egyptian history. Information provided by lists and annals of kings generally is notably unreliable for purposes of chronology, and even more caution is needed when dealing with Egyptian sources than with their counterparts in MESOPOTAMIA (the region between the Tigris and Euphrates Rivers). Historians have discovered that Egyptian records are not so much factual history as propaganda; they present the "official" view of events for the instruction of future Egyptian generations.

Historians have grouped the lists of Egyptian rulers into 31 dynasties. While this is a convenient way of looking at Egyptian history for the historian, the dates for events are not reliable until about the Saitic period (about 663–525 B.C.). Furthermore, both the First and Second Dynasties have "high" and "low" chronologies, the former supported by scholars who date the period between

5867 and 3100 B.C., and the latter supported by scholars who date the period between 2900 and 2760 B.C. Other difficulties in Egyptian dating include the Eighteenth Dynasty, which introduced the New Kingdom period (about 1570–1150 B.C.). This was the period of time during which pharaohs such as Amenhotep II, Akhenaton, Tutankhamen (and others) ruled.

In spite of all these confusions, some dates in Near Eastern history can be established reasonably well. The fall of SAMARIA in 722 B.C. (2 Kin. 17:6) is confirmed by a statement in the annals of SARGON of Assyria for that year. Again, the first Babylonian attack on Jerusalem, resulting in the CAPTIVITY of 597 B.C., occurred on March 15–16 of that year, as recorded in the Babylonian Chronicle, a contemporary CUNEIFORM text. Unfortunately, such points of contact are few. It was unusual in ancient times for a defeated nation to record its losses.

First of all, if the war resulted in the extinction of one nation—as happened when the Sea Peoples brought the Hittite Empire to an end about 1200 B.C.—the conquered nation usually was unwilling—or unable—to record its defeat. Furthermore, it was the common practice among Ancient Near Eastern nations—with the exception of the Hebrews—to exaggerate victories and to ignore defeats. In those instances where both sides fought to a standstill, each usually counted the battle as a victory.

Another practice that seems very strange to the modern reader was the practice in some Near Eastern countries of including an accession year as part of a king's reign. This period was not necessarily a full calendar year; often it consisted only of the interval between the accession of the new king and the beginning of the next calendar year. This is why it is so difficult to compare and make sense of the lists of kings in the books of 1 and 2 Kings and 1 and 2 Chronicles.

Another device that complicates the chronology of the Old Testament was the system of co-regencies. A king would begin his reign while his predecessor was still alive, governing with him several years before he died. This system is the reason for some of the obvious difficulties in harmonizing dates of kings in the Old Testament. Thus, in the history of Judah, Jehoshaphat (about 870–848 B.C.) actually was co-regent from 873 B.C., while Jehoram (Joram), who reigned from about 848–841 B.C., had been co-regent from 853 B.C.

But even after recognizing all these dating problems, the Bible student can rest assured that the ancient Near Eastern scribes worked with great care and precision in passing on the Old Testament. They furnish the patient modern interpreter with the information needed to gain a reliable picture of Old Testament history.

Time of the Patriarchs. Because of the problems involved, archaeological periods might be used to date the earliest history of the Old Testament. But these periods are general rather than precise, and archaeologists disagree about the length of each period. Therefore these archaeological descriptions may be used for the periods up to, and including, the Hebrew PATRIARCHS. These dates should be regarded as approximate.

A late period of the Old Stone Age known as Natufian (8000 B.C.) corresponds with the introduction of agriculture into the Near East. This period was followed by the pre-pottery Neolithic phase (8000–5000 B.C.) at Jericho and elsewhere. The Chalcolithic period (4500–3000 B.C.) was marked by the increasing use of metals in Mesopotamia and Egypt, and by weaving and pottery-making in Mesopotamia. The Sumerians began draining the southern Mesopotamian marshes during this period. This led to the beginning of a culture that has left its mark on the rest of humanity. This civilization reached its height in the Early Bronze Age

During the days of King Rehoboam about 920 B.C., a government building stood on this stone platform in the city of Lachish.
Photo by Howard Vos

(3000–2000 B.C.), when the first Semitic kingdom was established in Babylonia.

The Sumerian words and phrases in the early chapters of Genesis show there was an important cultural connection between Sumer and Israel. The Flood may well have occurred about the middle of this period, but actual data is lacking. According to some scholars, Abraham, Isaac, and Jacob lived at this time; but others place them in the Middle Bronze Age (2000–1500 B.C.). A few writers even think that they flourished toward the end of the Late Bronze Age (1500–1200 B.C.).

Four dates have been suggested for the Hebrew patriarchs. These are based upon two different dates for the EXODUS. The first is 2166–1805 B.C., assuming a fifteenth–century B.C. date for the Exodus and a 430–year Hebrew settlement in Egypt. The archaeological background material used to support this date comes from Mesopotamia and Syria. The second, also assuming a fifteenth–century B.C. Exodus but reckoning a 215–year Egyptian settlement by the Hebrews, is 1952–1589 B.C. Once more, Mesopotamian archaeological materials are claimed as evidence.

The third date, assuming a thirteenth–century B.C. period for the Exodus, is 1950–1650 B.C. Advocates of this theory argue from archaeological evidence from the Middle Bronze Age. The fourth date, also assuming a thirteenth–century B.C. Exodus, is 1500–1300 B.C. Advocates of this date support their position with evidence from the Late Amarna Age culture of the fourteenth–century B.C.

The Time of the Exodus. The two suggested dates for the Exodus must now be considered. The first is 1446 B.C., indicated by 1 Kings 6:1 and suggested by Judges 11:26. Mycenaean pottery from the Judges period at Hazor appears to support this date. The second is 1280 B.C., relying upon archaeological evidence indicating that the Egyptian cities of Pithom and Raamses (Ex. 1:11) were rebuilt in the thirteenth–century B.C., probably with Hebrew labor. Furthermore, the Merneptah stele, which describes that Pharaoh's campaign in Palestine about 1220 B.C., regarded Israel as an already settled nation. This suggests an exodus from Egypt some 60 years earlier. On the basis of these two dates there obviously will be two corresponding dates for the wilderness wanderings, namely 1446–1406 B.C. and 1280–1240 B.C. The date of the Exodus is one of the most difficult problems in Old Testament history. It is made worse by the fact that solid evidence can be produced to support both positions.

This situation not only affects the dating of the Exodus and the WANDERING OF ISRAEL in the wilderness; it also affects the dates for the Conquest and the period of the Judges. Alternate dates have been suggested for both these events. The first alternative is 1406–1050 B.C., to accommodate all the judges (assuming that the works of the judges follow one another historically); the second is a shorter interval of 1230–1025 B.C. (assuming that

their work overlapped). The earlier date is supported partly by the Mycenaean pottery at Hazor, which suggests a date for the Conquest shortly after 1400 B.C. The second date claims a great deal of evidence from archaeological studies at Bethel, Hazor, and several Philistine sites. In both instances the archaeological data are open to various interpretations.

The United Hebrew Kingdom. Few problems are associated with the date of the United Kingdom. Saul probably was made king in 1050 B.C. He ruled for 40 years (compare Acts 13:21), being succeeded by David in 1010 B.C. David was king for roughly the same length of time, as was Solomon his successor (970–931 B.C.). Following Solomon's death, it again becomes difficult to set precise dates, due to the different methods the scribes used in their work.

The Divided Kingdom. When the Kingdom divided, Israel followed the Egyptian system of not counting accession years until the ninth century B.C. Then it changed to the Babylonian system, which did count accession years.

Under Rehoboam, Judah began by using the accession year method, but in the ninth century B.C. it adopted the Egyptian system that Israel had abandoned. After a short interval, Judah returned to the accession year method and continued to use it until the Captivity. It also appears that the scribes also included co-regencies in their reckonings; in addition, two different calendars were involved. Israel's new year began in the spring (Nisan), and Judah's began in the autumn (Tishri).

Many of the kings in the separate nations of Judah and Israel also were mentioned in the annals or records of foreign nations. This proves their historicity and lays a foundation for an integrated system of Near Eastern dates.

The nation of Israel crumbled in 522 B.C. with their defeat by the Assyrians. Her sister nation, Judah, suffered the same fate about 150 years later, in 586 B.C., when Jerusalem fell to Babylon. The leading citizens of Judah were carried into captivity by the Babylonians, beginning their period of exile in a foreign land.

Return from Captivity. The Babylonian Captivity (597–538 B.C.) ended with Babylon's fall to CYRUS, founder of the Persian Empire, and his proclamation of freedom to the captive peoples in Mesopotamia. The captives returned to Judea between 535 and 515 B.C.; and the prophets HAGGAI and ZECHARIAH (520 B.C.) encouraged the rebuilding of the Temple, which was accomplished four years later (516 B.C.). The period of Xerxes (Ahasuerus) and Esther (486–465 B.C.) was followed in Judah by the work of Ezra and Nehemiah (458–444 B.C.). Together they rehabilitated the faithful community and established its life on the basis of the Law. Some scholars have tried to reverse the historical order of Ezra and Nehemiah by placing them in the reign of Artaxerxes II (404–359 B.C.), but this requires an unnecessary alteration of the Hebrew text of Ezra 7:7.

The Kings of Israel and Judah, Compared Chronologically

ISRAEL (Northern Kingdom)	JUDAH (Southern Kingdom)
931-910 B.C. Jeroboam I	931-913 B.C. Rehoboam
910-909 B.C. Nadab	913-911 B.C. Abijam
909-886 B.C. Baasha	911-869 B.C. Asa
886-885 B.C. Elah	Asa
885 B.C. Zimri	Asa
885-880 B.C. Tibni	Asa
880-874 B.C. Omri	870-848 B.C. Jehoshaphat
Omri	(co-regent from 873 B.C.)
874-853 B.C. Ahab	Jehoshaphat
853-852 B.C. Ahaziah	Jehoshaphat
852-841 B.C. Jehoram (Joram)	848-841 B.C. Jehoram (Joram)
Jehoram	(co-regent from 853 B.C.)
841-814 B.C. Jehu	841 B.C. Ahaziah
814-798 B.C. Jehoahaz	841-835 B.C. Athaliah
798-782 B.C. Jehoash (Joash)	835-796 B.C. Jehoash (Joash)
Jehoash	796-767 B.C. Amaziah
782-753 B.C. Jeroboam II	767-740 B.C. Uzziah (Azariah)
(co-regent from 793 B.C.)	(co-regent from 792 B.C.)
753-752 B.C. Zechariah	Uzziah
752 B.C. Shallum	Uzziah
752-742 B.C. Menahem	Uzziah
742-740 B.C. Pekahiah	740-731 B.C. Jotham
Pekahiah	(co-regent from 750 B.C.)
740-732 B.C. Pekeh	732-716 B.C. Jehoahaz I (Ahaz)
Pekeh	(co-regent from 744 B.C.)
732-722 B.C. Hoshea	716-686 B.C. Hezekiah
(end of the northern kingdom of Israel)	(co-regent from 729 B.C.)
	687-642 B.C. Manasseh
	(co-regent from 696 B.C.)
	642-640 B.C. Amon
	640-609 B.C. Josiah
	609 B.C. Jehoahaz II
	609-597 B.C. Jehoiakim
	597 B.C. Jehoiachin
	597-587 B.C. Zedekiah
	586-582 B.C. Gedaliah

Photo by Willem A. VanGemeren
The lush Jordan Valley, with the river flowing between Israel and the modern nation of Jordan.

From the Persians to the End of the Old Testament. The Persian period (539–331 B.C.) ended abruptly with the conquests of ALEXANDER the Great, and was replaced by the Greek period (331–65 B.C.). Alexander died in 323 B.C., and his empire was divided among his generals. Judah was controlled by the Egyptian PTOLEMIES until 205 B.C., when it was taken over by the SELEUCIDS of SYRIA, who were led by Antiochus III the Great. He died in 190 B.C. while resisting the Romans and was succeeded by his younger son ANTIOCHUS IV Epiphanes (175–163 B.C.).

The cruelty of Antiochus IV Epiphanes quickly caused a revolt by a Jewish family known as the MACCABEES (167–163 B.C.). This revolt ultimately secured Jewish independence from Syria. (The Dead Sea community at Qumran was probably founded about the time that Antiochus III died, although this is uncertain.) The Maccabees (or HASMONEANS) governed Judea for a century, from 143 B.C. Their rule was ended by the Roman occupation of Syria under Pompeii in 64 B.C. This meant the beginning of the Roman period in Palestine. For the next century Roman soldiers were stationed in Jerusalem. Under the watchful eye of Rome, Herod the Great (43–4 B.C.) became governor of Galilee and controlled political life in Judea; the religious affairs of the nation were governed by the PHARISEES and SADDUCEES.

With the defeat of Anthony and Cleopatra in 30 B.C., Octavius became the head of the Roman Empire. Under the title of AUGUSTUS, he brought a period of peace and prosperity to the Empire until his death in A.D. 14. During the reign of Augustus, and just before the death of Herod the Great, Jesus Christ was born (about 6 B.C.). With this event the chronology of the Old Testament formally comes to an end.

CHRYSOLITE, CHRYSOPRASE, CHRYSOPRASUS (see JEWELS AND PRECIOUS STONES).

CHUB [kub] — a people who allied with Egypt against the Babylonians in the time of Nebuchadnezzar (Ezek 30:5). Many scholars believe Chub is a textual error and should be read as in the SEPTUAGINT, Lub, that is, Libya (NIV, RSV).

CHUN [con] (meaning unknown) — a town in Syria from which David took bronze (1 Chr. 18:8; Cun, KJV).

CHURCH — a local assembly of believers as well as the redeemed of all the ages who follow Jesus Christ as Savior and Lord.

In the four gospels of the New Testament, the term church is found only in Matthew 16:18 and 18:17. This scarcity of usage in those books that report on the life and ministry of Jesus is perhaps best explained by the fact that the church as the body of Christ did not begin until the day of PENTECOST after the ASCENSION of Jesus (Acts 1:1–4).

That the church began on the day of Pentecost may be demonstrated in various ways: (1) Christ Himself declared the church to be yet future; (2) it was founded upon the death, resurrection, and ascension of Christ, and such an accomplished fact was not possible until Pentecost (Gal. 3:23–25); (3) there could be no church until it was fully purchased with Christ's blood (Eph. 1:20).

Nature. The Greek word for church is *ekklesia*. This word is used 115 times in the New Testament, mostly in the Book of Acts and the writings of the apostle Paul and the general epistles. At least 92 times this word refers to a local congregation. The other references are to the church general, or all believers everywhere for all ages.

When the church general is implied, church refers to all who follow Christ, without respect to locality or time. The most general reference to the church occurs in Ephesians 1:22; 3:10–21; 5:23–32. Since the church general refers to all believers of all ages, it will not be complete until after the judgment; and the assembly of all the redeemed in one place will become a reality only after the return of Christ (Heb. 12:23; Rev. 21—22).

Because the church general will not become a tangible reality until after Christ's return, the greatest emphasis in the New Testament is placed upon the idea of the local church. The local church is the visible operation of the church general in a given time and place.

Commission. Speaking to His followers after His resurrection, Jesus commissioned the church to make disciples and teach them what He had taught (Matt. 28:16). The entire Book of Acts is the story of the early church's struggle to be loyal to this commission. As one reads this book, he is impressed by the reality that Christ, through the presence of the Holy Spirit, continues to direct His church as it carries out its commission.

Activities. The early church met in the Temple and Jewish synagogues, as well as private homes of believers (Acts 5:42). Later, in recognition of Christ's resurrection on the first day of the week, Sunday became the principal time for public worship (1 Cor. 16:2). At these public worship services, missionary teachings and outreach in the name of Christ were offered to all within reach.

In the worship services of early Christians, prayer was offered, not only on the Lord's Day, but on special occasions as well (Acts 12:5), and Scripture was read (James 1:22; 1 Thess. 5:27). The breaking of bread and the sharing of the cup on the Lord's Day were observed as a continuing proclamation of Jesus' death, an anticipation of His return, and a participation in His "body and blood" (1 Cor. 11:20–29). Offerings for the needy were also received (1 Cor. 16:2).

Organization. At first, church organization was flexible to meet changing needs. As the church became more established, however, church officers came into existence. These included the APOSTLES, PROPHETS, EVANGELISTS, ELDERS, BISHOPS, MINISTERS or teachers, DEACONS, and DEACONESSES.

Although church organization varies from denomination to denomination today, the pattern and purpose of the New Testament remains a model for churches as they pursue their mission in the world.

CHURCH GOVERNMENT — the organization pattern by which a church governs itself. At first, church organization and government in the New Testament was flexible to meet changing needs. But as the church became better established, it gave attention to the right structures and procedures that would help it accomplish its mission. In the earliest days, the APOSTLES directed the work of the church. Then seven men were chosen to assist the needs (Acts 6). Later, PROPHETS, EVANGELISTS, ELDERS, BISHOPS, and DEACONS were chosen.

No single pattern of government in the early church can be discovered by reading the New Testament. Thus, numerous forms of church government are used today to provide order and structure for the work of churches. Present expressions of church government may be classified into six forms.

Congregational. This form of organization allows a local congregation the freedom to determine what it considers the will of Christ. Thus, each congregation governs its own affairs. Congregational freedom does not imply that the local bodies are self–governing apart from the Lordship of Christ. But the members of each congregation have the right to determine what they consider to be the will of Christ.

Presbyterian. This form of church government recognizes that Christ alone is Head of the Church, and that He rules His church by His Word and

In the early history of the church, believers used these underground catacombs as a meeting place as well as a burial site.

Photo: Levant Photo Service

Spirit. Thus, church officials have power, although it is ministerial and declarative, not legislative. They declare, explain, and apply Christ's will as the Spirit clarifies the Scripture to their understanding. They do not make new laws for the church. Presbyterians believe they find the authority for their form of church government in the Bible, but they do not claim that Presbyterian government is the only kind that God can bless.

Episcopalian. This system of church government views the bishop as the principal officer. Decisions are made at levels higher than the local church, but common sense often dictates that the will of God and the opinions of members should be given prayerful consideration.

Roman Catholic. Roman Catholics view the church as the continuing visible presence of Christ in the world. Christ maintains His life on earth through the church. The clergy form a hierarchy that governs the church with the pope as the highest authority. The pope is the "bishop" of Rome; his decisions are authoritative for the entire church. The papal office is believed to be passed from pope to pope. This authority is believed to have originated in Christ's declaration of Peter as the first pope, according to the Catholic interpretation of Matthew 16:18.

National Church Government. This form of government recognizes that the supreme authority for church matters is vested in the state and not the church itself. Supporters of this form of church government believe that representatives of the state have the right to rule on all religious matters connected with the church.

Quakers. The Quakers reject any type of church ruler or official and almost every form of physical organization. For the Quakers, everything depends on the inner light which any believer has the right and power to receive directly from God. They have no specific rules for receiving members. Decisions are arrived at by mutual agreement among the believers.

CHUZA [KOO zuh] (*little jug*) — a steward (business manager) of Herod Antipas and evidently a man of position and wealth. His wife, Joanna, was one of the women who "provided for Him [Jesus] from their substance" (Luke 8:3).

CILICIA [sih LISH ih uh] — a province in southeastern Asia Minor (modern Turkey, see Map 7, D–2). The capital of Cilicia was Tarsus, the birthplace of the apostle Paul (Acts 21:39; 22:3). Cilicia was bounded on the east by Syria, on the west by Pamphylia, and on the south by the Mediterranean Sea. On the north it is separated by the Taurus Mountains from Cappadocia, Lycaonia, and Isauria.

Geographically, Cilicia was divided naturally into two main regions: Cilicia Tracheia, a rugged mountainous area in the north and west, and Cilicia Pedias, a flat, fertile plain in the east.

The Jews of Cilicia formed part of a synagogue in Jerusalem called "the Synagogue of Freedmen" (Acts 6:9). Paul visited Cilicia soon after his conversion (Gal. 1:21) and again on his second missionary journey (Acts 15:41).

CINNAMON (see PLANTS OF THE BIBLE).

CINNEROTH [SIN uh roth] — a form of CHINNEROTH.

CIRCLE — to the ancient Hebrew mind, an invisible boundary that served as a line of separation be-

The falls of the Cydnus River just north of the city of Tarsus in the province of Cilicia.

Photo by Howard Vos

A stone carving from Egypt, about 2200 B.C., showing two boys being circumcised with flint knives.

tween the heavens and the earth. The Old Testament writers portrayed God as sitting "above the circle of the earth" (Is. 40:22) to emphasize His power and majesty (Job 22:14; Prov. 8:27).

CIRCUIT — a word with several different meanings in the Bible:

1. Samuel's regular tour of inspection of various communities (1 Sam. 7:16).

2. The construction of the city of Jerusalem "from the MILLO [a fortress or bastion built to resist siege] to the surrounding area" (1 Chr. 11:8, RSV).

3. The countryside around Jerusalem (Neh. 12:28, RSV).

4. The sun's "orbit"—that is, the apparent daily revolution of the sun around the earth (Ps. 19:6).

5. The periodical changes of the winds (Eccl. 1:6).

6. Jesus' teaching journeys around the villages of Galilee (Mark 6:6).

CIRCUMCISION — the surgical removal of the foreskin of the male sex organ. This action served as a sign of God's COVENANT relation with His people.

Circumcision was widely practiced in the ancient world, including the Egyptian and Canaanite cultures. But among these people the rite was performed at the beginning of puberty, or about 12 years of age, as a sort of initiation ceremony into manhood. In contrast, the Hebrew people performed circumcision on infants. This rite had an important ethical meaning to them. It signified their responsibility to serve as the holy people whom God had called as His special servants in the midst of a pagan world.

In the Bible's first mention of circumcision, God instructed Abraham to circumcise every male child in his household, including servants, "in the flesh of your foreskins" (Gen. 17:11). The custom was performed on the eighth day after birth (Gen. 17:12). At this time a name was given to the son (Luke 1:59; 2:21). In the early history of the Jewish people circumcision was performed by the father. But the surgical task was eventually taken over by a specialist.

Circumcision of the Jewish male was required as a visible, physical sign of the covenant between the Lord and His people. Any male not circumcised was to be "cut off from his people" (Gen. 17:14) and regarded as a covenant–breaker (Ex. 22:48).

Although circumcision was required by the Mosaic law, the rite was neglected during the days when the people of Israel wandered in the wilderness. Perhaps this was a sign that the nation had broken their covenant with God through their disobedience. The rite was resumed when they entered the land of Canaan, with Joshua performing the ritual on the generation born in the wilderness.

The Hebrew people came to take great pride in circumcision; in fact, it became a badge of their spiritual and national superiority. This practice fostered a spirit of exclusivism instead of a missionary zeal to reach out to other nations as God intended. A daily prayer of strict Jewish males was to thank God that he was neither a woman, a Samaritan, nor a Gentile.

Photo by Willem A. VanGemeren

A sheepherder draws water for his flock from a cistern in the Negev, the southern desert region of Palestine.

Gentiles came to be regarded by the Jews as the "uncircumcision," a term of disrespect implying that non-Jewish peoples were outside the circle of God's love. The terms circumcised and uncircumcised became emotionally charged symbols to Israel and their Gentile neighbors. This issue later brought discord into the fellowship of the New Testament church.

Moses and the prophets used the term circumcised as a symbol for purity of heart and readiness to hear and obey. Through Moses the Lord challenged the Israelites to submit to "circumcision of the heart," a reference to their need for repentance. "If their uncircumcised hearts are humbled, and they accept their guilt," God declared, "then I will remember My covenant" (Lev. 26:41–42; also Deut. 10:16). Jeremiah characterized rebellious Israel as having "uncircumcised" ears (6:10) and being "uncircumcised in the heart" (9:26).

In the New Testament circumcision was faithfully practiced by devout Jews as recognition of God's continuing covenant with Israel. Both John the Baptist (Luke 1:59) and Jesus (Luke 2:21) were circumcised. But controversy over circumcision divided the early church (Eph. 2:11), which included believers from both Jewish and Gentile backgrounds. Gentile believers regarded their Jewish brethren as eccentric because of their dietary laws, Sabbath rules, and circumcision practices. Jewish believers tended to view their uncircumcised Gentile brothers as unenlightened and disobedient to the law of Moses.

A crisis erupted in the church at Antioch when believers from Judea (known as Judaizers) taught the brethren, "Unless you are circumcised according to the custom of Moses, you cannot be saved" (Acts 15:1–2). In effect, the Judaizers insisted that a believer from a non-Jewish background (Gentile) must first become a Jew ceremonially (by being circumcised) before he could be admitted to the Christian brotherhood.

A council of apostles and elders was convened in Jerusalem to resolve the issue (Acts 15:6–29). Among those attending were Paul, Barnabas, Simon Peter, and James, pastor of the Jerusalem church. To insist on circumcision for the Gentiles, Peter argued, would amount to a burdensome yoke (Acts 15:10). This was the decision handed down by the council, and the church broke away from the binding legalism of Judaism.

Years later, reinforcing this decision, the apostle Paul wrote the believers at Rome that Abraham, "the father of circumcision" (Rom. 4:12), was saved by faith rather than by circumcision (Rom. 4:9–12). He declared circumcision to be of no value unless accompanied by an obedient spirit (Rom. 2:25, 26).

Paul also spoke of the "circumcision of Christ" (Col. 2:11), a reference to His atoning death which "condemned sin in the flesh" (Rom. 8:3) and nailed legalism "to the cross" (Col. 2:14). In essence, Paul declared that the new covenant of Christ's shed blood has provided forgiveness to both Jew and Gentile and has made circumcision totally unnecessary. All that ultimately matters for both Jew and Gentile, Paul says, is a changed nature—a new creation that makes them one in Jesus Christ (Eph. 2:14–18).

CIRCUMFERENCE — the distance around a round object. In Solomon's Temple the two bronze pillars named Jachin and Boaz each had a circumference of 12 cubits (1 Kin. 7:15; Jer. 52:21), or about 5.5 meters (18 feet); the BRONZE SEA had a circumference of 30 cubits (1 Kin. 7:23; 2 Chr. 4:2), or about 13.7 meters (45 feet).

CISTERN — an artificial reservoir for storing liquids (especially water); specifically, an underground tank for catching and storing rainwater. For about half the year, rainfall in Palestine is scarce, falling mainly during the winter months. As a result, it was important that water be stored during the rainy months for the long dry season.

Before about 1200 B.C., cisterns were dug out of the soft limestone rock found in many parts of Palestine. Because of the porous nature of limestone, however, these cisterns often broke and became unsatisfactory for holding rainwater. About the time of Israel's conquest of the land of Canaan, a remarkable advance in cisterns allowed the bottom and walls of the cistern to be sealed. This made it possible to build cisterns virtually anywhere and opened up many dry areas to permanent settlement.

A cistern differs from a well in that a well is fed by underground water seepage, while a cistern stores runoff rainwater. In most cities, each house generally had its own cistern. Rain falling on the roof was collected and channeled to the cistern, usually situated beneath the house. Cisterns were of great importance to fortified cities, enabling them to withstand a long military siege by an enemy.

Most references to cisterns in the Bible are symbolic. In writing of the peril of adultery, Proverbs 5:15 says, "Drink water from your own cistern, and running water from your own well." Jeremiah 2:13 describes God as a "fountain of living waters"—a cool, pure, natural spring. But Judah's unfaithfulness amounted to "broken cisterns that can hold no water."

Also see WELL.

CITADEL [sit uh DELL] — the inner or final defensive system of a walled city. Protected by its own wall within the city's outer wall, the citadel was usually built on a hill for even greater protection. Here is where the residents would make their last stand if the enemy should break through the outer defenses. In capital cities like Jerusalem and Samaria, the king's palace was situated within the citadel (2 Kin. 15:25; palace, KJV).

CITIES OF THE PLAIN — a term used for the five cities at the south end of the DEAD SEA (Gen. 14:2, 8). Because of their great wickedness, four of these cities—Sodom, Gomorrah, Admah, and Zeboiim (Gen. 19:28–29)—were completely destroyed. Only Zoar escaped destruction.

Prior to its destruction, this area was well-watered and productive; it was compared to the Garden of Eden and the rich Nile Delta of Egypt (Gen. 13:10). Today this area is totally barren and supports no life—an eloquent testimony of God's judgment upon the sin of these ancient peoples. Genesis 19 describes the complete destruction of

the area; even today earthquakes are common. Since most scholars believe these five cities were on land that now lies under the southern end of the Dead Sea, it is likely that a major earthquake (about 2000 B.C.) caused the area to be flooded.

CITIES OF REFUGE — six Levitical cities set aside to provide shelter and safety for those guilty of manslaughter. Of the 48 cities assigned to the Levites, six were designated as cities of refuge, three on either side of the Jordan River (Num. 35:6–7; Josh. 20:7–8). The three cities of refuge west of the Jordan were KEDESH in Galilee, in the mountains of Naphtali (Josh. 20:7; 21:32); SHECHEM, in the mountains of Ephraim (Josh. 20:7; 21:21; 1 Chr. 6:67); and HEBRON, also known as KIRJATH ARBA, in the mountains of Judah (Josh. 20:7).

The three cities east of the Jordan River were BEZER, in the wilderness on the plateau, or plain, of Moab, and assigned to the tribe of Reuben (Deut. 4:43; Josh. 20:8; 21:36); RAMOTH GILEAD, or Ramoth in Gilead, from the tribe of Gad (Deut. 4:43; Josh. 20:8; 21:38); and GOLAN, in Bashan, from the half–tribe of Manasseh (Deut. 4:43; Josh. 20:8; 21:27).

In the ancient Near East if a person were killed, it was the custom that the nearest relative became the "avenger of blood" (Num. 35:19, 21–27; Deut. 19:12). It became his duty to slay the slayer. However, if a person killed another accidentally or unintentionally, the cities of refuge were provided as an asylum, "that by fleeing to one of these cities he might live" (Deut. 4:42).

The regulations concerning these cities are found in Numbers 35, Deuteronomy 19:1–13, and Joshua 20. If the manslayer reached a city of refuge before the avenger of blood could slay him, he was given a fair trial and provided asylum until the death of the high priest. After that the manslayer was permitted to return home; but if he left the city of refuge before the death of the high priest, he was subject to death at the hands of the avenger of blood.

In the New Testament, the cities of refuge apparently became a type, or symbolic illustration, of the salvation that is found in Christ: "We...have fled for refuge to lay hold of the hope set before us" (Heb. 6:18). In other words, when the sinner flees to Christ Jesus for refuge he is safe from the divine Avenger of Blood. The apostle Paul wrote, "Having now been justified by his [Christ's] blood, we shall be saved from wrath through Him" (Rom. 5:9) and "There is therefore now no condemnation to those who are in Christ Jesus" (Rom. 8:1). Regardless of his sin, the sinner may find asylum and sanctuary in Christ; all who flee to Him find refuge: "The one who comes to Me I will by no means cast out" (John 6:37). The believer is safe forever in the heavenly city of refuge because the great High Priest, Jesus Christ, will never die: "He ever lives to make intercession for him" (Heb. 7:25).

CITIZENSHIP — the status of a native or adopted citizen—with its rights, privileges, and duties—as distinguished from a foreigner.

The word citizenship is found twice in the NKJV. When the Roman commander Claudius Lysias told the apostle Paul, "With a large sum I obtained this [Roman] citizenship," Paul said, "But I was born a [Roman] citizen" (Acts 22:28). And to the church at Philippi Paul wrote that all believers in Christ are citizens of the heavenly commonwealth (Phil. 3:20). Just as the city of Philippi was a colony of Rome, so the church at Philippi was a colony of heaven.

As a Roman citizen, Paul was entitled to the right to trial before punishment (Acts 16:35–39), freedom from interrogation by scourging (Acts 22:24–29), and the right to appeal to Caesar (Acts 24:10–12; 26:32).

CITRON (see PLANTS OF THE BIBLE).

CITY — an inhabited place of greater size, population, or importance than a town or village; a center of population, commerce, and culture. In biblical times the thing that distinguished a city from a town or village was not the size of its population but whether it had walls for defense (Lev. 25:29–31; Ezek. 38:11). But most cities also became known by their size and the magnificence of their buildings.

In ancient Israel a large city was often called a "mother" (2 Sam. 20:19) that was encircled by a cluster of villages—all its surrounding settlements (Num. 21:25, NIV; all its dependent villages, NEB). The original Hebrew word for villages literally means "daughters."

Cities were usually built on hills so they could be defended easily (1 Kin. 16:24; Matt. 5:14) and in areas where a supply of water was available (to help withstand a prolonged siege) and, preferably, where soil was fertile. City walls were often massive structures about 6 to 9 meters (20 to 30 feet) thick. The gates, just as massive, had bars with guardhouses atop the wall. Often the walls had towers (Deut. 1:28; Judg. 9:51; 2 Chr. 26:9).

Palestinian cities were probably relatively small with narrow, crooked, unpaved streets (Eccl. 12:4; Is. 10:6). In fact, many of the streets appear to have been partially blocked off by the projecting corners of houses. Near the gates, the social center of the city, merchants sold their wares and courts were held (Gen. 23:10; Ruth 4:1–11).

Jewish cities were governed by a council of elders composed of judges who were required to be priests (Deut. 16:18). During the period of David and Solomon's rule, cities seem to have had governors (1 Kin. 22:26; 2 Chr. 18:25). When Jerusalem was rebuilt after the Captivity, Ezra appointed magistrates and judges as city officials (Ezra 7:25).

In larger cities with palaces or temples, there was a recognizable street, a "broad way." This street probably was paved with stone. Many of the streets were divided into craftsmen's sections—copper and iron workers in one place and jewelers in another, etc. They were very much like today's eastern bazaars. Some streets had marketplaces reserved for foreign merchants (Jer. 37:21; Ezek. 17:4).

Jericho is the earliest Palestinian town to be discovered thus far. According to carbon 14 tests (a scientific method of establishing dates), archaeologists believe a nine–acre town existed at the site of Jericho as early as 5500 B.C., long before Abraham's time.

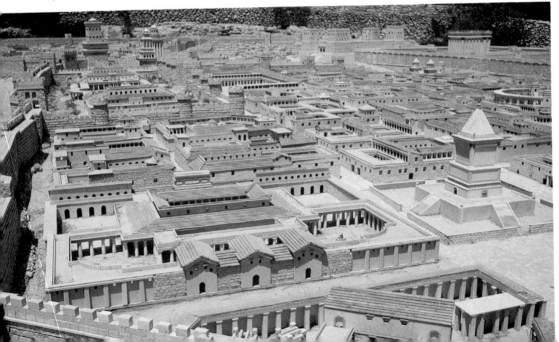

This model of Jerusalem shows how a typical walled city of the ancient world might have looked during the days of Jesus' ministry.

Photo by Ben Chapman

CITY CLERK (see OCCUPATIONS AND TRADES).

CITY OF DAVID — the name of two cities in the Bible:

1. The stronghold of ZION, the fortified city of the Jebusites, later known as Jerusalem. King David and his men captured it (2 Sam. 5:7, 9). The Jebusite fortress of Zion was situated on a hill overlooking the pool of Siloam, at the junction of the Kidron and Tyropoeon valleys (later in southeastern Jerusalem). The account of the capture of Zion implies that David's army entered the fortress by surprise (2 Sam. 5:8). The "water shaft" mentioned in this passage was apparently a tunnel leading from the underground spring of GIHON into the citadel. Joab was the one who went up the shaft first (1 Chr. 11:6); true to his promise, David made him the commander, or "chief," of the armies of Israel.

After the capture of Zion, "David dwelt in the stronghold, and called it the City of David" (2 Sam. 5:9). Not only did David establish his residence here, but he also strengthened the city's fortifications (1 Chr. 11:8). Solomon further strengthened the defenses of the city (1 Kin. 11:27). The site of Solomon's Temple was on the neighboring Mount Moriah, part of the same strong rock outcropping as Mount Zion.

2. Bethlehem, the birthplace or home of David (Luke 2:4, 11; John 7:42).

CITY, HOLY — another name for JERUSALEM, the religious center of the Jewish people (Neh. 11:1; Dan. 9:24).

CITY OF SALT — a city in the Wilderness of Judah (Josh. 15:62). It is mentioned with EN GEDI and probably was not far from that city. Some scholars identify the City of Salt with Khirbet Qumran, about 21 kilometers (13 miles) north of En Gedi and about 16 kilometers (10 miles) south of Jericho. Other scholars, however, place the City of Salt much farther south, near the southern or southwestern end of the Dead Sea, in the VALLEY OF SALT.

CITY OF WATERS — a phrase which refers to the lower part of the Ammonite city of RABBAH, as distinguished from the upper city, or CITADEL (2 Sam. 12:27, KJV, RSV).

CLAUDA [KLO duh] — a small island about 80 kilometers (50 miles) off the southwest coast of Crete (Acts 27:16; Cauda, NIV, RSV). When the apostle Paul was on his voyage to Rome, the ship on which he was traveling sought protection under its shelter when caught in a storm.

CLAUDIA [KLOW dih uh] (*lame*) — a Roman Christian who joined Paul in sending Timothy Christian greetings (2 Tim. 4:21). Some scholars suggest that Claudia was the wife of the Pudens mentioned in the same verse and that Linus, who would become a bishop of Rome, was their son.

CLAUDIUS [KLOW dih us] — the fourth emperor of the Roman Empire (A.D. 41–54), Tiberius Clau-

Bust of Claudius, Roman emperor who expelled all the Jewish people from the city of Rome (Acts 18:2).

dius Nero Germanicus, who suppressed the worship activities of the Jewish people in the city of Rome.

Early in his reign as emperor, Claudius was favorable toward the Jews and their practice of religion. But he later forbade their assembly and eventually "commanded all the Jews to depart from Rome" (Acts 18:2). This edict may have extended also to Christians, who were considered a sect of the Jews at that time.

Aquila and Priscilla, who became friends of the apostle Paul, were refugees from Italy because of this order of the Roman emperor (Acts 18:1–2). The Book of Acts also refers to a great famine which "happened in the days of Claudius Caesar" (Acts 11:28). Also see CAESAR.

CLAUDIUS LYSIAS [KLOW dih us LISS ih us] (see LYSIAS).

CLAW — the sharp, curved nail on the toe of a bird or animal. The word is found only once in the NKJV—A reference to Nebuchadnezzar, whose "nails [had grown] like birds' claws" (Dan. 4:33).

CLAY (see MINERALS OF THE BIBLE).

CLAY TABLETS — one of the world's oldest known writing materials, perhaps originating in Mesopotamia. Made of clean, smooth clay, the tablets were imprinted with CUNEIFORM signs or symbols (by means of a stylus) while still wet, then allowed to dry slowly. When baked in an oven, they hardened into a strong, durable material. Such tablets were used by the Sumerians, Akkadians, Elamites, Hittites, Hurrians, and Canaanites of Ugarit. These writing materials are a major source of our knowledge about these civilizations.

CLEAN, CLEANNESS — pure, clear, uncontaminated. The distinctions between clean and unclean foods, animals, and people is elaborated in Leviticus 11—15. "Clean" refers to physical health, especially in the case of the diseased, notably lepers (Lev. 13:1–14, 57; 2 Kin. 5; Matt. 8:2–3). Clean hands (Ps. 24:4) and a clean heart (Ps. 51:10) refer to moral purity. When Jesus admonished the religious rulers to cleanse the inside of the cup and dish, He stressed the priority of the inward condition of a person (Matt. 23:25–26; Is. 1:16; 2 Cor. 7:1).

The prophets spoke of an inner cleansing from sin (Jer. 33:8; Ezek. 36:33; 37:23). Jesus pronounced the disciples clean (John 13:10) "because of the word" (John 15:3). Cleansing from sin is possible through the blood of Jesus for all who confess their sins (1 John 1:7–9).

Also see UNCLEAN, UNCLEANNESS.

CLEFT — an opening or space made by a division, as a crack in a building (Amos 6:11, KJV), a hollow place in a rock (Ex. 33:22), or the split in the hoof of an animal (Deut. 14:6, KJV).

CLEMENT [KLEM ent] (*merciful*) — a Christian who worked with the apostle Paul, apparently at Philippi (Phil. 4:3). Writers such as Origen, Eusebius, and Jerome supposed this Clement to be the apostolic father known as Clement of Rome. Modern scholars, however, believe this identification is highly unlikely.

CLEOPAS [KLEE uh pus] (*renowned father*) — one of the two disciples with whom Jesus talked on the Emmaus Road on the day of His resurrection (Luke 24:18). Cleopas is apparently not the same person as Cleophas—or Clopas (RSV)—of John 19:25.

CLEOPHAS [KLEE uh fus] — a form of CLOPAS.

CLERK, CITY (see OCCUPATIONS AND TRADES).

CLOAK (see DRESS OF THE BIBLE).

CLOPAS [KLOE puhs] (meaning unknown) — the husband of Mary, one of the women who was present at the crucifixion of Jesus (John 19:25; Cleophas, KJV). According to tradition, Clopas was the same person as Alphaeus, the father of James the Less and of Joses (Matt. 10:3; Mark 15:40). Most scholars agree that Clopas is not the same person as CLEOPAS (Luke 24:18).

CLOSET — KJV word for a bridal chamber (Joel 2:16; dressing room, NKJV). The word also refers to the most private rooms in a home (Matt. 6:6; secret place, NKJV; Luke 12:3, inner rooms, NKJV). Also see HOUSE.

CLOTH — a fabric or material from which clothing is made. In biblical times cloth was made from the hair of goats, sheep, and camels and from linen, flax, hemp, and silk. Certain goats grew long black hair that produced a heavy waterproof cloth for making tents and outer garments.

The everyday clothing of the poor consisted of sheepskins and goatskins (Heb. 11:37). Cloaks of such material served as blankets (Ex. 22:26–27), saddle pads, and sleeping mats or pads. Perhaps it was such a garment that Paul asked Timothy to bring to him (2 Tim. 4:13). Goat–hair and camel–hair garments, being dark in color, were worn especially during a time of mourning and were called sackcloth (Gen. 37:34; 2 Sam. 3:31).

Perhaps the oldest and most common cloth of biblical times was made from wool—with the best wool coming from lambs. Judea was the wool-producing center of ancient Palestine, while Galilee was known for flax and linen. Wool was often prepared by a process of bleaching, rubbing, and dyeing and then spun into thread by means of a spindle. The rule against priests wearing wool suggests that woolen tunics (undergarments) were the garb of the common people (Ezek. 44:17).

Although cotton was known at an early time in China and India, most scholars question its use in ancient Palestine. They conclude that what is translated cotton in some Old Testament translations was really cloth made of flax or hemp.

Also see DRESS.

CLOTHES, CLOTHING (see DRESS OF THE BIBLE).

CLOUD — a visible mass of fine droplets of water or particles of ice suspended above the earth's surface. In the Bible, clouds are symbolic of many things.

The skies over Palestine are virtually cloudless from the beginning of May until the end of September. Thus, Samuel's calling forth the harvest rain (1 Sam. 12:17–18) was considered miraculous. The "cloud, as small as a man's hand, rising out of the sea" (1 Kin. 18:44) that Elijah saw when he prayed for rain probably came sometime during this five-month cloudless period.

The cloud was symbolic of God's presence. The pillar of cloud leading the Israelites in the wilderness (Ex. 13:21–22) was the same as God's presence leading the people. When God wanted to reveal Himself to the Israelites, He used a pillar of cloud to do so (Num. 12:5; Deut. 31:15). Clouds also revealed God's power and wisdom (Ps. 147:8; Prov. 8:28).

A "day of clouds" referred to a time marked by disaster and God's judgment (Ezek. 30:3; Joel 2:2). Clouds are symbolic of armies and multitudes of people (Jer. 4:13; Heb. 12:1). "Clouds without water" (Jude 12) are people who do not perform up to their capabilities. Jude probably had in mind Proverbs 25:14: "Whoever falsely boasts of giving is like clouds and wind without rain."

CLOUD, PILLAR OF — a miraculous cloud, representing the presence of God, that led the Israelites during their journey in the wilderness following their escape from slavery in Egypt (Ex. 13:21). At the Red Sea the pillar of cloud came between the camp of the Egyptians and the camp of Israel (Ex. 14:20). When the tabernacle was completed in the

Photo by Willem A. VanGemeren

Rain clouds in Upper Galilee, a mountainous region subject to sudden winds and severe storms.

wilderness, the cloud filled the building to show God's presence with His people (Ex. 40:34). Thereafter the cloud led Israel day and night on the journey toward the land of Canaan (Num. 9:22). Also see PILLAR OF FIRE AND CLOUD.

CLOUT — an obscure KJV word for a patch of cloth, leather, or other material hastily applied to mend a tear. Other translations are patched (Josh. 9:5) and rags (Jer. 38:11–12).

CLUB (see ARMS, ARMOR OF THE BIBLE).

CNIDUS [NYE dus] (*age*) — a city of the province of CARIA (see Map 8, C–2); it was situated on the extreme southwestern tip of ASIA MINOR and was between the islands of Cos and Rhodes in the Aegean Sea. On his journey to Rome, the apostle Paul passed the harbor at Cnidus after leaving Myra (Acts 27:7).

COAL (see MINERALS OF THE BIBLE).

COAST — an inaccurate KJV word for border or boundary. Occasionally, it refers to the seacoast (Num. 34:6; Judg. 5:17).

COAT (see DRESS OF THE BIBLE).

COAT OF MAIL (see ARMS, ARMOR OF the BIBLE).

COBRA, COCK, COCKATRICE (see ANIMALS OF THE BIBLE).

COCKCROWING — a period of time between midnight and three o'clock in the morning; the third watch of the night. This reflects the Roman custom of dividing the night into four watches: late, midnight, cockcrowing, and early. (The Jewish practice divided the night into three watches.) In His parable of a man going to a far country, Jesus said, "Watch therefore, for you do not know when the master of the house is coming—in the evening, at midnight, at the crowing of the rooster, or in the morning" (Mark 13:35). In this parable, the "crowing of the rooster" refers to the third watch of the night.

All other New Testament references, however, describe an actual rooster that crowed (Matt. 26:34; Mark 14:30; Luke 22:34; John 13:38). The crowing of a rooster reminded Peter how easy it is to deny the Savior.

COCKLE — KJV word for foul–smelling weeds (Job 31:40; stinkweed, NASB). The word may refer to any of several different species of such weeds in the land of Palestine. Also see PLANTS OF THE BIBLE.

CODEX [COE dex] — the forerunner of the modern book. A codex was formed by folding several sheets of papyrus in the middle and sewing them together along the fold. More convenient for reading than the SCROLL, the codex could also be written on both sides. Also see WRITING.

COFFER — KJV word for the CHEST in which the Philistines placed their guilt offering to the God of Israel (1 Sam. 6:8, 11, 15).

COFFIN — a stand on which a corpse, or a BIER containing a corpse, is placed before burial. The Hebrew word for coffin (or bier, KJV) is usually translated bed; it means coffin only when the context refers to a burial (2 Sam. 3:31; 2 Chr. 16:14).

COHORT (see REGIMENT).

COINS (see MONEY OF THE BIBLE).

COL–HOZEH [kole HOE zeh] (*wholly a seer*) — the name of two men in the Old Testament:

1. The father of Shallum, the man who repaired the Fountain Gate of Jerusalem after the Captivity (Neh. 3:15).

2. The father of Baruch of the tribe of Judah (Neh. 11:5). This is possibly the same person as Col–Hozeh No. 1.

COLLECTION — money gathered for two distinctive purposes:

1. In the Old Testament, the word collection refers to a nonvoluntary religious tax collected from the people by the Levites (2 Chr. 24:6, 9). The Mosaic law also referred to this tax as "ransom" (Ex. 30:12) and "atonement money" (Ex. 30:16).

2. In the New Testament, collection refers to a voluntary contribution gathered from the churches of Gentile territories for distribution to needy Christians in Jerusalem. In his letters to the churches at Corinth and Rome, the apostle Paul explained the need for this collection and encouraged the Gentile Christians to give liberally for this worthy cause (Rom. 15:25-27; 1 Cor. 16:1-4; 2 Cor. 8:1-15).

Paul also gave some helpful guidelines for Christian giving in his remarks. Giving should be on the first day of the week (Sunday) and according to a person's ability to give. Paul also taught that giving should be generous, voluntary, and in response to the grace of God and His "indescribable gift" (2 Cor. 9:15. These guidelines are still appropriate for all Christians.

COLLEGE (*second part*) — an inaccurate translation of the word *mishneh* (2 Kin. 22:14, KJV; 2 Chr. 34:22, KJV; Zeph. 1:10). The word refers to a district of JERUSALEM and actually means "Second Quarter" (NKJV).

COLONY — a group of emigrants or their descendants who settle in a distant land but remain subject to the parent country. In the New Testament the word occurs only once, in a reference to the city of Philippi (Acts 16:12). Here it has the specific meaning of a military settlement, or garrison city, of retired Roman legionaires and other Roman citizens who were stationed in an area to maintain control over a conquered people. PHILIPPI became a Roman colony in 30 B.C, with the legal rights of Roman citizens and freedom from control by the provincial governor.

COLORS OF THE BIBLE — Color as an abstract idea or concept is spoken of rarely in the Bible. The most common word translated as color actually means "eye," "appearance," or "aspect" (Lev. 13:55). It expresses color in terms of comparison with some other material. The word describing gems as "colorful" (Is. 54:11) means "antimony" or "stibium" and probably refers to the dark background that was generally used to set off precious stones. A few objects in the Bible are described as variegated or multicolored (Prov. 7:16; Ezek. 27:24).

This general lack of color terminology in the Bible may be a result of God's commandment to the Hebrews not to make any graven images or idols (Ex. 20:4). The Hebrews were never known as an artistic or art–loving people. Perhaps their background as an enslaved people also contributed to their lack of artistic and color appreciation.

Rather than specific coloration, a color's brightness or dimness, lightness or darkness, brilliance or somberness is more often emphasized in the Bible. Shade, rather than hue, seems to be considered more important by the biblical writers.

Natural Colors. Individual colors mentioned in the Bible fall into two major types—natural colors and artificial colors.

The Greeks painted their temples with bright colors, as demonstrated by this reconstruction of a section of the Parthenon in Athens.

Photo by Howard Vos

Blue—Blueness (Prov. 20:30, KJV) may describe the color of a wound, but usually the word refers to the wound itself.

Brown—Brown is a dark, blackish color applied only to sheep (Gen. 30:32-33, 35, 40).

Black—Black is one of the more commonly used colors in Scripture. Black describes the color of the middle of the night (Prov. 7:9); diseased skin (Job 30:30); healthy hair (Song 5:11, Matt. 5:36); the blackness of corpses' faces (Lam. 4:8); the sky (Jer. 4:28); the darkening of the sun and the moon (Joel 2:10); horses (Zech. 6:2, 6; Rev. 6:5); and marble (Esth. 1:6).

Gray—Gray is used only to describe the hair of the elderly (Gen. 42:38).

Green—The words for green normally describe vegetation of some type. It is used of pastures (Ps. 23:2); herbage (2 Kin. 19:26); trees in general (Deut. 12:2; Luke 23:31; Rev. 8:7); the marriage bed (in a figurative sense, Song 1:16); a hypocrite compared to a papyrus plant (Job 8:16); and grass (Mark 6:39). A word meaning "greenish" describes plague spots (Lev. 13:49; 14:37) as well as the color of gold.

Red—Several words for red describe natural objects such as Jacob's stew (Gen. 25:30); the sacrificial heifer (Num. 19:2); wine (Prov. 23:31); newborn Esau (Gen. 25:25); Judah's eyes (Gen. 49:12, KJV); the eyes of the drunkard (Prov. 23:29); and the dragon (Rev. 12:3).

White—The words translated as white describe the color of animals (Gen. 30:35); manna (Ex. 16:31); both hair and pustules located in plague sores (Lev. 13:3-39); garments (Eccl. 9:8; Dan. 7:9); the robes of the righteous (Rev. 19:8, KJV); horses (Zech. 1:8; Rev. 6:2; 19:11); forgiven sins (Ps. 51:7; Is. 1:18); a refined remnant (Dan. 11:35; 12:10); the beloved one (Song 5:10); the white of an egg (Job 6:6); the shining garments of angels (Rev. 15:6, KJV) and of the transfigured Christ (Matt. 17:2); hair (Matt. 5:36); gravestones (Matt. 23:27); and the great throne of judgment (Rev. 20:11).

Yellow—A word translated as yellow indicates the greenish cast of gold (Ps. 68:13). Another word for yellow describes the light-colored hair in a leprous spot (Lev. 13:30, 32).

In addition to black, red, and white horses, certain words suggesting color are used exclusively of horses. The term sorrel (Zech. 1:8; speckled, KJV; dappled, NEB) may refer more specifically to a pattern of reddish color mixed with white. Dappled (Zech. 6:3; grisled, KJV) probably speaks of a spotted pattern rather than color. The "pale" horse (Rev. 6:8; ashen, NASB) refers to the color of a corpse.

Artificial Colors. Artificial colors, such as paints and dyes, were used widely in the ancient world. In Babylonia, bricks were made in several different colors, some resulting from different kinds of clay, others from special manufacturing processes. Egyptians made dyes from numerous substances. The Israelites had an advanced textile industry.

They were skilled not only in weaving but also in dyeing.

Since dyes were made from vegetable sources or from shellfish, quality control was difficult. The completed colors were often impure and inexact. These problems were compounded by the fact that many dyes were closely guarded family recipes which were sometimes lost or changed.

The following dyes or artificial colors are mentioned in the Bible.

Purple—The most precious of ancient dyes was purple. In Ugarit, a city of the Canaanites, wool was often dyed this color. Phoenicia derived its name from the source of the dye. The word "Canaan" means "land of the purple." The dye itself was derived from a shellfish found in the Mediterranean Sea. A total of 250,000 mollusks was required to make one ounce of the dye, which partly accounts for its great price. It was highly valued within the nation of Israel.

The Lord prescribed the use of purple in several features of the tabernacle, such as the curtains (Ex. 26:1) and the hangings (Ex. 27:16). It was also an essential part of the Temple (2 Chr. 2:14).

Purple was the color of royal robes (Judg. 8:26), as well as the garments of the wealthy (Prov. 31:22; Luke 16:19), the vesture of the harlot (Rev. 17:4), and the robe placed upon Jesus (Mark 15:17, 20). Robes dyed purple were prescribed for the battle regalia of the Qumran priests, and purple was highly sought during the Maccabean period. In New Testament times, it was an important item of trade (Acts 16:14; Rev. 18:12).

Blue—During biblical times blue was another major dye, also derived from another species of shellfish. Fabric dyed this color was used as a part of the pattern for the tabernacle tapestries (Ex. 26:1) and for the hangings in the Temple (2 Chr. 2:7). The color was also used for royal trappings (Esth. 1:6; 8:15) and clothing for the rich (Jer. 10:9; Ezek. 23:6, KJV).

Red—Red existed in several shades, and the dye was extracted from the bodies of insects. One of the red colors was crimson. Linen of this color was used in the Temple trappings (2 Chr. 2:7, 14; 3:14). This artificial color must have been practically indelible or permanent (Jer. 4:30), since crimson is used figuratively of sin (Is. 1:18).

Another shade of red is called scarlet. It was the color of the cord tied around the wrist of Zerah (Gen. 38:28-30). Scarlet was used a great deal in the tabernacle (Ex. 25:4). It was the color of the cord extended from Rahab's window (Josh. 2:18). It was also a mark of prosperity (2 Sam. 1:24; Prov. 31:21). Scarlet also describes the robe placed upon Jesus (Matt. 27:28). Since the robe was also described as purple (Mark 15:17), these two colors were not always distinguished during New Testament times. The beast ridden by the harlot was scarlet in color (Rev. 17:3) as were some of the garments of the harlot herself (Rev. 17:4) and her followers (Rev. 18:16).

The mound of ancient Colosse, a city in Asia Minor where a church was established during the days of the apostle Paul.

Still another shade of red is called vermilion, used in decorating homes of the wealthy (Jer. 22:14) and in the painting of idols (Ezek. 23:14).

Certain colors have symbolic significance in the Scriptures. White portrays purity, righteousness, and joy, and a white horse symbolizes victory. Black is a picture of famine and death. Red, the color of blood, often symbolizes life; it is also a picture of the carnage of war. The color blue sometimes describes the sky, just as purple is a symbol of royalty.

COLOSSAE [kah luh SEE] — a form of COLOSSE.

COLOSSE [kah luh SEE] — a city in the Roman province of ASIA (western Turkey), situated in the Lycus River Valley about 160 kilometers (100 miles) east of Ephesus. The apostle Paul wrote a letter to the church at Colosse (Col. 1:2; Colossae, NASB, NEB, RSV). The Christian community at Colosse apparently grew up under the leadership of Epaphras (Col. 1:7; 4:12) and Archippus (Col. 4:17; Philem. 2). Philemon and Onesimus lived at Colosse (Col. 4:9).

Colosse formed a triangle with two other cities of the Lycus Valley, Hierapolis and Laodicea, both of which are mentioned in the New Testament. As early as the fifth century B.C., Colosse was known as a prosperous city; but by the beginning of the Christian era it was eclipsed by its two neighbors. Thereafter its reputation declined to a small town.

Shortly after the apostle Paul sent his epistle to Colosse, the cities of the Lycus Valley suffered a devastating earthquake in A.D. 61. They were soon rebuilt, even Laodicea, which had suffered the greatest damage. Although Colosse was increasingly overshadowed by Laodicea and Hierapolis, it retained considerable importance into the second and third centuries A.D. Later, the population of Colosse moved to Chonai (modern Honaz), three

miles to the south. The mound which marks the site of Colosse remains uninhabited today.

COLOSSIANS, EPISTLE TO THE — one of four shorter epistles written by Paul while he was in prison, the others being Philippians, Ephesians, and Philemon. The Epistle to the Colossians focuses on the person and work of Jesus Christ. It reaches heights of expression that rival anything said of Christ elsewhere in Scripture. Colossians shares many similarities in style and content with Ephesians. Colossians probably was written as a companion to the brief letter to Philemon (compare Col. 4:7-13 and Philem. 12, 24).

Structure of the Epistle. Colossians is neatly divided, as are most of Paul's epistles, into doctrinal (chaps. 1—2) and practical (chaps. 3—4) sections. Following the opening address (1:1-2), Paul expresses his thankfulness for the faith, love, hope, and example of the Colossians (1:3-8). He then develops a majestic hymn to Christ, emphasizing His role in both creation and redemption (1:9-23). In light of the surpassing worth of Christ and His work, Paul willingly accepts the obligation to proclaim Christ and to suffer for Him (1:24—2:5). He also appeals to the Colossians to take root in Christ rather than in confusing speculations (2:6-23).

In the second section, Paul urges the Colossian Christians to mold their behavior to fit their beliefs. Since believers share in Christ's resurrection (3:1-4), Paul encourages them to continue living to please God. He urges them to "put to death" various vices and to "put on" the character of Christ (3:5-17). True Christianity also works itself out in social relationships between wives and husbands (3:18-19), children and parents (3:20-21), and slaves and masters (3:22-4:1). Paul concludes with a note on witnessing to unbelievers (4:2-6) and his customary greetings (3:7-18).

Authorship and Date. Colossians was written by Paul (and Timothy, 1:1) to a Christian community (perhaps "house churches," 1:2; 4:15) which he had not visited (2:1). Paul had established a resident ministry in Ephesus, 100 miles west of Colossae. For more than two years the influence of his ministry reached "all who dwelt in Asia" (Acts 19:10). Epaphras must have heard Paul in Ephesus and then carried the gospel to Colosse (1:7-8; 4:12-13).

Paul wrote the epistle from prison (4:3, 10, 18), but he did not indicate where he was imprisoned. Caesarea and Ephesus have been suggested, but the most probable place is Rome (Acts 28:30). This would date the epistle in the late 50s or early 60s.

Historical Setting. False teaching had taken root in Colosse. This teaching combined Jewish observances (2:16) and pagan speculation (2:8); it is possible that this resulted in an early form of GNOSTICISM. This teaching pretended to add to or improve upon the gospel that, indirectly at least, had come from Paul. Some of the additions Paul mentions are feasts and observances, some of them related to ASTROLOGY (2:16), plus a list of rules (2:20). These practices were then included within a philosophy in which angels played a leading role (2:18); Paul calls this philosophy "the basic principles of the world" (2:8).

Theological Contribution. Paul unmasks the false teaching as "empty deceit...of men" (2:8), having the "appearance of wisdom" (2:23), but useless in fact. He declared that the addition of such things dilutes rather than strengthens the faith (2:20).

But Paul does more than denounce false teaching. The best medicine is a firm grip on who Jesus Christ is and what He did for our salvation. In Christ "are hidden all the treasures of wisdom and knowledge" (2:3), and "in Him all fullness" dwells (1:19). In fact, "He is the image of the invisible

COLOSSIANS: A Teaching Outline

God" (1:15). He has stripped every power opposed to Him (2:15), wiped out every accusation against us (2:14), and actually "reconciled all things to Himself" (1:20). He is not only head of the church (1:18); but He stands before all time and above every power, and at the end of all history (1:16).

This beautiful epistle on the majesty of Jesus Christ speaks to us today as much as to the Colossians. It reminds us that Jesus Christ is sufficient for every need and is still the most powerful force in the world.

COLT (see ANIMALS OF THE BIBLE).

COMFORTER (see HOLY SPIRIT).

COMMANDMENT — a law, edict, or statute; specifically, one of the Ten Commandments given by God through Moses (Ex. 20:3–17; Deut. 5:7–21). Also see COMMANDMENT, NEW; COMMANDMENTS, TEN.

COMMANDMENT, NEW — a commandment given by Jesus to His disciples, which is the commandment of Christian love—"that you love one another" (John 13:34).

COMMANDMENTS, TEN — the ten laws given by God as guidelines for daily living. They are part of a covenant between God and His people (Ex. 34:28; Deut. 4:13; 10:4). These laws are often called the *Decalogue*, from the Greek word which means "ten words."

Although God gave the Ten Commandments to His people through Moses at Mount Sinai more than 3,000 years ago, they are still relevant today. They have an abiding significance, for God's character is unchangeable. These laws originate from God and from His eternal character; therefore, their moral value cannot change.

About 1,300 years after God gave the laws, Jesus upheld them, calling them the "commandments" and listing five of them for the rich young ruler (Matt. 19:16–22). And in the Sermon on the Mount, Jesus showed that His coming had not canceled the Commandments. He specifically mentioned the laws against killing (Matt. 5:21) and committing adultery (Matt. 5:27).

Jesus actually placed these laws on a higher plane by demanding that the spirit as well as the legal aspects of the law be kept. Jesus placed His eternal stamp of approval on the law by declaring, "Do not think that I came to destroy the Law or the Prophets. I did not come to destroy but to fulfill" (Matt. 5:17–19).

The holy God uttered His Commandments from the top of Mount Sinai amid smoke and fire—visible expressions of His power, majesty, and authority (Ex. 19:16—20:17). Later the Commandments were engraved on two tablets of stone, "written with the finger of God" (Ex. 31:18). The awesome nature of the events surrounding the giving of the law is mentioned a number of times in the Bible, perhaps to emphasize the solemnity of the occasion (Ex. 19:16–19; Deut. 4:11–12).

The Ten Commandments form the heart of the special COVENANT between God and His people. He told them, "Now therefore, if you will indeed obey My voice and keep My covenant, then you shall be a special treasure to Me above all people. . . . And you shall be to Me a kingdom of priests and a holy nation" (Ex. 19:5). These verses also emphasize that their obedience to the Commandments was to be the basis of Israel's existence as the special people of God.

God never intended for the Ten Commandments to be a set of regulations by which the people of Israel would earn salvation. God's favor had already been freely granted! This was overwhelmingly demonstrated by His deliverance of Israel from Egyptian bondage (Deut. 4:37). Therefore, at the heart of the covenant relationship lay an act of divine GRACE. God even prefaced the Ten Commandments with a reminder of His deliverance (Ex. 20:2).

The Ten Commandments are still relevant today. The world desperately needs to see the name and character of God displayed in the lives of Christians who still take His Word seriously. These Commandments, particularly coupled with the teachings of Christ, are still the best guidelines for practical daily living known to man.

1. "You shall have no other gods before Me" (Ex. 20:3). Since God's character forms the basis of the covenant with His people, He demands absolute loyalty. And when the intent of the heart is to put God first, a person's outward actions will reveal it. Then others will see what God's character is like through the actions of His people.

2. "You shall not make for yourself a carved image" (Ex. 20:4). The second commandment is necessary because people do not always keep the first. The Israelites made a golden calf to worship even as the Lord gave the laws to Moses. And since Israel had so many contacts with people who did worship images, including replicas of their earthly rulers, God gave them this law. God has never been a tangible, visible Being (Deut. 4:12), but always a Spirit (John 4:24).

3. "You shall not take the name of the Lord your God in vain" (Ex. 20:7). God's name and His character are inseparable. Using His holy name lightly in a vain, empty manner is insulting and degrading. This could be done by perjuring oneself in a court of law or by cursing. However, this commandment also applies to hypocritical worship, using God's name in meaningless prayer and praise (Is. 29:13).

4. "Remember the Sabbath day, to keep it holy" (Ex. 20:8). Sabbath means "rest," but God intended for this day to stand for more than an absence of work. It was to be a day of worship as well—a day for setting aside all thoughts of materialistic gain and thinking about Him. God Himself set the pattern by ceasing from His labors after creating the world. Why, then, must modern-day Christians feel that being busy is equated with being spiritual?

5. "Honor your father and your mother, that your days may be long upon the land" (Ex. 20:12).

God established parents as the authority figures in the family unit. Children often get their first impressions about God from their parents. Parents who walk in the Spirit, honestly desiring to follow the guidelines of the Scriptures, will set better examples for their children. And children who want to please God will respect their parents, regardless of pressure from the world and their peers.

6. "You shall not murder" (Ex. 20:13). Commandments six through nine pertain to our relationships with one another. The breakdown of these guidelines has plunged many civilizations into decay. A person who cares about others, beginning with those in the home, does not want to harm them. This law reveals God's attitude toward people created in His image. No one has the right to take that life from another.

7. "You shall not commit adultery" (Ex. 20:14). Technically, this commandment refers to being sexually involved with a married person; but it is traditionally used to prohibit all sexual relationships outside of marriage. Again, this commandment involves a right relationship with God and with others. Adultery is possible only if people are prepared to hurt others, to enjoy themselves at the expense of other people. A right attitude toward keeping God first and not harming others is tied together in these commandments. A person who does not steal will not take another's mate. And he does not allow covetous thoughts to grow in his mind. He wants God to have his total allegiance.

8. "You shall not steal" (Ex. 20:15). Stealing involves taking something that does not belong to you. This could be another's life, marriage partner, or reputation. This law also emphasizes the importance of getting all you own through lawful channels.

9. "You shall not bear false witness against your neighbor" (Ex. 20:16). A good relationship demands honesty in speaking of another. The old saying, "A man's word is as good as his name" is sometimes a joke today. But God's people ought to cherish their own reputations and that of others. If a person is unwilling to speak ill of another, he is less likely to steal from him or to commit murder.

10. "You shall not covet" (Ex. 20:17). Jesus elaborated on this commandment by stating, "You shall love your neighbor as yourself" (Matt. 22:39). The negative and the positive work together. You do not harm people you care about.

This tenth commandment is an outgrowth of the first. If a person's heart is fixed on the Lord, he will have the right attitude toward others. Consequently, the desires that rise from his heart will not cause pain or loss to others. The right motive (pleasing God who is first in your life) will result in obeying the other commandments (not hurting others).

Jesus enlarged on the idea prevalent in the Ten Commandments by emphasizing the heart attitude: "Blessed are the pure in heart, for they shall see God" (Matt. 5:8). The Christian has blessed joy on earth when his priorities are straight.

COMMERCE — the buying, selling, and trading of goods, especially on a large scale (as between nations) involving transportation from place to place.

The harbor of Sidon, center of the commercial shipping activities of the Phoenicians during Old Testament times.

Photo by Howard Vos

Trade began well before recorded history in the ancient world. By the time of Abraham (about 2000 B.C.), trade was highly developed in such places as ancient Babylon and other cultures between the Tigris and Euphrates Rivers. Palestine contained important trade routes that connected Mesopotamia and Egypt; armies also made these trips as Egyptian and Mesopotamian rulers fought one another. Israel did not have many suitable harbors; so most of the sea trade went by way of the more northern parts like Tyre and Ugarit.

Israel did, however, export agricultural products such as wheat and olive oil (1 Kin. 5:11). Solomon was the most successful Israelite king in developing international trade relations with other nations (1 Kin. 5:10; 9:26–28), although later Ahab and Jehoshaphat also were apparently involved in trade (1 Kin. 20:34; 22:48). Ezekiel 27 (Tyre) and Revelation 18 ("Babylon") give the most complete picture of commerce to be found in the Bible.

Also see SOLOMON.

COMMON-LANDS — the open lands outside the wall of a city (Lev. 25:34; Num. 35:2–7; Josh. 21:2–42; 1 Chr. 6:55–81; pasturelands, NIV; suburbs, KJV). The Hebrew word means the place or area to which the city livestock could be driven.

COMMON LIFE — the mutual relationship among Christians that issues from their participation in Christ's body, the church. The words translated as "common," "communion," and "fellowship" express the idea of sharing. All Christians share together in the one living "body of Christ" (1 Cor. 12:27; Eph. 4:12) because they are joined to Jesus, their living Head. Also see COMMUNITY OF GOODS.

COMMUNION (see FELLOWSHIP; LORD'S SUPPER).

COMMUNITY OF GOODS — the voluntary practice through which some Christians of the New Testament made their possessions available to all believers (Acts 2:44–47; 4:32—5:11).

The Book of Acts reported that "all who were possessors of lands or houses sold them," giving the proceeds to the apostles for distribution (Acts 4:34–35). This does not necessarily mean that every Christian sold every piece of real estate he owned. The reference seems to be to houses and lands other than their family dwellings.

The tragic story of ANANIAS and SAPPHIRA shows that the selling of land and other possessions by these early Christians was partial and voluntary (Acts 5:1, 4). However, there is a profound truth that must not be missed. "Neither did anyone say that any of the things he possessed was his own, but they had all things in common" (Acts 4:32). The emphasis should be placed not on their selling of possessions but on the unselfish attitude of the believers (Acts 2:45; 4:34). This is the spirit of true unity in Jesus Christ.

Also see COMMON LIFE.

COMPASS (see TOOLS OF THE BIBLE).

COMPASSION (see MERCY).

COMPTROLLER (see OCCUPATIONS AND TRADES).

CONANIAH [kone ah NYE ah] (*Jehovah establishes*) — a chief of the Levites who assisted in the celebration of the Passover during the reign of King Josiah (2 Chr. 35:9).

CONCISION — a word for mutilation used by the apostle Paul to show his contempt for those who insisted a Gentile had to be circumcised before he could become a Christian (Phil. 3:2, KJV; mutilation, NKJV; those who mutilate the flesh, RSV; those mutilators of the flesh, NIV).

CONCOURSES — open spaces where roads or paths meet. The word is found only once in the NKJV (Prov. 1:21; at the head of the noisy streets, NIV, NASB). The word concourse also occurs in Acts 19:40 (KJV; commotion, RSV, NIV; uproar, NEB; disorderly gathering, NASB, NKJV) in Paul's description of the riot against him in Ephesus.

CONCUBINE [con cue BINE]— in Old Testament times, a female slave or mistress with whom a man was lawfully permitted to have sexual intercourse.

The first mention of a concubine occurs in Genesis 2:24, where Reumah is described as the concubine of Nahor, Abraham's brother. Other men in the Old Testament who had these female slaves included Abraham (Gen. 25:6), Jacob (Gen. 35:22), Eliphaz (Gen. 36:12), Gideon (Judg. 8:31), and Saul (2 Sam. 3:7).

Sarai presented HAGAR, her Egyptian maidservant, to Abram as a concubine so he could father children by Hagar (Gen. 16:2–3). This apparently was a common practice during the patriarchal period in Israel's history. The ancient Hebrews placed great value on having many children. If a couple remained childless after several years of marriage, the husband would often father children through a concubine.

By the time of the monarchy in Israel, the practice of keeping concubines apparently became a privilege of kings only. King SOLOMON is especially remembered for his many concubines (1 Kin. 11:3). Most of these concubines were foreign women. They led to Solomon's downfall, because they brought their pagan religions, which introduced idolatry into the land (1 Kin. 11:1–13).

In the ancient world concubines were protected by law; so they could not be sold if they were no longer of interest to the man. The Law of Moses also recognized the rights of concubines and guarded them from inhumane and callous treatment (Ex. 21:7–11; Deut. 21:10–14).

CONCUPISCENCE — strong, passionate desire, especially sexual desire or lust. This word is found three times in the KJV (Rom. 7:8; Col. 3:5; 1 Thess. 4:5). Various modern translations have evil desire (Rom. 7:8, NKJV; Col. 3:5, NKJV, RSV), passionate lust (1 Thess. 4:5, NIV), and covetousness (Rom. 7:8, RSV).

CONDEMN, CONDEMNATION — to declare a person guilty and worthy of punishment. Condemn and condemnation are judicial terms, the opposite of JUSTIFY and JUSTIFICATION (Matt. 12:37; Rom. 5:16, 18). God alone is the judge of men; in His demand for righteousness, sin leads invariably to condemnation and death.

The mission of Jesus was not to condemn the world but to save it by bearing on the cross the sin that belonged to His people (John 3:17–18). There is no condemnation for sinners who repent and believe in Him. Jesus not only bore the consequences of sin, but also condemned (destroyed) sin itself so that believers are released from its power (Rom. 8:1, 3). Since they have experienced a gracious pardon, believers are directed to practice forgiveness and to avoid vindictiveness: "Condemn not, and you shall not be condemned" (Luke 6:37).

CONDUIT — a water channel or tunnel. The biblical references to conduit describe the AQUEDUCT made by Hezekiah, king of Judah, to channel water from the upper pool, or spring, of Gihon to the southern part of Jerusalem (2 Kin. 18:17; Is. 7:3; 36:2, KJV; aqueduct, NKJV; also 2 Kin. 20:20, KJV; tunnel, NKJV).

CONEY (see ANIMALS OF THE BIBLE).

CONFECTIONER (see OCCUPATIONS AND TRADES).

CONFESSION — an admission of sins and the profession of belief in the doctrines of a particular faith. In the Bible most of the uses of the word confession fall into one of these two categories. Examples of confession of sin may be found in Joshua's words to Achan (Josh. 7:19), in the confession during the Passover during Hezekiah's reign (2 Chr. 30:22), and in Ezra's call to the people to admit wrongdoing in marrying pagan wives (Ezra 10:11).

The Bible also uses the word confession to describe an open, bold, and courageous proclamation of one's faith. The apostle Paul wrote: "If you confess with your mouth the Lord Jesus and believe in your heart that God has raised Him from the dead, you will be saved. For with the heart one believes to righteousness, and with the mouth confession is made to salvation" (Rom. 10:9–10).

CONFIRM, CONFIRMATION — to establish, ratify, or strengthen a covenant. In the Bible the word confirm or confirmation is used of a vow or binding oath (Num. 30:13–14), words (Ezek. 13:6), a transaction of redeeming or exchanging (Ruth 4:7), a covenant or statute (Dan. 9:27; Gal. 3:15, 17), a person (Dan. 11:1), promises (Rom. 15:8), the testimony of Christ (1 Cor. 1:6), the gospel (Phil. 1:7), and salvation (Heb. 2:3).

CONGREGATION — a gathering or assembly of persons for worship and religious instruction; a religious community, such as the people of Israel or the Christian church.

In the Old Testament the English word congregation is the translation of several Hebrew words that carry the idea of "an appointed meeting" or "an assembly called together." These words point to Israel as the community of the Law, a "sacred assembly" gathered together by God and appointed to be His covenant people. As such, the term congregation was a constant reminder to Israel of the hand of God upon its destiny. Each time the Law of God was read in the solemn assembly of the congregation, Israel's sacred privilege as His people under His covenant promises was renewed.

A phrase such as "the whole assembly of the congregation of Israel" (Ex. 12:6) refers to the largest unit of the Hebrew people. A Hebrew belonged, at the most basic level, to a house, then to a family (a collection of houses), then to a tribe (a collection of families), and then to the congregation (a collection of tribes). The "whole congregation of Israel," therefore, refers to the entire nation of Israel or the people of God as a whole.

In the New Testament the term congregation is used only three times in the NKJV (Acts 7:38; 13:43; Heb. 2:12). The two Greek words translated as congregation, however, occur often elsewhere in the New Testament. Originally these words—*ekklesia* and *synagoge*—were virtually interchangeable. But they began to take on separate and specialized meanings as the rift between the Christian church (*ekklesia*) and the Jewish synagogue (*synagoge*) became more antagonistic. The words soon referred to rival religious faiths.

Also see ASSEMBLY; CHURCH.

CONGREGATION, MOUNT OF — a phrase used by the prophet Isaiah, apparently referring to Mount Moriah, the site on which the Temple in Jerusalem was built (Is. 14:13).

CONIAH [koe NYE ah] — a form of JEHOIACHIN.

CONONIAH [kone oh NYE ah] (*Jehovah establishes*) — a Levite appointed overseer of the tithes and offerings at the Temple during the reign of King Hezekiah (2 Chr. 31:12–13; Conaniah, RSV).

CONSCIENCE — a person's inner awareness of conforming to the will of God or departing from it, resulting in either a sense of approval or condemnation.

The term does not appear in the Old Testament but the concept does. David, for example, was smitten in his heart because of his lack of trust in the power of God (2 Sam. 24:10). But his guilt turned to joy when he sought the Lord's forgiveness (Psalm 32).

In the New Testament the term conscience is found most frequently in the writings of the apostle Paul. Some people argue erroneously that conscience takes the place of the external law in the Old Testament. However, the conscience is not the ultimate standard of moral goodness (1 Cor. 4:4). Under both the old covenant and the new covenant the conscience must be formed by the will of God.

The law given to Israel was inscribed on the hearts of believers (Heb. 8:10; 10:16); so the sensitized conscience is able to discern God's judgment against sin (Rom. 2:14–15).

The conscience of the believer has been cleansed by the work of Jesus Christ; it no longer accuses and condemns (Heb. 9:14; 10:22). Believers are to work to maintain pure consciences. They also must be careful not to encourage others to act against their consciences. To act contrary to the urging of one's conscience is wrong, for actions that go against the conscience cannot arise out of faith (1 Cor. 8; 10:23–33).

CONSECRATION — the act of setting apart, or dedicating, something or someone for God's use. In the Old Testament, the Temple and its trappings were the most important objects consecrated to God (2 Chr. 7:5–9; Ezra 6:16–17); and Aaron and his sons were consecrated to the priesthood (Exodus 29; Leviticus 8). But even such items as the spoils of battle (Josh. 6:19; Mic. 4:13) and cattle could be consecrated (Lev. 27:28). Before the beginning of the priesthood in Israel's history, the first-born of men and beasts alike were consecrated (Ex. 13:2). But after the priesthood began, the tribe of Levi served as a substitute in this consecration (Num. 3:12).

In the New Testament, the supreme example of consecration is Christ himself (John 17:19; Heb. 7:28; 10:10). But believers are also consecrated by Christ (John 17:17; 1 Pet. 2:9), and are urged to consecrate themselves as well (Rom. 12:1; 2 Tim. 2:21). One of the results of our consecration by Christ is that we are now a priesthood of believers (1 Pet. 2:9) with direct access to our heavenly Father (Eph. 3:11–12).

CONSOLATION (see HOLY SPIRIT).

CONSTELLATIONS (see ASTRONOMY).

CONSUMMATION (see ESCHATOLOGY).

CONSUMPTION (see DISEASES OF THE BIBLE).

CONTENTMENT — freedom from anxiety or worry. The idea of contentment comes from a Greek word that means "independence" or "self-sufficiency." But the apostle Paul used the word in a Christian sense to show that real satisfaction or sufficiency comes from God: "I can do all things through Christ who strengthens me" (Phil. 4:13).

CONTRITE — the kind of spirit, or heart, pleasing and acceptable to God (Ps. 34:18; crushed, RSV, NIV, NEB, NASB; Ps. 51:17). The person with a contrite spirit weeps over wrongdoing and expresses genuine sorrow for his sin (see also Matt. 5:4; Luke 6:21; 2 Cor. 7:10).

CONTROLLER (see OCCUPATIONS AND TRADES).

CONVERSATION — communication from one person to another. The word is used only twice in the NKJV (Jer. 38:27; Luke 24:17). But conversation is used often in the KJV to describe one's conduct, behavior, or way of life. Thus, the writer of the Book of Hebrews declared, "Let your conversation be without covetousness" (Heb. 13:5, KJV).

CONVERSION — the initial change of attitude and will that brings a person into right relationship with God. The word conversion appears as a noun only once in the New Testament, referring to the conversion of the Gentiles (Acts 15:3). But the Bible is filled with examples of persons who experienced conversion.

The fullest description of conversion occurs in the words spoken to Saul of Tarsus at his own conversion: "To open their eyes, and to turn them from darkness to light, and from the power of Satan to God, that they may receive forgiveness of sins and an inheritance among those who are sanctified by faith in me" (Acts 26:18).

Conversion involves turning away from evil deeds and false worship and turning toward serving and worshiping the Lord. Conversion marks a person's entrance into a new relationship with God, forgiveness of sins, and his new life as a part of the fellowship of the people of God.

Closely related to conversion are repentance and faith. Repentance is turning from sin; faith is turning to God. Thus, conversion is more than the exchange of one set of beliefs for another; it is a wholehearted turning to God.

The inward experience of conversion is sometimes referred to as the new birth (John 3:3–8). This phrase was used by Jesus in His conversation with Nicodemus. New birth refers to a change so radical that it can be described only by the figure of birth into a new life. As an infant enters the physical world with a totally new existence, so conversion is a new spiritual beginning in a person's relationship to God.

The experience of conversion may differ with various individuals. The apostle Paul's conversion was sudden and radical, while the conversion of Lydia (Acts 16:14–15) was apparently gradual and gentle. But the results of conversion are always a clear change of attitude and a new direction for life.

CONVICTION — the process of being condemned by one's own conscience as a sinner because of God's demands. The idea of conviction is a major theme of Scripture, although the word is rarely used (Psalm 32; 51; Acts 2:37; Rom. 7:7–25). The agent of conviction is the Holy Spirit (John 16:7–11); and the means of conviction is either the Word of God (Acts 2:37) or God's general revelation of His demands through nature and man's inborn consciousness of a sense of right and wrong (Rom. 1:18–20; 2:15). The purpose of conviction is to lead a person to repent of his sins (Acts 2:37–38; Rom. 2:1–4) and to turn to God for salvation and eternal life.

CONVOCATION — a sacred assembly or calling together of the people of Israel for rest and worship (Lev. 23:2, 4, 37). Wherever the word convocation appears in the Bible, it is preceded by the word holy; hence, holy convocation. On the great feast days the people were called together by silver trumpets (Num. 10:2). These convocations included the weekly SABBATHS (Lev. 23:2–3), the PASSOVER and the Feast of Unleavened Bread (Lev. 23:7–8), PENTECOST (Lev. 23:15–21), the Feast of Trumpets (Num. 29:1), the Feast of Weeks (Num. 28:26), the Feast of Tabernacles (Num. 29:12), and the great feast day, the annual DAY OF ATONEMENT (Lev. 23:27).

Also see FEASTS AND FESTIVALS.

COOK (see OCCUPATIONS AND TRADES).

COOKING — preparation of food by the application of heat (Gen. 25:29). Roasting over an open fire was probably the first method of cooking used. But with the development of waterproof containers, boiling food became possible. The first Passover lamb was to be "roasted in fire" (Ex. 12:9), while during the period of the judges, some offerings were apparently boiled (1 Sam. 2:13). In the biblical period bread could be baked by placing the dough on a heated rock, or it might be cooked in a small, portable oven. No cooking took place on the Sabbath (Ex. 35:3). Also see FOOD.

COOS [KOE os] — a form of COS.

COPPER (see MINERALS OF THE BIBLE).

COPPERSMITH (see OCCUPATIONS AND TRADES).

COR (see WEIGHTS AND MEASURES).

COR ASHAN (kor AY shan) — a form of ASHAN.

CORAL (see JEWELS AND PRECIOUS STONES).

CORBAN [KAWR bahn] (*an offering*) — a word applied to a gift or offering in the Temple which declared that gift dedicated to God in a special sense. Once a gift was offered under the special declaration of Corban, it could not be withdrawn or taken back; it was considered totally dedicated for the Temple's special use.

Jesus condemned the Pharisees for encouraging the people to make such gifts to the Temple while neglecting their responsibility to care for their parents (Mark 7:11–13). According to Jesus, this was a clear violation of a higher commandment, "Honor your father and your mother" (Mark 7:10).

CORD — a long line of twisted fiber used to bind or secure. In Bible times, cord and rope were made from flax, date tree fibers, or even strips of camel hide. They were used for a number of different purposes, including rigging boats (Acts 27:32), drawing carts (Is. 5:18), and binding prisoners (Judg. 16:11). Cord or rope made from flax was especially strong and durable. It was often used to make fish nets.

A number of words in the original languages of the Bible are translated as rope, cord, or line, with the context determining the exact translation. When Rahab lowered two spies from her window (Josh. 2:15), or when Jehoiakim's servants lowered

Jeremiah into a cistern (Jer. 38:6, 11), a rope was required. But when the fine trappings of the court of Ahaseurus (Esth. 1:6) or the hangings of the tabernacle (Ex. 35:18) were described, cord carries the appropriate idea. Jesus made a whip of cords (John 2:15) to drive the moneychangers out of the Temple.

CORE [KOE reh] — Greek form of KORAH.

CORIANDER (see PLANTS OF THE BIBLE).

CORINTH [KAWR inth] — ancient Greece's most important trade city (Acts 18:1; 19:1; 1 Cor. 1:2; 2 Cor. 1:1, 23; 2 Tim. 4:20). Ideally situated on the Isthmus of Corinth between the Ionian Sea and the Aegean Sea (see Map 7, B–2), Corinth was the connecting link between Rome, the capital of the world, and the East. At Corinth the apostle Paul established a flourishing church, made up of a cross section of the worldly minded people who had flocked to Corinth to participate in the gambling, legalized temple prostitution, business adventures, and amusements available in a first-century navy town (1 Cor. 6:9–11).

Although the apostle Paul did not establish the church in Corinth until about A.D. 51 (Acts 18:1–18), the city's history dates back to 10,000 B.C., when ancient tribesmen first settled the site. Always a commercial and trade center, Corinth was already prosperous and famous for its bronze, pottery, and shipbuilding nearly 800 years before Christ. The Greek poet Homer mentioned "wealthy Corinth" in 850 B.C.

In the following centuries Corinth competed for power with Athens, its stronger neighbor across the isthmus to the north. And in 146 B.C. invading Roman armies destroyed Corinth, killing the men and enslaving the women and children. Only a token settlement remained until 44 B.C., when Julius Caesar ordered the city rebuilt. Not only did he restore it as the capital city of the Roman province of Achaia; he also repopulated it with freed Italians and slaves from every nation. Soon the merchants flocked back to Corinth, too.

The city soon became a melting pot for the approximately 500,000 people who lived there at the time of Paul's arrival. Merchants and sailors, anxious to work the docks, migrated to Corinth. Professional gamblers and athletes, betting on the Isthmian games, took up residence. Slaves, sometimes freed but with no place to go, roamed the streets day and night. And prostitutes (both male and female) were abundant. People from Rome, the rest of Greece, Egypt, Asia Minor—indeed, all of the Mediterranean world—relished the lack of standards and freedom of thought that prevailed in the city.

These were the people who eventually made up the Corinthian church. They had to learn to live together in harmony, although their national, social, economic, and religious backgrounds were very different.

Perched on a narrow strip of land connecting the

The ruins of Corinth, one of the wealthiest and most immoral of ancient cities (1 Cor. 5:1; 6:9-11).

Peloponnesus, a peninsula of southern Greece, with central Greece and the rest of Europe, Corinth enjoyed a steady flow of trade. The city had two splendid harbor cities — Cenchreae, the eastern port on the Saronic Gulf; and Lechaeum, the western port on the Corinthian Gulf.

In the outlying areas around Corinth, farmers tended their grain fields, vineyards, and olive groves. But the pulse of Corinth was the city itself, enclosed by walls ten kilometers (six miles) in circumference. Most of the daily business was conducted in the marble-paved agora, or marketplace, in the central part of the city. Although only one percent of the ancient city has been excavated by archaeologists, some interesting discoveries give ideas of what the city was like when Paul arrived.

A marble lintel or crosspiece of a door was found near the residential section of Corinth. It bore the inscription, "Synagogue of the Hebrews." This may have been the very synagogue in which Paul first proclaimed the gospel message to Corinth, accompanied by his new-found Jewish friends, Aquila and Priscilla (Acts 18:2).

Not far from the synagogue excavation site was the magnificient judgment seat, covered with ornate blue and white marble. There, the Roman proconsul of Achaia, Gallio, dismissed Paul's case (Acts 18:12-17).

South of the marketplace were the butcher stalls (shambles, KJV; meat market, NKJV, NASB, NIV, NEB, RSV) that Paul mentioned in 1 Corinthians 10:25. Corinthians purchased their meat from these butcher stalls. The meat was often dedicated to pagan idols before being sold. This presented a cultural problem for the Christians in Corinth (1 Corinthians 8).

Today the Temple of Apollo, partially in ruins, towers above the ancient marketplace. Each fluted Doric column, about seven meters (almost 24 feet) tall, was cut from a single piece of stone in one of several quarries outside Corinth's walls.

Rising 457 meters (1,500 feet) above the city itself and to the south is the acropolis, or citadel. From there, the acropolis at Athens, about 73 kilometers (45 miles) away, can be seen. Also, the infamous Temple of Aphrodite (or Venus) was located on top of this fortified hill. This pagan temple and its 1,000 "religious" prostitutes poisoned the city's culture and morals. For this reason, the apostle Paul sometimes had to deal harshly with the converts in the Corinthian church. Most of the Corinthians had lived in this godless society all their lives, and the idea of tolerating incest had not seemed so terrible to them (1 Corinthians 5).

In spite of Corinth's notorious reputation, God used the apostle Paul to establish a vigorous church in the city about A.D. 51 (Acts 18:1-18). Later, Paul wrote at least two letters to the church at Corinth (see CORINTHIANS, EPISTLES TO THE). Both deal with divisions in the church, as well as immorality and the abuse of Christian freedom.

The Corinth that Paul knew was partially destroyed by an earthquake in A.D. 521, then totally devastated by another in 1858. Modern Corinth, rebuilt about four kilometers (2.5 miles) from the ancient site, is little more than a town. It is certainly not a thriving trade center, but the inhabitants only need to look at the ancient ruins to recall the former glory of their city. The success of the gospel at Corinth—bittersweet though it was—illustrates that the grace of God comes not so much to the noble as to the needy.

CORINTHIANS, EPISTLES TO THE — two letters of the apostle Paul addressed to the church in Corinth. First Corinthians is unique among the Pauline letters because of the variety of its practical concerns. Second Corinthians is one of Paul's most personal letters, containing a wealth of insights into the heart of Paul the pastor. Both letters reveal the degree to which Paul identified with his churches, suffering in their shortcomings and celebrating in their victories. The Corinthian correspondence draws us into a world much like our own. Paul the anxious pastor wrote to young Christians who were concerned with problems involved in living the Christian life in a non-Christian environment.

Structure of the Epistles. Following the introduction (1 Cor. 1:1-9), Paul appealed to the Corinthians to mend the divisions within the church (chap. 1—4). Paul reminded the Corinthians that they all were united by the simple, but life-changing, preaching of the cross (1 Cor. 1:18—2:16). Indeed, each church leader builds on the one foundation of Jesus (chap. 3), and consequently labors in behalf of Christ (chap. 4). In chapters 5 and 6 Paul took up two moral abuses in Corinth. He judged a man who had sexual intercourse with his father's wife (chap. 5), and he reproved the believers for generating arguments that wound up in court before non-believing judges (1 Cor. 6:1-11).

Paul then addressed certain questions which were brought to him by the Corinthians: about sexuality (6:12-19), marriage (chap. 7), and eating food offered previously to idols (chap. 8). On such matters Paul appealed for a responsible use of Christian freedom—not for self-gain, but in consideration for the other. He reminded them that he conducted his own ministry in this way (chap. 9), and he warned against becoming fixed on anything that could lead to idolatry (chap. 10).

Paul then returned to other abuses, especially involving church order. In chapter 11 he developed the correct teaching on the Lord's Supper; in chapter 12 on spiritual gifts; in chapter 13 on love; in chapter 14 on the charismatic gifts of tongues and prophecy, and in chapter 15 on the resurrection. Finally, he reminded the Corinthians of the weekly collection for the saints in Jerusalem. He concluded with travel plans and greetings (chap. 16).

Second Corinthians is closely related to the circumstances that occasioned its writing. The letter begins with reference to a painful experience of rejection at Corinth (Paul's third visit). Paul gave thanks that the Corinthians were now reconciled to him (chap. 1), but he recalled his torment over their stubbornness (chap. 2). Chapters 3 and 4 are theological reflections on ministry, and chapters 5 and 6 on reconciliation. In chapter 7 Paul shared his joy at the church's repentance. Paul changed perspective in chapters 8 and 9 by turning to the matter of the collection for the church in Jerusalem.

The tone of 2 Corinthians changes in chapters 10—13. These chapters are laced with warnings to the Corinthians and Paul's opponents, defenses of his apostleship, and a rehearsal of Paul's sufferings as an apostle. If chapters 1—9 reveal Paul's joy and relief, chapters 10—13 let us see the wounds, both physical and emotional, which he bore as an apostle. The letter closes with the only trinitarian benediction in the Bible (2 Cor. 13:14).

Authorship and Date. First and Second Corin-

Ruins of the civil law court known as the Julian Basilica in ancient Corinth. Some of the charges of the Corinthian Christians against one another (1 Cor. 6:1-11) may have been reviewed on this very site.
Photo by Howard Vos

FIRST CORINTHIANS: A Teaching Outline

SECOND CORINTHIANS: A Teaching Outline

Part One: Paul's Explanation of His Ministry (1:1—7:16)

Part Two: Paul's Collection for the Saints (8:1—9:15)

Part Three: Paul's Vindication of His Apostleship (10:1—13:14)

The Temple of Apollo at Corinth and the acropolis of the city in the background.

thians bear unmistakable marks of Pauline authorship (1 Cor. 1:1; 2 Cor. 2:1). The first epistle was written from Ephesus (1 Cor. 16:8) during Paul's third missionary journey, perhaps in A.D. 56. The second letter followed some 12–15 months later from Macedonia, where Paul met Titus and received news of the church's repentance (2 Cor. 2:12–17).

Historical Setting. Acts 18:1–18 records the founding of the Corinthian church. During his second missionary journey, Paul went alone from Athens to Corinth in about A.D. 51. There he labored with a Jewish–Christian couple, Aquila and Priscilla, who recently had been expelled from Rome by the emperor Claudius because they were Jews. Silas and Timothy also joined Paul in Corinth. When Paul left Corinth 18 months later, a Christian congregation flourished. The congregation was composed primarily of former pagans (1 Cor. 12:2), most of them apparently from the lower classes (1 Cor. 1:26f.). Some were slaves (1 Cor. 7:21). A few wealthier persons (1 Cor. 11:22–32) and Jews, however, (8:1–13) were among the believers.

A bit of detective work enables us to reconstruct the circumstances of the Corinthian correspondence. It is reasonably certain that Paul wrote four letters and paid perhaps three visits to the church in Corinth.

During his third missionary journey, Paul received word about immorality in the young congregation at Corinth. He wrote a letter (which has since been lost) against mixing with fornicators (1 Cor. 5:9). The letter apparently failed to achieve its purpose. Some time later Paul learned (1 Cor. 1:11;

16:17) that the sexual problems persisted, along with many others. Paul responded by writing a second letter (probably 1 Corinthians), in which he referred to various points raised by the Corinthians (see the sections beginning, "Now concerning," 1 Cor. 7:1, 25; 8:1; 12:1; 16:1). In addition, he condemned the Corinthians for their divisions (1 Cor. 1:10) and their gross sexual violation (1 Cor. 5:1).

This letter also failed to correct the abuses at Corinth. Paul then apparently made a visit to Corinth, during which he was rebuffed (2 Cor. 2:1). From Ephesus Paul then wrote a third letter in which he spared no punches in his contest with the willful Corinthians. This letter, which he sent by Titus, has also been lost. Many scholars believe it has been attached to 2 Corinthians and preserved as chapters 10—13 of his epistle.

In anxiety over the possible effect of this drastic letter, and impatient over Titus' delay in returning, Paul traveled north from Ephesus to Macedonia. There Titus met him and, to Paul's relief and joy, reported that the Corinthians had punished the ringleader of the opposition and repented (2 Cor. 2:5–11). Paul then wrote a fourth letter (2 Corinthians), recounting his former anxiety and expressing his joy over the reform in Corinth.

Theological Contribution. The problems which Paul faced in the church at Corinth were complex and explosive. The correspondence which resulted is rich and profound in theological insight. While addressing the problems in Corinth, the apostle reaches some of the most sublime heights in all New Testament literature.

Corinth, like its neighboring city of Athens, symbolized Greek culture in its desire for wisdom and power. Paul must have been tempted to write to the Greeks as a Christian philosopher (1 Cor. 2:4). He rejected this tendency, however, and relied instead on the irony of the cross, "to the Jews a stumbling block and to the Greeks foolishness" (1 Cor. 1:23). The foolishness of the gospel—indeed, its offensiveness to cultured Greeks—was indication of its power to save. To those who respond, "Christ is the power of God and the wisdom of God" (1 Cor. 1:24). According to Paul, the preaching of the cross is not a human teaching but a revelation of the Spirit, who makes known the mind of Christ (1 Cor. 2:10-16). The centrality of the cross overcomes all divisions within the church.

Since many of the problems arising in Corinth concerned behavior and morals, Paul majored on ethical advice in his correspondence. The leading principle he uses is that "all things are lawful for me, but not all things are helpful" (1 Cor. 6:12; 10:23). Christians ought to use their freedom not for self-advantage, but for the glory of God and the good of their neighbors. This principle goes beyond legislating simple "do's and don'ts." Instead, it cultivates a mature and responsible faith which will provide guidance for every moral problem.

First Corinthians is also important because of its teaching on the gifts of the Spirit (chap. 12) and the resurrection of the dead (chap. 15). Paul recognized a variety of gifts (12:4-10), but insisted that "one and the same Spirit" gives them. The body consists of different parts, but remains one organism. Likewise, Christ's body of believers consists of members with different gifts, each given by the one Spirit.

First Corinthians 15 is our earliest record of the resurrection in the New Testament. Unless Christ has been resurrected, Paul maintained, the faith of Christians is empty (15:12-19). As death came through Adam, so new life comes through Christ (15:21, 45). The resurrection of Jesus is a "firstfruits" (15:20) of the victory to come. Because of the resurrection the believer can confess, "O death, where is your sting?" (15:55).

Second Corinthians is probably best known for its teaching on Christian ministry. Chapters 4 and 5 are unrivaled for their beauty of expression and grandeur of thought. Paul marvels at the treasure of the gospel which God entrusts to human servants. Indeed, the weakness of the servant only highlights the message of salvation (4:1-15). This message finds its most famous expression in 2 Corinthians 5:17, "If anyone is in Christ, he is a new creation; old things have passed away; behold, all things have become new." The voltage of this truth transforms Christian messengers into ambassadors for Christ.

Special Considerations. As in the case with the resurrection, Corinthians also contains the earliest record of the Lord's Supper (1 Cor. 11:23-26). The immortal last words of Christ, "This cup is the new covenant in my blood" (11:24-25), recall his past death and anticipate his future return.

First Corinthians also contains one of the best-known chapters in the New Testament. In poetic cadence Paul proclaims "the more excellent way" of *agape* (chap. 13). Love is not merely a feeling, but an attitude committed to patience, hope, and stability in the face of problems. Such love will outlast the world itself. Agape love is the greatest characteristic of the Christian life.

CORMORANT (see ANIMALS OF THE BIBLE).

CORN (see PLANTS OF THE BIBLE).

CORNELIAN (see JEWELS AND PRECIOUS STONES).

CORNELIUS [kor NEEL yus] (meaning unknown) — a Roman soldier stationed in Caesarea who was the first recorded Gentile convert to Christianity (Acts 10:1-33).

Cornelius was a God-fearing man strongly attracted to the Jewish teaching of monotheism (the belief in one God), as opposed to pagan idolatry and immorality, and to the concern expressed in the law of Moses concerning helping the poor and needy (Acts 10:2). He is introduced in the Book of Acts as a representative of thousands in the Gentile world who were weary of paganism and who were hungry for the coming of the Messiah—the Christ who would deliver them from their sins and lead them into an abundant, Spirit-filled life.

God sent a heavenly vision both to Cornelius and to Simon Peter. Obeying his vision, Cornelius sent some of his men to Joppa, about 58 kilometers (36 miles) south of Caesarea, to find Peter. Peter, in turn, obeyed his own vision (which he interpreted to mean that Gentiles were to be included in Christ's message) and went to Cornelius. While Peter was still preaching to Cornelius and his household, "the Holy Spirit fell upon all those who heard the word" (Acts 10:44). And Peter commanded them to be baptized in the name of the Lord.

This incident marked the expansion of the early church to include Gentiles as well as Jews (Acts 10:34-35; 11:18). Peter alluded to Cornelius' conversion at the Jerusalem Council (Acts 15:7-11).

Also see CENTURION; ITALIAN REGIMENT.

CORNER GATE (see GATES OF JERUSALEM AND THE TEMPLE).

CORNER, UPPER ROOM AT THE — a roof-chamber (NEB) at the junction of two walls at the northeast corner of the Temple in Jerusalem (Neh. 3:31-32; room above the corner, NIV). This upper chamber (RSV) was possibly a watchtower in Jerusalem's walls where Nehemiah finished his work of restoring the walls of Jerusalem.

CORNERSTONE — a stone placed at the corner, or the intersecting angle, where two walls of a building come together. In biblical times, buildings were often made of cut, squared stone. By uniting two intersecting walls, a cornerstone helped align the whole building and tie it together.

In his address before the Jewish SANHEDRIN, the apostle Peter quoted Psalm 118:22 and boldly proclaimed that "Jesus Christ of Nazareth," crucified and raised from the dead, was the stone rejected by the builders who has now become the chief cornerstone (Acts 4:11). This chief cornerstone, Jesus Christ, is the foundation of the church, because "there is no other name under heaven given among men by which we must be saved" (Acts 4:12) and in Him "the whole building, being joined together, grows into a holy temple in the Lord" (Eph. 2:21). All who believe in Jesus find a solid Rock on which to build their lives.

Also see CAPSTONE.

CORNET (see MUSICAL INSTRUMENTS).

CORRECTION — to reform or to punish. In the Old Testament, correction is equated with chastening (Prov. 3:11–12), reproof (Prov. 13:18; 15:10), and judgment (Hab. 1:12). The New Testament declares that all Scripture is profitable for correction (2 Tim. 3:16; reformation of manners, NEB). The Word of God (the Bible) teaches us what is true and false.

CORRUPTION — decay of the body (Acts 2:27, 31) and degradation of human life through the power of sin (2 Pet. 1:4). But because of the resurrection of Christ our bodies, sown in corruption (subject to the decay and dissolution of organic matter), will be raised in incorruption (1 Cor. 15:42, 50).

CORRUPTION, MOUNT OF (see MOUNT OF THE CORRUPTION).

COS [kahz] — a small island between Miletus and Rhodes, in the archipelago opposite the coast of Caria in Asia Minor (see Map 8, C–2). It was a place that the apostle Paul passed during his voyage to Jerusalem (Acts 21:1; Coos, KJV). Cos was famous for its wines, ointments, and purple dyes, and for its fine textured silk and cotton.

COSAM [KOE zam] (diviner) — a descendant of David and an ancestor of Jesus (Luke 3:28).

COSMETICS — items such as ointment, perfume, and eye paint used to enhance a person's appearance in Bible times. The biblical writers referred to disreputable women who used excessive eye paint (Jer. 4:30; Ezek. 23:40). Ointments or perfumes were expensive substances used for personal adornment as well as the anointing of bodies for burial (Song 1:13; Luke 7:37).

COTTAGE — KJV word for HUT.

COTTON — RSV word for LINEN. While cotton was known in ancient India, it apparently was never grown or used in Palestine during the biblical period.

COUCH — KJV word for BED.

COUNCIL — an assembly of people who meet to discuss important matters and to make decisions. The Greek words usually translated as council can refer to the place where a council meets, the group itself, or the meeting. In the New Testament, council is a technical term that often refers to the supreme Jewish council, the SANHEDRIN.

In Roman times, the Sanhedrin was the highest governing Jewish body in the province of Judea in southern Palestine. The council, or Sanhedrin, was composed of high priests, elders, and scribes. This council had the highest authority in legal, governmental, and religious matters; and it could exercise these powers as long as it did not infringe on Roman authority. Normally Rome confirmed and carried out death sentences passed by the Jewish Sanhedrin.

Most of the references in the New Testament to the Sanhedrin appear in connection with the trial of Jesus (Matt. 26:59; Mark 14:55; 15:1; John 11:47) and opposition to the work of the early church (Acts 5:21). The Sanhedrin became the focus of Jewish opposition to early Christianity (Acts 4:15; 5:21; 6:12; 22:30; 23:1; 24:20).

The council can also be a gathering of people, as in Matthew 12:14 where the Pharisees, indignant at the healing and teaching activities of Jesus, went out of the synagogue and "held a council against him" (KJV). During Paul's trial before Festus, Festus consulted with such a council. This group probably was made up of political advisors in the district which he governed.

COUNCIL OF JERUSALEM (see JERUSALEM COUNCIL).

COUNSELOR — one who gives counsel or advises (Prov. 11:14), especially the king's adviser (2 Sam. 15:12; 1 Chr. 27:33), or one of the chief men of the government (Job 3:14; Is. 1:26). In Mark 15:43 (KJV) and Luke 23:50 (KJV), the word designates a "council member" (of the SANHEDRIN). The HOLY SPIRIT is also called "the Counselor" in the RSV (John 14:16, 26; 15:26; 16:7). Also see OCCUPATIONS AND TRADES.

COUPLINGS — KJV word for stone or timbers used to tie a building together (2 Chr. 34:11; beams, NKJV). When the tabernacle was built in the wilderness, God also gave the Israelites detailed instructions on how the curtains around the altar were to be coupled, or joined, together (Ex. 26:3–24). Also see ARCHITECTURE.

COURAGE — the strength of purpose that enables one to withstand fear or difficulty. Physical courage is based on moral courage—a reliance on the presence and power of God and a commitment to His commandments (Josh. 23:6; 2 Chr. 19:11).

COURSE — a word in the Bible with many different meanings, including the passage of time (2 Chr. 21:19); a straight path, as of a ship (Acts 16:11; 21:1); the evil ways of this age (Eph. 2:2); and advancement or progress (2 Thess. 3:1).

COURT — an open space or courtyard enclosed by walls or buildings. Most of the references to court in the Bible are related to the TABERNACLE (Ex. 27:9–19) and the TEMPLE (1 Kin. 6:36). The tabernacle stood in a large courtyard approximately 44 meters (146 feet) long and 22 meters (73 feet) wide (Ex. 27:9–19). The sides of the courtyard were formed by a linen screen with an opening for a gate.

Solomon's Temple had an inner court (1 Kin. 6:36) and an outer court (Ezek. 10:5), as did the temple in the prophet Ezekiel's vision (Ezekiel 40—46). The Bible often used the plural form, referring to courts (Ps. 65:4; 84:2). The Jewish temple that Herod built had courts for Gentiles, women, Jewish men, and priests.

The word court also refers in Scripture to the yards of a prison (Jer. 32:2, 8, 12), a private house (2 Sam. 17:18), and a king's palace (Esth. 1:5).

Also see HOUSE.

COURT OF THE GENTILES — the outermost court of Herod's Temple in Jerusalem. The Temple consisted of a series of courts. As one entered the Temple precincts and proceeded toward the interior, each court was higher than the previous one. Non-Jews could enter the Court of the Gentiles but were prohibited from going farther. At Jesus' death, the veil that separated the inner court from the outer court was split, showing that all people had equal access to God through Jesus Christ, the great Mediator and Redeemer (Matt. 27:51; Eph. 2:14). Also see TEMPLE.

COURT, SANCTUARY (see TABERNACLE; TEMPLE).

COURTIER (see OCCUPATIONS AND TRADES).

COURTS, JUDICIAL (see LAW).

COUSIN — a child of one's aunt or uncle. The Greek word translated cousin (*anepsios*) occurs only once in Scripture: "Mark the cousin of Barnabas" (Col. 4:10; "sister's son," KJV). Elizabeth was not Mary's cousin (Luke 1:36, KJV), but her kinswoman (RSV, NEB) or relative (NKJV, NIV, NAS). Jeremiah and Hanameel were cousins (Jer. 32:7–9, 12). Esther was "the daughter of Abihail the uncle of Mordecai" (Esth. 2:15; also Esth. 2:7). Mordecai was therefore Esther's cousin and not, as sometimes erroneously stated, her uncle.

COVENANT — an agreement between two people or two groups that involves promises on the part of each to the other. The concept of covenant between God and His people is one of the most important theological truths of the Bible. By making a covenant with Abraham, God promised to bless His descendants and to make them His special people. Abraham, in return, was to remain faithful to God and to serve as a channel through which God's blessings could flow to the rest of the world (Gen. 12:1–3).

Even before Abraham's time, God also made a covenant with Noah, assuring Noah that He would not again destroy the world by flood (Genesis 9). Another famous covenant was between God and David, in which David and his descendants were established as the royal heirs to the throne of the nation of Israel (2 Sam. 7:12; 22:51). This covenant agreement reached its highest fulfillment when Jesus the Messiah, a descendant of the line of David, was born in Bethlehem about a thousand years after God made this promise to David the king.

A covenant, in the biblical sense, implies much more than a contract or simple agreement. A contract always has an end date, while a covenant is a permanent arrangement. Another difference is that a contract generally involves only one part of a person, such as a skill, while a covenant covers a person's total being.

The word for covenant in the Old Testament also provides additional insight into the meaning of this important idea. It comes from a Hebrew root word which means "to cut." This explains the strange custom of two people passing through the cut bodies of slain animals after making an agreement with each other (Jer. 34:18). A ritual or ceremony such as this always accompanied the making of a covenant in the Old Testament. Sometimes those entering into a covenant shared a holy meal (Gen. 31:54). Abraham and his children were commanded to be circumcised as a sign of their covenant with God (Gen. 17:10–11). Moses sprinkled the blood of animals on the altar and upon the people who entered into covenant with God at Mount Sinai (Ex. 24:3–8).

The Old Testament contains many examples of covenants between people who related to each other as equals. For example, David and Jonathan entered into a covenant because of their love for each other. This agreement bound each of them to certain responsibilities (1 Sam. 18:3). But the striking thing about God's covenant with His people is that God is holy, all-knowing, and all powerful; but He consents to enter into covenant with man, who is weak, sinful, and imperfect.

In the Old Testament, God's CHOSEN PEOPLE confirmed their covenant with God with oaths or promises to keep the agreement. At Mount Sinai, the nation of Israel promised to perform "all the words which the Lord has said" (Ex. 24:3). When the people later broke this promise, they were called by their leaders to renew their oath (2 Kin. 23:3). By contrast, God does not break promises. His oath to raise up believing children to Abraham (Gen. 22:16–17) is an "everlasting" covenant (Gen. 17:7).

The New Testament makes a clear distinction between covenants of Law and covenants of Promise. The apostle Paul spoke of these "two covenants," one originating "from Mount Sinai," the other from "the Jerusalem above" (Gal. 4:24–26). Paul also argued that the covenant established at Mount Sinai, the Law, is a "ministry of death" and "condemnation" (2 Cor. 3:7, 9)—a covenant that cannot be obeyed because of man's weakness and sin (Rom. 8:3).

But the "covenants of promise" (Eph. 2:12) are God's guarantees that He will provide salvation in spite of man's inability to keep his side of the agreement because of his sin. The provision of a Chosen People through whom the Messiah would be born is the promise of the covenants with Adam and David (Gen. 3:15; 2 Sam. 7:14–15). The covenant with Noah is God's promise to withhold judgment on nature while salvation is occurring (Gen. 8:21–22; 2 Pet. 3:7, 15). In the covenant with Abraham, God promised to bless Abraham's descendants because of his faith.

These many covenants of promise may be considered one covenant of grace, which was fulfilled in the life and ministry of Jesus. His death ushered in the new covenant under which we are justified by God's grace and mercy rather than our human attempts to keep the law. And Jesus Himself is the Mediator of this better covenant between God and man (Heb. 9:15).

Jesus' sacrificial death served as the oath, or pledge, which God made to us to seal this new covenant. He is determined to give us eternal life and fellowship with Him, in spite of our unworthiness. As the Book of Hebrews declares, "The word of the oath, which came after the law, appoints the Son who has been perfected forever" (Heb. 7:28). This is still God's promise to any person who turns to Him in repentance and faith.

Also see COVENANT, NEW.

COVENANT, BOOK OF THE — a name for the code of laws in Exodus 20:22—23:33, given to Moses at Mount Sinai immediately after the Ten Commandments. The Book of the Covenant was discovered in the Temple during the reign of King Josiah of Judah (641—609 B.C.), who used it in his restoration of true worship (2 Kin. 23:2–3, 21; 2 Chr. 34:30–31).

COVENANT, NEW — the new agreement God has made with mankind, based on the death and resurrection of Jesus Christ. The concept of a new covenant originated with the promise of the prophet Jeremiah that God would accomplish for His people what the old covenant had failed to do (Jer. 31:31). Under this new covenant, God would write His Law on human hearts. This promised action suggested a new level of obedience, a new knowledge of the Lord, and a new forgiveness of sin.

The New Testament, which itself means "new covenant," interprets the work of Jesus Christ as bringing this promised new covenant into being. In Luke 22:20, when Jesus ate the Passover meal at the Last Supper with His disciples, He spoke of the cup as "the new covenant in My blood." When the apostle Paul recited the tradition he had received concerning the Last Supper, he quoted these words of Jesus about the cup as "the new covenant in My blood" (1 Cor. 11:25).

But the Epistle to the Hebrews gives the new cov-

enant more attention than any other book in the New Testament. It includes a quotation of the entire passage from Jeremiah 31:31–34 (Heb. 8:8–12; also 10:16–17). Jesus is also referred to by the writer of Hebrews as "the Mediator of the new covenant" (Heb. 9:15; 12:24). The new covenant, a "better covenant...established on better promises" (Heb. 8:6), rests directly on the sacrificial work of Christ, according to Hebrews. The new covenant accomplished what the old could not: removal of sin and cleansing of the conscience (Heb. 10:2, 22). The work of Jesus Christ on the cross thus makes the old covenant "obsolete" (Heb. 8:13) and fulfills the promise of the prophet Jeremiah.

Also see COVENANT.

COVENANT PEOPLE — a name often used for the Hebrew people, Abraham's descendants. The Hebrews were chosen by God as instruments of His redemption of the world (Gen. 12:1–3).

In the New Testament, those who believe in Christ are people of a new and better covenant (Luke 22:20; 2 Cor. 3:6).

COVENANT OF SALT — an Old Testament expression for a covenant, or agreement, that was supposed to be honored forever (Num. 18:19). Salt apparently was used as a figure of speech for binding agreements because it was a basic part of the Hebrew diet and it was also used as a food preservative in the ancient world.

COVERING THE HEAD — the practice among women of wearing a veil in early Christian worship services. The apostle Paul argued that a woman participating in the services ought to have her head covered (1 Cor. 11:2–16). The veil covered the head but did not hide the face.

According to Paul, it was a "symbol of authority" (1 Cor. 11:10). The Christian woman had received a new freedom and spiritual authority from Christ (Gal. 3:28). Thus she was able to pray and prophesy in the services. By wearing the veil, however, she would show that her authority had come from God; she had not seized it herself. Without the veil she might offend recent Jewish converts or others who held to the ancient tradition that women ought always to be veiled in public as a sign of modesty.

COVETOUSNESS — an intense desire to possess something (or someone) that belongs to another person. The Ten Commandments prohibit this attitude (Ex. 20:17; Deut. 5:21). Covetousness springs from a greedy self-centeredness and an arrogant disregard of God's law. The Bible repeatedly warns against this sin (Josh. 7:21; Rom. 7:7; 2 Pet. 2:10).

Many examples of covetousness appear in the Bible: Gehazi's greed (2 Kin. 5:20–27), Judas' betrayal of Jesus (Matt. 26:14–15), the rich fool (Luke 12:13–21), the rich young ruler (Luke 18:18–25), and the deceit of Ananias and Sapphira (Acts 5:1–11). The apostle Paul labeled this sin as idolatry (Col. 3:5). He warned believers not to associate with a covetous brother (1 Cor. 5:10–11).

God the Creator, from a painting by Michelangelo in the Sistine Chapel in Rome.

The best way to avoid a self-centered, covetous attitude is to trust the Lord and to face one's responsibilities (Gal. 6:7–9; 2 Thess. 3:6–15). To those tempted by "covetousness" and "worthless things" (Ps. 119:36), Jesus declares, "Take heed and beware of covetousness, for one's life does not consist in the abundance of the things he possesses" (Luke 12:15).

COW (see ANIMALS OF THE BIBLE).

COZ [koz] — a form of KOZ.

COZBI [KOZ bih] (*lying, deceitful*) — a Midianite princess slain by Phinehas, the grandson of Aaron, because Zimri apparently took her to be his wife or concubine against the orders of Moses (Num. 25:15, 18).

COZEBA [ko ZEE buh] — a form of CHOZEBA.

CRACKNELS — KJV word for a kind of hard bread or cake (1 Kin. 14:3; KJV; cakes, NKJV; raisins, NEB). Also see FOOD.

CRAFTINESS — the use of trickery or underhanded means to achieve an objective. The serpent was more crafty (Gen. 3:1, NASB, NEB, NIV) than any wild creature that God made. The apostle Paul wrote, "The serpent deceived Eve by his craftiness" (2 Cor. 11:3).

CRAFTSMAN (see OCCUPATIONS AND TRADES).

CRANE (see ANIMALS OF THE BIBLE).

CREATION — God's action in creating the natural universe out of nothing. The writer of the Epistle to the Hebrews in the New Testament declared, "By faith we understand that the world was framed by the word of God, so that the things which are seen were not made of things which are visible" (Heb. 11:3).

People of the pagan nations of the ancient world believed that matter was eternal and that the gods evolved out of natural processes. But the Bible teaches that God existed before creation and called the physical world into existence out of nothing. The account of His act of creation is found in the first two chapters of the Book of Genesis.

God's first act of creation was to bring into being the great watery chaos described in Genesis 1:2: "The earth was without form and void; and darkness was on the face of the deep." His next creative act was to bring order out of chaos—to separate the land from the water. This set the stage for the creation of plant and animal life.

First God created inanimate life: grass, other vegetation, trees, and fruit trees. Then the sea was filled with living creatures, the air with flying things, and the earth with creeping things. Then God moved on in orderly fashion to create land animals.

The creation of man was left for the sixth and final day of creation because man was special and was to rule over the rest of creation. "Then God said, 'Let us make man in Our image, according to our likeness' " (Gen. 1:26). This statement has fascinated thinkers for centuries. Just what does the image of God in man mean? Since God is spirit—not a material substance—it must mean more than physical resemblance. To be created in God's image means that man, though a creature, is akin to God.

God is Creator—the only being capable of making something from nothing. Yet, on a lesser level, man also has capacity to be creative. This is one distinct meaning of the truth that we are created in God's image. God is speaker and a ruler. Man was also told to have dominion over the creation. God is holy, a moral and ethical God who is righteous. Man is also morally and ethically responsible and must make moral choices. God has revealed that he is a social being (Father, Son, and Holy Spirit). Man also is a social being who needs relationship with others. Human experience and the biblical record suggest that these are some ways in which man reflects the image of God.

The Genesis writer also declared that God created humanity as "male and female" (Gen. 1:27). This account of creation does not give priority to either male or female. Both are needed to reflect the image of God. The most fundamental difference in humanity is not race but sex. The Greeks said man once was androgynous—both male and female. Somehow he lost the female half and ever since has been looking for his other half. But the writer of Genesis pointed out that sex is an order of creation which is good and proper in God's sight.

Genesis 2 contains what some scholars call a second creation account. But others point out that it sets the stage for what follows in the accounts of man's temptation and sin. A major emphasis of chapter 2 is the creation of woman as a companion for man. Man's incompleteness apart from woman is shown in his loneliness and frustration. None of the animals could meet Adam's need. Then the Lord created woman from Adam's rib.

Bible students have long seen symbolic truth in this rib imagery. Woman was taken from under man's arm to symbolize his protection of her. She was taken from near his heart that he might love and cherish her. She was not made from a head bone to rule over man, nor from his foot to be trampled on and degraded. Like the man, she reflects God's image. Together they formed the blessed pair needed to replenish and subdue the earth.

Many Bible students wonder about the six days of creation. Were these 24-hour days or indefinite periods of time? It may help us in our interpretation if we remember that we use the word "day" in several ways, even as the ancient Hebrews did. We speak of the day of reckoning, the day of opportunity, and the day of trouble. These may signify more than a 24-hour day. In similar fashion, the biblical writers spoke of the "day of the Lord" and "day of visitation."

Skeptics have ridiculed the creation story in Genesis because it reports that the creation occurred in six days. But the indefinite meaning of day takes care of this objection. Besides, Scripture says that with the Lord, "A day is as a thousand years and a thousand years as a day" (2 Pet. 3:8). The biblical writer was not writing a scientific journal. He was moved by God's Spirit to give a revelation of spiritual reality. His primary emphasis was not on the process by which the world was created but on the Creator and His purpose.

Many of the pagan nations of the ancient world had their own creation stories. But in these stories, their gods evolved out of natural processes connected with the world itself. They believed the material universe was eternal, and it brought their gods into being. But Genesis declares that God existed before creation and is in full control of the physical universe. He called the world into being by His word. His power is absolute. He does not have to conform to nature and cannot be threatened by it. God is sovereign and does not have to share His power with other supernatural beings.

Since God created the universe out of nothing, it is His and will always serve His purpose. As He shaped creation without any interference from anyone, He will bring creation to its desired end. No power can frustrate God in His purpose to complete the process started in creation and revealed in Scripture. Our hope rests in the sovereign power of Him who created the world and then re-created us through the saving power of His Son, Jesus Christ.

CREATURE — any created being, man included, brought into existence as a result of God's power and authority. The Bible declares that the Redeemer God is the sovereign Creator of all things. Through His might and power He brought the universe into existence (Gen. 1:3–24; Ps. 33:6; Heb. 11:3). Therefore, all beings, even angels, are His creatures (John 1:3; 1 Cor. 8:6). The creaturely status of all finite beings and things reveals the sovereign rule of God and the dependence of man and the world on Him.

Man, the pinnacle of God's creation, was created to have dominion in the world (Gen. 1:26–28; Ps. 8:3–8). But man "exchanged the truth of God for the lie and worshiped and served the creature rather than the Creator" (Rom. 1:25). God's plan for man to rule His creation is now being fulfilled in Christ (1 Cor. 15:20–28; Phil. 2:5–11). He is establishing God's kingdom.

Redemption involves being made new creatures (2 Cor. 5:17), members of the new creation in Christ that God is bringing about through His power (Rom. 8:19). This universal kingdom of righteousness, peace, and joy will be fully revealed when Christ returns in triumph over all rebellious creatures and God creates a new heaven and earth (1 Cor. 15:20–28).

CREDITOR (see OCCUPATIONS AND TRADES).

CREED — a brief, authoritative, formal statement of religious beliefs. The word creed comes from the Latin word *credo* ("I believe"), the first word of both the Nicene Creed and the Apostles' Creed.

The following are the three classic, or most historically important, creeds of the church:

The Nicene Creed. A creed adopted by the First Council of Nicaea (A.D. 325) and revised by the First Council of Constantinople (A.D. 381). The First Council of Nicaea, convened by the Roman emperor Constantine the Great (ruled A.D. 306–337), rejected a heresy known as Arianism, which denied the divinity of Jesus. The Nicene Creed formally proclaimed the divinity and equality of Jesus Christ, the Son of God, in the Trinity.

The Athanasian Creed. A Christian creed originating in Europe in the fourth century and relating especially to the doctrines of the Trinity and the bodily INCARNATION of Christ. This creed was originally ascribed to Saint Athanasius (A.D. 293?–373), but it is now believed to be the work of an unknown writer of the time.

The Apostles' Creed. This well-known creed lies at the basis of most other religious statements of belief. Although it bears the name of the apostles, it did not originate with them. It was written after the close of the New Testament, and it held an important place in the early church. This creed has been appealed to by all branches of the church as a test of authentic faith.

Apostles' Creed

I believe in God the Father Almighty, Maker of heaven and earth.

And in Jesus Christ His only Son our Lord; who was conceived by the Holy Ghost, born of the Virgin Mary, suffered under Pontius Pilate, was crucified, died, and was buried. He descended into hell. The third day He rose again from the dead.

He ascended into heaven, and sitteth on the right hand of God the Father Almighty; from thence He shall come to judge the quick and the dead.

I believe in the Holy Ghost, the holy Catholic Church, the communion of saints, the forgiveness of sins, the resurrection of the body, and the life everlasting.

Nicene Creed

I believe in one God the Father Almighty, Maker of heaven and earth, and of all things visible and invisible.

And I believe in one Lord, Jesus Christ, the only-begotten Son of God, born of the Father before all ages. God of God, Light of Light, true God of true God; begotten, not made, of one substance with the Father. By whom all things were made. Who for us and for our salvation came down from heaven. And He became flesh by the Holy Spirit of the Virgin Mary and was made man. He was also crucified for us, suffered under Pontius Pilate, and was buried. And on the third day He rose again, according to the Scriptures. He ascended into heaven and sits at the right hand of the Father. He will come again in glory to judge the living and the dead. And of His kingdom there will be no end.

And I believe in the Holy Spirit, the Lord and Giver of life, who proceeds from the Father and the Son. Who together with the Father and the Son is adored and glorified, and who spoke through the prophets. And one holy, Catholic, and Apostolic Church. I confess one baptism for the forgiveness of sins. And I await the resurrection of the dead. And the life of the world to come. Amen.

Athanasian Creed

We believe and confess that our Lord Jesus Christ, the Son of God, is at once both God and Man. He is God of the substance of the Father, begotten before the worlds, and He is man, of the substance of his Mother, born in the world; perfect God; perfect man, of reasoning soul and human flesh consisting; equal to the Father as touching His Godhead; less than the Father as touching His manhood. Who, although He be God and man, yet He is not two, but is one Christ; one, however, not by change of Godhead into flesh but by taking of manhood into God; one altogether, not by confusion of substance, but by unity of person.

For as reasoning soul and flesh is one man, so God and man is one Christ; who suffered for our salvation, descended to the world below, rose again from the dead, ascended into heaven, and sat down at the right hand of the Father to come from thence to judge the quick and the dead. At whose coming all men shall rise again with their bodies, and shall give account for their own deeds. And they that have done good will go into life eternal; they that have done evil into eternal fire.

CREEPING THINGS — a phrase in the Bible that designates a teeming mass of miscellaneous animal life. It apparently refers to smaller mammals, reptiles, and insects. According to the Book of Genesis, God gave man dominion over birds, fish, and cattle as well as "every creeping thing" (Gen. 1:26). Also see ANIMALS OF THE BIBLE.

CRESCENS [KRESS enz] (*growing*) — a Christian mentioned by the apostle Paul (2 Tim. 4:10). For some reason, Crescens left Paul and departed for Galatia. Nothing else is known about him.

CRETANS [KREET uhns] — inhabitants of the island of CRETE in the Mediterranean Sea. The Book of Acts records that Cretans were among those present in Jerusalem on the Day of Pentecost (Acts 2:11). Cretan lifestyle was known for its excesses. In writing to Titus, Paul quoted from the Greek poet Epimenides of Knossos (about 600 B.C.) that "Cretans are always liars, evil beasts, lazy gluttons" (Titus 1:12). This must have presented a real challenge for Titus, who was assigned the responsibility to "set in order the things that are lacking" in the Cretan church (Titus 1:5).

CRETE [kreet] — an island in the Mediterranean Sea (see Map 7, C-2) where a ship on which the apostle Paul was sailing was struck by a storm. Crete is about 258 kilometers (160 miles) long and varies between 11 and 49 kilometers (7 and 30 miles) wide (Acts 27:7, 12–13, 21). It is probably to be identified with CAPHTOR (Deut. 2:23; Amos 9:7), the place from which the Philistines (Caphtorim) originated. A number of legends are associated with Crete, particularly those involving King Minos and the Minotaur (the half–bull, half-man monster).

The island was captured by the Romans in 68–66 B.C. and made a Roman province.

During his voyage to Rome, Paul's ship touched at Fair Havens, a harbor on the south coast of Crete (Acts 27:8). Not heeding Paul's advice about the weather, the Roman soldier who held Paul in custody agreed with the captain and set sail for Crete's large harbor at Phoenix. The result was a shipwreck at Malta (Acts 27:9—28:1).

Also see CRETANS.

CRIB — a feeding trough for livestock (Is. 1:3; manger, NIV, NASB; stall, NEB).

The central plain of the island of Crete, with the ruins of the royal palace of Knossos in the foreground.

Photo by Howard Vos

Photo by Gustav Jeeninga

Ruins of a church at Laodicea, showing engravings of two Latin crosses and the distinctive shape of a Greek cross in the foreground.

CRICKET (see ANIMALS OF THE BIBLE).

CRIME — any act forbidden by the civil law and punishable upon conviction. As used in the Bible, however, the word crime refers to any act against God's moral law as well as any transgression against God, or man, or both (Judg. 9:24; Ezek. 7:23; Acts 18:14). Specific crimes prohibited in the Bible include MURDER (Mark 15:7), theft (Josh. 7:21–25), LYING (Is. 28:15), FORNICATION (Gal. 5:19), and ADULTERY (Ex. 20:14).

CRIMINAL (see OCCUPATIONS AND TRADES).

CRIMINALS, TWO — two men who were crucified at the same time as Jesus, one on His right hand and the other on His left (Luke 23:32–33, 39). Other translations are malefactors (KJV) and criminals (NKJV, NIV, NASB, NEB, RSV). Apparently, these men not only broke the law but also were guilty of armed, violent rebellion against Roman rule.

CRIMSON (see COLORS OF THE BIBLE).

CRISPING PINS — KJV words for money bags (Is. 3:22, KJV; purses, NKJV, NIV; money purses, NASB; handbags, RSV).

CRISPUS [KRIS pus] (*curly*) — the ruler of the Jewish synagogue at Corinth who was converted to Christ (Acts 18:8) and personally baptized by the apostle Paul (1 Cor. 1:14).

CRITICISM (see BIBLICAL CRITICISM).

CROCODILE (see ANIMALS OF THE BIBLE).

CROCUS (see PLANTS OF THE BIBLE).

CROOKBACKED (see DISABILITIES AND DEFORMITIES).

CROP — a word in the Bible that means the gullet of a bird (Lev. 1:16), "to chop" or "pluck" (Ezek. 17:4, 22), and the harvest of a land (Ex. 9:32; Matt. 13:8, 26).

CROSS — an upright wooden stake or post on which Jesus was executed. Before the manner of Jesus' death caused the cross to symbolize the very heart of the Christian faith, the Greek word for cross referred primarily to a pointed stake used in rows to form the walls of a defensive stockade.

It was common in the biblical period for the bodies of executed persons to be publicly displayed by hanging them from the stakes of the stockade wall. This was done to discourage civil disobedience and to mock defeated military foes (Gen. 40:19; 1 Sam. 31:8–13). This gruesome practice may explain how the stake eventually came to be used as an instrument of civil and military punishment. Such stakes came to be used later with crossbeams as instruments of humiliation, torture, and execution for persons convicted as enemies of the state (foreign soldiers, rebels and spies, for example) or of civil criminals (such as robbers).

Usage in the Ancient World. During the Old Testament period, there is no evidence that the Jews fastened people to a stake or a cross as a means of execution. The Law directed death by stoning (Lev. 20:2; Deut. 22:24). But the Law did permit the public display (or "hanging") of a lawbreaker's body "on a tree" (Deut. 21:22) strictly commanding that the "body shall not remain overnight on the tree, but you shall surely bury him that day" (Deut. 21:23; also see John 19:31).

Grisly as such a practice seems today, it did set Israel apart from other nations. The degrading practice most often used throughout the ancient world was to allow the victim to rot in public. Persons so displayed (or "hanged") after execution by stoning for breaking Israel's Law were said to be "accursed of God." This helps explain the references to Jesus' being killed "by hanging on a tree" (Acts 5:30; 10:39) and the statement that Jesus was "cursed" in Galatians 3:13. Although Jesus died in a different manner, He was publicly displayed as a criminal and enemy of the state.

Ancient writers do not tell us much about how execution on a stake or cross was carried out. But excavated relief sculptures do show that the Assyrians executed their captured enemies by forcing their living bodies down onto pointed stakes. This barbaric cruelty was not crucifixion as we think of it today but impalement.

Scholars are not certain when a crossbeam was added to the simple stake. Jeremiah's mention of princes being "hung up by their hands" (Lam. 5:12) by the Babylonians may refer to the use of a crossbeam. But there is no way of knowing whether the prophet speaks of a method of execution or the dishonoring of bodies killed in battle. The classical Greek historians Herodotus and Thucydides refer to the stake or cross as a method of execution during the time of the Persians. But it is not clear whether the victim was tied or nailed to the wood or impaled.

Ezra 6:11 provides clear evidence that the Persians continued to use impalement as a method of execution. The references to "hanging" in Esther (2:23; 5:14) probably refer to either impalement or crucifixion. The "hangman's noose" was not commonly used in Persia during the biblical period. The word translated as gallows in the NKJV refers not to a scaffold for hanging with a rope, but a pole or stake.

Crucifixion on a stake or cross was practiced by the Greeks, notably Alexander the Great, who hung 2,000 people on crosses when the city of Tyre was destroyed. During the period between Greek and Roman control of Palestine, the Jewish ruler Alexander Jannaeus crucified 800 Pharisees who opposed him at Bethome. But these executions were condemned as detestable and abnormal by decent-minded people of Jannaeus's day as well as by the later Jewish historian, Josephus.

From the early days of the Roman Republic, death on the cross was used for rebellious slaves and bandits, although Roman citizens were rarely subjected to this method of execution. The practice continued well beyond the New Testament period as one of the supreme punishments for military and political crimes such as desertion, spying, revealing secrets, rebellion, and sedition. Following the conversion of the emperor Constantine to Christianity, the cross became a sacred symbol and its use by Romans as a means of torture and death was abolished.

Death on a Cross. Those sentenced to death on a cross in the Roman period were usually beaten with leather lashes—a procedure which often resulted in severe loss of blood. Victims were then generally forced to carry the upper crossbeam to the execution site, where the central stake was already set up.

After being fastened to the crossbeam on the ground with ropes—or, in rare cases, nails through the wrist—the naked victim was then hoisted with the crossbeam against the standing vertical stake. A block or peg was sometimes fastened to the stake as a crude seat. The feet were then tied or nailed to the stake.

The recent discovery near Jerusalem of the bones of a crucifixion victim suggests that the knees were bent up side-by-side parallel to the crossbeam and the nail was then driven through the side of the ankles. Death by suffocation or exhaustion normally followed only after a long period of agonizing pain.

The Shape of the Cross. In time the simple pointed stake first used for execution was modified. The four most important of the resulting crosses are: (1) the Latin cross (shaped like a lower case "t"), on which it seems likely that Jesus died for our sins, because of the notice placed above His head (Matt. 27:37); (2) the St. Anthony's cross, which has the crossbeam at the top (shaped like a capital "T"); (3) the St. Andrew's cross, which is shaped like a capital "X"; (4) the so-called Greek cross which has the crossbeam in the center (shaped like a plus sign).

Significance of the Cross. The authors of the gospels tell us that the Lord Jesus spoke of the cross before His death (Matt. 10:38; Mark 10:21; Luke 14:27) as a symbol of the necessity of full commitment (even unto death) for those who could be His disciples. But the major significance of the cross after Jesus' death and resurrection is its use as a symbol of Jesus' willingness to suffer for our sins (Phil. 2:8; Heb. 12:2) so that we might be reconciled (2 Cor. 5:19; Col. 1:20) to God and know His peace (Eph. 2:16).

Thus the cross symbolizes the glory of the Christian gospel (1 Cor. 1:17); the fact that through this offensive means of death (1 Cor. 1:23; Gal. 5:11), the debt of sin against us was "nailed to the cross" (Col. 2:14), and we, having "been crucified with Christ" (Gal. 2:20), have been freed from sin and death and made alive to God (Rom. 6:6–11).

The cross, then, is the symbol of Jesus' love, God's power to save, and the thankful believer's unreserved commitment to Christian discipleship. To those who know the salvation which Christ gained

Drawing: Gaalyah Cornfeld

This drawing of a crucifixion is based on the remains of a crucified man from the first century A.D. discovered in a cave in Jerusalem. Both of his feet had been pierced with a spike just below the heel.

for us through His death, it is a "wondrous cross" indeed.

Also see CRUCIFIXION OF CHRIST.

CROW (see ANIMALS OF THE BIBLE).

CROWN — special headgear used to symbolize a person's high status and authority. Several different words in the original Hebrew and Greek languages of the Bible are translated as crown. Persons in the Bible who are described as wearing crowns include Vashti (Esth. 1:11) and Esther (Esth. 2:17). The high priest and the king in the early history of the nation of Israel also apparently wore crowns as a mark of their office and authority (Lev. 8:9; 2 Sam. 1:10).

The wreath of leaves awarded the winner of an athletic competition in the Grecian games was also described by the apostle Paul as a crown (1 Cor. 9:25; 2 Tim. 4:8). The Roman soldiers mocked Jesus on the cross by placing a crown of thorns on His head, taunting Him as "King of the Jews" (Matt. 27:29; also Mark 15:17; John 19:2, 5).

The Book of Revelation portrays Christ with many crowns on His head, signifying His kingly authority (Rev. 19:12). Our inheritance as Christians who follow the will of our Lord is also described symbolically as a crown. As a reward for our faithfulness, we will receive an imperishable crown (1 Cor. 9:25), one that will not wither or fade away, and a crown of eternal life (James 1:12).

CROWN OF THORNS — a mock symbol of authority fashioned by the Roman soldiers and placed on Jesus' head shortly before His crucifixion (Matt. 27:29; Mark 15:17; John 19:2, 5). Crowns were symbols of honor and authority in the Greek and Roman worlds. Jesus' crown of thorns was probably meant to make Him an object of mockery and ridicule. "Hail, King of the Jews!" (Matt. 27:29; Mark 15:18; John 19:2) they scoffed, as they engaged in their cruel and brutal sport. But Jesus' love was so strong that He patiently endured this mockery to accomplish His mission on earth.

CRUCIFIXION OF CHRIST — the method of torture and execution used by the Romans to put Christ to death. At a crucifixion the victim usually was nailed or tied to a wooden stake and left to die.

Crucifixion was used by many nations of the ancient world, including Assyria, Media, and Persia. Alexander the Great of Greece crucified 2,000 inhabitants of Tyre when he captured the city. The Romans later adopted this method and used it often throughout their empire. Crucifixion was the Romans' most severe form of execution; so it was reserved only for slaves and criminals. No Roman citizen could be crucified.

Crucifixion involved attaching the victim with nails through the wrists or with leather thongs to a crossbeam attached to a vertical stake. Sometimes blocks or pins were put on the stake to give the victim some support as he hung suspended from the crossbeam. At times the feet were also nailed to the vertical stake. As the victim hung dangling by the arms, the blood could no longer circulate to his vital organs. Only by supporting himself on the seat or pin could the victim gain relief.

But gradually exhaustion set in, and death followed, although usually not for several days. If the victim had been severely beaten, he would not live this long. To hasten death, the executioners sometimes broke the victim's legs with a club. Then he could no longer support his body to keep blood circulating, and death quickly followed. Usually bodies were left to rot or to be eaten by scavengers.

To the Jewish people, crucifixion represented the most disgusting form of death: "He who is hanged is accursed of God" (Deut. 21:23). Yet the Jewish Sanhedrin sought and obtained Roman authorization to have Jesus crucified (Mark 15:13-15). As was the custom, the charge against Jesus was attached to the cross; He was offered a brew to deaden His senses, but He refused (Mark 15:23). There was no need for the soldiers to break His legs to hasten death. By the ninth hour (Mark 15:34, 37), probably 3:00 P.M.—in only six hours—Jesus was already dead (John 19:31-33). Jesus' body was not left to rot; the disciples were able to secure Pilate's permission to give Him a proper burial.

The cross has been a major stumbling block in the way of the Jews, preventing the majority of them from accepting Jesus as the MESSIAH. The apostle Paul summed up the importance of the crucifixion best: "We preach Christ crucified, to the

Photo by Gaalyah Cornfeld

The actual remains of the crucifixion victim discovered by archaeologists, with one spike driven through the victim's feet bones.

Jews a stumbling block and to the Greeks foolishness, but to those who are called, both Jews and Greeks, Christ the power of God and the wisdom of God" (1 Cor. 1:23–24). Out of the ugliness and agony of crucifixion, God accomplished the greatest good of all—the redemption of sinners.

Also see CROSS.

CRUSE [krooze] — KJV word for JAR or BOWL.

CRYSTAL (see JEWELS AND PRECIOUS STONES).

CUBIT (see WEIGHTS AND MEASURES).

CUCKOO (see ANIMALS OF THE BIBLE).

CUCUMBER (see PLANTS OF THE BIBLE).

CUD — partially digested food regurgitated from the first stomach of an animal and chewed again. The Hebrews were forbidden by the law of Moses from eating animals that chewed the cud (Lev. 11:3; Deut. 14:6).

CUDGEL (see ARMS, ARMOR OF THE BIBLE).

CUMI [KOO me] (see TALITHA CUMI).

CUMMIN (see PLANTS OF THE BIBLE).

CUN [kun] — a form of CHUN.

CUNEIFORM [kyu NAY uh form] (*wedge-shaped*) — a system of writing developed before 3000 B.C. in Mesopotamia (the lower Tigris and Euphrates Valley) probably by the Sumerians and then adopted and modified by the Akkadians, Hurrians, Hittites, and Elamites.

The wedge–shaped signs of cuneiform writing were carved on stone and metal or inscribed with a stylus on clay tablets. These clay tablets received the wedge-marks while soft and moist, but they became as hard as stone after they were dried in the sun or baked in a kiln. Thousands of such tablets were discovered by archaeologists at the ancient site of Ras Shamra, a Canaanite settlement.

Cuneiform was originally a pictographic form of writing, but it soon was used to signify syllables and consonants. Variations of cuneiform scripts were developed for Ugaritic (at Ras Shamra) and Old Persian writing.

Also see WRITING; WRITING MATERIALS.

CUP — a small container used for drinking water (Matt. 10:42), wine (Jer. 35:5), and other liquids. The cup is spoken of often in the Bible in a literal sense. Figuratively, the image of a cup also expresses several important ideas.

The cups described in the Bible may be of silver (Gen. 44:2, 12, 16–17) or gold (Jer. 51:7; Rev. 17:4) and have a decorated brim (1 Kin. 7:26; 2 Chr. 4:5). Kings had an official called a cupbearer (1 Kin. 10:5; 2 Chr. 9:4; Neh. 1:11) who prepared and handed him his drink (Gen. 40:11, 13, 21). His task was to sample the drink to make sure it contained no poison. Such an Assyrian official serving in a military capacity was called RABSHAKEH (2 Kin. 18:17; Is. 36:2).

According to the teachings of Jesus, the lowly service of giving a cup of cold water (Matt. 10:42; Mark 9:41) carries its reward. The "cup of consolation" is the drink shared with the grieving (Jer. 16:7). The "cup of blessing" (1 Cor. 10:16) refers to the cup over which a blessing is said.

For the wicked, the cup is a calamitous fate (Ps. 11:6; Ezek. 23:33). To experience the Lord's wrath is called drinking the cup of His wrath (Is. 51:17; Jer. 49:12). The Lord's judgment is spoken of as an intoxicating drink of wine from a cup, causing drunkenness and staggering (Ps. 75:8). The end of a nation comes by drinking this cup (Jer. 25:15, 17, 28; Lam. 4:21; Hab. 2:16). Babylon was the cup in the Lord's hand from which nations had to drink as she overran them (Jer. 51:7). But when the Lord finishes punishing Israel, He will take the cup of trembling from the hand (Is. 51:22). This figure of drinking the cup of the Lord's wrath is taken up in the New Testament to describe the punishment of the disobedient (Rev. 14:10).

The suffering and death of Jesus was His cup (Matt. 26:39–40; John 18:11). For Him, the endurance of suffering was to drink the cup (Matt. 20:22–23). But through this suffering, He provided a way for our salvation.

CUPBEARER (see OCCUPATIONS AND TRADES).

CURSE — a prayer for injury, harm, or misfortune to befall someone. Noah, for instance, pronounced a curse on Canaan (Gen. 9:25). Isaac pronounced a curse on anyone who cursed Jacob (Gen. 27:29). The soothsayer Balaam was hired by Balak, king of Moab, to pronounce a curse on the Israelites (Numbers 22—24). Goliath, the Philistine giant of Gath, "cursed David by his gods" (1 Sam. 17:43).

In Bible times, a curse was considered to be more than a mere wish that evil would befall one's enemies; it was believed to possess the power to bring about the evil the cursor spoke.

In the account of the temptation and Fall, God Himself is described as cursing the serpent (Gen. 3:14–15), as well as the ground (Gen. 3:17). Although the word curse is not used directly of Adam and Eve, the woman is sentenced to pain in childbirth and the man is condemned to earn his living by the sweat of his face. In the New Testament, Jesus cursed the fig tree, saying, " 'Let no fruit grow on you ever again.' And immediately the fig tree withered away" (Matt. 21:19; Mark 11:14). He also taught Christians how to deal with curses: "Bless those who curse you" (Luke 6:28).

The apostle Paul spoke of the law as a curse because it pronounces a curse upon everyone "who does not continue in all things which are written in

Gold cups discovered by archaeologists in tombs at the ancient city of Mycene on the island of Crete.
Photo by Howard Vos

Photo by Howard Vos

Ruins of a Greek gymnasium at the city of Salamis on the island of Cyprus. The apostle Paul visited Salamis on his first missionary journey (Acts 13:4-5).

the book of the law, to do them" (Gal. 3:10). By the grace of God, however, "Christ has redeemed us from the curse of the law, having become a curse for us (for it is written, 'Cursed is everyone who hangs on a tree')" (Gal. 3:13). John promised that the day is coming when "there shall be no more curse" (Rev. 22:3); all those whose names are written in the Lamb's Book of Life will enjoy the abundant blessings of God.

CURTAIN — a piece of cloth or similar material that acts as a decoration, shade, or screen. The inner part of the TABERNACLE (the Holy Place and the Holy of Holies) was made of ten blue, purple, and scarlet curtains (Ex. 26:1–13; 36:8–17). Eleven curtains made of goats' hair also covered the tabernacle.

Another curtain, or "veil," of blue, purple, and scarlet yarn and fine linen thread divided the Holy Place from the Holy of Holies (Ex. 26:31–33). Still another curtain of similar design functioned as a door to the tabernacle (Ex. 26:36–37).

In the New Testament the word curtain refers to the curtain of the Temple that covered the Holy of Holies, or Most Holy Place. This curtain was torn in two from top to bottom when Jesus died on the cross (Matt. 27:51; Mark 15:38; Luke 23:45; veil,

KJV, NKJV, NASB), symbolizing the opening of a new and living way to God (Heb. 6:19; 9:3; 10:20).

Also see VEIL.

CUSH [kush] (*black*) — the name of two men and two lands in the Old Testament:

1. A land that bordered the Gihon River, one of the four rivers of the Garden of Eden (Gen. 2:10–14). Since the Tigris (Hiddekel) and Euphrates are mentioned, this land must have been in or near Mesopotamia.

2. A son of Ham and grandson of Noah. His brothers settled in Egypt and Palestine and his famous son Nimrod lived in Mesopotamia (Gen. 10:6–12; 1 Chr. 1:8–10; also Mic. 5:6).

3. A man from the tribe of Benjamin who was an enemy of David (see the title of Psalm 7).

4. The land south of Egypt, also called Nubia, which includes part of the countries of Sudan and Ethiopia. Cush began just beyond Syene (modern Aswan; Ezek. 29:10). The Persian Empire of Ahasuerus (Xerxes, 486–465 B.C.) extended to this point, "from India to Ethiopia" (Esth. 1:1; 8:9). Precious stones came from Cush, "the topaz of Ethiopia" (Job 28:19), and the people were tall with smooth skin (Is. 18:2, 7) that could not be changed (Jer. 13:23). The prophets predicted that the distant

land of Cush would be judged by God (Is. 18:1–6; Zeph. 2:12). Other texts indicate, however, that some from Cush will bring gifts to God and worship Him as their king (Ps. 68:31; Is. 11:11; 18:7).

CUSHAN [KOO shan] (*belonging to Cush*) — a name referred to in Habakkuk 3:7. It is difficult to tell whether Cushan refers to a place (some suggest Ehtiopia, Mesopotamia, or the land of Midian) or to a person—perhaps the same as "Cushan-Rishathaim king of Mesopotamia" (Judg. 3:8, 10).

CUSHAN–RISHATHAIM [koo shan rish ah THAY im] (*double wickedness*) — a "king of Mesopotamia" who held Israel in bondage for eight years until its deliverance by Othniel (Judg. 3:8, 10).

CUSHI [KOO shy] (*black* or *Ethiopian*) — the name of two men in the Old Testament:
1. An ancestor of the Jehudi whom the Jewish leaders sent to ask Baruch to read the scroll of Jeremiah to them (Jer. 36:14).
2. A son of Gedaliah and the father of the prophet Zephaniah (Zeph. 1:1). Also see CUSHITE.

CUSHION (see PILLOW).

CUSHITE [KOO shyte] — a native or inhabitant of the ancient land of CUSH, identified by most scholars as Ethiopia, a country in northeastern Africa. Two people in the Bible are called "Cushites":
1. The wife of Moses (Num. 12:1, RSV). Some scholars, however, believe this usage of "Cushite" does not have to mean "Ethiopian" (KJV, NKJV); it also may refer to a person from northern Arabia.
2. A messenger sent by Joab to David to tell of his victory over Absalom (2 Sam. 18:21–23, 31–32; Cushi, KJV). He probably was an Ethiopian slave.

CUSTODIAN — RSV word for TUTOR.

CUTH, CUTHAH [kooth, KOO thuh] — a city of Babylonia, northeast of Babylon. When the king of Assyria conquered Israel, he deported the ten tribes of Israel and brought in colonists from Cuth (or Cuthah) to settle in Samaria (2 Kin. 17:24, 30).

CUTTINGS OF THE FLESH — the cutting of oneself during worship to attract the attention of the gods. This practice was strictly forbidden in ancient Israel: "You shall not cut yourselves nor shave the front of your head for the dead" (Lev. 19:28; 21:5; Deut. 14:1). A striking example of this pagan practice occurred during the ministry of the prophet ELIJAH. The priests of Baal "cut themselves...with knives and lances" (1 Kin. 18:28), but their pagan god paid no attention to their cries.
The folly of cutting one's flesh is that Jesus' body has already been sacrificed for us. Anything more would be an insult to the redemption He has already accomplished.

CYMBAL (see MUSICAL INSTRUMENTS).

CYPRESS (see PLANTS OF THE BIBLE).

CYPRUS [SIGH prus] — a large island in the northeastern corner of the Mediterranean Sea, about 97 kilometers (60 miles) off the coast of Syria and about 66 kilometers (41 miles) off the coast of Cilicia (modern Turkey; see Map 7, D–2). Although Cyprus is a rocky island, many nations sought its rich copper deposits and timber reserves (especially the cypress tree). Consequently, in the course of its history, Cyprus frequently was conquered by many powerful nations, including the Mycenaeans, Phoenicians, Assyrians, and Persians.
After Alexander the Great, the Egyptian Ptolemies controlled Cyprus until the Romans took it in 58 B.C. During the Roman period it was joined to the province of Cilicia, then made an independent imperial province; and in 22 B.C. it became a senatorial province, with a proconsul in charge at the capital city of Paphos.
The name Cyprus is not found in the Old Testament; but because extra–biblical texts refer to Alashiya as a primary source of copper, many believe that ELISHAH (Gen. 10:4; 1 Chr. 1:7; Ezek. 27:7) is Cyprus. KITTIM is another Old Testament name which may refer to Cyprus (Gen. 10:4; 1 Chr. 1:7). Another spelling is Chittim (Num. 24:24; Is. 23:1; Jer. 2:10, KJV).
The New Testament contains several references to Cyprus—all in the Book of Acts. Barnabas was a native "of the country of Cyprus" (Acts 4:36). The first Christians fled to Cyprus because of the persecution of the early church after the death of Stephen (Acts 8:1–4; 11:19–20). Barnabas, Mark, and Paul began their first missionary journey by stopping at Salamis, the largest city of Cyprus on the east coast of the island (Acts 13:4–5).
After the split between Paul and Barnabas, Barnabas took John Mark and returned to Cyprus to do missionary work there (Acts 15:39). Mnason, an early Christian, was from Cyprus (Acts 21:16). Later Paul sailed past the island (Acts 21:3; 27:4).

CYRENE [sigh RAY neh] — a city on the north coast of Africa founded by Dorian Greeks about 630 B.C. Cyrene was later the capital of the Roman province of Cyrenaica (ancient and modern Libya). Midway between Carthage and Alexandria—about 160 kilometers (100 miles) northeast of modern Benghazi—the city was built on a beautiful tableland nearly 610 meters (2,000 feet) above sea level.
Less than 16 kilometers (10 miles) from the sea, Cyrene attracted travelers and commerce of every kind. The city was renowned as an intellectual center; Carneades, the founder of the new Academy at Athens, and Aristippus, the Epicurean philosopher and friend of Socrates, were among its distinguised citizens. The city surrendered to Alexander the Great in 331 B.C. and passed into the hands of Rome in 96 B.C.
Although Cyrene is not mentioned in the Old Testament, it was an important city in New Testament times because of its large Jewish population. A Cyrenian named Simon was pressed into service to carry the cross of Jesus (Matt. 27:32; Mark 15:21; Luke 23:26). Cyrenians were present at Pen-

tecost (Acts 2:10) and were converted and subsequently scattered in the persecution that followed Stephen's death (Acts 11:19-20).

Once a very populous city, Cyrene declined for several reasons. In a Jewish revolt in A.D. 115-116, over 200,000 inhabitants of the city were killed in the rioting. A disastrous earthquake in A.D. 365 contributed to its further decline. With the Arab invasion of A.D. 642, the city came to an end. The site is now a wasteland occupied by Bedouins.

CYRENIUS [sigh REE nih us] — a form of QUIRINIUS.

CYRUS [SIGH russ] (meaning unknown) — the powerful king of Persia (559-530 B.C.), sometimes called "Cyrus the Great," who allowed the Jewish captives to return to their homeland in Jerusalem after he led the Persians to become the dominant nation in the ancient world. Within 20 years after becoming king of Persia, Cyrus had conquered the Medes, Lydians, and Babylonians (549, 547, and 539 B.C., respectively). He is praised most highly, in the Old Testament, in Isaiah 44:28 and 45:1, where he is called God's "shepherd" and His "anointed."

Cyrus first appears in the Old Testament in connection with the release of the Jewish captives (taken in the Babylonian captivity of Judah), when he proclaimed their return from CAPTIVITY (2 Chr. 36:22-23; Ezra 1:1-4). This restoration, which was highlighted by the rebuilding of the TEMPLE in Jerusalem, had been prophesied by Jeremiah (Jer.

29:10-14; also see Is. 44:28). The Book of Ezra contains a number of reports on the progress of the work related to the decree of Cyrus (Ezra 3:7; 4:3, 5; 5:13, 14, 17; 6:3, 14). The only other references to Cyrus occur in Daniel 1:21; 6:28; 10:1.

Cyrus was known in Persia as a wise and tolerant ruler. He was able to gain the goodwill of the varied ethnic and religious groups within his large empire, which extended from India to the western edge of Asia Minor (modern Turkey). The Old Testament describes him as chosen by the Lord God of Israel as the deliverer of His people. It was not that Cyrus became a follower of Israel's God; rather, he described himself as the one who received "all the kingdoms of the earth." He declared that God "commanded me to build Him a house at Jerusalem" (2 Chr. 36:23). The famous Cyrus Cylinder containing records of Cyrus' reign, revealed that Babylon's chief god, Marduk, had accepted Cyrus as "righteous prince," and had appointed him ruler "over the whole world."

Ezra 6:1-12 gives some idea of the careful organization carried out by Cyrus in relation to the rebuilding of the Jewish Temple in Jerusalem. Its dimensions and the materials and supplies required are carefully described, along with the specification of severe penalties for anyone who would change his orders regarding its construction.

Cyrus' reign ended in 530 B.C., when he was killed in battle. His tomb still stands at Pasargadae in southwestern Iran. He was succeeded by his son, Cambyses II.

D

DABAREH [DAB ah reh] — a form of DABERATH.

DABBASHETH [DAB bah shehth] (*camel hump*) — a border town of the tribe of Zebulun (Josh. 19:11; Dabbesheth, RSV).

DABBESHETH [DAB bah shehth] — a form of DABBASHETH.

DABERATH [DAB uh rath] (*pasture*) — a city of the tribe of Issachar assigned to the Levites (Josh. 19:12; 21:28; Dabareh, KJV; 1 Chr. 6:72). It is now identified as modern Daburiyeh at the northwest slope of Mount Tabor.

DAGGER (see ARMS, ARMOR OF THE BIBLE).

DAGON [DAY gun] (see GODS, PAGAN).

DAILY — occurring every day. The Israelite day lasted from one sunset to the next (Ex. 12:18). When Jesus said, "Give us this day our daily bread" (Matt. 6:11; Luke 11:3), he meant for us to trust God to provide for our needs every day.

DAILY OFFERING (see SACRIFICE).

DALAIAH [duh LIE ah] — a form of DELAIAH.

DALETH [DAH let] — the fourth letter of the Hebrew alphabet, used as a heading over Psalm 119:25–32. In the original Hebrew language, every line of these eight verses began with the letter daleth. Also see ACROSTIC.

DALMANUTHA [dal muh NEW thuh] — a place on the western shore of the Sea of Galilee (Mark 8:10). The parallel passage in Matthew 15:39 has Magdala (KJV, NKJV) or Magadan (RSV). Jesus came to this region after His miraculous feeding of the four thousand.

DALMATIA [dal MAY she uh] — a district of the Roman Empire north of Greece on the shore of the Adriatic Sea. The apostle Paul sent Titus to this mountainous region (2 Tim. 4:10), and Paul himself preached the gospel in Illyricum (Rom. 15:19), which was in roughly the same area as Dalmatia.

DALPHON [dal FON] (meaning unknown) — the second of the ten sons of Haman, who was the adviser to King Ahasuerus. All of Haman's sons were hanged like their father (Esth. 9:7).

DAMAGES (see LAW).

DAMARIS [DAM uh riss] (meaning unknown) — a woman of Athens converted as a result of Paul's sermon on Mars' Hill (Acts 17:34). The fact that she was singled out along with Dionysius the Areopagite, one of the court judges, may indicate she was a woman of distinction.

DAMASCENES [DAM uh scenes] (*belonging to Damascus*) — natives or inhabitants of Damascus, which is called "the city of the Damascenes" (2 Cor. 11:32).

DAMASCUS [duh MASS cuss] — the oldest continually–inhabited city in the world and capital of Syria (Is. 7:8), located northeast of the Sea of Galilee and Mount Hermon in northern Palestine (see Map 3, D–1).

Damascus was situated on the border of the desert at the intersection of some of the most important highways in the ancient Near Eastern world. Three major caravan routes passed through Damascus. Major roads extended from the city to the southwest into Palestine and Egypt, straight south to Edom and the Red Sea, and east to Babylon. Because of its ideal location, the city became a trade center. Its major exports included a patterned cloth called "damask" (Ezek. 27:18). Egypt, Arabia, and Mesopotamia, as well as Palestine, were some of the trade neighbors that made Damascus the "heart of Syria."

Damascus owed its prosperity to two rivers, the Abana and the Pharpar (2 Kin. 5:12). These rivers provided an abundant source of water for agriculture. The Syrian people were so proud of these streams that Naaman the Syrian leper almost passed up his opportunity to be healed when the prophet Elisha asked him to dip himself in the waters of the Jordan River in Israel. He thought of the Jordan as an inferior stream in comparison with these majestic rivers in his homeland (2 Kin. 5:9–14).

History. The founder of Damascus was Uz, grandson of Shem (Gen. 5:32; 6:10; 10:23). The Bible first mentions the city when Abraham traveled from Ur to Canaan, passing through Damascus on the way (Gen. 11:31; 12:4). Eliezer, Abraham's faithful servant, was from Damascus (Gen. 15:2).

Early Egyptian texts refer to Egypt's control over

Roman gate and entrance to the "street called Straight" in the ancient city of Damascus, Syria (Acts 9:10, 11).

Damascus, but this influence did not last long. The establishment of Syria (Aram) as a powerful state with Damascus as its capital (1 Kin. 11:23–25) took place shortly after David's rule over the United Kingdom of the Hebrew people. David defeated the Syrians and stationed his own troops in Damascus (2 Sam. 8:5–6; 1 Chr. 18:5–6). During Solomon's reign, however, God allowed Rezon, Solomon's enemy, to take Syria from Israel's control because of Solomon's sins. Rezon founded a powerful dynasty based in Damascus that lasted more than 200 years.

Shortly after Solomon's death, the king of Damascus formed a powerful league with other Aramean states. This alliance resulted in many years of conflict between Israel and Damascus. First, Ben-Hadad of Damascus defeated King Baasha of Israel (1 Kin. 15:16–20; 2 Chr. 16:1–4). Later, God miraculously delivered King Ahab of Israel and his small army from the superior Syrian forces (1 Kin. 20:1–30).

Even after this miraculous deliverance, Ahab made a covenant with Ben-Hadad II against God's will (1 Kin. 20:31–43). Ahab was killed a few years later in a battle with Syria (1 Kin. 22:29–38).

In the midst of these wars, the prophet Elijah was instructed by God to anoint Hazael as the new king of Damascus (1 Kin. 19:15). King Joram of Israel successfully opposed Hazael for a time (2 Kin. 13:4–5), but the situation was eventually reversed. Hazael severely oppressed both Israel and Judah during later years (2 Kin. 13:3, 22).

Much later, God sent Rezon II, king of Syria, and Pekah, king of Israel, against wicked King Ahaz of Judah (2 Kin. 16:1–6). Ahaz called on the Assyrians, who had become a powerful military force, for help (2 Kin. 16:7). The Assyrian King Tiglath-Pileser responded by conquering Syria, overthrowing the Aramean dynasty, killing Rezon II, and destroying Damascus, just as the prophets Amos and Isaiah had prophesied (Is. 17:1; Amos 1:4–5). This marked the end of Syria as an independent nation. The city of Damascus was also reduced to a fraction of its former glory.

The exact date of the reconstruction of Damascus is unknown, but such an excellent location could not long remain weak and insignificant. Damascus was the residence of Assyrian and Persian governors for five centuries after its conquest by Tiglath-Pileser. Still later, the city was conquered by Alexander the Great, who made it a provincial capital. In 64 B.C. the Romans invaded Syria, making it a province with Damascus as the seat of government.

All references to Damascus in the New Testament are associated with the apostle Paul's conversion and ministry. During this time, the city was part of the kingdom of Aretas (2 Cor. 11:32), an Arabian prince who held his kingdom under the Romans. The New Testament reports that Paul was converted while traveling to Damascus to persecute early Christians who lived in the city (Acts 9:1–8). After his dramatic conversion, Paul went to the house of Judas, where God sent Ananias, a Christian who lived in Damascus, to heal Paul of his blindness (Acts 9:10–22).

Paul preached boldly in the Jewish synagogues in

An altar for pagan worship at the city of Dan. Portions of the altar were constructed by King Ahab of Israel.

Damascus, but eventually he was forced to flee the city because of the wrath of those to whom he preached. The governor of Damascus tried to capture Paul, but the apostle escaped in a large basket through an opening in the city wall (Acts 9:25; 2 Cor. 11:32–33).

Little physical change has taken place in the city of Damascus since biblical times. The long streets are filled with open–air markets that sell the same type of ancient wares. But modern Damascus does show the strong influence of Muslim culture. The most important building in Damascus is the Great Mosque, a Moslem shrine built during the eighth century A.D. on the site of a former Christian church.

DAMN, DAMNATION (see CONDEMN, CONDEMNATION).

DAN [dan] (*a judge*) — the name of a man and a city in Israel named after him:

1. The fifth son of Jacob and the first born to Rachel's handmaid Bilhah (Gen. 30:1–6). Dan had one son—Hushim (Gen. 46:23), or Shuham (Num. 26:42). Jacob's blessing of Dan predicted:

Dan shall judge his people
As one of the tribes of Israel.
Dan shall be a serpent by the way,
A viper by the path,
That bites the horse's heels,
So that its rider shall fall backward (Gen. 49:16–17).

Nothing else is known of Dan himself.

2. A city in the northern territory of the tribe of Dan, identified as the modern ruin or archaeological site known as Tell el–Qadi (see Map 3, C–1). This city was located further north than any other village in Palestine during much of the Old Testament period. This explains the phrase, "from Dan to Beersheba" (Judg. 20:1), used to describe the entire territory of the Israelites from north to south.

DAN, CAMP OF — the name of two separate places in the Old Testament:

1. A place in southern Palestine where members of the tribe of Dan camped before settling permanently further to the north (Judg. 18:12).

2. A place "between Zorah and Eshtol" (Judg. 13:25) where God's Spirit stirred SAMSON before he became a judge among the Hebrew tribes.

DAN, TRIBE OF — the tribe of Dan, descended from the son of Jacob. This tribe never lived up to its promise. The area allotted to Dan included the towns of Aijalon, Ekron, Eltekeh, and Zorah in the west central part of Canaan (Josh. 19:40–46; 21:5, 23–24) and stretched to Joppa on the Mediterranean Sea. The Danites, however were unable to conquer much of the territory assigned to them. The original inhabitants, the Amorites, kept the Danites confined to the hill country of Ephraim and Benjamin. Unable to conquer their allotted territory, some members of the tribe of Dan migrated far to the northernmost area of the Promised Land and conquered the isolated city of LAISH, which they renamed Dan. The tribe's one glorious moment occurred when the mighty Danite SAMSON judged Israel (Judg. 13—17).

Apparently, Dan was among the tribes that were the least supportive of the Israelite tribes. The Song of Deborah, which celebrates the Israelite victory over the Canaanite king Jabin and his mighty general Sisera, reproves the tribes of Gilead, Dan, and Asher. Of Dan, Deborah asked: "And why did Dan remain on ships?" (Judg. 5:17). Dan's apparent lack of interest in assisting the other tribes suggests that Dan, situated on Israel's northernmost border, had more in common with its foreign neighbors to the north than with Israel's other tribes.

The exclusion of the tribe of Dan from the sealing of the twelve tribes (Rev. 7:5–8) should not be overlooked. It appears that Dan had been cut off from the other tribes of Israel. However, Ezekiel prophesied a "portion for Dan" (Ezek. 48:1).

DANCER (see OCCUPATION AND TRADES).

DANCING — rhythmic movement of the body, usually done to musical accompaniment. Among the Jews, dancing generally occurred among women, either singly or in groups. It was a way of celebrating joyous occasions. Indeed, dancing became a symbol of joy, the opposite of mourning (Ps. 30:11; Eccl. 3:4; Luke 15:25).

The Bible gives several examples of dancing. Groups of women danced at celebrations of military victories (1 Sam. 18:16). The dancing of the virgins at Shiloh was probably part of a religious celebration (Judg. 21:19–23). Occasionally, children imitated the dance in their play (Job. 21:11; Matt. 11:17).

The Bible also gives a well-known example of a man dancing. Wearing a linen ephod (the outer garment worn by priests), David "danced before the Lord with all his might" (2 Sam. 6:14) when the ARK OF THE COVENANT was brought up to Jerusalem from the house of Obed-Edom.

Dancing by the Israelites was usually accompanied by the rhythmic beating of timbrels—or tambourines (Judg. 11:34). On great national occasions, Israel also praised the Lord with stringed instruments, flutes, and cymbals (Ps. 150:4). Men and women never danced together. Even on those occasions where both sexes participated in the sacred professional dances, they always danced separately (Ps. 68:25; Jer. 31:13). Dancing for sensual entertainment was unheard of among the Hebrews.

Salome's infamous dance, which won her John the Baptist's head on a platter, was in the tradition of Greek dancing, a sensual art form rather than an act of worship (Matt. 14:6).

DANIEL [DAN yuhl] (*God is my judge*) — the name of three men in the Bible:

1. A son of David and Abigail (1 Chr. 3:1). He is also called Chileab (2 Sam. 3:3).

2. A priest of the family of Ithamar who returned with Ezra from the Captivity (Ezra 8:2). Daniel sealed the covenant in the days of Nehemiah (Neh. 10:6).

3. A prophet during the period of the Captivity of God's Covenant People in Babylon and Persia (Dan. 1:6—12:9; Ezek. 14:14, Matt. 24:15). Daniel also wrote the book in the Old Testament that bears his name.

Daniel was a teenager when he was taken from Jerusalem into captivity by the Babylonians in 605 B.C. He was in his 80s when he received the vision of the prophecy of the 70 weeks (Daniel 9). In more than 60 years of his life in Babylon, Daniel faced many challenges. But in all those years, he grew stronger in his commitment to God.

We know very little about Daniel's personal life. His family history is not mentioned, but he was probably from an upper-class family in Jerusalem. It seems unlikely that Nebuchadnezzar, the king of Babylon, would have selected a trainee for his court from the lower classes. Neither do we know whether Daniel married or had a family. As a servant in Nebuchadnezzar's court, he may have been castrated and made into a EUNUCH, as was common in those days. But the text does not specify that this happened. It does indicate that Daniel was a person of extraordinary abilities.

We tend to think of Daniel as a prophet because of the prophetic dimension of his book. But he also served as an advisor in the courts of foreign kings. Daniel remained in governmental service through the reigns of the kings of Babylon and into the reign of Cyrus of Persia after the Persians became the dominant world power (Dan. 1:21; 10:1).

Daniel was also a person of deep piety. His book is characterized not only by prophecies of the distant future but also by a sense of wonder at the

Egyptian dancers and musicians practice their skills, in this carving from a temple of Queen Hatshepsut at Karnak, Egypt.

presence of God. From his youth Daniel was determined to live by God's law in a distant land (see Daniel 1). In moments of crisis, Daniel turned first to God in prayer before turning to the affairs of state (2:14–23). His enemies even used his regularity at prayer to trap him and turn the king against him. But the grace of God protected Daniel (chap. 6).

After one of his stunning prophecies (chap. 9), Daniel prayed a noble prayer of confession for his own sins and the sins of his people. This prayer was based on Daniel's study of the Book of Jeremiah (Dan. 9:2). He was a man of true devotion to God.

So the Book of Daniel is more than a treasure of prophetic literature. It also paints a beautiful picture of a man of God who lived out his commitment in very troubled times. We should never get so caught up in the meanings of horns and beasts that we forget the human dimension of the book— the intriguing person whose name means "My God is Judge."

Also see DANIEL, BOOK OF.

DANIEL, APOCRYPHAL ADDITIONS TO (see APOCRYPHA).

DANIEL, BOOK OF — a major prophetic book of the Old Testament that emphasizes the truth that God is in control of world history. The book is named for Daniel, its author and central personality, who was rescued miraculously from a den of lions after he refused to bow down and worship a pagan king.

Structure of the Book. Daniel's 12 chapters may be divided naturally into three major sections: (1) introductory information about Daniel (chap. 1); (2) narratives about Daniel and his friends during their days of captivity among the Babylonians and the Persians (chaps. 2—7); and (3) Daniel's dreams and visions concerning the future of Israel and the end of time (chaps. 8—12).

The first chapter sets the stage for the rest of the book by introducing Daniel and his three friends, Hananiah, Mishael, and Azariah. These four young Hebrew men were taken captive in one of the Babylonian raids against Judah in 605 B.C. Intelligent and promising, they were placed in special training as servants in the court of King Nebuchadnezzar; then their names and diets were changed to reflect Babylonian culture in an attempt to take away their Jewish identity. But Daniel and his friends rose to the challenge, proving their Jewish food was superior to the diet of the Babylonians. The young men increased in wisdom and knowledge, gaining favor in the king's court.

In the second major section of the book (chaps. 2—7), Daniel and his friends met several additional tests to prove that although they were being held captive by a pagan people, the God whom they worshiped was still in control. Daniel's three friends (renamed Shadrach, Meshach, and Abed-Nego) refused to worship the pagan Babylonian gods. Cast into the fiery furnace, they emerged unharmed because of God's miraculous protection.

Daniel, refusing to bow down and worship Darius, the king of Persia, was also thrown into a den of lions. But he was also saved by God's direct intervention. These tests proved that the God whom they served was superior to the pagan gods of their captors.

Daniel's skill as an interpreter of dreams is also well established in this second section of his book. He interpreted several visions and dreams for King NEBUCHADNEZZAR of Babylon and his successor, BELSHAZZAR. As he revealed the meaning of the mysterious "handwriting on the wall," he made it plain that the Babylonian Empire would be defeated by the Medes and the Persians. This happened exactly as Daniel predicted (5:13–31), and he continued as a servant in the court of the conquering Persian king.

The final section of Daniel's book (chaps. 8—12) consists of a series of visions about succeeding kingdoms and the end of time. These visions came to the prophet during his years in captivity. Standing by the Tigris River in one of these visions, he saw a goat attack a ram. The goat symbolized the Persians, who would defeat the Babylonians. This goat had several different horns, representing the Greek Empire that would rise after the decline of the Persians and the subsequent division of the Greek Empire among the four generals of ALEXANDER the Great.

Daniel had another unusual look into the future known as the SEVENTY WEEKS PROPHECY. In this vision, the angel Gabriel revealed to Daniel that the nation of Israel would be restored to its homeland after their period of captivity. This would be followed many years later by the coming of the Messiah and then, finally, the final judgment and the end of time.

Daniel's spectacular book closes with a vision of the final judgment, when the righteous will receive everlasting life and the wicked will receive God's condemnation. But not even Daniel was blessed with perfect understanding of this mystery of the ages. "My Lord, what shall be the end of these things?" (12:8), he asked. To this God replied, "Go your way, Daniel, for the words are closed up and sealed till the time of the end" (12:9).

Authorship and Date. Most conservative scholars believe the Book of Daniel was written by the prophet and statesman of that name who lived as a captive of Babylon and Persia for more than 50 years after he was taken into captivity in 605 B.C. But this theory is rejected by some scholars, who object to the specific details of the prophetic visions that Daniel records.

Daniel predicted that the empires of Babylon and Persia, for example, would be succeeded by the Greeks under Alexander the Great. He also foresaw that the Greek Empire would be divided among the four generals of Alexander upon his death. Daniel also predicted that the Jewish people would suffer great persecution under an official who would come into power some time after Alexander's death.

Most interpreters identify this ruler, who would "destroy the mighty, and also the holy people" (8:24) as Antiochus Epiphanes, the Greek ruler of Syria. Antiochus persecuted the Jewish people unmercifully from 176–164 B.C. because of their refusal to adopt heathen religious practices. According to this line of thinking about Daniel and his prophecies, the book was written not by Daniel the prophet but by an unknown author about 400 years later than Daniel's time. This anonymous writer, according to this theory, wrote the book during the persecution of Antiochus Epiphanes to give the Jewish people renewed hope and religious zeal as they stood against their oppressors. Daniel's prophecies, according to these critics, are not "prophecies" at all, but were written after these events and were attributed to Daniel to show that these great events of world history would eventually happen.

Those who attack the authenticity of the Book of Daniel do not have enough evidence to support their charge. The speculation that it was written by zealous Jews to mobilize their countrymen in opposition to ANTIOCHUS Epiphanes is far-fetched and unconvincing. There's no valid reason to abandon the traditional view that it was written by the prophet Daniel. According to evidence in the book itself, Daniel's captivity lasted from the time of Nebuchadnezzar's reign in Babylon (1:1–6) into the reign of Cyrus of Persia (10:1), about 536 B.C. He must have written his book some time during this period or shortly thereafter.

Historical Setting. The Book of Daniel clearly belongs to that period among God's Covenant People known as the Babylonian CAPTIVITY. Nebuchadnezzar took captives from Judah on three separate occasions, beginning in 605 B.C. Among this first group taken were Daniel and his companions. Their courageous acts must have been a great enouragement to the other captives.

DANIEL: A Teaching Outline

Part One: The Personal History of Daniel (1:1–21)

Part Two: The Prophetic Plan for the Gentiles (2:1—7:28)

Daniel's own interest in the forthcoming close of the captivity is supported by his prophecy in chapter 9. His prayer to God is dated at 538 B.C., the very year that Cyrus of Persia issued his decree making it possible for some of the captives to return to Jerusalem to restore their land and rebuild the Temple (Ezra 1:1-4). The fact that some did choose to return may be a tribute to the effectiveness of Daniel's book. He wrote it to show that God was in charge of world history and that He had not yet finished with His Covenant People.

Theological Contribution. The major contribution of the Book of Daniel arises from its nature as apocalyptic prophecy. Highly symbolic in language, the prophecy was related to the events of Daniel's near future, but even today it contains a message for the future.

In apocalyptic prophecy, these close-at-hand and further-removed dimensions of the future often blend into each other. An example of this is the figure of Antiochus Epiphanes, prominent in chapters 8 and 11 of the book. In these passages the prophet Daniel moves from the nearer figure, who was to desecrate the Jewish Temple in 168 B.C., to his appearance at a remote time in the future as the Antichrist (8:23-26; 11:36-45; Rev. 13:1-10). This interplay between the near future and the distant future makes it difficult to interpret the book correctly.

In addition to its prophetic contribution, the Book of Daniel portrays a time in biblical history when miracles were abundant. Other periods when miracles were commonplace included the times of Moses, Elijah, Elisha, Jesus Christ, and the early church. In each of these periods, God was working in a spectacular manner to show His power and bring about a new era in His saving relationship to mankind.

Special Considerations. Chapter 9 of Daniel is a fascinating passage; it combines the best of biblical piety and biblical prophecy. Daniel's study of the prophecy of the 70 years of captivity from the prophet Jeremiah (Jeremiah 25) led him to pray for God's intervention on behalf of His people. He called on God to shorten the time of their grief (9:1–19). The Lord's answer came through the angel Gabriel, who gave Daniel the prophecy of the Seventy Weeks, or 70 sevens (9:20–27). The 70 sevens as envisioned by the prophet are usually interpreted as years. Thus, the prophecy deals with the next 490 years in the future of God's Covenant People. These 490 years are divided into three groups: 7 weeks (49 years), 62 weeks (434 years), and 1 week (7 years).

Various methods have been used to calculate these periods of years in this prophecy. Here's a general scheme of how it may be done:

During the first seven weeks (49 years), the returned exiles will complete construction of the city of Jerusalem.

The passing of the next 62 weeks (434 years) will mark the time for the cutting off of the Messiah (9:26).

The final or 70th week will bring the making and breaking of a covenant by a mysterious prince and the time of the ABOMINATION OF DESOLATION (9:27).

These verses contain a full scheme for the history of Israel from Daniel's time to the age of the Messiah. During the first period, the city of Jerusalem will be rebuilt. Then the Messiah will come, but He is destined to be cut off by a mysterious "people of the prince who is to come" (9:26). This prince will have authority during the final period; but his rule will then end, and God's purposes for His people will be realized.

Some scholars believe the 70 weeks or 490 years of this prophecy began with the decree of Ezra 7:11–26, in 458 B.C., when some of the exiles returned to rebuild the city of Jerusalem. They also believe the first 69 weeks (483 years) of this prophecy end roughly at the time of the beginning of the ministry of Christ, in A.D. 26. Others follow a more complex scheme and argue that the beginning point is the order of King Artaxerxes to Nehemiah in Nehemiah 2:5–8, which places the return of some of the exiles at 445 B.C. In this view, the first 69 weeks, or 483 years, of Daniel's prophecy end at the time of the triumphal entry of Jesus into Jerusalem.

Perhaps the round numbers in this prophecy (70 sevens) should be our clue that it is dangerous to try to pin its fulfillment to a specific day or year. But we can say for sure that the end of the 483 years spoken of by Daniel would bring us to the general period of the ministry of the Lord Jesus Christ. The final week in the prophecy is symbolic of the age between the ASCENSION of Jesus and His SECOND COMING. This part of Daniel's prophecy is yet to be fulfilled in the future TRIBULATION described so graphically in the Book of Revelation.

Also see APOCALYPTIC LITERATURE; DANIEL.

DANITES [DAN ites] — members of the tribe of Dan. David's army at Hebron included 28,600 Danites (1 Chr. 12:35). Also see DAN.

DAN JAAN [dan JAY un] (meaning unknown) — a town in northern Palestine visited by Joab as he took the census of Israel and Judah, which was ordered by King David (2 Sam. 24:6). The place may have been a suburb of Dan, located between Gilead and Sidon. Some scholars believe Dan Jaan is a textual corruption of "Dan and Ijon" ("Dan and Iyyon," NEB). Other versions render the text, "To Dan, and from Dan."

DANNAH [DAN nah] (*stronghold*) — a village in the hill country of Judah between Socoh and Kirjath Sepher (Josh. 15:49). Some writers identify it with modern Deir esh-Shemesh or Simya.

DARA [DARE uh] (*pearl of wisdom*) — a son of Zerah, of the tribe of Judah (1 Chr. 2:6). Also see DARDA.

DARDA [DAR duh] (*pearl of wisdom*) — a wise man with whom Solomon was compared (1 Kin. 4:31). He may have been the same as Dara (1 Chr. 2:6). As one of the "sons of MAHOL," Darda was a member of the musical guild.

DARIC [DARE ick] — a gold Persian coin used by the Jewish people (1 Chr. 29:7; drams, KJV). The name probably comes from the Persian King DARIUS I. The daric may also have been a unit of weight. Ezra spoke of 20 gold basins "worth" (or perhaps weighing) 1,000 darics each (Ezra 8:27, RSV, NIV, NASB).

DARIUS [duh RYE us] (meaning unknown) — the name of several kings of ancient Persia:

1. Darius I, the Great, who reigned from about 522 to 485 B.C. He was one of the most able Persian kings, and is also known as Darius Hystaspis, or Darius, son of Hystaspis.

Darius spent the first three years of his reign putting down rebellions in the far-flung regions of his empire. After he had secured his power, he divided the empire into 29 satrapies, or provinces, each ruled by Persian or Median nobles. He made SHUSHAN, or Susa, his new capital and created a code of laws similar to the Code of HAMMURABI; this code of Darius was in effect throughout the Persian Empire.

An effective organizer and administrator, Darius developed trade, built a network of roads, established a postal system, standardized a system of coinage, weights, and measures, and initiated fabulous building projects at Persepolis, Ecbatana, and Babylon.

Darius continued Cyrus the Great's policy of restoring the Jewish people to their homeland. In 520 B.C., Darius' second year as king, the Jews resumed work on the still unfinished Temple in Jerusalem. Darius assisted with the project by ordering it to continue and even sending a generous subsidy

Tombs of Darius I and Artaxerxes I at the royal city of Persepolis in ancient Persia.

to help restore worship in the Temple (Ezra 6:1–12). The Temple was completed in 515 B.C., in the sixth year of Darius' reign.

The final years of Darius' reign were marked by clashes with the rising Greek Empire in the western part of his domain. He led two major military campaigns against the Greeks, both of which were unsuccessful.

2. Darius II Ochus, the son of Artaxerxes I, who ruled over Persia from about 424 to 405 B.C. He was not popular or successful, and he spent much time putting down revolts among his subjects. His rule was marked by incompetence and misgovernment. Darius II may be the ruler referred to as "Darius the Persian" (Neh. 12:22).

3. Darius III Codomannus, the king of Persia from 336 to 330 B.C. This Darius is probably the "fourth" king of Persia mentioned by the prophet Daniel (Dan. 11:2). Darius III underestimated the strength of the army of ALEXANDER the Great when the Macedonians invaded Persia. He was defeated by Alexander in several major battles. He attempted to rally the eastern provinces of his empire, but he was hunted down in 330 B.C. and assassinated by his own followers. For all practical purposes, these events brought the Persian Empire to an end and marked the beginning of the period of Greek dominance in the ancient world.

4. Darius the Mede, successor of Belshazzar to the throne of Babylon (Dan. 5:31). He is called the "son of Ahasuerus, of the lineage of the Medes" (Dan. 9:1). Darius the Mede has not been identified

with certainty; he is not mentioned by Greek historians or in any Persian literature.

Darius the Mede was the Persian king who made Daniel a governor, or ruler, of several provincial leaders (Dan. 6:1–2). Daniel's popularity with his subjects caused the other governors and the satraps under them to become jealous of Daniel and to plot against him. It was Darius the Mede who had Daniel thrown into the den of lions (Dan. 6:6–9), but who ultimately issued a decree that all in his kingdom "must tremble and fear before the God of Daniel" (Dan. 6:26).

Much confusion and mystery have clouded the identity of Darius the Mede. Some scholars have denied the existence of such a ruler, concluding that the writer of the Book of Daniel was historically inaccurate in saying that Darius the Mede was the person who "received the kingdom" (Dan. 5:31) when Belshazzar, king of the Chaldeans, was slain. Persian cuneiform inscriptions show that Cyrus II ("the Great") was the successor of Belshazzar.

One possible answer to this problem is that "Darius the Mede" was an alternative title used by the writer of the Book of Daniel for Cyrus the Persian (Cyrus II, the Great). Indeed, in Daniel 11:1, the SEPTUAGINT—the Greek translation of the Old Testament—has Cyrus instead of Darius. Thus, a quite legitimate translation of Daniel 6:28 might read: "Daniel prospered during the reign of Darius, that is, the reign of Cyrus the Persian" (NIV, margin). Such a logical and reasonable interpretation silences the skepticism about this passage in the Book of Daniel.

DARKNESS — the absence of light. Darkness existed before the light of creation (Gen. 1:2). Since darkness was associated with the chaos that existed before the creation, it came to be associated with evil, bad luck, or affliction (Job 17:12; 21:17). Darkness was also equated with death. In SHEOL, the land of the dead, there is only darkness (Job 10:21–22; 38:17). Darkness symbolizes man's ignorance of God's will and, thus, is associated with sin (Job 24:13–17).

Darkness also describes the condition of those who have not yet seen the light concerning Jesus (John 1:4–5; 12:35; Eph. 5:14) and those who deliberately turn away from the light (John 3:19–20). Hating the light will bring condemnation (Col. 1:13; 2 Pet. 2:17). Living in extreme darkness describes those who at the end of time have not repented (Rev. 16:10; 18:23).

DARKON [DAR kahn] (*bearer* or *carrier*) — a servant of Solomon whose descendants returned to the land of Israel after the Captivity (Ezra 2:56; Neh. 7:58).

DART (see ARMS, ARMOR OF THE BIBLE).

DATHAN [DAY thun] (*strong*) — a chief of the tribe of Reuben who, along with Korah and others, tried to overthrow Moses and Aaron (Numbers 16; Deut. 11:6; Ps. 106:17). He and his conspirators and their households were swallowed up by the earth (Num. 16:31–33).

DAUGHTER — the female offspring of a husband and wife. The term daughter is also used in the Bible to designate a step–sister, niece, or any female descendant (Gen. 20:12; 24:48). Sometimes the word is used in an even more general sense to refer to the female branch of a family or the female portion of a community, as in "the daughters of Levi" (Num. 26:59). Also see FAMILY.

DAVID [DAY vid] (*beloved*) — second king of the United Kingdom of the Hebrew people, ancestor of Jesus Christ, and writer of numerous psalms. The record of David's life is found in 1 Samuel 19—31; 2 Samuel 1—24; 1 Kings 1—2; and 1 Chronicles 10—29.

David as a Youth. David's youth was spent in Bethlehem. The youngest of eight brothers (1 Sam. 16:10, 11; 17:12–14), he was the son of Jesse, a respected citizen of the city. His mother was tenderly remembered for her godliness (Ps. 116:16; 86:16). As the youngest son, David was the keeper of his father's sheep. In this job he showed courage and faithfulness by killing both a lion and a bear which attacked the flock.

As a lad, he displayed outstanding musical talent with the harp, a fact which figured prominently in his life. When Saul was rejected by God as king, the prophet Samuel went to Bethlehem to anoint David as the future king of Israel. Apparently, there was no public announcement of this event, although David and his father surely must have been aware of it.

David's Service Under Saul. King Saul, forsaken by God and troubled by an evil spirit, was subject to moods of depression and insanity. His attendants advised him to secure a harpist, whose music might soothe his spirit. David was recommended for this task. As harpist for Saul, David was exposed to governmental affairs, a task that prepared him for

Oasis at En Gedi where David hid from King Saul during his years as a fugitive (1 Sam. 23:29; 24:1).

Photo by Howard Vos

his later service as king of Israel. Apparently, David did not remain with Saul all the time, since the Bible indicates he returned to Bethlehem to continue caring for his father's sheep.

During one of these visits to his home, the PHILISTINES invaded the country and camped 24 kilometers (15 miles) west of Bethlehem. Saul led the army of Israel to meet the enemy. Three of David's brothers were in Saul's army, and Jesse sent David to the battle area to inquire about their welfare. While on this expedition, David encountered the Philistine giant, GOLIATH.

David as Warrior. Goliath's challenge for a Hebrew to do battle with him stirred David's spirit. Weighted with heavy armor, Goliath was equipped to engage in close-range combat. David's strategy was to fight him at a distance. Taking five smooth stones from a brook, David faced Goliath with only a sling and his unflinching faith in God. Goliath fell, struck by a stone from David's sling. For this feat, he became a hero in the eyes of the nation. But it aroused jealousy and animosity in the heart of Saul. Saul's son, JONATHAN, however, admired David because of his bravery, and they soon became good friends. This friendship lasted until Jonathan's death, in spite of Saul's hostility toward David.

Saul had promised to make the victor in the battle with Goliath his son-in-law, presenting one of his daughters as his wife. He also promised to free the victor's family from taxation. But after the battle, David was no longer allowed to return occasionally to his father's house. He remained at Saul's palace continually. Perhaps Saul realized that Samuel's prediction that the kingdom would be taken from him could reach fulfillment in David. On two occasions, he tried to kill David with a spear; he also gave his daughter, whom he had promised as David's wife, to another man. As David's popularity grew, Saul's fear increased until he could no longer hide his desire to kill him. David was forced to flee with Saul in pursuit.

David as Fugitive Hero. David gathered a handful of fugitives as his followers and fled from Saul. On at least two occasions, David could have killed Saul while the king slept, but he refused to do so. Perhaps David hesitated to kill Saul because he realized that he would be king one day, and he wanted the office to be treated with respect. If he had killed Saul, David also would have entered the office of king through his own personal violence. Perhaps this was a situation he wanted to avoid.

When the Philistines battled Saul and his army at Gilboa, they were victorious, killing Saul and his son, Jonathan, whom David loved as a dear friend. When David heard this news, he mourned their fate (2 Samuel 1).

David as King of Judah. At Saul's death the tribe of Judah, to whom David belonged, elected him as king of Judah and placed him on the throne in HEBRON. The rest of the tribes of Israel set up ISHBOSHETH, Saul's son, as king at Mahanaim. For the next two years civil war raged between these two

The Citadel or "Tower of David" in the Old City section of Jerusalem.

factions. It ended in the assasination of Ishbosheth, an event which saddened David.

David as King of All Israel. On the death of Ishbosheth, David was elected king over all the people of Israel. He immediately began work to establish a United Kingdom. One of his first acts as king was to attack the fortified city of Jebus. Although the inhabitants thought it was safe from capture, David and his army took it by storm. He then made it the capital city of his kingdom and erected his palace there. Also known as JERUSALEM, the new capital stood on the border of the southern tribe of Judah and the other tribal territories to the north. This location tended to calm the jealousies between the north and the south, contributing greatly to the unity of the kingdom.

After establishing his new political capital, David proceeded to re-establish and strengthen the worship of God. He moved the ARK OF THE COVENANT from Kirjath Jearim (Josh. 15:9) and placed it within a tabernacle which he pitched in Jerusalem. Next, he organized worship on a magnificient scale and began plans to build a house of worship. But God brought a halt to his plans, informing David that the building of the Temple would be entrusted to his successor.

Although David was a righteous king, he was subject to sin, just like other human beings. On one occasion when his army went to battle, David stayed home. This led to his great sin with BATHSHEBA. While Uriah, the Hittite, Bathsheba's husband, was away in battle, David committed adultery with her. Then in an effort to cover his sin, he finally had Uriah killed in battle. David was confronted by the prophet NATHAN, who courageously exposed his wrongdoing. Faced with his

The mound of Gibeah, where David allowed several of Saul's descendants to be executed and displayed in humiliation because of Saul's slaughter of the Gibeonites (2 Sam. 21:1-9).

sin, David repented and asked for God's forgiveness. His prayer of forgiveness is recorded in Psalm 51.

Although God forgave David of this act of adultery, the consequences of the sin continued to plague him. The child born to David and Bathsheba died. The example he set as a father was a bad influence on his sons. One son, Amnon, raped and humiliated his half-sister. Another son, ABSALOM, rebelled against David and tried to take away his kingdom by force.

One of David's deep desires was to build a temple in Jerusalem. But he was prevented from doing so. The prophet Nathan informed David that he should not build the temple because he had been a warrior. David did not build the temple, but he did gather material for the temple to be built later. It was Solomon, David's son and successor, who finally erected the first temple in Jerusalem.

David died when he was 71 years old, having been king for a total of over 40 years, including both his reign in Hebron and his kingship over the United Kingdom.

David as Psalmist. Early in his life David distinguished himself as the "sweet psalmist of Israel" (2 Sam. 23:1). Many of the psalms in the Book of Psalms are attributed to him.

David's fondness for music is recorded in many places in the Bible. He played skillfully on the harp (1 Sam. 16:18-23). He arranged worship services in the sanctuary (1 Chr. 6:31). He composed psalms of lament over Saul and Jonathan (2 Sam. 1:17-27). His musical activity was referred to by Amos (Amos 6:5), Ezra (Ezra 3:10), and Nehemiah (Neh. 7:24, 46).

David as Ancestor to Jesus Christ. Jesus was referred to as the Son of David. The genealogy of Jesus as recorded in the Gospels of Matthew and Luke traced Jesus back through the ancestry of David. God promised David a kingdom that would have no end. This prophecy was fulfilled in Jesus, who came to establish the Kingdom of God. Jesus was born in Bethlehem because this was the "city of David" (Luke 2:4), David's birthplace and boyhood home.

Although David committed deep sin, he still was known as a man who sought God's will. Certainly he was not perfect, but he was willing to repent of his wrongdoing and to follow God's leadership. His influence for good in the life of his nation was great, since every king after David was compared to the standard which he established.

A capable musician, David unquestionably gave great encouragement to this fine art in the life of his people. As a warrior and military man, he was resourceful and courageous. As a king, he was without equal in the life of his nation. As a religious leader, he was exceptional. Many of his writings will continue to be the favorite devotional literature for honest souls who seek a closer walk with God.

The Jewish historian Josephus praised David by saying, "This man was of an excellent character, and was endowed with all the virtues that were desirable in a king." But even higher praise came from God Himself through the speech of Stephen in the Book of Acts. Stephen quoted the Lord as declaring, "I have found David the son of Jesse a man after my own heart" (Acts 13:22).

DAVID, CITY OF — the name of two cities in the Bible:

1. The name given to Jebus or Zion, the fortified city of the Jebusites, after its capture by David's army (2 Sam. 5:6-9; 1 Chr. 11:4-7). David then moved his royal capital from HEBRON to his newly acquired stronghold, and it became known as the city of David. The city of David was a portion of the southeastern hill of Jerusalem, a triangular hill

wedged between the Tyropoeon and the Kidron Valleys. The "City of David" is mentioned often in the Old Testament (1 Kin. 3:1; 2 Kin. 8:24; 2 Chr. 5:2).

2. The town of BETHLEHEM in Judea, the birthplace of Jesus. Bethlehem is called the city of David (Luke 2:4, 11) because it was David's birthplace and boyhood home (1 Sam. 17:12). Jesus was born in Bethlehem, fulfilling the prophecy that the Messiah would spring from the line of David (Jer. 33:15–17). Bethlehem is about 10 kilometers (6 miles) south of Jerusalem.

Also see ZION.

DAVID, TOWER OF — a phrase in the Song of Solomon that probably refers to some fortress or fortified area of Jerusalem built by King David (Song 4:4; armoury, KJV; arsenal, RSV).

DAWN, DAWNING — the first appearance of light in the morning as the sun rises (Job 7:4; Is. 58:10; Acts 27:33). Matthew's account of the resurrection of Christ begins with these words: "Now after the Sabbath, as the first day of the week began to dawn, Mary Magdalene and the other Mary came to see the tomb" (Matt. 28:1). Matthew also quotes the prophet Isaiah, using the figure of the dawn as the beginning of a wonderful new era of hope and promise: "The people who sat in darkness saw a great light" (Matt. 4:16).

DAY — the 24–hour period between two successive risings of the sun. The Hebrew people reckoned their day from evening to evening, the period of time between two successive sunsets (Gen. 1:5, 8; Ex. 12:18; Lev. 23:32).

The Bible also uses the word day in a symbolic sense, as in "the day of His wrath" (Job 20:28), and "the day of the Lord" (Is. 2:12; 13:6, 9; Amos 5:18–20). The same phrase is used in the New Testament (1 Thess. 5:2; 2 Pet. 3:10), meaning "the day of the Lord Jesus" (1 Cor. 5:5), or His second coming. To those who scoff at the delay of the Lord's return, Peter declared, "With the Lord one day is as a thousand years, and a thousand years as one day" (2 Pet. 3:8). Also see TIME.

DAY OF ATONEMENT (see FEASTS AND FESTIVALS).

DAY OF CHRIST, THE — the period at the end of time when Jesus will return to claim faithful believers and members of His church as His own (1 Cor. 1:8; 5:5; 2 Cor. 1:14; Phil. 1:10). A related concept, DAY OF THE LORD, focuses on God's judgment against unbelievers. Also see ESCHATOLOGY.

DAY OF JUDGMENT (see ESCHATOLOGY).

DAY OF THE LORD, THE — a special day at the end of time when God's will and purpose for mankind and His world will be fulfilled. Many Bible students believe the Day of the Lord will be a long period of time rather than a single day—a period when Christ will reign throughout the world before He cleanses heaven and earth in preparation for the eternal state of all mankind. But others believe the Day of the Lord will be an instantaneous event when Christ will return to earth to claim His faithful believers while consigning unbelievers to eternal damnation.

Amos 5:18–20 is probably the earliest occurence in Scripture of the phrase, "Day of the Lord." According to Amos, that day would be a time of great darkness for any in rebellion against God, whether Jew or Gentile. The day would be a time of judgment (Is. 13:6, 9; Jer. 46:10), as well as restoration (Is. 14:1; Joel 2:28–32).

Also see DAY OF JESUS CHRIST.

DAY'S JOURNEY (see WEIGHTS AND MEASURES).

DAYSMAN — KJV word for MEDIATOR (Job 9:33).

DAYSPRING — a poetic way of speaking of the dawn. The term is also used figuratively to refer to Jesus as the Messiah who is the light to those who sit in darkness (Luke 1:78–79).

DEACON — a servant or minister; an ordained lay officer in many Christian churches.

The general concept of deacon as a servant of the church is well established in both the Bible and church history. But the exact nature of the office is hard to define, because of changing concepts and varying practices among church bodies through the centuries. Another problem is that the Bible passages associated with deacons are interpreted differently by various church groups.

The term deacon occurs in only two passages in the NKJV (Phil. 1:1; 1 Tim. 3:8–13). But the Greek word diakonos from which it is taken is found 30 times. In most cases diakonos is translated as "servant" rather than "deacon." In the Greek world, diakonos was used to describe the work of a servant—a person who waited on tables or ministered as a religious official. When the office of deacon was established in the New Testament church, it may have paralleled the function of the Jewish synagogue assistant—an official who took care of the administrative needs of the assembly.

The origin of the office of deacon is usually related to the events described in Acts 6:1–6. The young Christian church in Jerusalem was experiencing growing pains, and it had become increasingly difficult for the apostles to distribute charitable gifts to its needy members without neglecting their ministry of prayer and preaching. The widows of Greek or Gentile background complained to the apostles that they were not getting their just share of food and money. To meet this critical need, seven men were chosen by the congregation and presented to the apostles (Acts 6:1–6). Although these men were not called deacons at that time, the Greek word used to describe their work comes from the same Greek root word.

While these "table servers" were appointed to relieve an emergency and their assignment may sound somewhat menial, these men possessed the very highest moral and spiritual credentials. They are described as "men of good reputation, full of the Holy Spirit and wisdom" (Acts 6:3). They were formally installed or commissioned in a service of prayer and the LAYING ON OF HANDS by the apostles (Acts 6:6)—a practice regarded as the scriptural precedent for the ordination of deacons as church officials.

As a result of the selection of these seven men, harmony was restored in the congregation and the church continued to grow in number and spirit (Acts 6:5, 7). The later evangelistic work of two of these original "deacons," Stephen and Phillip, serves as a role model for the spiritual ministry of deacons today.

The list of qualifications for deacons given in 1 Timothy 3 shows that this servant of the church was to be equipped for a spiritual ministry to serve with the bishop or pastor: "Likewise deacons must be reverent, not double-tongued, not given to much wine, not greedy for money, holding the mystery of the faith with a pure conscience. But let these first be proved; then let them serve as deacons being found blameless" (1 Tim. 3:8-10).

The deacon was expected to have an exemplary home life (3:11, 12), to be a proven leader, and to possess flawless character.

The work of Stephen and Phillip strongly suggests that gifted deacons became a permanent part of the church's outreach to the world very early in its history. The thrilling activities of these servants of the church sound much like the work of a traveling evangelist, missionary, or lay preacher. Stephen is described as a man "full of faith and power" who "did great wonders and signs among the people" (Acts 6:8). So convincing were his words and miracles that "they were not able to resist the wisdom and Spirit by which he spoke" (Acts 6:10). While some responded in faith, Stephen's zeal for Christ stirred up powerful enemies (Acts 6:11-13). Undaunted by false witnesses, Stephen glorified the Lord even as he was put to death for his convictions (Acts 7:59-60). Phillip was also an evangelist who "preached the things concerning the kingdom of God and the name of Jesus Christ" (Acts 8:9-13). After preaching to eager crowds in Samaria, Phillip witnessed to a solitary Ethiopian in the desert and baptized him (Acts 8:26-38).

In the early years of the church, a difference of opinion arose about the role of deacons. Some church officials argued that no spiritual function had been assigned to deacons. But others insisted that deacons were a vital part of a church's ministry, with official duties to perform. Through the centuries deacons generally have served as assistants to the clergy in the service of the sanctuary.

In the modern church deacons exist as a distinct lower order of the clergy in the Roman Catholic, Church of England, Episcopal, United Methodist, and other liturgical churches. In other denominations, including Baptist, Presbyterian, and Congregational, deacons are ordained laymen who carry out a variety of practical and spiritual ministries that assist the pastor. Deacons are often given administrative and financial duties, such as reviewing

Photo by Howard Vos

An elaborate sarcophagus, or coffin, at the city of Tyre, dating from the Roman period.

budgets and recommending new church programs and personnel.

In some churches, each deacon is assigned "spiritual oversight" of several families in the congregation. The deacon keeps in close touch with the families in his charge to make certain they are involved in church life and are ministered to promptly at times of special need.

Paul wrote that the reward for faithfulness in the office of deacon is that they "obtain for themselves a good standing and great boldness in the faith which is in Christ Jesus" (1 Tim. 3:13). The selfless deacon may also feel close kinship with his Master, who walked the earth as "One who serves" (Luke 22:27). According to Jesus, the true heroes in the kingdom of God are those who assume the role of *diakonos*—a servant (Matt. 20:26).

Also see DEACONESS.

DEACONESS — a female believer serving in the office of DEACON in a church.

The only New Testament reference to deaconess as a church office is Paul's description of Phoebe as a deaconess of the church in Cenchrea (Rom. 16:1, RSV). The Greek word translated as deaconess in this passage is rendered as deacon and servant by other versions of the Bible. The office of deaconess was similar to the office of deacon. Their spiritual responsibility was essentially the same, except that deaconesses probably rendered a ministry exclusively to women, particularly in the early years of the church.

The office of deaconess became a regular feature of church organization as early as the first part of the second century. In A.D. 112, Pliny the Younger, governor of Bithynia, wrote a letter to the emperor

Trajan of Rome, indicating that in his investigation of Christians he had tortured two Christian maidens who were called deaconesses. The office of deaconess in the Eastern Church continued down to the 12th century. The widows of clergymen, who were not permitted to remarry, often served as deaconesses. Some scholars believe that Paul's standards for WIDOWS in 1 Timothy 5:9–12 were applied to these deaconesses.

No qualifications for the office of deaconess are specifically given in the New Testament. But tradition indicates that piety, discretion, and experience were required of deaconesses.

While controversy has centered around the ordination of women through the centuries, deaconesses apparently were installed in their office by the LAYING ON OF HANDS, just like deacons. However, there is no account of a deaconess ordination in the Bible. Church groups with both deacons and deaconesses customarily ordain women in the same manner as men. In the United States the office of deaconess is most prominent today among Lutherans, Episcopalians, United Methodists, Presbyterians, American Baptists, and in certain Reform bodies.

In the early centuries, deaconesses were especially called on to serve women in situations where custom forbade the ministry of the deacon. Deaconesses instructed female candidates for church membership, ministered to women who were sick and in prison, and assisted at their baptism, especially in the act of anointing. Through the years deaconesses have been assigned various types of educational, charitable, and social service work in their churches and communities. Deaconesses have traditionally served as doorkeepers in some churches. They may be seen frequently today as ushers and lay readers.

Also see DEACON.

DEAD, THE — those no longer alive; the deceased. The ancient Hebrews thought of the deceased as going to SHEOL, the abode of the dead, a netherworld where the dead have a shadowy existence. Apparently at death, according to the Old Testament view, even believers in God went to Sheol.

This belief would explain the view, prevalent in the early church, that Christ at His death descended into Sheol (Greek, *hades*) to bring the Old Testament believers to heaven with Him (1 Pet. 3:18–20).

Death is introduced in Genesis 2:17. God created man to live forever, both physically and spiritually. By man's disobedience, however, death became his lot (Rom. 5:12). The day Adam ate the forbidden fruit, he did not die physically but lived on and reached the age of 930 years (Gen. 5:5). However, with that act of disobedience he died spiritually and was separated from God's fellowship (Gen. 3:24). When the breath leaves the body, the body is dead. When man sins, he is separated from God and he becomes dead spiritually.

The Bible speaks of both types of death. Those outside of Christ are alive physically, but they are spiritually dead—"dead in trespasses and sins" (Eph. 2:1).

The Bible also speaks of eternal, or everlasting, death. Those who persist in their unbelief remain forever in spiritual death—eternal separation from God—which Scripture calls the "second death" (Rev. 2:11; 21:8).

Also see HELL.

DEAD, ABODE OF (see HELL).

DEAD, BAPTISM (see BAPTISM FOR DEAD).

DEAD SEA — a salt sea in southern Palestine (see Map 9, C–4) at the lowest point on earth. In the Old Testament it is called the Salt Sea (Gen. 14:3; Josh. 3:16); the Sea, or Plain, of Arabah (Deut. 3:17); and the East Sea (Ezek. 47:18; Joel 2:20). Josephus, the Jewish historian, referred to this bouyant body as Lake Asphaltitis. The Arabic name is

The Dead Sea, situated at the lowest point on earth, has a high salt content and no natural outlet.

Bahr Lut, meaning, "Sea of Lot." But from the second Christian century onward, Dead Sea has been the most common name for this unusual body of water.

The topography of the Middle East is dominated by a geologic fault that extends from Syria south through Palestine, all the way to Nyasa Lake in east–central Africa. The Dead Sea is located at the southern end of the Jordan valley at the deepest depression of this geologic fault. With a water level approximately 390 meters (1,300 feet) below sea level, the surface of the Dead Sea is the lowest point on earth. At the deepest point of the sea, on the northeast corner at the foot of the Moab mountains, the bottom is 390 meters (1,300 feet) deeper still.

The dimensions of the sea change from year to year. Many factors, such as rainfall and irrigation, contribute to this. In general, however, the Dead Sea measures approximately 80 kilometers (50 miles) in length and averages 15 to 16 kilometers (9 to 10 miles) in breadth, yielding a surface area of from 600 to 640 square kilometers (350 to 400 square miles).

A large peninsula known as El-Lisan ("the Tongue") protrudes into the sea from the southeast shore. It extends to within 3 kilometers (2 miles) of the western shore and is located some 24 kilometers (15 miles) from the southern tip. Throughout the centuries this tongue separated the sea into two parts with a channel of water flowing between them on the west. From the depths of the northeast corner, the bottom of the sea quickly shelves and rises southward. Thus the area of the sea south of El-Lisan is extremely shallow. It is here that the destroyed cities of Sodom and Gomorrah most probably lie (Gen. 19:24–29).

Except on the north where the Jordan River enters, the Dead Sea is nearly surrounded by hills and cliffs. From these hills, streams feed fresh water to the Salt Sea. In addition to these year–round streams and the Jordan River, waters flow into the sea from the winter torrents of several seasonal streams.

These water sources pour millions of gallons of water each day into the Dead Sea. However, the extreme hot temperatures and sparse rainfall (about two inches a year) cause an enormous evaporation rate which has kept the water level constant over the years. Due to the increased irrigation by the Israeli government, the volume of water flowing into the Dead Sea from the Jordan River is decreasing each year. Thus the level of the sea goes down proportionately. As a result, "the Tongue" currently stretches all the way across the sea, completely separating the northern portion from the southern portion. Evidence of a Roman road across the peninsula has been discovered, indicating that at other periods in its history the Dead Sea was shallow enough for traffic to cross its southern tip.

Because the Dead Sea has several watercourse entrances but no exits, it is indeed a "dead" sea. Although lush vegetation can be found at the mouths of these tributaries, the water itself is very salty. This is because it flows through nitrous soil and is fed by sulphurous springs. With the absence of an outlet, the water from the Dead Sea is left to evaporate, leaving behind most of its minerals. Thus it contains a very large supply of potash, bromine, magnesium chloride, salt, and other minerals. Although the value of these chemicals is enormous, making the Dead Sea the richest mineral deposit on earth, the cost of retrieving these minerals is also high. Potash extraction has been one of the most successful operations. But as technology increases, the interest in "mining" the Dead Sea will also increase.

The salt and mineral content of the Dead Sea constitutes more than twenty–five percent of the water. This compares with about six percent mineral content in the ocean. The specific gravity of the water is greater than that of the human body, making it next to impossible for any person to sink in the Dead Sea.

The Dead Sea formed part of Israel's eastern border (Num. 34:12; Ezek. 47:18). In addition to the destruction of Sodom and Gomorrah, many other historical and biblical events occurred along its shores. The springs of EN GEDI provided a refuge for David in his flight from King Saul (1 Sam. 24:1). In the Valley of Salt south of the sea, David and Amaziah won victories over the Edomites (1 Chr. 18:12; 2 Kin. 14:7). Here, too, Jehoshaphat encountered the Edomites (2 Chr. 20:1–2; 2 Kin. 3:8–9). The last days of Herod the Great were spent on the eastern shore of the Dead Sea at the hot sulphur springs of Callirhoe. At Machaerus, just to the southeast, his son Herod Antipas imprisoned John the Baptist.

The prophet Ezekiel (Ezek. 47:1–12) saw a vision of a river issuing from the Temple sanctuary in Jerusalem and flowing to the desert sea, the Dead Sea. And the prophet Zechariah wrote: "And in that day it shall be that living waters shall flow from Jerusalem, half of them toward the eastern sea [the Dead Sea] and half of them toward the western sea [the Mediterranean Sea]" (Zech. 14:8). Prophetically this is apparently a reference to the "pure river of water of life" said to flow from the throne of God in John's vision (Rev. 22:1–2).

The great fortress of Masada guarded the southern approaches toward Palestine, perhaps the road crossing from Moab to Judea at El-Lisan. Herod refortified this strong fortress, which finally fell in A.D. 73 to the Romans under Flavius Silva. He also refortified the Maccabean stronghold at Machaerus on the eastern shore.

The discovery of the DEAD SEA SCROLLS in caves on the northwest shore of the Dead Sea near QUMRAN has mustered renewed historical interest in this area. The remains of the ESSENE community at Qumran and the search for scrolls in the more than 250 surrounding caves focused the eyes of the world on a tiny sea devoid of marine life but bristling with mineral potential and archaeological promise.

Photo by John Trever

Interior of Cave 4 at Qumran. The archaeologist stands in a passageway to a lower room, where the thousands of manuscript fragments were stored.

This cave at Qumran, designated as Cave 4 by archaeologists, contained thousands of manuscript fragments.

DEAD SEA SCROLLS — the popular name for about 500 scrolls and fragments of scrolls which were found in 11 caves surrounding Khirbet ("ruin of") Qumran on the northwest shore of the Dead Sea in 1947 and shortly thereafter. Taken together, these leather and PAPYRUS (primitive paper) manuscripts were a find without precedent in the history of modern archaeology. The Dead Sea Scrolls have helped scholars to: (1) establish the date of a stabilized Hebrew Bible as no later than A.D. 70; (2) reconstruct the history of the Holy Land from the fourth century B.C. to A.D. 135; and (3) clarify the relationship between Jewish religious traditions and early Christianity.

The Dead Sea Scrolls were discovered when a Bedouin shepherd, who was looking for a stray goat, discovered several large clay pots containing ancient scrolls on the floor of a cave above Wadi Qumran. After some delay, several scholars were shown the manuscripts by dealers in antiquities. When it was determined that these manuscripts were extremely old, scholars began their search in earnest. Slowly other valuable scrolls were found, gathered, carefully unrolled, and published. It took 20 years (1947–1967) to bring together the various texts of the Dead Sea Scrolls. Because the Scrolls were written between 250 B.C. and A.D. 68, they offer an invaluable source for understanding the beliefs, community life, and use of the Bible of one group of Jews who were active during the time Jesus lived. Jericho, a town Jesus visited, is only 13 kilometers (8 miles) north of Khirbet Qumran. Some scholars believe that some of the early followers of Jesus or John the Baptist may have come from the Qumran Community. Some of the writ-

ings of this community remind the reader of the themes of "repentance" and the "coming of the new age" that were preached by John the Baptist and Jesus. However, there is no evidence that the followers of John or Jesus joined the Qumran group.

The writings are the work of Jewish sectarians, written mainly in Hebrew, with a few in Aramaic and some fragments in Greek. Some of the scrolls were written to protest the lawless priest who was in charge of the Temple worship in Jerusalem. It is likely that the main reason for building this monastic–like community near the Dead Sea was to get away from the "wicked priest" and to hear the words of the "teacher of righteousness." Not all of the Dead Sea Scrolls have been translated or published. Probably the most interesting ones were found in Cave I not far from Qumran. Seven scrolls were found preserved in fairly good condition. They had been carefully stored in large clay jars and include:

1. A complete manuscript of the Book of Isaiah in Hebrew.

2. A partial manuscript of Isaiah in Hebrew. (The two Isaiah scrolls are easy to read, even after 1920 years, and are the earliest copies of Isaiah in existence.)

3. *The Community Rule*, or *The Manual of Discipline*, from Cave I, reveal the laws that governed the life of the Qumran community.

4. *The Thanksgiving Psalms* are similar to the biblical psalms. They praise God the Creator for His protection against evil: "I give thanks unto thee, O Lord, for Thou hast put my soul in the bundle of life and hedged me against all the snares of corruption."

Photo by John Trever

The desolate wilderness of the Qumran area, with the Dead Sea in the background. Several of the caves where the manuscripts were found are situated in the cliffs in the center of the photo.

5. *The War Scroll* is an interesting collection of plans for the final battle between the "sons of light" and the "sons of darkness," or between the "army of God" and the "army of Belial" (the Evil One). Such information as that of religious offices during wartime, recruitment, the sequence of campaigns, and the order of deploying battle squadrons is included.

6. A commentary on the Book of Habakkuk known as the *Pesher on Habakkuk* was written to demonstrate how the prophet Habakkuk, who lived in the sixth century B.C., was actually writing for the battle of the last days, when the wicked would be defeated by the righteous. The author of the *Pesher on Habakkuk* made direct references from Habakkuk to his own day. One section has the following commentary: "And God told Habakkuk to write down that which would happen to the final generation, but He did not make known to him when time would come to an end. And as for that which He said, 'That he who reads may read it speedily' (Hab. 2:2); interpreted, this concerns the Teacher of Righteousness, to whom God made known all the mysteries of the words of His servants the prophets."

7. *The Genesis Apocryphon*, a "commentary" on the Book of Genesis, is only partially preserved. Written around 50 B.C. in Aramaic, the common language of the Jews, it begins with the birth of Noah and documents the life and adventures of Abraham.

These seven manuscripts are typical of the scrolls found in the other caves on the west side of the Dead Sea. The material discovered includes various kinds of literature. There are numerous biblical fragments, such as commentaries on Isaiah, Hosea, Micah, Nahum, Habakkuk, Psalm 37, Psalm 45, and Genesis. Twenty-four books of the Old Testament were found in part or in full.

Apocryphal (see APOCRYPHA) and pseudepigraphal (see PSEUDEPIGRAPHA) writings were found scattered in various caves. Fragments of Tobit and Ecclesiasticus from the Apocrypha give evidence of the importance of these works for the community. The Book of Jubilees, the Book of Enoch, some of the Testament of the Twelve Patriarchs, the Sayings of Moses, the Vision of Amram, the Psalms of Joshua, the Prayer of Nabonidus, and the Book of Mysteries are a few of the pseudepigraphal works discovered. A number of hymns or psalms that were found and are included in this category are: The Hymn of the Initiates, The Book of Hymns (The Thanksgiving Hymns), Psalm 151, Poems from a Qumran Hymnal, Lament for Zion, and Hymns of Triumph.

The writings which were found can be listed under the following categories:

Biblical Manuscripts: Isaiah Scroll (complete), Exodus, Leviticus, Numbers, and Deuteronomy.

Commentaries: Genesis Apocryphon, Job, Isaiah, Hosea, Micah, Habakkuk, Psalm 37, and Psalm 45.

Apocrypha: Epistle to Jeremiah, Tobit, and Ecclesiasticus.

Pseudepigrapha: Book of Jubilees, Book of Enoch, and The Testament of the Twelve Patriarchs (fragments).

Previously Unknown Pseudepigrapha: Sayings of Moses, Vision of Amram, Psalms of Joshua, Daniel cycle (The Prayer of Nabonidus), and Book of Mysteries.

Community Documents: The Manual of Discipline, Damascus Document, Thanksgiving Psalm, and War Scroll.

The examples listed here are meant to be suggestive, and not exhaustive, of the archaeological finds. Other manuscripts discovered in the Judean Wilderness, for instance, deal with a later era.

DEAF, DEAFNESS (see DISEASES OF THE BIBLE; DISABILITIES AND DEFORMITIES).

DEATH — a term which, when applied to the lower orders of living things such as plants and animals, means the end of life. With reference to human beings, however, death is not the end of life. The Bible teaches that man is more than a physical creature; he is also a spiritual being. For man, therefore, physical death does not mean the end of existence but the end of life as we know it and the transition to another dimension in which our conscious existence continues.

The Bible speaks of death in a threefold way: physical, spiritual, and eternal. The first physical death of a human being recorded in the Bible is that of Abel, who was murdered by his brother Cain (Gen. 4:8). However, death itself, in both the physical and spiritual sense, is first mentioned by God Himself (Gen. 2:17). In the Genesis account of the FALL both physical and spiritual death come as a result of sin (Rom. 5:12–21).

Various attitudes toward death are expressed in the Bible, from dread to anticipation. The ancient Hebrews regarded death as entrance into SHEOL, where they were cut off from everything dear in life, including God and loved ones. But God revealed to the psalmist that the Redeemer God is both in heaven and in Sheol (Ps. 139:7–8), and He is able to bring a person out of Sheol ("the grave"; 1 Sam. 2:6).

Because "all have sinned and fall short of the glory of God" (Rom. 3:23), all men are spiritually dead—separated from God who is the Source of spiritual life. Sin makes a person hate the light and despise the truth; it causes one to break God's laws and to become insensitive to holy things. Everyone who has not been redeemed by Christ is spiritually dead (Luke 15:32; Eph. 2:1–3; Col. 2:13).

The Bible also speaks of "the second death" (Rev. 2:11), which is eternal death, the everlasting separation of the lost from God in HELL. The "second death" is equated with "the lake of fire" (Rev. 20:14); "the lake which burns with fire and brimstone...is the second death" (Rev. 21:8).

The apostle Paul speaks of death as an enemy: "The last enemy that will be destroyed is death" (1 Cor. 15:26). In His resurrection, Jesus conquered death—physical, spiritual, and eternal. Through fear of death, men are subject to bondage (Heb. 2:15); but "our Savior Jesus Christ...has abolished death and brought life and immortality to light through the gospel" (2 Tim. 1:10).

DEATH, SECOND — the state of final condemnation and punishment to which unbelievers are condemned by God at the Last Judgment (Rev. 2:11; 21:8). To Smyrna, the persecuted church, the crucified and risen Christ delcared, "Be faithful unto death, and I will give you the crown of life...He who overcomes shall not be hurt by the second death" (Rev. 2:10–11). The meaning of this verse is that a person without Christ when he faces God's judgment will be condemned to eternal punishment in hell or "the second death." Also see ESCHATOLOGY.

DEBIR [duh BEER] (*speaker*) — the name of one man and three towns in the Old Testament:

1. A king of Eglon (Josh. 10:3). He was one of five allied Amorite kings who unsuccessfully attempted to halt Joshua's invasion of the land of Canaan (Josh. 10:1–27). Joshua soundly defeated these forces at GIBEON in the famous battle at the time of "Joshua's long day" (Josh. 10:12–13). The five kings were killed and hanged on five separate trees until evening. Their bodies were then placed in the cave where they had hidden (Josh. 10:16–27).

2. A town in Judah's hill country (Josh. 10:38–39), in the Negeb, or southland, and designated a city for the Levites (Josh. 21:15; 1 Chr. 6:57–58). In Joshua's time the town, also called Kirjath Sannah (Josh. 15:49) and Kirjath Sepher (Josh. 15:15–16; Judg. 1:11–12), was inhabited by the giant people, the ANAKIM, and was captured by Joshua (Josh. 10:38–39). Debir had to be recaptured later by the judge Othniel (Josh. 15:15–17; Judg. 1:11–13).

3. A town east of the Jordan River on Gad's border near Mahanaim (Josh. 13:26). This may be the same place as LO DEBAR (2 Sam. 9:4–5; 17:27).

4. A town on Judah's northern border near the Valley of Achor (Josh. 15:7).

DEBORAH [DEB uh rah] (*wasp*) — the name of two women in the Old Testament:

1. A nurse to Rebekah, Isaac's wife (Gen. 24:59; 35:8). Deborah accompanied Rebekah when she left her home in Mesopotamia to become Isaac's wife and lived with Jacob and Rebekah. She probably spent her years caring for their sons, Jacob and Esau. Deborah died at an advanced age. She was buried below Bethel under a tree which Jacob called Allon Bachuth (literally "oak of weeping")—a fitting name for the burial place of one who had served so long and so faithfully (Gen. 35:8).

2. The fifth judge of Israel, a prophetess and the only female judge (Judg. 4—5). The Bible tells us nothing about her family except that she was the wife of Lapidoth. Deborah's home was in the hill country of Ephraim between Bethel and Ramah. The palm tree under which she sat and judged Israel was a landmark; it became known as "the palm tree of Deborah" (Judg. 4:5).

Deborah summoned Barak (Judg. 4; 5:1; Heb. 11:32) and told him it was God's will that he lead her forces against the mighty warrior, Sisera. Sisera was the commander of the army of Jabin, king of Canaan, who had terrorized Israel for 20 years. Barak accepted on one condition: Deborah must accompany him. Deborah and Barak's army consisted of only 10,000, while Sisera had a multitude of fighters and 900 chariots of iron.

God was on Israel's side, however. When the battle ended, not a single man of Sisera's army survived, except Sisera himself, who fled on foot. When Sisera took refuge in the tent of Heber the Kenite, Jael (the wife of Heber) drove a tent peg through his temple (Judg. 4:21), killing him.

The "Song of Deborah" (Judges 5) is one of the finest and earliest examples of Hebrew poetry.

DEBT — borrowed money or property which a person is bound by law to pay back to another. In all periods of history, people have always had to borrow money. In Bible times many were willing to lend the desired money, but at a price. Excessive interest rates of 50 percent or higher per year were often charged.

When a financial need arose, the needy could borrow from relatives or professional lenders, but they had to pay interest for the privilege of the loan. In spite of this custom, Moses admonished the Israelites to give help to their own people without charging any interest (Ex. 22:25; Lev. 25:35–38; Deut. 23:19–20). However, they were allowed to charge interest to foreigners (Deut. 15:3, 6; 23:20). Apparently Moses' regulations either were not followed or fell into disuse (Neh. 5:6–13). The prophet Ezekiel condemned the Israelites for charging interest, or usury, to their fellow citizens (Ezek. 18:1–18; 22:12).

When a loan was made, something was usually put up for collateral (pledge or security) to guarantee that the debtor would pay his debt (Gen. 38:17–20; Deut. 24:10). But the creditor did not have the right forcefully to enter the debtor's house and claim the collateral. He was required to wait outside until the debtor brought out the pledge and presented it to him before witnesses (Deut. 24:10–11). Essential objects that were necessary to sustain life, such as the MILLSTONE, could not be taken as a pledge (Deut. 24:6).

A person's outer cloak, which was essential for warmth to the poor during the cold nights, could not be kept as a pledge overnight (Ex. 22:26; Amos 2:8). Thus the Mosaic law sought to preserve the worth and dignity of both the family and the individual debtor.

Occasionally a debtor would give his child or slave as the pledge for a debt (2 Kin. 4:1; Neh. 5:1–5). Sometimes a family member or a friend would guarantee the pledge for another (Prov. 6:1–5; 17:18).

The Mosaic law also provided for the SABBATICAL YEAR every seventh year (Deut. 15:1) and the Year of JUBILEE every 50th year (Lev. 25:8–55). These were times of release when debts were to be forgiven and all pledges returned.

Although Christ did not condemn investments to earn money (Matt. 25:27; Luke 19:23), he emphasized the need for every person to show love and grace toward his fellow human beings (Matt. 5:25–26; Luke 12:58–59). He taught us to pray, "Forgive us our debts, as we forgive our debtors" (Matt. 6:12). God has offered His grace in the form of his Son to pay the price for our debts (Heb. 7:22). Out of gratitude, we should show that love to others (Luke 7:36–50).

DECALOGUE [DECK uh log] (see COMMANDMENTS, TEN).

DECAPOLIS [dih CAP oh liss] (*ten cities*) — a district of northern Palestine, with a large Greek population, mostly on the east side of the Jordan River and embracing ten cities (see Map 6, C–3). Early in his ministry, Jesus was followed by "great multitudes," including people from Decapolis (Matt. 4:25). When Jesus healed the demon-possessed man from GADARA, he "began to proclaim in Decapolis all that Jesus had done for him" (Mark 5:20). Later, Jesus traveled through the midst of the region (Mark 7:31).

Pliny, the Greek historian, identified the ten cities of the Decapolis as: Damascus, Dion, Gadara, Gerasa (or Galasa), Hippos (or Hippo), Canatha (or Kanatha), Pella, Philadelphia (the Old Testament Rabbah or Rabbath Ammon and present–day Amman, the capital of Jordan), Raphana (or Rephana), and Scythopolis. Later other towns, such as Abila and Edrei, were added to this district.

DECISION, VALLEY OF (see JEHOSHAPHAT, VALLEY OF).

DECREE — an official order, command, or edict issued by a king or other person of authority. The decrees of kings were often delivered to distant towns or cities by messengers and publicly announced at city gates or other public places (Ezra 1:1; Amos 4:5). The Bible also refers to God's decrees, universal laws or rules to which the entire world is subject (Ps. 148:6).

DEDAN [DEE dun] (*low*) — the name of two men and a geographical region in the Bible:

1. A descendant of Cush (Gen. 10:7; 1 Chr. 1:9).
2. A son of Jokshan and a grandson of Abraham and Keturah (Gen. 25:3; 1 Chr. 1:32).
3. A district near Edom and the Dead Sea (Jer. 25:23; Ezek. 25:13; 27:15).

DEDANITES [DEAD un ites] — natives or inhabitants of DEDAN (Is. 21:13; Dedanim, KJV).

DEDICATE, DEDICATION — a religious ceremony in which a person or a thing is set aside or consecrated to God's service. In Bible times, many different things were included in such services: the Temple (2 Chr. 2:4), a field (Lev. 27:16), a house (Lev. 27:14), articles of precious metal (2 Sam. 8:10), even spoils won in battle (1 Chr. 26:27).

In one of the most beautiful passages in the Bible, Hannah presented her young son Samuel to God in an act of child dedication (1 Sam. 1:19–28). Hannah's prayer of thanksgiving to God (1 Sam. 2:1–10) is a model of praise and dedication for all who seek to honor God through their lives.

DEDICATION, FEAST OF (see FEASTS AND FESTIVALS).

DEEP, THE — a vast space, expanse, or abyss. The term is used in Scripture in several ways. The first use occurs in Genesis 1:2: "The earth was without form, and void; and darkness was on the face of the deep" (Gen. 1:2). The word may refer in this phrase to the chaos existing at creation, or it may indicate the vast expanse of waters which covered the earth at creation (Ps. 104:6; Prov. 8:28). The term is elsewhere used to refer to the oceans and to the volume of water that burst forth at the Flood (Gen. 7:11; 8:2). Jonah spoke of God's casting him "into the deep" (Jon. 2:3), or the Mediterranean Sea. The apostle Paul wrote, "Three times I was shipwrecked; a night and a day I have been in the deep" (2 Cor. 11:25). This was apparently a reference to his being cast adrift on the Mediterranean Sea.

The deep also refers to the ABYSS, the abode of the dead (Rom. 10:7) and evil spirits (Luke 8:31; Rev. 9:1–2, 11; 20:1). All of these references to the "bottomless pit" translate a Greek word for unfathomable depth.

Figuratively, the deep means that which is profound or mighty: the great judgments of God (Ps. 36:6; 92:5; Rom. 11:33) or the "deep things of God" (1 Cor. 2:10).

DEER, DOE (see ANIMALS OF THE BIBLE).

DEFECT (see DISABILITIES AND DEFORMITIES).

DEFILE — to make unclean or impure. At least five types of defilement are mentioned in the Old Testament: (1) ceremonial (Lev. 15:19); (2) ethical (Ezek. 37:23); (3) physical (Song 5:3); (4) religious (Jer. 3:1); and (5) sexual (Lev. 15:24). The purpose of the Old Testament laws about defilement was to preserve the holiness of God's chosen people. But the Jewish rabbis turned these laws into a legalistic system that emphasized ceremonial cleanliness while ignoring spiritual purity. Jesus reversed this situation by emphasizing the need for moral purity and ethical living (Mark 7:1–23).

DEGREES, SONG OF (see ASCENTS, SONG OF).

DEHAVITES [dih HAY vites] — one of the tribes that colonized Samaria after Israel was carried away into Captivity (Ezra 4:9). Herodotus, the fifth-century Greek historian, mentions that these people, known as Dai or Daoi, were among the nomadic tribes of Persia.

DELAIAH [dih LAY yah] (*God is Savior*) — the name of five men in the Old Testament:

1. The sixth son of Elioenai, a descendant of Zerubbabel and King David (1 Chr. 3:24; Dalaiah, KJV, NEB).

2. A descendant of Aaron and one of David's priests (1 Chr. 24:18).

3. One of the NETHINIM (Temple servants) who returned from the Captivity with Zerubbabel (Ezra 2:60; Neh. 7:62).

4. The father of a contemporary of Nehemiah (Neh. 6:10).

5. A son of Shemaiah who pleaded with King Jehoiakim not to destroy the scroll containing Jeremiah's prophecies (Jer. 36:12, 25).

DELILAH [dih LIE lah] (*dainty one*) — the Philistine woman loved by Samson, the mightiest of Israel's judges. She betrayed Samson to the lords of the Philistines for 1,100 pieces of silver (Judg. 16:5). Deluding Samson into believing she loved him, Delilah persuaded him to tell her the secret of his strength—his long hair, which was the symbol of his Nazirite vow. While Samson slept at her home in the Valley of Sorek, the Philistines entered and cut his hair. With his strength gone, Samson was easily captured and imprisoned, then blinded.

No biblical evidence supports the popular belief that Delilah was deeply repentant over her actions. She even may have been one of the 3,000 Philistines buried beneath the temple of Dagon which Samson destroyed when his God–given strength returned (Judg. 16:27–30).

DELUGE (see FLOOD).

DEMAS [DEE mus] (meaning unknown) — a friend and co–worker of the apostle Paul at Rome. Demas later deserted Paul, "having loved this present world" (2 Tim. 4:10; Col. 4:14; Philem. 24).

DEMETRIUS [dih ME tree us] — the name of two men in the New Testament:

1. A silversmith at Ephesus (Acts 19:24, 38) who made and sold silver models of the city's famed temple of the goddess Diana. Alarmed at what the spread of the gospel would do to his business, Demetrius incited a riot against the apostle Paul. For two hours, the mob cried, "Great is Diana of the Ephesians!" (Acts 19:28, 34). The mob was quieted by the city clerk (Acts 19:35–40). Later, Paul left Ephesus for Macedonia (Acts 20:1).

2. A Christian commended by John because he had "a good testimony from all " (3 John 12).

DEMONS — another name for fallen angels who joined the kingdom of Satan in rebellion against God.

Origin. The origin of demons is not explicitly discussed in the Bible. But the New Testament speaks of the fall and later imprisonment of a group of angels (1 Pet. 3:19–20; 2 Pet. 2:4; Jude 6). The group that participated in the fall apparently followed one of their own number, SATAN. The fall occurred before God's CREATION of the world, leaving Satan and his angels free to contaminate the human race with wickedness (Gen. 3; Matt. 25:41; Rev. 12:9).

Only part of the fallen angels took part in the wickedness at the time of the Flood (Gen. 6:1–4). These were the ones who were imprisoned. God left the rest free to try to undermine the cause of righteousness in the world.

A symbolic view of this "initial" fall appears in Revelation 12:3-4 where the dragon (a symbol for Satan) "drew a third of the stars of heaven" (a symbol for angels) and "threw them to the earth." Thus, Satan has his own angels, presumably these demons (Matt. 25:41; Rev. 12:9).

Demons in the Old Testament. Because the Jews believed God's power was unlimited, the Old Testament contains little information about demons. The primitive status of the understanding of demons during this time is perhaps reflected in the way the Old Testament relates the fallen angels to God. It was a "distressing (or evil) spirit from God" (1 Sam. 16:15-16, 23) that brought great distress to Saul the king. It was a "lying spirit" from the Lord about whom Micaiah, the prophet of the Lord, spoke (1 Kin. 22:21-23).

Pagan worship is also related to demon activity in the Old Testament (Lev. 17:7; Ps. 106:37). Demons delight in making heathen idols the focus of their activities.

Demons in the New Testament. The New Testament accepts the Old Testament teaching about demons and advances the doctrine significantly. Demons are designated in a number of different ways in the New Testament. Quite frequently they are called "unclean spirits" (Matt. 10:1; Mark 6:7). Another descriptive phrase for them is "wicked (or evil) spirit" (Luke 7:21; Acts 19:12-13). In his writings Paul calls them "deceiving spirits" (1 Tim. 4:1). John refers to "the spirit of error" (1 John 4:6) and "spirits of demons" (Rev. 16:14). Luke describes one demon as a "spirit of divination'" (Acts 16:16).

The only individual demon named in the New Testament (Satan himself is never referred to as a demon) is the one called Abaddon in Hebrew and Apollyon in Greek (Rev. 9:11). Some scholars believe this is another name for Satan or that this is an unfallen angel. But stronger evidence suggests he was a fallen angelic leader who is subject to the kingly authority of Satan. Legion (Mark 5:9; Luke 8:30) is probably a collective name for a group of demons rather than the name of a single demon.

A prime purpose of Jesus' earthly ministry was to overcome the power of Satan. This included His conquest of the demonic realm (Matt. 12:25-29; Luke 11:17-22; John 12:31; 1 John 3:8). This explains the fierce conflict between Jesus and these evil spirits while He was on earth.

Yet Jesus' enemies accused Him of being in alliance with Satan's kingdom, including his demons (Mark 3:22; John 8:48). This same accusation was made against His forerunner, John the Baptist (Matt. 11:18; Luke 7:33). But Jesus' works of goodness and righteousness showed that these claims were not true (Matt. 12:25-29; Luke 11:17-22).

Following the resurrection of Jesus and His return to heaven, these demonic principalities and powers have continued their warfare against those who are His followers (Rom. 8:38-39; Eph. 6:12). Yet Satan and his allies will finally be overthrown by God. After Christ returns, the devil and his angels will be defeated and thrown into the lake of fire

Photo by Gustav Jeeninga

The Assyrian desert demon Pazuza had the feet and wings of an eagle, a human body with claws for hands, and a misshapen head.

and brimstone (Matt. 25:41; Rev. 20:10). This is a doom with which demons are quite familiar (Matt. 8:29). God will achieve the ultimate victory in this conflict which has been going on since the beginning of time.

DEMON POSSESSION — an affliction of persons in the New Testament who were possessed or controlled by demons (Matt. 4:24; 8:33; demoniac, NASB).

The New Testament gives graphic descriptions of the effect of demons on people. Some of the diseases which they caused included muteness (Matt. 12:22; Mark 9:17, 25), deafness (Mark 9:25), blindness (Matt. 12:22), and bodily deformity (Luke 13:10-17). But demons were not responsible for all physical ailments. The gospel writers frequently distinguished between sickness and demon possession (Matt. 4:24; Mark 1:32; Luke 6:17-18). Sometimes a problem caused by demons appears to have another cause in another situation (Matt. 12:22; 15:30).

In New Testament times demons were also responsible for some mental problems (Matt. 8:28; Acts 19:13-16). The ranting and raving that they produced probably should be included with mental disorders (Mark 1:23-24; John 10:20). Uncontrolled fits were another form of demonic affliction

(Luke 9:37–42; Mark 1:26). Sometimes a demon also caused a person to behave in an antisocial manner (Luke 8:27, 35).

The method of Jesus and His disciples in casting out demons differed radically from the magical methods so often used in that time. Through His simple command Jesus expelled them (Mark 1:25; 5:8; 9:25). His disciples simply added the authority of His name to the command (Luke 10:17; Acts 16:18). Even some people who were not His followers invoked His power (Luke 9:49; Acts 19:13). In some instances prayer was necessary before a demon could be cast out (Mark 9:29).

By casting out demons, Jesus showed that the KINGDOM OF GOD—God's rule in the affairs of mankind—was a present reality. This was also a clear demonstration of His power over Satan and the demonic forces of sin and evil in the world.

DEN — the lair of a wild animal (Job 37:8). The prophet Daniel was cast into a den of lions (Dan. 6:7–24).

DEN OF LIONS — the lair (Job 38:40), thicket (Ps. 10:9), or cave (Nah. 2:12) where lions live. The most famous den of lions in the Bible is that into which Daniel was thrown (Daniel 6). This apparently was a deep cavern, either natural or artificial, sealed with a large stone (Dan. 6:17). The kings of Assyria kept lions in captivity, releasing them periodically for the royal sport of lion hunting. The lions of the Daniel story probably were kept by King Darius for this purpose. Daniel's preservation from the lions is an inspiring example of God's control of His world and His power to protect His people.

DENARIUS [dih NAIR e us] (see MONEY).

DENY, DENIAL — to be untrue or to disown. This word is used often in the Bible to express one's faithfulness to God or Christ. A person may deny God in word or deed. Denial in word often involves disowning or rejecting a relationship with, or knowledge of, God or Christ (Josh. 24:27; Matt. 10:33; 2 Pet. 2:1). Denial in deed especially refers to withholding something from someone (Prov. 30:7; 1 Tim. 5:8). It may even refer to self-denial—withholding or abstaining from the pleasures of the world for the sake of Christ (Matt. 16:24).

DEPOSIT — something entrusted to another for safekeeping; money given as a down payment. The Old Testament laid down specific laws concerning the protection of deposits (Ex. 22:7–13). The New Testament describes the gospel as a special trust given to Christians, who are responsible for proclaiming it faithfully (1 Cor. 9:17; 1 Tim. 6:20).

DEPRAVITY (see MAN).

DEPUTY (see OCCUPATIONS AND TRADES).

These columns completely surrounded an outdoor theater in Gerasa (modern Jerash) during the New Testament period. This is apparently not the same Gerasa (also spelled Gergesa) in the region where Jesus healed two demon-possessed men (Matt. 8:28-34).

Photo by Gustav Jeeninga

The unexcavated mound of Derbe, a city visited by the apostle Paul (Acts 14:20; 16:1).

DERBE [DUR bih] — a city in the southeastern part of LYCAONIA (see Map 7, D-2), a province of Asia Minor, to which Paul and Barnabas retreated when driven from Lystra (Acts 14:6–20), while on their first missionary journey. Paul also visited Derbe on his second missionary journey (Acts 16:1). Derbe is twice mentioned with Lystra; it was situated southeast of that city (Acts 14:6; 16:1). One of Paul's travel companions, Gaius, was a native of Derbe (Acts 20:4).

DESCENT INTO HADES — Christ's journey to the place of the dead on our behalf following His crucifixion. Some interpreters see this descent in Paul's reference to "lower parts of the earth" (Eph. 4:9). Both Peter (Acts 2:27) and Paul (Acts 13:35) quote Psalm 16:10, declaring that Jesus experienced death, but that He was kept from the corruption of the grave. God did not abandon His Son in hell, but raised Him from the dead (Acts 2:27). From the heights of heaven's throne Jesus descended to earth and even to death itself to provide for our REDEMPTION.

DESERT — a dry and barren wasteland; a solitary place which is uninhabited; or an arid pastureland. Different aspects of the desert (its wild beasts, barrenness, and death) are emphasized in various contexts in the Bible.

Many desert areas support green plant life in the wet season, but dry up in the heat of the long, hot summer (Jer. 23:10; Joel 1:19–20). The desert area south of Beersheba toward Mount Sinai is very barren with less than two inches of rain per year. Other desert areas of the Holy Land have sufficient rain to support plant life (Ps. 65:12; John 6:10).

The Bible refers to the Wilderness (desert) of Beersheba (Gen. 21:14), Beth Aven (Josh. 18:12), Damascus (1 Kin. 19:15), Edom (2 Kin. 3:8), En Gedi (1 Sam. 24:1), Red Sea (Ex. 13:18), Gibeon (2 Sam. 2:24), Jeruel (2 Chr. 20:16), Judah (Judg. 1:16), Kadesh (Ps. 29:8), Kedemoth (Deut. 2:26), Maon (1 Sam. 23:24), Moab (Deut. 2:8), Paran (Gen. 21:21), Shur (Ex. 15:22), Sin (Ex. 16:1), Sinai (Ex. 19:1), Tekoa (2 Chr. 20:20), Zin (Num. 13:21), and Ziph (1 Sam. 23:14).

One of the promises of God in the prophetic books is that the desert lands will be transformed into fertile and productive fields. God will put rivers in the desert (Is. 43:19–20), which will bloom and rejoice (Is. 35:1, 6–7). The fir trees will grow, and the deserts will look as lush as the Garden of Eden (Is. 51:3).

The New Testament usually refers to the desert as a solitary place. Jesus repeatedly withdrew from the large crowds (Luke 4:42; 9:10–12) to these places for privacy and a time of prayer with His Father.

DESIGNER (see OCCUPATIONS AND TRADES).

DESIRE OF ALL NATIONS, THE — a phrase interpreted by some translations of the Bible as a prophecy of the Messiah (Hag. 2:7; KJV, NKJV; wealth of all nations, NASB; treasure of all nations, NEB). The prophet Haggai envisioned a time when the choicest and costliest treasures of the Gentiles would be dedicated to the God of Israel. For the Christian, the Lord Jesus Christ is, indeed, "the Desire of all nations."

DESOLATION, ABOMINATION OF (see ABOMINATION OF DESOLATION).

DESTROYER — an enemy that invades the land of Israel (Is. 49:17; Jer. 22:7; 50:11), as well as a special agent used by God to accomplish judgment. In the account of the PASSOVER before the Hebrews were released from bondage by the Egyptians, the destroyer is first mentioned as distinct from the Lord (Ex. 12:23). In a few places in the Bible, Satan seems to be described as a divine agent of destruction (Job 15:21; Ps. 17:4; 1 Cor. 10:10).

DESTRUCTION (see ABADDON).

DEUEL [DEW el] (*knowledge of god*) — the father of Eliasaph, who was leader of the tribe of Gad when the people of Israel were numbered at Sinai (Num. 1:14; 7:42; 10:20). He is also called Reuel (Num. 2:14).

DEUTERONOMY, BOOK OF — an Old Testament book commonly identified as the farewell speech of Moses to the people of Israel just before his death. The title of the book comes from the Greek word *Deuteronomion*, which means "second law." In his address, Moses underscored and repeated many of the laws of God that the people received at Mount Sinai about 40 years earlier. He also challenged the people to remain faithful to their God and His commands as they prepared to enter the Promised Land.

Structure of the Book. Because it is written in the format of a series of warmhearted speeches, Deuteronomy is unique among the books of the Bible. Following a brief introduction of Moses as the speaker, the book begins with a series of speeches and addresses from Moses to the people. These speeches continue through chapter 33, with only brief narrative interruptions of his spoken words. The final chapter departs from the speech format to report on Moses' death and the selection of Joshua as his successor.

In his addresses, Moses reminded the people of their days of slavery in Egypt and how God had delivered them safely through the wilderness to the borders of the Promised Land. He also restated the Ten Commandments and indicated that these great moral principles should direct their lives. As God's special people, they were to be holy and righteous as an example for surrounding pagan nations. Moses also warned Israel of the perils of idolatry and called the people to worship the one true God, who demanded their total commitment: "Hear, O Israel: The Lord our God, the Lord is one! You shall love the Lord your God with all your heart, with all your soul, and with all your might" (6:4–5).

As he spoke to the people, Moses also repeated many of the laws and regulations that dealt with observance of the Sabbath, proper forms of worship, treatment of the poor, religious feasts and festivals, inheritance rights, sexual morality, property rights, treatment of servants, and the administration of justice. Finally, Moses ended his words of caution and counsel with a beautiful song of praise to God. Then he pronounced an individual blessing on each of the tribes of the nation that would go into Canaan with Joshua to possess the land.

Authorship and Date. Conservative Bible students are united in their conviction that Moses wrote this book. But many liberal scholars theorize that Deuteronomy was written several centuries after Moses' time by an unknown author who wanted to bring about the religious reforms of the nation of Judah under King Josiah (2 Kin. 22—23). These sweeping reforms began when a copy of the Book of Deuteronomy was discovered as workmen repaired the Temple in Jerusalem. According to this theory, Deuteronomy was placed in the Temple to call the Jewish people back to observance of the laws which God had revealed to Moses and the people of Israel many centuries earlier.

This theory unfortunately overlooks the statement of the book itself that Moses wrote Deuteronomy and directed that it be read regularly by the people (31:9–13). The first–person pronoun

This painting from a tomb at Thebes shows two women of the Egyptian nobility playing a board game. The Israelites were slaves of the ruling nobles of Egypt (Deut. 16:12).

DEUTERONOMY: A Teaching Outline

Part One: Moses' First Speech
"What God Has Done for Israel" (1:1—4:43)

Part Two: Moses' Second Speech
"What God Expects of Israel" (4:44—26:19)

Part Three: Moses' Third Speech
"What God Will Do for Israel" (27:1—34:12)

I appears throughout the book as Moses refers to himself and his experiences. The logical conclusion is that Moses wrote the first 33 chapters of the book. Chapter 34, about his death, probably was added by his successor Joshua as a tribute to Moses. The date of the writing must have been some time around 1400 B.C.

Historical Setting. The Book of Deuteronomy marks a turning point in the history of God's Chosen People. For the previous 40 years, they had been through many unforgettable experiences under the leadership of Moses. He had led them out of enslavement in Egypt and through the wilderness to receive God's laws at Mount Sinai. Then, because of their rebellion and unfaithfulness, they had wandered aimlessly in the desert for two generations. Now they were camped on the eastern border of Canaan, the land which God had promised as their homeland.

Moses sensed that the people would face many new temptations as they settled in the land and established permanent dwellings among the pagan Canaanites. He also realized that his days as their leader were drawing to a close. He used this occasion to remind the people of their heritage as God's special people and to challenge them to remain faithful to God and His laws. Thus, the Book of Deuteronomy becomes a stirring conclusion to the life of this great statesman and prophet. One of the final verses of the book pays this fitting tribute to Moses' visionary leadership: "Since then there has not arisen in Israel a prophet like Moses, whom the Lord knew face to face" (34:10).

Theological Contribution. The New Testament contains more than 80 quotations from Deuteronomy, so it must be rated as one of the foundational books of the Bible. Jesus Himself often quoted from Deuteronomy. During His temptation, He answered Satan with four quotations from Scripture. Three of these came from this key Old Testament book (Matt. 4:4, Luke 4:4—Deut. 8:3; Matt. 4:7, Luke 4:12—Deut. 6:16; Matt. 4:10, Luke 4:8—Deut. 6:13).

When Jesus was asked to name the most important commandment in the Law, He responded with the familiar call from Deuteronomy: "You shall love the Lord your God with all your heart, with all your soul and with all your might" (Matt. 22:37; Deut. 6:5; Mark 12:30; Luke 10:27). He then added some other important words from Leviticus to show that He was carrying the law one step further: "The second [commandment] is like it: 'You shall love your neighbor as yourself'" (Matt. 22:39; Lev. 19:18; Mark 12:31; Luke 10:27).

Another great truth underscored by the Book of Deuteronomy is that God is faithful to His Covenant People, those whom He has called to carry out His purpose of REDEMPTION in the world. The Hebrews were chosen as God's instruments not because they were a worthy, powerful people, but because He loved them and desired to bless the rest of the world through their influence (7:6, 11). This is still God's purpose as He continues to call people to follow Him and commit themselves to His purpose in their lives.

Special Considerations. Some people look upon the laws of God in the Old Testament as burdensome and restrictive. The Book of Deuteronomy, however, teaches that God's laws are given for our own good to help us stay close to Him in our attitudes and behavior. Thus, Moses called on the people to keep God's statutes, "which I command you today for your good" (10:13). The intention of God's law is positive; passages in the New Testament that seem to condemn the law must be interpreted in this light. It is the misuse of the law—trusting it rather than God's mercy as the basis of our salvation—that we should avoid. God's law is actually fulfilled in the person of our Lord and Savior Jesus Christ (Matt. 5:17, 20).

DEVIL *(accuser)* — the main title for the fallen angelic being who is the supreme enemy of God and man. Satan is his name, and devil is what he is—the accuser or deceiver. The title "devil" appears 35 times in the NKJV. In every case it is preceded by the article "the," indicating a title rather than a name. The term comes from a Greek word that means "a false witness" or "malicious accuser."

Several descriptive phrases applied to the devil in the New Testament point out the nature of his wicked personality and the extent of his evil deeds.

The Wicked or Evil One (Matt. 6:13; 13:19, 38; 1 John 2:13). This phrase depicts the devil's fundamental nature. He is in direct opposition to everything God is or all he wishes to do. He is the source of all evil and wickedness. While the KJV reads, "Deliver us from evil," the NKJV more accurately reads, "Deliver us from the evil one." Humanity needs this deliverance, for the devil "walks about like a roaring lion, seeking whom he may devour" (1 Pet. 5:8).

Enemy (Matt. 13:25, 28, 39). The devil is man's worst enemy. This is one enemy Jesus does not want us to love. He is an enemy of Christ, the church, and the gospel; and he is tireless in his efforts to uproot good and sow evil.

Murderer (John 8:44). "He was a murderer from the beginning" are strong words from the lips of Jesus. The devil killed Abel and the prophets, and he wanted to kill Jesus before His time (8:40).

Deceiver (Rev. 20:10). Starting with Eve, the devil has attempted to deceive every living soul. Evil men operating under the power of the evil one will continue to deceive (2 Tim. 3:13).

Beelzebub, Prince of Demons (Matt. 9:34; 12:24). The religious leaders of Jesus' time were guilty of blasphemy against the Holy Spirit because they claimed the miracles of Jesus were actually conducted by the devil. The KJV and some other versions incorrectly translate "demons" as "devils." There are many demons but only one devil. His name is Beelzebub, the chief leader of the fallen angels known as demons.

Ruler of This World (John 12:31; 14:30; 16:11). Three times Jesus called the devil the "ruler of this world." The devil offered the world to Jesus if He would worship him (Luke 4:5-7), but the Lord refused with these words, "Get behind me Satan" (4:8). At Calvary God dealt a death blow to this world ruler. It is only a matter of time before God will win the final victory at the end of time (1 John 3:8; Matt. 25:41; Rev. 12:7).

The devil is strong, but Christians are stronger through the Lord (Eph. 6:11). They have the protection needed to withstand his assaults. The devil tempts, but God provides a way of escape (1 Cor. 10:13); the devil tries to take advantage of people (2 Cor. 2:11), but he will flee if fought (James 4:7). The devil should not be feared, for Jesus is more powerful than this deceiving prince of the demons (1 John 4:4).

Also see SATAN.

DEW — condensed water that falls upon the vegetation during the cool nights of the summer months. The dew of Palestine is heaviest near the coast of the Mediterranean Sea and sea-facing slopes, and it does not occur at all in parts of the Jordan valley. The dew descends (2 Sam. 17:12) and departs (Hos. 6:4; 13:13) suddenly. It is vitally important in the summer when no rain falls, amounting to as much as 4'-5' (100-125 mm.) annually. A person can be drenched by the heavy dew (Song 5:2; Dan. 4:1). The dew on Gideon's fleece was so heavy that it filled a bowl with water (Judg. 6:37-38).

Like the rain, dew was regarded as God's gift (Gen. 27:28; Hos. 14:5). The dew brought good crops (Gen. 27:28; Deut. 33:13) and the manna during Israel's escape from Egypt (Ex. 16:13-14; Num. 11:9). It thus became a symbol of fruitfulness, and was associated with God's word (Deut. 32:2), the resurrection (Is. 26:19), and the remnant of God's people (Mic. 6:7; Zech. 8:12).

DIADEM [DIE uh dem] — a band or wrapping around the turban of a king or his queen signifying their royal authority. Rulers of the ancient Near East did not wear rigid gold crowns but cloth turbans wound around the head and decorated in turn with cloth diadems studded with gems.

Two Hebrew words translated as diadem in the Old Testament come from a word meaning "to wind around." One of these words refers to the high priest's headpiece (Lev. 8:9; 16:4) as well as the king's turban (Ezek. 21:26). The other word is also rendered as diadem in several Old Testament passages (Is. 62:3; Job 29:14).

The New Testament uses the Greek word for diadem only in the Book of Revelation (Rev. 12:3; 13:1; 19:12). The New Testament also makes a clear distinction between a diadem and a CROWN. A crown was a garland or a wreath awarded for faithfulness in service, such as a crown of righteousness (2 Tim. 4:8), while a diadem always symbolized royal authority.

DIAL (see SUN DIAL).

DIAL OF AHAZ (see SUNDIAL OF AHAZ).

DIAMOND (see JEWELS AND PRECIOUS STONES).

DIANA [die ANN uh] (see GODS, PAGAN).

DIASPORA [dee AS puh ruh] (see DISPERSION).

DIBLAH [DIB luh] (meaning unknown) — an unidentified place in the nation of Israel mentioned by the prophet Ezekiel (Ezek. 6:14; Diblath, KJV). It may be the same place as RIBLATH.

DIBLAIM [dib LAY im] (double cakes of figs)—the father-in-law of Hosea the prophet (Hos. 1:3).

DIBON [DIE bahn] (a wasting away) — the name of two settlements in Israel:

1. A city of the tribe of Gad (see Map 3, C-5) located east of the Jordan River and north of the River Arnon (Num. 21:30; 32:3; Is. 15:2; Jer. 48:18; Dimon, Is. 15:9). The Moabite (Mesha) Stone was discovered here in 1868. Dibon is now identified with the modern Dhiban.

2. A village of southern Judah near the boundary of Edom. Dibon was resettled following the Captivity (Neh. 11:25; Dimonah, Josh. 15:22).

DIBRI [DIB rye] (talkative) — a descendant of Dan whose daughter married an Egyptian. Her son was stoned to death for blaspheming the name of the Lord (Lev. 24:10-23).

DICE PLAYING — a game of chance. Although dice playing is never mentioned in the Bible, many cultures of the ancient world used dice in games of chance. Dice were used to determine moves in board games and as a form of gambling. The Egyptians used pyramid-shaped dice, probably introducing them to the Hebrew people while they were enslaved in Egypt.

The casting of lots is mentioned in the Bible as a form of decision making (Lev. 16:8; Acts 1:26). Just exactly how lots were cast is not known; this procedure could have involved dice. Soldiers at Jesus' crucifixion gambled for His clothes by casting lots (Matt. 27:35; John 19:24).

DIDACHE [DID uh kay] (teaching) — a writing of the early church probably used as a manual of instruction to train converts to Christianity in doctrine and discipline before they were baptized. The date of its writing is uncertain, but it was probably put into its final form between A.D. 50 and 225.

The Didache contained several important sections, including a discussion of the Two Ways—the ways of life and death; directions for worship; instructions concerning church officers and the conduct of congregational affairs; and a section on ESCHATOLOGY, or the end time. The Didache is important because it gives insights into church life during this early period of Christian history.

DIDRACHMA [dih DROCK muh] (see MONEY).

DIDYMUS [DID ih mus] (twin) — the Greek name of THOMAS, one of the twelve apostles of Christ (John 11:16; 20:24; 21:2).

DIGNITARIES — angelic beings who hold a posi-

Photo by Gustav Jeeninga

A city wall uncovered in the excavation of Dibon, one of the leading cities of Moab (Is. 15:1, 12).

tion of glory and honor (2 Pet. 2:10; Jude 8; dignities, KJV; the glorious ones, RSV; celestial beings, NEB, NIV; angelic majesties, NASB).

DIGNITIES — KJV word for DIGNITARIES.

DIKLAH [DICK la] (*palm grove*) — a descendant of the family of Shem (Gen. 10:27; 1 Chr. 1:21). Most likely, Diklah also was the name of an oasis in southern Arabia.

DILEAN [DILL ee un] (*cucumber* or *gourd*) — a town in the Shephelah (lowland) of Judah near Lachish (Josh. 15:38). It is possibly the same place as Tell en–Najileh.

DILL (see PLANTS OF THE BIBLE).

DIMNAH [DIM nah] (*dung heap*) — a border town in the territory of Zebulun assigned to the Levites of the Merari family (Josh. 21:35).

DIMON [DIE muhn] (*river bed*) — a city of Moab (Is. 15:9); the same place as DIBON No. 1. "The waters of Dimon" (Is. 15:9; Dibon, Is. 15:2) probably refers to the River Arnon.

DIMONAH [die MOW nuh]—a city in the Negeb (southern wilderness) of Judah, near Edom (Josh. 15:22). The same place as DIBON No. 2.

DINAH [DIE nah] (*one who judges*) — Jacob's daughter by Leah (Gen. 30:21; 34:1). When she was raped by Shechem, the son of Hamor the Hivite, her brothers were enraged. Later, when Shechem wanted Dinah for his wife, he asked his father to make arrangements for him to marry her. Dinah's brothers consented on the condition that all the Hivites be circumcised.

The Hivites agreed; but after they had been circumcised, Simeon and Levi, two of Dinah's brothers, suddenly attacked them "on the third day, when they were in pain" (Gen. 34:25) and killed all the males. Jacob did not condone the deed; in fact, upon his deathbed he denounced it (Gen. 49:5–7).

DINAITES [DIE nuh ites] (*judges*) — a people sent by OSNAPPER (Ashurbanipal), king of Assyria, to colonize the cities of Samaria after the Captivity (Ezra 4:9).

DINHABAH [DIN huh bah] (*give judgment*) — the capital city of Bela, king of Edom (Gen. 36:32; 1 Chr. 1:43). Its exact location is unknown.

DIONYSIUS THE AREOPAGITE [die oh NISS e us air e OP uh ghyte] — a member of the AREOPAGUS, the supreme court of Athens. Dionysius became a Christian after hearing the gospel preached by the apostle Paul (Acts 17:34). Nothing else is known about him except by tradition. One tradition says he was martyred in Athens during the reign of the Roman emperor Domitian.

DIOTROPHES [die OTT ruh fees] (*nourished by Jupiter*) — an unruly believer reprimanded by John (3 John 9, 10). He appears to have been a strong personality or a prominent church leader who rejected both John and certain of his followers. Diotrophes stands in contrast to both Gaius (verse 1) and Demetrius (verse 12).

DIPHATH [DIE fath] — the second son of Gomer (Gen. 10:3; 1 Chr. 1:6). He is probably the same person as RIPHATH.

DIRECTION — the line along which anything lies, in relationship to the point or region toward which it is directed. Several methods were used in the ancient world to determine direction. The Hebrews used at least three of these methods: basic direction, local geography, and the position of the sun. For the Hebrews, the terms north, south, east, and west carried certain characteristics. They were not, as in Western culture today, simply neutral terms telling direction only.

The Hebrews divided the world into four parts, which they termed "the four corners of the earth" (Is. 11:12; Rev. 7:1; 20:8). The basic direction for the Hebrews was the east—the direction of the rising sun. In determining direction, the Hebrews faced the point where they knew the sun rose each day. Thus, the east was the front, sometimes called the "place of dawning." All other directions received their designations relative to the east as the front. Thus, west was the "rear," north was on the left, and south was on the right. Directions such as northwest and southeast were seldom used in Bible times.

The Old Testament usually spoke of directions other than the east as definite geographic locations. The Hebrew word translated as north came from the Hebrew root word for "look out" and was the name of a high mountain in Syria.

The term south, from a Hebrew word meaning "dry country," usually referred to the NEGEV (Gen. 20:1), the dry region situated a few miles south of Hebron. The west was designated by two methods—the position of the sun ("place of the setting sun") and geographic location (the "sea" or "great sea," referring to the Mediterranean Sea).

DISABILITIES AND DEFORMITIES — bodily handicaps or defects in Bible times that marred a person's appearance or hindered his physical movement. Various kinds of physical disabilities are mentioned in the Bible, particularly in the gospels in the accounts of Jesus' healing miracles.

Jesus healed the blind (Mark 10:51-52), the lame (Matt. 21:14), the deaf (Mark 7:33-35), and the maimed (Matt. 15:30). The Greek word translated as maimed referred to a person who was missing an arm or a leg. On one occasion, Jesus also restored a person's withered hand (Matt. 12:9-13; shriveled, NIV)—an act of compassion that brought criticism from the Pharisees because He dared to heal on the Sabbath.

Another distinct disability in Bible times was impotence, or the inability of a male to father children. Sometimes a royal household servant was castrated as a precautionary measure, particularly if he worked with the members of the king's harem or other women of the royal palace. Such sterilized domestic servants were known as eunuchs (Acts 8:27-39). Sometimes impotence was caused by accident. But no matter what the cause, a person who was a eunuch (Lev. 21:20; broken stones, KJV; crushed testicles, RSV) was barred from serving as a priest under the Levitical law.

The Law also specifically stated that a person with an outward blemish or defect could not serve as a priest. This included "a man blind or lame,

who has a marred face (flat nose, KJV), or any limb too long, a man who has a broken foot or broken hand, or is a hunchback (crookbacked, KJV), or a dwarf, or a man who has a defect in his eye" (Lev. 21:18-20).

The reasoning behind these strict regulations was that only those who were physically perfect were worthy of serving at the altar of the Lord.

Also see DISEASES OF THE BIBLE.

DISCERNING OF SPIRITS — a gift of the Holy Spirit which enables a person to judge whether one who speaks in tongues or performs miracles does so by the power of the Holy Spirit or by a false spirit (1 Cor. 12:10). The apostle Paul suggested that a person led by the Holy Spirit will be concerned for those things which strengthen the church (1 Cor. 14:12, 26).

DISCIPLE — a student, learner, or pupil. In the Bible the word is used most often to refer to a follower of Jesus. The word is rarely used in the Old Testament. Isaiah used the term disciples to refer to those who are taught or instructed (Is. 8:16).

The word disciple is sometimes used in a more specific way to indicate the twelve apostles of Jesus (Matt. 10:1; 11:1; 20:17; Luke 9:1; the Twelve, NIV, NEB, NASB, RSV).

In general, apostles refers to a small, inner group of Jesus' followers; disciples refers to a larger group of Jesus' followers, such as the women who stood at Jesus' cross and discovered the empty tomb.

DISCIPLINE — to train by instruction and control (1 Cor. 9:27). The biblical concept of discipline has both a positive side (instruction, knowledge, and training) and a negative aspect (correction, punishment, and reproof). Those who refuse to submit to God's positive discipline by obeying His laws will experience God's negative discipline through His wrath and judgment. Also see CHASTEN, CHASTISEMENT.

DISEASES OF THE BIBLE — Disease and sickness have plagued man since God cast Adam and Eve out of the Garden of Eden. The Hebrews believed illness was caused by sin in the individual, which God had to punish (Gen. 12:17; Prov. 23:29-32), the sin of a person's parents (2 Sam. 12:14-15), or seduction by Satan (Matt. 9:34; Luke 13:16). However, some passages in the Bible show there is not always such a simple explanation for disease (Job 34:19-20).

The Bible contains many general references to illness and disease without naming a specific malady. For example, the words affliction (Ps. 25:18) and infirmity (Jer. 10:19) often refer to an overwhelming sense of pain or sorrow that may be caused by either illness or spiritual despair.

The words pestilence (Jer. 21:6) and plague (Num. 11:33) seem to refer to contagious diseases of epidemic proportions which God sent occasionally as instruments of judgment upon His people, as well as the pagan nations of the ancient world. In the NKJV the word pestilence is used of the mys-

Photo by Howard Vos

Ruins of the hospital used by the early Greek physician Hippocrates at Cos.

terious disease that struck the livestock of the Egyptians (Ex. 9:3; murrain, KJV).

Other words in the Bible that indicate the presence or effects of illness or disease include bruise (Is. 30:26), sore (Lev. 13:27), and wound (Job 34:6). A bruise occurs when the flesh beneath the skin is injured but the skin remains unbroken. But sores and wounds involve a puncture of the skin.

The following specific illnesses or diseases are mentioned or implied in the Bible. This list is keyed to the New King James Version of the Bible, with cross references from five additional popular English versions: KJV, NASB, NEB, NIV, AND RSV.

Ague (see *Fever*).

Blains (see *Boils*).

Blindness. Three types of blindness are mentioned in the Bible: sudden blindness caused by flies and aggravated by dirt, dust, and glare; the gradual blindness caused by old age; and chronic blindness. Paul suffered temporary blindness on the road to Damascus (Acts 9:8). Scripture often refers to old people whose eyes "grew dim" (Gen. 27:1; 48:10; 1 Sam. 4:15). But the Bible more often refers to chronic blindness.

The Israelites had compassion for the blind. In fact, God placed a curse upon those who made the blind wander out of their way (Deut. 27:18). Jesus ministered to many people who were blind. He said, "[God] has anointed me to preach the gospel to the poor. He has sent me to heal the brokenhearted, to preach deliverance to the captives, and

recovering of sight to the blind" (Luke 4:18). Jesus healed a man born blind (John 9:1–41); a blind man whose healing was gradual (Mark 8:22–24); two blind men sitting by the wayside (Matt. 20:30–34); and a great number of others (Mark 10:46–52; Luke 7:21).

Blindness was often understood to be a punishment for evil-doing. We find examples of this at Sodom (Gen. 19:11); in the Syrian army (2 Kin. 6:18); and in the case of Elymas at Paphos (Acts 13:6–11).

Blood, Flow of. According to the Mosaic Law, a woman suffering from menstrual disorders was to be considered ceremonially unclean (Lev. 15:25). One such woman who had suffered for 12 years (Luke 8:43–48) touched the hem of Jesus' garment and was healed immediately because of her great faith. The NASB refers to this condition as a hemorrhage.

Bloody Flux (see *Dysentery*).

Boils. This term probably refers to anthrax, a disease that can be transmitted to humans by cattle, sheep, goats, and horses. The disease is caused by a rod-shaped bacterium that forms spores. These spores, in turn, can infect humans, who develop a boil-like lesion with a pustule (blain). In the infectious stage, the blain is called a malignant pustule. God inflicted boils on the Egyptians when the Pharaoh refused to let the Hebrews go to the Promised Land (Ex. 9:9–10; blains, KJV). This was also one of the afflictions which God threatened to bring upon the Hebrew people because of their grumbling after the Exodus from Egypt (Deut. 28:27; botch, KJV).

Satan was permitted to afflict Job with boils from the top of his head to the tip of his toes (Job 2:7). King Hezekiah also was afflicted with boils (2 Kin. 20:7), which Isaiah cured by applying a poultice of figs. A fresh fig poultice has a drawing effect. Before the advent of antibiotics, this type of treatment for boils was common. Other words for boils used by different translations of the Bible are sores and scabs.

Botch (see *Boils*).

Bowels, Disease of (see *Dysentery*).

Cancer. This disease is mentioned only once in the Bible: "And their word will eat as doth a cancer" (2 Tim. 2:17; canker, KJV; gangrene, NASB, NEB, NIV, RSV). It refers to the circulatory deterioration known as gangrene, which spreads rapidly and eats up tissue.

Canker (see *Cancer*).

Consumption. Moses warned the rebellious Israelites, "The Lord shall smite thee with a consumption, and with a fever, and with an inflammation and with an extreme burning" (Deut. 28:22; wasting disease, NIV). This disease is probably tuberculosis, a consumptive infection of the lungs.

Dropsy. This describes an abnormal accumulation of serous fluid in the body's connective tissue or in a serous cavity. The accumulation causes swelling. Jesus met at least one victim of dropsy in a certain Pharisee's house. Asked by Jesus if he thought it lawful to heal on the Sabbath, the Pharisee declined to answer. Jesus then healed the sufferer (Luke 14:1–4).

Dumb, Dumbness (see *Muteness*).

Dumb Spirit (see *Mute Spirit*).

Dysentery. This is a disease that rots the bowels, or the intestines, in its advanced stage (2 Chr. 21:15–19). The fibrine separates from the inner coating of the intestines and is expelled. The KJV refers to a severe form of dysentery as the bloody flux. The father of a Christian named Publius lay sick with this disease (Acts 28:8). Paul prayed for him and the man was healed. Some scholars believe dysentery was also the strange malady which afflicted King Hezekiah of Judah (2 Kin. 20:1).

Eczema. A symptom of this disease was an inflammation of the skin, marked by redness, itching, and oozing lesions which become scaly, encrusted, or hardened (Lev. 21:20; 22:22; scurvy, KJV; itching disease, RSV).

Emerods (see *Tumor*).

Epilepsy (see *Mute Spirit*).

Feet, Diseased. Excessive uric acid in the blood causes this kidney ailment that manifests itself through painful inflammation of joints. Second Chronicles 16:12–13 says that King Asa had a foot disease, which apparently was gout.

Fevers. The KJV uses the word ague to describe a burning fever. Moses warned the rebellious Israelites that "I will ever appoint over you terror, panic, consumption and the burning ague that shall con-

A blind harpist practicing his skill, from an early Egyptian tomb carving.

sume the eyes" (Lev. 26:16).

When Jesus found Simon Peter's mother–in–law ill with this symptom, He rebuked the fever and she was able to rise from her bed and wait on the disciples (Luke 4:38–39). On another occasion, Jesus healed the feverish son of a government official (John 4:46–54). Many diseases in ancient Palestine would have been characterized by high fevers, the most common of which were malaria and typhoid.

Gangrene (see *Cancer; Feet, Disease of*).

Hemorrhage (see *Blood, Flow of*).

Insanity. King Saul seems to have had symptoms of manic depression (1 Sam. 16:14–23), and the Bible mentions others who may have suffered from mental or nervous disorders. King Nebuchadnezzar is an example (Dan. 4:33). The words mad and madness are also used by various translations to refer to this malady.

Intestines, Disease of (see *Dysentery*).

Itch. This is a curse which God threatened to send upon the Hebrew people if they departed from faith in Him (Deut. 28:27). Itch is caused by a microscopic mite which burrows into the skin, causing extreme discomfort.

Itching Disease (see *Eczema*).

Leprosy. One of the most dreaded diseases of the world, leprosy is caused by a bacillus and is characterized by formation of nodules that spread, causing loss of sensation and deformity. Now treated with sulfone drugs, leprosy is perhaps the least infectious of all known contagious diseases. Hansen's Disease, as it is more properly known, was often misdiagnosed in biblical times. People believed then that it was highly contagious and hereditary. Leviticus 13:1–17 condemned leprosy as a "plague."

On the basis of a hair in a scab, a pimple, or a spot on the skin that had turned white, the priest would declare a person to be a leper and would quarantine him for seven days. If no change in the spot occurred by then, the quarantine would be extended another week. At that time, if the spot had started to fade, the "leper" would be pronounced cured and returned to his normal life. However, if the spot remained or had spread, he was declared unclean and banished. The words scurf and scall are applied to these spots on the skin by various English translations of the Bible (Lev. 13:30).

Leprosy was very common in the Near East. If a Hebrew was healed of leprosy, he was expected to offer certain sacrifices and engage in rites of purification (Lev. 14:1–32). Jesus healed lepers on numerous occasions (Luke 5:12–13; 17:12–17).

Lunacy, Lunatick (see *Mute Spirit*).

Mad, Madness (see *Insanity*).

Muteness. This is the temporary loss of speech, usually caused by a brain lesion but sometimes attributed to an emotional upset. This happened to the prophet Ezekiel (Ezek. 33:22). When an angel told Zechariah that he would be the father of John the Baptist, the old man came out of the Temple and could not speak (Luke 1:22).

Mute Spirit. The NKJV uses this phrase for a disorder that was probably epilepsy. This is a disorder marked by erratic electrical discharges of the central nervous system and manifested by convulsive attacks. A certain man brought his epileptic son to Jesus for help (Mark 9:17–29). The KJV says the boy had a "dumb spirit." Jesus healed him. Among the scores of people brought to Jesus for healing were epileptics (Matt. 4:24; lunaticks, KJV).

An ancient theory held that epilepsy was caused by the moon; people referred to epileptics as being "moonstruck." Psalm 121:6 may reflect this idea when it says, "The sun shall not smite thee by day, nor the moon by night."

Palsy (see *Paralysis, Paralytic*).

Paralysis, Paralytic. These words refer to total paralysis. The Gospels record a well-known incident in which Jesus healed a paralyzed man at Capernaum (Mark 2:1–12). The Book of Acts describes how the apostles healed people with this disease (Acts 8:7; 9:33–34; palsy, KJV).

Scab, Scabs (see *Boils*).

Scall (see *Leprosy*).

Scurf (see *Leprosy*).

Scurvy (see *Eczema*).

Sore, Sores (see *Boils*).

Tumor. The specific nature of this disease is unknown, although some scholars believe the word refers to hemorrhoids (Deut. 28:27; 1 Sam. 6:11). Other versions prefer ulcers (RSV) or emerods (KJV).

Ulcer (see *Tumor*).

Wasting Disease (see *Consumption*).

Worms. The prophet Isaiah warned that the rebellious people of Israel would be afflicted with worms (Is. 51:8). He also predicted this fate for Babylon (Is. 14:11). This parasitic disease could be fatal because no medical remedies were available. Worms such as tapeworms and hookworms live as parasites in the human body and cause illness and disease.

The Bible says that "an angel of the Lord" struck Herod the Great. Worms ate him up and he died (Acts 12:23).

DISH — a utensil for holding or serving food. In biblical times dishes usually were made of earthenware, although the wealthy classes sometimes used dishes of precious metal.

Many different types of dishes and bowls were used by the people of the ancient world. Jael provided Sisera with food in a "lordly bowl" (Judg. 5:25)—apparently a bowl of unusual size or splendor. Jesus referred to a dish or large earthenware serving bowl used at the Last Supper (Matt. 26:23; Mark 14:20). A large, deep dish was used for carrying the bread of the presence in the tabernacle and Temple (Ex. 25:29). Also mentioned in the Bible are a flat dish (1 Kin. 21:13) and a platter of some sort (Luke 11:39).

The great variety of dishes discovered by archaelogists has been an invaluable aid in establishing dates for cities and biblical events.

DISHAN [DIE shan] (*antelope*) — the seventh son of Seir the Horite, a clan chief in Edom (Gen. 36:21, 1 Chr. 1:38). Also see DISHON.

DISHON [DIE shahn] (*antelope*) — the name given to two descendants of Seir the Horite:

1. The fifth son of Seir and a clan chief in Edom (Gen. 36:21, 26, 30; 1 Chr. 1:38).

2. A son of the Horite clan chief Anah and a grandson of Seir (Gen. 36:25; 1 Chr. 1:41). Also see DISHAN.

DISHONESTY — deceit, usually for the sake of profit. To God dishonesty is as despicable and morally destructive as sexual depravity (Ezek. 22:11–13). The fact that God struck Ananias and Sapphira dead for their deceit (Acts 5:1–11) shows His intolerance of dishonest Christians. For the unbeliever, the holiness of God is visible primarily in the behavior of His people. It is imperative that Christians be honest in their dealings with all people (2 Cor. 4:2).

DISOBEDIENCE — an unwillingness to comply with the guidance of authority, especially a neglect of God's will. The first and most crucial act of disobedience occurred when Adam and Eve ate of the forbidden fruit (Genesis 3). Like all later human disobedience, that act involved setting the desire of the flesh above the will of God. As a result of this, all men became "sons of disobedience" (Eph. 2:2). The Christian has no choice, therefore, but to engage in a kind of spiritual warfare against his own natural tendency to disobey God (2 Cor. 10:5–6). He should aim to be as obedient to God's will as

Christ was when He "became obedient to the point of death" (Phil. 2:8).

DISPENSATION — a period of time under which mankind is answerable to God for how it has obeyed the revelation of God which it has received. The term dispensation is found twice in the NKJV: "The dispensation of the fullness of the times" (Eph. 1:10) and "the dispensation of the grace of God" (Eph. 3:2). The KJV uses the term four times (1 Cor. 9:17; Eph. 1:10; 3:2; Col. 1:25).

Many Bible students believe all of history can be divided into several dispensations. According to this view, all of history has been pointing toward the SECOND COMING of Christ, when salvation will be made complete. Others reject this view, insisting that God has had faithful, loyal followers in all times who have lived according to His COVENANT with them.

Seven dispensations are commonly identified: *Innocence*, from Creation to the Fall of man and God's sending them out of the Garden of Eden (Gen. 3:24); *Conscience*, the covenant with Adam, ending with the judgment of the Flood (Genesis 9); *Human government*, the covenant with Noah, extending to the time of Abraham; *Promise*, from Abraham's call (Gen. 12:1) to Moses; *Law*, from the giving of the Law to Moses (Ex. 19:8; 20–31) to the death of Jesus Christ; *Grace*, from the death and resurrection of Christ to His Second Coming; *Kingdom*, the establishment of God's kingdom on earth and the thousand year reign of Christ over the nations.

DISPERSION OF THE JEWISH PEOPLE — a scattering of the Jewish people among other nations. Throughout their history, the Hebrew people have experienced many dispersions—a term which comes from a Greek word meaning "to scatter." Some of these dispersions have been voluntary, while others have been forced upon them.

Voluntary movements were sometimes made by the Jews to escape the threat of destruction, as with those Judeans who moved to Egypt in the time of the prophet Jeremiah. Others left the homeland on various occasions with the expectation of pursuing an easier and more profitable way of life, as with the brothers of Joseph. Some migrants were most probably traveling merchants who chose to settle in a new homeland for business reasons, whereas others found themselves on foreign territory in a military capacity (2 Sam. 8:14).

While all Jews regarded the land promised to them by God through Abraham as their natural home, no Jew was ever compelled to live in it for his entire life. In periods of economic hardship or political upheaval many Jews took advantage of the opportunity to leave and begin life afresh in another country.

But forced dispersion was another matter. Periods of captivity for the Hebrews may have begun as early as the invasion of Palestine by Shishak of Egypt, about 918 B.C. (1 Kin. 14:25–26). But most significant for Hebrew history were the fall of Israel to the Assyrians in 722 B.C. and the collapse of Judah before Babylonian and Chaldean attacks in 597–581 B.C. Already in 732 B.C. Tiglath Pileser III had carried Reuben, Gad, and the half–tribe of Manasseh captive to Mesopotamia when Damascus fell. A decade later the capture of Samaria resulted in the remaining Israelite tribes being carried away as captives to ASSYRIA.

The end of national life in JUDAH began with the first attack on Jerusalem by the BABYLONIANS in 597 B.C. The final attack in 581 B.C. marked the end completely. By the end of this period, a total of some 4,600 prominent persons had been deported from Judah (Jer. 52:28–30). This number probably did not include family members or servants. The total may well have been at least double the number recorded by Jeremiah. The dispersion actually began earlier in Judah, for early in his ministry Jer-

A stone carving from the palace of Tiglath-Pileser of Babylon, showing the deportation of conquered citizens of Judah who lived in the city of Ashtaroth.

emiah reported that a significant number of Jewish emigrants lived in such Egyptian cities as Migdol, Tahpanhes, and Noph (Memphis). The prophet ministered to these people even before Jerusalem fell (Jer. 43:8; 44:1).

But the settlement in Egypt was small compared to that in Assyria, Babylon, and Persia as a result of the deportation from Israel and Judah. Captives from the Northern Kingdom were apparently absorbed completely into their foreign surroundings. But a small group of Judeans ultimately returned from Persia to Judea as a result of the decree of Cyrus (538 B.C.). Those who remained behind in Babylonia formed the basis of the Dispersion that was well known in New Testament times (John 7:35).

This dispersed Jewish community in Mesopotamia flourished into the medieval Christian period, maintaining its distinctive religious practices. It was here that the Babylonian TALMUD, a work which formed the basis for law and faith in the community, was compiled. The Dispersion was certainly supported by conditions in the Persian Empire and in the later Greek Empire, as the character of the crowd at Pentecost illustrates (Acts 2:9–11).

Interesting light has been shed on a fifth century B.C. Jewish colony in Egypt by the discovery of the Elephantine papyri. These documents disclosed the existence of a Jewish trading community near Aswan that had its own temple worship. This community was also an important center for commerce in southern Egypt. With the rise of the Greek Empire, further Jewish settlements occurred in Egypt, along with a significant increase in the use of the Greek language across the Near East. One result of this was the translation of the Hebrew Scriptures into Greek at Alexandria, Egypt. This version (called the SEPTUAGINT) became so popular that the New Testament writers quoted the Old Testament from it instead of using the traditional Hebrew text.

By 139 B.C. Jews who had migrated to Italy and settled in Rome were being expelled from the capital city. Even so, they had gained a foothold in Italy. By the beginning of the Christian period, colonies of Jews were scattered across the Near East and southeastern Europe. Although they were often disliked and sometimes persecuted, they managed to survive and prosper. By the time of Philo Judaeus (30 B.C.—A.D. 45), a Jewish philosopher of Alexandria, an estimated one million Jews lived in Alexandria. An equal number had settled in both Persia and Asia Minor, and about 100,000 lived in Cyrenaica and Italy. The Jews who were dispersed throughout the world in this manner outnumbered the Jews who remained in their native land of Palestine.

These colonies provided useful bases for evangelistic efforts by the apostle Paul and later Christian preachers. Eventually Christian communities were established in those cities that had a large Jewish population. Thus, the Dispersion helped to prepare the world for the reception and growth of the gospel.

The terebinth tree, also referred to as the oak tree by some translations, was considered sacred by some pagan worshipers of the ancient world (Hos. 4:13).

DISPERSION OF THE NATIONS — the dividing and scattering of the people of earth after the FLOOD and the Tower of Babel through the three sons of Noah (Gen. 10:32; 11:9). Japheth's descendants were scattered to the north, Ham's to the south, and Shem's to the central regions between his two brothers.

DISQUALIFIED — the NKJV translation of the Greek word *adokimos* (1 Cor. 9:27; 2 Cor. 13:5-7; Titus 1:16). In three other references, the NKJV translates the Greek word as debased (Rom. 1:28), disapproved (2 Tim. 3:8), and rejected (Heb. 6:8). The literal sense of the word is "tested and proved to be false or unacceptable." Borrowed from the athletic games, the word describes a contestant who, because of some infraction of the rules, is disqualified from winning the prize (1 Cor. 9:27; castaway KJV). Another metaphor is possible: a "counterfeit faith" (2 Tim. 3:8, RSV). This suggests a coin that has been tested, proven false, and disapproved as legal tender.

DISSENSION — discord or strife that arises from a difference of opinion. The apostle Paul was accused of being "a creator of dissension" (Acts 24:5) because of His preaching of the gospel before the SANHEDRIN.

DISSIPATION — indulgent or wasteful living, especially excessive drinking. Drinking much wine leads to dissipation (Eph. 5:18). A bishop should not be guilty of dissipation (Titus 1:6-7). A Christian should separate himself from the dissolution that characterized his former life.

DISTAFF — a staff that holds unspun flax or wool for spinning into thread (Prov. 31:19).

DIVINATION (see MAGIC, SORCERY, AND DIVINATION).

DIVINE NAMES (see GOD, NAMES OF).

DIVINER (see MAGIC, SORCERY, AND DIVINATION; OCCUPATIONS AND TRADES).

DIVINER'S TEREBINTH TREE [TER uh binth] — a tree that could be seen from the entrance to the city gate of Shechem (Judg. 9:37). Some scholars believe this tree was the same one mentioned in Genesis 12:6 or Genesis 35:4. Apparently it was assumed to be the tree associated with Abram and Jacob. Those who practiced magic or sorcery at the tree considered it a sacred place (plain of Meonenim, KJV; diviners' oak, NAS, RSV; soothsayers tree, NIV; Soothsayers' Terebinth, NEB).

DIVORCE — the legal dissolution of a marriage.

The divine ideal for marriage is clearly a lifelong bond that unites husband and wife in a "one flesh" relationship (Matt. 19:5). The marriage union is a holy condition founded by God and is not to be dissolved at the will of man (Matt. 19:6). Separations of this bond displease God and pose a serious threat to the social order: "And let none deal treacherously with the wife of his youth. For the Lord God of Israel says that He hates divorce, for it covers one's garments with violence" (Mal. 2:15–16).

The Law of Moses allowed a man to divorce his wife when she found "no favor in his eyes, because he has found some uncleanness in her" (Deut. 24:1). The primary purpose of this legislation was to prevent him from taking her again after she had married another man—"an abomination before the Lord" (Deut. 24:4).

This law was intended to discourage, rather than encourage, divorce. A public document known as a "certificate of divorce" was granted the woman. This permitted her the right to remarry without civil or religious sanction. Divorce could not be done privately.

The Mosaic Law called for severe penalties for certain types of "uncleanness." Adultery carried the death penalty by stoning for the woman. If a man believed that his wife was not a virgin when he married her, he could have her judged by the elders of the city. If they found her guilty, she could be put to death (Deut. 2:13–21). Although a man was allowed to divorce his wife, the wife was not allowed to divorce her husband for any reason. Legally the wife was bound to her husband as long as they both lived or until he divorced her (1 Cor. 7:39).

In Jesus' day, confusion prevailed about the grounds for divorce. Even the rabbis could not agree on what constituted the "uncleanness" of Deuteronomy 24:1. Followers of Rabbi Shammai felt adultery was the only grounds for divorce. Those who followed Rabbi Hillel accepted many reasons, including such things as poor cooking.

The gospels record four statements by Jesus concerning divorce. In two of these He allowed divorce in the case of adultery. In Matthew 5:32 Jesus commented on the situation of both the woman and her new husband: "Whoever divorces his wife for any reason except sexual immorality causes her to commit adultery; and whoever marries a woman who is divorced commits adultery."

In another statement, Jesus described the position of the man who divorced his wife: "Whoever divorces his wife except for sexual immorality, and marries another, commits adultery; and whoever marries her who is divorced commits adultery" (Matt. 19:9). While these two statements seem to allow divorce because of unfaithfulness, two other statements of Jesus appear to make no provision for divorce (Mark 10:11–12; Luke 16:18).

Are Jesus' statements allowing divorce for infidelity in conflict with biblical statements that seem to forbid it entirely? Jesus' statements in Mark and Luke were made in conversations with Pharisees about the Mosaic Law, which they believed allowed divorce on grounds other than adultery (Deut. 24:1–4). Jesus' main point in these statements was that divorce is contrary to God's plan for marriage and should never be taken lightly. Even though Moses allowed divorce, this was an exception granted under the law because of their "hardness" of heart (Mark 10:5). Jesus desired to put "teeth" into the Law by declaring that, even if the divorced couple had not been sexually unfaithful to each other, they would commit adultery in God's sight if they now married other partners.

In allowing divorce for the single reason of "immorality," or illicit sexual intercourse, Jesus' thought is clearly that a person dissolves his marriage by creating a sexual union with someone other than the marriage partner. Such union violates the sacred "oneness" intended by God when he united Adam and Eve in the first marriage relationship (Gen. 2:18–25).

In the case of sexual unfaithfulness, the decree of divorce simply reflects the fact that the marriage has already been broken. A man divorcing his wife for this cause does not "make her an adulteress," for she already is one. Thus, divorce on the grounds of unchastity usually frees the innocent partner to remarry without incurring the guilt of adultery (Matt. 19:9). However, this is sometimes questioned. Although Jesus allowed divorce for adultery, He did not require it. On the contrary, He insisted that divorce disrupts God's plan for marriage and left the way open for repentance and forgiveness.

Paul was essentially in agreement with Jesus' teachings on marriage and divorce. However, the apostle dealt with new situations involving the marital conflict between believers and between a believer and a non–believer.

In the case of two Christians, Paul admonished them to follow the Lord's teachings and be reconciled. In any event, neither is to marry another (1 Cor. 7:10–11). In 1 Corinthians 7:15, Paul says that a Christian whose mate has abandoned the marriage should be free to formalize the divorce: "If the unbeliever departs, let him depart; a brother or a sister is not under bondage in such cases." Many authorities hold that the phrase "not under bondage" means that a deserted Christian spouse may lawfully go from divorce to remarriage. But other scholars disagree with this interpretation. In any event, Paul encourages the believer to keep the marriage together in hopes that the unbelieving partner might be saved (1 Cor. 7:16).

DIZAHAB [DIZ uh hab] (*abounding in gold*) — a place in the Arabian desert near the site where Moses gave his farewell address to the nation of Israel (Deut. 1:1). It may be Edh-Dheilbeh, east of Heshbon.

DOCTOR (see RABBI).

DOCTRINE — a body of beliefs about God, man, Christ, the church, and other related concepts considered authoritative and thus worthy of acceptance by all members of the community of faith.

Christ condemned the doctrine of the Pharisees because it was of human origin (Matt. 15:9; Mark 7:7). By contrast, Jesus' teaching was not systematic and repetitious. It was fresh and new (Matt. 7:28; Mark 1:22, 27; Luke 4:32).

After Pentecost, Christian doctrine began to be systematized (Acts 2:42). Doctrinal instruction was given by special teachers (1 Cor. 12:28–29; Gal. 6:6) to those who had responded to the gospel (Rom. 6:17). The earliest doctrine of the Christian church declared: (1) that Jesus was the Messiah, the Christ (Acts 3:18); (2) that God had raised Him from the dead (Acts 1:22; 2:24, 32); and (3) that salvation was by faith in His name (Acts 2:38; 2:16). These three truths were presented as a clear fulfillment of the promises of the Old Testament. Paul taught that true doctrine is essential for Christian growth (Eph. 4:11–16; 1 Tim. 4:6; 6:3; Titus 1:9) and that false doctrine destroys the church (Eph. 4:14; 2 Tim. 4:3).

DODAI [DOE die] — a form of DODO.

DODANIM [DOE dah nim] — a son of Javan (Gen. 10:4), also called Rodanim (1 Chr. 1:7). The reference may be to the people who lived on the island of RHODES, and on the neighboring islands in the Aegean Sea.

DODAVAH [DOE duh vah] (*beloved of Jehovah or Jehovah*) — the father of Eliezer of Mareshah (2 Chr. 20:37; Dodavahu, RSV, NIV, NASB, NEB). Eliezer prophesied the destruction of Jehoshaphat's ships.

DODO [DOE duh] (*beloved*) — a name given to three Old Testament men:

1. The grandfather of Tola, a judge of the tribe of Issachar (Judg. 10:1).

2. The father of Eleazar, one of David's mighty men (2 Sam. 23:9; 1 Chr. 11:12). Also spelled Dodai (1 Chr. 27:4).

3. The father of Elhanan of Bethlehem, one of David's mighty men (2 Sam. 23:24; 1 Chr. 11:26).

DOE (see ANIMALS OF THE BIBLE).

DOEG [DOE egg] (*timid*) — an Edomite who was the chief of Saul's herdsmen. Doeg betrayed David and, on Saul's orders, killed 85 priests of Nob (1 Sam. 21:7; 22:9).

DOG (see ANIMALS OF THE BIBLE).

DONKEY (see ANIMALS OF THE BIBLE).

DOOR — the covering over an entrance into a tent (Gen. 18:1), a permanent house (Judg. 19:22), or a public building (Ezek. 47:1). The doors of Bible times were made of a wide variety of material, ranging from animal hides to wood and metal. Doors are also spoken of symbolically in the Bible. In speaking of Himself as the Good Shepherd, Jesus declared, "I am the door of the sheep" (John 10:7). Also see HOUSE.

DOORKEEPER (see OCCUPATIONS AND TRADES).

DOORPOST — the two sides of a doorway, similar to a door frame. The Hebrews were ordered by the Lord to spread the blood of a sacrificial lamb on the doorposts of their houses during the PASSOVER while in captivity in Egypt. This was a sign of their loyalty to the Lord; it also was a sign for Him to pass over the houses of the Hebrews when the first-born of Egypt were killed in the tenth and final plague that struck the land (Ex. 12:7). The Hebrews were later told to write sacred words on the doorposts of their houses as a reminder of God's commands (Deut. 6:9; 11:20). Also see HOUSE.

DOPHKAH [DAHF kuh] (*drover*) — a place in the Wilderness of Sinai between the Red Sea and Rephidim. Dophkah was the site of the first camp of the Israelites after they left the Wilderness of Sin (Num. 33:12–13).

DOR [dor] (*habitation*) — a Canaanite town on the Mediterranean coast south of Mount Carmel and about 13 kilometers (8 miles) north of Caesarea (see Map 3, A–2). The town was captured by Joshua (Josh. 11:2; 12:23; 1 Chr. 7:29) and assigned to Manasseh (Josh. 17:11). However, its inhabitants could not be driven out (Judg. 1:27). The "regions of Dor" (Naphath–dor, RSV) was one of Solomon's tax districts (1 Kin. 4:11).

DORCAS [DOR cuss] (*a gazelle*) — a Christian woman from Joppa known for befriending and helping the poor (Acts 9:36–43); also called Tabitha (Acts 9:36–43). She was raised from the dead by the apostle Peter. The Bible tells us little about her background, but it is possible that she was a woman of some wealth, or at least had connections with the wealthy. Dorcas may well have been one of the early converts of Philip the evangelist, who established a Christian church at Joppa.

DOT — RSV word for TITTLE (Matt. 5:18; Luke 16:17; the least stroke of a pen, NIV).

DOTHAN [DOE thun] (*wells*) — a city of the tribe of Manasseh situated west of the Jordan River and 19 kilometers (12 miles) northeast of Samaria near Mount Gilboa (see Map 4, B–3). It was here that Joseph found his brothers tending their sheep. They put him in a pit and later sold him into slavery (Gen. 37:17). At Dothan the Syrians were blinded by God in the time of Elisha (2 Kin. 6:8–23). Dothan's modern name is Tell Dotha.

DOUBLE — twice as much in amount, number, or

The mound of Dothan (center), the Old Testament city where Joseph's brothers threw him into a pit and later sold him to slave traders (Gen. 37:17-28).

value (Gen. 43:12, Ex. 22:4-9). Elisha asked that a double portion of Elijah's spirit be given to him (2 Kin. 2:9). But to be double-tongued (1 Tim. 3:8) is to use double talk—to be insincere or hypocritical. To be double-minded (James 1:8; 4:8), literally "two-souled," is to be divided in thinking—to waver or falter between two opinions.

DOUBT (see UNBELIEF).

DOUGH (see BREAD).

DOVE (see ANIMALS OF THE BIBLE).

DOVE'S DUNG (see PLANTS OF THE BIBLE).

DOWRY — a gift given to the father of one's bride. In the ancient world, when a man married, he was expected to give something to the woman's father. This was not considered a payment or a purchase price for a wife, but compensation to the father for the loss of her help as a daughter. The dowry could be money or goods (Gen. 34:12; Ex. 22:16-17), service to make up for the loss (Gen. 29:15-30), or the performance of some assigned task (1 Sam. 18:25-27; Judg. 1:12). Through the trickery of Laban, JACOB was forced to give 14 years of labor as a dowry for Laban's daughter, Rachel (Gen. 29:15-30).

DOXOLOGY — a declaration of praise to God or a brief hymn expressing His power and glory. The word itself does not appear in the Bible, but the concept is certainly present. Several passages in the Bible are called doxologies because of their clear declaration of praise to God.

One such passage is called the *Gloria in Excelsis,* or "Greater Doxology" (Luke 2:14). The title comes from the opening words of the angels to the shepherds when they announced the birth of Jesus in Bethlehem: "Glory to God in the Highest." The words of another doxology are found at the end of the Lord's prayer: "For Yours is the Kingdom and the power and the glory forever" (Matt. 6:13). The *Gloria Patri,* "Glory be to the Father, and to the Son, and to the Holy Ghost, world without end, Amen," is known as the "Lesser Doxology." This statement is not found in the Bible, although it reflects scriptural teaching.

Similar expressions offering praise and glory to God are also found in the Old Testament (1 Chr. 29:11; Ps. 8:1). A strong statement of praise is also found in the stanza of a hymn, "Praise God from whom all blessings flow," which has come to be known as the Doxology.

DRACHMA [DROCK muh] (see MONEY OF THE BIBLE).

DRAGNET — a net in which fish are trapped as it is dragged along the bottom of a stream (Hab. 1:15-16; Matt. 13:47).

DRAGON (see ANIMALS OF THE BIBLE).

DRAGON, BEL AND THE (see APOCRYPHA).

DRAGON WELL (see SERPENT WELL).

DRAWERS OF WATER (see OCCUPATIONS AND TRADES).

DREAMS — a state of mind in which images, thoughts, and impressions pass through the mind of a person who is sleeping. Dreams have had a prominent place in the religious literature of ancient peoples. In ancient times, dreams—especially those of kings and priests—were thought to convey messages from God (Num. 12:6; Gen. 31:10-13). In the Bible these were sometimes prophetic in nature.

Elihu stated clearly his belief that God speaks through dreams (Job 33:14–15).

In a dream God warned Abimelech, the king of Gerar, not to touch Sarah, because she was Abraham's wife. The Lord spoke to Jacob in a dream in which He renewed the COVENANT and assured Jacob of His protection and presence.

Two special cycles of dreams in which expert interpretation was involved occur in the Old Testament. The first cycle related to Joseph (Gen. 37:5–10), or his officers. The second cycle involved Daniel (Dan. 2:14–45), with the dreams coming to Nebuchadnezzar of Babylon. The dreams in each case pertained to events of the future. God granted the ability to interpret these dreams to Joseph (Gen. 40:8; 41:12) and Daniel (Dan. 2:20–45).

In the Old Testament dreams were frequently associated with the Hebrew prophets (Deut. 13:1–5; Jer. 23:25–32). But dreams, with their proposed prophecies, were not accepted uncritically. The false prophet and his prophecy had to be recognized and rejected. Jeremiah, especially, denounced the prophets who spoke with lies.

In the New Testament, God appeared to Joseph in a dream after His announcement of the forthcoming birth of Jesus (Matt. 1:20). God also spoke through these dreams to protect the infant Jesus (Matt. 2:13–14).

DREGS — solid material settled to the bottom in a liquid, especially wine. The word is used symbolically to refer to the final amount of the Lord's wrath poured out in judgment (Is. 51:17; Ps. 75:8). The dregs are the worthless, bitter remnants left when the wine is gone. To drink the dregs is to swallow the bitter and undesirable, a fitting expression of judgment.

DRESS OF THE BIBLE — The warmth of Palestine's climate led the people to prefer loose-fitting clothes, while the drab landscape may have contributed to their preference for bright colors in their garments. Clothing styles remained essentially the same throughout the period covered by the Old and New Testaments.

Clothing was made from simple material, such as leather or goat's hair. In the early period of their history, the Hebrews were a people who tended flocks and herds. Thus, they wove most of their clothes from plentiful wool. The flax plant provided linen for the more formal clothing of the priests or the wealthier classes.

Every Jewish home had a loom for weaving cloth. Colorful embroidery enlivened the fancier clothes. Purple dye was taken from a Mediterranean shellfish. Red came from insects taken from oak trees. Pomegranate and other plants provided blue dye.

General terms for clothing in the Bible include attire and raiment. But many specific items of dress are also mentioned. The following list of specific items is keyed to the NKJV. But variant terms from five additional popular English versions—KJV, NASB, NEB, NIV, and RSV—are also cross-referenced to this list.

Any student who compares clothing terms in these six translations will notice many differences in the translation of the same Hebrew or Greek word from one version to another. This shows that scholars are not always sure about exactly how an item of clothing should be translated. For serious Bible study, be sure to compare the rendering of several different translations.

Apron (see *Belt*).

An Arab bedouin with a headdress for protection against the sun. The high priest of the nation of Israel also wore headgear, referred to by some translations as a turban (Ex. 28:40).

Photo by Gustav Jeeninga

Belt/Sash. The belt, made of leather, cloth, or cord, was worn around the waist, much like the belt of today. The Bible mentions belts worn by Elijah (2 Kin. 1:8) and John the Baptist (Matt. 3:4). The rich man's leather belt might hold his sword, dagger, knife, or an inkhorn for writing. The scribe's reed or pen was also carried in the belt (Ezek. 9:2, 11).

When Elijah "girded up his loins" (1 Kin. 18:46), he was probably tucking up the loose ends of his cloak, or outer garment, into his belt. Peter urged the early Christians to "gird up the loins of your mind" (1 Pet. 1:13)—to open themselves to Jesus' message. Agabus bound Paul's hands and feet with his own belt (Acts 21:11).

The sash was longer than the belt. It consisted of a piece of folded cloth or wool wound two or three times around the waist. When made into a pouch, it might serve as a pocket for carrying money, other valuables (Matt. 10:9; Mark 6:8), or even food. Shepherds might even carry a lamb in their sash.

Other words for belt or sash used by other translations are girdle (KJV) and apron (NEB).

Cloak (see *Mantle*).

Coat (see *Mantle; Tunic*).

Girdle (see *Belt/Sash*).

Mantle. This item of clothing was the distinctive Hebrew outer garment, made of two pieces of thick woolen material sewn together, with slits rather than sleeves for the arms. In Old Testament times the mantle was usually brightly colored. Joseph's "tunic of many colors" (Gen. 37:3) was probably a mantle of woven, bright strips.

The Lord commanded the people of Israel to add blue tassels to the corners of their outer garments, as reminders to obey His commandments (Num. 15:38). This custom degenerated into a mere outward show of piety, and it was condemned by Jesus (Matt. 23:5).

The typical Hebrew slept on the floor with his mantle used as a covering to keep him warm. This was especially true for travelers, shepherds, or poor people, so a person's mantle was not to be kept as collateral for a loan (Ex. 22:27). In times of anguish, the Hebrews often tore their mantles to show their distress (Job 2:12; Ezra 9:3).

A handy, one-piece garment, the mantle protected a person from the weather. Because it fitted loosely, it could also be used to conceal or carry items. The typical Jewish mantle hung below the knees and was decorated with fringe.

Other words for mantle used by various English translations are cloak, coat, robe, and wimple.

Robe (see *Mantle*).

Sandals. The sandals worn by the Hebrew people were of cloth, wood, or dried grass, held on the foot by a thong or strap (Is. 5:27; Mark 1:7). Sandals were worn by all classes in Palestine, unlike Egypt where some people went barefoot. Women wore them too, as in the Song of Solomon (7:1). A certain kind of sandal for females had two straps, one between the big toe and the second toe, and another circling the instep and heel.

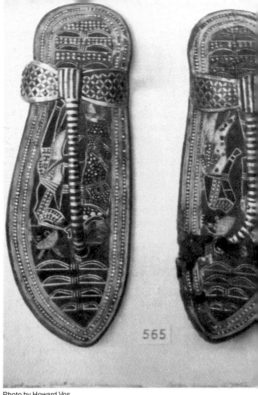

Photo by Howard Vos

Ornamental sandals, made of papyrus, discovered in the tomb of Pharaoh Tutankhamon (King Tut) of Egypt.

During mealtimes, the people apparently removed their sandals, as when Jesus washed His disciples' feet (John 13:5–6). However, the Israelites kept their sandals on their feet while eating the Passover meal, preparing to leave Egypt (Ex. 12:11). Sandals were to be taken off as a sign of reverence, as God said to Moses: "Take your sandals off your feet, for the place where you stand is holy ground" (Ex. 3:5).

Another word for sandals used by some English translations of the Bible is shoes.

Sash (see *Belt/Sash*).

Shirt (see *Tunic*).

Shoes (see *Sandals*).

Tunic. The tunic was a long piece of cloth folded in half, with holes for the arms and head. Also known as the inner garment, it was worn under the mantle, or outer garment. The tunic was generally made of leather, haircloth, wool, or linen. Jesus' tunic at the crucifixion was from one piece of cloth, since it had no seam (John 19:23). Women as well as men wore a tunic, often blue in color. Other words for tunic used by various English translations are coat and shirt.

Wimple (see *Mantle*).

Clothing for Special Occasions. In addition to the items of everyday dress used by the Hebrew people, the Bible also mentions the following specific clothes used for special occasions.

Mourning or repentance garments—Dark-colored sackcloth of coarse goat's hair was worn by Israel to lament the loss of his son Joseph (Gen. 37:34). Job wore sackcloth in his time of sorrow (Job 16:15). Eventually "sackcloth and ashes" became a symbol of repentance (Matt. 11:21). The dark sackcloth of the Israelites is similar to the western tradition of sombre colors at funerals.

Robe of honor—Special robes were worn by people of high political positions in the ancient world. Such a robe was given to Joseph by the Pharaoh of Egypt (Gen. 41:42).

Wedding garments—In New Testament times, the mother of the family often kept her wedding dress for her daughter to use at her wedding. She usually stored it in a box to protect it from moths alluded to by Jesus (Matt. 6:19). The wedding dress was usually white silk, perhaps embroidered. The bride also wore a veil and considerable jewelry. The bridegroom's attire resembled that of a king. He might also wear a garland. Festive robes were given to the guests at a wedding, as in Jesus' parable where a man was turned away for wearing inappropriate clothes (Matt. 22:11).

Winter clothing—The Hebrews wore fur dresses or animal-skin cloaks in winter time. The rich wore expensive robes, and the poor made do with common garments of "coarse hair" (Zech. 13:4), probably made from animal skins.

DRINK — the liquid necessary to sustain life. Water, milk, and wine were the most common forms of drink.

The hot, dry summers of Palestine required a dependable supply of water. Even travel routes were marked with watering places, usually WELLS or CISTERNS (Gen. 24:11; Ex. 15:27). During Israel's years of wandering in the wilderness, water from a rock furnished water for the people (Ex. 17:6). Later the psalmist David spoke of being led "beside still waters" (Ps. 23:2).

Because of the dry climate, it was necessary to store drinking water in cisterns. In unusually dry times water even had to be bought (Deut. 2:28; Lam. 5:4), and people might wander from city to city begging water (Amos 4:8). Families kept cows, sheep, goats, or camels for milk; they also kept vineyards for winemaking (1 Kin. 4:25; Zech. 3:10).

The Bible also speaks of drink in several symbolic ways. The earth "drinks" the rain (Heb. 6:7); killing one's enemy is to "drink blood" (Ezek. 39:18); evildoing is "drinking" evil (Job 15:16; Prov. 4:17; 26:6); and the sinful "drink" God's wrath (Rev. 14:10). In contrast, one can "drink" from the wells of salvation (Is. 12:3) and "drink" the blood of Jesus (John 6:54–55). The water of life satisfies all desires (John 4:14), and all who are thirsty are invited to come and "drink" (Is. 55:1; Rev. 22:17).

DRINK OFFERING (see SACRIFICIAL OFFERINGS).

DRINK, STRONG — any beverage that intoxicates. Strong drink was forbidden the priest when he was officiating at the altar of sacrifice (Lev. 10:9) and the Nazirite during his vow (Num. 6:3). It was also prohibited for princes (Prov. 31:4), but it was permitted the Israelite when eating at the sanctuary (Deut. 29:6). Samson's mother (Judg. 13:4, 7, 14), Hannah (1 Sam. 1:15), and John the Baptist (Luke 1:15) all abstained from taking strong drink. Those who drank excessively were called drunkards (Ps. 69:12).

The prophet Isaiah pronounced a woe on those who rose up early in the morning in order to follow strong drink (Is. 5:11). Israel's priests and prophets were accused of having erred through intoxicating drink (Is. 28:7). The people seemed to welcome false prophets who encouraged excessive drinking of wine and strong drink (Mic. 2:11).

In spite of all the commands against strong drink, it apparently had some medicinal value during Bible times. Along with wine, strong drink was listed as a sedative for the distressed (Prov. 31:6).

DRIVER (see OCCUPATIONS AND TRADES).

DROMEDARY (see ANIMALS OF THE BIBLE).

DROPSY (see DISEASES OF THE BIBLE).

DROSS — the residue left at the end of the smelting process after metal has been separated from the impurities. Dross was a symbol for the imperfection of sinful Israel. In the smelting process, heat is applied to ore that contains precious metal. This causes the imperfections to separate, leaving only the pure metal. The prophet Isaiah warned the nation of Israel that it had become impure and would require purging in this way (Is. 1:22–25).

DROUGHT (see FAMINE).

DRUNKENNESS — a drugged or deranged condition which results from drinking intoxicating beverages (1 Cor. 5:11; 6:10; Eph. 5:18). Drunkenness regularly appears in lists of vices in the New Testament (Luke 21:34; Rom. 13:13; Gal. 5:21).

Noah, who planted a vineyard and drank its wine after the Flood, is the first intoxicated man mentioned in the Bible (Gen. 9:20–21). While intoxicated, Lot fathered sons by his daughters (Gen. 19:32–38). People thought the apostles were drunk on the Day of Pentecost (Acts 2:15), and drunkenness was apparently a problem in the Corinthian church (1 Cor. 11:21).

Common symptoms associated with drunkenness and mentioned in the Bible include the drunkard and his songs (Ps. 69:12), his reeling and staggering (Job 12:25; Jer. 23:9), his vomiting (Is. 28:8; Jer. 25:27; 48:26), and his drugged condition (Joel 1:5).

Drunkenness is also spoken of figuratively in the Bible to describe a helpless people whose ways have brought them punishment from the Lord (Is. 29:9; Jer. 13:13; Ezek. 23:33). Symbolically, one may also be drunk from the Lord's fury (Is. 63:6; Jer. 25:27; Lam. 4:21) and the "wine" of fornication (Rev. 17:2).

DRUSILLA [droo SILL uh] (*watered by the dew*) — youngest daughter of Herod Agrippa I by his wife Cypros. Drusilla was the wife of Felix, the governor of Judea. While he was a prisoner, the apostle Paul pleaded his case before Felix and Drusilla: "Now as he [Paul] reasoned about righteousness, self-control, and the judgment to come, Felix was afraid" (Acts 24:25). The Scriptures do not record Drusilla's reaction.

According to the Jewish historian, Josephus, Drusilla was a Jewess who married Azizus, king of Emesa, who then converted to Judaism. Because of Drusilla's great beauty, Felix desired her for his wife. Drusilla then left Azizus and married the Gentile Felix in defiance of Jewish law (Acts 24:24).

DUKE (see OCCUPATIONS AND TRADES).

DULCIMER (see MUSICAL INSTRUMENTS).

DUMAH [DEW mah] (*silence*) — the name of one man and two places in the Old Testament:

1. A descendant of Ishmael and the ancestor of an Arabian tribe (Gen. 25:14; 1 Chr. 1:30).

2. A town in the hill country of Judah (Josh. 15:52). Its site is modern ed–Domeh, about 13 kilometers (8 miles) southwest of Hebron.

3. A symbolic name of EDOM or a place in Arabia (Is. 21:11).

DUMB, DUMBNESS (see DISEASES OF THE BIBLE).

DUNG — literally, waste produced by humans and animals as a part of the process of digesting food (Ex. 29:14; Lev. 4:11; Job 20:7). The word is also used in a general or symbolic way to describe what is useless, rejected, or despised (Jer. 16:4). It is in this sense that Paul evaluates the accomplishments of his life before Christ (Phil. 3:8), and the fate of Jezebel is described (2 Kin. 9:37).

Dung was used in Bible times as fertilizer. Dried dung was also used as a fuel. The prophet Ezekiel, for example, was commanded to bake his bread by using human dung. When he complained, God allowed him to use cow's dung (Ezek. 4:12, 15).

DUNG GATE (see GATES OF JERUSALEM AND THE TEMPLE).

DUNG HILL — KJV phrase for a heap or pit of human and animal wastes, used to fertilize plants in Bible times (Is. 25:10; refuse heap, NKJV).

DUNG PORT (see GATES OF JERUSALEM AND THE TEMPLE).

DUNGEON (see PRISON).

DURA [DEW ruh] (*circle* or *circuit*) — a plain in the province of Babylon where King Nebuchadnezzar set up a giant golden image (Dan. 3:1).

DUST — loose earth. God fashioned Adam out of the dust of the earth (Gen. 2:7). Because he led man to sin, the serpent was cursed to eat dust as he crawled on his belly (Gen. 3:14). Dust was poured upon the head as a sign of mourning. Dust is also used as a symbol for a numberless multitude (Gen. 13:16), for death (Job 10:9; Eccl. 12:7), and the grave (Dan. 12:2).

DUTY — obligatory tasks or service rendered to God. In the Old Testament, man's basic duty was contained in the Ten Commandments (Ex. 20:1–17). But Jesus summed up man's duty in His commandments to "love God" (Matt. 22:37) and "love your neighbor as yourself" (Matt. 22:39).

DWARF (see DISABILITIES AND DEFORMITIES).

DWELLING — the place where someone lives. This term could refer to a tent (Gen. 25:27), a HOUSE (2 Sam. 7:1), or God's dwelling, heaven (1 Kin. 8:30). The Hebrews lived in tents during their early history. They did not have permanent houses until they settled the land of Canaan under Joshua. The word dwelling is also used symbolically in the Bible. The Psalmist sang, "Lord, You have been our dwelling place in all generations" (Ps. 90:1).

DYER (see OCCUPATIONS AND TRADES).

DYSENTERY (See DISEASES OF THE BIBLE).

E

EAGLE (see ANIMALS OF THE BIBLE).

EAGLE OWL (see ANIMALS OF THE BIBLE).

EAR — an organ of hearing. The Bible speaks often of ears in a literal way (Gen. 35:4; Deut. 15:17). But far more significant is the use of the word ear in a figurative sense to speak of hearing and even of understanding. Thus the verb give ear means "to pay careful attention" (Job 32:11, KJV). Stopping up the ears means refusing to listen (Acts 7:57). To "turn the ear toward" suggests the desire to understand (Prov. 2:2). The "ears of the Lord" symbolize that He hears prayer, as opposed to idols which cannot hear (Ps. 18:6; 115:6).

EARNEST — a down payment or first installment given by a buyer to a seller to bind a contract, as a promise that the full amount will be paid at a later time. The apostle Paul wrote, "God has given us the Holy Spirit in our hearts as a deposit" (2 Cor. 1:22; earnest, KJV)—that is, as a guarantee of our inheritance (2 Cor. 5:5; Eph. 1:14; earnest, KJV; pledge, NASB, NEB). The Holy Spirit is not only the pledge of our complete salvation but also the foretaste of our future blessedness (Rom. 8:23).

EARRINGS — pieces of jewelry worn on the ear lobe in Bible times (Gen. 35:4). While these were generally worn only by Hebrew women, the men among the ancient ISHMAELITES apparently wore earrings (Judg. 8:24–25). Earrings were generally fashioned from silver or gold. Also see JEWELRY.

EARTH — the planet on which mankind lives. "The earth is the Lord's," wrote the psalmist, "and all its fullness" (Ps. 24:1). God is sovereign over the earth. All its living creatures, including mankind, are subject to His rule. The Israelites were promised that if they obeyed God's will and kept His laws, the earth would produce fruitful harvests; if they were disobedient, however, the crops would fail and famine would come (Deuteronomy 28).

After the FALL in the Garden of Eden, the earth was put under a curse. The Lord God said to Adam, "Cursed is the ground for your sake; in toil you shall eat of it all the days of your life. Both thorns and thistles it shall bring forth for you" (Gen. 3:17–18). The "earth" in this passage refers to the soil which brings forth food.

The apostle Paul wrote that the whole creation—including the earth and mankind—was "subjected to futility" and groans to "be delivered from the bondage of corruption" (Rom. 8:20–21). At the end of the age, however, the earth will be given renewed life, fertility, and productivity (Rev. 21:1).

EARTH, ENDS OF THE — the farthest regions of the world. The phrase is found often in the Old Testament (1 Sam. 2:10; Job 28:24), especially in the Psalms (59:13; 67:7), Isaiah (24:16; 40:28), and Jeremiah (31:8; 51:16). But the most important uses of this phrase occur in the Book of Acts: "You will be my witnesses in Jerusalem, and in all Judea and Samaria, and to the ends of the earth" (Acts 1:8, NIV). This reiterates the ancient promise made to Israel, now expressed in terms of the gospel of Christ, that the Gentiles will be brought to a saving knowledge of the Lord.

EARTH, FOUR CORNERS OF THE — a phrase found in Isaiah 11:12 and Revelation 7:1. To the people of Bible times the earth was flat and square. They knew nothing of a spherical earth which orbited the sun. The prophet Isaiah declared that "the Lord will...gather together the dispersed of Judah from the four corners of the earth" (Is. 11:11–12). The same thought might be expressed today as "from every point of the compass."

EARTH, THE NEW — the new physical universe that God will create at the end of time. After God created the heavens and the earth, humanity sinned and fell under God's curse (Genesis 3). One aspect of that curse was the desolation of the land of Israel when Israel rebelled against God. That desolation was described as a "waste and void" like the first unformed earth (Gen. 1:2). But God promised that He would create a new heaven and earth (Is. 65:17; 66:22). That promise will be fulfilled when the events foretold in Revelation 21—22 occur.

The occupation of the land was an important part of God's plan for man. Abraham and his descendants were promised a land, and Israel enjoyed the partial blessings of that land. But God always wanted to extend these blessings to all lands. This desire of God will be met when the new earth is created. For the present, the earth remains under God's curse, which brings much pain and suffering

(Rom. 8:19–22). But God's Spirit also groans in supportive prayer for the weakness of God's people until the new earth appears (Rom. 8:26–27).

EARTH, PILLARS OF THE — a phrase found in 1 Samuel 2:8: "For the pillars of the earth are the Lord's, and He has set the world upon them." A pillar is a support for holding up a building. The idea that the earth is supported by pillars, or upon foundations of some sort, is found often in the Old Testament. The eternal God was thought of as the certain foundation on which these pillars rested (Ps. 18:15; Jer. 31:37; Mic. 6:2).

EARTH, VAULT — a phrase used by some translations to show the view of the universe held by the ancient Hebrews. Many scholars believe the Israelites thought of the heavens as a solid dome above the earth—thus the description of God in some translations as founding "His vault upon the earth" (Amos 9:6; RSV, NASB). The Hebrew word translated as vault actually means "something held firmly together." The NKJV translates the phrase as "founded His strata in the earth."

EARTHQUAKE — a trembling or convulsion of the earth, often accompanied by volcanic eruptions. Earthquakes may cause fissures in the earth, avalanches, loud rumbling noises, and destructive fires (Num. 16:32; 1 Kin. 19:11).

A notable earthquake occurred during the reigns of Uzziah, king of Judah (792–740 B.C.), and Jeroboam II, king of Israel (793–753 B.C.). Amos dates his prophecy "two years before the earthquake" (Amos 1:1) and Zechariah writes of "the earthquake in the days of Uzziah king of Judah" (Zech. 14:5).

According to the Gospel of Matthew, an earthquake occurred at the crucifixion of Jesus (Matt. 27:51–54); another earthquake occurred at the resurrection of Jesus (Matt. 28:2). A great earthquake occurred in Macedonia when Paul and Silas were in jail at Philippi, "so that the foundations of the prison were shaken" (Acts 16:26).

The Bible uses earthquakes as symbols of God's power (2 Sam. 22:8), presence (Ps. 68:8), revelation (Ex. 19:18), and judgments (Ezek. 38:19–23).

Jesus said that "famines, pestilences, and earthquakes in various places...are the beginning of sorrows" (Matt. 24:7–8). All these events, he indicated, are "only the beginning" (Matt. 24:8) that will end in the catastrophic disasters of the last days. The Book of Revelation uses earthquakes as a symbol of the apocalyptic terrors of the endtimes—the upheavals in the religious and political realms which will precede and accompany the second coming of Christ (Rev. 6:12).

EAST (see DIRECTION).

EAST, CHILDREN OF — inhabitants of the lands east of Palestine, bordering on the desert (Judg. 6:3, 33).

EAST GATE (see GATES OF JERUSALEM AND THE TEMPLE).

EAST WIND (see WINDS).

EASTER — a feast or festival of the Christian church that commemorates the resurrection of Christ. It is observed and celebrated on the first Sunday following the full moon that occurs on or after March 21—or one week later if the full moon falls on Sunday. In other words, Easter falls be-

Mount Ebal, with the excavated remains of the city of Shechem in the foreground.

Photo: Levant Photo Service

Photo by Howard Vos

Excavated remains of Israelite houses at Ebenezer, where the Philistines captured the Ark of the Covenant from Israel (1 Sam. 4:1-22).

tween March 22 and April 25.

Easter was originally a pagan festival honoring Eostre, a Teutonic (Germanic) goddess of light and spring. At the time of the vernal equinox (the day in the spring when the sun crosses the equator and day and night are of equal length), sacrifices were offered in her honor. As early as the eighth century, the name was used to designate the annual Christian celebration of the resurrection of Christ.

The only appearance of the word Easter (KJV) is a mistranslation of *pascha*, the ordinary Greek word for "Passover" (Acts 12:4).

Also see PASSOVER.

EASTERN SEA — a lake on the southeastern boundary of the land of Israel (Ezek. 47:18), also known as the Salt Sea or the DEAD SEA.

EATING — the consumption of food at mealtime. The Israelites ate in the morning and in the evening (Ex. 16:12; John 21:4-5, 12). But this custom did not prohibit a snack at other times. For instance, laborers ate a light meal at noon (Ruth 2:14). Israelites were accustomed to wash their hands both before and after eating (Matt. 15:2; Luke 11:38), because food was lifted to the mouth with the fingers. Prayers were also offered before partaking of food (1 Sam. 9:13), in honor of God who sent the rain and harvest.

Like the ancient Egyptians and Greeks and modern Arabs, the Jewish people sat while eating, probably on mats spread on the floor or ground (Gen. 27:19; Judg. 19:6). They later adopted the practice of reclining upon cushions, couches, or divans (Esth. 1:6; 7:8).

Also see FOOD; HOSPITALITY; MEALS.

EBAL [EE buhl] (*bare*) — the name of two men and a mountain:

1. A son of Shobal and a descendant of Seir the Horite (Gen. 36:23).

2. A mountain north of Shechem and opposite Mount GERIZIM (Deut. 11:29; see map 3, B-3). Moses gave instructions to the Israelites about a religious ceremony they should observe after they crossed the Jordan River into the Promised Land. Moses also instructed that stones, whitewashed with lime, be set up on Mount Ebal, and an altar built to the Lord (Deut. 27:4-5).

At a later time, Joshua and the other leaders of the Israelites did all these things as Moses had commanded (Josh. 8:30-35). Joshua renewed the covenant by building "an altar to the Lord God of Israel in Mount Ebal" (v. 30), by offering "burnt offerings" and "peace offerings" to the Lord (v. 31), by writing on the stones the law of Moses (v. 32), and by reading the words of the law to the assembled multitude (vv. 33-35).

When Joshua read the blessings of the law, the people on Mount Gerizim responded with an "Amen;" when he read the curses of the law, the people on Mount Ebal responded with an "Amen." Hence, Mount Ebal became known as the Mount of Cursing. The tops of the two mountains are about three kilometers (two miles) distant from each other. The modern name of Mount Ebal is Jebel Eslamiyeh.

3. A son of Joktan, a descendant of Shem (1 Chr. 1:22; Obal, Gen. 10:28), possibly an ancestor of an Arabian tribe.

EBED [EH bed] (*servant*) — the name of two men in the Old Testament:

1. The father of Gaal (Judg. 9:26-35).

2. A descendant of Adin (Ezra 8:6). Ebed returned with Ezra from the Captivity.

EBED-MELECH [E bed ME leck] (*servant of the king*) — an Ethiopian eunuch who served Zedekiah, king of Judah. Ebed-Melech rescued the prophet Jeremiah from a dungeon (Jer. 38:7-13). Later, Jeremiah informed Ebed-Melech that he would be spared when the Babylonians captured Jerusalem (Jer. 39:15-18).

EBENEZER [ebb un EE zur] (*stone of help*) — the name of a place and a monument in Israel:

1. A place where Israel was defeated by the Philistines and the ARK OF THE COVENANT was captured (1 Sam. 5:1).

2. A stone erected by Samuel to commemorate Israel's victory over the Philistines. The stone may have been named after Ebenezer No. 1 to show that Israel's defeat there 20 years before had been reversed (1 Sam. 7:12).

EBER [EE bur] (*on the other side of*) — the name of six people or groups of people:

1. A descendant of Shem and an ancestor of Christ (Gen. 10:21, 24-25; Heber, Luke 3:35, KJV).

2. A name denoting the descendants of Eber; or, perhaps, a reference to those who lived "across" the River — on the other side of the Euphrates (Num. 24:24). Also see HEBER.

3. A family of the tribe of Gad (1 Chr. 5:13).

4. A family of the tribe of Benjamin (1 Chr. 8:12).

5. Another family of the tribe of Benjamin (1 Chr. 8:22).

6. A priest, the head of the house of Amok (Neh. 12:20).

EBEZ [EH bez] — a form of ABEZ.

EBIASAPH [eh BUY uh saf] (*the father has gathered*) — a Levite whose descendants were doorkeepers of the tabernacle (1 Chr. 6:23; 9:19; also spelled Abiasaph, Ex. 6:24).

EBONY (see PLANTS OF THE BIBLE)

EBRON [EE brun] (meaning unknown) — a town in the territory alloted to Asher (Josh. 19:28; Hebron, KJV). Ebron may be identical with Abdon (Josh. 21:30; 1 Chr. 6:74).

EBRONAH [ih BROH nah] — a form of ABRONAH.

ECBATANA [ECK bat uh nuh] — a form of ACHMETHA.

ECCE HOMO — the Latin translation of Pilate's words, "Behold the Man!" (John 19:5). "Ecce Homo" is also the name of a picture depicting Christ wearing a crown of thorns.

ECCLESIASTES, BOOK OF — a wisdom book of the Old Testament that wrestles with the question of the meaning of life. It takes its name from the Greek word, *ekklesiastes*, meaning "convener of an assembly." The book is often referred to by its Hebrew name, *qoheleth*, which means "preacher" or "speaker."

Structure of the Book. The second verse of Ecclesiastes, "Vanity of vanities, all is vanity" (1:2), eloquently summarizes the underlying theme of the book—that all human achievements are empty and disappointing when pursued as ends in themselves. Many passages in Ecclesiastes appear to be as pessimistic and depressing as this statement because they point out the folly of pursuing selfish goals. One after the other, the author shows how wisdom, pleasure, hard work, popularity, wealth, and fame fail to bring lasting satisfaction. But the book ends on a triumphant note as the reader is asked to consider life's highest good: "Fear God and keep His commandments, for this is the whole duty of man" (12:13).

Authorship and Date. King Solomon of Israel, a ruler noted for his great wisdom and vast riches, has traditionally been accepted as the author of Ecclesiastes. Evidence for this is strong, since Solomon fits the author's description of himself given in the book: "I, the Preacher, was king over Israel in Jerusalem. And I set my heart to seek and search out by wisdom concerning all that is done under heaven" (1:12–13). But some scholars claim that Solomon could not have written the book because it uses certain words and phrases that belong to a much later time in Israel's history. These objections by themselves are not strong enough to undermine

Solomon's authorship. The book was probably written some time during his long reign of 40 years, from 970 to 931 B.C.

Historical Setting. King Solomon amassed great riches during his long reign. He also developed a great reputation as a man of wisdom. He must have written Ecclesiastes as he looked back over his life and reflected on the meaning of all his accomplishments.

Theological Contribution. The Book of Ecclesiastes has a powerful message for our selfish, materialistic age. It teaches that great accomplishments and earthly possessions alone do not bring lasting happiness. True satisfaction comes from serving God and following His will for our lives.

But another important truth from Ecclesiastes, which we often overlook, is that life is to be enjoyed. The preacher of this book repeats this truth several times so it does not escape our attention: "There is nothing better for them than to rejoice, and to do good in their lives, and also that every man should eat and drink and enjoy the good of all his labor—it is the gift of God" (3:12–13). God wants us to enjoy life's simple pleasures. Our grateful acceptance of His daily blessings can bring a sense of joy and fulfillment to our lives.

Special Considerations. One of the most moving passages in the Bible is the poem from Ecclesiastes on the proper time for all events: "A time to be born, and a time to die" (3:2). This text, if taken seriously, can restore balance to our living. Another powerful passage is the figurative description of the aging process (12:1–7). The preacher realizes that old age with its afflictions looms ahead for every person. So he counsels his audience, "Remember now your Creator in the days of your youth, before the difficult days come" (12:1).

ECCLESIASTICUS (see APOCRYPHA).

ECLIPSE — a darkening of the earth that occurs when a planet or other heavenly body passes between the earth and the sun or moon. Several of the Old Testament prophets indicated that such a phenomenon in the sky was evidence of God's judgment (Is. 13:10; Joel 2:31). Also see ASTRONOMY.

ECZEMA (see DISEASES OF THE BIBLE).

ED [ed] (*witness*) — the name of an altar built by the Reubenites, Gadites, and the half-tribe of Manasseh who settled east of the Jordan River. This altar served as a witness of the loyalty of these tribes to the God of Israel and to the 10 tribes west of the Jordan (Josh. 22:34; translated *witness* by NKJV).

EDAR [E dar] — a form of EDER.

EDAR, TOWER OF [E dar] (see EDER).

EDEN [EE den] (*delight*) — the name of a garden, a man, and a region in the Old Testament:

1. The first home of Adam and Eve, the first man and woman. The concept "Garden of Delight" fits perfectly the setting of Genesis 2—3, a place of

ECCLESIASTES: A Teaching Outline

Part One: "All Is Vanity" (1:1–11)

Part Two: The Proof that "All Is Vanity" (1:12—6:12)

Part Three: The Counsel for Living with Vanity (7:1—12:14)

The Tigris River (shown here near Baghdad, Turkey) is commonly identified as the Hiddekel River referred to in the account of the Garden of Eden (Gen. 2:14).

God's blessing and prosperity.

A number of suggestions have been offered as to the location of Eden, including Babylonia (in Mesopotamia) or Armenia (north of Mesopotamia). Eden probably included the area of Mesopotamia (including Babylonia) and its immediate surroundings. The statement in Genesis 2:10 that four "riverheads" divided from the river that flowed out of the Garden of Eden (Gen. 2:10-14) supports this location.

Two of the rivers are clearly identified: the TIGRIS, which ran along the east side of Asshur (Assyria), and the EUPHRATES. The Pishon and Gihon rivers are hard to identify. The Gihon may have been in Mesopotamia, since Genesis 2:13 says it encompassed the whole land of Ethiopia, or "Cush" (possibly southeast Mesopotamia). Some think Pishon and Gihon represent the Indus and the Nile, respectively, suggesting that Eden included the whole of the Fertile Crescent from India to Egypt.

The Garden of Eden included many kinds of beautiful and fruitbearing trees, including "the tree of life" and "the tree of the knowledge of good and evil" located in the middle of the garden (Gen. 2:9). Man was to tend and keep the garden (Gen. 2:15) which, in addition to trees, could have contained other vegetation such as grain crops and vegetables (Gen. 1:11-12). The garden was also filled with all kinds of birds and land animals (Gen. 2:19-20), probably including many of the animals created on the sixth day of creation (Gen. 1:24-25). The garden was well-watered (Gen. 2:10), insuring lush vegetation and pasture.

After Adam and Eve sinned against God (Gen. 3:1-19), the Lord banished them from the garden. Cain, the son of Adam and Eve, is said to have lived in the land of Nod, "on the east of Eden" (Gen. 4:16).

In several Old Testament passages Eden is used as a symbol of beauty and fruitfulness, the place blessed by God (Is. 51:3). Revelation 22:1-2 alludes to the Garden of Eden by picturing a "river of water of life" and "the tree of life" in the heavenly Jerusalem.

2. A Levite who lived during the reign of King Hezekiah of Judah. He assisted in the religious reformation under Hezekiah, helping cleanse the Temple (2 Chr. 29:12) and overseeing the distribution of the freewill offerings (2 Chr. 31:15).

3. A region or city in Mesopotamia that supplied Tyre with choice items such as purple clothes, embroidered garments, chests of multicolored apparel, and strong twined cords (Ezek. 27:23-24). Called Bit-Adini on the Assyrian monuments, this place probably was near Damascus (Beth Eden, Amos 1:5; house of Eden, KJV).

EDER [EE dur] (*flock*) — the name of a tower, a city, and two men in the Old Testament:

1. A watchtower between Bethlehem and Hebron where Jacob once encamped (Gen. 35:21). The KJV has Edar.

2. A town of southern Judah, situated about seven kilometers (four or five miles) south of Gaza (Josh. 15:21).

3. A descendant of Elpaal and a son of Beriah, a Benjamite (1 Chr. 8:15). The KJV has Ader.

4. A descendant of Mushi and a Levite of the family of Merari (1 Chr. 23:23; 24:30).

EDOM [EE dum] (*red*) — the name of a person and a region (see Map 2, C-1) in the Old Testament:

1. The name given to ESAU after he traded his BIRTHRIGHT to his brother Jacob for a meal, which consisted of a red stew (Gen. 25:29-34).

2. The land inhabited by the descendants of Edom, or Esau (Gen. 32:3; 36:8). Ancient Edom in-

cluded the region beginning in the north at the River Zered, a natural boundary also for southern Moab, and extending southward to the Gulf of Aqabah. At times it included mountain ranges and fertile plateaus on the east and west of the Arabah, the Jordan River valley south of the Dead Sea.

The most significant area of ancient Edom was the mountain-encircled plain on the east of the Arabah. Mt. Seir, the highest of this range, rises to an elevation of nearly 1,200 meters (3,500 feet) above the Arabah. Edom's capital during the days of Israel's monarchy was Sela, situated at the southern end of a secluded valley that became the location of the city of PETRA in later times. Other important Edomite cities were Bozrah and Teman (Is. 34:6; Amos 1:12).

EDOMITES [EE dum ites] — descendants of Edom, or ESAU—an ancient people who were enemies of the Israelites. During the days of Abraham, the region which later became the home of the Edomites was occupied by more than one tribe of non-Israelite peoples. When Esau moved to this region with his family and possessions, the HORITES already lived in the land (Gen. 36:20).

Edom and Israel after Kadesh Barnea. After the years of wilderness wandering, Moses wanted to lead Israel northward to Canaan across Edom into Moab. The king of Edom, however, refused them passage (Num. 20:14–21), forcing them to bypass Edom and Moab through the desert to the east (Judg. 11:17, 18). Later in the journey northward to Abel Acacia Grove in the plains of Moab across from Jericho (Num. 33:48–49), Balaam prophesied that Israel would one day possess Edom (Num. 24:18).

From the Conquest Until the Division. In dividing the land of Canaan after the conquest, Joshua established Judah's border to the west of the Dead Sea and to the border of Edom (Josh. 15:1, 21). During the reign of Saul, Israel fought against Edom (1 Sam. 14:47). But Edomites at times served in Saul's army (1 Sam. 21:7; 22:9). David conquered Edom, along with a number of other adjacent countries, and stationed troops in the land (2 Sam. 8:13–14). In later years, Solomon promoted the building of a port on the northern coast of the Red Sea in Edomite territory. He also built a smeltery nearby as a significant part of his developing copper industry (1 Kin. 9:26–29).

After the Division. During the time of the Divided Kingdom, a number of hostile encounters occurred between the nations of Judah or Israel and Edom. During Jehoshaphat's reign, Edomites raided Judah but were turned back (2 Chr. 20:1, 8). An attempt to reopen the port at Ezion Geber failed (1 Kin. 22:48); and the Edomites joined forces with those of Judah in Jehoshaphat's move to put down the rebellion of Mesha of Moab (2 Kin. 3:4–5). During the reign of Joram, Edom freed herself of Judah's control (2 Kin. 8:20–22), but again came under Judah's control when Amaziah assaulted and captured Sela, their capital city. Edom became a vassal state of Assyria, beginning about 736 B.C.

Edom the Place of the Nabateans. After the downfall of Judah in 586 B.C., Edom rejoiced (Ps. 137:7). Edomites settled in southern Judah as far north as Hebron. Nabateans occupied old Edom beginning in the third century B.C., continuing their civilization well into the first century A.D. During the period from about 400–100 B.C., Judas Maccabeus subdued the Edomites and John Hyrcanus forced them to be circumcised and then made them a part of the Jewish people. The Herod family of New Testament times was of Edomite stock.

Since no written Edomite records have been found, knowledge of the Edomites comes mainly from the Bible, archaeological excavations of their ancient cities, and references to Edom in Egyptian, Assyrian and Babylonian sources.

EDREI [ED rih eye] (meaning unknown) — the name of two cities in the Old Testament:

1. A city of the kingdom of Og in BASHAN (see Map 3, D-2) and the site of Israel's defeat of Og's army (Num. 21:33–35; Josh. 12:4).

2. A fortified city allotted to the tribe of Naphtali. Edrei was between Kedesh and En Hazor, to the north of the Sea of Galilee (Josh. 19:37). It may be identical with present-day Tell Khureibeh.

EDUCATION — the transfer of knowledge, morals, and attitudes from one person to another, and usually from one generation to the next. In biblical times education did not follow the pattern with which we are now familiar. For the Hebrews, the goal of education was to prepare man to know God and to live peacefully among men (Luke 2:52); education did not emphasize the "three R's." The method of education was different, too, although by New Testament times, it had changed significantly. In the Old Testament period education was rather informal. Children were taught in the home by the parents, not in a formal classroom by a teacher. However, by New Testament times schools

Petra, situated in ancient Edom, is the site of numerous buildings carved from red sandstone cliffs by the Nabateans about 300 B.C.

Photo by Gustav Jeeninga

had been established to assist parents in the teaching of their children.

God gave the responsibility of teaching to parents (Deut. 11:19). To be a parent meant to teach. Both parents were involved in the child's education; however, the father was responsible to see that his children were properly educated (Prov. 1:8–9). A young son stayed with his mother when the father went to the fields to work. Therefore, a boy's first significant instruction came from his mother. As the boy grew, the father's involvement in his son's education increased, especially as they began to work together in the fields or in the father's trade. A daughter stayed on with her mother and continued under her instruction. In the close-knit family structure of that day, as parents became grandparents they also became involved in teaching their grandchildren (Deut. 4:9; 2 Tim. 1:5; 3:14–15). A parent's responsibility for instructing children continued until death.

The term "father" was applied to teachers outside the family, also, and teachers often called their students "sons." God made Joseph a "father" to the PHARAOH (Gen. 45:8), which means that the Pharaoh listened to Joseph as a pupil listens to his teacher and receives instruction from him. Throughout Proverbs the term "my son" indicates the same teacher–pupil relationship (Prov. 1:8, 10, 15; 2:1; 3:1, 11). And in the New Testament Paul spoke of Timothy as his son (1 Tim. 1:18).

During the period between the Old and New Testaments, SYNAGOGUES and schools were established. Generally, each rabbi taught in a village school supported by the parents of the children who attended. The teacher, or rabbi, of the school helped the parents by instilling religious truths in the boys' minds; however, the parents still were responsible for their children's education. In choosing a rabbi as a village teacher, the parents were more concerned with his personal character than with his ability to teach. His example was more important than his teaching skills. The ideal rabbi was a married man who also was industrious and serious. He would never joke with the boys, nor would he tolerate any wrongdoing. However, it was considered important that he be a patient man. Both rabbi and parents took God as their model for proper teaching. God was the Master Teacher (Is. 30:20–21), who taught by word and example (Ps. 78:1; Deut. 8:2–3).

Every father was expected to teach his son a trade. A Jewish proverb reads, "He who does not teach his son a useful trade teaches him to be a thief." Usually, a son followed in his father's occupation, with the father passing on his skills and trade secrets.

Scholars do not agree on how many Israelites could read and write in Old Testament times. By the New Testament period, however, almost every village had its own school where reading and writing were taught to the boys. Parents sent their sons to school for the purpose of learning to read the Scriptures; they continued in school from the age of 6 or 7 until about 12 years of age. If the parents wanted their son to receive more training, he was sent to Jerusalem, where a number of notable rabbis had schools. Young Paul (Saul of Tarsus) spent time there, studying under GAMALIEL (Acts 22:3). School was in session year-round, with the day beginning shortly after sunrise and continuing until about 10:00 A.M. On a hot day, the students would be dismissed for the remainder of the day. If the weather was more comfortable, classes reconvened about 3:00 P.M. for several more hours of study.

The school consisted of one classroom; all the students studied together. The teacher sat on a low platform (Luke 4:20); the students sat at his feet (Acts 22:3). Because the students were at different learning levels, the instruction had to be individualized. While the rabbi worked with one student or group, the others busied themselves with assignments. Because the rabbi believed that if the student did not voice his lessons, they would be forgotten, students spoke out loud as they read and memorized.

EGG, EGGS — an oval shell that contains the embryo of a bird. The Bible also speaks of eggs in symbolic fashion. The prophet Isaiah accused the people of Judah of hatching "vipers' eggs," a symbol of the evil schemes which they were plotting (59:5).

EGLAH [EGG la] — one of David's wives and the mother of David's son, Ithream (2 Sam. 3:5; 1 Chr. 3:3).

EGLAIM [EGG lay im] (*twin springs*) — a town on the border of Moab (Is. 15:8); site unknown.

EGLATH–SHELISHIYAH [EGG luth shell ih SHY ya] — an unknown city mentioned in the prophetic oracles pronounced against Moab (Is. 15:5; Jer. 48:34, NIV).

EGLON [EGG lahn] (*young bull*) — the name of a city (see Map 4, A–4) and a king in the Old Testament:

1. An Amorite city in the western SHEPHELAH (lowlands). Eglon was one of five allied cities that attacked Gibeon but were conquered by Joshua (Josh. 10:3).

2. An overweight Moabite king who reigned during the period of the judges (Judg. 3:12–25). Allied with the Ammonites and the Amalekites, Eglon invaded the land of Israel. His army captured Jericho, and he exacted tribute from the Israelites.

After 18 years of Eglon's rule, the Lord raised up EHUD the Benjamite, a left-handed man, to deliver Israel. Ehud stabbed Eglon in the belly with a dagger. Because Eglon was a very fat man, "even the hilt went in after the blade, and the fat closed over the blade, for he did not draw the dagger out of his belly" (Judg. 3:22).

Photo by Willem A. VanGemeren

Rameses II of Egypt ordered his craftsmen to carve these enormous statues out of solid rock in the 13th century B.C.

EGYPT [EE jipt] — the country in the northeast corner of Africa that extended from the Mediterranean Sea on the north to the first waterfall on the Nile River in the south (see Map 9, A–5)—a distance of about 880 kilometers (540 miles). The Israelites spent 430 years in this land (Ex. 12:40) between the time of Joseph and Moses. Jesus lived temporarily in Egypt during His infancy (Matt. 2:13–15).

The Egyptians called their country Tawy, "the two lands"—referring to Upper and Lower Egypt—or Kemyt, "the black land," which distinguished the fertile Nile valley from the red desert sand. In the Bible the word for Egypt is Mizraim, which is the name of one of the sons of Ham who founded the country (Gen. 10:6; 1 Chr. 1:8).

History of Egypt. Information about Egyptian history is found in the Bible, Egyptian and Greek historical books, various Egyptian papyrus documents and stone writings, and facts from archaeological investigations of ancient Egyptian cities, temples, and graves. One of the most helpful chronological surveys of the Egyptian kings was provided by the Egyptian priest Manetho. He divided the kings of Egypt into 30 different dynastic families who ruled from 3000–300 B.C. Some of these dynasties were strong, while others were comparatively weak.

The history of Egypt can be simplified by ordering these dynasties into three main periods of strength: the Old Kingdom (2700–2200 B.C.); the Middle Kingdom (2000–1800 B.C.); and the New Kingdom (1570–1100 B.C.). Each of these kingdoms

was followed by a period of weakness.

After the New Kingdom, Egypt was dominated by Libyan, Ethiopian, Persian, Greek and finally Roman powers during New Testament times. The dates for these periods and the length of the reigns of each king is not securely fixed. But Egyptologists have been able to reconstruct a fairly accurate chronology by using evidence from many different sources.

Archaeologists have found a number of small villages that date prior to the beginning of the Old Kingdom period of Egyptian history. These primitive hunting and farming communities were the descendants of Mizraim, the son of Ham (Gen. 10:6). Metal objects, tools, pottery, jewelry and religious objects were found in these early graves. Trade with Mesopotamia may have been an important factor in the development of a written Egyptian language, which used pictures in a system known as HIERO-GLYPHICS.

Around 3000 B.C., some 1000 years before Abraham, all of Egypt was joined together under one king at Memphis. The land was divided into districts called "nomes." Irrigation and the plow were introduced to increase the nation's agricultural productivity. Shortly thereafter, the Old Kingdom period of Egypt's history began. During this era, the famous pyramids of Egypt were built. Djoser's step pyramid at Saqqara and the three great pyramids at Giza are a testimony to the power and prosperity of the nation, as well as evidence of the people's belief in the divine character of the PHA-RAOH, the Egyptian ruler.

Several pyramids have long series of curses, magical spells, and ritual formulas written on the walls of the burial chambers. These were to be used by the dead Pharaoh for protection on his journey to the afterlife. Large open-air temples where various rituals in honor of the king were performed were built beside the pyramids.

The arts of painting, sculpturing, and architecture excelled in Egypt. One group of texts known as the "Memphite Theology" probably date back to this era. They describe how the god Ptah spoke and created all things, indicating that the Pharaoh was considered divine. Wisdom writings from Imhotep and Ptahhotep reveal something of the moral values and ideals of the nation and the high literary achievements of the educated classes.

As the government of Egypt expanded, noblemen from various parts of the nation began to gain greater power. This led to a decentralization of power and ultimately to the first intermediate period of weakness around 2200 B.C. This time was described as an epic of chaos, instability, poverty, and despair.

Two texts from this period describe man's disillusionment with life. Another expresses a strong desire for social stability and justice. These events led to a rethinking of man's ideals. As a result, the highly structured social order was re-evaluated and social justice for even the peasant was proclaimed as important. The possibility of life after death,

These two columns among the ruins of an ancient Egyptian building represented Lower Egypt (left) and Upper Egypt (right).

Photo by Howard Vos

which had been limited to the kings, became the goal of noblemen as they rose to higher power. Ultimately even the common person pursued this hope.

The Middle Kingdom era of Egypt's history (2000–1800 B.C.) parallels the time of Abraham's journey into Egypt (Gen. 12:10–20). Wisdom texts, one supposed prophecy, and stories about fishing and hunting depict life at this time. During this era, the new kings centralized the government, expanded agricultural production through new irrigation projects, established the security of the nation by defeating the Nubians from Cush, and set up a series of defensive fortresses on the southern and western borders.

Trade with Phoenicia, mining in the Sinai desert, and at least one military raid into Palestine to Shechem indicate that Egypt had close relationships with Palestine when the patriarchs such as Abraham and his descendants first came to the land. The "Story of Sinuhe" describes an Egyptian's trip to Palestine and the fertility of the land. A painting in a tomb from this period shows 37 men from Canaan who traveled to settle in Egypt. Texts containing magical curses (the Execretion Texts) on Egypt's enemies contains the names of the kings of Tyre, Beth-Shemesh and Jerusalem. These indicate that Egypt's stability was weakening and that the second intermediate period of weakness (1750–1570 B.C.) was about to begin.

During this time of weakness, many non-Egyptians entered the country. A group called the Hyksos ("ruler from a foreign land") took control of the nation. Joseph's rise to an important position in the house of Potiphar (Genesis 39) and his appointment to the task of collecting grain during the years of plenty (Genesis 41) were possible because other foreigners had significant places in the Hyksos government.

Some scholars once thought the Hyksos were the children of Israel, but few accept this view today. The Hyksos used the bow, body armor, the horse and chariot, and a new defensive wall system for Egyptian cities. But in spite of their military power, they were driven out of Egypt when the New Kingdom began.

The New Kingdom period (1575–1100 B.C.) parallels the biblical period just before the birth of Moses until the time of Samuel. The New Kingdom began when the Egyptians managed to drive out the Hyksos and reunite Egypt. This new dynasty was made of kings "who did not know Joseph" (Ex. 1:8). They began to persecute the Hebrews, forcing them to build the cities of Pithom and Rameses (Ex. 1:11). The Hebrews were seen as foreigners who were a threat to the security of the nation (Ex. 1:10), so they were enslaved.

The powerful Queen Hathshepsut carried out many building and reconstruction projects and expanded trade relations with several foreign countries. The next king was an aggressive warrior, and he conducted several campaigns into Palestine. Many believe his son, Amenhotep II, was the Pharaoh of the Exodus. Egyptian texts do not mention

The Sphinx and the Great Pyramid, timeless symbol of the land of Egypt and its people.

the ten plagues, the Exodus of the children of Israel from Egypt, or the defeat of Pharaoh and his army in the Red Sea (Exodus 7—15). But this would hardly be expected since the Egyptians seldom recorded any of their defeats. Before the Exodus, Egypt was at the height of its power; but God humbled the nation and taught its people that He was God—not Pharaoh or any of the other gods of Egypt (Ex. 7:5; 8:10, 22; 9:14, 29; 10:2; 12:12).

Many interesting stories come from this period of Egyptian history. "The Tale of Two Brothers" describes how the wife of one brother lied about the sexual advances of the other brother. This story is similar to the false accusation of Potiphar's wife against Joseph. Myths about the struggles between the gods Horus and Seth and the wisdom "Instructions of Amenemopet," which are in some ways similar to the book of Proverbs, are a few of the important literary compositions from Egypt during these years.

No one knows how the Exodus affected Egypt's religious beliefs. But several years later in the middle of the New Kingdom, King Akhenaten rejected the worship of Amon at Thebes and proclaimed that Aten, the solar disk of the sun, was the only god. A beautiful hymn of praise to Aten has been discovered. This shows clearly that Akhenaten was pushing the Egyptians to adopt belief in one god. Religious tension was very high because Akhenaten dismissed the priests at the other temples and moved his capital to El–Amarna.

About 350 letters from Babylon, the Hittites, and many cities in Palestine were found at this capital. These letters reveal that Palestine was under a great

deal of political unrest during the time of Joshua and the judges. A few years later the famous King Tut (Tutankhamen), whose burial chambers were found near Thebes, ruled for a few years. He brought the nation back to the worship of its traditional gods at Thebes, relieving much of the tension within the nation.

During the final 200 years of the New Kingdom, the capital of Egypt was moved from Thebes to the city of RAMESES in the delta area. Large construction projects at Thebes, Abydos, Abu Simbel, and in the delta stand as a memorial to the greatness and power of these kings. Some believe the Exodus took place during the reign of Rameses (1304–1238 B.C.), but this contradicts the statement of the Bible that the Exodus took place 480 years before Solomon began to build the temple in 955 B.C. (966 plus 480 equals 1446 B.C. for the Exodus). One king, Merneptah, described his defeat of several Canaanite countries and actually mentions his defeat of Israel.

There is a wealth of historical, literary, and religious writings from the New Kingdom period of Egyptian history. Papyri, ostraca, and tomb and temple accounts give a graphic picture of Egyptian life. A primitive alphabetic script was discovered on the rocks in the Egyptian mines in the Sinai desert. The New Kingdom ended because of government corruption, strikes, inflation, and the increasing power of the temple priests, who constantly contended for greater advantage.

After the New Kingdom came the Late Period of Egyptian history (1100–330 B.C.). The fragmentation of Egyptian power allowed David and Solo-

The step pyramid (right) near Cairo—the oldest known Egyptian pyramid (2700 B.C.)—with accompanying temple built in more modern times.

mon to establish Israel as a strong nation. The Egyptian story of Wen–Amon's trip to Byblos to secure cedar for the construction of a ship for the Pharaoh tells how he was robbed and then refused the needed lumber until proper payment could be made. Such incidents clearly indicate the low status of Egypt during this time. The nation was not a strong military power; so more emphasis was placed on trying to form peaceful trade relations with neighboring states.

Solomon married the daughter of an Egyptian Pharaoh (1 Kin. 3:1), but later in his reign a new king (probably Shishak) provided refuge for two of Solomon's enemies (1 Kin 11:17, 40). A few years after Solomon's death (930 B.C.), Shishak, a Libyan who had become Pharaoh, attacked Rehoboam, and plundered the gold from the king's palace and the temple in Jerusalem (1 Kin. 14:25–28). A monument of Shishak was discovered by archaeologists during their excavation of Megiddo. His record of this battle on the walls of a temple at Thebes indicates that he defeated 150 towns in Judah and Israel. Later Zerah, an Ethiopian general or Pharaoh (2 Chr. 14:9–15; 16:8), led an Egyptian army against Asa, king of Judah; but God miraculously gave victory to Asa.

Ethiopian and Saite dynasties controlled Egypt for several hundred years until the destruction of Israel by the Babylonian King, Nebuchadnezzar, in 587 B.C. These Pharaohs were not particularly powerful because of the political supremacy of the Assyrians and the Babylonians. The Israelite king Hoshea sought the help of Pharaoh So around 725 B.C. (2 Kin. 17:4) to fight against the Assyrians, but the Egyptians were of little value.

Around 701 B.C. Hezekiah was attacked by the Assyrian king Sennacherib. Tirhakah, the Ethiopian king of Egypt, came to Hezekiah's aid (2 Kin. 19:9; Is. 37:9). The Assyrians themselves marched into Egypt in 671 and 664 B.C., destroying the Egyptian forces as far south as Thebes. To strengthen the Egyptian army, the nation hired Greek mercenaries to fight in their army; but this still did not give them any great strength. Josiah, king of Israel, was killed by the Egyptian Pharaoh Necho in 609 B.C. because Josiah tried to interfere with the Egyptian efforts to help the Assyrians who were under attack by the Babylonians (2 Kin. 23:29). After Josiah's death, Judah came under the control of Egypt; but in 605 B.C. the Egyptians were crushed by the Babylonians. Many Jews fled to Egypt after the destruction of Jerusalem, although the prophet Jeremiah warned against it (Jeremiah 39—44). Nebuchadnezzar later defeated Egypt (Jer. 46:13); he was followed by the Persians (525 B.C.) and the Greeks (330 B.C.). After 330 B.C. a group of Ptolemaic kings ruled Egypt, developing the great city of Alexandria as a center of culture and learning.

Many Jews lived in Alexandria during this period. The Greek translation of the Old Testament from Hebrew to Greek was completed during this time so the Greek-speaking Jews would have a Bible in their language. The Romans took control of Egypt around 30 B.C. From the second century A.D. until the Muslim conquest of Egypt in 642 A.D., Egypt was primarily a Christian nation.

The Religion of Egypt. The Egyptians were polytheists, believing in many gods. Many of these gods were the personification of nature, such as the Nile, the sun and the earth. But other gods stood for abstract concepts such as wisdom, justice, and order. Some gods were worshiped on a national level, but others were local deities. Many cities had their favorite deity, which was the patron god of that locality (Ptah at Memphis or Amon at Thebes). But the cosmic gods like Nut (the goddess of the sky), Geb (the god of the earth), and Re (the sun god), were known throughout the nation.

The beliefs and practices of the Egyptians changed over their 3000-year history. Thus, any discussion of the Egyptian religion must involve generalizations that permeated most aspects of religious life, as well as the individual details and variations that changed within the nation's complex history.

One of the most confusing aspects of Egyptian religion was its ability to accept the process of syncretism. Through this process one god would take on the characteristics of another god and thus eliminate its distinctiveness. Another aspect of Egyptian religion, which is largely hidden, is the extent to which the official beliefs of the priests differed from those of the common peasants. Since most information is based on the official records kept in temples and the tombs of the kings, it is likely that these do not represent the beliefs of the poorer people.

The Egyptians believed that the gods were intimately involved with all aspects of life. The gods caused the rain, controlled the growth of crops, determined birth and death, and ultimately were behind everything. Nothing happened by chance. They did not give natural explanations to events, because they made no distinction between the secular and the sacred. The Israelites also believed that God was the force behind everything, but they had only one God who was not identified with any part of nature. The Egyptians confused the Creator with His creation.

Many of these nature deities were represented as animals (bull, crocodile, falcon, ram, jackal) or by a part-human and part-animal statue. These gods were worshiped in temples throughout the land. Huge temples that covered many acres were built for the great cosmic gods. These were cared for by a large company of priests. The priests were responsible for the regular festivals at the temples and for the daily care for the gods.

Since each god was the king of its own realm of influence, it was treated as a king in its temple. The deity would be awakened, washed, dressed, fed (by an offering), taken for walks, and put to bed. These practices were totally opposite the activities in the Israelite Temple, where God was separated from the priest in the Holy of Holies. God was considered the King of Israel and the head of the nation, but the sacrifices were for the removal of man's sin—not to provide food for God.

The Pharaoh himself was one of the most important Egyptian gods. While ruling, he was the incarnation of the god Horus and the son of Re. After his death, he was identified with the god Osiris. The Pharaoh was a mediator between the people and the cosmic gods of the universe. Thus the Pharaoh was a key factor in determining the fate of the nation. Israel's kings were never considered gods, because God was the true King of Israel (1 Sam. 8:7). Originally only the Egyptian kings had the possibility of eternal life after death, but later this hope was opened to all people. This possibility was dependent on one's character in this life.

The worship of Osiris was one of the most important aspects of Egyptian religion. Osiris was the king of the underworld, where people went after death, as well as the god of fertility. An Egyptian myth about the murder of Osiris by the god Seth and the subsequent avenging of his death by Horus was very popular in Egypt. It provided the basis for people's hope for prosperity and immortality in the next life because of fertility in this life.

Before the rise of the cult of Osiris, the worship of Ptah at Memphis was dominant. The "Memphite Theology" claimed that Ptah was the supreme god of Egypt who created the world and man. The god Amon came to prominence when the kings from Thebes came to power and the god Aten received special attention during the reign of the Pharaoh Akhenaten. Thus the significance and honor of the Egyptian gods rose and fell according to the religious convictions of the ruling Pharaoh and the political power of the priests at the various temples.

In the New Kingdom period three gods were given special status: Amon, Re, and Ptah. One text even talks about these three as different aspects of one great Egyptian god. It is astonishing how religious the Egyptians were and how close some of their beliefs came to the truth. But there is no sign that their contact with Moses and the children of Israel had a lasting effect on the religious beliefs or practices within Egypt.

EGYPT, BROOK OF — a dry stream bed, or wadi (see Map 4, A-4), which served as the dividing line between Canaan and Egypt (Josh. 15:4; Is. 27:12).

EHI [EE high] (*unity*) — a son of Benjamin (Gen. 46:21). Ehi is also called Ahiram (Num. 26:38).

EHUD [EE hud] (*strong*) — the name of two men in the Old Testament:

1. One of the judges of Israel (Judg. 3:15—4:1). This left-handed man of the tribe of Benjamin assassinated EGLON, king of Moab, who was Israel's oppressor. He then fled to the hill country of Ephraim, where he summoned the Israelites by blowing a trumpet. Under Ehud's leadership the Israelites descended into the Jordan Valley and captured the river crossing. They then killed 10,000

Moabites who attempted to cross the Jordan. After the victory, Ehud judged Israel the remainder of his life. During his leadership Israel remained faithful to God.

2. A son of Bilhan and a great-grandson of Benjamin (1 Chr. 7:10; 8:6).

EKER [EE cur] (*offspring*) — a son of Ram, of the tribe of Judah (1 Chr. 2:27).

EKRON [ECK ron] (*barren place*) — the northernmost of the five chief cities of the Philistines (see Map 3, A–4), near the Mediterranean Sea and about 66 kilometers (35 miles) west of Jerusalem (1 Sam. 6:16–17). Ekron was apportioned first to the tribe of Judah (Josh. 15:45–46), then given to the tribe of Dan (Josh. 19:40–43). After David killed Goliath, the Israelites pursued the Philistines to the very gates of their fortified stronghold, Ekron (1 Sam. 17:52).

The prophets pronounced God's judgment upon Ekron, along with her sister cities (Amos 1:8).

EKRONITES [ECK ron ites] — natives or inhabitants of EKRON (Josh. 13:3).

EL [EL] (see GOD, NAMES OF).

EL ELOHE ISRAEL [el e LOW he IHS ray el] (see GOD, NAMES OF).

EL OLAM [el OH lam] (see GOD, NAMES OF).

EL PARAN [el PAY ran] (*god of Paran*) — a place in the Wilderness of Paran in southern Palestine in Abraham's time (Gen. 14:6; El-paran, KJV, RSV, NEB, NASB). El Paran is probably an earlier name for Ezion Geber, today known as Elath.

EL SHADDAI [el SHAD eye] (see GOD, NAMES OF).

EL ELYON [el EL yun] (*God Most High*) — a Hebrew name for God. Translated into English, it means "God Most High" (Gen. 14:18–20). Melchizedek, king of Salem, was the priest of God Most High. Also see GOD, NAMES OF.

ELADAH [EL uh dah] (*God has adorned*) — a descendant of Ephraim (1 Chr. 7:20; Eleadah, RSV, NASB, NIV).

ELAH [EE la] (*oak*) — the name of six men and a valley:

1. A chieftain of Edom (Gen. 36:41).
2. The father of Shimei, one of Solomon's 12 governors who provided food for the royal household (1 Kin. 4:18).
3. A valley in Judah where David killed Goliath (1 Sam. 17:2; 21:9).
4. The fourth king of Israel. Elah was the son and successor of Baasha (1 Kin. 16:6–14). His wicked two-year reign ended when Zimri, one of his captains, murdered him while he was in a drunken stupor.
5. The father of Hoshea, king of Israel (2 Kin. 15:30; 17:1).
6. A son of Caleb and the father of Kenaz (1 Chr. 4:15).

7. A son of Uzzi, a Benjamite who returned from the Captivity to live in Jerusalem (1 Chr. 9:8).

ELAM [EE lum] (*highland*) — the name of eight or nine men and one geographical region in the Old Testament:

1. A son of Shem and grandson of Noah (Gen. 10:22). He was the ancestor of the Elamites (Ezra 4:9).
2. A geographical region east of Babylonia and the Tigris River (see Map 1, E–2). It was bounded on the north by Media and Assyria, on the east and southeast by Persia, and on the south by the Persian Gulf. In the time of Abraham, "Chedorlaomer, king of Elam" is described as the overlord of three other Mesopotamian kings (Gen. 14:1–17). The prophet Isaiah lists Elam as one of the places to which the Israelites were exiled (Is. 11:11). Elam is described as a people who "bore the quiver" (bow and arrow) and who had "chariots of men and horsemen" (Is. 22:6). Jeremiah lists Elam as one of the peoples who would be forced to drink of the cup of God's fury (Jer. 25:15, 25).

Ezekiel prophesies of a time when a funeral dirge will be chanted over the grave of Elam; the once-mighty nation shall be consigned to the Pit (Ezek. 32:24–25). When the Assyrians transported people from the east to settle them in Samaria, the Elamites were among those resettled (Ezra 4:9). CYRUS the Great, the founder of the Persian Empire who conquered Babylon and assisted the Jews, was from Anshan (a designation that apparently refers to eastern Elam with Susa, or SHUSHAN, as its capital). The Book of Esther records events which took place in Shushan (Esth. 1:2; 8:14–15). Daniel writes, "I was in Shushan, the citadel, which is in the province of Elam" (Dan. 8:2). Among the foreigners present in Jerusalem on the Day of Pentecost were "Parthians and Medes and Elamites" (Acts 2:9).

3. A son of Shashak, of the tribe of Benjamin (1 Chr. 8:24).
4. A son of Meshelemiah, a Levite from the family of Kohath (1 Chr. 26:3).
5. The ancestor of a family that returned with Zerubbabel from the Captivity (Ezra 2:1–2, 7).
6. Another person whose descendants returned from the Captivity (Ezra 2:31). Possibly the same as Elam No. 5.
7. One whose descendants returned with Ezra from the Captivity (Ezra 8:7).
8. The grandfather of Shechaniah, who confessed to marrying a pagan wife during the Captivity and proposed that all those who had done so "put away [divorce] all these wives" (Ezra 10:3).
9. One of the leaders who, with Nehemiah, sealed the new covenant after the Captivity (Neh. 10:14)
10. A priest in Nehemiah's time who helped dedicate the rebuilt walls of Jerusalem (Neh. 12:42).

ELAMITES [EE lum ites] — descendants of Elam; an ancient people who lived in the area east of the Tigris and Euphrates Rivers. During their history, the Elamites struggled with the Babylonians, Assyrians, and Persians for domination of the Mesopotamian region of the ancient world.

The great Babylonian dynasty of UR was brought to an end about 1950 B.C. by the Elamites, who destroyed the city and took its king prisoner. The capital of Elam during its entire history was Shushan (Susa). To it the Persian king, Darius I, transferred the Persian capital about 520 B.C. The city is therefore mentioned several times in the books of Nehemiah, Esther, and Daniel, since these books deal with events during the time of the Persian Empire (Neh. 1:1; Esth. 1:2; Dan. 8:2).

From about 2000 to 1800 B.C., the Elamites expanded their kingdom at the expense of the Mesopotamian states, until HAMMURABI (about 1728–1686 B.C.) put an end to Elamite expansion. Elam was a virtual province of Babylon until about 1200 B.C. Then from about 1200–1130 B.C. Babylon was ruled by Elam. Under the leadership of a succession of strong kings, the Elamites raided and defeated Babylon. In 1130 B.C., however, Nebuchadnezzar I of Babylon captured Elam. For almost three centuries thereafter the Elamites were again under Babylonian domination.

From about 740 B.C. onward, Assyria's power created a more serious threat to the Elamites. Finally, Ashurbanipal, king of Assyria, conquered Elam about 645 B.C. The Persians had already taken the part of Elam called Anshan; after the Assyrian Empire was destroyed (609 B.C.), the Medes annexed most of Elam. When the Persians, in turn, began to control Media, all of Elam became a Persian administrative district. After the sixth century B.C., Elam was never again an independent nation.

Genesis 10:22 identifies Elam, the ancestor of the Elamites, as a son of Shem. Chedorlaomer, who led a group of eastern kings on raids to Palestine about 2000 B.C., also was an Elamite. These kings defeated several cities in the Jordan River plain, including Sodom. Abraham and his allies—Aner, Eshcol, and Mamre, with their personal armies—finally defeated Chedorlaomer and his fellow kings and rescued Lot, regaining the wealth the easterners had captured (Genesis 14). Chedorlaomer himself was driven back to Elam.

After the Assyrians captured the northern kingdom of Israel in 722 B.C., they followed their usual practice of deporting the population as a means of strengthening their control. Elamites were among the national groups deported to Samaria. Some Samaritan Israelites were in turn deported to Elam (Ezra 4:9). Some of the Israelites returned from Elam when the Persians allowed the Jews to go back to Palestine after the Captivity.

Isaiah prophesied that Elam would be involved in the defeat of Babylon (Is. 21:2). By its connection with the Persians during their conquest of the Babylonian Empire, they fulfilled Isaiah's prophecy (Dan. 8:1–4). Elamites serving in the Assyrian army also took part in the siege of Jerusalem (Is. 22:6) in 701 B.C. The prophets Jeremiah and Ezekiel prophesied that Elam itself would eventually be destroyed (Jer. 49:34–39; Ezek. 32:24–25).

Elamites were among the pilgrims at Jerusalem on the Day of Pentecost (Acts 2:9). They probably were Jews from Elam, or descendants of those who had been exiled there in 722 B.C. This group may also have included native Elamites who had converted to Judaism.

ELASAH [el AH sah] (*God has made*) — the name of two Old Testament men:

1. A son of Pashhur the priest; following the return from the Captivity he divorced his pagan wife (Ezra 10:22).

2. One of two men whom Zedekiah sent as emissaries to Nebuchadnezzar and who carried Jeremiah's letter to the Babylonian captives (Jer. 29:3).

Also see ELEASAH.

ELATH [EE lath] (*palm grove*) — a seaport town on the northeast corner of the Gulf of Elath, or Aqa-

The Valley of Elah, site of the battle between David and Goliath (1 Sam. 17; 21:9).

bah, on the Red Sea (see Map 4, B-6). King David captured the city, where he established an extensive trade. King Solomon built a fleet at EZION GEBER, which is near Elath on the shore of the Red Sea, in the land of Edom (1 Kin. 9:26; Eloth, KJV, RSV). Subsequently the town was conquered by Rezin, king of Syria, and then held by the Syrians until it became a border station for the Roman legion (2 Kin. 16:6). During the Greek and Roman period the town was called Aila or Aelana.

ELDAAH [el DAY ah] (*whom God has called*) — the fifth of Midian's five sons. Midian was the son of Abraham and Keturah, Abraham's concubine (Gen. 25:4).

ELDAD [EL dad] (*God has loved*) — one of 70 elders chosen by Moses at the command of God to help "bear the burden of the people" (Num. 11:17). Eldad and MEDAD were absent from the tabernacle of meeting; nevertheless "the Spirit rested upon them [and]...they prophesied in the camp." When a young man told Moses, "Eldad and Medad are prophesying", Joshua was jealous. Moses refused to restrain them, however, answering, "Oh, that all the Lord's people were prophets and that the Lord would put his spirit upon them!" (Num. 11:26–29).

ELDER — a term used throughout the Bible but designating different ideas at various times in biblical history. The word may refer to age, experience, and authority, as well as specific leadership roles.

In ancient times authority was given to older people with wider experience. These were often considered the most qualified to hold places of leadership. The basic meaning of the Hebrew and Greek words for elder is "old age."

In the Old Testament those leaders associated with Moses in governing the nation of Israel were called "the elders of Israel" (Ex. 3:16; 24:1), "the elders of the people" (Ex. 19:7), or the "seventy elders" (Ex. 24:1). Moses called these elders together to give them instructions for the observance of the Passover before the Exodus from Egypt.

Later, after the years of wandering in the wilderness, bodies of elders ruled in each city. These elders were viewed as the representatives of the nation and its people. The term elder eventually came to be applied to those who governed in the local communities, the rulers of the various tribes, and those who ruled all of Israel. These leaders were responsible for legal, political and military guidance and supervision.

During the years of Israel's captivity in Babylon and the following centuries, elders again appeared as leaders who were responsible for governing in the Jewish communities. These elders became the upper class, forming a type of ruling aristocracy. Later in this period, a council of elders of 71 members, called the SANHEDRIN, emerged. This council had both religious and political authority among all the Jewish people in Palestine, particularly in New Testament times. The HIGH PRIEST was the chairman of the Sanhedrin. Local Jewish synagogues, which emerged in the period between the Old and New Testaments, were also governed by a council of elders.

A governing structure similar to the ruling elders among the Jews was followed in the early church. The title elder was continued, but the significance of the office changed. Thus, the term elder is used in the New Testament to refer to the Jewish elders of the synagogue, to the members of the Sanhedrin, and to certain persons who held office in the church. It also implied seniority by reason of age (1 Tim. 5:2; 1 Pet. 5:5).

The presence of elders in the church in the New Testament indicates that this office was taken over from the synagogue. Elders were associated with James in Jerusalem in the local church's government (Acts 11:30; 21:18) and, with the apostles, in the decision of the early church council (Acts 15). Elders were also appointed in the churches established during the apostle Paul's first missionary journey (Acts 14:23). Paul addressed the elders at Ephesus (Acts 20:17–35). Elders played an important role in church life through their ministry to the sick (James 5:14, 15). They were apparently also teachers in a local congregation. In addition to ministering to the sick, their duties consisted of explaining the Scriptures and teaching doctrine (1 Tim. 5:17; 1 Pet. 5:5).

ELEAD [EL e ad] (*God is witness*) — a son of Ephraim. Elead attempted to steal cattle near the Philistine city of Gath and was killed (1 Chr. 7:20–22).

ELEADAH [el ih AY duh] — a form of ELADAH.

ELEALEH [EE lih A leh] (*God is exalted*) — a city in Moab on the east side of the Jordan River. Elealeh was part of the allotment given to the tribe of Reuben (Num. 32:3). It is mentioned in oracles against Moab (Is. 15:4).

ELEASAH [el ee A sah] (*God has made*) — the name of two men in the Old Testament:

1. A son of Helez, of the tribe of Judah (1 Chr. 2:39–40).

2. A son of Raphah, a descendant of King Saul (1 Chr. 8:37; Rephaiah, 1 Chr. 9:43).

ELEAZAR [el e A zur] (*God is helper*) — a common name among the Hebrew people given to seven men in the Bible:

1. Aaron's third son by his wife, Elisheba (Ex. 6:23). Eleazar was the father of Phinehas (Ex. 6:25). Consecrated a priest, he was made chief of the Levites after his elder brothers, Nadab and Abihu, were killed for offering unholy fire (Lev. 10:1-7). Before Aaron died, Eleazar ascended Mount Hor with him and was invested with Aaron's high priestly garments (Num. 20:25-28). Eleazar served as high priest during the remainder of Moses' life and throughout Joshua's leadership. He helped in the allotment of the land of Canaan among the 12 tribes of Israel (Josh. 14:1), and was buried "in a hill that belonged to Phinehas his son...in the

mountains of Ephraim" (Josh. 24:33). Phinehas succeeded him as high priest (Judg. 20:28).

2. The son of Abinadab who was charged with keeping watch over the ark while it rested in Abinadab's house in Kirjath Jearim (1 Sam. 7:1).

3. The son of Dodo the Ahohite (1 Chr. 11:12). He was "one of the three mighty men with David when they defied the Philistines" (2 Sam. 23:9).

4. A man of the tribe of Levi, the family of Merari, and the house of Mahli (1 Chr. 23:21-22).

5. The Levite son of Phinehas (Ezra 8:33). He assisted the high priest.

6. A priest who acted as a musician when Jerusalem's rebuilt walls were dedicated (Neh. 12:27, 42).

7. Eliud's son and one of the ancestors of Jesus (Matt. 1:15).

Also see ELIEZER.

ELECT — a person or group chosen by God for special favor and for the rendering of special service to Him. In the Old Testament the Hebrew people were described as God's elect. The New Testament speaks of Christ as God's Chosen One (1 Pet. 2:4, 6) and of the church as God's new chosen people (Rom. 8:33; 2 John 1, 13). Also see ELECTION.

ELECT LADY — the person or church to which 2 John is addressed (2 John 1).

ELECTION — the gracious and free act of God by which He calls those who become part of His kingdom and special beneficiaries of His love and blessings. The Bible describes the concept of election in three distinct ways. Election sometimes refers to the election of Israel and the church as a people for special service and privileges. Election may also refer to the election of a specific individual to some office or to perform some special service. Still other passages of the Bible refer to the election of individuals to be children of God and heirs of eternal life.

Throughout the history of redemption, election has characterized God's saving activity. He chose and called Abraham from Ur to Canaan, making an everlasting covenant with him and his offspring (Gen. 11:31—12:7; Neh. 9:7; Is. 41:8). God also called Moses to lead His people out of bondage (Ex. 2:24—3:10; Deut. 6:21-23; Ps. 105). He chose Israel from among the nations of the world to be His special covenant people (Deut. 4:37; 7:6-7; Is. 44:1-2).

Election to salvation takes place "in Christ" (Eph. 1:4; 2:10) as a part of God's purpose for the human race. As part of His eternal plan, God allowed man to use his freedom to rebel against Him. Thus, it is gracious of God to save those who find salvation through Jesus Christ. It is not unjust of Him not to save everyone, since no one deserves to be saved (Matt. 20:14; Rom. 1:18; 9:15). Election is gracious; it is also unconditional and unmerited (Acts 13:48; Rom. 9:11; 1 Pet. 1:2). It is an expression of the eternal, sovereign will of God who cannot change (Rom. 8:29; 2 Thess. 2:13). Therefore, the salvation of the elect is certain (Rom. 8:28, 33).

Election is a necessary condition for salvation; faith is the sufficient condition. The elect inevitably believe, but they do not believe against their will. They have a God-given desire and ability to trust in Christ for salvation (Acts 13:48; 1 Cor. 15:10; Phil. 1:29; 2:13). The elect choose God because He effectively calls them through the proclamation of the gospel of Jesus Christ; they choose Him because He first chose and called them to Himself (Rom. 8:28). That initiating love of God is reflected in Jesus' statement, "You did not choose Me, but I chose you" (John 15:16).

A careful study of the Bible's doctrine of man cures any romantic notion of a human will that is free to choose for or against God. Those who are slaves to sin and its power (Rom. 6:6) neither understand nor seek after God in and of themselves (Rom. 3:11; John 14:17; 1 Cor. 2:14). Outside of Christ, men are spiritually dead rebels who neither desire to submit to the Lord Jesus Christ nor are able to. Apart from God's gracious, free, eternal, and sovereign choice of such sinful men to become His children, none would be saved but would abide forever under His wrath (Rom. 1:18).

Election is not to be a source of complacency (2 Pet. 1:12) or presumption (Rom. 11:19-22) on the part of Christians. They are to make their calling and election certain by growing in godliness (2 Pet. 1:2-11) as they respond to God's electing love with gratitude (Col. 3:12-17).

God has chosen Christians to bear the image and glory of Christ (Rom. 8:29; 2 Thess. 2:14). They have been elected to be holy in conduct, like Christ (Eph. 1:4). Like Him, they are also to be glorified in their whole being in the life to come (2 Cor. 3:18; Phil. 3:21). The ultimate goal of our election is that we might bring praise and glory to God (Eph. 1:6; Rom. 11:33; 2 Thess. 2:13).

Also see PREDESTINATION.

ELEMENTS — the essential substances of the physical world (2 Pet. 3:10, 12). The apostle Paul also used the word to refer to the demonic spirits or powers behind the physical universe (Gal. 4:3, 9).

ELEPH [E lef] — a town in Canaan allotted to the tribe of Benjamin (Josh. l8:28; Ha–Eleph, KJV).

ELEPHANT (see ANIMALS OF THE BIBLE).

ELEPHANTINE (see PAPYRI).

ELHANAN [el HAY nun] (*God is gracious*) — the name of one or two men in the Old Testament:

1. A son of Dodo the Bethlehemite and one of David's mighty men (2 Sam. 23:24; 1 Chr. 11:26).

2. A warrior who killed a giant during the time of David.

ELI [EE lie] (*Jehovah is high*) — a judge and high priest with whom the prophet Samuel lived during his childhood (1 Sam. 1—4; 14:3).

The first mention of Eli occurs when the childless Hannah poured out to him her unhappiness over her barren condition. Later, her prayers for a son were answered when Samuel was born. True to her word, she brought her son to the tabernacle and dedicated him to God. There the future prophet lived with the high priest Eli.

Eli was a deeply pious man whose service to the Lord was unblemished. However, he was a lax father who had no control over his two sons, Phinehas and Hophni. The two sons, both priests, took meat from sacrificial animals before they were dedicated to God. They also "lay with the women that assembled at the door of the tabernacle" (1 Sam. 2:22). God pronounced divine judgment on Eli because of his failure to discipline his sons.

God's judgment was carried out through the Philistines. Hophni and Phinehas carried the ARK OF THE COVENANT into battle to help the Israelites. Both were killed, and the ark was captured. When Eli, 98 years old and nearly blind, heard the news, he fell backward and broke his neck. God's final judgment against Eli and his descendants occurred when Solomon removed Abiathar, Eli's descendant, and put Zadok in his place as high priest of the nation (1 Kin. 2:35).

ELI, ELI, LAMA SABACHTHANI [EE lie, EE lie, LUH mah suh BOCK thuh NIE] — the bitter, anguished cry of Jesus from the cross. The first two words, Eli, Eli ("My God, My God"), are in Hebrew, while the final words are in Aramaic. With these words, Jesus identified with sinners, took their sins upon Himself, and experienced the righteous judgment of God against sin. In this moment of loneliness and despair, He cried out to His Father God by quoting these words from the Hebrew Old Testament (Ps. 22:1). Yet, even His cry portrayed His ultimate faith in God's deliverance.

ELIAB [e LIE ab] (God is Father) — the name of six men in the Old Testament:

1. A chieftain of the tribe of Zebulun during Israel's wandering in the wilderness (Num. 2:7; 7:24).

2. The father of Dathan and Abiram—Reubenites who rebelled against Moses.

3. David's oldest brother (1 Sam. 16:6-7). Eliab's bearing was so striking that when Samuel saw him, he thought Eliab must surely be God's chosen one. Eliab's daughter Abihail married one of David's sons (2 Chr. 11:18).

4. A Levite ancestor of Samuel (1 Chr. 6:27; Elihu, 1 Sam. 1:1; Eliel, 1 Chr. 6:34).

5. A Gadite warrior who joined David at ZIKLAG, where David was hiding from the jealous Saul (1 Chr. 12:8-9).

6. A Levite who served as a porter and musician in the tabernacle in David's time (1 Chr. 15:18; 16:5).

ELIADA [e LIE uh duh] (God knows) — the name of three men in the Old Testament:

1. A son of David born at Jerusalem (2 Sam. 5:16; Beeliada, 1 Chr. 14:7).

2. The father of Rezon of Zobah, the "captain over a band of raiders" who annoyed King Solomon (1 Kin. 11:23).

3. A Benjamite and one of Jehoshaphat's chief captains (1 Chr. 17:17).

ELIAHBA [e LIE a ba] (God conceals) — one of David's mighty men (2 Sam. 23:32; 1 Chr. 11:33).

ELIAKIM [e LIE uh kim] (God is setting up) — a notable name given to five Old Testament men:

1. A son of Hilkiah and overseer of the household of King Hezekiah of Judah (2 Kin. 18:18; 19:2). When the invading Assyrian army approached Jerusalem (701 B.C.), Eliakim was one of three men sent by Hezekiah to confer with Sennacherib's forces. Hezekiah then sent these men to report the Assyrians' answer to the prophet Isaiah, who praised Eliakim highly (Is. 22:20-23).

2. The original name of JEHOIAKIM, a son of King Josiah of Judah, who was made king of Judah by Pharaoh Necho (2 Chr. 36:4). Jehoahaz reigned only three months after Josiah's death before the Egyptian pharaoh carried him away captive. Pharaoh Necho then changed Eliakim's name to Jehoiakim.

3. One of the priests who took part in the cleansing of the rebuilt walls of Jerusalem (Neh. 12:41).

4. An ancestor of Christ descended from Zerubbabel (Matt. 1:13).

5. An ancestor of Christ, descended from David, who lived before the Captivity (Luke 3:30).

ELIAM [e LIE um] (people's God) — the name of two Old Testament men:

1. The father of Bathsheba, who became the wife of Uriah the Hittite and later, King David (2 Sam. 11:3; Ammiel, 1 Chr. 3:5).

2. One of David's mighty men (2 Sam. 23:34).

ELIAS [e LIE us] — Greek form of ELIJAH.

ELIASAPH [e LIE uh saf] (God has added) — the name of two men in the Old Testament:

1. The head of the tribe of Gad during Israel's wilderness journey (Num. 1:14; 2:14). He was the son of Deuel (or Reuel; Num. 2:14).

2. The head of the Gershonites during Israel's wilderness journey (Num. 3:24).

ELIASHIB [e LIE uh shib] (God restores) — the name of six or seven men in the Old Testament:

1. A son of Elioenai, a Judahite and descendant of Zerubbabel (1 Chr. 3:24).

2. A priest in David's time (1 Chr. 24:12).

3. One who helped Ezra resolve the problem of pagan wives following the Captivity (Ezra 10:6; Neh. 12:22-23). Possibly the same as Eliashib No. 7.

4. A Levite and singer who divorced his pagan wife after the Captivity (Ezra 10:27).

5. A son of Zattu who divorced his pagan wife after the Captivity (Ezra 10:36).

6. A son of Bani who divorced his pagan wife after the Captivity (Ezra 10:36).

7. The high priest in Nehemiah's time (Neh. 3:1; 13:4, 28).

ELIATHAH [e LIE uh thah] (God has come) — the head of a division of Temple musicians during David's reign (1 Chr. 25:4, 27).

ELIDAD [e LIE dad] (*my God is a friend*) — a chieftain of the tribe of Benjamin appointed to represent his tribe in the division of the land of Canaan (Num. 34:21).

ELIEHOENAI [el ih oh EE nigh] — a form of ELIOENAI No. 3 and ELIHOENAI.

ELIEL [e LIE el] (*God is God*) — the name of several Old Testament men:

1. A chief of the half-tribe of Manasseh (1 Chr. 5:24).

2. A Levite ancestor of the prophet Samuel (1 Chr. 6:34; Elihu, 1 Samuel 1:1).

3. A Benjamite son of Shimei (1 Chr. 8:20).

4. A Benjamite son of Shashak (1 Chr. 8:22).

5. One of David's captains and a Mahavite (1 Chr. 11:46).

6. One of David's mighty men (1 Chr. 11:47).

7. A Gadite who joined David at Ziklag when David was hiding from Saul (1 Chr. 12:11). Possibly the same as Eliel No. 5 or 6.

8. A Levite who helped bring the ark from the house of Obed-Edom during the reign of King David (1 Chr. 15:9).

9. A Levite overseer of the Temple tithes and offerings during the reign of King Hezekiah of Judah (2 Chr. 31:13).

ELIENAI [el ih EE nigh] (*my eyes are on my God*) — a son of Shimei, of the tribe of Benjamin (1 Chr. 8:20).

ELIEZER [el ih EE zur] (*God is helper*) — the name of 11 men in the Bible:

1. Abraham's chief servant (Gen. 15:2). If Abraham had never had a son, "Eliezer of Damascus" would have been his heir.

2. Moses' second son by Zipporah (Ex. 18:4; 1 Chr. 23:15).

3. A son of Becher, of the tribe of Benjamin (1 Chr. 7:8).

4. A priest who blew the trumpet before the ark when it was moved from Kirjath Jearim to Jerusalem (1 Chr. 15:24).

5. A son of Zichri and the officer over the tribe of the Reubenites during David's reign (1 Chr. 27:16).

6. A prophet who predicted that the ships of King JEHOSHAPHAT of Judah would be wrecked because he had joined forces with King AHAZIAH of Israel (2 Chr. 20:37).

7. A leader whom Ezra sent to bring Levites to Jerusalem (Ezra 8:16).

8, 9, 10. Three men who divorced their pagan wives after the Captivity. One was a priest (Ezra 10:18); one was a Levite (Ezra 10:23); and one was a son of Harim (Ezra 10:31).

11. An ancestor of Joseph, the husband of Mary (Luke 3:29).

Also see ELEAZAR.

ELIHOENAI [el ih oh EE nigh] (*my eyes are toward Jehovah*) — one of the sons of Pahath-Moab who returned with Ezra from the Captivity (Ezra 8:4; Eliehoenai, RSV, NIV, NASB).

ELIHOREPH [el ih HO ref] (*God of harvest rain*) — a son of Shisha and one of King Solomon's scribes (1 Kin. 4:3).

ELIHU [eh LIE hew] (*He is my God*) — the name of five men in the Old Testament:

1. The great-grandfather of the prophet Samuel (1 Sam. 1:1).

2. A captain of Manasseh who joined David at Ziklag to hide from the jealous King Saul (1 Chr. 12:20).

3. A Levite of the family of Kohath who served as a tabernacle gatekeeper during David's reign (1 Chr. 26:7).

4. The oldest son of Jesse and a brother of David (1 Chr. 27:18; Eliab, 1 Sam. 16:6).

5. The youngest of Job's "comforters." Elihu spoke to Job after the three friends—ELIPHAZ, BILDAD, and ZOPHAR—failed to give convincing answers to Job's questions. Elihu is called "the son of Barachel the Buzite "of the family of Ram" (Job 32:2). Like Job's other friends, Elihu was probably from the Transjordan area southeast of Palestine.

ELIJAH [ee LIE juh] (*the Lord is my God*) — the name of three or four men in the Old Testament:

1. A Benjamite, the son of Jeroham (1 Chr. 8:27).

2. An influential prophet who lived during the ninth century B.C. during the reigns of Ahab and Ahaziah in the northern kingdom of Israel. Elijah shaped the history of his day and dominated Hebrew thinking for centuries afterward.

Elijah's prophetic activities emphasized the unconditional loyalty to God required of the nation of Israel. His strange dress and appearance (2 Kin. 1:8), his fleetness of foot (1 Kin. 18:46), his rugged constitution that resisted famine (1 Kin. 19:8), and his cave-dwelling habits (1 Kin. 17:3; 19:9) all suggest that he was a robust, outdoors-type personality.

Elijah was opposed to the accepted standards of his day, when belief in many gods was normal. He appears in the role of God's instrument of judgment upon a wayward Israel because of the nation's widespread idolatry. The miracles that Elijah performed occurred during the period when a life-or-death struggle took place between the religion of Jehovah and BAAL worship.

Elijah's views were in conflict with those of King Ahab. Ahab had attempted to cultivate economic ties with Israel's neighbors, especially Tyre. One of the consequences was that he had married Jezebel, a daughter of Ethbaal, king of Tyre. Ahab saw no harm in participating in the religion of his neighbors, particularly the religion of his wife. Therefore, he established a center of BAAL worship at Samaria. Influenced by Jezebel, Ahab gave himself to the worship of Baal. Suddenly Elijah appeared on the scene.

Prediction of Drought. As punishment against Ahab for building the temple for Baal worship at Samaria, Elijah predicted that a drought would grip the land. Then he fled to the eastern side of the Jordan River and later to Zarephath on the Mediterra-

The fertile plain surrounding Mount Carmel, site of Elijah's victory over the prophets of Baal (1 Kin. 18; 19:1-2).

nean coast to escape Ahab's wrath. At both sites he was kept alive through miraculous means. While staying at a widow's home, he performed a miracle by bringing her son back to life (1 Kin. 17:1-24).

Contest on Mount Carmel. After the drought had lasted three years, the Lord instructed Elijah to present himself before Ahab with the message that the Lord would provide rain. Elijah then challenged the 850 prophets of Baal and Asheroth to a contest on Mount Carmel (1 Kin. 18:21). Each side would offer sacrifices to their God without building a fire. The ignition of the fire was left to the strongest god, who would thereby reveal himself as the true God.

While praying to God, Elijah poured water over his sacrifice to remove any possibility of fraud or misunderstanding about the offering. When Elijah's sacrifice was consumed by fire from heaven, the people of Israel responded strongly in favor of God (1 Kin. 18:39). Then the prophets of Baal and Asheroth were slaughtered at Elijah's command (1 Kin. 18:40), and God sent rain to end the drought (1 Kin. 18:41-46).

Flight from Jezebel. Queen Jezebel was furious over the fate of the prophets of Baal. She vowed that she would take revenge on Elijah. He was forced to flee to the desert south of Beersheba, eventually arriving at Mount Horeb—the mountain where Moses received the Ten Commandments. It is significant that this loyal follower of the Law came at last to the place where the commandments were first given. Like Moses, Elijah was sustained for 40 days and nights in the wilderness.

While Elijah was at Mount Horeb, the Lord re-vealed Himself in a low, murmuring sound. The prophet received a revelation of the coming doom on Ahab and Israel (1 Kin. 19:14). Then Elijah was given a threefold charge: he was instructed to anoint Hazael as king of Syria, Jehu as the future king of Israel, and Elisha as the prophet who would take his place (1 Kin. 19:16). These changes would bring to power those who would reform Israel in the coming years.

Naboth's Vineyard and Challenge of Ahaziah. In the years of war that followed between Ahab and Ben-Hadad of Syria, Elijah did not appear (1 Kings 20). But he did appear after Jezebel acquired a family-owned vineyard for Ahab by having its owner, Naboth, falsely accused and executed (1 Kin. 21:1-29). Elijah met the king in the vineyard and rebuked him for the act (1 Kin. 21:1-24). Ahab repented, and Elijah brought him word from the Lord that the prophesied ruin on his house would not come during his lifetime, but would occur in the days of his son.

Shortly after Ahaziah, the son of Ahab, took the throne from his father, he was involved in a serious accident. He sent messengers to inquire of Baal-Zebub, the god of Ekron, whether he would recover. Elijah intercepted the messengers and predicted his death because of his belief in other gods (2 Kin. 1:1-17). This event would also be a fulfillment of the doom pronounced earlier upon Ahab's house.

Twice King Ahaziah sent a detachment of soldiers to capture Elijah. But both times they were consumed by fire from heaven. The third group sent by the king begged for mercy, and an angel of God directed Elijah to go with the commander to see the king. Elijah repeated his message of doom to Ahaziah, who soon died (2 Kin. 1:9-17). Elijah's prophecy that Jezebel would meet a violent death was also fulfilled (2 Kin. 9:36).

Ascension to Heaven. The prophet Elijah did not die. He was carried bodily to heaven in a whirlwind (2 Kin. 2:1-11). This was an honor previously bestowed only upon ENOCH (Gen. 5:24). ELISHA, the only witness to this event, took up Elijah's mantle which fell from him as he ascended. He carried it during his ministry as a token of his continuation of Elijah's ministry (2 Kin. 2:13-14).

Elijah's influence continued even after his ascension into heaven. King Jehoram of Israel received a letter from the prophet seven years after his ascension, indicating that the king would be punished severely for his sins (2 Chr. 21:12-15).

Elijah's Contribution. The prophet Elijah understood that the nation of Israel had a mission to preserve its religious system—the worship of the one true God—in a pure form without any mixture with idol worship. Elijah was strongly opposed to the worship of pagan gods such as Baal and Asherah. This uncompromising stand often endangered his life by bringing him into conflict with those in positions of power, especially Queen Jezebel and her followers.

Elijah's impact on the prophetic movement among the Hebrew people was extensive. He stands as the transitional figure between Samuel (the adviser and anointer of kings) and the later writing prophets. Like the prophets who followed him, Elijah emphasized Israel's responsibility for total commitment to their God and the covenant responsibilities which God and His people had sworn to each other. Both these ideas are more fully developed in later prophets, such as Amos and Hosea.

In later Jewish thought, the messianic age was frequently associated with Elijah's return. The Old Testament spoke of the reappearance of Elijah. The prophet Malachi prophesied that the Lord would send Elijah before the day of the Lord arrived. According to the New Testament, this prophecy was fulfilled in the coming of JOHN THE BAPTIST (Matt. 11:4; 17:10–13; Luke 1:17). John the Baptist was similar to Elijah in his preaching as well as his dress and physical appearance (Matt. 11:7–8; Luke 7:24–28). During Jesus' earthly ministry, some identified him with Elijah (Matt. 16:14; Luke 9:8).

The New Testament also mentions the reappearance of Elijah in person. Along with Moses, he appeared with Jesus on the Mount of Transfiguration (Matt. 17:3).

Statue of the prophet Elijah on Mount Carmel, commemorating his victory over the pagan worshipers of Baal.

Photo: Levant Photo Service

3. A son of Harim (Ezra 10:21). Elijah divorced his foreign wife following the Captivity in Babylon.

4. An Israelite who divorced his foreign wife (Ezra 10:26). He may be the same as Elijah No. 3.

ELIKA [e LIE kuh] (*God has rejected*) — one of David's mighty men (2 Sam. 23:25).

ELIM [E lim] (*large trees*) — an encampment of the Israelites after they crossed the Red Sea (see Map 2, B–2). This encampment was famed for its "twelve wells [springs] of water and seventy palm trees" (Ex. 15:27; Num. 33:9). The exact location is uncertain.

ELIMELECH [e LIM uh leck] (*my God is king*) — the husband of Naomi and the father-in-law of Ruth (Ruth 1:2–3; 2:1). An Ephrathite of Bethlehem of Judah, he moved his family to Moab to escape famine. His two sons, Mahlon and Chilion, married Moabite women, Orpah and RUTH. After the death of Elimelech and his two sons, one of the Moabite daughters-in-law, Ruth, chose to return to Bethlehem with Naomi (Ruth 1:16–17).

ELIOENAI [el ih oh EE nigh] (*my eyes are toward Jehovah*) — the name of seven men in the Old Testament:

1. A descendant of David after the Captivity (1 Chr. 3:23–24).

2. A chief of the tribe of Simeon (1 Chr. 4:36).

3. A chief of the tribe of Benjamin (1 Chr. 7:8).

4. A gatekeeper of the Levitical family of Kore (1 Chr. 26:3, KJV; Eljehoenai, NKJV; Eliehoenai, RSV, NASB, NIV).

5. A priest of the sons of Pashhur (Ezra 10:22). Elioenai divorced his pagan wife after the Captivity.

6. One of the sons of Zattu (Ezra 10:27). Elioenai divorced his pagan wife.

7. A priest in the days of Nehemiah (Neh. 12:41). Perhaps the same as Elioenai No. 5.

Also see ELIHOENAI.

ELIPHAL [eh LIE ful] (*God is judge*) — a son of Ur and one of David's mighty men (1 Chr. 11:35).

ELIPHALET [e LIF uh let] — a form of ELIPHELET.

ELIPHAZ [EL ih faz] (*God is victorious*) — the name of two Old Testament men:

1. Esau's son by Adah, daughter of Elon the Hittite (Gen. 36:2, 4, 10–12). Eliphaz was the father, by his concubine Timna, of Amalek and thus was the ancestor of several Edomite tribes.

2. The chief and oldest of Job's three "friends" or "comforters" (Job 2:11). A very religious man, Eliphaz sought to uphold the holiness, purity, and justice of God; he became uneasy when Job questioned this understanding of God. Called "the Temanite," this Eliphaz may have been a descendant of Eliphaz No. 1, who had a son named TEMAN.

ELIPHELEH [e LIF uh leh] (*whom God makes distinguished*) — a Levite appointed to play the harp or lyre in the musical services of the tabernacle when David relocated the ARK OF THE COVENANT to Jerusalem (1 Chr. 15:18, 21; Eliphelehu, RSV).

ELIPHELEHU [e lif eh LEE hew] — a form of ELIPHELEH.

ELIPHELET [e LIF eh let] (*my God is deliverance*) — the name of six Old Testament men:

1. The last of David's 13 sons born in Jerusalem (2 Sam. 5:16; 1 Chr. 14:7; Eliphalet, KJV).

2. A son of Ahasbai and one of David's mighty men (2 Sam. 23:34). See ELIPHAL.

3. Another of David's sons born in Jerusalem (1 Chr. 3:6). Also spelled Elpelet (1 Chr. 14:5; Elpalet, KJV).

4. A son of Eshek and a Benjamite descendant of King Saul (1 Chr. 8:39).

5. A son or descendant of Adonikam who returned from the Captivity with Ezra (Ezra 8:13).

6. A son of Hashum who divorced his pagan wife after the Captivity (Ezra 10:33).

ELISHA — An early Hebrew prophet who succeeded the prophet Elijah when Elijah's time on earth was finished (1 Kin. 19:16). Elisha ministered for about 50 years in the northern kingdom of Israel, serving God during the reigns of Jehoram, Jehu, Jehoahaz, and Joash. Scholars have dated the period of his ministry from 850 B.C. to 800 B.C. Elisha's work consisted of presenting the Word of God through prophecy, advising kings, anointing kings, helping the needy, and performing several miracles.

Elisha was the son of Shaphat of Abel Meholah, a town between the Sea of Galilee and the Dead Sea on the western side of the Jordan River. Elijah found Elisha plowing with a team of oxen. As Elijah walked past Elisha, he threw his mantle over the younger man's shoulders. Elisha immediately recognized this as a call to ministry, leaving his family to follow Elijah.

The Bible indicates that Elisha "arose and followed Elijah, and became his servant" (1 Kin. 19:21), but Elisha is not mentioned again until 2 Kings 2:1, shortly before Elijah descended to heaven in a chariot of fire. Before taking his leave, Elijah fulfilled the final request of Elisha by providing him with a double portion of his spirit (2 Kin. 2:9–10). Upon receiving Elijah's mantle, Elisha demonstrated this gift by parting the waters of the Jordan River, allowing him to cross on dry land (2 Kin. 2:14). In this way, Elisha demonstrated that he had received God's blessings on his ministry as Elijah's successor.

Although Elisha continued Elijah's ministry of prophecy, he cultivated a different image from his predecessor. Instead of following Elijah's example as a loner and an outsider, Elisha chose to work within the established system. He assumed his rightful place as the head of the "official" prophetic order in Israel, where his counsel and advice were sought out by kings. In contrast to Elijah's strained relationship with the king and his officials, Elisha enjoyed the harmonious role of trusted advisor. This is not to say that Elisha never had a word of

Excavated remains of a house at the city of Dothan, where Elisha prayed for blindness to strike the Syrian army (2 Kin. 6:8-23).

Photo by Howard Vos

criticism for the government of Israel. Such criticism can be seen in the part Elisha played in the overthrow of Jezebel and the house of Ahab (2 Kin. 9:1–3).

Elisha displayed a contrast to Elijah in other ways. His appearance was much more typical and "average" than Elijah's. He was bald (2 Kin. 2:23), while Elijah had been an extremely hairy man (2 Kin. 1:8). Elisha did not wander as extensively as Elijah. Instead, he had a house in Samaria (2 Kin. 6:32). Much tension had existed between Elijah and his audience. Elisha's ministry provided a strong contrast as he was welcomed into virtually all levels of society from the courts of the king to the dwellings of the lowliest peasants.

In perhaps the most important part of his ministry, however, Elisha followed in Elijah's footsteps. This consisted of his performance of miracles. Elisha must have surely received a double portion of Elijah's spirit, because he performed twice as many miracles as Elijah. Elisha's miracles answered a wide variety of needs in every level of society. He carried out signs and wonders for high government officials, peasants, and the disadvantaged. He had a reputation for sympathizing with the poor and the oppressed. Elisha's activities and miracles as a prophet were often focused on those who were abused by officials in positions of power. In this way, Elisha demonstrated that religious commitment included a concern for all people.

One of Elisha's "community service" miracles was his purification of an unhealthy spring near Jericho. After learning that the spring was bad, Elisha threw a bowl of salt into it, making it pure (2 Kin. 2:19–21). The Bible reports that "the water remains healed to this day" (2 Kin. 2:22).

In another miracle, Elisha helped the widow of one of the sons of the prophets. To help her pay off creditors who intended to take the widow's two sons, Elisha multiplied the amount of oil in one jar to fill all available containers. This brought in enough money to pay off the debts and provided a surplus on which the widow and her sons could live (2 Kin. 4:1–7).

Elisha became a friend of a wealthy family in Shunem. The Shunnamite woman displayed hospitality toward the prophet by regularly feeding him and building a room onto their home where he could lodge. Elisha repaid the childless couple by promising them a son (2 Kin. 4:8–17). Later, when tragedy struck the child, Elisha raised him from the dead (2 Kin. 4:18–37). When Elisha learned that a famine would strike Israel, he warned the family to flee the land. When the family returned seven years later, the king restored their property because of their relationship with Elisha (2 Kin. 8:1–6).

Elisha also advised kings and performed miracles for them. He helped Jehoram, king of Israel; Jehoshaphat, king of Judah; and the king of Edom defeat Mesha—the king of Moab (2 Kin. 3:1–19).

Elisha ministered to all people, regardless of their nationalities. He cured Naaman, the commander of the Syrian army (2 Kin. 5:1–14), of leprosy, but he also advised the king of Israel of the plans (2 Kin. 6:8–10) of their Assyrian enemies. Even the bones of the dead Elisha had miraculous powers. When a corpse was hidden in Elisha's tomb, it came back to life as it touched the prophet's bones (2 Kin. 13:21).

ELISHAH [eh LIE shah] (*God is Savior*) — the oldest son of Javan and a descendant of Noah (Gen. 10:1–4). The home of his descendants is described as "the coasts of Elishah," which supplied the Phoenicians with dyes of "blue and purple" (Ezek. 27:7). The name may refer to the island of CYPRUS, which was known at one time as Alashiya.

ELISHAMA [e LISH uh muh] (*God is hearer*) — the name of several Old Testament men:

1. Leader of the tribe of Ephraim at the beginning of the Israelites' journey (Num. 2:18). This son of Ammihud was one of Joshua's ancestors (1 Chr. 7:26–27).

2. One of the sons born to David after he was crowned king at Jerusalem (2 Sam. 5:13–16).

3. The father of Nethaniah and the grandfather of Ishmael (Jer. 41:1).

4. A Judahite, a son of Jekamiah (1 Chr. 2:41).

5. One of the sons born to David at Jerusalem (1 Chr. 3:6). He may be the same as Elishama No. 2.

6. One of two priests sent by Jehoshaphat to teach the Law to the people in Judah (2 Chr. 17:8).

7. A scribe or secretary of King Jehoiakim (Jer. 36:12, 20–21).

ELISHAPHAT [e LISH uh fat] (*my God is judge*) — a son of Zichri and one who supported the revolt against Queen Athaliah in favor of seven–year–old Joash (2 Chr. 23:1).

ELISHEBA [ee LISH ih buh] (*my God is fullness*) — the wife of AARON and the mother of Nadab, Abihu, Eleazar, and Ithamar (Ex. 6:23). She was a daughter of Amminadab and a sister of Naashon.

ELISHUA [el ih SHOE uh] (*God is salvation*) — a son of David born at Jerusalem (2 Sam. 5:15; 1 Chr. 14:5; Elishama, 1 Chr. 3:6).

ELIUD [e LIE ud] (*God is majestic*) — a son of Achim and the father of Eleazar in the genealogy of Jesus (Matt. 1:14–15).

ELIZABETH [ee LIZ uh buth] (*God is my oath*) — the mother of John the Baptist (Luke 1). Of the priestly line of Aaron, Elizabeth was the wife of the priest ZACHARIAS. Although both "were...righteous before God, they had no child, because Elizabeth was barren" (Luke 1:6–7). But God performed a miracle, and Elizabeth conceived the child who was to be the forerunner of the Messiah.

Elizabeth was privileged in another way. When her cousin Mary visited her, Elizabeth, six months pregnant, felt the child move as if to welcome the child whom Mary was carrying. Elizabeth recognized the significance of this action and acknowledged the Messiah before He had been born.

ELIZAPHAN [el ih ZAY fun] (*my God has concealed*) — the name of two Old Testament leaders:

1. A Levite of the family of Kohath, a chief during the wilderness journey and a son of Uzziel (Num. 3:30). He helped remove the bodies of Nadab and Abihu, who had led a revolt against Moses, from the Israelite camp (Lev. 10:4; Elzaphan, Ex. 6:22).

2. A leader of the tribe of Zebulun during the wilderness journey (Num. 34:25). He was the son of Parnach.

ELIZUR [eh LIE zur] (*My God is a rock*) — a chief of the tribe of Reuben who assisted Moses in taking a census of Israel during the wilderness journey (Num. 1:1–5; 2:10).

ELKANAH [el KAY na] (*God has possessed*) — the name of eight Old Testament men:

1. A grandson of Korah (Ex. 6:24).

2. The husband of Hannah and Peninah and the father of the prophet Samuel (1 Sam. 1:1–23).

3. A Levite of the family of Kohath and a son of Joel (1 Chr. 6:25, 36).

4. A Levite of the family of Kohath and a son of Mahath (1 Chr. 6:26, 35).

5. A Levite who lived in a village of the Netophathites in Judah near Bethlehem (1 Chr. 9:16).

6. A Benjamite warrior who joined David at Ziklag (1 Chr. 12:6).

7. A doorkeeper of the ARK OF THE COVENANT during the time of King David (1 Chr. 15:23).

8. A high-ranking court official of Ahaz king of Judah (2 Chr. 28:7).

ELKOSHITE [EL koh shite] — a native or inhabitant of the village of Elkosh. The Bible has only one reference to Elkoshite (Nah. 1:1). Elkosh was the residence (and perhaps the birthplace) of the prophet Nahum. Elkosh itself is not mentioned in the Bible. Its location is unknown.

ELLASAR [el LAY sar] (meaning unknown) — a Mesopotamian country mentioned in the story of Abraham (Gen. 14:1, 9). Its king was Arioch. The traditional identification of Ellasar with the kingdom of Larsa, in southern Babylonia (or Chaldea), is questionable.

ELM (see PLANTS OF THE BIBLE).

ELMODAM [el MOE dam] (meaning unknown) — an ancestor of Jesus. He was a son of Er (Luke 3:28; Elmadam, NIV, RSV).

ELNAAM [el NAY am] (*God is pleasantness*) — the father of Jeribai and Joshaviah, two of David's mighty men (1 Chr. 11:46).

ELNATHAN [el NAY thun] (*God has given*) — the name of four men in the Old Testament:

1. The leader of the party sent to Egypt to bring back the prophet Uriah, who had displeased Jehoiakim by his prophecy (Jer. 26:22).

2, 3, 4. Three men sent by Ezra to invite priests and Levites to come to Jerusalem when the Israelites were in captivity in Babylon (Ezra 8:15).

ELOHIM [EL oh hihm] (see GOD, NAMES OF).

ELON [EE lahn] (*oak*) — the name of three men and one town in the Old Testament:

1. A Hittite and the father of Basemath, who became one of Esau's wives (Gen. 26:34).

2. A son of Zebulun and founder of a tribal family, the Elonites (Num. 26:26).

3. A border town in the tribe of Dan (Josh. 19:43). Its location is unknown.

4. A Zebulunite who judged Israel for ten years (Judg. 12:11–12).

ELON BETH HANAN [ee lahn beth HAY nen] (*oak of Hanan*) — a village of Dan, perhaps the same place as ELON (1 Kin. 4:9).

ELONITES [EL uhn ites] — the descendants of ELON, the second son of Zebulun (Num. 26:26).

ELOTH [E luth] — a form of ELATH.

ELPAAL [el PAY al] (*God is working*) — a descendant of Benjamin (1 Chr. 8:11–12, 18).

ELPALET [el PAY let] — a form of ELPELET.

ELPELET [el PEA let] (*God is deliverance*) — a son of David (1 Chr. 14:5; Elpalet, KJV). Also spelled Eliphelet (1 Chr. 3:6).

ELTEKEH [EL teh keh] (*meeting place*) — a town of the tribe of Dan assigned to the Levites of the family of Kohath (Josh. 19:44; 21:23). It was situated almost due west of Jerusalem.

ELTEKON [EL tuh con] (*founded by God*) — a village in the hill country of Judah between Bethlehem and Hebron (Josh. 15:59).

ELTOLAD [el TOE lad] (meaning unknown) — a town in southern Judah assigned to the tribe of Simeon (Josh. 15:30; Tolad, 1 Chr. 4:29).

ELUL [ee LOOL] — the sixth month of the Hebrew year, corresponding roughly to a lunar month during our August–September (Neh. 6:15). Also see CALENDAR.

ELUZAI [e LOO zuh i] (*God is my strength*) — a Benjamite warrior who left King Saul's forces to join David at Ziklag (1 Chr. 12:5).

ELYMAS [EL ih mas] (meaning unknown) — a false prophet who was temporarily struck blind for opposing Paul and Barnabas at Paphos on the island of Cyprus (Acts 13:8). Described as "a Jew whose name was Bar–Jesus" (Acts 13:6), he apparently had some influence with Sergius Paulus, the Roman proconsul, or governor, of the island. Elymas apparently was jealous of the gospel that Paul preached and sought to turn the proconsul away from accepting the Christian faith.

ELZABAD [el ZAY bud] (*God has given*) — the name of two men in the Old Testament:

1. A Gadite warrior who joined David at Ziklag (1 Chr. 12:12).

2. A gatekeeper in the Temple (1 Chr. 26:7).

ELZAPHAN [el ZAY fun] (see ELIZAPHAN).

EMBALMER (see OCCUPATIONS AND TRADES).

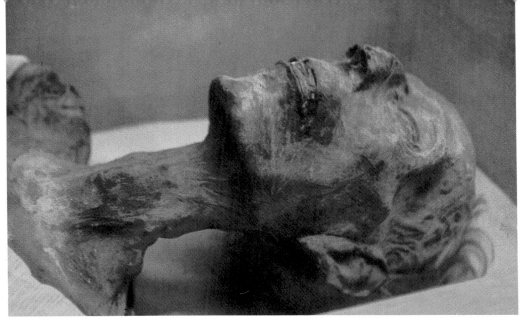

Mummy of an Egyptian Pharaoh from about 1400 B.C., demonstrating the remarkable way in which embalming preserved human bodies.

EMBALMING — a distinct method of preparing the dead for burial and preserving the body from decay which originated in ancient Egypt.

The practice of treating a corpse to preserve it from decay dates back more than 3,000 years. Mummification was invented by the Egyptians, who believed that the preservation of the body insured the continuation of the soul after death.

According to the Greek historian Herodotus, there were three different methods of embalming. The least expensive method involved emptying the intestines by flushing them with a cleaning liquid, after which the body was soaked in natron. The second method called for placing the body in natron after the stomach and intestines had been dissolved by an injection of cedar oil.

The most elaborate method of embalming required the removal of the brain and all internal organs except the heart. The inner cavity of the body was then washed and filled with spices. The corpse was soaked in natron, then washed and wrapped in bandages of linen soaked with gum. Finally, the embalmed body was placed in a wooden coffin.

The Bible mentions embalming only once, in reference to Joseph and his father Jacob (Gen. 50:2–3, 26). Even this single reference is surprising, since the ancient Hebrews did not generally embalm their dead because of laws concerning the touching of dead bodies (Num. 5:1–4; 19:11–22). But both Joseph and Jacob died in Egypt. They were apparently embalmed so their bodies could be taken back to Israel for burial.

Preparation for burial of the dead among the Hebrews usually consisted of washing the body (Acts 9:37) and then anointing it with aromatic oint-ments. Burial was usually on the day of death or the following day. The body was wrapped in cloth strips, with a separate cloth tied around the head. Spices were applied when the body was wrapped (Mark 16:1). Expensive spices were used to prepare Jesus' body for burial (John 19:39–42).

EMBROIDERER (see OCCUPATIONS AND TRADES; NEEDLEWORK).

EMBROIDERY (see NEEDLEWORK).

EMEK KEZIZ [EH meck KEH zeez] (*valley cut off*) — a city of the tribe of Benjamin, apparently near Jericho and Beth Hoglah (Josh. 18:21; Valley of Keziz, KJV).

EMERALD (see JEWELS AND PRECIOUS STONES).

EMERODS (see DISEASES OF THE BIBLE).

EMERY (see JEWELS AND PRECIOUS STONES).

EMIM [EE mim] (*frightful ones*) — an ancient people of the land of Canaan. The Emim lived in TRANSJORDAN, in an area later occupied by the Moabites. Like the ANAKIM, the Emim were regarded as giants; but their conquerors, the Moabites, called them Emim—"the Terrible." Chedorlaomer defeated them on the Plain of Kiriathaim (Gen. 14:5; Deut. 2:10–11).

EMMANUEL [em MAN you el] — a form of IMMANUEL.

EMMAUS [em MAY us] (*warm wells*) — a village in Judea where Jesus revealed Himself to two disciples after His resurrection (see Map 6, B-4). The disciples, Cleopas and an unidentified companion, encountered Jesus on the road to Emmaus, but they

Modern Emmaus, the village toward which Cleopas and another disciple were traveling when Jesus appeared to them after His resurrection (Luke 24:13-27).

did not recognize Him. Jesus accompanied them to Emmaus, and they invited Him to stay there with them. As He blessed and broke bread at the evening meal, the disciples' "eyes were opened and they knew Him" (Luke 24:31). The location of Emmaus is uncertain. Luke reported the village was 11 kilometers (7 miles) from Jerusalem, but he did not specify in which direction.

EMPEROR (see AUGUSTUS; CAESAR).

EMPEROR WORSHIP — a pagan custom of ancient times in which a ruler claimed for himself the qualities of a god and was so treated by those whom he ruled.

Many nations of the ancient world followed the custom of worshiping their rulers. The Egyptians, for example, claimed their Pharaohs had descended from the sun gods. The Greek conquerer ALEXANDER the Great, established a cult of such worship in Alexandria. The rulers of Syria and Egypt followed this tradition, calling themselves gods who ruled on earth.

Daniel 3 records an actual instance of emperor worship. King Nebuchadnezzar had a statue made. Then he ordered everyone to bow down to it. Those who refused were thrown into a fiery furnace. Later, the prophet Daniel was thrown to the lions for his refusal to pray to the Persian King Darius (Daniel 6).

When the Roman Empire conquered these ancient nations, the worship of the Roman state naturally replaced these pagan forms of worship. The conquered people began to worship outstanding Roman leaders, such as Mark Anthony and Julius Caesar.

Under Augustus Caesar as emperor of Rome, emperor worship grew in intensity. In the various Roman provinces, the subjects worshiped the Roman state and the emperor as a sign of their loyalty to Rome. Throughout the empire, Roman subjects incorporated emperor worship into their local religions. Leading citizens became priests in the emperor worship cult as evidence of their loyalty to the Roman Empire.

The New Testament never speaks of emperor worship as such, but it was practiced during that time. Secular history records that the Roman emperor Caligula (A.D. 37–41) proclaimed himself as a god, built temples for himself, and required his subjects to worship him. In A.D. 40, some Jews destroyed a statue that had been erected to him. Caligula retaliated by threatening to place a statue in the Jewish Temple, but the plan was never carried out because of Jewish opposition.

Open conflict between Christians and the Roman Empire over emperor worship came long after the close of the New Testament. Under Emperor Trajan, Christians who would not renounce their allegiance to Christ and pledge their worship of the emperor often were executed.

Emperor worship continued as the official religion of the Roman Empire until Christianity was recognized under the Emperor Constantine (reigned A.D. 305–337).

EN [in] (*fountain, spring*) — a Hebrew word used as a prefix to designate the location of specific springs of water (1 Sam. 24:1; Josh. 15:7).

EN DOR [IN dorr] (*fountain of habitation*) — a town of the tribe of Manasseh (see Map 3, B–2) where King Saul consulted a medium or spiritist about his future (Josh. 17:11; 1 Sam. 28:7). In a seance, the woman brought the spirit of the prophet Samuel up from the dead. En Dor is probably modern Indur on the northeastern shoulder of the Little Hermon Mountain about ten kilometers (six miles) southeast of Nazareth.

EN EGLAIM [in EGG la im] (*spring of two calves*)

— a place on the southeastern coast of the Dead Sea near Zoar (Ezek. 47:10).

EN GANNIM [in GAN im] (*spring of gardens*) — the name of two biblical cities:
1. A city in the lowlands of Judah near Zanoah and Tappuah (Josh. 15:34).
2. A city on the border of Issachar assigned to the Levites (Josh. 19:21; 21:29; Anem, 1 Chr. 6:73).

EN GEDI [in GEH die] (*spring of a kid*) — an oasis on the barren western shore of the Dead Sea about 54 kilometers (35 miles) southeast of Jerusalem (see Map 3, B–5). It lay on the eastern edge of the rugged Wilderness of Judah, which contained many hideouts where David sometimes hid when he was fleeing from King Saul (1 Sam. 23:29—24:1).

En Gedi was watered by a hot spring yielding an abundance of fresh water which burst forth three or four hundred feet above the base of a large cliff. Its ancient name was Hazezon Tamar—or Hazazon Tamar ("pruning of palms"), indicating that date palms may have grown there at one time. The plentiful supply of water from the hot spring created an oasis rich with semitropical vegetation. Vineyards also prospered at En Gedi (Song 1:14).

In Abraham's day CHEDORLAOMER conquered the Amorites who occupied this spot (Gen. 14:7). In Jehoshaphat's day, God overthrew invading enemies of Judah at En Gedi (2 Chr. 20:2).

EN HADDAH [in HAD ah] (*swift fountain*) — a city on the border of Issachar, near En Gannim (Josh 19:21).

EN HAKKORE [in HACK kuh ree] (*spring of the caller*) — a spring at Lehi that miraculously came out of a hollow place when Samson prayed (Judg. 15:19).

EN HAZOR [in HAY zur] (*spring of an enclosure*) — a fortified city in the territory of Naphtali (Josh. 19:37).

EN MISHPAT [en MISH puht] (*spring of judgment*) — an oasis where the Israelites camped during their years of wandering in the wilderness (Gen. 14:7). It is probably the same place as KADESH BARNEA.

EN RIMMON [in RIM mun] (*spring of the pomegranate*) — a city of Judah south of Jerusalem. It was one of the settlements of the tribe of Judah on their return from the Babylonian Captivity (Neh. 11:29). The city is usually identified with Khirbet Umm er–Ramamin, which was about 14 kilometers (9 miles) northeast of Beersheba.

EN ROGEL [in RO gull] (*fuller's well*) — a well on the border of Judah and Benjamin, east of Jerusalem, near the "Valley of the Son of Hinnom" (Josh. 15:7-8). Only the spring GIHON provided more water to Jerusalem. Jonathan and Ahimaaz stayed here in secret, ready to carry any message from Hushai to David about the revolt of Absalom (2 Sam. 17:17).

En Rogel was a man–made well 38 meters (125 feet) deep, walled for about half the way down, and cutting through solid rock for the remainder of the distance. It is identified today as Bir Ayyub ("Job's Well"), located near the juncture of the Kidron Valley and the Valley of Hinnom.

EN SHEMESH [in SHE mish] (*spring of the sun*) — a spring which served as an important landmark on the border between Judah and Benjamin (18:17). It is usually identified with 'Ain el–Hod, situated east of Bethany on the Jerusalem–to–Jericho road.

EN TAPPUAH [in top PEW ah] (*apple spring*) — a place of uncertain location, apparently on the border between Manasseh and Ephraim (Josh. 17:7). Some scholars identify it with the spring at Yasuf, located about 13 kilometers (8 miles) southwest of Shechem. It may also be identified with Tappuah, a city of Ephraim (Josh. 16:8).

ENAIM [ih NAY em] — a form of ENAM.

ENAM [E nahm] (*two fountains*) — a village in the lowland of Judah near Jarmuth (Josh. 15:34), probably the same place as Enaim (Gen. 38:14, 21, RSV).

ENAN [E non] (*fountains*) — the father of Ahira, leader of the tribe of Naphtali in the days of Moses. Ahira assisted in taking the first census of Israel during their years in the wilderness (Num. 1:15).

ENCAMPMENT (see CAMP).

The spring at En Gedi, where David hid from King Saul (1 Sam. 24:1).
Photo by Gustav Jeeninga

ENCHANTMENT — the practice of magic or sorcery. In the Bible, enchantment is used as a general word that can refer to several different types of supernatural experiences, including fortune telling, calling up devils, and controlling evil spirits. Most ancient civilizations believed in such magical approaches to religion, but the Mosaic Law referred to such practices as "abominations," forbidding them to the Hebrews (Deut. 18:10–12). The Law also provided that practitioners of such "black magic" should be stoned (Lev. 20:27).

ENEMY — one who opposes or mistreats another. This word occurs more frequently in the Old Testament than in the New Testament. The reason for this is that the Old Testament is concerned primarily with the existence of Israel as a nation over against the other countries of the ancient world. Before Israel could serve as the channel of God's grace to the world, its existence as a nation had to be securely established. The enemies of the Hebrew people were thus regarded as God's enemies, and the reverse was also true (Ps. 139:20–22). In the New Testament, by contrast, the enemies to be overcome are primarily spiritual in nature.

While the Old Testament does refer to charity toward one's enemy (Ex. 23:4–5; Prov. 24:17), the New Testament goes further by commanding love for one's enemy (Matt. 5:44; Rom. 12:20). The New Testament looks toward a day when all enemies of good and righteousness will be overcome because of the redemptive work of Christ (1 Cor. 15:25).

ENGINE (see ARMS, ARMOR OF THE BIBLE).

ENGLISH VERSIONS (see BIBLE VERSIONS AND TRANSLATIONS).

ENGRAVER (see OCCUPATIONS AND TRADES).

ENMITY — deep-seated animosity or hatred. The apostle Paul declared that the human mind in its natural state has a natural "enmity against God" (Rom. 8:7). This enmity can be changed only through the redemptive power of Christ.

ENOCH [EE nuck] (*initiated* or *dedicated*) — the name of two men and one city in the Bible:

1. The firstborn son of Cain (Gen. 4:17–18).
2. A city built by Cain in the land of Nod and named after his son (Gen. 4:17).
3. A son of Jared and the father of Methuselah (Gen. 5:18–24; Henoch; 2 Chr. 1:3, KJV). After living for years, Enoch was "translated," or taken directly into God's presence without experiencing death (Gen. 5:24).

ENOCH, BOOK OF (see PSEUDEPIGRAPHA).

ENOS [E nos] — a form of ENOSH.

ENOSH [EE nosh] (*man, mankind*) — a grandson of Adam, a son of Seth, and the father of Cainan (Gen. 5:6–11). He lived 905 years. Enosh is listed in Luke's genealogy of Jesus (Luke 3:38; Enos, KJV).

ENQUIRE OF THE LORD (see INQUIRE OF THE LORD).

ENROLLMENT — KJV word for the registration of the citizens of Palestine ordered by the Roman emperor Augustus (Luke 2:1–5). Augustus (Octavian) initiated a system of reforms, including a regular census of the populations of the various Roman provinces so they could be effectively taxed. Joseph probably owned some property in Bethlehem; so he returned there with Mary to be registered. God used this Roman edict to bring Jesus' parents to Bethlehem so the prophecy of Micah 5:2 might be fulfilled.

ENSIGN [IN sun] (see STANDARD).

ENVOY (see OCCUPATIONS AND TRADES).

ENVY — a feeling of resentment and jealousy toward another person because of his possessions or good qualities. James linked envy with self-seeking (James 3:14, 16; selfish ambition, RSV). Christians are warned to guard against the sin of envy (Rom. 13:13; 1 Pet. 2:1).

EPAENETUS [eh PEE nee tus] (*praiseworthy*) — a Christian, formerly from Asia, who later lived in Rome and was greeted by Paul (Rom. 16:5). He was the first convert to Christianity in Asia.

EPAPHRAS [EP uh frus] (*charming*) — a Christian preacher who spread the gospel to his fellow Colossian citizens (Col. 1:7; 4:12). When Paul was a prisoner in Rome, Epaphras came to him with a favorable account of the church at Colosse. He remained with Paul in Rome and was, in a sense, his "fellow prisoner" (Philem. 23). Epaphras should not be confused with EPAPHRODITUS, who was from Philippi (Phil. 2:25).

EPAPHRODITUS [ih paf ruh DIE tus] (*charming*) — a messenger sent by the church at Philippi with a gift for the apostle Paul, who was under house arrest in Rome (Phil. 2:25; 4:18). While in Rome Epaphroditus became ill and word of his sickness spread to Philippi. As soon as Epaphroditus was well enough, Paul sent him back home to relieve the church's anxiety and to deliver Paul's letter to the Philippians. Epaphroditus should not be confused with EPAPHRAS, who was from Colossae (Col. 4:12).

EPHAH [E fa] (*obscurity* or *darkness*) — the name of two men, one woman, one tribe and a unit of measurement in the Bible:

1. A son of Midian and a grandson of Abraham and Keturah, Abraham's concubine (Gen. 25:4).
2. A concubine of Caleb (1 Chr. 2:46).
3. A son of Jahdi (1 Chr. 2:47).
4. An Arabian tribe, a branch of Midianites living in northwest Arabia (Is. 60:6). This tribe was descended from Ephah No. 1.
5. A unit of measurement. See WEIGHTS AND MEASURES.

EPHAI [EE fie] (*birdlike*) — a resident of Netophah in Judah whose sons were among those who joined Gedaliah at Mizpah (Jer. 40:8–13). Ephai and his sons were promised protection and were subsequently murdered by Ishmael (Jer. 41:3).

EPHER [EE fur] (*gazelle*) — the name of three men in the Old Testament:

1. The second son of Midian and a grandson of Abraham and Keturah, Abraham's concubine (Gen. 25:4).

2. A descendant of Judah through Ezrah (1 Chr. 4:17).

3. A head of a family in the half–tribe of Manasseh east of the Jordan River (1 Chr. 5:24).

EPHES DAMMIM [EE fez DAM im] (*end of blood*) — a place in Judah between Socoh and Azekah where the Philistines camped at the time when David killed GOLIATH (1 Sam. 17:1; Pasdammim, 1 Chr. 11:13). This place is usually identified with Damun, about six kilometers (four miles) northeast of Socoh.

EPHESIANS [ee FEE zyuns] — natives or inhabitants of EPHESUS (Acts 19:35). Trophimus, one of Paul's co–workers, was an Ephesian (Acts 21:29).

EPHESIANS, EPISTLE TO THE — one of four shorter epistles written by the apostle Paul while he was in prison, the others being Philippians, Colossians, and Philemon. Ephesians shares many similarities in style and content with Colossians; it may have been written about the same time and delivered by the same person.

In the Epistle to the Ephesians, Paul is transported to the limits of language in order to describe the enthroned Christ who is Lord of the church, the world, and the entire created order. As the ascended Lord, Christ is completing what He began in His earthly ministry, by means of His now "extended body," the church. Christ's goal is to fill all things with Himself and bring all things to Himself.

Structure of the Epistle. Ephesians divides naturally into two halves: a lofty theological section (chaps. 1—3), and a section of ethical appeal and application (chaps. 4—6).

Paul begins by greeting his readers and assuring them that they have been blessed with God's gracious favor—redemption in Christ—from before the foundation of the world (1:1–14). Paul then prays that God may grant them an even greater measure of spiritual wisdom and revelation (1:15–23). Chapter two begins with perhaps the clearest statement of salvation by grace through faith in all the Bible (2:1–10). Although the Ephesians were once alienated from God, now they are reconciled both to God and to one another by Christ, who is "our peace" (2:11–22). Paul was made an apostle to proclaim the "mystery of Christ"—the inexhaustible riches of the gospel to the Gentiles (3:1–13). Paul brings the first half of the epistle to a close with a prayer that the Ephesians may understand the depth of Christ's love (3:14–19). A benediction concludes the doctrinal section (3:20–21).

An appeal to adapt one's life to one's faith (4:1) marks the transition to the second half of the epistle. The Christian fellowship should pattern itself after the unity of the Godhead (4:1–16), and the Christian should pattern himself after the example of Christ (4:17—5:20): as a new person in Christ he should walk in love, light, and wisdom. Paul cites Christ's relationship with the church as a model for wives and husbands (5:22–33), children and parents (6:1–4), and servants and masters (6:5–9). The epistle ends with an appeal to put on the whole armor of God and to stand against the forces of evil (6:10–20), followed by final greetings (6:21–24).

A beautiful column-lined marble street in ancient Ephesus.

Photo by Gustav Jeeninga

Authorship and Date. Ephesians bears the name of Paul (1:1; 3:1), and it sets forth many of the great Pauline themes, such as JUSTIFICATION by faith (2:1–10) and the body of Christ (4:15–16). Nevertheless, Ephesians has a number of notable differences from the undisputed letters of Paul. We know, for instance, that Paul spent three years in Ephesus (Acts 19:1–40), and it is clear that the Ephesians cherished his ministry among them (Acts 20:17–38). Strangely, however, Paul writes to the Ephesians as though they knew of his ministry only by hearsay (3:2). Moreover, with the exception of

Tychicus (6:21), Paul mentions no one by name in Ephesians. Because of the impersonal nature of the epistle, plus the fact that it contains a number of words and phrases not characteristic of Paul, some scholars suspect that Ephesians was written by someone other than the apostle Paul.

Although this is possible, it is not likely. If Ephesians were not written by Paul, then it was written by someone who understood Paul's thinking as well as the apostle himself. Moreover, it is unlikely that a person capable of writing Ephesians could have remained unknown to the church. Many scholars

---

EPHESIANS: A Teaching Outline

Part One: The Position of the Christian (1:1—3:21)

Part Two: The Practice of the Christian (4:1—6:24)

have resolved the problems of authorship by suggesting that while Ephesians was indeed written by Paul, it was intended as a circular letter, or "open letter," to a number of communities surrounding Ephesus.

In the oldest manuscripts of the epistle, the phrase "in Ephesus" (1:1) is absent. Perhaps this phrase was omitted to leave space in copies of the letter for the insertion of different place names. Paul is known to have used circular letters on occasion (Col. 4:16), and the circular theory would account for the general tone of the letter.

If Paul was the author of Ephesians, then he probably wrote it about the same time as the Epistle to the Colossians. Both Ephesians and Colossians agree to a large extent in style and content. Both these letters were also delivered by Tychicus (Eph. 6:21; Col. 4:7). Furthermore, Paul was in prison at the time, presumably in Rome. This would suggest a date in the late 50s or early 60s.

Historical Setting. The general nature of Ephesians makes it difficult to determine the specific circumstances that gave rise to the epistle. It is clear, however, that the recipients were Gentiles (3:1), who were estranged from citizenship in the kingdom of Israel (2:11). Now, thanks to the gracious gift of God, they enjoy the spiritual blessings that come from Christ.

Theological Contribution. The theme of Ephesians is the relationship between the heavenly Lord Jesus Christ and His earthly body, the church. Christ now reigns "far above all principality and power and might and dominion" (1:21) and has "put all things under His feet" (1:22). Exalted though He is, He has not drifted off into the heavens and forgotten His people. Rather, so fully does He identify with the church that He considers it His body, which He fills with His presence (1:23; 3:19; 4:10).

The marriage relationship between husband and wife is a beautiful analogy for expressing Christ's love, sacrifice, and lordship over the church (5:22–32). The enthroned Christ has reinvested Himself in the hearts of believers through faith (3:17) so they can marvel at His love. Absolutely nothing exists beyond His redeeming reach (1:10; 3:18; 4:9).

Christ's bond with His church is also portrayed in the oneness of believers. Those who were once "far off" and separated from God "have been made near by the blood of Christ" (2:13). In fact, believers are now raised with Christ and seated with Him in the heavenly places (2:5-6). Since believers are with Him, they are accordingly to be like Him— "endeavoring to keep the unity of the Spirit in the bond of peace" (4:3). "He [Christ] Himself is our peace" (2:14), says Paul, and He removes the walls and barriers that formerly divided Jews and Gentiles, and draws them together in one Spirit to the Father (2:14-22).

Having spoken of these marvelous spiritual blessings, Paul then appeals to believers "to have a walk worthy of the calling with which you were called" (4:1). This appeal is a helpful insight on Christian ethics. Rather than setting down laws and regulations, Paul says, in effect, *Let your life be a credit to the One who called you.* The Christian is set free by Christ; yet he is responsible to Christ. Paul makes several statements about how believers can honor Christ (4:17—5:9), but the goal is not to earn merit through morality. Instead of looking for nice people, Paul envisions new persons, the "perfect person," remade according to the stature of Christ Himself (4:13). This "mature manhood" (RSV) could refer to the desired, and still unattained unity of the church.

Special Considerations. The term "heavenly places" (1:3; 1:20; 2:6; 3:10; 6:12) is not the same as heaven, for in one instance Paul speaks of "spiritual hosts of wickedness in the heavenly places" (6:12). "Heavenly places" implies the unseen, spiritual world beyond our physical senses. It is the region where the most difficult, and yet authentic, Christian discipleship is lived out—the world of decisions, attitudes, temptations, and commitments. It is the battleground of good and evil (6:12).

Christ has raised believers to the heavenly places with the assurance that the One in whom we hope is more powerful, real, and eternal than the forces of chaos and destruction which threaten our world.

EPHESUS [EFF uh sus] — a large and important city on the west coast of Asia Minor where the apostle Paul founded a church (see Map 7, C-2). A number of factors contributed to the prominence which Ephesus enjoyed.

The first factor was economics. Situated at the mouth of the river Cayster, Ephesus was the most favorable seaport in the province of Asia and the most important trade center west of Tarsus. Today, because of silting from the river, the ruins of the city lie in a swamp 8 to 11 kilometers (5 to 7 miles) inland.

Another factor was size. Although Pergamum was the capital of the province of Asia in Roman times, Ephesus was the largest city in the province, having a population of perhaps 300,000 people.

A third factor was culture. Ephesus contained a theater that seated an estimated 25,000 people. A main thoroughfare, some 35 meters (105 feet) wide, ran from the theater to the harbor, at each end of which stood an impressive gate. The thoroughfare was flanked on each side by rows of columns 15 meters (50 feet) deep. Behind these columns were baths, gymnasiums, and impressive buildings.

The fourth, and perhaps most significant, reason for the prominence of Ephesus was religion. The Temple of Artemis (or Diana, according to her Roman name) at Ephesus ranked as one of the Seven Wonders of the Ancient World. As the twin sister of Apollo and the daughter of Zeus, Artemis was known variously as the moon goddess, the goddess of hunting, and the patroness of young girls. The temple at Ephesus housed the multi–breasted image of Artemis which was reputed to have come directly from Zeus (Acts 19:35).

The temple of Artemis in Paul's day was supported by 127 columns, each of them 60 meters

The great theater of the city of Ephesus, showing the marble boulevard leading to the nearby harbor, now silted in because of erosion.

(197 feet) high. The Ephesians took great pride in this grand edifice. During the Roman period, they promoted the worship of Artemis by minting coins with the inscription, "Diana of Ephesus."

The history of Christianity at Ephesus began probably about A.D. 50, perhaps as a result of the efforts of Priscilla and Aquila (Acts 18:18). Paul came to Ephesus in about A.D. 52, establishing a resident ministry for the better part of three years (Acts 20:31). During his Ephesian ministry, Paul wrote 1 Corinthians (1 Cor. 16:8).

The Book of Acts reports that "all who dwelt in Asia heard the word of the Lord Jesus" (Acts 19:10), while Paul taught during the hot midday hours in the lecture hall of Tyrannus (Acts 19:9). Influence from his ministry undoubtedly resulted in the founding of churches in the Lycus River valley at Laodicea, Hierapolis, and Colossae.

So influential, in fact, was Paul's ministry at Ephesus that the silversmith's league, which fashioned souvenirs of the temple, feared that the preaching of the gospel would undermine the great temple of Artemis (Acts 19:27). As a result, one of the silversmiths, a man named Demetrius, stirred up a riot against Paul.

During his stay in Ephesus, Paul encountered both great opportunities and great dangers. He baptized believers who apparently came to know the gospel through disciples of John the Baptist (Acts 19:1-5), and he countered the strong influence of magic in Ephesus (Acts 19:11-20).

After Paul departed from Ephesus, Timothy remained to combat false teaching (1 Tim. 1:3; 2 Tim. 4:3; Acts 20:29). Many traditions testify that the apostle John lived in Ephesus toward the end of the first century. In his vision from the island of Patmos off the coast of Asia Minor, John described the church of Ephesus as flourishing, although it was troubled with false teachers and had lost its first love (Rev. 2:1-7). In the sixth century A.D. the Roman emperor Justinian (A.D. 527-565) raised a magnificent church to John's memory in this city.

Ephesus continued to play a prominent role in the history of the early church. A long line of bishops in the Eastern church lived there. In A.D. 431 the Council of Ephesus officially condemned the Nestorian heresy, which taught that there were two separate persons, one divine and one human, in the person of Jesus Christ.

EPHLAL [EFF lal] (*judging*) — a descendant of Perez, of the tribe of Judah (1 Chr. 2:37).

EPHOD [EE fahd] (*oracular*) — the father of Hanniel. Hanniel was a leader of the tribe of Manasseh, and one of Moses' assistants in dividing the land of Canaan (Num. 34:23).

EPHOD OF HIGH PRIEST [EE fod] — a vest worn by the HIGH PRIEST when he presided at the altar (Ex. 28:4-14; 39:2-7). Worn over a blue robe (Ex. 28:31-35), the ephod was made of fine linen interwoven with some threads of pure gold and other threads that were blue, purple, and scarlet in color. The ephod consisted of two pieces joined at the shoulders and bound together at the bottom by a woven band of the same material as the ephod. This band perhaps served as a girdle.

Upon the shoulders of the ephod, in settings of gold, were two onyx stones. Upon these stones were engraved the names of the twelve tribes of Israel. The front of the vest, or the breastplate, was fastened to the shoulder straps by two golden chains (Ex. 28:14) and by a blue cord (Ex. 28:28).

In later years, ephods were worn by associate priests as well as the high priest (1 Sam. 22:18). Even the boy Samuel, dedicated to serve in the Shiloh temple, wore an ephod (1 Sam. 2:18). David, although not a priest, wore an ephod when he brought the ark to Jerusalem (2 Sam. 6:14; 1 Chr. 15:27).

Since Christ is our great High Priest (Heb. 8:1–6), the symbols in the ephod may be applied to Him. White linen speaks of His absolute righteousness. Scarlet (the color of blood) symbolizes His atoning work on the cross; purple, His royalty; gold, His divinity. Blue, the color of the sky, signifies Christ's origin with God the Father in heaven.

EPHPHATHA [EF fa thuh] — an Aramaic word spoken by Jesus when he healed a deaf-mute (Mark 7:34). The word means "Open!"

EPHRAIM [EE freh em] (*doubly fruitful*) — the second son of Joseph by Asenath and founder of one of the twelve tribes of the nation of Israel.

When Ephraim was born to Joseph in Egypt, he gave him his name meaning "fruitful" because "God has caused me to be fruitful in the land of my affliction" (Gen. 41:52). Even though Joseph was a foreigner (a Hebrew) in Egypt, he had been blessed by God as he rose to a high position in the Egyptian government and fathered two sons. Later this same theme of fruitfulness and blessing was echoed by Joseph's father, Jacob, as he accepted Ephraim as his grandson (Gen. 48:5). Eventually Ephraim's thousands of descendants settled in the land of Canaan as one of the most numerous of the twelve tribes of Israel (Gen. 48:19; Num. 1:10).

EPHRAIM, CITY OF (*double grainland*) — a city near the wilderness (see Map 6, B-4), northeast of Jerusalem, to which Jesus and His disciples retreated when threatened by the chief priests and Pharisees after He raised Lazarus from the dead (John 11:54). It has been identified with OPHRAH in the territory of Benjamin (Josh. 18:23; 1 Sam. 13:17) at present-day et-Taiyibeh, about 6 kilometers (4 miles) northeast of Bethel and about 22.5 kilometers (14 miles) northeast of Jerusalem.

EPHRAIM, FOREST OF — a thick forest in the hill country west of the Jordan River. Joshua gave this territory to the dissatisfied tribe of Ephraim (Josh. 17:14–18). Absalom's soldiers were defeated in this forest by David's army (2 Sam. 18:6–17).

EPHRAIM, GATE OF (see GATES OF JERUSALEM AND THE TEMPLE).

EPHRAIM, MOUNTAINS OF — a range of mountains west of the Jordan River, extending as far south as Ramah and Bethel (1 Sam. 1:1; 2 Chr. 13:4), named for the tribe of Ephraim which settled the region (Josh. 19:50).

EPHRAIM, TRIBE OF — descendants of EPHRAIM, who settled the land of Canaan as one of the twelve tribes of Israel. This tribe settled a territory bounded on the north by the territory of

Manasseh (west of the River Jordan) and on the south by the territories of Dan and Benjamin (Josh. 16:5–10).

From the early days, the tribe of Ephraim was an influential force in Israel, being highly commended by Gideon (Judg. 8:2), and including such key religious and political centers as Bethel and Shechem. At the time of the first census in their new land, the tribe contained 40,500 men eligible for military service.

Following the revolt of the ten tribes after Solomon's rule, Ephraim became a leader in the northern kingdom of Israel (1 Kin. 12:25–33). Often the name Ephraim was used for Israel because of the many members of this tribe and its leadership role. The Hebrew prophets, especially Hosea, chastised the tribe for idolatry (Hos. 4:17), spiritual unfaithfulness (8:9–10), and relationships with heathen nations (12:1). Ephraim was involved in an alliance with Syria against Judah and King Ahaz (2 Chr. 28:5–8; Is. 7:3–9).

In 722 B.C., the northern kingdom of Israel was taken into captivity in Assyria. This seemed to be the end of the tribe of Ephraim, but the Lord would not forget them. Through the prophet Jeremiah, He declared that these people were still His "dear son" and He would have mercy on them (Jer. 31:20). Years later, after God's people returned to their homeland following a long period of captivity in Babylon, "children of Ephraim" settled in Jerusalem (1 Chr. 9:3).

EPHRAIMITES [EE fruh im ites] — descendants of EPHRAIM, a son of Joseph, and inhabitants of the territory of Ephraim (Josh. 16:10; Judg. 12:4–6).

EPHRAIN [EE fruh in] — a city near Bethel which Abijah, king of Judah, took from Jeroboam, king of Israel (2 Chr. 13:19; Ephron, RSV).

EPHRATHAH [EF ray thah] (*fertility*) — the name of a woman and a city in the Old Testament:

1. A wife of Caleb, the son of Hezron (1 Chr. 2.19; 4:4). She was the mother of Hur and the grandmother of the Caleb who spied out the land of Canaan.

2. The ancient name of Bethlehem of Judah (Gen.48:7). The prophet Micah refers to the town as Bethlehem Ephrathah (Mic. 5:2). His prophecy that the Messiah would be born here was fulfilled in Jesus Christ (Matt. 2:6; Ephratah, KJV).

EPHRATHITE [EF ruh thite] — the title of two Old Testament men:

1. A native or inhabitant of Ephrath, or Bethlehem (Ruth 1:2; 1 Sam. 17:12).

2. An Ephraimite, one who belonged to the tribe of Ephraim (1 Sam. 1:1, KJV; 1 Kin. 11:26, KJV).

EPHRON [EE fron] (*dust*) — the name of a man and a place in the Old Testament:

1. A Hittite from whom Abraham purchased a field containing the cave of MACHPELAH. This cave became the burial place of the patriarchs Abraham, Isaac, and Jacob (and also of their wives, Sarah,

Rebekah, and Leah; Gen. 23:8–17; 25:9; 49:29–30; 50:13).

2. A ridge of mountains between Nephtoah and Kirjath Jearim on the boundary between Benjamin and Judah (Josh. 15:9).

EPICUREANS [epp uh cue REE anz] — Greek philosophers who belonged to a school founded by Epicurus about 306 B.C. The Epicureans were concerned with the practical results of philosophy in everyday life. Their chief aim in life was pleasure. They believed they could find happiness by seeking that which brought physical and mental pleasure, and by avoiding that which brought pain.

Only one reference to the Epicureans occurs in Scripture—in the New Testament account of the apostle Paul's encounter with "certain Epicurean and Stoic philosophers" at Athens (Acts 17:16–34). In contrast to these philosophers, Paul believed that true happiness was found in following the will of Jesus Christ.

EPILEPSY (see DISEASES OF THE BIBLE).

EPIPHANES [e PIFF uh knees] — a shorter name for Antiochus IV, the king of Syria (reigned 175–163 B.C.). He defiled the Jewish Temple in Jerusalem by sacrificing swine on the altar and by setting himself up as a god to be worshiped. Also see ANTIOCHUS.

EPISTLE — a letter of correspondence between two or more parties; the form in which several books of the New Testament were originally written. Epistle is generally synonymous with letter, although epistle sometimes is regarded as more formal correspondence, and letter as more personal.

There is no real precedent for the New Testament epistles in the Old Testament or Jewish literature. Rather, its 21 epistles (Romans through Jude) follow the general custom and form of letters, which became an important form of communication in the Greek-speaking world about 300 years before the birth of Jesus.

Greek letters may be roughly divided into six classes: (1) private letters, averaging slightly less than a hundred words in length, and written on PAPYRUS (an early form of paper); (2) correspondence between government officials; (3) letters intended for publication, such as the correspondence of the church fathers in the fourth century A.D.; (4) letters written to communicate ideas; (5) letters attributed to famous personalities; and (6) imaginary letters, somewhat like our modern historical novels, which were designed to entertain.

Ancient letters were written with a reed pen on either papyrus or PARCHMENT (scraped animal skins). A sheet of papyrus normally was about 10 to 12 inches in size, and accommodated about 200 words. For sending, it was folded or rolled, tied, and often sealed to insure privacy.

The Roman government provided postal service only for official documents. Private letters had to be sent by special messengers or friendly travelers. Letters normally were sent to designated parties, although some were "open" or circular letters. Paul's letters, with the possible exception of Ephesians, were addressed to specific congregations; but the non-Pauline letters, usually called "general" epis-

An epistle, or letter, in the Greek language from the third century A.D., written to a person named Aphrodite.

Photo: Pacific School of Religion

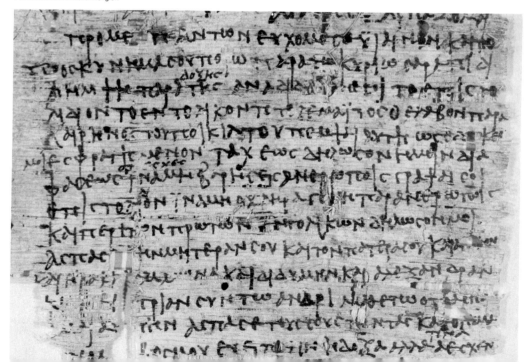

tles, included some letters which were circulated to several churches.

Most ancient letters were dictated to a secretary, or scribe. In Romans 16:22, Paul's secretary identifies himself as Tertius. When receiving dictation, a scribe could use a form of shorthand, in either Greek or Latin, which would later be converted to script and submitted to the author for approval. In addition to dictation, on occasion an author might provide a secretary with a summary of ideas and allow him to draft the epistle. This practice may have been followed in the case of 1 Peter.

Ancient letters normally followed a pattern which included: (1) an introduction, listing the names of sender and recipient, followed by a formal greeting inquiring about the recipient's health and a thanksgiving formula; (2) a body, or purpose for writing; and (3) a conclusion, consisting of appropriate remarks and a farewell. The farewell was normally written in the hand of the sender to show the recipient it was an authentic letter.

The apostle Paul's epistles follow this pattern, with the following exceptions. Paul replaced the bland greeting of inquiry about health with a salutation combining Christian grace and Hebrew peace. His thanksgiving was likewise more than a formality; it was a sincere expression of gratitude for the well-being of his congregations. He also omitted the farewell in favor of personal greetings or a benediction.

Paul's epistles were letters written to communicate ideas. But they were more than abstract essays. With the exception of Romans, Paul's letters were written as follow-ups to his missionary activity.

Their purpose was to further the spiritual growth of the churches he founded. The body of the Pauline epistles consisted of two parts: a theological or doctrinal section, and an ethical or practical section. These two sections flowed together in the same way that justification leads to sanctification in the life of the believer.

Paul's epistles illustrate his personality. Perhaps the most prominent impression Paul leaves with his readers is his pastoral concern. His life was intimately involved in the struggles of his churches. His sense of divine calling (Rom. 1:1–6; Gal. 1:12) shines through in every epistle. This leads Paul to assume a posture of authority when addressing his congregations. His authority, however, is not rooted in a superiority complex but in his devotion to his converts and churches.

The Pauline epistles are arranged in the New Testament according to length, from the longest (Romans) to the shortest (Philemon), and not by importance or the dates when they were written.

ER [ur] (*watchful*) — the name of three men in the Bible:

1. A son of Judah (Gen. 38:3, 6–7).
2. A son of Shelah, the youngest son of Judah (1 Chr. 4:21).
3. An ancestor of Jesus who lived between the time of David and Zerubbabel (Luke 3:28).

ERAN [EE run] (*watchful*) — a descendant of Ephraim through Shuthelah, Ephraim's oldest son and the founder of a tribal family, the Eranites (Num. 26:36).

ERASTUS [ih RAS tus] (*beloved*) — the name of

Reverse side of the letter to Aphrodite, showing how two pieces of papyrus were pressed together in crisscross fashion to produce a piece of writing material.
Photo: Pacific School of Religion

one or more Christians in the early church:

1. A Christian sent with Timothy from Ephesus into Macedonia while the apostle Paul stayed in Asia (Acts 19:22).

2. The "treasurer of the city" (Rom. 16:23) in Corinth who sent greetings to Rome.

3. One who remained at Corinth (2 Tim. 4:20).

Any two of the above—or perhaps all three— may be identical.

ERECH [EH wreck] (meaning unknown) — a city built by Nimrod on the Plain of Shinar. The city was situated between Ur and Babylon on the the Euphrates River. Its importance in ancient history is evident because no fewer than 11 names have been given to it. For example, the Babylonians and Assyrians called it Uruk, or Arku; the Arabs called it Warka; and the Greeks and Romans called it Orchoe. The Bible mentions Erech only once (Gen. 10:10).

ERI [EE rye] (*watchful*) — the fifth of the seven sons of Gad (Gen. 46:16) and leader of the Erites (Num. 26:16).

ERROR — deviation from the truth or an accepted code of behavior (Job 4:18; Eccl. 5:6; 10:5; Dan. 6:4). In the New Testament the Greek word translated as error means "a wandering from the way," "a straying from the path" (Rom. 1:27; 1 John 4:6). In the NKJV the same Greek word is also translated as "deception" (Matt. 27:64), or "deceit" (1 Thess. 2:3). James 5:19, 20 indicates that it is possible to wander from the truth. Since the Bible sees truth as moral in nature, error is more than incorrect thinking. It is a wrong way of life.

ESAIAS [eh ZAY yus] — Greek form of ISAIAH.

ESARHADDON [ee zar HAD un] — the favorite, though not the eldest, son of Sennacherib, who succeeded his father as king of Assyria. Sennacherib's favoritism toward Esarhaddon so enraged two other brothers, Adrammelech and Sharaezer, that they assassinated their father about 681 B.C., then escaped into Armenia (2 Kin. 19:36–37; 2 Chr. 37:21; Is. 37:37–38). At the time of the assassination, Esarhaddon was conducting a military campaign, probably in Armenia. He returned to Nineveh, the Assyrian capital, ended the civil strife, and assumed the Assyrian throne.

Esarhaddon was a wise ruler, both militarily and politically. He restored the city of Babylon, which his father had destroyed in an earlier campaign against Babylonia; and he successfully waged war against numerous groups that had been persistent in creating problems for the Assyrian Empire. Among his most notable military achievements was his conquest of Egypt, Assyria's competitor for world domination. In 677 B.C. Esarhaddon captured Memphis and then conquered the rest of Egypt. He then used native rulers and Assyrian advisers to rule the distant country.

Egypt rebelled in 669 B.C. On his way to Egypt to put down the rebellion, Esarhaddon became ill and died. As his father before him had done, Esarhaddon had provided for an orderly succession in the affairs of Assyria. His younger son, Ashurbanipal, ascended to the Assyrian throne.

Esarhaddon was the Assyrian king who resettled Samaria with foreigners after this capital city of the northern kingdom of Israel fell to Assyrian forces in 722 B.C. (Ezra 4:2). This was an example of the Assyrian policy of intermingling cultures in the nations which they conquered to make them weak and compliant.

ESAU [ee SAW] (meaning unknown) — a son of Isaac and Rebekah and the twin brother of Jacob. Also known as Edom, Esau was the ancestor of the Edomites (Gen. 25:24–28; Deut. 2:4–8).

Most of the biblical narratives about Esau draw a great contrast between him and his brother, Jacob.

A monument honoring Esarhaddon of Assyria, showing subjects kneeling before the king and symbols of his pagan gods in the upper corner.

Esau was a hunter and outdoorsman who was favored by his father, while Jacob was not an outdoors type and was favored by Rebekah (Gen. 25:27–28).

Even though he was a twin, Esau was considered the eldest son because he was born first. By Old Testament custom, he would have inherited most of his father's property and the right to succeed him as family patriarch. But in a foolish, impulsive moment, he sold his BIRTHRIGHT to Jacob in exchange for a meal (Gen. 25:29–34). This determined that Jacob would carry on the family name in a direct line of descent from Abraham and Isaac, his grandfather and father.

The loss of Esau's rights as first-born is further revealed in Genesis 27. In this account, Jacob deceived his blind father by disguising himself as Esau in order to receive his father's blessing. Esau was so enraged by his brother's actions that he determined to kill him once his father died. But Jacob fled to his uncle Laban in Haran and remained there for 20 years. Upon Jacob's return to Canaan, Esau forgave him and set aside their old feuds (Gen. 32:1–33:17). Years later, the two brothers together buried their father in the cave at Machpelah without a trace of their old hostilities (Gen. 35:29).

Esau in many ways was more honest and dependable than his scheming brother Jacob. But he sinned greatly by treating his birthright so casually and selling it for a meal. To the ancient Hebrews, one's birthright actually represented a high spiritual value. The oldest son was responsible to serve as a priest to the rest of his family by encouraging worship of the one true God. But Esau did not have the faith and farsightedness to accept this privilege and responsibility. Thus, the right passed by default to his younger brother.

ESAU'S WIVES — the six wives of Esau, oldest son of Jacob: (1) Judith (Gen. 26:34), (2) Basemath (Gen. 26:34), (3) Adah (Gen. 36:2), (4) Aholibamah (Gen. 36:2), (5) Basemath (Gen. 36:3), and (6) Mahalath (Gen. 28:9). Because of the large clan that came from these wives, Esau moved south and east of the Dead Sea to the area of Mount Seir sometimes referred to as Edom (Gen. 36:6–9). His descendants through these wives became known as the Edomites.

ESCHATOLOGY [es cuh TOL ih gih] — a theological term that designates the study of what will happen at the end of history, particularly the event known as the SECOND COMING of Christ. The word comes from two Greek words, *eschatos* (last) and *logos* (study)—thus its definition as "the study of last things."

The Curse. Genesis 3 shows God's response to human sin. Because of its sin and unrighteousness, He cursed the world which He had just made. At the other end of the Bible, Revelation 22:3 announces there will no longer be a curse. All that happens between Genesis 3 and Revelation 22 is related to God's efforts to reverse His curse and redeem His creation. This illustrates that eschatology is related

to salvation. Eschatology reveals the end of history and how God reverses His curse upon the world by separating the good from the bad.

The curse of God plunged the world into a long conflict. This conflict-strewn path leading up to God's final act in history can be traced from the Garden of Eden to Revelation. Just as God alone had cursed the creation, so only God can revoke the curse. He has chosen to revoke one aspect of the curse and its conflict through an event known as the Day of the Lord.

Because man was not obedient to God, the need for the Day of the Lord arose in biblical history. This was a day when all the world would be brought back under His rule (Amos 5:18–20; Joel 2:31). The final preparation for that rule was the elevation of Jesus to God's right hand (Ps. 110:1; Acts 2:34–35). We are now under the spiritual rule of Christ, awaiting His earthly rule and the defeat of all His enemies when He returns to reign.

Seed Conflict. The process that would eventually end with all of God's enemies in defeat begins in the first chapters of the Bible. Victory over evil was promised only through the conflict between the seed of the woman and the seed of the snake (Gen. 3:15). This conflict forms the guidelines for eschatological events throughout the Bible, especially for the end-time itself.

This curse set the pattern for all future conflicts between man and God (1 John 3:10–11; Gal. 4:28–29; Phil. 2:5–8). This conflict also typifies the conflict between flesh and spirit (Gal. 5:16–17; 2 Cor. 11:3, 14; Rom. 16:20). The battles of the end times are the climax of a long battle between the forces of good and evil that has been going on since the beginning of time.

The Flood. The universal Flood of Noah's time was an expression of God's hatred and judgment of sin. In this event, He plunged His creation back to its original state of darkness and chaos with the waters covering the deep (Gen. 7:17–24). Then He began again with a new head of the human race—His servant Noah. Although this particular act of God's wrath will not be repeated, the reminders of His judgment are still present in the rainbow and the creatures' fear of humans (Gen. 9:1–17).

The Flood became a sign of the future wrath of God, which would take place by fire (2 Pet. 3:5–9). The first heaven and earth will eventually fall away and be replaced with the new heaven and earth. This falling away will be a violent burning of the universe (2 Pet. 3:10–13). Jesus Himself thus defined the end-time judgment of His return in terms of the Flood and Noah's generation (Matt. 24:36–44).

God's Covenant with Abraham. The end of history is focused on the fulfillment of God's promise to Abraham. The Abrahamic covenant is specific in its explanation of how biblical conflict will end in the Day of the Lord. God promised to give Abraham a land and a lineage (Gen. 12:1–3). These two items, the result of God's blessing of Abraham, are the specific blessings promised the Hebrew people.

What began as a small national boundary for a small group of people (the Jews) became international in scope, including all races (Acts 3:25–26). Eschatology reveals that Abraham's land, ultimately, is the new heaven and earth and that Abraham's lineage is the redeemed community in Christ.

Abraham was also promised by God that those who blessed him would be blessed and those who cursed him would be cursed (Gen. 12:3). In eschatology this interplay between blessing and curse depends on how people respond to God's work through His people Israel, and ultimately through His work in Christ. Hell is the ultimate curse; heaven the ultimate blessing.

Abraham's Offspring. The idea of blessing and cursing by God is further seen through various events in the life of Abraham and his offspring, Israel. Plagues sent by God on Egypt in Abraham's time (Gen. 12:17) foreshadowed the plagues under Moses (Exodus 7—12) and the end-time plagues of the book of Revelation (Revelation 8—9). The enemies from Mesopotamia who captured Lot and were destroyed by Abraham (Gen. 14:1–17) foreshadowed God's destruction of Assyria and Babylon at the end of Israel's period of captivity (Is. 13—14; Dan. 5:13–31) and the end-time destruction of the pagan people represented by Babylon (Revelation 17—19).

Other foreshadowings of the wrath of the Day of the Lord are the downfall of Jericho with its seven trumpets, which announced the presence of God above the ark (Josh. 6:13), and the seven-trumpet judgments of the book of Revelation (Rev. 8:2–21; 11:15–19). These various destructions of Israel's enemies looked toward the final destruction of all of God's enemies in the Day of the Lord. Jesus' casting out of demons (Mark 5:29; Luke 8:31) also foreshadowed God's judgment on fallen angels (Jude 6; 2 Pet. 2:4; Rev. 20:10), who will be cast out in the Day of the Lord.

Final Judgments. In the end times, a basic order of judgment will prevail as the conflict between God and Satan comes to an end. There will be a time of great TRIBULATION (Matt. 24:4–26), followed by the SECOND COMING (Matt. 24:27–30) and the judgment of the nations (Matt. 25:31–46; 1 Cor. 15:20–24).

The Day of the Lord will reverse the curse upon the world by bringing judgment to all of God's enemies. The world will be judged by fire (Is. 66:16), and all nations will be included in this judgment (Amos 1:3—2:3; Ezek. 25:1–17). When the Lord spoke of the judgment of the people living at His arrival (Matt. 25:31–46), He pictured humanity as sheep or goats who inherit either everlasting punishment or ETERNAL LIFE. This concept of separation is expressed also through the figures of reaping harvest (Matt. 13:38–43; Rev. 14:14–20) and sorting out the good and the bad catch from a fishing net (Matt. 13:47–50).

Another judgment is portrayed in Revelation 20:11–15, commonly called the "Great White Throne" Judgment. This judgment is called the second death (Rev. 20:14). Those who are judged will be thrown into the lake of fire if their names are not found in the Book of Life.

The judgments of God at the end of history are preceded by resurrections of the just (Luke 14:13–14; Rev. 20:6) and the unjust (John 5:29; Rev. 20:5). Two specific resurrections are mentioned in the Bible. These will be separated by an interval of 1,000 years (Dan. 12:2–3; Rev. 20:4–6).

The Redeemer. Because God elected that some people would be saved in the day of His judgment, a saving event became necessary. This event is broadly defined as the seed of the woman (Gen. 3:15), which began the long process of conflict through which God introduced the Savior into the world.

Eschatology shows how God's Redeemer will establish His kingdom upon a rebellious earth. The long process through which God selected a righteous group to serve Him on earth came to a climax in the person of Christ. He is indeed "God with us" (Matt. 1:23). This phrase from Isaiah 7:14 spoke of God's presence in Jesus in order to save (Is. 9:6–7) and to judge (Is. 7:17; 8:6–8).

Christ's first coming was to save (Mark 10:45); His second will be primarily to judge. But His return will also spell relief to His faithful REMNANT. Eschatology shows that God's presence for the redeemed will be fully realized at Jesus' return, when He will dwell among all the redeemed in the new heavens and earth (Rev. 21:3).

The Cross. Above all, the cross is the decisive eschatological event. In it the curse that brought God's wrath was reversed. Ever since, God has been progressively accomplishing His judgment against the forces of wickedness in heaven and earth.

Psalm 110:1 is a key verse for understanding the redemptive side of eschatology. The King will reign until He defeats His enemies. As He returns to begin the final preparations for His reign, He will gather the ELECT to Himself. The redeemed will be evaluated by the Lord (Rom. 14:10; 1 Cor. 3:14–15) and will receive their reward of eternal life. The curse will be reversed, the Abrahamic covenant fulfilled, all earthly distinctions eliminated, and God's people will live in eternal fellowship with the Father and His Christ.

The point of eschatology throughout the Bible is to provide encouragement to believers in their witness for Jesus Christ (Matt. 24:14; 1 Cor. 15:58). It is not mentioned to encourage idle speculation or controversy. The reason God grants us a view of the future is to encourage us to witness for Christ and serve Him in the present.

ESDRAELON [ez dra EE lon] [*God sows*] — the great plain loosely identified as the Plain of Jezreel, about 89 kilometers (55 miles) north of Jerusalem (see Map 6, B–2). The word *Esdraelon* is the Greek form of the Hebrew word *Jezreel*. Esdraelon is a triangular plain approximately 24 by 24 by 32 kilometers (15 by 15 by 20 miles) in size, bounded along the southwest by the Carmel Mountain range and on the north by the hills of Nazareth.

The Plain of Esdraelon contains rich farmland because of the soil washed down into it from the mountains of Galilee and the highlands of Samaria. It is also the only east–west valley which divides the mountain ranges of western Palestine. Esdraelon has been the scene of numerous battles.

Here Deborah and Barak were victorious over Sisera (Judg. 4). Here, too, the Philistines were victorious over King Saul (1 Sam. 31:1–3). In this valley the Egyptians mortally wounded Josiah, king of Judah, when he attempted to intercept the army of Pharaoh Necho (2 Kin. 23:29).

But the greatest battle of this valley is yet to happen. The great battle of ARMAGEDDON will be fought here (Rev. 19:17). In this battle, the Lord of Glory, Jesus Christ, will triumph over the forces of Satan and "the kingdoms of this world [will] become the kingdoms of the Lord and of His Christ, and He shall reign forever and ever!" (Rev. 11:15).

ESDRAS, BOOKS OF [EZ drus] (see APOCRYPHA).

ESEK [EE seek] (*quarrel*) — a well dug by Isaac's servants in the Valley of Gerar (Gen. 26:20). When the herdsmen of GERAR quarreled over the well, Isaac abandoned it and had his servants dig another.

ESH–BAAL [esh BAY al] (*man of Baal*) — the original name of the son and successor of King Saul as king of Israel (1 Chr. 8:33; 9:39). He was also called Ishbosheth (man of shame) because Baal was a shameful deity (2 Sam. 2:8–15).

ESHBAN [ESH bun] (*meaning unknown*) — a son of Dishon (Gen. 36:26).

ESHCOL [ESH cuhl] (*cluster of grapes*) — the name of a man and a valley in the Old Testament:

1. A brother of Mamre and Aner. All three brothers helped Abraham defeat CHEDORLAOMER (Gen. 14:13, 24).

2. A valley north of Hebron, famous for its grapes (Num. 13:23–24). The Hebrew spies cut down a branch with one cluster of grapes from this valley and carried it to Moses to show the fertility of the land.

ESHEAN [ESH eh an] (*support*) — the name of a group of towns in Hebron during Joshua's time (Josh. 15:52).

ESHEK [EE sheck] (*oppressor*) — a Benjamite and a descendant of King Saul through Jonathan (1 Chr. 8:39).

ESHKALONITE [ESH ka lon ite] — a form of ASHKELONITE.

ESHTAOL [ESH tuh ole] (*meaning unknown*) — a town of the Danites situated in the Shephelah (lowland country) of Judah (Josh. 15:33). Near Eshtaol Samson began to feel the "Spirit of the Lord" (Judg. 13:24–25) and he was buried here after his death (Judg. 16:31). Eshtaol was the home of some of the Danites who attacked Laish (Judg. 18:1–11).

ESHTAOLITES [ESH tuh ole ites] — natives or inhabitants of ESHTAOL, a city of Judah (1 Chr. 2:53; Eshtaulites, KJV).

ESHTAULITES [esh tuh YOU lites] — a form of ESHTAOLITES.

ESHTEMOA [esh teh MOH uh] (*listening post*) — the name of two men and one town in the Old Testament:

1. A town about 15 kilometers (9 miles) south of Hebron in the hill country of Judah. Assigned to the priests, Eshtemoa was a city of refuge (1 Chr. 6:57; Eshtemoh, Josh. 15:50). David sent it some of the booty captured at Ziklag (1 Sam. 15:50; 30:28).

2. A descendant of Caleb, of the tribe of Judah (1 Chr. 4:17).

3. A Maachathite of the tribe of Judah (1 Chr. 4:19).

View of the fertile Esdraelon Valley from the mound of the ancient city of Megiddo.
Photo by Howard Vos

A section of the "Manual of Discipline," a scroll which contained strict regulations for the life of the Essene community at Qumran.

ESHTON [ESH ton] (meaning unknown) — a descendant of Judah through Caleb (1 Chr. 4:11–12).

ESLI [ES lie] (meaning unknown) — an ancestor of Jesus Christ (Luke 3:25).

ESPOUSAL (see BETROTHAL).

ESROM [ES rum] (see HEZRON).

ESSENES [es SEENZ] (meaning unknown) — a religious community that existed in Palestine from about the middle of the second century B.C. until the Jewish war with Rome (A.D. 66–70). The Essenes were noted for their strict discipline and their isolation from others who did not observe their way of life.

Although the Bible never mentions the Essenes, they are described by several ancient historians. The Essenes are an important part of the background to the New Testament, showing the beliefs and practices of one Jewish religious group at the time of John the Baptist and Jesus. People have been especially interested in the Essenes since the discovery of the DEAD SEA SCROLLS at QUMRAN. The people who lived at Qumran probably were a group of Essenes.

Individual Essenes did not own any private property. Instead, they shared all their possessions with others in their community. They avoided any show of luxury and ate very simple meals. They wore simple clothes until they hung in shreds.

The Essenes were also known for their careful observance of the laws of Moses as they understood them. They were stricter about keeping the Sabbath than any other Jews, even the PHARISEES.

They were concerned about being ritually clean themselves and about eating food that was ritually pure. For this reason they had priests prepare their food.

Essenes lived together in all the towns of Palestine in the days of Jesus. They were famous for their hospitality. An Essene traveling from one place to another knew he would be looked after by other Essenes, although he had never met them. The Essenes were also known for taking care of the sick and elderly. They were interested in medicines; in fact, some people think that the name Essenes means "healers."

The Essenes would arise before sunrise for prayer. Then they would work until about midday, when they would bathe—to make sure they were ritually clean—before eating. Afterwards they would work again until the evening meal.

Anyone who wanted to become an Essene was required to hand over all he owned to the community. He would then be given the typical Essene white robe. Only after he had shown that he was trustworthy for a full year would he be allowed to use the community's special water for purification. And he had to prove that he was reliable for two more years before he could become a full member. Then, after promising to keep the Essene rules, he became a full member and was allowed to take part in the community meals. But if he should break the Essene rule, he would be expelled from the community.

The Essenes believed that the souls of men were immortal and would be rewarded or punished after death. They had a special interest in angels, and some were known for making accurate predictions about the future. They avoided taking part in the services of the Temple in Jerusalem. Instead, they worshiped God in their own communities.

Some of the Essenes' beliefs and practices are similar to parts of the New Testament. The ritual washings of the Essenes bring to mind the baptism preached and practiced by John the Baptist. But John baptized people only once, while the Essenes' washings took place every day. And Jesus told his followers not to use oaths, just as the Essenes avoided oaths.

The Essenes' practice of COMMUNITY OF GOODS is also similar to what happened in the early church in Jerusalem (Acts 2:44–45). But again there is a difference. Christians sold their property of their own free will, while this was a requirement in the Essene community. Like the Essenes, the early Christians were soon known for their generous hospitality. A major difference was that the early Christians did not practice all the rules about the Sabbath and ritual purity that were so important to the Essenes. Above all, Christians believed that Jesus was the Messiah and Lord; Essenes continued to wait for God's salvation.

ESTHER [ESS ter] (*a star*) — the Jewish queen of the persian king AHASUERUS (Xerxes). Esther saved her people, the Jews, from a plot to eliminate them. A daughter of Abihail (Esth. 2:15; 9:29) and a cousin of Mordecai (Esth. 2:7, 15), Esther was raised by Mordecai as his own daughter after her mother and father died. Esther was a member of a family carried into captivity about 600 B.C. that later chose to stay in Persia rather than return to Jerusalem. Her Jewish name was Hadassah, which means "myrtle" (Esth. 2:7).

The story of Esther's rise from an unknown Jewish girl to become the queen of a mighty empire illustrates how God used events and people as instruments to fulfill His promise to His Chosen People. Following several days of revelry, the drunken king Ahasuerus—generally identified with Xerxes I (reigned 486–465 B.C.)—asked his queen, Vashti, to display herself to his guests. When Vashti courageously refused, she was banished from the palace. Ahasuerus then had "all the beautiful young virgins" (Esth. 2:3) of his kingdom brought to his palace to choose Vashti's replacement.

Scripture records that "the young woman [Esther] was lovely and beautiful" (Esth. 2:7). The king loved Esther more than all the other women. He appointed her queen to replace Vashti (Esth. 2:17).

At the time, HAMAN was Ahasuerus' most trusted advisor. An egotistical and ambitious man, Haman demanded that people bow to him as he passed—something which Mordecai, a devout Jew, could not do in good conscience. In rage, Haman sought revenge, not only on Mordecai but also on the entire Jewish population of the empire. He persuaded the king to issue an edict permitting him to kill all the Jews and seize their property.

With great tact and skill, Esther exposed Haman's plot and true character to the king. As a result, Ahasuerus granted the Jews the right to defend themselves and to destroy their enemies. With ironic justice, "they hanged Haman on the gallows that he had prepared for Mordecai" (Esth. 7:10).

Even today Jews celebrate their deliverance from this edict at the Feast of PURIM (Esth. 9:26–32), celebrated on the 14th and 15th days of the month of Adar.

Also see ESTHER, BOOK OF.

The royal titles of King Xerxes (possibly the biblical Ahasuerus of Esther 1:1) found at his palace at Persepolis, Persia.
Photo by Howard Vos

ESTHER, ADDITIONS TO (see APOCRYPHA).

ESTHER, BOOK OF — a historical book of the Old Testament that shows how God preserved His Chosen People. The book is named for its main personality, Queen Esther of Persia, whose courage and quick thinking saved the Jewish people from disaster.

Structure of the Book. The Book of Esther reports on actual events, but it is written like a short story.

The main characters in this powerful drama are King Xerxes of Persia; his wife Queen Esther, a Jewish woman; his second in command, Haman, recently promoted by the king; and Mordecai, a leader among the Jewish people who are scattered throughout the Persian Empire. In an attempt to stamp out the Jews, Haman manipulates the king into issuing an order calling for their execution. But Esther uses her royal favor to intervene and expose Haman's plot. Ironically, in a dramatic twist of

ESTHER: A Teaching Outline

Part One: The Threat to the Jews (1:1—4:17)

plot, Haman is hanged on the gallows he built for Mordecai's execution, and Mordecai is promoted to prime minister. The Jewish people are granted revenge against their enemies. They also celebrate by instituting the Feast of PURIM to mark their miraculous deliverance.

Authorship and Date. For centuries scholars have debated the question of who wrote the Book of Esther. The Jewish historian Josephus claimed it was written by Mordecai. But many modern scholars dispute this because Mordecai is mentioned in the past tense in the final chapter of the book. Until new evidence emerges, the author must remain unknown.

The question of date can be answered with greater certainty. The reign of the Persian king Xerxes (Esth. 1:1, NIV) lasted for about 20 years, beginning about 485 B.C. So Esther must have been written some time shortly after 465 B.C.

Historical Setting. The Book of Esther is valuable historically because it gives us a view of the Jewish people who were scattered throughout the ancient world about 475 B.C. The events in the book occurred about 100 years after the leading citizens of the Jewish nation were carried into exile by Babylon in 587 B.C. Shortly after the Persians overthrew the Babylonians, they allowed the Jewish exiles to return to their native land. Many did return to Jerusalem, but thousands of Jewish citizens chose to remain in Persia, probably because this had become home to them during their long separation from their native land. Thus, this book shows clearly that God protects His Chosen People, even when they are scattered among the nations of the world.

Theological Contribution. The Book of Esther is a major chapter in the struggle of the people of God to survive in the midst of a hostile world. Beginning with the Book of Genesis, God had made it clear that he would bless His Covenant People and bring a curse upon those who tried to do them harm (Gen. 12:1,3). The Book of Esther shows how God has kept this promise at every stage of history. Just as Haman met his death on the gallows, we can trust God to protect us from the enemy, Satan, and to work out His ultimate purpose of redemption in our lives.

Special Considerations. One unusual fact about this book is that it never mentions the name of God. For this reason some people believe Esther has no place in the Bible. They see it as nothing but a fiercely patriotic Jewish book that celebrates the victory of the Jews over their enemies.

This harsh criticism is unfair to Esther. A careful reading will reveal that the book does have a spiritual base. Queen Esther calls the people to prayer and fasting (4:16), and God's protection of His people speaks of His providence. The book also teaches a valuable lesson about the sovereignty of God: although the enemies of the Covenant People may triumph for a season, He holds the key to ultimate victory.

Also see ESTHER.

ETAM [E tum] (*place of birds of prey*) — the name of three or four places in the Old Testament:

1. A cave (Judg. 15:8, 11) in western Judah where Samson stayed after defeating the Philistines.

2. A place listed in Judah's genealogy (1 Chr. 4:3). It may be the same place as Etam No. 4.

3. A town of the tribe of Simeon (1 Chr. 4:32). It is likely modern 'Aitun, which is about 18 kilometers (11 miles) southwest of Hebron.

4. A resort town between Jerusalem and Hebron near Bethlehem, about 11 kilometers (7 miles) south of Jerusalem. Etam was decorated by Solomon with gardens and streams of water; he would often drive out to Etam in his chariot.

ETERNAL LIFE — a person's new and redeemed existence in Jesus Christ which is granted by God as a gift to all believers. Eternal life refers to the quality or character of our new existence in Christ as well as the unending character of this life. The phrase, *everlasting life*, is found in the Old Testament only once (Dan. 12:2). But the idea of eternal life is implied by the prophets in their pictures of the glorious future promised to God's people.

The majority of references to eternal life in the New Testament are oriented to the future. The emphasis, however, is upon the blessed character of the life that will be enjoyed endlessly in the future. Jesus made it clear that eternal life comes only to those who make a total commitment to Him (Matt. 19:16–21; Luke 18:18–22). Paul's letters refer to eternal life relatively seldom, and again primarily with a future rather than a present orientation (Rom. 5:21; 6:22; Gal. 6:8).

The phrase, *eternal life*, appears most often in the Gospel of John and the Epistle of 1 John. John emphasizes eternal life as the present reality and the present possession of the Christian (John 3:36; 5:24; 1 John 5:13). John declares that the Christian believer has already begun to experience the blessings of the future even before their fullest expression: "And this is eternal life, that they may know You, the only true God, and Jesus Christ whom You have sent" (John 17:3).

ETERNITY — infinite or unlimited time; time without beginning or end. The Bible speaks of the eternity of God (Ps. 90:2; Is. 57:15; Rev. 1:4). As Creator, He brought the world into being, even before the beginning of time itself (Gen. 1:1). He will also bring the world to its ultimate conclusion, in accordance with His will and purpose.

ETHAM [EE thum] (*fortress*) — a place "at the edge of the wilderness" (Ex. 13:20) between Succoth and the Wilderness of Sinai. This was the location of the second encampment of the children of Israel after they left Rameses in Egypt (Num. 3:5–8). Apparently, Etham was near the end of the eastern branch of the Red Sea, near Suez.

ETHAN [EE thun] (*long–lived*) — the name of three or four Old Testament men:

1. A renowned wise man in the time of Solomon called "Ethan the Ezrahite" (1 Kin. 4:31).

2. A son of Zerah, Judah's son by Tamar, and the father of Azariah (1 Chr. 2:6, 8). He may be the same person as Ethan No. 1.

3. A descendant of Gershon and an ancestor of Asaph (1 Chr. 6:42; perhaps Joah, 1 Chr. 6:21).

4. A descendant of Merari, son of Levi (1 Chr. 15:17, 19).

ETHANIM [ETH uh nim] (*ever-flowing streams*) — the seventh month of the Hebrew year, corresponding to our mid-September to mid-October (1 Kin. 8:2). Also see CALENDAR.

ETHBAAL [eth BAY al] (*with him is Baal*) — a king of Tyre and Sidon and the father of Jezebel, the idolatrous wife of King Ahab of Israel (1 Kin. 16:31). During his reign, a year-long drought occurred (1 Kings 17—18).

ETHER [EE thur] (*abundance*) — the name of two villages in the Old Testament:

1. A village of the tribe of Judah (Josh. 15:42).
2. A village of the tribe of Simeon (Josh. 19:7).

ETHICS, BIBLICAL (see BIBLICAL ETHICS).

ETHIOPIA [ee thih OH pih ah] (*burnt face*) — the ancient African nation south of Egypt, including the Egyptian territory south of Aswan (Syene; Ezek. 29:10), sometimes called Nubia or Cush. Ethiopia was known for its rivers, the Blue Nile and the White Nile (Is. 18:1), its papyrus boats (Is. 18:2), and its precious topaz gems (Job 28:19).

The early genealogies of the Bible identify Ham as the father of Cush (Ethiopia; Gen. 10:6; 1 Chr. 1:8–10), as well as of Mizraim (Egypt). These two nations were closely connected throughout their histories, and the biblical writers often mention the two together (Is. 20:3–5; Ezek. 30:4–5). Moses, who lived in Egypt for many years, married an Ethiopian woman from among the children of Israel (Num. 12:1).

Early Egyptian texts indicate that Ethiopia was controlled by Egypt until after the time of David (1000 B.C.). The Ethiopians frequently served as hired soldiers in the Egyptian army (2 Chr. 12:3). They were known for their black skin (Jer. 13:23), their tallness and smooth skin (Is. 18:2), and their fierceness in battle (Jer. 46:9). A Cushite soldier served as a runner in David's army and brought him the news of Absalom's death (2 Sam. 18:21–32).

Just after the time of Solomon, Zerah, an Ethiopian commander of a million soldiers and three hundred chariots, attacked the weaker forces of Asa, king of Judah. Asa, a righteous king, prayed to God for deliverance; and the forces of the Ethiopians were turned back (2 Chr. 14:9–13).

The Ethiopians attained their greatest strength during the time of Hezekiah (700 B.C.). This was possible because of internal disunity within Egypt. Egypt was defeated, and an Ethiopian dynasty ruled Egypt for 60 years. During this period, Sennacherib, king of Assyria, attacked Hezekiah in Jerusalem (2 Kin. 18:13; 2 Chr. 32:1–2; Is. 36:1). The

Assyrian commander discouraged any hope that the Egyptians (now ruled by an Ethiopian king) would come to the aid of Hezekiah (2 Kin. 18:21; Is. 36:6). But Tirhakah, king of Ethiopia and Egypt, did attack the Assyrian forces (2 Kin. 19:9; Is. 37:9).

Although the Ethiopians were defeated, God delivered Hezekiah by sending an angel to kill 185,000 of the Assyrian troops (Is. 37:36). Ethiopia was the strength of Egypt for this short time (Nah. 3:9), but an invasion by the Assyrian kings Esarhaddon and Ashurbanipal meant the end of Ethiopian power (Is. 20:2–6). An attack by Nebuchadnezzar, king of Babylon, was predicted by the prophets Ezekiel (30:4–10) and Jeremiah (46:9–10, 13–14). The prophet Isaiah also foretold the Persian conquest of Ethiopia (Esth. 1:1; 8:9; Is. 43:3).

In the midst of these judgments, there were promises of a return of God's people from Ethiopia (Is. 11:11). God was also concerned about the Ethiopians (Amos 9:7), for they would be included among those who came to Jerusalem to worship the true God (Ps. 68:31; Is. 45:14).

The New Testament records a partial fulfillment of these promises when an ETHIOPIAN EUNUCH who served Candace, the queen of Ethiopia, was converted to Christianity (Acts 8:26–40).

ETHIOPIAN EUNUCH [YOU nook] — a person baptized by Philip who held a responsible position as the royal treasurer in the court of Candace, queen of Ethiopia (Acts 8:26–40). The word eunuch refers to an emasculated servant who could rise to positions of power and influence in ancient times. The Ethiopian eunuch was apparently a convert to Judaism. A keen student of the Bible, he was probably a PROSELYTE who had come to Jerusalem to participate in worship at the Temple. On his return to his own country, he encountered Philip. On Philip's explanation of Isaiah 53, he confessed his faith in Christ and was baptized.

ETHIOPIAN VERSIONS (see BIBLE VERSIONS AND TRANSLATIONS).

ETH KAZIN [eth KAY zen] (meaning unknown) — a town on the eastern border of Zebulun, probably near Gath Hepher (Josh. 19:13; Ittah–kazin, KJV).

ETHNAN [ETH nan] (*gift*) — a descendant of Ashhur, of the tribe of Judah (1 Chr. 4:7).

ETHNI [ETH nigh] (*gift*) — an ancestor of Asaph, of the Gershomite branch of the Levites. David assigned him over the song service of the Lord's house (1 Chr. 6:41).

EUBULUS [you BYOU lus] (*well advised*) — a Christian of Rome who remained loyal to the apostle Paul during Paul's second imprisonment in that city (2 Tim. 4:21).

EUCHARIST [YOU kuh wrist] (see LORD'S SUPPER).

EUNICE [YOU niss] (*good victory*) — the daughter

of Lois and mother of Timothy. Although Eunice is a Greek name and her husband was a Gentile, Eunice was a Jewess, as was Lois her mother. Although Timothy had not been circumcised as a child, he had been brought up in the Jewish faith by Eunice and Lois. The "genuine faith" possessed by Timothy first existed in his grandmother Lois and later in his mother Eunice (2 Tim. 1:5).

EUNUCH [YOO nook] — a male servant of a royal household in Bible times. Such servants were often emasculated by castration as a precautionary measure, especially if they served among the wives in a ruler's harem (2 Kin. 9:32). The New Testament reported the conversion of a eunuch from Ethiopia under the ministry of PHILIP the evangelist (Acts 8:26–38).

EUODIA [you OH dih uh] (good journey) — a Christian woman at Philippi (Phil. 4:2; Euodias, KJV). Euodia and Syntyche, both of whom may have been deaconesses at Philippi, had an argument. The apostle Paul charged them to "be of the same mind in the Lord." The nature of their quarrel is not known.

EUODIAS [you OH dih us] — a form of EUODIA.

EUPHRATES [you FRAY tease] (meaning unknown) — the longest river of Western Asia and one of two major rivers in Mesopotamia (see Map 1, D-2). The river begins in the mountains of Armenia in modern–day Turkey. It then heads west toward the Mediterranean Sea, turns to the south, swings in a wide bow through Syria, and then flows some 1,000 miles southeast to join the Tigris River before it empties into the Persian Gulf.

The Euphrates is about 2,890 kilometers (1,780 miles) long and is navigable for smaller vessels for about 1,950 kilometers (1,200 miles). The ruins of many ancient cities are located along the river in Iraq. Among them are Babylon, Eridu, Kish, Larsa, Nippur, Sippar, and Ur.

In the Bible the Euphrates is referred to as "the River Euphrates," "the great river, the River Euphrates," or only as "the River." It is named as one of the four rivers that the river of the Garden of Eden divided and joined (Gen. 2:14). The Euphrates formed the northern boundary of the territories promised by God to Israel (Gen. 15:18; Josh. 1:4).

The biblical writer declared that the fathers of Israel had lived on "the other side of the River" (Josh. 1:2–3, 14–15; "beside the Euphrates," NEB), where they served other gods. But God took Abraham "from the other side of the River" (v. 3) and brought him to the land of Canaan. David attempted to expand the boundaries of his kingdom to this river (2 Sam. 8:3). The Euphrates also was the site of the great battle at Carchemish (605 B.C.) which led to the death of King Josiah (2 Chr. 35:20–24). "The great river Euphrates" is also mentioned in Revelation 9:14 and 16:12.

EUROCLYDON [you ROCK lih dun] (east wind) — a fierce, tempestuous wind often experienced by navigators, especially in the spring, in the eastern Mediterranean. Sometimes of hurricane or typhoon force, this tremendous wind (Acts 27:14; the Northeaster, RSV; Euraquilo, NASB) is so called because it blows from the northeast or east–north-east. The ship in which the apostle Paul was being transported to Rome was caught in this tempest (Acts 27:13–44).

EUTYCHUS [YOU tih cuss] (fortunate) — a young man of Troas who fell asleep while listening to a sermon by the apostle Paul and "fell down from the third story." When his friends reached him, he was "taken up dead." Paul miraculously brought Eutychus back to life (Acts 20:9–10).

EVANGELIST — a person authorized to proclaim the gospel of Christ. In a more narrow sense, the word refers to one of the gospel writers: Matthew, Mark, Luke, or John. Literally, however, the word means, "one who proclaims good tidings" (Eph. 4:11; 2 Tim. 4:5).

The evangelist was a gift of God to the early church (Eph. 4:11). These persons were not attached to any specific local church. They traveled over a wide geographical area, preaching to those to whom the Holy Spirit led them. The early disciples were also called evangelists (Acts 8:4) because they proclaimed the gospel.

All Christians today may continue the witness of the evangelists, Matthew, Mark, Luke, and John. As the evangelists spoke and wrote of Jesus, so may Christians bring His message to others.

EVE [eev] (life–giving) — the first woman (Gen. 3:20; 4:1), created from one of Adam's ribs to be "a helper comparable to him" (Gen. 2:18–22).

Adam and Eve lived together in innocence and happiness, enjoying sexual union ("one flesh") without guilt and sin (Gen. 2:25). However, the serpent tempted Eve to eat of the forbidden fruit (Gen. 2:17).

Eve succumbed to the serpent's temptation and ate the forbidden fruit. Then, "she also gave to her husband with her, and he ate" (Gen. 3:6). The result of this disobedience was the loss of innocence and the disturbing knowledge of sin and evil. "Then the eyes of both of them were opened, and they knew that they were naked; and they sewed fig leaves together and made themselves coverings" (Gen. 3:7) to conceal their shame.

In falling to temptation (Gen. 3:6), Eve knew sin and death (Gen. 2:17). She and her descendants experienced the animosity between Satan and Christ—the"seed of the serpent" and "the seed of the woman" (Gen. 3:15). Her pain in childbirth and Adam's authority over her were other results of her sin (Gen. 3:16).

The apostle Paul referred to Eve twice. By saying "the serpent deceived Eve by his craftiness," Paul gave an example of how easily a person can be led into temptation and sin, with disastrous consequences (2 Cor. 11:3; 1 Tim. 2:12–14).

EVEN, EVENING — the period between sunset and bedtime; the early part of the night. In the New

Testament the Greek word rendered as evening means "a period never earlier than sunset" (Matt. 8:16; Mark 1:32; John 6:16; even, KJV). For the Hebrew people, the old day ended and the new day began at evening, or sunset.

EVERLASTING — lasting forever; eternal. The Greek word translated as everlasting in the New Testament means "age-lasting," as contrasted with that which is brief and fleeting. The Bible speaks of the everlasting God (Is. 40:28), Father (Is. 9:6), King (Jer. 10:10), and Redeemer (Is. 63:16). The Lord is a God of everlasting kindness (Is. 54:8), love (Jer. 31:3), and mercy (Ps. 100:5; 103:17) who has established an everlasting covenant with His people (Heb. 13:20). His kingdom is everlasting (2 Pet. 1:11), as is His salvation (Ps. 45:17). Also see TIME.

EVI [EE vie] (perhaps *desire*) — one of five kings of Midian killed by the Israelites (Num. 31:8). The other four were Rekem, Zur, Hur, and Reba.

EVIL — a force that opposes God and His work of righteousness in the world (Rom. 7:8–19). The word is also used for any disturbance to the harmonious order of the universe, such as disease (Ps. 41:8). But the Bible makes it plain that even these so-called "physical evils" are the result of a far more serious moral and spiritual evil that began with the FALL of Adam and Eve in the Garden of Eden (Genesis 3).

The ultimate source of evil in the world is Satan, also called "the devil" (Luke 8:12) and "the wicked one" (Matt. 13:19). The Christian believer can rest assured that Jesus will triumph at the end of time, when Satan will be cast into a lake of fire and brimstone and evil will be overcome (Rev. 20:10).

Evil also comes from the hearts of men (Mark 7:20–23). It does not come from God, "for God cannot be tempted by evil, nor does He Himself tempt anyone" (James 1:13).

EVILDOER — one who does evil, wicked acts. The psalmist equates "evildoers" with "workers of iniquity" (Ps. 37:1). The word is used in this general sense also in Jeremiah 20:13 and 1 Peter 2:12. Generally, the word "evildoers" is applied to the enemies of God and his people (Is. 14:20). It also is applied to Israel when the people forsook the Lord (Is. 9:17).

EVIL EYE — a symbolic phrase which refers to the will of a grudging, selfish person (Deut. 15:9; Matt. 6:23; 20:15).

EVIL–FAVOREDNESS — a KJV term (Deut. 17:1) for any defect (NKJV, NASB), blemish (RSV, NEB), or flaw (NIV) that made an animal unfit for sacrifice.

EVIL–MERODACH [EE vil MARE uh dak] (*man of* [the god] *Marduk*) — king of the Neo-Babylonian Empire (562–560 B.C.) and son of Nebuchadnezzar II. When Evil-Merodach became king, he released King Jehoiachin of Judah, whom Nebuchadnezzar had kept imprisoned for 37 years (2

Kin. 25:27–30). Evil-Merodach's brother-in-law, Nergal-shar-usur (Neriglissar), formed a conspiracy against him and put him to death. Neriglissar then became king.

EVIL ONE (see DEVIL; SATAN).

EVIL–SPEAKING (see BLASPHEMY; SLANDER).

EVIL SPIRIT (see DEMON).

EWE (see ANIMALS OF THE BIBLE).

EXACTOR — KJV term for a ruler or overseer (Is. 60:17). An exactor was usually a government officer who collected customs, taxes, or tribute or a taskmaster who supervised manual laborers.

EXCOMMUNICATION — the expulsion of a member from the church because of a serious doctrinal or moral lapse. The concept of the CURSE or the BAN in the Old Testament is similar to excommunication. The curse signified divine judgment of sin (Num. 5:21; Jer. 29:18). It was considered God's agent in cleansing sin from the land (Deut. 27:11–26). To be under a curse meant to be excluded from society—thus removing a cancerous agent from the people (Lev. 20:17). When such a person refused to repent, he fell under the ban or curse (Mal. 4:6) and was no longer considered part of God's Covenant People (Lev. 27:28; Deut. 7:26).

The process of excommunication from the church was spelled out by Jesus (Matt. 18:15–18). The errant Christian should first be confronted about his behavior. If he refuses to heed the warnings, a representative of the church should return with witnesses. If that, too, is ineffective, the person should be brought before the church, which is to excommunicate him: "Let him be to you like a heathen or a tax collector" (Matt. 18:17). The apostle Paul often used the phrase "deliver to Satan" to speak of excommunication. This idea implies that God has removed His presence from the person's life and therefore Satan is free to afflict him (1 Cor. 5:5; 1 Tim. 1:20).

Apparently there were degrees of excommunication. The idle Thessalonian Christians who refused to heed Paul's admonition were to be socially shunned (2 Thess. 3:6). Then if they were still unrepentant, they were to be disassociated from the brethren (2 Thess. 3:14–15). But in neither case were the offenders to be considered under an absolute ban (v. 15).

Several purposes stood behind this extremely disciplinary tool. Primarily it was to protect the church from blatant evil in its midst (1 Cor. 5:6). It also had a redemptive function—to force the member to realize the seriousness of his offense and to return to Christ (1 Cor. 5:5). In this sense Paul admonished Timothy: "In humility correcting those who are in opposition, if God perhaps will grant them repentance, so that they may know the truth, and that they may come to their senses and escape the snare of the devil" (2 Tim. 2:25–26).

EXECUTIONER (see OCCUPATIONS AND TRADES).

EXEGESIS (see BIBLE INTERPRETATION).

EXERCISE, BODILY — physical training or athletic discipline such as that practiced by competitors in gymnastics (1 Tim. 4:8). The apostle Paul often referred to athletic contests to illustrate spiritual truths (1 Cor. 9:24–27; 2 Tim. 2:5; 4:7).

EXHORTATION — a message of warning or encouragement, designed to motivate persons to action. The apostle Paul often exhorted his fellow Christians to live out their calling as ministers of the Lord Jesus (Rom. 12:8; 2 Cor. 8:17).

EXILE (see DISPERSION).

EXODUS, THE — the departure of the Israelites from captivity in Egypt under the leadership of Moses. The actual Exodus was the final event in a series of miracles by which God revealed Himself to His people in bondage, humbled the pride of the Pharaoh who opposed the Israelites, and enabled Jacob's descendants to live in freedom once again.

The precise date of the Exodus from Egypt is uncertain, because the information in the Bible can be interpreted to support more than one date. Archaeological discoveries also present a confused picture. The result is that some scholars date the Exodus as early as 1446 B.C., while others place it later, about 1280 B.C.

The circumstances of Egyptian history are not very helpful either, because surviving Egyptian records do not mention either Joseph or Moses in any historical period. Neither does the Bible name the Pharaoh who ruled Egypt in Moses' day. The rise of a new king who "did not know Joseph," or, who refused to recognize Joseph's achievements (Ex. 1:8), might suggest a date from about 1314–1194 B.C.—a time when a great deal of rebuilding was begun in Egypt. There is no firm evidence for such a date.

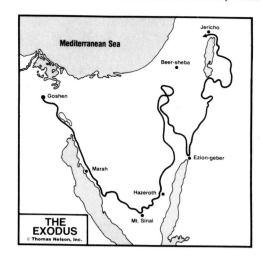

THE EXODUS
© Thomas Nelson, Inc.

The promise of the Exodus began with God's revelation of Himself to Moses at the burning bush (Ex. 3:2). This was followed by the commissioning of Moses and Aaron to stand before Pharaoh and demand the release of the Israelites. When he refused, a series of ten plagues began. Nine of these involved natural occurrences that were concentrated within a short period of time, affecting the Egyptians only and leaving the Israelites untouched. Each plague involved an Egyptian god in some manner, showing how powerless such deities were in comparison to Israel's God.

The final plague resulted in the death of all the Egyptian firstborn children and animals. Only when this had happened did Pharaoh agree to release the Hebrew people. They were spared from death by remaining in their houses and putting sac-

The rugged Sinai Desert, through which the Israelites passed during the Exodus from Egypt.
Photo by Howard Vos

rificial blood on the doorposts of their houses before they ate the newly–instituted PASSOVER meal (Ex. 12:6–13). The Egyptians were so glad to be relieved of what had become a great burden to them that they gave the departing Israelites gifts of gold, silver, and clothing (Ex. 12:35).

Then the Exodus from Egypt began, with the whole company under Moses being directed away from the northerly road leading from Egypt to Gaza in Canaan. From Rameses, probably near Qantir, they moved to Succoth, perhaps the ancient Tell el Maskhuta situated in the Wadi Tumilat in the southeastern region of the Nile delta. Then the Hebrews camped at Etham, on the edge of the Wilderness of Shur (Ex. 13:20), at a site still unknown but probably north of Lake Timsah close to the fortifications guarding Egypt's northeastern frontier. They were directed by a PILLAR OF CLOUD during the day. At night they were guided by a PILLAR OF FIRE, which led them away from Etham, probably in a northwesterly direction, to a site opposite Baal Zephon and Pi Hahiroth.

At this site a body of water stood in the way (Ex. 14:2). To the Egyptians this spelled the doom of a group of runaway slaves that had become thoroughly confused about their location as they struggled to get out of the Goshen area. This misunderstanding was part of God's plan to destroy the Egyptian armies (Ex. 14:3–4). They closed in on the Israelite camp, eager to recapture their escaped slaves. While the Hebrews assembled and rushed to the edge of the water, the pillar of cloud moved to the rear of the fleeing Hebrews, preventing the movement of the Egyptian armies.

A strong east wind from the desert began to blow on the surface of the water, which is also described

EXODUS: A Teaching Outline

Part One: Redemption from Egypt (1:1—18:27)

more fully as a "reed sea" (Ex. 15:22) or lake of papyrus reeds. English versions of the Bible mistakenly translated the phrase as "Red Sea," but this name describes a large oceanic gulf far to the southeast in which papyrus reeds do not grow. The concentrated, hot winds parted the shallow marsh waters and dried the bottom so the Israelites could flee across it.

As the Egyptians followed, the winds stopped and the waters drowned the pursuers. The miracles of the Exodus were thus completed by the destruction of the Egyptian armies. The jubilant Israelites sang a victory song with Moses to celebrate the event (Ex. 15:1–18). The women, led by Miriam the sister of Aaron, also danced and sang (Ex. 15:20–21) as they praised God for His deliverance.

Then the Israelites began to journey into the WILDERNESS OF SHUR (Ex. 15:22), known in Numbers 33:8 as the WILDERNESS OF ETHAM. They had traveled in a circular manner, except that now they were east of the body of water. Being free from the threat of capture, they traveled east and south into the Sinai peninsula in order to meet with God at Mount Sinai (Horeb). Here they would establish a COVENANT that would make them God's chosen nation. Etham contained very little water. But after God enabled Moses to locate a supply, the Hebrews arrived at an oasis named Elim.

The Exodus became for the Hebrews the supreme occasion when God acted to deliver His people from harsh captivity, binding them to Himself by a solemn covenant. Even today when the Jews celebrate the Passover, they are reminded of God's mighty deliverance in that long-ago time.

EXODUS, BOOK OF — key Old Testament book about Israel's beginning and early years as a nation.

It takes its name from the event known as the EXO-DUS, the dramatic deliverance of the Hebrew people from enslavement in Egypt under the leadership of Moses. Throughout Exodus we meet a God who is the Lord of history and the Redeemer of His people. These themes, repeated throughout the rest of the Bible, make Exodus one of the foundational books of the Scriptures.

Structure of the Book. Exodus begins where the Book of Genesis leaves off—with the descendants of Joseph who moved to Egypt to escape famine and hardship in their own land. For many years the Hebrew people grew and prospered with the blessings of the Egyptian ruler. But then with one transitional verse, Exodus explains the changing political climate that brought an end to their favored position: "Now there arose a new king over Egypt, who did not know Joseph" (1:8). The Hebrews were reduced to the status of slaves and put to work on the Pharaoh's building projects.

The Book of Exodus falls naturally into three major divisions: (1) Israel in Egypt (1:1—12:36); (2) Israel in the wilderness (12:37—18:37); and (3) Israel at Mt. Sinai (19:1—40:38).

Some of the major events covered by this rapidly moving book include God's call of Moses through the BURNING BUSH to lead His people out of bondage (3:1—4:17); the series of plagues sent upon the Egyptians because of Pharaoh's stubbornness (7:1—12:30); the release of the captives and their miraculous crossing of the Red Sea, followed by the destruction of Pharaoh's army (15:1-31); God's provision for the people in the wilderness through bread, quail, and water (16:1—17:7); the giving of the Ten Commandments and other parts of the Law to Moses at Mt. Sinai (20:1—23:33); and the renewal of the covenant between God and His people (24:1-8).

The book ends as Moses and the workmen under his supervision build a tabernacle in the wilderness around Mt. Sinai at God's command. A cloud, symbolizing God's presence, rests on the tabernacle; and the entire building is filled with His glory (36:1—40:38).

Authorship and Date. Exodus is one of the first five books of the Old Testament—books that have traditionally been assigned to Moses as author. (See PENTATEUCH.) But some scholars insist that Exodus was compiled by an unknown writer or editor who drew from several different historical documents. There are two sound reasons why Moses can be accepted without question as the divinely inspired author of this book.

First, Exodus itself speaks of the writing activity of Moses. In Exodus 34:27 God commands Moses to "write these words." Another passage tells us that "Moses wrote all the words of the Lord" in obedience to God's command (24:4). It is reasonable to assume that these verses refer to Moses' writing of material that appears in the Book of Exodus. Second, Moses either observed or participated in the events described in Exodus. He was well qualified to write about these experiences, since he had been

Photo by Willem A. VanGemeren

The Wilderness of Zin, a desert region through which the Israelites passed on their journey to the Promised Land (Num. 13:21).

educated in the household of the Pharaoh during his early life.

Since Moses wrote Exodus, it must be dated some time before his death about 1400 B.C. Israel spent the 40 years preceding this date wandering in the wilderness because of their unfaithfulness. This is the most likely time for the writing of the book.

Historical Setting. Exodus covers a crucial period in Israel's early history as a nation. Most conservative scholars believe the Hebrews left Egypt about 1440 B.C. Some believe it took place much later, around 1280 B.C. About two-thirds of the book describes Israel's experiences during the two years after this date. This was the period when Israel traveled through the wilderness toward Mt. Sinai and received instructions from God through Moses as he met with God on the mountain.

Theological Contribution. The Book of Exodus has exercised much influence over the faith of Israel, as well as Christian theology. The Bible's entire message of redemption grows out of the covenant relationship between God and His people first described in this book. In addition, several themes in the book can be clearly traced in the life and ministry of Jesus. Moses received the Law on Mt. Sinai; Jesus delivered the sermon on the Mount. Moses lifted up the serpent in the wilderness to give life to the people; Jesus was lifted up on the cross to bring eternal life to all who trust in Him.

The PASSOVER (see Exodus 12), first instituted by God for the deliverance of the Hebrews from slavery, became one of the focal points of Israel's faith. It also served as the base on which Jesus developed the Last Supper as a lasting memorial for His followers. With clear insight into Exodus, the message of the Bible and the meaning of the life of Jesus dawns with greater understanding for Christian believers.

Special Considerations. The Book of Exodus is a

dramatic testimony to the power of God. The signs and plagues sent by God to break Pharaoh's stubbornness are clear demonstrations of His power. In addition to setting the Israelites free, they also dramatize the weakness of Egypt's false gods. The puny idols of Egypt are powerless before the mighty God of Israel.

The crossing of the Red Sea is one of the most dramatic events in all of the Bible; the biblical writers repeatedly refer to it as the most significant sign of God's love for Israel. A helpless slave people had been delivered from their enemies by their powerful Redeemer God. They celebrated their victory with a song of praise that emphasizes the theme of the Book of Exodus:

I will sing to the Lord,
For He has triumphed gloriously!
The horse and its rider
He has thrown into the sea!
The Lord is my strength and song,
And He has become my salvation.

EXORCISM (see MAGIC, SORCERY AND DIVINATION).

EXORCIST (see OCCUPATIONS AND TRADES).

EXPEDIENT, EXPEDIENCY — doing what is necessary in a given circumstance to achieve a certain goal. During the plot to kill Jesus, Caiaphas the high priest declared, "It is expedient that one man [Jesus] should die for the people, and not that the whole nation should perish" (John 11:50; also 18:14). His argument was that it was better for an innocent man to be crucified than to give the Romans cause to destroy the whole nation.

EXPIATION — RSV word for PROPITIATION.

EXTORTION, EXTORTIONER — the act of obtaining property by force or underhanded means (Lev. 6:2; Is. 16:4). The apostle Paul mentions extortioners along with thieves, idolaters, and drunkards as those who will not inherit the kingdom of God (1 Cor. 5:10–11; 6:10).

EYE — the light–sensitive organ of vision in animals and humans. In Bible times, eyes were considered God's gifts (Prov. 20:12). Since early times, beautiful eyes have been part of physical attractiveness; women have long applied cosmetics to their eyes (2 Kin. 9:30). Cruel kings sometimes gouged out the eyes of conquered enemies, robbing them of any chance to rebel (2 Kin. 25:7).

In the Bible the eye is often described symbolically. "Evil eye" (Matt. 20:15) describes envy; "bountiful eye" (Prov. 22:9) refers to generosity; "wanton eyes" (Is. 3:16) mean pride; "eyes full of adultery" (2 Pet. 2:14) is symbolic of lust; "the lust of eyes" (1 John 2:16) means earthly temptation; and "the desire of your eyes" (Ezek. 24:16) refers to a loved one. "The apple [pupil] of His eye" (Deut. 32:10; Zech. 2:8) referred to the nation of Israel, implying its special place in God's plan.

EYE OF A NEEDLE — a figure of speech used by Jesus to illustrate the extreme difficulty of a wealthy person's attaining salvation: "It is easier for a camel to go through the eye of a needle than for a rich man to enter the kingdom of God" (Matt. 19:24; Mark 10:25; Luke 18:25). Much has been written in an attempt to explain this statement.

Some have suggested that the "Needle's Eye" was a particularly narrow gate adjacent to one of the main gates of Jerusalem. A camel could pass through this gate but only with great difficulty. First it had to be stripped of the goods it carried, and then it had to bow to its knees to get through the gate. However, this claim is unsupported by historical evidence.

Another suggestion is that "camel" (kamelos) should be translated "rope" (kamilos) or "ship's cable." Neither of these suggestions has received much support from scholars. It is probably best to understand this figure of speech as an example of Jesus' use of hyperbole, or exaggeration for effect. The image of a camel trying to climb through the eye of a needle would have been both vivid and amusing.

When Jesus' disciples heard this "hard saying" from their Lord, they asked, "Who then can be saved?" Jesus replied, "With man this is impossible, but with God all things are possible" (Matt. 19:25–26). Even man's best achievements cannot attain salvation which is granted as a gift of God.

EYE SALVE — an ointment of various compounds applied to the eyelids for medicinal purposes (Rev. 3:18). This salve was mentioned by the apostle John in the Book of Revelation in his message to the church at Laodicea. The medical school at Laodicea was famous for its eye salve; so in order to make his point that the Laodiceans were spiritually blind, John told them that the Lord would have to anoint their eyes with salve that they might see, or know the truth.

EYESERVICE — the outward show of service, in order to impress others—a form of deception condemned by the apostle Paul (Eph. 6:6; Col. 3:22).

EYEWITNESS — one who bears witness by giving a personal report of what he has seen. The apostles did not receive the gospel secondhand but "were eyewitnesses of the word" (Luke 1:2) which they received personally from Jesus Christ.

EYES, COVERING OF THE — a symbolic expression in the KJV (Gen. 20:16) which apparently refers to the practice of accepting a bribe or taking a gift from a person as a payment for wrongs committed. The night before Jacob was to meet his brother Esau, whom he had cheated years earlier, he sent a present to Esau's camp as a gesture of peace and goodwill (Gen. 32:21).

EYES, PAINTING OF — the practice of putting black cosmetic powder on a woman's eyelids to enhance her beauty. The arch of the eyebrow was lengthened and darkened, the edges of the eyelids were lined, and the eyelids were tinted in order to make the eyes appear larger (Jer. 4:30). Implements for this procedure, including boxes, horns, and slender reeds in which black cosmetic powder was kept, have been discovered by archaeologists. Generally it was only the wealthy who could afford such cosmetics (2 Kin. 9:30; Jer. 4:30; Ezek. 23:40).

EZAR [EE zur] — a form of EZER.

EZBAI [EZ ba eye] (*shining*) — the father of Naarai, one of David's mighty men (1 Chr. 11:37).

EZBON [EZ bun] — the name of two Old Testament men:
1. A son of Gad (Gen. 46:16; Ozni, Num. 26:16).
2. A grandson of Benjamin (1 Chr. 7:7).

EZEKIAS [ez eh KIE us] — Greek form of HEZEKIAH.

EZEKIEL [ih ZEEK e uhl] (*God will strengthen*) — a prophet of a priestly family carried captive to Babylon in 597 B.C. when he was about 25 years old. His call to the prophetic ministry came five years later. Ezekiel prophesied to the captives who dwelt by the River Chebar at Tel Abib. He is the author of the Book of Ezekiel.

In his book, Ezekiel identifies himself as a priest, the son of Buzi (1:3). He was married to a woman who was "the desire of his eyes" (24:16). One of the saddest notes of his life was the death of his wife. In Ezekiel 24:1-2, the prophet was told that on the very day he received this revelation, his wife would die as the armies of Babylon laid siege against the holy city of Jerusalem. Ezekiel's sadness at the death of his wife was to match the grief of God at the sin of Jerusalem. Ezekiel was commanded not to grieve her death; he was to steel himself for this tragedy even as God had prepared Himself for the death of His beloved city (24:15-22).

Perhaps no other event in the lives of the Old Testament prophets is as touching as this. The harshness of God's command to His prophet emphasizes the Lord's grief over the fate and sufferings of His rebellious people. Believers in God have been called upon to suffer many indignities through the ages, but in the suffering of Ezekiel, we learn some-

---

EZEKIEL: A Teaching Outline

Part One: The Commission of Ezekiel (1:1—3:27)

Part Two: Judgment on Judah (4:1—24:27)

thing of the suffering of God Himself.

Ezekiel shows us just how ugly and serious our sin is. Our rebellion brings grief and hurt to God, against whom our sin is directed. Perhaps this is why God acted so dramatically in dealing with the human condition—by sending His Son Jesus to die in our place and set us free from the bondage of sin.

Also see EZEKIEL, BOOK OF.

EZEKIEL, BOOK OF — a prophetic book of the Old Testament with vivid, symbolic language much like that in the Book of Revelation in the New Testament. The Book of Ezekiel is named for its author, the prophet Ezekiel, who received his prophetic messages from God in a series of visions. He addressed these prophecies to the Jewish exiles in Babylon.

Structure of the Book. Although Ezekiel is a long book of 48 chapters, it has a logical, orderly structure that makes it easy to analyze and understand. After a brief introductory section about Ezekiel and the nature of his mission, the book falls naturally into three main divisions: (1) judgment on the nation of Judah (chaps. 4—24); (2) judgment on the surrounding nations (chaps. 25—32); and (3) the future blessing of God's Covenant People (chaps 33—48).

Ezekiel was a priest who lived among the other citizens of the nation of Judah as a captive of Babylon during the years of the CAPTIVITY. In the very first chapter of the book, he describes an amazing vision of God which came to him at the beginning of his ministry. He saw four living creatures, each of which had the faces of a man, a lion, an ox, and an eagle. Clearly visible above these strange creatures was the likeness of a throne, symbolizing the might and power of God. The glory of the Lord was clearly visible to Ezekiel as He called the prophet to proclaim His message of judgment. This vision in the very first chapter sets the tone for the rest of Ezekiel. In other encounters with strange visions throughout the book, Ezekiel proclaims God's message for His Covenant People, as well as the Gentile nations surrounding the land of Israel.

In the first major section of the book (chaps. 4—24) Ezekiel describes God's judgment on the nation of Judah because of its rampant idolatry. Chapters 8—11 are especially interesting because their prophecies were delivered by Ezekiel in the city of Jerusalem after God transported him there during one of his visions (8:3). At the end of chapter 11, Ezekiel was taken back to Babylon, where he continued his messages (11:24–25).

The next major division of the book (chaps. 25—32) proclaims God's judgment against the Gentile nations surrounding the land of Israel. Included are judgments against Ammon, Moab, Edom, Philistia, Tyre and Sidon, and Egypt.

The final section of the book (chaps. 33—48) speaks of the future restoration of the people of Israel. It includes Ezekiel's famous vision of the valley of dry bones (chap. 37). At God's command, Ezekiel spoke to the bones and they arose. Then God declared to the bones, "I will put My spirit in you, and you shall live, and I will place you in your own land" (34:14). This was a clear promise from God that His Covenant People would be restored to their homeland after their period of exile in Babylon. This same theme is continued in chapters 40—48, which describe the restoration of the Temple in Jerusalem and the renewal of sacrifices and authentic worship. These chapters are similar in tone and content to the closing chapters of the Book of Revelation. Ezekiel points forward to the glorious kingdom of Jesus the Messiah.

Authorship and Date. The author of this book was clearly the prophet Ezekiel, a spokesman for the Lord who lived among the Jewish captives in Babylon. Some scholars have questioned Ezekiel's authorship, claiming instead that it was compiled by an unknown author from several different sources. But the book itself clearly states that Ezekiel delivered these prophecies. The prophet refers to himself with the personal pronoun "I" throughout the book. The uniformity of style and language in the book—including such phrases as "son of man" (2:1) and "as I live, says the Lord God" (5:11)—is also a convincing proof of authorship by a single person. There is no good reason to doubt the traditional theory that Ezekiel wrote the book.

The prophet identifies himself in the Book as "Ezekiel the priest, the son of Buzi" (1:3). He also tells us he began his prophetic ministry "in the fifth year of King Jehoichin's captivity" (1:2). This was the king of Judah who was taken captive by Babylon about 597 B.C. This would place the beginning of Ezekiel's prophecies at about 593 B.C. The last dates which he mentions in the book are the "twenty-seventh year" (29:17) and "the twenty-fifth year of our captivity" (40:1). So Ezekiel must have prophesied for at least 20 years among the captives, until 573 B.C. He probably wrote the Book of Ezekiel some time during this period or shortly thereafter.

Historical Setting. The Book of Ezekiel belongs to the early years of the Babylonian captivity of God's Covenant People. The Babylonians took captives from Jerusalem in three stages. In an early campaign about 605 B.C., the prophet Daniel was among the Jews taken to Babylon. A second attack against the city occurred in 597 B.C., when many additional captives were taken. Ezekiel must have been among those carried away at this time. Then in the extensive campaign of 587–586 B.C., Nebuchadnezzar destroyed Jerusalem and took most of the remaining inhabitants into exile.

In the early prophecies of the Book of Ezekiel, the author wrote as a captive in Babylon who expected Jerusalem to be destroyed. Chapter 24 describes the beginning of the final siege of the city. This date was so important that the Lord had the prophet write it down as a memorial of the dreaded event (24:2). This was followed by the symbol of the cooking pot with scum rising from the boiling meat, a clear judgment against Judah. On this day also the prophet's beloved wife died. Ezekiel was forbidden to mourn her death as a symbol of God's wrath upon the wayward nation (24:15–24).

Portions of the Book of Ezekiel were written during the long siege of Jerusalem. While Ezekiel and the other captives lived in Babylon, they must have heard of the suffering of their fellow citizens back home. At last they received word that the city had fallen, and Ezekiel translated this event into an unforgettable message for the people (33:21–29). Such were the perilous times in which Ezekiel prophesied.

Theological Contribution. One of the greatest insights of the Book of Ezekiel is its teaching of individual responsibility. This prophet proclaimed the truth that every person is responsible for his own sin as he stands exposed before God. In Ezekiel's time the Jewish people had such a strong sense of group identity as God's Covenant People that they tended to gloss over their need as individuals to follow God and His will. Some even believed that future generations were held accountable for the sins of their ancestors. But Ezekiel declared: "The soul who sins shall die. The son shall not bear the guilt of the father, nor the father bear the guilt of the son. The righteousness of the righteous shall be upon himself, and the wickedness of the wicked shall be upon himself" (18:20). This underscores the need for every person to make his own decision to follow the Lord. No person can depend on the faith of any ancestors to gain entrance into God's kingdom.

Ezekiel also paints a beautiful picture of the future age in which God will rule triumphantly among His people. Although God's people were suffering at the hands of a pagan nation when Ezekiel prophesied, better days were assured. God would establish His universal rule among His people through a descendant of David (37:24–25). This is a clear reference to the MESSIAH, a prophecy fulfilled when Jesus was born in Bethlehem more than 500 years later. The followers of Jesus became the

The road to Petra in ancient Edom in the vicinity of Ezion Geber—a region south of the Dead Sea.

"new Israel," or the church—those who seek to follow God and carry out His purpose in the world.

Special Considerations. In his use of parables, symbolic behavior, and object lessons to drive home his messages, the prophet Ezekiel reminds us of the great prophet Jeremiah. Through the use of parables, Ezekiel portrayed God's Covenant People as a helpless newborn child (16:12), as a lioness who cared carefully for her cubs (19:1–9), as a sturdy cedar (17:1–l0), and as a doomed and useless vine (chap. 15). He also used a clay tablet to portray the Babylonian siege against the city of Jerusalem (4:1–2), ate his bread "with quaking" and drank his water "with trembling and anxiety" (12:17) to symbolize God's wrath, and carried his belongings about to show that God would allow His people to be carried into exile by the Babylonians (12:1–16).

Ezekiel may have picked up this technique of acting out his messages from Jeremiah himself. For about 40 years before Jerusalem's fall in 587 B.C., Jeremiah prophesied in the capital city. As a young resident of Jerusalem, Ezekiel probably heard and saw this great prophet at work. When he was called to prophesy to the exiles in Babylon beginning about 593 B.C., he may have used Jeremiah's methods as a way to get attention and win a hearing for God's message.

EZEL [EE zel] (division) — the place where David hid until Jonathan brought back word of Saul's intentions. Apparently between Naioth (1 Sam. 20:1) and Nob (1 Sam. 21:1), this mound of stones was the scene of the final parting of Jonathan and David (1 Sam 20:19).

EZEM [EE zum] (*mighty*) — a village in the Negeb of Judah situated south of Beersheba, near the border of Edom (Josh. 15:29; 19:3; Azem, KJV; 1 Chr. 4:29).

EZER [EE zur] ([God is a] *help*) — the name of six Old Testament men:

1. A son of Seir the Horite (Gen. 36:21; Ezar, 1 Chr. 1:38, KJV). Also see ABIEZER and ROMAMTI-EZER.

2. A descendant of Judah through Caleb son of Hur (1 Chr. 4:4; perhaps Ezra, 1 Chr. 4:17).

3. A son of Ephraim killed by the people of Gath when he and his brother Elead attempted to steal cattle from the Philistines (1 Chr. 7:21).

4. A Gadite who joined David at Ziklag (1 Chr. 12:9).

5. A well-known priest of Nehemiah's time (Neh. 12:42).

6. A Levite who helped repair the wall of Jerusalem (Neh. 3:19).

EZION GEBER [EE zih on GHEE bur] (*backbone of a man*) — an archaeological site between the modern city of Eilat in Israel and the modern city of Aqaba in Jordan where King Solomon located his smelting industry (see Map 2, C–2). Situated on the northern shore of the Gulf of Aqaba—the eastern arm of the Red Sea—Ezion Geber was first mentioned in the Bible as the last stopping place for the children of Israel before they reached Kadesh (Num. 33:35–36; Deut. 2:8). At that time it was probably little more than a grove of palm trees and a few wells.

Ezion Geber's prominence came about during the golden age of Israel under Solomon. At this site Solomon built a port from which fleets of ships sailed to foreign ports along the coasts of Africa, Arabia, and the Far East (1 Kin. 9:26; 10:22; 2 Chr. 8:17). To the docks of Ezion Geber came gold of Ophir, silver, ivory, spices, precious stones, wood, apes, monkeys, and baboons (1 Kin. 10:11–12).

Archaeological research at the site has shown that the city was strategically located between the hills of Edom on the east and the hills of Palestine on the west. Thus, Solomon constructed an extensive system of smelting and refining furnaces situated so the north winds which blew down through the Wadi el-Arabah would provide the perfect draft for the fires.

From the smelting and refining of copper, Solomon gained most of the riches that made him the wealthiest king in the East. Also discovered nearby were copper mines which had been worked extensively by Solomon. These discoveries together prove the Israelite king made Ezion Geber the center of an elaborate smelting industry in Palestine.

EZNITE [EZ night] — the nickname of Josheb-Basshebeth the Tachmonite, who was "chief among the captains" of David's mighty men (2 Sam. 23:8).

EZRA [EZ ruh] (*God is a help*) — the name of three men in the Old Testament:

1. A descendant of Judah (1 Chr. 4:17; Ezrah, RSV).

2. A scribe and priest who led the returned captives in Jerusalem to make a new commitment to God's Law. A descendant of Aaron through Eleazar, Ezra was trained in the knowledge of the Law while living in captivity in Babylon with other citizens of the nation of Judah. Ezra gained favor during the reign of Artaxerxes, king of Persia. This king commissioned him to return to Jerusalem about 457 B.C. to bring order among the people of the new community. Artaxerxes even gave Ezra a royal letter (Ezra 7:11–16), granting him civil as well as religious authority, along with the finances to furnish the Temple, which had been rebuilt by the returned captives.

Ezra was a skilled scribe and teacher with extensive training in the Books of the Law (Genesis, Exodus, Leviticus, Numbers, and Deuteronomy). After his return to Jerusalem, he apparently did a lot of work on the Hebrew Bible of that time, modernizing the language, correcting irregularities in the text, and updating and standardizing expressions in certain passages. References to this work by Ezra are found in 2 Esdras, one of the apocryphal books of the Old Testament. He also refers to himself in his own book as a skilled scribe (Ezra 7:6, 12), whose task was to copy, interpret and transmit the books of the Law.

When he arrived in Jerusalem, Ezra discovered that many of the Hebrew men had married foreign wives from the surrounding nations (Ezra 9:1, 2). After a period of fasting and prayer (Ezra 9:3, 15), he insisted that these men divorce their wives (Ezra 10:1, 17). He feared that intermarriage with pagans would lead to worship of pagan gods among the restored community of Judah.

In addition to these marriage reforms, Ezra also led his countrymen to give attention to the reading of the Law. Several priests helped Ezra read the Law, translating and interpreting it for the people's clear understanding in their new language Aramaic. This reading process went on for seven days as the people focused on God's commands.

During this period, they also celebrated one of their great religious festivals, the Feast of Tabernacles, to commemorate their sustenance by God in the wilderness following their miraculous escape from Egyptian bondage (Nehemiah 8). The result of this week of concentration on their heritage was a religious revival. The people confessed their sins and renewed their covenant with God (Nehemiah 9—10).

Ezra must have been a competent scribe and priest, since he found favor with the ruling Persians. But he was also devoted to his God and the high standards of holiness and righteousness which the Lord demanded of His people.

As he communicated God's requirements to the captives in Jerusalem, Ezra also proved he was a capable leader who could point out shortcomings while leading the people to a higher commitment to God's law at the same time. Through it all, Ezra worked with a keen sense of divine guidance, "according to the good hand of His God upon him" (Ezra 7:9).

3. One of the priests who returned from the Captivity with Zerubbabel (Neh. 12:1, 13).

Also see EZRA, BOOK OF.

EZRA, BOOK OF — a historical book of the Old Testament that describes the resettlement of the Hebrew people in their homeland after their long exile in Babylon. The book is named for its author and central figure, Ezra the priest, who led the exiles in a new commitment to God's Law after their return.

Structure of the Book. The ten chapters of this book fall naturally into two main divisions, chapters 1—6, which report the return of the first wave of exiles to Jerusalem under the leadership of Zerubbabel, about 525 B.C., and chapters 7—10, which describe the return of a second group under Ezra's leadership, about 458 B.C. One of the most unusual facts about the Book of Ezra is that its two major sections are separated by a time gap of about 80 years.

The book opens with a brief introduction that explains how the first return from exile happened. Cyrus, king of Persia, issued a proclamation allowing the Jewish people to return to Jerusalem to rebuild their Temple and resettle their native land. About 50,000 of the people returned under the leadership of Zerubbabel, a Jewish citizen appointed by Cyrus as governor of Jerusalem (2:64–65). Arriving in about 525 B.C., they set to work immediately on the rebuilding project. In spite of some shrewd political maneuvering by their enemies, the work moved forward until the Temple was completed in 515 B.C. (6:14–15).

The second major section of the book (chaps. 7—10) reports on the arrival of Ezra in Jerusalem with another group of exiles about 60 years after the Temple had been completed. Just as Zerubbabel had led the people to rebuild God's house, Ezra's mission was to lead his countrymen to rebuild the Law of God in their hearts. Ezra worked with another Jewish leader, Nehemiah, to bring about several reforms among the Jewish people in Jerusalem

EZRA: A Teaching Outline

Part One: The Restoration of the Temple of God (1:1—6:22)

Part Two: The Reformation of the People of God (7:1—10:44)

during this period. From the Book of Nehemiah (Neh. 8:1-8), we learn that Ezra read the books of the Law (Genesis, Exodus, Leviticus, Numbers, and Deuteronomy) aloud to the people. This led to a great religious revival throughout Jerusalem as the people committed themselves again to God's Law, confessed their sins (Neh. 9:1-3), and renewed the covenant with their redeemer God (Nehemiah 10).

We also learn from the final chapter of his book that Ezra was distressed at the Jewish men who had married non-Jewish women. He led these men to repent of their sin and divorce their pagan wives (10:17-44).

Authorship and Date. Ezra has traditionally been accepted as the author of this book that bears his name, as well as the companion book of Nehemiah. In the Hebrew Old Testament, Ezra and Nehemiah appeared as one unbroken book, closely connected in theme and style to the books of 1 and 2 Chronicles. The last two verses of 2 Chronicles are repeated in the first three verses of the Book of Ezra, probably indicating that they belonged together in the original version. For this reason, many scholars believe Ezra served as writer and editor-compiler of all four of these books: 1 and 2 Chronicles, Ezra, and Nehemiah. He probably drew from official court documents to compile 1 and 2 Chronicles.

This compilation theory also helps explain the strange 80-year gap between the two major sections of Ezra's book. He probably wrote about Zerubbabel's return many years after it happened, drawing from official court records or some other account of the event. To this he added his own personal memoirs, now contained in chapters 7—10 of the Book of Ezra as well as chapters 8—10 of the Book of Nehemiah. The rest of the material in the Book of Nehemiah may have come from Nehemiah's memoirs, which Ezra incorporated into the book of Ezra-Nehemiah. The time for the final writing and compilation of all this material must have been some time late in the fifth century B.C.

Historical Setting. The Book of Ezra belongs to the post-exilic period. These were the years just after a remnant of the nation returned to Jerusalem following their exile of about 50 years in Babylon. The return came about after the defeat of Babylon by the Persian Empire. Unlike the Babylonians, the Persians allowed their subject nations to live in their own native regions under the authority of a ruling governor. The Persians also practiced religious tolerance, allowing each nation to worship its own god. This explains the proclamation of Cyrus of Persia, which allowed the Jewish people to return to Jerusalem and rebuild their Temple. Cyrus even returned the Temple treasures that the Babylonians took when they destroyed Jerusalem about 50 years earlier (1:7-11).

Theological Contribution. The theme of the Book of Ezra is the restoration of the remnant of God's Covenant People in Jerusalem in obedience to his Law. The book shows clearly that God had acted to preserve His people, even when they were being held captives in a pagan land. But in their absence, the people had not been able to carry on the true form of Temple worship. Only in their Temple in Jerusalem, they believed, could authentic worship and sacrifice to their redeemer God be offered. This is why the rebuilding of the Temple was so important. Here they could restore their worship of God and find their true identity as God's people of destiny in the world.

The Book of Ezra also teaches a valuable lesson about the providence of God. Several different Persian kings are mentioned in this book. Each king played a significant role in returning God's Covenant People to their homeland and helping them restore the Temple as the center of their religious life. This shows that God can use the unrighteous as well as the righteous to work His ultimate will in the lives of His people.

Special Considerations. Many scholars believe the Jewish people in Babylon and Persia must have numbered at least two million. Yet only about 50,000 chose to return to Jerusalem with the first group under Zerubbabel (2:64-65). This indicates that most of them probably had become comfortable with their lives in these foreign lands. Or perhaps the certainties of their present existence were more appealing than the uncertainties of life in Jerusalem—a city which most of them had never seen.

Some Bible readers are bothered by Ezra's treatment of the pagan women whom the Jewish men had married (10:10-19). How could he be so cruel as to insist that these wives be "put away" (divorced) with no means of support? His actions must be understood in light of the drastic situation that faced the Jewish community in Jerusalem following the Exile. Only a small remnant of the Covenant People had returned, and it was important for them to keep themselves from pagan idolatry and foreign cultural influences at all costs. Ezra must have realized, too, that this was one of the problems which had led to their downfall and captivity as a people in the first place. Yet even the horrors of defeat and exile by the Babylonians had failed to teach the people a lesson. He was determined to stamp out the problem this time before it became a widespread practice among God's Covenant People.

Also see EZRA.

EZRAH [EZ ruh] — a form of EZRA.

EZRAHITE [EZ ruh hite] — the title of ETHAN (1 Kin. 4:31) and HEMAN (Psalm 88 title). Ezrahites were descendants of Zerah, head of a Judahite family (1 Chr. 2:6).

EZRI [EZ rye] ([God is] *my help*) — a superintendent of farm workers in David's court (1 Chr. 27:26).

F

FABLE — a story in which animals and plants speak and act like human beings—as in the well-known *Aesop's Fables*. The Old Testament contains at least three good examples of the fable: (1) Jotham's story of the trees (Judg. 9:8–15)—a satire on the foolishness of choosing an unfit king; (2) Jehoash's story of the thistle and the cedar (2 Kin. 14:9)—a condemnation of Amaziah's presumption; and (3) Ezekiel's allegory of the two eagles and the cedar (Ezek. 17:1–24). The word fable appears in the New Testament as a translation of the Greek word *muthos* (1 Tim. 1:4). The word fable is used in a negative sense, as something to be avoided. Most modern translations translate *muthos* as "myth" (RSV, NEB, NIV)—an untruth designed to deceive and mislead.

FACE — that part of the human body which contains a person's unique, identifying characteristics; a term used in a symbolic way in the Bible to express the presence of God. In the Garden of Eden, Adam and Eve "hid themselves from the presence [literally, face] of the Lord God" (Gen. 3:8). Jacob said, "I have seen God face to face, and my life is preserved" (Gen. 32:30). God's presence and glory have been revealed fully in the face, or the person, of Jesus Christ (2 Cor. 4:6). In the future many things that are now puzzling to Christian believers will be made clear: "For now we see in a mirror, dimly, but then face to face" (1 Cor. 13:12).

FACES, BREAD OF — NEB, NIV word for SHOWBREAD, an UNLEAVENED BREAD placed in the tabernacle every Sabbath to symbolize God's presence among His people (Ex. 25:30; 2 Chr. 4:19).

FAIR — a word with several different meanings in the Bible:
1. Lovely or beautiful (Song 1:15).
2. Free from self-interest or prejudice (Ezek. 18:25, 29).
3. Clear and open, as in "fair weather" (Matt. 16:2).

FAIR HAVENS — a harbor on the south coast of Crete (see Map 8, C–2), near the city of Lasea (Acts 27:8–12). This harbor is virtually unprotected in the winter. This is why the ship carrying Paul to Rome left Fair Havens for Phoenix, a safer harbor to the west.

FAITH — a belief in or confident attitude toward God, involving commitment to His will for one's life.

According to Hebrews 11, faith was already present in the experience of many people in the Old Testament as a key element of their spiritual lives. In this chapter, the various heroes of the Old Testament (Abel, Enoch, Noah, Abraham, Sarah, Isaac, Jacob, Joseph, and Moses) are described as living by faith. In addition, the Old Testament itself makes the same point. Abraham "believed in the Lord" (Gen. 15:6); the Israelites "believed" (Ex. 4:31; 14:31); and the prophet Habakkuk taught that "the just shall live by his faith" (Hab. 2:4).

In the New Testament, "faith" covers various levels of personal commitment. Mere intellectual agreement to a truth is illustrated in James 2:19, where even demons are said to believe that there is one God. Obviously, however, they are not saved by this type of belief. Genuine saving faith is a personal attachment to Christ, best thought of as a combination of two ideas—reliance on Christ and commitment to Him. Saving faith involves personally depending on the finished work of Christ's sacrifice as the only basis for forgiveness of sin and entrance into heaven. But saving faith is also a personal commitment of one's life to following Christ in obedience to His commands: "I know whom I have believed and am persuaded that He is able to keep what I have committed to Him until that Day" (2 Tim. 1:12).

Faith is part of the Christian life from beginning to end. As the instrument by which the gift of salvation is received (Eph. 2:8–9), faith is thus distinct from the basis of salvation, which is grace, and from the outworking of salvation, which is good works. The apostle Paul declared that salvation is through faith, not through keeping the works of the law (Eph. 2:8, 9).

Finally, in the New Testament, faith can refer to the teachings of the Bible, the faith which was once for all delivered to the saints (Jude 3). In modern times, faith has been weakened in meaning so that some people use it to mean self-confidence. But in the Bible, true faith is confidence in God or Christ, not in oneself.

FAITHFULNESS — dependability, loyalty, and stability particularly as it describes God in His relationship to human believers. The faithfulness of God and His Word is a constant theme in the Bible. It is particularly prominent in Psalms 89 and 119. God is "the faithful God who keeps covenant" (Deut. 7:9) and chooses Israel (Is. 49:7); great is His faithfulness (Lam. 3:23).

It is not surprising that this aspect of God's nature should also belong to the Messiah, who would be clothed with faithfulness (Is. 11:5) and who is described as the Faithful one (Rev. 19:11), the "faithful witness" (Rev. 1:5; 3:14), and the "faithful High Priest" (Heb. 2:17; 3:2).

God's faithfulness is the source of the Christian's deliverance from temptation (1 Cor. 10:13); assurance of salvation (Heb. 10:23); and forgiveness of sins (1 John 1:9). He is faithful to His children because He is first of all faithful to Himself (2 Tim. 2:13).

God's faithfulness should be so deeply reflected in the lives of His people (Gal. 5:22) that they can be called simply "the faithful" (Ps. 31:23). The New Testament speaks of the faithfulness of Paul (1 Cor. 7:25), Abraham (Neh. 9:8), and Moses (Heb. 3:5).

Faithfulness is also expected in Christian believers. Faithfulness to one's fellowman is seen especially in relation to fulfilling an office. A steward must be found faithful (1 Cor. 4:2), just as Daniel and other persons in the Bible exercised their faithfulness toward God (Dan. 6:4; 2 Tim. 2:2).

FALCON (see ANIMALS OF THE BIBLE).

FALL, THE — the disobedience and sin of Adam and Eve that caused them to lose the state of innocence in which they had been created. This event plunged them and all of mankind into a state of sin and corruption. The account of the Fall is found in Genesis 3.

Adam and Eve were created by God in a state of sinless perfection so they could glorify God, reflecting His righteousness on the earth, and enjoy fellowship and union with Him. Their calling was to exercise dominion, or control, over God's creation through their own labors and those of their offspring in faithful response to the word of God. As a specific test of this loyalty, God commanded them not to eat of "the tree of the knowledge of good and evil" (Gen. 2:17). Adam and Eve were to demonstrate their willingness to live "by every word that proceeds from the mouth of the Lord" (Deut. 8:3; Matt. 4:4). God warned them clearly that their disobedience would result in death.

The fall from their original state of innocence occurred when Satan approached Eve through the serpent, who tempted her to eat of the forbidden fruit. Satan called into question the truthfulness of what God had spoken about the tree and its significance. He urged Eve to discover, through trial and error, whether it was in her best interest to do what God had forbidden. Eve's sin did not consist of being tempted, but in believing and acting on Satan's lie. Her rejection of God's command occurred when she ate of the forbidden fruit and persuaded her husband to do the same thing. The term Fall should

not be interpreted to suggest that their sin was accidental. The temptation was purposeful, and their submission to it involved their willing consent.

The immediate consequence of the Fall was death, symbolized by their loss of fellowship with God. For the first time, Adam and Eve experienced fear in the presence of the Lord God; and they hid when He approached (Gen. 3:8-10). Because of their unbelief and rebellion, they were driven from the garden that God had provided as their home. From that time on, man would experience pain and encounter resistance as he worked at the task of earning his daily bread. Physical death, with the decay of the body, is not a natural process. It entered the human experience as God's curse upon sin.

Adam and Eve did not sin simply as private persons, but as the representatives of all members of the human race. Their sin is the sin of all; and all persons receive from them a corrupt nature. It is this nature that stands behind all personal violations of the Lord's commandments. For this reason, the fall of Adam is the fall of the human race. The apostle Paul thought of Christ as the second Adam who would rebuild the old, sinful Adam through His plan of redemption and salvation. "As in Adam all die, even so in Christ all shall be made alive" (1 Cor. 15:22).

FALLOW DEER (see ANIMALS OF THE BIBLE).

FALLOW GROUND — farm land allowed to lie idle during a growing season to allow the fertility of the soil to be restored (Hos. 10:12).

FALSE CHRISTS — persons who pretend to be Christ but who are actually representatives of all that Christ opposes (Matt. 24:24; Mark 13:22). False Christs are similar to ANTICHRIST and his prophets, described in the Epistles of John (1 John 2:18; 2 John 7). These false Christs take their place in the long line of false prophets who have existed since Old Testament days.

FALSE PROPHET, THE — a religious leader of the end times who, along with the DRAGON (the devil) and the BEAST (the Antichrist), forms an unholy trinity in opposition to God (Rev. 16:13; 20:10). The Book of Revelation speaks of two beasts—The Antichrist (Rev. 13:1-10), a political ruler who sets up an evil empire in opposition to the kingdom of God; and the false prophet, a religious leader inspired by Satan who deceives the world into worshiping the Antichrist (Rev. 13:12). But they will be overthrown by Christ and cast into the lake of fire (Rev. 19:20).

FALSE PROPHETS — those who falsely claim to utter revelations that come from God, to foretell future events, or to have God's power to produce miracles, signs, and wonders. In the Bible, false prophets fell into three general categories: (1) those who worshiped false gods and served idols; (2) those who falsely claimed to receive messages from the Lord; and (3) those who wandered from the

Photo by Gustav Jeeninga

In biblical times the family was a closely knit group, the grandparents often living with their children and grandchildren in the same household.

truth and ceased to be true prophets.

In the Old Testament, Moses spoke of the punishment of those who betrayed the faith. He ordered that any prophet who advocated the worship of other gods be stoned to death (Deut. 13:1–18). During the reign of King Ahab of Israel, false prophets were officially approved by King Ahab and his queen, Jezebel. The writer of 1 Kings speaks of "the four hundred and fifty prophets of Baal, and the four hundred prophets of Asherah, who eat at Jezebel's table" (1 Kin. 18:19). Later, 400 false prophets spoke words they knew Ahab the king wanted to hear and assured him of victory at Ramoth Gilead. Micaiah, the true prophet, who warned Ahab of defeat and disaster, was put in prison on a diet of bread and water (1 Kin. 22:1–28).

A recurring characteristic of the false prophets is that they often are found in the employment of the powerful and that they are careful to speak pleasing, positive, and flattering words to their employers. Jeremiah condemned the false prophets who were always saying, "Peace, peace!" when there was no peace (Jer. 6:14). The false prophets preached a popular message: there would be victory against Babylon. Jeremiah said, "The prophets prophesy falsely...and My people love to have it so" (Jer. 5:31). Even though Jeremiah was a true prophet of the Lord, the false prophets were rewarded by the king and Jeremiah was cast into a dungeon (Jer. 38:6).

In the New Testament, Jesus said, "Woe to you when all men speak well of you, for so did their fathers to the false prophets" (Luke 6:26). He warned his disciples to beware of false prophets "who come...in sheep's clothing, but inwardly they are ravenous wolves" (Matt. 7:15). When speaking of

the signs of the times and the end of the age, He also said, "Then many false prophets will rise up and deceive many. For false christs and false prophets will arise and show great signs and wonders, so as to deceive, if possible, even the elect" (Matt. 24:11, 24).

Later, the false prophet Bar–Jesus, also called Elymas the sorcerer, was smitten with blindness by the apostle Paul because he tried to turn the Proconsul Sergius Paulus away from the Christian faith (Acts 13:6–12). In the Book of Revelation, the dragon (that is, the devil), the beast, and the false prophet make up an unholy trinity of evil that opposes Christ and His people (Rev. 16:13).

FAMILIAR SPIRITS (see MAGIC, SORCERY, AND DIVINATION).

FAMILY — a group of persons related by marriage and blood ties and generally living together in the same household. In the Western world, the family traditionally consists of a man and his wife and their children. In biblical times, however, the family units were often much larger than the primary family, especially if the man had more than one wife.

In the ancient world, the extended family could include any or all of the following relationships: the man and his wife or wives; his CONCUBINES or female slaves; his sons and unmarried daughters; the wives of the sons; grandchildren; aged parents and grandparents. Others living in the same home and considered as part of the family could include servants and their children and aliens, or strangers, who attached themselves to the family for a time before moving to another location.

The man making the decisions for the family was

designated as "father," although he may not have been the oldest male in the group. These family groups, therefore, could be very large. When Jacob's "family" moved to Egypt from the Promised Land, he was accompanied by at least 66 people (Gen. 46:26).

God's Design for the Family. The concept of the family as the basic social unit reaches back into the CREATION account found in Genesis 1—2. A man was to be the husband of one wife and was to leave his father and mother and be joined to his wife.

However, not everyone in the Old Testament measured up to God's ideal. Sometimes a man married more than one wife. Solomon is a prime example. He had 700 wives and 300 concubines (1 Kin. 11:3). In addition, the family system of the Old Testament, with the man serving as the absolute ruling authority, discouraged a man from leaving his parents; he and his wife usually lived with his parents in the same dwelling.

After God created Adam, He declared, "It is not good that man should be alone" (Gen. 2:18). Then He created woman and united the couple; and they became "one flesh" (Gen. 2:24). Thus the family was designed by God to provide companionship for the various members of the family. In addition, the institution of marriage was approved and sanctioned by the Lord (Matt. 19:4–6).

God's ideal for the family is that it be a harmonious unit, where love for God and neighbor are instilled into each member (Deut. 6:6–9). If the couple are divided, especially over religious beliefs, they can never have the harmony and sense of common purpose that God desires. Therefore, Old Testament believers were instructed not to marry foreigners who would hinder their faith and bring strife to the marriage (Ex. 34:13–16; Deut. 7:3–4). Likewise, the apostle Paul commanded the New Testament believers, "Do not be unequally yoked together with unbelievers" (2 Cor. 6:14).

The Bible describes situations where a man went contrary to the will of God and married an unbeliever. A prime example is Solomon, who disobeyed God's commandment and married 700 wives (1 Kin. 3:3–15). The tragedy of the final years of his life is summarized in one sentence: "For it was so, when Solomon was old, that his wives turned his heart after other gods; and his heart was not loyal to the Lord his God, as was the heart of his father David" (1 Kin. 11:4). His wives and their gods caused Solomon to take his eyes off the living God.

From time to time in the history of the nation of Israel, the very existence of the country was threatened because of the breakdown of the home. The prophet Micah described the decayed situation of his day when he proclaimed: "Do not trust in a friend; do not put your confidence in a companion; guard the doors of your mouth from her who lies in your bosom. For son dishonors father, daughter rises against her mother, daughter-in-law against her mother-in-law; a man's enemies are the men of his own house" (Mic. 7:5–6). Ezra took steps to remedy the family problems of his day (Ezra 9—

10), and the prophet Malachi condemned the men of his generation for being faithless to the wives of their youth (Mal. 2:14–15).

The Exalted Position of the Father. The social structure described in the Old Testament is known as a "patriarchal" society. The word patriarchy means "the rule of the father."

The father commanded a high position in the family of Old Testament times; his word was law. In addition, the Hebrew word translated into English as husband actually means "lord," "master," "owner," or "possessor" (Gen. 18:12; Hos. 2:16). Because of his position, shared to some degree with his wife, a man expected to be treated as royalty by the rest of his family. The fifth commandment carries this idea of the importance of the parents one step further when it states, "Honor your father and your mother" (Ex. 20:12). The word honor often refers to one's response to God. In other words, this commandment suggests that the parents should receive a recognition similar to that given to God.

Along with the honor of the position as head of the family, the father was expected to assume certain responsibilities. These responsibilities can be classified into three categories: spiritual, social, and economic.

First of all, the father was responsible for the spiritual well-being of the family, as well as the individual members of the family. In the earliest ages, the father functioned as the priest of his family, sacrificing on their behalf (Gen. 12:8; Job 1:5). Later, when a priesthood was established in Israel and the layman no longer functioned at an altar, the father's spiritual role was redefined. He continued to be the religious leader in the home. This involved the training of the children in godliness (Ex. 12:3, 26–27; Prov. 22:6; Eph. 6:4).

Socially, the father's responsibility was to see that no one took advantage of any member of his family. Those who were not protected by a father were truly disadvantaged persons. The two most common categories of "fatherless" people were widows and orphans. Four specific duties of a father toward his son, as stated in the Jewish writings, were to have the son circumcised; to pass on his inheritance to his firstborn son; to find his son a wife; and to teach him a trade.

Economically, the father was to provide for the needs of the various members of his family. From time to time, however, a lazy person failed to provide for his family. Conscientious men sought to mock the lazy man, shaming him to do what was expected of him (Prov. 6:6–11). The apostle Paul rebuked those who considered themselves Christian but who did not look after the needs of their families (1 Tim. 5:8).

From this background we can more fully appreciate God as the believer's Father. He knows all about His child, even numbering the hairs on his head (Matt. 10:30). He protects His child and rescues him when he gets into trouble (Is. 63:15–16). He teaches him the way that he should go (Hos. 11:1–3) and supplies all of his needs (Matt. 6:33). In

Photo by Willem A. VanGemeren

Wind, rain, and careless farming methods have caused extensive erosion such as this in Palestine.

turn, the Father expects honor from His child, although He does not always receive it (Mal. 1:6). Jesus sought to instill reverence and honor in the disciples when He taught them to pray: "Our Father in heaven" (Matt. 6:9–10).

The Clan. Each extended family was part of a larger group that was called a "clan." Often the male members of these clans numbered into the hundreds (Ezra 8:1–14). The members of the clan considered themselves to be relatives of the other members of the clan, because the members traced their lineage back to a common ancestor.

Each male member within the clan had one person designated as his *go'el,* or kinsman–redeemer. There were four specific tasks that the redeemer was to perform as his help was needed: (1) If his kinsman sold his property to pay his debts, the kinsman redeemed or bought back the property (Lev. 25:25; Ruth 4:1–6; Jer. 32:6–15); (2) The person who was captured and enslaved or who sold himself into slavery had every right to expect his kinsman to redeem him and set him free (Lev. 25:47–49); (3) If a person died childless, the redeemer married the dead man's widow and raised up a son to carry on the family line and to honor the deceased person, in a custom known as LEVIRATE MARRIAGE (Deut. 25:5–10); (4) If the person was murdered, his redeemer tracked down the killer and evened the score. In these passages that describe this custom, *go'el* is translated as "avenger of blood" (Deut. 19:12).

The term kinsman–redeemer is used of God to express His intimate relationship with His people (Is. 41:14; 43:14; 44:24). He is their "next of kin" who ransoms them from bondage (Is. 43:1–3); He pays the price to set them free. Paul reminded the believers at Corinth that God had bought them at a price; therefore, they were to glorify God (1 Cor. 6:19–20).

The Family of God. Biblical writers used other analogies from the family to describe various aspects of the gospel. To be brought into God's family, the believer must be "born from above" or "born again" (John 3:3, 5). Because a person has God as his Father, he must realize that other believers are his "fathers," "mothers," "brothers," and "sisters" (1 Tim. 5:1–2). The body of believers known as the church are also referred to as the "household of God" (Eph. 2:19) and the "household of faith" (Gal. 6:10). In addition, the concepts of ADOPTION and INHERITANCE are used to describe the position of believers in God's family (Gal. 4:5; 1 Pet. 1:4).

FAMINE — the lack of a supply of food or water. This word occurs often in the Bible in both literal and figurative senses. Since the line between famine and plenty in Palestine depends mainly on the rains coming at the right time and in the proper supply, famine was an ever-present threat. In the face of famine, Abraham migrated to Egypt (Gen. 12:10), Isaac went to Gerar in Philistine territory (Gen. 26:1), and Jacob moved to Egypt (Gen. 41—47).

The most famous famine recorded in the Bible is the seven-year famine in Egypt foretold by Joseph in interpreting Pharaoh's dream. Extending even into Canaan, it eventually brought the rest of Joseph's family to Egypt (Gen. 41—47; Ps. 105:16). During another famine Elijah was kept alive by the widow of Zarephath (1 Kin. 17:8; Luke 4:25–26).

Lack of rain and conditions of war brought famine to besieged cities (1 Kin. 18:2; Ezek. 6:12). Pathetic descriptions of famine conditions include people's resorting to cannibalism (2 Kin. 6:28–29), cries of hungry children (Lam. 4:4), and the fainting of people in the streets (Is. 51:20).

Famine was also one of the punishments sent by the Lord upon His people because of their sins (Is. 51:20; Ezek. 14:21). A famine in the time of David was caused by Saul's mistreatment of the Gibeonites (2 Sam. 21:1). A striking description of famine conditions was given by the prophet Amos in his phrase, "Cleanness of teeth" (Amos 4:6)—clean because there was no food to foul them.

A famine is one of the signs of the approaching fall of Jerusalem (Matt. 24:7), and one of the plagues coming upon "Babylon," as recorded in the Book of Revelation (Rev. 18:8).

Using figurative language, the prophet Amos described a famine of an entirely different sort—not one of lack of food or water, but a famine of hearing the word of the Lord (Amos 8:11). Those who had refused to hear the prophets would have no prophets to guide them in the perilous days when God's judgment would fall upon His people.

FAN (see TOOLS OF THE BIBLE).

FANNER (see OCCUPATIONS AND TRADES).

FARM, FARMING — the practice of growing livestock and crops for food or commercial purposes. Although the word farm occurs only in Matthew

22:5, farming was an important occupation in Bible times. Practically every family owned a piece of land in Israel, and many families farmed a small area of their own.

Outside the cities, most Israelites lived in villages rather than on farms. Cultivated land usually was outside the village, situated near the water supply or on western or northern slopes where rainfall was greatest. Crops grown included wheat, barley, vines, olives, and figs.

Farm animals lived in the houses with the families. All but the poorest owned at least one ox or ass as a work animal. Cattle, sheep, and goats were common, providing milk products as well as skins for clothes. Richer families and royal estates employed their own farm managers and workers (1 Chr. 27:25–31) and hired laborers for specialist tasks, particularly at harvest time (Matt. 20:1–16).

Frequent difficulties, such as hilly ground, stony soil, and unpredictable rainfall, did not make farming easy. But there were certain rewards, such as the joys of shearing animals and gathering the crops at harvest time (1 Sam. 25:2–8; Is. 9:3).

FARMER (see OCCUPATIONS AND TRADES).

FAST, FASTING — going without food or drink voluntarily, generally for religious purposes. Fasting, however, could also be done for other reasons. It was sometimes done as a sign of distress, grief, or repentance. The law of Moses specifically required fasting for only one occasion—the DAY OF ATONEMENT. This custom resulted in calling this day "the day of fasting" (Jer. 36:6) or "the Fast" (Acts 27:9).

Moses did not eat bread or drink water during the 40 days and 40 nights he was on Mount Sinai receiving the law (Ex. 34:28). Voluntary group fasts (not specified in the law) were engaged in during time of war, such as when the Benjamites defeated the other Israelites (Judg. 20:26), and when Samuel gathered the people to Mizpah during the Philistine wars (1 Sam. 7:6). It was at a called fast that witnesses accused Naboth, setting the stage for his death (1 Kin. 21:9, 12).

Jehoshaphat called for a fast in all Israel when opposed by the Moabites and Ammonites (2 Chr. 20:3). Reacting to Jonah's preaching, the men of Nineveh, at the king's order, fasted and put on sackcloth (Jon. 3:5). Those about to return with Ezra from the Captivity fasted at the river of Ahava in the face of the dangers faced on the journey (Ezra 8:21, 23). Esther and the Jews of Shushan (or Susa) fasted when faced with the destruction planned by Haman (Esth. 4:3, 16; 9:31).

In times of grief, people fasted. A seven-day fast was held when the bones of Saul and his sons were buried (1 Sam. 31:13; 1 Chr. 10:12). Fasting was done during the 70 years of the exilic period on the fifth and the seventh months, the date the siege of Jerusalem began and the date when Jerusalem fell to the Babylonians (Zech. 7:5).

Fasting was often done by individuals in times of distress. David fasted after hearing that Saul and Jonathan were dead (2 Sam. 1:12). Nehemiah

fasted and prayed upon learning that Jerusalem had remained in ruins since its destruction (Neh. 1:4). Darius, the king of Persia, fasted all night after placing Daniel in the lions' den (Dan. 6:18).

Going without food or water was not automatically effective in accomplishing the desires of those who fasted. In the prophet Isaiah's time, people complained that they had fasted and that God had not responded favorably (Is. 58:3–4). The prophet declared that the external show was futile. The fast that the Lord requires is to loose the bonds of wickedness, undo the heavy burdens, feed the hungry, shelter the poor, and clothe the naked (Is. 58:5–7).

Fasting also occurs in the New Testament. Anna at the Temple "served God with fastings and prayers night and day" (Luke 2:37). John the Baptist led his disciples to fast (Mark 2:18). Jesus fasted 40 days and 40 nights before His temptation (Matt. 4:2). Using a marriage–feast comparison, however, Jesus insisted that fasting was not suitable for His disciples as long as He, the Bridegroom, was with them (Matt. 9:14–15; Mark 2:18–20; Luke 5:33–35).

Cornelius was fasting at the time of his vision (Acts 10:30). The church in Antioch fasted (Acts 13:2) and sent Paul and Barnabas off on the first missionary journey with fasting and prayer (Acts 13:3). Paul and Barnabas prayed with fasting at the appointment of elders in the churches (Acts 14:23). Paul suggested that husbands and wives might abstain from sexual intercourse to give themselves to fasting and prayer (1 Cor. 7:5).

FAT — the richest part of an animal eaten as food or used as a sacrifice. In the ancient world, the fatty portions of the animal were eaten as a delicacy. While the fat of an animal offered to the Lord as a sacrifice could not be eaten, Deuteronomy 12:15–24 seems to imply that the fat of an animal slaughtered for food could be eaten.

In Old Testament times, being fat was considered a sign of personal success (Deut. 31:20; Prov. 15:30; Jer. 5:28). To a people for whom getting enough to eat was a constant problem, fat was a sign of abundance. It is easy to see why fat was a frequent symbol of excellence and desirability in the Old Testament. The spies were sent into Canaan to see if the land was "rich (Num. 13:20; fat, KJV) or poor."

Because of the high value placed on fat, it was only right that the fat of the sacrificial animal—the best part—belonged only to the Lord (Lev. 6:12).

FATHER — the male parent of a household in Bible times, charged with the responsibility of providing for the family and giving religious instruction to the children. Also see FAMILY.

FATHER, GOD THE (see GOD, NAMES OF).

FATHER–IN–LAW — the father of a person's husband or wife. The classic example of a father-in-law in the Bible is Jethro, father-in-law of Moses (Ex. 3:1). When Moses fled from Egypt to Midian,

A temporary booth, or shelter, near Jerusalem, set up to celebrate the Feast of Booths, also known as the Feast of Tabernacles (Ex. 34:22).

he married one of Jethro's daughters and was welcomed into his family.

FATHERLESS (see ORPHAN).

FATHER'S HOUSE — a way of designating families or households among the Israelites, sometimes referring to a family's physical dwelling place (Gen. 24:23), the family itself (Gen. 12:1), a specific tribe (Gen. 24:40), or the entire nation (Neh. 1:6).

FATHOM (see WEIGHTS AND MEASURES).

FATLING — a grain-fed lamb, calf, or kid raised for meat (1 Sam. 15:9). Because of the expense of feed, these animals were very valuable in Bible times and were probably a luxury not available to the poor. Also see FATTED.

FATTED — grain-fed livestock, probably grown mostly for use as sacrificial animals in the worship system of ancient Israel (2 Sam. 6:13; 1 Kin. 4:23). On special occasions, these prime animals, also called FATLINGS, were also used for food. When the prodigal son returned home, his father killed the fatted calf for a festive meal to celebrate the occasion (Luke 15:23, 24).

FAWN (see ANIMALS OF THE BIBLE).

FEAR — a feeling of reverence, awe, and respect, or an unpleasant emotion caused by a sense of danger. Fear may be directed toward God or man, and it may be either healthy or harmful.

A healthy fear is reverence or respect. The Bible teaches that children are to respect their parents (Lev. 19:3), wives are to respect their husbands (Eph. 5:33), and slaves are to respect their masters (Eph. 6:5). The Scriptures also declare that "the fear of the Lord is the beginning of knowledge" (Prov. 1:7) as well as "the beginning of wisdom" (Prov. 16:16).

A harmful fear is a sense of terror or dread. Believers are instructed not to fear human beings (Matt. 10:28; Phil. 1:28), because they cannot ultimately harm us. Wicked men, however, are constantly fearing other people, especially the righteous (Prov. 28:1; Matt. 14:5; Rom. 13:3–4). Such fear causes them to act deceitfully in an attempt to hide their sins (2 Sam. 11; Matt. 28:4–15).

On the other hand, the unbeliever has every reason to be panic-stricken at thoughts of God, for he stands condemned before Him (Matt. 10:28; John 3:18). And yet, this kind of fear of God does not often lead to repentance. It normally leads to a feeble attempt to hide from God (Gen. 3:8; Rev. 6:15–17) or worse, to a denial of God's existence and His claim on a person's life (Ps. 14:1; Rom. 1:18–28).

FEASTS AND FESTIVALS — the regular assemblies of the people of Israel for worship of the Lord.

The feasts and festivals of the Jewish nation were scheduled at specific times in the annual calendar and they were both civil and religious in nature. Some marked the beginning or the end of the agricultural year, while others commemorated historic events in the life of the nation. All of the feasts were marked by thanksgiving and joyous feasting.

Meat, a scarce item in the daily fare of the Hebrews, was eaten at these affairs, and wine was also consumed. The fat and the blood of the animals were reserved for sacrifice to God as a burnt offering. The libation (or offering) of wine may have been drunk by the worshipers as part of the meal ceremony. First the blood and the fat were offered to God; then the worshiper ate the meal.

The feasts and festivals of Israel were community observances. The poor, the widow, the orphan, the Levite, and the sojourner or foreigner were invited to most of the feasts. The accounts of these feasts suggest a potluck type of meal, with some parts of the meal reserved for the priests and the rest given to those who gathered at the Temple or the altar for worship. One of the feasts, Passover, originated in the home and later was transferred to the Temple. The rest were apparently observed at specific times during the year and in designated places.

The Hebrew word for "pilgrimage" seems to be reserved mostly for the three great annual feasts of the Hebrew people: the Feast of Unleavened Bread, the Feast of Weeks, and the Feast of Tabernacles. These feasts are discussed in Leviticus 23. They were very important in the Jewish faith, and every male was expected to observe them.

The religious pilgrimage from the various towns and cities to the Temple or to the LEVITICAL CITIES scattered throughout the land became annual events. This yearly event may also have progressed from an annual "pilgrimage" early in Israel's history to a "processional" at the Temple or at the Levitical center in later times. In all the feasts and festivals the nation of Israel remembered its past and renewed its faith in the Lord who created and sustained His people.

Following is a complete list of all the feasts and festivals observed by the Jewish people. Some of these were annual events, while others occurred weekly or once every several years.

Atonement, Day of. The tenth day of the seventh month was set aside as a day of public fasting and humiliation. On this day the nation of Israel sought atonement for its sins (Lev. 23:27; 16:29; Num. 29:7). This day fell in the month equivalent to our August, and it was preceded by special Sabbaths (Lev. 23:24). The only fasting period required by the Law (Lev. 16:29; 23:31), the Day of Atonement was a recognition of man's inability to make any atonement for his sins. It was a solemn, holy day accompanied by elaborate ritual (Lev. 16; Heb. 10:1–10).

The high priest who officiated on this day first sanctified himself by taking a ceremonial bath and putting on white garments (Lev. 16:4). Then he had to make atonement for himself and other priests by sacrificing a bullock (Num. 29:8). God dwelt on the MERCY SEAT in the Temple, but no person could approach it except through the mediation of the high priest, who offered the blood of sacrifice.

After sacrificing a bullock, the high priest chose a goat for a sin–offering and sacrificed it. Then he sprinkled its blood on and about the mercy seat (Lev. 16:12, 14, 15). Finally the scapegoat bearing the sins of the people was sent into the wilderness (Lev. 16:20–22). This scapegoat symbolized the pardon for sin brought through the sacrifice (Gal. 3:12; 2 Cor. 5:21).

Booths, Feast of (see *Tabernacles, Feast of*).

Dedication, Feast of. This feast, also known as Hanukkah and the Feast of Lights, is apparently mentioned only once in the Bible (John 10:22). It developed in the era of the MACCABEES and celebrated the cleansing of the Temple after its desecration by ANTIOCHUS EPIPHANES. The Feast of Dedication is observed on the 25th day of the ninth month.

Hanukkah (see *Dedication, Feast of*).

Harvest, Feast of (see *Weeks, Feast of*).

Jubilee, Year of. The references to the Year of Jubilee in the Bible include Leviticus 23:15–16; 25:8–55; 27:14–24, Jeremiah 34:8, 14–17, and Isaiah 61:1–2.

The Jubilee Year began with the blowing of the RAM'S HORN. This differed from the ordinary year, for which the Shofar was blown. It took place after seven Sabbatical years, or every 49 years; and the 50th year was thereby set aside as the Year of Jubilee. Once the Israelites entered and possessed the Promised Land, it became their obligation to observe this year.

The Year of Jubilee was a special year in family renewal. A man who was bound to another as a slave or indentured servant was set free and returned to his own family. If any members of his family were also bound, the entire family was set free. Houses and lands could also be redeemed in the Year of Jubilee. If they were not redeemed within a year, however, they became the permanent possession of the previous owner. The land owned by Levites was exempted from this law; they could redeem their land at any time.

The rights and privileges extended by the Hebrews to other Hebrews did not extend to non–Hebrews. Servants obtained by Hebrews from the non–Hebrew world were permanent slaves. And property purchased from non–Hebrews was not redeemable. The law of the Year of Jubilee favored the Hebrews.

Jeremiah 34:8, 14–17 warned Judah for first practicing the Jubilee and then taking away people's liberty. Apparently, those who gained wealth and power in Israel did not observe this festival willingly.

Lights, Feast of (see *Dedication, Feast of*).

New Moon. The references in the Bible to the New Moon celebration include Exodus 40:2, 17, Numbers 10:10; 28:1–10; 11–15, and Psalm 104:19. The law specified that two bullocks, one ram, seven lambs, and one kid were to be offered in connection with this celebration. Meal mixed with oil accompanied the offerings; a trumpet blast introduced this feast. The sins committed and not expiated during the previous month were covered by the offerings of the New Moon. Thus, sinners received atonement and were reconciled with the Lord.

Passover and the Feast of Unleavened Bread. References to the Passover and the Feast of Unleavened Bread include Exodus 12:1—13:16; 23:15; 34:18–20, 25; Leviticus 23:4–14; Numbers 28:16–25; Deuteronomy 16:1–8; Joshua 4:19–23; 5:10–12; and 2 Chronicles 30:2, 3, 13, 15.

The Passover was the first of the three great festivals of the Hebrew people. It referred to the sacrifice of a lamb in Egypt when the people of Israel were slaves. The Hebrews smeared the blood of the lamb on their doorposts as a signal to God that He should "pass over" their houses when He destroyed all the firstborn of Egypt to persuade Pharaoh to let His people go.

Passover was observed on the 14th day of the first month, Abib, with the service beginning in the evening (Lev. 23:6). It was on the evening of this day that Israel left Egypt. Passover commemorated this departure from Egypt in haste. Unleavened bread was used in the celebration because this showed that the people had no time to put leaven in their bread as they ate their final meal as slaves in Egypt.

Several regulations were given concerning the observance of Passover. Passover was to be observed "in the place which the Lord your God will choose." This implied the sanctuary of the tabernacle or the Temple in Jerusalem.

Joshua 5:10–12 refers to the observing of Passover in the plains of Jericho near Gilgal. Second Chronicles 30:1, 3, 13, 15 describes a Passover during the reign of Hezekiah. Messengers were sent throughout the land to invite the people to come to Jerusalem to observe the Passover. Many refused; some even scorned the one who carried the invitation. Because the people were not ready to observe the Passover, a delay of one month was recommended. That year the Passover was on the 14th day of the second month. Even after the delay many still were not ready to observe the Passover.

In New Testament times, Passover became a pilgrim festival. Large numbers gathered in Jerusalem to observe this annual celebration. Jesus was crucified in the city during one of these Passover celebrations. He and His disciples ate a Passover meal together on the eve of His death. Like the blood of the lamb which saved the Hebrew people from destruction in Egypt, His blood, as the ultimate Passover sacrifice, redeems us from the power of sin and death.

Pentecost (see *Weeks, Feast of*).

Purim, Feast of. References to Purim include Esther 3:7; 9:24, 26, 28–29, 31–32. This feast commemorates the deliverance of the Jewish people from destruction by an evil schemer named Haman during the days of their captivity by the Babylonians and Persians. It took its name from the Hebrew word *purim*, meaning "lots" because Haman cast lots to determine when he would carry out his plot against the Jews. The Feast of Purim took place on the 14th and 15th of Adar, and during its celebration the Book of Esther is read as a reminder of their deliverance. A happy ceremony, Purim is accompanied with the giving of gifts and much celebration.

Sabbath. The Sabbath is taught in many places, including Exodus 16:22–30; 20:8–11; 23:12; 31:12–16; 34:21; 35:2–3; Leviticus 23:3; 26:2; Numbers 15:32–36; 28:9–10; Deuteronomy 5:12–15. The Hebrew word for Sabbath means "to cease or abstain." Two reasons are given for observing the Sabbath: Creation and Exodus.

Exodus 20:8–11 reminded the nation of Israel to remember that God rested on the seventh day (Gen. 2:2). This grounds the observance of the Sabbath in the creation of the world. Deuteronomy 5:12–15 reminded Israel to remember its bondage years when there was no rest. This passage fixed the origin of the Sabbath in the bondage of the Hebrews in Egypt.

The Israelites were instructed to include the family, the hired servants, the stranger, and even their domestic animals in observance of this holy day. All were commanded to cease from normal labor. This included the command not to gather firewood (Num. 15:32–36) or to kindle a fire (Ex. 35:2–3). Stoning to death was apparently the penalty for gathering firewood on the Sabbath. Those who violated the Sabbath would be excommunicated from the community or could be put to death (Ex. 31:12–16).

The Sabbath became not only a day of rest but a convocation to the Lord as well. A specific sacrifice on the Sabbath is required in Numbers 28:9–10. It included a lamb, a meal offering mixed with oil, and a drink offering. This was to be offered as a burnt offering. In later periods of Hebrew history, prayer and other rituals became the procedure for observing the Sabbath.

The purpose of the Sabbath was twofold. It symbolized that the nation of Israel had been set apart by the Lord as His special people. The Sabbath was also a celebration of the fact that the land belonged to God. This is seen in His provision of a Sabbatical Year—one year out of every seven when the land should rest from cultivation in order to renew and replenish itself.

The observance of the Sabbath set the Hebrew people apart from their neighbors. Unfortunately, burdensome restrictions and heavy requirements eventually grew up around its observance. The day that was set apart for rest, renewal, and worship became a day filled with rules of many things that must not be done.

Jesus attempted to restore the purpose of the Sabbath (Matt. 12:1–14; Mark 2:23—3:6; Luke 6:1–11). He declared God's intention for the Sabbath by pointing out that "the Sabbath was made for man, and not man for the Sabbath" (Mark 2:27).

Sabbatical Year. The concept of the sabbatical year was that the land was to be given a rest every seventh year. This law included the fields of grain and the vineyards. Even that which grew from the planting and pruning of the sixth year was not to be consumed by the owner.

Eventually, the cancellation of debts was added to the land rest as a part of the sabbatical year. Debts to fellow Hebrews were to be forgiven during this year, although debts of non-Hebrews might be collected. But the spirit of generosity was encouraged even toward non-Hebrews. Indentured servants were to be granted their freedom. Not only were they to be freed; they were also to be provided with grain, meat, and drink in generous portions.

The purpose of the sabbatical year was renewal—renewal of the land, renewal of hope in the canceling of debts, and renewal of life in a new start.

Seventh Month Festival. This festival is mentioned in Leviticus 23:24–25, 27–32 and Numbers 29:1–40. It was introduced with the blowing of trumpets, the halt of labor, sacrifices, and a testing (Lev. 23:24–32; Num. 29:1–40). The exact reason for its observance is not clear. Some scholars believe it originated during the Babylonian Captivity as a way of counteracting the influence of the Babylonian New Year Festival. This feast is also known as the Feast of Trumpets.

Tabernacles, Feast of. References to the Feast of Tabernacles in the Bible include Exodus 23:16; 34:22; Leviticus 23:33–36; 39–43; Numbers 29:12–32; Deuteronomy 16:13–16; Ezra 3:4; and Zechariah 14:16, 18–19.

This festival was observed on the 15th day of the seventh month to commemorate the wandering of Israel in the wilderness. Features of the celebration included a holy convocation on the first and eighth days, and the offering of many animal sacrifices. The Israelites were also commanded to live in booths made of palm and willow trees during the festival to commemorate their period of wilderness wandering when they lived in temporary shelters. This feast is also known as the Feast of Booths.

Trumpets, Feast of (see *Seventh Month Festival*).

Unleavened Bread, Feast of. This feast began on the 15th day of the month as a part of the larger celebration of Passover (Ex. 13:3–10; Lev. 23:6–8). Manual labor was strictly forbidden. Strangers and native–born people alike were punished if they failed to keep this holy day. A convocation began the feast.

Only unleavened bread was to be eaten during this feast. Bread without leaven commemorated the haste with which Israel left Egypt. As the blood was drained from the sacrificial animal, so the life or the power of leaven was removed from the bread offered to God during this annual celebration.

Weeks, Feast of. Biblical references to the Feast of Weeks include Exodus 23:16; 34:22; Leviticus 23:15–21; Numbers 28:26–31; Deuteronomy 16:9–12; and 2 Chronicles 8:13. This feast was observed early in the third month on the 50th day after the offering of the barley sheaf at the Feast of Unleavened Bread. It included a holy convocation with the usual restriction on manual labor.

Numbers 28:26–31 describes the number and nature of offerings and Deuteronomy 16:9–12 describes those who were to be invited to this feast. They include servants, sons and daughters, Levites, the fatherless, the widow, and the stranger. Israelites were to be reminded of their bondage in Egypt on that day.

This feast was also known as the Feast of Harvest as well as Pentecost. The early Christian believers, who were gathered in Jerusalem for observance of this feast, experienced the outpouring of God's Holy Spirit in a miraculous way (Acts 2:1–4).

FEEBLE KNEES — a description of persons who are weak or exhausted (Job 4:4).

FEEBLE–MINDED — KJV word for fainthearted (1 Thess. 5:14; timid, NIV). The Greek word means "little spirited" or "small souled."

FEET, DISEASED (see DISEASES OF THE BIBLE).

FEET, WASHING (see FOOT WASHING).

FELIX [FEE lix] (*happy*) — Roman procurator, or governor, of Judea before whom the apostle Paul appeared.

Felix was an unscrupulous ruler. In addition to having three wives, he considered himself capable of committing any crime and avoiding punishment because of his influence with the courts. Because of Felix's tyranny, a group of Jewish revolutionaries, known as the Sicarii ("assassins"), flourished. Retaliation against the Sicarii by the Roman government eventually led to the downfall and destruction of Jerusalem.

Felix is best known for his encounter with the apostle Paul (Acts 23:23). Arrested in Jerusalem as a disturber of the peace, Paul was sent to Caesarea for judgment by Felix. After his initial appearance before Felix, Paul was confined to the judgment hall until his accusers arrived. After five days, they arrived under the leadership of Ananias, the Jewish

high priest. The case against Paul was managed by Tertullus, who sought to win Felix over by expressing gratitude on the part of the Jews (Acts 24:1–2).

Tertullus then proceeded to accuse Paul of committing rebellion against the Romans, being the ring–leader of a trouble-making religious sect, and profaning the Jewish Temple. The purpose of these accusations was to persuade Felix to surrender Paul to the Jewish courts, in which case he would have been assassinated.

When Felix gave Paul permission to speak, Paul refuted each of these charges; and Felix postponed his judgment. Several days later, Paul was brought before Felix a second time. On this occasion Paul gave his testimony as a Christian. Felix was visibly moved; and he dismissed Paul, indicating he would talk with him again on a more convenient day.

Felix kept Paul in suspense about his judgment because he hoped Paul would give him a bribe. He sent for Paul on several occasions. But his hopes for a bribe were unfulfilled, and he kept Paul a prisoner for two years.

Meanwhile, the atmosphere in Judea became more embarrassing, and Felix was finally removed as procurator by the Roman authorities. Because the Jews were making numerous accusations against Felix, Paul was left in prison in Caesarea for two years in an effort to appease the Jewish officials (Acts 24:27). Paul eventually appealed to Rome, which was his right as a Roman citizen, and finally was released from prison and taken to Rome.

FELLOES [FELL oze] — KJV word for RIMS (1 Kin. 7:33).

FELLOW — a word used in the Bible in both a positive and negative sense:

1. A worthless man or boy; a term of contempt for a person not worth mentioning (Matt. 26:61).

2. A friend, comrade, companion, or associate (Ex. 2:13).

The word fellow is also used in such phrases as fellow servant(s) (Col. 1:7), fellow disciples (John 11:16), and fellow workers (Phil. 4:3).

FELLOWSHIP — sharing things in common with others. In the New Testament, fellowship has a distinctly spiritual meaning. Fellowship can be either positive or negative.

Positively, believers have fellowship with the Father, Son, and Holy Spirit (John 17:21–26; Phil. 2:1; 1 John 1:3), as well as with other believers (Acts 2:42; 1 John 1:3, 7). The only reason why we dare to have fellowship with God, in the sense of sharing things in common with Him, is that He has raised our status through the death and resurrection of Christ (Eph. 2:4–7). What believers share in common with God is a relationship as well as God's own holy character (1 Pet. 1:15). Those who have fellowship with Christ should enjoy fellowship with other believers. This fellowship ought to illustrate the very nature of God Himself (John 13:35; Eph. 5:1–2; 1 John 1:5–10).

Negatively, believers should not have fellowship

with unbelievers. This means they should not share in unbelievers' sinful lifestyles (2 Cor. 6:14–18). This does not mean, however, that believers should have nothing to do with unbelievers. The Bible plainly teaches that believers are obligated to share the gospel with unbelievers (Matt. 28:16–20; Mark 16:15–16; 1 Cor. 9:16–17).

FENCE — a protective barrier around a house or field or an enclosure for livestock (Ps. 62:3). Job also used the word symbolically to express his futility at being closed in and having his freedom restricted by God (Job 19:8).

FENCED CITIES — KJV words for FORTIFIED CITIES.

FERRET (see ANIMALS OF THE BIBLE).

FERRYBOAT — a vessel used to transport people or objects across a body of water. When David returned to Jerusalem after Absalom's death, a ferryboat carried the king and his household across the Jordan River (2 Sam. 19:18).

FESTIVALS (see FEASTS AND FESTIVALS).

FESTUS, PORCIUS [FESS tuss POUR shih us] — the successor of FELIX as Roman procurator, or governor, of Judea (Acts 24:27). After Festus arrived at Caesarea, he went to Jerusalem and met with the high priest and other Jewish leaders. They informed him of Paul's confinement in prison. Paul had been left in prison when Felix was removed as procurator by the Roman authorities.

The Jewish leaders requested that Paul be brought from Caesarea to Jerusalem so he could be tried before the Jewish Sanhedrin (Acts 25:3). Their real intent, however, was to have Paul killed along the way. Festus refused and told the Jewish leaders they must meet with Paul in Caesarea.

A few days later, Paul was summoned before Festus, who asked if he would be willing to go to Jerusalem. Paul, knowing that danger awaited him on such a trip, used his right as a Roman citizen to appeal to Rome for trial (Acts 25:11).

About this time, Herod Agrippa, with his sister, Bernice, came to Caesarea to visit Festus. The result was a meeting between the three and Paul in which Paul was declared innocent. But because Paul had appealed to Caesar, he had to be sent to Rome (Acts 26:32).

FETTERS [FET turs] — shackles or chains attached to the ankles of prisoners to restrain movement (Ps. 105:18). Fetters were usually made of iron or bronze.

FEVER (see DISEASES OF THE BIBLE).

FIDELITY — faithfulness, loyalty. The word occurs only once (Titus 2:10). The apostle Paul wrote to Titus instructing him to exhort slaves to show "all good fidelity" to their own masters.

FIELD — a plot of open ground that might be used for many different purposes. The word field may refer to a place for hunting game (Gen. 27:5), a cultivated plot for planting crops (Ruth 2:3), or a place for grazing livestock (Gen. 34:5). A field could range in size from a small plot of land to a large territory.

Generally a field was not closed in; it was sometimes contrasted with enclosed land, such as a vineyard (Ex. 22:5). The boundaries separating fields were marked by stones that could be easily removed (Deut. 19:14). Because there were no fences to keep them in, the flocks and herds needed constant watching and tending to prevent them from straying. Fields were sometimes named for events, as in Field of Sharp Swords (2 Sam. 2:16) or for their uses, as in Fuller's Field (Is. 7:3) or potter's field (Matt. 27:7).

FIELD OF SHARP SWORDS — an area near the pool of Gibeon that became the scene of bloody combat between Israel and Judah (2 Sam. 2:16; Field of Blades, NEB; Helkath-hazzurim, RSV). Here 12 of Abner's men (servants of Ishbosheth, king of Israel) and 12 of Joab's men (servants of David, king of Judah) battled one another until every man was dead.

FIFE (see MUSICAL INSTRUMENTS).

FIG, FIG TREE (see PLANTS OF THE BIBLE).

FIGUREHEAD — a carved figure on the front of a ship. The Alexandrian ship on which the apostle Paul sailed to Rome had a figurehead (Acts 28:11; sign, KJV).

FILE (see TOOLS OF THE BIBLE).

FILLY — a young female horse or a lively, high-spirited girl. The Beloved in the Song of Solomon compared the Shulamite (a Palestinian young woman) to "a filly among Pharaoh's chariots" (Song 1:9; Pharaoh's chariot-horses, NEB; a company of horses, KJV; a mare, RSV, NASB, NIV). In the ancient world, where both horses and women were excessively adorned, this was considered a high compliment.

FILTH, FILTHINESS — in a literal sense, foul or dirty matter; in a figurative sense, ceremonial uncleanness or spiritual corruption. "All our righteousnesses," declared the prophet Isaiah, "are like filthy rags" (Is. 64:6). But God will forgive and cleanse the sinner who repents and believes in Christ (1 John 1:7–9).

FINE, FINES (see LAW).

FINER (see OCCUPATIONS AND TRADES).

FINGER — a part of the hand. In the Bible, the word can refer to the literal fingers of a human (Lev. 4:6) or, figuratively, to the power of God. The "finger of God" thus brought about the plagues in Egypt (Ex. 8:19), wrote the Ten Commandments on two tablets of stone (Deut. 9:10), and made the heavens (Ps. 8:3). In the New Testament, Jesus said, "If I cast out demons with the finger ("by the Spirit," Matt. 12:28) of God, surely the kingdom of God has come upon you" (Luke 11:20). Evidently, the "finger of God" refers to God's power working through the Holy Spirit to accomplish His work and will.

FINING POT — KJV words for REFINING POT.

FINISHER — a person who completes a project. The word is applied to Christ (Heb. 12:2). The Greek root refers to completing or bringing to an end or finish.

FINS — hard, scaly objects on fish, used as a distinguishing mark to separate fish into CLEAN and UNCLEAN foods under the law of Moses. Fish with fins could be eaten, while those without scales or fins were prohibited as foods (Lev. 11:9; Deut. 14:9, 10).

FIR, FIR TREE (see PLANTS OF THE BIBLE).

FIRE — the combustion of flammable materials. In the Bible, fire often appears as a symbol of God's presence and power.

The Israelites and other ancient cultures placed great value on fire. They used it to provide light, cook food, heat their houses, and forge their tools and weapons. The Israelites, particularly, thought of fire as a symbol of God's mystical presence as well as His power and judgment.

Fire worship was practiced in many cultures of the ancient world, including the Medes, the Persians, and the Canaanites. In an effort to appease their gods, the Canaanites even sacrificed their children on flaming altars (Deut. 12:31). God often warned Israel that this practice was an abomination to Him and that they should not participate in their neighbors' sin (Ezek. 16:20, 21; 2 Chron. 28:3).

In the Old Testament, fire and flame were closely associated with Israel's worship and religious life. On God's instructions, a fire was kept burning continuously on the altars where burnt offerings were sacrificed (Lev. 6:13). The consumption of offerings by flame assured them that God had accepted the people's sacrifices (Judg. 6:21; 1 Kin. 18:38).

God also used fire to guide His people. God spoke to Moses in the burning bush experience and called him to lead the children of Israel out of Egyptian bondage (Ex. 3:2–12). In their wilderness wanderings, the Israelites relied each night on a PILLAR OF FIRE from heaven to guide them in their travels (Ex. 13:21).

Numerous references to fire in the Bible emphasize God's judgment on wickedness and unbelief. God is represented as a "consuming fire" (Ex. 24:17; Deut. 4:24; Heb. 12:29). The prophet Amos warned Israel, "Seek the Lord and live, lest He break out like a fire in the house of Joseph and devour it" (Amos 5:6). In the New Testament, eternal damnation is pictured as an everlasting fire (1 Cor. 3:13; Rev. 21:8). Fire from heaven is described as an instrument of God's wrath to crush the satanic rebellion (Rev. 20:9, 10).

As a source of heat and light, fire is often pictured in the Bible as God's agent to purify and illuminate. The coming Messenger of the Lord is portrayed as a "refiner's fire" (Mal. 3:2). The tongues "as of fire" which came with the descent of the Holy Spirit at Pentecost underscored the purging and illuminating quality of God's truth (Acts 2:3).

FIRE BAPTISM (see BAPTISM OF FIRE).

FIRE, LAKE OF (see HINNOM, VALLEY OF).

FIREBRAND — a burning stick taken out of the fire. The prophet Amos described the nation of Israel as "a firebrand plucked from the burning" (Amos 4:11)—a figure of speech describing a narrow escape.

FIREPAN — a metal utensil to transport live coals used in starting a fire (Ex. 27:3). The firepans in the tabernacle were made of bronze. Also see CENSER.

FIRMAMENT — the expanse of sky and space in which the stars and planets are set. God made the firmament on the second day of creation to divide the waters that covered the earth from those which surrounded it (Gen. 1:16). But the firmament includes more than the atmospheric region between the seas of earth and the rain clouds of the sky; it is far more vast. In fact, on the fourth day of creation God placed the stars, the sun, and the moon in the "firmament of the heavens" (Gen. 1:15–18).

It is this vastness which the Hebrew writers tend to emphasize about the firmament. The writer of Psalm 150 pointed out that the firmament is "mighty" (v. 1). The prophet Ezekiel envisioned the firmament "like the color of an awesome crystal, stretched out over...[men's] heads" (Ezek. 1:22). What the firmament reflects, then, is the greatness of the God who created it. We are urged to praise God because "the firmament shows His handiwork" (Ps. 19:1). God's people can look forward to a day when they will "shine like the brightness of the firmament" (Dan. 12:3).

FIRST–BEGOTTEN (see FIRSTBORN).

FIRSTBORN — the first offspring of human beings or animals.

In memory of the death of Egypt's firstborn and the divine protection of Israel's firstborn in connection with the EXODUS, God placed a special claim on the firstborn of man and beast (Ex. 13:11–13). This meant that the nation of Israel attached unusual value to the eldest son and assigned special privileges and responsibilities to him.

Because of God's claim on the first offspring, the firstborn sons of the Hebrews were presented to the Lord when they were a month old. Since the firstborn was regarded as God's property, it was necessary for the father to redeem, or buy back, the child from the priest. The redemption price, established by the priest, could not exceed five shekels (Num. 18:16).

Early Hebrew laws also provided that the firstlings of beasts belonged to the Lord and were turned over to the sanctuary (Ex. 13:2; 34:19; Lev. 27:26). The clean animals—those that could be eaten under the law of Moses—were sacrificed to the Lord. The unclean beasts were either destroyed,

Fishermen with their catch in the Sea of Galilee.

Photo by Howard Vos

replaced, or redeemed at a price set by the priest.

In Israel, the firstborn son was loved in a special way by his parents and inherited special rights and privileges. His BIRTHRIGHT was a double portion of the estate and leadership of the family. As head of the home after his father's death, the eldest son customarily cared for his mother until her death, and provided for his unmarried sisters until their marriage. He was the family's spiritual head and served as its priest.

The inheritance rights of the firstborn son were sometimes transferred to a younger brother. Jacob, for example, stripped Reuben of his firstborn rights because of his incestuous conduct and transferred the birthright to his son Joseph (Gen. 48:20–22; 1 Chr. 5:1).

In figurative language, the term firstborn stands for that which is most excellent. This expression is applied to Jesus in several New Testament passages. All of them point to Jesus' high standing and His unique relationship to His Father and the Church.

In Colossians 1:15, Jesus is described as the "firstborn over all creation," indicating that He existed before creation and actually participated in the creation process (John 1:3). His unique birth to the Virgin Mary is depicted by the expression, "brought forth her firstborn son" (Matt. 1:25). The phrase, "firstborn from the dead" (Col. 1:18; Rev. 1:5), refers to Jesus' resurrection, which assures victory over sin and death to all who trust in Him.

Paul's description of Christ as "firstborn among many brethren" (Rom. 8:29) refers to His exalted position as head of the Church. Because of His atoning death and resurrection, Jesus Christ heads a new spiritual race of twice–born men and women (Col. 1:18). The author of Hebrews foresees a joyful gathering of "the church of the firstborn who are registered in heaven" (Heb. 12:23).

FIRSTFRUITS — the firstborn of the flocks and the first vegetables and grains to be gathered at harvest time. The Hebrew people thought of these as belonging to God in a special sense. They were dedicated or presented to God on the day of the firstfruits, a part of the celebration of PENTECOST (Num. 28:26; 2 Chr. 31:5).

FIRST GATE (see GATES OF JERUSALEM AND THE TEMPLE).

FIRSTLING — the firstborn of animals or the first of the harvest from a crop. Abel brought the firstlings of his flock as an offering to God (Gen. 4:4). The law of the FIRSTBORN is recorded in Exodus 13:11–16.

FISH (see ANIMALS OF THE BIBLE).

FISH GATE (see GATES OF JERUSALEM AND THE TEMPLE).

FISHERMAN (see OCCUPATIONS AND TRADES).

FISHER OWL (see ANIMALS OF THE BIBLE).

FISHHOOK — a special hook of bone or iron used for catching and holding fish. The prophet Amos warned the people of Samaria that God would "take you away with fishhooks, and your posterity with fishhooks" (Amos 4:2). This probably referred to the common practice among conquering nations, such as Egypt and Assyria, of placing fishhooks in the mouths of captives to make them easier to handle. This was a clear prediction by the prophet that the people of the northern kingdom of Israel would be carried into captivity.

FISHING — the practice of catching fish for food or for sale as a commercial product. Although the Jews were not really a seagoing people, fishing was an important industry and a source of considerable

Photo by Howard Vos

Engraved stone tablet from Babylon which describes a great flood. Unlike the Babylonian stories, the biblical account of the Flood emphasizes the sin of man and the power and moral judgment of God.

revenue. The Mediterranean Sea provided many different species of salt–water fish. Lake Huleh and the Sea of Galilee were the center of the fresh–water fishing business. Hunting and fishing for sport were unknown.

Many of the fish caught were used fresh. But the close proximity of the salt deposits at the Dead Sea made it possible to preserve large quantities of fish for shipping long distances. Taricheae on the western shore of the Sea of Galilee was the major center of the salting and preserving industry.

Commercial fishing was hard work and often was frustrating and ineffective (Luke 5:4–6; John 21:1–3). Lines and hooks (Job 41:1; Amos 4:10), as well as harpoons (Job 41:7) were used. But the most common method of fishing was with nets.

A small casting net could be handled by one man standing on the shore (Eccl. 9:12; Ezek. 47:10; Matt. 4:18). The larger drag nets required several people in boats for effective operation. Such drag nets had wooden floats on the top edge and stone or metal weights on the bottom. A cord was usually threaded along the bottom edge. This allowed the bottom to be drawn shut to trap the fish as the boat closed the circle of the net around them. Then they were either unloaded into the boats (Luke 5:6–8), or dragged to the shore where the fish were removed and sorted (Matt. 13:47–48).

According to the Jewish law (Lev. 11:9–12; Deut. 14:9–10), only fish that had fins and scales were ritually "clean" and could be eaten. All others, including catfish, eels, etc., and the various shellfish (clams, lobsters, etc.), were "unclean" and forbidden as food.

Of Jesus' first disciples, at least seven were fishermen—Peter, Andrew, Philip, James, John, Thomas, and Nathanael. At Jesus' call they left their nets to follow him and "catch men" (Luke 5:10).

FITCH (see PLANTS OF THE BIBLE).

FLAG (see STANDARD).

FLAGON [FLAY gon] — KJV word for RAISIN CAKES.

FLANGE — a connecting clamp or collar on the bronze carts in Solomon's Temple (1 Kin. 7:35–36; ledges, KJV; stays, RSV, NASB; supports, NIV).

FLANK — the fleshy part of the side between the ribs and the hip. The term refers to the part of an animal sacrifice burned along with the kidneys and the liver (Lev. 3:4). The Hebrew word for flank is used twice to refer to the corresponding part of man: "waist" (Job 15:27) and "loins" (Ps. 38:7).

FLASK — a container usually narrowed toward

the outlet and used for holding liquids such as oil, ointment, or perfume. Samuel used a flask of oil to anoint Saul as king of Israel (1 Sam. 10:1). Elisha the prophet sent one of his apprentice prophets with a flask of oil to anoint Jehu king of Israel (2 Kin. 9:1, 3).

The Lord told the prophet Jeremiah to take "a potter's earthen flask" and break it (Jer. 19:1, 10) as a sign of divine judgment against Jerusalem. In the house of Simon the leper, a woman of Bethany anointed the head of Jesus with a very expensive ointment, of pure nard, which she poured from an alabaster flask (Mark 14:3).

FLAT NOSE (see DISABILITIES AND DEFORMITIES).

FLAX (see PLANTS OF THE BIBLE).

FLEA (see ANIMALS OF THE BIBLE).

FLEECE — the coat of wool shorn from a sheep. Gideon used a fleece in a test to determine if God would deliver the nation of Israel from their enemies (Judg. 6:37–40).

FLESH — the physical bodies of humans or animals. When God removed a rib from Adam with which he created Eve, he closed up the place with flesh (Gen. 2:21). The apostle Paul spoke of the flesh of men, beasts, fish, and birds (1 Cor. 15:39).

The imagery of flesh expresses several different ideas in the Bible. Rather than only the "fleshy" parts of the body, the word could also refer to the entire body (Gal. 5:13). From this idea, the concept of a fleshly or human bond between people follows. A man and his wife "shall become one flesh" (Gen. 2:24), while a man can tell his family that "I am your own flesh and bone" (Judg. 9:2). "Flesh" is even used occasionally to describe all of mankind, and even animals (Gen. 6:3).

Biblical writers thought of the flesh as weak. The Psalmist sang, "In God I have put my trust; I will not fear. What can flesh do to me?" (Ps. 56:4). The weakness of the flesh was blamed for the disciples' inability to keep watch with Jesus in Gethsemane on the eve of His crucifixion (Mark 14:38).

In an even stronger sense, flesh is the earthly part of man, representing lusts and desires (Eph. 2:3). The flesh is contrary to the Spirit (Gal. 5:17). Those who are in the flesh cannot please God (Rom. 8:8). Galatians 5:19–23 contrasts works of the flesh with the fruit of the Spirit. The flesh is not completely condemned, however, for Christ Himself was described as being "in the flesh" (1 John 4:2). Christ alone is our salvation, since by the works of the law "no flesh shall be justified" (Gal. 2:16).

FLESH HOOK — an implement with three prongs used by the sons of Eli to handle meat provided for sacrifices in the tabernacle (1 Sam. 2:13, 14). The KJV also uses this word for an implement used in the Temple (Ex. 27:3; Num. 4:14; fork, NKJV). Both these tools were probably a three–pronged fork.

FLESH POT — KJV words for a large metal pot used for boiling water or cooking meat (Ex. 16:3; pots of meat, NKJV). These were used by the Hebrews during their years of slavery in Egypt (Ex. 16:3).

FLINT (see MINERALS OF THE BIBLE).

FLOCK — a herd of animals that consisted of a mixture of sheep and goats in Bible times. Both animals grazed and traveled together (Gen. 30:31–32). The animals in such mixed flocks were difficult to tell apart except at close range. This explains Jesus' teaching about separating sheep from goats at the last judgment (Matt. 25:32). In Old Testament times, the size of one's flocks and herds was a measure of wealth (1 Sam. 25:2; Job 1:3).

FLOOD, THE — the Lord's destruction of the world by water during the time of Noah.

The inspired writer of Genesis took two chapters to tell of the creation of the world and one chapter to portray sin, but he devoted four chapters to the Flood. Since the concern of the writer was to reveal the nature of God and His dealings with mankind, he evidently saw this story as a good vehicle for this truth. The Flood reveals both the judgment and the mercy of God.

Archaeologists have discovered a number of flood stories among pagan nations in the ancient world. One Sumerian and two Babylonian stories have survived. A comparison of these stories with the Flood account in Genesis is both interesting and significant.

In one of the Babylonian stories, the gods became irritated with the people because they grew too numerous and became too noisy; so they considered several different ways to get rid of these bothersome people. Finally, they decided on a flood. But the flood apparently got out of hand. For a while the gods were afraid they would be destroyed. They began to quarrel among themselves, shrinking in fear from the rising waters and crowding around a sacrifice like flies.

In stark contrast to this pagan story, the Book of Genesis presents the holy and sovereign God who acted in judgment against sin and yet mercifully saved Noah and his family because of their righteousness.

The Flood was not simply a downpour of ordinary rain. The text indicates a cosmic upheaval. "The fountains of the great deep" were broken up (Gen. 7:11). Perhaps there were earthquakes and the ocean floors may have been raised up until the waters covered the earth. By a supernatural upheaval, God returned the earth to the primitive chaos described in Genesis 1:2.

A Degenerate Humanity. The Flood was a drastic judgment, but the condition that brought it to pass was also serious. Society degenerated to the point that "every intent" of the thoughts of man's heart "was only evil continually" (Gen. 6:5). Violence raged upon earth. Instead of living responsibly as persons created in the image and likeness of God, people existed as beasts. Because the situation was hopeless, God chose to destroy that generation and make a new start with the family of righteous Noah.

The Divine Grief. While the minds of men were filled with every kind of evil, the heart of God was filled with grief and sorrow. Like a parent whose children have gone bad, God mourned for his wayward children. The Lord was sorry He had created man and "was grieved in his heart" (Gen. 6:6).

Since God knows the end from the beginning, how could He be sorry for what He had done? This was the biblical writer's way of showing the extreme disappointment of the Lord and the radical change in His attitude and action toward humanity. He had blessed the race, but now He would turn against the wicked people who refused to repent. Their failure to repent caused God to repent, or turn around, in his approach to humanity.

Righteous Noah. In stark contrast to the degenerate people among whom he lived, "Noah was a just man" who "walked with God" (Gen. 6:9). God's righteous judgment is seen in the destruction of the wicked, but His mercy and care are seen in His saving of Noah and, through him, the human race. God's judgment was accompanied by grief, but His grace was freely given to Noah and his family.

The Ark. The Lord revealed to Noah that His judgment was coming by way of a terrible flood. Noah could save himself and his family by building an ark of gopher, or balsam, wood. The ark was to be large enough to hold Noah, his wife, his three sons, and their wives. In addition, it must provide room for two of every kind of animal and bird. Plenty of time was allowed for this massive building project by Noah and his sons.

The dimensions of the ark were 140 meters (450 feet) long, 22 meters (75 feet) wide, and 14 meters (45 feet) high. There were three levels—lower, middle, and upper decks. The displacement or capacity of a vessel of these dimensions has been estimated as 43,300 tons.

The Long Voyage. The raging waters kept rising for 40 days, and the ark floated high above the hills and mountains. When the waters finally stopped rising, Noah and his passengers faced a long wait for the waters to go down. The total time spent in the ark was about one year and ten days. The ark came to rest on Mount Ararat in what is now Turkey. Numerous attempts across the centuries to find the ark or some trace of it have proved futile.

Noah released a raven and a dove to determine whether the waters were low enough to allow them to leave the ark. When the dove returned to the ark, he knew it had been unable to survive outside the ark. After seven days, he again released the dove. This time it came back with an olive leaf. This was good news, indicating that the waters had dropped further and the time when they could leave the ark was near. Finally the earth dried, and the people and animals left the ark (Gen. 8:7–19).

Worship and Covenant. The first act of the grateful Noah was to build an altar and worship God, thanking Him for deliverance from the Flood. Then the Lord made a covenant with Noah. Never again would He destroy the world by water. The rainbow was given as a pledge. The bow was an instrument of war, but the rainbow represents a bow with the string on the ground—a symbol of peace.

The Flood came upon the earth as a severe judgment of God against wickedness. But God's grace and mercy were also revealed in the preservation of Noah and, through him, the human race. The covenant was granted to reassure humanity about God's care.

New Testament References to the Flood. References to the Flood are found in Matthew 24:38; Luke 17:26, 27; Hebrews 11:7; 1 Peter 3:20; and 2 Peter 2:5. The Flood was used to illustrate the holy God's wrath against man's wickedness and the salvation of His people.

FLOOR — a stone or clay platform used for threshing grain (threshing floor, Num. 15:20) or the

Wheat—an important source of food in Palestine—growing in a terraced field on a Judean hillside.
Photo by Willem A. VanGemeren

part of a house on which the residents walked. In a house or building of Palestine, the floors were formed from beaten clay. Also see HOUSE.

FLOUR — ground grain from which bread is baked (Ex. 29:2; 1 Sam. 28:24). The flour of Bible times was a fine substance made from wheat, with all the bran removed. The Hebrew word for flour is often translated as "fine flour" (Lev. 14:10; Num. 29:14).

FLOWERS (see PLANTS OF THE BIBLE).

FLUTE (see MUSICAL INSTRUMENTS).

FLY (see ANIMALS OF THE BIBLE).

FOAL — the young offspring of a donkey—the animal on which Jesus rode in His triumphal entry into Jerusalem. By riding such a lowly animal, Jesus entered the city not as a conquering hero but as the Prince of Peace bearing the good news of a spiritual kingdom (Matt. 21:5).

FODDER — feed for livestock, consisting of a mixture of grains and vegetation left over after the most desirable parts of the harvest were gathered (Job 6:5).

FOLD (see SHEEPFOLD).

FOOD — nourishing substances eaten by man and animals. Palestine, the land of the Bible, was called a land of "milk and honey" (Ex. 13:5). Food was plentiful, although hard labor was required for its production. Lack of rainfall or other weather conditions sometimes caused meager crops.

After conquering and settling the land of Canaan, the Hebrew people became farmers. This was different from the nomadic life of their forefathers. Their diet reflected the change, because tillers of the soil eat differently than shepherds and herdsmen. The land which they worked produced foodstuffs in a variety pleasing to the palate and filling to the stomach. Among these were cereal grains, animal protein, vegetables, fruits and nuts, plus savory spices and herbs to make food tasty.

The cereal grains, often called corn in the KJV, are not to be confused with maize, a product of the western hemisphere unknown in Bible times. The word corn in the KJV should be translated as "wheat," "barley," and "millet." It also included spelt, a species of grain related to wheat but called fitch in the KJV.

In God's command to the prophet Ezekiel (4:9) to make bread, all these grains are mentioned, plus beans and lentils. This mixture for making bread sounds like the ingredients in a modern loaf on the grocer's shelf.

After the grain was harvested, it was ground into flour, mixed and kneaded into dough, and then baked into bread. In Isaiah (3:1) bread is called the "stock" and the "store." The clear meaning of these phrases is that bread was the principal food of the people—the stock and store of life.

But grain could be prepared and eaten in ways other than bread. It could be parched or roasted, or

Photo: Israel Government Press Office

Food was often stored underground in Bible times. Archaeologists discovered remains of grain, beans, and grapes in these underground storage silos that dated back to about 4000 B.C.

it could be cracked and made into a gruel (2 Sam. 17:28).

A distinctive feature of the agricultural economy of the Hebrew people was the provision for poor people to come into the fields of the wealthy to glean behind the harvesters. The story of Ruth reflects this custom. When Boaz, the wealthy kinsman of Naomi's departed husband, saw Ruth in his field, he told his reapers to leave grain for her to gather. At noon he invited her to share his parched grain (Ruth 2:14).

Protein is essential to life; it was readily available to everyone in the land of Palestine. Meat was part of every person's daily fare. Animal products such as milk, butter, and cheese were also readily available. A noon meal for a workman might consist of two loaves of barley bread—one filled with cheese, the other with olives.

Animals were divided into two distinct classes among the Hebrew people—clean and unclean (Lev. 11:1–47; Acts 10:9–15). The law governing this distinction dealt with four-footed animals as well as fish, birds, and insects. Only clean animals could be used for food. Clean animals were those that chewed the cud and had divided hooves (Lev. 11:3). Pigs have divided hooves, but they do not chew the cud. Therefore, they were ceremonially unclean and unfit for food. Camels chew the cud, but they do not have parted hooves. So they could not be eaten. Camel's milk and cheese from their milk, however, were not forbidden.

The effort to connect these unclean foods with modern practices of hygiene breaks down in details. But some forbidden foods did serve as health precautions. Pork is an example. It must be cooked at high temperatures to kill the dreaded parasite that can cause spiralis. The people of the land never heard of trichinosis, but they were protected from it by their food laws.

Animal fat was also forbidden as food (Lev. 3:16–17). While fat is essential to good health, it becomes extremely dangerous when eaten in large amounts that can cause a buildup of cholesterol. When Nehemiah urged the people to "eat the fat" (Neh. 8:10, NKJV), he used a word which is better translated as "dainties." He may have been referring to a rich confection or a tasty dessert. He neither forgot nor overlooked the dietary restrictions of the Hebrew food laws.

Fish of some types could be eaten (Lev. 11:9–12). A total of 20 different species of birds was rejected (11:13–19). Insects which had legs and leaped, such as the grasshopper, were fit for food.

Oysters and shrimp, which fell within the forbidden list, spoil quickly and become unfit for food in a hot atmosphere with no refrigeration.

Even the most humble people of Palestine had adequate protein in their diet. As is true in all agricultural societies, every family had land to till. The citizens of Palestine kept animals for heavy work and tended sheep for fiber. These animals yielded milk, cheese, and meat and even provided fiber such as wool for the making of clothing.

But bread, meat, milk, and cheese are not enough for a balanced diet. Other foods are necessary to maintain strong and healthy life. Other essential nutrients came from fruits, vegetables, and nuts which the land yielded in bountiful fashion.

While enslaved in Egypt, the Hebrew people learned to enjoy vegetables. During their years of wandering in the wilderness, they missed their cucumbers, melons, leeks, onions, and garlic (Num. 11:5). They also longed for their "pots of meat" (Ex. 16:3), which were stew pots, filled with simmering meat and vegetables.

Once settled in the land of Canaan, the Hebrew people cultivated these favorite vegetables, plus beans, lentils, and squash. The squash which they cultivated may have been one of the "melons" which they had learned to eat in Egypt many years before.

The abundance of food cultivated in Palestine is indicated by the list of provisions which Abigail furnished David in the desert of Paran (1 Sam. 25:18). Included was bread, wine, mutton, roasted grain, clusters of raisins, and cakes of figs.

Abigail's clusters of raisins were pressed into cakes with the stems still intact. Grapes or raisins might be made into a raisin cake, as she had done, but they could also be eaten fresh, or pressed for their juice. In time the fresh-pressed juice could be turned into vinegar or WINE.

Along with raisins Abigail brought figs, also dried and pressed into cakes. She may have brought apricots dried and pressed the same way, or fresh oranges. The land produced both of these fruits. Honey was also available, because the land had both wild and domesticated bees. Honey was made from dates as well. From a small garden she might have brought mint, anise, dill, and cummin. Certainly she could have brought almonds—or pistachios. These trees were common in Palestine. Olives were also plentiful. Olive orchards were

Watchtowers, like this one near Shiloh, were used by farmers to protect their crops from thieves and intruders.
Photo by Howard Vos

scattered throughout the land. The olive was eaten green or ripe. Or, it might be pressed for its oil. Olive oil was used for cooking and seasoning, and as fuel for lamps.

Perhaps Abigail brought salt; an abundant supply was available from the nearby Sea of Salt, or DEAD SEA. But she probably brought no pepper. This seasoning is not mentioned in either the Old or New Testament.

FOOL, FOOLISHNESS, FOLLY — a stupid person or a senseless act. In the Bible, the most foolish person of all is one who denies the reality of God the Father: "The fool has said in his heart, 'There is no God' " (Ps. 14:1; 53:1). Jesus also contrasted wise and foolish persons. Persons who keep His sayings are wise; those who do not are foolish (Matt. 7:24–27). The use of the word fool in Matthew 5:22 is a special case. Jesus warned against using the word fool as a form of abuse. This word expressed hatred in one's heart toward others; therefore, Jesus condemned the use of the word in this way.

The apostle Paul called the preaching of Christ crucified "foolishness" in the eyes of unbelievers. For believers, however, the message of the cross is the power and wisdom of God (1 Cor. 1:23–24).

FOOT — the lower extremity of the leg. The Bible uses the word both literally and symbolically.

Feet is used in the Bible in many symbolic ways. "To sit at the feet" of a teacher was a symbol of discipleship, recalling the practice of the Jewish schools and synagogues (Acts 22:3). "To fall at the feet" was a gesture of humility (1 Sam. 25:24). "To put under the feet" was symbolic of conquest (Josh. 10:24). In this way Egyptian monuments picture conquerors walking on the defeated. The Lord promised to tread the Assyrians under foot (Is. 14:25).

In Bible times, washing a guest's feet was an act of hospitality (Luke 7:44) and humility (John 13:4–15). To remove the sandals from one's feet was an expression of worship and reverence (Ex. 3:5). Before one entered a holy place, it was necessary for him to remove his shoes.

FOOTMAN (see OCCUPATIONS AND TRADES).

FOOTSTOOL — a piece of furniture for resting a person's feet. The word is often used symbolically in the Bible to signify God's promise to Israel to "make your enemies your footstool" (Ps. 110:1). This messianic promise is repeated six times in the New Testament (Matt. 22:44; Mark 12:36; Luke 20:43; Acts 2:35; Heb. 1:13; 10:13).

FOOT–WASHING — an expression of hospitality extended to guests in Bible times. People traveling dusty roads in Palestine needed to wash their feet for comfort and cleanliness. Foot–washing was generally performed by the lowliest servant in the household (Luke 7:44). Guests were often offered water and vessels for washing their own feet (Judg. 19:21).

At the Last Supper, Jesus washed His disciples' feet. He explained that this act was an example of the humble ministry that they must always be ready to perform for one another (John 13:5–17). First Timothy 5:10 suggests that the early church followed Christ's example in observing the ritual of foot–washing. But many churches reject this because the other duties mentioned in the verse are household tasks. Churches of some denominations continue to practice foot–washing even today.

FORBEARANCE — tolerance or mercy. Although man's sin deserves punishment, God in His forbearance, or longsuffering patience, gives an opportunity for REPENTANCE (Rom. 2:4). Also see LONGSUFFERING.

FORCES (see WAR, WARFARE).

FORD — a shallow place that provides easy passage across a body of water. Fords across three rivers are mentioned in the Bible:

1. The Jordan. Two different fords mentioned are the place where the Israelite spies crossed before the capture of Jericho (Josh. 2:7), and the ford where Israel's Moabite overlords suffered defeat (Judg. 3:28). Both fords were apparently in the region of Jericho.

2. The Jabbok, a narrow but cultivated valley in Transjordan, was crossed by Jacob and his family near Penuel (Gen. 32:22).

3. The Arnon, running westwards to the Dead Sea, and traditionally Moab's northern border (Num. 21:13), was a deep gorge crossed by a number of fords (Is. 16:2).

FOREHEAD — part of the face above the eyes. The forehead was one area where skin disease, such as leprosy, could be identified (Lev. 13:41–44). David killed Goliath with a stone to the forehead (1 Sam. 17:49).

Since the forehead is so prominent, it is a proper place for an identifying seal. It is the location of a holy mark for the Israelite high priest (Ex. 28:38), God's 144,000 end–time servants (Rev. 14:1), and people living in New Jerusalem (Rev. 22:4). The great harlot and the beast's followers will have evil marks on their foreheads (Rev. 13:16).

The Israelites were ordered to know God's law so well that it would be as if it was written across their foreheads (Deut. 6:8). Many Jews took this literally, and the custom of wearing PHYLACTERIES developed. Symbolically, the set of someone's forehead might mean rebellion (Ezek. 3:8–9).

FOREIGNER — a person whose citizenship and loyalty belong to a different country. The "foreigner" (or "outsider") mentioned often in the Bible was distinct from the "sojourner." The sojourner belonged to another nation; but, unlike the foreigner, he came to live (or sojourn) for a period of time away from his home country, perhaps taking on some obligations and enjoying some privileges in his new land.

In the English Bible it is not always easy to distinguish between these uses of the words, especially since stranger is sometimes used for foreigner, sometimes for sojourner. In Exodus 12, for instance, the "outsider"—the stranger who is a foreigner—is not to eat of the Passover (v. 43). But the stranger who sojourns among the Israelites, and whose males are circumcised, is allowed to eat the Passover (vv. 48–49). Other regulations dealing especially with foreigners may be found in Deuteronomy 14:21; 15:3; 23:20.

Usually the term foreigner in the Bible means someone who is foreign to the Hebrew people. Because Israel was to be a special nation, there was a great danger that the Israelites would be influenced by the ways of other nations and, in the process, lose something of their special identity. That is why the Old Testament is full of references to the perils of foreign or strange gods (Josh. 24:20, 23; Jer. 5:19) and foreign or strange women (1 Kin. 11:1; Prov. 2:16; 5:20). That is also why foreigners or outsiders were not permitted to take part in Israel's worship (Ex. 12:43; Ezek. 44:9). On the other hand, among the prophecies of a glorious future for Israel are some in which foreigners who come to worship the Lord are given an honored place (Is. 56:3–8).

In New Testament times, the lines between Jews and foreigners were sharply drawn. Jews were expected not to eat with foreigners (Acts 11:3; Gal. 2:12). Some Jewish Christians still insisted on these distinctions and were offended when other Jewish believers ate with Gentiles. But the apostle Paul insisted that the barriers between Jews and foreigners had been broken down in Jesus Christ (Eph. 2:11–3:6). Both Jews and Gentiles could belong to God's new people, the church, through faith in Christ (Rom. 1:16; 4:11–12; Gal. 3:26–29).

FOREKNOWLEDGE — the unique knowledge of God which enables Him to know all events, including the free acts of man, before they happen.

God's foreknowledge is much more than foresight. God does not know future events and the actions of men because He foresees them; He knows them because He wills them to happen (Job 14:5; Ps. 139:15–16). Thus God's foreknowledge is an act of His will (Is. 41:4; Rev. 1:8, 17; 21:6).

In Romans 8:29 and 11:2, the apostle Paul's use of the word foreknew means "to choose" or "to set special affection on." The electing love of God, not foresight of human action, is the basis of His predestination and salvation (Rom. 8:29–30, 33). This same idea is used to express the nation of Israel's special relationship to God (Acts 2:23; Rom. 11:2; 1 Pet. 1:2, 20).

FOREMAN (see OCCUPATIONS AND TRADES).

FORERUNNER — one who goes (literally, runs) before. The word is used only once in the New Testament to describe Jesus, who has opened a new and living way to God as our Savior and High Priest (Heb. 6:20).

FORESKIN — skin covering the end of the male sex organ. The foreskin was cut off in the rite of CIRCUMCISION, the sign of the Abrahamic covenant (Gen. 17:10–25). Males had their foreskin removed eight days after birth (Lev. 12:3). Because circumcision was a sign of the covenant with God, the word foreskin symbolically represented rebellion against God. Thus, the Israelites were told to "circumcise the foreskin of your heart" (Jer. 4:4); or to give up their disobedience.

FOREST — a grove or thicket of trees. Forests were far more common in ancient Israel than they are in the Holy Land today. Forests were especially abundant in the hills of Lebanon, Carmel, Bashan, the Sharon plain, and the Jordan valley. Extensive deforestation began even before the time of Abraham (around 2000 B.C.) with the continuing demand for timber, especially for building (2 Chr. 27:4; Neh. 2:8), fuel (Is. 44:14–15), and agriculture (Is. 29:17).

The forests spoken of in the Bible included everything from rough scrubland (Ezek. 20:46; rough country, NEB) to impenetrable jungle. The forest was a place of fear and of wild animals (Ps. 104:20), especially lions (Amos 3:4); but it belonged to God and would ultimately praise Him (Ps. 96:12; Is. 44:23).

The prophets often spoke of forests in a symbolic way. Forests represented both human pride (2 Kin. 19:23; Is. 10:34) and people who were ready for judgment, whether as the lion's prey (Is. 56:9; Jer. 5:6) or as fuel for the fire (Is. 9:18–19; 10:18–19). But the forest also was a picture of luxuriant growth, symbolizing the fruitfulness and glory of those on whom God poured His Spirit (Is. 32:15; 35:2).

FORGE (see TOOLS OF THE BIBLE).

FORGER (see OCCUPATIONS AND TRADES).

FORGIVENESS — the act of excusing or pardoning another in spite of his slights, shortcomings, and errors. As a theological term, forgiveness refers to God's pardon of the sins of human beings.

No religious book except the Bible teaches that God completely forgives sin (Ps. 51:1, 9; Is. 38:17; Heb. 10:17). The initiative comes from Him (John 3:16; Col. 2:13) because He is ready to forgive (Luke 15:11–32). He is a God of grace and pardon (Neh. 9:17; Dan. 9:9).

Sin deserves divine punishment because it is a violation of God's holy character (Gen. 2:17; Rom. 1:18–32; 1 Pet. 1:16), but His pardon is gracious (Ps. 130:4; Rom. 5:6–8). In order for God to forgive sin, two conditions are necessary. A life must be taken as a substitute for that of the sinner (Lev. 17:11, 14; Heb. 9:22), and the sinner must come to God's sacrifice in a spirit of repentance and faith (Mark 1:4; Acts 10:43; James 5:15).

Forgiveness in the New Testament is directly linked to Christ (Acts 5:31; Col. 1:14), His sacrificial death on the cross (Rom. 4:24), and His resurrection (2 Cor. 5:15). He was the morally perfect sacrifice (Rom. 8:3), the final and ultimate fulfillment of all Old Testament sacrifices (Heb. 9:11—

10:18). Since He bore the law's death penalty against sinners (Gal. 3:10–13), those who trust in His sacrifice are freed from that penalty. By faith sinners are forgiven—"justified" in Paul's terminology (Rom. 3:28; Gal. 3:8–9). Those who are forgiven sin's penalty also die to its controlling power in their lives (Rom. 6:1–23).

Christ's resurrection was more than proof of His deity or innocence; it was related in a special way to His forgiveness. Christ's resurrection was an act by which God wiped out the false charges against Him; it was God's declaration of the perfect righteousness of His Son, the Second Adam, and of His acceptance of Christ's sacrifice (1 Tim. 3:16). Because He has been acquitted and declared righteous, this is also true for those whom He represents. Thus, Christ's resurrection was a necessary condition for the forgiveness of man's sins (1 Cor. 15:12–28). To be forgiven is to be identified with Christ in His crucifixion and resurrection.

Christ has the authority to forgive sins (Matt. 1:21; Heb. 9:11—10:18). This forgiveness is an essential part of the gospel message (Acts 2:38; 5:31). But blasphemy against the Holy Spirit (attributing to Satan a deed done by Jesus through the power of God's Spirit) is an unpardonable sin (Mark 3:28–29)—not because God cannot or will not forgive such a sin but because such a hard-hearted person has put himself beyond the possibility of repentance and faith.

God's forgiveness of us demands that we forgive others, because grace brings reponsibility and obligation (Matt. 18:23–35; Luke 6:37). Jesus placed no limits on the extent to which Christians are to forgive their fellowmen (Matt. 18:22, 35; Luke 17:4). A forgiving spirit shows that one is a true follower of Christ (Matt. 5:43–48; Mark 11:25).

FORK — a three-pronged pitchfork, a farm tool used as a weapon by Saul's ill-equipped army (1 Sam. 13:21). Special forks of bronze and gold were also used by the priests to handle animal sacrifices in the tabernacle and Temple (Ex. 27:3; 1 Chr. 28:17; fleshhooks, KJV).

FORMER GATE (see GATES OF JERUSALEM AND THE TEMPLE).

FORNICATION [for nih KAY shun] — sexual relationships outside the bonds of marriage. The technical distinction between fornication and ADULTERY is that adultery involves married persons while fornication involves those who are unmarried. But the New Testament often uses the term in a general sense for any unchastity. Of the seven lists of sins found in the writings of the apostle Paul, the word fornication is found in five of them and is first on the list each time (1 Cor. 5:11; Col. 3:5). In the Book of Revelation, fornication is symbolic of how idolatry and pagan religion defiles true worship of God (Rev. 14:8; 17:4).

FORT, FORTIFICATION — the practice of erecting defensive walls around a city in Bible times to

A model of Jerusalem as it might have looked in the time of Jesus. The city was protected by massive walls, fortified gates, and defense towers built into the wall system.

Photo by E. B. Trovillion

protect it from enemy attacks. Such fortifications were not used widely in Palestine until the period of the United Kingdom under David and Solomon. Before that time, the Israelites hid from roving enemy bands in caves and mountain strongholds (Judg. 6:2). The first Israelite city to be fortified was Saul's capital at Gibeah. His successor David used fortifications extensively, especially at the capital city of Jerusalem.

The first fortifications were massive walls around cities. Material for these walls was plentiful in rocky Palestine. Usually these walls were from 5 to 8 meters (15 to 25 feet) thick, and about 8 meters (25 feet) high. Sometimes several of these walls were built around a city for even greater protection.

These massive walls were strengthened at regular intervals by supporting balconies and embankments. Towers were erected on the corners and at obvious points of attack (2 Chr. 14:7; Zeph. 1:16). The tops of these towers looked like rows of teeth with gaps between them. The protective towers were placed at regular intervals along the wall to give the city's defending archers a good vantage point for turning back an attack.

The walls were protected outside the city by a dry moat or an earth ramp heaped against the wall to make direct assault almost impossible. Most towns had only one or two gates. For even greater security, these massive gates were often reinforced with metal, usually bronze (Ps. 107:16; Is. 45:2).

Fortified cities were most often overcome by a prolonged siege from the enemy army. The enemy stationed their forces outside the walls so nothing could get in or out of the fortress. The greatest danger to a city under such a siege was a shortage of water. For this reason a city needed to be situated close to an abundant supply of water. If the water supply was not situated inside the walls, long underground tunnels were sometimes built to provide convenient access during times of siege.

Several methods were used by the attacking army to weaken a city's walls. The Assyrians built earthen causeways so their siege machines, or battering rams, could be rolled up to the wall to break it down. Attackers sometimes tunneled underneath to weaken the walls. Once the walls were weakened, a direct attack was made on the city.

Walled cities that served as Israelite defense posts included Lachish, Beth Horon, Samaria, Jezreel, Geba, and Mizpah. Solomon built fortresses around Jerusalem, Megiddo, Hazor, and Gezer (1 Kin. 9:15) as well as defense outposts across the kingdom for his army. His son Rehoboam fortified 15 more cities (2 Chr. 11:5–12).

FORTIFIED CITIES — cities strengthened by walls, towers, gates and bars (Deut. 3:5).

When the Israelites entered the Promised Land, they found many fortified cities belonging to the

Excavations at Hazor, a city in northern Palestine fortified by Solomon as a military stronghold (1 Kin. 9:15).

Photo by Willem A. VanGemeren

Canaanites and Amorites (Josh. 14:12). The strength of these fortifications is proven by the fact that the Canaanites resisted the Israelite invaders for a long time. Judges 1:27-36 describes the incomplete conquest. Jerusalem, for instance, was still held by the Jebusites until the time of David (1 Chr. 11:5).

After the Israelites occupied the land of Canaan, they rebuilt and improved the broken defenses. King Solomon built "the Millo, the wall of Jerusalem, Hazor, Megiddo, and Gezer" (1 Kin. 9:15). Rehoboam fortified 15 cities in Judah (2 Chr. 11:5-12). Asa fortified Geba and Mizpah (1 Kin. 15:22).

No city could hold out long against a siege without an adequate water supply. A city, therefore, was generally built near a river or a spring. Long tunnels were dug to supply water, as in the case of Hezekiah's tunnel, also called the Siloam tunnel (2 Chr. 32:30), cut through solid rock from the spring of Gihon to the pool of Siloam in Jerusalem—a distance of about 533 meters (1,749 feet).

FORTUNATUS [for chuh NAY tus] (*fortunate*) — a Christian of Corinth who, along with Stephanas and Achaicus, encouraged and comforted the apostle Paul at Ephesus (1 Cor. 16:17). These three men possibly carried Paul's letter (1 Corinthians) with them when they returned to Corinth.

FORTUNE–TELLING — predicting the future through magic and enchantment. At Philippi the apostle Paul healed a slave girl who had brought her masters much profit by fortune-telling (Acts 16:16; soothsaying, KJV, RSV). Also see MAGIC, SORCERY, AND DIVINATION.

FOUNDATION — the strong, stable base on which a building is built. Jesus talked figuratively about foundations in the Sermon on the Mount, teaching that believers should build their faith on the strong foundation of practicing His teachings (Matt. 7:24-27). The apostle Paul also referred to Christ as a foundation for believers (1 Cor. 3:11). Also see HOUSE.

FOUNDATION GATE (see GATES OF JERUSALEM AND THE TEMPLE).

FOUNDER (see OCCUPATIONS AND TRADES).

FOUNTAIN — a water source. Both the NKJV and the KJV use this word to translate several different Hebrew and Greek words. The two main types of fountains were the man–made well, or cistern, and the natural spring. To the Israelites, after 40 years of wandering in the dry wilderness of Sinai, the many fresh water springs of Canaan were a sign of real blessing. In this dry climate it was important that a spring was nearby before a city or village could be established. Thus the Hebrew word for spring, *En*, is preserved today in such biblical place names as En–dor, meaning "the spring of the town of Dor," or En–gedi, "the spring of the wild goat."

When the technique of plastering walls was developed, it made it possible to make storage places

to capture run–off water during a rain. This development made it possible to support larger populations, especially in cities. But the water from these cisterns was never as desirable as the "living water" of natural springs (Jer. 2:13).

FOUNTAIN GATE (see GATES OF JERUSALEM AND THE TEMPLE).

FOWL (see ANIMALS OF THE BIBLE).

FOWLER (see OCCUPATIONS AND TRADES).

FOX (see ANIMALS OF THE BIBLE).

FRANKINCENSE (see PLANTS OF THE BIBLE).

FREEDMAN — a free person, in contrast to a slave, who is still held in bondage. The apostle Paul used this word to describe a person who has been freed by Jesus Christ from bondage to sin (1 Cor. 7:22).

FREEDOM — the absence of slavery; the ability to do and go as one desires. The concept of freedom, both physical and spiritual, is expressed in several different ways in the Bible.

Only God has absolute freedom. He is not controlled from the outside. Human beings, while not totally free, can experience a measure of freedom in different areas of life: social, economic, political, and spiritual.

Slavery was common in biblical times. Many persons served others in bondage. The law of Moses provided for the Year of JUBILEE, when slaves were given the opportunity to gain their freedom (Leviticus 25; 27).

The EXODUS of the people of Israel from Egypt is an example of God's bringing His people into freedom. When the apostle Paul spoke of a free man (Col. 3:11), he referred to rights of citizenship. Politically, in Paul's day, one might be either a citizen of Rome, a free person (Acts 22:28), or a non–citizen, one who was not free under the Roman law. As a free person, Paul had certain rights, especially the right of a fair trial. In Christ, however, distinctions between citizens and non–citizens—"slave" and "free"—disappear (Gal. 3:28). In Christ, all have the glorious freedom of the sons of God.

In the spiritual realm, Jesus explained that when people know the truth, the truth will set them free (John 3:32). He Himself is the Truth (John 14:6). Jesus also declared that if He, the Son of God, set persons free, they would be truly free (John 8:36). Sin enslaves; Christ sets free. The believer in Jesus is released from the stranglehold of sin.

The apostle Paul pointed out that the law, when not properly understood, also enslaves. A mechanical sense of compulsion to obey the law binds and restricts one's freedom. Christ loosens the hold that the law has on Christians (Gal. 5:1, 13).

Set free from sin by Christ, the believer is able to choose service for God (Rom. 6:22). Using the phrase "the Lord's freedman," Paul emphasized the spiritual freedom which belongs to believers (1 Cor. 7:22). The spiritual freedom of other persons becomes the concern of those who have been set free by Christ.

FRIEND — a person whom one loves and trusts; close companion or comrade (Gen. 38:12). Perhaps the most famous friendship in the Bible was that of David and Jonathan (1 Sam. 18:1–4). Abraham was called God's friend (2 Chr. 20:7), and God spoke to Moses "face to face, as a man speaks to his friend" (Ex. 33:11). Jesus said we are His friends if we obey Him (John 15:14).

FRIEND OF THE BRIDEGROOM (see BRIDE-GROOM, FRIEND OF).

FRINGE — KJV word for TASSEL.

FROG (see ANIMALS OF THE BIBLE).

FRONTLET (see PHYLACTERIES).

FROST — a covering of small ice crystals, formed from frozen water vapor, that falls over the land at night during the winter months (Gen. 31:40). God once punished the rebellious nation of Israel by destroying their sycamore trees with frost (Ps. 78:47).

FRUIT (see PLANTS OF THE BIBLE).

FRYING PAN — KJV words for covered pan, a special pan used for baking bread for the meal offering in the TABERNACLE and the TEMPLE (Lev. 2:7).

FUEL — any material burned to produce heat or light. In Palestine, wood and other fuel sources were scarce. The people used almost any burnable substance for fuel. The Bible speaks of grass (Luke 12:28) and dung (Ezek. 4:15) as fuels used for cooking food. Olive oil was used as fuel for lamps (Ex. 25:6).

FULFILL (see PLEROMA).

FULLER (see OCCUPATIONS AND TRADES).

FULLER'S FIELD — a spot just outside the city walls of Jerusalem where fullers, or launderers, washed and dyed clothes and cloth and hung them out to dry (2 Kin. 18:17; Is. 36:2). The place was apparently close to the GIHON SPRING, where an ample supply of water was available. Also see OCCUPATIONS AND TRADES.

FULLER'S SOAP — an alkaline salt or natural lye extracted from Asiatic soap plants which are re-duced to ashes to obtain potash (Mal. 3:2; launderer's soap, NIV).

FULLNESS (see PLEROMA).

FUNERAL — a burial ceremony. The Bible provides few details about the actual rituals involved in burying the dead in ancient Palestine. Corpses were generally buried (Gen. 23:4, 6, 8), but only Joseph is said to have been embalmed and put in a coffin (Gen. 50:26). Mourners at funerals included family members (Gen. 37:34), acquaintances (1 Sam. 15:35) and, at times, professional mourners (Eccl. 12:5).

Mourning customs included weeping (Gen. 23:2), wearing sackcloth (Is. 15:3), cutting one's hair (Jer. 7:29), fasting (2 Sam. 1:11), and throwing ashes on oneself (Ezek. 27:30). A procession of mourners usually carried the corpse to the burial site (2 Sam. 3:31–34).

FURLONG (see WEIGHTS AND MEASURES).

FURNACE (see TOOLS OF THE BIBLE).

FURNACES, TOWER OF THE (see OVENS, TOWER OF THE).

FURNITURE — the furnishings of the tabernacle (Ex. 31:7–9). While this word is never used to describe the furnishings of a household, the furniture in a typical house in Palestine in Bible times included a bed, table, chair, and lampstand.

FURROW — a long, narrow trench in the ground made by a plow. The prophet Hosea declared that God's judgment would spring up against His people's sins "like hemlock in the furrows of the field" (Hos. 10:4).

FURY — violent and intense anger; rage. The Bible speaks often of the "fury of the Lord" (Is. 51:13, 22)—a phrase referring to the judgment of a holy God against man's sinful rebellion. Also see WRATH.

FUTURE — the time that is yet to come (Ps. 37:37–38). After the archangel Gabriel interpreted Daniel's vision, he said to Daniel, "Seal up the vision, for it refers to many days in the future" (Dan. 8:17–26). The Christian believer is confident of the future because he belongs to Jesus Christ.

G

GAAL [GAY al] (*rejection*) — a son of Ebed who led an unsuccessful rebellion by the inhabitants of Shechem against ABIMELECH. Abimelech defeated Gaal and demolished Shechem, sowing it with salt and making it uninhabitable (Judg. 9:26–45).

GAASH [GAY ash] (*trembling*) — a mountain in the hill country of Ephraim. On the north side of Mount Gaash was the village of Timnah Serah (Josh. 24:30), the place where Joshua was buried.

GABA [GAY buh] — a form of GEBA.

GABBAI [GAB eye] (*taxgatherer*) — a chief of the tribe of Benjamin who lived in Jerusalem after the captivity (Neh. 11:8).

GABBATHA [GAB ah thah] (*elevated place*) — the Aramaic name of the place from which Pontius Pilate—the Roman PROCURATOR, or governor, of Judea—pronounced the formal sentence of death by crucifixion against Jesus (John 19:13). Because the Aramaic word means "an elevated place," it was probably a raised platform. Gabbatha has been excavated and identified with a magnificent Roman pavement that made up the courtyard of the Tower of ANTONIA, at the northwest corner of the Temple area.

GABRIEL [GAY brih el] (*God is great*) — an ARCH-ANGEL who acts as the messenger of God; he appeared to Daniel (Dan. 8:16), Zacharias (Luke 1:19), and the Virgin Mary (Luke 1:26–38).

All appearances of Gabriel recorded in the Bible are connected with the promise about the coming of the Messiah. But one passage may link Gabriel with Christ's return. In Christian tradition, Gabriel is sometimes identified as the archangel whose voice is heard at the Second Coming of Christ (1 Thess. 4:16). Although Gabriel is not mentioned by name in this passage, he is sometimes depicted as the trumpeter of the Last Judgment.

GAD [gad] (*good fortune*) — the name of the founder of a tribe in Israel, a prophet, and a pagan god:

1. The seventh of Jacob's twelve sons. Gad was the firstborn of ZILPAH (Leah's maid) and a brother of Asher (Gen. 30:11). Moses praised Gad for his bravery and faithfulness to duty (Deut. 33:20–21). With the possible exception of Ezbon, Gad's seven sons all founded tribal families (Num. 26:15–18).

2. A prophet described as David's "seer" (1 Chr. 21:9). Gad commanded David to buy the threshing floor of Araunah the Jebusite, which became the site of the TEMPLE. Gad the prophet also helped arrange the tabernacle music (2 Chr. 29:25) and is credited with writing an account of David's reign (1 Chr. 29:29).

3. The name of a pagan god (Is. 65:11, NKJV). The name "Gad" appears in compound names, such as Baal Gad (Josh. 11:17) and Migdal Gad (Josh. 15:37).

Also see GODS, PAGAN.

GAD, TRIBE OF — the tribe that sprang from Gad and the territory this tribe inhabited, often referred to as Gilead (Num. 1:14). The territory of Gad lay east of the Jordan River between the half-tribe of Manasseh to the north and the tribe of Reuben to the south. Its western boundary was the Jordan River; on the east it faced the territory of the Ammonites. Gad had few major towns.

When Moses assigned the territory east of the Jordan River to the Gadites, he stipulated that they must cross over the river to help the other tribes in the conquest of Canaan (Num. 32:20–32). They did not always do this, however, most likely because the tribe experienced a great deal of trouble holding its own territory.

GAD, RAVINE OF — a place connected with David's census of the Hebrew nation (2 Sam. 24:5; river of Gad, KJV). The ravine of Gad is probably the Arnon River valley.

GADARA [GAD ah ruh] (*walls*) — a city of TRANSJORDAN about ten kilometers (six miles) southeast of the Sea of Galilee (see Map 6, C–2). Gadara was primarily a Greek city, one of the cities of the DECAPOLIS. It also was the capital city of the Roman province of Perea. The ruins of Gadara, present-day Um Qeis, include two theaters, a basilica, baths, and a street lined with columns. They indicate that at one time Gadara was a large and beautiful city.

Matthew 8:28–34 records that two demon-possessed men of the area of Gadara were healed by Jesus. Mark 5:1–20 and Luke 8:26–39 refer to only one man possessed by unclean spirits. He may have

Photo by Howard Vos

Remains of a church at ancient Gergesa which memorialized Jesus' healing of the demoniac (Matt. 8:28-34). This region along the Sea of Galilee was also known as Gadara and Gerasa.

been the more violent of these two.

Also see GADARENES.

GADARENES [gad uh REENZ] — the inhabitants of GADARA, the capital of the Roman province of Perea. The Gadarenes are mentioned in the account of Jesus' healing of the demon-possessed man (Mark 5:1-20) (or men) (Matt. 8:28-34, NIV, NAS, RSV, NEB). The city was on the east side of the Jordan River, about ten kilometers (six miles) from the Sea of Galilee, opposite Tiberias. Other translations of this name in different English versions are Gergesenes and Gerasenes.

GADDI [GAD dih] (*my fortune*) — one of the 12 spies sent by Moses to explore the land of Canaan (Num. 13:11).

GADDIEL [GAD ih ell] (*God is my fortune*) — one of the 12 spies sent by Moses to explore the land of Canaan (Num. 13:10).

GADI [GA dih] (*my fortune*) — the father of Menahem, king of Israel (2 Kin. 15:14, 17).

GADITES [GADD ites] — members of the tribe of GAD (Deut. 3:12; Josh. 1:12).

GAHAM [GAY ham] (*burning brightly*) — the second son of Nahor and his concubine Reumah (Gen. 22:24).

GAHAR [GAY hahr] (*concealment*) — the head of a family of Temple servants who returned from the Captivity with Zerubbabel (Ezra 2:47).

GAIUS [GAY US] — a common Roman name shared by several men in the New Testament:

1. A native of Macedonia and a companion of the apostle Paul (Acts 19:29).

2. A man of Derbe who accompanied Paul as far as Asia (Acts 20:4). He may be the same person as Gaius No. 3.

3. A Corinthian who was baptized under Paul's ministry (1 Cor. 1:14).

4. The person to whom John addressed his third letter. John commended him for his generosity and faithful service (3 John 1, 5). He may be the same person as Gaius No. 3.

GALAL [GAY lal] (*rolling*) — the name of two Levites who returned from the Babylonian Captivity:

1. A priest who served at Jerusalem (1 Chr. 9:15).

2. The father of Shemaiah (1 Chr. 9:16), or Shammua (Neh. 11:17)

GALATIA [guh LAY shih uh] — a region in central Asia Minor (modern Turkey) bounded on the east by Cappadocia, on the west by Asia, on the south by Pamphylia and Cilicia, and on the north by Bithynia and Pontus (see Map 7, D-2). The northern part of the region was settled in the third century B.C. by Celtic tribes that had been driven out of Gaul (France). From these tribes, the region derived its name, Galatia.

In 64 B.C. the Roman general Pompey defeated the king of Pontus, Mithradates VI, and established a foothold for Rome in the region. When the last Galatian king, Amyntas, died in 25 B.C., the Romans inherited the kingdom. Caesar Augustus then created the Roman province of Galatia, making Ancyra the capital and annexing a number of districts to the south and west, including Pisidia, Isauria, Phrygia, and Lycaonia. The term Galatia, consequently, is somewhat ambiguous. It may refer to the older ethnic region in north-central Asia Minor (north Galatia), or to the later and larger Roman province (including south Galatia).

On his first missionary journey (about A.D. 46–48), the apostle Paul and Barnabas evangelized the Galatian cities of Pisidian Antioch, Iconium, Lystra, and Derbe (Acts 13—14). Paul revisited the area on his second and third missionary journeys.

Although the point is debated, it appears that Paul's Epistle to the Galatians (Gal. 1:2; 3:1) was addressed to the churches founded by him in the southern part of the province of Galatia (south Galatian theory). No evidence exists to show that Paul visited the region of Galatia in north-central Asia Minor. Although Acts 16:6 and 18:23 are sometimes thought to refer to this more remote northern region, the context of these passages seems to point to southern Galatia (Acts 13—14).

Also see GALATIANS, EPISTLE TO THE.

GALATIANS [guh LAY shih uns] — the inhabitants of GALATIA (Gal. 3:1).

GALATIANS, EPISTLE TO THE — a brief but energetic letter from the apostle Paul to the Christians of Galatia. Galatians is one of Paul's most commanding epistles; its importance far exceeds its size. It provides valuable information about Paul's life between his conversion and missionary journeys (1:11—2:14). Beyond its autobiographical value, however, Galatians ranks as one of Paul's great epistles; in it he forcefully proclaims the doctrine of justification by faith alone. Martin Luther, the Reformer, claimed Galatians as "my epistle." So wedded was Luther to Galatians, both in interest and temperament, that, together, they shaped the course of the Reformation. Galatians has been called the "Magna Charta of Christian Liberty." The peals of its liberating truth have thundered down through the centuries, calling men and women to new life by the grace of God.

Structure of the Epistle. Galatians falls into three sections, each two chapters long. The first third of the letter is a defense of Paul's apostleship and gospel (chaps. 1—2). The middle section (chaps. 3—4) is devoted to the question of salvation. In it Paul uses a variety of means—logic (3:15-20), quotations from the Old Testament (3:7-14), metaphor (4:1-6), personal authority (4:12-20), and allegory (4:21-31)—to argue that salvation comes not through obeying the Mosaic law, but by receiving the grace of God through faith. The third section of Galatians concerns the consequences of saving

GALATIANS: A Teaching Outline

faith (chaps. 5—6). The Christian is free to love (5:1-15); the Holy Spirit produces fruit in his life (5:16-26); and the needs of others lay a rightful claim on his life (6:1-10). Paul concludes by summing up the main points of the letter (6:11-16), along with a closing admonition that he bears the marks of Jesus in his body (6:17), and a blessing (6:18).

Authorship and Date. No epistle in the New Testament has better claim to come from Paul than does Galatians. The epistle bears his name (1:1), tells his story (1:11—2:14), and expounds the truth that occupied his life—justification by faith in Jesus Christ (2:16).

The date of the epistle is less certain. It depends on another question: to whom is the epistle addressed? This question is difficult because the word GALATIA (1:2) is ambiguous. Ethnically, the word refers to a people of Celtic stock living in northern Asia Minor. Politically, however, it refers to the region throughout central Asia Minor, including various districts in the south, that were annexed to Galatia when it was made a province by the Romans in 25 B.C. It is impossible to say for sure which use of the term Paul intended, although the broader political usage seems more probable.

Paul was well acquainted with southern Galatia (Acts 13—14; 16:1-5), and we have no certain evidence that he ever visited northern Galatia (unless Acts 16:6 and 18:23 refer to that area).

Moreover, it seems unlikely that Paul would have addressed the Galatians in such a direct way unless he enjoyed a close relationship with them. These reasons indicate that the people to whom the letter was addressed probably lived in southern Galatia. If this is so, it probably was written before the Council of Jerusalem (Acts 15). If it had already occurred (about A.D. 49), Paul would undoubtedly have cited the decision of that council since it agreed with the thrust of his argument in the epistle. If this is so, Galatians may be Paul's earliest (surviving) epistle, written perhaps in A.D. 48.

If, on the other hand, "Galatia" refers to the northern ethnic region, which Paul could not have visited before his second (Acts 16:6) or third (Acts 18:23) missionary journeys, the letter could not have been written before the mid-fifties. But this viewpoint seems less likely to be true.

Historical Setting. After Paul had evangelized the churches of Galatia, he received disturbing news that they were falling away from the gospel he had taught them (1:6). Certain religious activists had visited Galatia after Paul's departure and had persuaded the Christians there that the gospel presented by Paul was insufficient for salvation (1:7). In addition to faith in Jesus Christ, they insisted that a person must be circumcised according to the law of Moses (5:12) and must keep the Sabbath and other Jewish holy days (4:10), including the Jewish ceremonial law (5:3). These "troublers" (1:7), as Paul calls them, may have included some GNOSTIC ideas (4:3, 9) in their teachings. These teachers are sometimes referred to as JUDAIZERS, since they

taught that both faith and works—belief in Jesus and obedience to the Law—are necessary for salvation.

Theological Contribution. News of the troublers' "perversion of the gospel" (1:7) was distressing to Paul. Paul quickly rose to the Judaizers' challenge and produced this letter. From the outset he was ready for battle; he abandoned his customary introduction and plunged immediately into the battle with the Judaizers. The Judaizers had suggested that Paul was an inferior apostle, if one at all, and that his gospel was not authoritative (1:10). Paul countered with an impassioned defense of his conversion (1:11-17) and of his approval by the leaders of the church at Jerusalem (1:18—2:10). Indeed, the gospel that Paul had delivered to the Galatians was not his own, nor was he taught it; but it came "through the revelation of Jesus Christ" (1:11-12). Those who presumed to change it were meddling with the very plan of God (1:7-8).

God's plan is that Jews and Gentiles are justified before God by faith alone. This plan can be traced to the beginning of Israel's history, for Abraham, "believed God, and it was accounted for righteousness" (Gal. 3:6; also Gen. 15:6). The law, which did not come until 430 years after Abraham (3:17), was never intended to replace justification by faith. Rather, the law was to teach us of our need for Christ (3:24-25). Christ, therefore, is the fulfillment of the promise to Abraham.

The result of justification by grace through faith is spiritual freedom. Paul appealed to the Galatians to stand fast in their freedom, and not get "entangled again with a yoke of bondage [that is, the Mosaic law]" (5:1). Christian freedom is not an excuse to gratify one's lower nature; rather, it is an opportunity to love one another (5:13; 6:7-10). Such freedom does not insulate one from life's struggles. Indeed, it may intensify the battle between the Spirit and the flesh. Nevertheless, the flesh (the lower nature) has been crucified with Christ (2:20); and, as a consequence, the Spirit will bear its fruit—such as love, joy, and peace—in the life of the believer (5:22-23).

Special Considerations. The letter to the Galatians was written in a spirit of inspired agitation. For Paul, the issue was not whether a person was circumcised, but whether he had become "a new creation" (6:15). If Paul had not been successful in his argument for justification by faith alone, Christianity would have remained a sect within Judaism, rather than becoming the universal way of salvation. Galatians, therefore, is not only Luther's epistle; it is the epistle of every believer who confesses with Paul:

"I have been crucified with Christ; it is no longer I who live, but Christ lives in me; and the life which I now live in the flesh I live by faith in the Son of God, who loved me and gave Himself for me" (Gal. 2:20).

GALBANUM (see PLANTS OF THE BIBLE).

GALEED [GAL ee ed] (*heap of witness*) — a pile of

Photo by Willem A. VanGemeren

A view from Mount Arbel, looking toward the mountains of Lower Galilee.

memorial stones erected by Jacob and his father-in-law Laban as a sign of their covenant of peace and as a boundary mark between their territories. Galeed was near Mount Gilead (Gen. 31:47).

GALILEAN [gal uh LEE un] — a native or inhabitant of GALILEE (Luke 13:1–2; John 4:45). After the Captivity, Galilee was only sparsely resettled by Jews. It came to be known as "Galilee of the Gentiles." Jesus (Luke 23:6) and 11 of His disciples were Galileans; only Judas Iscariot came from outside Galilee. Because of their distinctive accent, Galileans were easily recognized when they spoke. Thus, during the trial of Jesus, it was a simple matter for the servant girl to detect Simon Peter as one of Jesus' disciples. She knew he was a Galilean; his speech betrayed him (Mark 14:70).

The name Galilean was sometimes used as a term of contempt or reproach when applied to the disciples of Jesus (Luke 22:59; Acts 2:7). Flavius Claudius Julianus, the Roman emperor (A.D. 361–363), called Christ "the Galilean God" and made a law that all Christians must be called Galileans. He apparently hoped to end the use of the name Christian.

GALILEE [GAL ih lee] (*circle* or *circuit*) — a Roman province of Palestine during the time of Jesus (see Map 3, B–2). Measuring roughly 80 kilometers (50 miles) north to south and about 58 kilometers (30 miles) east to west, Galilee was the most northerly of the three provinces of Palestine—Galilee, Samaria, and Judea. Covering more than a third of Palestine's territory, Galilee extended from the base of Mount Hermon in the north to the Carmel and Gilboa ranges in the south. The Mediterranean Sea and the Jordan River were its western and eastern borders, respectively.

Originally a district in the hill country of Naphtali (2 Kin. 15:29; 1 Chr. 6:76), Galilee was inhabited by a "mixed race" of Jews and heathen. The Canaanites continued to dominate Galilee for many years after Joshua's invasion (Judg. 1:30–33; 4:2). It was historically known among the Jews as "Galilee of the Gentiles" (Is. 9:1; Matt. 4:15).

Galilee had such a mixed population that Solomon could award unashamedly to Hiram, king of Tyre, 20 of its cities in payment for timber from Lebanon (1 Kin. 9:11). After conquest by Tiglath-Pileser, king of Assyria, (about 732 B.C.), Galilee was repopulated by a colony of heathen immigrants (2 Kin. 15:29; 17:24). Thus the Galilean accent and dialect were very distinct (Matt. 26:69, 73). For this and other reasons, the pure-blooded Jews of Judea, who were more orthodox in tradition, despised the Galileans (John 7:52). Rather contemptuously Nathanael asked, "Can anything good come out of Nazareth?" (John 1:46).

Galilee consisted essentially of an upland area of forests and farmlands. An imaginary line from the plain of Acco (Acre) to the north end of the Sea of Galilee divided the country into Upper and Lower Galilee. Since this area was actually the foothills of the Lebanon mountains, Upper and Lower Galilee had two different elevations.

The higher of the elevations, Upper Galilee, was more than 1,000 meters (3,000 feet) above sea level; and in the days of the New Testament it was densely forested and thinly inhabited. The lower elevation, Lower Galilee, averaged between 500 to 700 meters (1,500 to 2,000 feet) above sea level; it was less hilly and enjoyed a milder climate than Upper Galilee. This area included the rich plain of Esdraelon and was a "pleasant" land (Gen. 49:15). Chief exports of the region were olive oil, grains, and fish.

Galilee was the boyhood home of Jesus Christ. He was a lad of Nazareth, as it was prophesied: "He shall be called a Nazarene" (Matt. 2:23). Here He attempted to begin His public ministry, but was rejected by His own people (Luke 4:16–30).

All the disciples of Jesus, with the exception of Judas, came from Galilee (Matt. 4:18; John 1:43–44; Acts 1:11; 2:7). In Cana of Galilee He performed His first miracle (John 2:11); in fact, 25 of His 33 great miracles were performed in Galilee. Capernaum in Galilee became the headquarters of His ministry (Matt. 4:13; 9:1). Of His 32 parables, 19 were spoken in Galilee. The first three gospels concern themselves largely with Christ's Galilean ministry. Most of the events of our Lord's life and ministry are set against the backdrop of the Galilean hills.

Photo by Willem A. VanGemeren

The Sea, or Lake, of Galilee, at the point where the Jordan River flows into the northern end of the lake.

When Herod the Great died in 4 B.C., Galilee fell to the authority of HEROD ANTIPAS, who governed until A.D. 39. He built his capital city at Tiberias on the Sea of Galilee and was succeeded by HEROD AGRIPPA I who took the title of "king." After Agrippa's death in A.D. 44 (Acts 12:23), Galilee became a ZEALOT stronghold until the Romans crushed Jewish resistance in Palestine between A.D. 70 and 73.

GALILEE, SEA OF — a fresh-water lake, fed by the Jordan River, which was closely connected with the earthly ministry of Jesus (see Map 6, C-2). This "sea" is called by four different names in the Bible: the "Sea of Chinnereth" [or "Chinneroth"] (the Hebrew word for "harp-shaped," the general outline of the lake; Num. 34:11; Josh. 12:3; 13:27); the "Lake of Gennesaret" (Luke 5:1), taking the name from the fertile Plain of Gennesaret that lies on the northwest (Matt. 14:34); the "Sea of Tiberias" (John 6:1; 21:1), because of its association with the capital of Herod Antipas; and the "Sea of Galilee" (Matt. 4:18; Mark 1:16).

Situated some 98 kilometers (60 miles) north of Jerusalem, the Sea of Galilee contains fresh water since it is fed by the cool waters of the Jordan. The lake itself is the deepest part of the northern Jordan Rift and thus the water collects there before it flows on its way. The surface of Galilee is about 230 meters (700 feet) below the Mediterranean Sea. The floor of the lake is another 25 to 50 meters (80 to 160 feet) lower. The lake itself is nearly 21 kilometers (13 miles) long and 13 kilometers (8 miles) wide at Magdala, the point of its greatest width.

The lake is surrounded, except on the southern side, by steep cliffs and sharply rising mountains. On the east these mountains rise to the Golan Heights and the fertile Hauran plateau as high as 900 meters (2,700 feet). As a result of this formation, cool winds frequently rush down these slopes and unexpectedly stir up violent storms on the warm surface of the lake. Waves such as these were easily calmed at the command of Jesus (Mark 4:35–41).

A fishing industry thrived on the Sea of Galilee. Jesus called His first disciples—Peter, Andrew, James, and John—from that industry (1:16–20). In spite of the steep hillsides around the lake, nine cities of 15,000 population or more thrived in the first century as part of an almost continuous belt of settlements around the lake. Of these cities, Bethsaida, Tiberias, and Capernaum were the most important. On and around the Sea of Galilee Jesus performed 18 of His 33 recorded miracles and issued most of His teachings to His disciples and the multitudes that followed Him.

GALL (see PLANTS OF THE BIBLE).

GALLERY — a word of uncertain meaning, describing an architectural feature of the Temple in Ezekiel's vision (Ezek. 41:15-16). Various scholars have suggested the word refers to "porticoes," "colonnades," "walk ways," "corridors," and "terraces."

GALLEY—a seagoing vessel of the ancient world propelled mainly by oars, sometimes with the aid of sails (Is. 33:21). Galleys were low vessels of shallow draft, used mostly for commercial shipping. Also see SHIP.

GALLIM [GAL eem] (heaps) — a village of Benjamin near Gibeah of Saul (Is. 10:30); Gallim is probably modern Khirbet Kakul, about one kilometer (half a mile) west of Anathoth (Anata).

GALLIO [GAL ih oh] (meaning unknown) — the Roman proconsul of Achaia before whom the apostle Paul appeared during his first visit to Corinth (Acts 18:12-17). When Gallio discovered that Paul's Jewish enemies had a religious grievance against him, he threw them out of his court. He also refused to take action when the mob took the synagogue ruler Sosthenes and beat him before the tribunal.

GALLON — a unit of liquid measure or capacity equal to 231 cubic inches or 3.785 liters (four quarts). Each of the six stone waterpots at the wedding in Cana of Galilee contained 20 to 30 gallons (John 2:6; two or three firkins apiece, KJV). Also see WEIGHTS AND MEASURES.

GALLOWS — a platform on which a person was hanged by the neck as a method of capital punishment. The gallows is mentioned several times in the NKJV in the Book of Esther (2:23; 7:9; 9:25). In an ironic turn of events, the wicked HAMAN was executed on the very gallows where he planned to hang the Jewish leader MORDECAI (Esth. 7:10).

GAMALIEL [guh MAY lih el] (God is my recompense) — the name of two men in the Bible:

1. A leader of the tribe of Manasseh chosen to help take the census during Israel's wandering in the wilderness (Num. 1:10).

2. A famous member of the Jewish SANHEDRIN and a teacher of the Law. Gamaliel, who had taught Paul (Acts 22:3), advised the Sanhedrin to treat the apostles of the young Christian church with moderation. Gamaliel's argument was simple. If Jesus was a false prophet, as many others had been, the movement would soon fade into obscurity. If, however, the work was "of God," he pointed out, "you cannot overthrow it" (Acts 5:39).

GAMES — activities conducted as a form of entertainment during Bible times. Games are seldom mentioned in the Bible and usually only indirectly to provide the setting for a historical event or to serve as an example for a theological or ethical teaching.

Many of the games and sports mentioned in the Old Testament were of a combative nature. The purpose of these games was probably to prepare young men to handle themselves in warfare.

The Bible mentions wrestling several times. Apparently, this was a popular sport or game in Bible times. Jacob, for example, wrestled with God (Gen. 32:24-26). Some believe that the combat between Joab's and Abner's forces was also a type of wrestling (2 Sam. 2:12-16).

Another game that also served to cultivate a person's battle skills was archery. Shooting at a target prepared the young men of Israel to fight in the army. The Old Testament mentions archery several times. Jonathan sent a message to his friend David by his skillful placement of arrows in the target as he practiced with his bow (1 Sam. 20:18-23). Job

The scholar Gamaliel, under whom Paul studied, taught on these steps of the Temple in Paul's day (Acts 5:33-40; 22:3). These steps have been uncovered in recent excavations in Jerusalem.
Photo by Howard Vos

A game board from Mesopotamia which dates back to about 2500 B.C. It was discovered in excavations at the city of Ur.

likened himself to a target that God was using for practice (Job 16:12).

Riddles, a type of word game, were well known and popular in the ancient world. One famous riddle in the Old Testament is the one Samson posed to his 30 Philistine companions (Judg. 14:12–14). Samson's use of a riddle is also an example of another type of sport well known in all times—gambling. Samson promised the person who could solve the riddle would receive 30 linen garments and 30 changes of clothing.

Brief mention is made in Zechariah 8:5 of children playing in the street. This verse is part of a description of the future blessing of Jerusalem, so no details are given of the type of play involved.

While descriptions of games and sports are indirect and fragmentary in the Old Testament, archaeological discoveries have filled out the picture a little more fully. For instance, many children's toys from Bible times have been discovered. These include dolls, rattles, and marbles. Board games of many types have been found at archaeological sites throughout the Near East, including Palestine (most notably at Gezer and Megiddo).

During the period between the Old Testament and the New Testament, quite a debate arose in the Jewish community when a GYMNASIUM was built in Jerusalem. The Jews who were in favor of at least partial acceptance of Greek culture joined in the activities of this gymnasium as both spectators and participants, while orthodox Jews saw it as a great sin. The building of this gymnasium is mentioned in the apocryphal books of 1 and 2 Maccabees and by the Jewish historian JOSEPHUS.

In the Old Testament, games provided the background to certain historical events. But in the New Testament, sports provide illustrations to important teachings. Sports involve a great deal of concentration, effort, and practice in order to win the prize.

This means it was natural for the apostle Paul and the other New Testament writers to refer to sports while urging believers to practice godliness. First Corinthians 9:24–27 develops this thought most fully as Paul compares the Christian's spiritual life to the training of a runner and a boxer. Other passages in the New Testament also refer to the foot race as a parallel to the Christian's life in Christ (Gal. 2:2; 5:7; Phil 2:16; Heb. 12:1, 2).

Jesus referred briefly to children playing in the public areas of the city (Luke 7:32). But perhaps the most notable example of games in the New Testament is the description of Roman soldiers engaged in "games of chance" over Christ's clothing just before He was crucified (Matt. 27:35).

GAMMAD [GAM add] (meaning unknown) — a city mentioned in the Book of Ezekiel. The reference is to the "men of Gammad," brave warriors who manned the towers of Tyre. (Ezek. 27:11; "men of Gamad," RSV; "Gammadim," KJV). Gammad may have been Kumidi in northern Syria.

GAMUL [GAY mool] (*weaned*) — a descendant of Aaron and a chief of the Levites (1 Chr. 24:17).

GANGRENE (see DISEASES OF THE BIBLE).

GARDEN — a plot of ground where flowers, vegetables, or ornamental shrubs are grown. But the word garden as used in the Bible also includes parks, plantations, and orchards. Gardens that belonged to kings (2 Kin. 25:4; Neh. 3:15) were actually royal parks. The garden of the Persian King Xerxes, for example, was large enough to hold a week–long feast for thousands (Esth. 1:5).

Mesopotamian kings kept and hunted wild animals in their gardens. They also used these plots of ground for cultivating a wide variety of plants. The author of Ecclesiastes apparently regarded the planting of gardens and orchards as a royal task, demonstrating the king's prosperity (Eccl. 2:4). Occasionally, however, parts of royal gardens might be used for other purposes, such as vegetable gardens (1 Kin. 21:2) or even burial grounds (2 Kin. 21:18, 26).

Ordinary people also owned gardens. These gardens were not generally attached to individual houses, but were in a separate area, often outside city walls and near a good water supply. Their main function was to produce food (Num. 24:6; Jer. 29:5).

Gardens are also spoken of symbolically as portraits of happiness and fruitfulness. For example, the lovers in the Song of Solomon compared one another to a garden of delights (Song 4:12; 5:1; 8:13). The Lord's blessings for His people are also described as a garden of delights (Is. 51:3; Ezek. 36:35; Amos 9:14).

The Garden of Eden represented God's ideal environment for man. Special characteristics of Eden were its wide variety of trees (Gen. 2:9; Ezek. 31:8–9), its precious stones and metals (Gen. 2:11–12; Ezek. 28:13–14), and its rivers (Gen. 2:10–14; Rev. 22:1–2), all of them portraying its richness and fertility. Eden is also sometimes referred to in the Bible as the garden of the Lord (Gen. 13:10; Is. 51:3) or the garden of God (Ezek. 28:13; 31:8–9). Some of this garden's features, especially its rivers and the TREE OF LIFE, are also used to portray God's final blessings for His people (Ezek. 47:12; Rev. 22:1–2, 14).

GARDEN HOUSE — a place south of the Valley of Jezreel toward which Ahaziah, king of Judah, fled when pursued by Jehu (2 Kin. 9:27, KJV, NASB; Beth Haggan, NKJV, NIV, NEB, RSV).

GARDENER (see OCCUPATIONS AND TRADES).

GAREB [GAY reb] (*reviler* or *despiser*) — the name of a man and a hill:
1. One of David's mighty men (2 Sam. 23:38).
2. A hill near Jerusalem (Jer. 31:39).

GARLAND — a wreath, usually woven of flowers or leaves, worn on the head (Acts 14:13; wreaths, NIV).

GARLIC (see PLANTS OF THE BIBLE).

GARMITE [GAR might] (*bony*) — a name applied to Keilah in the genealogy of Judah (1 Chr. 4:19).

GARNER — KJV word for BARN.

GARRISON — a fort or a company of soldiers stationed in a fort. During Saul's reign as king of the Hebrew nation, the Philistines had garrisons deep inside Israel—at Geba (1 Sam. 13:3) and Bethlehem (2 Sam. 23:14; 1 Chr. 11:16). In later years, David drove out the Philistines and placed his own garrisons in Damascus (2 Sam. 8:6) and Edom (2 Sam. 8:14; 1 Chr. 18:13).

In the New Testament, the word garrison always refers to a detachment of Roman soldiers who were stationed in Palestine (Matt. 27:27) or in one of the surrounding nations visited by the apostle Paul (2 Cor. 11:32). Paul was once rescued from an angry mob by a garrison of soldiers (Acts 21:31).

GASHMU [GASH mew] — a form of GESHEM.

GATAM [GAY tam] (*burnt valley*) — a descendant of Eliphaz. Gatam was a chief of an Edomite clan (Gen. 36:11; 1 Chr. 1:36).

GATE, CITY — a massive wooden door in a city wall through which traffic passed. Often reinforced with brass or iron for greater security, these gates were opened during the day to allow the city's citi-

Remains of the King Gate in the city wall of Hattusa, ancient capital of the Hittite Empire.

Photo by Howard Vos

The Golden Gate in the wall of Jerusalem in the Temple area. Scholars believe this gate was built in the fifth century A.D. on the site where Jesus made His triumphal entry into the city.

zens to come and go. But they were generally closed at night as a safety measure. In the event of attack, the gates were closed and barred to keep out the enemy.

Goods were often bought and sold and important legal matters were discussed just inside the city gate (Ruth 4:11). Because of their central location, gates were often spoken of in the Bible as symbols of power and authority. God promised Abraham that his descendants would possess the gates of their enemies (Gen. 22:17).

Also see GATES OF JERUSALEM AND THE TEMPLE.

GATES OF JERUSALEM AND THE TEMPLE — gates in the city wall of Jerusalem and the Temple area. The Bible mentions numerous gates by specific names. But keeping these names straight is complicated by the fact that as the walls of Jerusalem expanded to incorporate new areas, or were destroyed and rebuilt, different names were used for the same gate (or gate site). Unless the Bible gives a clear indication, as in the case of "the Beautiful Gate of the Temple" (Acts 3:10), it is difficult to distinguish between gates of the Temple and gates of the city wall.

Exactly how many gates the city of Jerusalem had is unknown. The number of gates probably varied from century to century. In John's vision of the New Jerusalem, the holy city had 12 gates— three gates on each of its four sides (east, north, south, and west). Each of these gates was inscribed with the name of one of the 12 tribes of Israel (Rev.

21:12–13). John's portrayal of the New Jerusalem seems to be based on the prophecy of Ezekiel (Ezekiel 48). The gates described in the Book of Revelation may not correspond to the number of gates of the Old Jerusalem.

As various modern versions of the Bible are compared, more than a dozen of the gates of Jerusalem are given different names by the different translations. A list of the gates of Jerusalem and the Temple, giving their names according to the NKJV, is as follows:

Beautiful Gate (Acts 3:10)
Benjamin's Gate (Jer. 38:7; Zech. 14:10)
Corner Gate (2 Kin. 14:13; 2 Chr. 25:23; 26:9; Jer. 31:38; Zech. 14:10)
East Gate (1 Chr. 26:14; 2 Chr. 31:14)
Ephraim, Gate of (2 Kin. 14:13; 2 Chr. 25:23; Neh. 8:16; 12:39)
First Gate (Zech. 14:10)
Fish Gate (2 Chr. 33:14; Neh. 3:3; 12:39; Zeph. 1:10)
Foundation, Gate of the (2 Chr. 23:5)
Fountain Gate (Neh. 3:15; 12:37)
Horse Gate (2 Chr. 23:15; Neh. 3:28; Jer. 31:40)
Joshua, Gate of (2 Kin. 23:8)
King's Gate (1 Chr. 9:18)
Middle Gate (Jer. 39:3)
Miphkad Gate (Neh. 3:31)
New Gate (Jer. 36:10)
North Gate (1 Chr. 26:14)
Old Gate (Neh. 3:6; 12:39)
Potsherd Gate (Jer. 19:2)
Prison, Gate of the (Neh. 12:39)
Refuse Gate (Neh. 2:13; 3:13–14; 12:31)
Shallecheth Gate (1 Chr. 26:16)
Sheep Gate (Neh. 3:1, 32; 12:39; John 5:2)
South Gate (1 Chr. 26:15)
Upper Gate (2 Kin. 15:35; 2 Chr. 23:20; 27:3)
Valley Gate (2 Chr. 26:9; Neh. 2:13, 15; 3:13)
Water Gate (Neh. 3:26; 8:1, 3, 16; 12:37)
West Gate (1 Chr. 26:16)

Translations of the Bible other than the NKJV have the following names of gates (not found in the NKJV):

Dung Gate (Neh. 2:13; 3:13–14; 12:31; RSV, NIV, NEB, KJV; Refuse Gate, NKJV)
Dung Port (Neh. 2:13, KJV; Refuse Gate, NKJV)
Former Gate (Zech. 14:10, RSV, NEB; First Gate, NKJV)
Guard, Gate of the (Neh. 12:39, RSV, NIV, NASB; Gate of the Prison, NKJV)
Guardhouse, Gate of the (Neh. 12:39, NEB; Gate of the Prison, NKJV)
High Gate (2 Chr. 23:20; 27:3; KJV; Upper Gate, NKJV)
Higher Gate (2 Kin. 15:35, KJV; Upper Gate, NKJV)
Inspection Gate (Neh. 3:31, NIV, NASB; Miphkad Gate, NKJV)
Jeshanah Gate (Neh. 3:6; 12:39; NIV, NEB; Old Gate, NKJV)
Muster Gate (Neh. 3:31, RSV; Miphkad Gate, NKJV)

Mustering Gate (Neh. 3:31, NEB; Miphkad Gate, NKJV)

Shalleketh Gate (1 Chr. 26:16, NIV; Shallecheth Gate, NKJV)

Sheep Market (John 5:2, KJV; Sheep Gate, NKJV)

Sheep-Pool (John 5:2, NEB; Sheep Gate, NKJV)

GATEKEEPER (see OCCUPATIONS AND TRADES).

GATH [gath] (*wine press*) — one of the five chief cities (see Map 3, A–4) of the Philistines (Judg. 3:3). Although Gath is frequently used as a prefix in combination with a proper name to refer to other cities — for example, Gath Hepher (Josh. 19:13) and Gath Rimmon (Josh. 19:45) — when it appears singly, it refers to the great Philistine city.

Gath was known as the residence of the ANAKIM, men of great stature (Josh. 11:22). GOLIATH and other giants belonged to this race and the city of Gath (1 Sam. 17:4). David captured Gath during his reign (1 Chr. 13:1). The residents of Gath, known as Gittites, were still subject to Israel during Solomon's reign, although they still had their own king (1 Kin. 2:39, 42).

Solomon's son, Rehoboam, later fortified Gath (2 Chr. 11:8), but the city returned to the hands of the Philistines. Later, it was recaptured by Hazael (2 Kin. 12:17), and Uzziah broke down its walls (2 Chr. 26:6).

GATH HEPHER [gath HEE fur] (*winepress of the well*) — a border town in the territory of Zebulun, about five kilometers (three miles) northeast of Nazareth (Josh. 19:13; Gittah-hepher, KJV). Gath Hepher was the hometown of the prophet JONAH (2 Kin. 14:25).

GATH RIMMON [gath-RIM un] (*winepress by the pomegranate*) — the name of two cities in the Bible:

1. A city of the tribe of Dan assigned to the Levites. Gath Rimmon probably was on the Plain of Joppa (Josh. 19:45).

2. A town of the half-tribe of Manasseh west of the Jordan River assigned to the Levites (Josh. 21:25). It was probably the same town as Bileam (1 Chr. 6:70) and Ibleam (Judg. 1:27).

GAULANITIS [goe luh NITE us] — a region or district east of the Sea of Galilee which received its name from its largest city, GOLAN (Deut. 4:43).

GAZA [GAY zuh] (*stronghold*) — one of the five principle cities of the Philistines (see Map 2, C–1). The southernmost city of Canaan, Gaza was situated on the great caravan route between Mesopotamia and Egypt, at the junction of the trade route from Arabia. This location made Gaza an ideal rest stop and a commercial center for merchants and travelers.

Gaza was originally inhabited by the Avim, a people who were replaced by the Caphtorim (Deut. 2:23). Gaza was allotted to the tribe of Judah by Joshua (Josh. 15:47); but it was not immediately occupied (Judg. 1:18), because the Anakim were still present in the city (Josh. 11:22; 13:3). Soon afterwards the Philistines recovered Gaza (Judg. 13:1). Here the mighty Samson was humiliated by being forced to grind grain as a blinded prisoner (Judg. 16:21). In a final victorious performance, Samson brought down the house of the pagan god Dagon, destroying many Philistines (Judg. 16:23–31).

Although Solomon ruled over Gaza, not until the reign of Hezekiah, king of Judah, was the decisive blow dealt to the Philistines (2 Kin. 18:8). Through the prophet Amos, God threatened Gaza with destruction by fire for its sins (Amos 1:6–7). This prophecy was fulfilled by the army of Alexander the Great in 332 B.C., when Gaza was destroyed and her inhabitants massacred (Zeph. 2:4; Zech. 9:5).

In the New Testament the evangelist Philip was directed by God to preach the gospel along the road from Jerusalem to Gaza (Acts 8:26). On this road the Ethiopian eunuch professed faith in Jesus and was baptized.

GAZATHITES [GAY zuh thites] — a form of GAZITES.

GAZELLE (see ANIMALS OF THE BIBLE).

GAZEZ [GAY zez] (*sheep shearer*) — the name of two men in the Bible:

1. A son of Caleb (1 Chr. 2:46).

2. A grandson of Caleb (1 Chr. 2:46).

GAZITES [GAY zites] — inhabitants of the Philistine city of Gaza (Judg. 16:2; Josh. 13:3; Gazathites, KJV).

GAZZAM [GAZ am] (*bird of prey*) — the founder of a family of NETHINIM (Temple servants) who returned from the Captivity with Zerubbabel (Neh. 7:51).

GEBA [GHEE buh] (*hill*) — a city of Benjamin assigned to the priests (1 Chr. 8:6). Situated in northern Judah (Zech. 14:10), about ten kilometers (six miles) northeast of Jerusalem, it was regarded as a strategic city. King Asa of Judah fortified Geba (1 Kin. 15:22). It is also called Gaba (Josh. 18:24). The city is identified with the present-day village of Jeba.

GEBAL [GHEE buhl] (*mountain*) — the name of a city and a region:

1. A mountainous region between Petra and the southern end of the Dead Sea. Inhabited by the Edomites, Gebal was one of the areas allied against Israel (Ps. 83:7).

2. An ancient and thriving seaport situated on a bluff in the foothills of Lebanon that overlooked the Mediterranean Sea. Gebal was about 32 kilometers (20 miles) north of Beirut between Sidon and Tripoli (Ezek. 27:9). One of the most important seaports of PHOENICIA, Gebal imported so much PAPYRUS from Egypt that its Greek name, *Byblos*, became synonymous with papyrus, or book.

Also see GEBALITES.

GEBALITES [GHEE buhl ites] — inhabitants of the city of GEBAL (Josh. 13:5; Giblites, KJV). The Gebalites were known for shipbuilding (Ezek. 27:9) and for stone–cutting (1 Kin. 5:18). They helped construct Solomon's Temple.

GEBER [GHEE buhr] (*strong one*) — the name of two governmental officials in Israel:
1. The father of one of Solomon's supply officers (1 Kin. 4:13, KJV).
2. A son of Uri (1 Kin. 4:19). Geber was one of Solomon's 12 governors. His district was in southern Gilead, east of the Jordan River.
Also see BEN–GEBER.

GEBIM [GHEE bem] (*ditches*) — a city of Benjamin, north of Jerusalem near Michmash and between Anathoth and Nob (Is. 10:31).

GECKO (see ANIMALS OF THE BIBLE).

GEDALIAH [gad uh LIE ah] (*Jehovah is great*) — the name of five Old Testament men:
1. A person of high birth appointed governor of Judah by Nebuchadnezzar (2 Kin. 25:22–25). Gedaliah governed Judah from Mizpah, where after only a two–month rule he was assassinated by Jewish nationalists led by Ishmael. Gedaliah's father had protected the prophet Jeremiah, and Gedaliah probably did the same.
2. A Levite musician of David's time. Gedaliah was one of the six sons of Jeduthun (1 Chr. 25:3, 9).
3. A priest who divorced his pagan wife after the Captivity (Ezra 10:18).
4. A son of Pashhur who called for the death of the prophet Jeremiah (Jer. 38:1, 4).
5. An ancestor of the prophet Zephaniah (Zeph. 1:1).

GEDER [GHEE duhr] (*fence*) — a town in southern Judah conquered by Joshua, along with Lachish and other cities (Josh. 12:13).

GEDERAH [GHED ah ruh] (*enclosure* or *sheepfold*) — the name of two towns in the Old Testament:
1. A town in the Shephelah, or lowlands, of Judah (Josh. 15:36), about 30 kilometers (20 miles) west of Jerusalem.
2. The hometown of Jozabad, a warrior who joined David at Ziklag (1 Chr. 12:4).

GEDERATHITE [GHED ah ruh thite] — a native or inhabitant of GEDERAH (1 Chr. 12:4).

GEDERITE [GHED uh rite] — a native or inhabitant of GEDER (1 Chr. 27:28).

GEDEROTH [ghe DARE oth] (*sheepfolds*) — an unidentified town in the SHEPHELAH, or lowlands, of Judah (Josh. 15:41).

GEDEROTHAIM [ghed eh row THAY em] (*two sheepfolds*) — a town of Judah (Josh. 15:36).

GEDOR [GHEE dawr] (*wall*) — the name of one person and four towns:
1. A town in the hill country of Judah (Josh. 15:58).
2. A person or family of the tribe of Benjamin (1 Chr. 8:31; 9:37).
3. A Calebite city in Judah founded by Jered (1 Chr. 4:18).
4. A town in the territory inhabited by the Simeonites (1 Chr. 4:39).
5. The hometown of Joelah and Zebadiah, two of David's warriors (1 Chr. 12:7).

GE–HARASHIM [gay hah RAH shem] (*valley of craftsmen*) — a valley in Judah (1 Chr. 4:14) inhabited after the Captivity by Benjamites (Neh. 11:35). It was near Lod and Ono, in the southern part of

Remains of the Phoenician city of Gebal on the Mediterranean Sea (Ezek. 27:9), also called Byblos by the Greeks.

Photo by Gustav Jeeninga

the Plain of Sharon, east of Joppa (modern Jaffa).

GEHAZI [geh HAH zih] (*valley of vision*) — a servant of the prophet Elisha (2 Kin. 4:8–37). Gehazi is first mentioned when Elisha asked how he could reward the Shunammite woman who had welcomed him into her home. Gehazi suggested that the childless woman and her husband might be given a child. A son was eventually born to the couple but after a few years he died. The Shunammite woman sought Elisha's help. In an attempt to show Gehazi that faith healed, and not magic, Elisha sent him to lay the prophet's staff on the dead child's head. Nothing happened. But when Elisha himself went to the child, the child revived.

Gehazi's true character came out in the story of NAAMAN the Syrian, whom Elisha cured of leprosy. Elisha refused any reward, but Gehazi ran after Naaman to claim something for himself. He told Naaman that Elisha wanted a talent of silver and two changes of clothing for the needy. Because of his greed, lying, and misuse of the prophetic office, Elisha cursed Gehazi with the same disease from which Naaman had been cured.

GEHENNA [ge HEN uh] (see HINNOM, VALLEY OF).

GELILOTH [geh LIH lohth] (*circles*) — a landmark on the border between Benjamin and Judah (Josh. 18:17). Apparently it was the same place as GILGAL on the road from Jerusalem to Jericho (Josh. 15:7).

GEM (see JEWELS AND PRECIOUS STONES).

GEMALLI [geh MAL ih] (*camel owner*) — the father of one of the spies who explored the land of Canaan (Num. 13:12).

GEMARA [geh MARE uh] (*completion* or *tradition*) — the second part of the TALMUD, the source from which the laws that govern orthodox Jews is derived. The MISHNAH, the text of Jewish oral law which was written in Hebrew, is the first part of the Talmud. The Gemara, which was written in Aramaic, is a commentary on the Mishnah. Together the Mishnah and the Gemara make up the Talmud. The Gemara contains historical information, sermons, ethical teaching, legal reports, legends, and other lore of the Jewish rabbis.

GEMARIAH [ghem ah RYE ah] (*Jehovah has accomplished*) — the name of two men in the Old Testament:

1. A citizen of Judah who carried tribute money to Nebuchadnezzar of Babylon and took a letter from Jeremiah to the Jews in Captivity (Jer. 29:3).

2. A son of Shaphan who tried to stop Jehoiakim, king of Judah, from destroying Jeremiah's scroll (Jer. 36:10–12, 25).

GENEALOGIES OF JESUS — the two distinct lists of the ancestors of Jesus found in the Gospels of Matthew and Luke.

The Gospel of Matthew (1:1–17) recorded Christ's descent from the patriarch Abraham, while Luke (3:28–38) reversed the recording process, contrary to biblical tradition, and traced the ancestry of Jesus back through Joseph, David, and Abraham to "Adam, the son of God." Both records reflect the Old Testament practices of selection and omission in such lists. (See GENEALOGY.)

Matthew used the SEPTUAGINT, the Greek translation of the Hebrew Old Testament, for his 41 names and grouped them in three units of 14 generations each, the latter being multiples of the sacred number seven. His divisions are: (1) Abraham to David, 14 names; (2) Solomon to the Captivity, 14 names; (3) Shealtiel to Jesus, 13 names. Luke catalogued almost twice as many names as Matthew and also used the number seven as a basis for organizing Christ's pedigree in terms of 77 names. Luke's groups are: (1) Jesus to Zerubbabel, 21 names; (2) Shealtiel to Nathan, 21 names; (3) David to Isaac, 14 names; and (4) Abraham to Adam, 21 names.

Some of the people named in Luke's record cannot be identified readily, although certain names may be Greek forms of the original Hebrew. Matthew's list also contains several persons not found elsewhere in the Old Testament. Matthew and Luke have the same names from Abraham to David, apart from Luke's addition of Arni and Admin; but beyond that point there are numerous variations. Matthew's genealogy is unusual in mentioning four women. By contrast, not even Jesus' mother was mentioned in Luke's genealogy.

Attempts have been made to explain how such different results can be arrived at by persons using the same sources of information, but no firm conclusions have emerged. Some writers suggest that both lists came from Joseph, but were compiled separately by different methods. Others believe that Matthew's list furnished a legal or "official" descent through the house of Joseph, while Luke's record actually reflected Mary's side of the family, since she herself probably was descended from David (Luke 1:27; 2:4). The absence of Mary's name from Luke's list argues against that theory, which would actually suit Matthew's genealogy better, since Mary is mentioned in it along with four other women.

Whatever the processes by which the two lists arose, their purpose was to show that Jesus Christ the Messiah was descended from the house of David. Matthew makes Jesus a legitimate heir through being "adopted" by Joseph, a member of the Davidic line. For Matthew the unfolding of Israelite history revealed Christ the Messiah, whose coming ushered in the age of grace. Luke's list reflects a wider concern by portraying Christ as the Savior of all peoples, not just the Jews. By reversing the normal order of listing, Luke may have intended to demonstrate the real nature of Jesus as the divine Son.

GENEALOGY [gene ee AL o gih] — a list of a person's ancestors that normally contains the members of each generation in succession. When compiled in the form of a "family tree," it begins at the bottom with the root stock from which the family came, then advances and branches out as the "tree" grows. When the genealogy records descent from ancestors by generations, the originating stock is listed first and all subsequent descendants are derived from it.

A technical term that means "family history," "record," or "genealogy" occurs in 11 places in the Book of Genesis in the phrase, "These are the generations of." This phrase divides the book in such a way as to suggest that the units thus formed were the actual sources from which the first 37 chapters of Genesis were compiled. These "family records" sometimes included genealogies (Genesis 10) in much the same way that tablets from ancient Babylonia would occasionally have "family trees" written on the back. This practice helped to date these tablets since they would obviously belong to the last generations to be mentioned.

Genealogical records probably began with the king–lists that were drawn up in ancient Mesopotamia. These lists preserved a record of personal history. They are interesting because they are sometimes dated by referring to historical personalities or to less familiar occurrences such as floods. For many people the information contained in the genealogies would be the only history they would know.

The people of the ancient world generally had far less access to written reference works than modern people do. Therefore, they committed a great deal of information to memory. To this day it is not uncommon for a Bedouin Arab to be able to recite a list of his ancestors from memory for an hour without making any mistakes. This emphasizes the importance that genealogical records had in the ancient Near East. In the Old Testament, no fewer than three of these dealt with the successors of Adam (Gen. 4:1-2, 17-22, 25-26; 5:1-32). This shows that compiling lists of descendants is a very ancient practice.

When the Hebrews began to manage large herds and flocks and to live together in families and tribes, genealogies became very important in deciding inheritance rights and land allotments. When land holdings had been distributed to the Israelite tribes in Canaan, a person could only lay claim legally to ancestral property by producing the proper genealogical records. When the Jewish captives returned from Babylonia to Jerusalem, a register of their genealogies was made (Neh. 7:5). These genealogies proved very useful in deciding who was qualified by birth to act as priests (Neh. 7:64). By the time of Christ, everyone who was a priest was expected to prove his descent from the tribe of Levi and the house of Aaron. For this purpose a proper written genealogy was of the greatest importance.

If this procedure was vital for the welfare of the priesthood, it was equally so for the royal succession in the kingdom of Judah, which traced its descent from the house of David. When the prophets proclaimed that the Messiah would also come from the stock of Jesse (Is. 11:1), the father of David, even greater precautions were taken to preserve the pattern of descent. The genealogies of Christ in the gospels show the way in which the details of our Lord's descent from the house of David has been preserved through the centuries.

Genealogies were important for still other reasons. In the period of Israel's wandering in the wilderness, genealogies were used in the military organization of the tribes (Num. 1:2-4), as well as for deciding the amount of taxes and offerings to be contributed to the service of the sanctuary (Num. 7:11-89). From the time when the Israelites were formed into tribes, the genealogies helped to give persons a special sense of identity within the nation and also to locate them broadly in terms of family holdings. Thus a man might be traveling away from home; but when asked about his identity, he would commonly reveal himself by name, ancestry, and tribe, along with the village or town from which he came.

In the period after the captivity of the Jewish people by Babylon, Greek paganism threatened the purity of their religion. Orthodox Jews compiled and maintained genealogies to remind them of the need to keep the faith pure. These genealogies helped them resist the paganism that had brought both Israel and Judah to their knees in earlier ages.

Biblical genealogies present some problems because of the ways in which they were compiled. Ancient genealogies frequently omitted the names of unimportant family members or those whose presence in a family tree might cause embarrassment. Such gaps can be illustrated by the pedigree of Moses. Only four generations are mentioned between Levi, the third son of Jacob and Leah (Gen. 29:34) and Moses. This is difficult to reconcile with the census of 22,000 males descended from Levi that was taken in Moses' day (Num. 3:39) some four centuries later (Ex. 12:40). More than four generations would have been required to produce this many descendants.

By contrast, the genealogy of Ephraim, Levi's nephew, as it was traced to the time of Joshua, recorded 18 generations (1 Chr. 7:20-27). Yet despite obvious omissions, the purpose of the genealogy of this family was accomplished because it demonstrated that Moses was descended from the tribe of Levi. A similar condensed record occurs in the case of Ezra (Ezra 7:1-2), which contained only five generations between Zadok (966 B.C.) and the time when Ezra returned to Judea, about 458 B.C. Even shorter was the opening verse of Matthew's gospel, which summarized Christ's genealogy in three major links. In the genealogies, the length of a generation is unknown.

Sometimes certain patterns in early genealogies are not evident in later ones. Thus in Genesis 5 and 11, the lists contain 10 units giving the age of the father when his first child was born and the remaining years of his life. Both lists end with the names of three brothers in a way that seems deliberate, and the entire pattern may have encouraged easy memorization in antiquity.

Modern readers of biblical genealogies also need

to be warned about the way in which such familiar terms as "father," "mother," "son," and "daughter" were used in the ancient Near East. A father was not always one who bore children. This term could simply denote a learned, older man who was not even a relative. The term mother could be a symbolic description of a woman who exercised the love and care normally given by mothers, such as the wise woman of Abel (2 Sam. 20:19). Just as father would also describe a grandfather or an even more remote ancestor, a son could actually be a grandson or a great–grandson. People could be brothers, not because they were siblings of one family, but because they were bound together by a treaty. Words such as son and daughter seem to have been used in the ancient world almost as widely as they are now. Thus caution is needed before they are taken at face value in Scripture.

The main purpose of genealogies was to establish the broad line of descent without furnishing all the details. Just because certain relatives were left out does not mean these records were inaccurate or invalid.

The vast majority of biblical genealogies occur in the Old Testament. An important one deals with the descent from Adam to Noah (Gen. 5:1–32). The descendants of Noah (Genesis 10), the line from Shem to Abraham (Gen. 11:10–26), and the long list of Abraham's offspring are extremely important for the early history of the Israelites.

The longest Old Testament genealogy contains a detailed list of persons from Adam to the time of Saul (1 Chronicles 1—9). This list was probably compiled at a later time in the history of the Hebrews to enable people to trace their descent from proven Israelite stock. The house of David was reckoned back to Judah (Gen. 46:12). This was an important genealogy because of the promises of the prophets about the Messiah.

GENERATION — a word with two distinct meanings in the Bible:

1. A body of people who live at the same time in a given period of history. Generation is used in this sense in, for example, Deuteronomy 32:5, where Moses calls his contemporaries "a perverse and crooked generation." Applied in this way, generation is roughly synonymous with the word age, as in this sentence: "Our age is characterized by its love of technology." See Matthew 11:16 and Luke 9:41 for further examples of this usage.

2. A single succession, made up of a set of individuals who share a common ancestor, in the line of descent. In this sense (Gen. 17:7; Ex. 1:6; Matt. 1:17), the word generation usually occurs when the Bible gives a genealogical or historical account of a family or tribe. First Chronicles 5:6–7, for instance, is the account of Beerah, his brothers, and "the genealogy of their generations."

While generation is sometimes used in the Bible to indicate a more or less specific span of time (Gen. 15:16), the word is far more frequently applied in an indefinite way. So it is best to avoid forc-

ing our English understanding of generation (the average period of time between the birth of a parent and the birth of his firstborn child, about 25–30 years) upon the word as it is used in the Bible.

GENEROSITY — liberality in spirit, especially in contributing to the needy. Christian giving should be "a matter of generosity and not as a grudging obligation" (2 Cor. 9:5). Also see ALMS.

GENESIS, BOOK OF — the first book of the Bible. Placed at the opening of the Hebrew Scriptures, Genesis is the first of the five books of Moses, known as the PENTATEUCH.

Genesis is the book of beginnings. The word Genesis means "the origin, source, creation, or coming into being of something." The Hebrew name for the book is *bereshith*, the first word in the Hebrew text, which is translated as "in the beginning" (Gen. 1:1). Genesis describes such important beginnings as the Creation, the fall of man, and the early years of the nation of Israel.

The beginning of salvation history—the story of God and man, sin and grace, wrath and mercy, covenant and redemption—also begins in the Book of Genesis. These themes are repeated often throughout the rest of the Bible. As the Book of Revelation is the climax and conclusion of the Bible, so the Book of Genesis is the beginning and essential seed-plot of the Bible. Thus, Genesis is an important book for understanding the meaning of the entire Bible.

Structure of the Book. The Book of Genesis may conveniently be divided into four major parts: (1) the Creation and the early days of mankind (Gen. 1:1—11:26); (2) the story of Abraham and Isaac (Gen. 12:1—25:18); (3) the story of Jacob and Esau (Gen. 25:19—36:43); and (4) the story of Joseph and his brothers (Gen. 37:1—50:26).

The first major part of the Book of Genesis (chaps. 1—11) contains five great events: (1) the history of creation and a description of life in the Garden of Eden before the Fall (Gen. 1:1—2:25); (2) the story of Adam and Eve in the Garden of Eden: the temptation and fall of man (Gen. 3:1–24); (3) the story of Cain and Abel (Gen. 4:1–16); (4) the story of Noah and the Flood: the wickedness and judgment of man (Gen. 6:5—9:29); and (5) the story of the Tower of Babel: the proud presumption of man, the confusion of tongues, and the scattering of mankind upon the earth (Gen. 11:1-9). Each of these great events relates to the whole of humanity, and each is filled with significance that continues throughout Scripture.

The rest of the Book of Genesis (chaps. 12—50) relates the narrative of the four great patriarchs of Israel: Abraham, Isaac, Jacob, and Joseph. The theme of these chapters is God's sovereignty in calling out a CHOSEN PEOPLE who would serve and worship Him.

Authorship and Date. The Book of Genesis gives no notice about its author. The early church, however, held to the conviction that Moses wrote the book, as did the Jerusalem Talmud and the first-century Jewish historian Josephus. In spite of the number of modern scholars who reject the Mosaic authorship of Genesis, the traditional view has much to commend it. Both the Old Testament and the New Testament contain frequent testimony to the Mosaic authorship of the entire Pentateuch (Lev. 1:1–2; Neh. 13:1; Matt. 8:4; Acts 26:22).

It would be difficult to find a person in Israel's life who was better prepared or qualified than Moses to write the history recorded in the Book of Genesis. A man who "was learned in all the wisdom of the Egyptians" (Acts 7:22), Moses was providentially prepared to understand and integrate, under the inspiration of God, all the avail-

GENESIS: A Teaching Outline

Part One: Primeval History (1:1—11:9)

Part Two: Patriarchal History (11:10—50:26)

able records, manuscripts, and oral narratives. Moses may have written the book during the years of the wilderness wandering to prepare the new generation to enter the land of Canaan.

As a prophet who enjoyed the unusual privilege of unhurried hours of communion with God on Mount Sinai, Moses was well equipped to record for all generations this magnificent account of God's dealings with the human race and the nation of Israel.

Historical Setting. Moses may have finished writing the Book of Genesis not long before his death on Mount Nebo (Deuteronomy 34). During this time the children of Israel, now led by Joshua, were camped east of the Jordan River, poised for the invasion of Canaan. In such a crucial historical context, the message of the Book of Genesis would have been of tremendous spiritual help to its first hearers. The creation of the world, the beginnings of sin and disobedience, the principle of judgment and deliverance, the scattering of the nations, the call and covenant God made with Abraham, the checkered careers of the first descendants of Abraham—all of these accounts would bear directly on the attitudes and faith of the new community.

The first readers, or hearers, of the Book of Genesis were the covenant community, the Chosen People of God. Like Abraham, they were on a journey—a great venture of faith into the unknown (Gen. 12:1–9). Like Abraham, they needed to respond to God in wholehearted faith and in the fear of the Lord (Gen. 22:1–19). They needed to hear such words as were spoken to Isaac: "I am the God of your father Abraham; do not fear, for I am with you. I will bless you and multiply your descendants for My servant Abraham's sake" (Gen. 26:24).

Theological Contribution. The Book of Genesis is a primary source for several basic doctrines of the Bible. The book focuses on God primarily in two areas: He is the Creator of the universe, and He is the one who initiates covenant with His people. Genesis ties creation and covenant together in a stunning manner: the God who initiates covenant is the same God who has created the entire universe. The eternal God and almighty Creator enters into covenant with His people! (Gen. 1:1; John 1:1).

God's covenant with Abraham is the basic plot of the Scripture. God's work from that day forward was to accomplish His plan for the nations of the world through His people Israel, the descendants of Abraham. God's covenant with Abraham (Gen. 12:1–3; 15:1–21) contains a number of personal blessings on the father of the faith. But the climax of the text is in the words of worldwide import: "And in you all the families of the earth shall be blessed" (Gen. 12:3).

This promise is realized in the person of the Lord Jesus Christ, the Seed of Abraham (Gal. 3:16, 19), through whom peoples of all nations and families may enter into the joy of knowing the God of Abraham. God's promise is realized also in the church, in those who believe in Christ, which the apostle Paul calls "the Israel of God" (Gal. 6:16). The true

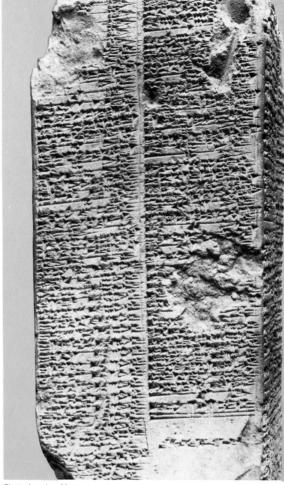

Photo: Asmolean Museum

This list of kings engraved in stone was discovered in ancient Mesopotamia. It contains the names of several kings who ruled before the Great Flood described in the Book of Genesis.

"seed," or descendants, of Abraham, Paul argued, are not Abraham's physical descendants but those who have the same faith as Abraham (Rom. 9:7–8; Gal. 3:29).

Genesis presents the creation of man as male and female in the image of God (Gen. 1:26–27; 5:3; 9:6), man's fall and ruin, his judgment, and his possible triumph in God's grace. In the context of man's judgment came the first whisper of the gospel message of the final triumph of Christ over Satan: "And I will put enmity between you [the serpent] and the woman, and between your seed and her seed; He shall bruise your head, and you shall bruise His heel" (Gen. 3:15). This prophecy was fulfilled by the death of Jesus on the cross, a sacrifice that destroyed the works of the devil (1 John 3:8).

The apostle Paul referred to the story of Adam's fall (Genesis 3) by comparing Adam to Christ (Rom. 5:12, 18). Christ is portrayed as a "second Adam" who, by His atonement, reverses the effects of the Fall. Some scholars see another type, or foreshadowing truth, of Calvary in the fact that God, in order to cover the nakedness of Adam and Eve (symbolic of sin, guilt, and shame), killed an animal (thereby shedding blood) and made tunics of skin with which to clothe them (Gen. 3:21). For, as the writer of the Book of Hebrews says, "Without shedding of blood there is no remission [of sin]" (Heb. 9:22).

Special Consideration. Some scholars organize the literary structure of the Book of Genesis around the Hebrew word *toledoth* (literally, genealogy), which Moses seems to use ten times in Genesis to indicate major blocks of material. The NKJV translates *toledoth* as "this is the history of" (Gen. 2:4) and "this is the genealogy of" (Gen. 5:1; 6:9; 10:1; 11:10; 11:27; 25:12; 25:19; 36:1; 37:2).

The Book of Genesis takes the reader to the moment when the Creator spoke into being the sun, moon, stars, planets, galaxies, plants, moving creatures, and mankind. Those who seek to discredit the Book of Genesis by pointing to alleged discrepancies between religion and science are blind to the exalted spiritual content of this work. If a student expects to find in Genesis a scientific account of how the world came into existence, with all questions concerning primitive life answered in technical language, he will be disappointed. Genesis is not an attempt to answer such technical questions.

Genesis is marked by exquisite prose, such as chapter 22 (the account of the binding of Isaac) and chapters 37—50 (the Joseph narrative). Literary critics often point to Genesis 24, the story of a bride for Isaac, as a classic example of great narrative style. Genesis also has poetic sections such as the solemn curses by God (Gen. 3:14–19) and the prophetic blessing of Jacob (Gen. 49:3–27). Genesis 1, the history of creation, is written in a highly elevated prose with a poetic tone.

At times attention is focused on the men in the Book of Genesis. But women of major significance also appear in the Book: Eve is the mother of all living (Gen. 3:20); Sarah had a faith that was complementary to Abraham's (Gen. 21:1–7); and Leah, Rachel, Bilhah, and Zilpah are the mothers of the 12 patriarchs of Israel (Gen. 29:31—30:24; 35:23–26).

Genesis is also a book of firsts. Genesis records the first birth (Gen. 4:1), the first death (Gen. 4:8), the first musical instruments (Gen. 4:21), and the first rainbow (Gen. 9:12–17). Genesis is indeed the book of beginnings. As the children of Israel read this book in the wilderness, or after they crossed the Jordan River, they knew that their experiences with God were just beginning.

GENITALS — the external organs of the human reproductive system (Deut. 25:11; the secrets, KJV; the private parts, RSV, NIV).

GENNESARET [geh NESS ah ray] (*garden of riches*) — the Greek form of the Hebrew name *Chinnereth* and the name of a lake, a district, and a city in the New Testament:

1. The town Gennesaret, on the west shore of the lake of the same name. This town was a fortified city of Naphtali (Josh. 19:35) commonly referred to as Chinnereth.

2. The district of Gennesaret, identified in the Bible as "the land of Gennesaret" (Mark 6:53). This district was a plain extending two kilometers (one mile) from the Sea of Galilee along a five kilometer (three mile) section of Galilee's north shore. Figs, olives, palms, and a variety of other types of trees were grown in this region's rich, loamy soil.

3. The "Lake of Gennesaret" (Luke 5:1). This lake is more commonly known as the Sea of Galilee (Matt. 4:18) and is sometimes simply referred to as "the lake" (Luke 5:2).

Also see GALILEE, SEA OF.

GENTILES — a term used by Jewish people to refer to foreigners, or any other people who were not a part of the Jewish race.

The Jews were the Chosen People of God who had entered a covenant with God. God initiated the

All nations surrounding Israel, including Egypt, were considered pagans and Gentiles by the Hebrew people.

Photo by Ben Chapman

The theater at Jerash (ancient Gerasa, one of the ten cities known as the Decapolis). Jerash is one of the best-preserved cities from the Roman era in Palestine.

covenant with Abraham (Gen. 12:1–7) and affirmed it repeatedly through Israel's leaders and prophets.

Because of this covenant relationship, a feeling of exclusivism gradually developed among the Jews over a period of several centuries. In early Hebrew history, Gentiles or non-Jews were treated cordially by the Israelites (Deut. 10:19; Num. 35:15; Ezek. 47:2). Men of Israel often married Gentile women, including Rahab, Ruth, and Bathsheba. However, after the Hebrews returned from their period of CAPTIVITY in Babylon, the practice of intermarriage was discouraged (Ezra 9:12; 10:2–44; Neh. 10:30). Separation between Jews and Gentiles became increasingly strict; by the New Testament period the hostility was complete. The persecution of the Jews by the Greeks and Romans from about 400 B.C. to the New Testament era caused the Jews to retaliate with hatred for all Gentiles and to avoid all contact with foreigners.

The life and teachings of Jesus set the ideal for positive relationships between Jews and Gentiles, as recorded in the apostle Paul's writings (Rom. 1:16; Eph. 2:14; Col. 3:11). But the process of such idealism becoming a reality was a struggle for the early church.

The Book of Acts pictures the struggle of the early church to include the Gentiles in its life. When Peter, taught by the vision at Joppa, broke with Jewish tradition by visiting and eating with the Gentile Cornelius, it gave offense even to the Christian Jews (Acts 10:28; 11:3).

The apostle Paul became an effective missionary to the Gentiles (Acts 13:46–49; 15:14). At first the early church was composed of converted Jews who accepted Jesus as the Messiah, God's Anointed One. But more and more Gentiles came to accept the teaching of the gospel. Some Jewish leaders warned that they could not enter the church unless they also submitted to the Jewish ritual of CIRCUMCISION (Acts 15:1–31). But Paul fought against this requirement as a denial of the gospel and ultimately convinced the churches. The only condition of sal-

vation is repentance from sin and faith in Christ Jesus (Acts 20:21). "There is neither Jew nor Greek...for you are all one in Christ Jesus" (Gal. 3:28).

GENTILES, COURT OF (see COURT OF THE GENTILES).

GENTLENESS — kindness, consideration, a spirit of fairness and compassion. The apostle Paul declared that Christians should have a spirit of gentleness toward all people (Phil. 4:5; 2 Cor. 10:1).

GENUBATH [geh NOO bath] (meaning unknown) — a son of Hadad (a fugitive Edomite prince) and his wife, who was the sister of Queen Tahpenes of Egypt (1 Kin. 11:20).

GERA [GHEE rah] (*sojourner, pilgrim*) — the name of four men from the tribe of Benjamin:
1. A son of Bela (Gen. 46:21).
2. The father or ancestor of the judge Ehud (Judg. 3:15).
3. The father or ancestor of Shimei, who cursed David when David fled from Absalom (1 Kin. 2:8).
4. A son or descendant of Bela (1 Chr. 8:3, 5, 7).

GERAH [GEE rah] (see MONEY OF THE BIBLE; WEIGHTS AND MEASURES).

GERAR [GEE rar] (*halting place*) — an ancient Philistine city in the NEGEB, in southern Palestine, between Kadesh Barnea and Shur (Gen. 10:19; 20:1). A wealthy city, Gerar probably controlled an important caravan route between Egypt and Palestine. Gerar was ruled by ABIMELECH, "king of the Philistines" (Gen. 26:1). During a famine, Abraham and his wife Sarah journeyed to Gerar. Fearing for his life, Abraham concealed the truth that Sarah was his wife, calling her his "sister." Abraham was reprimanded by Abimelech for his deception; eventually the two men concluded a treaty.

GERASA [GEAR ah sah] — a city situated in TRANSJORDAN about 56 kilometers (35 miles) southeast of the Sea of Galilee (see Map 6, C–3). One of the 10 cities of the DECAPOLIS, Gerasa is not men-

Photo by Howard Vos

Mount Gerizim in the district of Samaria, site of the Samaritan temple in Jesus' time (John 4:20-21).

tioned by name in the Bible, but it may be inferred from the use of Gerasenes (Mark 5:1; Luke 8:26, 37, RSV, NIV, NASB; Gadarenes, NKJV).

The Roman city of Gerasa was the same place as the Nabatean city of Jerash. Excavations at this site (the modern Jarash) have uncovered the best preserved Roman city in Palestine, (now Jordan), including ruins of the temple of Artemis, a triumphal arch (built in A.D. 129 to celebrate the visit of Emperor Hadrian), a forum with a street lined with columns, and a stairway leading to an older pagan temple. Archaeological evidence of at least a dozen churches indicate that Gerasa was also once a large Christian community.

GERASENES [GARE uh seens] — a form of GADARENES.

GERGESENES [GUR guh scenes] — a form of GADARENES.

GERIZIM [geh RUH zim] — a mountain in the district of Samaria (see Map 3, B–3). Gerizim was located southwest of Mount Ebal. The main north–south road through central Palestine ran between these two mountains. Thus, Gerizim was of strategic military importance.

When the Hebrew people reached the Promised Land, Moses directed them to climb Mount Gerizim and Mount Ebal. Six tribes stood on the slopes of each mountain (Deut. 27:11–14). Then Moses pronounced the blessings for keeping the Law from Mount Gerizim and the curses for not keeping it from Mount Ebal (Deut. 11:29; 27:4–26). A ledge halfway to the top of Gerizim is popularly called "Jotham's pulpit." The characteristics of the two mountains make it possible to speak from either mountain and be heard easily in the valley below.

When the Israelites returned from their years of CAPTIVITY in Babylon, they refused to allow the SAMARITANS, the residents of this mountain region, to assist in rebuilding Jerusalem (Ezra 4:1–4; Neh. 2:19–20; 13:28). In the days of Alexander the Great, a Samaritan temple was built on Mount Gerizim. Although it was destroyed by the Hasmonean king John Hyrcanus in 128 B.C., the Samaritans still worshiped on Mount Gerizim in Jesus' day (John 4:20–21). The small Samaritan community at Nablus continues to celebrate the Passover on Mount Gerizim to this day.

Jacob's Well is situated at the foot of Mount Gerizim, today called Jebel el-Tor. This is the well where Jesus met the woman of Samaria, discussed Samaritan worship practices on Mount Gerizim, and told her of Himself—"a fountain of water springing up into everlasting life" (John 4:14).

GERSHOM [GUR shom] (*sojourner*) — the name of four men in the Old Testament:

1. The firstborn son of Moses and Zipporah (Ex. 2:22).

2. The father of Jonathan, a Levite who became a priest to the Danites at Laish during the time of the judges (Judg. 18:30).

3. The oldest son of Levi (1 Chr. 15:7), also called GERSHON.

4. A descendant of Phinehas and a family leader who returned with Ezra from the Babylonian Captivity (Ezra 8:2).

GERSHOMITES [GUR shom ites] — the descendants of GERSHOM (1 Chr. 6:62, RSV; 1 Chr. 6:71, RSV).

GERSHON [GUR shun] (*exile, expulsion*) — the oldest of the three sons of LEVI; his brothers were

Kohath and Merari (Gen. 46:11; Num. 3:17). He is also called Gershom (1 Chr. 15:7). Gershon was the founder of the family called the GERSHONITES (Num. 26:57), one of the three main divisions of the Levitical priesthood. Gershon was apparently born to Levi before Jacob's family moved to Egypt to escape a famine (Ex. 6:16). Although Gershon was the oldest of Levi's sons, it was through the line of Gershon's younger brother, Kohath, that the priestly line of Aaron sprang years later after the EXODUS of the Hebrew people from Egypt.

GERSHONITES [GUR shon ites] — the descendants of GERSHON, son of Levi (Num. 3:21).

GESHEM [GEH shim] (*rain*) — an Arab who sought to hinder the building of the wall of Jerusalem by Nehemiah (Neh. 2:19; Gashmu, KJV).

GESHUR [GEH sure] (*bridge*) — a small Aramean kingdom on the eastern slopes of Mount Hermon. Geshur was situated north of Bashan and south of Syria, serving as a buffer state between Aram and Israel. David married MAACAH, the daughter of Talmai, king of Geshur; she became the mother of Absalom (2 Sam. 3:3).

GESHURI [gih SHOO rye] — a form of GESHURITES.

The Garden of Gethsemane, where Jesus agonized in prayer on the night before His crucifixion (Matt. 26:36-46). The roots of these giant olive trees may date from the time of Christ or before.

GESHURITES [GESH you rites] — the name of two groups in the Old Testament:
1. The inhabitants of GESHUR (Deut. 3:14, Geshuri; KJV).
2. A tribe which occupied the territory between Arabia and Philistia (Josh. 13:2; Geshuri, KJV).

GETHER [GHEE thur] (*fear*) — the name of two men in the Old Testament:
1. A son of Aram (Gen. 10:23).
2. A son or descendant of Shem (1 Chr. 1:17).

GETHSEMANE [geth SIMM uh nee] (*olive press*) — the garden where Jesus often went alone or with His disciples for prayer, rest, or fellowship, and the site where He was betrayed by Judas on the night before His crucifixion (Luke 21:37; John 18:1–2).

Gethsemane was situated on the Mount of Olives just east of Jerusalem, across the Kidron Valley and opposite the Temple (Mark 13:3; John 18:1). From its name scholars conclude that the garden was situated in an olive grove that contained an olive press. Attempts to locate the exact site of the garden have been unsuccessful. Many Christians have agreed on one site—the place which Constantine's mother Helena designated about A.D. 325. But at least two other sites are also defended by tradition and have their supporters. The gospel accounts do not provide enough details to show the exact site of the garden.

The four gospel writers focus special attention on Jesus' final visit to Gethsemane just before His arrest and crucifixion. After the Last Supper, Jesus returned there with His disciples for final instructions and a period of soul-searching prayer. All the disciples were instructed; but only Peter, James and John went to Gethsemane with Jesus to pray (Mark 14:26–32). Jesus urged them to stand watch while He prayed. Then He pleaded with God to deliver Him from the coming events (Mark 14:32–42). But His prayer was no arrogant attempt to resist God's will or even to change God's plan. His pleas clearly acknowledged His obedience to the will of the Father: "O My Father, if this cup cannot pass away from Me unless I drink it, Your will be done" (Matt. 26:42).

An important lesson can be learned from a study of Gethsemane. Jesus, no less than His disciples then and since, faced the temptation of Satan. He "was in all points tempted as we are, yet without sin" (Heb. 4:15). No wonder He cried, "My soul is exceedingly sorrowful, even to death" (Matt. 26:38). But He won the victory over Satan as He declared to His Father, "Your will be done."

Because Jesus has faced such powerful temptation Himself, we can relate to Him as a personal Lord and Savior. "For in that He Himself has suffered, being tempted, He is able to aid those who are tempted" (Heb. 2:18).

GEUEL [geh YOU ell] (*majesty of God*) — one of the 12 men sent by Moses to spy out the land of Canaan (Num. 13:15).

GEZER [GEZ ur] (*portion, division*) — an ancient

Canaanite city (see Map 3, A–4) 17 kilometers (20 miles) west of Jerusalem that was conquered by Joshua (Josh. 10:33; 12:12). Because the Hebrews never fully obeyed God's command to destroy the Canaanites in this city (Josh. 21:21; 1 Chr. 6:67), they eventually lost the city to the Philistines (2 Sam. 5:25; 1 Chr. 20:4).

During the reign of Solomon, an Egyptian Pharaoh conquered Gezer, burned the city, and killed its inhabitants. Pharaoh gave the city and his daughter to Solomon to establish peace between Egypt and Israel. Solomon rebuilt Gezer and turned it into a strategic military and economic center (1 Kin. 9:15, 17–19). Many years later, Gezer was destroyed by the Assyrian king, Tilgath-Pileser (2 Kin. 16:5–7) when he came to rescue Ahaz, king of Judah, from the attack of the Syrians and Israelites.

In the Jewish wars just before the time of Christ, Gezer was an important military fortress (1 Macc. 9:52, 13:53). The city is not mentioned in the New Testament because it was destroyed earlier by the Romans.

Major archaeological excavations at Gezer were conducted by R. A. S. Macalister from 1902–1909 and by W. G. Dever, J. D. Seger, and G. E. Wright from 1964–1973. The city covered an area of about 30 acres and was first established before the time of Abraham. Some of the most significant discoveries at Gezer were: (1) a Palestinian calendar based on the agricultural seasons. This inscription in the ancient Hebrew script is one of the oldest Hebrew documents (from the time of Solomon); (2) huge walls and gates that were characteristic of the construction methods of Solomon at Hazor and Megiddo; (3) an impressive sloping tunnel about 50 meters (150 feet) long that leads down to a large cistern under the city. This water supply was important to ancient walled cities if the people hoped to withstand an extended enemy siege; and (4) a row of eight huge stones standing on end. These stones may be a part of a High Place where heathen gods were worshiped.

GEZRITES [GEHZ rites] — a form of GIRZITES.

GHIMEL [GHEE muhl] — a form of GIMEL.

GHOST — an old English word used by the KJV to refer to one's spirit or the soul. In the KJV, "to give up the ghost" (Gen. 25:8; Job 3:11; Jer. 15:9) is to die or to give up one's spirit. The NKJV uses the expression, "to breathe one's last" or more simply, "to die." The other major use of "ghost" in the KJV is in referring to the Holy Ghost (John 7:39). The NKJV rightly renders this "Holy Spirit."

GHOST, HOLY (see HOLY SPIRIT).

GIAH [GIH ah] (*bubbling spring*) — an unidentified place in the territory of Benjamin (2 Sam. 2:24).

GIANTS — human beings of abnormal size and strength. Races of giants are first mentioned in the Old Testament in Genesis 6:4, where giant god-like beings were produced by the union of "the sons of God" and "the daughters of men." These giants, or NEPHILIM, became "mighty men…men of renown," probably a reference to their tremendous height. These abnormal unions displeased God (Gen. 6:5–6).

REPHAIM were primitive giants who lived in Canaan, Edom, Moab, and Ammon. They were also known as Emims (Deut. 2:11) and Zamzummims (Deut. 2:20). King Og of Bashan (Deut. 3:11) was the last of these giants. His iron bed was 13 cubits long and 4 cubits wide (about 19 feet by 6 feet).

When Moses sent 12 men to spy out the land of Canaan, they returned with the frightening report that they saw "giants" who made them feel like "grasshoppers" (Num. 13:33). These giants were descendants of Anak, "a people great and tall" (Deut. 9:2). This negative report by 10 of the spies caused the children of Israel to spend a night in murmuring and weeping. Only Joshua and Caleb urged the people to claim the land (Num. 14:38).

Goliath is the most famous giant in the Bible (1 Sam. 17:4), measuring six cubits and a span, which is more than three meters (nine feet) tall. Goliath taunted the Israelites and demanded a warrior to meet him in combat. David, the shepherd boy, with his sling and stone, dared to accept the challenge of the Philistine giant in full armor because he knew that God would direct him in the battle (1 Sam. 17:45). David's stone struck Goliath in a vulnerable spot, killing the giant and putting the Philistines to flight (1 Sam. 17:50, 51).

GIANTS, VALLEY OF (see REPHAIM).

GIBBAR [GIB bahr] (*mighty man*) — a man whose descendants returned from the Captivity with Zerubbabel (Ezra 2:20).

GIBBETHON [GIB uh thon] (*height*) — a village of the tribe of Dan (Josh. 19:44) assigned to the Levites (Josh. 21:23). Nadab, king of Israel, was assassinated by Baasha at Gibbethon (1 Kin. 15:27). This city is probably modern Tell el–Melat, east of Ekron.

GIBEA [GIB ee ah] (*hill*) — a grandson of Caleb, of the tribe of Judah (1 Chr. 2:49).

GIBEAH, GIBEATH [gibb ee AH, gibb ee ATH] (*hill*) — the name of four different places in the Old Testament:

1. Gibeath-Haaraloth, "the hill of the foreskins" (Josh. 5:3), a place in Canaan where male Hebrews were circumcised.

2. A small, unidentified city in the territory of Judah (Josh. 15:57). The location of this city is disputed. Suggested locations have been 11 to 16 kilometers (seven to ten miles) southwest of Jerusalem and the same distance southeast of Hebron.

3. A city belonging to Benjamin (Judg. 19:14). Scholars disagree over whether this is the same city called Gibeath in Joshua 18:28. Gibeah has been excavated at the modern site of Tell el-Ful, five kilometers (three miles) north of Jerusalem. This city figured prominently in two separate periods of Old

Photo by Howard Vos

The great pool in Gibeon (Jer. 41:12), 36 feet in diameter, extends 30 feet deep through solid rock. It was the center of a wine-making industry in Old Testament times.

Testament history. It first appeared in Judges 19—20 as the site of a crime of lewdness and obscenity. All the children of Israel came together to punish Gibeah for its crimes. After a prolonged and mostly unsuccessful war against the Benjamites, the Israelites completely destroyed Gibeah (Judg. 20:40). The Tel el–Ful excavations have uncovered the remains of a Hebrew village completely destroyed by fire.

Gibeah was apparently rebuilt after the fire. The birthplace of Saul, it became the capital of his kingdom (1 Sam. 14:16; 15:34). In many passages, it is even called "Gibeah of Saul" (1 Sam. 11:4; Is. 10:29). At Tell el–Ful, the remains of Saul's fortress, built around 1015 B.C., have been found. The fortress walls, 2.5 to 3.5 meters (8 to 10 feet) thick, enclosed an area of 52 x 47 meters (170 x 155 feet). The stronghold was made up of two stories joined by a stone staircase.

4. The KJV uses "Gibeah" instead of "hill" in some passages, such as "the house of Abinadab that was in Gibeah" (2 Sam. 6:4).

GIBEATH ELOHIM [GIB ee ath el oh HEEM] (*hill of God*) — the place where Saul was filled with the Spirit of the Lord after he was anointed king of Israel (1 Sam. 10:5, RSV).

GIBEATHITE [GIBB ih uh thite] — a native or inhabitant of GIBEAH, a city of the tribe of Benjamin (1 Chr. 12:3).

GIBEON [GIBB eh un] (*pertaining to a hill*) — a city in the territory of Benjamin about ten kilometers (six miles) northwest of Jerusalem (see Map 3, B–4). It was the chief city of the HIVITES.

The first reference to Gibeon in the Bible is Joshua 9:3. After the Israelites destroyed the cities of Jericho and Ai (Joshua 6—8), Gibeon's inhabitants, fearing the same fate, made a covenant with the Israelites. Although they established the treaty by deceit and thus were made slaves by the Israelites, the Gibeonites were still protected from the alliance of five Amorite kings. In a battle over Gibeon between Joshua and the Amorite alliance (Josh. 10:1–11), the sun stood still for a day and hailstones rained down on the fleeing Amorites.

Gibeon does not appear again in Scripture until about 1000 B.C. Then, in a gruesome contest of strength, 12 of David's men and 12 of the men of Ishbosheth (Saul's son) killed one another with their swords. The place was named "the Field of the Sharp Swords" (2 Sam. 2:16) because of this event. There followed a great battle in which David's forces were victorious (2 Sam. 2:12–17).

The prophet Jeremiah mentioned a "great pool that is in Gibeon" (Jer. 41:12). This pool was discovered in an excavation of the site, beginning in 1956. Archaeologists discovered a large open pit about 11 meters (33 feet) deep that had been dug into the solid rock. A large stone stairway descended into the pit, then continued another 12 meters (36 feet) down to a water chamber. This large vat or pit was apparently the center of a wine–making industry in ancient Gibeon during the seventh century B.C. The lower chamber provided water for the wine and also doubled as the city's water supply.

GIBEONITES [GIB ee un ites] — the Canaanite inhabitants of the city of GIBEON, probably also including the people of its three dependent towns (2 Sam. 21:1–9). When the Gibeonites heard of Joshua's victories at JERICHO and AI, they pretended to be ambassadors from a far country in order to make a peace treaty with the invading Israelites (Josh. 9:4–5). When the deception was discovered, the Israelites permitted the Gibeonites to live, according to their agreement. However, they were made slaves, "woodcutters and water carriers for all the congregation and for the altar of the Lord" (Josh. 9:21).

Apparently King Saul broke this covenant of peace with the Gibeonites in later years. During the reign of David, when a three–year famine blighted the land, it was discovered that the Lord was angry with the "bloodthirsty house" of Saul, who had "killed the Gibeonites" (2 Sam. 21:1) in a frenzy of patriotic zeal. To make up for this wrong, David allowed the Gibeonites to hang seven of Saul's descendants (2 Sam. 21:9).

GIBLITES [GIB lights] — a form of GEBALITES.

GIDDALTI [gih DAL tih] (*I have magnified God*) — a son of Heman and one of those in charge of the music services in the Temple in David's time (1 Chr. 25:4, 29).

GIDDEL [GID dell] (*magnified*) — the name of two men whose descendants returned from the Captivity to Jerusalem:

1. The ancestor of a family of Nethinim (Temple servants) who returned with Zerubbabel (Ezra 2:47).

2. The ancestor of a family of Solomon's servants (Neh. 7:58).

GIDEON [GIDD ee un] (*warrior*) — a military hero and spiritual leader who delivered Israel from the oppression of the Midianites.

As a young lad, Gideon had seen the land oppressed by the Midianites and Amalekites for seven years (Judg. 6:1). Like invading locusts, the roving bands camped on the land of the Israelites. At harvest time, they destroyed the crops and animals and plundered the farmers' houses. Israel's misfortune was apparently caused by their spiritual relapse into Baal worship (Judg. 6:1).

As young Gideon was threshing wheat, the angel of the Lord appeared with strong words of encouragement: "The Lord is with you, you mighty man of valor...Surely, I will be with you, and you shall defeat the Midianites as one man" (Judg. 6:12, 16).

Gideon then asked the messenger for a sign that God had selected him for divine service. He prepared an offering and placed it on an altar. The an-

gel touched the offering with his staff, and fire consumed it (6:19–21). Gideon then recognized his personal call to serve God.

Gideon's first assignment was to destroy his father's altar of Baal in the family's backyard (Judg. 6:25). This act required great courage, for Gideon feared his father's house and the men of the city who must have worshiped at the altar. For this reason, Gideon and ten servants destroyed the altar of Baal and a wood idol by night and erected an altar to the Lord. Gideon immediately presented an offering to the Lord on the altar (6:27–28). When they discovered that the altar to Baal had been destroyed, the household and the community were outraged. When it was learned that "Gideon the son of Joash has done this thing" (6:29), Joash was called to account for his son's behavior. To his credit, Joash defended Gideon by implying that an authentic god should require no defense. "If he (Baal) is a god, let him plead for himself" (6:31). From that day on, Gideon was called Jerubbaal, meaning "Let Baal plead" (6:25–32).

As the oppression of the Midianites intensified, Gideon sent out messengers to all Manasseh and the surrounding tribes to rally volunteers to Israel's cause (Judg. 6:35). When Gideon's volunteers assembled, about 32,000 citizen soldiers stood in the ranks (Judg. 7:1). Although there were 135,000 Midianites camped in a nearby valley, God directed Gideon to thin out the ranks. After dismissing the fearful and afraid, only 10,000 remained. Gideon's band was now outnumbered about 13 to 1.

"There are still too many," God told Gideon. "Bring them down to the water, and I will test them for you there" (7:4). Those who lapped the water with their hands, never taking their eyes from the horizon, were retained in Gideon's army; those who got down on their knees to drink, forgetting to keep watch for the enemy, were dismissed. Now only 300 soldiers remained (Judg. 7:5–7). The Midianites outnumbered Gideon's band 450 to 1. But God and Gideon had a secret plan!

Gideon divided the army into three companies. Then he gave each man a trumpet, a pitcher, and a torch. At the appointed time, 300 trumpets blasted the air, 300 hands raised their pitchers and smashed them to bits, 300 burning torches pierced the darkness, and 300 warriors cried, "The sword of the Lord and of Gideon" (Judg. 7:19–21).

The Midianites were thrown into panic. In the confusion, some committed suicide or killed their comrades. The remaining soldiers fled. The enemies of Israel were completely routed, and Israel's homeland was secure (Judg. 7:22; 8:10). It was a glorious victory for God and for Gideon, who became an instant hero (8:22).

Gideon and his men pursued the fleeing enemy. Many of them were killed or captured by Gideon's allies. Two Midianite kings, Zebah and Zalmunna, were captured and killed for their murderous deeds (Judges 8).

As a conquering warrior, Gideon was invited to become king (Judg. 8:22), but he declined. Modest

Photo by Howard Vos

A family fills their water jars at the Gihon Spring—a natural source of water for the residents of Jerusalem for many centuries (2 Chr. 32:30).

and devout, he was careful not to grasp at the power and glory that belonged to God. After he retired to his home, Israel was blessed with 40 years of peace (Judg. 8:28).

Through the life and exploits of Gideon, God reveals much about Himself and the preparation which His leaders need for divine service. Gideon shows that God calls leaders from unlikely situations. Gideon was a poor farmer's son who worked with his hands, and his father was an idol worshiper (Judg. 6:15, 25). Still, he was an effective leader in God's service.

Gideon also teaches that God prefers a few dedicated and disciplined disciples to throngs of uncommitted workers. God can win victories with a fully committed minority (Judg. 7:2, 4, 7).

Another leadership lesson from Gideon is that a leader's spiritual life is sustained by regular worship. Devout Gideon appears to have worshiped frequently—in times of personal crisis as well as celebration (Judg. 6:18–21; 7:15).

GIDEONI [gid ee OWN ih] (*feller*) — the father of Abidan, leader of the tribe of Benjamin in the wilderness (Num. 1:11).

GIDOM [GIE dum] (*desolation*) — a place in the territory of Benjamin which marked the farthest point of Israel's pursuit of the tribe of Benjamin during their civil war (Judg. 20:45).

GIER EAGLE (see ANIMALS OF THE BIBLE).

GIFT, GIVING — the act of bestowing a favor or an item on another person without expecting anything in return. The purpose of a gift may be to honor (2 Sam. 8:2; Dan. 2:48), celebrate (Rev. 11:10), or simply to bestow favor or help (Esth. 9:22). God is the giver of every good and perfect gift (Matt. 7:11; James 1:5, 17), including eternal life (Rom. 6:23), salvation (Eph. 2:8), the necessities of life (Matt. 6:11), ability to work (Eccl. 3:13; 5:19; Deut. 8:18), the Holy Spirit (Acts 2:38; 5:32), spiritual abilities (1 Cor. 12:4), and above all His indescribable gift (2 Cor. 9:15), His Son (John 3:16).

The Christian's gifts to God should not be bribes to obtain His favor, but grateful responses to what He has done in our lives. We are to give (Luke 6:30, 38), "for God loves a cheerful giver" (2 Cor. 9:7). Giving itself can be thought of as a gift from God: "Having...gifts...let us use them:...he who gives, with liberality" (Rom. 12:6, 8).

GIFT OF HEALING; GIFTS, SPIRITUAL (see SPIRITUAL GIFTS).

GIFT OF TONGUES (see TONGUES, GIFT OF).

GIHON [GIH hon] (*stream*) — the name of a river and a spring in the Old Testament:

1. One of the four rivers of the Garden of EDEN (Gen. 2:13). Some scholars believe the name Gihon implies a source in a large lake or cataract and that it refers to the NILE River. Others, however, believe Gihon refers to a smaller river in the Euphrates Valley system—perhaps a major irrigation ditch or canal.

2. A spring outside the walls of Jerusalem where the city obtained part of its water supply (2 Chr. 32:30). The Canaanite inhabitants of ancient Jerusalem, or JEBUS, had used and protected the spring in their fortifications, too. When David and his soldiers conquered Jebus, they entered the city through the water shaft that led from the spring into the city (2 Sam. 5:8). Israel continued to use Gihon and its water channel. King Hezekiah channeled the water more elaborately when he constructed the famous SILOAM tunnel in 701 B. C. as part of the city's preparation against the siege of the Assyrians.

Gihon was the site where Solomon was anointed and proclaimed king (1 Kin. 1:33, 38, 45). Some scholars believe it later became customary for the new king to drink of the waters of Gihon during his coronation ceremony (Ps. 110:7).

GILALAI [GILL ah lih] (*weighty*) — a Levite musician who participated in the dedication of the wall of Jerusalem following the Captivity (Neh. 12:36).

GILBOA [gill BOW ah] (perhaps *bubbling fountain*) — a ridge of mountains in the territory of Issachar at the east end of the Plain of Jezreel (see Map 3,

View of the Plain of Jezreel with the mountains of Gilboa in the background.

B–3). Gilboa was the site where King Saul and his sons died when the Philistines defeated Israel (1 Chr. 10:1, 8). Jebel Fuku'a, about five kilometers (three miles) southeast of Jezreel, represents the location today.

GILEAD [GILL ee ad] (*mound of stones*) — the name of three men, two mountains, and one city in the Old Testament:

1. A son of Machir and grandson of Manasseh (Josh. 17:1). He founded a tribal family, the GILE-ADITES.

2. A mountain region east of the Jordan River 915 meters (3,000 feet) above sea level. Extending about 97 kilometers (60 miles) from near the south end of the Sea of Galilee to the north end of the Dead Sea, Gilead is about 32 kilometers (20 miles) wide. It is bounded on the west by the JORDAN River, on the south by the land of Moab, on the north by the YARMUK River, and on the east by the desert.

The Jabbok River divides Gilead into two parts: northern Gilead, the land between the Jabbok and the Yarmuk, and southern Gilead, the land between the Jabbok and the Arnon (Josh. 12:2). The term Gilead, however, came to be applied to the entire region of Israelite TRANSJORDAN (Deut. 34:1).

This lush region receives an annual rainfall of from 71 to 81 centimeters (28 to 32 inches). Thus, much of it is thickly wooded today, as it was in Absalom's day (2 Sam. 18:6–9). Many fugitives fled to this region for safety. Jacob fled to Gilead from Laban his father–in–law (Gen. 31:21). The Israelites who feared the Philistines in King Saul's day fled here (1 Sam. 13:7), as did Ishbosheth (2 Sam. 2:8–9) and David (2 Sam. 17:22, 26) during Absalom's revolt. Gilead also contains rich grazing land (1 Chr. 5:9–10).

The BALM OF GILEAD, an aromatic resin used for medical purposes, was exported to Tyre and elsewhere (Ezek. 27:17). The Ishmaelites who carried Joseph into Egyptian bondage also traded in Gilead balm (Gen. 37:25).

When Canaan was being allocated to the Israelite tribes, Gilead fell to the Reubenites and Gadites because of its suitability for grazing cattle (Deut. 3:12–17). The half–tribe of Manasseh also shared in the land of Gilead.

3. A mountain on the edge of the Jezreel valley (Judg. 7:3). Gideon and his men were camped here when Gideon ordered a reduction in his troops before he fought the Midianites.

4. The father of JEPHTHAH, a judge of Israel (Judg. 11:1—12:7).

5. A chief of the family of Gad (1 Chr. 5:14).

6. A city in the region of Gilead condemned by the prophet Hosea (Hos. 6:8). The name Gilead in this passage is probably a poetic shortening of Ramoth Gilead or Jabesh Gilead, two of the cities of Gilead.

GILEAD, BALM OF — an aromatic gum or resin, reportedly having value as medicine (Jer. 8:22), exported from Gilead to Phoenicia and Egypt (Ezek. 27:17). Also see GILEAD.

GILEADITES [GILL ee ad ites] — descendants of Gilead (Num. 26:29; Judg. 10:3; 11:1, 40).

GILGAL [GILL gal] (*circle of stones*) — the name of a campsite and two cities in the Old Testament:

1. A village from which the prophet Elijah ascended into heaven (2 Kin. 2:1). Gilgal was perhaps in the hill country of Ephraim, about 13 kilometers (8 miles) northwest of Bethel.

2. The first campsite of the people of Israel after they crossed the Jordan River and entered the Promised Land (Josh. 4:19–20). They took stones from the Jordan and set them up at Gilgal as a memorial to God's deliverance. Many important events in Israel's history are associated with this city. The first Passover in Canaan was held at Gilgal (Josh. 5:9–10). It also became the base of military operations for Israel during the conquest of Canaan. From Gilgal Joshua led Israel against the city of Jericho (Josh. 6:11, 14) and conducted his southern campaign (Joshua 10). It was there that he began allotting the Promised Land to the tribes.

In later years, Gilgal was the site of King Saul's coronation as well as his rejection by God as king (1 Sam. 11:15; 13:4–12; 15:12–33). After Absalom's revolt, the Judeans gathered at Gilgal to welcome David back as their king (2 Sam. 19:15, 40). But during the days of later kings, Gilgal became a center of idolatry. Like Bethel, it was condemned by the prophets (Hos. 4:15; Amos 5:5). The presumed site of Gilgal is about two kilometers (one mile) northeast of Old Testament Jericho (Josh. 4:19).

3. A town between Dor and Tirzah (Josh. 12:23), probably Jiljulieh, a little town north of the brook Kanah and eight kilometers (five miles) northeast of Antipatris. It bordered on the Plain of Sharon west of Shechem.

GILOH [GIH low] (*circle*) — a town in the hill country of Judah (Josh. 15:51), the home of the traitorous Ahithophel and the place where he committed suicide (2 Sam. 15:12).

GILONITE [GIH low night] — a native or inhabitant of the town of GILOH (2 Sam. 23:34).

GIMEL [GHEE muhl] — the third letter of the Hebrew alphabet, used as a heading over Psalm 119:17–24. In the original Hebrew language, each line of these eight verses began with the letter gimel. Also see ACROSTIC.

GIMZO [GHIM zow] (*sycamores*) — a town in northern Judah, captured by the Philistines during the reign of King Ahaz of Judah (2 Chr. 28:18).

GINATH [GIH nath] (meaning unknown) — the father of Tibni, the unsuccessful rival of Omri. Tibni and Omri fought for the throne of Israel after the death of Zimri (1 Kin. 16:21–22).

GINNETHO [GHIN ee tho] — a form of GIN-NETHON.

GINNETHOI [GHIN ee thoy] — a form of GIN-NETHON.

GINNETHON [GHIN ee thun] (*gardener*) — the head of a priestly family who returned from the Captivity and sealed the covenant with Nehemiah (Neh. 10:6; 12:4; Ginnetho, KJV; Ginnethoi, RSV).

GIRDLE (see DRESS OF THE BIBLE; ARMS, ARMOR).

GIRGASHITE [GUR gah shite] (meaning unknown) — a member of an ancient tribe that inhabited Canaan before the Israelites drove them out (Josh. 3:10). Some scholars identify the Girgashites with the GADARENES.

GIRZITES [GUR zites] — a people who lived between Philistia and Egypt. The Girzites are mentioned with the Amalekites and the Geshurites (1 Sam. 27:8; Gezrites, KJV; Gizrites, NEB).

GISHPA [GISH puh] (*attentive*) — an overseer of the NETHINIM (Temple servants) in Nehemiah's time (Neh. 11:21). This name may be a different form of Hasupha (Ezra 2:43).

GITTAH HEPHER [GIT ah HEE fur] — a form of GATH HEPHER.

GITTAIM [GIT tah em] (*two winepresses*) — a village in Benjamin to which the Amorite inhabitants of Beeroth fled from King Saul (2 Sam. 4:3).

GITTITE [GIT tight] — a native or inhabitant of GATH (2 Sam. 15:18–19).

GITTITH [GITT ith] (*from Gath*) — the feminine form of Gittite (a native or inhabitant of Gath), used in the titles of Psalms 8, 81, and 84. At least three different meanings are possible:

1. A musical instrument used, or perhaps manufactured, in Gath—and to be used as an accompaniment to the singing of these psalms.

2. A "vintage song" whose tune was to be followed in the Temple music.

3. The tune of a military march used by Gittite warriors.

GIZONITE [GUY zoe nite] — a description applied to Hashem, one of David's mighty men (1 Chr. 11:34), indicating either the name of his family or his hometown.

GIZRITES [GIHZ rites] — a form of GIRZITES.

GLASS — a clear substance made of a mixture of minerals from which liquid-holding vessels, mirrors, and other useful objects are manufactured. Rarely mentioned in the Bible, glass was not a widespread commodity until Roman times. But it was developed much earlier in the history of the ancient world. Glass beads, datable to about 2500 B.C. or later, existed in Egypt.

Evidence of glass manufacturing has been found at the royal site of Tell el–Amarna in Eygpt. This was the center of a religious and artistic revolution under the Pharaoh Amenophis IV (1368–1351 B.C.), who later changed his name to AKHENATEN. Glass from this period is core-made. The desired shape of the vessel was first formed from clay or sand around a metal rod. On this core, or mold, the vessel was fashioned. These objects were constructed from coiled threads of colored glass which were reheated and frequently combed to produce zigzag patterns. Phoenicia was also a center of glass production during this period, undoubtedly being influenced by Egypt. Egyptian and Phoenician imports have been found at a number of sites in Palestine, such as Hazor, Gezer, Megiddo, and Samaria.

The Roman period witnessed unparalleled growth in the glassmaking industry. This was the result of the introduction of blown glass in the first century B.C. Vessels were fashioned on the end of a hollow metal tube by blowing a bulb of molten glass into a mold. Later the vessels were shaped without the use of molds.

Biblical references to glass are few. Its rarity in Palestine during the Old Testament period is reflected in its mention (translated "crystal") together with gold in Job 28:17. In several passages translated "glass" by the KJV, the reference is actually to highly polished metal surfaces—such as bronze—which served as mirrors (Ex. 38:8; 1 Cor. 13:12; James 1:23). The bottle for tears mentioned in Psalm 56:8 is a small glass vial which has been uncovered in tombs by archaeologists. Glass is also referred to in Revelation 21:18, 21.

GLASS, SEA (see SEA OF GLASS).

GLASS WORKER (see OCCUPATIONS AND TRADES).

GLEANING — the process of gathering grain or other produce left in the fields by reapers (Judg. 8:2; Ruth 2; Is. 17:6). The Old Testament Law required that property owners leave the gleanings of their produce in the fields so they might be gathered by "the poor and the stranger" (Lev. 19:9–10; 23:22). Also see AGRICULTURE.

GLEDE (see ANIMALS OF THE BIBLE).

GLORIFY — to magnify God through praising His name and honoring His commandments (Ps. 86:12). Jesus also glorified His father through His perfect obedience and His sacrificial death on our behalf (John 17:1).

GLORY — beauty, power, or honor; a quality of God's character that emphasizes His greatness and authority. The word is used in three senses in the Bible:

1. God's moral beauty and perfection of character. This divine quality is beyond man's understanding (Ps. 113:4). All people "fall short" of it (Rom. 3:23).

2. God's moral beauty and perfection as a visible presence. While God's glory is not a substance, at times God does reveal His perfection to man in a visible way. Such a display of the presence of God is often seen as fire or dazzling light, but sometimes as an act of power. Some examples from the Old Testament are the pillar of cloud and fire (Ex. 13:21), the Lord's deliverance of the Israelites at the Red Sea (Exodus 14), and especially His glory in the tabernacle (Lev. 9:23–24) and Temple (1 Kin. 8:11).

Since the close of the Old Testament, the glory of God has been shown mainly in Christ (Luke 9:29–32; John 2:11) and in the members of His church.

Christ now shares His divine glory with His followers (John 17:5–6, 22), so that in their lives Christians are being transformed into the glorious image of God (2 Cor. 3:18). Believers will be fully glorified at the end of time in God's heavenly presence (Rom. 5:2; Col. 3:4). There the glory of God will be seen everywhere (Rev. 21:23).

3. Praise. At times God's glory may mean the honor and audible praise which His creatures give to Him (Ps. 115:1; Rev. 5:12–13).

GLUTTON — a person who is debased and excessive in his eating habits. Gluttony is more than overeating. In its association with drunkenness (Prov. 23:21; Deut. 21:20), it describes a life given to excess. When Jesus was called a "gluttonous man" (Matt. 11:19), His critics were accusing Him of being loose and excessive by associating with tax collectors and sinners.

GNASH, GNASHING OF TEETH — to grate or grind one's teeth together as an expression of hatred and scorn (Job. 16:9). Jesus used the phrase to portray the futility of the wicked who will be judged by God at the end of time (Matt. 13:42, 50).

GNAT (see ANIMALS OF THE BIBLE).

GNOSTICISM [NOS tuh siz em] — a system of false teachings that existed during the early centuries of Christianity. Its name came from the Greek word for knowledge, *gnosis*. The Gnostics believed that knowledge was the way to salvation. For this reason, Gnosticism was condemned as false and heretical by several writers of the New Testament.

Sources. Our knowledge of Gnosticism comes from several sources. First, there are the Gnostic texts, which are known as the New Testament

Excavations at ancient Ashkelon, one of the five chief cities of the Philistines along the coast of the Mediterranean Sea.

Photo: Levant Photo Service

APOCRYPHA. These texts are not recognized as Scripture because they contain teachings which differ from those in the Bible. Then, there are the refutations of the Gnostics by the early church fathers. Some of the more important ones are Irenaeus, *Against Heresies*; Hippolytus, *Refutations of All Heresies*; Epiphanius, *Panarion*; and Tertullian, *Against Marcion*.

Still a third source about Gnosticism is the New Testament itself. Many Gnostic teachings were condemned by the writers of the New Testament. Paul emphasized a wisdom and knowledge that comes from God and does not concern itself with idle speculations, fables, and moral laxity (Col. 2:8–23; 1 Tim. 1:4; 2 Tim. 2:16–19; Titus 1:10–16). John, both in his gospel and in the epistles, countered heretical teaching which, in a broad sense, can be considered Gnostic.

Teachings of the Gnostics. The Gnostics accepted the Greek idea of a radical dualism between God (spirit) and the world (matter). According to their world view, the created order was evil, inferior, and opposed to the good. God may have created the first order, but each successive order was the work of anti-gods, archons, or a demiurge (a subordinate deity).

The Gnostics believed that the earth is surrounded by a number of cosmic spheres (usually seven) which separate man from God. These spheres are ruled by archons (spiritual principalities and powers) who guard their spheres by barring the souls who are seeking to ascend from the realm of darkness and captivity which is below to the realm of light which is above.

The Gnostics also taught that man is composed of body, soul, and spirit. Since the body and the soul are part of man's earthly existence, they are evil. Enclosed in the soul, however, is the spirit, the only divine substance of man. This "spirit" is asleep and ignorant; it needs to be awakened and liberated by knowledge.

According to the Gnostics, the aim of salvation is for the spirit to be awakened by knowledge so the inner man can be released from his earthly dungeon and return to the realm of light where the soul becomes reunited with God. As the soul ascends, however, it needs to penetrate the cosmic spheres which separate it from its heavenly destiny. This, too, is accomplished by knowledge. One must understand certain formulas which are revealed only to the initiated.

Ethical behavior among the Gnostics varied considerably. Some sought to separate themselves from all evil matter in order to avoid contamination. Paul may be opposing such a view in 1 Timothy 4:1–5. For other Gnostics, ethical life took the form of libertinism. For them knowledge meant freedom to participate in all sorts of indulgences. Many reasoned that since they had received divine knowledge and were truly informed as to their divine nature, it didn't matter how they lived.

Such an attitude is a misunderstanding of the gospel. Paul, on a number of occasions, reminded his readers that they were saved from sin to holiness. They were not to have an attitude of indifference toward the law. They had died to sin in their baptism into Christ (Rom. 6:1–11) and so were to walk "in newness of life." John reminded the Christians that once they had been saved they were not to continue living in sin (1 John 3:4–10).

These Gnostic teachings also had a disruptive effect on fellowship in the church. Those who were "enlightened" thought of themselves as being superior to those who did not have such knowledge. Divisions arose between the spiritual and the fleshly. This attitude of superiority is severely condemned in the New Testament. Christians are "one body" (1 Corinthians 12) who should love one another (1 Corinthians 13; 1 John). Spiritual gifts are for the Christian community rather than individual use; they should promote humility rather than pride (1 Corinthians 12—14; Eph. 4:11–16).

GOAD (see TOOLS OF THE BIBLE).

GOAH [GOE ah] — a form of GOATH.

GOAT (see ANIMALS OF THE BIBLE).

GOATH [GOE ath] (meaning unknown) — a place near Jerusalem, one of the boundaries prophesied for the rebuilt city (Jer. 31:39; Goah, NASB, NIV, RSV). The exact site is unknown.

GOATHERD (see OCCUPATIONS AND TRADES).

GOAT'S HAIR (see DRESS OF THE BIBLE).

GOB [gob] (*cistern*) — an unknown place where the Israelites battled the Philistines (2 Sam. 21:18–19). At Gob Jaare–Oregim killed the brother of the giant, Goliath.

GOBLET — any bowl–shaped container for holding liquids. The word is used symbolically in Song of Solomon 7:2, where the beloved's navel is compared to "a rounded goblet." The same Hebrew word is translated "cup" in Isaiah 22:24 and "basin" in Exodus 24:6.

GOD — the creator and sustainer of the universe who has provided humankind with a revelation of Himself through the natural world and through His Son, Jesus Christ.

The Bible does not seek to prove the existence of God; it simply affirms His existence by declaring, "In the beginning God…" (Gen. 1:1). God has revealed Himself through the physical universe (Ps. 19:1; Rom. 1:19–20). By observing the universe, one can find positive indications of God's existence. Creation reveals the results of a universal mind that devised a master plan and executed it. It makes more sense to accept the idea of God as Creator of the universe than to assume that our orderly universe came into existence apart from a divine being.

The greatest revelation of God, however, comes through the Bible. Through the inspired written record, both the existence of God and the nature of God are revealed in and through Jesus Christ. Jesus stated, "He that has seen me, has seen the Father" (John 14:9).

Although the full revelation of God was in Jesus Christ, the human mind cannot fully understand God. One reason for this is that Scripture does not record all the actions and teachings of Jesus (John 21:25). Another reason is the limitation of the human mind. How can man's finite mind understand the infinity of God? It is not possible.

Although we cannot fully understand God, we still can know Him. We know Him through a personal relationship of faith and through a study of what the Bible teaches about His nature.

God may be described in terms of attributes. An attribute is an inherent characteristic of a person or being. While we cannot describe God in a comprehensive way, we can learn about Him by examining His attributes as revealed in the Bible. The first group is known as the natural attributes of God.

God Is Spirit. Jesus taught that "God is Spirit" (John 4:24). God has no body, no physical or measurable form. Thus, God is invisible. He became visible in human form in the person of Jesus Christ, but His essence is invisible.

God Is Changeless. Progress and change may characterize some of His works, but God Himself remains unchanged (Heb. 1:12). He does not change; otherwise, He would not be perfect. Thus, what we know of God can be known with certainty. He is not different from one time to another.

God Is All Powerful. God's power is unlimited. He can do anything that is not inconsistent with His nature, character, and purpose (Gen. 17:1; 18:14). The only limitations on God's power are imposed by Himself (Gen. 18:25). "Impossible" is not in God's vocabulary. God creates and sustains all things; yet He never grows weary (Is. 40:27–31).

God Is All Knowing. God possesses all knowledge (Job 38:39; Rom. 11:33–36). Because God is everywhere at one and the same time, He knows everything simultaneously. That God has the power to know the thoughts and motives of every heart is evident from many Scripture passages, notably Job 37:16, Psalm 147:5, and Hebrews 3:13.

God Is Everywhere. God is not confined to any part of the universe but is present in all His power at every point in space and every moment in time (Ps. 139:7–12). Thus, God does not belong to any one nation or generation. He is the God of all the earth (Gen. 18:25).

God Is Eternal. Eternity refers to God's relation to time. Past, present, and future are known equally to Him (2 Pet. 3:8; Rev. 1:8). Time is like a parade that man sees only a segment at a time. But God sees time in its entirety.

The second group of attributes is called moral attributes. These refer to God's character, His essential nature.

God Is Holy. The word holy comes from a root word that means "to separate." Thus, it refers to God as separated from or exalted above other things (Is. 6:1–3). Holiness refers to God's moral excellence. Being holy, God demands holiness in His own children. And what He demands, He supplies. Holiness is God's gift that we receive by faith

Photo by Willem A. VanGemeren

The gorge of the Ayyun River, one of the many tributaries of the Jordan River.

through His Son, Jesus Christ (Eph. 4:24).

God Is Righteous. Righteousness as applied to God refers to His affirmation of what is right as opposed to what is wrong. The righteousness of God refers to His moral laws laid down to guide the conduct of humankind, as in the Ten Commandments. Righteousness also refers to God's administration of justice. He brings punishment upon the disobedient (Gen. 18:25; Deut. 32:4; Rom. 2:6–16). Finally, God's righteousness is redemptive. In the Book of Romans the righteousness of God refers to God declaring the believer to be in a state of righteousness as though he had never been unrighteous (Rom. 1:16–17; 3:24–26). This is possible because of the sacrificial death of Jesus on our behalf.

God Is Love. Love is the essential, self–giving nature of God. God's love for man seeks to awaken a responsive love of man for God. Divine love runs like a golden thread through the entire Bible. Nature is eloquent with the skill, wisdom, and power of God. Only in the Bible, however, do we discover God giving Himself and all He possesses to His creatures, in order to win their response and to possess them for Himself.

God loved and gave; He loved and sought—just as a shepherd seeks his sheep. God loved and suffered, providing His love by giving His all on the cross for the redemption of humanity. God, in His love, wills good for all His creatures (Gen. 1:31; Ps. 145:9; Mark 10:18).

God Is Truth. All truth, whether natural, physical, or religious, is grounded in God. Thus, any seemingly inconsistent teaching between natural and physical sciences and God's revelation of Himself is more apparent than real. Truth is magnified in an absolute way through God's revelation.

God Is Wisdom. God's wisdom is revealed in His doing the best thing, in the best way, at the best time for the best purpose.

Some people have knowledge, but little wisdom, while the most wise at times have little knowledge. But God is "the only wise God" (1 Tim. 1:17). In creation, history, human lives, redemption, and Christ, His divine wisdom is revealed. Man, lacking wisdom, can claim God's wisdom simply by asking (1 Kin. 3:9; James 1:5).

The believer's understanding of God continues to increase throughout his earthly pilgrimage. It will finally be complete in eternity when he stands in the presence of God.

GOD, CHILDREN OF (see SONS OF GOD).

GOD, IMAGE OF (see IMAGE OF GOD).

GOD, NAMES OF — the titles or designations given to God throughout the Bible. In the ancient world, knowing another's name was a special privilege that offered access to that person's thought and life. God favored His people by revealing Himself by several names which offered special insight into His love and righteousness.

Jehovah/Yahweh. One of the most important names for God in the Old Testament is Yahweh, or Jehovah, from the verb "to be," meaning simply but profoundly, "I am who I am," and "I will be who I will be." The four–letter Hebrew word YHWH was the name by which God revealed Himself to Moses

in the burning bush (Ex. 3:14). This bush was a vivid symbol of the inexhaustible dynamism of God who burns like a fire with love and righteousness, yet remains the same and never diminishes. Some English translations of the Bible translate the word as Jehovah, while others use Yahweh.

God is the author of life and salvation. His "I am" expresses the fact that He is the infinite and original personal God who is behind everything and to whom everything must finally be traced. This name, "I am who I am," signals the truth that nothing else defines who God is but God Himself. What He says and does is who He is. The inspired Scriptures are the infallible guide to understanding who God is by what He says about Himself and what He does. Yahweh is the all–powerful and sovereign God who alone defines Himself and establishes truth for His creatures and works for their salvation.

Moses was called to proclaim deliverance to the people and was told by God, "Thus you shall say to the children of Israel, 'I AM has sent me to you' " (Ex. 3:14). In the deliverance of the Hebrew people from slavery in Egypt, God revealed a deeper significance to His name. But He had already disclosed Himself to Abraham, Isaac, and Jacob as Yahweh. Each of them had called on the name of the Lord (Yahweh) (Gen. 12:8; 13:4; 26:25; Ex. 3:15) as the God who protects and blesses. Yet Exodus 6:3 shows that Abraham, Isaac, and Jacob did not know the fuller meaning of Yahweh, which was to be revealed to Moses and the Hebrew people in the Exodus experience.

The divine name Yahweh is usually translated Lord in English versions of the Bible, because it became a practice in late Old Testament Judaism not to pronounce the sacred name YHWH, but to say instead "my Lord" (Adonai)—a practice still used

The temple devoted to worship of the Roman Emperor Hadrian at Ephesus. This form of idolatry was condemned by the Lord God, who declared, "You shall have no other gods before Me" (Ex. 20:3).

Photo: Levant Photo Service

Excavations at the city of Dan, where King Jeroboam I of Israel set up a golden calf for pagan worship about 950 B.C.

today in the synagogue. When the vowels of Adonai were attached to the consonants YHWH in the medieval period, the word Jehovah resulted. Today, many Christians use the word Yahweh, the more original pronunciation, not hesitating to name the divine name since Jesus taught believers to speak in a familiar way to God.

The following are other names in honor of the Lord in the Old Testament that stem from the basic name of Yahweh:

Jehovah-jireh—This name is translated as "The-LORD-Will-Provide," commemorating the provision of the ram in place of Isaac for Abraham's sacrifice (Gen. 22:14).

Jehovah-nissi—This name means "The-LORD-Is-My-Banner," in honor of God's defeat of the Amalekites (Ex. 17:15).

Jehovah-shalom—This phrase means "The-LORD-Is-Peace," the name Gideon gave the altar which he built in Ophrah (Judg. 6:24).

Jehovah-shammah—This phrase expresses the truth that "The-LORD-Is-There," referring to the city which the prophet Ezekiel saw in his vision (Ezek. 48:35).

Jehovah-tsebaoth—This name, translated "The-LORD-of-hosts," was used in the days of David and the prophets, witnessing to God the Savior

who is surrounded by His hosts of heavenly power (1 Sam. 1:3).

Jehovah Elohe Israel—This name means "LORD-God-of-Israel," and it appears in Isaiah, Jeremiah, and the Psalms. Other names similar to this are Netsah Israel, "The Strength of Israel" (1 Sam. 15:29); and Abir Yisrael "The Mighty One of Israel" (Is. 1:24).

El. Another important root name for God in the Old Testament is El. By itself it refers to a god in the most general sense. It was widely used in ancient eastern cultures whose languages are similar to Hebrew and therefore may refer either to the true God or to false gods. The highest Canaanite god was El whose son was Baal. In the Bible the word is often defined properly by a qualifier like Jehovah: "I, the LORD (Jehovah) your God (Elohim), am a jealous God (El)" (Deut. 5:9).

Abraham planted a tamarisk tree at Beersheba "and there called on the name of the LORD (Yahweh), the Everlasting God (El Olam) (Gen. 21:33). Jacob built an altar on a piece of land he purchased at Shechem and called it "El Elohe Israel" ("God, the God of Israel"), commemorating his wrestling with the angel at the place he called Peni-el ("the face of God"), and receiving his new name Israel (Yisra-el, "God strives") (Gen. 32:28–30; 33:20). El Shaddai (God Almighty), signifying God as a source of blessing, is the name with which God appeared to Abraham, Isaac, and Jacob (Ex. 6:3).

Elohim. Elohim is the plural form of El, but it is usually translated in the singular. Some scholars have held that the plural represents an intensified form for the supreme God; others believe it describes the supreme God and His heavenly court of created beings. Still others hold that the plural form refers to the triune God of Genesis 1:1–3, who works through Word and Spirit in the creation of the world. All agree that the plural form Elohim does convey the sense of the one supreme being who is the only true God.

Several important names of God identify Him as Branch, King, Wisdom, Shepherd, and Servant:

Branch of Righteousness. Jeremiah 23:5–6 names the coming messianic figure, the "Branch of righteousness," who will descend from David and be raised up to reign as King to execute judgment and righteousness in the earth. Christians see in this linkage a prophecy about God the Son taking on human flesh to serve as righteous King.

King. This descendant of David will have several divine qualities. He will be a Branch of Righteousness, a King, and His name will be called "The Lord Our Righteousness" (Jehovah Tsidkenu).

Wisdom. This person also appears in Proverbs 8:1–36 as Wisdom, the speaker who always says and does what is righteous, is equal to Jehovah, and works with Him in the creation of the universe. Paul describes Christ in these terms in Colossians 1:13–19; 2:1–3.

Shepherd. God is also described in prophecy as the Shepherd who will feed His flock, gather the lambs in His arms, carry them in His bosom, and gently lead those with young (Is. 40:11; Jer. 31:10; Ezek. 34:11–16). Jesus applied this name to Himself (Luke 15:4–7; John 10:11–16), making Himself equal to God; and Jesus Christ is so named by His followers (Heb. 13:20; 1 Pet. 5:4; Rev. 7:17).

Servant. The name of Servant also identifies this divine person and His saving ministry on behalf of His people. God's Servant is described in terms that apply to Jesus. He is upheld and chosen by God; He delights in God; He receives God's Spirit. Like Wisdom in Proverbs 8, He is holy, just, and righteous. He will bring Jacob back to Him and will be a light to the nations since He is an offering for sin (Is. 42:1–4; 49:1–7; 53:1–12).

Word of God. The Word of God figures prominently in Scripture as another name of God. The Word is not as clearly a person in the Old Testament as in the New Testament where Jesus Christ is identified as the personal Word of God (John 1:1, 14). But it is evident from Psalm 33:4, 6, and 9 that the Word should be understood in a personal sense, for "the word of the Lord is right" indicating a personified Word. "By the Word of the Lord the heavens were made" (v. 6), echoing the creation in Genesis 1:3, 6. In the New Testament Jesus is seen to be both Word and Law personified.

Glory. God is described as Glory (Shekinah) in Exodus 16:7; Psalm 104:31; and Isaiah 60:1. In the New Testament Jesus shares the glory of God (Matt. 25:31; 1 Cor. 2:8; Heb. 1:3).

When the new age arrives with the birth of Jesus Christ, the names of the three persons who comprise the trinity are made more explicit. These names fulfill the deeper meanings of the Old Testament names for God.

In the New Testament God is known as Father (Matt. 5:16; 28:19) and Abba (Mark 14:36; Gal. 4:6). Jesus is known as Son (Matt. 11:27), Son of God (John 9:35), and Son of man (Matt. 8:20), Messiah (John 1:41), Lord (Rom. 14:8), Word (John 1:1), Wisdom (1 Cor. 1:30), Bridegroom (Mark 2:19), Shepherd (John 10:11), Vine (John 15:1), Light (John 1:9), and "I AM" (John 8:12). The Holy Spirit is known as the Helper (John 14:16).

GOD, SONS OF (see SONS OF GOD).

GOD, UNKNOWN — a god to whom the people of Athens, Greece, had erected a monument some time before the apostle Paul's visit to the city. After arriving in Athens, Paul argued daily in the synagogue and marketplace on behalf of Jesus and the resurrection. When he was taken to the AREOPAGUS for further questioning by the curious Athenians, Paul saw that in addition to the monuments erected in honor of named gods, there was an altar dedicated "to the unknown god" (Acts 17:23). The Athenians apparently wanted to make sure they missed no gods in their worship.

Paul seized this opportunity to tell them about the God who made Himself known in Jesus Christ. The truth of the Acts story is substantiated by several secular writers of the time who reported that altars dedicated to unknown gods were common in and around Athens. Other sources indicate that the custom was also practiced elsewhere.

GOD–WHO–FORGIVES — a name for God which appears once in the NKJV, emphasizing the forgiving nature of God toward His wayward people (Ps. 99:8).

GODDESS (see GODS, PAGAN).

GODHEAD — an old English term that is a synonym for God, with an emphasis on that which makes the triune God essentially one (Rom. 1:20; Col. 2:9). The apostle Paul used the term to show the contrast between God's sinless nature and the corrupt character of man and his tendency toward idolatry.

In Romans 1:20 Paul used the term Godhead to describe what mankind ought to see in nature as a result of God's creative handiwork—"His eternal power and Godhead," or "Deity." This entire passage in Romans describes how the human mind fails to understand the exalted Godhead because of its sinful rebellion and distortion of truth.

In the Colossians passage Paul declared that in Christ "dwells all the fullness of the Godhead bodily" (Col. 2:9), in contrast to the "tradition of men" (Col. 2:8). In the Son of God who took on human form, the essential quality and character of God are wholly present. This was Paul's way of emphasizing that Jesus is not a mere "divine man" like the heroes of the Greco–Roman world, but truly God—the Godhead or God Himself in human form.

GODLINESS — piety or reverence toward God (1 Tim. 2:2). Godliness means more than religious profession and a godly conduct; it also means the reality and power of a vital union with God.

GODS, PAGAN — the false gods and idols worshiped by people during Bible times—especially the false gods of Egypt, Mesopotamia (Assyria and Babylon), Canaan, Greece, and Rome.

Religion has always played an important part in civilization; in the ancient world it was a powerful force. The pagan civilizations of Bible times worshiped many gods. They had male and female deities, high and low gods, assemblies of gods, priests and priestesses, and temples and sacrifices. All the forces of nature that could not be controlled or understood were considered supernatural powers to be worshiped and feared.

Our knowledge of the pagan gods of the ancient world comes from the religious literature, idols, and other objects discovered by archaeologists. We have also learned from the meanings of names found in the literature from this period. People in Bible times were often named with sentences and phrases; sometimes they used the name of their favorite god in the compound name. Thus, names very often reflected popular religion. Most of the people of the ancient world were polytheistic; they worshiped more than one god.

The people worshiped these gods in the form of representative idols. This practice is called idolatry. The nation of Israel, however, was forbidden to make graven images of the one true and living God whom they worshiped (Ex. 20:3–6; Deut. 5:7–10). The pagan nations made statues or images to represent the powers which they worshiped. Most of these idols were in the form of animals or men. But sometimes these idols represented celestial powers like the sun, moon, and stars; forces of nature, like the sea and the rain; or life forces, like death and truth.

Belief in these false gods was characterized by superstition and magic. The people believed that what happened to their gods would also happen to them. Puzzled by the workings of nature, they assigned the causes of various natural happenings to their gods. Rain was absolutely essential to life in agricultural societies. If it rained, they believed this was caused by a rain god. If it did not rain, they thought this was because that god had not sent the rain. They prayed and sacrificed to the god to send it.

In time an elaborate system of beliefs in such natural forces was developed into mythology. Each civilization and culture had its own mythological structure, but these structures were often quite similar. The names of the gods may have been different, but their functions and actions were often the same. The most prominent myth to cross cultural lines was that of the fertility cycle. Many pagan cultures believed that the god of fertility died each year during the winter but was reborn each year in the spring. The details differed among cultures, but the main idea was the same.

According to the Old Testament, God was a jealous God who permitted no rivals: "You shall have no other gods before Me" (Ex. 20:3; Deut. 5:7). God's will is all–powerful and man must submit to it. He reveals Himself when He pleases and to whom He pleases, demanding that man obey His revelation. Nevertheless, the Hebrew people sometimes gave in to temptation and worshiped these pagan gods from the surrounding cultures.

The many pagan gods that served as a temptation to the Hebrew people may be conveniently grouped into four distinct types: the false gods of (1) Mesopotamia (Assyria and Babylon), (2) Egypt, (3) Canaan, and (4) Greece and Rome.

The Pagan Gods of Mesopotamia. The biblical references to pagan gods begin with the statement that Terah, Abraham, and Nahor, when they dwelt on the other side of the River (that is, in Mesopotamia), "served other gods" (Josh. 24:2). Ancient Mesopotamia covered the region that is roughly equivalent geographically to present–day Iraq and Iran.

The prominent gods in Mesopotamia were those over heaven, air, and earth, personified by Anu, Enlil, and Enki (Ea). Another group was made up of those that controlled the heavenly bodies: the sun, the moon, and the planet Venus (the "morning

Tomb painting which shows Pharaoh Seti I of Egypt making an offering to the sun god Ra, supreme god in the Egyptian religious system.

Photo by Howard Vos

Pagan Gods Mentioned in the Bible

Name of God in NKJV	Description	Biblical Reference	Name Used in Other Translations
Adrammelech	A Babylonian god worshiped by the Sepharvites	2 Kin. 17:31	
Anammelech	A Babylonian god worshiped by the Sepharvites	2 Kin. 17:31	
Asherah	The wife of Baal in Canaanite mythology	1 Kin. 18:19	prophets of the groves (KJV)
Ashima	A Hittite god worshiped by the people of Hamath	2 Kin. 17:30	
Ashtoreths	The plural form of Ashtoreth	Judg. 10:6	Ashtaroth (KJV, RSV, NEB, NASB)
Ashtoreth	The Syrian and Phoenician goddess of the moon, sexual love, and fertility	2 Kin. 23:13	
Baal	The chief male deity of the Phoenicians and Canaanites	Num. 22:41	
Baal-Berith	A name under which Baal was worshiped in the time of the judges	Judg. 9:4	
Baal of Peor	An idol of Moab, probably the same as Chemosh	Ps. 106:28	Baal-peor (KJV)
Baals	The plural form of Baal	Judg. 8:33	Baalim (KJV)
Baal-Zebub	A name under which Baal was worshiped at the Philistine city of Ekron	2 Kin. 1:2–3	
Beelzebub	A heathen god considered by the Jews to be the supreme evil spirit	Mark 3:22	
Bel	A god identified with Marduk, chief Babylonian god	Is. 46:1	
Chemosh	The national god of the Moabites and Ammonites	Jer. 48:7, 13	Kemosh (NEB)
Chiun	A star-god, identified with Saturn	Amos 5:26	Kiyyun (NASB) Kaiwan (RSV)
Dagon	The chief god of the Philistines	1 Sam. 5:2–7	
Diana	In Roman mythology, the goddess of the moon, hunting, wild animals, and virginity	Acts 19:24, 27–28	Artemis (RSV, NIV, NASB)
Gad	A pagan god worshiped by the Israelites along with Meni	Is. 65:11	Fortune (RSV, NIV, NASB)
Gold calf	An idol made by the Israelites in the wilderness	Exodus 32	
Hermes	The Greek god of commerce, science, invention, cunning, eloquence, and theft	Acts 14:12	Mercurius (KJV) Mercury (NEB)
Mammon	The Aramaic word for *riches*, personified by Jesus as a false god	Luke 16:9, 11	Worldly wealth (NIV, NEB)
Meni	A heathen deity worshiped by the Israelites along with Gad	Is. 65:11	Destiny (RSV, NIV, NASB) Fate (NEB)
Merodach	The Babylonian god of war and the patron deity of the city of Babylon	Jer. 50:2	Marduk (NIV, NEB, NASB)
Milcom	Another name for Molech	Zeph. 1:5	Malcham (KJV)
Molech	National god of the Ammonites whose worship involved child sacrifice	Lev. 18:21	
Moloch	Another name for Molech	Acts 7:43	
Nebo	The Babylonian god of literature, wisdom, and the arts	Is. 46:1	
Nehushtan	The name given to Moses' bronze serpent when people began to worship it	2 Kin. 18:4	
Nergal	The war god of the men of Cuth, in Media-Persia	2 Kin. 17:30	
Nibhaz	An idol worshiped by the Avites	2 Kin. 17:31	
Nisroch	An Assyrian god with a temple in Nineveh	Is. 37:38	
Remphan	An idol worshiped by Israel in the wilderness, perhaps the same as Chiun	Acts 7:43	Rephan (RSV, NIV, NEB) Rompha (NASB)
Rimmon	The Assyrian god of rain, lightning, and thunder	2 Kin. 5:18	
Sikkuth	A name given by the Babylonians to the planet Saturn	Amos 5:26	Sakkuth (RSV)
Succoth Benoth	A Babylonian goddess, the mistress of Marduk	2 Kin. 17:30	
Tammuz	A Babylonian fertility god	Ezek. 8:14	
Tartak	An idol worshiped by the Avites	2 Kin. 17:31	
Twin Brothers	In Greek mythology, the twin sons of Zeus	Acts 28:11	Castor and Pollux (KJV, NIV, NEB)
Zeus	The supreme god of the ancient Greeks	Acts 14:12–13	Jupiter (KJV, NEB)

A bust of Zeus in the Ephesus Museum. Zeus was the chief god of the ancient Greeks.

star"). In fact, Ur, the city from which Abraham came, was the center for worship of the moon god *Sin*. As Mesopotamian religion developed, each god had his own star, and the worship of the stars became popular with the development of ASTROLOGY. Many of the astrological texts and charts of the ancient Babylonians read like modern horoscopes.

The worship of the sun, moon, and stars eventually spread across the entire ancient world. The Egyptians, Canaanites, and Phoenicians all incorporated features of this form of worship. Place names in pre–Israelite Canaan reflect the practice. Beth Shemesh (Josh. 15:10) means house of the sun [god]. Jericho (Num. 22:1) probably means moon city. Joshua's miracle of the sun and the moon standing still takes on greater significance in light of this fact. It was a demonstration of the sovereign power of the Lord God of Israel over the pagan gods identified as the sun and the moon, worshiped in pagan cities (Josh. 10:12–13).

Another god of ancient Mesopotamia was Adad, who represented the storm—either the beneficial rains for the crops or the destructive storms with hurricanes. Identical with Adad, or Hadad, was Rimmon or Ramman, the Assyrian god of rain and storm, thunder and lightning. The two names, Hadad and Rimmon, were combined in one name, Hadad Rimmon, in one Old Testament reference (Zech. 12:11). In the Old Testament Rimmon was an Aramean (Syrian) god who had a temple at Damascus. Naaman and his royal master worshiped this pagan god (2 Kin. 5:18).

The ancient Babylonian and Assyrian goddess Ishtar symbolized Mother Earth in the natural cycles of fertility on earth. Many myths grew up around this female deity. She was the goddess of love, so the practice of ritual prostitution became widespread in the fertility cult dedicated to her name. Temples to Ishtar had many priestesses, or sacred prostitutes, who symbolically acted out the fertility rites of the cycle of nature. Ishtar has been identified with the Phoenician Astarte, the Semitic Ashtoreth, and the Sumerian Inanna. Strong similarities also exist between Ishtar and the Egyptian Isis, the Greek Aphrodite, and the Roman Venus.

Associated with Ishtar was the young god Tammuz, considered both divine and mortal (Ezek. 8:14). In Babylonian mythology Tammuz died annually and was reborn year after year, representing the yearly cycle of the seasons and the crops. This pagan belief later was identified with the pagan gods Baal and Anat in Canaan.

Another kind of god in both Babylonia and Assyria was a national god connected with politics. In Assyria it was Ashur, and in Babylonia it was Marduk, who became prominent at the time of HAMMURABI (about 1800 B.C.). The ancient ideas about the ordering and governing of the universe were taken over by these two gods. Marduk, for example, achieved his prominence by victory over Tiamat, goddess of the sea. This cosmic conflict, described also in ancient Sumerian, Indian, and Canaanite myths, was believed to have established order. Marduk established order by destroying the goddess Tiamat.

In contrast, the Bible makes it clear that the forces of nature are not pagan gods that war with one another annually to bring about an established order of the universe. They are part of the Lord's creation (Genesis 1).

The Babylonian god Bel (Is. 46:1; Jer. 50:2; 51:44) is the same as Marduk, the chief Babylonian god. The Babylonian god Merodach (Jer. 50:2), an alternate spelling of Marduk, was the god of war and the patron deity of the city of Babylon.

Nebo (Is. 46:1) was the Babylonian god of education, literature, writing, wisdom, the arts, and sciences. The special seat of his worship was at Borsippa, near Babylon. The Akkadian form of this name is Nabu.

Nisroch (2 Kin. 19:37; Is. 37:38) was an Assyrian god with a temple in Nineveh. The idol representing this pagan god had a human form with an eagle's head.

Sikkuth (Amos 5:26; Sakkuth, RSV) was a name given by the Babylonians to the planet Saturn.

Succoth Benoth (2 Kin. 17:30) was a Babylonian goddess, identified by some scholars with Zarpanitum, the mistress of Marduk. Other scholars believe this god is a designation of Marduk himself as Sakkut Binuti, the supreme judge of the world.

When SHALMANESER, king of Assyria, deported the inhabitants of Samaria to farflung regions of his empire, he also imported into Samaria settlers from afar to colonize this area of Palestine. These people brought their religion and their pagan gods with them. Among these gods were: Adrammelech (2 Kin. 17:31), an idol of the Sepharvites worshiped by child sacrifice; Anammelech (2 Kin. 17:31), another god revered by the Sepharvites; Ashima (2 Kin. 17:30), an idol worshiped by the people of Hamath; Nergal (2 Kin. 17:30), the war god of the men of Cuth; Nibhaz (2 Kin. 17:31), an idol of the Avites; and Tartak (2 Kin. 17:31), an idol also worshiped by the Avites.

The Pagan Gods of Egypt. The gods of Egypt were a constant threat to the Israelites, both during their years in bondage and afterwards. Their deliverance from Egypt was described by the Bible as a great spiritual victory, with the sovereign Lord of Israel defeating the gods of the Egyptians (Ex. 18:11; 2 Sam. 7:23).

Egyptian religion reflected the same pagan ideas that were popular in the ancient world, but with different figures. Horus was the god of Egypt's western delta; he was a human figure with a falcon's head. Hathor, the corresponding goddess, had a cow's body and a woman's head. The god Set had a man's body and an animal's head. Anubis had a man's body and the head of an ibis. Besides gods that were composite with animal forms and human forms, some Egyptian gods were portrayed as completely human. For instance, Min symbolized fertility. Amon, the famous god of Thebes, was the chief Egyptian god.

In ancient Egyptian religion Osiris was the god of the lower world and judge of the dead. He was the brother and husband of Isis and father (or brother) of Horus. Osiris was killed by Set, who was jealous of his power. Isis, the ancient Egyptian goddess of fertility, persuaded the gods to bring back Osiris, her dead husband. The myth is therefore an ancient vegetation cycle.

The Egyptians portrayed many of their gods with animal images. But they also had their cosmic deities. The Egyptians envisioned the earth as in the shape of a dish with their fertile region (Egypt) in the center. The Nile River flowed from under the earth, bringing fertility to the land. These elements of nature were personified as gods. Geb, earth, was portrayed as a god lying down. Nut, heaven, was a goddess who arched her body across from mountain to mountain. Shu, the air, stood erect, holding up the sky.

The Egyptians also worshiped the sun, moon, and stars. Ra (also Re), the sun god, was the supreme deity of the ancient Egyptians. He was represented as a man with the head of a hawk or a falcon, crowned with a solar disk and the figure of the sacred asp or cobra. Ra appears in the Old Testament in the name of Joseph's father-in-law, Poti-Pherah (Gen. 41:45, 50; 46:20), priest of On, a city called Heliopolis ("city of the sun") by the Greeks—the principal seat of the worship of the sun. When Ra is absent, Thoth, the moon, is prominent. But the moon is definitely inferior to the sun.

The Egyptians had many other pagan gods. Notable among them was Maat, representing the

Photo by Gustav Jeeninga

A sitting Ibis, representing the Egyptian god Thoth, who was the scribe, or secretary, of the pagan gods of Egypt.

abstract idea of truth, and Bes, a grotesque god who watched over childbirth. The worship of all the gods also involved magic and superstition. The purpose of these gods apparently was to explain the cycle and forces of life and to insure stability and fertility.

The great PLAGUES OF EGYPT before the EXODUS (Ex. 7:14—12:30) struck at the heart of Egypt's religion. Their fertile land was struck with plagues; their sacred river was turned to blood; their glorious sun was darkened; and even the son of the "divine" Pharaoh was killed. The wonders that God brought against Egypt clearly demonstrated that their gods were powerless before the true and living God of Israel.

The Pagan Gods of Canaan. The pagan peoples who inhabited the land of Canaan before the Israelites arrived also worshiped many gods and goddesses. The Canaanite literature discovered at RAS SHAMRA (on the site of the ancient city of Ugarit) on the Syrian coast provides abundant information about several gods mentioned in the Bible.

The Canaanite god most often referred to is Baal, which means "lord" or "master." The word could be used as a title for any person who owned something, or any god considered to be a lord or master. But the word *Baal* soon became identified with various regional gods that were thought to provide fertility for crops and livestock. As a god who symbolized the productive forces of nature, Baal was worshiped with much sensuality (Num. 22:41; Judg. 2:13; 1 Kin. 16:31-32).

Life-sized figures such as these were carved on the base of each of the 36 massive columns in the pagan temple of Diana in Ephesus.

Baal appeared in many forms and under many different names. The Bible often makes reference to the Baalim (the plural of Baal; KJV) or to the Baals (NKJV; Judg. 2:11; 1 Kin. 18:18; Jer. 2:23).

The word Baal was often used in forming names, such as Baal of Peor (Deut. 4:3; Baal-peor, KJV). Peor was the name of a mountain in Moab. Baal of Peor was an idol of Moab (probably to be identified with Chemosh) which Israel was enticed to worship with immoral practices. In several passages the idol is simply called Peor (Nu. 25:18; Josh. 22:17).

Baal–Berith, which means "lord of the covenant," is a name under which Baal was worshiped in the time of the judges at Shechem, where he had a temple. In Judges 9:46 he is called simply the god Berith.

Baal–Zebub, which means "lord of the fly," was "the god of Ekron" (2 Kin. 1:2–3, 6, 16)—the name under which Baal was worshiped at the Philistine city of Ekron. This god was worshiped as the producer of flies, and consequently as the god that was able to defend against this pest. In the New Testament, reference is made to Beelzebub, a heathen god considered the chief evil spirit by the Jewish people (Matt. 10:25; 12:27; Luke 11:18–19). The Pharisees called him "the ruler of the demons" (Matt. 12:24; Mark 3:22; Luke 11:15), and Jesus identified him with Satan.

This word Baal was also used in personal names, but when the worship of Baal became a problem in Israel, Baal was replaced by Bosheth, which means "shame" (probably because it was shameful to have the name of a pagan god as part of one's name and because Baal was a shameful god). For instance,

Merib–Baal (1 Chr. 8:34; 9:40), the name of the son of Jonathan, became Mephibosheth (2 Sam. 9:6–13), and Esh–Baal (1 Chr. 9:39) became Ishbosheth (2 Sam. 2:8).

The Canaanite god Baal was known as Zebel Baal ("prince Baal") or Aliyan Baal ("Baal the strong"), as well as by a number of other titles. Baal was considered the god who brought rain and fertility (especially good harvests and animal reproduction). In a number of passages in Canaanite literature he is identified as Hadad, another god believed to bring the rains, storms, and fertility. This god Hadad is the god Adad of Assyria.

Archaeologists have discovered rock carvings that show Baal holding a club in his right hand and a lightning flash with a spearhead in his left. These symbols identify him as the god of rain and storm. Baal is also known as the "rider of the clouds," a term showing his power over the heavens. Psalm 68:4, "Extol Him who rides on the clouds," gives this title to the God of Israel—a declaration that the Lord, and not the false god Baal, is ruler over the heavens.

Baal and related deities are also portrayed as a mating bull, symbolizing fertility. It is no surprise that while Moses was on Mount Sinai, receiving the Ten Commandments from the Lord, the disobedient Israelites fashioned a golden calf to worship (Exodus 32). Jeroboam I, king of Israel, acted in accordance with this pagan idea by making two calves of gold, setting up one at Bethel and the other at Dan (1 Kin. 12:26–30).

During the history of the Israelites, a rivalry developed between Baalism and the true worship of the Lord (Jer. 23:27). Perhaps the best example of this rivalry was the conflict between Elijah and the prophets of Baal on Mount Carmel (1 Kings 18). Elijah's challenge to them to bring down fire from heaven was appropriate, because the Canaanites believed that Baal could shoot lightning flashes from the sky. Elijah's mocking of Baal struck at the heart of their claims; he knew that Baal was powerless, that the prophets of Baal had misled the people, and that only the Lord God of Israel was alive and able to answer. In the struggle to the death between true religion and false religion, Elijah knew that Baalism and its prophets had to be destroyed.

In Canaanite mythological texts Baal is sometimes called the son of Dagon. Dagon (Judg. 16:23; 1 Sam. 5:2-7; 1 Chr. 10:10) was the chief god of the ancient Philistines, a grain and fertility god whose most famous temples were at Gaza and Ashdod. With the recent discovery of documents at ancient EBLA in Syria, it is clear that Dagon, or Dagan, was a much more ancient and prominent god. These texts show that Dagon was being worshiped before Abraham entered Canaan about 2000 B.C. Dagon continued to be worshiped by the Canaanites up to the time of Christ. In the APOCRYPHA mention is made of a temple of Dagon at Azotus in 147 B.C. (1 Macc. 10:83-84). Azotus was a later name for Ashdod, one of the five chief Philistine cities.

Like the myths of so many pagan religions, Canaanite stories claim that Baal came to prominence by defeating other gods. One of Baal's enemies was the sea monster known as Lotan. The Old Testament's reference to Leviathan (Job 3:8; 41:1; Ps. 104:26; Is. 27:1) corresponds to this word. But in the Bible Leviathan is simply a powerful creature in the sea that man cannot control, and not like Lotan—a pagan god in the form of a twisting serpent.

Baal's mistress or lover was Anat (or Anath), the goddess of war, love, and fertility. She was the virgin goddess who conceives and was also the victor over Baal's enemies. With the help of Shapash, the sun or luminary, Anat rescued Baal from Mot (the god of death). Her victories in battle were vicious; she is described as up to her hips in gore with heads and hands from the enemies stacked high. Thus, Anat was the driving force in the annual fertility cycle of Baal.

Anat is sometimes identified with the queen of heaven, to whom the Jews offered incense in Jeremiah's day (Jer. 7:18; 44:17-19, 25). But some scholars identify the "queen of heaven" with the Assyro–Babylonian goddess Ishtar. Anat was the patroness of sex and passion; lewd figurines of this nude goddess have been discovered at various archaeological sites in Palestine.

The goddess *Asherah* (1 Kin. 15:13; 2 Chr. 15:16; Asherahs, Judg. 3:7) was portrayed as the wife of El (or sometimes Baal) in Canaanite mythology. Asherah was a favorite deity of women. Some of the wives of David and Solomon worshiped her (1 Kin. 15:13), as Ahab's wife, Jezebel, also probably did (1 Kin. 16:31-33). King Asa suppressed the worship of Asherah (1 Kin. 15:13), and King Josiah destroyed "the articles that were made for Baal, for Asherah, and for all the host of heaven" (2 Kin. 23:4).

The word *asherah* also refers to a wooden pole, or cult pillar, that stood at Canaanite places of worship—perhaps the trunk of a tree with the branches chopped off—and associated with the worship of the goddess Asherah.

Other pagan gods in addition to Baal and his companions were worshiped by the Canaanites. *Molech* was the national deity of the Ammonites (Lev. 18:21; Jer. 32:35), whose worship was accompanied by the burning of children offered as a sacrifice by their own parents. The god *Molech* also appears in the Old Testament as *Milcom* (2 Kin. 23:13; Zeph. 1:5; Malcham, KJV) and in the New Testament as *Moloch* (Acts 7:43).

Chemosh (Judg. 11:24; 2 King. 23:13) was the national god of the Moabites and Ammonites. This deity was apparently compounded with *Athtar*, the Venus star, and so is thought to be a pagan god associated with the heavenly bodies. Chemosh has been identified with Baal of Peor, Baal–Zebub, Mars, and Saturn, as the star of ill–omen. Dibon (Num. 21:30), a town in Moab north of the River Arnon, was the chief seat of its worship.

Like Molech, Chemosh was worshiped by the sacrifice of children as burnt offerings, but scholars believe it is incorrect to identify Chemosh directly with Molech. Solomon sanctified Chemosh as a part of his tolerance of pagan gods (1 Kin. 11:7), but Josiah abolished its worship (2 Kin. 23:13). Human sacrifice was made to Chemosh, according to 2 Kings 3:27, which reports that Mesha, king of Moab, offered his eldest son as a burnt offering on

Bronze likeness of Baal, pagan god of war and fertility among the ancient Canaanites and Phoenicians.

the wall of Kir Hareseth, the ancient capital of Moab.

Ashtoreth (1 Kin 11:5, 33; 2 Kin. 23:13) was the ancient Syrian and Phoenician goddess of the moon, sexuality, sensual love, and fertililty. In the Old Testament Ashtoreth is often associated with the worship of Baal. The KJV word *Ashtaroth* is the plural form of Ashtoreth; the NKJV has *Ashtoreths* (Judg. 2:13; 1 Sam. 12:10; also see Ishtar above).

Remphan (Acts 7:43; Rephan, RSV, NIV, NEB; Rompha, NASB) was an idol worshiped by Israel in the wilderness. This may be the same pagan god as *Chiun* (Amos 5:26; Kiyyun, NASB; Kaiwan your star-god, RSV), or Saturn.

Nehushtan, literally "bronze serpent–idol," was the contemptuous name given by King Hezekiah to the bronze serpent made by Moses in the wilderness (Num. 21:8-9), when people began to worship it (2 Kin. 18:4).

Gad (Is. 65:11; Fortune, RSV, NIV, NASB; Fate, NEB) was a heathen deity worshiped along with *Meni* (Is. 65:11; Destiny, RSV, NIV, NASB; Fortune, NEB). Scholars are uncertain about the exact identity of these pagan gods.

The Pagan Gods of Greece and Rome. Only a few of the ancient Greek and Roman gods are mentioned in the New Testament.

Zeus (Acts 14:12-13: 19:35; Jupiter, KJV) was the supreme god of the ancient Greeks. According to Greek mythology, Zeus was the ruler of heaven and father of other gods and mortal heroes. He was identified by the Romans as *Jupiter.*

Hermes (Acts 14:12; Mercurius, KJV; Mercury, NEB) was the Greek god of commerce, science, invention, and cunning. He also served as messenger and herald for the other gods. Hermes was identified by the Romans with *Mercury,* who was generally pictured with winged shoes and hat, carrying a winged staff. He was the protector of roads and boundaries and he guided departed souls to Hades.

When the apostle Paul and Barnabas were in Lystra, the people of that city declared, "The gods have come down to us in the likeness of men!" They called Barnabas *Zeus* and Paul *Hermes,* because he was the chief speaker (Acts 14:11–12).

Diana (Acts 19:24, 27-28, 34-35), in Roman mythology, was the goddess of the moon, hunting, wild animals, and virginity. Diana is the same as the Greek goddess *Artemis* (RSV, NIV, NASB), virgin goddess of the hunt and the moon. When Paul preached in Ephesus, the Ephesians were in an uproar because the gospel threatened to destroy the profit of the artisans who crafted silver shrines of Diana.

The Twin Brothers (Acts 28:11; Castor and Pollux, KJV, NIV, NEB) is a translation of a Greek word which means "boys of Zeus." In Greek mythology, Castor and Pollux were the twin sons of Zeus. After Castor and Pollux died, they were transformed by Zeus into the constellation Gemini. They were regarded as the special protectors of distressed sailors. The Alexandrian ship in which Paul sailed from Malta to Puteoli had a carving of the Twin Brothers as its figurehead.

In both the Old Testament and the New Testament the people of God were surrounded by pagan gods. The apostle Paul declared to the philosophers of Athens, "I perceive that in all things you are very religious" (Acts 17:22). In the city of Athens, idols of pagan gods stood on every street corner. The Athenians, perhaps fearing that they had slighted some deity, had even erected an altar "to the unknown god" (Acts 17:23).

"The One whom you worship without knowing," said Paul, "Him I proclaim to you: God, who made the world and everything in it, since He is Lord of heaven and earth, does not dwell in temples made with hands" (Acts 17:23–24).

Only the sovereign Lord God has the power to rule the world; only the Lord Jesus Christ has the power to rise from the dead as the conqueror, establishing once and for all our everlasting life with Him.

GOG [gog] (*golden ornament*) — the name of two men in the Bible:

Amon, one of the principal gods of the Egyptians, may have been one of the false gods worshiped by the Israelites—a practice condemned by the prophet Jeremiah (Jer. 46:25, 26).

Photo by Howard Vos

Scholars point out the similarities between the golden calf worshiped by the Israelites (Ex. 7:14-25) and an Egyptian religious custom. Their god Hapi was represented by the figure of a bull.

1. A descendant of Joel, of the tribe of Reuben (1 Chr. 5:4).

2. The leader of a confederacy of armies that attacked the land of Israel. Described as "the prince of Rosh, Meshech, and Tubal," Gog is also depicted as being "of the land of Magog" (Ezek. 38:2-3), a "place out of the far north" of Israel. Ezekiel prophetically describes Gog and his allies striking at Israel with a fierce and sudden invasion (Ezekiel 38—39). According to Ezekiel's prophecy, Gog will be crushed on the mountains of Israel in a slaughter so great it will take seven months to bury the dead (Ezek. 39:12).

The vision of Gog and Magog that appears in the Book of Revelation is essentially a restatement of the prophecy of Ezekiel, although it places the events of this prophecy in the future (Rev. 20:7-8).

GOIIM [GOY yim] (*nations*) — the name of two groups in the Old Testament:

1. A people who were part of an attack against the cities of the plain (Gen. 14:1, 9).

2. One of the tribal groups conquered by Joshua (Josh. 12:23, RSV). The Goiim may have been a migrating group of tribes related to the Philistines.

GOLAN [GOE lan] (*circle*) — a city of Bashan in the territory of the half-tribe of Manasseh east of the Jordan River (see Map 3, C-2). Golan was assigned to the Gershonite Levites and was one of three cities of refuge east of the Jordan River. It is probably the site of modern Sahem el-Jaulan, about 27 kilometers (17 miles) east of the Sea of Galilee (1 Chr. 6:71). The area north and east of the Sea of Galilee is sometimes called the Golan Heights.

GOLD (see MINERALS OF THE BIBLE).

GOLD, PIECE OF (see MONEY OF THE BIBLE).

GOLDEN CALF — an idolatrous image of a young bull, probably made of wood and overlaid with gold, which the Israelites worshiped in the wilderness while Moses was on Mount Sinai receiving the Ten Commandments (Exodus 32). Another instance of this form of idolatry occurred years later in the history of God's people when King Jeroboam of Israel set up golden calves at Bethel and Dan (1 Kin. 12:26-33). Also see GODS, PAGAN.

GOLDSMITH (see OCCUPATION AND TRADES).

GOLGOTHA [GOL gah thuh] (*place of a skull*) — the place where Jesus was crucified, a hill just outside the walls of Jerusalem (Mark 15:22).

GOLIATH [goe LIE ahth] (*soothsayer*) — a Philistine giant whom David killed with a stone from his sling (1 Sam. 17:4-51). Goliath, who lived in the Philistine city of GATH, was probably a descendant of a tribe of giants known as the Anakim, or descendants of Anak (Num. 13:33). These giants probably served in a capacity similar to that of a foreign mercenary or soldier of fortune.

Based on the figures in the Bible (1 Sam. 17:4), Goliath was at least 9 1/2 feet tall and perhaps as tall as 11 feet. The magnificence of Goliath's armor and weapons—his bronze coat of mail, bronze greaves, bronze javelin, spear with an iron spearhead, and huge sword—must have made him appear invincible.

For 40 days this enormous man challenged Saul's army to find one man willing to engage in hand-to-hand combat. The winner of that one battle would determine the outcome of the war. The young David, chosen by God as Israel's next king, accepted the challenge, felling Goliath with a single stone to the forehead from his sling. When David beheaded the fallen giant, the Philistines fled in panic.

GOMER [GOAM ur] (*complete*) — the name of a man, a people, and a woman:

1. The oldest son of Japheth (Gen. 10:2-3).

2. The people descended from Gomer, son of Japheth. Apparently they lived to the far north, beyond the Black Sea (Ezek. 38:6). They were probably the Cimmerians of classical history.

3. A harlot who became the wife of the prophet HOSEA (Hos. 1:1-11). When Gomer left Hosea and became the slave of one of her lovers, Hosea bought her back at God's command for the price of a slave. Gomer's unfaithfulness and Hosea's forgiveness symbolized God's forgiving love for Israel.

GOMORRAH [guh MOR ruh] (*submersion*) — one of the five "cities of the plain" located in the Valley of Siddim (Salt Sea or Dead Sea). The other cities were Sodom, Admah, Zeboiim, and Zoar (Gen. 14:2-3). Gomorrah is associated closely with its twin city, Sodom. Because these cities became the site of intolerable wickedness, they were destroyed by fire (Gen. 19:24, 28).

The exact location of Sodom and Gomorrah has been a subject of much debate. In 1924 archaeologists W. F. Albright and M. G. Kyle undertook extensive surveys of the region south of the Dead Sea. This territory is now under water, but it may have been dry land when the cities were destroyed about 2000 B.C. during the days of Abraham.

The conclusion of these archaeologists was that Sodom and Gomorrah had to be located just east of Mount Usdum, a mountain of almost pure salt, on the western shores of the southernmost tip of the Dead Sea. Their research also showed that a violent explosion had occurred on the site at some time in the distant past—an event similar to the description of Gomorrah's destruction in the Book of Genesis.

GONG (see MUSICAL INSTRUMENTS).

GOOD — a word with two distinct meanings in the Bible:

1. As an adjective, good means "pleasant" (Prov. 15:23), "full measure" (Gen. 30:20), "kind" and "gracious" (1 Sam. 25:15).

2. As a noun, good means primarily God Himself (Mark 10:18). The Bible also speaks of God's works, gifts, and commands as good.

GOODMAN — KJV word for the male head of a family or master of a household (Luke 12:39; master of the house, NKJV; owner of the house, NIV).

GOODNESS — the quality of being good; praiseworthy character; moral excellence. The Bible speaks often of the goodness of God (Ex. 33:19; Rom. 2:4). God's goodness consists of righteousness, holiness, justice, kindness, grace, mercy, and love. Goodness is also one of the fruits of the Spirit that should characterize Christian believers (Gal. 5:22). Christians are called to goodness, even as God the Father is perfect and good (Matt. 5:48).

GOOSE (see ANIMALS OF THE BIBLE).

GOPHERWOOD (see PLANTS OF THE BIBLE).

GOSHEN [GOE shun] (*mound of earth*) — the name of two areas and one city in the Old Testament:

1. The northeastern territory of the NILE Delta in Egypt (see Map 2, A–1). Perhaps because it was situated so far from the Nile and its irrigation canals, Goshen was not highly valued by the Egyptians. Jacob and his family were granted permission to settle in this fertile section of Egypt during Joseph's rule as prime minister of Egypt (Gen. 46:28).

During the time of the Exodus, Goshen was protected from the plagues of flies (Ex. 8:22) and hail (Ex. 9:26) which engulfed the rest of Egypt. The district was not large, containing perhaps 900 square miles, and it had two principal cities: Rameses and Pithom. During its long history, Rameses had at least three other names: Zoan, Avaris, and Tanis. It was also the capital of the HYKSOS peoples for several centuries.

2. A district of southern Palestine between Gaza and Gibeon and the hill country and the Negeb (Josh. 10:41).

3. A town in the mountains of southwest Judah (Josh. 15:51).

GOSPEL — the joyous good news of salvation in Jesus Christ. The Greek word translated as gospel means "a reward for bringing good news" or simply "good news." In Isaiah 40:9, the prophet proclaimed the "good tidings" that God would rescue His people from captivity. In His first sermon in Nazareth, Jesus used a passage from the Old Testament to characterize the spirit of His ministry: "The Spirit of the Lord is upon Me, because He has anointed Me to preach the gospel to the poor" (Luke 4:18).

The gospel is not a new plan of salvation; it is the fulfillment of God's plan of salvation which was begun in Israel, was completed in Jesus Christ, and is made known by the church.

The gospel is the saving work of God in His Son Jesus Christ and a call to faith in Him (Rom. 1:16–17). Jesus is more than a messenger of the gospel; He *is* the gospel. The good news of God was present in His life, teaching, and atoning death. Therefore, the gospel is both a historical event and a personal relationship.

Faith is more than an intellectual agreement to a theoretical truth. Faith is trust placed in a living person, Jesus Christ. When the apostle Paul warned Christians of the dangers of following "another gospel" (2 Cor. 11:4), he was reminding them that any gospel different than the one he preached was no gospel at all.

In the second century, the word gospel came to

Bust of the Roman Emperor Tiberius, who was mentioned by Luke in his gospel account of the beginning of the ministry of Jesus (Luke 3:1).

Photo by Howard Vos

Photo by Gustav Jeeninga

These wild flowers in Palestine recall the words of Jesus to His followers: "Consider the lilies of the field, how they grow" (Matt. 6:28).

be used for certain writings in which the "good news" or story of Jesus Christ was told. These writings were written in the first century, but they became known as "gospels" much later. Mark was the first to write such a story (Mark 1:1), and in so doing he invented a literary form that we call a "gospel." The New Testament has four versions of the one gospel: the Gospels of Matthew, Mark, Luke, and John.

A gospel is more than a biography intended to provide information about a historical character. It is the presentation of the life of Jesus to show His saving significance for all people and to call them to faith in Him.

Also see GOSPELS.

GOSPELS — the four accounts at the beginning of the New Testament about the saving work of God in His Son Jesus Christ. The writers of the four gospels introduced a new literary category into literature. The gospels are not exactly biographies, because apart from certain events surrounding His birth, (Matt. 1—2; Luke 1—2) and one from His youth (Luke 2:41–52), they record only the last two or three years of Jesus' life.

Moreover, the material included is not written as an objective historical survey of Jesus' ministry. The gospels present Jesus in such a way that the reader realizes that God acted uniquely in Him. The authors of the gospels wrote not only to communicate knowledge about Jesus as a person, but also to call us to commitment to Him as Lord.

The gospels produce four distinctive portraits of Jesus rather than an exact photographic likeness. Thus, there are four gospels (accounts) of the one gospel (the good news of salvation in Jesus Christ).

The Gospel in Four Editions. Why, though, are there four versions of the same story? Why not one account? This question is as old as the church itself. Around A.D. 150, Tatian compiled a life of Christ, called the Diatessaron, by harmonizing the four gospels. His contemporary, Marcion, attempted to resolve the problem by choosing one gospel, Luke, and discounting the others.

The church, however, resisted Tatian's artificial life of Jesus and Marcion's choice of one gospel to the exclusion of the other three. Prior to Tatian and Marcion, the church had accepted each of the four gospels as a faithful and complementary witness to Jesus Christ. The church adopted symbols for the gospels—Matthew a lion, Mark an ox, Luke a man, John an eagle (or variations thereof)—from the fourfold witness to God in Scripture (Ezek. 1:5; 10:14; Rev. 4:7). At an early date the church realized that the combined witness of the four gospels was required to declare the full significance of Christ.

The Synoptic Problem. If one sets the four gospels side by side, it becomes apparent that Matthew, Mark, and Luke have much in common. Each gospel arranges its material in a similar fashion, and each gospel casts the life of Jesus within the framework of a Galilean ministry that extended from Jesus' baptism to His death, with emphasis on His final days in the flesh.

The similarity of the gospels also includes their content. The first three gospels recount many of the same incidents or teachings, and often in the same or related wording. A glance, for example, at the baptism of Jesus as related by Matthew (3:13–17), Mark (1:9–11), and Luke (3:21–22) will quickly demonstrate their agreement. Because of this similarity in arrangement, content, and wording, the first three gospels are called synoptic gospels (from the Greek *synopsis*, "a seeing together").

The Gospel of John presents a more independent account of Christ. John's relationship to the first three gospels can be considered only after a thorough discussion of Matthew, Mark, and Luke.

The synoptic problem arises from the attempt to explain the general similarity of Matthew, Mark, and Luke, while accounting for their individual differences. Two of the four gospel writers (Mark and Luke) were not eyewitnesses of the events they relate, and some question remains about the other two (see MATTHEW, GOSPEL OF; JOHN, GOSPEL OF). This means we cannot assume that the similarities and differences among the gospels come solely from their personal perspectives as interpreters of Jesus and His ministry. Other sources also probably contributed to the composition of the four gospels.

In the past 200 years, a great deal of scholarship has been devoted to recovering such possible sources, though it is doubtful whether the puzzle has been fully resolved. The theories advanced generally fit one of two categories. One possibility is that the synoptics depend on a prior source that is now lost, except as it is preserved in the synoptics themselves. A second possibility is that two of the synoptic gospels depend on the other gospel. Until about 1800, the church generally accepted the view, first advanced by Augustine, that Matthew wrote the first gospel, Mark abbreviated Matthew, and Luke used both to compose the third gospel.

Mark as a Source. Most scholars now agree that at least two, and perhaps as many as four, sources lie beneath the synoptic gospels. The first and most important of these is the Gospel of Mark—and not Matthew, as the church long assumed. Mark contains 666 verses (excluding 16:9-20, which many scholars consider later additions to the text). A total of 606 of these verses reappear in shortened form in Matthew's Gospel of 1,071 verses; 350 of Mark's verses reappear in Luke's Gospel of 1,151 verses. This means that more than one-half of Matthew and one-third of Luke are composed of material from Mark. Only 31 verses in Mark have no parallel in Matthew or Luke.

A number of observations show that Mark, and not Matthew or Luke, is the prior source. First, Matthew and Luke never agree in arrangement of material when compared against Mark. When either Matthew or Luke disagree in the sequence of events, the other follows Mark.

Second, certain details in Mark's gospel are either omitted or reworked in Matthew and Luke. The latter often refine Mark's awkward expressions; for example, compare Mark 4:1 with Matthew 13:1-2 and Luke 8:4. Inconsistencies in Mark are omitted by Matthew and Luke; for example, compare Mark 2:26 with Matthew 12:3 and Luke 6:3. Mark's frank assessments of the disciples (6:52; 9:32) are omitted by Matthew and Luke, apparently out of respect for their importance as apostles. Mark's references to Jesus' human emo-

tions—for example, grief (14:34), exasperation (8:12), anger (10:14), amazement (6:6), and fatigue (4:38)—are softened by the other synoptics; and examples of Jesus' ability to perform certain actions (Mark 6:6) are deleted by them, too (Matt. 13:58; Luke 4:23).

On the other hand, Matthew and Luke on occasion heighten Jesus' accomplishments in comparison with Mark (Mark 1:32, 34; Matt. 8:16). If we assume that Matthew and Luke reworked Mark in these instances, it is possible to explain the differences; but it is practically impossible to do so if we assume otherwise.

Q Source. When the remaining material in Matthew and Luke is examined, the reader discovers that more than 200 verses appear in them, while they have no parallel in Mark. This material, which consists mainly of Jesus' teachings, can be grouped into four categories: (1) Jesus and John the Baptist, (2) Jesus and His disciples, (3) Jesus and His opponents, and (4) Jesus and the future. Scholars assume that this material must have come from a source known only to Matthew and Luke.

For purposes of identification, this source is assigned the name "Q" (from the German, *Quelle*, "source"). Since Q passages agree closely, sometimes to the point of exact wording, it is reasonable to assume that this source was written rather than oral. Q material occurs scattered throughout Matthew 5—7; 10—11; 18:10, 23; and 24:37; but it is centralized in two sections of Luke (6:20—7:35; 9:57—13:34). Luke, therefore, probably more nearly preserves the original sequence of Q.

The "Q" document, of course, is theoretical, since no copy of it is known to exist. It is likely, however, that a document preserving the sayings of Jesus and fitting the description of Q was known to the early church. The church father, Papias, writing about 130 A.D., records, "Matthew collected the oracles in the Hebrew language, and each interpreted them as best he could." It is unlikely that these "oracles" are our present Gospel of Matthew, though it may be that they served as a source for the Gospel of Matthew (and Luke?). The sayings of Jesus were highly esteemed in the early church, especially for the instruction of converts; and it is possible that the more than 200 verses which Matthew and Luke have in common depend on a sayings source compiled by Matthew and known to Papias as "oracles."

Special M and Special L. When Mark and Q are accounted for, there remain more than one-fifth of Matthew and one-third of Luke for which there is no parallel in other gospels. Where each writer obtained this information is uncertain, although much of Luke's special material probably came from sources associated with his Pauline journeys, particularly in Caesarea. At any rate, each writer appears to have used unique materials in writing his gospel. These sources are sometimes labeled Special M (Matthew) and Special L (Luke).

Form Criticism. Following World War I, a new approach to gospel research arose in Germany. Its goal was to get behind the written sources (Mark, Q, L, or M) and investigate the forms (hence, form criticism) in which the gospel was transmitted by word of mouth in the period between the death of Jesus (A.D. 30) and the appearance of the first Christian writings of Paul (A.D. 50).

This school of thought rests on several assumptions. One assumption is that the tradition that was handed down about Jesus tended to become grouped into a number of broad categories: miracle stories, parables, pronouncements (Mark 2:27; 3:35), sayings of various kinds (Matt. 6:19–34), and most importantly, accounts of the death of Jesus.

Another assumption of form criticism is that the early church remembered, shaped, and passed on those aspects of Jesus' teachings and ministry which were relevant to its circumstances. This means that, in addition to telling us about Jesus, the gospels tell us something about the early church that passed on the stories about Jesus.

This assumption has resulted in the important awareness that the early church did not look upon Jesus merely as an historical figure of the past, but as the living Lord of the present. This second assumption is especially evident in the Gospel of John, which blends the remembrances called to mind by the Holy Spirit (John 14:26) with the events of Jesus' life. Since the early church maintained its treasure of tradition about Jesus primarily through preaching, the contents of the gospels are shaped significantly by the faith of the early church.

This is not to say that stories were "made up" by the early church in order to preach about a Jesus who was a figment of someone's vivid imagination. It means, instead, that the early church kept some memories about Jesus alive, while it did not continue others; and one of the reasons for this is that certain events and sayings were much more important in the early church's eyes than others were.

Although form criticism is still in its infancy stages, it has increased our appreciation of the role the early church played in the formation of the gospels. Some form critics, however, have erred in overstating the influence of the church on the gospel tradition, sometimes even implying that the gospels mirror the church instead of the Lord.

Is it possible to know whether the early church distorted or preserved the intent of the historical Jesus? Fortunately, the New Testament contains certain checks that provide reasonable certainty of careful handling on the part of the early church. We may be assured that eyewitnesses, including some of the apostles, were alive when the gospels appeared in writing. Such eyewitnesses would have encouraged historical accuracy and prevented distortion in the gospels.

Another important fact is that rabbis of Jesus' day trained their disciples to commit their teachings to memory, in fact, to the point of perfect recitation of long passages. We have no reason to assume that Jesus was less diligent about the transmission of His teaching than the rabbis were about theirs.

We also may be assured that the early church did not project upon the gospels any teachings or concerns foreign to Jesus. The synoptic gospels, for example, record more than 50 parables of Jesus, but not one parable is recorded in the remainder of the New Testament. This observation demonstrates that Jesus—and only Jesus—taught in parables, and the church was faithful to record them.

Expressed respect for the words of Jesus can also be found in the apostle Paul, who distinguishes between "commands of the Lord" and his own opinion (1 Cor. 7:10, 12, 25). In a similar vein, we have no instances where the words of Paul, Peter, John, or any of the "pillars" of the church (Gal. 2:9) are placed in Jesus' mouth. Nor do we find the teachings of the apostles included in the gospels. Jesus commands center stage, and He has no successors.

Furthermore, we know that the early church faced a series of crises as it began to evangelize the Gentile world. One such crisis concerned the conditions of accepting Gentiles into the church, and especially CIRCUMCISION. But such questions are scarcely mentioned in the gospels (Matt. 8:10).

Finally, inclusion in the gospels of confusing statements (such as the second coming; Mark 9:1), or matters unimportant to the early church (little children; Mark 10:13–16), or even embarrassing remembrances (Peter's denial; Mark 14:66–68), indicate that the early church was more intent on preserving the tradition it received than on improving its own image.

Redaction Criticism. Since World War II, some scholars have done gospel research in another area. These scholars focus on the role of the gospel writers as editors of the material received from the early church, and hence the name redaction criticism (from the German, *Redaktion,* "editing"). Whatever sources and traditions the writers may have inherited, redaction studies have revealed that the gospel writers were more than chroniclers or witless transmitters of the material they received. Each is an important link in the chain connecting us with Jesus. Each offers a unique and complementary portrait of Jesus, because each writes to a different audience and emphasizes different aspects of Jesus' life.

For Mark, Jesus is the Suffering Servant who reveals His divine Sonship on the cross. Matthew's major concern is to present Jesus as a teacher who is greater than Moses and continually present with the disciples. For Luke, Jesus is the keystone in the history of salvation, beginning with Israel, fulfilled in Jesus, and communicated by the church. The fourth gospel writer penetrates the mystery of the incarnation (Jesus as God in human form; John 1:14), who brings life to the world through trust in Him.

The Synoptics and the Gospel of John. It would be a mistake to imply that John is radically different from the other gospels and deserves no consideration with them. All four gospels portray Jesus Christ through selected events in His life, climaxing in His death and resurrection. But John features an independent, unique presentation of Jesus. In the synoptics, Jesus' ministry lasts less than a year, and is conducted mainly in Galilee; in John it extends to three or more years and centers more often in Judea.

The synoptics present Jesus as a man of action who paints word pictures for His hearers; John, however, portrays longer, less picturesque, and more speculative discourse coming from Jesus, and comparatively little action. In the synoptics, Jesus teaches in parables—nearly 60 in all—but in John no parables exist. In the synoptics, Jesus teaches mainly about the kingdom of God, whereas in John he teaches about Himself. In the synoptics, Jesus often demands silence of those who behold His miracles, but in John miracles are signs revealing Jesus and His mission.

These facts are sufficient to indicate that the synoptics present basically one perspective on the life of Jesus and that the Gospel of John presents another perspective, achieved most probably by profound meditation on the meaning of Jesus Christ.

The importance of the gospels for the early church may be indicated by noting that these four, which were collected perhaps as early as A.D. 125, were the first books of the New Testament to be accepted as authoritative by the early church. Today the four gospels remain our only reliable source of information about the central figure of the human race.

We may never fully understand how the gospels originated and what sources each writer used for his account. But a more important challenge than solving the literary mysteries of the gospels is learning to appreciate the unique portrait which each writer offers of Jesus and growing in our love and devotion to Him.

GOSSIP — a person who spreads rumors or idle, fruitless tales. The apostle Paul described some of the early believers as "not only idle but gossips [tattlers, KJV] and busybodies" (1 Tim. 5:13). Jesus said, "For every idle word men may speak, they will give account of it in the day of judgment" (Matt. 12:36).

GOTHIC VERSIONS (see BIBLE VERSIONS AND TRANSLATIONS).

GOURD (see PLANTS OF THE BIBLE).

GOVERNMENT — earthly authority; those who rule over others in order to keep society stable and orderly. Only God is the sovereign ruler of all. When human governments exalt themselves above God, they go beyond their legitimate function in society (Dan. 5:32). In Bible times God exercised government through many persons and institutions.

The basic unit of government among the Hebrews was the "father's house" or primary family (Gen. 12:1; Num. 1:4). Above this was the clan (Num. 36:6) and then the tribe, governed by a leader who was chosen by representatives from the tribes (Num. 1:4-16). Over all these units was a central leader. In early days, Moses or Joshua (and Aaron and his descendants in the religious sphere) served as central leaders among the Israelites. After Joshua's death, numerous local or tribal leaders known as JUDGES stepped forward to lead. These judges exercised many governmental functions, but no central leadership existed during those days. Only Samuel approached national status as a leader.

The possibility of a king as central leader of the nation was foreseen as early as Deuteronomy 17:14-20. The kings governed by using bureaucra-

The restored Senate Building in Rome, where civil officials met to conduct the affairs of the powerful Roman Empire.

Remains of the Pnyx, where the democratic assembly of ancient Athens met. Notice the speaker's stand for public meetings in front of the structure.

cies similar to those of other ancient Near Eastern kingdoms. Kings who overstepped the legitimate bounds of "government under God" were often confronted by prophets such as Elijah, Nathan, or Jeremiah (2 Sam. 12:1–15a). Isaiah the prophet pointed to the coming Messiah who would be the supreme ruling king and agency of God's government of His people (Is. 9:6–7).

After the fall of Jerusalem in 587 B.C., the Jews were ruled by foreign powers such as Babylon, Persia, Greece and Rome. During most of these times, however, the Jews were allowed a measure of self government. In time the office of HIGH PRIEST took on political as well as religious dimensions. At most times there was also a group of local Jewish leaders that formed a governing council. In Jesus' day, this body was called the SANHEDRIN. Made up of both SADDUCEES and PHARISEES, it was presided over by the high priest.

Jesus taught that earthly governments exist by God's will (John 19:11) and are legitimate as long as they do not take over the role reserved for God alone (Mark 12:13–17). Romans 13 discusses human government as ordained by God. Revelation 13, on the other hand, discusses it as degenerate and demonic. Christians live in the tension created by the fact that governments can be good (Romans 13) or evil (Revelation 13). When governments promote good and suppress evil, they fulfill their God–given function (1 Pet. 2:11–12). But if government exalts itself as sovereign over all life, then it has overstepped its bounds and is a handmaid of evil.

GOVERNOR — a regional agent or officer for the Roman emperor during New Testament times. This office gradually developed across a period of many years. The primary function of the governor was to serve as a financial officer. In a senatorial PROVINCE the governor was in charge of the emperor's properties within the province. In an imperial province he acted as the treasurer, collecting taxes and paying the troops in the Roman army. Later, in A.D. 53, Claudius gave governmental powers to governors in the third class provinces such as Judea. They had auxiliary troops to maintain order and were responsible to the Roman ruler based in Syria.

Before A.D. 53 the governor was officially called prefect as in the case of Pilate. After A.D. 53 he was called procurator as in the cases of Felix and Festus. There was much confusion at the time because after A.D. 53 the Jewish historian Josephus calls the ruler of Judea prefect, procurator, and governor. In the New Testament the political ruler of Judea was always called by the more general term "governor." The governors of Judea included Pilate (Matt. 27:2), Felix (Acts 23:24), and Festus (Acts 26:30–32).

GOZAN [GOE zan] (*quarry*) — a city or region in northern Mesopotamia, on the river Habor (or Khabur), to which the Israelites were deported by the King of Assyria after the destruction of Samaria (Is. 37:12). The KJV and NKJV refer to Gozan as a river, but the river mentioned is the Habor, and Gozan is the area through which it flows.

GRACE — favor or kindness shown without regard to the worth or merit of the one who receives it and in spite of what that same person deserves. Grace is one of the key attributes of God. The Lord God is "merciful and gracious, long–suffering, and abounding in goodness and truth" (Ex. 34:6). Therefore, grace is almost always associated with mercy, love, compassion, and patience as the source of help and with deliverance from distress.

In the Old Testament, the supreme example of grace was the redemption of the Hebrew people

Cemeteries, like this one in the Kidron Valley outside Jerusalem, were always located outside the city wall.

from Egypt and their establishment in the Promised Land. This did not happen because of any merit on Israel's part, but in spite of their unrighteousness (Deut. 9:5–6). Although the grace of God is always free and undeserved, it must not be taken for granted. Grace is only enjoyed within the COVENANT—the gift is given by God, and the gift is received by man through repentance and faith (Amos 5:15). Grace is to be humbly sought through the prayer of faith (Mal. 1:9).

The grace of God was supremely revealed and given in the person and work of Jesus Christ. Jesus was not only the beneficiary of God's grace (Luke 2:40), but He was also its very embodiment (John 1:14), bringing it to mankind for salvation (Titus 2:11). By His death and resurrection, Jesus restored the broken fellowship between God and His people, both Jew and Gentile. The only way of salvation for any person is "through the grace of the Lord Jesus Christ" (Acts 15:11).

The grace of God revealed in Jesus Christ is applied to human beings for their salvation by the HOLY SPIRIT, who is called "the Spirit of grace" (Heb. 10:29). The Spirit is the One who binds Christ to His people so that they receive forgiveness, adoption to sonship, and newness of life, as well as every spiritual gift or grace (Eph. 4:7).

The theme of grace is especially prominent in the letters of the apostle Paul. He sets grace radically over against the law and the works of the law (Rom. 3:24, 28). Paul makes it abundantly clear that salvation is not something that can be earned or merited; it can be received only as a gift of grace (Rom. 4:4). Grace, however, must be accompanied

by faith; a person must trust in the mercy and favor of God, even while it is undeserved (Rom. 4:16).

The law of Moses revealed the righteous will of God in the midst of pagan darkness; it was God's gracious gift to Israel (Deut. 4:8). But His will was made complete when Jesus brought the gospel of grace into the world (John 1:17).

GRAFT, GRAFTING — in horticulture, the process of uniting a shoot or bud with a growing plant so they grow as one. The apostle Paul used this procedure to illustrate the relationship between Jews and Gentiles in God's plan. The natural branches of the good olive tree (Israel) were broken off (because of Israel's unbelief) and the alien branches of a wild olive tree (the Gentiles) were grafted onto the root of the good olive tree (because of the Gentiles' faith; Rom. 11:17–24).

GRAIN (see AGRICULTURE).

GRANARY (see STOREHOUSE).

GRAPES (see PLANTS OF THE BIBLE).

GRASSHOPPER (see ANIMALS OF THE BIBLE).

GRATE, GRATING — a network of bronze on the altar in the TABERNACLE. Each of the four corners of the grating had a bronze ring by which the altar was carried (Ex. 27:4–7).

GRATITUDE (see THANKSGIVING).

GRAVE — a place where the dead are buried. In general, the Jewish people buried their dead in graves much as today, except that they were not as deep. In towns and cities the burial grounds were situated outside the city limits (Luke 7:12; John 11:30). Evidence of this may be seen today in the many graves in the Valley of Johoshaphat east of Jerusalem and at the Essene community overlooking the Dead Sea. Plain stones or a stone slab were used to cover the grave as a safeguard against animals and to mark the burial place (2 Sam. 18:17). In some instances hewn stones were used. Occasionally expensive pillars were used as memorials (2 Kin. 23:17); thus, Jacob erected a pillar over Rachel's grave (Gen. 35:20), which today is marked by a building over the site.

Natural caves were often used as family burial sites. The most famous of these is the cave of MACHPELAH (Genesis 23), which was purchased by Abraham for this purpose. It may still be seen in Hebron (Gen. 23:2).

Wealthy people, such as Joseph of Arimathea (John 19:38–42), sometimes hewed a family tomb out of solid rock. To cover the entrance, a large circular stone in a groove was rolled across the entrance and sealed. The "Garden Tomb" outside Jerusalem where Jesus was laid is a good example of this type of burial site.

Also see BURIAL.

GRAVECLOTHES — strips of cloth wrapped around a corpse in preparation for burial. When Lazarus was raised from the dead by Jesus, he emerged from the tomb "bound hand and foot by graveclothes" (John 11:44; bandages, RSV; wrappings, NASB; linen bands, NEB).

GRAVEN IMAGE (see IDOL, IMAGE).

GREAT LIZARD, GREAT OWL (see ANIMALS OF THE BIBLE).

GREAVES (see ARMS, ARMOR OF THE BIBLE).

GREECE — a region or country of city–states in southeastern Europe between Italy and Asia Minor. Greece was bounded on the east by the Aegean Sea, on the south by the Mediterranean Sea, on the west by the Adriatic Sea and Ionian Sea, and on the north by Mount Olympus and adjacent mountains. The Old Testament name for Greece was JAVAN (Gen. 10:2, 4; Is. 66:19).

In the early years of its history, Greece was a country of self–governing city–states. Politically and militarily, the Greek city–states were weak. Their varied backgrounds led to frictions and rivalries that kept them from becoming one unified nation.

In 338 B.C., Philip II, king of Macedon, conquered the southern peninsula of Greece. Under Philip's son, Alexander the Great (336–323 B.C.), the Greek Empire was extended from Greece through Asia Minor to Egypt and the borders of India. Alexander's military conquests and his passion to spread Greek culture contributed to the advancement of Greek ideas throughout the ancient world. This adoption of Greek ideas by the rest of the ancient world was known as HELLENISM. So thoroughly did Greek ideas penetrate the other nations that the Greek language became the dominant language of the known world.

Greek learning and culture eventually conquered the ancient Near East and continued as dominant forces throughout the New Testament era. Even after the rise of the Romans, about 146 B.C., the influence of Greek language, culture, and philosophy remained strong, even influencing the Jewish religion.

Greek religion included many gods. The religions of Egypt, Asia Minor, and Persia were more appealing than the old Greek gods because they promised immortality. However, the Greeks did not abandon their former gods; they simply adopted new gods and gave them old names. A renewed interest in astrology among the Greeks also led to widespread belief that the planets governed the lives and fates of human beings. The Greeks sought to control any turn of fate through worship. They even erected an altar inscribed "to the unknown god" in their capital city of Athens (Acts 17:23).

The peninsula of Greece fell to the Romans in 146 B.C. and later became the senatorial province of Achaia with Corinth as its capital. The apostle Paul visited this area on his second missionary journey, delivering his famous sermon to the Athenian philosophers (Acts 17:22–34). Later he appeared before the proconsul Gallio at Corinth (Acts 18:12–17). On his third missionary journey, he vis-

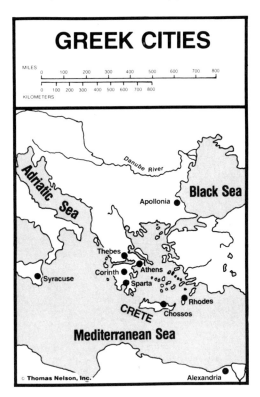

ited Greece for three months (Acts 20:2–3).

Greece is important to Christianity because of its language. In New Testament times Greek was the language spoken by the common people of the ancient world, as far west as Rome and the Rhone Valley, in South Eastern France. Most of the New Testament was written originally in Greek. This precise and expressive language provided the most capable vehicle for expressing thought of any in the ancient world.

Also see GREEKS; LANGUAGE.

GREEK (see LANGUAGES OF THE BIBLE).

GREEKS — natives of Greece or people of Greek descent. In the New Testament, Greeks is sometimes a general term for all who are not Jews.

Historically, the Greeks descended from four separate groups—the Acheans, Ionians, Aetolians, and Dorians—which immigrated into Greece and replaced the civilization that previously existed. Each group settled in different regions of Greece. Because these peoples did not mix very well, Greece developed into a group of city–states instead of a nation. They fought among one another for superiority, and even though they conquered isolated areas of the Mediterranean coastland, they were unable to establish a unified empire. Much later, Philip of Macedon conquered Greece, and his son

ALEXANDER the Great, extended Greek culture throughout most of the Mediterranean world. When Alexander died, his generals continued this policy of forcing Greek culture upon the people of his empire. The way of life they enforced is known as HELLENISM.

Centuries later when the Romans conquered the ancient world, they brought political organization to the Mediterranean, but they did little to change its Hellenistic culture. When the biblical writers use the term "Greeks," therefore, they do not merely mean natives of Greece; they are speaking of all who have been influenced by Greek culture and are not Jews (for instance, Mark 7:26, where a Syro–Phoenician woman is called a Greek).

By contrast, the term "Grecians" (KJV), Grecian Jews (NIV), or "Hellenists" (RSV, NKJV) refers to Greek–speaking Jews only (Acts 6:1; 9:29).

In the Old Testament, Greece is to be identified with Javan (Is. 66:19). The only Old Testament reference to Greeks occurs in Joel 3:6.

GREEK VERSIONS (see BIBLE VERSIONS AND TRANSLATIONS).

GREEN (see COLORS OF THE BIBLE).

GREEN FELDSPAR, **GREEN JASPER** (see JEWELS AND PRECIOUS STONES).

Remains of the Erechtheum, a temple devoted to worship of the pagan goddess Athena, in Athens.

GREETING — a SALUTATION on meeting a person (Matt. 26:49; hail, KJV) or an opening address in a letter or message (Acts 15:23).

GREYHOUND (see ANIMALS OF THE BIBLE).

GRIEF — an emotion of sorrow; the experience of emotional distress or pain. Today the word grief is usually used to express what a person feels in periods of intense sadness, as in the time of death. But the Bible uses the word more freely and, more often than not, in reference to things other than death. Grief is a response to the trouble one's enemies cause (Ps. 6:7; 31:10) or to the foolishness of a child (Prov. 10:1).

The Bible also tends to emphasize the cause of grief rather than the emotion itself. For example, in 1 Samuel 25:31, the word translated grief means literally a "stumbling block." To the Hebrew writers the importance of grief was not its psychological effect upon the individual. Grief was important to them because it is a response to the troubles of a fallen world.

The grief of Isaiah 17:10–11 is the result of man forgetting God. God Himself is sometimes grieved, or troubled, at man's sinfulness (Gen. 6:6–7; Is. 63:10). But if God and righteous men feel sorrow or pain about the world, there is hope in Christ, who "surely...has borne our griefs" (Is. 53:4).

GRIFFON (see ANIMALS OF THE BIBLE).

GRIND — to prepare grain for cooking by crushing it into a fine mixture. Wheat was ground into flour in Bible times by pulverizing the kernels between two large circular stones (Is. 47:2). Also see TOOLS OF THE BIBLE.

GRINDERS — a symbolic word for teeth (Eccl. 12:3), describing one of the common problems of old age—worn and decayed teeth.

GROVE (see WOODEN IMAGES).

GRUB (see ANIMALS OF THE BIBLE).

GUARANTEE — a promise or assurance; something given or held as security. The apostle Paul declared that the Holy Spirit, who lives in our hearts, is the guarantee that we shall receive our full inheritance from God (2 Cor. 5:5).

GUARD (see OCCUPATIONS AND TRADES).

GUARD, GATE OF THE; GUARDHOUSE, GATE OF THE (see GATES OF JERUSALEM AND THE TEMPLE).

GUARDIAN — a person legally responsible for the welfare and property of a minor (Gal. 4:2).

GUDGODAH [gud GOH dah] (*incision*) — a place where the Israelites camped in the wilderness, near Ezion Geber (Deut. 10:7). This place is also called Hor Hagidgad (Num. 33:32–33).

GUEST — a person who receives hospitality at the home or table of another (Zeph. 1:7; Matt. 22:10–11). The scribes and Pharisees were amazed that Jesus accepted the hospitality of Zacchaeus, a chief tax collector, and went to stay at his house. They murmured, "He has gone to be a guest with a man who is a sinner" (Luke 19:7).

GUEST ROOM — a room for the lodging of guests (Mark 14:14; Philem. 22). The Greek word translated as guest room means "a lodging or resting place." A few houses of Palestine had rooms set aside for use by guests.

GUILE — craftiness, cunning, deceit, or deception. Jesus commended Nathanael as a true Israelite, a man in whom there was no guile (John 1:47). The opposite of guile is truth, honesty, and sincerity.

GUILT, GUILTY — bearing responsibility for an offense or wrongdoing; remorseful awareness of having done something wrong (Lev. 4:3; Ezra 9:6, 13, 15). Although the word guilt is not specifically used, some classic examples of guilt in the Bible are: Adam and Eve (Gen. 3:7–8), Cain (Gen. 4:8–9), and David (2 Sam. 11; Ps. 51). One Greek word in the New Testament translated as guilty means "under justice," or answerable to the judgment and condemnation of God. Also see SIN.

GUILT OFFERING (see SACRIFICIAL OFFERINGS).

GULF — a deep gap or cleft separating two places. Jesus told about a rich man (traditionally called Dives, meaning "rich") and a beggar (Lazarus)—one in heaven and one in hell—who were separated by a great gulf (Luke 16:26; chasm, NASB, NEB, NIV, RSV).

GUM RESIN (see JEWELS AND PRECIOUS STONES).

GUNI [GOO nih] (*protected*) — the name of two Old Testament men:
1. A son of Naphtali and founder of the GUNITES (1 Chr. 7:13).
2. The father of Abdiel (1 Chr. 5:15).

GUNITES [GOO nights] — the descendants of GUNI No. 1 (Num. 26:48).

GUR, ASCENT TO [gure] (*lion's cub*) — a hill near IBLEAM, where Jehu's archers killed Ahaziah, king of Judah (2 Kin. 9:27).

GUR BAAL [gure BAY al] (*dwelling of Baal*) — a desert place, perhaps a town, inhabited by Arabians. Uzziah, king of Judah, numbered it among his conquests (2 Chr. 26:7).

GUTTER — a watering trough for livestock in which Jacob placed peeled branches of poplar, almond, and chestnut trees to influence the coloring of newborn lambs to his advantage (Gen. 30:38). In the KJV, gutter also refers to the water tunnel that David's army used to gain entrance into the city of Jerusalem for a decisive victory over the JEBUSITES (water shaft, NKJV). Apparently the Jebusites had dug a tunnel leading down to the GIHON SPRING so they could reach the water supply undetected.

Photo by Howard Vos

Reconstruction of the entrance to the Roman gymnasium at Sardis. Both the Greeks and the Romans built gymnasiums throughout the ancient world.

GYMNASIUM — an important institution in the culture of ancient Greece where young men were educated by the philosophers and trained in various physical routines. Although the word does not appear in the Bible, archaeologists have discovered evidence that gymnasiums did exist throughout the ancient world in Bible times. The gymnasium got its name from the fact that the men trained and performed naked. This and the fact that all activities were closely tied to Greek culture made the gymnasium repulsive to most of the Jewish people.

However, when Palestine came under Greek control, a gymnasium was built in Jerusalem early in the second century B.C. as part of an effort to make the Jews accept Greek culture. It continued in existence until Jerusalem was destroyed in A.D. 70 by the Romans.

HAAHASHTARI [hay uh HASH tur eye] (*courier*) — a descendant of Judah through Ashhur. His mother was Ashhur's second wife, Naarah (1 Chr. 4:6).

HABAIAH [huh BIGH yuh] (*Jehovah has hidden*) — the ancestor of a Jewish family whose name could not be found in the genealogical records (Ezra 2:61–62; Neh. 7:63; Hobaiah, RSV).

HABAKKUK [huh BAK uhk] (*embraced [by God]*) — a courageous Old Testament prophet and author of the Book of Habakkuk. The Scriptures say nothing of his ancestry or place of birth. A man of deep emotional strength, Habakkuk was both a poet and a prophet. His hatred of sin compelled him to cry out to God for judgment (Hab. 1:2–4). His sense of justice also led him to challenge God's plan to judge the nation of Judah by the pagan Babylonians (Hab. 1:12—2:1). His deep faith led him to write a beautiful poem of praise in response to the mysterious ways of God (Habakkuk 3). Also see HABAKKUK, BOOK OF.

HABAKKUK, BOOK OF — a short prophetic book of the Old Testament that deals with the age-old problems of evil and human suffering. The book is named for the prophet Habakkuk, who received this message from God in the form of a vision.

Structure of the Book. Habakkuk's book contains only three short chapters, but they present a striking contrast. In the first two, Habakkuk protests, complains, and questions God. But the final chapter is a beautiful psalm of praise. Habakkuk apparently used this complaining and questioning technique to drive home his powerful message about the approaching judgment of God.

Habakkuk begins his book with a cry of woe. Injustice is rampant, the righteous are surrounded by the wicked, the law is powerless, and God doesn't seem to care about the plight of His people (1:1–4). Habakkuk's prophecy is even introduced as a "burden" which the prophet saw (1:1). He wonders why God is allowing these things to happen.

God's reply brings little comfort to the prophet. He explains that the armies of Babylon are moving throughout the ancient world on a campaign of death and destruction. At the time when Habakkuk received this vision, the Babylonians had already defeated Assyria and Egypt. The implication is that Habakkuk's nation, Judah, will be the next to fall.

The prophet was shocked at the news. He reminded God of His justice and holiness (1:12–13). How could He use the wicked Babylonians to destroy His Chosen People? Surely He realized the sins of His people were as nothing, when compared to the pagan Babylonians (1:13). "Why do you...hold your tongue when the wicked devours one more righteous than he?" he asks (1:13). This

---

HABAKKUK: A Teaching Outline

direct question indicates Habakkuk's great faith. Only a person very close to God would dare question the purposes of the Almighty so boldly. God assures Habakkuk that the Babylonians will prevail not because they are righteous but because they are temporary instruments of judgment in His hands (2:4). Then he pronounces five burdens of woe against the Babylonians (2:6, 9, 12, 15, 19). God will not be mocked; the end of the Babylonians is as certain as the judgment they will bring on Judah. In all of this, God will vindicate His righteous character: "For the earth will be filled with the knowledge of the glory of the Lord, as the waters cover the sea" (2:14).

After this assurance, Habakkuk breaks out with the beautiful psalm of praise to God contained in chapter 3. This is one of the greatest testimonies of faith in the Bible.

Authorship and Date. Nothing is known about the prophet Habakkuk except his name. But he was surely a sensitive poet as well as a courageous spokesman for God. His little book is a literary masterpiece that points people of all ages to faith in God and His eternal purpose. Since the book speaks of the coming destruction of Judah, it had to be written some time before Jerusalem was destroyed by the Babylonians in 587 B.C. The most likely time for its composition is probably about 600 B.C.

Historical Setting. The Book of Habakkuk belongs to that turbulent era in ancient history when the balance of power was shifting from the Assyrians to the Babylonians. Assyria's domination came to an end with the destruction of its capital city, Nineveh, by the invading Babylonians in 612 B.C. Less than 20 years after Habakkuk wrote his book, the Babylonians also destroyed Jerusalem and carried the leading citizens of Judah into captivity. God used this pagan nation to punish His Covenant People for their unfaithfulness and worship of false gods.

Theological Contribution. The question-and-answer technique of the prophet Habakkuk teaches a valuable lesson about the nature of God. That God allows Himself to be questioned by one of His followers is an indication of His long-suffering mercy and grace.

The theme of God's judgment against unrighteousness also is woven throughout the book. God soon will punish His wayward people for their transgression, but He also will punish the pagan Babylonians because of their great sin. God always acts in justice. He will not forget mercy while pouring out his wrath (3:2). His judgment will fall on the proud, but the just will live in His faithfulness (2:4). God's acts of judgment are in accord with His holiness, righteousness, and mercy.

Special Considerations. The Protestant Reformation under Martin Luther was influenced by the Book of Habakkuk. Luther's discovery of the biblical doctrine that the just shall live by faith came from his study of the apostle Paul's beliefs in the Books of Romans and Galatians. But Paul's famous

declaration, "The just shall live by faith" (Rom. 1:17), is a direct quotation from Habakkuk 2:4. Thus, in this brief prophetic book, we find the seeds of the glorious gospel of our Lord and Savior Jesus Christ.

Also see HABAKKUK.

HABAZZINIAH [hab uh zih NIGH yuh] (meaning unknown) — the grandfather of Jaazaniah, leader of the RECHABITES (Jer. 35:3; Habaziniah, KJV).

HABERGEON (see ARMS, ARMOR OF THE BIBLE).

HABIRU [hah BIHR roo] — the people of a broad social movement that occurred throughout the ancient Near East from about 2000 to 1000 B.C. The word Habiru comes from the Akkadian language, and its equivalents appeared throughout the period in each of the known languages of the region. While scholars once thought that the word described an ethnic group, they now believe the word was merely a descriptive word that may very well have had the primary meaning of "immigrant." This conclusion agrees with the texts where the word appears, for they picture the Habiru as foreigners.

The Habiru apparently were thought of as a bad omen because they often hired themselves out as mercenaries, or soldiers of fortune. Although the word Habiru does not actually appear in the Bible, some scholars believe the reference to Abraham as "the Hebrew" in Genesis 14:13 may indicate that he was considered a part of the Habiru. See also Exodus 21:2.

HABITATION — a dwelling place. Solomon referred to the Temple as God's "house of habitation" (2 Chr. 6:2, KJV). The church is also called "a habitation of God in the Spirit" (Eph. 2:22).

HABOR [HAY bohr] (meaning unknown) — a tributary of the Euphrates River which flowed through Gozan, a region of Mesopotamia. Tiglath-Pileser (1 Chr. 5:26) and "the king of Assyria" (2 Kin. 17:6)—probably Sargon—settled some of the Israelites who had been deported from Samaria along the Habor. Habor is probably the modern Khabur River.

HACALIAH [hah kuh LIGH uh] (*Jehovah is hidden*) — the father of Nehemiah, the governor of Israel after the Captivity (Neh. 1:1; Hachaliah, KJV; Neh. 10:1).

HACHILAH [huh KIGH luh] (*gloomy*) — a hill in Judah opposite Jeshimon, a barren district in the Wilderness of Ziph. This site was one of David's hideouts from Saul (1 Sam. 23:19).

HACHMONI [hak MOE nigh] (*wise*) — the father of Jehiel (1 Chr. 27:32).

HACHMONITE [HAK muh night] — a member of a family founded by HACHMONI (1 Chr. 11:11).

HADAD [HAY dad] (*thunderer*) — a name of four men and one foreign god in the Old Testament:

1. A son of Bedada and king of Avith, a city of

Edom. Hadad defeated Midian in the field of Moab (Gen. 36:35–39; Hadar, NASB, NEB, KJV, RSV).

2. A prince of the Edomites. As a young child, Hadad escaped from Edom to Egypt during the six-month period when Joab, the leader of Israel's army, was killing every male in Edom. The pharaoh gave Hadad a house, land, and food. He also gave the sister of Queen Tahpenes to Hadad for a wife. After David and Joab died, Hadad became an enemy of Solomon (1 Kin. 11:14–25).

3. The eighth of the 12 sons of Ishmael and the grandson of Abraham (1 Chr. 1:30), also called Hadar (Gen. 25:15, KJV).

4. A king of Edom who ruled from the city of Pai (1 Chr. 1:50–51).

5. An ancient storm god. The Assyrians identified Hadad with their weather god Rimmon and the Canaanites identified him with Baal. The name is found in proper names such as Ben-Hadad and Hadadezer. See GODS, PAGAN.

HADADEZER [HAD uh DEE zur] (*Hadad is helper*) — the son of Rehob and king of Zobah in Syria. Hadadezer's army was defeated by the forces of David and Joab (2 Sam. 8:3–12). He is also called Hadarezer (2 Sam. 10:16, 19, KJV).

HADAD RIMMON [HAY dad RIM mahn] — a place in the plain of Megiddo, not far from Jezreel. At Hadad Rimmon King Josiah of Judah was killed and his army was defeated by Pharaoh Necho of Egypt (Zech. 12:11; 2 Chr. 35:24). Many scholars believe the name refers to a Canaanite vegetation god, since Hadad and Rimmon were pagan gods of the Syrians.

HADAR [HAY dahr] — a form of HADAD Nos. 1 and 3.

HADAREZER [HAY duh REE zur] — a form of HADADEZER.

HADASHAH [hah DAH shuh] (*new*) — a village in the lowlands of Judah (Josh. 15:37), location unknown.

HADASSAH [hah DAH suh] (*myrtle*) — the original Hebrew name for ESTHER (Esth. 2:7). Some scholars, however, see hadassah as a title ("bride") given to her—a title also used for the Babylonian fertility goddess Ishtar—when she became queen. Esther would then be the Hebrew form of Ishtar.

HADATTAH [hah DAH tuh] (*new Hazor*) — a word describing HAZOR, a city in the territory of Judah (Josh. 15:25; Hazor-hadattah, RSV, NAS, NEB, NIV). The KJV and the NKJV treat Hazor and Hadattah as two separate cities; however, the reference is probably to only one city.

HADES [HAY dees] — Greek word for HELL.

HADID [HAY did] (*sharp*) — a town of Benjamin named with Lod (Lydda) and Ono as a place inhabited by the Benjamites after the Captivity (Ezra 2:33). Hadid is identified as modern el-Haditheh, about five kilometers (three miles) northeast of Lydda.

HADLAI [HAD ligh] (*fat*) — the father of Amasa, a chief of the tribe of Ephraim (2 Chr. 28:12).

HADORAM [hah DOHR uhm] (*Haddu is exalted*) — the name of three Old Testament men:

1. A son of Joktan, who was descended from Shem and Noah (Gen. 10:27).

2. A son of Tou (or Toi), king of Hamath during David's reign (1 Chr. 18:10). Hadoram is also called Joram (2 Sam. 8:10).

3. The superintendent of forced labor under Rehoboam (2 Chr. 10:18). When the ten tribes revolted, Hadoram was sent to Israel as a messenger, but he was stoned to death (2 Chr. 10:18). He is also called Adoniram (1 Kin. 4:6; 5:14) and Adoram (1 Kin. 12:18).

HADRACH [HAY drak] (meaning unknown) — a city-state of northern Syria (Lebanon) mentioned with Damascus and Hamath (Zech. 9:1).

HAFT — KJV word for HILT.

HAGAB [HAY gab] (*locust*) — an ancestor of a family of NETHINIM (Temple servants) who returned to Jerusalem after the Captivity (Ezra 2:46).

HAGABA, HAGABAH [HAG uh buh] (*locust*) — the ancestor of a family of NETHINIM (Temple servants) who returned to Jerusalem after the Captivity (Ezra 2:45).

HAGAR [HAY gahr] (*flight*) — the Egyptian bond-woman of Sarah who bore a son, ISHMAEL, to Abraham (Gen. 16:1–16). After waiting ten years for God to fulfill his promise to give them a son, Sarah presented Hagar to Abraham so he could father a child by her, according to the custom of the day. Sarah's plan and Abraham's compliance demonstrated a lack of faith in God.

When Hagar became pregnant, she mocked Sarah, who dealt with her harshly. Hagar then fled into the wilderness, where, at a well on the way to Shur, she encountered an angel of the Lord. The angel revealed Ishmael's future to Hagar—that his descendants would be a great multitude. Tradition has it that Hagar is the ancestress of all the Arab peoples and of the prophet Muhammad. Hagar called the well Beer Lahai Roi, "The well of the Living One who sees me."

When Hagar returned to Abraham's camp, Ishmael was born and accepted by Abraham as his son. But when Ishmael was 14, Isaac, the promised son, was born. The next year Ishmael mocked Isaac at the festival of Isaac's weaning. At Sarah's insistence and with God's approval, Hagar and Ishmael were expelled from Abraham's family. Abraham grieved for Ishmael, but God comforted him by revealing that a great nation would come out of Ishmael.

Hagar and Ishmael wandered in the wilderness until their water was gone. When Hagar laid her son under the shade of a bush to die, the angel of the Lord appeared to Hagar and showed her a well. This is a beautiful picture of God's concern for the outcast and helpless.

HAGARENES [HAG uh reenz] — a form of HAGRITES.

HAGARITES [HAG uh rights] — a form of HAGRITES.

HAGGAI [HAG eye] (*festive*) — an Old Testament prophet and author of the Book of Haggai. As God's spokesman, he encouraged the captives who had returned to Jerusalem to complete the reconstruction of the Temple. This work had started shortly after the first exiles returned from Babylon in 538 B.C. But the building activity was soon abandoned because of discouragement and oppression. Beginning in 520 B.C., Haggai and his fellow prophet, Zechariah, urged the people to resume the task. The Temple was completed five years later, about 515 B.C. (Ezra 5:1). Also see HAGGAI, BOOK OF.

HAGGAI, BOOK OF — a short prophetic book of the Old Testament written to encourage the people of Israel who had returned to their native land after the captivity in Babylon.

Structure of the Book. The two short chapters of Haggai contain four important messages from the prophet to the people. He called on the people to rebuild the Temple, to remain faithful to God's promises, to be holy and enjoy God's great provisions, and to keep their hope set on the coming of the MESSIAH and the establishment of His kingdom.

Authorship and Date. This book was written by the prophet Haggai, whose name means "festive." Like those whom he encouraged, he probably spent many years in captivity in Babylon before returning to his native land. A contemporary of the prophet Zechariah, he must have worked constantly as a prophetic voice among his countrymen in Jerusalem. He delivered these messages of encouragement "in the second year of King Darius" (1:1), a Persian ruler. This dates his book precisely in 520 B.C.

Historical Setting. Haggai takes us back to one of the most turbulent periods in Judah's history—their captivity at the hands of a foreign power, followed by their release and resettlement in Jerusalem. For more than 50 years they were held captive by the Babylonians. But they were allowed to return to their native land, beginning in 538 B.C., after Babylon fell to the conquering Persians. At first, the captives who returned worked diligently at rebuilding the Temple, but they soon grew tired of the task and gave it up altogether. Haggai delivered his messages to motivate the people to resume the project.

Theological Contribution. Haggai urged the people to put rebuilding the Temple at the top of their list of priorities. This shows that authentic worship is a very important matter. The rebuilt Temple in Jerusalem was important as a place of worship and sacrifice. Centuries later, at the death of Jesus "the veil of the Temple was torn in two" (Luke 23:45), demonstrating that He had given Himself as the eternal sacrifice on our behalf.

Special Considerations. The Book of Haggai ends with a beautiful promise of the coming of the Messiah. Meanwhile, God's special servant, ZERUBBABEL, was to serve as a "signet ring" (2:23), a sign or promise of the glorious days to come. As the Jewish governor of Jerusalem under appointment by the Persians, Zerubbabel showed there was hope for the full restoration of God's Covenant People in their native land.

Also see HAGGAI.

HAGGEDOLIM [HAH guh doe lihm] (*the great ones*) — the father of the priest Zabdiel (Neh. 11:14, RSV).

HAGGERI [huh GHEE righ] — a form of HAGRI.

HAGGI [HAG eye] (*born on a feast day*) — a son of

HAGGAI: A Teaching Outline

Photo by Howard Vos

This stone engraving on the Tower of the Winds at Athens shows the northeast wind emptying a container filled with hailstones.

Gad and founder of a tribal family, the HAGGITES (Gen. 46:16).

HAGGIAH [hug EYE yuh] (*festival*) — a descendant of Merari, son of Levi (1 Chr. 6:30).

HAGGITES [HAG ights] — descendants of HAGGI (Num. 26:15).

HAGGITH [HAG ith] (*festival*) — the fifth wife of David and the mother of Adonijah, who later claimed the throne (1 Chr. 3:2).

HAGIOGRAPHA [HAG ee AHG ruh fuh] (*holy writings*) — the third division of the Hebrew Bible. The other two divisions are the Law and the Prophets. Also known as the Writings, the Hagiographa contained 11 books (13 in the English Bible) in the following order in the Hebrew Bible: Psalms, Proverbs, Job, Canticles (Song of Solomon), Ruth, Lamentations, Ecclesiastes, Esther, Daniel, Ezra–Nehemiah, and 1 and 2 Chronicles.

HAGRI [HAG righ] (*wanderer*) — the father of Mibhar, one of David's mighty men (1 Chr. 11:38; Haggeri, KJV, NEB).

HAGRITES [HAG rights] (*descendants of Hagar*) — a nomadic tribe of Aramean or Arabian origin that lived in TRANSJORDAN east of Gilead. The Hagrites were a pastoral BEDOUIN people rich in camels, donkeys, and sheep. During the reign of King Saul, the tribe of Reuben conquered the Hagrites (1 Chr. 5:10; Hagarites, KJV). The Hagrites are mentioned among the tribes that formed a confederacy against

Israel (Ps. 83:6; Hagarenes, KJV, NEB; Hagarites, NKJV).

HAHIROTH [hah HEAR ahth] — a form of PI HAHIROTH.

HAI [HAY eye] — a form of AI.

HAIL — a greeting which involves a wish for the good health and peace of the person addressed. Judas greeted Jesus hypocritically when he went up to Him in the Garden of Gethsemane and said, "Greetings [Hail, KJV], Rabbi!" and then kissed Him (Matt. 26:49). After His resurrection, Jesus met His disciples and said to them, "Rejoice!" (Matt. 28:9; All hail, KJV). Also see GREETING; SALUTATION.

HAILSTONES — precipitation in the form of pellets of ice. Although hailstones are not common in Palestine, they are reported in the Bible. The seventh plague that struck the land of Egypt before the Exodus was a destructive storm of hail (Ex. 9:18–34). In Joshua's day more men of the Amorite army were killed by "large hailstones from heaven" (Josh. 10:11) than by the sword of the Israelites. The Book of Revelation uses imagery similar to the seventh plague of Egypt to describe God's power. The fifth trumpet of judgment brought hail and fire mingled with blood (Rev. 8:7) and the seventh bowl of God's wrath was a plague of hail (Rev. 16:21).

HAIR — the hairy coating of an animal or the human body, especially the hairs covering a human head. In the Bible the word hair usually means the hair on a human head. In a few cases the word refers to animal hair or human hair other than on the head (Gen. 25:25; Mark 1:6).

In Old Testament times men as well as women wore long hair. Both Samson and Absalom were admired for their long, full hair (Judg. 16:13–14; 2 Sam. 14:25–26). Baldness was considered embarrassing (2 Kin. 2:23–24; Is. 3:24), and Israelite men were forbidden to cut the forelocks of their hair (Lev. 19:27). But men under a NAZIRITE vow shaved their entire heads when the vow was completed (Num. 6:18).

Women apparently left their hair loose. Both men and women groomed their hair (Is. 3:24), because leaving it unkempt was a sign of mourning (Ezra 9:3). Beautiful hair was prized by both men and women (Song 4:1; 5:11), while gray hair was desired by the aged (Prov. 16:31; 20:29).

In the New Testament era, men wore their hair much shorter than women's (1 Cor. 11:14–15). Christian women were instructed not to wear elaborately arranged hair (1 Pet. 3:3). In Palestine, honored guests often had their heads anointed. On two occasions Jesus' feet were anointed by women who then dried them with their hair (Luke 7:38–46; John 12:1–8). Jesus' statement that the Father has numbered each person's hairs (Matt. 10:30) shows God's concern for even the tiny and insignificant details of life.

HAKKATAN [HAK uh tan] (*the small one*) — the father of Johanan, who returned from the Captivity with Ezra (Ezra 8:12).

HAKKOZ [HAK ahz] (perhaps *the thorn*) — a priest and chief of the seventh course of service in the sanctuary (1 Chr. 24:10; Ezra 2:61; Neh. 3:4, 21). Also see KOZ.

HAKUPHA [huh KOO fuh] (*crooked*) — an ancestor of a family of NETHINIM (Temple servants) who returned from Babylon with Zerubbabel (Ezra 2:51).

HALAH [HAY luh] (meaning unknown) — a district of the Assyrian Empire to which SHALMANESER exiled some of the Israelites. Apparently the region included the basin of the Habor (Khabur) and Saorkoras Rivers (2 Kin. 17:6).

HALAK [HAH luhk] (*bald mountain*) — a mountain in southern Palestine which marked the southern limit of Joshua's conquests (Josh. 11:17). Halak is perhaps the modern Jebel Halaq, northeast of Abdeh.

HALF–SHEKEL [SHEK uhl] — the amount of payment required for the annual Temple tax of each Jew over 20 years of age (Ex. 30:13). A half–shekel was roughly equivalent to two day's pay for a common laborer. Also see MONEY OF THE BIBLE.

HALF–TRIBE — a term used in the Old Testament to refer to the two separate settlements of the tribe of Manasseh—one east of the Jordan River and the other in central Palestine west of the Jordan. During the days of Moses, half of the people of the tribe of Manasseh requested permission to settle the territory east of the Jordan after the land was conquered. Moses agreed to this request, on the condition that the entire tribe assist in the conquest of Canaan and that the other half of the tribe settle west of the Jordan (Num. 32:33–42; Deut. 3:12–13; Josh. 1:12–18).

HALHUL [HAL huhl] (meaning unknown) — a town in the hill country of Judah (Josh. 15:58), identified as modern Halhul, about six kilometers (four miles) north of Hebron.

HALI [HAY ligh] (*ornament*) — a border town in Asher, between Helkath and Beten (Josh. 19:25), location unknown.

HALL — a large open court in the Temple in Jerusalem, Solomon's palace, and other large buildings in Bible times (1 Kin. 7:50; 2 Chr. 4:22; Matt. 22:10). Other translations render the Hebrew word for hall as "porch" or "parlor."

HALL, JUDGMENT (see JUDGMENT).

HALLEL [hah LELL] (*praise thou the Lord*) — a song of praise celebrating God's mighty acts on behalf of His Chosen People, the nation of Israel. The complete text of the song is contained in Psalms 115—118. The Hallel was sung in Jewish homes at the PASSOVER meal and at other major FEASTS AND FESTIVALS during the Hebrew year.

HALLELUJAH — a form of ALLELUIA.

HALLOHESH [hah LOW hesh] (*the whisperer*) — the name of one or two men in Nehemiah:

1. The father of Shallum, who helped rebuild the walls of Jerusalem (Neh. 3:12; Halohesh, KJV).

2. A man who sealed the covenant with Nehemiah after the Captivity (Neh. 10:24). He may be the same person as Hallohesh No. 1.

HALLOW (see HOLINESS).

HALOHESH [ha LOW hesh] — a form of HALLOHESH.

HALT (see DISABILITIES AND DEFORMITIES).

HAM [hamm] (*hot*) — the name of a person and two places in the Old Testament:

1. The youngest of Noah's three sons (Gen. 5:32). Ham, along with the rest of Noah's household, was saved from the great Flood by entering the ark (Gen. 7:7). After the waters went down and Noah's household left the ark, Ham found his father, naked and drunk, asleep in his tent. Ham told his brothers, Shem and Japheth, who covered their father without looking on his nakedness. Noah was furious because Ham had seen him naked, and he placed a curse on Ham and his descendants. The offspring of Ham were to serve the descendants of Shem and Japheth (Gen. 9:21–27).

Ham had four sons: Cush, Mizraim, Put and Canaan (Gen. 10:6). The descendants of these four are

Aerial view of the mound of ancient Hamath, a city controlled by Solomon and later conquered by Jeroboam II of Israel (2 Kin. 14:28).

generally thought of as immoral and evil. The tribe of Mizraim settled in Egypt, while the tribes of Cush and Put settled in other parts of Africa. The tribe of Canaan populated Phoenicia and Palestine.

2. A city east of the Jordan River during the time of Abraham. It was attacked by Chedorlaomer and other allied kings (Gen. 14:5). The modern city of Ham lies six kilometers (four miles) south of Irbid.

3. Another name for Egypt, used in poetry (Ps. 78:51; 105:23, 27).

HAMAN [HAY mun] (meaning unknown) — the evil and scheming prime minister of Ahasuerus (Xerxes I), king of Persia (485–464 B.C.). When MORDECAI refused to bow to Haman, Haman plotted to destroy Mordecai and his family, as well as all of the Jews in the Persian Empire. But ESTHER intervened and saved her people. Haman was hanged on the very gallows he had constructed for Mordecai (Esth. 3:1—9:25). This shows that God is always in control of events, even when wickedness and evil seem to be winning out.

HAMATH [HAY math] (*fortress*) — the name of a city and a territory in the Old Testament:

1. An ancient city of Syria situated on the Orontes River about 78 kilometers (125 miles) north of Damascus. The city was on the main trade route that connected Mesopotamia to the east with Egypt to the south. The prophet Amos called Hamath great probably because the city's influence was spread over a wide area.

2. The territory that surrounded the city of Hamath in ancient Syria. In the days of David, the King of Hamath, Toi (or Tou), was friendly to Israel. He congratulated David for defeating their common enemy, King Hadadezer of Damascus (2 Sam. 8:9–10; 1 Chr. 18:9–10). King Solomon later controlled Hamath, where he built storage depots

(2 Chr. 8:4). Archaeological sources reveal that numerous kings of Syria–Palestine—including the king of Hamath, Ahab of Israel, and Ben–Hadad of Damascus—formed an alliance to stop the advance of King Shalmaneser III of Assyria in 853 B.C. at the battle of Karkor (Qarqar), a city east of Galilee in the Arabian desert.

About 780 B.C., Jeroboam II, king of Israel, took Hamath for Israel (2 Kin. 14:28). About 722 B.C., Syria–Palestine fell to Assyria. Sargon, king of Assyria, settled colonists from Hamath in cities of Samaria (2 Kin. 17:24; Is. 36:18–20; 37:13, 18–20). These colonists from Hamath worshiped an idol called Ashima (2 Kin. 17:30), which brought the Lord's anger upon them (2 Kin. 17:25). Likewise, some Israelites were deported from Samaria and settled in Hamath (Is. 11:11).

HAMATH ZOBAH [HAY meth ZOE buh] — a city of Syria captured by King Solomon (2 Chr. 8:3).

HAMATHITES [HAY meth ights] — the people of Hamath (Gen. 10:18).

HAMITES [HAM ites] — the descendants of HAM (1 Chr. 4:4).

HAMMATH [HAM eth] (*hot spring*) — the name of a city and a man:

1. A fortified city of Naphtali (Josh. 19:35). Hammath is probably identical with Hammon and Hammoth Dor which was assigned to the Levites. It is the modern Hamman Tabariyeh, situated on the western shore of the Sea of Galilee.

2. The founder of the house of Rechab, a family of the Kenites (1 Chr. 2:55).

HAMMEDATHA [ham ih DAY thuh] (*given by the moon*) — the father of Haman the Agagite (Esth. 3:1).

455

HAMMELECH [HAM uh lek] — the father of Jerahmeel and Malchiah (Jer. 36:26; 38:6, KJV). The Hebrew word is probably not a proper name, but a general title that means "the king." Hence, the NKJV has "the king's son."

HAMMER (see TOOLS OF THE BIBLE).

HAMMOLECHETH [huh MAH luh keth] — a form of HAMMOLEKETH.

HAMMOLEKETH [huh MAH luh keth] (*she who reigns*) — a daughter of Machir and sister of Gilead, the grandson of Manasseh (1 Chr. 7:18; Hammolecheth, NAS, RSV).

HAMMON [HAM uhn] (*hot spring*) — the name of two settlements in Israel:

1. A frontier village of Asher (Josh. 19:28), location uncertain.

2. A town of Naphtali allotted to the Levites (1 Chr. 6:76). It probably is the same place as Hammath (Josh. 19:35) and Hammoth Dor (Josh. 21:32).

HAMMOTH DOR [HAM uhth DOHR] (*warm springs of Dor*) — a fortified city of Naphtali allotted to the Gershonite Levites (Josh. 21:32). It is probably the same place as Hammon (1 Chr. 6:76) and Hammath (Josh. 19:35).

HAMMUEL [HAM yoo uhl] — a form of HAMUEL.

HAMMURABI, CODE OF [hah muhr RAH bee] — an ancient law code named after an early king of Babylon. These laws from the ancient world are valuable to Bible students because they are so similar to the Law as revealed to Moses in the first five books of the Old Testament.

The Code of Hammurabi was discovered in 1901–02 by the archaeologist V. Scheil at Susa, an early city of the ancient Babylonians. It was written on a seven-foot-high stone monument (called a stele) with the upper part picturing Hammurabi receiving a scepter and a ring, symbols of justice and order, from Shamash, the Babylonian sun–god and divine lawgiver. The rest of the monument contains the code; the direction of writing is from top to bottom. Hammurabi's law dates from about 300 years after Abraham and some 300 years before the events described in the books of Exodus, Leviticus, and Deuteronomy. This law code was written for a complex urban culture, in contrast to the simple agricultural culture of Palestine.

The contents of Hammurabi's Code are listed as follows:

1. Various offenses and crimes, including false witness, sorcery, corrupt judgment, theft, and kidnapping.

2. Property, with special reference to crown tenants, tenant farmers, and loans of money or seed. The king of Babylon owned crown–land in the Old Babylonian period, as did the God of Israel. According to the code, land owned by the king could not be sold.

3. Commercial law, related to partnerships and agencies.

4. Marriage law, including dowry settlements, bridal gifts, divorce, and matrimonial offenses.

5. The firstborn had special rights and privileges (compare Deut. 15:19).

6. Special cases involving women and priestesses, whose support was weakened by an increase in state and private ownership of land.

7. Adoption, as it relates to Genesis 17:17–18.

8. Assault and damage to persons and property, including pregnant women, a surgeon's liability in an eye operation, and the hire of boats.

9. Agricultural work and offenses, including goring by an ox (compare Ex. 21:28–32).

10. Rates and wages for seasonal workers, hire of beasts, carts and boats, and so forth.

11. An appendix concerning slaves, including their purchase and sale.

The content of the Code of Hammurabi and the Law of Moses is similar in many ways. This may be a result of the common cultural background the Babylonians and Israelites shared. Both were ancient peoples of the Near East who inherited their customs and laws from common ancestors. Yet it should be noted that much is different in the Old Testament revelation. For example, the Law given at Mount Sinai reflects a unique and high view of the nature of God, and the Old Testament law is presented as an expression of His holy nature, as Leviticus 19:2 clearly shows. Also, when com-

Hammurabi receives the laws in his famous code from the god of justice, Shamash, in this stone carving from ancient Babylon.
Photo by Howard Vos

pared with the Code of Hammurabi, the Old Testament law is much less harsh.

HAMONAH [huh MOE nuh] (*multitude*) — the symbolic name of a city in the Valley of HAMON GOG where the evil forces of GOG will be defeated (Ezek. 39:16).

HAMON GOG [HAY muhn GAHG] (*multitude of Gog*) — the name of a valley where the evil forces of GOG and his allies will be defeated in their final conflict with Israel (Ezek. 39:11, 15).

HAMOR [HAY mohr] (*donkey*) — the father of SHECHEM. Hamor was killed with Shechem in revenge by Levi and Simon after Shechem raped their sister Dinah (Gen. 34:2-26). Jacob purchased land from the sons of Hamor and built an altar upon it (Gen. 33:19). Later, Joseph was buried on this land (Josh. 24:32).

HAMRAN [HAM ran] — a form of HEMDAN.

HAMSTRING — to cripple by cutting the hamstrings, or leg tendons, of horses (1 Chr. 18:4; hough, KJV) or other animals (Gen. 49:6). When horses were captured from the enemy, the great muscles on their hind legs were clipped to render them useless for battle. Examples of hamstringing animals can be found in Genesis 49:6; Joshua 11:6, 9; 2 Samuel 8:4; and 1 Chronicles 18:4.

HAMUEL [HAM yoo el] (*God protects*) — a son of Mishma, a descendant of Simeon (1 Chr. 4:26; Hammuel, NAS, NIV, RSV).

HAMUL [HAY muhl] (*spared by God*) — a son of Perez, who was the son of Judah by Tamar (Gen. 46:12). Hamul was the founder of the HAMULITES.

HAMULITES [HAY muhl ights] — the descendants of HAMUL (Num. 26:21).

HAMUTAL [huh MYOO tuhl] (*father-in-law is protection*) — a daughter of Jeremiah of Libnah, one of King Josiah's wives, and the mother of Jehoahaz and Zedekiah (2 Kin. 23:31; 24:18).

HANAMEEL [huh NAM ih el] (*God is gracious*) — a son of Shallum and a cousin of Jeremiah the prophet. Jeremiah purchased a field from Hanameel during the siege of Jerusalem by the Babylonians (Jer. 32:7-9, 12; Hanamel, RSV, NEB, NIV).

HANAN [HAY nuhn] (*merciful*) — the name of several Old Testament men:
1. A son of Shashak and a chief of the tribe of Benjamin (1 Chr. 8:23).
2. A son of Azel and a descendant of Saul and Jonathan (1 Chr. 8:38).
3. A son of Maachah and one of David's mighty men (1 Chr. 11:43).
4. The founder of a family of NETHINIM (Temple servants) who returned from the Captivity with Zerubbabel (Ezra 2:46).
5. A Levite who helped Ezra interpret the law to the people (Neh. 8:7).
6. A Levite who sealed the covenant under Nehe-

miah (Neh. 10:10; 13:13). He may be the same person as Hanan No. 5.
7, 8. Two chiefs of the people who sealed the covenant under Nehemiah (Neh. 10:22, 26).
9. A son of Igdaliah and a prophet whose sons had a room in the Temple (Jer. 35:4).

HANANEEL [HAN uh neel] (*God is merciful*) — a tower on the north wall of Jerusalem near the Sheep Gate and the Tower of the Hundred (Jer. 31:38; Hananel, NIV, NAS, NEB, RSV).

HANANI [hah NAH nigh] (*gracious gift of the Lord*) — the name of six Old Testament men:
1. The father of Jehu (1 Kin. 16:1, 7).
2. A son of Heman and head of the 18th course of musicians appointed by David for the sanctuary (1 Chr. 25:4, 25).
3. A SEER who rebuked Asa for paying tribute money to Ben-Hadad, king of Syria (2 Chr. 16:7).
4. A priest who divorced his pagan wife after the Captivity (Ezra 10:20).
5. A brother of Nehemiah who brought news of Jerusalem to Susa and later was made governor of Jerusalem (Neh. 1:2; 7:2).
6. A Levite who played an instrument at the dedication of the repaired walls of Jerusalem (Neh. 12:36).

HANANIAH [han uh NIE uh] (*Jehovah is gracious*) — the name of 15 men in the Old Testament:
1. An ancestor of Jesus in Luke's genealogy (1 Chr. 3:19, 21; Luke 3:27).
2. A son of Shashak (1 Chr. 8:24).
3. Leader of a course of priests in David's time (1 Chr. 25:4, 23).
4. A commander in the army of King Uzziah of Judah (2 Chr. 26:11).
5. A son of Bebai. Hananiah divorced his foreign wife following the Captivity (Ezra 10:28).
6. A perfumer who helped rebuild Jerusalem's walls during Nehemiah's time (Neh. 3:8).
7. The son of Shelemiah. Hananiah helped rebuild Jerusalem's walls during Nehemiah's time (Neh. 3:30).
8. An official in Jerusalem during Nehemiah's time (Neh. 7:2).
9. A clan leader who sealed the covenant in Nehemiah's time (Neh. 10:23).
10. A clan leader in the days of the high priest Joiakim after the Captivity (Neh. 12:12).
11. A priest who blew the trumpet at the dedication of Jerusalem's rebuilt wall (Neh. 12:41).
12. A false prophet in the prophet Jeremiah's time (Jeremiah 28).
13. A prince under King Jehoiakim of Judah (Jer. 36:12).
14. An ancestor of the guard who arrested the prophet Jeremiah (Jer. 37:13).
15. The Hebrew name of Shadrach (Dan. 1:6-7).

HAND — the end of the arm that serves as a grasping and handling tool for man. The hand enables humans to use tools and to act in ways that are impossible for animals. The Bible speaks often of hands in the literal sense. In the ancient world hands were decorated with bracelets and rings (Gen. 24:22; Ezek. 23:42).

Because hands are involved in almost all of man's activity, the word is often used symbolically in the Bible. The "hand" of someone or some group can mean power. This gives rise to such expressions as "the hand of Saul," "the hand of the Egyptians," and "the hand of my enemies" (Ex. 3:8; 1 Sam. 23:17; Ps. 31:15). Because hands do the will of the entire person, hands may represent someone's "whole being" (Ps. 24:4; Acts 2:23).

The physical position of the hands suggest a person's attitude. Uplifted hands symbolize either praise and petition to God or violence against another person (1 Kin. 11:27; Ps. 63:4; 1 Tim. 1:8). Drooping hands mean weariness (Is. 35:3). To lay one's hands on another's head conveys blessing (Gen. 48:17). In the churches of the New Testament, the ordination of church officials regularly involved this custom (1 Tim. 5:22).

The expression "hand of God" refers to His great power (Deut. 2:15; Ezek. 1:3). Often the emphasis of this expression is on God's power in creation (Ps. 8:6; Is. 64:8). Sometimes His power in judgment is emphasized, especially in the phrase, "His hand is outstretched" (Ruth 1:13; Is. 9:12, 17). However, God may also extend His hand to express His mercy and forgiveness (Ps. 37:24).

HANDBREADTH — a linear measurement based on the width of the palm, four fingers closely pressed together. The psalmist used the word handbreadths to describe the brevity of human life (Ps. 39:5). Also see WEIGHTS AND MEASURES.

HANDKERCHIEF — a small cloth used by the Romans for wiping the hands and face. During the time of the Roman occupation of Palestine, the Jews started using handkerchiefs. In Jesus' parable of the minas (Luke 19:11–27), the wicked servant kept his master's mina put away in a handkerchief (v. 20). The same Greek word (*soudarion*) is used of the burial cloths used to cover the face of Lazarus in the grave (John 11:44) and the face of Jesus in the garden tomb (John 20:7). It was the custom to cover the face of the deceased with a handkerchief.

HANDLE — an ax handle (Deut. 19:5) or the knob of a sliding bolt or latch on a door (Song 5:5). Also see LOCK.

HANDPIKE, HANDSTAFF (see ARMS, ARMOR OF THE BIBLE).

HANDS, LAYING ON OF — the placing of hands upon a person by a body of believers in ceremonial fashion to symbolize that person's authority or his appointment to a special task.

The practice of laying hands on someone or something occurs frequently in the Old Testament—particularly the laying of hands on the head of an animal intended for sacrifice. In the account of the ritual of the DAY OF ATONEMENT, the priest

laid his hands on the SCAPEGOAT (Lev. 16:12). This probably symbolized the transferral of the sins and guilt of the people to the goat, which was taken away into the wilderness. The act of laying on of hands in the Old Testament was also associated with blessing (Gen. 48:18), installation to office (Deut. 34:9), and the setting apart of Levi (Num. 8:10). These passages seem to express the idea of transferral of authority and quality.

In the New Testament Jesus laid his hands on children (Matt. 19:13, 15) and on the sick when he healed them (Matt. 9:18). In the early church the laying on of hands was also associated with healing, the reception of the Holy Spirit (Acts 9:17), the setting apart of persons to particular offices and work in the church (Acts 6:6), the commissioning of Barnabas and Paul as missionaries (Acts 13:3), and the setting apart of Timothy (1 Tim. 4:14; 2 Tim. 1:6). The ritual was accompanied by prayer (Acts 6:6).

The laying on of hands was not a magical or superstitious rite that gave a person special power. It expressed the idea of being set apart by the entire church for a special task.

HANDWRITING (see WRITING).

HANES [HAY neez] (meaning unknown) — an unidentified place in Egypt (Is. 30:4).

HANGING — suspension of a person by the neck until dead. The usual method of capital punishment in Bible times, especially among the Hebrew people of the Old Testament, was stoning, not hanging (Ex. 19:13). Occasionally the Hebrews hung lawbreakers on trees, although such corpses were to be removed before nightfall (Deut. 21:22–23). In Egypt a beheaded corpse was occasionally left hanging for a longer period of time (Gen. 40:19). The Persians "hanged" persons by impaling them on a stake (Ezra 6:11; Esth. 6:4).

In the Bible only Ahithophel (2 Sam. 17:23) and Judas Iscariot died by hanging; each committed suicide.

Jesus' apostles applied the phrase "hanging on a tree" and the curse connected with it (Deut. 21:23) to Jesus' death (Acts 5:30; Gal. 3:13). Jesus transformed this dishonorable way of death into a beautiful picture of God's sacrificial and redeeming love.

HANIEL [HAN ee uhl] (*grace of God*) — a leader and warrior–hero of the tribe of Asher (1 Chr. 7:39; Hanniel, NIV, NAS, RSV). He was a son of Ulla.

HANNAH [HAN nuh] (*gracious*) — a wife of Elkanah, a Levite of the Kohathite branch of the priesthood (1 Sam. 1:1—2:21). Unable to bear children, Hannah suffered ridicule from Elkanah's second wife Peninnah, who bore the priest several children. Hannah vowed that if she were to give birth to a son, she would devote him to the Lord's service. The Lord answered her prayers, and to her was born the prophet Samuel.

Hannah was faithful to her promise. Making what must have been a heart–rending sacrifice,

Hannah took Samuel to the Temple after he was weaned, there to "remain forever" (1:21). God rewarded Hannah's piety and faithfulness with three more sons and two daughters. Hannah's beautiful thanksgiving psalm (2:1–10) is similar to the song of Mary when she learned she would be the mother of Jesus (Luke 1:46–55).

HANNATHON [HAN uh thahn] (*dedicated to grace*) — a town on the northern boundary of Zebulun (Josh. 19:14).

HANNIEL [HAN ee uhl] (*grace of God*) — a son of Ephod, of the tribe of Manasseh (Num. 34:23). Hanniel was a leader who helped distribute the land west of the Jordan River after the Israelite conquest of the land of Canaan.

HANOCH [HAY nahk] (*dedicated*) — the name of two Old Testament men:

1. A son of Midian. Hanoch was a descendant of Abraham by Keturah (Gen. 25:4; 1 Chr. 1:33; Henoch, KJV; Enoch, NIV).

2. The oldest son of Reuben and the founder of a tribal family, the Hanochites (1 Chr. 5:3).

HANOCHITES [HAY nahk ights] (*belonging to Hanoch*) — a family whose founder was HANOCH (Num. 26:5).

HANUKKAH [HAN uh kuh] (see FEASTS AND FESTIVALS).

HANUN [HAY nuhn] (*gracious*) — the name of three Old Testament men:

1. A son of Nahash, king of the AMMONITES. When David sent ambassadors to console Hanun on the death of Nahash, Hanun dishonored David's ambassadors by shaving off their beards and cutting off their clothes. Upon hearing of this disgrace, David declared war against the Ammonites (2 Sam. 10:1–4).

2. A man who helped repair the walls of Jerusalem after the Captivity (Neh. 3:13).

3. A son of Zalaph who helped repair the walls of Jerusalem (Neh. 3:30).

HAPHRAIM [haf RAY uhm] (*two pits*) — a frontier town of Issachar (Josh. 19:19; Hapharaim, RSV). It may be modern Khirbet el–Farriyeh, about ten kilometers (six miles) northwest of Megiddo.

HAPPIZZEZ [HAP uh zeez] (*scattering*) — a descendant of Aaron whose family became the 18th of David's 24 courses of priests (1 Chr. 24:15; Aphses, KJV, NEB).

HARA [HAIR uh] (*mountains*) — a place in Assyria to which some of the Israelites were taken into captivity by TIGLATH–PILESER (1 Chr. 5:26).

HARADAH [huh RAY duh] (*fear*) — a place where the Israelites camped in the wilderness (Num. 33:24–25), location unknown.

HARAN [HAIR uhn] (meaning unknown) — the name of three men and one city in the Old Testament:

1. The third son of Terah, Abraham's father, and the younger brother of Abraham. Haran was the father of Lot, Milcah, and Iscah (Gen. 11:26–31).

2. A city of northern Mesopotamia where Abraham and his father Terah lived for a time (Gen. 11:31–32; 12:4–5). The family of Abraham's brother Nahor also lived in this city for a time, as did Jacob and his wife Rachel (Gen. 28:10; 29:4–5). The city was on the Balikh, a tributary of the Euphrates River, 386 kilometers (240 miles) northwest of Nineveh and 450 kilometers (280 miles) northeast of Damascus. Haran lay on one of the main trade routes between Babylonia and the Mediterranean Sea. Like the inhabitants of Ur of the Chaldees, Haran's inhabitants worshiped Sin, the moon–god. Second Kings 19:12 records that the city was captured by the Assyrians. Today Haran is a small Arab village, Harran. Haran is also spelled as Charran (Acts 7:2, 4; KJV).

3. A son of Caleb by Ephah, Caleb's concubine.

Cone-shaped Syrian houses built near the mound of ancient Haran in Mesopotamia—the city where Abraham lived before journeying to Canaan (Gen. 11:31, 32).

Haran was the father of Gazez (1 Chr. 2:46).

4. A Levite from the family of Gershon and a son of Shimei. Haran lived during David's reign (1 Chr. 23:9).

HARARITE [HAIR uh right] (*mountaineer*) — a word used to characterize several of David's mighty men: Agee, Shammah, and Sharar (2 Sam. 23:11, 33). The term is thought to denote a native of the hill country of Judah or Ephraim.

HARBONA [hahr BOE nuh] (*donkey-driver*) — one of the eunuchs, or chamberlains, responsible for the harem of King Ahasuerus (Xerxes) of Persia (Esth. 1:10; 7:9).

HARD SAYING — a phrase in the Gospel of John (John 6:60) which John uses to indicate that Jesus' teaching was difficult to understand or to accept. In the Bible the word for hard, when used in reference to spoken language, has a figurative meaning: it is difficult to understand. Similar expressions in the Old Testament describe the words addressed to Abraham as displeasing (Gen. 21:11), refer to Joseph speaking harshly to his brothers (Gen. 42:7), and denote the words of a legal case as hard or difficult (Deut. 1:17). The phrase as used in the Gospel of John indicates that Jesus' disciples found His teaching about Himself difficult, unpleasant, or unacceptable.

HARDNESS OF HEART — to become stubborn and unyielding in opposition to God's will (1 Sam. 6:6; Job 38:30). The classic case in the Bible of such disobedience was the Pharaoh of Egypt, who refused to release the Hebrew people in spite of repeated displays of God's power (Ex. 4:21; 7:3; 14:4, 17).

HARE (see ANIMALS OF THE BIBLE).

HAREPH [HAIR ef] (*autumn*) — a son of Caleb and the founder of Beth Gader, a town in Judah (1 Chr. 2:51).

HARETH [HAIR eth] — a form of HERETH.

HARHAIAH [hahr HIGH uh] (meaning unknown) — the father of Uzziel (Neh. 3:8).

HARHAS [HAHR hass] — a form of HASRAH.

HARHUR [HAHR hur] (meaning unknown) — an ancestor of a family of NETHINIM (Temple servants) who returned from the Captivity (Ezra 2:51).

HARIM [HAIR em] (*dedicated to God*) — the name of four Old Testament men:

1. A priest in charge of the third division of Temple duties (1 Chr. 24:8).

2. An ancestor of many Israelites who returned from the Captivity (Ezra 2:32). Harim's descendants divorced their pagan wives (Ezra 10:31).

3. The head of a priestly family who sealed the covenant with Nehemiah (Neh. 10:5).

4. Another Israelite who sealed the covenant with Nehemiah (Neh. 10:27).

HARIPH [HAIR if] (*autumn*) — the name of two men in the time of Ezra and Nehemiah:

1. The founder of a family whose descendants returned from the Captivity (Neh. 7:24). He is also called Jorah (Ezra 2:18).

2. A leader who sealed the covenant, probably as a representative of his family (Neh. 10:19).

HARLOT — a prostitute. The term harlot is often used in a symbolic way in the Old Testament to describe the wicked conduct of the nation of Israel in worshiping false gods (Is. 1:21; Jer. 2:20; Ezek. 16).

In the New Testament, harlots were objects of Jesus' mercy (Matt. 21:31–32; Luke 15:30). The

A familiar harvest scene in Palestine is the winnowing, or separation, of grain from the chaff. This threshing floor for such an operation is situated at Samaria.

Photo by Howard Vos

apostle Paul used the term in a warning to the Corinthian church against the prevailing sexual immorality that had made Corinth a byword (1 Cor. 6:15–16). In the Book of Revelation, the term harlot is used symbolically of "Babylon the Great"—an apocalyptic image of great moral corruption (Rev. 17:1, 5, 15–16; 19:2).

When the spies entered the Promised Land and came to Jericho, they hid in the house of Rahab the harlot (Josh. 2:1). She made them promise that when the Lord gave Israel the land, she would be spared (Josh. 6:17–25). The New Testament records: "By faith the harlot Rahab did not perish with those who did not believe, when she had received the spies with peace" (Heb. 11:31). While Rahab was an important person in the life of Israel, her name always carries the label, Rahab the harlot. Placed among the heroes of faith (Heb. 11:1–40), Rahab brings into bold relief the power of God's love and mercy to transform a person's life. She is listed as one of the ancestors of Jesus (Matt. 1:1–16).

Also see PROSTITUTION.

HAR MAGEDON [hahr muh GED uhn] — a form of ARMAGEDDON.

HARMON [HAHR muhn] (meaning unknown) — an unknown place to which the people of Samaria were to be exiled (Amos 4:3).

HARNEPHER [HAHR nuh fur] (Horus is merciful) — a son of Zophah, of the tribe of Asher (1 Chr. 7:36).

HARNESS — the gear with which a domestic animal, such as a horse, is equipped for riding or for pulling a vehicle or farming tool (Ps. 32:9; Jer. 46:4).

HAROD [HAIR uhd] (terror) — a well or spring near the mountains of Gilboa (see Map 3, B–2) by which Gideon and his soldiers camped before they defeated the Midianites (Judg. 7:1; En-harod, NEB). Harod is commonly thought to be modern Ain Jalud on the northwest side of Mount Gilboa, about 1.5 kilometers (one mile) southeast of Jezreel.

HARODITE [HAIR uh dight] — a native or inhabitant of HAROD (Judg. 7:1). Two Harodites are mentioned in the Bible—Shammah and Elika (2 Sam. 23:25)—two of David's mighty men.

HAROEH [huh ROE uh] (the seer) — a son of Shobal, descended from Judah through Hezron (1 Chr. 2:52). Haroeh may be the same person as REAIAH (1 Chr. 4:2).

HARORITE [HAIR roe right] — a word used to describe Shammoth, one of David's mighty men (1 Chr. 11:27).

HAROSHETH HAGOYIM [huh ROE sheth huh GOY ihm] (forest of the Gentiles) — a town of Galilee on the north bank of the Kishon River about 26

kilometers (16 miles) northwest of Megiddo (Judg. 4:2; Harosheth-ha-goiim, RSV). Sisera, the commander of the army of Jabin, king of Canaan, lived in Harosheth Hagoyim.

HARP (see MUSICAL INSTRUMENTS).

HARPOONS — spearlike weapons with barbed heads used in hunting whales and large fish (Job 41:7; barbed irons, KJV). Neither harpoons nor fishing spears, according to Job, were powerful enough to kill LEVIATHAN, the mighty sea monster.

HARROW (see AGRICULTURE; TOOLS OF THE BIBLE).

HARSHA [HAHR shuh] (silent) — an ancestor of a family of NETHINIM (Temple servants), some of whom returned from the Captivity (Ezra 2:52).

HART (see ANIMALS OF THE BIBLE).

HARUM [HAIR uhm] (exalted) — the father of Aharhel, a descendant of Koz of the tribe of Judah (1 Chr. 4:8).

HARUMAPH [huh ROO mahf] (mutilated nose) — the father of Jedaiah (Neh. 3:10).

HARUPHITE [huh ROO fight] — a name applied to Shephatiah, a Benjamite warrior who joined David at Ziklag (1 Chr. 12:5). The reference may be to a descendant of Hareph (1 Chr. 2:51).

HARUZ [HAIR uz] (gold) — a man of Jotbah, a place in Judah (2 Kin. 21:19).

HARVEST — the period at the end of the growing season, when crops were gathered. Harvest was one of the happiest times of the year in Palestine (Ps. 126:5–6; Is. 9:3), marked with celebrations and religious festivals (Ex. 23:16). There were actually two harvests. Barley was gathered from mid–April onwards, and the wheat from mid–May.

The harvesting process began with the cutting of grain with a sickle (Deut. 16:9; Mark 4:29). Then it was gathered into sheaves (Deut. 24:5). Next the grain was taken to the threshing floor, an important local site with a hard surface and often situated on higher ground. Various tools, such as metal-toothed sledges drawn by oxen, were used for threshing (Is. 28:28; 41:15). Then the grain was winnowed, or tossed into the air, with a pitchfork. The wind carried off the chaff, but the heavier kernels and straw fell to the ground (Matt. 3:12).

Finally, the kernels were shaken in a sieve, made of a wooden hoop with leather thongs (Is. 30:28; Amos 9:9). Then the grain was stored.

Harvest became a picture of God's judgment (Jer. 51:33; Joel 3:13), and Jesus compared the Last Judgment with the harvest (Matt. 13:30, 39; Rev. 14:14–20). However, Jesus used the same metaphor for the gathering together of those who believed in Him (Matt. 9:37–38; Luke 10:2), indicating that the final harvest has already begun with His first coming (John 4:35).

HARVEST, FEAST OF (see FEASTS AND FESTIVALS).

HARVESTER (see OCCUPATIONS AND TRADES).

HASADIAH [hass uh DIGH uh] (*the Lord is faithful*) — a son of Zerubbabel and a descendant of Jehoiakim, king of Judah (1 Chr. 3:20).

HASENUAH [hass uh NOO uh] — a form of HASSENUAH.

HASHABIAH [hash uh BIGH uh] (*Jehovah has taken account*) — the name of 14 men in the Old Testament:
1, 2. Two Levites of the family of Merari (1 Chr. 6:45; 9:14).
3. A son of Jeduthun (1 Chr. 25:3, 19).
4. A Levite of the family of Kohath and a descendant of Hebron (1 Chr. 26:30).
5. A son of Kemuel and chief of the tribe of Levi during David's reign (1 Chr. 27:17).
6. A chief of the Levites in the time of King Josiah of Judah (2 Chr. 35:9).
7. A Levite who returned from the Captivity with Ezra (Ezra 8:19).
8. One of the 12 priests appointed by Ezra to take care of the gold, the silver, and the dedicated vessels of the Temple after the Captivity (Ezra 8:24).
9. An Israelite who helped repair the walls of Jerusalem (Neh. 3:17).
10. A Levite who sealed the covenant with Nehemiah (Neh. 10:11).
11. A Levite, a son of Bunni, who lived in Jerusalem in Nehemiah's time (Neh. 11:15).
12. A Levite descended from Asaph (Neh. 11:22).
13. A priest who was head of the house of Hilkiah during the high priest Jehoiakim's time (Neh. 12:21).
14. A Levite after the Captivity (Neh. 12:24).

HASHABNAH [hah SHAHB nah] (*Jehovah has considered*) — an Israelite who sealed the covenant after the Captivity (Neh. 10:25).

HASHABNIAH [hah shahb nee EYE uh] (*Jehovah has considered*) — the name of two men in the Book of Nehemiah:
1. The father of Hattush (Neh. 3:10; Hashabneiah, NAS, NIV, RSV).
2. A Levite who officiated at the feast under Ezra and Nehemiah when the covenant was sealed (Neh. 9:5).

HASHBADANA [hahsh buh DAH nuh] (*thoughtful judge*) — an Israelite who assisted Ezra in reading the Law (Neh. 8:4; Hashbaddanah, NEB, NIV, RSV).

HASHEM [HAY shem] (*shining*) — the father of several warriors who served in the bodyguard unit known as David's mighty men (1 Chr. 11:34).

HASHMONAH [hash MOE nuh] (*fruitfulness*) — a place in the wilderness where the Israelites camped (Num. 33:29–30).

HASHUB [HASH uhb] (*considerate*) — an Israelite who helped repair the wall of Jerusalem (Neh. 3:11; Hasshub, RSV, NIV, NAS, NEB).

HASHUBAH [huh SHOO buh] (*Jehovah has considered*) — a son of Zerubbabel and a descendant of Jehoiakim, king of Judah (1 Chr. 3:20).

HASHUM [HASH uhm] (*broad–nosed*) — the name of three Old Testament men:
1. An Israelite whose descendants returned with Zerubbabel after the Captivity (Ezra 2:19).
2. A priest who helped Ezra read the Law to the returned captives (Neh. 8:4).
3. The head of a family that sealed the covenant with Nehemiah (Neh. 10:18).

HASHUPHA [huh SOO fuh] — a form of HASUPHA.

HASMONEAN [haz moe NEE uhn] — the family name of a dynasty of Jewish rulers who held power in Palestine from 135 to 63 B.C. Simon Maccabeus, the leader and high priest of the Jews, established this family in power. He was followed by John Hyrcanus (135–104 B.C.), Aristobulus (104–103 B.C.), Alexander Janneus (103–76 B.C.), Salome Alexandra (76–67 B.C.) and Aristobulus II (67–63 B.C.).

Soon after the Greek conquest of the ancient Near Eastern world by ALEXANDER the Great, authority over Palestine was given to the Seleucid kings of Syria. Their attempts to force the Jews to adopt Greek ways led to a series of Jewish wars that are recorded in the apocryphal books of Maccabees and in the writings of the Jewish historian Josephus. Under Judas Maccabeus the Jews gained independence from their Syrian rulers. Simon, the brother of Judas Maccabeus, was appointed to the office of HIGH PRIEST. When Simon's son, John Hyrcanus, succeeded his father, it signaled the beginning of the Hasmonean dynasty.

The Hasmonean rulers gained recognition from Rome, but their period of rule was characterized by constant war with their neighbors, political infighting, murder, terrorism, and strong opposition between the Pharisees and the Sadducees. In 63 B.C. the Romans sent the famous general Pompey to end the Hasmonean rule and to establish their authority in Jerusalem.

Also see MACCABEES.

HASRAH [HAHZ rah] (*splendor*) — the grandfather of Shallum (2 Chr. 34:22), also called Harhas (2 Kin. 22:14).

HASSENAAH [hah suh NAY uh] (*thorny*) — an Israelite whose ancestors helped rebuild Jerusalem's wall (Neh. 3:3).

HASSENUAH [hass uh NOO uh] (*hated*) — the father of Hodaviah (1 Chr. 9:7; Hasenuah, KJV, RSV).

HASSHUB [HASH uhb] (*considerate*) — the name of three men in the Old Testament:
1. The father of Shemaiah (1 Chr. 9:14).
2. An Israelite who helped repair the walls of Jerusalem after the Captivity (Neh. 3:23; Hashub, KJV).

3. A head of a family who sealed the covenant after the Captivity (Neh. 10:23).

HASSOPHERETH [HASS soe FEAR eth] — a form of SOPHERETH.

HASUPHA [huh SOO fuh] (*swift*) — an ancestor of a family of NETHINIM (Temple servants), some of whom returned with Zerubbabel from the Captivity (Ezra 2:43). The name is also spelled Hashupha (Neh. 7:46, KJV).

HATACH [HAY tak] — a form of HATHACH.

HATE, HATRED — strong dislike, disregard, or even indifference toward someone or something. As such, hate may be seated in a person's emotions or will. Various degrees and types of hatred are described in the Bible. This makes it difficult to define hatred in simple, absolute terms.

The people of God are to hate what God Himself hates with an absolute hatred—sin (Deut. 12:31; Is. 61:8; Heb. 1:9). But God is also said to hate human beings, as when He declared, "Jacob I have loved but Esau I have hated" (Rom. 9:13). This is a relative hatred. It is not the opposite of love but a diminished love. God loved Jacob so much that He chose him to become the father of the nation Israel; He did not love Esau in the same way.

To hate our relatives for the sake of Christ (Luke 14:26) means to love them less than we love Christ (Matt. 10:37); it does not mean to hate them absolutely. Believers ought to love their enemies (Matt. 5:43–44) but hate their enemies' sins (Eph. 5:3–14; Rev. 2:6).

Wicked people, living under the power of Satan, will hate the Lord Jesus, His followers, and their righteous deeds (John 3:20; 8:44). It is the Christian's duty not to strike back but to do good to his enemies (Matt. 4:43–44; Luke 6:27).

HATHACH [HAY thak] (*good*) — a eunuch in the court of Ahasuerus (Xerxes), king of Persia, appointed to attend to Queen Esther (Esth. 4:5–6; Hatach, KJV).

HATHATH [HAY thath] (*terror*) — a son of Othniel (1 Chr. 4:13).

HATIPHA [huh TIGH fuh] (*seized*) — an ancestor of a family of NETHINIM (Temple servants), some of whom returned with Zerubbabel from the Captivity (Ezra 2:54).

HATITA [huh TIGH tuh] (meaning unknown) — a Temple gatekeeper whose descendants returned from the Captivity (Ezra 2:42).

HATS — KJV word for TURBANS (Dan. 3:21). Also see DRESS OF THE BIBLE.

HATTIL [HAT uhl] (*talkative*) — one of Solomon's servants. Members of Hattil's family returned from the Captivity with Zerubbabel (Neh. 7:59).

HATTIN, HORNS OF [HAT teen] (*depressions*) — a two-peaked hill on the road from Magdala, on the western shore of the Sea of Galilee, to Cana and Nazareth. This hill is the traditional site of Jesus' Sermon on the Mount (Matt. 5:1). One of the great battles of history took place near this hill. On July 4, 1187, at the battle of Hattin, the Crusaders suffered a decisive defeat at the hands of Saladin (1138–1193), a Muslim warrior and the sultan of Egypt and Syria. Saladin's victory at Hattin led to his capture of Jerusalem later in the same year, 1187.

HATTUSH [HAT uhsh] (*contender*) — the name of three Old Testament men:
1. A descendant of David who returned with Ezra from the Captivity (Ezra 8:2).
2. An Israelite who helped rebuild the walls of Jerusalem under Nehemiah (Neh. 3:10).
3. A priest who returned from the Captivity with Zerubbabel and signed the covenant (Neh. 10:4).

HAURAN [HOHR uhn] (*black land of basaltic rock*) — a region in TRANSJORDAN east of the Sea of Galilee, north of the Yarmuk River, and south of Damascus and Mount Hermon. According to Ezekiel's prophetic vision (Ezek. 47:16, 18), Hauran marked the northeastern limits of the land of Israel. Hauran had roughly the same boundaries as the Old Testament BASHAN (Num. 21:33). Noted for its rich and fertile volcanic soil, this region became the bread basket of the region because of its wheat production.

HAVEN — a harbor or port for ships (Gen. 49:13). The word is also used symbolically to describe God as a place of safety and refuge—a haven—for the believer (Ps. 107:30).

HAVENS, FAIR (see FAIR HAVENS).

HAVILAH [HAV uh luh] (*district*) — the name of two men and a land or region:
1. A land of uncertain location, perhaps a district in eastern Arabia (Gen. 2:11). King Saul's army attacked the Amalekites "from Havilah all the way to Shur, which is east of Egypt" (1 Sam. 15:7), suggesting a location somewhere in the northeastern Sinai Peninsula.
2. A son of Cush and a grandson of Ham (Gen. 10:7).
3. A son of Joktan and a grandson of Eber (Gen. 10:29).

HAVOTH JAIR [HAY vahth JAY uhr] — a group of villages, east of the Jordan River in Gilead and Bashan, captured by JAIR, son of Manasseh (Deut. 3:14; Havvoth-jair, NEB, NIV, RSV). According to Deuteronomy 3:4, there were 60 of these cities; but according to Judges 10:4, there were only 30.

HAWK (see ANIMALS OF THE BIBLE).

HAY (see PLANTS OF THE BIBLE).

HAZAEL [HAZ a el] (*God has seen*) — a Syrian official whom the prophet Elijah anointed king over Syria at God's command (1 Kin. 19:15). Sometime between 845 and 843 B.C., Ben-Hadad, king of Syria, sent Hazael to the prophet Elisha to ask whether the king would recover from an illness. Elisha answered that Hazael himself was destined to become king. The next day Hazael assassinated Ben–Hadad and took the throne (2 Kin. 8:7–15). Hazael immediately attacked Ramoth Gilead, seriously wounding King Joram of Israel (2 Kin. 8:28–29).

At the end of Jehu's reign over Israel, Hazael attacked the Israelites east of the Jordan River (2 Kin. 10:32). During the reign of Jehu's successor, Jehoahaz, Hazael oppressed Israel because "the anger of the Lord was aroused against Israel" (2 Kin. 13:3). A gift of the dedicated treasures of the Temple from King Jehoash of Judah prevented Hazael from attacking Jerusalem (2 Kin. 12:17–18).

As late as the first century A.D., Hazael and Ben–Hadad were worshiped in Damascus because of the way in which they had adorned their capital city. When Hazael died, his son Ben–Hadad II succeeded him.

HAZAIAH [huh ZIGH uh] (*Jehovah sees*) — a man of Judah, of the family of Shelah (Neh. 11:5).

HAZAR [HAY zar] — a term, meaning "villages which have no wall" (Lev. 25:31), used often as a prefix for geographical names in the Bible.

HAZAR ADDAR [HAY zur AY dahr] (*noble village*) — a fortress town on the southwestern border of Judah between Kadesh Barnea and Karkaa (Num. 34:4; Josh. 15:3; Adar, KJV, NKJV, RSV; Addar, NAS, NEB, NIV).

HAZAR ENAN [HAY zur EE nuhn] (*village of fountains*) — a place, perhaps an oasis, midway between Damascus and the land of Hamath (Num. 34:9–10; Ezek. 47:17; Hazar-enon, RSV).

HAZAR GADDAH [HAY zur GAH dah] (*village of Gad*) — a village in southern Judah, between Moladah and Heshmon (Josh. 15:27).

HAZAR HATTICON [HAY zar HAT tih kon] (*middle village*) — an unknown village named by the prophet Ezekiel as the northeast corner of the ideal boundary of Israel (Ezek. 47:16; Hazer-hatticon, NASB, RSV, NIV; Hazar-enan, NEB).

HAZARMAVETH [HAY zur MAY veth] (meaning unknown) — the third son of Joktan and a descendant of Shem (Gen. 10:26). The descendants of Hazarmaveth settled in the southern Arabian Peninsula.

HAZAR SHUAL [HAY zur SHOO uhl] (*village of the jackal*) — a town in southern Judah (Josh. 19:3; 1 Chr. 4:28).

HAZAR SUSAH [HAY zur SOO suh] (*village of horses*) — a village in southern Judah allotted to the tribe of Simeon (Josh. 19:5; 1 Chr. 4:31; Hazar Susim, NAS, NEB, NIV, KJV, NKJV, RSV).

HAZAR SUSIM [HAY zur SOO zim] — a form of HAZAR SUSAH.

HAZAZON TAMAR [HAZ uh zahn TAY mur] (*the palm tree*) — a city near the Dead Sea identified as EN GEDI (Gen. 14:7; Hazezon Tamar, NIV, KJV, NKJV).

HAZEL (see PLANTS OF THE BIBLE).

HAZELELPONI [haz ih lehl POE nigh] (*give shade*) — the daughter of Etam and the sister of Jezreel, Ishma, and Idbash in the genealogy of Judah (1 Chr. 4:3; Hazzelelponi, NAS, NIV, RSV).

HAZER–HATTICON [HAY zer HAT tih kon] — A form of HAZAR HATTICON.

HAZERIM [HAH zuh rim] — villages of the Avim in southwest Palestine, near Gaza (Deut. 2:23, KJV).

HAZEROTH [HAH zuh rahth] (*villages*) — a place in the WILDERNESS OF PARAN where the Israelites camped after leaving Egypt (Num. 11:35). Here Miriam and Aaron criticized Moses' marriage to an Ethiopian woman and rebelled against him (Num. 12:1–2). Hazeroth is possibly modern 'Ain Hadra, about 48 kilometers (30 miles) northeast of Mount Sinai.

HAZEZON TAMAR [hah ZEE zuhn TAY mur] — a form of HAZAZON TAMAR.

HAZIEL [HAY zee uhl] (*God sees*) — a Gershonite Levite of the family of Shimei in David's time (1 Chr. 23:9).

HAZO [HAY zoe] (*visionary*) — a son of Nahor and Milcah and a nephew of Abraham (Gen. 22:22).

HAZOR [HAH zohr] (*an enclosure*) — the name of three cities and one district in the Bible:

1. An ancient Canaanite fortress city in northern Palestine, situated about 16 kilometers (10 miles) northwest of the Sea of Galilee (see Map 3, C–1). When Joshua and the Israelites invaded Palestine, Hazor was one of the most important fortresses in the land (Josh. 11:10). This was due to its enormous size, its large population, and its strategic location on the main road between Egypt and Mesopotamia.

When the Israelites approached Palestine, Jabin, the king of Hazor, and several other kings formed an alliance against them. Through God's power the Israelites defeated these armies, killed all the people of Hazor, and burned the city (Josh. 11:1–14). The city regained its strength during the time of the JUDGES. Because of Israel's sinfulness, God allowed the armies of Hazor to oppress the Israelites for 20 years (Judg. 4:1–3). Sisera, the captain of the armies of Hazor, and his 900 chariots were miraculously defeated by God through the efforts of Deborah and Barak (Judg. 4:4–24). Later Solomon chose Hazor as one of his military outposts (1 Kin. 9:15). The rebuilt city continued to play an important part in the northern defenses of Israel until it was destroyed by the Assyrian king, Tiglath–Pileser (2 Kin. 15:29), about ten years before the collapse of the Northern Kingdom in 721 B.C.

Photo by Howard Vos

The mound of Hazor (center), a Canaanite city destroyed by Joshua during his conquest of the Promised Land (Josh. 11:1-13).

2. A city in the southern Judean desert (Josh. 15:23).

3. Hazor–Hadattah ("New Hazor") and Kerioth–Hazor ("City of Hazor"), which may be identical sites in southern Judea (Josh. 15:25).

4. A nomadic district or kingdom of villages in the Arabian desert (Jer. 49:28).

HAZOR HADATTAH [HAH zohr hah DAH tuh] — a form of HAZOR.

HAZZELELPONI [haz ih lehl POE nigh] — a form of HAZELELPONI.

HE [hay] — the fifth letter of the Hebrew alphabet, used as a heading over Psalm 119:33-40. In the original Hebrew language, each line of these eight verses began with the letter he. Also see ACROSTIC.

HEAD — the upper part of the human body containing the face and brain. In the Bible the head is more the center of sense experience (sight, hearing, etc.) than the center of thinking. To wound an enemy's head was to show his utter defeat, and to cut off someone's head was the ultimate disgrace (Ps. 68:21; Mark 6:14–28). Both priests and kings of Israel were initiated into office by having their heads anointed with oil (Lev. 8:12; 1 Sam. 10:1). In the New Testament those who were sick were also anointed (Mark 6:13; James 5:14). This custom apparently symbolized joy and well-being (Ps. 23:5; 45:7).

The position of a person's head symbolized various emotions. Wagging the head meant derision; bowing the head showed grief; covering the head with one's hand suggested shame (2 Sam. 13:19; Is. 58:5; Mark 15:29). To lift up a person's head was to elevate him to higher rank (Gen. 40:20; Jer. 52:31). For blood to be on the head of someone meant for that person to bear responsibility and guilt for some specified action (Josh. 2:19; Acts 18:6). To heap coals of fire on someone's head meant to make

an enemy ashamed by treating him well (Rom. 12:20).

The word head is often used of inanimate objects such as rivers to designate a beginning point or top part of the object (Gen. 2:10; Ps. 24:9). In this sense, several important messianic prophecies refer to Christ as the "head corner stone" (Ps. 118:22; Luke 20:17; 1 Pet. 2:7).

HEADBANDS — an article of feminine attire which the prophet Isaiah predicted would be taken away from the "daughters of Zion [Jerusalem]" (Is. 3:20). Some scholars believe this reference is to gold or silver head ornaments.

HEADDRESSES — ornamental head–coverings (Is. 3:20; bonnets, KJV; head–bands, NEB). The reference is probably to strips of material wound around the head in turban fashion. According to the prophet Isaiah, headdresses were one of the articles of feminine attire, or "finery," which would be taken away from the "daughters of Zion [Jerusalem]" (Is. 3:20) when the judgment of the Lord fell upon the city.

HEALING — the process of applying preventive and remedial practices to maintain good health. In the ancient world health was a highly prized possession. The Hebrews tended to think of health primarily in terms of physical strength and well-being. The land of Palestine apparently provided a relatively healthy environment, as compared to Egypt and Mesopotamia—probably because of its location as well as the various laws and practices prescribed by the Law of Moses.

Regulation of Diet. Most of the laws about food consumption are included in the first five books of the Old Testament. The restrictions involving meats were based on two simple tests. Only animals with separated hooves and that chewed the cud were suitable for eating (Lev. 11:3). This meant that pigs and rabbits were unsuitable for eating.

Excavations at the site of an ancient church in Jerusalem uncovered these twin pools believed to be the biblical Pool of Bethesda (John 5:1-15).

Modern medicine has demonstrated that these animals are especially liable to infections with parasites; they are safe only if well-cooked. Thus, the prohibition of these animals for food among the Hebrew people was beneficial to their health.

Rituals. Several rituals were observed among the Hebrew people to maintain sanitary conditions and to promote good health. One of these involved bodily discharge. Although not all bodily discharges are infectious, many are. Since the Hebrew people lacked ways to determine which bodily discharges were infectious, all were treated as potentially infectious. For example, sputum is mentioned as a possible cause of infection (Lev. 15:8)—a fact that was not positively validated until the 19th century.

Another good example of this principle is the instruction given in Deuteronomy 23:12 about the disposal of human excrement. A place was set off outside the camp for this purpose. The Hebrew people were required to carry a spade, dig a hole for the excrement, and cover it (Deut. 23:12–13).

Hygiene. The Law of Moses required that the body and clothes be washed after contact with a diseased or dead person. The regulations about contact with dead bodies specified a period of uncleanness lasting seven days. During this time, the person involved was isolated from other people and required to perform certain acts, including bathing his body and washing his clothes (Num. 19:1–22).

Sexual Perversion. The strict laws about sexual morality among the Hebrew people also promoted the prevention of venereal disease. CIRCUMCISION of males was not only a religious rite, but also a hygienic measure that reduced infection and cancer.

Medicine and Physicians. The first medicines probably were introduced to the Hebrews by the Egyptians while they were in bondage. In biblical times medicines were made from minerals, animal substances, herbs, wines, fruits, and other parts of plants. The Bible mentions numerous examples of these primitive medicines—notably the "balm of Gilead," which was probably an aromatic substance taken from an evergreen tree.

Wine mixed with myrrh was used to relieve pain by dulling the senses. This remedy was offered to Jesus when He was on the cross, but He refused to drink it (Mark 15:23). Olive oil and herbs often were used to anoint the sick. The early Christians continued this practice, anointing the sick as they prayed for them (James 5:14).

The Bible refers to the work of physicians (Gen. 50:2; 2 Chr. 16:12; Jer. 8:22). In the New Testament, Luke is mentioned as the "beloved physician" (Col. 4:14).

Medical treatment in the biblical world often included the use of MAGIC, SORCERY, AND DIVINATION. Such practices were prohibited by the Mosaic law; they were seen as inconsistent with the nature of the all-powerful God.

The Ministry of Jesus. The people of Old Testament times tended to think of sickness as punishment for sin. This concept is explored fully in the Book of Job. But Jesus was firmly convinced that His Father's purpose for humankind was health, wholeness, and salvation. He did not teach that disease was a punishment sent by God. And while He was always concerned to heal the sick in body, He also paid close attention to the mind and the spirit of those who suffered.

HEALING, GIFTS OF (see SPIRITUAL GIFTS).

HEART — the inner self that thinks, feels, and decides. In the Bible the word heart has a much broader meaning than it does to the modern mind. The heart is that which is central to man. Nearly all the references to the heart in the Bible refer to some aspect of human personality.

In the Bible all emotions are experienced by the heart: love and hate (Ps. 105:25; 1 Pet. 1:22); joy and sorrow (Eccl. 2:10; John 16:6); peace and bitterness (Ezek. 27:31; Col. 3:15); courage and fear (Gen. 42:28; Amos 2:16).

The thinking processes of man are said to be carried out by the heart. This intellectual activity corresponds to what would be called mind in English. Thus, the heart may think (Esth. 6:6), understand (Job 38:36), imagine (Jer. 9:14), remember (Deut. 4:9), be wise (Prov. 2:10), and speak to itself (Deut. 7:17). Decision-making is also carried out by the heart. Purpose (Acts 11:23), intention (Heb. 4:12), and will (Eph. 6:6) are all activities of the heart.

Finally, heart often means someone's true character or personality. Purity or evil (Jer. 3:17; Matt. 5:8); sincerity or hardness (Ex. 4:21; Col. 3:22); and maturity or rebelliousness (Ps. 101:2; Jer. 5:23)—all these describe the heart or true character of individuals. God knows the heart of each person (1 Sam. 16:7). Since a person speaks and acts from his heart, he is to guard it well (Prov. 4:23; Matt. 15:18–19). The most important duty of man is to love God with the whole heart (Matt. 22:37). With the heart man believes in Christ and so experiences both love from God and the presence of Christ in his heart (Rom. 5:5; 10:9–10; Eph. 3:17).

HEARTH — a dug-out depression in a house or tent where fires were built for heating or cooking. The smoke from the fire was let out through a hole in the wall, usually translated as CHIMNEY (Hos. 13:3). Also see HOUSE.

HEATH (see PLANTS OF THE BIBLE).

HEATHEN — one of several words used for the non-Jewish peoples of the world. The distinction between the Israelites and the other nations was important because God's relationship with Israel was unique. He chose Israel, rescued the people from Egypt, entered into a COVENANT with the Hebrews, and gave the nation His laws. God actually planned to bring light and salvation to all nations through Israel (Gen. 12:3; Is. 2:1–3), but this required that the Hebrews keep separate from the sinful ways of the surrounding nations (Lev. 18:24).

Following Israel's captivity in Babylon, the Jews were more rigid about their separation from the heathen. While the heathen often persecuted the Jews, the Jews generally had contempt for the heathen. These barriers between Jews and non-Jews were broken down in the early church as the gospel of Jesus Christ was taken to all the nations (Matt. 28:19), especially by Paul, the apostle to the Gentiles (Gal. 1:16; Eph. 2:11–22).

Also see GENTILES; NATIONS.

HEAVE OFFERING (see SACRIFICIAL OFFERINGS).

HEAVEN — a word that expresses several distinct concepts in the Bible:

1. As used in a physical sense, heaven is the expanse over the earth (Gen. 1:8). The tower of Babel reached upward to heaven (Gen. 11:4). God is the possessor of heaven (Gen. 14:19). Heaven is the location of the stars (Gen. 1:14; 26:4) as well as the source of dew (Gen. 27:28).

2. Heaven is also the dwelling place of God (Gen. 28:17; Rev. 12:7–8). It is the source of the new Jerusalem (Rev. 21:2, 10). Because of the work of Christ on the Cross, heaven is, in part, present with believers on earth as they obey God's commands (John 14:2, 23).

3. The word heaven is also used as a substitute for the name of God (Luke 15:18, 21; John 3:27). The kingdom of God and the kingdom of heaven are often spoken of interchangeably (Matt. 4:17; Mark 1:15).

At the end of time a new heaven will be created

to surround the new earth. This new heaven will be the place of God's perfect presence (Is. 65:17; 66:22; Rev. 21:1). Then there will be a literal fulfillment of heaven on earth.

HEAVENLY CITY, THE — the city prepared and built by God for those who are faithful to Him (Heb. 11:10, 16). Known as the heavenly Jerusalem (Heb. 12:22), this is the city that is to come (Heb. 13:14). These references in Hebrews find their fulfillment in Revelation 21—22. The New Jerusalem is illuminated by the glory of God. It serves as the dwelling place of God among His redeemed forever.

HEAVENS, NEW — a term which, when used with *new earth*, refers to the perfected state of the created universe and the final dwelling place of the righteous. The phrase is found in Isaiah 66:22, 2 Peter 3:13, and in a slightly modified form in Revelation 21:1.

Rooted deep in Jewish thought was the dream of a new heaven and a new earth, a re-creation of the universe that would occur following the Day of the Lord (Is. 13:10–13; Joel 2:1–2, 30–31). The concept of a re-created universe is closely related to the biblical account of the Creation and the Fall (Gen. 1:1) and the sin of Adam and Eve in the Garden of Eden (Genesis 3). Because of their sin, "the creation was subjected to futility.... [and] the bondage of corruption" (Rom. 8:19, 21). The need for a new heaven and a new earth arises from man's sin and God's judgment, not from some deficiency or evil in the universe (Gen. 3:17).

The apostle Paul referred to the Old Testament doctrine of the Day of the Lord and applied it to the events that will occur at the Second Coming of Christ (2 Pet. 3:10, 13). When Christ returns, this present evil age will give way to the age to come. The universe will be purified and cleansed by the power of God. This will be reminiscent of the purging of the earth in the days of Noah, but on a universal scale.

HEBER [HEE buhr] (*associate*) — the name of six men in the Bible:

1. A son of Beriah, of the tribe of Asher (Gen. 46:17).

2. The husband of Jael (Judg. 4:11–21).

3. A man of the tribe of Judah (1 Chr. 4:18).

4. The head of a family of Gadites (1 Chr. 5:13).

5. A Benjamite and a son of Elpaal (1 Chr. 8:17).

6. A Benjamite and a son of Shashak (1 Chr. 8:22; Eber, NAS, NIV, NKJV, RSV).

HEBERITES [HEE burr ites] — the descendants of HEBER, of the tribe of Asher (Num. 26:45; Gen. 46:17).

HEBREW (see LANGUAGES OF THE BIBLE).

HEBREW PEOPLE— an ethnic term designating the lineage of the Jewish people, the nation of Israel.

Abraham, or Abram, was the first person in the Bible to be called a Hebrew (Gen. 14:13). Thereaf-

Peasants appear before an Egyptian nobleman, in this painting from a royal tomb. In their early history, the Hebrew people were enslaved by the Egyptians.

ter, his descendants through Isaac and Jacob were known as Hebrews (Gen. 40:15; 43:32). The term is used five times in the story of Joseph (Gen. 39:14—43:32), including a reference to Joseph by Potiphar's wife as "the Hebrew servant" (Gen. 39:17). Joseph told Potiphar's chief butler, "For indeed I was stolen away from the land of the Hebrews" (Gen. 40:15).

The origin of the term Hebrew is a mystery to scholars. Later use of the words Israelite and Jew add to the confusion. Some believe the word came from a prominent man of the ancient Middle East known as Eber. Eber was a descendant of Noah through Shem and an ancestor of Abraham. Eber, literally meaning "on the other side of," may allude to Abraham's departure from Ur, a region east of the Euphrates River.

This possibility harmonizes with the statement made by God to the Hebrew people in Joshua's time: "Then I took your father Abraham from the other side of the River, led him throughout all the land of Canaan, and multiplied his descendants and gave him Isaac. To Isaac I gave Jacob and Esau" (Josh. 24:3-4). Of Eber's descendants, Abraham, Nahor, and Lot stand out. The genealogical list in Genesis 10 and other passages indicate that Abraham was the ancestor of the Hebrews; Nahor was the ancestor of the Arameans; and Lot was the ancestor of the Moabites and the Ammonites (Gen. 10:21, 24, 25; 11:14-27).

Still other scholars believe the Hebrew people sprang from a people known as the Habiru. These people are mentioned in clay tablets dating to the 18th and 19th centuries B.C. They are also featured in the Nuzian–Hittite and Amarna documents of the 14th and 15th centuries B.C. Some effort has even been made to identify Hebrew with *Hapiru*, a term which indicates that the Hebrews were donkey drivers.

There is considerable evidence in the Old Testament that the Hebrews regarded themselves as a composite race (Deut. 26:5). In their wandering tribal days and during their early years in Canaan, the Hebrews experienced a mixture of bloods through marriage with surrounding peoples. When Abraham sought a suitable wife for Isaac, he sent to Padan Aram, near Haran, for Rebekah, daughter of the Syrian Bethuel (Gen. 24:10; 25:20). Jacob found Rachel in the same location (Genesis 28–29).

Strains of Egyptian blood also appeared in the family of Joseph through Asenath's two sons, Ephraim and Manasseh (Gen. 41:50-52). Moses had a Midianite wife, Zipporah (Ex. 18:1-7), and an unnamed Ethiopian (Cushite) wife (Num. 12:1).

Although several unanswered questions about the origin of the Hebrews remain, no culture has equaled their contribution to mankind. In a pagan world with many gods, the Hebrews worshiped one supreme, holy God who demanded righteousness in His people. From the Hebrews also sprang Jesus Christ, our Great High Priest, who gave His life to set us free from the curse of sin.

HEBREWS, EPISTLE TO THE — the 19th book in the New Testament. Hebrews is a letter written by an unknown Christian to show how Jesus Christ had replaced Judaism as God's perfect revelation of Himself. Hebrews begins with a marvelous tribute to the person of Christ (1:1–3), and throughout the epistle the author weaves warning with doctrine to encourage his readers to hold fast to Jesus as the great High Priest of God. The author makes extensive use of Old Testament quotations and images to show that Jesus is the supreme revelation of God and the all–sufficient Mediator between God and man. Because of its literary style and the careful way it develops its argument, Hebrews reads more as an essay than a personal letter.

Structure of the Epistle. The letter begins by showing that Jesus is the Son of God and, therefore, is superior to angels (1:1—2:18) and to Moses (3:1–6). This section contains a warning not to lose the blessings, or "rest," of God because of unbelief, as the Israelites did under Moses (3:7—4:13).

The second section of the letter (4:14—10:18) attempts to show that Christ is the perfect High Priest because of His unmatched compassion for people and complete obedience to God (4:14—5:10). Following a second warning against renouncing the faith (5:11—6:20), the author then describes Jesus as a priest according to the order of Melchizedek (7:1–28). The emphasis on Melchizedek, who is mentioned only twice in the Old Testament (Gen. 14:18–20; Ps. 110:4), may seem far fetched to modern readers. However, there is a good reason for comparing Christ to Melchizedek; it is to show that Melchizedek, unlike Aaron, was unique. He had no predecessors and no successors. He was, therefore, a priest forever, like the Son of God (7:1–3). As a consequence of His being like Melchizedek, Jesus inaugurated a new and better covenant (8:1–13) because His sacrifice of Himself replaces the sacrifice of "bulls and goats" (9:1–10:18).

The final section of the epistle appeals to the readers not to give up the benefits of Christ's work as High Priest (10:19—13:17). In an attempt to offset spiritual erosion (10:19–39), the author recalls the heroes of faith (11:1–40). Let their example, he says, encourage the readers to "run with endurance the race that is set before us" (12:1). The letter closes with various applications of faith to practical living (13:1–19), a benediction (13:20–21), and greetings (13:22–25).

Authorship and Date. Other than 1 John, the Epistle to the Hebrews is the only letter in the New Testament with no greeting or identification of its author. Although the King James Version entitles the book "The Epistle of Paul the Apostle to the Hebrews," this title stems from later manuscripts which came to include it. It is highly doubtful, however, that Paul wrote Hebrews. The language, vocabulary, and style of Hebrews differ from Paul's

genuine letters. Such typically Pauline expressions as "Christ Jesus," "in Christ," or "the resurrection" are all but absent in Hebrews. When Hebrews and Paul treat the same subjects, they often approach them differently. For example, in Hebrews the "law" means the ritual law, whereas for Paul it means the moral law; "faith" in Hebrews is belief in the trustworthiness of God, whereas for Paul it is a personal commitment to a living Lord. The author of Hebrews sounds more like a Platonic philosopher than Paul when he speaks of the old covenant (8:5) and the law (10:1) as "shadows" of their originals.

There has been no shortage of suggestions concerning who the author may have been. The list includes Luke, Priscilla, Aquila, Clement of Rome, Silvanus, and Philip. Perhaps the two most likely candidates are Apollos and Barnabas. Both have characteristics which commend them, Apollos because he was an eloquent Alexandrian Jew who knew the Scriptures well (Acts 18:24), and Barnabas because he was a Levite (Acts 4:36). As with the others, however, this suggestion is only a possibility. The writer of the epistle remains anonymous.

One can only make an educated guess about the date and place of composition. Since the author's purpose was to show that Christianity had replaced Judaism, to have been able to point to the destruction of the Temple (which occurred in A.D. 70) as an indication that God had no further use for it would have been a decisive argument. Since the author does not make use of this information, it is reasonable to assume the destruction of the Temple had not happened yet, thus dating the letter sometime before A.D. 70. The only clue about where Hebrews was written is found in the closing remark, "Those from Italy greet you" (13:24). This may indicate that the author was writing from Italy, presumably Rome.

Historical Setting. The repeated use of Old Testament quotations and images in Hebrews suggests that the people who received this book had a Jewish background. The repeated warnings against spiritual unbelief reveal that the readers of this epistle were on the verge of renouncing the Christian faith and returning to their former Jewish ways (2:1–4; 3:7—4:14; 5:12—6:20; 10:19–39; 12:12–29). Negligence in good deeds and sloppy attendance at worship services (10:23–25) were evidence of a cooling in their faith. In an effort to rekindle the readers' flame of commitment to Christ, the author urges his readers not to retreat from persecution (10:32–39), but to hasten to the front lines. He calls for a new exodus (3:7–19); he holds before them examples of a pilgrim faith (chap. 11); and he tells them not to "draw back" (10:39), but to "go forth to Him, outside the camp, bearing His reproach" (13:13).

Theological Contribution. In a spirit similar to Stephen's defense before the Jewish Sanhedrin (Acts 7), Hebrews sets out to show that Christianity is superior to Judaism because of the person of Jesus Christ, who is the Son of God, the Great High

Priest, and the Author of salvation. Christ stands as the peak of revelation, superior to angels (1:1—2:9) and to Moses (3:1-6). He is the Son of God, the reflection of God's own glory and, indeed, the very character and essence of God (1:3). Whatever revelations appeared before Jesus were but shadows or outlines of what was to appear in Him.

Christ is also the Great High Priest (4:14). Whereas earthly priests inherited their office, Christ was appointed by the direct call of God (5:5-6). Whereas earthly priests followed in the lineage of Aaron, Christ, who has no successors, is a priest forever, according to the order of Melchizedek (7:17). Whereas earthly priests ministered within temples made with human hands, Christ ministers within the true sanctuary—the eternal house of God (8:2; 9:24). Whereas earthly priests offered animal sacrifices for their sins as well as for those of the people, Christ offered the one perfect sacrifice which never need be offered again—His sinless self (5:3; 10:4-14).

As the unique Son of God who made the supreme sacrifice of Himself to God, Jesus is described by the author of the book of Hebrews as the "author of their salvation" (2:10), the "finisher of our faith" (12:2), and the "great Shepherd of the sheep" (13:20). Christ saves His people *from* sin and death, and He saves them *for* fellowship with God. In Hebrews salvation is called the "rest" of God (4:1), "eternal inheritance" (9:15), the "Most Holy Place" (9:12). These three emphases—Jesus as Son, High Priest, and Savior—are drawn together in one key passage:

Though He was a *Son*, yet He learned obedience by the things which He suffered. And having been perfected, He became the *author of eternal salvation* to all who obey Him, called by God as *High Priest* "according to the order of Melchizedek" (5:8-10).

In light of Christ's preeminence, the author urges his readers to hold fast to the true confession and endure whatever suffering or reproach is necessary on its behalf (4:14; 6:18; 13:13).

Special Considerations. Two passages in Hebrews often trouble Christians. In 6:4-6 and 10:26 the author warns that if a person willingly turns from fellowship with Christ, he can no longer be forgiven. The intent of these verses is to cause Christians to remember the great cost of God's grace and to take

---

HEBREWS: A Teaching Outline

their profession of faith seriously. The intent of these verses is not to cause believers to doubt their salvation. There is no example in the Bible where anyone who desired the forgiveness of Christ was denied it.

The backbone of this epistle is the finality of Christ for salvation. This wonderful truth is no less urgent for us today than it was for the original readers of Hebrews. The rise of cults, with their deceptive claims of security, is but one example of the many things that appeal for our ultimate loyalty. Hebrews reminds us that "Jesus Christ is the same yesterday, today, and forever" (13:8). Because of His perfect sacrifice of Himself, He is still the only Mediator between us and God. Only Jesus is the true Author of our salvation.

HEBRON [HEE bruhn] (*alliance*) — the name of two cities and two men in the Bible:

1. A city situated 31 kilometers (19 miles) southwest of Jerusalem on the road to Beersheba (see Map 2, C-1). Although it lies in a slight valley, the city is 927 meters (3,040 feet) above sea level, which makes it the highest town in Palestine. Originally Hebron was called Kirjath Arba (Gen. 23:2). Numbers 13:22 speaks of Hebron being built seven years before Zoan (Tanis) in Egypt. This probably refers to the rebuilding of the city by the Hyksos rulers of Egypt. The 12 Hebrew spies viewed Hebron on their mission to explore the Promised Land.

The area surrounding Hebron is rich in biblical history. Abram spent much of his time in Mamre in the area of Hebron (Gen. 13:18). He was living in Mamre when the confederacy of kings overthrew the CITIES OF THE PLAIN and captured Lot (Gen. 14:1–13). Here, too, Abram's name was changed to Abraham (Gen. 17:5). At Hebron the angels revealed to Abraham that he would have a son who would be called Isaac (Gen. 18:1–15). Later, Sarah died at Hebron (Gen. 23:2); Abraham bought the cave of MACHPELAH as her burial place (Gen. 23:9).

During the period of the conquest of the land of Canaan, Joshua killed the king of Hebron (Josh. 10:3–27). Later, Caleb drove out the Anakim and claimed Hebron for his inheritance (Josh. 14:12–15). Hebron was also designated as one of the CITIES OF REFUGE (Josh. 20:7). David ruled from

---

Part Three: The Superiority of the Christian's Walk of Faith (10:19—13:25)

Photo by Howard Vos

Modern Hebron, successor to the ancient city of the same name where Abraham bought a burial cave for Sarah and his family (Genesis 23).

Hebron the first seven years of his reign (2 Sam. 2:11), after which he established Jerusalem as his capital.

When Absalom rebelled against his father David, he made Hebron his headquarters (2 Sam. 15:7–12). King Rehoboam fortified the city to protect his southern border (2 Chr. 11:10–12). The discovery of a jar handle stamped with the royal seal dating from the eighth or seventh century B.C. testifies that Hebron was a key storage city for rations of Uzziah's army (2 Chr. 26:10).

2. The third son of Kohath, the son of Levi (Ex. 6:18). Hebron was an uncle of Moses, Aaron, and Miriam. His descendants were called Hebronites (Num. 3:27).

3. A descendant of Caleb (1 Chr. 2:42–43).

4. A town in Asher (Josh. 19:28, KJV; Ebron, RSV, NKJV). This may be the same town as Abdon (Josh. 21:30).

HEBRONITES [HEE bruhn ites] — the descendants of HEBRON, the third son of Kohath (Num. 3:27; 1 Chr. 26:23, 30–31).

HEDGE — a thorn hedge (Is. 5:5), a stone wall (Ps. 80:12), or a fence or partition of any kind (Mark 12:1). Hedges helped protect vineyards from thieves and predators. They consisted of loose stones or thorny branches or bushes.

HEDGEHOG (see ANIMALS OF THE BIBLE).

HEEL — the back of the human foot (Gen. 49:17; Jer. 13:22). The psalmist spoke of a friend who had "lifted up his heel against me" (Ps. 41:9)—an apparent reference to treachery and denial. Jesus quoted this verse when Judas betrayed Him on the eve of His crucifixion (John 13:18).

HEGAI [HEG igh] (meaning unknown) — a eunuch under Ahasuerus (Xerxes), king of Persia, who had responsibility for the royal harem (Esth. 2:3; Hege, KJV).

HEGE [HEE gee] — a form of HEGAI.

HEIFER (see ANIMALS OF THE BIBLE).

HEIR (see INHERITANCE).

HELAH [HEE luh] (*necklace*) — a wife of Ashhur and the mother of Zereth, Zohar, and Ethan (1 Chr. 4:5, 7).

HELAM [HEE luhm] (*fortress*) — a place east of the Jordan River near the border of GILEAD where David's army defeated the Syrians (2 Sam. 10:16–17).

HELBAH [HEL buh] (*fertile*) — a town of the tribe of Asher whose Canaanite inhabitants could not be driven out by the Israelites (Judg. 1:31).

HELBON [HEL bahn] (*fruitful*) — a village of Syria known for its high–quality wines (Ezek. 27:18), probably the same place as Halbun (or

Khalbun), about 29 kilometers (18 miles) north of Damascus.

HELDAI [HEL digh] (*worldly*) — the name of two men in the Old Testament:

1. A captain of the Temple service and one of David's mighty men (1 Chr. 27:15). Heldai is also called Heled (1 Chr. 11:30, NAS, NIV, KJV, NKJV, RSV) and Heleb (2 Sam. 23:29, NAS, KJV, RSV).

2. An Israelite who brought gold and silver from Babylon to help the exiles who returned to Jerusalem with Zerubbabel (Zech. 6:10). Heldai is also called Helem (Zech. 6:14, NAS, KJV).

HELEB [HEE leb] — a form of HELDAI No. 1.

HELECH [HEE lek] — NIV, RSV word for the mercenaries who defended the walls of Tyre (Ezek. 27:11).

HELED [HEE led] — a form of HELDAI.

HELEK [HEE lek] (*portion*) — a son of Gilead and founder of the HELEKITES (Num. 26:30).

HELEKITES [HEE luh kights] — descendants of HELEK, a son of Gilead of the tribe of Manasseh (Num. 26:30).

HELEM [HEE lem] (*strength*) — the name of two Old Testament men:

1. A descendant of Asher (1 Chr. 7:35). Helem may be the same person as Hotham (1 Chr. 7:32).

2. A man mentioned by the prophet Zechariah (Zech. 6:14). Helem may be the same person as Heldai (Zech. 6:10).

HELEPH [HEE lef] (*meaning unknown*) — a town on the southern border of Naphtali (Josh. 19:33).

HELEZ [HEE lez] (*God has saved*) — the name of two Old Testament men:

1. One of David's mighty men (2 Sam. 23:26). He was a PELONITE or a PALTITE.

2. A son of Azariah (1 Chr. 2:39).

HELI [HEE ligh] (*God is high*) — the father of Joseph in Luke's genealogy of Jesus (Luke 3:23). Heli is the Greek form of Eli.

HELIOPOLIS [he lih OP oh lis] — Greek name for the Egyptian city of ON.

HELKAI [HEL kigh] (*Jehovah is my portion*) — the head of a priestly house in the days of Joiakim the high priest (Neh. 12:15).

HELKATH [HEL kath] (*portion*) — a town of Asher assigned to the Levites of the family of Gershon (Josh. 19:25). Helkath is also called Hukok (1 Chr. 6:75).

HELKATH–HAZZURIM [HEL kath hah ZUR im] — a Hebrew phrase which means "Field of Sharp Swords."

HELL — the place of eternal punishment for the unrighteous. The NKJV and KJV use this word to translate Sheol and Hades, the Old and New Testa-

ment words, respectively, for the abode of the dead.

Hell as a place of punishment translates *Gehenna*, the Greek form of the Hebrew word that means "the vale of Hinnom"—a valley just south of Jerusalem. In this valley the Canaanites worshiped Baal and the fire-god Molech by sacrificing their children in a fire that burned continuously. Even Ahaz and Manasseh, kings of Judah, were guilty of this terrible, idolatrous practice (2 Chr. 28:3; 33:6).

The prophet Jeremiah predicted that God would visit such destruction upon Jerusalem that this valley would be known as the "Valley of Slaughter" (Jer. 7:31–34; 19:2, 6). In his religious reforms, King Josiah put an end to this worship. He defiled the valley in order to make it unfit even for pagan worship (2 Kin. 23:10).

In the time of Jesus the Valley of Hinnom was used as the garbage dump of Jerusalem. Into it were thrown all the filth and garbage of the city, including the dead bodies of animals and executed criminals. To consume all this, fires burned constantly. Maggots worked in the filth. When the wind blew from that direction over the city, its awfulness was quite evident. At night wild dogs howled and gnashed their teeth as they fought over the garbage.

Jesus used this awful scene as a symbol of hell. In effect he said, "Do you want to know what hell is like? Look at the valley of Gehenna." So hell may be described as God's "cosmic garbage dump." All that is unfit for heaven will be thrown into hell.

The word *Gehenna* occurs 12 times in the New Testament. Each time it is translated as "hell." With the exception of James 3:6, it is used only by Jesus (Matt. 5:22, 29–30; 10:28; 23:15, 33; Mark 9:43, 45, 47; Luke 12:5). In Matthew 5:22; 18:9; and Mark 9:47, it is used with "fire" as "hell fire." So the word hell (*Gehenna*) as a place of punishment is used in the New Testament by Him who is the essence of infinite love.

In Mark 9:46 and 48, hell is described as a place where "their worm does not die and the fire is not quenched." Repeatedly Jesus spoke of outer darkness and a furnace of fire, where there will be wailing, weeping, and gnashing of teeth (Matt. 8:12; 13:42, 50; 22:13; 24:51; 25:30; Luke 13:28). Obviously this picture is drawn from the valley of Gehenna.

The Book of Revelation describes hell as "a lake of fire burning with brimstone" (Rev. 19:20; 20:10, 14–15; 21:8). Into hell will be thrown the beast and the false prophet (Rev. 19:20). At the end of the age the devil himself will be thrown into it, along with death and hades and all whose names are not in the Book of Life. "And they will be tormented day and night forever and ever" (Rev. 20:10b).

Because of the symbolic nature of the language, some people question whether hell consists of actual fire. Such reasoning should bring no comfort to the lost. The reality is greater than the symbol. The Bible exhausts human language in describing heaven and hell. The former is more glorious, and the latter more terrible, than language can express.

HELLENISM [HELL un is em] — a style of Greek civilization associated with the spread of Greek language and culture to the Mediterranean world after the conquests of Alexander the Great.

On the advice of Aristotle, his teacher, Alexander sought to instill a love for the Greek way of life within those whom he conquered. His generals adopted the same pattern of operation. Conflict soon arose between the Jews and his successors in Israel, the SELEUCIDS. The history of this conflict is detailed in the books of the MACCABEES.

In the Hellenistic period, Greek became the common language throughout the ancient world. So many Jews spoke Greek that an authorized Greek translation of the Old Testament, the SEPTUAGINT, was made at ALEXANDRIA, Egypt. In the Bible, the word "Hellenists" (NKJV) or "Grecians" (KJV) in Acts 6:1 and 9:29 refers to Greek–speaking Jews.

HELMET (see ARMS, ARMOR OF THE BIBLE).

HELMSMAN — a person who steers a ship (Acts 27:11; master, KJV; pilot, NIV; captain, RSV, NEB, NASB).

HELON [HEE lahn] (strength) — a Zebulunite and the father of Eliab (Num. 1:9).

HELP, HELPS — those able to help others (1 Cor. 12:28), or officers of the early church who performed helpful deeds for the poor and the sick.

HELPER — a word used by Jesus to describe the HOLY SPIRIT (John 14:16, 26; 15:26; 16:7). The Greek word has been translated into English by various versions of the Bible as comforter, advocate, and counselor, as well as helper. This Greek word is so filled with meaning that it is difficult to translate it with one English word. The basic meaning, however, is "helper."

The Holy Spirit is the one called to our side by Jesus to help us, to stand by us, to strengthen us and give assistance when needed. The Holy Spirit is the "other" helper (John 14:16). Just as Jesus was the Great Helper while on earth, the Holy Spirit is now our Helper, if we desire His help.

HELPMEET — KJV word for helper, companion, or mate, used by God to describe Eve before she was created as Adam's spouse (Gen. 2:18). The NKJV translates helpmeet as "a helper comparable to him."

HEM — KJV word for the border or fringe of a person's outer garment in Bible times (Ex. 28:33–34; 39:24–26). Tassels were worn by the Israelites on the hems of their garments to remind them of God's commandments (Num. 15:37–41). The scribes and Pharisees, because they prided themselves on keeping the Law, often enlarged their hems or added additional tassels to show how holy and pious they were. Jesus condemned them for this practice because they did it to be noticed and praised by others (Matt. 23:5).

HEMAM [HEE mam] (raging) — a son of Lotan and grandson of Seir (Gen. 36:22). This name is also spelled Homam (1 Chr. 1:39).

HEMAN [HEE muhn] (faithful) — the name of two Old Testament men:

1. A son of Zerah and grandson of Jacob. Heman composed a meditative psalm, a prayer for deliverance from sadness (Psalm 88, title).

2. A son of Joel and a grandson of Samuel the prophet (1 Chr. 6:33; 15:17). Presented as "the singer" or "the musician," he was the first of three chief Levites to conduct the vocal and instrumental music of the tabernacle during the reign of David (1 Chr. 16:41–42).

HEMDAN [HEM dan] (pleasant) — a descendant of Seir the Horite and the oldest son of Dishon (Gen. 36:26). Hemdan is also spelled as Hamran (1 Chr. 1:41, NKJV, NAS, RSV) and Amram (1 Chr. 1:41, NEB, KJV).

HEMLOCK (see PLANTS OF THE BIBLE).

HEMORRHAGE (see DISEASES OF THE BIBLE).

HEN (see ANIMALS OF THE BIBLE).

HEN [hen] (grace) — a son of Zephaniah (Zech. 6:14), also called Josiah (Zech. 6:10).

HENA [HEN uh] (meaning unknown) — a town of Syria captured by SENNACHERIB, king of Assyria (2 Kin. 18:34). Hena may be the same place as modern Anah, a town on the Euphrates River about 32 kilometers (20 miles) from Babylon.

HENADAD [HEN uh dad] (grace of Hadad) — a Levite whose descendants helped rebuild the walls of Jerusalem under Nehemiah (Neh. 10:9).

HENNA (see PLANTS OF THE BIBLE).

HENOCH [HEE nuhk] — a form of HANOCH.

HEPHER [HEE fur] (a well) — the name of three men and one town:

1. The youngest son of Gilead and founder of the tribal family of HEPHERITES (Num. 26:32; 27:1).

2. A town west of the Jordan River (Josh. 12:17) near the district of Sochoh (1 Kin. 4:10).

3. A descendant of Judah and a son of Ashhur by Naarah (1 Chr. 4:6).

4. One of David's mighty men (1 Chr. 11:36).

HEPHERITES [HEE fur ights] — the descendants of HEPHER, son of Gilead (Num. 26:32).

HEPHZIBAH [HEF zih buh] (my delight is in her) — the name of a queen of Judah and a symbolic name:

1. The wife of Hezekiah and the mother of Manasseh (2 Kin. 21:1).

2. A symbolic name used by the prophet Isaiah to refer to a Jerusalem restored to God's favor (Is. 62:4).

HERALD — an officer sent by a king or other high official to proclaim a message or announce good news (Dan. 3:4).

A beautiful view of Mount Hermon in northeastern Palestine—a familiar landmark along the border between the nations of Israel and Syria in Bible times.

HERB (see PLANTS OF THE BIBLE).

HERBS, BITTER — herbs eaten by the Jewish people in their celebration of the PASSOVER. These herbs symbolized the bitterness of the Israelites' years in bondage in Egypt. Jewish tradition identifies five plants, including lettuce, as the bitter herb; but modern Jews use horseradish in the Passover meal.

HERD — a group of cattle or other livestock in Bible times. Cattle herds were an important sign of wealth in Israel's agricultural society. Wealthy people, such as Abraham (Gen. 13:5) and Jacob (Gen. 32:7; 45:10), often owned vast herds. Herding was a common occupation in the ancient world, as references to the practice in Egypt (Gen. 47:17) and Amalek (1 Sam. 30:20) indicate. Israelite herdsmen are rarely mentioned in the Bible, although the best-known is the prophet Amos (Amos 1:1; 7:14).

Herds were kept for milk (Deut. 32:14) and meat (Luke 15:23), as well as for work such as plowing (1 Sam. 11:5; Job 1:14) and pulling carts (1 Sam. 6:7). They were fattened in the stalls (Amos 6:4; Hab. 3:17), as well as the fields. Herds from Bashan (in northeast Israel) were especially known for their fatness (Ezek. 39:18; Amos 4:1) and strength (Ps. 22:12). Cattle were also important as sacrificial animals (Lev. 27:32; Deut. 15:19), or for large public occasions such as Passover (2 Chr. 35:8) and the dedication of the Temple (2 Chr. 5:6; 7:5).

HERDSMAN (see OCCUPATION AND TRADES).

HERESH [HEAR esh] (*silent*) — a Levite among the captives who returned to Jerusalem (1 Chr. 9:15).

HERESY — false doctrine, or teaching which denies one of the foundational beliefs of the church, such as the Lordship or deity of Jesus. While the word itself is not used in the New Testament of the NKJV, the writings of the apostle Paul and other early church leaders make it clear that heretical teachings were a problem in the New Testament church.

In the Book of 2 Corinthians, Paul condemned certain "false apostles" and "deceitful workers" who claimed to be "apostles of Christ" (2 Cor. 11:13). These may have been the JUDAIZERS, who tried to force believers to observe the Jewish ritual of CIRCUMCISION before they could be accepted as members of the church. The writer of 1 John also condemned a heretical group known as the GNOSTICS, who denied the deity of Jesus (1 John 2:22).

HERETH [HEAR eth] (*thicket*) — a forest in the hill country of Judah near the cave where David hid from Saul (1 Sam. 22:5; Hareth, KJV, NEB).

HERETIC (see HERESY).

HERITAGE (see INHERITANCE).

HERMAS [HUR muhs] (*Mercury*) — a Christian in Rome to whom the apostle Paul sent greetings (Rom. 16:14).

HERMENEUTICS [hur meh NEWT icks] — the principles and methods used to interpret a given passage of Scripture. Bible scholars believe a biblical text must be interpreted according to the language in which it was written, its historical context, the identity and purpose of the author, its literary nature, and the situation to which it was originally addressed. Also see BIBLE, INTERPRETATION.

HERMES [HUR meez] (meaning unknown) — the name of a pagan god and an early Christian:

1. The Greek god of commerce who served as the messenger of the other gods. He corresponded to the Roman god Mercury (Acts 14:12; Mercurius, KJV).

2. A Christian to whom the apostle Paul sent greetings (Rom. 16:14).

HERMOGENES [hur MAH jih neez] (*offspring of Hermes*) — an Asian Christian who deserted the apostle Paul at Ephesus (2 Tim. 1:15).

HERMON [HUR mon] (*sacred mountain*) — the northern boundary of the land east of the Jordan River (see Map 3, C–1) that Israel took from the Amorites (Deut. 3:8; Josh. 12:1). The mountain is the southern end of the Anti-Lebanon range and is about 32 kilometers (20 miles) long. It has three peaks (Ps. 42:6), two of which rise over 2,750 meters (9,000 feet) above sea level.

Hermon was regarded as a sacred place by the Canaanites who inhabited the land before the Israelites (Judg. 3:3). Snow covers the mountain during most of the year. Patches of snow remain even through the summer in shaded ravines. The beautiful snow–covered peaks of Mount Hermon can be seen from the region of the Dead Sea, over 196 kilometers (120 miles) distant. The glaciers of Mount Hermon are the major source of the Jordan River, and water from its slopes ultimately flows into the Dead Sea.

The psalmist speaks of the "dew of Hermon" (Ps. 133:3). The snow condenses to vapor during the summer, so that a heavy dew descends on the mountain while the areas surrounding Hermon are parched.

Mount Hermon probably was the site of our Lord's transfiguration (Matt. 17:1–9; Mark 9:2–9; Luke 9:28–37). Jesus traveled with His disciples from Bethsaida, on the Sea of Galilee, to the area of Caesarea Philippi to the north and from there to a "high mountain." There, in the presence of His disciples, Jesus was transfigured. A late tradition identifies the "high mountain" as Mount Tabor, but Mount Hermon is nearer Caesarea Philippi.

HERMONITES [HUR muhn ights] — natives or inhabitants of Mount Hermon (Ps. 42:6, KJV).

HEROD — the name of several Roman rulers in the Palestine region during Jesus' earthly ministry and the periods shortly before His birth and after His resurrection.

The Herodian dynasty made its way into Palestine through Antipater, an Idumean by descent. The Idumeans were of Edomite stock as descendants of Esau. Antipater was installed as procurator of Judea by Julius Caesar, the emperor of Rome, in 47 B.C. He appointed two of his sons to ruling positions. One of these was Herod, known as "Herod the Great," who was appointed governor of Judea.

Herod the Great (37—4 B.C.). The title Herod the Great refers not so much to Herod's greatness as to the fact that he was the eldest son of Antipater. Nevertheless, Herod did show some unusual abilities. He was a ruthless fighter, a cunning negotiator, and a subtle diplomat. The Romans appreciated the way he subdued opposition and maintained order among the Jewish people. These qualities, combined with an intense loyalty to the emperor, made him an important figure in the life of Rome and the Jews of Palestine.

After Herod became governor of Galilee, he quickly established himself in the entire region. For 33 years he remained a loyal friend and ally of Rome. Later, he was appointed as king of Judea, where he was in direct control of the Jewish people. This required careful diplomacy because he was always suspect by the Jews as an outsider (Idumean) and thus a threat to their national right to rule.

At first Herod was conscious of Jewish national and religious feelings. He moved slowly on such issues as taxation, HELLENISM, and religion. He did much to improve his relationship with the Jews when he prevented the Temple in Jerusalem from being raided and defiled by invading Romans.

Herod the Great established his authority and influence through a centralized bureaucracy, well-built fortresses, and foreign soldiers. To assure his continued rule, he slaughtered all male infants who could possibly be considered legal heirs to the throne. His wife Mariamne also became a victim of his suspicion and brutality.

The territories under Herod's rule experienced economic and cultural growth. His business and organizational ability led to the erection of many important buildings. Hellenistic (Greek) ideas were introduced into Palestine through literature, art, and athletic contests. His major building project was the Temple in Jerusalem, which, according to John 2:20, took 46 years to build. From the Jewish perspective, this was his greatest achievement.

At times Herod implemented his policies with force and cruelty. His increasing fear of Jewish re-

Excavated remains of a structure in Jerusalem built by Herod the Great. This Herod was known as a builder of many magnificent buildings, including a Temple for use by Jewish worshipers.

volt led to suppression of any opposition. His personal problems also increased, and by 14 B.C. his kingdom began to decline. This decline was brought on mainly by his personal and domestic problems.

Herod's murder of his wife Mariamne I apparently haunted him. This was compounded when his two sons from that marriage, Alexander and Aristobulus, realized that their father was responsible for their mother's death. By 7 B.C., Herod had both of these sons put to death. Of Herod it was said, "It is better to be Herod's hog than to be his son."

As Herod became increasingly ill, an intense struggle for succession to his throne emerged within the family. His 10 marriages and 15 children virtually guaranteed such a struggle. One son, Antipater, poisoned Herod's mind against two other eligible sons, Archelaus and Philip. This resulted in his initial choice of a younger son, Antipas, as sole successor. However, he later changed his will and made Archelaus king. Antipas and Philip received lesser positions as TETRARCHS, or rulers, over small territories.

After Herod died, his will was contested in Rome. Finally Archelaus was made ethnarch over Idumea, Judea, and Samaria—with a promise to be appointed king if he proved himself as a leader. Antipas became tetrarch over Galilee and Perea. Philip was made tetrarch over Gaulanitis, Trachonitis, Batanea, and Paneas in the northern regions.

Jesus was born in Bethlehem during the reign of Herod the Great. The wise men came asking, "Where is he that is born King of the Jews?" This aroused Herod's jealous spirit. According to Matthew's account, Herod tried to eliminate Jesus by having all the male infants of the Bethlehem region put to death (Matt. 2:13-16). But this despicable act failed. Joseph and Mary were warned by God in a dream to take their child and flee to Egypt. Here they hid safely until Herod died (Matt. 2:13-15).

Herod Archelaus (4 B.C.—A.D. 6). Archelaus inherited his father Herod's vices without his abilities. He was responsible for much bloodshed in Judea and Samaria. Jewish revolts, particularly those led by the ZEALOTS, were brutally crushed. Antipas and Philip did not approve of Archelaus' methods; so they complained to Rome. Their complaints were followed by a Jewish delegation that finally succeeded in having Archelaus stripped of power and banished to Rome.

The only biblical reference to Archelaus occurs in Matthew 2:22. Matthew recorded the fear that Mary and Joseph had about going through Judea on their way from Egypt to Galilee because Archelaus was the ruler.

Herod Philip the Tetrarch. Philip, who inherited the northern part of his father Herod the Great's kingdom (Luke 3:1), must have been the best of Herod's surviving sons. During his long and peaceful rule, he was responsible for a number of building projects, including the city of Caesarea-Philippi. He also rebuilt Bethsaida into a Greek city and renamed it Julias in honor of Augustus Caesar's daughter, Julia.

Herod Antipas (4 B.C.—A.D. 39). Antipas, another of Herod the Great's sons, began as tetrarch over Galilee and Perea. He was the ruling Herod during Jesus' life and ministry. Herod Antipas was first married to the daughter of Aretas, an Arabian king of Petrae. But he became infatuated with Herodias, the wife of his half-brother, Philip I. The two eloped together, although both were married at the time. This scandalous affair was condemned severely by John the Baptist (Matt. 14:4; Mark 6:17-18; Luke 3:19).

Although Antipas apparently had some respect for John the Baptist, he had John arrested and imprisoned for his outspokenness. Later, at a royal birthday party, Antipas granted Salome, the daughter of Herod Philip, a wish. Probably at the prodding of Herodias (Mark 6:19), Salome requested the head of John the Baptist (Matt. 14:6-12; Mark 6:21-29). Since he was under oath and did not want to lose face before his guests, Herod ordered John's execution.

Antipas' contacts with Jesus occurred at the same time as the ministry of John the Baptist. Because of Jesus' popularity and miraculous powers, Antipas may have been haunted by the possibility that Jesus was John the Baptist come back to life.

The New Testament record shows that the relationship between Jesus and Antipas must have been strained. Jesus' popularity and teachings may have threatened Antipas who, according to the Pharisees, sought to kill Him (Luke 13:31). By calling Herod a "fox" (Luke 13:32), Jesus showed His disapproval of his cunning and deceitful ways.

The next encounter between Antipas and Jesus occurred at the trial of Jesus (Luke 23:6-12). Luke indicated that Herod could not find anything in the charges against Jesus that deserved death; so he sent Jesus back to Pilate for a final decision.

During this time of his rule, Antipas was experiencing political problems of his own. Aretas, the Nabatean king whose daughter had been Antipas' wife before he became involved with Herodias, returned to avenge this insult. Antipas' troops were defeated. This, together with some other problems, led to his political downfall. Antipas was finally banished by the Roman emperor to an obscure section of France.

Herod Agrippa I (A.D. 37—44). Agrippa took over Antipas' territory after Antipas fell from favor. Agrippa's power and responsibilities extended far beyond his ability. As a young person growing up in the imperial court, he developed an undisciplined and extravagant life-style. But Agrippa had enough charm and intelligence to stay on the good side of Rome.

After the Roman Emperor Caligula was murdered, Agrippa helped Claudius gain the throne. His loyalty was rewarded. Claudius confirmed Agrippa in his present position and added the territories of Judea and Samaria. This made Agrippa ruler of a kingdom as large as that of his grandfather, Herod the Great.

Very little about Agrippa I is recorded in Scripture. From the comments in Acts 12:1–23, we know that Agrippa sought to win the favor of his Jewish subjects by opposing the early Christian church and its leaders. The record of his death as recorded in Acts 12:20–23 shows the humiliating way he died. After his death, Palestine struggled through a number of chaotic years before Rome was able to establish order.

Herod Agrippa II (A.D. 50—100). Agrippa II was judged to be too young to assume leadership over all the territory of his father, Agrippa I. Thus, Emperor Claudius appointed Cuspius Fadus procurator of Palestine. But in A.D. 53, Agrippa II was appointed as the legitimate ruler over part of this territory.

The only reference to Agrippa II in the New Testament occurs in Acts 25:13—26:32, which deals with Paul's imprisonment in Caesarea. Agrippa listened to Paul's defense, but the apostle appealed to Rome. Agrippa had no power to set him free.

Agrippa was caught in the Jewish revolts that preceded the destruction of Jerusalem in A.D. 70 under the Roman Emperor Titus. He continued to rule by appointment of Vespasian until his death in A.D. 100. His death marked the end to the Herodian dynasty in the affairs of the Jewish people in Palestine.

HEROD, PALACE OF [HEHR ud] — a palace–fortress erected by Herod the Great, a Roman ruler in Palestine about 24/23 B.C. According to the Jewish historian Josephus, it was situated in JERUSALEM, at the northwest corner of the upper city, adjoined by three mighty towers. The palace was burned at the beginning of the Roman–Jewish war, but the three towers withstood the flames.

HERODIANS [heh ROW dih uns] — Jews of influence and standing who were favorable toward Greek customs and Roman law in New Testament times. Although the Herodians should not be equated with the SADDUCEES, they sided with the Sadducees in their pro–Roman sympathies and opposed the PHARISEES, who were anti–Roman. The Herodians joined forces with the Pharisees, however, in their opposition to Jesus.

In Galilee, the Herodians and the Pharisees plotted against Jesus' life (Mark 3:6). At Jerusalem, the Herodians and the Pharisees again joined forces, seeking to trap Jesus on the issue of paying tribute to Caesar (Matt. 22:16; Mark 12:13). Jesus warned his disciples, "Take heed, beware of the leaven [evil influence] of the Pharisees and...of Herod" (Mark 8:15).

HERODIAS [hih ROE dee uhs] — the queen who demanded John the Baptist's head on a platter (Matt. 14:1–12). The granddaughter of Herod the Great, Herodias first married her father's brother, Herod Philip I. One child was born to this union. Philip's half-brother, the tetrarch Herod Antipas, wanted Herodias for his own wife, so he divorced his wife and married Herodias while Philip was still living.

When John the Baptist denounced their immorality, Herodias plotted John's death. She had her daughter Salome gain Herod's favor by dancing seductively for him at a banquet. As a result, Herod promised her anything she wanted. Following her mother's wishes, Salome asked for the head of John the Baptist.

HERODION [hih ROE dee uhn] (*heroic*) — a Christian whom the apostle Paul called "my kinsman" (Rom. 16:11) and to whom he sent greetings.

HERODIUM [heh ROW dih um] — a fortress–palace near the Palestinian city of Tekoa built by Herod the Great (see Map 6, B–4). It is not mentioned in the Bible. Its modern name is Jebel el–Fureidis ("Hill of Paradise") about 6.5 kilometers (4 miles) southeast of Bethlehem. When Herod the Great died in Jericho, in 4 B.C., his body was borne in a funeral procession from Jericho, through Jerusalem, to Herodium, where it was interred. Herod's tomb has not yet been discovered.

Along with Machaerus and Masada, Herodium was one of the last strongholds of Jewish resistance to the Romans, who captured it in A.D. 72. Herodium was used as a supply depot by Simon Bar Kokba, who led a major but unsuccessful revolt against Rome (A.D. 132–135).

HERON (see ANIMALS OF THE BIBLE).

HESHBON [HESH bahn] (*stronghold*) — the former capital of SIHON, king of the Amorites (see Map 3, C–4). Situated in Transjordan about 80 kilometers (50 miles) east of Jerusalem and approximately 23 kilometers (14 miles) southwest of modern Amman, Jordan, Heshbon was captured by the Israelites (Josh. 12:1–2), then rebuilt and populated by the tribes of Reuben (Josh. 13:17) and Gad (1 Chr. 6:81). Later, it was captured by Mesha, King of Moab, and was denounced by the prophets (Is. 15:4; 16:8–9).

HESHMON [HESH mahn] (*fruitfulness*) — a town in southern Judah, between Moldah and Beersheba (Josh. 15:27).

HETH [hate] (*terrible*) — the name of an Old Testament man and a letter of the Hebrew alphabet:

1. The second son of Canaan, ancestor of the Hittites (Gen. 10:15; 1 Chr. 1:13). The Hittite Empire was centered in Anatolia, or Asia Minor.

2. The eighth letter of the Hebrew alphabet, used as a heading over Psalm 119:57–64. In the original Hebrew language, each line of these eight verses begins with the letter heth. Also see ACROSTIC.

HETHLON [HETH lahn] (meaning unknown) — a mountain pass on the northern boundary of Palestine, connecting the Plain of Hamath with the Mediterranean coast (Ezek. 47:15).

HEW — to cleave or cut with blows from a heavy cutting instrument. The words are used for chop-

Photo by Ben Chapman

Heshbon, a city of the Amorites conquered by the Israelites and assigned to the tribe of Reuben (Num. 21:25-34).

ping firewood (2 Chr. 2:10) and for quarrying and carving stone for building purposes (Amos 5:11).

HEWER (see OCCUPATIONS AND TRADES).

HEXATEUCH — the term for the first six books of the Old Testament (Genesis, Exodus, Leviticus, Numbers, Deuteronomy, and Joshua), viewed as a unit. The first five books of the Old Testament, known as the PENTATEUCH, have traditionally been regarded as the first division of the Jewish Old Testament. However, since the early 19th century many scholars who specialize in the literary criticism of the Old Testament have preferred to think in terms of a Hexateuch, or six-volumed book, as forming the first division. These scholars view the book of Joshua as closely linked with the preceding five, arguing that it came from essentially the same sources.

While Joshua is similar in some ways to the books that precede it, many scholars disagree with the concept of a Hexateuch. They argue that Joshua belongs with the Former Prophets, which includes Judges, Samuel, and Kings, rather than the Law.

HEZEKI [HEZ uh kigh] — a form of HIZKI.

HEZEKIAH [hez uh KIGH uh] (*Jehovah is strength*) — the name of three or four men in the Old Testament:

1. The 13th king of Judah. Born the son of Ahaz by Abi, daughter of Zechariah, Hezekiah became known as one of Judah's godly kings. That an ungodly man like Ahaz could have such a godly son can only be attributed to the grace of God. Hezekiah's father had given the kingdom over to idola-

try; but upon his accesion to the throne, Hezekiah decisively and courageously initiated religious reforms (2 Kin. 18:4).

In the first month of his reign, Hezekiah reopened the Temple doors that his father had closed. He also assembled the priests and Levites and commissioned them to sanctify themselves for service and to cleanse the Temple. Appropriate sacrifices were then offered with much rejoicing (2 Chr. 29:3–36).

Hezekiah faced a golden opportunity to reunite the tribes spiritually. In the north Israel had fallen to Assyria in 722 B.C. Hezekiah invited the remnant of the people to come to Jerusalem to participate in the celebration of the PASSOVER. Although some northern tribes scorned the invitation, most responded favorably (2 Chr. 30:1–27).

Hezekiah's reformation reached beyond Jerusalem to include the cleansing of the land, extending even to the tribes of Benjamin, Ephraim, and Manasseh. HIGH PLACES, images, and pagan altars were destroyed. The bronze serpent that Moses had made in the wilderness centuries earlier (Num. 21:5–9) had been preserved, and people were worshiping it. Hezekiah had it destroyed also (2 Kin. 18:4; 2 Chr. 31:1). The land had never undergone such a thorough reform.

When Hezekiah experienced a serious illness, the prophet Isaiah informed the king that he would die. In response to Hezekiah's prayer for recovery, God promised him 15 additional years of life. God also provided a sign for Hezekiah as evidence that the promise would be fulfilled. The sign, one of the most remarkable miracles of the Old Testament, consisted of the sun's shadow moving backward ten degrees in the SUNDIAL OF AHAZ (Is. 38:1–8).

Shortly after he recovered from his illness (Is. 39:1), Hezekiah received visitors from the Babylonian king, Merodach–Baladan (2 Kin. 20:12). They came with letters to congratulate Hezekiah on his recovery and to inquire about the sign (2 Chr. 32:31) in the land. But their real reason for visiting may have been to gain an ally in their revolt against Assyria. When they lavished gifts upon Hezekiah, he in turn showed them his wealth—an action that brought stiff rebuke from Isaiah (2 Kin. 20:13–18).

There is no evidence to indicate that Hezekiah formed an alliance with Babylon. Neither is there any indication that he joined the rebellion in 711 B.C. led by Ashdod, the leading Philistine city. However, Scripture does reveal that he finally did rebel. Sargon II had died in 705 B.C.; and his successor, Sennacherib, was preoccupied with trying to consolidate the kingdom when Hezekiah rebelled. With that accomplished, however, Sennacherib was ready to crush Hezekiah's revolt.

Anticipating the Assyrian aggression, Hezekiah made extensive military preparations. He strengthened the fortifications of Jerusalem, produced weapons and shields for his army, and organized his fighting forces under trained combat commanders. Realizing the importance of an adequate water supply, Hezekiah constructed a tunnel that channeled water from the Spring of Gihon outside the city walls to the Pool of Siloam inside the walls (2 Kin. 20:20). This waterway (now known as the famous "Hezekiah's Tunnel") was cut through solid rock, extending more than 520 meters (1,700 feet).

As Sennacherib captured the fortified cities of Judah, Hezekiah realized that his revolt was a lost cause and he attempted to appease the Assyrian king. To send an apology and tribute, he emptied the palace treasuries and the Temple, even stripping the gold from the doors and pillars. But this failed to appease Sennacherib's anger.

At the height of the Assyrian siege, the Angel of the Lord struck the Assyrian camp, leaving 185,000 dead (2 Kin. 19:35). In humiliation and defeat, Sennacherib withdrew to his capital city of Nineveh.

Little more is said about Hezekiah's remaining years as king, but his achievements are recorded in 2 Chronicles 32:27–30. When he died, after reigning for 29 years, the people of Jerusalem "buried him in the upper tombs of the sons of David" (2 Chr. 32:33), a place of honor.

2. A descendant of David's royal line, a son of Neariah (1 Chr. 3:23).

3. A head of a family who returned from the Captivity in Babylon (Neh. 7:21).

4. The great–great–grandfather of the prophet Zephaniah (Zeph. 1:1; Hizkiah, KJV; Berekiah, NIV).

HEZION [HEE zih ahn] (meaning unknown) — the father of Tabrimmon and the grandfather of Ben–Hadad I, king of Syria in the time of King Asa of Judah (1 Kin. 15:18).

HEZIR [HEE zur] (*swine*) — the name of two Old Testament men:

1. A Levite in the time of David (1 Chr. 24:15).

2. A leader of the people who sealed the covenant after the Captivity (Neh. 10:20).

HEZRAI [HEZ righ] (meaning unknown) — a CARMELITE and one of David's mighty men (2 Sam. 23:35; Hezro, NIV, NAS, RSV).

HEZRO [HEZ roe] — a form of HEZRAI.

HEZRON [HEZ rahn] (*enclosure*) — the name of two men and one town in the Old Testament:

1. A son of Reuben and founder of the HEZRONITES (Gen. 46:9).

2. A founder of a tribal family (Gen. 46:12) and an ancestor of Jesus (Matt. 1:3; Esrom, KJV).

3. A town on the southern border of Judah (Josh. 15:3).

HEZRONITES [HEZ ruh nights] — members of tribal families descended from HEZRON.

HIDDAI [HID day eye] (meaning unknown) — one of David's mighty men (2 Sam. 23:30), also called Hurai (1 Chr. 11:32).

HIDDEKEL [HID uh kel] (meaning unknown) — one of the rivers of the Garden of Eden (Gen. 2:14), known also as the TIGRIS (Dan. 10:4; Hiddekel, KJV).

Section of a stone carving, demonstrating the art of picture writing (hieroglyphics) developed by the Egyptians.

HIEL [HIGH uhl] (*God is living*) — a native of Bethel who fortified Jericho during the reign of Ahab (1 Kin. 16:34). Hiel also sacrificed his sons, in fulfillment of Joshua's curse (Josh. 6:26).

HIERAPOLIS [HIGH uh rap uh lis] (*priestly city*) — a city of the district of Phrygia in southwest Asia Minor (modern Turkey). One of the three major cities of the Lycus River Valley, it was about 16 kilometers (10 miles) northwest of Colossae (Col. 4:13). According to tradition, Philip the evangelist was the first Christian messenger to Hierapolis. Christianity apparently flourished in the city.

HIEROGLYPHICS [high roe GLIF iks] — a system of writing which used pictures to represent words and ideas. The ancient Egyptians developed picture writing to a refined art. Hieroglyphs (pictures) of objects such as birds, animals, trees, and tools represented phrases, words, syllables, or sounds. Also see WRITING.

HIGGAION [hih GAY ahn] (*meditation*) — a musical notation of uncertain meaning (Ps. 9:16). The context seems to connote a low, quiet, soft sound, hence "meditation."

HIGH GATE (see GATES OF JERUSALEM AND THE TEMPLE).

HIGH PLACES — elevated or hilltop sites dedicated to worship of pagan gods. Ancient peoples often built their shrines on hilltops. In Mesopotamia, where the land is flat, they built artificial mountains in the shape of step pyramids called ZIGGURATS. The TOWER OF BABEL (Gen. 11:1–9) was probably such a ziggurat.

Most of the Old Testament references to high places indicate a form of pagan worship forbidden to the Israelites. But sometimes the Lord's people, with His approval, worshiped Him at elevated altars. This happened between the time Shiloh was destroyed and before the ARK OF THE COVENANT was installed in Solomon's Temple. For instance, Samuel blessed the offerings made at the high place which perhaps was Ramah, a word which itself means "high place" (1 Sam. 9:12–14). At nearby Gibeon there was a high place. During the reign of David the tabernacle was there (1 Chr. 16:39; 21:29; 2 Chr. 1:3–4). At this "high place" Solomon made many sacrifices, had his dream, and asked God for wisdom (1 Kin. 3:4–15).

After this early period in Israel's history, all high places mentioned in the Bible were off limits to God's people. In Leviticus 26:30 God promised to destroy the high places, which He knew His people would later build. They probably got the idea for such shrines of worship from the native Canaanites.

In his waning years, Solomon established high places for his pagan wives (1 Kin. 11:7–8). After Solomon's death, the rebellious Northern Kingdom had its high places. The two major ones, containing golden calves, were at Dan and Bethel (1 Kin. 12:28–33). Then as bad kings came to the throne in

Judah they inaugurated high places, and successive good kings abolished them. During Rehoboam's reign high places appeared (1 Kin. 14:23), but Hezekiah broke them down (2 Kin. 18:4). Wicked Manasseh built them again (2 Kin. 21:3), but righteous Josiah dismantled them (2 Kin. 23:8).

The prophets condemned the high places (Jer. 17:1–3; 32:35; Ezek. 6:3; Amos 7:9). The authoritative word came from the prophet Isaiah: "Seek the Lord while He may be found, call upon Him while He is near" (Is. 55:6). Isaiah's message is that God is not found on a mountaintop or at a hilltop shrine. He is everywhere, always ready to listen to the prayers of those who call on him (John 4:21–24).

HIGH PRIEST (see PRIEST, HIGH).

HIGHER GATE (see GATES OF JERUSALEM AND THE TEMPLE).

HIGHEST — a name for God which appears only in the Gospel of Luke in the NKJV (Luke 1:32; 6:35), emphasizing the glory and majesty of God.

HIGHWAY (see ROADS).

HILEN [HIGH luhn] (*strong place*) — a town in the hill country of Judah (1 Chr. 6:58), also called HOLON (Josh. 15:51).

HILKIAH [hill KYE ah] (*Jehovah is my portion*) — the name of seven or eight Old Testament men:

1. The father of Eliakim (2 Kin. 18:18, 26, 37).

2. A high priest during the reign of King Josiah of Judah (2 Kin. 22:4–14). Hilkiah assisted Josiah in reforming Israel's religion.

3. A Levite and a son of Amzi (1 Chr. 6:45–46).

4. A son of Hosah (1 Chr. 26:11) and a tabernacle gatekeeper.

5. A priest who helped Ezra read the Book of the Law to the people (Neh. 8:4; 11:11). He may be the same person as Hilkiah No. 6.

6. A chief priest who returned from the Captivity with Zerubbabel (Neh. 12:7).

7. Father of Jeremiah the prophet (Jer. 1:1).

8. Father of Gemariah, a contemporary of Jeremiah (Jer. 29:3).

HILL — a rise in the land that is higher than a mound but lower than a mountain. The Bible contains many references to the hills of the land of Palestine (Josh. 24:33; 1 Kin. 11:7). Altars to pagan gods were often built on hills (Ezek. 6:13).

HILL COUNTRY — the hilly terrain of southern Palestine, referred to in the New Testament as the "hill country of Judea" (Luke 1:65).

HILL OF THE FORESKINS — a place near Gilgal (Josh. 5:9) where the Israelites who were born during the wilderness wandering were circumcised (Josh. 5:3). The NAS, NEB, NIV, and RSV translate the phrase as Gibeath–haaraloth.

HILL OF GOD — the place where Saul was filled with the Spirit of the Lord and prophesied with a group of prophets (1 Sam. 10:5).

HILLEL [HILL el] (*he has praised*) — the father of

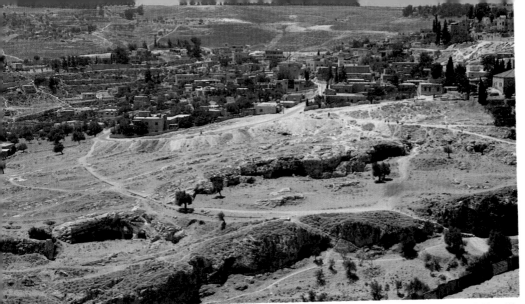

The Valley of Hinnom south of Jerusalem. In Jeremiah's time this valley was associated with worship of the pagan god Molech in rites that required infant sacrifices (Jer. 19:1-9).

Abdon (Judg. 12:13, 15). Abdon was one of the judges of Israel.

HILT — the handle of a weapon, especially a sword or dagger (Judg. 3:22; handle, NIV, NASB; haft, KJV). When Ehud assassinated Eglon, the king of Moab, he thrust a dagger into Eglon's stomach. Even the hilt of the dagger went in after the blade (Judg. 3:12–30).

HIN (see WEIGHTS AND MEASURES).

HIND (see ANIMALS OF THE BIBLE).

HINGE — a pin and socket arrangement on which a door of Bible times turned as it was opened and closed. Doors in ancient times did not have hinges as we know them today. Instead they had projecting pins at both the top and bottom on the side where the door swung open. These pins fitted into matching sockets in the door frame.

The doors of the Holy of Holies and the main hall in Solomon's Temple had gold hinges (1 Kin. 7:50). The lazy person turning back and forth in his bed is also compared in figurative fashion to a door turning back and forth on its hinges (Prov. 26:14).

HINNOM [HEN ohm] (*gratis*) — an unknown person, perhaps the original Jebusite owner, whose name appears only in the phrase, "the Valley of Hinnom" (Josh. 15:8; Neh. 11:30)—a valley outside Jerusalem. Also see HINNOM, VALLEY OF; HELL.

HINNOM, VALLEY OF [HEN nahm] — a deep, narrow ravine south of Jerusalem. At the HIGH PLACES of Baal in the Valley of Hinnom, parents sacrificed their children as a burnt offering to the pagan god Molech (2 Kin. 23:10). Ahaz and Manasseh, kings of Judah, were both guilty of this awful wickedness (2 Chr. 28:3; 33:6). But good

King Josiah destroyed the pagan altars to remove this temptation from the Hebrew people.

The prophet Jeremiah foretold that God would judge this awful abomination of human sacrifice and would cause such a destruction that "the Valley of the Son of Hinnom" would become known as "the Valley of Slaughter" (Jer. 7:31–32; 19:2, 6; 32:35). The place was also called "Tophet."

Apparently, the Valley of Hinnom was used as the garbage dump for the city of Jerusalem. Refuse, waste materials, and dead animals were burned here. Fires continually smoldered, and smoke from the burning debris rose day and night. Hinnom thus became a graphic symbol of woe and judgment and of the place of eternal punishment called HELL.

Translated into Greek, the Hebrew "Valley of Hinnom" becomes *gehenna*, which is used 12 times in the New Testament (11 times by Jesus and once by James), each time translated in the NKJV as "hell" (Matt. 5:22; Mark 9:43, 45, 47; Luke 12:5; James 3:6).

HIP — the part of the body where the thigh and torso are connected. When Jacob wrestled with God by the ford of the Jabbok the socket of his hip came "out of joint" as he wrestled (Gen. 32:25). The word hip is also used in connection with Samson's great slaughter of the Philistines (Judg. 15:8), Joab's armor (2 Sam. 20:8), Behemoth's strength (Job 40:16), and Belshazzar's fear (Dan. 5:6). Also see HIP AND THIGH.

HIP AND THIGH — literally, leg and thigh. The phrase occurs in Judges 15:8 describing one of Samson's successful attacks on his Philistine enemies that was particularly fierce, furious, and violent.

HIPPOPOTAMUS (see ANIMALS OF THE BIBLE).

HIRAH [HIGH ruh] (meaning unknown) — an Adullamite, the "friend" of Judah (Gen. 38:1, 12).

HIRAM [HIGH rum] (*brother is exalted*) — the name of two Old Testament men:

1. A king of Tyre and friend of both David and Solomon (2 Sam. 5:11; 1 Kin. 10:11, 22; 2 Chr. 8:2, 18). The Jewish historian Josephus records that Hiram succeeded his father, Abibaal, and reigned for 34 years. Hiram greatly enhanced the city of Tyre, building an embankment on its east side and a causeway to connect the city with the island where the temple of Baal–Shamem stood.

Hiram appears throughout the reigns of David and Solomon. He sent representatives to David after David captured Jerusalem. When David built a palace, Hiram furnished cedar from Lebanon and workmen to assist with the project. In later years, when Solomon built the Temple in Jerusalem, Hiram again sent cedar and skilled laborers—this time in return for wheat and olive oil. Hiram also supplied ships and sailors for Solomon's trade interests, probably for a share of the profits.

2. A skilled laborer who worked on Solomon's Temple (1 Kin. 7:13, 40, 45). He worked in bronze or copper. In Solomon's Temple he worked on the pillars, the laver, the basins, and the shovels. The title *father* given to him probably means he was a master workman. His name is also spelled Huram (2 Chr. 2:13–14).

HIRE (see WAGES).

HIRELING — a paid worker or employee in Bible times (John 10:11–12). A hireling could hire on for as little as one day, or he might also contract to work for longer periods. When speaking of Himself as the Good Shepherd, Jesus indicated that He had a personal interest in His sheep (or followers), unlike a hireling, who kept sheep for pay.

HISS, HISSING — to expel the air between the tongue and the teeth to express contempt, insult, and scorn (Job 27:23). Hissing often was accompanied by clapping the hands, wagging the head, and grinding the teeth (Lam. 2:15–16).

HISTORY — a narrative or chronological record of significant events (Gen. 2:4; story, NEB; account, NASB, NIV; generations, KJV, RSV). The Hebrew word translated as history literally means "genealogy."

HITTITES [HIT tights] — a people of the ancient world who flourished in Asia Minor (see Map 1, B–1), on the plateau of ANATOLIA, between about 1900 and 1200 B.C. The name Hittite comes from Hatti, another name for Anatolia, the capital of which was Hattushash. At a later date, the Hittites spread into northern Syria and populated such cities as Aleppo, Carchemish, and Hamath. The Old Testament contains numerous references to the Hittites (Gen. 15:20; Num. 13:29; 1 Kin. 10:29; Ezra 9:1; Ezek. 16:3, 45).

Hittites in the Bible. When Sarah died, Abraham purchased the field of Machpelah with a burial cave from Ephron the Hittite (Gen. 23:10–20). This first incident between a patriarch and a Hittite was followed later by Esau's act of taking two Hittite women as wives (Gen. 26:34).

Hittites were included among the peoples dwelling in the area from the river of Egypt to the River Euphrates—the region promised to Abraham. Hittites also occupied the land of Canaan while the Israelites were sojourning in Egypt. They were among the people who had to be driven out when Israel conquered Canaan under Joshua (Ex. 3:8, 17; Deut. 7:1; Judg. 3:5).

Hittites were particularly visible in Palestine during the reign of David. Ahimelech the Hittite was among the close associates and trusted companions

Remains of the Lion's Gate in the defensive wall of Hattusa, capital city of the ancient Hittite Empire.
Photo by Gustav Jeeninga

Photo by Gustav Jeeninga

Stone carving from a religious center of the ancient Hittites, showing a pagan god watching over King Tudhaliyas.

of David during his flight from Saul (1 Sam. 26:6). The most famous Hittite was Uriah, Bathsheba's husband, whom David sent to his death to cover his adultery with Uriah's wife (2 Sam. 11:15). The northern border of Israel during David's time was extended to the River Euphrates (2 Sam. 8:3) to include Syrian city-states. It is highly possible that "Hittites" of the Syrian region served in David's administration (2 Sam. 8:17; 1 Kin. 4:3).

Solomon had a Hittite wife (1 Kin. 11:1), apparently from another of his royal marriages to seal an alliance with a foreign power. After Solomon's time, the "kings of the Hittites" were powerful rulers in Syria during the time when Judah and Israel existed as separate kingdoms (2 Kin. 7:6; 2 Chr. 1:17).

Hittite Religion. The Hittites themselves described their array of pagan gods as "the thousand gods." Among this diversity of deities, there were many names which were Hattic, Hurrian, Sumerian, Nesite, and Canaanite in origin. The names of many gods occur in treaties of the Hittite people as guardian deities over the parties bound by treaty commitments. Each god was worshiped in its own native language. A storm god was the chief male god, and a solar goddess was his mistress.

The Hittites may have been one of the pagan influences that pulled the nation of Israel away from worship of the one true God during its long history. Students of the Old Testament point out that the Hittites formed treaties with other countries long before the Hebrew people developed a consciousness as a nation governed directly by God. Some scholars believe these treaties were used as a model for the covenant which God established with the Hebrews at Mt. Sinai. But this is only a speculative theory which other scholars do not accept.

HIVITES [HIGH vights] (*tent-villagers*) — a people descended from Canaan (Gen. 10:17) who lived in the land before and after Israel's conquest of the land of Canaan (Ex. 13:5; Deut. 7:1; Josh. 11:3; Judg. 3:5; 1 Kin. 9:20). No reference to the Hivites exists outside the Bible. Many scholars think the name "Hivite" is an early textual error for "Horite" (Hurrian). Other scholars suggest that the Hivites were a smaller group within the Horites.

The Bible indicates that the Hivites lived near Tyre and Sidon (2 Sam. 24:7), in the hill country of Lebanon (Judg. 3:3), in Mizpah near Mount Hermon (Josh. 11:3), in central Palestine at Shechem (Gen. 34:2), and in the town of Gibeon north of Jerusalem (Josh. 9:7; 11:19).

Many Hivites were murdered by Simeon and Levi, sons of Jacob, after a member of a Hivite clan assaulted their sister Dinah (Genesis 34). Later, the Israelites were commanded to take Canaan from various groups of Canaanites, including Hivites (Ex. 13:5; 23:23, 28). Hivites from Gibeon tricked Joshua and the Israelites into making a covenant with them (Joshua 9). Joshua spared the Hivites and made them servants (Josh. 9:27). Hivites were also among those Canaanites whom Solomon used as slave laborers for his building projects (1 Kin. 9:20–21; 2 Chr. 8:7–8).

HIZKI [HIZ kigh] (*Jehovah is strength*) — a son of Elpaal and a descendant of Benjamin (1 Chr. 8:17; Hezeki, KJV, NEB).

HIZKIAH [hiz KIGH uh] — a form of HEZEKIAH.

HOARFROST (see FROST).

HOBAB [HOE bab] (*beloved*) — the father-in-law of Moses (Num. 10:29; Judg. 4:11), apparently the same person as JETHRO.

HOBAH [HOE buh] (*hiding place*) — a town north of Damascus, the most distant point to which Abraham pursued the defeated army of Chedorlaomer (Gen. 14:15).

HOBAIAH [hoe BIGH uh] — a form of HABAIAH.

HOD [hahd] (*glory*) — a son of Zophah and a descendant of Asher (1 Chr. 7:37).

HODAIAH [hoe DIGH uh] — a form of HODAVIAH.

HODAVIAH [hoe duh VIGH uh] (*give honor to Jehovah*) — the name of four Old Testament men:
1. A son of Elioenai and a descendant of Zerubbabel and King David (1 Chr. 3:24; Hodaiah, KJV, NEB).
2. A head of the half-tribe of Manasseh, east of the Jordan River (1 Chr. 5:24).
3. A son of Hassenuah (1 Chr. 9:7).
4. Founder of the family of the "sons of Hodaviah" (Ezra 2:40), also spelled Hodevah (Neh. 7:43).

HODESH [HOE desh] (*new moon*) — a wife of Shaharaim, of the tribe of Benjamin (1 Chr. 8:9), also called Baara (1 Chr. 8:8).

HODEVAH [HOE duh vuh] — a form of HODAVIAH.

HODIAH [hoe DIE uh] (*splendor of Jehovah*) — a man who married Naham's sister (1 Chr. 4:19).

HODIJAH [hoe DIE juh] (*splendor of Jehovah*) — the name of two men in the Old Testament:
1. A Levite in the time of Ezra and Nehemiah (Neh. 8:7).
2. A chief of the people who sealed the covenant after the Captivity (Neh. 10:18).

HOE — a tool with a thin, flat blade on a long handle used for cultivating, weeding, or loosening the earth around plants (Is. 7:25; mattock, KJV). (Also see TOOLS OF THE BIBLE).

HOGLAH [HOG luh] (*partridge*) — a daughter of Zelophehad of the tribe of Manasseh (Num. 26:33).

HOHAM [HOE ham] (meaning unknown) — one of five Amorite kings killed by Joshua near the cave at Makkedah (Josh. 10:1–27).

HOLIDAY — a religious feast day or holy day (Esth. 2:18; a release, KJV; a remission of taxes, RSV). The "Feast of Esther" in this passage which King Ahasuerus proclaimed as a holiday was later referred to as the Feast of PURIM (Esth. 9:18–32). Also see FEASTS AND FESTIVALS.

HOLINESS, CEREMONIAL — a characteristic of the worship system of ancient Israel, which required that a person be ceremonially clean and pure before he could approach God. Many acts prohibited in Old Testament law were not immoral but they were considered ceremonially unclean. Ceremonial uncleanness resulted from eating forbidden foods or from contact with unclean objects such as a leper or a dead body (Lev. 11:24–47). Priests especially were restricted as to what they could handle or do (Leviticus 21).

Often ceremonial defilement required only washing. But penalties for such defilement could range from disbarment from the priesthood (Lev. 21:16–24) to exile from camp (Lev. 13:44–46). As our great High Priest, Jesus Christ has paid the penalty for our sin, taking away the need for the laws of ceremonial holiness (Hebrews 8—10).

HOLON [HOE lahn] (*sandy*) — the name of two towns in the Old Testament:
1. A town in the hill country of Judah west of Hebron (Josh. 15:51), also called Hilen (1 Chr. 6:58).
2. A town in Moab (Jer. 48:21) upon which the prophet Jeremiah pronounced judgment. It is possibly present-day Horon.

HOLY — moral and ethical wholeness or perfection; freedom from moral evil. Holiness is one of the essential elements of God's nature required of His people. Holiness may also be rendered "sanctification" or "godliness." The word holy denotes that which is "sanctified" or "set apart" for divine service.

God instructed Moses to "consecrate Aaron and his sons" (Ex. 29:9) to the priesthood. The children of Israel were admonished to "remember the Sabbath day, to keep it holy" (Ex. 20:8). The "Holy of Holies" (or "Holiest of All") was the most sacred place in the desert tabernacle and in the Temple at Jerusalem (Ex. 26:33; Heb. 9:1–9). Elisha was called a "holy man of God" (2 Kin. 4:9). Herod feared John the Baptist, "knowing that he was a just and holy man" (Mark 6:20).

While holy is sometimes used in a ceremonial sense, the main use is to describe God's righteous nature or the ethical righteousness demanded of His followers (Is. 1:10–14; Matt. 12:7). Originating in God's nature, holiness is a unique quality of His character. The Bible emphasizes this divine attribute. "Who is like you, O Lord?" (Ex. 15:11). "There is none holy like the Lord" (1 Sam. 2:2). "Who shall not fear You, O Lord...For You alone are holy" (Rev. 15:4). God's high expectations of His people flow out of His own holy nature: "You shall be to me a kingdom of priests and a holy nation" (Ex. 19:6); "sanctify yourselves therefore and be holy, for I am the Lord your God" (Lev. 20:7).

Jesus was the very personification of holiness; He reinforced God's demands for holiness by insisting that His disciples must have a higher quality of righteousness than that of the scribes and Pharisees (Matt. 5:20). Like the prophets Amos and Hosea, Jesus appealed for more than ceremonial holiness: "I desire mercy and not sacrifice" (Hos. 6:6; Matt. 12:7).

The theme of sanctification, or growing into God's likeness and being consecrated for His use, is prominent throughout the Bible. Like Jesus, the apostles taught that sanctification, or true holiness, expressed itself in patient and loving service while awaiting the Lord's return. Peter urged the suffering Christians of the Roman Empire to follow God's example of holiness in their trials: "As He who has called you is holy, you also be holy in all your conduct" (1 Pet. 1:15).

Paul's prayer for the saints at Thessalonica is timeless in its application to the church and individual believers: "And may the Lord make you increase in love and abound in love...so that He may establish your hearts blameless in holiness before our God and Father at the coming of our Lord Jesus Christ with all His saints" (1 Thess. 3:12-13).

HOLY CITY (see CITY, HOLY).

HOLY DAY — a term for the Sabbath (Ex. 35:2; Is. 58:13), as well as other days of special religious significance in the life of the Hebrew people. The day on which Ezra read the Law of God to the restored community in Jerusalem was described as a holy day (Neh. 8:9-11). In one passage, the people agree not to buy grain or wares from foreign traders "on the Sabbath, or on a holy day" (Neh. 10:31). In this case the term refers to any of the major religious festivals celebrated by the Jews.

HOLY GHOST (see HOLY SPIRIT).

HOLY OF HOLIES — KJV words for HOLY PLACE.

HOLY ONE OF ISRAEL (see GOD, NAMES OF).

HOLY PLACE — KJV term for the most sacred inner room in the TABERNACLE and the TEMPLE, where only the HIGH PRIEST was allowed to go. This room, separated from the rest of the worship area by a sacred veil, represented the visible presence of God in all His power and holiness. In this room was the ARK OF THE COVENANT, covered by the sacred MERCY SEAT (Ex. 25:10-22). Once a year on the DAY OF ATONEMENT, the high priest entered the Holy Place with sacrificial blood and made ATONEMENT before God for the sins of the people (Leviticus 16; holy of holies, KJV).

HOLY SPIRIT — the third person of the trinity, who exercises the power of the Father and the Son in creation and redemption. Because the Holy Spirit is the power by which believers come to Christ and see with new eyes of faith, He is closer to us than we are to ourselves. Like the eyes of the body through which we see physical things, He is seldom in focus to be seen directly because He is the one through whom all else is seen in a new light. This explains why the relationship of the Father and the Son is more prominent in the gospels, because it is through the eyes of the Holy Spirit that the Father-Son relationship is viewed.

The Holy Spirit appears in the Gospel of John as the power by which Christians are brought to faith and helped to understand their walk with God. He brings a person to new birth: "That which is born of the flesh is flesh, and that which is born of the Spirit is spirit" (John 3:6); "It is the Spirit who gives life" (John 6:63). The Holy Spirit is the Paraclete, or Helper, whom Jesus promised to the disciples after His ascension. The triune family of Father, Son, and Holy Spirit are unified in ministering to believers (John 14:16, 26). It is through the Helper that Father and Son abide with the disciples (John 15:26).

This unified ministry of the trinity is also seen as the Spirit brings the world under conviction of sin, righteousness, and judgment. He guides believers into all truth with what He hears from the Father and the Son (John 15:26). It is a remarkable fact that each of the persons of the trinitarian family serves the others as all defer to one another: The Son says what He hears from the Father (John 12:49-50); the Father witnesses to and glorifies the Son (John 8:16-18, 50, 54); the Father and Son honor the Holy Spirit by commissioning Him to speak in their name (John 14:16, 26); the Holy Spirit honors the Father and Son by helping the community of believers.

Like Father and Son, the Holy Spirit is at the disposal of the other persons of the triune family, and all three are one in graciously being at the disposal of the redeemed family of believers. The Holy Spirit's attitude and ministry are marked by generosity; His chief function is to illumine Jesus' teaching, to glorify His person, and to work in the life of the individual believer and the church.

This quality of generosity is prominent in the Gospels of Matthew, Mark, and Luke, where the Holy Spirit prepares the way for the births of John the Baptist and Jesus the Son (Matt. 1:20; Luke 1:15, 35, 41). At the baptism of Jesus, the Spirit of God is present in the form of a dove. This completes the presence of the triune family at the inauguration of the Son's ministry (Matt. 3:16-17; Mark 1:9-11; Luke 3:21-22; John 1:33). Jesus is also filled with the Holy Spirit as He is led into the wilderness to be tempted (Luke 4:1). He claims to be anointed by the Spirit of the Lord in fulfillment of Old Testament prophecy (Is. 61:1; Luke 4:18-19).

During His ministry, Jesus refers to the Spirit of God (Matt. 12:28-29; Luke 11:20) as the power by which He is casting out demons, thereby invading the stronghold of Beelzebul and freeing those held captive. Accordingly, the Spirit works with the Father and Son in realizing the redeeming power of the kingdom of God. God's kingdom is not only the reign of the Son but also the reign of the Spirit, as all share in the reign of the Father.

The person and ministry of the Holy Spirit in the Gospels is confirmed by His work in the early church. The baptism with the Holy Spirit (Acts 1:5) is the pouring out of the Spirit's power in missions and evangelism (Acts 1:8). This prophecy of Jesus (and of Joel 2:28-32) begins on Pentecost (Acts 2:1-18). Many of those who hear of the finished work of God in Jesus' death and resurrection (Acts 2:32-38) repent of their sins. In this act of repentance, they receive the gift of the Holy Spirit (Acts 2:38), becoming witnesses of God's grace through the Holy Spirit.

Paul's teaching about the Holy Spirit harmonizes with the accounts of the Spirit's activity in the gospels and Acts. According to Paul, it is by the Holy Spirit that one confesses that Jesus is Lord (1 Cor. 12:3). Through the same Spirit varieties of gifts are given to the body of Christ to ensure its richness and unity (1 Cor. 12:4–27). The Holy Spirit is the way to Jesus Christ the Son (Rom. 8:11) and to the Father (Rom. 8:14–15). He is the person who bears witness to us that we are children of God (8:16–17). He "makes intercession for us with groanings which cannot be uttered" (Rom. 8:26–27).

The Holy Spirit also reveals to Christians the deep things of God (1 Cor. 2:10–12) and the mystery of Christ (Eph. 3:3–5). The Holy Spirit acts with God and Christ as the pledge or guarantee by which believers are sealed for the day of salvation (2 Cor. 1:21–22), and by which they walk and live (Rom. 8:3–6) and abound in hope with power (Rom. 15:13). Against the lust and enmity of the flesh Paul contrasts the fruit of the Spirit: "Love, joy, peace, longsuffering, kindness, goodness, faithfulness, gentleness, self–control" (Gal. 5:22–23).

Since the Holy Spirit is the expressed power of the triune family, it is imperative that one not grieve the Spirit, since no further appeal to the Father and the Son on the day of redemption is available (Eph. 4:30). Jesus made this clear in His dispute with the religious authorities, who attributed His ministry to Satan rather than the Spirit and committed the unforgiveable sin (Matt. 12:22–32; John 8:37–59).

In Paul's letters Christian liberty stems from the work of the Holy Spirit: "Where the Spirit of the Lord is, there is liberty" (2 Cor. 3:17). This is a process of "beholding as in a mirror the glory of the Lord," and "being transformed into the same image from glory to glory, just as by the Spirit of the Lord" (2 Cor. 3:18). The personal work of the Holy Spirit is accordingly one with that of the Father and the Son, so Paul can relate the grace, love, and communion of the triune family in a trinitarian benediction: "The grace of the Lord Jesus Christ, and the love of God, and the communion of the Holy Spirit be with you all. Amen" (2 Cor. 13:14).

Among the other New Testament writings the Spirit's ministry is evident in the profound teaching of Hebrews 9:14, which shows the relationship of God, Christ, and the eternal Spirit. The Holy Spirit's work in the Old Testament in preparation for the coming of Christ is explained in this and other passages in Hebrews (3:7; 9:8; 10:15–17).

This leads us to consider the working of the Spirit in the Old Testament in light of His ministry in the New Testament. The Spirit is the energy of God in creation (Gen. 1:2; Job 26:13; Is. 32:15). God endows man with personal life by breathing into his nostrils the breath of life (Gen. 2:7). The Spirit strives with fallen man (Gen. 6:3), and comes

upon certain judges and warriors with charismatic power (Joshua, Num. 27:18; Othniel, Judg. 3:10; Gideon, Judg. 6:34; Samson, Judg. 13:25; 14:6). However, the Spirit departs from Saul because of his disobedience (1 Sam. 16:14).

In the long span of Old Testament prophecy the Spirit plays a prominent role. David declared, "The Spirit of the Lord spoke by me, And His word was on my tongue" (2 Sam. 23:2). Ezekiel claimed that "the Spirit entered me when He spoke to me" (Ezek. 2:2). The Spirit also inspired holiness in the Old Testament believer (Ps. 143:10). It also promised to give a new heart to God's people: "I will put My Spirit within you, and cause you to walk in My statutes" (Ezek. 36:27).

This anticipates the crucial work of the Spirit in the ministry of the Messiah. The prophecy of Isaiah 11:1–5 is a trinitarian preview of the working of the Father, the Spirit, and the Son, who is the branch of Jesse. Looking forward to the ministry of Jesus Christ, the Holy Spirit inspired Isaiah to prophecy: "The Spirit of the Lord shall rest upon Him" (Is. 11:2). The Holy Spirit inspired Jesus with wisdom, understanding, counsel, might, knowledge, fear of the Lord, righteousness, and faithfulness. Thus we come full cycle to the New Testament where Jesus claims the fulfillment of this prophecy in Himself (Is. 61:1–2; Luke 4:18–19).

Isaiah 42:1–9 summarized the redeeming work of the Father, Son, and Spirit in the salvation of the lost, as God spoke through the prophet: "Behold! My Servant whom I uphold, My Elect One in whom My soul delights! I have put My Spirit upon Him; He will bring forth justice to the Gentiles" (Is. 42:1). No clearer reflection of the intimate interworking of the triune family and the Spirit's powerful role can be found in the Old Testament than in this prophecy. It ties God's grace in Old and New together in remarkable harmony.

HOLY SPIRIT, SIN AGAINST — a sin that is often referred to as the "unpardonable sin" because, in the words of Jesus, "He who blasphemes [speaks evil] against the Holy Spirit never has forgiveness, but is subject to eternal condemnation" (Mark 3:29).

The context of Jesus' words about the sin against the Holy Spirit provides a clue to its nature. When a demon–possessed man came to Jesus, He was healed. The multitudes were amazed. But the scribes and Pharisees said He was healing through Satan's power (Matt. 12:24). Jesus had cast out the demons by the power of the Holy Spirit; His enemies claimed He cast them out by the power of the devil.

Such slander of the Holy Spirit, Jesus implied, reveals a spiritual blindness, a warping and perversion of the moral nature, that puts one beyond hope of repentance, faith, and forgiveness. Those who call the Holy Spirit Satan reveal a spiritual cancer so advanced that they are beyond any hope of healing and forgiveness.

HOMAGE — special honor, respect, or allegiance

shown to God (1 Kin. 1:16, 31; obeisance, RSV).

HOMAM [HOE mam] (*raging*) — a son of Lotan and grandson of Seir (1 Chr. 1:39), also called Hemam (Gen. 36:22).

HOME (see FAMILY).

HOMER (see WEIGHTS AND MEASURES).

HOMOSEXUAL — a person who is attracted sexually to members of his or her own sex. The apostle Paul listed homosexuals among "the unrighteous" who would not inherit the kingdom of God (1 Cor. 6:9), and declared that God's wrath stands against such behavior, whether practiced by men or women (Rom. 1:26–27).

HONESTY — the state of being honorable or truthful, upright and fair in dealing with others. When Joseph's brothers arrived in Egypt, they explained that they were "honest men...not spies" (Gen. 42:11).

HONEY — a sweet, liquid substance produced by bees or, artificially, from fruit. The Old Testament makes frequent reference to honey, using a Hebrew word that should be translated "sweet substance" since it can be applied to material that comes from sources other than bees.

Bible scholars have no way of knowing whether the word honey refers to the production of domestic or wild bees. In the description of Canaan as a "land which flows with milk and honey" (Num. 14:8), the connection with milk, obviously an agricultural product, may imply that the honey was also produced by domestic bees.

The story of Samson's riddle (Judges 14) is one passage where the Hebrew word must certainly refer to honey. Bees and honey are mentioned together in this text. It is also possible to interpret the honey in the story of Jonathan and Saul's vow (1 Samuel 14) as the product of bees.

The word honey can also refer to a thick syrup made from grapes and dates. In Arabic, the word used for this kind of fruit syrup is the same as the Hebrew word for honey from bees.

As a symbol, honey stands for abundance (Ex. 3:8; 13:5; 33:3), the believer's delight in God's word (Ps. 19:10; 119:103), and the rightness of God's word to His people (Ezek. 3:3).

HONOR — esteem and respect. To honor God is to give Him reverence and homage, for God alone is worthy of our highest honor (1 Chr. 16:27; Rev. 4:9–11). Second in honor would come the Son of God. Jesus makes it plain that one cannot honor the Father unless he also honors the Son (John 5:23). Esteem, honor, and respect should also be given to our spiritual leaders in the church (1 Tim. 5:17; Heb. 13:7, KJV).

The fifth of the Ten Commandments states, "Honor your father and your mother" (Ex. 20:12; Deut. 5:16). Jesus taught that to honor parents means to help them financially (Matt. 15:4–6).

HOOD, TURBAN (see DRESS OF THE BIBLE).

HOOK — a word used several different ways in the Bible:
1. A pin to which the curtains of the tabernacle were attached (Ex. 26:32).
2. A three–pronged fleshhook used by the priest's servant to handle sacrificial meat (1 Sam. 2:13–14).
3. A hook used for fishing (Matt. 17:27).
4. A vinedresser's pruning hook (Is. 2:4).
5. A ring such as one placed in an animal's nose to lead it about. Isaiah used the word in his prophecy against Sennacherib, king of Assyria (Is. 37:29). Later, the Assyrians took Manasseh, king of Judah, into captivity with nose hooks (2 Chr. 33:11).
6. Forked pegs upon which the carcasses of sacrificial animals were hung (Ezek. 40:43).

HOOPOE (see ANIMALS OF THE BIBLE).

HOPE — confident expectancy. In the Bible, the word hope stands for both the act of hoping (Rom. 4:18; 1 Cor. 9:10) and the thing hoped for (Col. 1:5; 1 Pet. 1:3). Hope does not arise from the individual's desires or wishes but from God, who is Himself the believer's hope: "My hope is in You" (Ps. 39:7). Genuine hope is not wishful thinking, but a firm assurance about things that are unseen and still in the future (Rom. 8:24–25; Heb. 11:1, 7).

Hope distinguishes the Christian from the unbeliever, who has no hope (Eph. 2:12; 1 Thess. 4:13). Indeed, a Christian is one in whom hope resides (1 Pet. 3:15; 1 John 3:3). In contrast to Old Testament hope, the Christian hope is superior (Heb. 7:19).

Christian hope comes from God (Rom. 15:13) and especially His calling (Eph. 1:18; 4:4), His grace (2 Thess. 2:16), His Word (Rom. 15:4) and His gospel (Col. 1:23). Hope is directed toward God (Acts 24:15; 1 Pet. 1:21) and Christ (1 Thess. 1:3; 1 Tim. 1:1). Its appropriate objects are eternal life (Titus 1:2; 3:7), salvation (1 Thess. 5:8), righteousness (Gal. 5:5), the glory of God (Rom. 5:2; Col. 1:27), the appearing of Christ (Titus 2:13) and the resurrection from the dead (Acts 23:6; 26:6–7).

HOPHNI [HOFF nigh] (meaning unknown) — a son of Eli the high priest who, along with his brother Phinehas, proved unworthy of priestly duties (1 Sam. 1:3; 2:34; 4:4–17). Their behavior was characterized by greed (1 Sam. 2:13–16) and lust (1 Sam. 2:22). Eli made only a halfhearted attempt to control his sons' scandalous behavior. Consequently, God's judgment was pronounced upon Eli and his household. Hophni and Phinehas were killed in a battle, and the ARK OF THE COVENANT was captured by the Philistines (1 Sam. 4:1–11). When Eli heard the news, he fell backward and died of a broken neck (1 Sam. 4:12–18).

HOPHRA [HAHF ruh] (*the heart of Ra endures*) — a king of Egypt who reigned 589–570 B.C. Early in his reign, Hophra marched against Nebuchadnezzar II who had besieged Jerusalem in 589 B.C. When the Babylonians turned from Jerusalem to challenge him, Hophra retreated to Egypt. Hophra's overthrow was foretold by the prophet Jeremiah (Jer. 44:30). Also see PHARAOH.

HOR HAGIDGAD [HOHR huh GID gad] (*cavern of Gidgad*) — a desert place where the Israelites camped, probably the same place as Gudgodah (Deut. 10:7).

HOR, MOUNT [hoer] (*hill, mountain*) — the name of two mountains in the Old Testament:

1. The mountain on the border of the Edomites where Aaron died and was buried (Num. 20:22–29; Deut. 32:50). The word Hor is usually regarded as an archaic form of Har, the Hebrew word for "mountain." Numbers 20:23 indicates that Mount Hor was situated by the border of the land of Edom. This was the place where the Hebrew people stopped after they left Kadesh (Num. 20:22; 33:37).

Early tradition established Jebel Harun, meaning "Aaron's Mountain," as the site of Mount Hor. It is a conspicuous mountain about 1,440 meters (4,800 feet) high on the eastern side of the Arabah, midway between the southern tip of the Dead Sea and the northern end of the Gulf of Aqaba. However, this peak is far from Kadesh. In recent years Jebel Madurah northeast of Kadesh on the northwest border of Edom has been suggested as the more likely site for Mount Hor.

2. A mountain in northern Palestine between the Mediterranean Sea and the approach to Hamath (Num. 34:7–8). The exact site of this mountain is unknown.

HORAM [HOHR em] (*height*) — a king of Gezer defeated by Joshua (Josh. 10:33).

HOREB, MOUNT [HOHR eb] (*waste*) — the "mountain of God" (Ex. 18:5) in the Sinai Peninsula where Moses heard God speaking through the burning bush (Ex. 3:1) and where the law was given to Israel (see Map 2, B–2).

HOREM [HOR em] (*sacred*) — a fortified town in the territory of Naphtali (Josh. 19:38).

HORESH [HOE resh] (*forest*) — a place in the Wilderness of Ziph, west of the Dead Sea, where David hid from King Saul (1 Sam. 23:15; in a forest, NKJV).

HORI [HOHR igh] (*noble*) — the name of two Old Testament men:

1. A son of Lotan and a descendant of Seir (Gen. 36:22).

2. The father of Shaphat, one of the 12 spies sent by Moses to spy out the land of Canaan (Num. 13:5).

HORITES [HOAR ites] — the inhabitants of Mt. Seir before its conquest by the Edomites (Gen. 14:6; Deut. 2:12, 22) and the descendants of Seir the Horite (Gen. 36:20).

Archaeological evidence has shed light on the Horites and their kingdom Mitanni. They lived in the Armenian and Kurdish mountains, infiltrating into the region along the Tigris and Euphrates Rivers in Mesopotamia before 2000 B.C. From 2100 to 1550 B.C., waves of Horites swept across a large part of the ancient world, including Canaan. Their kingdom reached its peak in the middle of the 15th century B.C., extending from Nuzi in upper Mesopotamia in the east to Ras Shamra in the west.

Study of Horite tablets from Nuzu shows a close parallel between many of their customs and the accounts of Abraham and the other patriarchs in the Book of Genesis.

HORMAH [HOHR muh] (*complete destruction*) — a Canaanite city in southern Judah, near Ziklag and the border of Edom. Originally called Zephath, the name was changed when it was captured by Judah and Simeon and utterly destroyed (Judg. 1:17).

The barren mountain traditionally identified as Mount Hor, the place where Aaron was buried along the border of ancient Edom (Num. 20:22-29).

Photo: Levant Photo Service

HORN — a word with several different meanings in the Bible:

1. The word often refers to the horns of various animals, such as the wild ox (Deut. 33:17) and the ram (Gen. 22:13). Animal horns served two purposes in Bible times. One was to carry oil. The second was as a musical instrument, created by cutting the tip off the horn and blowing through it. The curved horn of a ram or an ox was used for this purpose. This horn, called a SHOPHAR, was used to call the Israelites together for religious occasions and to signal them during battles (2 Chr. 15:14).

2. The altar in both the tabernacle and the Temple had four projections, or horns—one at each corner—on which the blood of the sacrificed animals was sprinkled (Ex. 29:12). Adonijah and Joab grabbed the horns of the altar, seeking refuge from King Solomon who was seeking their life (1 Kin. 1:50; 2:28).

3. The ink horn in Ezekiel 9:2-11 probably does not refer to a horn at all but to a palette-like board used by scribes to store their pens and cakes of ink. The Hebrew word used here closely resembles the Egyptian word for such a device.

4. Because the horn was used by animals as a weapon, it came to symbolize power and might. Zedekiah, a false prophet in Ahab's day, made horns of iron to portray how Ahab was going to defeat the Syrians (1 Kin. 22:11). God lifts up the horn of the righteous but cuts off the horn of the wicked (Ps. 75:10). Probably as an extension of this meaning of the word, horns in the visions of Daniel and John symbolized kingdoms and individual kings. David spoke of God as the horn, or strength, of his salvation (2 Sam. 22:3; Ps. 18:2).

HORNED OWL, HORNET (see ANIMALS OF THE BIBLE).

HORONAIM [hohr uh NAY uhm] (*two caves*) — a town of Moab, near Zoar (Is. 15:5), situated along the route the Assyrians followed when they invaded Israel.

HORONITE [HOHR uh night] — a title given to SANBALLAT, an enemy of Nehemiah (Neh. 2:10, 19). He was probably a native of Beth Horon in Samaria.

HORSE (see ANIMALS OF THE BIBLE).

HORSE GATE (see GATES OF JERUSALEM AND THE TEMPLE).

HORSELEECH (see ANIMALS OF THE BIBLE).

HORSEMAN (see OCCUPATIONS AND TRADES).

HOSAH [HOE suh] (*refuge*) — the name of a man and a village in the Old Testament:

1. A village of the tribe of Asher (Josh. 19:29).

2. A Levite gatekeeper of the family of Merari in David's time (1 Chr. 16:38).

HOSANNA [hoe ZAN nuh] (*save us now*) — the shout of the multitude at the time of Jesus' triumphal entry into Jerusalem (Matt. 21:9, 15; Mark 11:9-10; John 12:13). The word originally was a prayer requesting God's help, but it had become a cry of joy or a shout of welcome by this time in Jewish history.

The word Hosanna was also associated with Jewish hopes for deliverance by a political hero. When shouted to Jesus by pilgrims and children, it indicates they saw in him the fulfillment of their Messianic expectations. But Jesus came as a spiritual deliverer on a lowly donkey—not as a conquering military hero on a prancing horse.

HOSEA [hoe ZAY uh] (*deliverance*) — an Old Testament prophet and author of the Book of Hosea. The son of Beeri (Hos. 1:1), Hosea ministered in the northern kingdom of Israel during the chaotic period just before the fall of this nation in 722 B.C. The literary features within Hosea's book suggest he was a member of the upper class. The tone and contents of the book also show he was a man of deep compassion, strong loyalty, and keen awareness of the political events taking place in the world at that time. As a prophet, he was also deeply committed to God and His will as it was being revealed to His Covenant People.

Hosea is one of the most unusual prophets of the Old Testament, since he was commanded by God to marry a prostitute (Hos. 1:2-9). His wife Gomer eventually returned to her life of sin, but Hosea bought her back from the slave market and restored her as his wife (Hos. 3:1-5). His unhappy family experience was an object lesson of the sin or "harlotry" of the nation of Israel in rejecting the one true God and serving pagan gods. Although the people deserved to be rejected because they had turned their backs on God, Hosea emphasized that God would continue to love them and use them as His special people.

In his unquestioning obedience of God, Hosea demonstrated he was a prophet who would follow his Lord's will, no matter what the cost. He was a sensitive, compassionate spokesman for righteousness whose own life echoed the message that God is love.

Also see HOSEA, BOOK OF.

HOSEA, BOOK OF — a prophetic book of the Old Testament that emphasizes God's steadfast love for His COVENANT PEOPLE, in spite of their continuing sin and rebellion. The book is named for its author, the prophet Hosea, who demonstrated God's steadfast love in dramatic fashion through his devotion to his own unfaithful wife.

Structure of the Book. Hosea contains 14 chapters that are filled with some of the most powerful truths in all the Bible. After a brief introduction of himself as God's prophet, Hosea tells about his unusual family situation. God appeared to Hosea, instructing him, "Go, take yourself a wife of harlotry and children of harlotry" (1:2). The reason for this unusual request was to demonstrate that God's Covenant People, the nation of Israel, had been unfaithful to God because of their worship of false gods.

Hosea did as the Lord commanded, taking a prostitute named Gomer as his wife. The first three chapters of the book report their stormy relationship as husband and wife. Soon after their marriage, Gomer bore three children. Hosea gave them symbolic names—Jezreel (*God scatters*), Lo-Ruhamah (*Not Pitied*), and Lo-Ammi (*Not My People*)—to show that God was about to bring His judgment upon the nation of Israel because the people had fallen into worship of false gods. Just as the nation rejected God, Gomer eventually left Hosea and the children to return to her life of prostitution. But Hosea's love for his wife refused to die.

He searched until he found her at the slave market. Then he bought her back and restored her as his wife. This tender picture showed clearly that God had not given up on Israel, although the people had "played the harlot" many times by returning to their old life of pagan worship and enslavement to sin.

The second major division of Hosea's book, chapters 4—14, contains the prophet's messages of judgment against the nations of Israel and Judah.

The northern kingdom of Israel, Hosea's homeland, is singled out for strong rebuke because of its gross sin and immorality. But the book ends on a positive note. In tender language, the prophet reminds the nation of God's undying love. In spite of their unfaithfulness, He is determined to redeem them and restore them to their favored place as His Covenant People.

Authorship and Date. The undisputed author of this book is the prophet Hosea, who identifies himself in the book as "the son of Beeri" (1:1). His name, a variant form of Joshua and Jesus, means "salvation." The prophet also says that he lived and prophesied during the reign of King Jeroboam II of Israel while four successive kings—Uzziah, Jotham, Ahaz, and Hezekiah—were ruling in Judah. This means his prophetic ministry covered a period of about 40 years, from about 755 B.C. to about 715 B.C. His book was written some time during these years.

Historical Setting. Hosea prophesied during the twilight years of the northern kingdom of Israel, a time of rapid moral decline. Worship of false gods

HOSEA: A Teaching Outline

was mixed with worship of the one true God. Ritualism rather than righteousness was the order of the day as even the priests lost sight of the real meaning of worship. Although King JEROBOAM II was the instigator of many of these policies, at least his 40-year reign (793–753 B.C.) brought a measure of political stability to the nation. This stability came to an end when he died. In rapid succession, six different kings ruled Israel during the next 25 years; four were eliminated by assassination. Weakened by internal strife, Israel collapsed in 722 B.C. when the nation of Assyria destroyed Samaria, Israel's capital city. Hosea was probably an eyewitness to many of these events as his prophecy about God's judgment on Israel was fulfilled.

Theological Contribution. Through his marriage and prophetic message, Hosea presents a vivid picture of the steadfast love of God for His people. Because they have sinned and broken the covenant, God's people deserve His certain judgment. But because of His undying love for them, His mercy and lovingkindness will prevail. Many people believe the Old Testament portrays God's wrath, while the New Testament pictures his love. But the Book of Hosea includes tender expressions of deep love among this prophet's descriptions of judgment. Hosea ranks with Deuteronomy and the Gospel of John as major biblical treatises on the love of God. This love is not mere sentiment; it is rooted in compassion and bound in holiness. God's love makes demands, but it is also willing to forgive.

Special Considerations. The Book of Hosea is noted for its many references to the history of Israel, as well as its vivid poetic images. Throughout the book the prophet speaks tenderly of the nation of Israel as "EPHRAIM." This is a reference to the largest of the ten northern tribes of Palestine that made up the nation of Israel. Because of their superior numbers, Ephraim was a symbol of power and strength. This tribal name also reminded the nation of its history and tradition. Ephraim, after whom the tribe was named (Gen. 48:17–22), was the son of Joseph.

Few events in the Bible have been debated as strongly as Hosea's marriage. The command for a man of God to marry a harlot is so startling that interpreters have offered many different explanations. Some suggest that the story is meant to be read only as an allegory. Others believe Gomer was faithful at first but went astray after their marriage. Still others believe she was a prostitute from the very beginning but that Hosea did not learn this until later.

All of these approaches to the passage issue from our offended sense of right and wrong. The plain meaning of the text is that Hosea married a prostitute at God's direct command. In this way, through his own tormented life Hosea could present a striking picture of the pain in God's heart because of the harlotries of His Covenant People.

Also see HOSEA.

HOSEN — an archaic Old English word for "long

trousers" or "leggings" (Dan. 3:21, KJV). Other versions translate the word as "trousers" (NKJV) and "tunics" (RSV). Also see DRESS OF THE BIBLE.

HOSHAIAH [hoe SHAY uh] (*Jehovah has saved*) — the name of two Old Testament men:
1. An Israelite who participated in the dedication of the rebuilt wall of Jerusalem (Neh. 12:32).
2. The father of Jezaniah (Jer. 42:1) and Azariah (Jer. 43:2).

HOSHAMA [HOSH uh muh] (*Jehovah has heard*) — a son of Jeconiah, king of Judah, who was carried away captive by Nebuchadnezzar (1 Chr. 3:18).

HOSHEA [hoe SHEE ah] (*salvation*) — the name of four men in the Old Testament:
1. Another name of Joshua the son of Nun (Num. 13:8, 16).
2. The 19th and last king of Israel (2 Kin. 15:30; 17:1–6; 18:1, 9–10). Hoshea became king after he assassinated the former king, Pekah. Hoshea did evil in God's sight, but not to the extent of former kings. While he did not wipe out idolatrous worship, he at least did not give official approval to the practice. When Hoshea took the throne, he served as a puppet king under Assyria. But he eventually quit sending tribute money to Assyria and began negotiating an alliance with Egypt. When the Assyrian king, Shalmaneser V, learned of Hoshea's rebellion and conspiracy, he advanced toward Israel. Hoshea tried to buy off the king with tribute, but the capital city of Samaria was besieged and Hoshea was captured and imprisoned. After two years, Assyria finally captured Samaria, and its inhabitants were carried away to new locations in the Assyrian Empire (2 Kin. 17:18–23).
3. A son of Azaziah (1 Chr. 27:20) and an Ephraimite ruler in David's time.
4. A resident of Jerusalem during the rebuilding of Jerusalem's wall under Nehemiah (Neh. 10:23); he signed a covenant to keep God's law.

HOSPITALITY — the practice of entertaining strangers graciously. Hospitality was a very important trait in Bible times. In the New Testament, the Greek word translated as hospitality literally means "love of strangers." In the Old Testament, Abraham was the host to angels unaware; he invited strangers into his house, washed their feet, prepared fresh meat, had Sarah bake bread, and later accompanied them as they left (Gen. 18:1–15). Even today a traditional greeting to the guests among the Bedouin people of the Middle East is "You are among your family."

Hospitality was specifically commanded by God (Lev. 19:33–34; Luke 14:13–14; Rom. 12:13). It was to be characteristic of all believers (1 Pet. 4:9), especially bishops (Titus 1:–78; 1 Tim. 3:2). Jesus emphasized the importance of hospitality by answering the question of who should inherit the kingdom: "I was a stranger and you took Me in" (Matt. 25:35).

Several Old Testament personalities set a good

example for all believers in the practice of hospitality. These included Abraham (Gen. 18:1–8); David (2 Sam. 6:19); the Shunammite woman (2 Kin. 4:8–10); Nehemiah (Neh. 5:17–18); and Job (Job 31:17–20).

Psalm 23 concludes with a portrait of a host who prepares a table for the weary, anoints the head of the guest with oil, and shows every kindness so that the guest's cup runs over. The psalmist sees the Lord Himself as Host; His hospitality exceeds all others.

The New Testament also gives examples of gracious hospitality: Mary (Matt. 26:6–13); Martha (Luke 10:38); the early Christians (Acts 2:45–46); Lydia (Acts 16:14–15); and Priscilla and Aquila (Acts 18:26).

HOST — a person who entertains guests in his home and shows HOSPITALITY to strangers. Perhaps because of their own history as wanderers in the deserts, hospitality was important to the Hebrew people. Guests were welcomed and provided for (Gen. 18:1–8; 2 Kin. 4:8–17). A host would go to great lengths to protect his guests (Judg. 19:16–24). This was considered a sign of faithfulness to God (Job 31:32; Is. 58:7).

HOST OF HEAVEN — heavenly beings created by God and associated with Him in His rule over the world. God is a social being who brings other families into being and implants His divine image in them. The families of earth bear this image (Ps. 19:1–6; Rom. 1:19–20), as does the host of heaven (Is. 45:12). At the angel's announcement to the shepherds of the birth of Jesus, a multitude of the heavenly host praised God (Luke 2:13). They served as a great choir of created heavenly beings who glorified their Creator and participated in the background of the new age of salvation.

God is also called "the Lord of hosts" (Is. 1:9; 10:23; Rom. 9:29, RSV). The host of heaven consists of angelic beings and celestial bodies whom God has created and whose principal role, like ours, is to serve and glorify Him (1 Kin. 22:19; Ps. 103:19–21; Is. 40:26).

But the host of heaven can become demonic, rebel against God, and come under His judgment (Is. 24:21; 34:4). God's people must not give undue attention or worship to the host of heaven. Scripture warns of God's judgment upon those who love and serve created things like the host of heaven (2 Kin. 23:5; Acts 7:42; Gal. 4:3, 9). All things are created by God to demonstrate His glory and should be enjoyed as such. But these must never displace God the Creator.

HOSTAGE — a person held as a prisoner to insure good behavior, ransom payments, or certain other concessions from an opposing force. When Jehoash, king of Israel, defeated the nation of Judah, he took hostages back to Samaria to keep Judah from launching a counterattack (2 Kin. 14:14; 2 Chr. 25:24).

HOSTS, LORD OF (see GOD, NAMES OF).

HOTHAM [HOE tham] (*signet ring*) — the name of two men in the Old Testament:

1. A son of Heber (1 Chr. 7:32). Hotham is probably the same person as Helem (v. 35).

2. An AROERITE whose two sons Shama and Jeiel were among David's mighty men (1 Chr. 11:44; Hothan, KJV).

HOTHAN [HOE than] — A form of HOTHAM.

HOTHIR [HOE thur] (*abundance*) — a Levite in charge of the 21st division of singers in the tabernacle service (1 Chr. 25:4).

HOUGH [hok] — KJV word for HAMSTRING.

HOUND (see ANIMALS OF THE BIBLE).

HOUR — one of the 24 parts of a day. An hour was the shortest measurement of time among the people of the ancient world. It was a 12th part of the period from sunrise to sunset, and thus was of constantly changing length, according to the season of the year. The KJV phrase "the same hour" (Dan. 3:6, 15) occurs in the NKJV as "immediately." The word hour is sometimes used generally of time. For instance, Daniel was astonished for one hour (Dan. 4:19, KJV) or for a time (NKJV). A normal working day, from sunrise to sunset, was 12 hours (Matt. 20:1–12).

HOUSE, HOUSES — the structures in which people lived in Bible times. The word translated as house appears often in the Bible. It is used of any dwelling place, whether the hut of a peasant, the palace of a king, or the temple of God. Many different kinds and sizes of houses existed in biblical times. The style and size was dictated by tradition and the resources of the family. Those with money usually had two–story homes with a number of rooms. Local customs and available materials dictated the construction techniques used to build these houses.

Houses were not always built of stone or brick or made from mud. Many people in the Bible, such as Abraham and Moses, spent much of their lives in TENTS. Those whose livelihood depended upon sheep and goats moved their livestock from place to place to take advantage of the available pastureland. Obviously, such people had to live in tents. Others lived in tents for part of the year and in permanent houses for the rest. A farmer, for example, might live in the city for safety, except when he needed to be stationed close to his fields during the growing season.

Some people in all periods of Bible history lived in caves. Common in the limestone hills of central Israel, caves had several advantages over a house. Maintenance and upkeep was low. A cave is also cool in the summer and warm in the winter. Caves often served also as stables for livestock as well as a place to live. According to early Christian tradition, the stable in Bethlehem that became the place of Jesus' birth was located in such a cave.

Most people lived in walled villages and towns for protection from outlaws and foreign armies.

A full-size reconstruction, showing what a typical house of Palestine might have looked like about 750 B.C. Notice the holes in the walls, which let air and light in and allowed smoke to escape.

Conditions inside a town were crowded, with houses built next to each other, separated only by narrow streets. Town planning was rare during those times. It is sometimes difficult to tell from the archaeological remains of a group of houses just where one ended and another began. A particular room might belong to one house in one time, but when the city was rebuilt some time later, the same room might be joined to the house next door.

Roof. The typical roof of houses in Palestine throughout the biblical period was made by laying logs or beams across the top of the walls. Next, branches and thatch were laid on top of the beams, which were then covered by a layer of clay. To keep it waterproof, the clay was renewed by treatment with special rollers periodically. During Jesus' day, some houses of Palestine were built along Roman lines with sloping roofs covered with baked clay tiles; but such houses were rare.

Since it was flat, the roof became a vital part of the house. An outside staircase gave easy access, and a low wall around the roof kept members of the family from falling off. In a crowded city, the roof provided needed open space. It was a place to dry fruit and grains, wash clothes, and catch the cool evening breezes on hot nights. Sometimes an extra room was added on the roof to serve as a spare bedroom or as a storage room. The Shunammite woman prepared a room for the prophet Elisha, who frequently stayed at her house while visiting the area (2 Kin. 4:8–11).

Doors and Windows. Doorways within the house usually were covered with curtains, but the outside doorway generally had a wooden door. Doors turned on two pivots that fitted into sockets. In a two-story house, windows were located on the second floor. If the house had a central courtyard, most of the windows opened onto it. This provided security and privacy. Glass windows were unknown in Bible times. Most windows were left open, with perhaps a lattice or shutter providing security and reduced visibility from the outside.

Floor. The most common floor in houses during Bible times was packed clay. Other possibilities were a layer of plaster on top of the clay or thin pieces of limestone rock, called flagstones. During the time of Christ, mosaic floors were quite common among the wealthy. These were made by setting small cubes of stone in wet plaster. Usually white limestone cubes were used, but sometimes elaborate designs were made by using different colored stones.

Walls. The most common materials used for the walls of houses in Palestine were mud bricks or rough field stones.

These were often covered with a layer of plaster, which would be whitewashed. This brightened the interior of the home considerably. The walls of the wealthy were more elaborately decorated. The walls might be painted with different colors. Wood panels and inlays of ivory were also common in the houses of the wealthy.

Furnishings. The typical Israelite house was simply furnished, more like the homes of peasants a century or so ago than the modern homes of today. Mats covered the floors in some rooms, although the wealthy might have rugs. Inside lighting was poor, with small oil lamps providing some addi-

Reconstructed interior of a typical Palestinian house in Old Testament times. Notice the cooking stove, or clay oven, to the left of center; the horizontal loom (left); and the eating area, with mat and bowls, in the background.

tional light. Furniture was simple, consisting of chairs and a table for eating, perhaps a storage chest or two, and mats on a bed frame. The wealthy had more elaborate versions of this furniture, often with ivory inlays and trimming in gold and silver.

A central heating system, even a fireplace, was unheard of during these times. Because the climate in Palestine is mild, heat sources were not needed. Fires for cooking were usually built outside in the courtyard, or inside a room, with the smoke escaping from a window. Heat in the winter was sometimes provided by a small portable fire pan in which a fire was kept burning. King Jehoiakim of Judah probably cut up the scroll of Jeremiah's prophecies and burned it in such a fire pan (Jer. 36:23).

Food Preparation and Sanitation. Food was usually prepared in the courtyard outside the house. An oven and an open fire provided the normal means of cooking food. An oven consisted of a pile of stones and bricks. A fire in one part heated the whole oven to a high temperature. Food was then cooked by placing it in another part of the oven or on top of the fire.

Food storage was an important consideration, since most families grew their own food and stored it during the long, dry summer. Grains and dried fruits were stored in huge pottery jars kept in a special storage room in or near the house. Sometimes the jars were buried in the ground with only the mouth of the jars above ground. If the house did not have its own cistern, a large water jar was also kept nearby.

Most houses had their own cisterns. These were large chambers beneath the house, lined with plaster to make them waterproof. Rainwater falling on the roof was channeled to the cistern and stored there until the dry season. Drinking water was kept in a large pottery jar. These jars were excellent water coolers because the water seeped through the unglazed pottery and evaporated on the surface. This process cooled the rest of the water.

Sanitation measures varied considerably, depending upon the period of time and the particular city involved. Many cities had no provisions for the disposal of human waste. It may have been collected in chamber pots, carried outside the city, and used to fertilize the fields. Some rooms with toilets have been discovered by archaeologists. In some cities archaeologists have also discovered pipes buried in the ground, designed to carry water outside the city walls. Caesarea, the major port city in Palestine in the time of Christ, had a clever method of cleansing its sewers. The sewers, built at sea level and connected to the sea, were flushed twice each day by the incoming and outgoing tides.

Trash disposal was a problem in ancient times as it is today, although garbage did not exist in the volume our modern culture produces. Trash was usually carried outside the city and burned or dumped. Burning garbage was so common in the Hinnom Valley just south of Jerusalem that the valley became the source of the Greek word for hell used in the New Testament (*gehenna*).

Houses of the Patriarchal Period. The ancestors of Abraham came from the city of Ur. If this was the famous Ur of southern Iraq, it was a major city.

This Ur was partially excavated in the early 1900s. Large palaces, royal tombs, and many homes were uncovered. The typical house of Mesopotamia, the entire region between the Tigris and Euphrates Rivers, at this time was two stories tall, built right next to adjoining homes. The focus of the house was a central courtyard, surrounded by a series of rooms on both floors. The windows and doors opened onto this courtyard, thus giving privacy.

Rooms on the first floor were used for storage, servants' quarters, and animals. The second floor contained the bedrooms and living quarters of the owners.

Further west toward the Mediterranean Sea, the Canaanites of this time had divided the land into a number of small city–states, each consisting of one large town and several satellite villages. Excavations of these towns have uncovered evidence of a class-oriented society. A few large houses are evident, but the majority of the people lived in crowded quarters, with small homes built on top of one another. No typical layout for the small homes existed. The large houses tended to follow the plan of Mesopotamian homes of that time, with the rooms organized around a central courtyard.

Abraham and his immediate descendants did not live in such houses, since they were nomads, traveling from place to place and living in tents. They did visit towns frequently, however, and were probably familiar with such homes in Mesopotamia and ancient Canaan.

Houses of Israel and Judah. Although houses were built in a variety of styles and sizes during Bible times, there was a distinctly Israelite dwelling; it is usually called the four–room house. It consisted of an open courtyard, with rooms stretching along both sides of this open space. Another room or two was situated at one end so that the overall shape of the house was a rectangle. Entrance into the home was through a door leading into the courtyard. Sometimes one or both of the long rooms flanking the courtyard were open on the side that faced the courtyard. In these houses several large stone pillars supported the roof.

The houses averaged about 900 to 1000 square feet in area, with about one–fourth of that area as the courtyard. Many houses had second stories, almost doubling the size of the dwelling. This style of house has been found at sites all over Israel. Some towns, such as Tell Beit Mirsim, have many of these houses, all about the same size and well designed. This suggests that they were built at the same time following some overall plan.

Houses of New Testament Times. During this period the homes of the poor were not very different from what they had been centuries earlier. The building materials were similar; walls were built of rubble covered with plaster or mud bricks. Roofs were usually flat, serving also as living space.

The houses of the wealthy gave evidence of the long Persian occupation of the land of Palestine and the later influence of the Greeks. The floors of these more elaborate houses were often paved with mosaic tiles in beautiful designs. Arched roofs of bricks first appeared during the fifth century B.C. By the time of Christ, these were common throughout the land. Courtyards remained a vital part of the house, but they were often surrounded by porches. A few homes in Jerusalem from this time, with fragments of beautiful paintings of animals, have been uncovered by archaeologists.

HOUSEHOLD — all the people who lived together in the same family in Bible times. Israelite families were larger than ours today. The family included the immediate family and all who lived together in the same house. This included slaves, concubines, foreign residents, and servants. When Abraham circumcised all the males in his household (Gen. 17:23, 27), he included his servants and slaves. The household and their possessions moved as a unit (1 Sam. 27:3; 2 Sam. 15:16). When Obed-edom kept the ark, he and his household were given a special blessing by David (2 Sam. 6:11). In the New Testament, entire households were sometimes baptized together (Acts 16:15; 1 Cor. 1:16).

Household is also used in a spiritual or symbolic sense. United by God's election and salvation through Jesus Christ, Christians are included in God's household of faith (Gal. 6:10; Eph. 2:19).

HOUSEHOLDER — the owner of a house or head of a household (Matt. 13:52). The NKJV translates the same Greek word as owner (Matt. 13:27), landowner (Matt. 20:1), and master of the house (Mark 14:14).

HOUSETOP — the flat roof of a house. In Bible times, the housetop was used as a sitting area. Open to cool breezes in the evening, the housetop overlooked the streets of the city. It was an ideal place for proclaiming public messages; thus Jesus told the disciples to "preach on the housetops" (Matt. 10:27). Also see HOUSE.

HOZAI [HOE zay eye] (meaning unknown) — an unknown prophet who left a record of some of the events of King Manasseh's life (2 Chr. 33:19).

HUB — the center portion of a wheel to which the spokes are attached (1 Kin. 7:33).

HUKKOK [HUH kahk] (*ditch*) — a town on the border of Naphtali near Aznoth Tabor (Josh. 19:34). The site of Hukkok probably is identical with present–day Yakuk (or Yaquq), about ten kilometers (six miles) northeast of Tell Hum (Capernaum).

HUKOK [HUH kahk] (*hewn*) — a city on the boundary of Asher (1 Chr. 6:75), identical with HELKATH (Josh. 19:25).

HUL [huhl] (*circle*) — the second son of Aram and a grandson of Shem (Gen. 10:23).

HULDAH [HUHL duh] (*weasel*) — a prophetess consulted when the lost Book of the Law was found (2 Chr. 34:22–28). An indication of the esteem in which Huldah was held can be seen in Josiah's action. When the Book of the Law was found, he consulted her rather than Jeremiah. Huldah prophesied Jerusalem's destruction but added that because Josiah had done what was right in God's sight, it would not happen before Josiah died.

HUMAN SACRIFICE — a pagan rite in which a human being, often the firstborn child, was offered to a god to atone for sin or secure the god's favor. God distinctly prohibited the Hebrew people from imitating their heathen neighbors by offering up human beings as sacrifices (Lev. 20:2-5; Deut. 18:10). God's command to Abraham to sacrifice Isaac was no exception, because this was done to test Abraham and his faith (Gen. 22:1-19).

In times of rebellion and idolatry, the Israelites sometimes copied their neighbors in sacrificing children to Molech and other gods. The Valley of HINNOM was often the scene of these activities (Jer. 19:5-6; 32:35). Specific instances of human sacrifice mentioned in the Bible include the burning of his son on the city wall by the king of Moab (2 Kin. 3:26-27), and Kings Ahaz and Manasseh making their sons "pass through the fire" (2 Kin. 16:3; 21:6). Jephthah's offering of his daughter may be another example (Judg. 11:29-40).

HUMILITY — a freedom from arrogance that grows out of the recognition that all we have and are comes from God. The Greek philosophers despised humility because it implied inadequacy, lack of dignity, and worthlessness to them. This is not the meaning of humility as defined by the Bible. Jesus is the supreme example of humility (Matt. 11:29; Mark 10:45; John 13:4-17; Phil. 2:5-8), and He is completely adequate and of infinite dignity and worth. Biblical humility is not a belittling of

An oven in Carthage, where infants were sacrificed as a worship ritual. This practice was strictly forbidden among the Hebrew people because of the high value which God placed on human life (Lev. 20:1-5; Jer. 32:35).

Photo by Howard Vos

oneself (Matt. 6:16-18; Rom. 12:3), but an exalting or praising of others, especially God and Christ (John 3:30; Phil. 2:3). A humble person, then, focuses more on God and others than on himself.

Biblical humility is also a recognition that by ourselves we are inadequate, without dignity and worthless. Yet, because we are created in God's image and because believers are in Christ, we have infinite worth and dignity (1 Cor. 4:6-7; 1 Pet. 1:18-19). True humility does not produce pride but gratitude. Since God is both our Creator and Redeemer, our existence and righteousness depend on Him (John 15:5; Acts 17:28; Eph. 2:8-10).

HUMPS — the fleshy mounds on the backs of camels where reserve food is stored in the form of fat (Is. 30:6; bunches, KJV). These humps enable camels to make long trips with very little food or water.

HUMTAH [HUHM tuh] (*place of lizards*) — a town in the hill country of Judah near Hebron (Josh. 15:54).

HUNCHBACK (see DISABILITIES AND DEFORMITIES).

HUNDRED, TOWER OF THE — a tower on the wall of Jerusalem between the Sheep Gate and the Tower of Hananeel (Neh. 3:1; 12:39; Tower of Meah, KJV). It was one of the most important places on the wall restored by Nehemiah.

HUNGER — a strong need or intense desire for food (Prov. 19:15; Jer. 38:9). The Hebrew word translated hunger is also translated as famine to indicate a widespread and serious shortage of food (Gen. 12:10). Those who partake of Jesus, the Bread of Life, will never hunger (John 6:35).

HUNTER (see OCCUPATIONS AND TRADES).

HUPHAM [HOO fuhm] (*coast inhabitant*) — a descendant of Benjamin and the founder of a tribal family, the HUPHAMITES (Num. 26:39). He is also called Huppim, meaning "coast people" and Huram (Gen. 46:21).

HUPHAMITES [HOO fuhm ights] — members of a tribal family descended from HUPHAM (Num. 26:39).

HUPPAH [HUH puh] (*covering*) — a priest responsible for one of the divisions of service in the sanctuary in David's time (1 Chr. 24:13).

HUPPIM [HUH pim] — a form of HUPHAM.

HUR [her] (*noble*) — the name of six men in the Old Testament:

1. A leader who, with Aaron, held up Moses' hands at Rephidim so the army of Israel could defeat the forces of Amalek (Ex. 17:10, 12). Aaron and Hur were also left in charge of the people while Moses went up onto Mt. Sinai (Ex. 24:14).

2. A son of Caleb by Ephrath, grandfather of Bezaleel. Hur was filled with the Spirit by the Lord to work on the tabernacle (Ex. 38:22; 1 Chr. 2:19, 50; 2 Chr. 1:5).

3. One of the five kings of Midian. Hur was killed by the invading forces of Joshua (Num. 31:8; Josh. 13:21).

4. Father of Ben–Hur, an officer in Solomon's administration (1 Kin. 4:8).

5. A son of Judah (1 Chr. 4:1).

6. Father of Rephaiah, who helped repair Jerusalem's wall in Nehemiah's time (Neh. 3:9).

HURAI [HYUR igh] (*noble*) — one of David's mighty men (1 Chr. 11:32), also called Hiddai (2 Sam. 23:30).

HURAM [HUR uhm] (*lofty brother*) — the name of three Old Testament men:

1. A descendant of Bela and grandson of Benjamin (1 Chr. 8:5).

2. A king of Tyre who formed an alliance with David and Solomon (2 Chr. 2:13).

3. A master craftsman from Tyre employed by Solomon (2 Chr. 4:16), also called Hiram (1 Kin. 7:13).

HURI [HUR ree] (*linen weaver*) — the father of Abihail (1 Chr. 5:14).

HUSBAND — a woman's marriage partner. In Hebrew society, the husband was the absolute authority in the home. But the apostle Paul called on husbands to temper their authority with the higher value of love: "Husbands, love your wives" (Eph. 5:25). The apostle Paul compared the relationship between Christ and the church to the husband–wife union (Eph. 5:23). Also see FAMILY.

HUSBANDMAN (see OCCUPATIONS AND TRADES).

HUSHAH [HUH shah] (*haste*) — a son of Ezer and a member of the family of Judah (1 Chr. 4:4).

HUSHAI [HOO shigh] (*quick*) — a friend and wise counselor of King David (2 Sam 15:32, 37). During Absalom's revolt, Hushai remained faithful to David and became a spy for him in Jerusalem. He probably was the father of Baana, one of Solomon's 12 officers (1 Kin. 4:16).

HUSHAM [HYOO shuhm] (*hastily*) — a king of Edom (Gen. 36:34–35).

HUSHATHITE [HYOO shuh thight] (*dweller in Hushah*) — a native of HUSHAH (2 Sam. 21:18; 23:27).

HUSHIM [HYOO shim] (*hastily*) — the name of two men and one woman in the Old Testament:

1. A son of Dan (Gen. 46:23), also called Shuham (Num. 26:42).

2. A son of Aher, of the tribe of Benjamin (1 Chr. 7:12).

3. A Moabitess and one of the wives of Shaharaim (1 Chr. 8:11).

HUSK — KJV word for POD.

HUT — a shelter or lean–to made of tree limbs to provide temporary shelter. The prophet Isaiah

spoke of God's judgment as a strong wind that would flatten such flimsy buildings (Is. 1:8; 24:10; cottage, KJV).

HUZ [huhz] (*firmness*) — the oldest son of Nahor and Milcah (Gen. 22:21; Uz, NAS, NEB, NIV).

HUZZAB [HUH zuhb] (meaning unknown) — the name of an Assyrian queen, or more likely, a poetic reference to Nineveh, the "queen" city of Assyria (Nah. 2:7, KJV).

HYACINTH (see MINERALS OF THE BIBLE).

HYENA (see ANIMALS OF THE BIBLE).

HYKSOS [HICK soss] (*rulers of foreign countries*) — a people of the ancient Near East who ruled Egypt from about 1700–1550 B.C. The origin of the Hyksos is uncertain. They probably came from Asia. Some scholars believe they were Amorites from the Mesopotamian region. The Hyksos apparently also include Hurrian and Indo–European peoples.

While ruling in Egypt, their capital was situated at Avaris (the biblical Zoan), in the northwest corner of the Nile Delta (Num. 13:22; Is. 19:11, 13; Ezek. 30:14). The Hyksos introduced the horse and chariot into the Nile Valley. The Egyptians were quick to adopt this implement of warfare. While they were an important people, the Hyksos are not mentioned in the Bible. Also see EGYPT.

HYMENAEUS [high muh NEE uhs] (meaning unknown) — an early Christian who denied the faith (1 Tim. 1:19–20; 2 Tim. 2:16–17). His message was heretical because he claimed the resurrection of the dead was already past. His "profane and vain babblings...spread like cancer" and destroyed the faith of believers.

HYPOCRISY — pretending to be what one is not. The New Testament meaning of hypocrisy and hypocrite reflects its use in Greek drama. In the Greek theater, a hypocrite was one who wore a mask and played a part on the stage, imitating the speech, mannerisms, and conduct of the character portrayed.

Throughout His ministry, Jesus vigorously exposed and denounced the hypocrisy of many who opposed Him, especially the scribes and Pharisees. They paraded their charitable deeds, praying and fasting as a theatrical display to win the praise of men (Matt. 6:1–2, 5, 16). They sought to give the appearance of being godly, but they were actually blind to the truth of God (Luke 20:19–20).

The apostle Paul encountered hypocrisy among some Jewish Christians, who refused to eat with the Gentile converts. Paul pointed out that "sincere [literally, unhypocritical] love" is one of the marks of Christian ministry. And he exhorted his readers to behave like Christians: "Let love be without hypocrisy" (Rom. 12:9).

HYSSOP (see PLANTS OF THE BIBLE).

I

I AM (see GOD, NAMES OF).

IBEX (see ANIMALS OF THE BIBLE).

IBHAR [IB hahr] (*God chooses*) — a son of David born at Jerusalem (2 Sam. 5:15).

IBLEAM [IB lih uhm] (*he destroys the people*) — a town in the territory of Issachar assigned to the half-tribe of Manasseh west of the Jordan River (Josh. 17:11). The tribe failed to expel the inhabitants, and so the Canaanites continued to dwell in the land (Judg. 1:27). Ibleam may be the same place as Bileam (1 Chr. 6:70). The site is Khirbet Bel'ameh, about 16 kilometers (10 miles) southeast of Megiddo.

IBNEIAH [ib NEE uh] (*Jehovah builds*) — a son of Jeroham and the head of a Benjamite family that returned from the Captivity (1 Chr. 9:8).

IBNIJAH [ib NIGH juh] (*Jehovah builds*) — a Benjamite and the father of Reuel (1 Chr. 9:8).

IBRI [IB righ] (meaning unknown) — a Levite during the reign of King David (1 Chr. 24:27).

IBSAM [IB sahm] — a form of JIBSAM.

IBZAN [IB zan] (*swift*) — a judge who ruled over Israel, or a portion of it (Judg. 12:8–10). He had 30 sons and 30 daughters and was a man of wealth and influence.

ICE — frozen water. The Old Testament mentions ice in connection with God's power (Job 37:10; frost, KJV; 38:29). Because Palestine has a mild climate, ice, snow, and frost are rare except in the highest mountains. The summit of Mount Hermon is covered with SNOW all year round. Also see WEATHER.

ICHABOD [IK uh bahd] (*inglorious*) — a son of Phinehas and grandson of Eli, the high priest. Several national and family tragedies prompted the wife of Phinehas to name her child Ichabod, declaring, "The glory has departed from Israel!" (1 Sam. 4:21).

ICONIUM [eye KOE nih uhm] (meaning unknown) — the capital of the province of Lycaonia in central Asia Minor. Iconium was visited by Paul and Barnabas when they were expelled from Antioch of Pisidia (Acts 13:51). Paul's ministry at Ico-

nium was blessed by the salvation of many Jews and Gentiles (Acts 14:1). But persecution overtook them, and they had to flee for their lives (Acts 14:6; 19, 21). Iconium is known today as Konya, or Konia.

IDALAH [ID uh luh] (*memorial of God*) — a town in the territory of Zebulun (Josh. 19:15), known today as Khirbet el-Hawarah, near Nazareth.

IDBASH [ID bash] (*corpulent*) — one of the sons of the father of Etam (1 Chr. 4:3).

IDDO [IH doe] (*festal*) — the name of six or seven men in the Old Testament:
1. The father of Ahinadab, one of Solomon's 12 administrative officers (1 Kin. 4:14).
2. A Levite of the family of Gershon (1 Chr. 6:21; Gershom, KJV, RSV, NEB). He is also called Adaiah (1 Chr. 6:41).
3. A son of Zechariah. Iddo was a captain of the tribe of Manasseh in Gilead, east of the Jordan River, in David's time (1 Chr. 27:21).
4. A seer or prophet who wrote about three of the kings of Israel: Solomon (2 Chr. 9:29), Rehoboam (2 Chr. 12:15), and Abijah (2 Chr. 13:22).
5. The grandfather of the prophet Zechariah (Ezra 5:1; 6:14).
6. A leader of the Jews living at Casiphia, an unidentified place in Babylon (Ezra 8:17).
7. The head of a family of priests who returned to Jerusalem with Zerubbabel after the Captivity (Neh. 12:4, 16). He may be the same person as Iddo No. 5.

IDLE — useless, inactive, lazy. The Bible declares that the idle person will come to poverty and suffer hunger (Prov. 14:23; 19:15).

IDOL, IMAGE — a representation or symbol of an object of worship; a false god. In a few places in the Bible, the word image appears in a neutral sense, not referring to a man-made object of worship. Adam, created in the image of God (Gen. 1:26), or Christ, the visible image of the invisible God (2 Cor. 4:4; Col. 1:15) are examples of this.

Most of the time, however, image refers to a statue or something of human manufacture which people have substituted for the true and living God. Occasionally it appears in the same sentence with idol (Lev. 26:1; 2 Chr. 33:7).

Photo by Gustav Jeeninga

Remains of the temple of Artemis at Sardis, a lavish pagan shrine which symbolized the idolatry and false worship practices of the ancient world.

In biblical times idols were made in different ways and of various materials. Judges 17:3 speaks of "a carved image and a molded image." Some were made of metal or wood, and others were poured into a mold or shaped by hand. The silver or gold idols were poured, but the clay ones could also be shaped by hand. The image in Nebuchadnezzar's dream (Dan. 2:32–33) was of gold, silver, bronze, iron, and clay.

In a satire on idolatry, the prophet Isaiah provided considerable detail about the making of idols (Is. 44:9–20). He described the smith with his tongs and hammer and the carpenter with his ruler, line, planes, and compass. Isaiah also ridiculed the idolmakers by noting that such a statue has to be nailed down "that it might not totter" (Is. 41:7).

Perhaps the best definition of an idol is something we ourselves make into a god. It does not have to be a statue or a tree. It can be anything that stands between us and God or something we substitute for God.

IDOLATRY — the worship of something created as opposed to the worship of the Creator Himself. Scores of references to idolatry appear in the Old Testament. This shows that idolatry probably was the greatest temptation our spiritual forefathers faced. While we find bowing down to a statue no temptation, they apparently slipped into idolatry constantly. So serious was this sin that the prohibition against the making and worshiping of images was included as the second of the Ten Commandments (Ex. 20:4–6).

Israel's ancient neighbors believed there were many gods. They worshiped whatever gods were necessary at a given time. An equally erroneous notion was that these gods either were the idols themselves or were represented by idols. Some people probably insisted that the idol was only an aid to worship and not the object of worship itself. But this distinction must have been hard to keep in mind. That is why the Bible strictly forbids the making of images of any kind—because they themselves receive the worship—a worship which God jealously reserves for Himself.

Archaeologists have discovered idols of most of the pagan gods mentioned in the Bible, in addition to many unidentified ones. Since the Romans began emperor worship late in the New Testament period, some of the elegant statues of the Caesars discovered by archaeologists must have been idols to be worshiped.

Idolatry can take many forms, and it has persisted from the earliest times. Joshua 24:2 states that Abraham's father served idols. Perhaps the earliest reference in the Bible to idols is the "household idols" or TERAPHIM (small clay figurines) which Rachel stole from her father Laban (Gen. 31:34).

The next noteworthy instance of idolatry was Aaron's making of the golden calf at the foot of Mount Sinai. This happened when the Israelites lost their patience waiting for Moses to return with the revelation of the true and living God (Ex. 32:1–4). Some have tried to defend Aaron's action by saying that the calf was merely the seat which the invisible God occupied. Certainly Moses did not understand idolatry that way. The incident at Baal of Peor (Num. 25:1–3) also involved the worship of an idol.

The conquest of Canaan by the Hebrews brought new temptations to worship the object created rather than the Creator. Joshua 24:15 poses the classic question: Whom will you serve? The gods of Egypt where you have lived? The gods of the Amorites where you now dwell? Or Yahweh the God of Israel? As always, some made the wrong choices (Judges 17—18). A man made an idol for his personal use, but the tribe of Dan took it over for their own use. The Bible does not indicate what shape that statue was in or what god it represented.

Others tried the route of compromise: the mixing of idolatry with worship of the true God. So Gideon's ephod was made an object of worship (Judg. 8:24–27). Much later there was another instance of an otherwise good symbol of God's deliverance turned into an idol. In King Hezekiah's time the people worshiped Moses' bronze snake (Num. 21:9; 2 Kin. 18:4).

While idolatry was held in check during most of the period of the United Kingdom under David and Solomon, it burst forth again after the separation of the Israelites into two nations in 922 B.C. In fact, Jeroboam I made two calf idols and installed them at the major cities in the north and the south (Dan and Bethel) for the purpose of keeping his people's religious allegiance within the borders of the new kingdom (1 Kin. 12:27–30). He was afraid if they returned to Jerusalem they might also return to the Lord, and that would spell political disaster for him.

All the successive monarchs in the northern kingdom of Israel were bad. Invariably their sin involved idolatry. Starting with Elijah, the prophets called on the people to turn from the worship of false gods back to reverence for the true God. Ho-

Bronze idol of Baal, pagan god of war and fertility. Idols such as this were frequently plated with gold (Is. 40:19).

sea's entire book is devoted to preaching against idolatry. Under the figure of speech of divorcing the Lord and marrying Baal, he tied together the ideas of idolatry, spiritual adultery, and literal adultery (Hos. 2:2; 4:2, 13; 7:4; 8:5; 13:2).

Although there were some good kings in the southern kingdom of Judah, the bad ones invariably fell to idolatry. This prompted the major prophets—Isaiah, Jeremiah, and Ezekiel—and most of the minor prophets as well to ridicule, condemn, and warn against idolatry. A sampling of courageous declarations from these courageous preachers would include Isaiah 2:8; Jeremiah 50:2; Ezekiel 6:4–6; Micah 1:7; Habakkuk 2:18; and Zechariah 13:2.

The captivity of the people of Israel at the hands of the Babylonians produced a permanent cure for the sin of idolatry. Never again, even to the present time, has Judaism succumbed to idolatry.

In the gospels there is virtually nothing about idolatry, but in the letters of Paul and the other New Testament books Christians are frequently warned against idolatry. The Christians lived in a world filled with idols. Both the Romans and the Greeks used them. Paul's observation about Athens in Acts 17:16 tells it well: "He saw that the city was given over to idols."

In the New Testament period the term idolatry began to be used as an intellectual concept. Idolatry became not the actual bowing down before a statue but the replacement of God in the mind of the worshiper. Colossians 3:5 points in this direction: "Put to death...covetousness, which is idolatry." (See also Eph. 5:5.) At this point the modern believer must understand the vicious nature of idolatry. While we may not make or bow down to a statue, we must be constantly on guard that we let nothing come between us and God. As soon as anything does, that thing is an idol.

In addition to material objects such as houses, land, and cars, idols can be people, popular heroes, or those whom we love. Objects of worship can even include things like fame, reputation, hobbies, pride, and deeds done in the name of the Lord. Idolatry is a dangerous and deceitful sin. No wonder prophets preached against it so often and so strongly.

IDUMEA [id yoo MEE uh] (*land of the Edomites*) — the Greek name for the land of EDOM (Mark 3:8; also Is. 34:5–6, KJV; Ezek. 35:15, KJV; Ezek. 36:5, KJV). After the Babylonian Captivity, Idumea referred to the region south of Judea which was populated by Edomite refugees fleeing from the invasion of Arabs (see Map 6, A-5).

IGAL [EYE gal] (*Jehovah saves*) — the name of three men in the Old Testament:

1. One of the 12 spies sent by Moses to spy out the land of Canaan (Num. 13:7).

2. One of David's mighty men (2 Sam. 23:36).

3. A son of Shemaiah and a descendant of King David through King Jehoiachin (1 Chr. 3:22; Igeal, KJV, NEB).

IGDALIAH [ig duh LIGH uh] (*great is Jehovah*) — an ancestor of Hanan (Jer. 35:4).

IGEAL [IGH gih uhl] — a form of IGAL.

IIM [EYE em] — a form of IJIM.

IJE ABARIM [IGH jih AH buh rim] (*mounds or ruins*) — a place where the Israelites stopped in the wilderness on the southeastern frontier of Moab, between Oboth and the Valley of Zered (Num. 21:11; Iye–abarim, RSV, NIV, NEB).

IJIM [EYE yem] (*heaps, ruins*) — the name of an encampment and a city in the Old Testament:
  1. An encampment of the Israelites during their wilderness wandering, after the Exodus from Egypt (Num. 33:45; Iim, KJV; Iyim, NASB, NEB, NIV, RSV).
  2. A city in southern Judah (Josh. 15:29; Iim, KJV, RSV, NASB, NIV; Iyim, NEB).

IJON [IGH jahn] (*ruin*) — a fortified store–city in the hill country of Naphtali. Ijon was captured from King Baasha of Israel by King Ben–Hadad of Syria (2 Chr. 16:4). Later, the inhabitants of this city were captured by Assyria and carried into captivity (2 Kin. 15:29).

IKKESH [IK esh] (*subtle*) — a man of Tekoa and the father of Ira (2 Sam. 23:26).

ILAI [IGH ligh] (*elevated*) — one of David's mighty men (1 Chr. 11:29), also called Zalmon (2 Sam. 23:28).

ILEX (see PLANTS OF THE BIBLE).

ILLUSTRATION — something used to clarify or explain; an example that helps make something clear. Jesus used an illustration concerning the true shepherd (John 10:1–6; parable, KJV, NEB; figure, RSV; figure of speech, NIV, NASB).

ILLYRICUM [ih LIHR ih kuhm] — a Roman province in the Balkan Peninsula, stretching along the east coast of the Adriatic Sea from Italy to Macedonia (see Map 7, B–1). The apostle Paul preached the gospel of Christ "from Jerusalem and round about to Illyricum" (Rom. 15:19). Dalmatia (2 Tim. 4:10) was one of the two major divisions of Illyricum. Today, this region is known as Yugoslavia and Albania.

IMAGE (see IDOL, IMAGE).

IMAGE OF GOD — the characteristics of man with which God endowed him at creation, distinguishing him from the rest of God's creatures.
  The expression, "image of God," appears in Genesis 1:26–27; 9:6, and 1 Corinthians 11:7. Some also see a reference to this image in Romans 8:29, 2 Corinthians 3:18, and allusions to it in Psalm 8:5, 1 Corinthians 15:49, and Colossians 3:10. Jesus is referred to as being "the image of the invisible God" (Col. 1:15) and "the express image of His [God's] person" (Heb. 1:3).
  One understanding of the image of God in man is that it refers to qualities or attributes present in the

person. Thus, the image of God is identified as human reason, will, or personality. Others believe the image is something present when the person is in a relationship to God, and in fact, is that relationship. The image is present like a reflection in a mirror, rather than like a photo—a permanent image printed on paper. Still others believe the image is something which a person does. Immediately after God made man in His image, He gave man dominion or authority over the whole earth (Gen. 1:28). According to this view, this active tending and caring for God's creation constitutes the image of God in man.
  The Bible does not indicate exactly what the image of God in man is. It may involve all these ideas. Man alone has personal, conscious fellowship with God (Gen. 1:29–30; 2:15–16; 3:8). Man is to take God's place in ruling over and developing the creation (Gen. 1:26, 28). Yet these are possible only because of certain qualities of personality which man alone has (Ps. 139:14).
  To be created in the image of God means that we humans have the ability and the privilege of knowing, serving, and loving God, and that we are most fully human when fulfilling our spiritual potential. Every human life is precious to God, and this is exactly how we should treat the people with whom we share the world.

IMAGE, NEBUCHADNEZZAR'S — a human likeness seen by King Nebuchadnezzar in a dream; a gold statue set up by the King in the plain of Dura.
  In a dream, King Nebuchadnezzar of Babylon saw a frightening image, consisting of five different types of metal. The head was of fine gold, the breast and arms of silver, the abdomen and thighs of bronze, the legs of iron, and the feet of iron and clay (Dan. 2:32–33). These materials, representing four world empires, were inferior in quality from the head downward, terminating in clay. While the king was thinking about the meaning of the image, a stone broke loose from the mountains, struck against the lowest part of the image, broke the whole statue into pieces, and ground all of its material to powder (Dan. 2:34–35).
  Nebuchadnezzar's dream, as interpreted by the prophet Daniel, symbolized the ultimate end of Gentile world power at the second coming of Christ (Daniel 2 and 7; Luke 21:24; Rev. 16:19). One widely held view is that the four kingdoms represented by his dream were Babylon, Medo-Persia, Greece, and Rome. The stone that struck the image and became a great mountain symbolized the triumphant return of Christ as King of kings and Lord of lords (Dan. 2:35, 44).

IMAGERY — the products of a person's imagination. The word imagery is found only once in the NKJV: "the chambers of his imagery" (Ezek. 8:12, KJV; "room of His idols," NKJV). The Hebrew word translated as imagery may mean mental pictures or carved images, such as those of false gods.

IMAGINATION — the power of the mind to form

a mental image. The Bible uses the word imagination to refer to man's evil plans, purposes, and thoughts (Gen. 8:21; Jer. 7:24; Luke 1:51). It does not use the word to describe forming mental images of things that do not exist.

IMLA [IM luh] (*God fulfills*) — the father of Micaiah the prophet (2 Chr. 18:7-8), also spelled as Imlah (1 Kin. 22:8-9).

IMMANUEL [im MAN you ell] (*with us is God*) — a symbolic name from the prophecy of Isaiah applied in later years to Jesus the Messiah.

In the time of the prophet Isaiah, Syria and Israel were attacking Judah in an attempt to force King Ahaz of Judah to join a coalition against Assyria. Isaiah called on Ahaz to put his trust in the word of the Lord so the threat of Syria and Israel would come to nothing (Is. 7:1-9). Then the prophet announced God's intention to give Ahaz a sign that His word was true. Syria and Israel would lose their capacity to be a threat to Judah. But before this peace and prosperity becomes a reality, Isaiah announced there would be a drastic purging judgment at the hands of the king of Assyria. Only a remnant would experience the good future which God had intended for his people (Is. 7:10-25).

The sign that God promised to provide to Ahaz was the birth of a child within whose childhood years these events of promise and judgment would take place. The child would be given the name Immanuel, meaning "God with us," as a symbol of Judah's hope in the midst of adversity (Is. 8:8, 10). God would be with His people, in spite of the devastation wrought by the forces of the Assyrians (Is. 8:7-8). Immanuel offered a future and a hope for those who would place their trust in God.

The identity of this child and the circumstances of his birth are much disputed. This remarkable prophecy achieved its full meaning with the coming of Jesus. But there may have been an initial fulfillment in the eighth century B.C. when Hezekiah was born to the wicked King Ahaz. When Hezekiah took over the throne, he did lead many moral reforms that brought the people of Judah closer to God. Some scholars believe this may have been the child Isaiah had in mind when he announced this prophecy.

Regardless of Isaiah's intention, Matthew rightly recognized that hope for restoration through the house of David reached its ultimate fulfillment only with Jesus (Matt. 1:23). With the coming of Jesus, God is with us in the most profound sense. With the virgin birth God's pattern of working out His purposes through special births (Gen. 3:15; 1 Sam. 2:1-10; 2 Sam. 7:12-16) reaches its climax. And in Jesus God is with us always, even to the end of the age (Matt. 28:20).

IMMER [IM uhr] (*prominent*) — the name of a man and a place in the Old Testament:

1. A descendant of Aaron whose family had become a "father's house" by the time of David's reign (1 Chr. 24:14). The family was made the 16th of the 24 courses of priests serving the tabernacle. Some members of this family returned from the Captivity (Ezra 2:37) and lived in Jerusalem (Neh. 11:13).

2. A place in Babylonia from which Jewish exiles returned to Palestine (Neh. 7:61). They were unable to prove their genealogical lineage as Israelites.

IMMORALITY — behavior contrary to established moral principles. The word is used to describe Israel's worship of pagan gods (Ezek. 23:8, 17), an adulterous woman (Prov. 2:16), and sexual impurity (1 Cor. 5:1).

IMMORTALITY — exemption from death; the state of living forever. Thus, immortality is the opposite of mortality, or being subject to death. In the Bible, the word immortality refers primarily to the spirit, but is also used of the resurrected or transformed body.

The pagan Greeks had no concept of a bodily resurrection. Plato taught that spirit is everything and that matter is nothing. He believed the spirit lives on but the body returns to dust. In 1 Corinthians 15, Paul answered this idea. Paul also spoke of immortality and the resurrection in his sermon to the Greek philosophers on Mars Hill. Some mocked, while others said, "We will hear you again on this matter" (Acts 17:32).

The biblical concept of immortality is rooted in man's creation in God's image and likeness (Gen. 1:26-27). God is spirit. So the reference in Genesis is not to bodily form but to spiritual nature. As the Eternal, God is also immortal (1 Tim. 6:16). "And the Lord God formed man of the dust of the ground, and breathed into his nostrils the breath of life; and man became a living being" (Gen. 2:7). Like all other creatures, man has animal life. Only of man is it said that he "became a living being." God made man to live forever, physically and spiritually. At death the body returns to dust (Gen. 3:19), but the spirit lives on.

The ancient Hebrews believed in the survival of the spirit, although they thought of the afterlife as a shadowy existence. But the idea of a bodily resurrection gradually evolved (Job 19:26; Ps. 16:8-11; Dan. 12:2). In Jesus' time the Sadducees denied a bodily resurrection, while the Pharisees believed in it.

However, at least the tone of a hope of immortality pervades the entire Old Testament, including the faith of the patriarchs—Abraham, Isaac, and Jacob—in God's promises (Heb. 11:13). Abraham's near-sacrifice of Isaac (Genesis 22) is interpreted in Hebrews 11:17-9 as an act that involved faith in a resurrection.

In Jesus Christ we have God's full revelation about immortality of both body and spirit (John 11:23-26; Rom. 2:6-7; 2 Tim. 1:10). His bodily resurrection is proof of our immortality (1 Cor. 15:12-16).

The nature of the resurrection body is not clear. Some see it as like that of Jesus—a real body, but not subject to time, space, or density (Luke 24:31,

36–43; John 20:19–20, 26–29). But the matter should not be pressed too far. As our present bodies are fitted to conditions on earth, so will our resurrection bodies be suitable for conditions in heaven (1 Cor. 15:38–44).

Although death is an enemy (1 Cor. 15:26), Paul thought of death as necessary in order that believers may receive immortal, incorruptible bodies (1 Cor. 15:50–57). Those living at the Lord's return will receive transformed bodies (1 Cor. 15:51–54).

In 1 Thessalonians 4:14–17 Paul taught that "the dead in Christ will rise first. Then we who are alive and remain shall be caught up together with them in the clouds to meet the Lord in the air. And thus we shall always be with the Lord."

Jesus spoke of "the resurrection of life" and "the resurrection of condemnation" (John 5:29). Thus, we may assume that both believers and unbelievers will receive resurrection bodies—but their eternal destiny will be different. (Dan. 12:2).

IMMUTABILITY — a characteristic of God's nature which means that He does not change in His basic nature. In Him, "there is no variation or shadow of turning" (James 1:17). God does not "mutate" from being one kind of God to being another, nor is He subject to the limitations of time and space, since in Christ He upholds all things by the word of His power (Heb. 1:3). He is the Alpha and Omega, the Beginning and the End, "who is and who was and who is to come, the Almighty" (Rev. 1:8), Jesus Christ "the same yesterday, today, and forever" (Heb. 13:8), and the God of steadfast love (Deut. 5:10; Ps. 103:4; Is. 63:7).

IMNA [IM nuh] (*may he preserve*) — a son of Helem, of the tribe of Asher (1 Chr. 7:35).

IMNAH [IM nuh] (*good fortune*) — the name of two Old Testament men:

1. The oldest son of Asher (1 Chr. 7:30), also spelled Jimna (Num. 26:44) and Jimnah (Gen. 46:17).

2. The father of Kore, a Levite during the reign of King Hezekiah of Judah (2 Chr. 31:14).

IMPEDIMENT — a hindrance or obstruction. The phrase, *an impediment in his speech* occurs in the account of Jesus' healing of a deaf-mute (Mark 7:31–37). Jesus' healing of the sick and the disabled was viewed by the gospel writers as a fulfillment of the prophecy of Isaiah 35:5–6.

IMPORTUNITY — KJV word for persistence in making a request or demand. In Jesus' parable of the persistent friend (Luke 11:5–8), a man was rewarded for his importunity (persistence, NKJV, NASB, NIV; shamelessness, NEB) because he kept knocking on the door. Jesus applied this truth to the need for persistence in prayer.

IMPOTENCE (see DISABILITIES AND DEFORMITIES).

The village of Lubban (center of photo between the two highways) is the successor to the biblical city of Lebonah (Judg. 21:19). The surrounding valley is known as the Plain of Lebonah.

Photo: Levant Photo Service

IMPRECATORY PSALMS — individual psalms in the Book of Psalms in which the authors call for misfortune and disaster to strike their enemies. The writers of the psalms were often persecuted by ungodly men, so they prayed that God would pour out His wrath and righteous judgment upon their foes. Some examples of imprecatory psalms are Psalms 5, 11, 17, 35, 55, 59, 69, 109, 137, and 140. In contrast to this spirit of retaliation, Jesus taught that we should love our enemies (Matt. 5:43–48).

IMPURITY (see UNCLEAN, UNCLEANNESS).

IMPUTATION — charging or reckoning something to a person's account. A good example of the idea of imputation occurs in Philemon 18, where Paul says that any wrong or debt caused by the runaway slave, Onesimus, should be "put on my account." Three distinct theological truths in the Bible are directly related to the concept of imputation:

1. *The Imputation of Adam's Sin to His Descendants.* Romans 5:12–19 declares that God imputes the guilt of Adam's sin to all other members of the human race: "By one man's disobedience many were made sinners." "Through one's man's offense *judgment* came to all men, resulting in condemnation." "By the one man's offense death reigned through the one." This concept, also called "original sin," is touched on as well in 1 Corinthians 15:21–22.

2. *The Imputation of the Believer's Sin to Christ.* In addition to guilt imputed from Adam's sin, each individual is also charged with guilt for his personal sin. This Paul describes as "imputing their trespasses to them" (2 Cor. 5:19). The Lord Jesus, whose supernatural conception and birth freed Him from guilt from Adam's sin and who committed no personal sin, had no sin counted against Him. But when He died as our substitute, God "made Him who knew no sin to be sin for us" (2 Cor. 5:21) so that He "bore our sins in His own body on the tree" (1 Pet. 2:24). This is made explicit in the Book of Isaiah, where the prophet says of the Lord Jesus, "The Lord has laid on Him the iniquity of us all" (Is. 53:6).

3. *The Imputation of Christ's Righteousness to the Believer.* "The blessedness of the man to whom God imputes righteousness" is the theme of the fourth chapter of Romans (also 1 Cor. 1:30; 2 Cor. 5:21; Phil. 3:9). Jesus became the Holy and Just One (Acts 3:14) through His perfect obedience to God's Law (Rom. 5:19). These qualities are imputed in turn "to us who believe in Him who raised up Jesus our Lord from the dead" (Rom. 4:24). Because of this the believer will appear before God "faultless" (Jude 24). We can stand in God's presence because Jesus has imputed His righteousness and holiness to us through His sacrificial death on the Cross.

IMRAH [IM ruh] (*stubborn*) — a descendant of Zophah, of the tribe of Asher (1 Chr. 7:36).

IMRI [IM righ] (*Jehovah has promised*) — the name of two Old Testament men:

1. A son of Bani (1 Chr. 9:4). Imri may be identical with Amariah (Neh. 11:4).

2. The father of Zaccur (Neh. 3:2).

INCANTATION (see MAGIC, SORCERY, AND DIVINATION).

INCARNATION — a theological term for the coming of God's Son into the world as a human being. The term itself is not used in the Bible, but it is based on clear references in the New Testament to Jesus as a person "in the flesh" (Rom. 8:3; Eph. 2:15; Col. 1:22).

Jesus participated fully in all that it means to live a human life. But if Jesus were merely a man, no matter how great, there would be no significance in drawing attention to His bodily existence. The marvelous thing is that in Jesus, God Himself began to live a fully human life. As the apostle Paul declared, "In Him dwells all the fullness of the Godhead bodily" (Col. 2:9). The capacity of Jesus to reveal God to us and to bring salvation depends upon His being fully God and fully man at the same time.

Our human minds cannot understand how Jesus can be both fully God and fully man. But the Bible gives clear indication of how this works out in practice.

No person may see God and live (Ex. 33:20). He dwells in unapproachable light (1 Tim. 6:16). Can we, therefore, only know Him from a distance? No! God has come near in the person of Jesus (Matt. 1:23). He has taken on a form in which He can be seen, experienced, and understood by us as human beings (John 1:14, 18). Jesus reveals God to us perfectly since in His human life He is the image of God (2 Cor. 4:4), exhibiting full likeness with the Father (John 1:14). Jesus' godhood in His manhood is the key to our intimate knowledge of God.

This does not mean, however, that Jesus' humanity is only a display case for His divinity. Jesus lived out His human life by experiencing all the pressures, temptations, and limitations that we experience (Heb. 2:18; 4:15; 5:2, 7–8). That is why Jesus' life really is the supreme human success story (Heb. 5:8). Jesus was a pioneer (Heb. 2:10, RSV), showing in practical terms the full meaning and possibility of human life, lived in obedience to God. In this respect, Jesus is a kind of second Adam (Rom. 5:14–15), marking a new beginning for the human race.

Jesus would have performed a great work if He had done no more than set a perfect example. But His full humanity is also the basis on which it is possible for Him to represent us—indeed, take our place—in dying for us. The Bible makes this clear when it speaks of "one Mediator between God and men, the Man Christ Jesus, who gave Himself a ransom for all" (1 Tim. 2:5–6).

When He ascended to His Father after His resurrection, Jesus left behind some of the human restrictions experienced during His earthly life. He received at that time His original divine glory (John 17:5). But the joining together of deity and humanity that marks His incarnation did not come to an end with His ascension. Jesus took His resurrected body with Him back to heaven (Luke 24:51; Acts 1:9). In heaven now He is our divine Lord, our human leader, and the great High Priest who serves as a mediator between God and man (Heb. 3:1).

INCENSE — a sweet-smelling substance that was burned as an offering to God on the altar in the tabernacle and the Temple. The purpose of this incense offering was to honor God. Incense symbolized and expressed the prayers of the Hebrew people, which were considered a pleasant aroma offered to God.

The incense used in Israelite worship was of a specific composition, considered very sacred. The four substances from which it was made were stacte, onycha, galbanum, and pure frankincense (Ex. 30:34–35). Some of this was to be ground into powder and placed in front of the testimony in the tabernacle of meeting (Ex. 30:36). The use of any other composition of incense or of this particular compound for any other purpose was regarded as sin; this incense alone was to be considered holy (Ex. 30:36–38).

According to the law, only the priests descended from Aaron could offer incense (Lev. 2:2). The priest offered the compounded holy incense morning and evening on the altar of incense in front of the veil in the Holy Place in the tabernacle or Temple.

This incense formula specified for use in public ritual was not to be allowed for private use (Ex. 30:37, 38). Apparently some wealthy individuals were tempted to make their own private supply for personal use.

Incense is also mentioned in connection with certain pagan worship practices of the Israelites. The worship of Baal, the queen of heaven, and other foreign gods by means of incense was condemned in the Old Testament (1 Kin. 11:8). The Lord warned that he would destroy the pagan incense altars (Lev. 26:30; 2 Chr. 30:14). The burning of incense at the pagan shrines on "high places" and to other gods was strongly denounced (2 Kin. 22:17; 2 Chr. 34:25). The use of incense appeared widespread in connection with the Israelite lapses into pagan worship (Jer. 11:12, 17; 48:35).

Another misuse of incense is mentioned in 2 Chronicles 26:16–21. This passage describes how King Uzziah was afflicted by the Lord, who caused leprosy to break out on his forehead because he had attempted to burn incense in the temple. This duty was reserved for the priestly descendants of Aaron.

The New Testament church did not adopt the use of incense in worship. In fact, the use of it was considered a work of paganism and was banned by the first Christian emperors. However, later in church history incense was again widely used.

In a figurative use of the word, the psalmist requested that his prayer might be brought before the Lord as incense (Ps. 141:2). Incense possibly was also a symbol of a godly life, offered up to God as a pleasant aroma before him.

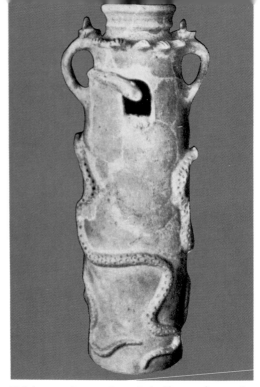

This incense burner, decorated with sacred serpents, was discovered in the excavation of the Canaanite temple at Beth Shan.

INCEST — RSV word for sexual relations with near kin, a sin expressly forbidden by the law of Moses (Lev. 20:12; perversion, NKJV). The word translated as incest by the RSV in this passage is a Hebrew word which expresses the idea of a mixing of unnatural elements. The Hebrew people were called to a higher code of sexual ethics than was practiced by their Canaanite and Egyptian neighbors. Intercourse was forbidden with one's mother, stepmother, sister, granddaughter, stepsister, aunt, daughter–in–law, sister–in–law, or stepdaughter/granddaughter.

INCH (see WEIGHTS AND MEASURES).

INDIA [IN dih uh] — a country of Asia south of the Himalaya Mountains and irrigated by the Indus River; it marked the eastern limit of the empire of Ahasuerus (Xerxes) king of Persia (Esth. 1:1; 8:9). Solomon's large fleet of ships may have visited India on their three-year voyages for "gold, silver, ivory, apes, and monkeys" (1 Kin. 10:22). This ancient country in Old Testament times covered essentially the same geographical region as the modern nations of India and Pakistan.

INFANT BAPTISM (see BAPTISM).

INFINITY — a theological term which implies that God is not bound by time and space (Col. 1:15; Heb. 1:3). God does experience everything that happens within the universe He has created. Not even a sparrow falls to the ground apart from His will. He numbers the very hairs of our head (Matt. 10:30). But at the same time, He is not limited to the process of finite space and time for His experience. God is the great and eternal I AM (Ex. 3:14) who, like the burning bush before Moses, burns with dynamic activity, yet is not consumed (Psalm 139; 147; Isaiah 45). Only an infinite God who is greater than His creation can determine the number of the stars and keep them in their courses.

INFIRMITY (see DISEASES OF THE BIBLE).

INHERITANCE — the receipt of property as a gift or by legal right, usually upon the death of one's father.

In ancient Israel the property of a deceased person was usually distributed according to law or tribal custom. Written wills were rarely used. The real and personal property of a father was normally divided among his sons. A larger amount, usually a double portion, went to the eldest son, who assumed the care of his mother and unmarried sisters.

The birthright of the firstborn son could be denied only because of a serious offense against the father, as in the case of Reuben (Deut. 21:15–17; 1 Chr. 5:1). The sons of concubines normally received presents of personal property. If there were no surviving sons, the inheritance went to daughters. The daughters had to marry within the tribe, however, or lose their inheritance. If a man died childless, his estate was received by his brothers or his father's brothers (Num. 27:9–11).

To the Hebrew mind, the term inheritance had strong spiritual and national associations extending far beyond the family estate. The land of Canaan was regarded as an inheritance from the Lord because God had promised the land to Abraham and his descendants (Num. 33:53). Both Moses and Joshua were told by the Lord to divide the land of Canaan among the tribes "as an inheritance" (Num. 26:52–53; Josh. 13:6). God directed that the land be distributed to each tribe by lot according to its population.

Each family, in turn, was assigned a parcel that was to remain in the family's possession. This sense of sacred birthright probably accounted for Naboth's refusal to sell his vineyard to King Ahab: "The Lord forbid that I should give the inheritance of my fathers to you!" (1 Kin. 21:3).

The Greeks relied more on wills for distributing an inheritance than did the Israelites. If a citizen died without a will, his sons in good standing inherited the property in equal parts, the eldest receiving the same as his brothers. Daughters received dowries, which reverted to other heirs if the daughter was divorced or remained childless. If a man had no sons, he usually adopted one to continue the family. If he had daughters, he would arrange for one of them to marry the adopted son. In that instance the major share of the inheritance fell to the daughter and her husband. If only daughters survived, the estate passed to them. If a man died

without a will and left no natural or adopted heirs, his closest male relatives received his property.

According to Roman law, the property of a man who died without a will went to his wife and children. But married daughters living with their husbands or children who had been emancipated from their father's authority did not share in the inheritance. If a man left no wife and children, the inheritance passed to his male relatives. The Romans held that a child became his father's heir the moment he was born and that the deceased lived through his heirs. Legally adopted children had full inheritance rights.

The apostle Paul's glorious concept of a spiritual inheritance for Christians is primarily of Jewish origin. But the doctrine was strongly influenced by Greek and Roman inheritance practices. Three of these influences were: (1) inheritance was regarded as immediate as well as ultimate, (2) all legitimate heirs usually shared the inheritance equally and jointly rather than a division favoring a firstborn son, and (3) legally adopted children enjoyed full inheritance rights along with natural offspring.

According to Paul, the Christian's spiritual inheritance is based strictly on our relationship to Christ. "For you are all sons of God through faith in Jesus Christ.... And if you are Christ's, then you are Abraham's seed, and heirs according to the promise" (Gal. 3:26, 29). This spiritual birthright cannot be inherited by sinners (1 Cor. 6:9–11). The present possession of the spiritual inheritance as well as its future glory is emphasized in Romans 8: "The Spirit Himself bears witness with our spirit that we are the children of God, and if children, then heirs—heirs of God and joint heirs with Christ, if indeed we suffer with Him, that we may also be glorified together" (Rom. 8:16–17).

Paul also declared that the Spirit's indwelling power is both the sign and seal that we are heirs of God's promise: "Having believed, you were sealed with the Holy Spirit of promise, who is the guarantee of our inheritance" (Eph. 1:13–14). Those who are redeemed, including the Gentiles, become God's adopted sons with full inheritance rights (Gal. 4:1–7).

Other New Testament passages present the Christian's spiritual inheritance as a reward for faithfulness and Christlikeness. Jesus invited those showing kindness in His name to "inherit the kingdom prepared for you from the foundation of the world" (Matt. 25:34). Peter counseled suffering saints in the Roman world to be patient in their trials, "That you may inherit a blessing" (1 Pet. 3:9). James declared that the poor of this world have been chosen "to be rich in faith and heirs of the kingdom" which God promised to those who love Him (James 2:5).

In a burst of joy, Peter celebrated every Christian's "living hope" of his heavenly inheritance: "To an inheritance incorruptible and undefiled and that does not fade away, reserved in heaven for you" (1 Pet. 1:3–4).

INIQUITY — unrighteousness, lawlessness. The Bible often uses this word to describe evil and wickedness. Iniquity can suggest different types of evil, such as transgressions of spiritual law and crimes against God (2 Pet. 2:16; Rev. 18:5), moral or legal wrongs (1 Cor. 13:6) or depravity and sin in general (Gen. 15:16; Ps. 51:1, 5, 9). Also see SIN.

INK — an ancient writing fluid made from powdered charcoal, lampblack, or soot mixed with water and sometimes tree resin (Jer. 36:18). In this form it could be erased with water. Iron or other metal oxides were added to make the ink more permanent and to change the color. Most ancient ink was black. Actual specimens of ink have been found in Palestine from as far back as the time of Ahab, about 850 B.C.

INKHORN — a horn or container that held writing ink. The inkhorn was apparently attached to the writer's belt (Ezek. 9:2–3).

INLET — a bay, cove, or other quiet recess along the seashore. According to the judges Deborah and Barak, "Asher continued at the seashore, and stayed by his inlets" (Judg. 5:17). This meant that the people of the territory of Asher were one of the tribes which failed to support Deborah and Barak when they battled against Sisera, the commander of the army of Jabin, king of Canaan.

INN — a lodging place for travelers. Hospitality was a religious duty in Bible times, so most travelers were guests in private residences. Inns were usually primitive shelters or enclosures for travelers and their animals. The word translated as inn means "loosing or untying," suggesting the releasing of animals upon arrival so they could rest.

In the Old Testament (Gen. 42:27, KJV), the word inn referred to a place to rest for the night or the act of pitching a tent. In New Testament times inns were usually built along trade routes. Pilgrims or merchants traveling together for safety would spend the night at these inns. A host or innkeeper provided basic lodging and some necessities such as food for the animals. Bazaars and markets offering provisions and entertainment for the weary traveler were usually located nearby.

Some synagogues had an adjacent inn where needy travelers could receive free food and a night's lodging. Joseph's brothers stayed at an inn near the Egyptian border (Gen. 42:27). The "Three Taverns" mentioned by Luke (Acts 28:15, RSV) were probably inns.

In the New Testament, two inns were the settings for very significant events.

Joseph and Mary were turned away by the innkeeper at Bethlehem, requiring them to seek refuge in a nearby cave where the Son of God was born (Luke 2:7). As Mary laid her Son in a cattle trough for a cradle, the Son of God was displayed in humiliation, identifying Him with all humanity.

The Good Samaritan carried a Jewish traveler who had been robbed and beaten by thieves to an inn where provision was made for his future care

(Luke 10:33–37). The Samaritan displayed a spirit of compassion and brotherhood that overcame the prejudices which usually separated the Jews and the Samaritans.

INNKEEPER (see OCCUPATIONS AND TRADES).

INNOCENCE — blamelessness, freedom from sin and guilt (Gen. 20:5; Ps. 26:6; Hos. 8:5). Since the Fall, when Adam and Eve brought disobedience into the world (Gen. 3:1–24), no one except Jesus has been totally sinless and blameless—innocent (Rom. 3:9–18; 2 Cor. 5:21). One may be called "innocent" only because he has been forgiven of sin and been declared a new creation through faith in Christ.

INNOCENTS, SLAUGHTER OF — Herod the Great's attempt to dispose of the infant Jesus by having all the male children of the region who were two years old and under put to death (Matt. 2:16–18). This event is not mentioned by Luke or the first-century Jewish historian Josephus. But such an act is in keeping with the cruelty that marked Herod's reign. He thought the security of his throne was threatened when he received news of one "born King of the Jews" (Matt. 2:2). But God protected His Son by directing Joseph in a dream to flee with his family to Egypt (Matt. 2:13–15).

Matthew compared this event with Pharaoh's slaughter of male Israelite babies at the time of Moses' birth (Ex. 1:15–22), and the tragedy of the Babylonian Captivity (Jer. 31:15). Such tragedy comes, even on the innocent, when leaders and people do not obey God (Matt. 27:25).

INQUIRE OF THE LORD — to seek God's counsel and guidance. The phrase occurs often in the Old Testament (Gen. 25:22; Judg. 20:27; 2 Sam. 2:1). Methods through which God made His will known included the PILLAR OF CLOUD AND FIRE, His SHEKINAH glory, the URIM and THUMMIM, and the words of the prophets.

INSANITY (see DISEASES OF THE BIBLE).

INSCRIPTION — words or letters carved, engraved, or printed on a surface. The term is applied to the words written on a placard above the head of Jesus as He hung on the cross (Mark 15:26; Luke 23:38; superscription, KJV). The inscription, which read "the King of the Jews," stated the crime for which Jesus was unjustly executed.

INSECTS (see ANIMALS OF THE BIBLE).

INSPECTION GATE (see GATES OF JERUSALEM AND THE TEMPLE).

INSPIRATION — a technical term for the Holy Spirit's supernatural guidance of those who received special revelation from God as they wrote the books of the Bible. The end result of this inspiration is that the Bible conveys the truths which God wanted His people to know and to communicate to the world.

Evangelical Christians agree that the primary

Photo by Howard Vos

The Good Samaritan Inn on the road from Jerusalem to Jericho (see Luke 10:25-37).

purpose of the Bible is to lead people to a personal relationship with God as Savior. But everything taught by the Bible on any subject is helpful and instructive for the complete Christian life (2 Tim. 3:16–17). Because Christianity does relate to the real world, the Bible's declarations about the earth and history are completely trustworthy.

Two terms often used in any discussion of the inspiration of the Bible are plenary and verbal. Plenary, a term meaning "full" or "complete," means that each book, chapter, and paragraph of the Bible is equally derived from God. Verbal inspiration emphasizes the truth that the wording of the text, as well as the ideas conveyed, is supernaturally inspired by God through the Holy Spirit.

Inerrancy is a term used along with plenary verbal inspiration to convey the view that the Bible's teaching is true on everything of which it speaks. The Bible is not just a useful body of human ideas. It makes clear the mind of God Himself.

Infallibility is a term often used as a synonym for inerrancy. However, the root meaning of infallibility is "not liable to fail in achieving its purpose." Truth, or inerrancy, is affirmed of the content of the Bible; infallibility refers to the effectiveness of the wording in conveying the reliable ideas, as well as the effectiveness of those ideas when used by the all–powerful Holy Spirit (Is. 55:11).

Important as biblical infallibility is, it is not enough without inerrancy. The reason why the all-powerful Spirit can use Scripture so effectively is that He directed its production from the beginning so that all of it is God's reliable information.

Inspiration, then, is a statement about God's greatness. God is intelligent and able to communicate with man, whom He created in His image. God knows everything about all reality in creation and is absolutely faithful and true (Rev. 3:7; 21:5). It follows that ideas communicated by divine revelation are true and conform to reality as God knows it. God overruled human limitations and sinful bi-

ases so that His spokesmen were able to write what He wanted written. God guided the thought conveyed so that it was without error, accomplishing the objectives He intended.

Exactly what role did the human writers of the Bible play in their transmission of God's message? They were not totally passive as those whose hands move automatically in an unconscious state. Their distinctive ways of writing stand out, as in the four gospels, which describe the life and ministry of Jesus Christ. Luke, the beloved physician, used many medical terms not found in Matthew, Mark, or John. Some biblical writers like Moses and Paul were highly educated; others were not.

Although some passages of Scripture may have been received by audible dictation (Ex. 4:12; 19:3–6; Num. 7:89), many were guided by a silent activity of the Holy Spirit (Luke 1:1–4). To err is human, and the conscious participation of finite, sinful authors would have led to error if not for this supernatural guidance by the Holy Spirit.

God gave these people the distinctive functions of prophets and apostles, originated what they wrote, and kept them from error in all the writing processes. All of Scripture has prophetic authority. None of it originated with the will of men. It came about through the will of God (2 Pet. 1:20–21). All Scripture was given by inspiration of God (2 Tim. 3:16).

Clear standards tested whether a person who claimed to speak for God was a true prophet or a false prophet (Deut. 13:1–5; 18:20–22). People who spoke out of their own hearts and by their own independent wills were subject to the death penalty (Deut. 13:6–10). But genuine prophets were inspired by the Holy Spirit as authentic spokesmen for God.

Although the Bible does not tell exactly how God inspired its writers, it was certainly not in a mechanical way. God the Holy Spirit is the third person of the trinity who is working with persons.

How does one person influence another person? Why do some have a more powerful impact upon people than others? Many factors are invoved. We do know for certain that the Scriptures originated with God and that the writers were "moved" or carried along by the Holy Spirit (2 Pet. 1:20–21) as they recorded God's message.

The Holy Spirit's work in the life of the Virgin Mary is a good example of how the Spirit worked with the biblical writers. A fully human, sinful woman bore a sinless child who would be called the Holy One, the Son of God (Luke 1:35). How could that be? The power of the Highest "overshadowed" her so that she conceived Jesus. Likewise, the power of the Highest "overshadowed" the biblical writers so that what they wrote could be called the Holy Bible, the Word of God.

Followers of Jesus Christ as Savior and Lord will follow Him in His view of the Old Testament Scriptures and the entire Bible. He endorsed all three sections of the Hebrew Bible: the Law, the Prophets, and the Psalms (Writings). He accepted as fact some of the most controversial historical details: Adam and Eve at the beginning of time (Matt. 19:4); Abel's murder of Cain (Luke 11:51); Noah, the ark, and the Flood (Matt. 24:37–39); the destruction of Sodom and Gomorrah and of Lot's wife (Luke 17:28–30); and Moses' authorship of the PENTATEUCH (John 5:46). "All things must be fulfilled," He said, "which were written in the Law of Moses and the Prophets and the Psalms concerning Me" (Luke 24:44). People were mistaken, Jesus said, "not knowing the Scriptures nor the power of God" (Matt. 22:29). He expressed His concern for unbelievers: "O foolish ones, and slow of heart to believe in all that the prophets have spoken!" (Luke 24:25).

The view that God's great mind had to accommodate itself to human errors in the production of the Bible does not fit the high view of Scripture which Jesus had. God did certainly adapt His truth to a human level of understanding. But a person can adapt truth about the origin of human life to a child's level of understanding without teaching errors about storks. In a similar way, God adapts His truth in part to our limited understandings, but neither He, nor His Son, nor His Spirit taught error in the name of God.

Belief in the Bible's inerrancy and infallibility best fits the claims of Jesus about the Bible and the claims which the Bible makes for itself. Salvation is the primary purpose of Scripture, but this is not its only function. It teaches truth about the world's origins, history, and the future.

Those who believe all that the Bible affirms should live faithfully according to its instruction in all personal relationships. Central to the Bible's teaching is love for God and love for neighbor. If believers in biblical inerrancy do not love God and their neighbors, their defense of scriptural authority will "become sounding brass or a clanging cymbal" (1 Cor. 13:1).

Also see BIBLE.

INSTANT — a brief unit of time; a split second. The prophet Isaiah warned the city of Jerusalem that God's judgment would fall in an instant unless the people turned from their sinful ways (Is. 29:5).

INSURRECTION — an act of rebellion against the established government (Ezra 4:19; Ps. 64:2; Acts 21:38). Barabbas, the criminal who was released by Pilate before Jesus' crucifixion, was guilty of insurrection against the Roman government (Mark 15:7).

INTEGRITY — honesty, sincerity, singleness of purpose. In the Old Testament, Noah (Gen. 6:9), Abraham (Gen. 17:1), Jacob (Gen. 25:27), David (1 Kin. 9:4), and Job (Job 1:1, 8; 2:3, 9; 4:6; 27:5; 31:6) were called people of integrity. Although Jesus did not use the word integrity, he called for purity of heart (Matt. 5:8), singleness of purpose (Matt. 6:22), and purity of motive (Matt. 6:1–6).

INTERCESSION — the act of petitioning God or praying on behalf of another person or group. The sinful nature of this world separates human beings from God. It has always been necessary, therefore, for righteous individuals to go before God to seek reconciliation between Him and His fallen creation.

One of the earliest and best examples of intercession of this type occurs in Genesis 18, where Abraham speaks to God on behalf of Sodom. His plea is compassionate; it is concerned with the well–being of others rather than with his own needs. Such selfless concern is the mark of all true intercession.

Another good example is the intercessory prayers of Moses. The leader of a nation and a righteous man, Moses successfully petitioned God on behalf of the Hebrew people (Ex. 15:25). Even the Pharaoh asked Moses to intercede for him (Ex. 8:28). But just as righteous men often succeeded in reconciling Creator and creation, the Bible also reminds us that the ongoing sinfulness of a people can hinder the effects of intercession (1 Sam. 2:25; Jer. 7:16).

The sacrifices and prayers of Old Testament priests (Ex. 29:42; 30:7) were acts of intercession which point forward to the work of Christ. Christ is, of course, the greatest intercessor. He prayed on behalf of Peter (Luke 22:32) and His disciples (John 17). Then in the most selfless intercession of all, He petitioned God on behalf of those who crucified Him (Luke 23:34).

But Christ's intercessory work did not cease when He returned to heaven. In heaven He intercedes for His church (Heb. 7:25). His Holy Spirit pleads on behalf of the individual Christian (Rom. 8:26–27). Finally, because of their unique relationship to God through Christ, Christians are urged to intercede for all people (1 Tim. 2:1).

INTEREST (see USURY).

INTERMEDIATE STATE — the period between a person's death and the final resurrection at the end of time. The Bible does not have a great deal to say about the intermediate state; its emphasis is upon the return of Christ, the final judgment, and the eternal state of man. What it does say is sketchy and open to various interpretations.

The New Testament sometimes describes the act of dying as a "falling asleep" and the state of death as a "sleeping" (Matt. 9:24; 11:11; 1 Cor. 15:20, 51). In 1 Thessalonians 4:13–15, the apostle Paul speaks of "those who have fallen asleep," "those who sleep in Jesus," and "those who are asleep." This should not be understood as "soul-sleeping"— a reference to the dead in an unconscious state. Death as sleep is a widely used biblical concept signifying rest from earthly care and labor, as is true of natural sleep (2 Pet. 3:4).

Jesus' story of the rich man and Lazarus (Luke 16:19–31) represents the rich man as conscious and tormented in Hades and Lazarus the beggar as conscious and blessed in Abraham's bosom. This passage of Scripture is a parable, which means that every point should not be pressed too far. The parable suggests that immediately after death the righteous are rewarded and the unrighteous receive punishment. The final degrees of both reward and punishment, however, are determined only at the final judgment (Rev. 20:11–15).

On the cross Jesus said to the repentant thief, "Today you will be with Me in Paradise" (Luke 23:43). The word paradise is of Persian origin. It suggests an orchard, park, or garden. The apostle Paul spoke of being "caught up into Paradise" (2 Cor. 12:4), evidently equating heaven and Paradise. In the Book of Revelation the crucified and resurrected Christ declared, "To him who overcomes I will give to eat from the tree of life, which is in the midst of the Paradise of God" (Rev. 2:7). The overall sense of these references identifies Paradise with heaven, to which the righteous go immediately after death.

The apostle Paul's clearest treatment of the intermediate state is found in 2 Corinthians 5:1–8: "For we know that if our earthly house, this tent, is destroyed, we have a building from God, a house not made with hands, eternal in the heavens" (v. 1). From this passage it is difficult to see Paul anticipating an unconscious, or even subconscious, state after death. He ends this passage by declaring, "We are confident, yes, well pleased rather to be absent from the body and to be present with the Lord" (v. 8). No in–between or intermediate state seems to be in mind here. In another place Paul says that when the Lord returns, "God will bring wth Him those who sleep in Jesus" (1 Thess. 4:14). This implies that believers who have died are with Jesus now.

INTERPRETATION (see BIBLE, INTERPRETATION OF).

INTERPRETATION OF TONGUES (see TONGUES, GIFT OF).

INTERTESTAMENTAL PERIOD (see ISRAEL, HISTORY OF).

INTESTINES — the lower part of the stomach through which waste is passed after food is digested by the human body. King Jehoram of Israel died with a mysterious disease of the intestines, just as the prophet Elijah predicted (2 Chr. 21:15–19).

INTESTINES, DISEASE OF (see DISEASES OF THE BIBLE).

IOB [IGH ahb] — a form of JASHUB No. 1.

IPHDEIAH [if DEE uh] (Jehovah redeems) — a son of Shashak (1 Chr. 8:25; Iphedeiah, KJV, NEB).

IPHTAH [IF tuh] — a form of JIPHTAH.

IPHTAHEL [IF tuh el] — a form of JIPHTHAH EL.

IR [ur] (donkey's colt) — the father of Shuppim and Huppim (1 Chr. 7:12). Ir may be the same person as Iri (1 Chr. 7:7).

IR–NAHASH [ur NAY hash] (city of the serpent) — a person or a town of the tribe of Judah (1 Chr. 4:12).

IR SHEMESH [ur SHEM esh] (city of the sun) — a city of the tribe of Dan near the border of Judah (Josh. 19:41). Ir Shemesh is apparently identical with BETH SHEMESH (Josh. 15:10; 21:16; Judg. 1:33).

IRA [IGH ruh] (young donkey) — the name of two or three men associated with David:

1. A "chief minister," or "priest" (RSV), under David (2 Sam. 20:26).

2. One of David's mighty men (2 Sam. 23:26).

3. An Ithrite who was one of David's mighty men (2 Sam. 23:38). He may be the same person as Ira No. 1.

IRAD [IGH rad] (wild donkey) — a grandson of Cain (Gen. 4:17–18).

IRAM [IGH ruhm] (meaning unknown) — an Edomite clan chief of the family of Esau (Gen. 36:43).

IRHA–HERES [UR hah HE rez] (city of destruction) — a term appearing in the Hebrew text of Isaiah 19:18, which stated that one of the five Egyptian cities will be called the City of Destruction (NKJV, KJV, NIV, NASB). Some English translations have Irha-hares, or City of the Sun (RSV, NEB), that is, Heliopolis (the biblical ON). The prophet Isaiah may have deliberately changed the name of Heliopolis to "City of Destruction" to denote the downfall of its idolatry.

IRI [IGH righ] (Jehovah is watcher) — a son of Bela (1 Chr. 7:7), possibly the same person as Ir (1 Chr. 7:12).

IRIJAH [igh RIGH juh] (Jehovah sees) — a sentry who arrested the prophet Jeremiah while Jerusalem was under siege by the Babylonian army (Jer. 37:11–14).

IRON (see MINERALS OF THE BIBLE).

IRON [EYE ron] (place of terror) — a fortified city in the territory of Naphtali (Josh. 19:38; Yiron,

RSV, NASB). It is probably present–day Yarun, about 16 kilometers (10 miles) northwest of Hazor, in northern Galilee.

IRONSMITH (see OCCUPATIONS AND TRADES).

IRPEEL [UR pee uhl] (*God heals*) — a city of the tribe of Benjamin (Josh. 18:27), near Jerusalem.

IRRIGATION — the watering of crops by artificial means. Irrigation is seldom mentioned in the Bible, because the nation of Israel was far less dependent on major rivers than Egypt and Mesopotamia. Much of Palestine had an adequate, though intermittent, rainfall, supplemented by the DEW, and many small springs were scattered through the land. Sometimes, however, irrigation was used to supplement the natural water supply, particularly for specialized agriculture such as vegetable gardens or orchards.

Water was often collected in CISTERNS for irrigation purposes (2 Kin. 18:31). Channels were constructed from these cisterns or from nearby streams to the fields and vineyards. Water was pumped to the fields by foot power (Deut. 11:10).

IRU [IGH roo] (*young donkey*) — the oldest son of Caleb (1 Chr. 4:15).

ISAAC [EYE zik] (*laughter*) — the only son of Abraham by his wife Sarah; father of Jacob and Esau. God promised to make Abraham's descendants a great nation that would become God's Chosen People. But the promised son was a long time in coming. Isaac was born when Abraham was 100 years old and Sarah was 90 (Gen. 17:17; 21:5). Both Abraham and Sarah laughed when they heard they would have a son in their old age (Gen. 17:17–19; 18:9–15). This explains why they named their son Isaac, which means "to laugh."

On the eighth day after his birth, Isaac was circumcised (Gen. 21:4). As he grew, his presence as Abraham's rightful heir brought him into conflict with Ishmael, Abraham's son by Sarah's handmaid Hagar. The strained relationship caused Sarah to send away Hagar and Ishmael (Gen. 21:9–21). God comforted Abraham by telling him that Ishmael would also become the father of a great nation (Gen. 21:13).

Birthright. Isaac's birthright was an important part of his life. The blessings which God gave to Abraham were also given to his descendants. Thus, to inherit this covenant with God was of far greater value than to inherit property or material goods.

Isaac's life gave evidence of God's favor. His circumcision was a sign of the covenant with God. God's favor toward him was also evident in Ishmael's disinheritance. The dismissal of the sons of Abraham's concubines to the "country of the east" is associated with the statement that Isaac inherited all that Abraham had, including God's blessing. Isaac was in a unique position historically because he would carry on the covenant.

When Isaac was a young man, God tested Abraham's faith by commanding him to sacrifice Isaac as an offering. But when Abraham placed Isaac upon the altar, an angel appeared and stopped the sacrifice, providing a ram instead. This showed clearly that Isaac was God's choice to carry on the covenant.

Marriage. Isaac married Rebekah when he was 40 years old. She became Isaac's wife when God directed one of Abraham's servants to her. The Bible reveals that Isaac loved Rebekah and that she was a comfort to him after his mother Sarah's death (Gen. 24:67). Isaac and Rebekah had twin sons, Jacob and Esau, who were born when Isaac was 60 years old (Gen. 25:20–26).

Famine prompted the family to move to Gerar, where God appeared to Isaac and reaffirmed the covenant. Moving through the Valley of Gerar, where he reopened the wells that Abraham had dug (Gen. 26:23; 28:10), Isaac made a camp at Beersheba. This place became his permanent home. There he built an altar just as his father had done (Gen. 26:24–25).

Jacob and Esau. The elder twin, Esau, was Isaac's favorite son, although God had declared that the older should serve the younger (Gen. 25:23). Jacob was Rebekah's favorite. Disagreement arose over which of the twins would receive the birthright and carry on the covenant which God had made with Abraham. Rebekah conspired with Jacob to trick the aging, blind Isaac into giving his blessing to Jacob rather than Esau.

Shortly thereafter, Isaac sent Jacob to Laban in Paddan–aram to find a wife and to escape Esau's wrath. Esau soon left his father's household. Many years passed before the two brothers were at peace with each other. But they were united at last in paying last respects to their father after his death. Isaac lived to be 180 years old. He was buried alongside Abraham, Sarah, and Rebekah in the cave of Machpelah (Gen. 35:28–29; 49:30–31).

Isaac's Character. The Bible contains many references to Isaac's good character. The Scripture gives evidence of his submission (Gen. 22:6, 9), meditation (Gen. 24:63), trust in God (Gen. 22:6, 9), devotion (Gen. 24:67), peaceful nature (Gen. 26:20–22), and his life of prayer and faith (Gen. 26:25; Heb. 11:11–17).

New Testament References. In the New Testament, Isaac is called a child of promise (Gal. 4:22–23). The Book of Acts points to his significance as the first to receive circumcision on the eighth day (Acts 7:8). His position as the first of the "elect" to receive God's blessing by birthright is also emphasized (Rom. 9:7).

In a famous passage, Paul uses Isaac and his mother as historical examples when discussing those who are justified by faith in God's promise (Gal. 4:21–31).

ISAIAH [eye ZAY uh] (*Jehovah has saved*) — a famous Old Testament prophet who predicted the coming of the Messiah; the author of the Book of Isaiah. Isaiah was probably born in Jerusalem of a family that was related to the royal house of Judah. He spent his early years as an official of King Uz-

Michelangelo's painting of the prophet Isaiah in the Sistine Chapel in Rome.

ziah (Azariah) of Judah (2 Chr. 26:22). When Uzziah died (740 B.C.), Isaiah received his prophetic calling from God in a stirring vision of God in the Temple (Is. 6). The king of Judah had died; now Isaiah had seen the everlasting King in whose service he would spend the rest of his life.

Isaiah was married to a woman described as "the prophetess" (Is. 8:3). They had two sons whom they named Shear–Jashub, "A Remnant Shall Return" (Is. 7:3) and Maher–Shalal–Hash–Baz, "Speed the Spoil, Hasten the Booty" (Is. 8:3). These strange names portray the two basic themes of the Book of Isaiah: God is about to bring judgment upon His people, hence Maher–Shalal–Hash–Baz; but after that there will be an outpouring of God's mercy and grace to the remnant of people who will remain faithful to God, hence Shear–Jashub.

After God called Isaiah to proclaim His message, He told Isaiah that most of his work would be a ministry of judgment. Even though the prophet would speak the truth, the people would reject his words (6:10). Jesus found in these words of Isaiah's call a prediction of the rejection of his message by many of the people (Matt. 13:14–15).

Isaiah's response to this revelation from the Lord was a lament: "Lord, how long?" (Is. 6:11). The Lord answered that Isaiah's ministry would prepare the people for judgment, but one day God's promises would be realized. Judah was to experience ut-

ter devastation, to be fulfilled with the destruction of the city of Jerusalem by the Babylonians in 587/ 586 B.C. (Is. 6:11). This destruction would be followed by the deportation of the people to Babylon (Is. 6:12). But although the tree of the house of David would be cut down, there would still be life in the stump (Is. 6:13). Out of the lineage of David would come a Messiah who would establish His eternal rule among His people.

Isaiah was a writer of considerable literary skill. The poetry of his book is magnificent in its sweep. A person of strong emotion and deep feelings, Isaiah also was a man of steadfast devotion to the Lord. His vision of God and His holiness in the Temple influenced his messages during his long ministry.

Isaiah's ministry extended from about 740 B.C. until at least 701 B.C. (Is. 37—39). His 40 years of preaching doom and promise did not turn the nation of Judah from its headlong rush toward destruction. But he faithfully preached the message God gave him until the very end.

According to a popular Jewish tradition, Isaiah met his death by being sawn in half during the reign of the evil king Manasseh of Judah. This tradition seems to be supported by the writer of Hebrews (Heb. 11:37). Certainly Isaiah is one of the heroes of the faith "of whom the world was not worthy" (Heb. 11:38).

Also see ISAIAH, BOOK OF.

ISAIAH, BOOK OF — a major prophetic book of the Old Testament, noted for its description of the coming Messiah as God's Suffering Servant. Because of its lofty portrayal of God and His purpose of salvation, the book is sometimes called "the fifth gospel," implying it is similar in theme to the gospels of the New Testament. The book is named for its author, the great prophet Isaiah, whose name means "God is salvation."

Structure of the Book. With its 66 chapters, Isaiah is the longest prophetic book of the Old Testament. Most scholars agree that the book falls naturally into two major sections, chapters 1—39 and chapters 40—66. One good way to remember the grand design of the book is to think of the sections as a parallel to the two main parts of the Bible. The first section of Isaiah contains the same number of chapters as the number of books in the Old Testament (39). The second part of the book parallels the New Testament in the same way—27 chapters for the 27 books of this section of the Bible.

The general theme of the first part of Isaiah's book is God's approaching judgment on the nation of Judah. In some of the most striking passages in all the Bible, the prophet announces that God will punish His people because of their sin, rebellion, and worship of false gods. But this message of stern judgment is also mixed with beautiful poems of comfort and promise. Although judgment is surely coming, better days for God's Covenant People lie just ahead. This section of Isaiah's book refers several times to the coming MESSIAH. His name will be called IMMANUEL (7:14). As a ruler on the throne of David, he will establish an everlasting kingdom (9:7).

Other significant events and prophecies covered in the first section of Isaiah's book include his call as a prophet (chap. 6), God's judgment against the nations surrounding Judah (chaps. 13—23), and a warning to Judah not to seek help through vain alliances with Egypt (chaps. 30—31).

During Isaiah's time, Judah's safety was threatened by the advancing Assyrian Empire. When the king of Judah sought to protect the nation's interests by forming an alliance with Egypt to turn back the Assyrians, Isaiah advised the nation to look to their God for deliverance—not to a pagan nation led by an earthly ruler. He also prophesied that the Assyrian army would be turned back by God before it succeeded in overthrowing the nation of Judah (30:27-33).

The second major section of Isaiah's book (chaps. 40—66) is filled with prophecies of comfort for the nation of Judah. Just as Isaiah warned of God's approaching judgment in the first part of his book, the 27 concluding chapters were written to comfort God's people in the midst of their suffering after His judgment had fallen. The theme of this entire section may be illustrated with Isaiah's famous hymn of comfort that God directed the prophet to address to the people: "Comfort, yes, comfort My people!" says your God. "Speak comfort to Jerusalem, and cry out to her, that her warfare is ended, that her iniquity is pardoned; for she has received from the Lord's hand double for all her sins" (40:1-2).

Isaiah's message in this part of his book is that after their period of judgment has passed, God's Covenant People will be restored to their place of responsibility in God's plan for the salvation of the world. The great suffering through which they were passing was their period of captivity as exiles of the pagan nation of Babylon. This theme of suffering on the part of God's people is demonstrated dramatically by Isaiah's famous description of the Suffering Servant. The nation of Israel was God's suffering servant who would serve as God's instrument of blessing for the rest of the world after their release from captivity and restoration as His Chosen People (42:1-9).

But Isaiah's prophecy also points beyond the immediate future to the coming of Jesus Christ as the Messiah several centuries later. The heart of this stunning prophecy occurs in chapter 53, as Isaiah develops the description of God's Servant to its highest point. The Servant's suffering and death and the redemptive nature of His mission are clearly foretold. Although mankind deserved God's

ISAIAH: A Teaching Outline

Part One: Prophecies of Condemnation (1:1—35:10)

Part Two: Historical Material (36:1—39:8)

Part Three: The Prophecies of Comfort (40:1—66:24)

The famous Isaiah Scroll is one of the best-preserved manuscripts discovered among the Dead Sea scrolls. It contains the entire text of the Book of Isaiah.

judgment because "we have turned, every one, to his own way" (53:6), God sent His Servant to take away our sins. According to Isaiah, it is through His suffering that we are made right with God, since "the Lord has laid on Him the iniquity of us all" (53:6).

Isaiah closes his book with a beautiful description of the glorious age to come (chaps. 60—66). In that day the city of Zion, or Jerusalem, will be restored. God's people will gather there to worship Him in all His majesty and glory. Peace and justice will reign, and God will make all things new.

Authorship and Date. The question of who wrote the Book of Isaiah is a matter of much disagreement and debate among Bible scholars. In one camp are those who insist the entire book was written by the famous prophet Isaiah who ministered in the southern kingdom of Judah for 40 years, from about 740–700 B.C. But other scholars are just as insistent that the entire book was not written by this prophet. They agree that chapters 1—39 of the book belong to Isaiah, but they refer to chapters 40—66 as "Second Isaiah," insisting it was written by an unknown author long after the ministry of this famous prophet of Judah.

Those who assign chapters 40—66 to a "Second Isaiah" point out that the two major sections of the book seem to be set in different times. Chapters 1—39 clearly belong to the eighth century B.C., a turbulent period in the history of Judah. But Isaiah 40—66, according to these scholars, seems to be addressed to the citizens of Judah who were being held as captives in Babylon about 550 B.C. This

was two centuries after Isaiah lived and prophesied. In addition, these scholars point to the differences in tone, language, and style between these two major sections as proof that the book was written by two different authors.

But the traditional view cannot be dismissed so easily. Conservative scholars point out that the two sections of the book do have many similarities, although they are dramatically different in tone and theme. Many phrases and ideas that are peculiar to Isaiah appear in both sections of the book. A good example of this is Isaiah's unique reference to God as "the Holy One of Israel" (1:4; 17:7; 37:23; 45:11; 55:5; 60:14). The appearance of these words and phrases can be used to argue just as convincingly that the book was written by a single author.

Conservative scholars also are not convinced that the two major sections of the book were addressed to different audiences living in different times. In the second section of his book, they believe Isaiah looked into the future and predicted the years of the Captivity and the return of the Covenant People to their homeland after the Captivity ended. If the prophet could predict the coming of the Messiah over 700 years before that happened, he could certainly foresee this major event in the future of the nation of Judah.

After all the evidence is analyzed, there is no convincing reason to question the traditional view that the entire book was written by the prophet whose name it bears. The most likely time for its writing was about 700 B.C. or shortly thereafter.

Isaiah gives us few facts about himself, but we do

Photo by Willem A. VanGemeren

Several Arabs haggle over a price with a Jewish merchant. The Arabs of the Middle East trace their ancestry to Ishmael, son of Abraham by Hagar.

know he was "the son of Amoz" (1:1). The quality of his writing indicates he was well educated and that he probably came from an upper-class family. Married, he had two children to whom he gave symbolic names to show that God was about to bring judgment against the nation of Judah. He was called to his prophetic ministry "in the year that King Uzziah [Azariah] died" (6:1)—about 740 B.C.—through a stirring vision of God as he worshiped in the Temple. He prophesied for about 40 years to the nation of Judah, calling the people and their rulers to place their trust in the Holy One of Israel.

Historical Setting. Isaiah delivered his prophecies during a time of great moral and political upheaval. In the early part of his ministry, about 722 B.C., Judah's sister nation, the northern kingdom of Israel, fell to the invading Assyrians. For a while, it looked as if Judah would suffer the same fate. But Isaiah advised the rulers of Judah not to enter alliances with foreign nations against the Assyrian threat. Instead, he called the people to put their trust in God, who alone could bring real salvation and offer lasting protection for the perilous times.

Theological Contribution. The Book of Isaiah presents more insights into the nature of God than any other book of the Old Testament.

To Isaiah, God was first of all a holy God. His holiness was the first thing that impressed the

prophet when he saw Him in all His glory in the Temple (6:1-8). But God's holiness also reminded Isaiah of his own sin and weakness. "Woe is me," he cried, "for I am undone! Because I am a man of unclean lips, and I dwell in the midst of a people of unclean lips" (6:5). After this confession, Isaiah's lips were cleansed by a live coal from the altar, and he agreed to proclaim God's message of repentance and judgment to a wayward people.

Isaiah also tells us about a God who is interested in the salvation of His people. Even the prophet's name, "God is salvation," emphasizes this truth. He uses the word salvation 28 times in his book, while all the other Old Testament prophets combined mentioned this word only 10 times. In Isaiah's thought, salvation is of God, not man. God is the sovereign ruler of history and the only one who has the power to save.

The Book of Isaiah also reveals that God's ultimate purpose of salvation will be realized through the coming Messiah, our Lord and Savior Jesus Christ. No other book of the Bible contains as many references to the coming Messiah as this magnificent book. Isaiah points us to a loving Savior who came to save His people from their sins. When Jesus began His public ministry in His hometown of Nazareth, He quoted from one of these beautiful messianic passages from Isaiah (61:1-2) to show that this prophecy was being fulfilled in His life and ministry. His purpose was "to set at liberty those who are oppressed, to preach the acceptable year of the Lord" (Luke 4:18–19).

Special Considerations. One unusual passage in the Book of Isaiah gives us a clue about how God views His work of judgment and salvation. The prophet describes God's judgment as "His unusual act" (28:21). If judgment is God's unusual act, does this not imply that salvation is the work more typical of Him as a loving God? It is an interesting question to think about as we express thanks to God for the marvelous insights of Isaiah and his important book.

Also see ISAIAH.

ISAIAH, MARTYRDOM OF (see PSEUDEPI-GRAPHA).

ISCAH [IZ kuh] (meaning unknown) — a daughter of Haran, Abraham's younger brother. Iscah was a sister of Milcah, the wife of Nahor (Gen. 11:29).

ISCARIOT [iss KER ee uht] (*man of Kerioth*) — the surname of Judas, one of the Twelve who betrayed Jesus (John 6:71; 12:4; 13:2, 26). Also see JUDAS IS-CARIOT.

ISHBAH [ISH buh] (meaning unknown) — the father of Eshtemoa, of the tribe of Judah (1 Chr. 4:17).

ISHBAK [ISH bak] (*free*) — a son of Abraham by Keturah (Gen. 25:2). Ishbak was probably the ancestor of a northern Arabian tribe.

ISHBI–BENOB [ISH bigh BEE nahb] (*dweller on the mount*) — a descendant of the Philistine giants of Gath. Ishbi–Benob was killed by Abishai, one of David's mighty men (2 Sam. 21:16).

ISHBOSHETH [ihsh BOE sheth] (*man of shame*) — a son of Saul whom Abner proclaimed king after Saul's death (2 Sam. 2:8–10). The tribe of Judah proclaimed David king after the death of Saul and Jonathan at Gilboa, but the 11 other tribes remained loyal to Saul's family. Ishbosheth reigned two turbulent years from Mahanaim, east of the Jordan River, while David ruled Judah from Hebron. Throughout the period, each side attempted unsuccessfully to gain control of the entire kingdom (2 Sam. 2:12—3:1).

Ishbosheth made a grave error in charging Abner with having relations with Saul's concubine, Rizpah. In anger, Abner changed his allegiance to David (2 Sam. 3:6–21). When Joab murdered Abner in Hebron (2 Sam. 3:27), Ishbosheth became discouraged (2 Sam. 4:1). Two captains of his guard, Baanah and Rechab, assassinated Ishbosheth as he lay napping. They carried Ishbosheth's severed head to David, who ordered it buried in the tomb of Abner in Hebron. Then David put the assassins to death (2 Sam. 4:5–12). Saul's dynasty ended with Ishbosheth's death.

ISHHOD [ISH hahd] (*man of vitality*) — a son of Hammoleketh, of the tribe of Manasseh (1 Chr. 7:18; Ishod, KJV).

ISHI [ISH igh] (*God has saved*) — the name of four men in the Old Testament and a symbolic name for God:

1. A son of Appaim and a member of the family of Jerahmeel (1 Chr. 2:31).

2. A descendant of Judah through Caleb (1 Chr. 4:20).

3. The father of four men, who were captains of the tribe of Simeon (1 Chr. 4:42).

4. A chief of the half-tribe of Manasseh, east of the Jordan River (1 Chr. 5:24).

5. A symbolic name for God used by the prophet Hosea (Hos. 2:16), signifying the close relationship which God desired with His people.

ISHIAH [ish IGH uh] — a form of ISSHIAH.

ISHIJAH [ish IGH juh] (*Jehovah exists*) — a son of Harum who divorced his pagan wife (Ezra 10:31; Isshijah, NAS, NEB, RSV).

ISHMA [ISH muh] (*may God hear*) — a brother of Jezreel and Idbash, of the tribe of Judah (1 Chr. 4:3).

ISHMAEL [IHSH may ell] (*God hears*) — the name of six men in the Old Testament:

1. The first son of Abraham, by his wife's Egyptian maid servant, Hagar. Although God had promised Abraham an heir (Gen. 15:4), Abraham's wife, Sarah, had been unable to bear a child. When Abraham was 85, Sarah offered her maid to him in order to help fulfill God's promise (Gen. 16:1–2).

After Hagar learned that she was pregnant, she grew proud and began to despise Sarah. Sarah complained to Abraham, who allowed her to discipline Hagar. Sarah's harsh treatment of Hagar caused her to flee into the wilderness. There she met the angel of God, who told her to return to Sarah and submit to her authority. As an encouragement, the angel promised Hagar that her son, who would be named Ishmael, would have uncounted descendants. Hagar then returned to Abraham and Sarah and bore her son (Gen. 16:4–15).

When Ishmael was 13, God appeared to Abraham to tell him that Ishmael was not the promised heir. God made a covenant with Abraham that was to be passed down to the descendants of Isaac—a son who would be conceived by Sarah the following year. Because Abraham loved Ishmael, God promised to bless Ishmael and make him a great nation (Gen. 17:19–20).

At the customary feast to celebrate Isaac's weaning, Sarah saw 16–year–old Ishmael making fun of Isaac. She was furious and demanded that Abraham disown Ishmael and his mother so Ishmael could not share Isaac's inheritance. Abraham was reluctant to cast out Ishmael and Hagar, but he did so when instructed by God (Gen. 21:8–13).

Hagar and Ishmael wandered in the wilderness of Beersheba. When their water was gone and Ishmael grew weary, Hagar placed him under a shrub to await death. The angel of God again contacted Hagar and showed her a well. After drawing water, she returned to Ishmael. Ishmael grew up in the wilderness of Paran and gained fame as an archer. Hagar arranged his marriage to an Egyptian wife (Gen. 21:14–21).

When Abraham died, Ishmael returned from exile to help Isaac with the burial (Gen. 25:9). As God promised, Ishmael became the father of 12 princes (Gen. 25:16), as well as a daughter, Mahalath, who later married Esau, son of Isaac (Gen. 28:9). Ishmael died at the age of 137 (Gen. 25:17).

Ishmael was the father of the ISHMAELITES, a nomadic nation which lived in northern Arabia. Modern-day Arabs claim descent from Ishmael.

2. The son of Nethaniah and a member of the house of David. After the Babylonian conquest of Judah, King Nebuchadnezzar appointed a Jewish captive, Gedaliah, as governor. Gedaliah promised to welcome all Jews who came under his protection. Ishmael and several others accepted Gedaliah's offer with the intent of killing him (2 Kin. 25:22–24). Gedaliah was warned that Ishmael was allied with the Ammonite king in plotting to kill him, but he refused to believe it (Jer. 40:14–16). When Gedaliah invited Ishmael and ten others to a banquet, they murdered everyone in attendance. The killers fled toward the Ammonite country with several hostages, but they were overtaken by pursuers in Gibeon. The hostages were rescued, but Ishmael and eight men escaped to the Ammonites (Jer. 41:1–15).

3. A descendant of Jonathan, son of Saul (1 Chr. 8:38; 9:44).

4. The father of Zebadiah, ruler of the house of Judah and the highest civil authority under King Jehoshaphat (2 Chr. 19:11).

5. A son of Jehohanan. Ishmael was one of five army officers recruited by Jehoiada to help overthrow Queen Athaliah of Judah in favor of the rightful heir, Joash (2 Chr. 23:1).

6. A priest of the clan of Pashhur who divorced his foreign wife after the Babylonian Captivity (Ezra 10:22).

ISHMAELITES [ISH may el ites] — descendants of Ishmael, Abraham's first son. His mother was Sarah's Egyptian servant, HAGAR (Gen. 16:1–16; 1 Chr. 1:28). The Ishmaelites, like the Israelites (Abraham's children through Sarah), were divided into 12 tribes (Gen. 25:16). Out of respect for Abraham, God made a great nation of the Ishmaelites, even though Ishmael was not Abraham's promised son (Gen. 21:12–13). Ishmael's 12 sons had many descendants who lived as nomads in the deserts of northern Arabia.

The Old Testament eventually used the term Ishmaelite in a broader sense, referring to all the Arabian merchants (Is. 13:20; Ezek. 27:20, 21). Any wild and war–like peoples of the desert could claim to be descendants of Ishmael (Gen. 16:12). This wider use of Ishmaelites is illustrated by an event in the life of Joseph. His older brothers sold him to some caravan traders who were called "a company of Ishmaelites" (Gen. 37:25) as well as "Midianite" traders (37:28). They were probably a minor clan

of the larger Ishmaelite tribe. Mohammed claimed Ishmael as his ancestor, as do most Arabs.

ISHMAIAH [ish MAY uh] (*Jehovah is hearing*) — the name of two men in David's time:

1. A Gibeonite who was one of David's mighty men (1 Chr. 12:4).

2. A son of Obadiah and a chief of Zebulun in David's time (1 Chr. 27:19).

ISHMERAI [ISH muh righ] (*Jehovah is protector*) — a son of Elpaal (1 Chr. 8:18).

ISHOD [IGH shahd] — a form of ISHHOD.

ISHPAH [ISH puh] — a form of ISPAH.

ISHPAN [ISH pan] (*strong*) — a son of Shashak (1 Chr. 8:22).

ISHTAR [ISH tahr] (see GODS, PAGAN).

ISH–TOB [ISH tahb] (*man of Tob*) — a small district east of the Jordan River (2 Sam. 10:6).

ISHUAH [ISH yoo uh] — a form of ISHVAH.

ISHUAI [ISH yoo igh] — a form of ISHVI.

ISHUI [ISH yoo igh] — a form of ISHVI.

ISHVAH [ISH vuh] (*to be like*) — the second son of Asher, descended from Jacob and Zilpah (Gen. 46:17), also called Ishuah (KJV).

ISHVI [ISH vigh] (*equal*) — the name of two men in the Old Testament:

1. The third son of Asher and founder of the tribal family of the Ishvites, also spelled Isui (Gen. 46:17, KJV), Ishuai (1 Chr. 7:30, KJV), and Jesui (Num. 26:44, NKJV).

2. A son of King Saul by Ahinoam (1 Sam. 14:49; Ishui, KJV; Ishyo, NEB; Jishui, NKJV). Some scholars believe Ishvi was the same person as ISHBOSHETH.

ISHYO [ISH yoe] — a form of ISHVI.

ISLAND — a tract of land completely surrounded by water and not large enough to be called a continent.

In the NKJV the word island is found only in the Book of Acts (13:6; 27:16, 26; 28:1) and in the Book of Revelation (1:9; 6:14; 16:20). A number of islands in the Mediterranean Sea are mentioned in connection with the missionary journeys of the apostle Paul; CHIOS (Acts 20:15); CAUDA (Acts 27:16); CRETE (Acts 27:7, 12–13, 21); CYPRUS (Acts 13:4; 15:39); MALTA (Acts 28:1–11); SAMOS (Acts 20:15); and SAMOTHRACE (Acts 16:11).

The KJV uses the word island in four ways: (1) an island as usually understood (Jer. 2:10); (2) dry land, or habitable places, as opposed to water (Is. 42:15); (3) a coastland, as the coastland of Palestine and Phoenicia (Is. 20:6); and (4) the farthest regions of the earth—the distant coastlands of people from afar (Ps. 72:10; Is. 11:11; Zeph. 2:11).

ISMACHIAH [is muh KIGH uh] (*Jehovah supports*) — an overseer of the Temple in Hezekiah's time (2 Chr. 31:13).

Tourists along the Jabbok River, where Jacob wrestled with an angel during the age of the patriarchs (Gen. 32:22-32).

ISPAH [IS pah] (*strong*) — a son or descendant of Beriah, of the tribe of Benjamin (1 Chr. 8:16; Ishpah, RSV).

ISRAEL [IS ray ell] (*prince with God*) — the name given to JACOB after his great struggle with God at Peniel near the brook Jabbok (Gen. 32:28; 35:10). The name Israel has been interpreted by different scholars as "prince with God," "he strives with God," "let God rule," or "God strives." The name was later applied to the descendants of Jacob, or the HEBREW people. The twelve tribes were called "Israelites," "children of Israel," and "house of Israel," identifying them clearly as the descendants of Israel through his sons and grandsons. Also see HEBREWS; ISRAEL, HISTORY OF.

ISRAEL, HISTORY OF — The ancient Hebrews were just one of a number of nations living in the ancient Near East. This region of the world included ancient Persia, Mesopotamia (the area between the Tigris and Euphrates Rivers), Syria, Anatolia, Palestine, and Egypt. Each of the nations in the area experienced at least one period in its history when it was more powerful or influential than its neighbors. But the nature of empires is such that all of them were destined to fall and to be replaced by a society that was more aggressive than those it overthrew.

The first of these great empires was that of the SUMERIANS. It consisted of about a dozen small city-states located in southern Mesopotamia in an area about 245 kilometers (150 miles) northwest of the Persian Gulf. The Sumerians established the first high culture in human society about 4000 B.C. They made fundamental discoveries in many important areas of life. They were at their height when a person named Sargon founded an aggressive culture at Agade, some 128 kilometers (80

miles) northwest in central Mesopotamia, adopting much of the Sumerian culture.

Sargon's dynasty was overthrown ultimately by a nation that was itself conquered after a century of rule by a powerful Babylonian king named HAMMURABI (about 1790-1750 B.C.). During Hammurabi's reign, the Sumerian cities were conquered and a large Semitic empire was established in Mesopotamia.

Abraham and the Patriarchs. It is difficult to assign an exact beginning to Hebrew history. But if we regard ABRAHAM as the forefather of the Israelites, it is clear that they had their roots in ancient Sumer. Abraham came from Ur, a Sumerian city (Gen. 11:31). Abraham became prosperous in HARAN in northwestern Mesopotamia, then later moved to the land of Canaan (Gen. 12:5), where he received God's assurance that he would be the ancestor of a mighty people.

Abraham's promised son ISAAC had two sons of his own, ESAU and JACOB. God chose Jacob for the renewal of His promise to Abraham (Gen. 28:13-15). Jacob later moved from Haran, where he had married LEAH and RACHEL, daughters of LABAN, and settled in Canaan. Jacob, whose name was changed to ISRAEL after an encounter with God (Gen. 32:24-30), had 12 sons. Eleven of these sons plotted to sell their youngest brother Joseph into slavery in Egypt.

Years in Egypt. When God prospered Joseph and made him a high official in Egypt, the brothers were forgiven, after being humiliated. They were instructed to bring their father and other family members to Egypt, where they settled in the fertile GOSHEN area for over two centuries. Then a Pharaoh who did not acknowledge Joseph's achievements came to power. The descendants of Israel, now known as HEBREWS or Israelites, were up-

Ramses II of Egypt bows before his gods with an offering. Many scholars believe this Ramses was the ruling Pharaoh at the time of the Exodus.

rooted from their land and forced to work on the rebuilding of great Egyptian cities.

After the Israelites experienced considerable suffering, God appointed Moses to liberate His people from bondage. Moses had been born to Hebrew slaves. He was set adrift in a basket on the Nile River in an attempt to prevent him from being killed by Pharaoh's troops. An Egyptian princess rescued him and brought him up as her own son.

Fleeing later from Egypt because of a crime that he had committed (Ex. 2:12), Moses experienced a divine revelation in the wilderness. He was ordered by God to return to Egypt where, with AARON his brother, he would confront Pharaoh and demand the release of the captive Israelites. Pharaoh's stubborn refusal finally resulted in the death of the Egyptian firstborn, after which Moses led the Israelites across the Red Sea to safety in the Sinai region.

The Covenant at Sinai. God appeared to Moses on Mount Sinai (Horeb) and entered into a relationship with the twelve tribes, which bound them to Himself and made them, in effect, the nation of Israel. The relationship was in the form of a COVENANT, or a written contract.

This covenant is fundamentally important for Israelite history. Through it a number of independent tribes were bonded together into one Hebrew nation and given a specific destiny as the people chosen by God as a channel for divine revelation. The Israelites, however, were not to behave just like any nation of the ancient world. All of these were pagan, following depraved and corrupt moral practices as part of their worship.

The Israelites were to live as a religious community in which each member cared for the others. The exploitation of such helpless persons as strangers, widows, and orphans was strictly forbidden under the Mosaic Law (Deut. 24:17), since God Himself was their champion (Deut. 10:18).

God promised to provide a land for the Hebrews in which they could settle in obedience to covenant law as a holy nation (Ex. 19:6), and be witnesses of His existence and power to all the neighboring nations.

Throughout their history, God's covenant people were meant to be an example of spirituality to the world. This, rather than political activity or territorial conquest, was to be their true destiny. Unfortunately, much of Israelite history was marked by

The mountain-top fortress of Masada, where a group of Jewish rebels made their last stand against the Roman army in A.D. 73. When the Romans finally scaled the mountain and broke through the defenses, the Jews committed suicide to avoid capture.

Photo by Ben Chapman

The Wailing Wall, part of the remains of Herod's Temple in Jerusalem. Modern Jews come here to mourn the loss of the Temple and to pray.

periodic disobedience of the covenant laws.

Israelite history began badly with an idolatrous act. The people made and worshiped a golden calf while Moses was still on Mount Sinai (Ex. 32:1-6). After their punishment, the covenant was renewed and work began on the building of the TABERNA-CLE. The structure was portable, and it moved with the Israelites whenever they wandered in the wilderness. Subsequent Hebrew temples were to reflect something of its structure.

The Wilderness Years. Because the Israelites disobeyed God by refusing to enter Canaan (Num. 14:30-35), they were compelled to wander for a generation in the wilderness. These aimless wanderings are summarized in Numbers 33. The people apparently moved between various oases in the Sinai wilderness. After Aaron's death (Num. 20:22-29), the Israelites moved steadily toward Moab in TRANSJORDAN and prepared to conquer Canaan. The tribes of Reuben, Gad, and half of the tribe of Manasseh, who owned large herds, were allowed to settle in the conquered Transjordan lands and to raise their cattle. The remainder of the Israelites prepared to cross the Jordan River at Jericho and occupy the Promised Land. Moses was not permitted to lead the Israelites to victory because he had not carried out God's will properly (Deut. 32:51). Instead he was allowed to view Canaan from the summit of Mount Nebo. After this, he died and was buried in Moab (Deut. 34:6).

Conquest of Canaan. Jericho was like a town un-der siege when JOSHUA, who had been commissioned as leader shortly before Moses died (Deut. 34:9), advanced to overthrow it. He obeyed God's instructions regarding the attack upon the fortress-like city that guarded the entrance to Canaan. The Hebrews marched around it daily for six days, and it collapsed dramatically on the seventh day (Josh. 6:12-20).

The next assault was on nearby Ai. This offensive, however, met with disaster because an Israelite named Achan had defied God's instructions about not taking plunder from Jericho. When his sin was discovered, he and his family were stoned to death (Josh. 7:25), after which Ai was overthrown.

Shortly afterwards, Joshua was tricked into sealing a covenant with the neighboring GIBEONITES. This was followed by a defense of the royal city of Gibeon against the attack of five Canaanite kings who resented the pact made with Joshua. The kings were captured and executed (Josh. 10:16-27). Then Joshua proceeded to conquer the southland, where Lachish and Hebron were important cities. JERUSA-LEM, however, was not captured at this time, nor was Megiddo in central Palestine.

The final phase of occupation involved northern Palestine, where Joshua was confronted by a military group led by Jabin, king of Hazor. Perhaps because the Israelites were anxious to keep the cities intact, none were destroyed except Hazor, the chief city of the north. This policy proved costly in later years. Although the Israelites had occupied the Promised Land, they had not conquered the people completely. Once the Canaanites were able to re-establish themselves, they presented serious problems for the Israelites.

Period of the Judges. After Joshua died, individual charismatic leaders known as judges provided leadership for the Hebrew nation. This event coincided with increasingly independent activity by the Israelite tribes, caused partly because of Canaanite resistance to the conquerors. This lack of centralized leadership meant that covenant law was not being observed, and it was being replaced by idolatry.

Although the judges tried hard to correct local problems, they were no match for the increasingly militant Canaanites, or for Eglon, a Moabite ruler who oppressed some of the Hebrew people for 18 years before being killed by a left–handed judge named Ehud (Judg. 3:15–30). By this time Hazor had been reoccupied by Canaanites under Jabin, their king, who made several northern tribes his subjects for 20 years (Judg. 4:2–3).

Jabin's forces were superior because they had iron–fitted, horse–drawn chariots. These chariots were effective on level ground, but they proved less threatening in the hill country. Jabin's general Sisera was defeated by the Hebrew commander Barak and slain by Jael, the wife of an ally named Heber (Judg. 4:21).

The Book of Judges shows clearly that Israel's troubles were the result of rejecting covenant law and adopting various forms of Canaanite idolatry. Canaanite religion was one of the most sensuous and morally depraved that the world has ever known; it contrasted dramatically with the holiness and moral purity demanded of the Israelites by the Sinai covenant.

Because of their persistent idolatry, the Hebrews were punished further by Midianite and Ammonite attacks. The most serious threat, however, came from the PHILISTINES. These war–like people had migrated to Canaan in small numbers in the time of Abraham. But they came in a body about 1175 B.C. and settled on the southwestern Palestinian coast. The Philistines established a group of five cities—Gaza, Gath, Ashkelon, Ashdod, and Ekron—and began to push the Israelites into the hill country.

The Philistines were superior in military power because they monopolized the manufacture and sale of iron implements and weapons. SAMSON had delivered the Israelites periodically from Philistine oppression, but after his death (Judg. 16:27–30) they were at the mercy of the enemy once more.

The United Kingdom Years. The social chaos described in the closing chapters of the Book of Judges came to a head in the religious corruption in Israel at the time of SAMUEL's childhood (1 Sam. 2:12–18, 22). Although Samuel himself exercised a wholesome ministry, the Israelites were more intent on being ruled by a king than in living as a holy nation in covenant with their God (1 Sam. 8:19–20). SAUL, son of Kish, was duly anointed by Samuel as

The Arch of Titus in the city of Rome, memorializing the victory of the Roman Emperors Vespasian and Titus over the Jewish rebellion, in A.D. 70.

a charismatic leader over the nation (1 Sam. 10:1).

But Saul had an unbalanced personality, which soon showed signs of paranoia. He disobeyed God's commands (1 Sam. 13:13), and a successor was chosen and anointed in the person of DAVID, son of Jesse. David gained popular favor by his defeat of the Philistine champion Goliath. Thereafter David was seen as Israel's savior, much to the dislike of Saul, who felt his own position threatened. Saul fought at intervals against both David and the Philistines, but was ultimately killed along with five sons at Mount Gilboa. The northern tribes then looked to Ishbosheth, the surviving son of Saul, who was made king at Mahanaim in Transjordan by Abner, his father's commander (2 Sam. 2:8–10).

David settled in Hebron (2 Sam. 2:11), and Abner tried to gain favor with him. But Abner was murdered by Joab, David's commander, at Hebron (2 Sam. 3:27). When Ishbosheth was also murdered (2 Sam. 4:5–6), the way was clear for David to assume sole rule of Israel and unify the kingdom. He established his capital at Jerusalem, which he captured from the Jebusites. He also brought the ARK OF THE COVENANT to the city, making it a religious as well as a political center.

For the remainder of his reign, David fought against the Ammonites and Syrians as well as the Philistines. His later years were clouded by family dissension and by a revolt among some of his subjects. In spite of his troubles, he behaved with great courage and managed to overcome all his enemies. Before his death, he proclaimed his son Solomon as

Photo: Levant Photo Service

Detail from the Arch of Titus, showing Romans carrying objects from the Temple in Jerusalem after the destruction of the city by the Roman army in A.D. 70.

his successor. Solomon was duly anointed at Gihon by Zadok the priest (1 Kin. 1:39).

Solomon became renowned for his wisdom. He brought the kingdom of Israel to great prominence at a time when other Near Eastern nations were weak politically. He renewed the alliance that David had made with Hiram, king of Tyre, engaging Hiram's workmen to construct a TEMPLE complex in Jerusalem. Although the finished building had some of the characteristics of the wilderness tabernacle, it also included some pagan features. These included the freestanding columns found in Syrian shrines, while certain aspects of the internal decoration reflected Canaanite religious symbolism.

The cost of Solomon's ambitious building projects in and around Jerusalem was high. Much of the agricultural productivity of the land was sent to Phoenicia to pay for materials and workmen's wages. Although Solomon levied tolls on the caravan trade that passed through his kingdom, he could not meet the rising costs that an increasingly lavish way of life involved. He attempted to replenish his depleted resources by increasing productivity in the mining industry of the Arabah and by building a fleet of ships near Elath for trading purposes (1 Kin. 9:26).

In desperation, Solomon finally began a program of forced labor which involved 30,000 men working by rotation (10,000 working every third month), laboring in the forests, mines, and cities under harsh conditions.

Rebellion of the Northern Tribes. As he grew older,

Solomon entered into political marriages with non–Israelites. These women brought with them the gods of their native lands (1 Kin. 11:7–8), adding to the problem of idolatry in Israel. Before Solomon died, he managed to antagonize almost all his subjects. When he was succeeded by his son Rehoboam, the ten northern tribes led by Jeroboam, a former head of the forced labor units, met with him and sought relief from the burdens of work and taxation.

Rehoboam followed bad advice and refused. The northern tribes declared independence and formed a separate kingdom with Jeroboam as head. They named their kingdom "Israel" (this sometimes causes confusion because the name is also used for the remnant of the Covenant People at a later time). The southern section of the divided kingdom was known as Judah. It soon attracted the attention of Shishak, pharaoh of Egypt (about 945–924 B.C.), who moved into Judah, robbed the Temple of its golden objects, and destroyed a number of Judah's fortresses. This event weakened still further an already vulnerable people.

Threat From Syria. Israel's troubles had also begun. The Arameans of Damascus were becoming powerful in Syria and were beginning to put pressure on Israel's northern borders. There was internal instability in the kingdom as well, indicated by the murder of King Nadab (about 908 B.C.), two years after his father Jeroboam's death. His murderer, Baasha, fortified a site close to Jerusalem (1 Kin. 15:17). Asa, the king of Judah (about 911–870 B.C.), appealed to the Syrians for help against

Baasha. Baasha's son Elah reigned for two years (about 886–884 B.C.); Elah was murdered by Zimri, who committed suicide after seven days and plunged the nation into civil war.

Four years later the army general Omri gained control of Israel and began his own dynasty. Omri moved Israel's capital from Tirzah to Samaria, which he fortified strongly. He allied with Phoenicia, and arranged a marriage between his son Ahab and Jezebel, a princess of Tyre. When Ahab (about 874–853 B.C.) became king, he continued Omri's policy of resistance to Syria. But his support of pagan Tyrian religion in Israel drew strong criticism from the prophet Elijah (1 Kin. 18:18). The nation was punished by famine, but this did little to halt the widespread spiritual and social corruption.

About 855 B.C. the Syrian Ben–Hadad attacked Samaria (1 Kin. 20:1) but suffered heavy losses, as he also did the following year at Aphek. Israel was saved by the appearance of the powerful Assyrian forces who, under Shalmaneser III (about 859–824 B.C.), attacked allied Syrian and Israelite forces in 853 B.C. at Qarqar on the Orontes River. The Assyrians were defeated decisively, but the victorious allies soon quarreled, and Ahab died while trying to recover Ramoth Gilead from Syrian control. Meanwhile Mesha, king of Moab, had refused to pay further tribute to Israel; consequently, he was attacked by Ahaziah (about 853–852 B.C.), Ahab's successor.

Jehoram (about 852–841 B.C.) of Israel enlisted Jehoshaphat of Judah (about 873–848 B.C.) in the struggle against Moab, which proved successful (2 Kings 3) as Elisha the prophet had predicted. About 843 B.C. Ben–Hadad was murdered by Hazel (2 Kin. 8:7–13); and two years later Jehu seized the throne of Israel, carrying out a vicious purge of Ahab's house and suppressing pagan religions.

At the same time, Athaliah, queen of Judah, exterminated the royal house except for Jehoash, who was proclaimed king six years later. Jehoash first banned idolatry, but then became attracted to it and subsequently killed the son of the high priest who had protected him earlier. In 841 B.C. Shalmaneser III again attacked a Syrian coalition. But Jehu wished to avoid fighting the Assyrians, so he paid heavy tribute to this powerful nation instead.

Prosperity and the Prophets. For both Israel and Judah the eighth century B.C. was marked by a period of prosperity. Jeroboam II (about 782–752 B.C.) was able to develop agriculture, trade, and commerce because the westward advance of Assyria compelled the Syrian armies to defend their eastern territories. In Judah, Uzziah (790–740 B.C.) raised the prosperity of the country to levels unknown since the time of David. In both nations there was a sense that the true "golden age" had arrived.

Unfortunately, however, idolatry and the rejection of covenant spirituality were prominent, especially in Israel. Prophets such as Amos, Hosea, Micah, and Isaiah spoke out against these abuses. They condemned the exploitation of the poor. They also rebuked the rich for accumulating land and wealth illegally, and for forsaking the simple Hebrew way of life for the luxurious living of pagan nations.

Fall of the Northern Kingdom. The end of all this for Israel occurred shortly after Jeroboam's death. The kingship was left to political opportunists. But they were dwarfed by the powerful Assyrian monarch Tiglath–Pileser III. About 745 B.C. he placed Menahem of Israel (752–741 B.C.) under tribute. But when Menahem died, Israel joined an alliance against Assyria.

Coin issued by the Roman Emperor Vespasian, showing a Roman soldier with a Jewish woman, who weeps over the destruction of Jerusalem in A.D. 70.

A stone monument from the days of Pharaoh Merneptah of Egypt, about 1220 B.C. The inscription contains the earliest known mention of Israel by another nation of the ancient world.

Ahaz of Judah, alarmed by this move, appealed to Tiglath–Pileser for help. Tiglath–Pileser overthrew Damascus in 732 B.C. (Is. 8:4; 17:1; Amos 1:4). He then carried people from the territory of Naphtali captive to Assyria (2 Kin. 15:29). But he still had to reckon with the resistance from Samaria under Pekah, whose murderer, Hoshea, was later made an Assyrian vassal.

On Tiglath–Pileser's death (727 B.C.), Hoshea of Israel rebelled. This brought the Assyrians to Samaria in a siege that ended three years later with the fall of Israel and the deportation of more northern tribesmen in 722 B.C. Isaiah's prediction that God would use Assyria as the rod of His anger upon Israel (Is. 10:5–6) had been fulfilled.

Fall of the Southern Kingdom. The Southern Kingdom under the godly Hezekiah (716–686 B.C.), son and successor of Jehoahaz I, prospered for a time. This was possible because Hezekiah took advantage of a developing power struggle between Assyria and Egypt to fortify Judah and build up its resources. Some 20 years after Samaria fell, Sennacherib, who succeeded Sargon, invaded Palestine and reduced the cities of Joppa, Ashkelon, Timnath, and Ekron in quick succession. An Egyptian army sent to relieve Ekron was defeated about 701 B.C., and the frontier fortress of Lachish came under heavy assault.

The Assyrians also threatened Jerusalem. To gain relief, Hezekiah offered to pay tribute to Sennacherib. In the end the Assyrians withdrew from Palestine, perhaps as the result of being devastated by a plague (2 Kin. 19:35). Hezekiah's successor, Manasseh (about 687–641 B.C.) encouraged idolatry and depravity in Judah, but he reformed toward the end of his life (2 Chr. 33:10–17).

Manasseh's grandson Josiah reigned until 609 B.C. He finally died at Megiddo while trying to prevent the Egyptians from helping the tottering Assyrian Empire. Assyria collapsed with the fall of Nineveh (612 B.C.) and Haran (610 B.C.) to Babylonian and Median forces. Later the Babylonians turned against Jerusalem. In the days of the prophet Jeremiah, they devastated the city in three assaults between 597 and 581 B.C.

The Captivity Years. With the removal of prisoners to Babylonia (Jer. 52:28–30), the Southern Kingdom collapsed and the shock of captivity began for the Hebrew people. The prophets Ezekiel and Daniel ministered in various ways to the distraught captives. For almost seven decades the Jewish people were occupied in building the Babylonian Empire under Nebuchadnezzar II (605–562 B.C.) and Nabonidus (556–539 B.C.). In this alien environment some Hebrew captives lost all hope for the future. But through a ministry of prayer, study of the law, memorial observances, worship, and personal testimony to God's power, Ezekiel was able to promote trust in divine mercy. He kept alive the hope that some day a faithful remnant would return to the ancestral homeland.

Return from Captivity. Magnificent as the Babylonian Empire appeared, it was fundamentally weak. It collapsed under the attack of the Persian ruler Cyrus II. Babylon fell in 538 B.C., and the same year Cyrus proclaimed liberty to all captives in Babylonia. The Hebrew remnant that longed to return home was able to do so between 536 and 525 B.C.

The returnees, however, found a desolate land claimed by Arab tribes and the Samaritans. They had to be urged by HAGGAI and ZECHARIAH to reconstruct the ruined Temple before they could expect divine blessing (Hag. 1:9–11). Even after this had been done, life was still insecure because Jerusalem lacked a defensive wall.

In 458 B.C. EZRA came from Persia as a royal commissioner to survey the situation and report to King Artaxerxes I (464–423 B.C.). Twelve years passed before action was taken, due to the initiative of NEHEMIAH, a high court official, who in 446 B.C. was appointed governor of Judea. As a preliminary step toward restoring regional security and prosperity, he supervised the reconstruction of Jerusalem's wall in the short period of 52 days, after which it was dedicated (Neh. 12:27).

Then Ezra led a ceremony of national confession and commitment to covenant ideals. He also instituted religious reforms which made the law central in community life, as well as reviving tithe–offerings and stressing Sabbath worship. He expelled non–Israelites from the community, regulated the priesthood carefully, and in general laid the foundations of later Judaism.

The Period of Greek Dominance. The restoration of the national life of the Jewish people was achieved quickly because of the peaceful conditions in the Persian Empire. But this phase ended with revolts under Artaxerxes II (404–359 B.C.) and the defeat of Darius III in 331 B.C. by ALEXANDER the Great of Greece. Thereafter Greek culture became firmly established in the ancient world, in spite of the premature death of Alexander in 323 B.C.

The small Judean community, which had faced extinction before because of Canaanite paganism, now reacted with fear lest it should become engulfed by the idolatry of Greek religion. The adoption of Greek traditions transformed the old Persian Empire. When Egypt became hellenized, the culture of Greece was represented strongly in cities such as ALEXANDRIA.

The chief threat to the Jewish community was not so much military or political as religious. Greek religion was coarse and superstitious, and its sensuous nature encouraged a wide following. The philosophy of Stoicism attracted some adherents because of its fatalism and the view that God was in everything, while a less rigorous view of life was taught by Epicurus (341–270 B.C.). He stressed the values of friendship, advising his followers to avoid sensual excesses if they wished to enjoy true pleasure.

By contrast, emphasis upon the teachings of the Jewish law became the hallmark of the SCRIBES, who had replaced the wise men as guardians of Jewish religious tradition. About the second century B.C., they were aided by the rise of a separatist or PHARISEE group, which taught scrupulous observance of the Mosaic Law, advocated synagogue worship, and professed belief in angels, demons, and the resurrection of the dead.

Another influential religious group during this period of Jewish history was the SADDUCEES, an aristocratic priestly minority that exercised close control over Temple ritual. The Sadducees accepted only the Law as Scripture. They would not allow any doctrine that could not be proved directly from the Law. This brought them into conflict with the Pharisees.

Revolt of the Maccabees. The political conflict in Palestine became critical under the Syrian ruler Antiochus IV Epiphanes (175–163 B.C.), who was determined to force Greek culture upon the Jewish community. Greek fashions were imposed upon Jerusalem. This provoked such unrest that Antiochus deliberately polluted the Temple in 168 B.C. and forbade traditional Jewish worship. A Jewish family near Jerusalem rebelled against Greek authority. Its leader, Mattathias, began what is known as the Maccabean revolt. This continued under his son, Judas Maccabeus, who finally won concessions from the Syrian regent Lysias.

Even after the Maccabean war ended, Greek culture exerted a considerable influence in Judea. The province came under Roman rule after 64 B.C. with the rise of the Roman Empire, but this did little to stop the threat presented by Greek religion. In spite of all adversity, the faithful remnant of God's people, Israel, struggled on in hope, looking for the long-promised Messiah who would deliver them from their enemies and bring God's kingdom upon earth.

Jesus and His Ministry. More than 600 years after the prophet Micah had foretold the birthplace of the Messiah (Mic. 5:2), the birth of a baby was announced by an angel to astonished shepherds in Bethlehem. The child was Jesus, God's Messiah (Anointed One), who would ultimately die for the sin of the world.

Jesus carried out a ministry of teaching, preaching, and healing for about three years. He came increasingly under suspicion by the Jewish authorities in Jerusalem. His work won for Him widespread acceptance, but He refused to allow His mission of salvation to be set aside in favor of following popular messianic expectations.

When Jesus condemned Jewish legalism (Mark 7:1–23), the Sadducees and Pharisees rose up in anger. The local Roman ruler Herod Antipas was also becoming concerned about Christ's activities (Luke 13:31). Matters came to a head when He was betrayed to the priests by one of His disciples. The Roman authorities took part in His trial and death, but even His disciples were unprepared for His dramatic resurrection on the first Easter morning.

After 40 days Jesus returned to heaven, leaving His disciples with an evangelistic commission (Matt. 28:18–20) which received a powerful impetus at the feast of Pentecost (Acts 2:1–4). The Christian church which came into being on this day spread across Palestine into Europe and ultimately throughout the world. At the forefront of evangelistic activity was a converted Jew, Paul of Tarsus, whose writings form a large part of the New Testament.

In Palestine, Pontius Pilate was removed from office just before Tiberius died in A.D. 37. Seven years later Herod Agrippa died. In the Roman Empire, Caligula followed Tiberius. Four years later he was succeeded by Claudius. During Paul's missionary journeys, Jews were expelled from Rome (about A.D. 49). About A.D. 52 Felix was made procurator of Judea. Seven years later he was succeeded by Porcius Festus, before whom Paul appeared (Acts 25:1–12).

There were threats of persecution of Christians in the Roman Empire, and these became a reality under Nero. He blamed a disastrous fire in Rome (A.D. 64) upon them to divert suspicion from himself. In A.D. 66 the first revolt against Roman power occurred in Judea. Four years later the Roman emperor Titus marched into Jerusalem, destroyed it, and brought the Jewish state to an end. Thereafter the Jews became a religious group that was scattered across Europe and Asia, while God's message of redemption and salvation was committed to the Christian church.

ISRAELITE [IZ rih uhl ight] — a descendant of Israel, or JACOB (Lev. 23:42–43). Israelites were considered to be children of the COVENANT, faithful servants of the Lord, and heirs to the promises made to Abraham (Rom. 9:4; 11:1). Also see ISRAEL, HISTORY OF.

ISSACHAR [IHZ ah car] (*there is hire* or *reward*) — the name of two men in the Old Testament:
1. The ninth son of Jacob; the fifth by his wife Leah (Gen. 30:17–18; 35:23). He fathered four sons: Tola, Puvah or Puah, Job or Jashub, and Shimron. He and his sons went with their father Jacob to Egypt to escape the famine (Gen. 46:13; Ex. 1:3; Num. 26:23–24; 1 Chr. 2:1; 7:1). Before his death, Jacob described Issachar as "a strong donkey lying down between two burdens" (Gen. 49:15). In other words, Jacob saw that Issachar could be a strong fighter but that his love of comfort could also cause him to settle for the easy way out.
2. A Levite gatekeeper in David's time (1 Chr. 26:5).

ISSACHAR, TRIBE OF — the tribe made up of Issachar's descendants. It consisted of four clans, the descendants of Issachar's four sons (Gen. 46:13; Num. 26:23–24; 1 Chr. 7:1). The territory allotted to this tribe was bounded on the north by Zebulun and Naphtali, on the south and west by Manasseh, and on the east by the Jordan River (Josh. 19:17–23). Most of the fertile Valley of JEZREEL, or Esdraelon, fell within Issachar's territory. Its fertile, flat plains were well-suited for the raising of cattle. In spite of its reputation for seeking comfort, the tribe did fight bravely against Sisera (Judg. 5:15).

Moses prophesied a quiet and happy life for Issachar (Deut. 33:18). At the first census, the tribe numbered 54,400 fighting men (Num. 1:28–29); at the second census 64,300 (Num. 26:25). By David's time it numbered 87,000 (1 Chr. 7:5). Its leaders mentioned in the Bible were Nethaneel (Num. 1:8; 2:8; 7:18; 10:15), and Paltiel (Num. 34:26; the judge Tola (Judg. 10:1), King Baasha (1 Kin. 15:27), and Omri (1 Chr. 27:18).

In accordance with Jacob's blessing, the tribe of Issachar showed an unusual insight into political situations. The tribe switched allegiance from Saul to David (1 Chr. 12:32). Although the tribe was a member of the Northern Kingdom, its members attended Hezekiah of Judah's Passover feast (2 Chr. 30:18).

ISSARON (see WEIGHTS AND MEASURES).

ISSHIAH [ih SHY ah] (*may Jehovah forget*) — the name of two men in the Old Testament:
1. A Levite, head of the house of Rehabiah (1 Chr. 24:21).
2. A Levite of the house of Uzziel (1 Chr. 24:25).

ISSHIJAH [is SHIGH juh] — a form of ISHIJAH.

ISUI [ISS yoo igh] — a form of ISHVI.

ITALIAN REGIMENT — a unit of the Roman army stationed in Caesarea (Acts 10:1), to which CORNELIUS was attached as a centurion. The Greek word translated as regiment refers to a COHORT, consisting of about 600 men under the command of a tribune.

ITALY [ITT uh lih] — a long, boot-shaped country (see Map 7, A–1) that juts into the Mediterranean

Sea (Acts 18:2; Heb. 13:24). It is bounded on the north by the Alps, on the east by the Adriatic Sea, on the south by Sicily and the straits of Messina, and on the west by the Tyrrhenian Sea. Its most important city is Rome. During New Testament times, Rome was the capital of the Roman Empire. Other places in Italy mentioned in the New Testament include RHEGIUM (Acts 28:13), PUTEOLI (Acts 28:13), APPII FORUM (Acts 28:15), and THREE INNS (Acts 28:15). Also see ITALIAN REGIMENT.

ITCH, ITCHING DISEASE (see DISEASES OF THE BIBLE).

ITHAI [IGH thay igh] — a form of ITTAI.

ITHAMAR [ITH uh mahr] (*oasis of palms*) — the youngest of the four sons of Aaron and Elisheba (Ex. 6:23). Ithamar was consecrated for the priestly office, along with his father and his three older brothers (Ex. 28:1). His duty was to number the articles collected for the tabernacle (Ex. 38:21) and to supervise two priestly families, the Gershonites and the Merarites (Num. 4:21–33). The priestly family founded by him included the high priest Eli and his descendants (1 Chr. 24:3–7). Although Ithamar's family eventually lost the high priesthood, it continued as a priestly family after the Captivity (Ezra 8:2).

ITHIEL [ITH ih el] (*God is with me*) — the name of two men in the Old Testament:
1. A Benjamite who returned from Babylon to Jerusalem after the Captivity (Neh. 11:7).
2. A person to whom AGUR addressed his oracle (Prov. 30:1).

ITHLAH [ITH luh] — a form of JETHLAH.

ITHMAH [ITH muh] (*orphan*) — one of David's mighty men (1 Chr. 11:46).

ITHNAN [ITH nan] (*constant*) — a city in southern Judah near Hazor (Josh. 15:23).

ITHRA [ITH ruh] — a form of JITHRA.

ITHRAN [ITH ran] (*excellence*) — a son of Dishon and grandson of Seir the Horite (Gen. 36:26). Also see JITHRAN.

ITHREAM [ITH ree uhm] (*remnant of the people*) — the sixth son born to David and his wife Eglah at Hebron (2 Sam. 3:5).

ITHRITE [ITH right] (*belonging to Jether*) — a family who lived at Kirjath Jearim (1 Chr. 2:53). Two of David's mighty men, Ira and Gareb, were Ithrites (1 Chr. 11:40).

ITTAH KAZIN — a form of ETH KAZIN.

ITTAI [IT uh eye] (*timely*) — the name of two of King David's supporters:
1. A native or inhabitant of the Philistine city of Gath who followed David during the dangerous period of Absalom's rebellion. Ittai, Abishai, and Joab each commanded a third of David's army in the battle of the woods of Ephraim, during which

This elaborate ivory carving discovered at Samaria recalls the words of the prophet Amos that Samaria's "houses of ivory" would be destroyed by God's judgment (Amos 3:12-15).

Absalom was killed (2 Sam. 15:18–22; 18:2, 5, 12). Joab and Abishai are mentioned after this battle, but Ittai is not. Ittai may have been killed during the battle.

2. A son of Ribai, from Gibeah of Benjamin, and one of David's mighty men (2 Sam. 23:29), also called Ithai (1 Chr. 11:31).

ITUREA [iht you REE ah] (*pertaining to Jetur*) — a small territory northeast of the Sea of Galilee at the base of Mount Hermon (see Map 6, C–1). Iturea is mentioned only once in Scripture, in Luke's description of the territory of Herod Philip (Luke 3:1). The name probably derives from the Jetureans, an Arab tribe descended from Jeter, a son of Ishmael (Gen. 25:15; 1 Chr. 1:31), who colonized the area. The Itureans were known as accurate archers and notorious robbers.

The little territory of Iturea was assigned to several different local rulers during the years of Greek dominance of Palestine. When the Romans came into power, Iturea was awarded to Herod the Great. At Herod's death, his son Herod Philip took over the territory. Some scholars believe that Iturea and TRACHONITIS referred to the same territory in New Testament times.

IVAH [IGH vuh] (*sky*) — a city-state of Samaria captured by the Assyrians. Ivah was mentioned by the envoys of Sennacherib in an attempt to break the resistance of Hezekiah to the Assyrian siege of Jerusalem (2 Kin. 18:34; Ivvah, NAS, RSV, NEB, NIV). Ivah may be the same place as Ava (2 Kin. 17:24) or Avva (NAS, RSV, NEB).

IVORY — decorative trim made from tusks of elephants. In Bible times, ivory was a rare and expensive item, found only in the palaces of kings and the homes of the very wealthy. Ornate carvings of ivory were inlaid in thrones, furniture, and the paneling used in expensive homes (1 Kin. 10:18; Ps. 45:8; Ezek. 27:6). The prophet Amos condemned the people of Samaria who lived in houses of ivory (Amos 3:15) and beds of ivory (Amos 6:4) because their wealth was gained through oppression of the common people of the nation of Israel.

Excavation of the royal city of Samaria has yielded evidence of the practice to which Amos referred. About 200 ivory plaques and fragments were discovered in the palace of King Ahab.

IVVAH [EYE vuh] — a form of IVAH.

IYE-ABARIM [igh ee AH buh rim] — a form of IJE ABARIM.

IYIM [EYE yem] — a form of IJIM.

IZHAR [IZ hahr] (*may the deity shine*) — a son of Kohath and the father of Korah (Ex. 6:18, 21). Izhar was the founder of a tribal family, the IZHAR-ITES (Num. 3:27). His name is also spelled Izehar (Num. 3:19, NKJV, KJV).

IZHARITES [IZ hahr ights] — descendants of IZHAR (1 Chr. 24:22; Num. 3:27; Izeharites, KJV).

IZLIAH [iz LIGH uh] — a form of JIZLIAH.

IZRAHIAH [is ruh HIGH uh] (*Jehovah will appear*) — a descendant of Issachar (1 Chr. 7:3). He may be the same person as Jezrahiah (Neh. 12:42).

IZRAHITE [IZ ruh hight] (*may the deity shine forth*) — a member of the family of Izrah or a native or inhabitant of the town of Izrah (1 Chr. 27:8).

IZRI [IZ righ] — a form of JIZRI.

IZZIAH [iz IGH uh] — a form of JEZIAH.

J

JAAKAN [JAY uh kan] (*meaning unknown*) — an ancestor of the "sons of Jaakan" around whose wells the Israelites camped during their wilderness wanderings (Deut. 10:6; Jakan, KJV). At the time of the Exodus, the "sons of Jaakan" lived on the borders of Edom near Mount Hor. Jaakan is also called Akan (Gen. 36:27).

JAAKOBAH [jay uh KOE buh] (*may God protect*) — a descendant of Simeon, the third son of Jacob (1 Chr. 4:36).

JAALA [JAY uh luh] (*ibex*) — the founder of a tribal family whose descendants returned from the Captivity (Ezra 2:56; Jaalah, KJV, RSV).

JAALAM [JAY uh luhm] (*to conceal*) — a son of Esau and Aholibamah, who became a chief of Edom (Gen. 36:18; Jalam, RSV).

JAANAI [JAY uh nigh] (*Jehovah answers*) — a chief of a family descended from Gad (1 Chr. 5:12; Janai, RSV).

JAAR [JAY ur] (*woods*) — poetic RSV word for a place where the ARK OF THE COVENANT rested for 20 years.

JAARE–OREGIM [JAY uh rih OHR uh jim] (*woodsmen*) — the father of Elhanan (2 Sam. 21:19), also called Jair (1 Chr. 20:5).

JAARESHIAH [jar uh SHIGH uh] (*Jehovah plants*) — a son of Jeroham (1 Chr. 8:27; Jaresiah, KJV).

JAASAI [JAY uh sigh] (*Jehovah is maker*) — a man of the family of Bani who divorced his pagan wife after the Captivity (Ezra 10:37; Jaasu, RSV; Jaasau, KJV, NEB).

JAASAU [JAY uh saw] — a form of JAASAI.

JAASIEL [jay AY zih uhl] (*God does*) — the name of two people in the Old Testament:
1. One of David's mighty men (1 Chr. 11:47; Jasiel, KJV).
2. A leader of the tribe of Benjamin during David's reign (1 Chr. 27:21, possibly the same person as Jaasiel No. 1.

JAASU [JAY uh soo] — a form of JAASAI.

JAAZANIAH [jay az uh NIGH uh] (*Jehovah is hearing*) — the name of four men in the Old Testament:

1. A son of Hoshaiah (2 Kin. 25:23), also called Jezaniah (Jer. 40:8; 42:1) and Azariah (Jer. 42:1; RSV).
2. A chief Rechabite (Jer. 35:3).
3. A son of Shaphan and leader of elders who were offering incense to idols (Ezek. 8:11).
4. A prince who gave wicked counsel to his people (Ezek. 11:1).

JAAZER [jay AZ ur] — a form of JAZER.

JAAZIAH [jay uh ZIGH uh] (*may Jehovah strengthen*) — a Levite, a descendant of Merari (1 Chr. 24:26–27).

JAAZIEL [jay AY zih uhl] (*may God nourish*) — a Temple musician in the time of David (1 Chr. 15:18), also called Aziel (1 Chr. 15:20).

JABAL [JAY buhl] (*nomadic*) — a son of Lamech and Adah (Gen. 4:20).

JABBOK [JAB uhk] (*meaning unknown*) — one of the main eastern tributaries of the Jordan River (Deut. 2:37). The stream rose in TRANSJORDAN, in

A hilly region through which the Brook of Jabbok flows. Along one stretch of this small stream, Jacob wrestled with an angel throughout the night (Gen. 32:22-32).

A wadi, or dry stream bed, on the road to Jabesh-Gilead, a city in central Palestine east of the Jordan River (Num. 32:33).

the hills of Bashan near Rabbah of the Ammonites (modern Amman) and entered the Jordan about 25 kilometers (15 miles) north of the Dead Sea (see Map 3, C–3). Near "the ford of Jabbok" Jacob "wrestled with God" and had his name changed to Israel (Gen. 32:22–32).

JABESH [JAY bish] (*dry place*) — the name of a man and a city in the Old Testament:

1. The abbreviated name of JABESH GILEAD, a city in the territory of Gad (1 Chr. 10:12).

2. The father of Shallum (2 Kin. 15:10, 13–14), a king of Israel.

JABESH GILEAD [JAY besh GIL ih add] (*Jabesh of Gilead*) — a town of Gilead (1 Sam. 31:11; 2 Sam. 2:4), situated about 16 kilometers (10 miles) southeast of Beth Shan and about three kilometers (two miles) east of the Jordan River (see Map 4, B–3). It was within the territory assigned to the half–tribe of Manasseh (Num. 32:29, 40).

Jabesh Gilead refused to join in the punishment of the Benjamites (Judg. 21:8–14), an offense for which every man was put to the sword. Four hundred young virgins of Jabesh were given to the Benjamites as wives.

During King Saul's reign, the king of Ammon besieged the city of Jabesh. He promised to spare the lives of those who lived in Jabesh if each of the men would submit to having his right eye put out. A seven–day truce was called and appeal was made to Saul, who mustered an army and defeated the Ammonites (1 Samuel 11).

The people of Jabesh Gilead never forgot this act of Saul. When Saul and his sons were slain at Gilboa, the men of Jabesh Gilead rescued their bodies, cremated them, and buried the ashes near Jabesh (1 Sam. 31:1–13).

Jabesh (1 Chr. 10:12) is the abbreviated name of Jabesh Gilead.

JABEZ [JAY biz] (*he will cause pain*) — the name of a place and a person in the Old Testament:

1. An unidentified place where several families of scribes lived (1 Chr. 2:55).

2. The head of a family of the tribe of Judah noted for his honorable character (1 Chr. 4:9–10).

JABIN [JAY bin] (*one who is perceptive*) — the name of two kings of the Canaanite kingdom of Hazor:

1. A king of Hazor defeated by Joshua at the waters of Merom (Josh. 11:1–14). Jabin organized a number of Canaanite princes against the Israelites.

2. A king of Hazor who oppressed Israel for 20 years. His army, led by SISERA, was defeated by DEBORAH and Barak at the River Kishon (Judg. 4:2).

JABNEEL [JAB nih uhl] (*God is builder*) — the name of two cities of the Old Testament:

1. A city on the northern border of Judah (Josh. 15:11), the same place as the Philistine city of Jabneh (2 Chr. 26:6).

2. A border city of the tribe of Naphtali (Josh. 19:33). This Jabneel is probably the same city as modern Khirbet Yemma, about eight kilometers (five miles) southwest of the Sea of Galilee.

JACAN [JAY kan] — a form of JACHAN.

JACHAN [JAY kan] (*afflicted*) — a clan leader of the tribe of Gad (1 Chr. 5:13; Jacan, RSV).

JACHIN [JAY kin] (*God will establish*) — the name of two Old Testament men:

1. A founder of a tribal family, the JACHINITES (Num. 26:12), also called Jarib (1 Chr. 4:24).

2. Head of the 21st course of priests during David's reign (1 Chr. 24:17). Jachin is also used as a family name (1 Chr. 9:10), describing Jachin's descendants who returned from the Captivity.

JACHIN AND BOAZ [JAY kin, BOE az] (meaning

---

unknown) — the names of twin pillars of cast bronze on each side of the entrance to Solomon's Temple in Jerusalem (2 Chr. 3:17). The pillars stood in front of the Temple and apparently had only decorative significance. When Jerusalem was defeated in 587 B.C., both pillars were destroyed and their metal was carried off to Babylon (2 Kin. 25:13).

JACHINITES [JAY ken ites] — descendants of JACHIN, the fourth son of Simeon (Num. 26:12).

JACINTH (see JEWELS AND PRECIOUS STONES; MINERALS OF THE BIBLE).

JACKAL (see ANIMALS OF THE BIBLE).

JACKAL'S WELL (see SERPENT WELL).

JACKDAW (see ANIMALS OF THE BIBLE).

JACOB [JAY cub] (*a supplanter*) — one of the twin sons of Isaac and Rebekah. The brother of Esau, he was known also as Israel (Gen. 32:28).

Jacob was born in answer to his father's prayer (Gen. 25:21), but he became the favorite son of his mother (25:28). He was nicknamed Jacob because, at the birth of the twins, "his hand took hold of Esau's heel" (25:26). According to the accounts in Genesis, Jacob continued to "take hold of" the possessions of others—his brother's birthright (25:29-34), his father's blessing (27:1-29), and his father-in-law's flocks and herds (30:25-43; 31:1).

The pattern of Jacob's life is found in his journeys, much like the travels of his grandfather ABRAHAM. Leaving his home in Beersheba, he traveled to Bethel (28:10-22); later he returned to Shechem (33:18-20), Bethel (35:6-7), and Hebron (35:27). At Shechem and Bethel he built altars, as Abraham had done (12:6-7; 12:8). Near the end of his life Jacob migrated to Egypt; he died there at an advanced age (Genesis 46—49).

The most dramatic moments in Jacob's life occurred at Bethel (Gen. 28:10-22), at the ford of the River Jabbok (32:22-32), and on his deathbed (49:1-33).

The experience at Bethel occurred when he left the family home at Beersheba to travel to Haran (a city in Mesopotamia), the residence of his uncle Laban (28:10). On the way, as he stopped for the night at Bethel, he had a dream of a staircase reaching from earth to heaven with angels upon it and the Lord above it. He was impressed by the words of the Lord, promising Jacob inheritance of the land, descendants "as the dust of the earth" in number, and His divine presence. Jacob dedicated the site as a place of worship, calling it Bethel (literally, House of God). More than 20 years later, Jacob returned to this spot, built an altar, called the place El Bethel (literally, God of the house of God), and received the divine blessing (35:6-15).

The experience at the ford of the River Jabbok occurred as Jacob returned from his long stay at Haran. While preparing for a reunion with his brother, Esau, of whom he was still afraid (32:7), he had a profound experience that left him changed in both body and spirit.

At the ford of the Jabbok, "Jacob was left alone" (32:24). It was night, and he found himself suddenly engaged in a wrestling match in the darkness. This match lasted until the breaking of the dawn. The socket of Jacob's hip was put out of joint as he struggled with this mysterious stranger, but he refused to release his grip until he was given a blessing. For the first time in the narrative of Genesis, Jacob had been unable to defeat an opponent. When asked to identify himself in the darkness, he confessed he was Jacob—the heel-grabber.

But Jacob's struggling earned him a new name. For his struggle "with God and with men" in which he had prevailed, his name was changed to Israel (literally, Prince with God). In return, he gave a name to the spot that marked the change; it would be called Peniel—"For I have seen God face to face, and my life is preserved" (32:30).

In these first two instances, a deep spiritual sensitivity is evident in Jacob. He appears outwardly brash and grasping, always enriching himself and securing his future. Yet he responded readily to these night experiences—the dream and the wrestling contest—because he apparently sensed "the presence of the holy" in each of them. He also proved to be a man of his word in his dealings with Laban (Gen. 31:6), and in the fulfillment of his vow to return to Bethel (35:1-3).

At the end of his life, Jacob—now an aged man (47:28)—gathered his 12 sons about his bed to tell them what should befall them "in the last days" (49:1). Jacob addressed his sons in the order of their birth.

The harshest language came against Reuben, the firstborn, who was rejected by his father for his sin (49:3-4), and Simeon and Levi, who were cursed for their anger and cruelty (49:5-7). The loftiest language was applied to Judah, who would be praised by his brothers and whose tribe would be the source of royalty, even the ruler of the people (49:8-12).

Words of warning were addressed to Dan, called "a serpent" and "a viper," a life which would be marked by violence (49:16-17). The longest speech was addressed to Joseph, Jacob's favorite son (49:22-26).

Following this scene, Jacob died and was embalmed by the physicians (Gen. 49:33; 50:2). By his own request Jacob was carried back to the land of Canaan and was buried in the family burial ground in the cave of the field of MACHPELAH (Gen. 49:29-32; 50:13).

JACOB, TESTAMENT OF (see PSEUDEPIGRAPHA).

JACOB'S WELL — the well where Jesus talked to the Samaritan woman (John 4:1-26). This is the earliest reference to Jacob's well; it is not mentioned in the Old Testament. The well, known today as Bir Ya'qub ("the well of Jacob"), is near Tell Balatah, regarded by some scholars as ancient Shechem.

JADA [JAY duh] (*God cares*) — a son of Onam and grandson of Jerahmeel (1 Chr. 2:28, 32).

JADDAI [JAD eye] (*friend*) — an Israelite who divorced his pagan wife after the Captivity (Ezra 10:43; Jadau, KJV).

JADDUA [JAJ oo uh] (*known*) — the name of two priests in the Book of Nehemiah:
1. A Levite who sealed the covenant with Nehemiah (Neh. 10:21).
2. A son of Jonathan and a descendant of the high priest Jeshua (Neh. 12:11, 22). Jaddua returned with Zerubbabel from the Captivity. He was the last HIGH PRIEST mentioned in the Old Testament.

JADE (see JEWELS AND PRECIOUS STONES).

JADON [JAY dahn] (*Jehovah judges*) — an Israelite who helped repair the walls of Jerusalem after the Captivity (Neh. 3:7).

JAEL [JAY uhl] (*mountain goat*) — the woman who killed Sisera, Israel's mighty enemy, by driving a tent peg through his temple while he slept (Judg. 4:17–22). Sisera accepted Jael's invitation to seek refuge in her tent. She covered him with a mantle, gave him milk to quench his thirst, and promised to stand guard against intruders. Instead, Jael killed Sisera as he slept. In her famous song, the prophetess Deborah honored Jael: "Most blessed above women is Jael" (Judg. 5:24).

JAGUR [JAY gur] (*dwelling*) — an unidentified town in southeastern Judah, near the border with Edom (Josh. 15:21).

JAHALELEEL [juh HAH luh leel] (*may God shine forth*) — a descendant of Judah through Caleb (1 Chr. 4:16; Jehallelel, NIV, RSV; Jehaleleel, KJV).

JAHATH [JAY hath] (*God will snatch up*) — the name of five men in the Old Testament:
1. A son of Reaiah (1 Chr. 4:2).
2. A son of Libni (1 Chr. 6:20, 43).
3. A son of Shimei (1 Chr. 23:10, 11).
4. A Levite of the family of Kohath (1 Chr. 24:22).
5. A Levite who helped repair the Temple during the reign of Josiah (2 Chr. 34:12).

JAHAZ [JAY haz] (*an open space*) — a city in the wastelands of Moab where Sihon, king of the Amorites, was defeated by the Israelites when he refused to allow them to pass through his territory (Num. 21:23). Jahaz was assigned to the tribe of Reuben (Josh. 13:18) and set apart for the Merarite Levites (Josh. 21:34–36). Later the city was captured by Mesha, king of Moab, and was part of Moab in the time of the prophets Isaiah and Jeremiah (Is. 15:4). Other spellings of Jahaz are Jahaza (KJV), Jahazah (KJV, NEB), and Jahzah (RSV, NEB).

JAHAZA [juh HAY zuh] — a form of JAHAZ (Josh. 13:18).

JAHAZAH [juh HAY zuh] — a form of JAHAZ.

JAHAZIAH [jay huh ZIGH uh] (*Jehovah reveals*) — a son of Tikvah and one of four men who opposed

Ezra's condemnation of improper marriages (Ezra 10:15, 44; Jahzeiah, NIV, RSV, NEB).

JAHAZIEL [juh HAY zih uhl] (*may God see*) — the name of five men in the Old Testament:
1. A Benjamite warrior who joined David's army at Ziklag (1 Chr. 12:4).
2. A priest who blew a trumpet before the ARK OF THE COVENANT as it was transported to Jerusalem (1 Chr. 16:6).
3. A Levite, the third son of Hebron (1 Chr. 23:19; 24:23).
4. A Levite who encouraged Jehoshaphat and his army to fight against the Ammonite, Edomite, and Moabite invaders (2 Chr. 20:14–17).
5. The father of a clan leader who returned with Ezra from the Captivity (Ezra 8:5).

JAHDAI [JAH digh] (*leader*) — a man of Judah, apparently of the family of Caleb (1 Chr. 2:47).

JAHDIEL [JAH dih uhl] (*may God rejoice*) — a leader in the half-tribe of Manasseh who lived in Transjordan (1 Chr. 5:24).

JAHDO [JAH doe] (*may God rejoice*) — a son of Buz the Gadite (1 Chr. 5:14).

JAHLEEL [JAH lih uhl] (*God waits*) — the third son of Zebulun (Gen. 46:14) and ancestor of the JAHLEELITES (Num. 26:26).

JAHLEELITES [JAY lih uhl lights] — descendants of JAHLEEL (Num. 26:26).

JAHMAI [JAH migh] (*Jehovah protects*) — a son of Tola and a clan leader of the tribe of Issachar (1 Chr. 7:2).

JAHZAH [JAH zuh] — a form of JAHAZ.

JAHZEEL [JAH zih uhl] (*may God distribute*) — a son of Naphtali and ancestor of the Jahzeelites (Gen. 46:24), also spelled Jahziel (1 Chr. 7:13).

JAHZEELITES [JAH zih uhl ights] — descendants of JAHZEEL (Num. 26:48).

JAHZEIAH [jah ZEE uh] — a form of JAHAZIAH.

JAHZERAH [JAH zuh ruh] (*prudent*) — a priest whose descendants lived in Jerusalem after the Captivity (1 Chr. 9:12), probably the same person as AHZAI (Neh. 11:13).

JAHZIEL [JAH zih uhl] — a form of JAHZEEL.

JAILER — a keeper of a prison (Acts 16:23). The same Greek noun (*desmophulax*) translated as jailer is also translated as keeper of the prison (Acts 16:27, 36).

JAIR [JAY ur] (*may Jehovah shine forth*) — the name of four people and one place in the Old Testament:
1. A descendant of Judah (Num. 32:41; Deut. 3:14).
2. An abbreviated form of HAVOTH JAIR ("towns of Jair" Josh. 13:30).
3. A Gileadite who judged Israel for 22 years (Judg. 10:3, 5).

4. The father of Elhanan (1 Chr. 20:5), also called Jaare-Oregim (2 Sam. 21:19).

5. A Benjamite, the father of Mordecai, Esther's cousin (Esth. 2:5).

JAIRITE [JAY ur ight] — a descendant of JAIR No. 1 (2 Sam. 20:26).

JAIRUS [jay EYE ruhs] (*he will awaken*) — a ruler of a synagogue near Capernaum and the Sea of Galilee. Jairus' daughter was miraculously raised from the dead by Jesus (Mark 5:21–23, 35–43).

JAKAN [JAY kuhn] — a form of JAAKAN.

JAKEH [JAY kuh] (meaning unknown) — an ancestor of Agur, the wise man who wrote the 30th chapter of the Book of Proverbs (Prov. 30:1).

JAKIM [JAY kim] (*may God establish*) — the name of two men in the Old Testament:

1. A son of Shimei (1 Chr. 8:19).
2. A head of a family of priests (1 Chr. 24:12).

JALAM [JAY luhm] — a form of JAALAM.

JALON [JAY lahn] (meaning unknown) — a son of Ezrah (1 Chr. 4:17).

JAMBRES [JAM breez] (see JANNES AND JAMBRES).

JAMES — the name of five men in the New Testament:

1. James, the son of Zebedee, one of Jesus' twelve apostles. James' father was a fisherman; his mother, Salome, often cared for Jesus' daily needs (Matt. 27:56; Mark 15:40–41). In lists of the twelve apostles, James and his brother John always form a group of four with two other brothers, Peter and Andrew. The four were fishermen on the Sea of Galilee. Their call to follow Jesus is the first recorded event after the beginning of Jesus' public ministry (Matt. 4:18–22; Mark 1:16–20).

James is never mentioned apart from his brother John in the New Testament, even at his death (Acts 12:2). When the brothers are mentioned in the Gospels, James is always mentioned first, probably because he was the older. After the resurrection, however, John became the more prominent, probably because of his association with Peter (Acts 3:1; 8:14). James was killed by Herod Agrippa I, the grandson of Herod the Great, some time between A.D. 42–44. He was the first of the twelve apostles to be put to death and the only one whose martyrdom is mentioned in the New Testament (Acts 12:2).

James and John must have contributed a spirited and headstrong element to Jesus' band of followers, because Jesus nicknamed them "Sons of Thunder" (Mark 3:17). On one occasion (Luke 9:51–56), when a Samaritan village refused to accept Jesus, the two asked Jesus to call down fire in revenge, as the prophet Elijah once had done (2 Kin. 1:10, 12). On another occasion, they earned the anger of their fellow disciples by asking if they could sit on Jesus' right and left hands in glory (Matt. 20:20–28; Mark 10:35–45).

James was one of three disciples—Peter, James, and John—whom Jesus took along privately on three special occasions. The three accompanied Him when He healed the daughter of Jairus (Mark 5:37; Luke 8:51); they witnessed His transfiguration (Matt. 17:1; Mark 9:2; Luke 9:28); and they were also with Him in His agony in Gethsemane (Matt. 26:37; Mark 14:33).

2. James, the son of Alphaeus. This James was also one of the twelve apostles. In each list of the apostles he is mentioned in ninth position (Matt. 10:3; Mark 3:18; Luke 6:15; Acts 1:13).

3. James the Less. This James is called the son of Mary (not the mother of Jesus), and the brother of Joses (Matt. 27:56; Mark 16:1; Luke 24:10). Mark 15:40 refers to him as "James the Less." The Greek word *mikros* can mean either "small" or "less." It could, therefore, mean James the smaller (in size), or James the less (well-known).

4. James, the father of Judas. Two passages in the New Testament refer to a James, the father of Judas (Luke 6:16; Acts 1:13). Judas was one of the twelve apostles; he was the last to be listed before his more infamous namesake, Judas Iscariot.

5. James, the brother of Jesus. James is first mentioned as the oldest of Jesus' four younger brothers (Matt. 13:55; Mark 6:3).

In the third and fourth centuries A.D., when the idea of the perpetual virginity of Mary gained ground, a number of church fathers argued that James was either a stepbrother to Jesus (by a former marriage of Joseph) or a cousin. But both options are forced. The New Testament seems to indicate that Mary and Joseph bore children after Jesus (Matt. 1:25; 12:47; Luke 2:7; John 2:12; Acts 1:14), and that the second oldest was James (Matt. 13:55–56; Mark 6:3). The gospels reveal that Jesus' family adopted a skeptical attitude toward His ministry (Matt. 12:46–50; Mark 3:31–35; Luke 8:19–21; John 7:5). James apparently held the same attitude, because his name appears in no lists of the apostles, nor is he mentioned elsewhere in the gospels.

After Jesus' crucifixion, however, James became a believer. Paul indicated that James was a witness to the resurrection of Jesus (1 Cor. 15:7). He called James an apostle (Gal. 1:19), though like himself, not one of the original Twelve (1 Cor. 15:5, 7).

In the Book of Acts, James emerges as the leader of the church in Jerusalem. His brothers also became believers and undertook missionary travels (1 Cor. 9:5). But James considered it his calling to oversee the church in Jerusalem (Gal. 2:9). He advocated respect for the Jewish law (Acts 21:18–25), but he did not use it as a weapon against Gentiles. Paul indicated that James endorsed his ministry to the Gentiles (Gal. 2:1–10).

The decree of the COUNCIL OF JERUSALEM (Acts 15:12–21) cleared the way for Christianity to become a universal religion. Gentiles were asked only "to abstain from things polluted by idols, from sexual immorality, from things strangled, and from blood" (Acts 15:20). The intent of this decree was practical rather than theological. It asked the Gentiles to observe certain practices which otherwise would offend their Jewish brethren in the Lord and jeopardize Christian fellowship with them.

Both Paul and Acts portray a James who was personally devoted to Jewish tradition but flexible enough to modify it to admit non-Jews into Christian fellowship. This James is probably the author of the Epistle of James in the New Testament.

JAMES, EPISTLE OF — the first of the general epistles of the New Testament and a book characterized by its hard-hitting, practical religion. The epistle reads like a sermon and, except for a brief introduction, has none of the traits of an ancient letter. Each of the five chapters is packed with pointed illustrations and reminders designed to motivate the wills and hearts of believers to grasp a truth once taught by Jesus: "A tree is known by its fruit" (Matt. 12:33).

Authorship and Date. The author identifies himself as "James, a servant of God and of the Lord Jesus Christ" (1:1). At least five personalities named JAMES appear in the New Testament. None has a stronger claim to being the author of this epistle than James, the brother of the Lord. Apparently neither a disciple nor an apostle during Jesus' lifetime, he is first mentioned in Mark 6:3, where he is listed as the first (oldest) of Jesus' four younger brothers. After the ascension of Jesus, James emerged as a leader of the church in Jerusalem (Acts 15:13; 1 Cor. 15:7; Gal. 2:9)—a position he must have occupied for nearly 30 years, until his martyrdom, according to church tradition.

This James is probably the author of the epistle that bears his name. He refers to himself simply as "James," with no explanation added. This indicates he was well-known to his readers. He calls himself a "servant" rather than an apostle; and he begins the epistle with the same "greetings" (1:1) with which he begins the apostolic decree following the Council of Jerusalem (Acts 15:23). These factors suggest one and the same James, the brother of the Lord.

The most important argument against authorship by the Lord's brother is that the Epistle of James was virtually unknown in the ancient church until the third century. It remains an unsolved mystery why it was neglected and then accepted into the New Testament canon at a relatively late date if James, the Lord's brother, were its author. Although this consideration cannot be overlooked, it does not overrule the Lord's brother as the most probable author of the epistle.

The Epistle of James gives few hints by which it might be dated. Estimates range from A.D. 45 to 150, depending on how one regards its authorship. If James, the Lord's brother, is its author, then it must have been written before A.D. 62 (the approximate time of his death). The epistle may have been written after Paul's letters were in circulation, because James' emphasis on works may be intended to offset Paul's emphasis on faith. This would date the epistle around A.D. 60.

Historical Setting. James addresses the epistle "to the twelve tribes which are scattered abroad" (1:1). This implies a readership of Jewish Chrstians living outside Palestine. Elsewhere in the epistle, however, James refers to hired field labor (5:4), and this locates his audience inside Palestine. In James' day only in Palestine did farmers employ hired rather than slave labor, as was customary elsewhere. The epistle makes frequent references or allusions to the Old Testament. Its style and language are reminiscent of the Old Testament, especially wisdom literature and the prophet Amos. All these factors

---

JAMES: A Teaching Outline

indicate that James was writing to persons of Jewish-Christian background. His emphasis was on the essentials of obedient living in accordance with the true intent of the law of God.

Theological Contribution. The Epistle of James is a sturdy, compact letter on practical religion. For James, the acid test of true religion is in the doing rather than in the hearing, "believing," or speaking. James exalts genuineness of faith, and is quick to encourage the lowly that God gives grace to the humble (4:6), wisdom to the ignorant (1:5), salvation to the sinner (1:21), and the kingdom to the poor (2:5). He is equally quick to condemn counterfeit religion which would substitute theory for practice, and he does so with biting sarcasm. True religion is moral religion and social religion. True religion is *doing* the right thing in one's everyday affairs. In this respect James echoes clearly the ethical teaching of Jesus, especially as it is recorded in the Sermon on the Mount (Matthew 5—7). "Not everyone who says to Me, 'Lord, Lord,' shall enter the kingdom of heaven, but he who does the will of My Father in heaven" (Matt. 7:21).

Special Considerations. Some Bible scholars suggest that James and Paul differ in their views on the saving significance of faith and works. Paul states, "A man is justified by faith apart from the deeds of the law" (Rom. 3:28), and James says, "A man is justified by works, and not by faith only" (James 2:19). A closer reading of the two, however, reveals that they differ more in their definition of faith than in its essence. James writes to readers who are inclined to interpret faith as mere intellectual acknowledgment (James 2:19). As a consequence he stresses that a faith which does not affect life is not saving faith; hence, his emphasis on works. Actually, this is quite close to Paul's understanding. For Paul, faith is the entrusting of one's whole life to God through Christ, with the result that one's life becomes renewed with the "fruit of the Spirit" (Gal. 5:22).

JAMES, PROTEVANGELIUM OF (see APOCRYPHA).

JAMIN [JAY min] (*right hand; south*) — the name of three men in the Old Testament:

1. Founder of a tribal family, the JAMINITES (Num. 26:12).

2. A son of Ram, of the tribe of Judah (1 Chr. 2:27).

3. A priest who helped interpret the law for the people after the Captivity (Neh. 8:7).

JAMINITES [JAY min ights] — descendants of JAMIN No. 1 (Num. 26:12).

JAMLECH [JAM lek] (*Jehovah rules*) — a chief of the tribe of Simeon (1 Chr. 4:34, 41).

JANAI [JAN eye] — a form of JAANAI.

JANGLING, VAIN — KJV phrase for the senseless, foolish, and empty chatter of those who talk contrary to God and God's revelation (1 Tim. 1:6; idle talk, NKJV; fruitless discussion, NASB; meaningless talk, NIV; a wilderness of words, NEB).

JANIM [JAY nim] — a form of JANUM.

JANNA [JAN uh] (meaning unknown) — an ancestor of Jesus (Luke 3:24; Jannai, NIV, RSV).

JANNES AND JAMBRES [JAN iz, jam BREZ] (*he who seduces; he who is rebellious*) — two men who, according to the apostle Paul, "resisted Moses" (2 Tim. 3:8). Although Jannes and Jambres are not named in the Old Testament, they are common figures in late Jewish tradition. According to legend, they were two Egyptian magicians who opposed Moses' demand that the Israelites be freed. They sought to duplicate the miracles of Moses in an attempt to discredit him before Pharaoh (Ex. 7:11–12, 22).

JANOAH [juh NOE uh] (*resting place*) — a town in northern Naphtali, in upper Galilee, captured by King Tiglath–Pileser of Assyria in 733 B.C. (2 Kin. 15:29).

JANOHAH [juh NOE huh] (*resting place*) — a town on the northern border of Ephraim (Josh. 16:6–7), possibly present–day Khirbet Yanun, about 11 kilometers (7 miles) southeast of Shechem.

JANUM [JAY nuhm] (*slumbering*) — a village in the hill country of Judah (Josh. 15:53; Janim, NIV, RSV, NEB).

JAPHETH [JAY fehth] — one of the three sons of Noah, usually mentioned after his two brothers Shem and Ham (Gen. 5:32; 6:10; 1 Chr. 1:4), and thus presumed to be the youngest. Japheth and his wife were two of the eight people who entered the ark and were saved from the destructive waters of the Flood (Gen. 7:7; 1 Pet. 3:20).

Japheth's descendants spread over the north and west regions of the earth: "The sons of Japheth were Gomer, Magog, Madai, Javan, Tubal, Meshech, and Tiras" (1 Chr. 1:5). The Medians, Greeks, Romans, Russians, and Gauls are referred to as his descendants. The Philistines, too, were descendants of Japheth (Gen. 9:27).

JAPHIA [juh FIGH uh] (*may God enlighten*) — the name of two people and one place in the Old Testament:

1. A king of Lachish, one of five Amorite kings who formed a military alliance to repel the Israelite invasion. They were defeated and executed by Joshua near the cave of Makkedah (Josh. 10:3).

2. A town on the border of Zebulun (Josh. 19:12), identified as Yafa, a site less than three kilometers (two miles) southwest of Nazareth.

3. A son of David, born during his reign in Jerusalem (2 Sam. 5:14–15).

JAPHLET [JAF lit] (*may God deliver*) — a son of Heber, an Asherite (1 Chr. 7:32–33).

JAPHLETI — [jaf LEE tie] a form of JAPHLETITES.

JAPHLETITES [JAF lih tights] — the descendants

Photo by Willem A. VanGemeren

Mount Gilboa, site of the battle in which King Saul and his three sons were killed. The account of this battle was recorded in the Bible (1 Sam. 31:8) as well as the lost book of Jasher.

of Japhlet (although apparently not the Japhlet mentioned in 1 Chr. 7:32–33). They lived near the southern border of Ephraim (Josh. 16:3; Japhleti, KJV).

JAPHO [JAY foe] — a form of JOPPA.

JAR — a container made of earthenware, used primarily for liquids but sometimes for dry goods. A jar could be used for both storage (1 Kin. 17:12) and serving (1 Kin. 19:6). Similar containers are called by several different names in the Bible. They are sometimes called "waterpots" (John 2:6), or "vessels" (Gen. 43:11).

JARAH [JAHR uh] — a form of JEHOADDAH.

JAREB [JAY rib] (*avenger*) — a figurative description, perhaps a nickname, of an Assyrian king who received tribute from Israel (Hos. 5:13; 10:6). The NIV, RSV and NEB translate as "the great king." The name may be a reference to Sargon II, who captured Samaria in 722 B.C.

JARED [JAY rid] (*servant*) — father of Enoch and an ancestor of Abraham and Jesus (Gen. 5:15–16; 1 Chr. 1:2; Jared, KJV; Luke 3:37).

JARESIAH [jar uh SIGH uh] — a form of JAARESHIAH.

JARHA [JAHR huh] (meaning unknown) — an Egyptian servant of a man of Judah, Sheshan (1 Chr. 2:34–35). Sheshan gave his daughter in marriage to Jarha, and she later gave birth to Attai.

JARIB [JAY rib] (*may God strive*) — the name of three men in the Old Testament:
1. A son of Simeon (1 Chr. 4:24), also called Jachin (Ex. 6:15).
2. A clan leader in Ezra's time (Ezra 8:15–16).
3. A priest who divorced his pagan wife after the Captivity (Ezra 10:18).

JARMUTH [JAHR muhth] (*a height*) — the name of two cities in the Old Testament:
1. A city in the lowlands of Judah, formerly belonging to the Amorites, whose king, Piram, was killed by Joshua (Josh. 10:3; 12:11).
2. A city in Issachar assigned to the Levites (Josh. 21:29), probably the same place as Remeth (Josh. 19:21) and Ramoth (1 Chr. 6:73).

JAROAH [juh ROE uh] (*new moon*) — father of Huri, of the tribe of Gad (1 Chr. 5:14).

JASHAR [JAY shur] — a form of JASHER.

JASHEN [JAY shuhn] (*sleepy*) — the father of one of David's mighty men (2 Sam. 23:32). Jashen was apparently the same person as Hashem (1 Chr. 11:34).

JASHER, BOOK OF [JAY shur] — an ancient collection of verse, now lost, which described great events in the history of Israel. The book contained Joshua's poetic address to the sun and the moon at the battle of Gibeon (Josh. 10:12–13) and the "Song of the Bow," which is David's lament over the death of Saul and Jonathan (2 Sam. 1:17–27; Jashar, NIV, RSV, NEB).

JASHOBEAM [juh SHOE bih uhm] (*the kinsmen return*) — the name of two of David's soldiers:
1. One of David's mighty men and a chief of his captains (1 Chr. 11:11; 27:2), also called Josheb–Basshebeth (2 Sam. 23:8).
2. A Benjamite who joined David's army at Ziklag (1 Chr. 12:6).

JASHUB [JAY shuhb] (*turning back*) — the name of two men in the Old Testament:
1. A son of Issachar and founder of a tribal family, the JASHUBITES (Num. 26:24). Jashub is also called Job (Gen. 46:13) and Iob, RSV.

2. A son of Bani who divorced his pagan wife after the Captivity (Ezra 10:29).

JASHUBI–LEHEM [juh SHOO bigh LEE hem] (*returning to Beth Lehem*) — a descendant of Judah, of the family of Shelah (1 Chr. 4:22).

JASHUBITES [JAY shuhb ights] — descendants of JASHUB (Num. 26:24).

JASIEL [JAY sih uhl] — a form of JAASIEL.

JASON [JAY suhn] (*healing*) — the name of one or two early Christians who worked with the apostle Paul:
   1. A Christian of Thessalonica who gave lodging to Paul and Silas in his home during their visit to his city (Acts 17:5–7, 9). A mob of "evil men from the marketplace," incited by "the Jews who were not persuaded," attacked the house of Jason. When they could not find Paul and Silas, they dragged Jason before the rulers of the city on charges of disturbing the peace.
   2. A "kinsman" or fellow countryman of the apostle Paul who sent greetings to Rome (Rom. 16:21). He may be the same person as Jason No. 1.

JASPER (see JEWELS AND PRECIOUS STONES; MINERALS OF THE BIBLE).

JATHNIEL [JATH nih uhl] (*God is giving*) — a son of Meshelemiah and a gatekeeper of the sanctuary (1 Chr. 26:2).

JATTIR [JAT ur] (*preeminence*) — a Levitical city in the hill country of Judah (Josh. 15:48). Jattir was one of the cities to which David sent spoils of war from Ziklag (1 Sam. 30:27). The site is known today as Khirbet Attir, about 21 kilometers (13 miles) southwest of Hebron.

JAVAN [JAY vuhn] (meaning unknown) — the name of a person and a place in the Old Testament:
   1. The fourth son of Japheth, son of Noah. Javan was the father of the Ionians, or Greeks (Gen. 10:2).
   2. A town or trading post in southern Arabia (see Map 1, A–1) from which the Syrians obtained wrought iron, cassia (cinnamon), and calamus (cane) (Ezek. 27:13, 19).

JAVELIN (see ARMS, ARMOR OF THE BIBLE).

JAZER [JAY zur] (*fortified*) — a fortified Amorite city east of the Jordan River, in or near the region of Gilead (Josh. 13:25). Israel captured Jazer from the Amorites, allotted it to the tribe of Gad, and then gave it to the Levites. Jazer was probably situated on the plain north of Heshbon. Noted for its pasture lands, Jazer and the surrounding region was a good place for livestock (Num. 32:1). It also produced luxuriant grapevines and fruit trees (Is. 16:8–9).
   The Ammonites, Amorites, Israelites, and Moabites all contested the possession of Jazer and its productive lands. The KJV also translates the name as Jaazer (Num. 21:32; 32:35).

JAZIZ [JAY ziz] (*shining*) — overseer of King David's flocks (1 Chr. 27:31).

JEALOUSY OFFERING — part of an adultery trial, also known as the ordeal of jealousy. If a man accused his wife of adultery but had no proof of her guilt, the Law provided a ritual to determine whether she was innocent or guilty (Num. 5:11–31). If she swore her innocence, the woman was forced to drink a potion made of holy water mixed with dust from the floor of the tabernacle (v. 17); and the priest burned the offering, made of barley meal, on the altar (v. 26).
   If she was guilty of adultery, she would suffer; but if she was innocent, she would be spared. In this way the decision was placed in the hands of God.

JEARIM, MOUNT [JEE uh rim] (*mountain of woods*) — a mountain on the northern border of Judah, probably the same place as Mount Seir, about 14.5 kilometers (9 miles) north of Jerusalem.

JEATHERAI [jee ATH uh righ] (*steadfast*) — a Levite of the family of Gershon (1 Chr. 6:21; Jeaterai, KJV).

JEBERECHIAH [jih bar uh KIGH uh] (*Jehova blesses*) — father of Zechariah (Is. 8:2), not to be confused with Zechariah the prophet.

JEBUS [JEE buhs] (meaning unknown) — an early name for the city of Jerusalem (Judg. 19:10–11). The citadel of Jebus, "the stronghold of Zion," was captured by the army of David, who called it "the City of David" (2 Sam. 5:7, 9). Also see JEBUSITES.

JEBUSITES [JEBB you sites] — the name of the original inhabitants of the city of JEBUS, their name for ancient Jerusalem (Judg. 19:10–11; 1 Chr. 11:4–6). When the Israelites invaded Palestine under the leadership of Joshua, the Jebusites were ruled by Adoni–Zedek (Josh. 10:1, 3), one of five Amorite kings who resisted the Hebrew conquest. These five kings were defeated and slain by Joshua (Josh. 10:16–27). But the Jebusites were not driven out of Jebus (Jerusalem).
   After David was anointed king, he led his army against the Jebusites. His military commander, Joab, apparently entered the city through an underground water shaft and led the conquest (2 Sam. 5:6–9; 1 Chr. 11:4–8). David then made this former Jebusite stronghold, now called the "City of David," the capital of his kingdom.
   The site on which Solomon's Temple was built in Jerusalem was previously a threshing floor that belonged to a Jebusite by the name of Araunah (2 Sam. 24:16–24), or Ornan (1 Chr. 21:24–25). David refused to accept this property as a gift from Araunah and paid him 50 shekels of silver for the land. Apparently David treated the defeated Jebusites humanely, but his son Solomon "raised forced labor" (1 Kin. 9:21) from their ranks.

JECAMIAH [jek uh MIGH uh] (*may Jehovah establish*) — a descendant of Jeconiah, king of Judah (1 Chr. 3:18; Jekamiah, NIV, RSV).

JECHILIAH, JECOLIAH [jek ih LIGH uh] — forms of JECHOLIAH.

JECHOLIAH [jek uh LIGH uh] (*Jehovah is able*) — the mother of Azariah (or Uzziah), king of Judah (2 Kin. 15:2; 2 Chr. 26:3; Jechiliah, NASB; Jecoliah, NIV, NEB, RSV). She was the wife of King Amaziah of Judah, the father and predecessor of Azariah.

JECONIAH [JEK uh nigh uh] — a form of JEHOIACHIN.

JEDAIAH [juh DAY uh] (*Jehovah has favored*) — the name of seven men in the Old Testament:
  1. A son of Shimri (1 Chr. 4:37).
  2. A priest in Jerusalem (1 Chr. 9:10; 24:7).
  3. A priest whose descendants returned from the Captivity (Neh. 7:39).
  4. An Israelite who helped repair the wall of Jerusalem (Neh. 3:10).
  5. A priest who returned from the Captivity with Zerubbabel (Neh. 11:10).
  6. Another priest who returned with Zerubbabel (Neh. 12:7, 21).
  7. One of the returned captives who brought gold and silver from Babylon to Jerusalem for the Temple (Zech. 6:10, 14).

JEDIAEL [juh DIGH uhl] (*known by God*) — the name of three or four men in the Old Testament:
  1. A son of Benjamin and founder of a family (1 Chr. 7:6, 10–11).
  2. One of David's mighty men (1 Chr. 11:45).
  3. A Manassite warrior who joined David's army at Ziklag (1 Chr. 12:20). He may be identical with Jediael No. 2.
  4. A gatekeeper of the tabernacle during David's reign (1 Chr. 26:2).

JEDIDAH [juh DIGH duh] (*beloved*) — the mother of King Josiah of Judah (2 Kin. 22:1–2). Jedidah was the wife of King Amon of Judah. Her son, Josiah, succeeded Amon as king.

JEDIDIAH [jed uh DIGH uh] (*beloved of the Lord*) — the name given to Solomon at his birth by Nathan the prophet (2 Sam. 12:25), symbolizing God's forgiveness of the wayward David.

JEDUTHUN [juh DOO thuhn] (*the praising one*) — the name of one or two men in the Old Testament:
  1. A Levite of the family of Merari (1 Chr. 9:16; 16:41–42), appointed a sanctuary musician in David's time. Apparently he was the same person as ETHAN (1 Chr. 6:44).
  2. The father of Obed-Edom (1 Chr. 16:38).

JEEZER [juh EE zur] — a form of ABIEZER.

JEEZERITES [juh EE zur ites] — descendants of JEEZER, the son of Gilead, of the tribe of Manasseh (Num. 26:30; Iezerites, RSV, NIV, NASB). Elsewhere Jeezer is referred to as Abiezer (Josh. 17:2; 1 Chr. 7:18), and his descendants are called Abiezrites (Judg. 6:11, 24).

JEGAR SAHADUTHA [JEE gur say uh DOO thuh] (*witness heap*) — a pile of stones set up by Jacob and Laban as a reminder of their agreement (Gen. 31:47).

JEHALELEEL [juh HAH luh leel] — a form of JAHALELEEL.

JEHALELEL [juh HAH lih lel] (*may God shine forth*) — a Levite who lived during the reign of King Hezekiah of Judah (2 Chr. 29:12; Jehallelel, RSV).

JEHALLELEL [juh HAH lih lel] — a form of JAHALELEEL; JEHALELEL.

JEHDEIAH [juh DEE uh] (*may Jehovah rejoice*) — the name of two men in the Old Testament:
  1. A Levite, a son of Shubael (1 Chr. 24:20).
  2. An official in charge of King David's donkeys (1 Chr. 27:30).

JEHEZEKEL [juh HEZ uh kel] (*Jehovah strengthens*) — a priest descended from Aaron (1 Chr. 24:16; Jehezkel, NIV, RSV).

JEHEZKEL [juh HEZ kel] — a form of JEHEZEKEL.

JEHIAH [juh HIGH uh] (*Jehovah lives*) — a Levite doorkeeper for the ARK OF THE COVENANT in David's time (1 Chr. 15:24).

JEHIEL [juh HIGH uhl] (*God lives*) — the name of 10 or 11 men in the Old Testament:
  1. A Levite who helped David transport the ARK OF THE COVENANT to Jerusalem (1 Chr. 15:18, 20; 16:5).
  2. A Levite of the family of Gershon. Jehiel supervised the treasury of the Temple (1 Chr. 23:8; 29:8).
  3. A companion of David's sons (1 Chr. 27:32).
  4. A son of King Jehoshaphat (2 Chr. 21:2).
  5. A son of Heman the singer in the time of King Hezekiah of Judah (2 Chr. 29:14; Jehuel, RSV).
  6. A Levite in Hezekiah's time who presided over gifts and dedicated items in the Temple (2 Chr. 31:13).
  7. A ruler of the Temple during Josiah's reformation (2 Chr. 35:8).
  8. The father of Obadiah (Ezra 8:9).
  9. The father of Shechaniah (Ezra 10:2).
  10. A priest who divorced his pagan wife after the Captivity (Ezra 10:21).
  11. A man of Elam's family who divorced his pagan wife after the Captivity (Ezra 10:26). He may be the same person as Jehiel No. 8.

JEHIELI [juh HIGH uh ligh] (*Jehovah lives*) — a Levite and a son of Laadan the Gershonite (1 Chr. 26:21–22).

JEHIZKIAH [jee hiz KIGH uh] (*Jehovah strengthens*) — a son of Shallum and one of the heads of the tribe of Ephraim during the reign of King Pekah of Israel (2 Chr. 28:12).

JEHOADDAH [juh HOE uh duh] (*Jehovah unveils*) — a descendant of King Saul of the tribe of Benjamin (1 Chr. 8:36; Jehoadah, KJV). He was also called Jarah (1 Chr. 9:42).

JEHOADDAN [juh HOE uh duhn] (*Jehovah gives delight*) — the mother of Amaziah and the wife of Joash, kings of Judah (2 Kin. 14:1–2; Jehoaddin, NIV, RSV).

JEHOAHAZ [juh HOE uh haz] (*God sustains*) — the name of a king of Israel and two kings of Judah:

1. The son and successor of Jehu and the 12th king of Israel (2 Kin. 10:35). His 17-year reign (815–798 B.C.) was a disaster for the nation of Israel. By not renouncing the idolatry of the golden calves set up by Jeroboam I at Dan and Bethel, Jehoahaz "did evil in the sight of the Lord." Hazael of Syria and his son Ben-Hadad severely punished Israel during Jehoahaz's reign. This drove Jehoahaz to the Lord, who heard his prayer and granted temporary deliverance from Syria (2 Kin. 13:2–5). Unfortunately, after the danger passed, Jehoahaz quickly abandoned his faith. After his death, Jehoahaz was succeeded by his son Joash (or Jehoash).

2. A son of King Josiah and ruler of Judah for three months (609 B.C.). At the battle of Megiddo, King Josiah was defeated and slain by the powerful Pharaoh Necho of Egypt. Jehoahaz was appointed king in his place at the age of 23, but he was deposed after only three months by Pharaoh Necho (2 Kin. 23:30–34; 36:1–4). Jehoahaz was also called Shallum (1 Chr. 3:15).

3. The youngest son of Jehoram, king of Judah (2 Chr. 21:17; 25:23). The sixth king of Judah, Jehoahaz was 42 years old at the beginning of his reign, which lasted only one year (842 or 841 B.C.). Jehoahaz is usually called Ahaziah (2 Kin. 8:24—14:13; 2 Chr. 22:1–11). Also, an inscription of the Assyrian king Tiglath-pileser III refers to Ahaz, king of Judah, as Jehoahaz; this was evidently his full name, but the Bible always uses the abbreviated form Ahaz.

JEHOASH [juh HOE ash] — a form of JOASH.

JEHOHANAN [jee hoe HAY nuhn] (*Jehovah is gracious*) — the name of eight men in the Old Testament:

1. A gatekeeper of the tabernacle in David's time (1 Chr. 26:3).

2. One of five captains in King Jehoshaphat's army (2 Chr. 17:15).

3. The father of Ishmael (2 Chr. 23:1).

4. A son of Eliashib (Ezra 10:6; Johanan, KJV).

5. A son of Bebai who divorced his pagan wife after the Captivity (Ezra 10:28).

6. A son of Tobiah the Ammonite, Nehemiah's opponent (Neh. 6:18; Johanan, KJV).

7. A priest who returned to Jerusalem with Zerubbabel after the Captivity (Neh. 12:13).

8. A priest who officiated at the dedication of the Jerusalem wall (Neh. 12:42).

JEHOIACHIN [juh HOI uh kin] (*the Lord establishes*) — the son and successor of Jehoiakim as king of Judah, about 598 or 597 B.C. (2 Chr. 36:8–9; Ezek. 1:2). Jehoiachin did evil in the sight of the Lord, like his father. But he had little opportunity to influence affairs of state, since he reigned only

three months. His brief reign ended when the armies of Nebuchadnezzar of Babylon besieged Jerusalem. When the city surrendered, Jehoiachin was carried into captivity in Babylon (2 Kin. 24:6–15).

Nebuchadnezzar then made Mattaniah, Jehoiachin's uncle, king in his place and changed Mattaniah's name to Zedekiah (v. 17). Zedekiah was destined to rule over a powerless land containing only poor farmers and laborers, while Jehoiachin was held a prisoner in Babylon.

In the 37th year of his captivity, Jehoiachin was finally released by a new Babylonian king, Evil-Merodach (Amel–Marduk). He must have been awarded a place of prominence in the king's court, since he ate his meals regularly in the presence of the king himself (2 Kin. 25:27–30).

Jehoiachin is also called Jeconiah (1 Chr. 3:16–17) and Coniah (Jer. 22:24). In the New Testament he is listed by Matthew as an ancestor of Jesus (Matt. 1:11–12).

JEHOIADA [juh HOI uh duh] (*The Lord knows*) — the name of six men in the Old Testament:

1. The father of Benaiah (2 Sam. 8:18).

2. A priest during the reigns of Ahaziah, Athaliah, and Joash of Judah (2 Kin. 11:1—12:16) who helped hide the young king Joash from the wrath of Queen Athaliah (2 Chr. 22:10–12). By his courageous action, Jehoiada was instrumental in preserving the line of David, since Joash was a descendant of David and an ancestor of Jesus. Jehoiada married Jehoshabeath, daughter of King Jehoram (2 Chr. 22:11). Even after Joash became king, Jehoiada was a powerful influence for good in his kingdom. Under his oversight, the temple of Baal was torn down and the influence of Baalism over the people was reduced. Under the prompting of the young king Jehoiada, the Temple of the Lord was restored to its former glory (2 Kin. 12; 2 Chr. 24). Jehoiada lived to be 130 years old. When he died, he was awarded the honor of burial in the royal tombs "because he had done good in Israel, both toward God and His house" (2 Chr. 24:15–16).

3. A leader of the Aaronites who joined David at Ziklag (1 Chr. 12:27).

4. One of David's aides, or counselors (1 Chr. 27:34).

5. A son of Paseah (Neh. 3:6; Joiada, RSV). After the Captivity, Jehoiada helped repair a gate in Jerusalem's wall.

6. A priest in Jerusalem in the prophet Jeremiah's time (Jer. 29:26).

JEHOIAKIM [juh HOI uh kim] (*Jehovah raises up*) — an evil king of Judah whose downfall was predicted by the prophet Jeremiah.

A son of the good king Josiah, Jehoiakim was 25 years old when he succeeded to the throne. He reigned 11 years in Jerusalem, from 609 B.C. to 598 B.C. During his reign Pharaoh Necho of Egypt exacted heavy tribute from the people of Judah (2 Chr. 36:3, 5). Jehoiakim was forced to levy a burdensome tax upon his people to pay this tribute.

The prophet Jeremiah described the arrogance of

Jehoiakim in great detail (Jer. 1:3; 24:1; 27:1, 20; 37:1; 52:2). He censured Jehoiakim for exploiting the people to build his own splendid house with expensive furnishings (Jer. 22:13–23). Unlike his father Josiah, Jehoiakim ignored justice and righteousness. Jehoiakim had no intention of obeying the Lord; he "did evil in the sight of the Lord" (2 Kin. 23:37). His 11-year reign was filled with abominable acts against God (2 Chr. 36:8). Because of this evil, Jeremiah predicted that no one would lament the death of Jehoiakim.

Jeremiah also told of Jehoiakim's execution of Urijah, a prophet of the Lord (Jer. 26:20–23). Perhaps Jehoiakim's most cynical act was his burning of Jeremiah's prophecies (Jer. 36:22–23). Jeremiah wrote a scroll of judgment against the king, but as this scroll was read, Jehoiakim sliced it into pieces and threw them into the fire.

Jehoiakim could burn the Word of God, but he could not destroy its power. Neither could he avoid Jeremiah's prophecy of his approaching destruction. Recognizing the power of the Babylonians, he made an agreement with Nebuchadnezzar to serve as his vassal king on the throne of Judah. After three years of subjection, he led a foolish rebellion to regain his nation's independence. The rebellion failed and Jerusalem was destroyed by the Babylonians. Jehoiakim was bound and carried away as a captive (2 Chr. 36:6).

JEHOIARIB [juh HOI uh rib] (*Jehovah contends*) — a descendant of Aaron whose name was given to a priestly house identified with the reign of King David. When David divided the priests into 24 courses for the service of the tabernacle, the family of Jehoiarib was made responsible for the first course (1 Chr. 24:7). He is also called Joiarib (Neh. 11:10; 12:6, 19).

JEHONADAB [juh HAHN uh dab] (*Jehovah is liberal*) — a son of Rechab (2 Kin. 10:15, 23). He was a zealous supporter of Jehu in the ruthless extermination of the house of Ahab and the violent suppression of Baal worship in Samaria. He is also called Jonadab (Jer. 35:6–19).

JEHONATHAN [juh HAHN uh thuhn] (*Jehovah gives*) — the name of three men in the Old Testament:
1. An overseer of the storehouses in the days of David (1 Chr. 27:25; Jonathan, NIV, RSV).
2. A Levite sent by Jehoshaphat to teach the law in the cities of Judah (2 Chr. 17:8).
3. Head of the family of Shemaiah in the days of the high priesthood of Joiakim (Neh. 12:18). He is also called Jonathan (Neh. 12:35).

JEHORAM [juh HOHR uhm] (*Jehovah is exalted*) — the name of three men in the Old Testament:
1. The fifth king of Judah, Jehoram was also called Joram. See JORAM No. 2.
2. The ninth king of Israel, Jehoram was also called Joram. See JORAM No. 3.
3. A priest sent by King Jehoshaphat to instruct the people in the law (2 Chr. 17:8).

JEHOSHABEATH [jee hoe SHAB ih ath] — a form of JEHOSHEBA.

JEHOSHAPHAT [juh HAH shuh fat] (*the Lord is judge*)—the name of five men in the Old Testament:
1. An official under David and Solomon (2 Sam. 8:16).
2. A son of Paruah and an official responsible for supplying food for King Solomon's table (1 Kin. 4:17).
3. A son of Asa who succeeded his father as king of Judah (1 Kin. 15:24). Jehoshaphat was 35 years old when he became king, and he reigned 25 years in Jerusalem (2 Chr. 20:31), from about 873 B.C. to about 848 B.C.

Jehoshaphat received an excellent heritage from his father Asa, who in the earlier years of his reign showed a reforming spirit in seeking God (2 Chr. 15:1–19). Jehoshaphat's faith in God led him to "delight in the ways of the Lord" (2 Chr. 17:6). He attacked pagan idolatry and he sent teachers to the people to teach them more about God (2 Chr. 17:6–9). In affairs of state, Jehoshaphat also showed a willingness to rely on the Lord. In a time of danger he prayed for God's help (2 Chr. 20:6–12).

Jehoshaphat showed a high regard for justice in his dealings (2 Chr. 19:4–11). He reminded the judges whom he appointed that their ultimate loyalty was to God. His attitude toward impartial justice is reflected in these words: "Behave courageously, and the Lord will be with the good" (2 Chr. 19:11).

But in his dealings with Ahab, king of Israel, Jehoshaphat made some serious mistakes. Through the marriage of his son, Jehoram, to Ahab's daughter, Jehoshaphat allied himself with Ahab (2 Chr. 21:5–6). This alliance led to even further dealings with the wicked king of Israel (2 Chr. 18:1–34), which the prophet Jehu rebuked (2 Chr. 19:1–3).

Jehoshaphat and his father Asa are bright lights against the dark paganism that existed during their time. Both father and son had certain weaknesses, but their faith in the Lord brought good to themselves as well as God's people during their reigns.
4. A son of Nimshi and father of Jehu, king of Israel (2 Kin. 9:2, 14).
5. A priest who helped move the ARK OF THE COVENANT from the house of Obed-Edom to Jerusalem (1 Chr. 15:24; Joshaphat, RSV).

JEHOSHAPHAT, VALLEY OF [juh HAH shuh fat] — a valley in which, according to Joel 3:2, 12, God will judge the nations at the end of this age. According to Jewish tradition, the Valley of Jehoshaphat was that part of the Kidron Valley between the Temple and the Mount of Olives. The name Jehoshaphat means "Jehovah is Judge." The name may refer to a symbolic "valley of decision" (Joel 3:14) which is connected with divine judgments instead of a literal geographical place.

JEHOSHEBA, JEHOSHABEATH [juh HAH shuh buh, juh hah SHAH bih uhth] (*Jehovah is her oath*) — the courageous woman who rescued her nephew

King Jehu of Israel bows before Shalmaneser III of Assyria, in this obelisk, or stone monument, discovered in ancient Assyria.

Joash from certain death at the hands of Athaliah, the wicked queen of Judah (2 Kin. 11:1–3; 2 Chr. 22:10–12). Jehosheba was the half-sister of King Ahaziah. When Ahaziah was killed in battle, his mother, Athaliah, attempted to kill all her grandsons and took the throne for herself. But Jehosheba rescued the youngest of Ahaziah's sons (2 Kin. 11:2) and hid him in the Temple for six years—until he was old enough to be proclaimed king.

Jehosheba's courageous act preserved "the house and lineage of David" (Luke 2:4), from which Jesus was descended.

JEHOSHUA [juh HAH shoo uh] — a form of JOSHUA.

JEHOVAH [jih HOE vuh] (see GOD, NAMES OF).

JEHOZABAD [juh HOE zuh bad] (*Jehovah bestows*) — the name of three men in the Old Testament:

1. A servant of Joash who conspired against his master and assisted in his assassination (2 Kin. 12:21).

2. A son of Obed-Edom (1 Chr. 26:4).

3. A Benjamite chief who was one of Jehoshaphat's military officers (2 Chr. 17:18).

JEHU [JAY hoo] (*the Lord is He*) — the name of five men in the Old Testament:

1. A prophet who announced a message of doom against Baasha, king of Israel (1 Kin. 16:12). Jehu also rebuked Jehoshaphat, king of Judah (2 Chr. 19:2).

2. The 11th king of Israel (2 Chr. 22:7–9). Jehu was anointed by Elisha the prophet as king; he later overthrew Joram (Jehoram), King Ahab's son and successor, and reigned for 28 years (841–813 B.C.). His corrupt leadership weakened the nation. He is known for his violence against all members of the "house of Ahab" as he established his rule throughout the nation.

At Jehu's command, Jezebel, the notorious wife of Ahab, was thrown out of the window of the palace to her death, as prophesied by Elijah (1 Kin. 21:23). Ahab's murder of Naboth and the subversion of the religion of Israel had brought terrible vengeance, but more blood was to be shed by Jehu. Next to feel the new king's wrath were the 70 sons of Ahab who lived in Samaria (2 Kin. 10). Jehu ordered them killed by the elders of Samaria. Jehu's zeal extended even further, commanding the death of Ahab's advisors and close acquaintances. This excessive violence led the prophet Hosea to denounce Jehu's bloodthirstiness (Hos. 1:4).

Jehu continued his slaughter against the family of Ahaziah, king of Judah (2 Kin. 10:12–14). Then he made an alliance with Jehonadab, the chief of the Rechabites, to destroy the followers of Baal. Jehu and Jehonadab plotted to conduct a massive assembly in honor of Baal. After assuring the Baal–worshipers of their sincerity and gathering them into the temple of Baal, Jehu had them all killed (2 Kin. 10:18–28). So complete was this destruction that Baalism was wiped out in Israel, and the temple of Baal was torn down and made into a garbage dump.

Although Jehu proclaimed his zeal for the Lord (2 Kin. 10:16), he failed to follow the Lord's will completely (2 Kin. 10:31). He did not completely eliminate worship of the golden calves at Dan and Bethel, and his disobedience led to the conquest of many parts of Israel by the Syrians (2 Kin. 10:32–33).

3. A son of Obed and a descendant of Hezron (1 Chr. 2:38). Jehu was descended from the family of Jerahmeel and the tribe of Judah.

4. A son of Joshibiah, of the tribe of Simeon (1 Chr. 4:35).

5. A Benjamite of Anathoth (1 Chr. 12:3) who joined David's army at Ziklag.

JEHUBBAH [juh HUH buh] (*God has hidden*) — a son of Shemer, of the tribe of Asher (1 Chr. 7:34).

JEHUCAL [juh HOO kuhl] (*Jehovah is mighty*) — a messenger sent to the prophet Jeremiah to ask for his prayers when the Babylonians besieged Jerusalem (Jer. 37:3), also called Jucal (Jer. 38:1).

JEHUD [JEE huhd] (*honorable*) — a town on the border of Dan (Josh. 19:45).

JEHUDI [juh HOO digh] (*Judahite*) — an officer of Jehoiakim, king of Judah (Jer. 36:14, 21, 23). Jehudi read Jeremiah's prophecies to the king, who destroyed the scroll.

JEHUDIJAH [jee huh DIGH juh] (*the Jewess*) — one of the two wives of Mered and the mother of Jered, Heber, and Jekuthiel (1 Chr. 4:18).

JEHUEL [juh HOO uhl] — a form of JEHIEL No. 5.

JEHUSH [JEE huhsh] — a form of JEUSH No. 3.

JEIEL [jih EYE uhl] (meaning unknown) — the name of nine or ten men in the Old Testament:
1. A chief of the tribe of Reuben (1 Chr. 5:7).
2. An ancestor of King Saul (1 Chr. 9:35; Jehiel, KJV, NEB).
3. One of David's mighty men (1 Chr. 11:44; Jehiel, KJV). He may be the same person as Jeiel No. 1.
4. A Levite gatekeeper of the tabernacle during David's reign (1 Chr. 15:18, 21; Jehiel, KJV, RSV, NEB).
5. A Levite of the sons of Asaph (2 Chr. 20:14).
6. A scribe who helped prepare the roll of military personnel for King Uzziah (2 Chr. 26:11).
7. A Levite of the family of Elizaphan in the time of King Hezekiah of Judah (2 Chr. 29:13; Jeuel, RSV).
8. A chief Levite at King Josiah's great Passover feast (2 Chr. 35:9).
9. A son of Adonikam who returned with Ezra from the Captivity (Ezra 8:13; Jeuel, RSV).
10. A member of the family of Nebo who divorced his pagan wife after the Captivity (Ezra 10:43).

JEKAMEAM [jek uh MEE uhm] (*raise up*) — the fourth son of Hebron and the head of a priestly house (1 Chr. 23:19; 24:23).

JEKAMIAH [jek uh MIGH uh] (*may Jehovah establish*) — a son of Shallum, of the tribe of Judah (1 Chr. 2:41).

JEKUTHIEL [juh KOO thih uhl] (*may God nourish*) — a descendant of Caleb the spy and the father of Zanoah (1 Chr. 4:18).

JEMIMAH [juh MIGH muh] (*dove*) — the first of Job's three daughters born after his great trial of suffering was over and his prosperity was restored (Job 42:14; Jemima, KJV).

JEMUEL [JEM yoo uhl] (*God is light*) — the oldest son of Simeon and a grandson of Jacob (Ex. 6:15), also called Nemuel (Num. 26:12).

JEPHTHAH [JEF thuh] (*God will set free*) — the ninth judge of Israel, who delivered God's people from the Ammonites (Judg. 11:1—12:7).

An illegitimate child, Jephthah was cast out of the family by his half-brothers, to prevent him from sharing in the inheritance. He fled to "the land of Tob," where he gathered a group of "worthless men" and soon engaged in raids throughout the surrounding countryside. When Israel was threatened by the Ammonites, the elders of Gilead asked Jephthah to free them from oppression by organizing a counterattack on Ammon. Jephthah showed shrewd foresight by insisting on a position of leadership in Gilead if he should succeed against the Ammonites. After this assurance (Judg. 11:10-11), he began his campaign.

Jephthah first tried the diplomatic approach, but Ammon wanted war. So Jephthah launched an attack through Mizpah of Gilead (Judg. 11:29) and defeated the Ammonites "with a very great slaughter" (Judg. 11:33). At this point, Jephthah made a rash vow, promising God that in exchange for victory in battle he would offer up as a sacrifice the first thing that should come out of his house to meet him on his return (Judg. 11:31).

The Lord delivered Ammon's army into Jephthah's hands. When he returned home, his daughter—his only child—came out to meet him (Judg. 11:34). Jephthah tore his clothing in distress as he realized the terrible rashness of his vow. The text seems to indicate that Jephthah followed through on his vow (Judg. 11:39), although a few scholars believe the verse means she was kept as a virgin dedicated to special service to the Lord for the rest of her life.

After this incident, Jephthah punished an arrogant group of Ephraimites at the Jordan River by using a clever strategy to confuse the enemy. He asked the soldiers to say "shibboleth." If they were Ephraimites, they would not be able to pronounce the word correctly and would say "sibboleth." Their accent would betray them as the enemy.

Jephthah was a man with remarkable abilities of leadership. In spite of rejection by his family, he exercised his many talents and rose to a position of great authority. His greatest weakness was his rash, thoughtless behavior. After his death, he was buried in a city of Gilead. The Book of Hebrews lists him as one of the heroes of faith (Heb. 11:32).

JEPHUNNEH [juh FUH nuh] (meaning unknown) — the name of two men in the Old Testament:
1. The father of CALEB the spy (Num. 13:6).
2. A son of Jether, of the tribe of Asher (1 Chr. 7:38).

JERAH [JIHR uh] (*moon*) — the fourth son of Joktan, of the family of Shem (1 Chr. 1:20).

JERAHMEEL [jih RAH mih uhl] (*God is compassionate*) — the name of three men in the Old Testament:
1. A son of Hezron of the tribe of Judah. Jerahmeel had many descendants, called Jerahmeelites (1 Chr. 2:9, 25–27, 33, 42).

2. A son of Kish, of the tribe of Levi (1 Chr. 24:29).

3. An official of King Jehoiakim of Judah (Jer. 36:26) sent to arrest Baruch the scribe and Jeremiah the prophet.

JERAHMEELITES [jih RAH mih uhl ights] — descendants of JERAHMEEL (1 Sam. 27:10; 30:29).

JERBOA (see ANIMALS OF THE BIBLE).

JERED [JEE red] (*flowing*) — a man of the tribe of Judah and the father of Gedor (1 Chr. 4:18).

JEREMAI [JER uh migh] (*Jehovah is high*) — a son of Hashum who divorced his pagan wife after the Captivity (Ezra 10:33).

JEREMIAH [jer uh MIGH uh] (*Jehovah lifts up*) — the name of nine men in the Old Testament:

1. The father of Hamutal (Jer. 52:1).

2. The head of a family of the tribe of Manasseh (1 Chr. 5:23–24).

3. A Benjamite who joined David at Ziklag (1 Chr. 12:4).

4. A Gadite who joined David at Ziklag (1 Chr. 12:10).

5. Another Gadite who joined David at Ziklag (1 Chr. 12:13).

6. A priest who sealed Nehemiah's covenant after the Captivity (Neh. 10:2).

7. A priest who returned from the Captivity with Zerubbabel (Neh. 12:1, 12, 34).

8. A son of Habazziniah and father of Jaazaniah, of the house of the Rechabites (Jer. 35:3).

9. The major prophet during the decline and fall of the southern kingdom of Judah and author of the Book of Jeremiah. He prophesied during the reigns of the last five kings of Judah.

Jeremiah was born in the village of Anathoth, situated north of Jerusalem in the territory of Benjamin (Jer. 1:1–2). He was called to the prophetic ministry in the 13th year of Josiah's reign, about 627 B.C. He must have been a young man at the time, since his ministry lasted for about 40 years— through the very last days of the nation of Judah when the capital city of Jerusalem was destroyed in 587/586 B.C.

Jeremiah's call is one of the most instructive passages in his book. God declared that he had sanctioned him as a prophet even before he was born (Jer. 1:5). But the young man responded with words of inadequacy: "Ah, Lord God!" (Jer. 1:6). These words actually mean "No, Lord God!" Jeremiah pleaded that he was a youth and that he lacked the ability to speak. But God replied that he was being called not because of age or ability but because God had chosen him.

Immediately Jeremiah saw the hand of God reaching out and touching his mouth. "Behold, I have put My words in your mouth," God declared (Jer. 1:9). From that moment, the words of the prophet were to be the words of God. And his ministry was to consist of tearing down and rebuilding, uprooting and replanting: "See, I have this day set you over the kingdoms, to root out and to pull down, to destroy and to throw down, to build and to plant" (Jer. 1:10).

Because of the negative nature of Jeremiah's ministry, judgmental texts abound in his book. Jeremiah was destined from the very beginning to be a prophet of doom. He was even forbidden to marry so he could devote himself fully to the task of

A woven tapestry which portrays the prophet Jeremiah, from the Church of San Vitale in Ravenna, Italy.
Photo by Howard Vos

preaching God's judgment (Jer. 16:1–13). A prophet of doom cannot be a happy man. All of Jeremiah's life was wrapped up in the knowledge that God was about to bring an end to the holy city and cast off His Covenant People.

Jeremiah is often called "the weeping prophet" because he wept openly about the sins of his nation (Jer. 9:1). He was also depressed at times about the futility of his message. As the years passed and his words of judgment went unheeded, he lamented his unfortunate state: "O Lord, You induced me, and I was persuaded; You are stronger than I, and have prevailed. I am in derision daily; everyone mocks me" (Jer. 20:7).

At times Jeremiah tried to hold back from his prophetic proclamation. But he found that the word of the Lord was "like a burning fire shut up in my bones" (Jer. 20:9). He had no choice but to proclaim the harsh message of God's judgment.

Jeremiah did not weep and lament because of weakness, nor did he proclaim evil because of a dark and gloomy personality. He cried out because of his love for his people and his God. This characteristic of the prophet is actually a tribute to his sensitivity and deep concern. Jeremiah's laments remind us of the weeping of the Savior (Matt. 23:37–39).

As Jeremiah predicted, the nation of Judah was eventually punished by God because of its sin and disobedience. In 587 B.C. Jerusalem was destroyed and the leading citizens were deported to Babylon. Jeremiah remained in Jerusalem with a group of his fellow citizens under the authority of a ruling governor appointed by Babylon. But he was forced to seek safety in Egypt after the people of Jerusalem revolted against Babylonian rule. He continued his preaching in Egypt (Jeremiah 43—44). This is the last we hear of Jeremiah. There is no record of what happened to the prophet during these years of his ministry.

In the New Testament (KJV) Jeremiah was referred to as Jeremy (Matt. 2:17; 27:9) and Jeremias (Matt. 16:14).

Also see JEREMIAH, BOOK OF.

JEREMIAH, BOOK OF — a major prophetic book of the Old Testament directed to the southern kingdom of Judah just before that nation fell to the Babylonians. The book is named for its author and central personality, the great prophet Jeremiah, who faithfully delivered God's message of judgment in spite of fierce opposition from his countrymen.

Structure of the Book. Jeremiah, consisting of 52 chapters, is one of the longest books in the Bible. It is also one of the hardest to follow and understand. Unlike most of the other prophetic books, which have a chronological arrangement, the material in Jeremiah seems to follow no logical pattern. Prophecies delivered in the final years of his ministry may appear at any point in the book, followed by messages that belong to other periods in his life. Mingled with his prophecies of God's approaching

judgment are historical accounts of selected events in the life of Judah, personal experiences from Jeremiah's own life, and poetic laments about the fate of his country. It is important to be aware of this if one wants to understand the message of this great prophetic book.

Perhaps the best way to get a big picture of the Book of Jeremiah is to break it down by types of literature. Basically, the first half of the book (chaps. 1—25) consists of poetry, while the second half (chaps. 26—52) is in prose or narrative–style writing. The poetry section of the book contains Jeremiah's prophecies of God's approaching judgment against Judah because of its sin and idolatry. The prose section contains a few of his prophecies, but the main emphasis is on Jeremiah and his conflicts with the kings who ruled in Judah during his ministry. Also included near the end of his book is a report on the fall of Jerusalem and Judah's final days as a nation (chaps. 39—41; 52), along with a narrative about Jeremiah's flight into Egypt with other citizens of Judah following its fall (chaps. 42—44).

Authorship and Date. Most conservative scholars agree that the author of the Book of Jeremiah was the famous prophet of that name who ministered in the southern kingdom of Judah during the final four decades of that nation's existence. But some scholars claim the book's disjointed arrangement proves it was compiled by an unknown author some time after Jeremiah's death. The book itself gives us a clue about how it may have taken its present form.

After prophesying against Judah for about 20 years, the prophet Jeremiah was commanded by God to put his messages in written form. He dictated these to his scribe or secretary, Baruch, who wrote them on a scroll (36:1–4). Because Jeremiah had been banned from entering the royal court, he sent Baruch to read the messages to King Jehoiakim. To show his contempt for Jeremiah and his message, the king cut the scroll apart and threw it in the fire (36:22–23). Jeremiah promptly dictated his book to Baruch again, adding "many similar words" (36:32) that had not been included in the first scroll.

This clear description of how a second version of Jeremiah came to be written shows the book was composed in several different stages during the prophet's ministry. The scribe Baruch was probably the one who added to the book at Jeremiah's command as it was shaped and refined over a period of several years. This is a possible explanation for the disjointed arrangement of the book. Baruch must have put the book in final form shortly after Jeremiah's death. This would place its final writing not long after 585 B.C.

We can learn a great deal about the prophet Jeremiah by reading his book. He was a sensitive poet who could weep over the sins of his nation: "Oh, that my head were waters, and my eyes a fountain of tears" (9:1). But he was also a courageous man of God who could endure persecution and affliction. He narrowly escaped death several times as he carried out God's command to preach His message of judgment to a wayward people. A patriot who passionately loved his nation, he drew the tough assignment of informing his countrymen that Judah was about to fall to a pagan power. Many of his fellow citizens branded him a traitor, but he never wavered from the prophetic ministry to which God had called him.

With the fall of Jerusalem in 587 B.C., most of the leading citizens of the nation were carried away as captives to Babylon. But Jeremiah was allowed to remain in Jerusalem with other citizens of Judah who were placed under the authority of a ruling governor appointed by Babylon. When the citizens of Jerusalem revolted against this official, Jeremiah and others were forced to seek safety in Egypt,

JEREMIAH: A Teaching Outline

where he continued his prophetic ministry (chaps. 43—44). This is the last we hear of this courageous prophet of the Lord.

Historical Setting. The Book of Jeremiah belongs to a chaotic time in the history of God's Covenant People. Jeremiah's native land, the southern kingdom of Judah, was caught in a power squeeze between three great powers of the ancient world: Egypt, Assyria, and Babylon. As these empires struggled for dominance with one another, the noose grew tighter around Judah's neck.

To protect its borders, Judah entered into an alliance with Egypt against the Babylonians. But Jeremiah realized the alliance was too little and too late. For years his beloved nation had risked disaster as it rejected worship of the one true God and turned to pagan gods instead. Immorality, injustice, graft, and corruption prevailed throughout the land. God revealed to the prophet that he intended to punish His Covenant People by sending the Babylonians to destroy Jerusalem and carry the people into captivity. Jeremiah preached this message of judgment faithfully for about 40 years.

At the beginning of his prophetic ministry, it appeared briefly that conditions might improve. King Josiah (ruled 641/40—609 B.C.) began reforms based on God's Law, but at his death the dark days of paganism returned. Josiah's successors continued their reckless pursuit of idolatry and foolish alliances with Egypt against the Babylonians. At the decisive battle of Carchemish in 605 B.C., the Egyptians were soundly defeated. About 18 years later the Babylonians completed their conquest of Judah by destroying the capital city of Jerusalem. Just as Jeremiah had predicted, the leading citizens of Judah were carried to Babylon, where they remained in captivity for half a century.

Theological Contribution. Jeremiah's greatest theological contribution was his concept of the new COVENANT (31:31-34). A new covenant between God and His people was necessary because the old covenant had failed so miserably; the captivity of God's people by a foreign power was proof of that. Although the old covenant had been renewed again and again throughout Israel's history, the people still continued to break the promises they had made to God. What was needed was a new type of covenant between God and His people—a covenant of grace and forgiveness written in man's heart, rather than a covenant of law engraved in stone.

As Jeremiah reported God's plan for this new covenant, he anticipated the dawning of the era of grace in the person of Jesus Christ more than 500 years in the future: "No more shall every man teach his neighbor, and every man his brother, saying, 'Know the Lord,' for they all shall know Me, from the least of them to the greatest of them," says the Lord. "For I will forgive their iniquity, and their sin I will remember no more" (31:34).

Special Considerations. Jeremiah was a master at using figures of speech, metaphors, and symbolic behavior to drive home his messages. He carried a yoke around his neck to show the citizens of Judah they should submit to the inevitable rule of the pagan Babylonians (27:1-12). He watched a potter mar a piece of clay, then reshape it into a perfect vessel. He applied this lesson to the nation of Judah, which needed to submit to the divine will of the Master Potter while there was still time to repent and avoid God's judgment (18:1-11).

The mound of ancient Jericho, believed by many archaeologists to be the oldest settlement in Palestine and possibly the oldest city in the ancient world.

But perhaps his most unusual symbolic act was his purchase of a plot of land in his hometown, Anathoth, about three miles northeast of Jerusalem. Jeremiah knew this land would be practically worthless after the Babylonians overran Jerusalem, as he was predicting. But by buying the plot, he symbolized his hope for the future. Even in Judah's darkest hour, Jeremiah prophesied that a remnant would return from Babylon after their years in captivity to restore their way of life and to worship God again in the Temple (32:26–44). God directed Jeremiah to put the deed to the land in an earthen vessel so it would be preserved for the future: "For thus says the Lord of hosts, the God of Israel: 'Houses and fields and vineyards shall be possessed again in this land' " (32:15).

Also see JEREMIAH.

JEREMIAH, EPISTLE OF (see APOCRYPHA).

JEREMIAH, LAMENTATIONS OF (see LAMENTATIONS OF JEREMIAH).

JEREMIAS, JEREMY [jer uh MIGH ass, JER uh mee] — forms of JEREMIAH.

JEREMOTH [JER e moth] (meaning unknown) — the name of eight men in the Old Testament:

1. A son of Becher, of the tribe of Benjamin (1 Chr. 7:8, NIV, RSV, and NEB).

2. A son of Beriah, of the tribe of Benjamin (1 Chr. 8:14). Jeremoth is probably the same person as Jeroham (1 Chr. 8:27).

3. A Levite of the family of Merari and house of Mushi (1 Chr. 23:23), also called Jerimoth (1 Chr. 24:30).

4. A descendant of Heman. Jeremoth was the head of the 15th course of musicians during David's reign (1 Chr. 25:22). He is also called Jerimoth (1 Chr. 25:4).

5. A son of Azriel and chief officer of the tribe of Naphtali during David's reign (1 Chr. 27:19, RSV). The KJV, NKJV, and NIV have Jerimoth.

6, 7, 8. Three Jews who, after the Captivity, divorced their pagan wives (Ezra 10:26, 27, 29). The name is spelled Ramoth in Ezra 10:29 (KJV and NKJV) instead of Jeremoth (NIV, RSV, and NEB).

JERIAH [juh RIGH uh] (*Jehovah sees*) — a Levite in the time of David (1 Chr. 23:19), also called Jerijah (1 Chr. 26:31).

JERIBAI [JER uh bigh] (*Jehovah contends*) — one of David's mighty men (1 Chr. 11:46).

JERICHO [JEHR ih coe] (meaning unknown) — one of the oldest inhabited cities in the world. Situated in the wide plain of the Jordan Valley (Deut. 34:1, 3) at the foot of the ascent to the Judean mountains, Jericho lies about 13 kilometers (8 miles) northwest of the site where the Jordan River flows into the Dead Sea, some 8 kilometers (5 miles) west of the Jordan.

Since it is approximately 244 meters (800 feet) below sea level, Jericho has a climate that is tropical and at times is very hot. Only a few inches of rainfall are recorded at Jericho each year; but the city is a wonderful oasis, known as "the city of palm trees" (Deut. 34:3) or "the city of palms" (Judg. 3:13). Jericho flourishes with date palms, banana trees, balsams, sycamores, and henna (Song 1:14; Luke 19:4).

There were actually three different Jerichos throughout its long history. Old Testament Jericho is generally identified with the mound of Tell es-Sultan, about 2 kilometers (a little more than a mile) from the village of er-Riha. This village is modern Jericho, located about 27 kilometers (17 miles) northeast of Jerusalem. New Testament Jericho is identified with the mounds of Tulul Abu el-'Alayiq, about 2 kilometers (a little more than a mile) west of modern Jericho and south of Old Testament Jericho.

By far the most imposing site of the three is Old Testament Jericho, a pear–shaped mound about 366 meters (400 yards) long, north to south, 183 meters (200 yards) wide at the north end, and some 67 meters (70 yards) high. It has been the site of numerous archaeological diggings and is a favorite stop for Holy Land tourists.

Old Testament Jericho. Jericho first appears in the biblical record when the Israelites encamped at Shittim on the east side of the Jordan River (Num. 22:1; 26:3). Joshua sent spies to examine the city (Josh. 2:1–24) and later took the city by perhaps the most unorthodox method in the history of warfare (Joshua 6). Joshua placed a curse on anyone who would attempt to rebuild Jericho (Josh. 6:26).

As the Israelites settled into the land, Jericho was awarded to the tribe of Benjamin, although it was on the border between Ephraim and Benjamin (Josh. 16:1, 7). Jericho is only incidentally mentioned in the reign of David (2 Sam. 10:5) and does not figure prominently again in Old Testament history until the reign of King Ahab (about 850 B.C.; 1 Kin. 16:34), when Hiel the Bethelite attempted to fortify the city and Joshua's curse was realized. During the days of Elijah and Elisha, Jericho was a community of the prophets (2 Kin. 2:5) and was prominently mentioned during this era (Ezra 2:34; Neh. 3:2; Jer. 39:5).

New Testament Jericho. In the early years of Herod the Great, the Romans plundered Jericho. But Herod later beautified the city and ultimately died here. Jesus passed through Jericho on numerous occasions. Near there He was baptized in the Jordan River (Matt. 3:13–17), and on the adjacent mountain range He was tempted (Matt. 4:1–11). Between Old Testament Jericho and New Testament Jericho Jesus healed blind Bartimaeus (Mark 10:46–52). Here too Zacchaeus was converted (Luke 19:1–10). And Jesus' parable of the Good Samaritan has the road from Jerusalem to Jericho as its setting (Luke 10:30–37).

Excavations at Jericho. From 1907 until 1911, the German scholars Ernst Sellin and Carl Watzinger excavated this site. But it was the British archaeologist John Garstang whose excavations from 1930 to

Remains of a house at Tirzah, the city which served as the capital of the northern kingdom of Israel under Jeroboam (1 Kin. 14:17, 18).

1936 yielded significant information. Garstang believed he had found ample evidence of Joshua's destruction of the city. He discovered an inner wall about 3.66 meters (12 feet) thick and an outer wall about 1.83 meters (6 feet) thick. Garstang was convinced that he had found the fabled walls of Jericho.

However, archaeologist Kathleen Kenyon began seven seasons of excavation at Jericho in 1952 and found evidence that conflicted with that of Garstang. Kenyon's findings indicated that little of the city in Joshua's day remained and thus the archaeologist must turn to Ai, Hazor, and other cities captured during Joshua's campaigns for information about this period. The most spectacular finds made by Kenyon were the Stone Age defenses, including a tower dating to about 7000 B.C.

JERIEL [JER ih uhl] (*God sees*) — a man of the tribe of Issachar (1 Chr. 7:2).

JERIJAH [juh RIGH juh] — a form of JERIAH.

JERIMOTH [JER ih mahth] (*elevation*) — the name of eight men in the Old Testament:
1. A son of Bela (1 Chr. 7:7).
2. A son of Becher (1 Chr. 7:8; Jeremoth, NIV, RSV).
3. A Benjamite who became one of David's mighty men (1 Chr. 12:5).
4. A Levite of the family of Merari (1 Chr. 24:30).
5. A descendant of Heman (1 Chr. 25:4).
6. A ruler of the tribe of Naphtali in the days of David (1 Chr. 27:19).
7. A son of David (2 Chr. 11:18).
8. A Levite overseer in the Temple during the reign of King Hezekiah of Judah (2 Chr. 31:13).

JERIOTH [JER ih ahth] (*tent curtains*) — the second wife, or perhaps a concubine, of Caleb, son of Hezron (1 Chr. 2:18).

JEROBOAM [jehr uh BOE ahm] (meaning unknown) — the name of two kings of the northern kingdom of Israel:

1. Jeroboam I, the first king of Israel (the ten northern tribes, or the Northern Kingdom), a state established after the death of Solomon (1 Kin. 11:26—14:20). The son of Nebat and Zeruah, Jeroboam reigned over Israel for 22 years (1 Kin. 14:20), from 931/30 to 910/09 B.C.

Jeroboam I first appears in the biblical record as Solomon's servant: "the officer over all the labor force of the house of Joseph" (1 Kin. 11:28). One day as Jeroboam went out of Jerusalem, the prophet Ahijah the Shilonite met him on the road and confronted him with an enacted parable. Ahijah, who was wearing a new garment, took hold of the garment and tore it into 12 pieces. He then said to Jeroboam, "Take for yourself ten pieces, for thus says the Lord, the God of Israel: 'Behold, I will tear the kingdom out of the hand of Solomon and will give ten tribes to you' " (1 Kin. 11:31).

When Solomon learned of Ahijah's words, he sought to kill Jeroboam. But Jeroboam fled to Egypt, where he was granted political asylum by Shishak I, the king of Egypt. Only after the death of Solomon did Jeroboam risk returning to his native Palestine (1 Kin. 11:40; 12:2–3).

Solomon's kingdom was outwardly rich, prosperous, and thriving. But the great building projects he undertook were accomplished by forced labor, high taxes, and other oppressive measures. Discontent and unrest existed throughout Solomon's kingdom. When the great king died, the kingdom was like a powder keg awaiting a spark.

The occasion for the explosion, the tearing of the ten northern tribes from Solomon's successor, came because of the foolish insensitivity of Solomon's son Rehoboam. Rehoboam had gone to Shechem to be anointed as the new king. A delegation led by Jeroboam, who had returned from Egypt following Solomon's death, said to Rehoboam, "Your father made our yoke heavy; now therefore, lighten the burdensome service of your father, and his heavy yoke which he put on us, and we will serve" (1 Kin. 12:4).

But Rehoboam followed the advice of his inexperienced companions, and replied, "Whereas my father laid a heavy yoke on you, I will add to your yoke; my father chastised you with whips, but I will chastise you with scourges!" (1 Kin. 12:11). After this show of Rehoboam's foolishness, the ten northern tribes revolted against Rehoboam and appointed Jeroboam as their king (1 Kin. 12:16–20).

Jeroboam was concerned that the people of Israel might return to the house of David if they continued to journey to Jerusalem for the festivals and observances at the Temple of Solomon. So he proposed an alternative form of worship that was idolatrous. He made two calves of gold that bore a close resemblance to the mounts of the Canaanite pagan god BAAL. The king told his countrymen: "It is too much for you to go up to Jerusalem. Here are your gods, O Israel, which brought you up from the land of Egypt!" (1 Kin. 12:28). One calf was erected in Bethel and one in Dan.

Once committed to this sinful direction, Jeroboam's progress was downhill. He next appointed priests from tribes other than Levi. He offered sacrifices to these images and gradually polluted the worship of Israel. The Lord confronted Jeroboam by sending him an unnamed prophet who predicted God's judgment on the king and the nation.

Although outwardly he appeared to be repentant, Jeroboam would not change his disastrous idolatry. His rebellious, arrogant attitude set the pattern for rulers of Israel for generations to come. Eighteen kings sat on the throne of Israel after his death, but not one of them gave up the golden calves.

2. Jeroboam II, the 14th king of Israel, who reigned for 41 years (793–753 B.C.). Jeroboam was the son and successor of Joash (or Jehoash); he was the grandson of Jehoahaz and the great–grandson of Jehu (2 Kin. 13:1, 13; 1 Chr. 5:17). The Bible declares that Jeroboam "did evil in the sight of the Lord" (2 Kin. 14:24).

Jeroboam was successful in his military adventures. His aggressive campaigns "recaptured for Israel, from Damascus and Hamath, what had belonged to Judah" (2 Kin. 14:28). The boundaries of Israel expanded to their greatest extent since the days of David and Solomon: "He restored the territory of Israel from the entrance of Hamath to the Sea of the Arabah" (2 Kin. 14:25). Jeroboam II was king during the prosperous interval between the economic reverses of other rulers. The prophets Hosea, Amos, and Jonah lived during his reign (Hos. 1:1; Amos 1:1–2). During this time of superficial prosperity, the prophet Amos especially spoke out against the many social abuses in Israel. A severe oppression of the poor had been instituted by the newly prosperous class. Justice was in the hands of lawless judges; dishonest merchants falsified the balances by deceit; and worship was little more than a pious smokescreen that covered the terrible abuses of the poor. Amos prophesied that the destructive fury of God would fall upon the house of Jeroboam (Amos 7:9).

After Jeroboam's death, his son Zechariah succeeded him on the throne of Israel (2 Kin. 14:29). Zechariah reigned in Samaria only six months before he was assassinated by Shallum (2 Kin. 15:10).

JEROHAM [juh ROE ham] (meaning unknown) — the name of several men in the Old Testament:

1. A Levite, the grandfather of the prophet Samuel (1 Sam. 1:1).
2. The head of a Benjamite family (1 Chr. 8:27).
3. A Benjamite (1 Chr. 9:8). He may be the same person as Jeroham No. 2.
4. A priest of Jerusalem (1 Chr. 9:12).
5. A Benjamite of Gedor (1 Chr. 12:7).
6. The father of Azarel (1 Chr. 27:22).
7. The father of Azariah (2 Chr. 23:1).
8. The father of Adaiah the priest (Neh. 11:12). He may be the same person as Jeroham No. 4.

JERUBBAAL [jer uh BAY uhl] (let Baal plead) — a name given to GIDEON, one of the judges of Israel, by his father after Gideon destroyed the altar of Baal at Ophrah (Judg. 6:32).

JERUBBESHETH [juh RUHB uh sheth] (contender with shame) — a name given to JERUBBAAL (or GIDEON) by those who wanted to avoid pronouncing Baal, which was associated with the idol worship of the Canaanites (2 Sam. 11:21).

JERUEL [juh ROO uhl] (founded by God) — a wilderness area between En Gedi and Tekoa (2 Chr. 20:16). A Levite named Jahaziel prophesied that Jehoshaphat would meet the armies of the Moabites and Ammonites and defeat them at Jeruel.

JERUSALEM [jeh ROO sah lem] (possession of peace) — sacred city and well–known capital of Palestine during Bible times. The earliest known name for Jerusalem was Urushalem. Salem, of which Melchizedek was king (Gen. 14:18), was a natural abbreviation for Jerusalem and probably referred to the city. Thus, Jerusalem appears in the Bible as early as the time of Abraham, although the city had probably been inhabited for centuries before that time.

The city of Jerusalem is mentioned directly in the Bible for the first time during the struggle of Joshua and the Israelites to take the land of Canaan (Josh. 10:1–4). Their efforts to take the city were unsuccessful, although the areas surrounding the city were taken and the land was given to the tribe of Judah. Still remaining in the fortress of the city itself

A narrow, twisting street in the Old City section of Jerusalem—a scene which amazes modern tourists who visit the area.

were the Jebusites. Thus, the city was called Jebus.

Jerusalem Under David. After the death of Saul, the first king of the United Kingdom of the Hebrew people, David was named the new king of Israel. One of his first efforts was to unite the tribes of the north and south by capturing Jerusalem from the

Jebusites, making the city the political and religious capital of the Kingdom (1 Chr. 11:4-9). It was David who gave the city the name of Jerusalem. Because it was captured during his reign, Jerusalem also came to be known as the "City of David." The city is often referred to by this title in the Bible.

David built a palace in the section of Jerusalem that served previously as the Jebusite stronghold. This section, situated in the highest section of the city, frequently is referred to as Mount Zion. The location was probably selected because it was easily defended from invaders.

Jerusalem has little to recommend it as a capital city, when compared to other major cities of the ancient world. It was an inland city not situated near a seaport. Moreover, it was not near the major trade routes used during that time. Why, then, did David select Jerusalem as the capital of his nation? The reasons are twofold.

First, Jerusalem was centrally located between the northern and southern tribes. Thus, it was geographically convenient for the nation. The central location of the capital city tended to unite the people into one kingdom.

Second, the topography of the city made it easy to defend. Jerusalem was situated on a hill. The eastern and western sides of the city consisted of valleys that made invasion by opposing forces difficult. The southern portion consisted of ravines that made an attack from this position unwise. The best point from which to attack Jerusalem was the north, which had the highest elevation of any portion of the city. It was from this position that attacks on the city were made in the years following the establishment of Jerusalem as the capital.

The Dome of the Rock in Jerusalem, an Islamic mosque built in the seventh century A.D. Some scholars believe it stands on the site where the original Jewish Temple built by Solomon was situated.

Photo by Gustav Jeeninga

Photo by Ben Chapman

The modern city of Jerusalem, showing the Dome of the Rock mosque and the hill on which Solomon's Temple was probably built. The hill in the distance is the site of the Mount of Olives.

David also made Jerusalem the religious capital of the nation. He moved the ARK OF THE COVENANT, which had been kept at Kirjath-jearim (Josh. 15:9) to Jerusalem. Then David proceeded to build a TABERNACLE, in which the ark was placed. One of his desires was to build a temple in the capital city, but he was prevented from completing this task. The prophet Nathan instructed him that God did not want him to build the temple because his hands had been involved in so much bloodshed (1 Chronicles 17). David did make preparation for the building of the temple, however, leaving the actual building task to Solomon, his son and successor.

During the reign of David, Jerusalem was firmly established politically and religiously as the capital city of the Hebrew nations The selection of this site resulted in the unification of the nation as David had hoped. But the selection of Jerusalem as the capital was more than a choice by a human king. Divine providence was also involved. Jerusalem was referred to as "the place which the Lord your God shall choose out of all your tribes to put his name there" (Deut. 12:5, 11, 14, 18, 21).

Jerusalem Under Solomon. The glory of Jerusalem, begun under David, reached its greatest heights under Solomon. Solomon proceeded to construct the Temple about which David had dreamed (2 Chronicles 3; 4). He also extended the borders of the city to new limits. Because surrounding nations were engaged in internal strife, Jerusalem was spared from invasions from opposing forces during Solomon's administration.

After completing the Temple, Solomon built the palace complex, a series of five structures.

These other buildings were the "house of the Forest of Lebanon," an assembly hall and a storage place for arms; an anteroom for the throne, where distinguished guests were received; the throne room, an ornately carved enclosure that contained the throne, which was made of carved ivory inlaid with gold; the king's palace, which was very large so as to hold the king's family; and the residence for Solomon's Egyptian wives, which adjoined the king's palace.

Solomon also planted vineyards, orchards, and gardens that contained all types of trees and shrubs. These were watered by streams and pools that flowed through the complex. Unfortunately, this splendor came to an end with the death of Solomon about 922 B.C. The division of the Hebrew kingdom into two separate nations after Solomon's reign resulted in the relapse of Jerusalem to the status of a minor city.

Jerusalem Under Siege. After the death of Solomon, the division that occurred in the kingdom resulted in the ten northern tribes establishing their own capital, first at Shechem and later at Samaria. The southern tribes, consisting of Judah and Benjamin, retained Jerusalem as the capital. Although separated politically from Jerusalem, the northern tribes continued their allegiance to the "holy city" by occasionally coming there for worship.

In 722 B.C., the northern tribes were conquered by the Assyrians. Many of the citizens of the northern kingdom of Israel were deported to the Assyrian nation, never to return to the "promised land."

But the Southern Kingdom, with Jerusalem as its capital, continued to exist as an independent nation. Although occasionally threatened and plundered by surrounding nations, Jerusalem remained intact until 587 B.C. At that time, Nebuchadnezzar, king of Babylon, ravaged the city and carried the inhabitants into captivity. During the siege of the city, Jerusalem's beautiful Temple was destroyed and the walls around the city were torn down. While a few inhabitants remained in the city, the glory of Jerusalem was gone.

The memory of Jerusalem among the Jewish people, however, would not die. They continued to grieve and to remember the City of David with affection. Psalm 137 is a good example of their expression of grief: "By the rivers of Babylon, there we sat down, yea, we wept, when we remembered Zion. We hanged our harps upon the willows in the midst thereof. For there they that carried us away captive required of us a song; and they that wasted us required of us mirth, saying, Sing us one of the songs of Zion. How shall we sing the Lord's song in a strange land? If I forget thee, O Jerusalem, let my right hand forget her cunning. If I do not remember thee, let my tongue cleave to the roof of my mouth; if I prefer not Jerusalem above my chief joy."

The Restoration. For more than half a century the Hebrews remained captives in Babylon, and their beloved Jerusalem lay in ruins. But this changed when Cyrus, king of Persia, defeated the Babylonians. He allowed the Jewish captives to return to Jerusalem to restore the city. Zerubbabel was the leader of a group that left Babylon in 537 B.C. to return to Jerusalem to rebuild the Temple. After a period of about 20 years, the Temple was restored, although it was not as lavish as Solomon's original Temple had been.

Under the leadership of NEHEMIAH, a second group of Jewish exiles returned to the holy city to restore the wall around the city. Through a masterful strategy of organization and determination, the wall was restored in 52 days (Neh. 6:15).

During the succeeding years of domination by the Persian Empire, Jerusalem apparently enjoyed peace and prosperity. The inhabitants were pleased with their status under Persian rule. When ALEXANDER the Great conquered Persia, the Jews were reluctant to pledge loyalty to the Greek ruler, preferring instead to remain under Persian rule. Only by tactful concessions of religious privileges was Alexander able to win the loyalty of the Jews.

Jerusalem During the Period Between the Testaments. The years that followed the death of Alexander brought many contending armies into conflict in the territory that surrounded Jerusalem. But the greatest threat to the Jews was the onslaught of Greek or Hellenistic culture, which threatened to erode the Jewish way of life. When the Jews resisted Greek cultural influence, the Greek leader ANTIOCHUS IV Epiphanes attacked the city and destroyed the Temple. Many of the inhabitants fled the city, taking refuge in the surrounding hills.

Led by JUDAS MACCABEUS, these inhabitants later recaptured Jerusalem and restored the Temple. The successors to Judas Maccabeus were able to gain independence and to set up Jerusalem as the capital of a newly independent Judea—a position the city had not enjoyed since its defeat by the Babylonians about three centuries before. This situation prevailed until the Roman Empire conquered Judea and reduced Jerusalem to a city-state under Roman domination. This was the situation that prevailed during New Testament times.

Jerusalem in the New Testament. The wise men who sought Jesus after His birth came to Jerusalem because this was considered the city of the king (Matt. 2:1-2). Although Jesus was born in Bethlehem, Jerusalem played a significant role in His life and ministry. It was to Jerusalem that He went when He was 12 years old. Here He amazed the Temple leaders with His knowledge and wisdom (Luke 2:47). In Jerusalem He cleansed the Temple, chasing away the moneychangers who desecrated the holy place with their selfish practices. And, finally, it was Jerusalem where He was crucified, buried, and resurrected.

The record of the New Testament church indicates that Jerusalem continued to play a significant role in the early spread of Christianity. After the martyrdom of Stephen, the early believers scattered from Jerusalem to various parts of the Mediterranean world (Acts 8:1). But Jerusalem always was the place to which they returned for significant events. For example, Acts 15 records that when the early church leaders sought to reconcile their differences about the acceptance of Gentile believers, they met in Jerusalem. Thus, the city became a holy city for Christians as well as Jews.

The Jerusalem of New Testament times contained a temple that had been built years before by Herod, the Roman leader. Although the main portion of the Temple was completed in 18 months, other areas of this building were still under construction during Jesus' ministry. In fact, the Temple was not completed until A.D. 67—only three years before it was finally destroyed by the Roman leader, Titus, and the Roman army.

As Jesus had prophesied in Matthew 23, the city of Jerusalem was completely destroyed in A.D. 70. The Temple was destroyed, and the high priesthood and the SANDHEDRIN were abolished. Eventually, a Roman city was erected on the site, and Jerusalem was regarded as forbidden ground for the Jews.

Modern Jerusalem. In 1919, under a ruling by British officials in Palestine, Jerusalem regained its status as a capital city. During the following three decades, numerous Jews, whose ancestors had been barred from the city, settled in and around Jerusalem. A new city, whose population was predominantly Jewish, was constructed west of the site of the old city. Following the Arab–Israeli War of 1948–49, the new city was allotted to the Jews, while the old city remained in Moslem hands. Less than two decades later, as a result of what has become known as the Six-Day War, the old city and

JERUZALEM
BEGIN 1ᵉ EEUW

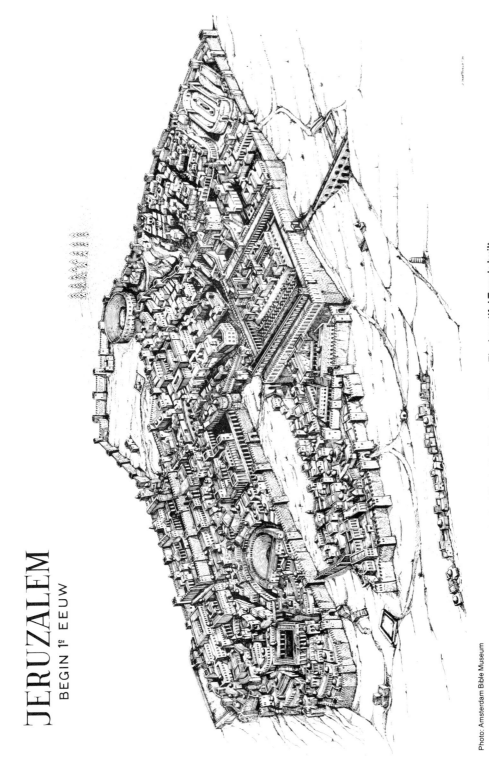

An artist's sketch of what Jerusalem might have looked like in New Testament times. The beautiful Temple built by Herod appears within the square wall structure in the foreground.

A view of modern Jerusalem, showing the El Aksa mosque (right) and excavations of Herod's Temple in the foreground.

the surrounding countryside were captured by Israel. It has remained occupied by the descendants of the biblical Israelites until the present day.

Topography. Unlike many other ancient cities, Jerusalem is neither a harbor city nor a city situated on trade routes. It sits about 800 meters (2,500 feet) above sea level in mountainous country about 60 kilometers (37 miles) from the Mediterranean Sea and 23 kilometers (14 miles) from the northern end of the Dead Sea. The site seems unattractive because it lacks an adequate supply of water, is surrounded by relatively infertile land, and is hemmed in by deep valleys and difficult roads.

But these disadvantages were probably the major factors that led to its establishment as a capital city. Its location made the city a fortress that could be easily defended against attack—a very important consideration in Old Testament times.

Topographically, Jerusalem was built on two triangle–shaped ridges which converge to the south. On the east lay the ravine known as the KIDRON Valley. On the west lay the deep gorge known as the Valley of HINNOM. At the southern border of the city, the two valleys converged. Only on the northern border was the city vulnerable to attack.

The lack of a water supply was solved by using a natural spring that flowed from the Kidron Valley. During the reign of Hezekiah in the Old Testament period, this spring was diverted underground so that it flowed into the city. Thus, the inhabitants of

the city had water, while invading armies did not. According to 2 Chronicles 32:30, "Hezekiah ...stopped the upper watercourse of Gihon, and brought it straight down to the west side of the City of David." Hezekiah's new water supply helped save the city when it was attacked by the Assyrians a short time later.

Jerusalem is considered a holy city not only by Jews and Christians but also by Moslems. The Book of Revelation speaks of a "new Jerusalem" (Rev. 21:2). This is not to be understood as an actual geographical location but as a heavenly city fashioned by God Himself for those who are known as His people.

JERUSALEM COUNCIL, THE — a conference held in about A.D. 49 between delegates (including Paul and Barnabas) from the church at Antioch of Syria and delegates from the church at Jerusalem. This council met to settle a dispute over whether Gentile converts to Christianity first had to identify with Judaism by being circumcised (Acts 15:1-29).

According to Luke, "Certain men came down from Judea and taught the brethren, 'Unless you are circumcised according to the custom of Moses, you cannot be saved' " (Acts 15:1). They insisted that Gentiles could not be received into the church unless they were circumcised and brought under the rules of the Mosaic Law. The apostle Paul, champion of Gentile freedom, said that all people—both

Jews and Gentiles—are saved by grace through faith in Jesus Christ, apart from the works of the Law. To require circumcision, he argued, would destroy the good news of God's grace.

The conclusion of the Jerusalem Council, which determined that Gentiles did not have to be circumcised, was a sweeping victory for Paul's understanding of Christianity. Speaking for the council, the apostle Peter declared, "We believe that through the grace of the Lord Jesus Christ we [Jews] shall be saved in the same manner as they [the Gentiles]" (Acts 15:11).

Why was the decision of the Jerusalem Council so important? Perhaps this question can be answered by considering another question: What would have happened to the gospel of Christ, and to Christianity, if the council had decided that circumcision is necessary for anyone to become a Christian? Such a decision would have been disastrous. It would have forced a condition that would have been unacceptable to the Gentiles. The missionary efforts would have become more difficult, and Christianity would have become nothing but a sect within Judaism. Furthermore, the truth of the gospel would have been compromised. Instead of a gospel based on salvation by grace through faith in Jesus Christ, it would have become one based on salvation by works (the Law).

The theological problem was solved, but a practical problem remained. Fellowship between the Jews and Gentiles in the early church remained on a shaky foundation. If the Gentile converts to Christianity flaunted their newfound freedom in Christ, without any concern for the sensitive feelings of the Jewish Christians, the unity of the church could be threatened. The Jerusalem Council decreed, therefore, that the Gentiles should make four reasonable concessions of their own: "We write to them to abstain from things polluted by idols, from sexual immorality, from things strangled, and from blood" (Acts 15:20; also 15:29; 21:25). In other words, Gentile converts should avoid offending the moral and religious convictions of the Jewish believers.

The Jerusalem Council was both a theological and a practical success. The concessions it called for were not "compromises"; indeed, they reaffirmed the integrity of the gospel of salvation by faith alone. They also dealt with a potentially explosive controversy by expressing concern for deeply held convictions. As the Jerusalem Council ended, the first great threat to the unity of the church brought rejoicing and encouragement instead (Acts 15:31).

JERUSALEM, NEW — the holy city described by John in Revelation 21—22; God's perfect and eternal order of the future. This New Jerusalem is not built by human hands; it is a heavenly city—one built and provided by God Himself (Rev. 21:2).

The New Jerusalem and the new Garden of Eden (symbols of righteousness, peace, and prosperity) are the dwelling place of God, Christ, and the church. John saw no temple in New Jerusalem, "for the Lord God Almighty and the Lamb are its temple" (Rev. 21:22).

In the Book of Revelation John draws a graphic contrast between the harlot city called "Babylon the Great" (Rev. 14:8; 16:19; 17:1—18:24), the earthly and temporal city of man, and the "New Jerusalem" (Rev. 21:2—22:5), the heavenly and eternal city of God. John identifies "the great city, the holy Jerusalem" (Rev. 21:10) as the church, which he calls "the bride, the Lamb's wife" (Rev. 21:9).

JERUSHA [juh ROO shuh] (*taken in marriage*) — the wife of Uzziah, king of Judah, and the mother of Jotham, who became king of Judah when Uzziah died (2 Kin. 15:33). The name is also spelled Jerushah (2 Chr. 27:1).

JERUSHAH [juh ROO shuh] — a form of JERUSHA.

JESAIAH [juh SIGH uh] — a form of JESHAIAH.

JESHAIAH [juh SHAY uh] (*salvation of Jehovah*) — the name of six men in the Old Testament:

1. A son of Hananiah (1 Chr. 3:21; Jesaiah, KJV).
2. A son of Jeduthun (1 Chr. 25:3, 15).
3. A Levite and a son of Rehabiah (1 Chr. 26:25).
4. A son of Athaliah who returned from the Babylonian Captivity (Ezra 8:7).
5. A Levite who returned from Babylon with Ezra (Ezra 8:19).
6. The father of Ithiel whose descendants lived in Jerusalem (Neh. 11:7; Jesaiah, KJV).

JESHANAH [juh SHAY nuh] (*ancient*) — a city in the hill country of Ephraim (2 Chr. 13:19), usually identified as present-day Ain Sinya, about six kilometers (four miles) north of Bethel.

JESHANAH GATE (see GATES OF JERUSALEM AND THE TEMPLE).

JESHARELAH [jesh uh REE luh] (*upright toward God*) — a musician who presided over the service of song during the reign of King David (1 Chr. 25:14; Asharelah, NEB).

JESHEBEAB [juh SHEB ih ab] (*may the father endure*) — head of the 14th course of priests in the sanctuary service in David's time (1 Chr. 24:13).

JESHER [JEE shur] (*uprightness*) — a son of Caleb (1 Chr. 2:18).

JESHIAH — [jih SHY uh] a form of JESSHIAH.

JESHIMON [juh SHIGH muhn] (*wasteland*) — the name of two wastelands in the land of Israel:

1. The name given in some translations to a wilderness north of the Dead Sea and east of the Jordan River (Num. 21:20, KJV).
2. A wilderness of Judah west of the Dead Sea (1 Sam. 23:19; 26:1, 3).

JESHISHAI [juh SHISH eye] (*venerable*) — a son of Jahdo (1 Chr. 5:14).

JESHOHAIAH [jesh oe HAY uh] (*Jehovah humbles*) — a leader of the tribe of Simeon (1 Chr. 4:36).

JESHUA [JESH oo uh] (*the Lord is salvation*)—the name of eight men and one city in the Old Testament:

1. Head of the ninth course of priests in David's time (Neh. 7:39; Jeshuah, KJV).

2. A Levite in the days of King Hezekiah of Judah (2 Chr. 31:15).

3. A priest who returned to Jerusalem from the Captivity (Ezra 2:2). Jeshua and his fellow priests and kinsmen built the altar of God to restore the burnt offerings and also began work on the restored Temple. He opposed the Samaritans in their efforts to discourage work on the Temple (Ezra 4:3–5). In Zechariah 3:1–9 and 6:11 he is called Joshua.

4. The father of Jozabad (Ezra 8:33).

5. A son of Pahath–Moab, whose descendants returned from the Captivity with Zerubbabel (Neh. 7:11).

6. The father of Ezer (Neh. 3:19).

7. A Levite who helped Ezra explain the Law to the people (Neh. 8:7).

8. A son of Azaniah (Ezra 2:40).

9. A city of southern Judah occupied by Israelites who returned from the Captivity (Neh. 11:26). It is identified with Tell es-Sa'wi, about 19 kilometers (12 miles) northeast of Beersheba.

JESHUAH [jih SHOO uh] — a form of JESHUA No. 1.

JESHURUN [JESH uh ruhn] (*the beloved one*) — a poetic term for the nation of Israel (Deut. 32:15; Is. 44:2; Jesurun, KJV). The term beloved suggests the election of Israel to a divine mission; the same Greek term is used of Christ (Matt. 3:17; Eph. 1:6) and the church (Col. 3:12; 1 Thess. 1:4).

JESIMIEL [juh SIM ih uhl] (*God establishes*) — a leader of the tribe of Simeon (1 Chr. 4:36).

JESSE [JES ee] (meaning unknown) — the father of King David (1 Sam. 16:18–19) and an ancestor of Jesus. Jesse was the father of eight sons—Eliab, Abinadab, Shimea (Shammah), Nethanel, Raddai, Ozem, Elihu, and David—and two daughters, Zeruiah and Abigail (1 Chr. 2:13–16). He is called a "Bethlehemite" (1 Sam. 16:1, 18).

On instructions from the Lord, the prophet Samuel went to Bethlehem to select a new king from among Jesse's eight sons. After the first seven were rejected, David was anointed by Samuel to replace Saul as king of Israel (1 Sam. 16:1–13). Later King Saul asked Jesse to allow David to visit his court and play soothing music on the harp. Jesse gave his permission and sent Saul a present (1 Sam. 16:20).

The title "son of Jesse" soon became attached to David. It was sometimes used in a spirit of insult and ridicule, mocking David's humble origins (1 Sam. 20:27; 1 Kin. 12:16). But the prophet Isaiah spoke of "a Rod from the stem of Jesse" (11:1) and of "a Root of Jesse" (11:10)—prophecies of the Messiah to come. For the apostle Paul, the "root of Jesse" (Rom. 15:12) was a prophecy fulfilled in Jesus Christ.

JESSHIAH [jesh EYE uh] (*Jehovah exists*) — the second son of Uzziel and the father of Zechariah (1 Chr. 23:20; Jeshiah, KJV), also called Isshiah (1 Chr. 24:25).

JESUI [JES yoo igh] (*Jehovah is satisfied*) — the third son of Asher and founder of a tribal family, the Jesuites (Num. 26:44). He is also called Isui (Gen. 46:17) and Ishvi (1 Chr. 7:30; Ishuai, KJV).

JESUITES [JEZ you ites] — descendants of JESUI, of the tribe of Asher (Num. 26:44; Ishvites, RSV, NIV, NEB, NASB).

JESURUN [JES oo ruhn] — a form of JESHURUN.

JESUS [GEE zus] (*Jehovah is salvation*) — the name of five men in the Bible:

1. Jesus BARABBAS, a prisoner released by the Roman governor Pontius Pilate before Jesus was crucified (Matt. 27:16–17, NEB; some manuscripts omit the word Jesus and have simply Barabbas).

2. An ancestor of Christ (Luke 3:29; Jose, KJV, NKJV; Joshua, NASB, NEB, NIV, RSV).

3. The KJV rendering of Joshua, the son of Nun (Acts 7:45; Heb. 4:8).

4. Jesus Justus, a Jewish Christian who, with the apostle Paul, sent greetings to the Colossians (Col. 4:11).

5. Jesus, the son of Mary. Also see JESUS CHRIST.

JESUS CHRIST — the human–divine Son of God born of the Virgin Mary; the great High Priest who intercedes for His people at the right hand of God; founder of the Christian church and central figure of the human race.

To understand who Jesus was and what He accomplished, students of the New Testament must study: (1) His life, (2) His teachings, (3) His person, and (4) His work.

The Life of Jesus. The twofold designation Jesus Christ combines the personal name Jesus and the title Christ, meaning "anointed" or "Messiah." The significance of this title became clear during the scope of His life and ministry.

Birth and upbringing—Jesus was born in Bethlehem, a town about ten kilometers (six miles) south of Jerusalem, toward the end of Herod the Great's reign as king of the Jews (37–4 B.C.). Early in His life He was taken to Nazareth, a town of Galilee. There He was brought up by His mother, Mary, and her husband, Joseph, a carpenter by trade. Hence He was known as "Jesus of Nazareth" or, more fully, "Jesus of Nazareth, the son of Joseph" (John 1:45).

Jesus was His mother's firstborn child; he had four brothers (James, Joses, Judas, and Simon) and an unspecified number of sisters (Mark 6:3). Joseph apparently died before Jesus began His public ministry. Mary, with the rest of the family, lived on and became a member of the church of Jerusalem after Jesus' death and resurrection.

The only incident preserved from Jesus' first 30 years (after his infancy) was His trip to Jerusalem with Joseph and Mary when He was 12 years old

(Luke 2:41–52). Since He was known in Nazareth as "the carpenter" (Mark 6:3), He may have taken Joseph's place as the family breadwinner at an early age.

The little village of Nazareth overlooked the main highway linking Damascus to the Mediterranean coast and Egypt. News of the world outside Galilee probably reached Nazareth quickly. During His boyhood Jesus probably heard of the revolt led by Judas the Galilean against the Roman authorities. This happened when Judea, to the south, became a Roman province in A.D. 6 and its inhabitants had to pay tribute to Caesar. Jews probably heard also of the severity with which the revolt was crushed.

Galilee, the province in which Jesus lived, was ruled by Herod Antipas, youngest son of Herod the Great. So the area where He lived was not directly involved in this revolt. But the sympathies of many Galileans were probably stirred. No doubt the boys of Nazareth discussed this issue, which they heard their elders debating. There is no indication of what Jesus thought about this event at the time. But we do know what he said about it in Jerusalem 24 years later (Mark 12:13–17).

Sepphoris, about six kilometers (four miles) northwest of Nazareth, had been the center of an anti-Roman revolt during Jesus' infancy. The village was destroyed by the Romans, but it was soon rebuilt by Herod Antipas. Antipas lived there as tetrarch of Galilee and Perea until he founded a new capital for his principality at Tiberias, on the western shore of the Lake of Galilee (A.D. 22). Reports of happenings at his court, while he lived in Sepphoris, were probably carried to Nazareth. A royal court formed the setting for several of Jesus' parables.

Scenes from Israel's history could be seen from the rising ground above Nazareth. To the south stretched the Valley of Jezreel, where great battles had been fought in earlier days. Beyond the Valley of Jezreel was Mount Gilboa, where King Saul fell in battle with the Philistines. To the east Mount Tabor rose to 562 meters (1,843 feet), the highest elevation in that part of the country. A growing boy would readily find his mind moving back and forth between the stirring events of former days and the realities of the contemporary situation: the all-pervasive presence of the Romans.

Beginnings of Jesus' ministry—Jesus began His public ministry when He sought baptism at the hands of John the Baptist. John preached between A.D. 27 and 28 in the lower Jordan Valley and baptized those who wished to give expression to their repentance (Matt. 3:13–17; Mark 1:9–11; Luke 3:21–22; John 1:29–34). The descent of the dove as Jesus came up out of the water was a sign that He was the One anointed by the Spirit of God as the Servant–Messiah of His people (Is. 11:2; 42:1; 61:1).

A voice from heaven declared, "You are My beloved Son; in You I am well pleased" (Luke 3:22). This indicated that He was Israel's anointed King, destined to fulfill His kingship as the Servant of the Lord described centuries earlier by the prophet Isaiah (Is. 42:1; 52:13).

In the Gospels of Matthew, Mark, and Luke, Jesus' baptism is followed immediately by His temptation in the wilderness (Matt. 4:1–11; Mark 1:12–13; Luke 4:1–13). This testing confirmed His understanding of the heavenly voice and His acceptance of the path which it marked out for Him. He refused to use His power as God's Son to fulfill His personal desires, to amaze the people, or to dominate the world by political and military force.

Apparently, Jesus ministered for a short time in

Terracing on hillside farmland outside Bethlehem, the Judean village where Jesus was born, in fulfillment of Old Testament prophecies.

Photo: Levant Photo Service

Modern Nazareth, the town in the province of Galilee where Jesus grew up (Luke 4:14-16, 33, 34).

southern and central Palestine, while John the Baptist was still preaching (John 3:22—4:42). But the main phase of Jesus' ministry began in Galilee after John's imprisonment by Herod Antipas. This was the signal, according to Mark 1:14-15, for Jesus to proclaim God's Good News in Galilee: "The time is fulfilled, and the kingdom of God is at hand. Repent, and believe in the gospel." What is the character of this kingdom? How was it to be established?

A popular view was that the kingdom of God meant throwing off the oppressive yoke of Rome and establishing an independent state of Israel. JUDAS MACCABEUS and his brothers and followers had won independence for the Jewish people in the second century B.C. by guerrilla warfare and diplomatic skill. Many of the Jewish people believed that with God's help, the same thing could happen again. Other efforts had failed, but the spirit of revolt remained. If Jesus had consented to become the military leader, which the people wanted, many would gladly have followed Him. But in spite of His temptation, Jesus resisted taking this path.

Jesus' proclamation of the kingdom of God was accompanied by works of mercy and power, including the healing of the sick, particularly those who were demon–possessed. These works also proclaimed the arrival of the kingdom of God. The demons that caused such distress to men and women were signs of the kingdom of Satan. When they were cast out, this proved the superior strength of the kingdom of God.

For a time, Jesus' healing aroused great popular enthusiasm throughout Galilee. But the religious leaders and teachers found much of Jesus' activity disturbing. He refused to be bound by their religious ideas. He befriended social outcasts. He insisted on understanding and applying the law of God in the light of its original intention, not according to the popular interpretation of the religious establishment. He insisted on healing sick people on the Sabbath day. He believed that healing people did not profane the Sabbath but honored it, because it was established by God for the rest and relief of human beings (Luke 6:6–11).

This attitude brought Jesus into conflict with the scribes, the official teachers of the law. Because of their influence, He was soon barred from preaching in the synagogues. But this was no great inconvenience. He simply gathered larger congregations to listen to Him on the hillside or by the lakeshore. He regularly illustrated the main themes of His preaching by parables. These were simple stories from daily life which would drive home some special point and make it stick in the hearer's understanding.

The mission of the Twelve and its sequel—From among the large number of His followers, Jesus selected 12 men to remain in His company for training that would enable them to share His preaching and healing ministry. When He judged the time to be ripe, Jesus sent them out two by two to proclaim the kingdom of God throughout the Jewish districts of Galilee. In many places, they found an enthusiastic hearing.

Probably some who heard these disciples misunderstood the nature of the kingdom they proclaimed. Perhaps the disciples themselves used language that could be interpreted as stirring political unrest. News of their activity reached Herod Antipas, ruler of Galilee, arousing His suspicion. He had recently murdered John the Baptist. Now he began to wonder if he faced another serious problem in Jesus.

On the return of His 12 apostles, they withdrew under Jesus' leadership from the publicity that surrounded them in Galilee to the quieter territory east of the Lake of Galilee. This territory was ruled by Antipas' brother Philip—"Philip the tetrarch"—who had only a few Jews among his subjects. Philip was not as likely to be troubled by Messianic excitement.

But even here Jesus and His disciples found themselves pursued by enthusiastic crowds from Galilee. He recognized them for what they were, "sheep without a shepherd," aimless people who were in danger of being led to disaster under the wrong kind of leadership.

Jesus gave these people further teaching, feeding them also with loaves and fishes. But this only stimulated them to try to compel Him to be the king for whom they were looking. He would not be the kind of king they wanted, and they had no use for the only kind of king He was prepared to be. From then on, His popularity in Galilee began to decline. Many of His disciples no longer followed Him.

He took the Twelve further north, into Gentile territory. Here He gave them special training to prepare them for the crisis they would have to meet shortly in Jerusalem. He knew the time was approaching when He would present His challenging message to the people of the capital and to the Jewish leaders.

At the city of Caesarea Philippi, Jesus decided the time was ripe to encourage the Twelve to state their convictions about His identity and His mission. When Peter declared that He was the Messiah, this showed that He and the other apostles had given up most of the traditional ideas about the kind of person the Messiah would be. But the thought that Jesus would have to suffer and die was something they could not accept. Jesus recognized that He could now make a beginning with the creation of a new community. In this new community of God's people, the ideals of the kingdom He proclaimed would be realized.

These ideals which Jesus taught were more revolutionary in many ways than the insurgent spirit that survived the overthrow of Judas the Galilean. The Jewish rebels against the rule of Rome developed into a party known as the Zealots. They had no better policy than to counter force with force, which, in Jesus' view, was like invoking Satan to drive out Satan. The way of nonresistance which He urged upon the people seemed impractical. But it eventually proved to be more effective against the might of Rome than armed rebellion.

Jerusalem: the last phase—At the Feast of Tabernacles in the fall of A.D. 29, Jesus went to Jerusalem with the Twelve. He apparently spent the next six months in the southern part of Palestine. Jerusalem, like Galilee, needed to hear the message of the

kingdom. But Jerusalem was more resistant to it even than Galilee. The spirit of revolt was in the air; Jesus' way of peace was not accepted. This is why He wept over the city. He realized the way which so many of its citizens preferred was bound to lead to their destruction. Even the magnificent Temple, so recently rebuilt by Herod the Great, would be involved in the general overthrow.

During the week before Passover in A.D. 30, Jesus taught each day in the Temple area, debating with other teachers of differing beliefs. He was invited to state His opinion on a number of issues, including the question of paying taxes to the Roman Emperor. This was a test question with the Zealots. In their eyes, to acknowledge the rule of a pagan king was high treason against God, Israel's true King.

Jesus replied that the coinage in which these taxes had to be paid belonged to the Roman emperor because his face and name were stamped on it. Let the emperor have what so obviously belonged to him, Jesus declared; it was more important to make sure that God received what was due Him.

This answer disappointed those patriots who followed the Zealot line. Neither did it make Jesus popular with the priestly authorities. They were terrified by the rebellious spirit in the land. Their favored position depended on maintaining good relations with the ruling Romans. If revolt broke out, the Romans would hold them responsible for not keeping the people under control. They were afraid that Jesus might provoke an outburst that would bring the heavy hand of Rome upon the city.

The enthusiasm of the people when Jesus entered Jerusalem on a donkey alarmed the religious leaders. So did his show of authority when he cleared the Temple of traders and moneychangers. This was a "prophetic action" in the tradition of the great prophets of Israel. Its message to the priestly establishment came through loud and clear. The prophets' vision of the Temple—"My house shall be called a house of prayer for all nations" (Is. 56:7)—was a fine ideal. But any attempt to make it measure up to reality would be a threat to the priestly privileges. Jesus' action was as disturbing as Jeremiah's speech foretelling the destruction of Solomon's Temple had been to the religious leaders six centuries earlier (Jer. 26:1-6).

To block the possibility of an uprising among the people, the priestly party decided to arrest Jesus as soon as possible. The opportunity came earlier than they expected when one of the Twelve, Judas Iscariot, offered to deliver Jesus into their power without the risk of a public disturbance. Arrested on Passover Eve, Jesus was brought first before a Jewish court of inquiry, over which the high priest Caiaphas presided.

The Jewish leaders attempted first to convict Him of being a threat to the Temple. Protection of the sanctity of the Temple was the one area in which the Romans still allowed the Jewish authorities to exercise authority. But this attempt failed. Then Jesus accepted their charge that He claimed to be the Messiah. This gave the religious leaders an occasion to hand Him over to Pilate on a charge of treason and sedition.

While "Messiah" was primarily a religious title, it could be translated into political terms as "king of the Jews." Anyone who claimed to be king of the Jews, as Jesus admitted He did, presented a challenge to the Roman emperor's rule in Judea. On this charge Pilate, the Roman governor, finally convicted Jesus. This was the charge spelled out in the inscription fixed above His head on the cross. Death by crucifixion was the penalty for sedition by one who was not a Roman citizen.

With the death and burial of Jesus, the narrative of His earthly career came to an end. But with His resurrection on the third day, He lives and works forever as the exalted Lord. His appearances to His disciples after His resurrection assured them He was "alive after His suffering" (Acts 1:3). These appearances also enabled them to make the transition in their experience from the form in which they had known Him earlier to the new way in which they would be related to Him by the Holy Spirit.

The Teachings of Jesus. Just as Jesus' life was unique, so His teachings are known for their fresh and new approach. Jesus taught several distinctive spiritual truths that set Him apart from any other religious leader who ever lived.

The kingdom of God—The message Jesus began to proclaim in Galilee after John the Baptist's imprisonment was the good news of the kingdom of God. When He appeared to His disciples after the resurrection, He continued "speaking of the things pertaining to the kingdom of God" (Acts 1:3). What did Jesus mean by the kingdom of God?

When Jesus announced that the kingdom of God was drawing near, many of His hearers must have recognized an echo of those visions recorded in the Book of Daniel. These prophecies declared that one day "the God of heaven will set up a kingdom which shall never be destroyed" (Dan. 2:44). Jesus' announcement indicated the time had come when the authority of this kingdom would be exercised.

The nature of this kingdom is determined by the character of the God whose kingdom it is. The revelation of God lay at the heart of Jesus' teaching. Jesus called Him "Father" and taught His disciples to do the same. But the term that He used when He called God "Father" was *Abba* (Mark 14:36), the term of affection that children used when they addressed their father at home or spoke about him to others. It was not unusual for God to be addressed in prayer as "my Father" or "our Father." But it was most unusual for Him to be called *Abba*. By using this term, Jesus expressed His sense of nearness to God and His total trust in Him. He taught His followers to look to God with the trust that children show when they expect their earthly fathers to provide them with food, clothes, and shelter.

This attitude is especially expressed in the Lord's Prayer, which may be regarded as a brief summary of Jesus' teaching. In this prayer the disciples were taught to pray for the fulfillment of God's eternal purpose (the coming of His kingdom) and to ask Him for daily bread, forgiveness of sins, and deliverance from temptation.

In Jesus' healing of the sick and proclamation of good news to the poor, the kingdom of God was visibly present, although it was not yet fully realized. Otherwise, it would not have been necessary for Him to tell His disciples to pray, "Your kingdom come" (Matt. 6:10). One day, He taught, it would come "with power" (Mark 9:1), and some of them would live to see that day.

In the kingdom of God the way to honor is the way of service. In this respect, Jesus set a worthy example, choosing to give service instead of receiving it.

The death and resurrection of Jesus unleashed the kingdom of God in full power. Through proclamation of the kingdom, liberation and blessing were brought to many more than could be touched by Jesus' brief ministry in Galilee and Judea.

The way of the kingdom—The ethical teaching of Jesus was part of His proclamation of the kingdom of God. Only by His death and resurrection could the divine rule be established. But even while the kingdom of God was in the process of inauguration during His ministry, its principles could be translated into action in the lives of His followers. The most familiar presentation of these principles is found in the SERMON ON THE MOUNT (Matthew 5—7), which was addressed to His disciples. These principles showed how those who were already children of the kingdom ought to live.

Jesus and the law of Moses—The people whom Jesus taught already had a large body of ethical teaching in the Old Testament law. But a further body of oral interpretation and application had grown up around the Law of Moses over the centuries. Jesus declared that He had come to fulfill the law, not to destroy it (Matt. 5:17). But He emphasized its ethical quality by summarizing it in terms of what He called the two great commandments: "You shall love the Lord your God" (Deut. 6:5) and "You shall love your neighbor as yourself" (Lev. 19:18). "On these two commandments," He said, "hang all the Law and the Prophets" (Matt. 22:40).

Jesus did not claim uniqueness or originality for His ethical teaching. One of His purposes was to explain the ancient law of God. Yet there was a distinctiveness and freshness about His teaching, as He declared His authority: "You have heard that it was said...But I say to you" (Matt. 5:21–22). Only in listening to His words and doing them could a person build a secure foundation for his life (Matt. 7:24–27; Luke 6:46–49).

In His interpretation of specific commandments, Jesus did not use the methods of the Jewish rabbis. He dared to criticize their rulings, which had been handed down by word of mouth through successive generations of scribes. He even declared that these interpretations sometimes obscured the original purpose of the commandments. In appealing to that original purpose, He declared that a commandment was most faithfully obeyed when God's

Traditional site of the baptism of Jesus in the Jordan River at the beginning of His public ministry (Matt. 3:13-17).

purpose in giving it was fulfilled. His treatment of the Sabbath law is an example of this approach.

In a similar way, Jesus settled the question of divorce by an appeal to the original marriage ordinance (Gen. 1:26–27; 2:24–25). Since husband and wife were made one by the Creator's decree, Jesus pointed out, divorce was an attempt to undo the work of God. If the law later allowed for divorce in certain situations (Deut. 24:1–4), that was a concession to men's inability to keep the commandment. But it was not so in the beginning, He declared, and it should not be so for those who belong to the kingdom of God.

Jesus actually injected new life into the ethical principles of the Law of Moses. But He did not impose a new set of laws that could be enforced by external sanctions; He prescribed a way of life for His followers. The act of murder, forbidden in the sixth commandment, was punishable by death. Conduct or language likely to provoke a breach of the peace could also bring on legal penalties. No human law can detect or punish the angry thought; yet it is here, Jesus taught, that the process which leads to murder begins. Therefore, "whoever is angry with his brother...shall be in danger of the judgment" (Matt. 5:22). But He was careful to point out that the judgment is God's, not man's.

The law could also punish a person for breaking the seventh commandment, which forbade adultery. But Jesus maintained that the act itself was the outcome of a person's internal thought. Therefore, "whoever looks at a woman to lust for her has already committed adultery with her in his heart" (Matt. 5:28).

Jesus' attitude and teaching also made many laws about property irrelevant for His followers. They should be known as people who give, not as people who get. If someone demands your cloak (outer garment), Jesus said, give it to him, and give him your tunic (undergarment) as well (Luke 6:29). There is more to life than abundance of possessions (Luke 12:15); in fact, He pointed out, material wealth is a hindrance to one's spiritual life. The wise man therefore will get rid of it: "It is easier for a camel to go through the eye of a needle than for a rich man to enter the kingdom of God" (Mark 10:25). In no area have Jesus' followers struggled more to avoid the uncompromising rigor of his words than in His teaching about the danger of possessions.

Jesus insisted that more is expected of His followers than the ordinary morality of decent people. Their ethical behavior should exceed "the righteousness of the scribes and Pharisees" (Matt. 5:20). "If you love [only] those who love you," He asked, "what credit is that to you? For even sinners love those who love them" (Luke 6:32). The higher standard of the kingdom of God called for acts of love to enemies and words of blessing and goodwill to persecutors. The children of the kingdom should not insist on their legal rights but cheerfully give them up in response to the supreme law of love.

The way of nonviolence—The principle of nonviolence is deeply ingrained in Jesus' teaching. In His references to the "men of violence" who tried to bring in the kingdom of God by force, Jesus gave no sign that He approved of their ideals or methods. The course which He called for was the way of peace and submission. He urged His hearers not to strike back against injustice or oppression but to turn the other cheek, to go a second mile when their services were demanded for one mile, and to take the initiative in returning good for evil.

But the way of nonviolence did not appeal to the people. The crowd chose the militant Barabbas when they were given the opportunity to have either Jesus or Barabbas set free. But the attitude expressed in the shout, "Not this man, but Barabbas!" (Matt. 27:15–26) was the spirit that would one day level Jerusalem and bring misery and suffering to the Jewish nation.

The supreme example—In the teaching of Jesus, the highest of all incentives is the example of God. This was no new principle. The central section of Leviticus is called "the law of holiness" because of its recurring theme: "I am the Lord your God...Be holy; for I am holy" (Lev. 11:44). This bears a close resemblance to Jesus' words in Luke 6:36, "Be merciful, just as your Father also is merciful." The children of God should reproduce their Father's character. He does not discriminate between the good and the evil in bestowing rain and sunshine; likewise, His followers should not discriminate in showing kindness to all. He delights in forgiving sinners; His children should also be marked by a forgiving spirit.

The example of the heavenly Father and the example shown by Jesus on earth are one and the same, since Jesus came to reveal the Father. Jesus' life was the practical demonstration of His ethical teaching. To His disciples He declared, "I have given you an example, that you should do as I have done to you" (John 13:15).

This theme of the imitation of Christ pervades the New Testament letters. It is especially evident in the writings of Paul, who was not personally acquainted with Jesus before he met Him on the Damascus Road. Paul instructed his converts to follow "the meekness and gentleness of Christ" (2 Cor. 10:1). He also encouraged them to imitate Him as he himself imitated Christ (1 Cor. 11:1). When he recommended to them the practice of all the Christian graces, he declared, "Put on the Lord Jesus Christ" (Rom. 13:14). Throughout the New Testament, Jesus is presented as the One who left us an example, that we should follow in His steps (1 Pet. 2:21).

The Person of Christ. The doctrine of the person of Christ, or Christology, is one of the most important concerns of Christian theology. The various aspects of the person of Christ are best seen by reviewing the titles that are applied to Him in the Bible.

Son of Man—The title Son of Man was Jesus' favorite way of referring to Himself. He may have done this because this was not a recognized title already known by the people and associated with popular ideas. This title means essentially "The Man." But as Jesus used it, it took on new significance.

Jesus applied this title to Himself in three distinct ways:

The Sea, or Lake, of Galilee, scene of many of Jesus' miracles and teachings (Matt. 14:13-33).
Photo by Gustav Jeeninga

First, He used the title in a general way, almost as a substitute for the pronoun "I." A good example of this usage occurred in the saying where Jesus contrasted John the Baptist, who "came neither eating bread nor drinking wine," with the Son of Man, who "has come eating and drinking" (Luke 7:33–34). Another probable example is the statement that "the Son of Man has nowhere to lay His head" (Luke 9:58). In this instance He warned a would-be disciple that those who wanted to follow Him must expect to share His homeless existence.

Second, Jesus used the title to emphasize that "the Son of Man must suffer" (Mark 8:31). The word *must* implies that His suffering was foretold by the prophets. It was, indeed, "written concerning the Son of Man, that He must suffer many things and be treated with contempt" (Mark 9:12). So when Jesus announced the presence of the betrayer at the Last Supper, He declared, "The Son of Man indeed goes just as it is written of Him" (Mark 14:21). Later on the same evening He submitted to His captors with the words, "The Scriptures must be fulfilled" (Mark 14:49).

Finally, Jesus used the title *Son of Man* to refer to Himself as the one who exercised exceptional authority—authority delegated to Him by God. "The Son of Man has power [authority] on earth to forgive sins" (Mark 2:10), He declared. He exercised this authority in a way that made some people criticize Him for acting with the authority of God: "The Son of Man is also Lord of the Sabbath" (Mark 2:28).

The Son of Man appeared to speak and act in these cases as the representative man. If God had given man dominion over all the works of His hands, then He who was the Son of Man in this special representative sense was in a position to exercise that dominion.

Near the end of His ministry, Jesus spoke of His authority as the Son of Man at the end of time. Men and women "will see the Son of Man coming in the clouds with great power and glory," He declared (Mark 13:26). He also stated to the high priest and other members of the supreme court of Israel: "You will see the Son of Man sitting at the right hand of Power, and coming with the clouds of heaven" (Mark 14:62). He seemed deserted and humiliated as He stood there awaiting their verdict. But the tables would be turned when they saw Him vindicated by God as Ruler and Judge of all the world.

Only once in the Gospels was Jesus referred to as the Son of Man by anyone other than Himself. This occurred when Stephen, condemned by the Jewish SANHEDRIN, saw "the Son of Man standing at the right hand of God" (Acts 7:56). In Stephen's vision the Son of Man stood as his heavenly advocate, in fulfillment of Jesus' words: "Whoever confesses Me before men, him the Son of Man also will confess before the angels of God" (Luke 12:8).

Messiah—When Jesus made His declaration before the high priest and His colleagues, He did so in response to the question: "Are You the Christ the Son of the Blessed?" (Mark 14:61). He replied, "I am" (Mark 14:62), "It is as you said" (Matt. 26:64).

The Christ was the MESSIAH, the Son of David—a member of the royal family of David. For centuries the Jewish people had expected a Messiah who would restore the fortunes of Israel, liberating the nation from foreign oppression and extending His rule over Gentile nations.

Jesus belonged to the family of David. He was proclaimed as the Messiah of David's line, both before His birth and after His resurrection. But He Himself was slow to make messianic claims. The reason for this is that the ideas associated with the Messiah in the minds of the Jewish people were quite different from the character and purpose of His ministry. Thus, He refused to give them any encouragement.

When, at Caesarea Philippi, Peter confessed Jesus to be the Messiah, Jesus directed him and his fellow disciples to tell no one that He was the Christ. After His death and resurrection, however, the concept of messiahship among His followers was transformed by what He was and did. Then He could safely be proclaimed as Messiah, God's Anointed King, resurrected in glory to occupy the throne of the universe.

Son of God—Jesus was acclaimed as the Son of God at His baptism (Mark 1:11). But He was also given this title by the angel Gabriel at the annunciation: "That Holy One who is to be born will be called the Son of God" (Luke 1:35). The Gospel of John especially makes it clear that the Father–Son relationship belongs to eternity—that the Son is supremely qualified to reveal the Father because He has His eternal being "in the bosom of the Father" (John 1:18).

At one level the title *Son of God* belonged officially to the Messiah, who personified the nation of Israel. "Israel is My Son, My firstborn," said God to Pharaoh (Ex. 4:22). Of the promised prince of the house of David, God declared, "I will make him My firstborn" (Ps. 89:27).

But there was nothing merely official about Jesus' consciousness of being the Son of God. He taught His disciples to think of God and to speak to Him as their Father.

But He did not link them with Himself in this relationship and speak to them of "our Father"—yours and mine. The truth expressed in His words in John 20:17 is implied throughout His teaching: "My Father and your Father...My God and your God."

As the Son of God in a special sense, Jesus made Himself known to the apostle Paul on the Damascus Road. Paul said, "It pleased God...to reveal His Son in me" (Gal. 1:15–16). The proclamation of Jesus as the Son of God was central to Paul's preaching (Acts 9:20; 2 Cor. 1:19).

When Jesus is presented as the Son of God in the New Testament, two aspects of His person are emphasized: His eternal relation to God as His Father and His perfect revelation of the Father to the human race.

Photo by Howard Vos

Ruins of the city of Tyre from the Roman period. Although Tyre was in Gentile territory, Jesus visited this region in His healing and teaching ministry (Matt. 15:21-28).

Word and Wisdom—Jesus' perfect revelation of the Father is also expressed when He is described as the Word (*logos*) of God (John 1:1–18). The Word is the self–expression of God; that self–expression has personal status, existing eternally with God. The Word by which God created the world (Ps. 33:6) and by which He spoke through the prophets "became flesh" in the fullness of time (John 1:14), living among men and women as Jesus of Nazareth.

Much that is said in the Old Testament about the Word of God is paralleled by what is said of the Wisdom of God: "The Lord by wisdom founded the earth" (Prov. 3:19). In the New Testament Christ is portrayed as the personal Wisdom of God (1 Cor. 1:24, 30)—the one through whom all things were created (1 Cor. 8:6; Col. 1:16; Heb. 1:2).

The Holy One of God—This title was given to Jesus by Peter (John 6:69, RSV) and remarkably, by a demon-possessed man (Mark 1:24). In their preaching, the apostles called Jesus "the Holy One and the Just" (Acts 3:14). This was a name belonging to Him as the Messiah, indicating He was especially set apart for God. This title also emphasized His positive goodness and His complete dedication to the doing of His Father's will. Mere "sinlessness," in the sense of the absence of any fault, is a pale quality in comparison to the unsurpassed power for righteousness which filled His life and teaching.

The Lord—"Jesus is Lord" is the ultimate Christian creed. "No one can say that Jesus is Lord except by the Holy Spirit" (1 Cor. 12:3). A Christian, therefore, is a person who confesses Jesus as Lord.

Several words denoting lordship were used of Jesus in the New Testament. The most frequent, and the most important in relation to the doctrine of His person, was the Greek word *kurios*. It was frequently given to Him as a polite term of address, meaning "Sir." Sometimes the title was used of Him in the third person, when the disciples and others spoke of Him as "The Lord" or "The Master."

After His resurrection and exaltation, however, Jesus was given the title "Lord" in its full, christological sense. Peter, concluding his address to the crowd in Jerusalem on the Day of Pentecost, declared, "Let all the house of Israel know assuredly that God has made this Jesus, whom you crucified, both Lord and Christ" (Acts 2:36).

The title "Lord" in the Christological sense must have been given to Jesus before the church moved out into the Gentile world. The evidence for this is the invocation "Maranatha" (KJV) or "O Lord, come!" (1 Cor. 16:22). The apostle Paul, writing to a Gentile church in the Greek–speaking world, assumed that its members were familiar with this Aramaic phrase. It was an early Christian title for Jesus which was taken over untranslated. It bears witness to the fact that from the earliest days of the church, the one who had been exalted as Lord was expected to return as Lord.

Another key New Testament text that shows the sense in which Jesus was acknowledged as Lord is Philippians 2:5–11. In these verses Paul may be quoting an early confession of faith. If so, he endorsed it and made it his own. This passage tells how Jesus did not regard equality with God as something which he should exploit to his own advantage. Instead, He humbled himself to become a man, displaying "the form of God" in "the form of a servant." He became "obedient to the point of death, even the death of the cross. Therefore God also has highly exalted Him and given Him the name which is above every name, that at the name of Jesus every knee should bow, ... and that every tongue should confess that Jesus Christ is Lord" (Phil. 2:8–11).

The "name which is above every name" is probably the title *Lord*, in the highest sense that it can bear. The words echo Isaiah 45:23, where the God of Israel swears, "To Me every knee shall bow, every tongue shall take an oath [or, make confession]." In the Old Testament passage the God of Israel denies to any other being the right to receive the worship which belongs to Him alone. But in the passage from Philippians He readily shares that worship with the humiliated and exalted Jesus. More than that, He shares His own name with him. When human beings honor Jesus as Lord, God is glorified.

God—If Jesus is called Lord in this supreme sense, it is not surprising that He occasionally is called God in the New Testament. Thomas, convinced that the risen Christ stood before him, abandoned his doubts with the confession, "My Lord and my God!" (John 20:28).

But the classic text is John 1:1. John declared that the Word existed not only "in the beginning," where He was "with God," but also actually "was God." This is the Word that became incarnate as real man in Jesus Christ, without ceasing to be what He had been from eternity. The Word was God in the sense that the Father shared with Him the fullness of His own nature. The Father remained in a technical phrase of traditional theology, "the fountain of deity." But from that fountain the Son drew in unlimited measure.

The Bible thus presents Christ as altogether God and altogether man—the perfect mediator between God and mankind because He partakes fully of the nature of both.

The Work of Christ—The work of Christ has often been stated in relation to His threefold office as prophet, priest, and king. As prophet, He is the perfect spokesman of God to the world, fully revealing God's character and will. As priest, Jesus has offered to God by His death a sufficient sacrifice for the sins of the world. Now, on the basis of that sacrifice, He exercises a ministry of intercession on behalf of His people. As king, He is "the ruler over the kings of the earth" (Rev. 1:5)—the one to whose rule the whole world is subject.

The work of Jesus can be discussed in terms of past, present, and future.

The finished work of Christ—By the "finished" work of Christ is meant the work of atonement or redemption for the human race which He completed by His death on the cross. This work is so perfect in itself that it requires neither repetition nor addition. Because of this work, He is called "Savior of the world" (1 John 4:14) and "the Lamb of God who takes away the sin of the world" (John 1:29).

In the Bible sin is viewed in several ways: as an offense against God, which requires a pardon; as defilement, which requires cleansing; as slavery, which cries out for emancipation; as a debt, which must be canceled; as defeat, which must be reversd by victory; and as estrangement, which must be set right by reconciliation. However sin is viewed, it is through the work of Christ that the remedy is provided. He has procured the pardon, the cleansing, the emancipation, the cancellation, the victory, and the reconciliation.

When sin is viewed as an offense against God, it is also interpreted as a breach of His law. The law of God, like law in general, involves penalties against the lawbreaker. So strict are these penalties that they appear to leave no avenue of escape for the lawbreaker. The apostle Paul, conducting his argument along these lines, quoted one uncompromising declaration from the Old Testament: "Cursed is everyone who does not continue in all things which are written in the book of the law, to do them" (Deut. 27:26; Gal. 3:10).

But Paul goes on to say that Christ, by enduring the form of death on which a divine curse was expressly pronounced in the law, absorbed in His own person the curse invoked on the lawbreaker: "Christ has redeemed us from the curse of the law, having become a curse for us (for it is written, 'Cursed is everyone who hangs on a tree')" (Deut. 21:23; Gal. 3:13).

Since Christ partakes in the nature of both God and humanity, He occupies a unique status with regard to them. He represents God to humanity, and He also represents humanity to God. God is both Lawgiver and Judge; Christ represents Him. The human family has put itself in the position of the lawbreaker; Christ has voluntarily undertaken to represent us. The Judge has made Himself one with the guilty in order to bear our guilt. It is ordinarily out of the question for one person to bear the guilt of others. But when the one person is the representative man, Jesus Christ, bearing the guilt of those whom He represents, the case is different.

In the hour of His death, Christ offered His life to God on behalf of mankind. The perfect life which He offered was acceptable to God. The salvation secured through the giving up of that life is God's free gift to mankind in Christ.

When the situation is viewed in terms of a law court, one might speak of the accused party as being acquitted. But the term preferred in the New Testament, especially in the apostle Paul's writings, is the more positive word justified. Paul goes on to the limit of daring in speaking of God as "Him who justifies the ungodly" (Rom. 4:5). God can be so described because "Christ died for the ungodly" (Rom. 5:6). Those who are united by faith to Him are "justified" in Him. As Paul explained elsewhere, "He made Him who knew no sin to be sin for us, that we might become the righteousness of God in Him" (2 Cor. 5:21). The work of Christ, seen from this point of view, is to set humanity in a right relationship with God.

When sin is considered as defilement that requires cleansing, the most straightforward affirmation is that "the blood of Jesus Christ His Son cleanses us from all sin" (1 John 1:7). The effect of His death is to purify a conscience that has been polluted by sin. The same thought is expressed by the writer of the Book of Hebrews. He speaks of various materials that were prescribed by Israel's ceremonial law to deal with forms of ritual pollution, which was an external matter. Then he asks, "How much more shall the blood of Christ, who through the eternal Spirit offered Himself without spot to God, purge your conscience from dead works to serve the living God?" (Heb. 9:14). Spiritual defilement calls for spiritual cleansing, and this is what the death of Christ has accomplished.

When sin is considered as slavery from which the slave must be set free, then the death of Christ is spoken of as a ransom or a means of redemption. Jesus Himself declared that He came "to give His life a ransom for many" (Mark 10:45). Paul not only spoke of sin as slavery; he also personified sin as a slaveowner who compels his slaves to obey his evil orders. When they are set free from his control by the death of Christ to enter the service of God, they find this service, by contrast, to be perfect freedom.

The idea of sin as a debt that must be canceled is based on the teaching of Jesus. In Jesus' parable of the creditor and the two debtors (Luke 7:40–43), the creditor forgave them both when they could make no repayment. But the debtor who owed the larger sum, and therefore had more cause to love the forgiving creditor, represented the woman whose "sins, which are many, are forgiven" (Luke 7:47). This is similar to Paul's reference to God as "having canceled the bond which stood against us with its legal demands" (Col. 2:14, RSV).

Paul's words in Colossians 2:15 speak of the "principalities and powers" as a personification of the hostile forces in the world which have conquered men and women and hold them as prisoners of war. There was no hope of successful resistance against them until Christ confronted them. It looked as if they had conquered Him too, but on the cross He conquered death itself, along with all other hostile forces. In His victory all who believe in Him have a share: "Thanks be to God, who gives us the victory through our Lord Jesus Christ" (1 Cor. 15:57).

Sin is also viewed as estrangement, or alienation, from God. In this case, the saving work of Christ includes the reconciliation of sinners to God. The initiative in this reconciling work is taken by God: "God was in Christ reconciling the world to Himself" (2 Cor. 5:19). God desires the well-being of sinners; so He sends Christ as the agent of His reconciling grace to them (Col. 1:20).

Those who are separated from God by sin are also estranged from one another. Accordingly, the work of Christ that reconciles sinners to God also brings them together as human beings. Hostile divisions of humanity have peace with one another through Him. Paul celebrated the way in which the work of Christ overcame the mutual estrangement of Jews and Gentiles: "For He Himself is our peace, who has made both one, and has broken down the middle wall of division between us" (Eph. 2:14).

When the work of Christ is pictured in terms of an atoning sacrifice, it is God who takes the initiative. The word propitiation, used in this connection in older English versions of the Bible (Rom. 3:25; 1 John 2:2; 4:10), does not mean that sinful men and women have to do something to appease God or turn away His anger; neither does it mean that Christ died on the cross to persuade God to be merciful to sinners. It is the nature of God to be a pardoning God. He has revealed His pardoning nature above all in the person and work of Christ. This saving initiative is equally and eagerly shared by Christ: He gladly cooperates with the Father's purpose for the redemption of the world.

The present work of Christ—The present work of Christ begins with His exaltation by God, after the completion of His "finished" work in His death and resurrection.

The first aspect of His present work was the sending of the Holy Spirit to dwell in His people. "If I do not go away," He had said to his disciples in the Upper Room, "the Helper will not come to you; but if I depart, I will send Him to you" (John 16:7). The fulfillment of this promise was announced by Peter on the Day of Pentecost: "Therefore being exalted to the right hand of God, and having received from the Father the promise of the Holy Spirit, He poured out this which you now see and hear" (Acts 2:33).

The promise of the Holy Spirit can be traced back to John the Baptist, who prophesied that the one who was to come after him, mightier than himself, would "baptize you with the Holy Spirit" (Mark 1:8).

But the present work of Christ that receives the main emphasis in the New Testament is His intercession. Paul, quoting what appears to be an early Christian confession of faith, spoke of "Christ who died, and furthermore is also risen, who is even at the right hand of God, who also makes intercession for us" (Rom. 8:34). So too, the writer to the Hebrews says that "He ever lives to make intercession" for His people (Heb. 7:25). He describes in detail Jesus' exceptional qualifications to be their high priest.

Jesus' presence with God as His people's representative provides the assurance that their requests for spiritual help are heard and granted. To know that He is there is a powerful incentive for His followers. No good thing that Jesus seeks for them is withheld by the Father.

The exaltation of Christ is repeatedly presented in the New Testament as the fulfillment of Psalm 110:1: "Sit at My right hand, till I make Your enemies Your footstool." This means that Christ reigns from His present place of exaltation and must do so until all His enemies are overthrown. Those enemies belong to the spiritual realm: "The last enemy

Photo by Howard Vos

An excavated area in ancient Jerusalem known as The Pavement, identified by some scholars as the place where Pilate rendered judgment against Jesus (John 19:13).

that will be destroyed is death" (1 Cor. 15:26). With the destruction of death, which occurred with the resurrection of Jesus, the present phase of Christ's work gives way to His future work.

The future work of Christ—During His earthly ministry, Jesus declared that He had even greater works to do in the future. He specified two of these greater works: the raising of the dead and the passing of final judgment. To raise the dead and to judge the world are prerogatives of God, but He delegated these works to His Son. While the Son would discharge these two functions at the time of the end, they were not unrelated to the events of Jesus' present ministry. Those who were spiritually dead received new life when they responded in faith to the Son of God. In effect, they were passing judgment on themselves as they accepted or rejected the life which He offered.

The raising of the dead and the passing of judgment are associated with the Second Coming of Christ. When Paul dealt with this subject, he viewed Christ's appearing in glory as the occasion when His people would share His glory and be displayed to the universe as the sons and daughters of God, heirs of the new order. He added that all creation looks forward to that time, because then it "will be delivered from the bondage of corruption into the glorious liberty of the children of God" (Rom. 8:21).

Both the present work of Christ and His future work are dependent on His "finished" work. That "finished" work was the beginning of God's "good work" in His people. This work will not be completed until "the day of Jesus Christ" (Phil. 1:6), when the entire universe will be united "in Christ" (Eph. 1:10).

JESUS JUSTUS (see JUSTUS).

JESUS, SON OF SIRACH — the author of the Book of Ecclesiasticus, also called The Wisdom of Jesus, Son of Sirach—one of the longer books of the APOCRYPHA.

JETHER [JEE thur] (*abundance*) — the name of five men in the Old Testament:

1. A son of Gideon, called his "firstborn" (Judg. 8:20–21).

2. An Ishmaelite (1 Chr. 2:17), also called "Jithra, an Israelite" (2 Sam. 17:25). He was the father of Amasa (1 Kin. 2:5).

3. One of the sons of Jada, a descendant of Judah through Jerahmeel (1 Chr. 2:32).

4. A son of Ezrah and a descendant of Caleb the spy (1 Chr. 4:17).

5. An Asherite and the father of Jephunneh, Pispah, and Ara (1 Chr. 7:38).

JETHETH [JEE theth] (meaning unknown) — a chief of Esau (Gen. 36:40), or Edom (1 Chr. 1:51).

JETHLAH [JETH luh] (*a hanging place*) — an unidentified village of the tribe of Dan (Josh. 19:42; Ithlah, NIV, RSV; Jithlah, NEB).

JETHRO [JETH roe] (*excellence*) — the father-in-law of Moses (Ex. 3:1), also called Reuel (Ex. 2:18), Hobab (Judg. 4:11), and Raguel (Num. 10:29).

After Moses fled from Egypt into the region of

the Sinai Peninsula, he married one of Jethro's daughters, Zipporah (Ex. 2:21). Then Moses tended Jethro's sheep for 40 years (Acts 7:30) before his experience at the burning bush (Exodus 3), when he was called to lead the Israelites from bondage in Egypt.

During the Exodus, Jethro and the rest of Moses family joined Moses in the wilderness near Mount Sinai (Ex. 18:5). During this visit, Jethro taught Moses to delegate his responsibilities. He noted that Moses was doing all the work himself and advised Moses to decide the difficult cases and to secure able men to make decisions in lesser matters (Ex. 18:13–23). Following this meeting, Jethro departed from the Israelites.

JETUR [JEE tuhr] (meaning unknown) — a son of Ishmael (Gen. 25:15). His tribe warred against the tribes of Reuben and Gad and the half–tribe of Manasseh (1 Chr. 5:19).

JEUEL [JOO uhl] (*God has healed*) — a descendant of Zerah. Jeuel and his clan lived in Jerusalem after the Captivity (1 Chr. 9:6).

JEUSH [JEE uhsh] (meaning unknown) — the name of five men in the Old Testament:

1. A son of Esau and Aholibamah (Gen. 36:5, 14, 18).

2. A Benjamite, son of Bilhan (1 Chr. 7:10).

3. A son of Eshek and a descendant of King Saul (1 Chr. 8:39; Jehush, KJV).

4. A son of Shimei and a Gershonite Levite (1 Chr. 23:10–11).

5. A son of King Rehoboam and grandson of King Solomon (2 Chr. 11:19).

JEUZ [JEE uhz] (*he who counsels*) — a son of Shaharaim and Hodesh (1 Chr. 8:10).

JEWELER (see OCCUPATIONS AND TRADES).

JEWELRY — objects of precious metals often set with gems and worn for personal adornment. Since the beginning of history, people have adorned themselves with various kinds of jewelry. To be elaborately decorated with jewelry in the ancient world was a symbol of wealth and status (2 Sam. 1:10; Dan. 5:7, 16, 29). The materials commonly used for jewelry were stone, metals, gems, ivory, shells, and carved horns.

The art of jewelry making probably developed very early in Egypt. It was known throughout the biblical world. The Hebrews learned this skill from foreign influences, probably from Egypt (Ex. 32:2–3), and obtained much of their jewelry from spoils of war.

The people of the ancient world placed much value on personal ornaments for political and religious purposes. The priestly garments of Aaron the HIGH PRIEST were elaborately decorated with jewels. The breastplate contained 12 engraved gems (Ex. 28:17–21). The shoulder pieces of the EPHOD were engraved onyx stones (Ex. 28:9–12). During Bible times, crowns were also set with gems (Zech. 9:16). Many ornaments were donated to build the

tabernacle (Ex. 35:22) and to decorate the Temple (1 Kin. 7:17).

Bracelets were worn by both men and women. They were made of bronze, silver, iron, and gold. Sometimes many bracelets were worn on each arm, covering the entire lower arm. Rebekah's gift from Abraham included a gold bracelet (Gen. 24:22). King Saul wore a bracelet or armlet (2 Sam. 1:10).

Ornaments for the ankles were worn by the women. These were usually made from the same material as the bracelets. Sometimes ANKLETS were fashioned to make a tinkling sound when walking, bringing more attention to the wearer. ANKLE CHAINS were often attached to the feet to encourage smaller steps. The prophet Isaiah disapproved of this practice among the women of Jerusalem (Is. 3:18–21).

Both men and women of Bible times wore necklaces (Judg. 8:25–26). They were made of various metals, often inlaid with precious stones. Necklaces of beads made from stone or jewels were strung with cord. Sometimes crescents, bottles, or other pendants were attached to the necklaces (Is. 3:18). Gold chains were given to Joseph (Gen. 41:42) and Daniel (Dan. 5:29), indicating their high positions in government.

Earrings were worn by men, women, and children in the ancient world (Ex. 32:2–3; Num. 31:50; Judg. 8:25–26). They were loops worn alone or with pendants attached. Earrings were made from various metals and stones and were sometimes inlaid with gems. Nose rings were worn mostly by

A ram in a thicket discovered at Ur. This artistic work is made of gold and lapis lazuli (sapphire). It dates from about 2500 B.C.

Photo by Howard Vos

women (Gen. 24:47) and were sometimes decorated with jewels (Is. 3:21).

Most men wore signet rings for business purposes. These rings were engraved with the owner's name or symbol to show authority or ownership (Gen. 38:18; Ex. 28:11; Esth. 8:8; Dan. 6:17). The signet rings were worn on the finger or strung around the neck. They were usually made of gold and set with an engraved gem. Signet rings were given as gifts for the tabernacle (Ex. 35:22).

In the New Testament jewels were worn much the same way as in the Old Testament. The Greeks emphasized fine, delicately worked jewelry, while the Roman jewelry was much heavier and more elaborate. In the early church the wearing of jewelry was not considered a Christian virtue by the apostle Paul, who exhorted women to modesty (1 Tim. 2:9). James apparently also had a dim view of jewelry (James 2:2).

Also see JEWELS AND PRECIOUS STONES.

JEWELS AND PRECIOUS STONES — Gems held a significant place in the life of the Hebrew people and the surrounding nations. In the ancient world the use of precious stones dates back thousands of years before Christ. Many myths and superstitions about their use existed. Early man attributed magical powers to many gems and even worshiped some of them. This practice, however, is not evident in the Old Testament; the Jewish people valued gems for their beauty, usefulness, and hardness.

No gem deposits existed in the land of Palestine. The Israelites secured their jewels from surrounding nations, which resulted in the art of cutting and engraving gems. Precious stones are mentioned 13 times in the Old Testament, and over 20 specific gems are named in the entire Bible. Since the Hebrews described gems by color or hardness, their precise identification is often difficult.

The majority of gems mentioned in the Old Testament are represented in Aaron's breastplate (Ex. 28:17–20; 39:10–13). Nine of them are mentioned in Ezekiel 28:13, the jacinth, agate, and amethyst being omitted. Jerome (fifth century A.D.) and others have attempted to establish a relationship between the 12 stones in Aaron's breastplate, the 12 months of the year, and the 12 signs in the zodiac; however, there is no indication of this in Scripture.

The Bible mentions gems used for personal adornment (Ex. 11:2; Is. 61:10) and as gifts (1 Kin. 10:2; Ezek. 16:11, 39). David's crown was set with gems (2 Sam. 12:30). Precious stones were also used to illustrate spiritual truths (Prov. 11:22; 20:15; Matt. 13:45–46). Amber, coral, and pearls are not actually gemstones, but were as highly prized among the ancients as precious stones.

The following gems and precious stones are mentioned in the Bible. This list is keyed to the NKJV, but cross references are included from five additional popular versions: KJV, NASB, NEB, NIV, and RSV.

Adamant. A hard stone of superior strength. The exact identity of this substance is unknown; but it is believed to be corundum, the hardest of all minerals next to the diamond. Corundum is not mentioned in the Bible. Pure corundum is colorless; it is the source of such gems as rubies and sapphires.

Because of its hardness, the prophet Ezekiel used adamant as a symbol of the stubborn will of the rebellious Israelites. God strengthened the prophet with a "forehead like adamant stone, harder than flint" to preach to the Israelites (Ezek. 3:9; emery, NASB). Other English translations of the Bible render the Hebrew word for adamant as diamond (Jer. 17:1, KJV, NASB, RSV) or flint (Jer. 17:1, NIV). Also see *Diamond.*

Agate. One of many fibrous varieties of quartz. Agate is a form of chalcedony with bands or patterns of various colors. The word comes from a Greek term for the river in Sicily where this stone was abundant. It was also found in Egypt, Arabia, and India. The agate was the middle stone in the third row of Aaron's breastplate (Ex. 28:19; 39:12). The agate was also useful for ornaments (beads) and was considered by the superstitious to possess magical powers. Also see *Chalcedony.*

Amber. Fossilized resin formed from the sap of various trees. The ancient Greeks and Romans regarded amber as a gem and used it for beads and other ornaments. Amber is yellowish–orange and can be polished to a high gloss. Apparently abundant in northern Europe, it reached other countries through trade.

The prophet Ezekiel mentioned amber three times. Each time he described it as a brilliant substance (Ezek. 1:4, 27; 8:2). Other English translations use the words gleaming bronze (RSV), brass (NEB), metal (NASB, NIV) or sapphire (NEB) rather than amber. Whatever the nature of this substance, Ezekiel compared its brilliance to the awe-inspiring glory of God.

Amethyst. A variety of the mineral corundum. Its color varied from light to deep violet and was used for jewelry. It was known in Egypt, India and Ceylon. Amethyst was the third stone in the third row of Aaron's breastplate (Ex. 28:19; 39:12; jasper, NEB). It was also included in the foundation of the New Jerusalem (Rev. 21:20).

Bdellium. A substance found in Havilah in Arabia, a land noted for its precious stones and aromatic gum. With the same color as manna, bdellium was considered to be a gum resin (Num. 11:7). In the Numbers passage, the word for bdellium is rendered as gum resin (NEB) and resin (NIV) by some translations. But in Genesis 2:12, bdellium was associated with gold and therefore it was considered a precious stone. Some scholars suggest that bdellium jewels were pearls from the Persian Gulf. The exact identification of this substance is not certain.

Beryl. A rare silver–white metal similar to aluminum. Beryl ranged in color from bluish green to yellow, white, pink and deep green. It was the first stone in the fourth row of Aaron's breastplate (Ex.

Photo by Howard Vos

This Sumerian jewelry discovered at Ur, dating from about 2500 B.C., is made of gold as well as lapis lazuli (sapphire) and carnelian.

28:20; 39:13). Other English translations render the word for beryl as chrysolite (NIV) and topaz (NEB). The wheels in the prophet Ezekiel's visions were described as resembling beryl (Ezek. 1:16; 10:9; Tarshish stone, NASB). The beryl was also the eighth foundation stone in the New Jerusalem (Rev. 21:20).

Carbuncle (see *Emerald; Turquoise*).

Carnelian (see *Sardius*).

Chalcedony. A translucent variety of quartz occurring in a variety of colors. Chalcedony received its name from Chalcedon, a city in Asia Minor. Agate, bloodstone, carnelian, chrysoprase, flint, jasper, and onyx are all varieties of chalcedony. The chalcedony was the third stone in the foundation of the New Jerusalem (Rev. 21:19; agate, RSV). Also see *Agate; Chrysoprase.*

Chrysolite. A yellow stone that could have been the same as topaz or some other yellow gem such as beryl, zircon, or a yellow quartz. Its name comes from a Greek word that means "gold stone." Chrysolite was the seventh stone in the foundation of the New Jerusalem (Rev. 21:20). The chrysolite known today is the peridot, an olive green silicate of magnesium and iron. This is not believed to be the same gem as that referred to by the Book of Revelation.

Chrysoprase. A variety of chalcedony. Chrysoprase had a light green color. Jewelry made from this precious stone has been found in ancient Egyptian graves. It was the tenth foundation stone of the New Jerusalem (Rev. 21:20; chrysoprasus, KJV). Also see *Chalcedony.*

Chrysoprasus (see *Chrysoprase*).

Coral. A limestone formation produced by certain kinds of marine life. Coral is not a mineral, but it does contain the mineral calcite because of its long exposure to sea water.

When the term coral was applied to jewelry, it referred to precious coral—a substance with a polished surface highly prized in the ancient world for various kinds of jewelry (Job 28:18; Ezek. 27:16). It was believed to possess magical powers.

Precious coral was formed in the shape of branches, or small bushes, and was found in the warm waters of the Mediterranean Sea and the Red Sea. The colors included many shades of red.

Cornelian (see *Onyx*).

Crystal. A colorless transparent quartz or rock (Job 28:17; Rev. 4:6). Crystal was used as jewelry for ornaments. In Roman times it was carved into various household utensils.

There are several different words for crystal in the original languages of the Bible. These words suggest that the pearl and glass (Job 28:17–18, RSV) may have been called crystal, too.

Diamond. Pure crystallized carbon, the diamond is the hardest mineral known. The Hebrew word which is rendered diamond in Exodus 28:18; 39:11; and Ezekiel 28:13 by the KJV and NKJV must have been some other hard stone. The diamond was not identifed in the Mediterranean lands until the first century. Other English translations render the word as emerald (NIV), jade (NEB), and jasper (RSV).

Emerald. A deep green variety of beryl. The emerald was found in Egypt, Cyprus, and Ethiopia. It was the third jewel in the first row of Aaron's breastplate (Ex. 28:17; 39:10). Emeralds were also an article of trade between Tyre and Syria (Ezek. 27:16). The emerald was the fourth foundation stone of the New Jerusalem (Rev. 21:19), and was used to describe the rainbow around the throne

(Rev. 4:3). Various other English translations render the word for emerald as carbuncle (KJV, RSV), beryl (NIV), green felspar (NEB), turquoise (NIV), and purple garnet (NEB).

Emery (see *Adamant*).

Flint (see *Diamond*).

Gem. Many precious gems were known in Bible times. Special value was attached to each because of its beauty, rarity, and durability. Although the modern method of cutting gems was not known during Bible times, ancient gem-cutters rounded and polished each stone, engraving some for seals or signet rings (1 Kin. 21:8; Esth. 3:10). They were also used for various kinds of jewelry (Ex. 11:2) and as gifts (Gen. 24:22). Precious stones in general are often referred to as gems in the Bible.

Glass (see *Crystal*).

Green Felspar (see *Emerald*).

Green Jasper (see *Jasper*).

Gum Resin (see *Bdellium*).

Jacinth. A yellow-orange variety of the mineral zircon. The jacinth was the first stone in the third row of Aaron's breastplate (Ex. 28:19; 39:12; ligure, KJV). In the New Testament the jacinth was the 11th foundation stone in the New Jerusalem (Rev. 21:20; turquoise, NEB).

Jade (see *Diamond*).

Jasper. An opaque variety of chalcedony, or quartz. Jasper is usually red because of the presence of iron, but it can be brown, yellow, or green. It was the third stone in the fourth row of Aaron's breastplate (Ex. 28:20; 39:13; green jasper, NEB). The Book of Revelation describes the one on the throne as "like a jasper" (Rev. 4:3). The brilliance of the New Jerusalem was "as a jasper, clear as crystal" (Rev. 21:11).

Lapis Lazuli (see *Sapphire*).

Ligure (see *Jacinth*).

Onyx. A form of chalcedony with contrasting layers of colors arranged in parallel lines. The colors are usually black and white or brown and white.

The onyx was used for engraving seals and for various ornaments. It was included in the treasures from Havilah, in Arabia (Gen. 2:12). The shoulder stones of Aaron's ephod were onyx with the names of six tribes of Israel engraved on each stone (Ex. 28:9). It was also the second stone in the fourth row of Aaron's breastplate (Ex. 28:20; 39:6). David included the onyx in the material he gathered for the Temple (1 Chr. 29:2). Job considered the wisdom from God a greater possession than even the precious onyx (Job 28:16). The NEB renders the word for onyx in all these passages as cornelian.

Pearl. A white translucent jewel created within certain species of mollusks. Although pearls are not minerals, they are composed of mineral substances; and they always have held an important place among the gemstones of the ancient world. Pearls were produced in the Persian Gulf, the Red Sea, and the Indian Ocean.

Pearls were considered valuable jewels and were used for various ornaments. Jesus referred to pearls in a figurative manner to speak of wise thoughts (Matt. 7:6; 13:45-46). The apostle Paul admonished women not to adorn themselves with pearls (1 Tim. 2:9). In John's vision of the New Jerusalem, "the twelve gates were twelve pearls: each individual gate was of one pearl" (Rev. 21:21). Jesus taught that man could possess the world's greatest treasure, the "one pearl of great price" (Matt. 13:46)—the spiritual wealth of the kingdom of heaven.

Purple Garnet (see *Emerald*; *Turquoise*).

Red Jasper (see *Ruby*).

Resin (see *Bdellium*).

Ruby. A variety of corundum, the hardest of all minerals next to the diamond. The ruby has a deep red color because of traces of chromium. Rubies may not have been known in the ancient world until the third century B.C. The Hebrew word translated rubies in the NKJV and KJV was probably pink pearl or red coral (Job 28:18; Prov. 3:15; 8:11; 20:15; 31:10; Lam. 4:7). Other words for ruby used by other English translations are agate (Is. 54:12, KJV, RSV); red jasper (Is. 54:12, NEB); and coral (Lam. 4:7, NASB, NEB, RSV).

Sapphire. The modern sapphire, a blue variety of corundum, was probably not used until the third century B.C. The Hebrew word for sapphire refers to lapis lazuli—a silicate of alumina, calcium, and sodium. It was highly regarded as an ornamental stone (Song 5:14; Lam. 4:7; Ezek. 28:13). Rich beds of sapphire were found in the mountainous regions of ancient Persia deposited in limestone rock.

Sapphire was the second jewel in the second row of Aaron's breastplate (Ex. 28:18; 39:11). It was also the second stone in the foundation of the New Jerusalem (Rev. 21:19).

Sardin (see *Sardius*).

Sardius. A red stone, considered by many to be carnelian, a reddish brown variety of chalcedony. Sardius was used for jewelry and for royal seals. Archaeologists have found many items of jewelry made from sardius in tombs and cities of Egypt and Palestine. It was the first stone in the first row of Aaron's breastplate (Ex. 28:17; 39:10) and was included as the covering of the King of Tyre (Ezek. 28:12-13). Sardius was also the sixth foundation stone of the New Jerusalem (Rev. 21:20).

Other words for sardius used by various English translations of the Bible are ruby, sardin, and carnelian.

Sardonyx. A red and white variety of chalcedony. Sardonyx is mentioned only once in the Bible as the fifth foundation stone of the New Jerusalem (Rev. 21:20; onyx, RSV). Sardonyx was obtained in Arabia and India and used by the Romans for cameos and signet rings. Some scholars believe the Hebrew word usually translated as *onyx* may refer to sardonyx. Also see *Onyx*.

Tarshish Stone (see *Beryl*).

Topaz. A yellowish-green form of chrysolite, the topaz was the second gem in the first row of Aaron's breastplate (Ex. 28:17; 39:10; chrysolite, NEB). The "topaz of Ethiopia" (Job 28:19) was famous for its quality. The topaz was also the ninth

Photo by Ben Chapman

A menorah, or seven-branched candlestick, symbolizes Judaism and the Jewish state of Israel.

foundation stone of the New Jerusalem (Rev. 21:20).

Turquoise. A deep green stone similar to the emerald. The only reference to turquoise in the NKJV occurs in the prophet Ezekiel's description of the covering of the King of Tyre (Ezek. 28:13; emerald, KJV; carbuncle, RSV; purple garnet, NEB). Many scholars believe this stone is essentially the same as the emerald. Also see *Emerald.*

JEWS — a name applied first to the people living in Judah (when the Israelites were divided into the two kingdoms of Israel and Judah); after the Babylonian Captivity, all the descendants of Abraham were called "Jews." The term is used in the New Testament for all Israelites as opposed to the "Gentiles," or those of non–Jewish blood. Since a number of Jews (especially the Jewish leaders) were hostile toward Jesus' ministry, the New Testament sometimes speaks simply of "the Jews" (John 6:41), when it really means "those Jews who did not believe in Jesus." This is especially true in John's Gospel (John 5:16, 18; 6:41, 52; 7:1).

Because the Jews were God's Chosen People, Paul could speak of the true "Jew" as being the person who pleases God, whatever his race (Rom. 2:28–29). In the Christian church, distinctions between "Jews" and "Greeks" (or Jewish people and foreigners) are wiped away (Gal. 3:28; Col. 3:11).

Also see HEBREWS.

JEZANIAH [jez uh NIGH uh] (*Jehovah hears*) — one of the Judean "captains" who allied himself with Gedaliah and remained at Mizpah after Judah was deported to Babylon. He was a son of Hoshaiah the Maachathite. He is also called Jaazaniah (2 Kin. 25:23).

JEZEBEL [JEZ uh bel] (meaning unknown) — the name of two women in the Bible:

1. The wife of Ahab, king of Israel, and mother of Ahaziah, Jehoram, and Athaliah (1 Kin. 16:31). Jezebel was a tyrant who corrupted her husband, as well as the nation, by promoting pagan worship.

She was reared in Sidon, a commercial city on the coast of the Mediterranean Sea, known for its idolatry and vice. When she married Ahab and moved to Jezreel, a city that served Jehovah, she decided to turn it into a city that worshiped BAAL, a Phoenician god.

The wicked, idolatrous queen soon became the power behind the throne. Obedient to her wishes, Ahab erected a sanctuary for Baal and supported hundreds of pagan prophets (1 Kin. 18:19).

When the prophets of Jehovah opposed Jezebel, she had them "massacred" (1 Kin. 18:4, 13). After Elijah defeated her prophets on Mount Carmel, she swore revenge. She was such a fearsome figure that the great prophet was afraid and "ran for his life" (1 Kin. 19:3).

After her husband Ahab was killed in battle, Jezebel reigned for 10 years through her sons Ahaziah and Joram (or Jehoram). These sons were killed by Jehu, who also disposed of Jezebel by having her thrown from the palace window. In fulfillment of the prediction of the prophet Elijah, Jezebel was trampled by the horses and eaten by the dogs (1 Kin. 21:19). Only Jezebel's skull, feet, and the palms of her hands were left to bury when the dogs were finished (2 Kin. 9:30–37).

One truth which emerges from Jezebel's life is that God always balances the scales of justice. Wickedness may prevail for a season, but His righteousness will eventually triumph over the forces of evil.

2. A prophetess of Thyatira who enticed the Christians in that church "to commit sexual immorality and to eat things sacrificed to idols" (Rev. 2:20). John probably called this woman "Jezebel" because of her similarity to Ahab's idolatrous and wicked queen.

JEZER [JEE zur] (*purpose*) — a son of Naphtali (Gen. 46:24) and founder of a tribal family, the JEZERITES (Num. 26:49).

JEZERITES [JEE zur ights] — descendants of JEZER (Num. 26:49).

JEZIAH [juh ZIGH uh] (*Jehovah unites*) — a son of Parosh who divorced his pagan wife (Ezra 10:25; Izziah, NIV, RSV).

JEZIEL [JEE zih uhl] (*God unites*) — a son of Azmaveth who, with his brother Pelet, joined David's army at Ziklag (1 Chr. 12:1-3).

JEZLIAH [jez LIGH uh] — a form of JIZLIAH.

JEZRAHIAH [jez ruh HIGH uh] (*Jehovah is shining*) — director of the singers at the rededication of the walls of Jerusalem (Neh. 12:42). He was the same person as IZRAHIAH (1 Chr. 7:3).

JEZREEL [JEZ reel] (*God scatters*) — the name of two people, two cities, and a valley or plain in the Old Testament:

1. A man of the tribe of Judah (1 Chr. 4:3).

2. A symbolic name given by the prophet Hosea to his oldest son (Hos. 1:4). The name Jezreel signified the great slaughter that God would bring on the house of Jehu because of the violent acts which he had committed (2 Kings 9).

3. A city in the hill country of Judah, near Jokdeam and Zanoah (Josh. 15:56). Apparently David obtained one of his wives from this place (1 Sam. 25:43). The site is probably present-day Khirbet Terrama on the Plain of Dibleh.

4. A city in northern Israel, on the Plain of Jezreel about 90 kilometers (56 miles) north of Jerusalem. The city was in the territory of Issachar, but it belonged to the tribe of Manasseh (Josh. 19:18). It was between Megiddo and Beth Shean (1 Kin. 4:12) and between Mount Carmel and Mount Gilboa. The palace of King Ahab of Israel was situated in Jezreel. Here Jezebel and all the others associated with Ahab's reign were assassinated by the followers of Jehu (2 Kings 9—10). The city of Jezreel has been identified with modern Zer'in.

5. The Old Testament name of the entire valley that separates Samaria from Galilee (Josh. 17:16). Some authors now refer to the western part of this valley as ESDRAELON (Greek for "Jezreel"), while the name Jezreel is restricted to the eastern part of the valley.

The entire valley is the major corridor through the rugged Palestinian hills. It was a crossroads of two major routes: one leading from the Mediterranean Sea on the west to the Jordan River Valley on the east, the other leading from Syria, Phoenicia, and Galilee in the north to the hill country of Judah and to the land of Egypt on the south. Throughout history, the Valley of Jezreel has been a major battlefield of nations.

Also see ARMAGEDDON.

JEZREELITE [JEZ reel ite] — a name applied to NABOTH, who had a vineyard in Jezreel (1 Kin. 21:1, 4, 6-7, 15-16). Jezebel conspired to murder Naboth and seize his vineyard (1 Kings 21).

JEZREELITESS [JEZ ree ehl eye tis] — a female inhabitant of JEZREEL, a town in Judah's hill country. One of the first two wives of David was Ahinoam the Jezreelitess (1 Sam. 27:3; 1 Chr. 3:1).

The Valley of Jezreel, which separated the province of Galilee from the district of Samaria. A rich agricultural district, it was the scene of many battles in the ancient world.

JIBSAM [JIB suhm] (*lovely scent*) — a son of Tola and a warrior in David's army (1 Chr. 7:2; Ibsam, NIV, RSV).

JIDLAPH [JID laf] (*melting away*) — a son of Nahor (Gen. 22:22).

JIMNAH [JIM nuh] (meaning unknown) — the firstborn son of Asher (Gen. 46:17) and the founder of the JIMNITES (Num. 26:44; Jimna). He is also called Imnah (1 Chr. 7:30) and Imna (Num. 26:44, NEB).

JIMNITES [JIM nights] — descendants of JIMNAH (Num. 26:44).

JIPHTAH [JIF tuh] (*breaking through*) — a city in the Shephelah (lowland plains) of Judah (Josh. 15:43; Iphtah, RSV).

JIPHTHAH EL [JIF thuh el] (*God breaks through*) — a valley in Zebulun, on the border between the land allotted to the tribes of Zebulun and Asher (Josh. 19:14, 27; Iphtah El, NIV; Iphtahel, RSV; Jiphtah–el, NEB; Jiphthah–el, KJV).

JISHUI [JISH yoo eye] (*man of Jehovah*) — a son of King Saul by his wife Ahinoam (1 Sam. 14:49), also called ABINADAB (1 Sam. 31:2). Other translations are Ishui, KJV; Ishvi, NIV, RSV; and Ishyo, NEB.

JISSHIAH [jish EYE uh] (*Jehovah exists*) — one of David's mighty men (1 Chr. 12:6; Jesiah, KJV; Isshiah, NIV, RSV, NEB).

JITHRA [JITH ruh] (*excellence*) — an Israelite who fathered Amasa by Abigail, David's sister or half–sister (2 Sam. 17:25; Ithra, KJV, RSV, NEB; Jether, NIV). Amasa later became the commander of Absalom's rebel army (2 Sam. 19:13; 20:4–12).

JITHRAN [JITH ran] (*abundance*) — a son of Zophah, of the tribe of Asher (1 Chr. 7:37; Ithran, KJV, NIV, RSV). Apparently, he is the same person as Jether (1 Chr. 7:38).

JIZLIAH [jiz LIGH uh] (*Jehovah delivers*) — a son of Elpaal (1 Chr. 8:18; Jezliah, KJV, NEB; Izliah, RSV, NIV, NAS).

JIZRI [JIZ righ] (*creator*) — a Levite and head of the fourth course of musicians for the sanctuary (1 Chr. 25:11; Izri, KJV). He is also called Zeri (1 Chr. 25:3), a son of Jeduthun.

JOAB [JO ab] (*Jehovah is father*)—the name of three men and one place in the Old Testament:

1. One of the three sons of Zeruiah (2 Sam. 2:13; 8:16; 14:1; 17:25; 23:18, 37; 1 Kin. 1:7; 2:5, 22; 1 Chr. 11:6, 39; 18:15; 26:28; 27:24) who was David's sister (or half sister). Joab was the "general" or commander–in–chief of David's army (2 Sam. 5:8; 1 Chr. 11:6; 27:34).

Joab's father is nowhere mentioned by name, but his tomb was at Bethlehem (2 Sam. 2:32). Joab's two brothers were named Abishai and Asahel. When Asahel was killed by Abner (2 Sam. 2:18–23), Joab got revenge by killing Abner (2 Sam. 3:22–27).

When David and his army went to Jerusalem, in an attempt to capture that city (then called Jebus), he said, "Whoever attacks the Jebusites first shall be chief and captain" (1 Chr. 11:6). Joab led the assault at the storming of the Jebusite stronghold on Mount Zion, apparently climbing up into the city by way of the water shaft. The city was captured and Joab was made the general of David's army (2 Sam. 5:8).

Other military exploits by Joab were achieved against the Edomites (2 Sam. 8:13–14; 1 Kin. 11:15) and the Ammonites (2 Sam. 10:6–14; 11:1–27; 1 Chr. 19:6–15; 20:1–3). His character was deeply stained, as was David's, by his participation in the death of Uriah the Hittite (2 Sam. 11:14–25). In putting Absalom to death (2 Sam. 18:1–14), he apparently acted from a sense of duty.

When Absalom revolted against David, Joab remained loyal to David. Soon afterward, however, David gave command of his army to Amasa, Joab's cousin (2 Sam. 19:13; 20:1–13). Overcome by jealous hate, Joab killed Amasa (2 Sam. 20:8–13).

Another of David's sons, Adonijah, aspired to the throne, refusing to accept the fact that Solomon was not only David's choice but also the Lord's choice as the new king. Joab joined the cause of Adonijah against Solomon. Joab was killed by Benaiah, in accordance with Solomon's command and David's wishes. Joab fled to the tabernacle of the Lord, where he grasped the horns of the altar. Benaiah then struck him down with a sword. Joab was buried "in his own house in the wilderness" (1 Kin. 2:34).

2. A village apparently situated in Judah near Bethlehem (1 Chr. 2:54). The KJV translation, "Ataroth, the house of Joab," is better rendered by the NKJV, "Atroth Beth Joab."

3. A son of Seraiah and grandson of Kenaz (1 Chr. 4:13–14). He was the "father of Ge–Harashim" (1 Chr. 4:14), or the founder of a place in Judah called the "Valley of Craftsmen."

4. A man of the house of Pahath–Moab, some of whose descendants returned from the Exile with Zerubbabel (Ezra 2:6; 8:9; Neh. 7:11).

JOAH [JOE uh] (*Jehovah is brother*) — the name of four men in the Old Testament:

1. A recorder in the time of King Hezekiah (Is. 36:3).

2. A descendant of Gershon, of the tribe of Levi (1 Chr. 6:21).

3. A gatekeeper in the tabernacle during David's time (1 Chr. 26:4).

4. A son of Joahaz who served as recorder in the time of King Josiah (2 Chr. 34:8).

JOAHAZ [JOE uh haz] (*Jehovah helps*) — the father of JOAH (2 Chr. 34:8).

JOANNA [joe AN uh] (*Jehovah has been gracious*) — the wife of Chuza, the steward of Herod Antipas. Along with Mary Magdalene, Susanna, and others, she provided for the material needs of Jesus and His disciples from her own funds (Luke 8:3).

Joanna was one of the women who witnessed the empty tomb and announced Christ's resurrection to the unbelieving apostles (Luke 24:1–10).

JOANNAS [joe AN us] (*God-given*) — a son of Rhesa and the father of Judah in the genealogy of Jesus (Luke 3:27; Joanan, NIV, RSV; Joanna, KJV; Johanan, NEB).

JOASH, JEHOASH [JOE ash, juh HOE ash] (*Jehovah supports*) — the name of eight men in the Old Testament:

1. The father of Gideon (Judg. 6:11). Apparently Joash was an idolater who built an altar to Baal on his land. Gideon pulled down his father's altar, and the men of the city of Ophrah demanded that Joash put his son to death. But Joash refused, saying, "If he [Baal] is a god, let him plead for himself" (Judg. 6:31). After this event, Joash called his son Jerubbaal, which means "Let Baal plead" (Judg. 6:32).

2. A man who was commanded by Ahab, king of Israel, to imprison the prophet Micaiah (1 Kin. 22:26).

3. The eighth king of Judah; he was a son of King Ahaziah (2 Kin. 11:2) by Zibiah of Beersheba (2 Kin. 12:1). Joash was seven years old when he became king, and he reigned 40 years in Jerusalem (2 Chr. 24:1), from about 835 B.C. until 796 B.C. He is also called Jehoash (2 Kin. 11:21).

After Ahaziah died, Athaliah killed all the royal heirs to the throne. But God spared Joash through his aunt, Jehosheba, who hid him for six years in the house of the Lord (2 Kin. 11:2–3). When Joash reached the age of seven, Jehoiada the priest arranged for his coronation as king (2 Kin. 11:4–16).

Early in his reign, Joash repaired the Temple and restored true religion to Judah, destroying Baal worship (2 Kin. 11:18–21). But the king who began so well faltered upon the loss of his advisor, Jehoiada. After Jehoiada died, Joash allowed idolatry to grow (2 Chr. 24:18). He even went so far as to have Zechariah, the son of Jehoiada, stoned to death for rebuking him (2 Chr. 24:20–22). God's judgment came quickly in the form of a Syrian invasion, which resulted in the wounding of Joash (2 Chr. 24:23–24). He was then killed by his own servants.

4. The 13th king of Israel; he was the son and successor of Jehoahaz, king of Israel, and was the grandson of Jehu, king of Israel. He is also called Jehoash (2 Kin. 13:10, 25; 14:8–17). Joash reigned in Samaria for 16 years (2 Kin. 13:9–10), from about 798 B.C. to 782/81 B.C.

Israel was revived during the reign of Joash (2 Kin. 13:7), following a long period of suffering at the hands of the Syrians. But while achieving political success, Joash suffered spiritual bankruptcy: "He did evil in the sight of the Lord; he did not depart from all the sins of Jeroboam the son of Nebat, who had made Israel sin; but he walked in them" (2 Kin. 13:11). He was succeeded by his son Jeroboam II.

5. A descendant of Shelah, of the family of Judah (1 Chr. 4:22).

6. A descendant of Becher, of the family of Benjamin (1 Chr. 7:8).

7. A commander of the warriors who left Saul and joined David's army at Ziklag (1 Chr. 12:3).

8. An officer in charge of David's olive oil supplies (1 Chr. 27:28).

JOATHAM [JOE uh tham] — a form of JOTHAM.

JOB [jobe] (*foe* or *hostile one*) — the name of two men in the Old Testament:

1. The third son of Issachar, and founder of a tribal family, the Jashubites (Gen. 46:13). He is also called Jashub (Num. 26:24; 1 Chr. 7:1).

2. The central personality of the Book of Job. He was noted for his perseverance (James 5:11) and unwavering faith in God, in spite of his suffering and moments of frustration and doubt. All the facts known about Job are contained in the Old Testament book that bears his name. He is described as "a man in the land of Uz" (Job 1:1) and "the greatest of all the people of the East" (Job 1:3). Uz is probably a name for a region in Edom (Jer. 25:20; Lam. 4:21).

A prosperous man, Job had 7,000 sheep, 3,000 camels, 500 yoke of oxen, 500 female donkeys, and a large household, consisting of seven sons and three daughters. He was also "blameless and upright, and one who feared God and shunned evil" (Job 1:1).

Satan suggested to God that Job would remain righteous as long as it was financially profitable for him to do so. Then the Lord permitted Satan to try Job's faith in God. Blow after blow fell upon Job: his children, his servants, and his livestock were taken from him and he was left penniless. Nevertheless, "In all this Job did not sin nor charge God with wrong" (Job 1:22).

Satan continued his assault by sneering, "Touch his bone and his flesh, and he will surely curse You to Your face!" (Job 2:5). The Lord allowed Satan to afflict Job with painful boils from the sole of his foot to the crown of his head, so that Job sat in the midst of ashes and scraped his sores with a piece of pottery. "Do you still hold fast to your integrity?" his wife asked him. "Curse God and die!" (Job 2:9). But Job refused to curse God. "Shall we indeed accept good from God," he replied, "and shall we not accept adversity?" (Job 2:10).

Job's faith eventually triumphed over all adversity, and he was finally restored to more than his former prosperity. He had 14,000 sheep, 6,000 camels, 1,000 yoke of oxen, and 1,000 female donkeys. He also had seven sons and three daughters. He died at the ripe old age of 140 years (Job 42:12–13, 16–17).

Job is a model of spiritual integrity—a person who held fast to his faith, without understanding the reason behind his suffering. He serves as a continuing witness to the possibility of authentic faith in God in the most troubling of circumstances.

Also see JOB, BOOK OF.

JOB, BOOK OF — an Old Testament book, written in the form of a dramatic poem, that deals with the age-old question of why the righteous suffer. The book takes its name from the main character in the poem, the patriarch Job. Because Job deals with one of man's universal questions, it is classified as one of the Wisdom Books of the Old Testament. Other books of this type are Proverbs, Ecclesiastes, and the Song of Solomon.

Structure of the Book. Job begins with two introductory chapters, in the form of a narrative or prologue, that set the stage for the rest of the book. Chapters 3 through 37 form the main body of the book. These chapters are poems in the form of dramatic dialogues between Job and his friends. Four additional chapters containing God's response to their arguments are also written in poetic form. The book ends with a final narrative or epilogue (42:7–17) that tells what happened to Job after these discussions had ended.

This prologue–poetry–epilogue format was used often in writings of this type in the ancient world. The author of Job was a literary craftsman who knew how to bring words together in dramatic fashion to drive home his message about the eternal purpose of life.

The story of Job opens with a brief description of the man, his possessions, and his family. "Blameless and upright" (1:1), he owned thousands of sheep, camels, oxen, and donkeys. He also had seven sons and three daughters. In simple terms, Job was considered a wealthy man in the tribal culture of the ancient world. But Satan insists that the integrity of this upright man has never been tested. He accuses Job of serving God only because God has protected him and made him wealthy. God granted permission for the testing to begin.

In rapid fashion, Job's sons and daughters are killed and all his flocks are driven away by his enemies. Finally, Job himself is stricken with a terrible skin disease. In his sorrow he sits mourning on an ash heap, scraping his sores with a piece of pottery while he laments his misfortune. This is when Job's three friends—Eliphaz, Bildad, and Zophar—arrive to mourn with him and to offer their comfort.

But instead of comforting Job, these friends launch into long lectures and philosophical debates to show Job the reason for his suffering. Their line of reasoning follows the generally accepted view of their time—that misfortune is always sent by God as punishment for sin. Job argues just as strongly that he is an upright man who has done nothing to deserve such treatment at the hand of God.

Finally, after Job and his friends have debated this question at length and have failed to arrive at a satisfactory solution, God himself speaks from a whirlwind. He does not enter their discussion about why the righteous suffer; He reveals Himself as the powerful, all-knowing God. God's message to Job is that He does not have to explain or justify His actions. He is the sovereign, all-powerful God who always does what is right, although His ways

The ostrich, which once lived in the Near East, is scorned in the Book of Job because of its nesting habits (Job 39:13-18).
Photo by Amikam Shoob

JOB: A Teaching Outline

Part One: The Dilemma of Job (1:1—2:13)

Part Two: The Debates of Job (3:1—37:24)

Part Three: The Deliverance of Job (38:1—42:17)

A mosaic of the prophet Joel, who prophesied about the outpouring of God's Spirit in the latter days (Joel 2:28).

may be beyond man's understanding.

Job is humbled by this outpouring of God's power, and he learns to trust where he cannot understand. This leads to his great affirmation of faith, "I have heard of You by the hearing of the ear, but now my eye sees You" (42:5). Then the book closes with the birth of more sons and daughters and Job's rise to a position of even greater wealth and prominence. Job lived out his additional years as a happy, contented man: "So Job died, old and full of days" (42:17).

Authorship and Date. No one knows who wrote the Book of Job. A few scholars have taken the position that it may have been written by Moses. Other have suggested that the patriarch Job himself may have written this account of his experiences. But these theories have no solid evidence to support them. The only thing we can say for certain is that the book was written by an unknown author.

The exact date of the book's writing is still something of a mystery. Some believe its unknown author put it in writing as late as the second century B.C. Others insist it must have been written about the time the people of Israel returned from the captivity in Babylon about 450 B.C. But many conservative scholars assign the writing of the book to the time of King Solomon, about 950 B.C. Historical evidence favors this date, since this was the golden age of biblical Wisdom literature.

Historical Setting. The events described in the Book of Job must have occurred many centuries be-

fore they were finally written. Job probably lived during the time of the patriarch Abraham, about 2000 to 1800 B.C. Like Abraham, Job's wealth was measured in flocks and herds. In patriarchal fashion, Job's married children were a part of his household, living in separate tents but subject to his rule as leader of the family clan.

This story of Job and his misfortunes was probably passed down by word of mouth from generation to generation for several hundred years. Finally, it was put in writing by an unknown writer during Solomon's time, thus assuring its preservation for all future generations.

Theological Contribution. The Book of Job teaches us to trust God in all circumstances. When we suffer, it usually is a fruitless effort to try to understand the reasons for the difficulty. Sometimes the righteous must suffer without knowing the reason why; that it why it is important to learn to trust God in everything.

This masterful book also shows very clearly that God is not captive to His world, His people, or our views of His nature. God is free; He is subject to no will but His own. He is not bound by our understanding or by our lack of it. Job also discovered that God is a God of great power and majesty. When we see how great He is, we realize just how little we are. Like Job, we want to bow down in humble submission.

The Book of Job also teaches us that God is good, just, and fair in His dealings. He restored Job's fortunes and gave him more than He had ever enjoyed. God always replaces the darkness of our existence with the light of His presence when we remain faithful to Him.

Special Considerations. The dialogue sections of the Book of Job are written in poetry. Great truths are often expressed in such poetic language. These great truths are worth the slow, reflective reading it sometimes takes to grasp their meaning. Great art like that in this book often challenges our understanding. That is why we need to come back to it again and again.

JOBAB [JOE bab] (meaning unknown) — the name of five men in the Old Testament:

1. A son of Joktan the Shemite (Gen. 10:29; 1 Chr. 1:23).

2. A king of Edom (1 Chr. 1:44–45).

3. A king of Madon, a royal city of the Canaanites (Josh. 11:1).

4. A son of Shaharaim and Hodesh (1 Chr. 8:9).

5. A son of Elpaal (1 Chr. 8:18).

JOCHEBED [JAH kuh bed] (*Jehovah is honor*) — a daughter of Levi and the mother of Aaron, Moses, and Miriam. To protect Moses from Pharaoh's command that every male Hebrew child be killed, she placed him in an ark of bulrushes on the river. After Pharaoh's daughter discovered the baby, Jochebed became his nurse. She is noted among the heroes of the faith (Hebrews 11).

JOED [JOE ed] (*Jehovah is witness*) — a Benjamite

who lived in Jerusalem after the Captivity (Neh. 11:7).

JOEL [JOE uhl] (*Jehovah is God*) — the name of 14 men in the Old Testament:

1. The oldest son of Samuel the prophet (1 Sam. 8:2; 1 Chr. 6:28; Vashni, KJV) and the father of Heman the singer (1 Chr. 6:33).

2. A leader of the tribe of Simeon (1 Chr. 4:35).

3. The father of Shemaiah, of the tribe of Reuben (1 Chr. 5:4).

4. A man of the tribe of Gad and a chief in the land of Bashan (1 Chr. 5:12).

5. A Levite ancestor of Samuel the prophet (1 Chr. 6:36).

6. A chief of the tribe of Issachar (1 Chr. 7:3).

7. One of David's mighty men (1 Chr. 11:38).

8. A Levite who helped bring the ark of the covenant from the house of Obed-Edom to Jerusalem (1 Chr. 15:7).

9. A keeper of the Temple treasuries in David's time (1 Chr. 26:22).

10. A son of Pedaiah who lived during the time of David (1 Chr. 27:20).

11. A Levite who helped cleanse the Temple during the reign of King Hezekiah of Judah (2 Chr. 29:12).

12. A son of Nebo who divorced his pagan wife after the Captivity (Ezra 10:43).

13. Overseer of the Benjamites in Jerusalem in Nehemiah's government (Neh. 11:9).

14. An Old Testament prophet and author of the Book of Joel. A citizen of Jerusalem, he spoke often of the priests and their duties (Joel 1:9, 13–14, 16). For this reason, many scholars believe he may have been a Temple prophet. He also had an ear for nature (Joel 1:4–7), and included imagery from agriculture and the natural world in his messages. Also see JOEL, BOOK OF.

JOEL, BOOK OF—a brief prophetic book of the Old Testament that predicted the outpouring of the spirit of God on all people—a prophecy fulfilled several centuries later on the Day of Pentecost (Joel 2:28–32; Acts 2:14–21). The title of the book comes from its author, the prophet Joel, whose name means *Jehovah is God*.

Structure of the Book. The three brief chapters of this book are divided into two major sections of about equal length. In the first section (1:1—2:11) the prophet Joel introduces himself and speaks to his readers about their need to turn from their sins. The speaker in the second part of the book (2:12—3:21) is the all-powerful God, who warns His people about the approaching day of judgment and assures them of His abiding presence, in spite of their unworthiness.

In the first section of the book, Joel calls attention to a devastating swarm of locusts that had recently swept through the land (1:4). These destructive locusts stripped the foliage from all trees, shrubs, and crops (1:7). The people and livestock of Judah were facing the threat of starvation because of the famine that followed this invasion (1:15–18). As bad as this natural catastrophe had been, the prophet declares it will be as nothing in comparison to the coming day of the Lord. This is the day of JUDGMENT, when God will vent His wrath upon His sinful and disobedient people. Joel also informs the people that this terrible day can be avoided. The way of escape is to turn to God "with all your heart, with fasting, and with mourning" (2:12).

After Joel delivers his pleas for repentance, God Himself speaks to His wayward people. In spite of the famine, He declares that there will be plenty to eat in the days of blessing to come (2:18–19). This day of renewal will be marked by the outpouring of His spirit on all people (2:28–29). All the nations of the world will take notice as God gathers His people together in the holy city of Jerusalem to serve as their ruler: "Judah shall abide forever, and Jerusalem from generation to generation" (3:20).

JOEL: A Teaching Outline

Authorship and Date. The author of this book was the prophet Joel, who identifies himself in the introduction as "the son of Pethuel" (1:1). This is all we know about this spokesman for the Lord. From evidence in the book itself, we can assume that he knew a great deal about Jerusalem, Judah's capital city, and the rituals associated with Temple worship (2:15). But he probably was not a priest, since he called upon the priests to go into mourning because of the sins of the nation (1:13). Indeed, Joel's many references to agriculture (1:7, 10–12) may indicate he was a farmer or a herdsman, although this is not certain.

It is difficult to determine the exact date of this book's writing. Unlike most of the other Old Testament prophets, Joel mentions no kings of Judah or Israel and no historical events that might give us some indication about when he wrote his prophecy. The one strong clue is the similarity of Joel's concept of the Day of the Lord to the language of the prophet Zephaniah (Joel 2:2; Zeph. 1:14–16). Zephaniah prophesied shortly before the fall of Jerusalem and the nation of Judah in 587 B.C. This also seems the most likely time for the writing of the Book of Joel.

Historical Setting. If Joel did write his book about 600 B.C., he would have lived in the frantic final years of the nation of Judah. After the Babylonian army destroyed Jerusalem in 587/586 B.C. the leading citizens of Judah were carried into captivity in Babylon. This invasion of the Babylonians must have given special significance to the terrible "day of the Lord" about which Joel warned his countrymen.

Theological Contribution. The Book of Joel is remarkable because it shows that a message from God can often come packaged in the form of a natural disaster. The truth of the book is rooted in the disastrous invasion of locusts, which Joel describes in such vivid language. This prophet teaches us that the Lord may use a natural disaster to stir in His people a renewed awareness of His will. Any traumatic event of nature—flood, fire, storm, or earthquake—should motivate the sensitive ear to listen again to the words of the Lord.

Special Considerations. Readers of Joel are always impressed with the prediction of the future outpouring of the Holy Spirit (2:28–32). The apostle Peter used this passage to explain the exciting events of PENTECOST to his hearers (Acts 2:16–21). Just as Joel predicted, the Holy Spirit was poured out on all these early followers of Jesus who were gathered in Jerusalem seeking God's will and praying for His divine guidance.

But there is still a future dimension to Joel's prediction. The gifts of the Spirit that began to flow through the people of God on Pentecost were not exhausted on that day. They are still available to all who believe in the Lord Jesus Christ and who anxiously await His return and the final establishment of His kingdom.

Also see JOEL.

JOELAH [joe EE luh] (*God is snatching*) — a son of Jeroham of Gedor (1 Chr. 12:7).

JOEZER [joe EE zur] (*Jehovah is help*) — a warrior who joined David's army at Ziklag (1 Chr. 12:6).

JOGBEHAH [JAHG buh huh] (*height*) — a fortified city in the land of Gilead east of the Jordan River (Num. 32:35). When he pursued the Midianites, Gideon passed Jogbehah (Judg. 8:11).

JOGLI [JAHG ligh] (*may God reveal*) — the father of BUKKI (Num. 34:22).

JOHA [JOE uh] (*Jehovah is living*) — the name of two men in the Old Testament:

1. A son of Beriah (1 Chr. 8:16).
2. A son of Shimri (1 Chr. 11:45).

JOHANAN [joe HAY nuhn] (*Jehovah is gracious*) — the name of eight or nine men in the Old Testament:

1. A captain of the Jews who joined forces with Gedaliah, governor of Judah, after the fall of Jerusalem (2 Kin. 25:23). When Gedaliah was murdered, Johanan pursued the assassin. He rescued several people, whom the assassin had taken as captives, including the prophet Jeremiah (Jeremiah 41—43). Against Jeremiah's protests, Johanan took these people to Egypt.

2. The oldest son of Josiah, king of Judah (1 Chr. 3:15).

3. A son of Elioenai, of the family of Jeconiah (1 Chr. 3:24).

4. A grandson of Ahimaaz and father of Azariah (1 Chr. 6:9–10).

5. A Benjamite soldier who joined David's army at Ziklag (1 Chr. 12:4).

6. A Gadite soldier who joined David's forces at Ziklag (1 Chr. 12:12).

7. Father of Azariah (2 Chr. 28:12).

8. A son of Hakkatan, of the clan of Azgad (Ezra 8:12).

9. A son of Eliashib the high priest (Neh. 12:22–23), also called Jonathan (Neh. 12:11). He may be the same person as Johanan No. 9.

JOHN THE APOSTLE — one of Jesus' twelve disciples, the son of Zebedee, and the brother of James. Before his call by Jesus, John was a fisherman on the Sea of Galilee, along with his father and brother (Matt. 4:18–22; Mark 1:16–20). His mother was probably Salome (Matt. 27:56; Mark 15:40), who may have been a sister of Mary (John 19:25), the mother of Jesus.

Although it is not certain that Salome and Mary were sisters, if it were so it would make James and John cousins of Jesus. This would help explain Salome's forward request of Jesus on behalf of her sons (Matt. 20:20–28). The Zebedee family apparently lived in Capernaum on the north shore of the Sea of Galilee (Mark 1:21). The family must have been prosperous, because the father owned a boat and hired servants (Mark 1:19–20). Salome the mother provided for Jesus out of her substance (Mark 15:40–41; Luke 8:3). John must have been

Photo by Howard Vos

Traditional tomb of the apostle John in the Church of St. John at Ephesus.

the younger of the two brothers, for he is always mentioned second to James in the Gospels of Matthew, Mark, and Luke.

The brothers Zebedee were the first disciples called by Jesus after His baptism (Mark 1:19–20). This happened immediately after the call of two other brothers, Simon Peter and Andrew (Mark 1:16–18), with whom they may have been in partnership (Luke 5:10). Three of the four—Peter, James, and John—eventually became Jesus' most intimate disciples. They were present when Jesus healed the daughter of Jairus (Mark 5:37; Luke 8:51). They witnessed His TRANSFIGURATION (Matt. 17:1–2; Mark 9:2; Luke 9:28–29), as well as His agony in Gethsemane (Matt. 26:37; Mark 14:33). Along with Peter, John was entrusted by Jesus with preparations for the Passover supper (Luke 22:8).

James and John must have contributed a headstrong element to Jesus' band of followers, because Jesus nicknamed them "Sons of Thunder" (Mark 3:17). On one occasion (Luke 9:51–56), when a Samaritan village refused to accept Jesus, the two offered to call down fire in revenge, as the prophet Elijah had once done (2 Kin. 1:10, 12). On another occasion, they earned the anger of their fellow disciples by asking if they could sit on Jesus' right and left hands in glory (Mark 10:35–45).

Following the ascension of Jesus, John continued in a prominent position of leadership among the disciples (Acts 1:13). He was present when Peter healed the lame man in the Temple. Together with Peter he bore witness before the Sanhedrin to his faith in Jesus Christ. The boldness of their testimony brought the hostility of the Sanhedrin (Acts 3—4). When the apostles in Jerusalem received word of the evangelization of Samaria, they sent Peter and John to investigate whether the conversions were genuine (Acts 8:14–25). This was a curious thing to do. The Samaritans had long been suspect in the eyes of the Jews (John 4:9). John himself had once favored the destruction of a Samaritan village (Luke 9:51–56). That he was present on this mission suggests he had experienced a remarkable change.

In these episodes Peter appears as the leader and spokesman for the pair, but John's presence on such errands indicates his esteem by the growing circle of disciples. After the execution of his brother James by Herod Agrippa I, between A.D. 42-44 (Acts 12:1-2), John is not heard of again in Acts. Paul's testimony to John as one of the "pillars," along with Peter and James (the Lord's brother, Gal. 2:9), however, reveals that John continued to hold a position of respect and leadership in the early church.

As might be expected of one of Jesus' three closest disciples, John became the subject of an active and varied church tradition. Tertullian (about A.D. 160–220) said that John ended up in Rome, where he was "plunged, unhurt, into boiling oil." A much later tradition believed that both James and John were martyred. The dominant tradition, however, was that the apostle John moved to Ephesus in Asia Minor, and that from there he was banished to the Island of Patmos (during Domitian's reign, A.D. 81–96). Tradition also held that he returned later to Ephesus, where he died some time after Trajan became emperor in A.D. 98.

Stories that John reclaimed a juvenile delinquent,

raised a dead man, and opposed the GNOSTIC heretic Cerinthus survive from this era in his life. It was also the general opinion of the time that from Ephesus John composed the five writings which bear his name in the New Testament (Gospel of John; 1, 2, and 3 John; and Revelation).

Only the Revelation identifies its author as John (1:1, 9). The second and third epistles of John identify the author as "the elder" (2 John 1; 3 John 1). Although 1 John and the Gospel of John do not name their author, he can be none other than "the elder," because style and content in these writings are unmistakably related. It may be, as tradition asserts, that the apostle John wrote all five documents. It appears more likely, however, that four of the five writings were actually penned not by John the apostle but by John the elder, a disciple and friend of John's who relied directly on the apostle's testimony as he wrote the documents. This would explain those passages in the gospel which speak about the beloved disciple (who presumably is John the apostle; John 19:35; 21:24), as well as the reference to "the elder" in 2 and 3 John. The Revelation, however, was probably written directly by the apostle John himself.

JOHN THE BAPTIST — forerunner of Jesus; a moral reformer and preacher of messianic hope. According to Luke 1:36, Elizabeth and Mary, the mothers of John and Jesus, were either blood relatives or close kinswomen. Luke adds that both John and Jesus were announced, set apart, and named by the angel Gabriel even before their birth.

As is true of Jesus, practically nothing is known of John's boyhood, except that he "grew and became strong in spirit" (Luke 1:80). The silence of his early years, however, was broken by his thundering call to repentance some time around A.D. 28–29, shortly before Jesus began His ministry. Exactly where John preached is not clear. Matthew reports the place as the wilderness of Judea (3:1), but it is more likely that the area was Perea east of the Jordan River. Perea, like Galilee, lay within the jurisdiction of Herod Antipas, under whom John was later arrested.

The four gospels are unanimous in their report that John lived "in the wilderness." There he was raised (Luke 1:80) and was called by God (Luke 3:2), and there he preached (Mark 1:4) until his execution. The wilderness—a vast badland of crags, wind, and heat—was the place where God had dwelled with His people after the Exodus. Ever since, it had been the place of religious hope for Israel. John called the people away from the comforts of their homes and cities and out into the wilderness, where they might meet God.

The conviction that God was about to begin a new work among this unprepared people broke upon John with the force of a desert storm. He was called to put on the prophet's hairy mantle with the resolve and urgency of Elijah himself. Not only did he dress like Elijah, in camel's hair and leather belt (2 Kin. 1:8; Mark 1:6); he understood his ministry to be one of reform and preparation, just as Elijah did (Luke 1:17). In the popular belief of the time, it was believed that Elijah would return from heaven to prepare the way for the Messiah (Mal. 4:5–6). John reminded the people of Elijah because of his dress and behavior (Matt. 11:14; Mark 9:12–13).

John was no doubt as rugged as the desert itself. Nevertheless, his commanding righteousness drew large crowds to hear him. What they encountered from this "voice...crying in the wilderness" (Mark 1:3) was a call to moral renewal, baptism, and a messianic hope.

The bite of John's moral challenge is hard for us to appreciate today. His command to share clothing and food (Luke 3:11) was a painful jab at a society that was hungry to acquire material objects. When he warned the tax collectors not to take more money than they had coming to them (Luke 3:12–13), he exposed the greed that had drawn persons to such positions in the first place. And the soldiers, whom he told to be content with their wages, must have winced at the thought of not using their power to take advantage of the common people (Luke 3:14).

John's baptism was a washing, symbolizing moral regeneration, administered to each candidate only once. He criticized the people for presuming to be righteous and secure with God because they were children of Abraham (Matt. 3:9). John laid an ax to the root of this presumption. He warned that they, the Jews, would be purged and rejected unless they demonstrated fruits of repentance (Matt. 3:7–12).

John's effort at moral reform, symbolized by baptism, was his way of preparing Israel to meet God. He began his preaching with the words, "Prepare the way of the Lord, make His paths straight" (Mark 1:3). He had a burning awareness of one who was to come after him who would baptize in fire and Spirit (Mark 1:7–8). John was a forerunner of this mightier one, a herald of the messianic hope which would dawn in Jesus.

John was a forerunner of Jesus not only in his ministry and message (Matt. 3:1; 4:17) but also in his death. Not until John's arrest did Jesus begin His ministry (Mark 1:14), and John's execution foreshadowed Jesus' similar fate. Imprisoned by Antipas in the fortress of Machaerus on the lonely hills east of the Dead Sea, John must have grown disillusioned by his own failure and the developing failure he sensed in Jesus' mission. He sent messengers to ask Jesus, "Are You the Coming One, or do we look for another?" (Matt. 11:3). John was eventually killed by a functionary of a puppet king who allowed himself to be swayed by a scheming wife, a loose daughter-in-law, and the people around him (Mark 6:14–29).

Josephus records that Herod arrested and executed John because he feared his popularity might lead to a revolt. The gospels reveal it was because John spoke out against Herod's immoral marriage to Herodias, the wife of his brother Philip (Mark 6:17–19). The accounts are complementary, be-

Remains of Machaerus, fortress of King Herod, where John the Baptist was beheaded, according to the Jewish historian Josephus.

cause John's moral righteousness must have fanned many a smoldering political hope to life.

Jesus said of John, "Among those born of women there has not risen one greater than John the Baptist" (Matt. 11:11). He was the last and greatest of the prophets (Matt. 11:13–14). Nevertheless, he stood, like Moses, on the threshold of the Promised Land. He did not enter the kingdom of God proclaimed by Jesus; and consequently, "he who is least in the kingdom of heaven is greater than he" (Matt. 11:11).

John's influence continued to live on after his death. When the apostle Paul went to Ephesus nearly 30 years later, he found a group of John's disciples (Acts 19:1–7). Some of his disciples must have thought of John in messianic terms. This compelled the author of the Gospel of John, writing also from Ephesus some 60 years after the Baptist's death, to emphasize Jesus' superiority (John 1:19–27; 3:30).

JOHN, EPISTLES OF — three epistles—one longer (1 John) and two shorter (2 and 3 John)— written by the author of the Gospel of John. These epistles read like a love letter from an elderly saint who writes from long years of experience with Christ and His message. Although unnamed, the author addresses his readers intimately as "little children" (1 John 2:1, 18, 28; 3:7, 18; 4:4; 5:21) and "beloved" (1 John 3:2, 21; 4:1, 7, 11). His tone changes, however, when he bears down on his opponents for making light of the bodily existence of Jesus (1 John 2:18–23; 4:1–3, 20).

Structure of the Epistles. None of the three epistles yields naturally to a structural outline. First John begins with an uncompromising testimony to the bodily existence of Jesus (1:1–4). Since God is light, fellowship with God must result in confession of our sin before Christ, our forgiveness, and our "walking in the light" (1:5—2:2). To know Christ is· to keep His commandments, or "to walk just as He walked" (2:6). One cannot be in the light and hate his brother or love the world (2:7–17).

The presence of antichrists, who deny that Jesus is the Christ, is a sign of the end times. But true be-lievers rest secure in the "anointing" of the Holy Spirit which they have from Christ (2:18–27). Since God is righteous, believers are to be righteous in their lives. When the Lord returns, His children will be like Him (2:28—3:3). Whoever abides in Christ does not continue to sin habitually or constantly (3:4–10).

Christian love is not something merely to talk about, but to do (3:11–18). Active love gives us confidence before God (3:19–24). A person must examine various spiritual manifestations to determine if they are of God; only teachers who confess that Jesus Christ has come in the flesh are of God (4:1–6). In His love God sent His Son as an atoning sacrifice for sin. As a consequence we are to love one another (4:7–21).

Faith is victory over the world (5:1–5), and there is a threefold witness to faith: the Holy Spirit, the water (baptism), and the blood (Holy Communion) (5:6–12). Christians may be assured that God hears and grants their requests (5:13–15). The letter concludes with assurance that the Son of God is sufficient to save (5:18–21).

Second John identifies its author as "the elder" and those to whom the letter is written as "the elect lady and her children" (v. 1). The "lady" and "children" are personified ways of referring to the church and its believers. Like 3 John, the letter has the character of a note from the elder, reminding his "children" to walk in truth and love (vv. 4–6). The elder also draws attention to false teachers who deny the bodily existence of Jesus Christ, and he warns against receiving them (vv. 7–11). He hopes to visit the church soon (vv. 12–13).

Third John, also from "the elder," is addressed to Gaius (v. 1), who has demonstrated his loyalty by offering hospitality to traveling missionaries (vv. 2–8). A certain Diotrephes had previously ignored a letter from the elder, and he receives some stiff criticism for doing so (vv. 9–11). In contrast to Diotrephes, a certain Demetrius is highly commended (v. 12). The elder expresses his hope to visit the church soon (vv. 13–15).

Authorship and Date. Although these three epistles were written by an anonymous author, he wrote affectionately to his readers as "little children" and referred to himself as "the elder" (2 John 1; 3 John 1). He must have been well-known and well-loved by those to whom he wrote.

Eusebius, an early church leader, mentions a John the elder (presbyter) who was a disciple and companion of John the apostle in Ephesus. Although we cannot say for sure, it may be that John the elder is the same "elder" mentioned in 2 and 3 John. If so, then he wrote the Gospel of John as well as these three letters; the style and content in each are very similar.

The inclusion of personal testimony (1 John 1:1–4) indicates that John the elder depended directly on the testimony of the apostle John in writing these documents. The epistles were probably written from Ephesus toward the close of the first century A.D.

Historical Setting. First John has none of the usual features of an epistle: no salutation or identification of author; no greetings; and no references to persons, places, or events. Ironically, although its format is impersonal, like a sermon or treatise, its tone is warm and personal. This suggests that it was written to a broad audience (probably in and around Ephesus) that was very dear to the author.

All three epistles were written to deepen the spiritual life of the churches while guarding against false teaching. The false teachers had arisen within the church, although the content of their teaching betrayed that they were not part of the church (1 John 2:19; 4:4). John fears that such a splinter group will lead true believers astray (1 John 2:26–27; 3:7; 2 John 7). He calls them "antichrists" (1 John 2:18, 22; 4:3; 2 John 7) for denying that Jesus had come in the flesh (1 John 4:1–13; 2 John 7; also 1 John 2:18–25; 4:15).

By emphasizing the divine nature of Jesus, the false teachers appeared to be Christians; but they showed their true colors by denying that God became a true human in Jesus. Claiming to have the Spirit of God, they were actually false prophets (1 John 4:1–6).

Theological Contribution. Like the Gospel of John, the epistles of John are built on the foundation blocks of love, truth, sin, world, life, light, and Paraclete. It emphasizes the great themes of knowing, believing, walking, and abiding. These words seem simple on the surface. But in the hands of one who had pondered the mystery and meaning of Jesus' existence in human form, they yield many deep truths.

For John, the keystone in the arch of the gospel is

FIRST JOHN: A Teaching Outline

that God has appeared in human form (1 John 1:1–4). The INCARNATION is life (1 John 1:2); and this life is available in the Son of God, Jesus Christ (1 John 5:11): "He who has the Son has life; he who does not have the Son of God does not have life" (1 John 5:12). The message of life is the alpha (1 John 1:2) and omega (1 John 5:20), the beginning and the end, of the epistle.

Jesus Christ has transferred us from death to life (1 John 3:14) by destroying the works of the devil (1 John 3:8). God made Jesus a "propitiation" (1 John 2:2; 4:10) in order to forgive sin (1 John 1:7–9; 2:12; 3:5). As a propitiation, Jesus is our "Advocate with the Father" (1 John 2:1) who takes away the guilt of our wrongdoing and gives us confidence to approach the judgment seat of God (1 John 2:28; 4:17). Jesus Christ is both the Son of God and the bearer of sin, the eternal demonstration of the love of God.

For John, love is not a feeling or attitude toward others. God is love (1 John 4:8, 16), and He acts in love on our behalf (1 John 4:9–10). Love, therefore, is something one does, by keeping God's commandments (1 John 2:2–5; 5:3), "in deed and in truth" (1 John 3:18), and, above all, by loving others (1 John 2:9–11; 3:10). John declares that it is hypocritical to profess love for God and to show hatred toward others (1 John 4:20). The love of God does not take us out of this world. Rather, it draws us into fellowship with God (1 John 1:3) and with others (1 John 1:7).

Fellowship with God is realized by knowing God and abiding in Him. To *know* God (the verb occurs 25 times in the epistles) is not to know about God, but to be joined to Him in righteousness (1 John 2:29), truth (1 John 3:19), and especially love (1 John 4:7–8). The permanence of such knowing is expressed in the word abide, which occurs 26 times in these epistles. To abide in God is to share the identity of Jesus Christ and to experience the characteristics of God: light (1 John 2:10), love (1 John 3:17; 4:12), and eternal life (1 John 3:15).

Special Considerations. Many Christians wonder about John's declaration, "Whoever abides in Him [Jesus Christ] does not sin" (1 John 3:6). This does not mean that if someone sins he is not a Christian. Indeed, in the epistles we are told that Christ came to forgive sins; and we are admonished to confess our sins to Him (1 John 1:6—2:2; 3:5; 4:10). The statement means that Christ has transferred us from death to life and has caused us to share in the nature of God. Consequently, we are no longer confined to darkness because Jesus Christ has broken the power of sin in our lives (1 John 3:8).

SECOND JOHN: A Teaching Outline

THIRD JOHN: A Teaching Outline

John says that believers may pray to God on behalf of others (1 John 5:16–17), unless their sins "lead to death." The exact meaning of such sin is unclear, although it probably refers to a denial of the bodily existence of Jesus (1 John 2:22; 4:3; 5:12).

JOHN, GOSPEL OF — the fourth and most theological of the gospels of the New Testament. The first three gospels portray mainly what Jesus did and how He taught, but the Gospel of John is different. It moves beyond the obvious facts of Jesus' life to deeper, more profound meanings. Events and miracles are kept to a minimum in the Gospel of John. They are used as springboards or "signs" for lengthy discussions that reveal important truths about Christ. On the other hand, John uses a host of key words that symbolize who Jesus is and how we may know God. John is a "spiritual" gospel— not because it is more spiritual than the other three—but because it expresses spiritual ideas in spiritual language. Among the gospels, therefore, John offers a unique portrait of Christ that has been cherished by believers through the centuries.

Structure of the Gospel. The fourth gospel consists basically of two parts: a book of "signs" and a book of "glory." The signs reveal Jesus' person (chaps. 1—12), and the glory results from Jesus' passion (chaps. 13–20). A prologue (1:1–18) and epilogue (chap. 21) serve as an introduction and conclusion to the gospel. Within this two–part structure, the gospel follows a pattern already presented in the prologue: revelation (1:1–5), rejection (1:6–11), and reception (1:12–18). The corresponding divisions of the gospel are: revelation (1:19—6:71), rejection (chaps. 7—12), and reception (chaps. 13—21).

Authorship and Date. Like the other gospels, John comes to us as an anonymous book. The question of authorship can be resolved only by observing clues within the gospel and by the tradition of the early church. Tradition agrees that the author was John the apostle, who was exiled to the island of Patmos in the Aegean Sea and who later died in Ephesus sometime after Trajan became emperor of Rome in A.D. 98. The gospel claims to come from an eyewitness (1:14; 1 John 1:1–4), and the author is familiar with the geography of Palestine. These external and internal evidences suggest that "the beloved disciple" (13:23; 19:26; 20:2; 21:7, 20), which appears as a title or nickname for John the apostle, composed the fourth gospel.

Other clues within the gospel and epistles of John, however, point beyond the apostle to another author. In 2 and 3 John, verses 1, the author identifies himself as "the elder." The similarities between the gospel and the epistles of John are too strong for us to conclude that the gospel was written by John the apostle and the epistles by John the elder. Early church tradition referred to an elder who was a disciple of John. Moreover, certain passages in the gospel of John tend to suggest that the writer was not the beloved disciple (19:35; 21:24).

Taking the evidence as a whole, it appears that the gospel was composed by a John the elder (*presbyter*), who was a disciple of John the apostle and who depended directly on the apostle's testimony for the content of the gospel. Both Johns are reputed to have lived in Ephesus. Some scholars identify John the Elder with John the Apostle and view the gospel as composed by the Apostle. Ephesus, therefore, becomes the most likely place for the gospel's origin, sometime around the close of the first century.

Historical Setting. It is difficult to say with certainty to whom this gospel was addressed. Unlike Luke (1:1–4), the author mentions no addressee. Unlike Matthew and Mark, he gives few hints of his intended audience. The gospel uses both Jewish and Greek thought forms in its presentation of Christ.

For John, Jesus goes beyond the bounds of Judaism. This gospel reports a fiercer conflict between Jesus and the Jews than the other gospels do. The gospel begins before time (1:1), and it shows that Jesus is timeless. Jesus speaks not to any one nation or ethnic group, but to the human condition. John portrays Jesus for the widest possible readership.

This ancient papyrus fragment, written in the Greek language, contains verses 1-14 of the first chapter of John's Gospel. It dates from about A.D. 200.
Photo by Howard Vos

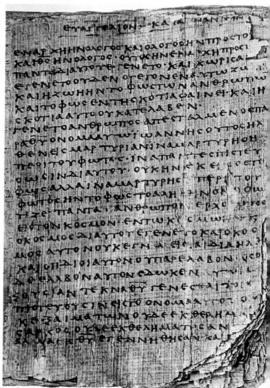

JOHN: A Teaching Outline

Part One: The Incarnation of the Son of God (1:1–18)

Part Two: The Presentation of the Son of God (1:19—4:54)

Part Three: The Opposition to the Son of God (5:1—12:50)

Part Four: The Preparation of the Disciples (13:1—17:26)

Part Five: The Crucifixion and Resurrection (18:1—21:25)

This is one reason why the fourth gospel has spoken so deeply to Christians in all ages.

If there is doubt to whom John writes, there can be little doubt about why John writes. The gospel contains a clear statement of purpose: "These [signs] are written that you may believe that Jesus is the Christ, the Son of God, and that believing you may have life in His name" (20:31).

For John, the sole purpose of life is that "you may know and believe that the Father is in me and I in Him" (10:38). Thus, John writes that we might know the Father and experience life eternal through faith in the Son.

Theological Contribution. John writes with a modest vocabulary, but his words are charged with symbolism. Terms like believe, love, truth, world, light and darkness, above and below, name, witness, sin, judgment (eternal) life, glory, bread, water, and hour are the key words of this gospel. In John 3:16–21, a passage of less than 150 words in Greek, seven of these terms occur.

The world is where God reveals truth (8:32), light (8:12), and life (14:6) in His Son Jesus Christ. The world is also where persons must decide for or against the witness of Christ, and the decision is judgment (3:18). Sin is to misjudge Jesus—to fail to receive Him as the bread of life (6:35), or not to walk in Him as the light of the world (8:12). The Son has come from above to glorify the Father (17:1), and He does so in His "hour" (12:23; 13:1)—through His suffering on the cross.

In the synoptic gospels—Matthew, Mark, and Luke—Jesus utters short sayings. Longer discourses, such as the Sermon on the Mount (Matthew 5—7), are either collections of sayings on various themes, or, like Matthew 13, mostly parables. John, on the other hand, records no parables and few of the brief sayings so common to the synoptics. Rather, he expands upon an incident; for example, Nicodemus (chap. 3), the woman at the well (chap. 4), the man born blind (chap. 9), Lazarus (chap. 11), or footwashing (chap. 13). Or he takes up an image; for example, bread (chap. 6), water (chap. 7), light (chap. 8), or shepherd (chap. 10). John then uses these words as symbols to reveal a fuller revelation of Christ. These discourses are blended so completely with John's own style that frequently the reader cannot tell whether it is John or Jesus speaking (3:16).

Why does John present such a different picture of Jesus? John may reveal Jesus as He taught in private, while the other three gospels may recall His public method of address (Mark 4:34). This may be a partial answer. A fuller explanation may be that the other gospels retain the actual form of Jesus' teaching, while John uncovers the essence of Jesus as a person.

This does not imply that John disregards historical truth. At some points his gospel probably preserves the facts of Jesus' life more accurately than the other gospels do. For example, Matthew, Mark, and Luke leave the impression that Jesus ministered mainly in Galilee, making only one Passover journey to Jerusalem. This leads one to assume that Jesus' ministry lasted less than one year. John, however, mentions at least three Passover journeys (2:13, 23; 6:4; 12:1) and longer periods of ministry in Judea. The other three gospels do hint of previous visits by Jesus to Jerusalem (Matt. 23:37; Luke 13:34). A longer ministry, therefore, as presented by John, is probably closer to the events of Jesus' life.

Nevertheless, it is clear that John is guided more by theological than historical interests. The gospels of Matthew, Mark, and Luke begin by showing Jesus' role as the fulfiller of the Old Testament promises of salvation. But John begins with the preexistence of Jesus: "In the beginning was the Word" (1:1). Jesus is divine ("the Word was God," 1:1), but He is also human ("the Word became flesh," 1:14). Only as such is He the revealer of the Father.

In the first chapter, John introduces Jesus by seven key titles: Word, Lamb of God, Rabbi, Messiah, King of Israel, Son of God, and Son of Man. Only in John do we find the "I am" sayings: "I am the bread of life" (6:35), "I am the light of the world" (8:12), "before Abraham was, I AM" (8:58), "I am the door of the sheep" (10:7), "I am the good shepherd" (10:11), "I and My Father are one" (10:30), "I am the way, the truth, and the life" (14:6), and "I am the vine" (15:5). In each of these sayings the "I" is emphatic in Greek. It recalls the name of God, "I AM," in the Old Testament (Ex. 3:14).

In the Old Testament God's words were to be reverently received. So it is with Jesus. In John He begins His messages by saying, "Truly, truly I say to you." Just as in the Old Testament God alone was to be worshiped, in John people are to believe in Jesus alone. Here John stresses his concept of "believing." The verb "to believe" is found nearly a hundred times in the gospel, though the noun "belief/faith" does not occur. For John, saving faith is a verb, carrying the sense of active trust in Jesus; it is not a static noun.

When one considers Jesus' moral teaching, another key word emerges. In John Jesus does not enter into questions of prayer, fasting, almsgiving, swearing, marriage, or wealth as he does in the other gospels. Rather, one's relationships to God, others, and the world are summed up in love. The love which God has for His beloved Son (3:35; 15:9) is passed on by the Beloved to "His own" (13:1). As recipients of God's love, Christians are to love God by loving one another (13:34). This love, which unites believers (17:1f.), is also a testimony to the world. The key verse of John expresses the basic theological truth of the gospel: "For God so loved the world that He gave His only begotten Son, that whoever believes in Him should not perish but have everlasting life" (3:16).

The Gospel of John expresses the uniqueness of the Son's relationship with the Father. The Son existed before the world with the Father; He was sent into the world by the Father; and He goes out of the world to the Father.

Special Considerations. Our present Gospel of John contains a story that probably was not written by the original author. The account of the woman caught in adultery (7:53—8:11) differs markedly in style from the rest of John. It is not found in the earlier and better manuscripts of the book. It was probably added at a later date by an unknown author under God's inspiration to express an important truth about Jesus and His attitude toward sinful people.

JOHN MARK (see MARK, JOHN).

JOHN, REVELATION OF (see REVELATION OF JOHN).

JOIADA [JOY uh duh] (*Jehovah knows*) — a high priest after the Captivity. He was succeeded by his son Jonathan (Neh. 12:10-11, 22).

JOIAKIM [JOY uh kim] (*Jehovah raises*) — a high priest after the Captivity, and the father of Eliashib (Neh. 12:10, 12, 26).

JOIARIB [JOY uh rib] (*Jehovah contends*) — the name of three men in the Old Testament:
1. A teacher sent by Ezra to Iddo to request ministers for Temple service (Ezra 8:16).
2. An ancestor of a family in Jerusalem in Nehemiah's time (Neh. 11:5).
3. A priest who returned from the Captivity and the father of Jedaiah (Neh. 11:10).

JOKDEAM [JAHK dee uhm] (meaning unknown) — a city in the hill country of Judah (Josh. 15:56).

JOKIM [JOE kim] (*Jehovah sets up*) — a descendant of Shelah, of the tribe of Judah (1 Chr. 4:22).

JOKMEAM [JAHK mee uhm] (*standing of the people*) — a city of the tribe of Ephraim given to the Levites. Jokmeam was in the Jordan Valley near the mouth of the River Jabbok (1 Chr. 6:68). It was probably the same place as Kibzaim (Josh. 21:22).

JOKNEAM [JAHK nee uhm] (*possession of the people*) — the name of two cities in the Old Testament:
1. A city in Zebulun allotted to the Levites (Josh. 21:34).
2. A city in Ephraim (1 Kin. 4:12; Jokmeam, NIV, RSV, NEB).

JOKSHAN [JAHK shan] (*fowler*) — a son of Abraham by his concubine Keturah (1 Chr. 1:32).

JOKTAN [JAHK tan] (*little*) — a son of Eber, of the family of Shem (Gen. 10:25-26, 29).

JOKTHEEL [JAHK thih uhl] (*God's reward of victory*) — the name of two cities in the Old Testament:
1. A city in the coastal lowlands of Judah (Josh. 15:38).
2. A name given to SELA, the ancient capital of the Edomites, by Amaziah after his army had captured it (2 Kin. 14:7).

JONADAB [JOE nuh dab] (*Jehovah is liberal*) — the name of two men in the Old Testament:

1. A son of Shimeah. Described as "a very crafty man" (2 Sam. 13:3), Jonadab suggested the plan that Amnon used to seduce Tamar. Later, when Absalom murdered Amnon, he reassured David that his other sons were still alive (2 Sam. 13:32-33). This suggests a prior knowledge of the crime.
2. A son of Rechab the Kenite and apparently the founder of the RECHABITES (Jer. 35:1-19), also called JEHONADAB (2 Kin. 10:15, 23). When Jehu suppressed Baal worship, Jonadab became his zealous supporter in exterminating the house of Ahab. Accompanying Jehu to Samaria, Jonadab assisted him in clearing the temple of Baal of all who were not priests of Baal. In this way Jonadab prepared the way for Jehu's massacre of the Baal worshipers (2 Kin. 10:15-28).

JONAH [JOE nuh] (*a dove*) — the prophet who was first swallowed by a great fish before he obeyed God's command to preach repentance to the Assyrian city of Nineveh. Jonah was not always a reluctant spokesman for the Lord. He is apparently the same prophet who predicted the remarkable expansion of Israel's territory during the reign of Jeroboam II (ruled about 793-753 B.C.; 2 Kin. 14:25). This passage indicates that Jonah, the son of Amittai, was from Gath Hepher, a town in Zebulun in the northern kingdom of Israel.

While Jonah is described as a servant of the Lord in 2 Kings 14:25, he is a sad and somewhat tragic figure in the book bearing his name. It is a mark of the integrity and reliability of the Bible that a prophet like Jonah is described in such a candid manner. The natural tendency of human writers would be to obscure and hide such a character. But the Spirit of God presents valiant heroes along with petty people to illustrate truth, no matter how weak and unpleasant these characters may have been. We know nothing of Jonah after he returned to Israel from his preaching venture in Nineveh.

Also see JONAH, BOOK OF.

JONAH, BOOK OF — a short Old Testament book that emphasizes God's love for all people—pagans and Gentiles as well as his Chosen People, the Israelites. The book is named for its central figure, the prophet Jonah, who learned about God's universal love as he struggled with God's call to service.

Structure of the Book. The book begins with God's call to Jonah to preach in the great city of Nineveh, capital of the Assyrian empire. As staunch political enemies of the Israelites and as worshipers of false gods, the Assyrians also were shunned as pagans and outcasts. But God's call to Jonah showed clearly that He had not given up on Assyria. The prophet was to call Nineveh to repentance, warning the nation of its approaching doom unless it turned to God.

Instead of obeying God's command and heading to Nineveh, Jonah caught a ship traveling in the opposite direction. At sea a great storm arose, and Jonah was tossed overboard by the superstitious sailors in an attempt to appease the prophet's God. Jonah escaped unharmed when he was swallowed by a great fish and was miraculously deposited on shore. This time he obeyed God's command and traveled to Nineveh to carry out his preaching assignment.

But the reluctant prophet was not prepared for the results of his message. The entire city repented, and Jonah sulked in anger because Nineveh escaped God's punishment.

To teach the prophet a lesson, God raised up a plant, perhaps a gourd vine, to shade Jonah from the sun, then allowed a worm to cut it down. A hot wind from the east added to Jonah's misery, and he whined and complained about the missing plant. Then God reminded Jonah that He was a God of compassion who had the right to love and forgive the pagan Assyrians or any other people who turned to Him in obedience and faith. Jonah had been fretting about a plant, while God had turned His attention to a much more important matter—the worth and salvation of people.

Authorship and Date. The traditional view is that the prophet Jonah wrote this book. This would place its writing at about 760 B.C., since this prophet—"the son of Amittai" (1:1)—is the same Jonah who prophesied during the reign of Jeroboam II of Israel, from 793 to 753 B.C. (2 Kin. 14:25). The only other thing we know about Jonah is that he was a native of the village of Gath Hepher in Israel.

Some scholars insist the book was not written until about three centuries later by an unknown author. According to this theory, the writer composed the story of Jonah and his prophecy to combat the narrow-minded views of the Jewish people after their return to Jerusalem following their years of captivity in Babylon. It is true that the Israelites went to extremes during these years as they tried to cast off all foreign influences and preserve the unique heritage of their faith. And Jonah certainly is a book that emphasizes the universal love of God. But the evidence put forth to support this theory is weak and inconclusive. There is no real reason to reject the traditional view that the prophet Jonah himself wrote the book after his visit to Nineveh about 760 B.C.

Historical Setting. The prophet Jonah visited Nineveh during the glorious days of the Assyrian empire. From about 885 to 625 B.C., the Assyrians dominated the ancient world. Numerous passages in the Old Testament report advances of Assyrian military forces against the neighboring kingdoms of Judah and Israel during these years. As early as 841 B.C., Jehu, king of Israel, was forced to pay tribute to the dominating Assyrian ruler, Shalmaneser III. This kind of harassment continued for over a century until Israel finally fell to Assyrian forces about 722 B.C. No wonder Jonah was reluctant to go to Nineveh; God had called him to visit the very heartland of enemy territory and to give the hated Assyrians a chance to repent! It was a radical order that would have taxed the obedience of any prophet. Jonah's grudging attitude should not blind us to the fact that he did carry out God's command.

Theological Contribution. One of the great truths emphasized by this book is that God can use people who do not want to be used by Him. Jonah was practically driven to Nineveh against his will, but his grudging message still struck a responsive chord in the Assyrians. This shows that revival and repentance are works of God's Spirit. Our task is to proclaim His message.

But the greatest insight of the book is that God desires to show mercy and grace to all the peoples of the world. No one nation or group can claim exclusive rights to His love. The task of the nation of Israel was to preach this message about God's universal love to all the world (Gen. 12:1–3). But they

---

JONAH: A Teaching Outline

forgot this missionary purpose and eventually claimed God and His blessings as theirs alone. The Book of Jonah cries out against this narrow-minded interpretation of God and His purpose. In the last verse of the book, God makes it plain to Jonah that His mercy and compassion is as wide as the world itself: "And should I not pity Nineveh, that great city, in which are more than one hundred and twenty thousand persons who cannot discern between their right hand and their left, and also much livestock?" (4:11).

Special Considerations. Too much attention has been focused on the "great fish" (1:17) that swallowed Jonah and then spat him out on the shore. We solve nothing by debating whether a fish could swallow a man or whether a person could remain alive for three days in the stomach of such a creature. The point of this part of the story is that God worked a miracle to preserve the life of His prophet so he could get to Nineveh to carry out God's orders. The text states that God "prepared" this fish specifically for that purpose (1:17). Other miracles that God "prepared" to teach Jonah His purpose for the city of Nineveh were the plant (4:6), the worm that cut the plant down (4:7), and the hot east wind that added to Jonah's misery (4:8).

Some Bible readers insist on interpreting this book as an allegory or a parable. But these approaches ignore Jesus' own literal interpretation of Jonah. In speaking of His death and resurrection, Jesus declared, "For as Jonah was three days and three nights in the belly of the great fish, so will the Son of Man be three days and three nights in the heart of the earth" (Matt. 12:40; also Luke 11:29–32). Thus, the Book of Jonah is much more than a fish story. It is a beautiful account of God's grace that lifts our sights to the greatest love story of all—the death of His Son Jesus Christ for the sins of the world.

Also see JONAH.

JONAM [JOE nuhm] — a form of JONAN.

JONAN [JOE nuhn] (*Jehovah has been gracious*) — an ancestor of Joseph in Luke's genealogy of Jesus (Luke 3:30; Jonam, NIV, RSV, NEB).

JONAS [JOE nuhs] — Greek form of JONAH.

JONATHAN [JAHN uh thuhn] (*Jehovah has given*) — the name of 14 men in the Old Testament:

1. A Levite from Bethlehem in Judah (Judg. 17:7–9) who was employed by Micah. Jonathan became the priest at Micah's idol shrine in the mountains of Ephraim. When the tribe of the Danites took Micah's graven image, ephod, household idols, and molded image (Judg. 18:18), Jonathan went with them. Jonathan and the Danites settled in the newly captured city of Dan (formerly Laish), and he became their priest (Judges 17—18).

2. The oldest son of King Saul and a close friend of David. The first time Jonathan is mentioned in Scripture he is described as a commander of 1,000 men (1 Sam. 13:2). When Jonathan attacked the

Philistine garrison at Geba, his action brought swift retaliation by the Philistines, who subdued and humiliated the Israelites. But Jonathan and his armorbearer courageously attacked the Philistine garrison at Michmash and were successful. This action inspired the Israelites to overthrow their oppressors (1 Sam. 14:1–23).

Perhaps the best-known fact about Jonathan is his close friendship with David. He made a covenant with David (1 Sam. 18:3–4) and warned David of Saul's plot against his life (1 Sam. 19:1–2). When Saul sought David's life, Jonathan interceded on behalf of David, and Saul reinstated David to his good favor (1 Sam. 19:1–7). Jonathan's loyalty to David was proven time after time as he warned David of Saul's threats of vengeance (1 Samuel 20) and encouraged David in times of danger (1 Sam. 23:16, 18).

The tragic end for Jonathan came at Mount Gilboa when he, his father Saul, and two of his brothers were slain by the Philistines (1 Sam. 31:1–2; 1 Chr. 10:1–6). When David heard of this, he mourned and fasted (2 Sam. 1:12). He then composed a lamentation, the "Song of the Bow," in which he poured out his grief over the death of Saul and Jonathan (2 Sam. 1:17–27).

Because David loved Jonathan, he treated Jonathan's lame son, Mephibosheth, kindly (2 Sam. 9:1–13). As a final act of love and respect, David brought the bones of Saul and Jonathan from Jabesh Gilead and buried them "in the country of Benjamin in Zelah, in the tomb of Kish his father" (2 Sam. 21:12–14). In this way David honored God's anointed king, Saul, and recognized the loyal, unselfish love of his friend. The story of David and Jonathan is a good example of the unselfish nature of love.

3. A son of Abiathar, a high priest in David's time (2 Sam. 15:27, 36; 17:17, 20). During Absalom's rebellion, when David and his supporters were forced to flee from Jerusalem, Jonathan relayed messages to David about developments in Jerusalem.

4. A son of Shimeah (2 Sam. 21:21), or Shimea (1 Chr. 20:7), one of David's brothers.

5. One of David's mighty men (1 Chr. 11:34).

6. A son of Jada (1 Chr. 2:32).

7. An uncle of David. Jonathan was "a counselor, a wise man, and a scribe" 1 Chr. 27:32).

8. The father of Ebed (Ezra 8:6).

9. A son of Asahel who opposed Ezra's proposal that pagan wives should be divorced (Ezra 10:15).

10. A descendant of Jeshua the high priest (Neh. 12:10–11).

11. A priest descended from Melichu (Neh. 12:14).

12. A priest descended from Shemaiah (Neh. 12:35).

13. A scribe in whose house Jeremiah the prophet was imprisoned (Jer. 37:15; 38:26).

14. A son of Kareah who joined Gedaliah after the fall of Jerusalem (Jer. 40:8).

Photo by Howard Vos

Modern Jaffa on the Mediterranean coast is the successor to the biblical city of Joppa (Acts 10:5-9). Today the city is part of the municipality of Tel-Aviv.

JONATH–ELEM–RECHOKIM [JOE nath EE luhm ruh KOE kim] (meaning unknown) — a term used in the title of Psalm 56 (KJV), probably referring to the tune to which the psalm was to be sung.

JOPPA [JAH puh] (*beautiful*) — an ancient seaport city on the Mediterranean Sea, about 56 kilometers (35 miles) northwest of Jerusalem (see Map 3, A–3).

A walled city, Joppa was built about 35 meters (116 feet) high on a rocky ledge overlooking the Mediterranean. It supposedly received its name (beautiful) from the sunlight which its buildings reflected.

The first mention of Joppa in the Bible indicates it was part of the territory inherited by the tribe of Dan (Josh. 19:46; Japho, KJV). The only natural harbor on the Mediterranean between Egypt and Acco, it was the seaport for the city of Jerusalem and the site of significant shipping in both Old and New Testament times. Rafts of cedar logs from the forests of Lebanon were floated from Tyre and Sidon to Joppa and then transported overland to Jerusalem to be used in building Solomon's Temple (2 Chr. 2:16).

In New Testament times Joppa was the home of a Christian disciple, Tabitha (or Dorcas), a woman "full of good works and charitable deeds" (Acts 9:36). After she became sick and died, she was raised to life by Simon Peter. As a result, many believed on the Lord (Acts 9:36–42).

Joppa was also the home of Simon the Tanner (Acts 10:32). Simon Peter stayed many days in Joppa with Simon. On the roof of Simon's house Peter received his vision of a great sheet descending from heaven (Acts 10:9–16)—a vision which indicated that all who believe in Christ, Gentiles as well as Jews, are accepted by God.

JORAH [JOHR uh] (*autumn rain*) — an Israelite whose descendants returned with Zerubbabel from the Captivity (Ezra 2:18). Jorah is also called Hariph (Neh. 7:24).

JORAI [JOHR eye] (*Jehovah has seen*) — a chief of the tribe of Gad (1 Chr. 5:13).

JORAM [JOHR uhm] (*Jehovah is exalted*) — the name of four men in the Old Testament:

1. A son of Toi, king of Hamath (2 Sam. 8:9–10). When David defeated the army of Hadadezer, Toi sent Joram—with gifts of gold, silver, and bronze—to greet and bless David.

2. The son and successor of Jehoshaphat as king of Judah (1 Chr. 3:10–11), also called JEHORAM (1 Kin. 22:50). Joram reigned eight years (2 Kin. 8:17) while his brother-in-law, also named Joram, reigned in Israel. His marriage to Athaliah, Ahab's daughter, marked the beginning of Joram's downfall. Athaliah influenced Joram to promote Baal worship in Judah. This illustrates the perils of an ungodly marriage.

In addition to promoting religious atrocities (2 Chr. 21:11), Joram is remembered for murdering his six brothers and chief nobles. This mass murder assured his position as king and probably added to his wealth (2 Chr. 21:4). Little else is noted of his reign, with the exception of revolts by Edom and Libnah (2 Chr. 21:8–10).

In spite of Joram's evil ways, "The Lord would not destroy the house of David, because of the covenant that He had made with David." But through a letter from Elijah, the Lord did warn Joram of coming judgment (2 Chr. 21:7, 12–15). The king soon lost nearly all his possessions, wives, and children at the hands of Philistine and Arabian raiders as Elijah had prophesied. Joram also contracted an excruciating intestinal disease. After two years of suffering, "he died in severe pain," for "his intestines came out because of his sickness" (2 Chr. 21:19).

Because of Joram's moral and religious depravity, no one mourned his death, and he was not buried in the tombs of the kings. Thus, at the age of 40, his reign was ended prematurely. Within a year, his wife had all of his descendants executed, except one grandson, Joash (2 Kin. 11:1-3).

3. The tenth king of Israel, slain by Jehu (2 Kin. 8:16-29; 9:14-29). The son of Ahab and Jezebel, Joram succeeded his brother, Ahaziah, as king. He was also called Jehoram (2 Kin. 1:17). His 12-year reign was characterized as an evil time, although he did manage to restrain Baal worship (2 Kin. 3:3).

One of Joram's first major projects was to enlist Jehoshaphat, king of Judah, and the king of Edom in a campaign against Moab. Joram also defended Israel against Syria. Through the aid of the prophet Elisha, Joram defeated the Syrian invaders. Later, however, Ben-Hadad of Syria besieged Samaria, leading to severe famine and even cannibalism (2 Kin. 6:8-29). In the darkest hour of the siege, however, the Lord miraculously delivered His people, just as Elisha had prophesied (2 Kin. 7:1-20).

When Hazael replaced Ben-Hadad as king of Syria, Joram made an alliance with his nephew Ahaziah, king of Judah, to occupy the city of Ramoth-Gilead by force. Joram was wounded in the battle, and he went back to Jezreel to recover. Jehu, the leader of his army, came to Jezreel and assassinated Joram. Joram's body was then thrown upon the very property which Ahab and Jezebel had stolen from Naboth, thus fulfilling Elijah's prophecy that the house of Ahab would come to an end (1 Kin. 21:21-29; 2 Kin. 9:21-29).

4. A Levite who worked as a treasury official in the tabernacle in David's time (1 Chr. 26:25).

Also see JEHORAM.

JORDAN [JORE dun] (*descending, flowing river*) — the name of the longest and most important river in Palestine (see Map 3, C-1). The river is part of the great rift valley that runs north to south into Africa. This rift valley is one of the lowest depressions on earth.

The headwaters of the Jordan River begin north of the Sea of Galilee. A number of rivers flow into Lake Huleh north of the Sea of Galilee. These waters emerge at the southern tip of the lake as the Jordan River. It is possible to ford the river just below the lake where the waters are low. In the ancient world trade caravans going from Damascus to Egypt probably crossed at this point.

At Lake Huleh the headwaters of the Jordan are about 70 meters (230 feet) above sea level. Some 16 kilometers (10 miles) south of the Sea of Galilee the river is about 213 meters (700 feet) below sea level. At the northern end of the Dead Sea (the end of the Jordan), the river has dropped to about 393 meters (1,290 feet) below sea level. This drastic drop is reflected in the name of the river, which means "the descender." The Jordan made a natural boundary as a serious obstacle in any east-to-west movement in the land of Palestine. A number of shallow spots, or fords, occur in the Jordan. Since bridges did not exist in the biblical period, possession of these fords was an important military factor.

The distance that the Jordan covers from the southern tip of the Sea of Galilee to the northern end of the Dead Sea is only about 113 kilometers (70 miles). But the winding, zigzag pattern of the river is such that it curves for about 323 kilometers (200 miles) as it weaves its way north to south. The river varies from 27 to 30 meters (90 to 100 feet) in width and between 1 and 3 meters (3 and 10 feet) deep. The water is not really navigable. With great difficulty flat-bottom boats are able to move along parts of the waterway; they must be towed, how-

The Jordan River in southern Palestine near Jericho.

Photo by Gustav Jeeninga

ever, through sandbars and must survive swift currents because of the descending nature of the valley. There are some 27 series of rapids in the Jordan.

At one time the Jordan valley may have been a large lake. Earthquakes and tremors over the centuries have dumped loose soil and gravel into the river, forcing new courses for the water that produced the switchback design of the Jordan. The northern part of the Jordan has numerous tributaries that flood their banks in winter and spring, allowing for good irrigation of the farmlands nearby. It was probably this fertile area that caught Lot's attention (Gen. 13:10). The middle and southern areas of Palestine that parallel the Jordan are the badlands with scarcely any rainfall. This type of land is only interrupted by an occasional oasis, such as those at Jericho.

The lower Jordan valley can be divided into three distinct regions. The first region is the Zor or thickets of underbrush that because of seasonal flooding has produced a jungle of vines, dense brush, shrubs, willows, and poplar trees. This area is sometimes referred to in the Bible as "Jordan's dense thickets" (Jer. 12:5; 49:19; Zech. 11:3, NEB; the jungle of the Jordan, RSV). The sons of the prophets were cutting down trees in the thickets of the Jordan when Elisha made an iron ax head float on the river, after it had been accidentally lost (2 Kin. 6:1–7).

The second area is called the Gattara, or badlands, on the outside of the Zor. This area is covered with sediment, probably from the period when the whole valley was flooded. Until the modern period, the soil was too salty for crops. But modern Israeli scientists have reclaimed the soil by washing it with river water.

The third region of the lower Jordan is the Ghor, or upper region. This area is steep but fertile. It has supported farming especially in the first 40 kilometers (25 miles) of the northern end of the river. The last 8 kilometers (5 miles) at the southern end is too barren for farming.

When the Hebrew tribes approached the Promised Land, they did so from the eastern side of the Jordan. To some degree the Jordan River served as the boundary for the tribes (Num. 34:12). Ancient Israel occupied territory on both sides of the river. The tribes of Reuben, Gad, and half of the tribe of Manasseh settled on the eastern side of the Jordan.

Weak parties often went east of the Jordan to escape from the pressures from their opponents. For instance, Abner took Ishbosheth, the son of Saul, to the eastern side of the Jordan in opposition to David (2 Sam. 2:8). David fled to the eastern side after Absalom's initial success (2 Sam. 17:22–24; 19:15–18). However, the crossing of the Jordan from east to west was symbolic of the arrival of the Hebrews in the Promised Land. The west side of the Jordan was the area generally thought to have been promised to Abraham.

It was probably at the south end of the river, near Jericho, that ancient Israel entered the region of Canaan (Joshua 3—4). At Gilgal, near the Dead

Sea, on the western side of the river about a mile from Jericho, an important shrine area was set up to commemorate the entrance of the Hebrews into the land (Josh. 4:19; 1 Sam. 7:16; 10:8).

In the period between the Old Testament and the New Testament, the Jordan River formed the main eastern boundary of the Persian and Greek province of Judea. The DECAPOLIS, a federation of ten Greek cities, was formed on the eastern side of the Jordan in the Greek period. John the Baptist carried out his ministry in the Jordan River region (Matt. 3:5–6; Mark 1:5; Luke 3:3; John 1:28; 3:26). Jesus' ministry was initiated by his baptism in the waters of the Jordan (Matt. 3:13; Mark 1:9; Luke 4:1). Jesus carried out His ministry on both sides of the Jordan (Matt. 4:15, 25; Mark 3:8; John 10:40).

JORIM [JOHR im] (*Jehovah is exalted*) — an ancestor of Jesus in Luke's genealogy (Luke 3:29).

JORKOAM [johr KOE uhm] (meaning unknown) — a son of Raham (1 Chr. 2:44; Jorkeam, NIV, RSV).

JOSABAD [JAHS uh bad] — a form of JOZABAD.

Aerial view of the twisting Jordan River in the region near the Dead Sea. Notice the tropical-like vegetation along the banks of the river in this fertile valley.

Photo by Howard Vos

Traditional tomb of Joseph at Shechem (Ex. 13:19).

JOSE [JOE see] (*Jehovah is savior*) — an ancestor of Jesus in Luke's genealogy (Luke 3:29; Joshua, NIV, NEB; Jesus, RSV).

JOSECH [JOE sek] (*may God increase*) — an ancestor of Jesus in Luke's genealogy (Luke 3:26).

JOSEPH [JOE zeph] (*may God add*) — the name of several men in the Bible:

1. The 11th son of Jacob (Gen. 30:24). Joseph was sold into slavery and later rose to an important position in the Egyptian government. The account of Joseph's life is found in Genesis 37—50.

Joseph was the first child of Rachel (30:24) and his father's favorite son (37:31). This is most clearly shown by the special coat which Jacob gave to Joseph. This favoritism eventually brought serious trouble for the whole family. Joseph's ten older brothers hated him because he was Jacob's favorite and because Joseph had dreams which he interpreted to his brothers in a conceited way. It is no surprise that Joseph's brothers hated him enough to kill him (37:4).

Joseph and his family were shepherds in the land of Canaan. One day Jacob sent Joseph to search for his brothers, who were tending the flocks in the fields. When Joseph found them, they seized upon the chance to kill him. The only opposing voice was Reuben's, but they finally sold Joseph into slavery to passing merchants.

To hide the deed from their father Jacob, Joseph's brothers took his coat and dipped it in animal blood. When Jacob saw the coat, he was convinced that Joseph had been killed by a wild animal (37:34–35).

Joseph was taken to Egypt, where he was sold to POTIPHAR, an officer of the ruling pharaoh of the nation. His good conduct soon earned him the highest position in the household. Potiphar's wife became infatuated with Joseph and tempted him to commit adultery with her. When he refused, she accused him of the crime and Joseph was sent to prison.

While in prison, Joseph's behavior earned him a position of responsibility over the other prisoners. Among the prisoners Joseph met were the Pharaoh's baker and his butler. When each of them had a dream, Joseph interpreted their dreams. When the butler left prison, he failed to intercede on Joseph's behalf, and Joseph spent two more years in prison.

When the Pharaoh had dreams that none of his counselors could interpret, the butler remembered Joseph and mentioned him to the Pharaoh. Then Joseph was called to appear before the Pharaoh. He interpreted the Pharaoh's dreams, predicting seven years of plentiful food, followed by seven years of famine. He also advised the Pharaoh to appoint a commissioner to store up supplies during the plentiful years.

To Joseph's surprise, the Pharaoh appointed him as food commissioner. This was a position of great prestige. Under Joseph's care, many supplies were stored and the land prospered (41:37–57). Joseph was given many comforts, including servants and a wife. He was called Zapenath–Paneah, which means "revealer of secrets." When the famine struck, Joseph was second only to the Pharaoh in power. People from all surrounding lands came to buy food from him.

Many years passed between Joseph's arrival in Egypt as a slave and his rise to power in the nation during the famine. The famine also struck Canaan, and Joseph's brothers eventually came to Egypt to buy grain. When they met Joseph, they did not recognize him. He recognized them, however, and decided to test them to see if they had changed. He accused them of being spies. Then he sold them grain only on the condition that Simeon stay as a hostage until they bring Benjamin, the youngest brother, to Egypt with them.

Upon returning to Canaan, the brothers told Jacob of their experiences. He vowed not to send Benjamin to Egypt. But the continuing famine forced him to change his mind. On the next trip Benjamin went with his brothers to Egypt.

When they arrived, Joseph treated them royally, weeping openly at the sight of his youngest brother. Simeon was returned to them. After purchasing their grain, they started home. On their way home, however, they were stopped by one of Joseph's servants, who accused them of stealing Joseph's silver cup. The cup was found in Benjamin's bag, where Joseph had placed it. The brothers returned to face Joseph, who declared that Benjamin must stay in Egypt. At this point Judah pleaded with Joseph, saying that it would break their father Jacob's heart if Benjamin failed to return with them. Judah's offer to stay in Benjamin's place is one of the most moving passages in the Old Testament.

Joseph was overcome with emotion. He revealed himself to them as their brother, whom they had sold into slavery years earlier. At first Joseph's brothers were afraid that Joseph would take revenge against them, but soon they were convinced that Joseph's forgiveness was genuine. Judah's plea on Benjamin's behalf was evidence of the change that Joseph had hoped to find in his brothers. He sent them back to Canaan with gifts for his father and invited the family to come live in Egypt.

The grace of God working in the family of Jacob is evident in the way Joseph dealt with his brothers. Joseph did not want revenge against them. He realized that his personal suffering had preserved the family as an instrument of God's will. Joseph also was aware that his rise to power was for the good of his family, not for his own glory (45:7–8).

Jacob accepted Joseph's offer and moved his entire family to Egypt. During the journey, God appeared to Jacob at Beersheba, blessing him and renewing His promise about the destiny of Jacob's sons. God promised that the family would return to Canaan some day. The families of Jacob settled in the land of Goshen, where they tended the Pharaoh's herds. They remained here until Joseph's death.

After the Exodus of the Hebrew people from Egypt years later, Joseph's faithfulness was rewarded. His two sons, Ephraim and Manassah, were counted as ancestral fathers of two tribes of Israel, although their mother was an Egyptian woman. In Psalm 80:1, the word "Joseph" is used as a poetic designation for these two tribes.

JOSEPHUS, FLAVIUS [joe SEE fis, FLAY vih us] — a Jewish historian and a general of the Galilean Jewish army in the war against Rome (A.D. 66–70). The historical works of Josephus provide important background information for the New Testament and the late intertestamental period. They include information on agriculture, geography, politics, religion, social traditions and practices, and insights into outstanding personalities such as HEROD, PILATE, and FELIX. He also refers to John the Baptist, James the Lord's brother, and Jesus.

JOSES [JOE seez] (meaning unknown) — the name of three men in the New Testament:
1. One of the four brothers of Jesus (Matt. 13:55; Mark 6:3), also called Joseph.
2. The brother of James the Less (Mark 15:40, 47), also called Joseph.
3. The original name of BARNABAS (Acts 4:36), also called Joseph.

JOSHAH [JOE shuh] (*Jehovah's gift*) — a son of Amaziah, of the tribe of Simeon (1 Chr. 4:34).

JOSHAPHAT [JAHSH uh fat] (*Jehovah judges*) — the name of two men in the Old Testament:
1. One of David's mighty men (1 Chr. 11:43).
2. A priest who preceded the ARK OF THE COVENANT when it was moved to Jerusalem (1 Chr. 15:24; Jehoshaphat, KJV).

JOSHAVIAH [jahsh uh VIGH uh] (*Jehovah is equality*) — one of David's mighty men (1 Chr. 11:46).

JOSHBEKASHAH [jahsh buh KAY shuh] (*seat of hardness*) — a son of Heman appointed by David as a singer (1 Chr. 25:4, 24).

JOSHEB–BASSHEBETH [JOE sheb bash EE beth] — a form of JASHOBEAM.

JOSHIBIAH [jah shuh BIGH uh] (meaning unknown) — a son of Seraiah (1 Chr. 4:35).

JOSHUA [JAHSH oo uh] (*the Lord is salvation*) — the successor to Moses and the man who led the nation of Israel to conquer the land of Canaan and settle the Promised Land.

Joshua was born in Egypt. He went through the great events of the Passover and the Exodus with Moses and all the Hebrew people who escaped from slavery in Egypt at the hand of their Redeemer God. In the Wilderness of Sinai, Moses took his assistant Joshua with him when he went into the mountains to talk with God (Ex. 24:13). Moses also gave Joshua a prominent place at the TABERNACLE. As Moses' servant, Joshua would remain at the tabernacle as his representative while the great leader left the camp to fellowship with the Lord (Ex. 33:11).

When Moses sent spies to scout out the land of Canaan, Joshua was selected as the representative of the tribe of Ephraim (Num. 13:8). Only Joshua and Caleb returned to the camp with a report that they could conquer the land with God's help. The other ten spies complained that they were "like grasshoppers" in comparison to the Canaanites (Num. 13:33). Because of their show of faith, Joshua and Caleb were allowed to enter the land at the end of their years of wandering in the wilderness. But all the other Israelites who lived at that time died before the nation entered the Promised Land (Num. 14:30).

Photo by Howard Vos

An excavated Canaanite high place, or pagan worship shrine, at Et Tell, identified by many archaeologists as biblical Ai. The city of Ai was defeated on the second attempt by Joshua and the invading Israelites (Joshua 7—8).

At Moses' death, Joshua was chosen as his successor (Josh. 1:1–2). He led the Israelites to conquer the land (Joshua 1—2), supervised the division of the territory among the 12 tribes, and led the people to renew their covenant with God (Joshua 13—22).

When Joshua died at the age of 110, he was buried in the land of his inheritance at Timnath Serah (Josh. 24:30). As Moses' successor, Joshua completed the work which this great leader began. Moses led Israel out of Egypt; Joshua led Israel into Canaan. Joshua's name, an Old Testament form of Jesus, means "the Lord is salvation." By his name and by his life, he demonstrated the salvation that comes from God.

Also see JOSHUA, BOOK OF.

JOSHUA, BOOK OF — an Old Testament book that describes the conquest and division of the land of Canaan by the Hebrew people. The book is named for its central figure, Joshua, who succeeded Moses as leader in this vigorous campaign.

Structure of the Book. The Book of Joshua has a natural, flowing structure that makes it a joy to read and study. In a brief prologue, the warrior Joshua is introduced as the capable leader selected by God to lead the people. Then the book launches immediately into narratives about the military victories of the Hebrews as they drove the Canaanites

out of the land. Joshua's strategy was to divide and conquer. He struck first in central Canaan by taking the city of Jericho and surrounding territory. Then he launched rapid attacks to the south and north. This strategy quickly gave the Covenant People a foothold in the land. After weakening the enemy's position with this strategy, Joshua led numerous minor attacks against them during the next several years.

These accounts of Joshua's military campaigns are followed by a long description of the division of the land among the 12 tribes of Israel. Finally, the book ends with the death of Joshua after he leads the people to renew the covenant and charges them to remain faithful to God.

Authorship and Date. Early Jewish tradition credited Joshua with writing this book. But this is disputed by many modern scholars. One of the strongest objections to his authorship is the final section of the book, which describes Joshua's death and burial (24:29–33). Obviously, Joshua could not have written this material.

But other sections of the book strongly suggest that they were written by Joshua. One passage declares that after giving his farewell address, "Joshua wrote these words in the Book of the Law of God" (24:26). Some of the battle narratives are also written with vivid description and minute detail, suggesting that they may have been composed by the commander on the scene, Joshua himself (see especially chaps. 6—8).

The most logical and believable theory about authorship is that Joshua wrote a major part of the book. But it probably did not reach its finished form until several years after his death. An editor must have added some additional narratives, such as the one about Joshua's death and burial, to complete this important book about Joshua and his contribution. A commonly accepted date for the death of Joshua is about 1375 B.C., so the book must have been completed shortly after this date.

Historical Setting. The Book of Joshua covers about 25 years in one of the most important periods of Israel's history—their conquest and final settlement of the land which God had promised to Abraham and his descendants many centuries earlier. The specific years for this occupation must have been from about 1400 to 1375 B.C.

Theological Contribution. One important message

of the Book of Joshua is that true and false religions do not mix. Joshua's orders were to destroy the Canaanites because of their pagan and immoral worship practices. But these people never were totally subdued or destroyed. Traces of their false religion remained to tempt the Israelites. Again and again throughout their history, the Hebrew people departed from worship of the one true God. This tendency toward false worship was the main reason for Joshua's moving farewell speech. He warned the people against worshiping these false gods and challenged them to remain faithful to their great deliverer Jehovah. The point of Joshua's message was, You cannot worship these false gods and remain faithful to the Lord: "But as for me and my house, we will serve the Lord" (24:15).

Special Considerations. Some people have difficulty with God commanding Joshua to destroy the Canaanites. But behind this command lay God's concern for his Covenant People. He wanted to remove the Canaanites' idolatrous worship practices

JOSHUA: A Teaching Outline

so they would not be a temptation to the Israelites. This command to Joshua also represented God's judgment against sin and immorality. God used Israel as an instrument of His judgment against a pagan nation.

Also see JOSHUA.

JOSHUA, GATE OF (see GATES OF JERUSALEM AND THE TEMPLE).

JOSIAH [joe SIGH uh] (meaning unknown) — the name of two men in the Old Testament:

1. The 16th king of Judah, the son of AMON, and the grandson of Manasseh (2 Kin. 21:23—23:30). The three decades of Josiah's reign were characterized by peace, prosperity, and reform. Hence, they were among the happiest years experienced by Judah. King Josiah devoted himself to pleasing God and reinstituting Israel's observance of the Mosaic Law. That a wicked king like Amon could have such a godly son and successor is a tribute to the grace of God. The Bible focuses almost exclusively on Josiah's spiritual reform, which climaxed in the 18th year of his reign with the discovery of the Book of the Law.

Josiah's reform actually occurred in three stages. Ascending to the throne at age eight, he apparently was blessed with God-fearing advisors who resisted the idolatrous influence of his father. More importantly, however, at the age of 16 (stage one), Josiah personally "began to seek the God of his father David" (2 Chr. 34:3).

At the age of 20 (stage two), Josiah began to cleanse Jerusalem and the land of Judah of idolatrous objects (2 Chr. 34:3-7). His reform was even more extensive than that of his predecessor, HEZEKIAH (2 Kin. 18:4; 2 Chr. 29:3-36). Josiah extended his cleansing of the land into the territory of fallen Israel; at the time Israel was nominally controlled by Assyria. Josiah personally supervised the destruction of the altars of the Baals, the incense altars, the wooden images, the carved images, and the molded images as far north as the cities of

Naphtali. Josiah's efforts were aided by the death of the great Assyrian king, Ashurbanipal, which brought about a serious decline in Assyria's power and allowed Josiah freedom to pursue his reforms.

At the age of 26 (stage three), Josiah ordered that the Temple be repaired under the supervision of Hilkiah, the high priest. In the process, a copy of the Book of the Law was discovered (2 Chr. 34:14–15). When it was read to Josiah, he was horrified to learn how far Judah had departed from the law of God. This discovery provided a new momentum for the reformation that was already in progress.

In 609 B.C. Josiah attempted to block Pharaoh Necho II of Egypt as he marched north to assist Assyria in her fight with Babylon for world supremacy. Despite the Pharaoh's assurance to the contrary, Josiah saw Necho's northern campaign as a threat to Judah's security. When he engaged Necho in battle at Megiddo, Josiah was seriously injured. He was returned to Jerusalem, where he died after reigning 31 years. His death was followed by widespread lamentation (2 Chr. 35:20-27). In the New Testament, Josiah is referred to as Josias (Matt. 1:10, KJV).

2. A captive who returned to Jerusalem from Babylon in Zechariah's day (Zech. 6:10).

JOSIAS [joe SIGH us] — a form of JOSIAH.

JOT [jaht] — the English rendering of the Greek word *iota* (Matt. 5:18), the smallest letter of the Greek alphabet. The word is used figuratively to express a matter that seems to be of small importance.

JOTBAH [JAHT buh] (*pleasantness*) — the home of Haruz, whose daughter Meshullemeth was the mother of King AMON of Judah (2 Kin. 21:19).

JOTBATHAH [JAHT buh thuh] (*pleasantness*) — a stopping place of the Israelites in the wilderness between Hor Hagidgad and Abronah (Num. 33:33–34).

JOTHAM [JOE thum] (*Jehovah is perfect*) — the

The Valley of Aijalon, where the sun stood still during a battle between Joshua and the Amorite kings (Josh. 10:1-15).

Photo by Howard Vos

name of three men in the Old Testament:

1. The youngest son of Gideon (Judg. 9:1–21). He escaped death at the hands of Abimelech, another son of Gideon. When the Shechemites made Abimelech king, Jotham stood on Mount Gerizim and pronounced judgment on Abimelech and the Shechemites by a parable of the trees (vv. 7–20). In fear for his life, Jotham fled to Beer. No more is recorded of him, except that his curse was fulfilled three years later (Judg. 9:57).

2. A son of Uzziah (or Azariah) and the 11th king of Judah (2 Kin. 15:32–38; 2 Chr. 26:21–23), who reigned from about 750–732 B.C. Jotham ruled as co-regent with his father when it was discovered that Uzziah had leprosy. His 18-year reign was a godly one, although the people persisted in idolatry. He was undoubtedly encouraged by the prophets Isaiah, Hosea, and Micah, who ministered during his reign (Is. 1:1; Hos. 1:1; Mic. 1:1).

Jotham built the Upper Gate of the Temple and strengthened the Jerusalem wall of Ophel. He also built cities and fortified buildings throughout the countryside to further strengthen Judah. He fought and defeated the Ammonites and exacted tribute from them for three years (2 Chr. 27:3–5).

Jotham's strength and prosperity were attributed to the fact that "he prepared his ways before the Lord his God" (2 Chr. 27:6). Jotham was an ancestor of Jesus (Matt. 1:9; Joatham, KJV).

3. A son of Jahdai and a descendant of Caleb (1 Chr. 2:47).

JOY — a positive attitude or pleasant emotion; delight. Many kinds of joy are reported in the Bible. This makes it difficult to give a simple definition of joy. Even the wicked are said to experience joy in their triumphs over the righteous (1 Cor. 13:6; Rev. 11:10). Many levels of joy are also described, including gladness, contentment, and cheerfulness.

But the joy which the people of God should have is holy and pure. This joy rises above circumstances and focuses on the very character of God. In the Psalms, for example, the psalmist rejoices over God's righteousness (71:14–16), salvation (21:1; 71:23), mercy (31:7), creation (148:5), word (119:14, 162), and faithfulness (33:1–6). God's characteristics as well as His acts are the cause of rejoicing.

The joy required of the righteous person (Ps. 150; Phil. 4:4) is produced by the Spirit of God (Gal. 5:22). This kind of joy looks beyond the present to our future salvation (Rom. 5:2; 8:18; 1 Pet. 1:4, 6) and to our sovereign God, who works out all things for our ultimate good, which is Christlikeness (Rom. 8:28–30). This kind of joy is distinct from mere happiness. Joy like this is possible, even in the midst of sorrow (1 Cor. 12:26; 2 Cor. 6:10; 7:4).

JOZABAD [JAHZ uh bad] (*Jehovah bestows*) — the name of several men in the Old Testament:

1. A Gederathite who joined David at Ziklag (1 Chr. 12:4; Josabad, KJV).

2, 3. Two captains of the tribe of Manasseh who

defected from Saul to join David's forces at Ziklag (1 Chr. 12:20).

4. A Levite overseer in the Temple during the reign of Hezekiah (2 Chr. 31:13).

5. A chief Levite during the reign of Josiah (2 Chr. 35:9).

6. A son of Jeshua (Ezra 8:33). He may be the same person as Jozabad No. 8, 9, or 10.

7. A descendant of Pashhur who divorced his pagan wife after the Captivity (Ezra 10:22).

8. A Levite who divorced his pagan wife after the Captivity (Ezra 10:23).

9. A Levite who helped Ezra interpret the Law to the people (Neh. 8:7–8).

10. A chief Levite in Jerusalem after the Captivity (Neh. 11:16).

Also see JOSABAD; JOZACHAR.

JOZACHAR [JAHZ uh kahr] (*Jehovah remembers*) — a son of Shimeath and one of two servants of Joash (Jehoash), king of Judah, who formed a conspiracy against Joash. Together they assassinated Joash (2 Kin. 12:20–21).

JOZADAK [JAHZ uh dak] (*Jehovah is just*) — the father of Jeshua (or Joshua), the high priest in Zerubbabel's time. Jozadak was among those who were carried into Babylonian captivity by Nebuchadnezzar.

JUBAL [JOO buhl] (*playing*) — a descendant of Cain, called "the father of all those who play the harp and the flute" (Gen. 4:21).

JUBILEE [JOO bah lee] (*blowing the trumpet*) — the 50th year after seven cycles of seven years, when specific instructions about property and slavery took effect (Lev. 25:8–55).

The word jubilee comes from the Hebrew *yobel*, which means to be "jubilant" and to "exult." The word is related to the Hebrew word for ram's horn or trumpet. The Jubilee year was launched with a blast from a ram's horn on the Day of Atonement, signifying a call to joy, liberation, and the beginning of a year for "doing justice" and "loving mercy."

The 50th year was a special year in which to "proclaim liberty throughout all the land" (Lev. 25:10). Specifically, individuals who had incurred debts and had sold themselves as slaves or servants to others were released from their debts and were set at liberty. Since all land belonged to God (Lev. 25:23), land could not be sold; but land could be lost to another for reasons of debt. In the Year of Jubilee such land was returned to the families to whom it was originally given.

Like the SABBATICAL YEARS, the Year of Jubilee was a year for neither sowing nor reaping (Lev. 25:11). The 50th year became important in Israel's economic life. If anyone wished to redeem a person in debt, the price for doing so was calculated on the basis of the number of years remaining until the Jubilee.

Part of the reason why God established the Jubilee Year was to prevent the Israelites from oppressing one another (Lev. 25:17). One effect of the Jubilee Year was to prevent a permanent system of classes. The Jubilee Year had a leveling effect on Israel's culture; it gave everyone a chance to start over, economically and socially. The Jubilee Year reminds one of God's interest in liberty; God wants people to be free (Luke 4:18–19). It also stands as a witness to God's desire for justice on earth and calls into question any social practices that lead to permanent bondage and loss of economic opportunity.

One may also see God's provision for the land's conservation in the call for the land to rest (Lev. 25:11, 18–22). The people were not to extract the earth's resources in a greedy manner.

The sabbatical year and presumably the Year of Jubilee were also characterized by instruction in the Law (Deut. 31:9–13). In this way the people learned that God's demand to love and obey Him was directly related to his concern for the welfare of all the people of Israel.

Also see FEASTS AND FESTIVALS.

JUBILEE, BOOK OF (see PSEUDEPIGRAPHA).

JUCAL [JOO kal] — a form of JEHUCAL.

JUDAEA [joo DEE uh] — a form of JUDEA.

JUDAH [JOO duh] (*praise*) — the name of seven men and a place in the Old Testament:

1. The fourth son of Jacob by his wife Leah and the founder of the tribal family out of which the messianic line came (Gen. 29:35; Num. 26:19–21; Matt. 1:2).

Judah was one of the most prominent of the 12 sons of Jacob. He saved Joseph's life by suggesting that his brothers sell Joseph to Ishmaelite merchants rather than kill him (Gen. 37:26–28). Later, in Egypt, it was Judah who begged Joseph to detain him (Judah) rather than Benjamin, Jacob's beloved son. In an eloquent speech Judah confessed what he and his brothers had done to Joseph; shortly thereafter, Joseph identified himself to his brothers (Gen. 44:14—45:1).

It appears that Judah was the leader of Jacob's sons who remained at home. Even though he was not the oldest son, Judah was sent by Jacob to precede him to Egypt (Gen. 46:28). Also Judah, rather than his older brothers, received Jacob's blessing (Gen. 49:3–10). In that blessing, Jacob foretold the rise of Judah: "Your father's children shall bow down before you... . the scepter shall not depart from Judah...until Shiloh comes" (Gen. 49:8, 10).

Judah had three sons: Er, Onan, and Shelah (Gen. 38:3–5). Er and Onan were killed by divine judgment because of their sins (Gen. 38:7–10). Judah also fathered twin sons, Perez and Zerah, by TAMAR, Er's widow (Gen. 38:29–30). The line of Judah ran through Perez to David and thus became the messianic line (Luke 3:30; Judas, KJV).

2. An ancestor of certain Israelites who helped rebuild the Temple after the Captivity (Ezra 3:9).

3. A Levite who divorced his pagan wife after returning from the Captivity (Ezra 10:23).

4. A son of Senuah (Neh. 11:9).

5. A Levite who returned from the Captivity with Zerubbabel (Neh. 12:8).

6. A leader of Judah who participated in the dedication of the Jerusalem wall (Neh. 12:34).

7. A musician and son of a priest (Neh. 12:36).

8. A place on the border of Naphtali (Josh. 19:34), location unknown.

JUDAH, KINGDOM OF — one of the two nations into which the united kingdom of Israel was divided following King Solomon's death in 922 B.C. (see Map 4, B-5). Judah consisted mostly of the tribes of Judah and part of Benjamin, although Simeon apparently was included later. The kingdom extended in the north as far as Bethel, while in the south it ended in the dry area known as the NEGEV. The Jordan River and the Mediterranean Sea formed the kingdom's eastern and western boundaries respectively. Jerusalem was its capital.

Judah was left suddenly independent when Rehoboam flatly refused to lighten the heavy load of forced labor and high taxation imposed on the Israelites by his father Solomon (1 Kin. 12:1–24). Upon Rehoboam's refusal, the ten tribes living north of Bethel promptly declared their independence. Under the leadership of Jeroboam, who once had been an overseer for Solomon, they followed their own way of life. Israel soon slipped into idolatry; and when the sensuous and depraved religion of the Phoenicians was introduced, this idolatry became increasingly worse.

Scarcely had this division occurred when a new and entirely unexpected blow devastated Judah. Shishak, Pharaoh of Egypt (about 945–924 B.C.), invaded the country, plundered the treasures of the Temple and the royal palace, and destroyed a num-

Statue of David, second and most beloved king of the Hebrew nation and ancestor of the Messiah, Jesus Christ (Matt. 1:1-17).

ber of newly built fortresses (2 Chr. 12:1–12). A damaged monument of Shishak recovered from MEGIDDO shows the extent of this conquest.

Judah never recovered from the sudden loss of her national wealth. Because her land was not as fertile as that of the northern kingdom of Israel, Judah never enjoyed the same degree of prosperity.

Rehoboam wanted to attack Israel and reunite the kingdom by force, but Shemaiah the prophet showed him how foolish the attempt would be (1 Kin. 12:21–24). Rehoboam's son Abijah (about 913–910 B.C.) regained a small area from Israel and tried to make an alliance with Syria against the Northern Kingdom, as did his successor Asa (about 910–869 B.C.). Asa rooted out much of the Canaanite paganism in Judah, and his reign was mostly peaceful and prosperous. He was followed (about 869 B.C.) by Jehoshaphat, who had co-ruled with Asa from about 873 B.C.

Judah prospered under the rule of Jehoshaphat, although he failed in his attempts to revive Solomon's seagoing trade. An alliance with Ahab of Israel against the Syrians at Ramoth Gilead proved to be even more disastrous (2 Chr. 18:31–32). Jehoshaphat's son Jehoram (about 848–841 B.C.) married Athaliah, daughter of Ahab and the wicked Queen Jezebel; and their marriage led to Baal worship also being established in Jerusalem (2 Kin. 8:18). Jehoram's son Ahaziah reigned only for one year (841 B.C.) before he was killed. The pagan queen–mother Athaliah (about 841–835 B.C.) seized the throne and nearly brought the Davidic line to extinction by killing most of Ahaziah's sons. Only the infant Joash escaped; he was rescued by his aunt Jehoshabeath and her husband Jehoiada, the godly high priest (2 Chr. 22:10–12).

After six years Joash was proclaimed the lawful king, and Athaliah was executed. The new king reigned well (about 835–796 B.C.) whenever he followed Jehoiada's advice. But following the death of the high priest, idolatry crept back into the nation's life. Joash was finally assassinated by his servants following a raid on Jerusalem by the army of Syria, which pillaged the city (2 Chr. 24:23–25).

Judah enjoyed modest prosperity under Amaziah (about 796–767 B.C.), the son and successor of Joash. Amaziah regained control of Edom, which had been independent since the days of Jehoram. Thus he was able to control the trading caravans of western Arabia as Solomon had done. With his victories, Amaziah became overconfident and he began worshiping the pagan gods of the Edomites instead of honoring the God of Sinai. Amaziah suffered a severe setback when he fought with Joash, king of Israel (about 798–781 B.C.), and was captured. His release came only after he had permitted Jerusalem's walls to be destroyed and the city's treasure to be removed. Consequently, Judah found it even more difficult to defend itself against Israel than in the days of Rehoboam. Amaziah was murdered at Lachish as the result of a conspiracy (2 Kin. 14:19), and he was succeeded by Azariah (Uzziah) about 767 B.C.

Uzziah had co–ruled with Amaziah from about 791 B.C., and he immediately set about restoring Judah's military and economic strength. He suppressed Baal worship in the kingdom and promoted the traditions of the Sinai covenant. He improved agricultural productivity by constructing cisterns, which increased available water supplies. Uzziah incorporated some Philistine and Ammonite territory into his own realm; he also built new defensive positions in Jerusalem and at the outposts on the borders of Judah. Uzziah became proud with his successes, which led him to take over the duties of the high priest (2 Kin. 15:5). For this he was struck with leprosy for the rest of his life.

Jotham succeeded his father Uzziah and continued to make the Southern Kingdom productive. His successor, Ahaz (about 732–715 B.C.), was faced with Assyria's rise to power under Tiglath-Pileser III; but Ahaz resisted the urgings of Rezin of Syria and Pekah of Israel to join an alliance against Assyria. Instead, Ahaz sought help from Assyria, against Isaiah's advice, and received assistance in return for heavy tribute. Syria and the kingdom of Israel were destroyed, leaving Judah at the mercy of the Assyrians.

When Hezekiah (about 714–686 B.C.) succeeded Ahaz, he also disregarded Isaiah's advice and became involved in a coalition with Babylonia and Egypt against Assyria. Assyria, now ruled by Sennacherib (about 705–681 B.C.), moved against Jerusalem in 701 B.C. It was at this time that Hezekiah constructed the SILOAM Tunnel to bring water from the Spring of GIHON into the city of Jerusalem (2 Chr. 32:30).

The Assyrians soon withdrew after suffering heavy losses, perhaps from a plague (Is. 37:36). The rest of Hezekiah's reign was marked by a renewal of covenant faith. Hezekiah's renewal was disrupted by his son Manasseh (about 687–641 B.C.), who reacted violently against his father's religious policies. Manasseh introduced a lengthy period of paganism that brought Judah to new depths of depravity (2 Chr. 33:1–20). He was deported to Babylon by Esarhaddon (about 681–669 B.C.) and later was allowed to return home. He then began a religious reformation, but with poor results.

Manasseh's son Amon (about 642–639 B.C.) continued in his father's depravity, but he soon was murdered. His successor Josiah (about 640–609 B.C.) restored traditional covenant religion, which was based on the Book of the Law newly discovered in a Temple storeroom (2 Chr. 34:14). Many did not follow Josiah's example, however; and the prophet ZEPHANIAH foretold disaster for the nation.

By 610 B.C. the Assyrian Empire had collapsed under Babylonian attacks, and the victors prepared to march against Egypt, which had been helping the Assyrians. Against Jeremiah's advice, Josiah intervened and was killed at Megiddo (2 Chr. 35:20–27). Pharaoh Necho deposed Jehoahaz (Shallum) in 609 B.C. and made Jehoiakim ruler of Judah, which was now firmly under Egyptian control. The Babylonians swept down upon Jerusalem in 597 B.C. and captured it. A second attack led to Jerusalem's second defeat in 586 B.C. Captives from both campaigns were taken to Babylonia to mark the captivity of the Southern Kingdom.

The Babylonians appointed Gedaliah, a court official in Judah, to oversee what was left of life in the land. After three years as governor, he was assassinated. Judah's kingdom reaped the reward of its idolatry and rebellion against the Lord and disappeared from history.

JUDAH, TRIBE OF — the tribe founded by JUDAH. Its five tribal families sprung from Judah's three sons—Shelah, Perez, and Zerah—and two grandsons, Hezron and Hamul (Num. 26:19–21). In the first census, the tribe of Judah numbered 74,600 men (Num. 1:26–27). In the second census, the tribe numbered 76,500 (Num. 26:22).

Except for Simeon, Judah was the southernmost tribe of the Israelites. However, Simeon seems to have been absorbed into Judah at an early date. Judah's eastern border was the Dead Sea, and its western border was the Mediterranean Sea, although the Philistines usually controlled the plain along the sea. Originally, Judah's northern boundary ran from just south of Jerusalem northwest to Kirjath Jearim and Jabneel. To the south Judah's border ran south to the Ascent of Akrabbim, to the Wilderness of Zin, and south from Kadesh Barnea to the Mediterranean. During the period of the divided kingdom, its northern boundary ran north of Jerusalem.

At its longest point Judah was about 153 kilometers (95 miles) in length. At its widest point it was about 73 kilometers (45 miles) wide, excluding the area controlled by the Philistines.

The tribe of Judah, along with Benjamin, remained true to David's line when the tribes split after Solomon's death. Together they formed the southern kingdom of Judah, which at one time included Edom to the southeast.

JUDAIZERS [joo dee EYE zurs] — early converts to Christianity who tried to force believers from non-Jewish backgrounds to adopt Jewish customs as a condition of salvation. Evidence of this movement within the early church first emerged about A.D. 49, when "certain men came down from Judea and taught the brethren, 'Unless you are circumcised according to the custom of Moses, you cannot be saved' " (Acts 15:1).

The apostle Paul denounced this idea, insisting that only one thing is necessary for salvation: faith in the Lord Jesus Christ (Acts 15:1–29). In the letter to the Galatians, Paul continued this same argument, insisting that the believer is justified by faith alone. To become a new person in Christ is to be set free from the requirements of the Jewish law: "For in Christ Jesus neither circumcision nor uncircumcision avails anything, but a new creation" (Gal. 6:15).

Also see GALATIANS, LETTER TO THE.

JUDAS [JOO duhs] (*praise of the Lord*) — the name of five men in the New Testament:

1. One of the four brothers of Jesus (Matt. 13:55; Mark 6:3; Juda, KJV). Some scholars believe he was the author of the Epistle of Jude.

2. One of the twelve apostles of Jesus. John is careful to distinguish him from Judas Iscariot (John 14:22). He is called "Judas the son of James" (Luke 6:16; Acts 1:13). In the list of the Twelve given in Mark, instead of "Judas...of James" a Thaddaeus is mentioned (Mark 3:18). Matthew has Lebbaeus, whose surname was Thaddaeus (Matt. 10:3). He was also called Judas the Zealot. Tradition says he preached in Assyria and Persia and died a martyr in Persia.

3. Judas of Galilee (Acts 5:37). In the days of the census (Luke 2:2), he led a revolt against Rome. He was killed, and his followers were scattered. According to the Jewish historian Josephus, Judas founded a sect whose main belief was that their only ruler and lord was God.

4. A man with whom the apostle Paul lodged in Damascus after his conversion (Acts 9:11).

5. A disciple surnamed Barsabas who belonged to the church in Jerusalem. The apostles and elders of that church chose Judas and Silas to accompany Paul and Barnabas to Antioch; together they conveyed to the church in that city the decree of the Jerusalem Council about circumcision.

JUDAS ISCARIOT [JOO duhs iss KAR ih uht] (*praise of the Lord*) — the disciple who betrayed Jesus. Judas was the son of Simon (John 6:71), or of Simon Iscariot (RSV). The term Iscariot, which is used to distinguish Judas from the other disciple named Judas (Luke 6:16; John 14:22; Acts 1:13), refers to his hometown of Kerioth, in southern Judah (Josh. 15:25). Thus, Judas was a Judean, the only one of the Twelve who was not from Galilee.

The details of Judas' life are sketchy. Because of his betrayal of Jesus, Judas, however, is even more of a mystery. It must be assumed that Jesus saw promise in Judas, or He would not have called him to be a disciple.

Judas' name appears in three of the lists of the Twelve disciples (Matt. 10:2–4; Mark 3:16–19; Luke 6:14–16), although it always appears last. His name is missing from the list of the 11 disciples in Acts 1:13; by that time Judas had committed suicide. Judas must have been an important disciple, because he served as their treasurer (John 12:6; 13:29).

During the week of the Passover festival, Judas went to the chief priests and offered to betray Jesus for a reward (Matt. 26:14–16; Mark 14:10–11). At the Passover supper, Jesus announced that He would be betrayed and that He knew who His betrayer was—one who dipped his hand with him in the dish (Mark 14:20), the one to whom He would give the piece of bread used in eating (John 13:26–27). Jesus was saying that a friend, one who dipped out of the same dish as He, was His betrayer. These verses in John indicate that Judas probably was reclining beside Jesus, evidence that Judas was an important disciple.

Jesus said to Judas, "What you do, do quickly" (John 13:27). Judas left immediately after he ate (John 13:30). The first observance of the Lord's Supper was probably celebrated afterward, without Judas (Matt. 26:26–29).

Judas carried out his betrayal in the Garden of Gethsemane. By a prearranged sign, Judas singled out Jesus for the soldiers by kissing him. The gospels do not tell us why Judas was needed to point out Jesus, who had become a well-known figure. It is possible that Judas disclosed where Jesus would be that night, so that He could be arrested secretly without the knowledge of His many supporters (Matt. 26:47–50).

Matthew reports that, realizing what he had done, Judas attempted to return the money to the priests. When the priests refused to take it, Judas threw the money on the Temple floor, went out, and hanged himself. Unwilling to use "blood money" for the Temple, the priests bought a potter's field, which became known as the "Field of Blood" (Matt. 27:3–10). But the Book of Acts reports that Judas bought the field himself with the money, fell headlong, and was disemboweled. This field is traditionally located at the point where the Kidron, Tyropoeon, and Hinnom valleys come together.

It is difficult to understand why Judas betrayed Jesus. Since he had access to the disciples' treasury, it seems unlikely that he did it for the money only; 30 pieces of silver is a relatively small amount. Some have suggested that Judas thought that his betrayal would force Jesus into asserting His true power and overthrowing the Romans. Others have suggested that Judas might have become convinced that Jesus was a false Messiah, and that the true Messiah was yet to come, or that he was upset over Jesus' apparent indifference to the law and His association with sinners and his violation of the Sabbath. Whatever the reason, Judas' motive remains shrouded in mystery.

Acts 1:20 quotes Psalm 109:8 as the basis for electing another person to fill the place vacated by Judas: "Let another take his office." When the 11 remaining apostles cast lots for Judas' replacement, "the lot fell on Matthias. And he was numbered with the eleven apostles" (Acts 1:26).

JUDAS MACCABAEUS [JOO duhs mak uh BEE uhs] (see MACCABEES).

JUDE [jood] (*praise*) — the author of the Epistle of Jude, in which he is described as "a servant of Jesus Christ, and brother of James" (Jude 1). Jude is an English form of the name Judas. Many scholars believe that the James mentioned in this passage is James the brother of Jesus. In Matthew 13:55 the people said concerning Jesus, "Is this not the carpenter's son? Is not His mother called Mary? And His brothers James, Joses, Simon, and Judas?" (Mark 6:3).

If Jude (Judas) was the brother of James and of Jesus, Jude did not believe in Him (John 7:5) until after Jesus' resurrection (Acts 1:14). The Bible tells nothing else about Jude.

JUDE, EPISTLE OF — the last of the general letters of the New Testament and the next to the last book of the Bible. Jude is a brief but hard-hitting epistle written by a man who believed in not allowing negative influences to destroy the church. Jude unmasks false teaching with pointed language and vivid images, while appealing to the faithful to remember the teachings of the apostles.

Structure of the Epistle. A salutation (vv. 1–2) is followed by a warning that "licentiousness" has found its way into the church (vv. 3–4). Such blasphemies will receive the judgment of God, as did sinful Israel (v. 5), rebellious angels (v. 6), and Sodom and Gomorrah (v. 7). Verses 8 through 13 note that the outrage of the blasphemers exceeds that of Satan himself and is similar to the rebellions of Cain (Gen. 4:3–8), Balaam (Numbers 22—24), and Korah (Num. 16:19–35). Their schemes are nothing new; Enoch of old prophesied their punishment (vv. 14–16). Christians need not be victimized by

---

JUDE: A Teaching Outline

Photo by Willem A. VanGemeren

The rugged, desolate Wadi Darga'n in the wilderness region of southern Judea.

such deceivers; their defense lies in remembering the words of the apostles and by working for the salvation of those caught in such errors (vv. 17–23). A famous benediction concludes the epistle (vv. 24–25).

Authorship and Date. The author of the epistle introduces himself as "Jude, a servant of Jesus Christ, and brother of James" (v. 1). There is no further identification, and the James mentioned is probably the Lord's brother (Gal. 1:19). Jude, therefore, would also be a brother of Jesus (Judas, Mark 6:3; Matt. 13:55), although not an apostle (Jude 17). The emphasis on remembering "the words which were spoken before the apostles" (v. 17) suggests that the epistle was composed sometime after the apostles had taught, thus favoring a date near the close of the first century.

Historical Setting. The Epistle of Jude has the character of a tract or brief essay written for a general Christian audience (v. 1). The author set out to write about "our common salvation" (v. 3), but the more pressing issue of false teachers launched him into a bitter attack on the "ungodly" (v. 15). Their ungodliness took the form of denying the lordship of Jesus Christ and, in the name of grace (v. 4), justifying a life that included immorality of all sorts (vv. 4, 7, 16), mercenary interests (v. 11, 16), cheap talk (v. 16), and utter worldliness (v. 19).

The false teachers attacked by Jude seem to have separated "spiritual " matters from behavior. Apparently they taught that the world is evil, and

therefore it makes little difference how one behaves. Like the Nicolaitans (Rev. 2:6, 15), the false teachers deserved the just punishment of God. They refused to recognize the implications of the incarnation—that if God cared enough to send His Son into the world, then He certainly cares how people behave in it.

Theological Contribution. Jude writes as a defender of the faith who is "contending earnestly for the faith which was once for all delivered to the saints" (v. 3). The "ungodly" are not the heathen outside the church; they are the false teachers inside (v. 12). Their association with the faith, however, does not mean they live in the faith: the ungodly have not the Spirit (v. 19), whereas the faithful do (v. 20); the ungodly remain in eternal darkness (v. 13), but the saints have eternal life (v. 21). Condemning his opponents in sharp imagery, Jude calls them "raging waves of the sea, foaming up their own shame; wandering stars for whom is reserved the blackness of darkness forever" (v. 13). The saints, on the other hand, must set their anchor in the teaching of the apostles (v. 17), and in the love of God (v. 21). They must work to retrieve those who have been deceived from certain destruction (vv. 22–23).

Special Consideration. Jude's last word on the problem of corruption in the church is preserved in a memorable benediction. Only God can keep us from error and bring us to Himself:

"Now to Him who is able to keep you from stumbling, and to present you faultless before the presence of His glory with exceeding joy, to God our Savior, who alone is wise, be glory and majesty, dominion and power, both now and forever. Amen."

JUDEA [joo DEE uh] — the Greco-Roman name for the land of Judah. Judea is first mentioned in Ezra 5:8 (Judaea, KJV), where it is used to designate a province of the Persian Empire. The word Judea comes from the adjective "Jewish," a term that was used of the Babylonian captives who returned to the Promised Land, most of whom were of the tribe of Judah.

Under the rule of the Persians, Judea was a district administered by a governor; usually this governor was a Jew (Hag. 1:14; 2:2). When Herod Archelaus was banished in A.D. 6, Judea ceased to exist as a separate district and was annexed to the Roman province of Syria. The governors of Judea, called PROCURATORS, were appointed by the Emperor; their official residence was at Caesarea. However, they were supervised by the proconsul of Syria, who ruled from Antioch (Luke 3:1). It was under this political arrangement that Jesus lived and ministered.

Judea extended from the Mediterranean Sea on the west to the Dead Sea on the east, and from a few miles south of Gaza and the southern tip of the Dead Sea north to about Joppa. Thus, Judea measured about 90 kilometers (56 miles) from north to south and from east to west. The region contained

Mount Tabor rises 1,300 feet above the Plain of Jezreel. The Book of Judges mentions this mountain in the account of Barak's attack against the army of Sisera (Judg. 4:14, 15).

four distinctive types of land: the coastal plains along the Mediterranean Sea, the lowlands in the south, the hill country, and the desert.

JUDGE (see OCCUPATIONS AND TRADES; LAW)

JUDGES, THE — military heroes or deliverers who led the nation of Israel against their enemies during the period between the death of Joshua and the establishment of the kingship. The stories of their exploits are found in the Book of JUDGES.

During the period of the judges, from about 1380—1050 B.C., the government of Israel was a loose confederation of tribes gathered about their central shrine, the ARK OF THE COVENANT. Without a human king to guide them, the people tended to rebel and fall into worship of false gods time and time again. "Everyone did what was right in his own eyes" (Judg. 17:6; 21:25) is how the Book of Judges describes these chaotic times. To punish the people, God would send foreign nations or tribes to oppress the Israelites.

These judges or charismatic leaders would rally the people to defeat the enemy. As God's agents for justice and deliverance, they would act decisively to free the nation from oppression. But the judges themselves were often weak, and their work was short-lived. The people would enter another stage of rebellion and idolatry, only to see the cycle of oppression and deliverance repeated all over again.

The judges themselves were a diverse lot. Some of them received only a brief mention in the Book of Judges. These minor judges were Shamgar (3:31); Tola (10:1-2), Jair (10:3-5), Ibzan (12:8-10), Elon (12:11-12), and Abdon (12:13-15).

The careers of other judges are explored in greater detail in the Book of Judges. Othniel, a nephew of Caleb, (3:7-11) was a warrior-deliverer who led the Israelites against the king of Mesopotamia. Ehud (3:12-30) was distinguished by left-handedness and his deftness with the dagger. Jephthah (11:1—12:7) was a harlot's son whose devotion to God was matched only by his rashness. Gideon (6:11—8:35) heeded many encouragements to act upon God's call. But he finally led 300 Israelites to defeat the entire army of the Midianites. The most interesting of the judges, perhaps, was Samson (13:1—16:31), whose frailties of the flesh led to his capture by the hated Philistines. The most courageous of the judges was Deborah, a woman who prevailed upon Barak to attack the mighty army of the Canaanites (4:1—5:31).

The stories of the judges make interesting reading because of their rugged personalities and the nature of the times in which they lived. The openness with which they are portrayed in all their weaknesses is one mark of the integrity of the Bible.

JUDGES, BOOK OF — a historical book of the Old Testament that covers the chaotic time between Joshua's death and the beginning of a centralized government under King Saul, a period of about 300 years. The "judges" for whom the book is named were actually military leaders whom God raised up to deliver His people from their enemies. Twelve of these heroic deliverers are mentioned in the book.

Structure of the Book. The introduction to Judges (1:1—3:6) describes the period after Joshua's death as a time of instability and moral depravity. Without a strong religious leader like Joshua to give them clear direction, the people of Israel fell into the worship of false gods. To punish the people, God delivered them into the hands of enemy nations. In their distress the people repented and cried out to God for help, and God answered their pleas by sending a "judge" or deliverer. In each instance after a period of faithfulness and security, the people once again forgot God, renewing the cycle of unfaithfulness all over again. This theme of sin-punishment-repentance-deliverance runs seven times throughout the book; it is introduced by the refrain, "The children of Israel again did evil in the sight of the Lord" (4:1).

The three best-known judges or deliverers described in the book are DEBORAH (4:1—5:31), GIDEON (6:1—9:57), and SAMSON (13:1—16:31). The other nine heroic figures from this period in Is-

JUDGES: A Teaching Outline

Part One: The Deterioration of Israel and Failure to Complete the Conquest of Canaan (1:1—3:4)

Part Two: The Deliverance of Israel (3:5—16:31)

Part Three: The Depravity of Israel (17:1—21:25)

rael's history are, OTHNIEL, EHUD, SHAMGAR, TOLA, JAIR, JEPHTHAH, IBZAN, ELON, and ABDON.

The Book of Judges contains some of the best-known stories in the Bible. One judge, Gideon, routed a Midianite army of several thousand with a group of 300 warriors. Under the cover of darkness, Gideon and his men hid lighted torches inside empty pitchers, then broke the pitchers and blew trumpets to catch the army by surprise. The mighty Midianites fled in panic (7:15–25).

An interesting part of the Gideon story is the way in which this judge of Israel tested what he perceived to be God's call. First, Gideon spread a piece of wool on the ground and asked God to saturate it with dew but leave the ground around it dry if he wanted Gideon to deliver Israel. This happened exactly that way. Still not satisfied, Gideon asked God to reverse this procedure the second night—to leave the wool dry with wet ground all around it. After this happened, Gideon agreed to lead his band of warriors against the Midianites (6:36–40).

Another famous story in the Book of Judges is about Samson and Delilah. A judge of superhuman strength, Samson defeated superior forces of the Philistine tribe several times by himself. They finally captured him after Delilah betrayed him by cutting his long hair, which was the secret of his strength. In captivity, Samson took thousands of his enemies to their death by pulling down the pillars of the temple where the Philistines were worshipping their pagan god Dagon (16:1–31).

Authorship and Date. Like the authors of several other historical books of the Old Testament, the author of Judges is unknown. But internal evidence gives us a clue about the probable date when it was written. The writer reminds us, "In those days there was no king in Israel; everyone did what was right in his own eyes" (17:6; 21:25). This statement tells us the book was written after the events described in Judges, probably during the days of King Saul or King David, about 1050 to 1000 B.C. Early Jewish scholars believed the book was written by Samuel, Israel's first prophet, who anointed Saul as the nation's first king. But this is impossible to determine from evidence presented by the book itself. At least we know that the unknown writer was a contemporary of Samuel.

Historical Setting. Israel's entry into the Promised Land under Joshua was not so much a total conquest as an occupation. Even after the land was divided among Israel's twelve tribes, the Israelites continued to face the possibility of domination by the warlike Canaanites who were never driven entirely out of the land. These were the enemies who threatened Israel repeatedly during the 300–year period of the judges, from about 1380 to 1050 B.C.

The Canaanite problem was intensified by Israel's loose form of tribal organization. The Israelites were easy targets for a well-organized enemy like the Canaanites. The first big task of the judges whom God raised up as deliverers was to rally the separate tribes behind them to rout the common enemy.

Theological Contribution. The Book of Judges points out the problems of the nation of Israel when the people had a succession of "judges" or military leaders to deliver them from their enemies. This is a subtle way of emphasizing the nation's need for a king or a strong, centralized form of government. But even the establishment of the kingship failed to lead to a state of perfection. Only after the right king, David, was placed on the throne did the nation break free of its tragic cycle of despair and decline. David, of course, as God's chosen servant, points to the great King to come, the Lord Jesus.

Judges also speaks of man's need for an eternal deliverer or a savior. The deliverance of the human judges was always temporary, partial, and imperfect. Some of the judges themselves were flawed and misdirected. The book points forward to Jesus Christ, the great Judge (Ps. 110:6), who is King and Savior of His people.

Special Considerations. Many readers are troubled by the rash vow of the judge Jephthah in the Book of Judges. He promised God that if he were victorious in battle, he would offer as a sacrifice the first thing to come out of his house to greet him on his return. The Lord did give Jephthah victory. On his return, his daughter came out of the house to greet him. And he was forced to carry out his terrible vow (11:29–40). This text is so troubling to some people that they seek to weaken it by claiming that Jephthah did not actually kill his daughter but only made her remain a virgin. This claim is based on the words, "She knew no man" (11:39). But the text indicates clearly that Jephthah did what he had vowed.

Human sacrifice was never sanctioned by the nation of Israel. Indeed, God condemned it as an evil of the surrounding nations. The point the author of Judges made in recording this deed is the same he had in mind as he recorded the sins and excesses of Samson. The period of the judges was a time of such religious and political chaos that even the best of God's servants were seriously flawed.

Deborah's song of victory (chap. 5) demonstrates a high degree of literary skill at this early period in Israel's history. It also shows clearly that women have made great contributions to God's work across the centuries. Another insight is that God deserves the praise when His people are victorious in battle.

Also see JUDGES, THE.

JUDGMENT — discernment or separation between good and evil. God judges among people and their actions according to the standards of His LAW. Judgment can refer either to this process of discernment or to the punishment meted out to those who fall under His wrath and condemnation (John 5:24).

In the Bible the most important judgment is the final judgment, the ultimate separation of good and evil at the end of history. The precise time of this judgment is appointed by God (Acts 17:31), but it

Painting depicting an Egyptian judgment scene. The dead man's heart is weighed on the scales in the afterlife, while the Egyptian god Thoth records the verdict.

Photo by Howard Vos

remains unknown to man (Matt. 24:36). The return of the Lord to earth, the resurrection of the dead, and the final judgment, together with the end of the world—all these may be thought of as belonging to a single complex of events at the end of time.

From earliest times it has been recognized that God Himself is the Judge of mankind (Gen. 18:25), and that He has the power and wisdom to judge with righteousness, truth, and justice (Ps. 96:13; 98:9). The final judgment is a task given specifically to God's Son (John 5:22; Acts 17:31) to conclude His work as mediator, deliver His people from sin, and destroy all God's enemies. God's people are associated with Christ in the exercise of this judgment (1 Cor. 6:2–3; Rev. 20:4).

The final judgment will be comprehensive in scope; it will include all people and nations from the beginning of the world to the end of history (Matt. 25:31–46; Rom. 14:10–12), as well as fallen angels (2 Pet. 2:4). Those who trust in the Lord, repent of sin, and walk in His ways will not be condemned but will enter into eternal life (Ps. 1). The purpose of the final judgment is the glory of God through the salvation of the ELECT and the condemnation of the ungodly (2 Thess. 1:3–10).

The final judgment has been anticipated throughout history in a series of judgments brought by God upon the wicked. The whole world was affected by the FLOOD and by the confusion of tongues at the Tower of BABEL (Gen. 6—8; 11:1–9). The heathen nations, such as the Egyptians and Canaanites, also experienced God's judgments, just as God's people, the Israelites, did when they persisted in rebellion. These judgments serve as a continual warning of the consequences of unbelief.

The death of Jesus Christ is unique among these judgments of history. Through His death God paid the judgment price demanded by mankind's sin. The death and resurrection of Jesus are the foundations on which sinners are saved (Is. 53:5) through their trust in Him as Lord and Savior.

God's role as judge is reflected in the leadership functions of political officials, who uphold order in society and execute judgment on evildoers (Rom. 13:1–7). The rulers of Israel bore special responsibility in this respect (Deut. 16:18–19), as do the leaders of the church today (Matt. 18:17–18). Believers also have a responsibility to judge matters of wrongdoing among themselves (Matt. 18:15), but this should always be done fairly and with compassion. Believers are never to take over the task of judgment that belongs to God alone (Heb. 10:30).

JUDITH [JOO dith] (*the praised one*) — one of the two Hittite wives of Esau (Gen. 26:34). Although she was a Hittite, her name is pure Hebrew, the feminine form of Judah.

JUDITH, BOOK OF (see APOCRYPHA).

JUG — a container of animal skins or earthenware, used for holding liquids (Judg. 4:17–21; bottle, KJV; skin, RSV, NEB, NIV).

JULIA [JOOL yuh] (meaning unknown) — a Christian woman at Rome to whom the apostle Paul sent greetings (Rom. 16:15).

JULIUS [JOOL yuhs) (meaning unknown) — a Roman centurion who conducted the apostle Paul and some other prisoners from Caesarea to Rome (Acts 27:1).

JUNIA [JOO nih uh] (*pertaining to Juno*) — a Jewish Christian at Rome to whom the apostle Paul sent greetings (Rom. 16:7; Junias, NIV, RSV, NEB).

JUNIPER (see PLANTS OF THE BIBLE).

JUPITER [JOO pih tur] (see GODS, PAGAN).

JUSHAB–HESED [JOO shub HEE sed] (*returner of kindness*) — a son of Zerubbabel (1 Chr. 3:20).

JUSTICE — the practice of what is right and just. Justice (or "judgment," KJV) specifies what is right, not only as measured by a code of law, but also by what makes for right relationships as well as harmony and peace.

The English term justice has a strong legal flavor. But the concept of justice in the Bible goes beyond the law courts to everyday life. The Bible speaks of "doing justice" (Ps. 82:3; Prov. 21:3), whereas we speak of "getting justice." Doing justice is to maintain what is right or to set things right. Justice is done when honorable relations are maintained between husbands and wives, parents and children, employers and employees, government and citizens, and man and God. Justice refers to brotherliness in spirit and action.

Kings, rulers, and those in power are to be instruments of justice (Ps. 72:1), as exemplified by David (2 Sam. 8:15) and Josiah (Jer. 22:15–16). The prophet Micah declared, "He has shown you, O man, what is good; and what does the Lord require of you but to do justly, to love mercy, and to walk humbly with your God?" (Mic. 6:8). The Book of Isaiah describes God's suffering servant, a description best fulfilled in Jesus, as one whose task as ruler will be to bring justice to the nations (Is. 42:1–4).

The prophets of the Old Testament were champions of social justice. During those days, justice was often perverted through bribery and favoritism or partiality (Deut. 1:17; Prov. 17:23). But God's rewards come to those who practice justice in all their dealings with others. In the words of the prophet Amos, "let justice run down like water, and righteousness like a mighty stream" (Amos 5:24).

JUSTICE OF GOD — God's fair and impartial treatment of all people. As a God of justice (Is. 30:18), He is interested in fairness as well as in what makes for right relationships. His actions and decisions are true and right (Job 34:12; Rev. 16:7). His demands on individuals and nations to look after victims of oppression are just demands (Psalm 82).

As Lord and Judge, God brings justice to nations (Ps. 67:4) and "sets things right" in behalf of the poor, the oppressed, and the victims of injustice (Ps. 103:6; 146:6–9). For the wicked, the unjust, and the oppressor, God as supreme Judge of the earth is a dreaded force. But for all who are unjustly treated, God's just action is reason for hope.

JUSTIFICATION — the process by which sinful human beings are made acceptable to a holy God.

Justification by Grace. Christianity is unique because of its teaching of justification by grace (Rom. 3:24). Justification is God's declaration that the demands of His Law have been fulfilled in the righteousness of His Son. The basis for this justification is the death of Christ. Paul tells us that "God was in Christ reconciling the world to Himself, not imputing their trespasses to them" (2 Cor. 5:19). This reconciliation covers all sin: "For by one offering He has perfected forever those who are being sanctified" (Heb. 10:14). Justification, then, is based on the work of Christ, accomplished through His blood (Rom. 5:9) and brought to His people through His resurrection (Rom. 4:25).

When God justifies, He charges the sin of man to Christ and credits the righteousness of Christ to the believer (2 Cor. 5:21). Thus, "through one Man's righteous act, the free gift came to all men, resulting in justification of life" (Rom. 5:18). Because this righteousness is "the righteousness of God" which is "apart from the law" (Rom. 3:21), it is thorough; a believer is "justified from all things" (Acts 13:39). God is "just" because His holy standard of perfect righteousness has been fulfilled in Christ, and He is the "justifier," because this righteousness is freely given to the believer (Rom. 3:26; 5:16).

Justification by Faith. Although the Lord Jesus has paid the price for our justification, it is through our faith that He is received and His righteousness is ex-

perienced and enjoyed (Rom. 3:25–30). Faith is considered righteousness (Rom. 4:3, 9), not as the work of man (Rom. 4:5), but as the gift and work of God (John 6:28–29; Phil. 1:29).

The New Testament sometimes seems to speak of justification by works. For example, Jesus spoke of justification (and condemnation) "by your words" (Matt. 12:37). Paul said, "the doers of the law will be justified" (Rom. 2:13). And James concluded that "a man is justified by works, and not by faith only" (James 2:24).

These statements seem to conflict with Paul's many warnings that "by the deeds of the law no flesh will be justified in His sight" (Rom. 3:20), and that the attempt to be justified through law is equivalent to being "estranged from Christ" and "fallen from grace" (Gal. 5:4).

The solution to this problem lies in the distinction between the works of the flesh and the fruit of the Spirit (Gal. 5:16–25). Not only is Christ's righteousness legally accounted to the believer, but Christ also dwells in the believer through the Holy Spirit (Rom. 8:10), creating works of faith (Eph. 2:10). Certainly God's works may be declared righteous (Is. 26:12). If this is true, then the order of events in justification is grace, faith, and works; or, in other words, by grace, through faith, resulting in works (Eph. 2:8–10).

The Results of Justification. The negative result of justification is what we are saved from: "Having now been justified…we shall be saved from wrath" (Rom. 5:9). The positive result is what we are saved to: "Whom He justified, these He also glorified" (Rom. 8:30).

Paul also notes "peace with God" (Rom. 5:1) and access to God's grace (Rom. 5:2) as positive benefits. The believer in Christ may look forward to the redemption of his body (Rom. 8:23) and an eternal inheritance (Rom. 8:17; 1 Pet. 1:4).

JUSTUS [JUHS tuhs] (*righteous*) — the name of three men in the New Testament:

1. A surname of Joseph, also called Barsabas, who was one of the two disciples the apostles considered to take the place of Judas Iscariot (Acts 1:23).

2. A godly man of Corinth with whom the apostle Paul lodged (Acts 18:7).

3. A Jewish Christian in Rome who sent greetings to the church at Colosse (Col. 4:11), also called Jesus.

JUTTAH [JUH tuh] (*extended*) — a town in the hill country of Judah (Josh. 15:55) given to the Levites as a city of refuge (Josh. 21:13–16). It is now called Yatta and is about nine kilometers (five miles) southwest of Hebron.

K

KAB [kab] (*a hollow vessel*) — a Hebrew dry measure (2 Kin. 6:25; cab, KJV). According to the Jewish rabbis, a kab was the 18th part of an ephah, or about 1.16 dry quarts. Other authorities, however, believe the kab was somewhat larger, between three pints and two English quarts. Also see WEIGHTS AND MEASURES.

KABZEEL [KAB zih uhl] (*God gathers*) — a city in southeastern Judah near the border of Edom (Josh. 15:21).

KADESH, KADESH BARNEA [kay DESH bar NEE uh] (*consecrated*) — a wilderness region between Egypt and the land of Canaan where the Hebrew people camped during the Exodus (see Map 2, C-1). Kadesh Barnea was situated on the edge of Edom (Num. 20:16) about 114 kilometers (70 miles) from Hebron and 61 kilometers (50 miles) from Beersheba in the Wilderness of Zin. Kadesh Barnea is also said to be in the Wilderness of Paran (Num. 13:26). Paran was the general name for the larger wilderness area, while Zin was the specific name for a smaller portion of the wilderness territory.

The first mention of Kadesh Barnea occurred during the time of Abraham. Chedorlaomer, king of Elam, and his allied armies waged war against the Amalekites and Amorites from Kadesh (Gen. 14:7). When Hagar was forced by Sarah to flee from Abraham's home, she was protected by the Angel of the Lord, who brought her to the well Beer Lahai Roi, between Kadesh and Bered (16:14). Later Abraham moved to Gerar, situated between Kadesh and Shur (20:1).

The most important contacts of the Israelites with Kadesh Barnea occurred during the years of the Exodus and wilderness wanderings. During the second year of the Exodus from Egypt, the Israelites camped around Mt. Horeb, or Sinai. God told them to leave Sinai and take an 11-day journey to Kadesh Barnea (Num. 10:11–12; Deut. 1:2). From here the people would have direct entry into the land of Canaan. Moses selected one man from each tribe as a spy and sent them to "spy out the land" (Num. 13:2). After 40 days they returned with grapes and other fruits, proving Canaan to be a fertile, plentiful land.

Ten of these spies reported giants in the land, implying that Israel was too weak to enter Canaan (Num. 13:33). But two of the spies, Joshua and Caleb, said, "Do not fear" (Num. 14:9). The people wanted to stone the two for their report (Num. 14:10), and they went so far as to ask for another leader to take them back to Egypt.

Because of their fear and rebellion at Kadesh (Deut. 9:23), the Israelites were forced to wander in the Wilderness of Paran for 38 years. Kadesh ap-

An exhausted traveler rests in the shade of a broom bush in the wilderness of Kadesh (1 Kin. 9:4).

parently was their headquarters while they moved about during these years. In the first month of the 40th year of the Exodus, the people again assembled at Kadesh for their final march to the Promised Land.

While they were still camped at Kadesh, a number of the leaders of the people rebelled against Moses and Aaron (Num. 16:1–3). They were killed in an earthquake (16:31, 32). Miriam, Moses' sister, also died and was buried (20:1). At Kadesh, Moses also disobeyed God by striking the rock to bring forth water (20:8–11). He had been told to speak, not strike the rock. Soon after Moses and the people began to move from Kadesh toward Canaan, Aaron died and was buried (20:23–29).

The events at Kadesh Barnea clearly demonstrate the peril of rebelling against God's appointed leaders, murmuring and complaining about God's directions, and refusing to follow God's orders.

KADMIEL [KAD mih uhl] (*God is first*) — the name of three men in the Old Testament:

1. A Levite whose descendants returned from the Captivity with Zerubbabel (Ezra 2:40).

2. A Levite who helped rebuild the Temple after the Captivity (Ezra 3:9).

3. A Levite who sealed the covenant after the Captivity (Neh. 9:4–5).

KADMONITES [KAD muh nights] (*people of the east*) — a nomadic Canaanite tribe that inhabited Palestine in Abraham's time (Gen. 15:19), living in the Syrian desert between Egypt and Mesopotamia.

KAIN [kayn] (*smith*) — the name of a tribe and a town in the Old Testament:

1. A tribe mentioned in Balaam's fourth prophecy (Num. 24:22).

2. A town in the mountain country of Judah (Josh. 15:57), also spelled Cain (KJV, NEB).

KAIWAN (see GODS, PAGAN).

KALLAI [KAL eye] (*swift*) — a priest who returned from the Captivity with Zerubbabel (Neh. 12:20).

KAMON [KAY muhn] — a form of CAMON.

KANAH [KAY nuh] (*brook of reeds*) — the name of a brook and a city in the Old Testament:

1. A brook (or "gorge," NEB) that served as a boundary between the territories of Ephraim and Manasseh.

2. A city on the northern border of the territory of Asher (Josh. 19:28).

KAPH [caf] — the 11th letter of the Hebrew alphabet, used as a heading over Psalm 119:81–88. In the original Hebrew language, every line of these eight verses began with the letter kaph. Also see ACROSTIC.

KAREAH [kuh REE uh] (*bald*) — the father of Johanan and Jonathan (Jer. 41:11–16; Careah, 2 Kin. 25:23, KJV).

KARKAA [KAHR kih uh] (*floor*) — an unknown

site on the southern border of the territory of Judah (Josh. 15:3).

KARKOR [KAHR kohr] (*level ground*) — a place in TRANSJORDAN where Gideon and his army defeated the remnants of the Midianite army (Judg. 8:1–21).

KARNAIM [kar NAY im] (*two peaks*) — a city in northern TRANSJORDAN (Amos 6:13). It is probably the same place as Ashteroth Karnaim (Gen. 14:5).

KARTAH [KAHR tuh] (*city*) — a city in the territory of Zebulun assigned to the Levites (Josh. 21:34).

KARTAN [KAHR tan] (*city*) — a city in the territory of Naphtali given to the Gershonite Levites (Josh. 21:32). Also called Kirjathaim (1 Chr. 6:76), Kartan was one of the CITIES OF REFUGE.

KATTATH [KAT ath] (*small*) — a city in the territory of Zebulun (Josh. 19:15), probably the same city as Kitron (Judg. 1:30).

KATYDID (see ANIMALS OF THE BIBLE).

KEDAR [KEE dur] (*mighty*) — the name of a man and a tribe in the Old Testament:

1. The second son of Ishmael (Gen. 25:13).

2. The tribe which sprang from Kedar, as well as the territory inhabited by this tribe in the northern Arabian desert (Is. 21:16–17).

KEDEMAH [KED eh muh] (*eastern*) — the youngest son of Ishmael and the name of an Arabian tribe (1 Chr. 1:31).

KEDEMOTH [KED uh mahth] (*ancient places*) — a city of the territory of Reuben assigned to the Levites (Josh. 13:18). From the Wilderness of Kedemoth, Moses sent messengers to Sihon the Amorite, requesting permission to pass through his land (Deut. 2:26–27).

KEDESH [KEE desh] (*holy*) — the name of three cities in the Old Testament:

1. A city in the territory of Naphtali allotted to the Levites and made a city of refuge (Judg. 4:6; Kedesh–naphtali, KJV).

2. A city in southern Judah (Josh. 15:23).

3. A Canaanite city conquered by Joshua allotted to the tribe of Issachar and given to the Levites (1 Chr. 6:72). This city is also called Kishion (Josh. 19:20) or Kishon (Josh. 21:28, KJV).

KEDESH–NAPHTALI [KEE desh NAF tuh ligh] — a form of KEDESH No. 1.

KEHELATHAH [kee uh LAY thuh] (*assembly*) — a desert camp of the Israelites between Egypt and the Promised Land (Num. 33:22–23).

KEILAH [kee EYE luh] (*fortress*) — the name of a man and a city in the Old Testament:

1. A descendant of Caleb, of the family of Judah (1 Chr. 4:19).

2. A fortified city in the lowland plain of the territory of Judah, about 29 kilometers (18 miles) southwest of Jerusalem (Josh. 15:44). David and

about 600 of his men attacked the Philistine army at Keilah and "struck them with a mighty blow" (1 Sam. 23:5), saving the city.

KELAIAH [kih LAY uh] (meaning unknown) — a priest who divorced his pagan wife after the Captivity (Ezra 10:23).

KELITA [kih LIGH tuh] (*dwarf*) — the name of two men in the Old Testament:
1. A priest who interpreted the Law to the people when it was read by Ezra (Neh. 8:7).
2. A Levite who sealed the covenant made by Nehemiah (Neh. 10:10). He may be the same person as Kelita No. 1.

KELUHI [keh LOU high] — A form of CHELUH.

KEMUEL [KEM yoo uhl] (*helper of God*) — the name of three men in the Old Testament:
1. The father of Aram (Gen. 22:21).
2. A leader of the tribe of Ephraim (Num. 34:24).
3. The father of Hashabiah (1 Chr. 27:17).

KENAN [KEE nuhn] — a form of CAINAN.

KENATH [KEE nath] (meaning unknown) — a city on the northeastern border of Israelite territory. Kenath was the easternmost city of the DECAPOLIS. It has been identified with Kanawat, on the western slope of Jebel Hauran (Mount Bashan), about 100 kilometers (62 miles) east of the Sea of Galilee.

KENAZ [KEE naz] (meaning unknown) — the name of three men in the Old Testament:
1. A son of Eliphaz (Gen. 36:11, 15).
2. The father of Othniel the judge (Judg. 1:13).
3. A son of Elah and grandson of Caleb (1 Chr. 4:15).

KENEZZITES [KEE nuh zights] — an Edomite tribe of Canaan in the time of Abraham (Gen. 15:19; Kenizzites, KJV, RSV, NEB, NIV, NAS). Before the conquest of Canaan by Joshua, the Kenezzites apparently lived in the NEGEV, the desert of southern Judah, and in the border regions of Edom, south of the Dead Sea. Some of the Kenezzites were absorbed by the tribe of Judah and others by the Edomites.

The Kenezzites were related to the Kenites and, like the Kenites, were skilled workers in metal. Their name probably comes from KENAZ, a descendant of Esau (Gen. 36:11, 15); he is listed among the Edomite chieftains (Gen. 36:42). Jephunneh the Kenezzite apparently married a woman of the tribe of Judah; their son CALEB (the spy) was a godly man who followed the Lord God of Israel.

KENITES [KEE nights] (*metalsmiths*) — the name of a wandering tribe of people who were associated with the Midianites (Judg. 1:16) and, later, with the Amalekites (1 Sam. 15:6). The Kenites lived in the desert regions of Sinai, Midian, Edom, Amalek, and the Negev. The Bible first mentions the Kenites as one of the groups that lived in Canaan during the time of Abraham (Gen. 15:19); their territory was to be taken by the Israelites (Num. 24:21–22).

The Kenites were metal craftsmen who may have traced their ancestry to TUBAL–CAIN (Gen. 4:22).

Around the time of Israel's exodus from Egypt, the Kenites showed kindness to Israel (1 Sam. 15:6). Moses' father–in–law, Jethro is called a Midianite (Ex. 18:1) and a Kenite (Judg. 1:16). Some scholars suggest the skill in smelting and casting the golden calf (Ex. 32) and the bronze serpent (Num. 21) may have been learned by Moses from the Kenites. Some Kenites were among those who entered the Promised Land along with the Israelites in the conquest led by Joshua (Judg. 1:16).

KENIZZITES [KEE nuh zights] — a form of KENEZZITES.

KENOSIS [keh NOE sis] — a theological term used in connection with the dual nature of Jesus as fully human and fully divine. The word comes from a Greek verb which means "to empty" (Phil. 2:7). The NASB translates this passage, "He emptied Himself," but the KJV and NKJV express it, "He made Himself of no reputation."

The Bible teaches that our Savior was both fully divine and completely human during His earthly life. But nowhere does Scripture explain exactly how Jesus' two natures co–existed. Theologians have struggled for years to explain this mystery. In the 1800s certain scholars formulated the Kenosis theory, which asserts on the basis of Philippians 2:7 that God's divine Son laid aside, or "emptied Himself," of certain divine attributes when He became human. However, these theories of Jesus' INCARNATION have been rejected by orthodox biblical scholars. Such views usually boil down to statements that when He became a man, Jesus stopped being God, or that He was first God, then became a man, and finally returned to being God after His resurrection.

Grammatically, Paul explains the "emptying" of Jesus in the next phrase: "Taking the form of a servant and coming in the likeness of men." He does not say that Jesus stopped being God or that He gave up any divine attributes. Although John 17:5 shows that Jesus' glory as God's eternal Son was veiled during His incarnation (Ex. 33:18, 20; 1 Tim. 6:16), we should take the phrase *He emptied Himself*, in a figurative sense as a reference to Christ's humility and willingness to "partake of flesh and blood" (Heb. 2:14). While not ceasing to be God's Son, Christ also became God's Servant.

KEREN–HAPPUCH [KER uhn HAP uhk] (*horn of antimony*) — the youngest of Job's three daughters, apparently born after his restoration to prosperity and health (Job 42:14). Also see JEMIMAH and KEZIAH.

KERIOTH [KER ih ahth] (*the cities*) — the name of two cities in the Old Testament:
1. A city of Judah in the Negev near Edom (Josh. 15:25). Judas, the disciple who betrayed Jesus, was probably a native of Kerioth since the name Iscariot means "man of Kerioth."
2. A fortified city in Moab (Jer. 48:24). Kerioth is

probably the same place as Ar, the ancient capital of Moab.

KEROS [KIR ahs] (*bent*) — one of the Temple servants whose descendants returned from the Captivity with Zerubbabel (Ezra 2:44).

KERYGMA [kay RIG mah] — the proclamation, or preaching, of the message of the gospel in the New Testament church. The word is a transliteration of the Greek word which means "proclamation," "preaching," or "message preached" (1 Cor. 1:21).

KESITAH [KESS ih tah] (see WEIGHTS AND MEASURES).

KETTLE — a cooking pot in which meat was prepared by worshipers before being offered to God as a SACRIFICE, or PEACE OFFERING (1 Sam. 2:14). Phinehas and Hophni, the evil and corrupt sons of Eli the high priest, were not content with the priest's portion (Lev. 7:14). They also reached into the worshiper's cooking pot with a fork to add to what was rightfully theirs. The kettle is only one of four different utensils mentioned in this passage. This may indicate that the meal prepared as a peace offering was conducted without specific regulations.

KETURAH [keh TUR uh] (*fragrance*) — a wife of Abraham (Gen. 25:1, 4), also called Abraham's concubine (1 Chr. 1:32–33). Some suggest that Keturah had been Abraham's "concubine-wife," before the death of Sarah. After Sarah died, Keturah was then elevated to the full status of Abraham's wife. Keturah bore to Abraham six sons: Zimran, Jokshan, Medan, Midian, Ishbak, and Shuah (Gen. 25:1–4). These men were the founders or ancestors of six Arabian tribes in southern and eastern Palestine. Late Arabian genealogies mention a tribe by the name of Katura dwelling near Mecca.

Keturah's sons were not on the same level as Abraham's promised son, Isaac. Through Isaac God would carry out His promise to Abraham to make of his descendants a CHOSEN PEOPLE. While he was still alive, therefore, Abraham gave Keturah's sons gifts and sent them to "the country of the east" (Gen. 25:6).

Abraham was already advanced in years when he married Keturah. She brought him both companionship and children in his old age. Keturah apparently outlived Abraham (Gen. 25:7).

KEVEH [keh VAY] — probably an ancient name for the province of CILICIA, in Asia Minor (modern Turkey). King Solomon imported horses from Egypt and Keveh (1 Kin. 10:28; 2 Chr. 1:16; Kue, RSV, NASB, NIV; Coa, NEB).

KEY — the tool that releases a lock (Judg. 3:25). The key is also spoken of symbolically in the Bible as a sign of authority. The prophet Isaiah described a time when Eliakim, son of Hilkiah, would be elevated as the king's steward (2 Kin. 18:18). The prophet declared that He would be given "the key of the House of David" (Is. 22:22), or the authority to act in the king's name. This is probably the background for a proper understanding of the statement of Jesus that the "keys of the kingdom of heaven" were being given to Peter (Matt. 16:19). As the Messiah from the line of David, Jesus was calling on Peter to take on leadership responsibility for the young church.

Jesus condemned the SCRIBES of His day because they had "taken away the key of knowledge" (Luke 11:52). According to their interpretation, only they had the right to explain the meaning of God's Law, or the Scriptures. They failed to share this knowledge with the common people.

KEYS, POWER OF — a phrase used by Jesus to describe the authority given by Him to His disciples. In ancient times a KEY expressed the idea of authority, power, or privilege. Jesus told Peter that He would give him "the keys of the kingdom of heaven" (Matt. 16:19). The result of this authority in Peter's life would be the power to bind or loose. These words for bind and loose stem from Aramaic words which carried the idea of excommunication and reinstatement, or determining objects either clean or unclean.

The general Protestant view is that the church is the agent of this power or authority to bind or loose, either through its official leaders or through all believers. This authority or power was best applied in New Testament times when the apostles announced the conditions for entrance into the

The Kidron Valley, just outside the walls of Jerusalem. Jesus and His disciples crossed this valley and its brook on their way to the Garden of Gethsemane (John 18:1).

kingdom. This authority was continued through the preaching of the gospel by Peter and the church as described in the Book of Acts.

KEZIAH [kih ZIE uh] (*cinnamon*) — a daughter of Job born after his restoration to prosperity and health (Job. 42:14; Kezia, KJV).

KEZIZ [KEE ziz] — a form of EMEK KEZIZ.

KIBROTH HATTAAVAH [KIB rahth huh TAY uh vuh] (*the graves of gluttony*) — a campsite on the Sinai Peninsula between the Wilderness of Sinai and Hazeroth (Num. 11:34–35). The name of this place came from the many Israelites who died from a plague in this region.

KIBZAIM [kib ZAY uhm] (*double gathering*) — a city of Ephraim assigned to the Kohathite Levites and made one of the CITIES OF REFUGE (Josh. 21:22).

KID (see ANIMALS OF THE BIBLE).

KIDNAPPER — one who captures a person by force (Ex. 21:16; 1 Tim. 1:10). In biblical times the motive for kidnapping was to sell into slavery and not to extort a ransom, as in modern times. According to the Law of Moses, the kidnapping of an Israelite, either to sell him into slavery or to treat him as a slave, was a crime punishable by death (Deut. 24:7).

KIDNEY — either of the organs in man and animals which discharges waste material into the urinary tract. The kidneys and the connected fat of sacrificial animals were burned on the altar as part of several of the offerings commanded in the Law (Lev. 3:4; 4:9; 7:4). When kidney refers to human beings, it is always used symbolically to mean someone's mind (Ps. 16:7; Jer. 12:2) or innermost being (Job 17:3; Prov. 23:16). Sometimes when kidney is used this way, it is translated "heart." A common biblical expression is that God examines the "kidneys and heart"—that He thoroughly knows a person's inner thoughts and motives (Ps. 7:9; 26:2; Jer. 11:20; Rev. 2:23; reins and heart, KJV).

KIDRON [KIH drun] (*gloomy*) — a valley on the eastern slope of Jerusalem through which a seasonal brook of the same name runs. The meaning of the name is fitting, in view of the great strife which has surrounded the Kidron throughout Bible times. A torrent in the winter rains, it contains little water in the summer months.

The ravine of the Kidron valley begins north of Jerusalem, running past the Temple, Calvary, the Garden of Gethsemane, and the Mount of Olives to form a well-defined limit to Jerusalem on its eastern side. From there the valley and the brook reach into the Judean wilderness, where the land is so dry that the brook takes the name of Wadyen-Nar or "fire wady." Finally its dreary course brings it to the Dead Sea.

Kidron was the brook crossed by David while fleeing from Absalom (2 Sam. 15:23, 30). While the brook is not large, the deep ravine is a significant geographical obstacle. When David crossed the Kidron and turned east to retreat from Absalom to the safety of Hebron, he signaled his abandonment of Jerusalem (2 Sam. 15:23).

On the west side of the Kidron is the spring of GIHON which King Hezekiah tapped for city water before the Assyrians besieged the city of Jerusalem. Hezekiah also blocked the Kidron and lesser springs in the valley to deny water to the besieging Assyrians.

Asa, Hezekiah, and Josiah, the great reforming kings of Judah, burned the idols and objects of worship of the pagan cults which they suppressed in the Kidron valley (1 Kin. 15:13). Beside the brook King Asa destroyed and burned his mother's idol of Asherah (1 Kin. 15:13). After this, the valley became the regular receptacle for the impurities and abominations of idol worship when they were removed from the Temple and destroyed (2 Kin. 23:4, 6, 12; 2 Chr. 29:16; 30:14).

From the Kidron valley Nehemiah inspected the walls of Jerusalem at night, probably because the walls were clearly visible along that side (Neh. 2:15). In the time of Josiah, this valley was the common cemetery of Jerusalem (2 Kin. 23:6; Jer. 26:23). When Jesus left Jerusalem for the Garden of Gethsemane on the night of His arrest, He must have crossed the Kidron along the way.

KILN — an oven or furnace used for hardening brick (Nah. 3:14). Brick kilns were rare in Palestine; some scholars believe, therefore, that in David's time the reference is likely to a brick mold rather than to a brick kiln.

KINAH [KIGH nuh] (*lamentation*) — a city on the southern boundary of Judah, probably not far from the Dead Sea (Josh. 15:22).

KINDNESS, LOVINGKINDNESS — God's loyal love and favor toward His people. In the Old Testament, the word translated as "kindness" or "lovingkindness" refers to God's long-suffering love—His determination to keep His promises to His chosen people in spite of their sin and rebellion (Deut. 7:12; Hos. 2:14–23). This attribute of God was shown through His divine mercy and forgiveness toward sinners when payment of sins through the sacrificial system was no longer effective (Deut. 22:22; Ps. 51:1).

In the New Testament, the Greek word translated as "grace" best represents the idea of God's kindness or lovingkindness. Because God has been gracious toward believers, they should treat all people with kindness or grace (Luke 6:35). All people are created in God's image and should be treated accordingly, no matter how badly they have twisted and deformed that image (Jas. 3:9). Kindness is not an apathetic response to sin, but a deliberate act to bring the sinner back to God (Hos. 2:14–23; Rom. 2:4).

KINDRED — blood kin or relatives. Family was important among the Hebrew people because the clan or tribe was the basic social unit, at least until the time of the United Kingdom under David and Solomon. The family had the responsibility for protecting and preserving its members from injustices at the hand of others (Gen. 34:1–31) or from slavery or loss of land due to poverty.

Protection against loss of land was provided for by the kinsman–redeemer, who would pay the loan or buy the land to keep it within the family group (Lev. 25:23–38, 47–53). If a member of the family was killed, another family member acted as the avenger of blood and retaliated against the killer (Ex. 21:14; Num. 35:19).

God Himself has special care for His family, which includes all who believe in Jesus Christ (John 1:12; 2 Cor. 6:18).

KINE (see ANIMALS OF THE BIBLE).

KING, KINGDOM — ruler of a nation or territory, especially one who inherits his position and rules for life; a state or nation with a form of government in which a king or queen serves as supreme ruler.

In the ancient world a king was generally the ruler over a specific region or city. His office was usually hereditary and his authority derived from it. In Egypt the king, or Pharaoh, was regarded as a god; in Assyria the king represented a god. Both the Canaanites and the Philistines had kings as early as the time of Abraham (Gen. 14:2; 20:2). Many of the other nations related to Israel—Edom, Moab, Midian, and Ammon—adopted the kingship form of government earlier than Israel (Gen. 36:31; Judg. 11:1).

Long before the Israelites chose Saul as their first king, Israel had been a religious community with God Himself as the ruler. God had promised Abraham that kings would come from him (Gen. 17:6). The same promise was given to Jacob (Gen. 35:11).

During the Exodus of the Hebrew people from Egypt and the conquest of Canaan several years later, Moses and Joshua exercised "royal" authority, but only as representatives of God. Following Joshua's death, various cities and villages had ELDERS (Josh. 24:31; Judg. 11:5) to whom the people looked for leadership. Occasionally God appointed certain leaders called JUDGES who would lead an army against foreign oppression (Judg. 2:16–19). These leaders, however, were not strong religious personalities. They had no official authority, and their rule was local and temporary.

At the insistence of the people of Israel, Samuel anointed Saul as the first king of the Hebrew nation (1 Sam. 10:1). Samuel regarded the demand for a king as an act of rebellion (1 Samuel 8), because the moral decline of the nation had created a desire for a monarchy that would be similar to the form of government of all the surrounding nations. Some scholars argue, however, that the introduction of the kingship in Israel was a historical necessity, brought about by a desperate political situation—oppression by the Philistines.

After establishment of the kingship under Saul

Photo by Howard Vos

The gold mask buried with Pharaoh Tutankhamon of Egypt about 1350 B.C., illustrating the wealth of his kingdom.

and David, SOLOMON became king of the United Kingdom. Under his administration, the Hebrew people reached new levels of prestige and power. Solomon entered trade agreements with other nations and completed many impressive building projects. But to pay for all these great accomplishments, Solomon placed burdensome taxes upon the people and even forced them to work as laborers on his building projects. At Solomon's death, the United Kingdom split into two separate nations—Judah in the south and Israel in the north. During the rest of their history, these two nations were ruled by their own individual kings. Accounts of the reigns of many of these kings are found in the books of 1 and 2 Kings in the Old Testament.

The New Testament speaks of several specific kings, including Herod the king (Matt. 2:1) and King Agrippa (Acts 25:24). They were actually governors or rulers over political provinces or territories of the ROMAN EMPIRE, serving under appointment by the Roman emperor.

A kingdom that would typify Christ's coming kingdom was in God's plan (Deut. 17:15). Israel's king was supposed to be responsible to God alone. This king was God's servant and only the earthly representative of the Lord, who was Israel's true king. In that office he was expected to know and do the Law of God (Deut. 17:18–20). He was to be a proclaimer and teacher of the law and one who judged wisely and righteously (1 Kin. 3:28; 2 Chr. 17:7).

David was clearly God's choice to be king (1 Sam. 16:7, 12–13). The hereditary kingship, therefore, began with him; from him would descend Jesus Christ, "the Lion of the tribe of Judah, the Root of David" (Rev. 5:5). In the light of the Messiah's descent from David, the meaning of God's COVENANT with David becomes clear: "I will establish the throne of his kingdom forever" (2 Sam. 7:13; also Ps. 2; 110; Is. 11:1–4).

The Bible used the title king not only of human rulers, but also of God as the Supreme Ruler of the world (Ps. 47:2, 7; Matt. 5:35). As the Creator of the world, it is His right to rule the universe. Only by His authority do earthly kings reign (Deut. 10:17; Dan. 4:17).

Christ Jesus the Messiah was born a king (Matt. 2:2), came preaching the kingdom of God (Mark 1:15), died as a king (Mark 15:32), and will yet be seen as King of kings and Lord of lords (1 Tim. 6:15; Rev. 19:16). He functions as a King–Priest (Heb. 5:6; 7:1; Rev. 11:15), enabling us to become heirs of the kingdom which He has established through His sacrificial death on the cross.

KINGDOM OF GOD, KINGDOM OF HEAVEN

KINGDOM OF GOD, KINGDOM OF HEAVEN — God's rule of grace in the world, a future period foretold by the prophets of the Old Testament and identified by Jesus as beginning with His public ministry. The kingdom of God is the experience of blessedness, like that of the Garden of Eden, where evil is fully overcome and where those who live in the kingdom know only happiness, peace, and joy. This was the main expectation of the Old Testament prophets about the future.

John the Baptist astonished his hearers when he announced that this expected and hoped-for kingdom was "at hand" in the person of Jesus (Matt. 3:2). Jesus repeated this message (Matt. 4:17; Mark 1:15), but He went even further by announcing clearly that the kingdom was already present in His ministry: "If I cast out demons by the Spirit of God, surely the kingdom of God has come upon you" (Matt. 12:28). Jesus was the full embodiment of the kingdom.

The entire ministry of Jesus is understood in relation to this important declaration of the presence of the kingdom. His ethical teachings, for example, cannot be understood apart from the announcement of the kingdom. They are ethics of the kingdom; the perfection to which they point makes no sense apart from the present experience of the kingdom. Participation in the new reality of the kingdom involves a follower of Jesus in a call to the highest righteousness (Matt. 5:20).

The acts and deeds of Jesus likewise make sense only in the larger context of proclaiming the kingdom. When John the Baptist asked whether Jesus was "the Coming One," or the Messiah, Jesus answered by recounting some of His deeds of healing (Matt. 11:5). The reference in these words to the expectation of a MESSIAH, especially of the prophet

Isaiah (Is. 29:18–19; 35:5–6; 61:1), could not have been missed by John. At the synagogue in Nazareth, Jesus read a passage from Isaiah 61 about the coming messianic age and then made the astonishing announcement, "Today this Scripture is fulfilled in your hearing" (Luke 4:21).

All that Jesus did is related to this claim that the kingdom of God has dawned through His ministry. His healings were manifestations of the presence of the kingdom. In these deeds there was a direct confrontation between God and the forces of evil, or Satan and his demons. Summarizing His ministry, Jesus declared, "I saw Satan fall like lightning from heaven" (Luke 10:18). Satan and evil are in retreat now that the kingdom has made its entrance into human history. This is an anticipation of the final age of perfection that will be realized at Christ's return.

Although the gospels of Matthew, Mark, Luke, and John focus on the present aspect of the kingdom of God, it is also clear that the kingdom will be realized perfectly only at the SECOND COMING. The kingdom that comes through the ministry of Jesus dawns in the form of a mystery. Although it is physically present in the deeds and words of Jesus, it does not overwhelm the world. The judgment of God's enemies is postponed. The kingdom that arrived with Jesus did not include the triumphal victory so longed for by the Jews. It arrived secretly like leaven, inconspicuously like a mustard seed, or like a small pearl of great value that can be hidden in one's pocket (Matt. 13:31–46).

The Jewish people expected the kingdom of God

A tourist examines a mustard bush in Palestine. The tiny black seed of this bush provided a good object lesson for Jesus' teaching about the Kingdom of God (Matt. 13:31-32).

Photo by Howard Vos

to bring the present evil age to an end. But it arrived mysteriously without doing so. The new reality of the kingdom overlapped the present age, invading it rather than bringing it to an end. The demons reflect this oddity when they ask Jesus, "Have you come here to torment us before the time?" (Matt. 8:29). The future kingdom will bring the present age to an end and usher in the perfect age promised in the prophets. The present kingdom is both an anticipation and a guarantee of this future bliss.

The expression kingdom of God occurs mostly in the gospels of Matthew, Mark, and Luke. The Gospel of John and the epistles of the New Testament refer to the same reality but in different language, using phrases such as eternal life or salvation. The apostle Paul identified the kingdom of God as "righteousness and peace and joy in the Holy Spirit" (Rom. 14:17). Perhaps one reason why he described it this way is that the kingdom of God was a Jewish expression unfamiliar and possibly misleading to Gentiles.

Some interpreters of the Bible have described the phrase kingdom of God as a more comprehensive term referring to both heaven and earth. Likewise, they believe kingdom of God is a more restricted term referring to God's rule on earth, especially in relation to the nation of Israel. In this view Jesus offered the literal kingdom of heaven to Israel, but the Jews refused to accept it. Thus, it has been postponed until the Second Coming of Christ.

A careful study of the gospels, however, shows that the two phrases are used interchangeably. In parallel passages, Matthew uses "kingdom of heaven" while Mark and Luke has "kingdom of God" (Matt. 4:17; Mark 1:15; Luke 13:28). Even in Matthew the two phrases are sometimes used interchangeably, as in Matthew 19:23-24, where they are used one after the other in the same connection.

KINGDOM OF ISRAEL (see ISRAEL, KINGDOM OF).

KINGDOM OF JUDAH (see JUDAH, KINGDOM OF).

KINGS, BOOKS OF — two Old Testament books that recount the history of God's Chosen People during four turbulent centuries, from 970 to 587 B.C. The narratives in these books of history are organized around the various kings who reigned during these centuries, thus explaining the titles by which the books are known.

Structure of the Books. As originally written in the Hebrew language, 1 and 2 Kings consisted of one unbroken book. It formed a natural sequel to the Books of 1 and 2 Samuel, which also appeared originally in the Hebrew Bible as a single book. The writer of Samuel traced the history of the Hebrew people up to the final days of David's reign. This is where the Book of 1 Kings begins—with the death of David and the succession of his son, Solomon, to the throne.

The first half of the Book of 1 Kings describes Solomon's reign. Included are accounts about his vast wealth, his great wisdom, his marriage to foreign wives, and his completion of the Temple in Jerusalem. But 1 Kings also reveals that all was not well in Solomon's empire. Many of the people grew restless and rebellious because of the king's excesses

FIRST KINGS: A Teaching Outline

Part One: The United Kingdom (1:1—11:43)

Part Two: The Divided Kingdom (12:1—22:53)

SECOND KINGS: A Teaching Outline

Part One: The Divided Kingdom (1:1—17:41)

Part Two: The Surviving Kingdom of Judah (18:1—25:30)

and the high taxes required to support his ambitious projects. At his death the people in the northern part of the empire rebelled and formed their own nation, known as the northern kingdom of Israel. Those who remained loyal to the house of David and Solomon continued as the Southern Kingdom, or the nation of Judah.

From this point on in the Books of 1 and 2 Kings, the narrative grows complex and difficult to follow. The historical writer traces the history of a king of Israel, then switches over to touch on the high points in the administration of the parallel king of Judah. This can be very confusing to the Bible reader unless this parallel structure is known.

But we do these books a great injustice if we assume they are filled with nothing but dry historical statistics and minute details. First and Second Kings contain some of the most interesting stories in the Bible. Here we come face to face with the fiery prophet ELIJAH, who challenged the false god BAAL and hundreds of his prophets in a dramatic

These tourists are overshadowed by a gigantic urn at Petra, a city built by the Nabateans in southern Palestine. They inhabited the land of the ancient Edomites, a people mentioned often in the Books of 1 and 2 Kings.

Photo by Denis Baly

showdown on Mount Carmel. The prophet's faith was verified as God proved himself superior to Baal by answering Elijah's fervent prayer.

In these books we also meet a proud Syrian commander, NAAMAN the leper, who almost passed up his opportunity to be healed by his reluctance to dip himself in the waters of the Jordan River. Fortunately, his servants convinced him to drop his pride, and he emerged from the river with his skin restored "like the flesh of a little child" (2 Kin. 5:14).

During the four centuries covered by these books, a total of 19 different kings ruled the nation of Israel, while 22 different kings (if David and Solomon are included) occupied Judah's throne. The writer covers some of these kings with a few sentences, while he devotes several pages to others. Apparently, this author selected certain kings for major attention because they illustrated the conditions that led to the eventual collapse of the nations of Judah and Israel.

Some of these kings were honest, ethical, and morally pure. But the good kings always were the exception. The majority of the rulers led the people astray, some even openly encouraging them to worship false gods. Thus, the most familiar refrain in 1 and 2 Kings is the phrase, "He did evil in the sight of the Lord" (2 Kin. 8:18).

Israel was the first nation to collapse under the weight of its disobedience and depravity. This kingdom ended in 722 B.C. with the fall of its capital city, Samaria, to the Assyrians. The citizens of the southern kingdom of Judah struggled on for another 136 years under a succession of kings before their nation was overrun by the Babylonians in 587 B.C. The Book of 2 Kings comes to a close with the leading citizens of Judah being held captive in Babylon.

Authorship and Date. These books cover, in chronological fashion, about 400 years of Judah and Israel's history. The last event mentioned in this chronology is the captivity of Judah's citizens by the Babylonians. This means the book had to be compiled in its final form some time after the Babylonians overran Jerusalem in 587 B.C.

Early tradition credited the prophet Jeremiah with the writing of these two books. Whether this is correct is uncertain. We do know that this famous prophet preached in Jerusalem before and after the fall of the city. Two chapters from 2 Kings also appear in the Book of Jeremiah (compare 2 Kings 24—25 and Jeremiah 39—42; 52). This led many scholars to the natural assumption that Jeremiah had written the book.

Most scholars today no longer hold to the Jeremiah theory. The evidence points to an unknown prophet who worked at the same time as Jeremiah to compile this long history of his nation's religious and political life. His purpose was to show that the two kingdoms fell because of their unfaithfulness and to call the people back to renewal of the COVENANT.

While this prophet–writer is not named in the

Books of 1 and 2 Kings, he does reveal the sources which he used. He speaks of "the chronicles of the kings of Israel" (1 Kin. 14:19) and "the chronicles of the kings of Judah" (1 Kin. 14:29). These were probably the official court documents and historical archives of the two nations. He must have drawn from them freely as he wrote.

Historical Setting. The four centuries covered by 1 and 2 Kings were times of change and political upheaval in the ancient world as the balance of power shifted from one nation to another. Surrounding nations that posed a threat to Israel and Judah at various times during this period included Syria, Assyria, and Babylon.

The Assyrian threat was particularly strong during the last 50 years of the Northern Kingdom. Under Tiglath-Pileser III, this conquering nation launched three devasting campaigns against Israel in 734, 733 and 732 B.C. It was a blow from which Israel never recovered, and the nation fell to Assyrian forces just 10 years later in 722 B.C.

While Syria and Assyria were threats to Judah at various times, their worst enemy turned out to be the nation of Babylon. The Babylonians took captives and goods from Jerusalem in three campaigns—in 605 and 597 B.C. and in a two-year siege beginning in 588 B.C. Jerusalem finally fell in 587 B.C. The Temple was destroyed, and thousands of Judah's leading citizens were carried into captivity in Babylon.

Theological Contribution. The Books of 1 and 2 Kings present an interesting contrast between King David of Judah and King Jeroboam I, the first king of the northern kingdom of Israel.

Jeroboam established a legacy of idol worship in this new nation by setting up golden calves at Bethel and Dan (1 Kin. 12:25-33). These were symbols of the fertility religion of Baal. His strategy was to mix this false religion with worship of the one true God in an attempt to win the loyalty and good will of the people and bind them together as a distinctive nation. This act of idolatry was condemned by the writer of 1 and 2 Kings. Each succeeding king of Israel was measured against the standard of Jeroboam's idolatry. Of each king who led the people astray, it was written, "He did not depart from the sins of Jeroboam the son of Nebat, who had made Israel sin" (2 Kin. 15:9).

Just as Jeroboam was used as a bad example by the writer of 1 and 2 Kings, King David was used as a standard of righteousness and justice. In spite of David's moral lapses, he became the measure of righteousness for all kings who followed him. The Northern Kingdom was marked by rebellion and strife as opposing factions struggled for the right to reign, but the house of David continued in the Kingdom of Judah without interruption for nearly four centuries. The writer explained that the evils of kings such as Abijam (or Abijah) did not cancel out the love and mercy that God had promised to the house of David: "Nevertheless for David's sake the Lord his God gave him a lamp in Jerusalem, by setting up his son after him and by establishing Je-

rusalem; because David did what was right in the eyes of the Lord" (1 Kin. 15:4-5).

Special Considerations. The writer of 1 Kings reported that Solomon had "seven hundred wives, princesses, and three hundred concubines" (1 Kin. 11:3). In the ancient world, the number of wives held by a ruler symbolized his might and power. Rulers also took on wives to seal political alliances and trade agreements. But Solomon cannot be totally excused for his excesses because of these cultural factors. According to the writer of 1 Kings, he let his foreign wives turn away his heart from worshiping the one true God (1 Kin. 11:1-3). This was a fatal flaw in his character that eventually led to rebellion and the separation of Solomon's empire into two opposing nations (1 Kin. 11:11-13).

The Books of 1 and 2 Kings describe several miracles wrought by God through the prophets Elijah and Elisha. In addition to proving God's power, these miracles are also direct attacks on the pagan worship practices of the followers of Baal. Elijah's encounter with the prophets of Baal on Mount Carmel, for example, was a test of the power of Baal—whether he could send fire from heaven (lightning bolts) to ignite the sacrifice and bring the rains that were needed to end the drought. Baal was silent, but God thundered—and the rains came, as Elijah had predicted (1 Kin. 18:20-46).

KING'S GATE (see GATES OF JERUSALEM AND THE TEMPLE).

KINSMAN —a male relative; a man sharing the same racial, cultural, or national background as another. In the Old Testament the word kinsman is most often used as a translation of a Hebrew word that means, "one who has the right to redeem."

Since an Israelite could sell himself, his family, or his land (Lev. 25:39-43) in cases of poverty, the kinsman-redeemer (Lev. 25:25) was provided to protect the clan. This person, a near relative, had the first option by law to buy any land being sold, thus allowing it to be kept within the clan (Lev. 25:23-28; Jer. 32:6-10).

The outstanding example of the kinsman-redeemer in the Old Testament occurs in the story of RUTH and BOAZ (Ruth 4). Boaz, a near kinsman of Naomi (Ruth's mother-in-law), acted as a redeemer in accordance with Jewish law, and married Ruth.

On another level, God is the "kinsman" who redeems. In the Old Testament the focus of God's redemptive activity is the EXODUS, the deliverance of Israel from slavery in Egypt (Deut. 7:8; 2 Sam. 7:23).

In the New Testament, Jesus is described as our brother (Heb. 2:11-12, 17), who redeems us from the power of sin.

KIR [kir] (*wall*) — the name of a region and a city in the Old Testament:

1. A city of Moab mentioned by Isaiah in his prophecy against Moab (Is. 15:1).

2. The original home of the Syrians (Amos. 9:7).

KIR HARASETH [kir HAHR uh seth] (*city of pottery*) — a fortified city of Moab (2 Kin. 3:25), also spelled Kir Hareseth (Is. 16:7), Kir Heres (Is. 16:11; Jer. 48:31, 36) and Kirharesh (Is. 16:11, KJV). Kir of Moab (Is. 15:1) is also thought to be identical with Kir Haraseth.

Mesha, king of Moab, fled to Kir Haraseth after he was defeated by Jehoram, king of Israel, and Jehoshaphat, king of Judah. Accompanied by the king of Edom, these two rulers crushed the rebellion Mesha had started (2 Kin. 3:4). Because Kir Haraseth was the only city of Moab that could not be overthrown, it was the last refuge of Mesha (2 Kin. 3:25).

The prophets foretold God's certain destruction of Kir Haraseth, a seemingly invincible city (Is. 16:7). Many commentators identify Kir Haraseth with present–day el–Kerak, about 80 kilometers (50 miles) southeast of Jerusalem (see Map 4, B–4).

KIR HARESHETH [kir HAHR uh sheth] — a form of KIR HARASETH.

KIR HERES — a form of KIR HARASETH.

KIR OF MOAB — a form of KIR HARASETH.

KIRHARESH [kir HAHR esh] — a form of KIR HARASETH.

KIRIATH–ARBA [KIR ih ath AHR buh] — a form of KIRJATH ARBA.

KIRIATH–BAAL [KIR ih ath BAY uhl] — a form of KIRJATH JEARIM.

KIRIATH–HUZOTH [KIR ih ath HUH zahth] — a form of KIRJATH HUZOTH.

KIRJATH [KIR jath] (*city*) — a city of the tribe of Benjamin (Josh. 18:25), sometimes equated with KIRJATH JEARIM (Josh. 18:14–15).

KIRJATH ARBA [KIR jath AHR buh] (*city of the four*) — the ancient name of HEBRON (Gen. 23:2; Kiriath–arba, NIV, RSV). Near this city was the Cave of Machpelah where, according to a Jewish tradition, Adam, Abraham, Isaac, and Jacob are buried (hence, "city of the four"). Caleb captured Kirjath Arba from the ANAKIM, after whose leader, Arba, the city was named (Josh. 14:15). Kirjath Arba was in the hill-country district of Judah, about 32 kilometers (20 miles) southwest of Jerusalem.

KIRJATH BAAL [KIR jath BAY uhl] — a form of KIRJATH JEARIM.

KIRJATH HUZOTH [KIR jath HUH zahth] (*city of streets*) — a city of Moab where BALAK, king of Moab, lived. Kirjath Huzoth was the first place to which Balak took BALAAM the soothsayer (Num. 22:39; Kiriath–huzoth, NIV, RSV).

KIRJATH JEARIM [KIR jath JEE uh rim] (*city of forests*) — a fortified city that originally belonged to the Gibeonites (see Map 6, B–4). Kirjath Jearim is first mentioned as a member of a Gibeonite confederation of four fortress cities, which also included Gibeon, Chephirah, and Beeroth (Josh. 9:17). Kirjath Jearim was also known as Baalah (Josh. 15:9), Baale Judah (2 Sam. 6:2), and Kirjath Baal (Josh. 15:60), and Kirjath (Josh. 18:28, NKJV, KJV). These names suggest that perhaps it was an old Canaanite "high place," a place of idolatrous worship.

Originally assigned to the tribe of Judah (Josh. 15:60), and later assigned to Benjamin (Josh. 18:14–15, 28), Kirjath Jearim was on the western part of the boundary line between Judah and Benjamin (Josh. 15:9). When the ARK OF THE COVENANT was returned to the Israelites by the Philistines, it was brought from Beth Shemesh to Kirjath Jearim and entrusted to a man named Eleazar (1 Sam. 7:1–2). The Ark remained in Kirjath Jearim, in the house of Abinadab, the father of Eleazar, for 20 years. It was from here that David transported the Ark to Jerusalem (2 Sam. 6:2–3).

The precise location of this ancient town is not known. It has been identified by some scholars with the area of Abu Ghosh, about 13 kilometers (8 miles) northwest of Jerusalem on the Jaffa Road.

KIRJATH SANNAH [KIR jath SAN uh] (*city of instruction*) — a city in the mountain country of Judah assigned to the Levites (Josh. 21:15). The city is also called Debir (Josh. 15:49).

KIRJATH SEPHER [KIR jath SEE fur] (*city of books*) — a city in the mountain country of Judah assigned to the Levites (Josh. 21:15). Kirjath Sepher was the former name of DEBIR (Josh. 15:15), which is equated with KIRJATH SANNAH (Josh. 15:49).

KIRJATHAIM [kir JATH ay uhm] (*double cities*) — the name of two cities in the Old Testament:

1. An ancient city of the EMIM occupied and rebuilt by the tribe of Reuben (Num. 32:37; Kiriathaim, NIV, RSV).

2. A city of refuge in the territory of Naphtali given to the Levites (1 Chr. 6:76; Kiriathaim, NIV, RSV).

KISH [kish] (meaning unknown) — the name of several men in the Old Testament:

1. The father of King Saul (1 Chr. 12:1).

2. A Levite who lived in David's time (1 Chr. 23:21–22; 24:29). He was a son of Mahli and a grandson of Merari.

3. A Levite who helped cleanse the Temple during the reign of King Hezekiah of Judah (2 Chr. 29:12).

4. A Benjamite ancestor of MORDECAI (Esth. 2:5).

KISHI [KISH eye] (*a gift*) — a Levite of the Merari family (1 Chr. 6:44), also called Kushaiah (1 Chr. 15:17).

KISHION [KISH ih uhn] (meaning unknown) — a city on the boundary of the tribe of Issachar assigned to the Levites and made a city of refuge (Josh. 19:20; 21:28; Kishon, KJV, NEB).

KISHON [KIGH shuhn] (*curving*) — a river in Palestine, which flows from sources on Mount Tabor and Mount Gilboa westward through the Plain of Esdraelon and the Valley of Jezreel, then empties into the Mediterranean Sea near the northern base of Mount Carmel (see Map 3, B-2). Because the Kishon falls slightly as it crosses the level plain, it often becomes swollen and floods much of the valley during the season of heavy rains.

At the River Kishon the Israelites won a celebrated victory over Sisera under the leadership of Deborah and Barak (Judg. 4:7). Fully armed with 900 chariots of iron (Judg. 4:13), the forces of Sisera became bogged down in the overflow of the Kishon (Judg. 5:21), and the Israelites defeated them. It was at the Brook Kishon, also, that the prophets of Baal were executed following their contest with Elijah on Mount Carmel (1 Kin. 18:40).

KISS — a symbolic act done to various parts of the body, especially cheeks, feet, forehead, and lips (Prov. 24:26). Ideally, a kiss shows a close relationship to another person, although the relationship and purpose may vary greatly.

Romantic kisses are mentioned infrequently in the Bible, whether genuinely loving (Song 1:2; 8:1) or seductive (Prov. 7:13). The most common type of kiss, however, was that between relatives (Gen. 29:11-13). A kiss could serve either as a greeting (Ex. 4:27) or a farewell (Ruth 1:9, 14; Acts 20:37). It can even express one's anticipation of departure by death (Gen. 48:10). The family kiss was extended in the New Testament to apply to the Christian family (1 Cor. 16:20; 1 Pet. 5:14).

Friends might kiss in greeting (1 Sam. 20:41; 2 Sam. 19:39) although occasionally such a kiss could be given insincerely (Prov. 27:6). Kissing also has figurative meaning when righteousness and peace are pictured as harmonious friends kissing each other (Ps. 85:10). A kiss can also mean betrayal. Judas' treachery is eternally symbolized by a kiss (Luke 22:47-48).

KITCHEN — one of four small subcourts at the corners of the outer court of the Temple in the prophet Ezekiel's vision (Ezek. 46:24; boiling places, NASB). People could have their sacrifices boiled here before they were offered in the Temple.

KITE (see ANIMALS OF THE BIBLE).

KITHLISH [KITH lish] (*a man's wall*) — a city in the Shephelah, or lowland plain, of Judah (Josh. 15:40; Chitlish, RSV; Kitlish, NIV).

KITLISH [KIT lish] — a form of KITHLISH.

KITRON [KIT rahn] (*shortened*) — a city in the territory of Zebulun inhabited by the Canaanites (Judg. 1:30).

KITTIM [KIT im] (meaning unknown) — the name of a man and an island in the Old Testament:

1. A son of Javan (Gen. 10:4). Tradition has it that the descendants of Kittim settled on CYPRUS and the nearby coasts and island and were called Kittim or Chittim.

2. The Hebrew name for Cyprus (Jer. 2:10). Kittim also became a symbol of Rome (Dan. 11:30).

The Hebrews must have been familiar with Kittim, or Cyprus (see Map 1, B-2). From the oracle of Balaam (Num. 24:24), it is evident that the Israelites associated Cyprus with ships. The prophet Jeremiah saw Kittim as the western boundary of the known world (Jer. 2:10), and Ezekiel reported that Cyprus supplied Phoenicia with pines for Phoenician ships (Ezek. 27:6).

KNAPSACK — a bag worn on the back in which supplies, equipment, and personal belongings were carried (2 Kin. 4:42; sack, RSV, NASB).

KNEAD, KNEADING — the mixing of flour, water, and oil in preparation for the baking of bread (Deut. 28:5). In Bible times, these ingredients were mixed in a wood or earthenware trough, with a piece of dough from the previous batch. This "sourdough" method provided raised bread through the activity of yeast or leaven in the old dough.

KNEADING BOWL — a shallow vessel—usually made of wood, baked clay, or bronze—in which dough was worked into a well-mixed mass in preparation for baking (Ex. 8:3; 12:34; troughs, KJV, NEB, NIV). After the dough was mixed and leavened, it was left in the kneading bowl to rise and ferment. The kneading bowl was among the objects of the Lord's blessing (Deut. 28:5).

KNEELING — falling to one's knees as a gesture of reverence, obedience, or respect. In the dedication of the Temple in Jerusalem, Solomon knelt before God (1 Kin. 8:54). Daniel knelt in prayer three times a day (Dan. 6:10).

KNIFE (see ARMS, ARMOR OF THE BIBLE; TOOLS OF THE BIBLE).

KNOB — an ornament that served as a detail of the seven-branched lampstand in the tabernacle (Ex. 25:31-36; knop, KJV). It was perhaps an imitation of the fruit of the almond. In other passages, the same Hebrew word (*kaphtor*) translated "ornamental knob" in the Book of Exodus refers to the capital of a column (Zeph. 2:14).

KNOP — a form of KNOB.

KNOWLEDGE — the truth or facts of life that a person acquires either through experience or thought. The greatest truth that a person can possess with the mind or learn through experience is truth about God (Ps. 46:10; John 8:31-32). This cannot be gained by unaided human reason (Job 11:7; Rom. 11:33). It is acquired only as God shows Himself to man—in nature and conscience (Ps. 19; Rom. 1:19-20); in history or providence (Deut. 6:20-25; Dan. 2:21); and especially in the Bible (Ps. 119; Rev. 1:1-3).

Mental knowledge by itself, as good as it may be, is inadequate; it is capable only of producing pride (1 Cor. 8:1; 13:2). Moral knowledge affects a person's will (Prov. 1:7; Phil. 3:11-12; 1 John 4:6). It is knowledge of the heart, not the mind alone. The Book of Proverbs deals primarily with this kind of knowledge. Experiential knowledge is that gained through one's experience (Gen. 4:1; 2 Cor. 5:21; 1 John 4:7–8).

The apostle Paul's wish for the church at Colosse was that they might increase in the "knowledge of God" (Col. 1:10).

KOA [KOE uh] (meaning unknown) — a people described as enemies of Jerusalem (Ezek. 23:23).

KOHATH [KOE hath] (meaning unknown) — the second son of Levi (Gen. 46:11). Kohath went to Egypt with Levi and Jacob (Gen. 46:11) and lived to the age of 133 (Ex. 6:18). He was the founder of the KOHATHITES.

KOHATHITES [KOE hath ights] (*belonging to Kohath*) — the descendants of KOHATH, son of Levi (Ex. 6:16). Kohath was the father of Amram, Izhar, Hebron, and Uzziel (Ex. 6:18). Consequently, the Kohathite family was subdivided into these four families (1 Chr. 26:23).

During Israel's journey after leaving Egypt, the Kohathites were responsible for caring for and transporting "the ark [of the covenant], the table, the lampstand, the altars, the utensils of the sanctuary with which they ministered, the screen, and [for doing] all the work related to them" (Num. 3:31).

When the Israelites camped, the Kohathites were stationed on the south side of the tabernacle (Num. 3:29, 31). At different times, the Bible specifies their numbers (Num. 3:28; 4:36). Aaron and Moses were Kohathites (Ex. 6:16, 18, 20).

KOHELETH [koe HEL eth] — the Hebrew title of the author of the Book of Ecclesiastes, translated as preacher in most English versions of the Bible (Eccl. 1:1). The Hebrew word actually means "speaker before an assembly." Also see ECCLESIASTES, BOOK OF.

KOLAIAH [koe LAY uh] (*voice of Jehovah*) — the name of two men in the Old Testament:
1. A son of Maaseiah whose descendants lived in Jerusalem after the Captivity (Neh. 11:7).
2. The father of AHAB, the false prophet condemned by Jeremiah (Jer. 29:21–23).

KOPH [cofe] (see QOPH).

KOR, KORS (see WEIGHTS AND MEASURES).

KORAH — the name of four men in the Old Testament:
1. The third son of Esau by his wife Aholibamah (Gen. 36:5, 14). Born in Canaan, Korah became a chief of an Edomite tribe (Gen. 36:18).
2. The grandson of Esau through Eliphaz. Korah was an Edomite chief (Gen. 36:16).
3. The Levite who, along with Dathan, Abiram, and On of the tribe of Reuben, led a revolt against the leadership of Moses and Aaron (Num. 16:1–49). Korah was the son of Izhar and a first cousin of Moses and Aaron (Ex. 6:21). He was equal in rank

with Aaron within the tribe of Levi.

Korah apparently was jealous that Aaron held the position of high priest. The Reubenites were the descendants of Jacob's eldest son. They thought the responsibility for leading Israel should rest with their tribe rather than the Levites. The four ringleaders gathered 250 leaders of the congregation, publicly charging Moses and Aaron with abusing their power. They claimed that all members of the congregation should have equal access to the Lord.

Moses placed the dispute in the hands of the Lord, directing Korah and his company to bring containers of incense as an offering to the Lord. Korah complied with this and went with his congregation to the door of the tabernacle where the Lord appeared, threatening to "consume them in a moment" (Num. 16:21). Moses and Aaron interceded, saving the nation of Israel from destruction. The decision of leadership was again placed before the Lord as Moses instructed the congregation to "depart from the tents of these wicked men" (Num. 16:26). The decision in favor of Moses was dramatized as "the earth opened its mouth" and swallowed all the men of Korah (Num. 16:32).

Apparently some of the descendants of Korah survived to become ministers of music in the tabernacle during the time of David (1 Chr. 6:31–37).
4. The eldest son of Hebron, a descendant of Caleb and Judah (1 Chr. 2:43).

KORAHITES [KOR uh hights] — that part of the Kohathite Levites descended from KORAH, son of Izhar and grandson of Levi. Many Korahites held responsible tabernacle positions (Ex. 6:24). The name is also spelled Korathites (Num. 26:58). The KJV translates as Korhites. Eleven psalms bear the title, "the sons of Korah" (Psalms 42; 44—49; 84—85; 87—88).

KORE [KOR ih] (*one who proclaims*) — the name of two men in the Old Testament:
1. The father of Shallum and Meshelemiah, who were gatekeepers at the tabernacle (1 Chr. 9:19).
2. A son of Imnah the Levite. Kore was the keeper of the East Gate of the Temple (2 Chr. 31:14).

KORHITES [KOR hights] — a form of KORAHITES.

KOROS (see WEIGHTS AND MEASURES).

KOZ [kahz] (*nimble*) — the name of three men in the Old Testament:
1. A descendant of Caleb, of the tribe of Judah (1 Chr. 4:8; Coz, KJV).
2. The ancestor of a priestly family that returned from the Captivity (Ezra 2:61). HAKKOZ (1 Chr. 24:10) may refer to the same person.
3. An ancestor of a person who helped repair the walls of Jerusalem (Neh. 3:4, 21).

KUSHAIAH [koo SHAY uh] — a form of KISHI (1 Chr. 15:17).

LAADAH [LAY uh duh] (meaning unknown) — a son of Shelah and grandson of Judah (1 Chr. 4:21).

LAADAN [LAY uh dan] (meaning unknown) — the name of two men in the Old Testament:

1. A descendant of Ephraim and an ancestor of Joshua (1 Chr. 7:26; Ladan, NIV, RSV).

2. A Levite of the family of Gershon (1 Chr. 23:7-9; Ladan, RSV), also called Libni (Ex. 6:17).

LABAN [LAY bihn] (*white*) — father-in-law of Jacob. Laban lived in the city of Nahor in Padan Aram where Abraham sent his servant to find a wife for Isaac. Laban, brother of Rebekah, is introduced when he heard of the servant's presence, saw the golden jewelry given Rebekah, and eagerly invited Abraham's emissary into their home (Gen. 24:29-60). Laban played an important role in the marriage arrangements. His stubbornness and greed characterized his later dealings with Rebekah's son, Jacob.

Over 90 years later, Jacob left home to escape Esau's wrath. At the well of Haran he met Rachel, Laban's daughter. Laban promised her to his nephew Jacob in return for seven years of labor from Jacob. Laban consequently dealt with Jacob with deception and greed; he gave him the wrong wife and then forced him to work seven more years for Rachel. Then he persuaded Jacob to stay longer, but the wages he promised were changed ten times in six years (Genesis 29—30).

When family situations became tense, Jacob quietly left with his wives, children, and possessions, only to be pursued by Laban (Genesis 31). Laban and Jacob eventually parted on peaceful terms, but they heaped stones as a mutual testimony that they would have no further dealings with one another. They called upon God as their witness that they would not impose upon one another again (Gen. 31:43-55).

LABORER (see OCCUPATIONS AND TRADES).

LACE — KJV word for twisted cord or thread used to bind items together. This word is used also of the cord that bound the priestly ephod to the breastplate (Ex. 28:28). It also refers to a rope (Judg. 16:9; yarn, NKJV), a tassel (Num. 15:38), or a belt (Gen. 38:18; cord, NKJV).

LACHISH [LAY kish] (meaning unknown) — an ancient walled city in the lowlands of Judah captured by Joshua and the Israelites. Lachish was situated about 49 kilometers (30 miles) southwest of Jerusalem and about 9.5 kilometers (15 miles) west of Hebron (see Map 3, A-4). The city covered about 18 acres and was inhabited for many years before the invasion by Joshua and the Israelites. The city is mentioned in early Egyptian sources as an important military stronghold.

After the Israelites overran the cities of Jericho and Ai, King Japhia of Lachish and four other kings formed an alliance against Israel (Josh. 10:1-4). God aided Israel against these five armies by causing the sun to stand still (Josh. 10:5-14). After a two-day siege, Lachish itself was captured (Josh. 10:31-33). It then was included in the allotment of the tribe of Judah (Josh. 15:39).

Little is known of the city until the time of Solomon, when Solomon's son Rehoboam rebuilt Lachish to protect Judah from Egypt (2 Chr. 11:5-12). Many years later Amaziah, king of Judah, fled from an uprising in Jerusalem to Lachish. Because Amaziah had turned away from following God, judgment was imposed upon him; he was killed while hiding in the city (2 Kin. 14:19; 2 Chr. 25:27).

During the time of Hezekiah (701 B.C.), Sennacherib, king of Assyria, attacked Lachish (2 Kin. 18:13-17; 2 Chr. 32:9). Its capture was so important to Sennacherib that he memorialized it in a magnificent relief on the wall of his palace at Nineveh. He also sent a letter to Hezekiah, demanding his surrender (2 Kin. 18:14, 17; 19:8).

About 100 years later, Lachish was again a stronghold in the nation of Judah. Nebuchadnezzar, king of Babylon, attacked and defeated the city when he took Judah into captivity in 586 B.C. (Jer. 34:7). When the Jews returned from their years of CAPTIVITY in Babylon, the city of Lachish was inhabited again (Neh. 11:30).

Archaeologists have excavated Lachish, and it has become one of the most significant sites in the Holy Land. A small temple with an altar for burnt offerings was discovered here; and the bones of many animals also were found—probably representing portions of the animals that the priests ate during sacrificial observances (Lev. 7:32-34). Also

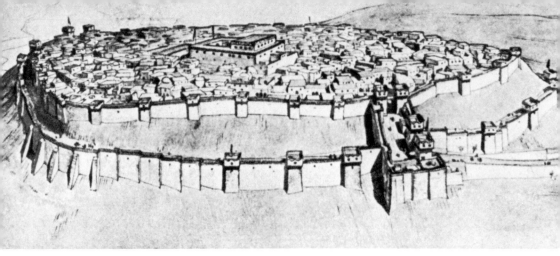

Drawing of Lachish, a walled city of the southern kingdom of Judah, which was destroyed by Nebuchadnezzar of Babylon in 587 B.C.

discovered was a deep well that probably provided water for the city when it was under siege.

Another important find consisted of early Hebrew writings on jars, bowls, seals, and a stone altar. Letters about the attack on Lachish and Jerusalem by Babylon in 586 B.C. were also found. Two of the letters refer to "the prophet"—possibly a reference to JEREMIAH, who prophesied in Jerusalem during this turbulent time in the city's history.

LADAN [LAY duhn] — a form of LAADAN.

LADDER — a device consisting of two long sidepieces, joined at intervals by parallel rungs, used for climbing up or down. This word occurs only once in Scripture—in the account of Jacob's dream at Bethel (Gen. 28:12). In this incident Jacob learned that in spite of all the underhanded things he had done, he had not been deserted by God. Communication between heaven and earth was still open, and God's messengers still visited a needy and sinful mankind.

LADLE — a long-handled spoon and a deep bowl that held incense for use in the tabernacle and the Temple (1 Kin. 7:50; 2 Chr. 4:22; spoons, KJV; saucers, NEB; dishes for incense, RSV). These ladles were among the bronze utensils carried away from the Temple by the conquering Babylonians in 586 B.C. (2 Kin. 25:14; Jer. 52:18–19).

LAEL [LAY uhl] (*belonging to God*) — a Levite of the family of Gershon (Num. 3:24).

LAHAD [LAY had] (*sluggish*) — son of Jahath (1 Chr. 4:2).

LAHAI ROI [luh HIGH roy] — a form of BEER LA-HAI ROI.

LAHMAS [LAH mahs] (meaning unknown) — a city in the SHEPHELAH, or lowland, of Judah (Josh. 15:40). It is possibly Khirbet el-Lahm, about 4 kilometers (2.5 miles) east of Lachish.

LAHMI [LAH migh] (*warrior*) — a brother of Goli-

ath, the Philistine giant killed by David (1 Chr. 20:5).

LAISH [LAY ish] (*lion*) — the name of one man and two places in the Old Testament:

1. A Canaanite city in northern Palestine conquered by the tribe of Dan. Its name was changed from Laish to Dan (Judg. 18:29). Dan was also called Leshem (Josh. 19:47).

2. Father of Palti (1 Sam. 25:44), or Paltiel (2 Sam. 3:15).

3. A village in the territory of Benjamin (Is. 10:30; Laishah, RSV).

LAKE OF GENNESARET (see GENNESARET).

LAKKUM [LAK uhm] (meaning unknown) — a border city in northeastern Naphtali near the Jordan River (Josh. 19:33; Lakum, KJV).

LAMA [LAH muh] — a Hebrew word meaning *why*. It is found twice in the New Testament (Matt. 27:46; Mark 15:34), as one of Jesus' "seven words" from the cross: "My God, My God, why have You forsaken Me?"—a quotation from Psalm 22:1.

LAMB (see ANIMALS OF THE BIBLE).

LAMB OF GOD — a phrase used by John the Baptist to describe Jesus (John 1:29, 36). John publicly identified Jesus as "the Lamb of God who takes away the sin of the world!" Elsewhere in the New Testament Jesus is called a lamb (Acts 8:32; 1 Pet. 1:19; Rev. 5:6). The Book of Revelation speaks of Jesus as a lamb 28 times.

John's reference to Jesus as the Lamb of God calls to mind the Old Testament sacrifical system. In the sacrifice God accepted the blood of animals as the means of atonement for sin. It is likely that John had many themes from the Old Testament in mind when he called Jesus the Lamb of God. These themes probably included the sin offering (Leviticus 4), the trespass offering (Leviticus 5), the sacrifice on the Day of Atonement (Leviticus 16), and the Passover sacrifice (Exodus 12).

But the strongest image from the Old Testament is the suffering servant who "was led as a lamb to the slaughter" (Is. 53:7) and who "bore the sins of many" (Is. 53:12). Thus, this vivid description of Jesus was a pointed announcement of the ATONEMENT He would bring about on man's behalf.

Also see JESUS CHRIST.

LAME, LAMENESS — a disability in one or more limbs, especially in a foot or leg, so that a person experiences difficulty in walking or moving freely. Lameness is one of the physical imperfections that excluded a priest from entering the holy place or offering sacrifices (Lev. 21:17–21). Jesus healed many lame people (Matt. 11:5; Luke 7:22). Peter and John also healed a man who had been lame from birth (Acts 3:1–11). Also see DISEASES OF THE BIBLE.

LAMECH [LAY mik] (meaning unknown) — the name of two men in the Old Testament:

1. A son of Methushael and a descendant of Cain (Gen. 4:18–24). Lamech is the first man mentioned in the Bible as having two wives (Gen. 4:19). By Adah he had two sons, Jabal and Jubal; and by Zillah he had a son, Tubal-Cain, and a daughter, Naamah.

2. The first son of Methuselah, and the father of Noah (Gen. 5:25–26, 28–31). Lamech lived to be 777 years old (Gen. 5:31). He is mentioned in the genealogy of Jesus (Luke 3:36).

LAMED [LAH mid] — the 12th letter of the He-

brew alphabet, used as a heading over Psalm 119:89–96. In the original Hebrew language, every line of these eight verses began with the letter lamed. Also see ACROSTIC.

LAMENT (see MOURN, MOURNING).

LAMENTATIONS, BOOK OF — a short Old Testament book, written in poetic form, that expresses deep grief over the destruction of the city of Jerusalem and the Temple. Its English title comes from a Greek verb meaning "to cry aloud," which accurately describes the contents of the book.

Structure of the Book. The book consists of five poems, one for each chapter. The first, second, and fourth poems are written as acrostics, with each successive verse beginning with the next letter of the Hebrew alphabet. The fourth poem is also an acrostic, although in an expanded form giving three verses to each of the 22 letters of the Hebrew alphabet. The fifth poem departs from the acrostic pattern, but it contains 22 verses, the same number as poems one, two, and four.

It is clear that the writer of Lamentations went to much trouble to compose this book. He wove several literary devices together, under the inspiration of God's Spirit, to give these poems a somber tone. Nothing less could express his deep sorrow over the plight of Jerusalem at the hands of the invading Babylonians.

Authorship and Date. Lamentations itself gives no clue concerning its author, but many conservative

LAMENTATIONS: A Teaching Outline

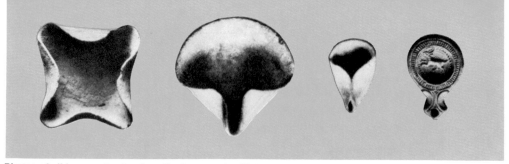

Photos of oil lamps, showing how the lamp evolved into a more efficient light-giving instrument from about 3000 B.C. to New Testament times.

Bible scholars agree on the prophet Jeremiah as the most likely candidate. The book is realistic in its portrayal of conditions in Jerusalem just before its fall, suggesting the author was an eyewitness of these events. This supports Jeremiah's authorship, since he prophesied in Jerusalem during this period of his nation's history.

Some of the language in Lamentations and the Book of Jeremiah is also similiar. For example, the phrase *daughter of* appears about 20 times in each book. In addition, Jeremiah was a very sensitive prophet who expressed his feelings about his nation's sins and approaching doom in rich symbols and metaphors. A deep outpouring of sorrow is characteristic of Lamentations as well as some sections of the Book of Jeremiah. All this evidence supports the traditional view that the prophet wrote the Book of Lamentations. The date of the writing was probably some time shortly after the fall of the city in 587 or 586 B.C.

Historical Setting. The fall of Jerusalem to Babylonian forces under NEBUCHADNEZZAR in 587/586 B.C. was one of Israel's most bitter experiences. Many of the nation's leading citizens were carried into captivity in Babylon. The people of Judah remained in that distant land for almost 50 years. Their idolatry and unfaithfulness had resulted in the loss of two of the focal points of their faith: Jerusalem and the Temple. Jeremiah must have expressed their collective shock and sorrow as he wrote this poetic book.

Theological Contribution. Why was there such despondency over the destruction of a city? The reasons become clear when we sense the importance of Jerusalem in the purpose of God.

Jerusalem was more than the capital of the nation or the city of Israel's beloved King David. Jerusalem was the site of the Temple of God, the place where God's presence dwelt and where sacrifice could be made to him. In later years Jerusalem became the focal point of God's final work of salvation in the person of Jesus Christ. The Book of Lamentations reminds us of the central role which this city has always played in God's work of redemption in the world.

Special Considerations. Lamentations has many strange expressions such as daughter of Zion (2:1), daughter of Judah (2:5), and daughter of Jerusalem (2:15). These do not refer to daughters of these cities but to the cities themselves as daughters of the Lord. In this context, these phrases refer to supreme grief. As such they remind us of the profound sorrow associated with God's judgment of His sinful people; yet, since they remain daughters, these cities speak of great hope during desperate times.

LAMP — a simple oil–burning vessel used for lighting houses and public buildings in Bible times. Pottery lamps either had lips or were completely enclosed, with a hole in the middle, or a spout in the rim, for the wick. Such lamps were often decorated, and many had handles for convenient carrying. Jewish lamps were decorated with the symbol of the MENORAH, the seven–branched lampstand. Christian lamps were decorated with Christian symbols such as crosses, fish, and the alpha and omega. The typical Palestinian lamp in Christ's day was plain and round, with a filling hole for oil and a spout for the wick.

Lamps could be held by hand or placed on a support, like a shelf or a lampstand. More light was provided by additional wicks. Lamps with up to seven spouts have been discovered by archaeologists. Some lamps were made of metal.

An elaborate, seven–branched lampstand of pure gold stood in the TABERNACLE (Ex. 25:31–40). Solomon made ten similar lampstands for the TEMPLE (1 Kin. 7:49).

Lamps burned olive oil or fat. Those with a single wick would burn from two to four hours. Occasionally the flax wick would have to be trimmed. WICK TRIMMERS were used for this purpose.

The lamp became a symbol of understanding (2 Sam. 22:29), guidance (Prov. 6:23), and life (Job 21:17). John the Baptist was "the burning and shining lamp" in whose light the Jews of his day rejoiced (John 5:35). In Jesus' parable of the wise and foolish virgins (Matt. 25:1–13), taking enough oil to keep the lamps burning represented good works done in obedience to Jesus' teaching. Not taking enough oil to keep the lamps burning represented disobedience to Christ.

LANCE, LANCET (see ARMS, ARMOR OF THE BIBLE).

LAND — a plot of ground, or soil, on which trees, vegetables, and shrubs grow; a portion of the earth. The Old Testament ideal was that every Hebrew family was to own a portion of land, where every person could sit under his own vine and fig tree (1 Kin. 4:25; Mic. 4:4). The land of Canaan belonged to the Lord, and He had given it to His people (Josh. 24:11–13). They were His tenants (Lev. 25:23).

After the conquest of the land under Joshua, the whole country was divided among the individual tribes and families (Joshua 13—22). Boundary stones were not to be removed (Deut. 19:14). Naboth's refusal to sell family land even to the king (1 Kings 21) illustrates the ideal that land should become a permanent family heritage. Although land could be sold in difficult times, a near relative had the right to buy this land back so it did not pass permanently from a family's hands. Land was eventually supposed to revert to the original family at the Year of the JUBILEE, every 50th year (Lev. 25:23–28). Inheritance laws also sought to ensure that property remained within the family or the tribe (Num. 27:7–11).

In practice, however, acquisition of property by the wealthier families increased throughout Bible history. The prophets condemned the practice (Is. 5:8; Mic. 2:2), because it led to wider divisions between rich and poor, depriving families of basic rights under the Mosaic law. Renting of land is first mentioned in Jesus' parable of the tenants (Matt. 21:33–41); when the practice began is unknown.

LANDMARK — a boundary line indicated by a stone or other monument. These monuments were erected to mark the separation of fields, territories, and nations. The law of Moses prohibited the removal of these landmarks (Deut. 19:14) and pronounced a curse upon those who did (Deut. 27:17). When Job complained of violence on the earth, the first crime he mentioned was the removal of landmarks (Job 24:2). Also, the prophet Hosea complained, "The princes of Judah are like those who remove a landmark" (Hos. 5:10); therefore, God's wrath would be poured out on them.

LANE — a narrow or constricted passageway in a town or city, crowded by buildings on both sides (Luke 14:21; alleys, NIV, NEB).

LANGUAGES OF THE BIBLE — the languages in which the Bible was originally written. The most famous of these are Hebrew, the original language of the Old Testament, and Greek, used in the writing of most of the New Testament. But several other ancient languages also had an important bearing on the writing or transmission of the original texts of the Bible.

Aramaic. Spoken from at least about 2000 B.C., Aramaic eventually replaced many of the languages of the ancient world in popularity and usage. Parts of the Book of Daniel were written in Aramaic. Aramaic was the common language spoken in Palestine in the time of Jesus. While the New Testament was written in the Greek language, the language which Jesus spoke was probably Aramaic. "Talitha, cumi" (Mark 5:41) and "Ephphatha" are two Aramaic phrases spoken by Jesus which have been preserved in English versions of the New Testament. Another name for the Aramaic dialect used in the early churches throughout Asia Minor is Syriac.

Latin. The New Testament also refers to Latin—the language which sprang from ancient Rome (Luke 23:38; John 19:20). Most of the Roman Empire also spoke Greek in Jesus' day. But as Roman

Examples of ancient writing in the Hebrew language. The bottom inscription, dating from about 700 B.C., was placed over a tomb near Jerusalem.

Photo by Gustav Jeeninga

A page from a codex, a primitive book, containing Romans 16:4-13 written in the Greek language.

power spread throughout the ancient world, Latin also expanded in use. The influence of Latin on the Mediterranean world in the time of Jesus is shown by the occurrence of such Latin words as denarii (Matt. 18:28) and praetorian (Phil. 1:13, RSV, NASB) in the New Testament.

Persian. This language was spoken by the people who settled the area east of the Tigris River in what is now western Iran. When the Jewish people were taken as captives to Babylon in 587 B.C., they may have been exposed to this distinctive language form, which used a combination of pictorial and phonetic signs in its alphabet. Scholars are uncertain if Persian was used in the writing of any parts of the Old Testament.

LANTERN — a light source mentioned in the account of the betrayal of Jesus (John 18:3). Scholars believe a lantern was much like a LAMP (Matt. 25:1). It probably had some type of simple globe or covering to keep it from being blown out by the wind.

LAODICEA [LAY ah duh SEE uh] — a city in the fertile Lycus Valley of the province of PHRYGIA where one of the seven churches of Asia Minor was situated (Rev. 3:14). About 65 kilometers (40 miles) east of Ephesus and about 16 kilometers (10 miles) west of Colossae, Laodicea was built on the banks of the river Lycus, a tributary of the Maeander River.

The words of the risen Christ to Laodicea in Revelation 3:14–22 contain allusions to the economic prosperity and social prominence of the city. Founded by the SELEUCIDS and named for Laodice, the wife of Antiochus II (261–247 B.C.), Laodicea became extremely wealthy during the Roman period. For example, in 62 B.C. Flaccus siezed the annual contribution of the Jews of Laodicea for Jerusalem amounting to 20 pounds of gold. Moreover, when the city was destroyed by an earthquake in A.D. 60 (along with Colossae and Hierapolis), it alone refused aid from Rome for rebuilding (compare the self-sufficient attitude of the church of Laodicea in Revelation 3:17). Laodicea was known for its black wool industry; it manufactured garments from the raven–black wool produced by the sheep of the surrounding area.

The apostle Paul does not seem to have visited Laodicea at the time he wrote Colossians 2:1. Epaphras, Tychicus, Onesimus, and Mark seem to have been the early messengers of the gospel there (Col. 1:7; 4:7-15). A letter addressed to the Laodiceans by Paul (Col. 4:16) has apparently been lost; some consider it to be a copy of the Ephesian letter. A church council was supposedly held at Laodicea (A.D. 344–363), but all that has come down to us are statements from other councils.

The site of Laodicea is now a deserted heap of ruins that the Turks call Eski Hisar, or "old castle."

According to the comments about the church at Laodicea in the Book of Revelation, this congregation consisted of lukewarm Christians (Rev. 3:14-22). The living Lord demands enthusiasm and total commitment from those who worship Him.

LAP — the top of the thighs of a person sitting. The term is not used often in the Bible. The two uses of the word in the NKJV refer to the clothes that cover the lap (2 Kin. 4:39; Prov. 16:33).

LAPIDOTH, LAPPIDOTH [LAP uh doth] (*flames*) — the husband of Deborah the prophetess, whose home appears to have been "between Ramah and Bethel in the mountains of Ephraim" (Judg. 4:4–5).

LAPIS LAZULI (see JEWELS AND PRECIOUS STONES).

LAPPED, LAPS — to drink by licking up liquid with the tongue. The Lord told Gideon this would be the standard by which his army would be tested. Those who lapped water with their tongues, as a dog laps, would be retained for battle. Those who got down on their knees to drink would be sent home (Judg. 7:5-7).

LAPWING (see ANIMALS OF THE BIBLE).

LASCIVIOUSNESS — KJV word for LICENTIOUSNESS.

LASEA [luh SEE uh] (meaning unknown) — a seaport on the southern coast of Crete. The ship that carried the apostle Paul toward Rome passed by Lasea (Acts 27:8).

LASHA [LAY shuh] (meaning unknown) — an ancient Canaanite site on the southeastern border of Palestine (Gen. 10:19), mentioned with Sodom and Gomorrah and other CITIES OF THE PLAIN. It was situated near the Dead Sea.

LASHARON [luh SHAR uhn] (meaning unknown) — a Canaanite city whose king was defeated by Joshua (Josh. 12:18). The NEB calls the city Aphek–in–Sharon.

LAST DAYS (see ESCHATOLOGY).

LAST SUPPER (see LORD'S SUPPER).

LATCHET — KJV word for a leather strap, thong, or cord used to fasten a sandal on the foot (Mark 1:7). Also see SANDAL.

LATIN (see LANGUAGES OF THE BIBLE).

LATIN VERSION (see BIBLE VERSIONS AND TRANSLATIONS).

LATTER DAYS (see ESCHATOLOGY).

LATTICE NETWORK — ornamental trim on the capitals, or tops, of JACHIN AND BOAZ, the twin pillars which stood before the porch of the Temple (1 Kin. 7:17; checker work, KJV).

LAUGH, LAUGHTER — to show mirth or joy. In the Bible, however, laughter is usually an expression of mockery or scorn. Both Abraham (Gen. 17:17) and Sarah (Gen. 18:12–15; 21:6) laughed when they were told they would become parents at an old age. God's laughter at man's pride and rebellion is also the laughter of mockery and scorn (Ps. 2:4).

LAUNDERER (see OCCUPATIONS AND TRADES).

LAUREL (see PLANTS OF THE BIBLE).

LAVER — a basin in which the priests washed their hands for purification purposes while officiating at

This laver on a stand with wheels dates to about the 12th century B.C. It was discovered in the excavation of a tomb on the island of Cyprus.

the altar of the TABERNACLE or the TEMPLE. Moses was commanded to make a laver, or basin, so Aaron and the Levitical priests could wash their hands and feet before offering sacrifices (Ex. 30:18–21). The laver and its base were made from the bronze mirrors of the serving women (Ex. 38:8). It stood between the Tent of Meeting and the altar.

Hiram made ten bronze lavers for Solomon's Temple (1 Kin. 7:27–39). Each laver rested on a bronze cart, and each cart rested on two pairs of wheels. The panels on the carts were decorated with lions, oxen, and cherubim. The lavers were di-

Ruins of the city gate in the wall of ancient Laodicea. The church of Laodicea was rebuked by John because of its lukewarm spirit (Rev. 3:14-22).

Photo by Gustav Jeeninga

Ancient Kish in Mesopotamia was apparently one of the first cities to be rebuilt after the Flood. Recent excavations have uncovered the city's impressive wall system.

vided into two groups of five and were used for washing sacrifices. The priests, however, washed in the BRONZE SEA (2 Chr. 4:6). Later in Judah's history, King Ahaz cut the panels off the carts and removed the lavers (2 Kin. 16:17).

The ten lavers are not mentioned in the prophet Ezekiel's description of the new Temple. The rebuilt Temples under ZERUBBABEL and HEROD each had a single laver.

LAW — an orderly system of rules and regulations by which a society is governed. In the Bible, particularly the Old Testament, a unique law code was established by direct revelation from God to direct His people in their worship, in their relationship to Him, and in their social relationships with one another.

Israel was not the only nation to have a law code. Such collections were common among the countries of the ancient world. These law codes generally began with an explanation that the gods gave the king the power to reign, along with a pronouncement about how good and capable he was. Then came the king's laws grouped by subject. The code generally closed with a series of curses and blessings.

The biblical law code, or the Mosaic Law, was different from other ancient near eastern law codes in several ways. Biblical law was different, first of all, in its origin. Throughout the ancient world, the laws of most nations were believed to originate with the gods, but they were considered intensely personal and subjective in the way they were applied. Even the gods were under the law, and they could suffer punishment if they violated it—unless, of course, they were powerful and able to conquer the punishers. The king ruled under the god whose temple and property he oversaw. Although he did

not live under a written law code, he had a personal relationship to the god. Therefore, law was decided ultimately case by case and at the king's discretion. For most of a king's lifetime, his laws were kept secret.

By contrast, the biblical concept was that law comes from God, issues from His nature, and is holy, righteous, and good. Furthermore, at the outset of God's ruling over Israel at Sinai, God the great King gave His laws. These laws were binding on His people, and He upheld them. Furthermore, His laws were universal. Ancient oriental kings often tried to outdo their predecessors in image, economic power, and political influence. This was often their motivation in setting forth law codes. God, however, depicts His law as an expression of His love for His people (Ex. 19:5–6).

In Israel all crimes were crimes against God (1 Sam. 12:9–10). Consequently, He expected all His people to love and serve Him (Amos 5:21–24). As the final judge, He disciplined those who violated His law (Ex. 22:21–24; Deut. 10:18; 19:17). The nation or community was responsible for upholding the law and insuring that justice was done (Deut. 13:6–10; 17:7; Num. 15:32–36).

God's law, unlike those of other nations of the ancient world, also viewed all human life as especially valuable, because man is created in God's image. Thus, biblical law was more humane. It avoided mutilations and other savage punishments. Victims could not inflict more injury than they had received. Neither could criminals restore less than they had taken or stolen simply because of a class distinction. Everyone was equal before God's law.

The "eye for eye" requirement of the Mosaic Law was not a harsh statement that required cruel punishment. Instead, it was a mandate for equality before the law (Ex. 21:24). Each criminal had to pay for his own crime (Num. 35:31). Under the law codes of some pagan nations, the rich often could buy their way out of punishment. God's law especially protected the defenseless orphan, widow, slave, and stranger from injustice (Ex. 21:2, 20–21; 22:21–23).

Some scholars refer to Leviticus 17—26 as the "holiness code." Although it does not contain all of God's directions for ceremonial holiness, it does set forth much of what God requires. These chapters contain moral and ritual specifications regarding the tabernacle and public worship as well as the command to love one's neighbor as oneself (19:18). The nation of Israel was to be characterized by separation from other nations. Several of these laws prohibited pagan worship. Because God is holy (21:8), Israel was to be holy and separated from other nations (20:26).

The Book of Deuteronomy is sometimes called the Deuteronomic Code. This book contains the command to love God with all one's heart, soul, and might (Deut. 6:5) as well as a second record of the Ten Commandments (Deuteronomy 5).

Biblical law is more than a record of human law. It is an expression of what God requires of man. It rests on the eternal moral principles that are consistent with the very nature of God Himself. Therefore, biblical law (the Ten Commandments) is the summary of moral law. As such it sets forth fundamental and universal moral principles.

What is often called the civil law includes those specific laws in the Pentateuch (first five books of the Old Testament) that regulate civil and social behavior. All such laws are fundamentally religious since God is the lawgiver and ruler over everything. There are eight distinct categories of civil law in the Old Testament: (1) laws regulating leaders, (2) laws regulating the army, (3) criminal laws, (4) laws dealing with crimes against property, (5) laws relating to humane treatment, (6) laws about personal and family rights, (7) laws about property rights, and (8) laws regulating other social behavior.

Laws Regulating Leaders. Several different types of laws in this category of civil law were designed to keep Israel's leadership strong and free of graft and corruption.

Exclusion laws—God commanded that several categories of people not be allowed to vote or serve in office. These included the physically handicapped, sexually maimed, those of illegitimate birth, and those of mixed race, such as Moabite or Ammonite (Deut. 23:1–3). These laws were another of the repeated attempts by God to teach Israel in a concrete manner that they were to be spiritually clean and perfect before Him.

Laws about the king—Long before Israel had a human king, God specified that if a king were to be appointed, he should follow all the laws God had given. Other specifications were that he should be a true Israelite, that he should not trust in a large army for protection, and that he should not be a polygamist or a greedy person (Deut. 17:14–20). The judges of the Book of Judges functioned as temporary military leaders. They also handled some of the functions of a modern judge. Israel's kings were different from these judges, in that they were permanent and they maintained a standing army, a governmental network, and a royal court supported by taxation.

Laws about judges—Judges were of two classes, priestly and non–priestly (elders). The priestly judges presided over religious law suits, and elders presided over civil law suits (Deut. 17:8–13; 2 Chr. 19:8, 11). Judges, also called elders, were to be elected from among heads of households (Ex. 18:13–26).

Laws about the judicial system—God commanded Israel to organize its ruling system into layers of courts (Ex. 18:21–22; Deut. 1:15), with lesser mat-

A cylinder seal from ancient Babylonia. Such seals were often used to validate decrees or legalize contracts in Bible times.

Photo by Gustav Jeeninga

Photo: Matson Photo Collection

Shepherd with his sheep at Jebel Musa (Arabic for "Mount Moses"), the mountain traditionally identified as Sinai, where Moses received the Law from God.

ters decided by lesser courts and greater matters decided by greater courts (Deut. 16:18). Matters that involved foundational principles or that were too hard for the lower courts were brought to the highest courts or the chief judge (2 Chr. 19:10-11). The highest court was God Himself (Ex. 22:21-24; Deut. 10:18).

Judges were charged not to be partial in favor of the rich or against the poor, widows, aliens, or others who might be helpless (Ex. 23:6-9; Deut. 16:18-20; 27:19). Consequently, they were to hear the witnesses carefully, examine the evidence, and make their decisions on the basis of what God had revealed in His written law. They also presided over making or nullifying all contracts.

Laws about witnesses—Witnesses were charged by God to tell the truth (Lev. 19:16). If they did not do so, they were judged by Him. If their deception was discovered, they were to bear the penalty involved in the case (Ex. 23:1-3; Deut. 19:15-19). Conviction of serious crimes required two or more witnesses (Num. 35:30). Indeed, no one could be convicted on the testimony of one witness. Written documents and other testimony could be used as evidence against the accused (Deut. 17:6; 19:18).

Laws about law enforcement—Refusal to comply with what the court decided (contempt of court) brought a sentence of death (Deut. 17:12-13). The citizens of ancient Israel were the policemen, bailiffs, etc. (Deut. 16:18). Usually executions were in the hands of the citizens (Deut. 13:9-10; 15:16). Later, the king's private army enforced his will,

while Levites also served as policemen (2 Chr. 19:11).

Laws about refuge cities—Judges controlled the entrance into the refuge cities. These were the cities where those who had committed accidental murder (manslaughter) could flee to safety. When the high priest of the nation died, refugees were free to go home without penalty (Ex. 21:12-14; Deut. 19:1-13). Israel was responsible for keeping the roads to such cities as safe as possible so the fugitive could outrun the avenger—the relative responsible for the fugitive's execution to repay the kinsman's death.

Laws about prophets—God's law strictly prohibited idolatry and provided for the death of those who would lead Israel into idolatry. The test of a true prophet was not his ability to work miracles but his faithfulness to God and His revelation (Deut. 32:1-5). On the other hand, Israel was to obey the words of true prophets. If they did not do so, God Himself would punish the people.

Laws Regulating the Army. The second category of civil law consisted of laws regulating the army. All Palestine belonged to God. Within its borders His people were commanded to wage war to gain and maintain the territory. To this end all Israelite males 20 years of age and older formed a militia (Num. 1:21-43), with 50 probably being the exemption age (Num. 4:3, 23). If only a small scale war was being fought, a selective service system operated by the casting of lots (Num. 31:3-6). Kings were to maintain only small standing armies. Their first defense from outside attack was to be the Lord Himself (Deut. 17:16; 23:9-14).

Certain citizens were exempt from the military: priests and Levites (Num. 1:48-49), the man who had not yet dedicated his newly built home (Deut. 20:5), anyone who had not gathered the first harvest from a field or vineyard (Deut. 20:6), a groom who had not yet consummated his recent marriage (Deut. 20:7), or any man who had been married within a year of the call to arms (Deut. 24:5).

All war was holy war—that is, it was fought under the lordship of God. Therefore, God promised to protect and fight for His army (Deut. 20:1-4), keeping them from harm and marshalling the forces of nature against the enemy (Josh. 10:11; 24:7). But God's protection required ritualistic separation from sin and death, dedication to God, and the following of His direction about the battle (Deut. 23:9-14). God was the commander-in-chief and the one to whom thanksgiving was due for the victory (Num. 10:9-10).

Within Palestine every non-Israelite was to be killed and all their possessions and goods offered to God (Deut. 20:16-18; 2:34; 3:6). Thus, they were to purify the territory and guard themselves from Canaanite idolatry. When the Israelites were fighting outside Palestine, the city being attacked was to be offered peace before the attack. Refusal triggered the attack. All the citizens and goods of that city then became rightful slaves and booty (Deut. 20:10-15).

Laws Respecting Criminals. The third category of

The majestic canopus of the Roman Emperor Hadrian's villa at Tivoli, Italy.

civil law consisted of laws against specific criminal offenses. In His law God defined what a criminal offense was and what the proper punishment for each offense was to be. All crimes were sins, or offenses, against God's law. Since there were degrees of punishments, there were degrees of sin under the law. God prohibited the Israelites from punishing criminals excessively (Deut. 25:1–3).

Crimes against God—Under God's law, all of life was religious, but some crimes were considered especially directed against the worship system which God had established. Conviction in these cases resulted in death, because such crimes struck out pointedly against God and life itself.

These crimes against God included worshiping other gods alongside God (Ex. 22:20; 34:14); turning from God to worship other gods (Deut. 13:1–18); seeking to control other people and future events by magic or sorcery (Ex. 22:18; Deut. 18:9–14); sacrificing children to false gods (Lev. 18:21; 20:2–5); blasphemy (Lev. 24:16); false prophecy (Deut. 18:18–20); and Sabbath labor other than that permitted by God (Ex. 35:2, 3; Matt. 12:1–8).

Crimes against society—Certain crimes struck at society as a whole. Among these were the perversion of justice through bribery, torture of witnesses, and false testimony or perjury (Ex. 23:1–7; Deut. 19:16–21). Judges were commanded to treat all people equally.

Crimes against sexual morality—Biblical law relating to sexual morality protected and sanctified the family. The sexual union of two persons made them one flesh, and this was the only such union they were to experience.

1. Fornication. In Israel the sexual union was most sacred. A newly married woman charged with premarital sex with a man other than her husband was to be put to death if the charge was proven. If the charge was not proven, her husband had to pay a large fine and keep her as his wife. Also, he could never divorce her (Deut. 22:13–21).

2. Adultery. Under God's law adultery was a serious crime, perhaps because tearing apart the two who had become one amounted to murder. Those convicted of adultery were to be put to death (Lev. 20:10–12; Deut. 22:22). A betrothed woman (virgin) was protected by the law, but she was also considered to be married in some cases. If she and some man other than her betrothed had sexual union, they were to be put to death (Deut. 22:23–24).

3. Homosexuality. Sodomy or male homosexuality was pointedly condemned and prohibited. It brought death under God's law (Lev. 20:13). By implication, the same penalty was probably also meted out for female homosexuality, or lesbianism.

4. Prostitution. Prostitutes of every guise (male or female, cultic or non–cultic) were to be put to death (Lev. 19:29; 21:9).

5. Incest. Sexual union with one's own offspring or near relative was to result in death (Lev. 20:11–14).

6. Bestiality. Having sex with a beast (a common feature of Canaanite worship) was an offense punishable by death (Ex. 22:19; Lev. 18:23; Deut. 27:21).

7. Transvestiture. The distinction between the sexes was to be retained in their outward appearance. Hence, transvestiture (wearing the clothing of the opposite sex) was forbidden.

Crimes against an individual's person—Crimes of

violence against others were serious criminal offenses. The following crimes are cited in biblical law.

1. Murder. The willful and premeditated taking of a human life was punishable by death. Accidental killing, killing as an act of war, and lawful executions were not considered murder (Ex. 21:12–14; Num. 35:14–34). The sixth commandment is, "You shall not murder." Jesus pointed to the spirit of this commandment when He expanded it to forbid hatred, anger, bitter insults, and cursing (Matt. 5:21–22).

2. Assault and battery. God's law expected people to live at peace with one another. But realizing that offenses might occur, God provided legislation about assault and battery. If injuring a person caused the victim to lose time but no further harm was done, the offender had to pay his victim for the time lost. Presumably the courts established the fine in such cases (Ex. 21:18–19). If someone maimed his foe in a struggle, he would pay for the lost time; but he would also suffer the same disfigurement at the hands of the court (Lev. 24:19). Some important exceptions to this punishment should be noted.

If the victim were a slave, disfigurement resulted in his freedom (a very heavy financial loss to the guilty party). If the slave died, the offender was to die. If the slave survived and was not disfigured, there was no penalty on the master, except that exacted for loss of time (Ex. 21:20–21, 26–27).

If a son or daughter attacked either parent, the attacker was to be put to death (Ex. 21:15). One law called for the severing of the hand of a woman who attacked a man's genitals, even though she may have been trying to protect her husband (Deut. 25:11–12).

3. Miscarriage. Miscarriage, or the death of the mother resulting from a blow by someone in a fight, brought death upon the attacker. Premature birth caused by this offense required a money fine determined by the husband as governed by the courts (Ex. 21:22).

4. Rape and seduction. A man who raped a betrothed woman was to be put to death (Deut. 22:25–27). However, if he raped or seduced an unattached woman, he was to pay a large fine and propose marriage. A girl's father could refuse the marriage and keep the money; but if he approved, the rapist had to marry the girl and could never divorce her (Ex. 22:16–17; Deut. 2:28–29). If the seduced girl was a betrothed slave, she was considered unattached (for she had not yet been released from slavery). Consequently, the attacker was not put to death. But the man had to bring a guilt offering before God to make restitution for his sin.

5. Oppression. In Israel the defenseless were to be defended. Those without rights or power to enforce their rights were protected by God. These included the alien passing through the area and the alien who was a temporary or permanent resident. The widow, orphan, deaf, blind, slave, hired hand, and poor were to be given just wages, paid immediately, given interest free loans (except aliens) in emergencies, gifts of food at festivals, and the privilege of gleaning, etc. (Ex. 22:21–24; Lev. 19:14, 33; Deut. 24:14; 27:18–19).

6. Kidnapping. Capturing a person to sell or use him as a slave was a capital offense (Deut. 24:7). This prohibition extended to foreigners, (unless they were prisoners of war; Ex 22:21–24), the blind and deaf (Lev. 19:14), and all people (Deut. 27:19).

7. Slander. Slander (making malicious statements about another person) was strictly forbidden and punished if the crime was committed during a trial (Ex. 23:1). This was viewed as a mortal attack on a person (Lev. 19:16).

Crimes Against Property. The fourth category of civil law consisted of laws dealing with crimes against property. Biblical law, unlike other ancient near Eastern codes, placed a higher value on human life than on possessions. But it also allowed people to have private possessions by protecting them from theft and fraud. The following crimes against property are dealt with in the Bible.

Stealing—God prohibited anyone from stealing from another. Heavy financial penalties were levied upon the thief. If he could not pay, he was required to serve as an indentured servant to pay the restitution price in labor (Ex. 22:1–3).

Blackmail and loan fraud—God's law counted these crimes as a kind of theft, mandating heavy penalties and possible indentured service as penalties (Ex. 22:1–3; Lev. 6:1–7).

Weights and measures—Ancient Israel did not use money; transactions were in measured, or weighed, precious metal. God prohibited anyone from juggling weights so the goods or metals would be measured out to favor the thief. Such a thief had to repay his victims (Lev. 19:35–36; Deut. 25:13–16).

Lost animals—"Finders, keepers" did not hold in ancient Israel. Straying animals were to be returned to the owner or cared for until claimed (Ex. 23:4–5; Deut. 22:1–4).

Boundaries—The land was marked into sections by ancient landmarks, according to the allotments made shortly after it was conquered. To move these landmarks resulted in God's curse. This act was considered stealing from one's neighbor as well as rebellion against God the great landowner (Deut. 19:14; 27:17).

Laws Relating to Humane Treatment. The fifth category of civil law consisted of laws about humane treatment. God's law regulated treatment of otherwise defenseless animals and people.

Protection of animals—Some of these laws were also environmental laws. For example, Israel was commanded not to work the land on the seventh year. Whatever grain or fruit grew up was to be left for the animals and the poor. This forced a crop rotation system on the Hebrew people so they would have some harvest every year (Ex. 23:11–12; Lev. 25:5–7). They were allowed to eat certain wild beasts and birds but were forbidden to take a mother. Presumably, they could take the young or

paid properly (Deut. 24:14–15, 19–22).

The respectable and responsible poor were to be extended interest free loans (Lev. 25:35–37). Their cloaks, which they used at night as blankets, could not be taken as collateral. Neither could a creditor forcibly enter a man's house to collect the debt (Deut. 24:10–13).

The elderly were to be respected, cared for, and protected (Lev. 19:32). Travelers could enter fields to harvest a meal for themselves, but they were forbidden to take more than they could eat (Deut. 23:24–25). If these provisions did not satisfy the needs of the poor, they could sell themselves into indentured service (temporary servitude). In cases like this, the law demanded that they be treated humanely (Lev. 25:39–43). In general, treatment of others was to be governed by the law of love (Lev. 19:18) or the Golden Rule (Matt. 7:12).

Laws Regulating Personal and Family Rights. Another broad category of civil law dealt with personal and family rights. The following situations were covered by these statutes.

Parents and children—The law of God assumed that parents would act responsibly and feed and clothe their children even as God fed and clothed them. Parents also were to discipline and teach their children (Deut. 6:6–7). A father was responsible for circumcising his sons (Gen. 17:12–13), redeeming his firstborn from God (Num. 18:15–16), and finding his children proper marriage partners (Gen. 24:4).

Children were commanded to respect and obey their parents (Ex. 20:12). Disrespect in the form of striking or cursing a parent and delinquency (stubbornness and disobedience expressed in gluttony and drunkenness) were punishable by death (Ex. 21:15, 17; Deut. 21:18–21). Minor children were under their parents' authority and could not make binding vows. Unmarried girls were not allowed to make binding vows without their fathers' or their male guardians' agreement (Num. 30:3–5).

Marriage—God prohibited the Israelites from marrying near relatives and members of their own immediate family (Lev. 18:6–18; Deut. 27:20–23). He also forbade intermarriage with the Canaanites because these pagans would lead their mates into idolatry (Deut. 7:1–4). But if Canaanites converted and became Israelites (members of God's covenantal community), no legal and religious bar prevented marriage with them. A man would marry a woman prisoner of war after she mourned her parents' deaths for a month. This did not necessarily mean her parents were actually dead, but only that this woman now became an Israelite. If her husband divorced her, she had to be set free. Her marriage had made her a full citizen under the law—an Israelite.

Special laws also regulated the marriage of priests. A priest was not to marry a former harlot, a woman who had been previously married, or one who had previously had sexual relations. His bride had to be a virgin Israelitess (Lev. 21:7, 13–15).

Within the marriage bond, women were pro-

Photo by Gustav Jeeninga

A Roman milestone which stood along a major Roman highway in Iconium. The marker told the traveler the distance to various cities along the highway.

the eggs, but they were required to let the mother live (Deut. 22:6–7). An ox or any working beast (or human being) was to be fed adequately to give him strength for doing the work (Deut. 25:4). Animals were not to be cruelly beaten or overloaded. They were to be rested on the Sabbath (Ex. 20:8–11; 23:12; Deut. 22:1–4).

Protection of human beings—The poor, widow, orphan, alien, sojourner, blind, deaf, etc., were to receive humane treatment from God's people (Ex. 22:21–25). To preserve their self-respect, they were to be given opportunities to earn a living by gleaning and working for wages. They were also to be tected from undue male harshness by the laws relating to the dowry, the large sum of money given to the girl and held in part by her father in case of their divorce or the husband's death. Laws also called for severe penalties for violent crimes (usually perpetrated by men), as well as severe penalties for the beating and maiming of household members. God also admonished the man to love the woman as his own body and to treat her accordingly (Deut. 21:10-14).

The wife and mother was to be honored by the children (Ex. 20:12). Sexual relations were forbidden during a woman's menstrual period—perhaps for sanitary reasons, but certainly to emphasize the sanctity of life and the life-giving process (Lev. 18:19; 20:18). A woman of child-bearing age left childless at the death of her husband was to be married to one of his surviving near relatives so she could bear children to carry on the family name (Deut. 25:5-10). This also provided her with an advocate and protector in the civil court (Deut. 22:13-19) and a representative before God's altar (Deut. 16:16).

Husbands were given primary authority in the family. His wife was under his authority in all matters. Obviously, this did not reduce her to a slave status or to an inferior position, since the two had become one. It did, however, establish a clear authority structure that minimized internal familial struggles and allowed the family to function socially, economically, and religiously (Num. 30:6-15).

Infidelity was punishable by death. Divorce was granted on many grounds other than the breaking of the one-flesh relationship through sexual union with man or beast and the willful abandonment of the marriage (Deut. 24:1-4). When a man wrongfully accused his wife of infidelity (22:17-19), he could not divorce her.

Hired servants—God especially protected the poor from the ravages of the rich. One such measure was the law requiring employees to pay their hired help a just and fair wage and to do so at the end of each work day (Lev. 19:13; Deut. 24:14).

Slaves—Slaves were of two classes, indentured and permanent. Hebrews who were unable to pay debts were indentured, or committed to temporary servitude. The indenture lasted only six years or until the year of JUBILEE. He might be given a wife while in this state, but the wife and children resulting from the union were bound to the master. Such a man could bind himself permanently to the master either for the master's sake or for that of his family (Ex. 21:2-6).

An Israelite indentured because of poverty was not to be thought of or treated as a slave. He could not be treated with the rigor of slavery. He was to be treated as a hired servant. For example, he was to be paid (Deut. 15:12-14). He could be bought out of the situation by his relatives, or by himself—presumably by savings resulting from his wages while indentured (Lev. 25:39-43, 47-55).

A girl sold to a man as a wife was especially protected. She could be redeemed by her family if the master was not satisfied with her. She could not be sold as a slave to foreign people. She was to be treated as a daughter and provided for in the same way as other wives. If these laws were disobeyed, her freedom was granted (Ex. 21:2-6).

Permanent slaves could be acquired by purchase or as prisoners of war. They were only to be taken from the nations and peoples outside Palestine (Lev. 25:44-46). Fugitive slaves were not to be returned to their owners or treated as slaves—a provision that worked to force masters to treat slaves humanely (Deut. 23:15-16).

Slaves were considered permanent members of their master's household, circumcised, and admitted to Passover (Ex. 12:43-44) and all the special meals eaten before the Lord, except the guilt offering (Deut. 12:17-18; 16:10-11). A slave could be forced to work; but if beaten severely, he was to be freed (Ex. 21:20-32). If a slave was killed, the master was to be put to death (Ex. 21:20).

Aliens—Aliens could convert to Judaism, be circumcised, and become full members of the covenant (Num. 9:14; 15:12-15). Even if aliens temporarily or permanently living as free people in Israel did not convert, they were to receive full privileges under the civil law (Num. 15:29-30). Unlike Jews, aliens ate foods declared unclean by God; such foods could be sold or given to them (Deut. 14:21).

Israelites were forbidden to take advantage of the poor Israelite by charging him interest for the loan of food, clothing, money, or anything else (Ex. 22:25; Lev. 25:35-37). But the poor and desperate alien could be charged interest, perhaps because the Israelites considered his state a result of God's judgment (Deut. 23:20).

Laws Regulating Property Rights. Another broad category of civil law consisted of those laws that regulated property rights. The following situations were covered by these laws.

Lost property—Under Mosaic law, all lost property was to be returned to its owner if the owner was known or held until claimed by him (Deut. 22:1-4).

Damaged property—Property held in trust was protected under the law. A person caught stealing had to restore to the owner double the value of the goods stolen. If the goods were stolen through carelessness by a trustee of the property, the trustee had to repay the full amount missing. If the loss was accidental or not due to the trustee's carelessness, that trustee was not liable for the loss, provided he was willing to swear before God that the loss was not his fault (Ex. 22:7-13). Borrowed goods had to be returned. If they were damaged or lost while borrowed, they had to be replaced by the borrower (Ex. 22:14-15).

Unsafe property—Owners were held responsible for unsafe property. Thus, if someone was hurt because of an owner's property, the owner had to pay a penalty. In the case of death, the owner of the property lost his life (Ex. 21:28-36; Deut. 22:8).

Land ownership—Ultimately, God owned all the land (Lev. 25:23). He demanded that His tenants rest the land every seventh year by not planting a crop (Lev. 25:1–7). During this seventh year, all travelers and the poor were allowed to eat of the produce of the land without paying for it. All parcels of land were assigned permanently to certain families; they reverted back to those original owners or their heirs every 50th year (Lev. 25:8–24). The land could also be purchased by those owners at its original selling price (Lev. 25:29–31) in the interim. Furthermore, it was a serious matter to move the ancient markers that designated the boundaries of the land. Within walled cities, only Levites owned houses in a permanent sense (Lev. 25:32–34).

Inheritance laws—Normally only legitimate sons were to inherit all the family's property. The first-born son received twice as much as the others (Deut. 21:15–17; 25:6). He was responsible for caring for elderly family members and providing a respectable burial for them. A wicked son could be disinherited. If no sons were born to a family, legitimate daughters were to inherit the property (Num. 27:7–8). Such heiresses had to marry within their own tribe or lose the inheritance (Num. 36:1–12).

Laws Regulating Other Social Behavior. The final category of civil law included those statutes that regulated specific social behavior. God commanded

Traditional tomb of Lazarus, who was raised from the dead by Jesus (John 11:1–44).

Photo by Howard Vos

the Hebrew people to keep themselves from pagan religious and cultic practices (Ex. 20:3–5; Lev. 19:27). Among these practices were boiling a kid in its mother's milk (Deut. 14:21), shaving one's head in a particular way (Lev. 13:33; 21:5), worshiping idols (Deut. 7:5, 25; 12:2–3), sacrificing children (Lev. 20:2), participating in homosexuality and temple prostitution (Lev. 19:29), slashing or tatooing one's body (Lev. 19:28), and practicing magic, sorcery, or divination (Lev. 19:26, 31).

God's people were to preserve and study the Lord's law (Deut. 4:2; 6:6–7), revere His name (Deut. 8:6; 10:12), be grateful and thankful (Deut. 8:10), and obey, love, and serve their redeemer God (Deut. 10:14–16; 6:4–5; 11:1, 13–14).

LAW, ROMAN (see ROMAN LAW).

LAWGIVER — one who gives a code of laws to a people. John wrote that the Law was given through Moses (John 1:17; 7:19). But above and beyond Moses stands God as the supreme Lawgiver, "For the Lord is our Judge, the Lord is our Lawgiver" (Is. 33:22).

LAWYER (see OCCUPATIONS AND TRADES).

LAYING ON OF HANDS (see HANDS, LAYING ON OF).

LAZARUS [LAZ ah russ] (*God has helped*) — the name of two men in the New Testament:

1. The beggar in Jesus' story about a rich man and a poor man (Luke 16:19–25). The wealthy man despised the beggar, paying no attention to his needs when he passed him each day. After the death of Lazarus, the poor man, he was carried by angels to Abraham's bosom, where he found comfort. But the rich man at death found himself in HADES, in eternal torment.

This story was not intended to praise the poor and condemn the rich. It shows the dangers of turning away from the needs of others. It teaches that our attitude on earth will result in an eternal destiny that parallels our attitude. This note is sounded frequently in the teaching of Jesus (Matt. 7:24–27; Luke 16:9).

2. The brother of Martha and Mary of Bethany (John 11:1). One long account in the Gospel of John tells about his death and resurrection at the command of Jesus (John 11). A second account in the same gospel describes him as sitting with Jesus in the family home after the resurrection miracle (John 12:1–2). Because of the publicity surrounding this event, the chief priest plotted to kill Lazarus (John 12:9–11).

Twice John's gospel records Jesus' love for Lazarus (John 11:3, 5). Yet, upon hearing of the sickness of his friend, Jesus delayed in returning to Bethany. When He finally arrived, both Martha and Mary rebuked Jesus for not coming sooner. Jesus showed His impatience at their unbelief (11:33) as well as His personal sorrow ("Jesus wept"). Then he brought Lazarus back to life (11:43).

Photo by Gustav Jeeninga

Cedars of Lebanon on the mountainsides of Lebanon. Reckless cutting of these magnificent trees across the centuries has almost eliminated them from the landscape.

LAZINESS — inactivity, idleness, or a refusal to work—a condition condemned by many biblical writers. "Because of laziness the building decays," wrote the author of Ecclesiastes, "and through idleness of hands the house leaks" (Eccl. 10:18). The New Testament speaks of a "wicked and lazy servant" (Matt. 25:26) and of "lazy gluttons" (Titus 1:12).

LEAD (see MINERALS OF THE BIBLE).

LEAGUE — an association of nations or states united by common interests (Dan. 11:23; alliance, RSV, NASB, NEB; agreement, NIV). The Hebrew word translated as league in this passage is usually translated as covenant; it can also mean confederacy, federation, or peace treaty.

LEAH [LEE uh] (*gazelle*) — the older daughter of Laban, who deceitfully gave her in marriage to Jacob instead of her younger sister Rachel (Gen. 29:16–30). Although Rachel was the more beautiful of the two daughters of Laban and obviously was Jacob's favorite wife, the Lord blessed Leah and Jacob with six sons—Reuben, Simeon, Levi, Judah (Gen. 29:31–35), Issachar, and Zebulun (Gen. 30:17–20)—and a daughter, Dinah (Gen. 30:21). Leah's maid, Zilpah, added two more sons: Gad and Asher (Gen. 30:9–13).

Leah was the less-favored of the two wives of Jacob, and she must have been painfully conscious of this during all the years of her marriage. But it was Leah rather than Rachel who gave birth to Judah, through whose line Jesus the Messiah was eventually born.

Apparently Leah died in the land of Canaan before the migration to Egypt (Gen. 46:6). She was buried in the Cave of Machpelah in Hebron (Gen. 49:31).

LEANNOTH (see MUSIC OF THE BIBLE).

LEATHER — the dressed and tanned hide of an animal used for making clothes, such as sheepskin, goatskin, and badger skin (Lev. 15:17; Num. 31:20). The trade of a TANNER, a person who tans hides, is mentioned in Acts 9:43 and 10:6, 32. Animal skins were sometimes used also as containers for liquids. Also see WINESKIN.

LEATHER WORKER (see OCCUPATIONS AND TRADES).

LEAVEN — a substance used to produce fermentation in dough and make it rise (Ex. 12:15, 19–20). In Bible times leaven was usually a piece of fermented dough retained from a previous baking that was placed in the new dough to cause it to rise.

The use of leaven was prohibited in food offerings dedicated to the Lord by fire (Lev. 2:11). However, leavened bread was required for the peace offering (Lev. 7:13) and for the two wave loaves offered at the Feast of Weeks, or Pentecost (Lev. 23:17). During the Exodus, the Israelites had eaten unleavened bread because of their hasty departure from Egypt (Ex. 12:34, 39). The practice of this first Passover was continued in all subsequent observances of the Passover. At the beginning of the Passover season every year, all leaven was expelled from the house (Ex. 12:15) and was kept from the house for seven days (Ex. 12:19). These days, called the "Days of Unleavened Bread" (Acts 12:3), commemorated the eating of unleavened bread at the time of departure from Egypt.

Leaven is used metaphorically in the Bible of an influence that can permeate whatever it touches. Leaven is used as a symbol of either good or bad influence. In one parable, Jesus used the word leaven in a good sense:

"The kingdom of heaven is like leaven, which a woman took and hid in three measures of meal till it was all leavened" (Matt. 13:33). The action of the leaven in the meal—hidden, yet powerful, relentless, and pervasive—is a symbol of the growth of God's spiritual rule in the world.

On the other hand, Jesus also used the word leaven in an evil sense to illustrate the "fermentation" of moral and political corruption: "Take heed and beware of the leaven [doctrine] of the Pharisees and the Sadducees" (Matt. 16:6, 12).

LEAVES — the foliage of plants or trees. Leaves are mentioned literally in the Bible as clothing for Adam and Eve (Gen. 3:7), as evidence of the earth's renewal following the Flood (Gen. 8:11), and as building material for constructing the booths required in the observance of the Feast of Tabernacles (Neh. 8:15).

Withered leaves serve as a metaphor for the Lord's judgment which brings death (Is. 1:30), or for unproductiveness in serving the Lord (Is. 64:6). Green and growing leaves are figures of speech for the righteous and their productivity in the kingdom (Ps. 1:3). Hence, trees that bear leaves which do not wither and which serve "for the healing of nations" symbolize the unending blessing of the age to come (Rev. 22:2).

LEBANA — [leh BAY nûh] a form of LEBANAH.

LEB KAMAI [leb KAY my] — a code name for Chaldea, or Babylonia (Jer. 51:1; Kambul, NEB; Chaldea, RSV; Leb-qamai, RSV margin).

LEBANAH [lih BAY nuh] (*whiteness*) — the head of a family of Nethinim (Temple servants). Some of his descendants returned from the Captivity with Zerubbabel (Ezra 2:45). The name is also spelled Lebana (Neh. 7:48).

LEBANON [LEB uh none] (*white*) — a nation of the Middle East which includes much of what was ancient PHOENICIA in Bible times (see Map 9, C–1). This territory has been an important trade center linking Europe and Asia for more than 4,000 years.

In ancient times the Phoenicians used the city-states of Byblos, Sidon, and Tyre as the base of a great sea-trading empire in what is now Lebanon. Over the years, these city-states were conquered by Egyptians, Assyrians, Persians, and the Greeks under Alexander the Great. Later still, Lebanon became part of the Roman Empire, and many inhabitants became Christians. But when the Arabs conquered Lebanon in the seventh century A.D., many turned to the Muslim religion.

Early in the 16th century, the Arabs were overthrown by the Turks. Then in 1918 the British and French forces broke up the Turkish or Ottoman Empire and placed Lebanon under French rule. In 1943, Lebanon achieved independence. The country has continued to be the scene of strife and turmoil involving Israelis, Syrians, and Palestinian guerrillas. Civil war at times between Muslims and Christians has also added to the strife of this war-torn country.

Lebanon takes its name from the Lebanon Mountains, which run parallel to the coast of the MEDITERRANEAN SEA for almost the length of the country. The range consists of snow–capped limestone peaks that rise sharply from the shore line, leaving just enough space for a coastal road. The 160–kilometer-long (100–mile–long) mountains are made up of two parallel ranges, the Lebanons and the Anti–Lebanons. Between the two is the fertile plain of el-Bekaa, measuring about 48 kilometers (30 miles) by 16 kilometers (10 miles), which was also called the Valley of Lebanon (Josh. 11:17).

The scenic beauty of the country has inspired many symbolic references in the Bible (Ps. 92:12; Song 4:15; 5:15). The rich vegetation of Lebanon became a symbol of fruitfulness and fertility (Ps. 72:16; Ps. 92:12).

Originally, the famed Cedars of Lebanon covered the region. But bands of marauding conquerors from Mesopotamia, Egypt, Israel, and Tyre destroyed the forests by using the wood for palaces, furniture, ships, coffins, and musical instruments. By the sixth century A.D., the beautiful groves were almost gone. Egyptian texts from many different periods refer to trade with the Phoenician cities that supplied them with lumber from Lebanon. Ugaritic and Mesopotamian texts mention that cedars from Lebanon were used in building their important temples and palaces.

In recent years a program of reforestation has been conducted in national parks. The prophets of the Old Testament used the destruction of these magnificient trees by aggressors as a symbol of Israel's destruction (Jer. 22:7; Ezek. 27:5; Zech. 11:2).

The climate of Lebanon ranges from the almost tropical heat and vegetation of the plain of Dan to heavy snow in the plain of el-Bekaa. Mainly it has a Mediterranean climate with cool, wet winters and hot, dry summers. In the spring or summer, a searing desert wind sometimes blows in from Syria. Lebanon is often called "the playground of the Middle East" because of summer sports along the coastline and winter sports in the snow-covered mountains and the el-Bekaa Valley.

The Lebanon Mountains formed the northwest boundary of the land of Palestine, the "Promised Land" to the Hebrew people (Deut. 1:7; 11:24). The original inhabitants of Lebanon were independent, warlike tribes of Phoenician stock. Further north were the HIVITES and the GEBALITES. It is occupied today by various sects of Christians and Muslims.

Archaeological discoveries have thrown light on the Canaanites who settled in neighboring Lebanon after Israel's gradual conquest of Canaan. Hundreds of clay tablets, dating from the 15th to the 14th centuries B.C., were uncovered in the ancient city of UGARIT, now modern RAS SHAMRA in Lebanon. Inscribed in wedge-shaped letters, the tablets reveal an advanced culture with depraved religious practices.

LEBAOTH [LEB ah ohth] — a form of BETH LEBAOTH.

LEBBAEUS [leh BEE uhs] (*man of heart*) — one of the 12 apostles, also called THADDAEUS (Matt. 10:3). According to a church tradition, Lebbaeus is the same person as "Judas the son [or brother] of James" (Luke 6:16).

LEBONAH [lih BOE nuh] (*incense*) — a town of Ephraim (Judg. 21:19), situated on the "highway" that led north from Jerusalem to Shechem.

LECAH [LEE kuh] (*addition*) — a son of Er, descended from Judah (1 Chr. 4:21).

LEECH (see ANIMALS OF THE BIBLE).

LEEK (see PLANTS OF THE BIBLE).

LEES — the sediments or settlings of wine during fermentation and aging; the dregs remaining in a skin of wine. In Bible times, the sediment or lees was often left in the wine to improve its flavor. "A feast of wines on the lees...of well-refined wines on the lees" (Is. 25:6) is a symbol of the happiness and enjoyment of the righteous in the age to come. But to drink the dregs, or lees, of the cup of God's wrath (Ps. 75:8) means to drain the cup, to endure the judgment and punishment that falls upon the wicked.

LEFT — the side of the body where the heart is located. In the Bible the word left is often used with the word hand. Among the Hebrews the left hand indicated the north (Gen. 14:15; Ezek. 16:46, KJV). Also see LEFTHANDED.

LEFT HAND — among the Hebrews a way of indicating the north. The Hebrew method of affixing directions assumed that a person was facing the sunrise, the east. The left hand, therefore, would indicate the north; and the right hand would indicate the south. In the Bible, the right hand is the hand of strength and blessing, but the left hand usually indicates deception and treachery (Judg. 3:15, 21).

When the Son of Man judges the nations, he will divide His sheep from the goats. His sheep, the righteous, will be placed at His right hand—the place of honor. But He will set the goats, the unrighteous, on His left hand—the place of condemnation.

LEFT-HANDED — favoring the left hand. The Bible indicates the tribe of Benjamin had more than its share of left-handed people (Judg. 20:16). Ehud, a left-handed Benjamite, assassinated Eglon, king of Moab, with a dagger (Judg. 3:15–22).

LEGACY — an inheritance (Prov. 3:35).

LEGION — the principal unit of the Roman army, consisting of 3,000 to 6,000 infantry troops and 100 to 200 cavalrymen. The New Testament does not use the word legion in its strict military sense, but in a general sense to express a large number. When Jesus healed a man possessed by unclean spirits or demons, He asked the man his name. He replied,

The Valley of Lebonah, situated between Shiloh and Shechem (Judg. 21:29).
Photo by E. B. Trovillion

"My name is Legion; for we are many" (Mark 5:9). The man was inhabited by many demons.

LEHABIM [lih HAY bim] (*red*) — a son of Mizraim (Gen. 10:13).

LEHI [LEE high] (*jawbone*) — a place in the hill country of Judah (Judg. 15:9, 14, 19) where Samson killed a thousand Philistines with the jawbone of a donkey. Lehi probably was about halfway between Jerusalem and the Mediterranean Sea.

LEMUEL [LEM yoo uhl] (*devoted to God*) — an unknown king who records "the utterance which his mother taught him" (Prov. 31:1). Some of the early Jewish rabbis identified Lemuel with Solomon. Other scholars believe he was Hezekiah, or even an anonymous Arabian prince.

LENTIL (see PLANTS OF THE BIBLE).

LEOPARD (see ANIMALS OF THE BIBLE).

LEPER — a person who suffers from a slowly progressing and incurable skin disease. In the Bible the word leprosy refers to a variety of symptoms. Modern medicine now recognizes that some of these symptoms belonged to diseases other than leprosy.

There are several types of leprosy. Biblical leprosy was most likely a severe type of psoriasis, a form of the disease relatively rare in modern times.

Old Testament Law was quite detailed in its instructions regarding recognition and quarantine of leprous persons. The Bible never implies that leprosy can be cured by non-miraculous means, even though it does contain guidelines for readmitting cured lepers into normal society. The Old Testament contains no references to treatment or remedy. Jehoram's exclamation (2 Kin. 5:7) implies the belief that leprosy could be cured only by a miracle.

Leprosy is a chronic, infectious disease characterized by sores, scabs, and white shining spots beneath the skin. Modern medicine has all but eliminated the disease after learning proper methods of treatment.

The Mosaic Law was very specific about the proper methods of purification where leprosy was concerned. The priest was the central figure in the Old Testament regulations for the care of patients and for sanitary precautions.

If the symptoms of leprosy showed up in a person, the priest was to decide if this was leprosy or some other disease. Because of the need to control the spread of a disease for which there was no cure, the law required that a leper be isolated from the rest of society (Lev. 13:45–46). While thus excluded, the leper was required to wear mourning clothes, leave his hair in disorder, keep his beard covered and cry "Unclean! Unclean!" so everyone could avoid him. As long as the disease lasted, he was to live in isolation away from other people (Lev. 13:45–46).

Leprosy in a house showed up in a greenish or reddish color on the walls. When the owner of a house noticed these symptoms, he reported them to the priest. The priest purified the dwelling if the disease could be controlled, or he ordered it destroyed if the signs of leprosy lingered on (Lev. 14:33–53).

In Old Testament times, linen and woolen garments were also said to be leprous when they had patches of mildew, mold, or fungus growth (Lev. 13:47–59). Leprosy in clothes, fabrics, and leather was also indicated by greenish or reddish spots. These spots were reported to the priest, who ordered the affected article to be purified or burned (Lev. 13:47–59).

Any contact with a leper defiled the person who touched him. Sometimes leprosy victims were miraculously cured. Moses (Ex. 4:7), Miriam, his sister (Num. 12:10), and Naaman (2 Kin. 5:1, 10) are prominent examples of such miracles.

King Uzziah was a leper from middle age until death (2 Chr. 26:19–21). The leprosy inflicted upon him (2 Kin. 15:5; 2 Chr. 26:23) for his unwarranted assumption of the priesthood began in his forehead.

In the New Testament, cleansing of lepers is mentioned as a specific portion of Jesus' work of healing. On one occasion Jesus healed ten lepers, but only one returned to thank him (Luke 17:11–15).

Also see DISEASES OF THE BIBLE.

LETTERS — written messages between persons separated by distance. In the Old Testament David wrote a letter to Joab, sending Uriah the Hittite into the heat of battle and insuring his death. In Bible times, letters consisted of three types: (1) sheets of PARCHMENT, or animal skins, which had been scraped and dried and then written on with ink; (2) fragments of inscribed pottery; and (3) CUNEIFORM (wedge-shaped) signs inscribed on clay tablets.

In the New Testament, Saul of Tarsus went to the high priest in Jerusalem and secured letters from him to the synagogues of Damascus. These letters authorized Saul to arrest Christians and bring them to Jerusalem (Acts 9:2; 22:5). The Jerusalem Council also sent a letter to Christians expressing their decision (Acts 15:23, 30).

Also see EPISTLE; WRITING; WRITING MATERIALS.

LETUSHIM [lih TOO shuhm] (*oppressed*) — a son of Dedan (Gen. 25:3).

LEUMMIM [LEE uh mim] (*people*) — a son of Dedan (Gen. 25:3).

LEVI [LEE vigh] (*joined*) — the name of four men and one tribe in the Bible:

1. The third son of Jacob and Leah (Gen. 29:34). His three sons were ancestors of the three main divisions of the Levitical priesthood: the GERSHONITES, the KOHATHITES, and the MERARITES (Gen. 46:11). Levi participated in the plot against Joseph (Gen. 37:4) and later took his family to Egypt with Jacob. On his deathbed Jacob cursed Simeon and Levi because of their "cruelty" and "wrath," and foretold that their descendants would be divided and scattered (Gen. 49:5–7). Levi died in Egypt at the age of 137 (Ex. 6:16).

2. A tribe descended from Levi (Ex. 6:19). Also see LEVITES.

3. Another name for MATTHEW, one of the twelve apostles (Mark 2:14). Levi was formerly a tax collector.

4. An ancestor of Jesus Christ (Luke 3:24). Levi was a son of Melchi and the father of Matthat.

5. Another ancestor of Jesus Christ (Luke 3:29). This Levi was a son of Simeon and the father of Matthat.

LEVIATHAN [lih VIE uh thuhn] (*the twisted one*) — a sea monster represented as a cruel enemy defeated by God (Job 3:8). Some interpreters see Leviathan as a symbol of the cruel enemies of God's people: as Egypt (Ps. 74:13–14) and as the Assyro-Babylonian Empire (Is. 27:1). In "that day"—the day of the Lord's judgment—the Lord "will punish Leviathan...that twisted serpent; and He will slay the reptile that is in the sea" (Is. 27:1).

LEVIRATE MARRIAGE — a form of marriage prescribed by the Law of Moses in which a man was required to marry the widow of a brother who died with no male heir. The term levirate means "husband's brother." The purpose of the law was to provide an heir for the dead brother, thereby preserving his name and estate. The law also was designed to provide for the welfare of the widows (Deut. 25:5–10).

The story of Ruth and Boaz, recorded in the Book of Ruth, is a good example of the levirate form of marriage. Reference to levirate marriage was also made by the Sadducees, who tested Jesus with a question about the resurrection (Matt. 22:23–33).

LEVITES [LEE vytes) — descendants of Levi who served as assistants to the PRIESTS in the worship system of the nation of Israel. As a Levite, AARON and his sons and their descendants were charged with the responsibility of the priesthood—offering burnt offerings and leading the people in worship and confession. But all the other Levites who were not descended directly from Aaron were to serve as priestly assistants, taking care of the tabernacle and the Temple and performing other menial duties (Num. 8:6).

The choice of the Levites as a people who would perform special service for God goes back to the days of the Exodus when the children of Israel were camped at Mount Sinai.

The people grew restless while they waited for Moses to return from talking with the Lord on the mountain. Breaking their covenant with God, they made a golden calf and began to worship it. The Levites were no less guilty than the other tribes. But when Moses returned and called for those on the Lord's side to come forward, the descendants of Levi were the only ones who voluntarily rallied to his side, showing zeal for God's honor (Ex. 32:26–28).

Even before this event, Aaron and his sons had been set apart for the priesthood. But many helpers were needed to attend to the needs of the tabernacle, which was built later at God's command in the Wilderness of Sinai. The Levites were chosen for this honor.

The designation of a tribe for special service to God grew out of an unusual concept of the Hebrew people known as the firstfruits. According to this principle, the first part of a crop to be harvested was dedicated to God. This principle even extended to the first children to be born in a family. Just before the Exodus from Egypt, when God sent the death angel to kill the firstborn of every Egyptian family, He instructed the Israelites to put blood on their doorposts, that their firstborn might be spared the same fate. Thus, the firstborn of every Israelite family became God's special property, dedicated to Him as a memorial. But because the Levites were the ones who voluntarily returned to their Lord after worshiping the golden image, they were chosen for service to the sanctuary, thus replacing the firstborn as God's representatives of the holiness of His people (Num. 3:12–13, 41).

A Levite's special service to God began with his consecration at about age 25. First he was sprinkled with the "water of purification" (Num. 8:7). Next, the hair was shaved from his entire body, his clothes were washed, and sacrifice was made of two young bulls, and a grain offering of fine flour mixed with oil (Num. 8:7–8). After this purification, he was brought before the door of the tabernacle and set apart for service by the laying on of the hands of the elders (Num. 8:9–15).

Young Levites began as assistants to the priests and chief Levites, then progressed through the higher duties and offices such as doorkeeper, member of the Temple orchestra, or administrator. In the days before the Temple was built and the people worshipped in the tabernacle, the Levites always transported the tabernacle and its furniture when the camp was moved. Then they erected and cared for the tent in its new location. They guarded it, cleaned it, and cleaned the furniture (Num. 1:50–53; 3:6–9; 4:1–33).

Since the Levites served under the priests, they were forbidden to touch any sacred furniture or the altar until it had been covered by the priests (Num. 4:15). Temple slaves often assisted the Levites in the heavier, more menial duties such as cutting wood and carrying water (Josh. 9:21; Ezra 8:20).

The Levites also prepared the SHOWBREAD and did whatever baking was needed in connection with the sacrifices. They helped the priests slaughter and skin the animals for sacrifices, examined the lepers according to the Law, and led music during worship. Retiring from active service at age 50, the Levites were free to remain in the Temple as overseers or to give assistance to their young successors (Num. 8:25–26).

Unlike the other tribes of Israel, the Levites received no territorial inheritance in the promised land of Canaan. Their portion was to be God Himself (Num. 18:20), who commanded that 48 cities be set apart for them, along with enough pasture

The mound of Gibeon (left), a city assigned to the Levites and priests at the time of Joshua's conquest of Canaan (Josh. 21:17). The modern village of Gibeon is on the right.

for their cattle (Num. 35:1–8). They were to receive the tithes due God from the fruits of the fields, the flocks and herds, the fruits of the firstborn, and certain portions of the people's sacrificial offerings (Num. 18:24). Of these tithes, the Levites had to turn over a tithe (a tenth part) to the priests (Num. 18:26).

The Levites were not required to devote all their time to the sanctuary. During most of the year, they lived in their own cities. Then at fixed periods they came to the tabernacle to take their turn at work. For example, during David's reign, the Levites were divided into four classes: (1) assistants to priests in the work of the sanctuary, (2) judges and scribes, (3) gatekeepers, and (4) musicians. Each of these classes, with the possible exception of the second, was subdivided into 24 courses or families who served in rotation (1 Chr. 24—25; Ezra 6:18).

During the long period of Old Testament history, the Levites waxed hot and cold in their devotion to God, just like the rest of the nation of Israel. During the period of the judges, for example, a Levite agreed to hire his services to a man who was known as a worshiper of false gods (Judg. 17:8–13). By New Testament times, both Levites and priests presided over a form of worship that had lost its warmth and human concern (John 1:19).

In His parable of the Good Samaritan, Jesus insisted that true worhip consisted of doing good to others. This is demonstrated by the lowly Samaritan traveler, who stopped to help a wounded man. What a contrast his compassion is to the hands–off approach of a priest and a Levite, both of whom "passed by on the other side" (Luke 10:31–32).

Also see PRIESTS.

LEVITICAL CITIES [luh VIT uh cull] — 48 cities assigned to the tribe of Levi. When the land of Canaan was divided among the tribes of Israel, each tribe, except Levi, received a specific region or territory for its inheritance. The tribe of Levi, however, was made up of priests who were to serve the religious and spiritual needs of the other tribes. Thus, instead of receiving a territory of their own, they were scattered throughout the entire land.

Numbers 35:1–8 sets forth a plan whereby the tribe of Levi was to live in 48 cities scattered throughout Palestine. (This plan was fulfilled according to assignments described in Josh. 20—21 and 1 Chr. 6:54–81.) The 48 cities were apportioned in this way: the AARONITES, one of the families of the Kohathites, received 13 cities (Josh. 21:4, 9–19; 1 Chr. 6:54–60); the rest of the KOHATHITES received 10 cities (Josh. 21:5, 20–26; 1 Chr. 6:61). The GERSHONITES received 13 cities (Josh. 21:6, 27–33; 1 Chr. 6:62), and the MERARITES received 12 cities (Josh. 21:7, 34–40; 1 Chr. 6:63). These 48 cities and their surrounding common-lands—pastures, fields, and vineyards— were to be used exclusively by the Levites.

Six of these Levitical cities were to be CITIES OF REFUGE (Num. 35:6, 9–34; Josh. 20—21). A person who caused the death of another could flee to one of these cities for protection from anyone who wanted to avenge the life of the person killed (see AVENGER OF BLOOD). The "refugee" thus was protected until he received a fair trial, or until the high priest of that particular city of refuge died (after which he was free to return home and claim the protection of the authorities).

Three of the cities of refuge were east of the Jordan River: Bezer (in the tribe of Reuben), Ramoth in Gilead (in Gad), and Golan (in Manasseh; Josh. 20:8). The other three cities of refuge were west of the Jordan: Kedesh (in the tribe of Naphtali), Shechem (in Ephraim), and Kirjath Arba, also known as Hebron (in Judah; Josh. 20:7). According to this plan, the Levites were situated throughout the land and could assist the other Israelites in spiritual matters. As a practical matter, since six of these Levitical cities were cities of refuge, citizens living in every part of Palestine had a refuge that was relatively near their homes. A look at a map will demonstrate how carefully the cities were spaced out to facilitate ease of access. Some of the ancient Levitical cities, such as Bethel and Gilgal, became an important part of the religious system of Israel (1 Kin. 3:4; Hos. 4:15; 12:11; Amos 4:4–5).

LEVITICUS, BOOK OF — an Old Testament book filled with worship instructions for God's Chosen People, the Hebrew nation. The Levites, members of the tribe of Levi, were the priestly family of the nation; the title of the book seems to indicate these instructions were given specifically for them. But Leviticus was actually a manual of worship for all the people. Because of its emphasis on holiness, sacrifice, and atonement, the book has an important message for modern believers.

Structure of the Book. Leviticus is difficult reading for most Bible students. It contains page after page of detailed instructions about strange worship rituals that seem to have no clear organizing principle. But with careful analysis, the book breaks down into six divisions.

The first several chapters of the book contain instructions about the ritual of sacrifice, including animal sacrifice, or the burnt offering—a key ingredient of Old Testament worship. Other segments of the book deal with the consecration of the priesthood, personal purification and dietary laws, laws of atonement, holiness of the people, and the redemption of tithes and vows.

Authorship and Date. Most conservative Bible students acknowledge Moses as the author of the Book of Leviticus. But some scholars insist the book was pulled together from many different sources by an unknown editor several centuries after Moses' death. This theory overlooks the dozens of instances in Leviticus where God spoke directly to Moses and Moses wrote down His instructions to be passed along to the people (4:1; 6:1; 8:1; 11:1).

In addition, nothing was more important to the nation of Israel in its earliest years than the development of its system of worship. Thus, worship rules would have been established at a very early stage in Israel's history. This argues convincingly for the early writing of these rules at the hand of Moses, probably about 1445 B.C.

Historical Setting. The Book of Leviticus belongs to the period in Israel's history when the people were encamped at Mount Sinai following their miraculous deliverance from slavery in Egypt. At Sinai Moses received the Ten Commandments and other parts of the Law directly from God. He also built and furnished the tabernacle as a place where the people could worship God (Ex. 40). Just after the tabernacle was filled with God's glory, Moses received instructions for the people regarding worship of God in this holy place. It is these instructions which we find in the Book of Leviticus.

Theological Contribution. The Book of Leviticus is important because of its clear teachings on three vi-

LEVITICUS: A Teaching Outline

Part One: The Laws of Acceptable Approach to God: Sacrifice (1:1—17:16)

Part Two: The Laws of Acceptable Walk with God: Sanctification (18:1—27:34)

Photo by Amikam Shoob

The Book of Leviticus instructed a woman who had given birth to offer a sacrifice which included a young pigeon (Lev. 12:6).

tal spiritual truths: ATONEMENT, SACRIFICE, and HOLINESS. Without the background of these concepts in Leviticus, we could not understand their later fulfillment in the life and ministry of Jesus.

Atonement—Chapter 16 of Leviticus contains God's instructions for observing the Day of Atonement. On that day the high priest of Israel entered the most sacred place in the tabernacle and offered an animal sacrifice to atone for his own sins. Then he killed another animal and sprinkled its blood on the altar to atone for the sins of the people. New Testament writers later compared this familiar picture to the sacrifice of Jesus on our behalf. But unlike a human priest, Jesus did not have to offer sacrifices, "first for His own sins and then for the people's, for this He did once for all when He offered up Himself" (Heb. 7:27).

Sacrifice—The Book of Leviticus instructs the Covenant People to bring many types of sacrifices or offerings to God: burnt offerings, grain offerings, peace offerings, sin offerings, and guilt or trespass offerings. These were considered gifts by which a worshiper expressed his loyalty and devotion to God. But a blood offering—presenting the blood of a sacrificed animal to God—went beyond the idea of a gift. It symbolized that the worshiper was offering his own life to God, since the Hebrews believed that "the life of the flesh is in the blood" (Lev. 17:11). Again, this familiar teaching assumed deeper meaning in the New Testament when applied to Jesus. He gave His life on our behalf when He shed His blood to take away our sins.

Holiness—The basic meaning of holiness as presented in the Book of Leviticus is that God demands absolute obedience of His people. The root meaning of the word is "separation." God's people were to be separate from, and different than, the surrounding pagan peoples. This is actually the

reason for God's instruction that His people were not to eat certain unclean foods. Only a clean, undefiled people could be used by Him to bring about His purpose of world redemption. Leviticus also makes it clear that the holiness demanded by God extended to the daily behavior of His people. They were expected to practice kindness, honesty, and justice and to show compassion toward the poor (Lev. 19:9–18).

Special Considerations. The blood of bulls and goats so prominent in Leviticus had no power to take away sin. But each of these rituals was "a shadow of the good things to come" (Heb. 10:1). They pointed forward to God's ultimate sacrifice, given freely on our behalf: "So Christ was offered once to bear the sins of many" (Heb. 9:28).

LEVY — forced labor or taxation. The word is found only once in the NKJV (Num. 31:28). It means "to impose a tax or fine." But the same Hebrew word translated levy in this passage is also used to describe the taskmasters set over Israel in Egypt (Ex. 1:11); conquered foreigners subjected to forced labor (Deut. 20:11); and the labor force of Israelites drafted by Solomon to build the Temple (1 Kin. 5:13–14). Also see TRIBUTE.

LEWDNESS — preoccupation with sex and sexual desire; lust (Judg. 20:6; Hos. 2:10; 6:9; Rom. 13:13). The Hebrew word translated as lewdness means an evil plan, purpose, or scheme; a wicked thought, especially with reference to sexual unchastity; ideas and practices that are indecent and disgraceful.

LIBERALITY — generosity and openhandedness, as opposed to stinginess. The apostle Paul taught that Christians should be liberal and generous in their financial giving (Rom. 12:8; 2 Cor. 8:2).

LIBERTINES — KJV word for FREEDMEN.

LIBNAH [LIB nuh] (*whiteness*) — the name of a campsite and a city in the Old Testament:

1. A place where the Israelites camped during their journey in the wilderness (Num. 33:20–21).

2. A Canaanite city captured by Joshua, allotted to the tribe of Judah, and later assigned to the Aaronites as a Levitical city (1 Chr. 6:57). When Jehoram was king of Judah, Libnah revolted against Judah's authority (2 Kin. 8:22). The city had been heavily fortified by the time Sennacherib of Assyria invaded Judah (2 Kin. 19:8).

LIBNI [LIB nigh] (*white*) — the name of two men in the Old Testament:

1. A son of Gershon and a grandson of Levi (Ex. 6:17), also called Laadan (1 Chr. 23:7–9).

2. A Levite descended from Merari (1 Chr. 6:29). He may be the same person as Libni No. 1.

LIBNITES [LIBB nights] — descendants of Libni (Num. 3:21; 26:58). Libni was a son of Gershon and the grandson of Levi (Ex. 6:17; 1 Chr. 6:17, 20).

LIBRARY — a collection of books for private or personal use. Libraries are depositories of culture; therefore, they are often the only link between the past and the present. For example, excavations of the libraries at Ras Shamra (UGARIT) and Qumran (DEAD SEA SCROLLS) have given scholars vital insights into the meaning of certain biblical words and incidents.

The Bible does not use the word library, but it does make specific references to a collection of books, scrolls, or parchments. King Solomon's complaint about the making of "many books" suggests that he had access to a large collection of manuscripts in his tenth-century B.C. library (Eccl. 12:12). Centuries later, when some enemies tried to stop the rebuilding of the Temple in Jerusalem, King Darius searched through Persia's archives or "house of scrolls" to find King Cyrus' official decree (Ezra 6:1). Also in the fifth century B.C., King Ahasuerus kept careful kingdom records, written in "the book of the chronicles" (Esth. 2:23; 10:2). This indicates a large collection of scrolls, or a library.

Many of the early libraries were located in religious sanctuaries. Hilkiah, the high priest under King Josiah, found the Book of the Law in the Temple at Jerusalem (2 Kin. 22:8; 2 Chr. 34:14). Also, Jesus read from Old Testament manuscripts in the synagogue (Luke 4:17). Some type of collection must have been housed here.

As early as A.D. 60, the apostle Paul owned too many manuscripts to carry around with him on his missionary journeys. He asked Timothy to bring "the books, especially the parchments" to him in Rome from Troas (2 Tim. 4:13). By this time libraries for personal and public use were common in the Greek and Roman societies.

The ancient world had a surprising number of libraries. Many of these collections contained thousands of volumes; others, only one manuscript. Some depositories were simple archives. Others housed documents on education, court records, business data, wills, probate, exploration, and worship.

A large library was established by Alexander the Great in Alexandria, Egypt, about 300 years before Christ. Tens of thousands of manuscripts from all over the Greek-dominated world were kept there. Later the ruler's general, Ptolemy I, built a library annex next to the temple of Jupiter. These 700,000 volumes accounted for the greatest artistic and literary collection of that time.

But libraries existed long before Greece ruled the world. Thousands of clay tablets have been unearthed in the Mesopotamian area between the Tigris and Euphrates Rivers. Some of them date back to 2600 B.C. Most of these tablets were written in the Sumerian and Akkadian languages.

These tablets are an important archaeological find because they help scholars in their translation of the Hebrew language. The tablets from the Babylonian area from the 15th century B.C. show many customs similar to Hebrew practices described in the Book of Genesis. The tablets from

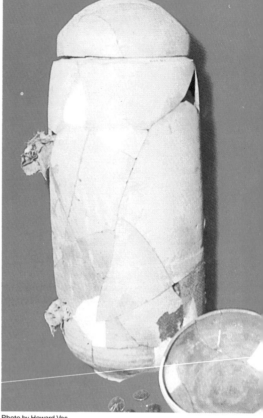

Photo by Howard Vos

A jar in which some of the Dead Sea Scrolls were stored in the caves of Qumran.

the period 1800 to 1700 B.C. reveal much about the time of Abraham, including geographical, historical, and religious information.

LIBYA [LIB ih uh] (meaning unknown) — a country of northern Africa west of Egypt (Ezek. 27:10), also called Phut (Ezek. 27:10, KJV) or Put (NIV, RSV). Some people who lived in "the parts of Libya adjoining Cyrene" (Acts 2:10) were in Jerusalem on the Day of Pentecost. Simon, the man who carried Jesus' cross, was from Cyrene, the New Testament name for Libya (Matt. 27:32).

LIBYANS [LIB ih uhnz] — the inhabitants of LIBYA (Jer. 46:9; Nah. 3:9; Lubim, KJV).

LICE (see ANIMALS OF THE BIBLE).

LICENTIOUSNESS — undisciplined and unrestrained behavior, especially a flagrant disregard of sexual restraints (Mark 7:22; 2 Cor. 12:21; lasciviousness, KJV). The Greek word translated as licentiousness means "outrageous conduct," showing that licentious behavior goes beyond sin to include a disregard for what is right.

LIE — any statement or act designed to deceive another person. The motivation for most lying is a desire either to hurt the one against whom the lie is directed (Gen. 3:1–13; Rom. 3:13) or to protect oneself, usually out of fear or pride (Matt. 26:69–75; Acts 5:1–11).

Lying is emphatically condemned in the Bible (Ex. 20:16; Eph. 4:25). It is wrong because it is contrary to the nature of God (Titus 1:2; Heb. 6:18) and because it shows a person is not in touch with reality (Rom. 1:25; 1 John 1:6).

On the other hand, it is possible to be truthful with the intention of hurting another person. The Bible teaches believers to be truthful in love (Eph. 4:25).

LIEUTENANT — another word for SATRAP.

LIFE — the physical functions of people, animals, and plants. In physical terms, life is the time between birth and death. Because God is the source of life, it is a gift from Him. He first filled Adam with the breath of life (Gen. 2:7), and He continues to be the source of all life. The Psalmist sang to God, "For with you is the fountain of life" (Ps. 36:9).

The New Testament expanded on the Old Testament idea of life. The word life began to refer to more than physical existence. It took on a strong spiritual meaning, often referring to the spiritual life that results from man's relationship with God.

Eternal life means more than eternal existence. Eternal life refers to eternal fellowship with God. "This is eternal life," Jesus declared, "that they may know You, the only true God, and Jesus Christ whom You have sent" (John 17:3).

Eternal life is the highest quality of life. According to the apostle Paul, it is freedom from sin, holiness, and a positive relationship with God. This is in contrast to spiritual death, which results from a life of sin (Rom. 6:21–23).

Eternal life comes through faith in Jesus Christ. He taught, "He who believes in Me has everlasting life" (John 6:47). This symbolic meaning of life appears frequently in the Gospel of John. Of Jesus, John wrote, "In Him was life and the life was the light of men" (John 1:4).

LIFE, BOOK OF (see BOOK OF LIFE).

LIFE, TREE OF (see TREE OF LIFE).

LIGHT — illumination; the opposite of darkness. The Bible also speaks of light as the symbol of God's presence and righteous activity.

Light has been associated with the presence, truth, and redemptive activity of God since creation. Before man was created, light was brought into being by the Creator: "Then God said, Let there be light; and there was light. And God saw the light, that it was good" (Gen. 1:3–4). Throughout the Bible, light represents truth, goodness, and God's redemptive work. Darkness, on the other hand, symbolizes error, evil, and the works of Satan (Gen. 1:4).

Several of the miracles recorded in the Bible are related to light and darkness: the "Pillar of Fire" that guided the Israelites in the wilderness (Ex. 3:21), the sun standing still at Gibeon at Joshua's request (Josh. 10:12–13), and the fall of darkness at midday when Jesus was being crucified (Matt. 27:45).

Man's misguided fascination with light caused some cultures of the ancient world to worship the sun and moon. Ur in Babylonia and several of the Canaanite cities had elaborate systems of moon worship. Use of light was common in the festivals of the Greek cults, especially those honoring Dionysus and Apollo.

Ruins of the library of Celsus at Ephesus from the second century A.D.

Photo by Howard Vos

God or God's Word, the Bible, are frequently represented as lights or lamps to enlighten and guide the believer (1 John 1:5). "Your word is a lamp to my feet and a light to my path" (Ps. 119:105). The Psalmist also declared, "The Lord is my light and my salvation; whom shall I fear?" (Ps. 27:1). Light is also used as a symbol of holiness and purity. Paul counseled the Christians at Rome to "put on the armor of light" (Rom. 13:12).

The New Testament presents Jesus as the personification of light or divine illumination: "I am the light of the world" (John 8:12). Jesus plainly stated that those who rejected this divine light would bring judgment upon themselves (John 3:19–21). Jesus and the New Testament writers extended the figure of light to include faithful Christian witnesses, who were called "children of light" (Eph. 5:8).

LIGHTNING — a high-tension electrical discharge in the atmosphere and the flash of light that goes with such a discharge. The biblical writers often associated thunder and lightning with the power and majesty of God (2 Sam. 22:15; Job 36:32; Ps. 18:14; Jer. 10:13). The giving of the Ten Commandments on Mount Sinai was accompanied by thundering, lightning flashes, and smoke (Ex. 19:16; 20:18), and Jesus compared His Second Coming to the lightning that comes from the east and flashes to the west (Matt. 24:27). He declared the startling revelation of God's kingdom that will be visible from horizon to horizon.

Electrical storms occur in Palestine especially in the spring and autumn months. Lightning is accompanied by thunder, wind squalls, and clouds of dust, and often by heavy rains and destructive hail (Ex. 9:23).

LIGHTS, FEAST OF (see FEASTS AND FESTIVALS).

LIGN ALOES (see PLANTS OF THE BIBLE).

LIGURE (see JEWELS AND PRECIOUS STONES).

LIKHI [LIK high] (*learned*) — a son of Shemida, of the tribe of Manasseh (1 Chr. 7:19).

LILY (see PLANTS OF THE BIBLE).

LILY–WORK — the architectural ornamentation on the crowns of JACHIN AND BOAZ, the two free-standing pillars in Solomon's Temple (1 Kin. 7:19, 22, RSV). Some scholars believe this lily–work was patterned after the Egyptian lotus.

LIME (see MINERALS OF THE BIBLE).

LINE — a tool similar to a tape measure for measuring or marking off distance. David divided the Moabites who would be executed from those who would be spared by measuring them off with a line (2 Sam. 8:2). The prophet Amos prophesied judgment by predicting, "Your land shall be divided by survey lines" (Amos 7:17). Zechariah encouraged Zerubbabel with his vision of the angel measuring the ruins of Jerusalem with a line before the process of rebuilding began (Zech. 2:1).

The word line is also used of the cord given to Rahab the harlot by the two spies (Josh. 2:18, 21).

LINEAGE (see GENEALOGY).

LINEN — a cloth woven from fibers of the flax or hemp plant. The word linen is also used to describe clothes or garments made from this cloth. The Hebrew word meaning "whiteness" also is used to represent linen, because bleached linen was so white.

In Bible times, the finest linen allowed free circulation of air, keeping the wearer cool in hot weather. Because it was so expensive, it was owned especially by the wealthy (Luke 16:19; Ezek. 16:10), the powerful (2 Sam. 6:14), and the priests. Fine linen was used in the clothing and headdress of the priests. Ordinary linen was used for less expensive clothing and items such as sheets, curtains, and sails of ships. Linen was the material from which the tunic, or undergarment, of Bible times was often made.

Fine linen garments were especially worn by kings and queens and members of their royal courts. Those who ministered in the TABERNACLE and TEMPLE also wore fine linen. These included the boy Samuel (1 Sam. 2:18), the temple singers (2 Chr. 5:12), and the priests (Ex. 28:39–42). They were surrounded in their places of worship by the veil and curtains, made of the finest linen (Ex. 26:1–37). At the end of time, the heavenly members of God's court will also wear fine white linen (Ezek. 9:2; Rev. 19:14), symbolizing that God provides them with the costliest and purest of garments.

After His death, the body of Jesus was wrapped in white linen (John 19:40; Luke 23:53). As a part of their burial customs, the Jews tore large linen sheets into strips and wrapped perfume inside them close to the body. Even centuries earlier, the Egyptians had wrapped their dead in the same way. Many Egyptian mummies now in museums are still wrapped in this fashion, although the linen has faded into a brownish tan color.

The weaving of linen fabric began with the lowly flax plant. These plants were usually pulled out by the roots, dried in the sun, then pounded until the fibers separated. Then the fibers were washed and bleached. This produced a fine fiber that at times was nearly invisible. Israel had craftsmen skilled in weaving fine linen, although the craft probably was first learned in Egypt (Ex. 35:35; 38:23). Guilds of linen weavers also existed in Bible times (1 Chr. 4:21). Palestinian weavers were so skilled that their fine linen was often preferred to that produced in Egypt.

LINTEL — a horizontal beam that supports the wall above the framework of a door or window. At the time of the first PASSOVER, the Lord told Moses to sprinkle the blood of a slain lamb on the doorposts and the lintels of the houses of the Israelites (Ex. 12:7). The blood of the lamb would be a sign of God's grace; and the Israelites would be spared as death spread throughout the land of Egypt. The word lintel is also applied to the entrance to the inner sanctuary of Solomon's Temple (1 Kin. 6:31).

LINUS [LIE nuhs] — a Christian man at Rome who joined the apostle Paul in sending greetings to Timothy (2 Tim. 4:21).

LION (see ANIMALS OF THE BIBLE).

LIPS — the fleshy, muscular folds that surround the mouth. Beautiful red lips were desirable for women in Bible times (Song 4:3). Lips covered by the hands symbolized mourning or trouble (Lev. 13:45). When Moses spoke of having "uncircumcised lips" (Ex. 6:12), he meant he lacked fluency as a speaker (Ex. 4:10). Telling lies was called "flattering lips" (Ps. 12:2) or "lying lips" (Ps. 31:18). On the other hand, the Bible mentions "joyful lips" (Ps. 63:5) and "righteous lips" (Prov. 16:13), or speech that honors and glorifies God.

LITERATURE — a body of writings on a particular subject. As captives of the Babylonians, Daniel and his three Hebrew friends—Shadrach, Meshach, and Abed-nego—were selected to receive instruction in their language, literature, and wisdom (Dan. 1:4, 17).

LITTER — a portable couch or chair, often enclosed with a cover or a curtain and mounted on shafts (Is. 66:20; wagons, NEB, NIV). Litters were widely used in the ancient world to carry a single passenger.

LITTLE OWL (see ANIMALS OF THE BIBLE).

LIVELIHOOD — a means of support or subsistence. The large offerings of the rich did not impress Jesus, because they gave out of their abundance an amount they would hardly miss. But He commended a poor widow who cast two small copper coins into the Temple treasury, because "she out of her poverty put in all that she had, her whole livelihood" (Mark 12:44; her whole living, RSV).

LIVER — an organ in the body that aids in digestion. The liver is referred to most often in connection with animal sacrifice. The "fatty lobe attached to the liver" (Ex. 29:13) was burned on the altar along with the kidneys and inner fat.

LIVING CREATURES — heavenly beings mentioned in the visions of the prophet Ezekiel and the apostle John. In Ezekiel's vision (Ezek. 1:1–28) these creatures had four faces (man, lion, ox, and eagle) and four wings. Later in his book (Ezekiel 10), the prophet identified the four living creatures as CHERUBIM. These four heavenly beings are probably the same as the four living creatures mentioned by John in the New Testament (Rev. 4:6–9).

LIZARD (see ANIMALS OF THE BIBLE).

LOAF (see BREAD).

LO–AMMI [loe AM eye] (*not my people*) — the symbolic name given by the prophet Hosea to his second son (Hos. 1:9–10; 2:23) to symbolize God's rejection of the nation of Israel (Rom. 9:25–26).

LO DEBAR [low DEE bahr] — a form of DEBIR No. 3.

LO–RUHAMAH [low roo HAY muh] (*not pitied*) — a daughter born to Gomer, the prophet Hosea's wife (Hos. 1:6, 8; not pitied, RSV). The name symbolized God's anger and His rejection of the nation of Israel. The faithful remnant of Israel is called Ruhamah, which means "pitied" (Hos. 2:1, 23).

LOCK, LOCKS — wooden bolts that slipped into slots in the doorpost in Bible times. These bolts were secured by wooden pins that dropped into holes in the moveable part of the bolt. Simple latch–type locks could be opened by hand through a hole in the door (Song 5:4–5; bolts, Neh. 3:3, 6, 15). More elaborate locks for use on large doors or city gates had multiple pins that were operated by large wooden or metal keys.

LOCUST (see ANIMALS OF THE BIBLE; PLANTS OF THE BIBLE).

LOD [lahd] (meaning unknown) — a city about 18 kilometers (11 miles) southeast of Joppa (1 Chr. 8:12) in the fertile Plain of Sharon (see Map 9, B–4). Its strategic location at the intersection of two great trade routes made Lod a rich prize of war among the nations of the ancient world. The prophet Nehemiah placed Lod in the "valley of craftsmen" (Neh. 11:35), referring to the various industries which produced the necessities for travel. The Greek name for the city in New Testament times was LYDDA. The apostle Peter healed a paralyzed man in Lydda (Acts 9:32–35, 38).

LODGE — to spend the night. The common thread that unites most of the words translated lodge in the Bible is the idea of a temporary resting place. The two Israelite spies lodged in the house of Rahab (Josh. 2:1); the Israelites lodged by the Jordan River before passing over into the Promised Land; and Peter lodged with Simon the tanner (Acts 10:18). The word lodge also refers to the temporary hut built by a watchman in a cucumber field (Is. 1:8).

LOFT — KJV word for UPPER ROOM, an upper story or small room built on the flat roof of a Palestinian house (1 Kin. 17:19; upper chamber, RSV; roof–chamber, NEB).

LOG (see WEIGHTS AND MEASURES).

LOGIA — a term applied to collections of sayings credited to Jesus and used as source materials by the gospel writers in the writing of their gospels. The Greek word *logia* literally means "oracles, divine responses, utterances, or sayings." Some scholars see many similarities between the Gospel of Matthew and the Gospel of Luke. They believe there existed an earlier source, now lost, upon which both Matthew and Luke drew in writing their gospels. Perhaps such a source was the logia, or collection of quotations attributed to Jesus.

When the apostle Paul spoke of "the words of the Lord Jesus" (Acts 20:35) he quoted a saying of Jesus not found in any of the four gospels. He may have been citing a quotation from the logia: "It is more blessed to give than to receive." An example of this type of literature, containing quotations from Jesus not found in the canonical gospels, is the Gospel of Thomas, an early APOCRYPHAL gospel.

LOGOS (see WORD, THE).

LOINS — the lower abdomen, including the reproductive organs. A man's loins are described as the source of his offspring (Gen. 35:11, KJV). When a man was ready to work, he put a belt around his waist; then he tucked up his robe so his legs would not be hindered. This is the meaning of "girded up his loins" (1 Kin. 18:46). To "gird up the loins of your mind" (1 Pet. 1:13) means to prepare for strenuous mental activity.

LOIS [LOE iss] (*desirable*) — the mother of Eunice and the grandmother of Timothy. A devout Jewess, Lois instructed both her daughter and her grandson in the Old Testament. Paul gave Lois and her daughter Eunice credit for Timothy's spiritual instruction (2 Tim. 3:15). Also see Acts 16:1.

LONGSUFFERING — a word in the KJV and NKJV that refers primarily to God's patient endurance of the wickedness of the sinful (Ex. 34:6). The purpose of God's longsuffering is to lead people to repentance (Rom. 2:4; 2 Pet. 3:9, 15). But since God is a God of justice, He cannot endure sin forever. He must ultimately punish all who do not repent and trust in Him for salvation (2 Thess. 1:5–10).

Believers are to imitate their heavenly Father in longsuffering (1 Cor. 13:4–5), because He has been patient with us (Eph. 4:31–32) and because vengeance belongs to God alone (Rom. 12:19).

LOOKING GLASS (see MIRROR).

LOOKOUT (see OCCUPATIONS AND TRADES).

LOOM (see WEAVING).

LOOP — a heavy thread ring used in the curtains of the tabernacle. Along the sides of the curtains were 50 loops of blue thread. These curtains were joined by gold clasps that passed through the corresponding loops on adjoining curtains.

LORD (see GOD, NAMES OF).

LORD GOD OF ISRAEL (see GOD, NAMES OF).

LORD OF HOSTS (see GOD, NAMES OF).

LORD–IS–MY–BANNER, THE — the name given to an altar built by Moses after a victory over the Amalekites at Rephidim (Ex. 17:15; Jehovah-nissi, KJV). Also see GOD, NAMES OF.

LORD–SHALOM, THE — the name given to an altar built by Gideon at Ophrah, in the territory of Manasseh, on the eve of his destruction of the altar of Baal (Judg. 6:24). Other translations are Jehovah-shalom (KJV, NEB) and The Lord is Peace (NIV, NAS, RSV). Also see GOD, NAMES OF.

LORD–WILL–PROVIDE, THE — the name given to an altar built by Abraham in the land of Moriah (Gen. 22:14; Jehovah–jireh, KJV, NEB). There the Angel of the Lord prevented Abraham from offering his only son Isaac as a sacrifice. Instead, the Lord provided a ram, caught in a thicket by its horns, which Abraham offered on the altar. Also see GOD, NAMES OF.

LORD'S DAY — the first day of the week, or Sunday; the day especially associated with the Lord Jesus Christ.

A special honor was reserved for Sunday, the first day of the week. This was the day on which Jesus was raised from the dead; every Lord's Day, therefore, is a weekly memorial of Christ's resurrection. Clearly the early church assembled for worship and religious instruction on Sunday, the Lord's Day (1 Cor. 16:2).

The Lord's Day is not to be confused with the SABBATH, the Jewish day of rest. The Jewish Sabbath corresponds with our Saturday, the seventh or last day of the week. This special day to the Jews commemorated the day on which God rested after the creation of the world. The Lord's Day is our Sunday, the first day of the week; it celebrates the resurrection of Jesus from the dead.

Under the new dispensation of grace, Christians are not to be trapped by the old legalism of observing days and seasons. The JERUSALEM COUNCIL did not include a demand for Sabbath observance in its rules for Gentile Christians (Acts 15:20, 28–29). Some members of the early church "esteemed every day alike"; they made no distinction between days, including Jewish festivals and Sabbaths and possibly also Sunday. The apostle Paul said they were not to be judged if they were acting in good conscience out of the fear of God.

Some Jewish Christians continued to observe the Sabbath and Jewish festivals. Neither should they be judged for "esteeming one day above another," Paul declared, for their behavior was guided by conscience in the fear of God. Paul believed such observance was a matter of Christian liberty, so long as the convert did not regard the observance as necessary for salvation (Rom. 14:5–6; Gal. 4:10; Col. 2:16–17).

Paul's principle of Christian liberty about holy places and holy days comes from the Lord Jesus Christ Himself. Jesus described Himself as one who is greater than the Temple (Matt. 12:6) and said, "The Son of Man is Lord even of the Sabbath" (Matt. 12:8; Luke 6:5). When accused by the Pharisees of breaking the Sabbath, Jesus replied, "The Sabbath was made for man, and not man for the Sabbath. Therefore the Son of Man is also Lord of the Sabbath" (Mark 2:27–28).

The phrase the Lord's Day occurs only once in the New Testament, in Revelation 1:10, where John declared, "I was in the Spirit on the Lord's Day." In Asia Minor, where the churches to which John wrote were situated, the pagans celebrated the first day of each month as the Emperor's Day. Some scholars also believe that a day of the week was also called by this name.

When the early Christians called the first day of the week the Lord's Day, this was a direct challenge to the emperor worship to which John refers so often in the Book of Revelation. Such a bold and fearless testimony by the early Christians proclaimed that the Lord's Day belonged to the Lord Jesus Christ and not the emperor Caesar.

LORD'S PRAYER — the model prayer which Jesus taught His disciples (Matt. 6:5–15; Luke 11:1–4). In the Gospel of Matthew the Lord's Prayer occurs in the Sermon on the Mount. He emphasized that prayer should not be an attempt to get God's attention by repeating words. Instead, it should be a quiet, confident expression of needs to our heavenly Father. Our attitude in prayer is important; in the Sermon on the Mount Jesus shows His disciples how to pray.

In the Gospel of Luke, the disciples saw Jesus praying, and they asked Him to teach them. The emphasis of this gospel is on what to pray (11:2). It is good to use the Lord's Prayer as a guide and to repeat its words as well.

The first part of the prayer concerns the glory of God. We call him "Father," a term which only His children by faith in Christ may rightly use. We request that God's name be "hallowed," or honored as holy. It is the mission of God's people to spread the reputation of His name throughout the world (Ezek. 36:22–23).

Next, we request that God's kingdom come. This means that we acknowledge God as ruler of the world and obey His will. His will shall be done perfectly when our Lord returns.

Requests relating to our own needs include food for each day, forgiveness, and help in temptation. Workers in Jesus' time often were hired day by day. They knew their daily need. Our forgiveness for sin comes only through the death of Christ on the cross. Our experience of that forgiveness requires us not to hold things against others and not to deny God's forgiveness.

"Lead us not into temptation, but deliver us from evil" means, "Do not let us be tested so that we fall into sin; save us from the power of the Evil One (Satan)."

The conclusion of the Lord's Prayer attributes all power and glory to God forever, through all eternity. This part of the prayer should be evident in our lives each day as we seek to do God's will on earth as His disciples.

LORD'S SUPPER — the ritualistic practice, usually during a worship service, in which Christians partake of bread and wine (or grape juice) with the purpose of remembering Christ, receiving strength from Him, and rededicating themselves to His cause. It is one of two sacraments or ordinances instituted by Christ to be observed by His church until He returns.

The term the Lord's Supper is used only in 1 Corinthians 11:20. The practice is also known as Communion (from 1 Cor. 10:16), the Lord's Table (from 1 Cor. 10:21), and the Eucharist (from the Greek word for "giving thanks"; Luke 22:17, 19; 1 Cor. 11:24). The expression breaking of bread (Acts 2:42, 46; 20:7, 11) probably refers to receiving the Lord's Supper with a common meal known as the LOVE FEAST (2 Pet. 2:13; Jude 12).

The institution of the Lord's Supper (Matt. 26:17–30; Mark 14:12–26; Luke 22:1–23; 1 Cor. 11:23–25) took place on the night before Jesus died, at a meal commonly known as the Last Supper. Although there is considerable debate over the issue, the Last Supper probably was the Jewish PASSOVER meal, first instituted by God in the days of Moses (Ex. 12:1–14; Num. 9:1–5).

Many of Jesus' actions and words at the Last Supper, such as the breaking and distributing of the bread, were part of the prescribed Passover ritual. But when Jesus said, "This is My body" and "This is My blood" while distributing the bread and the cup, He did something totally new. These words, which were intended for our blessing, have been the focus of sharp disagreement among Christians for centuries. In what sense are the bread and wine Christ's body and blood? What should the Lord's Supper mean to us? The answers to these questions are often grouped into four categories, although there are variations within these four broad views.

The Transubstantiation View. The first view is that of the Roman Catholic Church (especially before the Second Vatican Council of 1962–1965). This view holds that the bread and wine become the actual body and blood of Christ when the words of institution are spoken by the priest. This doctrine, known as transubstantiation, holds that while the physical properties (taste, appearance, etc.) of the bread and wine do not change, the inner reality of these elements undergoes a spiritual change.

While this view may help to foster a serious attitude toward the Eucharist, it fails to grasp the figurative nature of Jesus' language. Jesus could not have been holding His actual body and blood in His hands. He probably meant, "This bread represents My body" and "This wine represents My blood." Jesus often used figurative language (Luke 8:11, 21), just as a person does today when showing someone a photograph and saying, "This is my father."

The Consubstantiation View. The second viewpoint, developed by Martin Luther, is that Christ's body and blood are truly present "in, with, and under" the bread and wine. The elements do not actually change into Christ's body and blood. But in the same way that heat is present in a piece of hot iron, so Christ is present in the elements. The Lutheran position is often called consubstantiation.

This position can encourage the recipient of the Eucharist with the realization that Christ is actually present at the Supper. But it also misses the figurative use of Jesus' words. It also may tend to draw more attention to the bread and wine than to Christ Himself.

The Symbolic View. The third position, known as

the symbolic or memorial view, is derived from the teachings of the Swiss reformer, Ulrich Zwingli. Although his teaching is not completely clear, he basically held that the bread and wine were only symbols of the sacrificed body and blood of Christ. He taught that the Lord's Supper is primarily a memorial ceremony of Christ's finished work, but that it is also to be an occasion when God's people pledge their unity with one another and their loyalty to Christ. This is the viewpoint held by most Baptist and independent churches. While Zwingli's ideas are basically sound, this position tends to place more emphasis on what the Christian does and promises in the Supper than on what God does.

The Dynamic View. Finally, there is the view of John Calvin and the Reformed and Presbyterian churches which follow his teachings. Known as the dynamic or spiritual presence view, it stands somewhere between the positions of Luther and Zwingli.

Calvin agreed with Zwingli that the bread and wine are to be understood symbolically. Christ is not physically present in the elements, because His risen, glorified body is in heaven (Heb. 10:12–13). Still, He is dynamically and spiritually present in the Lord's Supper through the Holy Spirit.

In the worship service (but not at any one precise moment), when the Word of God is proclaimed and the Lord's Supper is received, the glorified Christ actually gives spiritual nourishment from His own glorified body to those who receive it. As bread nourishes the physical body, so Christ's glorified body enlivens the soul. Because of the organic union between Christ, the risen Head and the members of His body, the church (Eph. 1:18–23; 4:15–16; 5:23), this nourishment is conveyed to Christians by the Spirit who dwells in them (Rom. 8:9–11). Calvin admits that the way the Spirit does this is a genuine mystery. Yet, it is not contrary to reason—just above reason.

Calvin at times places more emphasis on Jesus' glorified flesh and blood than the Scriptures teach. But his position helps to explain why the Eucharist is so important for the Christian to observe, and why it is such a serious offense to misuse it. His view also corresponds well with those Scriptures that speak of God's nourishing and empowering work in His people (Eph. 3:14–21; Col. 2:6–10, 19).

Biblical Teachings. In 1 Corinthians 10:16, the apostle Paul rebuked the Corinthians for their involvement with idolatry. He referred to the cup as "the communion of the blood of Christ" and the bread as "the communion of the body of Christ." The Greek word for communion has the meaning of "fellowship, participating, and sharing." From the context it appears that Paul is saying that when Christians partake of the cup and the bread, they are participating in the benefits of Christ's death (referred to as His blood) and resurrection life (His glorified body). The most important of these benefits are the assurance of sins forgiven (through Christ's blood) and the assurance of Christ's presence and power (through His body).

The "one body" (the universal church) in 1 Corinthians 10:17 connects with the "body of Christ" in verse 16 in the sense that the entire church of Christ is organically related to the living, glorified human body of Christ now in heaven. The "one [loaf of] bread" (v. 17), representing Jesus the "bread of life" (John 6:35), is eaten by all believers at the Supper, symbolizing their unity and common participation in the one body of Christ. The great discourse of Jesus on the bread of life (John 6:25–68), while not intended to be a direct theological explanation of the Lord's Supper, helps to explain how receiving the Eucharist can be one way in which Christians "feed" on the Lord (John 6:55–57). Other important ways are by prayer and the hearing of God's Word through the Scriptures.

In 1 Corinthians 11:17–34 Paul rebuked the Corinthians for their pride and greed during the meal that accompanied the Eucharist (vv. 17–22). Then (vv. 23–25) he described the institution of the Lord's Supper and emphasized the need for Christians to partake in a worthy manner. Many of them who had not been doing so were weak and sick, and many had even died as a result of God's judgment (vv. 27–34).

Why does Paul use such strong language when speaking of the abuse of the Lord's Supper? The Corinthians were not properly discerning or recognizing the Lord's body. The wealthy Corinthians who shamed their poorer Christian brothers and sisters by their selfish eating practices (vv. 21–22) were not discerning the true nature of the church as Christ's body in which all distinctions of social class, race, etc. were blotted out (Gal. 3:28).

On the other hand, Christians who received the bread and the cup after behaving disgracefully were failing to discern that Christ would not automatically bless and empower those who received the sacrament in this manner. Such persons were guilty of sin against the body and blood of Jesus (v. 27).

Meaning for Today. When we ask how the Lord's Supper should be meaningful to the Christian today, three concepts—relating to the past, present, and future—can be helpful.

First, the Lord's Supper is a time of remembrance and Eucharist. Jesus said, "Do this in remembrance of Me" (Luke 22:19; 1 Cor. 11:24–25). This is not to be so much our dwelling on the agonies of the crucifixion as it is to be our remembering the marvelous life and ministry of our Savior. The Eucharist is to be an occasion for expressing our deepest praise and appreciation for all Jesus Christ has done for us.

Just as one step in the Jewish Passover meal was to proclaim the Hebrews' deliverance from Egyptian bondage (Ex. 12:26–27), so in the Supper Christians proclaim their deliverance from sin and misery through the death of "Christ, our Passover" (1 Cor. 5:7; 11:26).

Second, the Supper is a time of refreshing and communion. As we participate in the benefits of Jesus' death and resurrection life (Rom. 5:10; 1 Cor. 10:16), we are actually being nourished and empowered from the risen Christ through the Spirit.

John Wesley knew of this strengthening. On the average, he received communion every four or five days throughout his long and fruitful ministerial career. It is not that God cannot empower us without the Lord's Supper, but that He has instituted the Supper for us, even as He has designated prayer and the hearing of Scripture as means of communicating His grace. While the Bible does not tell us how often to observe the Eucharist, Wesley's guideline—"as often as you can"—deserves our serious consideration.

Third, the Supper is a time of recommitment and anticipation. We are to examine (literally "prove" or "test") ourselves and partake in a worthy manner (1 Cor. 11:28-29). In so doing we renew our dedication to Christ and His people, in hopeful anticipation "till He comes" (1 Cor. 11:26). After Christ's return we shall partake with Him—in His physical presence—in the kingdom (Matt. 26:29).

LOT [laht] (*concealed*) — Abraham's nephew. Lot accompanied Abraham from Mesopotamia to Canaan and to and from Egypt (Gen. 11:27-31; 12:4-5; 13:1). Both Lot and Abraham had large herds of cattle, and their herdsmen quarreled over their pasturelands. At Abraham's suggestion, the two decided to separate.

Abraham gave Lot his choice of land; and Lot chose the more fertile, well-watered site—the Jordan River valley—as opposed to the rocky hill country. Failing to take into account the character of the inhabitants, Lot "pitched his tent toward Sodom" (Gen. 13:12, KJV).

When the Elamite king Chedorlaomer invaded Canaan with his allies, Lot was taken captive. Abraham attacked Chedorlaomer's forces by night and rescued his nephew (Gen. 13:1—14:16).

When two angels were sent to warn Lot that God intended to destroy Sodom, Lot could not control the Sodomites, who wished to abuse the two visitors carnally. The angels struck the Sodomites blind to save Lot (Gen. 19:1-11), and Lot and his family fled the doomed city. Lot's wife, however, did not follow the angels' orders and looked back at Sodom. Because of her disobedience she was turned into a "pillar of salt" (Gen. 19:26). Our Lord Jesus warned, "Remember Lot's wife" (Luke 17:32) as a reminder of the disastrous results of disobedience.

Following his escape from Sodom, Lot lived in a cave near Zoar (Gen. 19:30-38). His two daughters served their father wine and enticed him into incest. They did this because "there is no man on the earth to come in to us as is the custom of all the earth" (Gen. 19:31). Out of that union came two sons, Moab and Ben-Ammi, the ancestors of the Moabites and the Ammonites respectively.

Lot's character is revealed by the major decisions which he made throughout his life. He chose to pitch his tent with the worldly SODOMITES, seeking riches and a life of ease rather than a path of obedience to God. He prospered for a while, but this decision eventually led to his humiliation and the tragic loss of his wife and other members of his family.

A formation of rock-salt, near the Dead Sea, associated for centuries with Lot's wife (Gen. 19:26).

LOTAN [LOE tan] (*covered*) — a son of Seir the Horite and a clan chief of a tribe of Horites in the land of Edom (Gen. 36:20, 22, 29).

LOTS, CASTING OF — a way of making decisions in Bible times, similar to drawing straws or casting a pair of dice to determine what course or direction to follow. The word lots occurs 70 times in the Old Testament and seven in the New Testament. Most of the occurrences were in the early period when little of the Bible was available and when God apparently approved of this means for determining His will.

For example, the high priest separated the SCAPEGOAT from the one he sacrificed by casting the lot (Lev. 16:8-10). The practice occurs most often in connection with the division of the land under Joshua (Joshua 14—21), a procedure that God directed several times in the Book of Numbers (Num. 26:55; 33:54; 34:13; 36:2).

Various offices and functions in the Temple were also determined by lot (1 Chr. 24:5, 31; 25:8-9; 26:13-14). The sailors on Jonah's ship (Jon. 1:7) also cast lots to determine who had brought God's wrath upon their ship. Only once in the New Testament did the casting of lots happen with God's approval. This occurred in the selection of Matthias to fill the spot vacated by Judas among the apostles (Acts 1:26).

In spite of the many references to casting lots in the Old Testament, nothing is known about the actual lots themselves. They could have been sticks of various lengths, flat stones like coins, or some kind of dice; but their exact nature is unknown.

LOTS, FEAST OF (see FEASTS AND FESTIVALS).

LOTUS (see PLANTS OF THE BIBLE).

LOVE — the high esteem which God has for His human children and the high regard which they, in turn, should have for Him and other people. Because of the hundreds of references to love in the Bible, it is certainly the most remarkable book of love in the world. It records the greatest love story ever written—God's unconditional love for us that sent His Son to die on the cross (John 3:16; 1 John 4:10).

Love is not only one of God's attributes; it is also an essential part of His nature. "God is love," the Bible declares (1 John 4:8, 16)—the personification of perfect love. Such love surpasses our powers of understanding (Eph. 3:19). Love like this is everlasting (Jer. 31:3), free (Hos. 14:4), sacrificial (John 3:16), and enduring to the end (John 13:1).

Two distinct Greek words for love appear in the Bible. The word *phileo* means "to have ardent affection and feeling"—a type of impulsive love. The other word *agapao* means "to have esteem" or "high regard." In the memorable conversation between Jesus and Peter, there is a play upon these two words (John 21:15-17). Jesus asked, "Simon, do you love [esteem] me?" But Peter replied, "You know that I love [have ardent affection for] You." Then Jesus asked, "Simon, do you love [have ardent affection for] Me?" And Peter responded that his love was *agape* love—a love that held Jesus in high esteem and which was more than a fleeting feeling.

The warm word *agape* is the characteristic term of Christianity. This word for love is used several different ways in the Bible.

1. *Agape* love indicates the nature of the love of God toward His beloved Son (John 17:26), toward the human race generally (John 3:16; Rom. 5:8), and toward those who believe on the Lord Jesus Christ (John 14:21).

2. *Agape* love conveys God's will to His children about their attitude toward one another. Love for one another was a proof to the world of true discipleship (John 13:34-35).

3. *Agape* love also expresses the essential nature of God (1 John 4:8). Love can be known only from the actions it prompts, as seen in God's love in the gift of His Son (1 John 4:9-10). Love found its perfect expression in the Lord Jesus. Christian love is the fruit of the Spirit of Jesus in the believer (Gal. 5:22).

Love is like oil to the wheels of obedience. It enables us to run the way of God's commandments (Ps. 119:32). Without such love, we are as nothing (1 Cor. 13:3). Such Spirit-inspired love never fails (1 Cor. 13:8) but always flourishes.

LOVE, BROTHERLY — love of brothers for each other (Rom. 12:10; Heb. 13:1; 2 Pet. 1:7). The phrase is used in a symbolic sense to express love of Christians for one another, since all are sons of the same Father. The Greek word translated as brotherly love implies more than love for one's "blood brothers," as in pagan writings; it means love for the broader brotherhood of true believers, for the members of the church, the "household of faith" (Gal. 6:10) and "of God" (Eph. 2:19; also 1 Pet. 2:17; 3:8; 5:9).

Christians are a brotherhood in the service of Christ (Matt. 23:8), a family made up of those who do the will of God (Matt. 12:50; Mark 3:35; Luke 8:21). "A new commandment I give to you," Jesus said to His disciples, "that you love one another; as I have loved you, that you also love one another. By this all will know that you are My disciples, if you have love for one another" (John 13:34-35).

A Christian's love should extend beyond the Christian brotherhood, however, to all people. "If you greet your brethren only," said Jesus in the Sermon on the Mount, "what do you do more than others?" (Matt. 5:47). The Christian is called not only to love his neighbor and his brother but also to love his enemy (Matt. 5:44).

LOVE FEAST — a meal shared by the early Christians when they met together for fellowship and the Lord's Supper. The term love feast is clearly used only in Jude 12 (feasts of charity; KJV). But some Greek manuscripts support "love feasts" instead of "deceptions" in 2 Peter 2:13. The love feast is also referred to in 1 Corinthians 11:17-34, and probably in Acts 6:1-3, although neither passage in English versions of the Bible uses the term. The Greek word for love feast also is the main New Testament noun for love, indicating that the meal was originally intended to be a rich experience of God's love. The purpose of the love feast was to remember Christ, to encourage His disciples, and to share God's provisions with the needy.

In the time of Christ, communal meals to express friendship and observe religious feasts were practiced in both Greek and Jewish cultures. The yearly Passover meal was the most important such event among the Jews. Jesus chose this occasion to institute the LORD'S SUPPER, or Eucharist (Matt. 26:17-30). Thus it was natural for the early Christians, whenever they celebrated the Lord's Supper, to do it in connection with a common meal. The "breaking of bread," which the very first disciples did daily, most likely refers to this dual experience of common meal and Eucharist (Acts 2:42, 46).

Because of such abuses as those described in the New Testament (1 Cor. 11:17-34; 2 Pet. 2:13), and probably for reasons of convenience, the meal and the Eucharist became separated in some regions by the second century. The meal—known as the love feast, the agape, and even the Lord's Supper—continued for several centuries. However, at times it became merely a charity supper for the poor and at other times a lavish banquet for the wealthy. After much controversy in the church, it was finally abolished at the end of the seventh century. A few Christian groups, however, still observe the agape.

LOVINGKINDNESS (see KINDNESS).

LOWLAND, THE — the southern division of the low area between the coastal plain of Philistia and the Mediterranean Sea on the west and the central highlands of Judah and Samaria on the east (1 Kin. 10:27; the Shephelah, RSV; low country, plain, vale, valley, KJV). The lowland, or Shephelah, contained the valleys of Aijalon, Sorek, Elah, and Zephathah. Some of the more important cities in the lowland were Lachish, Debir, Libnah, and Beth Shemesh.

LUBIM [LOU beam] (meaning unknown) — another term sometimes used for LIBYANS or the inhabitants of LIBYA, a region of North Africa west of Egypt and bordering on the Mediterranean Sea (2 Chr. 12:3; 16:8; Nah. 3:9). When Shishak, king of Egypt, invaded Palestine, part of his army consisted of the Lubim (2 Chr. 12:2–9).

LUCAS [LOO kuhs] — a form of LUKE.

LUCIFER [LOU see fur] (*morning star*) — the Latin name for the planet Venus. The word Lucifer appears only once in the Bible (Is. 14:12). Literally, the passage describes the overthrow of a tyrant, the king of Babylon. But many Bible scholars see in this passage a description of SATAN, who rebelled against the throne of God and was "brought down to Sheol, to the lowest depths of the Pit" (Is. 14:15). The same kind of interpretation is often given to Ezekiel 28:11–19. The description of the king of Tyre thus is believed to reach beyond that of an earthly ruler to the archangel who was cast out of heaven for leading a revolt against God.

Other scholars argue that Isaiah 14:12 should be interpreted as a reference to a Canaanite myth. "Helal, son of Shahar" is mentioned in an ancient text discovered at Ugarit, a Canaanite town. According to this view, Isaiah referred to the ancient Canaanite myth to dramatize the fall of the king of Babylon.

Also see DEVIL.

LUCIUS [LOO shuhs] (*luminous*) — the name of two men in the New Testament:

1. Lucius of Cyrene, a teacher in the church in Antioch of Syria (Acts 13:1). Lucius and other church leaders laid their hands on Barnabas and Paul and sent them forth on their first missionary journey.

2. A Jewish Christian, a kinsman of the apostle Paul, who sent greetings from Corinth to Rome (Rom. 16:21). He may be the same person as Lucius No. 1.

LUD [luhd] (meaning unknown) — the fourth son of SHEM (Gen. 10:22; 1 Chr. 1:17) and the ancestor of a people known as the LUDIM (1 Chr. 1:11).

LUDIM [LOU deam] (meaning unknown) — the first son of MIZRAIM, who was the second son of Ham (Gen. 10:13; 1 Chr. 1:11). Some scholars, however, believe this term refers not to an individual but to a people; in both passages the NEB translates Lydians and the NIV translates Ludites. Some scholars attempt to identify the Ludim with the LUBIM (2 Chr. 12:3; 16:8; Nah. 3:9), the plural of LIBYAN, a people of North Africa west of Egypt bordering the Mediterranean Sea.

There is no textual authority, however, for identifying Ludim with Lubim. Some confusion also exists because of the ambiguous way the Ludim are associated with both African and Asiatic nations.

LUHITH [LOO hith] (*tablets*) — a city of Moab probably near the south end of the Dead Sea. Luhith was one of the places to which the Moabites fled to escape the invading Babylonians (Is. 15:5).

LUKE — a "fellow laborer" of the apostle Paul (Philem. 24) and the probable author of the Gospel of Luke and the Acts of the Apostles. By profession he was a physician (Col. 4:14). During one of Paul's imprisonments, probably in Rome, Luke's faithfulness was recorded by Paul when he declared, "Only Luke is with me" (2 Tim. 4:11). These three references are our only direct knowledge of Luke in the New Testament.

A bit more of Luke's life and personality can be pieced together with the aid of his writings (Luke and Acts) and some outside sources. Tradition records that he came from Antioch in Syria. This is possible, because Antioch played a significant role in the early Gentile mission which Luke described in Acts (Acts 11; 13; 14; 15; 18). Luke was a Gentile (Col. 4:10–17) and the only non-Jewish author of a New Testament book. A comparison of 2 Corinthians 8:18 and 12:18 has led some to suppose that Luke and Titus were brothers, but this is a guess.

Luke accompanied Paul on parts of his second, third, and final missionary journeys. At three places in Acts, the narrative changes to the first person ("we"). This probably indicates that Luke was personally present during those episodes. On the second journey (A.D. 49–53), Luke accompanied Paul on the short voyage from Troas to Philippi (Acts 16:10–17). On the third journey (A.D. 54–58), Luke was present on the voyage from Philippi to Jerusalem (Acts 20:5—21:18). Whether Luke had spent the intervening time in Philippi is uncertain, but his connection with Philippi has led some to favor it (rather than Antioch) as Luke's home.

Once in Palestine, Luke probably remained close by Paul during his two-year imprisonment in Caesarea. During this time, Luke probably drew together material, both oral and written, which he later used in the composition of his gospel (Luke 1:1–4). A third "we" passage describes in masterful suspense the shipwreck during Paul's voyage to Rome for his trial before Caesar. Each of the "we" passages involves Luke on a voyage, and the description of the journey from Jerusalem to Rome is full of observations and knowledge of nautical matters.

Luke apparently was a humble man, with no de-

Photo by E. B. Trovillion

The pods of the carob tree, a fruit eaten by animals and the poor. This is probably the food which the lost son would have gladly eaten, in Jesus' parable of the prodigal in the Gospel of Luke (Luke 15:16).

sire to sound his own horn. More than one–fourth of the New Testament comes from his pen, but not once does he mention himself by name. He had a greater command of the Greek language and was probably more broad–minded and urbane than any New Testament writer. He was a careful historian, both by his own admission (Luke 1:1-4), and by the judgment of later history.

Luke's gospel reveals his concern for the poor, sick, and outcast, thus offering a clue to why Paul called him "the beloved physician" (Col. 4:14). He was faithful not only to Paul, but to the greater cause which he served—the publication of "good tidings of great joy" (Luke 2:10).

Also see LUKE, GOSPEL OF; ACTS OF THE APOSTLES.

LUKE, GOSPEL OF — the third gospel, in which the great truths of Jesus are communicated primarily through vivid stories. Luke is the first of a two–part work. In this work, the history of the gospel is traced from its beginnings in the life of Jesus (the Gospel of Luke) to the founding of the early church (the Acts of the Apostles).

The author of the Gospel of Luke is more interested in persons, especially those in trouble, than in ideas. He also is a skilled writer, and the literary quality of the Gospel of Luke is the highest of all four gospels. Luke often is the most interesting gospel to read. But he is also a serious historian who places Jesus within the context of world history. He presents Jesus and the church as the fulfillment of the history of salvation.

Structure of the Gospel. The literary structure of the Gospel of Luke is constructed primarily around Jesus' ministry in Galilee and in Jerusalem.

The first part of the gospel could be entitled Introduction and Infancy (chaps. 1—2). Here Luke declares his purpose in writing (1:1-4), and he tells the immortal stories of the births of John the Baptist and Jesus. The ministry of Jesus begins with a note of expectation in chapter 3. The rulers of the Roman world at that time are named. Next, accounts are given of the preaching of John the Baptist and of Jesus' baptism, genealogy, and temptation (3:1—4:13).

Between His TEMPTATION and Transfiguration (4:14—9:28), Jesus conducted His ministry in Galilee. Convinced of His approaching death (9:21-27, 43-45), Jesus steadfastly set His face to go to Jerusalem (9:51) where, like the prophets before Him, He would accept His fate. This journey occupies the central part of Luke (9:51—19:27). The reader is kept in dramatic tension as Jesus moves to Jerusalem and the shadow of the cross darkens His pathway. The cross, however, is not simply unlucky fate; on the contrary, "the Son of Man goes as it has been determined" (22:22) to fulfill the divine plan for which He came (note the use of *must* in 2:49; 4:43; 9:22; 17:25; 22:37; 24:7, 44).

Like Moses, Jesus accomplished for His people a deliverance—a deliverance from sin to salvation. The events of Jesus' final week in Jerusalem (19:28—24:53) conclude the gospel, and the ascension serves as a transition from the end of Luke to the beginning of Acts.

Authorship and Date. The author does not identify himself by name, but he does tell us a good deal about himself. Although not an eyewitness of the events he reports, he has followed them closely enough to write an orderly, reliable narrative (1:1-4). He is an educated man with the best command of Greek of any New Testament writer. He counts among his acquaintances a person of high social standing, the "most excellent" THEOPHILUS, to whom he addresses both Luke (1:3) and Acts (1:1). As a Gentile, the author is interested in Gentiles; he is equally disinterested in matters purely Jewish. At some point in his life he joined the apostle Paul. His experiences with Paul served as a firsthand source for his sequel to the Gospel of Luke.

For the author's name we are dependent on later tradition. Writing about A.D. 175, Irenaeus, bishop of Lyon, identified the author as LUKE, the companion of Paul. Eusebius agreed, adding that Luke was a native of Antioch. The importance of Antioch in Acts (13:1-3) lends credibility to Eusebius' statement. The few glimpses we get of Luke from Paul's epistles—a physician, both beloved and compassionate (Col. 4:14) who was with Paul during his Roman imprisonment (Philem. 24; 2 Tim. 4:11)—parallels what we gather from him in Luke–Acts. The logical conclusion is that Luke wrote Luke–Acts.

The date of Luke's writing can only be guessed from inferences. Luke tells us that he drew upon earlier accounts, some of which were written (1:2). It is likely that two such accounts were Q (about A.D. 50) and the Gospel of Mark (about A.D. 60). The Gospel of Luke probably was written sometime shortly after A.D. 70. (Also see GOSPELS.)

Historical Setting. Luke is written by a Gentile for Gentiles. The author substitutes Greek expressions for nearly all Jewish expressions (*amen* is one of the few exceptions), and he seldom appeals to Old Tes-

tament prophecy. When Luke occasionally quotes from the Old Testament, he usually uses quotations which show that "all flesh [Gentiles as well as Jews] shall see the salvation of God" (3:6). Furthermore, we know that Christianity encountered increasingly hostile opposition in the 50s and 60s. One ancient writer referred to "a class hatred for their abominations, called Christians." It appears that Luke intended to supply influential Romans, like Theophilus, with the solid truth about Christians. Luke shows that in every instance where Christians were suspected of sedition against Rome they were judged innocent (Luke 23:4, 14, 22; Acts 16:39; 17:9; 18:15-16; 19:37; 23:29; 25:25; 26:31).

Although Christianity was regarded by many pagans as a "mischievous superstition" which thrived on secrecy, Luke shows that Jesus associated with all sorts of people and that the early church openly proclaimed the gospel (Acts 2:14; 17:22). The truths of the Christian message did not happen in a corner (Acts 26:26), argued the apostle Paul. An

LUKE: A Teaching Outline

implicit argument of Luke–Acts is that if Judaism had earned the toleration of the Roman Empire, then Christianity, which was the fulfillment of the Old Testament, should be granted the same status. It is reasonably certain that one of Luke's reasons for writing his gospel was to show that Christianity was neither superstitious nor subversive.

Theological Contributions. Luke has the most universal outlook of all the gospels; he portrays Jesus as a man with compassion for all peoples. Whereas Matthew traces Jesus' genealogy back to Abraham, the father of the Jews (1:2), Luke traces it back to Adam, the father of the human race (3:38). In Matthew Jesus sends his disciples "to the lost sheep of the house of Israel" (10:6) only, but Luke omits this limitation.

Luke is also the most socially–minded of the gospels. When He was in the synagogue at Nazareth, Jesus gave the keynote of His ministry by reading from Isaiah:

"The Spirit of the Lord is upon Me,
Because He has anointed Me to preach the gospel to the poor.
He has sent Me to heal the brokenhearted,
To preach deliverance to the captives
And recovery of sight to the blind,
To set at liberty those who are oppressed,
To preach the acceptable year of the Lord." (Is. 61:1–2).

In Luke, Jesus' life is presented as a commentary on this passage of Scripture. He blesses the poor, the hungry, those who weep, and the excluded (6:20–23). In one parable He takes the side of a beggar who sits outside the gate of a rich man (16:19–31); and in another parable He celebrates a tax collector who shies away from the Temple because of his sinfulness (18:9–14). Jesus reaches out to a widowed mother who had lost her only son (7:11–17) and to a sinful woman (7:36–50). In another parable the hero of mercy is a despised Samaritan (10:25–37); and after a healing, a Samaritan is praised for his gratitude (17:11–19). The open arms of the Father, as in the parable of the Prodigal Son (15:11–32), await all who return to Him. Jesus' identification with sinners leads Him to open His arms to them on the cross, where "He was numbered with the transgressors" (22:37).

Jesus also criticizes the rich. "Woe to you who are rich" (6:24), He says; for the tables will turn. The rich are fools because they think life consists of possessing things (12:13–21). Those wealthy enough to throw dinner parties ought to invite those who cannot repay—"the poor, the maimed, the lame, the blind"—for God will repay "at the resurrection of the just" (14:13–14).

Special Considerations. For Luke the coming of Christ is good news; and his gospel is one of joy. The births of John and Jesus are echoed by songs of praise from Mary (1:46–55), Zacharias (1:67–79), the angels (2:14), and Simeon (2:29–32). Even the unborn leap for joy (1:44). Sad and cruel scenes will follow, but the note of joy that rings from Gabriel at the ANNUNCIATION (1:32–33) is repeated by

the apostles at the end of the gospel (24:52–53).

Second, Luke is a gospel of the Holy Spirit. Unlike the other evangelists, Luke emphasizes the activity of the Spirit in the ministry of Jesus. John the Baptist and his parents are filled with the Spirit (1:15, 41, 67), as is Simeon (2:25–35). Jesus begins His ministry "in the power of the Spirit" (4:14; also 4:1, 18; 10:21), and He promises the Spirit to His disciples in their hour of need (12:12). Jesus is not alone; the Spirit is always with Him, within Him, empowering Him to accomplish God's purpose.

Third, Luke is a gospel of prayer. The multitude prays as Zacharias serves at the altar (1:10). Mary prays at the news of salvation (1:46–55). Jesus prays at His baptism (3:21), when He chooses His disciples (6:12), at Peter's confession (9:18), and at His transfiguration (9:29). In the solitude of prayer Jesus takes the first steps of ministry (5:16) and falls to His knees on the Mount of Olives (22:39–46). He gives His final breath back to God in prayer, "Father, into Your hands I commend My spirit" (23:46).

LUKEWARM — mildly warm; neither hot nor cold; lacking in conviction. Jesus condemned the church at Laodicea because of its lukewarm faith and declared that He was about to spew them out of His mouth (Rev. 3:14–22). Lacking the courage to follow God or to rebel against Him, they were disgusting to Him.

LUNACY (see DISEASES OF THE BIBLE).

LUST — desire for what is forbidden; an obsessive sexual craving. Although there are legitimate desires for which God makes provision (Deut. 12:15, 20–21), lust refers to the desire for things that are contrary to the will of God. The "lust after evil things" (1 Cor. 10:6) of the Israelites in the wilderness serves as an example of the lusts that should be avoided by Christians.

Christians are able to resist lust through the power of the Holy Spirit. The flesh, with its passions and lusts, is to be crucified (Gal. 5:24; Titus 2:12).

LUTE (see MUSICAL INSTRUMENTS).

LUZ [luhz] (*almond tree*) — the name of two cities in the Old Testament:

1. A city of the Canaanites renamed BETHEL by Jacob (Gen. 28:19). Assigned to the tribe of Benjamin, Luz was near the border of Ephraim, about 18 kilometers (11 miles) north of Jerusalem.

2. A city of the Hittites (Judg. 1:26). The site is unknown, but some scholars suggest Luweiziyeh, about 7 kilometers (4.5 miles) northwest of Mount Hermon.

LXX — the abbreviation for the SEPTUAGINT, the Greek translation of the Hebrew Old Testament.

LYCAONIA [lik ih OE nih uh] (*she–wolf*) — a Roman province in south central Asia Minor visited by the apostle Paul (Acts 14:6). In apostolic times part of it (the part visited by Paul) was a region of the Roman province of Galatia. Lycaonia was bordered on the south by Cilicia, on the west by Phrygia and Pisidia, on the north by Galatia, and on the east by Cappadocia. Because of its remoteness, Lycaonia enjoyed political independence during much of its history. But it fell under Greek control and influence in the period following the conquests of Alexander the Great.

The apostle Paul visited the three main cities of Lycaonia—Iconium, Lystra, and Derbe—on his three journeys to Asia Minor (Acts 13:51—14:6; 2 Tim. 3:11). Timothy was from Lycaonia; apparently he was a native of Lystra (Acts 16:1).

LYCAONIAN [lick uh OHN ih un] — the language or speech of the people of LYCAONIA, a province of Asia Minor (Acts 14:11). When the apostle Paul healed a crippled man at Lystra, a city of Lycaonia, the people said in the Lycaonian language, "The gods have come down to us in the likeness of men!" (Acts 14:11). Some scholars believe that Lycaonian had its roots in the ancient Assyrian language. By Paul's time it probably was a corrupt Greek intermingled with Syriac.

LYCIA [LISH ih uh] — a mountainous country in southwest Asia Minor (modern Turkey; see Map 7, C-2). Shut in by rugged mountain ranges, Lycia made contact with the outside world mainly through its seaport cities. Lycia was united by a strong federation of cities. It enjoyed a measure of freedom and independence even under foreign rulers such as Persia, Greece, Egypt, and Rome.

The apostle Paul stopped at two of Lycia's coastal cities, PATARA (Acts 21:1) and at MYRA (Acts 27:5), during his ministry.

LYDDA [LID uh] — the Greek name for the Old Testament city of LOD (1 Chr. 8:12; Acts 9:38). When the apostle Peter visited Lydda (see Map 6, A-4), his cure of a paralyzed man encouraged many citizens to turn to the Lord (Acts 9:33–35).

LYDIA [LID ih uh] (meaning unknown)) — the name of a woman and a geographical region:

1. A prosperous businesswoman of the city of THYATIRA who became a convert to Christianity after hearing the apostle Paul speak (Acts 16:12-15, 40). Thyatira was noted for its "purple"—its beautifully dyed cloth. Lydia, who lived in Philippi, sold dyes or dyed goods from as far away as Thyatira. Already a worshiper of God, the usual designation for a PROSELYTE to Judaism, Lydia believed the gospel when Paul preached in Philippi. She became the first convert to Christianity in Macedonia and, in fact, in all of Europe. Lydia is a good example for Christians in the business world today. A devout Christian and a conscientious businesswoman, she used her work to help further God's purpose.

2. A large territory in western Asia Minor (modern Turkey) rich in natural resources (see Map 1, A-1). Its fertile land produced figs, grain, grapes, and olives. The Lydians are mentioned by the prophet Ezekiel as "men of war," or mercenaries, who fought to defend Tyre (Ezek. 27:10) and who made an alliance with Egypt (Ezek. 30:5; Lud, RSV).

LYDIANS [LID ih unz] — men who fought with the Egyptians (Ethiopians and Libyans) at the Battle of Carchemish (Jer. 46:9; men of Lydia, NIV; men of Lud, RSV). Some earlier scholars assumed these

The Chapel of Lydia on the riverside at Philippi. Lydia was converted to Christianity through the ministry of the apostle Paul (Acts 16:13-15).

Photo by Howard Vos

Photo by Howard Vos

The mound of ancient Lystra, a city in the province of Lycaonia where Paul was stoned by a mob (Acts 14:8-20).

soldiers, skilled with the bow, were a people of Africa. But many modern scholars believe they were natives of the Lydian kingdom in Asia Minor (modern Turkey), and were serving as hired soldiers in the Egyptian army. Also see LUD, LUDIM.

LYE — a mineral alkaline that was mixed with oil to produce soap in Bible times (Jer. 2:22; nitre, KJV). The one other biblical usage of the Hebrew word that is translated lye in Jeremiah 2:22 leaves a question about the exact nature of lye. Proverbs 25:20 says, "Like one who takes away a garment in cold weather, and like vinegar on soda, is one who sings songs to a heavy heart." The fact that the acid in vinegar would neutralize the lye or soda has led some modern versions (RSV) to translate this phrase, "like vinegar on a wound." However, since the proverb speaks of the unpleasant reaction of the unhappy person to joy around him, the violent foaming of an acid and an alkali when they are mixed makes a vivid image.

As a cleansing agent in Bible times, lye was effective but harsh. The clothes to be whitened with lye were trampled by the fuller, or launderer, in a vat to work this powerful agent thoroughly into the clothes. Jesus' robe, as witnessed by the three disciples on the Mount of Transfiguration, was gloriously white—whiter than a launderer using lye could have made it (Mark 9:3).

LYRE (see MUSICAL INSTRUMENTS).

LYSANIAS [lih SAY nih uhs] (meaning unknown) — the tetrarch or governor of the region of Abilene

in the 15th year of the reign of Tiberius Caesar, emperor of Rome (Luke 3:1). Lysanias was a contemporary of John the Baptist and Jesus.

LYSIAS, CLAUDIUS [LIS ih uhs, KLAW dih uhs] — the commander of the Roman garrison at Jerusalem who rescued the apostle Paul from an angry mob (Acts 21:31-38). Claudius Lysias sent Paul to Caesarea by night under military escort to the Roman governor, Felix (Acts 22:24—23:35). His letter to Felix (Acts 23:25-30) is an example of Roman military correspondence.

Claudius Lysias was a commander (commandant, NEB; tribune, RSV). The Greek noun is *chiliarchos* which means, "ruler of a thousand." A tribune was a Roman military officer commanding a cohort, a unit of from 600 to 1,000 men.

LYSTRA [LISS truh] — a city of LYCAONIA, in central Anatolia in modern Turkey, where Paul preached after being driven from Iconium (see Map 7, D-2). Lystra was built on a small hill about 46 meters (150 feet) above the plain that stretched northeastward to Iconium and southeastward to Derbe.

Apparently, Lystra was the home of Timothy (Acts 16:1-2). Paul wrote to Timothy mentioning his persecutions and afflictions at Antioch (of Pisidia), Iconium, and Lystra (2 Tim. 3:11). At Lystra, when Paul healed a crippled man, the people thought they were gods, calling Barnabas Zeus and Paul Hermes (Mercury). But Jews from Antioch and Iconium later came to the city, persuading the multitudes to stone the apostle Paul (Acts 14:19).

M

MAACAH [MAY ah kah] (*oppression*) — the name of four women, one man, and one place in the Old Testament:

1. One of David's wives and the mother of Absalom (2 Sam. 3:3; 1 Chr. 3:2).

2. Apparently, an Aramean king from whom the Ammonites hired a thousand men to fight David's army (2 Sam. 10:6).

3. A wife of Rehoboam and the mother of Abijah, kings of Judah (1 Kin. 15:2; 2 Chr. 11:20–22). Maacah was the favorite wife of Rehoboam and she bore him Abijah, Attai, Ziza, and Shelomith (2 Chr. 11:20–21). Abijah, or Abijam (1 Kin. 14:31— 15:8), her oldest son, succeeded Rehoboam as king of Judah. A strong-willed woman, Maacah maintained her position as queen mother until her grandson Asa (1 Kin. 15:8; 2 Chr. 14:1) removed her from that position. Maacah fell from favor "because she had made an obscene image of Asherah (a Canaanite goddess)" (1 Kin. 15:13; 2 Chr. 15:16).

4. The grandmother of Asa, king of Judah (2 Chr. 15:16; Maachah, 1 Kin. 15:10, 13).

5. A wife of Jeiel, the father of Gibeon (1 Chr. 8:29; 9:35). Maacah is mentioned in the genealogy of King Saul.

6. A small Aramean kingdom (2 Sam. 10:8).

MAACHAH [MAY ah kah] (meaning unknown) — the name of four men, two women, and one place in the Old Testament:

1. A son of Nahor by Reumah (Gen. 22:24) and a brother of Abraham. Maachah's descendants probably inhabited Maachah No. 3.

2. A small Aramean kingdom that joined Geshur on the western border of Bashan. Maachah probably was southwest of Mount Hermon and east of the Jordan River (1 Chr. 19:6). It was once called Syrian Maachah (1 Chr. 19:6). Together with the Syrian mercenaries from Beth Rehob, Zoba, and Ish-tob, 1,000 men from Maachah joined a military alliance with the Ammonites against the army of King David.

3. The father of Achish (1 Kin. 2:39). Achish was king of Gath during the reign of Solomon. Also see MAOCH.

4. A concubine of Caleb, son of Hezron (1 Chr. 2:48).

5. The sister of Huppim and Shuppim and the wife of Machir of the tribe of Manasseh (1 Chr. 7:15–16).

6. The father of Hanan (1 Chr. 11:43).

7. The father of Shephatiah (1 Chr. 27:16).

MAACHATHITES, MAACATHITES [may AK uh thights] — descendants of MAACAH, also called Maachah, or a native or inhabitant of the Aramean kingdom of Maacah. The Maacathites are often mentioned together with the Geshurites (Josh. 12:5). A number of Maacathites were among the mighty men of Israel (2 Sam. 23:34).

MAADAI [may uh DIE] (meaning unknown) — a son of Bani who divorced his pagan wife after the Captivity (Ezra 10:34).

MAADIAH [may uh DYE uh] (perhaps *God promises*) — a priest who returned with Zerubbabel from the Captivity (Neh. 12:5). Maadiah may be the same person as Moadiah (Neh. 12:17) or Maaziah No. 2 (Neh. 10:8).

MAAI [may AY eye] (meaning unknown) — a priest who participated in the celebration after the walls of Jerusalem were rebuilt (Neh. 12:36).

MAALEH–ACRABBIM [MAY uh leh ah KRAB im] (*ascent of scorpions*) — a hill in Judah near the Dead Sea (Josh. 15:3).

MAARATH [MAY uh rath] (meaning unknown) — a city in the hill country of Judah (Josh. 15:59), between the cities of Gedor and Beth Anoth.

MAASAI [MAY uh sye] (*work of Jehovah*) — an Aaronite priest whose family lived in Jerusalem after the Captivity (1 Chr. 9:12; Maasiai, KJV). He may be the same person as Amashai (Neh. 11:13).

MAASEIAH [may uh SYE uh] (*Jehovah is a refuge*) — the name of several men in the Old Testament:

1. A Levite who was a member of the second order of priests during David's reign (1 Chr. 15:18, 20).

2. A commander who helped Jehoiada overthrow Queen Athaliah and bring JOASH to the throne of Judah (2 Chr. 23:1).

3. An officer under King UZZIAH of Judah (2 Chr. 26:11).

4. A son of Judah's royal line (2 Chr. 28:7).

Maaseiah was probably the son of Jotham.

5. The governor of Jerusalem during the reign of King Josiah of Judah (2 Chr. 34:8).

6. A priest who divorced his pagan wife after the Captivity (Ezra 10:18).

7. Another priest of the family of Harim, who divorced his pagan wife (Ezra 10:21).

8. A priest of the family of Pashhur who divorced his pagan wife after the Captivity (Ezra 10:22).

9. A son of Pahath–Moab (Ezra 10:30).

10. The father of Azariah (Neh. 3:23).

11. A priest who helped Ezra read the Law to the people (Neh. 8:4).

12. A priest who explained the Law to the people after Ezra's reading (Neh. 8:7). He may be the same person as Maaseiah No. 11.

13. A leader of the Israelites who sealed the covenant after the Captivity (Neh. 10:25).

14. A man of Judah descended through Pharez (Neh. 11:5).

15. A man from the tribe of Benjamin whose descendants lived in Jerusalem after the Captivity (Neh. 11:7).

16. A priest who assisted at the dedication of Jerusalem's rebuilt wall (Neh. 12:41).

17. Another priest who took part in the dedication of the Jerusalem walls (Neh. 12:42).

18. A priest and the father of Zephaniah (Jer. 21:1).

19. The father of Zedekiah (Jer. 29:21).

20. The grandfather of Baruch (Jer. 32:12), Jeremiah's scribe.

21. A gatekeeper during the reign of King Jehoiakim of Judah (Jer. 35:4).

MAASIAI [may uh SYE eye] — a form of MAASAI.

MAATH [MAY ath] (*small*) — an ancestor of Jesus, listed in Luke's genealogy (Luke 3:26).

MAAZ [MAY az] (meaning unknown) — the oldest son of Ram, of the tribe of Judah (1 Chr. 2:27).

MAAZIAH [may uh ZYE uh] (*Jehovah is a refuge*) — the name of two men in the Old Testament:

1. Head of the 24th course of priests in David's time (1 Chr. 24:18).

2. A priest who sealed the covenant after the Captivity (Neh. 10:8).

MACCABEES [MACK uh bees] — the members of the Hasmonean family of Jewish leaders and rulers, made up of the sons of Mattathias and their descendants, which reigned in Judea from 167 to 37 B.C. This term is especially applied to Judas Maccabeus and his brothers, who defeated the Syrians under Antiochus IV Epiphanes (the Seleucid ruler of Syria, 175–164 B.C.) about 165 B.C. and who rededicated the Temple in Jerusalem.

In the spirit of an oriental tyrant, ANTIOCHUS IV Epiphanes fanatically determined to impose HELLENISM—the adoption of ancient Greek language, philosophy, customs, art—on all the subjects of his empire. The story of Antiochus' edict is told in the Old Testament apocryphal book of 1 Maccabees: "The king then issued a decree throughout his empire: his subjects were all to become one people and abandon their own laws and religion. The nations everywhere complied with the royal command, and many in Israel accepted the foreign worship, sacrificing to idols and profaning the Sabbath" (1 Macc. 1:41–43, NEB).

In seeking to unify his empire, Antiochus attacked Israel's religious practices. He prohibited the observance of the Sabbath and the traditional Jewish festivals and feast days. He also outlawed the reading of the law of Moses and gave orders that all copies should be burned. Temple sacrifices were forbidden, circumcision was outlawed, and other characteristic Jewish practices were declared illegal. The penalty for disobedience was death.

Antiochus' ultimate affront to the Jews occurred on the 25th day of the month of Kislev, in 167 B.C. He rededicated the Temple to the pagan Greek god Zeus, set up a statue of Zeus in the Holy of Holies, and sacrificed swine upon the altar. These outrages brought on the revolt of the Maccabees.

The home of Mattathias, a priest at Modein (or Modin), a town situated about 27 kilometers (17 miles) northwest of Jerusalem, quickly became the center of resistance against the Hellenizing policies of Antiochus. With Mattathias were his five sons: "John called Gaddis, Simon called Thassis, Judas called Maccabaeus, Eleazar called Avaran, and Jonathan called Apphus" (1 Macc. 2:3–5, NEB).

The title Maccabeus was first given to Judas, the third son of Mattathias, but it was soon transferred to the entire family. Some scholars believe the term is derived from the Hebrew word *makkebeth*, or from the related Aramaic word *makkaba*, meaning "hammer," probably in allusion to the crushing blows inflicted by Judas and his successors upon their enemies. Thus, Judas may have been called "the Hammer" or "the Hammerer," or, as some scholars prefer, "Extinguisher" or "Quencher" (of the enemy).

Antiochus had sent commissioners throughout

An ancient coin with the portrait of Antiochus IV Epiphanes, whose desecration of the Jewish Temple in Jerusalem set off the revolt of the Maccabees.

Photo by Gleason Archer

the entire country of Judea to enforce his decree. Appalled by the sacrilegious acts committed in Judea and Jerusalem and moved by his fervent zeal for the law of Moses, Mattathias killed one of the officers of the king sent to enforce pagan sacrifice. He and his five sons then fled from Modein, taking refuge in the rugged hills nearby. Joined by a growing number of sympathizers who detested the "abomination of desolation" set up on the altar by Antiochus, the Maccabees carried on guerilla warfare against the Syrians and the Jewish collaborators.

In December 164 B.C. Judas Maccabeus recaptured most of Jerusalem. Then he forced the loyal priests, those who had not collaborated with Antiochus, to cleanse the Holy Place and erect a new altar. On the 25th of Kislev, 164 B.C., precisely three years after Antiochus had defiled it, Judas rededicated the Temple.

According to Jewish tradition, only one undefiled cruse of oil could be found. This cruse contained oil for only one day. Miraculously, however, the cruse kept burning for eight days. The Hebrew word *Hanukkah*, which means "dedication," is the name still used today for the Jewish Festival of Lights that commemorates this event. Celebrated for eight days from the 25th day of the month of Kislev to the second day of Adar, Hanukkah occurs near or at the same time as the Christian celebration of Christmas. The Feast of Dedication is mentioned in the New Testament (John 10:22).

After a short time of peace, warfare broke out again between the Jews and the Syrians. Leadership of the Maccabees passed from Judas to Jonathan and then to Simon. (The two other brothers had been killed without assuming leadership.) After the death of Simon, the last remaining son of Mattathias, the succession of the Maccabees was maintained by Simon's son John, known later as John Hyrcanus or Hyrcanus I.

Although Judea was nominally still a province of Syria, practical independence was maintained until 63 B.C., when Pompey invaded the country and brought it under Roman domination. Mariamne, the wife of Herod the Great, was a descendant of the Maccabees.

The term Maccabees has gained wide acceptance and use. The proper name of the family, however, is Hasmoneans (or Asmoneans), a name probably derived from Chasmon, the great-grandfather of Mattathias.

Also see FEASTS AND FESTIVALS; HASMONEANS.

MACCABEES, BOOKS OF (see APOCRYPHA).

MACE (see ARMS, ARMOR OF THE BIBLE).

MACEDONIA [mass uh DOH neh uh] (meaning unknown) — a mountainous country north of Greece (Achaia) in the Balkan Peninsula (see Map 7, B-1). This area was visited twice, and perhaps three times, by the apostle Paul.

Macedonia was of little international significance until Philip II of Macedon (ruled 359-336 B.C.) es-

tablished his capital at PHILIPPI. He defeated the Greek city-states and united them into one kingdom. His son Alexander III of Macedon (ruled 336-323 B.C.), later known as ALEXANDER the Great, built an empire from Greece to the Nile River in Egypt and southeast to the Indus River.

After Alexander's death the generals divided the empire, and Macedonia declined in importance. But Macedonia regained its leading position and was made a colony after the Battle of Philippi (42 B.C.), at which Octavian (Augustus) and Antony defeated Brutus and Cassius on the plains near the city.

The first mention of Macedonia in the Bible is in Acts 16: the description of Paul's "Macedonian call." In a vision, a man appeared to Paul "and pleaded with him, saying, 'Come over to Macedonia and help us' " (Acts 16:9). Paul immediately set sail at Troas for NEAPOLIS (Acts 16:11), a seaport of Philippi in the extreme eastern part of Macedonia.

Luke gives a detailed account of Paul's journey through Macedonia (Acts 16:11—17:14). At Neapolis Paul picked up the Egnatian Way—the major road of Macedonia—and came to PHILIPPI, "the foremost city of that part of Macedonia, a colony" (Acts 16:12). At Philippi Paul made his first convert in Europe, "a certain woman named Lydia...[who] was a seller of purple" (Acts 16:14).

After Lydia's baptism and the healing of "a certain slave girl possessed with a spirit of divination" (Acts 16:16), and his imprisonment (Acts 16:23-24), Paul set out again on the Egnatian Way through AMPHIPOLIS and APOLLONIA to THESSALONICA (Acts 17:1)—the capital where the proconsul (governor) resided.

The final city Paul visited before leaving Macedonia for Athens was BEREA (Acts 17:10-14), where he left Silas and Timothy for a short time to assist in the work (Acts 17:15; 18:5).

At the close of this, his second missionary journey, Paul went on to Athens and Corinth and then back to Antioch of Syria (Acts 17:15—18:23). He revisited Macedonia at least once again (Acts 20:1-6), and perhaps twice (2 Cor. 2:13; 7:5; Phil. 2:24; 1 Tim. 1:3).

Several of Paul's travel companions and fellow workers were Macedonians: GAIUS (Acts 19:29), ARISTARCHUS (Acts 19:29; 27:2), SECUNDUS (Acts 20:4), and SOPATER (Acts 20:4). The Macedonian Christians' support of the needs of Paul and others is mentioned several times in Paul's letters (Rom. 15:26; 2 Cor. 8:1-5; Phil. 4:15-18).

MACEDONIANS [mass ih DOE nee unz] — natives or residents of MACEDONIA, a region of northern Greece (Acts 19:29; 2 Cor. 9:2).

MACHAERUS [ma KAY rus] (meaning unknown) — the place where JOHN THE BAPTIST was apparently imprisoned and put to death, according to the Jewish historian, Josephus. Machaerus is not mentioned in the Bible.

MACHBANAI [MAK buh nye] (meaning unknown) — a warrior who joined David at Ziklag (1 Chr. 12:13; Machbannai, RSV, NAS; Macbannai, NIV).

MACHBENAH [mak BEE nuh] (meaning unknown) — a son of Sheva mentioned in the genealogy of Judah. Machbenah was of the family of Caleb (1 Chr. 2:49).

MACHI [MAY kye] (meaning unknown) — one of 12 men sent by Moses to spy out the land of Canaan (Num. 13:15).

MACHIR [MAY kir] (sold) — the name of two men in the Old Testament:
1. The firstborn son of Manasseh (Gen. 50:23). The Machirites descended from Machir and were the only family of the tribe of Manasseh. They defeated the city of Gilead, which Moses gave to the Machirites as an inheritance (Josh. 17:1). In Judges 5:14 "Machir" is used poetically to refer to the whole tribe of Manasseh.
2. A son of Ammiel who lived in Lo Debar, east of the Jordan River (2 Sam. 9:4–5; 17:27). Machir provided for Saul's only surviving son, MEPHIBOSHETH, after David became king. He also brought provisions and supplies to David during Absalom's rebellion.

MACHIRITES [MAY kir ites] — the descendants of MACHIR No. 1 (Num. 26:29).

MACHNADEBAI [mak NAD eh bye] (liberality) — a son of Bani who divorced his pagan wife after the Captivity (Ezra 10:34, 40).

MACHPELAH [mahk PEE luh] (double) — a field, a cave, and the surrounding land purchased by Abraham as a burial place for his wife Sarah. The cave was to the east of Mamre, or Hebron (Gen. 23:19). At an earlier time, Abraham pitched his tent "by the terebinth trees of Mamre" (Gen. 13:18) and received three visitors who spoke of a child of promise to be born to Sarah (Gen. 18:1–15).

Abraham purchased the field of Machpelah from Ephron the Hittite. Abraham, Sarah, Isaac, Rebekah, Jacob, and Leah were all buried here (Gen. 49:31; 50:13).

Today the modern city of el-Khalil (Hebron) is built up around the site of Machpelah. The site of the cave was once covered by a Christian church but is now marked by a Moslem mosque. The Moslems held this site so sacred that for centuries Christians were forbidden to enter the ancient shrine. It is open to the public today.

MADABA [MAHD ah bah] — a form of MEDEBA.

MADAI [MAY dye] (middle land) — the third son of Japheth and a grandson of Noah (Gen. 10:2).

MADMANNAH [mad MAN nuh] (dunghill) — the name of a man and a town in the Old Testament:
1. A town in the southern wilderness of Judah near Ziklag (Josh. 15:20, 31), perhaps the same place as BETH MARCABOTH (1 Chr. 4:31).

2. A son of Shaaph, of the tribe of Judah (1 Chr. 2:49).

MADMEN [MAD men] (dunghill) — a city of Moab (Jer. 48:2) whose destruction was foretold by the prophet Jeremiah.

MADMENAH [mad MEE nuh] (dunghill) — a village north of Jerusalem in the territory of Benjamin (Is. 10:31).

MADNESS (see DISEASES OF THE BIBLE).

MADON [MAY dahn] (strife) — a Canaanite town in Galilee. The king of Madon, Jobab, was killed by Joshua in a battle at the waters of Merom (Josh. 11:1, 5, 7).

MAGADAN [MAG uh dan] — a form of MAGDALA.

MAGBISH [MAG bish] (fortress) — an unidentified town in the territory of Judah. The descendants of former residents of Magdish returned here after the Captivity (Ezra 2:30).

MAGDALA [MAG duh luh] (tower) — a place on the Sea of Galilee, perhaps on the west shore (see Map 6, C–2). Jesus and His disciples withdrew to this place after the feeding of the 4,000 (Matt. 15:39; Magadan, NIV, NAS, NEB, RSV). The parallel passage (Mark 8:10) has DALMANUTHA. Magdala was either the birthplace or the home of Mary Magdalene. Also see MAGDALENE.

MAGDALENE [mag de LEE nih] (of Magdala) — the designation given to a woman named Mary, one of Jesus' most prominent Galilean female disciples, to distinguish her from the other Marys. The first appearance of Mary Magdalene in the gospels is in Luke 8:2, which mentions her among those who were ministering to Jesus. Mary Magdalene has mistakenly been described as a woman of bad character and loose morals. There is no reason, however, to conclude that she was the same person as the sinful woman whom Simon the Pharisee treated with such disdain and contempt (Luke 7:36–50). Although such an identification is possible, the New Testament offers no evidence or proof for such an assumption.

Mary Magdalene was among the "many women who followed Jesus from Galilee, ministering to Him" (Matt. 27:55). She was one of the women at Calvary who were "looking on from afar" (Mark 15:40) when Jesus died on the cross (also John 19:25). She was at Joseph's tomb when the body of Jesus was wrapped in a fine linen cloth and a large stone was rolled against the door of the tomb (Matt. 27:61; Mark 15:47). And she was a witness of the risen Christ (Matt. 28:1; Mark 16:1; Luke 24:10; John 20:1). In fact, she was the first of any of Jesus' followers to see Him after His resurrection (Mark 16:9; John 20:11–18).

Apparently Mary is called "Magdalene" because she was a native or inhabitant of MAGDALA, a village on the west shore of the Sea of Galilee, about five kilometers (three miles) northwest of Tiberias.

These scarabs, shapes in the image of sacred beetles, were used as charms by the ancient Egyptians in their superstitious form of religion.

MAGDIEL [MAG deh el] (*renown of God*) — an Edomite clan chief, descended from Esau (1 Chr. 1:54).

MAGGOT (see ANIMALS OF THE BIBLE).

MAGI [MAY jie] (see WISE MEN).

MAGIC, SORCERY, AND DIVINATION — occult practices, such as fortune-telling and witchcraft, which were common among the pagan nations of the ancient world. But such attempts to control evil spirits were expressly forbidden to the Hebrew people. Deuteronomy 18:10–11 mentions the following specific occult practices which were forbidden by the law of Moses.

Passing a Son or Daughter Through the Fire. This phrase refers to the practice of child sacrifice. This seems incredible to us today, but the very fact that it was outlawed by God indicates it must have been done in Bible times (Deut. 18:10). Second Kings 16:3 records that King Ahaz sacrificed his son in this way. No doubt he thought that such a sacrifice would appease some pagan god. His grandson, King Manasseh, sacrificed his sons two generations later (2 Kin. 21:6; 2 Chr. 33:6). Second Kings 23:10 reveals that it was mainly the pagan god Molech who required this awful sacrifice. But other false gods apparently also demanded it (2 Kin. 17:31; Jer. 19:5).

Witchcraft. The practice of witchcraft, or divination, was a means for extracting information or guidance from a pagan god. The word describes the activity of Balaam the soothsayer, or professional prophet, who was hired to curse Israel (Num. 22:7; 23:23; Josh. 13:22). It also describes the woman at En Dor who brought up the spirit of Samuel. All the major prophets condemned divination (Is. 44:25; Jer. 27:9; 29:8; Ezek. 13:9).

The only places where information is given on the actual means people used in divination is in Genesis 44:5 and Ezekiel 21:21–23. In the case of Joseph's divining cup, the diviner apparently interpreted the shape of a puddle of oil floating on the water in the cup (Gen. 44:5). Ezekiel 21 describes the king of Babylon as he tried to decide which way to approach Jerusalem. It portrays him as throwing down a handful of arrows, hoping that a certain one will point to a route which he believes is the will of his god. It also records that "he consults the images, he looks at the liver" (Ezek. 21:21). Reading and interpreting the livers of sacrificial animals was another form of determining the will of the gods. All these forms of superstition, of course, were forbidden among the Hebrew people.

Soothsaying. Soothsaying is a relatively rare word in the Bible which describes some form of divination, the practitioner of which is also described by the KJV as "observer of times" (Deut. 18:10). Because it sounds like a Hebrew word for cloud, some scholars believe it refers to cloud reading. This may have been similar to tea leaf reading or astrology, which is a reading of the stars. God forbids the practice (Deut. 18:10, 14; Lev. 19:26). Wicked King Manasseh was also guilty of this sin (2 Kin. 21:6; 2 Chr. 33:6). The prophets of the Old Testament also condemned this occult practice (Is. 2:6; 57:3; Jer. 27:9; Mic. 5:12).

Interpreting Omens. Behind this phrase, also rendered as enchantments (KJV), lie four different Hebrew words. The most common of the four occurs in Genesis 30:27, in reference to Laban's "experience"; in Genesis 44:5 and 15, referring to Joseph's cup; and in Numbers 23:23 and 24:1, describing Balaam's activity. Leviticus 19:26 and Deuteronomy 18:10 specifically outlawed this practice as well. Another of the words used for the practice seems to mean "whisper," and it may indicate the way the enchanter lowered his voice. In Ecclesiastes 10:11 interpreting omens is connected with snake charming.

Sorcery. Sorcery or witchcraft is forbidden in the law of Moses (Ex. 22:18; Deut. 18:10). Sorcery was apparently practiced by the worst of the kings of Israel and Judah (2 Kin. 9:22; 2 Chr. 33:6), but it was denounced by the prophets (Nah. 3:4).

Conjuring Spells. This phrase, also translated as charm, appears in Deuteronomy 18:11, once in the Psalms (58:5), and twice in Isaiah (47:9, 12). Sometimes it is rendered as enchantments. A different Hebrew word lies behind this translation in Isaiah 19:3. Because it is related to a word for bind, it may mean casting a spell ("spell-binding"). One scholar suggests it has to do with tying a magic knot.

Consulting Mediums. This phrase may refer to the same thing as practicing wizardry. The word describes the witch at En Dor whom Saul engaged to conduct a seance and bring up the spirit of Samuel (1 Sam. 28:3, 9; familiar spirits, KJV). The woman

Photo: British Museum

Clay model of a sheep's liver, dating from about 1700 B.C., discovered in ancient Babylon. Pagan priests of the ancient world often used such livers from animals to try to foretell the future.

skillful person. But in the Bible it is always a forbidden thing, a kind of black magic. This is why most modern versions translate the word as spiritist, fortune-teller, or sorcerer.

Calling Up the Dead. Necromancy is another word used for this practice. The phrase occurs only in Deuteronomy 18:11, although this is exactly what an Old Testament witch did. The Bible gives us no indication that we can expect to talk with people who have died.

Magic. The Hebrew word translated as magic appears only in connection with Egyptian and Babylonian magicians. The first cluster of verses relates to Joseph in Egypt (Gen. 41:8, 24); the second appears in connection with the plagues (Ex. 7:11—9:11); and the third deals with Daniel and the various government-supported magicians of Babylon (Dan. 1:20; 2:2, 10, 27; 4:7, 9; 5:11). This term is never used in connection with the nation of Israel, so apparently it was not a threat or a temptation. In all the Old Testament contexts the ineffectiveness of magicians is underscored.

Magic actually comes from a Greek word which appears several times in the New Testament. Simon the sorcerer is one example (Acts 8:9–25). And Elymas the sorcerer is another (Acts 13:6–8). They may have been something like the "itinerant Jewish exorcists," also mentioned in the Book of Acts (Acts 19:13), who attempted to drive evil spirits out of people in the name of Jesus.

Still another New Testament word translated sorcery comes from the same Greek word as our English word, pharmacy. Quite obviously this has to do with drugs; a more relevant and contemporary application could hardly be found. The denunciations contained in Revelation 9:21; 18:23; 21:8; and

succeeded either by the power of God or the power of the Devil. As with other practices in this list, it was forbidden by the law of God, practiced by bad kings, and condemned by the prophets. In two places the prophet Isaiah hinted that consulting mediums may be a kind of ventriloquism (8:19; 29:4).

Spiritism. The word for spiritist always appears with witch. The root of the word in Hebrew is the verb "to know." In modern English wizard means someone very wise or inventive, a very clever or

The oracle of Delphi, a pagan object used to foretell the future, was kept in this shrine—the temple of Apollo in Delphi. Ruins of the temple are visible just beyond the amphitheater.

Photo by Howard Vos

22:15 apply to those who use drugs to bring on trances during which they claim to have supernatural knowledge or power.

MAGISTRATE (see OCCUPATIONS AND TRADES).

MAGNIFICAT [mag NIFF ih caht] (*it magnifies*) — Mary's song of praise when she was greeted by her cousin Elizabeth before the birth of Christ (Luke 1:46–55). In Latin the song begins with the word *magnificat*. Mary's song is modeled on the Song of Hannah (1 Sam. 2:1–10). Like Mary, HANNAH was a godly woman who miraculously bore a son through the intervention of God. Hannah's son, Samuel, anointed David as king in Israel (1 Samuel 16); Mary's Son would be the final and permanent Davidic King (Luke 1:32–33).

The Magnificat has two main sections. Verses 46–49 are very personal. They celebrate God's graciousness in choosing this humble maiden to be the mother of the Messiah. Verses 50–55 connect God's activity in the coming of Jesus with God's age–long pattern of putting down the proud, the mighty, and the rich, and of raising up the lowly and the hungry.

MAGOG [MAY gog] (*land of Gog*) — the name of a man and a people in the Bible:

1. The second son of Japheth and a grandson of Noah (Gen. 10:2).

2. The descendants of Magog (Ezek. 38:2), possibly a people who lived in northern Asia and Europe. The Jewish historian Josephus identified these people as the Scythians, known for their destructive warfare. Magog may be a comprehensive term which means "northern barbarians." The people of Magog are described as skilled horsemen (Ezek. 38:15) and experts in the use of the bow and arrow (Ezek. 39: 3, 9). The Book of Revelation uses Ezekiel's prophetic imagery to portray the final, apocalyptic encounter between good and evil at the end of this age. "Gog and Magog" (Rev. 20:8–9) symbolize the anti-Christian forces of the world.

Also see GOG.

MAGOR–MISSABIB [MAY gahr meh SAY bib] (*fear on every side*) — a symbolic name given by the prophet Jeremiah to PASHHUR, the chief governor of the temple (Jer. 20:3). Jeremiah prophesied that Pashhur and his family would be taken captive to Babylon (Jer. 20:1–6).

MAGPIASH [MAG peh ash] (meaning unknown) — an Israelite chief who sealed the covenant after the Captivity (Neh. 10:20).

MAHALAB [muh HAY lub] (meaning unknown) — a town in the territory of Asher (Josh. 19:29, RSV). The NKJV translates it "at the sea."

MAHALAH [muh HAY luh] — a form of MAHLAH.

MAHALALEEL [muh HAY luh lee el] (*God shines forth*) — the name of two men in the Bible:

1. A son of Cainan (1 Chr. 1:2), also spelled Maleleel.

2. An Israelite of the tribe of Judah (Neh. 11:4).

MAHALATH [MAY huh lath] (*mild*) — the name of two women and a musical term in the Old Testament:

1. A daughter of Ishmael and one of Esau's wives (Gen. 28:9), apparently the same person as BASEMATH (Gen. 36:3–4).

2. A daughter of Jerimoth (2 Chr. 11:18).

3. A musical term used in the titles of Psalm 53 and Psalm 88. Its meaning is uncertain. Also see MUSIC OF THE BIBLE.

MAHALATH LEANNOTH [MAY huh lath leh AN ahth] (see MUSIC OF THE BIBLE).

MAHALI [MAY huh lye] — a form of MAHLI.

MAHANAIM [may huh NAY im] (*two armies*) — an ancient town in Gilead, east of the Jordan River in the vicinity of the River Jabbok. Its exact location is disputed. Located on the border between the tribes of Manasseh and Gad (Josh. 13:26, 30), Mahanaim was later assigned to the Merarite Levites (Josh. 21:38).

On his way home after an absence of 20 years, Jacob was met by angels of God at this site. He named the place Mahanaim, meaning "two armies." This was a significant moment for Jacob, who was about to meet his estranged brother Esau. The knowledge that he was being accompanied by an angelic band undoubtedly brought him the confidence and assurance he needed.

Following the slaying of King Saul by the Philistines, his son Ishbosheth reigned for two years at Mahanaim (2 Sam. 2:8, 12, 29). Later, Mahanaim became the headquarters for David during the rebellion of his son, Absalom (2 Sam. 17:24). Solomon also made Mahanaim the capital of one of his 12 districts (1 Kin. 4:14).

MAHANEH DAN [MAY huh neh dan] (*camp of Dan*) — a place in Judah "between Zorah and Eshtaol" (Judg. 13:25)—and west of Kirjath Jearim (Judg. 18:12). The Danites rebuilt this city and called it "Dan, after the name of Dan their father" (Judg. 18:29).

MAHARAI [muh HAR ay eye] (*swift*) — one of David's mighty men. Maharai was captain over 24,000 men (2 Sam. 23:28; 1 Chr. 11:30; 27:13).

MAHATH [MAY hath] (*snatching*) — the name of two Temple servants in the Old Testament:

1. A priest who helped purify the sanctuary (1 Chr. 6:35).

2. A Levite overseer of Temple offerings in Hezekiah's time (2 Chr. 31:13). He may be identical with Mahath No. 1.

MAHAVITE [MAY huh vight] (meaning unknown) — the family name of Eliel, one of David's mighty men (1 Chr. 11:46).

MAHAZIOTH [muh HAY zeh ahth] (*visions*) — chief of the 23rd course of musicians in the Temple during David's reign (1 Chr. 25:4, 30).

MAHER–SHALAL–HASH–BAZ [MAY her SHAL al HASH baz] (*hasten the booty*) — the symbolic name of the second son of the prophet Isaiah (Is. 8:1, 3), signifying the doom of Damascus and Samaria and the destruction of Syria and Israel, who had formed a military alliance against Jerusalem (Is. 7:1).

MAHLAH [MAH luh] (*weak one*) — the name of two people in the Old Testament:
1. The oldest of the five daughters of Zelophehad (Num. 26:33). Because Zelophehad had no sons, his daughters were allowed to inherit their father's estate (Num. 36:1–13).
2. The third child of Hammoleketh (1 Chr. 7:18; Mahalah, KJV).

MAHLI [MAH leh] (*weak*) — the name of two men in the Old Testament:
1. The oldest son of Merari and founder of the Mahlites (Num. 3:33), also called Mahali (Ex. 6:19).
2. A son of Mushi (1 Chr. 23:23).

MAHLITES [MAH lights] — a tribal family of Levites descended from MAHLI, the son of Merari (Num. 3:33; 26:58).

MAHLON [MAH lahn] (*sickly*) — the husband of Ruth the Moabitess who died childless in the land of Moab (Ruth 1:1–5).

MAHOL [MAY hall] (*dance*) — an ancestor of Ethan, Heman, Chalcol, and Darda (1 Kin. 4:31)— men known for their wisdom during the reign of King Solomon.

MAHSEIAH [muh SIGH yuh] (*Jehovah is a refuge*) — the father of Neriah (Jer. 32:12; 51:59; Maaseiah, KJV).

MAID (see OCCUPATIONS AND TRADES).

MAIL, COAT OF (See ARMS, ARMOR OF THE BIBLE).

MAIMED (see DISABILITIES AND DEFORMITIES).

MAINSAIL — the principal sail of a ship (Acts 27:40; foresail, RSV, NIV, NEB, NASB).

MAKAZ [MAY kaz] (*boundary*) — a city that supplied food for Solomon and his royal household (1 Kin. 4:9).

MAKHELOTH [mak HEE lahth] (*assemblies*) — a campsite of the Israelites on their journey to Canaan (Num. 33:25–26), location unknown.

MAKKEDAH [ma KEE duh] (*place of shepherds*) — a royal city of the Canaanites (see Map 3, A–4). Near this city Joshua killed the five kings of the Amorites, who had formed a military alliance against the Israelites. The location of Makkedah is uncertain. Some scholars identify the site as el-Muqhar ("the caves"), southwest of Ekron. Others believe it was between Lachish and Hebron.

MAKTESH [MAK tesh] (*mortar*) — a place near Jerusalem where silversmiths and silver traders conducted their business during the reign of King Josiah of Judah (Zeph. 1:11). Literally, Maktesh means "the mortar" (NAS, RSV).

MALACHI [MAL ah kie] (*my messenger*) — Old Testament prophet and author of the prophetic book which bears his name. Nothing is known about Malachi's life except the few facts that may be inferred from his prophecies. He apparently prophesied after the CAPTIVITY, during the time when NEHEMIAH was leading the people to rebuild Jerusalem's wall and recommit themselves to following God's Law. The people's negligence in paying tithes to God was condemned by both Nehemiah and Malachi (Neh. 13:10–14; Mal. 3:8–10). Also see MALACHI, BOOK OF.

MALACHI, BOOK OF — a short prophetic book of the Old Testament written to rebuke the people of Israel for their shallow worship practices. The name comes from the Hebrew word *malachi* (1:1), meaning "my messenger" or "messenger of Jehovah."

Structure of the Book. Portions of Malachi are written in the format of a debate, unlike any other book of the Bible. God first makes a statement of truth that is then denied by the people. God then refutes their argument in great detail, restating and proving the truth of His original statement (1:2–7; 2:10–17; 3:7–10). Malachi also uses questions and answers freely to focus his accusations toward the priesthood as well as the people. These features make Malachi one of the most argumentative books of the Bible.

Authorship and Date. Some scholars believe the word Malachi should be interpreted as a description ("my messenger") rather than as the name of a specific person. This line of reasoning concludes that the book was written by an unknown author. But no other book of prophecy in the Old Testament was written anonymously. Although nothing else is known about this person, the weight of tradition has assumed the book was written by a prophet named Malachi. The prophecy can be specifically dated at about 450 B.C.

Historical Setting. Malachi was addressed to the nation of Israel about 100 years after its return from captivity in Babylon. At first the people had been enthusiastic about rebuilding Jerusalem and the Temple and restoring their system of worship. But their zeal soon began to wane. They wondered about God's love for them as His Chosen People. They began to offer defective animals as sacrifices and to withhold their tithes and offerings. Malachi was written to call the people back to authentic worship of their Redeemer God.

Theological Contributions. The prophecy of Malachi is noted for its vivid portrayal of the love of God as well as His might and power. Israel needed to be reminded of these truths at a time when widespread doubt had dashed its expectations of the Messiah.

Special Considerations. Malachi leaves us with the

feeling that the story is not yet finished, that God still has promises to fulfill on behalf of His people. After Malachi came 400 long years of silence. But when the time was right, heaven would burst forth in song at the arrival of the Messiah.

MALACHITE (see MINERALS OF THE BIBLE).

MALCAM [MAL kam] (*their king*) — a Benjamite, the fourth of the seven sons of Shaharaim by his wife Hodesh (1 Chr. 8:9; Malcham, KJV, NEB).

MALCHAM [MAL kam] — a form of MALCAM. Also used (Zeph. 1:5, KJV) as a form of Milcom. Also see GODS, PAGAN.

MALCHIAH [mal KYE ah] (*Jehovah is king*) — the name of two or three men in the Old Testament:

1. A son of Parosh (Ezra 10:25). He divorced his pagan wife after the Captivity.

2. The father of Pashhur (Jer. 38:1). King Zedekiah of Judah sent Pashhur to inquire of the Lord concerning the military situation with Nebuchadnezzar, king of Babylon. Malchiah is also called Melchiah (Jer. 21:1).

3. A royal prince—"the king's son" (Jer. 38:6)—in the time of Zedekiah, king of Judah. Jeremiah was cast into the dungeon of Malchiah. This is probably the same person as Malchiah No. 2.

MALCHIEL [MAL keh el] (*God is king*) — younger son of Beriah (Gen. 46:17) and founder of a tribal family, the MALCHIELITES (Num. 26:45).

MALCHIELITES [MAL keh el ites] — the descendants of MALCHIEL (Num. 26:45).

MALCHIJAH [mal KIE jah] (*Jehovah is king*) — the name of nine men in the Old Testament:

1. A Gershonite Levite and descendant of Asaph (1 Chr. 6:40).

2. A Levite descended from Aaron. Malchijah's descendants formed the fifth course of priests during David's time (1 Chr. 24:9).

3. A son of Parosh (Ezra 10:25). After the Captivity Malchijah divorced his pagan wife.

4. A son of Harim who divorced his pagan wife after the Captivity (Ezra 10:31).

5. A son of Rechab (Neh. 3:14).

6. A member of the guild of goldsmiths who helped repair the Jerusalem wall after the Captivity (Neh. 3:31).

7. One who helped Ezra explain the Law to the people (Neh. 8:4).

8. One of those who sealed the covenant in Nehemiah's time (Neh. 10:3).

9. A priest who officiated at the dedication of Jerusalem's wall (Neh. 12:42).

MALCHIRAM [mal KEH ram] (*my king is exalted*) — a son of King Jeconiah (Jehoiachin) of Judah and grandson of King Jehoiakim (1 Chr. 3:18).

MALCHISHUA [mal kye SHOO uh] (*my king is salvation*) — one of the four sons of King Saul killed by the Philistines at Mount Gilboa (1 Sam. 14:49; 31:2; Melchi-shua, KJV).

MALCHUS [MAL kus] (*ruler*) — a servant of the high priest who was present at the arrest of Jesus in the Garden of Gethsemane. Simon Peter struck Malchus with a sword and cut off his ear (John 18:10).

MALEFACTOR [MAL eh fak tur] — KJV translation of two Greek words meaning "evildoer" (John 18:30) and "evil worker" (Luke 23:32–33, 39). The two thieves crucified with Jesus were malefactors, or "criminals" (Luke 23:32–33, 39, NKJV).

MALACHI: A Teaching Outline

MALELEEL [muh LEE leh el] — a form of MA-HALALEEL No. 1.

MALICE — a vicious intention, or a desire of one person to hurt another (Titus 3:3). Malice is often irrational, usually based on the false belief that the person against whom it is directed has the same intention. It is contrary to love (1 Cor. 13:4–7). Christians are instructed to rid their lives of malice (Eph. 4:31–32).

MALKIJAH [mal KIE juh] — a form of MALCHIAH No. 2.

MALLOTHI [MAL oh thigh] (*Jehovah is speaking*) — a son of Heman who served in the Temple sanctuary during David's reign (1 Chr. 25:4, 26).

MALLOW (see PLANTS OF THE BIBLE).

MALLUCH [MAL uhk] (*counselor*) — the name of six men in the Old Testament:
1. A Levite of the family of Merari (1 Chr. 6:44).
2, 3. A son of Babi (Ezra 10:29) and a son of Harim (Ezra 10:32), each of whom divorced his pagan wife after the Captivity.
4, 5. A priest (Neh. 10:4) and a chief of the people (Neh. 10:27), both of whom sealed the covenant with Nehemiah after the Captivity.
6. A priest who returned to Jerusalem after the Captivity (Neh. 12:1–2). In Nehemiah 12:14, Malluch is also translated as Malluchi, NAS, RSV; Melichu, NKJV and Melicu, KJV.

MALLUCHI [mal LOU kih] — a form of MALLUCH No. 6.

MALTA [MAWL tuh] (*refuge*) — a small island in the Mediterranean Sea between Sicily and Africa, about 145 kilometers (90 miles) southwest of Syracuse (see Map 8, A–2). The apostle Paul was shipwrecked on Malta (Acts 28:1).

With its fine natural harbors, Malta was a convenient haven for ships. Colonized by the Phoenicians, it was captured by the Greeks (736 B.C.), the Carthaginians (528 B.C.), and the Romans (242 B.C.).

After the shipwreck, Paul stayed on Malta for three months (Acts 28:11; Melita, KJV) before he was able to board another ship to Rome. During this time he shared the gospel with the inhabitants of the island and started a church on Malta. Thus an incidental event in the life of Paul led to the expansion of the kingdom of God.

MAMMON [MAM mun] (*riches*) — a word that speaks of wealth (Matt. 6:24; Luke 16:9, 11, 13), especially wealth that is used in opposition to God. Mammon is a transliteration of the Aramaic word *mamon*, which means "wealth, riches," or "earthly goods." Modern versions have "money," "gold," and "material possessions." Jesus said that no one can serve two masters—God and money—at the same time. Nor can mammon (money) purchase security (see Jesus' parable of the rich fool in Luke 12:13–21). "For what is a man profited if he gains the whole world, and loses his own soul?" (Matt. 16:26; Mark 8:36; Luke 9:25).

MAMRE [MAM reh] (*firmness*) — the name of a man and a place in the Old Testament:
1. An Amorite chief who formed an alliance with Abraham against CHEDORLAOMER (Gen. 14:13, 24).
2. A place in the district of Hebron, west of Machpelah, where Abraham lived. It was noted for its "terebinth trees" (Gen. 13:18; 18:1), or "oaks" (RSV). Near Mamre was the cave of MACHPELAH, in which Abraham, Isaac, and Jacob—and their wives, Sarah, Rebekah, and Leah—were buried (Gen. 49:13). The site of ancient Mamre has been identified as Ramet el-Khalil, about three kilometers (two miles) north of Hebron.

MAN — God's highest creation, made in God's own image.

The Origin of Man. The Bible states that man was created by God. This truth is found especially in Genesis 1:26–31 and 2:7–25. These passages teach that God did not use any previously existing living creature in bringing man into being.

In the second account, God is described as using "dust of the earth" (Gen. 2:7) to form man. Some have understood this to represent some high form of life that was still sub-human. This view, sometimes called "theistic evolution," maintains that man's physical nature developed from other forms of life through evolution, but that God modified or adapted this previously existing creature by giving it a soul. This approach interprets the passage somewhat more symbolically. Others, however, have taken this passage literally and understand the reference to dust as meaning that God actually created man from dust.

The Age of Man. Some early students believed that by tracing the genealogies in the Bible and adding up the ages of the persons involved in the several generations, it was possible to establish a date for the creation of man. Perhaps the most extensive effort of this type was that done by Bishop James Ussher, who calculated the origin of man at 4004 B.C.

Closer study of the genealogies has revealed, however, that they cannot be used in quite this fashion. Thus, the apparent difference between the facts of Scripture and the great age which anthropologists assign to man is found not to be quite so serious. Attempts to relate Adam to any of the ancient specimens of man discovered by anthropologists will depend upon how we define humanity, because we know little about Adam's appearance, size, brain capacity, and so forth. Various Christian anthropologists assign dates for man's origin anywhere from 1,000,000 to 50,000 years ago.

The Makeup of Man. Some scientists believe man is composed of two or more components. They see man as made up of body and soul. Other scientists, basing their argument upon 1 Thessalonians 5:23, assign three parts—body, soul, and spirit—to man. It appears, however, from passages such as John 12:27 and 13:21 that soul and spirit may be used interchangeably in the Bible as terms meaning essentially the same thing.

More recently, biblical scholarship has declared

man to be more of a unity. Actions of man are not pictured as issuing from his body, soul, or spirit, but from the whole person.

The Role of Man. Man was created for fellowship or communion with God. Unlike any of the other creatures, he has a fundamental likeness to God: he is created in the "image of God" (Gen. 1:26–27). Man meets and talks with God in the Garden of Eden (Gen. 2:15–17). This was the original intention of God for man. It also becomes God's continuing intention, as He repeatedly intervenes to draw man back to Himself. Ultimately, the Redeemer—Jesus—was sent for this reason as well. Man is not only to have fellowship with God; he is to glorify Him, by what he is and what he does (1 Cor. 10:31; Eph. 1:12).

Man is also created to do God's will and work. Man was created in God's image so he might "have dominion" over the rest of creation (Gen. 1:26, 28), or perform God's work of ruling the creation in His place. This assignment of work to be done came before the FALL. As a result of the Fall, work took on its unpleasant or cursed character (Gen. 3:17–19).

The Restoration of Man. God has acted to restore man to his original state of innocence and fellowship with God. He has done this by sending His Son to die for man so man might be reconciled to God and be renewed or "born again" (John 3:3, 7). The aim of this is to restore man to a dynamic, vital relationship with God (Rom. 6:4; 2 Cor. 5:20).

Man is most fully human when fulfilling the intention of God for him: worshiping, serving, and loving God. Of all creatures, only man has been given this blessed privilege.

MAN OF SIN (see ANTICHRIST).

MANAEN [MAN uh en] (*comforter*) — a man listed as one of the "prophets and teachers" (Acts 13:1) in the church of Antioch of Syria. Luke records that Manaen "had been brought up with" Herod the tetrarch. Some scholars believe Manaen may have been a playmate of the young Herod, or may have been educated with him at Rome. In any case, his past association with Herod marked Manaen as a man of distinction.

MANAHATH [MAN uh hath] (*resting place*) — the name of a man and a city in the Old Testament:

1. A son of Shobal and a grandson of Seir the Horite (Gen. 36:23).

2. A city to which certain Benjamite descendants of Geba were forced to move (1 Chr. 8:6).

MANAHATHITES [man uh HATH eyts] — a form of MANAHETHITES.

MANAHETHITES [muh NAY heth eyts] — the descendants of a man or the inhabitants of a place named Manahath, presumably belonging to the tribe of Judah (1 Chr. 2:54). The RSV, NIV, and NAS translate as Manahathites. Other translations are MANUHOTH (NKJV) and Menuhoth (RSV).

MANASSEH [muh NASS uh] (*causing to forget*) — the name of five men in the Old Testament:

1. Joseph's firstborn son who was born in Egypt to Asenath the daughter of Poti-Pherah, priest of On (Gen. 41:50–51). Like his younger brother EPHRAIM, Manasseh was half Hebrew and half Egyptian. Manasseh's birth caused Joseph to forget the bitterness of his past experiences. Manasseh and Ephraim were both adopted by Jacob and given status as sons just like Jacob's own sons Reuben and Simeon (Gen. 48:5).

2. The grandfather of the Jonathan who was one of the priests of the graven image erected by the tribe of Dan (Judg. 18:30).

3. The 14th king of Judah, the son of HEZEKIAH

St. Paul's Bay at Malta. The beach on which Paul's ship ran aground (Acts 27:39—28:10) has eroded across the centuries, leaving this rocky shore.

Photo by Howard Vos

born to Hephzibah (2 Kin. 21:1–18). Manasseh reigned longer (55 years) than any other Israelite king and had the dubious distinction of being Judah's most wicked king. He came to the throne at the age of 12, although he probably co-reigned with Hezekiah for ten years. His father's godly influence appears to have affected Manasseh only negatively, and he reverted to the ways of his evil grandfather, Ahaz.

Committed to idolatry, Manasseh restored everything Hezekiah had abolished. Manasseh erected altars to Baal; he erected an image of Asherah in the Temple; he worshiped the sun, moon, and stars; he recognized the Ammonite god Molech and sacrificed his son to him (2 Kin. 21:6); he approved DIVINATION; and he killed all who protested his evil actions. It is possible that he killed the prophet Isaiah; rabbinical tradition states that Manasseh gave the command that Isaiah be sawn in two. Scripture summarizes Manasseh's reign by saying he "seduced them [Judah] to do more evil than the nations whom the Lord had destroyed before the children of Israel" (2 Kin. 21:9).

Manasseh was temporarily deported to Babylon where he humbled himself before God in repentance (2 Chr. 33:11–13). Upon Manasseh's return to Jerusalem, he tried to reverse the trends he had set; but his reforms were quickly reversed after his death by his wicked son Amon.

4. A descendant, or resident, of Pahath–Moab (Ezra 10:30). After the Captivity he divorced his pagan wife.

5. An Israelite of the family of Hashum. Manasseh divorced his pagan wife after the Captivity (Ezra 10:33).

MANASSEH, TRIBE OF [muh NASS uh] — the tribe that traced its origin to MANASSEH No. 1. The tribe of Manasseh descended through Manasseh's son, Machir; Machir's son, Gilead; and Gilead's six sons (Num. 26:28–34). During their first 430 years in Egypt, the tribe of Manasseh increased to 32,200 men of war (Num. 1:34–35). By the second census, 39 years later, it numbered 52,700 (Num. 26:34).

In the settlement of Canaan, land was provided for Manasseh on both sides of the Jordan River. Eastern Manasseh was able to occupy its land only after it had aided the other tribes in conquering their territories (Num. 32:1–33).

Because of the Canaanite fortresses and strong cities in the land (for example, Megiddo, En Dor, Taanach, Dor, Ibleam, and Beth Shean), western Manasseh had difficulty settling its territory. When it became strong, however, it did not expel the Canaanites but subjected them to tribute (Josh. 17:11–13).

The tribe of Manasseh was known for its valor, and it claimed two famous judges: Gideon (Judg. 6:11—8:35) and Jephthah (Judg. 11:1—12:7). During Saul's reign men from Manasseh joined David at Ziklag (1 Chr. 12:19–20). Later many people from both western and eastern Manasseh rallied to make David king at Hebron (1 Chr. 12:31, 37).

MANASSITES [muh NASS ites] — the descendants of MANASSEH, the older son of Joseph and Asenath (Deut. 4:43; Judg. 12:4).

MANDRAKE (see PLANTS OF THE BIBLE).

MANEH [MAN eh] (see MONEY; WEIGHTS AND MEASURES).

MANEIT (see WEIGHTS AND MEASURES).

MANGER — a feeding-trough, crib, or open box in a stable designed to hold fodder for livestock (Luke 2:7, 12; 13:15). In Bible times, mangers were made of clay mixed with straw or from stones cemented with mud. In the stables of King Ahab at Megiddo, a manger cut from a limestone block was discovered. Mangers were also carved in natural outcroppings of rock, such as livestock being stabled in a cave; some were constructed of masonry.

After Jesus' birth as the Son of God who would rule the kingdom from David's throne forever (Luke 1:32–35), he was placed in the humble obscurity of a manger (Luke 2:7). Baby Jesus lying in a manger was a sign to the shepherds (Luke 2:12, 16). Compare Jesus' statement in Luke 9:58: "Foxes have holes and birds of the air have nests, but the Son of Man has nowhere to lay His head."

MANNA — the food that God provided miraculously for the Israelites in the wilderness during their Exodus from Egypt (Ex. 16:15, 31, 33; Num. 11:6–9).

As long as the Hebrew people wandered in the Sinai Peninsula, they were able to gather manna from the ground each morning (Ex. 16:35). They ate the manna for 40 years, "until they came to the border of the land of Canaan" (Ex. 16:35). According to Joshua 5:12, the manna did not stop until the Israelites had crossed the Jordan River, had camped at Gilgal, had kept the Passover, and "had eaten the produce of the land."

"What is it?" (Ex. 16:15). This question, asked by the astonished Israelites, led to the name manna being applied to the "small round substance as fine as frost" (Ex. 16:14). Manna looked "like white coriander seed." It tasted like "wafers made with honey" (Ex. 16:31) or "pastry prepared with oil" (Num. 11:8).

The manna appeared with the morning dew. The Hebrews were instructed to gather only what was needed for one day, because any surplus would breed tiny worms and be spoiled. On the sixth day, however, the Israelites were permitted to gather enough for two days; they were forbidden to gather any manna on the Sabbath. Miraculously, the two days' supply of food gathered on the sixth day did not spoil.

Manna could apparently be baked, boiled, ground, beaten, cooked in pans, and made into cakes (Ex. 16:23; Num. 11:8). Moses even commanded Aaron to put a pot of manna in the ARK OF THE COVENANT (Ex. 16:32–34), so future generations might see the "bread of heaven" on which their ancestors had fed. The New Testament records

Photo by Howard Vos

A stone manger for feeding animals, built into the wall of the Good Samaritan Inn on the road to Jericho.

that inside the holy of holies in the Temple, the ark of the covenant contained, among other things, "the golden pot that had the manna" (Heb. 9:4).

Numerous attempts have been made to identify manna with substances found in the Sinai Peninsula. Insects living on the tamarisk bush produce a small, sweet substance during the early summer that has been identifed as manna by some scholars. But this substance does not fulfill all the biblical requirements for manna. Other suggestions have included resinous gums that drip from some wilderness shrubs. But such substances do not resemble the manna that the Hebrews gathered and ate. Manna certainly was nourishing, but it cannot be identified with any known food.

Manna was a visible reminder to the Hebrews of God's providential care for His people.

MANOAH [muh NOH uh] (*quiet*) — father of Samson the judge (Judg. 13:2–23). A Danite of the city of Zorah, Manoah and his wife tried to persuade Samson not to marry a Philistine woman, but he was determined to do so. They accompanied Samson to Timnah, where the ceremonies took place. Samson was buried "between Zorah and Eshtaol in the tomb of his father Manoah" (Judg. 16:31).

MANSERVANT (see SLAVERY).

MANSIONS — the translation of a Greek word in John 14:2 which means "rooms." Jesus did not describe HEAVEN as a neighborhood of beautiful country estates, where each person will have his own mansion. He promised many individual rooms, or dwelling–places, within the one house. In heaven the believer will experience the intimacy of dwelling with the Father and all other believers "under one roof."

MANSLAYER, MANSTEALER (see LAW).

MANTLE (see DRESS OF THE BIBLE).

MANUHOTH [man YOU hoth] (*resting places*) — the families of Shobal and Salma, two sons of Caleb, of the tribe of Judah (1 Chr. 2:52; Menuhoth, RSV; Manahathites, NIV, NASB; Manahethites, KJV, NEB).

MANUSCRIPTS (see BIBLE).

MAOCH [MAY ahk] (meaning unknown) — the father of Achish, king of Gath (1 Sam. 27:2). Maoch may be the same person as Maachah (1 Kin. 2:39).

MAON [MAY ahn] (*dwelling*) — the name of a city, a place, and a man in the Old Testament:
1. A city in the mountain country of Judah, near Carmel (Josh. 15:55).
2. A wilderness east of Maon and west of the Dead Sea (1 Sam. 23:24–25) where David and his men hid from King Saul.
3. A son of Shammai (1 Chr. 2:45).

MAONITES [MAY ahn ites] — a people who oppressed Israel (Judg. 10:12). The exact identification of this tribe is uncertain. They may have been the MEUNITES (2 Chr. 26:7), an Arab tribe south of the Dead Sea.

MARA [MAY ruh] (*bitter*) — the name which Naomi chose for herself after the death of her husband and sons to express her sadness and bereavement (Ruth 1:20).

MARAH [MAH rah] (*bitter*) — a pool, or well, of bitter water in the Wilderness of Shur (Num. 33:8–9). Marah was the first place where the Israelites stopped after crossing the Red Sea (see Map 2, B–2). The water from the well at Marah was so bitter it was undrinkable (Ex. 15:23–25).

MARALAH [marr ih LAH] (meaning unknown) — a place on the western border of Zebulun (Josh. 19:11; Mareal, RSV). Tell Ghalta, north of Megiddo in the Valley of Jezreel, may be the site.

MARANATHA [mar a NATH a] (*Our Lord, come!*) — an Aramaic expression written by the apostle Paul as he concluded his first letter to the Corinthians (1 Cor. 16:22, KJV). The meaning seems to be, "Our Lord is coming soon, and he will judge all those who do not love him." The fact that Paul used an Aramaic expression in addressing the Gentile Christians of Corinth indicates that maranatha had become a familiar expression of Christian hope—a watchword of the imminent SECOND COMING of the Lord.

MARBLE (see MINERALS OF THE BIBLE).

MARCUS [MAR kus] — Greek form of MARK (1 Pet. 5:13, KJV).

MARE (see ANIMALS OF THE BIBLE).

MAREAL [MAHR ih al] — a form of MARALAH.

MARESHAH [muh REE shuh] (*summit*) — the name of a city (see Map 3, A–4) and two men in the Old Testament:

1. A fortified city in the lowland of Judah (Josh. 15:44). King Rehoboam of Judah strengthened the fortifications of Mareshah (2 Chr. 11:8). King Asa of Judah defeated Zerah the Ethiopian and his huge army at Mareshah, in the Valley of Zephathah (2 Chr. 14:9–10).

2. The founder of Hebron (1 Chr. 2:42).

3. A son of Laadah, of the tribe of Judah (1 Chr. 4:21).

MARHESHVAN [mar HESH van] — the eighth month of the sacred Hebrew year, also called BUL (1 Kin. 6:38). Also see CALENDAR.

MARI [MAHR ee] — an ancient city of Mesopotamia on the west bank of the Euphrates River. It was the center of the Amorite kingdom that flourished about 1800–1700 B.C. Although the city is not mentioned in the Bible, Mari is of great archaeological importance. The most important finds at Mari were a ZIGGURAT; various temples dedicated to pagan gods and goddesses; and 25,000 clay tablets, which yielded much information about legal, economic, and diplomatic matters in the ancient world.

MARINER — one who directs or assists in the navigation of a ship; a seaman or sailor. The city of Tyre was depicted poetically by the prophet Ezekiel as a splendid ship made of materials from widespread lands and navigated by mariners from many places. When the great city falls, like a ship sinking in the midst of the sea, those on the shore lament its fate (Ezekiel 27). Also see SHIPS.

MARJORAM (see PLANTS OF THE BIBLE).

MARK, GOSPEL OF — the second book of the New Testament and the earliest of the four gospels, according to most New Testament scholars. The Gospel of Mark portrays the person of Jesus more by what He does than by what He says. It is characterized by a vivid, direct style that leaves the impression of familiarity with the original events.

Although Mark is the shortest of the four gospels, it pays close attention to matters of human interest. Mark is fond of linking the episodes of Jesus' ministry together with catchwords (for example, "immediately," "then"), rather than editorial comment; and frequently he interrupts a longer story by inserting a smaller one within it (Mark 5:21–43; 6:6–30; 11:12–25; 14:1–11).

Structure of the Gospel. The Gospel of Mark can be divided roughly into two parts: Jesus' ministry in Galilee (chaps. 1—9) and Jesus' ministry in Judea and Jerusalem (chaps. 10—16). Mark begins his gospel with the appearance of John the Baptist (1:2–8), followed by the baptism of Jesus (1:9–11). He comments on the temptation of Jesus only briefly (1:12–13) and concludes his introduction by a capsule of Jesus' message, "The time is fulfilled, and the kingdom of God is at hand. Repent, and believe in the gospel" (1:15). Then follows a series of 14 brief stories depicting Jesus as a teacher, healer, and exorcist in and around His hometown of Capernaum. In these stories Jesus often is in conflict with the Jewish authorities of His day.

In chapter four Mark assembles a number of Jesus' parables. In each parable Jesus uses common experiences to tell who God is and what man can become. Mark then resumes the activities of Jesus as an open-air preacher and healer with a series of 17 more episodes (4:35—8:26).

The first half of the gospel reaches a climax when Jesus is enroute to Caesarea Philippi and asks His disciples, "Who do men say that I am?" (8:27). Peter responds, "You are the Christ" (8:29); and Jesus then shocks the disciples by explaining that the Christ must suffer and die, and whoever desires to be His disciple must be prepared for the same (8:31—9:1). A glorious TRANSFIGURATION of Jesus immediately follows this pronouncement; it shows that the Father in heaven confirms Jesus' role as a suffering Messiah (9:2–13). Then follows another series of 23 stories as Jesus journeys to Jerusalem for the Passover.

In the various encounters included in the Gospel of Mark, Jesus tries to drive home the truth He taught at Peter's confession—that messiahship and discipleship involve suffering: "Whoever desires to become great among you shall be your servant…. For even the Son of Man did not come to be served, but to serve, and to give His life a ransom for many" (10:43, 45).

Chapter 13 contains a discourse of Jesus on the end of the age. Chapters 14—15 conclude the passion story, with accounts of Jesus' betrayal (14:1-11), His last supper with His disciples (14:12–31), His arrest (14:32–52), trial (14:53—15:20), and crucifixion (15:21–41). At the end, Jesus suffers passively "as a sheep before its shearers is silent" (Is. 53:7). In the oldest manuscripts the gospel ends with an angel announcing the resurrection of Jesus (16:1–8).

Authorship and Date. The Gospel of Mark nowhere mentions the name of its author. The earliest witness to identify the author was Papias (A.D. 60-130), a bishop of Hierapolis in Asia Minor (Turkey). Papias called him Mark, an interpreter of Peter. Papias then added that Mark had not followed Jesus during His lifetime, but later had written down Peter's recollections accurately, although not always in their proper order. Subsequent tradition unanimously agrees with Papias in ascribing this gospel to Mark.

MARK: A Teaching Outline

Part One: The Presentation of the Servant (1:1—2:12)

Part Two: The Opposition to the Servant (2:13—8:26)

Part Three: The Instruction by the Servant (8:27—10:52)

Part Four: The Rejection of the Servant (11:1—15:47)

Part Five: The Resurrection of the Servant (16:1–20)

The Mark believed to have written this gospel is JOHN MARK of the New Testament. He was a native of Jerusalem (Acts 12:12), and later became an associate of both Peter (1 Pet. 5:13) and Paul (2 Tim. 4:11). Eusebius tells us that Mark composed his gospel in Rome while in the services of Peter. There are good reasons to accept this report. The gospel has many characteristics of an eyewitness account, for which Peter would have been responsible (1:29–31). Moreover, it is unlikely that the early church would have assigned a gospel to a minor figure like John Mark unless he in fact were its author, since the books of the New Testament normally required authorship by an apostle to qualify for acceptance in the CANON.

It may be that as a youth Mark was present at the arrest of Jesus and that he has left an "anonymous signature" in the story of the young man who fled naked (14:51–52). If Mark composed his gospel while in the services of Peter, and Peter died in Rome between A.D. 64 and A.D. 68, then the gospel would have been written in Italy in the early 60's.

Historical Setting. The Gospel of Mark is evidently written for Gentiles, and for Romans in particular. Mark translates Aramaic and Hebrew phrases (3:17; 5:41; 7:34; 14:36); he transliterates familiar Latin expressions into Greek, for example, *legio* (5:9), *quadrans* (12:42), *praetorium* (15:16), *centurio* (15:39). Moreover, Mark presents Romans in a neutral (12:17; 15:1–10), and sometimes favorable (15:39), light. The emphasis on suffering in the gospel may indicate that Mark composed his gospel in order to strengthen Christians in Rome who were undergoing persecutions under Nero.

Theological Contribution. Mark begins his gospel with the statement, "The beginning of the gospel [good news] of Jesus Christ, the Son of God" (1:1); and the last human to speak in the gospel is the centurion who confesses at the cross, "Truly this Man was the Son of God!" (15:39). One of Mark's key objectives is to portray Jesus as God's Son. At decisive points in his story, he reveals the mystery of Jesus' person. At the baptism (1:11) and transfiguration (9:7) the Father in heaven calls Jesus "My beloved Son," thus indicating that Jesus shares a unique relationship with the Father. Demons recognize Jesus as God's Son, too (1:24; 3:11; 5:7), testifying that Jesus is equipped with God's authority and power.

Mark, however, is careful to avoid portraying Jesus as an unrealistic superstar whose feet do not touch the ground. The Son of God is not immune from the problems of life, but enters fully into them. He must be obedient to the will of the Father, even to death on a cross. Mark portrays Jesus according to the model of the Suffering Servant of Isaiah. Thus, Jesus tells a parable, which ultimately reflects His own fate: the only son of the owner of a vineyard suffers rejection and death at the hands of rebellious tenant farmers (12:1–12).

Furthermore, Mark does not emphasize Jesus' deity at the expense of His humanity. Jesus appears sorrowful (14:34), disappointed (8:12), displeased (10:14), angry (11:15–17), amazed (6:6), and fatigued (4:38). In no other gospel is Jesus' humanity presented as strongly as in the Gospel of Mark.

For Mark, faith and discipleship have no meaning apart from following the suffering Son of God. Faith is not a magic that works independently of the believer's participation (6:1–6); rather, it draws the believer into intimate union with Jesus as Lord (9:14–29). Jesus' disciples are to be with Him as He is with the Father, and they are given the same tasks of proclamation and power over the forces of evil as He had (3:13–15; 6:7).

As the Son of Man serves in self–abasement, so too must His disciples serve (10:42–45). Discipleship with Christ leads to self–denial and suffering: "Whoever desires to come after Me, let him deny himself, and take up his cross, and follow Me" (8:34). This, however, is not a matter of a religious desire to suffer; rather, when one loses his life, he finds it in Christ (8:35). Thus, one can only know and confess Jesus as God's Son from the vantage point of the cross (15:39). It is only through the Son of God who suffers and dies that we may see into the heart of God (symbolized by the tearing of the Temple curtain, thus exposing the Holy of Holies) and enter into fellowship with the Father.

Special Considerations. The ending of the Gospel of Mark poses a problem. The two oldest and most important manuscripts of the Greek New Testament (Sinaiticus and Vaticanus) end with the words, "For they were afraid" (16:8). Other manuscripts add, in whole or in part, the material making up verses 9–20. This longer ending, however, is unlike Mark 1:1—16:8 in style and content; it contains material presented exactly as it is in Matthew and Luke. It has long been debated whether Mark intended to end his gospel at 16:8, or whether the original ending was lost and a secondary ending (vv. 9–20) was later added.

The following observations suggest that Mark originally did not end at 16:8, and that the original ending was either lost (for example, the final section of a scroll or codex misplaced or destroyed) or left unfinished (for example, due to Mark's death).

First, it seems unlikely that, having begun the gospel with a bold introduction (1:10) Mark would end it on a note of fear (16:8). Considering the centrality of Jesus throughout the gospel, one would expect an appearance of the resurrected Christ rather than just an announcement of His resurrection.

Second, Mark's Gospel conforms in broad outline to the preaching pattern of the early church (see KERYGMA)—except for the shorter ending at 16:8. It would seem logical that one who drafted a gospel along the lines of the early Christian preaching would not have omitted a central feature like the resurrection (1 Cor. 15:3–26).

Third, the longer, later ending (vv. 9–20) testifies that the early tradition was dissatisfied with the shorter ending of Mark.

Finally, why would Matthew and Luke, both of

whom normally follow Mark's report (see GOS-PELS), depart from him at the resurrection appearances unless the ending of Mark was somehow defective? These reasons suggest that the shorter ending of Mark (at 16:8) is not the original (or intended) ending—for whatever reason—and that verses 9–20 are a later addition supplied to compensate for the omission.

Another special feature of Mark's Gospel concerns the "messianic secret." Often following a miracle, Jesus commands persons healed, onlookers, disciples, and even demons to silence (1:34; 1:44; 3:12; 5:43; 7:36; 8:26; 8:30; 9:9). It has long puzzled readers why Jesus, who came into the world to make Himself known, would work at cross-purposes with His mission by trying to remain hidden.

The puzzle can be explained in part by realizing that Jesus' command to silence was intended to protect Himself from false expectations of the Messiah that were current at that time. For most of Jesus' contemporaries, "messiah" brought up pictures of a military hero overthrowing the Roman rule of Palestine. Jesus had no intention to take up the warrior's sword; rather, He took up the servant's towel.

Another reason why Jesus tried to conceal His miraculous power was because He realized that faith could not be forced upon people by a spectacle (Matt. 4:5–7). Not sight but insight into Jesus' life and purpose could evoke true faith.

Finally, Jesus demanded silence because no title or label could convey Him adequately. Saving knowledge of Jesus needed to come through personal experience with Him. Indeed, until Jesus died on the cross He could not rightly be known as God incognito who reveals Himself to those who are willing to deny self and follow Him in costly discipleship.

MARK, JOHN — an occasional associate of Peter and Paul, and the probable author of the second gospel. Mark's lasting impact on the Christian church comes from his writing rather than his life. He was the first to develop the literary form known as the "gospel" (see GOSPEL) and is rightly regarded as a creative literary artist.

John Mark appears in the New Testament only in association with more prominent personalities and events. His mother, Mary, was an influential woman of Jerusalem who possessed a large house with servants. The early church gathered in this house during Peter's imprisonment under Herod Agrippa I (Acts 12:12). Barnabas and Saul (Paul) took John Mark with them when they returned from Jerusalem to Antioch after their famine–relief visit (Acts 12:25). Shortly thereafter, Mark accompanied Paul and Barnabas on their first missionary journey as far as Perga. He served in the capacity of "assistant" (Acts 13:5), which probably involved making arrangements for travel, food, and lodging; he may have done some teaching, too.

At Perga John Mark gave up the journey for an undisclosed reason (Acts 13:13); this departure later caused a rift between Paul and Barnabas when

This mosaic of a lion, symbolizing John Mark, hangs in the Church of San Vitale in Ravenna, Italy.
Photo by Howard Vos

Photo by Howard Vos

Remains of the Market of Trajan in Rome—an ancient outdoor trading mart named for a Roman emperor.

they chose their companions for the second missionary journey (Acts 15:37–41). Paul was unwilling to take Mark again and chose Silas; they returned overland to Asia Minor and Greece. Barnabas persisted in his choice of Mark, who was his cousin (Col. 4:10), and returned with him to his homeland of Cyprus (Acts 15:39; also Acts 4:36).

This break occurred about A.D. 49–50, and John Mark is not heard from again until a decade later. He is first mentioned again, interestingly enough, by Paul—and in favorable terms. Paul asks the Colossians to receive Mark with a welcome (Col. 4:10), no longer as an assistant but as one of his "fellow laborers" (Philem. 24). And during his imprisonment in Rome, Paul tells Timothy to bring Mark with him to Rome, "for he is useful to me for ministry" (2 Tim. 4:11). One final reference to Mark comes also from Peter in Rome; Peter affectionately refers to him as "my son" (1 Pet. 5:13). Thus, in the later references to Mark in the New Testament, he appears to be reconciled to Paul and laboring with the two great apostles in Rome.

Information about Mark's later life is dependent on early church tradition. Writing at an early date, Papias (A.D. 60–130), whose report is followed by Clement of Alexandria (A.D. 150–215), tells us that Mark served as Peter's interpreter in Rome and wrote his gospel from Peter's remembrances. Of his physical appearance we are only told, rather oddly, that Mark was "stumpy fingered." Writing at a later date (about A.D. 325), the church historian Eusebius says that Mark was the first evangelist to Egypt, the founder of the churches of Alexandria,

and the first bishop of that city. So great were his converts, both in number and sincerity of commitment, says Eusebius, that the great Jewish philosopher, Philo, was amazed.

MARKET, MARKETPLACE — an open space within cities that was used for business and other public transactions and assemblies. Archaeological investigations have shown that Israelite markets were primarily used as centers of business. Like the "bazaars" of present–day Oriental towns, they were places for buying and selling goods.

Greek marketplaces, such as those at Philippi (Acts 16:19) and Athens (Acts 17:17), contained more open spaces and were designed to be centers of public life. They were characteristically surrounded by temples, colonnades, public buildings, and numerous statues. Often these Greek marketplaces were carefully paved with stones and shaded by trees.

MARKING TOOL (see TOOLS OF THE BIBLE).

MAROTH [MAY roth] (*bitternesses*) — a town in the lowlands of Judah mentioned in connection with the invasion of the Assyrian army (Mic. 1:12), perhaps the same place as MAARATH (Josh. 15:59).

MARRIAGE — the union of a man and a woman as husband and wife, which becomes the foundation for a home and family.

Origin of Marriage. Marriage was instituted by God when He declared, "It is not good that man should be alone; I will make him a helper comparable to him" (Gen. 2:18). So God fashioned woman and brought her to man. On seeing the woman, Adam exclaimed, "This is now bone of my bones and flesh of my flesh; she shall be called Woman, because she was taken out of Man" (Gen. 2:23). This passage also emphasizes the truth that "a man shall leave his father and mother and be joined to his wife, and they shall become one flesh" (Gen. 2:24). This suggests that God's ideal is for a man to be the husband of one wife and for the marriage to be permanent.

Legislation. God's desire for His people was that they marry within the body of believers. The Mosaic Law clearly stated that an Israelite was never to marry a Canaanite. The Israelite would be constantly tempted to embrace the spouse's god as well (Ex. 34:10–17; Deut. 7:3–4). Likewise, the apostle Paul commanded the members of the church at Corinth, "Do not be unequally yoked together with unbelievers" (2 Cor. 6:14).

Marriages between Israelites were directed by law, and all incestuous relationships were outlawed (Lev. 18:6–8; 20:19–21). In addition, priests were forbidden to marry prostitutes and divorced women (Lev. 21:7, 13–14). Daughters who inherited their father's possessions had to marry within their tribe or lose their inheritance (Num. 27:8; 36:2–4).

Choosing the Bride. In Old Testament times, the parents chose the mate for their son. The primary reason for this was that the bride became part of the clan. Although they were married and became "one flesh," the couple remained under the authority of the bridegroom's father. The parents chose someone who would best fit into their clan and work harmoniously with her mother-in-law and sisters-in-law.

Sometimes the parents consulted with their children to see if they approved of the choice of mates being made for them. For example, Rebekah was asked if she wanted to marry Isaac (Gen. 24:58). Samson demanded that a certain girl be acquired for him. Although his parents protested, they completed the marriage contract for Samson (Judg. 14:1–4).

Frequently people married at a young age, a fact which made the parents' choice a practical matter. By New Testament times, the Jewish leaders had decided to establish minimum ages for which a marriage contract could be drawn up. The age was set at 13 for boys and 12 for girls.

Even if the young wife lost her husband in war or accident, she remained within the clan and was wed to her brother-in-law or next of kin. This arrangement is known as LEVIRATE MARRIAGE. It is the basis for the story of Ruth and Boaz (Deut. 25:5–10; Ruth 3:13; 4:1–12).

Concept of Love. Although romance before marriage was not unknown in Old Testament times, it played a minor role in the life of teenagers of that era. They did not marry the person they loved; they loved the mate they married. Love began at marriage. When Isaac married Rebekah, the Bible records that "she became his wife, and he loved her" (Gen. 24:67).

Marriage Customs. A number of customs and steps were involved in finalizing a marriage in Old Testament times. The first was agreeing on a price to be given to the father of the girl. The payment was compensation for the loss of a worker. The sum was mutually agreed upon (Gen. 34:12; Ex. 22:16–17). It could consist of services instead of money. For example, Jacob agreed to work for seven years for Rachel (Gen. 29:18–20). The giving and receiving of money was probably accompanied by a written agreement. After this agreement was made, the couple was considered engaged.

In biblical times, a betrothal for marriage was a binding agreement that set the young woman apart for the young man. The agreement was voided only by death or divorce; one could not get out of the betrothal in any other way. When Joseph discovered that Mary was pregnant, he did not want to make a "public example" of her; instead, he decided to divorce her secretly. However, he did not carry out the divorce, because an angel of the Lord convinced him that the baby to be born to Mary would be the Son of God (Matt. 1:18–25).

During the engagement period, the bridegroom had certain privileges. If war was declared, he was exempt from military duty (Deut. 20:7). He also knew that his bride-to-be was protected by Mosaic Law. If another man raped her, the act was treated as adultery; and the offender was punished accordingly (Deut. 22:23–27). This was considered a more serious crime than the rape of a girl not yet betrothed (Deut. 22:28–29).

The length of engagement varied. Sometimes the couple was married the same day they were engaged. Usually, however, a period of time elapsed between the betrothal and the marriage ceremony. During this time the young man prepared a place in his father's house for his bride, while the bride prepared herself for married life.

On the day of the wedding, the groom and his friends dressed in their finest clothes and went to the home of the bride. Together the couple went back to the groom's house. Their friends sang and danced their way back to his house.

Once at the groom's house, the couple was ushered into a bridal chamber. The marriage was consummated through sexual union as the guests waited outside. Once that fact was announced, the wedding festivities continued, with guests dropping by for the wedding feast. Usually the wedding party lasted for a week.

New Testament Teaching about Marriage. The New Testament does not contradict the teachings about marriage in the Old Testament. Most marriage teaching in the New Testament comes from Jesus and the apostle Paul.

Jesus' first miracle occurred in Cana in Galilee when He and His disciples were attending a wedding (John 2:1–11). Our Lord gave His blessing and sanction to the institution of marriage.

On another occasion, when Jesus was asked

about marriage and divorce, He quoted two passages from Genesis. "Have you not read that He who made them at the beginning 'made them male and female,' and said, 'For this reason a man shall leave his father and mother and be joined to his wife, and the two shall become one flesh'? So then, they are no longer two but one flesh. Therefore what God has joined together, let not man separate" (Gen. 1:27; 2:24; 5:2; Matt. 19:4-6). He taught that marriage was the joining together of two people so they become "one flesh." Not only did God acknowledge the marriage; He also joined the couple.

The church at Corinth struggled over a number of issues, including the proper view of marriage. In response to their questions, Paul gave an answer about marriage. From His answer, it seems that three faulty ideas about marriage were prominent among some believers in the church. The first was that marriage was absolutely necessary in order to be a Christian; another was that celibacy was superior to marriage; the third was that when a person became a Christian, all existing relationships such as marriage were dissolved. When chapter 7 of 1 Corinthians is read with that as background, the following teaching emerges.

First, Paul stated that celibacy is an acceptable lifestyle for a Christian; not all people need to marry. In fact, Paul declared that he himself preferred not to marry. However, the single life can be lived for God's glory only if God has given the gift of singlehood. If one does not have that gift, he should marry. And Paul expected most people to marry.

Next, Paul spoke to the problem faced by a Christian believer whose spouse does not believe. He reasoned that if the unbelieving partner is willing to live with the Christian, then the Christian should not dissolve the marriage. Remaining with the unbelieving partner could result in his or her salvation (1 Cor. 7:14).

In his letter to the Ephesians, Paul showed how a marriage relationship can best function. First, he said, "Wives, submit to your husbands, as to the Lord" (Eph. 5:22). The model for the wife's submission is the church, which is subject to Christ (Eph. 5:24). Second, husbands are to love their wives. The role that the husband plays is outlined by Jesus Christ, who loved His bride, the church, so much that He died for her (Eph. 5:25).

MARROW — the soft tissue inside the hollow cavities of bones. The Bible uses the word marrow figuratively. "Moist marrow" means good health and physical comfort (Job 21:24). To eat marrow refers to eating the choicest of foods (Is. 25:6). To fear the Lord and depart from evil is marrow (refreshment, medicine, strength) to one's bones (Prov. 3:8). The word of God divides the "joints and marrow" (Heb. 4:12), symbolizing the power of the Bible to penetrate to the inner depths of a person's thoughts and motives.

MARS' HILL (see AREOPAGUS).

MARSENA [mar SEE nuh] (*forgetful man*) — a high Persian official at Shushan, or Susa. Marsena was one of seven princes "who had access to the king's presence" (Esth. 1:14).

MARSH — the swamplands near the mouths of some rivers such as Kishon and at various places along the Jordan River and the Dead Sea (Ezek. 47:11).

MARSHAL — a military title given to a person in a position of honor and authority (Jer. 51:27; captain, KJV; commander, NIV).

MARTHA [MAR thuh] (*lady, mistress*) — the sister of Mary and Lazarus of Bethany (Luke 10:38-41; John 11:1-44; 12:1-3). All three were sincere followers of Jesus, but Mary and Martha expressed their love for Him in different ways. The account of the two women given by Luke reveals a clash of temperaments between Mary and Martha. Martha "was distracted with much serving" (Luke 10:40); she was an activist busy with household chores. Her sister Mary "sat at Jesus' feet and heard His word" (Luke 10:39); her instinct was to sit still, meditate, and receive spiritual instruction.

While Martha busied herself making Jesus comfortable and cooking for Him in her home, Mary listened intently to His teaching. When Martha complained that Mary was not helping her, Jesus rebuked Martha. "You are worried and troubled about many things," He declared. "But one thing is needed, and Mary has chosen that good part, which will not be taken away from her" (Luke 10:41-42). He told her, in effect, that Mary was feeding her spiritual needs. This was more important than Martha's attempt to feed His body.

Jesus recognized that Martha was working for Him, but He reminded her that she was permitting her outward activities to hinder her spiritually. Because of her emphasis on work and her daily chores, her inner communion with her Lord was being hindered.

MARTYR — a witness. Because the early Christians frequently suffered for their faith, the word martyr soon came to mean one who suffered or died because of his witness to Christ. Thus the apostle Paul calls Stephen a martyr (Acts 22:20), and the Book of Revelation mentions "the martyrs of Jesus" (17:6). Also see WITNESS.

MARY [MAIR ee] (meaning unknown) — the name of six women in the New Testament:

1. Mary, the mother of Jesus (Luke 1—2). We know nothing of Mary's background other than that she was a peasant and a resident of Nazareth, a city of Galilee. She must have been of the tribe of Judah and thus in the line of David (Luke 1:32), although the genealogies in Matthew 1 and Luke 3 do not say so, because they trace Joseph's genealogy rather than Mary's. We do know that Mary's cousin, Elizabeth, was the mother of John the Baptist.

When Mary was pledged to be married to Joseph

the carpenter, the angel Gabriel appeared to her. Calling her "highly favored one" and "blessed...among women" (Luke 1:28), the angel announced the birth of the Messiah. After Gabriel explained how such a thing could be possible, Mary said, "Let it be to me according to your word" (Luke 1:38). That Mary "found favor with God" and was allowed to give birth to His child indicates she must have been of high character and faith.

When Jesus was born in Bethlehem of Judea, Mary "wrapped him in swaddling cloths, and laid Him in a manger" (Luke 2:7). She witnessed the visits of the shepherds and the Wise Men and "pondered them in her heart" (Luke 2:19) and heard Simeon's prophecy of a sword that would pierce through her own soul (Luke 2:35). Joseph and Mary fled to Egypt to escape Herod's murder of all males under two years old (Matt. 2:13–18). Neither Mary nor Joseph appear again until Jesus is 12 years old, at which time He stayed behind in the Temple with the teachers (Luke 2:41–52). Both Mary and Joseph accepted Jesus' explanation, realizing He was Israel's Promised One.

Mary was present at Jesus' first miracle—the turning of water into wine at the wedding feast in Cana of Galilee (John 2:1–12). Mary seemed to be asking her Son to use His power to meet the crisis. Jesus warned her that His time had not yet come; nevertheless, He turned the water into wine. At another time Mary and Jesus' brothers wished to see Jesus while He was teaching the multitudes—perhaps to warn Him of impending danger. But again Jesus mildly rebuked her, declaring that the bond between Him and His disciples was stronger than any family ties (Luke 8:19–21).

The Scriptures do not mention Mary again until she stands at the foot of the cross (John 19:25–27). No mention is made of Joseph; he had likely been dead for some time. Jesus' brothers were not among His followers. Of His family, only His mother held fast to her belief in His messiahship—even though it appeared to be ending in tragedy. From the cross Jesus gave Mary over to the care of the beloved disciple, John. The last mention of Mary is in the upper room in Jerusalem, awaiting the coming of the Holy Spirit (Acts 1:14). We do not know how or when Mary died. The Tomb of the Virgin is in the Valley of Kidron in Jerusalem, southeast of the Temple area; but there is no historical basis for this site.

According to Scripture, Jesus had four brothers—James, Joses, Judas, and Simon—and unnamed sisters (Matt. 13:55–56; Mark 6:3). The Roman Catholic Church, however, claims that Mary remained a virgin and that these "brothers" and "sisters" were either Joseph's children by an earlier marriage or were cousins of Jesus. Legends concerning Mary began circulating in written form as early as the fifth century, but there is no valid historical evidence for them.

In reaction to the Roman Catholic teachings about Mary, many Protestants almost totally neglect her and her contribution. What can be said of her that is consistent with Holy Scripture?

God was in her womb. In conceiving and bearing the Lord Jesus Christ, she gave earthly birth not to mere man but to the Son of God Himself.

She conceived as a virgin through the mysterious power of the Holy Spirit.

We are to bless and honor her, for as she herself said under the inspiration of the Holy Spirit, "Henceforth all generations will call me blessed" (Luke 1:48).

As the first member of the human race to accept Christ, she stands as the first of the redeemed and as the flagship of humanity itself. She is our enduring example for faith, service to God, and a life of righteousness.

2. Mary Magdalene, the woman from whom Jesus cast out seven demons. The name Magdalene indicates that she came from Magdala, a city on the southwest coast of the Sea of Galilee. After Jesus cast seven demons from her, she became one of His followers.

The Scriptures do not describe her illness. Mary Magdalene has been associated with the "woman in the city who was a sinner" (Luke 7:37) who washed Jesus' feet, but there is no scriptural basis for this. According to the TALMUD (the collection of Rabbinic writings that make up the basis of religious authority for traditional Judaism), the city of Magdala had a reputation for prostitution. This information, coupled with the fact that Luke first mentions Mary Magdalene immediately following his account of the sinful woman (Luke 7:36–50), has led some to equate the two women.

Mary Magdalene is also often associated with the woman whom Jesus saved from stoning after she had been taken in adultery (John 8:1–11)—again an association with no evidence. We do know that Mary Magdalene was one of those women who, having "been healed of evil spirits and infirmities," provided for Jesus and His disciples "from their substance" (Luke 8:2–3).

Mary Magdalene witnessed most of the events surrounding the crucifixion. She was present at the mock trial of Jesus; she heard Pontius Pilate pronounce the death sentence; and she saw Jesus beaten and humiliated by the crowd. She was one of the women who stood near Jesus during the crucifixion to try to comfort Him. The earliest witness to the resurrection of Jesus, she was sent by Jesus to tell the others (John 20:11–18). Although this is the last mention of her in the Bible, she was probably among the women who gathered with the apostles to await the promised coming of the Holy Spirit (Acts 1:14).

3. Mary of Bethany, sister of Martha and Lazarus (Luke 10:38–42). As with Martha, we know nothing of Mary's family background. Martha was probably older than Mary since the house is referred to as Martha's; but she could have inherited it from an unmentioned husband. All we really know is that Mary, Martha, and Lazarus loved each other deeply. When Jesus visited their house in Bethany, Mary sat at Jesus' feet and listened to His

teachings while Martha worked in the kitchen. When Martha complained that Mary was no help, Jesus gently rebuked Martha. When Lazarus died, Mary's grief was deep. John tells us that when Jesus came following Lazarus' death Mary stayed in the house. After she was summoned by Martha, she went to Jesus, fell at His feet weeping, and, like Martha, said, "Lord, if You had been here, my brother would not have died" (John 11:21, 32).

Following Lazarus' resurrection, Mary showed her gratitude by anointing Jesus' feet with "a pound of very costly oil of spikenard" (John 12:3) and wiping His feet with her hair. Judas called this anointing extravagant, but Jesus answered, "Let her alone; she has kept this for the day of My burial" (John 12:7). Jesus called Mary's unselfish act "a memorial to her" (Mark 14:9).

4. Mary, the mother of the disciple James and Joses (Matt. 27:55–61). In light of her presence at Jesus' death and resurrection, it is likely that Mary was one of the women who followed Jesus and His disciples and provided food for them (Luke 8:2–3). Since Mark 15:40 tells us that this Mary, along with Mary Magdalene, observed Jesus' burial, the "other Mary" (Matt. 27:61) must refer to this mother of James and Joses. Mary was one of the women who went to the tomb on the third day to anoint Jesus' body with spices and discovered that Jesus was no longer among the dead (Mark 16:1–8).

5. Mary, the mother of John Mark (Acts 12:12). The mother of the author of the Gospel of Mark opened her home to the disciples to pray for the release of Peter, who had been imprisoned by Herod Antipas. When Peter was miraculously released, the angel immediately delivered him to Mary's house. Tradition has it that Mary's house was a primary meeting place for the early Christians of Jerusalem. We know that Barnabas and Mark were related (Col. 4:10), but whether through Mark's mother or through his father (who is never mentioned), we do not know.

6. Mary of Rome (Rom. 16:6). All we know about this Christian woman of Rome is found in Paul's salutation: "Greet Mary, who labored much for us."

MASCHIL [MAHS keel] (meaning unknown) — KJV word for a Hebrew term used in the titles of 13 psalms (Psalm 32, 42, 44, 45, 52, 53, 54, 55, 74, 78, 88, 89, 142; Maskil, RSV). Maschil may have been a term referring to a psalm sung at an annual festival, and accompanied by a special kind of music.

MASH [mash] (meaning unknown) — one of the four sons of Aram, and the name of an Aramean tribe descended from him (Gen. 10:23). Mash was the grandson of Shem and great–grandson of Noah.

MASHAL [MAY shal] (entreaty) — a city on the border of Asher assigned to the Levites (1 Chr. 6:74), also spelled Mishal (Josh. 19:26; Misheal, KJV).

MASKIL [MAHS keel] — a form of MASCHIL.

MASON (see OCCUPATIONS AND TRADES).

MASREKAH [MASS reh kuh] (meaning unknown) — an ancient city in Edom near Petra where Samlah, king of Edom, lived (1 Chr. 1:47).

MASSA [MASS uh] (oracle) — a son of Ishmael (Gen. 25:14) and founder of an Arabian tribe that is generally identified with the Masani—a people who lived near the Persian Gulf.

MASSAH [MASS uh] (testing) — a place in the Wilderness of Sin, near Mount Horeb. The Israelites murmured against Moses at Massah because of no water, indicating their lack of faith. At the command of God, Moses struck the rock with his rod to produce water. The place is also called MERIBAH, which means "rebellion, strife, contention" (Ex. 17:7).

MAST — a long pole that supports the sail and rigging on a ship (Prov. 23:34; rigging, NIV, NEB). Also see SHIPS.

MASTER — a person having authority, power, and control over the actions of other people. In the NKJV the word master is used to translate several Hebrew and Greek words. All these express the idea of human authority and control. Jesus was often called master by His disciples (Luke 5:5; 17:13). This title recognizes Jesus' right to command and implies an attitude of obedience. Literally the word means "superintendent," "overseer," or "one who stands over."

MASTICH [MAHS tick] (see PLANTS OF THE BIBLE).

MATHUSALA [muh THU suh luh] — a form of METHUSELAH.

MATRED [MAY tred] (thrusting forward) — the mother-in-law of Hadar (Gen. 36:39), or Hadad (1 Chr. 1:50), king of Edom.

MATRI [MAY try] (meaning unknown)—a family of Benjamin to which Saul, the first king of Israel, belonged (1 Sam. 10:21).

MATRIX — something within which something else originates, grows, develops, or is nurtured; the womb (Is. 49:1; bowels, KJV; body, RSV, NASB).

MATTAN [MAT un] (gift of God) — the name of two men in the Old Testament:

1. A priest of Baal in Jerusalem during the days of Queen Athaliah (2 Kin. 11:18).

2. The father of Shephatiah (Jer. 38:1).

MATTANAH [MAT uh nuh] (gift) — an encampment of the Israelites, between Beer and Nahaliel, during their years of wandering in the wilderness (Num. 21:18–19).

MATTANIAH [mat uh NYE uh] (gift) — the name of several men in the Old Testament:

1. A son of King Josiah of Judah (2 Kin. 24:17). After Mattaniah was made king of Judah, his name was changed to Zedekiah.

2. Founder of a tribal family and leader of the

Temple choir in the time of Nehemiah (Neh. 11:17).

3. A sanctuary singer during David's reign (1 Chr. 25:4, 16).

4. A descendant of Asaph who helped King Hezekiah of Jerusalem in the cleansing of the Temple (2 Chr. 29:13).

5. A descendant of Elam (Ezra 10:26). After the Captivity, Mattaniah divorced his pagan wife.

6. A son of Zattu who divorced his pagan wife (Ezra 10:27).

7. A son of Pahath–Moab who divorced his pagan wife (Ezra 10:30).

8. A son of Bani who divorced his pagan wife (Ezra 10:37).

9. A Levite whose descendant, Hanan, served under Nehemiah as a treasurer over the storehouse (Neh. 13:13).

MATTATHAH [MAT uh thah] (*gift*) — a descendant of King David listed in the genealogy of Jesus Christ (Luke 3:31; Mattatha, KJV, RSV, NEB, NIV).

MATTATHIAH [MAT uh thigh uh] (*gift of Jehovah*) — the name of two men in the New Testament:

1. A son of Amos, listed by Luke as an ancestor of Joseph in the genealogy of Jesus Christ (Luke 3:25; Mattathias, KJV, NASB, NIV, RSV).

2. A son of Semei, an ancestor of Jesus (Luke 3:26; Mattathias, KJV, NASB, NIV, RSV).

Also see MACCABEES, THE.

MATTATHIAS [mat uh THIGH us] — a form of MATTATHIAH.

MATTATTAH [MAT ah tah] (*gift of Jehovah*) — a son of Hashum (Ezra 10:33; Mattathah, KJV). Mattattah divorced his pagan wife after the Captivity.

MATTENAI [mat tuh NIGH] (*gift of Jehovah*) — the name of three men in the Old Testament:

1. One of the sons of Hashum who divorced his pagan wife after the Captivity (Ezra 10:33).

2. One of the sons of Bani who divorced his pagan wife after the Captivity (Ezra 10:37).

3. A priest in the days of Joiakim the high priest (Neh. 12:19).

MATTHAN [MAT than] (*gift* [of God]) — the grandfather of Joseph listed in Matthew's genealogy of Jesus Christ (Matt. 1:15).

MATTHAT [MAT that] (*gift* [of God]) — the name of two men in the New Testament:

1. An ancestor of Jesus listed in Luke's genealogy (Luke 3:24).

2. Another ancestor of Jesus listed in Luke's genealogy (Luke 3:29).

MATTHEW [MA thue] (*gift of Jehovah*) — a tax collector who became one of the twelve apostles of Jesus (Matt. 9:9). Matthew's name appears seventh in two lists of apostles (Mark 3:18; Luke 6:15), and eighth in two others (Matt. 10:3; Acts 1:13).

In Hebrew, Matthew's name means "gift of God," but we know from his trade that he delighted in the gifts of others as well. He was a tax collector (Matt. 9:9–11) who worked in or around Capernaum under the authority of Herod Antipas. In Jesus' day, land and poll taxes were collected directly by Roman officials, but taxes on transported goods were contracted out to local collectors. Matthew was such a person, or else he was in the service of one. These middlemen paid an agreed–upon sum in advance to the Roman officials for the right to collect taxes in an area. Their profit came from the excess

A model of Jerusalem as it might have appeared in Jesus' time. Jesus was distraught about the city because of its unbelief (Matt. 23:37).

Photo by Andy Schupack

they could squeeze from the people.

The Jewish people hated these tax collectors not only for their corruption, but also because they worked with the despised Romans. Tax collectors were ranked with murderers and robbers, and a Jew was permitted to lie to them if neccessary.. The attitude found in the gospels is similar. Tax collectors are lumped together with harlots (Matt. 21:31), Gentiles (Matt. 18:17), and, most often, sinners (Matt. 9:10). They were as offensive to Jews for their economic and social practices as lepers were for their uncleanness; both were excluded from the people of God.

It is probable that the Matthew mentioned in Matthew 9:9-13 is identical with the Levi of Mark 2:13-17 and Luke 5:27-32; the stories obviously refer to the same person and event. The only problem in the identification is that Mark mentions Matthew rather than Levi in his list of apostles (Mark 3:18), thus leading one to assume two different persons. It is possible, however, that the same person was known by two names (compare "Simon" and "Peter"), or, less likely, that Levi and James the son of Alphaeus are the same person, since Mark calls Alphaeus the father of both (Mark 2:14; 3:18). Following his call by Jesus, Matthew is not mentioned again in the New Testament.

MATTHEW, GOSPEL OF — the opening book of the New Testament. Matthew has had perhaps a greater influence on Christian worship and literature than any other New Testament writing. For 17 centuries the church took its readings for Sundays and Holy Days from Matthew, drawing from the other gospels only where it felt Matthew was insufficient.

Matthew offers the most systematic arrangement of Jesus' teaching in the New Testament, and the early church used it heavily for its instruction of converts. Because of its emphasis on the fulfillment of Old Testament prophecy, Matthew is well suited as the opening book of the New Testament. In it the promises of God are recalled and their fulfillment in Jesus Christ is announced.

MATTHEW: A Teaching Outline

Part One: The Presentation of the King (1:1—4:11)

Part Two: The Proclamation of the King (4:12—7:29)

Part Three: The Power of the King (8:1—11:1)

Part Four: The Progressive Rejection of the King (11:2—16:12)

Structure of the Gospel. The Gospel of Matthew contains five main sections. Each section consists of stories of Jesus' life, samples of His preaching and teaching, and a concluding refrain, "When Jesus had ended" (7:28; 11:1; 13:53; 19:1; 26:1). The story of Jesus' birth (chaps. 1—2) and the account of his betrayal, trial, and crucifixion (chaps. 26—28) stand outside this framework; they introduce and conclude the story of Jesus.

Section one begins with Jesus' baptism by John, His temptation, and the beginnings of His Galilean ministry (chaps. 3—4). The Sermon on the Mount (chaps. 5—7) follows; in it Jesus sets forth a new system of ethics, both individual and social, for the kingdom. Throughout the Sermon, Jesus contrasts the law, which was given by Moses, with the kingdom, which is present in Himself—showing the superiority of the kingdom. He highlights the contrast with two recurring phrases, "You have heard that it was said to those of old...but I say to you."

Section two begins with a series of miracles by Jesus (chaps. 8—9), continues with Jesus' teaching to His disciples concerning mission and suffering (chap. 10), and ends with the refrain (11:1). Section three contains stories that emphasize the difference between the ways of the kingdom and the ways of the world (chaps. 11—12) and parables on the nature of the kingdom (chap. 13). The refrain is repeated in 13:53, thus concluding the section.

Section four features further miracles, debates, and conflicts from Jesus' ministry (chaps. 14—17). It concludes with words of counsel directed by Jesus to His disciples about the Christian life (chap. 18). The section ends at 19:1. Section five is set in Jerusalem, and it recounts clashes between Jesus and the religious leaders (chaps. 19—22). In the discourses which follow, Jesus denounces the scribes and Pharisees (chap. 23), teaches of the end times (chap. 24), and tells three parables on judgment (chap. 25). The final refrain occurs in 26:1, and leads into the account of the betrayal, arrest, crucifixion, and resurrection of Jesus (chaps. 26—28).

The Gospel of Matthew concludes with Jesus'

command to go into all the world and make disciples, baptizing and teaching them in His name. He leaves His disciples with this assurance: "Lo, I am with you always, even to the end of the age" (28:20).

Authorship and Date. Matthew is an anonymous gospel. Like other gospel titles, the title was added in the second century A.D. and reflects the tradition of a later time. How, then, did the gospel acquire its name? Writing about A.D. 130, Papias, bishop of Hierapolis in Asia Minor (modern Turkey), records, "Matthew collected the oracles in the Hebrew (that is, Aramaic) language, and each interpreted them as best he could." Until comparative studies of the gospels in modern times, the church understood "oracles" to refer to the first gospel and considered Matthew, the apostle and former tax collector (9:9; 10:3), to be the author.

This conclusion, however, is full of problems. Our Gospel of Matthew is written in Greek, not Aramaic (as Papias records); and no copy of an Aramaic original of the gospel has ever been found. The Greek of the gospel cannot readily be translated back into Aramaic; and this strongly indicates that the gospel is not a Greek translation of an Aramaic original. Moreover, it is now generally agreed that Mark is the earliest of the four gospels and that the author of Matthew substantially used the Gospel of Mark in writing this gospel (also see GOSPELS).

If the apostle Matthew wrote the gospel, one would wonder why he quoted so extensively from Mark (601 of Mark's 678 verses appear in Matthew), who was not a disciple of Jesus. Such observations virtually eliminate the possibility of the apostle Matthew being the author of the gospel.

The most promising way out of this dead-end street is to understand the "oracles" mentioned by Papias, not as the Gospel of Matthew, but as a collection of Jesus' sayings collected by the apostle Matthew. Later these sayings were used by an unknown author as a source for the present Gospel. The actual author probably was a Palestinian Jew who used the Gospel of Mark, plus a Greek translation of Matthew's Aramaic "oracles," and composed the gospel in Greek. The name of the gospel, therefore, stems from the apostle Matthew on whom the author draws, in part, to compose his work. This interpretation has the benefit of paying Papias' testimony the respect it deserves, as well as honoring the problems mentioned above.

Historical Setting. The Gospel of Matthew is full of clues that it was written to convince Jewish readers that Jesus is the Messiah. First, the author makes no attempt to translate or explain Jewish words and practices. Also, the gospel quotes more frequently from the Old Testament than does any other gospel. Most important, however, Jesus is portrayed as a descendant of the three greatest personalities of the Old Testament, although he surpasses them. Matthew traces Jesus' genealogy back to Abraham (1:2), the father of the faith.

In the Sermon on the Mount (chaps. 5—7), Jesus appears as a royal teacher whose authority exceeds that of Moses, the founder of the faith. And Jesus fulfills the hopes of David, the greatest king of Israel. He is born in Bethlehem (mentioned five times in chap. 2), and like David he appears as a king (19:28). He is frequently recognized as "the son of David" (9:27; 12:23; 15:22; 21:9; 21:15), although in truth He is David's "Lord" (22:41–46).

Matthew appealed to a Jewish audience, but not exclusively. The visit of the wise men from the (Gentile) East (2:1–12) hints of the gospel's rejection by the Jews and its acceptance by the Gentiles (21:43; also 4:15–16; 8:5–13; 12:18–21; 13:38). Furthermore the Great Commission—the command to "make disciples of all the nations" (28:19)—indicates an interest beyond the confines of Judaism. We can conclude that Matthew was written to Jews and Jewish Christians to show that Jesus is the promised Messiah of the Old Testament. It also shows that the gospel does not lead to narrow Jewish concerns (chap. 23), but out into the Gentile world.

Theological Significance. Matthew's main subject is the "kingdom of heaven" or "kingdom of God." This kingdom is mentioned 51 times in the Gospel of Matthew, twice as often as in any other gospel. The kingdom is already here in Jesus (12:28), but it is not yet fulfilled (13:43; 25:34) .The kingdom cannot be earned (19:23); it can be received only by those who recognize that they do not deserve it (5:3; 21:31). The kingdom extends like a fishing net, gathering people from every part of society (13:47), offering new life in the life-changing presence of God (8:11). The kingdom is more valuable than a precious gem (13:45–46), and it excludes any and all competitors for its allegiance (6:33).

The kingdom of God means the rule or reign of God—in the entire universe, in the world, and in our hearts. The primary indication of the presence of the kingdom in the world is the transformation of life, both individually and socially. A person enters the kingdom not by saying the right words, but by doing "the will of My father in heaven" (7:21).

Special Considerations. The Gospel of Matthew has at least five special considerations that will be mentioned briefly here:

1. Matthew sought to prove to the Jews that Jesus was the Christ, the fulfillment of Old Testament prophecy. A recurring statement that occurs in this gospel is, "All this was done that it might be fulfilled which was spoken by the Lord through the prophet" (1:22; also 2:15, 17, 23).

2. Matthew has a special interest in the church, which by the time this gospel was written had become the dominant factor in the lives of Christians. Indeed, Matthew is the only gospel to mention the word "church" (16:18; 18:17).

3. Matthew has a strong interest in eschatology (the doctrine of last things)—that is, in the second coming of Jesus, the end of the age, and the final judgment (chap. 25).

4. Matthew has a great interest in the teachings of Jesus, especially concerning the kingdom of God

(chaps. 5—7; 10; 13; 18; 24—25).

5. Matthew writes to show that Jesus is the King to whom God has given power and authority to redeem and to judge mankind (1:1–17; 2:2; 21:1–11; 27:11,37; 28:18).

MATTHIAS [muh THIGH us] (*gift of Jehovah*) — a disciple chosen to succeed Judas Iscariot as an apostle (Acts 1:23, 26). Matthias had been a follower of Jesus from the beginning of His ministry until the day of His ascension and had been a witness of His resurrection. In this way he fulfilled the requirements of apostleship (Acts 1:21–22). Probably he was one of the "seventy" (Luke 10:1, 17). The New Testament makes no further mention of him after his election. One tradition says that Matthias preached in Judea and was stoned to death by the Jews. Another tradition holds that he worked in Ethiopia and was martyred by crucifixion.

MATTITHIAH [mat uh THIGH uh] (*gift of Jehovah*) — the name of several men in the Old Testament:

1. A son of Shallum the Korahite (1 Chr. 9:31).
2. A Levite musician and gatekeeper during the reign of David (1 Chr. 15:18).
3. A son of Jeduthun. Mattithiah was appointed to the service of song during the reign of David (1 Chr. 25:3, 21). He was probably the same person as Mattithiah No. 2.
4. A son of Nebo who divorced his pagan wife after the Captivity (Ezra 10:43).
5. An Israelite who helped Ezra read the Book of the Law to the people (Neh. 8:4).

MATTOCK (see TOOLS OF THE BIBLE).

MAUL (see ARMS, ARMOR; TOOLS OF THE BIBLE).

MAW — the KJV translation of a Hebrew word which refers to the fourth stomach of animals who chew the cud (Deut. 18:3). Considered a great delicacy by the ancients, the maw was one of the parts of a sacrificial animal given to the priests.

MAZZAROTH [MAZ uh roth] (*the scattered ones*) — a feature either of the starry heavens or the changing seasons (Job 38:32). The meaning of this term is uncertain. The NIV translates as "the constellations."

MEADOW — a tract of grassland. Meadows were rare in Israel but not in the river flats of Egypt. The pasture in which the seven fat cows of Pharaoh's dreams grazed is described as a meadow (Gen. 41:2, 18). The Psalmist says, "The enemies of the Lord, like the splendor of the meadows, shall vanish" (Ps. 37:20). In the hot, dry climate of Palestine, the image of a meadow's beauty vanishing quickly was a particularly effective way of picturing the dangerous situation in which the unrighteous live.

MEAH, TOWER OF (see HUNDRED, TOWER OF THE).

MEAL OFFERING (see SACRIFICIAL OFFERINGS).

MEALS — occasions of eating. At "mealtime"

Ruth was invited to eat with the harvesters in Boaz's field (Ruth 2:14). Her lunch consisted of bread dipped in vinegar and parched grain. Other occasions of eating are frequently mentioned in the Bible (Gen. 19:3; 27:17; 43:32). Eating customs varied during the long period covered by the Bible.

Palestinian people ordinarily ate in the morning and in the evening (Ex. 16:12; 1 Kin. 17:6). The evening meal was called "sitting at the table" (Matt. 9:10). It was scheduled when the day's work was over (Ruth 3:2–7; Luke 17:7–8). Early morning eating, however, was frowned on (Eccl. 10:16); and Peter could argue that the third hour (9 A.M.) was too early for drunkenness (Acts 2:15).

Knives, forks, and spoons were not used in Bible times. Food was served in a common bowl and eaten with the hands (Prov. 26:15; Matt. 26:23; Mark 14:20), or with bread which was dipped in the dish (John 13:26). Cups or goblets were used for wine. In earlier times people sat on the ground, later on chairs and stools (1 Sam. 20:5, 25); however, the prophet Amos refers to those who recline (Amos 6:4). At least by the Persian period reclining was common (Esth. 1:6; 7:8), and it continued through the New Testament period (John 21:20).

At mealtime the traveler might have only bread and water (Gen. 21:14) or bread, meat, and water (1 Kin. 17:6). A soldier's ration consisted of parched grain, bread, and cheese (1 Sam. 17:17–18; 25:18).

Special meals were held at times of rejoicing, such as sheepshearing (2 Sam. 13:23), the return of the prodigal (Luke 15:22–32), weddings (John 2:1–11), birthdays (Mark 6:21–23), or entertaining guests (Matt. 9:10–13). At a supper the host greeted the guest with a kiss (Luke 7:45), provided for his dusty feet to be washed (John 13:4–5), and anointed his head with oil (Luke 7:46). Guests were seated by age or importance (Gen. 43:33). The FOOD and the entertainment varied with the occasion and the host's wealth. There was music (Is. 5:12), singing (Amos 6:4–5), and dancing (Matt. 14:6). The guests could also be entertained with riddles (Judg. 14:12–18). Jesus stressed the need to include the poor, maimed, and blind (Luke 14:13) among those invited to meals.

Israel often committed idolatry by participating in sacrifice and eating to the gods at Baal of Peor (Num. 25:1–5). On the other hand, many of the sacrifices of the Old Testament, after the priests received their portion (Lev. 2:10; 7:6), were consumed by the worshiper, his family, and his slaves (Lev. 7:11–21; 1 Sam. 1:3–4). The worshiper often invited the widow, Levite, stranger, and orphan to share (Deut. 12:12). Samuel blessed the sacrifice before the people ate (1 Sam. 9:11–14). David's passing of the kingdom to Solomon was a sacrificial occasion (1 Chr. 29:21–22). The annual PASSOVER meal was shared by every Israelite and by those purchased with his money (Ex. 12:43–49; 13:5–10).

Covenant meals were sacred only as far as the Lord was witness to the agreement made. When making a covenant, Abimelech and Isaac (Gen. 26:28–30), Jacob and Laban (Gen. 31:45–54), Israel and Gibeon (Josh. 9:12–15), and David and Abner (2 Sam. 3:20) ate together. The making of the covenant at Sinai included a meal (Ex. 24:11). The violation of such an agreement, as Ishmael did when he murdered Gedaliah after eating with him (Jer. 41:1–2), was considered a lowly and disgraceful act (Ps. 41:9; John 13:18).

In New Testament times, the Pharisees did not eat with unwashed hands (Mark 7:2–5). They objected to Jesus' eating with tax collectors and sinners (Matt. 9:11). Jews criticized Peter for eating with Gentiles at the house of Cornelius (Acts 11:3).

Early Christians, though meeting in the Temple courts, took their meals at home (Acts 2:46). Abuses of the Lord's Supper led Paul to instruct that the hungry eat at home (1 Cor. 11:34).

The Lord's Supper was a communion, or sharing in the body and blood of Christ (1 Cor. 10:16–17). A person cannot eat at both the table of the Lord and the table of demons (1 Cor. 10:20–21).

MEARAH [meh AY ruh] (*cave*) — a place, possibly a cavern, in northern Canaan near Sidon (Josh. 13:4), exact location unknown.

MEASURE, CHOINIX (see WEIGHTS AND MEASURES).

MEASURING LINE (see TOOLS OF THE BIBLE).

MEASURING REED (see WEIGHTS AND MEASURES; TOOLS OF THE BIBLE).

MEAT — the edible flesh of animals, often referring to the flesh of mammals, as distinguished from fish and poultry (Num. 11:4; Deut. 12:15, 20).

Meat was often sacrificed on pagan altars and dedicated to pagan gods in Paul's day. Later this meat was offered for sale in the public meat markets. Some Christians wondered if it were morally right for Christians to eat such meat that had previously been sacrificed to pagan gods. Paul explained that they should not eat such meats if it would cause weaker Christians to sin (1 Cor. 8:13). Also see FOOD.

MEAT OFFERING (see SACRIFICIAL OFFERINGS).

MEATS, UNCLEAN — animals that were unfit for eating, according to the law of Moses. Leviticus 11 gives an extended list of foods that were forbidden to the Hebrew people, including the camel, the rock hyrax, the hare, the swine, anything in the seas or rivers that does not have fins and scales, 20 different species of birds, and most flying insects. The flesh of the swine was especially abominable to the Hebrews.

MEBUNNAI [meh BUN eh] (*building of Jehovah*) — a Hushathite, one of David's mighty men (2 Sam. 23:27). The name is probably a textual corruption of Sibbechai the Hushathite (2 Sam. 21:18). Also see SIBBECHAI.

MECHERATHITE [meh KEE rah thite] (*dweller in Mecherah*) — a name applied to Hepher, one of David's mighty men (1 Chr. 11:36).

MECONAH [meh KOH nuh] (*foundation*) — a city in southern Judah, between Ziklag and En Rimmon (Neh. 11:28; Mekonah, KJV). Meconah was inhabited by Israelites after the Captivity.

MEDAD [ME dad] (*beloved, friend*) — an Israelite who prophesied in the wilderness camp (Num. 11:26–27). When 70 elders assembled in the "tabernacle of meeting," the Spirit rested on them and they prophesied. Medad and Eldad had not gone to the tabernacle, but had remained in the camp. Nevertheless, the Spirit rested upon them also and they, too, prophesied. A young man ran and told Moses. Joshua asked Moses to forbid them; but Moses replied, "Oh, that all the Lord's people were prophets and that the Lord would put His Spirit upon them!" (Num. 11:29).

This story emphasizes the truth that God's Spirit can fill any person at any place at any time.

MEDAN [MEE dan] (*judgment*) — a son of Abraham and Keturah, Abraham's concubine (1 Chr. 1:32).

MEDEBA [MED eh buh] (*waters of quiet*) — an ancient Moabite city in TRANSJORDAN, about 24 kilometers (15 miles) southeast of the place where the Jordan River runs into the Dead Sea (see Map 3, C–4). It is mentioned with Heshbon and Dibon (Num. 21:30).

Medeba was a source of conflict between Moab and Israel. Apparently the Ammonites controlled the city in the time of David; for the Syrian mercenaries, allies of the Ammonites, "encamped before Medeba" (1 Chr. 19:7) before their defeat by Joab, the captain of David's army. The MOABITE STONE states that Omri, king of Israel, captured Medeba, probably from Moab, and the Israelites controlled the city for 40 years. Mesha, king of Moab, recaptured and rebuilt it.

Jeroboam II of Israel probably recaptured Medeba again, for "he restored the territory of Israel from the entrance of Hamath [in the north] to the Sea of the Arabah [in the south]" (2 Kin. 14:25). Jeroboam probably pushed the Moabites south of the River Arnon and regained control of the plain by Medeba. If so, it was a short–lived victory; for Isaiah's oracle against Moab (Is. 15:2) indicated that in Isaiah's time Medeba was once again under Moabite control.

Medeba, now known as Madeba or Madiyabah, is on the KING'S HIGHWAY, the main north–south highway through Transjordan.

MEDIA [MEE dih uh] — an ancient country of Asia situated west of Parthia, north of the Persian Gulf, east of Assyria and Armenia, and south of the Caspian Sea. The country is now included in parts of Iran, Iraq, and Turkey.

A mountainous country, Media contained some fertile sections; but much of it was cold, barren, and swampy. In the southern area lush plains were used as pasture land for the large herds of horses used in the Median cavalry.

The history of the Medes is complex, because it involves many entangling alliances and the rise and fall of several nations. The Medes were an Indo-European people who invaded the rough mountain terrain south of the Caspian Sea. In the ninth and eighth centuries B.C., Assyrian kings conducted campaigns against these people, forcing them to pay tribute. The mighty Tiglath-pileser (745–727 B.C.) invaded Media and added part of it to the Assyrian Empire. By 700 B.C., the era of the prophet Isaiah, a prosperous realm had been established.

Media is first mentioned in the Old Testament as the destination to which Shalmaneser, king of Assyria, deported the Israelites from Samaria around 721 B.C. (2 Kin. 17:6; 18:11). Medes are mentioned in Ezra in connection with Darius' search for the roll containing the famous decree of Cyrus that allowed the Jews to return to Jerusalem (Ezra 6:2). Laws of the Medes are mentioned in the Book of Esther (1:19) and in Daniel (6:8, 15).

The prophet Daniel prophesied that King Belshazzar's Babylonian kingdom would fall to "the Medes and Persians" (Dan. 5:28). Medes were also among the people from many different nations in Jerusalem on the day of Pentecost (Acts 2:9).

About 710 B.C. Sargon II of Assyria defeated the Medes and forced them to pay a tribute consisting of the thoroughbred horses for which Media was famous. The Medes, however, increased in strength and joined forces with Babylon. The Medes under Cyaxares and the Babylonians under Nabopolassar captured Asshur, the ancient capital of Assyria, in 614 B.C. In 612 B.C. this alliance overthrew Nineveh, the proud capital of Assyria, causing the crash of the Assyrian Empire. The seventh century Hebrew prophet Nahum expressed the great relief felt by neighboring nations at Nineveh's fall (Nah. 2:3; 3:19). Nabopolassar's son, Nebuchadnezzar, married Cyaxares' daughter, strengthening the bond between the two countries. During the era of Nebuchadnezzar and the time of Jeremiah (about 605–552 B.C.), the Median kingdom reached the height of its power.

Persia was dominated by Media until the time of Cyrus II who was founder of the Persian Empire. In 549 B.C. Cyrus defeated Media. Yet under the Persians, Media remained the most important province of Persia. As a consequence, the dual name, "Medes and Persians," remained for a long time (Esth. 1:19; Dan. 5:28). The expression, "The laws of the Medes and the Persians," depicted the unchangeable nature of Median law, which even the king was powerless to change (Esth. 1:19).

The Medes and Persians were Indo-European peoples known as Aryans. Their religion was Zoroastrianism. Its adherents believed that spiritual reality was divided between Ahura Mazdah, the god of light and goodness, and Angra Mainja, the god of darkness and evil.

Influenced by the moral teachings of his religion, Cyrus II of Persia was known for his humane attitude toward conquered peoples. He treated the vanquished Medes with respect. Medo-Persia, a dual nation, became a great empire that ruled Asia until it was conquered by Alexander the Great (330 B.C.). After Alexander's death, Medo-Persia became part of Syria and later a part of the Persian Empire.

MEDIATOR — one who goes between two groups or persons to help them work out their differences and come to agreement. A mediator usually is a neutral party, a go-between, intermediary, or arbitrator who brings about reconciliation in a hostile situation when divided persons are not able to work out their differences themselves.

A mediator can also be the negotiator of an agreement. After the agreement is made, he can then witness to its content and serve as the administrator or guarantor to make sure its provisions are followed. A mediator needs legal authority and recognized power to function effectively.

Mediation in the Old Testament. The concept of mediation is found throughout Scripture, but the actual term, mediator, seldom appears. The Hebrew verb meaning "to decide" is used in the sense of mediation in Genesis 31:37, "Set it here before my brethren and your brethren, that they may judge between us both." Later in Jewish history the idea of mediation became associated with the office of the priest, who stands between God and man in spiritual matters. This term was also applied to the prophet, who serves as intermediary in giving God's word to man, and the king, who serves as mediatorial administrator between God and men in government. These officers discharged their duties against the background of God's COVENANT with men expressed in the Law.

The central role of the covenant made Moses the supreme mediator in the Old Testament. Moses was the sole human mediator of the Sinai covenant (Ex. 20:19–22; Gal. 3:19; Heb. 3:2–5). And to some extent Moses assumed all three offices during his life. He offered sacrifice, consecrated the priestly house of Aaron, and interceded for the nation. He spoke the word of God as prophet and administered government for the nation. Moses is the figure whom the New Testament compares with Jesus as Mediator of the New Covenant (Heb. 3:2–5).

Jesus as Mediator in the New Testament. From the New Testament perspective, there is ultimately only "one Mediator between God and man" (1 Tim. 2:5)—Jesus the Messiah. He alone, being fully God, can represent God to man, and at the same time, being fully man, can represent man to God. He alone can bring complete reconcilation, because He alone can bring about complete payment for man's sin and satisfaction of God's wrath. He alone can bring everlasting peace (Acts 15:11; 2 Cor. 5:18; Eph. 1:7).

A major theme of the Book of Hebrews is that Jesus mediated a new and better covenant, an eternal covenant (7:27–28; 9:15; 10:1; 12:24). Speaking the words of God (John 14:24), Jesus fulfills the prophetic office. As High Priest over the house of God (Heb. 3:1-6), He sacrificed Himself to secure our redemption and continues to intercede on our behalf (Rom. 8:34; Heb. 7:25; 9:24; 1 John 2:1). Even our prayers are presented to God "through" His mediation (Rom. 1:8; Heb. 13:15). And He is also "King of Kings," having "all authority in heaven and on earth" (Matt. 28:18; Phil. 2:9-11; Rev. 19:11-16).

The Christian never need worry about the certainty of His salvation. The Mediator "is able to save to the uttermost those who come to God through Him" (Heb. 7:25).

MEDICINE (see DISEASES OF THE BIBLE).

MEDITATION — the practice of reflection or contemplation. The word meditation or its verb form, *to meditate*, is found mainly in the Old Testament. The Hebrew words behind this concept mean "to murmur," "a murmuring," "sighing," or "moaning." This concept is reflected in Psalm 1:2, where the "blessed man" meditates on God's law day and night. The psalmist also prayed that the meditation of his heart would be acceptable in God's sight (Ps. 19:14). Joshua was instructed to meditate on the Book of the Law for the purpose of obeying all that was written in it (Josh. 1:8).

The Greek word translated as meditate occurs only twice in the New Testament. In Luke 21:14 Jesus instructed His disciples not "to meditate beforehand" in answering their adversaries when the end of the age comes. The word may be understood in this passage as the idea of preparing a defense for a court appearance. Paul, in 1 Timothy 4:15, urged Timothy to meditate, or take pains with, the instructions he gives. The idea of meditation is also found in Philippians 4:8 and Colossians 3:2.

Meditation is a lost art for many Christians, but the practice needs to be cultivated again.

MEDITERRANEAN SEA [med ih ter RAIN ih un] — a large sea bordered by many important nations of the ancient world, including Palestine (see Map 9, B-3). The Hebrews referred to it by several different names. It was called "the Great Sea" (Num. 34:6), "the Western Sea" (Deut. 34:2), "the Sea of the Philistines" (Ex. 23:31), and simply "the sea" (Josh. 16:8; Jon. 1:4).

The Mediterranean Sea extends about 3,550 kilometers (2,200 miles) westward from the coast of Palestine to the Straits of Gibraltar. At its narrowest point, between Sicily and the coast of Africa, the sea is about 130 kilometers (80 miles) wide. Archaeologists believe that an open channel once existed, connecting the Mediterranean to the Red Sea, and that this channel was closed off by drifting desert sand and silt from the Nile River, providing a land connection between Asia and Africa.

Many ancient civilizations grew up around this sea and used it for trade and commerce. The Hebrews were afraid of the Mediterranean and usually hired others, often Phoenicians (1 Kin. 9:27), to conduct their seafaring business for them. Palestine itself had few good harbors.

The apostle Paul crossed the Mediterranean Sea during his missionary journeys. He tried to avoid sailing during the winter months, but was shipwrecked on his way to Rome while sailing in late autumn.

MEDIUM — a person thought to have the power to communicate with the spirits of the dead (Is. 8:19; 19:3; 29:4). According to the Law of Moses,

A beautiful view of the Mediterranean Sea near Patara in southwestern Asia Minor.
Photo by Howard Vos

A model of the ancient city of Megiddo, showing its impressive defensive wall built by King Solomon (1 Kin. 9:15).

anyone who professed to be a medium or a channel of communication to the spirit world was to be put to death by stoning (Lev. 20:27). Also see MAGIC AND SORCERY.

MEEKNESS — an attitude of humility toward God and gentleness toward men, springing from a recognition that God is in control. Although weakness and meekness may look similar, they are not the same. Weakness is due to negative circumstances, such as lack of strength or lack of courage. But meekness is due to a person's conscious choice. It is strength and courage under control, coupled with kindness.

The apostle Paul once pointed out that the spiritual leaders of the church have great power, even leverage, in confronting a sinner. But he cautioned them to restrain themselves in meekness (Gal. 6:1; 5:22–23). Even toward evil men, a man of God should be meek, knowing that God is in control.

Meekness is a virtue practiced and commended by our Lord Jesus (Matt. 5:5; 11:29). As such it is part of the equipment which every follower of Jesus should wear (2 Cor. 10:1; Gal. 5:23; 6:1; Eph. 4:1–2).

MEGIDDO [muh GID doe] (*place of troops*) — a walled city in the Carmel Mountain range where many important battles were fought in Old Testament times (see Map 3, B–2). Megiddo was situated on the main road that linked Egypt and Syria. Overlooking the Valley of Jezreel (Plain of Esdraelon), Megiddo was the most strategic city in Palestine. All major traffic through Palestine traveled past Megiddo, making it a strategic military stronghold.

Megiddo is first mentioned in the Old Testament in the account of the 31 kings conquered by Joshua (Josh. 12:21). In the division of the land of Canaan among the tribes of the Hebrew people, Megiddo was awarded to Manasseh. But the tribe was unable to drive out the native inhabitants of the city (Josh. 17:11; Judg. 1:27; 1 Chr. 7:29).

During the period of the judges, the forces of Deborah and Barak wiped out the army of Sisera "by the waters of Megiddo" (Judg. 5:19). During the period of the United Kingdom under Solomon, the Israelites established their supremacy at Megiddo. The city was included in the fifth administrative district of Solomon (1 Kin. 4:12). Along with Hazor, Gezer, Lower Beth Horon, Baalath, and Tadmor, Megiddo was fortified and established as a chariot city for the armies of King Solomon (1 Kin. 9:15–19).

The prophet Zechariah mentioned the great mourning which would one day take place "in the plain of Megiddo" (Zech. 12:11; Megiddon, KJV). The fulfillment of Zechariah's prophecy is the battle at the end of time known as the Battle of ARMAGEDDON. Armageddon is a compound word which means "mountain of Megiddo." This is the only New Testament reference to Megiddo.

In the end–times, God will destroy the armies of the Beast and the False Prophet in "the battle of that great day of God Almighty" (Rev. 16:14) when He shall gather them "together to the place called in Hebrew, Armageddon" (Rev. 16:16). Jesus Christ will ride out of heaven on a white horse (Rev. 19:11) as the "King of kings and Lord of lords" (Rev. 19:16). At this event, "The kingdoms of this world have become the kingdoms of our Lord and of His Christ, and He shall reign forever and ever" (Rev. 11:15).

MEGIDDON [meh GID ahn] — a form of MEGIDDO.

MEHETABEEL [meh HET uh beel] (*whose benefactor is God*) — father of Delaiah and grandfather of Shemaiah (Neh. 6:10; Mehetabel, RSV, NAS, NEB, NIV).

MEHETABEL [meh HET uh bel] (*benefited of God*) — the wife of Hadar (Gen. 36:39), or Hadad (1 Chr. 1:50), king of Edom. Mehetabel was a daughter of Matred.

MEHIDA [meh HIGH duh] (*renowned*) — founder of a family of NETHINIM (Temple servants) whose descendants returned from the Captivity with Zerubbabel (Ezra 2:52).

MEHIR [MEE hur] (*price*) — a son of Chelub, of the tribe of Judah (1 Chr. 4:11).

MEHOLATHITE [meh HO luh thite] — a native or inhabitant of Meholah, probably ABEL MEHOLAH, a city in the Jordan River Valley near Beth Shean (1 Sam. 18:19).

MEHUJAEL [meh HUE jay el] (*smitten by God*) — a son of Irad, of the family of Cain (Gen. 4:18).

MEHUMAN [meh HUE man] (*trusty*) — a eunuch or chamberlain who had charge of the harem of King Ahasuerus (Xerxes) of Persia (Esth. 1:10).

MEHUNIM [me HYOO nem] — a form of MEUNIM.

ME JARKON [mee JAHR kuhn] (meaning unknown) — a city or a river near Joppa (Josh. 19:46), probably the Wadi Nahr el-'Auja, which flows into the Mediterranean Sea.

MEKONAH [meh KOH nuh] — a form of MECONAH.

MELATIAH [mel uh TYE uh] (*Jehovah sets free*) — a GIBEONITE who helped repair the wall of Jerusalem in Nehemiah's time (Neh. 3:7).

MELCHI [mel KYE] (*my king*) — the name of two men in Luke's genealogy of Jesus Christ:
 1. A son of Janna and the father of Levi (Luke 3:24).
 2. A son of Addi and the father of Neri (Luke 3:28).

MELCHIAH [mell KIE ah] — a form of MALCHIAH No. 2.

MELCHISEDEC [mel KEZ uh dek] — a form of MELCHIZEDEK.

MELCHI–SHUA [mel kye SHU uh] — a form of MALCHISHUA.

MELCHIZEDEK [mel KIZ eh deck] (*king of righteousness*) — a king of Salem (Jerusalem) and priest of the Most High God (Gen. 14:18–20; Ps. 110:4; Heb. 5:6–11; 6:20—7:28). Melchizedek's sudden appearance and disappearance in the Book of Genesis are somewhat mysterious. Melchizedek and Abraham first met after Abram's defeat of Chedorlaomer and his three allies. Melchizedek presented bread and wine to Abraham and his weary men, demonstrating friendship and religious kinship. He bestowed a blessing on Abraham in the name of El Elyon ("God Most High"), and praised God for giving Abraham a victory in battle (Gen. 14:18–20).

A modern mud-brick village at the site of ancient Memphis in Egypt. This city is called Noph in the Bible (Is. 19:13).

Photo by Howard Vos

Abraham presented Melchizedek with a tithe (a tenth) of all the booty he had gathered. By this act Abraham indicated that he recognized Melchizedek as a fellow-worshiper of the one true God as well as a priest who ranked higher spiritually than himself. Melchizedek's existence shows that there were people other than Abraham and his family who served the true God.

In Psalm 110, a messianic psalm written by David (Matt. 22:43), Melchizedek is seen as a type of Christ. This theme is repeated in the Book of Hebrews, where both Melchizedek and Christ are considered kings of righteousness and peace. By citing Melchizedek and his unique priesthood as a type, the writer shows that Christ's new priesthood is superior to the old Levitical order and the priesthood of Aaron (Heb. 7:1–10; Melchisedek, KJV).

Attempts have been made to identify Melchizedek as an imaginary character named Shem, an angel, the Holy Spirit, Christ, and others. All are products of speculation, not historical fact; and it is impossible to reconcile them with the theological argument of Hebrews. Melchizedek was a real, historical king-priest who served as a type for the greater King-Priest who was to come, Jesus Christ.

MELEA [MEE lee uh] (meaning unknown) — an ancestor of Jesus (Luke 3:31).

MELECH [MEE lek] (*king*) — a Benjamite, the son of Micah and a descendant of King Saul (1 Chr. 8:35; 9:41).

MELICHU, **MELICU** [MEL eh kue] — forms of MALLUCH No. 6.

MELITA [MEL eh tuh] — a form of MALTA.

MELON (see PLANTS OF THE BIBLE).

MELZAR [MEL zahr] (*the overseer*) — KJV word for the title of an officer at the Babylonian court of Nebuchadnezzar (Dan. 1:11, 16). The NKJV translates as "the steward."

MEM [maim] — the 13th letter of the Hebrew alphabet, used as a heading over Psalm 119:97–104. In the original Hebrew language, every line of these eight verses began with the letter mem. Also see ACROSTIC.

MEMBER — a word with at least two different meanings in the Bible:
1. An organ of the human body, such as an arm or leg (Job 17:7; Matt. 5:29–30).
2. A Christian. In the New Testament the "members" of the "body" of Christ are described in a symbolic way as the individual Christians who together compose the church (Rom. 12:5; Eph. 4:25).

MEMORIAL — a monument, statue, holiday, or ritual which serves as a remembrance or reminder of a person or an event. The Feast of the Passover was a memorial of God's sparing the firstborn of the Israelites in Egypt and of Israel's deliverance from Egyptian bondage (Ex. 12:14).

When Israel crossed the Jordan River and occu-pied the Promised Land, Joshua commanded that 12 stones, representing the 12 tribes of Israel, be set up in the midst of the Jordan (Josh. 4:9). "These stones," he said, "shall be for a memorial to the children of Israel forever" (Josh. 4:7).

When Jesus was in the house of Simon the leper, a woman anointed His head with oil. "Wherever this gospel is preached in the whole world," said Jesus, "what this woman has done will also be told as a memorial to her" (Matt. 26:13; Mark 14:9).

On the eve of His crucifixion Jesus instituted the Lord's Supper (Luke 22:19). The observance of the Lord's Supper is an ongoing Christian memorial that helps the believer remember the sacrifice of Christ on his behalf (1 Cor. 5:7; 11:25–26).

MEMPHIS [MEM fis] (*haven of good*) — an ancient royal city (see Map 2, A–2) during the Old Kingdom period of Egypt's history (about 3000 B.C. to 2200 B.C.). It was situated on the west bank of the NILE RIVER about 21 kilometers (13 miles) south of Cairo. Today there is little left to mark the glorious past of the city.

In 670 B.C. Memphis was captured by the Assyrians, followed by a period of Persian dominance. After the Moslem conquest of the city, its ruins were used in the Middle Ages to build Cairo, Egypt's modern capital. The importance of Memphis is demonstrated by the multitude of pyramids and the celebrated Sphinx that are located near the site of the ancient city.

The word Memphis is found only once in the Bible—a translation of the Hebrew word *noph* (Hos. 9:6). In this passage the prophet Hosea condemned the Israelites for their sinfulness and predicted that some of them would be buried by Egyptians from Memphis. In seven other locations the word *noph* refers to Memphis (Is. 19:13; Jer. 2:16; 44:1; 46:14, 19; Ezek. 30:13, 16). In each passage the NIV has Memphis.

"The princes of Noph [Memphis] are deceived," wrote the prophet Isaiah (Is. 19:13). He prophesied that God would bring judgment on these deluded rulers. The prophet Jeremiah also warned the Jews to trust God and not flee to Memphis, because God was going to send destruction upon the land of Egypt (Jer. 2:16; 44:1; 46:14, 19).

MEMUCAN [meh MUE kan] (*sorcerer*) — a high Persian official in Shushan (Susa), one of seven princes "who had access to the king's presence" (Esth. 1:14). The "king" was Ahasuerus, generally identified as Xerxes I (485–464 B.C.).

MENAHEM [MEN ah him] (*comforter*) — a son of Gadi and 17th king of Israel (2 Kin. 15:14–23). Some scholars believe Menahem probably was the military commander of King Zechariah. When Shallum took the throne from Zechariah by killing him in front of the people, Menahem determined that Shallum himself must be killed. After Shallum had reigned as king of Israel for a month in Samaria, Menahem "went up from Tirzah, came to Samaria, and struck Shallum...and killed him; and he reigned in his place" (2 Kin. 15:14).

When the city of Tiphsah refused to recognize Menahem as the lawful ruler of Israel, Menahem attacked it and inflicted terrible cruelties upon its people (2 Kin. 15:16). This act of cruelty apparently secured his position, because Menahem remained king for ten years (752–742 B.C.). His reign was evil, marked by cruelty, oppression, and idolatrous worship. During his reign Menahem faced a threat from the advancing army of Pul (Tiglath-Pileser III), king of Assyria. To strengthen his own position as king and to forestall a war with Assyria, he paid tribute to the Assyrian king by exacting "from each man fifty shekels of silver" (2 Kin. 15:20). After Menahem's death, his son Pekahiah became king of Israel (2 Kin. 15:22).

MENAN [MEE nan] (meaning unknown) — an ancestor of Jesus (Luke 3:31; Menna, NIV, RSV).

MENE, MENE, TEKEL, UPHARSIN [MEE neh, MEE neh, TEK uhl, ue FAR sin] (*numbered, weighed, and divided*) — a puzzling inscription that appeared on the wall of the palace of Belshazzar, king of Babylon, during a drunken feast (Dan. 5:1–29). The king had just ordered that the gold and silver vessels which Nebuchadnezzar had stolen from the Temple in Jerusalem be used in the revelry. When the fingers of a man's hand had written the words, Belshazzar called his wise men, but they could neither read the inscription nor interpret its meaning. Daniel was then summoned. He deciphered the message and told the king what it meant.

The words of the inscription refer to three Babylonian weights of decreasing size and their equivalent monetary values. In his interpretation of this inscription, Daniel used a play on words to give the message God had for Belshazzar and Babylon.

"Mene: God has numbered your kingdom, and finished it." God had counted the days allotted to Belshazzar's rule and his time had run out. "Tekel: You have been weighed in the balances and found wanting." Belshazzar's character, his moral values and spiritual worth, had been evaluated and he was found to be deficient. "Peres: Your kingdom has been divided, and given to the Medes and Persians." Belshazzar's empire had been broken into bits and pieces, dissolved and destroyed.

Some scholars have suggested that in referring to three weights listed in declining order, Daniel may have been referring to the declining worth of various Babylonian kings. Thus, the great king Nebuchadnezzar probably was symbolized by the mina, Evil-Merodach by the shekel (in other words, only one 50th as great as Nebuchadnezzar), and Nabonidus and Belshazzar (father and son respectively, who reigned as co-regents) were half-shekels—implying that it took two "half-regents" to equal an Evil-Merodach.

The overall impact of Daniel's double meaning in these words was to point out that the degeneration of the rulers of Babylon cried out for God's judg-

ment. That very night Belshazzar was killed and Babylon was conquered by the Persians.

MENI [MEN eye] (see GODS, PAGAN).

MENNA [MEN uh] — a form of MENAN.

MEN–PLEASERS — those who cultivate the favor of their superiors through an outward show of service (Eph. 6:6; Col. 3:22). The Greek word translated as men–pleasers means "one who renders service to human beings." Also see EYESERVICE.

MENUHOTH [men YUE hawth] — a form of MANUHOTH.

MEONENIM, PLAIN OF [meh AHN eh nim] — KJV word (Judg. 9:37) for DIVINERS' TEREBINTH TREE.

MEONOTHAI [meh AHN oh thigh] (*habitations of the Lord*) — the father of Ophrah and a descendant of Judah (1 Chr. 4:14).

MEPHAATH [mef AY ath] (meaning unknown) — a city allotted to the tribe of Reuben (Josh. 13:18) and assigned to the Levites (Josh. 21:37). In Jeremiah's time Mephaath belonged to the Moabites (Jer. 48:21). It was in TRANSJORDAN, east of the Dead Sea.

MEPHIBOSHETH [meh FIB oh shehth] (meaning unknown) — the name of two men in the Old Testament:

1. A son of Jonathan and grandson of Saul. Mephibosheth was also called Merib–Baal (1 Chr. 8:34; 9:40), probably his original name, meaning "a striver against Baal." His name was changed because the word Baal was associated with idol worship.

Mephibosheth was only five years old when his father, Jonathan, and his grandfather, Saul, died on Mount Gilboa in the Battle of Jezreel (2 Sam. 4:4). When the child's nurse heard the outcome of the battle, she feared for Mephibosheth's life. As she fled for his protection, "he fell and became lame" (2 Sam. 4:4). For the rest of his life he was crippled.

After David consolidated his kingdom, he remembered his covenant with Jonathan to treat his family with kindness (1 Samuel 20). Through Ziba, a servant of the house of Saul, David found out about Mephibosheth. The lame prince had been staying "in the house of Machir the son of Ammiel, in Lo Debar" (2 Sam. 9:4). David then summoned Mephibosheth to his palace, restored to him the estates of Saul, appointed servants for him, and gave him a place at the royal table (2 Sam. 9:7–13).

When David's son Absalom rebelled, the servant Ziba falsely accused Mephibosheth of disloyalty to David (2 Samuel 16:1–4). David believed Ziba's story and took Saul's property from Mephibosheth. Upon David's return to Jerusalem, Mephibosheth cleared himself. David in turn offered Mephibosheth half of Saul's estates (2 Sam. 19:24–30), but he refused. David's return to Jerusalem as king was the only reward Mephibosheth desired.

Although Mephibosheth was often wronged and

his life was filled with tragedy, he never grew angry or embittered. Even material possessions had little appeal to him—an important lesson for all followers of the Lord.

2. A son of King Saul and Rizpah (2 Sam. 21:8).

MERAB [MEE rab] (*increase*) — the older daughter of King Saul (1 Sam. 14:49). When GOLIATH defied and taunted the Israelites, Saul promised that the man who killed him would be given great riches as well as Merab in marriage (1 Sam. 17:25). When David killed the giant, however, Saul changed his mind. David then married MICHAL, the younger daughter of Saul.

MERAIAH [meh RYE uh] (*revelation of Jehovah*) — head of the priestly family of Seraiah after the return from the Captivity (Neh. 12:12).

MERAIOTH [meh RAY yawth] (*revelations*)—the name of two men and a priestly house in the Old Testament:
1. A son of Zerahiah and the father of Amariah (1 Chr. 6:6–7).
2. A son of Ahitub and a priest of Jerusalem (Neh. 11:11).
3. A priestly house in the days of Joiakim the high priest (Neh. 12:15).

MERARI [meh RAY eye] (*bitter*) — the third and youngest son of Levi and the founder of the MERARITES, one of the three Levitical families. Merari was the father of MAHLI and MUSHI (Ex. 6:16–19), who, in turn, were the founders of the MAHLITES and the MUSHITES (Num. 3:33; 26:58).

MERARITES [meh RAY ites] — the descendants of MERARI (Num. 26:57). During the wilderness journey, the Merarites were stationed on the north side of the tabernacle. The Merarites (who included the MAHLITES and the MUSHITES) had the responsibility of transporting many of the materials that made up the tabernacle (Num. 3:35–37). To enable them to transport these materials they were assigned "four carts and eight oxen" (Num. 7:8). They were under the direction of ITHAMAR, Aaron's youngest son.

The Merarites were the smallest of the three Levitical families (also see GERSHONITES and KOHATHITES); at the first census they numbered 6,200 from a month old and above (Num. 3:34), or 3,200 males between the age of 30 and 50 (Num. 4:42–43).

Twelve cities were assigned to the Merarites: four from the tribe of Zebulun (Jokneam, Kartah, Dimnah, and Nahalal), four from the tribe of Reuben (Bezer, Jahaz, Kedemoth, and Mephaath), and four from the tribe of Gad (Ramoth in Gilead, Mahanaim, Heshbon, and Jazer). One of these cities, Ramoth in Gilead, also was a city of refuge (Josh. 21:34–40).

The Merarites made up six of the 24 courses of Temple musicians in David's time (1 Chr. 25:3). They aided in Hezekiah's cleansing of the Temple (2 Chr. 29:12). After the Captivity a small number of them returned to Jerusalem (Ezra 8:18–19).

MERATHAIM [mer uh THAY em] (*double rebellion*) — a symbolic name for Babylon (Jer. 50:21). Merathaim is a play in the Hebrew language on the words *mat marrati* (which means "Land of the Bitter River"), a region in southern Babylonia.

MERCHANDISER (see OCCUPATIONS AND TRADES).

MERCHANT (see COMMERCE; OCCUPATIONS AND TRADES).

MERCURIUS [mur KUE reh uhs] — a form of HERMES.

MERCURY (see GODS, PAGAN; MINERALS OF THE BIBLE).

MERCY — the aspect of God's love that causes Him to help the miserable, just as grace is the aspect of His love that moves Him to forgive the guilty. Those who are miserable may be so either because of breaking God's law or because of circumstances beyond their control.

God shows mercy upon those who have broken His law (Dan. 9:9; 1 Tim. 1:13, 16), although such mercy is selective, demonstrating that it is not deserved (Rom. 9:14–18). God's mercy on the miserable extends beyond punishment that is withheld (Eph. 2:4–6). Withheld punishment keeps us from hell, but it does not get us into heaven. God's mercy is greater than this.

God also shows mercy by actively helping those who are miserable due to circumstances beyond their control. We see this aspect of mercy especially in the life of our Lord Jesus. He healed blind men (Matt. 9:27–31; 20:29–34) and lepers (Luke 17:11–19). These acts of healing grew out of his attitude of compassion and mercy.

Finally, because God is merciful, He expects His children to be merciful (Matt. 5:7; James 1:27).

MERCY SEAT — the golden lid or covering on the ARK OF THE COVENANT, regarded as the resting place of God (Ex. 25:17–22; 1 Chr. 28:11; Heb. 9:5). Also see TABERNACLE.

MERED [MEE red] (*rebel*) — a son of Ezrah, of the tribe of Judah (1 Chr. 4:17).

MEREMOTH [MER eh moth] (*heights*) — the name of several men in the Old Testament:
1. A son of Uriah the priest who was assigned the task of weighing the gold and silver articles that Ezra brought back from Babylon (Ezra 8:33).
2. One of the "sons of Bani" (Ezra 10:34, 36) who divorced his pagan wife after the Captivity.
3. A priest who, with Nehemiah, sealed the covenant (Neh. 10:5). He may be the same person as Meremoth No. 1.
4. A priest who returned with Zerubbabel from the Captivity (Neh. 12:3).

MERES [MEE ress] (*forgetful man*) — a high Persian official at Shushan (Susa), one of seven princes "who had access to the king's presence" (Esth. 1:14).

MERIBAH [MEHR ih bah] (*contention*) — the name of two different places where Moses struck a rock with his rod and water gushed forth to satisfy the thirsty Israelites:

1. A place "in Rephidim" at the foot of Mount Horeb. The Israelites camped here near the beginning of their 40 years of wilderness wandering (Ex. 17:1–7).

2. A second place where Moses struck the rock and water gushed forth. This camp was in Kadesh, in the Wilderness of Zin. The Israelites camped here near the end of their period of wilderness wandering (Num. 20:2–13). In Deuteronomy 32:51, this place is referred to as Meribath-Kadesh.

MERIBATH–KADESH [MER eh buh KAY desh] — a form of MERIBAH No. 2.

MERIB–BAAL [MER ib BAY uhl] (*contender against Baal*) — a son of Jonathan (1 Chr. 8:34) and grandson of King Saul. Merib-baal is the same person as MEPHIBOSHETH No. 1 (2 Sam. 9:6).

MERODACH [meh ROH dak] (see GODS, PAGAN).

MERODACH–BALADAN [MEHR oh dack BAL ah dahn] (*the god Marduk has given an heir*) — the king of Babylon (721–710 and 704 B.C.) who sent emissaries to King Hezekiah of Judah (Is. 39:1; Berodach-Baladan, 2 Kin. 20:12).

To the Assyrians, Merodach–Baladan was a persistent rebel king. He appeared on the political scene during the days of TIGLATH–PILESER III of Assyria. He rallied the support of the ARAMEAN tribes in Babylonia and arranged an alliance with Elam. In 721 B.C., when SARGON II came to power in Assyria, Merodach–Baladan entered Babylon and claimed kingship to the country.

In 710 B.C., Sargon made a determined effort to expel Merodach–Baladan and make himself king. After submitting to Sargon, Merodach–Baladan was reinstated as king of the tribe of Bit–Yakin, a district near the mouth of the Euphrates River. Merodach–Baladan remained faithful to Sargon; but when Sennacherib came to power in 705 B.C., he grew restless. In 703 B.C., Merodach–Baladan returned to Babylon, killed the ruler there, and prepared to fight Assyria. Sennacherib reacted energetically and drove Merodach–Baladan into exile once again.

Merodach–Baladan sent ambassadors to Jerusalem to visit King Hezekiah of Judah, who had just recovered miraculously from a serious illness. He sent letters and presents (2 Kin. 20:12; Is. 39:1) and inquired of the "wonder that was done in the land" (2 Chr. 32:31). This probably was a reference to the sun's shadow moving backward ten degrees on the SUNDIAL OF AHAZ (2 Kin. 20:8–11). The real reason for his visit may have been to gain an ally in Hezekiah and to involve him in revolt against Assyria.

There is no indication that Hezekiah formed an alliance, but he showed the Babylonian ambassadors his wealth—an act that brought stiff rebuke from the prophet Isaiah (2 Kin. 20:13–18). Heze-

kiah later revolted from Assyria, a move that resulted in Sennacherib's invasion of Judah in 701 B.C.

Merodach–Baladan was never successful in his bid for Babylonian independence. The task was left for NABOPOLASSAR (626–605 B.C.), who was able to succeed where Merodach–Baladan had failed.

MEROM, WATERS OF [MEE rahm] (*high place*) — a place where Joshua defeated a coalition of Canaanites led by Jabin, king of Hazor (Josh. 11:5–7).

MERONOTHITE [meh RAHN uh thight] — an inhabitant of Meronoth. Two Meronothites are mentioned in the Old Testament: JEHDEIAH, who was over the royal stables of King David (1 Chr. 27:30), and JADON, who helped Nehemiah repair the wall of Jerusalem (Neh. 3:7).

MEROZ [MEE rahz] (*refuge*) — a place in northern Palestine near the Kishon River, in or near the Valley of Jezreel. In her song of victory (Judg. 5:23), Deborah pronounced a curse upon Meroz for its refusal to help the Israelites in their battle against Sisera.

MESECH [MEE sek] — a form of MESHECH.

MESHA [MEE shuh] (*freedom*) — the name of a boundary and three men in the Old Testament:

1. A boundary of the territory in Arabia occupied by the descendants of Joktan (Gen. 10:30).

2. A king of Moab who "regularly paid the king of Israel [Ahab] one hundred thousand lambs and the wool of one hundred thousand rams" (2 Kin. 3:4). After Ahab's death at Ramoth Gilead, Mesha refused to pay the tribute to Ahab's successor, Ahaziah (2 Kings 1:1). Mesha led the Moabites, Ammonites, and Edomites in an invasion of Judah after Jehoshaphat, Judah's king, began his religious reform. Mesha and his allies were defeated when the Lord caused them to turn on one another; Judah and Jehoshaphat won without a battle (2 Chr. 20).

When King Ahaziah died, Jehoram became king of Israel. Jehoram wanted Mesha to resume the tribute, and he asked Jehoshaphat to help him force Mesha to pay it (2 Kin. 3). The two kings, along with a king of Edom, moved around the southern end of the the Dead Sea to attack Mesha. The armies nearly died of thirst, but the prophet Elisha instructed them to dig trenches to reach water.

In the glare of the early–morning sun, Mesha mistook the water for blood. He carelessly moved to attack the armies of Israel and Judah. His army was beaten, and the cities of Moab were destroyed. In a last-ditch effort to avert total defeat, Mesha offered his oldest son as a burnt offering upon the wall of KIR HARASETH as a sacrifice to the god Chemosh. The human sacrifice apparently frightened or shocked the armies of Israel and Judah, so they pulled back from the city, lifting the siege and failing to capture Kir Haraseth.

Mesha is the king of whom the famous MOABITE STONE declares: "I am Mesha, son of Chemosh [Melech]...king of Moab, the Dibonite." Thus, he is the one who caused the Moabite Stone to be written and had it erected.

3. A man of the tribe of Judah (1 Chr. 2:42).

4. An ancestor of King Saul (1 Chr. 8:8-9).

MESHACH [MEE shak] (meaning unknown) — the Chaldean name given to Mishael, one of Daniel's companions (Dan. 1:7). Along with SHADRACH and ABED-NEGO, Meshach would not bow down and worship the pagan image of gold set up by Nebuchadnezzar. They were cast into "the burning fiery furnace," but were preserved from harm by the power of God.

MESHECH [MEE shek] (*drawn out*) — the name of two men and two tribes in the Old Testament:

1. A son of Japheth (1 Chr. 1:5).

2. A son of Shem (1 Chr. 1:17), or possibly an unknown Aramean tribe, also spelled Mash (Gen. 10:23).

3. A tribe mentioned in association with Kedar (Ps. 120:5; Mesech, KJV).

4. The descendants of the son of Japheth known as the Moschi or Moschoi (Ezek. 27:13).

MESHELEMIAH [meh SHEL uh mye] (*Jehovah repays*) — a Levite gatekeeper of the tabernacle during David's reign (1 Chr. 9:21). He is also called Shelemiah (1 Chr. 26:14), Shallum (Ezra 2:42), and Meshullam (Neh. 12:25).

MESHEZABEEL [meh SHEZ uh beel] (*God delivers*) — the name of three men in the Book of Nehemiah:

1. An ancestor of Meshullam (Neh. 3:4).

2. One of the "leaders of the people" who sealed the covenant with Nehemiah (Neh. 10:21).

3. A descendant of Judah through Zerah (Neh. 11:24).

Any two or perhaps all three of these men may be identical. The NIV, NAS, NEB, and RSV translate Meshezabel.

MESHEZABEL [meh SHEZ uh bell] — a form of MESHEZABEEL.

MESHILLEMITH [meh SHILL uh meth] — a form of MESHILLEMOTH No. 2.

MESHILLEMOTH [meh SHILL uh moth] (*acts of repayment*) — the name of two men in the Old Testament:

1. A man of the tribe of Ephraim (2 Chr. 28:12).

2. A priest of the family of Immer (Neh. 11:13), also called Meshillemith (1 Chr. 9:12).

MESHOBAB [meh SHOH bab] (*restored*) — a leader of the tribe of Simeon in the days of Hezekiah, king of Judah (1 Chr. 4:34).

MESHULLAM [meh SHUHL um] (*friendship*) — the name of 21 men in the Old Testament:

1. An ancestor of Shaphan (2 Kin. 22:3).

2. A son of Zerubbabel and descendant of King Jehoiakim's son, Jeconiah (1 Chr. 3:19).

3. A leader of the tribe of Gad during the reign of Jotham of Judah (1 Chr. 5:13).

4. A man of the tribe of Benjamin listed in the family tree of King Saul (1 Chr. 8:17).

5. The father of Sallu of the tribe of Benjamin (Neh. 11:7).

6. A son of Shephatiah, of the tribe of Benjamin (1 Chr. 9:8).

7. A priest and member of an important priestly family (Neh. 11:11).

8. A priest of the house of Immer (1 Chr. 9:12).

9. A Levite of the Kohath family who helped oversee Temple repairs under King Josiah of Judah (2 Chr. 34:12).

10. A man whom Ezra sent to find Levites willing to go to Jerusalem after the Captivity (Ezra 8:16).

11. A man who opposed Ezra in the matter of divorcing pagan wives married during the Captivity (Ezra 10:15).

12. A descendant of Bani who divorced his pagan wife after the Captivity (Ezra 10:29).

13. A son of Berechiah who helped repair two sections of the Jerusalem wall (Neh. 3:4, 30).

14. A son of Besodeiah who helped repair the Jerusalem wall (Neh. 3:6).

15. A leader of the people who helped Ezra read the Law of Moses (Neh. 8:4).

16. A priest who sealed the covenant with Nehemiah (Neh. 10:7).

17. A leader of the people who sealed the covenant with Nehemiah (Neh. 10:20).

18. A priest of the family of Ezra in the time of the high priest Joiakim (Neh. 12:13).

19. Another priest in the time of Joiakim (Neh. 12:16).

20. A gatekeeper during the time of Joiakim (Neh. 12:25).

21. A prince of Judah who participated in the dedication of the Jerusalem wall (Neh. 12:33).

MESHULLEMETH [meh SHUHL uh meth] (*restitution*) — the wife of Manasseh, king of Judah (2 Kin. 21:19). Meshullemeth was the mother of Amon, Manasseh's son who succeeded him to the throne of Judah.

MESOBAITE [meh SOH buh eyt] — a form of MEZOBAITE.

MESOPOTAMIA [mess oh poh TAME ih uh] (*land between the rivers*) — a region situated between the Tigris and Euphrates Rivers; the general area inhabited by the ancient Babylonians. In the New Testament the word Mesopotamia refers to the areas between and around the Tigris and Euphrates Rivers, including ancient Syria, Accad, Babylonia, and Sumer. But in the Old Testament, Mesopotamia usually translates a phrase that means "Aram of the two rivers."

Abraham sent his servant to Nahor in Mesopotamia to find a bride for Isaac (Gen. 24:10). If Nahor refers to a city, it may be the same city, Nahur, that is mentioned in the MARI texts. The Mari texts are over 20,000 clay tablets dating from about 1750 B.C. from the city of Mari (modern Tell Hariri) on the Euphrates River near the border between modern Syria and Iraq. Many scholars believe Nahur was situated near ancient Haran.

The pagan prophet Balaam came from Pethor of Mesopotamia (Deut. 23:4). In the days of the judges, God sent "Cushan–Rishathaim king of Mesopotamia" to afflict the rebellious Hebrew people (Judg. 3:8, 10). This king's ethnic background has been much debated. He has been identified by various scholars with the Hittites, Mitanni, Horites (Hurrians), and the Habiru.

Later, when the Ammonites waged war against King David, they hired chariot and cavalry troops from Mesopotamia (1 Chr. 19:6). These troops may have been members of the warrior class that lived throughout Mesopotamia at that time.

Acts 2:9 refers to the Jews present at the Feast of Pentecost as "those dwelling in Mesopotamia." These people were probably from Jewish settlements in Babylonia such as Pumbeditha, Neherdea, Babylon, Ctesiphon, and Nippur.

Stephen spoke of Abraham's original home, Ur of the Chaldeans, as being situated in Mesopotamia (Acts 7:2). Ur lay far to the south near the Persian Gulf. Today most of Mesopotamia is in Iraq with small parts in Turkey and Syria.

MESSENGER (see OCCUPATIONS AND TRADES).

MESSIAH [meh SIGH uh] (*anointed one*) — the one anointed by God and empowered by God's spirit to deliver His people and establish His kingdom. In Jewish thought, the Messiah would be the king of the Jews, a political leader who would defeat their enemies and bring in a golden era of peace and prosperity. In Christian thought, the term Messiah refers to Jesus' role as a spiritual deliverer, setting His people free from sin and death.

The word Messiah comes from a Hebrew term that means "anointed one." Its Greek counterpart is *Christos*, from which the word Christ comes. Messiah was one of the titles used by early Christians to describe who Jesus was.

In Old Testament times, part of the ritual of commissioning a person for a special task was to anoint him with oil. The phrase anointed one was applied to a person in such cases. In the Old Testament, Messiah is used more than 30 times to describe kings (2 Sam. 1:14, 16), priests (Lev. 4:3, 5, 16), the patriarchs (Ps. 105:15), and even the Persian King Cyrus (Is. 45:1). The word is also used in connection with King David, who became the model of the messianic king who would come at the end of the age (2 Sam. 22:51; Ps. 2:2). But it was not until the time of Daniel (sixth century B.C.) that Messiah was used as an actual title of a king who would come in the future (Dan. 9:25–26). Still later, as the Jewish people struggled against their political enemies, the Messiah came to be thought of as a political, military ruler.

From the New Testament we learn more about the people's expectations. They thought the Messiah would come soon to perform signs (John 7:31) and to deliver His people, after which He would live and rule forever (John 12:34). Some even

Photo by Howard Vos

King Sargon of Accad established the first great empire in Mesopotamia, about 3500 B.C.

thought that John the Baptist was the Messiah (John 1:20). Others said that the Messiah was to come from Bethlehem (John 7:42). Most expected the Messiah to be a political leader, a king who would defeat the Romans and provide for the physical needs of the Israelites.

According to the Gospel of John, a woman of Samaria said to Jesus, "I know that Messiah is coming." Jesus replied, "I who speak to you am He" (John 4:25–26). In the Gospels of Matthew, Mark, and Luke, however, Jesus never directly referred to Himself as the Messiah, except privately to His disciples, until the crucifixion (Matt. 26:63–64; Mark 14:61–62; Luke 22:67–70). He did accept the title and function of messiahship privately (Matt. 16:16–17). Yet Jesus constantly avoided being called "Messiah" in public (Mark 8:29–30). This is known as Jesus' "messianic secret." He was the Messiah, but He did not want it known publicly.

The reason for this is that Jesus' kingdom was not political but spiritual (John 18:36). If Jesus had used the title "Messiah," people would have thought he was a political king. But Jesus understood that the Messiah, God's Anointed One, was to be the Suffering Servant (Is. 52:13—53:12). The fact that Jesus was a suffering Messiah—a crucified deliverer—was a "stumbling block" to many of the Jews (1 Cor. 1:23). They saw the cross as a sign of Jesus' weakness, powerlessness, and failure. They rejected the concept of a crucified Messiah.

But the message of the early church centered around the fact that the crucified and risen Jesus is the Christ (Acts 5:42; 17:3; 18:5). They proclaimed the "scandalous" gospel of a crucified Messiah as the power and wisdom of God (1 Cor. 1:23–24). John wrote, "Who is a liar but he who denies that Jesus is the Christ [the Messiah]?" (1 John 2:22).

By the time of the apostle Paul, "Christ" was in the process of changing from a title to a proper name. The name is found mostly in close association with the name "Jesus," as in "Christ Jesus" (Rom. 3:24) or "Jesus Christ" (Rom. 1:1). When the church moved onto Gentile soil, the converts lacked the Jewish background for understanding the title, and it lost much of its significance. Luke wrote, "The disciples were first called Christians [those who belong to and follow the Messiah] in Antioch" (Acts 11:26).

As the Messiah, Jesus is the divinely appointed king who brought God's kingdom to earth (Matt. 12:28; Luke 11:20). His way to victory was not by physical force and violence, but through love, humility, and service.

MESSIAS [muh SYE uhs] — Greek form of MESSIAH.

METALSMITH (see OCCUPATIONS AND TRADES).

METAL WORKER (see OCCUPATIONS AND TRADES).

METALS OF THE BIBLE. The metals used in Bible times were gold (Gen. 2:11–12), silver (Gen. 13:2), bronze (Gen. 4:22; Ex. 25:3), copper (Deut. 8:9; Job 28:2), iron (Gen. 4:22; Lev. 26:19), tin (Num. 31:22), and lead (Ezek. 22:18, 20; 27:12).

Gold was almost certainly the first metal known and used by man. But it was too soft to be used for tools or weapons. It was used mainly for jewelry and decorative purposes. The same was true of silver.

Copper was especially famous and widely used in ancient times. Until the dawn of the Iron Age (about 1200 B.C.), copper was the most practical metal in the Old Testament era. Like gold, native copper is also soft. But the metal workers of the ancient world discovered it hardened appreciably when hammered, and especially when alloyed with tin to produce bronze or with zinc to produce brass. These copper alloys were used for making weapons such as daggers, tools such as sickles, and all kinds of utensils (Ex. 38:3; Num. 16:39; Jer. 52:18).

When the Israelites stood on the threshold of the Promised Land, Moses addressed them with these words: "The Lord your God is bringing you into a good land...a land whose stones are iron and out of whose hills you can dig copper" (Deut. 8:7, 9). In the nation's later history, King Solomon established a copper-smelting industry at EZION GEBER, a city on the Red Sea at the northern end of the Gulf of Aqaba (1 Kin. 9:26; 22:48; 2 Chr. 8:17; 20:36).

Solomon's copper-smelting refineries at Ezion Geber were built strategically between the hills of Edom (to the east) and the hills of Palestine (to the

Golden bowls from the Mesopotamian city of Ur, dating from about 2500 B.C.
Photo by Howard Vos

west). They were ideally situated to take advantage of the draft caused by the strong winds sweeping down from the north.

Not until the time of King David, who broke the Philistine stranglehold over the land of Israel, was iron available to any great degree among the Israelites. During the reign of King Saul, the Philistines still held a monopoly in iron–smelting. The story is told in 1 Samuel 13:19–22: "Now there was no blacksmith to be found throughout all the land of Israel, for the Philistines said, 'Lest the Hebrews make swords or spears.' But the Israelites would go down to the Philistines to sharpen each man's plowshare, his matttock, his ax, and his sickle…So it came about, on the day of battle, that there was neither sword nor spear found in the hand of any of the people who were with Saul and Jonathan."

According to archaeological findings, the first smelting of iron occurred about 1400 B.C., probably among the Hittites of Asia Minor. Before the Philistines, the Hittites held the iron monopoly; apparently the Phoenicians (including the Philistines) learned the secret of iron–smelting from them.

Archaeological excavations have established that iron ores were occasionally smelted in Mesopotamia, near the Tigris and Euphrates Rivers, perhaps as early as 2700 B.C. For some unknown reason, however, the use of iron was not pursued. This metal did not come into general use, at least on a wide scale, until about 1200 B.C., at the beginning of the Early Iron Age.

The primitive method of smelting iron ore involved the use of charcoal and forced air in pits or furnaces. By this method, iron ore was reduced to metallic iron. Then the glowing ball of iron was pulled out of the furnace and hammered vigorously to expel the impurities and give the metal its intended shape (Deut. 4:20; 1 Kin. 8:51; Jer. 6:29; 11:4).

METEYARD (see WEIGHTS AND MEASURES).

METHEG AMMAH [METH eg AM uh] (meaning unknown) — a phrase of uncertain meaning in 2 Samuel 8:1. No such place as Metheg Ammah is known.

METHUSELAH [meh THUE zuh luh] (*man of the javelin*) — a son of Enoch and the grandfather of Noah. At the age of 187, Methuselah became the father of Lamech. After the birth of Lamech, Methuselah lived 782 years and died at the age of 969. He lived longer than any other human. He was an ancestor of Jesus (Luke 3:37; Mathusala, KJV).

METHUSHAEL [meh THUE sheh el] (*man of God*) — a son of Mehujael and the father of Lamech (Gen. 4:18).

MEUNIM, MEUNITES [meh YU nem, meh YU nights] (*habitations*) — an Arabian tribe that lived in and around their capital at Maon (Josh. 15:55), about 19 kilometers (12 miles) southeast of Petra. In the days of Hezekiah, the Meunites lived as strangers in the eastern end of the Valley of Gedor.

Photo by Howard Vos

Bronze head of the Greek god Zeus. In ancient times, bronze was an alloy of copper and tin.

One group of the Meunites was attacked and destroyed by the Simeonites (1 Chr. 4:39–41). Uzziah also fought against the Meunites (2 Chr. 26:7). After the Captivity, some of the descendants of the Meunim were employed as Temple servants in the Jerusalem Temple (Neh. 7:52; 2 Chr. 26:7; Mehunim).

MEZAHAB [MEZ uh hab] (*waters of gold*) — the father of Matred and grandfather of Mehetabel. Mehetabel was the wife of Hadar (Gen. 36:39), or Hadad (1 Chr. 1:50), king of Edom.

MEZOBAITE [meh ZOH bay ite] — a title or description of Jaasiel, one of David's mighty men (1 Chr. 11:47; Mesobaite, KJV). The word probably means "from Zobah."

MEZUZAH [meh ZU zah] (*doorpost*) — a small parchment scroll inscribed with Deuteronomy 6:4–9 and 11:13–21, placed in a container, and attached to the doorpost, as commanded in these passages from Deuteronomy.

MIAMIN [MYE uh min] — a form of MIJAMIN No. 4.

MIBHAR [MEB har] (*elite*) — a "son of Hagri," probably meaning a Hagrite—one of the nomadic peoples of Gilead. Mibhar was one of David's mighty men (1 Chr. 11:38).

MIBSAM [MEB sam] (*fragrance*) — the name of two men in the Old Testament:

1. A son of Ishmael (Gen. 25:13).
2. A descendant of Simeon (1 Chr. 4:25).

MIBZAR [MEB zar] (*fortress*) — an Edomite clan chief descended from Esau (Gen. 36:42).

MICAH [MIE kuh] (*Who is like Jehovah?*) — the name of seven men in the Old Testament:

1. A man from the mountains of Ephraim during the period of the judges in Israel's history. Micah's worship of false gods led the Danites into idolatry (Judges 17—18).

2. A descendant of Reuben (1 Chr. 5:5).

3. A son of Merib-Baal listed in the family tree of King Saul of Benjamin (1 Chr. 8:34—35; 9:40—41). Micah was the father of Pithon, Melech, Tarea (or Tahrea), and Ahaz. His father Merib-Baal (also called Mephibosheth, 2 Sam. 4:4) was a son of Jonathan and a grandson of Saul.

4. A son of Zichri and grandson of Asaph (1 Chr. 9:15). Micah is also called "Micha, the son of Zabdi" (Neh. 11:17; also Neh. 11:22) and "Michaiah, the son of Zaccur" (Neh. 12:35).

5. The father of Abdon (2 Chr. 34:20) or Achbor (2 Kin. 22:12). Abdon was one of five men whom King Josiah of Judah sent to inquire of Huldah the prophetess when Hilkiah the priest found the Book of the Law. Micah is also called Michaiah (2 Kin. 22:12).

6. An Old Testament prophet and author of the Book of Micah. A younger contemporary of the great prophet Isaiah, Micah was from Moresheth Gath (Mic. 1:1, 14), a town in southern Judah. His prophecy reveals his country origins; he uses many images from country life (Mic. 7:1).

Micah spoke out strongly against those who claimed to be prophets of the Lord but who used this position to lead the people of Judah into false hopes and further errors: "The sun shall go down on the prophets, and the day shall be dark for them" (Mic. 3:6). Micah's love for God would not allow him to offer false hopes to those who were under His sentence of judgment.

Little else is known about this courageous spokesman for the Lord. He tells us in his book that he prophesied during the reigns of three kings in Judah: Jotham, Ahaz, and Hezekiah (Mic. 1:1). This would place the time of his ministry from about 750 to 687 B.C.

Also see MICAH, BOOK OF.

MICAH, BOOK OF — a brief prophetic book of the Old Testament, known for its condemnation of the rich because of their exploitation of the poor. Micah also contains a clear prediction of the Messiah's birth in Bethlehem, centuries before Jesus was actually born in this humble little village. The book

---

MICAH: A Teaching Outline

takes its title from its author, the prophet Micah, whose name means, "Who is like Jehovah?"

Structure of the Book. Micah is a short book of only seven chapters, but it stands as a classic example of the work to which the Old Testament prophets were called. Over and over again, Micah sounds the theme of God's judgment against his homeland, Judah, as well as her sister nation, Israel, because of their moral decline. Micah watched as the Assyrians grew in strength and marched their armies throughout the ancient world. It was clear to him that this pagan nation would serve as the instrument of God's judgment unless Judah and Israel turned back to God.

Micah also is known as the champion of the oppressed. He condemns wealthy landowners for taking the land of the poor (2:2). He also attacks dishonest merchants for using false weights, bribing judges, and charging excessive interest rates. Even the priests and prophets seemed to be caught up in this tidal wave of greed and dishonesty that swept his country. To a people more concerned about observing rituals than living a life of righteousness, Micah thundered, "He has shown you, O man, what is good; and what does the Lord require of you but to do justly, to love mercy, and to walk humbly with your God?" (6:8). This is one of the greatest passages in the Old Testament. It expresses the timeless truth that authentic worship consists of following God's will and dealing justly with other people.

In addition to the theme of judgment, Micah also emphasizes the reality of God's love. Practically every passage about God's wrath is balanced with a promise of God's blessing. The greatest promise in the book is a prophecy of the birth of the Messiah: "But you, Bethlehem Ephrathah, though you are little among the thousands of Judah, yet out of you shall come forth to Me the One to be ruler in Israel" (5:2). This messianic verse is stunning in its accuracy because it names the specific town where the Messiah was born—the village of Bethlehem in the territory of the tribe of Judah. This prophecy was fulfilled about 700 years after Micah's time with the birth of Jesus in Bethlehem.

The final two chapters of Micah's book are presented in the form of a debate between God and His people. God invites the nations of Israel and Judah to reason with Him on the subject of their conduct. He convinces them that their sin is deep and grievous, but He assures them of His presence in spite of their unworthiness.

Authorship and Date. This book was written by the prophet Micah, a native of the village of Moresheth (1:1) in southern Judah near the Philistine city of Gath. Since Micah championed the rights of the poor, he was probably a humble farmer or herdsman himself, although he shows a remarkable knowledge of Jerusalem and Samaria, the capital cities of the nations of Judah and Israel. Micah also tells us that he prophesied "in the days of Jotham, Ahaz, and Hezekiah, kings of Judah" (1:1). The reigns of these three kings stretched from

about 750 B.C. to 687 B.C.; so his book was probably written sometime during this period.

Historical Setting. The Book of Micah belongs to that turbulent period during which the Assyrians launched their drive for supremacy throughout the ancient world. Micah probably saw his prophecy of judgment against Israel fulfilled, since the Assyrians defeated this nation in 722 B.C. The fall of Israel to the north must have stunned the citizens of Judah. Would they be the next to fall before the conquering armies of this pagan nation? Still, the religious leaders retreated into a false confidence that no evil would befall them because the Temple was situated in their capital city of Jerusalem (3:11). Micah warned there was no magical saving power in their Temple or their rituals (3:12). They needed to turn back to God as their source of strength and power.

Theological Contribution. The mixture of judgment and promise in the Book of Micah is a striking characteristic of the Old Testament prophets. These contrasting passages give real insight into the character of God. In His wrath He remembers mercy; He cannot maintain His anger forever. Judgment with love is the ironic, but essential, work of the Lord. In the darkest days of impending judgment on Israel and Judah, there always was the possibility that a remnant would be spared. God was determined to maintain His holiness, and so He acted in judgment on those who had broken His covenant. But He was just as determined to fulfill the promises He had made to Abraham centuries earlier. This compelled Him to point to the fulfillment of the covenant in the kingdom to come.

Perhaps the greatest contribution of the Book of Micah is its clear prediction of a coming Savior. The future Messiah is referred to indirectly in some of the prophetic books of the Old Testament. But He is mentioned directly in the Book of Micah.

This prophecy of the Messiah's birth is remarkable when we think of the circumstances that were necessary to bring it to fulfillment. Although they were residents of Nazareth, Mary and Joseph happened to be in Bethlehem at the right time when the Messiah was born about 700 years after Micah's prediction. This is a valuable lesson on the providence of God. He always manages to work His will through a unique combination of forces and events.

Special Considerations. Micah begins his words of judgment with calls for the people to come to court. God is portrayed as the prosecuting attorney, the witness for the prosecution, and the sentencing judge. God is a witness against His people (1:2); He demands justice (3:1); He even calls upon the elements of creation to be His witnesses, since He has a legal dispute against His people (6:1–2). This type of language is also found in the Book of Isaiah (Is. 1:2). It is likely that Isaiah and Micah drew this terminology from the Book of Deuteronomy (Deut. 31:28). The clear implication is that God has the right to hold His people accountable for their behavior.

God insists that His people keep their part of the covenant agreement. But even while making His demands, He holds out the possibility of grace and forgiveness. This leads his Covenant People to declare: "You will cast all our sins into the depths of the sea. You will give truth to Jacob and mercy to Abraham, which You have sworn to our fathers from days of old" (7:19–20).

MICAIAH [mie KAY yah] (*who is like Jehovah?*) — the prophet who predicted the death of King Ahab of Israel in the battle against the Syrians at Ramoth Gilead (1 Kin. 22:8–28; 2 Chr. 18:7–27). Ahab gathered about 400 prophets, apparently all in his employment. They gave their unanimous approval to Ahab's proposed attack against the Syrian King, Ben-Hadad.

King Jehoshaphat of Judah was unconvinced by this display. He asked, "Is there not still a prophet of the Lord here, that we may inquire of Him?" (1 Kin. 22:7; 2 Chr. 18:6). Ahab replied, "There is still one man, Micaiah the son of Imlah, by whom we may inquire of the Lord; but I hate him, because he does not prophesy good concerning me, but evil" (1 Kin. 22:8; 2 Chr. 18:7). The prophet Micaiah was then summoned.

When Ahab asked this prophet's advice, Micaiah answered, "Go and prosper, for the Lord will deliver it into the hand of the king!" (1 Kin. 22:15; 2 Chr. 18:14).

Micaiah's answer was heavy with sarcasm, irony, and contempt. Ahab realized he was being mocked; so he commanded him to speak nothing but the truth. Micaiah then said, "I saw all Israel scattered on the mountains as sheep that have no shepherd" (1 Kin. 22:17; 2 Chr. 18:16). Ahab turned to Jehoshaphat and said, "Did I not tell you that he would not prophesy good concerning me, but evil?" (1 Kin. 22:18; 2 Chr. 18:17).

Zedekiah then struck Micaiah on the cheek and accused him of being a liar. Ahab commanded that Micaiah be put in prison until the king's victorious return from Ramoth Gilead. Then Micaiah said, "If you ever return...the Lord has not spoken by me" (1 Kin. 22:28; 2 Chr. 18:27).

Ahab did not return; he died at Ramoth Gilead, just as Micaiah had predicted.

MICE (see ANIMALS OF THE BIBLE).

MICHA [MY kuh] (*who is like Jehovah?*) — the name of three men in the Old Testament:
1. A son of Mephibosheth (2 Sam. 9:12).
2. A Levite who sealed the covenant with Nehemiah (Neh. 10:11).
3. A Levite descended from Asaph (Neh. 11:17, 22), also called Micah (1 Chr. 9:15).

MICHAEL [MIE kay el] (*who is like God?*) — the name of ten men and an archangel in the Bible:
1. The father of Sethur (Num. 13:13). Sethur was a representative of the tribe of Asher among the 12 spies sent by Moses to spy out the land of Canaan.
2. A descendant of Gad who settled in Bashan (1 Chr. 5:11–13).

3. Another descendant of Gad (1 Chr. 5:14).
4. A Levite of the family of Gershon (1 Chr. 6:40). He was an ancestor of Asaph the singer.
5. A chief man of the tribe of Issachar, family of Tola, house of Uzzi (1 Chr. 7:3).
6. One of the sons of Beriah (1 Chr. 8:16). Michael is mentioned in the family tree of King Saul of Benjamin.
7. A warrior from the tribe of Manasseh. He joined David at Ziklag (1 Chr. 12:20).
8. The father of Omri (1 Chr. 27:18).
9. A son of Jehoshaphat, king of Judah (2 Chr. 21:2). Michael was a brother of Jehoram, king of Judah.
10. The father of Zebadiah, of the family of Shephatiah (Ezra 8:8).
11. An archangel, or an angel of high rank, who served as prince or guardian over the destinies of the nation of Israel (Dan. 10:21; 12:1). According to the Epistle of Jude, Michael disputed with Satan over the body of Moses (Jude 9). This reference is a puzzle to scholars, because the incident to which Jude refers does not appear anywhere in the Old Testament. The Book of Revelation speaks of "Michael and his angels" (Rev. 12:7), who struggled with Satan when the devil rebelled against God at the beginning of time.

MICHAH [MY kuh] (*who is like Jehovah?*) — a Levite during David's reign (1 Chr. 23:20).

MICHAIAH [my KYE uh] (*who is like Jehovah?*) — the name of four men and one woman in the Old Testament:
1. An officer of King Josiah of Judah (2 Kin. 22:12).
2. The wife of King Rehoboam and mother of King Abijah (2 Chr. 13:1–2).
3. A leader sent by Jehoshaphat, king of Judah, to teach the Law in the cities of Judah (2 Chr. 17:7).
4. A priest who blew a trumpet during the celebration after Jerusalem's walls were rebuilt (Neh. 12:35, 41).
5. A son of Gemariah (Jer. 36:11, 13).

MICHAL [MY kul] (*who is like God?*) — the younger daughter of King Saul who became David's wife. After David had become a hero by slaying GOLIATH, Saul offered to give Michal to David as his wife. But instead of a dowry, Saul requested of David "one hundred foreskins of the Philistines" (1 Sam. 18:25), hoping that David would be killed by the Philistines.

Instead, David won an impressive victory. He and his warriors killed 200 Philistines and brought their foreskins to the king. Then Saul presented Michal to David to become his wife (1 Sam. 18:27–28).

After their marriage, the ARK OF THE COVENANT was brought from the house of Obed-Edom to the City of David. Caught up in an inspired frenzy of religious fervor, David was filled with joy at being able to bring the ark back to Jerusalem. "Then David danced before the Lord with all his might;

and David was wearing [only] a linen ephod [loincloth, kilt, or apron]" (2 Sam. 6:14). Whatever garment David was wearing, it apparently scandalized Michal, who accused him of lewd, base behavior—of "uncovering himself in the eyes of the maids" (2 Sam. 6:20).

Michal's withering sarcasm was met by David's devastating response. In effect he said, "My dance was a dance of joy, faith, and happiness in the Lord. Where is your joy in the Lord? Why do you not dance also?" By judging and condemning David, Michal had revealed a lack of love in her soul. Michal died barren (2 Sam. 6:21-23)—one of the most terrible fates that could befall a Hebrew woman.

MICHMASH [MICK mash] (*a hidden place*) — a city of Benjamin about 11 kilometers (7 miles) northeast of Jerusalem which figured prominently in the early history of Saul's reign.

According to 1 Samuel 13:2, Saul gathered an army of 3,000 men in an attempt to meet the Philistine threat. Two thousand of the men were under Saul's personal command at Michmash, and 1,000 men were under the command of Jonathan at nearby Gibeah of Benjamin.

When the Philistines moved toward Michmash, Saul fled to Gilgal where many of his soldiers deserted him. In a display of impatience and irreverence, Saul offered a sacrifice to the Lord and was severely rebuked by Samuel (1 Sam. 13:5-15). Saul then returned to Gibeah. While "Saul was sitting in the outskirts of Gibeah under a pomegranate tree" (1 Sam. 14:2), Jonathan and his armorbearer scaled the northern cliff of the gorge of Michmash. By this daring tactical maneuver, they were able to kill the enemy sentries and throw the entire Philistine camp into panic.

Several centuries later, Ezra recorded that 122 men of Michmash returned from the Captivity (Ezra 2:27; Michmas, NKJV).

MICHMETHATH [MICK meh thath] (meaning unknown) — an unknown place on the border of Ephraim and Manasseh.

MICHRI [MICK rye] (*purchase price*) — a descendant of Benjamin and an ancestor of Elah (1 Chr. 9:8).

MICHTAM [MICK tam] (meaning unknown) — a word occurring in the heading of six psalms (Psalm 16; 56—60; Miktam, RSV, NIV; Mikhtam, NAS). Its meaning is uncertain. The word may be a musical term indicating how the psalm should be sung.

MIDDAY — the middle part of the day; noon, or the time around noon (Neh. 8:3; Acts 26:13). Also see TIME.

MIDDIN [MID in] (*judgment*) — a town or village in the Wilderness of Judah, near the Dead Sea (Josh. 15:61).

MIDDLE GATE (see GATES OF JERUSALEM AND THE TEMPLE).

MIDDLE WALL — a barrier or partition that divided the inner court of the TEMPLE, open only to Jews, from the COURT OF THE GENTILES. The Jewish historian Josephus described this partition as a stone wall, inscribed with warnings to Gentiles not to enter the holy place of the Temple, under threat of death.

The "middle wall of partition" between Jews and Gentiles existed spiritually as well as physically. The Law of Moses, especially the practice of circumcision and the food laws, erected a barrier of hostility and contempt between the two peoples. The Jewish people scorned the Gentiles who were "without the law" and rejoiced in their superior religious traditions. Christ, however, "has made both one, and has broken down the middle wall of division between us" (Eph. 2:14).

MIDIAN [MID ee un] — the name of a man and a territory in the Old Testament:

1. A son of Abraham by his concubine Keturah (Gen. 25:1-6). Midian had four sons (1 Chr. 1:33). No other information about him is recorded in the Bible.

2. The land inhabited by the descendants of Midian. Situated east of the Jordan River and the Dead Sea, the land stretched southward through the Arabian desert as far as the southern and eastern parts of the peninsula of Sinai.

MIDIANITES [MID ee un ites] — a nomadic people who were enemies of the Israelites in Old Testament times. The Midianites were distantly related to the Israelites, since they sprang from MIDIAN, one of the sons of Abraham. But they usually were foes rather than friends of the Hebrew people. Abraham sent the children of Midian "to the country of the east" (Gen. 25:6) which probably included the desert fringes of Moab, Edom, and perhaps parts of the Sinai Peninsula. They are known thereafter in the Old Testament as one of the "people of the East" (Judg. 6:3, 33), or inhabitants of the desert regions of southern Syria and western Arabia.

The Midianites were at least loosely associated with others of this group, including the Ishmaelites (Gen. 37:28; Judg. 8:24). Midianite travelers bought Joseph from his brothers and resold him in Egypt (Gen. 37:25-36). Moses married into a Midianite family (specifically an associated group known as the Kenites) in "the land of Midian" (Ex. 2:15). His wife Zipporah and his father-in-law Jethro were Midianites (Ex. 2:21; 3:1). But this was the last friendly connection the Israelites had with the Midianites.

After the time of Moses, the Midianites consistently opposed the Israelites. They joined with the Moabites, in whose territory they had partly settled, in hiring the prophet-magician Balaam to curse Israel (Num. 22:4, 7). At Moab, just before the conquest of Canaan, the Midianites were among those who practiced sexual immorality as part of the ritual of their idolatrous religion. They involved some of the Israelites in this idolatry, caus-

Arab bedouin tents in the land of Midian, where Moses fled after killing an Egyptian (Ex. 2:11-15).

ing God's judgment to come upon His people (Num. 25:1-9). Because of this the Midianites were singled out for destruction (Num. 25:16-18).

Perhaps the most serious Midianite threat to Israel came during the days of the judges, about 1100 B.C., when Midianite warriors invaded Palestine. They came on camels, never before used in combat. The Israelites were driven into the hill country as the Midianites and other easterners raided their territory, plundering crops and cattle for seven years (Judg. 6:1-6).

Then God raised up Gideon to deliver Israel from the Midianites. He and the Ephraimites drove off the Midianites, capturing Oreb and Zeeb, two of their princes (Judg. 7:24-25), and pursuing escapees across the Jordan River to the desert fringes where their kings Zebah and Zalmunna were captured (Judg. 8:10-12). Gideon's great victory was mentioned in several later Old Testament passages as an example of God's deliverance of his people from oppression (Ps. 83:9, 11; Is. 9:4; 10:26).

MIDNIGHT — the middle of the night; specifically 12 o'clock at night (Judg. 16:3; Ps. 119:62; Acts 16:25). The word midnight is often used symbolically of a period resembling midnight, a time of intense darkness or extended gloom. It was at midnight that the Lord struck down all the firstborn in the land of Egypt (Ex. 11:4; 12:29). Also see TIME.

MIDRASH [MID rash] (*inquiry*) — any of a group of Jewish commentaries on the Hebrew Scriptures written between A.D. 400 and A.D. 1200. The word Midrash is based on a Hebrew word that means "to search out." The implication is that of discovering a thought or truth not seen on the surface—therefore a study, commentary, or homiletical exposition.

These commentaries are a collection of public sermons, stories, legal discussions, and meditations on the books of the Bible used during the festivals for public worship in the synagogues. Midrashim (plural of Midrash) were written in Israel and Babylon by the rabbis. Some Midrashim are contained in the Babylonian TALMUD; others are part of independent collections of commentaries.

There are two types of Midrash: Halakah ("law" or "tradition"), an interpretation of the laws of the Scriptures, and Haggadah ("narration"), the nonlegal, or homiletical, part of the Talmud.

MIDWIFE (see OCCUPATIONS AND TRADES).

MIGDAL EL [MIG dal el] (*tower of God*) — a fortified city in the territory of Naphtali (Josh. 19:38), listed between Iron (Yiron, NAS) and Horem. The exact site of Migdal El is unknown.

MIGDAL GAD [MIG dal gad] — (*tower of fortune*) — a town in or near the SHEPHELAH, or lowland plain, of Judah, perhaps near Lachish (Josh. 15:37).

MIGDOL [MIG dahl] (*watchtower, fortress*) — the name of two Egyptian sites in the Old Testament:

1. An encampment of the Israelites while they were leaving Egypt in the Exodus led by Moses (Ex. 14:2). It is impossible to identify this site precisely. But Migdol clearly lay west of the Red Sea in the eastern region of the Nile Delta.

2. A site in northeastern Egypt (Jer. 44:1; 46:14). After the destruction of Jerusalem by the Babylonians under Nebuchadnezzar, some Israelites fled to Egypt and lived in Migdol.

MIGHTY MEN — the brave warriors who risked their lives for David both before and after he became king of Israel. The names of David's mighty men are given in 2 Samuel 23:8–39 and 1 Chronicles 11:10–47. The term mighty men of valor is also used of the courageous warriors who served under Joshua (Josh. 1:14; 6:2).

MIGRON [MIG rahn] (*meaning unknown*) — the name of two towns in the Old Testament:

1. A town in Benjamin on the outskirts of Gibeah south of Michmash (1 Sam. 14:2).

2. A town of Benjamin (Is. 10:28). The prophet Isaiah mentioned this site in his account of the march of the Assyrian army upon Jerusalem.

MIJAMIN [MEJ uh min] (*on the right hand*) — the name of several men in the Old Testament:

1. A descendant of Aaron and leader of a course of priests in David's time (1 Chr. 24:9).

2. A son of Parosh (Ezra 10:25; Miamin, KJV) who divorced his pagan wife after the Captivity.

3. A priest who sealed the covenant (Neh. 10:7). Perhaps he was the Minjamin (Neh. 12:41) who was one of the trumpeters at the dedication of the wall of Jerusalem.

4. A chief of the priests who returned with Zerubbabel from Babylon (Neh. 12:5; Miamin, KJV), also called Minjamin (Neh. 12:17).

MIKHTAM [MICK tam] — a form of MICHTAM.

MIKLOTH [MICK lawth] (*sticks*) — the name of two men in the Old Testament:

1. A descendant of Jeiel, of the tribe of Benjamin (1 Chr. 8:32).

2. An officer who served under Dodai in David's army (1 Chr. 27:4).

MIKNEIAH [mick NYE uh] (*possession of Jehovah*) — a Levite harpist during the reign of David (1 Chr. 15:18, 21).

MIKTAM [MICK tam] — a form of MICHTAM.

MILALAI [MILL uh lye] (*eloquent*) — a musician who participated in the dedication of the wall of Jerusalem in Nehemiah's time (Neh. 12:36).

MILCAH [MILL kuh] (*queen*) — the name of two women in the Old Testament:

1. A daughter of Haran and the wife of Nahor (Gen. 22:20–22).

2. One of the five daughters of Zelophehad, of the tribe of Manasseh. Zelophehad had no sons. When he died, his daughters asked Moses for permission to share their father's inheritance. Their request was granted, providing they married within their own tribe in order to keep the inheritance within Manasseh (Num. 36:11–12).

MILCOM [MILL kahm] (see GODS, PAGAN).

MILDEW — a fungus that attacked the crops of Palestine in damp weather. This blight was interpreted as God's judgment upon the people's disobedience (Deut. 28:22). In King Solomon's prayer of dedication at the completion of the Temple, he prayed for deliverance from mildew and other calamities (2 Chr. 6:28).

MILE (see WEIGHTS AND MEASURES).

MILETUS [my LEE tuhs] — an ancient seaport in Asia Minor visited by the apostle Paul (Act 20:15, 17; 2 Tim. 4:20; Miletum, KJV). Situated on the shore of the Mediterranean Sea, Miletus was about 60 kilometers (37 miles) south of Ephesus and on the south side of the Bay of Latmus (see Map 8, C–2). Because of silting, the site is now more than eight kilometers (five miles) from the coast.

Colonized by Cretans and others, Miletus be-

A harbor monument on the site of ancient Miletus, a city visited by the apostle Paul (Acts 20:13-16).

Photo by Howard Vos

came a leading harbor during the Greek and Persian periods. It prospered economically and boasted a celebrated temple of Apollo. Although Miletus was still an important trade center in Roman times, the river was already silting in the harbor.

The apostle Paul visited Miletus on his journey from Greece to Jerusalem. In Miletus Paul delivered a farewell message to the elders of the church of Ephesus (Acts 10:18–35).

MILK — a nutritious foodstuff in liquid form that comes from goats, cows, sheep, and camels. Next to bread, dairy products were a staple item in the diet of the Hebrew people. Drunk fresh as a beverage, milk was also used in a variety of forms as a major food source.

Two different Hebrew words are translated as milk in English versions of the Bible. The first describes liquid milk, drunk by the Hebrews fresh, shortly after milking. Because of the high temperatures of Palestine, this kind of milk would not keep long without some kind of treatment.

Cultured milk, similar to yogurt, has a longer life in this climate. This is the kind of milk intended when English translations render the second Hebrew word as "butter" (Gen. 18:8), or "curds" (Is. 7:22). Milk is also used symbolically in the Bible to depict plenty and abundance (Ex. 3:17; Deut. 26:15).

MILL (see Tools of the Bible).

MILLENNIUM, THE — the thousand-year period mentioned in connection with the description of Christ's coming to reign with His saints over the earth (Rev. 19:11–16; 20:1–9). Many Old Testament passages refer to the millennium (Is. 11:4; Jer. 3:17; Zech. 14:9).

These and many other Old Testament passages are often taken to refer only to the thousand-year period itself. However, it is often difficult in these passages to see a clear dividing line between the earthly period of the millennium and the eternal state of new heavens and earth. Therefore, it is best to let one's teaching about the millennium be drawn specifically from the words in Revelation 20. The other great promises to Israel, while they have a temporary fulfillment in the thousand years, still await the fulness of the new heavens and new earth and the unhindered presence of Israel's king and the church's husband—Jesus Christ our Lord.

During that thousand-year period, Satan will be bound in the bottomless pit so he will not deceive the nations until his short period of release (Rev. 20:3, 7–8). The faithful martyrs who have died for the cause of Christ will be resurrected before the millennium. They will rule with Christ and will be priests of God and Christ (Rev. 5:10; 20:4). The unbelieving dead will wait for the second resurrection (Rev. 20:5). After the thousand years, Satan will be released and will resume his work of deceit (Rev. 20:7–8).

The most important aspect of the millennium is the reign of Christ. Peter taught that Christ now rules from the right hand of God (Acts 2:33–36). That rule will last until His enemies are made His footstool (Ps. 110:1). The apostle Paul also understood Christ to be presently reigning in a period designed to bring all of God's enemies underfoot (1 Cor. 15:25–27). Thus the impact of Christ's present rule over the earth from God's right hand must not be seen as unrelated to His future reign during the millennium.

The millennium is viewed by interpreters in several different ways. One position holds that the millennium only refers to Christ's spiritual rule today from heaven. This symbolic view is known as the amillennial interpretation. Another position views Christ's spiritual rule as working through preaching and teaching to bring gradual world improvement leading up to Christ's return. This is the postmillennial view.

The position that holds to an actual thousand-year period in the future is known as the premillennial view. This interpretation does not diminish the power of Christ's present rule from heaven or limit that rule to the church only. That position sees the need for a thousand-year place in history for an earthly fulfillment of Israel's promises of land and blessing. It stresses that the one thousand years in Revelation 20 are actual years and are not symbolic.

MILLET (see Plants of the Bible).

MILLO [MILL oh] (*mound*)—a fortification or citadel near Jerusalem. The Millo of Jerusalem was probably part of the fortification of the Jebusite city that David captured. It may have been either a solid tower full of earth or a bastion strengthening a weak point in the wall. It was already in existence when David's army captured the Jebusite city (2 Sam. 5:9).

The Millo was one of the building projects included in King Solomon's expansion program in Jerusalem in later years. He strengthened the Millo by using conscripted labor (1 Kin. 9:15). Centuries later, King Hezekiah had the Millo repaired in preparation for an invasion and siege by the Assyrians (2 Chr. 32:5). King Joash was killed "in the house of the Millo" (2 Kin. 12:20)—the victim of a conspiracy.

Also see Beth Millo.

MINA (see Weights and Measures).

MIND — the part of a person that thinks and reasons. Although the Hebrew language had no word for mind, several Hebrew words are sometimes translated as "mind." The word for Heart frequently means "mind" (Deut. 30:1; Jer. 19:5). The word for Soul is sometimes used similarly (1 Chr. 28:9), as is the word for Spirit (Ezek. 11:5). No Hebrew word is translated as brain in English versions of the Bible.

Four separate Greek words account for nearly all instances of "mind" in the New Testament. They all mean much the same thing: understanding, thought, mind, reason. While today we think of a person's mind in a morally neutral way, in the New Testament the mind was clearly thought of as either good or evil. Negatively, the mind may be "hardened" (2 Cor. 3:14), "blinded" (2 Cor. 4:4), "corrupt" (2 Tim. 3:8), and "debased" (Rom. 1:28). On the positive side, humans may have minds which are renewed (Rom. 12:2) and pure (2 Pet. 3:1). They may love God with all their minds (Matt. 22:37; Mark 12:30; Luke 10:27) and have God's laws implanted in their minds (Heb. 8:10). Since Christians have "the mind of Christ" (1 Cor. 2:16), they are instructed to be united in mind (Rom. 12:16; 1 Pet. 3:8).

MINER (see OCCUPATIONS AND TRADES; MINES, MINING).

MINERALS OF THE BIBLE. Minerals are inorganic substances found in the earth's crust. The Bible mentions many of these minerals, which include metallic and non–metallic rock, sand, clay, soils, salt, and most gemstones. Minerals existed in a variety of colors and degrees of hardness. They were often valued for these characteristics by the people of Bible lands. No one knows exactly how many minerals exist in the earth today, but estimates range between 1,500 and 3,000. Only a small percentage of these were known in the ancient world, and only a few are mentioned in the Bible.

The land of Palestine and surrounding areas were rich in minerals. These minerals provided the people of the Bible not only with food to eat but also with the material for houses, farming implements, household utensils, weapons, art, personal ornaments, medical supplies, and objects for religious purposes. The discovery and use of these minerals helped shape the cultural life of the ancient world.

The Bible mentions six metals known and used by the ancient Hebrews: gold, silver, bronze, iron, tin, and lead (Num. 31:22). Job's reference to metals "taken from the earth" (Job 28:2) seems to indicate a firsthand knowledge of mine operations. The smelting of ores was known apparently in very ancient times. Copper was the first metal smelted by the Egyptians, about 4500 B.C.

Palestine acquired much of its mineral resources through spoils of war (Josh. 22:8) and through trade with foreign countries. This trade reached its greatest height during Solomon's time (1 Kin. 10:10–11, 22, 27). These minerals proved to be a valuable asset to the physical, material, and spiritual welfare of the people of Bible lands.

The following minerals are mentioned in the Bible. This list is keyed to the New King James translation, with cross references from five additional popular versions: KJV, NASB, NEB, NIV, and RSV.

Alabaster. The most common form of alabaster is a fine textured variety of massive gypsum (sulfate of lime). It is very soft and therefore excellent for carving. The color is usually white; but it may be gray, yellow, or red.

Large quantities of gypsum were quarried in the Jordan Valley in the days before the Hebrew people occupied this territory. Many articles were fashioned from this stone, including vases, jars, saucers, bowls, lamps, and statues. Mary of Bethany anointed Jesus with costly oil from a flask made of alabaster (Matt. 26:7; Mark 14:3; Luke 7:37). Her willingness to express her love unselfishly won Christ's approval, just as He honors sacrificial expressions of love today.

The ancient variety of alabaster is known as "oriental alabaster" (carbonate of lime), a form of marble. It is much harder than the gypsum variety but is used for the same purpose. Ancient alabaster was found only in Egypt.

Antimony. A hard mineral, metallic gray in color, usually classed as a metal. In Bible times antimony was ground into a fine black powder, moistened with oil or water, and used as eye–paint to accent the eyelashes and make them appear larger (Jer. 4:30). This was an accepted custom in Egypt and Mesopotamia, but it was rejected by the Hebrew people, although Jezebel and other women of ill repute used it (2 Kin. 9:30).

The prophets Jeremiah and Ezekiel compared Israel to unfaithful women who adorned themselves with paint for their lovers (Jer. 4:30; Ezek. 23:40). The material which David furnished for the Temple included antimony. This was mixed with resin and used as a setting for gems (1 Chr. 29:2, RSV).

Ash (see *Lime*).

Asphalt. A black mineral substance, a form of bitumen, derived from crude petroleum (Gen. 11:3; Ex. 2:3). It was found in Mesopotamia and Palestine, especially in the Dead Sea region. Because of the abundance of asphalt around the Dead Sea, the Greeks and Romans referred to it as Lake Asphaltitis (Gen. 14:10). Other versions translate the word for asphalt as bitumen, slime, tar, or clay. Also see *Bitumen*; *Clay*.

Bitumen. A mineral substance consisting chiefly of hydrogen and carbon. Mineral pitch and asphalt are forms of bitumen. Highly flammable, its consistency varies from solids to semi–liquids (Is. 34:9). Large deposits of bitumen have been known to exist around the Dead Sea, and in Egypt and Mesopotamia since ancient times.

Bitumen was used as caulking to waterproof Noah's ark (Gen. 6:14) and the basket in which Moses was hidden (Ex. 2:3). It was also used as mortar (Gen. 11:3). The pits into which the kings of Sodom and Gomorrah fell were bitumen pits (Gen. 14:10, RSV). Various English versions of the Bible translate the word for bitumen as asphalt, slime, tar, or pitch. Also see *Asphalt*.

Brass. True brass is an alloy of copper and zinc. However, when brass is mentioned in the Bible, it generally refers to either copper or bronze (1 Cor. 13:1; Rev. 1:15; 2:18; 9:20). The three words, brass, bronze, and copper, are often used interchangeably in various English translations of the Bible.

Copper was in general use around 4500 B.C. Numerous refineries have been discovered in Sinai,

Photo by Gustav Jeeninga

An alabaster sphinx in Egypt. A type of marble, alabaster was often used in the construction of buildings and statues throughout the ancient world.

Armenia, Syria, and many other places in the ancient world. Although zinc was deposited in limestone and dolomite rock and was probably available in Bible lands, it is not certain when it first was alloyed with copper to make brass.

Many articles in the ancient world were fashioned from bronze, or brass. These included cooking utensils, shovels, spoons, musical instruments, weapons, and tools. Solomon used copper and bronze in many of the items in the Temple (1 Kin. 7:14). Also see *Copper*.

Brimstone. A bright yellow mineral usually found near active volcanoes. Large deposits of this substance are found in the Dead Sea region. Highly combustible, it burns with a very disagreeable odor.

The Hebrew and Greek words for brimstone denote divine fire (Gen. 19:24; Ezek. 38:22; Luke 17:29). Brimstone (burning stone) is often associated with fire (Rev. 9:17–18; 20:10; 21:8), and with barrenness and devastation (Deut. 29:23; Job 18:15). Brimstone was considered an agent of God's judgment (Gen. 19:24). In the New Testament it is used symbolically to represent God's wrath and the future punishment of the wicked (Rev. 9:17–18; 14:10; 20:10). Another word for brimstone used in various translations of the Bible is sulphur, or sulfur.

Bronze (see *Brass; Tin*).

Chalkstone. A variety of fine-grained limestone rock, chalkstone (or chalk) is a soft porous material consisting largely of calcite. It is usually white, but it can be yellow or gray. Limestone is the dominant stone in Palestine and other Bible lands. The He-

brews burned limestone in kilns to make lime (Is. 33:12). Also see *Lime*.

The prophet Isaiah spoke of chalkstone in a figurative sense to illustrate God's readiness to remove Israel's guilt if they would make their altars "like chalkstone beaten to dust" (Is. 27:9).

Chrysolite Marble (see *Marble*).

Clay. Soil that consists of extremely fine particles of sand, flint, or quartz. Some clays were formed of soft limestone with much grit and flint, while others included quartz which formed a much harder clay.

Clay was used widely in the ancient world. Archaeologists have found many clay objects dating from about 5000 B.C. at Jericho. Among its many uses, clay was an important building material. The Tower of Babel was constructed of clay bricks (Gen. 11:3). The poorest quality clay was used in making bricks. Both sun-baked and kiln-fired bricks were known (2 Sam. 12:31). Mortar was also usually made of clay. The Hebrew word for clay is translated by some English versions as asphalt.

Impressions were made into wet clay with signet rings or cylinder seals to prove ownership (Job 38:14; Dan. 6:17). Clay seals were placed on houses, vessels of various kinds, and perhaps on Christ's tomb (Matt. 27:66).

Clay tablets were used in Mesopotamia for cuneiform writing. Letters were pressed into soft clay with a stylus. The tablet was then sun-baked or kiln-fired to increase its strength. Various kinds of pottery were made of clay. These included lamps, cooking utensils, pots, vases, jars, dishes, and idols. Also see *Asphalt*.

Coal. A black, porous form of carbon (Lam. 4:8) or live embers of any kind (2 Sam. 22:9, 13). The Hebrew people learned to form charcoal by burning wood which had been covered by earth and leaves. The lack of air caused the wood to char. According to the prophet Isaiah, cedars, cypress, and oak were some of the trees used for fuel (Is. 44:14–16). Broom or juniper bushes were also used for charcoal (Ps. 120:4).

The intense heat of charcoal made it a valuable form of fuel in smelting furnaces (Song 8:6). The wealthy used charcoal to heat their homes (Jer. 36:22). It was also used for cooking (1 Kin. 19:6), by blacksmiths (Is. 44:12), and for heating (John 18:18).

Copper. A reddish–brown metal derived from many kinds of ores. One of the oldest metals known to man, copper was the first to be used for making tools. Gold and meteoric iron were probably used before copper. Pure copper was used until it was alloyed with zinc to form brass and tin to form bronze some time between 4500–3000 B.C.

Ancient copper refineries were located in Sinai, Egypt, Syria, Persia, the Phoenician coast, and Palestine. During Solomon's reign (about 971–931 B.C.), an elaborate mining operation existed at Ezion Geber in the Arabah, south of the Dead Sea (1 Kin. 9:26). Copper became Solomon's chief article of export.

Many useful articles were made from copper and its alloys, including tools of all kinds, utensils (Lev. 6:28), weapons (2 Sam. 21:16; 22:35; 2 Chr. 12:10), idols, musical instruments, and many furnishings for the Temple (2 Kin. 25:13). Also see *Brass; Tin.*

Crystal (see *Quartz*).

Flint. A very hard variety of quartz. Dark gray or brown in color, it is usually found in chalk or limestone rock. A form of silica, it sparks when struck by steel or another flint (2 Macc. 10:3). Because flint has a sharp edge when broken, tools such as knives, weapons, saws, sickles, and many other implements were made from flint by prehistoric man throughout the Stone Age.

Archaeologists have found many flint objects, especially knives, in Palestine. These were dated from the Neolithic or Late Stone Age (about 7000–4500 B.C.). Zipporah used a "sharp stone" to circumcise her children (Ex. 4:25; Josh. 5:2). The Bible refers to "rocks of flint" (Deut. 8:15); or "flinty rock" (Deut. 32:13).

Flint is also spoken of in a figurative manner in the Bible, denoting strength and determination (Is. 5:28; 50:7; Ezek. 3:9). This mineral is still abundant in the limestone rock of Syria, Palestine, and Egypt.

Glass (see *Quartz*).

Gold. A soft, bright yellow metal, gold was one of the first metals known to man. It could be used in its pure state without smelting. It never tarnishes—a property that makes it ideal for jewelry. This metal was extremely malleable; it could be hammered into thin strips and delicate objects (Ex. 39:3).

Gold is mentioned over 500 times in the Bible, more than any other metal. Rich deposits of gold were in Havilah (Gen. 2:11); Ophir (1 Kin. 22:48; 2 Chr. 8:18); Sheba (1 Kin. 10:1–2), Egypt, Armenia, Asia Minor, and Persia. Gold was at first hammered into desired shapes and sizes. In later periods it was refined and cast. Some scholars believe gold was not refined in Palestine until about 1000 B.C.

Many objects were made of gold, including the high priest's vest (Ex. 28:5), crowns (Ps. 21:3), chains (Gen. 41:42), rods (Song 5:14; rings, KJV), and coins (1 Chr. 21:25; Acts 3:6). Hiram brought gold to Israel for Solomon's palace (1 Kin. 10:16–21) and for furnishings for the Temple (1 Kin. 6:20; 10:2, 10). Gold was also taken as plunder in war (2 Kin. 24:13).

Hyacinth (see *Jacinth*).

Iron. This mineral is actually a metal obtained from certain rocks or ores. Iron occurs in a great variety of minerals. Much of the color of other minerals is due to the presence of iron, which has a steel-gray color with a metallic luster.

Meteoric iron is one of the oldest metals known to man. It existed in Egypt before 3100 B.C. The presence of nickel in meteoric iron distinguishes it from common iron ore. The ancient Egyptian word for this material meant "metal from heaven." Before the knowledge of smelting ores were known, ancient man fashioned small objects from this ore (Gen. 4:22; Deut. 8:9).

The Hittites in Asia Minor were the first to develop skills in the smelting of iron (about 1400 B.C.). Charcoal-fired furnaces were used for this purpose. Since much higher temperatures were required to cast iron, only wrought iron could be made at this time.

When the Philistines overthrew the Hittites (about 1200 B.C.), iron became widely used throughout the ancient world. Iron was definitely in use during the Israelite conquest of the land of Canaan (Josh. 6:24; Judg. 1:19; 4:3). The Philistines became skilled ironsmiths, eventually controlling most of Canaan and later conquering Israel, prohibiting their use of iron (1 Sam. 13:19, 22). After the Israelites' victory over the Philistines, iron became widespread in Palestine.

Iron ore was plentiful in Palestine, Syria, Cyprus, and Asia Minor. Extensive mining operations existed in Palestine, especially at Ezion Geber, south of the Dead Sea. Iron gradually replaced copper and bronze for farming implements, weapons, armor, and tools.

The reference to steel in Psalm 18:34 (KJV) means copper or bronze, because steel was not known at that time.

Jacinth. An orange or reddish gemstone. A variety of zircon, this mineral is widely distributed in crystal form in volcanic rocks and in fine granules in sand. Jacinth was the first stone in the third row of Aaron's breastplate (Ex. 28:19; ligure, KJV; turquoise, NEB). Jacinth was used to describe one of the colors in the breastplates of the riders in John's vision (Rev. 9:17; sapphire, RSV; sulfur, NIV; hyacinth, NKJV). Jacinth is also the 11th foundation stone in the heavenly Jerusalem (Rev. 21:20).

Jasper (see *Quartz*).

Lead. A soft, bluish–gray metal. Next to gold, lead is the heaviest of the common metals. Lead is easily worked, but it tarnishes very quickly. The ancient Roman name for lead was plumbum. The English word plumber (worker in lead) comes from this Latin word.

Lead is found in limestone and dolomite rock, usually deposited with other metals. Thus, it is sometimes mentioned in the Bible along with other metals (Num. 31:22; Ezek. 22:18, 20). Lead was never used extensively in Palestine, but it was mined in Egypt and the Sinai Peninsula. This metal was also imported from Tarshish (Ezek. 27:12).

Lead was used to purify silver (Jer. 6:29–30; Ezek. 22:18–20), as sinkers for fishing nets (Ex. 15:10), and as weights (Zech. 5:7–8). Job refers to his words being preserved permanently in lead (Job 19:24). Plumblines may also have been made of lead (Amos 7:7–8).

Ligure (see *Jacinth*).

Lime. A calcium oxide derived from limestone rock or chalk. Limestone was burned in lime–kilns and reduced to powder. Then it was used mainly for plastering floors and walls. The earliest mention of lime in the Bible is when God instructed Moses to whitewash stones with lime for a memorial of His covenant with Israel (Deut. 27:2, 4; plaster, KJV, NEB, NIV, RSV).

The Hebrew word for lime is also translated by various English versions as plaster, whitewash, or ash (Deut. 27:2, 4; Is. 27:9; 33:12; Dan 5:5; Amos 2:1). Lime was used by the Israelites for mortar and as plaster for floors (Dan. 5:5). The walls of cisterns were also waterproofed with plaster.

Lime may have been used in dyeing to give colors a permanent set in the fabric. Archaeologists have found stone jars containing lime and potash next to dyeing vats. Also see *Chalkstone*.

Lye. An alkaline material used as a cleansing agent. Both Egypt and Palestine produced some form of soap for washing the body as well as clothes. This may have been natron (niter), a sodium carbonate (soda) available in its natural state in southern Egypt. This substance could have been imported into Palestine.

The Hebrew word for lye is *nether*, referring to a mineral alkaline substance. Palestine produced potassium carbonate, an alkaline material made from the ashes of many scrubby plants and mixed with oil to form a soft soap. These plants grew in the Dead Sea region.

The prophet Jeremiah declared that the people of Judah were so full of iniquity that it could not be removed, "though you wash yourself with lye" (Jer. 2:22; nitre, KJV; soda, NIV).

Malachite (see *Marble*).

Marble. A crystallized form of limestone, marble is extremely hard and capable of a high polish. It is usually white, but is sometimes red or yellow.

The Hebrew and Greek words translated as marble means "brightness" or "glistening." Marble was obtained from most Bible lands in some form, but the choicest variety came from Arabia.

David supplied an abundance of marble for the Temple (1 Chr. 29:2). Solomon alluded poetically

This artistic gold lamp, excavated at Pompeii, dates back to the first century A.D.

Photo by Howard Vos

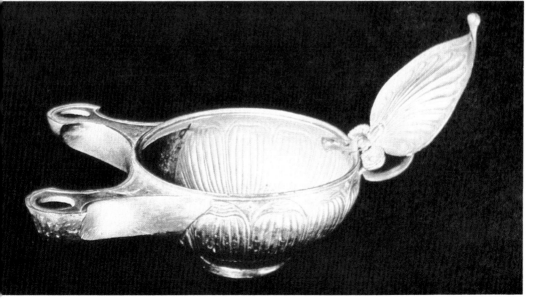

to the strength and beauty of marble (Song 5:15; alabaster, NASB, RSV; chrysolite marble, NIV). It was used in the palace of Shushan, or Susa (Esth. 1:6).

In the Greek and Roman periods many public buildings and homes of the wealthy contained marble. Archaeologists have found many marble beads and statues in Palestine. Marble is included in the merchandise of symbolic Babylon which will be destroyed (Rev. 18:12). Egyptian alabaster was also a form of marble. Also see *Alabaster*.

One distinct type of marble mentioned by several English translations is porphyry (Esth. 1:6; NASB, RSV; malachite, NEB). This was a purple rock with imbedded crystals of various sizes, used in the pavement of King Ahasuerus' palace at Susa.

Mercury. A silvery–white liquid metal, popularly called quicksilver. It is obtained from the ores of cinnabar. The Greek word for mercury means "water silver." It is used to extract gold and silver from their ores. This process, called amalgamation, was probably used in the ancient world. Pliny (A.D. 23–79) refers to mercury in this manner.

Mercury is not mentioned in the Bible by name, but it may be implied (Prov. 26:23; Is. 1:22; Ezek. 22:18–20) by the phrase, "silver dross." Also see *Vermilion*.

Mortar. A mixture of clay, sand, lime, and water used for building material. Mortar was sometimes made of clay alone or with chopped straw, sand, or crushed stone added for strength. The Hebrews in Egypt may have tempered their bricks and mortar with straw (Ex. 1:14; 5:7).

Lime mixed with sand or small stones was used in Palestine for mortar. This was used especially for more expensive houses. Mortar was spread on the walls, floors, and roofs of houses for more durability. The prophet Nahum suggested the usual method of mixing mortar was treading it (Nah. 3:14).

Nitre (see *Lye*).

Oil. In the Bible, the word oil usually refers to olive oil, although oil from myrrh, spikenard, and other varieties of trees was often used. Olive oil was one of the most important products in the economy of Palestine and in the daily life of the people. It became a symbol of peace and prosperity (Jer. 31:12), and was looked upon as a blessing from God.

Olives were harvested in the fall of the year, from September through the middle of November. Olives were gathered by shaking the trees (Is. 17:6) or by beating the trees with long sticks (Deut. 24:20). The oil harvested from them was stored in vats for later use. In homes it was stored in jars or flasks for domestic purposes (1 Kin. 17:12).

Every household was dependent upon a good supply of oil for their lamps (Ex. 25:6; Matt. 25:3–4, 8) and as an ingredient for bread (1 Kin. 17:12). Olive oil was also used as a medicine to treat wounds (Is. 1:6).

Ceremonial anointing was a common practice, especially for consecrating the high priest (Ex. 29:2) and anointing the king (1 Sam. 10:1). It was also used for personal cleanliness (Ruth 3:3; 2 Sam. 12:20). The early church practiced anointing with oil for healing (Mark 6:13; James 5:14). Oil was an article of trade especially during Solomon's time. Hiram, king of Tyre, received oil each year (1 Kin. 5:11) and it was also traded to Egypt.

Probably the most significant use of oil was in religious ceremonies. The best grade of oil was used for cereal offerings (Ex. 29:2; Deut. 12:17), sacrificial offerings (Ex. 29:40), and for the sanctuary lamp (Lev. 24:2).

Pearl (see *Quartz*).

Pitch (see *Asphalt*; *Bitumen*).

Plaster. A mixture of clay, lime, and water used to coat various surfaces. The Hebrew word for plaster means "to coat or overlay." At first plaster was probably made from clay and was used to coat floors, walls, and roofs of houses (Lev. 14:42, 45; Dan. 5:5). In later periods lime was mixed with clay or sand to waterproof cisterns and basins.

Porphyry (see *Marble*).

Quartz. A hard, glasslike mineral composed of oxygen and silicon. A common mineral, quartz is found in pure crystalline form in such other minerals as agate, flint, sand, and sandstone. Job indicated that wisdom was superior to all the precious gems and minerals of the earth, including quartz (Job 28:18; pearls, KJV; glass, NASB; alabaster, NEB; jasper, NIV; crystal, RSV).

Salt. This mineral is sodium chloride, a white crystalline substance used mainly for seasoning and as a preservative (Job 6:6). Salt is not only one of the most important substances mentioned in the Bible, but it is a necessity of life. The Hebrew people were well aware of the importance of salt to health (Job 6:6).

High concentrations of salt exist in the Dead Sea, a body of water that is nine times saltier than the ocean. The ancient cities of Sodom and Gommorah may have been located near the south end of the Dead Sea. Here Lot's wife was turned into a pillar of salt (Gen. 19:26).

An ancient method of extracting salt from sea water was to collect salt water in saltpits—holes dug in the sand; the water evaporated, leaving the salt behind (Zeph. 2:9). Saltpans were later used for this purpose.

Salt had a significant place in Hebrew worship. It was included in the grain offering (Lev. 2:13), the burnt offering (Ezek. 43:24), and the incense (Ex. 30:35). Part of the Temple offering included salt (Ezra 6:9). It was also used to ratify covenants (Num. 18:19; 2 Chr. 13:5). Newborn babies were rubbed with salt in the belief that this promoted good health (Ezek. 16:4).

During times of war, the enemies' lands were sown with salt to render them barren (Judg. 9:45). In Roman times salt was an important item of trade and was even used for money. Roman soldiers received part of their salary in salt.

Jesus described His disciples as the salt of the earth, urging them to imitate the usefulness of salt (Matt. 5:13; Col. 4:6).

Sand. Sand is made up of fine grains of rock which are worn away by wind and rain. Numerous minerals such as quartz, calcite, and mica are found in sand.

Sand was plentiful on the Mediterranean shores, along river banks, and in desert regions. It is usually mentioned in the Bible in a figurative manner, to symbolize a multitude (Gen. 22:17; Is. 10:22; Rev. 20:8), weight (Job 6:3), and weakness (Matt. 7:26). Sand was also used in mortar and in the manufacture of glass, which began in ancient Egypt or Phoenicia (Deut. 33:19).

Sapphire (see *Jacinth*).

Silver. This mineral is actually a silvery–white metal capable of a high polish. In ancient times it was valued next to gold. Silver was harder than gold, but not as hard as copper. It was usually extracted from lead ore, although it was also found in its native state. Silver never tarnishes when exposed to air, unless sulphur is present.

The main sources of silver were Asia Minor, Arabia, Mesopotamia, Armenia, and Persia. Palestine imported most of its silver from these countries, especially during Solomon's time (about 971–931 B.C.), when "the king made silver as common in Jerusalem as stones" (1 Kin. 10:27; 2 Chr. 9:27). Silver was refined and then cast into molds (Judg. 17:4; Ps. 12:6) by silversmiths (Jer. 10:9; Acts 19:24).

Abraham's wealth included silver (Gen. 13:2), which he used as a medium of exchange (Gen. 23:15). Other uses for silver were Joseph's cup (Gen. 44:2), idols (Ps. 115:4; Is. 40:19; Acts 19:24), various kinds of jewelry (Gen. 24:53; Ex. 3:22), and containers (Num. 7:13; 1 Chr. 28:17; Ezra 1:9–10). Many articles for the tabernacle were made of silver, including trumpets (Num. 10:2), lampstands (1 Chr. 28:15), and sockets (Ex. 26:19).

Slime (see *Asphalt, Bitumen*).

Soda (see *Lye*).

Steel. Steel was not known during Bible times until the first century A.D. The Hebrew word for copper and brass, or bronze, is incorrectly translated as steel in the KJV (2 Sam. 22:35; Job 20:24; Ps. 18:34; Jer. 15:12).

Sulfur, Sulphur (see *Brimstone*).

Tar (see *Asphalt, Bitumen*).

Tin. A soft, bluish–white metal smelted from cassiterite, its principle ore. Tin was used chiefly as an alloy with copper to produce bronze, a much harder material than either copper or tin. The Hebrew word for tin means "a substitute or alloy."

Phoenicia supplied the ancient Mediterranean world with tin obtained from Spain, its chief colony. Some scholars believe the Phoenicians sailed the Atlantic to Cornwall, England, the principle supplier of tin. Tyre received tin from Tarshish (Ezek. 27:12). Some think Persia and Armenia exported tin also.

Tin was among the spoils the Israelites took from the Midianites (Num. 31:22). The prophet Ezekiel pictured Jerusalem as being smelted as tin cast in a furnace (Ezek. 22:18–20; copper, NEB; bronze, NASB, RSV).

Turquoise (see *Jacinth*).

Vermilion. A red pigment obtained from cinnabar, the same mineral ore from which mercury or quicksilver is derived. Pure vermilion is a brilliant red, but it is brownish red when impurities such as clay, iron oxides, and bitumen are mixed. This ore is usually distributed in areas of volcanic rocks.

The prophet Jeremiah pronounced judgment on Shallum (Jehoahaz) for beautifying his own house with vermilion—decorating it in red (Jer. 22:14, NASB, NIV) while neglecting the poor and needy. Ezekiel saw the images of the Chaldeans painted in vermilion on the walls (Ezek. 23:14). Also see *Mercury.*

Whitewash (see *Lime*).

MINGLED PEOPLE — a reference to various foreign people used by the prophet Ezekiel (Ezek. 30:5). Elsewhere, the NKJV translates the same Hebrew expression as "MIXED MULTITUDE" (Jer. 25:20, 24) and "mixed peoples" (Jer. 50:37). The reference in Ezekiel may be to foreign mercenaries in the service of Egypt.

MINIAMIN [meh NYE uh min] (*on the right hand*) — a Levite in the days of King Hezekiah (2 Chr. 31:15).

MINING — the extraction of minerals or other valuable substances from the earth. Mining operations have been conducted in the biblical world since ancient times. It is not known exactly when people first began to dig into the earth to extract materials; but mining was known to have existed in Syria, Palestine, the Arabah, Sinai, Egypt, and in other Mediterranean lands. Mining was not limited to metallic ores such as gold, copper, silver, iron, lead, and tin. Mining also included other resources such as gems, salt, sand, clays, and many kinds of building stones. A vivid description of mining appears in Job 28.

The first mines were probably "placer mines" which involved panning or sifting by hand. Gold, the first metal mentioned in the Bible, was probably mined by this method. Open pit or surface mining was also used in Bible times.

The ancient Egyptians mined copper and turquoise in the Sinai Peninsula. Tunnels with shafts for ventilation were driven into the earth more than 30 meters (100 feet) with stone or beams of acacia wood used to support the roof. The ores were carried in baskets to the surface where it was smelted. Archaeologists have found crucibles, slag heaps, baskets, and other objects at many mining locations. Slaves, criminals, and prisoners of war worked these mines. Walled enclosures to house the prisoners have been found at some mines. The ancient trade route between Egypt and the Sinai Peninsula was traveled by these labor gangs. Moses was probably familiar with this route. He may have traveled it with the Israelites during the Exodus on their way to Mount Sinai.

Copper and iron were mined extensively in the Arabah (between the Gulf of Aqabah and the Dead Sea), especially at Ezion Geber during Solomon's time (1 Kin. 9:26–28). An elaborate mining and smelting system was discovered in this area in 1938–40.

The Hebrews learned mining and metallurgical skills early in their history (Gen. 4:22; Deut. 8:9). The KENITES, who were native to the Arabah, probably introduced the Israelites and the Edomites to the art of mining and metallurgy.

QUARRIES, which are actually mines, were operated in Palestine and Egypt. Masons usually quarried and shaped their own stone (1 Kin. 6:7; Is. 51:1). Deep channels were cut and wedges were driven into the openings and soaked with water. Sometimes these channels were cut along natural breaks by using iron axes.

Salt was also mined from the Dead Sea in "salt-pits" (Zeph. 2:9). These were holes or pits dug along the flat coastal area. When the sun evaporated the water, the salt remained.

MINISTER, MINISTRY — a distinctive biblical idea that means "to serve" or "servant." In the Old Testament the word servant was used primarily for court servants (1 Kin. 10:5; Esth. 1:10). During the period between the Old and New Testaments, it came to be used in connection with ministering to the poor. This use of the word is close to the work of the seven in waiting on tables in the New Testament (Acts 6:1–7).

In reality, all believers are "ministers." The apostle Paul urged the true pastor–teacher to "equip the saints" so they can minister to one another (Eph. 4:11–12). The model, of course, is Jesus, who "did not come to be served, but to serve" (Mark 10:45). His service is revealed in the fact that He gave "His life a ransom for many" (Matt. 20:28).

Jesus' servanthood radically revised the ethics of Jew and Greek alike, because He equated service to God with service to others. When we minister to the needs of the hungry or the lonely, we actually minister to Christ (Matt. 25:31–46). And when we fail to do so, we sin against God (James 2:14–17; 4:17). In this light, all who took part in the fellowship of service were ministers.

The concept is strengthened when the use of the Greek word *doulos* is noted. This was the term for a bondslave, one who was offered his freedom but who voluntarily surrendered that freedom in order to remain a servant. This idea typified Jesus' purpose, as described by Paul in Philippians 2:7. This passage alludes to the "servant of God" teaching of Isaiah 52—54. Truly Christ fulfilled this exalted calling, because His life was dedicated to the needs of others.

Following our Savior's example, all believers are bondslaves of God (Rom. 1:1; Gal. 1:10; Col. 4:12). We are to perform "good deeds" to all men, with a responsibility especially to fellow Christians (Gal. 6:10; Heb. 10:24).

Our unselfish service should especially be rendered through our spiritual gifts, which are given by God to the saints in order that they might minister to one another (1 Pet. 4:10). These gifts consist of both spiritual and practical gifts (1 Cor. 12:28). They are distributed to various members of the church so that the union of believers can be expressed in loving service. In Ephesians 4:7–11 the offices of apostles, prophets, evangelists, etc., are described as divine "gifts" to the church. This is the one place where the officers of the church might be linked with the term minister. In a special way these officers do "minister" to the church—the apostles through their inspired leadership; the prophets through their inspired preaching and even foretelling; the evangelists through their traveling missionary work; and the pastor–teachers through their service in local congregations. Yet their primary service was to equip all saints for ministry.

The concepts of minister and ministry must be broadened today to include all the members of a church. The common concept of the pastor as the professional minister must be discarded, because the biblical pattern is for him to be the one who trains the congregation for ministry. All the saints are responsible for loving and ministering in various ways to one another, using the spiritual gifts distributed to each by the Holy Spirit.

MINJAMIN [MEN juh men] (*on the right hand side*) — the name of two or three men in the Old Testament:

1. One who helped Kore the Levite distribute the freewill offerings collected in the reign of Hezekiah (2 Chr. 31:15; Miniamin, NKJV, KJV, RSV, NIV, NASB).

2. A priest who returned with Zerubbabel from the Captivity (Neh. 12:17; Miniamin, KJV, RSV, NASB, NEB, NIV). He is also called Mijamin (Neh. 12:5).

3. A priest who played the trumpet at the dedication of the rebuilt wall in Jerusalem (Neh. 12:41; Miniamin, KJV, RSV, NASB, NEB). He may be the same person as Minjamin No. 2.

MINNI [MIN eye] (meaning unknown) — a people and a state of ARMENIA in the area south of Lake Urmia and east of the Zagros Mountains, in what is present-day Iran. The Minni are mentioned only once in the Bible. The prophet Jeremiah called on them to make war against Babylonia (Jer. 51:27).

MINNITH [MIN ith] (*distribution*) — a city of the Ammonites that apparently marked the easternmost limit of Jephthah's military expansion and conquest. Minnith was famous for its high-quality wheat, which it exported to Tyre (Ezek. 27:17). The city was in TRANSJORDAN, about six kilometers (four miles) northeast of Heshbon.

MINSTREL (see OCCUPATIONS AND TRADES; MUSIC OF THE BIBLE).

MINT (see PLANTS OF THE BIBLE).

MIPHKAD GATE (see GATES OF JERUSALEM AND THE TEMPLE).

MIRACLES — historic events or natural phenomena which appear to violate natural laws but which reveal God to the eye of faith at the same time. A valuable way of understanding the meaning of miracles is to examine the various terms for miracles used in the Bible.

Both the Old Testament and the New Testament use the word sign (Is. 7:11, 14; John 2:11) to denote a miracle that points to a deeper revelation. Wonder (Joel 2:30; Mark 13:22) emphasizes the effect of the miracle, causing awe and even terror. A work (Matt. 11:2) points to the presence of God in history, acting for mankind. The New Testament uses the word power (Mark 6:7) to emphasize God's acting in strength. These terms often overlap in meaning (Acts 2:43). They are more specific than the more general term "miracle."

Miracles in the Old Testament. The readers of the Old Testament recognized that God is the Creator and sustainer of all life (Ex. 34:10; Ps. 33:6–7; Is. 40:26). This assumption permitted the Israelites the possibility of miracles. They thought of the world as God's theater for displaying His glory and love (Ps. 33:5; 65:6–13). Thus, the miracle was not so much a proof for God's existence as a revelation to the faithful of God's covenant love.

When God parted the water for the Israelites, or when He saved Israel in Egypt through the Passover, God revealed His character; and the Israelites were convinced that God was working for their salvation (Exodus 12:13–14). Miracles were expressions of God's saving love as well as His holy justice.

Miracles in the Old Testament are connected especially with the great events in Israel's history— the call of Abraham (Gen. 12:1–3), the birth of Moses (Ex. 1:1—2:22), the Exodus from Egypt (Ex. 12:1—14:31), the giving of the Law (Ex. 19:1—20:26), and entry into the Promised Land (Josh. 3:1—4:7), etc. These miracles are for salvation, but God also acts in history for judgment (Gen. 11:1–9).

The plagues of the Exodus showed God's sovereign power in judgment and salvation (Ex. 7:3–5). In parting the water, God showed His love and protection for Israel as well as His judgment on Egypt for its failure to recognize God (Ex. 15:2, 4–10). During the wilderness journey, God demonstrated His love and protection in supplying the daily MANNA (Ex. 16:1–36). Another critical period in Israel's history was the time of Elijah, the champion of Israel. Elijah controlled the rain and successfully challenged the pagan priests of Baal (1 Kin. 17:1; 18:1–40). God revealed Himself as Lord, as Savior of Israel, and as punisher of the nation's enemies.

Miraculous wonders like these were not as frequent during the days of the writing prophets. But one unusual miracle was the recovery of Hezekiah (2 Kin. 20:1–21; Is. 38:1–21) as well as the miracles in Jonah and Daniel. Prophecy itself can even be interpreted as a miracle. God revealed Himself during this time through the spoken and written Word.

Miracles in the New Testament. As with the Old Testament, the New Testament miracles are essentially expressions of God's salvation and glory.

Why did Jesus perform miracles? Jesus answered this question Himself. When in prison, John the Baptist sent some of his disciples to Jesus to see if He was the "one to come" (Matt. 11:3). Jesus told them to inform John of what He had done: "The blind receive sight, the lame walk, those who have leprosy are cured, the deaf hear, the dead are raised, and the good news is preached to the poor" (11:5). With these words, Jesus declared that His miracles were the fulfillment of the promises of the Messiah's kingdom as foretold by Isaiah (24:18–19; 35:5–6; 61:1). Jesus' miracles were signs of the presence of the kingdom of God (Matt. 12:39).

This theme of the miracles pointing to the kingdom of God was developed and deepened especially in the Gospel of John. John presented the miracles of Jesus as "signs" on seven occasions: John 2:1–11; 4:46–54; 5:1–18; 6:1–15; 6:16–21; 9:1–41; 11:1–57. He thought of these miracles as pointing to deep spiritual truth, demanding obedient faith (John 2:11, 23–25). Thus, Jesus' feeding miracle (6:1–15) was Jesus' presentation of Himself as the True Manna, the one who gives life and sustenance.

Jesus also understood His miracles as evidences of the presence of the kingdom in His ministry (Matt. 11:2–5; 12:28). Every miracle story was a sign that God's salvation was present. But not only did the kingdom come; it came in great power, because the dead were raised (Is. 26:19; Luke 7:11–15) and Satan was bound (Mark 3:27).

Jesus' miracles were also performed upon the most unlikely people. Jesus consciously brought the salvation of God to those who were rejected. He healed the lame (Matt. 9:1–8), the dumb (Matt. 9:32–33), and lepers (Luke 17:11–19). Jesus brought the kingdom to all, regardless of their condition.

But Jesus' miracles were not theatrical sensations. He demanded faith of others (Matt. 9:2). The hemorrhaging woman was healed because of her faith (Matt. 9:18–26). Furthermore, Jesus expected the disciples to do miracles and rebuked them for their "little faith" and unbelief (Matt. 17:20).

Jesus' demand of trust in Himself led regularly to opposition by Jewish leaders. John drew this out when he recorded Jesus' healing of a man born blind. Jesus' salvation comes even on the Sabbath, overturning Pharisaic legalism (John 9:16), and resulting in their blindness (John 9:39–41). Similarly, the Pharisees broke into a charge of blasphemy when Jesus healed the paralytic and pronounced him forgiven of sins (Mark 2:1–12). The miracles of Jesus, being God's offer of salvation, demanded a decision. As a result, a division of the Pharisees occurred (Matt. 9:32–34).

Finally, we gain a deeper understanding of Jesus in His miracles. He is Lord over nature (Mark 4:35–41) and death (Luke 8:41–56; John 11:1–44). He is the Suffering Servant who bears the infirmities of others (Matt. 8:16–17). He is the Messiah who was to come (Matt. 11:2–6). He fights the battle against evil (Mark 3:23-30; Luke 11:18-23).

Jesus did not work miracles to prove His deity or His messiahship. In fact, He clearly refused to work miracles as proofs (Matt. 12:38-42; Luke 11:29-32). His death was the proof to Israel. However, Jesus' miracles do give evidence that He was divine, that He was the Son of God, the Messiah.

The Acts of the Apostles is a book of miracles. Again, these miracles are a continuation of the miracles of Jesus, made possible through the Holy Spirit. The miracles of the apostles were done in the name of Jesus and were manifestations of God's salvation (Acts 3:11). This thread of continuity is seen in Peter's miracles which paralleled those of Jesus (Luke 7:22; 5:18-26; 8:49-56; Acts 3:1-16; 9:32-35; 9:36-42).

God began His church with a powerful display of miracles. At Pentecost, the Holy Spirit came on the people with great power (Acts 2:1-13), leading to conversions (Acts 2:41). When Philip went to Samaria, the Spirit of God anointed him with power (Acts 8:4-40), and the same happened with Peter and Cornelius (Acts 10:1-48). These powerful wonders were designed to convince the apostles and the Palestinian church that other cultures were to be part of the church. To these were added the stunning act of God through Peter with Ananias and Sapphira acted in hypocrisy (Acts 4:32—5:11), the church's power in prayer (Acts 4:23-31), and Paul's transforming vision (Acts 16:6-10).

Miraculous powers were also present in the apostles. Peter healed a lame man (Acts 3:1-6), a paralytic (Acts 9:32-35), and raised the dead (Acts 9:36-42). The apostles performed mighty miracles (Acts 5:12-16), and Peter was miraculously released from prison (Acts 12:1-11). Paul's conversion was a startling incident (Acts 9:1-19). Ability to work miracles was taken as a sign for apostleship by Paul (Romans 15:18-19; 2 Cor. 12:12). Thus, this ability to work miracles is not only an expression of God's salvation but also God's way of authenticating His apostles.

The lists of the gifts of the Spirit in the New Testament show miracles were one of the means by which believers ministered to others (Rom. 12:6-8; 1 Cor. 12:8-10, 28-30; Eph. 4:11-12).

MIRACLES, GIFT OF (see SPIRITUAL GIFTS).

MIRIAM [MER eh um] (*bitterness*) — the name of two people in the Old Testament:

1. A sister of Aaron and Moses and daughter of Amram and Jochebed (Num. 26:59; 1 Chr. 6:3). Called "Miriam the prophetess" (Ex. 15:20), she is described as one of the leaders sent by the Lord to guide Israel (Mic. 6:4). Although the Bible does not specifically say so, Miriam was probably the sister who watched over the infant Moses in the ark of bulrushes (Ex. 2:4-8). Miriam's song of victory after the Israelites' successful crossing of the Red Sea (Ex. 15:20-21) is one of the earliest fragments of Hebrew poetry.

Miriam was involved in a rebellion against Moses when he married an Ethiopian woman

Photo by Gustav Jeeninga

A typical mirror of Bible times, made of highly polished metal.

(Num. 12:1-2). Both she and Aaron claimed to be prophets, but God heard their claims and rebuked them. Because of her part in the rebellion against Moses' leadership, Miriam was struck with leprosy. However, Moses interceded for her, and she was quickly healed (Num. 12:1-16). She is not mentioned again until her death and burial at Kadesh in the Wilderness of Zin (Num. 20:1).

2. A daughter of Ezrah of the tribe of Judah (1 Chr. 4:17).

MIRMAH [MUR muh] (*height*) — a son of Shaharaim and Hodesh (1 Chr. 8:10; Mirma, KJV).

MIRROR — a polished metal surface intended to reflect objects. Mirrors of polished bronze, gold, and silver were used in ancient Egypt. Some of them may have been taken from Egypt by the Israelites at the time of the Exodus. Glass was not used in making mirrors until several centuries after Bible times.

In the tabernacle the bronze laver or pan where the priests washed their hands was made from bronze mirrors (Ex. 38:8). These highly polished metal mirrors gave surprisingly good images. But they did give a distorted reflection because of their imperfect surfaces. Perhaps this is why the apostle Paul declared, "We see in a mirror, dimly" (1 Cor. 13:12).

MISGAB [MISS gab] (*the height*) — KJV word for an unknown site in Moab (Jer. 48:1). The word may not be a proper noun. It could mean fortress (RSV), high stronghold, (NKJV), stronghold (NIV), or lofty stronghold (NAS).

MISHAEL [MISH eh uhl] (*who is what God is?*) — the name of three men in the Old Testament:

1. A son of Uzziel and grandson of Kohath, of the tribe of Levi (Lev. 10:4).

2. An Israelite who helped Ezra read the Book of the Law to the people (Neh. 8:4).

3. One of the three friends of Daniel who were cast into the fiery furnace. The Babylonians changed his name to MESHACH (Dan. 1:6–7).

MISHAL [MY shal] (*depression*) — a form of MASHAL.

MISHAM [MY sham] (meaning unknown) — a son of Elpaal, of the tribe of Benjamin (1 Chr. 8:12).

MISHEAL [MY sheh uhl] — a form of MISHAL.

MISHMA [MISH muh] (*fame*) — the name of two men in the Old Testament:
1. A son of Ishmael (Gen. 25:14). Mishma's name probably became the name of an Arabian tribe.
2. A descendant of Simeon (1 Chr. 4:25–26).

MISHMANNAH [mish MAN uh] (*strength*) — a warrior who joined David at Ziklag (1 Chr. 12:10).

MISHNAH [MISH nah] (*repetition*) — the first, and basic, part of the TALMUD and the written basis of religious authority for traditional Judaism. The Mishnah contains a written collection of traditional laws (halakoth) handed down orally from teacher to student. It was compiled across a period of about 335 years, from 200 B.C. to A.D. 135.

The Mishnah is grouped into 63 treatises, or tractates, that deal with all areas of Jewish life—legal, theological, social, and religious—as taught in the schools of Palestine. Soon after the Mishnah was compiled, it became known as the "iron pillar of the Torah," since it preserves the way a Jew can follow the TORAH.

For many Jews, the Mishnah ranks second only to the canon of the Hebrew Scriptures. Indeed, many Jews consider it part of the Torah. Because it is the core for both the Jerusalem and Babylonian Talmuds, the Mishnah serves as a link between Jews in the land of Israel and Jews scattered around the world.

MISHRAITES [MISH ray ites] — one of the four families of Kirjath Jearim, from whom the Zorathites and Eshtaolites descended (1 Chr. 2:53).

MISPAR [MISS par] (*writing*) — an Israelite who returned with Zerubbabel from the Captivity (Ezra 2:2; Mizpar, KJV). The feminine form of the name, Mispereth, is used in Nehemiah 7:7.

MISPERETH [MISS puh reth] — a form of MISPAR.

MISREPHOTH, THE BROOK [MIZ reh fahth] (*hot springs*) — a place near the Mediterranean Sea to which Joshua chased the Canaanites after defeating them at the waters of Merom (Josh. 11:8; Misrephoth–maim; Misrephoth on the west, NEB). Its location is uncertain.

MIST — water in the form of particles floating or falling in the atmosphere near the surface of the earth. Genesis 2:6 speaks of a mist going up from the earth and watering the ground. Some commentators believe the Hebrew word translated as mist in this verse refers to some subterranean water source, such as an underground spring or stream.

MITE (see MONEY OF THE BIBLE).

MITHCAH [MITH kuh] — a form of MITHKAH.

MITHKAH [MITH kuh] (*sweetness*) — a stopping place of the Israelites in the wilderness (Num. 33:28–29; Mithcah, KJV), site unknown.

MITHNITE [MITH night] — a term used to describe Joshaphat, one of David's mighty men (1 Chr. 11:43).

MITHRAISM [MYTH rah iz em] — a Persian religious cult that flourished in the late Roman Empire. In the second century A.D. it was stronger than Christianity in the Roman Empire. But it declined rapidly in the third century. Mithras was considered the god of light and wisdom and the guardian against evil by the Persians. Also see GODS, PAGAN.

MITHREDATH [MITH reh dath] (*gift of Mithra*) — the name of two men in the Book of Ezra:
1. The treasurer of King Cyrus of Persia. Mithredath delivered the Temple vessels that were to be returned to Jerusalem (Ezra 1:8).
2. A man who protested the rebuilding of the walls of Jerusalem by the Israelites (Ezra 4:7).

MITRE — KJV word for TURBAN. Also see DRESS OF THE BIBLE.

MITYLENE [mit uh LEE neh] (*purity*) — the wealthy chief city of Lesbos, an island in the Aegean Sea off the western coast of Asia Minor (see Map 8, C–2). On his third missionary journey, the apostle Paul stopped briefly at Mitylene while on his way from Troas to Miletus (Acts 20:14).

MIXED MULTITUDE — a collection of people of different races and nationalities (Ex. 12:38; Num. 11:4; Neh. 13:3; Jer. 25:20, 24). Each of the uses of this phrase, however, has a slightly different interpretation. In Exodus 12:38, the Hebrew expression means a group of people of different races. In Numbers 11:4, it refers to "rabble" or "riff–raff." These people may not be the same as those in Exodus 12:38. In Nehemiah 13:3, which refers to the situation after the return from Captivity, the term refers to the foreigners with whom Israel had made marriages and the children of those marriages (Ezra 9:1–2; Neh. 13:23–24). In Jeremiah 25:20, 24, the reference is to foreign nations which, like Judah, were to be conquered by Nebuchadnezzar, king of Babylon.

MIZAR [MY zar] (*little*) — a hill apparently east of the Jordan River, probably within sight of Mount Hermon, mentioned only in Psalm 42:6.

MIZPAH [MIZ pah] (*watchtower*) — the name of six sites in the Old Testament:
1. One of three names given to a mound of stones

erected as a memorial. Jacob set up this memorial in Gilead as a witness of the covenant between him and his father–in–law, Laban (Gen. 31:49). Both Jacob and Laban called this monument "heap of witness." The mound was also called Mizpah, meaning "watch [tower]." The stones were erected as a boundary marker between the two. God was the One who was to watch between them.

2. A district at the foot of Mount Hermon called "the land of Mizpah" and "the Valley of Mizpah" (Josh. 11:3, 8), exact location unknown.

3. A city of Judah (Josh. 15:38) in the Shephelah, or lowland plain.

4. A city of Benjamin in the region of Geba and Ramah (1 Kin. 15:22). At Mizpah Samuel assembled the Israelites for prayer after the ARK OF THE COVENANT was returned to Kirjath Jearim (1 Sam. 7:5–6). Saul was first presented to Israel as king at this city (1 Sam. 10:17). Mizpah was also one of the places that Samuel visited on his annual circuit to judge Israel (1 Sam. 7:16–17). Mizpah was one of the sites fortified against the kings of the northern tribes of Israel by King Asa (1 Kin. 15:22). After the destruction of Jerusalem in 587/86 B.C., Gedaliah was appointed governor of the remaining people of Judah; his residence was at Mizpah (2 Kin. 25:23, 25). After the fall of Jerusalem Mizpah became the capital of the Babylonian province of Judah. Mizpah also was reinhabited by Israelites after the Babylonian Captivity (Neh. 3:7, 15, 19).

5. A town or site in Gilead known as Mizpah of Gilead and the home of Jephthah the judge (Judg. 11:29, 34). This site was also probably known as Ramath Mizpah (Josh. 13:26)—the Ramoth in Gilead listed as one of the six cities of refuge (Josh. 20:8).

6. A city in Moab to which David took his parents for safety when King Saul sought to kill him (1 Sam. 22:3). Some scholars believe Mizpah of Moab was another name for Kir of Moab (present–day Kerak), the capital of Moab.

MIZPAR [MIZ pahr] — a form of MISPAR.

MIZRAIM [MIZ ray im] (meaning unknown) — the second son of Ham as well as the name of his descendants and the country where they lived. Mizraim apparently was the ancestor of the Egyptians. In the Old Testament the nation of Egypt is sometimes called Mizraim. The RSV gives Egypt in all places where the NKJV translates as Mizraim (Gen. 10:6, 13; 1 Chr. 1:8, 11).

MIZZAH [MIZ uh] (meaning unknown) — a son of Reuel and chief of a clan in the land of Edom (1 Chr. 1:37).

MNASON [NAY sohn] (*remembering*) — a Christian with whom the apostle Paul stayed on his final visit to Jerusalem (Acts 21:16). A native of Cyprus, Mnason was "an early disciple"—perhaps meaning that he was converted to Christianity on the Day of Pentecost or shortly thereafter. He may have been an acquaintance of Barnabas, who also was from Cyprus (Acts 4:36).

MOAB [MOE abb] (perhaps *of my father*) — the name of a man and a nation (see Map 2, C–1) in the Old Testament:

1. A son of Lot by an incestuous union with his older daughter (Gen. 19:37). Moab became an ancestor of the MOABITES.

2. A neighboring nation whose history was closely linked to the fortunes of the Hebrew people.

Ancient Egypt, often called Mizraim in the Bible, is famous for its mammoth pyramids, like this one at Giza.
Photo by Howard Vos

Moab was situated along the eastern border of the Dead Sea, on the plateau between the Dead Sea and the Arabian desert. It was about 57 kilometers (35 miles) long and 40 kilometers (25 miles) wide. Although it was primarily a high plateau, Moab also had mountainous areas and deep gorges. It was a fertile area for crops and herds. To the south and west of Moab was the nation of Edom; to the north was Ammon. After the Israelites invaded the land, the tribe of Reuben displaced the Moabites from the northern part of their territory and the tribe of Gad pushed the Ammonites eastward into the region.

General History. Moab was inhabited from prehistoric times. The KING's HIGHWAY, a major trade route from Syria to the Gulf of Aqabah, brought wealth and culture to Moab as early as 2500 B.C. Some time during the 15th century B.C., as the nomadic population settled down, the kingdom of Moab arose, along with the other kingdoms east of the Jordan River, such as Edom and Ammon. The Moabites built fortifications throughout their territory, especially on the south and east. Not long before the conquest of the region by the Hebrew people, Sihon, king of the Amorites, invaded Moab from the north and added much of Moab to his kingdom (Num. 21:27–30).

The Israelite tribes of Reuben and Gad settled the northern part of the territory of Moab. During most of Israel's history, the Moabites were Israel's enemies. In the late eighth century B.C. Moab became subject to Assyria, like many other nations in the region. When the Assyrian Empire fell in 609 B.C., Arab invasions intensified, and the kingdom of Moab was taken. Thereafter Moab was occupied increasingly by nomadic Arabs, until the NABATEANS established a settled culture from the first century B.C. to A.D. 106. After that, the entire region was made into a Roman province.

Connections with Israel. Moab, founder of the Moabites, was a son of Lot by incest (Gen. 19:30–38). Although the Moabites were of mixed ethnic stock, the influence of Moab's descendants among them was great enough to give the country its ancient name. The story in Genesis 14 of the raid of Chedorlaomer, king of Elam, and his fellow kings records the conquest of most of Moab about 2000 B.C.–1900 B.C.

Sihon's Amorite kingdom annexed much of Moab shortly before the Israelite conquest of Canaan (Num. 21:17–29). After the Israelites defeated Sihon, Balak, the king of the relatively weak Moabites, joined with the Midianites in hiring the prophet–magician Balaam to curse Israel so the Israelites could be defeated (Num. 22:1–20). Balaam's mission failed, but when the Israelites camped in Moab just before crossing the Jordan River, the women of Moab enticed the Israelites into a form of idolatry that involved ritual sexual immorality. This resulted in God's judgment against Israel (Num. 25:1–9).

Moses saw the Promised Land from Moab's Mount Nebo (Num. 27:12–23). Here he was buried after his death (Deut. 34:6). From the region of Acacia Grove in northwest Moab, the Israelites crossed the Jordan River into the Promised Land (Josh. 3:1). The tribes of Reuben and Gad actually settled in northern Moab (Num. 32:1–37).

The nation of Israel was relatively weak during the period of the judges, after the conquest. Eglon, a king of Moab, began to oppress Israel, capturing territory east of the Jordan River as far as Jericho. Ehud the judge delivered Israel from Eglon (Judg. 3:12–30). The events of the Book of Ruth occurred during this same general period. Ruth, a Moabite woman, became an ancestor of King David and therefore of Jesus himself (Ruth 2:6; 4:13–22; Matt. 1:5–16).

The Moabites also threatened Israel in the days of Israel's first king, Saul, who was apparently successful against them (1 Sam. 14:47). Although David had some early friendships among the Moabites (1 Sam. 22:3–4), he eventually conquered Moab (2 Sam. 8:2). The Moabites remained subject to Israel until after Solomon's death.

Omri, king of Israel (885–874 B.C.), kept Moab under his control, as did his son Ahab (874–853 B.C.), until Ahab was so occupied with wars against Syria and Assyria that Moab broke free. This was described by King Mesha of Moab in his monument, the MOABITE STONE. King Jehoram of Israel, King Jehoshaphat of Judah, and the king of Edom joined forces to attack Moab about 849 B.C. But they failed to conquer the Moabites because of a superstitious lack of faith when the king of Moab sacrificed his own son to show how deeply he believed in his cause (2 Kin. 3:1–27).

On another occasion, a coalition of Moabites, Ammonites, and Edomites invaded Judah, but they were destroyed by God (2 Chr. 20:1–30). The Moabites apparently raided Israelite territory during the eighth century B.C. (2 Kin. 13:20).

The Assyrians conquered Moab about 735 B.C., and invading Arabs conquered it about 650 B.C. The prophet Isaiah lamented over Moab's defeat (Isaiah 15—16), and Jeremiah predicted Moab's death at the end of the seventh century B.C. (Jeremiah 48). When Jerusalem was destroyed by the Babylonians in 587 B.C., some of the Jews fled to Moab to escape being taken into captivity (Jer. 40:11–12).

MOABITES [MOH uh bites] — natives or inhabitants of the land of MOAB (Num. 22:4).

MOABITESS [moe ab IGHT ess] — a description of several women from MOAB in the Old Testament:

1. RUTH, the wife of Boaz (Ruth 1:22; 2:2, 21; 4:5, 10).

2. Some of Solomon's wives (1 Kin. 11:1).

3. Shimrith, the mother of Jehozabad, who conspired to kill King Joash (2 Chr. 24:26).

MOABITE STONE — a black basalt memorial stone discovered in Moab by a German missionary in 1868. Nearly four feet high, it contained about

Photo by Gustav Jeeninga

The famous Moabite Stone, which celebrates the revolt of King Mesha of Moab against the rule of the Israelites.

34 lines in an alphabet similar to Hebrew. The stone was probably erected about 850 B.C. by the Moabite King Mesha.

King Mesha's story written on the stone celebrated his overthrow of the nation of Israel. This event apparently is recorded in 2 Kings 3:4–27, although the biblical account makes it clear that Israel was victorious in the battle. The passage shows clearly that Mesha honors his god Chemosh in terms similar to the Old Testament reverence for Jehovah. The inhabitants of entire cities were apparently slaughtered to appease this deity, recalling the similar practices of the Israelites, especially as described in the Book of Joshua. Besides telling of his violent conquests, Mesha boasted on the stone of the building of cities (with Israelite forced labor) and the construction of cisterns, walls, gates, towers, a king's palace, and even a highway.

The Moabite stone has profound biblical relevance. Historically, it confirms Old Testament accounts. It has a theological parallel to Israel's worship of one god. It is also valuable geographically because it mentions no less than 15 sites listed in the Old Testament. The writing on the stone also resembles Hebrew, the language in which most of the Old Testament was originally written.

Some pieces of the stone are now housed in the Louvre Museum in Paris.

MOADIAH [moh uh DYE uh] (*Jehovah promises*) — a priest and the head of a father's house in the time of the high priest Joiakim (Neh. 12:17). Moadiah may be the same person as Maadiah (Neh. 12:5).

MODERATION — self-control, not given to sudden impulses or excesses (1 Tim. 2:9). Although the term rarely occurs in the Bible, the concept of moderation is common. The Pharisees were not moderate. Jesus described them as those "who strain out a gnat to swallow a camel" (Matt. 23:24). They emphasized the minor aspects of the Law, neglecting the weightier matters. By contrast, Christian believers ought to be moderate in all things (1 Cor. 9:25; temperate, NKJV).

MODIOS (see WEIGHTS AND MEASURES).

MOLADAH [moh LAY duh] (*origin*) — a city in southern Judah, about 23 kilometers (14 miles) southwest of Beersheba. Moladah was assigned to the tribe of Simeon (Josh. 19:1–2) and was occupied by Israelites after the Captivity (Neh. 11:26).

MOLE (see ANIMALS OF THE BIBLE).

MOLECH (see GODS, PAGAN).

MOLID [MOH lid] (*begetter*) — a son of Abishur and a descendant of Judah through Perez (1 Chr. 2:3, 29).

MOLOCH [MOH lahk] (see GODS, PAGAN).

MOLTEN SEA (see LAVER).

MOMENT — a minute portion of time; an instant. The Hebrew word translated as moment means "a wink" or "a blink" (Ex. 33:5; Job 7:18). The Greek word translated as moment literally means "a pricking" or "a point." When Christ returns, "We shall all be changed in a moment [in a flash; NIV, NEB], in the twinkling of an eye" (1 Cor. 15:52). Also see TIME.

MONEY OF THE BIBLE. As soon as ancient people stopped living the lives of wandering hunters and began an agricultural system, a medium of exchange became necessary. A system of barter, or trading of property, preceded the creation of any formal currency that can be called money.

In Old Testament times, land itself became an immediate asset. It was a possession that could be traded. But produce, and especially livestock, was more convenient, because it was so moveable. The Pharaoh of Egypt supplied Abraham with oxen, sheep, camels, and female donkeys (Gen. 12:16). King Mesha of Moab exacted a tribute of 100,000 sheep and 100,000 rams (2 Kin. 3:4). The ritual sacrifice of animals underscored their value as a standard of barter—and thus encouraged commerce near the Temple area.

Grain, oil, and wine were also used in bartering, as when King Solomon traded wheat and olive oil

Photo by Howard Vos

A fifth century B.C. coin from Athens, Greece, showing the goddess Athena, with the sacred owl from the reverse side.

for the cypress trees needed to build the Temple (1 Kin. 5:11), or when the Israelites were taxed in the amount of one–tenth of their grain or wine (1 Sam. 8:15), or when the tribe of Levi (Levites) was directed by God to serve as priests in exchange for grain and wine (Num. 18:25–32). Spices were also an item of barter. These were offered by the queen of Sheba to Solomon (1 Kin. 10:2).

Gradually, as communities became more organized, tradesmen traveled between these settlements. Products circulated from one region to another. Soon metals began to replace goods and services as items of exchange. Copper or bronze was in demand for weapons (2 Sam. 21:16), for farming tools, and for offerings (Ex. 35:5). The early Egyptians, Semites, and Hittites shaped gold and silver into rings, bars, or rounded nodules for easier trading. The children of Jacob used "bundles of money" (Gen. 42:35), which may have been metal rings tied together with strings.

Silver generally was used in real estate transactions. Omri purchased the village and hill of Samaria for two talents of silver (1 Kin. 16:24). Gold was sometimes used, along with silver, in the payment of tribute, such as Hezekiah's payment to Sennacherib of Assyria (2 Kin. 18:14). Abraham bought the Cave of Machpelah for 400 shekels of silver (Gen. 23:15–16). David bought the threshing floor of Araunah for 50 shekels of silver (2 Sam. 24:24). Solomon purchased chariots and horses with silver (1 Kin. 10:28–29). Judas was paid for his betrayal of Jesus with 30 pieces of silver (Matt. 26:15). Silver was so commonly used as money that the Hebrew word for "silver" came to mean "money" (Gen. 17:13).

Gold, the most valuable of metals, was also used for major transactions. King Hiram of Tyre paid 120 talents of gold to Solomon for several cities near his land (1 Kin. 9:13–14). Later Hezekiah paid Sennacherib 300 talents of silver and 30 talents of gold to obtain peace (2 Kin. 18:14). Copper (proba-

bly a copper–bronze alloy, thus KJV "brass") was also used for barter but was considered less valuable (Ex. 35:5; 2 Sam. 21:16; Is. 60:17). Later these same three metals were used to mint the nation's first coins.

In their early use as money, metals were probably in their raw form or in varying stages of refinement. However, in that form it was difficult to transport them and to determine their true value. Thus the metals were soon refined into the form of a wedge or a bar (Josh. 7:21) or various forms of jewelry. Abraham's servant gave Rebekah a golden nose ring weighing half a shekel and two gold bracelets weighing ten shekels (Gen. 24:22). The spoil of the Midianites included many articles of jewelry (Num. 31:50). Gold and silver were also kept as ingots, vessels, dust, or small fragments that could be melted and used immediately. These small pieces of metal were often carried in leather

A Roman coin from New Testament times. Known as the lepton, it angered the Jewish people because it portrayed the staff, or wand, of a pagan priest.

Photo by Gleason Archer

pouches that could be easily hidden (Gen. 42:35).

The Bible frequently refers to "pieces" of silver or gold. The confusing term *shekel* did not denote any one value or weight at first, although it later became the name of a Jewish coin. For instance, there were heavy and light silver shekels (Phoenician), and heavy and light gold shekels (Babylonian). Fifteen heavy Phoenician shekels of silver equaled one heavy Babylonian gold shekel. Abraham paid pieces of silver, or shekels, for the cave of Machpelah (Gen. 23:16). David paid pieces of silver to Ornan the Jebusite (1 Chr. 21:22–25).

Fractions of the shekel are mentioned in the Old Testament as well: the half–shekel, or bekah (Ex. 38:26); the third part of a shekel as a convenant obligation (Neh. 10:32); the fourth part of a shekel, or rebah, proposed to Saul by the servant as a gift to the prophet Samuel (1 Sam. 9:8); and the 20th part of a shekel, or a gerah (Lev. 27:25). These pieces were probably fragments of gold or silver bars rather than shaped coins.

The talent was the largest unit of silver, shaped in pellets or rings, with approximately the value of one ox.

Before coins with stamped values were introduced, the pieces of precious metal for transactions had to be weighed on a scale. Abraham measured the shekels given to Ephron (Gen. 23:16). Such a system was certainly haphazard. Dishonest practices of weighing were banned (Deut. 25:13) in favor of a "perfect and just weight" (v. 15), because "a false balance is an abomination to the Lord" (Prov. 11:1).

Eventually pieces of metal were standardized, then stamped to designate their weight and value. Coins still had to be weighed, however, since their edges might have been trimmed or filed. Ancient coins often show other marks, indicating they may have been probed to assure their silver content.

The earliest coins were probably struck in Lydia by King Croesus (561–546 B.C), whose legendary Anatolian mines and stream beds supplied gold and silver. He was conquered by Cyrus the Great, who may have carried the idea of coined money back to Persia. The Persian Darius the Great (522–486 B.C.) minted coins of gold. The coin known as a daric which bore his name was common with the Israelites during the Captivity. It was similar to a U.S. five–dollar gold piece. Ten thousand darics were paid craftsmen for their work on the Temple built by Solomon (1 Chr. 29:7).

The Greeks soon adapted the Persian and Babylonian coinage, portraying animals, natural objects and Greek gods on the coins—which were called drachmas (Greek for "handful"). The tetradrachma or shekel of Tyre was about the size of an American half–dollar. It probably circulated among the Israelites. Archaeologists have uncovered coins of Greek design marked "YHD" (Judah), probably minted by the Persians for use by the Jews. However, these particular coins are not mentioned in the Bible.

Alexander the Great of Greece conquered the

Photo by Gleason Archer

The denarius coin was considered a day's wages for a laborer in the time of Jesus (Matt. 20:1-16). This particular denarius featured the image of the Roman Emperor Tiberius.

Persian Empire. In the period between the Old and New Testaments, Greek coins (especially the tetradrachma) began pouring into Palestine. After Alexander's death, his successors known as the Ptolemies added mints at Gaza, Jaffa, and Tyre for making coins.

The Seleucids seized Palestine (about 200 B.C.), forcing Greek culture upon the Jews until they rebelled against ANTIOCHUS IV around 167 B.C. The right to mint coins was an issue, but the Jewish revolt led by Simon Maccabeus was thwarted. Later Antiochus VII established a mint which struck coins bearing his name. But the Seleucids' domination lapsed as the Hasmoneans gained their freedom and began minting their own small bronze coins (one–half, one–third, and one–fourth shekel in weight). These were inscribed to a certain high priest of that time and "the community of Jews." Still the Selucids issued official gold and silver coins. This brief phase of freedom for the Jews ended when the Romans annexed Palestine in 63 B.C.

Roman coins common in New Testament times showed a profound Greek influence, including those issued by Herod the Great (36–4 B.C.) and his sons. But because of the Second Commandment which prohibited graven images, the coins displayed only traditional, stylized pictures. However, they did include the date of issue.

The basic unit of Roman coinage was the silver denarius, probably equal to a laborer's daily wage, as in the parable of the vineyard workers (Matt. 20:9–10, 13). It was also used for paying tribute, or taxes, to the Roman emperor, whose image it carried. Jesus was shown a denarius, in a ploy by the Pharisees to trick him into opposing the Roman taxation authority. But he replied, "Render therefore to Caesar the things that are Caesar's, and to God the things that are God's" (Matt. 22:15–22).

This silver shekel was issued by the Jewish people during their first revolt against Roman rule (A.D. 66-70). It portrayed the blossom of an almond tree on one side and a silver chalice on the other.

The golden aureus was worth about 25 denarii. The "copper coin" (assarion, equal to one–sixteenth of a silver denarius) was mentioned by Jesus as being worth no more than two sparrows, in his counsel about God's concern for the smallest creatures as well as the most powerful (Matt. 10:29; Luke 12:6). The "penny" (quadrans or kodrantes) was equal to one-fourth of the copper assarion. It was also mentioned by Jesus (Matt. 5:26).

Greek coins generally bore religious symbols. They may have been minted at pagan temples, which served as business centers for granting loans and receiving estates. The cult of Astarte may have had a strong influence on the production of coins. Silver for Greek coins was supplied by the rich mines of Laurium. Gold coins were less popular among the Greeks.

The basic Greek coin was the drachma, roughly equivalent to a Roman denarius, or one day's wages. Probably the drachma is the "lost coin" of Jesus' parable (Luke 15:8-10). The apostle Paul, when he practiced tent making at Corinth, probably exchanged his work for the Corinthian coins which pictured the winged horse Pegasus. (Corinth had minted coins as early as 650 B.C.) Paul later preached in Athens, Greece, where one archaeologist has excavated 80,000 coins.

The Greek didrachmon (two drachma piece) was used by the Jews for their half-shekel Temple tax (Matt. 17:24). The silver stater, or tetradrachma, was a four-drachma piece, used to pay the Temple tax (Matt. 17:27). The mina, equaling 100 drachmas, illustrated Jesus' parable about the wise use of resources (Luke 19:11-27).

The only Jewish coin mentioned in the New Testament is the "widow's mite" or lepton, called a mite by the NKJV. These were very small copper coins worth only a fraction of a penny by today's standards. Yet, Jesus commended the poor widow who gave two mites to the Temple treasury, because "she out of her poverty put in all that she had, her whole livelihood" (Mark 12:44).

MONEYBELTS — girdles, belts, or waistbands that bound together loose garments and also held money. When Jesus sent out the Twelve, He told them to take neither gold nor silver nor copper in their moneybelts (Matt. 10:9; Mark 6:8; belts, RSV, NIV; purses, KJV, NEB). They were to depend on the generosity of the people in the villages and towns through which they passed.

MONEYCHANGERS — bankers who exchanged one nation's currency, or one size of coin, for another. These people provided a convenience, charging a fee (often exorbitant) for their services. Some moneychangers operated in the Temple area (the Court of the Gentiles), because all money given to the Temple had to be in the Tyrian silver coin. According to Exodus 30:11-16, every Israelite 20 years old or older was required to pay an annual tax of a half-shekel into the Temple treasury.

On two different occasions Jesus cleansed the Temple of moneychangers: once at the beginning of His ministry (John 2:13-16) and once near the end of His ministry (Matt. 21:12-13).

According to the Gospel of John, Jesus made a whip of cords and drove out of the Temple those who sold oxen, sheep, and doves. He overturned the tables of the moneychangers and poured out the changers' money (John 2:13-14). It is not clear why Jesus was so angry with the moneychangers. His anger was not directed at the Temple tax, for He Himself paid it willingly (Matt. 17:24-27). Jesus' anger may have been directed at the commercialism within the Temple area that took advantage of the poor: "Do not make My Father's house a house of merchandise!" (John 2:16).

Also see OCCUPATIONS AND TRADES.

MONEYLENDER — one whose business is lending money at interest (Ex. 22:25; creditor, RSV, NASB; usurer, KJV). The Hebrew word translated as moneylender has the root meaning of "one who exacts" (Lev. 25:35–38; Prov. 28:8; Jer. 15:10).

MONITOR LIZARD, MONKEY (see ANIMALS OF THE BIBLE).

MONOTHEISM — worship of one supreme God, an important characteristic of the worship system of the Hebrew people. One of the central teachings in the Old Testament is Deuteronomy 6:4: "Hear, O Israel: The Lord our God, the Lord is one!" Against the idolatry of surrounding nations with their many gods (polytheism), God revealed this essential aspect of His nature to Israel in the Old Testament period. The Lord is one God.

In the New Testament God further revealed that He is One in Three and that His essential being is triune. God is the triune family of Father, Son, and Holy Spirit, united in will, purpose, holiness, and love. Accordingly, Christianity is both monotheistic and trinitarian.

Jesus' oneness with the Father is explicitly claimed in the fourth gospel: "In the beginning was the Word, and the Word was with God, and the Word was God" (John 1:1). Jesus Himself consciously laid claim to His oneness with the Father (John 5:17–24). This angered His opponents so much that they sought to kill Him (John 5:18). The absolute unity of Father, Son, and Holy Spirit is expressed throughout the New Testament (John 14:16; 16:13–15).

MONTH — one of the 12 divisions of a year, measured by the completed cycle in the changing of the MOON. Solomon had 12 governors over all Israel, who provided food for the king and his household; each made provision for one month of the year (1 Kin. 4:7). The military divisions of Israel were also 12 in number, one for each month of the year, each division consisting of 14,000 men (1 Chr. 27:1–15). Also see CALENDAR; TIME.

MOON — the "lesser light" of the heavens (Gen. 1:16) created by God to rule over the night. The moon had a special significance for the ancient Israelites. Their festival CALENDAR, which began each month with the rising of the new moon, was known as a lunar calendar. The day of the appearing of the new moon was signaled by the blowing of the ram's horn. This event was also observed with special sacrifices (Num. 10:10; 28:11–15). Since the lunar year is about 11 days shorter than the solar year, a 13th month was added to the Hebrew calendar every third year to keep the festival calendar on schedule with the changing seasons.

The accurate recording of the new moon as it arrived each month was important, because the moon governed the dates for other religious festivals. Clouds or fog could obscure the new moon on the night of its rising. When this happened, the Hebrew people would extend the festival days to be sure the correct day was observed. This is probably why the festival of the New Moon used by David to cover his absence from Saul's court seems to have lasted for two days (1 Sam. 20:5).

The prophet Amos condemned Israel's merchants for their impatience with the interruption to business caused by the festival of the New Moon (Amos 8:4–6). Speaking through the prophet Isaiah (1:13–15), God condemned the formal, but empty, observance of the New Moon festival.

Along with the sun and the planet Venus, the moon was worshiped as a cosmic god by many pagan nations of the ancient world. The moon was known as Sin in Babylon and Assyria, Nanna in Sumer, and Yarih at Ugarit. This last name is closely related to the Hebrew word for moon. While the worship of the moon and any other natural phenomenon was strictly forbidden among the Hebrews (Deut. 4:19, 17:3), the evil King Manasseh established the cults of "all the host of heaven," presumably including the moon, in the court of Solomon's Temple (2 Kin. 21:3–5).

MOON, NEW (see FEASTS AND FESTIVALS).

MORASTHITE [moh RASH thite] — a native of MORESHETH GATH.

MORDECAI [MAWR deh kie] (*related to Marduk*) — the name of two men in the Old Testament:

1. One of the Jewish captives who returned with Zerubbabel from Babylon (Ezra 2:2; Neh. 7:7).

2. The hero of the Book of Esther. Mordecai was probably born in Babylonia during the years of the CAPTIVITY of the Jewish people by this pagan nation. He was a resident of Susa (Shushan), the Persian capital during the reign of Ahasuerus (Xerxes I), the king of Persia (ruled 486–465 B.C.).

When Mordecai's uncle, Abihail, died (Esth. 2:5), Mordecai took his orphaned cousin, Hadassah (Esther), into his home as her adoptive father (Esth. 2:7). When two of the king's eunuchs, Bigthan and Teresh, conspired to assassinate King Ahasuerus, Mordecai discovered the plot and exposed it, saving the king's life (Esth. 2:21–22). Mordecai's good deed was recorded in the royal chronicles of Persia (Esth. 2:23).

Mordecai showed his loyalty to God by refusing to bow to Haman, the official second to the king (Esth. 3:2, 5). According to the Greek historian Herodotus, when the Persians bowed before their king, they paid homage as to a god. Mordecai, a Jew, would not condone such idolatry.

Haman's hatred for Mordecai sparked his plan to kill all the Jews in the Persian Empire (Esth. 3:6). Mordecai reminded his cousin, who had become Queen Esther, of her God–given opportunity to expose Haman to the king and to save her people (Esth. 3:1–4:17). The plot turned against Haman, who ironically was hanged on the same gallows that he had prepared for Mordecai (Esth. 7:10).

Haman was succeeded by Mordecai, who now was second in command to the most powerful man in the kingdom. He used his new position to encourage his people to defend themselves against the scheduled massacre planned by Haman. Persian officials also assisted in protecting the Jews, an event celebrated by the annual Feast of PURIM (Esth. 9:26–32).

MOREH [MOH reh] (*diviner*) — the name of two places in the Old Testament:

1. The site of a terebinth, or oak, tree near Shechem where Abraham built an altar (Gen. 12:6–7). The place probably was an old Canaanite sanctuary. The "terebinth tree of Moreh" was likely a sacred tree long before Abraham entered Canaan. This may have been the same tree under which Joshua set up a large memorial stone to commemorate Israel's renewed covenant with God (Josh. 24:26). The tree probably took its name from a "diviner" (a teacher or soothsayer who practiced DIVINATION) who lived here.

2. A hill in the territory of Issachar (see Map 3, B–2). In the time of the judges, the troops of the Midianites camped by the hill of Moreh. This hill apparently became the point of attack for the 300 Israelite warriors led by Gideon (Judg. 7:8). The site has been identified as present–day Jebel Dahi.

MORESHETH GATH [MOH reh sheth gath] (*possession of Gath*) — the birthplace, hometown, or residence of the prophet MICAH (Mic. 1:14). Micah is also called the Morasthite (Jer. 26:18, KJV; Mic. 1:1, KJV)—that is, a native or resident of Moresheth. The site of Moresheth Gath is identified with present–day Tell ej-Judeideh, in the lowland plain of Judah.

MORIAH [moh RYE uh] (*Jehovah provides*) — the name of two sites in the Old Testament:

1. A land to which God commanded Abraham to take his only son Isaac and to offer him as a burnt offering on one of the mountains. The mountains of this land were a three–day journey from Beersheba and were visible from a great distance (Gen. 22:2, 4).

2. The hill at Jerusalem where Solomon built "the house of the Lord," the Temple. Originally this was the threshing floor of Ornan the Jebusite (2 Chr. 3:1), also called Araunah the Jebusite (2 Sam. 24:16–24), where God appeared to David. David purchased the threshing floor from Ornan (1 Chr. 21:15—22:1), and built an altar on the site. It was left to David's son (Solomon) to build the Temple.

The Jews believe the altar of burnt offering in the Temple at Jerusalem was situated on the exact site of the altar on which Abraham intended to sacrifice Isaac. To them the two Mount Moriahs mentioned in the Bible are identical. The Muslim mosque, the Dome of the Rock in Jerusalem, presently is situated on this site.

MORNING — the first part of the day, extending from sunrise to noon (Gen. 1:5; Ps. 30:5; Matt. 16:3). Christ is called "the Bright and Morning Star" (Rev. 22:16) who brought a new day of hope and promise for the world. Also see TIME.

MORNING STAR (see LUCIFER).

MORROW — KJV word for the next day or to-morrow (Gen. 19:34; Luke 10:35; Acts 25:17). Also see TIME.

MORTAL — a biblical term that describes the weak, fleeting nature of human life, emphasizing man's weakness and limitation (Job 4:17; 10:5; Is. 13:12). The word carries the meaning of "one certain to die." In contrast, according to the apostle Paul, "Our Savior Jesus Christ has abolished death and brought life and immortality to light through the gospel" (2 Tim. 1:10).

MORTAR — a term which describes a cement used in building and a utensil for crushing grain:

1. A substance used to bond bricks or stones together (Ex. 1:14). The most common mortar of Bible times was a wet clay mixture, which was mixed by treading it by foot (Nah. 3:14). The second method was to use a natural tarlike substance, usually called pitch or bitumen (Gen. 11:3). In Mesopotamia and in Palestine around the Dead Sea, archaeologists have found buildings in which bitumen (a mineral pitch) was used for mortar.

2. A hollowed-out vessel—made of wood, stone, or metal—used to pulverize grain, spices, herbs, and other substances (Num. 11:8). Archaeologists have found many hollowed-out stones and pestles used for pounding.

Also see MINERALS; TOOLS OF THE BIBLE.

MORTAR, THE (see MAKTESH).

MORTAR AND PESTLE (see TOOLS OF THE BIBLE).

MORTIFY — KJV word for the practice of disciplining one's body and physical appetites through self-denial (Rom. 8:13; Col. 3:5; put to death, NKJV). The New Testament calls believers to be "crucified with Christ" by mortifying, or putting to death, the deeds of the body, such as fornication, uncleanness, passion, evil desire, and covetousness.

MOSERA [moh SEE ruh] (*bonds*) — a place in the wilderness where the Israelites camped on their journey from Egypt to Canaan. Situated between "the wells of Bene Jaakan" and Gudgodah, Moserah was the place where Aaron died and was buried (Deut. 10:6; Moserah, KJV; plural, Moseroth, Num. 33:30–31).

MOSEROTH [moh ZEE rawth] — a form of MOSERAH.

MOSES [MOE zez] (*drawn out*) — the Hebrew prophet who delivered the Israelites from Egyptian slavery and who was their leader and lawgiver during their years of wandering in the wilderness. He was the son of Amram and Jochebed (Ex. 6:18, 20; Num. 26:58–59), the grandson of Kohath, the great-grandson of Levi, and the brother of Aaron and Miriam.

Moses was a leader so inspired by God that he was able to build a united nation from a race of oppressed and weary slaves. In the covenant ceremony at Mount Sinai, where the TEN COMMANDMENTS were given, he founded the religious community known as Israel. As the interpreter of these covenant laws, he was the organizer of the community's religious and civil traditions. His story is told in the Old Testament—in the books of Exodus, Leviticus, Numbers, and Deuteronomy.

Moses' life is divided into three major periods:

The Forty Years in Egypt. The Hebrew people had been in slavery in Egypt for some 400 years. This was in accord with God's words to Abraham that his seed, or descendants, would be in a foreign land in affliction for 400 years (Gen. 15:13). At the end of this time, God began to set His people free from their bondage by bringing Moses to birth. He was a child of the captive Hebrews, but one whom the Lord would use to deliver Israel from her oppressors.

Moses was born at a time when the Pharaoh, the ruler of Egypt, had given orders that no more male Hebrew children should be allowed to live. The Hebrew slaves had been reproducing so fast that the king felt threatened by a potential revolt against his authority. To save the infant Moses, his mother made a little vessel of papyrus waterproofed with asphalt and pitch. She placed Moses in the vessel, floating among the reeds on the bank of the Nile River.

By God's providence, Moses—the child of a Hebrew slave—was found and adopted by an Egyptian princess, the daughter of the Pharaoh himself. He was reared in the royal court as a prince of the Egyptians: "And Moses was learned in all the wisdom of the Egyptians, and was mighty in words and deeds" (Acts 7:22). At the same time, the Lord determined that Moses should be taught in his earliest years by his own mother. This meant that he was founded in the faith of his fathers, although he was reared as an Egyptian (Ex. 2:1–10).

One day Moses became angry at an Egyptian taskmaster who was beating a Hebrew slave; he killed the Egyptian and buried him in the sand (Ex. 2:12). When this became known, however, he feared for his own life and fled from Egypt to the land of Midian. Moses was 40 years old when this occurred (Acts 7:23–29).

The Forty Years in the Land of Midian. Moses' exile of about 40 years was spent in the land of Midian (mostly in northwest Arabia), in the desert between Egypt and Canaan. In Midian Moses became a shepherd and eventually the son-in-law of Jethro, a Midianite priest. Jethro gave his daughter Zipporah to Moses in marriage (Ex. 2:21); and she bore two sons, Gershom and Eliezer (Ex. 18:3–4; Acts 7:29). During his years as a shepherd, Moses became familiar with the wilderness of the Sinai Peninsula, learning much about survival in the desert. He also learned patience and much about leading sheep. All of these skills prepared him to be the shepherd of the Israelites in later years when he led them out of Egypt and through the Wilderness of Sinai.

Near the end of his 40-year sojourn in the land of Midian, Moses experienced a dramatic call to ministry. This call was given at the BURNING BUSH in the wilderness near the mountain of Sinai. The Lord revealed to Moses His intention to deliver Israel from Egyptian captivity into a "land flowing with milk and honey" which He had promised centuries before to Abraham, Isaac, and Jacob. The Lord assured Moses that He would be with him, and that by God's presence, he would be able to lead the people out.

God spoke to Moses from the midst of a burning bush, but Moses doubted that it was God who spoke. He asked for a sign. Instantly his rod, which he cast on the ground, became a serpent (Ex. 4:3).

In spite of the assurance of this miraculous sign, Moses was still hesitant to take on this task. He pleaded that he was "slow of speech and slow of tongue" (Ex. 4:10), perhaps implying that he was a stutterer or a stammerer. God countered Moses' hesitation by appointing his brother Aaron to be his spokesman. Moses would be God's direct representative, and Aaron would be his mouthpiece and interpreter to the people of Israel. Finally Moses accepted this commission from God and returned to Egypt for a confrontation with Pharaoh.

Soon after his return, Moses stirred the Hebrews to revolt and demanded of Pharaoh, "Let My people go, that they may hold a feast to Me in the wil-

Michelangelo's statue of Moses, great lawgiver and leader of the Hebrew people.
Photo by Ben Chapman

derness" (Ex. 5:1). But Pharaoh rejected the demand of this unknown God of whom Moses and Aaron spoke: "Who is the Lord, that I should obey His voice to let Israel go? I do not know the Lord, nor will I let Israel go" (Ex. 5:2). He showed his contempt of this God of the Hebrews by increasing the oppression of the slaves (Ex. 5:5–14). As a result, the people grumbled against Moses (Ex. 5:20–21).

But Moses did not waver in his mission. He warned Pharaoh of the consequences that would fall on his kingdom if he should refuse to let the people of Israel go. Then followed a stubborn battle of wills with Pharaoh hardening his heart and stiffening his neck against God's commands. Ten terrible plagues were visited upon the land of Egypt (Ex. 7:14—12:30), the tenth plague being the climax of horrors.

The ultimate test of God's power to set the people free was the slaying of the firstborn of all Egypt, on the night of the PASSOVER feast of Israel (Ex. 11:1—12:30). That night Moses began to lead the slaves to freedom, as God killed the firstborn of Egypt and spared the firstborn of Israel through the sprinkling of the blood of the Passover lamb. This pointed to the day when God's own Lamb would come into the world to deliver, by His own blood, all of those who put their trust in Him, setting them free from sin and death (1 Pet. 1:19).

After the Hebrews left, Pharaoh's forces pursued them to the Red Sea (some scholars say *the Sea of Reeds*), threatening to destroy them before they could cross. A PILLAR OF CLOUD AND FIRE, however, stood between the Israelites and the Egyptians, protecting the Israelites until they could escape. When Moses stretched his hand over the sea, the waters were divided and the Israelites passed to the other side. When the Egyptians attempted to follow, Moses again stretched his hand over the sea, and the waters closed over the Egyptian army (Ex. 14:19–31).

The Forty Years in the Wilderness. Moses led the people toward Mount Sinai, in obedience to the word of God spoken to him at the burning bush (Ex. 3:1–12). During the long journey through the desert, the people began to murmur because of the trials of freedom, forgetting the terrible trials of Egyptian bondage. Through it all, Moses was patient, understanding both the harshness of the desert and the blessings of God's provision for them.

In the Wilderness of Shur the people murmured against Moses because the waters of Marah were bitter. The Lord showed Moses a tree. When Moses cast the tree into the waters, the waters were made sweet (Ex. 15:22–25). In answer to Moses' prayers, God sent bread from heaven—MANNA and quail to eat (Exodus 16). In the Wilderness of Sin, when they again had no water, Moses performed a miracle by striking a rock, at a place called Massah (Tempted) and Meribah (Contention), and water came out of the rock (Ex. 17:1–7). When they reached the land of Midian, Moses' father–in–law Jethro came to meet them. He gave Moses sound advice on how to exercise his leadership and authority more efficiently by delegating responsibility to subordinate rulers who would judge the people in small cases (Exodus 18).

When the Israelites arrived at Mount Sinai, Moses went up into the mountain for 40 days (Ex. 24:18). The Lord appeared in a terrific storm—"thunderings and lightnings, and a thick cloud" (Ex. 19:16). Out of this momentous encounter came the covenant between the Lord and Israel, including the Ten Commandments (Ex. 20:1-17).

In giving the Law to the Hebrew people, Moses taught the Israelites what the Lord expected of them—that they were to be a holy people separated from the pagan immorality and idolatry of their surroundings. Besides being the lawgiver, Moses was also the one through whom God presented the TABERNACLE and instructions for the holy office of the priesthood. Under God's instructions, Moses issued ordinances to cover specific situations, instituted a system of judges and hearings in civil cases, and regulated the religious and ceremonial services of worship.

When Moses delayed in coming down from Mount Sinai, the faithless people became restless. They persuaded Aaron to take their golden earrings and other articles of jewelry and to fashion a golden calf for worship. When he came down from the mountain, Moses was horrified at the idolatry and rebellion of his people. The sons of Levi were loyal to Moses, however; and he ordered them to punish the rebels (Ex. 32:28). Because of his anger at the golden calf, Moses cast down the two tablets of stone with the Ten Commandments and broke them at the foot of the mountain (Ex. 32:19). After the rebellion had been put down, Moses went up into Mount Sinai again and there received the Ten Commandments a second time (Ex. 34:1, 29).

After leaving Mount Sinai, the Israelites continued their journey toward the land of Canaan. They arrived at KADESH BARNEA, on the border of the Promised Land. From this site, Moses sent 12 spies, one from each of the 12 tribes of Israel, into Canaan to explore the land. The spies returned with glowing reports of the fruitfulness of the land. They brought back samples of its figs and pomegranates and a cluster of grapes so large that it had to be carried between two men on a pole (Num. 13:1–25). The majority of the spies, however, voted against the invasion of the land. Ten of them spoke fearfully of the huge inhabitants of Canaan (Ex. 13:31–33).

The minority report, delivered by Caleb and Joshua, urged a bold and courageous policy. By trusting the Lord, they said, the Israelites would be able to attack and overcome the land (Num. 13:30). But the people lost heart and rebelled, refusing to enter Canaan and clamoring for a new leader who would take them back to Egypt (Num. 14:1-4). To punish them for their lack of faith, God condemned all of that generation, except Caleb and Joshua, to perish in the wilderness (Num. 14:26-38).

During these years of wandering in the wilderness, Moses' patience was continually tested by the murmurings, grumblings, and complaints of the people. At one point, Moses' patience reached its breaking point and he sinned against the Lord, in anger against the people. When the people again grumbled against Moses, saying they had no water, the Lord told Moses to speak to the rock and water would flow forth. Instead, Moses lifted his hand and struck the rock twice with his rod. Apparently because he disobeyed the Lord in this act, Moses was not permitted to enter the Promised Land (Num. 20:1–13). That privilege would belong to his successor, Joshua.

When Moses had led the Israelites to the borders of Canaan, his work was done. In "the Song of Moses" (Deut. 32:1–43), Moses renewed the Sinai Covenant with the survivors of the wanderings, praised God, and blessed the people, tribe by tribe (Deut. 33:1–29). Then he climbed Mount Nebo to the top of Pisgah and viewed the Promised Land from afar and died. The Hebrews never saw him again, and the circumstances of his death and burial remain shrouded in mystery (Num. 34:1–8).

After his death, Moses continued to be viewed by Israel as the servant of the Lord (Josh. 1:1–2) and as the one through whom God spoke to Israel (Josh. 1:3; 9:24; 14:2). For that reason, although it was truly the Law of God, the Law given at Mount Sinai was consistently called the Law of Moses (Josh. 1:7; 4:10). Above all, Joshua's generation remembered Moses as the man of God (Josh. 14:6).

This high regard for Moses continued throughout Israelite history. Moses was held in high esteem by Samuel (1 Sam. 12:6, 8), the writer of 1 Kings (1 Kin. 2:3), and the Jewish people who survived in the times after the Captivity (1 Chr. 6:49; 23:14).

The psalmist also remembered Moses as the man of God and as an example of a great man of prayer (Ps. 99:6). He recalled that God worked through Moses (Ps. 77:20; 103:7), realizing that the consequence of his faithfulness to God was to suffer much on behalf of God's people (Ps. 106:16, 32).

The prophets of the Old Testament also remembered Moses as the leader of God's people (Is. 63:12), as the one by whom God brought Israel out of Egypt (Mic. 6:4), and as one of the greatest of the interceders for God's people (Jer. 15:1). Malachi called the people to remember Moses' Law and to continue to be guided by it, until the Lord Himself should come to redeem them (Mal. 4:4).

Jesus showed clearly, by what He taught and by how He lived, that He viewed Moses' Law as authoritative for the people of God (Matt. 5:17–18). To the two disciples on the road to Emmaus, Jesus expounded the things concerning Himself written in the Law of Moses, the Prophets, and the other writings of the Old Testament (Luke 24:27). At the TRANSFIGURATION, Moses and Elijah appeared to Jesus and talked with Him (Matt. 17:1–4; Mark 9:2–5; Luke 9:28–33).

In his message before the Jewish Council, Stephen included a lengthy reference to how God delivered Israel by Moses and how Israel rebelled against God and against Moses' leadership (Acts 7:20–44).

The writer of the Book of Hebrews spoke in glowing terms of the faith of Moses (Heb. 11:24–29). These and other passages demonstrate how highly Moses was esteemed by various writers of the Old and New Testaments.

The New Testament, however, shows that Moses' teaching was intended only to prepare humanity for the greater teaching and work of Jesus Christ (Rom. 1:16—3:31). What Moses promised, Jesus fulfilled: "For the law was given through Moses, but grace and truth came through Jesus Christ" (John 1:17).

MOST HIGH — a name for God which appears frequently in the Old Testament, particularly in the Psalms and the Books of Isaiah and Daniel (Ps. 92:1; Is. 14:14; Dan. 4:17). The name emphasizes the might and power of God. Also see GOD, NAMES OF.

MOTE — KJV word for SPECK.

MOTH (see ANIMALS OF THE BIBLE).

MOTHER — the female parent of a household. In the Hebrew family, the mother occupied a higher position than that enjoyed by women in many other nations. The mother's duties were primarily domestic, but she was held in high regard by her family and Hebrew society.

The concept of mother was sometimes used in other, more figurative ways. Nations were sometimes thought of as mothers. The prophet Ezekiel used mother as a metaphor for Israel. After being nurtured and cared for by their "mother," the "princes of Israel" brought shame upon her by their idolatrous practices (Ezek. 19:1–14). Jeremiah used the concept of Israel as mother to personify the nation's sin (Jer. 50:12–13), while Hosea made it a continuing theme of his prophecies.

The word mother was sometimes used to describe large and important cities. The city of Abel of Beth Maachah was called "a mother in Israel" (2 Sam. 20:19). A city was also a mother in terms of its influence. Babylon was called "the mother of harlots and of the abominations of the earth" (Rev. 17:5).

The figurative meaning of "mother" also included ancestry. Eve was the "mother of all living" (Gen. 3:20). God blessed Sarah by declaring, "She shall be a mother of nations" (Gen. 17:16). Rebekah was blessed to become "the mother of thousands of ten thousands" (Gen. 24:60).

The love and nurturing of God is sometimes compared to the love and caring a mother gives to a newborn child. Paul referred to new Christians as "babes in Christ" (1 Cor. 3:1), implying a connection to Jesus and God as mother as well as father (1 Thess. 2:7).

MOTHER–IN–LAW — the mother of a person's husband or wife. A classic example of a beloved mother-in-law is Naomi, mother-in-law of Ruth (Ruth 1:1–4). Also see FAMILY.

MOUNT, MOUNTAIN — elevations higher than hills, although the Hebrew words for hill and mountain are often used interchangeably. The mountains of Palestine consist of two main ridges.

The ridge west of the Jordan Rift (the Arabah) is the rugged hill country of Galilee, Samaria, and Judah.

The second ridge, east of the Jordan, includes the loftiest of the area's mountains—Mount Hermon (about 2,800 meters, 9,166 feet)—and runs through Gilead, Ammon, Moab, and Edom. The elevations of this range are not great: Ebal (940 meters, 3,084 feet); Gerizim (880 meters, 2,890 feet); Gilboa (517 meters, 1,696 feet); Nebo (800 meters, 2,630 feet); Tabor (590 meters, 1,930 feet); and Sinai, or Jebel Musa (2,300 meters, 7,500 feet). However, because these mountains are near the Dead Sea, which is about 400 meters (1,300 feet) below sea level, they appear higher than their elevations indicate.

In the KJV, the word mount also refers to a siege mound raised by an attacking army against a fortified city (2 Sam. 20:15).

MOUNT BAAL HERMON [BAY uhl HUR mun] — a mountain from which the Israelites were unable to expel the Hivites (Judg. 3:3). East of the Jordan River, the site marked the northern limit of the half-tribe of Manasseh. Some scholars believe the Hebrew text may originally have read "Baal Gad near Mount Hermon" (Josh. 13:5; 1 Chr. 5:23).

MOUNT OF THE BEATITUDES — a slope on the northwest shore of the Sea of Galilee where Jesus is believed to have delivered the Sermon on the Mount (Matt. 5:1—7:29), also known as the Sermon on the Plain (Luke 6:20–49). The "level place" (Luke 6:17) from which Jesus spoke was not necessarily on the plain, but could have been a plateau on the mountain. A church has been built on the site traditionally recognized as the Mount of Beatitudes. But the actual site cannot be identified with certainty.

MOUNT OF THE CONGREGATION — in Babylonian mythology, a mountain in the far north where the gods congregated (Is. 14:13; mount of assembly, NIV; the mountain where the gods meet, NEB). Apparently Isaiah knew of this Babylonian myth when he wrote his prophecy against the haughty king of Babylon (Is. 14:12).

MOUNT OF CORRUPTION — a hill on the southern ridge of the Mount of Olives. On the Mount of Corruption King Solomon built HIGH PLACES for his wives' pagan gods. These hill-shrines were destroyed in the religious reformation instituted by King Josiah (2 Kin. 23:13; Hill of Corruption, NIV; mount of destruction, NAS).

MOUNT EPHRAIM — [EE free im] (see EPHRAIN, MOUNT OF).

MOUNT HERES [HE reez] (*mountain of the sun*)

Photo: Matson Photo Collection

These magnificent cedars once covered the mountains of Lebanon. But only a few isolated groves remain today because of repeated cutting across the centuries.

— a mountain near Aijalon and Shaalbim on the border between Judah and Dan (Judg. 1:35; mountain of the sun, RSV).

MOUNT OF OLIVES — a north-to-south ridge of hills east of Jerusalem where Jesus was betrayed on the night before His crucifixion. This prominent feature of Jerusalem's landscape is a gently rounded hill, rising to about the height of 830 meters (2,676 feet) and overlooking the TEMPLE.

The closeness of the Mount of Olives to Jerusalem's walls made this series of hills a grave strategic danger. The Roman commander Titus had his headquarters on the northern extension of the ridge during the siege of Jerusalem in A.D. 70. He named the place Mount Scopus, or "Lookout Hill," because of the view which it offered over the city walls. The whole hill must have provided a platform for the Roman catapults that hurled heavy objects over the Jewish fortifications of the city.

In ancient times the whole mount must have been heavily wooded. As its name implies, it was covered with dense olive groves. It was from this woodland that the people, under Nehemiah's command, gathered their branches of olive, oil trees, myrtle, and palm to make booths when the Feast of

Tabernacles was restored after their years of captivity in Babylon (Neh. 8:15).

The trees also grew on this mountain or hill in New Testament times. When Jesus entered the city, the people who acclaimed him king must have gathered the branches with which they greeted His entry from this same wooded area.

Another summit of the Mount of Olives is the one on which the "men of Galilee" stood (Acts 1:11–12) as they watched the resurrected Christ ascend into heaven. Then there is the point to the south above the village of Silwan (or Siloam) on the slope above the spring. Defined by a sharp cleft, it faces west along the converging Valley of HINNOM. It is called the Mount of Offense, or the "Mount of Corruption" (2 Kin. 23:13), because here King Solomon built "high places" for pagan deities that were worshiped by the people during his time (1 Kin. 11:5–7).

Although the Mount of Olives is close to Jerusalem, there are surprisingly few references to this range of hills in the Old Testament. As David fled from Jerusalem during the rebellion by his son Absalom, he apparently crossed the shoulder of the hill: "So David went up by the ascent of the Mount of Olives" (2 Sam. 15:30). Support may be found in this account for the claim that the road from the Jordan Valley did not go around the ridge in Bible times but crossed over the ridge, allowing the city of Jerusalem to break spectacularly on the traveler's sight as he topped the hill.

The Mount of Olives is also mentioned in a reference by the prophet Zechariah to the future Day of the Lord: "In that day His feet will stand on the Mount of Olives, which faces Jerusalem on the east. And the Mount of Olives shall be split in two from east to west, making a very large valley; half of the mountain shall move toward the north and half of it toward the south" (Zech. 14:4). Christian tradition holds that when Christ returns to earth, His feet will touch first upon the Mount of Olives, the exact point from which He ascended into heaven (Acts 1:11–12).

In the New Testament the Mount of Olives played a prominent part in the last week of our Lord's ministry. Jesus approached Jerusalem from the east, by way of Bethphage and Bethany, at the Mount of Olives (Matt. 21:1; Mark 11:1). As He drew near the descent of the Mount of Olives (Luke 19:37), the crowd spread their garments on the road, and others cut branches from the trees and spread them before Him. They began to praise God and shout, "Hosanna to the Son of David!" (Matt. 21:9). When Jesus drew near Jerusalem, perhaps as He arrived at the top of the Mount of Olives, He saw the city and wept over it (Luke 19:41).

Jesus then went into Jerusalem and cleansed the Temple of the moneychangers; He delivered parables to the crowd and silenced the scribes and Pharisees with His wisdom. Later, as He sat on the Mount of Olives, the disciples came to Him privately, and He delivered what is known as "the OLIVET DISCOURSE," a long sermon that speaks of the signs of the times and the end of the age, the Great Tribulation, and the coming of the Son of Man (Matt. 24:3—25:46; Mark 13:3–37).

After Jesus had instituted the LORD'S SUPPER on the night of His betrayal, He and His disciples sang a hymn and went out to the Mount of Olives (Matt. 26:30; Mark 14:26), to the Garden of GETHSEMANE (Matt. 26:36; Mark 14:32). In this garden, on the slopes of the Mount of Olives, Jesus was betrayed by Judas and delivered into the hands of His enemies.

MOUNTAIN SHEEP (see ANIMALS OF THE BIBLE).

MOUNTAIN OF THE VALLEY — a mountain east of the Jordan River valley, in the territory of Reuben (Josh. 13:19; hill of the valley, NAS, RSV; hill in the valley, NIV; hill in the vale, NEB).

MOUNTAINS OF THE AMALEKITES — a place in the land of Ephraim connected with Pirathon, a town where Abdon died (Judg. 12:15).

MOUNTAINS OF THE AMORITES — the hill country of Judah and Ephraim (Deut. 1:7, 20).

MOURNER (see OCCUPATIONS AND TRADES).

MOURNING — the experience or expression of grief, as at a time of death or national disaster. In biblical times, the customs of most cultures encouraged a vivid expression of grief. The people of that time would be puzzled by our more sedate forms of mourning.

The Old Testament has many Hebrew words for mourning. These words range in meaning from anger and indignation to the more common idea of grief over a calamity or death. In addition to wailing and weeping, outward forms of mourning included tearing the clothes and wearing SACKCLOTH (Gen. 37:34), fasting (Ps. 35:13), and throwing dust upon the head (Lam. 2:10).

The period for mourning varied. The Egyptians mourned for Jacob for 70 days (Gen. 50:3), most likely out of respect for him. Israel mourned for Aaron 30 days (Num. 20:29), and the same time for Moses (Deut. 34:8). Jacob mourned for Joseph "many days" (Gen. 37:34). According to one Jewish tradition, after burial mourning was to take place on the third, seventh, and fortieth days, and on the anniversary of the burial.

Mourning began at the moment a person died. The family would begin its wailing, and neighbors would rush to the bereaved household and join in the wailing. If the family could afford them, hired mourners were employed to add their chants, lamentations, and shrieks. Such hired mourners were probably among those who scorned Jesus when He said that Jairus' daughter was "not dead, but sleeping" (Matt. 9:24). Dirge-songs were also played on flutes (Matt. 9:23–24). Amid such pandemonium, it is understandable that Jesus put the crowd outside the house before raising Jairus' daughter.

In the New Testament only three Greek words are rendered as mourn (Matt. 9:15; 11:17; 24:30). The few references to mourning suggests that

Christ's work removed the dread and pain of death (1 Cor. 15:55). Christians are not to "sorrow as others [unbelievers] who have no hope" (1 Thess. 4:13).

MOUSE (see ANIMALS OF THE BIBLE).

MOUTH — the opening by which food is taken into the body. In the Bible the mouth is mentioned primarily as the organ of speech. It means much the same as TONGUE. The mouth ought to be used for good, such as praising God (Ps. 34:1); but it also can be used for evil (Ps. 36:3).

To "open the mouth" means to speak; to "put one's hand on one's mouth" means to be quiet (Job 21:5). The word of God is described as coming from His mouth (Deut. 8:3), as symbolized in Revelation 1:16.

MOWING — the reaping or harvesting of mature grain (Amos 7:1). In Palestine the grain was cut by hand with a short sickle made of pieces of sharp flint or metal set in a wooden handle. After the stalks were cut, they were bound into SHEAVES for drying. Later the grain was stripped from the stalks in a threshing operation.

MOZA [MOH zuh] (*offspring*) — the name of two men in the Old Testament:

1. A son of Ephah, of the family of Hezron and the tribe of Judah (1 Chr. 2:46).

2. A descendant of King Saul (1 Chr. 8:36–37).

MOZAH [MOH zuh] (*unleavened*) — a city in the territory of Benjamin (Josh. 18:26). The site has been identified as the present–day Arab village of Kalunya, eight kilometers (five miles) northwest of Jerusalem.

MULBERRY (see PLANTS OF THE BIBLE).

MULE (see ANIMALS OF THE BIBLE).

MUPPIM [MUP em] (meaning unknown) — a descendant of Benjamin (Gen. 46:21), also called Shupham (Num. 26:39; Shephupham, RSV), Shuppim (1 Chr. 7:12, 15; Shuppites, NIV), and Shephuphan (1 Chr. 8:5).

MURDER — the unlawful killing of one person by another, especially with premeditated malice. After the Fall in the Garden of Eden (Gen. 3:1–24), it was not long before the first murder occurred (Gen. 4:8), as Cain killed Abel his brother.

According to the Book of Genesis, mankind is created in God's image (Gen. 1:26–27). Murdering a human being, therefore, is a serious crime and must be punished (Gen. 9:6). One of the Ten Commandments states, "You shall not murder" (Ex. 20:13; Deut. 5:17). This commandment is quoted several times in the New Testament (Matt. 19:18; Luke 18:20; Rom. 13:9).

Although a compensation—a "ransom" or payment of money—could be made for some crimes, this was not so in the case of murder (Num. 35:31). The "eye for eye, tooth for tooth" law (Ex. 21:24; Deut. 19:21) held that an appropriate punishment

must be given for a crime, but that the punishment must not be greater than the crime.

According to the Law of Moses, the person responsible for carrying out the death penalty, in revenge for a murder, was called the *go'el* or KINSMAN REDEEMER. He was the able–bodied male most closely related to the person who had been murdered. The normal means of execution apparently was stoning; the body was then hung on a tree (Deut. 21:21–22). A person who had accidentally killed another might flee to a CITY OF REFUGE for safety and protection.

In the New Testament, Jesus deepened the Old Testament teaching about murder by giving it a spiritual dimension. Whoever harbors anger and hatred against his brother is in danger of God's judgment (Matt. 5:21). Murder begins in the heart—one's thoughts and meditations—and proceeds out of the heart (Matt. 15:19; Mark 7:21).

But even murder can be forgiven (Matt. 12:31; Mark 3:28). Before his conversion, Saul of Tarsus launched "threats and murder" (Acts 9:1) against the church. But by the grace of God he was converted and became Paul the apostle, missionary to the Gentiles.

MURRAIN (see DISEASES OF THE BIBLE).

MUSHI [MUE shy] (*drawn out*) — a son of Merari and founder of the MUSHITES (Num. 3:20, 33).

MUSHITES [MOO shites] — descendants of Mushi (Num. 3:33; 26:58). Mushi was a son of Merari and grandson of Levi (Ex. 6:19; 1 Chr. 6:19, 47).

MUSIC — vocal or instrumental sounds with rhythm, melody, and harmony. Music was part of everyday life for the ancient Hebrew people. Music was a part of family merrymaking, such as the homecoming party for the prodigal son (Luke 15:25). Music welcomed heroes and celebrated victories. Miriam and other women sang, danced, and played timbrels when the Israelites miraculously escaped the Egyptians (Ex. 15:20), and the Song of Moses in Exodus 15 is the earliest recorded song in the Bible. Jephthah's daughter greeted him with timbrels to celebrate his victory over the Ammonites (Judg. 11:34). David's triumph brought music (1 Sam. 18:6).

Music was used in making war and crowning kings (Judg. 7:18–20; 1 Kin. 1:39–40; 2 Chr. 20:28). Wartime music–making was apparently little more than making noise, as in the fall of Jericho (Joshua 6). There was music for banquets and feasts (Is. 5:12; 24:8–9) and royal courts and harems (Eccl. 2:8). The Bible gives examples of occupational songs (Jer. 31:4–5), dirges and laments (Matt. 9:23), and cultic chants (Ex. 28:34–35; Josh. 6:4–20).

The Jews were apparently a very musical people. The Assyrian king, Sennacherib, demanded as tribute from King Hezekiah of Judah male and female Judean musicians—a most unusual ransom. Psalm 137 relates that the Babylonians demanded "songs of Zion" from the Israelites while they were in captivity (v. 3). During the period between the testaments, Strabo, a Greek geographer, called the female singers of Palestine the most musical in the world.

Music in the Old Testament. The Bible indicates that Jubal was "the father of all those who play the harp and flute" (Gen. 4:21). But professional musicians do not appear in the Bible before David's time. Even before professional musicians became the norm during David's reign, the concept of court musicians did exist. The young David was called to soothe Saul with music (1 Sam. 16:16–23). In this sense David was a minstrel (2 Kin. 3:15)—a player of stringed instruments.

The New Testament minstrels (Matt. 9:23) were flute–players employed as professional mourners. The transition from spontaneous music to professional male musicians chiefly associated with organized religion was a natural one. Israel's neighbors, Assyria and Egypt, had long had professional musicians. In spite of God's command to avoid other cultures, Israel was nevertheless strongly influenced by them—in music as well as religious practices.

Exactly how music was used in the tabernacle and Temple services is not known. But scholars are certain that it accompanied sacrificial rites. Sacrificial music was forbidden after the Romans destroyed the Temple in A.D. 70. The Levites, Temple assistants responsible for the music, seem to have kept this part of the service a secret.

David introduced music into the sanctuary worship. His son and successor Solomon later retained it after the Temple was built (2 Sam. 6:5; 1 Kin. 10:12). Music must have been considered an important part of the service, since Hezekiah and Josiah, the two reform kings, saw to it that music was included in the reformation (2 Chr. 29:25; 35:15).

Asaph, Heman, and Jeduthun (Ethan) helped David set up the sanctuary worship. Asaph headed a choir of singers and musicians who were stationed before the ARK OF THE COVENANT in Jerusalem. Heman and Jeduthun had similar choirs at the old tabernacle at Gibeon (1 Chr. 16:4–6, 39–42). These choirs had 4,000 members (1 Chr. 23:5); 288 of these were trained musicians who directed the lesser–skilled musicians (1 Chr. 25:7–8). All the musicians were divided into 24 courses, each containing 12 skilled musicians. An orchestra consisting of stringed instruments (harps and lyres) and cymbals accompanied the singers (1 Chr. 15:19–21).

Our greatest clue to Hebrew music lies in the Book of Psalms, the earliest existing hymnbook. As hymns, these individual psalms were suitable for chanting and singing in the worship of God.

The Bible gives a glimpse of musical terminology in the headings of the Psalms which appear in the Hebrew language, the language in which the Old Testament was originally written. Their meanings, however, are, to a large extent, obscure. These meanings were apparently lost as early as 250 B.C., the approximate date of the Greek translation of the Old Testament.

Photo by Gustav Jeeninga

A Jordanian flute player at Zaretan. The Jews and the Arabs of the Middle East are known as music-loving people.

Categories of psalm headings include the following:

Titles—These include titles such as "A Psalm [Hebrew, Mizmor] of" (Psalm 87) and "A Contemplation [Hebrew, Maschil] of" (Psalm 78). Mizmor seems to mean "to play, sing"; Maschil may indicate a meditation.

Directions for performance—Alamoth (Psalm 46) may mean "for the flutes" or for soprano voices. Sheminith (Psalms 6; 12) suggests a melodic pattern, perhaps an octave lower than Alamoth and, therefore, tenor or even bass. The NKJV translates, "On an eight–stringed harp." Neginoth (Psalms 4; 6; 54; 55; 61; 67; 76) is translated "stringed instruments" (NKJV), but in reference to most psalms it probably means simply "a song." Mahalath (Psalm 53) was probably a choreographic direction. In Psalm 88 Mahalath is coupled with Leannoth, the uncertain meaning of which has been interpreted as "for singing antiphonally."

Shiggaion (plural, *Shiggionoth*), a part of the Hebrew heading of Psalm 7 probably referred to an erratic, enthusiastic ode or to a psalm of lamentation. *Higgayon* (Ps. 9:16) refers to a solemn sound and may indicate soft music. The meaning of *Muth Labben* (Hebrew heading, Psalm 9) is a mystery. It may be a scribal error. If not, it may refer to a soprano melody for masculine voices.

Cue words—The majority of the psalm titles contain cue words. They direct the practice of setting new words to an old tune, an aspect of hymnology still practiced today. *Shoshannim*, a Hebrew word which means "lilies," occurs in the titles of Psalms 45 and 69 and in Psalm 80 as *Shoshannim Eduth*, "Lilies of testimony," and in Psalm 60 as *Shushan Eduth*, "Lily of the testimony." These expressions may have indicated the melody to which these songs were to be sung. These kinds of cue words appear before Psalms 22; 56—59; and 75, among others.

The heading *Shir–hammaloth* ("A Song of Ascents"; Latin, *cantus graduum*) above Psalms 120—134 has several interpretations. The most common are: (1) These 15 psalms were sung by Levites standing on the 15 steps between the court of the women and the court of the Israelites; and (2) These 15 psalms were sung at three pilgrimage festivals. The second explanation is more probable.

Selah—This word occurs 71 times in the Book of Psalms (also Hab. 3:3, 9, 13). Scholars agree that the term is a musical direction of some sort, but they are not agreed on what the direcion is. It may mean: (1) an interlude—a pause in the singing while the orchestra continues; (2) the equivalent of today's "Amen"; as such it would separate psalms or sections of psalms which have different liturgical purposes; and (3) an acrostic which means "a change of voices" or "repeat."

Music in the New Testament. The New Testament contains little information about music. But it does give some additional hymns to add to the Old Testament hymns—those of Mary (Luke 1:46–55) and Zacharias (Luke 1:68–79)—the Magnificat and the Benedictus. Early Christians sang Hebrew songs accompanied by music (2 Chr. 29:27–28). The apostle Paul refers to "psalms and hymns and spiritual songs" (Eph. 5:19; Col. 3:16). Matthew 26:30 records that Christ and His disciples sang a hymn after the Passover supper, probably the second half of the HALLEL, or Psalms 115—118.

The New Testament also contains accounts of the early Christians singing hymns for worship and comfort (Acts 16:25; Eph. 5:19; Col. 3:16). Some fragments of early Christian hymns also appear in the New Testament (Eph. 5:14; 1 Tim. 3:16). Pliny the Younger, at the beginning of the second century A.D., reported that Christians sang songs about Christ and their faith in Him.

Also see MUSICAL INSTRUMENTS OF THE BIBLE.

MUSICAL INSTRUMENTS OF THE BIBLE —

mechanical implements or devices used to produce harmonious sounds. Musical instruments used by the Hebrew people were of three types: (1) stringed instruments, which used vibrating strings to make sounds; (2) percussion instruments, which were struck to produce musical sounds; and (3) wind instruments, which made sounds either by passing air over a vibrating reed or by forcing air through the instrument.

Scholars have only a very general idea of the specific types of musical instruments intended by the Hebrew and Greek words in the original languages of the Bible. This is why there is such a great difference in the rendering of these words in various English translations. What one version calls a lyre may be rendered as harp, lute, or psaltery by other English translations.

Following is a description of all the musical instruments mentioned in the NKJV. Names of instruments from five other English translations (KJV, NASB, NEB, NIV, and RSV) are cross-referenced to these descriptions from the NKJV.

Bagpipe (see *Dulcimer*).

Bell. Bells were common in Palestine, but they are mentioned only twice in the Bible. These two references do not show that bells were used as musical instruments. Tiny bells of pure gold were fastened to the hem of the priest's robe (Ex. 39:25, 26). The prophet Zechariah also indicated that the Hebrew people put such tiny bells on the bridles or breast straps of their horses. Also see *Gong*.

Bugle (see *Trumpet*).

Cornet (see *Trumpet*).

Cymbals. Used in priestly functions, cymbals were played only by men, and perhaps only by priests. These instruments made a loud, distinctive sound when banged together. They were used to accompany trumpets (Ezra 3:10), the lyre when it was used for worship (1 Chr. 25:1; Neh. 12:27), and "the musical instruments of God" (1 Chr. 16:42). David's chief musician, Asaph, played the cymbals (1 Chr. 16:5).

Dulcimer. This instrument is mentioned only in the Book of Daniel. It was one of the Babylonian instruments that signaled the time for Daniel's three friends—Shadrach, Meshach, and Abed–Nego—to bow down before a golden image of King Nebuchadnezzar (Dan. 3:5, 7, 10, 15, KJV). Other English versions translate the Hebrew word for dulcimer as bagpipes (NASB, RSV) or pipes (NIV).

The exact nature of the dulcimer is unknown. Some scholars believe it may have been similar to a Greek instrument known as the symphonia, which consisted of two pipes thrust through a leather

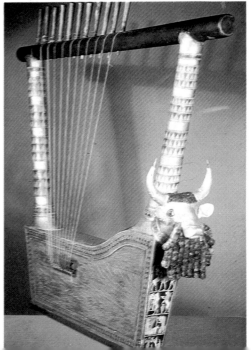

A reconstructed lyre from Mesopotamia. This was a popular musical instrument about 2500 B.C., several centuries before Abraham's time.

Photo by Howard Vos

A Canaanite musician with a zither, an ancient stringed instrument similar to a harp. This instrument was probably in use as early as about 2700 B.C.

sack. The pipes gave out a plaintive sound. The Scottish bagpipes of later centuries may have developed from this instrument. However, other scholars believe the dulcimer was similar to the flute in its construction and the sound which it produced.

Fife (see *Flute*).

Flute. A wind instrument that produced a high, shrill sound. Because of its unique sound, the flute was associated with fertility cults and was considered appropriate only in a secular setting to show both ecstatic joy and deep sorrow. The flute is mentioned in connection with the Temple only in the Psalms (Ps. 150:4). However, the Hebrew word *nehiloth* in the title of Psalm 5 means "[with] flutes." Some flutes were made of silver, while others were made of reeds, wood, or bones. Other words for flute used in various translations of the Bible are organ (Gen. 4:21, KJV); fife (1 Sam. 10:5, NEB); pipe (Job 21:11, RSV); and reed-pipe (Jer. 48:36, NEB).

Gong. Gong is the word used by some English translations for a type of bell sounded at weddings or other happy occasions (1 Cor. 13:1, RSV, NASB). The phrase "noisy gong" is rendered as "sounding brass" by the KJV and NKJV. The gong may have been similar to a handbell. Also see *Bell.*

Harp. The musical instrument mentioned more than any other in the Bible is the harp (2 Chr. 29:25; Ps. 147:7; Is. 23:16). Another word for this instrument used by various translations is lyre. Scholars believe these two instruments were similar in function and design, but the harp was probably a larger version.

The harp is the instrument that David used to soothe the "distressing spirit" which troubled King Saul (1 Sam. 16:16, 23). This smaller lyre, considered by some enthusiasts to be the most noble of all musical instruments, was used both for sacred (2 Chr. 29:25) and secular (Is. 23:16) purposes. Although David apparently plucked the strings with his fingers, the harp was usually played by stroking the strings with a pick, much as a guitar is played. The harp had anywhere from three to twelve strings. Considered an aristocratic instrument, the harp was often made of silver or ivory.

The harp and the lyre are often spoken of interchangeably in the Bible. Other words used for these two instruments by various translations of the Bible are psaltery, lute (1 Kin. 10:12), and viol (Is. 5:12). The lute was an even smaller version of the harp or lyre, consisting of only three strings. In the NKJV the phrase "stringed instruments" is often used to refer to all these instruments in a collective sense: harp, lute, lyre, psaltery, and viol.

Two specific types of harps or lyres are mentioned in some English translations of the Book of Daniel. Daniel's three friends—Shadrach, Meshach, and Abed-Nego—were commanded to bow down and worship an image of the Babylonian king at the sound of various Babylonian musical instruments. These instruments included a sackbut (Dan. 3:5, KJV; trigon, NASB, RSV; triangle, NEB) and a zither (Dan. 3:5, NIV). Some scholars believe the sackbut was the seven-stringed lyre used in Babylon, while the zither may have been a ten-stringed lyre or harp that gave its own distinctive sound.

Horn (see *Trumpet*).
Lute (see *Harp*).
Lyre (see *Harp*).
Organ (see *Flute*).
Pipe (see *Dulcimer*).
Psaltery (see *Harp*).
Ram's Horn (see *Trumpet*).
Reed-pipe (see *Flute*).
Sackbut (see *Harp*).
Shophar (see *Trumpet*).

Sistrums. Sistrums were small musical instruments with a U-shaped frame and a handle at the bottom. Strung on bars between the two parts of the U were small pieces of metal or other objects which could create a rattling sound. The collection of the Jewish oral law, known as the MISHNAH, recognized the sistrum, also called a rattler-sistrum, as the instrument used by women who mourned the death of a relative or friend. This instrument probably originated in Egypt. It was used to express great joy as well as deep sorrow (2 Sam. 6:5; cornets, KJV; castanets, NASB, NEB, RSV).

Tabret (see *Timbrel*).
Tambourine (see *Timbrel*).
Timbrel. A percussion instrument which was carried and beaten by hand. Considered inappropriate for the Temple, it was probably played primarily by women (Ps. 68:25). The timbrel may have been excluded from the Temple instruments because of its great popularity with the Canaanite fertility cults.

Among the Hebrew people, it was associated with merrymaking and processions (Gen. 31:27). Remnants of timbrels with pieces of bronze inserted in the rim have been uncovered by archaeologists. Thus, the instrument could be shaken as well as beaten.

The Hebrew word for timbrel is rendered by other English translations as tabret and tambourine.

Triangle (see *Harp*).

Trigon (see *Harp*).

Trumpet. The trumpet is mentioned several times in the Bible. This instrument was used by the priests during services of sacrifice, especially to signal the DAY OF ATONEMENT (Lev. 25:9). The trumpet was also used to rally troops on the battlefield (Josh. 6:4).

Made of metal or bones, the trumpet featured a sounding air column not quite two feet long. This short length gave this instrument a high, shrill sound. The tone of the trumpet apparently could be regulated (2 Chr. 5:12). Some trumpets were probably made from the horn of an animal; the word horn is used for this instrument in some English translations (1 Chr. 25:5, KJV). Other words used for trumpet include cornet (Ps. 98:6, KJV), and bugle (1 Cor. 14:8, NASB, RSV).

One distinctive type of trumpet or horn used by the Hebrew people was the ram's horn, also known by its Hebrew name, the shophar (Hos. 5:8). The shophar was the greatest of the Jewish ritual instruments. Eventually the horn of a mountain goat was used for this instrument, rather than the horn of a ram. The shophar, or trumpet, was basically a signaling instrument, used to assemble the army (Judg. 3:27; 1 Sam. 13:3), to sound an attack (Job 39:24–25), and to sound an alarm (Jer. 6:1; Amos 3:6).

The ram's horn signaled war and peace, the new moon, the beginning of the Sabbath, approaching danger, and the death of a dignitary. Some even believed the shophar had power to drive out evil spirits and to heal by magic. The sound of the shophar could be heard from a great distance (Ex. 19:16, 19). It can produce only the first two tones of the musical scale and those not very accurately. The ram's horn is rarely mentioned with other musical instruments. Its main function apparently was to make noise.

Viol (see *Harp*).

Zither (see *Harp*).

MUSICIAN (see OCCUPATIONS AND TRADES).

MUSTARD (see PLANTS OF THE BIBLE).

MUSTER GATE (see GATES OF JERUSALEM AND THE TEMPLE).

MUSTERING GATE (see GATES OF JERUSALEM AND THE TEMPLE).

MUTENESS (see DISEASES OF THE BIBLE).

MUTE SPIRIT (see DISEASES OF THE BIBLE).

MUTH LABBEN — [mooth LAH ben] (see MUSIC OF THE BIBLE).

MUZZLE — a leather or wire covering for the mouth of an animal that prevented it from eating or biting. The command in the Book of Deuteronomy, "You shall not muzzle an ox while it treads out the grain" (Deut. 25:4) implies that an animal helping with threshing must be allowed to eat some of the grain. The apostle Paul applied this verse symbolically to Christian workers (1 Cor. 9:9–10).

MYRA [MY ruh] (meaning unknown) — one of the chief cities of LYCIA, a province in southwestern Asia Minor (present–day Turkey). While a prisoner

Ruins of the theater at Myra, a city where Paul and his centurion escort boarded a ship bound for Italy (Acts 27:5,6).

Photo by Howard Vos

Photo by Howard Vos

Ruins of the initiation hall of the Eleusinian mystery religions near Athens, Greece.

on his way to Rome, the apostle Paul was transferred at Myra to an Alexandrian ship sailing to Italy (Acts 27:5-6). Myra was situated on the Andracus River, about 4 kilometers (2.5 miles) from the Mediterranean Sea (see Map 8, C-2).

MYRIAD — a large number; innumerable, beyond counting. The elders of the church of Jerusalem commented on "how many myriads of Jews there are who have believed, and they are all zealous for the law" (Acts 21:20).

MYRRH (see PLANTS OF THE BIBLE).

MYRTLE (see PLANTS OF THE BIBLE).

MYSIA [MISS ee uh] (meaning unknown) — a province in northwestern Asia Minor (present-day Turkey). Paul and Silas passed through Mysia on their way to TROAS, one of its main cities, during Paul's first missionary journey (Acts 16:7-8). Three other cities of Mysia are mentioned in the New Testament: ASSOS (Acts 20:13), ADRAMYTTIUM (Acts 27:2), and PERGAMOS (Rev. 1:11).

MYSTERY — the hidden, eternal plan of God that is being revealed to God's people in accordance with His plan.

In the Old Testament, mystery occurs only in the Aramaic sections of Daniel (Dan. 2:18, 27-30, 47; 4:9). Some of God's mysteries were revealed to Daniel and King Nebuchadnezzar.

In the New Testament, mystery refers to a secret that is revealed by God to His servants through His Spirit. As such, it is an "open secret." Mystery occurs three times in the Gospels. Jesus told His disciples, "To you it has been given to know the mystery of the kingdom of God" (Matt. 13:11; Mark 4:11; Luke 8:10). Jesus explained the mystery of God's kingdom to His disciples. But to others He declared, "All things come in parables" (Mark 4:11).

Most of the occurrences of the word mystery are in the Pauline Epistles. Mystery refers to the revelation of God's plan of salvation as that plan focuses in Christ. The gospel itself is a "mystery which was kept secret since the world began" (Rom. 16:25). This mystery was revealed by God through the prophetic Scriptures to Paul and the church (1 Cor. 2:7; Eph. 6:19; Col. 4:3).

Mystery also refers to the future resurrection of Christians (1 Cor. 15:51), the summing up of all things in Christ (Eph. 1:9), the inclusion of Gentiles in the church (Eph. 3:3-9), the future salvation of Israel (Rom. 11:25), the phenomenon of lawlessness (2 Thess. 2:7), and the godliness of Christ (1 Tim. 3:16).

MYSTERY RELIGIONS — secret religions that flourished in Syria, Persia, Anatolia, Egypt, Greece, Rome, and other nations several centuries before and after the time of Christ. The mystery religions were quite popular in the first century A.D. and thus provided strong religious competition for Christianity. They were called mysteries because their initiation and other rituals were kept secret. These religions included the cults of Eleusis, Dionysus, Isis and Osiris, Mithra, Cybele (the Magna Mater, or Great Mother), the Dea Syria, and many local deities, all of which promised purification and immortality.

By means of the secret rituals of these religions— which might involve ceremonial washings, blood-sprinkling, drunkenness, sacramental meals, passion plays, or even sexual relations with a priest or priestess—their followers became one with their god and believed that they participated in the life of that god.

Because of his contact with the Greek world, the apostle Paul was probably familiar with these mystery religions. But there is no evidence that his theological ideas were influenced by these pagan ideas and practices. Paul preached the gospel of salvation through Jesus Christ.

N

NAAM [NAY am] (*pleasantness*) — a descendant of Caleb, of the tribe of Judah (1 Chr. 4:15).

NAAMAH [NAY a mah] (*lovely, beautiful*) — the name of two women and a city in the Old Testament:

1. A sister of Tubal-Cain (Gen. 4:22), one of only four women who lived before the Flood whose names have been preserved.

2. A city in the lowlands of Judah (Josh. 15:41), probably present-day Khirbet Fered, about 36 kilometers (22 miles) west of Jerusalem.

3. The mother of Rehoboam, king of Judah (2 Chr. 12:13).

NAAMAN [NAY a man] (*pleasant*) — the name of several men in the Old Testament:

1. A son of Benjamin (Gen. 46:21).

2. A son of Bela and the founder of a family, the NAAMITES (Num. 26:40). He may be the same person as Naaman No. 1.

3. A commander of the Syrian army who was cured of leprosy by the prophet Elisha. Naaman was a "great and honorable man in the eyes of his master [Ben-Hadad, king of Syria]...but he was a leper" (2 Kin. 5:1–27). Although leprosy was a despised disease in Syria, as in Israel, those who suffered from the disease were not outcasts.

On one of Syria's frequent raids of Israel, a young Israelite girl was captured and became a servant to Naaman's wife. The girl told her mistress about the prophet Elisha, who could heal Naaman of his leprosy. Ben-Hadad sent a letter about Naaman to the king of Israel. Fearing a Syrian trick to start a war, the king of Israel had to be assured by Elisha that Naaman should indeed be sent to the prophet. To demonstrate to Naaman that it was God, not man, who healed, Elisha refused to appear to Naaman. Instead, he sent the commander a message, telling him to dip himself in the Jordan River seven times.

Naaman considered such treatment an affront and angrily asked if the Syrian rivers, the Abana and the Pharpar, would not do just as well. His servants, however, persuaded him to follow Elisha's instructions. Naaman did so and was healed. In gratitude, Naaman became a worshiper of God and

The Abanah River in downtown Damascus, Syria, known today as the Barada River. Naaman the leper looked upon the waters of this river as superior to "all the waters of Israel" (2 Kin. 5:1-19).
Photo by Howard Vos

carried two mule-loads of Israelite earth back to Syria in order to worship Jehovah "on Israelite soil," even though he lived in a heathen land.

Before he departed for Damascus, however, Naaman asked Elisha's understanding and pardon for bowing down in the temple of Rimmon when he went there with Ben-Hadad (2 Kin. 5:18). Elisha said to him, "Go in peace" (v. 19), thus allowing Naaman to serve his master, the king.

4. A son of Ehud, of the tribe of Benjamin (1 Chr. 8:7).

NAAMATHITE [NAY am a thite] (*dweller in Naamah*) — a native or inhabitant of Naameh, perhaps Djebel-el-Na'ameh, in northwestern Arabia. Zophar, one of Job's three friends, was a Naamathite (Job. 2:11).

NAAMITES [NAY a mites] (*the Naami*) — descendants of NAAMAN, of the tribe of Benjamin (Num. 26:40).

NAARAH [NAY a rah] (*girl or mill*) — the name of a woman and a city in the Old Testament:

1. A wife of Ashhur, a man of the tribe of Judah (1 Chr. 4:5-6).

2. A city in the territory of Ephraim (Josh. 16:7; Naarath, KJV), also called Naaran (1 Chr. 7:28). It was near the borders of Benjamin and Manasseh, about eight kilometers (five miles) northeast of Jericho.

NAARAI [NAY a rye] (*attendant of Jehovah*) — a son of Ezbai and one of David's mighty men (1 Chr. 11:37), also called Paarai the Arbite (2 Sam. 23:35).

NAARAN [NAY a ran] — a form of NAARAH No. 2.

NAARATH [NAY a rath] — a form of NAARAH No. 2.

NAASSON [nay AS on] — a form of NAHSHON.

NABAJOTH [nab ah JOHTH] — the first-born son of Ishmael (1 Chr. 1:29), also called NEBAJOTH.

NABAL [NAY bal] (*empty person*) — a wealthy sheepmaster of MAON and a member of the house of Caleb (1 Sam. 25:2-39). Nabal pastured his sheep near the Judahite town of CARMEL on the edge of the wilderness. Nabal was "harsh and evil in his doings" and was "such a scoundrel" that no one could reason with him (1 Sam. 25:3, 7).

While David was hiding from Saul, he sent ten men to Nabal to ask for food for himself and his followers. Nabal refused. David, who had protected people in the area from bands of marauding Bedouins, was so angered by Nabal's refusal that he determined to kill Nabal and every male in his household (1 Sam. 25:4-22).

Nabal's wife Abigail was "a woman of good understanding and beautiful appearance" (v. 3). She realized the danger threatening her family because of her husband's stupidity. "Then Abigail made haste and took two hundred loaves of bread, two skins of wine, five sheep already dressed, five seahs

of roasted grain, one hundred clusters of raisins, and two hundred cakes of figs, and loaded them on donkeys" (1 Sam. 25:18). She took these gifts of food to David, fell to the ground, and apologized for her husband's behavior. Her quick action soothed David's anger.

When Abigail returned home, she found a great feast in progress. Oblivious to his narrow brush with death, "Nabal's heart was merry within him, for he was very drunk" (1 Sam. 25:36). Abigail waited until the next morning to tell him of the destruction and death that he almost brought upon his household. Immediately, Nabal's "heart died within him, and he became like a stone" (1 Sam. 25:37). He died about ten days later, apparently from a heart attack or stroke that left him paralyzed.

When David heard that Nabal was dead, he proposed to Abigail; and she later became one of his wives. She is referred to as "Abigail the Carmelitess, Nabal's widow" (1 Sam. 27:3).

What a contrast they are—Abigail with her beauty and wisdom and Nabal with his beastly behavior and foolishness. Not only did her wisdom save her life and the lives of her family; it caught the heart of David so that he provided her with his love and protection.

NABATEA [nab uh TEE ah] — an Arabic territory situated between the Dead Sea and the Gulf of Aqaba. Nebajoth, son of Ishmael and brother-in-law of Edom (Gen. 25:13; 28:9), was possibly the ancestor of the Nabateans, although positive identification is impossible. Some time during the sixth century B.C. these peoples invaded the territory of the Edomites and Moabites. Their name first occurred in 646 B.C. when a people called the Nabaiate revolted against Ashurbanipal, king of Assyria. It took the Assyrians seven years to subdue these people.

In 312 B.C. Antigonus, one of the successors of Alexander the Great, sent an expedition against the Nabatean capital of PETRA. This rose-red city was situated more than 80 kilometers (50 miles) south of the Dead Sea in the wilderness and surrounded by mountains. Petra had only one entrance, a narrow passageway sometimes as little as eight feet wide, between the cliffs rising 60 to 90 meters (200 to 300 feet) above the road. The Greek army was unable to take the city.

At a later time the Nabateans took advantage of the turmoil of the Seleucid kingdom and extended their territory all the way to Damascus. During the first century B.C. they engaged in a war with the Maccabaean King Alexander Jannaeus. An officer of the Nabatean King Aretas IV attempted to detain the apostle Paul at Damascus (2 Cor. 11:32). Eventually the Romans, under Trajan, annexed Nabatea, and it became the province of Arabia in A.D. 106.

The Nabateans controlled the desert highways south of the Dead Sea, demanding outrageous fees from caravans before they allowed them to pass.

Photo by Gustav Jeeninga

Ruins of a temple of the ancient Nabatean civilization in southern Palestine.

They developed an advanced civilization in the middle of the desert wilderness. Out of the red sandstone cliffs they carved beautiful obelisks, facades, and HIGH PLACES, or altars, at which they worshiped pagan gods. They also developed a beautiful, thin pottery that was decorated with floral designs. With the rise of Palmyra, the trade that formerly passed through Petra was diverted; and the Nabateans were absorbed into the surrounding Arab population.

NABONIDUS [nab oh NIE duss] (*the God Nabu is exalted*) — the last king of the Neo–Babylonian, or Chaldean, Empire (556–539 B.C.). He is not mentioned in the Bible.

Nabonidus' wife Nitocris was the daughter of Nebuchadnezzar II. Their son, Belshazzar, was the king who saw the handwriting on the wall (Dan. 5:1–31). Belshazzar was co-regent with Nabonidus from the third year of Nabonidus' reign until the empire fell to the Persians in 539 B.C. During a major portion of that time, Nabonidus stayed away from the capital city of Babylon; thus little is known of his activities.

Among the DEAD SEA SCROLLS discovered at Qumran was a fragmentary document containing the "Prayer of Nabonidus." This document tells how Nabonidus was struck by a "dread disease of the most high God" and for seven years was "set apart from men." Apparently he was struck with a severe skin disease. Some scholars suggest that a nervous disorder, or psychological disturbance, may also have been involved. Nabonidus' mysterious illness has been compared with the madness of Nebuchadnezzar (Dan. 4:23–33).

NABOPOLASSAR [nab uh puh LASS ur] (*may the god Nabu protect the son*) — a king of Babylon (626–605 B.C.) who founded the Chaldean Dynasty. He was the father of NEBUCHADNEZZAR II, the Babylonian king who defeated Jerusalem and carried the Jewish people into captivity (2 Kin. 25:1–7). Nabopolassar brought Babylon to greatness by defeating the Assyrians. Nebuchadnezzar continued his father's policies by capturing other surrounding nations.

NABOTH [NAY bahth] (*a sprout*) — an Israelite of Jezreel who owned a vineyard next to the summer palace of Ahab, king of Samaria (1 Kin. 21:1). Ahab coveted this property. He wanted to turn it into a vegetable garden to furnish delicacies for his table. He offered Naboth its worth in money or a better vineyard. But Naboth refused to part with his property, explaining that it was a family inheritance to be passed on to his descendants.

Jezebel obtained the property for Ahab by bribing two men to bear false witness against Naboth and testify that he blasphemed God and the king. Because of their lies, Naboth was found guilty; and both he and his sons (2 Kin. 9:26) were stoned to death. Elijah the prophet pronounced doom upon Ahab and his house for this disgusting act of false witness (1 Kin. 21:1–29; 2 Kin. 9:21–26).

NACHON [NAY kon] (*firm, prepared*) — the name of the threshing floor where Uzzah (or Uzza) was struck dead for touching the ARK OF THE COVENANT (2 Sam. 6:6; Nacon, NIV, RSV). Whether the name is that of a person or a place is unclear. In a parallel account, the name is given as Chidon (1 Chr. 13:9).

NACHOR [NAY kor] — a form of NAHOR.

NACON [NAY kon] — a form of NACHON.

NADAB [NAY dab] (*liberal or willing*) — the name of four men in the Old Testament:

1. A son of Aaron and Elisheba (Ex. 6:23). Nadab is always mentioned in association with ABIHU, Aaron's second son. Nadab was privileged to accompany Moses, Aaron, Abihu, and 70 elders of Israel as they ascended Mount Sinai to be near the Lord (Ex. 24:1–10). Along with his father and brothers—Abihu, Eleazar, and Ithamar—he was consecrated a priest to minister at the tabernacle (Ex. 28:1).

Later, Nadab and Abihu were guilty of offering "profane fire before the Lord" in the Wilderness of Sinai; and both died when "fire went out from the Lord and devoured them" (Lev. 10:1–2).

2. A king of Israel (about 910–909 B.C.). Nadab was the son and successor of Jeroboam I (1 Kin. 14:20; 15:25). About the only noteworthy event that happened during Nadab's reign was the siege of GIBBETHON by the Israelites. During the siege, Nadab was assassinated by his successor, Baasha (1 Kin. 15:27–28).

3. A son of Shammai, of the family of Jerahmeel.

4. A Benjamite, son of Jeiel and Maacah (1 Chr. 8:30).

NAGGAI [NAG eye] (*splendor of the sun*) — an ancestor of Jesus Christ (Luke 3:25; Nagge, KJV).

NAGGE [NAG eh] — a form of NAGGAI.

NAG HAMMADI [nag ham MAH dih] — a town in Upper Egypt where an astonishing archaeological discovery of Coptic translations of ancient GNOSTIC writings was discovered in 1945. The find included such works as the Gospel of Thomas, the Gospel of the Egyptians, the Apocryphon ["secret book"] of John, the Secret Book of James, the Apocalypse of Paul, and the Apocalypse of Peter. Also see GNOSTICISM.

NAHALAL [nuh HAL al] (*pasture*) — a city allotted to the tribe of Zebulun (Josh. 19:15) and given to the Levites (Josh. 21:35). The city is also called Nahallal and Nahalol. Its site is uncertain.

NAHALIEL [nuh HAY li el] (*brook of God*) — a stopping place of the Israelites during their wilderness wandering (Num. 21:19). It was near Mount Pisgah, north of the River Arnon, but its exact location is uncertain.

NAHALLAL [nuh HAL al] — a form of NAHALAL.

NAHALOL [NAY huh lal] — a form of NAHALAL.

NAHAM [NAY ham] (*consolation*) — a chieftain of the tribe of Judah (1 Chr. 4:19).

NAHAMANI [nay huh MAY nigh] (*comforter*) — a leader of the tribe of Judah who returned with Zerubbabel from the Captivity (Neh. 7:7).

NAHARAI [NAY ha righ] (*intelligent*) — the armorbearer of Joab, commander-in-chief of David's army (2 Sam. 23:37; Nahari, KJV).

NAHARI [NAY ha rye] — a form of NAHARAI.

NAHASH [NAY hash] (*serpent*) — the name of three men in the Old Testament:

1. A king of the Ammonites who besieged Jabesh Gilead and was defeated by Saul (1 Sam. 12:12). When Nahash's men surrounded the city, the inhabitants of Jabesh Gilead sought peace (1 Sam. 11:1). Nahash refused to accept the tribute tax and threatened to put out all their right eyes. He allowed the people of Jabesh Gilead one week to appeal for help from the rest of Israel; after that they were to surrender to him. When Saul, the newly proclaimed king of Israel, heard about this, he was enraged. He quickly assembled an army and defeated the Ammonites (1 Sam. 11:4–11). The Nahash mentioned in 2 Samuel 10:2 and 1 Chronicles 19:1–2 was either this same Nahash or one of his descendants, probably a son.

2. Probably the father of Abigail and Zeruiah, David's half-sisters (2 Sam. 17:25). Some scholars feel that Nahash was a woman, one of Jesse's wives. But it is more likely that Nahash was a man whose widow married Jesse and bore him David.

3. A man of Rabbah of the Ammonites (2 Sam. 17:27), perhaps the same person as Nahash No. 1.

NAHATH [NAY hath] (*quietness*) — the name of three men in the Old Testament:

1. An Edomite clan chief (Gen. 36:17).

2. A descendant of Elkanah, of the tribe of Levi (1 Chr. 6:26). Nahath probably is the same person as Toah (1 Chr. 6:34) and Tohu (1 Sam. 1:1).

3. An overseer of Temple tithes and offerings during the reign of Hezekiah of Judah (2 Chr. 31:13).

NAHBI [NAH buy] (*fainthearted*) — one of the 12 spies sent by Moses to investigate the land of Canaan (Num. 13:14).

NAHOR [NAY hor] (meaning unknown) — the name of two men and a city in the Old Testament:

1. Father of Terah, grandfather of Abraham (Gen. 11:22–25), and an ancestor of Jesus Christ (Luke 3:34; Nachor, KJV).

2. A son of Terah and a brother of Abraham and Haran (Gen. 11:26–29). Nahor had 12 children, 8 by his wife Milcah and 4 by his concubine Reumah. One of his children was Bethuel, who became the father of Rebekah and LABAN (Gen. 28:5).

3. A city mentioned in Genesis 24:10. Some confusion exists about the phrase, "city of Nahor." This may refer either to a city called Nahor or to the city where Nahor lived. When Abraham and Lot migrated to Canaan, Nahor remained in Haran.

NAHSHON [NAH shun] (meaning unknown) — a son of Amminadab and a leader of the tribe of Judah during the wilderness wanderings (Num. 2:3). Nahshon was an ancestor of Boaz and of King David (Ruth 4:20–22) and, therefore, of Jesus Christ (Luke 3:32–33; Naasson, KJV).

NAHUM [NAY hum] (*compassionate*) — the name of two men in the Bible:

1. An Old Testament prophet and author of the Book of Nahum whose prophecy pronounced God's judgment against the mighty nation of Assyria.

Very little is known about Nahum. His hometown, Elkosh in the nation of Israel (Nah. 1:1), has not been located. But he must have lived some time shortly before 612 B.C., the year when Assyria's capital city, Nineveh, was destroyed by the Babylonians. Nahum announced that the judgment of God would soon be visited upon this pagan city.

The Book of Nahum is similar to the Book of Obadiah, since both these prophecies were addressed against neighboring nations. Obadiah spoke the word of the Lord against Edom, while Nahum prophesied against Assyria. Both messages contained a word of hope for God's Covenant People, since they announced that Israel's enemies would soon be overthrown.

While little is known about Nahum the man, his prophetic writing is one of the most colorful in the Old Testament. The Book of Nahum is marked by strong imagery, a sense of suspense, and vivid language, with biting puns and deadly satire. Nahum was a man who understood God's goodness, but he could also describe the terror of the Lord against His enemies. Also see NAHUM, BOOK OF.

2. An ancestor of Jesus (Luke 3:25).

NAHUM, BOOK OF — a short prophetic book of the Old Testament that foretells the destruction of the nation of Assyria and its capital city, Nineveh.

Structure of the Book. The book opens with a brief identification of the prophet Nahum. Then it launches into a psalm of praise that celebrates the power and goodness of God. This comforting picture is contrasted with the evil deeds of the Assyrians. With graphic language, Nahum presents a prophetic picture of the coming judgment of God. He informs the nation of Assyria that its days as a world power are drawing to a close. In an oracle of woe, the prophet describes Nineveh as a "bloody city, full of lies and robbery" (3:1). But soon the city of Nineveh will be laid waste, and Assyria will crumble before the judgment of God.

Authorship and Date. This book was written by a prophet known as "Nahum the Elkoshite" (1:1). This brief identification tells us all we know about this spokesman for the Lord. Even the location of his home, Elkosh, is uncertain, although some scholars believe he may have lived in northern Judah. The book can be dated with reasonable accuracy. Nineveh fell, as Nahum predicted, about 612 B.C. Therefore, the book was probably written shortly before this time.

Historical Setting. For more than 100 years before Nahum's day, Assyria had been one of the dominant powers of the ancient world. The northern kingdom of Israel fell to Assyrian forces in 722 B.C. Some prophets taught that this pagan nation was used as an instrument of God's judgment against His wayward people. But now it was Assyria's turn to feel the force of God's wrath. The armies of Nabopolassar of Babylon stormed Nineveh in 612 B.C. The entire Assyrian Empire crumbled three years later under the relentless assault of this aggressive Babylonian ruler. Thus, as Nahum prophesied, Assyria's day of dominance ended with their humiliation by a foreign power.

Theological Contribution. This book teaches the sure judgment of God against those who oppose His will and abuse His people. Acts of inhumanity are acts against God, and He will serve as the ultimate and final judge. God sometimes uses a pagan

NAHUM: A Teaching Outline

Ruins of an ancient temple at Thebes, Egypt, a city referred to by the prophet Nahum as No Amon (Nah. 3:8).

nation as an instrument of His judgment, just as He used the Assyrians against the nation of Israel. But this does not excuse the pagan nation from God's laws and requirements. It will be judged by the same standards of righteousness and holiness which God applies to all the other people of the world.

Special Considerations. By a strange irony, the city in Galilee most closely associated with the ministry of Jesus was Capernaum. The name Capernaum in the Hebrew language means "the village of Nahum."

Some people wonder about the gloomy, pessimistic tone of the Book of Nahum. How can this picture of God's wrath and judgment be reconciled with the God of grace and love whom we meet in the New Testament? As the sovereign, all-powerful God, He has the right to work His purpose in the world. Judgment against sin is a part of the work which He must do in order to remain a just and holy God.

Nahum's announcement of God's approaching judgment also carries a call for holy living and faithful proclamation by God's Covenant People. Our work is to carry the message of His salvation to those who are surely doomed unless they turn to God in repentance and faith.

Also see NAHUM.

NAIL (see TOOLS OF THE BIBLE).

NAIN [nane] (*delightful*) — a town in southwestern Galilee (see Map 6, B–2) where Jesus raised a widow's son from the dead (Luke 7:11–17). Nain was about eight kilometers (five miles) southeast of Nazareth on the northern edge of the Plain of Esdraelon. The present–day Arab village of Nein covers ruins of a much larger town.

NAIOTH [NAY oth] (*dwelling places*) — a place in RAMAH where Samuel lived and where David fled to escape the wrath of King Saul (1 Sam. 19:18). Apparently, Naioth was not a separate village but a section of Ramah. The Bible speaks four times of "Naioth [dwellings] in Ramah" (1 Sam. 19:19, 22–23; 20:1).

NAKED — without clothing. In the Garden of Eden, Adam and Eve were unashamed of their nakedness (Gen. 2:25). After eating from the tree of the knowledge of good and evil, however, they began to feel shame (Gen. 3:7–10). The shame associated with nakedness is dramatically presented in the account of Noah's drunkenness and exposure (Gen. 9:21–27).

The word naked is also used in the Bible to express the ideas of poverty (Matt. 25:36–44), desolation (Gen. 42:9), openness (Heb. 4:13), or moral bankruptcy (Rev. 3:17).

NAME — a label or designation that sets one person apart from another. But in the Bible a name is much more than an identifier as it tends to be in our culture. Personal names (and even place names) were formed from words that had their own meaning. Thus, the people of the Bible were very conscious of the meaning of names. They believed there was a vital connection between the name and the person it identified. A name somehow represented the nature of the person.

This means that the naming of a baby was very important in the Bible. In choosing a name, the parents could reflect the circumstances of the child's birth, their own feelings, their gratitude to God, their hopes and prayers for the child, and their commitment of the child to God. The name Isaac reflected the "laughter" of his mother at his birth (Gen. 21:6). Esau was named "hairy" because of his appearance. Jacob was named "supplanter" because he grasped his brother Esau's heel (Gen. 25:25–26). Moses received his name because he was "drawn out" of the water (Ex. 2:10).

A popular custom of Bible times was to compose names by using the shortened forms of the divine name El or Ya (Je) as the beginning or ending syllable. Examples of this practice are Elisha, which means "God is salvation"; Daniel, "God is my judge"; Jehoiakim, "the Lord has established"; and Isaiah, "the Lord is salvation."

Sometimes very specialized names, directly related to circumstances of the parents, were given to children. The prophet Isaiah was directed to name one of his children Maher-Shalal-Hash-Baz, meaning "speed the spoil, hasten the prey." This name was an allusion to the certain Assyrian invasion of the nation of Judah (Is. 8:3–4). Hosea was instructed to name a daughter Lo–Ruhamah, "no mercy," and a son Lo–Ammi, "not my people." Both these names referred to God's displeasure with His people (Hos. 1:6–9).

The change of a name can also be of great importance in the Bible. Abram's name was changed to Abraham in connection with his new calling to be "a father of many nations" (Gen. 17:5). God gave Jacob the new name Israel ("God strives") because he "struggled with God and with men, and prevailed" (Gen. 32:28; 35:10).

In the giving or taking of new names, often a crucial turning point in the person's life has been reached. Simon was given the name Peter because, as the first confessing apostle, he was the "rock" upon which the new community of the church would be built (Matt. 16:18). Saul was renamed Paul, a Greek name that was appropriate for one who was destined to become the great apostle to the Gentiles.

The connection between a name and the reality it signified is nowhere more important than in the names referring to God. The personal name of God revealed to Moses in the burning bush—"I AM WHO I AM"—conveyed something of His character (Ex. 3:14). According to Exodus 34:5–6, when the Lord "proclaimed the name of the Lord," He added words that described His character. The name of the Lord was virtually synonymous with His presence: "For your wondrous works declare that your name is near" (Ps. 75:1). To know the name of God is thus to know God Himself (Ps. 91:14). For this reason, to "take the name of the Lord your God in vain" (Ex. 20:7) is to act in any way that is inconsistent with the profession that He is the Lord God.

The New Testament writers also emphasized the importance of names and the close relationship between names and what they mean. A striking illustration of this is Acts 4:12: "For there is no other name under heaven by which we must be saved." In this instance the name is again practically interchangeable with the reality which it represents.

Jesus taught His disciples to pray, "Hallowed be Your name" (Matt. 6:9). Christians were described by the apostle Paul as those who "name the name of the Lord" (2 Tim. 2:19). A true understanding of the exalted Jesus is often connected with a statement about His name. Thus, Jesus "has by inheritance obtained a more excellent name" than the angels (Heb. 1:4). According to Paul, "God also has highly exalted Him and given Him the name which is above every name" (Phil. 2:9).

NAOMI [NAY oam ih] (*my joy*) — the mother-in-law of Ruth. After her husband and two sons died, Naomi returned to her home in Bethlehem, accompanied by Ruth. Naomi advised Ruth to work for a near KINSMAN, BOAZ (Ruth 2:1), and to seek his favor. When Boaz and Ruth eventually married, they had a son, whom they named Obed. This child became the father of Jesse, the grandfather of David, and an ancestor of Jesus Christ (Ruth 4:21–22; Matt. 1:5).

NAPHATH–DOR [NAY fath door] — a form of DOR.

NAPHISH [NAY fish] (meaning unknown) — a son of Ishmael (1 Chr. 1:31) and the founder of a clan against which the Israelite tribes east of the Jordan River were victorious (1 Chr. 5:19; Nephish, KJV).

NAPHTALI [NAF tuh lie] (*my wrestling*) — the sixth son of Jacob (Gen. 35:25). Because Jacob's wife Rachel was barren and her sister Leah had borne four sons to Jacob, Rachel was distraught. She gave her maidservant Bilhah to Jacob. Any offspring of this union were regarded as Rachel's. When Bilhah gave birth to Dan and Naphtali, Rachel was joyous. "With great wrestlings I have wrestled with my sister," she said, "and indeed I have prevailed" (Gen. 30:8). So she called his name Naphtali, which means "my wrestling." Little else is known about Naphtali.

NAPHTALI, MOUNT [NAF tuh lie] — KJV words for the mountains of Naphtali (Josh. 20:7).

NAPHTALI, TRIBE OF [NAF tuh lie] — the tribe that sprang from NAPHTALI and the territory it inhabited (Num. 1:15, 42–43). The tribe's four great families were descendants of Naphtali's four sons: Jahzeel, Guni, Jezer, and Shillem or Shallum (Num. 26:48–49). The first wilderness census numbered the tribe of Naphtali at 53,000 fighting men (Num. 2:29–30); the second census put it at 45,400 (Num. 26:50).

Along with Asher, Naphtali was the northernmost tribe of Israel, occupying a long, narrow piece of land—about 80 kilometers (50 miles) north to south and 16 to 24 kilometers (10 to 15 miles) from east to west. Naphtali was mountainous (Josh. 20:7) and very fertile. Fortified cities within the tribe's boundaries included Ramah, Hazor, Kedesh, Iron, and Beth Anath (Josh. 19:36–38). The three cities given to the Levites in Naphtali were Kedesh (a city of refuge), Hammoth Dor, and Kartan (Josh. 21:32).

The tribe of Naphtali did not drive out all the Canaanites, but it did receive tribute from them. Members of the tribe of Naphtali fought bravely under Deborah and Barak (Judg. 4:6, 10; 5:18) and responded to Gideon's call (Judg. 6:35; 7:23). When Saul's son Ishbosheth challenged David for the throne, 37,000 fighting men of Naphtali, led by 1,000 captains, joined David (1 Chr. 12:34).

A part of the Northern Kingdom after the Israelites divided into two kingdoms, Naphtali was ravaged by the Syrian king Ben-Hadad (1 Kin. 15:20). The Assyrian king Tiglath-Pileser III carried many from Naphtali into captivity (2 Kin. 15:29). Isaiah prophesied that one day the land of Naphtali, "in Galilee of the Gentiles," would see a great light (Is. 9:1–7). Indeed, Jesus made the cities of Chorazin, Capernaum, and Tiberias—all situated within the former territory of Naphtali—a focal point of His ministry (Matt. 4:12–16).

NAPHTUHIM [naf TOO heem] (*those of the Delta*) — a son of Mizraim, who was one of the four sons of Ham (Gen. 10:13). Some scholars, however, believe that the name Naphtuhim describes a tribal family that settled in the Egyptian Delta or west of Egypt.

NAPKIN — KJV word for HANDKERCHIEF.

NARCISSUS [narr SIS us] (meaning unknown) — a man to whose household the apostle Paul sent greetings (Rom. 16:11). Paul does not indicate if Narcissus was a Christian. Some scholars suggest he was a prominent freedman who served as secretary to the Emperor Claudius. But this theory cannot be proved.

NARD (see PLANTS OF THE BIBLE).

NARRATIVE — an orderly account that relates the details of a story (Luke 1:1; declaration, KJV; account, NASB, NEB, NIV). This is the word Luke used for the accounts of the life of Jesus that had been written.

NATHAN [NAY thun] (*gifted*) — the name of several men in the Old Testament:

1. A son of David and Bathsheba and an older brother of Solomon. Nathan was David's third son born in Jerusalem (2 Sam. 5:14). Six sons had been born to David earlier, while he was at Hebron. Through Nathan the line of descent passed from David to Jesus Christ (Luke 3:31).

2. A prophet during the reign of David and Solomon. Nathan told David that he would not be the one to build the Temple (1 Chr. 17:1–15). Using the parable of the "one little ewe lamb," Nathan confronted David ("You are the man!") with his double sin, the murder of Uriah the Hittite and his adultery with Bathsheba, Uriah's wife (2 Sam. 12:1–15). Nathan, as the Lord's official prophet, named Solomon Jedidiah, which means "Beloved of the Lord" (2 Sam. 12:25). Nathan was also involved in David's arrangement of the musical services of the sanctuary (2 Chr. 29:25).

When David was near death, Nathan advised Bathsheba to tell David of the plans of David's son Adonijah to take the throne. Bathsheba related the news to David, who ordered that Solomon be proclaimed king (1 Kin. 1:8–45). Nathan apparently wrote a history of David's reign (1 Chr. 29:29) and a history of Solomon's reign (2 Chr. 9:29).

3. A man from ZOBAH, an Aramean, or Syrian, kingdom between Damascus and the Euphrates River (2 Sam. 23:36).

4. Father of two of Solomon's officials (1 Kin. 4:5), perhaps the same person as Nathan No. 1 or Nathan No. 2.

5. A descendant of Jerahmeel, of the tribe of Judah (1 Chr. 2:36).

6. A brother of Joel (1 Chr. 11:38) and probably the same man as Nathan No. 3.

7. A leader sent by Ezra to find Levites for the Temple (Ezra 8:15–16).

8. A son of Bani (Ezra 10:34) who divorced his pagan wife after returning from the Captivity in Babylon (Ezra 10:39), probably the same person as Nathan No. 7.

NATHAN-MELECH [NAY thun MEH leck] (*the king has given*) — a Judean officer before whose chamber King Josiah removed the horses that previous "kings of Judah had dedicated to the sun" (2 Kin. 23:11).

NATHANAEL [nuh THAN ih el] (*God has given*) — a native of Cana in Galilee (John 21:2) who became a disciple of Jesus (John 1:45–49). Nathanael was introduced to Jesus by his friend Philip, who claimed He was the MESSIAH. This claim troubled Nathanael. He knew that Nazareth, the town where Jesus grew up, was not mentioned in the Old Testament prophecies. He considered Nazareth an insignificant town, hardly the place where one would look to find the Redeemer of Israel. "Can anything good come out of Nazareth?" he asked. Philip did not argue with him, but simply said, "Come and see." After Nathanael met Jesus, he acknowledged Him to be the Messiah, calling Him "the Son of God" and "the King of Israel" (John 1:46, 49).

Nathanael was one of those privileged to speak face to face with Jesus after His resurrection (John 21:1–14). Some scholars see Nathanael as a type, or symbol, of a true Israelite—"an Israelite indeed" (John 1:47)—who accepts Jesus as Lord and Savior by faith.

Many scholars believe Nathanael is the same person as BARTHOLOMEW (Matt. 10:3), one of the twelve apostles of Christ.

NATIONS — countries other than the nation of Israel. In the Bible the word nations means the Gentiles, in contrast to the Jews. God promised that He would make Abraham and his descendants a great nation. Thus, God's elect people were kept clearly distinct and separate from all other nations. The nations were regarded by the Hebrew people as godless and corrupt. Yet God intended ultimately to bless the nations through His people Israel: "And in you all the families of the earth shall be blessed" (Gen. 12:3). Israel was thus meant to be "a light to the Gentiles" (Is. 42:6; 49:6).

The prophecy that "the Gentiles shall come to your light" (Is. 60:3) was fulfilled in the Gentile response to Christ in the New Testament. The Great Commission refers to "all the nations" (Matt. 28:19); Cornelius, the first Gentile convert, was brought to faith through the preaching of Peter (Acts 10). The apostle Paul repeatedly quoted the Old Testament to justify the preaching of the gospel to the nations (Rom. 15:9–12; Gal. 3:8).

NATIVES — NKJV word for the people who lived on the island of Malta. It means foreigners who spoke an unknown foreign tongue, instead of the Greek or Latin language.

NATIVITY (see JESUS CHRIST).

NATURE — native, inborn, or inherent character; innate disposition.

In the NKJV the word nature is found only in the New Testament. In almost every occurrence it is a translation of a Greek word meaning "inherent nature" which describes the process of growth or normal characteristics. Thus, normal sexuality between men and women is the "natural use" (Rom. 1:26–27); perverse sexuality is "against nature" (Rom. 1:26).

Gentiles, who do not have the law of Moses, by nature may do the things contained in the law (Rom. 2:14). Gentiles were cut out of the olive tree, which is wild by nature, and were grafted, contrary to nature, into a good olive tree [the people of God] (Rom. 11:24).

NAVE — KJV word for RIM.

NAVEL — the scar or depression in the middle of the stomach where an unborn baby was attached to

Model of a merchant ship from King Solomon's fleet (1 Kin. 9:26).

the umbilical cord during the mother's pregnancy (Song 7:2; Ezek. 16:4). The prophet Ezekiel compared the city of Jerusalem to a newborn baby unloved and abandoned: "On the day you were born your navel cord was not cut...[and] you were thrown out into the open field" (Ezek. 16:4–5). Unless the Lord had shown pity on the city, it would have perished.

NAVY — KJV word for "fleet of ships" (1 Kin. 9:26–27). Solomon built a merchant fleet to sail from Ezion Geber, a port and refinery on the Red Sea. The Hebrews disliked the sea; so some of the crew members of Solomon's fleet were Phoenician sailors (1 Kin. 9:27). These ships sailed at times with King Hiram's Phoenician fleet (1 Kin. 10:22).

NAZARENE [nazz uh REEN] — an inhabitant or native of NAZARETH. The word Nazarene is used

A terraced hillside on the road to Petra, center of the ancient Nabatean kingdom south of the Dead Sea.

many times to identify Christ. Both demons (Mark 1:23, 24) and Jesus Himself spoke of Jesus as a Nazarene. When used by his friends, the word spoke of favor; when used by his enemies, it spoke of contempt. Matthew's Gospel stated that Jesus was raised as a boy in Nazareth, "that it might be fulfilled which was spoken by the prophets, 'He shall be called a Nazarene' " (Matt. 2:23).

This verse is one of the messianic prophecies in the Book of Isaiah, predicting that a descendant of King David would arise as the Messiah who would deliver His people. Christ Jesus is frequently referred to in prophecy as the Branch (Jer. 23:5; 33:15; Zech. 3:8).

A Nazarene was an obscure, insignificant place. Nathanael asked, "Can anything good come out of Nazareth?" (John 1:46). Thus the word Nazarene was a fitting title for the One who grew up "as a root out of dry ground, despised and rejected by men" (Is. 53:2–3).

NAZARETH [NAZ ah reth] (*watchtower*) — a town of lower Galilee (see Map 6, B–2) where Jesus spent His boyhood years (Matt. 2:23). For centuries Nazareth has been a beautifully secluded town nestled in the southernmost hills of the Lebanon Mountain range. Situated in the territory belonging to Zebulun, the city must have been of late origin or of minor importance. It is never mentioned in the Old Testament.

Nazareth lay close to the important trade routes of Palestine. It overlooked the Plain of Esdraelon through which caravans passed as they traveled from Gilead to the south and west. North of the city was the main road from Ptolemais to the Decapolis, a road over which the Roman legions frequently traveled. This fact may account for the possible source of the name Nazareth in the Aramaic word meaning "watchtower."

However, Nazareth itself was situated in something of a basin, a high valley about 366 meters (1,200 feet) above sea level overlooking the Esdraelon valley. To the north and east were steep hills, while on the west the hills rose to an impressive 488 meters (1,600 feet). Nazareth, therefore, was somewhat secluded and isolated from nearby traffic.

This apparent isolation of Nazareth as a frontier town on the southern border of Zebulun contributed to the reputation that Nazareth was not an important part of the national and religious life of Israel. This, coupled with a rather bad reputation in morals and religion and a certain crudeness in the Galilean dialect, prompted Nathanael, when he first learned of Jesus of Nazareth, to ask, "Can anything good come out of Nazareth?" (John 1:46).

Although it was not an important town before the New Testament era, Nazareth became immortal as the home town of Jesus the Messiah. It was here that the angel appeared to Mary and informed her of the forthcoming birth of Christ (Luke 1:26–38). Jesus was born in Bethlehem (Luke 2). But after their sojourn in Egypt (Matt. 2:19–22) to escape the ruthless murders of Herod the Great (Matt. 2:13–18), Joseph and Mary brought the baby Jesus to Nazareth where they had lived (Matt. 2:23). Here Jesus was brought up as a boy (Luke 4:16) and spent the greater part of His life (Mark 1:9). Apparently Jesus was well received as a young man in Nazareth (Luke 2:42; 4:16). But this changed after He began His ministry. His own townspeople twice rejected Him (Mark 6:1–6; Luke 4:28–30).

Because of His close association with this city, Christ became known as "Jesus of Nazareth" (Luke 18:37; 24:19; John 1:45). There is prophetic significance as well to His being known as a "Nazarene."

Modern Nazareth, successor to the village in lower Galilee where Jesus grew up (Luke 2:39; 4:16, 31-34).
Photo by Howard Vos

Matthew records that Joseph and Mary returned to their city during the reign of Herod Archelaus (ethnarch of Judea, Idumea, and Samaria, 4 B.C.—A.D.6) "that it might be fulfilled which was spoken by the prophets, 'He shall be called a Nazarene' " (Matt. 2:23).

NAZIRITE [NAZZ uh right] (*separated, consecrated*) — a person who took a vow to separate from certain worldly things and to consecrate himself to God (Num. 6:1–8). Among the Hebrew people anyone could take this vow; there were no tribal restrictions as in the case of the priest. Rich or poor, man or woman, master or slave—all were free to become Nazirites.

Nazirites did not withdraw from society and live as hermits; however, they did agree to follow certain regulations for a specified period of time. While no number of days for the vow is given in the Old Testament, Jewish tradition prescribed 30 days or a double period of 60 or even triple time of 90 to 100 days. Samson, Samuel, and John the Baptist were the only "Nazirites for life" recorded in the Bible. Before they were born, their vows were taken for them by their parents.

Once a person decided to make himself "holy to the Lord" (Num. 6:8) for some special service, he then agreed to abstain from wine and other intoxicating drinks. This prohibition was so strict that it included grapes, grape juice, and raisins. Perhaps this was to guard the Nazirite from being controlled by any spirit other than God's (Prov. 20:1; Eph. 5:17–18).

While under the Nazirite vow, a person also refused to cut his hair, including shaving (Num. 6:5). The purpose of this long hair was to serve as a visible sign of the Nazirite's consecration to the Lord (Num. 6:7).

A Nazirite also refused to touch or go near a dead body because this would make him ceremonially unclean. The Nazirite could not even help to bury his own relatives.

If a person accidentally broke his Nazirite vow, he had to undergo a ceremony of restoration for cleansing (Num. 6:9–12). He shaved his head, brought two turtledoves or two pigeons to the priest for offerings, and the priest made atonement for him. In addition, a Nazirite had to present a lamb for a trespass offering. It was as if he were starting all over again and the days already served under the vow did not count.

When the specified period of time was completed, the Nazirite could appear before the priest for the ceremony of release (Num. 6:13–21). After offering a male lamb for a burnt offering, he would then offer a ewe lamb for a sin offering. This was followed by a ram to be used as the peace offering. Next came the usual items for peace offerings (Num. 6:15). The prescribed sacrifices were completed with a meat offering and a drink offering. When the person cut off his hair and burned it on the altar, he was fully released from the vow.

The strong man of the Bible, Samson, was a Nazirite (Judg. 13:7; 16:17). His parents were told by an angel before his birth that he would "be a Nazirite to God from the womb to the day of his death" (Judg. 13:7).

While Samuel is not specifically called a Nazirite, 1 Samuel 1:11, 28 hints that he probably was. His mother, Hannah, made a vow before his birth, "No razor shall come upon his head" (1 Sam. 1:11). Samuel was probably a "Nazirite for life" like Samson and John the Baptist. John's refusal to drink wine (Matt. 11:18–19) is an indication that he was a Nazirite. His manner of living also indicates this probability (Luke 1:15).

The presence of many Nazirites was considered a sign of God's blessings on Israel. There were many Nazirites during the time of the prophet Amos. Amos strongly condemned the people for tempting the Nazirites to break their vows by offering them wine to drink (Amos 2:11–12).

The Nazirite vow was a part of the old law and is not imposed on modern Christians. But because it was personal and voluntary, we do have much to learn from this Old Testament practice. God wants us to live a separated, holy life and to abstain from things of the world. Christians must be dedicated to God's service not just for 30 days or one year but a lifetime.

NEAH [NEE ah] (*the settlement*) — a border town of Zebulun near Rimmon and the territory of Naphtali (Josh. 19:13), location unknown.

NEAPOLIS [nee AP oh lus] (*new city*) — a seaport in northeastern Macedonia near the border of Thrace which served as the port city of Philippi (see Map 7, C–1). On his second missionary journey, the apostle Paul landed at Neapolis as he traveled from Troas and Samothrace to Philippi (Acts 16:11). Paul may have visited this city again on his second tour of Macedonia (Acts 20:1–2).

NEARIAH [nee uh RYE uh] (*attendant of Jehovah*) — the name of two men in the Old Testament:
1. A son of Shemaiah (1 Chr. 3:22–23).
2. A son of Ishi, of the tribe of Simeon, who lived in the days of King Hezekiah of Judah (1 Chr. 4:42).

NEBAI [NEE buy] (*projecting*) — a leader of the people who sealed the covenant after the Captivity (Neh. 10:19).

NEBAIOTH [neh BUY yoth] (meaning unknown) — an Ishmaelite tribe descended from NEBAJOTH.

NEBAJOTH [neh BAY yoth] (meaning unknown) — Ishmael's firstborn son (1 Chr. 1:29; Nebaioth, KJV, RSV, NIV, NASB) and ancestor of an Arabian tribe named after him (Is. 60:7).

NEBALLAT [nih BAL uht] (*blessed with life*) — a settlement inhabited by the Benjamites after the Captivity (Neh. 11:34).

NEBAT [NEE bat] (*God has regarded*) — the father of Jeroboam I (1 Kin. 11:26), first king of the northern kingdom of Israel.

NEBO [NEE boe] (*elevation*) — the name of two towns, a mountain, a man, and a pagan god in the Old Testament:

1. A town in Moab east of the Jordan River that was captured and rebuilt by the tribe of Reuben (Num. 32:3, 38). Nebo is also mentioned on the MOABITE STONE as having been taken back to Mesha, king of Moab.

2. A mountain of the Abarim range (see Map 2, C–1) in Moab opposite Jericho (Num. 33:47). From Nebo Moses was permitted to view the Promised Land. He was buried in a nearby valley (Deut. 32:49, 50; 34:6).

3. A town mentioned immediately after Bethel and Ai in the lists of Israelites who returned from the Captivity (Ezra 2:29). Nehemiah calls it "the other Nebo," apparently to distinguish it from Nebo No. 1.

4. The ancestor of seven Israelites who divorced their pagan wives after the Captivity (Ezra 10:43).

5. KJV word for a Babylonian god (Is. 46:1; Nabu, NKJV) who was believed to preside over literature, the arts, and the sciences. Borsippa, near Babylon, was the seat of Nebo worship.

NEBUCHADNEZZAR [neb you kad NEZ ur] (*O god Nabu, protect my son*) — the king of the Neo–Babylonian Empire (ruled 605–562 B.C.) who captured Jerusalem, destroyed the Temple, and carried the people of Judah into captivity in Babylon. He plays a prominent role in the books of Jeremiah (21—52) and Daniel (1:1—5:18) and also appears in 2 Kings (24:1—25:22), Ezra (1:7—6:5), and Ezekiel (26:7—30:10).

Nebuchadnezzar was the oldest son of NABOPOLASSAR, the founder of the Neo–Babylonian, or Chaldean, dynasty of Babylon. Nabopolassar apparently was a general appointed by the Assyrian king. But in the later years of Assyria he rebelled and established himself as king of Babylon in 626 B.C. Nebuchadnezzar succeeded his father as king in 605 B.C., continuing his policies of conquest of surrounding nations.

In about 602 B.C., after being Nebuchadnezzar's vassal for three years, King Jehoiakim of the nation of Judah rebelled against the Babylonians. Nebuchadnezzar then "came up against him and bound him in bronze fetters to carry him off to Babylon" (2 Chr. 36:6). Apparently, however, Nebuchadnezzar's intention of carrying him to Babylon was abandoned; according to Jeremiah, Jehoiakim was "dragged and cast out beyond the gates of Jerusalem" and "buried with the burial of a donkey" (Jer. 22:19). After reigning for 11 years, Jehoiakim was succeeded by his son Jehoiachin.

Jehoiachin was only eight years old when he became king, and he reigned in Jerusalem about three months (2 Chr. 36:9). At that time Nebuchadnezzar took Jehoiachin captive to Babylon, "with the costly articles from the house of the Lord" (2 Chr. 36:10). He made Mattaniah, Jehoiachin's uncle (2 Kin. 24:17), king over Judah and Jerusalem, changing his name to Zedekiah.

For about eight years Zedekiah endured the Babylonian yoke and paid tribute to Nebuchadnezzar. In 589 B.C., however, in the ninth year of his reign, Zedekiah rebelled against the king of Babylon, perhaps trusting in the Egyptian promises of military aid. Nebuchadnezzar and his army came against Jerusalem and besieged the city for about two years (2 Kin. 25:2). The siege may have been temporarily lifted with the approach of the Egyptian army (Jer. 37:5).

In 586 B.C. Jerusalem fell to the army of Nebuchadnezzar. Under cover of darkness, Zedekiah and many of his men fled through a break in the city wall. But they were overtaken by the Chaldeans in the plains of Jericho and brought captive to Riblah, a city in the land of Hamath where Nebuchadnezzar was camped. Nebuchadnezzar ordered that the sons of Zedekiah be killed before his eyes. Then Zedekiah was bound and taken captive to Babylon, along with the leading citizens of Jerusalem (2 Kin. 25:1–7).

Nebuchadnezzar's policy of resettling conquered peoples and transporting them to other provinces of his empire provided him with slave labor for conducting his extensive building projects. He rebuilt many sanctuaries, including the temple of Nebo at Borsippa and the great temple of Marduk at Babylon. He accomplished an immense fortification of Babylon, including the building of its great wall.

Although the famous "hanging gardens" cannot be identified among the impressive ruins of Babylon, this fabulous construction project—one of the "seven wonders of the ancient world"—was built by Nebuchadnezzar on the plains of Babylon to cheer his wife, who was homesick for her native Median hills. Nebuchadnezzar also built a huge reservoir near Sippar, providing interconnecting canals in an elaborate irrigation system.

Nebuchadnezzar made an arrogant boast about all that he achieved (Dan. 4:30). But he was stricken at the height of his power and pride by God's judgment. Nebuchadnezzar was eventually driven out of office, living with the beasts of the field and eating grass like an ox (Dan. 4:32). Later, he was succeeded as king by his son, EVIL–MERODACH.

NEBUCHADREZZAR [neb you kad REZ ur] — a form of NEBUCHADNEZZAR.

NEBUSHASBAN [neb you SHAZ ban] (*Nebo delivers me*) — an officer of Nebuchadnezzar, king of Babylon, at the time of the siege of Jerusalem in 587 B.C. (Jer. 39:13; Nebushazban, NIV, NEB, NAS, RSV).

NEBUSHAZBAN [neb you SHAZ ban] — a form of NEBUSHASBAN.

NEBUZARADAN [neb you zar AY dan] (*Nebo has given offspring*)—the captain of Nebuchadnezzar's bodyguard who played an important part in the destruction of Jerusalem in 586 B.C. An important Babylonian official, Nebuzaradan may have been second in command to Nebuchadnezzar himself. When Jerusalem fell to the Babylonians, Nebuzaradan came to the city (2 Kin. 25:1, 8) and took charge of destroying it. He commanded the troops who burned the Temple, the palace, and all the houses of Jerusalem and tore down the walls of the city. He also was in charge of deporting the Israelites to Babylonia (2 Kin. 25:9–11).

After the fall of Jerusalem, Nebuchadnezzar told Nebuzaradan to take good care of the prophet Jeremiah (Jer. 39:11). Nebuzaradan showed kindness to Jeremiah and gave him the choice of remaining in Jerusalem or going to Babylon (Jer. 40:1–4).

NECHO [NEE koe] — a PHARAOH of Egypt who defeated Josiah in the Valley of Megiddo (609 B.C.). Pharaoh Necho was himself defeated by Nebuchadnezzar, king of Babylon, in the battle of CARCHEMISH (605 B.C.; 2 Chr. 35:20, 22). Variant spellings of this name in different passages and translations of the Bible include Neco, Necoh, and Nechoh.

NECHOH, NECO, NECOH [NEE koe] — forms of NECHO.

NECK — the part of the body that connects the head and the trunk. The word is often used figuratively in the Bible. To fall on the neck of someone was to embrace him in greeting or farewell (Gen. 33:4; Acts 20:37). To put a yoke on someone's neck suggested the person had been made a subject (Jer. 27:12). To put one's foot upon a neck expressed triumph over a foe.

The word neck is also used to speak of one's spiritual condition. To stiffen or harden one's neck means to rebel or resist (Deut. 31:27). A stiff-necked person is a stubborn, self-willed person determined to resist God's will (Acts 7:51).

NECKLACE — an ornament worn about the neck in Bible times. Necklaces were very popular throughout the ancient world. They frequently appear on monuments and paintings and many have been discovered by archaeologists. Moon-shaped or crescent-shaped pendants were worn around camels' necks, perhaps as amulets of the goddess ASTARTE. Many necklaces worn by people were probably amulets or charms as well. Necklaces were made of precious metals and strings of jewels (Song 1:10; Ezek. 16:11). Gold chains were worn by people of high rank (Gen. 41:42; Dan. 5:17; 5:29).

NECROMANCY (see MAGIC, SORCERY, and DIVINATION).

NEDABIAH [ned uh BUY uh] (*moved of Jehovah*) — a descendant of David through Solomon (1 Chr. 3:18).

NEEDLE (see TOOLS OF THE BIBLE).

NEEDLEWORK, EMBROIDERY — decorations on cloth sewn in with needle and thread. Archaeology has uncovered many ancient sculptures and paintings that depict garments beautifully decorated with lavish patterns. This art was widespread among the cultures of the ancient world.

In Exodus 35:35 the embroiderer appears alongside the weaver as a craftsman working on the tabernacle. Embroidery is mentioned mostly with reference to the tabernacle and priestly garments (Ex. 27:16; 26:36). Designs may have been sewn onto the high priest's clothes by applique. Embroidered work was valuable; it gave evidence of luxury (Ps. 45:14; Ezek. 27:16), the prized spoils of war (Judg. 5:30), and commercial goods.

NEGEV, THE [NEG ev] (*dry, parched*) — a term used by some English translations of the Bible for the southern desert or wilderness area of Judah (see Map 9, B–5), including about 4,500 square miles. Abraham journeyed in the Negev (Gen. 12:9; 13:1, 3; the South, NKJV). When the 12 spies explored the land of Canaan, they went up by way of the Negev (Num. 13:17, 22) and saw the Amalekites

An Arab bedouin family with their flocks moves slowly across the Negev, the desert area of southern Palestine.
Photo by Howard Vos

Photo: Levant Photo Service

Excavated section of the wall built by Nehemiah in Jerusalem after the Jewish people returned from the Captivity in Babylonia.

who lived there (Num. 13:29). The Canaanite king of Arad also lived in the Negev (Num. 21:1).

The prophet Isaiah described the Negev as a land of trouble and anguish, hardship and distress—a badland populated by lions and poisonous snakes (Is. 30:6). Through its arid wastes donkey and camel caravans made their way to and from the land of Egypt.

The Negev contained important copper deposits, and it connected Israel to trade centers in Arabia and Egypt. King Solomon built fortresses in the Negev to guard the trade routes. He also established at Ezion Geber, on the Gulf of Aqaba, a port from which he shipped copper to foreign lands. King Uzziah made great efforts to develop the region, building fortresses and expanding agriculture (2 Chr. 26:10).

In modern times, the desert is being made to "blossom as the rose" (Is. 35:1); the Israelis have built an impressive irrigation system which channels life-giving water from northern Galilee to the dry, parched region of the Negev.

NEGINOTH [neh GHEE nuh] (see MUSIC OF THE BIBLE).

NEHELAM [neh HELL um] — a form of NEHELAMITE.

NEHELAMITE [neh HELL uh mite] (*dweller of Nehelam*) — the designation of SHEMAIAH, a false prophet who went with the captives to Babylon (Jer. 29:24, 31–32).

NEHEMIAH [KNEE uh my ah] (*God is consolation*) — the name of three men in the Old Testament:

1. A clan leader who returned with Zerubbabel from the Captivity (Ezra 2:2; Neh. 7:7).

2. The governor of Jerusalem who helped rebuild the wall of the city (Neh. 1:1; 8:9; 10:1; 12:26, 47). Nehemiah was a descendant of the Jewish population that had been taken captive to Babylon in 587–586 B.C. In 539 B.C. Cyrus the Persian gained control over all of Mesopotamia. He permitted the Jewish exiles to return to the city of Jerusalem. Nearly a century later, in Nehemiah's time, the Persian ruler was Artaxerxes I Longimanus (ruled 465–424 B.C.). Nehemiah was his personal cupbearer (Neh. 1:11).

In 445 B.C. Nehemiah learned of the deplorable condition of the returned exiles in Jerusalem (Neh. 1:2–3). The wall of the city was broken down, the gates were burned, and the people were in distress. Upon hearing this, Nehemiah mourned for many days, fasting and praying to God. His prayer is one of the most moving in the Old Testament (Neh. 1:5–11).

Nehemiah then received permission from Artaxerxes to go to Judah to restore the fortunes of his people. He was appointed governor of the province with authority to rebuild the city walls.

Once in Jerusalem, Nehemiah surveyed the walls at night (Neh. 2:12–15). He gave his assessment of the city's condition to the leaders and officials and then organized a labor force to begin the work.

Nehemiah and his work crew were harassed by three enemies: Sanballat the Horonite (a Samaritan), Tobiah the Ammonite official, and Geshem the Arab (Neh. 2:10, 19; 6:1–14). But neither their ridicule (Neh. 4:3) nor their conspiracy to harm Nehemiah (Neh. 6:2) could stop the project. The builders worked with construction tools in one hand and weapons in the other (Neh. 4:17). To the taunts of his enemies, Nehemiah repled: "I am doing a great work, so that I cannot come down" (Neh. 6:3). Jerusalem's wall was finished in 52 days (Neh. 6:14)—a marvelous accomplishment for such a great task. Nehemiah's success stems from the fact that he kept praying, "O God, strengthen my hands" (Neh. 6:9).

Nehemiah's activities did not stop with the completion of the wall. He also led many social and political reforms among the people, including a return to pure worship and a renewed emphasis on true religion. Also see NEHEMIAH, BOOK OF.

3. A son of Azbuk and leader of half the district of Beth Zur (Neh. 3:16). After his return from the Captivity, Nehemiah helped with the repair work on the wall of Jerusalem.

NEHEMIAH, BOOK OF — a historical book of the Old Testament that describes the rebuilding of the city walls around Jerusalem. The book is named for its major personality, a Jewish servant of a Persian king and effective leader, who organized and guided the building project.

Structure of the Book. Nehemiah was serving as cupbearer to the Persian king Artaxerxes (1:11—2:1) in 444 B.C., when he received distressing news

about his native land. Jerusalem's wall was still in ruins, although the project to rebuild the city and its beautiful Temple had been under way for many years. So Nehemiah went to Jerusalem himself on special assignment from the king to oversee the building project. In spite of harassment by their enemies, Nehemiah rallied the people to the challenge and completed the wall in less than two months.

Nehemiah remained as Persian governor of Jerusalem for the next 12 years, leading the people in several important religious reforms. The priest Ezra assisted Nehemiah in interpreting God's Law for His people. He had accompanied a group of captives back to Jerusalem about 13 years before Nehemiah arrived on the scene.

Authorship and Date. As written originally in the Hebrew language, Nehemiah was connected to the books of First and Second Chronicles and Ezra. The material in these books formed one unbroken book, written probably by the priest Ezra. The purpose of this work was to show how God's blessings sustained his COVENANT PEOPLE after they returned to their native land following the years of captivity in Babylon and Persia. Most conservative scholars, however, believe Nehemiah contributed some of the material that appears in the book which bears his name. This is the only logical explanation for chapters 1—7 and 11—13, which are written by

NEHEMIAH: A Teaching Outline

Part One: The Reconstruction of the Wall (1:1—7:73)

Part Two: The Restoration of the People (8:1—13:31)

Nehemiah as a first-person report. Ezra could have picked up these passages from Nehemiah's personal diary.

Historical Setting. The Book of Nehemiah is set in that crucial time in Jewish history known as the post-exilic period. These were the years after the return of the Covenant People to their homeland in 536 B.C. following 70 years of CAPTIVITY in Babylon and Persia. At first the exiles were excited about rebuilding their lives and restoring their city; but the work was slow and tiring, and the living conditions were primitive. Their enemies often exploited them in their plight. These were the desperate circumstances that motivated Nehemiah to return to Jerusalem to encourage his countrymen.

Theological Contribution. Nehemiah is an excellent case study in courageous, resourceful leadership. Against overwhelming odds, he encouraged the people to "rise up and build" (2:18). Their rapid completion of the wall has been an inspiration to countless Christians across the centuries who have faced the challenge of completing some major task to the glory of God.

Nehemiah also teaches that prayer is an important part of the faith of every follower of God. At several crucial points in his book, he prayed for God's direction (1:5-11; 2:1-20; 4:1-14; 6:9-14). If this courageous leader needed to claim God's strength and guidance through prayer, how much more fervently should we pray for God's will to be done through us as we face the important decisions of life? Nehemiah is an excellent object lesson on the power of prayer for all believers.

Special Considerations. Scholars have debated who returned to Jerusalem first, Ezra or Nehemiah. But the Bible makes it plain that Ezra arrived about 13 years before Nehemiah. Ezra went back to Jerusalem in the seventh year of King Artaxerxes' reign (Ezra 7:8), while Nehemiah returned during this Persian king's 20th year (Neh. 2:1). The debate arises because of the account of the religious revival under Ezra, which is inserted as chapters 8—10 of Nehemiah.

Perhaps there is a simple reason why this "Ezra story" was included in the Book of Nehemiah. It was used to emphasize the truth that rebuilding the Law of God in the hearts of the people was just as important as rebuilding a wall of stone around the nation's capital city. This was a spiritual, life-sustaining wall that no enemy could batter down.

Also see NEHEMIAH.

NEHILOTH [neh hih LOWTH] (see MUSIC OF THE BIBLE).

NEHUM [NEE hum] (*consoled* [by God]) — a leader of the Jews who returned from the Captivity with Zerubbabel (Neh. 7:7), also called Rehum (Ezra 2:2).

NEHUSHTA [nih HUSH tuh] (*serpent*) — the wife of Jehoiakim, king of Judah, and the mother of Jehoiachin, king of Judah (2 Kin. 24:8).

NEHUSHTAN (see GODS, PAGAN).

NEIEL [nih EYE ul] (*dwelling place of God*) — a city in the territory of Asher near Zebulun (Josh. 19:27), probably present-day Khirbet Ya'nin, about 14 kilometers (8.5 miles) southeast of Akko.

NEIGHBOR — a friend, close associate, or a person who lives nearby. The Abrahamic Covenant (Gen. 12:1-3) established moral obligations among the Israelites. They were commanded to show concern for their neighbors. The ninth and tenth commandments (Ex. 20:16-17; Deut. 5:20-21) prohibited the defaming or slandering of a neighbor and condemned the envying of a neighbor's wife, servant, livestock, or other possessions.

A person was not to cheat or rob from his neighbor (Lev. 19:13). The maiming or disfigurement of a neighbor was punishable by "eye for eye, tooth for tooth" retribution (Lev. 24:19-20). Despising one's neighbor was sin (Prov. 14:21), as was leading him morally astray (Prov. 16:29-30) or deceiving him, then saying, "I was only joking" (Prov. 26:19). A person was not even permitted to think evil of his neighbor (Zech. 8:17).

Jesus extended the concept of neighbor to include strangers, as in the parable of the Good Samaritan (Luke 10:25-37), and hence all mankind. The apostle Paul declared that "love your neighbor as yourself" was a supreme commandment (Rom. 13:9-10).

NEKODA [nih KOE dah] (*speckled*) — the name of two men in the Old Testament:

1. The founder of a family of NETHINIM, or Temple servants (Ezra 2:48), whose descendants returned from the Captivity.

2. The founder of a family that could not prove their Israelite descent after the Captivity (Neh. 7:62).

NEMUEL [NIM you el] (meaning unknown) — the name of two men in the Old Testament:

1. A son of Eliab, of the tribe of Reuben (Num. 26:9).

2. A son of Simeon, a grandson of Jacob and Leah, and the ancestor of the NEMUELITES (Num. 26:12). Nemuel is also called Jemuel (Gen. 46:10).

NEMUELITES [NIM you uh lights] — the family or clan descended from NEMUEL, son of Simeon and grandson of Jacob and Leah (Num. 26:12).

NEPHEG [NEE feg] (*boaster*) — the name of two men in the Old Testament:

1. A son of Izhar, of the tribe of Levi (Ex. 6:21).

2. A son born to David in Jerusalem (2 Sam. 5:15).

NEPHEW — the son of one's brother or sister. But the term *nephew* when used in the Bible may mean "grandson" (Judg. 12:14), "descendant" (Job 18:19), "offspring" (Is. 14:22), or "grandchild" (1 Tim. 5:4). Also see FAMILY.

NEPHILIM [NEFF ih lem] — a word of uncertain meaning (Gen. 6:4; Num. 13:33, NIV, NEB, NASB, RSV), translated as giants by the KJV and

NKJV. Some scholars believe the Nephilim were descended from famous rulers, outstanding leaders, and mighty warriors who lived before the Flood. These men, so the theory goes, gathered great harems and were guilty of the sin of polygamy. The Nephilim were the product of these marriages. Also see GIANTS.

NEPHISH [NEH fish] — a form of NAPHISH.

NEPHISHESIM [neh FISH eh sim] — a family of NETHINIM, or Temple servants, who returned from the Captivity with Zerubbabel (Neh. 7:52; Nephushesim, RSV, NASB; Nephussim, NIV). This family may be the same as the NEPHUSIM mentioned in Ezra 2:50.

NEPHISIM [neh FUY sim] — a form of NEPHUSIM.

NEPHTOAH [nef TOE uh] (*an opening*) — a fountain or spring on the border of Benjamin and Judah (Josh. 15:9; 18:15).

NEPHUSHESIM [neh PHOOSH eh sim] — a form of NEPHISHESIM.

NEPHUSIM [neh FYOO sim] — a family of NETHINIM, or Temple servants, who returned from the Captivity with Zerubbabel (Ezra 2:50; Nephisim, NASB, RSV; Nephussim, NIV). This family may be the same as the NEPHISHESIM mentioned in Nehemiah 7:52.

NEPHUSSIM [neh FYOO sim] — a form of NEPHISHESIM; NEPHUSIM.

NER [nur] (*light*) — father of Abner, Saul's commander-in-chief (1 Sam. 14:50-51).

NEREUS [NEE roose] — a Roman Christian to whom the apostle Paul sent greetings (Rom. 16:15). An early tradition holds that Nereus was beheaded at Terracina about A.D. 97, probably during the reign of Nerva, emperor of Rome.

NERGAL (see GODS, PAGAN).

NERGAL-SAREZER, NERGAL-SHAREZER [nur GAL shah REE zur] (*may Nergal protect the king*) — a Babylonian officer who released the prophet Jeremiah from prison (Jer. 39:3, 13). Nergal-Sarezer had the title of Rabmag (Jer. 39:3, RSV, NASB), which means a high official with military authority—a commander or general. Nergal-Sarezer has been identified as Nergal-shar-usur, who married a daughter of Nebuchadnezzar and reigned as king of Babylon from 560–556 B.C.

NERI [NEE rye] (*lamp is Jehovah*) — an ancestor of Jesus Christ (Luke 3:27).

NERIAH [nih RYE uh] (*Jehovah is a lamp*) — the father of Baruch, the prophet Jeremiah's scribe (Jer. 32:12; 51:59).

NERO [NEE row] — the fifth emperor of Rome (ruled A.D. 54-68), known for his persecution of Christians. Nero began his reign with the promise that he would return to the policies of the great emperor Augustus. For several years he succeeded, thanks mainly to the guidance of Burrus and Seneca, two of his advisors. Under his reign Rome extended its borders, solidified certain territories of the Roman Empire, and incorporated some good qualities of Greek culture.

Nero had considerable artistic interests. He wanted to change the image of Rome from a violent society to one that was more humane. The Romans, however, despised his love for the Greek way of life. His extravagance, coupled with poor management, brought on heavy taxation, depreciation of the Roman currency, and the confiscation of large land holdings by the state.

Nero's personal life was filled with tragedy. His mother, Agrippina, and Octavia, his legal wife, were murdered. Many of his advisors and officials were either killed or exiled. Tension became so great that by A.D. 68, after several attempted conspiracies, the Praetorian guard revolted and Nero was forced to flee Rome. In that same year, at the age of 30, he took his own life.

Many of Nero's cruelties are linked to the time of the great fire in Rome (A.D. 64). Nero was accused of setting fire to the city in order to divert attention from himself, but this has never been proven with certainty. The Christians, however, were made the scapegoats for this arson. Many of them, possibly even Peter and Paul, lost their lives.

Nero became a kind of apocalyptic figure, a person associated with the end times. Rumors persisted that he was alive and would some day return and reign again. Some interpreters of Scripture believe that Nero is the beast from the sea whose "deadly wound was healed" (Rev. 13:3, 12). Some Bible students have found in the mysterious number 666 (Rev. 13:18), when decoded, the name

Bust of Nero, cruel emperor of the Roman Empire whose administration was marked by persecution of the Christians.

Nero Caesar. Possible references to Nero in the New Testament include Acts 25:11–12; 26:32; and Philippians 4:22.

NEST — a shelter made by a bird for its eggs and young. In addition to speaking of literal nests, the Bible also speaks of nests in a figurative way. Job spoke of the day when he would die in his "nest" (Job 29:18). Apparently he was hoping to die in the midst of his children and heirs who would carry on in his absence.

NET — a meshed fabric made of ropes, used for catching fish, birds, insects, or other animals (Job 18:8–9; Ps. 141:10; Ezek. 17:20). The net was used by the Hebrews for fishing, fowling, and hunting.

Fishing Nets. The Hebrew people were acquainted with the common dragnet of the Egyptians (Is. 19:8; Hab. 1:15–17), which was made of cords of flax. This type of net had floats of wood on the upper edge; it was weighted with lead on the lower edge so it would sink to the bottom. Sometimes the dragnet was lowered from a boat, while the men who pulled it often stood on the shore. In lake fishing the dragnet was cast from and drawn into the boat. If a large catch of fish was taken, the net was dragged behind the boat to the shore (John 21:6, 8, 11). A smaller net was sometimes used for fishing in shallow water (Matt. 4:18, 21).

Fowling Nets. The Hebrews, like the ancient Egyptians, used a device called the clap–net for catching birds (Prov. 1:17). Clap–nets commonly had two half frames or hoops covered with netting and attached to a common axis. The fowler spread the trap open flat and placed the bait in the center. When the bird disturbed the bait, the two sides closed suddenly and the bird was captured.

Hunting Nets. Such nets were cast about the game (Job 19:6) or laid to catch the feet (Ps. 9:15; 57:6; Lam 1:13). Long nets were sometimes placed on a path used by animals. The game was then chased into these nets so they could be easily subdued and killed.

The Bible often uses the word net in a figurative way, as of a snare or trap. The spreading of the net is an appropriate description of the subtle tricks and devious devices of one's enemies (Prov. 29:5; Eccl. 7:26).

NETAIM [nih TAY im] (*plants*) — a place in Judah where some royal potters lived (1 Chr. 4:23).

NETHANEAL [nih THAN e al] (*God has given*) — the name of two men in the Book of Nehemiah:

1. A priest in the days of the high priest Joiakim (Neh. 12:21; Nethaneel, KJV).

2. A musician who blew a trumpet when the walls of Jerusalem were dedicated after the Captivity (Neh. 12:35–36; Nethaneel, KJV).

NETHANEEL [neh THAN ih el] (*God gives*) — the name of six men in the Old Testament:

1. A chief of the tribe of Issachar and one of the ten spies sent to explore the land of Canaan (Num. 2:5).

A quail trapped in a net. This bird is probably similar to those provided miraculously to sustain the Israelites in the wilderness (Num. 11:31-32).
Photo by Amikam Shoob

2. A priest who blew the trumpet when the ARK OF THE COVENANT was brought to Jerusalem from the house of Obed–Edom (1 Chr. 15:24).

3. The father of Shemaiah (1 Chr. 24:6).

4. A prince of Judah sent by Jehoshaphat to teach the people of Judah (2 Chr. 17:7).

5. A chief Levite during the reign of Josiah of Judah (2 Chr. 35:9).

6. A son of Pashhur who divorced his pagan wife after the Captivity (Ezra 10:19, 22).

NETHANEL [nih THAN el] (*God gives*) — the name of two men in the Old Testament:

1. The fourth son of Jesse (1 Chr. 2:14–15; Nethaneel, KJV).

2. A son of Obed–Edom (1 Chr. 26:1, 4; Nethaneel, KJV). David appointed Nethanel a gatekeeper of the tabernacle.

NETHANIAH [neth uh NUY uh] (*Jehovah has bestowed*) — the name of four men in the Old Testament:

1. A son of Elishama, of the royal family of David (2 Kin. 25:25).

2. A leader of the fifth division of musicians and singers in the sanctuary during David's reign (1 Chr. 25:2, 12).

3. A Levite sent by King Jehoshaphat to teach the Law in the cities of Judah (2 Chr. 17:8–9).

4. Father of Jehudi (Jer. 36:14).

NETHINIM [NEHTH uh neam] — a group of people of non-Jewish background who served as Temple servants in Old Testament times. As assistants to the LEVITES, they performed such menial chores as cleaning the Temple, carrying water and wood to the altar, and scrubbing utensils used in the sacrificial ceremonies. Some of the Nethinim returned to Jerusalem with Ezra after the CAPTIVITY (Ezra 7:7).

NETOPHAH [neh TOE fuh] *(falling in drops)* — a city in Judah closely associated with Bethlehem. After the Captivity, 188 men of Bethlehem and Netophah returned to Palestine (Neh. 7:26).

NETOPHATHITE [neh TOE fuh thite] — a native or resident of NETOPHAH, a city in Judah near Bethlehem. Two of David's mighty men, Maharai and Heleb, were Netophathites (2 Sam. 23:28–29).

NETTLE (see PLANTS OF THE BIBLE).

NETWORK — a word with two distinct meanings in the Old Testament:
1. The grate of bronze that surrounded the altar of burnt offering before the tabernacle (Ex. 27:4; 38:4).
2. The ornamental network of bronze on the capitals of JACHIN AND BOAZ, the two great bronze pillars in Solomon's Temple (1 Kin. 7:18; 2 Chr. 4:12; Jer. 52:22–23). The system of latticework was built for Solomon by Hiram (or Huram), a craftsman from Tyre who specialized in producing skillful works of bronze.

NEW AGE — a future time when Jesus Christ will rule over the earth. The term new age does not appear in either the NKJV or KJV. However, Jeremiah prophesied of a new covenant (Jer. 31:31). Jesus Himself spoke of the regeneration when He would rule in His future kingdom (Matt. 19:28). The apostle Paul referred to this time as a "new creation" (2 Cor. 5:17).

NEW BIRTH — inner spiritual renewal as a result of the power of God in a person's life. The phrase new birth comes from John 3:3, 7, where Jesus told Nichodemus, "Unless one is born again, he cannot see the kingdom of God." Jesus meant that all people are so sinful in God's eyes that they need to be regenerated—recreated and renewed—by the sovereign activity of God's Spirit (John 3:5–8).

The activity of God's Spirit that regenerates sinful man comes about through faith in Jesus Christ (John 3:10–21). Without faith there is no regeneration, and without regeneration a person does not have eternal life. Regeneration occurs at the moment a person exercises faith in Christ. At that point, his sins are forgiven and he is born again by the power of the Holy Spirit working on behalf of Christ. The new birth is a decisive, unrepeatable, and irrevocable act of God.

Similar words are used elsewhere in the Bible to describe the same general concept. Paul said, "If anyone is in Christ, he is a new creation" (2 Cor. 5:17). Although our "outward man" is perishing, the Christian's "inward man is being renewed day by day" (2 Cor. 4:16).

NEW COVENANT (see COVENANT, NEW).

NEW GATE (see GATES OF JERUSALEM AND THE TEMPLE).

NEW HEAVENS (see HEAVENS, NEW).

NEW JERUSALEM (see JERUSALEM, NEW).

NEW MOON (see FEASTS AND FESTIVALS).

NEW TESTAMENT — the second major division of the Bible. It tells of the life and ministry of Jesus and the growth of the early church. The word testament is best translated as "covenant." The New Testament embodies the new covenant of which Jesus was MEDIATOR (Jer. 31:31–34; Heb. 9:15). This new covenant was sealed with the atoning death of Jesus Christ.

The 27 books of the New Testament were formally adopted as the New Testament canon by the Synod of Carthage in A.D. 397, thus confirming three centuries of usage by the church. Also see BIBLE, THE.

NEW YEAR — a solemn occasion that occurred in the month of TISHRI or Ethanim (1 Kin. 8:2), the first month in the Hebrew year. The law of Moses directed that this holiday should be observed by "blowing the trumpets" (Num. 29:1). Thus, this festival is also known as the feast of trumpets. Today this event is known as Rosh Hashanah (literally, beginning of the year), a Jewish high holy day that marks the beginning of the Jewish new year. Also see CALENDAR.

NEZIAH [nih ZIE uh] *(faithful)* — the founder of a family of NETHINIM (Temple servants) whose descendants returned to Jerusalem after the Captivity (Ezra 2:54).

NEZIB [NEE zib] *(standing place)* — a city in the SHEPHELAH, or lowland plain, of Judah (Josh. 15:43). Nezib has been identified as Khirbet Beit Nesib, about 40 kilometers (25 miles) southwest of Jerusalem.

NIBHAZ (see GODS, PAGAN).

NIBSHAN [NIB shan] *(prophecy)* — a town in the wilderness of Judah, on the shore of the Dead Sea (Josh. 15:62), location uncertain.

NICANOR [nie KAY nor] *(victorious)* — one of seven men in the church at Jerusalem chosen to serve tables (Acts 6:5). Apparently these seven servants (or DEACONS) were responsible for looking after the needs of the Greek–speaking widows, who had been neglected in the daily distribution of food.

NICODEMUS [nick oh DEE mus] *(conqueror of the people)* — a PHARISEE and a member of the SANHEDRIN who probably became a disciple of Jesus (John 3:1, 4, 9; 7:50). He was described by Jesus as "the teacher of Israel," implying he was well trained in Old Testament law and tradition.

Nicodemus was a wealthy, educated, and powerful man—well respected by his people and a descendant of the patriarch Abraham. Yet Jesus said to him, "You must be born again" (John 3:7). The Greek adverb translated again can also mean "from the beginning" (suggesting a new creation) and "from above" (that is, from God). In other words, Jesus told Nicodemus that physical generation was not enough, nor could his descent from the line of

Abraham enable him to be saved. Only as a person has a spiritual generation—a birth from above—will he be able to see the kingdom of God.

The next time Nicodemus appears in the Gospel of John, he shows a cautious, guarded sympathy with Jesus. When the Sanhedrin began to denounce Jesus as a false prophet, Nicodemus counseled the court by saying, "Does our law judge a man before it hears him and knows what he is doing?" (John 7:51).

Nicodemus appears a third and final time in the Gospel of John. Obviously a wealthy man, he purchased about a hundred pounds of spices to be placed between the folds of the cloth in which Jesus was buried (John 19:39). Nothing else is known of Nicodemus from the Bible. But there is reason to believe that he became a follower of Jesus.

Christian tradition has it that Nicodemus was baptized by Peter and John, suffered persecution from hostile Jews, lost his membership in the Sanhedrin, and was forced to leave Jerusalem because of his Christian faith. Further mention is made of him in The Gospel of Nicodemus, an apocryphal narrative of the crucifixion and resurrection of Christ.

NICOLAITANS [nick oh LAY ih tuns] — an early Christian heretical sect made up of followers of Nicolas, who was possibly the deacon of Acts 6:5. The group is mentioned explicitly only in Rev. 2:6, 14–15, where it is equated with a group holding "the doctrine of Balaam," who taught Israel "to eat things sacrificed to idols, and to commit sexual immorality."

Balaam probably was responsible for the cohabitation of the men of Israel with the women of Moab (Num. 25:1–2; 31:16). Therefore, the error of this group was moral rather than doctrinal. If the "Jezebel" of Revelation 2:20–23 was a teacher of this sect, as many believe, their sexual laxity was indeed strong. Most likely, they were a group of anti-law practitioners who supported a freedom that became self–indulgence. It may have been the same heresy condemned in 2 Peter 2:15 and Jude 11. Some early church leaders believed the Nicolaitans later became a GNOSTIC sect.

NICOLAS [NICK oh lus] (*conqueror of the people*) — one of the seven men chosen as DEACONS to serve tables in the church at Jerusalem. Nicolas is called "a proselyte from Antioch" (Acts 6:3, 5; Nicolaus, RSV). This means he was a Gentile who had converted to Judaism before becoming a Christian. The church fathers accused Nicolas of denying the true Christian faith and founding the heretical sect known as the NICOLAITANS (Rev. 2:6, 15).

NICOLAUS [nick uh LAY us] — a form of NICOLAS.

NICOPOLIS [nih COP oh liss] (*city of victory*) — a city in which the apostle Paul decided to spend the winter (Titus 3:12). Many cities in the first–century world were named Nicopolis. Most scholars believe the city of which Paul spoke was the Nicopolis in Epirus, a province in northwestern Greece. It was on the Adriatic Sea, about six kilometers (four miles) north of Actium.

NIGER [NIE jur] (meaning unknown) — the Latin surname of Simeon, one of the Christian prophets and teachers in the church of Syrian Antioch when Barnabas and Paul were called to missionary service (Acts 13:1–3). Some scholars believe he is the same person as Simon of Cyrene, who carried the cross of Christ (Matt. 27:32); but there is no evidence for this theory.

NIGHT — the period between sunset and sunrise, especially the hours of darkness. The night is often spoken of in the Bible as a symbol of evil. The apostle Paul contrasts the "sons of the day" with those who live in darkness (1 Thess. 5:5)—the faithful who live a righteous life with the unbelieving who practice deeds of depravity. Also see TIME.

NIGHT CREATURE, NIGHT HAG, NIGHTHAWK, NIGHTJAR, NIGHT MONSTER (see ANIMALS OF THE BIBLE).

NIGHT–WATCH (see WATCH).

NILE [nile] — the great river of Egypt that flows more than 5,700 kilometers (3,500 miles) from central Africa north through the desert to a rich delta area on the Mediterranean Sea (see Map 1, B–2). The source of the Nile is derived from two rivers: the Blue Nile from Ethiopia and the White Nile from Lake Victoria in central Africa.

The Blue Nile provides about twice as much water as the White Nile during the rainy season. This flood water, with the soil that it eroded, provided fertile top soil for the agriculture of northern Egypt. Low flood levels usually meant a famine year, while a high flood level would result in a year of plenty. The Aswan Dam and the High Dam now enable the modern nation of Egypt to control these floods and provide a more constant flow of water.

Because the Nile was so essential to the life and prosperity of Egypt, it was personified as a god called Hapi. Egyptians had religious celebrations at the beginning of the annual flooding of the Nile. One text discovered by archaeologists contains praises in adoration of the Nile for the blessings that it provides.

The river was also one of the chief methods of transportation for the Egyptians. The Nile delta produced papyrus which the Egyptians wove together to make household mats, baskets, sails for their boats, and paper. The Nile supported a fishing industry as well, and ancient drawings show the Pharaohs hunting wild game in the thick undergrowth of the Nile Valley.

The river in Pharaoh's dream (Gen. 41:1–36) was the Nile. The seven fat cows that pastured in the lush grass by the Nile represented seven years when the Nile would flood and there would be plenty of food. The seven thin cows represented years when there would be little grass because of low flood waters.

The prosperity that the river provided and the annual flooding of the Nile were spoken of symbolically in the prophetic writings (Is. 23:10; Jer. 46:7–8). The judgment on Egypt was often described in terms of the drying up of the Nile (Ezek. 29:10; 30:12; Zech. 10:11), because the Nile will fail, the papyrus will wither, the grain will wilt, and the fisherman will mourn (Is. 19:5–8). Yet in spite of this judgment, the day will come when some from Egypt will turn to God and become His people (Is. 19:18–25).

NIMRAH [NIM ruh] (*clear, flowing water*) — a fortified city east of the Jordan River built by the tribe of Gad (Num. 32:3). Nimrah is an abbreviated form of BETH NIMRAH (Num. 32:36).

NIMRIM, WATERS OF [NIM rim] (*basins of clear water*) — a fertile area in the land of Moab mentioned by the prophets Isaiah (Is. 15:6) and Jeremiah (Jer. 48:34). The exact identification and location of these waters are unknown.

NIMROD [NIM rahd] (meaning unknown) — a son of Cush and grandson of Ham, the youngest son of Noah (Gen. 10:8–12; 1 Chr. 1:10). Nimrod was a "mighty one on the earth"—a skilled hunter-warrior who became a powerful king. He is the first mighty hero mentioned in the Bible.

The principal cities of Nimrod's Mesopotamian kingdom were "Babel, Babylon, Erech, Accad, and Calneh, in the land of Shinar" (Gen. 10:10). From the land of Babylon he went to Assyria, where he built Nineveh and other cities (Gen. 10:11). In Micah 5:6 Assyria is called "the land of Nimrod."

The origin and meaning of the name Nimrod is uncertain, but it is doubtful that it is Hebrew. It is probably Mesopotamian, originating from the Akkadian (northern Babylonian) god of war and hunting, Ninurta, who was called "the Arrow, the mighty hero."

Some scholars believe Nimrod was Sargon the Great, a powerful ruler over Accad who lived about 2600 B.C. Others think he was the Assyrian king Tukulti–Ninurta I (about 1246–1206 B.C.), who conquered Babylonia. However, if Nimrod was indeed a Cushite, he may have been the Egyptian monarch Amenophis III (1411–1375 B.C.). He was more likely Assyrian. Nimrod's fierce agressiveness, seen in the combination of warlike prowess and the passion for the chase, makes him a perfect example of the warrior–kings of Assyria.

NIMSHI [NIM shy] (*weasel*) — the grandfather of JEHU (2 Kin. 9:2, 14, 20). Jehu killed Joram, son of Ahab, and reigned as king of Israel.

NINEVEH [NIN eh vuh] — ancient capital city of the Assyrian Empire, a place associated with the ministry of the prophet Jonah. The residents of this pagan city repented and turned to God after Jonah's preaching of a clear message of God's judgment (Jon. 3:5–10).

Founded by Nimrod (Gen. 10:8–10), Nineveh was the capital of the great Assyrian Empire for

Photo by Howard Vos

This ancient Nilometer, used for measuring the flood stages of the Nile River, was located at Elephantine Island at Aswan, Egypt.

Later when the Israelites were slaves under persecution by a Pharaoh who did not know Joseph, the king ordered that all male children born to the Israelites must be thrown into the Nile (Ex. 1:22). In an attempt to save her child, Moses' mother put him in a waterproofed papyrus basket and placed him among the papyrus reeds near where Pharaoh's daughter came to bathe (Ex. 2:1–5). When she saw the child, she had compassion on him; thus Moses was not killed.

Eighty years later Moses returned to Egypt to deliver the Israelites from slavery. In order that the children of Israel might believe that God had sent Moses, God gave him three signs to perform; the last was to pour water from the Nile on dry ground and have it turn to blood (Ex. 4:9). After hearing God's word and seeing these signs, the people believed God and worshiped Him (Ex. 4:29–31).

Because Pharaoh refused to let the Israelites leave Egypt, God sent ten plagues. Moses met Pharaoh at the Nile (Ex. 7:15) and turned the Nile to blood to prove to him that the Nile was not a god, but that Moses' God was the true God (Ex. 7:17–21; Ps. 78:44). Some believe the water was turned to a reddish–brown color from the eroded red soil in the flood water and that bacteria from the polluted water may have killed the fish. This naturalistic interpretation does not explain the intensity of the plague or the ability of Moses to start and conclude the plague on command. Since Pharaoh's magicians were able to reproduce a somewhat similar phenomenon, Pharaoh's heart was not moved to release the Israelites (Ex. 7:22–25).

The mound of Kuyunjik, one of the major mounds of the magnificent city of Nineveh in ancient Assyria.

many years. Its fortunes rose and fell as Babylonia and Assyria struggled with each other for the dominant position in the ancient world. During some periods Babylonia was stronger, while the Assyrians gained the upper hand at other times.

In 612 B.C. Nineveh was destroyed, as prophesied by the Hebrew prophets, especially Nahum. Many scholars questioned the existence of Nineveh until its discovery by A.H. Layard and H. Rassam in 1845-1854. The site has now been excavated thoroughly. Occupational levels on the site go back to prehistoric times, before 3100 B.C. Some of the pottery indicates the city may have originated with the SUMERIANS.

One of the exciting discoveries in this excavation was the great palace of the Assyrian King Sargon. Along with this find was a library of CUNEIFORM documents and many striking wall ornamentations. This clear evidence of Sargon's existence verifies the accuracy of the Book of Isaiah in the prophet's mention of this pagan king (Is. 20:1).

The wall around the city indicated that Nineveh was about two kilometers (three miles) long and less than half that distance wide. The Hebrews, however, perhaps like other foreigners, included other cities under the name of Nineveh. An example from today would be our reference to New York, which is actually made up of a complex of many cities. Cities included in references to Nineveh were Calah, Resen, and Rehoboth-Ir.

At the time of the greatest prosperity of Nineveh as described by Jonah, the city was surrounded by a circuit wall almost 13 kilometers (eight miles) long. This "great city" (Jon. 1:2) would have had an area sufficient to contain a population of 120,000, as indicated by Jonah 4:11 and 3:2. Evidence for this is provided by Calah to the south, where 69,754 persons lived in a city half the size of Nineveh. As a result, it would have required a "three day's journey" to go around the city, and a "day's journey" would have been needed to reach the city center from the outlying suburbs, just as the Book of Jonah reports (Jon. 3:4).

Several centuries before Jonah's preaching mission to the city, Nineveh became one of the royal residences of Assyrian kings. Sennacherib (705-681 B.C.) made it the capital of the Assyrian Empire to offset the rival capital of Dur-Sharrukin (Khorsabad), built by his father Sargon II (722-705 B.C.). He greatly beautified and adorned Nineveh. The splendid temples, palaces, and fortifications made it the chief city of the Empire (2 Kin. 19:36).

In Sennacherib's day the wall around Nineveh was 40 to 50 feet high. It extended for 4 kilometers (2 1/2 miles) along the Tigris River and for 13 kilometers (8 miles) around the inner city. The city wall had 15 main gates, 5 of which have been excavated. Each of the gates was guarded by stone bull statues. Both inside and outside the walls, Sennacherib created parks, a botanical garden, and a zoo. He built a water-system containing the oldest aqueduct in history at Jerwan, across the Gomel River. To bring new water supplies to the city, he cut channels for 20 kilometers (30 miles) from the Gomel River at Bavian and built a dam at Ajeila to control the flooding of the Khosr river.

In the years 1849-1851 archaeologist A. Layard unearthed the 71-room palace of Sennacherib. The mound also yielded the royal palace and library of Ashurbanipal, which housed 22,000 inscribed clay tablets. These tablets included Assyrian creation and flood accounts which furnished Old Testament scholars with valuable information for background studies on the Book of Genesis.

It was to Nineveh that Sennacherib brought the tribute which he exacted from King Hezekiah of Judah (2 Kin. 18:15). He also returned here after his campaign against Jerusalem and Palestine in 701 B.C. In 681 B.C. he was assassinated in the temple of Nisroch, which must have been situated within the city walls.

Esarhaddon, the younger son and successor to Sennacherib, recaptured Nineveh from rebels in 680 B.C. Here he built a palace for himself, although he spent much time in his other residence in Calah. One of his twin sons, Ashurbanipal, returned to live mainly at Nineveh where he had been crown prince during his school days. It was during his last days and the years of his sons Ahsur–etil–il-ani and Sin–shar–ishkun that Assyria's vassals revolted.

At the same time the Medes, with the help of the Babylonians, sacked Ashur and Calah in 614 B.C. Two years later Nineveh fell to these combined forces. Nineveh was left in ruins (Nah. 2:10, 13) and grazed by sheep (Zeph. 2:13–15), just as the Hebrew prophets of the Old Testament had predicted.

Nineveh is such a large site that it will probably never be fully excavated. A modern village covers one of its larger palaces. A nearby mound, named "Mound of the Prophet Jonah," contains the palace of Esarhaddon. The popular tradition is that Jonah is buried beneath the mosque at Nebi Yunas.

NINEVITES [NIN uh vights] — residents of NINEVEH, the capital of Assyria (Luke 11:30; men of Nineveh, RSV). In speaking to the people of His day, Jesus spoke favorably of the repentance of the people of Nineveh centuries earlier under the preaching of the prophet Jonah (Jon. 3:2–7; 4:11).

NISAN [NIE san] (meaning unknown) — the name given after the Captivity to ABIB, the first month of the Jewish sacred year (Esth. 3:7). Also see CALENDAR.

NISROCH (see GODS, PAGAN).

NITER, NITRE (see MINERALS OF THE BIBLE).

NO, NO AMON [noe, NO a mahn] — the royal city of southern Egypt at modern Luxor, about 565 kilometers (350 miles) south of Cairo. Some modern versions translate Thebes (NASB, NIV, RSV).

Thebes (or No) was of major importance from the time of Abraham about 2000 B.C. until it was sacked by the Assyrians in 663 B.C. Thebes not only was the capital of Egypt; it also served as the center of worship of the great Egyptian god Amon (Jer. 46:25) and as the place where many kings and queens were buried.

On the east bank of the Nile the huge temple complexes at Karnak and Luxor where the Egyptians worshiped their gods can still be seen. On the west bank are temples which contain the tombs of Pharaohs, queens, and noblemen. The most magnificent of all discoveries in this Valley of the Kings was the tomb of Tutenkhamon, or Tutankhamen (King Tut), a Pharaoh who flourished about 1358 B.C.

Nahum prophesied that Nineveh, the capital of Assyria, would be destroyed by God, just as No Amon was pillaged by the Assyrians in 663 B.C. (Nah. 3:8). Later Jeremiah (46:25) and Ezekiel (30:14–16) predicted that Nebuchadnezzar, king of Babylon, would punish the king of Egypt, destroy the gods of Egypt, and bring further desolation to Thebes. This was proof that God had power over all nations and that their gods were powerless.

NOADIAH [no uh DIE uh] (*Jehovah has met*) — the name of a man and a woman in the Old Testament:

1. A Levite, a son of Binnui (Ezra 8:33). Noadiah was responsible for "the silver and the gold and the articles" brought back to Jerusalem from Babylon after the Captivity.

2. A prophetess who tried to hinder Nehemiah's efforts to rebuild the walls of Jerusalem (Neh. 6:14).

NOAH [NOE uh] (*rest, relief*) — the name of a man and a woman in the Bible:

1. A son of Lamech and the father of Shem, Ham, and Japheth. He was a hero of faith who obeyed God by building an ark (a giant boat), thus becoming God's instrument in saving mankind

A portion of the great temple of Amon-Re at Luxor, Egypt. This city is called No in the Bible (Ezek. 30:15).
Photo by Howard Vos

from total destruction by the Flood (Gen. 5:28—9:29). The line of descent from Adam to Noah was as follows: Adam, Seth, Enosh, Cainan, Mahalaleel, Jared, Enoch, Methuselah, Lamech, and Noah (Gen. 5:1–32). If this GENEALOGY does not allow for any gaps, Noah was only nine generations removed from Adam; and his father, Lamech, was 56 years old at the time of Adam's death.

Noah lived at a time when the whole earth was filled with violence and corruption. Yet Noah did not allow the evil standards of his day to rob him of fellowship with God. He stood out as the only one who "walked with God" (Gen. 6:9), as was true of his great–grandfather Enoch (Gen. 5:22). Noah was a just or righteous man (Gen. 6:9). The Lord singled out Noah from among all his contemporaries and chose him as the man to accomplish a great work.

When God saw the wickedness that prevailed in the world (Gen. 6:5), He disclosed to Noah His intention to destroy the world by a flood. He instructed Noah to build an ark in which he and his family would survive the catastrophe. Noah believed God and obeyed Him and "according to all that God commanded him, so he did" (Gen. 6:22). He is therefore listed among the heroes of faith (Heb. 11:7).

With unswerving confidence in the Word of God, Noah started building the ark. For 120 years the construction continued. During this time of grace, Noah continued to preach God's judgment and mercy, warning the ungodly of their approaching doom (2 Pet. 2:5). He preached for 120 years, however, without any converts (1 Pet. 3:20). People continued in their evil ways and turned deaf ears to his pleadings and warnings until they were overtaken by the Flood.

When the ark was ready, Noah entered in with all kinds of animals "and the Lord shut him in" (Gen. 7:16), cut off completely from the rest of mankind.

Noah was grateful to the Lord who had delivered him from the Flood. After the Flood he built an altar to God (Gen. 8:20) and made a sacrifice, which was accepted graciously (Gen. 8:21). The Lord promised Noah and his descendants that He would never destroy the world again with a flood (Gen. 9:15). The Lord made an everlasting covenant with Noah and his descendants, establishing the rainbow as the sign of His promise (Gen. 9:12–17). The Lord also blessed Noah and restored the creation command, "Be fruitful and multiply, and fill the earth" (Gen. 9:1). These were the same words He had spoken earlier to Adam (Gen. 1:28).

Noah became the first tiller of the soil and keeper of vineyards after the Flood. His drunkenness is a prelude to the curse that was soon to be invoked on Canaan and his descendants, the Canaanites (Gen. 9:18–27). The Bible is silent about the rest of Noah's life after the Flood, except to say that he died at the age of 950 years (Gen. 9:28–29).

In the gospels of the New Testament, the account of Noah and the Flood is used as a symbol of the

Photo by Howard Vos

The modern village of Nob, the town where Saul massacred 85 priests because of their loyalty to David (1 Sam. 22:17-19).

end times. Warning His hearers about the suddenness of His return, Jesus referred to the sudden catastrophe that fell upon unbelievers at the time of the Flood: "As the days of Noah were, so also will the coming of the Son of Man be" (Matt. 24:37).

2. A daughter of Zelophehad (Josh. 17:3).

Also see ARK OF NOAH; FLOOD, THE.

NOB [knob] (meaning unknown) — a town allotted to the priests (1 Sam. 22:19) in the territory of Benjamin (Neh. 11:32), about three kilometers (two miles) northeast of Jerusalem, and apparently within sight of the Holy City (Is. 10:32). When David fled from King Saul, he went to Nob and obtained from Ahimelech the priest some showbread, or "holy bread," as provisions for his men (1 Sam. 21:1–9).

This incident was mentioned by Jesus when the Pharisees criticized His disciples for gathering grain to eat on the Sabbath (Matt. 12:1–8; Mark 2:23–28). It was not wrong, Jesus implied, for David and his men to eat the showbread, for they were hungry and in need.

A likely location of Nob is Mount Scopus, on the northern part of the Mount of Olives. The site is northeast of Jerusalem, overlooking the city. Three centuries after the time of David, the Assyrian army made its camp at Nob in preparation for an assault on Jerusalem (Is. 10:32).

NOBAH [NOE buh] (howling) — the name of a man and two cities in the Old Testament:

1. A chieftain of the tribe of Manasseh (Num. 32:42).

2. A city in Gilead (Num. 32:42), location unknown.

3. A city in eastern Gilead (Judg. 8:11). Gideon and his men went around Nobah to surprise the Midianite army at Karkor. The site is unknown.

NOBLE (see PRINCE).

NOD [nahd] (*wandering*) — an unidentified land east of the Garden of Eden where CAIN fled after he murdered his brother (Gen. 4:16).

NODAB [NOE dab] (*nobility*) — an Arabian tribe of the Syrian desert, east of the Jordan River (1 Chr. 5:19).

NOGAH [NO guh] (*brilliance*) — a son of David born in Jerusalem (1 Chr. 3:7; 14:6).

NOHAH [NO hah] (*rest*) — the fourth son of Benjamin (1 Chr. 8:2). Nohah is not mentioned among those who went with Jacob into Egypt (Gen. 46:21). He may have been born after the migration into Egypt.

NON [none] — a form of NUN.

NOON — twelve o'clock in the daytime; midday (2 Kin. 4:20; Jer. 6:4). The psalmist said that the person who abides in God "shall not be afraid of...the destruction that lays waste at noonday" (Ps. 91:5–6). Also see TIME.

NOOSE — a loop formed in a rope by a slipknot so that it binds tighter as the rope is pulled. Bildad, one of Job's friends, insisted that the wicked are punished for their wrongdoing, as surely as a noose captures and holds its prey (Job 18:10; snare, KJV; rope, RSV; cord, NEB).

NOPH [nohf] — the Hebrew name for MEMPHIS, an ancient Egyptian city on the western bank of the Nile and south of modern Cairo (Is. 19:13).

NOPHAH [NO fuh] (*blast*) — a city in Moab occupied by the Amorites, and then by the Israelites (Num. 21:30). Nophah may be another name for Nobah (Num. 32:42), situated northwest of modern Amman.

NORTH (see DIRECTION).

NORTHEASTER (see EUROCLYDON).

NORTH GATE (see GATES OF JERUSALEM AND THE TEMPLE).

NOSE — the part of the face between the eyes and the mouth and an organ of breathing (Gen. 7:22) and smelling (Gen. 27:27). In Bible times the side of a woman's nose was often pierced to allow a jewel or ring to be displayed (Ezek. 16:12). When someone was captured in war, a metal hook could be put through his nose to enforce obedience (Is. 37:29).

NOSE JEWEL, NOSE RING (see JEWELRY).

NOSTRILS — the external openings of the nose. The nostrils speak of both life and death. At the creation, life entered man when "God breathed into his nostrils the breath of life (Gen. 2:7). The Flood

drowned "all in whose nostrils was the breath...of life" (Gen. 7:22), except Noah and the others on the ark. When the Bible speaks of smoke from God's nostrils, it refers to God's holy anger against wickedness and the judgment and destruction that follows (2 Sam. 22:9).

NOVICE — a person newly converted to Christianity (1 Tim. 3:6; a recent convert, NIV, RSV). In the later history of the church, the term was applied to those being instructed in preparation for baptism.

NUMBER, NUMBERS — figures, characters, or symbols used for counting and enumerating in the special discipline known as mathematics. But the people of the Bible used numbers in a practical way rather than as part of a mathematical theory. They applied numbers to common problems of everyday life.

Numbers in the Old Testament. In the Old Testament, numbers are always spelled phonetically. But during the period between the Old and New Testaments, an alphabetic system of writing was used. Although this alphabetic system cannot be demonstrated in the Old Testament, it is interesting that the numerical value of the letters of David's name (14) seems to have determined the pattern of the genealogy in the first part of the Gospel of Matthew.

Archaeological excavations have yielded some evidence about the way the Hebrew people wrote numbers. Stone workers' marks and simple tallies have been discovered. Inscriptions such as the Gezer calendar, the MOABITE STONE, and the Siloam Inscription contain only numbers one through three; otherwise numbers are spelled out.

Conventional Use of Numbers. Little is known of the arithmetic of the Hebrews, but they seem to have had at least a practical awareness of the science. The Bible itself contains examples of addition (Num. 1:26), subtraction (Lev. 27:18), multiplication (Lev. 27:25), and division (Num. 31:27). A remarkable degree of accuracy in the use of fractions was achieved (Gen. 47:24; Lev. 5:16; Ezek. 4:11; 45:13). Scholars have noted that the proportions of the measurements of Ezekiel's Temple would have required considerable skill in mathematics on the part of the prophet as he interpreted this message from God.

Most of the numbers in the Bible indicate specific quantities. But in some cases writers of Scripture did not include exact, official, detailed enumerations or sums. They gave an estimate of the total which was rounded off. The most frequent numerical data given in the Old Testament are enumerations of census, age, or other statistics. These figures provide some difficult textual problems for the serious Bible students.

Ages of people mentioned in the Bible are close to the life span of people today, except in the case of the people before the Flood and the patriarchs. All of the pre-flood ages are either a multiple of five or a multiple of five plus seven. Scholars are not sure why this phenomenon exists, and they do not know what it means.

Another difficulty with numbers concerns the high census figures for the Hebrew people given in some books of the Bible. These high numbers have caused some scholars to question whether the translation of the word thousand is accurate. They suggest that its primary meaning in these contexts is something other than the literal number itself.

Rhetorical Use of Numbers. Old Testament numbers are often used for poetic or rhetorical impact. This usage is neither literal nor symbolic. Used in this way, these numbers may indicate such concepts as few or many, or they may be used to intensify a point. In Amos 1:9, the phrase, "For three transgressions of Tyre, and for four" provides not a catalogue but an emphatic statement of Tyre's sins. A similar usage is found in Proverbs 30:18. These are examples of a climactic formula, which builds stylistic progression and anticipation. The quantity itself, in such cases, is indefinite.

Some Bible students have devised intricate systems for foretelling the future which revolve around symbolic usages of numbers. Some uses of the number seven in the Bible itself fall into this category. Many times seven is important as a symbol rather than a number. It is used almost 600 times in the Bible. Often it expresses the idea of completeness or perfection. To identify any other number as a symbol leaves the interpreter on very shaky ground. The number 12 may be a primary number on which numbers or decimals were built, and the number 40 may have some significance as a round number.

Some interpreters use a system which attempts to find hidden meanings in the Bible by using elaborate codes based on the numerical values of the individual letters. A few interpreters have sought a mystical numerical pattern which establishes the correctness of the text, thus proving to their satisfaction the divine authority of the Bible.

Even considering its shorter length, the New Testament contains substantially less numerical data than the Old Testament. Most New Testament numbers are enumerations of groups of figures taken from the business world used to illustrate a point. With the possible exception of the genealogy in Matthew 1, there are no special signs for numbers in the New Testament. As they are in the Old Testament, numbers are always written out in full.

NUMBERS: A Teaching Outline

Part One: The Preparation of the Old Generation to Inherit the Promised Land (1:1—10:10)

Part Two: The Failure of the Old Generation to Inherit the Promised Land (10:11—25:18)

The only difficulty arises when numbers of the New Testament differ from numbers of the Old Testament, when both accounts refer to the same historical event.

The only mystical use of a number in the Bible occurs in Revelation 13:18. Attempts to identify the meaning of 666 (some manuscripts have 616) have generally been more clever than convincing. Like every other feature in God's Word, numbers should be studied with considerable care.

NUMBERS, BOOK OF — an Old Testament book that traces the Israelites through their long period of wandering in the wilderness as they prepared to enter the Promised Land. Numbers takes its name from the two censuses or "numberings" of the people recorded in the book (chaps. 1 and 26). But Numbers contains a great deal more than a listing of names and figures.

Structure of the Book. Numbers is actually a sequel to the Book of Exodus. Exodus follows the Hebrew people as they escape from slavery in Egypt and cross the wilderness, arriving finally at Mount Sinai, where they receive the Ten Commandments and other parts of God's Law. The Book of Numbers picks up this story with the people still encamped at Sinai. It follows their wanderings through the Wilderness of Sinai for the next 40 years until they finally arrive at Moab on the eastern side of the Jordan River, ready to occupy the land of Canaan. Thus, the books of Exodus and Numbers together show how an enslaved people were prepared to take possession of the land that God himself had promised many centuries earlier to Abraham and his descendants.

Just as Moses is the central figure in Exodus, he also is the dominant personality in Numbers. His leadership ability is pushed to the limit in Numbers as the people grumble about everything from the food they have to eat to the water supply. Time after time God supplied their needs by sending manna, quail, and water; but still they cried out in a stubborn spirit. Finally, in exasperation, Moses struck a rock with his rod to produce drinking water. This was a clear violation of God's command, since He had instructed Moses to *speak* to the rock. Because of his disobedience, Moses was not allowed to enter the Promised Land. He died shortly after viewing the land at a distance from atop Mount Nebo in Moab (Deut. 34).

Historical Setting. The events in the Book of Numbers cover a span of about 39 or 40 years in Israel's history—from 1445 B.C., when they left their encampment at Mount Sinai, to 1405 B.C., when they entered the land of Canaan by crossing the Jordan River near Jericho. These were years of preparation as well as punishment. Their harsh life in the desert wilderness prepared them for the task of pushing out the Canaanites.

The Book of Numbers clearly shows why the Israelites did not proceed immediately to take the land after leaving Mount Sinai. Moses chose 12 spies or scouts and sent them into Canaan along its southern border to explore the land and check its defenses. Ten of them returned with a pessimistic report about the warlike Canaanites who held the land. But two of the spies, Joshua and Caleb, encouraged the people to take the land; for God had promised to prepare the way. When the Israelites refused, God sentenced them to two generations of aimless wandering in the wilderness before they could enter the Promised Land (Num. 14:1–38).

Authorship and Date. Numbers is one of the first five books of the Old Testament—books that have traditionally been assigned to Moses as author. He is the central personality of the book, and it is reasonable to assume that he wrote about these events in which he played such a prominent role. One passage in Numbers states, "Now Moses wrote down the starting points of their journeys at the command of the Lord" (33:2). Other similar references to Moses' writings are found throughout Numbers, giving strong support to the conviction that he wrote the book.

Moses must have written Numbers some time just before his death as the Hebrew people prepared to enter the land. This would place the time of writing at about 1404 B.C.

Theological Contribution. The Book of Numbers presents the concept of God's correcting wrath upon His own disobedient people. Through their rebellion, the Hebrews had broken the covenant. Even Moses was not exempt from God's wrath when he disobeyed God.

But even in His wrath, God did not give up on His people. While He might punish them in the present, He was still determined to bless them and bring them ultimately into a land of their own. Even the false prophet Balaam recognized this truth about God's sovereign purpose. Balaam declares: "God is not a man, that He should lie, nor a son of man, that He should repent. Has He said, and will He not do it? Or has He spoken, and will He not make it good?" (23:19).

Special Considerations. The Israelite warriors counted in the two censuses in the Book of Numbers have been a puzzle to Bible scholars (see chaps. 1 and 26). In each case, they add up to an army of more than 600,000. If this is correct, then the total Israelite population must have been more than 2,000,000 people. Such a figure seems out of line for this period of ancient history when most nations were small.

One possible explanation is that the word translated thousands in English could have meant something like units, tents, or clans in the Hebrew language. If so, a much smaller number was in mind. But other scholars believe there is no reason to question the numbers, since the Israelites did increase dramatically during their years of enslavement in Egypt (Ex. 1:7–12).

NUN (*a fish*) — the name of a man in the Old Testament and of a letter of the Hebrew alphabet:

1. The father of Joshua (pronounced *none*) and an Ephraimite (Ex. 33:11; Num. 27:18).

2. The 14th letter of the Hebrew alphabet (pronounced *noon*), used as a heading over Psalm 119:105–112. In the original Hebrew language, every line of these eight verses began with the letter nun. Also see ACROSTIC.

NURSE, NURSING (see OCCUPATIONS AND TRADES).

NUTS — the edible seeds of several species of trees. When Jacob sought to win the favor of the ruler of Egypt, he sent as gifts some of the best produce of Palestine. The inclusion of "pistachio nuts and almonds" among "the best fruits of the land" (Gen. 43:11) indicates that these nuts were regarded as choice delicacies.

The "garden of nuts" mentioned by the Shulammite was probably a walnut orchard (Song 6:11). The walnut is native to the Near East. According to the Jewish historian Josephus, the walnut tree was cultivated extensively in Galilee and along the slopes of Hermon and Lebanon.

The almond tree figured prominently in Jeremiah's vision (Jer. 1:11), where the promise of God's faithfulness to His word is given through the vision of the almond branch.

Also see PLANTS OF THE BIBLE.

NUZI [NOO zi] — an ancient city of Mesopotamia which flourished from 2000–1000 B.C. The site is now 16 kilometers (10 miles) southwest of Kirkuk, east of the Tigris River, in the northern part of Iraq. Although Nuzi is not mentioned in the Bible, it is of great archaeological importance. It was excavated in 1925–31 by the American School of Oriental Research. Some 20,000 small clay tablets, inscribed with CUNEIFORM writing, and dating back as far as 2500 B.C., were discovered.

The Nuzi Tablets contain private contracts and public records, a list of goods which the city and the surrounding land produced, as well as tablets dealing with a wide range of other topics. These tablets describe an ancient civilization, perhaps partly contemporary with Abraham, in which installment buying was widely practiced.

NYMPHA [NEM fah] — a form of NYMPHAS.

NYMPHAS [NIM fuhs] (*gift of the nymphs*) — a Christian at Laodicea or Colossae in whose house the Christians had met and to whom the apostle Paul sent greetings (Col. 4:15; Nympha, NAS, NEB, NIV, RSV).

O

OAK (see Plants of the Bible).

OAR — a long pole with a broad blade at one end, used as a lever for rowing or steering a boat (Is. 33:21; Ezek. 27:6, 29).

OARSMEN — people who row or navigate a Ship. In Old Testament times the Phoenicians were the masters of the sea; hence, the mention of oarsmen in the prophet Ezekiel's lamentation for the Phoenician city of Tyre (Ezek. 27:8–9, 26; marines, KJV, RSV; rowers, NASB; sailors, NASB, NEB, NIV). Also see Ships.

OATH — a solemn statement or claim used to validate a promise. In Bible times, oaths were sometimes accompanied by protective curses to make sure the oaths were kept (1 Sam. 14:24; Gen. 24:41). Such curses were also used to protect property rights from thieves (Judg. 17:2) or from those who found a stolen object or knew of a theft (Lev. 5:1).

An oath was used to seal treaties, insuring that neither party broke their promise (Gen. 26:28). Oaths were also used in Israel's treaty with God at Sinai (Deut. 27:11—28:68; 29:11–20). In the Bible oaths were sometimes taken lightly, as if all parties expected them to be broken (Hos. 10:4). In legal cases oaths were sometimes used to make a person admit guilt (1 Kin. 8:31–32). However, oaths were not to be used in wrongful accusations of people (Ex. 20:7; Job 31:30; Ps. 10:7; Hos. 4:2).

Sometimes people pronounced a curse upon themselves in connection with an oath which they had taken. David vowed not to eat until evening with these words: "God do so to me, and more also, if I taste bread or anything else till the sun goes down" (2 Sam. 3:35). This was a strong pledge on his part that he expected to keep his promise.

Oaths could be taken with symbolic gestures such as raising the hand (Gen. 14:22; Dan. 12:7; Rev. 10:5–6) or touching the sex organs (Gen. 24:2; 47:29), possibly symbolizing a person's life and power. Oaths were taken very seriously (Ex. 20:7; Lev. 19:12). Lying about an oath could result in death (Ezek. 17:16–18). Jesus himself was bound by an oath (Matt. 26:63–64), as was Paul (2 Cor. 1:23; Gal. 1:20). Even God bound Himself by oath to keep His promises to Abraham (Heb. 6:13–18).

OBADIAH [oh bah DIE ah] (*servant of Jehovah*) — the name of 12 men in the Old Testament:

1. The governor of Ahab's palace (1 Kin. 18:3–7, 16).

2. A descendant of David and the head of a family (1 Chr. 3:21).

3. A son of Izrahiah, of the tribe of Issachar (1 Chr. 7:3).

4. A descendant of King Saul (1 Chr. 8:38).

5. A Levite, a son of Shemaiah (1 Chr. 9:16).

6. A Gadite captain who joined David at Ziklag (1 Chr. 12:9).

7. A leader of the tribe of Zebulun during the reign of David (1 Chr. 27:19).

8. A leader of Jehoshaphat commissioned to teach the Book of the Law (2 Chr. 17:7).

9. A Levite who supervised workmen repairing the Temple during the reign of King Josiah (2 Chr. 34:12).

10. A son of Jehiel, a descendant of Joab (Ezra 8:9).

11. A priest who sealed the covenant after the Captivity (Neh. 10:5).

12. A prophet of Judah (Obadiah 1). The fourth of the "minor" prophets, Obadiah's message was directed against Edom. Some scholars believe Obadiah was a contemporary of Jehoram, during whose reign (about 844 B.C.) Jerusalem was invaded by Philistines and Arabians (2 Chr. 21:16–17). Other scholars suggest a date following 587/86, the time of the destruction of Jerusalem by the Babylonians. Still others suggest an earlier Babylonian assault on Jerusalem, in 605 B.C.

Whatever date is assigned to Obadiah, he lived during a time of trouble for Jerusalem. His prophecy against Edom condemned the Edomites for taking sides against Jerusalem in its distress (Obadiah 15). The strongest mountain fortresses would be no defense for the Edomites against the Day of the Lord—the time when God would bring His final judgment upon the world.

OBADIAH, BOOK OF — a brief prophetic book of the Old Testament that pronounces God's judgment against the Edomites, ancient enemies of the nation of Israel. The book is the shortest in the Old Testament, containing one chapter of only 21 verses.

Structure of the Book. In a brief introduction, the author reveals himself as the prophet OBADIAH, a name meaning "servant of the Lord" or "worshiper of Jehovah." He makes it clear that he has received this message directly from God. The Lord has announced that He will destroy the Edomites because they have sinned against Israel. They mocked God's Covenant People in their hour of misfortune and even participated in the destruction and looting of the capital city, Jerusalem, when it fell to a foreign power. Because of this great sin, Edom will be destroyed. But Israel, the prophet declares, will be blessed by God and restored to its native land.

Authorship and Date. The author clearly identifies himself as the prophet Obadiah, but this is all we know about him. Several Obadiahs are mentioned in the Old Testament (1 Kin. 18:3; Ezra 8:9; Neh. 12:25), but none of these can be identified for sure as the author of this book. But at least his prophecy can be dated with greater certainty. Most scholars believe the great humiliation of Israel which the prophet mentions was the siege of Jerusalem by the Babylonians, beginning in 605 B.C. and ending with its final destruction in 586 B.C. Thus, the book must have been written shortly after the fall of the city, perhaps while the Israelites were still in Captivity in Babylon.

Historical Setting. This book's condemnation of the Edomites is understandable when we consider the bitter feelings that had always existed between these two nations. It began centuries earlier when the twin brothers, Jacob and Esau, went their separate ways (Genesis 27; 36). Esau's descendants settled south of the Dead Sea and became known as the Edomites. Jacob's descendants settled farther north, eventually developing into the Covenant People known as the nation of Israel. The Bible reports many clashes between these two factions.

One notable example was the refusal of the Edomites to let the Israelites cross their land as they traveled toward the land of Canaan (Num. 20:14–21). But the final insult to Israel must have been Edom's participation in the looting of Jerusalem after the city fell to the Babylonians. This led the prophet Obadiah to declare, "For your violence against your brother Jacob, shame shall cover you, and you shall be cut off forever" (v. 10).

Theological Contribution. The Book of Obadiah makes it clear that God takes His promises to His Covenant People seriously. He declared in the Book of Genesis that He would bless the rest of the world through Abraham and his descendants. He also promised to protect His special people against any who would try to do them harm (Gen. 12:1–3). This promise is affirmed in the Book of Obadiah. God is determined to keep faith with His people, in spite of their unworthiness and disobedience.

Special Considerations. Verses 1–9 of Obadiah and Jeremiah 49:7–22 express essentially the same idea. Many of the words and phrases in these two passages are exactly alike. Some scholars believe Jeremiah drew from the Obadiah passage to emphasize God's impending judgment on Edom. If this is true, it indicates the little Book of Obadiah was taken seriously by Jeremiah, one of the great prophetic figures in Israel's history.

OBAL [OH bahl] (*stout*) — a son of Joktan and a descendant of Shem (Gen. 10:28), also called Ebal (1 Chr. 1:22, 40).

OBED [OH behd] (*worshiper*) — the name of five men in the Old Testament:

1. A son of Boaz and Ruth (Ruth 4:17–22; 1 Chr. 2:12) and an ancestor of Jesus (Matt. 1:5).

2. A son of Ephlah (1 Chr. 2:37–38).

3. One of David's mighty men (1 Chr. 11:47).

4. A Levite gatekeeper in the time of David (1 Chr. 26:7).

5. The father of Azariah (2 Chr. 23:1).

OBED–EDOM [OH bed EE dum] (*servant of Edom*) — the name of two or three men in the Old Testament:

1. A Gittite, possibly a Levite from Gath Rimmon, a Levitical city in Dan (2 Sam. 6:10–12; 1 Chr. 13:13–14; 15:25). Some scholars believe, however, that the word Gittite indicates he was a native of the Philistine city of Gath. If so, Obed–Edom was probably a member of David's bodyguard. David stored the ARK OF THE COVENANT in the house of Obed–Edom for three months before moving it on to Jerusalem. During this time, Obed–Edom and all his household were blessed.

2. A Levite gatekeeper who helped transport the

OBADIAH: A Teaching Outline

Photo by Howard Vos

An obelisk in honor of Queen Hatshepsut at Karnak, Egypt.

ark to Jerusalem (1 Chr. 15:18–24; 26:4, 8, 15).

3. A Levite musician who ministered before the ark when it was placed in the tabernacle (1 Chr. 16:5, 38). He may be the same person as Obed–Edom No. 2.

4. The guardian of the sacred vessels in the Temple (2 Chr. 25:24).

OBEDIENCE — carrying out the word and will of another person, especially the will of God. In both the Old and New Testaments the word obey is related to the idea of hearing. Obedience is a positive, active response to what a person hears. God summons people to active obedience to His revelation. Man's failure to obey God results in judgment. In the Old Testament covenant between God and man, obedience was the basis for knowing God's blessing and favor (Ex. 19:5; 24:1–8). Samuel emphasized that God's pleasure was not in sacrifice but in obedience (1 Sam. 15:22). Even the promise of a new covenant emphasized obedience as God's gift (Jer. 31:33).

In the New Testament, the obedience of Christ stands in contrast to the disobedience of Adam. The disobedience of Adam brought death, but the perfect obedience of Christ brought grace, righteousness, and life (Rom. 5:12–21).

OBEISANCE — the KJV translation of a Hebrew verb *shachah*, which means "to bow down." The NKJV translates as bowed down to (Gen. 37:7, Ex. 18:7), prostrated (2 Sam. 1:2), and did homage (1 Kin. 1:16).

OBELISK [AHB uh lisk] — a stone monument or PILLAR. These stones are generally associated with Egyptian religion (Jer. 43:13). Stone pillars were raised as monuments to honor Rachel and Absalom (Gen. 35:20; 2 Sam. 18:18).

OBIL [OH bill] (*tender*) — an Ishmaelite camel driver appointed keeper of David's royal camels (1 Chr. 27:30).

OBLATION (see SACRIFICIAL OFFERINGS).

OBOTH [OH bowth] (*water skins*) — a place where the Israelites camped during their wanderings in the wilderness.

OBSCENE — indecent or immoral. The word is used in the NKJV to describe the image of the pagan god ASHERAH which King Asa's grandmother set up in the nation of Judah (1 Kin. 15:13; 2 Chr. 15:16). Asa cut down the obscene image and burned it by the Brook Kidron.

OBSERVING TIMES (see MAGIC, SORCERY, AND DIVINATION).

OCCUPATIONS AND TRADES. The ancient Near East is often called the "cradle of civilization." Highly developed cultures flourished in this region of the world long before Abraham's day (about 2100 B.C.). Many skills which developed into occupations and trades originated here very early in history. By Abraham's day civilization was quite complex. Indeed, Abraham himself was a herder of vast flocks of sheep, goats, donkeys, cattle, and perhaps even camels. Many modern scholars think he was also a trader, managing donkey caravans and doing business from Turkey to Egypt.

Throughout their history, the inhabitants of Palestine ranged from primitive to quite advanced peoples. Many skills were required to sustain and promote life in every period of its history.

Palestine was a dry region where water was carefully handled. Palestinians dug wells and from about 1200 B.C. constructed cisterns lined with plaster. These processes required a great variety of skill.

The gathering of food was an important aspect of life in Palestine. Food was secured from the water, forest, and farm. Each of these sources of food demanded a separate set of skills and abilities.

In early history, each wandering family or tribe relied on its members to supply its needs. As society became more complex, however, tribes began to settle into specific areas with larger groups. As this happened, people became more dependent on each other. Skills and occupations became more and more specialized. Farms and other businesses grew in size, demanding servants and hired hands.

As society developed, the skills needed began to

change. The early wandering Hebrew herdsmen lived in tents of animal skins which they could prepare by themselves. When they started to move into houses in towns, they needed a wider variety of skilled laborers. They needed builders, carpenters, brick layers, and many other trades and occupations to build and maintain the houses. The more civilized society had a wider variety of needs. It demanded occupations and trades which could fill its clothing needs, provide health care, education, and other needed products and services. Ultimately, it needed skilled rulers and government officials to govern and maintain order.

Just as in our world, the civilizations of Palestine required specific people to perform certain tasks and hold specific occupations. Young people learned the trades which were needed through apprenticeships. Older tradesmen would take the youngster in as an assistant, teaching him everything he would need to know to be able to continue the trade.

Many necessary occupations and trades existed during Bible times. The following list is keyed to the NKJV. But variant names from five additional translations—KJV, NASB, NEV, NIV, and RSV—are cross-referenced to this listing.

Ambassador. An official representative of kings and rulers. In ancient times many kings and rulers spoke to other nations through official representatives who congratulated (1 Kin. 5:1), sought favors (Num. 20:14), made treaties (Josh. 9:4–6), and registered protests (Judg. 11:12). How the other nations treated the ambassador represented how they related to the ruler. If one treated the ambassador rudely, it was an insult to the ruler and could lead to war (2 Sam. 10:4–6). In the New Testament the apostle Paul called himself Christ's ambassador (Eph. 6:20)—an idea which he applied to all Christian ministers (2 Cor. 5:20). An ambassador is sometimes called an envoy.

Apothecary (see *Perfumer*).

Archer. One who shot an arrow from a bow. Ancient armies had archers who were trained from childhood. Deadly accurate, these warriors were the first to contact the enemy by shooting from a distance. To draw ancient war bows required a pull of 100 pounds. The arrows could pierce almost all armor. The Bible notes how effective archers could be (1 Sam. 31:3; 2 Sam. 11:24; 1 Chr. 10:3).

Armorbearer. A servant who carried additional weapons for commanders. Abimelech (Judg. 9:54), Jonathan (1 Sam. 14:6–17), and Joab (2 Sam. 18:15) had armorbearers. David was once Saul's armorbearer (1 Sam. 16:21). Armorbearers were also responsible for killing enemies slain by their masters. After enemy soldiers were wounded with javelins or bows and arrows, armorbearers finished the job by using clubs and swords. After the time of David, commanders fought from chariots and armorbearers are no longer mentioned.

Armorer. One who made armor. Armorers (smiths skilled in making armor and leather workers skilled in making shields) were primarily Philistines in the days of Saul. While armorer is not mentioned directly in the Bible as an occupation, ancient Hebrew soldiers did use shields, helmets, breastplates of scale-like plates, and greaves (leg armor). God is the great armorer for the Christian soldier (Eph. 6:14–17).

Artificer (see *Metalsmith*).

Artisan (see *Metalsmith*).

Astrologer. One who gained or sought information from the positions of the sun, moon, and stars in relation to one another and to the Zodiac. Astrology and astrologers were widespread in the ancient world, being documented as early as 2000 B.C. in Mesopotamia. From there it spread to Egypt, Greece, China, India, and throughout the ancient world.

The Bible clearly warns against astrologers (Deut. 4:19; 17:2–7; Is. 47:13–15). Many scholars believe the "magi" who came to honor Jesus were astrologers. Other names for astrologers used by other translations are prognosticator, sage, and stargazer.

Attendant (see *Servant*).

Baker. One who baked bread. Bread was a major food among the ancients, and baking and bakers were common. Home bakers prepared dough from cereal grains and baked it on a rock or in an oven. Towns and villages probably had public bakers who baked bread from dough prepared in their customers' homes. Kings had their own royal bakers (Gen. 40:2). A street in Jerusalem was occupied by bakers and their shops (Jer. 37:21).

Banker. Someone involved with keeping, loaning, changing, or issuing money. Banking and bankers appeared among the Jews during the Babylonian Captivity. There is no mention of banking in the

A potter at Hebron fashions a large jar from a lump of clay.

Photo by Gustav Jeeninga

Old Testament, because lending to other Jews for profit was forbidden (Deut. 23:19-20). Loans were permitted if extended to foreigners. Creditors are mentioned in the Mosaic Law (Deut. 15:2). Temples and palaces (citadels and homes of the wealthy) safeguarded much wealth, while others hid their treasures and valuables.

By Roman times bankers were common among the Jews (Matt. 25:27) with "moneychangers" setting up open-air banks to change foreign currency into local money. Moneychangers often cheated their customers—a practice especially irksome when money changing was necessary to present an offering to God (John 2:13-20). Bankers were usually very wealthy. Under Roman law bankers could put a debtor in prison (Matt. 18:25).

Barber. One who shaved or trimmed a man's hair or beard. Tomb pictures of Egyptian barbers at work have been found. The Hebrew word for barber occurs only in Ezekiel 5:1, where the Lord commanded the prophet to shave his hair and beard. Male Israelites normally let their hair grow long, although they did not let it go uncut as the women did. Barbers most likely served royalty and the rich.

Basketmaker. One who made baskets. Women members of the household wove baskets from some kind of natural fiber such as fronds of palms, straw, reeds, rushes, sedges, and grasses. Ancient Near Eastern societies had a great need for light-weight containers. Israel used such containers throughout its history. Baskets came in all sizes and shapes, although the shape resembling earthenware pots was very common. Basketmakers made containers large enough to hold a man (Acts 9:25) or a human head (2 Kin. 10:7), and small enough to house birds (Jer. 5:27) and carry bread (Ex. 29:3).

Beggar. A person who begged for a living. There are very few biblical references to beggars and no term in biblical Hebrew to describe the professional beggar. A person was reduced to begging by divine judgment or wickedness (1 Sam. 1:7-8; Ps. 109:10; Luke 16:3), a physical handicap (Mark 10:46; Luke 18:35; John 9:8), or laziness (Prov. 20:4). God commanded Israel to care for the poor and handicapped, so the presence of beggars indicated Israel's disobedience (Deut. 15:1-11; 8:4, 6-10). In New Testament times beggars were commonplace. Almsgiving, giving to beggars, was praised as good work contributing to a person's righteousness.

Blacksmith (see *Metalsmith*).

Bleacher (see *Fuller*).

Brewer. One who made strong drink. While brewers are not mentioned in the Bible, scholars know that ancient brewers produced beers from various cereals starting over 8,000 years ago. Beer was known in Egypt and the Mesopotamian valley. Barley was buried in pots to force it to germinate, then it was mixed with water and fermented naturally. Sometime between the tenth and seventh centuries B.C. hops began to be added to the process. Strong drink is mentioned in 21 Old Testament passages, starting from the Exodus period.

Photo by Howard Vos

Mosaic of an archer, discovered at ancient Susa. He may have been a professional soldier in the Persian army.

Brickmaker. One who made bricks. The first record of brickmaking occurs in Genesis 11:3. Israel made clay bricks in Egypt, a process depicted on Egyptian wall paintings. Chemicals released by decomposed straw made clay bricks much stronger (Ex. 5:6-19). Such bricks have been found at Pithom. The Israelites who served as slaves in Egypt worked mostly as brickworkers (Ex. 1:11-14).

Brick Worker (see *Brickmaker*).

Bronze Worker (see *Metalsmith*).

Builder. One who constructed a building. Building is a very ancient task, beginning with Cain who built a walled dwelling to protect himself (Gen.

4:17). Later, the descendants of Noah built a tower to climb into heaven so they might make a name for themselves (Gen. 11:4). In Egypt the Hebrew people became a slave corps of builders who built storage cities for Pharaoh (Ex. 1:11). While inhabiting Palestine, the Israelites built walled towns (cities) and unwalled towns (villages), houses, palaces, temples, and many other structures.

The more humble structures of Palestine may have employed skilled carpenters for certain tasks, but most of the work was done by the prospective owner or other unskilled laborers. Larger, more extravagant projects were headed by a master builder, who chose the site and laid out the project with a measuring line. He usually recorded the results in a plan and in writing. Isaiah referred to this process as a symbol of God's judgment (Is. 28:17). The master builder checked the work of the skilled and unskilled workers. He used a plumb line to check if it was truly vertical (Zech. 4:10). The most skilled builders employed in Israel came from Phoenicia. These skilled builders included masons, carpenters, and others (2 Sam. 5:11).

God is often symbolically portrayed as a master builder. He built the throne of David (Ps. 89:4), Jerusalem (Ps. 147:2), and the church (1 Cor. 3:9; 1 Pet. 2:4-6). In 1 Corinthians 3 Paul compared himself to God's master builder and others to brick layers building a symbolic living Temple. The foundation of this living Temple is "the apostles and prophets, Jesus Christ Himself being the chief cornerstone" (Eph. 2:20).

Butler (see *Cupbearer*).

Camel Driver. One who herded and rode camels. The existence of camels in Abraham's day is widely questioned. However, the remains of wild camels found in Palestine, Egyptian sculptures of camels from the third and fourth centuries B.C., and simi-

lar evidence, supports the scriptural reports (Gen. 12:16, 24). Camels were used to cross the desert between Mesopotamia and Palestine about 1800 B.C. The Midianites were desert nomads and camel drivers (Judg. 6:5), as was the Queen of Sheba (1 Kin. 10:2).

Carpenter (see *Builder; Woodworker*).

Carver. One skilled at whittling, cutting, or chipping wood, stone, ivory, clay, bronze, gold, silver, or glass. Skilled wood carvers were rare. Carved panels, windows, and woodwork were signs of great wealth. The tabernacle and Temple (1 Kin. 6:15-39) were lavishly adorned with such work. Ivory carving—for signet rings and inlays for wooden panels (2 Chr. 9:17), jewelry, furniture, and figurines—was an ancient and highly skilled art.

Caulker. Men skilled in applying tar to hulls of ships to make them watertight. Mentioned only in Ezekiel 27:27, caulkers plugged cracks in and between a ship's planks. These caulkers were Phoenicians, the most noted nation in the Old Testament for ships and sea trade. Also see *Shipbuilder*.

Centurion (see *Soldier*).

Chamberlain. One responsible for guarding the king's bedroom and harem. This man, usually a eunuch to remove all possibility of unfaithfulness, was employed by ancient kings. He was a highly trusted and influential official (Acts 8:27). Also see *Eunuch*.

Chancellor (see *Government Official*).

Charioteer (see *Soldier*).

City Clerk. An official of a Greek city state. The city clerk held an important political position. He was responsible for the city archives; taking minutes at the council meetings; handling official communications, including public readings; serving on a number of boards; handling many administrative

A stone carving from Egypt showing carpenters at work, probably from about 2500 B.C.
Photo by Howard Vos

Photo by Howard Vos

Brickmaking near Memphis, Egypt, utilizing the ancient method of hardening the bricks in the sun.

details; and even annually distributing money to the poor. The Ephesian city clerk (Acts 19:35; townclerk, KJV) was also president of the assembly. His importance and prominence are shown by the fact that his name frequently appeared on coins.

Commander (see *Soldier*).

Commissioner (see *Government Official*).

Comptroller (see *Government Official*).

Confectioner (see *Perfumer*).

Controller (see *Government Official*).

Cook. One who prepared food for eating. The Hebrew word translated cook literally means "slaughterer"—one who kills and dresses animals. The king's cooks apparently killed the animals to be prepared for his table. Cooks may have been either women servants (1 Sam. 8:13) or male professionals (Luke 17:8). In the average household, cooking was the women's job (Gen. 18:6; 27:9), although men did the slaughtering and dressing (Gen. 18:7). Gideon was a cook and a baker (Judg. 6:19).

Coppersmith (See *Metalsmith*).

Counselor. One who gave advice. Ancient kings often had trusted officials who served as counselors (1 Chr. 27:32; Ezra 4:5). Not all counselors, however, were professionals (2 Chr. 22:3). Isaiah 9:6 describes the coming Messiah as a Counselor. Joseph of Arimathea is called a "counsellor" (Mark 15:43; Luke 23:50, KJV). He was a member of the Jewish council, the SANHEDRIN.

Courtier (see *Government Official*).

Craftsman (see *Metalsmith*).

Creditor (see *Banker*).

Criminal. A lawbreaker. The first criminal was Cain, who murdered his brother (Gen. 4:8). A criminal mentality and rebellion against God's law apparently characterized Cain's descendants (Gen. 4:23–24). Men began to use their own system of laws and "criminal" came to mean one who violated such a system. Divine law again became the ruling system of Hebrew society after the Exodus from Egypt. God distinguished between sacred and civil law. Criminals were to be punished by death, mutilation, scourging, paying monetary damages and fines, and enslavement.

Both thieves and robbers fall into the category of criminal. Both thieves and robbers took the possessions of others. But while thieves stole secretly, robbers stole openly and often violently. The Hebrew language does not differentiate between robber and thief, but Greek does. Jesus was crucified between two robbers (Matt. 27:38).

Cupbearer. One who tasted and served wine to the king. Ancient kings had to be very cautious about what they ate and drank. They used trusted servants to taste everything before they consumed it. If the servant lived or did not get sick, the king and queen then ate or drank. The "chief butler" in the Joseph account (Genesis 40) headed the king's cupbearers. Nehemiah held this highly trusted position under King Artaxerxes (Neh. 1:11), influencing the king politically. King Solomon also used employed cupbearers (1 Kin. 10:5).

Dancer. One who dances. Professional dancers apparently did not exist among the Hebrew people as they did in Egypt, Babylon, and other pagan nations. However, children danced in play (Job 21:11) and adults danced in joy (2 Sam. 6:14). One could dance before God as an act of joy in worship (Ex. 15:20; Ps. 149:3; 150:4). The original Hebrew words reveal that this dancing involved skipping about, whirling, and leaping.

Dealer (see *Merchant*).

Deputy (see *Government Official*).

Designer. One who designed artistic work. Designer is often mentioned with engraver and weaver (Ex. 35:35; 38:23). Artisans during Old Testament times may have been knowledgeable in several crafts.

Disciple. A follower and a pupil. It was common in the ancient world for students or apprentices to attach themselves to a teacher and follow him in learning and discipline (Is. 8:16). The Pharisees (Mark 2:18), John the Baptist (Matt. 11:2), and Jesus gathered such disciples, or learners. Jesus chose twelve, the number of tribes in Israel, to be his special disciples.

Diviner. One who practiced MAGIC, SORCERY, AND DIVINATION. Diviners used the trance, dreams, clairvoyance, and many mechanical means such as inspecting the livers of animals to gain information which could not be found by ordinary means. This is the tool of false prophets, although at least once in the Old Testament it is a proper tool used by the godly (Prov. 16:10). Divination was widely spread in the ancient Near East from earliest times and non–biblical literature contains directions on its pursuit. Pagan divination and diviners are soundly condemned (Lev. 19:26; Deut. 18:9–14), but the Israelites resorted to it at times (2 Kin. 17:17; 21:6).

Doorkeeper (see *Porter*).

Drawer of Water (see *Water Carrier*).

Driver (see *Overseer*).

Duke (see *Prince*).

Dyer. One skilled in permanently coloring cloth. While this is not mentioned as a specific occupation in the Bible, scholars know that dyeing was an ancient craft which often used secret formulas passed on from previous generations. The tabernacle materials were dyed with purple dye that was probably imported from Phoenicia.

Embalmer. One who prepared the dead for burial by treating the body to prevent decay. The Egyptians were well-known for this practice. The Hebrews, however, did not practice embalming because they were prevented by divine law from touching dead bodies (Num. 19:11–19). Joseph, a high official in the Egyptian court and an adopted member of the royal family, was embalmed (Gen. 50:26) and had his father Jacob embalmed (Gen. 50:2–3). This was probably done to preserve the bodies for the trip to the family burial grounds in Palestine (Gen. 50:13–14; Josh. 24:32).

Embroiderer. One skilled in decorative ornamental needlework. Ancient embroiderers decorated clothes by using geometrical and stylized designs. The rich and powerful wore clothes beautifully embroidered (Ps. 45:14). Embroiderers participated in decorating tabernacle garments and hangings (Ex. 27:1, 16; 28:4, 15). The embroiderer and the weaver were separate and distinct occupations, but some translations use the terms interchangeably. Also see *Weaver*.

Engraver (see *Metalsmith*).

Envoy (see *Ambassador*).

Eunuch. A male officer of a court or royal household. Frequently, the Hebrew word translated eunuch also means a man who was castrated to assure he would not become involved sexually with the members of the king's harem (Is. 56:3). In many passages, however, the word refers simply to an officer. Castrated males were not permitted to approach God's altar (Deut. 23:1).

Executioner. One who legally takes another person's life. The Old Testament clearly distinguishes between murder, or illegally taking another's life (Ex. 20:13), and execution. In God's law many crimes were met with the death penalty (Gen. 9:6; Deut. 13:10; 21:22). It was the executioner's task to exact that penalty. Personal vengeance was prohibited (Deut. 24:16). The New Testament records several executions which were legal under Roman law but not under divine law (Matt. 14:10). The most famous execution in the Bible is the crucifixion of Jesus (John 18).

Exorcist. One who cast out demons. The people of the ancient world believed in spirit powers and that a person could be taken over by an evil power. Many methods were used to cast out the demons. These included potions, spells, and chants. The New Testament also tells of the existence of evil powers and describes Christ's total victory over them. Jesus expelled demons quickly and easily (Mark 1:23–27). He did not practice the mysterious and often complicated acts of the exorcist (Matt. 12:24–28).

Fanner. One who winnows, or separates, grain. The grain was beaten to loosen the kernels. These kernels were then trampled underfoot to loosen the chaff covering the grain. After each stage, the fanner would throw the grain into the air. The wind blew the chaff away and the grain fell to the ground. The fanner used a six–pronged pitchfork in the first stage and a shovel for the second stage (Is. 30:24). In the same way, God separates the wheat, or true believers, from the chaff, or hypocrites, at the last day (Matt. 3:12; Luke 3:17).

Farmer. One who tills the soil and raises food. Terms in the Bible which refer to farmer include plowman (Is. 28:24), husbandman (KJV), vinedresser (Is. 61:5), gardener (John 20:15), and tiller (Gen. 4:2). This was one of the major occupations of the ancient Hebrews, along with shepherding. The farmer of ancient times was responsible for all aspects of farming. All the plowing, planting, tending, and harvesting was done by the farmer and his family. More prosperous farmers were able to hire helpers for their farm. In the New Testament a farmer is one who owns the land or rents it and raises crops (Matt. 21:33). In John 15:1–8, Jesus refers to Himself as the true vine and His Father as the vinedresser.

Finer (see *Metalsmith*).

Fisherman. One who catches fish for food. Both amateur and professional fishermen existed in Bible times. They used various kinds of nets, hooks, and lines (Is. 19:8). Sometimes fishermen used spears (Job 41:7). Several of Jesus' disciples were professional fishermen.

Footman. A runner or messenger. The footmen in Jeremiah 12:5 were couriers. The KJV often uses footmen to refer to foot soldiers or infantrymen. Also see *Herald.*

Foreman (see *Overseer*).

Forger (see *Metalsmith*).

Fowler. One who hunts and captures birds. The Egyptians were especially known for their taste for bird meat. Ancient fowlers used all kinds of implements and devices such as decoys, traps, nets, bait, bows and arrows, slings, lures, setting dogs, and bird lime smeared on branches to catch their prey. The Mosaic Law forbade taking a mother bird and her young together; only the young were to be taken (Deut. 22:6–7). Wicked, scheming enemies of the righteous are called fowlers (Ps. 91:3; 124:7).

Founder (see *Metalsmith*).

Fuller. One who cleans, shrinks, thickens, and sometimes dyes newly cut wool or cloth. The Hebrew word rendered as fuller means "to trample" or "to tread," suggesting that action as a major part of the craft. The fuller removed the oily and gummy substances from material before it could be used by washing it in some alkaline such as white clay, putrid urine, or nitre, as there was no soap in those days. The alkaline was washed out by treading on the material repeatedly in running or clean water. The material was then dried and bleached by the sun.

The fuller's process created an unpleasant odor. Therefore, it was usually done outside the city gates in an area named Fuller's Field (2 Kin. 18:17; Is. 7:3). God is compared to fuller's "soap" (Mal. 3:2). Jesus' garments at His transfiguration were described as whiter than any human fuller could make them (Mark 9:3; launderer, NASB; bleacher, NEB).

Gardener (see *Farmer*).

Gatekeeper (see *Porter*).

Glassworker. One who made glass and formed it into useful or ornamental objects. Glass was known by 2600 B.C. and so glassworkers date from at least this date. While glassworkers are not mentioned specifically in the Bible, Egyptian glassworkers (about 1400 B.C.) made vessels similar to pottery and small perfume vessels by winding hot glass rods around a sand core and then joining the layers by reheating them.

Gleaner (see *Laborer*).

Goatherd (see *Shepherd*).

Goldsmith (see *Metalsmith*).

Government Official. A worker for a government. Many different officials are mentioned in the Bible. Little is known, however, about many of these official positions. These officials may have been government administrators (Gen. 41:34), religious or military overseers (1 Kin. 4:5), secretaries (Ex. 5:6–8), commanders (Num. 11:16), or assistants to the king (Esth. 1:8). Government officials referred to in the Bible by specific title include chancellor, com-

missioner, comptroller, controller, courtier, deputy, magistrate, officer, prefect, president, procurer, recorder, treasurer, trustee, and viceroy. A quartermaster was an official who made lodging arrangements for the king during his official travels.

Guard (see *Soldier*).

Harvester (see *Laborer*).

Hewer of Stone (see *Stoneworker*).

Herald. One responsible for bearing a message, often in preparation for the appearance of a king or other royal figure. The heralds ran before the king's chariot to announce his coming. Heralds also were responsible for announcing the king's messages (Dan. 3:4). The Aramaic word for herald is sometimes translated "to preach" (Matt. 3:1; 4:17). Hence, New Testament preachers are heralds of the King. Heralds are also sometimes referred to as messengers. Also see *Footman; Government Official.*

Hewer (see *Woodworker*).

Horseman (see *Soldier*).

Hunter. One who pursues wild animals as a source of food, to protect crops, or for sport. Hunting for sport was common among ancient kings. It is often depicted on monuments in Egypt and Assyria. In earliest times Nimrod was a noted hunter, adept at using weapons (Gen. 10:9). Later, Esau was a hunter (Gen. 27:3).

The Mosaic Law allowed Israel to hunt and consume some wild animals (Lev. 17:13). Other Old Testament accounts of hunting have to do with defending homes (Judg. 14:5–6). Hunters used bows and arrows (Gen. 27:3), nets (Prov. 1:17), traps (Amos 3:5), and pits (Is. 24:17) to capture or kill wild animals. Hunters who used traps were called trappers.

Husbandman (see *Farmer*).

Innkeeper. One who managed an inn. In Old Testament times, most travelers stayed in private dwellings or slept in the open. By New Testament times some people managed inns (Luke 10:35) which were often not very comfortable or safe. Mary and Joseph stopped at a larger private dwelling, because it was the custom for such homeowners to rent out dwelling quarters during festival times (Luke 2:7).

Ironsmith (see *Metalsmith*).

Jeweler. One who made jewelry. People of the ancient world were fond of jewelry. In Old Testament times, jewelry was a sign of wealth and blessing (Ezek. 23:26; Is. 61:10). It was given to brides as presents (Gen. 24:22, 30, 53) or as part of her dowry.

Judge. One who governs and dispenses justice, judgment, and protection. The first judge mentioned in the Old Testament is God Himself (Gen. 18:25). This divine model is first manifested in human beings in the head of a household (Genesis 21; 22; 27). It was then seen in Moses who judged over all Israel, and in elders appointed to be judges under Moses (Ex. 18:13–27). Israel was ruled by a system of judges described in the Book of Judges. The power of judgment was later passed on to the king.

An ancient bakery at Pompeii, showing an oven (left) and mills for grinding wheat into flour (right).

Israel had both a civil and ecclesiastical system (2 Chr. 19:11). In the New Testament the high court of Israel was the SANHEDRIN, although there were also judges in every town (Luke 18:2). None of the New Testament judges "protected" the people by leading them into battle.

Laborer. One who worked at manual, or physical, labor. Almost everyone in the Bible worked and worked hard. There were relatively few skilled occupations such as potters, metalsmiths, masons, scribes, dyers, weavers, and jewelry makers. For the most part the life of the average person consisted of long hours of very hard work and small incomes (Ps. 90:10). Some laborers worked in the fields at harvest times as harvesters, gleaners, and reapers.

Launderer (see *Fuller*).

Lawyer. One who knew and practiced law. Lawyers are mentioned only in the New Testament. By Jesus' day the Law, the first five books of the Old Testament, had been expanded by the Jewish leaders. Their intent was to give the people an adequate interpretation and application of divine law to every situation of life. Added to the Law was a vast body of explanation, commentary, and application which was held to be just as binding as the actual writings of Moses.

New Testament lawyers were experts in this large body of material. They spent their time studying, interpreting, and expounding this law and acting as court judges. Also referred to as "teachers of the law" or "scribes," Jewish lawyers generally opposed both John the Baptist (Luke 7:30) and Jesus (Luke 14:3) and tried to discredit Jesus (Matt. 22:34-40).

Leatherworker (see *Tanner*).

Lookout (see *Watchman*).

Magistrate (see *Government Official*).

Maid/Maidservant. A female servant. Two Hebrew words are translated maid and maidservant. Often they refer to a girl or woman whose task was to see to the needs of a wife or daughter of a rich or important man (Gen. 16:1). The Hebrew words may also refer to a female servant (1 Sam. 1:11) or bondservant (Lev. 25:44) whose duties are quite diverse (Ex. 11:5), and a female servant who serves as a concubine (Judg. 19:9). The New Testament uses words which mean "young girl" to signify maid. Also see *Servant*.

Mason (see *Builder; Stoneworker*).

Merchandiser (see *Merchant*).

Merchant. One who earns a living by buying items from one person and selling them to another. Merchants are referred to by various translations as traders, dealers, and merchandisers. The Old Testament recognizes a difference between international merchants (Gen. 37:28; Prov. 31:14) and merchants in general (Ezek. 17:4). In Jerusalem in Nehemiah's time, merchants selling similar or the same items located close to one another (Neh. 3:22; 13:16). Only in the New Testament was being a merchant as normal as being a farmer (Matt. 22:5).

Messenger (see *Footman; Herald*).

Metalsmith. One who worked with metal. This occupation included those who dug the ore from the ground, refined the metal, and worked the metal into useful objects. Refining metal was a very ancient skill which was well developed by the time of Abraham.

During Abraham's day, smiths were using bellows to increase the heat of their furnaces to melt iron ore for extraction from the metal. Long before this time, copper was mixed with tin to form bronze, and copper was mixed with zinc to form brass. Iron and other metals such as gold and silver were often hammered or forged into desired shapes by metalworkers even before 4000 B.C. The refining process became quite well developed so that ancient metalworkers produced a high quality of gold, silver, and other precious metals.

Ancient metalsmiths were skilled in making ornamental objects of precious metals. Israel was relatively ignorant of metalworking skills before the time of David, about 1000 B.C. Recognizing the importance of metalworking, David moved to conquer Edom and its iron and copper mines (2 Sam. 8:14). Solomon brought Israel into a high stage of metalworking by importing experts from other more advanced nations (1 Kin. 7:13–14).

The first metalworker mentioned in the Bible was Tubal-Cain, a descendant of Cain (Gen. 4:22). The smith was often named for the metal he refined, cast, or molded. Goldsmiths worked with gold, silversmiths with silver, coppersmiths with copper, and ironsmiths with iron. Various translations use several different terms to describe metalworkers: artificer, artisan, blacksmith, bronze worker, craftsman, engraver, finer, forger, founder, refiner, and smelter.

Midwife. A woman who helped other women give birth to their children (Gen. 35:17). Midwives were sometimes relatives or friends. Their task involved cutting the umbilical cord, bathing the baby, rubbing it down with salt, and swaddling it (Ezek. 16:4). In swaddling, the baby was wrapped snugly in cloth which bound its arms to its body. The midwife also marked which twin was the first to come forth or the firstborn (Gen. 38:28). In Egypt, Pharaoh ordered the Hebrew midwives, apparently professionals, to kill all the boy babies at birth, but the women refused to do so (Ex. 1:15–22).

Mourner. One who grieved over the dead. Paid professional mourners worked in the ancient world from very early times. They are called "mourning women" and "skilled wailing women" (Jer. 9:17), "singing men" and "singing women" (2 Chr. 35:25). These mourners sang or chanted funeral songs or dirges (Amos 5:16), accompanied by musical instruments (Matt. 9:23).

Noble (see *Prince*).

Nurse. A woman who breast fed an infant or helped raise the child. Pharaoh's daughter hired Moses' mother to suckle him (Ex. 2:7–9), while Naomi helped raise her grandson Obed (Ruth 4:16). Some nurses were respected members of households, even after the child became an adult (Gen. 24:59; 35:8).

Officer (see *Government Official*).

Orator. A teacher of speech making or a professional writer of speeches. The Jews found an orator's services very necessary whenever they appeared before a Gentile court. Such courts operated according to given rules of etiquette and oratory (Acts 24:1). One could lose his case simply by the crudeness of his speech. Paul was a capable orator himself and thus defended himself before Felix (Acts 24:10–21). A careful study of Paul's speech at the Areopagus (Acts 17:22–31) further shows Paul's oratory abilities, even though he notes in 1 Corinthians 2:4 that the power of his preaching did not depend on such a skill.

Overseer. One responsible for controlling and managing a group of people or a task. In the Old Testament, overseer refers to those responsible for getting a job done (2 Chr. 2:8) and to those who helped rule a people (Neh. 11:9). A captain in Pharaoh's guard made Joseph the overseer of his house (Gen. 39:4–5). When an overseer was responsible for slaves, he was sometimes called a taskmaster. The taskmasters over the Israelite slaves in Egypt were particularly cruel (Ex. 1:11–14). Overseers were also sometimes called drivers, foremen, and slavemasters. In the New Testament an overseer is an officer in the church. Some scholars equate this officer with the "elder," while others see it as a distinct office. Some translations do not agree with one another and do not consistently translate the Greek word as overseer. This word appears in Acts 20:28, Philippians 1:1, 1 Timothy 3:2, and Titus 1:7. Jesus is the great Overseer of the church (1 Pet. 2:25).

Perfumer. One who made perfume. Perfume making is an ancient art. People of the ancient world loved perfumes and used them to cover up unpleasant body odors. The rich, especially royalty, used perfumers (1 Sam. 8:13). Perfumers and cooks are frequently associated in ancient literature, since the skills of both were closely related.

Flower perfume was made by dipping and heating the flowers in oils and by squeezing out the perfume. Egyptian tomb paintings of the 15th century B.C. depict these processes. Tabernacle and temple worship required the services of professional perfumers to make perfumes for the priests as well as incense to burn before God (Ex. 30:25, 35; 1 Chr. 9:30). Guilds of perfumers existed in Old Testament days (Neh. 3:8). Perfumers are sometimes called apothecaries and confectionaries by the KJV.

Pilot (see *Sailor*).

Plasterer. One who put plaster on the walls of a home (Lev. 14:42–43) to form a smooth surface. Plastering is a very ancient and widespread craft, but homeowners often did their own plastering. Good quality plaster was made by heating broken limestone and gypsum. The lowest quality plaster consisted of clay and straw and was used only in very dry climates. Plaster, called "whitewash" in Deuteronomy 27:2–4, was applied to the altar in the tabernacle and engraved while still wet. God's finger inscribed a message in the dry plaster in Belshazzar's palace (Dan. 5:5).

Plowman (see *Farmer*).

Poet. One who composed poetry. This involves expressing ideas about things in imagery. Biblical

This stone carving from Assyria shows King Ashurnasirpal (center) on his throne between his cupbearer (left) and another servant (right).

poets used simile, comparing one subject to another (Ps. 125:1); metaphor, referring to a subject in terms of another subject (Ps. 62:2); and other figures of speech. The most famous Old Testament poets are probably Moses (Exodus 15), David (Psalms) and Solomon (Proverbs, Ecclesiastes, Song of Solomon). Several New Testament writers, including Paul (Rom. 8:31–39) and John (Rev. 18:2–24), wrote poetry.

Porter. A keeper of the door. This person guarded the entrance to a city, public building (John 18:17), temple, rich man's house (Mark 13:34), and sheepfold (John 10:3). A guard was stationed at any entrance through which someone unwanted might enter, especially at night. This must have been a lowly job because of the contrast implied in Psalm 84:10, where "doorkeeper" is the opposite of the most luxurious and favorable position. Porters were also called gatekeepers.

Potter. One who made and decorated pottery. Pottery is a very ancient and developed craft. The pottery wheel appeared about 4000 B.C. In its early history, the nation of Israel had professional potters who sat on the edge of a small pit, turning the pottery wheel with their feet. In treading the clay or kneading it by foot it was very important to get the right consistency for a good end product. Many potters probably treaded the clay themselves (Is. 41:25).

The remains of potter's shops at Lachish (about 1200 B.C.), Megiddo, Gezer, and Hazor (after 1000 B.C.) have been found. These remains include the nearby clay fields, potters' wheels and kilns, and the dump for unusable pottery. Such a workshop was mentioned by the prophet Jeremiah. The potter's total control over the clay is likened to God's control over men (Jer. 18:1–12).

Prefect (see *Government Official*).

President (see *Government Official*).

Prince, Princess. A son or daughter of royalty, or a person in a position of authority and responsibility. Prince is sometimes translated duke or noble by some English versions.

Procurer (see *Government Official*).

Prognosticator (see *Astrologer*).

Quarryman (see *Stoneworker*).

Quartermaster (see *Government Official*).

Reaper (see *Laborer*).

Recorder (see *Government Official*).

Refiner (see *Metalsmith*).

Robber (see *Criminal*).

Sage (see *Astrologer*).

Sailor. One who manned a ship. The nation of Israel was never a seafaring power. But the PHOENICIANS were the best known and perhaps most skilled sailors who toiled at sea. The prophet Jonah traveled on a Phoenician ship (Jon. 1:3). Phoenician sailors were skilled as navigators, pilots, oarsmen, and sailmen who sailed their sturdy ships to distant lands in international trade.

Scribe (see *Secretary*).

Sculptor (see *Stoneworker*).

Seamster (see *Weaver*).

Secretary. A man who did the writing and corresponding for another. In Old Testament society this job was done by a scribe (Jer. 36:26, 32). By New Testament times scribal duties had increased considerably. The non-Jewish New Testament world featured public and private secretaries who wrote, usually in shorthand, from dictation, or received the general sense from the author and filled in the rest with appropriate language. The apostle Paul may have dictated his letters (Rom. 16:22; Gal. 6:11; 2 Thess. 3:17).

Sentry (see *Watchman*).

Sergeant (see *Soldier*).

Serpent Charmer. One skilled in hypnotizing snakes. This skill was used by the priests and magicians of Egypt before the Exodus (Ps. 58:4; Eccl. 10:11; Jer. 8:17).

Servant. One under another's authority. In Bible times, a servant could be a slave, a person not free to do his own bidding. Or, he could also be a domestic or hired hand who was paid for his work but free to leave the job. He could also be neither of these, but a volunteer choosing to do someone else's bidding. This idea may be rooted in and governed by the idea of a covenant. Thus, individual believers (Ps. 78:70-72) or God's people as a whole (Is. 41:8-10) are His servants. A servant is sometimes referred to in the Bible as an attendant.

Sheepbreeder (see *Shepherd*).

Sheepshearer (see *Shepherd*).

Shepherd. One who tends sheep. Abel was the first shepherd mentioned in the Bible. Later Abraham, Isaac, and Jacob became shepherds (Gen. 13:7; 26:20; 30:36). When Israel went into Egypt, the Egyptian rulers isolated them because they considered shepherds unclean (Gen. 46:34). Shepherding and goatherding were among the major occupations of Palestine throughout its history. Sheep and goats were sometimes herded together and sometimes herded separately. Either way, the methods were the same. Shepherding had many other occupations which grew up around it, including sheepbreeders, and sheepshearers, who cut the sheep's wool.

Ancient shepherds went before their flocks (John 10:4-5). A flock knew its shepherd's voice and would follow only him. Often for protection flocks were lodged together at night and separated in the morning when the shepherds called their flock by name. They provided their flocks with water and food (Ps. 23:2; Jer. 31:10). They knew each sheep and lamb. When one was lost, they went out to find it (Ezek. 34:12; Luke 15:4-5). Small lambs, unable to keep up with the flock, were often carried next to a shepherd's breast inside the fold of his outer garment (Is. 40:11). The shepherd also protected his flock, risking his life if necessary (Amos 3:12; John 10:12).

In the Old Testament God is often called a shepherd. David used this beautiful metaphor for God in Psalm 23. The prophet Isaiah used the same image, probably with Psalm 23 in mind, comparing God's care of Israel to a shepherd feeding his flock and bearing lambs in "his bosom" (Is. 40:11). According to Jeremiah, God the shepherd protected His flock (Jer. 31:10), while the prophet Ezekiel spoke of the divine shepherd who seeks out His flock (Ezek. 34:12). Jesus declared that He is the good shepherd who cares for, protects, and redeems His flock—the people of God (John 10:2-16). He is the good shepherd who suffers for the sheep (Matt. 26:31) and divides His own from the goats at the day of judgment (Matt. 25:32). He is the "great Shepherd of the sheep" (Heb. 13:20).

In the Old Testament, leaders of God's people are called shepherds (Num. 27:17; 1 Kin. 22:17). Poor leaders, rebellious against God, are called irresponsible shepherds who desert, mislead, and misfeed God's flock (Jer. 23:1-4). New Testament leaders are also called shepherds of God's flock and are admonished to lead and protect His people (Acts 20:28-30).

Shipbuilder. One who built ships. While they were never a seafaring people, the Hebrews were acquainted with ships, as their historical and poetic literature demonstrates (1 Kin. 9:27; Is. 33:21; Ezek. 27:25). The primary shipbuilders of Old Testament days were the Phoenicians, who supplied ships for Solomon's trading fleet at Ezion Geber (1 Kin. 9:26-27). In the time between the Old and New Testaments, the Greeks and Romans gained prominence as shipbuilders. Smaller fishing boats with a capacity of about 12 men may have been constructed by craftsmen or by the fishermen themselves (Mark 4:1). Shipbuilders were sometimes called shipwrights. Also see *Caulker*.

Shipwright (see *Shipbuilder*).

Silversmith (see *Metalsmith*).

Singer. A professional vocalist, usually trained. David organized 4,000 Levites as Temple musicians (1 Chronicles 25). Many of these were probably choir members. Temple singers originally were all men between the ages of 30 and 50. After the Captivity, women participated in the choirs (Ezra 2:65).

Slave. One held in bondage by another. In the Old Testament, slaves were both Jewish and Gentile. Jews became slaves through their inability to pay their debts or because of poverty and theft. The Old Testament law protected all slaves and granted them certain rights (Ex. 21:2-11; Lev. 25:39-55; Deut. 21:10-14).

The economy of classical Greece and imperial Rome was based on slave labor, and slaves had fewer rights than under Old Testament law. Christianity, by teaching the equality of all people as God's creatures and objects of the gospel call, has led to the extinction of slavery wherever society is dominated by Christian thought.

Christians, since they are purchased by Christ (1 Cor. 6:20), are to be slaves of Christ (Rom. 6:16-22). On the other hand, the Old Testament calls God's people his servants in a covenantal rather than a purchased sense (Is. 41:8-10; Matt. 12:18).

Slavemaster (see *Overseer*).

Smelter (see *Metalsmith*).

Smith (see *Metalsmith*).

Soldier. A member of a military force. Before SAUL, Israel had no professional soldiers, although each tribe specialized in training its adult males in the use of a particular weapon (1 Chronicles 12). With a few exceptions (Deut. 20:5–8), all men over the age of 20 were liable to be called to arms in emergencies (Num. 1:3). In addition to the militia, Saul chose certain capable fighters to serve him permanently (2 Sam. 13:15). David followed Saul's example in this (1 Sam. 22:2). Solomon boasted a large professional soldiery including cavalrymen, or troops on horseback—the first in Israel's history (1 Kin. 10:26).

These professional soldiers were sometimes referred to in more specific terms. A guard was a soldier assigned to protect a particular person or thing. A charioteer was a soldier who fought from a chariot. As warfare became more developed, chariots were made to hold a driver and one or more fighting soldiers (1 Kin. 22:34; 2 Chr. 18:33). A commander was a soldier who led other soldiers.

During New Testament times, the Romans had a very elaborate and detailed army. Specific Roman soldiers are sometimes mentioned in the Bible. A centurion was a non-commissioned officer commanding at least 100 men. A sergeant was often the local policeman, enforcing the law, with punishment pronounced by the magistrate.

Stargazer (see *Astrologer*).

Steward. One entrusted with caring for a superior's goods. In the Old Testament a steward was over an entire household. He was responsible for managing the householder's material goods (Gen. 43:19). In the New Testament the word steward refers to a guardian or curator (Matt. 20:8; Gal. 4:2) in addition to its Old Testament meaning as a manager or superintendent of a household (Luke 8:2–3; 1 Cor. 4:1–2).

The apostle Paul called himself a steward of Christ's household, responsible to Christ the Master for carrying out an assigned task—to preach the gospel to the Gentiles. All Christians are stewards under Christ (1 Pet. 4:10).

Stonecutter (see *Stoneworker*).

Stonemason (see *Stoneworker*).

Stoneworker. One who fashioned stone into usable or ornamental items. These included quarrymen or stonecutters who cut stones or slabs of stone in quarries (1 Kin. 5:17; 6:7), stonemasons who shaped the stones and joined them into walls of buildings (2 Kin. 22:6; 1 Chr. 22:2; 2 Chr. 24:12), and sculptors. The most skilled stoneworkers in Old Testament times were from Phoenicia (2 Sam. 5:11; 1 Chr. 14:1). Stoneworkers also hewed out wine vats, cisterns, tombs, and water tunnels.

Many skills were necessary for stoneworkers. Masons used hammers and wooden pegs in quarrying out rock, then sawed it and trimmed it with a pick or an ax. Quarrymen drove wooden wedges into the stone and soaked them until they expanded, causing the rock to crack. The quarryman's hammer is compared to the Word of God (Jer. 33:29). Stoneworkers are sometimes called stonecutters and hewers of stone.

Tailor. One who made clothing. This occupation is implied rather than specifically mentioned in the Bible. In Israel most women made all the family's clothing. This work included preparing the thread or yarn and doing the weaving. Clothing was loose fitting, requiring little design work. The rich, no doubt, had others sew and decorate their clothing for them. The first "tailors" were Adam and Eve (Gen. 3:7) who made loincloths for themselves.

Tanner. One who converted animal skins into leather and made useful or ornamental items from it. Tanning was widespread in the ancient world. Early Israelite families tanned their own hides. But with the growth of cities, leather craftsmen arose. Peter once stayed with a tanner named Simon (Acts 10:6).

Tanning animal skins was an involved process requiring much skill. The hides were soaked until all fat, blood, and hair was removed. After the leather was tanned, it was used for many purposes, including tents (Ex. 26:14), sandals (Ezek. 16:10), hats, skirts, and aprons.

Tapestry Maker (see *Weaver*).

Taskmaster (see *Overseer*).

Tentmaker. One who made tents. An ancient craft, tentmaking consisted of cutting and sewing together cloth, frequently of goat's hair, and attaching ropes and loops. Such crafts were passed from father to son. Paul's native city of Cilicia exported Cilician cloth, a cloth of goat's hair. The only direct reference to tentmakers in the Bible occurs in Acts 18:2–3, where Paul, Aquila, and Priscilla are called tentmakers.

Thief (see *Criminal*).

Tiller (see *Farmer*).

Town Clerk (see *City Clerk*).

Trader (see *Merchant*).

Trapper (see *Hunter*).

Treasurer (see *Government Official*).

Trustee (see *Government Official*).

Viceroy (see *Government Official*).

Vinedresser (see *Farmer*).

Watchman. One who guarded or watched over a city or harvest field. Because of the danger of being raided, every Palestinian city or village had a watchman, especially at night. These watchmen were stationed on the city walls (2 Sam. 18:24), a watchtower (2 Kin. 9:17), or a hilltop (Jer. 31:6). Watchmen were responsible for reporting any hostile action or approaching suspicious person. These watchmen sometimes patrolled the city, called out the hours of the night, and especially looked forward to dawn (Is. 21:11–12).

At harvest times watchmen guarded the crops at night. Israel's prophets were responsible for watching for impending divine judgment or blessing (Is. 21:6; 52:8; Jer. 6:17) and bringing the news to the people. Watchmen are sometimes referred to as sentries and lookouts.

Water Carrier. One who went to the well or spring to bring back a household's water. A lowly job, it was assigned to young men (Ruth 2:9) and women (Gen. 24:13; 1 Sam. 9:11), but preferably to the lowliest slaves (Josh. 9:21–27). Some translations refer to this occupation as drawer of water. Wells and springs were generally situated outside the city gates. Water was carried home in water pots and goatskin bags, sometimes borne by a donkey.

Weaver. One who fashioned threads into cloth. Weaving was known in the ancient world from about 2000 B.C. Almost every household had a loom, and women spent much time at this task (Prov. 31:13, 19, 22, 24). A woman sat before her loom and passed the shuttle back and forth through the warp thread while manipulating the loom. She also made her own yarn or thread from animal hair or plant fibers. For instance, flax was made into linen. In other countries, such as Egypt and Assyria, weaving was done by men. Such professional weavers worked in urban areas. Even urban areas in Israel boasted professional weavers.

Well Digger. One who dug wells. During most of the year there is relatively little rain in Palestine, so having wells and cisterns was quite important. Most scholars believe well diggers were relatively skilled workers. The wells that they dug were considered very valuable. The wells bore specific names (Gen. 26:20–22) and were sometimes fought over by rivals (Gen. 21:25–30).

Starting about the time of the Exodus, people of the ancient world also built cisterns which were usually pear–shaped holes lined with plaster and filled with rain water. They were considerably more skilled in digging through rock and earth and engineering than is often realized. One example of this is Hezekiah's SILOAM tunnel in Jerusalem. It was cut through 5,334 meters (1,750 feet) of solid rock, with workers starting at both ends and meeting in the middle.

Woodcutter (see *Woodworker*).

Woodworker. One who worked to make wood into usable items. Archaeology has demonstrated that ancient Palestine had forests, and yet wood was scarce and quite expensive. Woodworkers included lumberjacks and woodcutters who felled trees (1 Kin. 5:6); hewers who trimmed and readied them for transportation (1 Kin. 5:13–14); laborers who transported them (1 Kin. 5:13–14); carpenters who fashioned them into houses, furniture, tools, and other useful items (2 Kin. 22:6); and those who carved wood into bas–relief and statue artistry (Is. 40:20; Jer. 10:3–4). Also see *Builder*.

OCHRAN [OCK ran] — a form of OCRAN.

OCRAN [OCK ran] (*troubler*) — the father of Pagiel (Num. 1:13; Ochran, KJV).

ODED [OH dead] (*counter*) — the name of two men in the Old Testament:

1. The father of Azariah the prophet (2 Chr. 15:1).

2. A prophet of Samaria during the reign of Pekah, king of Israel (2 Chr. 28:9). Pekah invaded Judah and defeated the army of Ahaz. Pekah then

Photo by Howard Vos

The beautiful handiwork of stoneworkers on the massive stairway of a temple in ancient Persepolis.

carried 200,000 captives to Samaria, the capital of the northern kingdom of Israel. As the victorious army drew near the city, Oded the prophet met them, urging a policy of mercy and forgiveness toward the Judean captives. His request had a transforming effect on the Israelites, who fed and clothed the captives, brought them to Jericho, and gave them their freedom.

ODOR (see SWEET INCENSE).

OFFAL — the waste or castoff parts of a butchered animal. In the sin offering of Israel's system of worship, the offal was burned outside the camp (Ex. 29:14; Lev. 4:11–12; Num. 19:5; dung, KJV, RSV).

OFFENSE — a word with two distinct meanings in the Bible:

1. That which prompts a person to bristle with indignation or disgust. This type of offense may in fact be from God, according to its usage in the

Bible. The apostle Paul spoke of "the offense of the cross" (Gal. 5:11). The Jews were offended because faith without Jewish legal observances was offered as the only means of salvation.

2. Offense also refers to those things which cause a person to do something against his conscience. This type of offense may be from Satan or from men. Its effect is to entice a person to sin (Matt. 5:29; 17:23; 18:6–9). It is this kind of offense which can be produced by the "grey" areas of the Christian life—those practices which are right for some but wrong for others (Rom. 14:13; 1 Cor. 8:13).

OFFERINGS (see SACRIFICE; SACRIFICIAL OFFERINGS).

OFFICER (see OCCUPATIONS AND TRADES).

OFFICES OF CHRIST (see JESUS CHRIST).

OFFSCOURING — a coating of filth or refuse; something vile and worthless. The prophet Jeremiah lamented that Jerusalem was left as "an offscouring and refuse" in the midst of her enemies (Lam. 3:45; scum, NIV).

OG [ahg] (meaning unknown) — a king of the Amorites of the land of Bashan, a territory east of the Jordan River and north of the River Jabbok (Num. 21:33; 32:33). Og was king over 60 fortified cities, including Ashtaroth and Edrei. He was defeated by Moses and the Israelites (Deut. 3:6). Then his kingdom was given to the tribes of Reuben, Gad, and the half-tribe of Manasseh.

Og was the last survivor of the race of giants (Deut. 3:11). His huge iron bedstead was kept on display in Rabbah Ammon long after his death (Deut. 3:11).

OHAD [OH had] (meaning unknown) — a son of Simeon (Gen. 46:10; Ex. 6:15).

OHEL [OWE hell] (*shelter*) — a son or descendant of Zerubbabel (1 Chr. 3:20).

OHOLAH [oh HOH lah] (*her own tent*) — a symbolic name for Samaria, capital of the Northern Kingdom, and the ten tribes which made up this nation (Ezek. 23:4–5, 36, 44). The prophet Ezekiel used the allegorical figure of two harlot sisters: Oholah (Aholah, KJV), and Oholibah (Aholibah, KJV), to represent Jerusalem and the kingdom of Judah. Oholah and Oholibah are pictured as lusting after the Assyrians, Babylonians, and Egyptians.

OHOLIAB [o HOLE ih ab] — a form of AHOLIAB.

OHOLIBAH [o HOLE ih bah] (*my tent is in her*) — a symbolic name given by the prophet Ezekiel to Jerusalem, the capital of Judah (Ezek. 23:4–44), to signify its unfaithfulness to God.

OHOLIBAMAH [oh HOLE ih bah mah] — a form of AHOLIBAMAH.

OIL, OIL TREE (see *Olive* under PLANTS OF THE BIBLE).

OINTMENT — a perfumed oil, sometimes used in Bible times to anoint people as well as bodies for burial.

The term ointment frequently means oil, particularly olive oil mixed with aromatic ingredients such as spices, myrrh, and extracts of the nard plant. Many of these ingredients were expensive, leading the prophet Amos to associate those who used "the best ointment" with a life of self-indulgence (Amos 6:6). The use of ointment originated with the Egyptians, and it eventually spread to neighboring nations, including Israel. Ointment was often imported from Phoenicia in small alabaster boxes that best preserved its aroma. Some of the better ointments were known to keep their distinctive scents for centuries.

Perfumed ointments were widely used in warm climates of the ancient world to combat perspiration odor. Ointment had a cosmetic use among the Greeks, Romans, Egyptians, and probably the Jews. It was customary to anoint the head and clothing on festive occasions; and ointment containing myrrh was used to anoint the dead before burial (Luke 23:56). In ancient times, as today, ointment was also used to soothe wounds and bruises.

Ointments, or perfumed oil, are often mentioned in the Bible for both their practical and ceremonial uses. God instructed Moses to compound a "holy anointing oil" composed of pure myrrh, sweet cinnamon, sweet calamus, cassia, and olive oil (Ex. 30:25). The vessels in the tabernacle were anointed with this holy ointment. It was also used to consecrate Aaron and his sons to the priesthood (Exodus 26—30). Ointments were also used by the Hebrew prophets to anoint new kings (2 Kin. 9:3). It was also used in anointing the sick (James 5:14) and in preparing bodies for burial (Mark 14:8; Luke 23:56).

Jesus was deeply touched on more than one occasion by people who anointed Him with perfumed ointment. He seemed to accept these deeds as acts of worship (Matt. 26:6–13; Luke 7:36–50; John 12:1–8). At the home of Simon the leper in Bethany, Mary poured ointment of costly nard on Jesus' head. This spontaneous expression of love moved the Master to silence her critics with His beautiful tribute: "Let her alone…She has done a good work for me…She has come beforehand to anoint my body for burial" (Mark 14:6, 8).

OLD GATE (see GATES OF JERUSALEM AND THE TEMPLE).

OLD TESTAMENT — the first of the two major sections into which the Bible is divided, the other being the New Testament. The title "Old Testament" apparently came from the writings of the apostle Paul, who declared, "For until this day the same veil remains unlifted in the reading of the Old Testament, because the veil is taken away in Christ" (2 Cor. 3:14).

The word testament is best translated "covenant." God called a people, the nation of Israel, to live in covenant with Him. The Old Testament begins with God's creation of the universe and continues by describing the mighty acts of God in and through His people. It closes about 400 years before the coming of Jesus Christ, who established a NEW COVENANT as prophesied by the prophet Jeremiah (Jer. 31:31-34). Also see BIBLE.

OLD TESTAMENT CHRONOLOGY (see CHRONOLOGY, OLD TESTAMENT).

OLIVE (see PLANTS OF THE BIBLE).

OLIVES, MOUNT OF (see MOUNT OF OLIVES).

OLIVET DISCOURSE — Jesus' discussion on the Mount of Olives about the destruction of Jerusalem and the end of the world (Matt. 24:1—25:46; Mark 13:1-37; Luke 21:5-36).

In response to Jesus' prophecy that the Temple would be destroyed, the disciples asked when this would occur and how they would know it was about to happen. The disciples believed that the Temple would be destroyed at the end of the world when, among other things, Jesus would return. That is why Matthew records the two questions, "When will these things [the destruction of the Temple] be? And what will be the sign of Your coming, and of the end of the age?" (Matt. 24:3). What makes the Olivet discourse difficult to understand is that Jesus intermingles His answers to these two questions.

The key to unraveling His answers is the repetition of the key phrase *take heed* (Mark 13:5, 23, 33). The disciples' first question was, "When will these things be? And what will be the sign when all these things will be fulfilled?" (Mark 13:4). Jesus began by saying, "Take heed that no one deceives you" (Mark 13:5); then He described the events leading up to the Temple's destruction (vv. 6–22). He then said, "But take heed; see, I have told you all [these] things beforehand" (Mark 13:23). By repeating the phrase *these things* He provides a conclusion to the first answer.

The key note in this first answer is the warning "take heed": there will be persecutions (Mark 13:9-13), wars and famines (13:7-8), false prophets, and false messiahs (13:6), all of which will lead up to the destruction of Jerusalem (13:14-23). But despite all these woes, the disciples must "take heed" because "the end [of the world] is not yet" (13:7). Mark 13:6-23 is therefore the answer to the question of when the Temple will be destroyed. Furthermore, it is an accurate picture of the havoc that existed in Jerusalem during the Roman siege of A.D. 70 when the city and the Temple were finally destroyed. Jesus' prophecy was therefore fulfilled in the years leading up to the Temple's destruction (although some would say it is also a picture of what will be fulfilled again at the end of time).

The disciples had assumed that the Temple would be destroyed only at the end of the world. They were mistaken, and Jesus said that despite all the woes leading up to the Temple's destruction, when it happens the end of the world still will not be in sight. Therefore in Mark 13:24-27 He answered the next logical question: what signs will precede the end of the world? The phrase *in those days* is a common Old Testament expression used when speaking of the end times. In those days there will be signs in the heavens; and then Jesus, the Son of Man, will come.

We must be prepared for His coming and must not be taken by surprise. In Mark's Gospel, Jesus remarked that no one except the Father knows exactly when "that day"—Christ's return at the end of time—will be. Therefore we must be on our guard. Matthew and Luke close with further warnings to wait carefully in anticipation.

OLYMPAS [oh LIMP us] (meaning unknown) — a Christian in Rome to whom the apostle Paul sent greetings (Rom. 16:15).

OMAR [OH mer] (*commander*) — a son of Eliphaz and grandson of Esau (Gen. 36:11, 15; 1 Chr. 1:36).

OMEGA [oh MAY gah] — the last letter of the Greek alphabet, used figuratively in the phrase "the Alpha and the Omega" as a title describing both God the Father and the Lord Jesus Christ (Rev. 1:8, 11).

OMEN — a sign used by magicians and fortune tellers to predict future events. God commanded the Israelites not to allow one who interprets omens (Deut. 18:10; an augur, RSV) to live among them. Also see MAGIC, SORCERY, AND DIVINATION.

OMER (see WEIGHTS AND MEASURES).

OMNIPOTENCE [om NIP oh tunce] — a theological term that refers to the all-encompassing power of God. The almighty God expects human beings to obey Him, and He holds them responsible for their thoughts and actions. Nevertheless, He is the all-powerful Lord who has created all things and sustains them by the Word of His power (Gen. 1:1-3; Heb. 1:3).

God reveals in the Bible that He is all-powerful and in the final sense is the ruler of nature and history. Before Him "the nations are as a drop in a bucket, and are counted as the small dust on the balance" (Is. 40:15). Yet He has so fashioned humankind that He graciously appeals to every person to return to Him.

OMNIPRESENCE [om nih PRES ence] — a theological term that refers to the unlimited nature of God or His ability to be everywhere at all times. God is not like the manufactured idols of ancient cultures that were limited to one altar or temple area. God reveals Himself in the Bible as the Lord who is everywhere. God was present as Lord in all creation (Ps. 139:7-12), and there is no escaping Him. He is present in our innermost thoughts. Even as we are formed in the womb, He knows all the days of our future.

God sees in secret and rewards in secret, as Jesus taught His disciples; He looks not only on outward actions, but especially on the inner attitudes of a person's heart (Matt. 6:1-18). Because God is the Creator and Sustainer of time and space, He is everywhere. Being everywhere, He is our great Comforter, Friend, and Redeemer.

OMNISCIENCE [om NISH unce] — a theological term that refers to God's superior knowledge and wisdom, His power to know all things. God is the Lord who knows our thoughts from afar. He is acquainted with all our ways, knowing our words even before they are on our tongues (Ps. 139:1–6, 13–16). He needs to consult no one for knowledge or understanding (Is. 40:13–14). He is the all-knowing Lord who prophesies the events of the future, including the death of His Son (Isaiah 53) and the return of Christ at the end of this age when death will be finally overcome (Rom. 8:18–39; 1 Cor. 15:51–57).

Only the all–knowing and all–powerful God can guarantee real freedom from sin, decay, and death. He can begin a process of change in believers during the present age; for "where the Spirit of the Lord is, there is liberty" (2 Cor. 3:17).

OMRI [UM rih] (*pilgrim of God*) — the name of four men in the Old Testament:

1. The sixth king of the northern kingdom of Israel (885—874 B.C.). Omri is first mentioned as the commander of the army of Israel under King Elah. While Omri besieged the Philistine city of Gibbethon, another military figure, Zimri, conspired against Elah, killed him, and established himself as king. Zimri, however had little support in Israel, and the army promptly made Omri its king. Omri returned to the capital with his army, besieged the city, and Zimri committed suicide. Tibni, the son of Ginath, continued to challenge Omri's reign; but after four years Tibni died and Omri became the sole ruler of Israel.

Omri was a king of vision and wisdom. From Shemer he purchased a hill on which he built a new city, Samaria, making it the new capital of Israel. Samaria was more defensible than Tirzah had been. Because it was strategically located, Omri was able to control the north–south trade routes in the region. Archaeological excavations at Samaria revealed buildings of excellent workmanship—an indication of the prosperity the city enjoyed during his reign.

The MOABITE STONE tells of Omri's success against King Mesha of Moab (2 Kin. 3:4). But Omri's conflict with Syria proved to be less successful, and he was forced to grant a number of cities to the Syrians (1 Kin. 20:34).

2. A member of the tribe of Benjamin and a son of Becher (1 Chr. 7:8).

3. A member of the tribe of Judah and a son of Imri (1 Chr. 9:4).

4. The son of Michael and a prince of the tribe of Issachar during the time of David (1 Chr. 27:18).

ON [own] (*strength*) — the name of a man and a city in the Old Testament:

1. A son of Peleth, of the tribe of Reuben (Num. 16:1). On joined Korah, Dathan, and Abiram in a rebellion against Moses and Aaron.

2. An ancient city of Lower Egypt in the Nile Delta on the east bank of the Nile River, about 31 kilometers (19 miles) north of Memphis and about 10 kilometers (6 miles) northeast of Cairo. Because On was the principal seat of the cult of Ra whose devotees worshiped the sun–god, the Greeks called the city Heliopolis, or "City of the Sun" (Is. 19:18, RSV). On was also called Aven (Ezek. 30:17), which means "nothingness" or "emptiness," probably because of its idolatry. At the time of the Greek historian Herodotus (fifth century B.C.), the priests of On were considered the most learned men in the history of Egypt. Associated with the temple of the sun were a medical school and a training center for the priests of On. Greek philosophers who studied in Egypt attended these institutions. Asenath, the Egyptian wife of Joseph, was the daughter of Poti-Pherah, a priest of On (Gen. 41:45, 50; 46:20).

ONAGER (see ANIMALS OF THE BIBLE).

ONAM [OH namm] (*vigorous*) — the name of two men in the Old Testament:

1. A son of Shobal (1 Chr. 1:40).

2. Founder of a clan in Judah (1 Chr. 2:26, 28).

ONAN [OH nan] (*strong*) — the second son of Judah by the daughter of Shua the Canaanite (Gen. 38:2,4).

ONESIMUS [oh NESS ih muss] (*useful*) — a slave of Philemon and an inhabitant of Colossae (Col. 4:9; Philem. 10). When Onesimus fled from his master to Rome, he met the apostle Paul. Paul witnessed to him, and Onesimus became a Christian. In his letter to Philemon, Paul spoke of Onesimus as "my own heart" (Philem. 12), indicating that Onesimus had become like a son to him.

Paul convinced Onesimus to return to his master, Philemon. He also sent a letter (the Epistle to Philemon) with Onesimus, encouraging Philemon to treat Onesimus as a brother rather than a slave. Paul implied that freeing Onesimus was Philemon's Christian duty, but he stopped short of commanding him to do so. Onesimus accompanied Tychicus, who delivered the Epistle to the Colossians as well as the Epistle to Philemon.

Some scholars believe this Onesimus is Onesimus the bishop, praised in a letter to the second–century church at Ephesus from Ignatius of Antioch.

ONESIPHORUS [on ee SIF oh rus] (*profitable*) — a Christian from Ephesus who befriended the apostle Paul (2 Tim. 1:16–18; 4:18). Not only did Onesiphorus minister to Paul while the apostle was in Ephesus; he also ministered to Paul during his imprisonment in Rome (2 Tim. 1:17). Onesiphorus overcame any fears he had for his own safety to visit and minister to Paul in prison. Unable to repay Onesiphorus for his "mercy," Paul prayed that he might "find mercy from the Lord in that Day" (2 Tim. 1:18), referring to the Judgment Day.

ONION (see PLANTS OF THE BIBLE).

ONLY BEGOTTEN — a title used by John to des-

Photo by Gustav Jeeninga

The temple of Apollo at Delphi. The oracle of Delphi was revered throughout the ancient world because people believed it had the power to foretell the future.

ignate Jesus' uniqueness (John 1:14, 18; 3:16, 18; 1 John 4:9). This title comes from combining two Greek words that mean "single kind." Therefore, it means "the only one of its kind" or "unique."

ONO [OH noh] (*grief*) — a fortified city in the territory of Benjamin, rebuilt by the sons of Elpaal (1 Chr. 8:12). The site of Ono is generally identified with present-day Kefr 'Ana, about 49 kilometers (30 miles) northwest of Jerusalem.

ONYCHA (see PLANTS OF THE BIBLE).

ONYX (see JEWELS AND PRECIOUS STONES).

OPHEL [OH fell] (*knoll*) — the northeast part of the triangular hill in ancient Jerusalem on which the CITY OF DAVID stood. Situated south of the Temple area, the hill was the site of the original city of the JEBUSITES. Surrounded on three sides by deep valleys, the ancient city was so strongly fortified that it was considered unconquerable. But David captured this center of Canaanite power and made it his new capital city (2 Sam. 5:6–9).

Usually the name Ophel is given to the entire hill. But it is more accurate to identify the hill of Ophel with the fortifications built on the eastern ridge of the hill that overlooks the Kidron Valley. Jotham, king of Judah (750–732 B.C.), built extensively on the wall of Ophel (2 Chr. 27:3). Manasseh, king of Judah (696–642 B.C.), built a high wall outside the City of David; and it enclosed Ophel (2 Chr. 33:14). The NETHINIM, or Temple servants, lived in Ophel after the Captivity (Neh. 3:26–27; 11:21).

OPHIR [OH fur] (meaning unknown) — the name of a man and a land in the Old Testament:

1. A son of Joktan (Gen. 10:29; 1 Chr. 1:23). The name may possibly refer to a tribe that inhabited modern Somaliland.

2. A region from which David and Solomon obtained gold (1 Kin. 9:28; 1 Chr. 29:4). Although Ophir is mentioned several times in the Old Testament, its exact location remains a mystery. Some believe Ophir was an island situated in the Red Sea; others think it was in India; still others believe it was in Africa, perhaps Somaliland, or on the southwest corner of the Arabian peninsula, perhaps in the land of Sheba.

Ophir is consistently associated in the Old Testament with gold, probably its most noteworthy product. The gold may have come from Ophir itself, or it may have simply passed through Ophir from its place of origin. King Solomon sent ships to Ophir for gold (2 Chr. 8:17–18). In addition, they brought a great abundance of almug trees (sandalwood) and precious stones from Ophir (1 Chr. 9:10). Near the end of his life, David announced that he had collected 3,000 talents of gold of Ophir for the building of the Temple (1 Chr. 29:4). Later, Jehoshaphat unsuccessfully attempted to send ships to Ophir for gold (1 Kin. 22:48).

The air of mystery about Ophir adds to its significance when spoken of in a symbolic way in the Bible. Psalm 45:9 speaks of "the queen in gold from Ophir." Job 28:16 says that wisdom "cannot be valued in the gold of Ophir," suggesting its incomparable worth.

OPHNI [AHF nih] (*the high place*) — a city in the territory allotted to the tribe of Benjamin (Josh. 18:24), site unknown.

OPHRAH [AHF rah] (*fawn*) — the name of two cities and a man in the Old Testament:

1. A city of the tribe of Benjamin (Josh. 18:23; 1 Sam. 13:17).

2. A city west of the Jordan River, occupied by the Abiezrites, a family of the tribe of Manasseh (Judg. 6:24). Ophrah was the place where GIDEON lived (Judg. 8:32). Its exact site is unknown.

3. A son of Meonothai, of the tribe of Judah (1 Chr. 4:14).

ORACLE [OR uh cull] — a prophetic speech, utterance, or declaration. In Greek religion, an oracle was a response given by a pagan god to a human question. Oracles were uttered by persons entranced, by those who interpreted dreams, and by those who saw or heard patterns in nature. The most famous oracle, in this sense, was the Oracle at Delphi. Delphi was the shrine of Apollo—the

The Orontes River in downtown Antioch of Syria.

Greek god of the sun, prophecy, music, medicine, and poetry.

The word oracle is used in several ways in the Bible. In the Book of Numbers it is used to describe the prophecies of Balaam the son of Beor, the soothsayer (Numbers 23—24; Josh. 13:22). The Hebrew word translated oracle means a "similitude, parable, or proverb." In 2 Samuel 16:23 the word oracle is a translation of a Hebrew word that means "word" or "utterance." It refers to a communication from God given for man's guidance.

A different Hebrew word is translated oracle in Jeremiah 23:33–38 (burden, KJV). This word means "a thing lifted up"; it can refer to a prophetic utterance as well as a physical burden. Jeremiah plays upon this double meaning and speaks of the prophetic oracle as a burden that is difficult to bear.

When the New Testament speaks of oracles, it sometimes refers to the Old Testament or some portion of it (Acts 7:38; Rom. 3:2). Hebrews 5:12 uses the term to speak of both the Old Testament revelation and the Word made flesh, Jesus Christ. First Peter 4:11 warns that the teacher of Christian truths must speak as one who utters oracles of God—a message from God and not his own opinions.

ORACLES, SIBYLLINE (see APOCALYPTIC LITERATURE).

ORATOR (see OCCUPATIONS AND TRADES).

ORCHARD — a grove of fruit or nut trees (Eccl. 2:5; Song 4:13). In the ancient Near East, plantations of fruit trees, especially POMEGRANATES, were well–known. Orchards also contained olives, nuts, figs, and various spice trees. Also see PLANTS OF THE BIBLE.

ORDAIN, ORDINATION — the process of "commissioning" a pastor or other officer of the church. This process is seldom mentioned in the New Testament. Some scholars doubt whether the solemn service we know today as ordination was practiced in the time of Christ. However, while the technical sense of the term does not occur in the New Testament, several references do indicate an official commissioning ceremony.

The Twelve were "chosen" and "sent" by Christ (Mark 3:13–19; Luke 6:12–16), but without any ordination service. The same is true of the election of Matthias (Acts 1:26). The seven were commissioned by the "laying on of hands" (Acts 6:6). Paul and Barnabas were commissioned by the Antioch church in the same manner (Acts 13:3). However, the laying on of hands was widespread in the ancient world and does not necessarily point to an ordination service.

The primary evidence of an ordination service comes from 1 Timothy 4:14, where Paul apparently speaks of an official ceremony. Timothy's special spiritual "gift" was given to him "by prophecy with the laying on of the hands of the presbytery." From 2 Timothy 1:6 it would seem that Paul joined with them in this service.

The ordination of a Christian leader is an act of the church by which the responsibility of an office is passed on to an individual. Ordination is a solemn affair for the one who is commissioned and the church which commissions.

OREB [OH reb] (*raven*) — the name of a man and a place in the Old Testament:

1. One of two Midianite princes defeated by Gideon and beheaded by the Ephraimites near the Jordan River (Judg. 7:25; 8:3; Ps. 83:11). Also see ZEEB.

2. A rock near Beth Bareh near the Jordan River where the Midianite prince Oreb was killed (Judg. 7:25; Is. 10:26).

OREN [OH ren] (*cedar*) — a son of Jerahmeel, of the tribe of Judah (1 Chr. 2:25).

ORGAN (see MUSICAL INSTRUMENTS).

ORION [oh RYE un] (*the strong one*) — the name of a constellation, consisting of thousands of stars, which is mentioned in the Old Testament (Job 9:9; 38:31; Amos 5:8). The constellation is near Gemini and Taurus, and contains the giant red star Betelgeuse and Rigel, a blue–white star of first magnitude. Most of the stars of Orion cannot be seen without the aid of a telescope. Also see ASTRONOMY.

ORNAMENTS — decorative or religious jewelry and other items attached to the clothing or body in Bible times. The Bible speaks often of various kinds of ornaments worn by both men and women (Gen. 24:22; Ex. 12:35). These ornaments were worn for dignity (Gen. 41:42), as well as decoration (Song 1:10). Rich women were especially adorned in a lavish way (Is. 3:16, 18–23), but the prophet Jeremiah pointed out that every Jewish maid was attracted to jewelry (Jer. 2:32).

Among Jewish women, ornaments consisted of rings worn on the nose (Is. 3:21; Ezek. 16:12), ears, upper and lower arm, and legs. ANKLETS and ANKLE CHAINS were worn on the ankles. Hebrew men did not wear nose rings.

Egyptian mummies with as many as nine rings on a single hand have been discovered. Some rings were SIGNET RINGS bearing the legal seal of an individual. The king's seal was his signature. It bore his personal authority (Gen. 41:42; Dan. 6:17). It could be worn on the finger, on a cord around the neck, or attached to an armlet.

Often jewelry was amulets, or charms to ward off evil spirits or to please the gods (Gen. 35:4; Judg. 8:24). These might be earrings or pendants around one's neck. Some amulets were prayers or curses written on papyrus or parchment, wrapped in linen, and attached to one's body.

Among the Jews, men wore PHYLACTERIES or FRONTLETS, which consisted of passages of Scripture wrapped in leather and attached to the arm or forehead. These were worn while praying.

Both men and women took considerable pains with arranging and caring for their hair. This was true of men with their beards. Women wore their hair very long, braided, held in place with combs and pins, and often ornamented with gold coins, chains, and other jewelry.

ORNAN [AWR nan] (*prince*) — a Jebusite prince who owned a threshing floor on Mount Moriah. David purchased the property, where he built an altar to the Lord.

ORONTES [oh RAHN tez] — the chief river of Syria, in southwest Asia. Three important cities of the Old Testament period were on the Orontes: Riblah (2 Kin. 23:33–35), Hamath (1 Kin. 8:65), and Kadesh. The Orontes River is not mentioned in the Bible.

ORPAH [AWR pah] (*neck*) — a Moabite woman who married Chilion, one of the two sons of Elimelech and Naomi (Ruth 1:4). When Elimelech and his sons died in Moab, Orpah accompanied Naomi, her mother-in-law, part of the way to Bethlehem and then returned "to her people and to her gods" (Ruth 1:14) in Moab.

ORPHAN — a child deprived by death of one or both parents (Lam. 5:3; John 14:18; James 1:27). Jesus used the word symbolically, promising His followers, "I will not leave you orphans" (comfortless, KJV; desolate, RSV; bereft, NEB). In His absence, Jesus promised to send the Holy Spirit, who would serve as the believer's teacher, guide, guardian, and protector. In the Bible, the fatherless, or orphans, are included among the needy who need mercy and compassion (Deut. 10:18; Job 22:9; James 1:26–27).

ORYX (see ANIMALS OF THE BIBLE).

OSEE [OH zee] — Greek form of HOSEA.

OSHEA [oh SHAY ah] — a form of HOSHEA.

OSNAPPER [oz NAP purr] — the biblical name for ASHURBANIPAL, a king of Assyria.

OSPREY, OSSIFRAGE (see ANIMALS OF THE BIBLE).

OSTIA [AHS tih ah] (*mouth*) — the seaport for the city of Rome. An ancient city of Italy at the mouth of the Tiber River, Ostia was about 25 kilometers (15.5 miles) from Rome.

OSTRACA [OSS treh kuh] (*potsherds*) — the plural of *ostrakon*, a Greek word for potsherd (broken pieces of pottery). Less expensive than PAPYRUS sheets or parchment, pottery fragments were commonly used in the ancient world as a writing material. Inscribed with ink, potsherds were widely used for letters, receipts, notes, inventory lists, brief memoranda, and school lists. Although the word ostraca is not used in the Bible, potsherds are mentioned in the Old Testament (Job 2:8; Ps. 22:15; Is. 45:9), but not as writing materials. Archaeologists have unearthed thousands of ostraca in Egypt and Palestine.

This ostracon from the Dead Sea caves at Qumran contains writing in Hebrew—the language in which most of the Old Testament was originally written.

OSTRICH (see ANIMALS OF THE BIBLE).

OTHNI [OATH nih] (*Jehovah is force*) — a Levite gatekeeper of the tabernacle in the days of David (1 Chr. 26:7).

OTHNIEL [OATH nih el] (*powerful one*) — the name of two men in the Old Testament:
1. The first judge of Israel (Judg. 1:13; 3:9, 11). Othniel was a son of Kenaz and probably was a nephew of Caleb. When the Israelites forgot the Lord and served the pagan gods of Canaan, the king of Mesopotamia oppressed them for eight years. When the Israelites repented of their evil and cried out to the Lord for deliverance, Othniel was raised up by the Lord to deliver His people. Othniel was one of four judges (the other three were Gideon, Jephthah, and Samson) of whom the Scripture says, "The Spirit of the Lord came upon him" (Judg. 3:10).
2. An ancestor of Heldai (1 Chr. 27:15).

OUCHES — an Old English word, used by the KJV, which denoted sockets or cavities in which gems were set (Ex. 28:11; settings of gold, NKJV).

OUTCASTS — a word used in the Old Testament to refer to refugees or exiles from the land of Israel (Ps. 147:2; Is. 11:12; 56:8). The modern idea of outcasts refers to those who are rejected by society. In the Bible, however, the word corresponds to our refugees—those forced from their homes by terror of war (Is. 16:3–4; Jer. 40:12; 49:5, 36). It is used also of those who were taken into captivity for breaking God's covenant (Is. 11:12; 56:8). Thus, "the outcasts" is a technical term for the DISPERSION OF THE JEWISH PEOPLE.

OVEN (see BREAD; TOOLS OF THE BIBLE).

OVENS, TOWER OF THE — a tower on the wall of Jerusalem restored by Nehemiah (Neh. 3:11; 12:38; tower of the furnaces, KJV, NASB).

OVERSEER (see OCCUPATIONS AND TRADES).

OWL, OX (see ANIMALS OF THE BIBLE).

OX–GOAD (see GOAD).

OZEM [OH zim] (*irritable*) — the name of two men in 1 Chronicles:
1. The sixth son of Jesse and a brother of David (1 Chr. 2:15).
2. A son of Jerahmeel (1 Chr. 2:25).

OZIAS [oh ZIE us] — a form of UZZIAH.

OZNI [AHZ nih] (*my hearing*) — a member of the tribe of Gad and the ancestor of a tribal family, the OZNITES (Num. 26:16), also called Ezbon (Gen. 46:16).

OZNITES [AHZ nites] — the descendants of OZNI (Num. 26:16).

P

PAARAI [PAY uh righ] (*revelation of Jehovah*) — one of David's mighty men (2 Sam. 23:35), also called Naarai the son of Ezbai (1 Chr. 11:37).

PADAN, PADDAN [PAD uhn] — forms of PADAN ARAM.

PADAN ARAM [PAD uhn AH rem] (*the plain of Aram*) — the area of Upper Mesopotamia around Haran and the home of the patriarch Abraham after he moved from Ur of the Chaldeans (Gen. 25:20; Paddan–aram, RSV). Abraham later sent his servant to Padan Aram to find a bride for his son Isaac (Gen. 25:20). Much later, Isaac's son Jacob fled to Padan Aram to avoid the wrath of his brother Esau and dwelt there with Laban (Gen. 28:2, 5–7). The region was also referred to as Padan (Gen. 48:7; Paddan, RSV).

PADON [PAY duhn] (*redemption*) — a family of Temple servants who returned with Zerubbabel after the Captivity (Ezra 2:44).

PAGAN — a follower of a false god or a heathen religion; one who delights in sensual pleasures and material goods. After the return from the Captivity, Ezra and Nehemiah carried on a vigorous campaign against the practice of marriage between Israelites and the pagan women of the land (Ezra 10:2, 10–18, 44; Neh. 13:26–27, 30).

PAGIEL [PAY gih uhl] (*God intervenes*) — leader of the tribe of Asher during the wilderness wanderings (Num. 7:72; 10:26). Pagiel helped take the first census of Israel.

PAHATH–MOAB [PAY hath MOE ab] (*governor of Moab*) — the name of two men in the Old Testament:
1. The founder of a clan or family, members of which returned to Jerusalem after the Captivity. Under Zerubbabel's leadership, 2,812 members of the family returned (Ezra 2:6). Under Ezra's leadership, another company of 200 males of Pahath–Moab also returned from the Captivity (Ezra 8:4).
2. A man who sealed the covenant with Nehemiah (Neh. 10:14). Evidently he represented the entire clan of Pahath–Moab.

PAI [PAY eye] (*groaning*) — a city in Edom and home of King Hadad (1 Chr. 1:50). In Genesis 36:39 the king is called Hadar and his city is referred to as Pau.

PALAL [PAY luhl] (*God judges*) — a son of Uzai (Neh. 3:25). Palal helped Nehemiah repair the wall of Jerusalem after the Captivity.

PALANQUIN [puh LAN kwin] — a portable chair or throne with a canopy carried by four servants. Kings of the ancient world used such chairs as a symbol of their rank and power. The chair sat in the center of two long poles, one on each side, which rested on the shoulders of the servants. Solomon had a luxurious palanquin, which featured silver poles, a golden base, and a purple seat (Song 3:9–10; chariot, KJV; carriage, NIV; sedan chair, NASB).

PALESTINA [pal ess TIE nuh] — the west coast of Canaan, from the Brook of Egypt to Joppa (Ex. 15:14; Philistia, RSV, NASB, NEB, NIV). Palestina is apparently an alternate name for PHILISTIA and PALESTINE.

PALESTINE [PAL ess tyne] — the land promised by God to Abraham and his descendants and eventually the region where the Hebrew people lived (see Map 7, D–2).

Palestine (or Palestina) is a tiny land bridge between the continents of Asia, Africa, and Europe. The word itself originally identified the region as "the land of the Philistines," a war–like tribe that inhabited much of the region alongside the Hebrew people. But the older name for Palestine was CANAAN, the term most frequently used in the Old Testament. The AMARNA Letters of the 14th century B.C. referred to "the land of Canaan," applying the term to the coastal region inhabited by the PHOENICIANS. After the Israelites took the land from the Canaanites, the entire country became known as the "land of Israel" (1 Sam. 13:19; Matt. 2:20) and the "land of promise" (Heb. 11:9).

The term Palestine as a name for the entire land of Canaan, beyond the coastal plains of the Phoenicians, was first used by the fifth century B.C. historian Herodotus. After the Jewish revolt of A.D. 135, the Romans replaced the Latin name *Judea* with the Latin *Palaestina* as their name for this

The Judean Desert near Jerusalem, showing the rugged topography of this region in southern Palestine.

province. Although the prophet Zechariah referred to this region as the "Holy Land" (Zech. 2:12), it was not until the Middle Ages that this land became popularly known as the Holy Land.

Location. The medieval concept that Palestine was the center of the earth is not as farfetched as one might expect. This tiny strip of land not only unites the peoples and lands of Asia, Africa, and Europe but also the five seas known as the Mediterranean Sea, the Black Sea, the Caspian Sea, the Red Sea, and the Persian Gulf. Palestine was sandwiched in between two dominant cultures of the ancient world—Egypt to the south and Babylon-Assyria-Persia between the Tigris and Euphrates Rivers to the northeast.

Palestine is also the focal point of the three great world religions: Judaism, Christianity, and Islam. It has been the land corridor for most of the world's armies and, according to the Book of Revelation, will be the scene of the final great conflict of history, the battle of Armageddon (Rev. 16:16).

The boundaries of Palestine were not clearly defined in ancient times—a problem which plagues the area even today. Generally, the Hebrews occupied the land bordered on the south by the Wadi el–'Arish and Kadesh Barnea and on the north by the foothills of Mount Hermon. The Mediterranean Sea formed a natural western boundary and the Jordan River a natural eastern boundary, except that several of the Israelite tribes occupied the region known as TRANSJORDAN, the land east of the Jordan River.

At certain times in Israel's history, the territory they occupied was much larger. During the days of the United Monarchy under David and Solomon, Israel controlled Hamath, Damascus, and the region beyond as far as the Euphrates River. They also held dominion over Ammon, Moab, and Edom, stretching the nation's borders from the mountains of Lebanon to the waters of the Red Sea.

The boundaries of the Promised Land defined in Numbers 34, as promised to Moses, were much more extensive than the region in which the Hebrews eventually settled. The southern boundary was placed at Kadesh Barnea and the northern boundary at "the entrance of Hamath" (Num. 34:8), which may either be the entrance to the Biqa Valley between the Lebanon and Anti-Lebanon Mountains or farther north near modern Lebweh, some 23 kilometers (14 miles) north of historic Baalbek.

It is also clear that the land promised to Abraham and his descendants for an everlasting possession included an area similar to that seen by Moses and greater than that area actually inhabited by the Israelites. This covenant promise to Abraham is the basis for the modern Israeli claim to Palestine (Gen. 12:7; 28:4; 48:4).

Size. To the jet–age traveler Palestine seems quite small. The expression "from Dan to Beersheba" (1 Sam. 3:20) refers to a north–south distance of only about 240 kilometers (150 miles). The width of the region is even less impressive. In the north, from Acco on the coast to the Sea of Galilee is a distance of only 45 kilometers (28 miles). In the broader south, from Gaza on the coast to the Dead Sea is a distance of only 88 kilometers (54 miles). The distance between Jaffa and Jericho is only 72 kilometers (45 miles); Nazareth to Jerusalem is only 98 kilometers (60 miles).

The land area from Dan to Beersheba in Cis–Jordan (the region west of the Jordan River) is approximately 6,000 square miles—a region smaller than Hawaii. If the area east of the Jordan River is included, the maximum total area of Palestine amounts to only 10,000 square miles—an area smaller than the state of Maryland.

People. The history of Palestine is complicated by the many different cultures and civilizations that have flourished in the region. The first historical reference to the inhabitants of Canaan occurs in Genesis 10. Canaan, the son of Ham and the grandson of Noah (Gen. 10:6; 5:32), is said to have fathered most of the inhabitants of the land. These include Sidon (the Phoenicians), Heth (the Hittites), and the Jebusites (who lived near Jerusalem), the Amorites (in the hill country), the Girgashites (unknown), the Hivites (peasants from the northern hills), the Arkites (from Arka in Phoenicia), the Sinites (from the northern coast of Lebanon), the Arvadites (from the island of Arvad), the Zemarites (from Sumra), and the Hamathites (from Hamath; Gen. 10:15–18).

The native inhabitants of Canaan were tall, giant–like, and stalwart races known as the Anakim (Josh. 11:21–22), the Rephaim (Gen. 14:5), the Emim, Zamzummim, and Horites (Deut. 2:10–23). They lived in the hill country, and traces of their primitive population continued as late as the days of the United Monarchy under David and Solomon (2 Sam. 21:16–22). When Abraham arrived in the Promised Land it was almost entirely inhabited by the Canaanites, with a mixture of Edomites, Ammonites, and Moabites.

History. The history of Palestine gains its significance for the Bible student with the beginning of the biblical period. But the region was inhabited by other cultures long before Abraham and his family arrived.

Prebiblical Period (Tower of Babel—2000 B.C.)—As the human race was scattered over the earth, a number of cultures emerged. Small city–states began to be organized in Mesopotamia, the land between the Tigris and Euphrates Rivers. A Sumerian civilization (about 2800–2360 B.C.) was one of the earliest, classical civilizations of the world. The Akkadians as well built their cities in the Tigris-Euphrates plain. Almost at the same time Egypt emerged as a unified nation. In the 29th century B.C. the kingdoms of Upper and Lower Egypt were united, and a world power was born. Palestine witnessed the same urban development and population increases during this period. The cities of Jericho, Megiddo, Beth Shan, Ai, Shechem, Gezer, Lachish, and others were all in existence at this time.

Old Testament Period (Abraham—2000 B.C. and after)—About 2000 B.C. the patriarch Abraham arrived in Canaan from Ur of the Chaldees and found the land controlled by Amorites and Canaanites. Abraham lived for a while in Egypt, where he was exposed to this great culture of the ancient world. He saw the great pyramids of Egypt and eventually returned to Palestine, where the wealth and influence of his family and his descendants expanded through the land.

For 430 years the descendants of Abraham were in Egyptian bondage, but God raised up a champion in Moses to lead them back to the Land of Promise (Exodus 3). God strengthened the new leader of Israel, Joshua (Josh. 1:1–9), and he led the people in successful campaigns to win control of Palestine (Josh. 11:16–23). The period of the judges which followed indicated the continuous struggle which Israel had with the peoples of the land (Judg. 2:16–23).

With the rise of the United Monarchy under David (2 Sam. 8:1–18) and Solomon (1 Kin. 9:15—11:13), the Hebrew people extended their influence over more of Palestine than ever before. But about 920 B.C. Israel was divided into two segments, the northern kingdom of Israel, and the southern kingdom of Judah. These were turbulent times in the history of the Jewish people. The Old Testament period came to an end with the fall of Samaria, the capital of Israel, in 721 B.C. The Assyrians took Israel into captivity and this nation ceased to exist (2 Kin. 17:1–6).

Babylonian Period (605–562 B.C.)—The influence of the Babylonians in the land of Palestine was swift and deadly. In 605 B.C. Nebuchadnezzar, king of Babylon, annihilated the Egyptian army, effectively controlling all of Palestine to the Egyptian border. In 597 B.C. Jerusalem fell to the Babylonians. Jehoiachin the king was carried into captivity. Ten years later the city of Jerusalem was destroyed and nearly all the Jewish inhabitants of Palestine were carried away as captives to Babylon (2 Kin. 25:1–21).

Persian Period (549–332 B.C.)—When Cyrus, the king of Persia, conquered Babylon, he allowed the Jews to return to Jerusalem. In 536 B.C. the first group of Jews returned to Jerusalem under Sheshbazzar (Ezra 1:1–11). As a Persian province, the region was governed by regional rulers under Persian authority.

The barren, mountainous region of eastern Palestine known as the Wilderness of Judah, with the Dead Sea in the background.
Photo by Werner Braun

Greek Period (332–167 B.C.)—During this period Alexander the Great conquered Palestine. Upon his death the land fell to the Ptolemies of Egypt and the Seleucids of Syria. In 167 B.C. the Seleucid king Antiochus IV (Antiochus Epiphanes) polluted the Jewish Temple by offering swine on the altar and putting up a statue of a pagan god.

Maccabean Period (167–63 B.C.)—Under the leadership of the aged priest Mattathias and his sons, the Jewish people revolted against the Seleucids and enjoyed nearly 100 years of independence.

Roman Period (63 B.C.—A.D. 300)—In 63 B.C. Pompey conquered Palestine for Rome. From 37 B.C. until 4 B.C. Herod the Great ruled the land as the Roman king under the Caesars. During the reign of this Herod, Jesus was born in Bethlehem. During Roman rule also, Christianity was born. In A.D. 70 Jerusalem was destroyed by the Roman general Titus as he crushed a revolt by the Jewish people.

Pre-Modern Period (A.D. 330–1917)—During these years, Palestine was under the successive rules of the Byzantines (330–634), the Persians (607–29), the Arabs (634–1099), the Crusaders (1099–1263), the Mamelukes (1263–1516) and the Turks (1517–1917). The most important historical events during this period were Saladin's consolidation of his control of Egypt, Syria, Mesopotamia, and most of Palestine in A.D. 1187 by his victory over the crusader kingdom of Jerusalem and the establishment of the Turkish Ottoman Empire in A.D. 1517.

Modern Period (1917—Present)—In 1917 the Balfour Declaration liberated Palestine from Turkish rule and placed the land under the control of Great Britain. On May 14, 1948, the modern State of Israel was established, and the British withdrew. Almost immediately the Jews and Arabs began their struggle for control of the land of Palestine. The borders of Palestine have been in a state of flux ever since.

The Geography of Palestine. The geography of Palestine falls naturally into five regions: the coastal plain, the central highlands, the Rift Valley, the Transjordan plateau, and the Negev.

The coastal plain—The coastal lowlands run along the western border of Palestine at the Mediterranean Sea. The plain varies in width from less than 5 kilometers (3 miles) to more than 40 kilometers (25 miles), but it forms an almost straight line for more than 320 kilometers (200 miles) north to south.

At the famous Ladder of Tyre in Upper Galilee, the hills reach the coast and divide the Plain of Phoenicia from the Plain of Acco. The Plain of Acco is about 13 kilometers (8 miles) wide and 40 kilometers (25 miles) long. It was the region allotted to the tribe of Asher (Josh. 19:24–31). At the foot of Mount Carmel the coastal plain is only a few hundred feet wide, but it quickly widens into the Plain of Dor and, at the Crocodile River (the Wadi Zerqa), into the marshy Plain of Sharon. The Plain of Sharon is some 64–80 kilometers (40–50 miles) in length and 13–16 kilometers (8–10 miles) wide. A fertile region, it was once covered with oak forests. Through it flow five streams, including the river Kanah, which in ancient Israel divided the territories of Ephraim and Manasseh. South of the Plain of Sharon is the triangle known as the Philistine Plain where the five lords of the Philistines build their great cities: Ekron, Gath, Ashdod, Ashkelon, and Gaza (1 Sam. 6:17).

One problem with this coastal plain is that it did not have a natural harbor. Joppa was a precarious harbor formed by offshore reefs (2 Chr. 2:16; Acts 9:36). Caesarea was built by Herod the Great, who created an artificial harbor. This territory was of lit-

The Hasbani Brook in northern Palestine—one of the tributaries of the Jordan River—with Mount Hermon in the background.

Photo by Gustav Jeeninga

tle value to the ancient Israelites, a fact which may have contributed to Philistine dominance of the coastal plains long after the Israelites conquered Canaan.

The central highlands—Between the coastal plain and the hill country of Judea and Samaria runs a series of foothills known as the Shephelah. These hills were the scene of many battles between the Philistines and the Israelites. It is divided by three valleys: the Valley of Aijalon on the north, the Valley of Sorek in the middle, and the Valley of Elah on the south. At Aijalon Joshua commanded the sun to stand still (Josh. 10:12–14). And in Elah young David killed the giant Goliath (1 Sam. 17:2, 19; 21:9).

The central highlands are a mountain range running north to south the length of Palestine. In Lebanon the range rises to over 2,740 meters (9,000 feet) above sea level at Mount Hermon. The highest peak in Palestine is Jebel Jermaq, 1,200 meters (3,960 feet), in Upper Galilee.

The highlands consist of several distinct regions. The northernmost region is Galilee, customarily divided into Upper and Lower Galilee. Upper Galilee is almost double the altitude of its lower counterpart with corresponding differences in climate and vegetation. Lower Galilee has outcrops of chalk and marl that give the region a rugged beauty. Even today it is populated with small villages, many of which are mentioned in the New Testament. To the east lies the Sea of Galilee, separated from Lower Galilee by a series of hills and valleys.

South of Galilee is the Plain of Jezreel or Esdraelon. This plain is actually a low plateau of the hill country stretching from Mount Carmel on the west to Mount Gilboa on the east. This was an important corridor between the Via Maris, one of the main roads through Palestine, and the road to Damascus to the north. Many notable battles have been fought here (Josh. 17:16; 2 Chr. 35:22). Here too will be fought the Battle of Armageddon (Rev. 16:16; 19:11–21).

South of the central highlands is the hill country of Ephraim. This broad limestone upland consists of fertile valleys, tree–laden hills, and north–south, east–west highways. This easy access to Samaria explains this region's greater receptivity to foreign influences in religion and politics than that of Galilee to the north or Judea to the south. The highest of these Samaritan hills are Mount Ebal (940 meters; 3,084 feet) and Mount Gerizim (881 meters; 2,890 feet).

Unlike the broken terrain of Samaria, the Judean highlands present a solid barrier that practically shuts off east–to–west traffic. Judea is subdivided into the Shephelah, the central hills, and the eastern wilderness. The terrain of these three divisions reflects quite a contrast, just like the annual rainfall (16–32 inches in the foothills, 32 inches in the highlands, and 12 inches or less in the wilderness).

Most of the towns in this region are built on a series of hills, just as Jerusalem is. All the land to the south is "down," although the central highlands

continue to climb until they reach the area of Hebron, Palestine's highest town (927 meters; 3,040 feet). As one continues south in these highlands, however, the elevation begins to drop. Thus at Beersheba, a few miles south, the region becomes a triangular depression between the hills of Judea and the hills of the Negev.

The central highlands are the most important natural region in Palestine, boasting of such towns as Nazareth, Shechem, Samaria, Bethel, Jerusalem, Bethlehem, Hebron, and Beersheba. This region is known as the heartland of Palestine.

The Rift Valley—Between the western hills of Israel and the hills east of the Jordan River lies the world's deepest depression, known as the Rift Valley. Beginning in the valley between the Lebanon and Anti–Lebanon Mountains and running south through Palestine, through the Arabah, through the Gulf of Aqaba and the Red Sea and on south through eastern Africa, this is the deepest geological fault on earth. The contrast in elevation is striking. Mount Hermon is a majestic 2,814 meters (9,232 feet) above sea level, while the Sea of Galilee just below it is 212 meters (695 feet) below sea level. The Jordan River, which flows from the foothills of Hermon to the Sea of Galilee and then on south to the Dead Sea, is derived from a word which means "the descender." The river is appropriately named. In one nine–mile stretch the Jordan plunges 284 meters (850 feet). North of the Sea of Galilee the river drops an average of 12 meters (40 feet) per mile. The Jordan is unique in that it is the world's only major river that runs below sea level along most of its course.

The distance between the Sea of Galilee and the Dead Sea is approximately 105 kilometers (65 miles). In the Rift Valley, or the Jordan Valley, the river has carved a narrow channel called the Zor. A haven for wildlife, this appears as a snakelike path of green vegetation when viewed from the air.

In the southern extremity of the Rift Valley, between the Dead Sea and the Red Sea, is the Arabah. This valley, from three to nine miles wide but 169 kilometers (105 miles) in length, features terrain varying from salt flats to badlands. It is watered only by the flowing of seasonal streams in the rainy season. From the Gulf of Aqaba the floor of this valley rises to 230 meters (755 feet) on a steep ridge. From there it drops dramatically, over 152 meters (500 feet) in two miles, toward the Dead Sea.

The Transjordan plateau—The beautiful hills of the Transjordan tableland are cut by four important rivers as they wind their way to the Rift Valley. They are the Yarmuk, Jabbok, Arnon, and Zered Rivers. These rivers provide natural boundaries for four discernible regions of Transjordan.

North of the Yarmuk River is Bashan, a plateau rising from 213 meters (700 feet) in the west to 914 meters (3,000) feet in the east. South of the Yarmuk to the Jabbok is Gilead. This is the most fertile region of Transjordan. The rainfall of 28 to 32 inches a year provides sufficient water for rich agricultural land and pasture land. This is where the Greco–Roman cities of the region known as the Decapolis were located. Here, too, the famous "balm of Gilead" was found. South of the deep Jabbok gorge to the southern tip of the Dead Sea lay the kingdoms of Ammon and Moab. Located here were the capital of the Ammonite kingdom, Rabbah, and Mount Nebo (802 meters; 2,631 feet), the commanding site from which Moses viewed the Promised Land (Deut. 34:1). The Arnon River was the approximate border between Ammon and Moab, with the Zered River to the south serving as the border between Moab and Edom.

Edom stretches for a hundred miles above the Arabah. In the Shera Mountains of Edom the reddish sandstones may have given rise to the biblical name adom, which means "red." In a basin secluded in these mountains is Petra, the famous capital of the Nabatean kingdom. The conquest of Edom for a brief time during the days of David and Solomon enabled Solomon to build the port of Ezion Geber on the Red Sea and to exploit the copper mines in the area (1 Kin. 9:26–28).

The Negev—Directly south of Palestine lies the Negev, a barren wilderness. Shaped like a triangle with its apex pointing toward the Sinai Peninsula, the steppe of the Negev is situated immediately south of the Valley of Beersheba. It encompasses over 12,500 square miles, more than all of Palestine itself. The inhabitable sector of the area is a small strip about 49 kilometers (30 miles) wide from north to south, centered at Beersheba. The rest of the Negev is a rocky wilderness with the desert pushing in from all sides.

Because of its long desert frontier, the Negev has been inhabited mostly by tribal herdsmen known as the Bedouins, including the Amalekites (Num. 13:29; 1 Sam. 30:1). In the Old Testament this area was known as the Wilderness of Zin and the Wilderness of Paran. Occasionally permanent settlements would be found here in the days of Abraham and especially in the days of the Nabatean kingdom. The Negev is crisscrossed with caravan routes. The important route to Egypt, known as "the way of Shur" (Gen. 16:7), went southwest from Beersheba through this area.

Geological Formations. Palestine has a wide variety of geological formations for a small 10,000 square-mile area. A band of Nubian or Petra sandstone, red and soft, stretches along the eastern coast of the Dead Sea. Above this band is the most important geological formation in Palestine, the limestone, which makes up most of the tableland on both sides of the Jordan River. This limestone is particularly evident at Jerusalem; reservoirs, sepulchers, and cellars abound under the city.

The Philistine country north of Mount Carmel consists of sandstone. Between this sandstone and the sand dunes of the seacoast is a sedimentary bed. On the eastern side of the Jordan, from Mount Hermon to south of the Sea of Galilee, is volcanic rock, frequently found in other parts of the land. Another notable feature of the region is the blowing sand from Egypt and the Sinaitic deserts, which

frequently invades the cultivated sections of Palestine.

On the west shore of Galilee as well as along both shores of the Dead Sea are hot springs. At the hot springs of Callirrhoe on the eastern shore of the Dead Sea, Herod the Great sought relief from his illness. Earthquakes also played a vital role in Palestinian life. David interpreted an earthquake as a sign of the anger of the Lord (Ps. 18:7). Jonathan's attack at Michmash was accompanied by an earthquake (1 Sam. 14:15). A memorable quake occurred during the days of Uzziah in the eighth century B.C. (Amos 1:1). An earthquake also accompanied the crucifixion of Jesus in Jerusalem (Matt. 27:51–54).

The presence of these phenomena—plus volcanic activity, basalt, sulphur, petroleum, salt, bromide, phosphate, potash, and other chemicals in and around the Dead Sea—make Palestine a geologist's paradise. It is indeed one of the most unique regions of the world.

The Climate and Vegetation of Palestine. The latitude of Palestine is approximately the same as southern California or Georgia. It is therefore marginally subtropical. Situated between the cool winds of the Mediterranean and the hot winds of the desert, Palestine has a variety of weather patterns.

Temperature—The sea breeze has a moderating effect on the coastal plain. The average temperature at Haifa in January is 56 degrees F. and in August 83 degrees. However, the elevation at Jerusalem (777 meters, or 2,550 feet, above sea level), brings cooler temperatures, a 48 degrees F. average in January and a 75 degrees average in August.

In contrast, the temperatures in the Rift Valley are much hotter year round. This makes the region comfortably warm in winter but unbearably hot in summer. Jericho has an average winter temperature of 76 degrees F., but the temperature consistently climbs well over 100 in the summer. Such temperature extremes are noted in the Bible. The midday sun caused the death of a lad in Elisha's day (2 Kin. 4:18–20), but King Jehoiakim sat in his winter house with a fire on the hearth (Jer. 36:22).

Precipitation—Two seasons characterize Palestine: winter, which is moist, rainy, and mild (November to April), and summer, which is hot with no rain (May to October). The exact time when the rainy season begins each year is not predictable. It usually begins about mid–October and includes our winter months plus some additional weeks (Song 2:11). Rainfall usually occurs three to four days in a row, alternating with three to four days of chilling winds from the desert.

The Bible frequently refers to "the early rain and the latter rains" (Deut. 11:14). This designation does not indicate the period of greatest rainfall, which was frequently in January and February (Lev. 26:4; Ezra 10:9, 13), but the period of the most important rainfall for agriculture. The initial autumn rains soften the hard Palestinian soil, making plowing and sowing an easier task. The latter

The plains of Jericho and the lush oasis at Jericho in the region north of the Dead Sea.

rains fall in March and April when rain is needed to make the fruit and grain luscious and healthy (Hos. 6:3; Zech. 10:1).

The greatest amount of precipitation falls on the region of Galilee (28–40 inches a year). Average rainfall for other areas of Palestine are: Haifa (24 inches); Tiberias (17 inches); Beth Shean (12 inches); Jerusalem (25 inches); and Jericho (4 inches or less). In the summer the humidity is twice as intense as during other times of the year. Thus Jericho, with high temperatures and humidity and little rainfall, is almost unbearable in summer. However, the summer humidity condenses as the ground cools during the night. The result is a heavy dew each morning in Palestine.

Gideon was able to collect a bowl of water from dew on a fleece (Judg. 6:38). Dew was essential for the growing of grapes during the summer (Zech. 8:12). Without dew a devastating drought would occur (2 Sam. 1:21; Hag. 1:10). Frequently God's grace is compared to the dew (Gen. 27:28; Hos. 14:5).

Occasionally Palestine would be the victim of violent precipitation in the form of hail. Such hail would flatten the standing grain and destroy the tender vines (Ps. 78:47; Ezek. 13:11, 13). Sometimes hailstones big enough to kill a man would fall (Josh. 10:11). But occasionally the higher elevations of Palestine are covered with a light snow during the winter. In David's time Benaiah slew a lion on a day when snow fell (2 Sam. 23:20).

Vegetation—In areas with adequate precipitation, the abundance of sunshine and fertile soil make Palestine a garden paradise. More than 3,000 varieties of flowering plants exist in the region—a large number for such a small country. So plentiful were flowers in Bible times that floral patterns adorned the branches of the golden lampstand (Ex. 25:31–34) and the walls and doors of the Temple (1

Kin. 6:18, 29, 32). The rim of the huge laver in the Temple was shaped like the flower of a lily (1 Kin. 7:26; 2 Chr. 4:5).

Trees also grow in abundance in Palestine. Grains and other crops are also plentiful. The land also produced fruits and vegetables of all kinds, spices, herbs, aromatics, perfumes, and preservatives. Although it was the scene of many fierce and bloody battles, and yet will be, still Palestine is a special place: the Holy Land.

Also see ANIMALS OF THE BIBLE; MINERALS OF THE BIBLE; PLANTS OF THE BIBLE; WEATHER.

PALLET — KJV word for a straw–filled mattress, light enough to be carried; the mat of a poor man (John 5:8–11; Acts 5:15; bed, NKJV; mat, NIV).

PALLU [PAL oo] (*distinguished*) — father of Eliab (Num. 26:8) and founder of the PALLUITES (Num. 26:5), also called Phallu (Gen. 46:9, KJV).

PALLUITES [PAL oo ights] — a tribal family descended from PALLU (Num. 26:5).

PALM TREE (see PLANTS OF THE BIBLE).

PALMERWORM (see ANIMALS OF THE BIBLE).

PALSY (see DISEASES OF THE BIBLE).

PALTI [PAL tigh] (*delivered*) — the name of two men in the Old Testament:

1. One of 12 men sent by Moses to spy out the land of Canaan (Num. 13:9).

2. A son of Laish, of the tribe of Benjamin (1 Sam. 25:44; Phalti, KJV; Paltiel, NIV). Palti is the same person as PALTIEL No. 2 (2 Sam. 3:15).

PALTIEL [PAL tih uhl] (*God delivers*) — the name of two men in the Old Testament:

1. A son of Azzan, of the tribe of Issachar (Num. 34:26). Paltiel helped Joshua divide the land west of the Jordan River.

A barren shore on the island of Cyprus near the site of Paphos, a city visited by the apostle Paul (Acts 13:6-13).

2. A son of Laish, of the tribe of Benjamin (2 Sam. 3:15; Phaltiel, KJV).

PALTITE [PAL tight] — a family name of Helez, one of David's mighty men (2 Sam. 23:26). The term Paltite refers to a native of BETH PELET, a city in southern Judah (Josh. 15:27).

PAMPHYLIA [pam FIL ih uh] (*a region of every tribe*) — a Roman province on the southern coast of central Asia Minor (modern Turkey; see Map 7, D-2). The province consisted mainly of a plain about 130 kilometers (80 miles) long and up to about 32 kilometers (20 miles) wide. The capital city of Pamphylia, its largest city, was Perga (Acts 13:13-14).

Pamphylia is first mentioned in the New Testament in Acts 2:10. People from Pamphylia were among those present in Jerusalem on the Day of Pentecost. In Pamphylia the apostle Paul first entered Asia Minor (Acts 13:13) during his first missionary journey. It was also at Pamphylia that John Mark left Paul and Barnabas (Acts 15:38). On his voyage to Rome, Paul sailed off the coast of Pamphylia (Acts 27:5).

PAN — a shallow container, usually of metal and without a lid, used for liquids, for cooking, and for other domestic purposes (Ex. 25:29; 2 Sam. 13:9; 2 Chr. 35:13). The pan mentioned in Leviticus 6:21 and 1 Chronicles 23:29 was a thin, flat plate used for baking bread. A larger pan was a kettle or pot for boiling meat (1 Sam. 2:14).

The most frequent occurrence of the word pan in the NKJV is in the Book of Numbers: "One gold pan of ten shekels full of incense" (Num. 7:14).

This was a utensil presented as a gift for use in the tabernacle. The Hebrew word in this verse is translated by various versions as spoon (KJV), ladle (NIV), dish (RSV), and saucer (NEB).

PANNAG [PAN ag] (*sweet*) — KJV word for a product of Palestine exported to the markets of Tyre (Ezek. 27:17; millett, NKJV; cakes, NASB; confections, NIV; early figs, RSV; meal, NEB). The name probably refers to some kind of sweet pastry or confection, perhaps fig cakes.

PANTHER (see ANIMALS OF THE BIBLE).

PAPER (see PAPYRUS; WRITING).

PAPHOS [PAY fuhs] (meaning unknown) — a city on the southwestern extremity of the island of Cyprus (see Map 7, D-2). Paul, Barnabas, and John Mark visited Paphos during Paul's first missionary journey, about A.D. 47 or 48 (Acts 13:6-13). Two settlements in the same general area of Cyprus are known as Old Paphos (modern Konklia), and New Paphos, about 16 kilometers (10 miles) to the northwest. New Paphos is the Paphos mentioned in the Book of Acts (modern Baffa). At Paphos, Paul met the Roman proconsul Sergius Paulus, who believed the gospel (Acts 13:12) when he witnessed Paul's rebuke of Elymas the sorcerer.

PAPS — KJV translation of breasts (Ezek. 23:21; Luke 11:27) and chest (Rev. 1:13).

PAPYRUS [puh PIE russ] — the name of a plant and a writing material:

1. A tall aquatic plant of southern Europe and northern Africa, especially of the Nile River valley. This plant is now unknown in its wild state in Egypt; but it still grows plentifully in the Sudan. Extensive growths of papyrus may also be found in the marshes at the northern end of Lake Huleh in Palestine. The Roman naturalist Pliny the Elder (A.D. 23-79) wrote in his encyclopedic *Natural*

History about the papyrus plant and its many uses:

"The papyrus grows in the swamps of Egypt or else in the sluggish waters of the Nile where they have overflowed and lie stagnant in pools not more than three feet in depth; it has a sloping root as thick as a man's arm, and tapers gracefully up with triangular sides to a length of not more than fifteen feet. The roots are used by the natives for timber, serving not only as firewood but also for making various utensils and vessels. Indeed the papyrus itself is woven to make boats, and the inner bark is woven into sailcloth and matting, and also cloth, as well as blankets and ropes. It is also used as chewing gum, both in the raw state and when boiled, although only the juice is swallowed."

The Hebrew word translated as papyrus in Job 8:11 is also used in Exodus 2:3. Apparently the "ark of bulrushes" in which Moses was hidden by his mother was woven from papyrus plants. The Egyptians made blankets, boats, shoes, and other articles from papyrus.

2. A paper made from the pith, or the stems, of the papyrus, used in ancient times as a writing material; also a written scroll made of papyrus. In the same passage from *Natural History*, Pliny the Elder wrote:

"The process of making paper from papyrus is to split it with a knife into very thin strips made as broad as possible....Paper of all kinds is 'woven' on a board moistened with water from the Nile, muddy liquid supplying the effect of glue. First an upright layer is smeared onto the table, using the full length of papyrus available after the trimmings have been cut off at both ends, and afterwards cross strips complete the latticework. The next step is to press it in presses, and the sheets are dried in the sun and then joined together, the next strip used always diminishing in quality down to the worst of all. There are never more than twenty sheets to a roll."

The story of the cutting and burning of Jeremiah's scroll by King Jehoiakim (Jer. 36:20–23) suggests papyrus rather than leather; indeed, the Septuagint assumes it was a papyrus scroll. Scholars believe that John's reference to "paper and ink" (2 John 12) is to papyrus writing material because the Greek noun used in this verse refers to the papyrus roll or sheet used in writing a letter.

The ancient Egyptians did not burn their paper rubbish; they simply piled it in the sand and let the blowing sand cover it layer upon layer. Thousands of pages of papyrus documents were found in rubbish heaps by the British archaeologists Grenfell and Hunt, who explored ancient Egyptian tombs in search of documents. They knew that the Egyptians believed that since man lived on in another world, all of his comforts should be buried with him for further use, including his books. Whenever these books were discovered, they were an archaeologist's treasure. On one occasion a tomb yielded little reading matter; it contained only mummified crocodiles (in ancient Egypt the crocodile was worshiped as a god). When the workmen were ordered to abandon their digging, one of them broke through the skin of one of these crocodiles. Out spilled rolls and rolls of papyrus, which were dated at three centuries before Christ.

The first recorded notice of papyrus documents was in 1778. An unknown European dealer in antiquities saw peasants setting fire to nearly 50 sheets of papyrus to obtain the aromatic scent of the smoke. The papyrus purchased included documents from the year A.D. 191–192. Between 1820 and 1840, large numbers of papyrus documents were discovered in Egypt, but most scholars ignored these finds as unimportant.

In the year 1891 the great era of papyrus discoveries was born, when Sir Flinders Petrie and E. Wallis Budge discovered some leaves or rolls of outstanding literary merit. Most of these documents were dated in the third century B.C. Perhaps the most important discovery of the period was by Adolf Deissmann, who realized that the language

Several stalks of papyrus, reed-like plants used for making a primitive type of paper in Bible times.

Photo by Willem A. VanGemeren

Elephantine Island in the Nile River near Aswan, Egypt. A series of Aramaic papyri and ostraca, written by a colony of Jews stationed here during the Persian era, was found at this site.

was identical to that of his Greek New Testament. Clearly New Testament Greek was not a special biblical language created by the Holy Spirit as many had claimed.

The oldest manuscripts of the Old Testament and the New Testament, the majority of the DEAD SEA SCROLLS, and the large collection of GNOSTIC documents at the NAG HAMMADI library were written on papyrus. The English word paper comes from the word papyrus.

PARABLE — a short, simple story designed to communicate a spiritual truth, religious principle, or moral lesson; a figure of speech in which truth is illustrated by a comparison or example drawn from everyday experiences.

A parable is often no more than an extended metaphor or simile, using figurative language in the form of a story to illustrate a particular truth. The Greek word for parable literally means "a laying by the side of" or "a casting alongside," thus "a comparison or likeness." In a parable something is placed alongside something else, in order that one may throw light on the other. A familiar custom or incident is used to illustrate some truth less familiar.

Although Jesus was the master of the parabolic form, He was not the first to use parables. Examples of the effective use of parables are found in the Old Testament. Perhaps the best known of these is Nathan's parable of the rich man who took the one little ewe lamb that belonged to a poor man (2 Sam. 12:1–4). By means of this parable, Nathan reproved King David and convicted him of his sin of committing adultery with Bathsheba (2 Sam. 12:5–15). A

wise woman of Tekoa also used a parable (2 Sam. 14:5–7) to convince King David to let his son return to Jerusalem.

Jesus' characteristic method of teaching was through parables. His two most famous parables are the parable of the lost son (Luke 15:11–32) and the parable of the Good Samaritan (Luke 10:25–37). Both parables illustrate God's love for sinners and God's command that we show compassion to all people. Actually, the parable of the lost son (sometimes called the parable of the prodigal son or the parable of the loving father) is the story of two lost sons: the younger son (typical of tax collectors and prostitutes) who wasted possessions with indulgent living and the older son (typical of the self-righteous scribes and Pharisees) who remained at home but was a stranger to his father's heart.

Some entire chapters in the Gospels are devoted to Jesus' parables; for instance, Matthew 13—which contains the parables of the sower (vv. 1–23), the wheat and the tares (vv. 24–30), the mustard seed (vv. 31–32), the leaven (vv. 33), the hidden treasure (v. 44), the pearl of great price (vv. 45–46), and the dragnet (vv. 47–52).

Although parables are often memorable stories, impressing the listener with a clear picture of the truth, even the disciples were sometimes confused as to the meaning of parables. For instance, after Jesus told the parable of the wheat and the tares (Matt. 13:24–30), the disciples needed interpretation in order to understand its meaning (Matt. 13:36–43). Jesus sometimes used the parabolic form of teaching to reveal the truth to those who followed Him and to conceal the truth from those who

The Parables of Jesus

Parables which appear only in the Gospel of Matthew
The Wheat and the Tares . . . . (13:24–30)
The Hidden Treasure . . . . (13:44)
The Pearl of Great Price . . . . (13:45–46)
The Dragnet . . . . (13:47–50)
The Unforgiving Servant . . . . (18:21–35)
The Workers in the Vineyard . . . . (20:1–16)
The Two Sons . . . . (21:28–32)
The Wedding Feast . . . . (22:1–14)
The Wise and Foolish Virgins . . . . (25:1–13)
The Talents . . . . (25:14–30)

Parables which appear only in the Gospel of Mark
The Growing Seed . . . . (4:26–29)
The Watchful Doorkeeper . . . . (13:32–37)

Parables which appear only in the Gospel of Luke
The Creditor Who Had Two Debtors . . . . (7:40–47)
The Good Samaritan . . . . (10:25–37)
The Friend Who Came at Midnight . . . . (11:5–8)
The Rich Fool . . . . (12:13–21)
The Faithful Servant and the Evil Servant . . . . (12:35–48)
The Barren Fig Tree . . . . (13:6–9)
The Unfinished Tower . . . . (14:25–34)
The Lost Coin . . . . (15:8–10)
The Lost Son . . . . (15:11–32)
The Unjust Steward . . . . (16:1–13)
The Condescending Master . . . . (17:7–10)
The Persistent Widow . . . . (18:1–8)
The Pharisee and the Tax Collector . . . . (18:9–14)
The Minas . . . . (19:11–27)

Parables which appear in Matthew and Luke
The Two Builders . . . . (Matt. 7:24–27; Luke 6:47–49)
The Leaven . . . . (Matt. 13:33; Luke 13:20–21)
The Lost Sheep . . . . (Matt. 18:10–14; Luke 15:1–7)

Parables which appear in Matthew, Mark, and Luke
The Lamp and the Lampstand . . . . (Matt. 5:15–16; Mark 4:21; Luke 8:16)
New Cloth on Old Garments . . . . (Matt. 9:16; Mark 2:21; Luke 5:36)
New Wine in Old Wineskins . . . . (Matt. 9:17; Mark 2:22; Luke 5:37–39)
A House Divided Against Itself . . . . (Matt. 12:25–29; Mark 3:23–27; Luke 11:17–22)
The Sower and the Seed . . . . (Matt. 13:1–23; Mark 4:1–20; Luke 8:4–15)
The Mustard Seed . . . . (Matt. 13:31–32; Mark 4:30–32; Luke 13:18–19)
The Wicked Vinedressers . . . . (Matt. 21:33–41; Mark 12:1–12; Luke 20:9–18)
The Fig Tree . . . . (Matt. 24:32–35; Mark 13:28–31; Luke 21:29–33)

Parables which appear only in the Gospel of John
The Bread of Life . . . . (John 6:32–58)
The Shepherd and the Sheep . . . . (John 10:1–18)
The Vine and the Branches . . . . (John 15:1–8)

did not (Matt. 13:10-17; Mark 4:10-12; Luke 8:9-10). His parables thus fulfilled the prophecy of Isaiah 6:9-10. Like a double-edged sword, they cut two ways—enlightening those who sought the truth and blinding those who were disobedient.

Most of Jesus' parables have one central point. Thus, Bible students should not resort to fanciful interpretations that find "spiritual truth" in every minute detail of the parable. The central point of the parable of the Good SAMARITAN is that a "hated" Samaritan proved to be a neighbor to the wounded man. He showed the traveler the mercy and compassion denied to him by the priest and the Levite, representatives of the established religion. The one central point of this parable is that we should also extend compassion to others—even those who are not of our own nationality, race, or religion (Luke 10:25-37).

In finding the central meaning of a parable, the Bible student needs to discover the meaning the parable had in the time of Jesus. We need to relate the parable to Jesus' proclamation of the kingdom of God and to His miracles. This means that parables are more than simple folk stories; they are expressions of Jesus' view of God, man, salvation, and the new age which dawned in His ministry. A good example of this approach are the parables dealing with the four "lost" things in Luke 15:3-32: the lost sheep, the lost coin, and the two lost sons. The historical context is found in Luke 15:1-2: Jesus had table fellowship with tax collectors and sinners. The Pharisees and scribes, the "religious experts" of Jesus' day, saw such action as disgusting because, in their view, it transgressed God's holiness. If Jesus truly were a righteous man, they reasoned, then He would not associate with such people; He would keep Himself pure and separate from sinners.

In response to their murmuring, Jesus told them these parables. God rejoices more, He said, over the repentance of one sinner (those sitting with Him at table) than over "ninety-nine just persons who need no repentance" (Luke 15:7)—that is, than over the religious professionals who congratulate themselves over their own self-achieved "goodness" (compare the parable of the Pharisee and the tax collector; Luke 18:9-14). Likewise, the prodigal son (Luke 15:11-24) represents the tax collectors and sinners; the older son (Luke 15:25-32) represents the scribes and Pharisees.

A major theme in Jesus' parables is the demand of following Him in authentic discipleship. In the parable of the great supper (Luke 14:15-24), Jesus showed clearly that the time for decision is now. In the parable of the unfinished tower and the king going to war (Luke 14:28-32), Jesus demanded that His followers be prepared to give up all. In the parables of the hidden treasure and the pearl of great price (Matt. 13:44-46), Jesus stated that the kingdom of heaven is of such value that all other treasures in life are of secondary worth. Jesus' parables are a call to a radical decision to follow Him, regardless of the cost.

PARACLETE [pair uh KLEET] — a transliteration of the Greek word *parakletos*, which means "one who speaks in favor of," as an intercessor, advocate, or legal assistant. The word appears only in the Gospel of John. Jesus applied the term to the HOLY SPIRIT, who would be an advocate on behalf of Jesus' followers after His ascension; the Spirit would plead their cause before God (John 14:16, 26; 15:26; 16:7).

Sheep on a Judean hillside. Jesus often used such commonplace scenes from daily life to illustrate spiritual truths, as in His parable of the lost sheep (Matt. 18:10-14).
Photo by Gustav Jeeninga

PARADISE (*park, garden*) — a place of exceptional blessedness, happiness, and delight; a descriptive name for heaven. Originally paradise was a Persian word meaning "a wooded park," "an enclosed or walled orchard," or "a garden with fruit trees." Traditional Hebrew theology held that the dead descended to SHEOL. After the emergence of belief in the resurrection, however, this view was drastically modified. In the period between the Old and New Testaments, the Jews believed that, after the resurrection, the righteous would go to Paradise, a place much like the Garden of Eden before the Fall.

In the NKJV the word paradise occurs only three times (Luke 23:43; 2 Cor. 12:4; Rev. 2:7). To the repentant thief on the cross Jesus said, "Today you will be with Me in Paradise" (Luke 23:43). Various commentators have pointed out that when a Persian king wished to bestow upon one of his subjects a special honor, he made him a "companion of the garden." The subject was chosen to walk in the king's garden as a special friend and companion of the king. Thus, Jesus promised the thief that he would be a companion of the King of kings, walking with Christ in the garden of heaven.

PARAH [PAH ruh] (*young cow*) — a city in the territory of Benjamin (Josh. 18:23), apparently identical with Khirbet el–Farah, about nine kilometers (5.5 miles) northeast of Jerusalem.

PARALLELISM (see POETRY).

PARALYSIS (see DISEASES OF THE BIBLE).

PARAMOUR — an adulterous lover, either male or female; a mistress. In Ezekiel 23:20 the word paramours in the NKJV refers to male lovers (male prostitutes, NEB). In all other occurrences in the NKJV, however, the Hebrew word for paramours is translated as CONCUBINES.

PARAN [PAH ruhn] — a wilderness region in the central part of the Sinai Peninsula (see Map 2, C–1). Although the boundaries of this desert region are somewhat obscure, it probably bordered the ARABAH and the Gulf of Aqaba on the east.

Paran is frequently mentioned in the Old Testament. Chedorlaomer, one of the four kings who attacked Sodom, conquered as far as "El Paran, which is by the wilderness" (Gen. 14:6). After Hagar was driven from Abraham's household (Gen. 21:21), she fled to this wilderness with her son Ishmael. The Israelites crossed Paran during their Exodus from Egypt (Num. 10:12; 12:16), and Moses dispatched spies from Paran to explore the land of Canaan (Num. 13:3). After their mission, these spies returned "unto the wilderness of Paran, to Kadesh" (Num. 13:26).

Much later, after the death of Samuel, David fled to Paran (1 Sam. 25:1). After revolting from King Solomon, Hadad went through Paran on his flight to Egypt (1 Kin. 11:18).

PARAPET — a railing, wall, or latticework around the edge of the flat roofs of Palestinian houses, required by Mosaic law as a protection against accidents (Deut. 22:8; battlement, KJV).

PARBAR [PAHR bahr] (meaning unknown) — a word that refers to an area in the outer court of the Temple (1 Chr. 26:18). Apparently, it refers either to a section of the Temple courtyard or to a place west of the courtyard where horses dedicated to the sun were stabled during the reign of King Manasseh.

PARCHED GRAIN — grain roasted in a fire and eaten as a snack in Bible times (Josh. 5:11; Ruth 2:14; parched corn, KJV). Seeds, lentils, and beans were also roasted and eaten in the same way (2 Sam. 17:28).

PARCHMENT (see WRITING).

PARDON — to forgive; to release a person from punishment. The Bible portrays God as "ready to pardon" (Mic. 7:18). Also see FORGIVENESS; JUSTIFICATION.

PARENTS — those who give birth to children and provide nurture and guidance during their childhood years. Children were to honor their parents (Ex. 20:12) and to obey and honor them (Lev. 19:3; Deut. 5:16). Failure to do this could result in punishment or death (Deut. 21:18–21). Parents were also taught to "train up a child in the way he should go" (Prov. 22:6). In the New Testament, Paul instructed parents to bring up their children in "the training and admonition of the Lord" (Eph. 6:4). Also see FAMILY.

PARLOR — KJV word for an inner room in the Temple in Jerusalem (1 Chr. 28:11; inner chamber, NKJV). This word also refers to a room on the flat roof of a house, used in the summer as a cool retreat (Judg. 3:20–25). Also see HOUSE.

PARMASHTA [par MASH tah] (*strong–fisted*) — a son of HAMAN, hanged like his father (Esth. 9:9).

PARMENAS [PAHR muh nuhs] (*faithful*) — one of seven men chosen by the church in Jerusalem to assist the apostles in distributing food to the needy (Acts 6:5).

PARNACH [PAHR nak] (meaning unknown) — father of Elizaphan (Num. 34:25).

PAROSH [PAHR ahsh] (*a flea*) — the founder of a family, 2,172 of whom returned from the Captivity with Zerubbabel (Ezra 2:3; Pharosh, KJV; Neh. 7:8). Another group of this family returned from the Captivity with Ezra (Ezra 8:3).

PAROUSIA [puh ROO· sih ah] — a transliteration of a Greek word that refers to the SECOND COMING, or the return of the Lord Jesus Christ at the end of this age to set up His kingdom, judge His enemies, and reward the faithful. The Greek word literally means, "a being alongside," hence "appearance" or "presence." Christians are "looking for the blessed hope and glorious appearing of our great God and Savior Jesus Christ" (Titus 2:13). This blessed hope of the Parousia, or Second Coming, sustains believers in a godless age.

PARSHANDATHA [pahr SHAN duh thuh] (*inquisitive*) — the first of the ten sons of Haman, adviser to Ahasuerus (Xerxes), king of Persia (Esth. 9:7).

PARSIN [PAHR sin] (see MENE, MENE, TEKEL, UPHARSIN).

PARTHIANS [PAHR thih uhns] — a tribal group from Parthia, a region southeast of the Caspian Sea in ancient Persia (Iran). Parthians are mentioned in Acts 2:9 as one of the many national and language groups gathered in Jerusalem for the Feast of Pentecost.

Parthia was one of the original Persian administrative districts established by Darius I (Dan. 6:1). Late in the fourth century B.C., the Persian Empire fell to Alexander the Great and his successors, the Macedonian emperors known as the SELEUCIDS. In the middle of the third century B.C., the Parthians revolted from the Seleucids under the leadership of King Arsaces. The kings who followed Arsaces gradually built a great empire; it extended from the Euphrates River in Mesopotamia to the Indus River in (modern) Pakistan. Fierce warriors, the Parthians were formidable in battle; their archers fought while mounted on horseback. Even the Roman armies were largely unsuccessful against the Parthians.

The Babylonians settled some citizens of the nation of Judah in Parthia after their deportation from Judah in 587 B.C. (2 Chr. 36:20). The Jewish historian Josephus reported that some of the Jews who settled in Parthia continued to practice the Israelite faith, apparently without harassment from the natives. Thus the "Parthians" in Jerusalem on Pentecost (Acts 2:9) may have included remnants of these deported Jewish people as well as converts to Judaism from among native Parthians.

PARTIALITY — to favor one person or party more than another and thus to act in a prejudiced or biased manner. In the Old Testament, the Hebrew people were reminded that just as God shows no partiality, so should they show no favoritism to the rich or poor, great or small (Lev. 19:15; Deut. 16:19; 2 Chr. 19:7). The New Testament declares that salvation is freely given to all who believe in Jesus Christ, whether Jew or Gentile, male or female, bondslave or free man (Gal. 3:28).

PARTITION — KJV word for VEIL, a curtain that separated the general worship area from the Holy of Holies in the tabernacle and Temple. Once a year the priest passed through this partition, or veil, to make atonement first for his own sins and then the sin of the people (Ex. 26:31–35).

PARTRIDGE (see ANIMALS OF THE BIBLE).

PARUAH [puh ROO uh] (*blossoming*) — the father of Jehoshaphat (1 Kin. 4:17).

PARVAIM [pahr VAY uhm] (meaning unknown)

— an unidentified place, rich in minerals, from which Solomon obtained gold to decorate the Temple (2 Chr. 3:6).

PARZITES [PAHR zights] — a tribal family descended from Perez, son of Judah (Num. 26:20; Perezite, NASB, NIV, RSV; Pharzites, KJV).

PASACH [PAY sak] (*divider*) — a son of Japhlet, of the tribe of Asher (1 Chr. 7:33).

PASDAMMIM [pass DAM mim] (*boundary of blood*) — a place in the territory of Judah, scene of a victory of David over the Philistines (1 Chr. 11:13).

PASEAH [puh SEE uh] (*lame*) — the name of two or three men in the Old Testament:

1. A son of Eshton, of the tribe of Judah (1 Chr. 4:12).

2. The founder of a family of Temple servants who returned from the Captivity with Zerubbabel (Neh. 7:51; Phaseah, KJV).

3. The father of Jehoiada (Neh. 3:6). He may be the same person as Paseah No. 2.

PASHHUR [PASH ur] (meaning unknown) — the name of three or more men in the Old Testament:

1. The founder of a priestly family whose members returned from the Captivity (Ezra 2:38; Neh. 7:41). Members of this family divorced their pagan wives after the Captivity (Ezra 10:22). This Pashhur may be the Pashur of 1 Chronicles 9:12.

2. A priest who sealed the covenant after the Captivity (Neh. 10:3).

3. A son of Immer the priest (Jer. 20:1–6). Pashhur put Jeremiah in the stocks because Jeremiah's prophecies were so unfavorable.

4. A son of Melchiah and one of several officials who opposed Jeremiah because of his unpopular prophecies (Jer. 21:1; 38:1, 4).

5. The father of Gedaliah (Jer. 38:1) and a person who opposed Jeremiah. He may be the same person as Pashhur No. 3 and No. 4. The KJV consistently spells his name as Pashur.

PASHUR [PASH ur] (meaning unknown) — the founder of a priestly family whose descendants returned from the Captivity (1 Chr. 9:12). Pashur may be the Pashhur mentioned in Ezra 2:38 and Nehemiah 7:41.

PASSAGE — a word used by the NKJV in two ways:

1. A right of way; the right to travel through an area. The Edomites refused to give the Israelites passage through their territory (Num. 20:21).

2. A ford or river crossing (Jer. 51:32).

PASSION OF CHRIST — KJV words referring to the suffering and death of Jesus Christ by crucifixion (Acts 1:3). The NKJV refers to Jesus' ordeal on the cross by using the word suffering in its translation of the verse.

PASSOVER, FEAST OF (see FEASTS AND FESTIVALS).

PASTOR — the feeder, protector, and guide, or shepherd, of a flock of God's people in New Testament times. In speaking of spiritual gifts, the apostle Paul wrote that Christ "gave some to be apostles, some prophets, some evangelists, and some pastors and teachers" (Eph. 4:11). The term pastor by this time in church history had not yet become an official title. The term implied the nourishing of and caring for God's people.

The Greek word translated pastors in Ephesians 4:11 is used elsewhere in the New Testament of sheepherders, literally or symbolically (Matt. 25:32); of Jesus, the Good Shepherd (John 10); and of "shepherds," or leaders, of the church (Eph. 4:11). The NKJV uses the word pastor only in this verse. Also compare Jeremiah 23:1-2 (KJV).

PASTORAL EPISTLES — the name given to three letters of the apostle Paul: 1 Timothy, 2 Timothy, and Titus. They are called the pastoral epistles because they clearly show Paul's love and concern as pastor and administrator of several local churches.

Historical Setting. The occasion for Paul's writing these three letters was the need to maintain the faith and to insure the faithfulness of the church. He charged the young pastor Timothy, "Guard what was committed to your trust" (1 Tim. 6:20). This declaration is the heart of the pastoral epistles. Here Timothy, with all the church, is charged to keep the deposit of faith—the written record or message to be carried on by the indwelling power of the Holy Spirit.

The more immediate need of the first two epistles—1 Timothy and Titus—lay in the fact that many things in Ephesus and Crete, where Timothy was serving, needed adjustment and correction. Paul, intending to advise Timothy and Titus in the faith, determined to advise others at the same time. Paul charged them to avoid heresy, hold to sound doctrine, and maintain purity and piety of life.

Authorship. In the 19th century doubts were expressed about whether Paul actually wrote these three letters. A group of German scholars noted alleged differences in style and vocabulary, church organization, heresies, biographical and historical situations, and theology from those found in the letters that were undisputedly written by Paul.

Linguistic objections to Pauline authorship of the pastoral epistles include certain words, phrases, or forms which appear about twice as often in the pastorals as in Paul's other letters. But this argument is inconclusive because it is impossible to prove. Paul may have chosen to speak in a different vocabulary because he was writing on other subjects and to specific church situations.

Theological objections point to an emphasis on works in the pastorals rather than on grace and faith and an apparent attack on second-century GNOSTICISM. Good works, however, are mentioned as the "fruit" (the natural outgrowth) of the "tree" of faith, and grace is celebrated in several passages (1 Tim. 1:14; 2 Tim. 1:9; Titus 2:11—3:7). Moreover, it is reasonable to assume that in these

epistles Paul may not have been fighting a Gnosticism as advanced as some have argued.

Ecclesiastical objections have also been raised to the view that Paul wrote the pastorals. Some scholars charge that a highly structured hierarchical organization, later than the time of Paul, is reflected in the pastoral epistles. However, the elements of church organization found in the pastorals are also described elsewhere in the New Testament (Acts 20:28; Phil. 1:1).

Chronological objections revolve around the discrepancies that supposedly exist between the pastoral epistles and the Book of Acts, with the assumption that Paul was put to death at the end of his one and only Roman imprisonment. The charge is a very good reason for extending the life of Paul beyond the events recorded in Acts. The pastoral epistles would then be the product of Paul's fourth missionary journey and second imprisonment (1 Tim. 3:14; 2 Tim. 1:8, 16).

All the pastorals are to be taken as written by Paul because their internal evidence reflects the character and temperament of the great apostle. The evidence of the writings themselves indicates that Paul is the writer, since his name appears in the salutation of each letter (1 Tim. 1:1; 2 Tim. 1:1; Titus 1:1).

Date. The first letter to Timothy and the one to Titus were written during travel and missionary work between Paul's two Roman imprisonments. A date somewhere between A.D. 61 and 63 can be set, because the Second Epistle to Timothy contains Paul's farewell address (2 Tim. 4:6-8), the last words from the apostle shortly before his martyrdom, generally set between A.D. 65 and 68.

Summary of Theme. The purpose of the pastoral epistles is to admonish, instruct, and direct the recipients in their pastoral duties. These letters deal with the care and the organization of the church, the flock of God. They contain common injunctions to guard the Christian faith, to appoint qualified officials, to conduct proper worship, and to maintain discipline both personally and in the churches. They give instructions in the work of the church and show how threats to the doctrinal and moral purity of Christians should be overcome.

Also see TIMOTHY, EPISTLES TO; TITUS, EPISTLE TO.

PATARA [PAT uh ruh] — a seaport of LYCIA (see Map 8, C-2). The apostle Paul visited Patara on his third missionary journey. At Patara he transferred to a ship bound for Tyre (Acts 21:1-3). Patara was famous for a magnificent temple dedicated to Apollo. Many remains of its other impressive structures can still be seen today.

PATH — any road or way. When the word path is used literally, it refers to a footpath (Gen. 49:17). However, it usually is used figuratively for a way of life. A person's path may lead him to a life of forgetting God (Job. 8:13) and unrighteousness (Prov. 2:13). A person's path may also be lighted by the Word of God (Ps. 119:105).

Photo by Howard Vos

An arch erected in honor of the Roman Emperor Hadrian at Patara, a seaport city visited by the apostle Paul (Acts 21:1).

PATHROS [PATH rahs] (*the southern land*) — the Hebrew name for Upper Egypt, roughly the southern region of the Nile River Valley between Cairo and Aswan (Is. 11:11). After the fall of Jerusalem (597 B.C.), the idolatrous Jews who offered incense to other gods fled to Pathros and formed a Jewish colony in Egypt. The prophet Jeremiah predicted that their disobedience would be judged by the king of Babylon (Jer. 44:1, 15). Ezekiel also prophesied that Pathros would be humiliated by Nebuchadnezzar (Ezek. 30:10–14), but that the Jews would recognize their sins and turn to God (Ezek. 29:14).

PATHRUSIM [puh THROO zim] (*southerners*) — the fifth son of MIZRAIM (1 Chr. 1:12) and founder of a people known by this name.

PATIENCE — forebearance under suffering and endurance in the face of adversity. Two Greek words are translated as patience: *makrothymia* (Heb. 6:12; James 5:10) and *hypomone* (Matt. 18:26, 29). The former word generally expresses patience with regard to people. It is also translated longsuffering as a quality of God (Rom. 2:4; 2 Pet. 3:9) and is listed by the apostle Paul as one of the nine fruits of the Holy Spirit (Gal. 5:22).

The second word, *hypomone*, generally expresses patience with regard to things. It may be described as the quality that enables a person to be "patient in tribulation" (Rom. 12:12). The Christian has for his example the patience of Jesus, who "endured the cross" (Heb. 12:2). The Christian is challenged to run with endurance the race that is set before him (Heb. 12:1).

PATMOS [PAT muhs] — a small rocky island to which the apostle John was banished and where he wrote the Book of Revelation (Rev. 1:9). The island, about 16 kilometers (ten miles) long and ten kilometers (six miles) wide, lies off the southwest coast of Asia Minor (modern Turkey). Because of its desolate and barren nature, Patmos was used by the Romans as a place to banish criminals, who were forced to work at hard labor in the mines and quarries of the island. Because Christians were regarded as criminals by the Roman emperor Domitian (ruled A.D. 81–96), the apostle John probably suffered from harsh treatment during his exile on Patmos. An early Christian tradition said John was in exile for 18 months.

PATRIARCHS [PAY trih arks] (*head of a father's house*) — the founder or ruler of a tribe, family, or clan; the forefathers of the Israelite nation. The phrase *the patriarchs* usually refers to the tribal leaders of Israel who lived before the time of Moses. Specifically, it is used of Abraham, Isaac, Jacob, and the 12 sons of Jacob. Therefore, the patriarchs were the ancestors of the Israelites from Abraham to Joseph (Acts 7:8–9; Heb. 7:4).

In Peter's sermon in Jerusalem on the Day of Pentecost, the apostle expanded the term to include King David (Acts 2:29). Peter's point was that, in contrast to Jesus Christ, the patriarch David died and remained buried in the tomb. There is no hope in David: "His tomb is with us to this day" (Acts 2:29). In his sermon before the council, Stephen stressed that the patriarchs were sinners—they sold Joseph into slavery in Egypt (Acts 7:9)—and that

---

804

they all needed to be redeemed from their sin.

The author of Hebrews reminded his readers that the patriarch Abraham gave a tenth of the spoils of battle to MELCHIZEDEK, king of Salem (Heb. 7:1–4). He also compared Melchizedek to Jesus Christ. In all uses of the term patriarch, the New Testament says the patriarchs were sinners, were limited in their power, and were greatly inferior to the Lord Jesus Christ.

When Jesus sought to teach the Pharisees their need of Him, they implied they did not need Him. They had pride in the claim, "We are Abraham's descendants" (John 8:33). They were the "children" of Abraham (the patriarch *par excellence*). With such an illustrious ancestor, what need did they have of a prophet from Nazareth? They found their security in Abraham, not in Jesus; and thus the man whose faithfulness was the cornerstone of Israel's faith became the stone against which his descendants stumbled.

PATRIARCHS, TESTAMENTS OF THE TWELVE (see APOCALYPTIC LITERATURE).

PATRIMONY — KJV and RSV words for an inheritance (Deut. 18:8). Other translations are family possessions (NIV) and what he may inherit from his father's family (NEB). Also see INHERITANCE.

PATROBAS [PAT ruh buhs] (*having life from father*) — a Christian at Rome to whom Paul sent greetings (Rom. 16:14).

PAU [PAY oo] (meaning unknown) — a city in Idumea, or Edom, where King Hadar of Edom was born or reigned (Gen. 36:39). In 1 Chronicles 1:50 the king is called Hadad, and the name of his city is Pai. The location of this city is unknown.

PAUL, THE APOSTLE — the earliest and most influential interpreter of Christ's message and teaching; an early Christian missionary; correspondent with several early Christian churches.

The Life of Paul. Paul was born at Tarsus, the chief city of Cilicia (southeast Asia Minor). He was a citizen of Tarsus, "no mean city," as he called it (Acts 21:39). He was also born a Roman citizen (Acts 22:28), a privilege which worked to his advantage on several occasions during his apostolic ministry. Since Paul was born a Roman citizen, his father must have been a Roman citizen before him. Paul was part of his Roman name. In addition to his Roman name, he was given a Jewish name, Saul, perhaps in memory of Israel's first king, a member of the tribe of Benjamin, to which Paul's family belonged.

His Jewish heritage meant much more to Paul than Roman citizenship. Unlike many Jews who had been scattered throughout the world, he and his family did not become assimilated to the Gentile way of life which surrounded them. This is suggested when Paul describes himself as "a Hebrew of the Hebrews" (Phil. 3:5), and confirmed by Paul's statement in Acts 22:3 that, while he was born in Tarsus, he was brought up in Jerusalem "at the feet of Gamaliel," the most illustrious rabbi of his day (Acts 5:34). Paul's parents wanted their son to be well-grounded in the best traditions of Jewish orthodoxy.

Paul proved an apt pupil. He outstripped many of his fellow students in his enthusiasm for ancestral traditions and in his zeal for the Jewish law. This zeal found a ready outlet in his assault on the infant church of Jerusalem. The church presented a threat to all that Paul held most dear. Its worst of-

The rocky, barren island of Patmos in the Mediterranean Sea—the place where John received the messages from God which he included in the Book of Revelation (Rev. 1:9-11).

Photo: Religious News Service

fense was its proclamation of one who had suffered a death cursed by the Jewish law as Lord and Messiah (Deut. 21:22–23). The survival of Israel demanded that the followers of Jesus be wiped out.

The first martyr of the Christian church was Stephen, one of the most outspoken leaders of the new movement. Luke told how Paul publicly associated himself with Stephen's executioners and then embarked on a campaign designed to suppress the church. Paul himself related how he "persecuted the church of God beyond measure and tried to destroy it" (Gal. 1:13).

Conversion and apostolic commission—At the height of Paul's campaign of repression, he was confronted on the road to Damascus by the risen Christ. In an instant his life was reoriented. The Jewish law was replaced as the central theme of Paul's life by Jesus Christ. He became the leading champion of the cause which he had tried to overthrow.

The realization that Jesus, whom he had been persecuting, was alive and exalted as the Son of God exposed the weakness of the Jewish law. Paul's zeal for the law had made him an ardent persecutor. He now saw that his persecuting activity had been sinful; yet the law, instead of showing him the sinfulness of such a course, had really led him into sin.

The law had lost its validity. Paul learned that it was no longer by keeping the law that a person was justified in God's sight, but by faith in Christ. And if faith in Christ provided acceptance with God, then Gentiles might enjoy that acceptance as readily as Jews. This was one of the implications of the revelation of Jesus Christ which gripped Paul's mind. He was assured that he himself had received that revelation in order that he might proclaim Christ and His salvation to the Gentile world.

Paul began to carry out this commission not only in Damascus but also in the kingdom of the Nabatean Arabs, to the east and south. No details are given of his activity in "Arabia" (Gal. 1:17), but he did enough to attract the hostile attention of the authorities there, as the representative of the Nabatean king in Damascus tried to arrest him (2 Cor. 11:32–33).

After leaving Damascus, Paul paid a short visit to Jerusalem to make the acquaintance of Peter. During his two weeks' stay there, he also met James, the Lord's brother (Gal. 1:18–19). Paul could not stay in Jerusalem because the animosity of his former associates was too strong. He had to be taken down to Caesarea on the Mediterranean coast and put on a ship for Tarsus.

Paul spent the next ten years in and around Tarsus, actively engaged in the evangelizing of Gentiles. Very few details of those years have been preserved. At the end of that time BARNABAS came to Tarsus from Antioch and invited Paul to join him in caring for a young church there. A spontaneous campaign of Gentile evangelization had recently occurred at Antioch, resulting in the formation of a vigorous church. Barnabas himself had been com-

missioned by the apostles in Jerusalem to lead the Gentile evangelization in the city of Antioch.

About a year after Paul joined Barnabas in Antioch, the two men visited Jerusalem and conferred with the three "pillars" of the church there—the apostles Peter and John, and James the Lord's brother (Gal. 2:1–10). The result of this conference was an agreement that the Jerusalem leaders would concentrate on the evangelization of their fellow Jews, while Barnabas and Paul would continue to take the gosepl to Gentiles.

The Jerusalem leaders reminded Barnabas and Paul, in conducting their Gentile mission, not to forget the material needs of the impoverished believers in Jerusalem. Barnabas and Paul (especially Paul) readily agreed to bear those needs in mind. This may have been the occasion when they carried a gift of money from the Christians in Antioch to Jerusalem for the relief of their brethren who were suffering hardship in a time of famine (Acts 11:30).

Apostle to the Gentiles—The way was now open for a wider Gentile mission. Barnabas and Paul were released by the church of Antioch to pursue a missionary campaign which took them first through Barnabas' native island of Cyprus and then into the highlands of central Asia Minor (modern Turkey), to the province of Galatia. There they preached the gospel and planted churches in the cities of Pisidian Antioch, Iconium, Lystra, and Derbe. The missionaries then returned to Antioch in Syria.

The great increase of Gentile converts caused alarm among many of the Jewish Christians in Ju-

Entrance to the street called Straight in the ancient city of Damascus, Syria. After his conversion, the apostle Paul visited a man on this street (Acts 9:1-19).
Photo: Matson Photo Collection

dea. They feared that too many Gentiles would hurt the character of the church. Militant Jewish nationalists were already attacking them. A movement began which required that Gentile converts become circumcised and follow the Jewish law. The leaders of the Jerusalem church, with Paul and Barnabas in attendance, met in A.D. 48 to discuss the problem. It was finally decided that circumcision was not necessary, but that Gentile converts should conform to the Jewish code of laws in order to make fellowship between Jewish and Gentile Christians less strained (Acts 15:1–29).

After this meeting, Barnabas and Paul parted company. Paul chose SILAS, a leading member of the Jerusalem church and a Roman citizen like himself, to be his new colleague. Together they visited the young churches of Galatia. At Lystra they were joined by TIMOTHY, a young convert from Barnabas and Paul's visit some two years before. Paul in particular recognized qualities in Timothy which would make him a valuable helper in his missionary service. From that time to the end of Paul's life, Timothy was his most faithful attendant.

Paul and Silas probably planned to proceed west to EPHESUS, but they felt the negative guidance of the Holy Spirit. They instead turned north and northwest, reaching the seaport of TROAS. Here Paul was told in a vision to cross the north Aegean Sea and preach the gospel in MACEDONIA. This Paul and his companions did. By now their number had increased to four by the addition of Luke. The narrative reveals his presence at this point by using "we" instead of "they" (Acts 16:10).

Their first stop in Macedonia was the Roman colony of PHILIPPI. Here, in spite of running into trouble with the magistrates and being imprisoned, Paul and his companions planted a strong church. They moved on to THESSALONICA, the chief city of the province, and formed a church there, as well. But serious trouble broke out in Thessalonica. The missionaries were accused of rebelling against the Roman emperor by proclaiming Jesus as his rival. They were forced to leave the city quickly.

Paul moved south to BEREA, where he was favorably received by the local synagogue, but his opponents from Thessalonica followed him, making it necessary for him to move on once more. Although churches of Macedonia would later give Paul much joy and satisfaction, he felt dejected at this time from being forced to flee city after city.

Paul, alone now, moved south into the province of ACHAIA. After a short stay in ATHENS, he came "in weakness, in fear, and in much trembling" (1 Cor. 2:3) to CORINTH, the seat of provincial administration. Corinth had a reputation as a wicked city in the Greco-Roman world and it did not seem likely that the gospel would make much headway there. Surprisingly, however, Paul stayed there for 18 months and made many converts. While he was there, a new Roman proconsul, GALLIO, arrived to take up residence in Corinth. The beginning of his administration can be accurately dated as July 1, A.D. 51. Paul was prosecuted before Gallio on the

Photo by Gustav Jeeninga

Statue of Diana of the Ephesians, a pagan goddess of the ancient Greeks. During one of his preaching missions, the apostle Paul was almost mobbed by a group of silversmiths who made artifacts for Diana worshipers (Acts 19:1, 21-41).

charge of preaching an illegal religion, but Gallio dismissed the charge. This provided other Roman magistrates with a precedent which helped the progress of the gospel over the next ten years.

The church of Corinth was large, lively, and talented but deficient in spiritual and moral stability. This deficiency caused Paul much anxiety over the next few years, as his letters to the Corinthians reveal.

After his stay in Corinth, Paul paid a brief visit to Jerusalem and Antioch and then traveled to Ephesus, where he settled for the next three years. Paul's Ephesian ministry was perhaps the most active part of his apostolic career. A number of colleagues shared his activity and evangelized the city of Ephesus as well as the whole province of Asia (western Asia Minor).

Ten years earlier there had been no churches in the great provinces of Galatia, Asia, Macedonia, or Achaia. Now Christianity had become so strong in them that Paul realized his work in that part of the world was finished. He began to think of a new area where he might repeat the same kind of missionary program. He wanted to evangelize territories where the gospel had never been heard before, having no desire to "build on another man's foundation" (Rom. 15:20). He decided to journey to Spain, and to set out as soon as he could. This journey would also give him a long-awaited opportunity to visit ROME on the way.

Before he could set out, however, an important task had to be completed. Paul had previously organized a relief fund among the Gentile churches to help poorer members of the Jerusalem church. Not only had he promised the leaders in Jerusalem to do such a thing, but he hoped it would strengthen the bond of fellowship among all the churches involved.

Before leaving, Paul arranged for a member of each of the contributing churches to carry that church's donation. Paul himself would go to Jerusalem with them, giving the Jerusalem Christians an opportunity to see some of their Gentile brethren face to face in addition to receiving their gifts. Some of Paul's hopes and misgivings about the trip are expressed in Romans 15:25-32. His misgivings were well founded.

A few days after his arrival in Jerusalem, Paul was attacked by a mob in the area of the Temple. He was rescued by a detachment of Roman soldiers and kept in custody at the Roman governor's headquarters in Caesarea for the next two years. At the end of that period he exercised his privilege as a Roman citizen and appealed to Caesar in order to have his case transferred from the provincial governor's court in Judea to the emperor's tribunal in Rome. He was sent to Rome in the fall of A.D. 59. The great apostle spent a further two years in Rome under house arrest, waiting for his case to come up for hearing before the supreme tribunal.

Paul, the prisoner of Jesus Christ—The restrictions under which Paul lived in Rome should have held back his efforts to proclaim the gospel, but just the opposite actually happened. These restrictions, by his own testimony, "actually turned out for the furtherance of the gospel" (Phil. 1:12). Although he was confined to his lodgings, handcuffed to one of the soldiers who guarded him in four-hour shifts, he was free to receive visitors and talk to them about the gospel. The soldiers who guarded him and the officials in charge of presenting his case before the emperor were left in no doubt about the reason for his being in Rome. The gospel actually became a topic of discussion. This encouraged the Christians in Rome to bear more open witness to their faith, allowing the saving message to be proclaimed more fearlessly in Rome than ever before "and in this," said Paul, "I rejoice" (Phil. 1:18).

From Rome, Paul was able to correspond with friends in other parts of the Roman Empire. Visitors from those parts came to see him, bringing news of their churches. These visitors included EPAPHRODITUS from Philippi and EPAPHRAS from Colossae. From Colossae, too, Paul received an unexpected visitor, ONESIMUS, the slave of his friend PHILEMON. He sent Onesimus back to his master with a letter commending him "no longer as a slave but...as a beloved brother" (Philem. 16).

The letters of Philippi and Colossae were sent in response to the news brought by Epaphroditus and Epaphras, respectively. At the same time as the letter to Colossae, Paul sent a letter, which has been lost, to Laodicea and a more general letter which we now know as Ephesians. The Roman captivity became a very fruitful period for Paul and his ministry.

We have very little information about the rest of Paul's career. We do not know the outcome of his trial before Caesar. He was probably discharged and enjoyed a further period of liberty. It is not known whether he ever preached the gospel in Spain.

It is traditionally believed that Paul's condemnation and execution occurred during the persecution of Christians under the Roman Emperor NERO. The probable site of his execution may still be seen at Tre Fontane on the Ostain Road. There is no reason to doubt the place of his burial marked near the Basilica of St. Paul. There, beneath the high altar, is a stone inscription going back to at least the fourth century: "To Paul, Apostle and Martyr."

The Teaching of Paul. Paul is the most influential teacher of Christianity. More than any other disciple or apostle, Paul was given the opportunity to set forth and explain the revelations of Jesus Christ. Because Paul was called to teach Gentiles rather than Jews, he was in the unique position of confronting and answering problems which could only be presented by those completely unfamiliar with Jewish traditions. Several themes come through in his writings.

Christ, the Son of God—Paul knew that the one who appeared to him on the Damascus Road was the risen Christ. "Last of all He was seen by me also," he says (1 Cor. 15:8), counting this as the last of Christ's appearances.

Paul seems to have entertained no doubt of the validity of the appearance or of the words, "I am Jesus" (Acts 9:5). Both the appearance and the words validated themselves in his later life. His whole Christian outlook on the world, like the gospel which he preached, stemmed from that "revelation of Jesus Christ" (Gal. 1:12).

Christ was, in a unique sense, the Son of God. Other human beings became sons and daughters of God through their faith-union with Christ and their reception of the Spirit of Christ. From this point of view the Spirit was "the Spirit of adoption," enabling them to address God spontaneously as "Abba, Father" (Rom. 8:15).

Another token of the indwelling Spirit was giving Jesus the designation "Lord": "No one can say that Jesus is Lord except by the Holy Spirit" (1 Cor. 12:3). This designation is given by Paul to Jesus in the highest sense possible. It was bestowed on Jesus by God Himself when He rose to supremacy over the universe after His humiliation and death on the cross.

One striking designation which Paul gives to Christ—"the image of God" (2 Cor. 4:4) or "the image of the invisible God" (Col. 1:15)—appears to be closely associated with his conversion experience. Paul emphasizes the heavenly light which was such a memorable feature of that experience. Paul

Modern Antalya, the port site for the city of Perga. Paul and Barnabas stopped at Perga during the apostle's first missionary journey (Acts 13:13-15).

speaks of the minds of unbelievers being darkened to keep them from seeing "the light of the gospel of the glory of Christ, who is the image of God" (2 Cor. 4:4). This suggests that when "the glory of that light" (Acts 22:11) dispelled the darkness from Paul's own mind, he recognized the one who appeared to him as being the very image of God.

Christ is presented by Paul as the one "through whom are all things, and through whom we live" (1 Cor. 8:6), and in whom, through whom, and for whom "all things were created" (Col. 1:16).

Displacement of the law—After his conversion Paul said, "To me, to live is Christ" (Phil. 1:21). Before his conversion he might well have said, "To me, to live is law." In his mind he had judged Christ according to the Jewish law, finding Him condemned by it. Since the law pronounced a curse on one who was hanged on a tree (Deut. 21:23; Gal. 3:13), Paul took the side of the law and agreed that both Christ and His people were accursed.

After his conversion, Paul recognized the continuing validity of the Scripture which declared the hanged man to be accursed by God, but now he understood it differently. If Christ, the Son of God, subjected Himself to the curse pronounced by the law, another look at the law was called for. The law could not provide anyone with righteous standing before God, however carefully he kept it. Paul knew that his life under the law stood condemned in the light of his Damascus–Road experience. It was not the law in itself that was defective, because it was God's law. It was instead the people with which the law had to work who were defective.

The righteous standing which the law could not provide was conferred on believers through their faith in Christ. That righteous standing was followed by a righteous life. In one tightly packed sentence Paul declared that God has done what the law, weakened by the flesh, could not do, "sending His own Son in the likeness of sinful flesh, on account of sin: He condemned sin in the flesh, that the righteous requirement of the law might be fulfilled in us who do not walk according to the flesh but according to the Spirit" (Rom. 8:3-4).

The law could lead neither to a righteous standing before God nor to a righteous life. Paul, while faithfully keeping the law, was condemned before God rather than justified. His life was not righteous but was sinful because he "persecuted the church of God" (1 Cor. 15:9). This situation radically changed when Paul believed in Christ and knew himself to "be found in Him, not having my own righteousness, which is from the law, but that which is through faith in Christ, the righteousness which is from God by faith" (Phil. 3:9).

Christ, then, "is the end of the law for righteousness to everyone who believes" (Rom. 10:4). The word "end" is ambiguous: it may mean "goal" or "completion." As the law revealed the character and will of God, it pointed to Christ as the goal. He was the fulfillment of all the divine revelation that had preceded Him: "All the promises of God in Him are Yes" (2 Cor. 1:20). But when the law came to be regarded as the way of salvation or the rule of life, Christ put an end to it. The law pronounced a curse on those who failed to keep it; Christ redeemed His people from that curse by undergoing it Himself. He exhausted the curse in His own person through His death.

According to Paul, the law was a temporary provision introduced by God to bring latent sin into the open. When they broke its individual commands, men and women would realize their utter dependence on divine grace. Centuries before the law was given, God promised Abraham that through him and his offspring all nations would be blessed. This promise was granted in response to Abraham's faith in God. The later giving of the law did not affect the validity of the promise. Instead, the promise was fulfilled in Christ, who replaced the law.

The law had been given to the nation of Israel only, providing a privilege which set it apart from other nations. God's original promise embraced all nations and justified Paul's presentation of the gospel to Gentiles as well as Jews. The promise had wide implications: "Christ has redeemed us from the curse of the law...that the blessing of Abraham might come upon the Gentiles in Christ Jesus, that we might receive the promise of the Spirit through faith" (Gal. 3:13–14).

The age of the Spirit—Those who believe God as Abraham did are not only justified by faith but also receive the Holy Spirit. The blessing promised to Abraham, secured through the redemptive work of Christ, is identified with the gift of the Spirit. The age of the Spirit has replaced the age of law.

It is common teaching in the New Testament that the age of the Spirit followed the completion of Christ's work on earth. Paul presents this teaching with his own emphasis. His negative evaluation of the place of law in Christian life naturally caused others to ask how ethical and moral standards were to be maintained. Paul answered that the Spirit supplied a more effective power for holy living than the law could ever supply. The law imposed bondage but "where the Spirit of the Lord is, there is liberty" (2 Cor. 3:17). The law told people what to do, but could provide neither the will nor the power to do it; the Spirit, operating within the believer's life, can provide both the will and the power.

The Spirit is called not only the Spirit of God but also the Spirit of Christ. He is the Spirit who dwelled within Christ during His earthly ministry, empowering Him to accomplish merciful works and to teach wisdom and grace. The qualities which characterized Christ are reproduced by His Spirit in His people: "love, joy, peace, longsuffering, kindness, goodness, faithfulness, gentleness, self-control" (Gal. 5:22–23).

John the Baptist predicted that Christ would baptize men and women with the Holy Spirit (Matt. 3:11; Mark 1:8; Luke 3:16). The New Testament teaches that this prediction was fulfilled with the coming of the Holy Spirit at Pentecost (Acts 2:2–12). Paul accepted this teaching about baptism with the Spirit, but linked it with his teaching about the church as the body of Christ. "For by one Spirit," he wrote to his converts in Corinth, "we were all baptized into one body—whether Jews or Greeks, whether slaves or free" (1 Cor. 12:13).

In various ways Paul views the present indwelling of the Spirit as an anticipation of the coming glory. The Spirit's work in the lives of Christ's people differs in degree, but not in kind, from their full sharing of Christ's glory at His advent. It is through the work of the Spirit that they, "beholding...the glory of the Lord, are being transformed into the same image from glory to glory" (2 Cor. 3:18).

The Spirit is referred to by Paul as the one who identifies the people of God to secure them "for the day of redemption" (Eph. 4:30), as the "firstfruits" of the coming glory (Rom. 8:23), as the "deposit," "guarantee," or initial down-payment of the resurrection life which is their assured heritage (2 Cor. 1:22; 5:5).

The body of Christ—Paul is the only New Testament writer who speaks of the church as a body. The members of the church, he suggests, are as interdependent as the various parts of the human body, each making its contribution in harmony with the others for the good of the whole. Just as a body functions best when all the parts follow the direction of the head, the church best fulfills its purpose on earth when all the members are subject to the direction of Christ. He is, by divine appointment, "head over all things to the church, which is His body" (Eph. 1:22–23). The Spirit of Christ not only dwells within each member but also dwells within the church as a whole, continually giving His life to the entire body together. The body cannot be thought of without the Spirit. "There is one body and one Spirit," and when the members show one another the love of God they "keep the unity of the Spirit in the bond of peace" (Eph. 4:3–4).

The source of Paul's concept of the church as the body of Christ has been long debated. One source

This landmark known as the tomb of Caecilia Metella (wife of a Roman official) stood on the Appian Way when Paul went to Rome to appear before Nero (Acts 28:15,16).

Photo by Howard Vos

may have been the Old Testament principle of "corporate personality"—the principle of regarding a community, nation, or tribe as a person to the point where it is named and described as if it were an individual. God said to Pharaoh through Moses, "Israel is My Son, My firstborn...Let My son go that he may serve Me" (Ex. 4:22–23).

Perhaps the most satisfactory source of Paul's concept can be found in the words of the risen Christ who appeared to him on the Damascus Road: "Why are you persecuting me?" (Acts 9:4). Paul did not think he was persecuting Jesus, who was beyond his direct reach. But that is exactly what he was doing when he persecuted Jesus' followers. When any part of the body is hurt, it is the head that complains. Jesus' words may have sown the seed of that doctrine in Paul's mind. The Lord told Ananias of Damascus that He would show Paul "how many things he must suffer for My name's sake" (Acts 9:16). Paul later echoed this in his statement, "If one member suffers, all the members suffer with it" (1 Cor. 12:26).

The first time Paul wrote of this subject (1 Cor. 12:12–27), his purpose was to impress on his readers the fact that, as Christians, they have mutual duties and common interests which must not be neglected. When he next expounded on it (Rom. 12:4–8), he wrote of the variety of service rendered by the various members of the church. In accordance with their respective gifts, all members build up the one body to which they belong. The health of the whole body depends on the harmonious cooperation of the parts.

In his later letters, Paul dealt with the relation which the church, as the body of Christ, bears to Christ as head of the body. The well-being of the body depends on its being completely under the control of the head. It is from Christ, as head of the church, that "all the body, nourished and knit together by joints and ligaments, grows with the increase which is from God" (Col. 2:19).

Paul's doctrine of the church as the body of Christ is closely bound up with his description of believers as being "in Christ" at the same time as Christ is in them. They are in Him as members of His body, having been "baptized into Christ" (Gal. 3:27). He is in them because it is His risen life that animates them. Jesus once used another organic analogy when He depicted Himself as "the true vine" and His disciples as the branches (John 15:1–6). The relationship is similar to that between the head and the body. The branches are in the vine and the vine at the same time is in the branches.

Eschatology—Eschatology is the teaching about things to come, especially things to come at the end times.

Paul originally held the views of eschatology which were taught in the Pharisaic schools. When Paul became a Christian, he found no need to abandon the eschatological teaching which he had received at the feet of Gamaliel. But his experience of Christ did bring about some important modifications of his views.

The distinction between the present age and the age to come was basic to this teaching. The present age was subject to evil influences which affected the lives and actions of men and women. The God of righteousness and truth, however, was in control of the situation. One day He would bring in a new age from which evil would be banished.

The Pharisees taught that the end of the present age and beginning of the new age would be marked by the resurrection of the dead. Whether all the dead would be raised or only the righteous among them was a matter of debate. In Acts 24:15 Paul stated before the governor, Felix, that he shared the hope "that there will be a resurrection of the dead, both of the just and the unjust." In his letters he spoke only of the resurrection of believers in Christ, perhaps because it was to such people that his letters were written.

An important question was the relation of this framework to the messianic hope. When would the Messiah, the expected ruler of David's line, establish his kingdom? His kingdom might mark the closing phase of the present age; it might be set up with the inauguration of the age to come; or it might occupy a phase between the two ages. There was no general agreement on this question. Another question on which there was no general agreement concerned the extent to which the Messiah would revoke or replace the law of Moses.

When Paul was confronted with the risen Christ on the Damascus Road, he realized that the Messiah had come and that in Him the resurrection had begun to take place. Having been raised from the dead, Christ had now entered upon His reign. The age of the Spirit for His people on earth coincided with the reign of Christ in His place of exaltation in the presence of God. There "He must reign till He has put all enemies under His feet" (1 Cor. 15:25). The present age had not yet come to an end, because men and women, and especially the people of Christ, still lived on earth in mortal bodies. But the resurrection age had already begun, because Christ had been raised.

The people of Christ, while living temporarily in the present age, belong spiritually to the new age which has been inaugurated. The benefits of this new age are already made good to them by the Spirit. The last of the enemies which are to be subdued by Christ is death. The destruction of death will coincide with the resurrection of the people of Christ. Paul wrote, "Each one in his own order: Christ the firstfruits, afterward those who are Christ's at His coming" (1 Cor. 15:23). The eternal kingdom of God will be consummated at that time.

The resurrection of the people of Christ, then, takes place at His coming again. In one of his earliest letters Paul said that, when Christ comes, "the dead in Christ will rise first. Then we who are alive and remain shall be caught up together with them in the clouds to meet the Lord in the air. And thus we shall always be with the Lord" (1 Thess. 4:16–17).

Further details are provided in 1 Corinthians

15:42–57. When the last trumpet announces the Second Coming of Christ, the dead will be raised in a "spiritual body" replacing the mortal body which they wore on earth. Those believers who are still alive at the time will undergo a similar change to fit them for the new conditions. These new conditions, the eternal kingdom of God, are something which "flesh and blood cannot inherit"; they make up an imperishable realm which cannot accommodate the perishable bodies of this present life (1 Cor. 15:50).

The assurance that the faithful departed would be present at the Second Coming of Christ was a great comfort to Christians whose friends and relatives had died. But the question of their mode of existence between death and the Second Coming remained to be answered. Paul's clearest answer to this question was given shortly after a crisis in which he thought he faced certain death (2 Cor. 1:8–11).

Paul answered that to be "absent from the body" is to be "present with the Lord" (2 Cor. 5:8). Whatever provision is required for believers to enjoy the same communion with Christ after death as they enjoyed before death will certainly be supplied (2 Cor. 5:1–10). Or, as he put it when the outcome of his trial before Caesar was uncertain, "To live is Christ, and to die is gain," for to die would mean to "be with Christ, which is far better" (Phil. 1:21, 23).

The church as a whole and its members as individuals could look forward to a consummation of glory at the Second Coming of Christ. But the glory is not for them alone. In a vivid passage, Paul describes how "the creation eagerly waits for the revealing of the sons of God" (Rom. 8:19). This will liberate it from the change and decay to which it is subject at present and allow it to obtain "the glorious liberty of the children of God" (Rom. 8:21). In Genesis 3:17–19 man's first disobedience brought a curse on the earth. Paul looked forward to the removal of that curse and its replacement by the glory provided by the obedience of Christ, the "second Man" (1 Cor. 15:47).

This prospect is integrated into Paul's message, which is above all a message of reconciliation. It tells how God "reconciled us to Himself through Jesus Christ" (2 Cor. 5:18) and calls on people to "be reconciled to God" (2 Cor. 5:20). It proclaims God's purpose through Christ "to reconcile all things to Himself,…whether things on earth or things in heaven, having made peace through the blood of His cross" (Col. 1:20).

Paul and the Message of Jesus. Some critics charge that Paul corrupted the original "simple" message of Jesus by transforming it into a theological structure. But the truth is completely otherwise. No one in the apostolic age had a surer insight into Jesus' message than Paul.

A shift in perspective between the ministry of Jesus and the ministry of Paul must be recognized. During His own ministry Jesus was the preacher; in the ministry of Paul He was the one being preached. The gospels record the works and words of the earthly Jesus; in Paul's preaching Jesus, once crucified, has been exalted as the heavenly Lord. Jesus' earthly ministry was confined almost entirely to the Jewish people; Paul was preeminently the apostle to the Gentiles. Paul's Gentile hearers required that the message be presented in a different vocabulary from that which Jesus used in Galilee and Judea.

The gospel of Jesus and the gospel preached by Paul are not two gospels but one—a gospel specifically addressed to sinners. Paul, like Jesus, brought good news to outsiders. This was the assurance that in God's sight they were not outsiders, but men and women whom He lovingly accepted. In the ministry of Jesus, the outsiders were the social outcasts

Ruins of the judgment seat in the marketplace at Corinth, where Paul appeared before the Roman official Gallio (Acts 18:12-17).
Photo by Howard Vos

of Israel. In the ministry of Paul the outsiders were Gentiles. The principle was the same, although its application was different.

Paul's achievement was to communicate to the Greco–Roman world, in terms which it could understand, the good news which Jesus announced in His teaching, action, and death. Paul did not have before him the gospels as we know them, but he knew the main lines of Jesus' teaching, especially parts of the Sermon on the Mount. This teaching was passed orally among the followers of Jesus before it circulated in written form. If Jesus summed up the law of God in the two great commandments of love toward God and love toward one's neighbor, Paul echoed Him: "All the law is fulfilled in one word, even in this: 'You shall love your neighbor as yourself' " (Gal. 5:14; also Rom. 13:9).

Paul's Legacy. Paul was a controversial figure in his lifetime, even within the Christian movement. He had many opponents who disagreed with his interpretation of the message of Jesus. In the closing years of his life, when imprisonment prevented him from moving about freely, Paul's opponents were able to make headway with their rival interpretations. Even though Asia had been Paul's most fruitful mission field, at the end of his life he wrote, "All those in Asia have turned away from me" (2 Tim. 1:15).

In the following generation, however, there was a resurgence of feeling in Paul's favor. His opponents were largely discredited and disabled by the dispersal of the church of that city shortly before the destruction of Jerusalem in A.D. 70. Throughout most of the church Paul became a venerated figure. His letters, together with the gospels, became the foundation of the Christian movement.

Paul's liberating message has proved its vitality throughout the centuries. Repeatedly, when the Christian faith has been in danger of being shackled by legalism or tradition, Paul's message has allowed the gospel to set man free.

The relevance of Paul's teaching for human life today may be brought out in a summary of four of his leading themes:

1. True religion is not a matter of rules and regulations. God does not deal with men and women like an accountant, but He accepts them freely when they respond to His love. He implants the Spirit of Christ in their hearts so they may extend His love to others.

2. In Christ men and women have come of age. God does not keep His people on puppet strings but liberates them to live as His responsible sons and daughters.

3. People matter more than things, principles, and causes. The highest of principles and the best of causes exist only for the sake of people. Personal liberty itself is abused if it is exercised against the personal well–being of others.

4. Discrimination on the ground of race, religion, class, or sex is an offense against God and humanity alike.

PAULUS, SERGIUS (see SERGIUS PAULUS).

PAVEMENT, THE — the official place in Jerusalem where Pilate passed sentence on Jesus (John 19:13; Stone Pavement, NIV). Archaeologist L. H. Vincent identified The Pavement with a splendid Roman pavement uncovered when an extensive area of the Tower of ANTONIA was excavated. Also see GABBATHA.

PAVILION — any kind of temporary shelter, such as a tent, tabernacle, or booth (2 Kin. 16:18; Ps. 27:5; 31:20; Jer. 43:10). Psalm 31:20 refers to the pavilion of God in which the righteous are sheltered. But usually the Hebrew word *sukkah* refers to a tent or similar kind of shelter. Leviticus 23:42 mentions booths, or dwellings made of branches, in which the Jews lived during the Feast of Tabernacles.

PE [pay] — the 17th letter of the Hebrew alphabet, used as a heading over Psalm 119:129–136. In the original Hebrew language, every line of these eight verses began with the letter pe. Also see ACROSTIC.

PEACE — a word with several different meanings in the Old and New Testaments.

The Old Testament meaning of peace was completeness, soundness, and well–being of the total person. This peace was considered God–given, obtained by following the Law (Ps. 119:165). Peace sometimes had a physical meaning, suggesting security (Ps. 4:8), contentment (Is. 26:3), prosperity (Ps. 122:6–7) and the absence of war (1 Sam. 7:14). The traditional Jewish greeting, *shalom*, was a wish for peace.

In the New Testament, peace often refers to the inner tranquility and poise of the Christian whose trust is in God through Christ. This understanding was originally expressed in the Old Testament writings about the coming MESSIAH (Is. 9:6–7). The peace that Jesus Christ spoke of was a combination of hope, trust, and quiet in the mind and soul, brought about by a reconciliation with God. Such peace was proclaimed by the host of angels at Christ's birth (Luke 2:14), and by Christ Himself in His SERMON ON THE MOUNT (Matt. 5:9) and during His ministry. He also taught about this kind of peace at the Lord's Supper, shortly before His death (John 14:27).

The apostle Paul later wrote that such peace and spiritual blessedness was a direct result of faith in Christ (Rom. 5:1).

PEACE OFFERING (see SACRIFICIAL OFFERINGS).

PEACOCK (see ANIMALS OF THE BIBLE).

PEARL (see JEWELS AND PRECIOUS STONES).

PECULIAR —an archaic term used by the KJV to describe Israel, God's "special treasure" (Ex. 19:5; Deut. 14:2) — the valuable property or costly possession of their redeemer God.

PEDAHEL [PED uh hel] (*God delivers*) — a leader of the tribe of Naphtali who assisted Joshua in dividing the land of Canaan (Num. 34:28).

PEDAHZUR [pih DAH zur] (*the Rock delivers*) — the father of Gamaliel (Num. 1:10; 7:54).

PEDAIAH [pih DAY uh] (*Jehovah delivers*) — the name of seven men in the Old Testament:
1. Father of Zebudah (2 Kin. 23:36).
2. A descendant of Jeconiah (1 Chr. 3:18–19) and the father of Zerubbabel (1 Chr. 3:19).
3. Father of Joel (1 Chr. 27:20).
4. A son of Parosh (Neh. 3:25). Pedaiah helped repair the wall of Jerusalem after the Captivity.
5. A Levite who stood with Ezra when the Book of the Law was read to the people (Neh. 8:4).
6. A son of Kolaiah, of the tribe of Benjamin (Neh. 11:7).
7. A treasurer of the Temple in Nehemiah's time (Neh. 13:13).

PEG — a bronze tent pin driven into the ground to secure the cords of the tabernacle court (Ex. 27:19; Num. 3:37; 4:32). JAEL killed Sisera with a tent peg and a hammer (Judg. 4:21–22; 5:26).

PEKAH [PEE kuh] (*God has opened the eyes*) — the son of Remaliah and 18th king of Israel (2 Kin. 15:25–31; 2 Chr. 28:5–15). Pekah became king after he assassinated King Pekahiah. Pekah continued to lead Israel in the idolatrous ways of Jeroboam (2 Kin. 15:28).

Pekah took the throne at the time when Tiglath-Pileser III, king of Assyria, was advancing toward Israel. To resist this threat, Pekah formed an alliance with Rezin, king of Syria. He also hoped to enlist the sister Jewish nation of Judah in the alliance. Under the counsel of the prophet Isaiah, however, Judah's kings, Jotham and later Ahaz, refused. Pekah and Rezin attempted to enlist Judah by force, marching first against Jerusalem. They were unsuccessful, and so they divided their armies.

Rezin successfully captured Elath, and Pekah slew thousands in the districts near Jericho, taking many prisoners into Samaria. Later, these prisoners were returned to Jericho upon the advice of the prophet Oded. Pekah probably was unaware that he was God's instrument to punish Judah (2 Chr. 28:5–6).

As Tiglath-Pileser III of Assyria advanced, King Ahaz of Judah met him to pay tribute and ask his help against Syria and Israel (2 Kin. 16:10). Assyria planned to march against Syria, and so Damascus was taken and Rezin was killed. The Assyrians also invaded northern Israel, with city after city taken and their inhabitants deported to Assyria. Through the Assyrian army God brought His judgment on Israel and Syria, even as the prophet Isaiah had warned (Is. 7:8–9).

Pekah was left with a stricken nation, over half of which had been plundered and stripped of its inhabitants. Soon Hoshea, son of Elah, conspired against Pekah and assassinated him. However, in his own writings Tiglath-Pileser III claimed that he was the power that placed Hoshea on the throne of Israel, possibly indicating he was a force behind the conspiracy. Pekah's dates as king of Israel are usually given as 740–732 B.C.

PEKAHIAH [pek uh HIGH uh] (*Jehovah has opened*) — a son of Menahem and the 17th king of Israel (2 Kin. 15:22–26). Pekahiah assumed the throne after his father's death. He was an evil king who continued the idolatrous worship first introduced by King Jeroboam. After reigning only two years (about 742–740 B.C.), Pekahiah was killed by his military captain, PEKAH, and 50 Gileadites. Pekah then became king.

PEKOD [PEE kahd] (*visited by judgment*) — a minor Aramean tribe in eastern Babylonia. The prophet Jeremiah applied the name symbolically to the entire land of Babylonia (Jer. 50:21), indicating they would be judged by God.

PELAIAH [peh LIE yuh] (*Jehovah is wonderful*) — the name of three men in the Old Testament:
1. A son of Elioenai, descended from David through Shechaniah (1 Chr. 3:24).
2. A priest who explained the Law as Ezra read it to the people (Neh. 8:7).
3. A Levite who sealed the covenant after the Captivity (Neh. 10:10). He may be the same person as Pelaiah No. 2.

PELALIAH [pel uh LIGH uh] (*Jehovah has intervened*) —a priest whose grandson returned from the Captivity (Neh. 11:12).

PELATIAH [pel uh TIE uh] (*Jehovah sets free*) — the name of three or four men in the Old Testament:
1. A descendant of David (1 Chr. 3:21).
2. A captain of the Simeonites who destroyed the Amalekites who lived at Mount Seir during King Hezekiah's reign (1 Chr. 4:42).
3. A chief of the people who sealed the covenant after the Captivity (Neh. 10:22).
4. A son of Benaiah (Ezek. 11:1–13).

PELEG [PEE leg] (*division*) — a descendant of Noah through Shem and a son of Eber (Gen. 10:25). Peleg was an ancestor of Jesus (Luke. 3:35; Phalec, KJV). He was named Peleg (meaning "division"), because "in his days the earth was divided" (Gen. 10:25; 1 Chr. 1:19), probably referring to the scattering of Noah's descendants as God's judgment following the attempt to build the Tower of Babel (Gen. 11:8, 16–19).

PELET [PEE let] (*liberation*) — the name of two men in the Old Testament:
1. A son of Jahdai (1 Chr. 2:47).
2. A son of Azmaveth (1 Chr. 12:3).

PELETH [PEE leth] (*swiftness*) — the name of two men in the Old Testament:
1. Father of On (Num. 16:1).
2. A son of Jonathan (1 Chr. 2:33).

PELETHITES [PEE leth ights] (meaning unknown) — a select company of soldiers who, along with the CHERETHITES, formed David's bodyguard (2 Sam.

8:18; 15:18). Some scholars believe the Pelethites and the Cherethites refer to Philistines and Cretans, respectively.

PELICAN (see ANIMALS OF THE BIBLE).

PELLA [PEL uh] — a city of the DECAPOLIS in TRANSJORDAN. Pella is not mentioned in the Bible, but it is referred to by the Jewish historian Josephus as one of the "Ten Cities," which the Romans called *Decapolis* (Matt. 4:25; Mark 5:20; 7:31).

PELONITE [PEL uh night] — a designation for Helez (1 Chr. 11:27) and Ahijah (1 Chr. 11:36), two of David's mighty men. Helez is also called the PALTITE (2 Sam. 23:26), or a native of Beth Pelet.

PEN (see WRITING).

PENDANT — an ornament suspended from a necklace. Pendants were among the articles of gold captured from the Midianites by Gideon (Judg. 8:26; collars, KJV). Gold pendants, resembling medallions, have been excavated at Shechem. Pendants of various shapes have been found at Megiddo. Also see JEWELRY.

PENIEL [pih NIGH uhl] — a form of PENUEL.

PENINNAH [pih NIN uh] (*pearl*) — a wife of Elkanah (1 Sam. 1:2, 4). Peninnah taunted Hannah, Elkanah's other wife, because Peninnah had given birth to sons and daughters while Hannah had remained barren. When Hannah prayed for a child, the Lord answered her prayer by sending Samuel.

PENKNIFE (see SCRIBE'S KNIFE).

PENTATEUCH [PIN tuh tuke] — a Greek term meaning "five-volumed" which refers to the first five books of the Old Testament. The Jews traditionally refer to this collection as "the Book of the Law," or simply "the Law." Another word for this collection, Torah, apparently means "instruction, teaching, or doctrine." It describes such basic sections of the Pentateuch as Exodus, Leviticus, and Deuteronomy.

This ancient division of the Law into five sections is supported by the SEPTUAGINT, a third-century B.C. translation of the Hebrew Old Testament into Greek, and also by the SAMARITAN PENTATEUCH, which is even earlier. The five books together present a history of humanity from creation to the death of Moses, with particular attention to the development of the Hebrew people. The activity of God receives special emphasis throughout, and the Pentateuch reveals a great deal about God's nature and His purposes for mankind.

The Pentateuch is generally divided into six major sections: (1) the creation of the world and its inhabitants (Genesis 1—11); (2) the period from Abraham to Joseph (Genesis 12—50); (3) Moses and the departure of the Israelites from Egypt (Exodus 1—18); (4) God's revelation at Sinai (Exodus 19—Numbers 10); (5) the wilderness wanderings (Numbers 11—36); and (6) the addresses of Moses (Deuteronomy 1—34).

From the time it was written, the Pentateuch was consistently accepted as the work of Moses. His specific writing or compiling activity is mentioned in the Pentateuch (Ex. 17:14; 24:4; 34:27), while in the post–exilic writings the Law, or Torah, was often attributed directly to Moses (Neh. 8:1; 2 Chr. 25:4; 35:12). This tradition was supported by Christ in New Testament times (Mark 12:26; John 7:23).

The Pentateuch was also called the Law of the Lord (2 Chr. 31:3; Luke 2:23–24) and "the Book of the Law of God" (Neh. 8:18). The word book should not be understood in its modern sense, for several different writing materials were used by Old Testament SCRIBES, including papyrus and leather scrolls or sheets, pieces of broken pottery, clay tablets, and stone. The word book has two important usages in connection with the Law. First, it indicates that the material referred to was in written form at an early period. Second, it shows the combination of divine authorship and human transmission that gave the Law its supreme authority and made it *The Book* for the ancient Hebrews.

The Mosaic authorship of the Pentateuch was accepted without question for centuries by both Jews and Christians. Occasionally, the account of Moses' death (Deut. 34:5–8) was questioned, but in the Jewish TALMUD, a collection of rabbinical laws and interpretations of the Torah, the section was said to have been written by Joshua. In the Middle Ages Jewish and Christian scholars began to point to supposed contradictions and insertions in the Law, some of the latter being credited to Ezra.

In spite of these objections, most people believed unquestioningly in Moses as the author; but criticism took on a new appearance in 1753 with a theory by Jean Astruc, a French physician, that Moses had used two principal literary sources from which he composed the Book of Genesis: one contained the divine name Elohim and the other contained the divine name Jehovah (or Yahweh).

With the expansion of this suggestion by later authors came the increasing abandonment of belief in Mosaic authorship, and support for the view that the Pentateuch was compiled by unknown editors from a number of documents. It became common to attribute sections of the Pentateuch to late periods in Israel's history. Even the main documents from which the Pentateuch had supposedly been compiled were assigned to periods long after the time of Moses.

In the 19th century the Book of Deuteronomy began to be regarded as the law-scroll found in the time of Joshua (2 Kin. 22:8–10), and written about that period, according to many scholars.

While more conservative thinkers rejected these conclusions, the liberal humanism of the day pushed forward with its suppositions. Allied with the views of organic evolutionists, it presented its opinions about the authorship of Genesis as "scientific." Actually, these liberal scholars were using procedures that were the exact opposite of true scientific method. But this did not prevent them from making pronouncements that amounted to rewriting history. Thus, all priestly materials in the Pentateuch were assigned to one main documentary source and regarded as late rather than early.

According to the liberal view, the tabernacle could no longer be dated in the days of Moses. It was regarded instead as a much later invention, based on the design of the Jerusalem Temple, that had been put back into the Mosaic period by an anonymous compiler or editor. Israelite religion was interpreted in evolutionary terms as originating in the worship of spirits in nature, then advancing slowly from simple family sacrifices to the high view of God as the one and only true God.

This type of approach was aided by the 19th century emphasis on evolution. The liberal view found its fullest development in the supposition that the Pentateuch was compiled from four principal documents, none of which was in writing before about 850 B.C. This theory of composition, popularized by Julius Wellhausen in 1878, is still held by liberal scholars, but with slight changes in emphasis because of the pressure of more recent discoveries.

This view of the compilation of the Pentateuch has had its critics at every stage. Some of the presuppositions of the liberal position are incorrect. One example is the notion that writing was only invented about the time of David (about 1000 B.C.). Evidence to the contrary already existed in Wellhausen's day, but it was ignored. Most recently, the EBLA Tablet discoveries show that a sophisticated language was in use in the ancient world about 2500 B.C.

It is now known that all priestly pronouncements dealing with social organization in the ancient world are always early rather than late, because priests were originally responsible for such matters. Furthermore, exhaustive comparative studies have shown that no other composition of the ancient Near East was assembled in the manner that liberal scholars claimed was the case with the Pentateuch. Archaeological and linguistic studies have confirmed many old customs recorded in the Pentateuch. These discoveries have provided an excellent background against which we can understand the Law of Moses.

To date, no articles that would prove the existence of such persons as Abraham, Isaac, and Jacob have been recovered. But if the traditions about the nature and location of the cave of Machpelah (Gen. 23:17) are correct, we know the actual burial place of Abraham, Sarah, Isaac, Rebekah, and Jacob.

Studies in Genesis have shown that the book was compiled from genuine literary sources. But these are vastly different from those imagined by liberal scholarship. Generally speaking, the liberal view has failed to take account of ancient methods of compiling and transmitting information. Liberal scholars have supposed that Western editorial methods can be applied equally well to Near Eastern compositions, which is simply not true.

Whereas the 19th–century critics relied heavily upon the handing down of material by word of mouth, subsequent studies have shown that anything of importance in the ancient world was written down when it happened or shortly afterward. Furthermore, this record was quite independent of any verbal accounts passed on to later generations. Not all written or spoken material survived, of course; but enough did to provide us with the Pentateuch, as well as other Scriptures.

Finally, any suggestion that the five books of Moses are basically fraudulent in nature, not actually having been compiled or written by Moses, is contrary to Jewish tradition, as well as the nature of God as revealed in the Torah.

The five books of the Pentateuch can be described as follows:

Genesis. This "book of beginnings" contains very ancient material, describing man's place in God's creation and the unfolding of human history. It begins with an account of how the universe came into existence (1:1—2:4), followed by narratives about Adam and Eve and their sin of disobedience (2:5—3:24). The descendants of Adam are described (4:1—5:32), and after this the reasons for a disastrous flood and its consequences (6:1—9:29). Nations spread across the Near East after the Flood (10:1—11:32), and Abraham became prominent after obeying God's call (12:1—25:11). Thereafter the narratives continue with Ishmael, Isaac, and Jacob (25:12—36:43), concluding with the story of Joseph's career (37:1—50:26).

Genesis is important for its theology of creation, sin, and the divine plan of salvation because it provides answers about these matters. If Scripture did not begin in this way, New Testament theology would have little foundation in history. Genesis deals with real people. Near Eastern archaeological discoveries provide an important background to the narratives which describe their activities. The covenants between God and persons such as Noah and Abraham point forward to the covenant under Moses at Mount Sinai. They also point to the new covenant in Jesus Christ.

No author is named for the Book of Genesis, although it has always been regarded as a cornerstone of the Law, and therefore probably written by Moses. In contrast to the artificial sources proposed by liberal criticism, genuine blocks of source material can be recognized in the narratives. Eleven such units can be recovered by stopping at the phrase, "These are the generations [that is, family histories] of" and regarding that as the conclusion of a section rather than as a heading. These units are written according to the pattern of ancient Mesopotamian writings.

Genesis was apparently compiled by placing these units end-to-end and adding the stories of Joseph. Most probably the latter were written by Moses, who attached them to the ancient narratives and transferred the completed Book of Genesis to a leather scroll. There is no actual proof that the book was assembled in this manner, but it seems most probable.

Exodus. This book deals with the miracle of Israel's deliverance from Egypt and with God's covenant relationship with the Israelites at Mount Sinai. Preliminaries to the departure from Egypt (Ex. 1:1—4:28) are followed by the circumstances leading up to the Exodus, including the ten PLAGUES OF EGYPT and the celebrating of the first PASSOVER (4:29—12:36). The deliverance from Egypt and the subsequent journey to Sinai (12:37—19:2) precede the giving of the Law of God through Moses (19:3—31:8), in spite of intervals of idolatry (32:1—33:23). A renewal of the covenant relationship is followed by narratives describing the construction of the tabernacle.

The Book of Exodus continues Hebrew history from the death of Joseph, showing how the sons of Jacob became a distinctive nation. The COVENANT was central to this event. It bound God and Israel in an agreement by which God undertook to provide for all His people's material needs, including a land in which to live, if they would worship Him alone as the one true God and live as a holy community. Central to the rules of the covenant were the Ten Commandments, which are still fundamental to any relationship with God. The tabernacle was a portable place of worship which was placed in the center of Israel's wilderness encampment, symbolizing God's presence in their midst.

Leviticus. This is a book for both priests and people. The priests were responsible for teaching the Law to the people, conducting sacrificial worship in the tabernacle according to the directions given by God, and ordering the life of the community. Because Israel was meant to live as a holy people (Ex. 19:6), Leviticus contained regulations for both the spiritual and material aspects of life. These rules can be divided into five sections: (1) sacrificial laws (Leviticus 1—7); (2) laws governing ordination (Leviticus 8—10); (3) laws about impurities (Leviticus 11—16); (4) laws about holiness (Leviticus 17—26); and (5) rules governing vows (Leviticus 27).

All this material was divinely revealed to the nation of Israel directly from God. No part of it has been adopted from any other nation. The Year of Jubilee legislation (Lev. 25:8-17) is unique in the Near East. Leviticus continues the narrative of Exodus, but it emphasizes the way in which God is to be worshiped and the manner in which His people are to live. Holiness must govern the community (Lev. 11:44); and this must be reflected by everyone, not just the priesthood.

Numbers. This book follows the lead given by Leviticus in emphasizing the holiness of Israel. All the various elements that make up the book bear upon this important concept. The book can be divided into three broad sections: (1) the departure from Sinai (1:1—11:11); (2) the journey to Kadesh (10:11—20:21); and (3) the journey from Kadesh to Moab (20:22—30:13). The holiness of the tabernacle is central, as is the important place that the Levites occupied (8:5-26) in relation to the Aaronic priesthood. The description of the wilderness wanderings shows how quickly divine blessing could

turn to severe judgment whenever God's commandments were broken.

The disobedience and idolatry of the Israelites is a sad theme in Numbers. Even Moses was not totally obedient to God. Although he brought Israel to Moab and within sight of the Promised Land, he was not privileged to lead the nation across the Jordan River. The book ends with the nation looking forward to the settlement of Canaan.

Deuteronomy. This book may be described as a covenant-renewal document that begins with a review of Israel's departure from Sinai (1:1—4:40); describes the religious foundation of the nation (4:44—26:19); reestablishes the covenant (27:1—30:20); and narrates the final days of Moses (31:1—34:12). In Deuteronomy Moses looks back upon God's blessing and provision while looking forward to the time when Israel will occupy the Promised Land.

The language of the book is noble oratory that glorifies the righteous and faithful God of Sinai and encourages the response of His people in obedience and faithfulness. The God revealed in Moses' addresses is not only the Judge of all the earth, but also the loving Father of mankind. Israel is reminded that the privileges of covenant relationship with Him also carry responsibilities. Moses predicts a dark future for the nation if it does not follow the covenant principles and remain faithful to God.

PENTATEUCH, SAMARITAN (see SAMARITAN PENTATEUCH).

PENTECOST, FEAST OF (see FEASTS AND FESTIVALS).

PENUEL [pih NOO uhl] *(face of God)* — the name of a place and two men in the Old Testament:

1. A place north of the River Jabbok where Jacob wrestled with "a Man" until daybreak. Hosea 12:4 calls the "man" an "Angel." Jacob called the place Penuel, "For I have seen God face to face" (Gen. 32:30). A city was built there later, not far to the east of Succoth. When Gideon and his band of 300 men pursued the Midianites, the people of Succoth and Penuel insulted Gideon, refusing to give supplies to his army. Gideon later killed the men of the city (Judg. 8:17). Penuel is about 65 kilometers (40 miles) northeast of Jerusalem. It is also called Peniel (Gen. 32:30).

2. A son of Hur and grandson of Judah (1 Chr. 4:4).

3. A son of Shashak, of the tribe of Benjamin (1 Chr. 8:25).

PEOPLE OF GOD — the Hebrew people or the nation of Israel; all people who are part of the COVENANT relationship which God has established with His chosen ones.

In the Old Testament, the nation of Israel is referred to as the people of God. The Hebrew people are the Lord's "special treasure" (Ex. 19:5), His "inheritance" (Deut. 4:20), His "servant" (Is. 48:20), His "son" (Ex. 4:22-23), His "sheep" (Ps. 95:7), and His "holy people" (Deut. 14:2). The concept of the

Photo by Howard Vos

Ruins of the walls and city gate at Perga, a city visited by Paul and Barnabas on their first missionary journey (Acts 13:13, 14).

people of God is closely related to the concept of ELECTION, which stresses the truth that Israel is God's possession because of His gracious choosing—not because of Israel's merit or worth. The phrase *the people of God* refers to the special relationship of Israel with Jehovah through His Covenant with Abraham (Gen. 12:1–3).

In the New Testament, the phrase *the people of God* is used occasionally to describe the "old Israel" (Heb. 1:25). But there is a definite transition to a new covenant and a new people of God, the church, who are now "His own special people" (Titus 2:14) and "a chosen generation, a royal priesthood, a holy nation, His own special people" (1 Pet. 2:9). Peter and Paul applied Old Testament passages describing Israel to the church.

The church, then, is seen as the new Israel, or true Israel, of God (Rom. 9:6; Gal. 6:16), the true seed of Abraham (Gal. 3:29), and the new people of God (2 Pet. 2:9). Each person who believes in the Lord Jesus Christ is chosen of God, set apart as an object of His covenant love and faithfulness.

PEOR [PEE ohr] (*the opening*) — the name of a mountain and a pagan god in the Old Testament:

1. A mountain near Mount Nebo, northeast of the Dead Sea, in the land of Moab. Balak took Balaam to the summit of Peor (Num. 23:28) to encourage Balaam to curse the Israelites.

2. A false god, more fully called Baal of Peor, which was worshiped by the Moabites. By the counsel of Balaam (Num. 31:16), the Israelites were enticed to worship this idol. Also see GODS, PAGAN.

PERAZIM [pih RAY zim] (*breaches*) — a mountain in central Palestine (Is. 28:21), also called BAAL PERAZIM.

PERDITION — destruction, ruin, or waste, especially through the eternal destruction brought upon the wicked by God (Heb. 10:39; 2 Pet. 3:7). Jesus contrasted the broad way that leads to life with the difficult way that leads to destruction (Matt. 7:13). The apostle Paul contrasted perdition with salvation (Phil. 1:28). The "desire to be rich" may lead one to "destruction and perdition" (1 Tim. 6:9). Peter speaks of "the day of judgment and perdition of ungodly men" (2 Pet. 3:7), a perishing far worse than those destroyed in the Flood.

The New Testament twice uses the phrase *the son of perdition:* once of Judas Iscariot (John 17:12) and once of "the man of sin [or lawlessness]," whom some scholars identify with the Antichrist (2 Thess. 2:3). The phrase portrays the progression of an evil character who produces ruin in others, and is headed toward final judgment (Rev. 17:8, 11). Perdition in this passage refers to a place of eternal punishment, the final state of the damned.

PEREA [peh REE ah] (*the land beyond*) — the Greek term for TRANSJORDAN (see Map 6, C–3). The name Perea does not occur in the New Testament (except in a variant reading of Luke 6:17), but it is used regularly by the Jewish historian Josephus to describe the area east of the Jordan River. The New Testament refers to this area by using the phrase *beyond the Jordan* (Matt. 4:25; Mark 3:8). Josephus described Perea as the region between the Jabbok and the Arnon rivers, east of the Jordan.

PERES [PEA rez] (*dissolved*) — one of the mysterious words that appeared in the handwriting on the wall in King Belshazzar's palace in Babylon (Dan. 5:28). Daniel interpreted this word to mean that Belshazzar's kingdom had been divided (*peres*) and given to the Medes and Persians. Also see MENE, MENE, TEKEL, UPHARSIN.

PERESH [PIR esh] (*separate*) — a son of Machir and Maachah (1 Chr. 7:16).

PEREZ [PIR ez] (*breakthrough*) — the name of a man and a tribal family in the Old Testament:

1. The firstborn of the twin sons of Judah by Tamar (Gen. 38:29; Pharez, KJV). Perez was an ancestor of David and Jesus (Ruth 4:12, 18; Matt. 1:3; Luke 3:33). The New Testament (KJV) calls him Phares.

2. A tribal family that took its name from Perez (1 Chr. 27:3). After the Captivity, 468 valiant men of the "sons of Perez" lived in Jerusalem (Neh. 11:4, 6).

PEREZ UZZAH, PEREZ UZZA [PIR iz UHZ uh] (*breakthrough*) — the name of the place where God struck Uzzah (or Uzza) dead for touching the ARK OF THE COVENANT (2 Sam. 6:7). Angry at "the Lord's outbreak against Uzzah" (2 Sam. 6:8), David named the place Perez Uzzah.

PEREZITES [PIR eh zights] — a form of PARZITES.

PERFECT, PERFECTION — without flaw or error; a state of completion or fulfillment. God's perfection means that He is complete in Himself. He lacks nothing; He has no flaws. He is perfect in all the characteristics of His nature. He is the basis for and standard by which all other perfection is to be measured (Job 36:4; Ps. 18:30; 19:7; Matt. 5:48).

By contrast, man's perfection is relative and dependent on God for its existence. As applied to a person's moral state in this life, perfection may refer either to a relatively blameless lifestyle (Gen. 6:9; Job 1:1; James 3:2) or to a person's maturity as a believer (Phil. 3:15; James 1:4). Because perfection in this life is never reached, man will continue to sin (Phil. 3:12, 15; 1 John 1:8). A believer's perfection in the next life, however, will be without sin (Eph. 5:27; Col. 1:28; 1 Thess. 5:23).

PERFUME — liquid substances with a pleasant smell. Perfume, also known as incense, was used widely throughout the ancient world in Bible times. Making perfume was a highly developed skill, and some were known to retain their smell for centuries. Israel's first perfumer made incense for use in the tabernacle (Ex. 37:29), a task performed in later years by the priests (1 Chr. 9:30).

Perfumes were made from many different herbs and plants. These plants were imported from such places as Arabia, India, Persia, Ceylon, and Egypt. Perfumes were used especially, but not exclusively, by the rich to cover the unpleasant body odors that resulted from the hot temperatures of Palestine and surrounding regions. Thus, they were applied to the feet (Luke 7:38), the freshly washed body (Ruth 3:3), clothing (Ps. 45:8), couches or beds (Prov. 7:17), the priest's head (so he would be presentable to God; Ps. 133:2), and even dead bodies (2 Chr. 16:14; John 19:39–40).

PERFUMER (see OCCUPATIONS AND TRADES).

PERGA [PUR guh] (meaning unknown) — the capital city of Pamphylia, a province on the southern coast of Asia Minor, twice visited by the apostle Paul (see Map 7, C–2). During Paul's first missionary journey, he sailed to Perga from Paphos, on the island of Cyprus (Acts 13:13–14). Some time later, Paul and Barnabas stopped a second time at Perga (Acts 14:25).

PERGAMOS [PURR guh mos] (*citadel*) — the chief city of Mysia, near the Caicus River in northwest Asia Minor (modern Turkey) and the site of one of the seven churches of Asia (Rev. 1:11; 2:12–17; Pergamum, RSV, NIV, NEB, NASB). The city, situated opposite the island of Lesbos, was

The modern city of Pergamum, or Pergamos, with the ruins of the Basilica of St. John in the center.
Photo by Howard Vos

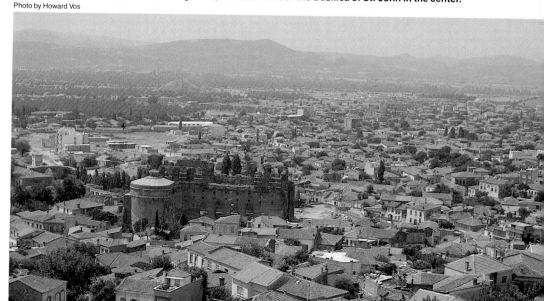

Remains of the stately audience hall at the Persian city of Persepolis—a structure begun by King Darius I and completed by Xerxes.

about 24 kilometers (15 miles) from the Aegean Sea.

In its early history Pergamos became a city-state, then a powerful nation after Attalus I (241-197 B.C.) defeated the Gauls (Galatians). It stood as a symbol of Greek superiority over the barbarians. Great buildings were erected and a library containing over 200,000 items was established. The Egyptians, concerned with this library which rivaled their own at ALEXANDRIA, refused to ship papyrus to Pergamos. As a result, a new form of writing material, Pergamena charta, or parchment, was developed.

In the days of Roman dominance throughout Asia Minor, Pergamos became the capital of the Roman province of Asia. In a gesture of friendship, Mark Antony gave Pergamos' library to Cleopatra; its volumes were moved to Alexandria.

Not only was Pergamos a government center with three imperial temples, but it was also the site of the temple of Asklepios (the Greco-Roman god of medicine and healing), and the medical center where the physician Galen worked (about A.D. 160). Here also was a temple to Athena and a temple to Zeus with an altar showing Zeus defeating snake-like giants. In the Book of Revelation, John spoke of Pergamos as the place "where Satan's throne is" (Rev. 2:13). This could be a reference to the cult of EMPEROR WORSHIP, because Pergamos was a center where this form of loyalty was pledged to the emperor of the Roman Empire.

PERGAMUM [PUR guh muhm] — a form of PERGAMOS.

PERIDA [pih RIGH duh] — a form of PERUDA.

PERIZZITES [PER uh zights] (*villagers*) — inhabitants of the "forest country" (Josh. 17:15) in the territory of the tribes of Ephraim, Manasseh, and Judah (Judg. 1:4-5). The Perizzites, who lived in Canaan as early as the time of Abraham and Lot (Gen. 13:7), were subdued by the Israelites. After the conquest of the land of Canaan under Joshua, the Perizzites were allowed to live. They entered into marriages with their conquerors and seduced the Israelites into idolatry (Judg. 3:5-6). In the time of the judges, Bezek was their stronghold and Adoni-Bezek was their leader (Judg. 1:4-5). In the days of King Solomon the Perizzites were recruited for the king's forced-labor force (1 Kin. 9:20).

PERJURY (see OATH).

PERSECUTION — the hatred and affliction that follows the witness and holy life of God's people in a hostile world. The concept is stressed in many of the Old Testament prophetic books, such as Isaiah. The New Testament also teaches that God's people will suffer persecution. Jesus taught that God's prophets always faced persecution (Matt. 5:12); so His disciples should expect the same (Matt. 10:23).

In the early church, two ideas were taken over from Judaism to express the meaning of persecution. The Jewish theologians taught that the death of the righteous sufferer had redemptive value. While this idea was applied primarily to Jesus by the early Christians, the persecution of His followers was seen as a participation in Jesus' suffering: filling up "what is lacking in the afflictions of Christ" (Col. 1:24). A good statement of this is that of Tertullian: "The blood of the martyrs is the seed of the Church."

The idea of the coming Messiah held that the suffering of God's people was part of the coming of the kingdom—evidence that a person is truly one of God's own. Therefore they are "blessed" (Matt. 5:10) and should "rejoice" and "glorify God" since "the time has come for judgment to begin at the house of God" (1 Pet. 4:13–17).

Jewish opposition to Christianity arose primarily among the Sadducees (Acts 4:1; 5:17). At first the common people and the Pharisees did not oppose the church strongly (Acts 5:14, 34; 23:6). The first persecution came because Stephen spoke out about the inadequacy of the land of Israel and the Temple for salvation. This intensified when the apostle Paul began to proclaim the salvation of the Gentiles through Jesus Christ alone. Both Jew and Christian began to realize that the two were now separate religions, rather than sects of a single religion.

Roman opposition to Christianity also developed gradually. The Book of Acts emphasized Roman tolerance for the new religion. But this began to change with the Jewish riots against Christians in Rome, resulting in the Emperor Claudius banning both groups from Rome in A.D. 49. This set the stage for the intense opposition of later years that allowed Nero to make Christians the scapegoats for the fire which leveled Rome in A.D. 64. During this persecution the apostles Paul and Peter were martyred.

PERSEPOLIS [purr SEP oh liss] (*city of Persia*) — the ceremonial capital of the Persian Empire under Darius the Great (522–486 B.C.), his son Xerxes (486–465 B.C.), and their successors. The city was second in importance to Shushan (or Susa), the administrative capital. Persepolis was destroyed in 330 B.C. by Alexander the Great. Its ruins are situated about 49 kilometers (30 miles) northeast of the modern city of Shiraz in southwestern Iran. Although Persepolis is not mentioned in the Bible, it appears in the apocryphal book of 2 Maccabees (2 Macc. 9:1–2).

PERSEVERANCE — the steadfast effort to follow God's commands and to do His work. The New Testament makes it clear that faith alone can save. But it makes it equally clear that perseverance in doing good works is the greatest indication that an individual's faith is genuine (James 2:14–26). Indeed, perseverance springs from a faithful trust that God has been steadfast toward His people. Through persevering in God's work, the Christian proves his deep appreciation for God's saving grace (1 Cor. 15:57–58).

As a result of perseverance, the Christian can expect not only to enhance the strength of the church, but also to build up the strength of his own character (Rom. 5:3–4). In short, he can expect to become closer to God. He learns that he can persevere primarily because God is intimately related to him (Rom. 8:25–27) and especially because he has the assurance of a final reward in heaven (1 John 5:13).

PERSIA [PURR zyah] — an ancient world empire that flourished from 539–331 B.C (see Map 1, E–2). The Babylonian Empire fell to the Persians, setting the stage for the return of the Hebrew people to Jerusalem about 538–445 B.C., following their long period of captivity by the Babylonians.

The Old Testament contains many references to the nation of Persia and its representatives. Ezra 9:9 refers to the "kings of Persia." Ezra 6:14 cites "Cyrus, Darius, and Artaxerxes king of Persia." Daniel 8:20 speaks of the "kings of Media and Persia." Daniel 10:13 mentions the "prince of the kingdom

Cliffside tomb of the Persian king Xerxes I, the ruler generally identified as King Ahasuerus of the Book of Esther (Esth. 1:1).

Photo by Gustav Jeeninga

of Persia." The Book of Esther refers to the "powers of Persia and Media" (1:3), the "seven princes of Persia and Media" (1:14), and the "ladies of Persia and Media" (1:18). Daniel 5:28 prophesied that Belshazzar's kingdom would be "given to the Medes and Persians."

The Persians apparently sprang from a people from the hills of Russia known as Indo–Aryans. As early as 2000 B.C., they began to settle in Iran and along the Black Sea coast. Two of these Indo–European tribes settled on the Elamite border and to the east of the Zagros mountain range. The first references to them are made in the inscriptions of Shalmaneser III (858–824 B.C.). They are noted as the Parsua (Persians) and Madai (Medes).

The first mention of a Persian chieftain refers to his role as an ally aligned against Sennacherib of Assyria. His son was called "King, Great King, King of the City of Anshan." His grandson fathered Cyrus II, who was one of the most celebrated kings of history. He is called by the prophet Isaiah "My shepherd" (Is. 44:28). In another passage he is referred to as "His [the Lord's] Anointed" (Is. 45:1), a term used in the Old Testament of the Messiah.

Cyrus II, founder of the mighty Persian Empire, ascended the throne in Anshan in 559 B.C. He conquered the Median King Astyages. Then he defeated Lydia (about 546 B.C.) and Babylon (about 539 B.C.), finally establishing the Persian Empire. This last conquest is referred to in Daniel 5. Cyrus' rule was a result of the sovereignty of God. In contrast to previous rulers, especially the Assyrians, Cyrus was humane and benevolent toward those whom he defeated. Cyrus was the Persian king who issued the decree restoring the Jews to their homeland, following their long period of captivity by the Babylonians (2 Chr. 36:22–23; Ezra 1:1–4).

Cyrus was the founder of the system under which each province, or Persian satrapy, was governed by an official who answered to the great king. However, he allowed a remarkable degree of freedom of religion and customs for the vassal states, including Palestine. He developed roads, cities, postal systems, and legal codes, and treated the subject nations kindly and humanely. Cyrus accomplished all of this because he was God's tool—just as Assyria, who conquered Israel, was God's rod of anger. Hence the Bible refers to Cyrus in favorable terms (Is. 44:28—45:3).

Cambyses II (530–522 B.C.), the son of Cyrus, reigned after his father. During his reign, Egypt was added to the list of nations conquered by Persia. According to the Greek historian Herodotus, Cambyses accidentally wounded himself with his own sword in 522 B.C. Some believe he committed suicide.

The next Persian king, Darius I (521–486 B.C.), was not a direct descendant of Cyrus but was of royal, Achaemenid blood. He defeated nine kings to claim all 23 Persian satrapies. This was recorded on the famous Behistun Inscription, which was written in the Akkadian, Elamite, and Old Persian languages.

Photo by Gleason Archer

This golden Persian coin known as the daric shows King Artaxerxes kneeling with bow and arrow.

Darius I further unified the Persian Empire by using an efficient gold coinage, state highways, and a more efficient postal system. He was defeated by the Greeks at the Battle of Marathon in 490 B.C. This is the same Darius who, in his second year, ordered the Jewish Temple at Jerusalem to be rebuilt after work on it had been discontinued for 14 years (Ezra 4:24; 6:1). He also gave a generous subsidy that made it possible to complete the Temple. The extent of the Persian Empire under Darius is reflected in Esther 1:1 and 10:1. The vast territory was nearly 4,900 kilometers (3,000 miles) long and 800–2,400 kilometers (500 to 1,500 miles) wide.

Xerxes ruled Persia from 486 to 465 B.C. He was the Ahasuerus of the Book of Esther. Esther did not become queen until the seventh year of his reign, which would be about 478 B.C. This was two years after his devastating defeat at Salamis (480 B.C.), which ended Persia's last hope for conquering Greece.

Another Persian king, Artaxerxes I Longimanus (464–424 B.C.), illustrates one of the ironies of history. This minor Persian king was of major importance because of his connection with the Hebrew people. Apparently two of the three returns of the Jewish people from captivity in Babylon occurred during his reign. The second return was apparently under Ezra. This was made possible because of the generosity of Artaxerxes. The third return occurred in 445 B.C. (Neh. 1:1). The specific purpose of this return to Jerusalem was to rebuild the city walls.

Among the kingdoms of the ancient world, Persia is remembered because it built many important cities. PERSEPOLIS was a showpiece of Persian power. Pasargadae was the ancestral capital rapidly supplanted in importance. ECBATANA served as the capital of the Median Empire and became a resort area for the Persians. SUSA (the Shushan of Esther) was the former capital of the Elamite Empire.

The religion of the Persians centered around a reformation of the old Iranian religions developed by Zoroaster. He believed in a dualism in which Ahura Mazda (or Ormazd) headed the gods of goodness (Amesha Spentas) and Angra Mainyu (or Ahriman) headed the gods of evil (daevas). Some of this is revealed in the Jewish apocryphal literature which developed from the fifth century B.C. to the time of Christ.

PERSIS [PUR sis] (*Persian*) — a Christian at Rome who "labored much in the Lord" and to whom Paul sent greetings, calling her "beloved" (Rom. 16:12).

PERSON OF CHRIST (see JESUS CHRIST).

PERUDA [pih ROO duh] (*unique*) — one of Solomon's servants whose descendants returned with Zerubbabel from the Captivity (Ezra 2:55), also called Perida (Neh. 7:57).

PESHITTA [puh SHEE tuh] (see BIBLE VERSIONS AND TRANSLATIONS).

PESTILENCE (see DISEASES OF THE BIBLE).

PETER, APOCALYPSE OF (see APOCRYPHA).

PETER, EPISTLES OF — two New Testament epistles bearing the name of "Peter, an apostle of Jesus Christ" (1 Pet. 1:1) and "Simon Peter, a servant and apostle of Jesus Christ" (2 Pet. 1:1), though otherwise having little in common.

First Peter, the longer of the two epistles, is written in fine Greek and refers frequently to the Old Testament. It is an epistle for the downhearted, written to give encouragement in times of trial and disappointment. First Peter anchors the Christian's hope not on logic or persuasion, but on the matchless sacrifice of Jesus Christ, who "suffered for us, leaving us an example, that you should follow His steps" (2:21).

In contrast to 1 Peter, 2 Peter is briefer and written in a forced style. It rails against false teachers, while reminding believers of their election by God and assuring them of Christ's return.

Structure of the Epistles. Following a greeting (1:1-2), 1 Peter begins on a positive note, praising God for the blessings of a "living hope" which He has reserved for believers (1:3-12). This Doxology of praise sets a triumphant tone for the remainder of the letter, which can be divided into three parts: blessings, duties, and trials. The blessings extend from 1:3 to 2:10. Because of the "inheritance incorruptible and undefiled...reserved in heaven for you" (1:4), Peter calls on his readers to live a life holy and blameless, reminding them that they are a "holy nation, His [God's] own special people" (2:9).

The second part of 1 Peter extends from 2:11 to 3:22. This section consists of guidance for social duties. The Christian's life-style ought to be a testimony to non-believers (2:11-17); slaves ought to obey their masters—even unjust ones—bearing their humiliation as Christ bore His (2:18-25); the silent example of a Christian wife has great effect on a non-Christian husband (3:1-6); Christian husbands are to treat their wives as joint-heirs of the grace of life (3:7). In all things, let a blameless lifestyle bring shame on whomever would show opposition (3:8-22).

The third and final part of 1 Peter addresses the question of trials (4:1—5:11). In light of the nearness of the end, Christians must be "good stewards of the manifold grace of God" (4:1-11). They can rejoice in sharing Christ's sufferings because of the glory that awaits them (4:12-19). In their pastoral duties, church elders are to follow the example of Jesus, who perfects, establishes, and strengthens the flock (5:1-11). The epistle closes with mention of Silvanus, the secretary who wrote the letter, and with greetings from "Babylon" (5:12-14).

Second Peter begins with a greeting (1:1-2), enjoining believers, because they have been chosen by God, to develop noble characters (1:3-11). Recognizing that his own death is near, the author sees in the transfiguration of Jesus a forecast of the brilliant day when Christ will come again (1:16-21). Chapter two is a condensation of material from the letter of Jude, condemning false teachers and prophets. The final chapter deals with the future coming of the Lord and the reasons for its delay (3:1-18).

Authorship and Date. First Peter identifies its author as "Peter, an apostle of Jesus Christ" (1:1). His frequent references to Christ's suffering (2:21-24; 3:18; 4:1; 5:1) show that the profile of the Suffering Servant was etched deeply upon his memory. He calls Mark his "son" (5:13), recalling his affection for the young man and family mentioned in Acts 12:12. These facts lead naturally to the assumption that the apostle Peter wrote this letter.

Authorship of the epistle by the apostle Peter has been challenged, however, on the following grounds: (1) no official persecutions of the church took place during Peter's lifetime; (2) the epistle echoes some of Paul's teachings; and (3) the literary quality of the Greek seems too refined for a Galilean fisherman.

Valid as these objections are, they do not seriously challenge Peter's authorship of the epistle. The sufferings mentioned in the epistle need not refer to official persecutions, which did not begin until the time of the Roman emperor Domitian (A.D. 81-96), but to earlier local incidents. The last two questions are neatly resolved by recognizing the role that Silvanus (5:12) played in composing the epistle.

As a former associate of the apostle Paul, and as one who doubtlessly came to the Greek language as a native, Silvanus may have played an important role in bringing this epistle to completion. We might say of 1 Peter that the ideas came from Peter, but the design from Silvanus. The reference to "Babylon" (5:13), a common image for civil power opposed to God, indicates that the epistle was written from Rome.

The question of authorship of 2 Peter is more difficult. Although the epistle claims to come from the apostle Peter (1:1; 3:1-2), who witnessed the transfiguration of Christ (1:18) and at the time of writing was nearing his death (1:14), few scholars believe Peter wrote the letter. Reasons for this judgment stem from a number of factors.

The style of 2 Peter is inferior to that of 1 Peter. Nearly the whole of Jude 4–18 has been reproduced in the second chapter; if Jude were not written until late in the first century, then 2 Peter obviously could not have been written before it. Again, 2 Peter refers to Paul's epistles as a part of "the Scriptures" (3:16). This suggests a date, perhaps early in the second century, when Paul's epistles had reached a level of authority in the early church. Finally, the Epistle of 2 Peter seems to have been unknown to the early church, and it was one of the last books to be included in the New Testament.

These factors suggest that 2 Peter was written by an anonymous author but attributed by someone to the apostle Peter in order to assure a hearing for a message in a time well after Peter's death.

Historical Setting. First Peter is addressed to Christians living in "Pontus, Galatia, Cappadocia, Asia, and Bithynia" (1:1)—places in the northern and western parts of Asia Minor (modern Turkey). The readers appear to have been Gentiles (1:14, 18; 2:10; 4:3), although they probably had not been evangelized by Peter himself (1:12). The letter was obviously written to believers undergoing trials and persecutions, to give them courage in the face of their adversities (5:10).

Since it makes no mention of its audience, 2 Peter was probably intended for a general readership. Its primary purpose was to combat false teachers. Widespread in the ancient world was the view that sparks of eternal light lay trapped within the prisons of human bodies. These sparks of light, which longed to return to their primal home, could be liberated only by *gnosis*, or knowledge. Second Peter uses "knowledge" (1:5–6; 3:18) to show that only in Jesus Christ is the knowledge of God and salvation fully revealed. These false teachers also must have been critical of the delay in Christ's return. To this challenge the author devoted the entire third chapter.

Theological Contribution. First Peter was written by one who sensed the triumphant outcome of God's purpose for the world (1:4). The triumph of the future depends in no way on what we have done but on the resurrection of Jesus Christ. Because God has raised Jesus from the dead, God is deserving of praise; for "His abundant mercy has begotten us again to a living hope" (1:3).

The unshakableness of our hope in Jesus Christ, which awaits us in heaven, resounds like a clap of thunder throughout this epistle. Because Christ has been raised from the dead, His suffering and death have meaning. The believer can gain courage in present adversity by looking to the example of Christ in His suffering. We have a sure hope for the future because of Christ's resurrection. This truly is a "living hope," for it is one we can live by, even in the midst of "various trials" (1:6).

If 1 Peter is an epistle of hope, the accent falls not on wishful thinking, but on present help. No biblical writer shows the connection between faith and conduct in a clearer manner than does Peter. "Conduct," in fact, is a key word in this epistle (1:15, 17–18; 2:12; 3:1–2, 16). For Peter, practice is not simply the most important thing; it is the only thing.

Peter's stress on behavior, however, is not an appeal to some vague sense of "moral goodness" in people. The conduct Peter describes is the result of a life reclaimed by the perfect power of Jesus Christ. Christ has redeemed believers (1:18–19); Christ upholds and guides them (1:8; 2:25); and Christ will reward them (5:4). Christ is both the model and goal of the redeemed life. Consequently, believers may move forward on the pilgrim way, confident that the end will rise up to meet them with joy and salvation (2:11; 4:13–14).

Jesus said, "Blessed are those who are persecuted for righteousness' sake, for theirs is the kingdom of heaven" (Matt. 5:10). There is no better commentary on this Beatitude than the Epistle of 1 Peter. Here is no pale, tight-lipped religion. Rather, "living from the end" cultivates an abiding joy even in the trials of the present. Here, too, Jesus is our sole help and our sure Lord, "who for the joy that was set before Him endured the cross" (Heb. 12:2).

Second Peter shifts the emphasis from a hope by which one can live to a hope on which one can count. The epistle speaks to the assurance of salvation in chapter one by making the extraordinary claim that Christians are "partakers of the divine nature" (1:4). The second chapter deals with false teachers. The unique contribution of 2 Peter, however, comes in chapter three.

In chapter three the "day of the Lord" (3:10) or the "day of God" (3:12) breaks through the gloom of the doubters who taunt the hopeful: "Where is the promise of His coming? For since the fathers fell asleep, all things continue as they were from the beginning of creation" (3:4). Such persons may be assured that God does not delay in coming because he lacks power or concern. Rather, what the unfaithful interpret as delay, the faithful know to be patience; for God is "not willing that any should perish but that all should come to repentance" (3:9).

PETER, GOSPEL OF (see Apocrypha).

PETER, SIMON — the most prominent of Jesus' twelve apostles. The New Testament gives a more complete picture of Peter than of any other disciple, with the exception of Paul. Peter is often considered to be a big, blundering fisherman. But this is a shallow portrayal. The picture of his personality portrayed in the New Testament is rich and many sided. A more fitting appraisal of Peter is that he was a pioneer among the twelve apostles and the early church, breaking ground that the church would later follow.

The First Apostle to be Called. Peter's given name was Symeon or Simon. His father's name was Jonah (Matt. 16:17; John 1:42). Simon's brother,

FIRST PETER: A Teaching Outline

Part One: The Salvation of the Believer (1:1—2:12)

Part Two: The Submission of the Believer (2:13—3:12)

Part Three: The Suffering of the Believer (3:13—5:14)

SECOND PETER: A Teaching Outline

Andrew, also joined Jesus as a disciple (Mark 1:16). The family probably lived at Capernaum on the north shore of the Sea of Galilee (Mark 1:21, 29), although it is possible they lived in Bethsaida (John 1:44).

Peter was married, because the gospels mention that Jesus healed his mother–in–law (Matt. 8:14–15). The apostle Paul later mentioned that Peter took his wife on his missionary travels (1 Cor. 9:5). Peter and Andrew were fishermen on the Sea of Galilee, and perhaps in partnership with James and John, the sons of Zebedee (Luke 5:10). In the midst of his labor as a fisherman, Peter received a call from Jesus that changed his life (Luke 5:8).

The Gospel of John reports that Andrew and Peter were disciples of John the Baptist before they joined Jesus. John also reports that Peter was introduced to Jesus by his brother Andrew, who had already recognized Jesus to be the Messiah (John 1:35–42). Whether Andrew and Peter knew Jesus because they were disciples of John is uncertain. But it is clear that they followed Jesus because of His distinctive authority.

The First Among the Apostles. Jesus apparently gathered His followers in two stages: first as disciples (learners or apprentices), and later as apostles (commissioned representatives). Peter was the first disciple to be called (Mark 1:16–18) and the first to be named an apostle (Mark 3:14–16). His name heads every list of the Twelve in the New Testament. He was apparently the strongest individual in the band. He frequently served as a spokesman for the disciples, and he was their recognized leader (Mark 1:36; Luke 22:32). Typical of Peter's dominant personality was his readiness to walk to Jesus on the water (Matt. 14:28), and to ask Jesus the awkward question of how often he should forgive a sinning brother (Matt. 18:21).

An inner circle of three apostles existed among the Twelve. Peter was also the leader of this small group. The trio—Peter, James, and John—was present with Jesus on a number of occasions. They witnessed the raising of a young girl from the dead (Mark 5:37; Luke 8:51); they were present at Jesus' transfiguration (Matt. 17:1–2); and they were present during Jesus' agony in Gethsemane (Matt. 26:37; Mark 14:33). During Jesus' final week in Jerusalem, two of the three, Peter and John, were sent to make preparations for their last meal together (Luke 22:8).

The First Apostle to Recognize Jesus as Messiah. The purpose of Jesus' existence in the flesh was that people would come to a true picture of who God is and what He has done for man's salvation. The first apostle to recognize that was Peter. He confessed Jesus as Lord in the region of Caesarea Philippi (Matt. 16:13–17).

Jesus began the process which would lead to Peter's awareness by asking a non–threatening question, "Who do men say that I, the Son of Man, am?" (Matt. 16:13). After the disciples voiced various rumors, Jesus put a more personal question to them, "But who do you say that I am?" (Matt.

Photo by Willem A. VanGemeren

Jaffa, the biblical Joppa, where Peter received the heavenly vision about God's acceptance of the Gentiles (Acts 10:1–23).

16:15). Peter confessed Jesus to be the Messiah, the Son of God. According to Matthew, it was because of this confession that Jesus renamed Simon, Cephas (in Aramaic) or Peter (in Greek), meaning "rock."

Why Jesus called Simon a "rock" is not altogether clear. Peter's character was not always rock–like, as his denial of Jesus indicates. His new name probably referred to something that, by God's grace, he would *become*—Peter, a rock.

The First Apostle to Witness the Resurrection. How ironic that the one who denied Jesus most vehemently in His hour of suffering should be the first person to witness to His resurrection from the dead. Yet according to Luke (Luke 24:34) and Paul (1 Cor. 15:5), Peter was the first apostle to see the risen Lord. We can only marvel at the grace of God in granting such a blessing to one who did not seem to deserve it. Peter's witnessing of the resurrection was a sign of his personal restoration to fellowship with Christ. It also confirmed His appointment by God to serve as a leader in the emerging church.

The First Apostle to Proclaim Salvation to the Gentiles. The earliest information about the early church comes from the Book of Acts. This shows clearly that Peter continued to exercise a key leadership role in the church for a number of years. Indeed, the first 11 chapters of Acts are built around the activity of the apostle Peter.

When the Holy Spirit visited the church in Samaria, the apostles sent Peter and John to verify its authenticity (Acts 8:14-25). But this event was only a prelude to the one event which concluded Peter's story in the New Testament: the preaching of the gospel to the Gentiles (Acts 10—11). The chain of events that happened before the bestowal of the Holy Spirit on Gentile believers—beginning with Peter's staying in the house of a man of "unclean" profession (Acts 9:43), continuing with his vision of "unclean" foods (Acts 10:9-16), and climaxing in his realization that no human being, Gentile included, ought to be considered "unclean" (Acts 10:34-48)—is a masterpiece of storytelling. It demonstrates the triumph of God's grace to bring about change in stubborn hearts and the hardened social customs of Jewish believers.

Following the death of James, the brother of John, and Peter's miraculous release from prison (Acts 12), Peter drops out of the narrative of Acts. Luke reports that he "went to another place" (Acts 12:17). We know, however, that Peter did not drop out of active service in the early church.

Peter probably broadened his ministry, once the mantle of leadership of the Jerusalem church fell from his shoulders to those of James, the Lord's brother. Peter played a key role at the Council of Jerusalem (Acts 15; Galatians 2), which decided in favor of granting church membership to Gentiles without first requiring them to become Jews. Paul mentioned a visit of Peter to Antioch of Syria (Gal. 2:11), and he may even refer to a mission of Peter to Corinth (1 Cor. 1:12). Peter dropped into the background in the Book of Acts not because his ministry ended. Luke, the writer of Acts, simply began to trace the course of the gospel's spread to Gentile Rome through the ministry of the apostle Paul.

Peter in Rome: The First to Inspire the Writing of a Gospel. According to early Christian tradition, Peter went to Rome, where he died. Only once in the New Testament do we hear of Peter's being in Rome. Even in this case, Rome is referred to as "Babylon" (1 Pet. 5:13). Little is known of Peter's activities in Rome, although Papias, writing about A.D. 125, stated that Peter's preaching inspired the writing of the first gospel, drafted by Mark, who was Peter's interpreter in Rome.

This early and generally reliable tradition supports the pioneer role played by Peter throughout his life and ministry. A number of other works—the Preaching of Peter, the Gospel of Peter, the Apocalypse of Peter, the Acts of Peter, and the Epistle of Peter to James—are apocryphal in nature. They cannot be accepted as trustworthy sources of information for the life and thought of the apostle.

Peter the First Pope? Whether Peter was the first pope of Rome is a question which can be answered by a study of church history, not by the New Testament. Jesus' statement to Peter in Matthew 16:18, "You are Peter, and on this rock I will build My church," does not mention papal succession. But it does emphasize Peter's prominent role in the founding of the church.

PETHAHIAH [peth ah HIGH ah] (*Jehovah opens*) — the name of three or four men in the Old Testament:

1. A priest whose family was appointed by David as sanctuary priests (1 Chr. 24:16).

2. A Levite who divorced his pagan wife after the Captivity (Ezra 10:23).

3. A Levite who helped regulate the devotions of the people (Neh. 9:5). He may be the same person as Pethahiah No. 2.

4. An official of the Persian king for those who had returned from the Captivity (Neh. 11:24).

PETHOR [PEE thohr] (*soothsayer*) — a city in northern Mesopotamia in which Balaam lived (Num. 22:5; Deut. 23:4). Balak, king of the Moabites, sent to Pethor to summon Balaam (Josh. 13:22) to curse Israel. Pethor has been identified with Tell Ahmar, about 19 kilometers (12 miles) south of CARCHEMISH.

PETHUEL [pih THOO uhl] (*vision of God*) — father of the prophet Joel (Joel 1:1).

PETITION (see PRAYER).

PETRA [PET ruh] (*rock*) — the capital of Edom and later of Nabatea, situated about 275 kilometers (170 miles) southwest of modern Amman and about 80 kilometers (50 miles) south of the Dead Sea. Petra is not mentioned by name in the Bible, but many scholars believe it was the same place as SELA (Judg. 1:36; 2 Kin. 14:7).

Petra is one of the most spectacular archaeological ruins in the Near East and is a popular attraction on Holy Land tours. Most of the buildings and tombs of Petra are cut into the rose–red rock cliffs of the area.

A pagan temple, commonly called "the Treasury," built by the Roman Emperor Hadrian in honor of the goddess Isis. This is one of many buildings at Petra carved into the rock cliffs.

Photo by Gustav Jeeninga

A glimpse of "the Treasury" through the Siq, the narrow rock entranceway to the city of Petra.

Petra's ruins consist of about 750 monuments, most of them dating from the second half of the first century B.C. to the second century after Christ. Most of these structures date from the Roman period. In A.D. 131 the Roman emperor Hadrian (ruled A.D. 117–38) visited the city and ordered construction to begin on the treasury, which has been called "Petra's gem"—a temple to Isis.

Many ruins of Roman construction may be seen at Petra: a triumphal arch, an amphitheater, remains of baths, temples, tombs, and sections of a road. Above the city is the great high place, containing sacrificial altars hewn from the solid rock. Such open–air sanctuaries have thrown light on the HIGH PLACES mentioned in the Old Testament.

Petra is reached from the west by ascending the Wadi Musa and passing through a narrow, high-walled gorge, known as the SIQ. Over a mile in length, this gorge provided Petra with excellent defense. The city is situated in a basin that is about 900 meters (3,000 feet) wide and about 1,600 meters (one mile) long. The city is surrounded by massive sandstone cliffs of a dark red color.

PEULLETHAI [pee UHL thigh] — a form of PEUL-THAI.

PEULTHAI [pee UHL thigh] (*wages of the Lord*) — a gatekeeper of the tabernacle in the time of David (1 Chr. 26:5; Peullethai, RSV, NIV, NASB).

PHALEC [PAY lek] — a form of PELEG.

PHALLU [FAL oo] — a form of PALLU.

PHALTI [FAL tigh] — a form of PALTI.

PHALTIEL [FAL tih uhl] — a form of PALTIEL.

PHANUEL [fuh NOO uhl] (*face of God*) — an Asherite and father of Anna (Luke 2:36). Anna gave thanks in the Temple for having lived long enough to see the Messiah.

PHARAOH [PHAY row] — the title of the kings of Egypt until 323 B.C. In the Egyptian language the word Pharaoh means "great house." This word was originally used to describe the palace of the king. Around 1500 B.C. this term was applied to the Egyptian kings. It meant something like "his honor, his majesty." In addition to this title, the kings also had a personal name (Amenhotep, Rameses) and other descriptive titles (King of Upper and Lower Egypt).

The Pharaoh was probably the most important person in Egyptian society. The Egyptians believed he was a god and the key to the nation's relationship to the cosmic gods of the universe. While the Pharaoh ruled, he was the Son of Ra, the sun god, and the incarnation of the god Horus. He came from the gods with the divine responsibility to rule the land for them. His word was law, and he owned everything. Thus there were no law codes, because the king upheld order and justice and insured the stability of society.

When the Pharaoh died, he became the god Osiris, the ruler of the underworld and those who live after death. The Pharaoh was the head of the army as well as a central figure in the nation's religious life. As an intermediator between gods and men, the Pharaoh functioned as a high priest in the many temples in Egypt. Because the Egyptian people believed their fate was dependent on that of the Pharaoh, they seldom attempted to overthrow the government, although some pharaohs were very cruel.

In several instances the Israelites came into contact with a Pharaoh. Abram (Abraham) went to Egypt around 1900 B.C. because of a famine in the land of Palestine. Because Abram lied about Sarai (Sarah) being his sister, Pharaoh wanted to take her into his harem; but God stopped him by sending a plague (Gen. 12:10–20). About 200 years later Joseph was thrown into prison in Egypt because the wife of Potiphar, the captain of Pharaoh's guard, lied about Joseph's behavior (Genesis 39).

While in prison Joseph met two of Pharaoh's servants, the butler and the baker, who had been put in prison because they displeased the powerful Pharaoh (Genesis 40). Joseph correctly interpreted the dream of the butler and baker and later was brought from prison to interpret the dream of the Pharaoh (Genesis 41). The Egyptian priestly magicians could not interpret Pharaoh's dream. But because God told Joseph the meaning of the dream, Joseph was appointed as second in command to collect one-fifth of the nation's crops during the seven years of plenty.

Because of the severity of the seven years of famine, the Egyptians had to sell their cattle, their property, and themselves to the Pharaoh for grain; thus the Pharaoh owned everything (Gen. 47:13–20). The Pharaoh sent carts to bring Joseph's broth-

Entrance to the tomb of Pharaoh Tutankhamon of Egypt in the foreground with the tomb of Ramses VI just behind it.

ers to Egypt (Gen. 45:16–20) and settled them in the fertile land of Goshen (Gen. 47:1–6).

After about 300 more years in Egypt, a new dynasty came to power. Its kings did not acknowledge Joseph and his deeds to save Egypt (Ex. 1:8). Therefore all the Israelites but Moses were enslaved. He was raised in the Pharaoh's own court (Ex. 1:11–2:10; Acts 7:21–22). At 80 years of age Moses returned to Pharaoh to ask permission to lead the Israelites out of Egypt. Pharaoh did not know or accept the God of the Israelites and refused to obey Him (Ex. 5:1–2). On a second visit Moses functioned as God to Pharaoh by delivering a divine message (Ex. 7:1), but the miracles and initial plagues only hardened Pharaoh's heart (Ex. 7:8–13, 22; 8:15, 32). Each plague was carried out so the Israelites, the Egyptians, and the Pharaoh would know that Israel's God was the only true God and that the Egyptian gods and their "divine pharaoh" were powerless before Him (Ex. 7:5, 17; 8:10, 22; 9:14, 29–30; 10:2).

Eventually Pharaoh admitted his sin, but before long he again hardened his heart (Ex. 9:27, 34; 10:16, 20). When Pharaoh's own "divine" firstborn son was killed in the last plague, he finally submitted to God's power and let the people go (Ex. 12:29–33). Pharaoh later chased the Israelites to bring them back, but he and his army were drowned in the Red Sea (Ex. 14:5–31).

Solomon formed an alliance with an Egyptian Pharaoh through marriage with his daughter (1 Kin. 3:1; 7:8; 9:24). This Pharaoh later gave the city of Gezer to his daughter (1 Kin. 9:16). The next Pharaoh had less friendly relationships with Solomon and gave refuge to Solomon's enemy, Hadad the Edomite (1 Kin. 11:14–22). This may have been the Pharaoh Shishak who protected Jeroboam (1 Kin. 11:40) and captured Jerusalem in the fifth year of Rehoboam (1 Kin. 14:25–28). Hoshea, the king of Israel, had a treaty with So, the king of Egypt (2 Kin. 17:4). The Pharaoh Tirhakah may have had a similar relationship with Hezekiah, whom he rescued from the Assyrian attack on Hezekiah (2 Kin. 19:9).

In 609 B.C. the Pharaoh Necho marched north through Palestine to save the Assyrians who were being attacked by Babylon and Media. King Josiah opposed this move, so Necho killed him (2 Kin. 23:29). Nebuchadnezzar later defeated Necho and took control of Palestine (Jer. 46:2). It was possibly Pharaoh Hophra who challenged the Babylonians during the siege of Jerusalem in 587 B.C. (Jer. 37:5–10; 44:30; Ezek. 17:17).

The prophets Isaiah, Jeremiah, and Hosea condemned Pharaoh and the Israelites who trusted in him and his army (Is. 30:1–5; 31:1; Jer. 42:18; Hos. 7:11). But the prophecies of Ezekiel are by far the most extensive (Ezekiel 29—32). Pharaoh is quoted as saying, "My River is my own; I have made it for myself" (Ezek. 29:3). Because Pharaoh claimed the power and authority of God, Ezekiel declared, God will destroy Pharaoh and Egypt by delivering them into the hands of Nebuchadnezzar, king of Babylon (Ezek. 29:19). God will break Pharaoh's arm of strength (Ezek. 30:21) and remove his pride (Ezek. 31:2; 32:2, 12).

The "king of the South" in (Dan. 11:5, 9, 11, 14, 25, 40) probably refers to one or more of the Greek kings, called Ptolemy, who ruled Egypt after the line of Pharaohs ended in 323 B.C.

PHARES, PHAREZ [FAR eez] — forms of PEREZ.

PHARISEES [FARE uh sees] (*separated ones*) — a religious and political party in Palestine in New Testament times. The Pharisees were known for insisting that the law of God be observed as the scribes interpreted it and for their special commitment to keeping the laws of tithing and ritual purity.

The Pharisees had their roots in the group of faithful Jews known as the Hasidim (or Chasidim). The Hasidim arose in the second century B.C. when the influence of HELLENISM on the Jews was particularly strong and many Jews lived little differently than their Gentile neighbors. But the Hasidim insisted on strict observance of Jewish ritual laws.

When the Syrian King ANTIOCHUS IV tried to do away with the Jewish religion, the Hasidim took part in the revolt of the MACCABEES against him. Apparently from this movement of faithful Hasidim came both the Essenes—who later broke off from other Jews and formed their own communities—and the Pharisees, who remained an active part of Jewish life. Indeed, during the period of independence that followed the revolt, some of the Greek rulers who controlled Palestine favored the Pharisaic party.

As a result of this favoritism, Pharisees came to be represented on the SANHEDRIN, the supreme court and legislative body of the Jews. At times, the Pharisees even dominated the assembly. In New Testament times, Pharisaic scribes, though probably in the minority, were still an effective part of the Sanhedrin.

One distinctive feature of the Pharisees was their strong commitment to observing the law of God as it was interpreted and applied by the scribes. Although the priests had been responsible for teaching and interpreting the Law (Lev. 10:8–11; Deut. 33:8–10) in Old Testament times, many people had lost all respect for the priests because of the corruption in the Jerusalem priesthood. They looked to the scribes instead to interpret the Law for them. Some scribes were priests; many were not. Still, they lived pious, disciplined lives; and they had been trained to become experts in the Law. It was natural, then, for people to follow their leading rather than that of the priests.

The way in which the scribes spelled out the meaning of the Mosaic Law, the ways in which they adapted that Law to suit the needs of their day, the time–honored customs which they endorsed—all these became a part of the "tradition of the elders" (Mark 7:3). Although these traditions were not put into writing, they were passed on from one scribe to another and from the scribes to the people. From this tradition, they claimed, the Jewish people could know the way God's law should be observed. The Pharisees agreed, and they were known for supporting and keeping the "tradition of the elders."

The Pharisees also believed it was important to observe all the laws of God. But they were especially known for their commitment to keep the laws of tithing and ritual purity. These were the laws that other people were less careful about observing.

According to the New Testament, the Pharisees were concerned about strictly interpreting and keeping the law on all matters (Acts 26:5), including the Sabbath (Mark 2:24), divorce (Mark 10:2), oaths (Matt. 23:16–22), the wearing of PHYLACTERIES and FRINGES (Matt. 23:5), and so on. But they showed special zeal in insisting that laws of tithing and ritual purity be kept (Matt. 23:23–26; Mark 7:1–13; Luke 11:37–42; 18:12).

Since Pharisees found that other Jews were not careful enough about keeping the laws of tithing and ritual purity, they felt it was necessary to place limits on their contacts with other Jews as well as with Gentiles. For example, they could not eat in the home of a non–Pharisee, since they could not be sure that the food had been properly tithed and kept ritually pure.

Unlike the SADDUCEES, the Pharisees did believe in the resurrection of the dead. On this point, they were on common ground with the early Christians (Acts 23:6–9). The scribe in Mark 12:28 who thought that Jesus had answered the Sadducees well concerning the resurrection was probably a Pharisee.

The Pharisees and their scribes enjoyed a good deal of popular support. In one way this is surprising, since the Pharisees kept apart from other Jews. They always seemed to be ready to criticize others for not keeping the laws, and they often looked down on "sinners" who showed no interest in God's law (Mark 2:16; Luke 7:39; 15:2; 18:11).

Still, unlike the Sadducees, who were mostly rich landowners and powerful priests, many Pharisees were ordinary people. And even though other Jews could not be bothered with observing all the details of the law, they respected the Pharisees for making the effort. Even Paul credited unbelieving Jews with having a "zeal for God" (Rom. 10:2)—even though it was misguided. He probably was thinking primarily of the Pharisees when he wrote these words.

In the New Testament, the Pharisees appear frequently in the accounts of Jesus' ministry and the history of the early church. In these passages a number of the typical failings of the Pharisees are evident. Of course, not all Pharisees failed in all these points—and the same failings can be found among religious people of any age.

Pharisees observed the Law carefully as far as appearances went, but their hearts were far from God. Their motives were wrong because they wanted the praise of men (Matt. 6:2, 5, 16; 23:5–7). They also had evil desires that were hidden by their pious show (Matt. 23:25–28). That is why Pharisees are often called hypocrites: their hearts did not match their outward appearance.

The Pharisees thought they could match God's standards by keeping all the outward rules. Luke 18:9 says they "trusted in themselves that they were righteous." This can easily happen when people think God's will is the same thing as their list of what they can and cannot do. Their desire to keep all of God's laws was commendable, but sometimes they put the emphasis on the wrong places. Minor details became a major preoccupation, and they forgot the more important things (Matt. 23:23).

Finally, because Pharisees thought they were doing their best to keep God's laws while others were not, they often looked down on such "sinners"—especially people like tax collectors and prostitutes. Religious people need to remember that they, too, are sinners in God's eyes, and that Christ died for everyone.

PHAROSH [FAY rahsh] — a form of PAROSH.

PHARPAR [FAHR pahr] (meaning unknown) — a river of southern Syria near Damascus (2 Kin. 5:12) mentioned by Naaman, the Syrian leper (2 Kin. 5:12). The Abana probably is the modern Nahr el-Awaj, formed by several streams that descend from Mount Hermon. The river empties into Lake Bahret Hijaneh, east of Damascus.

PHARZITES [FAHR zights] — a form of PARZITES.

PHASEAH [fuh SEE uh] — a form of PASEAH.

PHEBE [FEE bih] — a form of PHOEBE.

PHENICE [fuh NIH seh] — a form of PHOENIX.

PHENICIA [fuh KNEE shuh] — a form of PHOENICIA.

PHICHOL [FIGH kuhl] (meaning unknown) — the commander of the army of Abimelech who made covenants with Abraham (Gen. 21:22, 32) and Isaac (Gen. 26:26; Phicol, NASB, NEB, NIV, RSV).

PHICOL [FIGH kuhl] — a form of PHICHOL.

PHILADELPHIA [fill ah DELL fih uh] (*brotherly love*) — a city of the province of Lydia (see Map 6, C-4) in western Asia Minor (modern Turkey) and the site of one of the seven churches of Asia to which John wrote in the Book of Revelation (Rev. 1:11).

Philadelphia was situated on the Cogamus River, a tributary of the Hermus (modern Gediz) and was about 45 kilometers (28 miles) southeast of Sardis. It was founded by Attalus II (Philadelphus), who reigned as king of Pergamos from 159 B.C. until 138 B.C. Philadelphia was a center of the wine industry. Its chief deity was Dionysus, in Greek mythology the god of wine (the Roman Bacchus).

In the Book of Revelation, John describes the church in Philadelphia as the faithful church and the church that stood at the gateway of a great opportunity (Rev. 3:7-13). Christ said to this church, "See, I have set before you an open door and no one can shut it" (v. 8). The "open door" means primarily access to God, but it also refers to opportunity for spreading the gospel of Jesus Christ. Still a city of considerable size, Philadelphia is known today as Alasehir, or Allah-shehr ("the city of God").

PHILEMON [fie LEE mun] — a wealthy Christian of Colossae who hosted a house-church. Philemon was converted under the apostle Paul (Philem. 19), perhaps when Paul ministered in Ephesus (Acts 19:10). He is remembered because of his runaway slave, Onesimus, who, after damaging or stealing his master's property (Philem. 11, 18), made his way to Rome, where he was converted under Paul's ministry (Philem. 10).

Accompanied by Tychicus (Col. 4:7), Onesimus

The modern Turkish city of Alasehir, the biblical Philadelphia, on the Hermus River. John commended the Christians at Philadelphia for their faithfulness (Rev. 1:11; 3:7-13).

Photo by Gustav Jeeninga

later returned to his master, Philemon. He carried with him the Epistle to the Colossians, plus the shorter Epistle to Philemon. In the latter, Paul asked Philemon to receive Onesimus, not as a slave but as a "beloved brother" (Philem. 16). Nothing further is known of Philemon.

PHILEMON, EPISTLE TO — the shortest and most personal of Paul's epistles. Philemon tells the story of the conversion of a runaway slave, ONESIMUS, and the appeal to his owner, PHILEMON, to accept him back. The letter is warm and masterful, reminding us that the presence of Christ drastically changes every relationship in life.

Structure of the Epistle. Philemon consists of one chapter of 25 verses. A greeting, addressed to Philemon and the church which meets in his house (vv. 1–3), is followed by four verses in praise of Philemon's love and faith (vv. 4–7). Paul comes to his point in verses 8–16, where he tells of his affection for Onesimus and entreats Philemon to receive him back as a "beloved brother" (v. 16). Paul is so confident that Philemon will do even more than he asks that he offers to pay any expenses Philemon has incurred and asks him to prepare the guest room for a forthcoming visit (vv. 17–22). Final greetings conclude the letter (vv. 23–25).

Authorship, Date, and Historical Setting. The Epistle to Philemon is a companion to the Epistle to the Colossians. Both were written during Paul's imprisonment, probably in Rome (Col. 4:18; Philem. 9). They contain the names of the same greeters (compare Col. 4:7–17 with Philem. 23–25) and were delivered at the same time by Tychicus and Onesimus (Col. 4:7–9). The date for the two letters is the late 50s or early 60s.

Theological Contribution. The Epistle to Philemon is a lesson in the art of Christian relationships. No finer example of "speaking the truth in love" (Eph. 4:15) exists than this beautiful letter. While it was Philemon's legal right in the ancient world to punish or even kill a runaway slave, Paul hoped—indeed expected (v. 19)—that Philemon would receive Onesimus back as a brother in the Lord, not as a slave (v. 16). From beginning to end Paul addresses Philemon as a trusted friend rather than as an adversary (v. 22); he appeals to the best in his character (vv. 4–7, 13–14, 17, 21). In spite of Paul's subtle pressures for Philemon to restore Onesimus, he is careful not to force Philemon to do what is right; he helps him choose it for himself (vv. 8–9, 14).

Special Considerations. Although Paul never, so far as we know, called for an end to slavery, the Epistle to Philemon laid the ax at the root of that cruel and deformed institution—and to every way of treating individuals as property instead of persons. If there is "one God and Father of all" (Eph. 4:6), and if all are debtors to Him (Rom. 3:21–26), then no person can look on another person as something to be used for his own ends. In Christ that person has become a "beloved brother."

PHILETUS [fih LEE tuhs] (*beloved*) — a false teacher of the early church. Along with Hymenaeus, Philetus was condemned by the apostle Paul because he claimed the resurrection was already past (2 Tim. 2:17). Undoubtedly, Philetus advocated a GNOSTIC teaching which held that the body is evil and only the spirit will be saved. Because it upset the faith of some, such teaching is dangerous, Paul declared.

PHILIP [FILL ihp] (*lover of horses*) — the name of four men in the New Testament:

1. One of the twelve apostles of Christ (Matt. 10:3· Mark 3:18; Luke 6:14) and a native of Bethsaida in Galilee (John 1:44; 12:21). According to the Gospel of John, Philip met Jesus beyond the Jordan River during John the Baptist's ministry. Jesus called Philip to become His disciple. Philip responded and brought to Jesus another disciple, named Nathanael (John 1:43–51) or Bartholomew (Mark 3:18). Philip is usually mentioned with Nathanael.

Before Jesus fed the five thousand, He tested Philip by asking him how so many people could possibly be fed. Instead of responding in faith, Philip began to calculate the food it would take to feed them and the cost (John 6:5–7).

When certain Greeks, who had come to Jerusalem to worship at the Feast of Passover, said to Philip, "Sir, we wish to see Jesus" (John 12:21), Philip seemed unsure of what he should do. He first told Andrew, and then they told Jesus of the request. Philip was one of the apostles who was present in the Upper Room following the resurrection of Jesus (Acts 1:13).

2. A son of Herod the Great and Mariamne; first husband of Herodias (Matt. 14:3; Luke 3:19). He

---

PHILEMON: A Teaching Outline

Photo by Howard Vos

Ruins of the agora, or marketplace, of Philippi, with a pagan temple in the foreground.

was either the brother or half-brother of Herod Antipas. Since he is not called the tetrarch, scholars believe him to be a different Philip from Philip the tetrarch, a half-brother of Herod Antipas. Most scholars agree that this Philip was Herod Philip the first husband of Herodias. Herodias left him for Herod Antipas. He did not actually reign, but lived as a private citizen in Rome. According to the Jewish historian Josephus, although Philip was in the line of succession, he was passed over in the wills of Herod the Great.

3. Philip the tetrarch, a son of Herod the Great by Cleopatra of Jerusalem. Luke 3:1 records that Philip was "tetrarch of Iturea and the region of Trachonitis" at the time when John the Baptist began his ministry. He married Salome, the daughter of Herod Philip and Herodias. According to Josephus, Philip's character was exceptional and his rule of 37 years (4 B.C.—A.D. 34) was just and fair. He improved the town of Paneas and renamed it Caesarea. It was later called Caesarea Philippi (Matt. 16:13) to avoid confusion with Caesarea on the Mediterranean Sea. He also turned the village of Bethsaida into a city and renamed it "Julias," in honor of Julia, the daughter of Augustus Caesar.

4. Philip the evangelist, one of the seven men chosen to serve the early church because they were reported to be "full of faith and the Holy Spirit" (Acts 6:5). Their task was to look after the Greek-speaking widows and probably all of the poor in the Jerusalem church. Following the stoning of Stephen, the first Christian martyr, many Christians scattered from Jerusalem (Acts 8:1). Philip became an evangelist and, in Samaria, preached the gospel, worked miracles, and brought many to faith in Christ (Acts 8:5-8).

Probably the most noted conversion as a result of Philip's ministry was the ETHIOPIAN EUNUCH, an official of great authority under Candace, the queen of the Ethiopians. Philip met the Ethiopian eunuch on the road from Jerusalem to Gaza. The eunuch was reading from Isaiah 53, the passage about the SUFFERING SERVANT. Philip used this great opportunity to preach Jesus to him. The eunuch said, "I believe that Jesus Christ is the Son of God" (Acts 8:37). Then Philip baptized the eunuch.

After this event, Philip preached in Azotus (the Old Testament Ashdod) and Caesarea (Acts 8:40). He was still in Caesarea many years later when the apostle Paul passed through the city on his last journey to Jerusalem (Acts 21:8). Luke adds that Philip had "four virgin daughters who prophesied" (Acts 21:9).

PHILIP HEROD (see HEROD).

PHILIPPI [FIL uh pie] (*city of Philip*) — a city in eastern Macedonia (modern Greece) visited by the apostle Paul (see Map 7, C-1). Situated on a plain surrounded by mountains, Philippi lay about 16 kilometers (10 miles) inland from the Aegean Sea. The Egnatian Way, the main overland route between Asia and the West, ran through the city. Philippi was named for Philip II of Macedonia, the father of Alexander the Great. In 356 B.C. Philip enlarged and renamed the city, which was formerly known as Krenides ("wells, springs"). Philip resettled people from the countryside in Philippi and built a wall around the city and an acropolis atop the surrounding mountain. Although they date from later periods, other points of interest in Philippi include a forum the size of a football field, an open-air theater, two large temples, public

— 833 —

buildings, a library, and Roman baths.

In 42 B.C. Mark Antony and Octavian (later Augustus Caesar) combined forces to defeat the armies of Brutus and Cassius, assassins of Julius Caesar, at Philippi. In celebration of the victory, Philippi was made into a Roman colony; this entitled its inhabitants to the rights and privileges usually granted those who lived in cities in Italy. Eleven years later, Octavian defeated the forces of Antony and Cleopatra in a naval battle at Actium, on the west coast of Greece. Octavian punished the supporters of Antony by evicting them from Italy and resettling them in Philippi. The vacated sites in Italy were then granted to Octavian's own soldiers as a reward for their victory over Antony.

The apostle Paul visited Philippi on his second missionary journey in A.D. 49 (Acts 16:12; 20:6). Evidently the city did not have the necessary number of Jewish males (ten) to form a synagogue, because Paul met with a group of women for prayer outside the city gate (Acts 16:13).

French excavations at Philippi between 1914 and 1938 unearthed a Roman arch which lay about one mile west of the city. This arch may have served as a zoning marker to restrict undesirable religious sects (Jewish perhaps?) from meeting in the city. One of the women of Philippi who befriended Paul, named LYDIA, was a dealer in purple cloth (Acts 16:14). A Latin inscription uncovered in excavations mentions this trade, thus indicating its economic importance for Philippi. Philippi also is mentioned or implied in Acts 20:16; Philippians 1:1; and 1 Thessalonians 2:2.

PHILIPPIANS [fih LIP ih anz] — natives or inhabitants of PHILIPPI (Phil. 4:15), a city of Macedonia situated about 113 kilometers (70 miles) northeast of Thessalonica (Acts 16:12; Phil. 1:1)

PHILIPPIANS, EPISTLE TO THE — one of four shorter epistles written by the apostle Paul while he was in prison. The other three are Ephesians, Colossians, and Philemon. Paul founded the church at Philippi (Acts 16:12–40). Throughout his life the Philippians held a special place in his heart. Paul writes to them with affection, and the epistle breathes a note of joy throughout. When Paul first came to Philippi, he was thrown in jail. In the deep of the night, bound and beaten, he sang a hymn to God (Acts 16:25). A decade later Paul was again in prison, and he still was celebrating the Christian's joy in the midst of suffering, "Rejoice in the Lord always. Again I will say, rejoice!" (Phil. 4:4).

Structure of the Epistle. Paul begins the epistle by giving thanks for the love of the Philippians and by praying for its increase (1:1–11). Even though Paul is in prison, the gospel is not confined; on the contrary, it is increasing. Whether Paul lives or dies, "Christ is preached" (1:18); and this results in salvation (1:12–26). Following these reflections, Paul introduces a series of exhortations: to remain faithful in suffering (1:27–30); to remain considerate of others, as Jesus Christ was (2:1–11); and to avoid evil and live blamelessly (2:12–18).

Paul then turns to news of two companions. Once a decision has been reached about his trial, Paul will send Timothy to the Philippians with the news (2:19–24). For the present, he is sending back Epaphroditus, who had brought the Philippians' gift to him and who in the meantime has been critically ill (2:25–30). In chapter 3 Paul discusses the difference between true and false righteousness. Whereas the JUDAIZERS would say, "If you do not live rightly you will not be saved," Paul teaches, "If you do not live rightly you have not been saved."

The final chapter summarizes several miscellaneous matters. Paul exhorts quarrelsome church members to rise above their differences (4:2–50). He also leaves two important lessons, on substituting thankful prayer for anxiety (4:6–7), and on the characteristics of a noble and godly life (4:8–9). He concludes with thanks for the Philippian's gift and includes final greetings (4:10–23).

Authorship and Date. There can be little doubt that Philippians comes from Paul. The entire epistle bears the stamp of his language and style; the setting pictures Paul's imprisonments; and the recipients correspond with what we know of the church at Philippi.

During his second missionary journey, in A.D. 49, Paul sensed the Lord calling him to visit Macedonia (Acts 16:6–10). At Philippi he founded the first Christian congregation on European soil (Acts 16:11–40). A lifelong supportive relationship developed between the Philippians and Paul (Phil. 1:5; 4:15). He visited the church again during his third missionary journey (Acts 20:1, 6).

At the time he wrote Philippians, Paul was in prison awaiting trial (Phil. 1:7). The Philippian Christians came to Paul's aid by sending a gift, perhaps of money, through Epaphroditus (4:18). During his stay with Paul, Epaphroditus fell desperately ill. But he recovered, and Paul sent him back to Philippi. He sent this letter with him to relieve the anxiety of the Philippians over their beloved fellow-worker (2:25–30).

Historical Setting. The location of Paul's imprisonment has been long debated. Much can be said for Ephesus or Caesarea but still more for Rome. Paul refers to "the whole palace guard" (1:13), and he even sends greetings from "Caesar's household" (4:22). These references suggest Rome, as does the description of his confinement in 1:12–18. This description is similar to Clement's description of Paul's Roman imprisonment written near the close of the first century. Paul also considers the possibility of his death (1:23). This prospect was more likely toward the end of his life in Rome than earlier. The epistle, therefore, should probably be dated about A.D. 60.

Theological Contribution. The focus of Paul's thoughts in this epistle is the Christ–centered life, the hallmark of which is joy. Paul has surrendered everything to Christ and can say, "For to me, to live is Christ" (1:1), "to be a prisoner for Christ" (1:13), "to live and die in Christ" (1:20), "and to give up all to win Christ" (3:7–8)." Christ has laid hold of Paul

(3:12), and Paul's sole passion is to glorify Christ (3:8–9). Paul longs for his experience of Christ to be repeated in the lives of the Philippians. He prays that they will abound in the love of Christ (1:9), will lay hold of the mind of Christ (2:5–11), and, like himself, will know the experience of Christ—His sufferings, death, and resurrection (3:10–11).

Because Paul's only motive is to "know Him" (3:10), he shares in the power of Christ and "can do all things through Christ," who is his joy and strength (4:13).

Several times in the epistle Paul exhorts the Philippians to translate their relationship with Christ into daily life by being "like-minded" with Christ or "setting their minds on Christ." In the face of opposition, Paul tells them to "stand fast...with one mind striving together for the faith of the gospel" (1:27). Differences between Christians can be overcome when the parties have "the same mind in the Lord" (4:2). Paul exhorts the believers to set their mind on the high calling of God in Jesus Christ (3:14–15) and to meditate on whatever is true, noble, just, pure, lovely, and of good report (4:8). To have the mind of Christ is to see life from Christ's perspective and to act toward other people with the intentions of Christ.

Special Considerations. Nowhere is the mind of Christ presented to the Christian more strongly that in Philippians 2:1–11. Appealing to the Philippians to be of "one mind" (2:2) in pursuing humility, Paul cites the example of the incarnation of God in Jesus Christ. "Let this mind be in you which was also in Christ Jesus" (2:5), urges Paul. Unlike Adam, who sought to be equal with God (Gen. 3:5), Christ did not try to grasp for equality with God. Instead, being God, he poured Himself out and took upon Himself the form of a slave, to the point of dying the death of a common criminal. "Therefore," glories Paul, "God...has highly exalted Him, and given Him the name which is above every name" (2:9).

This is the Christ whose attitude and intention all believers must share. To be identified with Christ in humility and obedience is the noblest achievement to which anyone can aspire.

PHILISTIA [fih LIS tih uh] (meaning unknown) — the land of the PHILISTINES (see Map 3, A–4), as used in the poetry of the Book of Psalms (60:8; 108:9). This land lay between Joppa and Gaza on the coastal plain of Palestine. Also see PALESTINE.

PHILISTIM [fih LIS tim] — KJV translation of PHILISTINES (Gen. 10:14).

PHILISTINES [fih LIS teens] — an aggressive tribal group that occupied part of southwest Palestine (see Map 3, A–4) from about 1200 to 600 B.C. The name Philistine was used first among the Egyptians to describe the sea people defeated by Rameses III in a naval battle about 1188 B.C. Among the Assyrians the group was known as Pilisti or Palastu, but the origin of the term is uncertain. The Hebrew word *pelishti* actually comes from the territory they occupied, Philistia. This is

PHILIPPIANS: A Teaching Outline

the basis of the name Palestine, the country occupied by God's Covenant People.

Little is known about the origins of the Philistines except what is contained in the Bible—that they came from Caphtor (Gen. 10:14), generally identified with the island of Crete in the Mediterranean Sea. Crete also was supposed to be the home of the Cherethites, who were frequently associated with the Philistines (Ezek. 25:16). Philistine territory was considered Cherethite in 1 Samuel 30:14, suggesting that both peoples were part of the invading group defeated earlier by Rameses III of Egypt.

Liberal scholars have assumed that references to the Philistines during Abraham's time are incorrect historically and that the Philistine occupation actually occurred in the 12th century B.C. More careful examination indicates there were two Philistine settlements in Canaan, one early and another later. Both these settlements were marked by significant cultural differences. The Philistines of Gerar, with whom Abraham dealt (Genesis 20—21), evidently were a colony of the early settlement located southeast of Gaza in southern Canaan. This colony was situated outside the area occupied by the five Philistine cities after 1188 B.C. Gerar was also a separate city–state governed by a king who bore the name or title of Abimelech.

That Abimelech's colony was the chief one in the area seems probable from his title, "king of the Philistines" (Gen. 26:1, 8). This is different from a later period when the Philistines were governed by five lords. Unlike the later Philistines who were Israel's chief foes in the settlement and monarchy periods, the Gerar Philistines were peaceful. They encouraged the friendship of Abraham and Isaac. Finally, Gerar was not included among the chief cities of Philistia (Josh. 13:3). It was not mentioned as one of the places conquered by the Israelites. It is best, therefore, to regard the Genesis traditions as genuine historical records.

The early Philistine settlements in Canaan took on a new appearance when five cities—Ashkelon, Ashdod, Ekron, Gath, and Gaza—and the areas around them were occupied by the Philistines in the 12th century B.C. Probably all of these except Ekron were already in existence when the sea peoples conquered them. These five Philistine cities formed a united political unit. Archaeological discoveries in the area have illustrated how they expanded to the south and east. Broken bits of Philistine pottery were found at archaeological sites in those areas.

The Philistines possessed superior weapons of iron when they began to attack the Israelites in the 11th century B.C. The tribe of Dan moved northward to escape these Philistine attacks, and Judah also came under increasing pressure (Judges 14—18). In Samuel's time the Philistines captured Shiloh, where the ARK OF THE COVENANT was located. Although the ark was recovered later, the Philistines continued to occupy Israelite settlements (1 Sam. 10:5).

The threat of the Philistines prompted Israel's demands for a king. But even under Saul the united nation was still menaced by the Philistines—a threat which ultimately resulted in Saul's death. David's slaying of Goliath, a giant from Gath, was a key factor in his rise to fame. By this time the Philistines had moved deep into Israelite territory. Archaeological evidence shows they had occupied Tell Beit Mirsim, Debir, Beth Zur, Gibeah, Megiddo, and Beth Shan. Yet by the end of David's reign their power had begun to decline significantly. By the time Jehoshaphat was made king of Judah (873–848 B.C.), the Philistines were paying tribute (2 Chr. 17:11), although they tried to become independent under Jehoshaphat's son, Jehoram (2 Chr. 21:16–17).

When the Assyrians began to raid Palestine in later years, the Philistines faced additional opposition. The Assyrian Adad–Nirari III (about 810–783 B.C.) placed the Philistine cities under heavy tribute early in his reign, while Uzziah of Judah (791–740 B.C.) demolished the defenses of several Philistine strongholds, including Gath. When he became king, Ahaz of Judah (732–715 B.C.) was attacked by Philistine forces, and cities in the Negev and the Judean lowlands were occupied. The Assyrian king Tiglath–Pileser III responded by conquering the chief Philistine cities.

In 713 B.C. Sargon, king of Assyria, invaded Philistia and conquered Ashdod. The following year he launched another campaign against other Philistine cities. Hezekiah of Judah (716–686 B.C.)

A Philistine sarcophagus, or coffin. After the body was placed inside, the opening was sealed with a matching lid (left) on which stylized human features were engraved.

Photo by Gustav Jeeninga

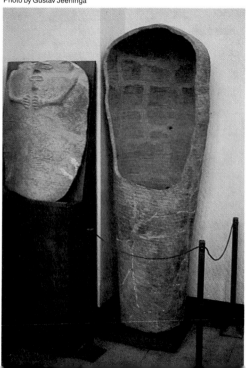

attacked Gaza (2 Kin. 18:8), supported by the people of Ekron and Ashkelon; but in 701 B.C. Sennacherib brought Philistine territory under his control to prevent any Egyptian interference. When Nebuchadnezzar came to power in Babylon, the Philistines formed an alliance with Egypt; but when the Judeans were exiled to Babylonia between 597 and 587 B.C., the Philistines, too, were deported.

No Philistine literature has survived, making it difficult to reconstruct their religious beliefs or rituals. Old Testament records indicate they worshiped three gods, Ashtoreth, Dagon, and Baal-Zebub—each of which had shrines in various cities (Judg. 16:23; 1 Sam. 5:1-7). Sacrifices were offered to Dagon, a god represented with the head and hands of a man and the tail of a fish (Judg. 16:23). Philistine soldiers apparently carried images of this god into battle, perhaps as standards (2 Sam. 5:21). Like other Near Eastern peoples, the Philistnes were superstitious. They respected the power of Israel's ARK OF THE COVENANT (1 Sam. 5:1-12).

As depicted on an Egyptian inscription, Philistine soldiers wore short tunics, were clean-shaven, had crested or decorated helmets, carried round shields, and fought with iron weapons such as spears and swords. In the days before David's reign, the Philistine cities were governed by a representative from each city. These authorities exercised complete power in both peace and war. This centralized control made the Philistines strong, in contrast to the loosely organized Israelites.

The Philistines were important culturally because they adopted the manufacture and distribution of iron implements and weapons from the Hittites. Goliath's equipment was obviously of Philistine manufacture. The golden objects that were offered to Israel's God (1 Sam 6:4-5) show that the Philistines were skilled goldsmiths as well.

The remains of Philistine furnaces have been uncovered at Tell Jemmeh and Ashdod. The area around Ashdod has produced some examples of typical Philistine pottery. This pottery reflected Greek as well as Egyptian and Palestinian styles. The Philistines loved beer. Large beer mugs decorated with red and black geometric designs were some of their important pottery products, along with large cups, beakers, and bowls. Some Philistine burial places discovered at Tell Far'ah reveal bodies encased in clay coffins shaped to match the human body. The coffin lid was decorated with crude figures of the head and clasped arms of the deceased.

PHILO JUDAEUS [FIE low joo DEE us] — a Jewish philosopher and teacher who is known for his allegorical interpretation of Scripture; also known as Philo of Alexandria. He was born into one of the most influential Jewish families in Alexandria, Egypt, around 20 B.C. and died in A.D. 50. Thus, he was teaching and writing during the time of Jesus. Philo was schooled in the Greek philosophers and dramatists as well as his own Jewish traditions. Most scholars agree that he was not familiar with the Hebrew Bible and did most of his work in the Greek translation known as the SEPTUAGINT.

Philo was very active in the synagogues of Alexandria and he learned from the numerous teachers and preachers who visited there. The stories and scholarly lectures he heard were incorporated into his writings. During the reign of the Roman Emperor, Gaius Caligula, Philo visited Rome to plead for the protection of the Jews of Alexandria. The persecution of Jews in Egypt made it impossible for Philo to isolate himself from diplomatic service.

Philo's writings were preserved by the Christian church. Many Jews thought his writings were suspect because they reflected Greek philosophy rather than Hebrew tradition, while the church viewed his works as close to the thoughts of the church fathers. Many Christian writers saw parallels between Philo and the Gospel of John, for example—especially in his idea of the Word, or Logos, of God being in the beginning with God (John 1:1).

Philo's writings dealt mainly with the Pentateuch and various themes within the writings of Moses. Among his many writings are: *On the Creation*, which says that the creation (the laws of nature) is in harmony with the law as written in the first five books of Moses (the Pentateuch). *Allegorical Interpretation* is a comment on the first 17 chapters of Genesis. He does not deal with the text of Genesis itself so much as he uses it as a springboard to various themes from the rest of the Pentateuch. *On Dreams* is a series of sermons Philo gave in the synagogue; it is based on the dream stories in Genesis.

On the Ten Commandments is Philo's interpretation of the Ten Commandments; and *On the Special Laws* is a summary of the laws in the Pentateuch placed into the ten categories given in the Ten Commandments. Philo also wrote lives of the patriarchs, Abraham, Joseph, and Moses. These "Lives" deal with the patriarchs as models of righteous people.

PHILOLOGUS [fih LAHL uh guhs] (*talkative*) — a Christian to whom the apostle Paul sent greetings (Rom. 16:15).

PHILOSOPHY — the love of wisdom (from *phileo*, "to love," and *sophia*, "wisdom"). At the sporting events of ancient Greece, the philosopher Pythagoras said, there were three types of people: lovers of money (selling refreshments), lovers of fame (sports heroes), and lovers of wisdom (seekers of wisdom in sports and life in general). Everyone who has some convictions by which he lives is a philosopher. However, those called philosophers in a formal sense consciously seek well-founded convictions by which to live.

Teachers of philosophy give their lives to examining convictions by which people live in order to develop a consistent world view and way of life based on reliable evidence. The Bible warns against philosophies whose highest realities and concerns are atoms, energy, cosmic laws, or humanity—those founded on "the basic principles of the world, and

An inscribed altar to unknown gods, perhaps similar to the one Paul saw at Athens (Acts 17:22-24).

not according to Christ" (Col. 2:8). Christians ought to beware that their minds not be taken captive by such philosophies as secular humanism, communist materialism, and capitalist materialism. But these philosophies are best fought with spiritual weapons (2 Cor. 10:4–5).

Christian wisdom appears to be foolishness to the people of the world (1 Cor. 1:18). But it is wiser than the philosophy of this age, which comes to nothing (1 Cor. 1:25; 2:6). Christians "speak the wisdom of God" (1 Cor. 2:7), which is revealed through His Spirit (1 Cor. 2:10) and received by His Spirit (1 Cor. 2:12–14). Christians have the highest and most complete wisdom in Christ (Col. 2:8–10).

The chief biblical example of how to help students of philosophy who do not accept biblical authority is found in Paul's ministry to the EPICUREAN and STOIC philosophers at Athens. Paul commended their zeal, quoted them favorably on a point of agreement, declared the truth about the living Lord of all, announced their accountability to Christ (not to Socrates, Plato, Aristotle, Epicurus, or Zeno), and called on them to repent and trust Jesus Christ (Acts 17:16–34).

PHINEHAS [FIN ih uhs] *(the Nubian)* — the name of three men in the Old Testament:

1. A son of Eleazar and grandson of Aaron (Ex. 6:25). During the wilderness wandering, Phinehas killed Zimri, a man of Israel, and Cozbi, a Midianite woman whom Zimri had brought into the camp (Num. 25). This action ended a plague by which God had judged Israel for allowing Midianite women to corrupt Israel with idolatry and harlotry. For such zeal Phinehas and his descendants were promised a permanent priesthood

(Num. 25:11–13). Phinehas became the third high priest of Israel, serving for 19 years. His descendants held the high priesthood until the Romans destroyed the Temple in A.D. 70, except for a short period when the house of Eli served as high priests.

2. The younger of the two sons of Eli the priest (1 Sam. 1:3). Phinehas and his brother, Hophni, were priests also; but they disgraced their priestly office by graft, irreverence, and immorality (1 Sam. 2:12–17, 22–25). The Lord told Eli his two sons would die (1 Sam. 2:34). They were killed in a battle with the Philistines. When Phinehas' wife heard the news, she went into premature labor and died in childbirth. The child was named ICHABOD, which means "The glory has departed from Israel!"(1 Sam. 4:22). Because of the evil actions of Phinehas and Hophni, the high priesthood later passed from Eli's family.

3. The father of Eleazar (Ezra 8:33).

PHLEGON [FLEG ahn] *(zealous)* — a Christian of Rome to whom the apostle Paul sent greetings (Rom. 16:14).

PHOEBE [FEE bih] *(radiant)* — a servant of the church in Cenchrea, the eastern port of Corinth (Rom. 16:1; Phebe, KJV). The apostle Paul tells us little about Phoebe, other than "she has been a helper of many and of myself also" (Rom. 16:2). The Greek words he used to describe her suggest that Phoebe was a wealthy businesswoman. Many scholars believe she delivered Paul's letter to the Romans.

PHOENICIA [foe KNEE shih uh] — the land northwest of Palestine on the eastern shore of the Mediterranean Sea (see Map 4, B–2), between the

Litani and Arvad Rivers. Phoenicia is a Greek word, a direct translation of the Hurrian word *Canaan*, which means "land of purple." The area was famous from early times for its purple dyes, produced from shellfish. In the KJV, Phoenicia is spelled either Phenice or Phenicia.

Phoenicia was a long, narrow country on the seacoast covering much of the territory that today is called Lebanon and southern Latakia (coastal Syria). Like Israel, much of it is mountainous, with only a narrow coastal plain. The low hills and plain are very fertile. Phoenicia was famous in biblical times for its lush plant life (Hos. 14:5–7), which included fruit, flowers, and trees.

The cedars of Phoenicia were cut and shipped as far away as Egypt and eastern Mesopotamia, because most other nations in this part of the world had very few trees suitable for timber. Many direct land and sea routes connected Phoenicia to northern Israel. The Phoenicians had many contacts with the Israelites. During their long history, the Hebrew people often fell into paganism and idolatry because of the influence of Phoenician religion.

Also see PHOENICIANS.

PHOENICIANS [foe KNEE shih uns] — inhabitants of PHOENICIA, the ancient nation along the Mediterranean Sea northwest of Palestine. The Phoenicians were known for their trade and commerce and their skill as a seafaring people. There were three major reasons why Phoenicia became a major trading power.

First, the Phoenicians were crowded onto a narrow strip of coastland after being conquered by the Israelites around 1380 B.C. Thus hemmed in, they took to the sea in order to expand their empire, eventually becoming one of the most distinguished seafaring peoples in history.

Second, the mountains that approach the Phoenician coast made travel by land unusually difficult; travel by sea was the logical alternative.

Finally, the plentiful supply of pine, cypress, and cedar trees in Phoenicia made shipbuilding an ideal pursuit for the Phoenician people. The men of Byblos were noted shipbuilders (Ezek. 27:9), and the people of the Phoenician city of Sidon were experts at felling trees (1 Kin. 5:6).

Phoenicia's two major ports, Tyre and Sidon, were semi–independent city–states. Besides these two, several other Phoenician cities grew in influence as the merchant fleets brought wealth into the country. The nation increasingly became independent of foreign domination. By its "golden age" (about 1050–850 B.C.) the Phoenicians achieved their height of prosperity and influence. Phoenicia founded many colonies along shipping routes, so that Phoenicians lived in Crete, Cyprus, Sardinia, Sicily, North Africa (especially the important colony of Carthage), and even Spain.

In the course of their travels, Phoenician merchants developed many skills that had a lasting influence on world culture. They are usually given credit for originating the alphabet and for pioneering the skills of glass–making and the dyeing of cloth. Scholars believe Solomon's Temple and many of its furnishings were based on a Phoenician design. Some archaeologists believe that the Phoenicians were extremely skilled in working with gold, iron, and copper, and that they were skilled jewelers. Also, Phoenician designs possibly inspired much of Greek, Assyrian, and Etruscan architecture.

As the Assyrians began to dominate the ancient world in the eighth century B.C., Phoenicia's influence declined. Phoenicia was progressively weak-

Model of a type of long-range Phoenician merchant ship called a "Hippos."
Photo: Haifa Maritime Museum

ened in wars with Assyria during the seventh century B.C. In 587 B.C. the Babylonians, who had conquered Assyria only two decades earlier, laid siege to Tyre—the last remaining independent Phoenician city.

After 13 years of siege (585–572 B.C.), the mainland city of Tyre was captured. There was also an island city of Tyre, which did not fall until 332 B.C. when Alexander the Great built a causeway over half a mile long in order to reach it. Alexander destroyed the city, but Tyre was later rebuilt. The city was an important outpost in the Greek and Roman period.

Like its neighbor Israel, Phoenicia finally ceased to be an independent nation. It was dominated in turn by the Persians, Greeks, Seleucids, and Romans.

Phoenician Religion. Phoenician gods were male and female representations of nature. Their primary god was called Baal. He combined the attributes of several other Phoenician deities, including Hadad, the storm god; Shamash, the sun god; and Reshep, god of the earth and the netherworld. The Phoenician goddess honored as the "great mother" was called Ashtoreth. Additionally, Eshmun, the god of healing, was especially honored in Sidon. The Phoenician religion survives today in folk festivals in Lebanon near Byblos.

Connections with the Old Testament. When David completed the conquest of the Promised Land and made Israel the strongest power in the area, the Phoenicians under Hiram of Tyre (981–947 B.C.) became involved commercially with the Israelites (2 Sam. 5:11). The Phoenicians of Tyre helped supply materials and laborers for the building of Solomon's Temple (1 Kin. 5:1–12). In later years, Solomon bought Hiram's help by transferring ownership of large tracts of real estate in Galilee from Israel to Tyre (1 Kin. 9:11).

The Phoenicians also helped the Israelites in Solomon's kingdom to learn the shipping trade and to construct a merchant fleet that brought wealth to Israel (1 Kin. 9:26–28). Regrettably, Solomon fell under the influence of foreign religions later in his life. These problems included worship of the Phoenician idol Ashtoreth, the supreme goddess of the Sidonians (1 Kin. 11:1–8). His turning from the Lord to the beliefs of people such as the Phoenicians resulted in the division of the nation—an act of judgment by God (1 Kin. 11:9–13).

Phoenician religious influence in Israel was given a dramatic boost by King Ahab, who married the Phoenician princess Jezebel, the daughter of the king of the Sidonians. Ahab gave Jezebel the freedom to put prophets of Baal on the government payroll in Israel (1 Kin. 18:19) and to try to convert the nation to idolatry.

Although the Bible mentions Phoenicia rarely, it often refers to the major Phoenician cities of Tyre and Sidon. Isaiah (23:1–18), Jeremiah (25:22; 47:4), Ezekiel (26:2—28:23), and other Old Testament prophets predicted the judgment of God on Tyre and Sidon. This judgment came in large measure when the Babylonians captured these cities along with the rest of Phoenicia in the early sixth century B.C.

Connections with the New Testament. Phoenicians were among those who came to hear Jesus teach about the kingdom of God (Luke 6:17). After the death of Stephen, some Christians escaped persecution by going to Phoenicia, where they preached the gospel (Acts 11:19). The apostle Paul traveled through Phoenicia on more than one occasion (Acts 15:3; 21:2–3).

PHOENIX [FEE niks] *(date palm)* — a harbor in the southern part of CRETE, west of Fair Havens (Acts 27:12; Phenice, KJV). On his trip to Italy the ship on which the apostle Paul and 275 other passengers were traveling anchored in the harbor of Fair Havens.

PHRYGIA [FRIJ ih uh] *(dry, barren)* — a large province of the mountainous region of Asia Minor (modern Turkey; see Map 7, C–2), visited by the apostle Paul (Acts 2:10; 16:6; 18:23). Because of its size, Phrygia was made a part of other provinces. In Roman times the region was split between two provinces. The cities of Colossae, Laodicea, and Hierapolis belonged to Asia, while Iconium and Antioch belonged to Galatia.

The apostle Paul visited Phrygia on three journeys (Acts 13:14—14:5, 21; 16:6; 16:23). He apparently also passed through Phrygia on his third journey (Acts 18:22–24), although his letter to the Colossians suggests he did not found a church there (Col. 2:1). Jews who were at Jerusalem on the Day of Pentecost may have been the first Phrygian converts (Act 2:10). Jews settled in Phrygia during the SELEUCID period. Some of them apparently adopted non-Jewish practices. Consequently, strict Jews became hostile to new ideas (Acts 13:44—14:6).

PHURAH [FYUR uh] — a form of PURAH.

PHUT [fuht] — a form of PUT.

PHUVAH [FOO vuh] — a form of PUVAH.

PHYGELLUS [FIGH juh luhs] *(fugitive)* — a Christian who deserted the apostle Paul in his hour of need (2 Tim. 1:15). He was probably afraid of being condemned by the Roman authorities.

PHYLACTERIES [fie LACK tuh rees] — small square leather boxes or cases, each containing four strips of parchment inscribed with quotations from the Pentateuch, the first five books of the Old Testament (Ex. 13:1–10; 13:11–16; Deut. 6:4–9; 11:13–21). In Bible times, phylacteries were worn by every male Israelite above 13 years of age during morning prayer, except on the Sabbath and holidays. Although orthodox Jews still observe this practice, reformed Judaism has discontinued it.

Phylacteries consisted of two small hollow cubes made of the skin of clean animals. These boxes were attached to leather straps which were used to fasten them to the left hand and to the forehead

This inscription from a theater in Caesarea mentions Pontius Pilate, procurator of Judea who pronounced the death sentence against Jesus (Mark 15).

during morning worship. The custom of wearing phylacteries can be traced to Deuteronomy 6:8, "You shall bind them as a sign upon your hand, and they shall be as frontlets between your eyes."

The discovery of portions of phylacteries in the Dead Sea caves reveals they were not standardized before the time of Christ. Certainly not all the people wore them, but the Pharisees possibly wore them constantly during the time of Jesus.

The word phylacteries occurs only once in the New Testament: "They [the scribes and Pharisees] make their phylacteries broad and enlarge the borders of their garments" (Matt. 23:5). In this passage Jesus criticized the display of some religious leaders who wanted to impress people with their piety.

PHYSICIAN — a person skilled in the art of healing the sick. Both the Old and New Testaments frequently mention the curing of ailments, but specific details about how this was done are few.

In the ancient world, primitive medical practices were performed by magicians or priests. This was especially true in ancient Egypt, where even elementary brain surgery was attempted. Some of the Egyptian procedures were adopted by the Hebrews. These included embalming (Gen. 50:2, 3, 26) or obstetrics, as with the midwives Shiphrah and Puah (Ex. 1:15).

Specific medical remedies are often recorded in the Bible. These include the application of bandages (Is. 1:6), oil (James 5:14), roots and leaves (Ezek. 47:12), wine (1 Tim. 5:23), and salves—particularly the BALM OF GILEAD (Jer. 8:22).

In the New Testament, the Good Samaritan treated the wounded traveler's injuries with oil and wine (Luke 10:34). Luke, one of the twelve disciples of Jesus and author of the Gospel of Luke, is called "the beloved physician" by the apostle Paul (Col. 4:14).

PI BESETH [pie BEE zith] (*house of Bastet*) — an ancient city in the Nile River delta which became the capital of Egypt at one time in its past. Pi Beseth is mentioned only once in the Bible. In Ezekiel 30:17 it is the place where young men were to fall by the sword and from which others were to be carried into captivity. The city was about 49 kilometers (30 miles) southwest of ancient Zoan and about 73 kilometers (45 miles) northeast of modern Cairo.

PI HAHIROTH [pie huh HIGH rahth] (meaning unknown) — the site of the final Israelite encampment in Egypt before they crossed the RED SEA. Pi Hahiroth is described as being "between Migdol and the sea" and "opposite" Baal Zephon (Ex. 14:2). Numbers 33:8 has Hahiroth, probably a shortened form of Pi Hahiroth.

PICK (see TOOLS OF THE BIBLE).

PIECE OF GOLD, MONEY, SILVER (see MONEY OF THE BIBLE).

PIETY — a word usually defined as religious devotion and reverence to God. In its only occurrence in the NKJV, however, it means faithfulness in performing one's responsibilities to the family, especially to parents (1 Tim. 5:4).

PIG, PIGEON (see ANIMALS OF THE BIBLE).

PILATE, PONTIUS [PIE lat, PON chus] — the fifth Roman procurator of Judea (ruled A.D. 26–36), who issued the official order sentencing Jesus to death by crucifixion (Matthew 27; Mark 15; Luke 23; John 18—19).

Pilate's Personal Life. The Jewish historian Josephus provides what little information is known about Pilate's life before A.D. 26, when Tiberius appointed him procurator of Judea. The sketchy data suggests that Pilate was probably an Italian-born Roman citizen whose family was wealthy enough for him to qualify for the middle class. Probably he held certain military posts before his appointment in Judea. He was married (Matt. 27:19), bringing his wife, Claudia Procula, to live with him at Caesarea, the headquarters of the province. Pilate governed the areas of Judea, Samaria, and the area south as far as the Dead Sea to Gaza. As procurator he had absolute authority over the non-Roman citizens of the province. He was responsible to the Roman governor who lived in Syria to the north (Luke 2:2).

Pilate never became popular with the Jews. He seemed to be insensitive to their religious convictions and stubborn in the pursuit of his policies. But when the Jews responded to his rule with enraged opposition, he often backed down, demonstrating his weakness. He greatly angered the Jews when he took funds from the Temple treasury to build an aqueduct to supply water to Jerusalem. Many Jews reacted violently to this act, and Pilate's soldiers killed many of them in this rebellion. It may be this or another incident to which Luke refers in Luke 13:1-2. In spite of this, Pilate continued in office for ten years, showing that Tiberius considered Pilate an effective administrator.

Pilate's later history is also shrouded in mystery. Josephus tells of a bloody encounter with the Samaritans, who filed a complaint with Pilate's superior, Vitellius, the governor of Syria. Vitellius deposed Pilate and ordered him to stand before the emperor in Rome and answer for his conduct. Legends are confused as to how Pilate died. Eusebius reports that he was exiled to the city of Vienne on the Rhone in Gaul (France) where he eventually committed suicide.

Pilate's Encounter with Jesus. Since the Jews could not execute a person without approval from the Roman authorities (John 18:31), the Jewish leaders brought Jesus to Pilate to pronounce the death sentence (Mark 14:64). Pilate seemed convinced that Jesus was not guilty of anything deserving death, and he sought to release Jesus (Matt. 27:24; Mark 15:9-11; Luke 23:14; John 18:38-40; 19:12). Neither did he want to antagonize the Jews and run the risk of damaging his own reputation and career. Thus, when they insisted on Jesus' crucifixion, Pilate turned Jesus over to be executed (Matt. 27:26; Mark 15:12-15; Luke 23:20-25; John 19:15-16).

Pilate's Character. Pilate is a good example of the unprincipled achiever who will sacrifice what is right to accomplish his own selfish goals. Although he recognized Jesus' innocence and had the authority to uphold justice and acquit Jesus, he gave in to the demands of the crowd rather than risk a personal setback in his career. This is a real temptation to all people who hold positions of power and authority.

PILDASH [PIL dash] (meaning unknown) — the sixth son of Nahor and Milcah (Gen. 22:22).

PILEHA [PIL ih huh] — a form of PILHA.

PILGRIMAGE — a word with three distinct meanings in the Bible:

1. The course of life on earth (Gen. 47:9; Ex. 6:4). Jacob summed up his entire life to that point—130 years—as a pilgrimage (Gen. 47:9).

2. A journey of a pilgrim to a sacred place or shrine, especially of the worshipers of the Lord who went up to the Temple in Jerusalem for special feasts (Ps. 84:5; 119:54).

3. A long journey or search, especially one of exalted purpose and moral significance. The heroes of faith are described as "strangers and pilgrims on the earth" (Heb. 11:13). The Christian's true citizenship, or permanent home, is in heaven (Phil. 3:20). While on earth, he or she is but a pilgrim, a traveler, a temporary resident.

Sacred pillars located at a pagan high place at Gezer.
Photo by Howard Vos

PILHA [PIL huh] (*millstone*) — a leader of the people who sealed the covenant after the Captivity (Neh. 10:24; Pileha, NIV, NEB, RSV, NASB).

PILLAR — a word with several different meanings in the Bible:

1. The word pillar can refer to an architectural element that supports a roof. Use of pillars was common in the Near East long before the time of Abraham. Pillars were usually made of wood or stone. References to pillars as a part of a building occur throughout the Old Testament but not in the New Testament.

Wooden pillars were a prominent part of the tabernacle (Ex. 27:11). But the only mention of pillars in the construction of Solomon's Temple were the two that flanked the main entrance (1 Kin. 7:15–22). Solomon built a "Hall of Pillars" as part of his palace complex (1 Kin. 7:6). A famous reference to pillars occurs in Judges 16:25–30, where Samson brought down the roof of a pagan temple by knocking out two key pillars. Excavators have found the remains of a Philistine temple that had two pillars supporting the roof, probably like the one Samson destroyed.

2. Pillars, or upright standing stones with religious significance, were used by both the Canaanites and the Israelites. In Canaanite worship places, a stone pillar was used as a symbol for the male god, usually Baal (2 Kin. 17:10). Moses erected twelve pillars, representing the twelve tribes of Israel, beside the altar he built to call upon the COVENANT (Ex. 24:4). Pillars could also serve as boundary markers (Gen. 31:45) or as tombstones (Gen. 35:20).

3. The Bible also contains many figurative references to pillars. For instance, the physical demonstration of God's presence during the Exodus was described as a "pillar of fire" and a "pillar of cloud" (Ex. 13:21). In other places, the importance of persons or things is emphasized by referring to them as pillars (Gal. 2:9). That which holds something up, either figuratively or literally, can also be called a pillar (1 Sam. 2:8; 1 Tim. 3:15).

PILLAR OF FIRE AND CLOUD — the phenomenon by which God guided the Israelites during their travels through the wilderness after leaving Egypt (Ex. 14:24). The pillar of fire and cloud is first mentioned in Exodus 13:21–22, where some of its characteristics are described. In the form of cloud by day and fire by night, the pillar was constantly visible to the Israelites. By this phenomenon, God led the people on their journey from the border of Egypt as they marched toward the Promised Land. As a pillar of fire, it gave enough light for the people to travel by night.

The pillar of fire and cloud was also a visible sign or representation of God's presence with His people. In a sense God could be said to be "in" the pillar (Ex. 14:24); in it He "came down" to the tabernacle of meeting (Num. 12:5), and "appeared" at the tabernacle (Deut. 31:15).

After the TABERNACLE was built in the wilderness, it was covered by a cloud which had the appearance of fire by night. Although this cloud was not described as a pillar, it must have been the same phenomenon. While the cloud remained over the tabernacle, the people did not break camp. But they set out when the cloud was taken up. Wherever it settled down again was to be the next stopping place.

PILLARS OF SALT — odd–shaped natural rock–salt formations near the Dead Sea, in the area of Sodom and Gomorrah. In spite of the warning by the angels, Lot's wife looked back longingly at the wicked cities of the plain. She was transformed immediately into a pillar of salt. Also see LOT.

PILLOW — a leather–covered cushion on which a person's head rests while at sleep (Mark 4:38; cushion, RSV, NIV, NEB, NASB). Jesus rested in the stern of a boat on the Sea of Galilee, asleep on a pillow that may have belonged to the owner of the boat. This is the only occurrence of the word pillow in the NKJV. In the KJV, Jacob put a stone under his head for a pillow (Gen. 28:11, 18).

PILOT (see OCCUPATIONS AND TRADES).

PILTAI [PIL tigh] (*my deliverance*) — the head of a household in the time of the high priest Joiakim (Neh. 12:17).

PIM [pim] (see WEIGHTS AND MEASURES).

PIN — KJV word for PEG. The pin or peg was a part of the structure of the tabernacle (Ex. 27:19; 39:40; Num. 4:32). A peg was also a symbol of the worthlessness of a fruitless vine (Ezek. 15:3). God compared the inhabitants of Jerusalem to the wood of a vine which, if it does not bear fruit, is good only for burning.

PINE (see PLANTS OF THE BIBLE).

PINNACLE — a part of the Temple mentioned in the temptation of Jesus (Matt. 4:5; Luke 4:9). The pinnacle was an elevated part of the Temple now unknown. It probably was either the battlement or the roof of Solomon's Porch. Whatever its exact location, the pinnacle offered a vast view of Jerusalem.

PINON [PIE nahn] (*meaning unknown*) — a chief of Edom, of the family of Esau (1 Chr. 1:52).

PIPE (see MUSICAL INSTRUMENTS).

PIRAM [PIE ruhm] (*meaning unknown*) — the king of JARMUTH, a city southwest of Jerusalem in the lowlands of Judah (Josh. 10:3). Piram was one of five Amorite kings who formed a military alliance to resist the invasion of the Israelites.

PIRATHON [PIR uh thahn] (*princely*) — a city in which Abdon died after judging Israel eight years (Judg. 12:13–15). Pirathon is now called Ferata. It is about 12 kilometers (7.5 miles) southwest of Shechem.

PIRATHONITE [PIR uh thuh night] — a native or inhabitant of PIRATHON (Judg. 12:13; 1 Chr. 11:31).

PISGAH [PIZ guh] (*cleft*) — a word that refers to the rugged ridge that crowns a mountain. As a proper noun, the word Pisgah was sometimes identified with Mount Nebo. But the word more likely refers to the entire ridge of the Abarim Mountains, which extends from the Moabite plateau toward the Dead Sea.

Nebo is the highest peak of this "pisgah." From the top of the Pisgah Moses was permitted to survey the Promised Land. The particular peak upon which he stood was on or near Mount Nebo (Num. 21:20; 23:14; Deut. 3:27; 34:1).

Balaam offered sacrifices upon seven altars at the field of Zophim on the top of Pisgah (Num. 23:14). From the Pisgah ridge steep slopes drop about 792 meters (2,600 feet) into the Jordan valley below (Deut. 3:17). Ashdoth-Pisgah, "the slopes of Pisgah" (translated "the springs of Pisgah" in Deut. 4:49, KJV), was allotted to the tribe of Reuben (Josh. 13:20, KJV). This ridge originally marked the southern limites of the territory of Sihon, king of the Amorites (Josh. 12:3).

PISHON [PIE shahn] (*freely flowing*) — an unknown stream named in connection with the river that watered the Garden of EDEN (Gen. 2:11–12; Pison, KJV).

PISIDIA [pih SID ih uh] (meaning unknown) — a mountainous province in central Asia Minor (modern Turkey; see Map 7, C–2), twice visited by the apostle Paul (Acts 13:14; 14:24). Pisidia was a wild, mountainous country infested with bandits. When Paul wrote that he had been "in perils of robbers" (2 Cor. 11:26), he may have been referring to his dangerous journey through the mountains of Pisidia. While in Perga Paul intended to travel north through this rugged and dangerous mountain terrain to Antioch of Pisidia. The synagogue in Antioch of Pisidia was the scene of one of Paul's most impressive sermons (Acts 13:16–41).

PISON [PIGH sahn] — a form of PISHON.

PISPAH [PIS puh] (meaning unknown) — a son of Jether (1 Chr. 7:38; Pispa, RSV, NASB).

PISTACHIO NUTS (see PLANTS OF THE BIBLE).

PIT — a deep hole in the ground, either natural (Gen. 14:10) or man-made (Gen. 37:20). This word translates 12 Hebrew words in the Old Testament and two Greek words in the New Testament. The Hebrew word used most often denotes a cistern in which rainwater was collected (Lev. 11:36).

Another Hebrew word referred to a pit sometimes used to trap animals or people (Ezek. 19:4, 8). These verses reflect this practice, either literally describing a snare or figuratively describing temptation (Ps. 35:7).

The word pit is used in a theological way in both the Old Testament and the New Testament. As a deep underground place, "the Pit" became synonymous for SHEOL, the abode of the dead, the netherworld of departed spirits (Job 33:18, 24; Ps. 30:3; Is. 14:15).

In the New Testament, the phrase *the bottomless pit* refers to the abode of the demons. Satan will be bound and cast into the bottomless pit (Rev. 20:2–3). Then he will be released from this pit or prison after a thousand years of captivity (Rev. 20:4–7).

PITCH (see MINERALS OF THE BIBLE).

PITCHER — a vessel for holding liquids; an earthenware jar or water jug. In the ancient world, pitchers ordinarily had one or two handles, were usually carried on the head or shoulders, and were used mainly by women for carrying water or drawing water from wells (Gen. 24:14–46). The pitcher used by Rebekah at the well may have been made of pottery, but leather buckets were also used.

This was the same kind of jug used by Gideon's warriors in their battle with the Midianites (Judg. 7:16–20). The men hid their torches inside their pitchers until the time of their surprise attack. The fact that they broke the pitchers (v. 19) indicates these vessels were clay or earthenware jars.

PITHOM [PIE thuhm] (*temple of Tem*) — one of the supply cities, or store cities (see Map 2, A–1), in Lower Egypt built by the Israelites while they were slaves in Egypt (Ex. 1:11). Pithom was in the general area of RAAMSES, but the Bible gives no further details about its location. Some archaeologists suggest that the temple, fortress, and storage chambers discovered at Tell el–Maskhutah, in the valley connecting the Nile River and Lake Timsah, are the remains of biblical Pithom. Others believe that Pithom should be identified with Tell er– Ratabah, about 16 kilometers (10 miles) to the west and closer to the land of Goshen.

It is possible that Pithom and Raamses (Ex. 1:11) were built during the reign of Pharaoh Rameses II (who ruled from about 1292–1225 B.C.). Rameses II, however, often made claims to "build" a city, when actually he "rebuilt" it, or strengthened its fortifications. Pithom is supposed by some scholars to be identical with Succoth (Ex. 12:37)—Pithom being the sacred, or religious name and Succoth being the secular or civil name.

The site of Pithom remains a subject of doubt and debate. Generally, the site chosen depends on one's opinion about the route of the Exodus. Since Tell el–Maskhutah is close to Tjeku (biblical Succoth), which was the Israelites' first stop after leaving Raamses, a more westerly site seems a more logical location for Pithom.

PITHON [PIE thahn] (meaning unknown) — a son of Micah, of the tribe of Benjamin (1 Chr. 8:35).

PITY — a sense of sympathetic sorrow for the unfortunate. In this respect, pity is the emotional side of mercy, which is the desire to help people in this state. Pity may come from God, especially in His role as heavenly Father to His children (Ps. 103:13). Pity for others may also be expressed by man (Ps. 103:13; Matt. 18:33; Luke 10:33). Also see MERCY.

PLACENTA — a protective sack that surrounds an unborn baby during the mother's pregnancy (Deut.

28:57; young one, KJV; afterbirth, RSV, NASB, NEB, NIV). God called the Hebrew people to worship Him as the one true God. They were warned that if they failed to do so, the Lord would judge them. In their desperate situation mothers might become so hungry that they would eat the placentas that are expelled during birth.

PLAGUE — an affliction sent by God as punishment for sin and disobedience. In most cases in the Bible the affliction is an epidemic or disease. The Greek word for plague literally means a blow or a lash, implying punishment or chastisement.

Plagues appear throughout the biblical record. The first mention of a plague in Scripture was that sent on Pharaoh for the protection of Sarah, Abraham's wife (Gen. 12:17). The next plagues were the ten afflictions experienced by the Egyptians when the Pharaoh refused to release the Hebrew people from bondage. While these plagues were phenomena with which the Egyptians were familiar, they exhibited miraculous features that were characteristic of God's judgment.

Later, during the years of the EXODUS, a plague was sent upon the Hebrews for making and worshiping a golden calf (Ex. 32:35). Another occurred because of their murmuring against the food which God provided for them (Num. 11:33–34). The spies who brought faithless reports about the Promised Land were inflicted with a plague (Num. 14:37).

When the Hebrews complained about the righteous punishment of the rebels Korah, Dothan, and Abiram, 14,700 people died of a plague (Num. 16:46–50). In another plague sent upon the Hebrews because of idolatry at Baal–peor, 24,000 people died (Num. 25:9; Josh. 22:17; Ps. 106:29–30).

The plagues were sometimes miraculous events. At other times they appeared as natural phenomena. But always they represented God's aggressive acts to punish sin and disobedience among His people.

PLAGUES OF EGYPT — the series of afflictions used by God to break the will of Pharaoh and to bring about the release of the Hebrew people from slavery in Egypt.

After the Hebrews had been in Egypt for about 400 years, "there arose a new king over Egypt, who did not know Joseph" (Ex. 1:8). This new king enslaved the Hebrews and forced them to labor in his extensive building projects (Ex. 5:7–19). When the Hebrews cried out for deliverance, God sent Moses to lead them from bondage. The Pharaoh resisted the release of the Hebrew people. The plagues of Egypt occurred as God's action to change the mind of the Pharaoh, thus bringing the Hebrew's freedom.

A total of ten plagues occurred. Scholars generally agree that the first nine plagues were regular, natural occurrences in Egypt. They were remarkable only in their intensity and in the timing with which they happened. But this does not mean that they were purely natural phenomena. They were miraculous in that God used natural forces to achieve His purpose. A sovereign God can use whatever methods He chooses to bring about a miracle. The method does not diminish the miraculous nature of the occurrence.

The tenth plague, the death of the firstborn of Egypt, was altogether supernatural. There is no known natural phenomenon closely related to this plague.

The sequence of the plagues has been studied and compared with the observations of travelers to Egypt. Many scholars point out that the first nine plagues are logical consequences of an unusually

The Nile River near Luxor, Egypt. God turned the waters of this river into blood to punish the Egyptians for not freeing His people (Ex. 7:14-25).

Photo by Howard Vos

high flooding of the NILE RIVER. Such flooding usually occurred in July, August, and September. Based on the best estimates that can be made from the biblical account, the plagues probably occurred over a period of about seven to nine months, beginning in July or August and continuing until around April or May.

The plagues may be viewed as God's intervention to seek the release of the Hebrew people. They also represented God's challenge to the Egyptian religious system. To the Egyptians, the Nile River was a god. From it came the power and life of the Egyptian culture. They worshiped the Nile and the abundance of resources that it provided. Since the first nine plagues seem to be a natural progression of God's attack on the Nile River, all of these plagues relate to God's challenge to the Egyptian religious system.

Following are the ten plagues, as recorded in Exodus 7:14—12:30:

1. *The Water of the Nile Turned into Blood* (Ex. 7:14-25). This first plague probably was the pollution of the Nile River by large quantities of fine, red earth, brought down from the Sudan and Ethiopia by abnormal flooding. The pollution of the water provided a favorable environment for the growth of micro-organisms and parasitic bacteria. Their presence could have led to the death of the fish in the river (Ex. 7:21).

In addition to depriving Egypt of water and fish—an important part of their diet—the plague also had a religious effect. The Nile River, god of the Egyptians, had been confronted by the power of the Redeemer God of the Hebrew people.

2. *Frogs Cover the Land* (Ex. 8:1-15). Seven days after the first plague, frogs came out of the river and infested the land. The frogs would have been driven from the Nile and its canals and pools by the polluted water. When Moses prayed to God, the frogs died in the houses, courtyards, and fields. The frogs were symbols of the Egyptian goddess, Heqt, who was supposed to help women in childbirth. This plague was another demonstration of the superior power of God over the gods of Egypt.

3. *Lice Throughout the Land* (Ex. 8:16-19). Insects of various kinds are common in Egypt. It is not easy to identify the exact pests involved in the third and fourth plagues. Various translations have lice (KJV, NKJV), gnats (NASB, RSV, NIV), maggots (NEB), and sand flies and fleas (RSV).

4. *Swarms of Flies* (Ex. 8:20-32). Many kinds of flies are common in Egypt. The mounds of decaying frogs would have provided an ideal breeding ground for these pests. Some scholars suggest that the swarms mentioned here were a species known as the stable-fly, a blood feeder that bites man as well as cattle. This fly is a carrier of skin anthrax, which is probably the disease brought on by the sixth plague.

5. *Pestilence of Livestock* (Ex. 9:1-7). Either the frogs or the insects may have been the carriers of this infection. The livestock of the Israelites were miraculously protected (Ex. 9:6-7). This was the

Statue of Rameses II of Egypt. Many scholars believe he was the ruling Pharaoh at the time of the Exodus.

second time God had made a distinction between the Israelites and the Egyptians in the plagues which He sent (Ex. 8:22-23).

6. *Boils on Man and Beast* (Ex. 9:8-12). This infection was probably skin anthrax, carried by the flies of the fourth plague. The festering boils broke into blisters and running sores.

7. *Heavy Hail, with Thunder and Lightning* (Ex. 9:13-35). Egypt was essentially an agricultural country. By destroying the crops, this plague and the next struck at the heart of Egypt's economy. Moses' warning gave the Egyptians a chance to save their remaining livestock, and some acted upon it (Ex. 9:19-20). The severe storm caused great destruction (Ex. 9:24-25). The flax and barley were ruined, but not the wheat because it had not yet been planted (Ex. 9:31-32). This would suggest early February as the time of this plague. Again the Israelites received special protection. There was no hail in the land of Goshen, where the Hebrews lived (Ex. 9:26).

8. *Swarm of Locusts* (Ex. 10:1-20). The destruction from the previous plague was fresh in the minds of Pharaoh's advisors (Ex. 10:7). The eighth plague must have followed the hail very closely. Heavy rainfall in July–September would have produced conditions favorable for locusts in March.

These locusts, swarms of foliage–eating grasshoppers, probably were driven into the Egyptian delta by strong winds. They wiped out the vegetation that had survived the earlier destruction. Again, as after the seventh plague, Pharaoh confessed "I have sinned" (Ex. 10:16). But again, after the plague was withdrawn, Pharaoh hardened his heart and would not let the children of Israel go (Ex. 10:20).

9. *Three Days of Darkness* (Ex. 10:21–29). This darkness could have been caused by a severe dust storm. For three days darkness covered the land (Ex. 10:23). This storm would have been intensified by fine earth deposited over the land by previous flooding. This plague probably occurred in March. Again, the Israelites were spared the effects (Ex. 10:23). By showing God's power over the light of the sun—represented by one of Egypt's chief deities, the sun-god Ra—this plague was a further judgment on the idolatry of the Egyptians.

10. *Death of Egyptian Firstborn* (Ex. 11:1—12:30). The tenth plague was the most devastating of all—the death of the firstborn in Egyptian families. The Hebrews were spared because they followed God's command to sprinkle the blood of a lamb on the doorposts of their houses. The death angel "passed over" the houses where the blood was sprinkled—hence, the name PASSOVER for this religious observance among the Jewish people. Only a supernatural explanation can account for the selective slaughter of the tenth plague.

Some people might wonder if such a massive slaughter was really necessary. But Pharaoh had been given ample warning (Ex. 4:23). He had seen many demonstrations of God's reality and power, and yet he had refused to acknowledge Him. Although Pharaoh wavered at times and promised to release the Israelites (Ex. 8:8, 28; 9:28), once the danger passed he changed his mind (Ex. 8:15, 32; 9:34–35). Because he rejected the power of God, Pharaoh was forced to face one final, terrible manifestation of God's power. The deliverance of the Hebrews from slavery in Egypt was one of the most memorable occasions in Hebrew history. The Passover Feast was observed annually as a celebration of God's deliverance of His people from bondage.

PLAIN — a level stretch of land, as a valley or a tableland. In the Old Testament plains were especially important to military strategy. Since they were flat and open, they were the likely sites of conflicts involving large numbers of warriors. Plains were particularly suited for chariot warfare (Joshua 11; 1 Kings 20).

There are seven words which the KJV translates as plain. Four of these are general terms for level terrain, but three refer to specific regions in the Holy Land. The word *shephelah*, for instance, refers to a plain in southern and central Palestine (1 Chr. 27:28; 2 Chr. 9:27; Jer. 17:26; Obad. 19; Zech. 7:7). Bounded on the west by the Mediterranean Sea, these "lowlands"—as the word is translated in the NKJV and other versions—were particularly crucial to maritime trade.

The second word, *arabah*, refers to the plain which runs along the Jordan River from north of the Sea of Galilee to south of the Dead Sea (Num. 22:1; 36:13; Deut. 1:1; 34:8). In this plain the Hebrew people of the Exodus found the Promised Land.

The final term, *kikkar*, meaning circle or circuit, refers to the Plain of Jordan which lies east of the Jordan River (Gen. 13:10–12; 1 Kin. 7:46). The city of Succoth was at the northern extreme of this plain. The cities of Sodom and Gomorrah (Genesis 19) lay at its southern edge.

PLANE (see TOOLS OF THE BIBLE).

PLANE TREE (see PLANTS OF THE BIBLE).

PLANK — a beam (KJV) or log (RSV, NASB). Jesus used this word in Matthew 7:3–5 and Luke 6:41–42 when he said a person should not criticize the speck of sawdust in another's eye while disregarding the plank in his own eye.

PLANTS OF THE BIBLE — The land which God promised to Abraham and his descendants was extremely fertile. Because of its diverse climate, the world of the Bible contained many varieties of plants. Botanists have identified 3,500 species of plant life in Palestine and Syria. Plants or plant products are mentioned in almost every book of the Bible.

The flora of the Bible has been the subject of much discussion and research. Accurately identifying many of these plants has taken many years of scientific research. The Bible writers were not botanists, and they seldom bothered to describe or identify the plants they mentioned.

In the 16th century Levinus Lemmens wrote the first book on the plants of Scripture. It was not until the middle of the 18th century, however, that a botanist traveled to Palestine for firsthand knowledge of its vegetation. Since then much valuable information has been learned about the plants of the Bible.

Many of the Bible writers often used general terms to refer to plants. Sometimes a reference is no more specific than "tree," "grass," or "grain." Even if an individual grain such as "corn" or "wheat" is named, it is referring to all grains in general.

Although many types of flowers grow in Palestine and other Bible lands, very few are mentioned by name in the Bible. Some of the flowers found in the Holy Land are irises, roses, anemones, lilies, tulips, hyacinths, and narcissus.

Some of the other general terms referring to plant life include bush, herb, grass, cockle, fruit, and verdure.

The Hebrew people were certain that God provided the Promised Land for their use, but they were not careful to take good care of it. The land was cultivated continuously for thousands of years without rest until much of the soil was depleted and many areas became devastated wastelands. The great forests of Lebanon and Hermon were eventually destroyed and the soil was eroded. The people of that time did not know how to manage their environment intelligently. Eventually the land that once flowed with "milk and honey" became barren of much of its vegetation. Today many of these barren regions of the Holy Land are being turned again into fertile farmland. Effort is being made to restore the richness of the land as God intended it to be.

The following specific plants are mentioned in the Bible. This listing is keyed to the NKJV, but variant names from five additional popular translations—KJV, NASB, NEB, NIV, and RSV—are cross-referenced throughout the listing.

Acacia. A large thorny tree with rough gnarled bark. The orange–brown wood was hard–grained, and it repelled insects. It bore long locust–like pods with seeds inside and produced round, fragrant clusters of yellow blossoms. Many species of acacia grew in the desert of Sinai, in southern Palestine, and in Egypt.

Acacia wood was used to build the ark of the covenant and the first tabernacle (Ex. 36:20; 37:1). The acacia is called shittim and shittah in the KJV (Ex. 25:5, 10; Is. 41:19).

Algum, Almug. A large leguminous tree native to India and Ceylon. While its identity is uncertain, many consider it to be the red sandlewood. Its blossoms were pea–like, and its wood was close grained, dark outside, and red within. It was highly scented, making it resistant to insects. Most authorities believe that algum and almug are two forms of the same wood.

Solomon ordered the algum wood from Orphir and Lebanon (1 Kin. 10:11–12; 2 Chr. 9:10–11). The wood was well suited for making musical instruments, cabinet work, and pillars for the Temple.

Almond. A large tree resembling the peach tree in both size and fruit. The almond was chiefly valued for the nuts it produced, which were used for making oil used in the home and as medicine. The Hebrew word for almond means "awakening," an allusion to the almond blossom, which is first to bloom in the spring. The almond's pinkish–white blossoms always appear before its leaves.

The almond played an important role in the history of the Hebrews. Jacob included almond nuts in his gifts to Joseph in Egypt (Gen. 43:11). The decorations on the lampstands were modeled after the almond blossom (Ex. 25:33), and Aaron's rod was an almond twig (Num. 17:8). The almond also symbolized the dependability of God (Jer. 1:11–12). Many scholars think the hazel of Genesis 30:37 (KJV) is the almond tree.

Almug (see *Algum*).

Aloes. Two plants, one a tree and the other a flower.

1. The aloes mentioned in Psalm 45:8, Proverbs 7:17, and Song of Solomon 4:14 came from a large tree known as "eaglewood," a plant native to India. The wood of the aloe tree is fragrant and highly valued for perfume and incense. Many authorities believe the lign aloe to be the same tree (Num. 24:6, KJV).

2. The aloes brought by Nicodemus to wrap the body of Jesus (John 19:39) were probably the true aloes of the lily family, a beautiful plant with thick, fleshy leaves and red flowers. The aloin derived from the pulp of the aloe leaf was an expensive product used in embalming.

Amaranth. A large family of plants that includes weeds and garden plants. Goodspeed translates the amaranth, also called the "rolling thing," of Isaiah 7:13 as the tumbleweed. It is also called the "resurrection plant" and the "rose of Jericho." The Greek word for amaranth means "unfading." This describes the bloom's ability to retain its color when dried. This meaning is used symbolically in 1 Peter 1:4 and 5:4, where the inheritance of the faithful is described as unfading. Thus, the amaranth became a symbol of immortality.

Anise. An annual herb which bears yellow flowers and fragrant seeds. The anise mentioned in the Bible is generally thought to be dill. Anise (dill) was used as medicine and for cooking. It grows in Palestine today both cultivated and wild.

Jesus used the anise as an illustration when He scolded the Pharisees for keeping part of the law in detail while ignoring the rest (Matt. 23:23; also Deut. 14:22).

Apple. A tree that grows about 9 meters (30 feet) high and has rough bark and pink blossoms. Many authorities believe the apple of Scripture actually is the apricot, a native of Armenia. Other authorities suggest the quince, peach, citron, orange, or some other fruit; some believe it was the apple.

The apple was described as sweet and fragrant (Song 7:8; apricot, NEB), golden (Prov. 25:11), and suitable for shade (Song 2:3). This fruit was used figuratively to show how precious we are to God, and how extremely sensitive He is to our needs (Deut. 32:10; Ps. 17:8; Lam. 2:18; Zech. 2:8).

Apricot (see *Apple*).

Ash (see *Pine*).

Aspen (see *Mulberry*).

Asphodel (see *Rose*).

Balm (see *Balsam*).

Balsam. A thorny tree growing 3 to 5 meters (10–15 feet) tall with clusters of green flowers, also known as the Jericho balsam. Some think the lentisk or mastic tree, a shrubby evergreen growing one to three meters (3–10 feet) tall, is meant.

Balsam was highly valued during Bible times (Gen. 37:25; 43:11; Jer. 8:22; 46:11; 51:8; Ezek. 27:17). It produced a fragrant, resinous gum called balm. This was an article of export (Gen. 37:25) and was given as a gift by Jacob (Gen. 43:11). Balm was used as a symbol in Jeremiah 8:22 to refer to spiritual healing.

Barley. A grain known since early times. It was well adapted to varied climates, ripening quickly and resistant to heat; it usually was harvested before wheat. Because barley was considered a food for slaves and the very poor, however, it was held in low esteem as a grain.

In the Bible barley was first associated with

Photo by Gustav Jeeninga

The long roots of the broom tree enable it to reach ground water even in the driest months (1 Kin. 19:4).

Egypt (Ex. 9:31). It was used as an offering of jealousy (Num. 5:15), for fodder (1 Kin. 4:28), and for food (Judg. 7:13; John 6:5, 13).

Bay Tree. The laurel, a tree native to Canaan. The laurel grew to heights of 12 to 18 meters (40–60 feet) and produced small greenish–white flowers and black berries. Parts of the tree were used in medicine, while its leaves were used as seasoning. The Hebrew word means "a tree in its native soil"; this was a fitting way for David to describe the natural prosperity of the wicked (Ps. 37:35, KJV; native green tree, NKJV).

Beans. A hardy plant about one meter (three feet) tall with pea–shaped fragrant blooms, large pods, and black or brown beans, which were eaten alone or cooked with meat. Beans have always been an important part of the Hebrew diet, especially among the poor, and they have been known since ancient times. When beans were threshed and cleaned, they were often mixed with grains for bread (Ezek. 4:9).

Bitter Weed (see *Wormwood*).

Black Cummin (see *Cummin; Fitches*).

Box Tree. A tree of very hard wood and glossy leaves, which grew to a height of about 6 meters (20 feet). A native of northern Palestine and the Lebanon mountains, the box tree was well suited to beautify the Temple (Is. 60:13). The box tree was used since Roman times for wood engravings and musical instruments. Isaiah symbolically used the box tree, along with other trees, to remind the Hebrews of God's perpetual presence (Is. 41:17–20).

Some scholars have suggested that the box tree of Scripture may instead be the cypress or plane. Also see *Chestnut*.

Bramble (see *Thistle/Thorns*).

Brier (see *Thistle/Thorns*).

Broom. A dense, twiggy bush, almost leafless, which grew to about 3.6 meters (12 feet). It has small white blooms. Common in the desert regions of Palestine, Arabia, and Egypt, it was used as charcoal (Ps. 120:4) and provided shade for the prophet Elijah (1 Kin. 19:4–5). The roots which Job ate were not from the broom, which was not edible, but may have been an edible parasite which infested the bush (Job 30:4). The broom is sometimes referred to as juniper in the NKJV, KJV, and NASB. Many scholars believe this to be the shrub or heath referred to in Jeremiah 17:6 and 48:6.

Bud (see *Gourd*).

Bulrush (see *Reed/Rush*).

Calamus. A fragrant, reed–like grass growing along streams and river banks (Song 4:14), also referred to as sweet cane (Is. 43:24; Jer. 6:20). Calamus leaves are fragrant and ginger–flavored when crushed. It is named with other aromatic substances (Ezek. 27:19) and as one ingredient for the anointing oil (Ex. 30:23). It is believed to be a plant native to India (Jer. 6:20). Also see *Reed/Rush*.

Camel–thorn (see *Cypress*).

Camphire (see *Henna*).

Cane (see *Calamus; Reed/Rush*).

Caperberry. A plant with large white, berry–producing flowers, which grows in clefts of rocks and on walls. Only the NEB and NASB refer to the caper. Other versions translate the Hebrew word as "desire" (Eccl. 12:5). Also see *Hyssop*.

Caraway (see *Cummin*).

Cassia. A plant with a flavor and aroma similar to cinnamon, but considered inferior. Some believe it could be the Indian perfume, orris. Moses included cassia in the anointing oil (Ex. 30:24). It was also an article of trade (Ezek. 27:19).

Cedar. An evergreen tree which sometimes grows more than 30 meters (100 feet) tall with a trunk circumference of 12 to 15 meters (40–50 feet). It grows in western Asia, the Himalayas, and Cyprus as well as Lebanon.

The cedar's fragrant wood was rot–resistant and knot–free, making it ideal for building purposes (2

Photo by Howard Vos

Once plentiful in the mountains of Palestine, the cedars of Lebanon have suffered from centuries of reckless cutting. Only a few isolated groves remain today.

Sam. 5:11; 1 Kin. 6:9), ship building (Ezek. 27:5), and fashioning idols (Is. 44:14). The reference to cedar in Leviticus 14:4 and Numbers 19:6 is generally understood to be the juniper which grew in the Sinai. Also see *Fir; Pine.*

Chestnut. A tree of Syria and Lebanon thought by many scholars to be the plane tree. It grew to a height of about 21 to 27 meters (70–90 feet) and had a massive trunk. This tree is translated chestnut in the NKJV and KJV, but is translated plane by the RSV, NIV, NEB, and NASB.

Cinnamon. A member of the laurel family, the cinnamon tree grew to be more than 9 meters (30 feet) tall with white flowers and wide-spreading branches. A native of Ceylon, the cinnamon tree produced bark and oil which was used for the anointing oil (Ex. 30:23) and as perfume (Prov. 7:17; Rev. 18:13).

Citron. A fragrant wood from the sandarac tree. Citron is sometimes referred to as "sweet" or "scented" wood. The sandarac tree grew to a height of no more than about 9 meters (30 feet) tall. Citron is translated as thyine by the KJV (Rev. 18:12).

Coriander. An annual herb, growing from one-half to one meter (two to three feet) tall, which produced grayish seeds used to flavor foods, for confections, and in medicine. The dried leaves of coriander were also used to flavor foods.

Corn (see *Wheat*).

Crocus (see *Rose; Saffron*).

Cucumber. A climbing vine which produces vegetables. The cucumber was one of the vegetables which the Israelites longed for after leaving Egypt (Num. 11:5).

Cummin. An annual seed-producing herb with pinkish-white blooms. Cummin is native to the eastern Mediterranean lands. When harvested, cummin was threshed with sticks (Is. 28:25, 27), a method still used today. Cummin was used to flavor foods, in medicine, and was subject to the tithe (Matt. 23:23).

The NKJV also mentions black cummin, which is translated dill (RSV, NEB, NASB), caraway (NIV), and fitches (KJV).

Cypress. A tall evergreen tree of hard and durable wood. Cypress wood was suitable for building, and was used to fashion idols (Is. 44:14). The word rendered gopherwood by the NKJV, KJV, RSV, and NASB in Genesis 6:14 is thought to be cypress. This was the wood which Noah used to build his ark. The word for cypress is also renderd as camel-thorn (Is. 55:13) and ilex (Is. 44:14) by the NEB.

Darnel (see *Tares*).

Date Palm (see *Palm*).

Dill (see *Anise; Cummin*).

Dove Droppings/Dove Dung. A bulbous plant which was edible after being boiled or roasted. Dove's dung was mentioned as food eaten during the siege of Samaria (2 Kin. 6:25). Some believe this was excrement from pigeons and doves, while others interpret it as an edible plant (seed pods, NIV; locust-beans, NEB).

Dove dung was also referred to as the Star of Bethlehem. Syrians are known to have used this plant as food. Also see *Locust.*

Ebony. A large tree which produces edible fruit similar to the persimmon. The hard, black wood from the inner portion of the tree is quite valuable and is used for fine furniture. It is also known to have been inlaid with ivory. Idols were sometimes carved from ebony wood.

Elm (see *Terebinth*).

Fig. A fruit-producing plant which could be either a tall tree or a low-spreading shrub. The size of the tree depended on its location and soil. The blooms of the fig tree always appear before the leaves in spring. When Jesus saw leaves on a fig tree, He expected the fruit (Mark 11:12-14, 20-21). There were usually two crops of figs a year.

Figs were eaten fresh (2 Kin. 18:31), pressed into cakes (1 Sam. 25:18), and used as a poultice (Is. 38:21). Jeremiah used the fig tree as a symbol of desolation (Jer. 8:13). It also signified security and hope for Adam and Eve (Gen. 3:7), the 12 spies (Num. 13:23), and the poets and prophets.

Fir. An evergreen tree of uncertain identity. Although this tree is mentioned several times in Scripture, biblical authorities question whether this was the true fir or some other evergreen of Palestine. Many suggest the aleppo pine would fit this description, while others think the cypress, juniper, or cedar could be meant.

The Israelites valued the timber of the fir tree for building the Temple (1 Kin. 6:15, KJV), for ship building (Ezek. 27:5), and for making musical instruments (2 Sam. 6:5). The fir is used symbolically to describe the blessings of God for His people (Is. 41:19; 55:13, KJV).

Fitches. Two different plants mentioned in the KJV:

1. An annual herb one-half meter (one to two feet) tall with finely cut leaves and blue flowers,

which produces black poppy seeds used in curries and sprinkled on breads. It is translated black cummin in the NKJV (Is. 28:25, 27).

2. A plant apparently mislabeled by the KJV in Ezekiel 4:9. The correct identification is spelt. Also see *Spelt*.

Flag (see *Reed/Rush*).

Flax. A plant growing one meter (three feet) tall with pale blue flowers, and used for making cloth. When mature, the entire flax plant was pulled and placed in water to separate the fibers from the stems. It was then laid on housetops to dry (Josh. 2:6), and later woven into linen. Flax was also used as wicks for lamps in Bible times (Is. 42:3). Also see *Reed/Rush*.

Frankincense. An aromatic gum resin obtained from the Boswellia tree. These trees are large with small, white, star-shaped flowers and leaves resembling the mountain ash. The gum is obtained by cutting into the bark and collecting the resin from the tree. When this substance hardens, it is gathered and used as incense.

Frankincense was part of the sacred anointing oil (Ex. 30:34). It was used in sacrificial offering (Lev. 2:1), as a fumigant during animal sacrifices (Ex. 30:7), and as perfume (Song 3:6). It was a gift to baby Jesus (Matt. 2:11).

The trees are native to India, Arabia, and Africa. Palestine probably obtained this product through foreign trade (Is. 60:6).

Galbanum. The gum from an herb which grew one to one and one-half meters (three to five feet) high and had greenish-white flowers. Galbanum was the milky substance extracted from the stems which quickly hardened. It was used in perfume and anointing oil (Ex. 30:34).

Gall. A bitter, poisonous herb. This may have been the poppy or some other wild poisonous plant. Gall is used figuratively to mean a bitter pun-

A fig tree loaded with its small green fruit. Jesus pronounced a curse on a fig tree because of its lack of fruit (Mark 11:12-14).

Photo by Gustav Jeeninga

ishment (Jer. 8:14; 9:15; 23:15) or any bitter experience (Acts 8:23). Gall and vinegar were offered to Jesus on the cross (Matt. 27:34), but He refused the drink.

Garlic. A strong-flavored herb, resembling the onion. Garlic was eaten with bread and used to flavor food and is still highly favored today. Garlic was highly esteemed in Egypt and was believed to have been used as wages for the workers who built the pyramids. The Hebrews yearned for garlic after leaving Egypt (Num. 1:5).

Gopherwood (see *Cypress*).

Gourd. A fast-growing shrub which grew to a height of three to four meters (10–12 feet). One of Elisha's servants put the fruit of the gourd into a pot of stew (2 Kin. 4:39).

The gourd (Jon. 4:6–10; KJV, NEB) is identified as the plant under which Jonah found shade. Some biblical scholars suggest this may have been pumpkin, squash, or ivy.

Many types of wild gourds also flourished in the Mediterranean region. Some of these were poisonous. The decorations used on the Temple called ornamental buds (1 Kin. 6:18; 7:24) are thought to be a type of wild gourd.

Grapes. A luscious fruit cultivated on vines. Large clusters of grapes weighing about five kilograms (12 pounds) each (Num. 13:23) have been reported in Palestine.

Grapes were used in a variety of ways. They were eaten fresh or dried and were made into wine or vinegar. Dried grapes were called raisins. The first suggestion of grapes in Scripture was in connection with Noah's vineyard (Gen. 9:20).

The soil and climate of Palestine was well suited for vineyards, where grapes were grown. They were cultivated here long before the Israelites occupied the land (Gen. 14:18). The vineyards of Palestine produced immense clusters of grapes (Num. 13:20, 23–24).

Vineyards were hedged or fenced as protection from wild animals (Song 2:15). In each vineyard a tower was erected and a guard placed to protect the vines from robbers (Matt. 21:33).

Vinedressers were hired to care for the vines and prune them yearly (Lev. 25:3; Is. 61:5). The grapes were gathered in baskets in September and October with much festivity (Judg. 9:27; Is. 16:10). Provision was made for the poor to glean the fields (Lev. 19:10; Deut. 24:21). The choicest grapes were dried or eaten fresh and the rest were placed in presses to extract the juice (Is. 61:5; Hos. 9:2-4). This was drunk fresh or fermented.

Jesus alluded to His relationship with His followers by referring to Himself as the vine and to them as the branches (John 15:5). The fruit of the vine symbolized Jesus' shed blood (Matt. 26:27–29). He also used the vineyard in many of His parables (Matt. 9:17; 20:1-6; 21:28-32; Luke 13:6-9).

Hazel (see *Almond*).

Heath (see *Broom*).

Hemlock. A poisonous plant that grows to about two meters (five feet) tall and has small white flowers. Hemlock is referred to only once in the NKJV (Hos. 10:4). Other translations use the more general term weeds. Also see *Wormwood*.

Henna. A plant used to produce a valuable orange-red dye. It was two to three meters (seven to ten feet) tall and bore fragrant white flowers. Solomon compared his beloved to a cluster of henna (Song 1:14; 4:13; camphire, KJV).

Hyssop. A species of marjoram and a member of the mint family. Hyssop was an aromatic shrub under one meter (three feet) tall with clusters of yellow flowers. It grew in rocky crevices and was cultivated on terraced walls (1 Kin. 4:33). Bunches of hyssop were used to sprinkle blood on the doorposts in Egypt (Ex. 12:22), and in purification ceremonies (Lev. 14:4, 6, 51–52). David mentioned it as an instrument of inner cleansing (Ps. 51:7). It was used at the crucifixion to relieve Jesus' thirst (John 19:29).

The hyssop was very similar to the caper plant. It is sometimes rendered marjoram by the NEB.

Ilex (see *Cypress*).

Juniper (see *Broom*).

Laurel (see *Bay Tree*).

Leek. A bulbous vegetable resembling the onion which grows 15 centimeters (about six inches) high. The stems and bulbs of leeks were eaten raw and used to flavor foods. Named with garlic and onions, the leek was a food which the Hebrew people ate in Egypt (Num. 11:5).

Lentil. A small annual plant with white, violet-striped flowers. The seeds of lentils grew in pods similar to the pea. During Bible times lentil was threshed like wheat and boiled into a reddish-brown pottage. This was the dish which Esau purchased with his birthright (Gen. 25:34). Lentils could also be used as an ingredient for bread (Ezek. 4:9).

Lign Aloe (see *Aloe*).

Lily. A flower with white or rosy-purple blooms measuring up to 30 centimeters (12 inches) across. Many scholars think the lily is sometimes a term applied to flowers in general. Others believe specific types such as the Turks Cap, the Madonna, or the lotus is referred to.

The lily was used as an ornament for the Temple (1 Kin. 7:22). The Beloved and the Shulamite used lilies to describe their love (Song 2:1; 2:16; 4:5; 5:13; 6:3).

Locust. An evergreen tree growing about 6 to 9 meters (20–30 feet) tall and having small glossy leaves. A native of Syria and Palestine, it bears long pods known as carob or locust beans (Luke 15:16; husks, KJV). These may have been used for food in dire circumstances (2 Kin. 6:25, NEB).

Lotus (see *Lily*).

Mallow. A shrub growing one and one-half to three meters (five to ten feet) high and having thick, succulent leaves and small purple flowers. The Hebrew word for mallow means "salt plant." It thrived in dry, salty regions especially around the Dead Sea. Although the leaves were sour and had little nutritive value, they were boiled and eaten by the poor in dire circumstances.

Mentioned only once in the Bible (Job 30:4), mallow is also translated as salt herbs in the NIV and saltwort in the NEB.

Mandrake. A fruit-producing plant with dark green leaves and small bluish-purple flowers. The mandrake is a relative of the potato family which grew abundantly throughout Palestine and the Mediterranean region.

The yellow fruit of the mandrake was small, sweet-tasting, and fragrant. It had narcotic qualities and may have been used medicinally. The fruit of the mandrake was also referred to as the "love apple." It was considered a love potion.

Marjoram (see *Hyssop*).

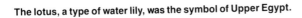

The lotus, a type of water lily, was the symbol of Upper Egypt.

Photo by Howard Vos

Melon. A type of gourd which bears sweet fruit. Both cantaloupes and watermelons may have grown along the banks of the Nile River in Egypt. Melons were used as food and medicine. An intoxicating drink was made from their juice.

The Hebrews had become accustomed to eating melons and other tasty foods in Egypt. They looked back on these fondly while in the wilderness (Num. 1:5). This word is translated watermelon by the NEB.

Millet. An annual grain–producing grass which was under one meter (three feet) high and produced many seeds. The seeds of millet were smaller than other cereal grains. Millet has been known since ancient times in Palestine and Egypt. It was used for bread (Ezek. 4:9) and eaten raw, especially by the poor.

Millet is referred to in several different ways in Ezekiel 27:17. It is translated pannag in the KJV, confections in the NIV, meal in the NEB, and cakes in the NASB.

Mint. A sweet–smelling herb which grew to a height of one meter (three feet) and produced spikes of lilac flowers. Mint was used in medicine and to flavor foods.

Mulberry. A tree which grew to a height of about eight to ten meters (25–30 feet) and produced red berries. A refreshing drink was prepared from the fruit. Jesus used the mulberry tree as an illustration when teaching about faith (Luke 17:6). It is called sycamine in the KJV and RSV, and aspen in the NEB. The mulberry trees mentioned in 2 Samuel 5:23-24 and 1 Chronicles 14:14-15 are believed to be a species of poplar.

Mustard. A plant which grew wild along roadsides and in fields, reaching a height of about 4.6 meters (15 feet). The black mustard of Palestine seems to be the species to which Jesus referred (Matt. 13:31–32; Mark 4:31–32; Luke 13:19). It was cultivated for its seeds which were used as a condiment and for oil.

The mustard seed was the smallest seed known in Jesus' day (Matt. 13:32). Nevertheless, Jesus said that if one has faith as a mustard seed, he can move mountains (Matt. 17:20) or transplant a mulberry tree in the sea (Luke 17:6).

Myrrh. An extract from a stiff–branched tree with white flowers and plum–like fruit. After myrrh was extracted from the wood, it soon hardened and was valued as an article of trade. It was an ingredient used in anointing oil (Ex. 30:23), and was used as perfume (Ps. 45:8; Prov. 7:17; Song 3:6), in purification rites for women (Esth. 2:12), as a gift for the infant Jesus (Matt. 2:11), and in embalming (John 19:39). According to the Gospel of Mark (15:23), the drink offered to Jesus before His crucifixion was "wine mingled with myrrh." Matthew, however, has "sour wine mingled with gall" (Matt. 27:34).

The reference to myrrh in Genesis 37:25 and 43:11 is thought to be ladanum, sometimes called onycha, from a species of rockrose and not the true myrrh. Also see *Onycha.*

Myrtle. An evergreen tree with dark glossy leaves and white flowers. The leaves, flowers, and berries of the myrtle were used for perfume and as seasoning for food. The myrtle tree had a religious significance for the Hebrews (Zech. 1:8–11) and was a symbol of peace and joy. Queen Esther's Hebrew name (Esth. 2:7) meant myrtle.

Nard (see *Spikenard*).

Nettle. Two different plants referred to in the Bible:

1. The nettles mentioned in Isaiah 34:13 and Hosea 9:6 are believed to be the true nettle. It is a spiney leaf plant sometimes growing to a height of about two meters (six feet).

2. The nettles referred to in Job 30:7 and Proverbs 24:31 are considered by some to be the acanthus, a stinging plant common in Palestine.

The nettles of Zephaniah 2:9 (KJV) are translated weeds by the NKJV.

Oak. A large tree with a massive trunk that grew abundantly in Palestine and the surrounding countries. Many Hebrew words refer to the oak. Some scholars think these words could have referred to any large tree such as the terebinth or elm.

The oak tree was an important historical landmark to the Hebrews. Some specific oak trees are mentioned in the Bible. These include the oaks of Bashan (Is. 2:13; Zech. 11:2), the oak of Bethel (Gen. 35:8, KJV; terebinth tree, NKJV), and the oaks of Mamre (Gen. 13:18, RSV; terebinth trees, NKJV).

Oak wood was also used in shipbuilding (Ezek. 27:6), and for fashioning idols (Is. 44:14). Also see *Tamarisk; Terebinth.*

Oil Tree. A tree of uncertain identity. Many oil-producing trees mentioned in the Bible could be identified as the oil tree. Many authorities believe the oleaster or wild olive is the tree meant. It grew to a height of about 4.5 to 6 meters (15–20 feet) and produced small bitter fruit resembling an olive. The oleaster yielded an inferior oil which was used medicinally.

The oil tree of Isaiah 41:19 is translated olive tree in the RSV, NIV, NEB, and NASB. Also see *Olive.*

Olive. A fruit–bearing tree about six meters (20 feet) tall with a gnarled, twisted trunk, white flowers, and berries that ripen to a black color. The olive tree grew slowly and continued to bear fruit after reaching a great age. Before it died, new branches sprouted from its roots.

The fruit was harvested by beating the boughs of the olive tree with a stick (Deut. 24:20), or by shaking the tree (Is. 17:6). The ripe fruit was enjoyed fresh or the green fruit was often pickled or made into a relish.

The best oil was obtained from the green olive fruit. It was used as fuel for lamps (Ex. 27:20), as anointing oil (Lev. 2:1), as an article of commerce (1 Kin. 5:11), and for dressing wounds (Luke 10:34).

Olive trees were cultivated in groves or orchards (Ex. 23:11; Josh. 24:13). The most famous olive garden mentioned in the Bible is Gethsemane,

Photo by Ben Chapman

Palm trees in southern Palestine. The leaves of palm trees were used as tokens of peace and victory (John 12:12-13; Rev. 7:9).

meaning "oil press" (Matt. 26:36).

Onion. A plant with a large, edible bulb. The onion is mentioned only once in the Bible, as one of the foods the Hebrews longed for in the wilderness (Num. 11:5). The onion was known in Egypt from ancient times. Drawings of the onion have been found on Egyptian tombs.

Onycha. A dark brown gum resin which was obtained from the stem and leaves of a species of the rockrose, also known as ladanum. Onycha was used as an ingredient in the holy anointing oil (Ex. 30:34). It was highly valued for its fragrance and medicinal qualities.

The rockrose was a bush growing to a height of about one meter (three feet) and having large white flowers measuring eight centimeters (three inches) across. Some scholars believe the substance referred to as myrrh in Genesis 37:25 and 43:11 was onycha.

Palm. A tree which grew to a height of about 18 to 30 meters (60–100 feet) and had long feathery leaves (branches; Neh. 8:15; John 12:13; Rev. 7:9). These branches were about two to three meters (six to eight feet) long and grew from the top of the trunk. Also called the date palm, this tree is believed to grow from 100 to 200 years old.

Palm branches were considered a symbol of victory (John 12:13; Rev. 7:9). Many places in the Bible were identified by the abundance of palm trees (Ex. 15:27; Deut. 34:3; Judg. 1:16). One of the Hebrew words for palm, Tamar, was often used as a woman's name (Gen. 38:6; 2 Sam. 13:1).

Pannag (see *Millet*).

Papyrus (see *Reed/Rush*).

Pine. An evergreen tree of uncertain identity. Biblical scholars believe pine refers to either the Brutian or the Aleppo pine (Is. 41:19; 60:13). The Brutian pine grew to a height of about 9 to 11 me-

ters (30–35 feet). It is smaller and has longer needles than the Aleppo pine, which grew to a height of about 27 meters (90 feet). Both trees grew in Lebanon and in Palestine.

Bible scholars are not agreed on the identity of the many evergreens mentioned in the Bible. Other trees suggested for these references are the ash, fir, cypress, cedar, or juniper.

Pistachio Nut. A product of the pistacia tree, which was about nine meters (30 feet) tall with wide spreading branches. The pistachio nut is about 2.5 centimeters (one inch) long and has a thin, hard outer shell. The smooth husk or skin which shields the green kernel is red. These nuts were sweet and considered a luxury. Jacob included them in the gifts sent to Egypt (Gen. 43:11).

Plane (see *Chestnut*).

Pomegranate. A round, sweet fruit about ten centimeters (four inches) across with a hard rind. It is green when young and turns red when ripe. There are numerous edible seeds inside the pomegranate.

The pomegranate tree has been cultivated in Palestine and Egypt since ancient times (Num. 13:23; Deut. 8:8). It grew as a bush or small tree, sometimes reaching a height of about 9 meters (30 feet) with small, lance-shaped leaves. The blossoms were bright red. The fruit usually ripened in August or September.

Pomegranates were highly esteemed during Bible times. The hem of Aaron's robe was decorated with blue, purple, and red pomegranates (Ex. 28:33–34; 39:24–26). It was listed among the pleasant fruits of Egypt (Num. 20:5). Solomon decorated the Temple with the likeness of the pomegranate (1 Kin. 7:18, 20). A spiced wine was made from the juice (Song 8:2).

Poplar. A tree which grew to a height of about 9 to 18 meters (30–60 feet) and had wide spreading branches. The leaves were green with white undersides. Jacob stripped the bark from poplar branches to reveal the white wood. This was supposed to control the color of his cattle (Gen. 30:37).

Hosea refers to the Israelites worshiping idols in the shade of poplar trees. This brought God's condemnation for their sin (Hos. 4:13). Also see *Willow*.

Raisin (see *Grapes*).

Reed/Rush. Gigantic hollow-stemmed grasses which grew along river banks and in moist areas of Egypt and Palestine. Many different Hebrew words refer to the marsh plants of the Bible. They form a large order of plants, such as flax, flags, bulrush, cane, calamus, and papyrus.

Reeds and rushes grew anywhere from one to six meters (3–20 feet) high and had long, narrow leaves. A cluster of white flowers formed at the top of each stem.

The reeds were used in various ways, including walking sticks, fishing poles, musical instruments, and pens. People also used them for weaving baskets, mats, and for other domestic purposes. Moses' basket was woven from reeds. Papyrus, a particular reed, was used to make paper.

Reeds were a symbol of weakness. Jesus refers to them as shaking in the wind (Matt. 11:7). A reed was placed in Jesus' hand as He was mocked by the Roman soldiers (Matt. 27:29).

Rose. The name of two different plants of the Bible:

1. Most authorities think that the rose referred to in Song of Solomon 2:1 and Isaiah 35:1 is not what we know as the rose today, but a low-growing bulbous plant producing from two to four yellow

A flowering pomegranate. In biblical times pomegranates were widely cultivated in Palestine (Num. 13:23; Deut. 8:7-8). The juice of the fruit made a pleasant drink (Song 8:2).

Photo by Gustav Jeeninga

flowers on each stalk. This flower is noted for its fragrance. Other scholars have suggested the mountain tulip, anemone, saffron, or crocus as the flower in question. All of these flowers grew wild in Palestine. This particular flower is translated crocus by the RSV, NIV, and NASB (Is. 35:1) and asphodel by the NEB (Song 2:1; Is. 35:2). The flower we call the "Rose of Sharon" is a native of China and is not the one mentioned by Solomon (Song 2:1).

2. The rose of Ecclesiastes 24:14; 39:13 (NEB) is thought to be the oleander. This shrub grows to a height of about 3.6 meters (12 feet) and has pink or white flowers.

Rue. A garden herb growing one-half to one meter (two to three feet) high with gray-green foliage and clusters of small yellow flowers. Rue had a strong odor. It was valued for its antiseptic and disinfectant qualities. It was also used to flavor foods.

Rye (see *Spelt*).

Saffron. The product of many varieties of crocus, a flower which grew from a bulb and produced light-blue flowers.

Crocus blooms were gathered, dried, and pressed into cakes of saffron. Saffron was used as a coloring for curries and stews. It was also used as a perfume for the floors of theaters and for weddings. Solomon was the only Bible writer to refer to saffron (Song 4:14).

Salt Herb (see *Mallow*).

Saltwort (see *Mallow*).

Shittah Tree (see *Acacia*).

Shittim Wood (see *Acacia*).

Spelt. An inferior kind of wheat. Although the bread made from this grain was of a poorer quality than that made from wheat, spelt was preferred over barley by many in the ancient world. The KJV translates this word as rye in Exodus 9:32 and Isaiah 28:25, and as fitches in Ezekiel 4:9. Spelt was sown later than wheat. It thrived in poor soil and under adverse conditions.

Spikenard. A costly oil derived from the dried roots and stems of the nard, an herb of Asia. This oil was used as a liquid or made into an ointment. Solomon praised the fragrance of spikenard (Song 1:12; 4:13–14).

Spikenard was imported from India in alabaster boxes. These were stored and used only for special occasions. When household guests arrived, they were usually anointed with this oil. Jesus was anointed on two occasions as an honored guest (Mark 14:3; John 12:3).

Many spikes grew from a single nard root which produced clusters of pink flowers. The stems were covered with hair, giving them a woolly appearance. Some translations of the Bible refer to spikenard as nard.

Stacte. A resin believed to be an extract of the stems and branches of the storax tree. Stacte was highly prized as perfume and as incense. It was one of the ingredients of anointing oil (Ex. 30:34).

The storax was a small, stiff shrub growing to a height of about 3 to 6 meters (10–20 feet), which grew abundantly in Lebanon and throughout Palestine. Its leaves were dark with grayish–white undersides. In spring the storax flowered profusely with highly fragrant white blooms which resembled the orange blossom.

Straw. The dried stalks of various grains such as spelt, barley, millet, or many kinds of wheat. Straw could also include stalks of wild grasses. Straw was mixed with grain and used as fodder (Gen. 24:25; Judg. 19:19; 1 Kin. 4:28). The Egyptians mixed straw with clay for stronger bricks (Ex. 5:7).

Sycamine (see *Mulberry*).

Sycamore. A huge evergreen tree growing to a height of about 12 to 15 meters (40–50 feet) with a trunk circumference of over 6.5 meters (20 feet). The trunk forked near the ground, and the branches grew outward.

The leaves of the sycamore, sometimes called the sycamore fig, were heart–shaped, resembling the leaves of the mulberry. The fruit was similar to the true fig but was inferior in quality. These yellow figs grew in clusters close to the branches.

Sycamores were trees of the plains (1 Kin. 10:27) and could not tolerate colder climates (Ps. 78:47). The sycamore was the tree which Zacchaeus climbed to gain a better view of Jesus (Luke 19:4).

Tamarisk. A small tree with thick foliage and spikes of pink blooms. It provided ample shade for desert travelers (1 Sam. 22:6). The word for tamarisk is translated tree, grove, or oak by the KJV.

Tares. A poisonous grass resembling wheat, but with smaller seeds. The tares were usually left in the fields until harvest time, then separated from the wheat during winnowing. Jesus used tares growing with wheat as a parable to illustrate evil in the world (Matt. 13:25–30, 36–40). Tares is translated weeds in the RSV and NIV, and darnel in the NEB.

Teil (see *Terebinth*).

Terebinth. A large spreading tree which grew to a height of about 6 to 8 meters (20–26 feet) with red-dish–green leaves and red berries in clusters. The terebinth is mentioned several times in the Bible. It is sometimes translated as teil (Is. 6:13), elm (Hos. 4:13), or oak (Gen. 35:4) by the KJV.

Thistles/Thorns. General terms for any spiney plant. Such plants are characteristic of arid and desert regions. Some of these were brambles, briers, thorny bushes, small trees, weeds, and prickly herbs. They grew abundantly in Palestine and other Bible lands, especially along roadsides, in fields, and in dry places.

The most noted use of thorns in the Bible was the crown of thorns placed on the head of Jesus on the cross (Matt. 27:29). This was done by the Romans as a form of mockery.

Some of the thorns and thistles were annuals, scattering their seed in autumn. The industrious farmer would destroy the plants before he seeded (Matt. 13:7). Many of them were used as fuel for ovens (Ps. 58:9; Eccl. 7:6; Is. 33:12).

Thorny shrubs were used as hedges to guard fields and vineyards (Prov. 15:19; Mark 12:1). The prophet Micah declared that even the most upright person is "sharper [more destructive] than a thorn hedge" (Mic. 7:4).

Thyine (see *Citron*).

Vine (see *Grapes*).

Watermelon (see *Melon*).

Wheat. The most important cereal grass mentioned in the Bible. This was the bearded variety belonging to the genus Triticum. It was cultivated in Bible lands from early times (Gen. 30:14). Egyptian wheat was the many–eared variety called "mummy wheat." This was the wheat of Pharaoh's dream (Gen. 41:5–57). It was also depicted on Egyptian monuments.

Wheat was sown after barley in November or December. It was usually broadcast and then either plowed or trodden into the soil by oxen or other animals (Is. 32:20). This grain was used for bread (Ex.

Wheat, the main field crop of biblical times, was a staple food as well as a trade item for the Israelites (1 Kin. 5:10, 11).

29:32), and was also eaten parched (Lev. 23:14; Ruth 2:14). It was used in ceremonial offerings (Lev. 2:1; 24:5–7) and as an article of commerce (Ezek. 27:17; Acts 27:38).

When corn is mentioned in the Bible, it refers to wheat, as corn was not known in Bible times (Ps. 72:16; Matt. 12:1; Mark 4:28). Jesus compared His death to a grain of wheat which must die to produce fruit (John 12:24).

Willow. A tree which grew to about 9 to 12 meters (30–40 feet) and had reddish–brown bark; narrow, pointed leaves; and flowers or catkins which hung downward. Willow branches were used to construct the booths for the Feast of Tabernacles (Lev. 23:40). The Israelites hung their harps on willows while in Babylon.

Some biblical scholars think the willow mentioned in the Bible was actually the poplar or Euphrates Aspen. The word for willow is consistently translated as poplar by the NIV. Isaiah 44:4 is translated poplar by the NEB and NASB as well. Also see *Poplar.*

Wormwood. A woody shrub covered with small green leaves, with greenish–yellow flowers growing in clusters. Wormwood grows in the desert regions of Palestine and Syria. This plant is mentioned many times in the Bible. It had a bitter taste and a strong aroma (Jer. 9:15).

Wormwood was used symbolically to refer to any calamity or bitter experience (Deut. 29:18; Prov. 5:4; Amos 5:7; Rev. 8:10–11). An intoxicating drink could also be made from this plant (Lam. 3:15). Wormwood is sometimes translated as bitter weeds or hemlock (Amos 6:12, KJV).

PLASTER (see Minerals of the Bible).

PLASTERER (see Occupations and Trades).

PLATE (see Dish).

PLATTER — a large, shallow dish or plate, used especially for serving food. Most of the references to platters in the Bible occur in Numbers 7. They refer to the silver plates or dishes presented by the twelve tribal leaders at the dedication of the altar of the Tabernacle (Num. 7:13–85). The platters of Ezra 1:9 were probably basins for receiving the blood of sacrifices. In the New Testament, John the Baptist's head was brought to Salome, the daughter of Herodias, on a platter (Matt. 14:11; Mark 6:28; charger, KJV).

PLAY (see Games).

PLEDGE — something held as security to guarantee fulfillment of an obligation. As proof of his intention to send Tamar a young goat from his flock, Judah left his signet, cord, and staff with her as a pledge (Gen. 38:17–18, 20). The giving of pledges is regulated in Deuteronomy 24:6, 10–13, 17–18. The abuse of this custom is mentioned by the prophet Ezekiel (18:7, 12). He classified this abuse with such crimes as idolatry, robbery, murder, and adultery. Amos also makes reference to the oppression of the poor through the misuse of the pledge (Amos 2:8).

PLEIADES [PLEE uh deez] — a brilliant cluster of stars seen in the shoulder of Taurus (the Bull). The name Pleiades comes from the seven daughters of Atlas and Pleione in Greek mythology. This constellation consists of several hundred stars, although the naked eye can usually see only six or seven. Job declared that God made the Pleiades (Job 9:9) and bound them in a cluster (Job 38:31).

PLEROMA [pleh RAUH muh] — a Greek word meaning "fullness." In the New Testament *pleroma* is used with two basic senses: (1) something that fills or completes, such as a patch in Matthew 9:16 or love in Romans 13:10; (2) fullness or the state or fact of being filled, such as the completed number of saved Gentiles (Rom. 11:25) or the "full measure" of Christ's blessing (Rom. 15:29, NIV). In some places in the Bible, distinguishing between these two meanings is difficult.

First Corinthians 10:26 (the earth's fullness) and Galatians 4:4 (the fullness of the time; Eph. 1:10) suggest God's sovereign appointment of events in both space and time. In Romans 11:12 pleroma refers to the completion of God's plan for the nation of Israel. The Lord Jesus Christ possesses the complete fullness of God's divine nature and attributes. "In Him dwells all the fullness of the Godhead bodily" (Col. 2:9).

The apostle Paul also used the phrase, "all the fullness of God" (Eph. 3:19), to show that Christ embodied the love of God. In Ephesians 4:13, "the fullness of Christ" means that state of Christian maturity in which believers are no longer "tossed to and fro and carried about with every wind of doctrine, by the trickery of men" (v. 14). There are other practical implications of this idea of the fullness of Christ. Knowing that He has been made full and "complete" in Christ (Col. 2:10), each Christian must be willing to accept whatever edifying suffering God may send to "fill up in my flesh what is lacking in the afflictions of Christ" (Col. 1:24).

PLOWMAN (see Occupations and Trades).

PLOWSHARE — the blade of a plow used for tilling the soil. In early times plows were constructed of wood; but with the development of metallurgy, metal tips were placed over the wood. The prophets Micah and Isaiah spoke of making plowshares from weapons as a sign of the peace to be accomplished in the coming reign of God (Is. 2:4; Mic. 4:3). Also see Tools of the Bible.

PLUMB LINE, PLUMMET (see Tools of the Bible).

POCHERETH–ZEBAIM [POCK eh reth zeh BAY im] *(binder of gazelles)* — a servant of Solomon whose descendants returned from the Captivity with Zerubbabel (Ezra 2:57; Neh. 7:59; Pokereth-Hazzebaim, NIV). Some scholars believe this reference may be to Zeboim (Neh. 11:34), a town occupied by Benjamites after the Captivity. It was situated in the hills bordering the Plain of Sharon, north of Lydda.

PODS — the rough seed cases of the carob tree, commonly called the acacia or locust tree. The prodigal son became so destitute after he squandered his inheritance that "he would gladly have filled his stomach with the pods that the swine ate" (Luke 15:16; husks, KJV). The rabbis frequently mention the pods and beans of the carob tree as fodder for domestic animals in their writings. It was eaten by humans as food only by the poorest classes, or in times of great famine.

POET (see OCCUPATIONS AND TRADES).

POETRY — lofty thought or impassioned feeling expressed in imaginative words. Beautiful poetry occurs in both the Old Testament and the New Testament of the Bible.

Poetry in the Old Testament. At a very early date poetry became part of the written literature of the Hebrew people. Many scholars believe the song of Moses and the song of Miriam (Ex. 15:1–21), celebrating the destruction of Pharaoh's army in the sea, is the oldest existing Hebrew hymn or poetic work, dating perhaps from the 12th century B.C. Three of the greatest poetic masterpieces of the Old Testament are the Song of Deborah (Judges 5); the Song of the Bow—David's lament over the death of Saul and Jonathan (2 Sam. 1:17–27)—and the Burden of Nineveh (Nah. 1:10—3:19).

Approximately one-third of the Old Testament is written in poetry. This includes entire books (except for short prose sections), such as Job, Psalms, Proverbs, the Song of Solomon, and Lamentations. Large portions of Isaiah, Jeremiah, and the Minor Prophets are also poetic in form and content. Many scholars consider the Book of Job to be not only the greatest poem in the Old Testament but also one of the greatest poems in all literature.

The three main divisions of the Old Testament—the Law, the Prophets, and the Writings—contain poetry in successively greater amounts. Only seven Old Testament books—Leviticus, Ruth, Ezra, Nehemiah, Esther, Haggai, and Malachi—appear to have no poetic lines.

Poetic elements such as assonance, alliteration, and rhyme—so common to poetry as we know it today—occur rarely in Hebrew poetry; these are not essential ingredients of Old Testament poetry. Instead, the essential formal characteristic of Hebrew poetry is parallelism. This is a construction in which the content of one line is repeated, contrasted, or advanced by the content of the next—a type of sense rhythm characterized by thought arrangement rather than by word arrangement or rhyme. The three main types of parallelism in biblical poetry are synonymous, antithetic, and synthetic.

Synonymous parallelism—A parallel segment repeats an idea found in the previous segment. With this technique a kind of paraphrase is involved; line two restates the same thought found in line one, by using equivalent expressions. Examples of synonymous parallelism are found in Genesis 4:23: "Adah and Zillah, hear my voice; / Wives of Lamech, lis-

Photo by Gustav Jeeninga

Wild flowers near Jerusalem, in the Kidron Valley. The psalmist probably had flowers such as these in mind when he spoke of the fleeting nature of life (Ps. 103:15, 16).

ten to my speech! / For I have killed a man for wounding me / Even a young man for hurting me." Another example is found in Psalm 2:4: "He who sits in the heavens shall laugh; / The Lord shall hold them in derision." Yet a third example is Psalm 51:2–3: "Wash me thoroughly from my iniquity, / And cleanse me from my sin. / For I acknowledge my transgressions, / And my sin is always before me." (Also see Ps. 24:1–3; 103:3, 7–10; Jer. 17:10; Zech. 9:9.)

Antithetic parallelism—By means of this poetic construction, the thought of the first line is made clearer by contrast—by the opposition expressed in the second line. Examples of antithetic parallelism may be found in Psalm 1:6: "The Lord knows the way of the righteous, / But the way of the ungodly shall perish"; in Psalm 34:10: "The young lions lack and suffer hunger; / But those who seek the Lord shall not lack any good thing"; and in Proverbs 14:20: "The poor man is hated even by his own neighbor, / But the rich has many friends."

Synthetic parallelism—Also referred to as climactic or cumulative parallelism, this poetic construction expands the idea in line one by the idea in line two. In synthetic parallelism, therefore, there is an ascending (or descending) progression, a building up of thought, with each succeeding line adding to the first.

Here is one good example of this poetic technique: "He shall be like a tree / Planted by the rivers of water, / That brings forth its fruit in its season, / Whose leaf also shall not wither; / And whatever he does shall prosper" (Ps. 1:3).

Another poetic form found in the Old Testament

is the alphabetical acrostic, a form used often in the Book of Psalms (Psalm 9; 10; 25; 34; 37; 111; 112; 119; 145). In the alphabetical psalms the first line begins with the first letter of the Hebrew alphabet, the next with the second, and so on, until all the letters of the alphabet have been used. Thus, Psalm 119 consists of 22 groups of eight verses each. The number of groups equals the number of letters in the Hebrew alphabet. The first letter of each verse in a group is (in the original Hebrew text) that letter of the alphabet which corresponds numerically to the group.

Many of the subtleties of Hebrew poetry, such as puns and various play-on-word allusions, are virtually untranslatable into English and may be fully appreciated only by an accomplished Hebrew scholar. Fortunately, many good commentaries are available to explain to the layperson these riches of Hebrew thought.

The Bible is full of numerous figures of speech, such as metaphors and similes. For example, the psalmist metaphorically described God by saying, "The Lord is my rock and my fortress and my deliverer; My God, my strength, in whom I will trust; My shield and the horn of my salvation, my stronghold" (Ps. 18:2).

Moses gave this remarkable simile describing God's care of Israel in the wilderness: "As an eagle stirs up its nest, / Hovers over its young, / Spreading out its wings, taking them up, / Carrying them on its wings, / So the Lord alone led him" (Deut. 32:11–12).

Such figures of speech are not to be interpreted literally but as poetic symbolism for God. He is the firm ground of life and a solid defense against evil. The worshiper sings for joy because of His protecting presence and the soaring power of His loving care.

Poetry in the New Testament. Very little poetry is found in the New Testament, except poetry quoted from the Old Testament or hymns which were included in the worship services of the early church. The Beatitudes (Matt. 5:3–10; Luke 6:20–26) have a definite poetic form. The Gospel of Luke contains several long poems: Zacharias' prophecy, known as the *Benedictus* (Luke 1:68–79); the song of Mary, known as the *Magnificat* (Luke 1:46–55); the song of the heavenly host, known as the *Gloria in Excelsis* (Luke 2:14); and the blessing of Simeon, known as the *Nunc Dimittis* (Luke 2:29–32).

Examples of parallelism may be found in the New Testament. For instance, synonymous parallelism occurs in Matthew 7:6: "Do not give what is holy to the dogs, nor cast your pearls before swine." Antithetic parallelism occurs in Matthew 8:20: "Foxes have holes and birds of the air have nests, but the Son of Man has nowhere to lay His head." Synthetic parallelism occurs in John 6:32–33: "Moses did not give you the bread from heaven, but My Father gives you the true bread from heaven. For the bread of God is He who comes down from heaven and gives life to the world."

In the writings of the apostle Paul several poetic passages may be found: his lyrical celebration of God's everlasting love (Rom. 8:31–39); his classic hymn to love (1 Corinthians 13); his glorious faith in the triumph of the resurrection (1 Cor. 15:51–58); and his thoughts on the humbled and exalted Christ (Phil. 2:5–11).

Who can deny the poetic passion in Paul's words to the Corinthians? "We are hard pressed on every side, yet not crushed; / we are perplexed, but not in despair; / persecuted, but not forsaken; / struck down, but not destroyed" (2 Cor. 4:8–9).

POISON — a chemical substance that causes injury or death when taken into the body. The Bible contains many references to the poison of "serpents" (Deut. 32:24, 33), "cobras" (Job 20:16), and "asps" (Ps. 140:3; Rom. 3:13). When the apostle Paul was on the island of Malta, a viper bit him, but he suffered no ill effects from the snakebite (Acts 28:1–6).

Poisonous plants are also mentioned in the Bible. These include hemlock (Hos. 10:4) and wormwood (Deut. 29:18). At Gilgal, in a time of famine, the prophet Elisha purified a pot of stew which contained poisonous "wild gourds" (2 Kin. 4:38–41).

POLE — the staff or standard upon which Moses put a bronze serpent, when the Israelites were bitten by fiery serpents in the wilderness. Everyone who looked at the serpent on the pole lived, in spite of their snakebites (Num. 21:4–9). The Gospel of John treats this event as a type, or symbol, of the lifting up of the Son of Man (John 3:14–15)—the death of Jesus on the cross.

POLLUTE — to make ceremonially unclean or morally impure; to defile, profane, or corrupt. Allowing a murderer to go unpunished polluted the land of Israel (Num. 35:33). So did participation in a pagan religion that practiced human sacrifice (Ps. 106:38; Jer. 7:30). The prophet Zephaniah charged the wicked and corrupt leaders of Jerusalem with polluting the holy city (Zeph. 3:1–4). Worship of the one true God was the way to keep oneself holy and morally pure.

POLYGAMY — the practice of having several spouses, especially wives, at one time. Polygamy includes polygyny (marriage to more than one woman) and polyandry (marriage to more than one man). The term polygamy is more often used, however, as a synonym for polygyny, which was common throughout the ancient world.

According to the custom of the times, Abraham took Hagar, the Egyptian maidservant of his wife Sarah, to be his wife when Sarah was unable to bear a child (Gen. 16:1–4). Abraham's son, Isaac, had only one wife; but Abraham's grandson, Jacob, took two wives (Leah and Rachel) and two CONCUBINES, Zilpah and Bilhah (Gen. 29:15—30:13).

The Bible presents monogamy as the divine ideal. The Creator made marriage as a union between one man and one woman (Gen. 2:18–24; Matt. 19:4–6; 1 Cor. 6:16). Apparently polygamy, like divorce, was tolerated because of the hardness of peoples' hearts (Matt. 19:8).

After the time of Moses, polygamy continued to be practiced, especially by wealthy individuals, such as Gideon, Elkanah, Saul, and David (1 Sam. 1:2; 2 Sam. 5:13; 1 Kin. 11:3). But the most famous polygamist in the Bible was King Solomon: "And he had seven hundred wives, princesses, and three hundred concubines; and his wives turned away his heart" (1 Kin. 11:3). The criticism of polygamy expressed in Deuteronomy 17:17, therefore, is not surprising: the ideal king to whom Israel's obedience can be rightly given shall not "multiply wives for himself, lest his heart turn away."

Also see MARRIAGE.

POMEGRANATE (see PLANTS OF THE BIBLE).

POMMEL – KJV word for CAPITAL.

POND (see POOL).

PONTIUS PILATE (see PILATE, PONTIUS).

PONTUS [PONN tus] (*the sea*) — a province in northern Asia Minor (modern Turkey) mentioned in the Book of Acts (see Map 7, D–1). Pontus was situated on the southern shore of the Pontus Euxinus, or the Black Sea. A mountainous area broken by fertile plains, Pontus produced olives, grain, and timber.

Pontus was made part of the Galatian–Cappadocian province of the Roman Empire by Nero in A.D. 64. It is mentioned twice in the Book of Acts. Men from Pontus were in Jerusalem on the Day of Pentecost (Acts 2:9) and it was the birthplace of Aquila, the husband of Priscilla (Acts 18:2). The First Epistle of Peter is addressed to "the pilgrims of the Dispersion in Pontus, Galatia, Cappadocia, Asia, and Bithynia" (1 Pet. 1:1). From this we may assume that Christians were living in Pontus. But no information is given concerning the beginnings and the growth of Christianity in that region.

POOL — a large open receptacle fed either by springs or by rainwater; a pond or reservoir for holding water. Because rainfall is not plentiful in Palestine, storage of water is crucial. Most cities developed near a spring or similar water supply, but this was not always adequate as the city grew. It became necessary to store water to provide for the dry season and to prepare for the possibility of a prolonged siege against the city.

Individual families or groups sometimes stored water in cisterns, which are plaster–lined pits in the ground. Another method was to collect water in open–air pools. The pools could be quite large, and frequently they took advantage of natural features. For instance, a narrow valley might be dammed to create a pool. Pools were frequently fed by underground springs.

Several pools are mentioned in the Bible, but the location of most of these remains unknown today. One famous pool in Jerusalem was the "pool of Siloam" (John 9:7, 11), which is still in use today. It was originally built by King Hezekiah shortly be-

fore 700 B.C. to provide an adequate water supply during an expected siege by the Assyrians. A tunnel, dug through the ridge upon which Jerusalem was built, allowed the water of the Gihon Spring to flow to the pool of Siloam (2 Kin. 20:20; 2 Chr. 32:30). In the New Testament, Jesus sent a blind man to wash his eyes at the pool of Siloam (John 9:7).

Pools of water came to be used as figures of God's blessing upon the land of Israel. In Isaiah 35:7 and 41:18, God promised that He would once again bless the land. Part of that blessing would be abundance of water.

POOR — having little or no wealth and few or no possessions; lacking in financial or other resources. Although the poor will remain a part of society (Deut. 15:11; Matt. 26:11), the Bible instructs the righteous to show concern for them.

God takes up the cause of the poor. The psalms repeatedly emphasize that God helps them. He will "spare the poor and needy" (Ps. 72:13). He promises, "I will satisfy her poor with bread" (Ps. 132:15). The poor of the world can take comfort in the fact that God cares for them.

The divine compassion for the poor is demonstrated by Jesus (Luke 6:20). Luke, who especially emphasizes concern for the poor, relates Christ's mission statement from Isaiah, "He has anointed Me to preach the gospel to the poor" (Is. 61:1; Luke 4:18). The rich young man was instructed by Jesus to sell his possessions and "to distribute to the poor" (Luke 18:22). Jesus' followers cannot remain unconcerned about the poor of the world.

Instructions about considerate treatment of the poor are found in the Law, the Prophets, the Writings, and the New Testament. The Law, as well as the Prophets, warned against oppressing the poor and crushing the needy (Deut. 24:14; Prov. 14:31; Amos 2:6; 4:1). People of means were warned not to take advantage of the poor, especially in court: "You shall not pervert the judgment of your poor in his dispute" (Ex. 23:6; Amos 5:12). Help was to be given to the poor (Deut. 15:7–8; Is. 58:7). Such help was to be motivated by God's own action of providing the underprivileged with food and clothing (Deut. 10:18).

The extent to which God identifies with the poor is clear from Proverbs 19:17 and Matthew 25:34–40. Jesus instructed that the poor should be invited when a feast is prepared (Luke 14:12–14; Gal. 2:10). James warned against discrimination against the poor (Lev. 19:15; James 2:2–4).

POOR IN SPIRIT — those who admit their spiritual inadequacy and cast themselves on the mercy of God (Matt. 5:3). The poor in spirit are the opposite of the proud, the arrogant, the self–righteous who boast of their own goodness. Jesus' parable of the Pharisee and the tax collector (Luke 18:9–14) illustrates this contrast.

The Gospel of Luke declares, "Blessed are you poor for yours is the kingdom of God" (Luke 6:20). The poor in spirit are those who look to the Lord

Photo by Ben Chapman

The Pool of Siloam (John 9:7-11), a reservoir inside the walls of Jerusalem which held the city's water supply.

for justice, mercy, and deliverance, and not to themselves.

POPLAR (see PLANTS OF THE BIBLE).

PORATHA [poe RAY thuh] (*bounteous*) — a son of Haman, hanged like his father (Esth. 9:8).

PORCH — an open veranda, vestibule, or portico on the outside of a building (Joel 2:17; John 5:2). Few homes in Bible times had porches. Most references to porches in the Bible refer to the Temple or to Solomon's palace. Solomon's palace featured a veranda that was open in front and on the sides, but it could be closed off with curtains. Also see HOUSE.

PORCIUS [POHR shih uhs] (see FESTUS PORCIUS).

PORCUPINE (see ANIMALS OF THE BIBLE).

PORPHYRY (see MINERALS OF THE BIBLE).

PORPOISE (see ANIMALS OF THE BIBLE).

PORTER (see OCCUPATIONS AND TRADES).

PORTION — an allowance, ration, or part that is allotted to a person or group, including the following ideas:

1. An allowance of food or clothing (Gen. 14:24). Daniel refused his portion of the king's delicacies (Dan. 1:8–16).

2. One's family inheritance, the part of an estate received by an heir (Gen. 31:14; Luke 15:12).

3. A parcel of ground (2 Kin. 9:10).

4. Metaphorically, a person's destiny or lot in life (Job. 3:22).

5. One's spiritual or religious heritage (2 Chr. 10:16), especially in the sense of one's personal relationship to the Lord (Ps. 119:57).

6. The judgment that is the lot of the wicked (Matt. 24:51).

POSSESSION, DEMON (see DEMON POSSESSION).

POST, POSTS — words used in the Bible in a number of ways: a command post (1 Kin. 20:12, 16); an observation post, or watchtower (Is. 21:8); guard posts (Acts 12:10); a person's position or station of employment (Eccl. 10:4); and the doorposts of a building (Prov. 8:34; Eccl. 10:4). The prophet Ezekiel used the word several times to describe the doorway of the new Temple. The NKJV uses gateposts (Ezek. 40:9–38) and doorposts (Ezek. 40:48–49; 41:1, 3).

Posts also referred to runners (2 Chr. 30:6, 10; Job 9:25; Jer. 51:31) and couriers (Esth. 3:13, 15; 8:10, 14)—men usually employed by a king to deliver letters swiftly on horseback (Esth. 8:10).

POTENTATE [POTE un tate] — one who has the power, position, and authority to rule over others. The apostle Paul called the Lord "the blessed and only Potentate, the King of kings and Lord of lords" (1 Tim. 6:15; Sovereign, RSV, NASB; Ruler, NIV). This way he expressed reverence for the Lord as ruler of the universe.

POTIPHAR [PAHT uh fur] (*dedicated to Ra*) — the Egyptian to whom the Ishmaelites (Gen. 39:1) sold Joseph when he was brought to Egypt as a slave. Potiphar was a high officer of Pharaoh and a wealthy man (Gen. 37:36). In time, he put Joseph in charge of his household. But Potiphar's wife became attracted to Joseph and attempted to seduce him. When he rejected her advances, she falsely accused him and had him imprisoned (Gen. 39:6–19).

POTI–PHERAH [poh TIFF eh rah] (*he whom Ra has given*) — a priest of ON (Heliopolis) and father–in–law of Joseph (Gen. 41:45). Asenath, Potipherah's daughter, bore Joseph two sons. Other spellings of the name are Potipherah (KJV) and Potiphera (RSV, NEB, NASB, NIV).

POTSHERD [POTT shurd] — a fragment of broken pottery; a shard found in an archaeological excavation. Job used a potsherd to scrape the sores of his body (Job 2:8). The sharp points of a potsherd are compared to the scales of LEVIATHAN (Job 41:30). The dryness of a potsherd is likened to one whose strength is totally gone (Ps. 22:15). Larger fragments of broken pottery were used to "take fire from the hearth"—that is, carry hot coals from one house to another—and "take water from the cistern" (Is. 30:14). The same Hebrew word translated as potsherd can also refer to unbroken earthenware pots (Lev. 6:28; Jer. 19:1).

A careful analysis of the make–up, style, and

method of pieces of pottery gives archaeologists an important clue for dating different levels of occupation of ancient cities. Potsherds were also used as a writing material in Bible times. These potsherds, called ostraca, contained tax receipts, military correspondence, and other short bits of information. The famous Lachish ostraca were potsherds containing correspondence between the city of Lachish and its military outposts.

POTSHERD GATE (see GATES OF JERUSALEM AND THE TEMPLE).

POTTAGE (see STEW).

POTTER (see OCCUPATIONS AND TRADES).

POTTER'S FIELD — the field bought with the 30 pieces of silver paid to Judas for his betrayal of Jesus (Matt. 27:7, 10). Since the field was purchased with blood money, it was considered good for nothing but a cemetery in which foreigners were buried. According to tradition, the potter's field was at the eastern end of the Valley of Hinnom. Also see AKEL DAMA.

POTTER'S GATE (see GATES OF JERUSALEM AND THE TEMPLE).

POTTERY — vessels or other objects manufactured from clay and hardened by fire. In modern usage, the term pottery generally refers only to vessels (bowls, plates, jars, etc.). But the products of the potter's craft were very diverse in Bible times.

The Making of Pottery. Clay is the basic material from which pottery is produced. It has two important characteristics: it can be shaped and will retain its form, and it hardens when exposed to a high temperature. A clay vessel that has been sun–dried will eventually collapse if filled with water. But if the clay is heated to a temperature of at least 500 degrees C (900 degrees F), its chemical composition and physical characteristics change. It hardens and no longer can be molded.

Clay, in its natural state, was seldom fit for use in making pottery. Several stages of preparation were usually necessary. The clay was mixed with water, then sifted to remove stones and larger particles. This was accomplished with the use of settling basins, a series of refining pits that produced gradually finer grades of clay. Straw, sand, shell, or pulverized POTSHERDS were often added to the clay. These ingredients minimized shrinkage and helped to prevent cracking of the vessel during the drying or firing process. A final step was to knead the clay with hands or feet to remove air bubbles and assure the right consistency.

A number of techniques for shaping a vessel were developed by the potters of the ancient world. Fashioning by hand was probably the earliest pottery–making technique. But this method was inadequate for larger and more complex vessels. Before the invention of the potter's wheel, such pottery was produced by the technique of coil construction. By this method a vessel was built up by coiling long rolls of clay on top of one another. More elaborate forms were possible by varying the thickness of the coils. The irregular surface created by the coils was smoothed over as the vessel was formed.

Another common technique was the use of molds to form figurines and vessels. Oil lamps, small statuettes, and plaques were among the most common clay objects manufactured in molds. One of the most beautiful ceramic products from the ancient world, known as "Arretine ware," was produced from molds. This pottery generally features scenes of people, plants, animals, and geometric designs.

Pottery–making was revolutionized with the invention of the potter's wheel. A primitive wheel, called a turntable or tournette, is datable in Palestine to about 3000 B.C. This device consisted of a single horizontal disk which was turned by hand. The slow rotation created the centrifugal force that allowed the potter to "throw" the vessel. The true potter's wheel added a second disk or kick wheel, operated by foot, that increased the speed of rotation. The development of the potter's wheel evolved in several stages from the tournette to the kick wheel.

Pottery was sometimes produced by a combination of techniques. The bodies of certain jars, bottles, and teapots were produced by the technique of coil construction, while the necks and rims were wheelmade.

Because a vessel has no function until hardened by exposure to high temperatures, the drying or firing process was the crucial step in the production of pottery. Although pottery could be sun–dried, as the earliest vessels were, they could only be used for storing dry materials. A pot will sufficiently harden to hold liquid and retain its shape if exposed to a minimum temperature of 500 degrees C (900 degrees F). An open fire will produce temperatures in the range of 700–800 degrees C, adequate to fire

A potter, using his foot to power a revolving turntable, forms a jar from a lump of clay.
Photo: Matson Photo Collection

Photo by Gustav Jeeninga

This piece of pottery, known as a bilbil, is a type of Cypriote pot. It was common in the ancient world about 1500 B.C.

clay vessels, but a vessel fired in this way is brittle, porous, and black from the smoke.

Efficient firing finally was accomplished in a kiln. The earliest kiln in Palestine dates to about 3000 B.C. Although there are variations, the basic form of the kiln remained unchanged throughout the biblical period. A beehive–shaped structure was divided into two chambers by a horizontal partition, which was perforated with holes. The vessels were placed in the upper chamber. The fuel, consisting of wood or dung, was placed in the lower chamber. Heat reached the upper chamber through the holes in the floor. Firing was a delicate process. It required well–prepared clays, thoroughly–dried vessels, adequate temperatures, and firing time.

Many decorating techniques were developed by the potters of ancient times. These included painting, incising, burnishing, stamping, glazing, and the application of slip.

Pottery as a Dating Tool. Pottery is the most common artifact from the ancient world. It was found in the poorest houses and in the most luxurious palaces, on the surfaces of ancient streets and in building foundations. Burials, from the simplest to the most elaborate, yield quantities of pottery, usually whole vessels. An archaeological excavation will produce thousands of sherds (fragments of pottery) and many intact vessels. The fact that pottery finds far outnumber any type of archaeological artifact is due mainly to its indestructibility. Fired clay will not disintegrate even if buried for thousands of years. Most other materials, like metal or wood, will disappear.

Apart from its functional value to the people of ancient times, pottery has a special importance for the study of these cultures. Pottery has changed through the centuries. These changes are reflected in form, decoration, clay composition, manufacturing technique, and quality of firing. Pottery is, therefore, one of the indicators of the technical and artistic achievements of a culture. The presense of imported pottery, clearly distinguishable from the styles and wares of local pottery, enables the archaeologist to identify and study foreign influence, such as trade relations, population movements, and conquest. The most important contribution of pottery to the study of ancient cultures is its value as a dating tool.

Pottery is usually found in every level of an ancient TELL—an artificial mound which is formed by the accumulation of ancient ruins. A tell may be described as one city or occupational level on top of another, producing a mound of considerable height. Each occupational level has its own level or layer of debris. The study of these various layers presents the archaeologist with a complicated task. In the absence of written materials, pottery is the most reliable tool for determining the chronology of a site or its individual levels.

Ceramic Typology. Mastery of ceramic typology, the ability to date potsherds, is the result of many years of study and constant exposure to the pottery forms of the various archaeological periods. Textbooks alone are inadequate for the study of pottery typology. There are many features which have potential significance for the dating of pottery, such as the quality and texture of the clay, the kind of matter included for strength, the type and quality of decoration, numerous considerations relative to the firing process and, most importantly, the vessel's form or shape.

The shape of the vessel's rim or base, the curvature of the body, the presence or absence of handles, the type of handle, the manner and point of a handle's attachment—these are among the distinctives of pottery that have chronological significance. The shape of a vessel's rim most often provides the best dating criterion. The cooking pot, for instance, has very distinctive rim shapes as this vessel changes through the archaeological periods. Some pottery shapes change dramatically and rapidly while others, like the lamp, change more slowly and subtly.

Also of great value as chronological indicators are the various types of burnishing, painting, and glazing. Clay composition and firing technique can be significant. The retrieval of this data is achieved through various scientific tests.

The earliest pottery dates back to the Neolithic period (New Stone Age), about 7500–4000 B.C. This archaeological period is divided into two phases at about 5000 B.C. by the first appearance of pottery: pre–Pottery Neolithic and Pottery Neolithic. The second, ceramic, phase of the Neolithic culture has been studied at a number of sites, including Catal Huyuk in Anatolia, Jericho, and in the Yarmuk Valley. The pottery of this period is handmade and is characterized by simple and primitive forms. The ware or fabric is often soft and

A decorated Phoenician juglet (left) with a plain and utilitarian high-footed vase.

Photo by Gustav Jeeninga

crumbly—the result of firing the clay at a low temperature.

During this period, straw was frequently mixed with the clay as a temper. In addition to these coarse wares, finer pottery was also used in this period. The clay is of better quality, the firing is at a higher temperature, and the pottery was frequently decorated with a burnished red slip in a design of triangles or chevrons. The most common forms are small bowls, deeper bowls with gently curving sides, and globular jars with flat bases. The handles are basically of three types: simple loop handles, small pierced lug handles, and small ledge or knob handles. The ledge handle is a most distinguishing feature of Early Bronze Age pottery.

The transition from the Neolithic period to the Chalcolithic period, from about 4000–3000 B.C., is not well–understood. The site of Tuleilat el–Ghassul in the southern Jordan Valley and several sites in the region of Beersheba have contributed significantly to our understanding of the culture and pottery of the Chalcolithic period.

Two pottery forms characteristic of the Chalcolithic period are churns and cornets. The cornet is shaped much like an ice–cream cone, often painted with horizontal bands, and it has small lug handles. Its distinctive shape makes it a hallmark of Chalcolithic pottery. The churn is an oddly shaped vessel whose function is not completely understood. The form is horizontal, barrel–shaped, with tapered ends. Small loop handles are mounted on the top of each end, allowing the vessel to be hung much like a goat skin. The neck, sometimes containing a strainer, is located in the middle of the body. The overall shape gives the general impression of a submarine. The larger churns are decorated with red painted bands.

Although there is some controversy, the Early Bronze Age (3200–2200 B.C.) may be divided into three phases, each of which has characteristic pottery types and distinctive decoration. One of the most common features of Early Bronze pottery is the ledge handle, which has distinctive shapes for each of the phases of this period. Vessels with parallel lines of red paint covering the entire body are one of the common ceramic types of the Early Bronze I period.

The most typical pottery shape of Early Bronze II is an oval jug which is designated "Abydos ware" after the name of the site in Egypt where it was first discovered. A typical pottery type of Early Bronze III, designated "Khirbet Kerak ware" after the site of its discovery, is one of the most beautiful ceramics of ancient Palestine. Though the forms set this pottery apart from local ceramic traditions, the decoration is the distinguishing feature. This handmade ware is a red and/or black burnished pottery. It differs also from local pottery in terms of clay quality, manufacturing technique, and firing. Although the origins of this import are not clear, Khirbet Kerak ware is widely distributed throughout northern and central Palestine.

The period traditionally designated Middle Bronze I, now Early Bronze IV–Middle Bronze I (2200–2000 B.C.), was an interlude between the urban cultures of the preceding Early Bronze Age and the following Middle Bronze II period. New pottery forms appeared. Among the most common were four-spouted lamps, jars with flat bases, and spouted pots (teapots).

The widespread use of the potter's wheel in the Middle Bronze II period (2000–1500 B.C.) is, in large measure, responsible for technical improvements in pottery–making. A wide range of forms, some quite elaborate, appeared in this period. One of the distinctive forms was a carinated, or sharply curved, bowl which may have been patterned after a metal vessel. Another common pottery type is the so-called "Tell el-Yahudiyeh ware," named after the site of its first discovery in the Nile Delta. Found primarily on juglets, this ware is characterized by white-filled punctures, making up geometric patterns.

The Late Bronze Age (1500–1200 B.C.) is divided into two main phases with further subdivision of each phase. The variety of local and imported ceramic traditions is rich. Characteristic of Late Bronze I is a beautiful pottery, called "bichrome painted ware," which is decorated with pictures of birds, animals, fish, and geometric designs. Imported Cypriot wares and pottery from Mycenae are common in this period.

The Iron Age spans the period from about 1200 B.C. to the destruction of Jerusalem in 586 B.C. Two fundamental problems associated with the study of this period are the nature of the transition from the Late Bronze to the Iron Age and the division of the Iron Age into phases. As with all of the archaeological periods, the constant flow of new pottery from recent excavations is helping to clarify the picture. The Iron Age has generally been divided into two periods with the division of the kingdom under Solomon's son Rehoboam (918–900 B.C.) constituting the datum which separates Iron I and Iron II. Both periods are further subdivided.

Iron Age pottery is characterized by technical sophistication and an abundance of types with numerous variants. Finish and decoration in this period are distinctive. Vessels are commonly covered with a red, black, brown, or yellow slip (a coat of watery clay which is applied to the surface of a pot before firing) which is burnished to a high lustre. Pottery of this period clearly reflects ancient Israel's relations with Phoenicia, Cyprus, Egypt, Assyria, and other nations. One of the outstanding traditions of the early Iron Age is Philistine pottery, which is decorated with red and black geometric designs and stylized birds.

A vast variety of pottery forms are characteristic of Iron II, including various sizes of burnished bowls, kraters, jugs, juglets, cups, and large storage jars. These storage vessels often bear royal seal impressions on the handles. Contemporary with the wheelmade wares of the Iron Age is the tradition of handmade pottery which is known as "Negevite ware." It is attested throughout this period in a wide variety of forms which often look like wheelmade types of pottery.

The Exilic–Persian period (about 586–332 B.C.) is distinguished by many unique forms, including jars with stump bases and "basket" handles, shallow lamps which are distinguished by wide rims and the so-called "sausage" jars. An imported black–glazed pottery, commonly small bowls and plates, is the hallmark of the Hellenistic period (about 332–63 B.C.). The Roman period, in addition to the usual ceramic repertoire, has produced two beautiful pottery traditions. "Nabatean ware,"

These beautiful Corinthian vases discovered at Athens date from about the seventh century B.C.

Photo by Howard Vos

common in the Negev and Transjordan, is a thin, delicate, well-fired pottery with painted floral designs. "Terra sigillata" is a red–glazed pottery, stamped with roulettes, which was produced in Italy and the Roman provinces. This ware was imitated by local potters.

Pottery and Pottery–Making in the Bible. The potter's craft is alluded to in numerous biblical passages. This is especially true of the Old Testament, which contains a large ceramic vocabulary, including terms not well–understood. Among the numerous references are those to bowls of varying sizes (Ex. 8:3; 12:34; kneading trough, KJV; Judg. 6:38; 2 Kin. 2:20; cruse, KJV; Matt. 26:23; dish, KJV; cooking pots (Judg. 6:19; 2 Kin. 4:38); jars and pitchers (Gen. 24:14; 1 Sam. 26:11; cruse, KJV; 2 Kin. 4:2; pot, KJV; Jer. 35:5; pots, KJV; John 4:28; waterpot, KJV); juglets (1 Kin. 17:12; cruse, KJV); and lamps (Ex. 27:20; Prov. 31:18; candle, KJV). The list of ceramic types in the Bible, together with the actual vessels found in archaeological excavations, have provided a clear picture of the pottery of biblical times.

Jeremiah 18:1–6 is the most vivid passage about pottery–making in the Bible. It contains a realistic description of the potter's workshop (18:1–4), and it uses figurative language for the potter's craft. The image of God as the Master Potter also appears in Genesis 2:7; Isaiah 29:16; 64:8; Job 10:8–9, and Romans 9:20–24.

POUND (see MONEY OF THE BIBLE; WEIGHTS AND MEASURES).

POVERTY (see POOR).

POWDERS — aromatic spices pulverized and used as perfume or burned as incense (Song 3:6). Solomon's palanquin (a portable couch) was perfumed by powders.

POWER — the ability or strength to perform an activity or deed. Power is sometimes used with the word authority. If power suggests physical strength, authority suggests a moral right or privilege. One can have power to perform a task but not authority to do it. Jesus Christ had both power and authority (Luke 4:36), and He bestowed these upon His followers (Luke 10:19).

PRAETORIUM, PRAETORIAN GUARD — a special group of Roman soldiers in New Testament times, established to guard the emperor of the Roman Empire. Originally, they were restricted to the city of Rome, but later they were sent to the Roman provinces as well. This guard was an elite corps of soldiers whose salaries, privileges, and terms of service were better than the other soldiers of the Roman Empire.

In the NKJV, Praetorium is mentioned with reference to place (Matt. 27:27; Mark 15:16; John 18:28, 33; 19:9). The implication from the Gospels is that the Praetorium was part of Herod's palace or the governor's residence in Jerusalem. Paul, when he was in prison in Caesarea, was "kept in Herod's Praetorium" (Acts 23:35).

Philippians 1:13 refers to the "whole praetorian guard" (RSV) or to the "whole palace guard" (NKJV). Commentators are not sure whether this reference is limited to the guard or whether it may refer to the imperial high court as well.

The Praetorium guard was discontinued in the third century A.D. because they had become too powerful, threatening the authority of the Roman emperor himself.

PRAISE — an act of worship or acknowledgment by which the virtues or deeds of another are recognized and extolled. The praise of man toward man, although often beneficial (1 Cor. 11:2; 1 Peter 2:14), can be a snare to man (Prov. 27:21; Matt. 6:1–5). But the praise of God toward man is the highest commendation a person can receive. Such an act of praise reflects a true servant's heart (Matt. 25:21; 1 Cor. 4:5; Eph. 1:3–14).

The praise of man toward God is the means by which we express our joy to the Lord. We are to praise God both for who He is and for what He does (Ps. 150:2). Praising God for who He is is called adoration; praising Him for what He does is known as thanksgiving. Praise of God may be in song or prayer, individually or collectively, spontaneous or prearranged, originating from the emotions or from the will.

The godly person will echo David's words, "My praise shall be continually of You…And [I] will praise You yet more and more" (Ps. 71:6, 14).

PRAYER — communication with God. Because God is personal, all people can offer prayers. However, sinners who have not trusted Jesus Christ for their salvation remain alienated from God. So while unbelievers may pray, they do not have the basis for a rewarding fellowship with God. They have not met the conditions laid down in the Bible for effectiveness in prayer.

Christians recognize their dependence upon their Creator. They have every reason to express gratitude for God's blessings. But they have far more reason to respond to God than this. They respond to the love of God for them. God's love is revealed through the marvelous incarnation and life of Christ, His atoning provision at the Cross, His resurrection, as well as His continuing presence through the Holy Spirit.

Prayer cannot be replaced by devout good works in a needy world. Important as service to others is, at times we must turn away from it to God, who is distinct from all things and over all things. Neither should prayer be thought of as a mystical experience in which people lose their identity in the infinite reality. Effective prayer must be a scripturally informed response of persons saved by grace to the living God who can hear and answer on the basis of Christ's payment of the penalty which sinners deserved. As such, prayer involves several important aspects.

Faith. The most meaningful prayer comes from a heart that places its trust in the God who has acted and spoken in the Jesus of history and the teachings of the Bible. God speaks to us through the Bible, and we in turn speak to Him in trustful, believing prayer. Assured by the Scripture that God is personal, living, active, all–knowing, all–wise, and all–powerful, we know that God can hear and help us. A confident prayer life is built on the cornerstone of Christ's work and words as shown by the prophets and apostles in the Spirit–inspired writings of the Bible.

Worship. In worship we recognize what is of highest worth—not ourselves, others, or our work, but God. Only the highest divine being deserves our highest respect. Guided by Scripture, we set our values in accord with God's will and perfect standards. Before God, angels hide their faces and cry, "Holy, holy, holy is the Lord of hosts" (Is. 6:3).

Confession. Awareness of God's holiness leads to consciousness of our own sinfulness. Like the prophet Isaiah, we exclaim, "Woe is me, for I am undone! Because I am a man of unclean lips, and I dwell in the midst of a people of unclean lips; for my eyes have seen the King, the Lord of hosts" (Is. 6:5). By sinning we hurt ourselves and those closest to us; but first of all, and worst of all, sin is against God (Ps. 51:4). We must confess our sins to God to get right with Him. We need not confess them to another being. But we should confess them directly to God, who promises to forgive us of all our unrighteousness (1 John 1:9).

Adoration. God is love, and He has demonstrated His love in the gift of His Son. The greatest desire of God is that we love Him with our whole being (Matt. 22:37). Our love should be expressed, as His has been expressed, in both deeds and words. People sometimes find it difficult to say to others and to God, "I love you." But when love for God fills our lives, we will express our love in prayer to the one who is ultimately responsible for all that we are.

Praise. The natural outgrowth of faith, worship, confession, and adoration is praise. We speak well of one whom we highly esteem and love. The one whom we respect and love above all others naturally receives our highest commendation. We praise Him for His "mighty acts...according to His excellent greatness!" (Ps. 150:2), and for His "righteous judgments" (Ps. 119:164). For God Himself, for His works, and for His words, His people give sincere praise.

Thanksgiving. Are we unthankful because we think we have not received what we deserve? But if we got what we "deserved," we would be condemned because of our guilt. As sinners, we are not people of God by nature. We have no claim upon His mercy or grace. Nevertheless, He has forgiven our sins, granted us acceptance as His people, and given us His righteous standing and a new heart and life. Ingratitude marks the ungodly (Rom. 1:21). Believers, in contrast, live thankfully. God has been at work on our behalf in countless ways. So in everything, even for the discipline that is unpleasant, we give thanks (Col. 3:17; 1 Thess. 5:18).

Dedicated Action. Christ's example does not require us to withdraw from society, but to render service to the needy in a spirit of prayer. He wept over Jerusalem in compassionate prayer, and then He went into the city to give His life a ransom for many. Authentic prayer will be the source of courage and productivity, as it was for the prophets and apostles.

Request. Prayer is not only response to God's grace as brought to us in the life and work of Jesus and the teaching of Scripture; it is also request for our needs and the needs of others.

For good reasons God's holy and wise purpose does not permit Him to grant every petition just as it is asked. Several hindrances to answered prayer are mentioned in the Bible: iniquity in the heart (Ps. 66:18), refusal to hear God's law (Prov. 28:9), an estranged heart (Is. 29:13), sinful separation from God (Is. 59:2), waywardness (Jer. 14:10–12), offering unworthy sacrifices (Mal. 1:7–9), praying to be seen of men (Matt. 6:5–6), pride in fasting and tithing (Luke 18:11–14), lack of faith (Heb. 11:6), and doubting or double–mindedness (James 4:3).

More positively, God has promised to answer our requests when we start helping the hungry and afflicted (Is. 58:9–10), when we believe that we will receive what we ask (Mark 11:22–24), when we forgive others (Mark 11:25–26), when we ask in Christ's name (John 14:13–14), and when we abide in Christ and His words (John 15:7), pray in the Spirit (Eph. 6:8), obey the Lord's commandments (1 John 3:22), and ask according to His will (1 John 5:14–15). Until we have properly responded to God and His Word, He cannot entrust us with His powerful resources.

Prayer is request to a personal Lord who answers as He knows best. We should not think that we will always have success in obtaining the things for which we ask. In His wisdom, God hears and answers in the way that is best.

Effectiveness. Prayer has power over everything. God can intelligently act in any part of the universe or human history. Although some people think prayer is a waste of time, the Bible declares that "the effective, fervent prayer of a righteous man avails much" (James 5:16).

Prayer meets inner needs. One who prays will receive freedom from fear (Ps. 118:5–6), strength of soul (Ps. 138:3), guidance and satisfaction (Is. 58:9–11), wisdom and understanding (Dan. 9:20–27), deliverance from harm (Joel 2:32), reward (Matt. 6:6), good gifts (Luke 11:13), fullness of joy (John 16:23–24), peace (Phil. 4:6–8), and freedom from anxiety (1 Pet. 5:7).

Is prayer effective only in the inner lives of those who pray? No, prayer can make a difference in the lives of others. Biblical writers believed prayer for others could result in greater wisdom and power (Eph. 1:18–19); inward strength, knowledge of Christ's love, filling with God's fullness (Eph. 3:16–19); discernment, approval of what is excellent, filling with the fruits of righteousness (Phil. 1:9–11); knowledge of God's will, spiritual understanding, a life pleasing to God, fruitfulness, endurance, patience, joy (Col. 1:9–12); a quiet, peaceable life (1 Tim. 2:1–2); love for one another and all people, holiness before God (1 Thess. 3:10–13); comfort and establishment in every good word and work (2 Thess. 2:16–17); love for God, steadfastness in Christ (2 Thess. 3:5); the sharing of one's faith, promotion of the knowledge of all that is good (Philem. 6); and equipment for every good work that is pleasing to God (Heb. 13:20–21).

Some people who think prayer can affect others question the ability of God to change His usual patterns in the physical world. But some prayers in the Bible changed nature and physical bodies.

Jabez prayed for enlarged borders and protection from harm (1 Chr. 4:10). Other people in the Bible prayed for deliverance from trouble (Ps. 34:15–22), deliverance from both poverty and riches (Prov. 30:7–9), deliverance from the belly of a great fish (Jon. 2:7–10), daily bread (Matt. 6:11), preservation and sanctification of spirit, soul, and body (1 Thess. 5:23), the healing of the sick (James 5:14–15), and the ending of the rain and its beginning again (James 5:17–18).

When the disciples prayed, the building around them shook (Acts 4:31) and an earthquake opened the doors of their prison (Acts 16:25–26). Our prayers do make a difference in how God acts in the world!

PRAYER OF AZARIAH, PRAYER OF MANASSEH (see Apocrypha).

PRAYER, LORD'S (see Lord's Prayer).

PREACHER, PREACHING — one who proclaims the gospel; proclamation of God's saving work through Jesus Christ.

The Old Testament mentions several prominent preachers. Noah, who warned of the impending flood and proclaimed God's ark of safety, was called a "preacher of righteousness" (2 Pet. 2:5). Solomon described himself as a preacher who taught "words of truth" (Eccl. 1:2; 12:9–10). At God's direction, Jonah made a preaching mission to Nineveh, declaring God's judgment and mercy (Jon. 3:2). Like Jonah, all the prophets of the Old Testament were regarded as preachers, particularly Isaiah, Jeremiah, Amos, and Micah.

In the New Testament, the gospel advanced on the wings of preaching. The zeal generated by Pentecost, coupled with growing persecution of the young church, led the disciples to preach everywhere in the known world (Mark 16:20). With a sense of urgency, Jesus and the apostles preached in homes, by the seaside, on the Temple steps, and in the synagogues. John the Baptist called for repentance in preparation for the Messiah's appearance (Matt. 3:11–12).

At His home synagogue in Nazareth, Jesus connected His ministry with that of the prophets (Is. 61:1) and identified His mission as one of proclaiming deliverance: "The Lord has anointed Me to preach good tidings to the poor...to preach deliverance to the captives" (Luke 4:18–19).

Jesus was under a divine order to spread the gospel by means of preaching (Luke 4:43–44). Philip, the preaching deacon, "preached the things concerning the kingdom of God and the name of Jesus Christ" (Acts 8:12). In sending out the Twelve, Jesus commanded them, "As you go, preach, saying, The kingdom of heaven is at hand" (Matt. 10:7). The apostle Paul proudly declared his credentials as one whom God "appointed a preacher and an apostle" (1 Tim. 2:7).

Virtually all New Testament preaching carries an evangelistic thrust. Paul declared, "It pleased God through the foolishness of the message preached to save those who believe" (1 Cor. 1:21). The redemptive mission of Christ as fulfillment of prophecy— particularly His death and resurrection—was the main theme of apostolic preaching (1 Cor. 1:2–3; 15:14). The preacher's personal testimony to Christ's power in his own life was also featured in many sermons (Acts 4:20). As a consequence of such evangelistic passion, thousands were saved when Peter preached at Pentecost (Acts 2:41).

The distinction between preaching and teaching made in the church today is not evident in the New Testament. Both Jesus and Paul regarded themselves as preacher–teachers and were so regarded by others. Luke reports that Jesus "taught the people and preached the gospel" (Luke 20:1). Paul testified that he was appointed "a preacher, an apostle, and a teacher of the Gentiles" (2 Tim. 1:11). The best New Testament preaching, while aimed at motivating sinners to receive Christ, had a strong element of teaching. Paul charged young Timothy to "preach the word!...Convince, rebuke, exhort, with all longsuffering and teaching..." (2 Tim. 4:2).

The Great Commission has a broad application that calls all believers to participate in preaching the gospel (Mark 16:15). The piercing question, "How shall they hear without a preacher?" (Rom. 10:14), challenges all Christians to share with others the good news of the gospel of Jesus Christ.

PRECIOUS STONES (see Jewels and Precious Stones).

PREDESTINATION — the biblical teaching that declares the sovereignty of God over man in such a way that the freedom of the human will is also preserved.

Two major concepts are involved in the biblical meaning of predestination. First, God, who is all-powerful in the universe, has foreknown and predestined the course of human history and the lives of individuals. If He were not in complete control of human events, He would not be sovereign and, thus, would not be God.

Second, God's predestination of human events does not eliminate human choice. A thorough understanding of how God can maintain His sovereignty and still allow human freedom seems to be reserved for His infinite mind alone. Great minds have struggled with this problem for centuries.

Two views of predestination are prominent

among church groups today. One view, known as Calvinism, holds that God offers irresistible grace to those whom he elects to save. The other view, known as Arminianism, insists that God's grace is the source of redemption but that it can be resisted by man through his free choice. In Calvinism, God chooses the believer; in Arminianism, the believer chooses God.

Although the term predestination is not used in the Bible, the apostle Paul alludes to it in Ephesians 1:11: "We have obtained an inheritance, being predestined according to the purpose of Him who works all things according to the counsel of His will."

All Christians agree that creation is moving within the purpose of God. This purpose is to bring the world into complete conformity to His will (Rom. 8:28). From the very beginning of time, God predestined to save humankind by sending His Son to accomplish salvation. Thus, "God would have all men to be saved and come to the knowledge of the truth" (1 Tim. 2:4).

The doctrine of predestination does not mean that God is unjust, deciding that some people will be saved and that others will be lost. Mankind, because of Adam's FALL in the Garden of Eden, sinned by free choice. Thus, no person deserves salvation. But God's grace is universal. His salvation is for "everyone who believes" (Rom. 1:16).

Paul also declared that he was a debtor under obligation to take the message of the gospel to other people (Rom. 1:14) so they might hear and obey. Paul clearly meant that no one is saved apart from the will of God and no one is lost apart from the will of God. But the will of God functions within an order which God Himself has established.

Predestination is a profound and mysterious biblical teaching. It focuses our thinking on man's freedom and responsibility as well as God's sovereignty.

PREFECT (see GOVERNOR).

PREPARATION DAY — the day immediately before the Sabbath and other Jewish festivals. Preparation Day always fell on Friday among the Jewish people, because all religious festivals began on the Sabbath, or Saturday (Matt. 27:62; John 19:14, 31).

With a week of holidays ahead, the Preparation Day for the PASSOVER was especially busy. The details for preparing the Passover supper had to be completed by afternoon. Preparations included baking the unleavened bread, gathering festive garments to wear for the occasion, and taking a ceremonial bath.

But above all, the paschal lamb had to be slain. Slaughtering began an hour or more earlier than for the usual daily evening sacrifice. At the Temple, the priests slaughtered thousands of lambs brought in by the people. Their blood was poured at the foot of the altar. Then the lambs were roasted whole in preparation for the Passover meal in each home that evening.

PRESBYTER — a leader in one of the Jewish communities (especially a member of the SANHEDRIN), or of the early Christian churches. The Greek word *presbuteros*, translated elders in most English translations of the Bible, basically means an older person and is sometimes used with that sense (1 Tim. 5:1–2). The word may also refer to the lay members of the Jewish Sanhedrin (Mark 14:43, 53) or to the spiritual leaders in each Christian church (Acts 14:23). A number of presbyters together constitute a "presbytery" (1 Tim. 4:14), a council or assembly of Christian elders. Regardless of what the chief governing body in a local church is called today, the members of that body should have the same high qualifications (Titus 1:5–9) and perform the same essential duties of teaching (1 Tim. 5:17; Titus 1:9), serving (James 5:14), decision making (Acts 15:2, 6, 22–29), and shepherding (Acts 20:17, 28) as the New Testament presbyters. Also see ELDERS.

PRESBYTERY — an assembly of elders in one of the early Christian churches (1 Tim. 4:14). The same Greek noun translated presbytery (*presbuterion*) is also used twice in the New Testament to refer to the Jewish Sanhedrin (Luke 22:5, 66). Also see PRESBYTER.

PRESIDENT (see OCCUPATIONS AND TRADES).

PRESS (see WINE PRESS).

PRIEST, HIGH — a chief priest of the Hebrew people, especially of the ancient Jewish Levitical priesthood traditionally traced from AARON. Head priest, the great one from his brothers, and ruler of the house of God are literal translations of references to this officer (Lev. 21:10; 2 Chr. 19:11). The high priest was the supreme civil head of his people. Aaron held this position above his sons that was to continue in the firstborn of successive holders of the office. The high priest was distinguished from his fellow priests by the clothes he wore, the duties he performed, and the particular requirements placed upon him as spiritual head of God's people.

Character and Conduct. Although the office of high priest was hereditary, its holder had to be without physical defect as well as holy in conduct (Lev. 21:6–8). He must not show grief for the dead—even his father or mother—by removing his headdress or letting his hair go unkempt. He must not tear his clothes in grief or go near a dead body. Leaving his duties unperformed because of a death would "profane the sanctuary" (Lev. 21:12). He could marry only a "virgin of his own people" (Lev. 21:14), or a believer in God. She could not be a widow, a divorced woman, or an impure woman. He must not, by a bad marriage, spoil his own holiness or endanger the holiness of his son who would succeed him.

Consecration. A high priest was consecrated (installed in office) by an elaborate seven-day service at the tabernacle or Temple (Exodus 29; Leviticus 8). He was cleansed by bathing, then dressed in the garments and symbols he must wear in his ministry and anointed with special oil. Sacrifices of sin offering, burnt offering, and consecration offering were made for him; and he was anointed again with oil and blood of the sacrifice. Thus "sanctified" to serve as a priest and "consecrated" to offer sacrifice (Ex. 28:41; 29:9), he became "the saint [holy one] of the Lord" (Ps. 106:16).

Dress. The high priest's special dress represented his function as mediator between God and man. Over the trousers, coat, girdle, and cap, worn by all priests, the high priest wore an EPHOD, a two-piece apron reaching to his hips, made of royal colors (blue, purple, and scarlet), and sewed with gold thread. By two onyx stones bearing the names of the twelve tribes of Israel fastened to the shoulders of the ephod, he brought the whole nation before God in all his priestly acts (Ex. 28:5–14).

The "breastplate of judgment," made of the same material, was attached to the front of the ephod (Ex. 28:15–30). On its front were 12 precious stones engraved with the names of the 12 tribes. In its pocket, directly over his heart, were the URIM AND THUMMIM (Ex. 28:30), the medium through which God could communicate His will. By this the high priest was Israel's advocate before God and God's spokesman to them.

Over the breastplate he wore the blue "robe of the ephod" (Ex. 28:31). Around its hem were pomegranates, pointing to the divine law as sweet and delicious spiritual food (Deut. 8:3), and bells that would ring as he went "into the holy place before the Lord...that he may not die" (Ex. 28:35). The bells announced God's gracious salvation for He had accepted the people in the person of their advocate, the high priest.

On his forehead the high priest wore "the holy crown" of gold engraved with the words, "Holiness to the Lord" (Ex. 28:36–37). Thus he was represented as bearing "the iniquity of the holy things" (Ex. 28:38) which Israel offered to God and crowned mediator, making atonement for the nation so God might accept their gifts and show them favor.

All these garments stood for the "glory and beauty" (Ex. 28:40) which God placed upon his priests, sanctifying them to minister in His name (Ex. 28:3).

Particular Services. The high priest held a leadership position in seeing that all responsibilities of the priests were carried out (2 Chr. 19:11). He could participate in all priestly ministry, but certain functions were given only to him. As he alone wore the Urim and the Thummim, Israel came to him to learn the will of God (Deut. 33:8). For this reason Joshua was to "ask counsel" of Eleazar regarding the movements of the army in the conquest of the land of Canaan (Num. 27:21). Even John recognized prophecy as a gift belonging to the high priest (John 11:49–52). The high priest had to offer a sin offering for his own sins and the sin of the whole congregation (Lev. 4:3–21). At the death of the high priest freedom was granted to all who were confined to the CITIES OF REFUGE for accidentally

causing the death of another person (Num. 35:28).

The most important responsibility of the high priest was to conduct the service on the DAY OF ATONEMENT, the tenth day of the seventh month each year. On this day he alone entered the Holy Place inside the veil before God. Having made sacrifice for himself and for the people, he brought the blood into the Holy of Holies and sprinkled it on the mercy seat, "God's throne." This he did to make atonement for himself and the people for all their sins committed during the year just ended (Ex. 30:10; Leviticus 16). It is with this particular service that the ministry of Jesus as high priest is compared (Heb. 9:1–28).

Historical Development. ELEAZAR succeeded Aaron (Num. 20:28) and served at Shiloh where the tabernacle was erected after the conquest of Canaan by the Israelites (Josh. 18:1). He was followed by his son PHINEHAS (Num. 25:11–12; Josh. 24:33). ELI, a descendant of Ithamar, the younger brother of Eleazar, held the office by the Lord's choice (1 Sam. 2:28) at the end of the period of the judges, the change being unexplained. Because of the sins of Eli's sons, SAMUEL appears to have succeeded Eli (1 Sam. 2:12–36; 7:5, 9–10, 17), although he is not called a high priest, and did not regularly function at the tabernacle. Eli's sons cared for the tabernacle at Nob after the destruction of Shiloh (1 Samuel 21—22). ABIATHAR, a descendant of Eli, escaped Saul's slaughter of the priests at Nob (1 Sam. 22:19–21) taking the ephod with him and serving with David (1 Sam. 23:9; 30:7).

David appointed ZADOK, a descendant of Eleazar, to serve at the tabernacle at Gibeon (1 Chr. 16:39) at the same time that he took the ark to Jerusalem. Zadok and Abimelech, the son of Abiathar, are listed as priests among David's officers. Zakok crowned Solomon (1 Kin. 1:39) and was appointed by him as high priest in the place of Abiathar when the latter was banished for supporting Adonijah's claim to the throne (1 Kin. 2:26–27, 35). This made him the first high priest to minister in the Temple. His line of high priests served there until the Babylonian Captivity (1 Chr. 6:3–15).

Mutual support and encouragement characterized the Davidic kings and high priests. David organized 24 groups of priests to serve by turn at the Temple, supervised by both Zadok and Abiathar (1 Chr. 24:6, 31). Solomon confirmed the appointments of his father (2 Chr. 8:14–15). Jehoshaphat organized priests, Levites, and chief men of Israel under the leadership of the high priest to go through the land teaching the people the law, encouraging them to faithful, reverent service (2 Chronicles 19). The high priest Jehoiada protected Joash from Athaliah's murder of the king's sons and organized his coronation and the destruction of Athaliah (2 Chr. 22:10—23:21).

Kings Hezekiah and Josiah assisted the high priests in reform and restoration of the Temple and its worship after its desecration by Ahaz and Manasseh (2 Chronicles 30—31, 34—35). Ezekiel announced that the sons of Zadok would be priests

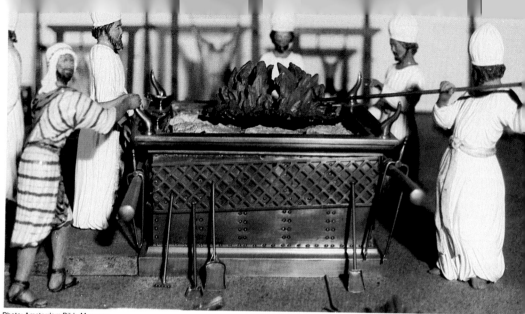

Photo: Amsterdam Bible Museum

Model of a priest offering a sacrifice in the tabernacle in the wilderness.

in the new Temple (Ezek. 44:15–16) because they had not rejected God when Israel went astray (1 Kin. 12:31; 2 Chr. 11:13–15; 13:9).

After the Captivity, JOSHUA the high priest, of the sons of Zadok (Hag. 1:1) and ZERUBBABEL of the house of David—the governor appointed by Cyrus—led the rebuilding of the Temple. As no further governors were appointed, the high priest became sole political and religious leader. Great care was taken by Ezra and Nehemiah to restore the Mosaic order in purity, but interference by unprincipled civil rulers took a sad toll on the purity and influence of the high priest. The Syrian, ANTIOCHUS IV, removed the Zadokite high priest and replaced him with a man from a non-priestly family.

In the revolt that followed and the consequent independence, the Hasmoneans, a family of ordinary priests, took political control. In 153 B.C. one of them, Jonathan, assumed the high priest's office, and later the royal title. When Herod came to power under Rome in 37 B.C. he arbitrarily deposed and appointed high priests as he pleased, and did away with anointing them.

During this period until the destruction of the Temple in Jerusalem in 70 A.D., five prominent families of high priests held power. ANNAS was the leader of one of these. His son-in-law CAIAPHAS, five of his sons, and a grandson held the office. Although Annas had been replaced by Caiaphas before the time of Jesus' ministry, his influence continued (Luke 3:2; John 18:13, 24).

New Testament Times. In the New Testament as in the Old, the "high priest was appointed to offer both gifts and sacrifices" (Heb. 8:3), and was referred to as "God's high priest" and "ruler of [the] people" (Acts 23:4–5). He was the president of the SANHEDRIN, the highest ruling body of the Jews (Matt. 26:3). But the office ceased to be hereditary, and it was subject to the whim of the political power, Rome. The high priests' religious influence was weakened by the rising power of the scribes and Pharisees, and they became known for their materialism and thirst for power.

Above all, the high priest and his fellow priests were threatened by the presence of Jesus in His Father's house, for they had changed it from a "house of prayer for all nations" (Mark 11:17) to a place of merchandise, a "den of thieves" (Matt. 21:12–13; Luke 19:45–48; John 2:14–16).

The "chief priests" were the holders of the priestly offices of higher rank in the Temple and, along with the high priest, were leaders in the Sanhedrin. That they had administrative authority in the Temple is indicated by their agreement with Judas concerning his betrayal of Jesus (Matt. 27:6; Luke 22:4–5). The chief priests led the opposition to Jesus at His trial (Mark 15:3, 11; Luke 23:23). They were equally prominent in their opposition to the apostles and the Christian church (Acts 4:6; 9:14, 21). Along with all the council, the high priest and chief priests condemned Jesus to death (Matt. 26:65–66), mocked Him as He was dying (v. 41), and sealed His grave (Matthew 26—27).

Jesus as High Priest. The New Testament's most important references to the high priest are found in the Epistle to the Hebrews, referring to Jesus. Qualifying Himself to be a merciful and faithful high priest by becoming man of the seed of Abraham (Heb. 2:11–18), He is sympathetic with our weaknesses (Heb. 4:15). He did not assume the office of high priest for glory (Heb. 5:5), but was called by God to the office, and not of the order of Aaron, but of Melchizedek (Heb. 5:10). He had no need, as the sons of Aaron, to offer sacrifices for His own sins, and then for the sins of the people; for He had no sin (Heb. 7:27–28). They offered animal blood that could never take sin away (Heb. 10:1–4). But he offered His own blood (Heb. 9:12) once for all (Heb. 9:26; 10:10, 12). They were many priests, because they died (Heb. 7:23); His is an eternal priesthood because He lives forever (Heb. 7:25). Their priesthood was performed in an earthly model of the real sanctuary (Heb. 8:5); He performs His ministry in heaven itself (Heb. 4:14; 9:11), seated at the right hand of God (Heb. 10:12). By His one offering He has achieved His goal—the sanctification of His people. We may therefore come directly into the presence of God through the "one Mediator between God and men, the man Christ Jesus" (1 Tim. 2:5).

PRIESTS — official ministers or worship leaders in the nation of Israel who represented the people before God and conducted various rituals to atone for their sins. This function was carried out by the father of a family (Job 1:5) or the head of a tribe in the days before Moses and his brother Aaron. But with the appointment of Aaron by God as the first High Priest, the priesthood was formally established. Aaron's descendants were established as the priestly line in Israel. They carried out their important duties from generation to generation as a special class devoted to God's service.

The Bible often speaks of priests and Levites as if these two offices were practically the same (1 Chr. 23:2; 24:6, 31). They were closely related, in that both priests and Levites sprang from a common ancestor. They traced their lineage back to Levi, head of one of the original twelve tribes of Israel. But these two offices were different, in that priests (a specific branch of Levites descended through Aaron) and Levites (all descendants of Levi in general) performed different duties.

Priests officiated at worship by offering various offerings on behalf of the nation and by leading the people to confess their sins. The Levites were assistants to the priests. They took care of the tabernacle and the Temple and performed other menial tasks, such as providing music, serving as doorkeepers, and preparing sacrifices for offering by the priests.

In their function of offering sacrifices at the altar, the priests acted as mediators between man and God, offering sacrifices so that sin might be forgiven (Lev. 4:20, 26, 31). Each sacrifice was a demonstration that the penalty of sin is death (Ezek. 18:4, 20), and that there can be no forgiveness of sin without the shedding of BLOOD (Heb. 9:22).

The first priest mentioned in the Bible was Melchizedek, "king of Salem" and "the priest of God Most High" (Gen. 14:18). Abraham paid tithes to Melchizedek and was blessed (Gen. 14:18–20). Next mentioned was Jethro, Moses' father-in-law and the priest of Midian, who joined Moses, Aaron, and the elders of Israel for a sacrificial meal (Ex. 18:1, 12).

But true priesthood began many years before their time in the Garden of Eden. After Adam and Eve sinned against God, He made them tunics of skin and clothed them. Thus, the death of animals became a symbol of the removal of man's guilt (Gen. 3:21).

After this event, Abel offered a sacrifice that pleased God (Gen. 4:4). Still later Noah (8:20), Abraham (12:7–8), Isaac (26:25), Jacob (35:1–7), and Job (Job 1:5) all acted as priests, offering sacrifices to God. In fact, each family in Israel killed the PASSOVER lamb, offering it as sacrifice to God (Ex. 12:6; 34:25). But when God established Israel as His Chosen People at Mount Sinai after their deliverance from slavery in Egypt (Ex. 6:7; 19:5–6), He established a formal priesthood through Aaron and his descendants. As descendants of Levi, they were to represent the nation of Israel in service to God at the tabernacle and altar (Num. 8:9–18).

The priesthood was given to Aaron and his descendants "as a gift for service" (Num. 18:7) and as "an everlasting priesthood throughout their generations" (Ex. 40:15). Since the office was hereditary, the descendants of Aaron were obligated to accept the responsibility and meet the qualifications. No person with a physical defect or disqualifying disease could serve as a priest (Lev. 21:16–21). Bodily perfection was to symbolize the priest's spiritual wholeness and holiness of heart. Even the priest's home life and relationship with his wife were to show his consecration to God (Lev. 21:7).

Aaron and his sons were consecrated for the priesthood in an elaborate seven-day ceremony (Ex. 29:30, 35, 37). Their bodies were bathed to symbolize the purifying of their souls from sin. Then they were clothed in their priestly garments and anointed with oil as sacrifices were made on their behalf. The entire dedication procedure was as an outward sign of their SANCTIFICATION in God's service (Ex. 29:9).

The clothes which the priests wore also carried great significance. Their white linen garments symbolized holiness and glory. They also wore a coat woven in one piece without a seam to indicate their spiritual integrity, wholeness, and righteousness. The four-cornered cloth of the coat signified that the priest belonged to the kingdom of God. The cap, resembling an opening flower, symbolized the fresh, vigorous life of the one who wore it. The girdle, or sash, a belt which encircled the priest's body, was the priestly sign of service. It showed that the wearer was an office bearer and administrator in the kingdom of God (Exodus 39).

The priests had several responsibilities as mediators between the sinful people and their holy God. They lit the incense and cleaned, trimmed, and lit the lamps. Ministering before God at the altar, the priests had to make sure the offerings of the people were correct and that the sacrificial rituals were carried out correctly. Otherwise, the people could not be cleansed of their sin until the priests had made atonement for the error (Num. 18:1).

As "messengers of the Lord" (Mal. 2:7), the

priests also were to teach the Law to the people of Israel. In addition to instructing in the Law year by year, they were also responsible for reading the Law at the Feast of Tabernacles every seventh year (Deut. 31:9–13).

By their example, the priests also taught the people how to "distinguish between holy and unholy, and between unclean and clean" (Lev. 10:10). Living in cities scattered throughout the nation of Israel, the priests were in a good position to fulfill this function (Joshua 21). In addition, the priests served as judges, acting as a kind of supreme court for Israel (Deut. 17:8–13). In special cases, the high priests declared the will or judgment of God through the URIM AND THUMMIN, the medium through which God sometimes communicated His divine will (Ex. 28:30; Lev. 8:8; Deut. 33:8).

When the land of Canaan was conquered and divided among the tribes of Israel, 13 cities with their surrounding land were allotted to the priests as residences for their families and pasturelands for their flocks (Josh. 21:10–19). Across the centuries, the priests increased to a numerous body. King David divided them into 24 groups (1 Chr. 24:1–19). Except for the great festivals when all the groups served at the tabernacle at the same time, each group of priests officiated for a week at a time on a rotating basis.

As long as the king and the people of Israel remained loyal to God and His Law, the priests were highly respected and exercised a healthy influence in the land. But the priests eventually sank to immorality, departed from God, and worshiped idols, along with the rest of the people (Ezek. 22:26).

In the final book of the Old Testament, the prophet Malachi pointed to the neglect, corruption, and false teaching of the priests. According to Malachi, this was the reason why the people began to neglect the offerings and festivals of the Temple. They lost their respect for the persons who held the office, and finally the office itself (Mal. 1:6; 2:7–9). Thus, the Old Testament closes with the announcement that God in His judgment "will suddenly come to His temple...like a refiner's fire" to purify the priests (Mal. 3:1–3). God was determined to preserve His human priests until the appearance of His true Priest, Jesus Christ.

By the New Testament period, the position of priests in the nation of Israel had changed considerably. The Temple functions were taken over by the "chief priests." Rank-and-file priests were also overshadowed by the SCRIBES and PHARISEES, two special groups that arose to present the Law and interpret its meaning for the people. But in spite of the diminished role of priests, Jesus respected the office and called upon the priests to witness His healing of lepers in keeping with the Law of Moses (Mark 1:44; Luke 17:12–14). But the priests themselves were some of the most zealous opponents of Jesus. As leaders of the SANHEDRIN, the Jewish high court, they bore much of the responsibility for His crucifixion. They also led the opposition to the apostles and the early church.

The office of priest was fulfilled in Jesus Christ. The Son of God became a man (Heb. 2:9–14) so that He might offer Himself as sacrifice "once to bear the sins of many" (Heb. 9:28). Hence, there is no longer a need for priests to offer a sacrifice to atone for man's sin. A permanent sacrifice has been made by Jesus Christ through His death on the Cross.

Priesthood and holiness were meant to be inseparable. But the sinful nature of the priests allowed corruption to enter the God-ordained office. However, the priesthood to which the nation of Israel was called at Mount Sinai continues today in the church. "You are a chosen generation, a royal priesthood, a holy nation, His own special people, that you may proclaim the praises of Him who called you out of darkness into His marvelous light" (1 Pet. 2:9).

PRINCE — a leader or ruler. The common elements in the many different words translated as prince in the Bible are leadership and authority. The word often denotes royalty, but it just as frequently describes leadership in general. Both Abraham (Gen. 23:6) and Solomon (1 Kin. 11:34) were called princes. Tribal leaders of early Israel were often designated as princes. Jesus, the coming Messiah, was referred to by the prophet Isaiah as the Prince of Peace (Is. 9:6).

In the New Testament, Jesus is called the Prince (Author, NIV) of life (Acts 3:15) and a Prince (Leader, RSV) and Savior (Acts 5:31).

PRINCESS — a woman of royal rank. The NKJV uses this word to refer to Solomon's wives (1 Kin. 11:3) and to Jerusalem as the "princess among the provinces" (Lam. 1:1; queen of cities, NIV, NEB), which was made a slave and carried into Babylonian captivity. The Hebrew word translated princess is also translated as lady and queen. Thus, Esther 1:18 refers to the noble ladies of Persia, and Judges 5:29 refers to the ladies of Sisera's mother (Judg. 5:29).

PRINCIPALITY — a powerful ruler, or the rule of someone in authority. The word (often found in the plural) may refer to human rulers (Titus 3:1, KJV), demonic spirits (Rom. 8:38; Eph. 6:12; Col. 2:15), angels and demons in general (Eph. 3:10; Col. 1:16), or (especially when used in the singular) any type of rule other than God Himself (Eph. 1:21; Col. 2:10). While Christians must often wrestle against evil principalities (Eph. 6:12), they can be victorious because Christ defeated all wicked spirits (Col. 2:15).

PRINTING — the process of applying ink to a prepared surface, then transferring that ink to paper or some other material, making an exact copy of the original. The Old Testament speaks of one ancient printing form, which consisted of coloring a person's body with various shapes. The art of tatooing was practiced by ancient man in pagan worship (Lev. 19:28; Job 13:27; Ezek. 9:3–6). Another ancient form of printing was the branding of characters on the flesh. Many scholars believe Cain was marked with such a brand (Gen. 4:15).

Early manuscripts of the Bible were not printed or reproduced by mechanical means. Each copy was an original which had to be done by hand. Scribes produced copies of the Bible text under close supervision to insure quality and a minimum of errors. The modern process of printing did not begin until the middle of the 15th century.

The love of God for His people is everlasting. His constant remembrance of the believer is compared to a permanent, tatooed inscription on a person's hands (Is. 49:16).

PRISCA [PRIS kuh] — a form of PRISCILLA.

PRISCILLA [prih SIL uh] (meaning unknown) — the wife of AQUILA and a zealous advocate of the Christian cause (Rom. 16:3; 1 Cor. 16:19). Her name is also given as PRISCA (2 Tim. 4:19). Aquila and Priscilla left their home in Rome for Corinth when the emperor Claudius commanded all Jews to depart from the city (Acts 18:2). Thus, they were fellow passengers of the apostle Paul from Corinth to Ephesus (Acts 18;18), where they met Apollos and instructed him further in the Christian faith (Acts 18:26).

PRISON — a place of forcible restraint or confinement. Most prisons of the ancient world were crude and dehumanizing. Persons guilty of violating the laws of a community were detained in several different types of prisons.

Most common were natural pits or cavelike dungeons, where prisoners survived on the bread and water "of affliction" (1 Kin. 22:27). Prison pits provided places in which to conceal the slain (Jer. 41:7). The prophet Jeremiah may have been cast into a dungeon because this was a convenient way to kill him without bloodshed (Jer. 38:6). Another example of a natural pit used for holding prisoners is the one on the plain of Dothan, into which Joseph's jealous brothers threw him (Gen. 37:20–28).

Less common were manmade structures or prison houses like the one in which Samson was held at Gaza (Judg. 16:21, 25) and the one provided by King Ahab at Samaria (1 Kin. 22:26–27).

Old Testament kings were usually held in prison by conquering armies (Jer. 52:11). Hebrew prophets who were at odds with the policies of their kings were often thrown into prison, notably Hanani the seer under King Asa of Judah (2 Chr. 16:10).

During the wandering of the Hebrews in the desert after their escape from Egypt, some of the people were held "in custody" or "under guard" (Lev. 24:12; Num. 15:34). Since imprisonment was not specifically called for by Mosaic Law, it was not practiced in Israel until the time of the monarchy, when the prison is mentioned as a special part of the king's house (Neh. 3:25; Jer. 32:2; 37:21).

The New Testament uses four related terms that are translated as prison. The cell of John the Baptist was a "place of bonds" (Matt. 11:2). The apostles

were arrested in Jerusalem and placed in the common prison ("place of custody or public watching") by the Sadducees (Acts 5:18). The apostle Peter was imprisoned in a "house" (Acts 12:7). Paul and Silas were thrown into a prison ("place of guarding") at Philippi (Acts 16:23–40).

Jewish prisons mentioned in the New Testament were used to detain persons awaiting trial or execution (Acts 5:21, 23; Acts 4:3; 5:18). Imprisonment as a form of punishment was also known (Acts 22:19).

Because of the number of times the apostles were imprisoned, Roman prisons are more fully described in the New Testament than the prisons of other nations. Roman authorities used imprisonment to control behavior (Matt. 18:30) and as punishment for minor lawbreakers (Matt. 11:2; Acts 16:26). Prisons were usually part of the government headquarters: examples are the PRAETORIUM at Jerusalem (Mark 15:16) and the Caesarea prison in Herod's judgment hall, where Paul was detained for two years (Acts 23:35; 24:27).

Paul had so many prison experiences that he called himself a "prisoner of the Lord" (Eph. 4:1). When Paul and Silas were cast into the Roman prison at Philippi, the jailer bound their feet in stocks (Acts 16:23–24). Under Roman military rule, the soldier who guarded the prison was responsible for the safety of the prisoners. After Paul and Silas were miraculously released by God (Acts 16:25–34), their jailer would have killed himself if Paul had not prevented it. Paul was bound with chains at the Jerusalem Tower of Antonia (Acts 21:33, 37), from which his declaration of Roman citizenship freed him. He was also imprisoned in Rome, but under lenient surveillance in his own dwelling.

In a symbolic way, the Book of Revelation refers to the imprisonment of persecuted Christians (Rev. 2:10) and to the binding of Satan in a bottomless pit for a thousand years (Rev. 20:3, 7).

Christ showed concern for prisoners (Matt. 25:36). He made several references to prisons (Matt. 5:25; 18:30; 25:36). His parable of the unmerciful debtor reveals the custom of casting men and their families into prison for their debts (Matt. 18:24–35). Jesus himself became Jerusalem's most notable prisoner, detained at first by the Sanhedrin and later at the Praetorium.

PRISON, GATE OF THE (see GATES OF JERUSALEM AND THE TEMPLE).

PROCHORUS [PRAHK uh ruhs] (*leader of the dance*) — one of the seven men chosen by the early church to provide for the Greek–speaking widows and the poor among the Christians (Acts 6:5).

PROCLAMATION (see PREACHER, PREACHING).

PROCONSUL [pro CON suhl] — a title given to the governor of a senatorial province in the Roman Empire. Under the Roman system of government, the Empire was divided into senatorial provinces and imperial provinces. Imperial provinces were administered by representatives of the emperor.

Photo by Howard Vos

This inscription at the city of Tyre contains the names of nine Greek generals who accompanied Alexander the Great when he destroyed the city about 333 B.C. More than 200 years before, Ezekiel had prophesied Tyre's destruction (Ezek. 26:1-5).

The senatorial provinces were presided over by proconsuls appointed by the Roman senate. Two proconsuls are mentioned in the New Testament: Sergius Paulus (Acts 13:7-8, 12), and Gallio (Acts 18:12; deputy, KJV; governor, NEB). Also see OCCUPATIONS AND TRADES.

PROCURATOR (see GOVERNOR).

PRODIGAL — reckless and extravagant. When Jesus told the parable of the two lost sons, He devoted the first part of the story to the younger son who "wasted his possessions with prodigal living" (Luke 15:13; loose living, RSV, NASB; riotous living, KJV; wild living, NIV). The lesson of the prodigal son is that when one abandons the Father's house to venture into the far country, he ends up with an empty purse, an empty stomach, and a starving soul.

PROFANE — to treat anything holy with disrespect. In the Bible, many things could be profaned by disregarding God's laws about their correct use: the Sabbath (Is. 56:6), the Temple (Acts 24:6), the covenant (Mal. 2:10), and God's name (Ex. 19:22). The term profane is often applied to foolish or irresponsible people. Esau, who sold his birthright, was a "profane" person (Heb. 12:16).

PROGNOSTICATOR — one who predicts future events by using present signs and omens as a guide. According to the prophet Isaiah, one of the superstitions of the Chaldeans, or Babylonians, was that of the monthly prognosticators (Is. 47:13), who foretold the future by observing the phases of the moon. This pagan superstition probably was related to the practice of constructing horoscopes based on signs of the planets in the heavens. Isaiah made it plain that this type of fortune telling would not save the Babylonian nation from God's certain judgment.

PROMISE — a solemn pledge to perform or grant a specified thing. God did not have to promise anything to sinful man. But the fact that almost all biblical promises are those made by God to man indicates that His nature is characterized chiefly by grace and faithfulness.

Grace prompted God to promise a new land to the Israelites (Ex. 12:25). His faithfulness urged Him to fulfill that promise, in spite of the nation's disobedience. And as Paul pointed out (Gal. 3:15–29), God's faithfulness and grace are particularly evident in His promise to Abraham. This promise was eventually fulfilled in the work of Christ. Christians should trust completely that God's promise of eternal life (Heb. 9:15) is secure.

PROPHECY — predictions about the future and the end–time; special messages from God, often uttered through human spokesmen, which indicate the divine will for mankind on earth and in heaven.

The focus of all prophetic truth is Jesus Christ (Heb. 1:2; Luke 24:25-27), who was destined to be the greatest prophet (Deut. 18:15-18). He declared God's truth in this age (John 3:31-33) and the age to come (Is. 2:2-4). As the embodiment of truth (John 1:1), Christ fully radiated the brilliance of God which the earlier prophets reflected only partially.

Earlier prophets anticipated Jesus Christ by reflecting His person and message in their own life and ministry (Ex. 34:29-35; 1 Kin. 19:10; 2 Chr. 24:20-21). Each contributed a portion of the truth, sharing in the Spirit that would be completely expressed in Jesus Christ (John 6:68).

Prophecy was technically the task of the prophet. But all truth or revelation is prophetic, pointing to some future person, event, or thing. The full panorama of God's will takes many forms; it may be expressed through people, events, and objects. Historical events such as the PASSOVER anticipated Jesus Christ (John 1:29), as did various

Photo by Howard Vos

An almond tree in full bloom in Palestine. The prophet Jeremiah had a vision of a blossoming almond, symbolizing God's coming judgment against His sinful people (Jer. 1:11-12).

objects in the tabernacle, including MANNA (John 6:31-35) and the inner VEIL (Matt. 27:51; Heb. 10:20).

Prophecy may also be expressed in many different forms through the prophet himself, whether by his mouth or some bodily action. The prophets received God's messages from the voice of an angel (Gen. 22:15-19), the voice of God, a dream (Daniel 2), or a vision (Ezek. 40:2ff.). The prophetic speech might range from the somber reading of a father's last will (Genesis 49) to an exultant anthem to be sung in the Temple (Ps. 96:1, 13).

Sometimes a prophet acted out his message symbolically. Isaiah's nakedness (Isaiah 20) foretold the exile of the Egyptians and the Cushites. Hosea's marriage symbolized God's patience with an unfaithful wife, or the nation of Israel. Ahijah divided his garment to foretell the division of the monarchy (1 Kin. 11:30-31). Even the names of some of the prophets are symbolic, matching their message. Hosea means "salvation"; Nahum, "comfort"; Zephaniah, "the Lord hides"; and Zechariah, "the Lord remembers."

Prophecy declared God's word for all time, so the time of fulfillment of a prophecy is rarely indicated in the Bible. Exceptions to this rule include the timetable assigned to Daniel's seventy weeks' prophecy (Dan. 9:24-27), the prophecy of Peter's denial (Matt. 26:34), and predictions of someone's death (Jer. 28:16-17). The common problem of knowing the time for the fulfillment of a prophecy is acknowledged by Peter (2 Pet. 1:11). This problem is due to several factors. First, some prophecies appear together, as if they would be fulfilled simultaneously. For example, Isaiah 61:1-2 has already been fulfilled, according to Luke 4:18-19; but Isaiah 61:2, which adjoins it, awaits fulfillment. The

same is true of Zechariah 9:9-10. The prophets saw the mountain peaks of prophetic events but not the valleys of time in between.

Another factor that complicates the problem is the ambiguity of tenses in the Hebrew language, which distinguishes *type* of action but not *time* of action. The prophets focused on the reality of their prophecies and not the time of their fulfillment. In their minds their prophecies were already accomplished, primarily because they knew God was in charge of history.

Finally, since the prophets' messages had eternal force, it is often difficult to tell whether they applied their messages to their day or the future. For example, Isaiah 7:14 promised a son who could be a contemporary of Isaiah (perhaps the prophet's son in 8:3, and 18 or the son of Hezekiah the king in Isaiah 36—39) or Jesus (Matt. 1:23), or both.

Several questions are raised when there appears to be more than one possible fulfillment for a prophecy. Does a primary fulfillment in one passage rule out a secondary application to another passage? Not necessarily. Did the author intend both fulfillments with one as an analogy or illustration for the other? Did the author intend a dual fulfillment for two different audiences at two different times? Joel 2:30, speaking about signs on the earth, was applied by the apostle Peter to the tongues of fire at PENTECOST (Acts 2:3-4, 18-19). But Jesus seemed to apply this prophecy to His SECOND COMING (Mark 13:24; Luke 11:25).

In the same way, the destruction of Gog and Magog in Ezekiel 38 and 39 may be fulfilled in Revelation 20:8 after the MILLENNIUM. But similarities of this prophecy to earlier invasions from the north before the millennium seem to allow for its multiple fulfillment. The earlier parallels with Ezekiel 38 and

39 are two invasions from the north in Daniel 11:40, 44 and a third in Revelation 19:17–18, where the birds consume the carcasses as in Ezekiel 39:17–20.

The problem of understanding when a prophecy is fulfilled is compounded if the modern reader has a theological bias about who is to fulfill a prophecy. For example, premillennialists believe that a 1,000-year reign by Christ (Rev. 20:2–7) will exalt the nation of Israel and the Jewish people in the future (Rom. 11:24–26). But amillennialists believe the promises to Israel in the Old Testament have been taken from Israel and transferred to the church (Gal. 6:16). Such a disagreement does not deny that Abraham's descendants will inherit Palestine from the River of Egypt to the Euphrates River (Gen. 15:18). But the premillennialist looks for a future revival of Israel as a nation (Ezek. 37:11–28), while the amillennialist claims the promise of the land was fulfilled in the past in the days of Joshua (Josh. 21:43–44) or Solomon (2 Chr. 9:26).

Prophecy presents volumes about the future kingdom of God, particularly information about the MESSIAH and His chosen people, Israel. Much prophecy also foretells the destiny of the nations and their relationship to the kingdom of God. The New Testament identifies Jesus as the King (John 1:49) who spends much of His ministry describing His kingdom and its establishment (Matthew 13; 24—25). The battleground is the world; and the arch-foe of Christ is Satan, whose intrigue in Eden gave him control of the nations (Matt. 4:9). Most prophecy is concerned with undoing Satan's work; it elaborates upon the initial promise of Genesis 3:15, which announced that Christ, the seed of the woman (Gal. 4:4), would crush the great Serpent, the Devil (Rom. 16:20; Rev. 20:2). All prophecy testifies about Jesus (Rev. 19:10).

Over 300 prophecies in the Bible speak of Jesus Christ. Specific details given by these prophecies include His tribe (Gen. 49:10), His birthplace (Mic.

5:2), dates of His birth and death (Dan. 9:25–26), His forerunner John the Baptist (Mal. 3:1; 4:5; Matt. 11:10), His career and ministry (Is. 52:13—53:12), His crucifixion (Ps. 22:1–18), His resurrection (Ps. 16:8–11; Acts 2:25–28), His ascension (Psalm 2; Acts 13:33), and His exaltation as a priest-king (Psalm 110; Acts 2:34). The kingly magnificence of His second coming is also graphically portrayed. Psalms 2, 45, and 110 picture His conquest and dominion over the nations. His kingdom is characterizd in Psalm 72. Events leading up to and including the first and second advents of Christ are described in the two burdens of the prophet Zechariah (Zechariah 9—11, 12—14).

Premillennialists point to many Bible passages to support their belief in the national resurrection of Israel. Many prophecies graphically portray Israel's history (Leviticus 26; Deuteronomy 27—28; Amos 6—9). Her bounty as a nation is prophesied in Deuteronomy 30 and Isaiah 35. Just as the nation had received a double punishment (Jer. 16:18), so it would receive a double blessing (Is. 61:7). Temple worship would be restored (Ezekiel 40—48); Israel would be the center of world government (Zechariah 1—6); and the Davidic line would be set up as a permanent dynasty (2 Sam. 7:12–16; Luke 1:32–33).

Much controversy surrounds the roles of the church and Israel in the final days preceding Christ's Second Coming, known as the "day of Jacob's trouble" (Jer. 30:7), "the great tribulation" (Matt. 24:21), or "the great day of His wrath" (Rev. 6:17). This will be a period of seven years (9:27) with the most intense trial in the last three and one-half years of this time (Dan. 12:11–12; Rev. 12:6; 13:5).

As Christ's Second Coming approaches, many difficult prophecies about the Tribulation will be understood more clearly (Jer. 30:24; Dan. 11:32–35; 12:3, 9–10). Premillennialists point to the establishment of the state of Israel in 1948 as just one of

Prophecies of the Messiah in Zechariah

Passage	Prophecy	Fulfillment
2:10–13	The ruler on the throne	Rev. 5:13; 6:9; 21:24; 22:1–5
3:8	A holy priesthood	John 2:19–21; Eph. 2:20–21; 1 Pet. 2:5
6:12–13	A heavenly high priest	Heb. 4:4; 8:1–2
9:9–10	The ruler on a donkey	Matt. 21:4–5; Mark 11:9–10
11:12–13	The price of 30 pieces of silver	Matt. 26:14–15
11:13	The silver used to buy a potter's field	Matt. 27:9
12:10	Piercing of the Messiah's body	John 19:34, 37
13:1, 6, 7	Wounding of the Shepherd Savior and scattering of the sheep	Matt. 26:31; John 16:32

these signs of Christ's approaching return.

While premillennialists agree upon the restoration of Israel in the earthly reign of Jesus Christ, many are divided over the relation of Israel to the church, particularly just before Christ's appearance at the end of the Tribulation. Covenant theologians see Israel and the church as one people who go through the Tribulation together. Dispensational theologians believe Israel and the church are always separated in the Bible. As a result, dispensationalists believe the church will not join Israel in its days of tribulation, but will be transported to heaven before it begins, at the beginning of the seven years.

Three theories exist about the time of the church's departure to meet the Lord in the air (1 Thess. 4:13–17): the pre-tribulational rapture, the mid-tribulational rapture, and the post-tribulational rapture. These three theories place the rapture at the time of John's ascension to heaven (Rev. 4:1), at the time when the two prophets ascend to heaven (Rev. 11:11–12), and at the end of the series of seven bowls (Rev. 16:15), respectively.

PROPHET — a person who spoke for God and who communicated God's message courageously to God's Chosen People—the nation of Israel.

The Prophet's Call. A prophet received his call or appointment directly from God. Some prophets, like Jeremiah or John the Baptist, were called before birth (Jer. 1:5; Luke 1:13–16), but their privilege was not a birthright. Their authority came from God alone whose message they bore (Ex. 7:1). Who can match the eloquence and brilliance of Isaiah, the depth of emotion and melancholy of Jeremiah, or the dramatic and dogged spirit of Ezekiel? A prophetic call was a call to liberty and freedom to be oneself (John 8:31–32). It enabled the prophet to be unaffected by human bias and criticism. The call of the prophet required that he not be intimidated or threatened by his audience (Jer. 1:7–8; Ezek. 2:6).

A prophet sometimes became quite dramatic and acted out his message. Isaiah went naked and barefoot for three years (Is. 20:2–3). Ezekiel lay on his left side for 390 days and on his right side for 40 more (Ezek. 4:1–8). Zechariah broke two staffs (Zech. 11:7–14). Making themselves a spectacle, prophets not only aroused curiosity but also invited the scorn of their peers (Jer. 11:21).

Except for God's call, prophets had no special qualifications. They appeared from all walks of life and classes of society. They included sheepbreeders and farmers like Amos (Amos 7:14) and Elisha (1 Kin. 19:19) but also princes like Abraham (Gen. 23:6) and priests like Ezekiel (Ezek. 1:3). Even women and children became prophets (1 Sam. 3:19–20; 2 Kin. 22:14). In rare circumstances, God used the hesitant or unruly to bear his message. Balaam prophesied (Num. 22:6—24:24) the Lord's message but was actually an enemy of God (2 Pet. 2:15–16; Rev. 2:14). Saul certainly was not in fellowship with God when he prophesied (1 Sam. 10:23–24).

Some prophets were called for a lifetime. But sometimes prophets spoke briefly and no more (Num. 11:25–26). In either case, a prophet spoke with the authority of the Holy Spirit (Num. 11:29; 24:4). One trait characterized them all: a faithful proclamation of God's word and not their own (Jer. 23:16; Ezek. 13:2). Jesus' reference to Himself as a prophet in John 12:49–50 rests upon this standard of faithfully repeating God's word to man.

Many scholars deny that prophecy includes the prediction of future events, but fulfillment was, in fact, the test of a prophet's genuineness (Deut. 18:20–22). Whether a prophet's words were fulfilled within his lifetime or centuries later, they were fulfilled to the letter (1 Kin. 13:3; 2 Kin. 23:15–16). But regardless of the time of fulfillment, the prophet's message applied to his generation as well as to ours.

The main role of the prophet was to bear God's word for the purpose of teaching, reproving, correcting, and training in righteousness (2 Tim. 3:16). Whether warning of impending danger or disclosing God's will to the people, they were similar in function to the modern preacher in the church. Prophets were referred to as messengers of the Lord (Is. 44:26; Hag. 1:13), servants of God (Amos 3:7), shepherds (Zech. 11:4, 7; Jer. 17:16), and watchmen (Is. 62:6).

Important Prophets of the Bible. God has used people in every age to fill the prophetic role of proclaiming His word. Noah was a "preacher of righteousness" to his generation (2 Pet. 2:5). Abraham was considered a prophet (Gen. 20:7). So was his son Isaac (Ps. 105:9, 14–15) and his grandson Jacob (Genesis 49). Moses was eulogized as the greatest prophet of all, due to his major accomplishments as well as his many writings (Deut. 34:10–12). His successor, Joshua, received the commission to continue Moses' work and so assumed the prophetic role also (Deut. 34:9; Josh. 1:1, 5).

Following the entrance of the Hebrew people into the land of Canaan, many prophets appeared throughout Israel's history to aid and protect the nation. The prophets mentioned in the Bible probably represent only a small portion of the total number of prophets. Most of the prophets remain obscure because they never wrote down their message. This indicates their task required face–to–face confrontations and a spoken rather than a written message. Many times the prophet stood alone and spoke to an unsympathetic or even antagonistic audience. Great courage and independence of spirit was required. The prophet was not a man of routine like the priest; he charted new paths for the people.

It is appropriate that the first prophet mentioned after Joshua is unnamed (Judg. 6:7–10). Prophets were to exalt God's word and not seek their own glory. This unnamed prophet appeared in the time of Gideon when Israel was falling back into idolatry. Rather than speak of the future, he called Israel to remember the Lord who delivered them from Egypt.

The modern village of Anata is situated near the site of ancient Anathoth, home of the prophet Jeremiah (Jer. 1:1; 11:21).

The next prophet was Samuel, whose vocation was apparent to all from his youth (1 Sam. 3:19–20). Samuel's life was spent serving diligently as a judge (1 Sam. 7:15), leading the army to victory (1 Sam. 7:9–10), and establishing the religious and civil life of the nation (1 Sam. 10:25). He both appointed (1 Sam. 12:1) and recalled the first king of Israel (1 Sam. 15:26–28). Samuel provided a model for other prophets to follow (1 Sam. 19:20).

Four prophets appeared in the time of David, who himself demonstrated the traits of a prophet (2 Sam. 23:2–3). They were Gad (1 Sam. 22:5), Nathan (2 Sam. 12:1–15), Zadok (2 Sam. 15:27), and Heman (1 Chr. 25:5).

Four prophets also appeared during the time of Jeroboam: Ahijah, a man of God, an old prophet, and Iddo the seer. Iddo apparently had visions, but he confined his revelations to writing (2 Chr. 9:29; 12:15; 13:22). A man of God confronted Jeroboam for his intrusion into the priestly office at the altar and prophesied the coming of Josiah by name (1 Kin. 13:1–9); but his rival, the old prophet in Bethel, deceived him and brought about his death (1 Kin. 13:11–32). Even though the old prophet lied, God revealed the death sentence of the man of God to him (1 Kin. 13:21–23).

The prophet Shemaiah appeared to Solomon's successor, Rehoboam, to stop him from attempting to reunite the country by force (2 Chr. 11:2–4). The prophet Iddo recorded the acts of Abijah, the successor of Rehoboam (2 Chr. 13:22), who himself raised a prophetic voice, although he was a wicked king (1 Kin. 15:1–5). The king correctly anticipated victory over Jeroboam's troops (2 Chr. 13:12).

The next king, Asa, was promised God's blessing by the prophet Azariah when the king was returning from his victory over Zerah, the Ethiopian (2 Chr. 15:1–7). But Asa did not remain faithful, seeking help instead from the Syrians when Baasha threatened him. The prophet Hanani was imprisoned for rebuking Asa for not relying upon the Lord alone as in the earlier victory (2 Chr. 16:7–10). The son of Hanani, Jehu, played a more prominent role than his father. He condemned the wickedness of Baasha and declared his dynasty would end (1 Kin. 16:1–4).

Jehoshaphat was promised victory over the alliance of Moab, Ammon, and Edom by the prophet Jahaziel (2 Chr. 20:14–17). God alone would supply the victory. After these two lessons about alliances, Jehoshaphat allied with Ahab's son, Ahaziah, in order to build a southern fleet. The prophet Eliezer proclaimed the alliance caused God to destroy the fleet (2 Chr. 20:37).

Five prophets appeared during the reign of Ahab. These included the famous prophets ELIJAH and ELISHA. Elijah was the most unforgettable and dynamic of the Hebrew prophets. He dominated the scene under Ahab in 1 Kings 17—19 and 21, but his ministry continued until the reigns of Ahaziah (2 Kings 1) and Jehoram (2 Kings 2). His impact and eminence was compared with Moses, as their joint appearance with Christ in His transfiguration suggests (Matt. 17:1–13). Elijah's spectacular success over the prophets of Baal in the bringing of rain defies comparison. His volatile and dynamic temperament stands in stark contrast to Elisha, who realized that his quieter personality needed some help if he was to follow a prophet like Elijah. So he asked for a double portion of Elijah's spirit (2 Kin. 2:9).

Although he was called by Elijah in the reign of Ahab, Elisha really only succeeded him in the reign of Jehoram (2 Kings 2—9). Doubly blessed, Elisha performed 14 miracles to Elijah's seven (2 Kin. 13:21).

Three prophets confronted kings in person. A man of God told Amaziah of Judah to dismiss his Israelite mercenaries (2 Chr. 25:7–10), while another prophet rebuked Amaziah for saving the idols after defeating Edom (2 Chr. 25:15). Finally, Oded secured the release of Judaeans captured by Israelites during the time of Ahaz (2 Chr. 28:9–15).

These prophets in Joshua, Judges, 1 and 2 Samuel, and 1 and 2 Kings provided those books with the name of former prophets in the Hebrew canon. They actually overlapped in time with the "latter" or "writing" prophets, known commonly as the major and minor prophets. The former prophets dealt more with daily problems and the current state of affairs, while the latter prophets wrote down for later generations what would happen in the future.

A few passages in the writing prophets give biographical material about the prophets themselves. While most of the writing prophets simply present God's message, there are biographical chapters in Isaiah (6—7; 20; 37—39), Jeremiah (1; 13; 19—21; 24—29; 32; 34—35), Daniel (1—6), Hosea (1, 3), Amos (7:10–17), Jonah (1—4), Haggai (1—2), and Zechariah (7—8). Other parts of Zechariah and Ezekiel tell about the prophets' receiving visions, but these passages have lesser value in portraying the prophets' personalities.

The writing prophets do not appear to be in chronological order, but they provide clues that can be matched with historical facts which suggest their proper sequence. Obadiah spoke against Edom; his ministry may have occurred in the time of Jehoram (853–41 B.C.) when Edom revolted against Judah (2 Kin. 8:20–22). Joel can be dated to the time when Judah's enemies were Tyre and Sidon along with Philistia (Joel 3:4), Egypt, and Edom (Joel 3:19). Since no king is mentioned, the book has been dated to the time of Joash's childhood when Jehoida the high priest was his guardian. The dates of Joash's reign are 835–796 B.C.

In the following century five prophets can be dated to the reigns of various kings. Hosea probably prophesied from about 760 B.C. to past 715 B.C. or from the time of Uzziah and Jeroboam II to Hezekiah. Amos prophesied when Uzziah and Jeroboam II ruled. Their reigns overlapped for at least 15 years (767–753 B.C.) and even longer if Uzziah's co-regency with his father Amaziah is counted.

Jonah was a contemporary of Jeroboam II (793–753 B.C.), but his trip to Nineveh may have been before or after Jeroboam's reign. Since Assyrian power and spirit fell during the weak reign of Ashurdan III (773–755 B.C.), especially after the plague of 765 B.C. and the total eclipse of the sun in 763 B.C., Jonah may have undertaken his successful mission shortly afterwards around 760 B.C.

Isaiah 1:1 says that Isaiah's ministry spanned four kings from the death of Uzziah (Is. 6:1) through Hezekiah, about whom Isaiah wrote a history (2 Chr. 32:32). That Isaiah ministered after Hezekiah's death in 686 B.C. is evident from his recording of Sennacherib's death which occurred in 681 B.C.

Micah began his ministry under Uzziah's successor, Jotham, and finished it some time in the reign of Hezekiah (Mic. 1:1). This would suggest his ministry began some time after Uzziah's death in 739 B.C. Since Micah does not mention Sennacherib's invasion of 701 B.C., he must have concluded his ministry before that date.

Nahum, Zephaniah, Habakkuk, and Jeremiah appeared in the next century. Nahum probably wrote his prophecy in the latter half of the seventh century, since Nahum 3:8–10 refers to the destruction of Thebes in 663 B.C. Nahum probably prophesied the 612 B.C. destruction of Nineveh before the ministry of Zephaniah, who also predicted the fall of Nineveh and dates himself to the time of Josiah (640–609 B.C.), according to Zephaniah 1:1. Zephaniah's attack on idolatry suggests he wrote

his work before the reforms of Josiah in 621 B.C.

Habakkuk's prophecy should be dated after 612 B.C., since he made no reference to Assyria. The prophet was concerned about the coming invasion of Babylon, probably the first one of 605 B.C. in the reign of Jehoiakim (609-598 B.C.). Thus his work can be dated about 609–606 B.C.

Jeremiah began his work in 627 B.C. (Jer. 1:2-3) and continued ministering in Egypt after the fall of Jerusalem in 586 B.C.

Daniel and Ezekiel ministered during the Captivity in Babylon. Daniel was taken to Babylon in 605 B.C. at the time of Nebuchadnezzar's first invasion of Judah. Ezekiel was taken there in 597 B.C. at the time of the second invasion. Daniel ministered until the third year of Cyrus of 536 B.C. (Dan. 10:1). Ezekiel was called to begin his ministry in 592 B.C. (Ezek. 1:2) and continued until at least 571 B.C. (Ezek. 29:17).

Haggai, Zechariah, and Malachi ministered after the Captivity when the people returned to Judah. Haggai dates his prophecy to 520 B.C. (Hag. 1:1, 15; 2:1, 20). Zechariah began his prophecy two months after Haggai (Zech. 1:1) with his first message. His other revelations came later in the year, two years later (Zech. 1:7; 7:1), and at a later period of time (Zech. 9:1). Malachi was probably written after 432 B.C. when Nehemiah wrote his book because Nehemiah 13 faces the same problems mentioned by Malachi: priestly carelessness (Mal. 1:6—2:9), intermarriage with foreigners (Mal. 2:10—3:6), and lack of tithing (3:7—4:3).

PROPHET, FALSE (see FALSE PROPHET).

PROPHETESS — a female prophet. Women were also blessed with prophetic abilities in Bible times. Miriam, the sister of Moses, led the women with her chorus in response to the great song of her brother (Ex. 15:20). Deborah joined with Barak in song and exulted in their great victory (Judg. 5:2-31). Hannah's prayer was remarkable, foretelling how David's dynasty would be founded (1 Sam. 2:1-10).

Luke reported the prophetic activity of the elderly Anna in the Temple (2:36–38), as well as that of Elizabeth and Mary (1:41-45, 46-55). First Corinthians 11:5 assumes the female role in prophesying, seen again in Philip's four virgin daughters (Acts 21:9). Other prophetesses such as Noadiah gained a bad reputation (Neh. 6:14).

PROPITIATION [pro PISH ih a shun] — the atoning death of Jesus on the cross, through which He paid the penalty demanded by God because of man's sin, thus setting mankind free from sin and death. The word comes from an old English word, propitiate, which means "to appease." Thus, propitiation expresses the idea that Jesus died on the cross to pay the price for sin which a holy God demanded of man the sinner.

Although Jesus was free of sin, He took all our sins upon Himself and redeemed us from the penalty of death which our sins demanded. As the writer of 1 John declared, "He Himself is the propitiation for our sins, and not for ours only but also for the whole world" (1 John 2:2; expiation, RSV).

PROSELYTE [PROS eh lite] (*one who has drawn near*) — a convert from one religious belief or party to another. In the New Testament (Matt. 23:15; Acts 2:10), the term is used in a specific sense to designate Gentile converts who had committed themselves to the teachings of the Jewish faith or who were attracted to the teachings of Judaism. A full-fledged proselyte, or convert, to Judaism underwent circumcision and worshiped in the Jewish Temple or synagogue. They also observed all rituals and regulations concerning the sabbath, clean and unclean foods, and all other matters of Jewish custom.

By the New Testament period, when communities of Jews were widely scattered over the Gentile world, many Gentiles came into contact with Judaism. They found worship of one God and its wholesome ethical teaching attractive. Tired of pagan gods and heathen immorality, the Gentiles came to the synagogues to learn of the one true God and of His call to holiness, justice, and mercy. Many of them accepted the religion, morality, and life-style of the Jews. Not all Gentile sympathizers went so far as to be circumcised, but by New Testament times proselytes were nevertheless a significant part of Judaism, as the references to them in the Book of Acts (2:10; 6:5; 13:43) make clear.

These "halfway proselytes" proved to be a rich mission field for the early church. Unable to accept the binding requirements of the Jewish law, many of them turned to Christianity. This new faith welcomed all people, regardless of their background, culture, or religious tradition.

This universal appeal of Christianity was largely the result of the pioneering work of the apostle Paul. He taught that Gentiles did not have to become Jews—or submit to circumcision—in order to embrace the truths of the gospel. With this barrier removed, many proselytes who were attracted to Judaism turned instead to the Christian faith.

PROSTITUTION — the act or practice of promiscuous sexual relations, especially for money. Several words are used for a woman who engages in illicit sexual activity for pay, including HARLOT, whore, and prostitute.

Several classes of harlots existed in the ancient world. One type was the temple prostitute, who performed sexual acts at a heathen temple (Hos. 4:12–14). Both male and female cult prostitutes presided at these temples. Whenever Judah was ruled by a righteous king, this king sought to remove the temple prostitutes from the land (2 Kin. 23:4–14).

A second class of prostitutes consisted of those who owned bars or inns and had sexual relations with the patrons who desired their services. Rahab of Jericho was such a woman (Josh. 2:1; 6:17–25). God had mercy on her, and she was delivered and transformed. Her name is included in the genealogy of the Messiah (Matt. 1:5).

Jerusalem is pictured as playing the part of a har-lot. But instead of being paid for her services, she paid others! (Ezek. 16:15–59). Those who worshiped idols were also referred to in a symbolic way as harlots (Judg. 2:17).

PROVERB — a short, pithy statement about the nature of man and life. In the Bible Solomon is singled out for his use of proverbs (1 Kin. 4:32). His wisdom was shown by his ability to make clear, true commentaries upon the nature of things. The Hebrew word most frequently translated as proverb means literally "a similitude," or loosely, "a representation." So when God declared that Israel would be "a proverb...among all peoples" (1 Kin. 9:7), He implied that the name Israel would come to symbolize disobedience. Proverbs are designed to make God's truth accessible to all people, so they might direct their lives in accordance with His will.

PROVERBS, BOOK OF — one of the "wisdom books" of the Old Testament, containing instructions on many of the practical matters of daily life. The PROVERB was a familiar literary form in all ancient cultures; it was a very suitable device for collecting and summarizing the wisdom of the centuries. But the Book of Proverbs has one important difference: it points the believer to God with instructions on how to live a holy, upright life.

Structure of the Book. The Book of Proverbs has the longest title of any Old Testament book, covering the first six verses of chapter one. The author introduces himself as a teacher, one of the Wise Men of Israel, who has written this book as a manual of instruction on the ways of wisdom. His declaration, "The fear of the Lord is the beginning of knowledge" (1:7), summarizes the theme of Proverbs, a point which he emphasizes again and again throughout the book.

In its 31 chapters, Proverbs discusses many practical matters to help the believer live in harmony with God as well as his fellowman. Subjects covered in this wise and realistic book include how to choose the right kind of friends, the perils of adultery, the value of hard work, dealing justly with others in business, the dangers of strong drink, treating the poor with compassion, the values of strong family ties, the folly of pride and anger, and the characteristics of genuine friendship.

Scholars agree that Proverbs is a compilation of material from several different sources. This gives the book a unique internal structure. But the book itself tells us which parts were written by one author and which came from another's hand.

Authorship and Date. The name of Solomon as author is associated with the Book of Proverbs from the very beginning. Verse 1 of chapter 1 states: "The proverbs of Solomon the son of David." We also know that Solomon was noted throughout the ancient world for his superior wisdom (1 Kin. 4:29–34). Additional evidence of his authorship is found within the book itself, where Solomon is identified as author of the section from 10:1–22:16 as well as writer of chapters 25—29.

But what about those portions of Proverbs that

clearly are attributed to other writers, such as "the wise" (22:17), Agur (30:1), and King Lemuel (31:1)? Although Solomon wrote a major portion of Proverbs, he did not write the entire book. Many scholars believe he wrote the basic core of Proverbs but added some writings from other sources, giving proper credit to their writers.

Another interesting fact about this book and its writing is that the second collection of proverbs attributed to Solomon (chaps. 25—29) were not added to the book until more than 200 years after his death. The heading over this material reads: "These also are proverbs of Solomon which the men of Hezekiah king of Judah copied" (25:1). Perhaps these writings of Solomon were not discov-

ered and inserted into the book until Hezekiah's time.

Because of the strong evidence that the Book of Proverbs is, indeed, a compilation, some scholars dismiss the idea that Solomon wrote any of the material. But evidence for his authorship of some sections is too strong to be dismissed that lightly. In its original version the book must have been written and compiled by Solomon some time during his reign from 971 B.C. to 931 B.C. Then, about 720 B.C. the material now contained in chapters 25—29 was added to the book.

Historical Setting. The Book of Proverbs is the classical example of the type of writing in the Old Testament known as WISDOM LITERATURE. Other

PROVERBS: A Teaching Outline

Photo by Amikam Shoob

The writer of one of the proverbs praised the rock badger (or rock hyrax) for nesting in places where they were hidden from their enemies (Prov. 30:26).

books so categorized are Job, Ecclesiastes, and the Song of Solomon. These books are called wisdom writings because they were written by a distinctive group of people in Israel's history who grappled with some of the eternal questions of life. This type of writing flourished especially during Solomon's time, and he was known as the wisest of the wise throughout the ancient world. "Thus Solomon's wisdom excelled the wisdom of all the men of the East and all the wisdom of Egypt. For he was wiser than all men...and his fame was in all the surrounding nations" (1 Kin. 4:30–31).

Theological Contribution. Israel's distinctive contribution to the thinking of the wise men of all nations and times is that true wisdom is centered in respect and reverence for God. This is the great underlying theme of the Book of Proverbs.

Special Considerations. In reading the Book of Proverbs, we need to make sure we do not turn these wise sayings into literal promises. Proverbs are statements of the way things generally turn out in God's world. For example, it is generally true that those who keep God's commandments will enjoy "length of days and long life" (3:2). But this should not be interpreted as an ironclad guarantee. It is important to keep God's laws, no matter how long or short our earthly life may be.

PROVIDENCE — the continuous activity of God in His creation by which He preserves and governs. The doctrine of providence affirms God's absolute lordship over His creation and confirms the dependence of all creation on the Creator. It is the denial of the idea that the universe is governed by chance or fate.

Through His providence God controls the universe (Ps. 103:19); the physical world (Matt. 5:45); the affairs of nations (Ps. 66:7); man's birth and destiny (Gal. 1:15); man's successes and failures (Luke 1:52); and the protection of His people (Ps. 4:8).

God preserves all things through His providence

(1 Sam. 2:9; Acts 17:28). Without His continual care and activity the world would not exist. God also preserves His people through His providence (Gen. 28:15; Luke 21:18; 1 Cor. 10:13; 1 Pet. 3:12).

Divine government is the continued activity of God by which He directs all things to the ends He has chosen in His eternal plan. God is King of the universe who has given Christ all power and authority to reign (Mat. 28:18–20; Acts 2:36; Eph. 1:20–23). He governs insignificant things (Matt. 10:29–31), apparent accidents (Prov. 16:33), as well as man's good (Phil. 2:13) and evil deeds (Acts 14:16).

God acts in accordance with the laws and principles that He has established in the world. The laws of nature are nothing more than man's description of how we perceive God at work in the world. They neither have inherent power nor do they work by themselves.

Man is not free to choose and act independently from God's will and plan; he chooses and acts in accordance with them. In His sovereignty, God controls man's choices and actions (Gen. 45:5; Deut. 8:18; Prov. 21:1). God's actions, however, do not violate the reality of human choice or negate man's responsibility as a moral being.

God permits sinful acts to occur, but He does not cause man to sin (Gen. 45:5; Rom. 9:22). He often overrules evil for good (Gen. 50:20; Acts 3:13).

PROVINCE — an administrative district of the government or civil ruling authority. The word province is used only four times of rulers in Israel. All these occurrences come from the time of King Ahab (1 Kin. 20:14–15, 17, 19). The other occurrences of the word refer to the administrative districts during the Babylonian and Persian rules (Ezra 2:1; 4:15; Neh. 1:3). The term occurs only twice in the New Testament (Acts 23:34; 25:1).

During New Testament times the government of the Roman Empire had senatorial and imperial provinces. The senatorial provinces were the ten

— 883 —

older provinces of the Empire, which had no need of a large military force. These were ruled by proconsuls like Sergius Paulus of Cyprus (Acts 13:7) and Gallio of Achaia (Acts 18:12). The proconsuls were appointed for one year.

The imperial provinces of the Roman Empire consisted of frontier provinces that had large installations of Roman troops under the leadership of the emperor. Each of these provinces was governed by a military leader. The second kind of imperial provinces were those consisting of special cases such as rugged terrain (Alpine districts) or difficult people to rule (Judea and Egypt). They were ruled by an imperial governor appointed by the emperor.

These regional governors were responsible to both the emperor and the local provincial military ruler. In Jesus' day Judea was governed by the governor or prefect Pilate (Luke 3:1). In Paul's day it was ruled by the governors Felix (Acts 23:24) and Festus (Acts 25:1).

PROVOCATION — anything that provokes, excites, incites, or stimulates. The reference in Hebrews 3:8, 15 to "the provocation" (KJV), or "the rebellion" (NKJV), is a quotation from Psalm 95:7–11. This passage points back to a specific time when the Israelites provoked God by their rebellion against Moses during the Exodus (Ex. 17:1–7). The name of that place was called MASSAH (testing, temptation) and MERIBAH (strife, contention). The word provocation generally describes the ungrateful spirit and rebellious conduct of Israel that stirred the Lord's anger.

PROW — the front section of a ship or boat (Acts 27:30, 41; bow, RSV, NIV, NEB).

PRUDENCE — skill, good judgment, and common sense. Both David and Solomon are described as men of prudence and wisdom (1 Sam. 16:18; 2 Chr. 2:12). The Book of Proverbs has good words for the prudent person (Prov. 1:4; 12:16, 23; 18:15).

PRUNING HOOKS — small knives with curved blades used for pruning grapevines. The prophets Isaiah, Joel, and Micah contrasted pruning hooks with spears in a way that allowed these knives to become symbols of peace, not war (Is. 2:4; Joel 3:10; Mic. 4:3).

PSALMIST — a writer or composer of a psalm. David is called "the sweet psalmist of Israel" (2 Sam. 23:1). Also see MUSIC OF THE BIBLE; POETRY; PSALMS, BOOK OF.

PSALMS, BOOK OF — a collection of prayers, poems, and hymns that focus the worshiper's thoughts on God in praise and adoration. Parts of this Book were used as a hymnal in the worship services of ancient Israel. The musical heritage of the psalms is demonstrated by its title. It comes from a Greek word which means "a song sung to the accompaniment of a musical instrument."

Structure of the Book. With 150 individual psalms, this Book is clearly the longest in the Bible.

It is also one of the most diverse, since the psalms deal with such subjects as God and His creation, war, worship, wisdom, sin and evil, judgment, justice, and the coming of the Messiah. In the original Hebrew manuscripts, this long collection of 150 psalms was divided into five sections: Book 1 (1—41); Book 2 (42—72); Book 3 (73—89); Book 4 (90—106); and Book 5 (107—150). Each of these major sections closes with a brief prayer of praise. Many modern translations of the Bible, including the NKJV, retain this fivefold division.

Scholars are not sure exactly why the Book of Psalms was organized in this manner. One theory is that it was divided into five sections as a sort of parallel to the Pentateuch—the first five books of the Old Testament (Genesis, Exodus, Leviticus, Numbers, and Deuteronomy). But other scholars believe the five sections were different collections of psalms that circulated at different times in Israel's history. These five small collections were finally placed together, they believe, to form the large compilation which we know today as the Book of Psalms.

The second theory does seem to make sense when we examine the content of the psalms themselves. Individual psalms attributed to David appear in all five of these sections of the Book. Within these five sections, different types of psalms also appear. These include songs of thanksgiving, hymns of praise, psalms of repentance and confession, psalms which invoke evil upon one's enemies, messianic psalms, and songs sung by pilgrims as they traveled to Jerusalem to observe one of the great festivals of their faith. Such variety among the psalms within these five sections may indicate they were complete collections within themselves

Short-lived wild flowers such as these in the Jordan Valley provided the Psalmist with a striking analogy of the brevity of life (Ps. 103:15-16).

before they were placed with other groups of psalms to form this larger body of material.

But no matter how the present arrangement of the book came about, these individual psalms were clearly inspired by God's Spirit. Through these hymns of praise, we come face to face with our Maker and Redeemer. In the glory of His presence, we are compelled to exclaim along with the psalmist, "O Lord, our Lord, how excellent is Your name in all the earth!" (8:9).

Authorship and Date. Most people automatically think of David when they consider the question of who wrote the Book of Psalms. A shepherd boy who rose to become the most famous king of Judah, he was also known as "the sweet psalmist of Israel" (2 Sam. 23:1). He lived during the most creative age of Hebrew song and poetry. As king, he organized the services of worship in the tabernacle, appointing priests and Levites for the specific purpose of providing songs and music. So it is not surprising that his name should be clearly associated with this beautiful book of praise.

The brief descriptions that introduce the psalms have David listed as author in 73 instances. But some scholars believe the phrase, "A psalm of David," should not be interpreted as a certain indication that David actually wrote all these psalms. They point out the Hebrew word translated as *of* can also be translated *to* or FOR. Thus, these psalms could have been written by anonymous authors and dedicated to David or even written on his behalf (for David) and added to a special collection of his material already being used in the sanctuary.

While this is an interesting theory, there is no strong reason to question the traditional view that David actually wrote all the psalms that are attributed to him. David's personality and identity are clearly stamped on many of these psalms. For example, Psalm 18 is a psalm of David which sings praises to God as the sovereign Savior. The title indicates it was written after David was delivered "from the hand of all his enemies and from the hand of Saul." The same psalm in almost identical wording appears in 2 Samuel 22. This passage indicates that David sang this song after the death of Saul and upon his succession to the throne as the new king of Judah.

While it is clear that David wrote many of the individual psalms, he is definitely not the author of the entire collection. Two of the psalms (72 and 127) are attributed to Solomon, David's son and successor. Psalm 90 is a prayer assigned to Moses. Another group of 12 psalms (50 and 73—83) is ascribed to the family of Asaph. The sons of Korah wrote 11 psalms (42, 44—49, 84—85, 87—88). Psalm 88 is attributed to Heman, while Psalm 89 is assigned to Ethan the Ezrahite. With the exception of Solomon and Moses, all these additional authors were priests or Levites who were responsible for providing music for sanctuary worship during David's reign. Fifty of the psalms designate no specific person as author. They were probably written by many different people.

A careful examination of the authorship question, as well as the subject matter covered by the psalms themselves, reveal they span a period of many centuries. The oldest psalm in the collection is probably the prayer of Moses (90), a reflection on the frailty of man as compared to the eternity of God. The latest psalm is probably 137, a song of lament clearly written during the days when the Hebrews were being held captive by the Babylonians, from about 586 to 538 B.C.

It is clear that the 150 individual psalms were written by many different people across a period of a thousand years in Israel's history. They must have been compiled and put together in their present form by some unknown editor shortly after the Captivity ended about 537 B.C.

Historical Setting. Some of the psalms written by David grew out of specific experiences in his life. For example, Psalm 3 is described as "a Psalm of David when he fled from Absalom his son" (see also 51, 52, 54, 56, 57, 59). But others seem to be general psalms that arose from no specific life situation (53, 55, 58). Knowing the particular historical background of a psalm can help the student interpret it correctly and apply its message to life today.

Theological Contribution. We may think of the psalms as a description of our human response to God. At times God is presented in all His majesty and glory. Our response is wonder, awe, and fear: "Sing to God, you kingdoms of the earth" (68:32). But other psalms portray God as a loving Lord who is involved in our lives. Our response in these cases is to draw close to His comfort and security: "I will fear no evil; for You are with me" (23:4).

God is the same Lord in both these psalms. But we respond to Him in different ways, according to the specific needs of our lives. What a marvelous God we worship, the psalmist declares—One who is high and lifted up beyond our human experiences but also one who is close enough to touch and who walks beside us along life's way.

Other psalms might be described as outcries against God and the circumstances of life rather than responses to God because of His glory and His presence in our lives. The psalmist admits he sometimes feels abandoned by God as well as his human friends (88). He agonizes over the lies directed against him by his false accusers (109). He calls upon God to deliver him from his enemies and to wipe them out with His wrath (59). Whatever else we may say about the psalms, we must admit they are realistic about human feelings and the way we sometimes respond to the problems and inequities of life.

But even in these strong psalms of lament, the psalmist is never totally engulfed by a feeling of despair. The fact that he uttered his protest to the Lord is a sign of hope in God and His sense of justice. This has a significant message for all believers. We can bring all our feelings to God, no matter how negative or complaining they may be. And we can rest assured that He will hear and understand. The psalmist teaches us that the most profound prayer of all is a cry for help as we find ourselves overwhelmed by the problems of life.

The psalms also have a great deal to say about the person and work of Christ. Psalm 22 contains a remarkable prophecy of the crucifixion of the Savior. Jesus quoted from this psalm as He was dying on the cross (Ps. 22:1; Matt. 27:46; Mark 15:34). Other statements about the Messiah from the psalms that were fulfilled in the life of Jesus include these predictions: He would be a priest like Melchizedek (Ps. 110:4; Heb. 5:6); He would pray for His enemies (Ps. 109:4; Luke 23:34); and His throne would be established forever (Ps. 45:6; Heb. 1:8).

Special Considerations. The Book of Psalms is the best example in the Bible of the nature of Hebrew poetry. The principle upon which this poetry is based is not rhythm or rhyme but parallelism. In parallelism, one phrase is followed by another that says essentially the same thing but in a more creative, expressive way. Here is a good example of this poetic technique:

The Lord of hosts is with us;
The God of Jacob is our refuge (46:11).

This example is known as synonymous parallelism because the second phrase expresses the same thought as the first. But sometimes the succeeding line introduces a thought that is directly opposite to the first idea. This is known as antithetic parallelism. Here is a familiar couplet that demonstrates this form:

For the Lord knows the way of the righteous,
But the way of the ungodly shall perish (1:6).

A third kind of parallelism in Hebrew poetry may be called progressive, or climbing—in which part of the first line is repeated in the second, but also something more is added. For example:

The floods have lifted up, O Lord,
The floods have lifted up their voice (93:3).

Another literary device which the Hebrew writers used to give their psalms a peculiar style and rhythm was the alphabetical acrostic. The best example of this technique is Psalm 119—the longest in the collection—which contains 22 different sections of eight verses each. Each major section is headed by a different letter of the Hebrew alphabet. In the original language, each verse in these major divisions of the psalm begins with the Hebrew letter which appears as the heading for that section. Many modern translations of the Bible include these Hebrew letters as a part of the structure of this psalm. Writing this poem with such a structure required a high degree of literary skill.

The peculiar poetic structure of the 150 psalms make them ideal for believers who like to create their own devotional exercises. You can easily combine the lines from many different psalms into a fresh, authentic expression of praise to God. Here is an example of such a combined psalm:

Oh, give thanks to the Lord, for He is good!
For His mercy endures forever (136:1).
He has not dealt with us according to our sins,
Nor punished us according to our iniquities (103:10).

For You, O God, have heard my vows;
You have given me the heritage of those who fear Your name (61:5).
Your testimonies are very sure;
Holiness adorns Your house, O Lord, forever (93:5).
So teach us to number our days,
That we may gain a heart of wisdom (90:12).
The fear of the Lord is the beginning of wisdom;
A good understanding have all those who do His commandments (111:10).
Oh, give thanks to the God of heaven!
For His mercy endures forever (136:26).

PSALMS OF SOLOMON (see Pseudepigrapha).

PSALTERY (see Musical Instruments).

PSEUDEPIGRAPHA — a collection of Jewish books containing various forms of literature, using names of famous people in Israel's history for the titles of the books. The real authors are unknown. Such names as Ezra, Baruch, Enoch, Solomon, Moses, and Adam are used to add authority to the writing.

A few of these books are folk tales or sacred legends. These include the Letter of Aristeas, the Book of Adam and Eve, and the Martyrdom of Isaiah. One book of psalms, the Psalms of Solomon, has been included in the Pseudepigrapha. Ethical and wisdom writings are also part of this collection.

One problem addressed by the pseudepigraphal books is, Why do the wicked seem to prosper and the righteous suffer? Books like Jubilee, Enoch, and IV Ezra develop a careful scheme of history that shows the power of the world in the hands of the ruler of this age. The ruler of this age is Satan or Belial. The present age will end with God as Lord of all nations.

The books in the Pseudepigrapha were written by pious Jews living in either Palestine or Egypt. They were concerned that the Jews live according to the law of Moses.

The Book of Jubilee describes a conversation which took place on Mt. Sinai between Moses and an angel of the Lord. The Martyrdom of Isaiah reports the sad news of the death of the great prophet. Through this story, the writer (using Isaiah's name) emphasizes how far Israel has gone astray. To protest against the growing secularization of the Pharisees, The Assumption of Moses was written around A.D. 7 to 29.

The Book of Adam and Eve, written in the middle of the first Christian century, is probably a protest against Christians. It tells about the future resurrection which was promised to Adam. The Testament of the Twelve Patriarchs is a book with many sub-books, describing the patriarch Jacob blessing his twelve sons before his death. Written around 105 B.C. by a Pharisee, it tells about the intense hope for a Messiah held by some Jews during this period (100–50 B.C.). The value of this book is the contribution it makes to an understanding of forgiveness, the two great commandments, the

Messianic expectation, the resurrection, the Antichrist, demonology, and other teachings which were later developed in the New Testament.

Some collections of pseudepigraphal works include The Sayings of the Fathers. This work is actually a collection of wisdom sayings from the rabbis that is included in the MISHNAH and TALMUD.

PTOLEMAIS [tahl uh MAY iss] — a seaport in northern Palestine between Tyre and Caesarea (see Map 6, B-2). The apostle Paul visited Ptolemais for one day on his return to Jerusalem during his third missionary journey (Acts 21:7). In the Old Testament the city is known as ACCO (Judg. 1:31; Accho, KJV). Today the city is about 15 kilometers (nine miles) north of Haifa and about 19 kilometers (12 miles) south of Lebanon.

PTOLEMY [TOL eh mih] — a general title (similar to Pharaoh) of the 14 Greek kings who ruled Egypt between the conquest of Alexander the Great (323 B.C.) and the Roman conquest of Egypt in 30 B.C.

After the death of Alexander the Great in 323 B.C., his empire eventually fell into the hands of two of his generals, Seleucus I and Ptolemy I Soter. Seleucus established a dynasty in Syria, Asia, and the east, while Ptolemy I Soter and his descendants ruled in Egypt. During this period the Ptolemies engaged in many wars with the Seleucid rulers in Syria over the control of Palestine. Many scholars believe that Daniel 11 contains a prediction of many of these events.

Ptolemy I Soter (323–285 B.C.) conducted three campaigns in Palestine against the SELEUCIDS (Dan. 11:5), and by 301 B.C. he controlled Phoenicia and Palestine, which his successors retained for a century. His capital, Alexandria, situated on the northern coast of Egypt, became the center of intellectual life for the eastern Mediterranean. Ptolemy settled many Jewish prisoners of war in Alexandria.

Ptolemy's son, Ptolemy II Philadelphus (285–246 B.C.) continued to battle the Seleucids (Dan. 11:6). At Alexandria he established a famous library and museum which comprised a university promoting the spread of Greek culture throughout the ancient world. Along with prisoners of war, many Jews chose to migrate to Alexandria and elsewhere in Egypt. In Alexandria they eventually adapted the prevailing culture, producing learned Jewish writings in the fields of philosophy, history, and biblical interpretation.

Ptolemy II Philadelphus commissioned 70 Jewish students of the Bible to translate the Old Testament from Hebrew to Greek (this is called the SEPTUAGINT). This translation was the Bible for many Greeks and Greek-speaking Jews for years to come.

Judea, a state ruled by a high priest and his council, the SANHEDRIN, was content under Ptolemaic rule; it was allowed a certain measure of self-rule as long as it paid taxes to the Ptolemy and abided under his ultimate rule. There was an influx of Greeks and Hellenistic culture into Palestine during this era.

During the reign of Ptolemy III Euergetes (246–

222 B.C.), the fighting between the Ptolemies and the Seleucids continued (Dan. 11:7-9). During this time synagogues were established for the Jews who lived in Egypt.

Ptolemy IV Philopater (222–205 B.C.) defeated Antiochus III (Dan. 11:11-12), but his successor, Ptolemy V Epiphanes (205–180 B.C.), brought about a measure of peace by forming an alliance through intermarriage (Dan. 11:14-16). It was this Ptolemy who wrote the ROSETTA STONE which led to the decipherment of the mysterious Egyptian HIEROGLYPHICS.

Judea passed into Seleucid control in 200 B.C. From that time on, Egypt began to decline in power.

During the reign of Ptolemy VI Philometor (180–146 B.C.), the Jewish priest Onias III from Jerusalem was allowed to build a Jewish temple in Egypt at Leontopolis. The Egyptian and Seleucid wars continued (Dan. 11:25-29). Some of these events are described in the apocryphal books of Maccabees, and by Josephus and Aristobulus. Murder, revolt, bribery, and trickery characterized the last group of Ptolemies.

During the reign of Ptolemy VI Philometor, Egypt was attacked by Antiochus IV. Only Roman intervention forced his withdrawal. This was the beginning of the end for the Ptolemies. Externally, Egypt was doomed to be incorporated into Rome's spreading sphere of influence and power. Internally, native revolts grew more frequent in response to crippling taxation and injustice in bureaucratic, nationalized Egypt.

The line of Ptolemies came to an end with Cleopatra VII (51–30 B.C.)—the daughter of Ptolemy XI—and her son by Julius Caesar, Ptolemy XIV Caesarion (36–30 B.C.), when Cleopatra committed suicide. Egypt then passed into Roman hands (30 B.C.) and became a lucrative province of the Roman Empire. The Ptolemies had ruled Egypt with selfish motives without gaining much support from the native population.

The clashes between Seleucid Syria and Ptolemaic Egypt are mentioned in Daniel 11 to illustrate God's control over His people. "The king of the South" is the representative Ptolemy, as the references to Egypt in verses 8, 42, and 43 indicate: Ptolemy I (v. 5), Ptolemy II (v. 6), Ptolemy III (vv. 7-9), Ptolemy IV (v. 11), Ptolemy V (vv. 14-15), and Ptolemy VI (vv. 25, 27). Daniel's descriptions of these events long before they took place is proof of God's sovereign control over nations.

PUA [POO uh] — a form of PUAH.

PUAH [POO uh] (*girl*) — the name of two men and one woman in the Old Testament:

1. The second son of Issachar (1 Chr. 7:1), also called Puvah (Gen. 46:13, RSV), Phuvah (KJV), and Pua (Num. 26:23, KJV).

2. One of two midwives whom Pharaoh ordered to kill Hebrew males at their birth (Ex. 1:15). The midwives courageously disobeyed Pharaoh's command.

3. The father of Tola, of the tribe of Issachar (Judg. 10:1).

PUBLICAN — KJV word for TAX COLLECTOR.

PUBLIUS [PUHB lih uhs] (*pertaining to the people*) — the leading citizen of the island of Malta (Melita, KJV) who showed hospitality to the apostle Paul and his companions when they were shipwrecked (Acts 28:1–10). Publius may have been a native official or perhaps the chief Roman official on Malta, which at that time was part of the province of Sicily. The apostle Paul healed Publius' father, who suffered from a fever and dysentery (Acts 28:8).

PUDENS [POO denz] (*modest*) — a Christian at Rome who joined Claudia, Eubulus, Linus, and the apostle Paul in sending greetings to Timothy (2 Tim. 4:21).

PUHITES [POO hights] — a form of PUTHITES.

PUL [pool] (meaning unknown) — the name of a man and a place in the Old Testament:

1. An Assyrian king who invaded Israel during the reign of King Menahem. When Menahem paid tribute to Pul, giving him 1,000 talents of silver (2 Kin. 15:19), Pul withdrew his army from Israel (v. 20). Pul did, however, carry the tribes east of the Jordan River into captivity (1 Chr. 5:26). Pul is the same person as TIGLATH–PILESER. Tiglath-Pileser was the throne–name he bore as king of Assyria; Pul was the throne–name he bore in Babylonia as king of Babylon.

2. An African country and its people (Is. 66:19), identical with Libya.

PULPIT — KJV word for a raised platform reached by steps, or a desk used for preaching and teaching in a service of worship (Neh. 8:4; platform, NKJV). Such a platform is mentioned in connection with the gathering of the people of Israel to hear the reading of the Law of God and its interpretation.

PULSE — a KJV word for vegetables, or edible seeds—a simple diet which Daniel and his friends requested instead of the rich dishes offered by the Babylonians (Dan. 1:12, 16; vegetables, NKJV).

PUNISHMENT — payment for crime or sin. Punishment of sin is one of the basic truths of the Old Testament. Mosaic Law spelled out the proper punishments for each crime. The punishments generally took the form of retribution, "eye for eye" (Ex. 21:24) and other punishment in kind being the most memorable. Retribution such as this was only a small part of the ideas of compensation and restitution of value emphasized under the Old Testament law (Ex. 21:18–36). For example, if one person injured another in a fight, he was required to repay the victim for any time lost from his job because of the injury. In the case of disfigurement, the person committing the crime might also suffer the same violence as a punishment handed down by the court.

Since punishment was tied so closely to crime and sin, it was only natural that this concept should extend from the temporal world into the spiritual world. God meted out His own punishment to those who broke His moral law, notably against Sodom and Gomorrah (Gen. 19:12–29) and the Hebrew people wandering in the wilderness (Num. 14:26–35).

In the New Testament, the concern with temporal punishment became secondary to Christ's message of redemption. An eternal spiritual punishment falls upon those who refuse to accept God's message.

PUNISHMENT, EVERLASTING — the final judgment of God upon the wicked. The classic example of eternal punishment in the Old Testament is the destruction of Sodom and Gomorrah (Gen. 19:15–28). While speaking about wicked angels who are being held in "everlasting chains," the writer of Jude in the New Testament likened these wrongdoers to the wicked men of Sodom and Gomorrah, who "are set forth as an example, suffering the vengeance of eternal fire" (Jude 7).

In his second letter to the Thessalonians, the apostle Paul wrote about the final judgment. He explains that those who do not know God "shall be punished with everlasting destruction from the presence of the Lord and from the glory of His power" (2 Thess 1:9). This same idea was expressed by Jesus in the parable of the sheep and the goats (Matt. 25:31–46). After separating the two, Jesus blessed the sheep—those who have cared for the unfortunate and poor. Then he pronounced judgment upon the goats—those who did not have compassion: "Depart from Me, you cursed, into the everlasting fire" (v. 41).

The essential meaning of the phrase everlasting punishment involves banishment from the presence of God and Christ forever—a fate made vivid by the image of eternal fire (Rev. 19:20; 21:8).

Also see HELL.

PUNITES [PUE nites] — the descendants of PUAH, of the tribe of Issachar (Num. 26:23; the Puite family, NEB).

PUNON [POO nahn] (*ore pit*) — an Israelite encampment (see Map 2, C–1) occupied during the last part of the wilderness wandering (Num. 33:42–43). Punon is probably modern Khirbet Feinan on the east side of the Arabah about 40 kilometers (25 miles) south of the Dead Sea.

PURAH [PYUR uh] (*beauty*) — one of Gideon's servants, probably his armor–bearer, who went with Gideon under cover of darkness to scout the enemy camp of the Midianites (Judg. 7:10–11); Phurah, KJV).

PURGE — to cast out whatever is impure or undesirable; to refine or free from impurities (Dan. 11:35; 1 Cor. 5:7; Heb. 9:14). In his religious reformation King Josiah purged the Temple of Jerusalem and the land of Judah by destroying the altars of the Baals and all idolatrous images (2 Chr. 34:1–8). After he had committed adultery with Bathsheba and sent her husband to his death, David prayed,

"Purge me with hyssop, and I shall be clean; wash me, and I shall be whiter than snow" (Ps. 51:7). In His atonement Christ purged our sins by His own blood (Heb. 1:3; 9:22).

PURIFICATION — the act of making oneself clean and pure before God and men. The Mosaic Law provided instructions for both physical and spiritual purification. These laws and regulations were much more than sanitary instructions. The act of purification also involved religious and spiritual cleansing.

The Mosaic Law recognized and detailed purification rituals for three distinct categories of uncleanness. These were leprosy (Leviticus 13—14), sexual discharges (Leviticus 15), and contact with a dead body (Num. 19:11-19).

By the time of Jesus, much had been added to the laws of purification, making them a burden to the people. Jesus denounced such rituals, teaching that defilement and uncleanness came from within, or the inner motives of the mind and heart (Mark 7:14-23). He taught that genuine purification is possible only by following Him and giving heed to His message of love and redemption (John 15:3).

PURIM [POOR im] (*lots*) — a Jewish holiday observed on the 14th and 15th of the month of Adar, a month before Passover, in commemoration of the deliverance of the Jews, by ESTHER and MORDECAI, from a massacre plotted by HAMAN (Esth. 3:7; 9:24-32). Also see FEASTS AND FESTIVALS.

PURITY — the quality or state of being free from mixture, pollution, or other foreign elements. The term purity may refer to things (gold, Ex. 25:17; oil, Lev. 24:2) or people. Purity with reference to people may be racial (Phil. 3:5), ceremonial (Lev. 19:16-33; Luke 2:22), ethical (Prov. 22:11), or spiritual (1 Tim. 1:5; 4:12).

The Jews of Jesus' day often took ceremonial purity beyond what Scripture commanded. They considered ceremonial purity more valuable than spiritual purity (Mark 7:3-4; Luke 11:39-41). For this error they were soundly rebuked by Jesus (Mark 7:1-13; Luke 11:39-41). The purity which a Christian should strive for is spiritual in nature (Matt. 5:8; James 1:27).

PURPLE (see COLORS OF THE BIBLE).

PURPLE GARNET (see JEWELS AND PRECIOUS STONES).

PURSE, BAG — containers for carrying money or other objects. In the Old Testament the word for purse is used of a small bag or of the gold carried in such a bag (Is. 46:6). A second word is used of the money bags belonging to Joseph's brothers (Gen. 42:35). David's shepherd pouch (1 Sam. 17:40, 49) was probably a leather bag which Palestinian shepherds threw over their shoulders and in which they carried food.

The New Testament uses several words to describe bags and purses. One refers to the shepherd's bag carried over the shoulder (Luke 10:4) and to a smaller money purse (Luke 12:33). Another word represents the money box in which Judas kept the disciples' funds (John 12:6; 13:29).

PUT [put] (meaning unknown) — the name of a man and a land or people mentioned in the Old Testament:

1. One of the sons of Ham (Gen. 10:6; Phut, KJV; 1 Chr. 1:8). Put was a grandson of Noah.

2. The land where Put's descendants lived (see Map 1, A-2). This nation is mentioned in the Bible in connection with Egypt and Ethiopia (Cush). Some scholars identify this land with Punt, an area on the eastern shore of Africa (possibly Somaliland), famous for its incense. Since Put and Punt are not identical in spelling and because Put was known for its warriors rather than its incense, other scholars believe Put refers to certain Libyan tribes west of Egypt.

Men from Put and LUBIM (Libya) were used as mercenary soldiers by the King of Tyre (Ezek. 27:10) and Magog (Ezek. 38:5). But most references in the Bible picture them as allies with Egypt (Jer. 46:9; Ezek. 30:5; Nah. 3:9). Although the warriors of Put were hired to help these different nations secure their borders and win their wars, the prophets point to the futility of such forces in the face of God's mighty power and judgment.

PUTEOLI [poo TEE uh lih] (*little wells*) — a seaport on the western shore of southern Italy (see Map. 8, A-1) visited by the apostle Paul (Acts

The modern wharf at Puteoli surrounds the site where Paul landed on his way to Rome (Acts 28:13-14).

Photo by Howard Vos

Aerial view of the giant pyramid of Khafre (Chefren) at Giza, Egypt.

28:13). Puteoli was one of the most important harbors in Italy. At Puteoli the great grain ships from Alexandria were unloaded. Paul stayed with the Christians at Puteoli for a week before he travelled overland toward Rome (Acts 28:14).

Puteoli is now known as the modern city of Pozzuoli, across the Bay of Naples from Pompeii and Mount Vesuvius. The city boasts an ancient Roman amphitheater, built like the Colosseum of Rome. With a capacity of 40,00 to 60,000 people, it was overshadowed in size only by the Colosseum and the amphitheater at nearby Capua.

PUTHITES [POO thights] — a family of the tribe of Judah in Kirjath Jearim (1 Chr. 2:53; Puhites, KJV).

PUTIEL [POO tih uhl] (*he whom God has given*) — the father–in–law of Aaron's son Eleazar (Ex. 6:25).

PUVAH [POO vuh] — a form of PUAH.

PYGARG (see ANIMALS OF THE BIBLE).

PYRAMID — an ancient massive structure of Egypt with a rectangular base, outside walls in the form of four triangles that meet in a point at the top, and inner chambers used as tombs for Egyptian royalty. Such monuments were constructed over about 80 royal tombs in ancient Egypt.

The first pyramid was the Step Pyramid of King Djoser (about 2600 B.C.). The structure was made of six ascending "steps," each one smaller than the one below. Most of the other pyramids were built during the Old Kingdom (2600–2200 B.C.), before the time of Abraham and well before the Israelite sojourn in Egypt.

The Great Pyramid of Khufu, or Cheops, is the largest of the pyramids. One of the seven wonders of the ancient world, it covered 13 acres and was originally 768 feet square and 482 feet high. It is situated at Giza, a city of northern Egypt, on the Nile River near Cairo. Some blocks of the Great Pyramid are estimated to weigh more than 54,400 kilograms (60 tons).

As a sacred symbol, the pyramid played an important part in the religious beliefs of the Egyptians. A text inside one pyramid suggests they were considered stairways to heaven for the buried pharaoh, who would be reunited with the sun god Ra.

The pyramids of Egypt are not mentioned in the Bible. Some scholars, however, believe the Tower of Babel (Gen. 11:1–9) was a step pyramid somewhat like those of the Egyptians.

PYRRHUS [PIR uhs] (*flame–colored*) — the father of Sopater of Berea (Acts 20:4, NASB, NEB, NIV, RSV). Sopater was a friend and companion of the apostle Paul. Some ancient Greek manuscripts do not contain the name Pyrrhus; the name is omitted by the KJV and NKJV.

Q — the letter Q (from the German word QUELLE, meaning "source") refers to a hypothetical document that contained material from which Matthew and Luke drew as they wrote certain sections of their gospels. This document supposedly consisted mostly of sayings of Jesus in narrative form. Not all scholars accept the existence of Q as a background document to these gospels. Also see GOSPEL.

QOPH [kofe] — the 19th letter of the Hebrew alphabet, used as a heading over Psalm 119:145–152. In the original Hebrew language, every line of these eight verses began with the letter qoph. Also see ACROSTIC.

QUAIL (see ANIMALS OF THE BIBLE).

QUARRY — an open excavation from which stone is cut, usually for building purposes. Archaeologists have discovered quarries throughout Palestine. The most notable quarries built during the Old Testament period are those near Megiddo, Samaria, Jerusalem, and Ramat Rahel. These four quarries date to about 850 B.C.

The most common method of quarrying was to cut deep, vertical slits on the four sides of the desired block. The stones then were separated from the stone underneath by wedges. While building stones were occasionally finished at the quarry (1 Kin. 6:7), the final dressing was usually completed at the building site.

QUARRYMAN (see OCCUPATIONS AND TRADES).

This massive cut stone was never removed from an ancient quarry at the Phoenician city of Baalbek, perhaps because of its weight and size.

Photo by Howard Vos

Cave Four at Qumran, where several of the Dead Sea Scrolls were discovered, is visible at upper right. The Dead Sea looms in the background.

QUARTERMASTER (see OCCUPATIONS AND TRADES).

QUARTUS [KWOR tus] *(fourth)* — a Christian who probably lived in Corinth and who sent greetings to the church in Rome (Rom. 16:23). According to early church tradition, Quartus was one of the 70 disciples whom Jesus sent out and who eventually became a bishop at Berytus.

QUARTZ (see MINERALS OF THE BIBLE).

QUATERNION [kwah TURN ih on] — KJV translation of the Greek word *tetradion*, meaning a guard of four soldiers (Acts 12:4; squad, NKJV).

QUEEN — a female member of the royal house, either the wife of a king, or a woman who reigns by her own power. The term may refer to an actual ruler of state, such as the queen of Sheba (1 Kings 10), or Candace the queen of the Ethiopians (Acts 8:27). BATHSHEBA and JEZEBEL are not called queens, but certainly they ruled with their husbands (1 Kin. 1:21). On the other hand, a queen might be simply the king's favorite mate or wife— as probably was the case with both Vashti and Esther (Esther 1—2).

The term is also used for the queen mother (1 Kin. 15:13, NKJV). The queen mother's name is consistently included in the summaries of the reigns of the Judean kings (1 Kin. 15:1-2). MAACHAH, King Asa's grandmother, served as queen mother until she was removed by her grandson (1 Kin. 15:9-13). Some years later, Athaliah was a queen mother who seized the throne and ruled in Judah for about six years (2 Kings 11; 2 Chronicles 22—23).

QUEEN OF HEAVEN — a fertility goddess to whom the Israelites, especially the women, offered sacrifice and worship in the days before the fall of the southern kingdom of Judah (Jer. 7:18; 44:17-19, 25). In the time of Jeremiah, many people in Jerusalem and other cities of Judah worshiped the queen of heaven. Their worship included burning incense and pouring out drink offerings to her (Jer. 44:17). This was obviously a form of idolatry, but it is not clear exactly which pagan god was worshiped.

The phrase queen of heaven may be a title for the goddess Ishtar (perhaps the same goddess as the biblical ASHTORETH); or it may refer to the Canaanite goddess Anat. Cakes were also baked in honor of the "queen of heaven" (Jer. 7:18). These cakes may have been in the shape of stars, crescent moons, or the female figure. The worship of this goddess was one of the evils that brought God's judgment upon Judah (Jer. 7:20).

QUEEN OF SHEBA (see SHEBA).

QUICK, QUICKEN — KJV translation of several Hebrew and Greek words translated by the NKJV as alive (Ps. 55:15), living (Acts 10:42), revive (Ps. 119:25), and gives life to (John 5:21).

QUICKSANDS, THE (see SYRTIS SANDS)

QUIRINIUS [kwy REN ih us] (meaning unknown) — Roman governor of Syria at the time of Jesus' birth (Luke 2:1-5; Cyrenius, KJV). Quirinius is mentioned in connection with a census taken for tax purposes. The census was not a local affair; the Roman emperor Augustus (ruled 31 B.C.–A.D. 14) had decreed that all the world, or the Roman Empire, should be taxed. For this purpose, Joseph and Mary made their pilgrimage to Bethlehem. While they were there, Jesus was born.

The Gospel of Luke reports that Quirinius was governor of Syria at a time when HEROD THE GREAT was still alive. According to historians, the governor of Syria at this time was Quintilius Varus. Quirinius may have been a military commander who shared civil duties with Varus.

QUIVER (see ARMS, ARMOR OF THE BIBLE).

QUMRAN, KHIRBET [KIR beht KOOM rahn] — an ancient ruin on the northwestern shore of the Dead Sea (see Map 6, B-4). In 1947 a wandering goatherder looking for his goats in caves above the dry river bed, or wadi, of Qumran found several large jars. These jars contained ancient scrolls that have since become known as the DEAD SEA SCROLLS. Following this discovery, the area was opened for extensive archaeological research.

From 1951 to 1956 excavation of the area revealed more scrolls, as well as dated coins, pottery, and fragments from scrolls. These items made it possible to connect the Dead Sea Scrolls discovered in nearby caves to the Qumran Community, which lived in Khirbet Qumran.

Excavations reveal that Khirbet Qumran was a Jewish community that was active from 130 B.C. to A.D. 135. In 31 B.C. an earthquake destroyed the settlement and made it uninhabitable. In 4 B.C. another group of Jews rebuilt on the site, enlarged it, and occupied it until the war with Rome in A.D. 68, when the Roman garrison sent to destroy Jericho took command of this outpost in the desert. Jewish zealots reestablished themselves at Qumran in A.D. 90 and defended their position until A.D. 135, when the Romans again fought and conquered Jewish resistance.

Some of the remains of walls and pottery in Khirbet Qumran date to the eighth and seventh centuries B.C— the time of King Uzziah of Judah. The significant period is much later, around 50 B.C. to A.D. 68, when a group of pious Jews built and oc-

The Qumran community was situated on this plateau (center) and separated from the surrounding territory by a deep gorge.

Photo by John Trever

cupied the fortress, or monastery–like dwelling, at Qumran. The people who occupied the fortress committed themselves to a disciplined life of obedience to the Law as interpreted by the leader of the community, known as the Teacher of Righteousness. Some of the writings found here may be a collection of teachings from the Teacher of Righteousness himself.

The exact identity of the people who lived in Qumran in this later period is not known. Scholars have suggested that they were a small group of Jews who were disgusted with the corruption and lawlessness of the priests and leaders responsible for worship at the Temple in Jerusalem. The Qumran community sought to purify itself from the sin of those who distorted the law. Large baths or pools were found in Khirbet Qumran and were probably used for daily ritual baths. Twelve hundred grave sites were found just east of the ruin. The skeletal remains were simply laid to rest in the ground without any burial objects. This indicates that a large number of people inhabited Qumran at one time.

Josephus and Philo, both first–century A.D. Jewish writers, describe a group known as ESSENES who occupied communities similar to Qumran. This has led some scholars to the conviction that Essenes were the residents of Khirbet Qumran and were the authors of the Dead Sea Scrolls. During the Jewish wars with Rome (A.D. 66–73 and A.D. 135) ZEALOTS joined the people of Qumran for what they believed to be the final war with evil. The Romans won the war and destroyed the memory of these people until the discovery of the caves at Qumran in 1947.

QUOTATIONS IN THE NEW TESTAMENT. Several different kinds of quotations appear in the New Testament. It includes quotations of pagan authors (Acts 17:28; 1 Cor. 15:33; Titus 1:12) and at least one quotation of a statement of Jesus that is not recorded in any of the four gospels (Acts 20:35).

The New Testament also contains statements that parallel non–canonical literature from the New Testament era. For example, Jude 14 and 15 parallel 1 Enoch 1:9, a book of the APOCRYPHA. The New Testament also quotes itself (Luke 10:7; 1 Tim. 5:18). But more than anything else, it quotes the Old Testament. This indicates how important each testament is for an understanding of the other.

The number of quotations from and allusions to the Old Testament in the New varies with the counter. Direct quotations have been numbered from 150 to 300. When allusions are added to this number, the total number rises to anywhere from 600 to more than 4,000, again according to the person doing the counting.

A number of verses from the Old Testament are quoted more than once in the New Testament. The majority of quotations are taken from the SEPTUAGINT, the Greek translation of the Old Testament.

The New Testament authors used the Old Testament scripture to do several things: (1) to provide authority for their statements or conclusions, (2) to answer questions or to rebuke opponents' claims, (3) to provide further interpretations of the Old Testament, (4) to call attention to parallel situations, and (5) to show continuity in the revelation of God.

R

RAAMA, RAAMAH [RAY uh muh] (*trembling*) — the name of a man and a place in the Old Testament:

1. A son of Cush (Gen. 10:7). Raama's sons were Sheba and Dedan.

2. A country or region in southwest Arabia. The merchants of Sheba and Raamah traded in the markets of Tyre (Ezek. 27:22).

RAAMIAH [ray uh MIGH uh] — a form of REELAIAH.

RAAMSES [ray AM sez] — a form of RAMESES.

RABBAH [RAB uh] (*great*) — the name of two cities in the Old Testament:

1. The chief city of the Ammonites. Known as Rabbah of the people of Ammon (Deut. 3:11; 2 Sam. 12:26), Rabbah is the only Ammonite city mentioned in the Bible (see Map 3, C–4). Rabbah was at the headwaters of the Jabbok River, 37 kilometers (23 miles) east of the Jordan.

Rabbah is first mentioned as the place where the giant King Og had his massive iron bedstead (Deut. 3:11; Rabbath, KJV). Rabbah remained the capital of Ammon during David's reign, when the Ammonites and Arameans joined forces to fight against Israel. While Joab and the Israelites camped before the gate of Rabbah, the Arameans marched to MEDEBA (1 Chr. 19:7). In the decisive battle the Israelite armies defeated both the Arameans and the Ammonites, also subjecting the Ammonites to forced labor (2 Sam. 12:27–31; 1 Chr. 20:1–3). During this conflict, Uriah the Hittite was killed at David's orders (2 Sam. 11:1, 15). Later the Ammonites recovered the city. Throughout its history Israel's prophets denounced Rabbah (Jer. 49:2–6; Ezek. 21:20; Amos 1:14).

Sitting astride the King's Highway, Rabbah's strategic location put it in the middle of most of the conflicts and wars of the biblical period. Consequently, it repeatedly was destroyed and rebuilt.

This Roman amphitheater at Amman, Jordan, is an excellent example of the architecture that dominated Palestine at the time of Jesus. In Old Testament times Amman was known as Rabbah (Amos 1:14).
Photo by Willem A. VanGemeren

Under Ptolemy Philadelphus (285–246 B.C.) the city became an important trading center renamed Philadelphia. It was the southernmost of the ten cities of the DECAPOLIS. During the Byzantine period of the fourth century A.D., Rabbah ranked in importance with Gerasa (Jerash). Destroyed during the Muslim conquest, Rabbah has once again gained its ancient splendor. Today it is one of the most important Arab cities of the Middle East—Amman, Jordan.

2. A city in the Judaean hill country mentioned with Kirjath Jearim (Josh. 15:60). Although the exact location is unknown, some archaeologists have equated it with Rubute of the Amarna Letters and have identified it with Khirbet Bir el–Hilu, eight kilometers (five miles) east of Gezer on the road to Jerusalem.

RABBI [RAB igh] (*my teacher*) — a title of honor and respect given by the Jews to a teacher of the Law. In our day rabbi means a Jew trained for professional religious leadership. The ordained spiritual leader of a Jewish congregation, the rabbi is an official formally authorized to interpret Jewish law. In Jesus' day, however, the term had not yet become a formal title. Instead, it was a term of dignity given by the Jews to their distinguished teachers. The Pharisees loved to be called "Rabbi," but Jesus told his disciples, "Do not be called 'Rabbi'; for One is your Teacher, the Christ, and you are all brethren" (Matt. 23:7–8).

The word rabbi comes from a Semitic root word meaning "great" or "head." It is only used in the gospels, usually of Jesus. The disciples of John the Baptist also addressed him as rabbi (John 3:26).

RABBIT (see ANIMALS OF THE BIBLE).

RABBITH [RAB ith] (*great*) — a border town in the territory of Issachar (Josh. 19:20), perhaps the present village of Raba, about 13 kilometers (8 miles) south of Mount Gilboa.

RABBONI [rab BOE nigh] — a form of RABBI.

RABMAG, THE [RAB mag] (meaning unknown) — the title of Nergal–Sharezer, a chief officer in the army of Nebuchadnezzar (Jer. 39:3, 13). Rabmag is not a proper name; it is an official position. The Rabmag wielded great power in the Babylonian government.

RABSARIS, THE [RAB suh ris] (meaning unknown) — the title of two men in the Old Testament:

1. One of three officials sent from Lachish by Sennacherib, king of Assyria (2 Kin. 18:17).

2. An officer under Nebuchadnezzar, king of Babylon, and possibly the one who ordered the release of Jeremiah (Jer. 39:3, 13).

Rabsaris was a title of a high government official. The official in Nebuchadnezzar's court known as "the master of his eunuchs" (Dan. 1:3) probably held this office.

RABSHAKEH, THE [RAB shuh kuh] (meaning unknown) — the title of an Assyrian military official under Sennacherib, king of Assyria (2 Kin. 18:17–37; Is. 36:2–22). The Rabshakeh accompanied the RABSARIS and the TARTAN from Lachish to Jerusalem. They presented Sennacherib's demand that Hezekiah, king of Judah, surrender the city of Jerusalem.

RACA [RAH kah] (*stupid*) — an expression of contempt (Matt. 5:22). The word appears often in the writings of the Jewish rabbis with the meaning of "ignorant, senseless." To say raca to a person was like saying, "You idiot!"

RACAL [RAY kal] —a form of RACHAL.

RACE — a contest of speed, as in running or riding. The Greek games in New Testament times featured several sports, including chariot racing, horse racing, and foot racing. The apostle Paul may have had these athletic events in mind when he spoke of a person's life as a racecourse to run (Acts 13:25; Phil. 3:14) and of running well (Gal. 5:7). The writer of the Book of Hebrews also spoke eloquently of the race of faith that Christians must run with endurance (Heb. 12:1–2). Also see GAMES.

RACHAB [RAY kab] — a form of RAHAB.

RACHAL [RAY kal] (*trade*) — a town in southern Judah to which David sent some of the spoils of battle taken from the Amalekites (1 Sam. 30:29; Racal, RSV). The site is unidentified.

RACHEL [RAY chuhl] (*lamb*) — the younger daughter of Laban; the second wife of Jacob; and the mother of Joseph and Benjamin.

Jacob met Rachel, the beautiful younger daughter of his uncle Laban, at a well near Haran in Mesopotamia as he fled from his brother Esau (Gen. 29:6, 11). Jacob soon asked Laban for Rachel as his wife (Gen. 29:15–18). However, it was customary in those days for the groom or his family to pay the bride's family a price for their daughter. Having no property of his own, Jacob served Laban seven years for Rachel, only to be tricked on the wedding day into marrying Rachel's older sister, Leah (Gen. 29:21–25). Jacob then had to serve another seven years for Rachel (Gen. 29:26–30).

Although Rachel was Jacob's favorite wife, she envied Leah, who had given birth to four sons—Reuben, Simeon, Levi, and Judah—while she herself had remained childless (Gen. 29:31–35). Her response was to give her handmaid Bilhah to Jacob. According to this ancient custom, the child of Bilhah and Jacob would have been regarded as Rachel's. Bilhah bore Dan and Naphtali (Gen. 30:1–8), but Rachel named them, indicating they were her children. Rachel's desperate desire to become fruitful is illustrated by her asking for Reuben's mandrakes, which she believed would bring fertility (Gen. 30:14–16). Mandrakes were considered love potions or magic charms by people of the ancient world.

Only after Zilpah, Leah's handmaid, produced two sons—Gad and Asher (Gen. 30:9–13)—and after Leah had borne two more sons and a daugh-

Ancient tomb near Bethlehem, traditionally identified as the burial place of Rachel (Gen. 48:2, 7).

ter—Issachar, Zebulun, and Dinah (Gen. 30:17–21)—did Rachel finally conceive. She bore to Jacob a son named Joseph (Gen. 30:22–24), who became his father's favorite and who was sold into Egypt by his jealous brothers. Rachel died following the birth of her second son, whom she named Ben–Oni (son of my sorrow). But Jacob later renamed him Benjamin (son of the right hand). Jacob buried Rachel near Ephrath (or Bethlehem) and set a pillar on her grave (Gene. 35:16–20). Jews still regard Rachel's tomb with great respect. The traditional site is about a mile north of Bethlehem and about four miles south of Jerusalem.

Although Rachel was Jacob's favorite wife, the line of David and ultimately the messianic line passed through Leah and her son Judah, not Rachel. "Rachel weeping for her children" (Jer. 31:15; Rahel, KJV; Matt. 2:18) became symbolic of the sorrow and tragedy suffered by the Israelites. Matthew points out that the murder of all the male children in Bethlehem, from two years old and under, by Herod the Great, was the fulfillment of Jeremiah's prophecy (Matt. 2:16–18).

RADDAI [RAD igh] (*Jehovah rules*) — a son of Jesse (1 Chr. 2:14) and brother of David.

RAFT — a collection of logs or timber fastened together for transportation by water. In the days of King Solomon of Israel and King Hiram of Tyre, cedar and cypress logs were hauled down from Mount Lebanon, floated in rafts southward to Joppa, and then carried overland to Jerusalem (1 Kin. 5:9, floats, KJV). In Jerusalem they were used in the construction of Solomon's TEMPLE. These logs may have been conveyed to Joppa not in a raft, but as a raft—roped together for easy transportation.

RAGAU [RAG oe] — a form of REU.

RAGUEL [RAG yoo uhl] — a form of REUEL.

RAHAB [RAY hab] (*spacious*) — a harlot of Jericho who hid two Hebrew spies, helping them to escape, and who became an ancestor of David and Jesus (Josh. 2:1–21; 6:17–25; Matt. 1:5). Rahab's house was on the city wall of Jericho. Rahab, who manufactured and dyed linen, secretly housed the two spies whom Joshua sent to explore Jericho and helped them escape by hiding them in stalks of flax on her roof (Josh. 2:6).

Rahab sent the king's messengers on a false trail, and then let the two spies down the outside wall by a rope through the window of her house (Josh. 2:15). When the Israelites captured Jericho, they spared the house with the scarlet cord in the window—a sign that a friend of God's people lived within. Rahab, therefore, along with her father, her mother, her brothers, and all her father's household, was spared. Apparently she and her family were later brought into the nation of Israel.

Matthew refers to Rahab as the wife of Salmon (Ruth 4:20–21; Matt. 1:4–5; Luke 3:32; Salma, 1 Chr. 2:11). Their son Boaz married Ruth and became the father of Obed, the grandfather of Jesse, and the great–grandfather of David. Thus, a Canaanite harlot became part of the lineage of King David out of which the Messiah came (Matt. 1:5; Rachab, KJV)—perhaps an early sign that God's grace and forgiveness is extended to all, that it is not limited by nationality or the nature of a person's sins.

The Scriptures do not tell us how Rahab, who came out of a culture where harlotry and idolatry were acceptable, recognized Jehovah as the one true God. But her insights recorded in Joshua 2:9–11 leave no doubt that she did so. This Canaanite woman's declaration of faith led the writer of the Epistle to the Hebrews to cite Rahab as one of the heroes of faith (Heb. 11:31), while James commended her as an example of one who has been justified by works (James 2:25).

According to rabbinic tradition, Rahab was one of the four most beautiful women in the world and was the ancestor of eight prophets, including Jeremiah and the prophetess Huldah.

RAHAB–HEM–SHEBETH [RAY hab hem SHIH beth] (*Rahab sits idle*) — a name given by the prophet Isaiah to Egypt (Is. 30:7), comparing that nation to RAHAB THE DRAGON, a mythological sea monster or primeval dragon of chaos. The context of this passage is that Israel had sought to establish a political and military alliance with Egypt under the threat of Assyrian aggression. The prophet Isaiah warned that such an alliance was worthless. Trust in God alone, warned Isaiah; Egypt cannot save others, for she cannot even save herself.

RAHAB THE DRAGON [RAY hab] (*agitated*) — a mythological sea monster or dragon representing the evil forces of chaos that God subdued by His creative power. The name Rahab as it occurs in Job 9:13 (NIV), Job 26:12 (NIV), Psalm 87:4 and 89:10, Isaiah 30:7 (NIV), and Isaiah 51:9 has no connection with the personal name of Rahab, the harlot of Jericho, in Joshua 2:1–21. The reference to Rahab in the books of Job, Psalms, and Isaiah speak of an evil power overcome by God.

God's smiting of Rahab is described in Job 26:12 (NIV) to signify God's power over the chaos of primeval waters at the Creation. The NKJV translates as the storm for Rahab.

Because the Rahab–dragon imagery was used in describing the deliverance from Egypt, the name Rahab also became a synonym for Egypt itself (Ps. 87:4; Is. 30:7; RAHAB–HEM–SHEBETH, NKJV). In its widest sense, the dragon can represent any force that opposes God's will. It is a fitting symbol for Satan (Rev. 20:2).

RAHAM [RAY ham] (*pity*) — a son of Shema, of the family of Caleb (1 Chr. 2:44).

RAHEL [RAY huhl] — a form of RACHEL.

RAIL — KJV spelling of Hebrew and Greek words rendered by the NKJV as revile (2 Chr. 32:17; 1 Sam. 25:14), blasphemed (Mark 15:29; Luke 23:39), reviling (1 Tim. 6:4; 1 Pet. 3:9; 2 Pet. 2:11; Jude 9), and reviler (1 Cor. 5:11). Also see REPROACH.

RAIMENT (see DRESS OF THE BIBLE).

RAIN — liquid precipitation that provides essential moisture for plants, animals, and man. The biblical writers believed that only the Lord, and not the pagan gods, had control over the rain. This belief was strikingly confirmed several times in the Old Testament, especially through the predictions of Moses (Ex. 9:33–34) and Samuel (1 Sam. 12:17–18), the prayers of Elijah (1 Kin. 18:42–45), and God's announcement of the Flood (Gen. 7:4, 10–12).

In addition to these special occasions, God promised to send rain at the proper time (Lev. 26:4; Deut. 11:14), a promise which applied to all nations (Matt. 5:45; Acts 14:17). The rain was a sign of God's blessing to the Israelites (Deut. 28:12), al-

The modern village of Ramah, successor to the Old Testament city where the prophet Samuel was born and buried.

Photo by Howard Vos

though He could also hold back the rain, either as a warning (Amos 4:6–7) or as an expression of His judgment (1 Kin. 17:1; Jer. 3:3).

Belief in God's power to send the rain was not easy in an area like Palestine, where the timing, quantity, and distribution of rainfall were uncertain. The rainy season was synonymous with winter (Song 2:11; Prov. 26:1), but it could begin any time from mid–October to January. It generally ended in April or early May. The early and latter rains were especially significant in the Old Testament period (Deut. 11:14; Joel 2:23). The people longed for the rain (Jer. 14:4), and waterless clouds were the source of frustration and irritation (Prov. 25:14; Jude 12).

Rainfall was much heavier in the north, the west, and on sea-facing hills. For example, in modern times the average annual rainfall in the mountains of Upper Galilee is 738 millimeters (29 inches); at Jerusalem, 560 millimeters (22 inches); but only 50 millimeters (2 inches) at Sodom at the southern end of the Dead Sea. Storms were often very heavy. This truth is reflected in Jesus' parables (Matt. 7:25, 27) and in the experiences of Elijah (1 Kin. 18:45) and Ezra (Ezra 10:9, 13).

Rain is often a symbol of abundance in the Bible, a further testimony to the occasional heaviness of Palestine's rain. This abundance is compared with the effectiveness of God's Word (Deut. 32:2; Is. 55:10), with the righteousness and peace of God's kingdom (Ps. 72:6–7; Hos. 10:12), and with God's provision of food in the wilderness (Ex. 16:4; Ps. 78:24, 27). But rain could also be destructive (Prov. 28:3; Is. 4:6). The Bible sometimes speaks of the rain as a sign of God's judgment, when He might rain down hail, fire, or brimstone (Ex. 9:18).

RAINBOW — an arch of colors in the sky, caused by light passing through moisture in the air. The most important reference to the rainbow in the Bible occurs in Genesis 9:13–17, where the rainbow serves as a sign of God's covenant with Noah. This covenant was a promise by God to the world that it would never again be destroyed by a flood. The rain clouds and the rainbow were never again to be regarded by man as a threat of ultimate judgment, but as an unchanging indicator of God's mercy. This passage does not state that this was the first rainbow, but that it gained this new significance after the Flood.

The remaining references to the rainbow in the Bible develop this symbolism. They all occur in passages where judgment is to be announced, notably in Revelation 4:3 and 10:1 in connection with God's judgment of the world (Ezek. 1:28). In all these cases, however, the rainbow is a sign of the glorious presence of God. It is a reminder that His mercy and grace will finally triumph.

RAISIN CAKE — a dessert or delicacy in Solomon's time (Song 2:5; flagon, KJV). These cakes were made from dried raisins. Raisin cakes were also connected by the prophet Hosea with sacrifices made to the pagan god Ishtar (Hos. 3:1).

RAISINS — dried grapes prepared by soaking grapes in water and oil and drying them in the sun. Raisins were usually made into cakes. Slow to spoil and high in sugar, raisin cakes were ideal food for fighting men and travelers (1 Sam. 30:12).

RAKEM [RAY kem] (*friendship*) — a descendant of Manasseh (1 Chr. 7:16).

RAKKATH [RAK uhth] (meaning unknown) — a fortified city in the territory of Naphtali, on the west shore of the Sea of Galilee, apparently situated between Hammath and Chinnereth (Josh. 19:35).

RAKKON [RAK ahn] (*narrow place*) — a city in the original territory of Dan (Josh. 19:46).

RAM [ramm] (*high, exalted*) — the name of three men in the Bible:

1. The father of Amminadab of the tribe of Judah (Ruth 4:19; 1 Chr. 2:9–10). Ram was an ancestor of Jesus Christ through King David (Matt. 1:3–4; Luke 3:33; Aram, KJV).

2. The firstborn son of Jerahmeel of Judah (1 Chr. 2:25, 27). This Ram is apparently the nephew of Ram No. 1.

3. The founder of a family or clan that included Elihu, one of the friends of Job (Job 32:2).

RAMA [RAY muh] — Greek form of RAMAH.

RAMAH [RAY mah] (*height*) — the name of six cities in the Old Testament:

1. Ramah of Benjamin, one of the cities allotted to the tribe of Benjamin (Josh. 18:25) in the vicinity of Bethel (Judg. 4:5) and Gibeah (Judg. 19:13). According to Judges 4:5, Deborah lived between Ramah and Bethel.

Shortly after the division of the nation of Israel into two kingdoms, King Baasha of Israel fortified Ramah against King Asa of Judah (1 Kin. 15:16–17). Ramah lay on the border between the two kingdoms. The fortification was done to guard the road to Jerusalem so no one from the Northern Kingdom would attempt to go to Jerusalem to worship. Baasha was also afraid these people would want to live in the Southern Kingdom.

When Asa learned that Baasha was fortifying the city, he bribed the Syrians to invade northern Palestine (1 Kin. 15:18–21) so Baasha's attention would be turned away from Ramah. Meanwhile, Asa dismantled Ramah and used the stones to build two forts of his own nearby at Geba and Mizpah (1 Kin. 15:22; 2 Chr. 16:6).

When Nebuchadnezzar invaded Judah, he detained the Jewish captives, including Jeremiah, at Ramah (Jer. 40:1). The captives who were too old or weak to make the trip to Babylonia were slaughtered here. This was the primary fulfillment of the prophecy, "A voice was heard in Ramah, lamentation and bitter weeping, Rachel weeping for her children" (Jer. 31:15), although Matthew also applies it to Herod's slaughter of children after the birth of Christ (Matt. 2:18). This city also figures in the prophecies of Isaiah (10:29) and Hosea (5:8).

2. Ramah of Ephraim, the birthplace, home, and burial place of the prophet Samuel (1 Sam. 7:17; 19:18–23; 28:3). It is elsewhere referred to as Ramathaim Zophim (1 Sam. 1:1). The exact location of this Ramah is unknown. It was at Ramah that the elders of Israel demanded a king (1 Sam. 8:4) and Saul first met Samuel (1 Sam. 9:6, 10). David sought refuge from Saul in Ramah as well (1 Sam. 19:18; 20:1). In New Testament times the name of this town was ARIMATHEA, situated northwest of Jerusalem.

3. Ramah of Naphtali, one of the fortified cities of Naphtali (Josh. 19:36). Ramah appears to have been in the mountainous country northwest of the Sea of Galilee. It is identified with Khirbet Zeitun er–Rama, about three kilometers (two miles) southwest of the modern village of er–Rama.

4. Ramah of Asher, a town on the border of Asher (Josh. 19:29). Ramah is mentioned only once in the Bible and was apparently near the seacoast. It has been identified both with er–Ramia, about 21 kilometers (13 miles) south of Tyre, and with an unknown site north of Tyre but south of Sidon.

5. Ramah of the South, a town of Simeon in the Negev (South country) of Judah (Josh. 19:8; Ramah in the Negev, NIV; Ramah of the Negeb, RSV; Ramah of the Negev, NASB; Ramath-negeb, NEB; Ramath of the south, KJV). The exact site is unknown. Joshua 19:8 identifies this town as BAALATH BEER.

6. Ramah of Gilead (2 Kin. 8:29; 2 Chr. 22:6), elsewhere known as Ramoth Gilead. This was an important town on the Syrian border, about 40 kilometers (25 miles) east of the Jordan River. King Ahab was killed in a battle for this site after failing to heed the prophet Micaiah's warning (1 Kin. 22:1–40). Ahab's son Joram was wounded in a battle at Ramah (2 Kin. 8:28). Here too Jehu was anointed to succeed Joram as king of Israel (2 Kin. 9:1–13).

RAMATH [RAY math] — a form of RAMAH.

RAMATH LEHI [RAY muhth LEE high] (*the high place of the jawbone*) — a place in Judah where Samson killed a thousand Philistines with the jawbone of a donkey (Judg. 15:17). The place is also called LEHI (Judg. 15:9, 14, 19), which means jawbone or cheek. This site was probably northwest of Bethlehem.

RAMATH MIZPAH [RAY muhth MIZ puh] (*high place of the watchtower*) — a city in TRANSJORDAN, in the territory of Gad (Josh. 13:26; Ramath-mizpeh, NASB, RSV; Ramoth-mizpah, NEB).

RAMATH–MIZPEH [RAY muhth MIZ puh] — a form of RAMATH MIZPAH.

RAMATH–NEGEB [ray math NEG ebb] — a form of RAMAH.

RAMATH OF THE SOUTH [RAY math] — a form of RAMAH.

RAMATHITE [RAY muhth ight] — a native or inhabitant of RAMAH. Shimei the Ramathite was overseer of the vineyards of David (1 Chr. 27:27).

RAMESES, RAAMSES [RAM uh seez, RAM seez] (*house of Ramses*) — the royal city of the Egyptian kings of the 19th and 20th dynasties (about 1300–1100 B.C.) situated in the northeastern section of the Nile Delta. While the children of Israel were slaves in Egypt, they were forced to work on at least two of Pharaoh's vast construction projects—building the supply cities of Pithom and Raamses (Ex. 1:11, KJV, RSV, NASB, NKJV; Rameses, NIV, NEB).

The reference to "the land of Rameses" (Gen. 47:11) in the story of Joseph, well before Ramses II lived, suggests that the author of Genesis used the "modern" name (Rameses)—the name which was common in his day and not the earlier name of the city, which was used during the time of Joseph. This may also be true of the use of Rameses in the account of the Exodus, because the Hebrews apparently left Egypt around 1446 B.C., well before the time of King Ramses.

"The land of Rameses" (Gen. 47:11) was "the best of the land"—the most fertile district of Egypt. This almost certainly refers to the Land of Goshen, in the northeastern Nile Delta.

RAMIAH [ruh MIGH uh] (*Jehovah is exalted*) — a son of Parosh who divorced his pagan wife after the Captivity (Ezra 10:25).

RAMOTH [ray MOTH] — a form of RAMAH.

RAMOTH GILEAD [RAY muhth GIL ee uhd] (*heights of Gilead*) — an important fortified city in the territory of Gad near the border of Israel and Syria (see Map 4, C–3). It was approximately 40 kilometers (25 miles) east of the Jordan River. Ramoth Gilead was designated by Moses as one of the CITIES OF REFUGE (Deut. 4:43; Josh. 20:8). In the time of Solomon, one of the king's 12 district officers was stationed at Ramoth Gilead to secure food for the king's household, since it was a commercial center.

Because of its strategic location near the border of Israel and Syria, Ramoth Gilead was frequently the scene of battles between the two nations. The Jewish historian Josephus says that the city was captured by King Omri from Ben–Hadad I. It then changed hands several times. King Ahab enlisted the aid of King Jehoshaphat to retake the city, but he was mortally wounded in the attempt (2 Chr. 28–34). Ahab's son Joram was likewise wounded while attacking Ramoth Gilead (2 Kin. 8:28). While Jehu was maintaining possession of Ramoth Gilead, Elisha sent his servant to anoint Jehu king of Israel (2 Kin. 9:1–13).

RAMOTH–MIZPAH [RAY muhth MIZ puh] — a form of RAMATH MIZPAH.

RAMOTH–NEGEB [RAY moth NEG ebb] — a form of RAMAH.

RAMPART — a fortification consisting of an elevation or embankment, often provided with a wall to protect soldiers. A rampart was used as a protective

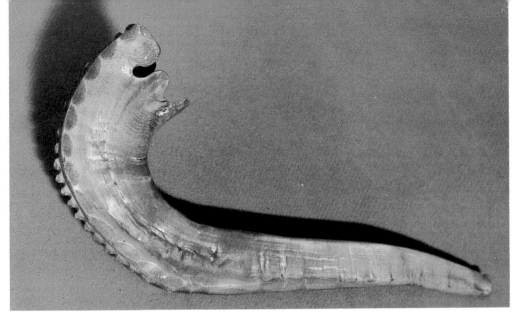

A ram's horn, or shofar, used by the Israelites as a trumpet to summon the people to battle or to gather for worship.

barrier against an attacking army. The Hebrew word translated as rampart (Lam. 2:8; Nah. 3:8) means encirclement; it is variously translated by the KJV as army, bulwark, host, rampart, trench, and wall. The general sense of the word is that of the outer fortification, or the front line of defense, encircling a city (2 Sam. 20:15; Hab. 2:1). This fortification included moats and towers as well as walls and earthworks. Also see FORT, FORTIFICATION; WAR, WARFARE.

RAM'S HORN (see MUSICAL INSTRUMENTS).

RAMS' SKINS — the tanned hides of male sheep, usually dyed. Ram skins were worn as garments by shepherds. They were also used as the inner covering of the TABERNACLE.

RANSOM (see REDEMPTION).

RAPE — the crime of forcing another person to submit to sexual intercourse. The word rape does not occur in many English translations of the Bible (KJV, RSV, NKJV). The NIV and the NEB, however, do use the word (Judg. 20:5; Zech. 14:2). The account given in the Book of Judges tells of the "filthy outrage" (Judg. 20:6) of the men of Gibeah who assaulted and abused a woman so that she died.

Zechariah the prophet predicted that Jerusalem would be captured, "the houses plundered and the women raped" (Zech. 14:2, NEB). This prophecy did come true. The Book of Lamentations records that "women were raped in Zion, virgins raped in the cities of Judah" (Lam. 5:11, NEB).

The Mosaic laws concerning rape and seduction are recorded in Exodus 22:16–17 and Deuteronomy 22:25–29.

RAPHA [RAY fuh] (*God has healed*) — the name of two men in the Old Testament:

1. An ancestor of four Philistines from Gath who fell at the hands of David (2 Sam. 21:15–22).

2. The fifth son of Benjamin (1 Chr. 8:2).

RAPHAH [RAY fah] (*God has healed*) — a descendant of King Saul of the tribe of Benjamin (1 Chr. 8:37; Rapha, KJV), also spelled Rephaiah (1 Chr. 9:43).

RAPHU [RAY foo] (*healed*) — the father of Palti (Num. 13:9). Palti was one of 12 men sent by Moses into Canaan as spies.

RAS SHAMRA [rahs SHAHM ruh] (*fennel mound*) — the modern name of the mound (Minet el–Beida) which marks the site of the ancient city of UGARIT. The site is on the coast of Syria, opposite the island of Cyprus.

Beginning in 1929 a team of French archaeologists worked at excavating Ras Shamra–Ugarit. Many clay tablets, inscribed in CUNEIFORM, were unearthed. These tablets were written in Ugaritic, a Semitic language closely related to Phoenician and Hebrew. They contain mythological texts and religious poetry of the ancient Canaanite religions, indicating that although El was the head of the Canaanite gods, he was being replaced by Baal.

The excavations at Ras Shamra–Ugarit also brought to light a great palace and two temples, dedicated to the pagan gods Baal and Dagon. Ras Shamra–Ugarit disappeared about 1200 B.C.

RAT, RAVEN (see ANIMALS OF THE BIBLE).

RAZOR (see TOOLS OF THE BIBLE).

REAIA [ree AY uh] — a form of REAIAH No. 2.

REAIAH [ree AY uh] (*Jehovah sees*) — the name of three men in the Old Testament:

1. A son of Shobal (1 Chr. 4:2), also called Haroeh (1 Chr. 2:52).

2. A son of Micah (1 Chr. 5:5; Reaia, KJV).

3. The founder of a family of Temple servants whose descendants returned with Zerubbabel from the Captivity (Ezra 2:47; Neh. 7:50).

REAPING — the practice of harvesting grain. A sickle, with a short handle and a curved blade, was normally used for reaping. These tools were made of flint, bone, bronze, and iron. A supervisor organized the reapers (Ruth 2:5), who were often hired for daily wages (Deut. 24:15; Matt. 20:1–16) and provided with food (Job 24:10–11). The workers were followed by the poor and the foreigners such as RUTH, who gathered the leftover grain from the harvest (Deut. 24:19).

REBA [REE buh] (*offspring*) — one of five Midianite kings killed by the Israelites in the plains of Moab (Num. 31:8).

REBECCA [ruh BEK uh] — a form of REBEKAH.

REBEKAH [ruh BEK uh] (*cow*) — the wife of Isaac and the mother of Esau and Jacob. The story of Rebekah (Genesis 24) begins when Abraham, advanced in age, instructs his chief servant to go to Mesopotamia and seek a bride for Isaac. Abraham insisted that Isaac marry a young woman from his own country and kindred, not a Canaanite.

When Abraham's servant arrived at Padan Aram, he brought his caravan to a well outside the city. At the well he asked the Lord for a sign that would let him know which young woman was to be Isaac's bride. When Rebekah came to the well carrying her water pitcher, she not only gave the servant a drink of water from her pitcher but she also offered to draw water for his camels. These actions were the signs for which the servant had prayed, and he knew that Rebekah was the young woman whom the Lord God had chosen for Isaac.

When the servant asked Rebekah her name and the name of her family, he learned that she was the granddaughter of Nahor (Abraham's brother) and, therefore, was the grand-niece of Abraham. The servant then told Rebekah and her father the nature of his mission, and she chose to go to Canaan and become Isaac's wife.

When a famine struck the land of Canaan, Isaac took Rebekah to Gerar, a city of the Philistines (Gen. 26:1–11). Fearful that Rebekah's beauty would lead the Philistines to kill him and seize his wife, he told them she was his sister. Abimelech, king of the Philistines, criticized Isaac for this deception. A similar story is told of Abraham and Sarah, who were scolded for their deception by Abimelech, king of Gerar (Gen. 20:1–18).

Nor was Rebekah above deception. When the time came for Isaac to give his birthright to Esau, she conspired with Jacob and tricked Isaac into giving it to Jacob instead. Jacob was forced to flee to Padan Aram to escape Esau's wrath.

As a result of her scheming, Rebekah never again saw her beloved son. Apparently she died while Jacob was in Mesopotamia. She was buried in the cave of Machpelah (Gen. 49:30–31), where Abraham, Isaac, Jacob, Sarah, and Leah were also buried.

Rebekah's name is spelled Rebecca in the New Testament (Rom. 9:10).

RECAH [REE kuh] — a form of RECHAH.

RECHAB [REE kab] (*charioteer*) — the name of three men in the Old Testament:

1. A son of Rimmon, a Benjamite from Beeroth (2 Sam. 4:2, 5, 9). Rechab and his brother Baanah were both captains in the army of Ishbosheth (the son of King Saul), with whom David struggled for Israel's throne after Saul's death. While Ishbosheth was lying in his bed, Rechab and Baanah stabbed him in his stomach and beheaded him. The next day they brought Ishbosheth's head to David, thinking he would be pleased and would reward them. Instead, "David commanded his young men, and they executed them, cut off their hands and feet, and hanged them by the pool in Hebron" (2 Sam. 4:12).

2. The father of JEHONADAB (2 Kin. 10:15, 23). Jehonadab assisted Jehu in his violent purge of the house of Ahab and zealous war against Baal worshipers. Jehonadab was the ancestor of the RECHABITES (Jer. 35:1–19).

3. The father of Malchijah (Neh. 3:14). Malchijah may have been the head of the Rechabites after the Captivity. Malchijah helped Nehemiah rebuild the wall of Jerusalem.

RECHABITES [REE kab ights] — a Kenite tribe founded by Jonadab, the son of Rechab (Jer. 35:1–9). The Rechabites were convinced it was easier to live a godly life as nomads than in the settled life of the cities, where they would be tempted to compromise with idolatry and immorality. They did not drink wine or any other intoxicating drink; they chose to live in tents rather than houses; and they refused to plant crops or own vineyards. This strict life-style was similar to the law of the NAZIRITE (Num. 6:1–21).

The only biblical description of the Rechabites occurs in Jeremiah 35. When Nebuchadnezzar's army attacked Judah and besieged Jerusalem, the Rechabites sought refuge in the city (Jer. 35:11). Jeremiah tested them to see if they would live up to their vows. He set wine before them and encouraged them to drink, but they refused. Jeremiah praised them and held them up as an object lesson to the people of Judah who had disobeyed the laws of God.

Because of their faithfulness, Jeremiah promised that the Rechabites would never cease to exist (Jer. 35:18–19). A rabbinic tradition says that the daughters of the Rechabites were married to the sons of the Levites and that their children ministered in the Temple. Professed followers of this group still live in the Middle East—in Iraq and Yemen.

RECHAH [REE kuh] (meaning unknown) — a village in Judah (1 Chr. 4:12; Recah, NASB, NIV, RSV), location unknown.

RECONCILIATION — the process by which God and man are brought together again. The Bible teaches that God and man are alienated from one another because of God's holiness and man's sinfulness. Although God loves the sinner (Rom. 5:8), it is impossible for Him not to judge sin (Heb. 10:27). Therefore, in biblical reconciliation, both parties are affected. Through the sacrifice of Christ, man's sin is atoned and God's wrath is appeased. Thus, a relationship of hostility and alienation is changed into one of peace and fellowship.

The initiative in reconciliation was taken by God—while we were still sinners and "enemies," Christ died for us (Rom. 5:8, 10; Col. 1:21). Reconciliation is thus God's own completed act, something that takes place before human actions such as confession, repentance, and restitution. God Himself "has reconciled us to Himself through Jesus Christ" (2 Cor. 5:18).

Paul regarded the gospel as "the word of reconciliation" (2 Cor. 5:19). And knowing "the terror of the Lord," Paul pleaded, implored, and persuaded men: "Be reconciled to God" (2 Cor. 5:20).

RECORDER (see OCCUPATIONS AND TRADES).

RED (see COLORS OF THE BIBLE).

RED HEIFER — a young cow "without blemish" that was slaughtered outside the camp of the Israelites and then burned in the fire. Its ashes were used as a SIN OFFERING to bring about PURIFICATION from uncleanness. The need for purification from uncleanness would arise when a person touched a corpse, a human bone, or a grave (Num. 19:2–17).

The entire heifer—its hide, flesh, blood, and intestines—was to be burned. A priest would cast into fire cedar wood (symbolic of durability), hyssop (symbolic of healing, cleansing power), and scarlet thread (probably symbolic of the blood that atones for sin). When a case of uncleanness arose, the ashes of the red heifer were to be mixed in a vessel with "living" (fresh spring) water and sprinkled with hyssop over the unclean person and his dwelling.

Also see SACRIFICIAL OFFERINGS.

RED JASPER (see JEWELS AND PRECIOUS STONES).

RED SEA — a narrow body of water (see Map 1, B-3) that stretches in a southeasterly direction from Suez to the Gulf of Aden for about 2,100 kilometers (1,300 miles). It is an important section of a large volcanic split in the earth that goes southward into east Africa and continues north along the Jordan Valley to the Lebanon mountain range.

The Red Sea separates two large portions of land. On the east are Yemen and Saudi Arabia. On the west are Egypt, the Sudan, and Ethiopia. From ancient times the Red Sea has been an impressive sea covering some 169,000 square miles. It measures about 310 kilomers (190 miles) at its widest part

and almost 2,900 meters (about 9,500 feet) at its greatest depth. The Red Sea branches at its northern end into two distinct channels, the northeasterly one being the Gulf of Aqaba and the northwesterly one named the Gulf of Suez. The Suez branch is fairly shallow and has broad plains on either side. By contrast, the Gulf of Aqaba is deep and clear, with a narrow shoreline.

The Red Sea is usually bright turquoise, but periodically algae grows in the water. When they die, the sea becomes reddish-brown, thus giving it the name, the Red Sea. This body of water has the reputation of being one of the hottest and saltiest on earth. The reason for this is the presence of volcanic slits in the ocean floor that have become filled with salt deposits and other minerals. The sea is heavily traveled because the Suez Canal links it with the Mediterranean. But navigation is difficult at the southern end because of outcroppings of coral reefs that force ships into a narrow channel of water. No large rivers flow into the Red Sea, and there is little rainfall in the area which it crosses.

The name Red Sea has found its way into the Bible as a translation of the Hebrew *yam suph*, which means "sea of reeds" and not "Red Sea." The term *suph* comes from the Egyptian *twf*, meaning "papyrus." This confusion is unfortunate because papyrus reeds and similar vegetation do not grow in the Red Sea or in the Gulf of Suez. This fact excludes them as the area that witnessed the deliverance of the Hebrew captives at the time of the EXODUS.

The term *yam suph*, however, seems to have been applied from the time of Solomon onwards to some area near to, or identical with, the Gulf of Aqaba. In 1 Kings 9:26 Ezion Geber, Solomon's port in the Gulf, is described as being on the shore of the *yam suph* in the land of Edom. A further probable reference to the Gulf of Aqaba is in Jeremiah 49:21. In this prophecy dealing with Edom, Jeremiah spoke of their desolation being heard as far as the *yam suph*.

Perhaps the place-name Suph in Deuteronomy 1:1, where Moses spoke God's words to the Israelites, was either a shortened form of *yam suph*, indicating the Gulf of Aqaba, or some settlement in that area. Just before Korah, Dathan, and Abiram met their end as the result of an earthquake, the Israelites had been instructed to go into the wilderness by way of the *yam suph* (Deut. 1:40). At a later stage, after the death of Aaron, the Hebrews left Mount Hor by a route near the *yam suph* to go around hostile Edomite territory (Num. 21:4). Such a journey would have brought them to the northeast of the Gulf of Aqaba, which might suggest that this body of water was being described by the term *yam suph*.

There is a strong argument against identifying the Gulf of Aqaba with the *yam suph*, or "Red Sea," that the fleeing Israelites crossed under the leadership of Moses. A crossing of the Gulf of Aqaba would have taken the Israelites much too far from the Goshen area. To reach the gulf they would have

Photo by Howard Vos

A rocky shore along the Red Sea, at a point north of where the Israelites crossed during the Exodus (Exodus 14).

had to skirt the western edge of the Wilderness of Shur and make a direct southeast journey through the rugged central Sinai region and the Wilderness of Paran. Having crossed this *yam suph*, the Israelites would then have had to go north and then return to the Sinai Peninsula to meet with God at Mount Horeb.

An alternative suggestion is to regard the term *yam suph* not merely as describing a specific body of water, but as a general title that could be applied to any marshy area where reeds and papyri grew. The Egyptians used such terms in a wide sense. In the 15th century B.C. they spoke of both the Mediterranean and the Red Sea as the "Great Green Sea." Since there were several marshes in the Nile Delta, *yam suph* could apply to any one of them. It is even possible that the *yam suph* of Numbers 33:10–11 referred to the Gulf of Suez but that the Israelite visit there occurred after the Exodus. If that part of the Red Sea was actually meant, the description was not completely accurate since reeds do not flourish in the Gulf of Suez. The view that the Gulf of Suez extended much further northward into the area of the Bitter Lakes during the time of the Exodus cannot be supported by archaeological evidence or other studies.

The best understanding of *yam suph* is that it does not refer to the Red Sea or any of its branches. Instead, it probably refers to a shallow amount of water bordered by papyrus reeds and located somewhere between the southern edge of Lake Menzaleh and the lakes close to the head of the Gulf of Suez that were drained when the Suez Canal was constructed. Such a location for the Exodus would be directly opposite the Wilderness of Shur, which was the first encampment of the Israelites after crossing the *yam suph* (Ex. 15:22).

REDEEM (see REDEMPTION).

REDEEMER — one who frees or delivers another from difficulty, danger, or bondage, usually by the payment of a ransom price. In the Old Testament the redeemer could function in several ways. He could buy back property (and even enslaved people) sold under duress (Lev. 25:23–32). He (usually as owner, not as a relative) often redeemed from the Lord dedicated property and firstborn livestock (Lev. 27:1–33; also Ex. 21:28–30). He could (as "legal avenger") take the life of one who had murdered his relative as a blood price (Num. 35:12–28).

Boaz's function as redeemer for Ruth (Ruth 3:13—4:10) is well known, as is Job's resurrection hope in God, his Redeemer (Job 19:25). God Himself is the Redeemer of Israel, a fact mentioned 18 times—especially by the prophet Isaiah (Ps. 78:35; Is. 41:14).

In the New Testament, Christ is viewed as the ultimate Redeemer, although the Greek word for redeemer is not used. Jesus gave His life as "a ransom for many" (Mark 10:45). Thus, the apostle Paul speaks of believers as having "redemption through His blood" (Eph. 1:7).

REDEMPTION — deliverance by payment of a price. In the New Testament, redemption refers to salvation from sin, death, and the wrath of God by Christ's sacrifice. In the Old Testament, the word redemption refers to redemption by a KINSMAN (Lev. 25:24, 51–52; Ruth 4:6; Jer. 32:7–8), rescue or deliverance (Num. 3:49), and ransom (Ps. 111:9; 130:7). In the New Testament it refers to loosing (Luke 2:38; Heb. 9:12) and loosing away (Luke 21:28; Rom. 3:24; Eph. 1:14).

In the Old Testament redemption was applied to property, animals, persons, and the nation of Israel as a whole. In nearly every instance, freedom from obligation, bondage, or danger was secured by the payment of a price, a ransom, bribe, satisfaction, or sum of money paid to obtain freedom, favor, or reconciliation. Men may redeem property, animals, and individuals (slaves, prisoners, indentured relatives) who are legally obligated to God or in bondage for other reasons. God alone, however, is able to redeem from the slavery of sin (Ps. 130:7–8), enemy oppressors (Deut. 15:15), and the power of death (Job 19:25–26; Ps. 49:8–9).

The New Testament emphasizes the tremendous cost of redemption: "the precious blood of Christ" (1 Pet. 1:19; Eph. 1:7), which is also called an atoning sacrifice, "a propitiation by His blood" (Rom. 3:25). Believers are exhorted to remember the "price" of their redemption as a motivation to personal holiness (1 Cor. 6:19–20; 1 Pet. 1:13–19). The Bible also emphasizes the result of redemption: freedom from sin and freedom to serve God through Jesus Christ our Lord.

How can we fail to rejoice, having been freed from the oppressive bondage of slavery to sin (John 8:34; Rom. 6:18), the law (Gal. 4:3–5; 5:1), and the fear of death (Heb. 2:14–15)? "Therefore if the Son makes you free, you shall be free indeed" (John 8:36).

REED (see PLANTS OF THE BIBLE; WEIGHTS AND MEASURES).

REED–PIPE (see MUSICAL INSTRUMENTS).

REED, VESSELS OF — boats or seagoing vessels made of reed (Is. 18:2; vessels of papyrus, RSV; vessels of bulrushes, KJV). Some boats on the Nile River, apparently used for fishing, were made by tying together long bundles of papyrus or reeds and daubing them with pitch. In Mesopotamia similar vessels were made of reeds, caulked with bitumen, and used on the Tigris and Euphrates Rivers.

REELAIAH [ree uh LIGH uh] (*Jehovah has caused trembling*) — an Israelite chief who returned from the Captivity with Zerubbabel (Ezra 2:2), also called Raamiah (Neh. 7:7).

REFINE — to separate pure metal from the impurities in the ore in the smelting process. This procedure is spoken of in the Old Testament as a symbol of God's purification of the nation of Israel when he sent hardship and affliction upon them in punishment for their sins (Jer. 9:7; Zech. 13:9).

REFINER (see OCCUPATIONS AND TRADES).

REFINING POT — a vessel used in the production of silver (Prov. 17:3; 27:21). The smelting done in this pot could have been either the last of several steps in the refining process or the remelting of scraps to recover precious metals.

REFORMATION — an improvement by change or correction. The Old Testament priesthood and sacrifices, along with its food laws and ritual washings, was "imposed until the time of reformation" (Heb. 9:10; the new order, NIV). The reformation

referred to in this verse is the NEW COVENANT established by Jesus Christ, who is both the eternal High Priest and the sacrifice offered once and for all for our sins.

REFUGE, CITIES OF (see CITIES OF REFUGE).

REFUSE GATE (see GATES OF JERUSALEM AND THE TEMPLE).

REGEM [REE guhm] (*a friend*) — a son of Jahdai, of the tribe of Judah (1 Chr. 2:47).

REGEM–MELECH [ree guhm MEE lek] (*friend of the king*) — one of a group of men sent to the Temple to ask about a day of national mourning (Zech. 7:2). They were instructed to ask the priests and prophets whether they should continue to observe fasts in remembrance of the destruction of the Temple.

REGENERATION — the spiritual change brought about in a person's life by an act of God. In regeneration a person's sinful nature is changed, and he is enabled to respond to God in faith.

The word regeneration occurs only in the New Testament (Matt. 19:28; Titus 3:5), but the concept or idea is common throughout the Bible. The literal meaning of regeneration is "born again." There is a first birth and a second birth. The first, as Jesus said to Nicodemus (John 3:1–12) is "of the flesh"; the second birth is "of the Spirit." Being born of the Spirit is essential before a person can enter the kingdom of God. Every biblical command to man to undergo a radical change of character from self–centeredness to God–centeredness is, in effect, an appeal to be "born again" (Ps. 51:5–11; Jer. 31:33; Zech. 13:1).

Great religious experiences like that of Jacob at Jabbok (Gen. 32:22–32), Moses at the burning bush (Ex. 3:1), Josiah on hearing the reading of the Law (2 Kin. 22:8–13), or Isaiah in the Temple (Is. 6:1–8) might well be regarded as "new birth." Thus, regeneration involves an enlightening of the mind, a change of the will, and a renewed nature. It extends to the total nature of man, changing a person's desires and restoring him to a right relationship with God in Christ.

The need for regeneration grows out of humanity's sinfulness. It is brought about through God's initiative. God works in the human heart, and the person responds to God through faith. Thus, regeneration is an act of God through the Holy Spirit, resulting in resurrection from sin to a new life in Jesus Christ (2 Cor. 5:17).

REGIMENT — one of ten divisions of an ancient Roman legion. The traditional Roman legion consisted of 6,000 soldiers. A regiment, or cohort, consisted of about 600 men, although this number varied. The Book of Acts mentions the ITALIAN REGIMENT (Acts 10:1; band, KJV; cohort, RSV, NEB, NASB) and the AUGUSTAN REGIMENT (Acts 27:1; band, KJV)

REGISTER (see CENSUS).

REHABIAH [ree uh BIGH uh] (*Jehovah widens*) — a son of Eliezer and grandson of Moses (1 Chr. 23:17; 26:25).

REHOB [REE hahb] (*open space*) — the name of three cities and two men in the Old Testament:

1. A city in northern Palestine in the upper Jordan River Valley (Num. 13:21). Rehob is the same place as BETH REHOB (Judg. 18:28; 2 Sam. 10:6).

2. A city in the territory of Asher, near Sidon (Josh. 19:28).

3. Another city in the territory of Asher (Josh. 19:30). The Israelites did not drive the Canaanites out of one of these Rehobs; the other Rehob was occupied by the Gershonite Levites.

4. The father of Hadadezer (2 Sam. 8:3:12), king of Zobah.

5. A Levite who sealed Nehemiah's covenant (Neh. 10:11).

REHOBOAM [ree uh BOE uhm] (*the people is enlarged*) — the son and successor of Solomon and the last king of the united monarchy and first king of the southern kingdom, Judah (reigned about 931–913 B.C). His mother was Naamah, a woman of Ammon (1 Kin. 14:31).

Rehoboam became king at age 41 (1 Kin. 14:21) at a time when the northern tribes were discontented with the monarchy. They were weary of Solomon's heavy taxation and labor conscription. To promote unity, Rehoboam went to Shechem—center of much of the discontent among the northern tribes—to be made king officially and to meet with their leaders. They in turn demanded relief from the taxes and conscription.

Rehoboam first sought advice from older men who were of mature judgment and who had lived through Solomon's harsh years. They assured him that if he would be the people's servant, he would enjoy popular support. When he also sought the counsel of younger men, his arrogant contemporaries, he received foolish advice that he should rule by sternness rather than kindness. Misjudging the situation, he followed the foolish advice. The northern tribes immediately seceded from the kingdom and made JEROBOAM king.

When Rehoboam attempted to continue his control over the northern tribes by sending Adoram to collect a tax from the people (1 Kin. 12:18), Adoram was stoned to death. Rehoboam fled in his chariot to Jerusalem. The prophet Shemaiah prevented Rehoboam from retaliating and engaging in civil war (1 Kin. 12:22–24).

To strengthen Judah, Rehoboam fortified 15 cities (2 Chr. 11:5–12) to the west and south of Jerusalem, undoubtedly as a defensive measure against Egypt. The spiritual life of Judah was strengthened, too, by the immigration of northern priests and Levites to Judah and Jerusalem because of the idolatrous worship instituted at Bethel and Dan by Jeroboam (2 Chr. 11:13–17).

Rehoboam's military encounters were primarily with Jeroboam and Egypt. No specific battles with Jeroboam are described in the Bible, but "there was war between Rehoboam and Jeroboam all their days" (1 Kin. 14:30). This warring probably involved border disputes over the territory of Benjamin, the buffer zone between the two kingdoms.

In Rehoboam's fifth year Judah was invaded by Shishak (Sheshonk I), king of Egypt, who came against Jerusalem and carried away treasures from the Temple and from Solomon's house. When Shemaiah told him that this invasion was God's judgment for Judah's sin, Rehoboam humbled himself before God and was granted deliverance from further troubles (2 Chr. 12:1–12).

Rehoboam did not follow the pattern of David. Instead, he was an evil king (2 Chr. 12:14). During his 17–year reign, the people of Judah built "high places, sacred pillars, and wooden images" (1 Kin. 1:23) and permitted "perverted persons" to prosper in the land (1 Kin. 14:24). When he died, he was buried in the City of David (1 Kin. 14:31).

REHOBOTH [rih HOE buhth] (*broad places*) — a well dug by Isaac in the Valley of Gerar (Gen. 26:22). Rehoboth is probably present–day Wadi Ruheibeh, about 31 kilometers (19 miles) southwest of Beersheba.

REHOBOTH–BY–THE–RIVER [rih HOE buhth] (*broad places*) — a city somewhere in northern Edom (Gen. 36:37; 1 Chr. 1:48), location unknown. The city was the home of Saul, an early king of Edom.

REHOBOTH IR [rih HOE buhth ur] (*broad places of the city*) — a suburb or outlying area of the city of Nineveh (Gen. 10:11) in Assyria.

REHUM [REE huhm] (*compassion*) — the name of five men in the Old Testament:

1. A chief Israelite who returned from the Captivity with Zerubbabel (Ezra 2:2), also called Nehum (Neh. 7:7).

2. A Persian official in Samaria during the reign of Artaxerxes I (king of Persia, 465—425 B.C.). Rehum opposed the rebuilding of the walls and the Temple of Jerusalem (Ezra 4:8–9, 17, 23).

3. A leader of the Levites who helped repair the wall of Jerusalem (Neh. 3:17).

4. A leader of the people who sealed the covenant after the Captivity (Neh. 10:25).

5. A group of priests and Levites who returned with Zerubbabel from the Captivity (Neh. 12:3).

REI [ree] (*friendly*) — a man who supported Solomon when Adonijah, the son of David, tried to take over the throne (1 Kin. 1:8).

REINS — KJV word for KIDNEYS when kidneys are spoken of in a symbolic rather than a literal sense. For God to examine a person's reins and heart (Jer. 11:20) means that He knows a person's inner thoughts and motives.

REKEM [REE kuhm] (*friendship*) — the name of two men and a city in the Old Testament:

1. A king of Midian killed by the Israelites during the time of Moses (Num. 31:8).

2. A city in the territory of Benjamin (Josh. 18:27), location unknown.

3. A son of Hebron, of the tribe of Judah (1 Chr. 2:43–44).

RELEASE, YEAR OF — a term applied to the Year of JUBILEE, the end of a cycle of seven sabbatical years. To safeguard against a small group gaining control of much land and people falling into poverty because of high interest, the Year of Jubilee was established (Lev. 25:8–17; 23–55). It fell every 50 years.

During this year, land that had been sold during the past 50 years was returned to its original owner, and Israelite slaves were released. The principle behind this custom was the belief that land does not belong to Israel but to God, who permits its use (Lev. 25:23). Another principle was that human beings are not to be in life–long service to other people, but to God, who freed all Israel from slavery in Egypt (Lev. 25:38, 55).

RELIGION — belief in and reverence for God or some supernatural power that is recognized as the creator and ruler of the universe; an organized system of doctrine with an approved pattern of behavior and a proper form of worship. The classic New Testament passage on religion is James 2:17. Faith divorced from deeds, says James, is as lifeless as a corpse.

REMALIAH [rim uh LIE uh] (*Jehovah increases*) — the father of King Pekah of Israel (2 Kin. 15:25–37; Is. 7:1–9).

REMETH [REE mith] (*height*) — a border town in the territory of Issachar (Josh. 19:21). Remeth is probably the same place as Ramoth (1 Chr. 6:73) and Jarmuth (Josh. 21:29).

REMISSION — to be released or set free from sin (Acts 2:38; Heb. 9:22). The active nature of the word for remission in the Greek language indicates that forgiveness is more than a passive act on God's part. Through the death of His Son, God has taken the initiative to break the grip of sin and set man free for a new way of life in God's Spirit. Also see FORGIVENESS; REPENTANCE.

REMMON [REM ahn] — a form of RIMMON No. 1.

REMMON–METHOAR [REM uhn mih THOE ahr] — a form of RIMMON No. 2.

REMNANT — the part of a community or nation that remains after a dreadful judgment or devastating calamity, especially those who have escaped and remain to form the nucleus of a new community (Is. 10:20–23). The survival of a righteous remnant rests solely on God's providential care for His Chosen People and His faithfulness to keep His COVENANT promises.

The concept of the remnant has its roots in the Book of Deuteronomy (4:27–31; 28:62–68; 30:1–10), where Moses warned the people of Israel that they would be scattered among the nations. But God also promised that He would bring the people back from captivity and establish them again in the land of their fathers. This concept was picked up by the prophets, who spoke of the Assyrian and Babylonian captivities. The concept was extended to apply also to the gathering of a righteous remnant at the time when the Messiah came to establish His kingdom.

In Amos and Isaiah the remnant consisted of those chosen by God who were rescued from the impending doom of the nation (Is. 1:9; Amos 5:14–

Excavations at ancient Succoth, an Old Testament city in the territory of Gad in eastern Palestine.
Photo: Levant Photo Service

15). As such, they were labeled "the poor," those who suffer for God (Is. 29:19; 41:17). At the same time, they serve God and stand before the nation as witnesses, calling the people to repent of their rebellion.

In the New Testament the apostle Paul picked up the teaching of Isaiah and other prophets about the remnant and applied it to the church (Rom. 11:5). Paul showed that God's purpose is seen in the "remnant" out of Israel who have joined the Gentiles to form the church, the new people of God. Further, Jesus' choice of twelve apostles built upon remnant themes. Symbolizing the twelve tribes, the apostles became the remnant who erected a new structure, the church, upon the foundation of Israel. In the church, both Jews and Gentiles, circumcised and uncircumcised, find their true spiritual home when they believe in Christ.

REMPHAN [RIM fan] — KJV word for Rephan, a pagan god of the Babylonians. Also see GODS, PAGAN.

REND — to tear or pull apart. In the ancient world, rending one's garments was a sign of grief, despair, or sorrow. To "rend your heart" (Joel 2:13) signified inward, spiritual repentance and sorrow for sin. God's primary requirement from sinners is "a broken and a contrite heart" (Ps. 51:17). Also see MOURN.

REPENTANCE — a turning away from sin, disobedience, or rebellion and a turning back to God (Matt. 9:13; Luke 5:32). In a more general sense, repentance means a change of mind (Gen. 6:6–7) or a feeling of remorse or regret for past conduct (Matt. 27:3). True repentance is a "godly sorrow" for sin, an act of turning around and going in the opposite direction. This type of repentance leads to a fundamental change in a person's relationship to God.

In the Old Testament the classic case of repentance is that of King David, after Nathan the prophet accused him of killing Uriah the Hittite and committing adultery with Uriah's wife, Bathsheba. David's prayer of repentance for this sin is found in Psalm 51.

In the New Testament the keynote of John the Baptist's preaching was, "Repent, for the kingdom of heaven is at hand" (Matt. 3:2). To the multitudes he declared, "Bear fruits worthy of repentance" (Matt. 3:8; Luke 3:8). When Jesus began His ministry, He took up John's preaching of the message of repentance, expanding the message to include the good news of salvation: "The time is fulfilled, and the kingdom of God is at hand. Repent and believe in the gospel" (Matt. 4:17; Mark 1:15).

In Jesus' preaching of the kingdom of God is seen the truth that repentance and faith are two sides of the same coin: by repentance, one turns away from sin; by faith, one turns toward God in accepting the Lord Jesus Christ. Such a twofold turning, or conversion, is necessary for entrance into the kingdom (Matt. 18:3). "Unless you repent," said Jesus, "you will all likewise perish" (Luke 13:3, 5). This is the negative, or judgmental, side of Jesus' message.

The positive, or merciful, side is seen in these words: "There is joy in the presence of the angels of God over one sinner who repents" (Luke 15:10).

After Jesus' crucifixion and resurrection, His disciples continued His message of repentance and faith (Acts 2:38; 3:19; 20:21; 26:20). Repentance is a turning from wickedness and dead works (Acts 8:22; Heb. 6:1) toward God and His glory (Acts 20:21; Rev. 16:9), eternal life (Acts 11:18), and a knowledge of the truth (2 Tim. 2:25).

Repentance is associated with prayer (1 Kin. 8:47), belief (Mark 1:15), baptism (Acts 2:38), and conversion (Acts 3:19) and is accompanied by humility (Matt. 11:21). Repentance is God's will and pleasure (Luke 15:7–10; 2 Pet. 3:9), as well as His command (Mark 6:12; Acts 17:30). It is a gift of His sovereign love (Acts 5:31; 11:18; Rom. 2:4; 2 Tim. 2:25), without which we cannot be saved (Luke 13:3).

REPHAEL [REF ay el] (*God heals*) — gatekeeper of the sanctuary during the time of King David (1 Chr. 26:7).

REPHAH [REE fuh] (*agreeable*) — a descendant of Ephraim (1 Chr. 7:25) who became an ancestor of Joshua.

REPHAIAH [rih FAY uh] (*Jehovah heals*) — the name of five men in the Old Testament:
1. The head of a family of the house of David (1 Chr. 3:21).
2. A son of Ishi, of the tribe of Simeon (1 Chr. 4:41–43).
3. A son of Tola, of the tribe of Issachar (1 Chr. 7:2).
4. A son of Binea (1 Chr. 9:43), also called Raphah (1 Chr. 8:37).
5. A son of Hur (Neh. 3:9) who helped Nehemiah rebuild the wall of Jerusalem.

REPHAIM [REF ih yuhm] (*lofty men*) — the name of a race of giants and a valley in the Old Testament:
1. A race of giants who lived in Palestine before the time of Abraham (Gen. 14:5; 15:20). The last survivor of the Rephaim was OG, king of Bashan (Deut. 3:11). The kingdom of Og—Gilead, Bashan, and Argob—was called "the land of the giants [Rephaim]" (Deut. 3:13).
2. A valley in Judah where David defeated the Philistines (2 Sam. 5:17–22). Rephaim lies between Jerusalem and Bethlehem (2 Sam. 23:13).

REPHAN (see GODS, PAGAN).

REPHIDIM [REF uh dim] (*refreshments*) — an Israelite encampment in the wilderness (Ex. 17:1–7). The Amalekites attacked the Israelites at Rephidim (Ex. 17:8–16). During the battle Moses stood on a hill and held the rod of God aloft. Aaron and Hur supported his arms until sundown, and the Israelites won the battle.

REPROACH — to suffer scorn, rebuke, or shame (1 Tim. 3:7). On the cross Christ bore the shame of our sin. Followers of Jesus are called to bear the reproach of Christ and to suffer for His name (2 Cor. 12:10; 1 Pet. 4:14).

REPROBATE — one who fails to pass a test and is rejected. While the word reprobate only appears in the KJV, it speaks graphically of those whom God has rejected and left to their own corruption (Rom. 1:28). The word is also found once in the Old Testament, where the prophet Jeremiah speaks of "reprobate silver" (Jer. 6:30, KJV).

REPTILE (see ANIMALS OF THE BIBLE).

REPUTATION — the general estimation in which a person is held by others. A person's reputation may be ruined by careless deeds or words (Prov. 25:8-10). The apostle Paul declared that Christ "made Himself of no reputation" by dying on the cross for our sins (Phil. 2:7).

RESEN [REE zuhn] (meaning unknown) — an ancient Assyrian city built by NIMROD between Calah and Nineveh (Gen. 10:12). Its exact location is unknown.

RESERVOIR — any large storage place for water. The frequent threat of an extended siege and the infrequent rain in Palestine made it necessary for the people to store water in large quantities. The normal way to do this was to catch rainfall and channel it to a storage area.

There were basically two types of reservoirs. One was a large, open pool for public use. The other type was an underground pit or cistern, lined with plaster, to which the rain that fell on the roof was diverted.

RESH [raysh] — the 20th letter of the Hebrew alphabet, used as a heading over Psalm 119:153-160. In the original Hebrew language, every line of these eight verses began with the letter resh. Also see ACROSTIC.

RESHEPH [REE shef] (a flame) — the name of a man and a pagan god in the Old Testament:
1. A son of Beriah (1 Chr. 7:25).
2. A Canaanite god worshiped as the lord of the underworld.

RESIN (see JEWELS AND PRECIOUS STONES).

RESPECT OF PERSONS — showing favoritism or partiality toward some people as opposed to others (Acts 10:34; James 2:1, 9). Also see PARTIALITY.

RESTITUTION — the act of restoring to the rightful owner something that has been taken away, stolen, lost, or surrendered. Leviticus 6:1-7 gives the Mosaic Law of restitution; this law establishes the procedure to be followed in restoring stolen property.

Full restitution of the property had to be made and an added 20 percent (one-fifth of its value) must be paid as compensation (Lev. 5:16). If a man stole an ox or donkey or sheep, and the animal was recovered alive, the thief had to make restitution of double the value stolen (Ex. 22:4). If the thief had killed or sold the animal, however, he had to make a fourfold (for a sheep) or a fivefold (for an ox) restitution (Ex. 22:1).

In the New Testament, the word restitution is not used, but the idea is expressed. Zacchaeus, a chief tax collector, said to Jesus, "If I have taken anything from anyone by false accusation, I restore fourfold" (Luke 19:8).

Also see LAW.

RESURRECTION — being raised from the dead. Resurrection has three primary meanings in the Bible.

1. *Miraculous healings.* In this usage, resurrection refers to individuals who have been brought back to life (resuscitated) in this present world. Such raisings were performed by Elijah on the Zarephath widow's son (1 Kin. 17:20-24), by Elisha on the Shunammite woman's son (2 Kin. 4:32-37) and the dead man who touched Elisha's bones (2 Kin. 13:21), by Jesus on Jairus' daughter (Mark 5:41-43) and Lazarus (John 11:43-44), by Peter on Dorcas (Acts 9:40-41), and by Paul on Eutychus (Acts 20:9-12). In these raisings there is no suggestion that the person will not again experience death.

2. *Our Lord's resurrection.* This resurrection is clearly linked with the overcoming of the powers of evil and death. For Paul, Christ's resurrection is the basis for the doctrine of general resurrection (1 Cor. 15:12-19). (See RESURRECTION OF JESUS CHRIST.)

3. *The hope of a general resurrection.* Many of the Greek philosophers, such as Plato, believed that an immortal soul inhabited a body and that at death the soul left its bodily prison and soared upward to the divine spirit. In the Old Testament Sheol is the place of the rephaim (shades), the Hebrew term for a weakened existence (Is. 14:9-11). These beings, however, are not souls without bodies. Therefore, the psalmist expected that God would ransom his soul from Sheol (Ps. 49:15). It was Israel's firm belief in the goodness of God that led the Jewish people to believe that the righteous dead would yet see God (Job 19:26). This expectation was the foundation upon which the Jewish ideas concerning the resurrection were built.

By the time of Jesus, two positions were firmly entrenched within Judaism. The SADDUCEES, who were oriented to this world, rejected any belief in the resurrection. They believed that such an idea was irrelevant to this life and was not part of the revelation which God gave to Moses. When they encountered Jesus, the Sadducees sought to trap Him by their question concerning the seven brothers who married one woman. Jesus criticized their view of resurrection life by indicating that earthly marriage patterns are not repeated in heaven. He also condemned their understanding of Moses and the Scriptures (Mark 12:18-27).

The PHARISEES, in contrast, believed in a resurrection. The Jewish historian Josephus reported that the Pharisees held that the good dead are transferred into other bodies. Although this report is not totally clear, it is certain that the Pharisees proclaimed a life after death that required a resur-

A tomb carved out of limestone rock, similar to the tomb in which Jesus was buried. A large stone was rolled across the entrance to seal the tomb (Mark 15:46).

rection. It was from the ranks of these scholarly Pharisees that the apostle Paul came (Phil. 3:5). Luke records that in his defense before the Sanhedrin (Jewish Council), Paul stressed that he was a Pharisee of Pharisaic descent and that he was on trial for affirming the resurrection (Acts 23:6).

Israel's concepts of the resurrection were born out of her relationship to God in her tumultuous history. At first glance the prophet Isaiah seems to express a view that the resurrection is for the faithful and that the wicked may not arise (Is. 26:10–19). The Jewish loyalist of the apocryphal book of 2 Maccabees apparently agreed that for some there will be no resurrection to life. But Daniel announced, "Many of those who sleep in the dust of the earth shall awake, some to everlasting life, some to shame and everlasting contempt" (Dan. 12:2).

The New Testament consistently teaches hope in the resurrection of the believer based upon the resurrection of Christ as the "firstborn from the dead" (1 Cor. 15:12–58; Col. 1:18; 1 Thess. 4:14–18; 1 Pet. 1:3–5). This idea of resurrection is expressed in terms of such images as a transformed body (Phil. 3:21), a new dwelling (2 Cor. 5:2), and new clothing (2 Cor. 5:4; Rev. 6:11). The New Testament also contrasts resurrection to life with resurrection to judgment (John 5:29; Acts 24:15). Apparently a similar contrast lies behind the statements in Revelation 20 about "the first resurrection" (20:5) and "the second death" (20:14).

But not all who sought identification with the Christian church proclaimed a future resurrection. Some preached a spiritual awakening, or resurrection, that was already past. Such a view, adopted by Hymenaeus and Philetus and adopted by later Gnostic heretics, was sternly condemned by Paul (2 Tim. 2:17–19).

RESURRECTION OF JESUS CHRIST — a central doctrine of Christianity that affirms that God raised Jesus from the dead on the third day. Without the resurrection, the apostle Paul declared, Christian preaching and belief are meaningless (1 Cor. 15:14). The resurrection is the point at which God's intention for Jesus becomes clear (Rom. 1:4) and believers are assured that Jesus is the Christ.

So significant is the resurrection of Jesus that without it there would be no church or Christianity, and we would still be in our sins (1 Cor. 15:17). In spite of the centrality of the resurrection, however, scholars have frequently debated a number of the elements in the resurrection accounts in the New Testament.

Empty Tomb. Some critics argue that because Paul does not speak of an empty tomb, the idea of the resurrection of Jesus must have developed years after His earthly life and ministry was over. But Paul refers to the burial (1 Cor. 15:4), which argues both for a proper tomb and against the body being dumped into a pit or a common criminal's grave.

Critics have also pointed to variations in the accounts of Jesus' resurrection in the gospels, such as how many women came to the tomb and who they were. Why did they come: to anoint the body (Mark and Matthew) or to see the tomb (Matthew)? Was there one angel (Mark and Matthew) or were there two (Luke and John) at the tomb? Did the angel say, "He is going before you into Galilee" (Mark and Matthew) or "Remember how He spoke...when He was still in Galilee" (Luke)? Did the women say "nothing to anyone" (Mark) or did they report the message to the disciples (Matthew)? (Note that most ancient manuscripts of Mark do not have 16:9–20—a fact noted in many modern English translations.)

It is well to remember that these variations were recognized by early Christians and were not discovered by recent critics. As early as the second century, Tatian wrote his *Diatessaron*, or harmony of the gospels, expecting that Christians would gladly accept his work as a substitute for the four gospels. But while Christians read Tatian, they refused to substitute his harmony for the witnesses of the four gospel writers. The faithfulness of these writers in transmitting to us the gospel texts is a testimony to Christian integrity. It is also a witness to their early understanding that the gospels were Holy Scripture, inspired by God.

Furthermore, these writers knew the tomb was empty; because if it had not been empty, the body would soon have been supplied. The only other alternative is that the disciples stole the body as the Jews (Matt. 28:13) and some modern critics have suggested. But such a view is self-defeating because the gospel accounts themselves witness to the surprise of both the women and the disciples about the empty tomb.

Moreover, while it may seem incredible to us, the gospel writers generally refrain from using the empty tomb as a basis for faith! Furthermore, the stone was not rolled away to let Jesus out; he did not need open doors to move about (Luke 24:31, 36; John 20:19, 26). The stone was removed to begin communicating the resurrection to the followers of Jesus. But the empty tomb did not convince them that Jesus was alive! It was at first frustrating to the disciples and "seemed to them like idle tales" (Luke 24:11). Would anyone contructing a story and trying to *prove* the resurrection use such an approach? These testimonies have an element of authenticity that inventors of stories seldom duplicate.

The Appearances. While the above testimonies about the empty tomb seem to have little to do with the faith of these early Christians, the appearances of Jesus are clearly at the heart of early Christian belief. The consistent witness of the New Testament is that in the appearances of Jesus something incredible happened. The two followers in Emmaus, upon realizing it was the risen Jesus, forgot their concern with the lateness of the hour and rushed back to Jerusalem to tell the others (Luke 24:29–33). The doubting Thomas uttered Christianity's greatest confession when he realized that the risen Christ was actually addressing him (John 20:27). Peter left his fishing nets for good when the risen Savior asked him, "Do you love Me?" (John 21:15). And at a later time (1 Cor. 15:8), the persecutor Paul was transformed into a zealous missionary as the result of a special appearance by the risen Lord (Acts 9:1–22).

But what was the nature of these appearances? Some have suggested that the appearance of Jesus to Paul seemed to be of a spiritual nature, similar to the revelation of Jesus to Christians today. Since Paul lumps all of the appearances together in 1 Corinthians 15:5–8, these critics argue that all the appearances must be spiritual in nature. They reject the idea that the risen Jesus could be touched (Matt. 28:9; Luke 24:39; John 20:27) or that He could eat (Luke 24:41–42).

Such a line of argument not only judges the witnesses on the basis of rationalistic assumptions, but it flies in the face of Paul's own admission that his experience was somewhat irregular. Another approach is that advocated by the German theologian Rudolph Bultmann, who speaks of an "Easter faith" of the disciples rather than an actual bodily resurrection of Jesus. Accordingly, he splits the Jesus of history from the spiritual experience of the Christ of faith.

But when the New Testament writers speak of the resurrection of Jesus, they are bearing witness not to what God did for them but what God did to Jesus. Certainly, as a result of the resurrection of Jesus human lives were transformed. For Paul this transformation of Christians is not termed resurrection but salvation. "In Christ" is the expression which Paul uses for the spiritual experience of the living Christ.

Finally, the resurrection of Jesus, His exaltation to the right hand of the Father (Acts 2:33), and the giving of the Spirit (John 20:22) are all to be seen as a single complex of events. Although the elements may be viewed as separate happenings, the New Testament writers see them as closely integrated theologically. Together they represent the firstfruits of the new age.

RETRIBUTION — the act of receiving what one deserves. While retribution may be used in the sense of a reward for doing good, it usually refers to punishment for doing evil, especially in the world to come. The word retribution is not found in the KJV, and it appears only once in the NKJV (2 Chr. 6:23). Other translations use the word more frequently (Rom. 11:9; Heb. 2:2, RSV; Deut. 32:35; 2 Thess. 1:8, NASB; Rom. 1:18; Rev. 11:18, NEB).

The principle of retribution is found often in the Bible; it is indicated by words such as wrath, vengeance, punishment, judgment, and hell. Retribution is the judgment of a holy God upon sin. Eventually it becomes the eternal punishment of the ungodly— unless the sinner turns in faith to Christ, who took the punishment the sinner deserves upon Himself on the cross.

Also see LAW.

RETURN OF CHRIST (see ESCHATOLOGY; SECOND COMING).

REU [roo] (*friend*) — a son of Peleg and father of Serug (Gen. 11:18–21; 1 Chr. 1:25). Reu is listed in Luke's genealogy of Jesus (Luke 3:35; Ragau, KJV).

REUBEN [ROO ben] (*behold a son*) — the firstborn son of Jacob, born to Leah in Paddan Aram (Gen. 29:31–32; 35:23). Leah named her first son Reuben because the Lord had looked upon her sorrow at being unloved by her husband. By presenting a son to Jacob, she hoped he would respond to her in love.

The only reference to Reuben's early childhood is his gathering of mandrakes for his mother (Gen. 30:14). Years later, as the hatred of Jacob's sons for Joseph grew, it was Reuben who advised his brothers not to kill their younger brother. He suggested that they merely bind him, which would have allowed him to return later to release Joseph to his father (Gen. 37:20–22). It also was Reuben who reminded his brothers that all their troubles and fears in Egypt were their just reward for mistreating Joseph (Gen. 42:22).

When Jacob's sons returned from Egypt, Reuben offered his own two sons as a guarantee that he would personally tend to the safety of Benjamin on the next trip to Egypt (Gen. 42:37). In view of these admirable qualities, it is tragic that he became involved in incest with Bilhah, his father's concubine (Gen. 35:22).

As the firstborn, Reuben should have been a leader to his brothers and should have received the birthright—the double portion of the inheritance (Deut. 21:17). His act of incest, however, cost him dearly. He never lost his legal standing as firstborn, but he forfeited his right to the birthright. When Reuben made his descent into Egypt with Israel, he was father of four sons who had been born to him in Canaan (Gen. 46:9).

REUBEN, TRIBE OF — the tribe whose ancestor was Reuben (Num. 1:5). During 420 years in Egypt, the descendants of Reuben increased from four sons to 46,500 men of war (Num. 1:20–21). In the wilderness the tribe of Reuben was represented in a conspiracy against Moses. As representatives of the tribe, Dathan and Abiram tried to assert their legal rights as descendants of Jacob's oldest son to a role of leadership in Israel (Num. 16:1–3), but their efforts failed.

The Reubenites were a pastoral people. The tribe requested an early inheritance east of the Jordan River where the land was suitable for cattle (Num. 32:1–33). They helped the other tribes claim their land, however, and Joshua commended them for their efforts (Josh. 22:9–10). The tribe also built an altar—along with the tribe of Gad and the half-tribe of Manasseh—in the Jordan Valley as a witness to their unity with the tribes west of the Jordan (Josh. 22:11–34).

Later, members of the tribe of Reuben refused to assist Deborah and Barak in fighting the Canaanite Sisera (Judg. 5:16), although the tribe apparently assisted the other tribes in their war against Benjamin (Judg. 20:11). During Saul's reign, Reuben joined Gad and Manasseh in fighting the Hagrites (1 Chr. 5:18–22). When the kingdom divided under Rehoboam, Reuben joined the Northern Kingdom under Jeroboam.

While never prominent, the tribe of Reuben was never forgotten. Ezekiel remembered Reuben in his description of Israel (Ezek. 48:6). The tribe is also represented in the 144,000 sealed—12,000 from each of the twelve tribes of Israel (Rev. 7:5).

REUBENITES [ROO ben ights] — the descendants of REUBEN, the oldest son of Jacob (Num. 26:7). The Reubenites were taken into exile by Tiglath-Pileser III, king of Assyria (1 Chr. 5:6, 26).

REUEL [ROO uhl] (*friend of God*) — the name of four men in the Old Testament:
1. A son of Esau and Basemath, the daughter of Ishmael (Gen. 36:4, 10; 1 Chr. 1:35).
2. A priest of Midian who became Moses' father-in-law (Num. 10:29; Raguel, KJV). Reuel is also called Jethro (Ex. 3:1).
3. The father of Eliasaph (Num. 2:14), also called Deuel (Num. 10:20).
4. A son of Ibnijah (1 Chr. 9:8).

REUMAH [ROO muh] (*coral*) — a concubine of Nahor, Abraham's brother (Gen. 22:24).

REVELATION — God's communication to people concerning Himself, His moral standards, and His plan of salvation.

God is a personal Spirit distinct from the world; He is absolutely holy and is invisible to the view of physical, finite, sinful minds. Although people, on their own, can never create truth about God, God has graciously unveiled and manifested Himself to mankind. Other religions and philosophies result from the endless human quest for God; Christianity results from God's quest for lost mankind.

God has made Himself known to all people everywhere in the marvels of nature and in the human conscience, which is able to distinguish right from wrong. Because this knowledge is universal and continuous, by it God has displayed His glory to everyone (Ps. 19:1–6).

Some Christians think that only believers can see God's revelation in nature, but the apostle Paul said that unbelievers know truth about God: The unrighteous must have the truth to "suppress" it (Rom. 1:18); they "clearly see" it (Rom 1:20); knowing God, they fail to worship Him as God (Rom. 1:21); they alter the truth (Rom. 1:25); they do not retain God in their knowledge (Rom. 1:28); and knowing the righteous judgment (moral law) of God, they disobey it (Rom. 1:32). The reason the ungodly are "inexcusable" (Rom. 2:1) before God's righteous judgment is that they possessed but rejected the truth which God gave them.

What can be known of God from nature? God's universal revelation makes it clear that God exists (Rom. 1:20), and that God, the Creator of the mountains, oceans, vegetation, animals, and mankind, is wise (Ps. 104:24) and powerful (Psalm 29; 93; Rom. 1:20). People aware of their own moral responsibility, who know the difference between right and wrong conduct and who have a sense of guilt when they do wrong, reflect the requirements of God's moral law (the Ten Commandments) that is written on their hearts (Rom. 2:14–15).

What is the result of divine revelation in nature? If anyone lived up to that knowledge by loving and obeying God every day of his life, he would be right with God and would not need salvation. However, no one loves God with his whole being and his neighbors as himself. People worship and serve things in creation rather than the Creator (Rom. 1:25). The problem does not lie with the revelation, which like the Law is holy, just, and good (Rom. 7:12); the problem is with the sinfulness of human lives (Rom. 8:3). The best human being (other than Jesus Christ) comes short of the uprightness God requires.

Because of God's universal revelation in nature, the philosopher Immanuel Kant could say, "Two things fill the mind with ever new and increasing admiration and awe... the starry heavens above me and the moral law within me."

When Christians defend justice, honesty, and decency in schools, homes, neighborhoods, businesses, and governments, they do not impose their special beliefs upon others. They merely point to universal principles that all sinners know but suppress in their unrighteousness (Rom. 1:18).

As valuable as general revelation is for justice, honesty, and decency in the world today, it is not enough. It must be completed by the good news of God's mercy and His gracious gift of perfect righteousness. Nature does not show God's plan for saving those who do wrong: that Jesus was the Son of God, that He died for our sins, and that He rose again from among the dead. The message of salvation was seen dimly throughout Old Testament sacrifices and ceremonies. It was seen more clearly as God redeemed the Israelites from enslavement in Egypt and as God disclosed to prophetic spokesmen the redemptive significance of His mighty acts of deliverance.

The full and final revelation of God has occurred in Jesus Christ. "God, who at various times and in different ways spoke in time past to the fathers by the prophets, has in these last days spoken to us by His Son, whom He has appointed heir of all things, through whom also He made the worlds" (Heb. 1:1-2). Christ has "declared" God to us personally (John 1:18). To see Christ is to see the Father (John 14:9). Christ gave us the words which the Father gave Him (John 17:8). At the cross Jesus revealed supremely God's self-giving love. There He died, "the just for the unjust, that He might bring us to God" (1 Pet. 3:18). And the good news is not complete until we hear that He rose again triumphantly over sin, Satan, and the grave, and is alive forevermore.

Christ chose apostles and trained them to teach the meaning of His death and resurrection, to build the church, and to write the New Testament Scriptures. We are to remember the words of these eyewitnesses to Christ's resurrection. The content of God's special revelation concerning salvation, given to specially gifted spokesmen and supremely revealed in Christ, is found in "the words which were spoken before by the holy prophets, and of the commandment of...the apostles of the Lord and Savior" (2 Pet. 3:2). "The Holy Scriptures...are able to make you wise for salvation through faith which is in Christ Jesus" (2 Tim. 3:15).

REVELATION OF JOHN — the last book of the Bible, and the only book of APOCALYPTIC LITERATURE in the New Testament. *Apocalypse*, the title of this book in the original Greek, means "unveiling" or "disclosure" of hidden things known only to God. Other examples of apocalyptic literature can be found in the Old Testament in Daniel (chaps. 7—12), Isaiah (chaps. 24—27), Ezekiel (chaps. 37—41), and Zechariah (chaps. 9—12).

Like its counterparts, the Book of Revelation depicts the end of the present age and the coming of God's future kingdom through symbols, images, and numbers. These symbols include an angel whose legs are pillars of fire, men who ride on horses while smiting the earth with plagues of destruction, and a fiery red dragon with seven heads and ten horns who crouches before a heavenly woman about to deliver a child.

Why was apocalyptic literature written in such imagery? One reason is that these books were written in dangerous times when it was safer to hide one's message in images than to speak plainly. Moreover, the symbolism preserved an element of mystery about details of time and place. The purpose of such symbolism, however, was not to confuse, but to inform and strengthen believers in the face of persecution.

Although the keys to some symbols have been lost, the overall message of this book is clear: God is all-powerful. No countermoves of the devil, no matter how strong, can frustrate the righteous purposes of God.

Structure of the Book. The Book of Revelation contains seven visions.

The first vision (chaps. 1—3) is of Christ Almighty exhorting His earthly church to remain loyal against all hostile attacks.

The second vision (chaps. 4—7) is of Christ the Lamb standing with a sealed scroll before God in heaven. As the Lamb opens each of the seven seals, which symbolize knowledge of the destinies of individuals and nations, a series of disasters befall the earth.

A series of seven angels blowing seven trumpets forms vision three (chaps. 8—11). At the sound of these trumpets more disasters occur.

The fourth vision (chaps. 12—14) consists of the persecution of the church—symbolized by a heavenly woman and by two witnesses (Moses and Elijah)—by Satan and the beast.

Vision five (chaps. 15—16) is another series of seven: seven bowls pouring out God's wrath.

The judgment of Babylon (a symbol for Rome) forms the sixth vision (chaps. 17:1—19:10).

The final victory, final judgment, and final blessedness form the seventh and final vision (chap. 19:11—22).

The consummation of God's eternal kingdom finds expression in the word new. Christ comes with the promise to make all things new: a new heaven, a new earth, and a new Jerusalem (21). The book closes with the sigh and longing of all Christians, "Come, Lord Jesus!" (22:20).

Remains of the altar for worship of the pagan god Zeus at Pergamos. The writer of Revelation may have had this idolatrous shrine in mind when he spoke of "Satan's throne" at Pergamos (Rev. 2:12-13).

Authorship and Date. The author identifies himself as John (1:4, 9; 21:2; 22:8), a prophet (1:1-4; 22:6-7). He was familiar enough with his readers to call himself their "brother and companion in tribulation" (1:9). He indicates that he was exiled to the island of Patmos (1:9) off the west coast of Asia Minor (modern Turkey) and that on the "Lord's Day" (Sunday) he was caught up "in the Spirit" (1:10) and saw the visions recorded in his book. An examination of the Greek language of the book of Revelation reveals that it has some strong similarities with the Gospel and Epistles of John, but also some striking stylistic differences. The author seems to think in Hebrew and write in Greek.

As a whole, this evidence points to John the Apostle, who spent his latter years in Ephesus or on the island of Patmos. The earliest church tradition was unanimous in attributing the Book of Revelation to John. Although later voices have found problems with this identification, the apostle John remains the strongest candidate for authorship. The Book was probably written during the latter years of the reign of the Roman Emperor Domitian (A.D. 81-96).

Historical Setting. John tells us, "The seven heads [of the beast] are seven mountains" (17:9), undoubtedly a reference to the famed seven hills of Rome. Chapter 13 tells us that the dragon (Satan) gave authority to the beast (Rome) to exact worship from its inhabitants (v. 4). The first Roman emperor to demand that his subjects address him as "Lord and God" on an empire-wide basis was Domitian. It was under Domitian that the apostle John was banished to Patmos. Christians, of course, were forbidden by the First Commandment (Ex. 20:3) to worship anyone other than God. In the Book of Revelation, John sounded the trumpet alert to Domitian's challenge.

Theological Contribution. The grand theme of the Book of Revelation is that of two warring powers, God and Satan, and of God's ultimate victory. It would be a mistake to consider the two powers as equal in might. God is stronger than Satan, and Satan continues his scheming plots only because God permits him to do so. Thus, at the final battle Satan and his followers are utterly destroyed—without a contest—by fire from heaven (20:7-10).

John portrays God's majesty and power through two key words. The first is the image of the throne. Elsewhere in the New Testament this word is found 15 times, but in Revelation it occurs 42 times! The throne stands for the rightful reign of God over the course of history. Angelic choruses bow before God's throne and chant, "Holy, holy, holy, Lord God Almighty" (4:8).

The second term is Almighty. Outside Revelation this term is found only once in the New Testament (2 Cor. 6:18), but here it occurs nine times (once as Omnipotent in 19:6). Almighty means "without contenders." No matter how fierce and wicked Satan may be, he cannot defeat God. In God's time and in His way He will fulfill His promises and accomplish His sovereign purpose in history.

The central figure in the army of God the King is Jesus Christ. The Book of Revelation begins with the words, "The Revelation of Jesus Christ" (1:1). This is not a book of revelations, but of one revelation—Jesus Christ. John's first vision is of Christ

REVELATION: A Teaching Outline

Part One: "The Things Which You Have Seen" (1:1–20)

Part Two: "The Things Which Are" (2:1—3:22)

Part Three: "The Things Which Will Take Place after This" (4:1—22:21)

standing in the midst of His churches with eyes like fire (all-seeing), feet like fine brass (all-powerful), hair like wool, white as snow (eternal and all-knowing), and with a sharp two-edged sword coming out of His mouth (the word of truth). Christ is "the First and the Last" (1:11; 22:13), whose final promise is "Surely I am coming quickly" (22:20).

Throughout the Book of Revelation Christ appears in various images, each illuminating a special function or characteristic. He appears as a lion (5:5), representing royal power. As a root (5:5; 22:16), He represents Davidic lineage. As the rider on a white horse (19:11), He symbolizes victory over evil. Most important is the symbol of the Lamb who was slain (5:6). By His sacrifice on the cross, Christ has redeemed humankind (1:5). Because of His humble obedience to the will of the Father, He alone is worthy to open the sealed book that discloses events to come (5:6-10).

This Lamb is victorious. He shares in the power of God's throne (7:17). At the end of time, He will come in judgment (19:11). Then He will reveal Himself as the Lord of the world who was foretold in the Old Testament (2:26; 12:5; 19:15) and the source of new life with God in the heavenly Jerusalem (21:22; 22:1).

In its own way, each metaphor tells an important truth about Christ. Christ is before all things, and all things were created in Him and for Him. This is the abiding message of Revelation: Jesus Christ is the fulfillment of the hopes of believers, no matter how grim circumstances may appear.

Special Considerations. Revelation was written originally for first-century Christians who faced severe trials under a totalitarian political system. Its imagery reflects the historical realities of that time. This is not to say, however, that it is not also addressing succeeding generations, including our own. As is true of all biblical prophecy, God's Word comes to a particular situation; but it yields a harvest to later generations as they receive it. Thus, Revelation assures us that God is present, purposeful, and powerful today, no matter what forms the beast may take.

One of the unique characteristics of Revelation is its use of four, twelve, and seven. Thus, we find four living creatures, four horsemen, and four angels; twelve elders, twelve gates to the city of God, twelve foundations, and twelve varieties of fruit on the tree of life; and seven churches, seven spirits of God, seven thunders, seven seals, seven trumpets, seven bowls, and seven beatitudes. In apocalyptic literature these numbers represent completeness and perfection. Conversely, 3 1/2 is a number frequently associated with Satan (11:2; 13:5; 42 months or 3 1/2 years); this number symbolizes a fracturing and diminishing of God's unity.

With this in mind, the 144,000 elect in chapter seven should not be taken literally. Immediately following this passage (v. 9), John mentions that he saw "a great multitude [of the redeemed] which no one could number." Actually, the 144,000 refers to martyrs—12,000 from each of the twelve tribes of Israel. One hundred and forty-four thousand (a multiple of 12,000 times 12) stands for totality. This means that no martyr will fail to see God's reward.

Finally, the number of the beast, 666 (Rev. 13:18), probably refers to Nero, or more specifically to the idea that Nero would return alive to lead the armies of Satan against God. In Hebrew and Greek, letters of the alphabet also served as numbers, and in this case the numerical value of "Nero Caesar" amounts to 666, the number of the beast.

REVELRY — boisterous merrymaking or noisy partying. This word means any form of indulgence, usually in connection with the worship of pagan gods (Rom. 13:13; 1 Pet. 4:3; carousing, NASB; orgies, NIV).

REVENGE — inflicting punishment or harm on another to pay back for an injury or insult. Revenge was a way of life among the Hebrew people in Old Testament times. But Jesus taught that we should love our enemies (Luke 6:27).

REVERENCE — a feeling of profound awe and respect. Because of His majesty and holiness, God arouses a feeling of reverence in those who worship and serve Him (Heb. 12:28-29).

REVILE (see SCORN).

REWARD — something offered in return for some service or benefit received. In the Bible, a reward can refer to something given for either a good or bad act. The psalmist, for example, speaks of "a reward for the righteous" (Ps. 58:11) and of "the reward of the wicked" (Ps. 91:8). When the Son of Man returns in glory, "He will reward each according to his works" (Matt. 16:27).

REZEPH [REE zef] (*glowing coal*) — a city in eastern Syria, mentioned in the message of Sennacherib to King Hezekiah of Judah (Is. 37:12).

REZIA [ree ZIGH uh] — a form of RIZIA.

REZIN [REE zin] (*dominion*) — the name of two men in the Old Testament:

1. The last king of Syria. Rezin was killed by Tiglath-Pileser III, king of Assyria, in 732 B.C. Rezin allied himself with Pekah, king of Israel, to try to take away Judah's throne from Ahaz and the line of David (2 Kin. 15:37; 16:5-9). Together Rezin and Pekah besieged Jerusalem, but they were unable to capture Ahaz's stronghold. The prophet Isaiah counseled Ahaz not to fear Rezin and Pekah (Is. 7:4).

Instead of trusting the Lord, however, Ahaz panicked. He appealed for help to Tiglath-Pileser III, king of Assyria, by sending him silver and gold from the Temple and Ahaz's palace. The Assyrian king marched against Damascus and besieged it in 734 B.C. After a two-year siege, Damascus fell to the Assyrians, Rezin was killed by Tiglath-Pileser, and the Syrians were carried away as captives to Kir (2 Kin. 16:9). In the Assyrian records, Rezin is called Rasannu.

St. Paul's Harbor at Rhodes where Paul's ship landed on its way back to Palestine after his third missionary journey (Acts 21:1).

2. The founder of a family of NETHINIM, or Temple servants, whose descendants returned from the Captivity with Zerubbabel (Ezra 2:48).

REZON [REE zuhn] (*noble, prince*) — a son of Eliadah (1 Kin. 11:23). Rezon was a subject of Hadadezer, king of Zobah; he fled from Hadadezer, perhaps at the time of his defeat by David (2 Sam. 8:3). Rezon then became captain over a band of raiders and went to Damascus, where he founded a dynasty. He opposed Israel in Solomon's time (1 Kin. 11:23–25).

RHEGIUM [REE jee uhm] (*breach*) — a seaport on the coast of southern Italy, across the Strait of Messina from the island of Sicily (see Map 8, A–2). The apostle Paul stopped at Rhegium, apparently staying for only one day (Acts 28:13), on his way from Syracuse to Puteoli, before continuing on to Rome.

RHESA [REE suh] (*prince*) — a son of Zerubbabel and an ancestor of Jesus (Luke 3:27).

RHODA [ROE duh] (*rose*) — a servant girl in the home of Mary, the mother of John Mark (Acts 12:13). According to tradition, this house in Jerusalem was the site of the Last Supper; it may also have been the headquarters of the early church in Jerusalem. Following his miraculous release from prison, the apostle Peter went to Mary's house. Rhoda answered his knock and was filled with such surprise and joy that she forgot to let him in and ran back to tell the others. Peter had to continue knocking until someone let him in (Acts 12:16).

RHODES [roedz] (*a rose*) — a large island in the Aegean Sea off the southwest coast of ASIA MINOR (see Map 8, C–2) visited by the apostle Paul (Acts

21:1). The island is about 68 kilometers (42 miles) long and about 24 kilometers (15 miles) wide; it lies about 19 kilometers (12 miles) off the coast of the province of CARIA.

On the northeast corner of the island was the city of Rhodes, an important commercial, cultural, and tourist center for the Greeks as well as the Romans. At the entrance to the harbor of Rhodes stood the famous Colossus of Rhodes, a huge bronze statue of the sun–god Apollo built by the Greek sculptor Chares between 292 and 280 B.C. This towering statue was one of the seven wonders of the ancient world.

Because the island of Rhodes was on the natural shipping route from Greece to Syria and Palestine, the ship on which Paul traveled during his third missionary journey stopped at Rhodes (Acts 21:1). There is no evidence that Paul conducted any missionary activity on the island during his brief visit; he was in a hurry to get to Jerusalem for the Day of Pentecost (Acts 20:16).

RIBAI [RIGH bigh] (*Jehovah contends*) — the father of Ittai (2 Sam. 23:29) or Ithai (1 Chr. 11:31).

RIBLAH [RIB luh] (*fertility*) — the name of a city (see Map 4, C–1) and a landmark in the Old Testament:

1. A Syrian city in the land of Hamath (2 Kin. 23:33; 25:21). Situated at the headwaters of the Orontes River in the broad plain between the Lebanon and the Anti–Lebanon Mountains, Riblah was approximately 105 kilometers (65 miles) north of Damascus and about 57 kilometers (35 miles) northeast of Baalbek. This area was blessed with abundant water, fertile lands, and the famous cedar

forests of the nearby Lebanon Mountains. Consequently, it was an ideal campsite for the armies that regularly invaded the land of Israel. Riblah was easy to defend, and it commanded a main route from Egypt to the Euphrates.

Following Josiah's defeat at Megiddo and the sack of Kadesh-on-the-Orontes in 609 B.C., Pharaoh Necho made Riblah his headquarters. Here he deposed King Jehoahaz, appointed Eliakim (Jehoiakim) as king in his place, and forced Judah to pay him tribute (2 Kin. 23:31–34). A few years later (605 B.C.), Nebuchadnezzar, king of Babylon, defeated the Egyptians at Carchemish (2 Chr. 35:20). He, too, chose Riblah as his command post. He directed the capture of Jerusalem in 587/86 B.C. from Riblah. Once he had subdued the city, he brought King Zedekiah to Riblah in captivity. There he forced Zedekiah to watch his sons killed, after which he was blinded (2 Kin. 25:6–21; Jer. 52:9–11).

2. A landmark on the eastern boundary of Israel (Num. 34:11).

RICHES (see WEALTH).

RIDDLE — a puzzling question posed as a problem to be solved or guessed; an enigma. Riddle is a translation of a Hebrew word that means "something twisted, bent, or tied in a knot." While the word riddle appears in the Old Testament occasionally, other words are also used to translate the Hebrew word (for instance, dark sayings, Ps. 49:4; hard questions, 1 Kin. 10:1; and sinister schemes, Dan. 8:23).

The classic use of riddle in the Old Testament occurs in the story of Samson. Samson posed it to the Philistines at Timnah: "Out of the eater came something to eat/and out of the strong came something sweet" (Judg. 14:14). This riddle was suggested to Samson by a swarm of bees and honey that he saw in the carcass of a lion (v. 8).

When the Queen of Sheba heard of the fame of Solomon, she came to Jerusalem "to test him with hard questions" (1 Kin. 10:1; 2 Chr. 9:1). Literally, she tested his wisdom with riddles. According to the Jewish historian Josephus, King Solomon was particularly fond of riddles; he and Hiram, king of Tyre, engaged in a contest of riddles.

The "riddle" or "parable" of the eagles and the vine posed by Ezekiel (Ezek. 17:1–21) actually is an allegory. Ezekiel's parable may have been a riddle to some, had he not chosen to give its interpretation.

The word riddle does not occur in the New Testament (NKJV). There is, however, one instance where the Greek word often translated riddle is used: "For now we see in a mirror, dimly [ainigma], but then face to face" (1 Cor. 13:12). Our present life, and even God's revelation to us, contains riddles; but one day the riddles will be solved.

RIGHTEOUSNESS — holy and upright living, in accordance with God's standard. The word righteousness comes from a root word that means "straightness." It refers to a state that conforms to

an authoritative standard. Righteousness is a moral concept. God's character is the definition and source of all righteousness (Gen. 18:25; Deut. 32:4; Rom. 9:14). Therefore, man's righteousness is defined in terms of God's.

In the Old Testament the term righteousness is used to define man's relationship with God (Ps. 50:6; Jer. 9:24) and with other people (Jer. 22:3). In the context of relationships, righteous action is action that promotes the peace and well-being of human beings in their relationships to one another.

For example, Adam and Eve would have acted righteously in their relationship with God if they had obeyed Him, because His commands defined that relationship. The Ten Commandments and related laws defined Israel's relationship with God. To obey those laws was to act righteously, because such obedience maintained the covenant relationship between God and His people.

The sacrificial system in the Old Testament and the cross of Jesus in the New Testament show man's need for righteousness. Sin is disobedience to the terms that define man's relationship with God and with other people. Since the FALL in the Garden of Eden, man is inherently unrighteous. As the prophet Isaiah said, "We are all like an unclean thing, and all our righteousnesses are like filthy rags; we all fade as a leaf, and our iniquities, like the wind, have taken us away" (Is. 64:6). Man cannot be righteous in the sight of God on his own merits. Therefore, man must have God's righteousness imputed, or transferred, to him.

The cross of Jesus is a public demonstration of God's righteousness. God accounts or transfers the righteousness of Christ to those who trust in Him (Rom. 4:3–22; Gal. 3:6; Phil. 3:9). We do not become righteous because of our inherent goodness; God sees us as righteous because of our identification by faith with His Son.

RIM — the inner part of the wheels of a cart in Bible times (1 Kin. 7:33). The word is also used for the outer edges of the altar in the tabernacle and Temple (Ex. 38:4).

RIMMON [RIM uhn] (*pomegranate*) — the name of two towns, a rock, a man, and a pagan god in the Old Testament:

1. A town in southern Judah allotted to the tribe of Simeon (Josh. 19:7; Remmon, KJV). Today it is identified with Khirbet Umm er–Ramamim, about 14.5 kilometers (nine miles) northeast of Beersheba.

2. A town on the border of Zebulun assigned to the Levites (Josh. 19:13; Rimmon–methoar, KJV; 1 Chr. 6:77).

3. A rock near Gibeah, in the territory of Benjamin, where 600 Benjamites took refuge for four months (Judg. 20:45, 47).

4. A man from Beeroth in the territory of Benjamin. His two sons, BAANAH and RECHAB, murdered Saul's son Ishbosheth, beheaded him, and took his head to David—an act for which they were executed (2 Sam. 4:1–12).

5. A Syrian god whose temple was at Damascus. NAAMAN the Syrian and his lord, the king of Syria, worshiped Rimmon (2 Kin. 5:18). Rimmon was the god of rain and storm, lightning and thunder. Also see GODS, PAGAN.

RIMMON–METHOAR [RIM uhn meh THOW ahr] — a form of RIMMON.

RIMMON–PAREZ [RIM uhn PAR iz] — a form of RIMMON PEREZ.

RIMMON PEREZ [RIM uhn PIR iz] (*pomegranate of the breach*) — a campsite of the Israelites during their wilderness wanderings (Num. 33:19–20; Rimmon-parez, NEB, KJV).

RIMMON, ROCK OF [RIM uhn] — a form of RIMMON No. 3.

RING (see JEWELRY).

RINGLEADER — a troublemaker; one who leads others in disruptive activities. The apostle Paul was accused by his enemies of being "a ringleader" of a sect referred to in contempt as "the Nazarenes," or followers of Jesus (Acts 24:5).

RINNAH [RIN uh] (*a loud cry*) — a son of Shimon, of the tribe of Judah (1 Chr. 4:20).

RIPHATH [RIH fath] (meaning unknown) — a son of Gomer and grandson of Japheth (Gen. 10:3). The name also appears as Diphath (1 Chr. 1:6, NKJV, RSV, NEB, NASB; Riphath, KJV, NIV).

RISSAH [RIS uh] (*heap of ruins*) — a campsite of the Israelites during their wilderness wanderings (Num. 33:21–22).

RITHMAH [RITH muh] (*wild broom bush*) — a campsite of the Israelites during their wilderness wandering (Num. 33:18–19).

RITUAL — the prescribed order of conducting a religious ceremony. The people who were resettled in Samaria by the king of Assyria did not know "the rituals of the God of the land" (2 Kin. 17:26–27; law, RSV; custom, NASB; manner, KJV; established usage, NEB). They contined to serve their own gods according to their former customs.

RIVER — a large stream of water emptying into an ocean, lake, or other body of water and usually fed along its course by smaller streams. Rivers served as ideal places for cities and settlements, as well as religious events, such as John's baptism (Matt. 3:6; Mark 1:5), or Naaman's dipping (2 Kin. 5:14) in the Jordan.

In the Old Testament the Euphrates River has a distinct place; it is often called simply "the River" (Ezra 4:10). It served as the ideal eastern boundary of Israel (Gen. 15:18; Deut. 1:7), briefly achieved under David and Solomon (2 Sam. 8:3; 1 Kin. 4:21). This frontier was soon lost, but it was reaffirmed by the prophets as a national promise (Is. 27:12; Mic. 7:12). The Euphrates also served as a geographical marker for the border between Mesopotamia (Josh. 24:3, 14–15) and Assyria (Is. 7:20; 8:7).

The rivers of the Garden of Eden, including the Euphrates and the Tigris (or Hiddekel), represent God's rich provision for the fertility of the garden (Gen. 2:10–14). The idea is transferred to Zion as a source of divine blessing (Ps. 46:4; Ezek. 47:5–12) and to the heavenly Jerusalem (Rev. 22:1–2).

The word river is also used to symbolize God's delights (Ps. 36:8), peace (Is. 48:18; 66:12), life

The Jordan River, shown here near the traditional site of Jesus' baptism (Matthew 3), is the only river in the world that flows for most of its course below sea level.

(John 7:38), and tears (Lam. 3:48). It also illustrates God's providential control over nature (Ps. 107:33; Is. 42:15).

RIVER OF EGYPT (see EGYPT, RIVER OF).

RIZIA [rih ZIGH uh] (*delight*) — a son of Ulla (1 Chr. 7:39; Rezia, KJV).

RIZPAH [RIZ puh] (*a glowing stone*) — a daughter of Aiah who became a concubine of King Saul (2 Sam. 3:7; 21:8, 10–11). She bore two sons, Armoni and Mephibosheth. After Saul's death, Abner had sexual relations with Rizpah (2 Sam. 3:7)—an act that amounted to claiming the throne of Israel. Ishbosheth (also called Esh–Baal), one of Saul's sons by another woman, accused Abner of immorality and, by implication, of disloyalty to Ishbosheth's authority. This accusation so enraged Abner that he transferred his loyalty from Saul to David.

Rizpah is a good example of the undying devotion of a mother. After the death of her sons, she kept vigil over their bodies for several months. When David heard of this, he ordered that Saul and Jonathan's bones, still unburied, be mingled with those of Saul's sons and grandsons and that they be buried "in the country of Benjamin in Zelah, in the tomb of Kish his [Saul's] father" (2 Sam. 21:14).

ROAD — an open public way for the passage of vehicles, persons, and animals. Three types of roads existed in Palestine: (1) international roads which passed through the land, giving armies and caravans access to the great empires of the ancient world; (2) an internal system of roads which provided communication between the many regions of the country; and (3) the local roads, which were often little more than paths or trails.

The most important international highways were "the way of the sea," which followed the coastline of the MEDITERRANEAN SEA, and the "King's Highway," which ran north–south through TRANSJORDAN. The coastal route is designated "the way to the sea" (Is. 9:1), as well as "the way of the land of the Philistines" (Ex. 13:17). This route was later known as the *Via Maris* because of the way Latin versions of the Bible translate the Isaiah passage.

The *Via Maris*, the most important international highway throughout the biblical period, originated in Egypt and then ran north by way of the Plain of Philistia and the Plain of Sharon. The road crossed the Carmel ridge at Megiddo, passed through the Valley of Jezreel, and continued by way of Hazor to Damascus. Some of the most important cities in this region of the world were situated along this road and its branches.

The King's Highway (Num. 20:17; 21:22) was next in importance to the *Via Maris*. The northern section of the King's Highway was also called "the way to Bashan" (Num. 21:33) or "the road to Bashan" (Deut. 3:1). This route ran the length of the Transjordanian Highlands, beginning at the Gulf of Aqaba and continuing north to Damascus. The campaign of Abraham against Chedorlaomer and his allies (Genesis 14) was conducted along the King's Highway. It was along this road also that the Israelites were refused permission to pass on their march from Kadesh Barnea to the plains of Moab (Num. 20:19; 21:22).

The King's Highway, which gave access to the spice routes from Arabia, was often controlled by semi-nomadic people who prevented the founding of settlements along its length. In certain periods, however, the route was guarded by a network of fortresses. Another north–south route was located to the east of the King's Highway, along the fringe

A section of the Roman road in Syria between Aleppo and Antioch. The road is paved with carefully cut blocks of limestone.
Photo by Ben Chapman

of the desert in order to avoid the four great dry stream beds whose deep canyons divide the Trans-jordanian Highlands into its main geographical regions.

The *Via Maris* and the King's Highway were joined by roadways that connected regions within the country. Thus, the network of roadways among the various regions was also used as part of the system for international travel. Regional roads mentioned in the Bible include "the way to the mountains of the Amorites" (Deut. 1:19), "the road...to Beth Shemesh" (1 Sam. 6:9), "the road to Beth Horon" (1 Sam. 13:18), and "the way of the wilderness" (Josh. 8:15).

ROBBER (see Occupations and Trades).

ROBE (see Dress of the Bible).

ROCK — a large mass of stone which formed a cliff or peak as well as broken pieces of such masses. Rocks abounded in the rough terrain of Palestine, especially in the Central Highlands. Some had specific names, including "the rock of Oreb" (Judg. 7:25) and "the rock of Etam" (Judg. 15:8). Huge rocks were used to construct the walls of fortified cities.

The word rock is often used figuratively in the Bible to speak of God and Christ. As Rock, God is the Creator (Deut. 32:18), His people's strength (Deut. 32:4), His people's defense and refuge (Ps. 31:2–3; 94:22), and His people's salvation (Deut. 32:15; Ps. 89:26). In the New Testament, Christ is the Rock from whom the Spirit of life flows (John 4:13–14; 1 Cor. 10:4), the foundation of the church (Matt. 16:18) and its cornerstone (Eph. 2:20).

ROCK BADGER, ROCK GOAT, ROCK HYRAX (see Animals of the Bible).

ROD — a staff, pole, or stick with many uses: a staff upon which a person may lean (Gen. 32:10; staff, KJV; Ex. 4:2); a club-like weapon (Ex. 21:20; 1 Sam. 14:27; Ps. 23:4); an instrument of punishment (2 Sam. 7:14; 1 Cor. 4:21); a shepherd's crook (Ezek. 20:37); a mark of authority, a scepter—such as Moses' rod (Ex. 4:20) and Aaron's rod (Num. 17:2–10); a measuring stick (Ezek. 40:3; Rev. 11:1); and a tool used to thresh grain (Is. 28:27).

RODANIM [ROE duh nim] — a tribe descended from Javan (1 Chr. 1:7; Dodanim, KJV). The NKJV refers to these people as Dodanim in Genesis 10:4 (Rodanim, NIV, NEB). The Rodanim were probably the inhabitants of the island of Rhodes.

ROE, ROEBUCK (see Animals of the Bible).

ROGELIM [ROE guh lim] (*place of fullers*) — a city in East Gilead probably near the River Jabbok (2 Sam. 17:27). It was the hometown of Barzillai the Gileadite (2 Sam. 19:31–39).

ROHGAH [ROE guh] (meaning unknown) — a son of Shemer, of the tribe of Asher (1 Chr. 7:34).

ROLL (see Scroll.)

ROMAMTI–EZER [roe MAM tigh EE zur] (*I have exalted help*) — a singer in the 24th course of sanctuary musicians during David's reign (1 Chr. 25:4, 31).

ROMAN EMPIRE — the powerful pagan empire that controlled most of the known world during New Testament times.

Rome was founded in 753 B.C. by Romulus, who became its first king. The little kingdom grew in size and importance, absorbing its immediate neighbors through the reign of seven kings, until the tyranny of Tarquinius Superbus drove the people to revolt and to take the government into their own hands. A republic was established, and Roman citizens had a voice in governmental affairs. During the period of the republic, Rome extended her borders throughout all of Italy and the known world.

In 63 B.C., Judea became formally subject to Rome and this was the case during the entire New Testament period.

The republic was subject to internal strife which eventually led to the decline of a people–oriented government. The emperor Octavian, who was also known as Augustus, became emperor in 27 B.C. He was still reigning at the time of Jesus' birth.

Roman Religion. The religion that was native to Rome was basically primitive in nature. The Romans believed that impersonal spirits or supernatural powers inhabited such natural objects as trees, streams, and earth. They believed that these spirits affected one's personal life for good or evil.

But the most striking feature of Roman religion was its ability to merge the best features of several religions. As the empire expanded, it imported and assimilated many religious ideas and pagan gods from Greece and the Orient. Roman gods were fused and identified with the gods of the Greeks. Buildings, temples, and monuments to these gods were erected. Astrological beliefs and magical practices flourished.

An "imperial ruler cult" developed in the first century B.C. when the Roman senate voted to deify Julius Caesar and to dedicate a temple to his honor. Among all the emperors, only Julius Caesar, Augustus, and Claudius were deified. This phenomenon apparently had more political than religious meaning.

Throughout the entire New Testament period, various emperors ruled over the Roman Empire. During the reign of Augustus, Christ was born. His crucifixion occurred during the reign of the succeeding emperor Tiberius. The martyrdom of James, the brother of John, took place in the reign of the emperor Claudius (Acts 11:28; 12:1–2). It was to the emperor Nero that Paul appealed (Acts 25:11). The destruction of Jerusalem prophesied by Jesus (Matthew 24; Mark 13; Luke 19:41–44) was accomplished in the year A.D. 70 by Titus, who later became emperor. Thus, all of the New Testament story unfolded under the reign of Roman emperors.

The Roman Empire reached the height of its power from about A.D. 100 to 175. By the end of

Model of a Roman warship, used by the Romans in their campaign of conquest throughout the ancient world.

the century, however, the Romans and their power had begun to decline. Because of the vast expanse of its territory, the Empire grew increasingly difficult to administer. High taxation and political infighting also took their toll.

Morally, Rome was also a sick society; its life of sin and debauchery served to hasten its collapse from within, even as barbaric tribes moved in to challenge the Romans' military rule. By A.D. 450 the Roman Empire was only a skeleton of its former self, reduced to a third-rate power among the nations of the ancient world.

The Jews Within the Empire. Contact between Rome and the Jews took place when some of the Jews were scattered to various parts of the Mediterranean world and when Rome moved into Palestine as a part of its eastern expansion. Technically, however, contact between the Romans and the Jews began in 63 B.C., when Pompey marched into the land of Palestine.

From the time of the Captivity in Babylon—or perhaps even earlier—many Jews made their homes outside Palestine. While some of them did this for economic reasons; others had been deported as prisoners of war to such places as Assyria and Babylon. The prophet Jeremiah indicated that some Jews had settled in Egypt during his time (Jer. 44:1).

Under Roman rule the Jews were given a special status with certain legal rights. They were permitted to practice their own religion and to build their synagogues. They also were exempt from military service and were not required to appear in court on the Sabbath.

Relationships between the Jews and the Romans were mostly positive. But a few major disturbances did occur. The emperor Caligula alienated the Jews by opposing their belief in one God and forcibly erecting a statue of himself in their synagogues. Also, in A.D. 19, the emperor Tiberius expelled some Jews from Italy. This edict was renewed under Claudius in A.D. 49 (Acts 18:2). Apparently this edict did not last long, because Jews were living in Rome when Paul arrived there about A.D. 62.

The situation of the Jews varied considerably under the different Roman rulers. Basically, the Romans treated the Jews fairly. Herod the Great rebuilt the Temple in 20 B.C., and Herod Agrippa sought Jewish favor by persecuting the Christians (Acts 12:1–3). Archelaus, on the other hand, was a cruel and tyrannical ruler who massacred many Jews (Matt. 2:22).

Resentful of the presence of these foreign oppressors, the Jews refused to recognize anyone but God as sovereign. Revolutionary activities of Jewish nationalists such as the ZEALOTS increased and threatened the peace in Palestine. By A.D. 66, Rome was forced to subdue a Jewish revolt in Judea. And in A.D. 70, Titus, a Roman general who later became emperor, marched on the city of Jerusalem to destroy Jewish resistance. Many Jews lost their lives by crucifixion and other violent means. A small group of freedom fighters held out at Masada, but they took their own lives just before the Roman soldiers broke into their fortress.

The destruction of Jerusalem did not wipe out the Jewish state or religion. In some ways, it made the Jews more determined to resist. During the next 60 years Rome and the Jews clashed on a number of occasions. From A.D. 132–135 a second rebellion was led by a self-proclaimed messiah, Simon Bar Cochba. Hadrian, emperor at the time, issued an edict which virtually destroyed Judaism. Jerusalem was rebuilt as a Roman colony, complete with a pagan Roman temple, erected on the site of the Jewish

Temple. The province of Judea was replaced by Syria Palestine. In this rebellion, some 500,000 Jews were killed and many others were sold into slavery. Those who survived were scattered beyond this new province.

Christianity Within the Empire. The birth and development of Christianity took place within the borders of the Roman Empire. The New Testament contains several references to Romans who were ruling at this time. Among them were CAESAR AUGUSTUS (Luke 2:1), QUIRINIUS (Luke 2:2), and TIBERIUS CAESAR (Luke 3:1; 20:22). Other minor officials ruled on behalf of Rome, particularly those of the Herodian dynasty.

The Book of Acts shows how Christianity spread throughout the Roman Empire. Under Paul, the great missionary to the Gentiles, the gospel may have been preached as far west as Spain (Rom. 15:28). A Christian church existed in Rome as early as A.D. 50 (Acts 18:2–3). By the time Paul wrote his Epistle to the Romans (A.D. 58), a large Christian community existed in the imperial city.

Paul's appearance in Rome was ironic, because he came as a prisoner and not as a missionary (Acts 25:12; 27:1; 28:19–31). Here he was held in confinement awaiting a trial that apparently never took place. According to tradition, Paul lost his life under Nero's persecution about A.D. 64.

In its early stages, Christianity was regarded by Rome as a sect of Judaism. This is why it was ignored during its early years. On several occasions, Roman authorities viewed conflicts between Jews and Christians as an internal matter, not worthy of their attention (Acts 18:12–17). When Christians were accused by the Jews of breaking the law, they were acquitted (Acts 16:35–39). Rome even protected Christians from Jewish fanatics (Acts 19:28–41; 22:22–30; 23:23–24) and assured Paul the right of a proper trial (Acts 23:26; 28:31).

Most Christians had a positive and respectful attitude toward Roman authority. They were careful not to promote any revolutionary or treasonous acts. Jesus spoke about paying taxes (Mark 12:17). Paul reminded his readers to respect, pray for, and honor governing authorities (Rom. 13:1–7; 1 Tim. 2:1–2; Titus 3:1). Peter admonished the churches: "Honor all people. Love the brotherhood. Fear God. Honor the king" (1 Pet. 2:17).

The first known persecution of Christians by the Roman authorities took place under Nero. But this was an isolated case and not a general policy. Many Christians, including Paul, lost their lives at this time. Tacitus, a Roman historian, refers to vast multitudes of Christians who were arrested, tortured, crucified, and burned.

Hardships came to Christians in parts of Asia while Domitian was emperor. Later, under Trajan, there were further problems, especially in Bithynia, where Pliny was governor (A.D. 112). Ignatius, bishop of Antioch, was martyred during this persecution. Rome may have feared that Christians could become a political threat because they would not acknowledge Caesar as lord.

Marcus Aurelius took official action against Christianity. As emperor, he was responsible for the death of Justin Martyr (A.D. 165). Celcius (A.D. 249–251) launched attacks against Christians and, like Nero, used them as scapegoats for his own failures.

Under Diocletian intense persecution of the church took place for three years (A.D. 303–305). Many churches were destroyed. Bibles were burned, and Christians were martyred. With the coming of Constantine, however, this policy of per-

Ruins of the Forum in the city of Rome. The Forum was the meetingplace, marketplace, and religious and political center of the Roman Empire's capital city.

Photo by Gustav Jeeninga

A theater inscription at Corinth, mentioning the name Erastus. This may have been the same Erastus, "the treasurer of the city" (Rom. 16:23), who sent greetings to the Christians in Rome.

secution was reversed. His Edict of Milan in A.D. 313 made Christianity the official religion of the Roman Empire.

ROMAN LAW — the unique laws and judicial codes by which the Roman Empire governed itself and the various nations and foreign provinces under its control.

Judicial authority ranged from the absolute power of the emperor to the function of the senate and the imperial civil service (GOVERNORS, PROCURATORS, prefects, magistrates, etc.). Judicial procedure in Rome generally included appearance before a magistrate, a trial, and the selection of a judge who would then render judgment on a case.

In the provinces, Roman law was administered by Roman officials. Pontius Pilate, for example, was the Roman governor involved in the trial of Jesus. The gospel accounts of this episode give considerable insight into the judicial procedure of the Romans and how they related to local Jewish officials (Matthew 27; Mark 15; Luke 23; John 18—19).

The apostle Paul's Roman citizenship granted him certain privileges as well as protection from Jewish and Roman fanaticism (Acts 16:35–39; 22:22–29). His imprisonment in Caesarea and defense before Felix, Festus, and King Agrippa (Acts 23:26—26:32), as well as his specific appeal to plead his case before Caesar (25:10–12), are good examples of Roman civil and legal law.

Christianity began in Roman territory and expanded into additional areas controlled by Rome. Christians were expected to observe Roman law and not to get involved in any disorderly, suspicious, or treasonous activity.

The Book of Acts shows that the early Christians were protected and acquitted by the Roman authorities. They recognized Christianity as a legal and valid religion with the right to exist. Paul affirmed that he had not broken any Jewish, religious, or Roman law (Acts 25:8).

ROMANS, EPISTLE TO THE — the most formal and systematic of Paul's epistles. The main theme of Romans is that righteousness comes as a free gift of God and is receivable by faith alone. Romans stands at the head of the Pauline epistles because it is the longest of his letters, but it is also Paul's most important epistle.

Repeatedly in its history, the church has found in this epistle a catalyst for reform and new life. In the fourth century a troubled young man, sensing a divine command to open the Bible and read the first passage he came to, read these words: "Not in revelry and drunkenness, not in licentiousness and lewdness, not in strife and envy. But put on the Lord Jesus Christ, and make no provision for the flesh, to fulfill its lusts" (13:13–14).

"In an instant," says St. Augustine, "the light of confidence flooded into my heart and all the darkness of doubt was dispelled." In the 16th century a young monk found release from his struggles with God by claiming salvation by grace through faith (Rom. 1:17; 3:24). This truth caused Martin Luther to launch the greatest reform the church has ever known. Romans, perhaps more than any single book of the Bible, has exerted a powerful influence on the history of Christianity.

Structure of the Epistle. The Epistle to the Romans consists of two halves, a doctrinal section (chaps. 1—8) and a practical section (chaps. 12—16), separated by three chapters on the place of Israel in the history of salvation (chaps. 9—11).

Paul declares his main theme in the first chapter—that the gospel is the power of salvation to everyone who believes (1:16–17). This declaration is then held in suspension until 3:21, while Paul di-

ROMANS: A Teaching Outline

Part One: The Revelation of the Righteousness of God
(1:1—8:39)

Part Two: The Vindication of the Righteousness of God
(9:1—11:36)

Part Three: The Application of the Righteousness of God
(12:1—16:27)

gresses to show that all peoples are in need of salvation: the Gentiles have broken the law of conscience, and the Jews the law of Moses (1:18—3:20).

Paul then returns to his opening theme. In a classic statement of the Christian gospel, he explains that righteousness comes by the grace of God through man's trust in the saving work of Christ (3:21-31). The example of Abraham testifies that the promise of God is realized through faith (4:1-25). The benefits of JUSTIFICATION are peace and confidence before God (5:1-11). Thus, Christ's ability to save is greater than Adam's ability to corrupt (5:12-21).

Paul then takes up the problem of SIN in the Christian life. Rather than acting as a stimulus to sin, GRACE draws us into a loyal union with Christ (6:1-14). Christ has freed us from slavery to sin so that we may become slaves of righteousness (6:15—7:6). Paul admits that the law brings sin to light, but sin convinces us of our need for a Savior (7:7-25). Paul concludes the doctrinal section by one of the most triumphant chapters in all the Bible: believers are not condemned by God, but are raised by the power of the Holy Spirit to face all adversity through the redeeming love of God (8:1-39).

In chapters 9—11 Paul discusses the question of why Israel rejected the Savior sent to it.

Paul then discusses a number of practical consequences of the gospel. A proper response involves the sacrifice of one's entire life to the gospel (12:1-2). The gifts of grace to the church are complementary, not competitive or uniform (12:3-8). He lists insights for Christian conduct (12:9-21). Christians are instructed on the attitudes they should have toward the government (13:1-7), neighbors (13:8-10), the Second Coming (13:11-14), and judging (14:1-12) and cooperating with others (14:13—15:13). Paul closes with his travel plans (15:14-33) and a long list of greetings (16:1-27).

Authorship and Date. There can be no doubt that Romans is an exposition of the content of the gospel by the strongest thinker in the early church—the apostle Paul. The epistle bears Paul's name as author (1:1). Throughout, it reflects Paul's deep involvement with the gospel. Paul most likely wrote the epistle during his third missionary journey as he finalized plans to visit Rome (Acts 19:21). His three-month stay in Corinth, probably in the spring of A.D. 56 or 57, would have provided the extended, uninterrupted time needed to compose such a reasoned commentary on the Christian faith.

Historical Setting. Romans was written to a church that Paul did not found and had not visited. He wrote the letter to give an account of his gospel in preparation for a personal visit (1:11). Paul wrote most probably from Corinth, where he was completing the collection of money from the Macedonian and Achaian Christians for the "poor saints" in Jerusalem. After delivering the money, he planned to visit Rome and, with the Roman's support, to travel to Spain. The epistle, therefore, served as an advanced good-will ambassador for Paul's visit to Rome and his later mission to Spain (15:22-33).

Theological Contribution. The great theme of Romans is God's power to save. The Romans understood power; when Paul wrote this epistle to the capital of the ancient world, Rome ruled supreme. The gospel, however, is nothing to be ashamed of in comparison; for it, too, is power—indeed the "power of God to salvation for everyone" (1:16). In the gospel both Jews and Gentiles find access to God, not on the basis of human achievement, but because of God's free grace bestowed on those who accept it in faith.

Paul emphasizes that everyone stands in need of God's grace. This was apparent in the case of the Gentiles, who, instead of worshiping the Creator, worshiped the things created (1:25). But the Jews, in spite of their belief that they were superior to Gentiles, were also bankrupt. The Jews knew the revealed will of God and they judged others by it; but they failed to see they were condemned by the very law under which they passed judgments (2:1—3:8). Thus, "there is no difference, for all have sinned and fall short of the glory of God" (3:22-23).

But "good news" is that God's love is so great that it reaches humankind even in their sin. The form it took was the death of the beloved Son of God on the cross. The righteous one, Jesus, died on behalf of the unrighteous. Therefore, God pronounces persons justified, not when they have attained a certain level of goodness—thus excluding justification by works—but in the midst of their sin and rebellion (5:8-10). Such grace can be received only by grateful and trusting surrender, which is FAITH.

In light of this magnificent salvation, Paul urged the Romans not to return to their old human nature, which always stands under condemnation of the law. Rather, he called on them to live free from sin and death through the power of the indwelling presence of the Holy Spirit (8:10-11).

Special Considerations. Romans reflects Paul's deep concern with the relation between Jew and Gentile (chaps. 9—11). The Jews are indeed God's Chosen People, although their history is one of rebellion against God. Their rejection of Christ is consistent with their history, although a remnant does remain faithful. The rejection of the Jews, ironically, has increased the truly faithful because the cutting off of the native olive branch (Israel) has allowed a wild branch (Gentiles) to be grafted onto the tree (11:13).

Paul also declared that the inclusion of the Gentiles in the household of God aroused the Jews to jealousy, moving them to claim God's promised blessings. Thus, the hardened response of the Jews to the gospel is only temporary, until the Gentiles are fully included into the faith. At some future time the Jews will change and, like the remnant, "all Israel will be saved" (11:26).

Paul's wrestling with this problem caused him

not to doubt or condemn God, but to marvel at God's wisdom (11:33). This marvelous epistle has kindled the same response in Christians of all generations.

ROME, CITY OF — capital city of the ancient Roman Empire and present capital of modern Italy (see Map 8, A–1).

Founded in 753 B.C., Rome was situated 24 kilometers (15 miles) from where the Tiber River flows into the Mediterranean Sea. From its initial settlement on the Palatine Hill near the river, the city gradually grew and embraced the surrounding area. Ultimately, the city was situated on seven hills: Capital, Palatine, Anentine, Caelian, Esquiline, Viminal, and Quirinal.

As capital of the Roman Empire, the city was the seat of Roman government. During its long history, Roman government went through the forms of a monarchy, a republic, and an empire.

The monarchy occurred from 753 to 510 B.C. when Rome was ruled by kings. After Romulus, the first king (ruled 753–714 B.C.), Rome was ruled by six other princes until the decline of the monarchical form of government in 510 B.C.

As a republic, Rome was governed by elected consuls who in turn presided over the senate. Under the republic, Rome expanded its borders and engaged in major internal reforms. The period of the republic lasted until 31 B.C. when Caesar Augustus became the first emperor. He developed Rome into a beautiful and stately city.

During the reign of Augustus as emperor in Rome, Jesus was born in Bethlehem of Judea. At that time and during the entire New Testament period, Judea was under Roman rule. Roman influence penetrated the entire Jewish community and continued to be felt in the life and mission of the New Testament church. During the reign of Tiberius, successor to Augustus, Jesus' public ministry occurred. And the great missionary endeavors of the apostle Paul took place during the reign of Claudius. Under Nero, the city of Rome was burned, Christians were persecuted, and the apostle Paul was martyred.

The Book of Acts describes the thrilling story of the early church as it shared the gospel, beginning at Jerusalem and finally reaching Rome.

The apostle Paul's first known connection with Rome was when he met Aquila and Priscilla at Corinth (Acts 18:2). They had left Rome when Claudius expelled all the Jews from the city. Some few years after meeting Aquila and Priscilla, Paul decided that he "must also see Rome" (Acts 19:21). When he wrote his letter to the Christians at Rome, his plan was to visit friends in the city on his way to Spain (Rom. 15:24).

However, Paul actually went to Rome under very different conditions than he had originally

The Roman Forum looking toward the east, with the famous Colosseum of the city in the distance.
Photo by Howard Vos

planned. To keep from being killed by hostile Jews in Jerusalem, Paul appealed to Caesar. The binding effect of that appeal ultimately brought him to the capital city as a prisoner. Here he waited for his trial. The Book of Acts closes at this point, and one must rely on secular history and references in the Pastoral Epistles for the rest of the story. Tradition holds that Paul was ultimately martyred by Nero during the emperor's persecution of Christians.

The city to which Paul came was very similar to a modern city. The public buildings and other structures were lavishly constructed. A new senate house and a temple to honor Caesar had been constructed in A.D. 29. In A.D. 28 the senate had authorized Augustus to rebuild or restore some 82 temples which were in need of repair. In the process, he built a great temple to Apollo near his palace on the Palatine Hill. Other buildings included the Coliseum, where Roman games occurred.

The houses of the wealthy people of Rome were elaborately constructed and situated on the various hills, but most of the people lived in tenements. These crowded apartment dwellings were multi-storied buildings that engulfed the city. Over a million people lived in these tenements, which were surrounded by narrow and noisy streets with a steady flow of traffic day and night.

The people of Rome were provided with food and entertainment by the state. Wine was also plentiful and cheap. Admission to the games was free. Large crowds attended these games, which included chariot racing, gladiatorial contests, and theatrical performances.

Like Babylon, the city of Rome became a symbol of paganism and idolatry in the New Testament. The Book of Revelation contains several disguised references to the pagan city. Most scholars agree that Revelation 17—18 should be interpreted as predictions of the fall of Rome.

ROOF — the top of a house. The roof of a typical house in Palestine usually was flat and often was used as a sitting area. The roof was used as a place both to relax and to observe the surrounding area (2 Sam. 11:2). The phrase, "Under my roof," suggested hospitality. Thus, when the centurion whose servant Jesus healed did not feel worthy of having Jesus "under my roof" (Matt. 8:8), he was saying that he had no right to entertain Him. Also see HOUSE.

ROOF-CHAMBER (see CHAMBER).

ROOMS — separate compartments into which buildings were divided. Typical houses in Bible times had few rooms. The upper room, enclosed on the housetop, was the most desirable one in the house, and it usually was given to house guests. Jesus probably held the Last Supper in a room like this (Mark 14:14; Luke 22:11). The houses of the poor did not feel such special rooms. They usually contained only one all-purpose room. Also see HOUSE.

ROOSTER — the adult male of the common do-

Photo: British Museum

The famous Rosetta Stone, showing the three distinct ancient languages with which the stone was inscribed.

mestic fowl. All four gospels tell how Jesus predicted Peter's denial: "Assuredly, I say to you that this night, before the rooster crows [or crows twice, Mark 14:30], you will deny Me three times" (Matt. 26:34; also Luke 22:34; John 13:38).

ROOT — the part of a plant which provides stability and nourishment for the plant. Most of the references to root in the Bible are symbolic, based on this important relationship of the root to the plant. As a metaphor, to be rooted means to be established; to be uprooted means to be dispossessed.

The highest use of the metaphor of the word root comes in the messianic passages that refer to Jesus as the descendant of David: "And in that day there shall be a Root of Jesse who shall stand as a banner to the people" (Is. 11:10). The Book of Revelation speaks of Christ as "the Root of David" (5:5) and "the Root and Offspring of David" (22:16), indicating that Jesus is both human and divine, both the Offspring and the Origin of the messianic line.

ROPE (see CORD).

ROSE (see PLANTS OF THE BIBLE).

ROSETTA STONE — a black basalt tablet unearthed in August, 1799, near the village of Rosetta, Egypt, then taken to the British Museum in 1802. The stone was inscribed in three languages: hieroglyphic, Demotic Egyptian, and Koine Greek. This stone was the key which the brilliant young French scholar and Egyptologist, Jean Francois

Champollion, needed to decipher Egyptian hieroglyphics. Champollion broke the hieroglyphic code by comparing it with the other two languages, which were translations of the same text. The discovery of this stone made it possible for scholars to translate Egyptian texts and to understand the historical background of Israel's history.

ROSH [rahsh] (*chief*) — the name of a man and a tribe in the Old Testament:

1. A descendant of Benjamin (Gen. 46:21) and one of those who went to Egypt with Jacob and Jacob's sons.

2. A northern people mentioned with Meshech and Tubal (Ezek. 38:2–3; 39:1). Some scholars believe Rosh was the name of one of the three northern tribes over which Gog ruled.

ROYAL CITY — a headquarters or capital city, or the center of a king's royal rule in Bible times. Notable capital cities of the Bible included JERSUALEM (Judah), SAMARIA (Israel), and DAMASCUS (Syria). The term royal city is also applied to RABBAH, capital of the AMMONITES (2 Sam. 12:26).

RUBY (see JEWELS AND PRECIOUS STONES).

RUDDER — a flat piece of wood or metal attached to a ship's stern that causes the ship to turn as it is moved (Acts 27:40; steering-paddles, NEB; James 3:4; helm, KJV). "Look also at ships," James wrote. "Although they are so large and are driven by fierce winds, they are turned by a very small rudder wherever the pilot desires. Even so the tongue is a little member and boasts great things" (James 3:4–5). Also see SHIPS.

RUDDY — a healthy, reddish color. In two places in the Bible the word refers to the rosy complexion of vigorous health (Song 5:10; Lam. 4:7). As a boy, David was also described as ruddy (1 Sam. 16:12; 17:42). Some scholars believe the word in this case may mean that David had red hair.

RUDIMENTS — KJV word for fundamental elements, principles, or skills (Col. 2:8, 20; basic principles, NKJV). The word rudiments may refer to "the elemental spirits of the universe" (RSV), demons (1 Cor. 10:20–21), or to principles of human philosophy in contrast to the truths of Christ. In Galatians 4:3, 9, the apostle Paul uses the same word to refer to the "weak and beggarly elements" to which believers were in bondage before they came to Christ.

RUE (see PLANTS OF THE BIBLE).

RUFUS [ROO fuhs] (*red-haired*) — the name of one or two men in the New Testament:

1. A son of Simon of Cyrene (Mark 15:21). Simon was the man who was compelled by the Romans to carry the cross of Jesus (Matt. 27:32; Luke 23:26).

2. A Christian in Rome to whom Paul sent greetings (Rom. 16:13).

RUHAMAH [roo HAH muh] (*mercy is shown*) — a symbolic name given to Israel by the prophet Hosea to indicate the return of God's mercy (Hos. 2:1, KJV, NAS; mercy is shown, NKJV).

RUIN, RUINS — a total disintegration or collapse; the remains of something destroyed. The Bible also speaks of moral and spiritual ruin, which can come to those who worship idols (2 Chr. 28:23) or who hear the words of Christ and do nothing (Luke 6:46–49).

RULER OF THE SYNAGOGUE — the leader or president of a SYNAGOGUE. As an administrator, he was charged with supervision of all matters pertaining to the synagogue. He was not a dictator over the congregation. He was elected by the board of elders to oversee the worship services and the upkeep of the building. He chose the men to read the Scriptures, to offer prayer, and to preach or explain the Scripture for each meeting.

If discipline was called for, the ruler of the synagogue could reprimand or excommunicate a member (John 9:22; 16:2), or even order that a scourging or a whipping be carried out (Matt. 10:17; Mark 13:9). Rulers of the synagogue mentioned by name in the New Testament are JAIRUS (Mark 5:22; Luke 8:41), CRISPUS (Acts 18:8), and SOSTHENES (Acts 18:17).

RUMAH [ROO muh] (*elevated*) — the hometown of Pedaiah (2 Kin. 23:36), location unknown.

RUSH (see PLANTS OF THE BIBLE).

RUST — corrosion of metal. This term is often used symbolically in the Bible. In the Old Testament, the prophet Ezekiel's parable of the corroded copper cauldron (Ezek. 24:6–13, RSV, NAS) speaks of the rust (or scum, NKJV, KJV) that has become encrusted on the cooking pots as a symbol of the ingrained filthiness of the unbelievers in Jerusalem. In the New Testament, Jesus contrasted "treasures on earth" that moth and rust destroy with "treasures in heaven" (Matt. 6:19–20).

In an indictment of the rich who have oppressed the poor, James said that the rich would be judged: "Your gold and silver are corroded and their corrosion will be a witness against you" (James 5:3).

RUTH [rooth] (*friendship*) — the mother of Obed and great-grandmother of David. A woman of the country of Moab, Ruth married Mahlon, one of the two sons of Elimelech and Naomi. With his wife and sons, Elimelech had migrated to Moab to escape a famine in the land of Israel. When Elimelech and both of his sons died, they left three widows: Naomi, Ruth, and Orpah (Ruth's sister-in-law). When Naomi decided to return home to Bethlehem, Ruth chose to accompany her, saying, "Wherever you go, I will go" (Ruth 1:16).

In Bethlehem, Ruth was permitted to glean in the field of Boaz, a wealthy kinsman of Elimelech (Ruth 2:1). At Naomi's urging, Ruth asked protection of Boaz as next of kin—a reflection of the Hebrew law of LEVIRATE MARRIAGE (Deut. 25:5–10). After a nearer kinsman waived his right to buy the family property and provide Elimelech an heir, Boaz married Ruth. Their son, Obed, was considered one of Naomi's family, according to the custom of the day.

Ruth's firm decision—"Your people shall be my people, and your God, my God" (Ruth 1:16)—brought a rich reward. She became an ancestor of David and Jesus (Matt. 1:5).

RUTH, BOOK OF — a short Old Testament book about a devoted Gentile woman, Ruth of Moab, who became an ancestor of King David of Israel.

Structure of the Book. The Book of Ruth tells the story of a Moabite woman who married into a family of Israelites. But her husband and all the other men of the family died, leaving Ruth and her mother-in-law Naomi in a desperate situation. Ruth accompanied Naomi back to Judah, where they scratched out an existence by gathering leftover grain in the fields. This led to Ruth's encounter with Boaz, a wealthy Israelite and distant kinsman of Naomi, who eventually married the Moabite woman. Their son became the father of David's father, making Ruth and Boaz the great-grandparents of Judah's most famous king.

Authorship and Date. The author of Ruth is unknown, although some scholars credit it to the prophet Samuel. The book had to be written some time after David became king of Judah, since it refers to his administration. This would place its writing at some time around 990 B.C.

Historical Setting. The events in the book occurred at a dark time in Israel's history—in "the days when the judges ruled" (1:1), according to the historical introduction. This was a period when the nation lapsed again and again into worship of false gods. What a contrast this is to Ruth, who remained faithful to God, although she was a Moabite by birth—one considered an alien by God's Chosen People.

Theological Contribution. Ruth's life gives us a beautiful example of the providence of God. He brought Ruth to precisely the right field where she could meet Boaz. God is also portrayed in the book as the model of loyal and abiding love (2:20).

Special Considerations. The name Ruth means "friendship," and this book contains one of the most touching examples of friendship in the Bible. Ruth's words to her mother-in-law are quoted often as a pledge of love and devotion. "Entreat me not to leave you, or to turn back from following after you; for wherever you lodge, I will lodge; your people shall be my people, and your God, my God" (1:16).

RYE (see PLANTS OF THE BIBLE).

RUTH: A Teaching Outline

Part One: Ruth's Love Is Demonstrated (1:1—2:23)

Part Two: Ruth's Love Is Rewarded (3:1—4:22)

S

SABACHTHANI [suh BAHK thuh nigh] — one of the final words spoken by Jesus from the cross (Matt. 27:46; Mark 15:34), meaning "you have forsaken me." Also see SEVEN WORDS FROM THE CROSS.

SABAOTH [SABB a ohth] — a name for God which means, literally, "God of hosts" (Rom. 9:29; James 5:4). This name refers specifically to God's control over all creation. Also see GOD, NAMES OF.

SABBATH [SAB bahth] — the practice of observing one day in seven as a time for rest and worship. This practice apparently originated in creation, because God created the universe in six days and rested on the seventh (Genesis 1). By this act, God ordained a pattern for living—that man should work six days each week at subduing and ruling the creation and should rest one day a week. This is the understanding of the creation set forth by Moses in Exodus 20:3–11, when he wrote the Ten Commandments at God's direction.

History of the Sabbath. The practice of the weekly Sabbath is suggested at several places in the Bible, long before the Ten Commandments were given at Mt. Sinai. In Genesis, for example, starting with Seth (Gen. 4:26), men began to call upon the name of the Lord in acts of worship. Thus, periods of seven days play a prominent role at crucial points throughout Genesis (Gen. 7:4, 10; 8:10, 12). The mention of a seven-day week and a seven-year cycle in the life practice of Laban, Abraham's relative, is striking. The patriarch Job worshiped God every seventh day (Job 1:4–5).

The formal institution of the Sabbath is a basic part of the Mosaic Law system. Each division of the law contains specific sections relating to the practice of the Sabbath: the moral law (the Ten Commandments), the civil law (Ex. 31:14), and the ceremonial law (Lev. 23:3). The keeping of the Sabbath was a sign that God truly ruled Israel. To break His Sabbath law was to rebel against Him—an action meriting death (Ex. 21:14). Society was not to seek advancement outside of submission to God. Therefore, all work except acts of mercy, necessity, and worship were forbidden on the Sabbath (Is. 58:13; Matt. 12:1–13).

The Old Testament prophets recounted God's blessings upon those who properly observed the Sabbath (Is. 58:13). They called upon the people to observe the Sabbath (Neh. 10:31; 13:15–22), while soundly condemning those who made much of external observance and ignored the heart and moral issues to which the Sabbath bound them (Is. 1:13; Hos. 2:11; Amos 8:5). During the period between the Old and New Testaments, Jewish religious leaders added greatly to the details of Sabbath legislation. They sought to insure proper and careful observance by making certain that people did not even come close to violating it. This substituted human law for divine law (Matt. 15:9), made the law a burden rather than a rest and delight (Luke 11:46), and reduced the Sabbath to little more than an external observance (Matt. 12:8). Jesus, like the Old Testament prophets, kept the Sabbath Himself (Luke 4:16) and urged others to observe the day (Mark 2:28). But He condemned the pharisaical attitude that missed the deep spiritual truth behind Sabbath observance (Matt 12:14; Mark 2:23; Luke 6:1–11; John 5:1–18).

The Christian Sabbath. Many Christians feel that God still expects His people to set aside one day in seven to Him. They argue that such an observance is a creation ordinance which is binding until this creation comes to an end and our ultimate rest as Christians is realized in heaven (Hebrews 4). They also believe that as part of the moral system known as the Ten Commandments, the Sabbath is morally binding upon all people for all time.

Historically, Christians of this persuasion usually observe Sunday, the first day of the week, as the Christian Sabbath. They note that Christ arose on the first day of the week (Matt. 28:1) and, thereafter, the New Testament church regularly worshiped on Sunday (Acts 20:7; 1 Cor. 16:2; Rev. 1:10). This day on which Jesus arose was called the LORD'S DAY (Rev. 1:10).

Meaning of the Sabbath. The Sabbath is a means by which man's living pattern imitates God's (Ex. 20:3–11). Work is followed by rest. This idea is expressed by the Hebrew word for Sabbath, which means "cessation."

Sabbath rest is also a time for God's people to think about and enjoy what God has accomplished. Another Hebrew word meaning "rest" embodies this idea (Deut. 5:14). God's people are directed to keep the Sabbath because God delivered and redeemed His people from the bondage in Egypt. Thus, the Sabbath is an ordinance that relates redemption directly to history.

Sabbath rest also holds promise of the ultimate salvation that God will accomplish for His people. As certainly as He delivered them from Egypt through Moses, so will He deliver His people from sin at the end of the age through the Great Redeemer (Gen. 3:15; Hebrews 4).

Finally, the Sabbath includes the idea and practice of celebrating rest, or salvation. To this end, God declared that His Sabbath was a day for public convocation (Lev. 23:3), a special time for His people to gather together in public worship to signify their submission to His lordship over them and their way of living (Ex. 31:13; Ezek. 20:12). The idea of Sabbath celebration includes the Sabbath as a sacrament—a gift of God that allows man to enter into God's rest (salvation).

The concept of celebration also presents the Sabbath as a delight (Ps. 92; Is. 58:13; Hos. 2:11). The sabbatical holy days (holidays) prescribed rest from work for everyone (Ex. 23:21; Num. 15:32). These holy days also were to be characterized by great rejoicing before the Lord. To this end the daily morning and evening sacrifices were doubled on the weekly Sabbath day (Num. 28:9; Ps. 92).

On the Sabbath the SHOWBREAD, which reminded Israel of God's daily and bounteous blessings, was to be renewed (Lev. 24:8). The people were to meet together to praise God and to be instructed in His law (Lev. 10:11; Deut. 14:29; 33:10).

Also see FEASTS AND FESTIVALS.

SABBATH DAY'S JOURNEY — the distance a Jew could travel on the Sabbath without breaking the law. This phrase occurs in the Bible in Acts 1:12, where Mount Olivet is described as being "near Jerusalem, a Sabbath day's journey." This distance is usually reckoned to be about a thousand yards (Josh. 3:4, NIV, NEB; two thousand cubits, NKJV), because of the distance between the ARK OF THE COVENANT and the rest of the Israelite camp in the wilderness.

The idea behind the Jewish law (see Ex. 16:29) was that every person within the camp or city would be close enough to the center of worship to take part in the services without having to travel such a great distance that the Sabbath became a harried and busy day. This law, although noble in intent, was soon abused by a strict legalism. In the New Testament, Jesus often clashed with the Pharisees because of their blind legalism over observance of the Sabbath (Matt. 12:1-9).

SABBATICAL YEAR — a year of rest and redemption that occurred every seven years in the Hebrew nation. By God's prescription, Israel was to set apart every seventh year by letting the land go uncultivated (Lev. 25:4-5). The crops and harvest that were reaped during this year were considered the

Photo: Levant Photo Service

Pompey's Pillar in Alexandria, Egypt—a monument erected in honor of a famous Roman general and statesman Pompey the Great.

common possession of all men and beasts (Ex. 23:11; Deut. 15:1-18). None of this harvest was to be stored for future use.

During a sabbatical year, Israelites were to cancel all debts owed to them by their fellow Israelites (Deut. 15:1-5). At the least, a period of grace was to be set aside in which payment was not required. The people of Israel were also to free their Hebrew slaves, remembering that they were also slaves in the land of Egypt at one time and that God had redeemed them by His goodness.

God's anger fell on Israel because the sabbatical year was not observed from the time of Solomon (Jer. 34:14-22). This was one reason why Israel spent 70 years in bondage at the hands of the Babylonians.

Also see FEASTS AND FESTIVALS.

SABEANS [suh BEE uhnz] — the inhabitants of SHEBA, an ancient country of southwest Arabia, now known as Yemen (Job 1:15).

SABTA, SABTAH [SAB tuh] (meaning unknown) — the third son of Cush and grandson of Ham (Gen 10:7; Sabtah; 1 Chr. 1:9; Sabta). Sabta's descendants lived in Arabia, perhaps along the southwestern coast of the Red Sea.

SABTECA [SAB tuh kuh] — a form of SABTECHA.

SABTECHA [SAB tuh kuh] (meaning unknown) — the youngest son of Cush and grandson of Ham (Gen. 10:7, Sabtechah, Sabteca, NAS, RSV; 1 Chr. 1:9, Sabteca, NAS, RSV).

SACAR [SAY kahr] (*reward*) — the name of two men in the Old Testament:
1. The father of Ahiam (1 Chr. 11:35; Sachar, RSV). Sacar is also called Sharar (2 Sam. 23:33).
2. A son of Obed-Edom (1 Chr. 26:4).

SACHAR [SAY kahr] — a form of SACAR.

SACHIA [suh KIGH uh] — a form of SACHIAH.

SACHIAH [suh KIGH uh] (*captive of the Lord*) — a descendant of Benjamin (1 Chr. 8:10; Sachia, RSV, NASB; Sakia, NIV; Shachia, KJV, NEB).

SACKBUT (see MUSICAL INSTRUMENTS).

SACKCLOTH — a rough, coarse cloth, or a bag-like garment made of this cloth and worn as a symbol of mourning or repentance. In the Bible sackcloth was often used to symbolize certain actions. In the case of mourning, either over a death (Gen. 37:34; Joel 1:8) or another calamity (Esth. 4:1–4; Job 16:15), the Israelites showed their grief by wearing sackcloth and ashes. This was done also in instances of confession and grief over sin (1 Kin. 21:27).

Sackcloth was often worn by prophets, perhaps to show their own brokenness in the face of their terrible message of judgment and doom (Is. 20:2; Rev. 11:3). The word for sackcloth in the Bible can also mean sack. Joseph ordered that the sacks of his brothers be filled with grain (Gen. 42:25). Rizpah spread sackcloth on a rock, using it as bedding material (2 Sam. 21:10). But sackcloth was most commonly used as an article of clothing.

SACRAMENT — a formal religious act in which the actions and materials used are the channels by which God's grace is communicated, either actually or symbolically. The word sacrament is not used in most English versions of the Bible. It comes from the Latin *sacramentum*, which was the word for a soldier's oath of allegiance. The word also came to have the idea of mystery associated with it. The Eastern Orthodox churches usually refer to the sacraments as mysteries.

Roman Catholics and the Orthodox have seven sacraments: the Eucharist (Lord's Supper), baptism, confirmation, penance (the forgiveness of sins), matrimony, holy orders, and extreme unction (the anointing of those in danger of death). They hold that these sacraments are means of grace, or channels through which God imparts spiritual blessedness.

Protestant Christians, who generally prefer to use the word ordinances rather than sacraments, consider baptism and the Lord's Supper the only true sacraments instituted by the Lord Jesus. These are the only two actions involving visible symbols (the water, and the bread and wine) that were clearly observed by Christ (Luke 22:14–20) and commanded by Him (Matt. 28:19–20). Some Christians object to calling baptism and the Lord's Supper sacraments, insisting that these "ordinances" are not means to grace but symbols of grace.

SACRIFICE — the ritual through which the Hebrew people offered the blood or the flesh of an animal to God as a "substitute payment" for their sin. Sacrifice and sacrificing originated in the Garden of Eden immediately following the FALL of man. Adam and Eve made loincloths of leaves to cover their sinfulness, then hid from God because their provision was inadequate in their own minds. God then killed animals and made larger tunics for Adam and Eve. God's covering covered men adequately, while man's covering was insufficient.

These coverings were declared acceptable by God, because they covered more of man's body and they were produced by the shedding of blood. Furthermore, the curses and the promise of a redeemer (Gen. 3:14–19) fell between man's attempt to cover his sin (Gen. 3:7) and God's adequate covering (Gen. 3:21). Man's reaction to God's provision (3:14–19) was faith and hope in the Lord. Adam called his wife Eve, which means "the mother of all living" (Gen. 3:20). God's provision of adequate coverings for Adam and Eve symbolized that man could come before God, the source of all life, in the confidence that he would not die.

These principles of sacrifice are confirmed in the account of Cain and Abel (Gen. 4:3–5). Abel offered a better sacrifice than Cain for two reasons (Heb. 11:4). First, he conformed to the provisions and concepts which God had previously established with Adam and Eve. Second, Abel's offering recognized the just penalty for sin—death—and God's gracious provision of an acceptable substitute. To Abel God's provision was a sacrifice—the substitution of a living being for himself. Abel received God's approval because He believed God and had faith in what God promised (Gen. 4:4–5).

When Noah came out of the ark, his first act was to build an altar upon which he sacrificed animals to God. This pleased God not because God was hungry but because Noah's act was a recognition that God understood his sinfulness, its penalty, and the necessity of blood sacrifice as a divine provision (Heb. 11:39–40). Noah represented all mankind who now recognized God's gracious provision and promise. God pledged never again to curse the ground (Gen. 8:20–22), and He blessed Noah because of his faith.

Eventually, God called Abraham, who rejoiced in anticipation of the appearance of a promised redeemer (John 8:56). Abraham regularly worshiped God by offering sacrifices to Him. God taught Abraham that the ultimate sacrifice would be the sacrifice of a human being, one of Adam's descendants—an only son provided miraculously by God.

The fullest explanation of the concept of sacrifice is found in the Mosaic Law. In this code sacrifice has three central ideas: consecration, expiation (covering of sin), and propitiation (satisfaction of divine anger). Only consecration had a kind of sacrifice which spoke of it alone. This was the vegetable or meal offerings. These could not be brought to God, however, unless they were preceded by an expiatory offering, or an animal or bloody sacrifice. There was no consecration (commitment) to God apart from expiation (dealing with the penalty and guilt of sin). Man could not approach God and be right with Him without the shedding of blood.

The general word for sacrifices in the Mosaic Law was *qorban*—literally "that which is brought near." The fuller designation of these sacrifices was a gift of holiness (Ezek. 20:40). The word *qorban* was used of anything given or devoted to God, so it included more than sacrifices presented at the altar. Sacrifice, however, referred to items placed on the altar to be consumed by God. Hence, there was no sacrifice apart from the altar.

The Old Testament also referred to sacrifices as food for Jehovah (Lev. 3:11, 16; 22:7) and an offering made by the fire for the satisfaction of Jehovah (Lev. 2:2, 9). As a spiritual being, God did not need physical food. Nevertheless, He did insist that these sacrifices be given to Him. Sacrifice as worship is man giving back to God what God has previously given him as a means of grace. Ultimately, these sacrifices speak of the one final and perfect sacrifice of Jesus Christ (Heb. 10:11–18).

The gift aspect of sacrifice was emphasized by the many divine regulations determining what was acceptable to God. For man to determine what pleased God would put man in the place of God. Therefore, God determined what was pleasing to Him. Whatever was offered had to be "clean" (acceptable, or symbolically without sin). Not everything designated "clean," however, was to be offered as a sacrifice. Of the clean animals, only oxen, sheep, goats, and pigeons were acceptable offerings. Likewise, of the clean vegetables, only corn, wine, and oil were proper.

These materials were selected perhaps to teach that man should give to God from that which sustains his life. In short, man was required to give God the gift of his life. Therefore, God repeatedly emphasized that He did not need or desire food and sacrifices themselves. He wants man's love, commitment, and service (Deut. 6:5; 1 Sam. 15:22).

Both the Old Testament and the New Testament confirm that sacrifices were presented as a symbolic gesture. Man was obligated, because of his sin, to present offerings by which he gave another life in place of his own. These substitutes pointed forward to the ultimate substitute, Jesus Christ (Heb. 10:1–18).

According to God's command, the animal sacrificed had to be physically perfect in age and condition. Through the perfection of this animal, perfection was presented to God. Ultimately, this symbolized the necessity for man to present himself perfect before God by presenting the perfect one in his place (1 Pet. 1:18–19). The true Lamb of God, innocent of all sin, took away sin (John 1:29).

After the animal was selected and presented at the altar, the first act was the laying on of hands by the person presenting the offering. By this act the worshiper symbolically transferred his sin and guilt to the sacrificial animal which stood in his place. The sacrifice symbolically pointed to the Savior who would do for the believer what he could not do for himself. He would take upon Himself sin and guilt and accomplish redemption for His people (Is. 53:4–12; Matt. 1:21).

In the great atonement festival, two goats de-

Sacrificial altar for wine and fruit at the Nabatean city of Petra in southern Palestine.

Photo by Gustav Jeeninga

picted this redemptive act. One goat died, its death symbolizing how the ultimate sacrifice in the future would pay the penalty for the believer's sin. Its blood was applied to the MERCY SEAT in the HOLY OF HOLIES, symbolizing how the great sacrifice would cover man's sin, bring unworthy man into God's presence, and make full restitution to God. On the head of the second goat the priest symbolically conferred the sin of God's people. Then this goat, known as the SCAPEGOAT, was sent into the wilderness to symbolize the removal of the people's sin.

In the second act of the ritual, the offerer killed the animal on the north side of the altar. Details such as the stipulation of the north side taught the worshiper that this act must be done exactly as God prescribed in order to be acceptable to Him. This slaying was an important element in the whole process of making sacrifice. By it the offerer acted out his guilt and involvement in the death of the victim and in the death of the promised redeemer.

SACRIFICE, HUMAN (see HUMAN SACRIFICE).

SACRIFICIAL OFFERINGS — offerings to God in Old Testament times by which man hoped to atone for his sins and restore fellowship with God. The Bible depicts man as a sinner abiding in death and destined for death. He abides in death because he is separated from fellowship with God and unable to restore that life-giving fellowship (Rom. 5:12; 8). The sentence of death hangs over man because of his identity with Adam's fall (Rom. 5:14), his enmity toward God, and his constant sinning (Gen. 6:5; 8:21; Rom. 3:10). Ultimately, this will result in physical death and eternal suffering in hell.

God, however, provided a method by which man's penalty can be paid and fellowship with God can be restored. This method is the sacrificial offering of Jesus Christ (Hebrews 9—10). This perfect offering was anticipated throughout the Old Testament by various sacrificial offerings. These Old Testament sacrifices were effective only when offered in faith in the promised sacrifice (Gen. 3:15; Heb. 9:8–9; 10:8–9, 16–17).

The first sacrifice was made by God; it consisted of animals slain to cover man's sin. This was followed by the offerings of Cain and Abel. Only Abel's offering was a true sacrifice made in faith because Abel recognized his unworthiness and the divine promise of a true and perfect redeemer (Gen. 4:3–5; Heb. 1:4).

After this first sacrifice provided by God, godly people offered similar blood sacrifices looking forward to the sacrifice of Jesus Christ (Heb. 11:17–19, 23). The sacrifice of Christ is most clearly and fully anticipated in the Mosaic system of sacrifical offerings. The following specific sacrificial offerings were provided for in the Mosaic Law:

Burnt Offering. This kind of offering was described as "that which goes up (to God)." It was termed "whole" (Lev. 6:22) because the entire offering was to be burnt upon the altar. It was termed "continual" (Ex. 29:38–42) to teach the nation of Is-

rael that their sinfulness required a complete and continual atonement and consecration. This sacrifice, offered every morning and evening, pointed to Christ's atoning death for sinners (2 Cor. 5:21) and His total consecration to God (Luke 2:49). The burnt offering spoke of Christ's passive obedience and His submission to the penalty required by man's sinfulness. It also refers to His perfect obedience to God's law by which He did for us what we are unable to do for ourselves.

Cereal Offering (see *Meal Offering*).

Guilt Offering (see *Sin Offering*).

Heave Offering (see *Peace Offering*).

Meal Offering. This offering is translated meat offering in some versions, but since this offering was bloodless and meatless, it is more meaningfully rendered meal (NKJV) or cereal offering (RSV). Meal offerings were prepared and presented to God as a meal, symbolically presenting the best fruits of human living to be consumed or used as He desired (Heb. 10:5–10). A notable exception to this is that poor people could present meal offerings as sin offerings.

In the meal offering a person presented to God a vicarious consecration of the perfect life and total property of another (Christ). There is no ground in this offering for human boasting as though the offerer were received by God on the grounds of his own human effort. Rather, the recognition of the person's unworthiness is emphasized by the fact that meal offerings must always be accompanied by a whole burnt offering or a peace offering (Lev. 2:1; Num. 15:1–16). Both offerings were made to atone for man's sin.

Meat Offering (see *Meal Offering*).

Peace Offering. This sacrificial offering was also called a heave offering and a wave offering. This was a bloody offering presented to God. Part of the offering was eaten by the priest (representing God's acceptance) and part was eaten by the worshiper and his guests (non-officiating priests or Levites and the poor, Deut. 12:18; 16:11). Thus, God hosted the meal, communing with the worshiper and other participants. This sacrifice celebrated covering of sin, forgiveness by God, and the restoration of a right and meaningful relationship with God and with life itself (Judg. 20:26; 21:4).

There were three kinds of peace offerings: (1) thank offerings in response to an unsolicited special divine blessing; (2) votive (vowed) offerings in pursuit of making a request or pledge to God; and (3) freewill offerings spontaneously presented in worship and praise.

Sin Offering. This bloody offering, also known as a guilt offering, was presented for unintentional or intentional sins for which there was no possible restitution (Lev. 4:5–13; 6:24–30). If the offering was not accompanied by repentance, divine forgiveness was withheld (Num. 15:30). Expiation or covering (forgiveness) of sin was represented by the blood smeared on the horns of the altar of incense or burnt offering and poured out at the base of the altar.

The size (value) and sex of the beast offered depended on the rank of the offerer. The higher his post the more responsibility he bore. The penalty for all sin, death, was vicariously inflicted on the sacrificial animal. Guilt for the worshiper's sin was transferred symbolically to the animal through the laying on of the offerer's hands.

Thank Offering (see *Peace Offering*).

Trespass Offering. This was a bloody offering presented for unintentional or intentional sins of a lesser degree and for which the violater could make restitution (Lev. 5:15). The sprinkling of the blood on the sides of the altar rather than on its horns gave further evidence that this offering addressed sins of a lesser degree. Special provisions were made for the poor by allowing less valuable offerings to be substituted in this kind of sacrifice.

The amount of restitution (money paid) was determined by the officiating priest. Restitution declared that the debt incurred was paid. Significantly, Christ was declared a trespass offering in Isaiah 53:10. He not only bore the sinner's penalty but made restitution, restoring the sinner to right standing with God.

Wave Offering (see *Peace Offering*).

SACRILEGE (see ABOMINATION OF DESOLATION).

SADDLE — a seat for a rider, strapped to the back of an animal (Lev. 15:9). The saddle of Old Testament times had little resemblance to the modern saddle. It probably consisted of little more than a flat piece of leather or cloth.

SADDUCEES [SAJ uh seez] — members of a Jewish faction that opposed Jesus during His ministry. Known for their denial of the bodily resurrection, the Sadducees came from the leading families of the nation—the priests, merchants, and aristocrats. The high priests and the most powerful members of the priesthood were mainly Sadducees (Acts 5:17).

Some scholars believe the name Sadducees came from Zadok, the high priest in the days of David (2 Sam. 15:24) and Solomon (1 Kin. 1:34–45). Many of the wealthy lay people were also Sadducees. This may be the reason why the Sadducees gave the impression of wanting to preserve things as they were. They enjoyed privileged positions in society and managed to get along well under Roman rule. Any movement that might upset order and authority was bound to appear dangerous in their eyes.

The Sadducees rejected "the tradition of the elders," that body of oral and written commentary which interpreted the law of Moses. This automatically placed them in direct conflict with another Jewish group, the PHARISEES, who had made the traditions surrounding the Law almost as important as the Law itself. The Sadducees insisted that only the laws that were written in the law of Moses (the PENTATEUCH, the first five books of the Old Testament) were really binding. The Sadducees thought this way because of religious practices that had taken place for several centuries.

For many years the priests were in charge of teaching the law of God to the Israelites; they were the authorities to go to for interpretation or application of the law (Deut. 17:8–13). Unfortunately, the leading priests lost the respect of the people by becoming corrupt. When this happened, many Jews began to respond to the SCRIBES, people who had become experts in God's law and who usually lived pious, disciplined lives, although many of them were not priests. People began to follow the teaching of the scribes and to let the scribes interpret the law of God for them. The "tradition of the elders" which followed was made up of customs, rulings, and interpretations that the scribes passed on as the authoritative way in which God's law should be applied.

The Sadducees rejected this approach to authority in favor of the written law of Moses. They felt the original law alone could be trusted. Naturally, they felt Saducean priests should be the ones to serve as the law's interpreters.

The Sadducees did not believe in the resurrection of the dead or the immortality of the soul, since these doctrines are not mentioned in the law of Moses. Neither did they believe in rewards or punishments handed out after death, as in the doctrines of heaven and hell. Acts 23:8 indicates that they did not believe in angels or spirits, either. They also believed in free will—that man is responsible for his own prosperity or misfortune. They interpreted the law literally and tended to support strict justice as opposed to mercy toward the offender.

Only a few references are made to the Sadducees in the New Testament. They opposed the early church (Acts 4:1–3; 5:17–18), much more so than even the Pharisees (Acts 5:34–39; 15:5; 23:6–9). Since the chief priests usually came from among the Sadducees, it is clear that they played a major role in the arrest of Jesus and the preliminary hearing against Him (Mark 14:60–64), and that they urged Pilate to crucify Him (Mark 15:1, 3, 10–11). Jesus warned His disciples about the "leaven"—the "doctrine" or teaching—of the Sadducees (Matt. 16:1–12). John the Baptist was suspicious of their supposed "repentance" (Matt. 3:7–12).

One incident when Jesus clashed with the Sadducees is recorded in all three of the synoptic gospels (Matt. 22:23–33; Mark 12:18–27; Luke 20:27–40). Apparently one of the favorite sports of the Sadducees was to make fun of their opponents by showing how their beliefs led to ridiculous conclusions. They approached Jesus with a "what if" question, designed to show the absurd consequences that can arise from believing in the resurrection of the dead. "Suppose," they asked, " a woman had seven husbands in this life, and each of them died without leaving children? Whose wife would she be in the world to come?"

Jesus replied with a two–part answer. First, He said that they were wrong to suggest that earthly relationships, such as marriage, will continue after the resurrection. Second, Jesus pointed out that they were wrong in not believing in the resurrection at all: "Have you not read what was spoken to you

Photo by Howard Vos

Harbor at the New Testament city of Salamis, where Paul and Barnabas landed on their first missionary journey (Acts 13:4-5).

by God, saying, 'I am the God of Abraham, the God of Isaac, and the God of Jacob'? God is not the God of the dead, but of the living" (Matt. 22:31-32; also Ex. 3:6,15–16).

Jesus' argument was that God told Moses that He was the God of Abraham, Isaac, and Jacob. Of course, these three men had died long before the time of Moses. Yet, if they were not "alive" at the time of Moses (that is, if they did not live on after their deaths), then God would not have called Himself their God, for "God is not the God of the dead, but of the living." Abraham, Isaac, and Jacob must live on if God is still their God; therefore, it is wrong to deny life after death and the resurrection of the dead.

After posing His reasons, Jesus stated clearly that the Sadducees were "greatly mistaken" in their beliefs (Mark 12:27). The multitude who heard Jesus' argument were "astonished at His teaching" (Matt. 22:33) and the Sadducees were "silenced" (Matt. 22:34).

SADOC [SAY dahk] — a form of ZADOK.

SAFFRON (see PLANTS OF THE BIBLE).

SAGE, SAILOR (see OCCUPATIONS AND TRADES).

SAINTS — people who have been separated from the world and consecrated to the worship and service of God. Followers of the Lord are referred to by this phrase throughout the Bible, although its meaning is developed more fully in the New Testament. Consecration (setting apart) and purity are the basic meanings of the term. Believers are called "saints" (Rom. 1:7) and "saints in Christ Jesus"

(Phil. 1:1) because they belong to the One who provided their sanctification.

When Christ returns, the saints will be clothed in their "righteous acts" (Rev. 19:8) because they will have continued to live in faith through God's power (1 Sam. 2:9) and Christ's praying for them (Rom. 8:27). The saints are also those to whom the privilege of revelation (Col. 1:26; Jude 3) and the task of ministry (Eph. 4:12) are committed.

SAKIA [suh KIGH uh] — a form of SACHIAH.

SAKKUTH [SACK kuth] (see GODS, PAGAN).

SALAH [SAY luh] (*a sprout*) — a son of Arphaxad (Gen. 10:24). A grandson of Shem, Salah was the father of Eber and an ancestor of Christ. He is also called Shelah (1 Chr. 1:18,24; Luke 3:35) and Sala (Luke 3:35, KJV).

SALAMIS [SAL uh mis] — a thriving port city on the east coast of the island of Cyprus visited by the apostle Paul and Barnabas during Paul's first missionary journey (see Map 7, D–2). These two missionaries preached in several Jewish synagogues at Salamis, assisted by John Mark (Acts 13:5). The city has traditionally been recognized as the birthplace of Barnabas. According to an early tradition, Barnabas was stoned to death here by a Jewish mob. Salamis was famous for its copper mines, flax, wine, fruit, and honey.

SALATHIEL [suh LAY thih uhl] — a form of SHEALTIEL.

SALCAH [SAL kuh] (*wandering*) — a city in the territory of Gad near the eastern border of Bashan.

Part of the former kingdom of Og, Salcah was conquered by the Israelites before they settled the land of Canaan (Deut. 3:10; Salecah, NIV, RSV; Salchah; KJV). The site is now known as Salkhad, about 106 kilometers (66 miles) east of the Jordan River, opposite Beth Shean in Samaria.

SALCHAH, SALECHAH [SAL kuh] — forms of SALCAH.

SALEM [SAY luhm] (*peaceful*) — a city ruled by Melchizedek, the king to whom Abraham gave a tithe (Gen. 14:18). Salem is usually identified with ancient Jerusalem, or Jebus, the Jebusite city captured by David and turned into the capital city of the nation of Judah (1 Chron. 11:4–9).

SALIM [SAY lim] (*peaceful*) — a place near Aenon, where John the Baptist baptized (John 3:23). The phrase, "beyond the Jordan," in this passage probably indicates the city was located east of the Jordan River in Perea.

SALIVA — the watery secretion of the saliva glands (1 Sam. 21:13; John 9:6). Job spoke of saliva in a figurative sense when he indicated he was tormented continuously by God, unable even to swallow his saliva in peace (Job 7:19).

SALLAI [SAL eye] (meaning unknown) — the name of two men in the Old Testament:
1. A leading Benjamite who lived in Jerusalem after the Captivity (Neh. 11:8).
2. A priest who returned to Jerusalem with Zerubbabel after the Captivity (Neh. 12:20). He is also called Sallu (Neh. 12:7).

SALLU [SAL oo] (*contempt*) — the name of two men in the Old Testament:
1. A chief of a family living at Jerusalem after the Captivity (Neh. 11:7).
2. A chief priest who came to Jerusalem with Zerubbabel after the Captivity (Neh. 12:7). He is also called Sallai (Neh. 12:20).

SALMA [SAL muh] (*strength*) — the name of two men in the Old Testament:
1. The father of Boaz and an ancestor of Jesus (1 Chr. 2:11). Salma is also called Salmon (Ruth 4:20–21; Matt. 1:4–5) and Sala (Luke 3:32, RSV).
2. A son of Hur, of the family of Caleb (1 Chr. 2:51).

SALMAI [SAL migh] (meaning unknown) — a Temple servant whose descendants returned to Jerusalem after the Captivity (Neh. 7:48). Salmai is also called Shalmai (Ezra 2:46) and Shamlai (Ezra 2:46, NEB, RSV).

SALMON [SAL muhn] (*peaceable*) — the name of a man and a mountain in the Old Testament:
1. The father of Boaz and an ancestor of Jesus (Ruth 4:20–21; Matt. 1:4–5). He is also called Salma (1 Chr. 2:11) and Sala (Luke 3:32, RSV).
2. A wooded mountain in Samaria near Shechem (Ps. 68:14, KJV). Salmon is also called Zalmon (Judg. 9:48).

SALMONE [sal MOE nih] (*peace*) — a high cliff on the shore of Crete, around which Paul sailed on his voyage to Rome (Acts 27:7). Salmone is now known as Cape Sidero.

SALOME [suh LOE mee] (*peace*) — the name of two women in the New Testament:
1. The daughter of HERODIAS by her first husband Herod Philip, a son of Herod the Great. The New Testament identifies her only as Herodias' daughter (Matt. 14:6–11; Mark 6:22–28). At the birthday celebration of Herod Antipas, who was now living with Herodias, Salome danced before the king and pleased him greatly. He offered to give her anything she wanted. At her mother's urging, Salome asked for John the Baptist's head on a platter. Salome later married her uncle Philip, tetrarch of Trachonitis (Luke 3:1) and then her cousin Aristobulus.
2. One of the women who witnessed the crucifixion of Jesus and who later brought spices to the tomb to anoint His body (Mark 15:40; 16:1). Salome apparently was the mother of James and John, two of the disciples of Jesus. She is pictured in the Gospel of Matthew as asking special favors for her sons (Matt. 20:20–24). Jesus replied that Salome did not understand what kind of sacrifice would be required of her sons.

SALT (see MINERALS OF THE BIBLE).

SALT, CITY OF — a city near the Dead Sea allotted to the tribe of Judah (Josh. 15:62; Ir-melach, NEB). Many scholars identify this city with Khirbet Qumran, about 13 kilometers (8 miles) south of modern Jericho—a site made famous by the discovery of the DEAD SEA SCROLLS.

SALT, COVENANT OF — an Old Testament expression for an everlasting covenant (Num. 18:19). Salt was an important commodity in the ancient world. It was used for seasoning foods as well as to purify and preserve certain substances. Thus, a covenant of salt indicated faithfulness, dependability, and durability. Nomads of the Middle East still eat "bread and salt" together as the sign and seal of a covenant of brotherhood.

SALT HERB (see PLANTS OF THE BIBLE).

SALT, PILLAR OF (see LOT).

SALTPITS — pits from which salt is obtained. The prophet Zephaniah predicted that MOAB and the people of AMMON would become like Sodom and Gomorrah, "overrun with weeds and saltpits, and a perpetual desolation" (Zeph. 2:9). This was a bitter picture of the barrenness that would befall these peoples who rebelled against the Lord.

SALT SEA — an Old Testament name for the body of water at the southern end of the Jordan Valley (Gen. 14:3). It contains no marine life because of its heavy mineral content. The Salt Sea is also called the Sea of the Arabah (Deut. 3:17). Its modern name is the DEAD SEA.

SALT, VALLEY OF — a barren valley, probably south of the Dead Sea, where the nation of Israel won two important victories over the Edomites. The army of King David killed 18,000 Edomites (2 Sam. 8:13; Syrians, KJV, NKJV; Arameans, NASB) in the Valley of Salt. Two centuries later the army of King Amaziah of Judah killed another 10,000 Edomites in this valley (2 Kin. 14:7).

SALTWORT (see PLANTS OF THE BIBLE).

SALU [SAY loo] (meaning unknown) — a Simeonite and the father of Zimri (Num. 25:14).

SALUTATION — an expression of greeting or the word or phrase of greeting with which a letter begins.

In the Old Testament, people often were greeted with the phrase, "God be gracious to you" (Gen. 43:29) or some similar expression (Ps. 129:8). Another typical Hebrew greeting was the word peace. In the New Testament, Jesus criticized the scribes and Pharisees for their elaborate salutations, or greetings, in the marketplaces (Mark 12:38). Apparently the rabbis claimed such public recognition on the basis of their office. When Jesus sent out the 70 disciples, He told them, "Greet no one along the road" (Luke 10:4). The work of the disciples was so important that they had no time for idle ceremonies and prolonged greetings; they must hasten to carry out their mission.

The apostle Paul used the word salutation three times in his writings (1 Cor. 16:20-21; Col. 4:18; 2 Thess. 3:17). Each time he indicated that he had written the salutation in his own hand. Paul must have had his letters transcribed by a secretary or scribe. But at the end he often included a few words in his own handwriting. This added a personal touch and established the letter as his own.

SALVATION — deliverance from the power of sin; redemption.

In the Old Testament, the word salvation sometimes refers to deliverance from danger (Jer. 15:20), deliverance of the weak from an oppressor (Ps. 35:9-10), the healing of sickness (Is. 38:20), and deliverance from blood guilt and its consequences (Ps. 51:14). It may also refer to national deliverance from military threat (Ex. 14:13) or release from captivity (Ps. 14:7). But salvation finds its deepest meaning in the spiritual realm of life. Man's universal need for salvation is one of the clearest teachings of the Bible.

The need for salvation goes back to man's removal from the Garden of Eden (Gen. 3). After the Fall, man's life was marked by strife and difficulty. Increasingly, corruption and violence dominated his world (Gen. 6:11-13). When God destroyed the world with the Flood, He also performed the first act of salvation by saving Noah and his family. These eight people became the basis of another chance for mankind. The salvation of Noah and his family was viewed by the apostle Peter as a pattern of that full salvation which we receive in Christ (1 Pet. 3:18-22).

The central Old Testament experience of salvation is the Exodus (Ex. 12:40-14:31). Much of Israel's worship of God was a renewal of this mighty experience that brought them from tyranny in Egypt to freedom in the Promised Land (Ex. 13:3-16). The mighty saving power of God was demonstrated dramatically as the Israelites formed a holy nation of priestly servants of the Lord (Ex. 19:4-6). The Exodus became a pattern of salvation by which God's future deeds of redemption would be understood.

But just as the Exodus symbolized their salvation, the Captivity of the Israelites in Babylon was a disastrous return to bondage. The people responded to this plight with expectations of a new and better Exodus (Is. 43:14-16) in which God would forgive their sins and restore their hearts to faithfulness (Jer. 31:31-34).

This hope for a new Exodus merged with expectation of a full realization of the rule of God (Ezek. 36:22-38). Since God was Lord and had shown Himself to be righteous and faithful, He must one day overpower His enemies and perfect the life of His people. This hope is expressed through the concept of the "day of the Lord" as described by the Old Testament prophets (Joel 2:1-11; Amos 9:11-15). But this hope also focused on the role of the Anointed King and the coming of the Messiah (Psalm 2).

Even Israel's return from the Captivity, however, failed to fulfill all their hopes (Hag. 2:3). So a new understanding arose: the full realization of God's purpose of salvation would involve the coming of a completely new age (Is. 65:17-25). This doctrine of salvation reached its fulfillment in the death of Christ on our behalf. Jesus' mission was to save the world from sin and the wrath of God (Matt. 1:21; John 12:47; Rom. 5:9). During His earthly ministry, salvation was brought to us by His presence and the power of faith (Luke 19:9-10). Now, our salvation is based on His death and resurrection (Mark 10:25).

The salvation that comes through Christ may be described in three tenses: past, present, and future. When a person believes in Christ, he is saved (Acts 16:31). But we are also in the process of being saved from the power of sin (Rom. 8:13; Phil. 2:12). Finally, we shall be saved from the very presence of sin (Rom. 13:11; Titus 2:12-13). God releases into our lives today the power of Christ's resurrection (Rom. 6:4) and allows us a foretaste of our future life as His children (2 Cor. 1:22; Eph. 1:14). Our experience of salvation will be complete when Christ returns (Heb. 9:28) and the kingdom of God is fully revealed (Matt. 13:41-43).

Also see ADOPTION, ATONEMENT, CONVERSION, FORGIVENESS, JUSTIFICATION, RANSOM, RECONCILIATION, REDEMPTION, REGENERATION.

SALVE — a medical ointment used to soothe the eyes (Rev. 3:18; ointment, NEB; eyesalve, KJV, NASB). A popular eye medicine known as "Phrygian powder" was one of Laodicea's sources of

Photo by Howard Vos

The hill on which King Omri of the Northern Kingdom built the city of Samaria. It remained the capital city of Israel until the fall of the nation in 722 B.C.

wealth. The medical school at Laodicea was famous for the preparation and use of this eye salve. The lukewarm church at Laodicea, however, needed something greater than eye salve to heal its faltering spiritual vision.

SAMARIA, CITY OF [suh MAR ih uh] (*lookout*) — the capital city of the northern kingdom of Israel (see Map 6, B–3).

Built about 880 B.C. by Omri, the sixth king of Israel (1 Kin. 16:24), Samaria occupied a 91–meter (300–foot) high hill about 68 kilometers (42 miles) north of Jerusalem, and 40 kilometers (25 miles) east of the Mediterranean Sea. This hill was situated on the major north–south road through Palestine. It also commanded the east–west route to the Plain of Sharon and the Mediterranean Sea. Because of its hilltop location, Samaria could be defended easily. Its only weakness was that the nearest spring was a mile distant, but this difficulty was overcome by the use of cisterns.

Samaria withstood an attack by Ben–Hadad, king of Syria (2 Kin. 6:24–25), but it finally fell to the Assyrians, in 722–21 B.C., and its inhabitants were carried into captivity. The city was repopulated by "people from Babylon, Cuthah, Ava, Hamath, and from Sepharvaim" (2 Kin. 17:24), all bringing their pagan idolatries with them. Intermarriage of native Jews with these foreigners led to the mixed race of SAMARITANS so despised by full–blooded Jews during the time of Jesus (John 4:1–10).

In excavations of Samaria, archaeologists have uncovered several different levels of occupation by the Israelites. The first two levels, from the reigns of Omri and Ahab, show careful construction, apparently by Phoenician craftsmen. At this time, the city may have been 20 acres in extent, enclosed by an outer wall 6 to 8 meters (20 to 30 feet) thick, with a more narrow inner stone wall about 2 meters (5 feet) thick. A two–story palace was constructed at the higher western end of the hill around some courtyards. In one of these courtyards a pool about 5 by 9 meters (17 by 33 feet) was discovered. This may have been the pool where the blood of Ahab was washed from his chariot after he was killed in a battle against the Syrians (1 Kin. 22:38).

The palace was described as an "ivory house" (1 Kin. 22:39; Amos 3:15). Excavations near the pool uncovered a storeroom housing 500 plaques or fragments of ivory used for inlay work in walls and furniture.

The third level of the city, from the period of Jehu (about 841–813 B.C.), gave evidence of additions and reconstruction. Levels four to six covered the period of Jereboam II and showed that repairs had been made to Samaria before the Assyrians captured it in 722/21 B.C. From this period came several pieces of pottery inscribed with administrative records describing shipments of wine and oil to Samaria. One potsherd recorded the name of the treasury official who received the shipment, the place of origin, and the names of the peasants who had paid their taxes. Structures from the Greek period can still be seen in ruined form. A series of round towers are magnificent monuments of the Hellenistic age in Palestine. Roman remains include a colonnaded street leading from the west gate, an aqueduct, a stadium, and an impressive theater.

The small village of Sebastiyeh—an Arabic corruption of the Greco-Roman name Sebaste—now occupies part of the ancient site of this historic city. Even after the Israelite residents of Samaria were deported, the city continued to be inhabited by several different groups under the successive authority of Assyria, Babylon, Persia, Greece and Rome. Herod the Great, Roman procurator in Palestine (ruled 37 B.C.—A.D. 4) when Jesus was born, made many improvements to Samaria and renamed it Sebaste—the Greek term for Augustus—in honor of the emperor of Rome. This Herodian city is probably the "city of Samaria" mentioned in the book of Acts (8:5).

SAMARIA, REGION OF [suh MAR ih uh] — a territory in the uplands of central Palestine that corresponded roughly with the lands allotted to the tribe of Ephraim and the western portion of Manasseh. Samaria consisted of about 1,400 square miles of attractive, fertile land, bounded by the Valley of Jezreel on the south and Mount Carmel on the north. Its rich alluvial soil produced valuable grain crops, olives, and grapes. This productivity was made all the more important by the presence of two north-south and three east-west roads. Samaria was able to engage in commerce with neighboring Phoenicia as well as the more distant nations of Syria and Egypt.

Because Samaritan soil was considerably more fertile than the soil in Judah, the Northern Kingdom was always more prosperous. But the very attractiveness of the territory brought invaders, while trade with such pagan nations exposed the people to corrupt foreign religions. The prophets strongly condemned the wickedness of Samaria—its idolatry, immorality, idle luxury, and oppression of the poor (Hos. 7:1; 8:5-7).

In the time of Jesus, Palestine west of the Jordan River was divided into the three provinces of Galilee, Samaria, and Judea. Because of their intermarriage with foreigners, the people of Samaria were shunned by orthodox Jews. Situated between Galilee and Judea, Samaria was the natural route for traveling between those two provinces. But the pure blooded Jews had no dealings with the Samaritans (John 4:9). They would travel east, cross the Jordan River, and detour around Samaria.

Also see SAMARITANS.

SAMARITAN PENTATEUCH — an ancient version of the first five books of the Old Testament as preserved by the Samaritans. The manuscript copies of the Samaritan Pentateuch use a form of letters similar to that which was in general use before the Captivity—the old Hebrew, or "Phoenician script." The origin of this version of the Law is difficult to determine, but the events recorded in 2 Kings 17:24-28 suggest that the Law was the basis of the instruction given by the exiled priest which enabled the newly settled Samaritans to worship the God of Israel.

Since only the PENTATEUCH (the first five books of the Old Testament) was accepted as authentic Scripture by the Samaritans, it must have been available in complete form as early as 681 B.C. Some scholars claim that the Samaritans had no copy of the Law before about 450 B.C. But there is no reason why copies of the Law should not have been circulating in Israel during Jeroboam II's rule (about 793-753 B.C.). This means they could have been taken to Assyria when the citizens of Samaria were deported by this pagan nation in 722 B.C. Nor is there any difficulty in supposing that the priest who returned to Samaria brought with him a copy of the Law for traditional teaching purposes.

Because of their differences with the pure He-

Terraced hillsides in the region of Samaria—a territory noted for its rich, fertile farmlands.
Photo by Willem A. VanGemeren

brew tradition, the Samaritans occasionally changed the wording of their books of the Law to give preference to Mount GERIZIM to show that their temple there was the authentic place for worship. In other respects the Samaritans promoted their own ceremonies and beliefs, but they emphasized the place of Moses as the lawgiver who acted by direct divine command. Despite scribal additions and variations in spelling, the Samaritan Pentateuch is very similar to the Hebrew Pentateuch.

Several fragments related to the text of the Samaritan Pentateuch were discovered among the Dead Sea Scrolls. These prove that this text was handed down in Samaritan circles in the same way that the Hebrew Law and other parts of the Old Testament were preserved by the Jews. Certain groups among the Samaritans probably made copies of individual books as well as the entire Pentateuch. These valuable manuscript fragments support the idea of such activity without actually indicating that the Samaritan Pentateuch's text was earlier than that of the traditional Hebrew Bible.

SAMARITANS [suh MAR ih tuhns] — natives or inhabitants of Samaria, a distinct territory or region in central Palestine.

Until the rise of Assyrian power in the ancient Near East, Samaria was occupied by the tribes of Ephraim and the western portion of the tribe of Manasseh. Many of the sites in Samaria held important places in Israelite history. Mount Gerizim and Mount Ebal were the scene of the covenant–renewal ceremony in Joshua's time (Josh. 8:30–35). Shechem, situated near Mount Gerizim, was an ancient Canaanite town that regained its earlier prosperity during the monarchy. It became capital of the northern kingdom of Israel briefly under Jeroboam I (about 931–910 B.C.; 1 Kin. 12:25), but it was replaced by Penuel and then Tirzah.

Construction on the city of Samaria was begun by Omri about 880 B.C. and completed by his son Ahab (about 874–853 B.C.). Samaria became the new capital of Israel, and successive kings added to it and rebuilt sections to make it a well–fortified capital. But the city fell to the Assyrians in 722–721 B.C. Most of the leading citizens of the Northern Kingdom were deported to places in Syria, Assyria, and Babylonia.

Sargon replaced the deported Israelites with foreign colonists (2 Kin. 17:24). These newcomers intermarried among the Israelites who remained in Samaria. Later their numbers were increased when Esarhaddon and Ashurbanipal (the biblical Osnapper; Ezra 4:10) sent more Assyrian colonists to the district of Samaria. These people took the name Samaritans from the territory and attempted to settle the land. However, "they did not fear the Lord, and the Lord sent lions among them, which killed some of them" (2 Kin. 17:25). In despair they sent to Assyria for "one of the priests" who would "teach them the rituals of the God of the land" (2 Kin. 17:27). Thereafter the Samaritans worshiped the God of Israel. But they also continued their idola-

Photo by Howard Vos

A Samaritan priest displays a scroll of the five books of Moses, the only Old Testament books which they accept as authoritative.

try, worshiping the pagan gods imported from foreign lands (2 Kin. 17:29).

So the Samaritans were a "mixed race" contaminated by foreign blood and false worship. The Jewish historian Josephus indicates that the Samaritans were also opportunists. When the Jews enjoyed prosperity, the Samaritans were quick to acknowledge their blood relationship. But when the Jews suffered hard times, the Samaritans disowned any such kinship, declaring that they were descendants of Assyrian immigrants.

When a group of Jews, led by Zerubbabel, returned from the Babylonian Captivity, the Samaritans offered to help Zerubbabel rebuild the Temple. When their offer was rejected, they tried to prevent the Jews from finishing their project (Ezra 4:1–10). When Nehemiah attempted to rebuild the wall of Jerusalem, he was opposed by Arabic and Samaritan groups (Neh. 2:10—6:14). The breach between the Samaritans and the Jews widened even further when Ezra, in his zeal for racial purity, pressured all Israelite men who married during the Captivity to divorce their pagan wives (Ezra 10:18–44).

The final break between the two groups occurred when the Samaritans built a rival temple on Mount Gerizim, claiming Shechem rather than Zion (Jerusalem) as the true "Beth–el" (house of God), the site traditionally chosen and blessed by the Lord.

The Samaritans trace their beginnings to the time of Eli, who established the sanctuary for worship of God in Shiloh. They also believe their religion is distinctive because they base their beliefs and practices on the Torah, or the Law—the first five books of the Old Testament. They recognize no other Hebrew Scriptures as authoritative.

At what stage the pagan elements of Mesopotamian religion were removed from Samaritan belief is impossible to determine. But probably by the time of Nehemiah (about 450 B.C.), the Samaritans considered themselves orthodox. The Samaritans also claimed that Ezra changed the Hebrew text to favor Jerusalem over Mount Gerizim as the site for the second temple. But the Samaritans themselves may also be guilty of changing the wording of the Law to reflect favorably on their traditions.

In the Roman period the Samaritans appeared to prosper. Their religion was made legal in the Empire, being practiced in synagogues in Italy and Africa. Suffering persecution from Christians, they finally revolted in the fifth and sixth centuries. The Roman emperor Justinian (ruled A.D. 527–565) suppressed the Samaritans and brought them almost to extinction, a condition from which they never recovered. But two small units of Samaritans survive until the present time—one group in Nablus (ancient Shechem) and a second group near Tel Aviv.

The pride of the modern Samaritan community at Nablus is a large scroll of the books of the Law, inscribed in an angular script much as Hebrew was written long before the time of Christ.

The Samaritans retained their belief in God as the unique Creator and Sustainer of all things. They also worshiped Him in the three feasts prescribed in the books of the Law—Passover, Pentecost, and Booths (or Tabernacles)—and the solemn Day of Atonement. But their faith was influenced in later periods by Islamic and other beliefs, unlike the orthodox Jewish community. To this day they sacrifice one or more lambs on Mount Gerizim during the Feast of Passover.

SAMECH, SAMEKH [SUM mik] — forms of SAMEK.

SAMEK [SUM mik] — the 15th letter of the Hebrew alphabet, used as a heading over Psalm 119:113–120. In the original Hebrew language, every line of these eight verses began with the letter Samek (Samech, KJV; Samekh, NAS). Also see ACROSTIC.

SAMGAR–NEBO [SAM gahr NEE boe] (meaning unknown) — a Babylonian prince, an officer of King Nebuchadnezzar, who participated in the siege (588–586 B.C.) and capture of Jerusalem (Jer. 39:3). He took his seat with other nobles in the Middle Gate of Jerusalem after the Chaldean army had taken the city.

SAMLAH [SAM luh] (*a garment*) — the fifth of the ancient kings of Edom (Gen. 36:36–37).

SAMOS [SAY muhs] (*lofty place*) — an island of Greece in the Aegean Sea (see Map 8, C–2), about 1.61 kilometers (1 mile) off the coast of Lydia in Asia Minor (modern Turkey). On his voyage from Assos to Miletus, the apostle Paul sailed between Samos and the mainland as he returned to Jerusalem at the end of his third missionary journey (Acts 20:15).

SAMOTHRACE [SAM uh thrays] (meaning unknown) — a small island in the Aegean Sea, about 50 kilometers (31 miles) off the southern coast of

Samaritans celebrating the Passover on Mount Gerizim, a site which they have considered sacred since before the time of Jesus.

Photo by Howard Vos

Thrace. Samothrace is mentioned in connection with the second missionary journey of the apostle Paul (Acts 16:11). The most important archaelogical find on the island was the famous Winged Nike (or Victory) of Samothrace, now housed in the Louvre, Paris.

SAMSON [SAM suhn] (*distinguished*) — a hero of Israel known for his great physical strength as well as his moral weakness. The last of the "judges," or military leaders, mentioned in the Book of Judges, Samson led his country in this capacity for about 20 years.

Samson lived in a dark period of Israelite history. After the generation of Joshua died out, the people of Israel fell into a lawless and faithless life. The author of the Book of Judges summarized these times by declaring, "There was no king in Israel; everyone did what was right in his own eyes" (Judg. 17:6; 21:25). The standard of God's Word, His Law as handed down by Moses, was ignored.

Samson was a product of that age, but his parents gave evidence of faith in the Lord. During a time when the Philistines were oppressing the Israelites (Judg. 13:1), the Lord announced to Manoah and his wife that they would bear a son who would be raised as a NAZIRITE (Judg. 13:5). This meant that Samson should serve as an example to Israel of commitment to God. Through most of his life, however, Samson fell far short of this mark.

Samson's mighty physical feats are well-known. With his bare hands he killed a young lion that attacked him (Judg. 14:5–6). He gathered 300 foxes (jackals; Judg. 15:4, NEB) and tied them together, then sent them through the grain fields with torches in their tails to destroy the crops of the Philistines.

On one occasion, he broke the ropes with which the enemy had bound him (Judg. 15:14). He killed a thousand Philistine soldiers with the jawbone of a donkey (Judg. 15:15). And, finally, he carried away the massive gate of Gaza, a city of the Philistines, when they thought they had him trapped behind the city walls (Judg. 16:3).

But in spite of his great physical strength Samson was a foolish man. He took vengeance on those who used devious means to discover the answer to one of his riddles (Judg. 14). When deceived by his enemies, his only thought was for revenge, as when his father-in-law gave away his wife to another man (Judg. 15:6–7). He had not learned the word of the Lord, "Vengeance is mine" (Deut. 32:35).

Samson's life was marred by his weakness for pagan women. As soon as he became of age, he fell in love with one of the daughters of the Philistines. He insisted on marrying her, in spite of his parents' objection (Judg. 14:1–4). This was against God's law, which forbade intermarriage of the Israelites among the women of Canaan. On another occasion he was almost captured by the Philistines while he was visiting a prostitute in the city of Gaza.

Samson eventually became involved with DELILAH, a woman from the Valley of Sorek (Judg. 16:4), who proved to be his undoing (Judges 16).

The Philistines bribed her to find out the key to his strength. She teased him until he finally revealed that the secret was his uncut hair, allowed to grow long in accord with the Nazirite law. While Samson slept, she called the Philistines to cut his hair and turned him over to his enemies. Samson became weak, not only because his hair had been cut but also because the Lord had departed from him (Judg. 16:20).

After his enslavement by the Philistines, Samson was blinded and forced to work at grinding grain. Eventually he came to his senses and realized that God had given him his great strength to serve the Lord and his people. After a prayer to God for strength, he killed thousands of the enemy by pulling down the pillars of the temple of Dagon (Judg. 16:28–31). That one great act of faith cost Samson his life, but it won for him a place among the heroes of faith (Heb. 11:32). Out of weakness he was made strong by the power of the Lord (Heb. 11:34).

Samson was a person with great potential who fell short because of his sin and disobedience. Mighty in physical strength, he was weak in resisting temptation. His life is a clear warning against the dangers of self–indulgence and lack of discipline.

SAMUEL [SAM yoo uhl] (*name of God*) — the earliest of the great Hebrew prophets (after Moses) and the last judge of Israel. Samuel led his people against their Philistine oppressors. When he was an old man, Samuel anointed Saul as the first king of Israel and later anointed David as Saul's successor. Samuel is recognized as one of the greatest leaders of Israel (Jer. 15:1; Heb. 11:32).

Samuel's birth reveals the great faith of his mother, HANNAH (1 Sam. 1:2–22; 2:1). Unable to bear children, she prayed earnestly for the Lord to give her a child. She vowed that if the Lord would give her a son she would raise him as a gift of God and would dedicate him to the Lord's service. Eventually, Samuel was born as an answer to Hannah's prayer.

Hannah made good on her promise to dedicate her son to the Lord's service. At a very early age, Samuel went to live with Eli the priest, who taught the boy the various duties of the priesthood. Here Samuel heard the voice of God, calling him to special service as a priest and prophet in Israel (1 Sam. 3:1–20). After Eli's death, Samuel became the judge of Israel in a ceremony at Mizpah (1 Samuel 7). This event was almost turned to disaster by an attack from the Philistines, but the Lord intervened with a storm that routed the enemies and established Samuel as God's man. The godly Samuel erected a memorial stone which he called "Ebenezer," meaning "Stone of Help." "Thus far the Lord has helped us," he declared (1 Sam. 7:12).

In the early part of his ministry, Samuel served as a traveling judge. With his home in Ramah, he made a yearly circuit to Bethel, Gilgal, and Mizpah. In the person of Samuel, the judgeship developed into something more than a military leader

The tomb of Absalom (far left), the tomb of Bene Hezir (center) and the tomb of Zechariah (far right) in the Kidron Valley just outside Jerusalem.

called upon for dramatic leadership in times of national crises. He became a judge with a permanent leadership office, an office approaching that of a king.

When the people clamored for a king like the surrounding nations (1 Sam. 8:5), Samuel was reluctant to grant their request. He took this as a rejection of his long years of godly service on behalf of the people. He also was aware of the evils that went along with the establishment of a royal house. But the Lord helped Samuel to see the real issue: "Heed the voice of the people in all that they say to you; for they have not rejected you, but they have rejected Me, that I should not reign over them" (1 Sam. 8:7).

The person whom Samuel anointed as first king of Israel turned out to be a poor choice. Saul was handsome, likeable, and tall. But he had a tragic flaw that led ultimately to his own ruin. He disobeyed God by taking spoils in a battle rather than wiping out all living things, as God had commanded (1 Sam. 15:18–26). Saul's false pride and extreme jealousy toward David also led him into some serious errors of judgment.

When God rejected Saul as king, He used Samuel to announce the prophetic words (1 Sam. 15:10–35). Samuel was faithful in presenting the stern words of rejection. Although he had no further dealings with Saul, Samuel mourned for him and for the death of the dream (1 Sam. 15:35). Samuel was then sent by the Lord to Bethlehem, to the house of Jesse, where he anointed the young man David as the rightful king over His people (1 Sam. 16:1–13).

In addition to his work as judge, prophet, and priest, Samuel is also known as the author of the Books of First and Second Samuel. He apparently wrote much of the material contained in these books during the reigns of Saul and David. After Samuel's death, these books were completed by an unknown writer, perhaps Abiathar, the priest who served during David's administration.

When Samuel died, he was buried in his hometown of Ramah and was mourned by the nation (1 Sam. 25:1; 28:3). But he had one more message to give. After Samuel's death, Saul visited a fortune teller at Endor (1 Sam. 28). This fortune teller gave Saul a message that came from the spirit of Samuel: "The Lord has departed from you and has become your enemy" (1 Sam. 28:16). Even from the grave Samuel still spoke the word of God!

In many ways Samuel points forward to the person of the Savior, the Lord Jesus Christ. In the story of Samuel's birth, the direct hand of the Lord can be seen. In his ministry as judge, prophet, and priest, Samuel anticipates the ministry of the Lord as well as the work of his forerunner, John the Baptist. As Samuel marked out David as God's man, so John the Baptist pointed out Jesus as the Savior.

Also see SAMUEL, BOOKS OF.

SAMUEL, BOOKS OF — two historical books of the Old Testament that cover the nation of Israel's transition from a loose tribal form of government to a united kingship under Saul and David. The books are named for the prophet Samuel, who anointed these two leaders.

Structure of the Books. In the Bible used by the Hebrew people during Old Testament days, the books of Samuel consisted of one continuous narrative. This long book was divided into 1 and 2 Samuel when the Hebrew Bible was translated into the Greek language in the second century B.C. All Bibles since that time have followed the two-book pattern.

First Samuel covers the lives of the prophet Samuel and King Saul, introducing David as a warrior and a possible successor to the throne. Second Samuel picks up the story at David's anointing and focuses on his career as Israel's greatest king.

Some of the most dramatic stories in the Bible are found in these two Old Testament books. First Samuel reports Samuel's own experience as a boy when he heard God's call to a prophetic ministry (chap. 2). It also reveals that David was a shepherd boy destined for greatness when he defeated the Philistine giant Goliath with nothing but a slingshot and a stone (1 Sam. 17:19-51).

Contrast this triumphant moment, however, with David's great sin, when he committed adultery with Bathsheba, then arranged for the killing of her husband, Uriah. David repented of his sin and claimed God's forgiveness, but from that day on his fortunes were clouded and his family was troubled.

Authorship and Date. Since the name of the great prophet Samuel is associated with these books, it is logical to assume that he wrote 1 and 2 Samuel. But the problem with this theory is that all of 2 Samuel and a major portion of 1 Samuel deal with events that happened after Samuel's death. However, there is strong support for Samuel's authorship of some of the material, since the Book of 1 Chronicles refers to "the book of Samuel the seer" (1 Chr. 29:29).

Before Samuel's death about 1000 B.C., he must have written accounts of the kingship of Saul and the early life of David that appear as part of 1 Samuel. Many scholars believe that Abiathar the priest wrote those parts of these two books that deal with the court life of David. He served as a priest during David's administration; so he may have had access to the royal records that provided the historical facts for these accounts.

Historical Setting. The Books of 1 and 2 Samuel describe a turning point in Israel's history. This was a time when the people became dissatisfied with

FIRST SAMUEL: A Teaching Outline

Part One: Samuel, the Last Judge (1:1—7:17)

Part Two: Saul, the First King (8:1—31:13)

their loose tribal form of organization and insisted on a united kingdom under the ruling authority of a king. For hundreds of years they had existed as a tribal society, with each tribe living on its own portion of the land and minding its own affairs. If a superior enemy threatened the entire nation, they depended on deliverance at the hands of JUDGES, those military leaders described in the Book of Judges, who would raise a volunteer army to make their borders secure.

This system of defense, however, proved woefully inadequate when the Philistines began to flex their muscles against the nation with renewed intensity about 1100 B.C. These warlike people boasted of iron chariots, a well-organized army, and other superior weapons which they used with military precision against the poorly organized Israelites. The threat of this superior force led the nation to clamor for a king—a ruler who could unite all the tribes against a common enemy.

Saul was anointed by Samuel about 1050 B.C. to serve as first king of the nation. A gifted young man of great promise, he ruled for 40 years (Acts 13:21) before taking his life by falling on his own sword when the Philistines prevailed against him in a decisive battle (1 Sam. 31:1-7). David, his successor, also ruled 40 years (2 Sam. 5:4; 1 Chr. 29:27), from 1010 to 971 B.C. Building on Saul's beginning,

SECOND SAMUEL: A Teaching Outline

Photo by Howard Vos

A fragment of 1 Samuel 23:9-16 discovered at Qumran. It dates from the third century B.C.

David succeeded in driving out the Philistines, unifying the people, and conquering or establishing peaceful relationships with surrounding nations.

Theological Contribution. The major theological contribution of 1 and 2 Samuel is the negative and positive views of the kingship which they present. On the negative side, the books make it clear that in calling for a king the people were rejecting God's rule. Because Israel was unable to live under God's rule through the judges, God gave in to their demands and granted them a king. But He also warned them about the dangers of the kingship (1 Sam. 8:9–21).

On the positive side, 1 and 2 Samuel portray the kingship as established through David as a clear picture of God's purpose for His people. The COVENANT that God established with David demonstrated God's purpose through David's family line; David's ancestors would be adopted as the sons of God in a special sense (2 Samuel 7). David's line would continue through the centuries, and his throne would be established forever (2 Sam. 7:13). In the person of Jesus Christ the Messiah, this great covenant came to its fulfillment.

Special Considerations. The story of David and Goliath (1 Samuel 17) presents more than a dra-

matic encounter between two warriors. It also points up the contrast between David and Saul. Since he was tall himself, Saul should have been the one to face the giant (1 Sam. 9:2). By his failure to meet Goliath, Saul demonstrated both his folly and his inability to rule. By rising to the challenge, David demonstrated his wisdom and faith, proving that he was God's man for the throne of Israel.

In addition to its stories, the books of 1 and 2 Samuel contain several poems, or psalms of praise to God. One such poem is the lovely Psalm of Hannah (1 Samuel 2), in which Hannah rejoices in God's goodness in allowing her to conceive. The dramatic Psalm of the Bow (2 Samuel 1), in which David laments the death of Saul and Jonathan, is another of these poems.

Also see SAMUEL.

SANBALLAT [san BAL uht] (*the god sin has given life*) — a leading opponent of the Jews after their return from the Captivity; he tried to hinder Nehemiah in his work of rebuilding the walls of Jerusalem (Neh. 2:10, 19–20; 4:1–23; 6:1–19; 13:28).

Sanballat's designation as the Horonite probably indicates the town of his origin, possibly Horonaim of Moab (Is. 15:5; Jer. 48:3, 5, 34) or Beth Horon in Ephraim near Jerusalem (2 Chr. 8:5). In papyri found at the Jewish settlement in Elephantine, Egypt, Sanballat is called the governor of Samaria. His daughter married "one of the sons of Joiada, the son of Eliashib the high priest" (Neh. 13:28). Nehemiah viewed such a "mixed marriage" as a defilement of the priesthood, so he drove Joiada away.

Sanballat's opposition to Nehemiah's work may have stemmed from jealousy. He may have felt that his authority was threatened by the reawakening of the land of Judah. After mocking Nehemiah and his crew, he tried to slip through the broken wall of Jerusalem with people from other enemy nations to kill the Jews. Nehemiah thwarted this plot, setting up guards of half the people while the other half worked (Neh. 4:7–23). Neither did he fall for Sanballat's ploy to come outside the wall for a "friendly" discussion (Neh. 6:3).

In spite of Sanballat's open opposition and trickery, Nehemiah carried out the task which he felt called by God to accomplish. After the wall was completed, he reported that even the enemies of the project realized "this work was done by our God" (Neh. 6:16).

SANCTIFICATION — the process of God's grace by which the believer is separated from sin and becomes dedicated to God's righteousness. Accomplished by the Word of God (John 17:7) and the Holy Spirit (Rom. 8:3–4), sanctification results in holiness, or purification from the guilt and power of sin.

Sanctification as separation from the world and setting apart for God's service is a concept found throughout the Bible. Spoken of as "holy" or "set apart" in the Old Testament were the land of Canaan, the city of Jerusalem, the tabernacle, the Temple, the Sabbath, the feasts, the prophets, the priests, and the garments of the priests. God is sanctified by the witness of believers (1 Pet. 3:15) and by His judgments upon sin (Ezek. 38:16). Jesus also was "sanctified and sent into the world" (John 10:36)

Sanctification in the Atonement. As the process by which God purifies the believer, sanctification is based on the sacrificial death of Christ. In his letters to the churches, the apostle Paul noted that God has "chosen" and "reconciled" us to Himself in Christ for the purpose of sanctification (Eph. 1:4; 5:25–27; Titus 2:14).

Old Testament sacrifices did not take away sin, but they were able to sanctify "for the purifying of the flesh" (Heb. 9:13). The blood of the new covenant (Heb. 10:29), however, goes far beyond this ritual purification of the body. The offering of Christ's body (Heb. 10:10) and blood (Heb. 13:12) serves to purge our conscience from "dead works to serve the living God" (Heb. 9:14). Because our cleansing from sin is made possible only by Christ's death and resurrection, we are "sanctified in Christ Jesus" (1 Cor. 1:2; Acts 20:32; 1 Cor. 1:30; 6:11).

Sanctification: God's Work. We are sanctified by God the Father (Jude 1), God the Son (Heb. 2:11), and God the Holy Spirit (2 Thess. 2:13; 1 Pet. 1:2). Perfect holiness is God's command (1 Thess. 4:7) and purpose. As Paul prayed, "Now may the God of peace Himself sanctify you completely" (1 Thess. 5:23). Sanctification is a process that continues during our lives as believers (Heb. 10:14). Only after death are the saints referred to as "perfect" (Heb. 12:23).

Sanctification: The Believer's Work. Numerous commands in the Bible imply that believers also have a responsibility in the process of sanctification. We are commanded to "be holy" (Lev. 11:44; 1 Pet. 1:15–16); to "be perfect" (Matt. 5:48); and to "present your members as slaves of righeousness for holiness" (Rom. 6:19). Writing to the church of the Thessalonians, the apostle Paul made a strong plea for purity: "This is the will of God, your sanctification: that you should abstain from sexual immorality; that each of you should know how to possess his own vessel in sanctification and honor, not in passion of lust, like the Gentiles who do not know God" (1 Thess. 4:3–5).

These commands imply effort on our part. We must believe in Jesus, since we are "sanctified by faith in Him" (Acts 26:18). Through the Holy Spirit we must also "put to death the evil deeds of the body" (Rom. 8:13). Paul itemized the many "works of the flesh" from which we must separate ourselves (Gal. 5:19–21). Finally, we must walk in the Spirit in order to display the fruit of the Spirit (Gal. 5:22–24).

SANCTUARY — a holy place set apart for worship of God or refuge from danger. The word has at least five different meanings in the Bible:

1. Israel's earliest sanctuary was the portable tent known as the TABERNACLE, where the ARK OF THE COVENANT containing the Ten Commandments was housed (Ex. 25:8; 36:1). After the conquest of the land of Canaan by Joshua, the tabernacle with its sanctuary was placed at Shiloh, a town in central Palestine (Josh. 18:1).

2. When David became king he planned the TEMPLE in Jerusalem and it was eventually built by his son Solomon. This became a more permanent place of worship (1 Chr. 22:19).

3. The prophets refer to the heathen sanctuaries, where pagan gods were worshiped (Is. 16:12).

4. The word sanctuary is applied also to the most holy place, or the Holy of Holies, in the tabernacle and the Temple (Lev. 4:6).

5. The word is also used of God's holy habitation in heaven (Ps. 102:19). In the New Jerusalem there will be no sanctuary, "for the Lord God Almighty and the Lamb are its temple" (Rev. 21:22). Where all is made sacred, consecrated, and holy by God's presence, there is no need for one specific holy place.

SAND (see MINERALS OF THE BIBLE).

SAND FLY, SAND LIZARD, SAND PARTRIDGE, SAND VIPER (see ANIMALS OF THE BIBLE).

SANDALS, SHOES — footwear of Bible times. The sandal and shoe were very important cultural and status symbols.

Although the word shoe is sometimes used in the NKJV (Ps. 60:8; 108:9), sandal is a much better description of biblical footwear. A basic sandal was made up of a flat piece of leather, wood or matted grass, with a leather strap attached on both sides to secure it to the foot. Depending on the use of the sandal or the rank of the wearer, many variations were possible. Wealthy people often wore sandals made from badger skin (Ezek. 16:10). Shepherds needed a tougher, more durable sandal to wear outside in the fields.

Poorer people sometimes did not have sandals at all (Luke 15:22). The absence or removal of sandals was a sign of humiliation (Is. 20:2–4). People who entered the presence of God to stand on holy ground were ordered to remove their sandals (Ex. 3:5; Josh. 5:15). When a person refused to bear responsibility for other family members, part of his public humiliation and condemnation was the removal of his sandal (Deut. 25:9).

Because a sandal did not completely cover the foot, the feet became quite dirty when a person traveled. It was a customary expression of hospitality for the lowest slave of a household to remove the traveler's sandals and wash his feet (1 Sam. 25:41). Jesus washed the feet of His disciples to demonstrate His attitude of humility and service (Luke 7:44).

Also see DRESS OF THE BIBLE.

SANHEDRIN [SAN hee drun] (*a council* or *assembly*) — the highest ruling body and court of justice among the Jewish people in the time of Jesus.

Headed by the high priest of Israel, the Sanhedrin was granted limited authority over certain religious, civil, and criminal matters by the foreign nations that dominated the land of Israel at various times in its history. The Sanhedrin was exercising this limited power when it charged Jesus with the crime of blasphemy but then sent him to Pilate, the Roman official, for a formal trial and sentencing.

The word Sanhedrin is not found in the NKJV; instead the word council is used. Usually the assembly itself is meant, although the word may also refer to the assembly meeting (John 11:47) or to the place where the assembly met (Luke 22:66; Acts 4:15). The same word is also used for smaller, local courts of justice (Matt. 10:17; Mark 13:9). The Sanhedrin is also implied in Bible passages that mention a meeting of the various groups which made up the council: the chief priests, the elders, and the scribes (Mark 14:53-55). Sometimes some of the members of the Sanhedrin are simply called rulers (Luke 24:20; Acts 4:5).

The Sanhedrin had 71 members. The New Testament mentions some of them by name: Joseph of Arimathea (Mark 15:43), Gamaliel (Acts 5:34), Nicodemus (John 3:1; 7:50), the high priests Annas and Caiaphas (Luke 3:2) and Ananias (Acts 23:2). The high priest was always president of the Sanhedrin. Some scholars suggest that the apostle Paul was a member of the Sanhedrin before his conversion to Christianity, but this is not known for sure.

The Sanhedrin grew out of the council of advisors for the high priest when the Jewish people lived under the domination of the Persian and Greek empires. In the beginning, the council was made up of the leading priests and the most distinguished aristocrats among the lay people. Later, however, as the influence of the scribes grew, they were also given some positions on the Sanhedrin. In this way, the Sanhedrin came to include both Sadducees—or "chief priests" and "elders"—and Pharisees or scribes. These were the two main groups within Judaism, and the Sanhedrin usually tried to maintain a balance of power between them. But Acts 23:1-10 shows that the Sanhedrin would sometimes divide along party lines. As he stood before the Sanhedrin, the apostle Paul was shrewd enough to pit the Pharisees against the Sadducees to his own advantage.

After A.D. 6 the official authority of the Sanhedrin extended only to the province of Judea in southern Palestine. Still, Jews living elsewhere respected the Sanhedrin highly and would often be guided by its decisions. Within the province of Judea, which included the city of Jerusalem, the Romans left most of the business of governing the Jews to the Sanhedrin. The Sanhedrin even had its own police force, or Temple police, so it could make arrests on its own. This is the force that arrested Jesus in the Garden of Gethsemane (Mark 14:43; Acts 4:1-3).

The Sanhedrin also served as the supreme court of the Jews. This does not mean that people who were dissatisfied with the verdict of the lower court could appeal to the Sanhedrin for a different decision. But matters of special importance and other matters that lower courts were unable to resolve were brought to the Sanhedrin. The Roman rulers did, however, reserve the right to interfere with what the Sanhedrin was doing, as happened in the case of Paul (Acts 23:10; 24:7), but this probably happened very seldom. The Romans denied the power of capital punishment to the Sanhedrin. This is why the Jews said to Pilate after they had tried Jesus, "It is not lawful for us to put anyone to death" (John 18:31).

In the New Testament the Sanhedrin was involved in hearings against Jesus (Matt. 26:59; Mark 14:55), Peter and John and the other apostles (Acts 4:1-23; 5:17-41), Stephen (Acts 6—7), and Paul (Acts 22—24). Jesus probably was not officially tried by the Sanhedrin. It is more likely that He was given a preliminary hearing to establish the charges against Him and then taken to Pilate. It is also not clear whether Stephen was officially condemned and executed by the Sanhedrin or simply was stoned by an angry mob without due process of law (Acts 7:54-60).

SANSANNAH [san SAN uh] (*thorn bush*) — a city in the Negev, the extreme southern part of Judah (Josh. 15:31). It is probably present-day Khirbet esh-Shamsaniyat.

SAPH [saf] (meaning unknown) — a Philistine giant killed by one of David's mighty men (2 Sam. 21:18), also called Sippai (1 Chr. 20:4).

SAPHIR [SAY fur] — a form of SHAPHIR.

SAPPHIRA [suh FIGH ruh] (*beautiful*) — a dishonest woman who, along with her husband Ananias, held back goods from the early Christian community after they had agreed to share everything. Because of their hypocrisy and deceit, they were struck dead by God (Acts 5:1-11). This may seem like a severe punishment for such an offense. But it points out the need for absolute honesty in all our dealings with God.

SAPPHIRE (see JEWELS AND PRECIOUS STONES).

SARAH, SARAI [SAR uh, SAR eye] (*noble lady*) — the name of two women in the Bible:

1. The wife of ABRAHAM, and the mother of ISAAC. Sarah's name was originally Sarai, but it was changed to Sarah by God, much as her husband's name was changed from Abram to Abraham. Ten years younger than Abraham, Sarah was his half-sister; they had the same father but different mothers (Gen. 20:12).

Sarah was about 65 years old when she and Abraham left Haran (Gen. 12:5; 17:7). Passing through Egypt, Abraham introduced Sarah as his sister, apparently to keep himself from being killed by those who would be attracted by Sarah's beauty (Gen. 12:10-20; 20:1-18).

In spite of God's promise to Abraham that he would become the father of a chosen nation, Sarah remained barren. When she was 75, she decided that the only way to realize God's promise was to present Abraham her Egyptian maidservant, HAGAR, by whom he could father a child. Hagar bore a son named ISHMAEL (Gen. 16:1–16).

When Sarah was 90 years old, far beyond her childbearing years, she gave birth to a son, Isaac—the child of promise (Gen. 21:1–7). After Isaac was born, Sarah caught Ishmael mocking the young child and, with God's approval, sent both Ishmael and Hagar into the wilderness.

At the age of 127, Sarah died at Kirjath Arba (Hebron) and was buried by Abraham in the cave of Machpelah (Gen. 23:1–20). Sarah is the only woman in the Bible whose age was recorded at death—a sign of her great importance to the early Hebrews. The prophet Isaiah declared Abraham and Sarah as the father and mother of the Hebrew people: "Look to Abraham your father, and to Sarah who bore you" (Is. 51:2).

In the New Testament the apostle Paul pointed out that "the deadness of Sarah's womb" (Rom. 4:19) did not cause Abraham to waver in his faith; he believed the promise of God (Rom. 9:9). The apostle Peter cited Sarah as an example of the holy women who trusted in God, possessed inward spiritual beauty, and were submissive to their husbands (1 Pet. 3:5–6). The writer of the Epistle to the Hebrews also includes Sarah as one of the spiritual heroines in his roll call of the faithful (Heb. 11:11).

2. A daughter of Asher (Num. 26:46, KJV; Serah, NKJV).

SARAPH [SAR if] (*burning*) — a descendant of the tribe of Judah. At one time Saraph ruled in Moab (1 Chr. 4:22).

SARDIN, SARDIUS (see JEWELS AND PRECIOUS STONES).

SARDIS [SARR dis] — the capital city of Lydia in the province of Asia, in western Asia Minor (modern Turkey). The church at Sardis was one of the seven churches mentioned by John in the Book of Revelation (Rev. 3:1–6).

Sardis was situated on the east bank of the Pactolus River about 80 kilometers (50 miles) east of Smyrna; it occupied a rocky spur of Mount Tmolus and a valley at the foot of this mountain. In ancient times Sardis was well fortified and easily defended. It became the capital of the ancient Lydian empire, then passed successively to the Persians, the Greeks, and the Romans during their respective dominance of the ancient world.

During its days as a Roman city, Sardis became an important Christian center. However, the church at Sardis was evidently affected by the complacency of the city and its reliance on past glory: "You have a name that you are alive, but you are dead" (Rev. 3:1). Sardis, the dead church, was like "whitewashed tombs which…appear beautiful outwardly, but inside are full of dead men's bones" (Matt. 23:27). Its thriving, healthy appearance masked an inner decay.

The most impressive building of ancient Sardis must have been its magnificent Temple of Artemis, built in the fourth century B.C. The temple was 100 meters (327 feet) long and 50 meters (163 feet) wide and had 78 Ionic columns, each 17.7 meters (58 feet) high. Some of these columns remain standing until this day.

SARDITES [ZAR dights] — a tribal family (Num. 26:26; Seredites, RSV) founded by SERED (Gen. 46:14).

SARDONYX (see JEWELS AND PRECIOUS STONES).

SAREPTA [suh REP tuh] — a form of ZAREPHATH.

Ruins of the Temple of Artemis at Sardis. The Romans referred to this goddess as Diana (Acts 19:24-35).

SARGON [SAHR gahn] (*the king is legitimate*)– the name of three kings of ancient Mesopotamia:

1. Sargon, king of Akkad (or Agade) in Mesopotamia. He began ruling about 2360 B.C. and ruled for about 56 years, according to the Sumerian king list. His kingdom, extending from the Mediterranean Sea to the Persian Gulf, was the first true world empire in history. He is not mentioned in the Bible.

2. Sargon I, king of Assyria (about 1850 B.C.). He is not mentioned in the Bible. The only reference to this king is the impression of his seal on old Akkadian tablets from Cappadocia.

3. Sargon II (722–705 B.C.), king of Assyria and Babylonia, whose military campaigns are important for understanding the prophecies of Isaiah. Sargon claimed to have besieged and captured Samaria, capital city of the northern kingdom of Israel. Actually, Sargon's predecessor Shalmaneser had besieged Samaria for three years (2 Kin. 17:3–6; 18:9–12) and apparently died shortly before its fall in 722–721 B.C. Nevertheless, Sargon claimed credit for the victory. On an inscription found in his palace he says: "The city of Samaria I besieged, I took; 27,290 of its inhabitants I carried away; fifty chariots that were among them I collected."

According to Assyria's policy of dealing with conquered nations, the people of Samaria were deported to Mesopotamia, where they were resettled; and people from the east were brought to Samaria (2 Kin. 17:6, 24). In 720 B.C. the kingdom of Judah, under King Ahaz, paid tribute to Sargon II, along with Edom, Moab, and Philistia.

At about this same time (720 B.C.) Sargon II also defeated the Egyptian king So (2 Kin. 17:4). So had come to the aid of the people of Gaza, who also were defying the Assyrians. In 717 B.C. Sargon put down a rebellion by the vassal state of Carchemish in Syria and destroyed that ancient center of Hittite culture.

The city of Ashdod rebelled in 713 B.C. under the promise of Egyptian aid (Isaiah 20). Egyptian ambassadors tried to enlist the aid of Hezekiah, king of Judah (Is. 18). But Isaiah the prophet opposed such action, symbolizing the folly of trusting in Egypt by walking about Jerusalem "naked and barefoot" (Is. 20:1–6). Apparently Judah listened to Isaiah's wise counsel, because the nation escaped harm during the time of Ashdod's rebellion.

Merodach–Baladan, a king of Babylon, convinced the nations subject to Sargon to revolt against Assyrian rule. In 712 B.C., Sargon sent troops against Ashdod, capturing it the following year (Is. 20:1). In 710 B.C. Sargon captured Merodach–Baladan's capital and took the title "king of Babylon."

After a reign of 16 years, Sargon apparently was murdered by one of his own soldiers. His son, Sennacherib, succeeded him as king of Assyria.

SARID [SAR id] (*refugee*) — a landmark in the territory of Zebulun on its southern border near Issachar (Josh. 19:10, 12). It is present-day Tell

Sargon II of Assyria had this prism engraved. It lists his victories, including his claim that he destroyed the city of Samaria.

Shadud, a small mound about eight kilometers (five miles) southwest of Nazareth.

SARSECHIM [SAHR suh kim] (meaning unknown) — a prince under King Nebuchadnezzar of Babylon. Sarsechim was present at the capture of Jerusalem about 587 B.C. (Jer. 39:3).

SARUCH [SAR uhk] — a form of SERUG.

SASH (see DRESS OF THE BIBLE).

SATAN [SAY tuhn] (*adversary*) — the great opposer, or adversary, of God and man; the personal name of the devil.

The Hebrew word from which Satan comes sometimes refers to human enemies (1 Sam. 29:4; Ps. 109:6). Once it refers to the angel of the Lord who opposed Balaam (Num. 22:22). But whenever this word is used as a proper name in the Old Testament, it refers to the great superhuman enemy of God, man, and good (1 Chr. 21:1; Job 1—2). This use of the word also occurs frequently in the New Testament.

Another common name for Satan in the New Testament is " the devil," meaning "slanderer" or "false accuser." Other titles by which Satan is identified in the New Testament include "the tempter" (1 Thess. 3:5); "Beelzebub" (Matt. 12:24); "the wicked one" (Matt. 13:19, 38); "the ruler of this world" (John 12:31); "the god of this age" (2 Cor. 4:4); "Belial" (2 Cor. 6:15); "the prince of the power of the air" (Eph. 2:2); and "the accuser of our brethren" (Rev. 12:10).

History. Two Old Testament passages—Isaiah 14:12–15 and Ezekiel 28:11–19—furnish a picture of Satan's original condition and the reasons for his loss of that position. These passages were addressed originally to the kings of Babylon and Tyre. But in their long-range implications, many scholars believe, they refer to Satan himself. They tell of an exalted angelic being, one of God's creatures, who became proud and ambitious. He determined to take over the throne of God for himself. But God removed him from his position of great dignity and honor.

Building upon this foundation, Revelation 12 sketches the further stages in Satan's work of evil. In his fall from God's favor, Satan persuaded one third of the angels to join him in his rebellion (Rev. 12:3–4). Throughout the Old Testament period he sought to destroy the messianic line. When the Messiah became a man, Satan tried to eliminate Him (Rev. 12:4–5). During the future period of tribulation before the Messiah's second coming, Satan will be cast out of the heavenly sphere (Rev. 12:7–12). Then he will direct his animosity toward the Messiah's people (Rev. 12:13–17). Revelation 20 notes the final phases of Satan's work. He will be bound for a thousand years and then finally cast into the lake of fire (Rev. 20:2, 10).

Characteristics. As a result of his original status and authority, Satan has great power and dignity. So great is his strength that Michael the archangel viewed him as a foe too powerful to oppose (Jude 9).

Satan's influence in worldly affairs is also clearly revealed (John 12:31). His various titles reflect his control of the world system: "the ruler of this world" (John 12:31), "the god of this age" (2 Cor. 4:4), and "the prince of the power of the air" (Eph. 2:2). The Bible declares, "The whole world lies under the sway of the wicked one" (1 John 5:19).

Satan exercises his evil power through demons (Matt. 12:24; 25:41; Rev. 12:7, 9). An outburst of demonic activity occurred when Jesus came to earth the first time because of the Savior's attack against Satan's kingdom (Matt. 12:28–29; Acts 10:38). Another such outburst is expected just before the second coming of Christ, because this will bring about the downfall of Satan and his angels (Rev. 9:3–17; 12:12; 18:2).

Satan also has high intelligence. Through it he deceived Adam and Eve and took over their rule of the world for himself (Gen. 1:26; 3:1–7; 2 Cor. 11:3). His cleverness enables him to carry out his deceptive work almost at will.

Yet Satan's attributes, impressive as they are, are not limitless. His power is subject to God's restrictions (Job 1:12; Luke 4:6; 2 Thess. 2:7–8). The reins of God on his activities are illustrated by Satan's request to God for permission to afflict Job (Job 1:7–12).

Satan is permitted to afflict God's people (Luke 13:16; 1 Thess. 2:18; Heb. 2:14). But he is never permitted to win an ultimate victory over them (John 14:30–31; 16:33).

A part of Satan's continuing ambition to replace God is his passionate yearning to have others worship him (Matt. 4:8–9; Rev. 13:4, 12). Since God has frustrated this desire and put down Satan's rebellion, he has become God's exact opposite. He is "the wicked one" (Matt. 13:19, 38), while God is "the Holy One" (Is. 1:4).

Satan's nature is malicious. His efforts in opposing God, His people, and His truth are tireless (Job 1:7; 2:2; Matt. 13:28). He is always opposed to man's best interests (1 Chr. 21:1; Zech. 3:1–2). Through his role in introducing sin into the human

family (Gen. 3), Satan has gained the power of death—a power which Christ has broken through His crucifixion and resurrection (Heb. 2:14–15).

Methods. Of the various methods used by Satan in carrying out his evil work, none is more characteristic than TEMPTATION (Matt. 4:3; 1 Thess. 3:5). Satan leads people into sin by various means. Sometimes he does it by direct suggestion, as in the case of Judas Iscariot (John 13:2, 27); sometimes through his agents who disguise themselves as messengers of God (2 Thess. 2:9; 1 John 4:1); and sometimes through a person's own weaknesses (1 Cor. 7:5). He tempted Christ directly, trying to lead Him into compromise by promising Him worldly authority and power (Luke 4:5–8).

Along with his work of tempting mankind, Satan also delights in deception (1 Tim. 3:6–7; 2 Tim. 2:26). His lying nature stands in bold contrast to the truth for which Christ stands (John 8:32, 44). The great falsehood which he uses so frequently is that good can be attained by doing wrong. This lie is apparent in practically all his temptations (Gen. 3:4–5). As the great deceiver, Satan is an expert at falsifying truth (2 Cor. 11:13–15).

Satan's methods are designed ultimately to silence the gospel. He seeks to stop the spread of God's Word (Matt. 13:19; 1 Thess. 2:17–18). When the gospel is preached, Satan tries to blind people's understanding so they cannot grasp the meaning of the message (2 Cor. 4:3–4; 2 Thess 2:9–10). At times he opposes the work of God by violent means (John 13:2, 27; 1 Pet. 5:8; Rev. 12:13–17). He brings disorder into the physical world by afflicting human beings (Job 1—2; 2 Cor. 12:7; Heb. 2:14). Sometimes God allows him to afflict His people for purposes of correction (1 Tim. 1:20).

Defeat. Satan is destined to fail in his continuing rebellion against God. His final defeat is predicted in the New Testament (Luke 10:18; John 12:31; Rev. 12:9; 20:10). The death of Christ on the cross is the basis for Satan's final defeat (Heb. 2:14–15; 1 Pet. 3:18, 22). This event was the grand climax to a sinless life during which Jesus triumphed over the enemy repeatedly (Matt. 4:1–11; Luke 4:1–13). The final victory will come when Jesus returns and Satan is cast into the lake of fire (Rev. 20:1–15).

Strength for a Christian's victory over sin has also been provided through the death of Christ. We have assurance that "the God of peace will crush Satan under your feet" (Rom. 16:20). But such personal victory depends on our will to offer resistance to Satan's temptations (Eph. 4:25–27; 1 Pet. 5:8–9). To help Christians win this battle against Satan, God has provided the power of Christ's blood (Rev. 12:11), the continuing prayer of Christ in heaven for believers (Heb. 7:25), the leading of the Holy Spirit (Gal. 5:16), and various weapons for spiritual warfare (Eph. 6:13–18).

Reality. Some people have trouble admitting the existence of such an enemy as Satan. But his presence and activity are necessary to explain the problems of evil and suffering. The Bible makes it plain that Satan exists and that his main work is to op-

Photo by Howard Vos

The mound of Beth Shan, the city where King Saul's body was hung by the Philistines, overlooks the ruins of a Roman theater (1 Sam. 31:7-10) in the foreground.

pose the rule of God in the affairs of man.

Many wonder why God would allow Satan, this great embodiment of evil, to exist in His creation. No completely satisfying answer to this question has been found. Perhaps He allows it to show that evil and wrongdoing do not provide the key to the ultimate meaning of life which man so desperately desires.

Also see DEVIL.

SATAN, SYNAGOGUE OF — a phrase used by John to describe the Jews who opposed the church (Rev. 2:9; 3:9).

SATISFACTION (see ATONEMENT).

SATON (see WEIGHTS AND MEASURES).

SATRAP [SAY trap] (*lieutenant*) — the governor of a province in the ancient Persian Empire; a subordinate ruler who ruled over a region on behalf of the emperor (Ezra 8:36; Esth. 3:12; lieutenants, KJV). For all practical purposes, a satrap was a vassal king who had great authority.

SATYR (see ANIMALS OF THE BIBLE; GODS, PAGAN).

SAUL [sawl] (*asked*) — the name of three men in the Bible:

1. The sixth of the ancient kings of Edom (Gen. 36:36-38; 1 Chr. 1:48-49).

2. The first king of Israel (1 Sam. 9:2—31:12; 1 Chr. 5:10—26:28). Saul lived in turbulent times. For many years, Israel had consisted of a loose organization of tribes without a single leader. In times of crisis, leaders had arisen; but there was no formal government. SAMUEL was Saul's predecessor as Israel's leader; but he was a religious leader, not a

king. Threatened by the war-like Philistines, the people of Israel pressured Samuel to appoint a king to lead them in their battles against the enemy. Samuel gave in to their demands and anointed Saul as the first king of the nation of Israel.

Saul's Qualifications. Saul had several admirable qualities that made him fit to be king of Israel during this period in its history. He was a large man of attractive appearance, which led to his quick acceptance by the people. In addition, he was from the tribe of Benjamin, situated on the border between Ephraim and Judah. Thus, he appealed to both the northern and southern sections of Israel. Furthermore, he was a capable military leader, as shown by his victories early in his career.

One of the most important episodes of Saul's career was his first encounter with the Philistines. Saul took charge of 2,000 men at Micmash, leaving his son Jonathan with 1,000 men at Gibeah. After Jonathan made a successful, but unplanned, attack on a company of Philistines at Geba, the reaction of the Philistine forces drove the Israelites back to Gilgal. The Philistines gained control of central Palestine, and Saul's defeat seemed imminent.

But Jonathan burst in unexpectedly upon the Philistines at Micmash, succeeding in starting a panic in their camp. Saul took advantage of this and routed the Philistines. This victory strengthened Saul's position as king.

Saul's Mistakes. Saul's first sin was his failure to wait for Samuel at Gilgal (1 Sam. 13:8-9). There he assumed the role of a priest by making a sacrifice to ask for God's blessing. His second sin followed soon afterward. After defeating Moab, Ammon, and Edom, Saul was told by Samuel to go to war against the Amalekites and to "kill both man and woman, infant and nursing child, ox and sheep, camel and donkey" (1 Sam. 15:3). Saul carried out his instructions well except that he spared the life of Agag, the king, and saved the best of the animals. When he returned, he lied and told Samuel that he had followed instructions exactly.

Saul's disobedience in this case showed that he could not be trusted as an instrument of God's will. He desired to assert his own will instead. Although he was allowed to remain king for the rest of his life, the Spirit of the Lord departed from Saul. He was troubled by an evil spirit that brought bouts of madness. Meanwhile, Samuel went to Bethlehem to anoint DAVID as the new king.

Saul and David. Saul's last years were tragic, clouded by periods of depression and gloom. David was brought into Saul's court to play soothing music to restore him to sanity. Saul was friendly toward David at first, but this changed as David's leadership abilities emerged. Enraged by jealousy, Saul tried to kill David several times. But David succeeded in eluding these attempts on his life for many years, often with the aid of Saul's son JONATHAN and his daughter Michal.

Saul's Death. The closing years of Saul's life brought a decline in his service to his people and in his personal fortunes. Rather than consolidating his gains after his early victories, Saul wasted his time trying to kill David. Meanwhile, the Philistines sensed Israel's plight and came with a large army to attack the Hebrew nation. Saul's army was crushed, and three of his sons, including Jonathan, were killed. Wounded in the battle, Saul committed suicide by falling on his own sword.

An Appraisal of Saul. Saul is one of the most tragic figures in the Old Testament. He began his reign with great promise but ended it in shame. As Israel's first king, he had the opportunity to set the pattern for all future leaders. His weakness was his rebellious nature and his inability to adapt to the necessity of sharing power and popularity.

Saul also used his power to pursue unworthy purposes and wasted much time and energy in fruitless attempts on David's life. Commercial enterprises were not encouraged during his reign. As a result, the economic condition of the nation was not good. Saul also failed to unite the various tribes into one nation.

Saul allowed the religious life of his people to deteriorate as well. However, he did provide distinct services to his people through his military actions. His victories paved the way for the brilliant career of his successor David.

3. The original name of PAUL, a persecutor of the church, who became an apostle of Christ and a missionary of the early church (Acts 7:58—9:26; 11:25—13:9).

SAVIOR — a person who rescues others from evil, danger, or destruction. The Old Testament viewed God Himself as the Savior: "There is no other God besides Me, a just God and a Savior" (Is. 45:21). Because God is the source of salvation, He sent hu-

man deliverers to rescue His people, Israel (Ps. 106:21; Is. 43:3, 11). This word was also used to describe the judges of Israel, those "saviors" or "deliverers" who rescued God's people from oppression by their enemies (Judg. 3:9, 15).

In the New Testament the word for savior describes both God the Father (1 Tim. 1:1; Jude 25) and Jesus Christ the Son (Acts 5:31; Phil. 3:20). The apostles rejoiced that in Christ, God had become the "Savior of all men" (1 Tim. 4:10). He was the Savior of Gentiles as well as Jews. As Christians, we are exhorted to "grow in the grace and knowledge of our Lord and Savior Jesus Christ" (2 Pet. 3:18).

Also see JESUS CHRIST.

SAVOR (see SWEET INCENSE).

SAW (see TOOLS OF THE BIBLE).

SCAB (see DISEASES OF THE BIBLE).

SCALE — a word used in the Bible at least four different ways:

1. The outer covering of fish or reptiles (Lev. 11:9–12). The scales of LEVIATHAN are described as impenetrable, a reference to his pride (Job 41:15).

2. A balance for determining weight. The prophet Isaiah pictured God weighing out the mountains on a scale like a merchant weighing a portion of grain (Is. 40:12).

3. A scaly substance peeled off the body, as the scales that fell from the eyes of the apostle Paul (Acts 9:18).

4. Used as a verb, to scale means to climb up or over, as the wise man scales a mighty city in the wisdom and power of God (Prov. 21:22).

SCALL (see DISEASES OF THE BIBLE).

SCAPEGOAT — a live goat over whose head AARON confessed all the sins of the children of Israel. The goat was then sent into the wilderness on the Day of Atonement, symbolically taking away their sins (Lev. 16:8, 10, 26; azazel, RSV).

The derivation of the term scapegoat is not completely clear. Scholars suggest it communicates such ideas as "passing away in his strength," "strength of God," "loneliness," or "desert." But the most probable meaning is the idea of "far removed" or "going far away."

The scapegoat was one of two goats that served as a sin offering on the Day of Atonement (Lev. 16:5). One of the goats was sacrificed as a part of the sin offering (Lev. 16:9). The other was kept alive so it could be taken into the wilderness by an escort (Lev. 16:10, 21). The person who released the goat was to wash his clothes and bathe afterwards (Lev. 16:26). The goat symbolized the removal of the sins of the people into an uninhabited land (Lev. 16:21–22). The process represented the transfer of guilt from the people of Israel, the complete removal of guilt from their midst.

Also see FEASTS AND FESTIVALS.

SCARLET (see COLORS OF THE BIBLE).

SCENT (see SWEET INCENSE).

SCEPTER — the official staff of a ruler, symbolizing his authority and power. Originally the scepter was the shepherd's staff, since the first kings were nomadic princes (Mic. 7:14). In some instances the scepter was a strong rod (Ezek. 19:11, 14).

Sometimes the symbolism of a scepter refers to the Messiah who will rule from Israel, from the tribe of Judah in particular (Gen. 49:10). In the New Testament, the Book of Hebrews describes Christ as the Son who rules with a scepter of righteousness.

The breaking of a scepter signified the downfall of the one who possessed it. This symbolism was used by several of the Old Testament prophets to predict what would happen to the enemies of the nation of Israel (Is. 14:5; Ezek. 19:1–14).

When the Roman soldiers mocked Jesus before His crucifixion, they placed a reed in His hand as a mock scepter and saluted Him as "King of the Jews" (Matt. 27:29).

SCEVA [SEE vuh] (meaning unknown) — a Jewish chief priest at Ephesus during Paul's time (Acts 19:14). Sceva's seven sons attempted to cast out an evil spirit in the name of Jesus. But they were wounded instead by the demon–possessed man and had to flee naked and humiliated.

SCHIN [shin] — a form of SHIN.

SCHISM — a separation or division into factions, especially a break in church fellowship (1 Cor. 12:25; discord, RSV; division, NASB, NIV). The apostle Paul was concerned about the divisions within the church at Corinth (1 Cor. 1:10, 11:18). Jealousy, mistrust, and party strife must be replaced, said Paul, by mutual respect and unity of mind and heart in the Holy Spirit.

SCHOLAR — a person who has done advanced study in a special field (Eccl. 12:11). A footnote to this verse (NKJV) points out that scholars means, literally, "masters of the assemblies."

SCHOOLMASTER — KJV word for TUTOR. Also see OCCUPATIONS AND TRADES.

SCHOOLS (see EDUCATION).

SCIENCE — the systematic organization of knowledge about the laws which govern the world and the universe. The word science occurs twice in the KJV (Dan. 1:4; 1 Tim. 6:20), but in both cases the NKJV renders the word as knowledge. All truth, whether revealed in Scripture or gained from experimentation and observation of God's creation, is God's truth. Ultimate knowledge comes from God and His Word.

SCOFFER — one who shows contempt by mocking, sneering, or scorning (Gen. 21:9; Ps. 73:8). Unlike the good man, who walks the path of wisdom, the scoffer is a wicked man who follows the path of folly, refusing to listen to the wisdom of others.

SCORN — mockery, ridicule, or contempt. This concept appears in several passages in the Bible. Among the more significant is Psalm 22:7, where Jesus Christ is prophesied as One who will become the object of scorn. This is because of the seeming contradiction between His claims and His death in suffering and disgrace. In the same way, those who continue to follow the Lord in the midst of adverse circumstances are scorned by others (Ps. 44:13; 79:4). Nevertheless, the righteous will be vindicated as Christ was in His resurrection. Therefore, God's blessing rests on those who refuse to join with the scornful (Ps. 1:1).

The scourging place at St. Peter's in Jerusalem. Prisoners were suspended for flogging by tying their hands through holes in the stone wall above the doorway.

Photo by Howard Vos

Restored writing tables and benches used by scribes in the settlement at Qumran. Many of the Dead Sea Scrolls discovered at Qumran may have been written on tables such as these.

SCORNFUL — the act of expressing contempt toward others (Ps. 1:1). The scornful are proud, arrogant people who scoff at the way of peace and make mockery of goodness. Also see SCOFFERS.

SCORPION (see ANIMALS OF THE BIBLE).

SCOUNDREL — a wicked or worthless person. Nabal, a foolish man who refused to provide food for David and his men, was called a scoundrel (1 Sam. 25:17, 25; a son of Belial, KJV; a wicked man, NIV).

SCOURGE — a whip used as a means of punishment. In the Old Testament, scourge is generally a word that describes punishment, either by man (1 Kin. 12:11) or by God (Is. 10:26). The Mosaic Law prescribed that a wicked person could be beaten with forty blows (Deut. 25:2–3).

In the New Testament, to be "examined under scourging" (Acts 22:24) referred to an investigation which began with the beating of the prisoner. Another word describes the "whip of cords" with which Jesus cleansed the Temple (John 2:15). It also graphically describes the beating which Jesus received before His crucifixion (Matt. 27:26).

The whip used for this type of punishment consisted of a handle to which one or more leather cords or thongs were attached. Sometimes these cords were knotted or weighted with pieces of metal or bone to make the whip more effective as a flesh–cutting instrument. In his prediction of the

coming of the Messiah, the prophet Isaiah declared, "He was wounded for our transgressions; He was bruised for our iniquities" (Is. 53:5), referring to the scourging of Jesus.

SCREECH OWL (see ANIMALS OF THE BIBLE).

SCRIBES — members of a learned class in ancient Israel through New Testament times who studied the Scriptures and served as copyists, editors, and teachers.

In the Old Testament the Hebrew word translated as scribe identified a person who numbered or mustered the troops (Jer. 52:25). Such a steward controlled the access of the people to the throne rooms of David and Solomon (2 Sam. 8:17). Gradually, the word came to refer to those who chose a profession of literary studies.

Hezekiah, king of Judah, chose a body of men who transcribed the ancient records for preservation, including the proverbs of Solomon (Prov. 25:1). The nature of the scribe's work had changed by this time. He was no longer an officer of the king's court; he had become a person who interpreted the Scriptures. The scribes soon became known for their study and knowledge of the Mosaic Law.

After the Jews returned from the Captivity in Babylon, the era of the scribes began. The reading of the Law before the nation of Israel by Ezra (Nehemiah 8—10) signaled the nation's return to exact observance of all the laws and rites that had been given. Following the Law and the traditions that had grown up around it became the measure of devotion and spirituality.

At first the priests were responsible for the scientific study and professional communication of this legal code. But this function eventually passed to the scribes. Their official interpretation of the meaning of the Law eventually became more important than the Law itself.

This position of strength allowed these early scribes to enforce their rules and practices with a binding authority. To speak of the scribes as interpreters of Scripture means that they provided rules for human conduct out of their study.

By the time of Jesus, the scribes were a new upper class among the Jewish people. Large numbers of priests in Jerusalem before A.D. 70 served as scribes. One of these was JOSEPHUS, the Jewish historian. Some scribes came from among the SADDUCEES. Others came from the ordinary priestly ranks. But the largest group of scribes came from among every other class of people, including merchants, carpenters, flax combers, tent makers, and even day laborers, like HILLEL, who became a famous Jewish teacher.

The young Israelite who devoted his life to become a scribe went through a set course of study for several years. Josephus began his preparation when he was 14. Students were in continual contact with the teacher, listening to his instruction. The disciple–scribe first had to master all the traditional material and the unique method of interpretation of the Jewish Halakah. The aim was to give the apprentice competence in making decisions on questions of religious legislation and penal justice.

According to the traditon of the scribes, there were "secrets" of interpretation, forbidden degrees of knowledge, which were not to be expounded before three or more persons. Some chapters in the Bible were to be explained only to sages (2 Esdras 14:1–5).

The apocalyptic writings of late Judaism contained great theological systems that were understood only by the specially initiated. This was left to the confidential teaching of the scribes. They believed that God intended to leave the mass of people ignorant of His reasons for requiring certain things under the Law. These truths were hidden from the masses because they could not be trusted to understand and apply the Law.

The city of Jerusalem was the center of this scribal knowledge and interpretation of the Law. Only ordained teachers could transmit and create the tradition; this was the matter studied to perfection by students often beginning at age 14. When they completed their study at the age of 40, they could be ordained. As members with full rights, they could act as judges, be called rabbis, and occupy positions in administration of justice, government, and education. They joined the chief priests and aristocratic families who made up the SANHEDRIN. The scribes were held in greatest esteem by the people.

Sometimes the gospels refer to the scribes as lawyers (Matt. 22:35; Luke 7:30)—a title that identifies them as experts in the Mosaic Law. This Law was regarded as the sole civil and religious authority governing Jewish life. In Jesus' day, the scribes were usually associated with the PHARISEES (Matt. 12:38; Mark 7:5; Luke 6:7). In the gospels, they are sometimes called "the scribes of the Pharisees" (Mark 2:16, RSV, NASB; the teachers of the law who were Pharisees, NIV). This phrase identifies scribes who were members of the Pharisaic party.

Many of the scribes were members of the SANHEDRIN, the highest legal and administrative body in the Jewish state in Roman times. Gamaliel was one of these (Acts 5:34), as was Nicodemus (John 3:1). They sat as administrators of the Law "in Moses' seat" (Matt. 23:2). This administration intensified after the destruction of Jerusalem by the Romans in A.D. 70.

Since a scribe was not paid for his services, he had to earn a livelihood in another way. This rule may have been enforced to keep down the problem of bribery among the scribes in their application of the Law. The scribes often developed attitudes based on their professional privileges, and this often resulted in pride (Matt. 23:5–7). Jesus warned against these excesses, and He boldly attacked the religious hypocrisy of the scribes (Matthew 23).

SCRIBE'S KNIFE — a small knife used by scribes to sharpen their writing pens and cut PAPYRUS scrolls. King Jehoiakim used such a knife to destroy the scroll containing Jeremiah's prophecies (Jer. 36:23; penknife, KJV).

SCRIPT — an ancient system of characters used in writing (Ezra 4:7; Esth. 1:22). From the Aramaic script the square characters of the Hebrew alphabet were developed. Also see LANGUAGES OF THE BIBLE.

SCRIPTURE — the Old and New Testaments, which make up the Bible, God's written word. God gave to the world His living Word, Jesus Christ, and His written Word, the Scriptures. Although the Bible was written by prophets and apostles, the Bible originated not with their wills, but with God's (2 Pet. 1:20–21). "All Scripture," Paul wrote, "is given by inspiration of God" (2 Tim. 3:16).

After Jesus, God's living Word, returned to heaven, the Bible, God's written Word, remained on earth as God's eternal guide for mankind. The written Word is durable and universally available and has remained essentially unchanged in its message since it was first inspired by God.

Because the Bible is God's inspired Word, it is able to make us "wise for salvation through faith which is in Christ Jesus" (2 Tim. 3:15). The Scriptures testify of Christ (John 5:39) and are understood and received as He opens our understanding to the revealed will of His Father (Luke 24:27). Like the Berean Christians, we should search the Scriptures daily (Acts 17:11) to discover God's message for our lives.

Also see BIBLE; BIBLE VERSIONS AND TRANSLATIONS.

SCROLL — a roll of papyrus, leather, or parchment on which an ancient document—particularly a text of the Bible—was written (Ezra 6:2). Rolled up on a stick, a scroll was usually about 11 meters (35 feet) long—the size required, for instance, for the Book of Luke or the Book of Acts. Longer books of the Bible required two or more scrolls.

One of the scrolls written by the prophet Jeremiah was read in the Temple and in the king's palace, then destroyed by King Jehoiakim. The king cut it into pieces and threw it into the fire to show his contempt for God's prophet. But Jeremiah promptly rewrote the scroll through his scribe, Baruch (Jer. 36:1–32).

Books did not exist until the second or third century A.D., when the CODEX was introduced. The codex had a page arrangement much like our modern books.

SCRUPLES — a conviction of conscience that causes a person to hesitate about participating in some action. More mature Christians, said the apostle Paul, ought to bear with the tender scruples of weak Christians, by always acting in love and unselfishness (Rom. 15:1).

SCUM — rust, symbolizing sin (Ezek. 24:6–12; rust, RSV, NASB; corrosion, NEB; deposit, NIV). The prophet Ezekiel compared the sin of Jerusalem to rust on a cooking pot. To remove the rust, the pot was heated on a fire. This action was to symbolize the purging fire of God's judgment (Ezek. 24:13).

SCURVY (see DISEASES OF THE BIBLE).

SCYTHIANS [SITH ee uhns] — a barbaric race who lived in Scythia, an ancient region of southeastern Europe and southwestern Asia (see Map 1, D-1), now generally identified as the Soviet Union. In biblical times, the Scythians were a tribe of nomadic raiders notorious for their cruelty and barbarism.

Originally from western Siberia, the Scythians migrated to southern Russia about 2000 B.C. Several centuries later they moved into northern Persia. Eventually they became allies of the Assyrians and oppressed western Persia for almost three decades. After the Medes became a world power, they finally drove the Scythians back to southern Russia.

Famous as raiders, the Scythians carried out a major campaign of plunder against Syria and Palestine in the late seventh century B.C. The prophets Zephaniah and Jeremiah may have referred to this raid. Jeremiah spoke of waters that would rise out of the north and eventually become "an overflowing flood" of God's judgment against the nations of that region of the world (Jer. 47:2).

SEA — a major body of water that served as an important shipping route in the ancient world. But biblical writers had several different meanings in mind when they spoke of "the sea."

1. The phrase usually refers to the MEDITERRANEAN SEA off the western coast of Palestine (Gen. 49:13; Ps. 80:11).

2. In Genesis, the phrase *the sea* refers to the ocean, the "gathering together of the waters" (Gen. 1:10) as distinguished from the dry land.

These copper scrolls were discovered among the Dead Sea Scrolls at Qumran. Most scrolls in ancient times were written on papyrus, parchment, or leather.

Photo by Howard Vos

3. Sometimes the phrase refers to a large river, with its network of branches, channels, and irrigating canals, such as the Nile (Is. 19:5; Ezek. 32:2).

4. *The sea* is also used of the Red Sea (Ex. 14:16, 27; 15:4; Josh. 24:6) or one of its gulfs (Num. 11:31; Is. 11:15), and perhaps the sea crossed by Solomon's fleet (1 Kin. 9:26; 10:22).

5. In the New Testament, the large lake in Galilee, an inland fresh-water lake, is also called the Sea of Galilee (Matt. 4:18).

6. The phrase is also used of the Dead Sea, variously known as the Salt Sea (Gen. 14:3), the Eastern Sea (Joel 2:20), and the Sea of the Arabah (Deut. 3:17).

The Hebrews were a land-loving people who distrusted a large body of water such as the Mediterranean Sea. To them the sea was a perilous and forbidding place. The sea therefore became a symbol of the seething nations of the world and of the troubled lives of the unrighteous (Dan. 7:2-3; Matt. 13:47; Rev. 13:1). Perhaps this is why the apostle John spoke of the glorious new heaven and new earth as a place in which "there was no more sea" (Rev. 21:1).

SEA, BRAZEN (see SEA, MOLTEN).

SEA, CHINNERETH (see CHINNERETH).

SEA COW, SEA GULL, SEA MEW, SEA MONSTER (see ANIMALS OF THE BIBLE).

SEA, DEAD (see DEAD SEA).

SEA, MOLTEN — a large laver, or basin, of cast bronze used in Solomon's Temple. The KJV uses the term molten sea (1 Kin. 7:23), describing its method of manufacture. The bronze was melted and cast into the proper mold.

The molten sea was larger than a normal laver. It measured 5 meters (15 feet) in diameter, 2 1/2 meters (7 1/2 feet) in height and 15 meters (45 feet) in circumference (1 Kin. 7:23). Its thickness was "a handbreadth," estimated at 7 1/2 centimeters (3 inches). It contained 2,000 baths, or about 38,000 liters (10,000 gallons) of water (1 Kin. 7:26).

Below the brim, shaped "like a lily blossom" (1 Kin. 7:26), were two rows of gourd-shaped "ornamental buds" (1 Kin. 7:24). The sea rested on the backs of 12 oxen. The oxen were separated into four groups of three, facing north, south, east and west (1 Kin. 7:25).

SEA OF GALILEE (see GALILEE, SEA OF)

SEA OF GLASS — a sea which stood before God's throne in the Book of Revelation, symbolizing the Lord's holiness and purity. This sea is "like crystal" (Rev. 4:6), and it is also "mingled with fire" (Rev. 15:2). These descriptions are similar to the language used in the Old Testament, when the Lord revealed Himself in all His glory to the people of Israel (Ex. 24:10), and in the prophet Ezekiel's vision of God's throne (Ezek. 1:22-28). The message of this image is that the Lord is a God of holiness who demands righteous living from His people.

SEA, THE GREAT — another name for the MEDITERRANEAN SEA, a major body of water along the western coast of the land of Palestine (Josh. 15:47).

SEA OF JAZER [JAY zur] — a lake in Gilead, east of the Jordan River (Jer. 48:32). Also see JAZER.

SEA, SALT (see DEAD SEA).

SEA, TIBERIAS (see TIBERIAS).

SEAH [SEE uh] (see WEIGHTS AND MEASURES).

SEAL — a device such as a signet ring or cylinder, engraved with the owner's name, a design, or both (Ex. 28:11; Esth. 8:8). A medallion or ring used as a seal featured a raised or recessed signature or symbol so it could be impressed on wax or moist clay to leave its mark (Job 38:14).

The seal was strung on a cord and hung around the neck or worn on one's finger (Gen. 38:18, RSV; Jer. 22:24). A seal usually served to certify a signature or authenticate a letter or other document (Neh. 9:38; Esth. 8:8; John 3:33).

In the New Testament, Pilate authorized a guard to be sent to secure the tomb where the body of Jesus had been laid: "So they went and made the tomb secure, sealing the stone and setting the guard" (Matt. 27:66).

The word seal is used also in a figurative sense of an outward condition (John 6:27; 1 Cor. 9:2; 2 Tim. 2:19). The Book of Revelation uses the word frequently in this sense (Rev. 5:1; 7:2-8; 10:4).

SEAMSTER (see OCCUPATIONS AND TRADES).

SEANCE — a ritual in which persons try to communicate with the dead. King Saul of the Israelites asked a medium (the woman of En Dor) to conduct a seance so he could communicate with the spirit of the deceased prophet Samuel (1 Sam. 28:8-11). Also see MAGIC AND SORCERY.

SEAR — to burn with an iron. Warning of the danger of adultery, the writer of Proverbs asked, "Can one walk on hot coals, and his feet not be seared?" (Prov. 6:28; burned, KJV; scorched, NASB, NIV, RSV). The apostle Paul warned Timothy of the denial of Jesus that would be prevalent in the end times. False teachers, whose consciences will be burned away or "seared with a hot iron" (1 Tim. 4:2), will abound. Christians must beware of the doctrine of such teachers even today.

SEASON — one of the four natural divisions of the year: spring, summer, autumn, and winter (Lev. 26:4; Deut. 11:14). Basically, however, there are only two seasons in the Palestinian year: the dry season, which is hot, and the wet season, which is cool or cold. Also see WEATHER.

SEAT — a sitting place of great importance. The mercy seat on the ARK OF THE COVENANT was reserved only for the Lord (Ex. 25:22). A seat could also refer to a royal throne (Judg. 3:20; Esth. 3:1). In the New Testament, the word often refers to a judgment seat, sometimes Christ's judgment seat in particular (Rom. 14:10; 2 Cor. 5:10).

SEBA [SEE buh] (meaning unknown) — the name of a man and a place in the Old Testament:
1. The oldest son of Cush (Gen. 10:7). Seba was a grandson of Ham and a great-grandson of Noah.
2. A country, probably in northeastern Africa, since it is mentioned along with Egypt and Ethiopia (Is. 43:3). Some scholars believe Seba refers to the Sudan or northern part of Ethiopia.

Also see SABEANS.

SEBAM [SEE bam] — a form of SHEBAM.

SEBAT [SEE bat] — a form of SHEBAT.

SECACAH [sih KAY kuh] (*thicket*) — a city in the Valley of Achor in the Wilderness of Judah (Josh. 15:61). Secacah has been identified with Khirbet es-Samrah, near the northwest shore of the Dead Sea.

SECHU [SEE koo] (*watchplace*) — a place in the territory of Benjamin between Gibeah (Saul's residence) and Ramah (Samuel's residence). Sechu was noted for its "great well." When King Saul arrived at Sechu, in pursuit of David, he was directed to NAIOTH (1 Sam. 19:22; Secu, RSV). Some scholars identify Sechu as Khirbet Shuweikeh, about five kilometers (three miles) northwest of er-Ram (perhaps ancient Ramah), but this is uncertain.

Some Greek and Latin texts of 1 Samuel 19:22 do not treat Sechu as a proper name but translate it "on the bare hilltop." The "great well" at Sechu may have been a large cistern that served as a gathering place.

SECOND COMING — Christ's future return to the earth at the end of the present age. Although the Bible explicitly speaks of Christ's appearance as a "second time," the phrase "second coming" occurs nowhere in the New Testament. Many passages, however, speak of His return. In fact, in the New Testament alone it is referred to over 300 times.

The night before His crucifixion, Jesus told His apostles that He would return (John 14:3). When Jesus ascended into heaven, two angels appeared to His followers, saying that He would return in the same manner as they had seen Him go (Acts 1:11). The New Testament is filled with expectancy of His coming, even as Christians should be today.

Various opinions exist about what is meant by the Second Coming. Some regard it as the coming of the Holy Spirit on the day of PENTECOST. Others regard it as the coming of Christ into the heart at conversion. Christ's coming for the believer at the time of death is still another view. Careful examination of the New Testament, however, makes it clear that the Second Coming will be a climactic historical event. The Lord will return in the same manner in which He left. His coming will be personal, bodily, and visible.

The time of the Second Coming is unknown. In fact, Jesus stated that only the Father knew the time. Therefore, the return of the Lord should be a matter of constant expectancy. As He came the first time, in the "fullness of time" (Gal. 4:4), so will the

Second Coming be. The believer's task is not to try to determine the time of the Second Coming. We should share the gospel message diligently until He returns (Acts 1:8–11).

SECOND DEATH (see ESCHATOLOGY).

SECOND QUARTER, THE — a district of Jerusalem in which Huldah the prophetess lived (2 Kin. 2:14). This district lay in the angle formed by the west wall of the Temple and the ancient wall of the city. It was later included within the wall restored by Nehemiah.

SECOND SABBATH — a term found only in Luke 6:1: "On the second Sabbath after the first" (KJV, NKJV). The Greek word means literally "the second–first (sabbath)." Scholars are not certain about the exact meaning of this term.

SECRET (see MYSTERY).

SECRETARY (see OCCUPATIONS AND TRADES).

SECT — a small faction or party united by common interests or beliefs. Before the apostle Paul became a Christian, he was a Pharisee, a member of the strictest sect (party, RSV; group, NEB) of the Jewish religion (Acts 26:5). The early Christians were also criticized by the Jewish people because they were members of a hated sect known as the WAY—an early name for Christianity (Acts 24:14).

SECU [SEE koo] — a form of SECHU.

SECUNDUS [sih KUN duhs] (*second*) — an early Christian who lived in Thessalonica (Acts 20:4). Secundus was one of seven friends and companions who accompanied the apostle Paul from Greece to Asia Minor, as Paul returned from his third missionary journey.

SEDITION — conduct or language inciting rebellion against the authority of a state or other lawful government (Ezra 4:15; revolt, NASB; rebellion, NIV).

SEDUCTRESS — a female seducer; a woman who induces men to have sexual intercourse with her. The Book of Proverbs is filled with warnings against the temptations of such a woman (Prov. 2:16; 7:5; 27:13).

SEED — a fertilized and ripened egg cell of a plant, capable of sprouting to produce a new plant. The word seed is also used figuratively in the Bible to express several important truths. It refers to human descendants or offspring (Gen. 21:12). The apostle Paul explained that the seed of Abraham not only referred to his physical descendants, "but also to those who are of the faith of Abraham" (Rom. 4:16). In Galatians 3:16, Paul went even further, stating that Abraham's seed is Jesus Christ rather than the nation of Israel.

Jesus often used the imagery of seeds in His parables. In the 13th chapter of Matthew, He told three different parables involving seeds: the parable of the sower (Matt. 13:3–9, 18–33), the parable of the

wheat and the tares (Matt. 13:24–30, 36–43), and the parable of the mustard seed (Matt. 13:31–32). He compared His own death and resurrection in a figurative sense to the sowing of seeds (John 12:24).

SEEDTIME — the time for planting seeds (Gen. 8:22). In Palestine grain crops were sown in late October or November. The seed for summer produce, such as beans, cucumbers, and melons, were sown between January and March.

SEGUB [SEE guhb] (meaning unknown) — the name of two men in the Old Testament:
1. The youngest son of Hiel of Bethel (1 Kin. 16:34). Segub may have been buried beneath the city gate as a foundation sacrifice when his father rebuilt the city of Jericho.
2. A son of Hezron and a grandson of Judah (1 Chr. 2:21–22).

SEIR [SEE ur] (*hairy, rough*) — the name of two places and one person in the Old Testament:
1. The mountainous country stretching from the Dead Sea to the Red Sea, east of the gorge called the Arabah (Gen. 14:6). The elevations of Seir range from 183 meters (600 feet) to 1,830 meters (6,000 feet). Two of Seir's outstanding features are Mount Hor, where Aaron died (Num. 20:27–28), and the ancient city of rock, Petra or Sela (Is. 16:1). The region was named after a Horite (Hurrian) patriarch whose descendants settled in this area.

God gave this land to Esau and his descendants, who drove out the Horites, or Hurrians (Deut. 2:12). Esau and his descendants, the Edomites, lived in Seir (Deut. 2:29). This explains why God directed the children of Israel not to invade this territory when they moved from Egypt toward the Promised Land (Deut. 2:4–5).

Although Seir was originally the name of the mountain range in Edom, the name came to signify the entire territory of Edom south of the Dead Sea (2 Chr. 20:10). King David made these people his servants (2 Sam. 8:14). Later, in the days of King Jehoshaphat of Judah, the people of Mount Seir (the EDOMITES) joined the Ammonites and the Moabites in an invasion against Judah (2 Chr. 20:10, 22–23). Later, the prophet Ezekiel predicted God's destruction of "Mount Seir" because of their strong hatred of Israel and their desire to possess the lands of Israel and Judah (Ezek. 35:1–15).
2. The grandfather of Hori, ancestor of the Horites (1 Chr. 1:39).
3. A mountain on the northern border of the territory of Judah (Josh. 15:10). Some have identified Seir with the rocky point near Chesalon on which the present–day village of Saris stands, about 19 kilometers (12 miles) west of Jerusalem. Other scholars insist the mountain has not been identified.

SEIRAH [SEE uh ruh] (*woody district*) — an unknown city in the mountains of Ephraim west of Jericho (Judg. 3:26; Seirath, KJV). Seirah was the place to which Ehud the judge escaped after murdering Eglon, king of Moab.

SEIRATH [SEE uh rath] — a form of SEIRAH.

SELA [SEE luh] (*rock, cliff*) — the name of three places in the Old Testament:

1. A fortress city, the capital of Edom, situated on the Wadi Musa ("the Valley of Moses") between the Dead Sea and the Gulf of Aqaba (2 Kin. 14:7; Selah, KJV). A rock formation about 1,160 meters (3,800 feet) above sea level, now known as Umm el-Bayyarah, the great acropolis of the Nabatean city of PETRA dominates the site.

Sela was near Mount Hor, close to the Wilderness of Zin. Its name was changed to Joktheel by Amaziah, king of Judah, after he captured it (2 Kin. 14:7). Amaziah's men took 10,000 of the people of Seir (Edomites), "brought them to the top of the rock, and cast them down...so that they all were dashed in pieces" (2 Chr. 25:12).

2. A place apparently in the territory of Judah near the boundary of the Amorites (Judg. 1:36; the rock, KJV). Some scholars believe the site was in Amorite territory. Its exact location is unknown.

3. An unidentified site in Moab mentioned by Isaiah in a prophecy of doom (Is. 16:1).

SELAH [SEE luh] — a form of SELA No. 1. Also see MUSIC.

SELA-HAMMAHLEKOTH [SEE luh huh MAH luh kahth] (*rock of divisions*) — a cliff in the Wilderness of Judah, where David escaped from Saul (1 Sam. 23:28; the Rock of Escaping, NKJV; the Dividing Rock, NEB). Scholars have identified this site with a gorge at Wadi el-Malaki, about 13 kilometers (8 miles) northeast of Maon, toward En Gedi.

SELED [SEE led] (*leaping for joy*) — a descendant of Jerahmeel, of the tribe of Judah (1 Chr. 2:30).

SELEUCIA [sih LOO shuh] (meaning unknown) — a seaport near Antioch of Syria from which Paul and Barnabas began their first missionary journey (see Map 7, D–2). Apparently they also landed at Seleucia when they returned to Antioch (Acts 14:26). Seleucia was an important Roman city because of its strategic location on the trade routes of the Mediterranean Sea.

SELEUCUS [sih LOO kuhs] — the name of six different kings who ruled ancient Syria during the period between the close of the Old Testament and the beginning of the New Testament.

SELF-CONTROL — control of one's actions or emotions by the will. The New Testament teaches that self-control is a fruit of the Spirit (Gal. 5:22–23). The Christian is to be governed by God, not by self.

SELF-DENIAL — the act of refusing to partake of anything not necessary for life or service to God. Sometimes self-denial can become extreme, in which case it is called asceticism.

SELF-INDULGENCE — excessive indulgence of one's sensual appetites and desires. The Pharisees were hypocrites, Jesus declared, because they cleansed the outside of the cup—or their lives—but inside they were full of extortion and self-indulgence (Matt. 23:25; excess, KJV; rapacity, RSV).

SELF-SUFFICIENCY — the capability of providing for oneself without the help of others. In the view of the Bible, a sinner is a self-sufficent person who declares his independence of God and boasts of his own accomplishments. In his sermon on the wicked man, Zophar declared, "In his self-sufficiency he will be in distress" (Job 20:22).

SELF-WILL — the act of stubbornly and arrogantly insisting on one's own way, as opposed to following the will of God. In the New Testament, the idea of self-will appears twice. In Titus 1:7 Paul indicated that a candidate for bishop, or pastor, must not be self-willed. And in 2 Peter 2:10 those persons "who walk according to the flesh" are said to be "presumptuous" as well as "self-willed."

SELVEDGE [SELL vij] (*end, extremity*) — a narrow border of different or heavier threads around the edge of a piece of fabric or cloth. Both references to selvedge in the NKJV (Ex. 26:4; 36:11) describe the fringe of the curtains in the tabernacle.

SEM [sim] — a form of SHEM.

SEMACHIAH [sem uh KIGH uh] (*Jehovah sustains*) — a gatekeeper of the tabernacle in the days of David (1 Chr. 26:7).

SEMEI [SEM ih eye] (meaning unknown) — a man in Luke's genealogy of Jesus Christ (Luke 3:26; Semein, RSV, NEB, NASB, NIV). Semei is apparently not mentioned in the Old Testament.

SEMEIN [SEM ih in] — a form of SEMEI.

SEMEN — a fluid filled with sperm and secreted by the male reproductive organs (Lev. 15:16–18, 32; 22:4; seed of copulation, KJV). Semen is mentioned in the section of Leviticus that deals with bodily discharges.

SENAAH [sih NAY uh] (*thorn hedge*) — the head of a family that returned from the Captivity. According to Ezra, 3,630 of the "people of Senaah" returned to Jerusalem with Zerubbabel (Ezra 2:35). The name Senaah is probably identical with HAS-SENAAH, an ancestor of the people who built the Fish Gate in the rebuilt wall of Jerusalem (Neh. 3:3). This group may also be the same as the SENUAH (Neh. 11:9; Hassenuah, NAS, NEB, NIV, RSV)—a clan of the tribe of Benjamin.

SENEH [SEE nuh] (*thornbush*) — one of two sharp rocks in the mountain pass between Michmash and Gibeah. Jonathan and his armorbearer climbed this pass to attack the Philistines (1 Sam. 14:4). Seneh was the southern rock, while BOZEZ was the northern rock. These rocks were situated along the Wadi es-Suweinit, about 11 kilometers (7 miles) northeast of Jerusalem.

SENIR [SEE nur] (meaning unknown) — the Amo-

rebellion against the Assyrians, but he refused. During the reign of Sennacherib, Hezekiah went against the wise counsel of the prophet Isaiah and joined a coalition against Assyria led by Tyre and Egypt.

Sennacherib began his western military campaign in 701 B.C., when Tyre and Sidon refused to pay tribute to Assyria. He marched down the Phoenician coast and captured Sidon and many other cities. The cities that refused to submit were destroyed. After the Assyrians defeated the Egyptians, they laid siege to LACHISH, which, along with Jerusalem, was one of the best-fortified cities in Judah. The account of his campaign in Judah is found in 2 Kings 18:13—19:37 and Isaiah 36—37. After a cruel siege, Lachish fell. Sennacherib sacked 46 towns and villages in Judah, taking away thousands of prisoners and much spoil. Hezekiah refused Sennacherib's demand to surrender Jerusalem (2 Kin. 18:17; Is. 36:1-21), but he did agree to pay 300 talents of silver and 30 talents of gold in tribute.

The siege of Jerusalem proved unsuccessful for two reasons: (1) Hezekiah protected his water supplies (2 Kin. 20:20) and (2) Hezekiah steadfastly trusted in God rather than in material and military support from his allies (2 Kin. 19:32-34).

Although Sennacherib, in his description of the siege of Jerusalem, boasts of shutting up Hezekiah "like a bird in a cage," he makes no reference to the outcome of the siege—evidence that his campaign failed. The Bible narrates what happened in dramatic words: "And it came to pass on a certain night that the angel of the Lord went out, and killed in the camp of the Assyrians one hundred and eighty-five thousand; and when people arose early in the morning, there were the corpses—all dead" (2 Kin. 19:35).

The ancient Greek historian Herodotus tells of a similar incident, although he sets the scene in Egypt: "Thousands of field-mice swarmed over them during the night, and ate their quivers, their bowstrings, and the leather handles of their shields, so that on the following day, having no arms to fight with, they abandoned their position and suffered severe losses during their retreat."

The "field-mice" mentioned by Herodotus may have been plague-carrying rodents, instruments of the Lord's judgment. An army of mice bearing the "Black Death" (the bubonic plague) would have been more than a match for the mighty Assyrian army.

After the destruction of his army, Sennacherib returned to Nineveh. While worshiping in the temple of his god Nisroch, he was assassinated by his sons Adrammelech and Sharezer. He was succeeded by Esarhaddon, another son (2 Kin. 19:36-37; Is. 37:37-38).

SENSUAL — pertaining to or given to life according to one's physical appetites and desires rather than in obedience to the Holy Spirit (James 3:15; Jude 19).

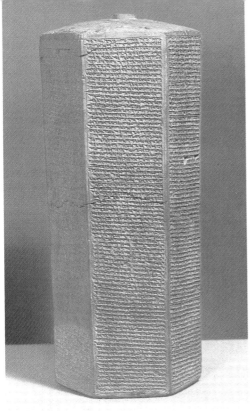

Photo by Howard Vos

This stone monument, known as the prism of Sennacherib, gives the Assyrian account of Sennacherib's invasion of Jerusalem (Isaiah 36—37).

rite name for Mount Hermon, the highest mountain in the Anti-Lebanon range. Senir was famous for its fir trees used in shipbuilding (Ezek. 27:5). Psalm 29:6 uses the name Sirion to refer poetically to this mountain.

SENNACHERIB [suh NAK uh rib] (*Sin* [the moon-god] *has compensated me with brothers*) — an Assyrian king (705-681 B.C.) noted for his military campaigns against the southern kingdom of Judah. He was the son and successor of Sargon II and was succeeded by his son Esarhaddon in 681 B.C. after a reign of 24 years.

Upon taking the throne, Sennacherib led his armies south, removing Merodach-Baladan (Is. 39:1), also called Berodach-Baladan (2 Kin. 20:12), from the throne of Babylon and reducing the city to ruins in 689 B.C. Sennacherib then marched his army east against the Kassites in the Zagros mountain range.

Sennacherib's military campaigns in the west have caused a great deal of controversy because his account and the Bible's (2 Kin. 18:13—19:37; 2 Chr. 32:1-22; Is. 36:1—37:38) describe the events so differently. Earlier, during the military campaign of Sargon II in 711 B.C., King Hezekiah of Judah (reigned 716-687 B.C.) had been asked to join the

SENTRY (see Occupations and Trades).

SENUAH [suh NOO uh] (*hated one*) — a Benjamite whose son Judah was second in command in Jerusalem after the Captivity (Neh. 11:9; Hassenuah, NAS, NEB, NIV, RSV). Also see Senaah.

SEORIM [see OHR im] (meaning unknown) — a priest in the fourth division of priests in the sanctuary at Jerusalem in David's time (1 Chr. 24:8).

SEPARATION — the state of being set apart; avoidance of contact. The NKJV uses the word separation only in Numbers 6:4–21, in a passage describing the law of the Nazirite. During the days of the Nazirite's vow, he was to drink no wine nor eat anything produced by the grapevine; he was to place no razor upon his head; and he was to separate himself from all dead bodies (Num. 6:1–21).

The KJV uses the word separation in several other places (Lev. 12:2, 5; Num. 19:9–21; Ezek. 42:20). Various defilements rendered a person unclean and separated him or her from the sanctuary or from association with others: child–bearing (Leviticus 12), leprosy (Leviticus 13—14), certain bodily discharges (Leviticus 15), and contact with a corpse (Num 19:11–22).

SEPHAR [SEH fur] (*border country*) — an unknown city or "mountain of the east" (Gen. 10:30). Some scholars believe Sephar may have been the ancient city of Zhafar between the Red Sea and the Persian Gulf.

SEPHARAD [seh FA rid] (*descending*) — an unknown place where Jewish exiles lived during the days of the prophet Obadiah (Obad. 20). Sepharad may be Sardis, in the province of Lydia in western Asia Minor, or perhaps Sparta in Greece. Spanish Jews today are called Sephardim, which causes speculation that Sepharad may have been in Spain.

SEPHARVAIM [seh fur VAY uhm] (meaning unknown) — a city conquered by Assyria, and one of the places from which Sargon II sent people to colonize Samaria, capital of Israel (2 Kin. 17:24, 31; Is. 36:19). Some scholars believe Sepharvaim was the Syrian city of Sibraim, situated between Hamath and Damascus (Ezek. 47:16). Other scholars believe the reference in Ezekiel is to two Babylonian cities. Sepharvaim's exact location is unknown.

SEPHARVITES [SEH fur vights] — natives or inhabitants of Sepharvaim. These people apparently sacrificed their children to their gods, even after being resettled by the king of Assyria in Samaria (2 Kin. 17:31).

SEPTUAGINT [SEP tuh jint] (see Bible Versions and Translations).

SEPULCHER, SEPULCHRE (see Tomb).

SERAH [SEE ruh] (*the one who extends*) — a granddaughter of Jacob by Zilpah, the handmaid of Jacob's wife Leah (Gen. 46:17; 1 Chr. 7:30). Serah was a daughter of Asher. With her four brothers she went into Egypt with Jacob.

SERAIAH [sih RAY uh] (*soldier of the Lord*) — the name of several men in the Old Testament:

1. David's scribe, or secretary (2 Sam. 8:17).

2. A son of Azariah and chief priest at Jerusalem when this city was captured by Nebuchadnezzar of Babylon (2 Kin. 25:18). Nebuchadnezzar executed Seraiah at Riblah. Seraiah was the father of Jehozadak, the grandfather of the high priest Jeshua; he was an ancestor of Ezra.

3. A son of Tanhumeth, from Netophah in southern Judah (Jer. 40:8).

4. A son of Kenaz, brother of Othniel, and father of Joab (1 Chr. 4:13–14).

5. A Simeonite, son of Asiel (1 Chr. 4:35).

6. A priest who returned with Zerubbabel from the Captivity (Ezra 2:2). In Nehemiah 7:7, he is called Azariah.

7. A priest and clan leader who signed the new covenant under Nehemiah (Neh. 10:2). He is probably the same as Seraiah No. 6.

8. A son of Hilkiah (Neh. 11:11). A priest, Seraiah was a ruler of the house of God after the Captivity.

9. A chief priest who returned from Babylon with Zerubbabel (Neh. 12:1). He may be the same person as Seraiah No. 6.

10. A priest, son of Azriel. Seraiah was sent by Jehoiakim to capture Jeremiah and his secretary-scribe, Baruch (Jer. 36:26).

11. A son of Neriah. Seraiah was the "quartermaster" who accompanied Zedekiah, king of Judah, to Babylon (Jer. 51:59, 61; staff officer, NIV)

SERAPHIM [SER uh fim] (*fiery, burning ones*) — angelic or heavenly beings associated with the prophet Isaiah's vision of God in the Temple when he was called to his prophetic ministry (Is. 6:1–7). This is the only place in the Bible that mentions these mysterious creatures. Each seraph had six wings. They used two to fly, two to cover their feet, and two to cover their faces (Is. 6:2). The seraphim flew about the throne on which God was seated, singing His praises as they called special attention to His glory and majesty.

These beings apparently also served as agents of purification for Isaiah as he began his prophetic ministry. One placed a hot coal against Isaiah's lips with the words, "Your iniquity is taken away and your sin is purged" (Is. 6:7).

SERED [SIR ed] (*escape*) — the oldest son of Zebulun (Gen. 46:14) and founder of the Sardites (Num. 26:26; Seredites, RSV).

SEREDITES [SIR eh dights] — a form of Sardites.

SERGEANT (see Occupations and Trades).

SERGIUS PAULUS [SUR jee uhs PAW luhs] — the Roman proconsul, or governor, of Cyprus who was converted to Christianity when the apostle Paul visited that island on his first missionary journey, about A.D. 46 (Acts 13:7). Luke describes Sergius Paulus as an intelligent man. This Sergius Paulus may have been the same man as L. Sergius Paulus, a Roman official in charge of the Tiber during the reign of the emperor Claudius (ruled A.D. 41–54).

SERMON ON THE MOUNT — the title given to Jesus' moral and ethical teachings as recorded in Matthew 5 through 7.

The Sermon on the Mount was brought on by Jesus' growing popularity (Matt. 4:25). At first, the people were attracted to Him because of His healing ministry. When Jesus began to teach, the people remained to hear what He said. They also were impressed with the authority with which He taught. Although many people heard the Sermon on the Mount, it was primarily directed to Jesus' followers or disciples.

The central theme of the Sermon is summarized in Matthew 5:48, "You shall be perfect just as your Father in heaven is perfect." The word perfect does not refer to sinless or moral perfection. It means completeness, wholeness, maturity—being all that God wants a person to be. It is a goal that is never attained in our earthly life, but it continuously challenges us to greater achievements for the Lord.

The Beatitudes (5:2–12). Jesus began His teachings by stating the way to happiness. The word blessed is appropriately translated as "happy." The poor in spirit, those who recognize their spiritual poverty, will attain the kingdom of heaven. Those who mourn, who are truly sorry for their sins, will receive comfort. The meek, those who have disciplined strength, will inherit the earth. The quest for righteousness will be satisfied. The merciful will receive mercy; the pure in heart will see and understand the heart of God; the peacemakers shall be called God's children. And those who endure persecution for doing God's commands will inherit the kingdom of God.

Influence (5:14–16). Jesus used two symbols, salt and light, to describe the influence that His followers should have on the world. Salt has a preserving quality, and light clears away the darkness. Salt and light bring about noticeable changes, but they are seldom noticed themselves.

Righteousness (5:17–48). Jesus did not come to give a new law. He came to uncover the intentions of the law and the prophets and to bring them to their fullest expression. He gave five illustrations of what it means to fulfill the law: (1) Murder is wrong, but so is the hateful attitude that leads to it. (2) The act of adultery is wrong, but so is the lustful look. (3) The marriage relationship should be permanent. (4) We should be honest in our words and deeds. (5) We should love our enemies. Each of these righteous admonitions was contrasted with the legalistic teachings of the Pharisees.

Giving, Praying, and Fasting (6:1–18). Good religious practices may be done for the wrong reasons. Jesus called attention to three: (1) Almsgiving, kind deeds to help the needy, should be done, but not for the personal recognition the giver might receive; (2) prayer should be offered, but not in a way to seek the recognition of others; (3) fasting should be a sincere spiritual experience and not an attempt to impress others with our goodness and spirituality.

Material Resources (6:19–24). Jesus used three concepts—treasures, light, and slavery—to remind us that we cannot serve two masters. We must have single–minded devotion to the values of God's kingdom if we are to be his loyal followers.

Anxiety (6:25–34). Worldly people are those who live only for material things: food, drink, clothes. Jesus' disciples are to place God's kingdom first and to live with faith that God will provide for their needs.

Chapel on the Mount of Beatitudes, the site where Jesus delivered His Sermon on the Mount, according to many scholars.
Photo: Levant Photo Service

Judgment: Right and Wrong (7:1–6). The disciple should not be judgmental in his attitude toward others. He should continuously judge himself in terms of God's expectations.

Persistence (7:7–12). Jesus challenged His followers to maintain persistence in their commitment to God, to ask God to empower them to persevere, and to take the initiative to treat other people as they would like to be treated.

Choosing (7:13–14). Jesus stated that there are two life–styles, or roads, which a person can take. The broad road leads to destruction; the narrow road leads to life. Every person is on one or the other of these two roads.

Performance (7:15–23). As Jesus neared the end of His teachings, He began to focus on the need to put His teachings into action. He warned against following false teachers and instructed His followers to put truth into action.

Life's Foundation (7:24–27). Although much attention has been focused on the two houses in this story, Jesus emphasized the builders. The difference between the two builders is the obedience of one and the other's failure to obey God's command.

SERPENT — a crawling reptile, or snake, often associated in the Bible with temptation, sin, and evil.

A serpent appears early in the Scriptures in the account of the temptation and fall of Adam and Eve (Genesis 3). Satan, or the Devil, is the Tempter; but he made his approach to Eve by speaking through a serpent, which is described as "more cunning than any beast of the field which the Lord God had made" (Gen. 3:1). Because of the serpent's role in the temptation, God pronounced a curse on the animal, sentencing it to crawl on its belly and eat dust "all the days of your life" (Gen. 3:14).

This account of the temptation and fall of man helps us understand many of the references to serpents throughout Scripture. Serpents are mentioned under various names (for example, asp, cobra, and viper), and they pose a life–threatening danger to man because of their poisonous bite (Deut. 8:15). They are also mentioned as instruments of God's wrath upon rebellion or apostasy (Jer. 8:17). The best–known incident of this kind happened during the wilderness journey to the Promised Land when "the Lord sent fiery serpents among the people" (Num. 21:5–6). Wicked and rebellious persons are addressed as "serpents" or are compared to serpents because of their destructive influence (Ps. 58:4; Matt. 3:7).

In line with the theme of Genesis 3:15, redemption is sometimes described as the destruction or subduing of serpents (Is. 27:1; Mic. 7:17). In Numbers 21, the threat of the fiery serpents was overcome when, at the command of the Lord, Moses fashioned a serpent of bronze and put it on a pole: "And so it was, if a serpent had bitten anyone, when he looked at the bronze serpent, he lived" (Num. 21:9). The bronze serpent raised up by Moses in the wilderness serves as a symbol of the saving power of Christ on the cross (John 3:14). By His crucifixion and resurrection, Christ has bruised the head of the serpent (Gen. 3:15).

The prophet Isaiah used the taming of the serpent to describe the peace that will prevail in the messianic kingdom (Is. 11:8; 65:25). And Jesus gave His disciples "authority to trample on serpents and scorpions" (Luke 10:19).

Also see ANIMALS OF THE BIBLE.

SERPENT, BRONZE (see BRONZE SERPENT).

SERPENT CHARMERS (see OCCUPATIONS AND TRADES).

SERPENT WELL — a well, fountain, or spring between the Valley Gate and the Refuse (Dung) Gate in Jerusalem in Nehemiah's time (Neh. 2:13; dragon well, KJV; Jackal's Well, RSV).

SERUG [SIR uhg] (*branch*) — a son of Reu and the father of Nahor (Gen. 11:20–23). Serug is listed as an ancestor of Jesus in Luke's genealogy (Luke 3:35; Saruch, KJV).

SERVANT (see OCCUPATIONS AND TRADES; SLAVE, SLAVERY).

SERVANT OF THE LORD — a theological concept in the Book of Isaiah which points forward to Jesus the Messiah. Passages in the book which express this idea are Isaiah 42:1–4; 49:1–6; 50:4–9; and 52:13—53:12.

But even before Isaiah's time, the concept of God's servant was deeply rooted in the history of the nation of Israel. The term servant was frequently applied to those who performed some service, task, or mission for the Lord. The term servant was applied to Abraham (Gen. 26:24), Isaac (Gen. 24:14), Jacob (Ezek. 28:25), and Moses (Deut. 34:5), as well as many of the prophets of the Old Testament.

But in the "Servant Songs" of his book, the prophet Isaiah used the phrase *Servant of the Lord* in a specialized or messianic sense. The Servant of the Lord not only would encounter and accept suffering in the course of His work, but He also would realize that His vicarious suffering would become the means by which He would give His life as a ransom for others.

The New Testament writers are unanimous in stating that the Servant of the Lord is a messianic figure and that Jesus is that Servant. The first of Isaiah's "Servant Songs" (Is. 42:1–4) was quoted by Matthew as being fulfilled in Jesus (Matt. 12:18–21). The Book of Acts emphasized the suffering and hostility which the Messiah underwent to accomplish redemption (Acts 3:13, 26; 4:27, 30). In these passages Jesus is referred to as "His Servant Jesus" (Acts 3:13, 26) and "Your holy Servant Jesus" (Acts 4:27, 30). The violent treatment suffered by Jesus was precisely what the "Servant Songs" of Isaiah prophesied about God's Servant. Jesus saw His role as that of a servant (Mark 10:45, in fulfillment of Isaiah 53:10–11). He taught His followers to view His mission, and theirs as well, in terms of servanthood. Thus the Servant of the Lord, spoken of by

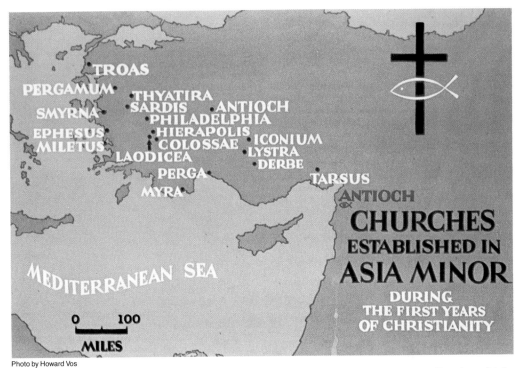

Photo by Howard Vos

This map of early churches connected with the ministry of Paul and John shows the Seven Churches of Asia Minor.

Isaiah the prophet, is preeminently Jesus Himself.

According to Isaiah, the Servant of the Lord would "bring forth justice to the Gentiles" (Is. 42:1) and establish "justice in the earth" (Is. 42:4). He would bring Jacob back to the Lord (Is. 49:5) and would be "a light to the Gentiles" (Is. 49:6). He would not hide His face from shame and spitting (Is. 50:6). He would be the sin–bearing Servant, giving His life for the redemption of His people (Is. 52:13—53:12).

Through Jesus the ancient mission given by God to Abraham—to be a blessing to all the families of the earth (Gen. 12:1-3)—is now entrusted to the church. The church's responsibility is to preach the gospel to Jew and Gentile, bondslave and freeman, male and female, rich and poor. To be a servant of God is to serve Him continually (Dan. 6:20). As His mission was that of a servant, so must ours be (Mark 10:42-45).

SERVICE, SERVITUDE (see SLAVE, SLAVERY).

SETH [seth] (appoint, compensate) — the third son of Adam and Eve, born after Cain murdered Abel (Gen. 4:25-26; 5:3-8; Sheth, KJV). The father of Enosh (or Enos) and an ancestor of Jesus Christ (Luke 3:38), Seth died at the age of 912.

SETHUR [SEE thur] (hidden) — a spy, representing the tribe of Asher, sent by Moses to spy out the land of Canaan (Num. 13:13).

SETTINGS OF GOLD — sockets or cavities in which gems were set (Ex. 28:11; ouches, KJV). The Hebrew word translated settings of gold comes from a verb meaning to weave; thus, it probably refers to a filigree setting—woven gold wire or thread. Most of the Old Testament references deal with the gold settings of the engraved stones in the EPHOD, or breastplate, of the high priest (Ex. 28:13-14).

SEVEN CHURCHES OF ASIA — the seven Christian congregations to which John addressed special messages in the Book of Revelation. From the Isle of Patmos John wrote seven messages to "the seven churches which are in Asia" (Rev. 1:4, 11). These seven messages, found in Revelation 2—3, were to Ephesus, the Loveless Church (2:1-7); Smyrna, the Persecuted Church (2:8-11); Pergamos, the Compromising Church (2:12-17); Thyatira, the Corrupt Church (2:18-29); Sardis, the Dead Church (3:1-6); Philadelphia, the Faithful Church (3:7-13); and Laodicea, the Lukewarm Church (3:14-22).

The Roman province of Asia included more churches than these seven. Why did John single them out?

One theory is that these seven cities may have been centers of seven postal districts. These seven churches all stand on the great circular road which formed a rough circle around the west central part of the Roman province of Asia. As such, these seven sites served as good centers of communication for the surrounding districts. Letters in the first century had to be handwritten, and a letter sent to one church would be passed on to be read by Christians in other congregations.

The letters to the seven churches called for the Christians to repent of sin and return to faithfulness and good works; encouraged them to stand firm for Christ against the temptations, trials, and persecutions of the Roman Empire; and promised specific rewards to the martyrs who faced death without denying Christ.

SEVEN, SEVENTH — a sacred number to the ancient Hebrew people. The word is used often in the Bible to symbolize perfection, fullness, abundance, rest, and completion. This number was also considered holy or sacred by other cultures of the ancient world. It may have received its significance from the seven "planets" visible in the heavens—the sun and moon and the five planets known to the ancients.

The first mention of the number seven occurs in Genesis 2:2–3. God created the world in six days, but on the seventh day he rested from His work, setting aside the seventh day as holy. The fourth of the Ten Commandments states, "Remember the Sabbath day [that is, the seventh day], to keep it holy" (Ex. 20:8).

The number seven also had a ritual importance to the Hebrews. Several of the religious acts of the Old Testament received a sevenfold repetition, for instance, the sprinkling of blood (Lev. 4:6), or the dipping of Naaman the leper in the Jordan River (2 Kin. 5:10, 14). Periods of time composed of seven units are often used in the Old Testament (Gen. 2:2; Dan. 9:25). Within visions and dreams, the number seven often plays a prominent part. Pharaoh dreamed of two herds composed of seven animals each. These symbolized the seven years of famine and the seven years of plenty, as did the two groups of seven heads of grain (Gen. 41:1–36).

In the New Testament, Jesus cast seven demons out of Mary Magdalene (Luke 8:2) and fed the 4,000 with seven loaves of bread and a few small fish (Matt. 15:32–39). The number seven appears frequently in the Book of Revelation.

Also see NUMBER; SEVENTY.

SEVEN WORDS FROM THE CROSS — the seven different utterances of Jesus while He hung on the cross:

1. "Father, forgive them, for they do not know what they do" (Luke 23:34). Jesus taught that we should forgive those who sin against us. How appropriate that His first words from the cross should be words of forgiveness.

2. "Assuredly, I say to you, today you will be with Me in Paradise" (Luke 23:43). As He hung on the cross, Jesus certainly did not appear to be a king. Yet, what faith the repentant thief displayed when he asked, "Lord, remember me when You come into Your kingdom" (Luke 23:42). Jesus' reply

was good news indeed to this dying sinner.

3. "Woman, behold your son!...Behold your mother!" (John 19:26–27). In spite of His grief and pain, Jesus continued to think of others. His earthly father, Joseph, probably had died by this time. Jesus asked his beloved disciple, John, to take care of His mother, Mary.

4. "Eli, Eli, lama sabachthani?...My God, My God, why have You forsaken Me?" (Matt. 27:46; Mark 15:34). These words came from Jesus' lips about 3 P.M., after He had hung on the cross for nine hours. Death was near, and Jesus was feeling the pain and loneliness that sin causes. But the sin in this case was our sin and not His. To express His anguish and grief, Jesus quoted the opening words of Psalm 22, using the same words that King David had used many years earlier (Ps. 22:1).

5. "I thirst!" (John 19:28). The Old Testament had prophesied that Jesus would suffer for the sins of the world. In His death, that prophecy was being fulfilled. Jesus suffered spiritual torment as well as physical agony as He hung on the cross. His spirit thirsted to win the spiritual battle against evil while His body thirsted for water.

6. "It is finished!" (John 19:30). The word translated "finished!" shows clearly that Jesus' victory has been achieved. It carries the idea of perfection or fulfillment. God's plan of salvation had been accomplished through Jesus' sacrifice on the cross.

7. "Father, into Your hands I commend My spirit" (Luke 23:46; also see Ps. 31:5; Matt. 27:50; Mark 15:37). Jesus did not die a failure. He died a victorious Savior. He finished His work triumphantly and entrusted His spirit to God His Father.

SEVENTH MONTH FESTIVAL (see FEASTS AND FESTIVALS).

SEVENTY — a number of great significance in the Bible because it is a multiple of the number seven, considered a sacred number by the Hebrew people (Ex. 1:1–5). Seventy is the number of persons of the house of Jacob who went to Egypt (Gen. 46:27). And when Jacob (Israel) died, he was mourned 70 days (Gen. 50:3). Seventy elders of Israel accompanied Moses to Mount Sinai (Ex. 24:1). Psalm 90:10 says that the days of our lives are 70. In His teachings, Jesus emphasized that we should forgive others not seven times but "up to seventy times seven" (Matt. 18:22). Also see SEVEN.

SEVENTY, THE — in Luke's Gospel, a group of 70 disciples sent out by Jesus to heal the sick and preach the good news of the kingdom of God (Luke 10:1–17). Jewish writings often spoke of the Gentile nations as numbering 70. Among the four gospels, Luke is known as the one with a universal, worldwide view. By speaking of the 70 disciples, Luke probably wanted to show that the gospel of Christ is not only for Jews, the 12 tribes of Israel, but also for the Gentiles, the "70 nations" of the world.

SEVENTY WEEKS — a term that the prophet Daniel used in his prophecy of the future (Dan. 9:24–27). In Daniel's vision, God revealed that the

Captivity of His people in Babylon would come to an end and they would be restored to glory as a nation within a period of 70 weeks of seven years each—or a total of 490 years.

Scholars interpret this seventy weeks prophecy in different ways. Some insist that Daniel is not a book of prophecy at all but that he was writing about events that had already happened. Others believe the 490–year period came to a grand climax with Jesus' death on the cross. Still others believe this prophecy is yet to be fulfilled in the future.

Also see DANIEL, BOOK OF.

SEVENTY YEARS (see CAPTIVITY).

SEX — the concept of male and female; pertaining to the reproductive function of human beings; sexual intercourse.

Although the idea and fact of sex repeatedly appear in Scripture, the word sex never appears (KJV and NKJV). The NKJV, however, does refer often to "sexual immorality" (Matt. 5:32; Acts 15:20) and to the "sexually immoral" (1 Cor. 5:9–10; Rev. 22:15).

God created mankind in His own image as "male and female" (Gen. 1:27; 5:2). The act of sexual intercourse is part of God's first command to mankind: "Be fruitful and multiply; fill the earth" (Gen. 1:28). Although the primary reason for intercourse was procreation, God created mankind with a capacity to enjoy sex.

The Old Testament records legislation that sought to restrict premarital and extramarital sex (Ex. 20:14; Lev. 20:10). In addition, homosexuality, bestiality, and incest were condemned (Lev. 18:6–18, 22–23). Distinctions between the sexes also involved clothing; articles of clothing of the opposite sex were not to be worn (Deut. 22:5).

Sexual intercourse within marriage was considered "honorable" (Heb. 13:4). According to the Old Testament, however, a couple was to refrain from sex during the wife's monthly menstruation (Lev. 15:19–24). In addition, if the husband was involved in war, he was to abstain until God gave them the victory (1 Sam. 21:4; 2 Sam. 11:11). In the New Testament, the apostle Paul stated that since sex is such an integral part of marriage, the spouse always should be sexually available. If the couple refrains from intercourse, the decision should be mutual, should be for a spiritual reason, and should be only for a stated period (1 Cor. 7:1–5).

Sex played an important role in the religious beliefs and practices of the Canaanites. For instance, Baal was considered to be the god of fertility, and both male and female prostitutes were kept at the temples dedicated to Baal. Through sexual intercourse with these prostitutes, the Canaanites believed they could influence Baal to give them large herds, abundant crops, and many children. While these beliefs attracted a number of the Israelites (1 Kin. 14:24), these practices were condemned by those who continued to believe that the Lord alone was God and that only He was the giver of life (1 Kin. 15:12).

A number of sexual taboos are declared in Scripture. The Jewish people believed it wrong for sexual organs to be exposed. For instance, Noah's son placed a covering over his father to conceal his nakedness, and David was denounced by his wife for exposing himself while dancing before the Lord (2 Sam. 6:20).

The vocabulary dealing with sexual matters is often veiled in Scripture. The male sexual organs are variously referred to as a man's "feet" (Ex. 4:25), "nakedness" (Ex. 28:42), "privy member" (Deut. 23:1, KJV), and "unpresentable parts" (1 Cor. 12:23). The female sexual organs are called "nakedness" (Lev. 18; 20) and "feet" (Deut. 28:57). To "become one flesh" (Gen. 2:24), to "know" (Gen. 4:1), and to "lie with" (Lev. 18:20, 22) are euphemisms for sexual intercourse.

SHAALABBIN [shay AHL uh bin] (*place of foxes*) — an Amorite city in the territory of Dan (Josh. 19:42), also called Shaalbim (Judg. 1:35). The Amorites did not give up this city until long after the Israelites had settled the area (Judg. 1:35). Shaalabbin was about 24 kilometers (15 miles) west of Jerusalem.

SHAALBIM [shay AHL bim] — a form of SHAALABBIN.

SHAALBON [shay AHL bahn] — the home of Eliahba, one of David's mighty men (2 Sam. 23:32). It may be the same place as SHAALABBIN.

SHAALBONITE [shay AHL bahn ight] — a native or inhabitant of SHAALBON (2 Sam. 23:32).

SHAALIM [SHAY uh lim] (*foxes*) — an unidentified region, perhaps in the territory of Ephraim or Benjamin, where Saul searched for his father's donkeys (1 Sam. 9:4; Shalim, KJV).

SHAAPH [SHAY af] (*friendship*) — the name of two men in the Old Testament:

1. A descendant of Caleb through Jahdai (1 Chr. 2:47).

2. A son of Caleb by his concubine Maachah (1 Chr. 2:49).

SHAARAIM [shay uh RAY uhm] (*two gates*) — the name of two cities in the Old Testament:

1. A city in the lowland hills of Judah (1 Sam. 17:52), also called Sharaim (Josh. 15:36).

2. A Simeonite city in southern Judah (1 Chr. 4:31). It is identified with Tell el–Far'ah, southeast of Gaza.

SHAASHGAZ [shay ASH gaz] (*lover of beauty*) — a servant (chamberlain, KJV) in the household of Ahasuerus, king of Persia (Esth. 2:14).

SHABBETHAI [SHAB uh thigh] (*born on the Sabbath*) — a Levite mentioned in connection with Ezra's order to the people to divorce their foreign wives (Ezra 10:15). Shabbethai probably was the same man who helped the people understand the Law after Ezra read it to them (Neh. 8:7).

SHACHIA [shah KIGH uh] — a form of SACHIAH.

SHACKLE — a metal clamp that holds the ankle or wrist of a prisoner or captive. The demon-possessed man of Gadara, whom Jesus healed, had broken the shackles with which he was bound (Mark 5:4; Luke 8:29; fetters, KJV, RSV).

SHADDAI [SHAD eye] (see GOD, NAMES OF).

SHADOW — the dark figure cast by a solid object when it intercepts the rays from a source of light. Shadow symbolizes the brevity of life and the impermanent nature of things (Eccl. 6:12); physical weakness and death (Job 14:2); God's protection of His people (Ps. 17:8); and the Messiah's blessings— "as the shadow of a great rock in a weary land" (Is. 32:2). The Bible also uses the word to contrast the Jewish and Christian periods. The Jewish regulations, rituals, and rules are "a shadow of things to come, but the substance is of Christ" (Col. 2:17).

SHADRACH [SHAD rak] (command of Aku) — the name that Ashpenaz, the chief of Nebuchadnezzar's eunuchs, gave to Hananiah, one of the Jewish princes who were carried away to Babylon in 603 B.C. (Dan. 1:7; 3:12–30).

Shadrach was one of the three faithful Hebrews who refused to worship the golden image that King Nebuchadnezzar of Babylon set up (Dan. 3:1). Along with his two companions, MESHACH and ABED–NEGO, Shadrach was "cast into the midst of a burning fiery furnace" (Dan. 3:11, 21). But they were protected by a fourth "man" in the fire (Dan. 3:25), and they emerged without even the smell of fire upon them (Dan. 3:27).

SHAGE, **SHAGEE** [SHAY gih] — forms of SHA-GEH.

SHAGEH [SHAY gih] (wandering) — the father of one of David's mighty men (1 Chr. 11:34; Shage, KJV, NEB; Shagee, NASB, NIV, RSV). Shageh may be the same person as Agee (2 Sam. 23:11).

SHAHAR [SHAY hahr] (the dawn) — a word used in the title of Psalm 22 (KJV). In Canaanite mythology, Shahar was the god of dawn. He and his twin brother, Shalem (the god of sunset), were sons of El, the chief god of the Canaanites.

SHAHARAIM [shay uh RAY uhm] (double dawn) — a Benjamite whose nine sons became the heads of tribes (1 Chr. 8:8–11).

SHAHAZIMAH [shay uh ZIH muh] (meaning unknown) — a northern border town of the territory of Issachar, between Mount Tabor and Beth Shemesh (Josh. 19:22; Shahazumah, RSV, NASB).

SHAHAZUMAH [shay uh ZOO muh] — a form of SHAHAZIMAH.

SHALEM [SHAY luhm] (peaceful, safe) — according to the KJV, a city near Shechem (Gen. 33:18). Most modern versions, however, do not regard the word as a proper name. They translate the word for Shalem as "peace."

SHALIM [SHAY lim] — a form of SHAALIM.

SHALISHA [SHAL uh shuh] (a third part) — a region through which Saul passed when searching for his father's donkeys (1 Sam. 9:4; Shalishah, NASB). It was probably the district of Baal Shalisha (2 Kin. 4:42) in the Plain of Sharon.

SHALISHAH [SHAL uh shuh] — a form of SHALISHA.

SHALLECHETH GATE, **SHALLEKETH GATE** (see GATES OF JERUSALEM AND THE TEMPLE).

SHALLUM [SHAL uhm] (the requited one) — the name of several men in the Old Testament:
1. A son of Jabesh (2 Kin. 15:10). Shallum be-

This stone obelisk was erected by Shalmaneser of Assyria to commemorate his achievements during the first 31 years of his reign.

Photo by Gustav Jeeninga

came the 16th king of Israel by assassinating Zechariah and claiming the throne.

2. The husband of Huldah the prophetess in the days of Josiah, king of Judah (2 Chr. 34:22).

3. A son of Sismai (1 Chr. 2:40–41).

4. A son of King Josiah of Judah (1 Chr. 3:15). Shallum is better known by the name JEHOAHAZ, given to him when he became king of Judah after his father's death. After reigning three months in Jerusalem, Jehoahaz was deposed by Pharaoh Necho and replaced by Eliakim (whose name was changed to Jehoiakim), another of the sons of Josiah. Pharaoh Necho took Jehoahaz to Egypt, where he died.

5. A son of Shaul (1 Chr. 4:24–25). Shallum was the father of Mibsam and a descendant of Simeon.

6. A son of Zadok (1 Chr. 6:12–13). Shallum was the father of Hilkiam and an ancestor of Ezra (Ezra 7:2).

7. A son of Naphtali (1 Chr. 7:13), also called Shillem (Gen. 46:24).

8. Chief of the gatekeepers of the sanctuary in David's time (1 Chr. 9:17).

9. The father of Jehizkiah (2 Chr. 28:12).

10. A Levite and gatekeeper of the sanctuary in Ezra's time (Ezra 10:24). During the Captivity, Shallum had married a pagan wife and was told to divorce her.

11. A son of Bani (Ezra 10:42). During the Captivity, Shallum had married a pagan wife and was told to divorce her.

12. A son of Hallohesh (Neh. 3:12). A leader in Jerusalem, Shallum helped Nehemiah repair the city wall.

13. The uncle of Jeremiah the prophet (Jer. 32:7). He may be the same person as Shallum No. 2.

14. The father of Maaseiah (Jer. 35:4).

SHALLUN [SHAL uhn] (*recompenser*) — a ruler of part of Mizpah who repaired the Fountain Gate at Jerusalem (Neh. 3:15; Shallum, RSV, NASB).

SHALMAI [SHAL migh] (meaning unknown) — a Temple servant whose descendants returned to Jerusalem after the Captivity (Ezra 2:46). He is also called Salmai (Neh. 7:48) and Shamlai (Ezra 2:46, NEB, RSV).

SHALMAN [SHAL muhn] (meaning unknown) — an unidentified king or conqueror mentioned by the prophet Hosea (Hos. 10:14). This name may be an abbreviated form of Shalmaneser, king of Assyria. But other scholars believe it refers to a ruler of Moab or even to Shallum, a king of Israel.

SHALMANESER [shal muh NEE zur] (*Shulmanu is chief*) — the name of five Assyrian kings, only one of whom is mentioned in the Bible. Another is important because he mentions an Israelite king in an inscription:

1. Shalmaneser I (1274–1245 B.C.), son of Adadnirari I, restored Assyrian power after it had been overshadowed by the Hittites and by the kingdom of Mitanni.

2. Shalmaneser II (1031–1020 B.C.), son of Ashurnasirpal I. Although he was a weak king, he took action to strengthen Assyria after a period of domination by Aramean tribes.

3. Shalmaneser III (859–824 B.C.), son of Ashurnasirpal III, and first Assyrian king to come into direct contact with Israel. He is not mentioned in the biblical narrative about the reign of Ahab of Israel (2 Chr. 18:1–34), but he does appear in an inscription that recounts a coalition composed principally of Syria (Hadadezer of Damascus, the biblical Ben-Hadad II) and of Israel ("Ahab, the Israelite"), a coalition that Shalmaneser met and presumably defeated at the famous Battle of Qarqar, on the Orontes River (853 B.C.). According to this inscription, Ahab supplied 2,000 chariots and 10,000 men.

This reference to Ahab is one of the most important non-biblical archaeological references to a person mentioned in Scripture. The famous Black Obelisk mentions "Jehu, son of Omri" and shows him paying tribute to Shalmaneser. Jehu or his representative is portrayed on his hands and knees, kissing the ground at the feet of Shalmaneser. Jehu's Israelite servants are portrayed as bearing bars and vessels of precious metals, extended as presents for the Assyrian king.

4. Shalmaneser IV (783/82–772 B.C.), son of Adad-nirari III, and the first of three weak rulers who preceded the reign of the great Tiglath-Pileser III.

5. Shalmaneser V (727–722 B.C.), the son and successor of Tiglath-Pileser III (745–727 B.C.; called "Pul" in 2 Kin. 15:19). He is the only Assyrian king named Shalmaneser mentioned in the Bible (unless SHALMAN of Hosea 10:14 is a contraction of the name). Shalmaneser received tribute from Hoshea, king of Israel. Then he imprisoned Hoshea and besieged Samaria for three years (2 Kin. 17:3–6; 18:9–10), until it fell in 723/22 B.C. This marked the end of the northern kingdom of Israel.

SHAMA [SHAY muh] (*hearer*) — one of David's mighty men (1 Chr. 11:44).

SHAMARIAH [sham uh RIGH uh] (*whom Jehovah guards*) — a son of Rehoboam (2 Chr. 11:19; Shemariah, RSV, NIV, NEB, NASB).

SHAME — a negative emotion caused by an awareness of wrongdoing, hurt ego, or guilt. In the Bible, the feeling of shame is normally caused by public exposure of one's guilt (Gen. 2:25; 3:10). Shame may also be caused by a hurt reputation or embarrassment, whether or not this feeling is due to sin (Ps. 25:2–3; Prov. 19:26; Rom. 1:16).

Joseph, not wishing to shame Mary, desired to divorce her secretly (Matt. 1:19). Ultimately, God will expose the guilt of the ungodly, putting them to shame (Dan. 12:2). God also puts to shame the wise of the world by exposing their guilt before Him and by choosing to save the foolish of this world by a "foolish" message (1 Cor. 1:18–31).

Finally, our Lord Jesus suffered the shame of the Cross because He was put on public display as the recipient of God's wrath (2 Cor. 5:21; Heb. 12:2).

SHAMED [SHAH med] — a form of SHEMED.

SHAMER [SHAY mur] ([God is] *preserver*) — the name of two men in the Old Testament:
1. A son of Mahli (1 Chr. 6:46; Shemer, NIV, NASB, RSV).
2. A son of Heber, of the tribe of Asher (1 Chr. 7:34, KJV; Shemer, NKJV, RSV, NASB). He is also called Shomer (1 Chr. 7:32).

SHAMGAR [SHAM gahr] (meaning unknown) — the third judge of Israel (Judg. 3:31) who delivered the nation from oppression by the Philistines. Using an ox goad as a weapon, Shamgar killed 600 Philistines who were terrorizing the main travel routes. Shamgar was a "son of Anath"—which may mean he was a resident of Beth Anath (Judg. 1:33), a fortified city in the territory of Naphtali.

SHAMHUTH [SHAM huhth] (*desolation*) — a captain of David's army who commanded 24,000 men. Shamhuth is probably the same person as Shammah the Harodite (2 Sam. 23:25) and Shammoth the Harorite (1 Chr. 11:27).

SHAMIR [SHAY mur] (*hard stone*) — the name of two cities and a man in the Old Testament:
1. A city in the hill country of Judah (Josh. 15:48), identified with Khirbet Somerah, about 21 kilometers (13 miles) southwest of Hebron.
2. A city on Mount Ephraim, the home and burial place of Tola the judge (Judg. 10:1–2).
3. A son of Michah (1 Chr. 24:24) and a Levite who lived in David's time.

SHAMLAI [SHAM ligh] — a form of SALMAI, SHALMAI.

SHAMMA [SHAM uh] (*fame*) — a son of Zophah, of the tribe of Asher (1 Chr. 7:37).

SHAMMAH [SHAM uh] (*fame*) — the name of several men in the Old Testament:
1. A son of Reuel and a descendant of Esau (1 Chr. 1:37).
2. The third son of Jesse and a brother, or half-brother, of David (1 Sam. 16:9; 17:13; Shimea, 1 Chr. 2:13).
3. A son of Agee the Hararite (2 Sam. 23:11). Shammah was one of David's mighty men.
4. Another Hararite and also one of David's mighty men (2 Sam. 23:33). He may be the same person as Shammah No. 3.
5. A Harodite and another of David's mighty men (2 Sam. 23:25). He is also called Shammoth the Harorite (1 Chr. 11:27).

SHAMMAI [SHAM eye] (meaning unknown) — the name of three men in the Old Testament:
1. A son of Onam and great-grandson of Judah (1 Chr. 2:28, 32).
2. A son of Rekem, of the tribe of Judah (1 Chr. 2:44–45).
3. A descendant of Judah (1 Chr. 4:17).

SHAMMOTH [SHAM ahth] (*desolation*) — one of David's mighty men (1 Chr. 11:27). Shammoth is

probably the same person as Shamhuth (1 Chr. 27:8) and Shammah the Harodite (2 Sam. 23:25).

SHAMMUA [sha MOO uh] (*heard by God*) — the name of four men in the Old Testament:
1. The representative of the tribe of Reuben among the 12 spies who explored the land of Canaan (Num. 13:4).
2. A son of David by Bathsheba (2 Sam. 5:14; Shammuah, KJV; 1 Chr. 14:4). Shammua is also called Shimea (1 Chr. 3:5).
3. The father of Abda (Neh. 11:17). Shammua is also called Shemaiah (1 Chr. 9:16).
4. A priest in the days of Nehemiah (Neh. 12:18).

SHAMMUAH [sha MOO uh] — a form of SHAMMUA No. 2.

SHAMSHERAI [SHAM shuh righ] (*heroic*) — a son of Jeroham, of the tribe of Benjamin (1 Chr. 8:26).

SHAPHAM [SHAY fuhm] (*vigorous, youthful*) — a chief of the tribe of Dan (1 Chr. 5:12).

SHAPHAN [SHAY fuhn] (*rock badger*) — the name of several men in the Old Testament:
1. A scribe during the reign of King Josiah of Judah who helped Josiah carry out his religious reform (2 Kin. 22:3–14). He is probably the same person as Shaphan No. 2, 3, or 4.
2. The father of Ahikam (2 Kin. 22:12). A chief officer in Josiah's court during the prophet Jeremiah's time, Ahikam protected Jeremiah from death (Jer. 26:24).
3. The father of Elasah, who carried a letter from Jeremiah to the Babylonian captives (Jer. 29:3).
4. The father of Gemariah (Jer. 36:10–12). It was in the house of Gemariah that Baruch the scribe read Jeremiah's scroll to the people during the reign of Jehoiakim.
5. The father of Jaazaniah (Ezek. 8:11).

SHAPHAT [SHAY fat] (*judge*) — the name of five men in the Old Testament:
1. A representative of the tribe of Simeon sent by Moses to spy out the land of Canaan (Num. 13:2, 5).
2. The father of Elisha the prophet (1 Kin. 19:16).
3. A son of Shemaiah of the family of Jeconiah and a descendant of David (1 Chr. 3:22).
4. A descendant of Gad in the days of Jotham of Judah (1 Chr. 5:12).
5. An overseer of David's herds (1 Chr. 27:29).

SHAPHER [SHAY fur] — a form of SHEPHER, MOUNT.

SHAPHIR [SHAY fur] (*beautiful*) — a place, probably a city, which Micah prophesied against (Mic. 1:11; Saphir, KJV). Some scholars identify it as Khirbet el–Kom in Judah and others as Tell es–Sawafir in Philistine territory.

SHARAI [SHAR eye] (*Jehovah is deliverer*) — an Israelite who divorced his pagan wife after the Captivity (Ezra 10:40).

SHARAIM [shuh RAY uhm] (*two gates*) — a city in the lowland hills of Judah, apparently west of Azekah and Socoh (or Sochoh) and southwest of Jerusalem (Josh. 15:36; Shaaraim, NASB, NEB, NIV, RSV). It probably is Tell Zakariya in the Valley of Elah.

SHARAR [SHAH rur] (*strong*) — the father of Ahiam the Hararite (2 Sam. 23:33). Sharar is also called Sacar (1 Chr. 11:35; Sachar, KJV, RSV).

SHARD — a fragment of broken pottery (Is. 30:14; sherd, KJV; fragment, NIV). When archaeologists excavate sites where ancient peoples lived, they usually find such broken pieces of earthenware pottery.

SHAREZER [shuh REE zur] (*protect the king*) — a son of the Assyrian king Sennacherib (2 Kin. 19:37). In 681 B.C. Sharezer killed his father and fled to the land of Ararat.

SHARON [SHAR uhn] (meaning unknown) — the name of a plain and a district in the Old Testament:
1. The chief coastal plain of Palestine, running approximately 80 kilometers (50 miles) from south of the Carmel Mountain range to the vicinity of Joppa (1 Chr. 27:29). This lowland region was extremely fertile and it was known for its agriculture (Is. 33:9). In ancient times, an important caravan route ran along the Plain of Sharon, connecting Egypt, Mesopotamia, and Asia Minor. The flowers of Sharon (Is. 35:2), particularly the rose of Sharon (Song 2:1), were beautiful. Sharon is also called Lasharon (Josh. 12:18).
2. A district in Transjordan, the area east of the Jordan River, occupied by the tribe of Gad (1 Chr. 5:16).

SHARONITE, THE [SHAR uhn ight] (*of Sharon*) — a term applied to Shitrai, King David's chief herdsman in the Plain of Sharon (1 Chr. 27:29).

SHARUHEN [shuh ROO uhn] (meaning unknown) — a city in the territory of Judah assigned to the tribe of Simeon (Josh. 19:6). Sharuhen may be identical with Shilhim (Josh. 15:32) and Shaaraim (1 Chr. 4:31).

SHASHAI [SHAY shigh] (*noble*) — a son of Bani who married a pagan wife during the Captivity (Ezra 10:40).

SHASHAK [SHAY shak] (*runner*) — an ancestor of King Saul (1 Chr. 8:14, 25).

SHAUL [shahl] (*asked of God*) — the name of two men in the Old Testament:
1. The founder of a tribal family known as the Shaulites (Num. 26:13).
2. A Levite descended from Kohath (1 Chr. 6:24).

SHAULITES [SHAHL ights] — a tribal family descended from SHAUL (Num. 26:13).

SHAVEH [SHAY vuh] (*level place*) — a valley near Salem where Abraham was met by the king of Sodom and by Melchizedek after the defeat of Che-

dorlaomer (Gen. 14:17–18). This valley was the place where Abraham erected a monument to himself, a pillar that came to be called "Absalom's Monument" (2 Sam. 18:18).

SHAVEH KIRIATHAIM [SHAY vuh kir ih uh THAY uhm] (*the plain of Kiriathaim*) — a plain in Transjordan near the city of Kiriathaim of Moab (Gen. 14:5). The Emim were defeated on this plain by Chedorlaomer in the days of Abraham and Lot.

SHAVING — removal of the beard or other body hair, as with a razor. Among the Jewish people, beards were common, especially in early times when the Hebrews lived as wandering shepherds. But the Egyptians shaved their faces closely and preferred short hair. The Greeks and Romans also preferred the clean-shaven style.

Shaving was a part of the ritual by which a Levite was set apart for priestly service (Num. 8:7). Shaving was also required for those unclean with plague (Lev. 13:33) or leprosy (Lev. 14:8). Refusing to allow a man-made instrument to touch their heads, a group of Hebrews known as the NAZIRITES kept their hair uncut until a particular vow had been fulfilled (Num. 6:18; Acts 18:18). But if a Nazirite touched a dead body, he was required to cut his hair immediately (Num. 6:9).

Although shaving the head was often a sign of mourning (Deut. 14:1; Job 1:10), priests did not follow this practice (Lev. 21:5).

SHAVSHA [SHAV shuh] (*nobility*) — the scribe, or state secretary, in David's administration (1 Chr. 18:16; secretary, NIV, NASB, RSV). Some scholars believe Shavsha was a person of foreign birth whose language skills qualified him to serve as David's secretary of state or foreign correspondent.

SHEAF — stalks of grain gathered and tied into a bundle after harvesting. The reapers either gathered the cut grain into sheaves themselves (Ruth 2:7) or left it to be collected by the sheaf-binder (Jer. 9:22). The sheaves were then gathered into stacks (Ex. 22:6) and loaded into carts (Amos 2:13). The ancient Jewish law directed that some stray stalks and sheaves should be left in the field for the poor and hungry to glean (Deut. 24:9).

The first sheaves of harvest were to be given as a firstfruit offering to the Lord (Lev. 23:10). The grain was threshed from the remainder for grinding into flour.

SHEAL [SHEE uhl] (*may God grant*) — an Israelite who divorced his foreign wife after the Captivity (Ezra 10:29).

SHEALTIEL [shee AL tih uhl] (*I asked of God*) — a son of Jehoiachin (Jeconiah), king of Judah (1 Chr. 3:17; Matt. 1:12; Salathiel, KJV). Shealtiel apparently was an ancestor of Zerubbabel, the Jewish governor of Jerusalem after the Captivity. Shealtiel may have been Zerubbabel's father (Ezra 3:2), or his uncle or grandfather (1 Chr. 3:17–19). In the New Testament, Shealtiel is listed in the genealogy of Jesus Christ (Luke 3:27; Salathiel, KJV). He was

Ruins of a gate and the entrance to a temple in the northwest portion of the city of Shechem. This gate was built during the Hyksos period about 1650 to 1550 B.C.

a descendant of David through his son Nathan (2 Sam. 5:14).

SHEAR–JASHUB [shee ur JAY shuhb] (*a remnant shall return*) — a symbolic name given to a son of the prophet Isaiah in the days of King Ahaz of Judah (Is. 7:3). The name emphasized Isaiah's prophecy that a remnant of the nation would return to the land after their years of captivity in a foreign country.

SHEARIAH [shee uh RIGH uh] (*esteemed of the Lord*) — a son of Azel, of the tribe of Benjamin (1 Chr. 8:38). Sheariah was a descendant of King Saul.

SHEARING HOUSE — KJV form of BETH EKED OF THE SHEPHERDS (2 Kin. 10:12–14).

SHEATH — the carrying case for a knife, dagger, or sword. The Bible mentions the sheaths of Goliath (1 Sam. 17:51), Joab (2 Sam. 20:8), and Simon Peter (John 18:11), and symbolically the sheath from which God's sword is drawn in judgment (1 Chr. 21:27; Ezek. 21:3–5, 30).

SHEBA [SHEE buh] (*oath*) — the name of five men, a city, and a country in the Old Testament:

1. A descendant of Ham. Sheba's descendants are believed to have settled on the shores of the Persian Gulf (Gen. 10:7).

2. A son of Joktan of the family of Shem, whose descendants have been traced to southern Arabia (Gen. 10:28).

3. A grandson of Abraham (Gen. 25:3). Sheba was a son of Jokshan, who was a son of Abraham by Keturah. Sheba and his descendants probably lived in Edom or northern Arabia.

4. A city of the territory of Judah assigned to the tribe of Simeon (Josh. 19:2). Some modern translations of the Bible (NKJV, NIV, NASB) equate Sheba with Beersheba.

5. A son of Bichri, of the tribe of Benjamin (2 Sam. 20:1–22). After the death of Absalom, Sheba led a short–lived rebellion against King David and was forced to retreat inside the city of Abel of Beth Maachah. This city was then besieged by Joab, the captain of David's army. In order to save their city, the people of Abel cut off Sheba's head and threw it over the wall to Joab (2 Sam. 20:1–22).

6. A mountainous country in southwest Arabia (1 Kin. 10:1–13), identified as the land of "the queen of the South" (Luke 11:31) who came to investigate Solomon's fame and wisdom. By means of its international trade and control of trade routes through its land, Sheba developed into a strong commercial power. Its trade specialties were perfumes and incense. Camel caravans followed routes northward across its dry regions, bearing their precious commodities for the royal courts of the countries bordering the Mediterranean Sea. Thus the Queen of Sheba's visit to Solomon may have been motivated also by her interest in trade and in the unhindered movement of her caravans into the large territory under Solomon's control.

7. A chief of the tribe of Gad who lived in Gilead in Bashan during the reign of Jeroboam II of Israel (1 Chr. 5:13).

SHEBA, QUEEN OF — a queen who came to visit King Solomon. She tested him with "hard questions" and found that Solomon's wisdom and prosperity exceeded his fame (1 Kin. 10:1–13). Some scholars believe she represented the region of Ethiopia, south of Egypt. But others insist she ruled among the tribes of southwestern Arabia. In the

New Testament, Jesus referred to her as "the queen of the South," who "came from the ends of the earth to hear the wisdom of Solomon" (Matt. 12:42). Also see SHEBA.

SHEBAH [SHEE buh] (*well of seven*) — the famous well from which Beersheba derived its name; it was dug by Isaac's servants near Beersheba in Judah (Gen. 26:33; Shibah, NASB, NEB, NIV, RSV).

SHEBAM [SHEE bam] (meaning unknown) — a city east of the Jordan River in the Plain of Moab near Heshbon. After the conquest of the land of Canaan, Shebam was assigned to the tribes of Reuben and Gad (Num. 32:3; Sebam, NAS); but it fell back under Moabite control. It probably was the same place as Shibmah (Num. 32:38) and Sibmah (Josh. 13:19).

SHEBANIAH [sheb uh NIGH uh] (*the Lord is powerful*) — the name of four men in the Old Testament:
1. A Levite trumpeter who helped transport the ARK OF THE COVENANT to the Temple in Jerusalem (1 Chr. 15:24).
2. A Levite who helped at the Feast of Tabernacles after the Captivity (Neh. 9:4–5).
3. A priestly family that lived one generation after the Captivity (Neh. 12:14). A representative of this family sealed the covenant with Nehemiah (Neh. 10:4).
4. A priest who sealed the covenant with Nehemiah after the Captivity (Neh. 10:12).

SHEBARIM [SHEB uh rim] (*broken places*) — a place where the Israelites fled after their defeat at Ai (Josh. 7:5).

SHEBAT [SHEE bat] (meaning unknown) — the fifth month of the civil year in the Hebrew calendar (Zech. 1:7; Sebat, KJV). Also see CALENDAR.

SHEBER [SHEE bur] (*breach*) — a son of Caleb and a descendant of David (1 Chr. 2:48).

SHEBNA [SHEB nuh] (meaning unknown) — a high official in the court of Hezekiah, king of Judah (2 Kin. 18:18, 26; Shebnah, RSV; 18:37; 19:2; Is. 36:3, 11, 22; 37:2). Shebna is described as a scribe (NKJV, NASB), a secretary (NIV, RSV), and an adjutant–general (NEB), probably indicating he held an office similar to secretary of state. Shebna was one of three ambassadors who represented Hezekiah before the messengers of Sennacherib, king of Assyria, whose army was besieging Jerusalem. As the administrator of Hezekiah's palace, Shebna was a man of great influence. But the prophet Isaiah predicted he would fall from power and die as an outcast because of his pride (Is. 22:15–25).

SHEBUEL [shih BOO uhl] (meaning unknown) — the name of two men in the Old Testament:
1. A son of Gershon (also spelled Gershom) and grandson of Moses (1 Chr. 23:16). Shebuel was ruler of the tabernacle treasury in the time of David (Shubael, 1 Chr. 24:20).

2. A son of Heman the musician (1 Chr. 25:4; Shubael, 1 Chr. 25:20).

SHECANIAH [shek uh NIGH uh] (*Jehovah is a neighbor*) — the name of three men in the Old Testament:
1. A priest whose descendants were organized for special service during David's reign (1 Chr. 24:11).
2. A priest during the reign of King Hezekiah of Judah (2 Chr. 31:15). Shecaniah helped distribute the Temple offering among the priests.
3. The descendant of a family, perhaps that of Shecaniah No. 1, that returned from the Captivity (Ezra 8:3; Shechaniah, KJV).

SHECHANIAH [shek uh NIGH uh] (*Jehovah is a neighbor*) — the name of six men in the Old Testament:
1. The head of a family in the lineage of David (1 Chr. 3:21–22).
2. A person who returned with Ezra from the Captivity (Ezra 8:5).
3. A son of Jehiel (Ezra 10:2). Shechaniah divorced his foreign wife after the Captivity.
4. The father of Shemaiah (Neh. 3:29). Shemaiah was the keeper of the East Gate in Jerusalem in Nehemiah's time.
5. The father-in-law of Tobiah the Ammonite (Neh. 6:17).
6. A chief priest who returned from the Captivity with Zerubbabel (Neh. 12:1–3).

SHECHEM [SHEK uhm] (*shoulder*) — the name of a city and three men in the Bible:
1. An ancient fortified city in central Palestine and the first capital of the northern kingdom of Israel (see Map 4, B–3). Its name means "shoulder," probably because the city was built mainly on the slope, or shoulder, of Mount Ebal. Situated where main highways and ancient trade routes converged, Shechem was an important city long before the Israelites occupied Canaan. The city has been destroyed and rebuilt several times through the centuries.

Shechem is first mentioned in connection with Abraham's journey into the land of Canaan. When Abraham eventually came to Shechem, the Lord appeared to him and announced that this was the land He would give to Abraham's descendants (Gen. 12:6; Sichem, KJV). This fulfilled God's promise to Abraham at the time of his call (Gen. 12:1–3). In response, Abraham built his first altar to the Lord in Canaan at Shechem (Gen. 12:7). Because of this incident, Shechem is an important place in the religious history of the Hebrew people.

Upon his return from Padan Aram, Jacob, a grandson of Abraham, also built an altar to the Lord at Shechem (Gen. 33:18–20). This marked Jacob's safe return to the Promised Land from the land of self–imposed exile. According to Jewish tradition, Jacob dug a deep well here (John 4:12). Jacob's Well is one of the few sites visited by Jesus that is identifiable today.

After the Israelites conquered Canaan under the leadership of Joshua, an altar was built at Shechem. Its building was accompanied by a covenant ceremony in which offerings were given and the blessings and curses of the Law were recited (Josh. 8:30–35). This was done in obedience to the command of Moses, given earlier in Deuteronomy 27:12–13. Because Shechem was situated between Mount Ebal and Mount Gerizim, this covenant ceremony took on a symbolic meaning. To this day Mount Gerizim is forested while Mount Ebal is barren. Thus the blessings of faithfully keeping the covenant were proclaimed from Mount Gerizim, while the curses of breaking the covenant were proclaimed from Mount Ebal.

At the close of his life, Joshua gathered the tribes of Israel at Shechem. Here he reviewed God's gracious dealings with Israel and performed a covenant–renewing ceremony on behalf of the nation. He closed his speech with his famous statement, "Choose for yourselves this day whom you will serve...but as for me and my house, we will serve the Lord" (Josh. 24:15).

The significance of Shechem in Israel's history continued into the period of the Divided Kingdom. Rehoboam, successor to King Solomon, went to Shechem to be crowned king over all Israel (1 Kin. 12:1). Later, when the nation divided into two kingdoms, Shechem became the first capital of the northern kingdom of Israel (1 Kin. 12:25). Samaria eventually became the permanent political capital of the Northern Kingdom, but Shechem retained its religious importance. It apparently was a sanctuary for worship of God in Hosea's time in the eighth century B.C. (Hos. 6:9).

At Shechem (sometimes identified with Sychar) Jesus visited with the Samaritan woman at Jacob's Well (John 4). The SAMARITANS had built their temple on Mount Gerizim, where they practiced their form of religion. To this outcast woman of a despised sect Jesus offered salvation. This is a vivid example of the truth that the gospel of Christ is meant for all people.

2. A son of Hamor, a Hivite prince (Gen. 33:19; 34:1–31). Shechem raped Dinah, the daughter of Jacob. When Shechem later wanted to marry her, Dinah's half–brothers, Simeon and Levi, agreed to give Shechem permission only if "every male of you is circumcised" (Gen. 34:15). When Hamor, Shechem, and their followers agreed to the procedure, Simeon and Levi killed them before the circumcision operations had healed.

3. A son of Gilead and grandson of Manasseh (Num. 26:31; Josh. 17:2).

4. A son of Shemida, of the tribe of Manasseh (1 Chr. 7:19).

SHECHEMITES [SHEK uhm ights] — the descendants of SHECHEM, a son of Gilead of the tribe of Manasseh (Num. 26:31; Josh. 17:2).

SHEDEUR [SHEH dih ur] (*shedder of light*) — the father of the Reubenite chief Elizur (Num. 1:5). Elizur helped Moses take a census of the people in the wilderness.

SHEEP (see ANIMALS OF THE BIBLE).

SHEEP BREEDER (see OCCUPATIONS AND TRADES).

SHEEPCOTE — KJV word for SHEEPFOLD.

In all periods of biblical history sheep were important because they provided wool, milk, meat, and leather for the Hebrew people.
Photo by Gustav Jeeninga

SHEEPFOLD — a pen or shelter for protecting sheep (Num. 32:16; sheepcote, KJV). A permanent sheepfold was enclosed by stone walls. The Old Testament declares that the Lord took David from the sheepfold to be ruler over the Lord's people (1 Chr. 17:7). The New Testament portrays Jesus as the Good Shepherd who protects His sheep (John 10:7–30).

SHEEP GATE, SHEEP MARKET, SHEEP POOL (see GATES OF JERUSALEM AND THE TEMPLE).

SHEEP SHEARER (see OCCUPATIONS AND TRADES).

SHEERAH [SHEE uh ruh] (*blood relationship*) — a female descendant of Ephraim (1 Chr. 7:24; Sherah, KJV, NEB). Sheerah built or fortified three villages: Lower Beth Horon, Upper Beth Horon, and Uzzen Sheerah.

SHEET — a word with two different meanings in the NKJV:
1. Thin sheets of gold from which threads for the making of the EPHOD were formed (Ex. 39:3).
2. A large piece of cloth made of fine linen. While in a trance, Simon Peter had a vision of an object coming down out of heaven that looked like a "great sheet" (Acts 10:11).

SHEHARIAH [shee uh RIGH uh] (*Jehovah is the dawn*) — a tribal chief who lived in Jerusalem after the Captivity (1 Chr. 8:26).

SHEKEL (see MONEY; WEIGHTS AND MEASURES).

SHEKINAH [shuh KIGH nuh] (*dwelling*) — a visible manifestation of the presence of God (also spelled Shechinah and Shekhinah). Although the word is not found in the Bible, it occurs frequently in later Jewish writings. It refers to the instances when God showed Himself visibly, as, for example, on Mount Sinai (Ex. 24:9–18) and in the Holy of Holies of the tabernacle and in Solomon's Temple. The Shekinah was a luminous cloud which rested above the altar in the place of worship and lit up the room. When the Babylonians destroyed the Temple, the Shekinah glory vanished. There was no Shekinah in the temples rebuilt later under Zerubbabel and Herod.

SHELAH [SHEE luh] (*prayer*) — the name of two men and a pool in the Bible:
1. The youngest son of Judah, by the daughter of Shua the Canaanite (Gen. 38:5).
2. A son of Arphaxad (1 Chr. 1:18). He was the father of Eber and an ancestor of Christ (Luke 3:35; Sala, KJV).
3. A pool in Jerusalem (Neh. 3:15; Siloah, KJV; Siloam, NIV). Also see SILOAM.

SHELANITES [SHEE luh nights] — the descendants of SHELAH, son of Judah (Num. 26:20).

SHELEMIAH [sheh luh MIGH uh] (*Jehovah has recompensed*) — the name of nine men in the Old Testament:
1. A Levite who was a tabernacle gatekeeper dur-

ing David's reign (1 Chr. 26:14). He is also called Meshelemiah (1 Chr. 26:1–2).
2, 3. Descendants of Bani who divorced their foreign wives after the Captivity (Ezra 10:39, 41).
4. The father of Hananiah (Neh. 3:30).
5. A priest and treasurer appointed by Nehemiah to distribute the tithes among the Levites (Neh. 13:13).
6. A son of Cushi and ancestor of Jehudi (Jer. 36:14).
7. A son of Abdeel (Jer. 36:26).
8. The father of Jehucal (Jer. 37:3).
9. The father of Irijah (Jer. 37:13). Irijah was the captain of the guard who arrested Jeremiah before he left Jerusalem.

SHELEPH [SHEE lif] (*a drawing forth*) — a son of Joktan, of the family of Shem (Gen. 10:26).

SHELESH [SHEE lish] (*triplet*) — a son of Helem and head of a clan in the tribe of Asher (1 Chr. 7:35).

SHELOMI [shih LOE migh] (*God is my peace*) — the father of Ahihud (Num. 34:27). Ahihud helped divide the land of Canaan west of the Jordan River.

SHELOMITH [shih LOE mith] (*peacefulness*) — the name of seven people in the Old Testament:
1. A daughter of Dibri, of the tribe of Dan (Lev. 24:11).
2. A daughter of Zerubbabel, of the family of Jeconiah (1 Chr. 3:19).
3. A son of Shimei (1 Chr. 23:9; Shelomoth, RSV).
4. A descendant of Izhar, a Levite of the Kohathite family (1 Chr. 23:18). He is also called Shelomoth (1 Chr. 24:22).
5. A keeper of the tabernacle treasures in David's time (1 Chr. 26:25–26; Shelomoth, RSV).
6. A child of Rehoboam by Maacah, the granddaughter of Absalom (2 Chr. 11:20).
7. A son of Josiphiah and the ancestor of a family that returned from the Captivity with Ezra (Ezra 8:10).

SHELOMOTH [sheh LOE mahth] (*peacefulness*) — a Levite of the Izharite family (1 Chr. 24:22).

SHELUMIEL [shih LOO mih uhl] (*God is peace*) — a leader of the tribe of Simeon who helped Moses take the first census of Israel in the wilderness (Num. 1:6).

SHEM [shim] (*renown*) — the oldest son of Noah and brother of Ham and Japheth. Shem was born when Noah was 500 years old (Gen. 5:32). He was one of eight people who entered Noah's ark and survived the Flood (Gen. 7:7, 13). Shem was married at the time of the Flood but had no children. After the Flood he became the father of Elam, Asshur, Arphaxad, Lud, and Aram (usually identified by scholars as Persia, Assyria, Chaldea, Lydia, and Syria, respectively). Thus Shem was the ancestor of the people of the ancient Near East generally, and the Hebrews specifically.

Shem died at the age of 600 (Gen. 11:10–11). He is listed by Luke as an ancestor of Jesus Christ (Luke 3:36; Sem, KJV).

SHEMA [SHEE muh] (*repute*) — the name of four men and one city in the Old Testament:

1. A city in the NEGEV, in southern Judah, near the border of Edom (Josh. 15:26).

2. A son of Hebron, of the tribe of Judah (1 Chr. 2:43–44).

3. A son of Joel and father of Azaz (1 Chr. 5:8).

4. A son of Elpaal (1 Chr. 8:13), also called Shimei (1 Chr. 8:21; Shimhi, KJV).

5. One of the priests who assisted Ezra in the public reading of the Law (Neh. 8:4).

SHEMA, THE [shuh MAH] (*hear thou*) — the Jewish confession of faith which begins, "Hear, O Israel: The Lord our God, the Lord is one!" (Deut. 6:4). The complete Shema is found in three passages from the Old Testament: Numbers 15:37–41, Deuteronomy 6:4–9 and 11:13–21.

The first of these passages stresses the unity of God and the importance of loving Him and valuing His commands. The second passage promises blessing or punishment according to a person's obedience of God's will. The third passage commands that a fringe be worn on the edge of one's garments as a continual reminder of God's laws. This collection of verses makes up one of the most ancient features of worship among the Jewish people. According to the Gospel of Mark, Jesus quoted from the Shema during a dispute with the scribes (Mark 12:28–30).

SHEMAAH [shih MAY uh] (*fame*) — a Benjamite of Gibeah whose sons joined David's army at Ziklag (1 Chr. 12:3).

SHEMAIAH [shih MAY uh] (*Jehovah has heard*) — the name of several men in the Old Testament:

1. A prophet who directed King Rehoboam of Judah to stop fighting the ten northern tribes that had revolted and formed their own nation (1 Kin. 12:22).

2. A son of Shechaniah, who founded a family apparently in the line of David (1 Chr. 3:22).

3. The head of a family of the tribe of Simeon (1 Chr. 4:37).

4. A son of Joel (1 Chr. 5:4), perhaps the Shema of 1 Chronicles 5:8.

5. A Levite who supervised work on the Temple during Nehemiah's time (Neh. 11:15).

6. A Levite and father of Obadiah (1 Chr. 9:16).

7. A Levite who helped move the ark to Jerusalem (1 Chr. 15:8, 11).

8. A Levite and son of Nethaneel (1 Chr. 24:6).

9. A tabernacle gatekeeper in David's time (1 Chr. 26:6–7).

10. A Levite sent by Jehoshaphat to teach the law to the people of Judah (2 Chr. 17:8).

11. A Levite and descendant of Jeduthun who helped purify the Temple under King Hezekiah (2 Chr. 29:14). He may be the same person as Shemaiah No. 6. He may also be the person called Shammua in Nehemiah 11:17.

12. A Levite who distributed firstfruits, tithes, and gifts to the priests in Hezekiah's time (2 Chr. 31:15).

13. A chief Levite during the reign of Josiah in Judah (2 Chr. 35:9).

14. A head of a family who returned from the Captivity with Ezra (Ezra 8:13).

15. A messenger for Ezra after the Captivity (Ezra 8:16).

16. A son of Harim who divorced his foreign wife (Ezra 10:21).

17. A son of another Harim. This Shemaiah also divorced his foreign wife (Ezra 10:31).

18. A Levite who helped repair Jerusalem's wall under Nehemiah (Neh. 3:29).

19. A false prophet hired by Tobiah and Sanballat to frighten Nehemiah (Neh. 6:10).

20. A priest who sealed the covenant under Nehemiah (Neh. 10:8).

21. A chief priest who returned from the Captivity with Zerubbabel (Neh. 12:6).

22. A prince of Judah who helped dedicate Jerusalem's wall after the Captivity (Neh. 12:34).

23. A Levite descended from Asaph (Neh. 12:35).

24. A Levite musician at the dedication of the Jerusalem wall (Neh. 12:36).

25. A priest who helped dedicate Jerusalem's wall. He may be the same person as Shemaiah No. 24 (Neh. 12:42).

26. The father of Urijah (Jer. 26:20).

27. A false prophet in Jeremiah's time (Jer. 29:24–32).

28. The father of Delaiah (Jer. 36:12).

SHEMARIAH [shem uh RIGH uh] (*whom Jehovah guards*) — the name of three men in the Old Testament:

1. A Benjamite warrior who joined David's army at Ziklag (1 Chr. 12:5).

2. A son of Harim who divorced his foreign wife (Ezra 10:32).

3. A son of Bani who divorced his foreign wife (Ezra 10:41).

SHEMEBER [shem EE bur] (meaning unknown) — the king of Zeboiim who was defeated by Chedorlaomer in the days of Abraham (Gen. 14:2).

SHEMED [SHEE mid] (*destruction*) — a son of Elpaal, of the tribe of Benjamin (1 Chr. 8:12; Shamed, KJV). Shemed rebuilt the cities of Ono and Lod after the Captivity.

SHEMER [SHEE mur] (*God is a keeper*) — the name of two men in the Old Testament:

1. The man from whom Omri bought the hill on which he built Samaria (1 Kin. 16:24).

2. A son of Heber, of the tribe of Asher (1 Chr. 7:34; Shamer, KJV), also called Shomer (1 Chr. 7:32).

SHEMIDA [shih MIGH duh] (meaning unknown) — a son of Gilead, of the tribe of Manasseh (Josh.

17:2; Shemidah, KJV). Shemida was the founder of a tribal family, the SHEMIDAITES (Num. 26:32).

SHEMIDAH [shih MIGH duh] — a form of SHEMIDA.

SHEMIDAITES [shih MIGH day ights] — the descendants of SHEMIDA (Num. 26:32).

SHEMINITH (see MUSIC OF THE BIBLE).

SHEMIRAMOTH [shih MIR uh mahth] (*fame of the highest*) — the name of two men in the Old Testament:
1. A Levite singer during David's reign (1 Chr. 15:18).
2. A Levite who instructed the people in the law in Jehoshaphat's time (2 Chr. 17:8).

SHEMUEL [SHEM yoo uhl] (*name of God*) — the name of three men in the Old Testament:
1. A representative of the tribe of Simeon in the division of the land of Canaan (Num. 34:20).
2. Another name for Samuel the prophet, the father of Joel (1 Chr. 6:33, KJV).
3. A son of Tola (1 Chr. 7:2).

SHEN [shen] (*tooth*) — an unknown place near the site where Samuel erected a stone memorial to commemorate Israel's victory over the Philistines (1 Sam. 7:12; Jeshanah, RSV, NEB).

SHENAZAR [shih NAZ ur] — a form of SHENAZZAR.

SHENAZZAR [shih NAZ ur] (*may* [the god] *Sin protect*) — a descendant of the exiled King Jehoiachin (Jeconiah or Coniah; 1 Chr. 3:18, Shenazar, KJV).

SHEOL [SHE ole] (meaning unknown) — in Old Testament thought, the abode of the dead. Sheol is the Hebrew equivalent of the Greek *Hades*, which means "the unseen world."

Sheol was regarded as an underground region (Num. 16:30, 33; Amos 9:2), shadowy and gloomy, where disembodied souls had a conscious but dull and inactive existence (2 Sam. 22:6; Eccl. 9:10). The Hebrew people regarded Sheol as a place to which both the righteous and unrighteous go at death (Gen. 37:35; Ps. 9:17; Is. 38:10), a place where punishment is received and rewards are enjoyed. Sheol is pictured as having an insatiable appetite (Is. 5:14; Hab. 2:5).

However, God is present in sheol (Ps. 139:8; hell, NKJV). It is open and known to Him (Job 26:6; Prov. 15:11). This suggests that in death God's people remain under His care, and the wicked never escape His judgment. Sheol gives meaning to Psalm 16:10. Peter saw the fulfillment of this messianic psalm in Jesus' resurrection (Acts 2:27).

Also see HELL.

SHEPHAM [SHEE fuhm] (meaning unknown) — a site near Riblah and Mount Hermon (Num. 34:10–11) mentioned by Moses when he outlined the borders of the Promised Land. Its exact location is unknown.

SHEPHATIAH [shef uh TIGH uh] (*Jehovah has judged*) — the name of nine men in the Old Testament:
1. David's fifth son born at Hebron. His mother was Abital (2 Sam. 3:4).
2. A Benjamite and the father of Meshullam (1 Chr. 9:8; Shephathiah, KJV).
3. A Benjamite who joined David's army at Ziklag (1 Chr. 12:5).
4. A son of Maachah and chief of the tribe of Simeon during David's reign (1 Chr. 27:16).
5. A son of King Jehoshaphat (2 Chr. 21:2).
6. A family whose descendants returned from the Captivity with Zerubbabel (Neh. 7:9) and Ezra (Ezra 8).
7. A family of Temple servants whose descendants returned from the Captivity with Zerubbabel (Ezra 2:57).
8. A descendant of Perez, of the tribe of Judah (Neh. 11:4).
9. A prince and son of Mattan (Jer. 38:1). Shephatiah urged King Zedekiah of Judah to put the prophet Jeremiah to death.

SHEPHER, MOUNT [SHEE fur] (*brightness*) — a mountain encampment of the Israelites during their wanderings in the wilderness (Num. 33:23–24; Shapher, KJV, NEB).

SHEPHERD — a person who takes care of sheep. Figuratively, the Old Testament pictures God as Israel's Shepherd–Leader (Ps. 80:1; Ezek. 34:14). The New Testament reveals Jesus as the Good Shepherd who gave His life for His sheep. When He said, "I am the good shepherd" (John 10:11), Jesus linked His own divine nature with one of the most ordinary occupations in Israel.

Abel is the first shepherd mentioned in the Bible (Gen. 4:2). Kings who led Israel (Jer. 6:3; 49:19) and certain ministers (Jer. 23:4) are also called shepherds. The sons of Abraham, Isaac, and Jacob herded sheep (Gen. 13:7; 26:20; 30:36). Rachel was a shepherdess (Gen. 29:3). David (2 Sam. 5:2; Ps. 78:70–72), Moses (Ex. 3:1), and Amos (Amos 1:1) found herding to be excellent preparation for future leadership roles.

Jesus' life exemplifies these leadership traits. Jesus knows each of His sheep intimately (John 10:3–5). Sometimes several shepherds will pen their sheep together in a cave or a sheepfold at night. The next morning each shepherd calls to his own sheep with his own unique gutteral cry. Each sheep knows his shepherd's voice and responds immediately. Even in a large flock, one individual sheep will run to his shepherd when his own pet name is called (John 10:27).

Sheep are curious but dumb animals, often unable to find their way home even if the sheepfold is within sight. Knowing this fault, the shepherd never takes his eyes off his wandering sheep (Ps. 32:8). Often a sheep will wander into a briar patch or fall over a cliff in the rugged Palestinian hills. The shepherd tenderly searches for his sheep and carries it to safety on his shoulder, wrapped in his

This fresco from a catacomb in Rome portrays Jesus as the Good Shepherd who takes care of His sheep (John 10:14).

own long cloak (Luke 15:6).

In water–hungry Syria and Palestine, shepherds have always had to search diligently for water, sometimes for hours every day. Sheep must be watered daily. The shepherd might find a bubbling stream for the sheep that are always on the move and needing fresh pastures every day (Ps. 23:2). An old well with a quiet pool or trough close by might provide the water (Gen. 29:7; 30:38; Ex. 2:16). Often the shepherd carries a small pail with him, patiently filling it many times for the thirsty sheep who cannot reach the available water.

A trusted shepherd also provides loving protection for his flock. Shepherds on the Bethlehem hillsides still use a sling, made of goat's hair or leather and immortalized by David against Goliath (1 Sam. 17:49). At times the shepherd will throw his rod at a stubborn, straying sheep that refuses to hear his voice. At other times he gently nudges the stray with the end of his six–foot staff, crooked at one end to fit his strong hand. Both the rod and the staff work together to protect the sheep (Ps. 23:4).

The presence of the shepherd also offers comfort to the flock. David recognized this in Psalm 23. Sheep are content merely to be in the same field with their shepherd; Christians are comforted by the very presence of the Lord. This thought is especially comforting when darkness overshadows the believer. Jesus is our Door; nothing can touch our lives without touching Him first. This is a perfect picture of the shepherd. He literally becomes the living door of the sheepfold. He curls up in the door or in the entrance of a cave. He puts his body between the sleeping sheep and ravenous animals or thieves.

One day Jesus the Chief Shepherd will return,

gather His whole flock into one fold, and divide the sheep from the goats (Matt. 25:31–33). Until that time, Jesus continues His search for every lost sheep (Matt. 18:12–14). His sheep are to yield themselves to Him for His useful service until, at last, they "will dwell in the house of the Lord forever" (Ps. 23:6).

Also see OCCUPATIONS AND TRADES.

SHEPHI, SHEPHO [SHEE fie, SHEE foe] (*bare*) — one of the sons of Shobal (Gen. 36:23; 1 Chr. 1:40).

SHEPHUPHAM [shih FOO fuhm] — a form of SHEPHUPHAN.

SHEPHUPHAN [shih FOO fan] (*serpent*) — a son of Bela, of the tribe of Benjamin (1 Chr. 8:5). The name is also given as Muppim (Gen. 46:21), Shupham (Num. 26:39; Shephupham, NASB), and Shuppim (1 Chr. 7:12).

SHERAH [SHEE ruh] — a form of SHEERAH.

SHERD (see POTSHERD).

SHEREBIAH [sher uh BIGH uh] (*flame of the Lord*) — the name of three men in the Old Testament:

1. The head of a family of Levites who returned with Ezra from the Captivity (Ezra 8:18).

2. A Levite who assisted Ezra in reading the law to the people (Neh. 8:7). He may be the same person as Sherebiah No. 1.

3. A Levite head of a family who returned with Zerubbabel from the Captivity (Neh. 12:8).

SHERESH [SHIR esh] (meaning unknown) — a son of Maachah (1 Chr. 7:16).

SHEREZER [sheh REE zur] — a man sent by the people of Bethel to ask about the observance of the anniversary feast commemorating the destruction of Jerusalem (Zech. 7:2; Sharezer, NASB, NIV, RSV).

SHESHACH [SHEE shak] — a code word for Babel, or Babylon. The code operates according to the ancient Hebrew system known as atbash (a word made of four different letters of the Hebrew alphabet). This code word was used by the prophet Jeremiah when he predicted the downfall of the Babylonian Empire (Jer. 25:26).

SHESHAI [SHEE shigh] (meaning unknown) — a son of Anak. Sheshai and his tribe were defeated by Caleb during the conquest of the land of Canaan (Josh. 15:14).

SHESHAN [SHEE shan] (meaning unknown) — a son of Ishi, of the tribe of Judah (1 Chr. 2:31).

SHESHBAZZAR [shesh BAZ ur] (meaning unknown) — a governor of Judah appointed by Cyrus, king of Persia. Sheshbazzar was given authority to return the gold and silver articles taken by the Babylonians to the Temple in Jerusalem (Ezra 1:8, 11). Sheshbazzar may have been the same person as Shenazzar (1 Chr. 3:18), the son of Jehoiachin.

SHETH [sheth] (meaning unknown) — the name of two men in the Old Testament:
1. A Moabite chief, (Num. 24:17).
2. The third son of Adam and Eve, born after the murder of Abel by Cain (1 Chr. 1:1, KJV; Seth, NKJV). Also see SETH.

SHETHAR [SHEE thahr] (*commander*) — a high Persian official, one of seven princes "who had access to the king's presence" (Esth. 1:14).

SHETHAR–BOZENAI [SHEE thahr BAHZ uh nigh] — a form of SHETHAR–BOZNAI.

SHETHAR–BOZNAI [SHEE thahr BAHZ nigh] (meaning unknown) — an official, perhaps a royal scribe, of the Persian Empire (Ezra 5:3; Shethar–Bozenai, RSV). Shethar–Boznai attempted to hinder the returned Jewish exiles from rebuilding the Temple.

SHEVA [SHEE vuh] (meaning unknown) — the name of two men in the Old Testament:
1. A scribe in King David's administration (2 Sam. 20:25). Sheva is also called Seraiah (2 Sam. 8:17), Shavsha (1 Chr. 18:16), and Shisha (1 Kin. 4:3).
2. A son of Maachah (1 Chr. 2:49).

SHEWBREAD (see SHOWBREAD).

SHIBAH [SHIGH buh] — a form of SHEBAH.

SHIBBOLETH [SHIBB oh lehth] (*flowing stream*) — the password used by the Gileadites at the fords of the Jordan River to detect the fleeing Ephraimites (Judg. 12:6). In a conflict between the people of Ephraim, who lived west of the Jordan, and the people of Gilead, who lived east of the Jordan, the Gileadites were victorious. Led by the judge Jeph-

thah, the Gileadites seized the fords of the Jordan, where they met the fleeing invaders and asked them to say "Shibboleth."

Because of a difference in dialect, an Ephraimite "could not pronounce it right" (v. 6), saying "Sibboleth" instead. Betrayed by his own speech, the unlucky Ephraimite was then killed at the fords of the Jordan by Jephthah and his men.

SHIBMAH [SHIB muh] — a form of SHEBAM.

SHICRON [SHIH krahn] (*drunkenness*) — a city west of Jerusalem on the northern border of Judah (Josh. 15:11; Shikkeron, NASB, NIV, RSV), probably modern Tell el–Ful, north of the Valley of Sorek.

SHIELD (see ARMS, ARMOR OF THE BIBLE).

SHIGGAION, SHIGGIONOTH [shih GAY ahn, shih gay ah NOHTH] (see MUSIC OF THE BIBLE).

SHIHON [SHIGH hahn] — a form of SHION.

SHIHOR, SIHOR [SHIGH hohr, SIGH hohr] (*black*) — a body of water situated "east of Egypt" (Josh. 13:3) or "in Egypt" (1 Chr. 13:5) that ideally was to be Israel's southwestern boundary. Some scholars believe Shihor (or Sihor) is the Brook of Egypt, the Wadi el–'Arish. Others believe Shihor refers to an eastern branch of the Nile River (Is. 23:3, NASB; Jer. 2:18, NASB, RSV).

SHIHOR LIBNATH [SHIGH hohr LIB nath] (*turbid stream of Libnath*) — a brook that served as the southwestern boundary of the territory of Asher (Josh. 19:26; the swamp of Libnath, NEB).

SHIKKERON [SHIK uh rohn] — a form of SHICRON.

SHILHI [SHIL high] (*dart-thrower*) — the maternal grandfather of Jehoshaphat, king of Judah (1 Kin. 22:42).

SHILHIM [SHIL him] (meaning unknown) — a city in southern Judah (Josh. 15:3), location uncertain.

SHILLEM [SHIL uhm] (*repayment*) — the youngest son of Naphtali (Gen. 46:24) and the founder of a tribal family known as the SHILLEMITES (Num. 26:49).

SHILLEMITES [SHILL em ites] — a tribal family descended from SHILLEM, the fourth son of Naphtali (Num. 26:49).

SHILOAH, WATERS OF [shigh LOE uh] (*sent*) — a water channel in Jerusalem (Is. 8:6), carrying water from the spring of Gihon to the lower pool of SILOAM.

SHILOH [SHIGH loe] (meaning unknown) — a city in the territory of Ephraim which served as Israel's religious center during the days before the establishment of the United Kingdom (see Map 3, B–3). Shiloh was "north of Bethel, on the east side of the highway that goes up from Bethel to Shechem, and south of Lebonah" (Judg. 21:19). This pinpoints Khirbet Seilun, about 16 kilometers (10 miles) northeast of Bethel.

At Shiloh the tabernacle received its first permanent home, soon after the initial conquest of Canaan by the children of Israel (Josh. 18:1). This established Shiloh as the main sanctuary of worship for the Israelites during the period of the judges (Judg. 18:31). Here the last seven tribes received their allotments of land (Josh. 18:8–10).

Hannah prayed for a son at Shiloh (1 Sam. 1:3, 11). God granted her request by giving her SAMUEL, a godly man who became a famous prophet and priest in Israel. The TABERNACLE, with the ARK OF THE COVENANT, was still located in Shiloh during Samuel's early years as priest and prophet (1 Sam. 1:9; 4:3–4). However, during a battle with the Philistines, the ark was captured by Israel's enemies because God had forsaken Shiloh as the center of worship (Ps. 78:60). When the ark was returned to the Israelites by the Philistines, it was not returned to Shiloh (2 Sam. 6:2–17).

After the ark was moved to another city, Shiloh gradually lost its importance. This loss was made complete when Jerusalem was established as capital of the kingdom. After the division of the kingdom, Jeroboam, the king of the ten northern tribes, established worship centers at Dan and Bethel; but Ahijah, the prophet of the Lord, still remained at Shiloh (1 Kin. 14:2, 4). From here, Ahijah pronounced the doom of Jeroboam's rule (1 Kin. 14:7–16).

In the days of the prophet Jeremiah, Shiloh was in ruin (Jer. 7:12, 14), although some people continued to live on the site of this former city (Jer. 41:5). Shiloh became an inhabited town again in the days of the Greeks and Romans several centuries later.

SHILONI [shih LOE nigh] (*a Shilonite*) — the father of Zechariah (Neh. 11:5; the Shelonite, RSV;

the Shilonite, NASB; a descendant of Shelah, NIV). Zechariah was an ancestor of Maaseiah, one of the Jewish princes who lived in Jerusalem in Ezra's time.

SHILONITE [SHIH loe night] — a name given to Ahijah the prophet, who was a native or resident of Shiloh (1 Kin. 11:29). The references to Shilonites in Nehemiah 11:5 (RSV) and 1 Chronicles 9:5 probably should be Shelanites, to indicate a descendant of Shelah (Gen. 38:5; Num. 26:20).

SHILSHAH [SHIL shuh] (*triad*) — a son of Zophah, of the tribe of Asher (1 Chr. 7:37).

SHIMEA, SHIMEAH [SHIM ih uh] (*God has heard*) — the name of five men in the Old Testament:

1. The third son of Jesse and brother of David (2 Sam. 13:3). Shimeah was the father of Jonadab (2 Sam. 13:3, 32) as well as Jonathan, who slew a Philistine giant (2 Sam. 21:21). Shimeah is also called Shammah (1 Sam. 16:9) and Shimma (1 Chr. 2:13, KJV).

2. A son of David born in Jerusalem (1 Chr. 3:5). Shimea is also called Shammua (2 Sam. 5:14; 1 Chr. 14:4).

3. A Levite of the family of Merari (1 Chr. 6:30).

4. A Levite of the family of Gershon (1 Chr. 6:39).

5. A Benjamite, descendant of Jeiel (1 Chr. 8:32). He is also called Shimeam (1 Chr. 9:38).

SHIMEAM [SHIM ih uhm] (*hearing*) — a son of Mikloth, of the tribe of Benjamin (1 Chr. 9:38), also called Shimeah (1 Chr. 8:32).

SHIMEATH [SHIM ih ath] (*hearing*) — an Ammonitess, the mother of one of the assassins of King Joash. Her son's name is given as Jozachar (2 Kin. 12:21) or Zabad (2 Chr. 24:26).

Remains of an early sanctuary at the Old Testament city of Shiloh (1 Sam. 1:3, 9).
Photo by Howard Vos

SHIMEATHITES [SHIM ih uth ights] — a Kenite family of scribes who lived at Jabez in Judah. They were descendants of Hammath (1 Chr. 2:55).

SHIMEI [SHIM ih uh] (*Jehovah is fame*) — the name of several men in the Old Testament:

1. A son of Gershon and grandson of Levi (Num. 3:18; Zech. 12:13), also called Shimi (Ex. 6:17).

2. A son of Gera of Saul's family and the tribe of Benjamin (2 Sam. 16:5-13; 1 Kin. 2:8). Shimei grew bitter because David had taken the throne from the family of Saul. He insulted David when the king was fleeing from his own son, Absalom. When David finally won the struggle for the throne, Shimei repented. David accepted Shimei's apology and promised to let him live. After David's death, his son and successor, Solomon, would not allow Shimei to go beyond Jerusalem's walls. Shimei obeyed Solomon's command at first, but eventually he left the city and was promptly executed at Solomon's command.

3. One of David's officers. Shimei remained loyal to David and Solomon when Adonijah attempted to seize the throne (1 Kin. 1:8).

4. One of Solomon's 12 supply officers who provided food for the king and his household (1 Kin. 4:18).

5. A son of Pedaiah and brother of Zerubbabel (1 Chr. 3:19). A member of the royal house, Shimei was the great-grandson of King Jehoiakim of Judah (1 Chr. 3:16-19).

6. A son of Zacchur (1 Chr. 4:26-27).

7. The son of Gog (1 Chr. 5:4).

8. A Levite and the son of Libni (1 Chr. 6:29).

9. A Levite, the son of Jahath (1 Chr. 6:42).

10. A descendant of Benjamin and head of a family in Aijalon (1 Chr. 8:21; Shimhi, KJV).

11. Head of a family of Levites in David's time (1 Chr. 23:9).

12. A Levite who headed the tenth course of sanctuary singers during David's reign (1 Chr. 25:3, 17).

13. A supervisor of David's vineyards (1 Chr. 27:27).

14. A descendant of Heman who helped cleanse the Temple in King Hezekiah's time (2 Chr. 29:14).

15. A Levite with responsibility for the tithes and offerings in Hezekiah's time (2 Chr. 31:12-13). He may be the same person as Shimei No. 14.

16. A Levite who divorced his foreign wife (Ezra 10:23).

17. A member of the family of Hashum who divorced his foreign wife (Ezra 10:33).

18. A son of Bani who divorced his foreign wife (Ezra 10:38).

19. A son of Kish and grandfather of Mordecai (Esth. 2:5).

SHIMEITES [SHIM ee ites] — a form of SHIMITES.

SHIMEON [SHIM ih uhn] (*hearing*) — a son of Harim who divorced his foreign wife after the Captivity (Ezra 10:31).

SHIMHI [SHIM high] — a form of SHIMEI No. 10.

SHIMI — a form of SHIMEI No. 1.

SHIMITES [SHIM ites] — a tribal family descended from SHIMEI, son of Gershon (Num. 3:21; Shimeites, NASB, NIV, RSV).

SHIMMA [SHIM muh] — a form of SHIMEA No. 1.

SHIMON [SHIGH muhn] (meaning unknown) — a Judahite, father of four sons (1 Chr. 4:20).

SHIMRATH [SHIM rath] (*guard*) — the ninth son of Shimei, of the tribe of Benjamin (1 Chr. 8:21).

SHIMRI [SHIM righ] (*Jehovah watches*) — the name of four men in the Old Testament:

1. A son of Shemaiah, of the tribe of Simeon (1 Chr. 4:37).

2. The father of Jediael (1 Chr. 11:45).

3. A tabernacle gatekeeper during David's time (1 Chr. 26:10; Simri, KJV).

4. A Levite who assisted in the cleansing of the Temple during Hezekiah's religious reformation (2 Chr. 29:13).

SHIMRITH [SHIM rith] (*God preserves*) — a Moabitess, the mother of Jehozabad (2 Chr. 24:26), also called Shomer (2 Kin. 12:21).

SHIMROM [SHIM rahm] — a form of SHIMRON No. 1.

SHIMRON [SHIM rahn] (*guard*) — the name of a man and a city in the Old Testament:

1. A son of Issachar (Gen. 46:13; Shimrom, KJV) and founder of the SHIMRONITES (Num. 26:24).

2. A royal city of the Canaanites whose king entered a military alliance with Jabin, king of Hazor, against Joshua and the invading Israelites (Josh. 11:1).

SHIMRON MERON [SHIM rahn MIR ahn] (meaning unknown) — an ancient royal city of the Canaanites whose king was killed by Joshua (Josh. 12:20). Shimron Meron is possibly the full name of the city of Shimron (Josh. 11:1).

SHIMRONITES [SHIM ruhn ights] — the descendants of SHIMRON No. 1 (Num. 26:24).

SHIMSHAI [SHIM shigh] (*the shining one*) — the scribe or secretary of Rehum, a Samaritan official in the Persian Empire. Rehum and Shimshai opposed the rebuilding of the Temple and the wall of Jerusalem (Ezra 4:8-9, 17, 23).

SHIN [sin] — the 21st letter of the Hebrew alphabet, used as a heading over Psalm 119:161-168. In the original Hebrew language, every line of these eight verses began with the letter shin. Also see ACROSTIC.

SHINAB [SHIGH nab] (*Sin is my father*) — the king of Admah defeated by Chedorlaomer and his allies in the time of Abraham (Gen. 14:2).

SHINAR [SHIGH nahr] — the land of southern

Photo by Howard Vos

Model of an Egyptian ship with a double mast discovered in the tomb of Pharaoh Sahure. These ships were used by the Egyptians about 2550 B.C.

Mesopotamia, later known as Babylonia or Chaldea, through which the Tigris and Euphrates Rivers flow (Gen. 10:10; 11:2). Secular historians usually refer to the area as SUMER.

Nimrod's kingdom in Shinar consisted of the cities of Babel (Babylon), Erech (Uruk), Accad (Akkad or Agade), and Calneh (Gen. 10:10). It was here that the Tower of Babel was situated (Gen. 11:2). In the days of Abraham, Amraphel, a king of Shinar, was involved in the attack and defeat of five kings of Canaan, including the kings of Sodom and Gomorrah (Gen. 14:1, 9).

In about 606 B.C. Nebuchadnezzar, king of Babylon, took the Temple vessels from Jerusalem to Shinar (Dan. 1:2), from where Isaiah had predicted God's people would return to Israel (Is. 11:11). After the return from the Captivity, the prophet Zechariah saw a vision of the removal of a woman from Israel to Shinar (Zech. 5:11). Some scholars associate this woman with the great harlot, "Babylon the great" (Rev. 17:5), a symbol of imperial Rome.

SHION [SHIGH uhn] (meaning unknown) — a border city in the territory of Issachar (Josh. 19:19; Shihon, KJV). It may be Sirin, about 23 kilometers (14 miles) southeast of Mount Tabor.

SHIP BUILDER (see OCCUPATIONS AND TRADES).

SHIPHI [SHIGH figh] (*Jehovah is abundance*) — a Simeonite who lived in the time of Hezekiah, king of Judah (1 Chr. 4:37).

SHIPHMITE [SHIF might] — a native or inhabitant of Shepham (Num. 34:10–11), a city in northeast Canaan, or perhaps of Siphmoth (1 Sam. 30:28), a city in southern Canaan.

SHIPHRAH [SHIF ruh] (*splendor*) — one of two Hebrew midwives (also see PUAH) in Egypt at the time of the birth of Moses. These women defied Pharaoh's command to kill all the male babies of the Hebrew people (Ex. 1:15).

SHIPHTAN [SHIF tuhn] (*judging*) — the father of Kemuel (Num. 34:24). Kemuel assisted Moses in dividing the land west of the Jordan River among the tribes of Israel.

SHIPMASTER — the person responsible for the navigation of a ship (Rev. 18:17; sea captain, NEB, NIV). The shipmaster often was the owner of the ship which he piloted.

SHIPS — sea-going vessels used mainly for carrying cargo in Bible times. The Jews were never a seafaring people. For them, the sea was a barrier and danger to be feared. Note the hope expressed in Revelation 21:1. In the heavenly realm there will be "no more sea." Yet both the Old and New Testaments do contain many references to ships and shipping.

By about 2800 B.C., the nations of Egypt and Babylon, as well as Assyria, were involved in traffic on the Nile and the Tigris and Euphrates Rivers. From these rivers they eventually ventured into the Persian Gulf and the Mediterranean Sea. But the most venturesome sailors and international traders were the Phoenicians, who worked out of the port cities of Acco, Tyre, Sidon, and Byblos.

The judgment on Tyre recorded in Ezekiel 27, while coming a thousand years after the beginning of Tyrian trade, reflects the wealth this trade provided. Verses 12 to 25 list many nations that Tyre traded with and the many cargoes they brought.

Verses 5 to 11 describe the various parts of the ships and the materials from which they were made.

Merchant Ships. Merchant ships were of varying size. The smaller costal traders were from 19 to 22 meters (50 to 60 feet) long and 5 to 7 meters (15 to 20) feet wide. The larger ones that sailed the open water were frequently well over 38 meters (100 feet) long—sometimes as long as 66 meters (180 feet)—and up to 19 meters (50) feet wide. These ships were usually made of fir, pine, or cedar boards over a hardwood frame. The whole structure was held together with hardwood dowels.

Early Egyptian ships had no central keel. They were strengthened by a heavy rope fastened to the bow and stern and supported on three or four vertical posts stretching throughout the ship and kept taut with wooden levers. Keeled hulls appear to have been introduced by the Phoenicians.

Cargo ships usually had little space for passengers. Occasionally they would carry voyagers either on the open deck or in the hold with the cargo (Jon. 1:5). The biblical "ships of Tarshish" (2 Chr. 9:21, KJV) were these merchant vessels, large enough to carry considerable cargo and sturdy enough to survive the stormy open sea.

Egyptian ships usually had a single mast and a large rectangular sail, while Phoenician ships were usually double-masted with a large square sail on the mainmast and a smaller square sail on the foremast. Since the wind could be contrary, these ships were also equipped with banks of oars, although Phoenician ships in the 13th century B.C. still relied exclusively on sail power and used oars only for steering.

Egyptian cargo-vessels, since they were primarily river ships, made use of oars much earlier than those of the Phoenicians. Raised platforms at the bow for the navigator and the rear for the helmsman were usual features. Steering was done with one or two large paddles over the stern.

Warships. Warships (Is. 33:21) were of similar construction but of very different proportions, being anywhere from 38 to 55 meters (100 to 150 feet) long, but less than 7 meters (20 feet) wide. This ratio of length to width with as many as 50 oars in two rows on each side made for a very fast ship. Some of the older vessels were powered by five banks of oars on each side, but these were difficult to maneuver in the heat of battle. These multiple rows of oars soon gave way to three banks and eventually two.

Except for the Egyptian craft, warships usually had single or double rams built into the prow at the water line. With two or even three decks to carry armed soldiers, these war vessels could be formidable instruments of destruction.

Warships as well as cargo vessels frequently had carved or painted figureheads of animals, plants, or pagan gods on the bow and stern.

Israelite Ships. Israel did not have a naval fleet except for a short time during the reign of Solomon. As part of the great expansion in international trade during his reign, Solomon contracted with Hiram of Tyre to build the nation of Israel a fleet of cargo and naval vessels and to provide sailors to man them (1 Kin. 9:26–28; 10:22; 2 Chr. 8:18; 9:21).

Solomon's maritime trade took his ships down the coast of Africa and as far east as India. This trade probably continued, although on a smaller scale, until the fleet was wrecked in fulfillment of the prophecy of Eliezer (2 Chr. 20:37).

The fishing vessels used on the Sea of Galilee in Jesus' time were large enough to accommodate all

Model of a grain ship, used by the Romans in commercial trading.

Photo: Haifa Maritime Museum

the disciples (Matt. 8:23–27), but small enough to be in danger of sinking under the weight of a large catch of fish (Luke 5:7). There is no record of how these boats were constructed. But it appears from some biblical accounts (Mark 6:48) that they did not have sails. They apparently depended upon the rowing efforts of the crew to maneuver the vessel. Luke 5:2, John 6:17–22, and John 21:8 distinguish between "boats" and "little boats," but scholars are not sure of the exact difference between the two.

Paul's Shipwreck. Paul's trip to Rome recorded in Acts 27 is one of the most complete accounts of a sea voyage from ancient times. The account indicates that the ship they traveled on was carrying a cargo of grain (v. 38) from Alexandria to Rome. In addition to the cargo, it carried a total of 276 passengers and crew, including the guard under the centurion Julius (vv. 1, 37).

The ship was probably a double–master (vv. 17, 40), with possibly an extra topsail on the main mast. Four anchors were carried in the stern (v. 29). An additional two or more anchors were carried on the prow (v. 30). A small skiff or rowboat (vv. 16, 30) was standard equipment for use when the ship was in harbor. Normally it was towed behind the ship. But it would be brought on board during storms to keep it from being destroyed or swamped (v. 16).

Navigation depended on visual sightings of the sun or stars (v. 20). The depth of the water was checked by a sounding line (v. 28).

The heavy seas threatened to break up the ship. The hull was strengthened by passing ropes around the beam and tightening them with wooden levers. Ships may have carried net-like webs for use in such emergencies, although ordinary ropes could be pressed into service if needed. A similar arrangement is known from Egyptian ships as early as 2500 B.C.

When the ship finally did run aground, the passengers escaped by using broken pieces of the ship as life preservers (v. 44). The dangers of winter navigation are clearly indicated in this account. But God's providence in rescuing Paul and the other people on the ship also comes through clearly in the graphic narrative.

SHIPWRECK — the destruction or loss of a ship at sea. The apostle Paul declared that he had been involved in three shipwrecks (2 Cor. 11:25). The same word is also used figuratively of an irretrievable loss or a complete failure by those who renounced Christianity (1 Tim. 1:19).

SHIPWRIGHT (see OCCUPATIONS AND TRADES).

SHIRT (see DRESS OF THE BIBLE).

SHISHA [SHIGH shuh] (meaning unknown) — the father of Elihoreth and Ahijah, scribes in Solomon's administration (1 Kin. 4:3). Also see SHAVSHA.

SHISHAK [SHIGH shak] — a Libyan war chieftain who became Pharaoh of Egypt (reigned from about 940 B.C. to about 915 B.C.). Shishak is known for his expedition against the southern kingdom of Judah after the United Kingdom split into two nations following Solomon's death about 920 B.C.

In about 926 B.C., in the fifth year of the reign of King Rehoboam (reigned about 931–913 B.C.), Shishak invaded Judah and captured many of its fortified cities (1 Kin. 14:25). He then marched against Jerusalem, Rehoboam's capital city, forcing Rehoboam to pay tribute and plundering the treasures of the Temple and Rehoboam's palace (1 Kin. 14:25–26).

The Egyptian account of Shishak's invasion of Judah was recorded on the wall of the temple of the Egyptian god Amon at Karnak (ancient Thebes), in southern Egypt. More than 150 cities captured or destroyed by Shishak are listed, including Adoraim, Aijalon, and Socoh. Cities from the northern kingdom of Israel, such as Shechem, Beth Shean, and Megiddo, are also listed on this monument as being captured by Shishak.

SHITRAI [SHIT righ] (*Jehovah is deciding*) — the chief shepherd over the royal herds in Sharon during David's administration (1 Chr. 27:29).

SHITTAH TREE (see PLANTS OF THE BIBLE).

SHITTIM [SHIT em] (see ACACIA GROVE).

SHITTIM WOOD (see PLANTS OF THE BIBLE).

SHIZA [SHIGH zuh] (meaning unknown) — father of Adina (1 Chr. 11:42).

SHOA [SHOE uh] (meaning unknown) — an unknown people mentioned by the prophet Ezekiel as one of many who would rise against Judah (Ezek. 23:23).

SHOBAB [SHOE bab] (*backsliding*) — the name of two men in the Old Testament:
1. A son born to David by Bathsheba after he became king (2 Sam. 5:14).
2. A member of the family of Hezron, of the house of Caleb (1 Chr. 2:18).

SHOBACH [SHOE bak] (meaning unknown) — commander of the army of HADADEZER, king of Zobah in David's time (2 Sam. 10:16, 18). Israel was victorious in battle, and Shobach was killed. Shobach is also called Shophach (1 Chr. 19:16, 18).

SHOBAI [SHOE bigh] (meaning unknown) — a Levite who founded a family of tabernacle gatekeepers. Shobai's descendants returned from the Captivity with Zerubbabel (Neh. 7:45).

SHOBAL [SHOE buhl] (meaning unknown) — the name of two or three men in the Old Testament:
1. A son of Seir the Horite (Gen. 36:20).
2. A son of Hur (1 Chr. 2:50, 52). Shobal was the founder of Kirjath Jearim (1 Chr. 2:50, 52).
3. A descendant of Judah (1 Chr. 4:1–2). He may be the same person as Shobal No. 2.

SHOBEK [SHOE bek] (*free*) — a Jewish chief who

sealed the covenant under Nehemiah after the Captivity (Neh. 10:24).

SHOBI [SHOE bigh] (meaning unknown) — a son of Nahash from Rabbah of the Ammonites (2 Sam. 17:27). Shobi provided supplies for David's army in their campaign against Absalom.

SHOCHO, SHOCHOH, SHOCO [SHOW koe] — forms of SOCHOH.

SHOE (see DRESS OF THE BIBLE).

SHOFAR [show FAR] (see RAM'S HORN).

SHOHAM [SHOW ham] (*a precious stone*) — a Levite who served in the tabernacle sanctuary during David's reign (1 Chr. 24:27).

SHOMER [SHOW mur] (*God is preserver*) — the name of a man and a woman in the Old Testament:
1. The mother of Jehozabad (2 Kin. 12:21), also called Shimrith (2 Chr. 24:26).
2. A son of Heber (1 Chr. 7:32), also called Shamer and Shemer (1 Chr. 7:34, KJV, RSV, NASB).

SHOPHACH [SHOW fack] — a form of SHOBACH.

SHOPHAN [SHOW fan] (meaning unknown) — a fortress city east of the Jordan River (Num. 32:35), exact site unknown.

SHOPHAR [show FAR] (see RAM'S HORN).

SHORE — land at the edge of a body of water. The word shore is used to describe the number of descendants that God promised to Abraham: "As the sand which is on the seashore" (Gen. 22:17). This speaking of people as grains of sand to indicate a host beyond counting is used vividly to describe the battle between Israel and the Canaanites (Josh. 11:4) and Saul's first major battle with the Philistine army (1 Sam. 13:5). Solomon's "largeness of heart," or the breadth and scope of his knowledge, is also compared to the sand on the seashore (1 Kin. 4:29).

SHOSHANNIM [show SHAN em] (see MUSIC OF THE BIBLE).

SHOULDER — the place on the human body where the arm is joined to the trunk. The shoulder is spoken of both literally and figuratively in the Bible. Abraham placed a waterskin on Hagar's shoulder before she departed for the Wilderness of Beersheba (Gen. 21:14). Rebekah bore a pitcher of water on her shoulder (Gen. 24:15, 45–46).

People who "shrugged their shoulders" also "stiffened their necks" and "stopped their ears so that they could not hear" (Neh. 9:29; Zech. 7:11). Such people refused the responsibility of keeping the law, preferring to rebel against God. The word shoulder is also used figuratively of destruction (Ezek. 29:7), servitude (Is. 10:27), deliverance from bondage (Ps. 81:6), and security (Deut. 33:12).

The New Testament uses the Greek word for shoulder only twice. Jesus said that the scribes and the Pharisees "bind heavy burdens, hard to bear,

and lay them on men's shoulders" (Matt. 23:4). In His parable of the lost sheep, Jesus described the joy of the shepherd when the sheep is found: "He lays it on his shoulders, rejoicing" (Luke 15:5).

SHOULDER PIECE — the shoulder straps which joined the front and back halves of the EPHOD, an apron–like garment worn by the high priest of Israel. The shoulder straps were engraved with the names of the twelve tribes of Israel (Ex. 28:5–14). Also see PRIEST, HIGH.

SHOVELS — ceremonial instruments used by priests in the tabernacle (Ex. 27:3) and in the Temple (Jer. 52:18) for placing coals on the altar and for removing the fat–soaked ashes. Archaeologists who excavated Megiddo found a 22-inch bronze shovel with a rectangular shape and a long, thin handle.

SHOWBREAD — holy or consecrated bread placed in the sanctuary of the tabernacle or Temple every Sabbath to symbolize God's presence and His provision for His people. The ritual always involved 12 loaves of bread, representing the 12 tribes of the nation of Israel. It was called showbread because it was kept continually before God's presence in the tabernacle.

The Levites descended through the family of Kohath were in charge of preparing the showbread each week. On each Sabbath they placed fresh bread on the table of showbread and removed the week–old bread from the sanctuary (1 Chr. 9:32). The older bread was eaten by the priests; whatever was left was burned with incense as an offering to the Lord (Lev. 24:5–9).

When David fled from King Saul, he and his men came to Nob, where the tabernacle was located. David and his men were hungry, but Ahimelech, the high priest, had no ordinary food. So David asked for the "holy bread," the showbread that had been taken from the Holy Place (1 Sam. 21:1–6).

When the Pharisees criticized Jesus' disciples for harvesting grain to eat as they walked through the fields on the Sabbath, Jesus reminded them of what David had done (Mark 2:25–26). In this situation, Jesus and His disciples were also hungry and in need of nourishment. This illustrated perfectly His teaching that human need often was more important than a legalistic keeping of the law. Or, as He declared to the Pharisees, "The Sabbath was made for man, and not man for the Sabbath" (Mark 2:27).

The showbread symbolized the continual presence of the Lord—a presence more vital than one's daily bread—and the people's dependence on God's provision for their spiritual and physical needs.

SHRINE — a sanctuary or sacred place set apart for worship. The Israelites worshiped God first in the tabernacle and later in the Temple after its completion by Solomon. But they never spoke of worshiping God in a shrine. This word was always used to describe the temples or sacred places where pagan gods were worshiped (Judg. 17:1–5). The prophet Ezekiel spoke of adulterous and idolatrous Jerusalem erecting a pagan shrine at every road and building (Ezek. 16:24, 31).

SHRIVELED HAND (see DISABILITIES AND DEFORMITIES).

SHUA [SHOO uh] (*prosperity*) — the name of two women in the Old Testament:
 1. The mother of one of Judah's wives (Gen. 38:2, 12; Shuah, KJV; 1 Chr. 2:3; Bathshua, NEB).
 2. A daughter of Heber (1 Chr. 7:32).

SHUAH [SHOO a] (*bow down*) — the name of two men in the Old Testament:
 1. A son of Abraham and Keturah, Abraham's concubine (1 Chr. 1:32).
 2. A brother of Chelub, of the tribe of Judah (1 Chr. 4:11, KJV, NEB; Shuhah, RSV, NIV, NASB).

SHUAL [SHOO al] (*fox*) — the name of a district and a man in the Old Testament:
 1. A district toward which the Philistines marched in the time of King Saul (1 Sam. 13:17).
 2. A son of Zophah, of the tribe of Asher (1 Chr. 7:36).

SHUBAEL [SHOO bale] (*captive of God*) — the name of two men in the Old Testament:
 1. A son of Amram (1 Chr. 24:20). Shubael had charge of the Temple treasures in David's time. He is also called Shebuel (1 Chr. 23:16; 26:24).
 2. One of the sons of Heman, of the tribe of Levi (1 Chr. 25:20). Shubael served as a sanctuary musician in David's time. He is also called Shebuel (1 Chr. 25:4).

SHUHAH [SHOO ha] (*bow down*) — a brother of Chelub (1 Chr. 4:11; Shuah, KJV, NEB).

SHUHAM [SHOO ham] (*depression*) — a son of Dan and founder of the SHUHAMITES (Num. 26:42), also called Hushim (Gen. 46:23).

SHUHAMITES [SHOO hum ites] — the descendants of SHUHAM, of the tribe of Dan (Num. 26:42).

SHUHITE [SHOO hite] — a descendant of SHUAH, son of Abraham and Keturah (Gen. 25:1–2; 1 Chr. 1:32). In the Bible the word Shuhite always occurs in the phrase Bildad the Shuhite (Job 2:11; 8:1; 18:1), one of Job's friends. The Shuhites may have lived in Suhu, a district in northern Syria.

SHULAMITE [SHOO lum ite] — a young woman mentioned in Song of Solomon 6:13 (Shulammite, RSV, NIV, NEB, NASB). Many scholars interpret Shulamite as Shunammite—a woman from the city of SHUNEM (1 Sam. 28:4). Others believe this woman was ABISHAG, the lovely young Shunammite brought to David in his old age (1 Kin. 1:1–4, 15) and who later apparently was a part of Solomon's harem (1 Kin. 2:17–22).

SHULAMMITE [SHOO lum ite] — a form of SHULAMITE.

SHUMATHITES [SHOO muh thites] — a family of Kirjath Jearim descended from Hur (1 Chr. 2:53).

SHUNAMMITE [SHOO nam ite] — a female native or inhabitant of SHUNEM. Two different Shunammites are mentioned in the Bible:
 1. ABISHAG, a lovely young woman who ministered to King David in his old age (1 Kin. 1:3, 15).
 2. A woman who befriended the prophet Elisha (2 Kin. 4:8–36).

SHUNEM [SHOO num] (*meaning unknown*) — a border city (see Map 3, B–2) allotted to the tribe of Issachar (Josh. 19:18). Shunem was about five kilometers (three miles) north of Jezreel, near Mount Gilboa. The site is present-day Solem or Sulam.

SHUNI [SHOO nih] (*meaning unknown*) — a son of Gad (Gen. 46:16) and founder and chief of a tribal family, the SHUNITES (Num. 26:15).

SHUNITES [SHOO nights] — a tribal family founded by SHUNI (Num. 26:15).

SHUPHAM [SHOO fam] (*serpent*) — a son of Benjamin (Num. 26:39; Shephupham, RSV) and founder of a tribal family, the SUPHAMITES (Num. 26:39). His name is also spelled Shephuphan (1 Chr. 8:5), Shuppim (1 Chr. 7:12, 15), and Muppim (Gen. 46:21).

SHUPHAMITES [SHOO fum ites] — the descendants of SHUPHAM (Num. 26:39).

SHUPPIM [SHUP em] (*serpent*) — the name of two men in the Old Testament:
 1. A descendant of Benjamin (1 Chr. 7:12, 15), also called Shupham (Num. 26:39), Shephuphan (1 Chr. 8:5), and Muppim (Gen. 46:21).
 2. A Levite gatekeeper of the tabernacle in David's time (1 Chr. 26:16).

SHUR [shoor] (*enclosure*) — a desert in the northwest part of the Sinai Peninsula (see Map 2, A–2) where the Angel of the Lord found Hagar by a spring in the wilderness (Gen. 16:7). Shur was probably a caravan route from Beersheba to Egypt known as Darb el Shur.
 The Wilderness of Shur must have been immediately east of the Red Sea. As soon as Moses brought the people of Israel from the Red Sea, they went out into the Wilderness of Shur (Ex. 15:22). Some scholars believe the name Shur (wall) comes from a series of fortifications built by the Egyptians on their northeastern frontier as a defense against invaders.

SHUSHAN [SHOO shan] (*meaning unknown*) — the ancient capital of Elam, in southwestern Iran; later a royal residence and capital of the Persian Empire (Neh. 1:1; Susa, NASB, NIV, RSV). The site is present-day Shush, about 240 kilometers (150 miles) north of the Persian Gulf.
 Long before the time of Abraham in the Old Testament, Shushan was the center of Elamite civilization. Some scholars believe it was a cult city

Photo by Howard Vos

Human headed winged sphinxes in enameled brick from a palace at Shushan.

centering around worship of one of the chief Elamite gods. The city had frequent contacts with Mesopotamia.

The Assyrian King Ashurbanipal (the biblical OSNAPPER, Ezra 4:10) led a military campaign against Shushan about 642–639 B.C. In about 640 B.C. he sacked the city and carried some of its inhabitants (Susanchites, Ezra 4:9, KJV) into exile in Samaria (v. 10).

When Cyrus the Great (reigned 550–529 B.C.) established the Persian Empire, he made Shushan its capital. At Shushan Darius the Great (ruled about 521–486 B.C.) built his magnificient royal palace. This palace, when occupied by Artaxerxes II (404–359 B.C.), figured prominently in the story of Esther. In fact, most of the events recorded in the Book of Esther took place in Shushan (Esth. 1:2–5; 2:3–8; 3:15; 4:8–16; 8:14–15; 9:6–18). It was in Shushan also that the prophet Daniel had his vision of the ram and the goat (Dan. 8:2) and where Nehemiah lived in exile (Neh. 1:1).

According to a tradition of the Shiite Muslims, the present–day village of Shush (ancient Shushan) is the site of the tomb of the prophet Daniel.

SHUSHAN EDUTH [SHOO shan EE duth] (see MUSIC OF THE BIBLE).

SHUTHALHITES [SHOO thul hites] — descendants of SHUTHELAH (Num. 26:35; Shuthelahites, RSV).

SHUTHELAH [SHOO thuh lah] (meaning unknown) — the name of two men in the Old Testament:

1. A son of Ephraim and founder of a tribal family, the SHUTHALHITES (Num. 26:35–36).

2. A descendant of Ephraim (1 Chr. 7:21).

SHUTHALHITES [SHOO thal hites] — the descendants of SHUTHELAH, of the tribe of Ephraim (Num. 26:35–36; 1 Chr. 7:20).

SHUTTLE — an instrument on a LOOM to which thread or yarn was attached and which was used to pull the thread back and forth for the weaving of fabric. Two men were required to operate the large upright Egyptian–type looms. Job used the word in a figurative sense: "My days are swifter than a weaver's shuttle" (Job 7:6).

SIA, SIAHA [SEE ah, SEE a hah] (*congregation*) — a family of NETHINIM (Temple servants) who returned with Zerubbabel from the Captivity (Siaha, Ezra 2:44; Sia, Neh. 7:47).

SIBBECAI [SIB uh kie] — a form of SIBBECHAI.

SIBBECHAI [SIB uh kie] (*Jehovah intervenes*) — one of David's mighty men (1 Chr. 11:29; Sibbecai, RSV). Sibbechai killed the giant Saph during a battle with the Philistines. Sibbechai is also called Mebunnai (2 Sam. 23:27).

SIBBOLETH [SIB oh lehth] — a form of SHIBBOLETH.

SIBMAH [SIB mah] — a form of SHEBAM.

SIBRAIM [sib RAH em] (*double hope*) — a city of Syria on the northern border of Palestine (Ezek. 47:16).

SIBYLLINE ORACLES [sib uh LEAN] (see APOCALYPTIC LITERATURE).

SICARII [sih KAH rih eye] — a word for ASSASSINS.

SIKKUTH [SICK kuhth] (see GODS, PAGAN).

SICK (see DISEASES OF THE BIBLE).

SICKLE (see TOOLS OF THE BIBLE).

SIDDIM [SID em] (*tilled fields*) — a valley at the southern end of the Dead Sea where Chedorlaomer and his allies defeated the kings of the five cities of the plain—Sodom, Gomorrah, Admah, Zeboiim, and Zoar (Gen. 14:3, 8, 10). The Valley of Siddim was full of asphalt pits (bitumen pits, RSV), which became a death–trap to those who fled from Chedorlaomer.

The most likely site of this valley is the area south of the peninsula that juts out from the east shore of the Dead Sea. Some scholars believe this peninsula once extended all the way across the Dead Sea and that the area south of it was the Valley of Siddim.

SIDE — the right or left part of the trunk of the body. Warriors wore their swords at their sides (Neh. 4:18). God ordered the prophet Ezekiel to lie on his side as a symbolic action (Ezek. 4:4–9). Blood and water gushed from Jesus' side when He was pierced with a spear, proving He was truly dead (John 19:34).

SIDON [SIGH dun] (*a fishery*) — an ancient Phoenician city on the Mediterranean coast in northern Palestine (see Map 3, B–1). Sidon dominated the coastal plain in the area of the Lebanon Mountains. Built on a hill across several small islands, it was connected by bridges.

Sidon was the oldest of the Phoenician cities. Founded by the son of Canaan (Gen. 10:15), it became a principal Canaanite stronghold (Gen. 10:19; 1 Chr. 1:13; Zidon, KJV). So dominant was Sidon originally that Sidonian and Phoenician became interchangeable terms. Even after the city of Tyre on the coast to the south assumed a position of dominance, Ethbaal, king of Tyre, was called king of the Sidonians (1 Kin. 16:31).

After the Israelites settled the land of Canaan, Sidon was near the territory of Zebulun (Gen. 49:13) and Asher (Josh. 19:28). But the tribe of Asher failed to drive out the inhabitants of Sidon (Judg. 1:31). This indicates something of the strength of the city. Sidon, however, frequently was destroyed by foreign invaders during the next several centuries. But it was rebuilt following each defeat and restored to a position of prominence.

By the time of ALEXANDER the Great in the third century B.C., Sidon was still a major Phoenician city. Alexander was received by the Sidonians as a deliverer, and they assisted Alexander as he besieged their neighboring city of Tyre. Later, under Roman rule Sidon was given the privilege of self–government, which it enjoyed during New Testament times.

Not only did the city of Sidon resist the efforts of the tribe of Asher to inhabit that region, but it also oppressed Israel during the period of the judges (Judg. 10:12). Once they were settled in the land, the Israelites began to worship the gods of Sidon, including their chief god Baal (1 Kin. 16:31) but especially Ashtoreth, the goddess of fertility (2 Kin. 23:13). Ethbaal, the king of Sidon, was the father of JEZEBEL (1 Kin. 16:31), who was mainly responsible for introducing the worship of pagan gods into Israel.

The people of Sidon came to Galilee to hear the preaching of Christ and to be healed by His touch (Mark 3:8; Luke 6:17). Jesus even went to the borders of Tyre and Sidon (Matt. 15:21–28; Mark 7:24–31), where He healed the Syro–Phoenician woman's daughter. Herod Agrippa I was displeased by the people of Tyre and Sidon, but they won over his servant Blastus and begged for peace "because their country was supplied with food by the king's country" (Acts 12:20).

The apostle Paul stopped briefly at Sidon on his way to Rome, meeting with Christian friends there (Acts 27:3). In early Christian history, the city became an important Christian center, sending a bishop to the Council of Nicea in A.D. 325.

Frequently Sidon was the subject of prophecies of judgment. Isaiah predicted that Sidon would pass into the hands of Cyprus (Is. 23:12). Jeremiah predicted its defeat by Nebuchadnezzar, king of Babylon (Jer. 27:3, 6). Ezekiel denounced Sidon (Ezek. 28:20–24) because her inhabitants had been "a pricking brier [and] a painful thorn for the house of Israel" (Ezek. 28:24). Joel denounced Sidon for helping to plunder Jerusalem (Joel 3:4–6).

In the eighth century B.C. Sidon was noted for its artistic metalwork and skilled tradesmen who made objects of silver and gold. Like the citizens of Tyre, the Sidonians were also known for their purple dye. The art of glass blowing was in evidence in the first century B.C. at Sidon. In the first century learned Sidonians were also noted for their study in the sciences of astronomy and arithmetic. Sidon also had a law school that was famed throughout the ancient world.

SIDONIANS [sigh DAWN ih uns] (see SIDON).

SIEGE — a prolonged military blockade of a city

Modern harbor of Sidon. The ancient Phoenician city of Sidon was one of the most important seaports on the Mediterranean coast.

Photo by Gustav Jeeninga

or fortress to force it to surrender. The purpose of a siege was to take away the advantage of the city's massive defensive walls by cutting off its supplies and contacts from the outside. Without supplies, the defending city would be forced to surrender or to attack the besieging army.

The attacking army would sometimes press the siege by trying to scale the walls with ladders or ramps. Other techniques included battering down the walls or tunneling under them. But attack was dangerous because the city's defenders were well protected and could carry on the battle from a superior position.

A siege might continue for several months. To shorten a siege, the attacking army usually tried to capture a city's water supplies. These were usually situated outside the city walls.

Much of the warfare described in the Old Testament is siege warfare. For instance, Joab laid siege to Rabbah (2 Sam. 12:26–31) and Sennacherib besieged Jerusalem and all the fortified cities of Judah (Is. 36:1). In the New Testament Jesus predicted the Roman siege of Jerusalem (Luke 19:43–44).

SIEVE (see TOOLS OF THE BIBLE).

SIGN — something that points to, or represents, something larger or more important than itself. The word is used in this way to refer to a wide variety of things in the Bible. But by far the most important use of the word is in reference to the acts of God. Thus, it is often linked with "wonders." In the Old Testament most references point to the miracles produced by God to help deliver the Hebrew people from slavery in Egypt (Ex. 7:3; Is. 8:18).

In the New Testament the word signs is linked with both "wonders" and "miracles" (Acts 2:22; 2 Cor. 12:12; Heb. 2:4). Signs point primarily to the powerful, saving activity of God as experienced through the ministry of Jesus and the apostles. The word occurs frequently in the Gospel of John, pointing to the deeper, symbolic meaning of the miracles performed by Jesus. Throughout the Bible the true significance of a sign is understood only through faith.

SIGNET — a seal or ring used by an official much like a personal signature to give authority to a document. The Old Testament indicates several uses of the ring seal.

Pharaoh gave his ring to Joseph (Gen. 41:42) as a badge of his delegated authority. Ahasuerus gave his ring to the wicked Haman (Esth. 3:10, 12), then gave it to Mordecai after Haman's treachery was exposed (Esth. 8:2). King Darius of Persia sealed the lion's den after Daniel was placed in it (Dan. 6:17).

The signet was an emblem of royal authority (Gen. 41:42). Zerubbabel, who had been chosen by God to lead the returned captives in Jerusalem (Hag. 2:23), was compared to a signet ring, signifying that God had invested him with the highest honor.

Also see SEAL.

SIGNPOST — a sign with information or direc-

tions for travelers. The prophet Jeremiah encouraged the citizens of Judah to set up signposts (Jer. 31:21; waymarks, KJV, RSV; road signs, NIV) to mark their route into Babylon so they could return to Israel by the same route once the CAPTIVITY was over.

SIHON [SIGH hun] (meaning unknown) — a king of the Amorites defeated by the Israelites during their journey toward the land of Canaan. Moses asked Sihon to let the Israelites pass peacefully through his kingdom, located east of the Jordan River. Sihon refused and later attacked the Israelites at Jahaz. In the battle that followed Sihon and his army were killed (Num. 21:21–32), and his territory was given to the tribes of Gad and Reuben (Num. 32:33). Sihon's defeat is mentioned often in the Old Testament (Deut. 1:4; Josh. 2:10; Ps. 135:11; Jer. 48:45).

SIHOR [SIGH hawr] — a form of SHIHOR.

SIKKUTH [SICK uth] — a Babylonian god mentioned by the prophet Amos (Amos 5:26; Sakkuth, RSV). Some scholars identify Sikkuth with Ninurta, the god of war and chase. Also see GODS, PAGAN.

SILAS [SIGH lus] (*person of the woods*) — a prominent member of the early church at Jerusalem and companion of the apostle Paul. Silas accompanied Paul to Antioch of Syria to report the decision of the Jerusalem Council to accept Gentile Christians into the church (Acts 15:22, 27, 32).

Paul chose Silas as his companion on his second missionary journey. During their travels, Paul and Silas were imprisoned at Philippi (Acts 16:19, 25, 29). Silas and Paul were also together during the riot at Thessalonica (Acts 17:4). Later they were sent to Berea, where Silas remained with Timothy; both Silas and Timothy soon followed Paul to Athens (Acts 17:14–15), although they may not have caught up with him until reaching Corinth (Acts 18:5). Silas played an important role in the early Christian work in Corinth.

In his letters, Paul referred to Silas as Silvanus (1 Thess. 1:1, 2 Thess. 1:1). The time, place, and manner of his death are unknown.

SILENCE — the absence of noise or sound. The word silence is used in the Bible to symbolize death (Ps. 94:17) and SHEOL (Ps. 115:17). Silence can express a mood of gloom and despair, as after the destruction of Jerusalem (Lam. 2:10). Silence can also express fear and reverence: "The Lord is in His holy temple. Let all the earth keep silence before Him" (Hab. 2:20).

SILK — cloth woven from thread that was made from the Chinese silk worm. Although the word silk occurs a few times in the KJV and the NKJV, many scholars think the Hebrew word for silk should be rendered "fine linen" or "costly fabric" (Ezek. 16:10, 13; Prov. 31:22).

The use of silk among the Egyptians is unknown, but it did appear among the Chinese and other people of ancient Asia. From the earliest times trade existed between India and China on the one hand and India and the Mesopotamian valley on the other. So it is possible that Solomon's extensive trade could have brought silk to Palestine. Certainly after the campaigns of Alexander the Great, silk reached the Near East.

As one of the finest and most vividly colored fabrics, silk was highly prized. The rich and powerful people called the Babylonians wore it, according to Revelation 18:12. At one time people of the ancient world bought silk for its weight in gold (around A.D. 275).

SILLA [SILL ah] (meaning unknown) — an unknown place near Jerusalem where Joash (or Jehoash), king of Judah, was killed by his servants (2 Kin. 12:20).

SILOAM [sigh LOW um] (*sent*) — a storage pool and water tunnel that provided a water supply for early residents of the city of Jerusalem. The pool and tunnel drew water from the GIHON spring outside the city wall.

Under the peril of an impending invasion by the armies of Sennacherib, king of Assyria (reigned about 705–681 B.C.), King Hezekiah of Judah "made a pool and a tunnel [or conduit] and brought water into the city" (2 Kin. 20:20). The parallel account in 2 Chronicles says he "stopped the water outlet of Upper Gihon, and brought the water by tunnel to the west side of the City of David" (2 Chr. 32:30).

Hezekiah's tunnel was discovered accidentally in 1838 and was explored by the American traveler, Edward Robinson, and his missionary friend, Eli Smith. They found the Siloam tunnel to be about 518 meters (1,750 feet) long, although the straight line distance between the storage pool and the Gihon spring is only 332 meters (1,090 feet). The course has numerous twists and turns. Some scholars have suggested that by following such a crooked course, the tunnel builders were trying to avoid the royal tombs cut into the same area through which the conduit was cut. But it is just as possible that more accurate surveying methods were unavailable to Hezekiah's technicians. By any standards, however, Hezekiah's tunnel was a notable achievement.

The tunnel was explored in 1867, but it was not until 1880 that an important Hebrew inscription was discovered near the entrance to the reservoir. It gave a graphic description of how the tunnel was built. Two work crews cut the tunnel through solid rock, working from opposite ends until they met in the middle.

It may have been through another tunnel or gap such as this that David's warriors entered the ancient city of Jerusalem about 1002 B.C. The city was known as Jebus at that time. David captured it and turned it into the capital city of his kingdom.

The Bible does contain some puzzling references to a more ancient pool. The prophet Isaiah, for instance, speaks of Hezekiah's "reservoir between the

The tunnel of Siloam was dug through solid rock to insure a supply of water to Jerusalem in case of an Assyrian attack.

two walls for the water of the old pool" (Is. 22:11). Perhaps Hezekiah and his craftsmen used an existing reservoir and linked it to his tunnel and pool.

SILOAM, TOWER OF [sigh LOW um] — a tower near the Pool of Siloam inside the walls of Jerusalem. The exact site of this tower is unknown. In the time of Christ, a local disaster in which 18 lives were lost by a collapse of this structure was fresh in the minds of the people (Luke 13:4). Also see SILOAM.

SILOAM, VILLAGE OF [suh LOW ahm] — although this village is not mentioned in the Bible, there exists today a village of Siloam (Silwan), situated across the valley from the Gihon spring. Some scholars believe the tower of Siloam (Luke 13:4) was located at this site. Also see GIHON; SILOAM, TOWER OF.

SILVANUS [sill VAIN us] — a form of SILAS.

SILVER (see MINERALS OF THE BIBLE).

SILVERLING — another word for the standard silver coin used as a medium of exchange during Bible times. The word appears only once in the Bible (Is. 7:23, KJV). Also see MONEY.

SILVER, PIECE OF (see MONEY OF THE BIBLE).

SILVERSMITH (see OCCUPATIONS AND TRADES).

SIMEON [SIM ih un] (*God hears*) — the name of four men in the Bible:

1. The second son of Jacob and Leah (Gen. 29:33). Simeon's descendants became one of the twelve tribes of Israel. He and his brother Levi tricked the Hivites of Shechem and massacred all the males because one of them had raped Dinah, their sister (Gen. 34:2, 25, 30). Simeon was the brother whom Joseph kept as security when he al-

lowed his brothers to leave Egypt and return to their father Jacob in the land of Canaan (Gen. 42:24).

2. A devout Jew who blessed the infant Jesus in the Temple (Luke 2:25, 34). The Holy Spirit had promised Simeon that he would not die until he had seen the long-awaited Messiah. Simeon recognized the child as the Messiah when Mary and Joseph brought him to the Temple to present Him to the Lord.

3. An ancestor of Joseph listed in the genealogy of Jesus Christ (Luke 3:30).

4. A Christian prophet or teacher in the church at Antioch of Syria (Acts 13:1). Some scholars believe Simeon was the same person as Simon of Cyrene, who bore Jesus' cross (Luke 23:26).

SIMEON, TRIBE OF — One of the twelve tribes of Israel, descended from Simeon No. 1 (Rev. 7:7). Simeon had six sons—Jemuel (Nemuel), Jamin, Ohad, Jachin (Jerib), Zohar (Zerah), and Shaul—and all but Ohad founded tribal families (Ex. 6:15).

The tribe of Simeon numbered 59,300 fighting men at the first census in the wilderness (Num. 1:23; 2:13) and 22,200 at the second (Num. 26:12–14). This tribe was omitted in Moses' blessing of the nation of Israel (Deut. 33). A comparison of the cities assigned to Simeon with those assigned to Judah (Josh. 15:20–63; 19:1–9; 1 Chr. 4:28–33) makes it appear that the tribe of Simeon had been assimilated into the tribe of Judah, thus fulfilling Jacob's prophecy (Gen. 49:5–7).

When the land of Canaan was divided, the second lot fell to Simeon. The tribe received land in the extreme southern part of Canaan, in the middle of Judah's territory (Josh. 19:1–9). Simeon united with Judah in fighting the Canaanites (Judg. 1:1, 3, 17). Among the Simeonite cities were Beersheba, Hormah, and Ziklag (Josh. 19:1–9). Although the descendants of Simeon disappeared as a tribe, Ezekiel mentions it in his prophecies about a future land of Canaan (Ezek. 48:24–25, 33). The Book of Revelation mentions 12,000 of the tribe of Simeon who were sealed (Rev. 7:7).

SIMEONITES [SIMM ee un ites] — the descendants of SIMEON, the second son of Jacob and Leah (Gen. 29:33; Num. 25:14; 1 Chr. 27:16).

SIMILITUDE — a similarity or resemblance. James pointed out that with the tongue, we sometimes both bless and condemn people "who have been made in the similitude of God" (James 3:9). This is a reference to the image of God in man (Gen. 1:26–27). By referring to the original creation story, James emphasized the seriousness of the sin of the tongue; it violates God's creation.

SIMON [SIME un] (*God has heard*) — the name of nine men in the New Testament:

1. Simon Peter, the Galilean fisherman who became an apostle of Christ (Matt. 4:18; 10:2). Simon was the son of Jonah (Matt. 16:17; John 21:15) and a brother of the apostle ANDREW (John 1:40). Also see PETER, SIMON.

2. Another of the Twelve, called the Canaanite to distinguish him from Simon Peter. The name may also indicate he was a member of a fanatical Jewish sect, the ZEALOTS (Matt. 10:4; Mark 3:18; Luke 6:15; Acts 1:13). Members of this group were fanatical opponents of Roman rule in Palestine. As a Zealot, Simon would have hated any foreign domination or interference.

3. One of Jesus' brothers (Matt. 13:55).

4. A former leper in whose house Mary, the sister of Lazarus, anointed Jesus' feet with a precious ointment (Matt. 26:6–13; Mark 14:3–9; John 12:1–8). Mary, Martha, and Lazarus were present when this happened, and Martha took an active part in serving the dinner. This has led to speculation that Simon was a member of the family or at least was a very close friend.

5. A man of Cyrene who was forced to carry Jesus' cross (Matt. 27:32; Mark 15:21; Luke 23:26). Simon was the father of Alexander and Rufus, men who were known to the early Christians in Rome (Rom. 16:13).

6. A Pharisee in whose house Jesus ate (Luke 7:36–50). On that occasion a woman who was a sinner anointed Jesus' feet. Simon felt that Jesus should not have allowed her to come near Him. But Jesus explained that sinners like her were the very ones who needed forgiveness.

7. The father of Judas Iscariot (John 13:2). Both father and son are called Iscariot. The RSV has "Judas the son of Simon Iscariot" (John 6:71; 13:26).

8. A sorcerer known as Simon Magus, or Simon the magician, who tried to buy spiritual powers from the apostle Peter (Acts 8:9–24). Simon's feats were so impressive that the people of Samaria declared, "This man is the great power of God" (Acts 8:10) and followed him. But when Philip the evangelist preached, the Samaritans believed and were baptized. Simon also believed and was baptized.

Later the apostles Peter and John visited Samaria to make sure these believers received the power of the Holy Spirit. When Simon saw that the Holy Spirit was bestowed by the laying on of hands, he attempted to buy this power. Peter rebuked him, "Your money perish with you, because you thought that the gift of God could be purchased with money! You have neither part nor portion in this matter, for your heart is not right in the sight of God" (Acts 8:20–21).

9. A tanner of Joppa and friend of the apostle Peter (Acts 9:43; 10:6, 17, 32).

SIMON MACCABAEUS [mack kuh BEE us] (see MACCABEES, THE).

SIMON PETER (see PETER, SIMON).

SIMPLICITY— NKJV word used in both a negative and a positive way:

1. A lack of good sense or intelligence; foolishness or ignorance (Prov. 1:22).

2. The absence of pretense and hypocrisy (Acts 2:46; 2 Cor. 1:12; 11:3).

SIMRI [SIM rih] — a form of SHIMRI.

SIN — lawlessness (1 John 3:4) or transgression of God's will, either by omitting to do what God's law requires or by doing what it forbids. The transgression can occur in thought (1 John 3:15), word (Matt. 5:22), or deed (Rom. 1:32).

Mankind was created without sin, morally upright and inclined to do good (Eccl. 7:29). But sin entered into human experience when Adam and Eve violated the direct command of God by eating the forbidden fruit in the Garden of Eden (Gen. 3:6). Because Adam was the head and representative of the whole human race, his sin affected all future generations (Rom. 5:12–21). Associated with this guilt is a corrupted nature passed from Adam to all his descendants. Out of this perverted nature arise all the sins that people commit (Matt. 15:19); no person is free from involvement in sin (Rom. 3:23).

God is holy and cannot sin (James 1:13). Jesus Christ, the Son of God who came to earth in human form, is also sinless. His perfection arises from His divine nature, as well as His human nature (1 Pet. 2:22). Although the story of the Bible focuses on the sin of mankind and God's provision for our redemption, the angels are also described as capable of sinning. Some have fallen away from God's service (Jude 6). But animals are not morally responsible creatures; so they cannot sin.

Mankind originally fell into sin at the temptation of Satan. As the tempter, he continues to lure people into sin (1 Pet. 5:8); nevertheless, people remain fully responsible for what they do. God is not the author of sin, but His plan for world redemption does include His dealing with the reality of sin (2 Sam. 24:1; 1 Chr. 21:1). This truth is dramatically witnessed in the death of Jesus Christ. The crucifixion happened according to God's will; but at the same time, it was the worst crime of human history (Acts 2:23).

Sin is not represented in the Bible as the absence of good, or as an illusion that stems from our human limitations. Sin is portrayed as a real and positive evil. Sin is more than unwise, inexpedient, calamitous behavior that produces sorrow and distress. It is rebellion against God's law—the standard of righteousness (Ps. 119:160).

Since God demands righteousness, sin must be defined in terms of mankind's relation to God. Sin is thus the faithless rebellion of the creature against the just authority of his Creator. For this reason, breaking God's law at any point involves transgression at every point (James 2:10).

Violation of the law of God in thought, word, and deed shows the sinfulness of the human heart. Sin is actually a contradiction to the holiness of God, whose image mankind bears. This depraved condition is called "original sin" because it comes from Adam and characterizes all persons from the moment of their birth.

The moral depravity of mankind is total in that "the carnal mind is enmity against God; for it is not subject to the law of God, nor indeed can be" (Rom. 8:7). Apart from Christ, all are "dead in trespasses and sins" (Eph. 2:1). But this does not mean that people behave as wickedly as they might, for God restrains the outworkings of the sinful heart. At times He even helps sinners to do things that conform to the law (Gen. 20:6). The corruption of sin is not developed or expressed to the same degree in every person. Neither is it expressed in the same way in any person at all times.

Sin involves the denial of the living God from whom human beings draw their life and existence (Acts 17:28); the consequence of this revolt is death and the torment of hell. Death is the ultimate penalty imposed by God for sin (Rom. 6:23).

Against this dark background of sin and its reality, the gospel comes as the good news of the deliverance that God has provided through His Son. Jesus bears the penalty of sin in place of His people (Mark 10:45). He also redeems us from lawlessness and makes us long for good works in service to God and others (Titus 2:14).

SIN [sin] (*the moon–god*) — the name of a wilderness and a city in the Old Testament:

1. A wilderness through which the Israelites passed on their journey toward Mount Sinai (Ex. 16:1; 17:1; Num. 33:11–12). In the Wilderness of Sin the children of Israel murmured against Moses and Aaron. The Lord sent quail and manna to feed the people. The Wilderness of Sin should not be confused with the Wilderness of Zin (Num. 13:21; 27:14; Josh. 15:1, 3).

2. A city of Egypt on the eastern side of the Nile (Ezek. 30:15–16). It is possibly Pelusium (Ezek. 30:15–16, RSV), or Tell Farama; but it also has been identified with Syene (Ezek. 30:16, NEB), which is present–day Aswan in Egypt.

SIN, MAN OF (see ANTICHRIST).

SIN OFFERING (see SACRIFICIAL OFFERINGS).

SIN, UNPARDONABLE (see HOLY SPIRIT, SIN AGAINST).

SIN, WILDERNESS OF (see SIN No. 1).

SINAI [SIGH nih eye] (meaning unknown) — the name of a peninsula, a wilderness, and a mountain in the Bible (see Map 9, B–5). All three of these played a prominent role in the life of God's Covenant People as they searched for the Land of Promise following their miraculous deliverance from enslavement in Egypt.

The Peninsula. Shaped like a triangle, the peninsula of Sinai is an area of great contrasts. It appears to hang from the southeast corner of the Mediterranean Sea with its base serving as the land bridge between Egypt and Israel. The peninsula is bounded on the west by the Gulf of Suez and on the east by the Gulf of Aqaba.

The Sinai peninsula is about 240 kilometers (150 miles) wide at the northern end and about 400 kilometers (250 miles) long. Its land area is wilderness and a tableland rising to about 762 meters (2,500

Photo by Ben Chapman

The Wilderness of Sinai. Three months after leaving Egypt, the Israelites arrived in this rugged, barren region (Ex. 19:1-2).

feet). On the north the Sinai plateau slopes away to the Mediterranean Sea. Near the south end of the peninsula a series of granite mountains rise 1,209 to 2,743 meters (4,000 to 9,000 feet) high, in striking contrast to the surrounding wastelands.

The Wilderness. Exodus 19:1 indicates that "in the third month after the children of Israel had gone out of the land of Egypt, on the same day, they came to the Wilderness of Sinai." This phrase may refer only to the particular wilderness which lies at the foot of Mount Sinai and in which the Israelites pitched their camp. But the phrase may also refer in a broader sense to the entire wilderness area of the Sinai Peninsula. If this is the case, it would include the Wilderness of Sin, through which the Israelites passed between Elim and Mount Sinai (Ex. 16:1); the Wilderness of Paran, in the central Sinaitic Peninsula (Num. 10:12); the Wilderness of Shur, east of Egypt in the northern Sinai (Gen. 16:7); and the Wilderness of Zin, close to the border of Canaan (Num. 13:21).

The Mountain. Perhaps the most frequent use of the word "Sinai" is in connection with the mountain. This was the mountain where God met Moses and gave him the Law (Ex. 19:3, 20). This mountain is to be identified with Mount Horeb (Ex. 3:1), or perhaps Horeb refers to a mountain range or ridge and Sinai to an individual summit on that ridge. The name Sinai is used at the time when the Israelites were actually at the foot of the mountain (Ex. 19:11), whereas Horeb is used upon reflection about the events that happened here.

Although several mountains have been identified as possibilities, there are only two serious contenders for the title—Jebel Serbal (2,070 meters; 6,791 feet) in central Sinai and Jebel Musa (2,286 meters; about 7,500 feet) in southern Sinai. One of a cluster of three peaks, Jebel Musa has a broad plain at its base, where the Israelites may have camped.

Biblical References. After the Israelites left Egypt, they camped first in the Wilderness of Sin, then at Rephidim, and finally at Sinai. Moses climbed the mountain and received the tablets of the Law from God. When he came down, a thick cloud shielded the glory that shone from his face (Ex. 19:11, 16). A stirring atmospheric disturbance accompanied God's meeting with the people (Ex. 19:17—20:18).

During their years of wandering in the Sinai wilderness, the census was taken (Num. 1:1-46), the firstborn were redeemed (Num. 3:40-51), the office and duties of the Levites were established (Num. 4:1-49), and the first tabernacle was built (Num. 9:15).

SINCERITY — freedom from hypocrisy; purity of motive. The apostle Paul compared sincerity to unleavened bread (1 Cor. 5:8), a biblical symbol of purity. The sincerity with which a Christian conducts his life is a testimony to his godliness (2 Cor. 1:12).

SINEW — fibrous tissue that connects muscles to bones in the body. The word sinew is used literally in passages such as Job 10:11; 30:17 (KJV); 40:17;

and Ezekiel 37:6, 8. In Isaiah 48:4 an "iron sinew" is a figure of speech for rebellion. The Israelites' custom was to cut away the sinew of the thigh joint of meat before cooking it (Gen. 32:32, KJV, RSV). This was in memory of Jacob's wrestling with the angel, in which the angel injured Jacob's thigh to gain an advantage in the struggle (Gen. 32:24–31).

SINGER (see OCCUPATIONS AND TRADES; MUSIC).

SINGING (see MUSIC OF THE BIBLE).

SINGLENESS OF HEART — undivided purpose; total dedication and commitment (2 Chr. 30:12; one heart, KJV, RSV, NASB; unity of mind, NIV).

SINIM [SIH nem] (meaning unknown) — a land from which the scattered Israelites were to be gathered, according to the prophet Isaiah (Is. 49:12). It probably refers to Syene, present–day Aswan in southern Egypt.

SINITE [SIGH night] — a tribe of Canaanites in northern Phoenicia (modern Lebanon; 1 Chr. 1:15). Some scholars believe the Sinites were inhabitants of Sin, a city near Arka at the foot of Mount Lebanon, now in ruins.

SINNER — any person who sins. Because sin is natural to man, every person sins and must be considered a sinner (Rom. 3:23).

Many times in the Bible, the word sinner is contrasted with the term righteous. God told Noah he was righteous (Gen. 7:1), but, by definition, Noah was also a sinner. Although Noah did fall into sin (Gen. 9:21), his attitude toward God and what is right made him a "righteous" man.

Jesus also contrasted sinner with righteous. He said, "I did not come to call the righteous, but sinners, to repentance" (Mark 2:17). In this verse the term sinner refers to those who consciously make a lifestyle of sin, rather than the righteous who occasionally fall into sin. In the Sermon on the Mount, Jesus taught that sin lies within a person's attitude rather than his actions (Matt. 5:21–30). Thus, the person with the sinful attitude has separated himself from God, while those with righteous attitudes and trust in Christ have united with God.

SION [SIGH un] (*elevated*) — the name of a mountain and a city in the Bible:

1. The peak of Mount Hermon (Deut. 4:48), perhaps identical with Sirion (Deut. 3:9).

2. The Greek form of Mount Zion, referring specifically to the Temple mount and generally to the city of Jerusalem (Rom. 9:33; KJV; Zion, NKJV).

SIPHMOTH [SIF mahth] (*fruitful*) — a city in southern Judah where David hid from King Saul (1 Sam. 30:28). The site is unknown.

SIPPAI [SIP pih eye] — a form of SAPH.

SIR — a title of respect for gentlemen of rank, position, or power. The Philippian jailer asked Paul and Silas, "Sirs, what must I do to be saved?" (Acts 16:30). John also used this word in addressing one of the 24 elders (Rev. 7:14).

SIRAH [SIH rah] (*turning*) — a well (cistern, RSV; pool, NEB) near Hebron where Abner was murdered by Joab and Abishai (2 Sam. 3:26). The well of Sirah is probably present–day 'Ain Sarah, about 2.5 kilometers (1.5 miles) northwest of Hebron.

SIRION [SEAR ih un] (*breastplate*) — the Sidonian (Phoenician) name for Mount Hermon in northern Palestine (Deut. 3:9).

SISAMAI [SIS ah my] — a form of SISMAI.

SISERA [SIS uh rah] (meaning unknown) — the name of two men in the Old Testament:

1. The commander of the army of Jabin, king of Canaan. Deborah and Barak defeated Jabin's army under Sisera's command at the River Kishon. Sisera was later killed by a Kenite woman who drove a tent peg into his temple (Judg. 4:1–22).

2. One of the NETHINIM (Temple servants) who returned from the Captivity with Zerubbabel (Neh. 7:55).

SISMAI [SIS my] (meaning unknown) — a son of Eleasah and father of Shallum (1 Chr. 2:40; Sisamai, KJV).

SISTER — a female offspring of one's parents or of one's father or mother. The word sister was also used by the Hebrews to indicate a female relationship comparable to the brotherly male relationship. Sometimes the term was applied to any blood female relative, such as a niece or a cousin (Matt. 13:56). Also see FAMILY.

SISTRUM (see MUSICAL INSTRUMENTS).

SITHRI [SITH rih] — a form of ZITHRI.

SITNAH [SIT nah] (*enmity*) — a well dug by the servants of Isaac near the Philistine city of Gerar after a dispute over water rights (Gen. 26:21). Some scholars identify Sitnah with present–day Shutneh, about 32 kilometers (20 miles) south of Beersheba.

SIVAN [sih VAN] — the third month of the sacred Hebrew year (Esth. 8:9). Sivan went from the new moon of May to the new moon of June. Also see CALENDAR.

SIX, SIXTY (see NUMBER).

SKIFF — a small rowboat (Acts 27:16–32; boat, KJV, RSV; lifeboat, NIV).

SKIN — the outer protective covering of the bodies of man and animals. When the Bible speaks of skin, it always does so literally. This is in contrast to the word for FLESH, which is often used symbolically to refer to man's sinful nature. Animal skin (leather) was used to make the first garments worn by man, but it was generally used this way only in unusual situations (Gen. 3:21; Mark 1:6; Heb. 11:37). The most prominent mention of animal skins is in the description of the various coverings over the tabernacle (Ex. 25:5; 35:7; 39:34; Num. 4:6–25).

Human skin is fragile, and it deteriorates in the sick or the elderly (Job 7:5; Lam. 3:4). Various skin diseases of Bible times were referred to by the general term LEPROSY. Many references to skin occur in Leviticus 13, where the diagnosis and treatment of leprosy are described.

SKINK (see ANIMALS OF THE BIBLE).

SKIRT — an item of dress in Bible times whose exact nature is unknown. Other translations have collar (NKJV, NASB, RSV). Also see DRESS OF THE BIBLE.

SKULL — the bony foundation of the human face. Three of the gospels state that Jesus was crucified at Golgotha, or Place of a Skull (Matt. 27:33; Mark 15:22; John 19:17). Some scholars believe this name was given to the site because it looks like a skull from a distance. Also see CALVARY; GOLGOTHA.

SKY — the upper atmosphere, appearing as a great vault or arch above the earth. In the Bible the sky is the home of the sun (Job 37:21), moon (Ps. 89:37), and stars (Heb. 11:12). Sailors and navigators knew how to "discern the face of the sky" for weather signs (Matt. 16:2–3). Also see FIRMAMENT; HEAVEN.

SLABS — huge pieces of stone, or marble, gathered by David for the building of the Temple in Jerusalem (1 Chr. 29:2). These materials were later used by Solomon in the actual construction of the building.

SLACK, SLACKNESS — not lively or moving; sluggish. The Greek word translated as slackness occurs only in 2 Peter 3:9: "The Lord is not slack [slow, NIV] concerning His promise, as some count slackness [slowness, NIV], but is longsuffering toward us, not willing that any should perish, but that all should come to repentance." Unbelievers scoff at the Lord's delay in returning, not knowing that His "tardiness" is a mark of His mercy and grace.

SLANDER — evil, malicious talk intended to damage or destroy another person (Ps. 31:13; 50:20; Ezek. 22:9). Slander is prohibited in the ninth commandment: "You shall not bear false witness against your neighbor" (Ex. 20:16; Deut. 5:20). The greatest slanderer of all is the DEVIL, or SATAN—the adversary who opposes God's people and accuses them before God (Job 1:9–11; Rev. 12:10).

SLAUGHTER OF THE INNOCENTS (see INNOCENTS, SLAUGHTER OF).

SLAUGHTER, VALLEY OF (see TOPHET).

SLAVE, SLAVERY — a person bound in servitude to another human being as an instrument of labor; one who has lost his liberty and has no rights.

An ancient practice (Gen. 9:25), slavery existed in several different forms in biblical times. Household or domestic slavery was its most common form; this is illustrated by HAGAR, who lived in the home of Abraham and Sarai (Gen. 16:) and by Jesus in His parables (Matt. 13:24–30; 21:33–44). State slavery, another common form, is illustrated by the Israelites' experience under their Egyptian taskmasters (Ex. 5:6–19; 13:3), and later by Solomon, who enslaved some of the Canaanite peoples (1 Kin. 9:20–21). Temple slavery is illustrated by the practice of Moses and Joshua, who assigned certain people as slaves to the Levites for Temple service (Num. 31:25–47; Josh. 9:21–27).

One could purchase slaves, as in the case of Joseph. He was sold into slavery by his brothers for 20 shekels of silver (Gen. 37:28). Israelites could also buy foreign slaves (Lev. 25:44). People captured in war frequently became slaves (Gen. 14:21; Num. 31:9). Occasionally those who wanted slaves might kidnap them, but this practice was forbidden by the Jewish law (Ex. 21:16; 1 Tim. 1:10).

People could become slaves in several ways. The poor who were unable to pay their debts could offer themselves as slaves (Ex. 21:2–6; Neh. 5:1–5). A thief who could not repay what he had stolen could also be sold as a slave. Children born of slave parents became "house-born slaves" (Gen. 15:3; 17:12–13). Sometimes children would be taken as slaves in payment for debts (2 Kin. 4:1–7).

Treatment of slaves generally depended on the

Stone carving of a servant of King Tiglath-Pileser III of Assyria, from the king's palace at Calah.

Photo by Howard Vos

The modern city of Izmir, Turkey, covers the site of biblical Smyrna. The excavated square in the center is the Roman marketplace from New Testament times.

character of the master (Gen. 24; 39:1-6). But a set of regulations governed the treatment of domestic slaves (Ex. 21; Deut. 15). Repeatedly, Israel was instructed by the law not to rule over a fellow Israelite harshly (Lev. 25:39; Deut. 15:14). If a master beat a slave or harmed him, the law provided that the slave could go free (Ex. 21:26-27); and the killing of a slave called for a penalty (Ex. 21:20).

Slaves were allowed to secure their freedom. Under the Jewish law, no Hebrew was to be the permanent slave of another Hebrew. After six years of service, a slave was to be released (Ex. 21:2; Deut. 15:12). In the Year of JUBILEE, no matter how long a slave had served, he was to be released (Lev. 25:37-43). If a slave desired to continue with his master, he would have a mark made in the ear; this mark would signify that he had chosen to remain a slave (Ex. 21:5-6). A slave could also buy his freedom, or another person could buy his freedom for him (Lev. 25:47-49).

Among the Romans in New Testament times, freedom for a slave could be arranged if ownership was transferred to a god. The slave could then receive his freedom in return for contracting his services. He would continue with his master, but now as a free man.

The Bible contains warnings about the practice of slavery. The prophet Amos spoke woe to Gaza and Tyre for their practices of slave-trading entire populations (Amos 1:6-9). The Book of Revelation declares that disaster awaits those who sell slaves (Rev. 18:13). As for Christians, the apostle Paul ad-

vised slaves to obey their masters (Eph. 6:5; Col. 3:22; Titus 2:9). Paul appealed to Philemon to receive back Onesimus, a runaway slave who was now a Christian and therefore a brother (Philem. 1:16). Elsewhere Paul counseled believing slaves to seek freedom if they could (1 Cor. 7:21). Since slave practices were part of the culture in biblical times, the Bible contains no direct call to abolish slavery. But the implications of the gospel, especially the ethic of love, stand in opposition to slavery.

Both slave and free are called upon to receive the gospel of Jesus Christ. In Christ, social distinctions such as slavery no longer apply (Gal. 3:28; Col. 3:11); in Christ all are brothers and sisters. The excitement of such new relationships is expressed by Paul: "Therefore you are no longer a slave but a son, and if a son, then an heir of God through Christ" (Gal. 4:7).

In a spiritual sense, people apart from Christ are slaves to sin. To commit sin is to demonstrate that sin has control of one's life (John 8:34). Christ can set us free from this kind of slavery (John 8:36)—to be obedient to Christ and to do righteousness (Rom. 6:16-18).

Paul spoke of himself as a "servant," a word sometimes rendered as "bondservant" but frequently also as "slave" (Rom. 1:1; Titus 1:1). Christians, especially ministers, are not hired servants but slaves committed to service to Jesus. A slave does not manage his own life. The person who calls himself a slave of Christ acknowledges that the Savior has power over him.

SLEEP — a natural period of rest during which consciousness is suspended. In the Bible, sleep is a common metaphor for death. In 1 and 2 Kings, especially, the phrase, "he rested (slept, KJV) with his fathers," occurs many times (1 Kin. 2:10; 11:43). The Christian dead "sleep in Jesus" (1 Thess. 4:14). Sleep also can symbolize physical laziness, which brings poverty (Prov. 6:9–11). In the New Testament sleep often suggests spiritual or moral laziness (1 Thess. 5:6). On the other hand, sleep can be a symbol of living in safety (Ezek. 34:25). God gives sleep to the righteous and to the hard worker (Ps. 4:8; Eccl. 5:12).

SLIME (see Minerals of the Bible).

SLING (see Arms, Armor of the Bible).

SLINGSTONES — stones hurled from a sling by shepherds and warriors (Job 41:28; Zech. 9:15). Slingstones were usually small stones or clay pebbles. But sometimes they were made of limestone or flint and were as large as a baseball. Also see Arms, Armor of the Bible.

SLOOPS — small, single–masted sailing boats (Is. 2:16).

SLOTHFUL — idle, lazy, sluggish (Prov. 15:19; 26:13–15). The Book of Proverbs contrasts two paths, or ways of life: the way of wisdom and the way of folly. The slothful man is foolish, while the diligent, hard-working person is wise.

SMELTER — a large container for heating ore and separating the metal from the dross; a person engaged in the smelting industry. The people of Jerusalem and Judea were so corrupted with the impurity of wickedness that they were almost beyond redemption. The prophet Jeremiah declared, "The smelter refines in vain" (Jer. 6:29).

SMITH (see Occupations and Trades).

SMYRNA [SMER nuh] (*myrrh*) — a city in western Asia Minor (modern Turkey) where one of the seven churches in the Book of Revelation was situated (Rev. 1:11; 2:8–11). Smyrna's superb natural harbor made the city an important commercial center. In spite of keen competition from the neighboring cities of Ephesus and Pergamum, Smyrna called itself "the first city of Asia."

As early as 195 B.C., Smyrna foresaw the rising power of Rome and built a temple for pagan Roman worship. In 23 B.C., Smyrna was given the honor of building a temple to the Emperor Tiberius because of its years of faithfulness to Rome. Thus, the city became a center for the cult of emperor worship—a fanatical "religion" that later, under such emperors as Nero (ruled A.D. 54–68) and Domitian (ruled A.D. 81–96), brought on severe persecution for the early church. The apostle John encouraged the persecuted Christians of Smyrna to be "faithful unto death" and they would receive a "crown of life" (Rev. 2:10).

Smyrna, known today as Izmir, is the chief city of Anatolia and one of the strongest cities in modern Turkey. Excavations in the central part of Izmir have uncovered a Roman marketplace from the second century A.D.

SNAIL, SNAKE (see Animals of the Bible).

SNARE — a device for trapping birds and small animals; figuratively, anything alluring and attractive that entangles the unwary (Job 18:8–10). In the Old Testament, the pagan gods of the Canaanites became a snare to Israel (Judg. 2:3). In the New Testament, the leaders of the church were warned not to fall into the "snare of the devil" (1 Tim. 3:7).

SNOW — solid precipitation in the form of white crystals originating in the upper atmosphere. Snow is relatively rare in the land of Israel. Although snow is mentioned frequently, the Bible records only one instance where snow actually fell. Benaiah, the son of Jehoiada, "went down and killed a lion in the midst of a pit on a snowy day" (2 Sam. 23:20).

Snow-covered Mount Hermon was visible year-round from many parts of the Holy Land. This served as the source of the Jordan River and much of Israel's water supply (Jer. 18:14). Snow is noted for its whiteness (Num. 12:10), cleanness (Job 9:30), and refreshing coolness (Prov. 25:13). The Bible uses snow as a symbol of cleansing (Job 9:30), purity (Is. 1:18), and brilliance (Dan. 7:9).

SNUFFDISHES, SNUFFERS (see Wick–trimmers, Trimmers).

SO [soh] (meaning unknown) — a king of Egypt whom Hoshea, the last king of Israel (ruled about 732–23 B.C.), tried to enlist as an ally against Assyria (2 Kin. 17:4). Some scholars identify So with Sib'e. In 720 B.C. this Egyptian king allied himself with Hanunu, the king of Gaza, against Sargon of Assyria. Sargon soundly defeated this coalition at the Battle of Raphia, about 32 kilometers (20 miles) south of Gaza. Other scholars regard So as the name of a city, Sais, in the western delta of Egypt. This was the residence of Tefnakhte, an Egyptian ruler during the days of King Hoshea. If this theory is correct, then the text would read: "He had sent messengers to So [Sais], to the king of Egypt."

SOAP — an alkaline substance used as a cleaning agent. The prophet Jeremiah referred to soap as a symbol of man's inability to purify himself: Soap can accomplish an external cleansing, but more is required (Jer. 2:22). Malachi spoke of God as a fuller, or laundryman, who would purge his sinful people with soap (Mal. 3:2). Job felt that God was determined to find him guilty and that no amount of washing or cleansing with soap or water could cleanse him (Job 9:30).

The exact nature of the soap used in Bible times is open to question. Most scholars believe the alkaline used to make it came from plants.

SOBER — marked by self–control; of sound moral judgment. A sober Christian denies himself worldly pleasures (Titus 2:12). This allows him to be always alert, able to guard against Satan's attacks (1 Pet. 5:8) and ready to receive the revelation of Christ (1 Pet. 1:13).

SOCHOH, SOCO, SOCOH [SOW koe] (*thorn-hedge*) — the name of three cities and one man in the Old Testament:

1. A city in the lowland of Judah (Josh. 15:35), also spelled Soco (2 Chr. 11:7; 28:18; NASB, NEB, NIV, RSV); Shochoh (1 Sam. 17:1, KJV), and Shoco (2 Chr. 11:7, KJV). It has been identified with Khirbet 'Abbad, about 23 kilometers (14 miles) southwest of Bethlehem.

2. A city in the hill country of Judah (Josh. 15:48). Its site is Khirbet Shuweikeh, about 16 kilometers (10 miles) southwest of Hebron. Other translations have Socoh (KJV, NASB, NIV, RSV).

3. A city in one of Solomon's administrative districts (1 Kin. 4:10; Socoh, NASB, NEB, NIV, RSV). It is present-day Tell er-Ras, about 16 kilometers (10 miles) northwest of Samaria.

4. A son of Heber listed in the genealogy of Judah (1 Chr. 4:18; Socho, KJV; Soco, NASB, NEB, NIV, RSV). A comparison with Joshua 15:48–56, however, suggests that Sochoh (1 Chr. 4:18) may be a city rather than a person. If so, this Sochoh would be identical with Sochoh No. 2.

SODA — a form of sodium bicarbonate. According to Proverbs, a person who sings songs to a person with a heavy heart is like one who pours vinegar on soda (Prov. 25:20; nitre, KJV).

SODI [SOW dih] (*God is my secret counsel*) — the father of Gaddiel (Num. 13:10).

SODOM [SOD um] (*place of lime*) — a city at the southern end of the Dead Sea destroyed because of its wickedness (Gen. 10:19; Rom. 9:29). Together with her sister cities—Gomorrah, Admah, Zeboim, and Zoar—Sodom formed the famous pentapolis of the plain or circle of the Jordan (Gen. 10:19; 13:10; 14:2) in the valley that surrounded the Dead Sea (Gen. 14:3).

Although Sodom was a notoriously wicked city, when Lot separated himself and his herdsmen from Abraham, he chose to pitch his tent toward Sodom (Gen. 13:5–13). This was because the fertile plain that surrounded the city "was well watered everywhere" (Gen. 13:10).

When Sodom was plundered by CHEDOR-LAOMER, the goods and captives which he carried away had to be rescued by Abraham (Gen. 14:11, 21–24). However, the wickedness of the people of the city continued, and God finally had to destroy Sodom. Fire and brimstone fell from heaven and consumed Sodom and Gomorrah and the other cities of the plain. When Lot's wife looked back at Sodom, she was instantly changed into a pillar of salt (Gen. 19:26).

Early tradition held that the northern end of the Dead Sea was the Valley of Sodom. But the geological conditions of the southern end of the Dead Sea match those of the area around Sodom. Salt formations, asphalt, and sulfur are found in large quanti-

ties here. Many scholars believe the cities of the plain may be located beneath the shallow end of the Dead Sea. The basin surrounding the shallow southern end of the Dead Sea is fed by five streams, including the Wadi Zered (Num. 21:12), which would have provided for a fertile, well-watered plain. In addition, Zoar, one of the cities of the plain (Gen. 13:10), is reported by the Jewish historian Josephus to have been visible during his time at the southern end of the sea.

The sin, vice, and infamy of Sodom and the judgment of God on this city is referred to often throughout the Bible (Is. 1:9–10; Ezek. 16:46–49; Amos 4:11; Rom. 9:29).

SODOM, VINE OF (see VINE OF SODOM).

SODOMITE, SODOMY [SAHD um ite, SAHD uh me] — one who practices sodomy; unnatural sexual intercourse, especially that between two males. These English words are derived from SODOM, an ancient city in the land of Canaan noted for such depraved activities.

All the men of Sodom came to Lot's house, demanding that he allow them to have sexual relations with two people inside (Gen. 19:5). But Lot refused. The next day Lot escaped from Sodom and God destroyed the city because of its great sin (Gen. 19). Sodomy was prohibited by the law of Moses (Deut. 23:17) and condemned by the apostle Paul (Rom. 1:27; 1 Cor. 6:9).

SOJOURNER (see FOREIGNER).

SOLDIER (see ARMY; OCCUPATIONS AND TRADES).

SOLOMON [SAHL uh mun] (*peaceful*) — the builder of the Temple in Jerusalem and the first king of Israel to trade commercial goods profitably to other nations; author of Proverbs, the Song of Solomon, and Ecclesiastes.

Solomon succeeded David his father as king of Israel. Solomon's rise met with widespread approval from the people, but David's officials were slow to accept the new king. They did warm up considerably, however, when they realized David was determined to anoint Solomon as his heir. Solomon became Israel's king because God had told David that Saul's heirs would not follow him to the throne. Thus, Solomon became king although there was no clear precedent for his succession.

According to the chronology in 1 Kings 11:42, Solomon was about 20 years old when he was crowned. He assumed leadership of Israel at a time of great material and spiritual prosperity. During his 40-year reign (970–930 B.C.), he expanded his kingdom until it covered about 50,000 square miles—from Egypt in the south to Syria in the north to the borders of Mesopotamia in the east.

Great Beginnings. One of the first things Solomon did as king was to go to Gibeon to offer sacrifices to the Lord. God appeared to the new king at night and asked him, "What shall I give thee?" Solomon asked for an understanding heart to judge the people of Israel and the ability to tell good from evil. God not only granted Solomon's request, but He also promised him riches and honor if he would walk in the steps of his father, David (1 Kin. 3:4-15).

Solomon organized Israel much as David had done, but he enlarged and expanded its government. He divided the country into 12 districts, each of which was responsible for providing the court with regular supplies, with a supply officer in charge of each district. As the years passed, Solomon's court reached a standard of luxury that had never existed in Israel's history.

Wisdom. Solomon is usually remembered as a wise man. His Proverbs and his "Song of Songs" demonstrate his deep knowledge of the natural world (plants, animals, etc.). He also had a profound knowledge of human nature, as demonstrated by the two women who claimed the same child. His suggestion that the child be physically divided between the two was a masterful strategy for finding out who was the real mother (1 Kin. 3:16-28). Solomon's concern with the ethics of everyday life is evident in his Proverbs. They show that Solomon loved wisdom and was always trying to teach it to others. They also indicate he was a keen observer who could learn from the mistakes of others.

Solomon's sayings in these Proverbs are so true that they sound almost trite today. Their clarity sometimes hides their depth. During his lifetime, Solomon's fame as a man of wisdom spread to surrounding lands, and leaders came from afar to hear him speak. When the Queen of Sheba came to test his wisdom, he answered all her questions with ease. After she saw the extent of his empire and the vastness of his knowledge, she confessed that she had underestimated him (2 Chr. 9:1-12).

Solomon's Temple. One of Solomon's first major feats was the construction of the TEMPLE in Jerusalem as a place for worship of the God of Israel. The task was enormous, involving much planning and many workmen. A work force of 30,000 was employed in cutting timber from the cedars of Lebanon. Also working on this massive project were 80,000 cutters of stone in the quarries of Jerusalem, 70,000 ordinary workmen, and many superintendents. Gold, silver, and other precious metals were imported from other lands. Hiram, king of Tyre, sent architects and other craftsmen to assist with the project. The building was completed after seven years. The Temple was famous not for its size—since it was relatively small—but for the quality of its elaborate workmanship (1 Kings 6—7).

After the Temple was completed, Solomon planned an elaborate program of dedication. He invited the leaders of all twelve tribes to attend as he presided over the ceremony. The ARK OF THE COVENANT was brought into the most sacred place in the Temple as a cloud filled the room to hide God's presence. King Solomon then blessed the crowd, recounted the history of the building of the Temple, and offered long prayers of dedication while standing at the altar. This reveals the admirable spirit of devotion in Solomon's heart. The dedication cere-

mony lasting seven days was followed by observance of the Feast of Tabernacles (1 Kings 8—9).

Immediately after the dedication, the Lord appeared to Solomon once again. He assured the king that his prayers had been heard and that the Temple had been blessed. He also warned Solomon that the divine favor and protection which had been bestowed upon Israel would continue only if their faith remained uncorrupted by other beliefs. If idolatry should be introduced, Israel would be punished and the Temple would be destroyed (1 Kin. 9:1-9).

Other Buildings. After completing the Temple, Solomon built the palace complex, a series of five structures that took 13 years to complete. He also built many cities to assist the development of his trade empire. Among these were Tadmor (also called Palmyra) and Baalath (also called Baalbek) in Syria. To protect his kingdom, he built fortresses and lodgings for his army. These fortifications, especially the ones at Gezer, Megiddo, and Hazor, had strong double walls and massive gateways.

Commercial Enterprises. Trade with other nations was another of Solomon's contributions to the nation of Israel. The international situation was favorable for a strong leader to emerge in Palestine; traditional centers of strength in Egypt and Syria were at an all-time low. Solomon entered into trade agreements with a number of nations, increasing Israel's wealth and prestige.

Although Solomon had a strong army, he relied upon a system of treaties with his neighbors to keep the peace. Egypt was allied with Israel through the marriage of Solomon to the daughter of the Pharaoh. The sea-faring cities of Tyre and Sidon were also united to Israel by trade agreements.

Some of Israel's trade was conducted overland by way of camel caravans. But the most significant trade was by sea across the Mediterranean Sea through an alliance with Tyre. Solomon's ships apparently went as far west as Spain to bring back silver. Archaeologists have discovered an old mine in ancient Ethiopia that is believed to have been one of Solomon's sources of silver.

Soon Solomon became the ruler of a huge commercial empire. Archaeologists believe that Solomon's trading may have brought him into conflict with the Queen of Sheba. One purpose of her famous visit to Solomon may have been to establish trade agreements between Solomon's kingdom and her own nation (1 Kin. 10:1-13).

Solomon's Sins. Solomon's reign brought changes not only to Israel but also to his own life. Near the end of his life, the king lost the ideals of his youth, becoming restless and unsatisfied. His writings in Ecclesiastes, proclaiming that "all is vanity," support the view that the world's wisest man had become a pathetic figure in his old age.

Solomon's greatest sin was his loss of devotion to the God of the Hebrew people. In this, he fell victim to his own trade agreements. By custom, beautiful women were awarded to the most powerful member of a treaty to seal the covenant. The con-

Remains of the massive gate complex at Gezer. Solomon rebuilt the entire city and its defenses (1 Kin. 9:15-17).

stant influx of wives and concubines in Solomon's court led eventually to his downfall. Thus, Solomon broke the Mosaic Law and violated the warning not to stray from the path of his father David.

The large number of foreign women in Solomon's court made many demands upon the king. He allowed these "outsiders" to practice their pagan religions. The result was that Jerusalem, and even its holy Temple, was the scene of pagan practices and idol worship (1 Kin. 11:1-13).

Solomon's own faith was weakened. Eventually he approved of, and even participated in, these idolatrous acts. The example he set for the rest of the nation must have been demoralizing. This unfortunate error was a severe blow to the security of Solomon's throne and to the nation he had built.

The End of Solomon's Throne. Years before Solomon's death, his heavy taxation of the people brought unrest and rebellion. Surrounding nations began to marshal their forces to free themselves of Israel's tyranny, but the most serious uprising came from within the nation itself. Jeroboam, a young leader who had the support of Egypt, led ten of the twelve tribes out of Israel to the North. When Solomon's son Rehoboam ascended the throne after his father, Jeroboam returned to lead a successful civil war against him. The result was a division of Solomon's United Kingdom into two separate nations—the southern kingdom of Judah and the northern kingdom of Israel.

Solomon's Character. In many ways, Solomon's 40-year reign as king of the Hebrew people is a puzzle. In his early years he was both noble and humble—undoubtedly one of the best rulers of his day. Although he was surrounded by wealth and luxury as a young man, he seemed to be a person of

honor and integrity. He was the first king in Israel who was the son of a king. The glory of his empire was a reflection of his own royal tastes, which he satisfied through a shrewd and successful foreign policy.

Unfortunately, Solomon was not strong enough to withstand the temptations that go along with a long life of luxury. His contribution to the nation of Israel is figured largely in material terms. He made Jerusalem one of the most beautiful cities of the ancient world, and he will always be remembered as a great builder. The tragedy is that after the building of the Temple, Solomon did very little to promote the religious life of his people.

SOLOMON, PSALMS OF (see PSEUDE-PIGRAPHA).

SOLOMON, WISDOM OF (see APOCRYPHA).

SOLOMON'S POOLS — three storage reservoirs. probably constructed some time after the reign of King Solomon, to provide water for the capital city of Jerusalem (Eccl. 2:6).

SOLOMON'S PORCH — the name of two porches associated with the Temple in Jerusalem:
1. The outer corridor of Solomon's Temple (1 Kin. 6:3, KJV).
2. A roofed portico on the east side of Herod's Temple in Jerusalem (John 10:23; Solomon's Portico, NEB; Solomon's Colonnade, NIV).

SOLOMON'S SERVANTS — Canaanites who served as forced laborers during the reign of King Solomon of Judah (1 Kin. 9:20-22). These people labored in the stone quarries and did much of the difficult construction work on Solomon's massive building projects. The descendants of Solomon's servants returned with the NETHINIM (Temple servants) from the Captivity in the time of Zerubbabel (Ezra 2:55–58). On their return from Babylon, they did lowly jobs in the Temple.

SON — the male offspring of a husband and wife. The birth of a son brought great joy to the Hebrew family, because a family's heritage and inheritance was preserved through its sons. The word son is also used in a figurative sense in the Bible. Occasionally it refers to remote relatives and dwellers in a specific place, as in the "sons of Javan" (Gen. 10:4). Also see FAMILY.

SON OF GOD, SON OF MAN (see JESUS CHRIST).

SONG (see MUSIC OF THE BIBLE).

SONG OF DEGREES (see DEGREES, SONG OF).

SONG OF SOLOMON, THE — an Old Testament book written in the form of a lyrical love song. Some interpreters believe this song speaks symbolically of the love of God for the nation of Israel. But others insist it should be interpreted literally—as a healthy expression of romantic love between a man and a woman. No matter how the book is interpreted, it is certainly one of the most unusual in the Bible. Its subtitle, "the song of songs" (1:1), implies it was the loveliest and best-known of all the songs of Solomon.

Structure of the Book. The Song of Solomon is a brief book of only eight chapters. But in spite of its brevity, it has a complicated structure that sometimes confuses the reader. Several different characters or personalities have speaking parts within this long lyrical poem. In most translations of the Bible, these speakers change abruptly with no identification to help the reader follow the narrative. But the NKJV clears up this confusion by publishing identification lines within the text. This helps the reader gain a clearer understanding of this beautiful song.

The three main parties with speaking parts in this long poem are: (1) the groom, King Solomon; (2) the bride, a woman referred to as "the Shulamite" (6:13); and (3) the "daughters of Jerusalem" (2:7). These women of Jerusalem may have been royal servants who served as attendants to Solomon's Shulamite bride. In this love song, they serve as a chorus to echo the sentiments of the Shulamite, emphasizing her love and affection for Solomon.

In addition to these main personalities, the brothers of the Shulamite bride are also mentioned in the poem (8:8–9). These may have been her step-brothers. The poem indicates she worked under their command as "the keeper of the vineyards" (1:6).

This beautiful love song falls naturally into two major sections of about equal length—the beginning of love (chaps. 1—4) and the broadening of love (chaps. 5—8).

In the first section, the Shulamite tells about Solomon's visit to her home in the country in the springtime (2:8–17). She also recalls the many happy experiences of their courtship when she visited Solomon in his palace in Jerusalem (2:4–7). She thinks about the painful separations from his love during this time (3:1–5), as well as the joyous wedding procession to Jerusalem to become the king's bride (3:6–11). Solomon also praises his bride-to-be in a beautiful poem on the magic and wonder of love (chap. 4).

In the second section of the book, the love of the

SONG OF SOLOMON: A Teaching Outline

Shulamite and Solomon for each other continues to deepen after their marriage. She has a troubled dream when he seems distant and unconcerned (5:2–8). But Solomon assures her of his love and praises her beauty (6:4—7:9). Longing to visit her country home (7:10—8:4), she finally makes the trip with Solomon; and their love grows even stronger (8:5–7). The song closes with an assurance of each to the other that they will always remain close in their love.

Authorship and Date. Traditionally, authorship of the Song of Solomon has been assigned to Solomon, since the book itself makes this claim (1:1). But some scholars reject this theory. They insist it was a later collection of songs attributed to Solomon because of his reputation as a writer of psalms and proverbs (1 Kin. 4:32). A careful analysis of the internal evidence, however, gives strong support to the view that Solomon wrote the book.

Solomon is mentioned by name several times in the song (1:1, 5; 3:7, 9, 11; 8:11–12), and he is specifically identified as the groom. The book also gives evidence of wealth, luxury, and exotic imported goods (3:6–11)—a characteristic of his administration. The groom of the song also assures the Shulamite bride that she is "the only one" (6:9) among his "sixty queens and eighty concubines" (6:8)—probably a reference by Solomon to his royal harem. At the height of his power and influence, Solomon was known to have 700 wives and 300 concubines (1 Kin. 11:3).

This strong internal evidence clearly supports the traditional view that Solomon himself wrote this song that bears his name. It must have been written early in his reign, probably about 965 B.C.

Historical Setting. With his large harem, how could King Solomon write such a beautiful love song to one specific wife? Perhaps his union with the Shulamite woman was the only authentic marriage relationship which Solomon ever knew. Most of his marriages were political arrangements, designed to seal treaties and trade agreements with other nations. In contrast, the Shulamite woman was not a cultured princess but a lowly vineyard keeper whose skin had been darkened by her long exposure to the sun (1:6). Yet, she was the bride to whom Solomon declared, "How much better than wine is your love, and the scent of your perfumes than all spices!" (4:10).

This has a real message about the nature of true love. Authentic love is much more than a surface relationship; it extends to the very core of one's being. Love like this cannot be bought and sold like some commodity on the open market. Solomon had many wives, but the Shulamite may have been the only one with whom he enjoyed a warm, enriching relationship.

Theological Contribution. The great message of the Song of Solomon is the beauty of love between a man and a woman as experienced in the relationship of marriage. In its frank but beautiful language, the song praises the mutual love which husband and wife feel toward each other in this highest of all human relationships.

The sexual and physical side of marriage is a natural and proper part of God's plan, reflecting His purpose and desire for the human race. This is the same truth so evident at the beginning of time in the Creation itself. God created man and woman and brought them together to serve as companions and to share their lives with one another: "Therefore a man shall leave his father and mother and be joined to his wife, and they shall become one flesh" (Gen. 2:24). Like the Book of Genesis, the Song of Solomon says a bold yes to the beauty and sanctity of married love.

But this book also points beyond human love to the great Author of love. Authentic love is possible in the world because God brought love into being and planted that emotion in the hearts of His people. Even husbands and wives should remember that the love which they share for one another is not a product of their human goodness or kindness. We are able to love because the love of God is working in our lives: "In this is love, not that we loved God, but that He loves us and sent His Son to be the propitiation for our sins. Beloved, if God so loved us, we also ought to love one another" (1 John 4:10–11).

Special Considerations. The symbols and images that the groom uses to describe the beauty of his Shulamite bride may seem strange to modern readers. He portrays her hair as "a flock of goats, going down from Mount Gilead" (4:1). Her neck, he says, is like "the tower of David, built for an armory, on which hang a thousand bucklers" (4:4). Such compliments today would certainly not be flattering to most women!

In his use of these symbols, the groom is reflecting the cultural patterns of the ancient world. To those who lived in Solomon's time, the rippling effect of a flock of goats moving down a hillside was, indeed, a thing of beauty. And a stately tower atop a city wall reflected an aura of stability and nobility. The Shulamite woman would have been very pleased at such creative compliments from her poetic groom.

Scholars are not certain of the exact meaning of the phrase, "the Shulamite" (6:13), which has come to be used as a title for the bride in this song. No city or region known as Shulam has been identified in Palestine or any of the surrounding territories. Because the poem makes several references to Lebanon (3:9; 4:8, 11, 15; 5:15; 7:4), some scholars believe she came from this mountainous territory along the Mediterranean coast in northwestern Palestine.

SONG OF SONGS (see Song of Solomon).

SONG OF THE THREE YOUNG MEN (see Apocrypha).

SONS OF GOD — a phrase with three different meanings in the Bible:

1. In the Book of Job the phrase is used for angelic or non–human beings (Job 1:6; 2:1). These

sons of God presented themselves before God in what might be called a heavenly assembly. Satan appeared with them, although this does not necessarily mean he was one of the "sons of God." Thus the stage was set for the telling of the story of Job.

2. The phrase, *sons of God*, appears in the New Testament as a name for people who are in a covenant relationship with God. This exact phrase never appears with this meaning in the Old Testament, although the idea is implied. For example, God referred to the scattered children of Israel, whom He promised to gather together again, as His sons and daughters (Is. 43:6; 45:11).

The classic New Testament passage where this phrase occurs is Romans 8:12-19. The apostle Paul encouraged the Christians at Rome to live not "according to the flesh," but "by the Spirit," because those who "are led by the Spirit of God, these are sons of God" (v. 14). The process is described as one of adoption, by which the believer becomes a child of God, and thus an heir of God, a joint-heir with Christ (Gal. 4:5; Heb. 2:10; 12:7). Other passages use the phrase *children of God*, with the same basic meaning (John 1:12; Phil. 2:15; 1 John 3:1-2).

3. The third usage of the phrase occurs in Genesis 6:1-4. Certain "sons of God saw the daughters of men, that they were beautiful; and they took wives for themselves of all whom they chose" (v. 2). The offspring of these unions are described as "giants," "mighty men," and "men of renown" (v. 4). The question centers on the identity of these "sons of God" mentioned in this passage. There are two basic possibilities. The phrase could refer to non-human beings such as those mentioned in Job (1:6; 2:1). Or, the phrase may be an unusual way of referring to human beings.

The context of the verse gives important clues that the "sons of God" in this case are not angelic beings. One clue is found in the total biblical context. Nowhere else in the Bible is there even a hint that non-human and human beings can mate. There are many parallels in pagan thought, but none in biblical thought. A second clue occurs right in the passage itself. The Hebrew verb in verse two translated as "took them wives" is the standard verb in the Old Testament for marriage. In the New Testament, Jesus stated that angels do not marry (Matt. 22:30). Thus, *sons of God* in this passage must refer to human beings.

SOOT — the fine, black powder, consisting chiefly of carbon, that gives smoke its distinct color. The Nazirites of Jerusalem, once "brighter [purer, RSV] than snow and whiter than milk," became degraded, said the prophet Jeremiah, so that "now their appearance is blacker than soot" (Lam. 4:7-8; a coal, KJV).

SOP — KJV word for a piece of bread which Jesus dipped in the common dish and then handed to Judas at the Last Supper (John 13:26-30, KJV; piece of bread, NKJV). In Bible times, a small piece of bread like this often served as a makeshift spoon (Ruth 2:14).

SOPATER [SOW pa tur] (*savior of his father*) — a Christian from Berea who accompanied the apostle Paul from Greece to the province of Asia (Acts 20:4; son of Pyrrhus, RSV). Sopater may be the Sosipater who joined Paul in sending greetings to fellow Christians (Rom. 16:21).

SOPHERETH [so FEH reth] (*scribe*) — a servant of Solomon whose descendants returned from the Captivity with Zerubbabel (Ezra 2:55; Hassophereth, RSV; Neh. 7:57).

SORCERY, SORCERER (see MAGIC, SORCERY, AND DIVINATION).

SORES (see DISEASES OF THE BIBLE).

SOREK [SOW reck] (*choice vine*) — the valley in southern Palestine where DELILAH, Samson's mistress, lived (Judg. 16:4). The valley contained such sites as Timnah, where another of Samson's lovers lived; Zorah, Samson's birthplace; and Beth Shemesh, a fortified outpost near the border of Philistia and Palestine.

SORREL — a color of a distinct reddish-brown shade or an animal of this color (Zech. 1:8). Also see COLORS OF THE BIBLE.

SORROW — extreme sadness or mental distress; the opposite of joy. The psalmist spoke of the shadows of sorrow that hung over his life when he felt persecuted by people (Ps. 16:4) or rejected by God (Ps. 38:17). In the New Testament, the apostle Paul spoke of a "godly sorrow" (2 Cor. 7:10) for sin that can lead to repentance and a renewed relationship with God.

SOSIPATER [soh SIP ah tur] (*saving one's father*) — a believer who joined the apostle Paul in sending greetings to the Roman Christians (Rom. 16:21). Sosipater may be the same person as SOPATER (Acts 20:4).

SOSTHENES [SOS thuh knees] (*of sound strength*) — the ruler of the synagogue at Corinth during the apostle Paul's first visit to this city (Acts 18:17). When the Roman ruler of the area refused to deal with the angry mob's charges against Paul, they beat Sosthenes. This may be the same Sosthenes as the one greeted by Paul in one of his Corinthian letters (1 Cor. 1:1). If so, he must have become a Christian some time after the mob scene in his city.

SOTAI [SOW tih] (*Jehovah is turning aside*) — a servant of Solomon (Ezra 2:55) whose descendants returned from the Captivity with Zerubbabel.

SOUL — a word with two distinct meanings in the Bible:

1. That which makes a human or animal body alive. This usage of the word soul refers to life in the physical body. The best example of this usage are those passages in the New Testament in which the Greek word for soul is translated as life. "For whoever desires to save his life [soul] will lose it," Jesus declared, "but whoever loses his life [soul] for My sake and the gospel's will save it. For what will

it profit a man if he gains the whole world, and loses his own soul?" (Mark 8:36–37).

This idea is also present in the Old Testament. For example, the soul of a dying person departed at death (Gen. 35:18). The prophet Elijah brought a child back to life by stretching himself upon the child three times and praying that God would let the child's soul come back into him (1 Kin. 17:19–23).

2. The word soul also refers to the inner life of man, the seat of his emotions, and the center of human personality. The first use of the word soul in the Old Testament expresses this meaning: "And the Lord God formed man of the dust of the ground, and breathed into his nostrils the breath of life; and man became a living being (soul)" (Gen. 2:7). This means more than being given physical life; the biblical writer declares that man became a "living soul," or a person, a human being, one distinct from all other animals.

The soul is described as the seat of many emotions and desires: the desire for food (Deut. 12:20–21), love (Song 1:7), longing for God (Ps. 63:1), rejoicing (Ps. 86:4), knowing (Ps. 139:14), and memory (Lam. 3:20).

In the New Testament, Jesus spoke of his soul as being "exceedingly sorrowful" (Matt. 26:38). Mary, the mother of Jesus, proclaimed that her soul "magnifies the Lord" (Luke 1:46). John prayed that Gaius would "prosper in all things and be in health, just as your soul prospers" (3 John 2).

SOUTH (see DIRECTION).

SOUTH GATE (see GATES OF JERUSALEM AND THE TEMPLE).

SOUTH RAMOTH [RAY mahth] — a form of RAMAH.

SOUTH, THE (see NEGEV).

SOVEREIGNTY OF GOD — a theological term which refers to the unlimited power of God, who has sovereign control over the affairs of nature and history (Is. 45:9–19; Rom. 8:18–39). The Bible declares that God is working out His sovereign plan of redemption for the world and that the conclusion is certain. Immediately after the Fall He talked about the curse of human sin and specified the cure for man's sin. To the serpent He said, "I will put enmity between you and the woman, and between your seed and her seed; He shall bruise your head, and you shall bruise His heel" (Gen. 3:15). The whole redemptive story of the Bible is the fulfillment of this prophecy by the sovereign God, as Paul clearly teaches in Romans 8—11.

The story of redemption from Genesis to Revelation is possible only because the sovereign God loves the created world, fallen though it is, and is able to do something about it. Without the sovereign love of the Father ministered to us through the Son and the Holy Spirit, there would be no real human freedom and no hope of everlasting life.

Also see GOD; OMNIPOTENCE; OMNIPRESENCE; OMNISCIENCE.

SOW (see ANIMALS OF THE BIBLE).

SOWER, SOWING (see AGRICULTURE).

SPAIN [spane] (meaning unknown) — the large peninsula of Europe, now comprising Spain and Portugal, at the western end of the Mediterranean Sea. The Phoenicians had established trading posts here by the time the Israelites conquered Canaan. The Greeks called this peninsula Iberia and the Romans referred to it as Hispania.

By New Testament times Spain was a part of the Roman Empire. The apostle Paul had a deep desire to visit Spain and preach the gospel (Rom. 15:24, 28). This reflects his plan to preach the gospel and establish the church throughout the Roman Empire. But whether he actually visited Spain is uncertain.

SPAN [see WEIGHTS AND MEASURES].

SPARKS — fiery particles thrown from a fire or burning substance (Is. 1:31; 50:11). Eliphaz, one of Job's friends, remarked, "Man is born to trouble as the sparks fly upward" (Job 5:7).

SPARROW (see ANIMALS OF THE BIBLE).

SPEAR (see ARMS, ARMOR OF THE BIBLE).

SPECK — a splinter or chip of wood (Matt. 7:3–5; Luke 6:41–42; mote, KJV; speck of sawdust, NEB). Jesus used the word in his parable about self-righteous people who looked for specks of dust in the eyes of other people while ignoring entire planks—logs or beams of wood—in their own eyes. He was referring to the hypocrisy of a person who tries to improve others while remaining blind to his own faults.

SPECKLED — several different colors mixed together; spotted or mottled in appearance. As payment for Jacob's work, Laban gave Jacob all the speckled livestock from his herds (Gen. 30:32–39; 31:8, 12; dappled, NEB).

SPECTACLE — an object of curiosity or contempt (Nah. 3:6; Heb. 10:33). The apostles of Christ were made a spectacle to the world and ridiculed because of their faith (1 Cor. 4:9). The same Greek word translated as spectacle here is translated as theater in Acts 19:29, 31. The verb form of this word is used in Hebrews 10:33. It means to make a public show of, to expose to public shame.

SPELT (see PLANTS OF THE BIBLE).

SPHERE — a field or range of influence. God assigned to the apostle Paul his sphere of work (2 Cor. 10:13–16), an area of activity (v. 15, NIV) that included Corinth.

SPICE, SPICES — sweet-smelling vegetable substances used as incense, holy anointing oil, cosmetics, and perfume. Such spices were also used to prepare bodies for burial.

Myrrh, cinnamon, calamus (or aromatic cane), and cassia were mixed with pure olive oil to make a holy anointing oil (Ex. 30:23–33). This was used to

The Valley of Eshcol, where the 12 spies sent out by Moses picked huge clusters of grapes (Num. 13:17, 23).

anoint items of worship in the Temple or tabernacle sanctuary. Holy anointing oil was also used to consecrate Aaron, the high priest, and his sons for their service in the priesthood.

Stacte, onycha, and galbanum were mixed with pure frankincense to make incense or perfume. This was placed in the tabernacle of the congregation where God would meet with Moses (Ex. 30:34–36).

Spices were also used to prepare bodies for burial (2 Chr. 16:14). Nicodemus brought "a mixture of myrrh and aloes, about a hundred pounds" (John 19:39), with which he prepared the body of Jesus for burial after His death on the cross.

Most spices used in Palestine came from Southern Arabia (Ezek. 27:22), but some came from Syria (Gen. 37:25). Spices were valuable and expensive, and they were considered a luxury among the Jewish people. The disciples rebuked a woman for her indulgence when she anointed Jesus with a costly oil. But Jesus replied, "Let her alone....She has done what she could. She has come beforehand to anoint my body for burial" (Mark 14:6, 8).

Also see BURIAL; EMBALMING.

SPIDER (see ANIMALS OF THE BIBLE).

SPIES — agents who operate in undercover fashion to obtain information about the enemy. Spies are mentioned in two specific places in the Old Testament.

In Numbers 13—14 Moses sent 12 men into the land of Canaan to gather information about its manpower, defenses, and fertility. They returned 40 days later with samples of fruit and produce of the land. Their opinion was unanimous concerning the fertility of Canaan: "It truly flows with milk

and honey" (Num. 13:27). But they were divided on whether the land should be invaded. Because of their lack of faith in God, the Hebrew people were forced to wander for 40 additional years in the wilderness.

Spies are also mentioned in Joshua 2. After the Israelites had crossed the Jordan, Joshua sent two men to gather information about the city of Jericho (Heb. 11:31; James 2:25).

SPIKENARD (see PLANTS OF THE BIBLE).

SPINDLE — a round stick with tapered ends used to form and twist the yarn in hand spinning. The spindle and the DISTAFF are the most ancient of all instruments used in the craft of spinning (Prov. 31:19). About 8 to 12 inches long, spindles were used to guide the thread as it was fashioned into cloth. The weaver sometimes turned the spindle by rolling it across her thigh. Also see CLOTH.

SPINNING — the art of twisting natural fibers and converting them into yarn or thread for making cloth. Among the Hebrew people, as in many ancient cultures, spinning was the work of women. Spinning was done by hand, because the spinning wheel was unknown at that time. In hand spinning the DISTAFF and SPINDLE were used.

The wool or flax was wound on the distaff, which was stuck upright in the ground or held under the arm, and the thread was drawn out by hand. The spindle, which had a circular rim to steady it when revolving, was attached to the thread being drawn out from the distaff. By rotating the spindle, the spinner twisted the thread.

Also see CLOTH.

SPIRIT — a word with three distinct meanings in the Bible:

1. The word is used as a general reference in the New Testament to the spirit of human beings (Matt. 5:3; Rom. 8:16; Heb. 4:12). Jesus made several specific references to His spirit in a human sense (Mark 2:8; John 11:33), as did Paul (Acts 17:16; 2 Cor. 2:13). Paul sometimes referred to the spirits of those to whom he wrote (Gal. 6:18; 2 Tim. 4:22).

2. A second common usage of the word is in reference to good and evil spirits, meaning the beings other than God and humans. An example of a good spirit is an angel (Ps. 104:4). The Bible also contains many references to evil spirits (Mark 9:25; Acts 19:12-17; Rev. 18:2).

3. The word spirit also refers to the Spirit of God, the Holy Spirit. In the Old Testament, the Spirit occasionally came upon people to give them power to do God's will or to enable them to serve God in a special way. For example, the Spirit of the Lord enabled Samson to kill a young lion with his bare hands (Judg. 14:5-6). Earlier the Spirit of God had given Bezaleel wisdom and skill to build the tabernacle (Ex. 31:3). The Spirit of the Lord also enabled the judges to lead Israel to military victory (Judg. 3:10; 11:29) and the prophets to prophesy (Num. 24:2; Ezek. 11:5).

In the New Testament, the Holy Spirit was an even more active presence among the people of God. The Holy Spirit was the agent of fulfillment of Old Testament prophecies (Acts 1:16; 2:16-21; 3:18; 28:25-27), and He continued to inspire Christian prophets and workers in order to work His will on earth (Acts 2:4; 19:6). The Holy Spirit came upon new Christians (Acts 10:44-48), purified and sanctified them (2 Cor. 3:18; 2 Thess. 2:13), and guided the direction of early Christian missionary work (Acts 10:19-20; 16:6-7).

This Holy Spirit is the Spirit of Jesus (2 Cor. 3:17). A person can relate to Jesus only by means of the Holy Spirit (Rom. 8:9; Gal. 4:6). In the Gospel of John, He is called the Helper (John 14:16-17).

SPIRIT, HOLY (see HOLY SPIRIT).

SPIRITS, FAMILIAR (see MAGIC, SORCERY, AND DIVINATION).

SPIRITS IN PRISON — those to whom Jesus preached in connection with His death and resurrection (1 Pet. 3:19). Several interpretations have been suggested for this puzzling passage.

Some believe the reference is to departed human spirits, especially those of Noah's day who heard preaching by the Spirit or by the preincarnate Christ through Noah. These spirits, who are disembodied, now await final judgment. Others believe the phrase refers to the spirits of the departed saints of the Old Testament to whom Christ, at His death, proclaimed liberty from the bonds of death. However, the Greek word for spirits used in this verse is never applied to human spirits. It is always used to refer to supernatural beings, both good and evil (Luke 10:20; Heb. 1:14).

The most logical explanation of this passage is that Jesus made a proclamation of His victory over death to the rebellious angels who had been placed in prison. His proclamation was also a form of judgment on them because of their sin and rebellion. This idea also seems to be supported by 2 Peter 2:4 and Jude 6.

SPIRITUAL — of the spirit or non-material. The word spiritual refers to non-material things, including a spiritual body (1 Cor. 15:44-46) and spiritual things as distinct from earthly goods (Rom. 15:27; 1 Cor. 9:11). But the most important use of the word is in reference to the Holy Spirit. The Spirit gave the law (Rom. 7:14) and supplied Israel with water and food (1 Cor. 10:3-4).

The Christian's every blessing is from the Spirit (Eph. 1:3), as is his understanding of truth (1 Cor. 2:13-15; Col. 1:9). His songs should be sung in the Spirit (Eph. 5:19; Col. 3:16), and his ability to understand Scripture correctly is given by the Spirit (Rev. 11:8). He is to be so dominated by the Spirit that he can be called spiritual (1 Cor. 2:15; Gal. 6:1).

SPIRITUAL BLESSINGS (see BLESSINGS).

SPIRITUAL BODY (see BODY, SPIRITUAL).

SPIRITUAL GIFTS — special gifts bestowed by the Holy Spirit upon Christians for the purpose of building up the church. The list of spiritual gifts in 1 Corinthians 12:8-10 includes wisdom, knowledge, faith, healing, miracles, prophecy, discerning of spirits, speaking in tongues, and interpretation of tongues. Similar lists appear in Ephesians 4:7-13 and Romans 12:3-8.

The apostle Paul indicated that these gifts are equally valid but not equally valuable. Their value is determined by their worth to the church. In dealing with this matter, he used the analogy of the human body. All members of the body have functions, Paul declared, but some are more important than others. The service of each Christian should be in proportion to the gifts which he possesses (1 Corinthians 12—14).

Since these gifts are gifts of grace, according to Paul, their use must be controlled by the principle of love—the greatest of all spiritual gifts (1 Corinthians 13).

SPIRITUALITY — sensitivity or commitment to religious values and sacred matters. In the New Testament a person is spiritual because of the indwelling presence and power of the Holy Spirit and the spiritual gifts which He imparts to the believer (1 Cor. 12:1; Col. 1:9).

SPIT, SPITTLE — saliva, the liquid formed in the mouth. Under the Mosaic Law, the spit of certain sick persons was recognized as unclean (Lev. 15:8). Lack of control of one's own saliva indicated insanity (1 Sam. 21:13).

Spitting in the face was a gesture of contempt, a deliberate insult (Num. 12:14; Job 17:6; 30:10). Isaiah prophesied that our Lord would be so humiliated, as indeed He was (Is. 50:6; Matt. 27:30; Mark 15:19). Jesus Himself had spoken of such humiliation (Mark 10:34; Luke 18:32).

SPLINT — a rigid device, such as a piece of wood or other hard material, used to immobilize a broken bone or to maintain any part of the body in a fixed position. Through the prophet Ezekiel, the Lord declared that He would break the arm of Pharaoh, king of Egypt, and would not allow it to be treated with a splint (Ezek. 30:21). This broken arm refers to the defeat of Pharaoh Hophra, who sent an army to relieve the siege of Jerusalem in 588 B.C. Nebuchadnezzar, the king of Babylon, withdrew from the battle just long enough to smash the Egyptian army.

SPOIL (see BOOTY).

SPOKES — the rods or braces that connect the hub and the rim of a wheel (1 Kin. 7:33).

SPOKESMAN — a person who speaks as a representative of another person. When Moses balked at obeying God's call to be a leader of the Hebrews because of his lack of speaking ability, God replied that Aaron would be his spokesman (Ex. 4:14, 16).

SPONGE (see ANIMALS OF THE BIBLE).

SPOONS — KJV word for PANS.

SPORTS (see GAMES).

SPOT — KJV word for a discoloration or blemish on the skin. In Old Testament times, a certain spot on a person's body could indicate the presence of leprosy—a dreaded skin disease. The word is also used in connection with sacrificial animals. Only perfect animals—those without spot or blemish—were to be offered to God. This Old Testament terminology is echoed in the New Testament, where Jesus is described as "a lamb without blemish and without spot" (1 Pet. 1:19)—the perfect sacrifice for our sin. Also see DISEASES OF THE BIBLE.

SPRING (see FOUNTAIN).

SPRINKLING — a ceremonial act of consecration. God often commanded that an unclean object be sprinkled with water, olive oil, or blood (Lev. 14:48–52; Num. 19:18–20). Sprinkling signified that an impurity had been recognized and then cleansed. In symbolic recognition that blood would be required to cleanse man's sinful heart, the Old Testament priests would sprinkle the blood of an unblemished lamb around the altar (Lev. 3:7–8). These acts were in preparation for the sacrifice of Christ. In His death, Christ would "sprinkle many nations" (Is. 52:15), thus cleansing the hearts of all people who accept Him and ending the necessity for ceremonial sprinkling (Heb. 9:13–14).

SPRINKLING–BOWLS — large bowls, made of bronze, silver, or gold, used in the tabernacle and the Temple for holding the grain offering and for receiving the blood of sacrifices (2 Kin. 12:6–14).

SQUAD — a group of four Roman soldiers on guard duty (Acts 12:4; quaternion, KJV). Herod the king (Herod Agrippa I) captured the apostle Peter, put him in prison, and delivered him to "four squads of soldiers." Each squad of soldiers guarded Peter for a WATCH, which lasted three hours. There were four such watches in any night. Peter was chained between two soldiers; the other two stood guard at the door (Acts 12:6).

STABLE (see STALL).

STACHYS [STAY kis] (*ear of grain*) — a Christian at Rome to whom the apostle Paul sent greetings (Rom. 16:9).

STACTE (see PLANTS OF THE BIBLE).

STADION, FURLONG (see WEIGHTS AND MEASURES).

STAFF — a short pole or stick used for many different purposes in Bible times. A staff was used much like a walking cane by travelers (Gen. 32:10), the elderly (Heb. 11:21), and the lame (2 Sam. 3:29); but it could also serve as a simple weapon, especially in the hands of a SHEPHERD (1 Sam. 17:40). A staff also symbolized a leader's authority (Is. 14:5), as well as God's protection of the believer (Ps. 23:4). Also see ROD.

STAG (see ANIMALS OF THE BIBLE).

STAIRS — a series of steps for passing from one level to another. In Bible times, the typical house had a flat roof where many family activities took place. A flight of stairs outside the house provided access to the roof. Stairs, or wide steps on the city streets, also made travel between various levels of the city easier (Neh. 12:37). Archaeologists have discovered stairs leading down into deep wells or cisterns at such sites as Beth Zur, Gezer, Gibeon, Megiddo, and Qumran.

STAKES — long, pointed pegs used to anchor tents, such as the tabernacle (Is. 33:20). The stakes of the tabernacle were made of bronze. Stakes could be made of metal (such as bronze, iron, or silver), but wood was by far the most common substance used.

STALL — a place where livestock were kept and fed. In biblical times, the animal quarters were usually connected to the house, rather than in separate buildings. In two–story houses domestic animals were usually kept on the ground level; the family lived upstairs. King Solomon's stables had stalls for thousands of horses (2 Chr. 9:25). King Hezekiah had "stalls for all kinds of livestock" (2 Chr. 32:28).

The Greek word for stall appears only once in the New Testament: Mary wrapped the baby Jesus in swaddling clothes and laid him in a "stall." This word is rendered as manger in most translations.

STAMMER, STAMMERING — to speak with spasmodic repetitions of syllables and sounds (Is. 32:4; 33:19). The prophet Isaiah realized that the people of Jerusalem had closed their ears to the plain words of God. Therefore, "with stammering lips and another tongue He will speak to this people" (Is. 28:11). Isaiah declared that a barbarian conqueror, uttering a strange, jabbering language, would eventually capture Jerusalem and take God's people into Captivity. This prophecy was fulfilled when the Babylonians overran Jerusalem in 586 B.C.

STANDARD — a symbol carried on a pole and raised high in the air, much like a flag, to rally a tribe or a group of warriors in battle (Num. 2:10; Is. 59:19). These standards or ensigns were probably carvings or likenesses of animals raised on a spear or pole (Num. 21:8-9). These were usually set on a hill and often were accompanied by the sound of a trumpet. The Bible does not describe Israel's official standard; so we have no idea of its appearance.

The eagle was one of the earliest known standards. In fact, it became the official standard or symbol of the Roman Empire. Other popular animal standards were stags, steers, horses, lions, unicorns, serpents, and wolves. Assyrian armies carried the moon sickle mounted on a spear in honor of their god, Ashur.

STAR — any of the heavenly bodies visible in the night sky. In the Bible the word star is used as a generic term for all the heavenly bodies—including stars, planets, comets, and meteors—but excluding the sun and the moon. In this general sense, the phrase the host of heaven sometimes refers to all the astronomical phenomena visible in the night sky (2 Kin. 17:16; 21:3–5; 23:4–5). Stars are usually referred to either in connection with God's power in creation (Gen. 1:16), the promised number of Abraham's descendants (Gen. 22:17), or God's power exhibited in judgment (Joel 2:10; Matt. 24:29).

The word star is also used as a figure of speech for angels. Job 38:7 speaks of "the morning stars" singing together and all "the sons of God" shouting for joy. The morning stars are a poetic way of speaking of angels. This symbolic usage is most obvious in the Book of Revelation (Rev. 8:10–11; 9:1–2).

STAR OF BETHLEHEM — the heavenly sign by which God announced the birth of Christ. The star is mentioned only in the Book of Matthew in connection with the visit of the wise men (Matt. 2:2, 7, 9–10). This star, observed by wise men from the East (probably Mesopotamia), may be what the Mesopotamian prophet Balaam refers to in Numbers 24:17: "A Star shall come out of Jacob."

Various attempts have been made to explain the star in scientific terms. Since the wise men were Babylonian astrologers, it is reasonable to assume they were men who had seen the star during their regular observations of the heavens. Men who were familiar with the night sky would readily identify any new object.

Some scholars suggest that a supernova, or exploding star, recorded by Chinese astronomers at about the time of Christ, might have led the wise men to Bethlehem. Others argue that a rare alignment of planets in the sky signaled a highly unusual event to the astrologers. The appearance of a meteor or an unidentified comet has also been suggested.

The event as recorded in Matthew indicates the star was a supernatural phenomenon. The Bible clearly declares that the star "went before them, til it came and stood over where the young Child was" (Matt. 2:9). None of the proposed natural explanations fits this description adequately. Matthew obviously understood the star as an occurrence beyond the reach of rationalistic explanations. At the same time, our attention should be focused not on the Star of Bethlehem, but on the Messiah, Jesus Christ, whose birth the star proclaimed.

STARGAZER (see MAGIC, SORCERY, AND DIVINATION).

STARS, THE ELEVEN — a symbolic reference to the 11 brothers of Joseph. Of all his 12 sons, Jacob loved Joseph the most "because he was the son of his old age" (Gen. 37:3). This favoritism aroused the jealousy of Joseph's brothers. Joseph did not help the situation when he related his dreams of greatness. He told his brothers he had a dream in which "the sun, the moon, and the eleven stars bowed down to me" (Gen. 37:9). This dream came true years later when Joseph arose to become a high official in the Egyptian government. Because of a famine in Palestine, his brothers were forced to go to Egypt to ask Joseph for grain (Genesis 42—45).

STATURE — a person's height. Jesus increased in wisdom and stature (Luke 2:52). Zacchaeus was of short stature (Luke 19:3). The apostle Paul encouraged his readers to measure up to the "stature of the fullness of Christ" (Eph. 4:13). Stature can also refer to one's age, or span of life. When Jesus said, "Which of you by worrying can add one cubit to his stature?" (Matt. 6:27), He may have been saying that one cannot prolong life by worrying about the time of death.

STATUTE — a decree or law issued by a ruler or governing body, or especially by God as the supreme ruler (Gen. 26:5; Ps. 18:22; Ezek. 5:6).

STAVE — KJV word for POLE.

STEADFASTNESS — stability in commitment or belief. The apostle Paul referred to "the steadfastness of your faith in Christ" (Col. 2:5). The loss of stability may be avoided if one will "grow in the grace and knowledge of our Lord and Savior Jesus Christ" (2 Pet. 3:18).

STEALING (see LAW).

STEALTH — to act in a secret, undercover way. The apostle Paul said that certain false believers had come into the church by stealth (privily, KJV; secretly, RSV) to spy out the liberty of the Christian fellowship and make them slaves to the old Jewish law (Gal. 2:4).

STEEL (see MINERALS OF THE BIBLE).

STEPHANAS [STEFF ah nus] (*crown-bearer*) — a Christian in the church at Corinth who was baptized by the apostle Paul (1 Cor. 1:16). The church at Corinth sent Stephanas, Fortunatus, and Achaicus to Paul while he was at Ephesus, informing him of the situation in Corinth. Paul apparently was encouraged by the good news which they brought (1 Cor. 16:17).

STEPHEN — one of the first seven deacons of the early church and the first Christian martyr. The story of Stephen is found in Acts 6:7—7:60.

In the period following PENTECOST, the number of Christians in the New Testament church grew steadily. Followers were eventually recruited not only from among the Jews in Palestine but also from among the Jews in Greek settlements. The church had to appoint several men to handle the work of providing aid to these needy Christians.

Stephen was one of the first seven "good and worthy men" chosen to provide relief to these needy Christians from Greek backgrounds. Since Stephen is mentioned first in the list of the seven administrators, he was probably the most important leader in this group. Although they are not specifically named as deacons, these seven men are considered to be the forerunners of the office of deacon that developed later in the early church. Stephen assumed a place of prominence among these seven leaders as the church grew (Acts 6:7).

Stephen was probably critical of the system of Old Testament laws, claiming they had already lost their effectiveness because they had reached fulfillment in Christ. This viewpoint, which Stephen argued very skillfully, brought him into conflict with powerful leaders among the Jewish people. Stephen became well-known as a preacher and a miracle-worker (Acts 6:8). His work was so effective that renewed persecution of the Christians broke out.

Members of certain Jewish synagogues felt that Stephen had blasphemed Moses and God. They accused him of being disloyal to the Temple and rejecting Moses. He was also accused of hostility toward Judaism—a charge that had never been made before against other disciples. In debates the Jews were no match for Stephen; even Saul was outwitted by him. Thus, they resorted to force.

Stephen was arrested and brought before the SANHEDRIN, the Jewish council, where charges were placed against him. False witnesses testified against him. The high priest then asked Stephen if these things were true. Stephen was not dismayed. When he stood before them his face was "as the face of an angel" (Acts 6:15).

The lengthy speech which Stephen made in his own defense is reported in detail in Acts 7:2-53. Stephen summarized Old Testament teachings, showing how God had guided Israel toward a specific goal. He reviewed Israel's history in such a way that he replied to all the charges made against him without actually denying anything. This amounted to a criticism of the Sanhedrin itself. Stephen de-

nounced the council as "stiff-necked and uncircumcised in heart and ears" and accused them of resisting the Holy Spirit. Then he charged that they had killed Christ, just as their ancestors had killed the prophets. He accused them of failing to keep their own law (Acts 7:51-53).

Stephen's speech enraged the Sanhedrin so that they were "cut to the heart, and they gnashed at him with their teeth" (Acts 7:54). At this moment Stephen had a vision of God in heaven, with Jesus on His right hand. Stephen's fate was sealed when he reported this vision to his enemies. The crowd rushed upon him, dragged him out of the city, and stoned him to death (Acts 7:55-58).

Among the people consenting to Stephen's death that day was Saul, who later became the apostle Paul—great Christian missionary to the Gentiles. As he was being stoned, Stephen asked God not to charge his executioners with the sin of his death (Acts 7:59-60).

Stephen's martyrdom was followed by a general persecution which forced the disciples to flee from Jerusalem into the outlying areas. This scattering led to the preaching of the gospel first to the Samaritans and then to the Gentiles in the nations surrounding Palestine.

STEW — a dish of boiled food, usually of vegetables such as lentils, legumes, beans, or peas (Gen. 25:29-30, 34; pottage, KJV, RSV; broth, NEB). Jacob bought Esau's birthright for a red stew made of lentils, a dish that would have been part of the everyday diet of that time. Such a stew provided an inexpensive source of protein. A stew, or thick vegetable soup, was eaten by Elisha's disciples (2 Kin. 4:38-40); such a broth was mentioned by the prophet Haggai, along with bread and wine, as a common food (Hag. 2:12).

STEWARD (see OCCUPATIONS AND TRADES).

STEWARDSHIP — the management of another person's property, finances, or household affairs. As far as Christians are concerned, stewardship involves the responsibility of managing God's work through the church. God has appointed all Christians to be His stewards on earth. Stewardship is not an option, as Paul points out about his own call. Being a steward is a necessary part of believing the gospel, even if it involves sacrificing personal rewards (1 Cor. 9:17).

As the parable of the talents (Matt. 25:14-30) shows, Christians will be held accountable for the way in which they manage God's affairs as stewards. These matters include extending the church's ministry through the preaching of the gospel (Col. 1:24-28), supporting the church financially (Acts 4:32-37), and ministering to the sick and needy (Matt. 25:31-46).

STIFF-NECKED — stubborn, unyielding, arrogant, and proud. The phrase *a stiff-necked people* is a figure of speech for rebellion and disobedience taken from stubborn domestic animals, such as oxen that turn their shoulders away from the yoke and refuse to follow directions. Israel was stiff-necked in refusing to obey the Word of God and in following after idolatry and immorality (Deut. 31:27; Neh. 9:16–17, 29; Jer. 17:23).

STOCKS — an instrument of confinement and punishment. Stocks were heavy wooden frames with holes into which a person's arms and legs were clamped to hold the prisoner in a sitting position. A collar was also used at times to hold the head in place. The prophet Jeremiah was put into stocks (Jer. 20:2–3; 29:26) as was (probably) Hanani the seer (2 Chr. 16:10, NEB; prison, NKJV). The author of the Book of Job spoke of stocks as a symbol of suffering (13:27; 33:11).

In New Testament times, stocks used by the Romans had a number of holes so the prisoner's legs could be spread widely, causing great discomfort. Paul and Silas were thrown into prison and put in stocks at Philippi. Instead of moaning in pain, they sang hymns and praised God until they were freed by an earthquake (Acts 16:24–26).

STOICISM [STOW uh siz em] — the doctrine of the Stoics, a Greek school of philosophy which taught that human beings should be free from passion, unmoved by joy or grief, and submissive to natural law, calmly accepting all things as the result of divine will.

Stoicism was one of the most influential Greek schools of philosophy in the New Testament period. It took its name from the *Stoa Poikile*, the portico or lecture place in Athens where its founder, Zeno, taught.

The Stoics believed that man is part of the universe which itself is dominated by reason. God is identified with the world–soul and so inhabits everything. Therefore, man's goal is to identify himself with this universal reason which determines his destiny, to find his proper place in the natural

order of things. Since man cannot change this grand design, it is best for him to cooperate and to take his part in the world order. Moreover, he must live above any emotional involvement with life, exemplifying a detached virtue in serving others. Above all, he must be self–sufficient, living life with dignity and pride.

The apostle Paul used the word self–sufficient in a radically different sense in Philippians 4:11. Here Paul spoke of the believer's self–sufficiency in God. Paul's speech on the AREOPAGUS, or Mars' Hill (Acts 17:16–34), interacts with Stoic ideas, arguing that the highest good is not internal (in man's union with nature) but external (in a right relationship with God).

In his address, Paul quoted one of the Stoic poets (Aratus), who said, "For we are also His offspring" (Acts 17:28). Some of these philosophers ridiculed Paul, but others invited him to address them again about the Christ in whom he believed so strongly (Acts 17:32).

STOMACH — the digestive tract of the body. The word BELLY was preferred by the KJV translators. Stomach occurs in the KJV only in 1 Timothy 5:23. Modern versions have used stomach instead of belly in many instances (for example, Matt. 15:17; Luke 15:16; Rev. 10:9–10).

STONE — a hardened, granite–like mass formed from soil, clay, and minerals. The soil of Palestine was rough and rocky. The most common stones were limestone (Is. 27:9) and flint. Because wood was scarce, city walls, houses (Lev. 14:45; Amos 5:11), palaces (1 Kin. 7:1, 9), temples (1 Kin. 6:7), courtyards, columns, and streets were built of hewn stone.

The abundance of stones cleared from fields (Is. 5:2) provided the people with excellent weapons against their enemies. Stones were thrown on an enemy's field to ruin it and were used to stop up his wells (2 Kin. 3:19, 25; Eccl. 3:5). Knives were made from flint stones. Larger weapons of war, such as slings (1 Sam. 17:40, 49), catapults (2 Chr. 26:14), and bows also made use of stones. Stoning was a common form of capital punishment. Stones served also as boundary and treaty markers (Gen. 31:46; Deut. 19:14; 27:17; Job 24:2) for individuals and nations.

In addition to their practical uses, stones were also used for sacred, spiritual purposes. Memorials were built from large stones to mark an unusual event (Gen. 28:18; 31:45; Josh. 4:9; 1 Sam. 7:12). Stone mounds also marked graves (2 Sam. 18:17). Small, smooth stones occasionally became a part of the Israelites' idol worship (Is. 57:6). The Hebrew people were apparently influenced by surrounding pagan cultures and believed that meteorites were sacred. While the Gentiles believed that meteorites talked and served as protection from evil, the Israelites often dedicated them to God (Gen. 28:18–22; Is. 19:19) but did not worship them as heathen nations did.

In a figurative way, stones imply firmness and

Both large and small stones were used in the construction of walls, fortresses, residences, and public buildings in Bible times.

An iron stove from the first century A.D. excavated at Pompeii.

strength (Gen. 49:24), as well as insensibility and hardness (1 Sam. 25:37; Ezek. 11:19). "Jesus Christ Himself being the chief cornerstone" (Eph. 2:20) describes best the stone's symbolism for Christ as the strength and foundation of Christianity. The references to the cut stone from the mountainside in Daniel 2:34–35, 45 have been interpreted to represent Christ and the church.

STONECUTTER, STONEMASON, STONE-WORKER (see OCCUPATIONS AND TRADES).

STONES, PRECIOUS (see JEWELS AND PRECIOUS STONES).

STONING — the usual method of capital punishment in ancient Israel. People who broke specific statutes of the law of Moses were put to death by stoning. Stoning was usually carried out by the men of the community (Deut. 21:21), upon the testimony of at least two witnesses, who cast the first stones (Deut. 17:5–7; John 8:7; Acts 7:58). Stoning usually took place outside the settlement or camp (Lev. 24:14, 23; 1 Kin. 21:10, 13).

Acts punishable by stoning were certain cases of disobedience (Josh. 7:25), child sacrifice (Lev. 20:2), consultation with magicians (Lev. 20:27), blasphemy (John 10:31–32), Sabbath-breaking (Num. 15:32–36), the worship of false gods (Deut. 13:10), rebellion against parents (Deut. 21:21), and adultery (Ezek. 16:40).

Jesus once encountered a woman who was about to be stoned because she had been found guilty of adultery. Her accusers walked away when He declared, "He who is without sin among you, let him throw a stone at her first" (John 8:7).

STOOL (see BIRTHSTOOL).

STOREHOUSE, STORAGE CITY — a supply depot or warehouse for the storage of government supplies, such as food, treasures, and military equipment (1 Chr. 26:15; 27:25; 2 Chr. 11:11). The difference between a storehouse and a storage city may be only one of size or complexity.

The Hebrew slaves in Egypt were forced to build PITHOM and RAAMSES, "supply cities" for Pharaoh (Ex. 1:11; store cities, RSV, NEB, NIV; treasure cities, KJV; storage cities, NASB). Various kings of the Israelites also built storage cities. These included Solomon (1 Kin. 9:19; 2 Chr. 8:4, 6), who built facilities to house his chariots, horses, and cavalry; Baasha (2 Chr. 16:5–6); Jehoshaphat (2 Chr. 17:12); and Hezekiah (2 Chr. 32:27–29).

The concept of the storage city or storehouse is at least as old as the time of Joseph. He established a food reserve that saved Egypt from famine (Genesis 41). During seven years of plenty, Joseph had the Egyptian farmers store one-fifth of their produce. Then, when seven years of famine struck, the grain in the storehouses kept starvation from the land.

In the ancient world, storehouses were sometimes situated underground. Oil and wine were often kept in cellars. At Megiddo archaeologists discovered a large underground silo pit for grain storage. This pit, with a capacity of almost 13,000 bushels of grain, apparently dates back to the time of King Solomon.

The prophet Malachi accused the people of his day of robbing God by withholding from Him their tithes and offerings (Mal. 3:8–9). Then he said, "Bring all the tithes into the storehouse" (Mal. 3:10). "Storehouse" apparently refers to a special treasury-chamber, probably within the Temple precincts and administered by LEVITES.

STORK (see ANIMALS OF THE BIBLE).

STOVE — an oven for cooking (Lev. 11:35). Stoves as such were not used in biblical times, since cooking was done over an open fire or in an oven. Ovens ranged from a heated stone on which dough was spread to cone-shaped earthenware structures. The bread dough was spread on the heated surface of these ovens for cooking.

STRAIGHT STREET — a main thoroughfare in the ancient city of Damascus where the apostle Paul was visited by Ananias (Acts 9:11).

STRAIN OUT — to separate impurities from a liquid, such as wine (Matt. 23:24; strain at, KJV; strain off, NEB). In this verse, Jesus criticized the hypocrisy of the Pharisees. He described them as zealously trying to strain a gnat out of a liquid before they drank it, while at the same time swallowing a camel—a graphic picture of their sin and self-righteousness.

STRANGER (see FOREIGNER).

STRANGLING — to kill an animal without bloodshed by choking or squeezing its throat and cutting off its oxygen supply. According to the law of Moses, the Israelites were forbidden to eat "flesh with its life, that is, its blood" (Gen. 9:4). Therefore, they could not eat strangled animals because these still contained blood.

STRAW (see PLANTS OF THE BIBLE).

STREETS — roadways through cities and villages. In Bible times, streets were little more than twisting paths, dusty or muddy and unpaved. The psalmist spoke of taking revenge against his enemies, whom he cast out "like dirt in the streets" (Ps. 18:42).

Business streets of biblical cities were lined with open–front stores, each devoted to one kind of trade or selling items of one specific type. Proof of this comes from the time of the prophet Jeremiah. King Zedekiah threw Jeremiah in prison with the sarcastic words, "Give him daily a piece of bread from the bakers' street, until all the bread in the city [is] gone" (Jer. 37:21).

A few of the larger cities of Bible times had wide streets or major thoroughfares, similar to modern boulevards. Three rows of columns divided the street called Straight in Damascus (Acts 9:11) into three avenues. Similar boulevards also existed in such major cities as Babylon in Babylonia and Alexandria in Egypt.

STRINGED INSTRUMENTS (see MUSICAL INSTRUMENTS).

STRIPES — blows or lashes dealt out as punishment during Bible times. Stripes could be inflicted with blows from a rod or lashes from a whip. Mosaic Law spelled out that no more than 40 blows should be given to a condemned person (Deut. 25:3). Isaiah's prophecy of the future Messiah declared, "By His stripes we are healed" (Is. 53:5). Jesus fulfilled this prophecy (1 Pet. 2:24).

STRONG DRINK (see DRINK, STRONG).

STUBBLE — that part of grain plants left in the ground after the crop has been harvested. God's judgment upon unrighteousness is often pictured as a destroying fire raging through a field of stubble (Ex. 15:7; Joel 2:5). In several places, the NKJV translates as straw (Job 21:18; 41:29; 1 Cor. 3:12) or chaff (Ps. 83:13).

STUMBLING BLOCK — a cause of stumbling; anything that leads others to sin. The word is used literally (Lev. 19:14) as well as symbolically (Jer. 6:21; Zeph. 1:3). Christ was a stumbling block to the unbelieving people of His own nation, just as He continues to be a stumbling block today to all those without faith in Him (1 Cor. 1:23). Christians may also be stumbling blocks when they exercise their freedom at the expense of those who are weak (1 Cor. 8:9). Also see OFFENSE.

SUAH [SUE ah] (meaning unknown) — a son of Zophah, of the tribe of Asher (1 Chr. 7:36).

SUBURBS (see COMMON–LANDS).

SUCATHITES [SUE kuh thites] — a form of SUCHATHITES.

SUCCOTH [SUK oth] (*booths*) — the name of a town and a district in the Bible:

1. An ancient town in Transjordan where Jacob built booths for his cattle and a dwelling for his family after he and Esau separated (Gen. 33:17). During the period of the judges, this town was severely punished by Gideon for refusing to help him

This street in the Roman city of Pompeii had raised stepping stones that allowed pedestrians to avoid standing rain water. The stones were spaced to allow chariot wheels to pass between them.

The mound of Tell Deir Alla, identified as Succoth—a city where Jacob lodged (Gen. 33:17).

as he chased the defeated Midianites (Judg. 8:5–16).

2. A district or region where the people of Israel pitched their first encampment after leaving Rameses in Egypt (Ex. 12:37). Succoth may be the same place as Thuku, the area around the Egyptian city of PITHOM. Some scholars identify this Succoth with Tell el–Maskhutah, west of the Bitter Lakes, in the northeastern part of the Nile delta.

SUCCOTH BENOTH [SUK oth bih NAHTH] (see GODS, PAGAN).

SUCHATHITES [SUE kah thites] — a family of scribes who lived at Jabez in the territory allotted to Judah (1 Chr. 2:55; Sucathites, NASB, NIV, RSV). The Suchathites were descendants of Caleb.

SUFFERING — agony, affliction, or distress; intense pain or sorrow. Suffering has been part of the human experience since man's fall into sin (Genesis 3). The Psalms, one-third of which are laments, include graphic descriptions of suffering (Psalm 22). The theme of the Book of Job is the problem of suffering and why God permits the righteous to suffer.

The Bible makes it clear that some suffering is the result of evil action or sin in the world. This type of suffering came upon man after the FALL in the Garden of Eden (Gen. 3:16–19). But some suffering is not related to the past. It is forward–looking in that it serves to shape and refine God's children (1 Pet. 1:6–7; 5:10). The Book of Hebrews declares that Jesus learned obedience by the things which He suffered (Heb. 5:8), and that He was perfected through suffering (Heb. 2:10). Suffering has the potential of demonstrating God's power (2 Cor. 12:7). Those who suffer are in a position to comfort others (2 Cor. 1:3–6).

Suffering also helps believers to identify with Christ, which is more than suffering for Christ. Through persecution and tortures, people have suffered for the sake of Christ and His kingdom (Phil.

1:29; 2 Thess. 1:5; 2 Tim. 3:12). To suffer *with* Christ, however, is another matter. Paul speaks of the "fellowship of His [Christ's] sufferings" (Phil. 3:10). Believers share in the suffering of Christ in the sense that through suffering they identify with Christ. To be a disciple involves suffering like the Master. Christ as Lord and His believers as disciples are bonded even further through the experience of suffering.

Another type of suffering is that endured for the sake of others. The prophet Isaiah portrayed the Suffering Servant as sin–bearer when he declared, "By His stripes we are healed" (Is. 53:5). Jesus announced repeatedly that His suffering was His mission (Matt. 17:12; Luke 24:46). Looking back to the cross, Peter explained that "Christ also suffered once for sins, the just for the unjust, that He might bring us to God" (1 Pet. 3:18).

SUFFERING SERVANT (see SERVANT OF THE LORD).

SUICIDE — the act of taking one's own life. The word suicide does not occur in the Bible. Neither are there any laws relating to it. But the Bible does give several examples of suicide, including Saul and his armorbearer (1 Sam. 31:4–5); and Zimri, king of Israel, who "burned the king's house down upon himself with fire" (1 Kin. 16:18), when Tirzah was besieged. In the New Testament, Judas killed himself because of his shame and grief at betraying Jesus (Matt. 27:5).

Human life is sacred, since we are created in God's image (Gen. 1:27). God as the Creator has power over all existence. He alone should control life, whether it continues or stops (Job 1:21; 1 Cor. 6:19).

SUKKIIM [SOOK ih eem] (meaning unknown) — a tribe that fought in the army of Shishak, king of Egypt (2 Chr. 12:3; Sukkims, KJV; Sukkites, NIV).

Along with the Lubim and Ethiopians, the Sukkiim were part of Shishak's army when he attacked Jerusalem in the days of King Rehoboam of Judah (about 926 B.C.).

SUKKIMS [SOOK eems] — a form of SUKKIIM.

SUKKITES [SOOK ites] — a form of SUKKIIM.

SULPHUR (see MINERALS OF THE BIBLE).

SUMER [SOO mehr] — the southern division of ancient BABYLONIA, consisting primarily of the fertile plain between the Tigris and Euphrates Rivers. This area is now the southern part of modern Iraq.

In the Old Testament Sumer is the territory referred to as Shinar (Gen. 10:10; Is. 11:11; Zech. 5:11) or Chaldea (Jer. 50:10; Ezek. 16:29). The term Shinar is also used to describe the land of the great tyrant and empire builder Nimrod, who founded his kingdom in Babel, Erech (Sumerian Uruk), Accad (Akkad or Agade), and Calneh, "in the land of Shinar" (Gen. 10:10). The Tower of Babel was also built "in the land of Shinar" (Gen. 11:2), or Sumer.

Archaeologists believe the inhabitants of ancient Sumer, or the Sumerians, developed the first high civilization in the history of mankind, about 3000 B.C. The Sumerians were the first people to develop writing, consisting of a form of CUNEIFORM script. Major cities of ancient Sumer included the biblical UR (Gen. 11:28, 31; 15:7), the city from which Abraham migrated.

About 2100 B.C. Sumer was conquered by invading tribesmen from the west and north. A mighty warrior named Sargon (later known as Sargon I, Sargon the Great, and Sargon of Akkad), conquered this area and extended his empire from the Persian Gulf to the Mediterranean Sea. He founded a new capital city, Agade, which was, for more than half a century, the richest and most powerful capital in the world. This magnificent capital was destroyed during the reign of Naram-Sin, Sargon's grandson, by the Guti, semibarbaric mountain tribes.

Sumer enjoyed a brief revival at Ur (about 2050 B.C.), only to decline before the rise of the Elamites, a people to their east. Finally, in about 1720 B.C., HAMMURABI of Babylon united Sumer (the southern division of ancient Babylon) and Akkad (the northern division of ancient Babylon) into one empire. This conquest by Hammurabi marked the end of ancient Sumer. But the cultural and intellectual impact of the Sumerians continued until after the PERSIANS became the dominant force in this part of the ancient world.

SUN — a star that sustains life on the earth, being the source of heat and light. Usually the word sun, as used in the Bible, refers to the heavenly body that rises in the morning, shines through the day, and sets in the evening (Gen. 19:23; Ps. 121:6). But the biblical writers also used "sun" in a symbolic or figurative sense. In Psalm 19:4–6 and Isaiah 45:6, the sun speaks of universality. And in Psalm 84:11, God is called "a sun and shield," meaning He sends light and heat and also gives protection.

God created the sun (Gen. 1:16), and therefore it was not worthy of worship by man. Along with the moon, the sun's duty was to regulate the days and the seasons. The sun was also under God's control. On at least two occasions, He interrupted the sun's regular course for His purposes. The sun stood still for Joshua at Gibeon (Josh. 10:13), and it went backwards for Hezekiah when he prayed for an extension of his life (Is. 38:8).

God also has the power to darken the sun. The prophet Joel predicted He would do that on the day of the Lord (Joel 2:31). Three of the gospel writers (Matt. 27:45; Mark 15:33; Luke 23:44–45) tell us that the sun grew dark at the crucifixion. At the end of the world, God will extinguish the sun (Rev. 6:12; 9:2; 21:23; 22:5).

SUN, WORSHIP OF — a form of pagan idolatry commonly practiced in the ancient world, especially by the Assyrians, Chaldeans (Babylonians), Egyptians, and Phoenicians. Worship of the sun and other heavenly bodies was specifically forbidden among the Hebrew people (Deut. 4:19). But a few cases of this form of idolatry did occur among the nation of Israel during their long history.

King Manasseh of Judah built altars for worship of "all the host of heaven" during his administration (2 Kin. 21:5). The prophet Ezekiel also portrayed the abomination of men who had rejected the Temple of the Lord and had turned their faces toward the east to worship the rising sun (Ezek. 8:15–16).

SUNDAY (see LORD'S DAY).

SUNDIAL — a device for measuring time by the position of the sun in the sky. The word dial (KJV), or sundial (NKJV), occurs only twice in the Old Testament, both times in connection with the miracle of the healing of King Hezekiah (2 Kin. 20:11; Is. 38:8). The word itself is derived from a Hebrew verb that means "to go up." This root word appears frequently in the Old Testament in its usual meaning of "step" or "stair."

Some scholars suggest that the sundial mentioned in the Bible actually is not a dial at all but a stairway. This stairway may have been constructed in such a way that a shadow cast by a stationary post or pillar climbed the stairs at the rate of one every half hour. The Greek historian, Herodotus, writing several hundred years after Hezekiah, mentions the use among the Babylonians of a sundial marked off in this fashion.

SUNDIAL OF AHAZ — time-keeping device by which God gave Hezekiah the sign that he would be healed (2 Kin. 20:1–11; Is. 38:4–8). Hezekiah asked that the sun's shadow go backward ten degrees or steps as a sign of his healing. This "dial" was probably not a small disk, as modern readers might suppose, but an escalating stairway on which the sun cast its shadow higher and higher during the day. The biblical writers identified this stairway with Ahaz, probably because it was constructed during his reign. Also see SUNDIAL.

SUPERSCRIPTION (see INSCRIPTION).

SUPERSTITIOUS — KJV word used by the apostle Paul in his famous speech at Athens for the religious beliefs of the Greeks (Acts 17:22; very religious, NKJV). While the Athenian philosophers worshiped many pagan gods, Paul did compliment them because of their respect for divine matters and challenged them to exercise faith in Jesus Christ.

SUPH [soof] (*reeds*) — an unidentified place in the wilderness where Moses explained the Law to the Israelites before they entered the Promised Land (Deut. 1:1; Red Sea, KJV).

SUPHAH [SOO fah] (meaning unknown) —an unknown place near the border of Moab associated with the years of the wilderness wandering in Israel's history (Num. 21:14).

SUPPER, LORD'S (see LORD'S SUPPER).

SUR [soor] (*turning aside*) — an unidentified gate in Jerusalem, probably leading from the king's palace to the Temple area (2 Kin. 11:6). The parallel passage calls it the Gate of the Foundation (2 Chr. 23:5). Also see GATES OF JERUSALEM AND THE TEMPLE.

SURETY — a pledge made to secure against default; one who contracts to assume the debts of another in the event of default. The practice of one man standing as surety for another apparently was prevalent in Old Testament times, judging from the frequency with which the Book of Proverbs warns against its dangers (Prov. 17:18; 22:26). And certainly as financial advice, the proverbial warnings are sound.

But there is a surety more significant than a financial pledge. Judah, for example, pledged to be surety for Benjamin (Gen. 43:9), thus taking responsibility for the life of his brother. This is the kind of far-reaching responsibility which the psalmist had in mind when he asked God to stand as surety for him in the face of his oppressors (Ps. 119:122). This is the kind of responsibility which Christ took by dying and becoming for all men "a surety of a better covenant" (Heb. 7:22; guarantee, NIV, NASB; guarantor, NEB).

SURNAME — a nickname added to a person's formal name. It often is derived from one's physical characteristics, temperament, occupation, or hometown. Jesus gave Simon the surname, Peter ("a rock"). To James and John He gave the surname, Boanerges, meaning "Sons of Thunder" (Mark 3:16–17). Judas, the disciple who betrayed Jesus, was surnamed Iscariot, which may mean, "Man from Kerioth." Also see NAME.

SUSA [SUE suh] — a form of SHUSHAN.

SUSANCHITES [SOO san kites] — the inhabitants of SHUSHAN, a nation of foreigners who repopulated Samaria after the city fell to the Assyrians (Ezra 4:9, KJV).

SUSANNA [SUE zan nah] (*a lily*) — a woman who provided food for Jesus and His disciples during His early ministry in Galilee (Luke 8:3). No further details of her life are known. Also see APOCRYPHA.

SUSI [SOO sih] (*horselike*) — the father of Gaddi, of the tribe of Manasseh (Num. 13:11).

SWADDLE — to wrap in swaddling clothes. These were long, narrow strips of cloth wrapped around a newborn infant to restrict movement (Job 38:9; Luke 2:7, 12). Also see SWADDLING BAND.

SWADDLING BAND — a long, narrow strip of cloth used to wrap a newborn baby. To swaddle a child was to wrap an infant in strips of cloth, much like narrow bandages. This was believed to ensure the correct early development of the limbs. Thus, swaddling was a mark of parental love and care, while the need for swaddling symbolized the humble, dependent position of the newborn child (Ezek. 16:4).

Although she could offer Jesus no better crib than an animal's manger, Mary showed her mother's love by wrapping her baby in swaddling clothes (Luke 2:7, 12). The baby Jesus in swaddling bands reminds us of the great humility of our Lord in becoming a human being for our sakes.

SWALLOW, SWAN (see ANIMALS OF THE BIBLE).

SWEARING (see OATH).

SWEAT — perspiration of the human body, caused by heat, physical labor, or emotional strain. In the Garden of Eden, Adam and Eve disobeyed God by eating the fruit of the forbidden tree. Because of this sin, God cursed the ground with thorns and thistles and said to Adam: "In the sweat of your face you shall eat bread till you return to the ground" (Gen. 3:19). Sweat symbolized the curse placed on mankind at the Fall.

In the Garden of Gethsemane, Jesus was in agony, or great fear, as he approached the cross. As he prayed earnestly, "His sweat became like great drops of blood" (Luke 22:44). Scholars are not sure whether this means Jesus perspired heavily or whether His sweat was actually mixed with blood. Such "bloody sweat" is a rare condition known medically as diapedesis—the passing of blood through the intact walls of blood vessels.

Also see BLOODY SWEAT.

SWEET INCENSE — a fragrant substance usually offered with animal sacrifices and burned daily at the altar of the tabernacle and the Temple in connection with the morning and evening sacrifices (Ex. 30:1–10). Sweet incense was also burned on special occasions such as the Day of Atonement (Lev. 16:12).

The ingredients for sweet incense are given in Exodus 30:34–36 as stacte, onycha, galbanum, and frankincense. Stacte is probably myrrh. If so, stacte and frankincense became two of the three precious gifts brought by the wise men at Christ's birth.

Myrrh, galbanum, and frankincense were obtained from desert plants by stripping bark from

Photo by Howard Vos

Sychar, the Samaritan town where Jesus taught a woman the true nature of worship (John 4:4-42).

the bush to let the sap ooze out. The sap became a resinous gum which yielded fragrant odors when burned. Onycha was a portion of the shell of a sea mollusk which gave off a fragrant odor when roasted.

SWELLING — a discoloration or inflammation of the skin. Under the leprosy laws of the Book of Leviticus, a certain swelling of the skin could indicate the presence of this disease (Lev. 13:2-43; 14:56). The priests were charged with the responsibility of examining these inflammations to diagnose the disease. Also see DISEASES OF THE BIBLE.

SWIFT, SWINE (see ANIMALS OF THE BIBLE).

SWORD (see ARMS, ARMOR OF THE BIBLE).

SYCAMINE, SYCAMORE (see PLANTS OF THE BIBLE).

SYCHAR [SIGH car] (meaning unknown) — a city of Samaria (see Map 6, B-3) mentioned in connection with Jesus' visit to Jacob's Well (John 4:5). The reference indicates it was not a well-known spot— "a city of Samaria which is called Sychar." The fame of Sychar is associated with Jesus' conversation with the woman who came there to draw water, her conversion, and the conversion of many of the Samaritans during His two days in the area. Many scholars identify Sychar with ancient SHECHEM (Gen. 33:18). Jacob's Well, one of the best attested sites in Palestine, is situated on the eastern edge of the valley which separates Mount Gerizim from Mount Ebal.

SYENE [sigh EE neh] (meaning unknown) — a city in southern Egypt on the east bank of the Nile River near the border of Ethiopia (Ezek. 29:10). Syene is the site of modern Aswan, about 890 kilometers (550 miles) south of Cairo.

SYMBOL — an object or signal that stands for something else; usually a visible image which represents a concept. Obviously, concepts are invisible. We cannot point to the idea of democracy as we can point to a car or a dog. A symbol, however, gives us a visible point of reference for these invisible things.

Thus, the American flag is a symbol of those democratic ideas which unite 50 states under one government. Similarly, the rose has long been used by poets to symbolize the idea of beauty; and the lion has come to symbolize courage and strength. The Christian tradition has as its greatest symbol the cross, an object which represents the redeeming work of Christ.

In the Bible we should distinguish between three main kinds of symbols. The first, the poetic symbol, is found throughout the Bible, but especially in the Book of Psalms and the Song of Solomon. These symbols help define the way in which the writer views himself and his world. For instance, David—recognizing that man is vulnerable to the attack of sin—sees God as a "fortress of defense" (Ps. 31:2, 71).

The second kind of symbol, the symbol of religious ceremony, occurs most often in the PENTATEUCH, particularly in the Book of Exodus. These symbols were directly ordained by God for the benefit of the Israelites as they worshiped Him. They served as daily reminders of God's invisible presence and plan. Thus, the cherubim placed on the ARK OF THE COVENANT (Ex. 25:18-19) were symbols of God's presence among His people. The daily sacrifices ordered in Exodus 30 were acts symbolic of God's plan of redemption.

The third kind of symbol, the symbol of prophetic vision, is found in books of prophecy, and in particular in the books of Ezekiel, Daniel, Zechariah, and Revelation. Like the ceremonial symbols, these symbols serve to reveal God's plan for man; but their emphasis is the future rather than the present. These symbols are generally very colorful images which evoke the mystery of the unseen future.

SYNAGOGUE — a congregation of Jews for worship or religious study. The word synagogue comes from the Greek *sunagoge* (literally, "a leading or bringing together"), which refers to any assembly or gathering of people for secular or religious purposes. Eventually the term came to refer exclusively to an assembly of Jewish people.

The synagogue was a place where local groups of Jews in cities and villages anywhere could gather for the reading and explanation of the Jewish sacred Scriptures and for prayer. The original emphasis was not on preaching but instruction in the law of Moses.

Function. A distinction must be made between synagogue worship and tabernacle or Temple worship. The tabernacle of Moses' day was enclosed by a fence of curtains. None but the priests dared enter this area. The people brought their animals for sacrifice to the gate of the court but could go no further. The later temples of Solomon, Zerubbabel, and Herod (the Temple of Jesus' day) did have courts or porches where the people could pray or have discussions (Matt. 26:55; Luke 2:46; Acts 2:46), but the Temple precincts proper were for the priests only.

In synagogues, on the other hand, the people took part in worship, reading of the Scriptures, and prayer. By New Testament times synagogues were very numerous and popular. They became centers of community activity, playing a number of roles.

Sometimes they were local courts of justice which could sentence the offender as well as inflict the punishment of scourging (Matt. 10:17; 23:34). The synagogue was also an elementary school for teaching children to read. It was, no doubt, a center of social life for the Jewish community.

Origin. The Jewish captives in Babylon did not have a temple or an altar, but they longed for communion with God. This longing is clearly reflected in Psalm 137 and Daniel 9. It was only natural for them to meet in local groups for prayer and the reading of the Scriptures.

When the Jews returned to their land, Ezra the scribe promoted the reading of the Law and prayer (Nehemiah 8). But Zerubbabel had rebuilt the Temple, giving the Palestinian Jews a worship center. Many Jews, however, lived in Persia (see ESTHER, BOOK OF) and others had fled to many countries. By about 300 B.C. a large community of Jews lived in Alexandria, Egypt. A marble slab found near Alexandria bears an inscription dedicating a synagogue to Ptolemy III (Euergetes), who ruled Egypt from 246–221 B.C., and his queen Berenice. This is the first solid evidence of a true synagogue. Within Palestine the oldest known synagogue is the one uncovered at Herod's palace fortress on the rock of Masada near the Dead Sea, built 36–30 B.C.

Eric Meyers, in a team study of some 60 synagogues in Palestine, says he and his fellow archaeologists found no synagogues earlier than the first century A.D. In Jesus' day, however, synagogues were common even in the villages. They must have been well-established with the customary officials and order of worship (Luke 4:14–30; 8:41). Paul found synagogues in cities throughout the Roman Empire (Acts 9:2, Damascus; 13:5, Salamis; 13:14, Antioch in Pisidia; 14:1, Iconium; 17:1, Thessalonica; 17:10, Berea; 17:16–17, Athens; 19:1, 8, Ephesus). This shows that the synagogue had existed for a long time.

The Building. Three types of synagogue architecture developed. The earliest was the basilica. This was a rectangular building with one of the narrower ends facing Jerusalem. The door on this side

A synagogue at Masada. The synagogue was a place of worship, instruction, teaching of Scripture, and prayer for the Jewish people (Acts 13:13-15).

Photo by Gustav Jeeninga

Remains of a synagogue at Capernaum. It was probably built during the second or third century A.D.

was a triple door with elaborate stone carvings above the doors. Inside were two rows of three or four pillars each. This made a large central seating area with two smaller areas, one on each side, beyond the pillars.

Along the side walls were some stone benches, but not enough to seat the congregation. Probably the people sat cross-legged on the floor as they still do in Eastern mosques. At the far end of the room was a platform which held the Torah Ark, a cabinet or chest which contained the scrolls of the sacred Scriptures, wrapped in linen. Here too were the lamps and the lectern on which the scrolls were laid to be read in the service. Arranged in front were the "best seats" of the elders (Matt. 23:6).

The basilica had an awkward problem. Prayer and the reading of the Scripture had to be done facing Jerusalem, but the entrance door was toward Jerusalem; therefore, the Torah Ark had to be carried or wheeled to the other end of the building. The congregation had to stand up and turn around during the reading and prayer.

The broadhouse solved this problem by making the long side of the building face Jerusalem. This created room on each side of the door for a platform for the Torah Ark and the bema or lectern. Most broadhouses did not have pillars.

The apsidal synagogue was arranged like a modern church or synagogue. On the side toward Jerusalem was a platform with a niche or alcove back of it for the Torah Ark. The main door was at the rear.

The Officials. A synagogue could not be formed unless there were at least ten Jewish men in the community. Some synagogues paid ten unemployed men a small sum to be present at every service to be sure this rule was met. The following officials served in a synagogue.

Elders—A board of elders made up of devout and respected men of the community regulated the policies of the synagogue.

Ruler of the synagogue—There could be one or more rulers. They were appointed by the elders. Their duty was to attend to matters concerning the building and the planning of the services.

Minister—The minister (*chazzan*) had several duties. He had charge of the sacred scrolls which were kept in the Ark; he attended to the lamps; and he kept the building clean. If an offender was found guilty by the council of elders, the chazzan administered the number of lashes prescribed for the scourging. During the week the chazzan taught elementary children how to read.

Delegate of the congregation—This was not a permanent office. Before each service the ruler chose a capable person to read the Scripture lesson, to lead in prayer, and to preach or comment on the Scripture. Jesus was selected for this office in the synagogue in Nazareth (Luke 4:16–20).

Interpreter—The Scriptures were written in ancient Hebrew. By Jesus' day the people spoke Aramaic, a language related to Hebrew but different enough to call for an interpreter.

Almoners—These were two or three persons who received money or other necessities for the poor.

Order of Worship. The customary seating order placed the elders in the chief seats at the platform. Jesus rebuked some of those who loved the best seats merely for the praise and honor they conferred (Matt. 23:6). The front seats in the congregation were for the older spiritual leaders. The younger people and other individuals sat to the rear. A special section was reserved for lepers.

The service began with the recitation of the SHEMA by the people. Shema ("Hear") is the first Hebrew word in the passage in Deuteronomy 6:4–9: "Hear, O Israel: The Lord our God, the Lord is one!" The Shema includes Numbers 15:37–41 and Deuteronomy 6:4–9; 11:13–21.

The speaker for the day then led the congregation in prayer as they stood facing Jerusalem with hands extended. At the close of the prayer the people said "Amen."

Before the service the minister took from the Torah Ark the scrolls containing the lesson for the day and placed them on the lectern. The chosen speaker stood and read the lesson from the law of Moses and the interpreter translated it verse by verse into Aramaic. Then the passage from the Prophets was read and translated. For the commentary or sermon the speaker usually sat down (Luke 4:20). After the sermon, a priest, if one was present, pronounced a benediction and the people said "Amen." If no priest was present, a closing prayer was offered.

Influence. Synagogue worship has influenced both Christian and Moslem worship. The earliest Christians were Jews. Therefore, church worship followed the synagogue pattern with Scripture reading, prayer, and a sermon. In the seventh century A.D. Muhammad learned much from Jewish customs and also spent some time at Bosora or Bostra in the desert east of Gilead where a Christian bishopric was located. Hence, the mosques of Islam reflect worship patterns from both Jewish and Christian services.

SYNAGOGUE, GREAT — in Jewish tradition, an assembly of noted rabbis called together by the scribe Ezra or beginning with him (Nehemiah 8—10). This group supposedly determined what books belonged in the Old Testament. They also originated the prayers and benedictions used in synagogue worship. The Great Synagogue apparently began in the Persian period, an obscure time in Jewish history. Those who were supposed to be members of the group are spread over a period of some 200 years. Members of the Great Synagogue included Zerubbabel, Haggai, Zechariah, Malachi, Mordecai, and Simon the Just. Many scholars doubt the whole tradition.

SYNTYCHE [SIN tih keh] (*fortunate*) — a woman in the church at Philippi who apparently was in conflict with another church member. The apostle Paul called upon them to settle their differences (Phil. 4:2).

SYRACUSE [SEAR ih coos] — a Greek city (see Map 8, A–2) on the southeast coast of the island of Sicily (Acts 28:12). The apostle Paul spent three days in Syracuse before he proceeded on to Rome as a prisoner.

SYRIA [SIHR ih uh] — a major nation northeast of Palestine which served as a political threat to the nations of Judah and Israel during much of their history (see Map 4, C–2). The name Syria comes from the Greek language. The Hebrew language of the Old Testament uses the word *Aram* for the region which is translated in turn as Syria in most English versions of the Bible.

The boundaries of Syria changed often in biblical times. Often a particular group of Syrians such as those of Damascus or Zobah or else some combination of cities or regions are referred to as "Syria" or "the Syrians" in the Old Testament. Most of these references designate the region that makes up the southeastern part of the modern nation of Syria.

The Syrians (Arameans) were part of the massive migrations of population groups that occurred from about 3000 to 2100 B.C. They eventually settled in several parts of the ancient world, including much of northern Mesopotamia. One group, probably semi-nomads from the Arabian desert fringes, settled in force in the area north and east of Canaan. It is this group that the Israelites had most contact with during the time of the Israelite kings.

Gradually, these settlements produced the Aramean states known as Hamath, Zobah, and Damascus, each of which was an independent city-state. At times, all of these states were allied together against a common threat, such as that posed by the Assyrians. One or another of these "states" was often at war with Israel, until the Assyrians, under one of their kings, Tiglath–Pileser III (745–727 B.C.), defeated Syria and annexed it to the Assyrian Empire.

After this conquest, many Syrians were exiled to various parts of the Assyrian Empire, just as many citizens of the northern kingdom of Israel were carried away (2 Kin. 17:23). Some Syrians were even forced to settle in Samaria (2 Kin. 17:24). Thereafter Syria was ruled as a province by Babylonia, Persia, the Seleucids, and Rome in successive conquests by these ancient world powers.

In New Testament times Syria was a Roman province, linked with Cilicia. Syrians were among those who first responded to Jesus' preaching and healing ministry (Matt. 4:23–24). The gospel spread rapidly in Syria. Many of the places mentioned in the Book of Acts (Damascus, Antioch, Seleucia, Caesarea Philippi) were located in Syria.

Saul of Tarsus (the apostle Paul) was converted in Syria, while he was on the road to Damascus (Acts 9:3). His first missionary journey began from the great church at Antioch of Syria (Acts 13:1–3), and he traveled through Syria on several occasions (Acts 15:41; 18:18; Gal. 1:21).

SYRIAC VERSIONS (see BIBLE VERSIONS AND TRANSLATIONS).

SYRIANS [SIHR ih uns] — inhabitants or citizens of SYRIA, the ancient nation northeast of Palestine. The Hebrew people had many contacts with these people during their history.

Abraham was a Syrian (Deut. 26:5). His family was part of the Aramean ethnic stock who left Ur of the Chaldees around 2000 B.C. Many of the people and places mentioned in the stories about Abraham, Isaac, and Jacob are Syrian (Gen. 1:28–32; 24:1–67; 28:2–5).

During the period of the JUDGES, one of the foreign oppressors of the Israelites was a Syrian (Aramean), Cushan-Rishathaim. He was king of Aram-Naharaim, a kingdom of Syrians in Mesopotamia. The NKJV and the KJV translate the term simply as Mesopotamia (Judg. 3:8, 10). The "gods of Syria" (Judg. 10:6) are mentioned among the various idols which the Israelites began to worship at this time, as their faithfulness to the Lord faltered and they were influenced by the Syrians living in Canaan (Josh. 13:13).

David (1011–971 B.C.) fought against and either conquered or subdued several of the Syrian states, including Zoba, Rehob, Ish-Tob, Maacah, and Abel of Beth Maachah (2 Sam. 10:8; 20:15). Eventually David made even Damascus a part of his kingdom (2 Sam. 8:5), and he had influence over Toi, king of Hamath (2 Sam. 8:9–10). In fact, David's victories over the Syrians were probably his most famous military achievements. He killed 18,000 Syrians in the Valley of Salt (2 Sam. 8:13).

Solomon (971–931 B.C.) won a military victory against Hamath Zobah, which some scholars interpret as the allied Syrian city-states of Hamath and Zobah (2 Chr. 8:3–4). He used the area of Hamath as a place to build storage cities—something he would not have done if he did not have military control of the area. Some time later in Solomon's reign, however, a Syrian named Rezon seized power in Damascus and became an enemy of Solomon (1 Kin. 11:23–25; Rezon is probably to be identified with Hezion, the grandfather of Ben-Hadad, 1 Kin. 15:18).

The Bible says that Rezon "reigned over Syria" (1 Kin. 11:25). This can only mean that Solomon's power began to wane so that he lost control of Syria. God caused Israel's kingdom to weaken in order to punish Solomon and Israel for their idolatry (1 Kin. 11:14–40), and the Syrians were part of this process.

Once Rezon (or Hezion) had come to power, most of Syria, except for the area around Hamath, was under the control of Damascus. His son, Tabrimmon, and his grandson, Ben-Hadad I, succeeded him as kings over Syria, reigning in succession through the middle of the ninth century B.C. (1 Kin. 15:18). Ben-Hadad fought major wars with Israel, but was defeated by Ahab (ruled 874–853 B.C.) each time (1 Kin. 20:1–34).

Later in Ahab's reign, however, Israel and Syria put aside their differences long enough to join a coalition in battle against the Assyrians at Qarqar (853 B.C.), on the Orontes River—a battle which kept the Assyrians from adding Syria and Palestine to the Assyrian Empire. But Ahab's unwillingness to crush Ben-Hadad I and the Syrians brought on the wrath of God (1 Kin. 20:35–43).

After Hazael (843–796 B.C.) became king of Syria in Damascus by assassinating Ben-Hadad (2 Kin. 8:7–15), the Syrians again were at war with Israel (2 Kin. 8:28) and gained more and more against Israel as God planned (2 Kin. 10:32–33). King Joash of Judah had to pay tribute to Hazael to keep him from destroying Jerusalem (2 Kin. 12:17–18). God had caused the Syrians to turn the tables on Israel (2 Kin. 13:13).

In His mercy, however, God delivered Israel (2 Kin. 13:4) when Jehoahaz (ruled 814–798 B.C.) was king, probably by causing the Assyrians to attack the Syrians, thus relieving Israel. King Joash, or Jehoash (ruled 798–782 B.C.) of Israel was successful in battle against Ben-Hadad II of Syria, as the prophet Elisha had prophesied on his deathbed (2 Kin. 13:14–19, 25). Thereafter, Israel ruled over Syria once again (2 Kin. 14:28) under the powerful Israelite King Jeroboam II (ruled 793–753 B.C.).

When Rezin became king in Damascus, he threw off Israelite control. Then, in alliance with Pekah (740–732 B.C.), king of Israel, he attacked Judah, because King Ahaz (735–715 B.C.) of Judah refused to join a group of allies in rebelling against the control of the Assyrians. The war that followed is called the Syro–Ephraimite War (734–732 B.C.). Ahaz turned directly to the Assyrians for help. The Assyrians captured and annexed Syria (and most of Israel), thus ending the threat to Judah and ending Syria's existence as an independent nation (2 Kin. 16:9).

SYRIAC [SEER ih ack] (see LANGUAGES OF THE BIBLE).

SYRO–PHOENICIAN [sigh row feh KNEE shun] — a Gentile woman whose daughter was healed by Jesus (Mark 7:26). She was from Phoenicia, a nation northeast of Palestine which had been incorporated into the Roman province of Syria—thus the term, Syro–Phoenician. Although she was not a citizen of the Jewish nation, she believed Jesus could heal her daughter. Jesus commended her because of her great faith.

SYRTIS SANDS, THE [SUR tis] — the sandbanks of the northern coast of Africa which posed a danger to ships in Bible times. The ship on which the apostle Paul was traveling was in danger of running aground on these banks (Acts 27:17; the quicksands, KJV; the Syrtis, RSV; the sandbars of Syrtis, NIV; the shallows of Syrtis, NASB, NEB).

T

TAANACH [TAY uh nak] (meaning unknown) — an ancient royal city of the Canaanites (see Map 4, B–3) whose king was conquered and slain by Joshua, but whose inhabitants were not driven out of the land (Josh. 12:21; Judg. 1:27). Tanaach was occupied by the tribe of Manasseh and was assigned to the Levites of the family of Kohath (Josh. 17:11–13; 21:25, Tanach, KJV). According to the Song of Deborah, the kings of Canaan fought against Deborah and Barak at Taanach, but they were defeated (Judg. 5:19).

The ruins of Taanach, Tell Taannak, are on the southwestern edge of the Valley of Jezreel about eight kilometers (five miles) southeast of Megiddo.

TAANATH SHILOH [TAY uh nahth SHY loe] (*approach to Shiloh*) — a city between Michmethath and Janohah (Josh. 16:16). The site has been identi-

fied as Khirbet Ta'nah el–Foqa, about 11 kilometers (7 miles) southeast of Shechem.

TABBAOTH [TAB ih ahth] (*signets*) — the head of a family of Temple servants who returned from the Captivity (Neh. 7:46).

TABBATH [TAB uhth] (meaning unknown) — a place near Abel Meholah mentioned in connection with Gideon's pursuit of the Midianite army (Judg. 7:22).

TABEEL [TAB ih uhl] (*God is good*) — the name of two men in the Old Testament:

1. An Aramean in Samaria who protested the rebuilding of the walls of Jerusalem (Ezra 4:7).

2. The father of the man proposed by Rezin (king of Syria) and Pekah (king of Israel) to be the puppet king of Judah (Is. 7:6).

Remains of the city walls on the mound of Taanach, where Deborah defeated the Canaanites (Judg. 5:1, 19).
Photo by Howard Vos

Model of the tabernacle as it might have looked soon after it was built in the wilderness.

TABERAH [TAB uh ruh] (*burning*) — an encampment of the Israelites in the Wilderness of Paran where the Lord burned portions of the camp as punishment for their complaints (Num. 11:3).

TABERING — an archaic English word that means beating, as on a drum. Thus, "tabering upon their breasts" (Nah. 2:7, KJV) is translated "beating their breasts" (NKJV). The action expressed deep anguish.

TABERNACLE [TAB ur nack el] — the tent which served as a place of worship for the nation of Israel during their early history.

On Mount Sinai, after the Lord had given the commandments, judgments, and ordinances to Moses, He instructed Moses to construct the tabernacle. This was to be a center for worship and a place where the people could focus upon the presence of the Lord. This tabernacle was to replace the temporary tent that had been pitched outside the camp (Ex. 33:7–11). God began the description of this building by giving His people the opportunity to participate in its construction. They did this by giving an offering of the needed materials, including a combination of rare and beautiful fabrics and precious metals, along with supplies easily available in the wilderness.

After describing the offering (Ex. 25:1–9), the Lord proceeded to specify in minute detail the pattern for the tabernacle. He began by giving a description of the holiest item in the entire structure: the ARK OF THE COVENANT (Ex. 25:10–22). Other items in the tabernacle for which the Lord gave minute construction details included the seven-branched lampstand (Ex. 25:31–39); the intricate curtains of the tabernacle (Ex. 26:1–25); the veils, and the screen (Ex. 26:1–37); the large altar of burnt offering, and the brazen or bronze altar (Ex. 27:1–8); and the hangings for the courtyard (Ex. 27:9–19).

A brief recipe for the oil to be used in worship is given in Exodus 27:20–21, followed by a description of the priests' garments and consecration (Exodus 28—29). Directions for making the incense altar and the golden altar are given in Exodus 30:1–10. After a brief statement about a tax assessment (Ex. 30:11–16), the Lord told Moses to build a bronze laver (Ex. 30:17–21).

Mixed in with these instructions about specific items of the tabernacle are plans for the architecture and design of the building. The tabernacle was in the form of a tent 10 cubits wide and 30 cubits long. It was to be set up with its only entrance toward the east. The tent consisted of a wooden framework made of 46 identical planks 10 cubits long and 1 1/2 cubits wide; there were 20 planks each on the north and south sides. Six of the planks were on the west end, along with two additional planks which were 1/2 cubit wide. All of these planks were acacia wood plated with gold.

Over this framework were four separate coverings that made up the roof of the structure. The first covering was made of fine–twined linen of blue, scarlet, and purple with intricately portrayed CHERUBIM. The second covering was of pure white goats' hair. The third was of rams' skins dyed red. The topmost covering was of material referred to in the NKJV as badger skins. Other English translations suggest that this should be translated porpoise skins, or possibly leather.

The tent constructed in this manner was then divided into two rooms divided by an intricate veil of blue, scarlet, and purple linen embroidered with cherubim.

The inner, western room was called the HOLY OF HOLIES. It was 10 cubits square, and it contained only one piece of furniture—the holiest item in the tabernacle, the ark of the covenant. The ark was a chest made of acacia wood covered with gold, 2 1/2 cubits long and 1 1/2 cubits in width and height.

In addition, a gold border extended above the top of the ark to keep the lid stationary. The ark also had golden rings on each side so it could be transported with poles that were placed through the rings. The lid of the ark was called the MERCY SEAT. Upon it were two gold cherubim that faced each other. The ark contained a copy of the stone tablets with the TEN COMMANDMENTS, a copy of the entire law of Moses or the PENTATEUCH; a gold pot filled with MANNA; and Aaron's rod that budded.

The outer, eastern room was called the Holy Place. Ten cubits wide and 20 cubits long, it was entered through the blue, scarlet, and purple linen curtains which served as a door. This door was always aligned toward the east. It contained three items. On its western side, next to the veil, was the altar of incense, or golden altar, one cubit square and two cubits high. Upon this altar, made of acacia wood overlaid with gold, the morning and evening incense was burned.

On the northern side of the Holy Place was the seven-branched golden lampstand, or candlestick, comprised of a pedestal, a shaft, and three branches extending to both sides of the shaft. This lampstand was made of a talent of fine gold. On the southern side of the Holy Place was the table for the SHOWBREAD, or bread of the presence. This table was made of gold-covered acacia wood two cubits long, one cubit wide, and one and one-half cubits high.

Surrounding the main building of the tabernacle was a spacious courtyard 100 cubits long in its east-west direction and 50 cubits wide from north to south. This courtyard was surrounded by a fence five cubits high, formed of pillars with silverwork, resting in brass sockets, placed five cubits apart, and hung with fine linen. In the western half of this courtyard the tabernacle itself was to be pitched, and in the eastern half stood two items—the altar of burnt offering or the great bronze altar, and the laver.

The description of the actual building of the tabernacle is recorded in Exodus 35—40. The workers were first enlisted as God had commanded. Following that enlistment, recorded in Exodus 35, the building of each item of the tabernacle is described in Exodus 36—39. The record of the tabernacle's construction occurs in Exodus 40. Up to this time, the nation of Israel had used a temporary tent called the tabernacle of the congregation; this temporary meeting tent is mentioned in Exodus 33:7-11. Just how central the tabernacle was in the life of Israel is graphically portrayed in the Book of Numbers. When the Israelites pitched camp in the wilderness, the tabernacle was to be placed in the center, with the Levites camping next to it (Num. 1:53). Then the tribes were to be arrayed in specific order on the four sides of the tabernacle (Numbers 2).

Responsibilities for the care and moving of the tabernacle were delegated to various families of the tribe of Levi (Num. 1:50-52; Numbers 3—4). The Levitical family of Kohath was to disassemble the structure and cover the tabernacle furnishings with the badger skin. The tapestries were the responsibility of the family of Gershon. Merari's family had charge of the boards, pillars, foundations, pins, and cords. All these Levitical families were commissioned to care for the sanctuary.

The first day of tabernacle worship is described in Numbers 7—9. The guiding pillar of cloud and fire rested upon the tabernacle when the people were encamped. When the people were on the march, with the pillar serving as their guide, the tribes which camped on the east of the tabernacle were first in marching order. These were Judah, Issachar, and Zebulun. The tabernacle was carried by the assigned family members of Gershon and Merari.

The next group in the marching order were the tribes which camped on the south of the tabernacle. These were Reuben, Simeon, and Gad. Following these, the family of Kohath carried the holy objects of the tabernacle.

Then came the tribes which camped on the west of the tabernacle. These were Ephraim, Manasseh, and Benjamin.

The rear guard of the march was composed of the tribes which camped on the north of the tabernacle. These were Dan, Asher, and Naphtali.

When the tribes were camped, two silver trumpets were used to summon the tribes to gather at the tabernacle. The tabernacle was also the place where the 70 elders advised and counseled the people (Num. 11:16). It was also the place of specific judgments (Num. 12:4) and appointments (Deut. 31:14).

During the conquest of the land of Canaan by the Israelites, the tabernacle remained at Gilgal, while the ark of the covenant was evidently carried from place to place with the armies of Israel. The ark was reported at the crossing of the Jordan (Josh. 3:6), at Gilgal (Josh. 4:11), at the conquest of Jericho (Josh. 6:4), at the campaigns against Ai (Josh. 7:6), and at Mount Ebal (Josh. 8:33). The tabernacle was finally placed on the site which it was to occupy during the duration of the period of conquest and judges, at Shiloh (Josh. 18:1). Here the tribes were assigned their territorial allotments.

As the years passed, certain other structures were added to the tabernacle while it remained at Shiloh. These included living quarters for the priests and Levites who served at the tabernacle. By the end of the period of the judges, during the administration of Eli, at least some of the attendants lived on the premises (1 Sam. 3:3).

During the Israelites' battle against the Philistines at Aphek, the ark of the covenant was removed from the tabernacle and taken into battle. Lost to the Philistines, it finally came to rest at Kirjath Jearim (1 Sam. 4:1—7:1). It remained here until the time of David's reign.

With the departure of the ark, the tabernacle lost some of its esteem in the eyes of the Hebrew people (Ps. 78:60). During the reign of Saul, the tabernacle

The Valley of Jezreel, as seen from Mount Tabor. The valley separates Samaria from Galilee (Judg. 6:33; Hos. 1:5).

was at Nob (1 Sam. 21:1). From the latter part of David's reign throughout the fourth year of Solomon's reign, the tabernacle was at the high place of Gibeon (1 Chr. 16:39; 21:29). When the Temple was completed, Solomon had the Levites bring the tabernacle to Jerusalem (1 Kin. 8:4; 2 Chr. 5:5), presumably to be stored in the Temple area.

The New Testament uses some terminology and concepts drawn directly from the tabernacle. The supreme event of all the ages is the existence of God's son in human form. The Bible declares that the Word became flesh and "tabernacled" (Greek word rendered as "dwelt" in the NKJV) among us (John 1:14). In his final speech, Stephen accepted the Old Testament account of the tabernacle as historical (Acts 7:44). In Romans 3:25, Paul used the word propitiation which might also be translated "mercy seat." Titus 3:5 probably refers to the laver. Revelation 8:3–5 speaks of the golden incense altar. In Revelation 13:6 and 15:5, reference is made to the heavenly tabernacle. Practically every feature of the tabernacle is found in the Book of Hebrews.

TABERNACLE OF THE CONGREGATION (see TABERNACLE OF MEETING).

TABERNACLE OF MEETING — the tent which Moses pitched outside the camp before the TABERNACLE was built (Ex. 33:7). After the tabernacle itself was built, it also was often called by this name (Ex. 38:8), signifying the meeting of God with His people. The phrase is also translated tabernacle of the congregation (Ex. 27:21, KJV) and tent of meeting (RSV). Most of the references to the tabernacle of meeting occur in the books of Exodus, Leviticus, and Numbers.

TABERNACLES, FEAST OF (see FEASTS AND FESTIVALS).

TABITHA [TAB ih thuh] — a form of DORCAS.

TABLE — an article of furniture used for ritual, eating, and money changing. The tabernacle had a table of acacia wood overlaid with gold on which the showbread was placed (Ex. 25:23; Num. 3:31; Heb. 9:2). A table of gold was in the Temple (1 Kin. 7:48). Tables for the burnt offering were furnishings of Ezekiel's temple (Ezek. 40:39–43). There was also a table before the sanctuary (Ezek. 41:22; 44:16). The prophet Malachi spoke of the altar as the Lord's table (Mal. 1:7, 12).

Tables were used for serving meals (Judg. 1:7; Is. 28:8). The table depicted on an ivory piece found at Megiddo had legs quite similar to a modern table. Rulers had large groups at their tables. David offered places at his table to those to whom he felt indebted (2 Sam. 9:7–13; 1 Kin. 2:7). Solomon's table was supplied each month by separate officials (1 Kin. 4:27).

In the New Testament period, people reclined at the table (Luke 7:37) during meals. "Serving tables" (Acts 6:2) referred to looking after the material needs of the poor. The tables on which the moneychangers exchanged money were overthrown by Jesus when He cleansed the Temple (Matt. 21:12; Mark 11:15; John 2:15).

In a symbolic way, the word table is sometimes used to describe abundant provision. The psalmist declared of God, "You prepare a table before me in the presence of my enemies" (Ps. 23:5).

TABLET — a word with several different meanings in the Bible:

1. The tablets of stone on which God wrote the law given to Moses at Mount Sinai (Ex. 24:12; Deut. 10:1–5).

2. Ordinary writing tablets made of clay or wood (Ezek. 4:1; Luke 1:63).

3. The Bible also uses the word tablet to speak of God's law written on the heart (Prov. 3:3; Jer. 17:1; 2 Cor. 3:3).

TABOR [TAY buhr] (*height*) — the name of a mountain (see Map 3, B–2), a terebinth tree, and a city in the Old Testament:

1. A mountain of limestone in the northeastern part of the Valley of Jezreel (Josh. 19:22). Now called Jebel et–Tur, Tabor is 8.8 kilometers (5.5 miles) southeast of Nazareth and about 16 kilometers (10 miles) southwest of the Sea of Galilee. Mount Tabor rises some 411 meters (1,350 feet) above the plain. It rises steeply to form a dome-shaped summit. No other mountains are adjacent to Mount Tabor.

Because of its strategic location and commanding height, Mount Tabor frequently was fortified with protective walls. In 218 B.C. Antiochus III captured a town on the summit and fortified it. As a Jewish general, Josephus added a defensive rampart to the fortress in A.D. 66. The remains of this structure can still be seen today.

Situated where the borders of Issachar, Zebulun, and Naphtali meet (Josh. 19:22), Mount Tabor played an important role in Israel's history. Here Barak gathered 10,000 men of Naphtali and Zebulun and attacked the Canaanite armies of Sisera at Megiddo (Judg. 4:6, 12, 14; 5:18). Also at Tabor the Midianite kings Zebah and Zalmunna killed the brothers of Gideon (Judg. 8:18–19). During the time of the prophets, the top of the mountain was a sanctuary for idolatry (Hos. 5:1). In fact, the mountain may have been the site of a pagan sanctuary from ancient times (Deut. 33:19).

2. The "plain of Tabor" (1 Sam. 10:3, KJV), or more correctly, the "terebinth tree of Tabor" (NKJV), where Samuel told Saul he would find men bearing gifts as a sign of God's favor. It was situated in the territory of Benjamin by the road leading from Rachel's tomb to Gibeah.

3. A Levite city of the sons of Merari in the territory of Zebulun (1 Chr. 6:77).

TABRET (see MUSICAL INSTRUMENTS).

TABRIMMON [tab RIM uhn] (*Rimmon is good*) — father of Ben–Hadad I, king of Syria (1 Kin. 15:18; Tabrimon, KJV).

TACHES [TACH ez] — KJV word for clasps (Ex. 26:6; 35:11). These clasps were hooks upon which the tabernacle curtains were hung.

TACHMONITE [TAK muh night] — the family name of Josheb-Basshebeth, chief captain in David's army (2 Sam. 23:8; Tahchemonite, NASB, RSV; Tahkemonite, NIV).

TACKLE, TACKLING — the gear or rigging of a ship used to work the sails and handle cargo (Is. 33:23; Acts 27:19; tacklings, KJV; gear, NEB). When a storm threatened to sink the ship on which the apostle Paul was traveling to Rome, the tackle was thrown overboard to lighten the vessel (Acts 27:18–19). Also see SHIPS.

TADMOR [TAD mohr] (*palm tree*) — a city known to the Greeks and Romans as Palmyra, about 193 kilometers (120 miles) northeast of Damascus (1 Kin. 9:18). The city was built on an oasis in the Syrian desert, astride the main east–west trade route which ran from Mesopotamia to Canaan.

Ruins of the temple of Bel in Palmyra, or ancient Tadmor (2 Chr. 8:4).
Photo by Howard Vos

The city was also situated on the main north–south trade route. Because of its strategic location, Tadmor became an important commercial center and military outpost.

According to 2 Chronicles 8:4, Solomon "built Tadmor in the wilderness." This city, which marked the northeastern boundary of his empire, helped Solomon control the entire region. After Solomon's death, Tadmor came under the control of the ARAMEANS.

In its subsequent history, Tadmor became the center of the kingdom ruled by Septimius Odaenathus and his wife, the legendary Queen Zenobia. The armies of the Roman Empire brought an end to Tadmor, laying siege to the city in A.D. 272.

Tadmor is one of the most impressive ruins of the ancient Near Eastern world. Here archaeologists have excavated an outer wall that enclosed the city—a wall dating from the time of Zenobia. The ruins of a great colonnade, an agora (marketplace), a theater, a senate building, and a huge sanctuary of Bel have been unearthed.

TAHAN [TAY han] (*graciousness*) — the name of two men in the Old Testament:
1. A descendant of Ephraim (Num. 26:35).
2. An ancestor of Joshua (1 Chr. 7:25–27).

TAHANITES [TAY han ights] — descendants of TAHAN, son of Ephraim (Num. 26:35).

TAHAPANES [TAH puh neez] — a form of TAHPANHES.

TAHASH [TAY hash] — a form of THAHASH.

TAHATH [TAY hath] (*that which is beneath*) — the name of one place and three men in the Old Testament:
1. A desert encampment of the Israelites after they left Egypt (Num. 33:26–27).
2. A Kohathite Levite, a son of Assir (1 Chr. 6:24, 37).
3. A descendant of Ephraim (1 Chr. 7:20).
4. Another descendant of Ephraim (1 Chr. 7:20). He apparently was a grandson of Tahath No. 3.

TAHCHEMONITE, TAHKEMONITE [TAK uh muh night] — forms of TACHMONITE.

TAHPANHES, TEHAPHNEHES [TAH puh neez, tuh HAH fuh neez] — a city on the eastern frontier of lower Egypt, in the area of the Nile delta (Jer. 2:16; Tahapanes, KJV; Ezek. 30:18, Tehaphnehes). This city was probably named for a powerful general who brought the surrounding area under firm Egyptian control in the 11th century B.C.

Tahpanhes became a place of refuge for Jews who fled their homeland after the assassination of GEDALIAH, the Babylonian governor of Judah. Jeremiah warned the Jews against this move, declaring that they would not escape the judgment of God so easily (Jer. 42:16). He dramatically visualized this for them by hiding stones at Tahpanhes for the foundation of the throne of Nebuchadnezzar, the king of Babylon (Jer. 43:9–10).

Tahpanhes is identified with the modern Tell Defneh, a small mound bordering Lake Manzaleh in northern Egypt.

TAHPENES [TAH puh neez] (meaning unknown) — a queen of Egypt who lived during the time of David and Solomon (1 Kin. 11:19–20). The Pharaoh gave Tahpenes' sister in marriage to HADAD the Edomite. But she died shortly after giving birth to her son, Genubath. Tahpenes raised the child in Pharaoh's house.

TAHREA [tuh REE uh] — a form of TAREA.

TAHTIM HODSHI [TAH tim HAHD shy] (meaning unknown) — a district between Gilead and Dan Jaan, east of the Jordan River, visited by Joab and his officers during the census of Israel (2 Sam. 24:6).

TAILOR (see OCCUPATIONS AND TRADES).

TALEBEARER — a person who spreads idle rumors or gossip that is likely to cause trouble or harm (Prov. 18:8; whisperer, NASB, RSV).

TALENT (see MONEY; WEIGHTS AND MEASURES).

TALITHA CUMI [TAL uh thuh KOO migh] — an Aramaic phrase spoken by Jesus when He raised the daughter of Jairus from the dead. The phrase means, "Little girl, arise" (Mark 5:41).

TALMAI [TAL migh] (meaning unknown) — the name of two men in the Old Testament:
1. One of the three sons of Anak (Num. 13:22; Josh. 15:14; Judg. 1:10). They were known as ANAKIM, a race of giants who were driven out of Hebron by Caleb's army and were finally killed by the tribe of Judah.
2. A king of Geshur whose daughter Maacah was one of David's wives and the mother of Absalom (2 Sam. 3:3).

TALMON [TAL muhn] (meaning unknown) — a Levite gatekeeper whose descendants returned from the Captivity with Zerubbabel (1 Chr. 9:17; Neh. 7:45).

TALMUD — a collection of books and commentary compiled by Jewish rabbis from A.D. 250—500. The Hebrew word *talmud* means "study" or "learning." This is a fitting title for a work that is a library of Jewish wisdom, philosophy, history, legend, astronomy, dietary laws, scientific debates, medicine, and mathematics.

The Talmud is made up of interpretation and commentary of the Mosaic and rabbinic law contained in the MISHNAH, an exhaustive collection of laws and guidelines for observing the law of Moses. As a guide to following the law, the Talmud also serves as a basis for spiritual formation. More than 2,000 scholars or rabbis worked across a period of 250 years to understand the meaning of God's word for their particular situation. Out of these efforts they produced the Talmud.

The wide variety and comprehensive detail of the Talmud's subject matter conveys a deep thirst for learning. Questions as minute as why God created a gnat and as universal as the origin of the universe filled the teachers of Israel with wonder. A passion for truth and understanding led the Jewish teachers deep into the marvels of the human experience.

The Pharisees were the first to give greater attention to the laws of Moses. The Roman historian Josephus reported that their oral tradition included regulations that were not recorded in the Mosaic Law at all. The Mishna collected all of these oral regulations into one permanent record. In response to the Mishna, wide discussions concerning its content and meaning began, resulting in the Talmud.

The centers for these learned discussions were the academies in Babylonia and Israel. As a result, two Talmuds, the Babylonian Talmud and the Jerusalem Talmud, were created. Because the Babylonian rabbis were far more thorough in word–by–word interpretation of the Mishnah than were the rabbis in Israel, the Babylonian Talmud is much more complete. An English edition of this work fills 36 volumes and almost 36,000 pages.

The Talmud is divided into six major sections. The first of these deals with agriculture and crops and the offerings, tithes, and prayers associated with them. The second section is about holidays and festivals such as the Sabbath, Passover, Rosh Ha–Shanah and others. A third section discusses laws about marriage, divorce, property, and related subjects. Another section concerns the rules governing the courts. The next section deals with the laws pertaining to the Temple and the sacrifices and Jewish foods. The final section discusses the laws of ritual purity.

At some points during Jewish history, traditions and the Talmud have been considered equal to or better than the Scripture itself. Jesus encountered such an attitude among the Pharisees even before the existence of the Talmud (Matt. 15:3). Christians must be careful not to make the same mistake in regard to our own traditions.

TAMAH [TAH muh] (meaning unknown) — one of the Nethinim (Temple servants) whose descendants returned from the Captivity with Ezra (Ezra 2:53; Thamah, KJV; Neh. 7:55).

TAMAR [TAY mur] (palm) — the name of three women and a city in the Bible:

1. The widow of Er and Onan, sons of Judah (Gen. 38:6–30; Matt. 1:3; Thamar, KJV). According to the law of LEVIRATE MARRIAGE, Judah's third son, Shelah, should have married Tamar; their first child would have been regarded as his brother's and would have carried on his name. However, Judah withheld his third son from marrying Tamar. Undaunted, Tamar disguised herself as a harlot and offered herself to Judah. Twin sons, Perez and Zerah, were born of their union. Judah and Tamar became ancestors of Jesus through Perez (Matt. 1:3).

2. The lovely daughter of David by Maacah and sister of Absalom (2 Sam. 13:1–22, 32; 1 Chr. 3:9). Tamar was raped by her half–brother Amnon. She

fled to Absalom, who plotted revenge. Two years later Absalom got his revenge for Tamar by arranging Amnon's murder.

3. Absalom's only surviving daughter, possibly named after his sister Tamar (2 Sam. 14:27).

4. A place southwest of the Dead Sea (Ezek. 47:19; 48:28).

TAMARISK (see PLANTS OF THE BIBLE).

TAMBOURINE (see MUSICAL INSTRUMENTS).

TAMMUZ (see CALENDAR; GODS, PAGAN).

TANACH [TAY nak] — a form of TAANACH.

TANHUMETH [tan HOO mith] (comfort) — a Netophathite whose son Seraiah remained with Gedaliah after the Captivity (2 Kin. 25:23).

TANNER (see OCCUPATIONS AND TRADES).

TAPESTRY MAKER (see OCCUPATIONS AND TRADES).

TAPHATH [TAY fath] (a drop) — one of Solomon's daughters (1 Kin. 4:11). She married the son of Abinadab, Solomon's supply officer in the district of Naphath–dor.

TAPPUAH [TAP yoo uh] (apple) — the name of two cities and one man in the Old Testament:

1. A city in the lowland of Judah (Josh. 12:17).

2. A border city of Ephraim (Josh. 16:8; 17:8).

3. A son of Hebron, of the tribe of Judah (1 Chr. 2:43).

TAR (see MINERALS OF THE BIBLE).

TARAH [TAY ruh] — a form of TERAH.

TARALAH [TAR uh luh] (strength) — a city in the territory of Benjamin between Irpeel and Zelah (Josh. 18:27).

TAREA [tuh REE uh] (meaning unknown) — a son of Micah and a descendant of Saul (1 Chr. 8:35; Tahrea, 1 Chr. 9:41).

TARES (see PLANTS OF THE BIBLE).

TARGUM — translations of parts of the Old Testament from the original Hebrew language into Aramaic. The word Targum is related to a Hebrew term meaning "translation." These translations were sometimes literal and exact, but often were paraphrased. Many translators took the opportunity to comment upon the Hebrew texts. In a sense, some Targumim (plural) are a form of commentary on the Bible.

Scholars question when and why the Old Testament was first translated. Some suggest that the Hebrew language had changed so much that an explanation of Mosaic Law helped the Israelites understand its true meanings. Ezra sometimes provided such explanations (Neh. 8:8). Other scholars think the Israelites adopted the Aramaic language during the Babylonian Captivity. The Targumim, then, translated the Old Testament into a more understandable language.

By the time of Christ, Aramaic was the common language in Israel. During a synagogue service, one verse of the Hebrew text was read, followed by a translation and explanation in Aramaic. By the second or third century A.D., the common practice was to read only the Aramaic translation.

The best-known Targum was probably the Targum Onkelos which translated the Pentateuch, or the first five books of the Old Testament, quite literally. The Targumim are helpful today in understanding ancient Jewish interpretations of the Old Testament. Because they are paraphrased, they cannot be used to identify original Hebrew texts.

TARPELITES [TAR puh lights] — members of an Assyrian tribe transported to Samaria by Shalmaneser of Assyria (Ezra 4:9).

TARSHISH [TAR shish] (*yellow jasper*) — the name of a type of ship, a city or territory, a man, and a precious stone in the Old Testament:

1. The Hebrew name for a type of cargo ship fitted for long sea voyages (1 Kin. 10:22; Tharshish, KJV).

2. A city or territory in the western portion of the Mediterranean Sea with which the Phoenicians traded (2 Chr. 9:21; Ps. 72:10). Tarshish is believed to be modern Tartessus, in southern Spain, near Gibraltar. When the prophet Jonah fled from God's instruction to go to Nineveh, he boarded a ship bound for Tarshish, in the opposite direction from Nineveh (Jon. 1:3; 4:2). Tarshish was famous for its ships (Ps. 48:7; Is. 2:16) which carried gold, silver, iron, tin, lead, ivory, apes, and monkeys (1 Kin. 10:22; Jer. 10:9).

Because the ships of Tarshish carried such great riches, they became symbols of wealth, power, and pride. When God judged the nations for their sinful ways, He destroyed their "ships of Tarshish" to humble them and to demonstrate His great power (2 Chr. 20:35–37; Is. 2:16–17).

3. A high official at SHUSHAN (Susa). He was one of seven princes of Persia and Media "who had access to the king's presence" (Esth. 1:14). Tarshish was one of those present at the royal banquet of King Ahasuerus which Vashti, the queen, refused to attend.

4. The Hebrew name of a precious stone (Ex. 28:20; Ezek. 28:13). Its brilliant color is associated with the glorious appearance of God Himself (Ezek. 1:16; Dan. 10:6). Also see JEWELS AND PRECIOUS STONES.

TARSHISHAH [TAR shish uh] — a son of Javan and great-grandson of Noah (Gen. 10:4; Tarshish, KJV).

TARSUS [TAHR suss] — the birthplace of the apostle Paul (Acts 21:39; 22:3), formerly known as Saul of Tarsus (Acts 9:11). Tarsus was the chief city of CILICIA, a province of southeast Asia Minor (modern Turkey; see Map 7, D–2). This important city was situated on the banks of the Cydnus River about 16 kilometers (10 miles) north of the shore of the Mediterranean Sea.

Because of its strategic location, protected on the north by the Taurus Mountains and open to navigation from the Mediterranean, the city of Tarsus was a prize location for the Hittites, Mycenean Greeks, Assyrians, Persians, Seleucids, and Romans. In the post–Roman period it dwindled to a small city in the wake of battles between various Christian and Muslim powers.

During the Seleucid period, however, Tarsus became a free city (about 170 B.C.), and was open to Greek culture and education. By the time of the Romans, Tarsus competed with ATHENS and ALEXANDRIA as the learning center of the world. "I am a Jew

St. Paul's Gate at Tarsus. The chief city of Cilicia in eastern Asia Minor, Tarsus was the birthplace of the apostle Paul (Acts 21:39).

Photo by Gustav Jeeninga

from Tarsus, in Cilicia," wrote the apostle Paul, "a citizen of no mean city" (Acts 21:39).

North of Tarsus were the famous Cilician Gates, a narrow gorge in the Taurus Mountains through which ran the only good trade route between Asia Minor and Syria. The location of Tarsus in a fertile valley relatively close to the Cilician Gates brought great wealth to the city.

The apostle Paul spent his early years at Tarsus (Acts 9:11; 21:39; 22:3) and revisited it at least once after his conversion to Christianity (Acts 9:30; 11:25).

TARTAK (see GODS, PAGAN).

TARTAN [TAR tan] — the title of the commander-in-chief of the Assyrian army. Two Tartans are mentioned in Scripture:

1. A messenger sent by Sennacherib to Hezekiah, demanding the surrender of Jerusalem (2 Kin. 18:17).

2. A general of Sargon sent to besiege and capture Ashdod (Is. 20:1).

TASKMASTER (see OCCUPATIONS AND TRADES).

TASSEL — a decorative ornament around the hems of the clothes of the Hebrew people, worn to remind them of God's commandments in the Law (Deut. 22:12) and to encourage them to do His will.

TATTENAI [TAT uh nigh] (meaning unknown) — the Persian governor of Samaria during the reign of Darius the Great (ruled 521–486 B.C.). When Tattenai sent a letter to Darius (Ezra 5:7–17), asking whether the work of restoring the Temple was authorized, the decree of King Cyrus ordering that it should be rebuilt was found.

TATTOO — a permanent mark or design fixed upon the body by a process of pricking the skin and inserting an indelible color under the skin. The moral and ceremonial laws of Leviticus declare, "You shall not make any cuttings in your flesh for the dead, nor tattoo any marks upon you" (Lev. 19:28). Any kind of self-laceration or marking of the body was prohibited among the Hebrew people. Such cuttings were associated with pagan cults that tattooed their followers while they mourned the dead.

TAU [taw] — the 22nd letter of the Hebrew alphabet, used as a heading over Psalm 119:169–176. In the original Hebrew language, every line of these eight verses began with the letter tau. Also see ACROSTIC.

TAUNT–SONG — a song of contempt or mockery. Job said of his enemies, "And now I am their taunt–song" (Job 30:9; the target of their taunts, NEB). Job's tormentors believed that if he was suffering, he must have sinned to deserve such punishment. This is why they ridiculed Job's claim of righteousness.

TAVERNS, THREE (see THREE INNS).

TAWNY OWL (see ANIMALS OF THE BIBLE).

TAX, TAXES — a compulsory fee or financial contribution for the maintenance of government. Taxes may have originated with the custom of giving presents for protection from harm (Gen. 32:13–21; 33:10; 43:11). When Joseph revealed to the Pharaoh in Egypt that there would be seven years of famine after seven years of abundance, Pharaoh put him in charge of raising revenues. During the time of famine as well as plenty, he collected a 20 percent tax to store up food and then to buy land for Pharaoh (Gen. 47:20–26).

During the time of the Exodus, Moses asked for voluntary revenues for the construction of the tabernacle (Ex. 25:2; 35:5, 21). The Mosaic Law prescribed that every male over the age of 20 was to give half a shekel for the service of the tabernacle (Ex. 30:11–16).

With the establishment of the United Kingdom under David and Solomon, several avenues of taxation were established: a 10 percent tax on the produce of land and livestock (1 Sam. 8:15, 17); compulsory military service for one month each year (1 Chr. 27:1); and import duties (1 Kin. 10:15). Tribute was also paid by subject peoples (2 Sam. 8:6; 2 Kin. 3:4). The oppressive taxation by Solomon was one of the causes of the split of the kingdom after his death (1 Kin. 12:4).

When the Persians came into power and ruled over Palestine, they set up a new system of taxation. Instead of paying tribute to a foreign master, each province in the Persian Empire was required to collect its own taxes. Each Persian SATRAP was to collect for his own province. The decree of Darius Hystaspis states that the satraps paid a fixed amount into the royal treasury. The revenue collected was derived from tribute, custom, and toll (Ezra 4:13). Priests and others involved in religious service were exempted from these taxes (Ezra 7:24). Beyond the central government's tax, a tax was also collected for the maintenance of the governor's household. The taxes were so heavy that many people were forced to mortgage their fields and vineyards. Some even sold their own sons and daughters into slavery (Neh. 5:1–5).

During the period between the Old and the New Testament, the Jews were first under the Egyptian Ptolemaic rule (301–198 B.C.) and later under the Syrian Seleucid rule (198–63 B.C.). Under the Ptolemies taxes were not collected by an Egyptian representative. Instead, taxing privileges were farmed out to the highest bidders. From the various provinces people would come to Alexandria to bid for the privilege of collecting taxes from their own people. The bidder who won the contract would tax the people up to double the amount required by law in order to make a handsome profit. These contracted tax collectors were given military assistance to enable them to enforce their demands.

This same type of taxation system probably continued in Palestine under Syrian rule. A poll tax, a salt tax, and a crown tax were enforced during this time. The Syrians taxed as much as one–third of the grain, one–half of the fruit, and a portion of the

Photo: Levant Photo Service

The mound of Tekoa south of Jerusalem—home of the prophet Amos (Amos 1:1).

tithes which the Jews paid to support the Temple.

When the Romans under Pompey captured Jerusalem in 63 B.C., a tax of 10,000 talents was temporarily imposed on the Jews. The tax–contracting system was reformed by Julius Caesar, who reduced the taxes and levied no tax in the sabbatic years. But soon after the Herods came to power in Palestine, they demanded heavy taxes.

The Herods instituted a poll tax and a tax on fishing rights in the rivers and lakes. Customs were collected on trade routes by men like Levi, who collected in Capernaum (Matt. 9:9; Mark 2:14; Luke 5:27). This city may have also been a place for port duties and fishing tolls. Some items sold for 1000 per cent above their original prices because of all the taxes. There may have been sales tax on slaves, oil, clothes, hides, and furs. Over and above these taxes were the religious dues. These were generally between 10 and 20 percent of a person's income before government tax.

During Jesus' time, the Jews were probably paying from 30 to 40 percent of their income on taxes and religious dues.

TAX COLLECTOR — an agent or contract worker who collected taxes for the government during Bible times. The Greek word translated tax collector (tax gatherer, NASB, NEB) is incorrectly rendered publican by the KJV. Publicans were wealthy men, usually non–Jewish, who contracted with the Roman government to be responsible for the taxes of a particular district of the imperial Roman state. These publicans would often be backed by military force.

By contrast, the tax collectors to which the New Testament refers (with the possible exception of ZACCHAEUS) were employed by publicans to do the actual collecting of monies in the restricted areas where they lived. These men were Jews, usually not very wealthy, who could be seen in the Temple (Luke 18:13). They were probably familiar to the people from whom they collected taxes.

These tax collectors gathered several different types of taxes. Rome levied upon the Jews a land tax, a poll tax, even a tax for the operation of the Temple. The distinctions between the kind of rule which a given province received dictated the kinds of taxes its people had to pay. For example, since some provinces, like Galilee, were not under an imperial governor, taxes remained in the province rather than going to the imperial treasury at Rome. These differences within the taxation system prompted the Pharisees in Judea (an imperial province) to ask Jesus, "Is it lawful to pay taxes to Caesar, or not?" (Matt. 22:17).

As a class, the tax collectors were despised by their fellow Jews. They were classified generally as "sinners" (Matt. 9:10–11; Mark 2:15), probably because they were allowed to gather more than the government required and then to pocket the excess amount. John the Baptist addressed this when he urged tax collectors to gather no more money than they should (Luke 3:12–13). But even further, the tax collectors were hated because their fellow countrymen viewed them as mercenaries who worked for a foreign oppressor of the Jewish people.

Jesus, however, set a new precedent among the

Jews by accepting and associating with the tax collectors. He ate with them (Mark 2:16), He bestowed His saving grace upon them (Luke 19:9), and He even chose a tax collector (Matthew) as one of His twelve disciples (Matt. 9:9). By His attitude toward the tax collectors, Jesus showed that God's covenant of grace extends to all people—not simply the righteous who observed the Law of the Old Testament. In fact, His message was that God would welcome the repentant and humble tax collector, while He would spurn the arrogant Pharisee (Luke 18:9-14). His mission was to bring sinners—people like the tax collectors of His day—into God's presence (Matt. 9:11-13).

TEACHING — the act of instructing students or imparting knowledge and information. As used in the New Testament, the concept of teaching usually means instruction in the faith. Thus, teaching is to be distinguished from preaching, or the proclamation of the gospel to the non-Christian world. Teaching in the Christian faith was validated by Jesus, who was called "teacher" more than anything else.

Since sound instruction in the faith is essential to the spiritual growth of Christians and to the development of the church, the Bible contains numerous passages which deal with teaching (Matt. 4:23; Luke 4:14; Acts 13:1-3; Rom. 12:6-8; Gal. 6:6).

Special attention is directed to the danger of false teachings. Christians are warned to test those who pervert the true gospel (2 Tim. 3:1-7; 1 Pet. 2:1-3).

Sound teaching was a concept deeply engrained in the Jewish mind since Old Testament times. Moses and Aaron were considered teachers of God's commandments (Ex. 18:20). Parents were also directed to teach their children about God and His statutes (Deut. 4:9-10).

TEARS (see MOURN).

TEBAH [TEE buh] (meaning unknown) — a son of Nahor and Reumah (Gen. 22:24).

TEBALIAH [tee buh LIE uh] (Jehovah has dipped) — a Temple gatekeeper after the Captivity (1 Chr. 26:11).

TEBETH [TEE beth] — the tenth month of the sacred year in the Jewish calendar (Esth. 2:16). Also see CALENDAR.

TEETH (see TOOTH).

TEHAPHNEHES [teh HAP nuh hez] — a form of TAHPENES.

TEHINNAH [tih HIN uh] (supplication) — a son of Eshton, of the tribe of Judah (1 Chr. 4:12).

TEIL TREE (see PLANTS OF THE BIBLE).

TEKEL (see MENE, MENE, TEKEL, UPHARSIN).

TEKOA [tuh KOE uh] (trumpet blast) — the birthplace of the prophet Amos (see Map 4, B-4). Situated in Judah (1 Chr. 2:24; 4:5), Tekoa is identified today with Khirbet Taqu'a, about 10 kilometers (6

miles) southeast of Bethlehem and about 16 kilometers (10 miles) south of Jerusalem. It was built on a hill in the wilderness of Tekoa toward En Gedi (2 Chr. 11:6; 20:20).

Tekoa is first mentioned in the Bible in connection with Joab employing a "wise woman" (v. 2) to bring reconciliation between David and Absalom (2 Sam. 14:2, 4, 9; Tekoah, KJV). Later Rehoboam, king of Judah (ruled 931/30-913 B.C.), fortified the site in order to prevent an invasion of Jerusalem from the south (2 Chr. 11:6).

Because of its elevation—about 850 meters (2,790 feet) above sea level—Tekoa became a station for warning Jerusalem of the approach of its enemies (Jer. 6:1). From Tekoa a person can see the Mount of Olives in Jerusalem and Mount Nebo beyond the Dead Sea. About two miles from Tekoa, Herod the Great (ruled 37-4 B.C.) built the fortress, the Herodium, in the Judean wilderness.

TEKOAH [tuh KOE uh] — a form of TEKOA.

TEKOITE [tuh KOE ight] — a native or inhabitant of TEKOA (2 Sam. 23:26; Neh. 3:5).

TEL ABIB [tel uh BIB] (mound of grain) — a locality in Babylonia near "the River Chebar" (a great irrigation canal) where the prophet Ezekiel stayed among the captives for seven days (Ezek. 3:15). These captives had been taken prisoner in Judah and had been deported to Babylon in 597 B.C. The largest city in modern Israel, Tel Aviv, derives its name from Tel Abib.

TEL-HARESHA [tel ha RESH ah] — a form of TEL HARSHA.

TEL HARSHA [tel HAHR shuh] (hill of workmanship) — a Babylonian city where the Jews gathered to return to Jerusalem after the Captivity (Ezra 2:59; Tel-harsa, KJV; Neh. 7:61; Tel-haresha, KJV).

TEL MELAH [tel MEE luh] (hill of salt) — a place in Babylon from which the Israelites returned after the Captivity (Ezra 2:59).

TELAH [TEE luh] (breach) — a son of Resheph and the father of Tahan (1 Chr. 7:25).

TELAIM [tuh LAY uhm] (young lambs) — a place where Saul gathered his fighting men before his campaign against the Amalekites (1 Sam. 15:4). The site probably was in southern Judah.

TELASSAR [tel ASS uhr] (hill of Asshur) — a city and district of Mesopotamia inhabited by "the people of Eden" (2 Kin. 19:12; Thelasar, KJV; Is. 37:12). Telassar may have been in Bit-Adini, a small Aramean kingdom on the upper Euphrates River.

TELEM [TEE lem] (a lamb) — the name of a city and a man in the Old Testament:

1. A city in southern Judah (Josh. 15:24).

2. A gatekeeper who divorced his pagan wife after the Captivity (Ezra 10:24).

A tell in Palestine. A tell is an artificial hill or mound built up by the rubble and debris of successive stages of occupation.

TELL — a mound of rubble that marks the site of an ancient city. When a city was destroyed, a new city would often be built on the rubble. Thus, these mounds grew higher and higher across the centuries. The ultimate prophetic judgment on a city was that it would become a "desolate mound" (Jer. 49:2).

The typical tell has a flat top and sloping sides. The largest tells in Palestine are at MEGIDDO, HAZOR, JERICHO, and BETH SHEAN.

TELL EL AMARNA (see AMARNA, TELL EL).

TEMA [TEE muh] (*south country*) — the name of a man and a city in the Old Testament:

1. The 9th of the 12 sons of Ishmael (Gen. 25:15; 1 Chr. 1:30).

2. An oasis, or desert city, in northwest Arabia (Job 6:19; Is. 21:14; Jer. 25:23). Tema was situated at the intersection of two important caravan routes—one from the Persian Gulf to the Gulf of Aqaba and the other from Damascus to Medina and Mecca—about midway between Babylon and Egypt. The site is present-day Teima.

TEMAN [TEE muhn] (*on the right hand*) — the name of a man and a city in the Old Testament:

1. A son of Eliphaz and a grandson of Esau (Gen. 36:11). Teman was an Edomite chief (Gen. 36:15; 1 Chr. 1:36) who gave his name to the region where his descendants settled (Gen. 36:34).

2. An important city (see Map 4, B-5) in southern Edom (Gen. 36:34; Hab. 3:3). Some scholars identify Teman with Tawilan, about eight kilometers (five miles) east of Petra.

TEMANITE [TEE mun ite] — a descendant of TEMAN or an inhabitant of the region occupied by the clan of Teman, in the land of Edom (Gen. 36:34; Temani, KJV; 1 Chr. 1:45). Eliphaz, one of Job's friends, was a Temanite (Job 2:11).

TEMENI [TEM uh nie] (meaning unknown) — a son of Ashhur and Naarah (1 Chr. 4:6).

TEMPERANCE — control over sensual desires. The meaning of the word temperate in English translations of the Bible should not be restricted to the kind of self-control a person exerts by abstaining from alcoholic beverages. The temperance of which the Bible speaks is far more inclusive. It indicates a self-control that masters all kinds of sensual desires, such as sexual desire or the desire for material comfort. Through temperance the Christian disciplines body and spirit, so that he is more capable of striving for his spiritual reward (1 Cor. 9:24–27).

TEMPLE — a building in which a god (or gods) is worshiped. The Old Testament describes temples as some of man's oldest buildings. The Tower of Babel (Gen. 11:4) is the first recorded example of a structure that implies the existence of a temple, although this tower was not a temple itself. A temple was thought of as the building where the god manifested his presence, so the place the temple occupied was holy, or sacred. Because the god was thought to dwell in the temple, the Old Testament had no specific word for temple. It refers instead to the "house" of a deity.

Abraham was from Mesopotamia, where each city had a temple for its patron god. The Mesopotamians believed that the god owned their land, that the king was the vassal of the god, and that the land had to be blessed by the god in order to be fruitful. Their religious practices were, in part, designed to win the god's favor.

Several Canaanite temples are mentioned in the Old Testament. They include the temples of the god Berith in Shechem (Judg. 9:46), Dagon in Ashdod (Judg. 16:23–30; 1 Sam. 5:2–5; 1 Chr. 10:10), and Beth Shan on Mount Gilboa (1 Sam. 31:12).

Because they were wandering herdsmen, the patriarchs such as Abraham and Jacob did not build temples. However, they did have shrines and altars in places where God had revealed Himself to them, such as by the oak of Moreh (Gen. 12:6–7; 33:20), at Bethel (Gen. 12:8; 28:18–22), and at Beersheba (Gen. 21:33; 26:23–25).

Even after Solomon's Temple was completed, rival sanctuaries at Bethel and Dan (1 Kin. 12:28–33) competed with it. Later the Samaritans had a temple on Mount Gerizim (John 4:20). A Judeo–Aramaic colony founded a temple at Elephantine in Upper Egypt. According to the Jewish historian Josephus, Ptolomy VI Philometor (181–145 B.C.) granted Jewish refugees in Egypt the use of an ancient temple in the delta region.

Solomon's Temple. Once the land was fully conquered and all the tribes were properly settled, it was important that the worship of God be centralized. Because he was a man of war, David was not allowed to build the temple, but he was allowed to gather the materials for it and to organize the project (1 Chr. 22:1–19). The actual work began "in the four hundred and eightieth year after the children of Israel had come out of the land of Egypt, in the fourth year of Solomon's reign over Israel" (1 Kin. 6:1). Solomon began to reign about 971 B.C., so his fourth year would have been about 967 B.C. The temple was completed about 960 B.C., seven years later (1 Kin. 6:37–38).

In biblical times three temples were built on the same site: Solomon's, Zerubbabel's, and Herod's. Solomon built the temple on the east side of Jerusalem on Mount Moriah, "where the Lord had appeared to his father David, at the place that David had prepared on the threshing floor of Ornan the Jebusite" (1 Chr. 21:28; 2 Chr. 3:1). The highest part of Mount Moriah is now the site of the build-

ing called The Dome of the Rock in Jerusalem.

Solomon contacted Hiram, king of Tyre, to supply workmen and materials to help construct the Temple (2 Chr. 2:3). First Kings 5:6 calls those workmen Sidonians. Additionally, Solomon "raised up a labor force out of all Israel" of 30,000 men to assist Hiram in the forests of Lebanon (1 Kin. 5:13). According to 1 Kings 5:15, "Solomon had seventy thousand who carried burdens, and eighty thousand who quarried stone in the mountains." The Gebalites also helped to quarry stones (1 Kin. 5:18). Those who quarried stones were overseen by 3,300 of Solomon's deputies (1 Kin. 5:16).

Solomon's Temple is described, though incompletely, in 1 Kings 6—7 and in 2 Chronicles 3—4. The description of Ezekiel's Temple (Ezek. 40–43), an elaborate version of Solomon's, may supplement those accounts. Solomon's Temple was in the shape of a rectangle that ran east and west. Like Ezekiel's Temple (Ezek. 41:8), it may have stood on a platform. The accounts in Kings and Chronicles suggest that there was an inner and an outer courtyard.

Three main objects were situated in the inner courtyard. The bronze altar that was used for burnt offerings (1 Kin. 8:22, 64; 9:25) measured 20 cubits square and 10 cubits high (2 Chr. 4:1). Between that and the porch of the Temple stood the bronze laver, or molten sea, that held water for the ritual washings (1 Kin. 7:23–26). It was completely round, 5 cubits high, 10 cubits in diameter, and 30 cubits around its outer circumference (1 Kin. 7:23). Twelve bronze oxen, in four groups of three, faced outward toward the four points of the compass, with the bronze laver resting on their backs (1 Kin. 7:25; Ahaz removed the bronze laver from the oxen; 2 Kin. 16:17).

Finally, at the dedication of the Temple, Solomon is said to have stood on a "bronze platform five cu-

A model of Herod's Temple in Jerusalem. Begun in 19 B.C., it was not completed until A.D. 63, long after Herod's death.

Photo by Ben Chapman

Photo by Ben Chapman
Massive Roman ruins at Baalbek—a large, prosperous city in the first century A.D.

bits long, five cubits wide, and three cubits high" that stood in the middle of the courtyard (2 Chr. 6:12–13).

The interior dimensions of the Temple were 60 cubits long, 20 cubits wide, and 30 cubits high (1 Kin. 6:2). The ten steps to the porch of the Temple were flanked by two bronze columns, Jachin and Boaz, each 25 cubits high (including the capitals) and 12 cubits in circumference (1 Kin. 7:15–16; 2 Chr. 3:15). The porch was 10 cubits long, 20 cubits wide, and, supposedly, 120 cubits high (2 Chr. 3:4). But since the rest of the building was only 30 cubits high, some scholars question this figure of 120 cubits.

To the west of the porch was the Holy Place, a room 40 cubits long, 20 cubits wide, and 30 cubits high where ordinary rituals took place. Windows near the ceiling provided light. In the Holy Place were the golden incense altar, the table for the showbread, five pair of lampstands, and the utensils used for sacrifice. Double doors, probably opened once a year for the high priest on the Day of Atonement, led from the west end of the Holy Place to the Holy of Holies, a 20-cubit cube. In that room two wooden cherubim, each ten feet tall, stood with outstretched wings. Two of the wings met above the ark of the covenant and two of them touched the north and south walls of the room (1 Kin. 6:27). God's presence was manifested in the Holy of Holies as a cloud (1 Kin. 8:10–11).

The outside of the Temple building, excluding the porch area, consisted of side chambers, or galleries, that rose three stories high (1 Kin. 6:5). The rooms of the Temple were paneled with cedar, the floor was cypress, and the ornately carved doors and walls were overlaid with gold (1 Kin. 6:20–22).

Not a stone could be seen.

Shishak, king of Egypt, took away the Temple treasures during the reign of Rehoboam, Solomon's son (1 Kin. 14:26). Asa used the Temple treasure to buy an ally (1 Kin. 15:18) and to buy off an invader (2 Kin. 16:8). Manasseh placed Canaanite altars and a carved image of Asherah, a Canaanite goddess, in the Temple (2 Kin. 21:4, 7). Ahaz introduced an altar patterned after one he saw in Damascus (2 Kin. 16:10–16). By about 640 B.C., Josiah had to repair the Temple (2 Kin. 22:3–7). After robbing the Temple of its treasures and gold during his first attack (2 Kin. 24:13), in 587 B.C. the Babylonian King Nebuchadnezzar looted, sacked and burned the Temple (2 Kin. 25:9, 13–17), but people still came to the site to offer sacrifice (Jer. 41:5).

Ezekiel's Temple. Ezekiel's vision of a future Temple (Ezekiel 40—43) comforted the Jewish captives in Babylon (Psalm 137) who remembered the glory of Solomon's Temple and its destruction by the Babylonians. The Temple in Ezekiel's vision differs little in its physical configuration and dimensions from Solomon's.

The Second Temple. Cyrus, king of Persia, authorized the return of the Jewish captives, the return of the Temple vessels Nebuchadnezzar had looted, and the reconstruction of the Temple (about 537 B.C.), which was finished about 515 B.C. The completed Temple was smaller than and inferior to Solomon's (Ezra 3:12). The ark of the covenant was never recovered, and so the Second Temple (and Herod's Temple) had no ark. Neither were Solomon's ten lampstands recovered. One seven-branched candelabrum, the table of showbread, and the incense altar stood in the Holy Place of the

The temple of Bacchus at Baalbek. Bacchus, also called Dionysus, was the Greek god of wine.

second Temple (as they did in Herod's Temple), but these were taken by Antiochus IV Epiphanes (about 175–163 B.C.), who defiled the altar in 167 B.C. The Maccabees cleansed the Temple, restored its furnishings (164 B.C.; 1 Macc. 4:36–59), and later turned it into a fortress.

Herod's Temple. King Herod, an Idumean, sought to appease his Jewish subjects by constructing an enormous, ornate, cream–colored Temple of stone and gold that began in 19 B.C. The main building was finished by 9 B.C., but the entire structure was not completed until A.D. 64. The Romans destroyed it in A.D. 70. The gold and white stone shone so brightly in the sun that it was difficult to look directly at the Temple.

The Temple building occupied an area that measured about 446 meters (490 yards) from north to south and 296 meters (325 yards) from east to west. The entire Temple complex was enclosed by a massive stone wall, the southeast corner of which stood about 45 meters (50 yards) above the floor of the Kidron ravine. The parapet above this corner may have been the "pinnacle of the temple" referred to in the gospels (Matt. 4:5). There was one gate in the north wall, one in the east wall, two in the south wall, and four in the west wall facing the city.

The Fortress of Antonia, the Jerusalem residence of the Roman procurators, stood at the northwest corner of the complex. The fortress housed a Roman garrison (Acts 21:31) and, as a symbol of submission, the robes of the High Priest.

Double porticos, 30 cubits wide and supported by shining marble columns 25 cubits high, were constructed along the inside of the main walls, surrounding the outer court of the Temple, the Court of the Gentiles. Including the Tower of Antonia, these porticos were about 11,800 meters (3,600 feet) in circumference. The Royal Porch, along the south wall, had four rows of columns. Solomon's Porch, located along the east wall, had two rows of columns (John 10:23; Acts 3:11; 5:12). This was the place where the scribes had their debates (Mark 11:27; Luke 2:46; 19:47) and where the merchants and moneychangers transacted business (Luke 19:45–46; John 2:14–16).

Inside of and slightly higher than the outer court (the Court of the Gentiles) was a smaller enclosure surrounded by a ballustrade three cubits high. This enclosure was posted with recurring notices in Greek and Latin that any Gentile who entered the inner area was subject to death. After passing through one of several openings in the ballustrade, 14 steps led up to the inner area, which was surrounded by a wall 25 cubits high. This wall was separated from the steps by a terrace 10 cubits wide. Flights of five steps led from the terrace to eight gates in the wall, four on the north and four on the south side.

The inner area of Herod's Temple contained three courts. The easternmost court was the Court of Women, and it contained the Temple treasury where people donated their money (Mark 12:41–44). Three gates led into this court, one on the north, one on the south, and a third on the east. This third gate was probably the "Beautiful Gate" (Acts 3:2, 10). A fourth, larger, more massive and ornate gate led from the Court of the Women west into the Court of Israel (for male Jews), which was elevated 15 steps above the Court of Women.

Inside the Court of Israel was the innermost court, the Court of the Priests. During the Feast of Tabernacles, men could enter the Priest's Court to walk around the altar. The Court of Priests immediately surrounds the Temple building itself (the Holy Place and the Holy of Holies) and the altar of burnt offering.

The layout of Herod's Temple was patterned after Solomon's. The two-story temple building was in the shape of a "T." The porch of the building (the cross member of the "T") was a vestibule 100 cubits long and 100 cubits high, with an opening 70 cubits high and 25 cubits wide. In front of the porch at the foot of the steps, surrounded by a cubit-high stone barrier, was the altar of burnt offering (15 cubits high and 50 cubits square). At the back of the vestibule were the main double doors (16 cubits wide and 55 cubits high) that led into the Holy Place.

The Holy Place was 40 cubits long, 20 cubits wide, and 60 cubits high. It contained the table of showbread, the seven-branched lampstand, and the altar of incense. The Holy Place was divided from the Holy of Holies by a curtain that stretched from floor to ceiling (Matt. 27:51; Mark 15:38; 2 Cor. 3:14). The Holy of Holies was 20 cubits by 20 cubits by 60 cubits high. It contained no furniture. The temple was surrounded on the north, south, and west sides by three stories of rooms that rose 60 cubits.

Temple in the New Testament. The New Testament uses two words for Temple. One of these words refers to the collection of buildings that made up the Temple in Jerusalem, while the other usually refers to the sanctuary of the Temple.

Jesus related to the Temple in four distinct ways. First, as a pious Jew who was zealous for the Lord, Jesus showed respect for the Temple. He referred to it as "the house of God" (Matt. 12:4) and "My Father's house" (John 2:16). He taught that everything in it was holy because of the sanctifying presence of God (Matt. 23:17, 21).

Second, Jesus' zeal led Him to purge the Temple of the moneychangers (Mark 11:15–17; John 2:16) and to weep over it as He reflected on its coming destruction (Mark 13:1; Luke 19:41–44). Because Malachi 3:1 prophesied the cleansing of the Temple as something the Lord and His Messenger would do, Jesus' act implied His deity and messiahship. Consequently, the hard-hearted scribes and chief priests "sought how they might destroy Him" (Mark 11:18; Luke 19:47).

Third, because He was the Son of God incarnate, Jesus taught that He was greater than the Temple (Matt. 12:6). Jesus' teaching that if the temple of His body was destroyed in three days He would raise it up (John 2:19) likewise affirms His superiority to the Temple building. That saying of Jesus may have provided the basis for the claim of the two false witnesses at His trial who stated that Jesus said, "I am able to destroy the temple of God and to build it in three days" (Matt. 26:60–61; 27:40; Mark 14:57–58; 15:29).

Finally, Jesus taught that the church (Matt. 16:18) is the new, eschatological temple (Matt. 18:19–20; John 14:23).

At the moment of Jesus' death, the veil of the Temple was torn from top to bottom (Matt. 27:51; Mark 15:38; Luke 23:45). By His death, Jesus opened a new way into the presence of God. A new order replaced the old. No longer was the Temple in Jerusalem to be the place where men worshiped God. From now on they would worship Him "in spirit and truth" (John 4:21–24).

The first Christians were converted Jews. They continued to worship at the Temple as Jesus had (Luke 24:52; Acts 2:46; 3:1; 5:12, 20–21, 42). As they began to understand the meaning and significance of Jesus' person, work, and teaching, they realized they were the new people of God, infused by

The temple of Hephaestus (Vulcan) in Athens is one of the best-preserved Greek temples from ancient times.
Photo by Howard Vos

God's Spirit. As such, they were a new, living Temple. A new order had replaced the old. Stephen, a Christian of Gentile background (Acts 6:1–5), was the first person to understand that the church had replaced the Temple as the place where God's presence was manifested in a special way among His people.

In Acts 15:13–18 Stephen's insight was carried forward by James, who identified the church with Amos' prophecy about the "tabernacle of David, which has fallen" (v. 16). According to James' application of Amos' prophesy about the end times, the restoration of David's tabernacle, the Temple, would serve as the rallying point for Gentiles who wished to come to the Lord (Amos 9:11–12). James understood the church as the new temple that fulfilled that prophecy.

According to the apostle Paul, "All the promises of God" are "Yes, and...Amen" in Christ (2 Cor. 1:20). Ezekiel and other prophets had prophesied a new temple (Ezekiel 40—43), and Paul understood the church as the fulfillment of those prophesies. Individually the Christian's body is "the temple of the Holy Spirit" (1 Cor. 6:19). Corporately the church is "the temple of God" where the Spirit of God dwells (1 Cor. 3:16; 2 Cor. 6:16). Christians are growing "into a holy temple in the Lord...a dwelling place of God in the Spirit" (Eph. 2:21–22). Because we are God's new temple where the Holy Spirit dwells, Christians are to be holy (1 Cor. 6:18–20; 2 Cor. 7:1).

Because God dwells in us, Christians are holy to God, and He will destroy anyone who defiles us (1 Cor. 3:16–17). Because there is only one new temple and all Christians—regardless of race or religious background—are members of it, all Christians have equal access to God (Eph. 2:19–22). Paul understood the church, then, as the eschatological temple to which God is gathering Israel and the other nations of the world (Is. 2:2–4; Mic. 4:1–5).

Paul used the metaphor of the temple to express the unity of the new people of God that God is bringing about through the preaching of the gospel. The members of this new race are Jews and Gentiles who formerly were separated by the "middle wall of separation" and the "ordinances" that forbade them to mix (Eph. 2:14–15). Christ's sacrificial death on the cross ushered in a new age in God's relationship with mankind and abolished the enmity between Jew and Gentile by abolishing the validity of the ordinances that gave expression to it (v. 15). He abolished those ordinances in order to create "one new man," a new race composed of Jewish and Gentile Christians at peace with one another (v. 15, 17). This "new man" is a living temple (v. 21) that is based on the teaching of the New Testament apostles and prophets and on the teaching, work, and person of Christ (v. 20).

Jesus Himself is the chief cornerstone of the building and so gives it shape and character (v. 20). The building is holy because it is growing "in the Lord" (v. 21) and because God dwells there in the

Spirit (v. 22). "Lord," "God," and "Spirit" define this new temple in a trinitarian fashion. The metaphors of God's new people being a temple ("building") and being a body ("growing") are blended in verse 21.

In a similar way, Peter used the word house to describe Christians as members of a new, spiritual temple (1 Pet. 2:4–10). Christ is the chief cornerstone (v. 6). He is "a stone of stumbling and a rock of offense" (v. 8), a "living stone, rejected...by men, but chosen by God and precious" (v. 4). Like Christ, Christians are "living stones" who are being built into a "spiritual house," or temple (v. 5). The metaphor of the "spiritual house" is combined with that of the "holy priesthood" that offers "spiritual sacrifices" (v. 5). And this "royal priesthood" of believers is a "holy nation," God's new people who proclaim His praises (vv. 9–10), the New Israel (Ex. 19:6).

In addition to understanding the church as the new, spiritual temple of God on earth that replaced the Temple in Jerusalem, the New Testament alludes to a heavenly temple in whose life the church participates. John (John 1:51; 14:2) and Paul (Gal. 4:26; Phil. 3:20) both allude to the heavenly temple, but the idea is most developed in Hebrews and Revelation.

The author of Hebrews was concerned to demonstrate that Christianity is better than Judaism. Among other things, Christians have a better covenant, a better sacrifice, a better high priest, and a better temple. The Temple in Jerusalem was only a "copy and shadow," a type, of the true temple, which is in heaven (Heb. 8:5). Therefore the true, heavenly sanctuary into which Christ has entered on our behalf is better than its earthly copy (9:24). Because Christ our High Priest dwells in this heavenly sanctuary (9:24; 10:12; 19–22), we can enter the heavenly Holy of Holies and participate in the worship of the heavenly temple (10:19–22; 12:18–24). The author appears to define the heavenly temple as "the general assembly and church of the firstborn" (12:23).

According to John, the author of Revelation, there is a celestial Mount Zion (14:1; 21:10), a heavenly Jerusalem (3:12; 21:2), and a heavenly temple (11:19; 15:5—16:1). Christians who overcome temptation and trials are made pillars in the heavenly temple of God (3:12). As in Ephesians, then, the heavenly temple grows.

From this heavenly temple God will issue His judgments on the nations during the Tribulation (11:19; 14:14–20; 15:5—16:1). The martyrs of the Tribulation will serve God "day and night in His [heavenly] temple" (7:15). The temple in Jerusalem will be measured and judged during that time (11:1–2).

In the New Jerusalem there will not be a temple because "the Lord God Almighty and the Lamb are its temple" (Rev. 21:22). In that perfect city nothing will come between God and man, and we "shall see His face" (22:4). In the new heaven and earth "the tabernacle of God" will be "with men, and He will dwell with them, and they shall be His people. God Himself will be with them and be their God" (21:3).

Paul identified the new temple with the church, but John and the author of Hebrews identified it with the heavenly realm where Christ dwells. Furthermore, just as there was no temple before the fall, so John anticipated a new heaven and earth without a temple. These different ways of understanding the relation of the temple to the new people of God are complementary, not contradictory.

TEMPLE SHEKEL (see WEIGHTS AND MEASURES).

TEMPTATION — an enticement or invitation to sin, with the implied promise of greater good to be derived from following the way of disobedience. In this sense, God does not tempt man, nor can He Himself as the holy God be tempted (James 1:13). God cannot be induced to deny Himself (2 Tim. 2:13). The supreme tempter is Satan (Matt. 4:3; 1 Cor. 7:5; 1 Thess. 3:5), who is able to play upon the weakness of corrupted human nature (James 1:14) and so to lead people to destruction.

The gospel of Jesus Christ directs man to resist temptation, promising blessedness to those who do (James 1:12). The gospel also directs us to pray for deliverance from exposure to temptation and from surrender to it (Matt. 6:13; Luke 11:4). The Lord will not allow His people to encounter temptation beyond their Spirit–given ability to resist (1 Cor. 10:13; 2 Pet. 2:9).

In the Old Testament, temptation can best be understood as testing or proving. The context is the covenant relation of mutual love and faithfulness between God and His people. The Lord tests Israel to prove the true nature of her faithfulness to Him (Gen. 22:1; Deut. 8:2, 16). His purpose is not to induce His people to sin but to confirm their faith (James 1:2-4). As in the case of Job, Satan the tempter can serve the Lord's purpose. Satan's temptation of Adam in the Garden of Eden was also the Lord's testing of Adam's faith.

The nation of Israel also "tempts," or tests, the Lord by calling into question the Lord's unswerving loyalty to His people (Ex. 17:2, 7; Ps. 78:18, 41, 56). God has promised to preserve Israel as His own everlasting possession, but His righteousness requires that He destroy a rebellious nation. His people's disobedience tempts the Lord to break His promise to be their God.

In the temptation of Jesus (Matt. 4:1-11; Luke 4:1-13), Satan enticed the Son of God to forsake His messianic commitment. Jesus, however, did not prove to be a disloyal Son. He did not put the Lord to the test, or tempt God, like Israel of old. He lives "by every word that proceeds from the mouth of God" (Matt. 4:4). Having resisted satanic temptation Himself, Christ is able to comfort and aid His followers who are tempted in similar fashion (Heb. 2:18; 4:15).

TEMPTATION OF CHRIST — the 40–day period in the wilderness when Jesus was tempted by the devil (Matt. 4:1-13; Mark 1:12-13). Jesus' first temptation (to turn stones to bread) was to use His

Photo by Howard Vos

A cut through the mound of Old Testament Jericho, with the traditional site of the Mount of Temptation in the distance (Matt. 4:1-11).

divine power to satisfy His own physical needs. The second (to jump off the Temple) was to perform a spectacular feat so the people would follow Him. The third was to gain possession of the world by worshiping Satan.

One motive lay behind all these temptations: Satan wanted to destroy Jesus' mission. Because Jesus' death would destroy Satan's power, Satan wanted Jesus to pollute His life and ministry. The ultimate issue behind these temptations was idolatry. The real purpose of Satan's temptation was that he might be worshiped instead of God.

TEN (see NUMBER).

TEN COMMANDMENTS (see COMMANDMENTS, TEN).

TENDERHEARTED — easily moved by another's distress. The Greek noun translated tenderhearted (Eph. 4:32) literally means "having strong, kindly bowels." In the Bible the BOWELS are regarded as the source of kindness (Gen. 43:30, KJV; Phil. 1:8, KJV).

TENON — a projection on the end of a piece of wood shaped to fit into a socket. The tabernacle boards had tenons that fitted into sockets of silver (Ex. 26:17).

TENT — a temporary shelter made of cloth, supported usually by poles and ropes. In biblical times tents were frequently made of a cloth woven out of black goat's hair. The cloth was woven on a loom in long strips, which were then sewn together until the desired length was reached. Poles and rope held the tent upright and in the desired position. The ropes were usually tied to tent pegs driven into the ground. While tents came in a variety of sizes and shapes, the traditional shape has been a rectangle. The side and end walls were made of the same material, reed mats, which were removable to catch the breeze.

The interior of a tent was quite plain. The floor was covered with mats or a rug upon which the people sat. A chest or two and a low table might be the only furniture. Since a family's belongings had to be packed and moved frequently, even the wealthy did not accumulate numerous pieces of furniture.

Tents have been the housing of nomadic and semi-nomadic people in the Middle East since the beginning of history. The patriarchs—Abraham, Isaac, and Jacob—all lived in tents as they crisscrossed the Promised Land. For 40 years after they left Egypt, the Israelites lived in tents. The tabernacle, where the Israelites worshiped God before the building of Solomon's Temple, is frequently called the "tent of meeting" (Ex. 29:32, 40). Tents continued to have several uses even after the Israelites settled into villages. The Rechabites continued to dwell in tents (Jer. 35:7), and armies used tents during military campaigns.

In later years, a tent came to stand symbolically for a number of abstract ideas. The most common usage is as a general term for a home or dwelling (Luke 16:9; Ps. 15:1). The apostle Paul used the word to refer to our bodies, calling them "earthly tents" (2 Cor. 5:1).

TENT OF MEETING (see TABERNACLE OF MEETING).

TENTMAKER (see OCCUPATIONS AND TRADES).

TERAH [TEE ruh] (meaning unknown) — the name of a man and a place in the Bible:

1. The father of Abraham and an ancestor of Christ (Gen. 11:26–27; Luke 3:34; Thara, KJV). Descended from Shem, Terah also was the father of Nahor and Haran. He lived at Ur of the Chaldeans most of his life; apparently at Ur he worshiped gods other than the one true God (Josh. 24:2). From Ur, Terah migrated with his son Abraham, his grandson Lot (Haran's son), and his daughter–in–law Sarah (Abraham's wife) to Haran, a city about 800 kilometers (500 miles) north of Ur and about 445 kilometers (275 miles) northeast of Damascus. Terah died in Haran at the age of 205 (Gen. 11:24–32).

2. An encampment of the Israelites in the wilderness, after the Exodus from Egypt (Num. 33:27–28; Tarah, KJV).

TERAPHIM [TEHR uh fim] (meaning unknown) — figurines or images in human form used in the ancient world as household gods. *Teraphim* is a Hebrew word for idols which appears in the NKJV only once (Hos. 3:4). But the Hebrew word appears 14 additional times in the Old Testament. It is translated in these various usages as household idols (Gen. 31:19, 34–35), household gods (2 Kin. 23:24), idolatry (1 Sam. 15:23), idols (Zech. 10:2), image (1 Sam. 19:13, 16), and images (Ezek. 21:21).

Teraphim were probably of Mesopotamian origin, but apparently they were widespread in Hebrew households. Possibly made of clay, these objects may have been similar to the objects in Rome that were connected with superstition, idolatry, and magic.

The term teraphim, translated as household idols (NKJV) occurs in Judges 17:5 and 18:14, 17–18, 20, where it is linked with an EPHOD and with carved images and molded images. All of these items formed part of the equipment of Micah's idolatrous

Tents used by the Arab bedouin people. Frequently made of black cloth woven from goat hair, tents were used by nomads, shepherds, and soldiers (Gen. 4:20; Judg. 8:11).

Photo by Gustav Jeeninga

shrine. In Hosea 3:4 teraphim is again linked with ephod in a reference to the absence of all forms of religion from Israel during her time of punishment.

The household gods (teraphim) of Genesis 31:19, 34–35 were probably idolatrous images which Rachel wanted to bring with her to Palestine, perhaps for the safety they might provide on the perilous journey and in a strange land.

In other contexts teraphim are directly related to idolatry. The idols that speak delusion (Zech. 10:2) and the idolatry that is linked with iniquity (1 Sam. 15:23) both are translations of the word teraphim. In his reformation of religion, King Josiah of Judah sought to restore true worship by abolishing the practices of consulting mediums and spiritists and using household gods (teraphim) and images (2 Kin. 23:24).

TEREBINTH (see PLANTS OF THE BIBLE).

TERESH [TEE resh] (solid) — one of the two eunuchs who conspired against King Ahasuerus (Xerxes) of Persia. When Mordecai discovered their plot, they were hanged (Esth. 2:21).

TERRACE — a type of landing or outer courtyard. King Solomon built terraces for the Temple and his royal palace (2 Chr. 9:11, KJV). Ezekiel also mentioned terraces several times in his prophecy (Ezek. 17:7, 10; 41:9, 11). Also see HOUSE.

TERROR — a state of intense fear or dread (Gen. 35:5; Ps. 91:5; Rom. 13:3). The apostle Paul referred to the SECOND COMING of Christ as the "terror of the Lord" for those who have not professed Christ as Savior and Lord (2 Cor. 5:11).

TERTIUS [TUR shee uhs] (third) — the scribe or secretary to whom the apostle Paul dictated his letter to the Romans (Rom. 16:22).

TERTULLUS [tur TUHL uhs] (third) — a professional orator hired to prosecute the Jews' case against the apostle Paul (Acts 24:1–2). Tertullus accompanied Ananias the high priest and the elders from Jerusalem to Caesarea to accuse Paul before Felix, the Roman governor of Judea.

Tertullus' speech followed the common Roman pattern of his day. He began by flattering the judge, the "most noble Felix," for the peace and prosperity he had brought to the nation. He then charged Paul with crimes which the apostle had not committed (Acts 21:26–40; 23:26–30; 24:10–21).

TESTAMENT — a written document that provides for the disposition of one's personal property after death; a bequest. The word testament occurs only two times in the NKJV (2 Cor. 3:14; Heb. 9:16–17). In the KJV the word appears in several additional places (Matt. 26:28; 2 Cor. 3:6; Rev. 11:19)—translated in all these cases as covenant by the NKJV.

The word testament also refers to either of the two main divisions of the Bible: the Old Testament and the New Testament, or, more accurately, the Old Covenant and the New Covenant (2 Cor. 3:14). Thus, testament is generally used to refer to

the spiritual COVENANT between God and His people.

TESTAMENTS OF THE TWELVE PATRIARCHS (see PSEUDEPIGRAPHA).

TESTICLES, CRUSHED (see DISABILITIES AND DEFORMITIES).

TESTIMONY (see WITNESS).

TESTIMONY, ARK OF THE (see ARK OF THE TESTIMONY).

TETH [tate] — the ninth letter of the Hebrew alphabet, used as a heading over Psalm 119:65–72. In the original Hebrew language, every line of these eight verses began with the letter teth. Also see ACROSTIC.

TETRARCH [TEH trahrk] (ruler of a fourth part) — the ruler or governor of the fourth part of a country, which was divided into these parts for efficient government, especially under the Roman Empire. According to the Jewish historian Josephus, before Herod the Great was named king he was first named tetrarch. The title was also given to Herod Antipas, ruler of Galilee and Perea (Matt. 14:1; Acts 13:1). Philip, the brother of Herod Antipas, was tetrarch of Iturea and the region of Trachonitis; and Lysanias was tetrarch of Abilene (Luke 3:1).

TEXTS AND MANUSCRIPTS (see BIBLE).

THADDAEUS [tha DEE uhs] (breast) — one of the twelve apostles of Jesus (Matt. 10:3; Mark 3:18; Thaddeus, KJV), also called Lebbaeus (Matt. 10:3) and Judas the son of James (Luke 6:16; Acts 1:13). He is carefully distinguished from Judas Iscariot (John 14:22). Nothing else is known about this most obscure of the apostles, but some scholars attribute the Epistle of Jude to him.

THAHASH [THAY hash] (dolphin) — the third son of Reumah, the concubine of Nahor (Gen. 22:24; Tahash, NASB, NIV, RSV). Nahor was the brother of Abraham.

THAMAH [THAY muh] — a form of TAMAH.

THAMAR [THAY mahr] — a form of TAMAR.

THANK OFFERING (see SACRIFICIAL OFFERINGS).

THANKSGIVING — the aspect of praise that gives thanks to God for what He does for us. Ideally, thanksgiving should spring from a grateful heart; but it is required of all believers, regardless of their initial attitude (1 Thess. 5:18). We should be grateful to God for all things (Eph. 5:20; Col. 3:17; 1 Thess. 5:18), but especially for His work of salvation and sanctification (Rom. 7:25; Col. 1:3–5; 1 Thess. 1:2–7; 2:13). We ought also to thank God in anticipation of His answering our prayers (Phil. 4:6), knowing that His answers will always be in accord with His perfect will for our lives (Rom. 8:28–29). Also see PRAISE.

THARA [THAR uh] — a form of TERAH.

Remains of the spectacular Roman theater at Pergamos. Built into the steep face of a hill, it had 78 rows of seats.

THARSHISH [THAHR shish] — a son of Bilhan, of the tribe of Benjamin (1 Chr. 7:10).

THEATER — a semicircular structure with stone seats used as a place for dramatic productions. The theater was often the largest building in a city, capable of seating many people. Thus, it was often used for public meetings and for conducting public business. The apostle Paul was prevented by the disciples from entering the theater at Ephesus, because of the hostile crowd (Acts 19:29, 31).

In biblical times the theater was a strictly Greek and Roman institution. The earliest Greek theaters took advantage of naturally sloping land for the typical outdoor semicircular seating arrangement.

The Greek theaters had rows of seats cut from rock, stone, or marble. Arranged in concentric semicircles, these seats were divided into two or more sections by gangways. Most theaters featured a raised wooden stage and a round space for the chorus or orchestra.

The beginning of the theater must be credited to the Greeks in the sixth and fifth centuries B.C. The Greek theaters were sites for dramatic performances taken from songs and dances in honor of the Greek god Dionysus, the god of wine, and to the fertility of nature (identified with the Roman god Bacchus).

In contrast to Greek theaters, Roman theaters were partly roofed. Theaters were built in Palestine under Roman rule. Herod the Great, a patron of Roman culture, built theaters in Caesarea, Damascus, Gadara, Philadelphia, and other cities. Herod built both a theater and an amphitheater in Jerusa-

lem. Games were held every four years to honor the Roman emperor in the chief towns of Palestine. Remains of Greek and Roman theaters survive in cities visited by the apostle Paul, including Athens, Corinth, Ephesus, Miletus, and Philippi.

THEBES [theebz] — a form of No, No Amon.

THEBEZ [THEE biz] (meaning unknown) — a fortified city of Manasseh about 21 kilometers (13 miles) southwest of Beth Shean (Scythopolis). At Thebez Abimelech was killed by a woman who dropped a millstone on his head (Judg. 9:50–54).

THEFT (see Law).

THELASAR [thih LAY zur] — a form of Telassar.

THEOCRACY [the OCK rih see] — direct government of the nation of Israel by God Himself or His earthly representatives. Although theocracy is not a biblical word, the concept of God's rule on earth is thoroughly biblical. In a theocracy human rulers interpret and carry out the divine ruler's will. In Israel's early days God ruled through men such as Moses, Aaron, and Joshua. Later, He ruled by using a group called the judges.

Deuteronomy 17:14–20 allows for an Israelite monarchy under God and in cooperation with other ruling officials. Later, when Israel finally demanded a king, it was their attitude of being "like all the nations" rather than the request itself that God considered a rejection of His kingship (1 Sam. 8:5). Samuel, the last judge and a great prophet, insisted that having an earthly king did not excuse Israel from obedience to the divine king (1 Sam.

12:1–25). The human king was not an absolute monarch.

After the return from the Babylonian Captivity (about 539 B.C.), the priest became a more important agent of God's rule. Prophets such as Zechariah and Haggai mention the high priest as a ruler (Zech. 6:9–15). Apparently some Jews expected the Messiah to exercise priestly as well as kingly functions (Gen. 14:17–18; Ps. 110:4).

One of the purposes of the New Testament is to show God's kingly rule reestablished in Jesus Christ, the Prophet, Priest, and King appointed by God (Luke 24:19; Heb. 7:17; Rev. 19:16).

THEOPHANY [the AHF ih knee] — any direct, visual manifestation of the presence of God. The key word is visual, since God makes His presence and power known throughout the Bible in a variety of ways. But even in a theophany a person does not actually see God Himself. This is an impossibility, according to Exodus 33:20; 1 Timothy 6:16; and 1 John 4:12. What a person sees are the effects of God's unmediated presence.

Theophanies proper are limited to the Old Testament. They are most common in the books of Genesis and Exodus; but they also occur in the writings of the prophets, especially in connection with the calling of a prophet. The most frequent visible manifestation of God's presence in the Old Testament is the "Angel of the Lord." Other theophanies are the burning bush (Ex. 3:1–6), the pillar of cloud and the pillar of fire (Ex. 13:21–22), the cloud and fire of Sinai (Ex. 24:16–18), and the cloud of the glory of the Lord (Ex. 40:34–38).

The SHEKINAH glory that dwelt in the Holy of Holies in the tabernacle and the Temple may also be thought of as a specialized, permanent theophany. Theophanies are never given for their own sake, to satisfy a curiosity about God, but to convey some revelation or truth about Him.

In the New Testament Jesus as the physical expression of God is a kind of theophany (John 1:14, 18; 14:9). But such is the uniqueness of His Incarnation that the word is not entirely appropriate.

The word theophany does not appear in the Bible.

THEOPHILUS [thih AHF uh luhs] (*lover of God*) — a Christian to whom Luke dedicated the Gospel of Luke and the Book of Acts (Luke 1:3; Acts 1:1). The fact that Luke spoke of Theophilus as "most excellent" indicates that he was a prominent man of high rank and possibly a Roman. He may have chosen the name when he was converted to Christianity. According to tradition, both Luke and Theophilus were natives of Antioch in Syria. Much speculation surrounds Theophilus, but little is known for certain about him.

THESSALONIANS, EPISTLES TO THE — two letters written by the apostle Paul, which are among the earliest of Paul and of the New Testament. The major theological theme of 1 and 2 Thessalonians is the return of Christ to earth. Im-

portant as this theme is, however, the Thessalonian letters leave the reader wide awake to the responsibilities of the present, not gazing into the future. Both epistles aim to establish and strengthen a young church in a stormy setting (1 Thess. 3:2, 13; 2 Thess. 2:17; 3:3). In neither epistle does Paul fight any grave errors in the church. In both epistles the reader feels the heartbeat of Paul the pastor as he identifies with a young congregation taking its first steps in faith.

Structure of the Epistles. Paul begins the first epistle by thanking God for the faith, hope, and love of the Thessalonians, and marveling that they have become "examples to all in Macedonia and Achaia" (chap. 1). Paul recalls his sacrificial labor for the gospel (2:1–12), and the suffering the Thessalonians endured (2:13–16). Longing to see them again (2:17—3:5), Paul expresses his relief and encouragement upon hearing Timothy's report of their well-being (3:6–10). He prays for their growth in the gospel (3:11–13).

In chapters four and five Paul addresses three concerns. He reminds his converts that in sexual matters a Christian must conduct himself differently from a pagan (4:1–8). He adds a gentle reminder to work diligently and thus earn the respect of "those who are outside" (non–Christians, 4:9–12). Paul then devotes extended consideration to the most pressing questions in Thessalonica, the Second Coming of Christ (4:13—5:11).

The first letter concludes with a number of memorable exhortations and a charge to read the epistle "to all the holy brethren" (5:12–28).

Second Thessalonians is both shorter and simpler than 1 Thessalonians. Paul follows a nearly identical opening (1:1) with an assurance that when Christ returns He will punish those who persecute the Thessalonians (chap. 1). Chapter two brings Paul to the purpose of the letter—to clarify and expand his teaching on the Second Coming (4:13—5:11). Certain signs will precede the return of Christ, in particular, an outbreaking of lawlessness, followed by the appearance of "the man of sin," or "lawless one" (Antichrist), who will escort to their doom those who have no love for the truth (2:1–12). In contrast to those who are perishing, believers can give thanks to God for their call to salvation (2:13–17).

Paul concludes by requesting the prayers of the Thessalonians (3:1–3) and encouraging idlers to earn their living rather than live off their neighbors (3:6–15). He ends with a benediction in his own hand (3:16–18).

Authorship and Date. The vocabulary, style, and thought of the Thessalonian correspondence are genuinely Pauline. In 1 Thessalonians 2:1—3:10 Paul shares his point of view on some of the events described in Acts 16:16—18:7, thus supporting Luke's description of Paul's ministry in Acts. Both letters bear Paul's name as author (1 Thess. 1:1; 2 Thess. 1:1). Paul's co-workers, Silvanus (Silas) and Timothy, are both mentioned along with Paul in the opening greeting of both epistles.

It is possible to date the Thessalonian letters with some precision. Paul wrote both from Corinth (1 Thess. 1:1; 2 Thess. 1:1; Acts 18:5) while Gallio was proconsul (governor of a Roman province) of Achaia. We know from an inscription discovered at Delphi that Gallio ruled in Corinth from May, A.D. 51, to April, A.D. 52. If Paul spent 18 months in Corinth (Acts 18:11), and yet was brought to trial before Gallio (Acts 18:12–17), he must have arrived in Corinth before Gallio became proconsul. If he wrote to the Thessalonians shortly after leaving them, which seems probable, the letters would have to be dated in late A.D. 50 or early A.D. 51.

Historical Setting. Paul founded the church at Thessalonica in A.D. 49 or 50 during his second missionary journey (Acts 17:1–9). The church con-sisted of a few Jewish converts and a larger number of former pagans (1 Thess. 1:9; Acts 17:4). Desiring not to handicap the young church, Paul worked at his own job as a tentmaker—and at some sacrifice to himself, he adds (1 Thess. 2:7–12)—twice receiv-ing aid from the ever-faithful Philippians (Phil. 4:16).

Paul's stay in Thessalonica was cut short, how-ever, when the Jews gathered some local trouble-makers and accused him before the city fathers of "turning the world upside down" by favoring Jesus as king instead of Caesar (Acts 17:1–7). This accu-sation was no small matter; it was a matter of trea-son, which in the Roman Empire was punishable by death. Not surprisingly, an uproar broke out; and Paul was escorted out of town, leaving Timothy to

FIRST THESSALONIANS: A Teaching Outline

SECOND THESSALONIANS: A Teaching Outline

patch up the work (Acts 17:10, 15). Separated so suddenly from the infant church, Paul describes his feelings as one who had been "orphaned" (Greek text, 1 Thess. 2:17).

Once he was safe in Athens, Paul sent Timothy (who apparently had since rejoined him) back to Thessalonica to strengthen and encourage the believers (1 Thess. 3:2). When Timothy returned to Paul, who had since moved on to Corinth (Acts 18:1–5), he brought news of the love and faith of the Thessalonians. Paul was greatly relieved at this news.

In response to Timothy's encouraging report, Paul wrote the first epistle to Thessalonica. Evidently the Thessalonians were unsettled over the Second Coming of Christ, because Paul discusses the issue in both letters. In the first letter he informs them that at Christ's coming the dead in Christ must be raised first, then the living (1 Thess. 4:13–18). Since the time of Christ's coming will be as secretive as a thief's, Paul admonishes the believers to keep alert and be watchful (1 Thess. 5:1–11). Some, however, may have been too watchful, assuming that Christ would come any moment. In his second letter, therefore, Paul reminds the Thessalonians that certain events, namely, a rebellion against faith and the appearance of a "lawless one" (Antichrist), must happen before Christ returns (2 Thess. 2:8–9). In the meantime, Paul tells them to get back to work: "If anyone will not work, neither shall he eat" (2 Thess. 3:10).

Theological Contributions. Three themes appear in the Thessalonian correspondence: thanksgiving for their faith and example in the past; encouragement for those undergoing persecution in the present; and exhortation to further work and growth in the future.

Paul writes the epistles in the spirit of a true pastor. He is overjoyed with their enthusiastic response to the gospel (1 Thess. 1). He longs for the day when they will stand with him in the presence of the Lord Jesus (1 Thess. 2:19–20). At the same time, Paul is grieved at unjust charges leveled against him that his gospel is more talk than action (1 Thess. 1:5; 2:1–8). Cut off from his flock, he is anxious for their well-being (1 Thess. 2:17–3:5).

Paul compares himself to a nursing mother caring for her children (1 Thess. 2:7), and to a father working in behalf of his family (1 Thess. 2:9–12). He gives himself body and soul to the Thessalonians (1 Thess. 2:8) and dares to hope that they will give themselves likewise to God (1 Thess. 5:23). Such is the concern of a dedicated pastor.

Paul addresses the question of the return of Christ as a concerned pastor. He reminds them that confidence in Christ's return enables believers to be patient (1 Thess. 1:10), creates hope and joy (1 Thess. 2:19), and spurs them to pursue pure and blameless lives (1 Thess. 3:13; 5:23). Uncertainty as to when Christ will return demands alertness and watchfulness (1 Thess. 5:1–11), but the certainty that He will return makes present trials and sufferings bearable (2 Thess. 1:3–11). His return will come as a surprise, like a thief in the night (1 Thess. 5:4); but it will not be disorderly: those who have died first in Christ will proceed first to Christ, followed by the living, "And thus we shall always be with the Lord" (1 Thess. 4:17).

There is no mention in either letter of a MILLENNIUM, followed by a battle between Christ and Satan (Rev. 20:1–10). Paul simply states that at His coming Jesus will destroy the "lawless one" and will judge the unrighteous (2 Thess. 2:8–12). The end, however, will follow widespread rebellion and abandonment of the faith. Paul appeals for them to be levelheaded during the time of trouble and warns Christians not to despair when they see the Antichrist pretending to be God (2 Thess. 2:4). The schemes of "the man of sin" or "man of lawlessness" (2 Thess. 2:6, NIV) will be restrained until his treachery is fully disclosed, and then Christ will utterly destroy him (2 Thess. 2:8).

On the subject of the Second Coming, Paul assures the Thessalonians what will happen, but not when it will happen. His discussion throughout is dominated by an emphasis on practical living, rather than on speculation. The best way to prepare for Christ's return is to live faithfully and obediently now.

THESSALONICA [thes uh luh NIGH kuh] — a city in Macedonia (see Map 7, B–1) visited by the apostle Paul (Acts 17:1, 11, 13; 27:2; Phil. 4:16). Situated on the Thermaic Gulf, Thessalonica was the chief seaport of Macedonia. The city was

The ancient walls of Thessalonica, a city in Macedonia where Paul founded a church (Acts 17:1-4; 1 Thess. 1:1).
Photo by Howard Vos

founded in about 315 B.C. by Cassander, who re-settled the site with inhabitants from 26 villages that he had destroyed. He named the city after his wife, Thessalonica, the sister of Alexander the Great and daughter of Philip II of Macedonia. The Egnatian Way, the main overland route from Rome to the East, ran directly through the city.

Under Roman rule, Thessalonica achieved prominence. In 167 B.C. the Romans divided Macedonia into four districts, Thessalonica becoming capital of the second district. Some 20 years later, in 148 B.C., Macedonia became a Roman province with Thessalonica as its capital. After the battle of Philippi in 42 B.C., when Octavian (later Augustus Caesar) and Mark Antony defeated Brutus and Cassius, the assassins of Julius Caesar, Thessalonica became a free city. It was the most populous city of Macedonia.

In the third century A.D. Thessalonica was selected to oversee a Roman temple, and under Decius (ruled A.D. 249-251), infamous for his persecution of Christians, the city achieved the status of a Roman colony, which entitled it to the rights and privileges of the Roman Empire. The city was surrounded by a wall, stretches of which still stand. Archaeologists have uncovered a paved Roman forum some 63 by 99 meters (70 by 110 yards) in size, dating from the first or second centuries A.D.

The apostle Paul visited Thessalonica in A.D. 49 or 50 during his second missionary journey (Acts 17:1-9). Paul's evangelistic efforts met with success. Within a short time a vigorous Christian congregation had blossomed, consisting of some members of the Jewish synagogue as well as former pagans.

The Book of Acts leads us to assume that Paul stayed in Thessalonica only a few weeks before being forced to leave because of Jewish opposition. But in reality he probably stayed at least two or three months. A shorter stay would scarcely account for Paul's receiving two gifts of aid from the Philippians (Phil. 4:16), or for the depth of affection which developed between Paul and the Thessalonians (1 Thess. 2:1-12). Thessalonica was also the home of two of Paul's co-workers, Aristarchus and Secundus (Acts 20:4; 27:2).

THEUDAS [THOO duhs] (*gift of God*) — a false leader of whom Gamaliel spoke before the Sanhedrin, about A.D. 32. According to Gamaliel's account, about 400 men joined Theudas, but "he was slain, and all who obeyed him were scattered and came to nothing" (Acts 5:36).

Scholars are uncertain of the identity of Theudas. Luke records that Judas the Galilean rose up in the days of the census. It is certain that this Judas was Judas the Gaulanite who, according to the Jewish historian Josephus, incited a riot over the census in the time of Quirinius, about A.D. 6. Then Josephus mentions a magician named Theudas who, acting as a false prophet, persuaded many people to cross the Jordan River and was beheaded for his efforts by the Romans. But this

Theudas lived about 44 B.C., after Judas.

Josephus has rarely been found in error, but Luke has also been established as a reliable historian. It is not unlikely then that there were two insurrectionists named Theudas who lived about 40 years apart. Perhaps Luke's Theudas was one of the many revolutionaries who arose during the turbulent last year of Herod the Great's rule. Or Theudas may have been the Greek name for one of the three revolutionaries named by Josephus: Judas, Simon, or Matthias.

THIEF — any person who takes something which he does not own. Mosaic Law provided strict penalties for thieves. A thief who slaughtered a stolen ox was required to pay back five. When a thief was killed while robbing a house, his killer was without guilt (Ex. 22:1-2). Jesus was crucified between two thieves who reviled Him. One later feared God and asked forgiveness. Jesus forgave this repentant sinner, assuring Him of salvation (Luke 23:32-43).

THIEVES, TWO (see CRIMINALS, TWO).

THIGH — the part of the leg between the knee and the hip. A person struck his own thigh as a sign of sorrow, an action similar to beating his breast (Jer. 31:19; Ezek. 21:12). During the time of the patriarchs, it was a custom that when one made an oath, he was to put his hand under the thigh of the one who required him to swear by his word (Gen. 24:2, 9; 47:29). When Jacob wrestled with the angel, his thigh joint at the hip was injured (Gen. 32:24-32).

For certain Israelite sacrifices, the right thigh of the slain animal was given to the priest for food (Lev. 7:32-34; 10:14-15). To smite "hip and thigh" (Judg. 15:8) indicated a violent, widespread slaughter. The Hebrews sometimes used the word thigh as a euphemism for the sexual organs.

THIMNATHAH [THIM nuh thuh] — a form of TIMNAH.

THIRD PART OF A SHEKEL (see MONEY OF THE BIBLE).

THISTLES, THORNS (see PLANTS OF THE BIBLE).

THOMAS [TAHM uhs] (*twin*) — one of the twelve apostles of Jesus; also called *Didymus*, the Greek word for "twin" (Matt. 10:3; Mark 3:18; Luke 6:15). Thomas is probably best known for his inability to believe that Jesus had indeed risen from the dead. For that inability to believe, he forever earned the name "doubting Thomas."

Thomas was not present when Jesus first appeared to His disciples after His resurrection. Upon hearing of the appearance, Thomas said, "Unless I see in His hands the print of the nails, and put my finger into the print of the nails, and put my hand into His side, I will not believe" (John 20:25). Eight days later, Jesus appeared again to the disciples, including Thomas. When Jesus invited him to touch the nail prints and put his hand into His side, Thomas' response was, "My Lord and my God!" (John 20:28). Of that incident the great church fa-

A threshing floor in Samaria. The oxen are dragging a weighted sled over the harvest to separate the grain from the stalk.

ther Augustine remarked, "He doubted that we might believe."

Thomas appears three other times in the Gospel of John. (Except for the listing of the disciples, Thomas does not appear in the other three gospels.) When Jesus made known his intention to go into Judea, where only a short time before the Jews had threatened to stone Him, Thomas urged his fellow disciples, "Let us also go, that we may die with Him" (John 11:16). Knowing that His earthly life would soon end, Jesus said He was going to prepare a place for His followers and that they knew the way. Thomas asked, "Lord, we do not know where You are going, and how can we know the way?" (John 14:5). To that Jesus gave his well-known answer: "I am the way, the truth, and the life" (John 14:6).

After the resurrection, Thomas was on the Sea of Galilee with six other disciples when Jesus signaled to them from the shore and told them where to cast their net (John 21:2). Thomas was also with the other disciples in the Jerusalem upper room after the ASCENSION of Jesus.

According to tradition, Thomas spread the gospel in Parthia and Persia, where he died. Later tradition places Thomas in India, where he was martyred.

THOMAS, GOSPEL OF (see APOCRYPHA).

THORN IN THE FLESH — a reference to some extreme difficulty "in the flesh" which the apostle Paul encountered in his ministry (2 Cor. 12:7). The context of this reference is Paul's experiences of visions and revelations that came to him from the Lord (2 Cor. 12:1–6). The purpose of this difficulty was to prevent Paul from being "exalted above measure." The thorn was designated as a "messenger of Satan," perhaps to indicate that Satan, as an adversary, resisted Paul's ministry. The Greek word for

thorn may be used to refer to a stake, on which a person could be impaled.

Many explanations have been offered about the nature or identity of Paul's "thorn in the flesh." If the best translation is "in the flesh," referring to the physical flesh, the thorn may refer to some physical infirmity such as epilepsy, malaria, or bad eyesight. An eye ailment seems to be supported by Galatians 4:13–15. If the translation is "for the flesh," referring to the Pauline concept of man's lower nature, the thorn may refer to some painful experience which was spiritual in nature, such as temptation or the opposition of the Jews.

The purpose of the thorn, however, was to eliminate spiritual arrogance in Paul. Although Paul prayed for its removal, the Lord said to him, "My grace is sufficient for you, for My strength is made perfect in weakness" (2 Cor. 12:9). Thus Paul could boast in his "infirmities," because of the victorious power of Christ in his life (2 Cor. 12:9).

THOUSAND — a number with deep spiritual significance that occurs often in the Bible (Ps. 84:10; Dan. 7:10; Jude 14). In the Old Testament, according to some scholars, thousand is often used as a round or approximate number for an innumerable multitude (1 Sam. 21:11; Eccl. 6:6). The Book of Revelation declares that Satan will be bound for a thousand years at the end of time in connection with the Second Coming of Christ (Rev. 20:2).

THREE (see NUMBER).

THREE CHILDREN, SONG OF THE (see APOCRYPHA).

THREE INNS — a village or town on the Appian Way (see Map 8, A–1) about 53 kilometers (33 miles) south of Rome (Acts 28:15; Three Taverns, NIV, KJV, RSV). At Three Inns Christians met Paul as he approached Rome.

THREE TAVERNS (see THREE INNS).

THRESHING — removing the kernel of grain from its stalk. Different methods were used to accomplish this. The most basic method, beating the grain, was used by farmers with a small amount of grain to thresh. These farmers sometimes would walk their animals over the grain to thresh it.

For larger operations, animal–drawn machines were used. The most common of these was the threshing sledge (Is. 41:15). Made of planks with rocks or metal attached to its underside, the sledge was pulled back and forth over the grain. Weight was added by using stones or the weight of the driver and his children.

While threshing was an important part of the everyday life of the ancient Israelites, it formed an important backdrop for Old Testament picture language. Threshing is mentioned frequently as a symbol for destruction (2 Kin. 13:7; Amos 1:3) or divine judgment (Is. 28:27–28).

THRESHING FLOOR — a flat surface prepared for the threshing of grain. The threshing floor was usually located at the edge of a village, frequently on a large flat rock outcropping. When no flat rock was available, the threshing floor would be prepared by leveling the ground and pounding the earth to create a hard surface. Also see THRESHING.

THRESHING SLEDGE (see TOOLS OF THE BIBLE).

THRESHOLD — the sill of a doorway and the place of entrance to a building. Because the threshold was part of a house's foundation, it was sometimes spoken of symbolically to represent the house as a whole. When the glory of the Lord "paused over the threshold of the temple," it filled the entire court with "the brightness of the Lord's glory" (Ezek. 10:4). Also see HOUSE.

THRONE — the chair of a king. The word may mean either "throne" or "chair" (stool, KJV), depending on the context (2 Sam. 3:10; 2 Kin. 4:10). The throne is a symbol of royal government and may refer to the king's role as a judge (Ps. 122:5; Is. 16:5). Since God alone is the true King, it is natural that the word throne should apply to His royal authority (Ps. 11:4; 45:6), especially His authority as Judge (Ps. 9:4, 7).

The image of God's throne is carried into the New Testament (Acts 7:49; Rev. 4:2). Here God's royal authority is given to Jesus, the heir to David's throne (Luke 1:32; Acts 2:30). Jesus shares this throne with the Father (Rev. 3:21). Believers also will share in Christ's authority and government (Rev. 3:21).

THROWING STICK (see ARMS, ARMOR OF THE BIBLE).

THRUSH (see ANIMALS OF THE BIBLE).

THUMMIM [THUHM im] (see URIM AND THUMMIM).

THUNDER — the sound that follows a flash of lightning. Thunder seldom occurred during Palestine's long, dry summer (mid–April through mid–September). This scarcity meant that it naturally became a symbol of God's power, wrath, and vengeance.

When Samuel called upon the Lord, thunder and rain came during the wheat harvest (a notoriously dry season), and the people greatly feared the Lord (1 Sam. 12:17–18). When Moses stretched his rod toward heaven, the Lord sent thunder and hail (Ex. 9:23–34); this was the seventh plague upon the land of Egypt. The Lord sent thunder at the giving of the law at Mount Sinai (Ex. 19:16; 20:18), when the Philistines drew near to battle against Israel (1 Sam. 7:10), and at David's deliverance (2 Sam. 22:14–15).

In the New Testament, Jesus gave the nickname "Sons of Thunder" to two of His apostles, James and John, the sons of Zebedee (Mark 3:17). This name probably referred to their fiery, hot–tempered, stormy temperaments. When Jesus predicted His death on the cross, a voice came from heaven as a seal of approval upon His redemptive mission. Some people who heard the heavenly voice said that it had thundered; others said, "An angel has spoken to Him" (John 12:27–29).

Most of the New Testament references to thunder are in the Book of Revelation (Rev. 4:5; 14:2; 19:6). The imagery of thunder speaks of the powerful presence of God.

THUNDER, SONS OF (see THUNDER).

THYATIRA [thigh uh TIE ruh] — a city of the province of LYDIA in western Asia Minor (modern Turkey) situated on the road from Pergamos to Sardis. The city was on the southern bank of the Lycus River, a branch of the Hermus River.

Although never a large city, Thyatira was a thriving manufacturing and commercial center during New Testament times. Archaeologists have uncovered evidence of many trade guilds and unions here. Membership in these trade guilds, necessary for financial and social success, often involved pagan customs and practices such as superstitious worship, union feasts using food sacrificed to pagan gods, and loose sexual morality.

The Book of Revelation refers to a certain woman known as "Jezebel" who taught and beguiled the Christians at Thyatira to conform to the paganism and sexual immorality of their surroundings (Rev. 1:11; 2:18–29). In the church in Thyatira, one of the "seven churches which are in Asia" (Rev. 1:4), Jezebel's followers seem to have been a minority because the majority of Christians in this church are commended.

The apostle Paul's first convert in Europe was "a certain woman named LYDIA...a seller of purple from the city of Thyatira" (Acts 16:14). The modern name of Thyatira is Akhisar, which means "white castle."

THYINE (see PLANTS OF THE BIBLE).

Modern Tiberias, situated on the western shore of the Sea of Galilee.

TIBERIAS [tigh BEER ee uhs] — the name of a city (see Map 6, C–2) and a lake in the New Testament:

1. A city on the western shore of the Sea of Galilee. Tiberias stands on a rocky cliff about 19 kilometers (12 miles) south of where the Jordan River flows into the Sea of Galilee. Still, Tiberias is 208 meters (682 feet) below the level of the nearby Mediterranean Sea, and it has a semitropical climate that is mild in winter but humid in summer.

The city was founded by Herod Antipas (about A.D. 20) and named after the emperor, Tiberius Caesar. It was said to have occupied the site of Rakkath, an old town of Naphtali (Josh. 19:35), and to have been built over a graveyard. Because of this, it was declared unclean by the Jews, who would not enter the city. Although Tiberias was an important city in the days of Christ, there is no record that He ever visited it. In fact, it is only mentioned once in the New Testament (John 6:23).

The city enjoyed a commanding view of the lake. Because of the numerous hot springs just south of the city, it was a popular resort for the Romans. Pliny the Elder mentions the healthful nature of the springs. Today the city contains a number of health spas.

Although the Jews would not enter the ancient Roman town, after the fall of Jerusalem in A.D. 135, Tiberias ironically became the center of rabbinic learning. Here the Mishnah was completed about A.D. 200 and the Jerusalem (or Palestinian) Talmud was finished about A.D. 400. The pointing system later used by the Masoretes to add vowels to the Hebrew text was first developed in Tiberias.

2. A lake in northern Galilee (John 6:1; 21:1), the same lake as the Sea of Galilee. Also see GALILEE, SEA OF.

TIBERIAS, SEA OF (see TIBERIAS; GALILEE, SEA OF).

TIBERIUS [tie BEER ih us] (*son of the Tiber*) — Tiberius Claudius Nero Caesar (42 B.C.—A.D. 37),

the second emperor of Rome (A.D. 14–37). The adopted son and son-in-law of Octavian (Augustus Caesar), Tiberius succeeded Augustus as emperor.

Tiberius is mentioned by name only once in the Bible. Luke 3:1 states that John the Baptist began his ministry "in the fifteenth year of the reign of Tiberius Caesar," or A.D. 28. Luke 3:1 is very important in helping to establish the chronology of the life and ministry of Jesus. Tiberius is also frequently referred to simply as "Caesar" (Luke 23:2; John 19:12, 15). The Pharisees and Herodians sought to entrap Jesus by asking him a question concerning tribute to Caesar: "Tell us...is it lawful to pay taxes to Caesar, or not?" The "Caesar" in question is Tiberius, and the coin which they brought to Jesus bore Tiberius' image (Matt. 22:15–22; Mark 12:13–17; Luke 20:20–26). Jesus began his ministry and was crucified during the reign of Tiberius.

Born in Rome on November 16, 42 B.C., Tiberius became emperor in his 55th year and reigned for 23 years, until his death in March, A.D. 37, at the age of 78. Some historians believe that Caligula, the mad successor to Tiberius, hastened Tiberius' death.

The city of TIBERIAS, on the Sea of Galilee, was built in the emperor's honor, about 20 B.C., by Herod Antipas, Roman governor of Galilee and Perea.

TIBHATH [TIB hath] (*place of slaughter*) — a city in ZOBAH, a kingdom in central Syria (1 Chr. 18:8). David captured Tibhath from Hadadezer, king of Zobah.

TIBNI [TIBB nie] (*intelligent*) — a man who is sometimes listed as the sixth king of Israel (884–880 B.C.). He and Omri were rival kings for three years, but Omri eventually emerged as victorious (2 Kin. 16:21–22).

TIDAL [TIE duhl] (meaning unknown) — the

"king of nations" (king of Goiim, NASB, NIV, RSV) who joined an alliance with three other kings—Chedorlaomer, Amraphel, and Arioch—and attacked the cities of the plain (Gen. 14:1, 9).

TIGLATH-PILESER [TIG lath puh LEE zur] (meaning unknown) — a king of Assyria (ruled 745-727 B.C.) and, under the name Pul (2 Kin. 15:19), king of Babylonia (729-727 B.C.). He is also called Tilgath-Pilneser (1 Chr. 5:6, 26; 2 Chr. 28:20).

The accession of Tiglath-Pileser to the throne ended a period of political and military weakness in Assyrian history. He moved first to reestablish Assyrian dominance in Babylon and also attacked his powerful opponent to the north, Urartu. In 740 B.C. he conquered Arpad in northern Syria. The effect of this victory was far-reaching (2 Kin. 19:13; Is. 37:13). Tribute came in from Tyre, Damascus, Cilicia, and Carchemish. During this period, Tiglath-Pileser penetrated all the way to Israel, where he received tribute from Menahem. The fabulous sum of 1,000 talents of silver "from all the very wealthy" probably resulted in the unpopularity of Menahem (2 Kin. 15:17-22). When Pekahiah, Menahem's son, succeeded to the throne, he ruled for only two years before he was assassinated. In all likelihood, the murder was a result of his father's unpopular policy of submission to Assyria (2 Kin. 15:23-26).

While serving as king of Israel, Pekah adopted a strong anti-Assyrian policy by aligning himself with Rezin, king of Syria. Both Pekah and Rezin sought to force Ahaz, king of Judah, to join the revolt. But Ahaz appealed to Tiglath-Pileser for help. In 734 B.C. Tiglath-Pileser moved south along the coast to cut off possible Egyptian aid to the revolt. In 733 B.C. he marched into Israel, devastating much of Galilee and deporting many Israelites (2 Kin. 15:29). Finally, he moved against the real power of the region, Damascus, which fell in 732 B.C.

After devastating the countryside, Tiglath-Pileser captured the city of Damascus, executed Rezin, and sent much of the Syrian population into exile. Meanwhile, Hoshea had assassinated Pekah to become the new king of Israel (2 Kin. 15:30). Hoshea paid tribute to Tiglath-Pileser, as did the kings of Ashkelon and Tyre. When Tiglath-Pileser died in 727 B.C., the borders of his country had been dramatically enlarged and every enemy of Assyria had been severely weakened.

TIGRIS [TIE gris] — a major river of southwest Asia (see Map 1, C-1). Flowing about 1,850 kilometers (1,150 miles) from the Taurus Mountains of eastern Turkey, the Tigris joins the Euphrates River north of Basra. The Tigris and Euphrates flow roughly parallel to each other for hundreds of miles in the "Land of the Two Rivers," or Mesopotamia. The Tigris is considered by most scholars to be identical with Hiddekel (Gen. 2:14, KJV, NKJV), one of the four branches of the river that flowed from the Garden of Eden.

TIKVAH [TICK vah] (*expectation*) — the name of two men in the Old Testament:

1. The father-in-law of Huldah the prophetess, wife of Shallum (2 Kin. 22:14; Tokhath, NASB, NIV, RSV; Tikvath, KJV). Tikvah is also spelled as Tokhath in the NKJV (2 Chr. 34:22).

2. The father of Jahaziah (Ezra 10:15).

TIKVATH [TIK vath] — a form of TIKVAH.

TILGATH-PILNESER [TIL gath pil NEE zur] — a form of TIGLATH-PILESER.

TILING — a surface of tiles, expecially a roofing made of slabs or tablets of baked clay. Although clay tile roofs were common in Greek and Roman houses of the first century, they were rare in Palestine. The typical roof in Palestine was made of packed clay laid over thatch and branches.

Some men brought a friend who was paralyzed to Jesus, hoping he might be healed. When they saw the crowd around Jesus in a house, they went up on the roof, removed the tiles, and then lowered the friend. Jesus healed the man, who departed to his own house, glorifying God (Luke 5:19).

TILLER (see OCCUPATIONS AND TRADES).

TILON [TIE luhn] (meaning unknown) — a son of Shimon, of the tribe of Judah (1 Chr. 4:20).

TIMAEUS [tih MEE uhs] (*highly prized*) — the father of the blind beggar Bartimaeus (Mark 10:46; Timeus, KJV).

TIMBREL (see MUSICAL INSTRUMENTS).

TIME — a measurable period during which an action or condition exists or continues. Among the Hebrew people, units of time were measured in hours, days, weeks, months, and years. The more abstract concept of time is also mentioned in the Bible.

Present Time. The Bible speaks of God who exists

A stone carving of Tiglath-Pileser III of Assyria, from his excavated palace at Nimrud.
Photo by Howard Vos

eternally as well as man who lives in a time–space framework. A key passage for the present time is Ecclesiastes 3:1–11, which declares, "There is . . . a time for every purpose under heaven." This passage goes on to note that there is a time for birth and death, mourning and dancing, keeping and throwing away, silence and speaking, and war and peace. Man does not know his time (Eccl. 9:12), and his times are in the Lord's hands (Ps. 31:15). Man is warned not to plan his time as if it belonged to him, but to do what the Lord wills in his life (James 4:13–17).

The accepted time of salvation is now (2 Cor. 6:2). Man is to seek (Hos. 10:12) and trust the Lord at all times (Ps. 62:8) and practice righteousness during his life on earth (Ps. 106:3). Since the days are evil, the Christian is to make the most of his opportunity (Eph. 5:16). God is honored in these things. Scripture bears testimony that God is working out His purposes in man's time. He promised Abraham that he and Sarah would have a child (Gen. 18:10, 14), and the promise was fulfilled (Gen. 21:1–4). God also told the wicked Pharaoh of a plague that would come to him the next day (Ex. 9:18). God is working in our present time–space world; therefore, the present time is to be used for God's purposes and glory.

Fulfillment of Time. The fulfillment of time is an important concept, because it shows God's sovereign control of time in order to bring His promises to pass. Only the Lord knows the times and seasons for fulfillment (Acts 1:7; 1 Thess. 5:1). God has indicated that what He promised long ago would be fulfilled (Is. 37:26; Titus 1:3). God warned that Jerusalem would be destroyed if His people continued in disobedience. The prophet Jeremiah lamented after their downfall that their time was fulfilled (Lam. 2:17).

In the New Testament Jesus announced that the promised kingdom of God was at hand (Matt. 4:17). Jesus continually stated that His hour, or time, had not yet come (John 2:4; 7:6, 8, 30; 8:20); it was to be fulfilled when He was crucified (John 12:23; 13:1; 17:1). In fact, when Jesus came into Jerusalem in His triumphal entry, He stated that Israel should have known the time of the visitation of the Messiah (Luke 19:44). Jesus' death was prophesied in the Old Testament and the fulfillment of this was seen in His death at the appointed time (Rom. 5:6; Gal. 4:4; 1 Tim. 2:6).

The Future and the End Times. The future and the end times are in God's control. Many references to future time are related to judgment. Daniel's prophecy outlines the succession of world empires, and this prophecy involved judgments (Dan. 2:28–29). The nations will face a time of doom in the future (Ezek. 30:3; Dan. 8:17, 19). Israel will also suffer in "the time of Jacob's trouble" (Jer. 30:7). During that time many will fall (Matt. 24:10). Nations as well as individuals will face the future time of judgment (Ps. 81:15; Jer. 10:15). In fact, the demons realize that they will face a time of torment in the future (Matt. 8:29).

Photo by Willem A. VanGemeren

A beautiful sunset scene on the Sea of Galilee. In their system of measuring time, the Jewish people began a new day at sunset.

However, the future will not be all doom, because in that time Israel will be a restored kingdom (Joel 3:1; Zeph. 3:20). Messiah will endure forever (Dan. 2:44). The future of the unbeliever will be judgment (Rev. 11:18), while the believer will be exalted by God (1 Pet. 5:6). The believer eagerly awaits for the time of the SECOND COMING (Heb. 9:28), which is nearer than when he first believed (Rom. 13:11). The future is in God's hands. This means the future is filled with fear and uncertainty for the unbeliever but with hope and certainty for the believer.

Eternity. The Bible portrays God as existing eternally (Ex. 3:14; Ps. 90:2; Rev. 1:4; 15:7). This is also true for Christ, His Son (Is. 9:6; John 1:1–3, 18; Heb. 13:8). The unbelievers will face an eternity of punishment (Matt. 25:41; Rev. 14:11; 20:10–15). The believer's eternal life begins the moment he believes (John 3:16, 36; 5:24; 1 John 5:11). After this present time the believers will live eternally with God and His kingdom (Dan. 7:18, 27; Rev. 22:5).

Although man now lives within a time–space framework, he will live eternally. God who exists eternally will remove time and space, and man will relate to God in an eternal relationship.

TIMES, LAST (see ESCHATOLOGY).

TIMES, OBSERVING (see MAGIC, SORCERY, AND DIVINATION).

TIMEUS [tih MEE us] — a form of TIMAEUS.

TIMNA [TIM nuh] (*holding in check*) — the name of a woman and a man in the Old Testament:

1. A daughter of Seir the Horite and sister of Lotan (Gen. 36:22; 1 Chr. 1:39).

2. A son of Eliphaz and grandson of Esau (1 Chr. 1:36), also spelled Timnah (Gen. 36:40; 1 Chr. 1:51).

TIMNAH [TIM nuh] (*allotted portion*) — the name of a man and two cities in the Old Testament:

1. A chief of Edom (Gen. 36:40; 1 Chr. 1:51), also spelled Timna (1 Chr. 1:36).

2. A city on the northern border of Judah near Beth Shemesh (Josh. 15:10). Timnah was allotted to the tribe of Dan (Josh. 19:43; Thimnathah, KJV). Some scholars identify it with Tell el-Batashi, about six kilometers (four miles) northwest of Beth Shemesh. At Timnah Samson married a Philistine woman and later told her his riddle of the lion and the honey (Judges 14).

3. A city in the hill country of Judah (Josh. 15:57). This Timnah is probably the same place to which Judah was traveling when he met Tamar (Gen. 38:12–14). Timnah is probably to be identified with present-day Tibnah, about six kilometers (four miles) east of Beit Nettif.

TIMNATH HERES [TIM nath HEAR eez] (*portion of the sun*) — a city in the mountains of Ephraim that was both the inheritance and burial place of Joshua (Judg. 2:9). The meaning of the name Timnath Heres suggests that this site was once a place of sun worship. It is the same place as Timnath Serah (Josh. 19:50; 24:30). Some scholars suggest that the consonants for Heres (hrs) were deliberately written backwards as Serah (srh) as a reminder of these pagan worship practices. Also see TIMNATH SERAH.

TIMNATH SERAH [TIM nath SIR uh] (*remaining portion*) — a city in the mountains of Ephraim that was the inheritance and burial place of Joshua (Josh. 19:50; 24:30). It is probably present-day Khirbet Tibneh, about 28 kilometers (17 miles) southwest of Shechem. Timnath Serah is the same place as TIMNATH HERES (Judg. 2:9).

TIMNITE [TIM night] — a native or inhabitant of TIMNAH (Judg. 15:6).

TIMON [TIE muhn] (*honorable*) — one of the seven original "deacons" appointed to serve tables in the early church in Jerusalem (Acts 6:5).

TIMOTHY [TIM uh thih] (*honored of God*) — Paul's friend and chief associate, who is mentioned as joint sender in six of Paul's epistles (2 Cor. 1:1; Phil. 1:1; Col. 1:1; 1 Thess. 1:1; 2 Thess. 1:1; Philem. 1).

Timothy first appears in the second missionary journey when Paul revisited Lystra (Acts 16:1–3). Timothy was the son of a Gentile father and a Jewish-Christian mother named Eunice, and the grandson of Lois (Acts 16:1; 2 Tim. 1:5). Timothy may have been converted under Paul's ministry, because the apostle refers to him as his "beloved and faithful son in the Lord" (1 Cor. 4:17) and as his "true son in the faith" (1 Tim. 1:2). Timothy was held in high regard in Lystra and Iconium, and Paul desired to take him along as a traveling companion (Acts 16:3).

Timothy played a prominent role in the remainder of the second missionary journey. When Paul was forced to leave Berea because of an uproar started by Jews from Thessalonica, Silas and Timothy were left behind to strengthen the work in Macedonia (Acts 17:14). After they rejoined Paul in Athens (Acts 18:5), Paul sent Timothy back to the believers in Thessalonica to establish them and to encourage them to maintain the faith (1 Thess. 3:1–9). Timothy's report of the faith and love of the Thessalonians greatly encouraged Paul.

During Paul's third missionary journey, Timothy was active in the evangelizing of Corinth, although he had little success. When news of disturbances at Corinth reached Paul at Ephesus, he sent Timothy, perhaps along with Erastus (Acts 19:22), to resolve the difficulties. The mission failed, perhaps because of fear on Timothy's part (1 Cor. 16:10–11). Paul then sent the more forceful Titus, who was able to calm the situation at Corinth (2 Cor. 7). Later in the third journey, Timothy is listed as one of the group that accompanied Paul along the coast of Asia Minor on his way to Jerusalem (Acts 20:4–5).

Timothy also appears as a companion of Paul during his imprisonment in Rome (Col. 1:1; Phil. 1:1; Philem. 1). From Rome, Paul sent Timothy to Philippi to bring back word of the congregation that had supported the apostle so faithfully over the years.

Timothy's strongest traits were his sensitivity, affection, and loyalty. Paul commends him to the Philippians, for example, as one of proven character, faithful to Paul like a son to a father, and without rival in his concern for the Philippians (Phil. 2:19–23; also 2 Tim. 1:4; 3:10). Paul's warnings, however, to "be strong" (2 Tim. 2:1) suggests that Timothy suffered from fearfulness (1 Cor. 16:10–11; 2 Tim. 1:7) and perhaps youthful lusts (2 Tim. 2:22). But in spite of his weaknesses, Paul was closer to Timothy than to any other associate.

Writing about A.D. 325, Eusebius reported that Timothy was the first bishop of Ephesus. In 356 Constantius transferred what was thought to be Timothy's remains from Ephesus to Constantinople (modern Istanbul) and buried them in the Church of the Apostles, which had been built by his father Constantine.

Also see TIMOTHY, EPISTLES TO.

TIMOTHY, EPISTLES TO — two letters of the apostle Paul which, along with the Epistle to Titus, form a trilogy called the Pastoral Epistles. These letters are called Pastoral Epistles because they deal with matters affecting pastors and congregations. In these letters to Timothy, Paul's primary concern is to instruct his young associate to guard the spiritual heritage that he has received (1 Tim. 6:20; 2 Tim. 1:12–14; 2:2) by establishing sound doctrine in the church.

Structure of the Epistles. First Timothy begins with a warning against false doctrine (1:1–11) and a reminder of God's mercy, illustrated by Paul's experience of salvation (1:12–20). This is followed by instructions on church practices: on prayer (2:1–7), on public worship (2:8–15), and on the qualifications of bishops (3:1–7) and deacons (3:8–13). A salute to Christ concludes the section (3:14–16).

Continuing with Timothy's responsibilities, Paul warns that false teachers will infiltrate the church (4:1–5). He instructs Timothy on the characteristics of a fit minister of the gospel (4:6–16), as well as his duties toward others (5:1–2), widows (5:3–16), elders (5:17–25), and servants (6:1–2). Following another warning against false teaching (6:3–10), Paul exhorts Timothy to "fight the good fight of faith" (6:11–21).

After a brief greeting (1:1–2), the second Epistle to Timothy begins by recalling Timothy's spiritual heritage (1:3–7), exhorting him to be strong under adversity and to keep the faith (1:8–18). In chapter two Paul uses the metaphors of soldier (2:3–4), farmer (2:6), experienced worker (2:15), and household utensils (2:20–21) as models for Timothy to imitate as a strong and worthy servant of the gospel. Paul declares what people will be like in the last days (3:1–9), although Timothy can take encouragement in the face of adversity from Paul's example and from the Scriptures (3:10–17).

The final chapter of 2 Timothy takes on a solemn tone as Paul appeals to Timothy to press forward in fulfilling his pastoral calling (4:1–5). Writing in the shadow of his impending death (4:6–8), Paul closes with personal greetings (4:9–22).

Authorship and Date. The authorship and date of the Pastoral Epistles remain an unresolved question in New Testament studies. On the one hand, the epistles bear the name of Paul as author (1 Tim. 1:1; 2 Tim. 1:1; Titus 1:1) and preserve personal references to him (1 Tim. 1:3, 12–16; 2 Tim. 4:9–22; Titus 1:5; 3:12–13). Other considerations, however, pose problems for Paul's authorship of the Pastorals. These can be listed under the following categories:

Historical—The Book of Acts makes no mention of a situation in which Paul goes to Macedonia, leaving Timothy behind in Ephesus (1 Tim. 1:3), or Titus in Crete (Titus 1:5).

Ecclesiastical—The description of church order in the Pastorals (for example; bishops, elders, deacons, an enlistment of widows) appears rather advanced for Paul's time.

Theological—Some ideas in the Pastorals differ from Paul's thought. For example, "faith" (Titus 1:13; 2:2) suggests orthodoxy or "sound doctrine," rather than a saving relationship with Christ; "righteousness" (Titus 3:5) suggests "good deeds," rather than a status of being justified before God. Likewise, the understanding of law (1 Tim. 1:8–11) differs from Paul's usual teaching on the subject (compare Rom. 3:19–20).

Literary—The vocabulary and style of the Pastorals differ from Paul's other writings. A significant number of words that appear in the Pastorals are not found in Paul's genuine letters, and the tone of the letters is uncharacteristically harsh at places (for example, Titus 1:12–13).

Each of these objections is not of equal weight, although taken as a whole they are impressive. If one assumes, as church tradition often has, that Paul was released following the Roman imprison-

ment mentioned in Acts 28 (2 Tim. 4:16) and later went to Spain (1 Clement 5, writing about A.D. 96), or revisited points eastward, many of the problems listed above are lessened. In this view, the circumstances of the Pastorals would fall after the events described in Acts. Thus, confronted by a rise in false teaching and by a need to increase church discipline and order, Paul could have written the Pastorals with the help of a secretary who expressed Paul's ideas in somewhat un-Pauline ways. This would date the letters between Paul's first and second Roman imprisonments, or about A.D. 65.

On the other hand, it may be that an admirer of Paul, using genuine notes or letters of the apostle, drafted the Pastorals to address the problems of a later day in the spirit of Paul. This view would date the letters at the close of the first century.

Historical Setting. First and Second Timothy differ in historical context. In the first epistle Paul writes from Macedonia to young Timothy (1 Tim. 4:12), who has been left in Ephesus to oversee the congregation (1 Tim. 1:3). The second epistle, also written to Timothy in Ephesus (2 Tim. 1:18), comes from Rome where Paul is undergoing a second (2 Tim. 4:16) and harsher imprisonment (2 Tim. 1:18, 16; 2:9). Paul is alone (except for Luke, 2 Tim. 4:11), and he knows the end of his life will come soon (2 Tim. 4:6). One can almost hear the plaintive echo of the apostle's voice as he bids Timothy to "come quickly before winter" (2 Tim. 4:9, 21).

The occasion for both epistles is much the same. Paul is deeply troubled by false teaching (1 Tim. 1:3–11; 2 Tim. 2:23) and apostasy (1 Tim. 1:6; 4:1; 2 Tim. 3:1–9) which endanger the church at Ephesus. He warns Timothy to beware of fables and endless genealogies (1 Tim. 1:4; 4:7; 2 Tim. 4:4), idle gossip (1 Tim. 5:13; 2 Tim. 2:16), rigid lifestyles based on the denial of things (1 Tim. 4:3), the snares of wealth (1 Tim. 6:9–10, 17–19), and religious speculations (1 Tim. 6:20). He warns that apostasy, in whatever form, will spread like cancer (2 Tim. 2:17). Paul urges Timothy to combat its malignant growth by teaching sound doctrine, promoting good works, and accepting one's share of suffering for the sake of the gospel (2 Tim. 1:8; 2:3, 11–13).

Theological Contribution. The message of 1 and 2 Timothy can be summed up by words like remember (2 Tim. 2:8), guard (1 Tim. 6:20), be strong (2 Tim. 2:1), and commit (1 Tim. 1:18; 2:2). For Paul, the best medicine for false teaching and apostasy is "sound doctrine" (1 Tim. 1:10; 4:3). The gospel is a spiritual inheritance to be received from faithful witnesses and passed on to such (2 Tim. 2:2). It brings about wholeness or health (which is the meaning of "sound" in Greek), not only in belief, but also in good deeds. So vital is sound doctrine to the health of the church that it is something to be pursued (1 Tim. 6:11), fought for (1 Tim. 6:12), and even suffered for (2 Tim. 1:8; 2:3, 11–13).

Special Consideration. The Epistles to Timothy might be considered our earliest manual of church organization. Within them we find guidelines for

FIRST TIMOTHY: A Teaching Outline

SECOND TIMOTHY: A Teaching Outline

the selection of church leaders (1 Tim. 3:1–13). They also reveal an awareness of the need for standard forms of expressing the faith. For example, the words, "This is a faithful saying," appear four times in the epistles (1 Tim. 1:15; 3:1; 4:9; 2 Tim. 2:11). Two creeds, or perhaps hymns, also appear (1 Tim. 3:16; 2 Tim. 2:11–13). Finally, 2 Timothy presents the first (and only) pronouncement in the New Testament on the Bible as "Scripture" (referring to the Old Testament, 2 Tim. 3:14–17).

In Greek, the word for "inspiration" (2 Tim. 3:16) means "breathed into by God." As God breathed life into Adam (Gen. 2:7), so he breathes life into the written word, making it useful for teaching, reproof, and correction. Paul leaves us, therefore, not with a theory about Scripture, but with a description of its purpose and its power for salvation (2 Tim. 3:15).

Also see PASTORAL EPISTLES; TIMOTHY.

TIN (see MINERALS OF THE BIBLE).

TINDER — a highly combustible material, such as dry twigs or wood shavings, used to kindle fires (Is. 1:31).

TINKLING — a series of short jingling sounds. The word is found twice in the Bible. Isaiah refers to the wanton daughters of Jerusalem whose anklets make a tinkling noise (Is. 3:16, KJV). The apostle Paul said that the gift of tongues without love is like a "tinkling [clanging, NKJV] cymbal" (1 Cor. 13:1).

TIPHSAH [TIF suh] (*passage*) — the name of two cities in the Old Testament:

1. A city on the west bank of the Euphrates River that marked one of the boundaries of Solomon's kingdom (1 Kin. 4:24). Situated about 160 kilometers (100 miles) northeast of Tadmor (Palmyra), Tiphsah was an important caravan center.

2. A city in Judah defeated by Menahem, king of Israel (2 Kin. 15:16; Tappuah, RSV). Tiphsah is believed by many scholars to be Tafsah, about 10.5 kilometers (6.5 miles) southwest of Shechem.

TIRAS [TIRE us] (meaning unknown) — a son of Japheth (Gen. 10:2; 1 Chr. 1:5). Nothing else is known about Tiras. Some scholars believe Tiras' descendants were also an ancient people known by this name, but they are not mentioned in the Bible.

TIRATHITES [TIH ruh thights] — a family of scribes who lived in Jabez, probably in Judah (1 Chr. 2:55).

TIRE — Archaic KJV word for TURBAN.

TIRHAKAH [tur HAY kuh] (meaning unknown) — the third king of the 25th dynasty of Egypt (reigned 689–664 B.C.). During his reign he opposed three Assyrian kings—Sennacherib, Esarhaddon, and Ashurbanipal (the biblical Osnapper)—in a struggle for control of Palestine. Tirhakah is mentioned twice in the Bible (2 Kin. 19:9; Is. 37:9). In both instances Tirhakah gave military aid to Hezekiah, king of Judah (reigned 715–686 B.C.) to aid his resistance against Sennacherib.

TIRHANAH [tur HAY nuh] (meaning unknown) — a son of Caleb and his concubine Maachah (1 Chr. 2:48).

TIRIA [TIR igh uh] (*fear*) — a son of Jahaleleel, of the tribe of Judah (1 Chr. 4:16).

TIRSHATHA [tur SHAY thuh] (*feared*) — a title given to Zerubbabel (Ezra 2:63, KJV) and Nehemiah (Neh. 7:65, 70; 8:9; 10:1, KJV) as governors of Judah under Persian rule.

TIRZAH [TUR zuh] (*delightfulness*) — the name of a woman and a city in the Old Testament:

1. The youngest of the five daughters of Zelophehad (Num. 26:33; Josh. 17:3).

2. One of 31 ancient Canaanite cities west of the Jordan River (see Map 3, B–3) conquered by Joshua (Josh. 12:24). Tirzah was the capital of the northern kingdom of Israel from the time of Jeroboam I until the time of Omri (reigned 885–874 B.C.), who moved the capital to Samaria after reigning in Tirzah six years (1 Kin. 16:23).

TISHBITE [TISH bite] — a name applied to Elijah the prophet (1 Kin. 17:1; 21:17; 2 Kin. 9:36). Some scholars believe Elijah was from a town named Thisbe, in Galilee (Naphtali). Most scholars, however, believe Elijah was from TRANSJORDAN, an area east of the Jordan River, specifically in the land of Gilead.

TISHRI [TISH rih] (*beginning*) — the seventh month of the religious year in the Jewish calendar, also called Ethanim (1 Kin. 8:2). Also see CALENDAR.

TITHE — the practice of giving a tenth of one's income or property as an offering to God. The custom of paying a tithe was an ancient practice found among many nations of the ancient world.

The practice of giving a tenth of income or property extends into Hebrew history before the time of the Mosaic Law. The first recorded instance of tithing in the Bible occurs in Genesis 14:17–20. After returning from rescuing Lot and defeating his enemies, Abraham met MELCHIZEDEK, the "king of Salem" and "priest of God Most High." The text states simply that Abraham gave Melchizedek a tithe of all the goods he had obtained in battle. The author of the Book of Hebrews, in recounting this episode, considered the Levitical priests who descended from Abraham and who appeared centuries later as having paid tithes to Melchizedek through Abraham (Heb. 7:1–10). There is no recorded demand of Abraham for a tenth. Neither is an explanation given about why Abraham gave a tithe to Melchizedek. Jacob also, long before the law of Moses, promised that he would give to the Lord a tenth of all he received (Gen. 28:22).

The law of Moses prescribed tithing in some detail. Leviticus 27:30–32 stated that the tithe of the land would include the seed of the land and the fruit of the tree. In addition the Hebrew people

Photo by Willem A. VanGemeren

Modern Tirzah, successor to the ancient Canaanite city which served for a time as capital of the northern kingdom of Israel.

were required to set apart every tenth animal of their herds and flocks to the Lord.

Mosaic legislation on tithing is also found in two other passages. Numbers 18:21–32 stated that the tithes in Israel would be given to the Levites, because the Levites did not receive a land inheritance like the other tribes of Israel. The Levites, in turn, were to offer a heave offering to the Lord. This would constitute a tithe on their part of the goods which they received. The rest of the goods which the Levites received would provide their living as the reward for their work in the tabernacle.

The third passage dealing with the tithe is Deuteronomy 12:5–7, 11–12, 17–18. This passage instructed Israel to take their tithes to the place the Lord prescribes, or the city of Jerusalem. In Deuteronomy, only a vegetable tithe is mentioned. In 2 Chronicles 31:6, however, the tithe of cattle is mentioned.

In Deuteronomy 26:12–15 the third year is called the year of tithing. This may indicate that the tithes were not collected annually. Apparently in this year only the goods which were given as tithes could be offered and stored locally. The offering of the tithe also took the form of a ritual meal (Deut. 12:7, 12). Some suggest that there were three tithes, but this seems unlikely. There is no mention of a tithe in Exodus but only the giving of the FIRSTFRUITS (Ezek. 44:29–30). Finally, the prophet Malachi indicated that Israel had robbed God in withholding tithes and offerings. Thus the Israelites were exhorted to bring their tithes into the storehouse in order to enjoy the Lord's blessing (Mal. 3:8–12).

In the Old Testament the purpose of the giving of a tenth was to meet the material need of the Levite, the stranger, the fatherless (the orphan), and the widow (Deut. 26:12–13). The tithe was an expres-

sion of gratitude to God by His people. Basic to tithing was the acknowledgment of God's ownership of everything in the earth.

In the New Testament the words tithe and tithing appear only eight times (Matt. 23:23; Luke 11:42; 18:12; Heb. 7:5–6, 8–9). All of these passages refer to Old Testament usage and to current Jewish practice. Nowhere does the New Testament expressly command Christians to tithe. However, as believers we are to be generous in sharing our material possessions with the poor and for the support of Christian ministry. Christ Himself is our model in giving. Giving is to be voluntary, willing, cheerful, and given in the light of our accountability to God. Giving should be systematic and by no means limited to a tithe of our incomes. We recognize that all we have is from God. We are called to be faithful stewards of all our possessions (Rom. 14:12; 1 Cor. 9:3–14; 16:1–3; 2 Cor. 8—9).

TITIUS [TISH ee uhs] — a man of Corinth who worshiped God. His house was next door to the synagogue (Acts 18:7; Titius Justus, RSV, NIV, NEB, NASB; Justus, KJV, NKJV). Also see JUSTUS.

TITLE — a placard that Pilate ordered fastened to Jesus' cross (John 19:19–20; inscription, NASB, NEB; notice or sign, NIV). The words, "Jesus of Nazareth, the King of the Jews," were written in three languages (Hebrew, Greek, and Latin) so that all who passed by could understand its meaning.

TITTLE — an ornamental stroke decorating the letters of the Hebrew alphabet (Matt. 5:18; Luke 16:17; dot, RSV; the smallest stroke, NASB; the least stroke of a pen, NIV). The word tittle comes from a Greek word that means "little horn." Jesus meant that even the smallest detail of the law of Moses would never fail or pass away. Also see JOT.

TITUS [TIGH tuhs] (*pleasant*) — a "partner and fellow worker" (2 Cor. 8:23) of the apostle Paul. Although Titus is not mentioned in the Book of Acts, Paul's letters reveal that he was the man of the hour at a number of key points in Paul's life.

Paul first mentions Titus in Galatians 2:1-3. As an uncircumcised Gentile, Titus accompanied Paul and Barnabas to Jerusalem as a living example of a great theological truth: Gentiles need not be circumcised in order to be saved.

Titus next appears in connection with Paul's mission to Corinth. While Paul was in Ephesus during his third missionary journey, he received disturbing news from the church at Corinth. After writing two letters and paying one visit to Corinth, Paul sent Titus to Corinth with a third letter (2 Cor. 7:6-9). When Titus failed to return with news of the situation, Paul left Ephesus and, with a troubled spirit (2 Cor. 7:5), traveled north to Troas (2 Cor. 2:12-13).

Finally, in Macedonia, Titus met the anxious apostle with the good news that the church at Corinth had repented. In relief and joy, Paul wrote yet another letter to Corinth (2 Corinthians), perhaps from Philippi, sending it again through Titus (2 Cor. 7:5-16). In addition, Titus was given responsibility for completing the collection for the poor of Jerusalem (2 Cor. 8:6, 16-24; 12:18).

Titus appears in another important role on the island of Crete (Titus 1:4). Beset by a rise in false teaching and declining morality, Titus was told by Paul to strengthen the churches by teaching sound doctrine and good works, and by appointing elders in every city (Titus 1:5). Paul then urged Titus to join him in Nicopolis (on the west coast of Greece) for winter (Titus 3:12). Not surprisingly, Titus was remembered in church tradition as the first bishop of Crete.

A final reference to Titus comes from 2 Timothy 4:10, where Paul remarks in passing that Titus has departed for mission work in Dalmatia (modern Yugoslavia).

Titus was a man for the tough tasks. According to Paul, he was dependable (2 Cor. 8:17), reliable (2 Cor. 7:6), and diligent (2 Cor. 8:17); and he had a great capacity for human affection (2 Cor. 7:13-15). Possessing both strength and tact, Titus calmed a desperate situation on more than one occasion. He is a good model for Christians who are called to live out their witness in trying circumstances.

TITUS, EPISTLE TO — one of three PASTORAL EPISTLES among Paul's writings, the others being 1 and 2 Timothy. The Pastoral Epistles are so named because they deal with matters concerning pastors and congregations. They are the only letters of Paul addressed to individuals (Philemon is addressed "to the church in your house," 1:2). The purpose of the epistle to Titus was to warn against false teaching and to provide guidance for one of Paul's younger associates on sound doctrine and good works.

Structure of the Epistle. Following an extended greeting (1:1-4), Paul advises Titus on the qualifications for church elders or bishops (1:5-9) and warns against false teachers (1:10-16). He proceeds to list ideal characteristics of older men (2:1-2), older women (2:3-5), younger men (2:6-8), and slaves (2:9-10) in the church. The grace of God as it is shown in Jesus Christ provides the foundation for such qualities of life (2:11-15). The final chapter lists ideal characteristics for Christians in society as a whole (3:1-2), again based on the goodness and grace of God (3:3-7); right beliefs thus lead to right actions (3:8-11). The letter closes with personal news and greetings (3:12-15).

Authorship and Date. The circumstances were the same as those under which the apostle Paul wrote the letters to Timothy. (See TIMOTHY, EPISTLES TO).

Historical Setting. According to Titus 1:5, Paul left Titus on the island of Crete to continue establishing churches by appointing "elders in every city." As soon as Artemas or Tychicus relieved him, Titus was to meet Paul in Nicopolis (on the west coast of Greece) where the apostle planned to spend the winter (Titus 3:12).

The occasion for the letter was clear enough—to warn against false teachers (1:10-16). The precise nature of the teaching was less clear, although it included "Jewish fables," legalism, and disputes over genealogies (1:10, 14; 3:9-10). Paul urged Titus to

TITUS: A Teaching Outline

avoid such traps, for anyone associated with them would get caught in his own schemes (3:11).

Theological Contribution. Titus emphasizes sound doctrine (1:9, 2:8, 10) and challenges believers to good works (1:16; 2:14; 3:14). Paul summons Titus "to affirm constantly that those who have believed in God should be careful to maintain good works" (3:8). This letter will allow no separation between belief and action. We often hear it said that it makes no difference what we believe, as long as we do what is right. The truth, however, is that we become what we think, and all action is shaped by belief.

Two passages (2:11–14; 3:4–7) remind us of this truth. In a world such as ours, we cannot be reminded too often to hold fast to the truth of the gospel of our salvation.

TIZITE [TIGH zight] — a name of Joha, one of David's mighty men (1 Chr. 11:45).

TOAH [TOE uh] (*humility*) — the great-great grandfather of Samuel the prophet (1 Chr. 6:34), also called Tohu (1 Sam. 1:1).

TOB [tahb] (*good*) — a land east of the Jordan River between Gilead and the Syrian desert. Jephthah fled to Tob from his half-brothers, who did not want him to share in their inheritance. And it was from Tob that Jephthah was called to lead the eastern tribes of Israel against the Ammonites (Judg. 11:3, 5).

TOBADONIJAH [tahb ad uh NIGH juh] (*good is Jehovah*) — a Levite sent by King Jehoshaphat to teach the law of Moses in the cities of Judah (2 Chr. 17:8).

TOBIAH [toe BIGH uh] (*Jehovah is good*) — the name of two men in the Old Testament:
1. The founder of a tribal family whose descendants returned from the Captivity but could not trace their genealogy (Ezra 2:60).
2. An Ammonite official who tried to prevent the Jews from rebuilding the wall of Jerusalem (Neh. 2:10; 4:3; 6:1–19).

TOBIJAH [toe BIGH juh] (*Jehovah is good*) — the name of two men in the Old Testament:
1. A Levite sent by Jehoshaphat to teach the law of Moses in the cities of Judah (2 Chr. 17:8).
2. A Jewish captive from whom the prophet Zechariah received a gift of silver and gold to make an elaborate crown for Joshua the high priest (Zech. 6:10, 14).

TOBIT, BOOK OF (see APOCRYPHA).

TOCHEN [TOE kuhn] (*measure*) — a city of the tribe of Simeon in southern Judah (1 Chr. 4:32).

TOGARMAH [toe GAHR muh] (meaning unknown) — the name of a man and a country in the Old Testament:
1. A son of Gomer (Gen. 10:3; 1 Chr. 1:6). Togarmah's descendants inhabited the country described in Togarmah No. 2.

Photo by Ben Chapman

Cliffside tomb of Bene Hezir, member of an influential priestly family in Palestine about 150 B.C.

2. A country in the "far north" (Ezek. 38:6) whose people traded horses and mules (Ezek. 27:14) for the wares and merchandise of Tyre (see Map 1, C–1). This country is often thought to be Armenia.

TOHU [TOE hoo] — a form of TOAH.

TOI [TOE eye] (*error*) — a king of HAMATH who sent his son as a friendly ambassador to King David (2 Sam. 8:9–10). He is also called Tou (1 Chr. 18:9–10).

TOKEN — a sign or symbol. Rahab the harlot begged the two spies to give her a "true token" that her family would be spared when Joshua attacked Jericho (Josh. 2:12).

TOKHATH [TOE kath] — a form of TIKVAH.

TOLA [TOE luh] (*crimson worm*) — the name of two men in the Old Testament:
1. A son of Issachar (Gen. 46:13; 1 Chr. 7:1–2) and the ancestor of the TOLAITES (Num. 26:23).
2. A man of the tribe of Issachar who judged Israel 23 years (Judg. 10:1–2).

TOLAD [TOE lad] — a form of ELTOLAD.

TOLAITES [TOE lay ights] — the descendants of TOLA (Num. 26:23).

TOLL (see TAX).

TOMB — an elaborate burial place for the dead. In Palestine ordinary people were buried in shallow graves covered by stones or a stone slab. People of importance and wealth were placed in tombs.

The most elaborate examples of tombs are the pyramids of Egypt, which served as burial places for the Pharaohs. Other and more conventional tombs are found in the Valley of the Kings near Luxor, Egypt. Placed in the tomb with the body were items needed in the afterlife—treasures often later taken by grave robbers. Such treasures were found in the tomb of Tutankhamen. His tomb escaped the robbers because another tomb was built over it; its location was unknown until the 1920s.

Josephus, the Jewish historian, tells of the riches placed in David's tomb (1 Kin. 2:10) in Jerusalem, which was robbed centuries later. The sepulcher consisted of several chambers. The traditional site of the tomb of Herod the Great is Herodium, about six kilometers (four miles) southeast of Bethlehem. Originally it was one of a series of strongholds built by Herod. At his request he was buried there in 4 B.C. This tomb is situated beneath an imposing structure with a sloping passage leading down to the burial place.

Tombs were of two types—natural caves and those hewn out of rock. The most famous natural tomb is the cave of Machpelah, which Abraham purchased from Ephron the Hittite as a burial place for Sarah (Genesis 23). Abraham himself was later buried there (Gen. 25:9–10). It was apparently used as a family burial place, because Isaac, Rebekah, Leah, and Jacob were also buried in this cave (Gen. 49:29–33; 50:12–13). Rachel, Jacob's other wife, died in childbirth near Bethlehem. She was buried in a grave upon which Jacob set a pillar (Gen. 35:16–20). Today a building stands over the site.

Tombs were usually at a distance from the places where the living dwelt. In special cases, such as David and other kings, they might be situated within the city walls (1 Kin. 2:10) or in a garden near a person's house (2 Kin. 21:18). Usually they were outside a city or town (Luke 8:27), but they might be in a garden (John 19:41).

If burial caves were not large enough to accommodate the number of bodies, they were enlarged by excavation (Gen. 50:5). In smaller families places for the bodies were hewn out of the cave or tomb floor. For instance, to the right of the entrance to the Garden Tomb are places for two bodies side-by-side with a bone receptacle or niche between the two at the head. To the left of the entrance beyond a dividing wall, the tomb is unfinished. Since there is room for two bodies, perhaps it was a family tomb for the parents and two children.

TONGS (see TOOLS OF THE BIBLE).

TONGUE — the organ of taste and speech. In addition to its many references to the tongue in a literal sense, the Bible also uses the word tongue for a particular language or dialect (Deut. 28:49; Acts 1:19). The word tongue also refers to a people or race with a common language (Is. 66:18; Rev. 11:9).

Figuratively speaking, the tongue can be sharpened like a sword (Ps. 64:3) or like a serpent (Ps. 140:3)—a reference to its ability to utter caustic, poisonous words. Like a bow, the tongue can project lies (Jer. 9:3), or like an arrow, can be shot out, striking down with its deceit (Jer. 9:8). The tongue can be used as a weapon for attack (Jer. 18:18), wounding like a sharp sword (Ps. 57:4). The tongue can be used viciously for flattery (Ps. 5:9; Prov.

28:23), backbiting (Ps. 15:3; Prov. 25:23), deceit (Ps. 50:19), unrestrained speech (Ps. 73:9), lying (Ps. 109:2; Prov. 26:28), strife (Ps. 31:20), cursing (Hos. 7:16), destruction (Ps. 52:2), and craftiness (Job 15:5).

People may use the tongue to sin (Ps. 39:1) or to speak of the Lord's righteousness (Ps. 35:28) and sing praises to God (Ps. 126:2). The tongue of the wise promotes health (Prov. 12:18). The tongue of the righteous is a treasure, like choice silver (Prov. 10:20). The Bible speaks of keeping the tongue from evil (Ps. 34:13), of guarding the tongue (Prov. 21:23), and of bridling the tongue (James 1:26).

The tongue is an indicator of a person's spirit: it reveals what is in the heart (Matt. 12:33–37; 15:18; Luke 6:43–45). In the classic New Testament passage on the tongue, James warns specifically against the evil of an uncontrolled and uncharitable tongue (James 3:1–12).

TONGUES, CONFUSION OF (see BABEL, TOWER OF).

TONGUES, GIFT OF — the Spirit–given ability to speak in languages not known to the speaker or in an ecstatic language that could not normally be understood by the speaker or the hearers.

Apparently the only possibly direct reference in the Old Testament to speaking in another tongue or language is found in Isaiah 28:11: "For with stammering lips and another tongue He will speak to this people." This seems to be a reference to an invasion of the Assyrians. They apparently would speak in another language, one probably unknown to the people of Israel. The apostle Paul later applied this verse to speaking in tongues (1 Cor. 14:21). The apostle Peter considered the phenomenon of speaking in tongues that occurred on the Day of Pentecost (Acts 2) as the fulfillment of Old Testament prophecy (Joel 2:28–32).

In an appearance to His disciples after His resurrection, Jesus declared, "And these signs will follow those who believe: In My name they will cast out demons; they will speak with new tongues" (Mark 16:17).

On the Day of Pentecost, the followers of Christ "were all filled with the Holy Spirit and began to speak with other tongues, as the Spirit gave them utterance" (Acts 2:4). The people assembled in Jerusalem for this feast came from various Roman provinces representing a variety of languages. They were astonished to hear the disciples speaking of God's works in their own languages. Some have suggested that the miracle was in the hearing rather than in the speaking. This explanation, however, would transfer the miraculous from the believing disciples to the multitude who may not have been believers.

Tongues as a gift of the Spirit is especially prominent in 1 Corinthians 12 and 14. In 1 Corinthians 12 the phenomenon of tongues is listed with other gifts of the Spirit under the term gifts. As one of the several gifts given to believers as a manifestation of the Holy Spirit, tongues is intended, with the other gifts, to be exercised for the building up of the church and the mutual profit of its members. In 1 Corinthians 13 the apostle Paul puts the gift of tongues in perspective by affirming that though we "speak with the tongues of men and of angels" (v. 1), if we do not have love, the gift of tongues has no value.

In 1 Corinthians 14 Paul deals more specifically with the gift of tongues and its exercise in the church. In this chapter the tongue is not an intelligible language, for it cannot be understood by the listeners. Therefore, a parallel to the gift of tongues is the gift of interpretation. The gift of tongues was used as a means of worship, thanksgiving, and prayer. While exercising this gift, the individual addresses God not man; and the result is to edify himself and not the church (1 Cor. 14:2, 4). This gift is never intended for self-exaltation but for the praise and glorification of God. Paul does not prohibit speaking in tongues in a public service (14:39). But he seems to assign it to a lesser place than the gift of prophecy. Paul claims for himself the gift of tongues-speaking, but apparently he exercised this gift in private and not in public (14:18–19).

The gift of tongues is to be exercised with restraint and in an orderly way. The regulations for its public use are simple and straightforward. The person who speaks in an unknown tongue is to pray that he may interpret (1 Cor. 14:13). Or, someone else is to interpret what he says. Only two or three persons are to speak, with each having an interpretation of what he says. Each is also to speak in turn. If these criteria are not met, they are to remain silent (1 Cor. 14:27–28). The gifts of speaking in tongues and their interpretation are to be Spirit-inspired. Paul also points out that tongues are a sign to unbelievers. If these guidelines are not observed, unbelievers who are present will conclude that the people of the church are out of their minds.

The phenomenon of speaking in tongues described in the New Testament is not some psychological arousal of human emotions that results in strange sounds. This is a genuine work of the Holy Spirit.

TOOLS OF THE BIBLE — Tools in Bible times were used to form, shape, cut, measure, move, or fasten materials. Various types of knives, saws, hammers, drills, and other tools were common in the ancient world.

In the earliest times—long before Abraham—people used stone tools fixed to wooden handles. Many of these were naturally-shaped stones. Others were shaped by people for specific purposes. Flint, a very hard stone that can be shaped into sharp-edged blades by hammering or pressing it with another stone, was in use from the earliest days of man.

By about 3200 B.C., techniques for smelting copper had been discovered, and metalworking tools made their first appearance in Palestine. Copper is relatively soft and does not hold an edge well. It was soon replaced by bronze, an alloy of copper

and tin that was much harder and more efficient. The older versions of the Bible use the term brass to refer to this alloy. But true brass, an alloy of copper and zinc, was not in use in Bible times.

Bronze tools and weapons were used by the Hebrews right down to the time of the judges and Saul (about 1050 B.C.). By then the secrets of smelting iron had been learned from the Philistines, and iron farm implements were available in Israel.

The Philistines tried to keep the secrets of the technology from the Israelites who had no iron spears or swords (1 Sam. 13:19–22). But with David's victory over the Philistines, iron became readily available to the Hebrews (1 Kin. 6:7).

Many specific tools—from general and household tools to those used by specialists such as metalsmiths—are mentioned in the Bible. The following alphabetical list is keyed to the NKJV. But variant names from five additional translations—KJV, NASB, NEB, NIV, and RSV—are cross-referenced to this list.

Anvil. A large iron block on which metal was hammered and shaped. The only use of this word in the Bible occurs in Isaiah 41:7 where the word usually translated foot or foundation is translated as anvil. Metalsmiths, whether working in delicate jewelry making or in heavy construction work, used anvils as bases on which to shape metal.

Awl. Awls were used by carpenters and leatherworkers to punch holes. The only biblical references to awls are in regard to the ceremony by which a slave had an ear lobe pierced as a sign of his willingness to serve his master all his life (Ex. 21:6; Deut. 15:17). Archaeologists have found many samples of such tools. They are usually about 15 centimeters (six inches) long, made of iron or bronze, and come to a sharp conical point.

Ax. A cutting and chopping tool. Eight different Hebrew words and one Greek word are translated ax in English versions of the Bible. Several of these axes were tools designed for specific jobs. One type of ax was a sort of pruning tool (Jer. 10:3) with a curved blade that could also be used by a blacksmith to pick up hot metal (tongs, Is. 44:12).

Iron axes were used to clear forests and cut wood (Deut. 19:5; Is. 10:15; Matt. 3:10). Sometimes the iron head would separate from the wooden handle and either be lost, as in the miracle of the floating axe head (2 Kin. 6:5–6), or possibly injure someone standing nearby. Deuteronomy 19:5 provides for this sort of accident. First Samuel 13:20–21 records the prices which the Philistines charged for sharpening iron axes and agricultural tools.

Battle axes of various sorts are also mentioned in the Bible. They were used either as weapons or as tools to destroy captured cities (Ps. 74:5–6; Jer. 46:22; Ezek. 26:9). Some versions translate this tool as hatchet.

Another special type of ax was used by stonecutters to break out the large sawn blocks from a quarry or to shape the stone after it was quarried.

One other Hebrew word, translated ax (NKJV) in 2 Chronicles 34:6 (mattock, KJV) and Ezekiel

26:9 is more properly a weapon, either a large sword (Gen. 3:24; 1 Sam. 17:51) or a smaller dagger (Judg. 3:16). This word suggests a sturdy blade that could be used to cut down enemies as an ax cuts a tree.

Bellows. A device which provided a gust of air when squeezed. These small blowing instruments were made of leather and pottery and were operated by either hand or foot. To raise the temperature in the furnace high enough to work bronze or iron, it was necessary to get a good supply of air into the fire. The earliest furnaces were built so the prevailing wind blew through, increasing the draft. Later, in order to make it possible to work without the wind, bellows were used to force the air into the fire. The only biblical reference to this tool is in Jeremiah 6:29.

Brazier (see *Oven*).

Chisel. A chisel has a sharp metal blade and is commonly used for cutting and shaping wood or stone. Examples of chisels with bronze or iron blades from biblical times have been found. The only reference to a chisel in the Bible is as a stonecutter's tool (1 Kin. 6:7). The NIV uses chisel in Isaiah 44:13 for a word translated plane by the NKJV and other translations.

Compass. A device for drawing circles or parts of circles. The only mention of a compass in the Bible is in Isaiah 44:13. A primitive compass can be made by using a length of cord fixed at one end to a nail or pin and a marking instrument at the other. More accurate wooden or metal holders for the marking tool were also used.

Fan. The fan mentioned in the Old Testament was probably a type of long-handled fork used to toss the threshed grain into the air. The wind blew the chaff away, allowing the heavier grain to fall into a separate pile (Is. 30:24; Jer. 15:7). Some versions translate this tool as fork or winnowing fork.

John the Baptist's description of the Messiah as one who would separate good from evil in the last days uses this illustration (Matt. 3:12; Luke 3:17).

File. The file was probably some sort of stone used to sharpen the edge of metal blades. This word

appears only in the KJV (1 Sam. 13:21).

Fire Pot (see *Oven*).

Forge (see *Tongs*).

Fork (see *Fan*).

Furnace. Many tradesmen needed the fiery heat provided by the furnace to perfect their goods. Furnaces made of stone or brick were used mostly by potters and metalsmiths. The word used for household furnaces or stoves in Bible times is usually translated as oven.

Clay pots and jars were of limited use unless they had been "fired" by being raised to a very high temperature. The heat changed the chemical makeup of the clay, leaving it very strong but brittle. By carefully controlling the amount of fuel and the air supply, the proper temperature was reached and maintained until the clay was cured.

Special furnaces were also necessary for smelting metal ores. Finely ground ores were mixed with charcoal and fluxes of limestone or crushed seashells, and placed into the fire. Bellows kept the fire hot enough to melt the ore. As it melted, the liquid metal sank to the bottom of the furnace, allowing the waste slag to float to the top. This waste was removed through a small pipe. The metal was allowed to cool and then remelted in a crucible for purification. It was then cast into molds to be shaped into many useful items.

Large furnaces big enough for several people to walk into were used in Babylon to make bricks. This is probably the "burning fiery furnace" of Daniel 3:15-30. Also see *Oven*.

Goad. A sharpened metal point on the end of a long pole. Goads were used by farmers to prod animals to keep them moving, but they could also be dangerous weapons (Judg. 3:31). Ecclesiastes 12:11 notes that the wise instruction of a good teacher acts like a goad.

Hammer. Hammers and mauls were very useful to the people of the Bible. Four different Hebrew words are translated by these two English words. One refers to the small hammer used by stonecutters or carpenters to drive nails or shape stones (1 Kin. 6:7; Jer. 10:4). This same word is used in

This wooden model, dating from about 2000 B.C., shows an Egyptian farmer guiding a two-handled plow drawn by a pair of oxen.

Ancient grain mills at Pompeii. Poles were inserted through the holes in the mills, which were then turned to grind the grain.

Judges 4:21 of the hammer which Jael used to kill the Syrian general Sisera. When the incident is related in Judges 5, the RSV translates this word as mallet.

Another word translated as hammer is what would be known today as a sledgehammer. This tool was used to break up rocks (Jer. 23:29) or shape iron (Is. 41:7).

Harrow. A toothed bar, dragged by oxen, which was used to level plowed ground for planting. The harrow is not mentioned in the NKJV, but it does appear in the KJV (2 Sam. 12:31) and other translations (Job 39:10, RSV, NEB; Is. 28:24, NIV, NASB). No examples of this tool have been identified from the ancient world.

Hatchet (see *Ax*).

Hoe (see *Mattock*).

Knife. Three Hebrew words are sometimes translated as knife. The first describes either flint blades used for ritual circumcision or self–mutilation (Josh. 5:2–3; 1 Kin. 18:28), or short metal swords or daggers used in battle (Gen. 3:24; 34:25–26). The second word describes a knife used for the slaughter of animals for food or sacrifice (Gen. 22:6, 10; Judg. 19:29; Prov. 30:14). The third word occurs only in Proverbs 23:2. This tool was apparently similar to the second type of knife.

Knives were usually bronze or iron blades with the handle and the blade consisting of one piece of metal. Sometimes the blade was fastened to a wooden or bone handle with rivets.

Level (see *Plumb Line/Plummet*).

Mallet (see *Hammer*).

Marking Tools. Isaiah 44:13 describes a carpenter marking out divisions on a piece of wood. The Hebrew word occurs only here in the Bible, so the exact nature of the tool is not certain. It appears to be some sort of sharp–pointed instrument that was used to scratch marks in wood.

Mattock. A mattock was similar to a hoe. It was a flat iron head fastened to a wooden handle, used to weed the terraced gardens and fields. Mattock appears in only one passage in the NKJV (1 Sam. 13:20–21). The KJV translates two other Hebrew words as mattock (axes, 2 Chr. 34:6; hoe, Is. 7:25).

Maul (see *Hammer*).

Measuring Line (see *Measuring Tools*).

Measuring Rod (see *Measuring Tools*).

Measuring Tools. Both builders and surveyors used measuring tools. These were of two types: a solid rule, rod, or straight edge, up to three meters (ten feet) long; and a flexible rope, cord, or line that could be used to measure longer distances or irregularly shaped objects.

The prophet Ezekiel mentioned a measuring rod that was "six cubits long" (Ezek. 40:5). The ordinary cubit was about 45 centimeters (18 inches) long and the "long" cubit about 55 centimeters (22 inches), so Ezekiel's rod was about 3.3 meters (11 feet) long.

Measuring lines were probably much longer. No definite length is mentioned, although 1 Kings 7:23 suggests at least 30 cubits, or 13.5 meters (45 feet), or more. According to Ezekiel 40:3, these lines were made of flax or linen, although other fibers were probably also used. The measuring line was used as a symbol of God's judgment on evil (Lam. 2:8) or as a sign of His blessing and restoration (Jer. 31:39).

Mill. Mills and millstones were tools used to grind grain. The most common household mills of Bible times were flat stones on which grain was placed and crushed as other stones rolled over the grain.

Commercial mills were of different construction

and considerably larger. One type was made of two round flat stones. A wooden peg was firmly fastened in the center of the bottom stone. The upper stone, which had a funnel–shaped hole through the center, was placed over the peg. Grain was poured between the stones and around the peg through the hole. The upper stone was turned by a peg handle placed near the outside edge, crushing the grain. Some of these larger mills required two operators.

A second type of commercial mill was similar in operation but of a different shape. The lower stone was in the shape of an upside–down cone. The upper stone, with a cone–shaped hollow cut into the bottom side, was placed over the lower stone. Grain was poured through a hole in the top. The upper stone was turned either by animals hitched to wooden arms attached to the stone or by slaves or prisoners (Judg. 16:21).

A third type of mill consisted of a large circular stone set on its edge and rolled around in a trough in the lower stone. This was also operated by animals or slaves.

The sound of grinding was heard constantly in the villages and towns. Its absence was a prophetic sign of famine and death (Jer. 25:10; Rev. 18:22). The loss of a millstone could mean disaster for a family (Deut. 24:6).

Mirror. Many examples of small bronze mirrors on decorated handles are known from ancient times. It was impossible to get a perfectly flat surface on these metal mirrors, so the reflection was always somewhat distorted, like the mirrors in a fun house. Paul's comment in 1 Corinthians 13:12 recognized this problem.

Since glass mirrors were not made until after the time of the New Testament, the KJV references in 1 Corinthians 13:12, James 1:23, and Isaiah 3:23 are mistranslations.

Mortar and Pestle. Used by masons and builders, mortar was a material which held bricks together in construction. This substance was a mixture of asphalt (Gen. 11:3), clay, straw, mud, and other elements, depending on the location where it was made. The Israelites wandering in the wilderness included manna in their mortar (Num. 11:8). The various elements used in mortar were ground together with a pestle (Prov. 27:22) or trod by workers (Nah. 3:14). Mortar was usually treated in some way, probably by heat, to allow it to harden for safer masonry. The prophet Ezekiel compared the security which Israel sought in false prophets to a boundary wall plastered with "untempered mortar" which would fall before the Lord (Ezek. 13:10–16).

Nail. Metal nails of either bronze or iron were commonly used by carpenters and cabinet makers. They were usually hand–forged and about the same size as our modern cut nails. First Chronicles 22:3 and 2 Chronicles 3:9 describe the large quantities of iron and bronze nails gathered by David for use in constructing the Temple in Jerusalem. Jeremiah 10:4 describes fancy work done by craftsmen and goldsmiths, and the use of nails for decoration by these people. Archaeologists have found many

samples of decorative nails with gold or silver heads.

A different word than the one for nail described the large iron spikes used in the crucifixion of Jesus (John 20:25). Another word, translated nail in the KJV, is translated peg by the NKJV and other translations (Ex. 35:18; Judg. 4:21–22; Zech. 10:4).

Needle. The Old Testament has many references to needlework or embroidery, particularly the woven linen used in the tabernacle hangings (Ex. 26:1–13) and the fine clothes of wealthy Israelites (Ezek. 16:10–18; 27:7, 16, 24). Needles must have been used also for sewing and repairing family clothing (Gen. 3:7; Job 16:15; Eccl. 3:7; Ezek. 13:18). Samples of needles found in numerous archaeological excavations are made of bone, bronze, or iron. They are of various sizes, from very fine to the size of large darning needles. Their shape is similar to the common needles of today.

Jesus' words in Matthew 19:24 (also Mark 10:25; Luke 18:25), that it is easier for a rich man to enter heaven than "for a camel to go through the eye of a needle," reflect an idea found in early rabbinic writing. There is no archaeological or historical support for the common idea that the "needle's eye" was a small pedestrian gate through the city wall. The statement simply means that humanly speaking, this is an impossible thing. Only a divine miracle can make it possible.

Oven. Cooking was usually done on small clay or stone ovens (Lev. 2:4; 26:26; Hos. 7:4). The word translated oven by the NKJV is translated in the KJV as furnace in Genesis 15:17 and Nehemiah 3:11 and 12:38. The NEB translates Genesis 15:17 as brazier, while the RSV and NIV use fire pot.

Ovens were either rectangular or circular, about 60 centimeters (two feet) in diameter and about 30 centimeters (one foot) high, with the top flattened and slightly hollow. The food was cooked on the flat top, with the fire inside the oven or stove. The usual fuel was animal dung or wood, but straw was used to make a quick fire and to rekindle the embers.

Malachi 4:1 describes the day of judgment when the evildoers will be destroyed in a day "burning like an oven." Nehemiah 3:11 and 12:28 mention the "Tower of the Ovens" on the city wall. This may have been a section of the city where commercial baking was carried on, but more likely it is a reference to either potter's or brickmaker's kilns or to metal smelters.

Peg (see *Nail*).

Pick. An iron tool of uncertain use. It is listed, along with saws and axes, as a tool used by the conquered people of Rabbah (2 Sam. 12:31; 1 Chr. 20:3).

Plane. The word plane occurs only in Isaiah 44:13. The exact nature of ancient Hebrew planes is not certain, but they were used to shape wood by scraping or shaving motions. The NIV translates this word as chisel.

Plow/Plowshare. The earliest plows were probably simple wooden sticks used to scratch furrows in

Photo by Howard Vos

Drawings of several householder's tools excavated at Pompeii and dating to the first century A.D.

the ground for planting seeds. Eventually, larger forked branches drawn by animals were used. These "single-handed" plows were light enough for one man to lift around obstructions. They had the advantage of leaving one hand free for the farmer to guide the animals.

By the time of David (about 1000 B.C.), iron tips were commonly fastened to the wooden plows. This made it easier to cultivate the stony soil of Palestine. The Philistines were concerned that the Israelites not learn the secrets of iron smelting. They apparently recognized it would be easy to make "plowshares into swords" for warfare (Joel 3:10). On the other hand, the age of the Messiah, the "Prince of Peace," was to be a time when "they shall beat their swords into plowshares" (Is. 2:4; Mic. 4:3).

Plumb Line/Plummet. A small heavy weight on the end of a long cord, used to make sure a wall is standing vertically (2 Kin. 21:13; level, Is. 28:17, NASB). In a vision, the prophet Amos saw the Lord measuring the nation of Israel with a plumb line. The people were not considered true and straight in their devotion to God because they had fallen into worship of false gods (Amos 7:7-8).

Press. A device used to crush fruits in order to make oil or juice. The cultivation of olives was an important part of the agricultural activity in Israel, since olive oil was a major item of trade and export. To extract the oil from the fruit, olives were placed in large shallow presses hewn out of rock and

crushed with a large stone roller operated by two people. The oil was collected in a container, then strained to remove impurities before being bottled in clay pottery jars.

The New Testament name Gethsemane (Matt. 26:36; Mark 14:32) is a compound word meaning "oil press." Gethsemane was the place where the olives from the groves on the Mount of Olives were processed.

Wine presses were deep pits dug out of the rock. The grapes were put in and trampled by the workers with their bare feet (Amos 9:13). If the harvest was good, this was a joyous occasion and a time of singing and celebration (Is. 16:10; Jer. 25:30). The juice was channeled to another pit where it was allowed to settle before being put into skin bags or pottery jars for fermentation.

The description of Gideon threshing wheat in a winepress illustrates how carefully he had to hide the crop from the invading Midianites. Threshing such as this was normally done on the high ground to take advantage of the wind. But he was threshing in a pit in the valley (Judg. 6:11).

Pruninghook. A sickle-shaped knife used by the keepers of the vineyards to prune grapevines in the spring (Is. 18:5). This regular cutting was essential if the vines were to continue to produce good crops.

Razor. Razors of the ancient world were usually bronze or iron blades fastened to wooden handles. Those used by kings or for ritual purposes often had more elaborate bone or ivory handles. The prophet Isaiah predicted the Assyrians would conquer the northern kingdom of Israel, shaving Israel with a razor and bringing judgment on His people. The prophet Ezekiel (5:1-2) used a similar picture to illustrate the destruction of Jerusalem by the Babylonians.

Rule (see *Measuring Tools*).

Saw. Saws were metal blades with a toothed edge. They were used by ancient peoples to cut wood or stone. Prisoners of war were sometimes put to work in the quarries cutting stone with saws. Marks left by the stonecutter's saws can still be seen in many of the ancient quarries of Palestine.

Hebrews 11:37 describes the faithful Israelites who were killed for their faith. Some were "sawn in two," a common method of execution among the Greeks. It is traditionally believed that the prophet Isaiah was killed in this way.

Shovel. According to Isaiah 30:24, shovels were sometimes used in the winnowing process. This was in addition to winnowing fans. Shovels were usually wooden paddle-type implements with long handles. These were different from the metal shovels used in the tabernacle and Temple to remove the ashes from the altar (Ex. 27:3; 1 Kin. 7:40).

Sickle. A small hand tool used for cutting stalks of grain. The oldest known examples have flint teeth set in wood or bone handles. Later, metal blades were used. The grain was held in one hand and cut off near the ground by the sickle. The final judgment is sometimes pictured in terms of reaping with a sickle (Joel 13:13; Rev. 14:14-19).

Sieve. Scholars are not certain what kind of tool a sieve was. Two unrelated words, used once each in the Old Testament, are translated as sieve (Is. 30:28; Amos 9:9). In both places the word for sieve is used with a verb meaning "to sift."

Sledge (see *Threshing Sledge*).

Threshing Sledge. The purpose of threshing was to separate usable grain from the waste straw or chaff. This was usually done by spreading the stalks of grain several inches deep on a smooth flat area which was on a high piece of ground open to the wind. Specially shod animals walked around on the stalks until the grain separated from the hulls.

Frequently threshing sledges (Is. 28:27) made of wood (2 Sam. 24:22) with stone or metal teeth embedded in the bottom side were dragged over the grain by these animals.

The city of Damascus was called under judgment because that nation "threshed Gilead with implements of iron" (Amos 1:3–5) or behaved with unnecessary cruelty against a conquered people. God promised to make His people into a "new threshing sledge" with sharp teeth and use them to bring judgment on those who oppress the godly (Is. 41:15).

Tongs. Tongs were a type of tool with a hook or a blade. They were used by blacksmiths to handle hot metal (Is. 44:12). These are called forges by the NIV and RSV. The same Hebrew word is translated ax in Jeremiah 10:3.

Wheel. The potter's wheel was a device used by potters to make their pottery even and symmetrical. It was invented about 4000 B.C. Before that time pots and jars were built up of coils of clay smoothed and shaped by hand. The "slow wheel" was a small flat disk on a spindle, with a larger stone disk on the other end. It was spun by hand as the potter alternated between keeping the wheel in motion and shaping the clay.

The "fast wheel" made its appearance about a thousand years later. It was really two wheels, one above the other, with an axle joining them. The potter sat on a bench and turned the lower wheel with his feet. This way, he could keep it going rapidly, yet still have both hands free to shape the clay on the upper wheel.

The most symbolic and descriptive use of a potter's wheel in the Bible appears in the Book of Jeremiah. Jeremiah visited a potter at his wheel. He compared the potter who molds his clay to God who has the power to mold the nation of Israel (Jer. 18:2–8).

Winnowing Fork (see *Fan*).

Yoke. A type of harness which connected a pair of animals to a plow or similiar tool. Oxen were the most common animals in working the land. A yoke of oxen was a pair (1 Sam. 11:7; Luke 14:19). Using a pair to pull a plow required a yoke to link them together so they could work efficiently. Yokes were usually made of a wooden beam shaped to fit over the necks of the two animals and held in place by wooden or leather fasteners.

The yoke was also used as a symbol of the burden or oppression of heavy responsibility, duty,

sin, or punishment (1 Kin. 12:4–14; Jer. 27:8–12; Acts 15:10). In New Testament times the phrase *take the yoke of* was used by the Jewish rabbis to mean, "Become the pupil of a certain teacher." Jesus gave a gentle invitation to His disciples: "Take My yoke upon you and learn from Me, for I am gentle and lowly in heart, and you will find rest for your souls. For My yoke is easy and My burden is light" (Matt. 11:29–30).

TOOTH, TEETH — bonelike structures in the mouth used for chewing. In Bible times, clean, white teeth were desired for beauty (Song 4:2; 6:6). Many wild animals used their teeth to catch their prey (Deut. 32:24; Joel 1:6). This led naturally to biblical phrases which suggested that when one person destroyed another, it was through sharp teeth (Ps. 57:4; Prov. 30:14).

Teeth is also a familiar figure of speech in the Bible. "By the skin of my teeth" (Job 19:20) means a narrow escape; "children's teeth...set on edge" (Jer. 31:29; Ezek. 18:2) means children suffering for the sins of their "fathers," or ancestors—a doctrine which the prophets Jeremiah and Ezekiel repudiated. "Cleanness of teeth" means famine, hunger, or starvation (Amos 4:6). To break an enemy's teeth was a sign of his defeat (Ps. 3:7).

Gnashing one's teeth can symbolize intense anger (Job 16:9; Acts 7:54). Jesus described hell as an "outer darkness" and a "furnace of fire," a place of "weeping [wailing] and gnashing of teeth" (Matt. 8:12; 13:42; Luke 13:28). This is a graphic picture of the anguish and suffering of those excluded from the kingdom of God.

TOPAZ (see JEWELS AND PRECIOUS STONES).

TOPHEL [TOE fuhl] (meaning unknown) — a place in the Wilderness of Sinai near Paran (Deut. 1:1). It has been identified with et–Tafileh, an Arab village about 23 kilometers (14 miles) southeast of the Dead Sea.

TOPHET [TOE fet] (meaning unknown) — a place southeast of Jerusalem, in the Valley of Hinnom, where child sacrifices were offered and the dead bodies were buried or consumed (Is. 30:33; Jer. 7:31–32; 19:6, 11–14; Topheth, 2 Kin. 23:10). Chemosh, a Moabite god (1 Kin. 11:7, 33; 2 Kin. 23:13) and Molech, an Ammonite god (1 Kin. 11:7; 2 Kin. 23:10) were worshiped at Tophet through a practice despised by God—infant sacrifice (2 Kin. 16:3; Jer. 7:31; 19:5; 32:35).

Two kings of Judah—Ahaz, or Jehoahaz (2 Kin. 16:3) and Manasseh (2 Kin. 21:6)—made their own sons "pass through the fire." Godly King Josiah stopped this horrible practice (2 Kin. 23:10), possibly by dumping the garbage of Jerusalem at Tophet.

The prophet Isaiah used Tophet as a symbol of the death and destruction which God would use as judgment against the king of Assyria (Is. 30:33). Jeremiah proclaimed that God's judgment would fall upon the Judeans for sacrificing their infants to Baal (Jer. 19:5–6). The burial of slaughtered Judeans at this place would be so great, said Jeremiah, that the name Tophet would be changed to "Valley of Slaughter" (Jer. 7:31–32; 19:6). Jeremiah also announced that God would make Jerusalem itself a defiled place like Tophet because of the idolatry of the city (Jer. 19:6, 11–14).

Also see HINNOM, VALLEY OF; GEHENNA.

TOPHETH [TOE fet] — a form of TOPHET.

TORAH [toe RAH] — guidance or direction from God to His people. In earlier times, the term Torah referred directly to the five books of Moses, or the PENTATEUCH. Moses told the people, "Command your children to observe to do, all the words of this law." While the English word law does not suggest this, both the hearing and the doing of the law made the Torah. It was a manner of life, a way to live based upon the COVENANT that God made with His people.

Later the Hebrew Old Testament included both the books of wisdom and the prophets, but this entire collection was spoken of as the Torah. Jesus quoted Psalm 82:6, calling it a part of the law (John 10:34). Following the return from Babylon, the development of the synagogue gave rise to interpretations of the law by leading rabbis, which after a time were collected into 613 precepts. Considered part of the Torah, they were as binding as the law itself. Jesus referred to these additions to the original law of Moses as "the traditions of men."

The Torah, both then and now for Jewish people, should be seen as a total way of life. It requires

This massive stone tower was part of the defense system of the ancient city of Jericho. It dates back to before 4000 B.C., long before Joshua and his army destroyed the city.

complete dedication because it is seen as God's direction for living the covenant relationship.

TORCH — a light source consisting of a flaming stick of wood. Torches were used by the mob that arrested Jesus in the Garden of Gethsemane (John 18:3).

TORMENT — to inflict physical pain or mental agony. Job cried out against his three friends who had come to comfort him, "How long will you torment my soul" (Job 19:2). The rich man in Jesus' account of the rich man and Lazarus also described hell as a "place of torment" (Luke 16:28).

TORSO — the trunk of the human body. When the Philistines captured the ARK OF THE COVENANT, they took it into the temple, which contained a statue of their pagan god, Dagon. Later they found the statue fallen on its face before the ark; its head and hands had broken off and only the torso remained (1 Sam. 5:4; trunk, NASB, RSV; stump, KJV; body, NIV, NEB). This showed the powerlessness of the heathen idol and the strength of Jehovah, the true God of Israel.

TORTOISE (see ANIMALS OF THE BIBLE).

TOU [TOE oo] — a form of TOI.

TOW — KJV word for the refuse of flax produced in the manufacture of linen (Judg. 16:9; yarn, NKJV; Is. 1:31, KJV; tinder, NKJV).

TOWER — a tall building erected for defense. Some landowners used towers to protect their crops (Is. 5:2; Matt. 21:33; Mark 12:1). In the wilderness, towers were used to watch for approaching marauders (2 Kin. 17:9; 2 Chr. 26:10). In cities towers were part of the walls built for defensive purposes (2 Chr. 14:7; Neh. 3:1). They were erected at the corners of the wall, beside the city gates, and at intervals along the walls (2 Chr. 26:9). Watchmen secured the towers (2 Kin. 9:17), and military machines which threw arrows and stones could be mounted on the massive structures (2 Chr. 26:15).

The defensive nature of a tower led naturally to figurative references in the Bible. God is pictured as a high, strong tower sheltering His people from the enemy (Ps. 61:3; 144:2; Prov. 18:10).

TOWER OF BABEL (see BABEL, TOWER OF).

TOWER OF THE FURNACES (see FURNACES, TOWER OF THE).

TOWN — a cluster of homes which, in terms of size and organization, lies somewhere between a city and a village. A town is larger and more independent than a village, but it lacks many of the services (for example, a wall) which characterize a city.

While the English language preserves a neat distinction between city, town, and village, the same is not true for Hebrew and Greek. The main distinction in the Old Testament is between cities, which have defensive walls and are self–contained, and villages, which are without a wall and depend on

A Roman road near Aleppo in Syria. Roads were important for trade, as well as military travel, in ancient times. The Romans built and maintained extensive systems of roads throughout their empire.

large cities for protection. Many English translations confuse the issue by rendering various Hebrew words for city or village as town.

TOWN CLERK (see OCCUPATIONS AND TRADES).

TRACHONITIS [trak uh NIGH tuhs] (*hilly region*) — a district in the tetrarchy of Philip (see Map 6, C–1), properly belonging to Arabia and not to Canaan (Luke 3:1). It was bordered by Iturea on the south, Bashan on the west, Damascus on the north, and the Arabian desert on the east. Trachonitis abounded with rocks and craggy mountains and, according to the Jewish historian Josephus, was infested with robbers and other predators who earned their living by violence.

TRADE AND TRAVEL — commercial buying and selling in Bible times and the travel required to conduct these activities.

The nation of Israel had little in the way of natural resources. But its geographic situation made the nation a strategic corridor through which all military and economic traffic between Europe, Asia, and Africa had to pass. Important roads from Egypt crossed the southern wilderness to Kadesh-Barnea and Elath and then proceeded north along the edge of the desert through Moab, Heshbon, Amman, and Ramoth–Gilead to Damascus. Numerous secondary roads ran along the mountain ridge from Beersheba and Hebron to Jerusalem, Dothan, and Beth–Shean, then along the Jordan Valley from Jericho to Galilee. Several east–west roads linked the coast with the inland towns and cities.

The major route through Palestine was the "Way of the Sea," an important highway that ran along the coast from Egypt through Gaza and Ashkelon to Joppa. Because of the swamps along the central coast, this road then swung inland to Aphek and up through the Aruna Pass through the Carmel mountains to Megiddo. At Megiddo the road divided, the western branch continuing along the coast to the Phoenician ports of Acco, Tyre, and Sidon. The eastern branch cut across the Esdraelon plain in Lower Galilee to Capernaum, Hazor, Dan, and Damascus, where it joined the highway coming up from Gilead.

The strategic military importance of this road meant that the nations struggled to control the key cities and passes at Megiddo and Hazor. Because of this constant ebb and flow of armies and traders, Israel was greatly influenced by neighboring nations. In turn, the Hebrew nation became a major factor in international trade and commerce.

Israel's wealth was primarily agricultural. Grain, especially wheat and barley, grew abundantly in the shallow valleys along the foothills of Judea and Samaria. These were major export crops. Figs, grapes, and olives were plentiful in the hill country of Judea.

The land around Hebron produced magnificent grapes (Num. 13:23–24). Large quantities of raisins and wine were produced around Hebron for home

Photo by Howard Vos

The Cilician Gates north of Tarsus was one of the main passes through the Taurus Mountains.

consumption and export. Olives were used either as food or crushed for cooking oil. Olive oil was also used in lamps or as a body rub, making it a major item in the economy of the region.

Large herds of sheep and goats were raised in Palestine (1 Sam. 16:11; John 10:1–16). Wool and the cloth made from this product were important sources of revenue.

Fish were taken along the Mediterranean Sea coast and in the Sea of Galilee. The northern part of the Mediterranean coast was also the source of the murex shell, which was used to make a very valuable purple dye. Extensive textile industries, using both wool and the linen made from the flax grown in the coastal plain, produced the distinctive Tyrian purple cloth that was in great demand all around the Mediterranean. Lydia of Philippi and Thyatira was engaged in this business (Acts 16:14).

The southern end of the Jordan Valley and the Dead Sea area was the source of a large and profitable salt-mining industry. The city of Jericho appears to have been involved in this trade as early as 7000 B.C.

Asphalt or bitumen was easily obtained from the tar pits in the Dead Sea area (Gen. 11:3; 14:10). This substance was used as caulk in boats and rafts, as mortar in building, and for making monuments and jewelry. Timber from the Lebanon mountains was also a significant trade item.

Little pottery was exported from Israel, except for simple containers for wine and oil. Israelite pottery was more practical and less artistic than Philistine and Greek pottery.

Neither did Israel export a great deal of metals, except during the time of Solomon when the copper mines in Sinai and the iron mines in Syria were worked commercially.

One major industry was the manufacture of mill stones from the high-quality basalt stone found in the volcanic hills of northern Gilead. These were shipped as far away as Spain, Italy, and North Africa.

During the early days of the United Kingdom under David and Solomon, Israel controlled all the major trade routes through the area. It was impossible to ship anything anywhere between Asia Minor, the Mesopotamian Valley, and Egypt without going through Israelite-controlled territory. Heavy excise taxes and import and export duties on all goods traveling through Israel produced huge sums of money. These revenues went into the construction of elaborate palaces and temples and extensive public works and military projects (1 Kings 5—7; 1 Chr. 29:1–5; 2 Chr. 1:14–17).

Ezekiel 27:1–24 lists a number of products that were traded through the city of Tyre. Israel probably also traded in these items. Much of the material was carried by camel or donkey, but ox-drawn wagons were also extensively used (Gen. 37:25).

By New Testament times, travel was relatively simple and considerably safer than in the earlier periods. The establishment of Roman control over the Mediterranean Sea and the lands around it put an effective end to piracy and highway robbery in the Empire. The Roman road system linked every part of the Empire and made travel much easier.

For long distances, ship travel was common (Jonah 1; Acts 13:4; 27:1–44). Government officials and the wealthy frequently used various types of chariots (Acts 8:28) and portable chairs (Song 3:6–10). Horses were mostly used for military purposes (Acts 23:23–24).

But for most people, the only way of traveling was on foot or donkey back. Foot travelers could average about 16 miles a day. Under normal circumstances Mary and Joseph's trip from Nazareth to Bethlehem (Luke 2:1–7) probably took at least five days. With Mary unable to travel easily because of her pregnancy, that trip could well have taken two weeks or more.

TRADER (see OCCUPATIONS AND TRADES; COMMERCE).

TRADITION — customs and practices from the past which are passed on as accepted standards of behavior for the present. Jesus criticized the Pharisees for slavishly following their traditions and making them more authoritative than the Scripture (Matt. 15:2; Mark 7:3).

TRAIN — the lowest and back hem of the outer garment (Is. 6:1). The outermost garment worn by the Hebrew people was a long, loosely fitting robe. Usually sleeveless, its rear skirt was drawn up through the legs and attached around the waist by a belt or girdle when the person was working. This long skirt is called a train when it is not girded. To have a robe or cloak with a long train was a sign of favor and wealth (Ex. 28:33). Also see DRESS OF THE BIBLE.

TRAJAN [TRAY jan] (meaning unknown) — emperor of Rome, A.D. 98–117. Trajan is not mentioned in the New Testament. But scholars identify him as a bitter foe of Christianity soon after the close of the age of the apostles. Many Christians were martyred during his reign. When it was speculated that believers were engaging in a secret rite when they gathered for the Lord's Supper, Trajan outlawed such meetings.

TRANCE — an ecstatic state of mind that gives a person a sense of detachment from his physical surroundings.

The Greek word for trance literally means "standing outside" or "being put outside" of one's normal state of mind. Peter had been in prayer when he "fell into a trance," receiving the vision indicating that the Gentiles were to be included in the church (Acts 10:10). In his defense to the people in Jerusalem, the apostle Paul declared that after his conversion, he fell into a trance and Christ commanded him to leave the city and evangelize the Gentiles (Acts 22:17).

The trances of Peter and Paul involved their seeing and hearing senses. They saw and heard the Lord speaking to them. Both trances took place as they were in prayer, and in both cases the recipients were awake. Neither trance was self–induced; God revealed Himself in both.

Paul's vision on the Damascus Road (Acts 9:3–9), the experience recorded in 2 Corinthians 12:2–4, and John's experience of being "in the Spirit" (Rev. 1:10) are other examples of revelatory trances in the Bible.

In the Old Testament the word translated as blindness (Gen. 19:11; 2 Kin. 6:18) suggests that God caused a trancelike state to fall on the men at Lot's house and on the Syrians. Trances are experiences through which God communicates His will and purpose to man.

Also see VISION.

TRANSFIGURATION — a display of God's glory in the person of His Son, Jesus Christ (Matt. 17:1–8; Mark 9:2–8; Luke 9:28–36). Peter cites the Transfiguration as historical proof of the true gospel of Christ (2 Pet. 1:16–18).

It is hard to imagine what Jesus looked like when He was transfigured, or changed in form. The gospel writers speak of His face becoming bright like the sun, and of His clothes being dazzling white. Peter explains that God gave Him honor and glory (2 Pet. 1:17).

Moses and Elijah appeared also. Both of these were Old Testament figures who did not have a normal death and burial. Luke indicates they discussed Jesus' approaching death which He was going to accomplish at Jerusalem (Luke 9:31). Throughout his gospel, Luke emphasizes that Jerusalem was the city of destiny for Jesus, who carefully accomplished all that the Old Testament prophesied and all that God wanted him to do. Jesus was destined for the cross.

Peter offered to make three tabernacles—one for Jesus, one for Moses, and one for Elijah. He may have been thinking that the Jews would have a final great celebration of the Feast of Tabernacles when the Messiah came. However, this was not the time for that, because Jesus still had to endure the cross.

A cloud overshadowed Jesus during His Transfiguration. This has symbolic as well as historical significance. It is a subtle reminder of the Exodus and the appearance of God to Moses on Mount Sinai (Exodus 24), when God also spoke from a cloud. The Transfiguration occurred about a week after Peter's confession of Jesus as the Messiah at Caesarea Philippi; Moses had to wait on the Mount about that long. Both Moses and Jesus were accompanied by three companions on their respective experiences. The word decease (Luke 9:31; exodus, KJV) occurs in the conversation of Moses and Elijah. Thus the Old Testament Exodus points forward to Christ and His redeeming work.

At the same time, symbols of the SECOND COMING of Christ are also present in the Transfiguration account. Jesus will come with clouds and be revealed as God's chosen one. He will stand on a mountain, the Mount of Olives. The Feast of Tabernacles was associated in Jewish thinking with the return of the Messiah as well as with the journey in the wilderness after the Exodus. Moses gave the Law, yet also symbolized Jesus, the great prophet of the last days (Deut. 18:15). Elijah too, was expected by the Jews to come in the last days (Mal. 4:5-6). The Transfiguration calls to mind both God's redemption through the Exodus and the future return and glory of Christ, His Son.

The Transfiguration concludes with God's voice speaking from the cloud, which marked God's presence (Ex. 40:34-38). When the disciples heard that Jesus was God's beloved Son, the chosen one with whom He was well pleased, they probably remembered Psalm 2:7, Isaiah 42:1, and possibly Genesis 22:2. All Scripture focuses on the person of the Lord Jesus Christ.

In the Transfiguration God showed clearly that Jesus is His one and only Son, superior even to the two great Old Testament figures, Moses and Elijah. His disciples are to listen to Him. At the conclusion of the Transfiguration, no one is seen but Jesus. He alone is worthy.

TRANSFORM — to change radically in inner character, condition, or nature. In Romans 12:2 the apostle Paul exhorted Christians, "Do not be conformed to this world, but be transformed by the renewing of your mind." Followers of Christ should not be conformed, either inwardly or in appearance, to the values, ideals, and behavior of a fallen world. Believers should continually renew their minds through prayer and the study of God's Word, by the power of the Holy Spirit, and so be transformed and made like Christ (2 Cor. 3:18). When He returns, Christ will "transform our lowly body that it may be conformed to His glorious body" (Phil. 3:21).

In 2 Corinthians 11:13-15 Paul warned his readers to beware of "false apostles, deceitful workers, transforming themselves into apostles of Christ" (v. 13). One should not be surprised, said Paul, at such false apostles—people who are counterfeit and phony but who wear masks to deceive others—for "Satan himself transforms himself into an angel of light" (v. 14). Satan's workers, in imitation of their ruler, also disguise themselves as agents of good.

TRANSGRESSION — the violation of a law, command, or duty. The Hebrew word most often translated as transgression in the Old Testament means "revolt" or "rebellion." The psalmist wrote, "Blessed is he whose transgression is forgiven, whose sin is covered" (Ps. 32:1). In the New Testament every occurrence of the word transgression (NKJV) is a translation of a Greek word which means "a deliberate breach of the law" (Rom. 4:15; 1 Tim. 2:14; Heb. 2:2). Also see SIN.

TRANSJORDAN [trans JORE dahn] — a large plateau east of the Jordan River, the Dead Sea, and the Arabah. The term Transjordan is not used in the NKJV, KJV, or RSV, but the general area is often called "beyond the Jordan" (Gen. 50:10-11; Deut.

3:20; Judg. 5:17; Is. 9:1; Matt. 4:15; Mark 3:8). The KING'S HIGHWAY (Num. 20:17; 21:22) crossed the entire length of Transjordan from north to south.

Before the time of Joshua, Transjordan was made up of the kingdoms of AMMON, BASHAN, EDOM, GILEAD, and MOAB. After the conquest, this area was occupied by the tribes of REUBEN, GAD, and MANASSEH.

Also see DECAPOLIS; PEREA.

TRANSLATE, TRANSLATION — to remove a person or thing from one condition, place, or state to another. In the Bible, the word translation or the concept of translation is used in three senses: (1) the physical translation of Enoch (Gen. 5:24; Heb. 11:5) and Elijah (2 Kin. 2:11) to heaven without the intervening experience of death; (2) the spiritual translation of Christians in their present experience from "the power of darkness" into "the kingdom of the Son of His love" (Col. 1:13); and (3) the future, physical translation and transformation of Christians at the SECOND COMING of Christ (1 Cor. 15:51-57; Phil. 3:21; 1 Thess. 4:13-18).

Translation is a special act of God. It is permanent in its results; it occurs in response to faith; and it has heaven as its reward.

TRANSLITERATION — the process by which letters or words are spelled in the corresponding characters of another alphabet. For example, Hades is a transliteration of a Greek word meaning "the unseen world" (Matt. 11:23; Luke 10:15; Acts 2:27). Amen is the transliteration of a Hebrew word meaning "so be it" or "let it be so" (Num. 5:22).

TRAP — a mechanical device such as a snare with bait, a striker-bar, a net, or a noose usually laid on the ground in which animals, birds, and even human beings are caught (Job 18:9; Ps. 140:5; 141:9; Is. 8:14; Amos 3:5). Also see SNARE.

TRAPPER (see OCCUPATIONS AND TRADES).

TRAVAIL — physical or mental pain or anguish. Rachel travailed in childbirth, dying as she gave birth to Benjamin (Gen. 35:16-19). The prophet Isaiah spoke of the Suffering Servant: "He [God] shall see the labor of His soul, and be satisfied" (Is. 53:11). Our salvation has been secured through the pain and suffering of God's Son.

TRAVEL (see TRADE AND TRAVEL).

TREASURE, TREASURY — something of value; a place for storing valuables. In the Old Testament a treasure was described as something "laid aside," "possessed," or "hidden," and thus valuable (Gen. 43:23; Deut. 32:34). A treasury is a place to keep such valuables (Esth. 3:9; 4:7). A place where royal records are stored might, therefore, be called a "treasure house" (Ezra 5:17). Sometimes the term is used figuratively of the place where God keeps snow and hail (Job 38:22) or wind (Jer. 10:13; 51:16). Wisdom is called "hidden treasure" (Prov. 2:4).

The New Testament often uses the term literally to indicate something of value (Matt. 2:11). Or, it may be used in a figurative sense, as Jesus does to describe priorities as "treasures in heaven," (Matt. 6:19–21). The apostle Paul also uses the term figuratively to speak of Jesus as the one "in whom are hidden all the treasures of wisdom and knowledge" (Col. 2:3).

The Temple at Jerusalem had treasuries, or rooms, for storing various kinds of treasures (1 Kin. 7:51; 1 Chr. 28:11–12). In Jesus' day, Herod's Temple also had a treasury, where taxes and tithes were paid. Once Jesus sat opposite the treasury so he could see the rich and the poor putting in their contributions. He commended a poor widow for her contribution because she "put in all that she had, her whole livelihood" (Mark 12:44).

TREASURE CITY — KJV words for STORAGE CITY.

TREASURER (see OCCUPATIONS AND TRADES).

TREATY (see ALLIANCE; COVENANT).

TREE OF KNOWLEDGE — one of two special trees planted by God in the Garden of Eden. The other was the tree of life (Gen. 2:9). Since "the tree of the knowledge of good and evil" symbolized the all-powerful nature of God, its fruit was forbidden to Adam and Eve (Gen. 2:17). But the tempter suggested to them that, by adding to their knowledge, the tree's fruit would make them "as Gods" (Gen. 3:5). So they chose to disobey God. This act of rebellion marked the entrance of sin into the world.

The result was quite different than Adam and Eve expected. Instead of gaining superior knowledge that made them equal with God, they gained awareness or knowledge of their guilt, shame, and condemnation.

TREE OF LIFE — the tree in the Garden of Eden that bestowed continuing life (Gen. 2:9, 17; 3:1–24). Before Adam and Eve sinned, they had free access to the tree of life; after their act of rebellion, two CHERUBIM guarded the way to its fruit.

Adam and Eve's inability to eat from this tree after their sin showed that they failed to gain immortality, or eternal life. Because of their sin, they were subject to death and dying. This condition lasted until the coming of Jesus Christ, the second Adam, who offers eternal life to all who believe in Him (1 John 5:11–12).

TRESPASS — the violation of a law. The Hebrew word translated as trespass means "a stepping aside from the (correct) path" (Gen. 31:36; Ex. 22:9). In the New Testament trespass is often a translation of a Greek word which means "a falling aside" (Mark 11:25–26; Eph. 2:1, 5). The apostle Paul wrote: "God was in Christ reconciling the world to Himself, not imputing their trespasses to them" (2 Cor. 5:19). Also see SIN.

TRESPASS OFFERING (see SACRIFICIAL OFFERINGS).

TRIAL — a temptation or an adversity, the enduring of which proves the merit of an individual's faith. For the Christian, to encounter adversity is to undergo a trial in which his faith is proved either true or false before God, the highest judge. Since many positive things come about through such trials, Christians are urged to rejoice at their occurrence (James 1:2; 1 Pet. 4:13). Christ Himself set the example in how trials should be endured when He defeated Satan's temptations by appealing to the word and will of God (Luke 4:1–13).

TRIAL OF JESUS (see JESUS CHRIST).

TRIANGLE (see MUSICAL INSTRUMENTS).

TRIBE, TRIBES — a social group composed of many clans and families, together with their dependents, outside the ties of blood kinship, who had become associated with the group through covenant, marriage, adoption, or slavery. The nation of ancient Israel, especially at the time of the events recorded in the Book of Judges, was a tribal society (Numbers 1; 2; 26; Joshua 13—21; Judges 19—21). Several neighboring nations also were organized along tribal lines (Gen. 25:13–16).

Israel was an association of twelve tribes, designated by the names of the ancestors from whom they were descended (Deut. 27:12–13; Ezek. 48:1–35). The historical origins of the tribal units may be traced to the Book of Genesis. Jacob, whose name was later changed to Israel (Gen. 32:28), was the father of 12 sons (Gen. 29:31—30:24; 35:18, 22–26). The sons of Jacob, excluding Joseph but including Joseph's sons, Manasseh and Ephraim, were the ancestors of the later tribal units in the nation's history. The development of the tribes begins with the events described in the Book of Exodus.

The sons of Jacob, together with their father and families, migrated to Egypt to join their brother Joseph and to escape the famine in Canaan (Gen. 46:1–27; Ex. 1:16). They grew significantly in number for the next 400 years (Gen. 15:13; Ex. 12:40). Then the descendants of Jacob's sons left Egypt in the EXODUS under the leadership of Moses. They were joined by many who were not descendants of Jacob. The Exodus people are thus characterized as a "mixed multitude" (Ex. 12:38; Num. 11:4).

The number of dependents, those not of blood kinship, continued to increase as the tribal units developed. Moses' father-in-law, whose clan joined Israel in the wilderness, was a Midianite (Num. 10:29). Caleb, who figured prominently in the conquest of the land of Canaan, was called a Kenizzite (Josh. 14:13–14). Later the Calebites were given an inheritance among the tribe of Judah (Josh. 15:13).

The tribal confederation with its institutions reached its highest form during the period recorded in the books of Joshua and Judges. The rigidity of Israel's tribal structure did weaken somewhat with the establishment of the United Kingdom under David and Solomon. But tribal organization and association was maintained throughout later biblical history (Luke 2:36; Acts 4:36; Rom. 11:1; Heb. 7:14).

TRIBULATION — great adversity and anguish; intense oppression or persecution. Tribulation is linked to God's process for making the world right again. His Son underwent great suffering, just as His people undergo a great deal of tribulation from the world (Rom. 5:3; Acts 14:22). This tribulation has its source in the conflict between God and the devil (Gen. 3:15) which will end with the devil being cast into the lake of fire to suffer eternal tribulation (Rev. 20:10). Also see TRIBULATION, THE GREAT.

TRIBULATION, THE GREAT — a short but intense period of distress and suffering at the end of time. The exact phrase, *the great tribulation*, is found only once in the Bible (Rev. 7:14). The great tribulation is to be distinguished from the general tribulation a believer faces in the world (Matt. 13:21; John 16:33; Acts 14:22). It is also to be distinguished from God's specific wrath upon the unbelieving world at the end of the age (Mark 13:24; Rom. 2:5–10; 2 Thess. 1:6).

The great tribulation fulfills Daniel's prophecies (Daniel 7—12). It will be a time of evil from false christs and false prophets (Mark 13:22) when natural disasters will occur throughout the world.

Also see ANTICHRIST; MILLENNIUM.

TRIBUTE — a compulsory fee or financial contribution levied on an inferior by a superior ruler or nation. Before the establishment of the United Kingdom under David and Solomon, the judge Ehud brought tribute money to Eglon, the king of Moab (Judg. 3:15–18). During the time of the United Kingdom, Israel was strong and received tribute. David received tribute from Moab and Syria (2 Sam. 8:2, 6; 1 Chr. 18:2, 6), and Solomon accepted tribute from "all kingdoms from the River [Euphrates] to the land of the Philistines, as far as the border of Egypt" (1 Kin. 4:21).

After the division of the kingdom in 931 B.C., King Ahab of the northern kingdom of Israel received tribute from the king of Moab (2 Kin. 3:4–5). In the southern kingdom of Judah, Jehoshaphat received tribute from the Philistines and the Arabians (2 Chr. 17:11). Uzziah also forced the Ammonites to pay tribute to Judah (2 Chr. 26:8).

Even more is reported in the Bible about Israel and Judah paying tribute to foreign nations. Israel's king Jehoash paid tribute to Hazael of Syria to prevent attack (2 Kin. 12:17–18). Hoshea paid tribute to Shalmaneser of Assyria (2 Kin. 17:3). Judah's King Ahaz sent tribute to Tiglath–Pileser III of Assyria (2 Kin. 16:7–8). King Hezekiah paid tribute to Sennacherib of Assyria (2 Kin. 18:13–16). Jehoiakim paid tribute to Pharaoh Necho of Egypt just before Judah was captured by Babylon (2 Kin. 23:33–35). Although Israel was supposed to depend only on God for protection, the nation occasionally depended on foreign kings, paying heavily in tribute.

TRIBUTE MONEY (see MONEY OF THE BIBLE).

TRIFLES — rich, sweet desserts, usually fruit cakes topped with jam and soaked in wine (Prov. 18:8; 26:22; choice morsels, NIV; dainty morsels, NASB; delicious morsels, RSV).

TRIGON (see MUSICAL INSTRUMENTS).

TRIMMERS (see WICK–TRIMMER).

TRINITY — the coexistence of the Father, the Son, and the Holy Spirit in the unity of the Godhead (divine nature or essence). The doctrine of the trinity means that within the being and activity of the one God there are three distinct persons: Father, Son, and Holy Spirit. Although the word trinity does not appear in the Bible, the "trinitarian formula" is mentioned in the Great Commission (Matt. 28:19) and in the benediction of the apostle Paul's Second Epistle to the Corinthians (2 Cor. 13:14).

God revealed Himself as one to the Israelites: "Hear, O Israel: The Lord our God, the Lord is one!" (Deut. 6:4). This was a significant religious truth because the surrounding nations worshiped many Gods and had fallen into idolatry, worshiping the creation rather than the true Creator (Rom. 1:18–25). "But when the fullness of the time had come," Paul wrote (Gal. 4:4), "God sent forth His Son, born of a woman, born under the law." In the New Testament God revealed that He is not only one but a family of persons—an eternal, inexhaustible, and dynamic triune family of Father, Son, and Holy Spirit, who are one in will and purpose, love and righteousness.

The relationship of Father and Son is prominent in the gospels because Jesus, the eternal Son who takes on human flesh, is most visible to us as He strikes a responsive chord through the Father–Son relationship. All the while the Holy Spirit is in the background, serving as our eyes of faith. The unity of Father, Son, and Holy Spirit is portrayed by Jesus' trinitarian teaching (John 14—16). This truth is expressed in the total ministry of Jesus as recorded in all four gospels as well as in the rest of the New Testament. The triune family cooperates as one in bringing the lost person home again into a redeemed family of believers.

The most distinctive characteristic of the persons of the triune family is their selfless love for one another. Each esteems and defers to the other in a way that makes the original family of the trinity a model for the Christian family of believers in the church.

The Father gives all authority to the Son and bears witness to Him, as does Jesus to Himself (John 8:18). Yet the Son claims nothing for Himself; He gives all glory to the Father who has sent Him (John 12:49–50). The key to unlocking the mystery of the trinity is to observe how the persons of the triune family give themselves to one another in selfless love. They are always at one another's disposal.

The Father serves the Son; the Son serves the Father; Father and Son defer to the Holy Spirit, who in turn, serves and defers to the Father and Son in a oneness that is eternally dynamic and inexhaustible. The mutual love of the triune persons spills over into the creation and is seen in their generous cooperation in saving the lost (John 14:15-17, 25-26).

Since God is the original family-in-unity, so Christians are urged by Jesus and the apostles to imitate the divine family in the believing fellowship, as Jesus taught so clearly when He washed the disciples' feet (John 13:14-15). The principal trait of the triune family is speaking the truth in love; this encourages a spirit of generosity among Christians as they reflect the divine family in calling the lost to come home.

The trinity was at work in the incarnation of Jesus, the Son of the Most High, as He was conceived in the womb of Mary by the power of the Holy Spirit (Luke 1:30-35). At His baptism Jesus the Son received approval from the Father in the presence of the Holy Spirit (Luke 3:21-22), fulfilling two Old Testament prophetic passages (Ps. 2:7; Is. 42:1). The trinity was also present in the temptation, as Jesus, full of the Holy Spirit, was led by the Spirit for 40 days in the wilderness. The devil recognized Jesus as the Son of God (Luke 4:3), but he tried to destroy the faithful relationship of the divine family.

In His preaching in the synagogue at Nazareth Jesus fulfilled Isaiah 61:1-2, claiming that "the Spirit of the Lord is upon Me" (Luke 4:18) and indicating that the triune family was at work in Him as the servant Son. At the transfiguration, the voice of the Father spoke again in approval of Jesus the Son to the innermost circle of disciples (Luke 9:35).

Jesus rejoiced in the Holy Spirit and in the Father who had delivered all things to the Son (Luke 10:21-22). He claimed to be acting in the place of God and through the power of the Holy Spirit, who is the "finger" of God (Matt. 12:28; Luke 11:20). Jesus' cleansing of the Temple was a claim of identification with the house of God His Father (Luke 19:45-46) that paralleled His concern for being in His Father's house at a much younger age (Luke 2:41-51).

Jesus witnessed further to His authority as He sent forth the disciples, following His resurrection, with the words, "Behold, I send the promise of My Father upon you" (Luke 24:49). He also told them to wait until they were empowered by the Holy Spirit (Acts 1:5, 8). Jesus claimed His Sonship not only from David but from David's Lord (Matt. 22:42-45), indicating His deity.

Following His resurrection, Jesus sent the disciples to baptize "in the name of the Father and of the Son and of the Holy Spirit" (Matt. 28:19). The fulfillment of Jesus' prophecy as spokesman for the Father and the Holy Spirit (Acts 1:4-8) occurred at Pentecost. This continued throughout the Book of Acts when the Holy Spirit inspired Peter and the apostles to preach a trinitarian gospel of Father, Son, and Holy Spirit (Acts 2:32-33; 5:29-32; 10:38).

Paul wrote from a sense of the triune family in Galatians, speaking often of Father, Son, and Holy Spirit (Gal. 3:13-14; 4:6; 5:5-6, 22-24). In Romans he used a threefold, trinitarian pattern to describe the plan of salvation (Rom. 1:18—3:20; 3:21—8:1; 8:2-30). All the remaining New Testament books contain trinity teaching except James and 3 John.

The triune family is God's revelation of Himself as the ultimate truth about reality. This family is the original pattern from which God creates all the families of earth with their unity and diversity. The family of mankind, after losing its intimate relationship with the divine family at the Fall, is restored to fellowship by God's action. This happens when its members acknowledge the generosity originating in the Father, expressed by the Son, and energized by the Holy Spirit.

TRIUMPH — the joy or exultation of victory. In the Bible the word triumph usually refers to God's triumph—in the Old Testament His triumph over Israel's enemies and in the New Testament His victory through Christ on the cross. Examples of God's triumph over Israel's enemies include the song of Moses (Ex. 15:1) and the song of Miriam (Ex. 15:21). In the Old Testament the word triumph is found most often in the Book of Psalms (25:2; 60:8; 108:9).

In the New Testament the Greek verb which means "to make a show or spectacle of" is twice translated as triumph (2 Cor. 2:14; Col. 2:15). The figure of speech is drawn from the ceremony that greeted a Roman general who had won a decisive victory over a foreign enemy. This ceremony usually featured a display of captives and spoil following the general's chariot.

The apostle Paul used such a triumphal procession as an analogy of Christ's victory on the cross. By His triumph He conquered supernatural foes and "made a public spectacle of them" (Col. 2:15). Through Christ we also can claim the victory: "Now thanks be to God who always leads us in triumph in Christ" (2 Cor. 2:14).

TROAS [TROW as] (*the region around Troy*) — an important city on the coast of Mysia (see Map 7, C-2), in northwest Asia Minor (modern Turkey), visited at least three times by the apostle Paul (Acts 16:8, 11; 20:5-6; 2 Cor. 2:12; 2 Tim. 4:13). Troas was situated about 16 kilometers (ten miles) southwest of Hissarlik, the ruins of ancient Troy.

At Troas, on his second missionary journey, the apostle Paul saw a vision of a "man of Macedonia" inviting him to preach the gospel of Christ in Europe (Acts 16:8-9). After ministering in Greece (Acts 20:2), Paul returned to Troas. Here he restored to life a young man named Eutychus, who had fallen from a third-story window while Paul preached late into the night (Acts 20:5-12).

The ruins of Troas extend over many miles. The city walls, about ten kilometers (six miles) in length, can still be traced. Remains of a stadium, baths, and a harbor are also still visible.

TROGYLLIUM [troe JIL ee uhm] (meaning unknown) — a city near the foot of Mount Mycale opposite the island of Samos in Caria. The apostle

Photo by Howard Vos

Ruins of Roman baths at Troas—the city where Paul received a vision to evangelize Macedonia (Acts 16:6-10).

Paul stayed at Trogyllium on his return to Jerusalem after his third missionary journey (Acts 20:15). Trogyllium was about 32 kilometers (20 miles) south of Ephesus.

TROPHIMUS [TROF ih muss] (*nourishing*) — a Gentile Christian who lived in Ephesus and who accompanied the apostle Paul to Jerusalem at the end of Paul's third missionary journey (Acts 20:4). When certain Jews from Asia saw Trophimus the Ephesian with Paul in Jerusalem, they supposed that Paul had brought "Greeks" (uncircumcised Gentiles) into the Court of Israel (an inner court beyond the Court of the Gentiles), defiling the Temple (Acts 21:28–29).

The people seized Paul, dragged him out of the Temple, and tried to kill him. But Paul was rescued by the commander of the Roman garrison and sent to Rome for trial. Apparently Trophimus accompanied Paul on the trip toward Rome. In his Second Epistle to Timothy, Paul revealed, "Trophimus I have left in Miletus sick" (2 Tim. 4:20).

TROUSERS — a distinctive item of dress worn by the priests of the nation of Israel. These trousers were similar to a loin cloth which covered their hips and thighs (Ex. 28:32). Other versions translate the Hebrew word as breeches and girdle. Also see PRIEST; PRIEST, HIGH.

TRUMPET (see MUSICAL INSTRUMENTS).

TRUMPETS, FEAST OF (see FEASTS AND FESTIVALS).

TRUSTEE (see OCCUPATIONS AND TRADES).

TRUTH — conformity to fact or actuality; faithfulness to an original or to a standard.

In the Old and New Testaments, truth is a fundamental moral and personal quality of God. God proclaimed that He is "merciful and gracious, longsuffering, and abounding in goodness and truth" (Ex. 34:6). He is a "God of truth...without injustice" (Deut. 32:4). Furthermore, all of His paths are "mercy and truth" (Ps. 25:10). Frequently in the psalms, God's mercy and His truth are joined together (Ps. 57:3; 89:14; 115:1). All of God's works, precepts, and judgments are done in righteousness and truth (Ps. 96:13; 111:8).

Truth is a moral and personal characteristic of God: He is "the God of truth" (Is. 65:16). The psalmist declared, "Your law is truth" (119:142), "all Your commandments are truth" (119:151), and "the entirety of Your word is truth" (119:160). Because of His perfect nature and will, God has to speak and act in truth; He cannot lie (1 Sam. 15:29; Heb. 6:18; James 1:17–18).

Jesus is the Word of God who became flesh, "the only begotten of the Father, full of grace and truth" (John 1:14). All Jesus said was true, because He told the truth which He heard from God (John 8:40). He promised His disciples that He would send "the Spirit of truth" (John 14:17; 15:26; 16:13)—a Helper who would abide in Christians forever (John 14:16), testify about Jesus (John 15:26), guide Christians into all truth (John 16:13), and glorify Jesus (John 16:14).

God is truth; the Spirit is truth; and Jesus is truth. Jesus said, "I am the way, the truth, and the life. No one comes to the Father except through Me" (John 14:6). Jesus and the revelation which the Spirit of truth gave through His apostles are the final, ultimate revelation and definition of truth about God, man, redemption, history, and the world. "The law was given through Moses, but grace and truth came through Jesus Christ" (John 1:17).

TRYPHAENA [trigh FEE nuh] — a form of TRY-PHENA.

TRYPHENA [trigh FEE nuh] (*dainty*) — a woman at Rome to whom the apostle Paul sent greetings (Rom. 16:12; Tryphaena, RSV, NEB, NASB). Tryphena is mentioned with another woman, Tryphosa. They may have been sisters, twins, or perhaps fellow deaconesses. Paul described them as women "who have labored in the Lord." Also see TRYPHOSA.

TRYPHOSA [trigh FOE suh] (*delicate*) — a woman in Rome to whom the apostle Paul sent greetings (Rom. 16:12), along with another woman, TRY-PHENA.

TSADDE [SOD dy] — the 18th letter of the Hebrew alphabet, used as a heading over Psalm 119:137–144. In the original Hebrew language, every line of these eight verses began with the letter tsadde. Also see ACROSTIC.

TUBAL [TOO buhl] (meaning unknown) — the name of a man and a country or people in the Old Testament:
1. The fifth son of Japheth and grandson of Noah (Gen. 10:2; 1 Chr. 1:5).
2. A people who lived in the Cappadocian region of eastern Asia Minor (modern Turkey). The prophet Isaiah mentions Tubal along with JAVAN (Is. 66:19), and Ezekiel mentions Tubal, Javan, and MESHECH as some of those who traded with Tyre (Ezek. 27:13).

TUBAL–CAIN [too buhl KANE] (*the smith*) — a son of Lamech and Zillah. Tubal–Cain was the "father" of all metalworkers (Gen. 4:22).

TUMOR (see DISEASES OF THE BIBLE).

TUNIC (see DRESS OF THE BIBLE).

TUNNEL — an underground passage. King Hezekiah of Judah stopped the water outlet of Upper Gihon, thereby making a pool, and brought the water of this pool by tunnel to the west side of Jerusalem (2 Kin. 20:20; 2 Chr. 32:30).
Also see HEZEKIAH'S TUNNEL.

TURBAN — a long piece of linen cloth wound around the head and fastened in the back to form a type of headdress worn by Hebrew men in Bible times (Job 29:14). Such a turban was a distinctive form of headdress worn by the priests of the nation of Israel (Ex. 28:39). The Hebrew word for turban is rendered as tire, bonnet, and mitre by some English translations of the Bible. Also see DRESS OF THE BIBLE.

TURQUOISE (see JEWELS AND PRECIOUS STONES).

TURTLE, TURTLEDOVE (see ANIMALS OF THE BIBLE).

TUSK — a long tooth, usually one of a pair, which extends outside the mouth of certain animals, such as the elephant, walrus, or wild boar. The merchants of Tyre received ivory tusks and ebony as payment for their wares (Ezek. 27:15; horns of ivory, KJV).

TUTOR — a trusted slave among wealthy Greek and Roman families whose responsibility was to supervise their son's activities, acting as his guide and guardian. When the boy reached 16 he was considered to be of age and no longer needed his tutor.
The apostle Paul compared the law to a tutor, because it guided people to Christ (Gal. 3:24–25; schoolmaster, KJV; custodian, RSV). Until Christ came the law confined us and kept us in custody. But when Christ came, we attained the freedom and maturity of faith. Those who live under the law thus have an inferior status to those who live by faith—"for the law was given through Moses, but grace and truth came through Jesus Christ" (John 1:17).

TWELVE (see NUMBER).

TWELVE, THE — a term for the band of Jesus' closest disciples (Mark 4:10). Early in His ministry Jesus selected 12 of His followers and named them "apostles" (Luke 6:12–16). They are also referred to as the "twelve disciples" (Matt. 10:1). Jesus appointed them to travel with Him, preach, heal, and cast out demons (Mark 3:14–15).
Although the terms disciple and apostle may refer to someone other than one of the Twelve (John 8:31; 1 Cor. 15:9), the Twelve appears to be a term restricted to the original dozen selected by Jesus, and to Matthias who took the place of Judas (Acts 1:15–26). There was a symbolic significance to the Twelve, similar to that of the twelve children of Israel (1 Cor. 15:5; Rev. 21:14), whose descendants became the twelve tribes of the Hebrew nation.

TWIN BROTHERS, THE — the figurehead of an Alexandrian ship which took the apostle Paul from Malta to Puteoli (Acts 28:11). In Greek mythology, Castor and Polydeuces (Latin *Pollux*) were sons of Zeus and Leda; they were protectors of sailors and were hostile to pirates. The Greek word translated "the Twin Brothers," or "Castor and Pollux" (KJV), is *dioskourois* (from *dios kouroi*, "sons of Zeus"). The Dioscuri were identified with the constellation Gemini (the Twins), which is the third sign of the Zodiac. Castor and Pollux, the Twin Brothers, are the brightest stars of this constellation. Also see GODS, PAGAN.

TWO (see NUMBER).

TYCHICUS [TIKE ih kuhs] (*fortuitous*) — a Christian of the province of ASIA (Acts 20:4). Tychicus was a faithful friend, fellow worker, and messenger of the apostle Paul (Eph. 6:21–22; Col. 4:7–8). Along with other disciples, Tychicus traveled ahead of Paul from Macedonia to Troas, where he waited for the apostle's arrival (Acts 20:4).
Paul also sent Tychicus to Ephesus to deliver and

Roman ruins at the ancient city of Tyre, with buildings of the modern city in the background.   Photo by Bernice Johnso

perhaps to read his epistle to the Christians in that city (Eph. 6:21). He did the same with the Epistle to the Colossians (Co. 4:7). Paul sent him as a messenger to Titus in Crete (Titus 3:12) and afterward to Ephesus (2 Tim. 4:12).

TYPE — a figure, representation, or symbol of something to come, as an event in the Old Testament foreshadows another in the New Testament. Types generally find their fulfillment in the person and ministry of Christ, but they sometimes relate to God, His people, or some other reality.

Scholars using typology range over a wide spectrum of interpretation. On the one extreme is that method which makes practically every item in the Old Testament find a greater fulfillment in the New Testament. At the other extreme are those scholars who insist on the word type being explicitly mentioned in the New Testament before they recognize any Old Testament type. Between those extremes, many scholars feel that there are some Old Testament correspondences to New Testament truths which are indeed typical, although the word type is not specifically used.

For instance, Melchizedek, the king–priest of Salem (Gen. 14:18–20 and Ps. 110:4) is said to be typical of Christ (Heb. 6:20). Jesus said the brazen serpent in the wilderness (Num. 21:4–9) was in some sense typical of His own crucifixion (John 3:14–15). The writer of Hebrews (Hebrews 9—10) pointed out that the tabernacle typically foreshadowed the person and work of Jesus Christ.

The NKJV uses the word type in only one place; in Romans 5:14 the apostle Paul mentions Adam as "a type of Him [Jesus] who was to come" (pattern, NIV).

Also see ANTITYPE.

TYRANNUS [tigh RAN uhs] (*a tyrant*) — a man of Ephesus who owned a school or lecture hall at which the apostle Paul reasoned daily for two years (Acts 19:9–10). Tyrannus was either a teacher of rhetoric and philosophy or a Jewish rabbi who taught the law in his private synagogue. He allowed Paul to speak of Jesus so that people from throughout the province of Asia heard of Him.

TYRE [tire] (*a rock*) — an ancient seaport city of the Phoenicians situated north of Palestine (see Map 3, B–1). Tyre was the principal seaport of the Phoenician coast, about 40 kilometers (25 miles) south of Sidon and 56 kilometers (35 miles) north of Carmel. It consisted of two cities: a rocky coastal city on the mainland and a small island city. The island city was just off the shore. The mainland city was on a coastal plain, a strip only 24 kilometers (15 miles) long and 3 kilometers (2 miles) wide.

Behind the plain of Tyre stood the rocky mountains of Lebanon. Tyre was easily defended because it had the sea on the west, the mountains on the east, and several other rocky cliffs (one the famous "Ladder of Tyre") around it, making it difficult to invade.

History. Tyre was an ancient city. According to one tradition, it was founded about 2750 B.C. However, SIDON—Tyre's sister city—was probably older (Gen. 10:15), perhaps even the mother city (Is. 23:2, 12). The Greek poet Homer mentioned "Sidonian wares," without reference to Tyre. This seems to confirm that Sidon was older. About 1400 B.C. Sidon successfully besieged the city of Tyre and maintained supremacy over it. However, when sea raiders left Sidon in ruins about 1200 B.C., many people migrated to Tyre. The increasing greatness of Tyre over Sidon, and its closer location to Israel, caused the order of mentioning Tyre first and then Sidon to be established by biblical writers (Jer. 47:4; Mark 3:8).

The period from 1200 to 870 B.C. was largely one of independence for Phoenicia. This enabled Tyre to realize her expansionist dreams. Hiram I, the ruler of Tyre (980–947 B.C.), apparently began a colony at Tarshish in Spain. He fortified Tyre's two harbors, one on the north of the city and one on the south. Tyrian ships began to dominate Mediterranean commerce. Their merchants were princes, the honorable of the earth (Is. 23:8). In the ninth century B.C. a colony from Tyre founded the city of Carthage on the north coast of Africa.

The most celebrated product of Tyrian commerce was the famous purple dye made from mollusks found on the shores near Tyre. This dye became a source of great wealth for Tyrians. In addition they produced metal work and glassware, shipping their products to and buying wares from peoples in remote parts of the earth (1 Kin. 9:28).

Friendly relations existed between the Hebrews and the Tyrians. Hiram was on excellent terms with both David and Solomon, aiding them with materials for the building of David's palace (1 Kin. 5:1; 1 Chr. 14:1), Solomon's Temple, and other buildings (1 Kin. 4:1; 9:10–14; 2 Chr. 2:3, 11). Hiram and Solomon engaged in joint commercial ventures (1 Kin. 9:26–28).

The dynasty of Hiram came to an end early in the ninth century B.C. when a priest named Ethbaal revolted and assumed the throne. Still, cordial relations between the Tyrians and Israelites continued. Ethbaal's daughter Jezebel married Ahab of Israel (1 Kin. 16:31). From this union Baal worship and other idolatrous practices were introduced into Israel.

While the people of Tyre were mostly interested in sea voyages, colonization, manufacturing, and commerce, they were frequently forced into war. Phoenician independence ended with the reign of Ashurnasirpal II (883–859 B.C.) of Assyria. More than a century later Shalmaneser IV laid siege to Tyre and it fell to his successor, Sargon. With the decline of Assyria after the middle of the seventh century B.C. Tyre again prospered.

Tyre in Prophecy. Several prophets of the Old Testament prophesied against Tyre. They condemned the Tyrians for delivering Israelites to the Edomites (Amos 1:9) and for selling them as slaves to the Greeks (Joel 3:5–6). Jeremiah prophesied Tyre's defeat (Jer. 27:1–11). But the classic prophecy against Tyre was given by Ezekiel.

Ezekiel prophesied the destruction of Tyre (Ezek. 26:3–21). The first stage of this prophecy came true when Nebuchadnezzar, king of Babylon, besieged the mainland city of Tyre for 13 years (585–572 B.C.) and apparently destroyed it. However, Nebuchadnezzar had no navy; so he could not flatten the island city. But losing the mainland city was devastating to Tyre. This destroyed Tyre's influence in the world and reduced her commercial activities severely.

The second stage of Ezekiel's prophecy was fulfilled in 332 B.C., when Alexander the Great besieged the island city of Tyre for seven months. He finally captured it when he built a causeway from the mainland to the island. Hauling cedars from the mountains of Lebanon, he drove them as piles into the floor of the sea between the mainland and the island. Then he used the debris and timber of the ruined mainland city as solid material for the causeway. Hence, the remarkable prophecy of Ezekiel was completely fulfilled.

Tyre in the New Testament. During the Roman period Tyre again was rebuilt, eventually achieving a degree of prosperity. A Roman colony was established at the city. Herod I rebuilt the main temple, which would have been standing when Jesus visited the coasts of Tyre and Sidon (Matt. 15:21–28; Mark 7:24–31). People of Tyre listened to Jesus as He taught (Mark 3:8; Luke 6:17). The Lord Jesus even cited Tyre as a heathen city that would bear less judgment than the Galilaean towns in which He had invested so much of His ministry (Matt. 11:21–22; Luke 10:13–14).

In the New Testament period a Christian community flourished at Tyre. At the close of Paul's third missionary journey he stopped at Tyre and stayed with the believers there for a week (Acts 21:1–7).

TYROPOEON VALLEY [tie ROW pih un] (*valley of the cheesemakers*) — a small valley in the city of Jerusalem which divides the hill of Ophel—site of the original City of David—from the site known as the Western Hill, or Upper City. This valley, not mentioned by name in the Bible, exists today only as a slight depression because it has been filled in by debris and waste throughout the centuries.

U

UCAL [YOU cal] (meaning unknown) — an unknown person to whom Agur addressed his proverbs along with Ithiel (Prov. 30:1). Some scholars, however, do not believe Ithiel and Ucal are proper names. Therefore, "to Ithiel—to Ithiel and Ucal" (Prov. 30:1, NKJV) becomes "I am weary, O God, I am weary and worn out" (NEB).

UEL [YOU ehl] (*will of God*) — a son of Bani who married a pagan wife and then divorced her after the Captivity (Ezra 10:34).

UGARIT [YOU guh rit] — an ancient Canaanite city (modern RAS SHAMRA) in northern Syria. Ugarit was situated about 40 kilometers (25 miles) southwest of Antioch, about one–half mile from the Mediterranean Sea and directly east of the island of Cyprus. Although Ugarit is not mentioned in the Bible, it is important to Bible students because of the archaeological discoveries made at this site.

The excavation of Ugarit began in 1929 under the direction of Claude F. A. Schaeffer. Although interrupted by World War II, the excavation resumed in 1948. These excavations reveal that the city of Ugarit reached the height of its importance between the time of Abraham and David (2000 to 1000 B.C.).

The discoveries at Ugarit have had a great impact on the understanding of the Old Testament. The language of Ugarit is similar to biblical Hebrew. The Ugaritic myths describe the false religion of Baal that the prophets of Israel condemned. Several of the religious institutions in Ugarit are similar to those found in the Bible.

These details are known because the archaeologists discovered a library containing a large number of clay tablets written in several ancient Near Eastern languages. The texts in the Ugaritic language contain many words, grammatical forms, and idioms which are common to the Hebrew language.

Entrance to Ras Shamra, the ancient city of Ugarit, in northern Syria. Clay tablets discovered at Ugarit have helped scholars understand the religious practices of the ancient Canaanites.

Photo by Gustav Jeeninga

The poetic texts are especially similar to the style and imagery of the Book of Psalms.

One of the Ugaritic texts is a myth about the struggles of the gods to gain control of the earth. Mot, the god of death and the dry season, struggles with Baal, the god of life and the wet season. The Baal worshiper hoped to encourage Baal to bless his crops with rain and fertility by offering sacrifices to Baal and by his involvement with the sacred prostitutes at the Baal temples and high places. The drought that God sent during the time of Elijah (1 Kin. 17:1, 7) proved that the God of Israel, not Baal, was in charge of fertility and rain. Later Elijah prayed and God sent the rain (1 Kin. 18:41–45). This false religion was especially encouraged by Ahab and Jezebel who built an altar and temple for Baal in Samaria (1 Kin. 16:29–33), and Athaliah and Manasseh who built altars to Baal in Jerusalem (2 Kin. 11:13–20; 21:1–4).

The prophets condemned the Israelites for their worship of Baal, but the Israelites never listened. God destroyed both Israel (2 Kin. 17:1–20) and Judah (2 Chr. 36:9–21) because of their sinful worship of this false god.

UKNAZ [UHK naz] — the marginal reading of 1 Chronicles 4:15 (KJV; Kenaz, NKJV). Also see KENAZ.

ULAI [YOU lie] (meaning unknown) — a wide, artificial irrigation canal near SHUSHAN (Susa), a winter capital of the Persians. The classical Greek writers called it Eulaeus, and it is known today as Karun. Some scholars, however, are skeptical of a positive identification because of centuries of erosion and shifting of the waterways. On the banks of the River Ulai the prophet Daniel received his vision of the ram and the male goat (Dan. 8:2, 16).

ULAM [YOU lamm] (*leader*) — the name of two men in the Old Testament:

1. A son of Sheresh, of the tribe of Manasseh (1 Chr. 7:16–17).

2. A son of Eshek, of the tribe of Benjamin (1 Chr. 8:39). The sons of Ulam were "mighty men of valor—archers" (1 Chr. 8:40).

ULCER (see DISEASES OF THE BIBLE).

ULLA [UHL uh] (*burden, yoke*) — a descendant of Asher who became the father of three tribal leaders: Arah, Haniel, and Rizia (1 Chr. 7:39).

UMMAH [UHM uh] (*kindred*) — a city in the territory allotted to the tribe of Asher, near Aphek and Rehob (Josh. 19:30).

UNBELIEF — lack of belief or faith in God and His provision. While unbelief does not hinder God's faithfulness (Rom. 3:3), it does affect the individual's capacity to receive the benefits of that faithfulness. The unbelief of many Israelites, for example, kept them from seeing the Promised Land (Heb. 3:19). The unbelief of the Nazarenes prevented them from witnessing Christ's miracles (Matt. 13:58). The skeptic is limited in what he

might see or know, while "all things are possible to him who believes" (Mark 9:23).

UNCHASTITY (see ADULTERY; FORNICATION).

UNCIRCUMCISED — a word with several different meanings in the Bible:

1. Not circumcised; a man who has not gone through the Jewish rite of CIRCUMCISION.

2. Not Jewish; Gentile (Ex. 12:48).

3. Spiritually impure; a heathen; one who has closed his ears and heart to God's call (Acts 7:51).

The issue is not whether a man has been circumcised but whether he has faith in Christ (1 Cor. 7:18–19).

UNCLE — the brother of a person's father or mother. In Hebrew society, an uncle could redeem a nephew who had sold himself into slavery, because of poverty, to a stranger or sojourner (Lev. 25:49). Uncles mentioned in the Bible include Laban, uncle of Jacob (Gen. 24:29); Abner, uncle of Saul (1 Sam. 10:14–16); and Abraham, uncle of Lot (Gen. 11:27, 31). Also see FAMILY.

UNCLEAN, UNCLEANNESS — to be defiled, foul, unfit. To be unclean refers to foods that are unfit, to defilement of a moral or religious character, and to spiritual impurity. The Old Testament distinguishes between what is clean and helpful and what is unclean and unacceptable (Lev. 10:10; 11:47). The priest was to teach the people the difference (Ezek. 44:23).

The teaching about uncleanness springs from the concept of God's holiness (Lev. 11:44–45). Freedom from uncleanness and guilt is possible through God's gracious work (Ps. 51:7). Holiness within, purity of heart, is possible through the exercise of faith in Christ's redemption (Titus 2:41; Pet. 1:2) and obedience to His word of truth (John 15:3; 17:17; 1 Pet. 1:22).

There were different kinds of uncleanness. One type was unclean food. Several kinds of birds—such as ravens and vultures—and certain animals—such as swine, camels, and hares—were labeled unclean (Lev. 11:1–19). Besides foods, persons were designated unclean under certain conditions. Through a discharge or because of menstruation, men and women were considered unclean (Lev. 15:2–13, 19–24). Puss-type body emissions from open sores also rendered the person unclean. A leprous person was unclean (Lev. 13:11).

Serious uncleanness was connected with dead bodies, including both humans and animals (Lev. 11:25–31). Anything on which a dead thing fell would become unclean (Lev. 11:32). Severe defilement came from a dead human body: "He who touches the dead body of anyone shall be unclean seven days" (Num. 19:11). Indeed, when a person died in a tent, the whole tent was regarded as unclean (Num. 19:14). To be unclean was to be disqualified for divine worship.

The land could be defiled through idolatry (Ezek. 36:18) or through the sacrifice of innocent children (Ps. 106:38). God's Temple was defiled be-

Photo by Amikam Shoob

The law of Moses made clear distinctions between clean and unclean animals. The vulture was considered unclean because it was a scavenger (Lev. 11:13).

cause of the entry of pagans (Ps. 79:1). The prophet Haggai used the notion of uncleanness of things to speak of immoral behavior of people (Hag. 2:13–14).

In the gospels, the word unclean describes those who are possessed by undesirable or even demonic spirits. Jesus exercised command over these unclean spirits (Luke 4:36) and effectively rebuked them (Luke 9:42). The disciples were also given power over unclean spirits (Mark 6:7; Acts 5:16). Jesus often cast out unclean spirits (Mark 1:23, 26–27; 5:2).

The word defilement described a sinful and unfit condition (Is. 6:5). Because of sin, "we are all like an unclean thing" (Is. 64:6). The New Testament lists uncleanness or moral defilement along with fornication and other sins, such as covetousness, as works of the flesh (Gal. 5:19; Col. 3:5). Believers are not called to uncleanness, but they are to live in holiness (1 Thess. 4:7). They are not to yield their members to uncleanness but to righteousness and holiness (Rom. 6:19).

Unclean things and people can be purified. Temple articles were purified through sprinkling of blood (Lev. 16:19). For those who touched dead bodies, washing with water provided cleansing (Lev. 15:27). Sprinkling with hyssop and water made clean the tent in which someone had died (Num. 19:18). For a woman with an issue of blood, a priest could offer sacrifice and make atonement (Lev. 15:30).

The uncleanness of sin to which the prophet Isaiah referred (Is. 6:5) is an uncleanness that is removed through God's actions. To Isaiah's lips the angel applied coals of fire and said, "Your iniquity is taken away" (Is. 6:6). John explained that the blood of Jesus Christ, God's Son, cleanses us from the defilement of sin (1 John 1:7). God fully provides for the cleansing of that which is unclean.

UNLEAVENED BREAD, FEAST OF

The reason why food and other things were designated unclean is not always fully clear. But there was a connection between the regulations about uncleanness and God's holiness. Following the list of unclean foods, God declared, "You shall be holy; for I am holy" (Lev. 11:44).

The great concern for dead things causing uncleanness may point to the notion that dead things were the very opposite of God. He is the living God. Death and dead things are opposite to who God is and what He desires. Thus, to be in contact with dead bodies was to be defiled. The human corpse represents an absence of life, and thus an absence of God. The laws about uncleanness are a powerful statement of the living God of the universe. Those made clean through His provision, however, will enjoy eternal life.

UNCLEAN DEMON, UNCLEAN SPIRIT (see DEMONIAC).

UNCTION — KJV word for the act of anointing, referring to the gift of the Holy Spirit (1 John 2:20; anointing, NKJV, RSV, NIV, NASB). In the Old Testament, kings (1 Sam. 10:1), priests (Num. 35:25), and prophets (1 Kin. 19:16) were anointed with holy oil; in the New Testament believers were anointed with the Holy Spirit.

UNDEFILED — unstained, unsoiled, not tainted with evil; clean, pure, faultless. The word undefiled is used of the sinless Christ (Heb. 7:26), of sex in marriage (Heb. 13:4), of a pure and faultless religion (James 1:27), and of our incorruptible inheritance in heaven (1 Pet. 1:4).

UNDERSETTERS — KJV word for the supports at the four corners of each of the ten bronze lavers in King Solomon's Temple (1 Kin. 7:30, 34; supports, NKJV).

UNICORN (see ANIMALS OF THE BIBLE).

UNITY — oneness, harmony, agreement. Unity was apparent on the day of Pentecost when the believers "were all with one accord in one place" (Acts 2:1). The church is a unity in diversity, a fellowship of faith, hope, and love that binds believers together (Eph. 4:3, 13).

UNKNOWN GOD (see GOD, UNKNOWN).

UNLEAVENED BREAD — bread baked from unfermented dough, or dough without yeast or "leaven" (Gen. 19:3; Josh. 5:11; 1 Sam. 28:24). Unleavened bread was the flat bread used in the PASSOVER celebration and the priestly rituals (Lev. 23:4–8). The tradition of eating unleavened bread goes back to the time of the Exodus, when the Hebrews left Egypt in such haste that they had no time to bake their bread (Ex. 12:8, 15–20, 34, 39; 13:6–7). Leaven was produced by the souring of bread dough. Its exclusion from ceremonial breads probably symbolized purity.

UNLEAVENED BREAD, FEAST OF (see FEASTS AND FESTIVALS).

UNNI [UHN eye] (*answered*) — the name of two men in the Old Testament:

1. A Levite musician who accompanied the ARK OF THE COVENANT brought by David from the house of Obed–Edom to Jerusalem (1 Chr. 15:18, 20).

2. A Levite who returned from the Captivity with Zerubbabel (Neh. 12:9; Unno, RSV).

UNNO [UHN oh] — a form of UNNI.

UNPARDONABLE SIN (see SIN, UNPARDONABLE).

UPHARSIN (see MENE, MENE, TEKEL, UPHARSIN).

UPHAZ [YOU faz] (meaning unknown) — a place from where gold was brought (Jer. 10:9). Some scholars believe Uphaz is a misspelling of OPHIR, a famous gold–bearing region. If Uphaz was distinct from Ophir, its location is unknown.

UPPER CHAMBER (see CHAMBER).

UPPER GATE (see GATES OF JERUSALEM AND THE TEMPLE).

UR — Abraham's native city in southern Mesopotamia; an important metropolis of the ancient world situated on the Euphrates River. Strategically situated about halfway between the head of the Persian Gulf and Baghdad, in present–day Iraq, Ur was the capital of Sumer for two centuries until the Elamites captured the city. The city came to be known as "Ur of the Chaldees" after the Chaldeans entered southern Babylonia after 1000 B.C.

Abraham lived in the city of Ur (Gen. 11:28, 31) at the height of its splendor. The city was a prosperous center of religion and industry. Thousands of recovered clay documents attest to thriving business activity. Excavations of the royal cemetery, from about 2900 to 2500 B.C., have revealed a surprisingly advanced culture, particularly in the arts and crafts. Uncovered were beautiful jewelry and art treasures, including headwear, personal jewelry, and exquisite china and crystal.

The Babylonians worshiped many gods, but the moon god Sin was supreme. Accordingly, the city of Ur was a kind of theocracy centered in the moon deity. Ur–Nammu, the founder of the strong Third Dynasty of Ur (around 2070–1960 B.C.), built the famous ZIGGURATS, a system of terraced platforms on which temples were erected. The Tower of BABEL (Gen. 11:3–4) was a seven–story ziggurat made of brick. It is a miracle of God's providence that Abraham resisted Ur's polluted atmosphere and set out on a journey of faith to Canaan that would bless all mankind.

Ur's glory was suddenly destroyed about 1900 B.C. Foreigners stormed down from the surrounding hills and captured the reigning king, reducing the city to ruins. So complete was the destruction that the city was buried in oblivion until it was excavated centuries later by archaeologists.

URBANE [UHR bain] — a form of URBANUS.

URBANUS [uhr BAIN us] (*refined, polite*) — a Christian in Rome to whom the apostle Paul sent greetings as "a fellow worker in Christ" (Rom. 16:9; Urbane, KJV).

URI [YOU rye] (*God is my light*) — the name of three men in the Old Testament:

1. A son of Hur and father of Bezaleel (Ex. 31:2). Bezaleel was the chief architect of the tabernacle.

2. The father of Geber (1 Kin. 4:19). Geber was one of 12 governors in charge of providing food for Solomon and his household.

3. A gatekeeper who, at Ezra's urging, divorced the wife whom he had married during the Captivity (Ezra 10:24).

URIAH [you RYE uh] (*flame of Jehovah*) — the name of three men in the Old Testament:

1. A Hittite married to Bathsheba. Uriah was one of David's mighty men (2 Sam. 11:3–26; 12:9–10, 15; 1 Kin. 15:5; Matt. 1:6; Urias, KJV).

Judging from the usual interpretation of his name and good conduct, Uriah was a worshiper of God. David's adultery with Uriah's wife, Bathsheba, occurred while Uriah was engaged in war at Rabbah, the Ammonite capital. Uriah was immediately recalled to Jerusalem to hide what had happened, but his sense of duty and loyalty only frustrated the king. Failing to use Uriah as a shield to cover his sin with Bathsheba, David ordered this valiant soldier to the front line of battle, where he was killed.

2. A priest, the son of Koz and father of Meremoth. Uriah helped rebuild the wall of Jerusalem under Nehemiah. He stood with Ezra the scribe as Ezra read the law and addressed the people (Ezra 8:33). The NKJV spells his name Urijah in Nehemiah 3:4, 21; 8:4.

3. A priest, one of two faithful witnesses to a scroll written by the prophet Isaiah (Is. 8:2).

URIEL [YOU rih ehl] (*flame of God*) — the name of three men in the Old Testament:

1. A Levite of the family of Kohath (1 Chr. 6:24).

2. A chief of the Kohathites (1 Chr. 15:5, 11). Uriel was one of many priests employed by David when the ARK OF THE COVENANT was brought to Jerusalem from the house of Obed–Edom. He may be the same as Uriel No. 1.

3. A man of Gibeah and father of a daughter named Michaiah (2 Chr. 13:2).

Ruins of ancient Ur on the Euphrates River in Mesopotamia—the city from which Abraham migrated (Gen. 11:31).

URIJAH [you RYE jah] (*flame of Jehovah*) — the name of two men in the Old Testament:

1. A priest in Jerusalem who built an altar according to the pattern provided by King Ahaz (2 Kin. 16:10–16). When the wicked Ahaz sought help from the Assyrian King Tiglath–Pileser, he embraced pagan worship at an Assyrian altar and instructed Urijah to build a replica for his worship in Jerusalem. The priest fashioned the heathen altar, placing it in the court of the Temple in the place of the bronze altar of God. Without protest, he complied with Ahaz's instructions, offering all sacrifices and offering on the new altar.

2. A prophet, the son of Shemaiah of Kirjath Jearim and a contemporary of Jeremiah (Jer. 26:20–23). Like Jeremiah, this prophet of God was faithful to the Word of God, prophesying against Jerusalem and Judah. When King Jehoiakim tried to kill him, he sought asylum in Egypt. The king, however, had Urijah returned to Jerusalem, where he was killed.

URIM AND THUMMIM [YOU rim, THUME em] (*lights and perfections*) — gems or stones carried by the high priest and used by him to determine God's will in certain matters. Many scholars believe these gems were cast, much as dice are thrown, to aid the high priest in making important decisions.

The Urim and Thummim were either on, by, or in the high priest's breastplate. For this reason the breastplate is often called the breastplate of judgment, or decision. In the instructions for making the breastplate, the linen was to be doubled to form a square (Ex. 28:16). If the top edge was not stitched together, the breastplate would be an envelope or pouch. Many scholars believe the Urim and Thummim were kept in this pouch and were stones or gems with engraved symbols that signified yes-no or true-false. By these the high priest reached a decision, according to this theory.

The Jewish historian Josephus (A.D. 37–100?), a contemporary of the apostle John, believed that the Urim and Thummim had to do with the flashing of the precious stones in the breastplate. Later Jewish writers believed that the letters in the names of the twelve tribes of Israel engraved on the stones stood out or flashed in succession to spell out God's answer. This theory does imply that the Urim and Thummim could produce answers to questions which called for more than a mere yes or no reply. Another theory is that by staring at the glow of the Urim and Thummim, the high priest went into a state of ecstasy or trance during which God spoke to him.

The student or Bible teacher should bear in mind that all of these theories are pure guesswork. No one knows the exact nature of the Urim and Thummim or precisely how they were used.

There are few allusions to the Urim and Thummim in the Bible. They are first mentioned in the description of the breastplate of judgment (Ex. 28:30; Lev. 8:8). When Joshua succeeded Moses, he was to have answers from the Urim through Eleazar the priest (Num. 27:21). They are next mentioned in Moses' dying blessing upon Levi (Deut. 33:8). There are places in the Bible where Urim and Thummim may be implied but are not named (Josh. 7:14–18; 1 Sam. 14:37–45; 2 Sam. 21:1).

Saul sought direction from the witch of En–dor when he could receive no answer from the Lord, "either by dreams or by Urim or by the prophets" (1 Sam. 28:6). Another interesting reference to the Urim and Thummim occurred during the period after the return of the Jewish people from their years in captivity by the Babylonians. The Persian governor of Jerusalem denied the people permission to observe some of their ancient Jewish food laws until "a priest could consult with the Urim and Thummim" (Ezra 2:63).

USURY [YOU zhu ree] — interest paid on borrowed money. In the Bible the word usury does not necessarily have the negative connotations of our modern meaning of lending money at an excessive interest rate. Instead, it usually means the charging of interest on money that has been loaned.

The Old Testament prohibited charging usury to fellow Israelites; the need of one's countryman was not to become an opportunity for profit (Ex. 22:25; Deut. 23:19–20; Neh. 5:1–13). However, foreigners were traders and merchants, and usury was a part of their everyday lives. Thus they could be charged usury (Deut. 23:20).

By the time of the New Testament, Israel's economy had changed so much from Old Testament days that usury was common practice, even among God's people. Therefore, Jesus did not condemn receiving usury. But He did insist that the rates be fair and justly applied (Matt. 25:27; Luke 19:23). Usury, as all other aspects of life, was to be handled in a spirit of love and genuine concern for the welfare of others (Luke 6:31).

UTHAI [YOU thigh] (*Jehovah is help*) — the name of two men in the Old Testament:

1. A son of Ammihud of the tribe of Judah (1 Chr. 9:4). Uthai lived in Jerusalem after the Captivity.

2. A son of Bigvai (Ezra 8:14). With his brother Zabbud and 70 males, Uthai returned to Jerusalem with Ezra.

UZ [uhz] (*counsel* or *firmness*) — the name of four men and a place in the Old Testament:

1. A son of Aram and grandson of Shem (Gen. 10:23). The name may refer to an Aramean tribe or people.

2. A son of Nahor and Milcah (Gen. 22:21, NASB, NIV, RSV; Huz, KJV, NKJV).

3. A son of Dishan, a Horite in the land of Edom (Gen. 36:28).

4. One of the sons (or descendants) of Shem (1 Chr. 1:17).

5. The land where Job lived (Job 1:11). Two possible locations are Hauran, south of Damascus, and the area between Edom and northern Arabia. The exact location of the land of Uz is unknown, but it was probably east of the Jordan River in the Syrian or Arabian desert.

UZAI [YOU zie] (*hoped for*) — the father of Palal (Neh. 3:25). Palal helped rebuild the walls of Jerusalem.

UZAL [YOU zal] (meaning unknown) — a son of Joktan (Gen. 10:27). The name Uzal may refer to an Arabian tribe or settlement (Ezek. 27:19, RSV). Recent scholarship identifies Uzal with a town named Azalla, in the neighborhood of Medina.

UZZA, UZZAH [UHZ uh] (*strength*) — the name of five men in the Old Testament:

1. A man who was struck dead by God because he touched the ARK OF THE COVENANT (2 Sam. 6:3–8; 1 Chr. 13:7–11).

2. A person in whose garden Manasseh, king of Judah, and Amon (Manasseh's son), also king of Judah, were buried (2 Kin. 21:18, 26).

3. A Levite of the family of Merari (1 Chr. 6:29).

4. A descendant of Ehud mentioned in the family tree of King Saul (1 Chr. 8:7).

5. An ancestor of a family of NETHINIM (Temple servants) who returned with Zerubbabel from the Captivity (Ezra 2:49; Neh. 7:51).

UZZEN SHEERAH [UHZ en SHE uh rah] (*tip of Sheerah*) — a town or village built by Sheerah (1 Chr. 7:24; Uzzen–sherah, KJV), a female descendant of Ephraim. She also built Lower and Upper Beth Horon. The site of Uzzen Sheerah is still uncertain, although some scholars identify it with Beit Sira, about 21 kilometers (13 miles) northwest of Jerusalem.

UZZI [UHZ eye] (*Jehovah is strong*) — the name of seven men in the Old Testament:

1. A high priest descended from Aaron, Eleazar, and Phinehas (1 Chr. 6:5–6, 51). Uzzi was an ancestor of Ezra (Ezra 7:4).

2. A grandson of Issachar and father of Izrahiah (1 Chr. 7:2–3).

3. A son of Bela (1 Chr. 7:7).

4. The father of Elah, a Benjamite (1 Chr. 9:8). He may be the same person as Uzzi No. 3.

5. An overseer of the Levites in Jerusalem after the Captivity (Neh. 11:22).

6. A priest, head of the house of Jedaiah in the days of the high priest Joiakim (Neh. 12:19).

7. A priest who helped dedicate the rebuilt walls of Jerusalem (Neh. 12:42). He may be the same person as Uzzi No. 6.

UZZIA [you ZIE ah] (*Jehovah is strong*) — a native of Ashtaroth, an ancient city of Bashan, and one of David's mighty men (1 Chr. 11:44).

UZZIAH [you ZIE uh] (*my strength is Jehovah*) — the name of five men in the Old Testament:

1. The son of Amaziah and Jecholiah; ninth king of Judah and father of Jotham (2 Kin. 15:1–7; 2 Chr. 26). Uzziah is also called Azariah (2 Kin. 14:21; 15:1–7).

Uzziah ascended the throne at age 16 and reigned longer than any previous king of Judah or Israel—52 years. He probably co–reigned with his father and definitely had his son Jotham as his co–regent

during his final years as a leper. A wise, pious, and powerful king, he extended Judah's territory and brought the nation to a time of great prosperity. In the south he maintained control over Edom and rebuilt port facilities at Elath on the Gulf of Aqaba. To the west he warred against the Philistines, seizing several cities. He also apparently defeated and subdued the Ammonites.

The foolishness of Uzziah's father Amaziah in fighting Joash, the king of Israel, had left the city of Jerusalem in a vulnerable position (2 Chr. 25:23). So Uzziah focused his attention on securing the defenses of both his capital and his country. He reinforced the towers of the city gates. On these towers and walls he placed huge catapults which were capable of shooting arrows and hurling stones at the enemy (2 Chr. 26:15). He also maintained a well-equipped army and fortified strategic places in the desert. His successes were directly related to his spiritual sensitivity, because he sought the Lord through a prophet who encourged him to honor and obey God (2 Chr. 26:5).

However, Uzziah's heart was lifted up in pride. No longer satisfied to be a mortal king, he desired to be like some of his contemporaries—a divine king. He entered the Temple to burn incense. When Azariah the high priest and 80 associates confronted him, he responded in anger instead of repentance. God judged him by striking him with leprosy. Uzziah was forced to live the rest of his life in a separate place, with his son Jotham probably acting as king. At Uzziah's death the prophet Isaiah had a transforming vision of the Lord, high and lifted up on a throne (Is. 1:1; 6:1–13; 7:1).

2. A Levite of the family of Kohath. Uzziah was the son of Uriel and the father of Shaul (1 Chr. 6:24).

3. The father of Jehonathan (1 Chr. 27:25). Jehonathan was an officer of David over the storehouses.

4. A priest commanded by Ezra to divorce his pagan wife (Ezra 10:21).

5. The father of Athaiah (Neh. 11:4).

UZZIEL [uh ZEYE el] (*God is strong*) — the name of six men in the Old Testament:

1. A Levite, son of Kohath, and founder of a tribal family (Ex. 6:18; Lev. 10:4). Uzziel was the ancestor of the UZZIELITES (Num. 3:27; 1 Chr. 26:23).

2. One of four sons of Ishi, of the tribe of Simeon (1 Chr. 4:42).

3. A son of Bela and grandson of Benjamin (1 Chr. 7:7).

4. One of the sons of Heman (1 Chr. 25:4).

5. A Levite, son of Jeduthun (2 Chr. 29:14). Uzziel helped cleanse the Temple during King Hezekiah's religious reformation.

6. The son of Harhaiah (Neh. 3:8). Uzziel was a goldsmith who helped repair a part of the damaged wall of Jerusalem.

UZZIELITES [uh ZEYE el ights] — members of the tribal family of UZZIEL (Num. 3:27; 1 Chr. 26:23).

V

VAGABOND — one who moves from place to place without a permanent home; an aimless wanderer (Ps. 109:10).

VAIN (see VANITY).

VAINGLORY (see PRIDE).

VAJEZATHA [vah HEZ ah thah] (*son of the atmosphere*) — one of the ten sons of Haman, all of whom were hanged like their father after he tried to destroy all the Jews in the Persian Empire (Esth. 9:9–10, 13).

VALE (see VALLEY).

VALLEY — a depression in the earth's surface between ranges of mountains, hills, or other uplands. In the NKJV the word valley is the translation of several different Hebrew and Greek words.

1. One Hebrew word refers to a split or cleft place, more like a plain than a valley. This word is used of the valleys of Aven (Amos 1:5), Jericho (Deut. 34:3), Lebanon (Josh. 11:17), Megiddo (2 Chr. 35:22), and Mizpah (Josh. 11:8).

2. Another Hebrew word, meaning "a deep place," refers to a long, broad sweep of land between parallel hill or mountain ranges. In the NKJV this particular Hebrew word is used of several valleys, including Achor (Josh. 7:24, 26), Hebron (Gen. 37:14), and Succoth (Ps. 60:6; 108:7).

3. Another Hebrew word, meaning "gorge," refers to a deep, narrow ravine, usually with a stream at the bottom. Some of the valleys to which this word applies are Hamon Gog (Ezek. 39:11, 15) and Hinnon (Josh. 15:8; Neh. 11:30).

4. A fourth Hebrew word, which means "a ravine," refers to the bed or channel of a stream that is usually dry except during the rainy season, when it may become a rushing torrent. Some of the "valleys" to which this word applies are the Arabah (Amos 6:14), Gerar (Gen. 26:17), and Sorek (Judg. 16:4).

5. A Greek word translated as valley means "a precipice." This word occurs only once in the New Testament of the NKJV: "Every valley shall be filled and every mountain and hill brought low" (Luke 3:5).

The lush Esdraelon Valley as viewed from the site of the ancient city of Megiddo.

Photo by Howard Vos

The valleys of Palestine vary considerably in shape and size. Some are deep canyons or narrow gorges, while others are broad, fertile plains.

Also see PLAIN; SHEPHELAH.

VALLEY GATE (see GATES OF JERUSALEM AND THE TEMPLE).

VALLEY OF SLAUGHTER — a variant translation of TOPHET.

VANIAH [vah NIE ah] (meaning unknown) — one of the sons of Bani who divorced his pagan wife after returning from the Captivity (Ezra 10:36).

VANITY — emptiness, worthlessness, or futility. The word occurs about 37 times in the Old Testament (NKJV), most frequently in Ecclesiastes. The word vanity as used in the Bible does not mean conceit or a "superiority complex," like the modern meaning of the term. When applied to persons, it means emptiness or futility of natural human life (Job 7:3; Eccl. 1:2; 2:1; 4:4; 1:10).

When applied to things, vanity is especially used to describe idols, because there is no spiritual reality to them (Is. 41:29). Believers are urged to stay away from vain things and to live their lives in the reality of their relationship to Christ. Anything short of God Himself which a person trusts to meet his deepest needs is vanity (Eph. 4:17–24).

VASHNI [VASH nie] (the second) — KJV word for the firstborn son of Samuel the prophet (1 Chr. 6:28). Most modern versions, however, have Joel instead of Vashni.

VASHTI [VASH tie] (one who is desired) — the beautiful queen of King Ahasuerus (Xerxes I, reigned 486–465 B.C.) who was banished from court for refusing the king's command to exhibit herself during a period of drunken feasting (Esth. 1:11). Her departure allowed Esther to become Ahasuerus' new queen and to be used as God's instrument in saving the Jewish people from destruction.

VASSAL — a slave or a person in a subservient position. Hoshea, king of Israel, became the vassal of Shalmaneser, king of Assyria, and paid him tribute money (2 Kin. 17:3). Jehoiakim, king of Judah, became the vassal of Nebuchadnezzar, king of Babylon, for three years (2 Kin. 24:1).

VEIL — an article of clothing and a curtain in the tabernacle or Temple:

1. A woman's head covering, generally consisting of a piece of muslin or fine linen, sometimes adorned with embroidery and precious metals (Gen. 24:65; 38:14; Is. 3:23).

2. A curtain in the tabernacle or Temple that separated the Holy Place from the Holy of Holies (or Most Holy Place). Only the high priest could go behind the veil, and this occurred only one day each year—on the Day of Atonement (Lev. 16:2). But when Jesus died on the cross, "the veil of the temple was torn in two from top to bottom" (Matt. 27:51), showing that Jesus had opened a new and living

way into the presence of God through His death (Heb. 6:19; 9:3).

VENGEANCE — punishment in retaliation for an injury or offense; repayment for a wrong suffered. The Levitical law prescribed, "You shall not take vengeance" (Lev. 19:18). Only God was qualified to take vengeance, because His acts were based on His holiness, righteousness, and justice which punishes sin and vindicates the oppressed and the poor in spirit (Deut. 32:35; Rom. 12:19).

VENISON — wild game of any kind taken in hunting (Gen. 25:28; 27:3; game, NKJV).

VENOM — a poisonous secretion transmitted by the bite or sting of an animal, such as a snake, spider, or scorpion (Deut. 32:33; Job 20:14).

VERILY — KJV word for truly (Gen. 42:21; Gal. 3:21), surely (Jer. 15:11), actually (2 Kin. 4:14), certainly (Ps. 66:19), assuredly (Matt. 5:18), indeed (Acts 16:37), and yes (Luke 11:51).

VERMILION (see COLORS OF THE BIBLE; MINERALS OF THE BIBLE).

VESSEL — any kind of container or receptacle. The vessels of the Hebrew people were usually earthenware. But vessels of glass, metal, leather, wicker, and stone were not uncommon. They were used to hold everything from documents (Jer. 32:14) to wine, fruits, and oil (Jer. 40:10).

In a broader sense, ships are sometimes referred to as vessels (Is. 18:2) since they are the receptacles of people. In an even broader sense, vessel refers to people who carry within them the knowledge of God (2 Cor. 4:6–7). Just as any clay vessel reflects the craftsmanship of its potter, so people reflect the craftsmanship of God. Man is in God's hands and is formed in accordance with His plan (Rom. 9:21–23).

VESTIBULE (see ARCHWAY).

VIA DOLOROSA (way of sorrows) — the traditional route taken by our Lord Jesus on His way from Pilate's judgment hall to GOLGOTHA, or CALVARY, the place of crucifixion. Although tradition marks out 14 stations of the cross, or the events which transpired during that exhausting journey, it is almost impossible to locate the exact route taken because the ancient streets of Jerusalem were destroyed several years after the crucifixion by the Roman army. The Via Dolorosa is not mentioned by name in the Bible.

VIAL — KJV word for juglet, a vessel that held oil for the anointing of a king (1 Sam. 10:1; 1 Kin. 9:1, 3; flask, NKJV). The word is also used for a broad, shallow bowl, mentioned in the Book of Revelation, that held the wrath of God (Rev. 15:7; bowl, NKJV).

VICE — wicked or depraved conduct. The apostle Peter said that Christians are free from the law, but not free to do wrong. We should not use our Christian freedom "as a cloak for vice" (1 Pet. 2:16).

VICEROY (see OCCUPATIONS AND TRADES).

VIGIL — a time of watchfulness during the normal hours of sleeping (Job 21:32).

VILLAGE — a settlement larger than a hamlet and smaller than a town. A village may be distinguished from a city by its smaller size and its lack of defenses, particularly a wall (Ezek. 38:11). Villages were located in open spaces, but usually a city was situated nearby. When a region was threatened by hostile troops, the inhabitants of the local villages would seek refuge within the walls of a nearby city.

Villages were primarily centers for agriculture, but the term village could also refer to what is known as suburbs today. Villages were ruled on a local level by ELDERS (Ruth 4:2).

Also see CITY.

VINE, VINEYARD (see PLANTS OF THE BIBLE).

VINE–DRESSER (see OCCUPATIONS AND TRADES).

VINE OF SODOM — an unknown plant. Scholars disagree on whether the single reference to the plant (Deut. 32:32) should be understood literally or symbolically. Most interpret it symbolically as a reference to the bitterness and unfruitfulness of pagan gods and religious practices. If the reference is to a real fruit, its identification remains obscure. The most likely suggestions are either the solanum, an orange–colored, inedible fruit, or the colocynth, a wild gourd with bitter fruit which grows on sandy ground near the Dead Sea.

VINEGAR — a drink made from wine that had been soured or overfermented. In accordance with their vow, the NAZIRITES separated themselves from any product of the grapevine, including vinegar (Num. 6:3). The psalmist complained that his enemies had given him gall for food and vinegar to drink (Ps. 69:21). Vinegar was used by farm families as a relish in which to dip parched grain (Ruth 2:14; wine vinegar, NIV; sour wine, NEB).

In the New Testament, the word vinegar is used only in reference to Jesus' crucifixion (Matt. 27:34, 48; Mark 15:36; Luke 23:36; John 19:29–30, KJV; sour wine, NKJV). Before Jesus was nailed to the cross, "they gave Him sour wine mingled with gall to drink" (Matt. 27:34). He was offered the same drink again shortly before He died (Luke 23:36). After Jesus had hung on the cross for three hours, and shortly before He yielded up His spirit, He was again offered sour wine, which He received (Matt. 27:48; Mark 15:36; Luke 23:36; John 19:29–30).

VINEYARD, PLAIN OF THE (see PLAIN OF THE VINEYARD).

VIOL (see MUSICAL INSTRUMENTS).

VIOLENCE — the use of physical force, usually with an intent to violate or destroy. Violence is a violation of God's perfect order. Thus the Greek word translated as violent force applies to the disorderly mob of Acts 21:35. But if godly men are subject to the human instability that causes violence, they also have the hope of seeking refuge in God's stability (2 Sam. 22:3). Faith in Him can lead to a quenching of the violence of fire (Heb. 11:34).

VIPER (see ANIMALS OF THE BIBLE).

VIRGIN — a person who has not had sexual intercourse. Leviticus 21:7, 14 specified that a priest must not marry a widow, a divorced woman, or a prostitute, but only a virgin. The term was sometimes used to describe the nation of Israel (Is. 37:22; Jer. 31:4) to emphasize its purity and holiness as the CHOSEN PEOPLE of God.

But the most important use of the word virgin is as a description of the mother of Jesus. The prophet Isaiah foretold that the mother of the one to be known as Immanuel ("God with us") would be a virgin (Is. 7:14). The Hebrew word for virgin used by Isaiah (*almah*), although different from that usually used for virgin in the Old Testament (*bethulah*), nonetheless means a young woman not yet married. When Mary, a virgin (Luke 1:27), conceived Jesus, the prophecy of Isaiah 7:14 was fulfilled (Matt. 1:23).

The doctrine of the virgin birth of Christ is also found in other New Testament passages (Matt. 1:18, 20, 25; Luke 1:34–35).

Also see VIRGIN BIRTH.

VIRGIN BIRTH — the theological doctrine that Jesus was miraculously begotten by God and born of Mary, who was a virgin. The term virgin birth explains the way in which the Son of God entered human existence; it means that Mary had not had sexual relations with any man when she conceived Jesus.

This unparalleled act of God is described beautifully in Luke 1:26–38. The angel of God appeared to a virgin who was engaged to Joseph. In those days engagement was a legal arrangement in which a woman was betrothed, or pledged, to a man. But engagement did not permit sexual relations.

Since Mary had not "known" Joseph sexually, she wondered how she could bear a child. The angel explained that this would be encouraged by "the power of the Highest" as the Holy Spirit would "overshadow her." There was nothing physical about this divine act; this is emphasized by the statement that the child would be the "Holy One" (Luke 1:35).

The angel also declared that the child would be called "the Son of God." This clearly teaches that it was only through the virgin birth that Jesus, a human being, could also be properly identified as the Son of God. The one person, Jesus, has two natures—divine and human. The eternal, divine nature of the Son of God was joined, in Mary's womb, with a human nature by the direct act of God.

The parallel account in Matthew 1:18–25 views the virgin birth from Joseph's perspective. Because of the legal nature of engagement, a man who found his fiancee pregnant would normally divorce her. Because Joseph was a fair and just man, he did not want to shame Mary by divorcing her publicly; so he decided to do so privately. But the angel prevented this by assuring him that Mary was still a virgin. Her child was conceived by the Holy Spirit, as predicted in Isaiah 7:14.

After this revelation, Joseph took Mary as his wife but did not unite with her sexually until Jesus was born. This implies (but does not prove) that Joseph and Mary later united sexually and had other children.

Some scholars claim that the reference in Luke 2:27, 33, and 41 to Jesus' parents (Joseph and Mary) implies that the virgin birth was not a part of early Christian tradition. But these words were written by the same writer who described the annunciation of the virgin birth in Luke 1:26–38. Some Bible students also express concern over the lack of reference to the virgin birth elsewhere in the New Testament. However, the other gospels say nothing about Jesus' birth, so it is not strange that they do not speak of the virgin birth. Since the gospel message concerns the death, burial, and resurrection of Christ (1 Cor. 15:1–3), the virgin birth is not a natural part of its proclamation. But the virgin birth is a wonderful and personal truth that clearly belongs to Christian doctrine.

VIRTUE — moral excellence or goodness (Phil. 4:8). Virtue is considered a necessary ingredient in the exercise of faith (2 Pet. 1:3, 5). Sometimes the Greek word for virtue is used to express the idea of power or strength (Luke 6:19).

VISIONS — experiences similar to dreams through which supernatural insight or awareness is given by revelation. But the difference between a dream and a vision is that dreams occur only during sleep, while visions can happen while a person is awake (Dan. 10:7).

In the Bible, people who had visions were filled with a special consciousness of God. The most noteworthy examples in the Old Testament of recipients of visions are Ezekiel and Daniel. Visions in the New Testament are most prominent in the Gospel of Luke, the Book of Acts, and the Book of Revelation.

The purpose of visions was to give guidance and direction to God's servants and to foretell the future. Daniel's vision, for example, told of the coming of the Messiah (Dan. 8:1, 17).

Also see DREAMS.

VOCATION — a call or an invitation to a profession or way of life. But in theological discussions, the word vocation is not used in reference to the professional trade which one pursues. Vocation refers to the invitation God has given to all people to become His children through Christ's work. This vocation, or calling, does not come to people because they deserve it; it comes strictly as a result of God's GRACE (2 Tim. 1:9). However, it is up to the individual to decide whether he will accept and act upon the vocation.

Just as excellence in any professional vocation requires faithful study and work, so God requires that Christians labor to be worthy of their divine vocation (Eph. 4:1). If any person accepts the Christian vocation and labors in it, he can expect—just as he might expect from his professional vocation—a great reward (Eph. 1:18).

VOID — an emptiness; a great desolation. When the earth was first created, it was void and formless (Gen. 1:2). This means it was a desolate place, not yet filled with the plants and creatures which God later created. In a similar vein, the prophet Jeremiah envisioned an earth "without form, and void" (Jer. 4:23), indicating that invading armies would turn the nation of Israel into an uninhabited wasteland.

Since the word chaos is often used to describe what the Bible means by void, it should be noted that only the original meaning of the Greek word *chaos* (vast space) applies. Our modern understanding of chaos as confusion is not the meaning intended by the biblical writers.

VOPHSI [VAHF sigh] (*fragrant, rich*) — the father of Nahbi, of the tribe of Naphtali (Num. 13:14).

VOW — a solemn promise or pledge that binds a person to perform a specified act or to behave in a certain manner. The first mention of a vow in the Bible is of Jacob at Bethel (Gen. 28:20–22; 31:13). Other people who made a vow are Jephthah (Judg. 11:30–31, 39), Hannah (1 Sam. 1:11), David (Ps. 132:2–5), and Absalom (2 Sam. 15:7–8).

In the New Testament the apostle Paul, probably at the end of a 30–day period of abstinence from meat and wine, had his hair cut off at Cenchrea, "for he had taken a vow" (Acts 18:18). The vow that Paul had taken was probably the NAZIRITE vow (Num. 6:1–21). Samson was an Old Testament hero who had also taken the Nazirite vow (Judg. 13:5, 7; 16:17).

All vows were made to God as a promise in expectation of His favor (Gen. 28:20) or in thanksgiving for His blessings (Ps. 116:12–14). Vowing might be a part of everyday devotion (Ps. 61:8) or the annual festivals (1 Sam. 1:21). Vows must be paid to God in the congregation at the tabernacle or Temple (Deut. 12:6, 11; Ps. 22:25).

Vowing was voluntary. But after a vow was made, it had to be performed (Deut. 23:21–23; Eccl. 5:4–6). Vows, therefore, were to be made only after careful consideration (Prov. 20:25) and in keeping with what pleased God (Lev. 27:9–27). Sinful man does not know what will please God; he needs God's direction in making vows.

Vowing is joyful worship in faith and love (Ps. 61:4–5, 8), often associated with the proclamation of God's salvation (Ps. 22:22–27; 66:13–20). For this reason, deception in vowing is an affront to God and brings His curse (Mal. 1:14).

VULGATE (see BIBLE VERSIONS AND TRANSLATIONS).

VULTURE (see ANIMALS OF THE BIBLE).

W

WADI [WAH dih] — a valley, ravine, or riverbed that usually remains dry except during the rainy season; a stream that flows through such a channel. While the word wadi does not occur in most translations, they are often called by other names, such as brook (Josh. 15:47; 2 Kin. 23:12) and torrent (Judg. 5:21).

At the conclusion of the Sermon on the Mount, Jesus probably had a wadi in mind when He told the parable of the two builders and the houses they built (Matt. 7:24–27; Luke 6:47–49). In Palestine the pleasant, bone–dry valley of summertime frequently becomes an angry, turbulent flood that demolishes everything in its path during the winter rains.

Also see CHERITH; EGYPT, BROOK OF; and KIDRON.

WAFERS — the thin cakes of unleavened bread prepared by the Levites for the cereal offering. Wafers were used in the consecration of Aaron and his sons to the priesthood (Ex. 29:2, 23; Lev. 8:26), in the sacrifice of the peace offering (Lev. 2:4; 7:12), and in the consecration of the Nazirite (Num. 6:15, 19). As with the unleavened bread of PASSOVER, these wafers probably symbolized a person's separation from sin.

WAGES — compensation for performing work or service. In Bible times, wages were often paid in the form of property or privileges, not money. Such "in kind" payment for tasks completed especially suited the nomadic peoples of the Old Testament.

For instance, Jacob worked for Laban seven years to earn the hand of Rachel. Instead, he was

The Wadi Zered, marking the boundary between Moab and Edom. The Israelites crossed this wadi on the way to the Promised Land (Num. 21:12).

Photo by Gustav Jeeninga

The Wilderness of Zin, a desert region through which the Israelites passed on their journey to the Promised Land (Num. 13:21; 34:3-4).

tricked into a marriage with her sister Leah. But he willingly accepted this, toiling another seven years to win Rachel as well (Gen. 29:15-20). He also labored six years to earn a flock of goats and sheep (Gen. 31:41). Because of Jacob's efforts, Laban prospered; but when wage disputes occurred between them, God directed Jacob to depart (Gen. 31:7, 41).

This sort of concern for full, prompt wages is a recurring legal and ethical theme in the Bible. Mosaic Law required payment each evening: "You shall not cheat your neighbor, nor rob him. The wages of him who is hired shall not remain with you all night until morning" (Lev. 19:13). Frequently prophets and religious leaders severely denounced those who withheld wages.

In Jesus' parable of the vineyard–workers, a landowner agreed to pay the laborers one denarius a day. Even workers who had served only an hour received a full day's wages, thanks to the landowner's generosity. This parable illustrates God's grace. He rewards each believer far more than he deserves.

The term wages also denotes the consequences of a person's acts or deeds, as in Paul's immortal declaration, "The wages of sin is death" (Rom. 6:23).

WAGON — a vehicle of two or four wheels used for hauling. The wagons mentioned in the Bible had wheels of wood; and they were drawn usually by oxen, although sometimes by horses. Wagons were used to transport people (Gen. 45:19; carts, NKJV) or supplies, occasionally military supplies (Ezek. 23:24). Also see CART.

WAHEB [WAY heb] (meaning unknown) — an unknown place near the border of Moab and close by "the brooks of the Arnon" (Num. 21:14).

WAIL — a mournful cry of grief, sorrow, or lamentation. In ancient funeral processions, wailing relatives, often accompanied by professional mourners and musicians, preceded the body to the grave. The prophet Jeremiah called for "the mourning women" and "skillful wailing women" (Jer. 9:17) to cry because of the coming destruction of Jerusalem as a punishment for the people's idolatry. On the DAY OF THE LORD, declared Amos, "There shall be wailing in all streets" (Amos 5:16). Also see MOURN.

WAIT — to remain in readiness or expectation. In Scripture, the word wait normally suggests the anxious, yet confident, expectation by God's people that the Lord will intervene on their behalf. Such waiting may be for answers to prayer (Ps. 25:5), for the coming of the Holy Spirit (Acts 1:4), for salvation (Gen. 49:18), or especially for the coming of the Messiah to bring salvation to His people and to establish His kingdom on earth (Ps. 37:34; Luke 12:36; Rom. 8:23; 1 Thess. 1:10). Waiting, therefore, is the working out of hope.

WALK — to move at a pace slower than a run; one's conduct of life. The literal sense predominates in the Old Testament, but the figurative meaning of the word does occur (Gen. 5:24; 6:9; Eccl. 11:9). In the New Testament the word usually is used literally in the gospels, while it is usually used figuratively in Paul and John's letters.

The figurative sense has decidedly spiritual overtones. One either walks (conducts his life) as a Christian or as a non–Christian (Rom. 8:4; Eph. 2:2, 10; 1 John 1:6–7). The believer can walk "in darkness" or "in the light," and constantly is urged to choose the latter; only such a path is "worthy of the calling with which you were called" (Eph. 4:1).

WALKWAYS — passages for walking, especially those connecting various areas of a building. Solomon made walkways of algum wood for the Temple and his palace (2 Chr. 9:11).

WALL — a thick, high, continuous structure of stones or brick that formed a defensive barricade around an ancient city. Walls of houses in Palestine were also made of bricks or stones, but these were usually plastered over to give them a smooth surface.

The walls of public buildings and royal palaces were often made of squared stone blocks, cut by skilled craftsmen and carefully fitted together. Solomon employed 80,000 workmen to cut and place the stones for the Temple in Jerusalem (1 Kin. 5:15).

WANDERINGS OF ISRAEL — the activities of the Israelite tribes during the period between their departure from Egypt under Moses and the time when they were encamped by the Jordan River, ready to be led into Canaan by Joshua. The period of time covered by these events is traditionally 40 years, much of which was spent in the area of KADESH-BARNEA.

The Israelite journeyings are commonly spoken of as "wilderness wanderings," because they took the people through some areas that were known as wilderness. In order to understand the nature of the wanderings, it is important to realize the difference between a wilderness and a desert. A desert is best imagined as a barren expanse of sand dunes or a rocky area that does not support any vegetation.

Although a wilderness may also have barren areas, it has grassy upland plains, oases, springs, and vegetation such as flowers, shrubs, and trees that can support a surprising variety of animal life. The Sinai Mountain range where the Hebrew people wandered appears rugged and inhospitable when viewed from the air. But when approached by land, it shows it has sizeable grassy areas and upland plains.

Even the central Sinai area is not completely lacking in surface water. The Wadi el Arish, which is most probably the Old Testament "brook of Egypt," is a seasonal watercourse which reaches as far south as Serabit el-Khadem. South and west of that site is another prominent watercourse, the Wadi Feiran, the best oasis in Sinai, which sustains a considerable amount of vegetation. Thus, it was possible for the Israelites to survive and feed their flocks under wilderness conditions.

The wanderings of the Hebrew people began with the crossing of the Red Sea, a papyrus-reed marsh probably situated in the region of the Bitter Lakes. Immediately thereafter they entered the Wilderness of Shur, an area in northwest Sinai lying south of the coastal road from Egypt to Philistia and bounded on the east by the Wadi el-Arish. This was the first stage of the journey to Mount Sinai (Ex. 15:22), which was probably followed in a southwesterly direction along the east coast of the Gulf of Suez. In this region the watertable is high

and many springs and wells are available. In spite of this, the Israelites experienced many difficulties (Ex. 15:23-25). They were relieved when they arrived at the oasis of Elim.

It is extremely difficult to identify most of the encampments of the wilderness period. This is partly because many of the names may have been given to the locations by the Israelites themselves as a result of specific happenings (for example, Marah, Ex. 15:23; Taberah, Num. 11:3), and not because those were the local names. Even if they had been named before the Hebrews arrived, only the most important of them would have survived in modern Arabic. An example of one place name that has survived is Jebel Musa ("Mountain of Moses") as one possible location of Mount Sinai. This imposing peak in the Sinai range is the traditional site of the covenant with Israel, although two other locations, Jebel Serbal and Ras es Safsafeh, have also been suggested.

The Israelites encamped in the Wilderness of Sin at Rephidim, possibly the Wadi Refayid in southwest Sinai, and drove off an Amalekite attack (Ex. 17:8-16) before reaching Mount Sinai. There they received the Law, and settled for nearly a year (Num. 1:1; 10:11) while Moses worked at organizing the new nation. At this stage of the wanderings the construction of the tabernacle and the regulations governing its use were given careful attention because of their importance for the future life of the Israelites.

Even these precautions, however, were not enough to stop dissatisfaction among the wandering Israelites as they traveled toward Kadesh. The people complained about the lack of food in the wilderness. Even when God provided manna, they soon began to dislike it. To punish them God sent a flock of quail for food, which made the people ill and caused many deaths (Num. 11:32-33).

From the Wilderness of Paran Moses sent spies into Canaan, but they returned with discouraging reports about the inhabitants (Num. 13:32-33). The people then refused to enter Canaan and rebelled against their leaders. God was angry with them. With the exception of Joshua and Caleb, all the people alive at that time were condemned to spend the rest of their lives in the wilderness. Korah, Dathan, and Abiram accused Moses and Aaron of assuming too much priestly authority. They were punished by being swallowed up in a spectacular earthquake (Num. 16:32-33). The Israelites became angry at this, and God would have killed them all if Moses had not interceded on their behalf.

Because of an act of disobedience at Kadesh (Num. 20:8-12), Moses and Aaron were forbidden to enter the Promised Land. Nevertheless, they and the Israelites attempted to go to Canaan along the King's Highway which passed through Edomite territory. But they were refused permission. The people then journeyed to Mount Hor on the border of Edom, where Aaron died (Num. 20:28). A skirmish with the Canaanite king of Arad took place before the Hebrews moved toward the wilderness area east of Moab (Num. 21:1–3). When the Amorite King Sihon refused them access to the King's Highway, he was defeated in battle (Num. 21:21–32). Shortly afterwards Og, king of Bashan, suffered the same fate (Num. 21:33–35).

The Israelites now occupied a large area of territory in Transjordan. This alarmed Balak, king of Moab. He hired Balaam, a Mesopotamian soothsayer, to curse the Israelites, but by divine intervention he blessed them instead (Numbers 22—24). Unfortunately the Israelites committed sin with the Moabite women, and this was to prove an indication of what lay ahead in Canaan.

While the people were in the plains of Moab, across the Jordan River from Jericho, a second census of the people was taken, apparently in preparation for the crossing into Canaan, for which Joshua was appointed leader (Num. 27:18–23). Perhaps because of the immorality with the Moabite women, Moses proclaimed a series of regulations involving offerings and festivals that would be observed once the Israelites were in Canaan (Numbers 28—29).

The hold of the Israelites on Transjordanian territory was consolidated by a successful attack upon the Midianites. This resulted in a great deal of plunder. The conquered lands were ideal for raising herds and flocks, so the tribes of Gad and Reuben and half of the tribe of Manasseh were given that territory as their own. Moses then issued instructions for the conquest of Canaan, and appointed leaders who would divide the land among the tribes.

After reviewing Israel's wilderness wanderings (Num. 33:1–49) and composing a victory song (Deut. 32:1–43), Moses climbed Mount Nebo to see the land that he had been forbidden to enter. With a final blessing upon Israel, Moses died on Mount Nebo. With his death the wilderness wanderings ended and the occupation of Canaan began.

WAR, WARFARE — armed conflict with an opposing military force. From the perspective of the Hebrew people, a holy war was one which God Himself declared, led, and won. The concept was at its height during the period of the judges. By the time of the United Kingdom under David and Solomon, however, political concerns began to cloud the concept of holy war. The prophets saw war as God's judgment against Israel. Those looking for a violent end to man's existence saw war as a sign of the end times, both in the Old and New Testaments. Jesus emphasized peace instead of war, and the New Testament church saw war as a spiritual battle between good and evil.

The concept of holy war required that God declare the war (Ex. 17:16; Num. 31:3). Every warrior considered himself consecrated to God (Is. 13:3). Before and during a war, soldiers abstained from certain activities to sanctify themselves (Judg. 20:26; 2 Sam. 11:11). Those who fought under a divinely ordained leader (Judg. 6:34) had to be singleminded in their devotion to God. Those who

were frightened, newly married, or beset by domestic or financial problems were asked to go home (Deut. 20:5–9). The ARK OF THE COVENANT, the symbol of God's presence, went with Israel's army into battle (2 Sam. 11:11).

The Israelites determined the right moment to enter into battle and sought guidance in battle by casting the sacred lot or by heeding the words of a prophet (Judg. 1:1; 1 Sam. 23:2; 1 Kin. 22:5). King Ahab was killed when he failed to heed the warning of Micaiah, the Lord's prophet (2 Chronicles 18).

In Numbers 21:14, Moses mentioned a book which has remained a mystery to biblical scholars—"the Book of the Wars of the Lord." This was probably a collection of records or songs celebrating the victories of Israel over its enemies. The Old Testament contains many references to God's role in battle against Israel's foes (Ex. 15:3; Ps. 24:8). God struck Israel's enemies with terror, overtaking and killing all fugitives (Ex. 15:1–27; Josh. 10:10–11). The judge Deborah, in her famous "Song of Deborah," cursed those who did not come to the Lord's aid against mighty Sisera (Judg. 5:23). As Israel's king, David fought "the Lord's battles" (1 Sam. 18:17). The prophet Jeremiah cursed those who refused to fight the Lord's battles (Jer. 48:10).

According to 2 Samuel 11:1, wars were usually waged "in the spring of the year." The trumpet or ram's horn, symbolic of the voice of God, called Israel into battle (Judg. 3:27; 1 Sam. 13:3). The number of soldiers whom Israel mustered for battle made no difference, for God fought alongside them (Judges 7; 1 Sam. 14:6). Indeed, the Israelites were forced to wander 40 years in the wilderness because they did not believe God could help them win over the Canaanites, who outnumbered the Israelites in both manpower and equipment (Num. 14:1–12).

The tactics of war were simple. They included surprise, ambush, pretended flight, and surrounding the enemy (Gen. 14:15; Josh. 8:2–7; 2 Sam. 5:23). On occasion a representative of each army met in combat (1 Samuel 17).

According to Deuteronomy 20:10–20, three outcomes of a holy war were possible. If the besieged city surrendered, the occupants' lives were spared, but all were enslaved. If the city refused to agree to peace terms and had to be taken by force, all males were killed by the sword. An exception to both these policies occurred when the captured city lay within Israel's boundaries. Then all occupants and their possessions were utterly destroyed. Known as the ban, this custom was intended to keep Israel free of any heathen influence (Josh. 6:17; 1 Sam. 15:3).

Besieging a city required elaborate planning. If possible, the city's water supply was cut off. Often the towers and gates of the city were set on fire (Judg. 9:52). In order for armies to use their battering rams and catapults that propelled arrows or stones, mounds were built to raise the weapons to appropriate height. From the mound, scaling ladders were laid against the wall so soldiers could get inside the city. All the while, the city's defenders were using their own similar weapons to kill the enemy and destroy their war machinery (2 Sam. 11:21, 24; 2 Chr. 26:15).

A famous battle using these techniques was the Roman siege of Masada, a rock fortress about 1.6 kilometers (one mile) west of the Dead Sea. Masada had been considered impregnable. In fact, it took the Romans nearly three years to gain entry into Masada, only to find its some 960 inhabitants, all Jewish ZEALOTS, dead as a result of a suicide pact.

By the time of Solomon, warfare was the result of national policy set by the ruling king who supposedly was acting at God's direction. Court prophets, when asked about the advisability of entering into war, rarely went against the king's wishes—although Micaiah the son of Imlah did so (1 Kin. 22:8-28; 2 Chr. 18:7-27). Israel entered into international treaties with the great earthly powers rather than relying on God's strength for security (1 Kin. 15:18-19; 2 Kin. 17:4). After the Captivity, the concept of holy war was applied to any revolt against the current ruling power.

The early prophets accepted the holy war concept and even stirred up war. But the later prophets often condemned war, because they felt Israel's wars did not meet the qualifications for a holy war. The one thing necessary for a holy war was that Israel trust in God without any doubt or reservations. But the nation increasingly put its trust in the powers of the day, wealth, and political alliances.

WAR CLUB (see ARMS, ARMOR OF THE BIBLE).

WASHING (see ABLUTION).

WASHPOT — a pot used for washing or bathing. The psalmist declared, "Moab is my washpot" (Ps. 60:8; 108:9; washbasin, NIV, RSV; washbowl, NASB, NEB). The meaning is that Moab (with its sea, the Dead Sea) is to be despised and held in contempt, like a washpot in which soiled hands and feet are washed.

WASP (see ANIMALS OF THE BIBLE).

WASTING DISEASE (see DISEASES OF THE BIBLE).

WATCH — either a group of soldiers or others posted to keep guard (Neh. 4:9; 7:3; 12:25) or one of the units of time into which the night was divided (Ps. 63:6; Lam. 2:19; Luke 12:38).

Because of the mention of the "middle watch" (Judg. 7:19), there must have been three such units in the Old Testament period. The "beginning of the watches" (Lam. 2:19) was apparently the first of these and the "morning watch" was the third (Ex. 14:24; 1 Sam. 11:11). However, by the New Testament period the Roman system of four watches had been adopted (Matt. 14:25; Mark 6:48). These were apparently named as follows: evening, midnight, cockcrow (RSV; the crowing of the rooster, NKJV), and morning (Mark 13:35).

Also see TIME.

WATCHTOWER — an observation tower upon which a guard or lookout was stationed to keep watch; an elevated structure offering an extensive view (2 Kin. 17:9; 18:8; Is. 21:8). Also see TOWER.

WATER OF BITTERNESS — part of a ceremonial test, or trial by ordeal, of a woman accused of adultery (Num. 5:11-31). When a Hebrew man suspected his wife of infidelity but he had no proof, he would bring her before the priest with the charge. The priest would mix "holy water"—probably water from a sacred spring—with dust from the tabernacle floor and curses scraped from a book. This potion, known as the Water of Bitterness, would be

Herod the Great, fearing revolt by the Jews, built several military strongholds in Palestine, such as this one, Machaerus, located in the Transjordan area.

Photo by Gustav Jeeninga

A plentiful source of water was crucial for the survival of an ancient city. This massive well at Gibeon was cut through more than 30 feet of solid rock.

drunk by the woman after she had sworn her innocence under oath.

If the woman had lied to the priest and to God, this potion would turn bitter in her mouth and cause her belly to swell and her thigh to rot. If she was not guilty, the mixture would not harm her.

Also see JEALOUSY, ORDEAL OF; OATH.

WATER CARRIER (see OCCUPATIONS AND TRADES).

WATER OF JEALOUSY (see WATER OF BITTERNESS).

WATERMELON (see PLANTS OF THE BIBLE).

WATERPOOLS — reservoirs which hold water for irrigation purposes (Eccl. 2:6). Solomon's pools were part of an elaborate irrigation system built by the king to store water for Jerusalem.

WATERPOT — a jar for carrying or storing water. These vessels ranged from those large enough to hold 114 liters (30 gallons) (John 2:6–7) to those small enough for a woman to carry on her shoulder or head (John 4:28).

WATERS OF MEROM (see MEROM).

WATERSPOUTS — KJV word for a descent of water over a steep surface (Ps. 42:7; waterfalls, NASB, NIV, NKJV; cataracts, NEB, RSV). The psalmist, apparently an exile from the Temple (vv. 2–3), compares the roaring waters of snowcapped Mount Hermon with the anguish of his own soul.

WAVE OFFERING (see SACRIFICIAL OFFERINGS).

WAW [waw] — the sixth letter of the Hebrew alphabet, used as a heading over Psalm 119:41–48. In the original Hebrew language, every line of these eight verses began with the letter waw. Also see ACROSTIC.

WAX — a sticky substance secreted by bees to build the honeycomb, also called beeswax. The wicked melt like wax before God's judgment (Ps. 68:2).

WAY — a thoroughfare for travel, such as a path, road, or highway. Figuratively, the word way is used in the Old Testament as a synonym for God's divine will and manner of dealing with man (Ps. 1:6). In the New Testament, the word is often used as a metaphor for man's moral course (Matt. 7:13–14; 2 Pet. 21:15).

Jesus reminded His disciples that the single road to God was through Himself: "I am the way, the truth, and the life. No one comes to the Father except through Me" (John 14:6). In the Book of Acts, the phrase *the Way* was a scornful label for the early Christian movement used by the enemies of the church. Like the word Christian, this term of derision was borne with pride by the followers of Jesus (Acts 9:2; 24:14, 22).

WEALTH — an abundance of possessions or resources. During the times of the PATRIARCHS, wealth was measured largely in livestock—sheep, goats, cattle, donkeys, and camels. This was true of Abraham (Gen. 13:2), Isaac (Gen. 26:12–14), and Jacob (Gen. 30:43; 32:5). People of the ancient world also measured wealth in terms of land, houses, servants, slaves, and precious metals. The prime example is King Solomon, whose great wealth is described in 1 Kings 10:14–29.

Wealth is a major theme in the WISDOM LITERATURE of the Bible (Prov. 10:15; 13:11; 19:4). The most important observation of these writings is that wealth comes from God (Prov. 3:9–10). The possession of wealth is not always the sign of God's favor. "Why does the way of the wicked prosper?" (Jer. 12:1) became a familiar theme to the writers of the Old Testament. The popular view that wickedness brings poverty and goodness brings wealth is strongly opposed by the Book of Job.

The prophet Amos thundered against the rich and prosperous inhabitants of Israel, who sold "the righteous for silver, and the poor for a pair of sandals" (Amos 2:6). Their wealth was corrupt and under a curse because it was founded on exploitation of the poor.

In the New Testament, many warnings are given of the dangers of letting money and things possess a person's heart. In the Sermon on the Mount, Jesus spoke of "treasures on earth" and "treasures in heaven" and called upon His followers to be careful of which treasure they chose (Matt. 6:19-21, 24).

Many of Jesus' parables, such as the rich fool (Luke 12:13-21) and the rich man and Lazarus (Luke 16:19-31), deal with people who made the wrong choice, choosing earthly wealth over heavenly wealth. But the only true and lasting wealth is the spiritual riches of God's grace (Matt. 13:44-46).

WEAPONS (see ARMS, ARMOR OF THE BIBLE).

WEASEL (see ANIMALS OF THE BIBLE).

WEATHER — the state of the atmosphere, which varies from time to time in temperature, moisture, and wind velocity. Palestine's climate varies between three zones: the coastal area along the Mediterranean Sea, the hills, and the desert. Winters are warmest near the oceans and coldest on the Lebanon mountains. But virtually everywhere in Palestine the summers are painfully hot. Searing winds often blow in from the south (Job 37:9-11; Luke 12:55).

In spite of the severity of the elements in Palestine, the Israelites endured worse in their 40 years of wandering in the desert before they entered the land of Canaan. No wonder this new land appeared to be "a land flowing with milk and honey" (Num. 16:13).

WEAVER (see OCCUPATIONS AND TRADES).

WEAVING — the skill of making cloth from threads. Egyptian paintings from as early as 2,000 B.C. depict weaving as an advanced skill. This skill was widely practiced throughout the ancient world long before this time. About 2500 B.C. the city of Ebla boasted a highly developed textile industry, and weavers of this city traded their goods widely. The Hebrews practiced weaving probably as early as Abraham's time, about 2000 B.C. The great skill required to weave the tabernacle curtains (Exodus 26) and priestly garments (35:35) was probably learned in Egypt.

Ancient families often manufactured all their own cloth, although professionals labored in the urban areas. Family looms were primitive and inefficient, requiring much of a woman's time. According to the Book of Proverbs, the godly woman spends every spare moment at the weaving task (31:13-27). In forbidding the Israelites to mix two different kinds of materials, God taught them the necessity of keeping the faith pure (Lev. 19:19; Deut. 22:11).

WEB — a word in the Old Testament with two distinct meanings:

1. A textile fabric, especially one woven on a loom. Delilah wove the seven locks of Samson's head into the web of a loom, hoping to trap him. But Samson easily broke free from the web (Judg. 16:13-14).

2. A pattern of threadlike filaments, characteristically spun by spiders (Job 8:14; Is. 59:5).

WEDDING — a marriage ceremony with its accompanying festivities (Luke 12:36; 14:8). Among the Jewish people a wedding was a festive occasion in which the whole community participated.

When the day for the wedding arrived, the bride put on white robes (often richly embroidered),

A mosaic of the wedding procession of the virgins (Matt. 25:1-13) in an ancient church in Ravenna, Italy.
Photo by Howard Vos

decked herself with jewels, fastened a bridal girdle about her waist, covered herself with a veil, and placed a garland on her head. The bridegroom, dressed in his best clothes, with a handsome head-dress on his head, set out for the house of the bride's parents. He was accompanied by his friends, by musicians and singers, and by persons bearing torches if the procession moved at night.

The groom received his bride from her parents with their blessings and the good wishes of friends. Then he conducted the whole party back to his own house or his father's house with song, music, and dancing. On the way back they were joined by ad-ditional friends of the bride and groom. A feast was served and celebrated with great joy and merry-making. In the evening the bride was escorted to the nuptial chamber by her parents, and the groom by his companions or the bride's parents. On the next day the festivities were resumed, continuing for seven days.

Also see MARRIAGE.

WEEK — any seven consecutive days; the interval between two sabbaths (Lev. 12:5; Jer. 5:24; Luke 18:12). The Jews observed the seventh day of the week, from Friday evening (beginning at sunset) to Saturday evening, as their SABBATH, or day of rest and worship (Ex. 16:23–27).

The early Christians, to commemorate the resur-rection of Christ, worshiped not on the old Jewish Sabbath, but on the Lord's Day (the first day of the week, or Sunday), which became the new Christian "sabbath" (Mark 16:2, 9; Acts 20:7; 1 Cor. 16:2).

Also see TIME.

WEEKLY SABBATH (see SABBATH).

WEEKS, FEAST OF (see FEASTS AND FESTIVALS).

WEEKS, SEVENTY (see SEVENTY WEEKS).

WEEPING (see MOURN).

WEIGHTS AND MEASURES OF THE BIBLE. Early in the development of society, man learned to measure, weigh, and exchange commodities. At first this trade was simple barter, the exchange of one type of goods for another type. As society be-came more complex, the need for standardized trade values became apparent. Yet each city set up its own standards of weights and measures, thus creating great confusion in trade between different peoples and cultures.

Weighing (pounds) and measuring (volume, length, and area) are two distinct functions in the Bible. The various units by which these two func-tions were expressed in Bible times are discussed in this article under these two major divisions.

Weights

The balance was an early method of determining weight. The balance consisted of a beam of wood supported in the middle with a pan suspended by cords on each end. A known quantity of weight would be placed in the pan on one side of the bal-ance and the object to be weighed on the other side. By adding or removing known weights until each

Photo by Gustav Jeeninga

Ancient weights were frequently cast in the shapes of animals such as turtles, ducks, and lions to make them easily recognizable and easy to handle.

side was equal, the weight of the object could be determined.

Most of the weights in the ancient world were made of stone, metal, or clay. The weights ap-peared in many forms, such as cubes, spheres, cones, cylinders, domes, or animal shapes. Some of these weights were inscribed with the amount of their weight, but most were not. Since these weights varied from one place to the next, many people carried pouches which contained their own weights (Deut. 25:13; Prov. 16:11), so they could see if they were receiving just value.

These ancient weights were sometimes used as money. Instead of referring to a talent of gold or sil-ver or a shekel of gold or silver, people would merely refer to a talent or a shekel (2 Kin. 7:1; Matt. 25:15–28).

In Palestine, both the Canaanites and the Israel-ites used the Mesopotamian weight system. Each level of weight had four separate standards—the common, the heavy (twice the common weight), the common royal (5 percent heavier than the com-mon weight), and the heavy royal (5 percent heavier than the heavy weight). Several of these weights are mentioned in the Bible.

Talent. The heaviest unit of weight in the Hebrew system. The talent was used to weigh gold (2 Sam. 12:30), silver (1 Kin. 20:39), iron (1 Chr. 29:7), bronze (Ex. 38:29), and many other commodities. The common talent weighed about 3000 *shekels* or the full weight that a man could carry (2 Kin. 5:23). In Revelation 16:21 giant heavenly hailstones are described as heavy as a talent.

Kesitah. The second heaviest weight in the He-brew system (Gen. 33:19, piece of money; Josh. 24:32, piece of silver). The kesitah weighed about

125 shekels. Since the root meaning of the word is lamb, this particular weight may have been shaped like a lamb. Jacob paid Hamor of Shechem a hundred kesitah for a parcel of land (Gen. 33:19; sheep, NEB). At the end of Job's encounter with God, his friends brought him a kesitah and a ring of gold (Job 42:11).

Mina. A weight equal to about 50 common shekels, similar to the Canaanite system (1 Kin. 10:17; Ezra 2:69; pound, KJV). Ezekiel 45:12 seeks to redefine the weight (maneh, KJV, NASB), to equal 60 shekels, as in the Mesopotamian system. In Daniel 5:25 the words MENE, MENE, TEKEL, UPHARSIN may be interpreted as a play on monetary values of that day ("Mina, mina, shekel, and a half shekel"). The phrase, then, would refer to the Babylonian rulers Nabopolassar, Nebuchadnezzar, Nabonidus, and Belshazzar, implying that they were decreasing in importance.

The mina is used in Luke 19:13, 16 (pound, RSV, NEB) to refer to approximately a pound of money.

Pound. A Roman weight of about 340 grams, or 12 ounces (John 12:3). This term is used in the NKJV to designate the pound of precious ointments used to anoint Christ. The same word is also used to describe the amount of myrrh and aloes used to anoint the body of Christ in John 19:39.

Shekel. The most common weight in the Hebrew system (Josh. 7:21; Ezek. 4:10). The shekel weighed about 11.4 grams, or less than an ounce. Its use was so common that in Genesis 20:16, the Hebrew text states "a thousand pieces of silver" without even bothering to specify shekel.

The shekel of the sanctuary (Ex. 30:13; Ezek. 45:12) was said to weigh 20 gerahs, the same weight as the common shekel. It is possible that the standard for the common shekel was kept at the sanctuary and became known as the sanctuary shekel. There is no clear reference to the use of the heavy shekel in Israel, but the shekel of the king's standard (the royal shekel) is referred to in 2 Samuel 14:26.

Pim. A weight which apparently weighed about two-thirds of a shekel (1 Sam. 13:21). This verse is difficult to translate accurately, but it probably should read "and the charge...was a pim for the ploughshares." This charge is not mentioned in the KJV.

Bekah. One-half shekel. The bekah was the weight in silver that was paid by each Israelite as a religious tax (Ex. 30:13; 38:26). The bekah, spelled beka in some translations, is named only once in English translations (Ex. 38:26), but is referred to more often (Gen. 24:22; Ex. 30:13, 15).

Gerah. The smallest of the Israelite weights. The Bible defines it as one-twentieth of a shekel (Ex. 30:13; Lev. 27:25).

Measures

Measurements recorded in the Bible are of three types: (1) measures of volume, which told the amount of dry commodity (for example, flour) or liquid (for example, oil) that could be contained in a vessel; (2) measures of length, for height, width,

and depth of an object or person; and (3) measures of total area, which described the size of a building, field, or city.

Measures of Volume. Measurements of volume were originally made by estimated handfuls. Eventually containers (jars, baskets, etc.), which held an agreed upon number of handfuls were used as the standard measure. The terms used for such measures were frequently taken from the name of the containers.

The Israelites adapted the Mesopotamian system of measure of volume from the Canaanites. Their system contained several major designations for measuring dry volume.

Homer—The standard unit for dry measure (Ezek. 45:11-14; Hos. 3:2). This unit contained about 220 liters (6 1/4 bushels). It was a large measure weighing the equivalent of the normal load a donkey could carry. In Leviticus 27:16, a homer of barley is worth 50 shekels of silver. In Numbers 11:32 God provided quail so generously for his people that they could gather ten homers of them. Isaiah's prophecy of only an ephah of wheat from a homer of seed was a sign of God's judgment (Is. 5:10).

Kor—The same size as the homer (Ezek. 45:14, cor; measure, KJV). The kor was used to measure flour (1 Kin. 4:22), wheat, and barley (2 Chr. 2:10; 27:5).

Ephah—a unit equal to one-tenth of a homer (Ex. 29:40; deal, KJV; Is. 5:10).

Seah—a unit of uncertain capacity, but one-third of an ephah is probably correct (1 Sam. 25:18; 1 Kin. 7:1; measure, KJV, RSV, NEB, NASB).

Omer—a unit equal to one-tenth of an ephah (Ex. 16:36). Another Hebrew word, *issaron*, translated "one-tenth of an ephah," (Ex. 29:40; Lev. 14:10; Num. 15:4) was a dry measure of similar size to the omer.

Kab—a unit containing about 1.2 liters or 1.16 quarts. The kab is mentioned only once in the Bible (2 Kin. 6:25). During the Syrian siege of Samaria, prices were inflated so badly that one-fourth of a kab of dove's dung was sold for five pieces of silver.

The New Testament contains four major designations for measuring dry capacity. These Greek words are not mentioned in the English translations of the New Testament.

Koros (Luke 16:7; measure, NKJV, KJV, RSV, NASB; bushel, NEB, NIV), was a measure of wheat equal to about 453 liters (13 bushels).

Modios (Matt. 5:15; Mark 4:21; Luke 11:33; basket, NKJV; bushel, KJV, RSV), contained about 9 liters (1/4 bushel).

Saton (Matt. 13:33; Luke 13:21; measure, NKJV, KJV, RSV; hundredweight, NEB; peck, NASB; large amount, NIV) contained about 13 liters (3/8 bushel).

Choinix (Rev. 6:6; quart, NKJV; measure, KJV) contained about 1.1 liters (1 quart).

The Old Testament contained five major designations for liquid measure. The homer (Ezek. 45:11-14) containing 10 baths, was the largest liquid measure. The kor was the same size as the homer (Ezek. 45:14). The bath was the equivalent in liquid measure to the ephah in dry measure (Ezek. 45:11, 14). It was the standard liquid measure, equaling about 22 liters (5.83 gallons). It was used to measure water (1 Kin. 7:26), wine (Is. 5:10), and oil (2 Chr. 2:10). The hin, equal to one-sixth of a bath, was used to measure water (Ezek. 4:11), oil (Ex. 29:40), and wine (Lev. 23:13). One-sixth of a hin was considered the daily ration of water (Ezek. 4:11). The log, found only in Leviticus 14:10–24, was a measure of oil in the ceremony for the purification of a leper. The log was equal to one-twelfth of a hin.

The New Testament contains three major terms for liquid measure. These words appear in Greek manuscripts but are translated by different words in English versions of the Bible.

The largest of these measures was the metretes (John 2:6; gallon, NKJV; firkin, KJV; water-jar, NEB). Batos (Luke 16:6; measures, NKJV, KJV; gallons, NEB, NIV) was the next smaller measure. Xestes (Mark 7:4, 8; pitcher, NKJV; pot, KJV; copper pot, NASB; copper bowl, NEB; kettles, NIV; vessels of bronze, RSV) was the smallest unit of liquid measure.

Measures of Length. Linear measure, as with other units of measure, was originally based upon parts of the body, such as the hand, arm, or foot. Sometimes the unit was named for the part of the body it represented (palm, finger, etc.). Early linear distances were also based upon common but difficult-to-define objects, such as the step, bowshot, or a day's journey. By New Testament times, the Greek and Roman influences had caused these measures to be defined quite clearly.

Lengths were measured by various devices, including the measuring line (Zech. 2:1), measuring rod or measuring reed (Ezek. 40:5) and the mete-yard (Lev. 19:35, KJV).

Several units expressing measurements of length are mentioned in the Bible.

Cubit—The distance from the elbow to the finger tip—about 45 centimeters (18 inches). The cubit was the standard unit of length. It was the common designation of the height of a man (1 Sam. 17:4) or an object (Ezek. 40:5). There was more than one size cubit, for the bed of Og, king of Bashan, is described "according to the standard cubit" (Deut. 3:11), while Ezekiel's measuring rod extended "six cubits long, each being a cubit and a handbreadth" (Ezek. 40:5). The long cubit was probably 51.8 centimeters (20.4 inches). The cubit is mentioned several times in the New Testament (Luke 12:25; Rev. 21:17). In each case it probably refers to the common cubit.

Rod/Reed—Units of measure equal to six cubits. The rod (Ezek. 40:5) and the reed (Ezek. 29:6) appear to be interchangeable. (Ezekiel 40:5 specifies that this measure is according to the long cubit.)

Span—The distance between the extended thumb and the little finger (1 Sam. 17:4). The span was equivalent to one-half cubit.

Handbreadth—The width of the hand at the base of the four fingers (1 Kin. 7:26; 2 Chr. 4:5). The handbreadth was considered to be one-sixth of a cubit.

Finger—The smallest subdivision of the cubit, equal to one-fourth of a handbreadth (Jer. 52:21). The finger is also called the cubit.

Fathom—A Greek unit equal to the length of the outstretched arms, about 1.8 meters (six feet), or four cubits (Acts 27:28).

Furlong—A distance equal to about 200 meters, or one-eighth of a mile (Rev. 14:20; stadia, RSV).

Mile—A Roman measurement of 1000 paces (five Roman feet to the pace), equaling about 1,477.5 meters, or 1,616 yards (Matt. 5:41).

Several less definite distances are expressed in the Bible. Before the Babylonian Captivity, distance was expressed variously as "a bowshot" (Gen. 21:16), "the area plowed by a yoke (of oxen in a day)" (1 Sam. 14:14, footnote), "a day's journey" (Num. 11:31; 1 Kin. 19:4), "three days' journey" (Gen. 30:36; Ex. 3:18; 8:27; "a journey of three days", Num. 10:33), " seven days' journey" (Gen. 31:23), or even "eleven day's journey" (Deut. 1:2). No one knows for sure the amount of these distances, but a "day's journey" has been estimated to be approximately 32 to 40 kilometers (20 to 25 miles).

The "Sabbath day's journey" (Acts 1:12) was the product of rabbinical exegesis of Exodus 16:29 and Numbers 35:5. The rabbis fixed the legal distance for travel on the Sabbath at 2,000 cubits.

Many modern English translations of the Bible often use modern measurements of length, such as feet and inches (Gen. 6:15–16, NIV), and yards (John 21:8, NASB, NEB, NIV, RSV).

Measures of Area. Measures of area are not well defined in the Bible. Sometimes an area was determined by the amount of land a pair of oxen could plow in a day (1 Sam. 14:14). According to the NKJV, this was considered to be about one-half of an acre. Another method of designating area was to estimate the space by the amount of seed required to sow it (Lev. 27:16).

WELL — a pit or hole sunk into the earth to provide water. References in English versions of the Bible sometimes confuse wells, natural springs, and cisterns. Many different types of wells are mentioned in the Bible. These include a cistern dug in the ground (Gen 16:14; 2 Sam. 17:18); a spring (Ps. 84:6); a fountain, also called a living spring (Neh. 2:13); and a pit or hole (John 4:11–12).

Wells in Palestine were dug from solid limestone rock. Sometimes they were furnished with descending steps that allowed a person to dip directly from the pool of water (Gen. 24:16). The brims of still other wells had a curb or low wall of stone that often bore the marks of the furrows worn over the years by ropes in drawing water. Jesus sat on a curb of this sort when he talked to the woman of Samaria (John 4:6).

There is no information on how biblical wells

Photo by Gustav Jeeninga

Long staircases were sometimes built to provide convenient access to wells, such as this one at the ancient city of Zaretan.

were dug. But the process must have been very difficult, because only crude tools were available. Isaac (Gen. 26:18–22) and Uzziah (2 Chr. 26:10) are the most active well-diggers mentioned in the Bible. Many ancient wells descended to a great depth. Jacob's Well is still 75 feet deep and at one time it may have been twice as deep. These deep wells were necessary because of the problem of shallow wells running dry in the summer.

Even in very favorable locations, the water in Palestine almost vanishes during the summer drought. Some wells are not covered because the soil in the area is not likely to drift and fill them up, but desert wells are always covered. They taper to a point so that the opening is easily closed.

Wells were often situated outside towns, where they became local landmarks and meeting places (Gen. 24:11,20; John 4:6–8). Sometimes they were in isolated locations, enabling livestock to be grazed nearby (Gen. 29:3,8–10; Ex. 2:15–18). Both the ownership and the use of wells could become matters of dispute (Gen. 21:25; Ex. 2:17–19). Occasionally, old dry wells were used as prisons (Gen. 27:24; Jer. 38:6).

The Bible's most famous wells were at Bethlehem, for whose water David longed (2 Sam. 23:15–

16), and at Sychar in Samaria, where Jesus spoke about His free gift of unfailing living water.

WELL DIGGER (see Occupations and Trades).

WEST (see Direction).

WEST GATE (see Gates of Jerusalem and the Temple).

WHALE (see Animals of the Bible).

WHEAT (see Plants of the Bible).

WHEEL — a solid disk connected by spokes to a hub, designed to turn around in an axle passed through the center. Wheels are first mentioned in Exodus 14:25, a reference to the chariot wheels of the Egyptians.

The original wheels were probably pieces cut from wooden logs. Illustrations from Ur about 2500 B.C. show large wheels made from solid pieces of wood pegged together with crosspieces on either side of the axle. Sometimes these had a leather strip around the rim. Later, solid metal rims were used.

By about 1500 B.C., war chariots from Canaan and Egypt were equipped with spoked wheels.

The wheels of the Assyrian chariots about 900 B.C. were of much heavier construction. In order to carry the weight of an armor-bearer in addition to the driver and the armed soldier, six- and eight-spoked wheels were developed and the rims were thickened considerably over the Egyptian types. These heavy vehicles were more cumbersome to operate than the lighter models. The noise of these heavy wheels rumbling over the ground and raising huge clouds of dust signaled the approach of the enemy forces (Jer. 47:3; Nah. 3:2).

The word wheels is also used in reference to the four bonze wheels on each of the ten bronze carts in Solomon's Temple. On each of the ten carts was a laver containing 40 baths, or about 392 gallons. First Kings 7:33 states: "The workmanship of the wheels was like the workmanship of a chariot wheel; their axle pins, their rims, their spokes, and their hubs were all of cast bronze."

WHELP — a young offspring of various carnivorous mammals, such as a dog, wolf, or lion; a puppy or cub. In the Bible the word whelp always refers to a lion cub and is always used figuratively, for instance, of the tribes of Judah (Gen. 49:9) and Dan (Deut. 33:22).

WHIP —an instrument for flogging, usually consisting of a rod with a lash on one end. The whip was used for driving animals or administering corporal punishment. Jesus made a whip of cords and used it to drive the moneychangers out of the Temple (John 2:15). Also see Scourge, Scourging.

WHIRLWIND —any violent storm or destructive wind. Windstorms are common in Palestine, especially in the northern Jordan River Valley and around the Sea of Galilee, because of the proximity of these bodies of water to the hot desert.

The Lord took Elijah into heaven by a whirlwind (1 Kings 2:1, 11) and answered Job out of the whirlwind (Job 38:1; 40:6). The whirlwind is often symbolic of God's wrath and destructive fury visited upon the wicked (Ps. 58:9; Nah. 1:3).

WHITE (see COLORS OF THE BIBLE).

WHITEWASH (see MINERALS OF THE BIBLE).

WHORE (see HARLOT).

WICKED ONE, THE — another name for SATAN or the DEVIL (1 John 2:13–14; 3:12; 5:18–19). In Jesus' parable of the sower, Satan (Mark 4:15) is equated with the devil (Luke 8:12) and the wicked one (Matt. 13:19). The apostle Paul also equates *the devil* (Eph. 6:11) with the wicked one (Eph. 6:16).

WICK–TRIMMER — a gold tong used to snuff out the wicks of the lamps in the tabernacle and Temple (Ex. 25:38; 2 Chr. 4:21; tongs, KJV).

WIDOW — a woman whose husband has died and who has not remarried. If a man died in Bible times, his widow often suffered at the hands of the powerful (Job 24:21). This was especially true if she had no family to provide for her and her children.

God was concerned about the plight of the widow (Ps 68:5; 146:9). Through the Mosaic Law, God provided her with the opportunity to glean in the fields, orchards, and vineyards after the harvesters had taken most of the crop (Deut. 24:19–22). She shared with the Levite in the third–year tithe (Deut. 26:12).

True believers followed the model that God had established. Job noted that he had shared his food with widows (Job 31:16). James wrote: "Pure and undefiled religion before God and the Father is this: to visit orphans and widows in their trouble, and to keep oneself unspotted from the world" (James 1:27).

WIFE — a man's marriage partner. After God created Adam, He declared, "It is not good that man should live alone" (Gen. 2:18). Then He created woman and united the couple and they became "one flesh" (Gen. 2:24). The wife is to honor her husband (Eph. 5:22), and the husband is to love his wife as Christ loved the church (Eph. 5:25–33). Also see FAMILY.

WILD ASS, WILD BEASTS, WILD BOAR, WILD DONKEY, WILD GOAT, WILD OX (see ANIMALS OF THE BIBLE).

WILDERNESS — a land not suited for farming. Wilderness land was too dry, rough, or rocky to be cultivated, but it was sufficient for grazing (Gen. 14:6; Ex. 3:18). Occasionally, the word wilderness means "desert." John the Baptist preached in the wilderness of Judea (Matt. 3:1; Luke 3:2–4), and Jesus was in the wilderness when He was tempted by the devil (Mark 1:12; Luke 4:2). In both instances a desert area is intended.

WILDERNESS OF WANDERING (see WANDERINGS OF ISRAEL).

WILE — a trick or strategy intended to entice or deceive. The apostle Paul warned Christian believers to beware of "the wiles of the devil" (Eph. 6:11; schemes, NASB, NIV).

WILL — a word with two distinct meanings in the Bible:

1. Wishing, desiring, or choosing especially in reference to the will of God. In the gospels, primarily in John, Jesus is said to be acting not according to His own will, but according to the will of the heavenly Father (John 5:30; 6:38). Indeed, doing the will of the Father is Jesus' nourishment (John 4:34), and Jesus does nothing apart from the Father's will (John 5:19). Luke confirms this when he quotes Jesus' statement in the Garden of Gethsemane: "Father, if it is Your will, remove this cup from Me; nevertheless not my will, but yours, be done" (Luke 22:42).

2. A legal declaration of how a person wishes his possessions to be disposed after his death. No written Israelite wills existed until the first century B.C. They were unnecessary because of the strict inheritance customs of the Hebrew people. Land belonged to the family, and it was passed on to the sons, the oldest receiving a double portion. If there were no sons, the land passed in the following order—daughters, brothers, father's brothers, and next of kin (Num. 27:8–11).

This mosaic from ancient times personifying the four winds was discovered at the Roman city of Ostia.

Photo by Howard Vos

WILLOW (see PLANTS OF THE BIBLE).

WILLOWS, BROOK OF THE — a brook or stream mentioned by the prophet Isaiah in his proclamation against Moab (Is. 15:7). This brook was near Zoar (Is. 15:5), a city at the southern end of the Dead Sea, and was at or near the boundary between Moab and Edom. Isaiah warned that when the people of Moab fled their land, they would carry their wealth with them to this brook.

WIMPLE — KJV word for a cloth covering wound around the head, framing the face, and drawn into folds beneath the chin (Is. 3:22). Other translations are veil (KJV), mantle (RSV), and shawl (NKJV, NIV). Also see DRESS.

WIND — the natural movement of air as a part of the weather pattern. The hot, dry climate of Palestine made the winds very important to the Hebrew people. The winds of this region included cool daytime winds, evening sea breezes bearing essential moisture, and hot blasts from the desert.

The dry north wind is the coldest wind in Palestine, blowing from June until September. Today the Arabs call this wind the Simoom (from *samm* or "poison"). Its combined cold, wind, and heat cause headache, fever, and neuralgia. The "north wind" of Proverbs 25:23 which "brings forth rain" is really the northwest wind.

The violent east wind blows from the desert. This is the wind most often mentioned in the Bible. It scorched the grain (Gen. 41:6, 23, 27), withered the vine (Ezek. 17:9), and parched the fruit (Jon. 4:8). The east wind also brought the plague of locusts (Gen. 10:13). Blowing "from the wilderness," it dried up the springs of water (Hos. 13:15).

Generally, all such violent gusts of wind were attributed to the east. These winds were also called winds of the wilderness. The blast that struck the home of Job's sons and killed them was probably the east wind (Job 1:19). An east wind from God parted the Red Sea (Ex. 14:21) and shattered the ships of Tarshish (Ps. 48:7). Probably it was an east wind that wrecked Paul's ship (Acts 27:14).

The west wind carries moisture from the Mediterranean Sea over Palestine between November and February. A west wind drove off the locusts in Egypt (Ex. 10:19). The rain-bearing west wind also ended a severe drought in the days of the prophet Elijah (1 Kin. 18:43–44).

The south wind blew Paul's ship gently (Acts 27:13), before a fiercer wind demolished his ship. God "quiets the earth" with the south wind (Job 37:17). The Arabs call the south wind off the desert *sirocco*. It blows for about one day at a time during the spring (February–June).

Winds were used to separate the grain from the chaff in the winnowing process (Job 21:18; Ps. 1–4). A wind from God brought quail to Moses and his people (Num. 1:31). Squalls from the Sea of Galilee are also mentioned (Mark 4:37; Luke 8:23). But this wind and the raging waters were stilled by Jesus.

In a figurative sense, war is compared to the east wind (Jer. 18:17). The wind, or breath, is used as a metaphor for the brevity of life. Persons of uncertain faith are said to be tossed about on "every wind of doctrine" (Eph. 4:14).

Also see EUROCLYDON; RAIN; WEATHER.

WINDOW — an opening in the wall of a building. Windows varied in size, ornamentation, and style. They usually were protected by wooden latticework or grills. Some windows were large enough for a person to go through (Josh. 2:15; 1 Sam. 19:12). Windows were often spoken of symbolically in the Bible, as at the time of the flood when "the windows of heaven were opened" (Gen. 7:11). Also see HOUSE.

WINE — the fermented juice of grapes. Wine is first mentioned in the Bible when Noah became intoxicated after the Flood (Gen. 9:20–21). Wine was a common commodity in Hebrew life and was regularly included in summaries of agricultural products (Gen. 27:28; 2 Kin. 18:32; Jer. 31:12).

In Palestine, grape harvesting occurred in September and was accompanied by great celebration. The ripe fruit was gathered in baskets (Jer. 6:9) and carried to winepresses. The grapes were placed in the upper one of two vats that formed the winepress. Then the grapes were trampled or "treaded." The treading was done by one or more men, according to the size of the vat. These grape treaders encouraged one another with shouts (Is. 16:9–10; Jer. 25:30; 48:33).

Sometimes the juice from the grapes was served in an unfermented state, but generally it was bottled after fermentation. If the wine was to be kept for some time, a substance was added to give it body (Is. 25:6). Consequently, the wine was always strained before it was served (Is. 25:6).

A watchtower, or leaf–covered wooden booth, was often built on a high place overlooking the vineyard (Mark 12:1). This booth was occupied by members of the family during the growing season to protect their crop (Job 27:18) and sometimes by a watchman during the winter. Often a cottage or hut was built in the vineyard. The family lived here during the summer to protect the grapes but abandoned the hut in the winter (Is. 1:8).

Wine was stored in either clay jars or wineskins, which were made by tying up the holes of skins taken from goats. Old wineskins could not be used a second time because the fermentation process would cause the old skins to burst and the wine would be lost (Matt. 9:17; Mark 2:22; Luke 5:36–38).

Uses of Wine. Wine was a significant trade item in Palestine. Solomon offered Hiram 20,000 baths of wine in exchange for timber (2 Chr. 2:10, 15). Damascus was a market for the "wine of Helbon" (Ezek. 27:18). Fines were sometimes paid with wine (Amos 2:8).

Wine was also used in worship. Libations to false gods were condemned (Deut. 32:27–38; Is. 57:6; 65:11; Jer. 7:18; 19:13), but the drink offering pre-

A modern vineyard at the foot of the mound of ancient Lachish. As in biblical times, winemaking is still an important industry in Palestine.

scribed by the Law of Moses was a libation of wine offered to the Lord. The daily offering (Ex. 29:40; Num. 28:7), the offering of the FIRSTFRUITS (Lev. 23:13), the burnt offering, and the freewill offering (Num. 15:4) required one-fourth of a hin of wine. The sacrifice of a ram was accompanied by a hin of wine (Num. 15:6–7). In the temple organization set up by David, Levites were appointed to supervise these wine offerings (1 Chr. 9:29).

Wine was also used as a common beverage, or drink, in Palestine. A part of the daily fare of the Hebrew people, wine was a creation of the Lord to cheer the hearts of men (Ps. 104:15), a gift given by Him and not by Baal (Hos. 2:8), as the idol worshiper thought.

Wisdom is said to have mixed her wine (Prov. 9:2) in furnishing her table. Wine might be drunk with milk (Song 5:1). Melchizedek brought wine and bread to Abraham when Abraham returned from battle (Gen. 14:18). Wine was offered by the old man of Gibeah to the traveling Levite (Judg. 19:19). Jesse sent David with bread, a skin of wine, and a young goat as a present when Saul was fighting the Philistines (1 Sam. 16:20). Abigail brought David two skins of wine (1 Sam. 25:18).

The tribes of Issachar, Zebulun, and Naphtali brought wine to David (1 Chr. 12:40) when David was made king. Ziba brought David wine as he fled from Abasalom (2 Sam. 16:1–2). Job's children were drinking wine at their brother's house when disaster struck (Job 1:13, 18). Wine was on the list of supplies that the Persians furnished the captive Hebrew people when they returned to Jerusalem (Ezra 6:9; 7:22). These are but a few of the many references to the use of wine as food among the Hebrew people.

Wine was also used as medicine. It was said to re-vive the faint (2 Sam. 16:2) and was suitable as a sedative for people in distress (Prov. 31:6). Mixed with a drug, it was used to ease suffering (Matt. 27:34; Mark 15:23). The Samaritan poured oil and wine on the wounds of the injured traveler (Luke 10:34). The apostle Paul charged Timothy, "No longer drink only water, but use a little wine for your stomach's sake" (1 Tim. 5:23).

Misuses of Wine. The dangers of drunkenness are abundantly recognized in the Bible (Prov. 20:1; 23:29–35). Wine often enslaved the heart (Hos. 4:11). The prophets accused Israel of being overcome with wine (Is. 28:1), of drinking wine by bowlfuls (Amos 6:6), and of wanting prophets who spoke of wine (Mic. 2:11). Leaders were interested in drinking and were not concerned about the ruin of the country (Is. 5:11–12; 22:13). The list of those drunken with wine in the Bible begins with Noah and includes Lot, Nabal, and Ammon (Gen. 9:21; 1 Sam. 25:36–37; 2 Sam. 13:28).

While the use of wine continued in New Testament times, Paul admonished his readers to be filled with the Holy Spirit rather than with wine (Eph. 5:18). Wine was a basic commodity in biblical times. But there is no biblical justification for the heavy liquor traffic of modern times.

WINEBIBBERS — those who drink too much wine. The Bible warns against associating with such persons (Prov. 23:20). Jesus' enemies accused Him of being a winebibber (Matt. 11:19; Luke 7:34). Unlike John the Baptist, who "came neither eating bread nor drinking wine" (Luke 7:33), Jesus "came eating and drinking" (Matt. 11:18). His association with those who ate and drank freely brought the rebuke of the religious leaders who had decided to get rid of Him. Also see DRUNKENNESS; WINE.

An ancient winepress in Capernaum, used for crushing grapes and olives in Bible times (Is. 5:2).

Photo by Gustav Jeeninga

WINEPRESS — a vat in which the juice is pressed from grapes in the process of making wine (Deut. 16:13; Judg. 6:11). A winepress was made by digging a square basin in the rock (Neh. 13:15). At a slightly lower level on the slope was a second basin where the juice could be collected in clay jars or in WINESKINS for storage. Digging a winepress was a fixed part of the preparation of a vineyard (Is. 5:2; Matt. 21:33; Mark 12:1). Winepresses were owned by common people (Num. 18:27, 30; Deut. 15:14), as well as kings (Judg. 7:25; Zech. 14:10).

The time for making wine in Palestine was August and September. This was a time of joy, and the work of treading the winepress was lightened by shouts of joy (Jer. 48:33).

Egyptian art depicts men treading the winepress. In figurative language, treading the winepress was a picture of God's judgment (Lam. 1:15; Joel 3:13). The Lord is presented as coming from Edom after treading down the peoples, leaving His clothing splattered with their blood (Is. 63:2–3). This same figure occurs in the Book of Revelation. The Word of God "treads the winepress of the fierceness and wrath of Almighty God" (Rev. 19:15).

Also see TOOLS OF THE BIBLE.

WINESKIN — a bag for holding and dispensing WINE, made from the skin of a goat or another animal (Job 32:19). In Bible times, wineskins were manufactured from whole animal hides.

Jesus used the analogy of wineskins to show that the Jewish legalism of the Old Testament was inflexible and outdated: "No one puts new wine into old wineskins; or else the new wine bursts the wineskins, the wine is spilled, and the wineskins are ruined" (Matt. 9:17; Mark 2:22; Luke 5:37–38). The "old wineskins" of Judaism could not contain the dynamic new faith of Christianity.

WING — a specialized organ of flight in a bird. But the word is generally used in a symbolic sense in the Bible. God is described as protecting His people "under [His] wings" (Ruth 2:12; Ps. 17:8). Jeremiah describes God's judgment of Moab in terms of a great bird of prey, an eagle swooping down on its target (Jer. 48:40; 49:22). God brought His people out of Egypt on eagle's wings (Ex. 19:4; Deut. 32:11). In the same way He will lift up the weary faithful returning from the years of CAPTIVITY in Babylon, giving them renewed strength (Is. 40:31).

WINNOWING — the process of separating the kernels of threshed grain, such as wheat or barley, from the CHAFF with a current of air. The grain and its mixture of straw and husks were thrown into the air. The kernels of wheat or barley would fall into a pile on the THRESHING FLOOR; and the chaff, or refuse, would be blown away by the wind (Ps. 1:4). Also see AGRICULTURE.

WINNOWING FORK (see TOOLS OF THE BIBLE).

WINTER — the season between autumn and spring. In Palestine winters usually were short and mild, but snow and hail sometimes occurred in higher elevations (Jer. 18:14). Winter is also known as the rainy season in Palestine (Song 2:11).

WINTER HOUSE — a section of the palace of King Jehoiakim exposed to the sun and used in wintertime because of its warmth (Jer. 36:22; winter apartments, NEB, NIV).

WISDOM — ability to judge correctly and to follow the best course of action, based on knowledge and understanding. The apostle Paul declared that the message of the cross is foolishness to the Greeks and a stumbling block to the Jews. But to those who believe, said Paul, this "foolishness of God" is "the wisdom of God" (1 Cor. 1:18–25).

Against the wisdom of God Paul contrasted "the wisdom of this world" (1 Cor. 1:20; 3:19), "human wisdom" (1 Cor. 2:4), "the wisdom of men" (1 Cor. 2:5), "the wisdom of this age" (1 Cor. 2:6), and "man's wisdom" (1 Cor. 2:13).

The biblical concept of wisdom, therefore, is quite different from the classical view of wisdom, which sought through philosophy and man's rational thought to determine the mysteries of existence and the universe. The first principle of biblical wisdom is that man should humble himself before God in reverence and worship, obedient to His commands. This idea is found especially in the WISDOM LITERATURE: the books of Job, Psalms, Proverbs, and Ecclesiastes.

In the Old Testament, the best example of a "wise man" is King Solomon (1 Kin. 10:4, 6–8; 2 Chr. 1:7–12). And yet the same book that heaps such lavish, warm, and glowing praise upon Solomon for his reputed wisdom (1 Kin. 4:29–34) also points out how Solomon's heart turned away from the Lord (1 Kin. 11:1–13).

WISDOM LITERATURE — a type of literature, common to the peoples of the ancient world, that included ethical and philosophical works. The wisdom literature of the Old Testament consists of the books of Job, Proverbs, and Ecclesiastes, and certain of the psalms (Psalm 1; 19; 37; 49; 104; 107; 112; 119; 127; 128; 133; 147; 148).

In general, two principal types of wisdom are found in the wisdom literature of the Old Testament—practical and speculative. Practical wisdom consists mainly of wise sayings that offer guidelines for a successful and happy life. These are maxims of commonsense insight and observation about how an intelligent person should conduct himself.

The Book of Proverbs is a good example of practical wisdom; it encourages the pursuit of wisdom and the practice of strict discipline, hard work, and high moral standards as the way to happiness and success. Proverbs is an optimistic book. It assumes that wisdom is attainable by all who seek and follow it. The book also declares that those who keep God's moral and ethical laws will be rewarded with long life, health, possessions, respect, security, and self-control.

Speculative wisdom, such as that found in the books of Job and Ecclesiastes, goes beyond practical maxims about daily conduct. It reflects upon the deeper issues of the meaning of life, the worth and value of life, and the existence of evil in the world.

The Book of Job seeks to explain the ways of God to man. The theme of the book is the suffering of the righteous and the apparent prosperity of the wicked. The answer to such questions is that the prosperity of the wicked is brief and illusory (Job 15:21–29; 24:24) while the righteous, although presently suffering, will eventually receive God's reward.

Like the Book of Proverbs, the Book of Ecclesiastes also contains rules for living and sayings of practical wisdom. But Ecclesiastes is more than a collection of discourses and observations designed to instruct a person on how to conduct his life. Because of its skeptical and pessimistic tone, the Book of Ecclesiastes is the most "philosophical" book of the Bible. As such, it must be classified among the works of speculative wisdom.

The wisdom psalms are similar in tone and content to the books of Job and Proverbs. Some of these psalms struggle with the problem of evil and sin in the world. Others give practical advice for daily living.

Also see ECCLESIASTES, BOOK OF; JOB, BOOK OF; PROVERBS, BOOK OF; WISDOM.

WISDOM OF SOLOMON (see APOCRYPHA).

WISE MEN — the men from the East who were led by a star to come to Palestine to worship the infant Christ (Matt. 2:1, 7, 16). The Greek word for wise men in this account (*magoi*) is rendered as astrologers where it occurs in the SEPTUAGINT, the Greek translation of the Old Testament (Dan. 1:20; 2:2) and as sorcerer in its other occurrences in the New Testament (Acts 13:6, 8).

The Greek historian Herodotus, writing in the

fifth century B.C., identified the Magi as a caste of Medes who had a priestly function in the Persian Empire. In the Book of Daniel the "astrologers" (*magoi*) are grouped with magicians, sorcerers, and Chaldeans as advisers to the court of Babylon with responsibility for interpreting dreams.

The role of the star in Matthew 2 suggests a connection with astrology. These astrologers, pursuing their observations of the stars in the heavens, encountered a sign of God (Matt. 24:29–30). God broke through their misguided system to make the great event known.

The joy, rejoicing, worship, and gifts which mark the response of these wise men to the birth of Jesus is quite a contrast to the troubled state and murderous intent of Herod and his Jewish advisers in Jerusalem (Matt. 2:1–12).

WITCH, WITCHCRAFT (see MAGIC, SORCERY, AND DIVINATION).

WITHERED HAND (see DISABILITIES AND DEFORMITIES).

WITNESS — a person who gives testimony; testimony given for or against someone, often in a law-court setting, where there is considerable concern for the truth of the testimony. "You shall not bear false witness against your neighbor" (Ex. 20:16; Deut. 17:6; Prov. 25:18).

A witness can also be a guarantee of the accuracy of a transaction (Jer. 32:10, 12, 25, 44). The Old Testament prophets often pictured God either as bearing witness against Israel (Mic. 1:2) or as challenging Israel to bear witness against Him (Mic. 6:3). God is also seen in the Old Testament as witnessing covenants between individuals (Gen. 31:50) as well as covenants between Himself and the nation of Israel or individuals (Deut. 31:19–26).

In addition to these general uses, witness is also used in connection with the distinctively religious message of the Bible. God witnesses to the believer about His assurance of salvation: "The Spirit Himself bears witness with our spirit that we are children of God" (Rom. 8:16).

The Bible also declares that God has not left Himself without witness (Acts 14:17). Witness to Christ is borne by the prophets (Acts 10:43), John the Baptist (John 1:7), the Father (John 5:37; 8:18), the works of Christ (John 5:36; 10:37–38), and Christ Himself (John 8:18).

The believer's life and word also serve as a witness to the world. Sometimes this witness to the world is represented in the witness of the apostles, who are Christ's special witnesses—witnesses of His resurrection (Acts 1:22; 2:32; 10:41; 13:31). However, the command to witness in Acts 1:8 has implications for all believers. It applies to the new Christian community the similar command that was given to ancient Israel (Is. 43:10, 12). The believer's model in witness is none other than Christ Himself (1 Tim. 6:13; Rev. 1:5).

WIZARD (see MAGIC, SORCERY, AND DIVINATION).

WOE — deep sorrow, grief, or affliction. In the Bible the word woe is often used, particularly by the Old Testament prophets, as an exclamation expressing dismay or misfortune (Is. 3:9, 11; Jer. 10:19; Amos 5:18). In the New Testament Jesus pronounced woes on the cities of Chorazin and Bethsaida (Matt. 11:21), on the scribes, Pharisees, and lawyers (Luke 11:42–44), and on the one who betrayed Him (Mark 14:21).

WOLF (see ANIMALS OF THE BIBLE).

WOMAN — a female adult. However, the word woman is sometimes used in the Bible to refer to a weak and helpless man (Is. 3:12; 19:16).

In order to understand the Old Testament view of woman, one must turn to the Book of Genesis. When God created mankind, He created both "male and female" (Gen. 1:27; 5:2). Both were created in God's image and both were given the responsibility of exercising authority over God's creation. The man was created before the woman. Because the man needed companionship and a helper, God caused the man to sleep. From him He created a woman, "a helper comparable to him" (Gen. 2:18, 20). Man is incomplete without woman. Because she is called a "helper" does not imply that she is inferior to man. The same Hebrew word translated as helper is used of God in His relationship to Israel (Ps. 33:20; 70:5).

The culture that developed around the Israelites in ancient times did not always have this perspective of woman. Certain Old Testament passages tend to reflect an attitude that woman was little more than a thing and that a woman should be entirely subordinate to man. This tendency became pronounced before the coming of Christ. One of the Jewish prayers that dated from that era declared, "I thank Thee that I am not a woman."

Jesus lived and taught a better way—the way of love. He allowed women to accompany Him and His disciples on their journeys (Luke 8:1–3). He talked with the Samaritan woman at Jacob's Well and led her to a conversion experience (John 4). Jesus did not think it strange that Mary sat at His feet, assuming the role of a disciple; in fact, He suggested to Martha that she should do likewise (Luke 10:38–42). Although the Jews segregated the women in both Temple and synagogue, the early church did not separate the congregation by sex (Acts 12:1–17; 1 Cor. 11:2–16).

The apostle Paul wrote, "There is neither Jew nor Greek, there is neither slave nor free, there is neither male nor female; for you are all one in Christ Jesus" (Gal. 3:28). Within the writings of Paul, however, other statements restrict women from participating in church leadership as freely as men. Women were to keep silent in church; they were to be submissive to the male leaders (1 Cor. 14:34–35; 1 Tim. 2:11–12).

How does one reconcile these two seemingly opposing views? In Galatians Paul was stating a general principle that men and women were equal, just as the slave is equal to his master in the sight of God. However, Paul did not require or teach that the slaveholder had to release his slaves. In the same manner, Paul requested the women to be submissive to their husbands—to preserve order within the church and to be a witness to outsiders.

Some of the finest leaders in Israel were women, in spite of the fact that the culture was male-dominated. Military victories were sometimes won because of the courage of one woman (Judges 4—5; 9:54; Esth. 4:16). God revealed His Word through PROPHETESSES (Judg. 4:4; Luke 2:36; Acts 21:9). God used Priscilla and her husband Aquila to explain "the way of God more accurately" to Apollos the preacher (Acts 18:26). The heroes of faith mentioned in Hebrews 11 include Sarah (v. 11), Moses' mother (v. 23), and Rahab the harlot (v. 31).

WOODCUTTER, WOODWORKER (see OCCUPATIONS AND TRADES).

WOODEN IMAGES — images or idols or false gods. The Hebrew word which the NKJV translates as wooden image (Ex. 34:13; Deut. 7:5; grove, KJV) is *Asherah*. Asherah was the name which the Canaanites gave to their goddess of fertility. Thus, the wooden images were idols erected in honor of her. Usually these images were tree trunks or simple poles that the people placed next to the altar of the storm god, Baal.

The disobedience and wickedness of the Israelites is shown in their repeated opposition to the Lord's will by bowing down to these images (1 Kin. 16:33; 2 Chr. 33:3). Their idolatry, however, did not go unpunished (1 Kin. 14:15). God's wrath at this

Stone carving of Nefertiti, the queen of Pharaoh Akhenaten of Egypt. She was considered one of the most beautiful and influential women of her time.

form of disobedience should remind His people of the necessity of tearing down all images which hinder the proper worship of the one true God.

WOOL — the thick, soft hair forming the fleece, or coat, of sheep and certain other mammals, valued as a fabric for making cloth (Deut. 22:11; Is. 51:8; Heb. 9:19). Gideon placed a fleece of wool on the threshing floor to receive a sign from the Lord (Judg. 6:37). In a country where snow was seldom seen, wool became the common symbol for whiteness and purity (Ps. 147:16). "Though your sins are like scarlet," wrote the prophet Isaiah, "they shall be as white as snow; though they are red like crimson, they shall be as wool" (Is. 1:18). Also see CLOTH.

WORD, THE — a theological phrase which expresses the absolute, eternal, and ultimate being of Jesus Christ (John 1:1–14; 1 John 1:1; Rev. 19:13). The Old Testament spoke of the word of God as the divine agent in the creation of the universe: "By the word of the Lord the heavens were made" (Ps. 33:6). In the New Testament, the Gospel of John declared, "And the Word became flesh and dwelt among us" (John 1:14). Through the incarnation of Christ, God has come to dwell in our midst. Through the life and ministry of Jesus, a unique and final revelation of God has been given—one superior to the revelation given through the law and the prophets. In Christ, the word of God, God's plan and purpose for mankind is clearly revealed (2 Cor. 4:4; Heb. 1:1–3). Also see LOGOS.

WORD OF GOD — the means by which God makes Himself known, declares His will, and brings about His purposes. The phrases such as word of God, and word of the Lord are applied to the commanding word of God that brought creation into existence (Genesis 1; 2 Pet. 3:5) and also destroyed that same world through the waters of the Flood (2 Pet. 3:6); to God's announcement of an impending or future act of judgment (Ex. 9:20–21; 1 Kin. 2:27); to the word that declares God's commitment and promises His blessing (Gen. 15:1, 4); and to a particular instruction from God (Josh. 8:27).

The term word of God is also used of the Ten Commandments given from Mount Sinai (Deut. 5:5); of the whole Mosaic Law (Is. 2:3); of specific parts of the Old Testament (Rom. 9:6; 1 Tim. 4:5); of a more personal communication from God (1 Sam. 3:21; 15:10); of the directive of God that set in motion John the Baptist's ministry (Luke 3:2); of Jesus' message of the kingdom of God (Luke 8:11); of the gospel as preached in the early church (Acts 4:31); and finally of the Lord Jesus Christ Himself (Rev. 19:13).

God's word is the primary means by which He is present and working in the world. He is not Himself part of this world, but He acts in it by means of His word. He becomes personally known through His word (1 Sam. 3:21). His word is powerfully creative (Ezek. 37:4) and its purposes are irresistible (Is. 55:11; Jer. 23:29). God's word is totally dependable; it represents His permanent commitment (Is. 40:8). When heard and responded to, His word meets deep needs in the human heart and provides joy, satisfaction, and confident direction which can be achieved in no other manner (Deut. 8:3; Ps. 119:162; Jer. 15:16). God's word has the power to penetrate all pretense and discern "the thoughts and intents of the heart" (Heb. 4:12).

God's speaking of His word reaches a culmination in the sending of His Son (John 1:1, 14; Heb. 1:1–2). All that is true of God's earlier word is supremely true of Jesus. The gospel of Jesus Christ is, in a special way, the word of God as it makes known and brings into operation the reconciliation with God which is His purpose for mankind (2 Cor. 5:18–19). So central is the gospel to the purpose of God in this world that the successful spread of the gospel is the growth of the word of God (Acts 12:24).

Not only Jesus' message, but also all that He is communicates God to us. He Himself is described as the word of God (John 1:1; Rev. 19:13). Jesus brings the presence of God to a new level—the personal presence of God in the world in a human life.

WORK — physical or mental activity directed toward the accomplishment of a task; the labor by which a person earns his livelihood.

Man as created was intended to work. One of his primary tasks in the Garden of Eden was to "till [work] the ground" (Gen. 2:5). Although work was ordained by God as a blessing, it became a curse as a result of the FALL (Gen. 3:17–19). Man would now have to work for his food and much of his produce would be frustration. The Book of Ecclesiastes teaches that work, no matter how noble and diligently pursued, is rendered meaningless in a world cursed at the Fall (Eccl. 4:4). Work in a fallen world is frequently reduced to exploitation and oppression.

Nevertheless, through redemption, work finds meaning. God ordained that six days be spent in work with one day of rest (Ex. 20:9). The people of God in the Old Testament are frequently encountered performing works in service to God, for instance, in the building of the tabernacle in the wilderness (Exodus 26) and the Temple (1 Chr. 28:10). Much of the WISDOM LITERATURE of the Old Testament praises hard work (Prov. 14:23; 31:27), while it condemns and ridicules laziness (Prov. 6:6–11; 21:25). The same attitude is found in the New Testament. Paul and his associates worked (1 Cor. 4:12; 9:6), and they expected other believers to work and earn their own support (2 Thess. 3:10).

In the Bible God's mighty acts are called works. Creation (Ps. 8:3, 6; 19:1; 102:25), redemptive acts in history like the Exodus (Judg. 2:7, 10), and even wrath (Is. 28:21) are referred to as God's work. Jesus Christ's work was given to Him by His Father. His task was to accomplish redemption for man on the Cross (John 4:34; 5:36; 9:4; 10:38; 15:24; 17:4). Also see WORKS.

WORKS — acts or deeds. God's works are praised often in the Book of Psalms (Ps. 33:4; 92:5; 104:24) and Christ's works are thoroughly discussed in the Gospel of John (John 10:25–38). Man's works are either good or bad, and these two categories are often mentioned together (Rom. 13:3, 12; Heb. 6:1, 10). Christians are taught to display good works (Matt. 5:16; Rev. 3:8).

On the other hand, works are viewed negatively when they are either bad in themselves, works of darkness (Rom. 13:12; Eph. 5:11), works of the flesh (Gal. 5:19), idolatry (Acts 7:41), hypocrisy (Matt. 23:3–5), or works of the law. Although works of the law are good in themselves, they do not bring salvation (Rom. 4:2, 6; Gal. 2:16). Romans 4:2 (Abraham *not* justified by works) and James 2:21 (Abraham justified by works) are not contradictory but complementary; works were the evidence of Abraham's faith (James 2:14–26).

Also see WORK.

WORLD — the heavens and the earth which form the universe and the place where man and animals live. Among both the Jewish people and the Greeks the terms world and earth were used interchangeably to mean the created universe, the fruitful and habitable earth. The biblical declaration, "The earth is the Lord's, and all its fullness thereof; the world and those who dwell therein" (Ps. 24:1), denotes the whole of created nature.

According to the New Testament, the world was created by God's word, identified with Christ in John 1:1–14. John says of Christ in John 1:10, "He was in the world, and the world was made through Him."

World is also associated with mankind. Christ said of His disciples, "Ye are the light of the world" (Matt. 5:14a). Often world is used to indicate "the men of this world" who are said to lie in wickedness (Eph. 2:2; 1 John 5:19). The men are called "the world," not only because they compose the greater part of the world's population, but mainly because they pursue and cherish the things of this world. The Psalmist describes these men "as having their portion in this life" (Ps. 17:14).

World may also denote the fleeting character of life's riches and pleasures and the folly of making them of central importance in life. "Will a person gain anything if he wins the whole world, but loses his life?" (Matt. 16:26).

Jesus states, "You belong to the world here below but I come from above" (John 8:23). Jesus was living in this world as a sphere of habitation, but He was separated from its atmosphere that was temporal and worldly. The term world also denotes the condition of human affairs, with man alienated from and opposed to God. Jesus wants His followers to live in the world to serve and to witness but not get caught up in the godless pleasures and perversitites of life. "I do not ask you to keep them out of the world, but I do ask you to keep them safe from the Evil One" (John 17:15).

The Old Testament world extended from Spain to Persia and from Greece to Ethiopia. The New Testament world also included the southern portions of the Roman Empire. Our world has expanded greatly since biblical times, but the final commands of Jesus to His disciples are as urgent and relevant as ever: "Go therefore and make disciples of all the nations" (Matt. 28:19–20).

WORM, WORMS (see ANIMALS OF THE BIBLE; DISEASES OF THE BIBLE).

WORMWOOD — any of several aromatic plants which yield a bitter, dark green oil (Deut. 29:18; Rev. 8:11).

WORSHIP — reverent devotion and allegiance pledged to God; the rituals or ceremonies by which this reverence is expressed. The English word worship comes from the Old English word worthship, a word which denotes the worthiness of the one receiving the special honor or devotion.

In Old Testament times Abraham built altars to the Lord and called on His name (Gen. 12:8; 13:18). This worship of God required no elaborate priesthood or ritual.

After God's appearance to Moses and the deliverance of the Israelites from slavery in Egypt, the foundations of Israelite ritual were laid. This worship took place in the light of history, especially the Exodus of the Hebrew people from Egypt. Through Moses, God established the form and principles of Israelite worship (Exodus 25—31; 35—40).

After the occupation of the Promised Land, Israel's exposure to Canaanite worship affected the nation's own worship. The Old Testament reveals clearly that Israel adopted some of the practices of the pagan people around them. At various times God's people lapsed into idolatry. Some idols were placed on pedestals and sometimes they were adorned or fastened with silver chains (Is. 40:19) or fastened with pegs lest they totter and fall (Is. 41:7). Shrines and altars were sometimes erected to these pagan gods. But such idolatry was condemned by God and His special spokesmen, the PROPHETS of the Old Testament.

New Testament worship was characterized by a joy and thanksgiving because of God's gracious redemption in Christ. This early Christian worship focused on God's saving work in Jesus Christ. True worship was that which occurred under the inspiration of God's Spirit (John 4:23–24; Phil. 3:3).

The Jewish Sabbath was quickly replaced by the first day of the week as the time for weekly public worship (Acts 20:7; 1 Cor. 16:2); it was called the Lord's Day (Rev. 1:10). This was the occasion for celebration of the resurrection of Jesus, since He arose on the first day of the week (Mark 16:2).

At first worship services were conducted in private houses. Possibly for a time the first Christians worshiped in the synagogues as well as private homes. Some scholars believe the Jewish Christians would go to the synagogues on Saturday and to their own meeting on Sunday.

Many early Christians of Jewish background

continued to follow the law and customs of their people. They observed the Sabbath and the Jewish holy days, such as the great annual festivals. However, the apostle Paul held himself free from any obligation to these and never laid an obligation to observe them on his converts (Col. 2:16). The New Testament itself contains no references to any yearly Christian festivals. The KJV mention of Easter (Acts 12:4) is a mistranslation; the NKJV has Passover.

Although the New Testament does not instruct worshipers in a specific procedure to follow in their services, several elements appear regularly in the worship practices of the early church.

Prayer apparently had a leading place in Christian worship. The letters of Paul regularly open with references to prayer for fellow–Christians who are instructed to "pray without ceasing" (1 Thess. 5:17). Praise, either by individuals or in hymns sung in common, reflects the frequent use of psalms in the synagogue. Also, possible fragments of Christian hymns appear scattered through the New Testament (Acts 4:24–30; Eph. 5:14; 1 Tim. 3:16; Rev. 4:8, 11; 5:9–10, 12–13).

Lessons from the Bible to be read and studied were another part of the worship procedure of the New Testament church. Emphasis was probably given to the messianic prophecies which had been fulfilled in Jesus Christ. His teachings also received a primary place.

Prophecy, inspired preaching by one filled with the Holy Spirit, helped build up the church, the body of Christ (Eph. 12:6). Contributions were also collected on the first day of each week (1 Cor. 16:2). Other details about the worship procedures of the early Christians in the New Testament times are spotty. But these elements must have been regularly included in the weekly worship service.

WORSHIP, EMPEROR (see EMPEROR WORSHIP).

WRANGLINGS — angry, noisy, or prolonged disputes or quarrels. The apostle Paul advised Timothy to withdraw from association with those given to "useless wranglings" (1 Tim. 6:5; disputings, KJV; friction, NASB, NIV). In contrast, godliness expresses itself in peace, gentleness, and contentment.

WRATH — the personal manifestation of God's holy, moral character in judgment against sin. Wrath is neither an impersonal process nor is it irrational and fitful like anger. It is in no way vindictive or malicious. It is holy indignation—God's anger directed against sin.

God's wrath is an expression of His holy love. If God is not a God of wrath, His love is no more than frail, worthless sentimentality; the concept of mercy is meaningless; and the Cross was a cruel and unnecessary experience for His Son.

The Bible declares that all people are "by nature children of wrath" (Eph. 2:3) and that "the wrath of God is revealed from heaven against all ungodliness and unrighteousness of men, who suppress the truth in unrighteousness" (Rom. 1:18). Since Christians have been "justified by His blood, we shall be saved from wrath through Him" (Rom. 5:9). The magnitude of God's love is manifested in the Cross, where God's only Son experienced wrath on our behalf.

"The day of the Lord's wrath" (Zeph. 1:18) is identical with "the great day of the Lord" (Zeph. 1:14). These terms refer to "the wrath of the Lamb" (Rev. 6:16), Jesus Christ, that will fall on the ungodly at His Second Coming (1 Thess. 1:10; 5:9; 2 Thess. 1:7–10).

WRITING — language symbols or characters written or imprinted on a surface with a marking instrument. Archaeological discoveries of the last century or so have revolutionized our knowledge of ancient writing methods and the materials that were used.

Development of Writing. The art of writing was practiced in the ancient world as early as 4000 B.C. This art developed through a number of stages before the use of a written alphabet emerged. Early writing was done in HIEROGLYPHICS, or the use of symbols and pictures to represent words.

Early inscriptions, although fragmentary and damaged, were discovered in temple ruins at Serabit in the Sinaitic Peninsula. These were dated at about 1500 B.C. The text was the work of laborers who had been employed to work an Egyptian turquoise mine.

Many of the signs used in this writing show a distinct resemblance to Egyptian picture writing. The signs are too few in number to serve as an alphabet.

Later excavations at GEZER and SHECHEM yielded POTSHERDS belonging to the same period or slightly earlier. Digging at LACHISH produced inscriptions on a dagger blade. The writing had many of the same letters that were discovered at Serabit in the Sinai Peninsula. Four pieces of pottery found at Lachish, dated at about 1250 B.C., bore the same kind of writing.

From Byblos (Gebal) on the coast north of Beirut came a number of inscriptions about kings who lived there from the thirteenth to the ninth centuries B.C.

All this evidence indicates that alphabetic writing, with a recognizable continuous script, was in use in and near Palestine at about the same time that Egyptian hieroglyphics and Babylonian cuneiform were also being used.

A calendar from the archaeological dig at Gezer is the oldest important Israelite document as well as the earliest completely intelligible text found on Palestinian soil. It presents a "farmer's almanac" of agricultural operations by months. This calendar has been dated as early as the tenth century B.C.

Another celebrated discovery was the MOABITE STONE. When it was found (1868), it was the earliest known example of the Phoenician alphabetic script. This small column of black basalt records the story of Mesha's war against the kings of Israel and Judah. It is the only surviving record of the an-

A sheet of papyrus from the third century A.D., showing parts of Ephesians and Galatians written in the Greek language.

cient MOABITES and their kingdoms.

The SILOAM Inscription, carved on the tunnel connecting the Virgin's Spring with the Pool of Siloam in Jerusalem, comes from the reign of King Hezekiah of Judah (about 700 B.C.). Discovered in 1880, it describes the successful junction made when opposite ends of the work were joined.

Finally, there are the LACHISH Letters discovered in 1935 and 1938. These were potsherds containing part of the military correspondence between the governor of Lachish and an officer of a Hebrew outpost when Babylon's army was overrunning the ancient world in 587–586 B.C.

The Canaanite or Old Semitic (Phoenician) alphabet was widely used among the countries between the Nile and the Euphrates Rivers. The model on which it was built probably came from Egypt. The Phoenicians exploited and perfected this alphabet, then carried it to Greece in their shipping and trading activities.

Several significant archaeological finds have yielded valuable information about ancient writing and how it developed.

The Ras Shamra Tablets. Ras Shamra is a site on the coast of northwest Syria opposite Cyprus. The site was identified as the ancient city of Ugarit, a Phoenician city which served as a gateway of commerce between Asia and the Mediterranean lands as early as about 2000 B.C. Among its buildings

was an extensive library of clay tablets of cuneiform writing. The building also included a writing school for scribes. The language of most of the texts found was similar to the Phoenician language.

Several items found at this site were dictionaries and lexicons, including some written in Sumerian-Babylonian (Akkadian) and Hurrian (Horite) vocabularies. In that day Sumerian was used only by scholars; Babylonian was the diplomatic and commercial language. Inscriptions in Egyptian hieroglyphics, Hittite and Cypriot were also discovered. Commercial, medical, legal, diplomatic, and private documents were discoverd, although the greatest part of the find consisted of religious writings.

The religious tablets were written in an alphabetic script of 29 or 30 letters. The words are written from left to right. This evidence shows the Ugaritic alphabet was invented by people who were aware of the Phoenician or a similar alphabetic system. They adapted this system into an alphabet of their own.

The Dead Sea Scrolls. These scrolls are the greatest archaeological discovery about the text of the Bible ever made. They have been dated at about two centuries before Christ. The find included two scrolls of Isaiah, the Manual of Discipline of the ESSENE community, the Habakkuk Commentary, The War Scroll, Thanksgiving Psalms, and two manuscripts of Daniel. Nearby finds yielded a palimpsest written in Phoenician script, fragments of the Minor Prophets, phylacteries, and parts of two letters from the Jewish revolutionary Simon Bar Kochba. In addition a copper scroll and thousands of manuscript fragments were found. Their importance includes a firsthand view of what a Hebrew scroll looked like at the beginning of the Christian era.

The Nag Hammadi Documents. An entire library of papyrus documents was accidentally discoverd by peasants north of Luxor, Egypt, in 1946. These manuscripts were written in the Sahidic dialect of the Coptic language. The leather covers in which they were wrapped probably account for their excellent preservation. The find included 13 codices with nearly 1,000 pages. They have been dated in the third and fourth centuries A.D.

Originally produced by a sect known as the GNOSTICS, these manuscripts represent a wide variety of literature, including a number of otherwise unrecorded sayings of Jesus. Many quotations are genuinely biblical. These writings show familiarity with the New Testament, but they contain little of abiding spiritual or moral value. Their understanding of the person and work of Christ is not in agreement with the teaching of the New Testament.

The Eblaite Discoveries. A group of tablets discovered in 1974–77 represents the royal archives in a civilization that flourished in northwestern Syria around 2500 B.C. Seventy–five percent of their contents deal with economic and administrative matters. This culture rivaled those of Egypt and Sumer during the same period. The language was an early form of Canaanite belonging to the same lin-

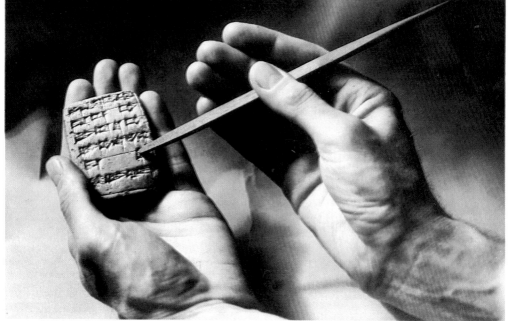

Ancient cuneiform characters were impressed on soft clay tablets with a pointed stylus. These tablets were then baked to form a piece of writing that was virtually indestructible.

guistic branch as Hebrew. They used the characters of Sumerian but wrote in an old Phoenician language. This discovery has helped Old Testament scholars determine the meaning of certain words in the Hebrew texts of the Old Testament.

These tablets also show that the world of the 14th century B.C. was not primitive but highly urbanized, cosmopolitan, and literate. They also throw a great deal of light on the languages of both the Old and New Testaments. The language is closer to Hebrew than Phoenician or Ugaritic.

Study of all these ancient writings reinforces our confidence in the history and culture of the Old Testament. For example, the Eblaite tablets support the list of the five cities of the plain in Genesis 14, which had previously been questioned by some scholars.

WRITING MATERIALS — ancient surfaces, such as animal skins and stone, on which information was recorded in Bible times. The earliest writing materials were clay tablets or stone (Ex. 32:16; Job 19:23–24). An engraving tool or a chisel was used to write on stone, bricks, and tablets (Is. 8:1). A reed pen (3 John 13), a metal pen, or a brush–like tool was used to write on softer materials (Job 19:24; Jer. 17:1).

The ink used was black, sometimes of metallic content. Usually it was made of soot, mixed with oil and gum of balsam. This permitted erasure by a water–bearing sponge. Inkhorns were carried by scribes. Inkwells discovered at QUMRAN were of brass and earthenware.

Many materials were used throughout the ancient world to receive writing—stone, ivory, leaves, bark, wood, metals, linen, baked clay, wax, and potsherds. But the three main materials on which the text of the Bible was written were skins, papyrus, and vellum. Prepared skins were used to record state documents as early as 3000 B.C. The ancient Persians used leather as a writing material; so did the Assyrians in the eighth century B.C. Jeremiah's scroll, cut up by King Jehoiakim, was leather (Jer. 36:23).

Papyrus met the needs of the Greco–Roman world for nearly a thousand years. The Phoenicians used Egyptian papyrus in the tenth century B.C. It was easily obtained, relatively inexpensive, and durable. Unfortunately, it becomes brittle with age. The first papyrus document, an employee list, was not found until 1778. The bulk of papyrus discoveries took place near the turn of this century. Some papyrus finds in CODEX form are as much as 59 sheets before being folded.

Vellum (parchment) is a material prepared from the skin of cattle, sheep, goats, and sometimes deer. However, papyrus was the preferred material for books until vellum replaced it in the fourth century A.D. (2 Tim. 4:13).

Christian Scriptures in Greek were written in capital letters, separately formed often without spaces between words. These were called uncial letters. The word uncial probably means "inch high." In the ninth century A.D. a new style known as miniscule, or cursive, came into general use. The letters were smaller and often more quickly formed than the uncial characters. The Scriptures continued to be reproduced in this smaller script until the invention of printing.

WRYNECK (see ANIMALS OF THE BIBLE).

X-Y-Z

XERXES [ZURK sees] — the Greek name of AHA-SUERUS, the king mentioned in the Book of Esther (Esth. 1:1; 2:1; 3:1, NIV). Known as Xerxes the Great, he was the king of Persia from 486–465 B.C.

YAH [yah] — an abbreviation or contraction of JE-HOVAH (Ps. 68:4; Jah, KJV).

YAHWEH, YAHWEH ELOHIM [YAH way, ell oh HEEM] (see GOD, NAMES OF).

YARMUK [YAHR muck] — a river, or WADI, on the eastern side of the Jordan River valley close to the southern end of the Sea of Galilee. The Yarmuk is not mentioned in the Bible, although numerous biblical events happened in its vicinity.

YARN — a continuous strand of twisted threads used to form cloth. In Bible times, yarn was spun on a simple hand spindle from linen and wool fiber as well as the hair of camels and goats (Ex. 35:25–26).

Lamb's wool was considered the finest for yarn, although wool from sheep kept clean from dirt and manure was especially valued for the sparkling white yarn it produced. Woolen yarn was also rubbed and bleached, and even dyed. Linen yarn made from flax or hemp (Ex. 9:31; Judg. 2:1, 6) was made especially into inner garments.

Most of the references to yarn in the Bible refer to the furnishings of the tabernacle—the curtains, veils, and screens—and to the clothes of the priests (Ex. 25:4; 26:36; 27:16; 38:23).

The Yarmuk, a dry stream bed on the eastern side of the Jordan River, close to the southern end of the Sea of Galilee.

YEA — an obsolete or poetic word meaning "yes, indeed, truly" (Ps. 23:4). The word is also used to introduce a more explicit or emphatic phrase: not only so but (Ps. 19:10; 137:1).

YEAR — the period of time required for the earth to complete a single revolution around the sun. The year of the Hebrew people consisted of 12 months (1 Kin. 4:7; 1 Chr. 27:1–5). Apparently these months were based on the changing cycles of the moon. Such a year would contain about 354 days. Periodically a 13th month had to be added to the Hebrew calendar to make up for this discrepancy of time. Also see TIME.

YEAR OF JUBILEE (see FEASTS AND FESTIVALS).

YHWH — the Hebrew name of the God of Israel, probably originally pronounced Yahweh. Eventually the Jews gave up pronouncing it, considering the name too holy for human lips. Instead they said Adonai or "Lord." This oral tradition came to be reflected in the written Greek translation of the Old Testament as *kurios* or "Lord," and it is often so quoted in the New Testament (Mark 1:3; Rom. 4:8). English versions of the Old Testament also tend to translate this word as "LORD." There is also a shorter form, YAH (Ps. 68:4; Is. 12:2; 26:4; 38:11). In Exodus 3:14–16 YHWH is linked with the verb *hayah*, "to be," probably referring to the presence of God with His people (Ex. 3:12).

YIRON [YIHR on] — a form of IRON.

YOD [yode] — the tenth letter of the Hebrew alphabet, used as a heading over Psalm 119:73–80. In the original Hebrew language, every line of these eight verses began with the letter yod. Also see ACROSTIC.

YOKE (see TOOLS OF THE BIBLE).

YOKEFELLOW — a fellow laborer of the apostle Paul (Phil. 4:3, RSV, NIV, KJV; companion, NKJV). The word implies one who is yoked in harness with another — the two working as a team. Various persons have been suggested as Paul's yokefellow: Luke, Epaphroditus, Barnabas, Silas, Timothy, or even Paul's wife. But the actual identity of this person is unknown.

ZAANAIM [zay ah NAY ihm] — a form of ZAANANNIM.

ZAANAN [ZAY ah nan] (*going out*) — a city of Palestine, apparently situated in the lowland plain of western Judah (Mic. 1:1). The site is unknown.

ZAANANNIM (zay uh NAN ihm] (meaning unknown) — a place on the southeastern border of the territory of Naphtali (Josh. 19:33), the same place as Zaanaim (Judg. 4:11). Near the terebinth tree at Zaanannim, which is beside Kedesh, Heber the Kenite pitched his tent. When Sisera, the commander of the army of Jabin, king of Canaan, went to sleep in the Kenite's tent, he was killed by Jael, Heber's wife, who drove a tent peg into his head (Judg. 4:21).

ZAAVAN [ZAY ah van] (*quake, terror*) — a son of Ezer the Horite (Gen. 36:27).

ZABAD [ZAY bad] (*gift, endowment*) — the name of seven men in the Old Testament:

1. A Judahite of the family of Hezron, of the house of Jerahmeel (1 Chr. 2:36–37). Zabad was a son of Nathan and the father of Ephlal.

2. An Ephraimite of the family of Shuthelah (1 Chr. 7:21). Zabad was a son of Tahath and the father of Shuthelah.

3. One of David's mighty men (1 Chr. 11:41) and a son of Ahlai.

4. One of two servants of King Joash of Judah who conspired against their king and murdered him (2 Chr. 24:26). Zabad was the son of Shimeath the Ammonitess.

5, 6, 7. Three Hebrews who were persuaded by Ezra to divorce their pagan wives (Ezra 10:27, 33, 43).

ZABBAI [ZAB ay eye] (*wanderer, pure*) — the name of two men in the Old Testament:

1. One of the sons, or descendants, of Bebai (Ezra 10:28). Zabbai divorced his pagan wife after the Captivity.

2. The father of a certain Baruch (Neh. 3:20). Baruch helped repair the wall of Jerusalem after the Captivity. Zabbai may be the same person as Zaccai (Ezra 2:9; Neh. 7:14) or the same person as Zabbai No. 1.

ZABBUD [ZAB uhd] (*mindful, remembered*) — one of the sons, or descendants, of Bigvai (Ezra 8:14; Zaccur, NIV). Zabbud returned from the Captivity with Ezra.

ZABDI [ZAB die] (*gift of Jehovah*) — the name of four men in the Old Testament:

1. The grandfather of Achan (Josh. 7:1, 17–18). Achan took spoils of battle from Jericho and was responsible for Israel's defeat at AI in the days of Joshua. Zabdi is also called Zimri (1 Chr. 2:6).

2. A Benjamite mentioned in the family tree of King Saul (1 Chr. 8:19).

3. A state official in David's administration. Zabdi was custodian of the royal wine–cellars (1 Chr. 27:27).

4. The grandfather of Mattaniah (Neh. 11:17). Mattaniah led a prayer of thanksgiving after the return from the Captivity. Zabdi is also called Zichri (1 Chr. 9:15).

ZABDIEL [ZAB dih ehl] (*my gift is God*) — the name of two men in the Old Testament:

1. The father of Jashobeam, a descendant of Perez of the tribe of Judah (1 Chr. 27:2).

2. An overseer of the priests in Jerusalem in the days of Nehemiah (Neh. 11:14).

ZABUD [ZAY bud] (*bestowed* or *endowed*) — an official in Solomon's administration (1 Kin. 4:5). He was a "principal officer" (KJV) and "a personal advisor to the king" (NIV).

ZABULON [ZAB you lon] (*habitation*) — Greek form of ZEBULUN (Rev. 7:8, KJV).

Photo by Willem A. VanGemeren

The mound of New Testament Jericho, the home of Zacchaeus the tax collector who became a disciple of Jesus (Luke 19:1-10).

ZACCAI [ZACK cay eye] (*pure*) — a person whose descendants returned from the Captivity with Zerubbabel (Ezra 2:9; Neh. 7:14).

ZACCHAEUS [zack KEY us] (*pure*) — a chief tax collector of Jericho who had grown rich by over-taxing the people for the hated Roman government. When Jesus visited Jericho, Zacchaeus, who was "of short stature" (Luke 19:3) climbed a tree in order to see Jesus. Jesus asked him to come down and then went to visit Zacchaeus as a guest. As a result of Jesus' visit, Zacchaeus became a follower of the Lord, repented of his sins, and made restitution for his wrongdoing. He gave half of his goods to the poor and restored fourfold those whom he had cheated through over-collection of taxes. In associating with people like Zacchaeus, Jesus showed that He came to call sinners to repentance.

ZACCHUR [ZACK coor] (*well remembered*) — a Simeonite, descended through Mishma (1 Chr. 4:26; Zaccur, NIV, RSV).

ZACCUR [ZACK cure] (*well remembered*) — the name of six men in the Old Testament:
1. The father of Shammua (Num. 13:4).
2. A Merarite Levite, a son of Jaaziah (1 Chr. 24:27).
3. A Gershonite Levite, head of a course of musicians set up by King David (1 Chr. 25:2; Neh. 12:35).
4. A son of Imri (Neh. 3:2). Zaccur helped rebuild the wall of Jerusalem after the Captivity.
5. A Levite who sealed the covenant after the Captivity (Neh. 10:12).
6. An administrator who helped Nehemiah in his reforms (Neh. 13:13).

ZACHARIAH [zack ah RYE uh] — a form of ZE-CHARIAH.

ZACHARIAS [zack ah RYE us] (*God has remembered*) — the name of two men in the New Testament:
1. The son of Berechiah whom the Jews "murdered between the temple and the altar" (Matt. 23:35, KJV) because he rebuked them for breaking God's commandments (Luke 11:51, KJV). This may be a reference to Zechariah, the son of Jehoiada—the priest who was stoned to death in the court of the house of the Lord (2 Chr. 24:20-22).
2. The father of John the Baptist (Luke 1:13; 3:2). Zacharias was a priest of the division of Abijah. His wife, Elizabeth, was one "of the daughters of Aaron" (Luke 1:5), meaning she also was of priestly descent.
Also see ZECHARIAH.

ZADOK [ZAY dock] (*just, righteous*) — the name of ten men in the Bible:
1. A high priest in the time of David. Zadok was a son of Ahitub (2 Sam. 8:17) and a descendant of Aaron through Eleazar (1 Chr. 24:3). During David's reign he served jointly as high priest with Abiathar (2 Sam. 8:17). Both Zadok and Abiathar fled from Jerusalem with David when the King's son Absalom attempted to take over the throne. They brought the ARK OF THE COVENANT out with them. After Absalom had been killed, David asked Zadok and Abiathar to urge the people to recall David to the throne (2 Sam. 19:11).
When David was dying, another of his sons, Adonijah, tried to take the throne. This time only Zadok remained faithful to the king. When David

heard of the plot, he ordered Zadok and the prophet Nathan to anoint Solomon king (1 Kin. 1:7-8, 32-45). Consequently, Abiathar was deposed and Zadok held the high priesthood alone (1 Kin. 2:26-27). In this way the high priesthood was restored to the line of Eleazar, son of Aaron.

2. The grandfather of Jotham, king of Judah (2 Kin. 15:33; 2 Chr. 27:1).

3. A high priest in Solomon's Temple (1 Chr. 6:12; 9:11).

4. A valiant warrior who joined David's army at Hebron (1 Chr. 12:28).

5. A son of Baana who helped repair part of the Jerusalem wall after the Captivity (Neh. 3:4). He may be the same person as Zadok No. 7.

6. A son of Immer who helped repair Jerusalem's wall (Neh. 3:29). He may be the same person as Zadok No. 9.

7. An Israelite who sealed the covenant with Nehemiah (Neh. 10:21). He may be the same person as Zadok No. 5.

8. A son of Meraioth (Neh. 11:11).

9. A scribe in the time of Nehemiah (Neh. 13:13). Zadok was appointed a treasurer over the storehouse.

10. An ancestor of Jesus (Matt. 1:14; Sadoc, KJV).

ZAHAM [ZAY ham] (*loathing*) — a son of King Rehoboam of Judah (2 Chr. 11:19).

ZAIR [ZAY ihr] (*narrow place*) — a place in or near Edom where King Joram (Jehoram) of Judah camped before attacking the Edomites (2 Kin. 8:21).

ZALAPH [ZAY lahf] (*caper-plant*) — the father of Hanun (Neh. 3:30). Hanun helped repair a section of the wall of Jerusalem in the time of Nehemiah.

ZALMON [ZAL muhn] (*ascent, terrace*) — the name of a man and two mountains in the Old Testament:

1. A wooded mountain near Shechem in Samaria where Abimelech and his men cut branches from trees to burn the stronghold, or tower, of Shechem (Judg. 9:48). It may have been the southern peak of Mount Gerizim, now called Jebel Sulman.

2. One of David's mighty men (2 Sam. 23:28). He is also called Ilai (1 Chr. 11:29).

3. A hill covered with snow where kings who were enemies of Israel were defeated (Ps. 68:14; Salmon, KJV).

ZALMONAH [zal MOAN nah] (*dark*) — the first desert camp of the Israelites after Mount Hor and before they reached Punon (Num. 33:41-42). Zalmonah was probably one of the desert wells or oases south of Punon, about 40 kilometers (25 miles) south of the Dead Sea.

ZALMUNNA [zal MUN nah] (see ZEBAH, ZALMUNNA).

ZAMZUMMIM [zam ZAHM mem] (*mumblers*) — the Ammonite name for the people called REPHAIM (giants) by the Jews in their narrative of the conquest of Canaan (Deut. 2:20; Zamzummims, KJV). The Zamzummin inhabited the region east of the Jordan River until they were driven out by the Ammonites.

ZANOAH [zah NO ah] (*broken district*) — the name of two cities in the Old Testament:

1. A city in the Shephelah, or low hill country, of Judah (Josh. 15:34; Neh. 11:30), whose inhabitants repaired the wall of Jerusalem (Neh. 3:13). It has been identified as Khirbet Zanu or Zanuh, about five kilometers (three miles) southeast of Beth Shemesh.

2. A city in the highlands of Judah (Josh. 15:56). Some scholars locate it about two kilometers (1.3 miles) northwest of Yatta (Juttah).

ZAPHNATH-PAANEAH [ZAF nath pay ah NEE ah] (meaning unknown) — the Hebrew form of the Egyptian name given to Joseph by Pharaoh when the king of Egypt raised Joseph to the rank of "prime minister" of the kingdom (Gen. 41:45; Zaphenath-paneath, NASB, NEB, NIV, RSV).

ZAPHON [ZAY fun] (*north*) — a city situated east of the Jordan River (see Map 3, C-3), in the territory of Gad (Josh. 13:27; Judg. 12:1; northward, KJV). It is also called Shophan (Num. 32:35). Zaphon was probably a shrine of Baal-zephon, one of the chief Canaanite gods, before the city was annexed by the Hebrews.

ZARA, ZARAH [ZAY rah] — forms of ZERAH.

ZAREATHITES [ZARE ih uh thites] — a form of ZORATHITES.

ZARED [ZAY rehd] — a form of ZERED.

ZAREPHATH [ZAR eh fath] (*place of dyeing*) — a Phoenician coastal city situated between Tyre and Sidon (see Map 4, B-2), where the prophet Elijah lodged with a widow (1 Kin. 17:9-10; Obad. 20; Luke 4:26; Sarepta, KJV). The widow of Zarephath showed great faith in feeding Elijah during a time of severe drought and famine. Her faith was rewarded, for her "bin of flour was not used up, nor did the jar of oil run dry" (1 Kin. 17:16).

ZARETAN [ZAR eh tan] (perhaps *cooling*) — a city situated east of the Jordan River valley, apparently in the territory of Manasseh—although some scholars believe it was west of the river, in the territory of Ephraim (Josh. 3:16; 1 Kin. 4:12; Zartanah, KJV; 1 Kin. 7:46, Zarethan, KJV).

At Zaretan the waters of the Jordan River rose up in a heap so the people could cross over toward Jericho (Josh. 3:16).

ZARHITES [ZAR heights] — the name of two families in the Old Testament:

1. A family of Simeonites (Num. 26:13; Zerahites, RSV).

2. A family of Judahites (Num. 26:20; Zerahites, RSV). Achan (Josh. 7:17) and two of David's mighty men belonged to this family (1 Chr. 27:11).

ZARETH–SHAHAR [zay RETH SHAY hahr] — a form of ZERETH SHAHAR.

ZARETHAN [ZAHR eh than] — a form of ZARETAN.

ZARTANAH [ZAHR tay nah] — a form of ZARETAN.

ZATTU [ZAT two] (meaning unknown) — the founder of a family of Israelites who returned from the Captivity with Zerubbabel (Ezra 2:8; Neh. 7:13). Some men of this family had married pagan wives, but Ezra convinced them to divorce these women (Ezra 10:27). The leader of this family signed the pledge of reform in Nehemiah's time (Neh. 10:14).

ZAYIN [ZIE yin] — the seventh letter of the Hebrew alphabet, used as a heading over Psalm 119:49-56. In the original Hebrew language, every line of these eight verses began with the letter zayin. Also see ACROSTIC.

ZAZA [ZAY zah] (meaning unknown) — a son of Jonathan and descendant of Jerahmeel, of the tribe of Judah (1 Chr. 2:33).

ZEAL, ZEALOUS — enthusiastic devotion; eager desire; single-minded allegiance (2 Sam. 21:2; 2 Kin. 10:16; 19:31). The psalmist wrote, "Zeal for Your house has eaten me up" (Ps. 69:9). When Jesus cleansed the Temple, His zeal reminded the disciples of the psalmist's words (John 2:17). Even before he became a Christian, Paul was zealous toward God and the law of Moses (Acts 22:3; Phil. 3:6).

ZEALOT [ZELL uht] (*devoted supporter*) — a nickname given to Simon, one of Jesus' twelve apostles (Luke 6:15; Acts 1:13), perhaps to distinguish him from Simon Peter. Simon the Zealot is also called Simon the Canaanite (Matt. 10:4; Mark 3:18; Cananaean, RSV; a member of the Zealot party, NEB). The Aramaic form of the name means "to be jealous" or "zealous."

Simon was given this name probably because he had been a member of a Jewish political party known as the Zealots. A Zealot was a member of a fanatical Jewish sect that militantly opposed the Roman domination of Palestine during the first century A.D. When the Jews rebelled against the Romans and tried to gain their independence, a group of the most fervent Jewish nationalists called themselves "Zealots." They thought of themselves as following in the footsteps of men like Simon and Levi (Gen. 34:1-31), Phinehas (Num. 25:1-13), and Elijah (1 Kin. 18:40; 19:10-14) who were devoted supporters of the Lord and His laws and who were ready to fight for them.

Like the PHARISEES, the Zealots were devoted to the Jewish law and religion. But unlike most Pharisees, they thought it was treason against God to pay tribute to the Roman emperor, since God alone was Israel's king. They were willing to fight to the death for Jewish independence.

The Zealots eventually degenerated into a group of assassins known as SICARII (Latin, daggermen). Their increasing fanaticism was one factor that provoked the Roman-Jewish war. The Zealots took control of Jerusalem in A.D. 66, a move that led to the siege of Jerusalem and its fall in A.D. 70. The last stronghold of the Zealots, the fortress of Masada, fell to the Romans in A.D. 73.

ZEBADIAH [zebb ah DIE ah] (*Jehovah has given*) — the name of nine men in the Old Testament:

1. A Benjamite, one of the sons of Beriah (1 Chr. 8:15).

Remains of the Roman camp at Masada. From this site the Romans laid siege against a band of Jewish zealots who were entrenched on the plateau above.

Photo by William White, Jr.

2. A Benjamite, one of the sons of Elpaal (1 Chr. 8:17).

3. A son of Jeroham of Gedor (1 Chr. 12:7). With his brother, Zebadiah joined David at Ziklag.

4. A gatekeeper of the sanctuary in David's time (1 Chr. 26:2).

5. A captain of the fourth division of David's army (1 Chr. 27:7). Zebadiah took command of this division after Asahel was killed by Abner.

6. A leader sent by King Jehoshaphat to teach the Law in the cities of Judah (2 Chr. 17:7–8).

7. A son of Ishmael in the time of King Jehoshaphat (2 Chr. 19:11).

8. A son of Michael who returned with Ezra from the Captivity (Ezra 8:8).

9. A priest of the house of Immer (Ezra 10:20) who divorced his foreign wife.

ZEBAH, ZALMUNNA [ZEE bah, zal MOON uh] (*shelter is denied*) — two Midianite kings who were killed by the army of GIDEON (Judg. 8:5–21; Ps. 83:11). The execution of Zebah and Zalmunna was a blood revenge, because these Midianite kings had previously killed Gideon's brothers at Tabor (Judg. 8:18–19). Gideon's victory over Zebah and Zalmunna was a turning point for the Israelites in their struggle against the Midianites. It was long remembered in Israel (Ps. 83:11; Is. 9:4; 10:26).

ZEBAIM [zeh BAY em] (*gazelles*) — the home of Pochereth, whose descendants returned from the Captivity (Ezra 2:57; Neh. 7:59). Its location is unknown.

ZEBEDEE [ZEBB uh dee] (*gift of Jehovah*) — the father of James and John, two of Jesus' twelve apostles (Matt. 4:21–22; Mark 1:19–20). Apparently Zebedee's wife was named Salome (Matt. 20:20; Mark 15:40). He was a fisherman on the Sea of Galilee, perhaps living in Capernaum or Bethsaida. Zebedee was probably wealthy since he had "hired servants" (Mark 1:20). In later references to Zebedee in the gospels, he appears only in the phrase "sons [or son] of Zebedee" (Matt. 10:2; Mark 10:35; Luke 5:10; John 21:2).

ZEBIDAH [zeh BUY dah] — a form of ZEBUDAH.

ZEBINA [zeh BUY nah] (*purchased*) — a descendant of Nebo who divorced his foreign wife after the Captivity (Ezra 10:43).

ZEBOIIM [zeh BOY yim] (meaning unknown) — one of the five cities of the plain in the Valley of Siddim destroyed along with Sodom and Gomorrah (Gen. 10:19; 14:2) The prophet Hosea used Admah and Zeboiim (Hos. 11:8; Zeboim, KJV) as examples of God's judgment on wicked cities. Although its exact location is unknown, many scholars believe Zeboiim was situated near the southern end of the Dead Sea in an area presently covered by water.

ZEBOIM [zeh BOY yim] (meaning unknown) — the name of a town and a valley in the Old Testament:

1. A valley in Benjamite territory southeast of Michmash toward the wilderness (1 Sam. 13:18).

2. One of the towns occupied by the Benjamites after the return from the Captivity (Neh. 11:34). Although the exact site is not known, it probably was in the hills bordering the Plain of Sharon, north of Lydda.

ZEBUDAH [zeh BOO dah] (*gift*) — the mother of Jehoiakim, king of Judah (2 Kin. 23:36; Zebidah, NASB, NEB, NIV, RSV). Zebudah was a daughter of Pedaiah of Rumah and the wife of Josiah, king of Judah.

ZEBUL [ZEE buhl] (*habitation*) — the ruler of the city of Shechem under Abimelech (Judg. 9:28–41). When Zebul warned Abimelech of a plot to seize control of the city, Abimelech destroyed Shechem and killed its entire population. He then sowed the city's ruins with salt.

ZEBULUN [ZEBB you lun] (*dwelling*) — the name of a man and the territory inhabited by the tribe of Zebulun in the Old Testament:

1. The tenth of Jacob's 12 sons; the sixth and last son of Leah (Gen. 30:19–20; 35:23; 1 Chr. 2:1). Zebulun had three sons: Sered, Elon, and Jahleel (Gen. 46:14; Num. 26:26–27). These are the only details about Zebulun that appear in the Bible.

2. The territory in which the tribe of Zebulun lived. The land allotted to Zebulun after the conquest of Canaan was bounded by Issachar and Manasseh on the south, by Asher on the west, and by Naphtali on the north and east (Josh. 19:10–16, 27, 34). Zebulun was fertile. It included part of the mountainous area of lower Galilee and the

A painting of the prophet Zechariah by Michelangelo, in the Sistine Chapel in Rome.
Photo by Howard Vos

northwest corner of the fertile Plain of Esdraelon (Valley of Jezreel).

ZEBULUN, TRIBE OF — the tribe that sprang from Zebulun, son of Jacob (Num. 1:9; Deut. 27:13; Josh. 19:10, 16; Judg. 1:30). The tribe was divided into three great families headed by Zebulun's three sons (Num. 26:26–27). At the first census taken in the wilderness, the tribe numbered 57,400 fighting men (Num. 1:30–31). The second census included 60,500 members of the tribe of Zebulun (Num. 26:27).

Zebulun played an important role in Israel's history during the period of the JUDGES. Its fighting men were an important part of Barak's force against Sisera (Judg. 4:6–10; 5:14, 18) and of Gideon's army against the Midianites (Judg. 6:35). ELON the Zebulunite judged Israel for ten years (Judg. 12:12). At Hebron, 50,000 Zebulunites joined the other tribes in proclaiming David king (1 Chr. 12:33, 40).

Although Zebulun suffered during the Assyrian wars, when Tiglath-Pileser carried away captives to Assyria (2 Kin. 15:29), Isaiah prophesied that in the future Zebulun would be greatly blessed: "The land of Zebulun and the land of Naphtali…in Galilee of the Gentiles. The people who walked in darkness have seen a great light; those who dwelt in the land of the shadow of death, upon them a light has shined" (Is. 9:1–2). According to the Gospel of Matthew, this prophecy was fulfilled when Jesus began His Galilean ministry (Matt. 4:12–17). Nazareth, Jesus' hometown, and Cana, where He performed His first miracle, both lay in the territory of Zebulun.

ZEBULUNITE [ZEBB you lunn ite] — a member of the tribe of ZEBULUN, or one who lived within its territory. Elon the Zebulunite judged Israel for ten years (Judg. 12:11–12; Zebulonite, KJV). In the second census of Israel in the wilderness "the families of the Zebulunites" numbered 60,500 (Num. 26:27).

ZECHARIAH [zack ah RIE a] (*Jehovah remembers*) — the name of several men in the Bible:

1. The 15th king of Israel (2 Kin. 14:29; 15:8, 11; Zachariah, KJV), the last of the house of Jehu. The son of Jeroboam II, Zechariah became king when his father died. He reigned only six months (about 753/52 B.C.), before being assasinated by Shallum.

2. The father of Abi or Abijah, mother of Hezekiah (2 Kin. 18:2; Zachariah, KJV; 2 Chr. 29:1).

3. A chief of the tribe of Reuben (1 Chr. 5:7).

4. A son of Meshelemiah (1 Chr. 9:21; 26:2, 14) and a Levite doorkeeper in the days of David.

5. A son of Jeiel, of the tribe of Benjamin (1 Chr. 9:37), also called Zecher (1 Chr. 8:31).

6. A Levite musician in the days of David (1 Chr. 15:18).

7. A priest and musician in the days of David (1 Chr. 15:24).

8. A descendant of Levi through Kohath (1 Chr. 24:25).

9. A descendant of Levi through Merari (1 Chr. 26:11).

10. A Manassite of Gilead and the father of Iddo (1 Chr. 27:21).

11. A leader sent by King Jehoshaphat to teach the people of Judah (2 Chr. 17:7).

12. The father of Jahaziel, a Levite who encouraged Jehoshaphat against Moab (2 Chr. 20:14).

13. A son of King Jehoshaphat (2 Chr. 21:2).

14. A son of Jehoiada (2 Chr. 24:20). This Zechariah was stoned to death at the command of Joash, king of Judah (v. 21).

15. A prophet in the days of Uzziah, king of Judah (2 Chr. 26:5).

16. A Levite who helped cleanse the Temple during the reign of King Hezekiah of Judah (2 Chr. 29:13).

17. A Levite who supervised Temple repairs during Josiah's reign (2 Chr. 34:12).

18. A prince of Judah in the days of Josiah (2 Chr. 35:8).

19. A prophet in the days of Ezra (Ezra 5:1; 6:14; Zech. 1:1, 7; 7:1, 8) and author of the Book of Zechariah. A leader in the restoration of the nation of Israel following the Captivity, Zechariah was a contemporary of the prophet Haggai, the governor Zerubbabel, and the high priest Joshua. Zechariah himself was an important person during the period of the restoration of the community of Israel in the land of Palestine after the Captivity.

The Book of Zechariah begins with a note concerning the prophet. He is named as a grandson of Iddo, one of the heads of the priestly families who returned with Zerubbabel from Babylon (Zech. 1:1, 7; also Ezra 5:1; 6:14). This means that Zechariah himself was probably a priest and that his prophetic activity was in close association with the religious center of the nation. His vision of Joshua the high priest (Zech. 3:1–5) takes on added importance, since he served as a priest in association with Joshua. Zechariah began his ministry while still a young man (Zech. 2:4) in 520 B.C., two months after Haggai completed the prophecies that are recorded in the Book of Haggai. Also see ZECHARIAH, BOOK OF.

20. A leader of the Jews who returned to Palestine with Ezra after the Captivity (Ezra 8:3).

21. A son of Bebai who returned with Ezra from the Captivity (Ezra 8:11).

22. A leader of Israel after the Captivity (Ezra 8:16). He may be the same person as Zechariah No. 20 or No. 21.

23. An Israelite who divorced his pagan wife after the return from the Captivity (Ezra 10:26).

24. A man who stood with Ezra at the public reading of the law (Neh. 8:4).

25. A descendant of Perez, of the tribe of Judah (Neh. 11:4).

26. A person whose descendants lived in Jerusalem after the Captivity (Neh. 11:5).

27. A priest descended from Pashhur (Neh. 11:12).

28. A Levite who led a group of musicians at the

dedication of the rebuilt wall of Jerusalem (Neh. 12:35–36).

29. A priest who took part in the dedication ceremony for the rebuilt wall of Jerusalem (Neh. 12:41).

30. A son of Jeberechiah (Is. 8:2) and a witness who recorded a prophecy given to Isaiah.

31. A prophet whom the Jews stoned (Matt. 23:35; Luke 11:51). The exact identity of this prophet is unknown.

ZECHARIAH, BOOK OF — an Old Testament prophetic book that portrays the coming glory of the MESSIAH. Many scholars describe Zechariah as "the most Messianic of all the Old Testament books" because it contains eight specific references to the Messiah in its brief 14 chapters.

Structure of the Book. The 14 chapters of Zechariah fall naturally into two major sections: chapters 1—8, the prophet's encouragement to the people to finish the work of rebuilding the Temple, and chapters 9—14, Zechariah's picture of Israel's glorious future and the coming of the Messiah.

In the first section, Zechariah introduces himself as God's prophet and calls the people to repent and turn from their evil ways. Part of their sin was their failure to finish the work of rebuilding the Temple after returning from the Captivity in Babylon. In a series of eight symbolic night visions that came to the prophet (1:7—6:8), Zechariah encourages the people to finish this important task. These visions are followed by a coronation scene (6:9–15), in which a high priest named Joshua is crowned as priest and king, symbolizing the Messiah who is to come. This is considered one of the classic Messianic prophecies of the Old Testament.

Chapters 7 and 8 also continue another important element of the Messianic hope: the One to come will reign in justice from Zion, the city of Jerusalem (8:3, 15–16).

The second major section of Zechariah's book, chapters 9—14, contains God's promises for the new age to come. Chapter 9 has a remarkable description of the manner in which the ruling Messiah will enter the city of Jerusalem: "Behold, your King is coming to you; He is just and having salvation, lowly and riding on a donkey, a colt, the foal of a donkey" (9:9). These were the words used by

ZECHARIAH: A Teaching Outline

Matthew to describe Jesus' triumphant entry into Jerusalem about 400 years after Zechariah made this startling prediction (Matt. 21:5; Mark 11:7–10).

Other promises for the future in this section of the book include the restoration of the nation of Israel (chap. 10) and Jerusalem's deliverance from her enemies (chap. 12), as well as her purification as the holy city (chap. 13). Like the Book of Revelation, Zechariah closes on the theme of the universal reign of God. All nations will come to worship Him as He extends His rule throughout the world (chap. 14).

Authorship and Date. Most conservative scholars agree that the entire book of Zechariah was written by the prophet of that name, who identifies himself in the book's introduction as "the son of Berechiah" (1:1). But some scholars insist the second major section of the book, chapters 9—14, was written by an unknown author. These scholars believe this section was added to the book about 30 or 40 years after Zechariah the prophet wrote chapters 1—8.

It is true that these two sections of the Book have their own unique characteristics. In the first section Zechariah encourages the people to finish the Temple, while in the second section he is more concerned about the glorious age of the future. The language and style of these two sections of Zechariah are also quite different. And the prophecies in these two sections seem to be set in different times.

Chapters 1—8, Zechariah tells us, were delivered as prophecies "in the eighth month of the second year of Darius" (1:1), and "in the fourth year of King Darius" (7:1). These references to Darius I of Persia (ruled 521–486 B.C.) date these prophecies clearly from 520 to 518 B.C. But chapters 9—14 contain a reference to Greece (9:13), probably indicating it was written after 480 B.C., when the balance of world power was shifting from the Persians to the Greeks. How can these major differences between these two sections of the book be explained unless we accept the theory that they were written by two different people?

One possible explanation is that Zechariah was a young man when he delivered his prophecies in the first section of the book. The book itself contains a clue that this may have been the case. In one of his visions, two angels speak to one another about the prophet, referring to him as "this young man" (2:4). Thus, it is quite possible that Zechariah could have encouraged the Jewish captives in Jerusalem in the early part of his ministry and could have delivered the messages about the future, contained in the second section of the book, during his final years as a prophet.

After all the evidence is examined, there is no convincing reason to dispute the traditional view that Zechariah the prophet wrote the entire book that bears his name. These prophecies were first delivered and then reduced to writing over a period of about 45 years—from 520 to 475 B.C.

As for the prophet himself, very little is known about him beyond the few facts he reveals in his

book. He was a descendant, perhaps the grandson, of Iddo the priest (1:1)—one of the family leaders who returned from the Captivity in Babylon (Neh. 12:16). This means that Zechariah probably was a priest as well as a prophet—an unusual circumstance because most of the prophets of Israel spoke out against the priestly class. Since he was a young man when he began to prophesy in 520 B.C., Zechariah was probably born in Babylon while the Jewish people were in captivity. He probably returned with his family with the first wave of captives who reached Jerusalem under Zerubbabel about 536 B.C.

Historical Setting. The setting at the beginning of the Book is the same as the setting of the Book of Haggai. The prophet Haggai spoke directly to the issue of the rebuilding of the Temple, encouraging those who returned from captivity in Babylon to finish the task. Zechariah spoke to that issue as well, according to the Book of Ezra (Ezra 5:1). But Zechariah wished to bring about a complete spiritual renewal through faith and hope in God. He spoke about the nature of God's Law and of the hope which God promised to those who were faithful to Him.

The second portion of Zechariah was written in the period between the times of the prophets Haggai (520 B.C.) and Malachi (450 B.C.). The Persian Empire was ruled by two great kings during these years, Darius I (522–486 B.C.) and Xerxes I (585–465 B.C.). This was a period when the Jewish people in Jerusalem were settled in their new land with a walled city and their beloved Temple. But they were unhappy and dissatisfied. Some of the people had expected that Zerubbabel, governor of Jerusalem, might be the Messiah, but this had proven to be false. The people needed a new word concerning God's future for them. This message from God was given in a most dramatic fashion by the great prophet Zechariah.

Theological Contribution. One of the greatest contributions of the Book of Zechariah is the merger of the best from the priestly and prophetic elements in Israel's history. Zechariah realized the need for both these elements in an authentic faith. He called the people to turn from their sins. He also realized that the Temple and religious ritual played an important role in keeping the people close to God. Because he brought these elements together in his own ministry, Zechariah helped prepare the way for the Christian community's understanding of Christ as both priest and prophet.

Zechariah is also noted for his development of an apocalyptic-prophetic style—highly symbolized and visionary language concerning the events of the end-time. In this, his writing resembles the Books of Daniel and Revelation. The visions of lampstands and olive trees, horsemen and chariots, measuring lines and horns place him and these other two books in a class by themselves. Zechariah also has a great deal to say about the concept of God as warrior. While this was a well-established image among biblical writers, Zechariah ties this idea to the concept of the Day of the Lord (see Joel 2). His description of the return of Christ to earth as the great Warrior in the Day of the Lord (14:1–9) is one of the most stirring prophecies of the Old Testament.

On that day, according to Zechariah, Christ will place His feet on the Mount of Olives, causing violent changes throughout the land (14:3–4). The day will be changed to darkness and the darkness to light (14:5–8). The entire world will worship Him as the Lord spreads His rule as King "over all the earth" (14:9).

Special Considerations. Zechariah 12:10 is a remarkable verse that speaks of the response of the nation of Israel to Jesus Christ as Savior and Lord. It describes a day in the future when the Jewish people (the house of David and the inhabitants of Jerusalem) will recognize the significance of the death of Jesus. This recognition will lead to mourning, repentance, and salvation (compare Rom. 11:25–27).

But the most startling thing about this verse is the phrase, "Then they will look on Me whom they have pierced." In speaking through the prophet Zechariah, the Lord identifies Himself as the one who will be pierced. Along with Psalm 22 and Isaiah 53, these words are a wonder of inspiration as they describe the result of Jesus' death as well as the manner in which He died to deliver us from our sins.

Also see ZECHARIAH.

ZECHER [ZEE ker] — a form of ZECHARIAH.

ZEDAD [ZEE dad] (*mountainside*) — a place, probably a tower, on the northern boundary of Palestine (Num. 34:8; Ezek. 47:15). It has been identified with the ruins of Sadad, about 105 kilometers (65 miles) northeast of Damascus; but this is uncertain.

ZEDEKIAH [zedd eh KIE ah] (*Jehovah my righteousness*) — the name of five men in the Old Testament:

1. A false prophet, son of Chenaanah, who advised King Ahab of Israel to attack the Syrian army at Ramoth Gilead (1 Kin. 22:11). Zedekiah's flattery and unfounded optimism proved to be lies; the king was mortally wounded in the battle.

2. The last king of Judah (597–586 B.C.). The son of Josiah, Zedekiah was successor to Jehoiachin as king (2 Kin. 24:17–20; 25:1–7; 2 Chr. 36:10–13). After Jehoiachin had reigned only three months, he was deposed and carried off to Babylon. Nebuchadnezzar installed Zedekiah on the throne as a puppet king and made him swear an oath that he would remain loyal (2 Chr. 36:13; Ezek. 17:13). Although he reigned in Jerusalem for 11 years, Zedekiah was never fully accepted as their king by the people of Judah.

Because Zedekiah was a weak and indecisive ruler, he faced constant political unrest. Almost from the first he appeared restless about his oath of loyalty to Babylon, although he reaffirmed that commitment in the fourth year of this reign (Jer.

51:59). However, he was under constant pressure from his advisors to revolt and look to Egypt for help. A new coalition composed of Edom, Moab, Ammon, and Phoenicia was forming against Babylon, and they urged Judah to join (Jer. 27:3). Adding to the general unrest was the message of false prophets who declared that the yoke of Babylon had been broken (Jeremiah 28).

In his ninth year Zedekiah revolted against Babylon. King Nebuchadnezzar invaded Judah and besieged Jerusalem. While Jerusalem was under siege, other Judean cities were falling to the Babylonians (Jer. 34:7).

The final months of the siege were desperate times for Zedekiah and the inhabitants of Jerusalem. The king made frequent calls on the prophet Jeremiah, seeking an encouraging word from the Lord. Jeremiah's message consistently offered only one alternative: surrender to Nebuchadnezzar in order to live in peace and save Jerusalem. To his credit, Zedekiah was not arrogant and heartless (Jer. 36:22–23). But he regarded God's prophetic word superstitiously and "did not humble himself before Jeremiah the prophet, who spoke from the mouth of the Lord" (2 Chr. 36:12).

In July, 586 B.C. the wall of Jerusalem was breached, and Zedekiah fled the city. The army of the Babylonians pursued the king, overtaking him in the plains of Jericho. He was brought before Nebuchadnezzar and forced to watch the slaying of his sons. Then his own eyes were put out and he was led away to Babylon (2 Kin. 25:6–7). Zedekiah died during the years of the CAPTIVITY of the Jewish people in Babylon. His reign marked the end of the nation of Judah as an independent, self-governing country.

3. A prominent Jewish official who sealed the covenant with Nehemiah after returning from the Captivity (Neh. 10:1; Zidkijah, KJV).

4. A false prophet denounced by the prophet Jeremiah (Jer. 29:21).

5. A prince of Judah, son of Hananiah, in the days of the prophet Jeremiah and Jehoiakim, king of Judah (Jer. 36:12).

ZEEB [ZEE ebb] (*a wolf*) — one of two princes of the Midianites defeated by the army of Gideon. The men of Ephraim beheaded Oreb and Zeeb and brought their heads to Gideon on the other side of the Jordan River (Judg. 7:25; 8:3).

ZELAH [ZEE lah] (*slope*) — a town in the territory of Benjamin (Josh. 18:28). Zelah was the site of the tomb of Kish, the father of King Saul. The site of this town is not known, but it probably was in the hill country northwest of Jerusalem (Josh. 18:25–28).

ZELEK [ZEE lehk] (*cleft*) — an Ammonite, one of David's mighty men (2 Sam. 23:37; 1 Chr. 11:39).

ZELOPHEHAD [zeh LOW fee had] (*shadow of fear*) — a man of the tribe of Manasseh who died during the wilderness wandering, leaving five daughters. Because Zelophehad had no male heirs, his daughters—Mahlah, Noah, Hoglah, Milcah, and Tirzah—went to Moses and requested that they inherit their father's property. Moses allowed this, with one stipulation; they were to marry within their father's tribe (Num. 26:33; 27:1–11; 36:2–11).

ZELOTES [zeh LOW tees] (*full of zeal*) — a nickname of Simon, one of the twelve apostles of Jesus (Luke 6:15; Acts 1:13, KJV), to distinguish him from Simon Peter. Modern versions translate as the Zealot.

Also see SIMON; ZEALOT.

ZELZAH [ZEHL zah] (*noontide*) — an unidentified site in the territory of Benjamin, near Rachel's tomb (1 Sam. 10:2). Samuel the prophet told Saul that he would receive the first of three signs from the Lord at Zelzah (1 Sam. 10:1–9). These would confirm his selection as king of Israel.

ZEMARAIM [zim ah RAY im] (*double peak*) — the name of a city and a mountain in the Old Testament:

1. A city in the territory of Benjamin (Josh. 18:22), location unknown.

2. A mountain in the hill country of Ephraim (2 Chr. 13:4). The site is uncertain. Mount Zemaraim was where Abijah, king of Judah, stood when he addressed the army of Jereboam, king of Israel, before defeating Israel (2 Chr. 13:4–12).

ZEMARITES [ZEM ah rights] — a Canaanite tribe (Gen. 10:18; 1 Chr. 1:16), probably living in northern Phoenicia in a town now called Sumra. This town is situated on the Mediterranean coast between Arvad and Tripolis.

ZEMER [ZEE mehr] — a Phoenician city mentioned only in the RSV (Ezek. 27:8).

ZEMIRAH [zeh MY rah] (*melody*) — a Benjamite of the family of Becher (1 Chr. 7:8; Zemira, KJV, NEB).

ZENAN [ZEE nan] (*place of flocks*) — a city of Judah in the SHEPHELAH of Lachish (Josh. 15:37). It is probably the same place as Zaanan (Mic. 1:11).

ZENAS [ZEE nahs] (*gift of Zeus*) — a Christian missionary who worked with Titus on the island of Crete (Titus 3:13). The apostle Paul called Zenas a lawyer, or a man skilled in the Jewish law, an expert in the TORAH. According to church tradition, Zenas was the first bishop of Diospolis (Lydda) in Palestine and the author of the apocryphal Acts of Titus.

ZEPHANIAH [zeff ah NIE ah] (*the Lord has hidden*) — the name of four men in the Old Testament:

1. A son of Maaseiah (2 Kin. 25:18; Jer. 21:1; 29:25, 29; 37:3).

2. A Levite of the family of Kohath (1 Chr. 6:36).

3. An Old Testament prophet and the author of the Book of Zephaniah (Zeph. 1:1). As God's spokesman to the southern kingdom of Judah, Zephaniah began his ministry about 627 B.C., the same year as the great prophet JEREMIAH. Zepha-

niah was a member of the royal house of Judah, since he traced his ancestry back to King Hezekiah. He prophesied during the reign of King Josiah (ruled 641–609 B.C.). One theme of his message was that through His judgment God would preserve a remnant, a small group of people who would continue to serve as His faithful servants in the world (Zeph. 3:8–13). Also see ZEPHANIAH, BOOK OF.

4. Father of Josiah (Zech. 6:10).

ZEPHANIAH, BOOK OF — a brief prophetic book of the Old Testament that emphasizes the certainty of God's judgment and the preservation of a remnant, a small group of people who will continue to serve as God's faithful servants in the world. The book takes its title from its author, the prophet Zephaniah, whose name means "the Lord has hidden."

Structure of the Book. Zephaniah contains only three short chapters, but these chapters are filled with some of the most vivid pictures of God's judgment to be found in the Bible. After a brief introduction of himself as God's spokesman, the prophet launches immediately into a description of God's approaching wrath. He portrays this great "day of the Lord" as a time of "trouble and distress," "darkness and gloominess," "trumpet and alarm" (1:14–15).

Zephaniah's prophecy makes it clear that the nation of Judah, as well as surrounding countries, will feel the sting of God's wrath. Judah's capital city, Jerusalem, is soundly condemned for its wickedness, rebellion, and injustice. The prophet even portrays God with searchlamps as He exposes the corruption of the city and marks it for His certain judgment (1:12).

In spite of its underlying theme of judgment and punishment, the Book of Zephaniah closes on a positive note. After God judges the wayward nations, the prophet announces He will raise up a remnant of the faithful who will continue to serve as His Covenant People in the world. The book ends with a glorious promise for the future, a time when God will "quiet you in His love" and "rejoice over you with singing" (3:17).

Authorship and Date. Scholars are in general agreement that Zephaniah the prophet wrote this book that bears his name. In his introduction (1:1), the author traces his ancestry back four generations to Hezekiah, a former king of Judah noted for his faithfulness to God. Zephaniah must have been proud that he was the great–great–grandson of this beloved ruler, who had led his people back to worship of the one true God.

The book also tells how Zephaniah the prophet ministered during the days of Josiah, a godly king who reigned over the nation of Judah from about 641 to about 609 B.C. Most scholars place the writing of the book at about 627 B.C.

Historical Setting. This book belongs to a dark period in Judah's history. About 100 years before Zephaniah's time, Judah's sister nation, the northern kingdom of Israel, had fallen to a foreign power because of its sin and idolatry. Zephaniah sensed that the same thing was about to happen to the southern kingdom of Judah—and for precisely the same reason.

Under the leadership of two successive evil kings, Manasseh and Amon, the people of Judah had fallen into worship of false gods. Zephaniah delivered his prophecy and wrote this book to warn the people of God's approaching wrath and judgment. As Zephaniah predicted, God punished His people and the surrounding pagan nations through a superior foreign power. Not even a brief religious renewal under the good king Josiah was enough to turn the tide of paganism and false worship that carried Judah toward certain destruction. Judgment came to the nation in 587 B.C., when the invading Babylonians destroyed the city of Jerusalem and carried its leading citizens into CAPTIVITY in Babylon.

Theological Contribution. The judgment of the Lord portrayed by the prophet Zephaniah springs from His nature as a God of holiness. Because God demands holiness and righteousness in His people, He will judge those who continue to sin and rebel (1:17). But the Lord also is merciful and faithful to His promise. To the committed remnant He offers encouragement and protection from the approaching dark day (2:1–3). And to the righteous He promises the final realization of the covenant which He sealed with Abraham hundreds of years earlier. People of all nations will gather to worship the Lord (2:11; 3:9). His own people will be renewed in righteousness (3:11–13). And the King of Kings Himself will rule in their midst (3:15).

Special Considerations. The prophet Zephaniah shows keen familiarity with the city of Jerusalem (1:10–11). Since he was a member of the royal line, he was probably a resident of Jerusalem. It must have troubled him deeply to pronounce God's prophecies of judgment against his beloved city.

One of the most beautiful passages in the book is the description of the joy of the Lord (3:8–20). His song of joy will join the happy singing of His people. The dark day of doom will not last. A happy day is coming for those who, like Zephaniah, are "hidden in the day of the Lord's anger" (2:3).

Also see ZEPHANIAH.

ZEPHATH [ZEE fath] (*watchtower*) — a Canaanite city in southern Judah, destroyed by the men of Judah and Simeon and renamed HORMAH (Judg. 1:17).

ZEPHATHAH [ZEFF ah thah] (*watchtower*) — a valley in the territory of Judah, near Mareshah (2 Chr. 14:10), where Asa crushed Zerah the Cushite and his army (2 Chr. 14:9–13).

ZEPHI, ZEPHO [ZEE fie, ZEE foe] (*watchtower*) — the third son of Eliphaz the Edomite, descended from Esau (Zepho, Gen. 36:11; Zephi, 1 Chr. 1:36).

ZEPHON [ZEE fun] (*expectation*) — one of the seven sons of Gad and founder of a tribal family, the ZEPHONITES (Num. 26:15). He is also called Ziphion (Gen. 46:16).

ZEPHONITES [ZEFF oh nights] — a Gadite family descended from ZEPHON (Num. 26:15).

ZER [zehr] (*flint, rock*) — a walled city west of the Sea of Galilee (Josh. 19:35). Some scholars believe Zer was the Israelite name for Madon (Josh. 11:1; 12:19), but this is uncertain.

ZEPHANIAH: A Teaching Outline

ZERAH [ZEE ruh] (*sprout*) — the name of seven men in the Old Testament:

1. An Edomite chief descended from Esau and also from Ishmael (Gen. 36:13, 17; 1 Chr. 1:37).

2. The father of Jobab (Gen. 36:33; 1 Chr. 1:44). Jobab was one of the early kings of Edom.

3. One of the twins born to Judah by Tamar, his daughter-in-law (Gen. 38:30; 46:12, Zarah, KJV; KJV Zara; Matt. 1:3,). He founded a tribal family of Judah, the ZARHITES (Num. 26:20).

4. A son of Simeon, second son of Jacob and Leah (Num. 26:13; 1 Chr. 4:24), also called Zohar (Gen. 46:10; Ex. 6:15). He was the founder of a tribal family, the ZARHITES (Num. 26:13).

5. A Gershonite Levite (1 Chr. 6:21).

6. The father of Ethni, a Levite (1 Chr. 6:41).

7. A Cushite (2 Chr. 14:9, NIV, NEB), or Ethiopian (KJV, NKJV, RSV, NASB), who led a large army against King Asa of Judah. Zerah's warriors were defeated by Asa's smaller army.

ZERAHIAH [zehr ah HIGH ah] (*the Lord shines forth*) — the name of two men in the Old Testament:

1. A son of Uzzi and father of Meraioth (1 Chr. 6:6, 51–52; Ezra 7:3–4). A priest, Zerahiah was a descendant of Phinehas and an ancestor of Ezra.

2. The father of Elihoenai (Ezra 8:4).

ZERAHITES [ZEE rah heights] — a form of ZARHITES.

ZERED [ZEE red] (*brook*) — a brook and a valley (see Map 2, C–1) that ends at the southeastern corner of the Dead Sea (Num. 21:12; Zared, KJV; Deut. 2:13–14). Zered was south of the River Arnon, probably the Wadi el-Hesa, and was the boundary between Moab and Edom. When the Israelites crossed the Zered, they marked an end to their years of wandering in the wilderness.

ZEREDA [ZEHR eh dah] (*ambush*) — a city of Mount Ephraim. Zereda was the birthplace or hometown of Jeroboam I, the first ruler of the northern kingdom of Israel (1 Kin. 11:26; Zeredah, RSV, NIV, NASB).

ZEREDAH [ZEHR eh dah] (*cold*) — a city in the Jordan River valley where Solomon erected foundaries and where Huram (or Hiram, 1 Kin. 7:13) of Tyre, a master craftsman in metallurgy, made the great castings of bronze for Solomon's Temple (2 Chr. 4:17; Zeredathah, KJV).

ZERERAH [ZER eh rah] (meaning unknown) — a town in the Jordan River valley through which the Midianite army fled when defeated by Gideon and his band of 300 men (Judg. 7:22; Zererath, KJV).

ZERERATH [ZER ih rath] — a form of ZERARAH.

ZERESH [ZEE resh] (meaning unknown) — the wife of HAMAN the Agagite (Esth. 5:10, 14; 6:13). Zeresh advised Haman to satisfy his hatred for the Jews by building a gallows for Mordecai (Esth. 5:14). Later, however, when she learned that Mordecai was of Jewish descent, she warned Haman that Mordecai would prevail. She predicted Haman's downfall.

ZERETH [ZEE reth] (*splendor*) — the first son of Helah, the wife of Asshur (1 Chr. 4:5, 7).

ZERETH SHAHAR [zee RETH SHAY har] (*splendor of the dawn*) — a town in the territory of Reuben (Josh. 13:19; Zareth-shahar, KJV).

ZERI [ZEE rye] (*balsam*) — one of the "sons of Jeduthun," a group of Levitical singers established during the reign of David. Apparently Zeri was the head of this family after the return from the Captivity (1 Chr. 25:3).

ZEROR [ZEE rohr] (*particle*) — an ancestor of King Saul (1 Sam. 9:1).

ZERUAH [zeh ROO ah] (*smitten*) — the mother of Jeroboam, the first king of the northern kingdom of Israel, and wife of Nebat (1 Kin. 11:26).

ZERUBBABEL [zeh RUB uh buhl] (*offspring of Babylon*) — head of the tribe of Judah at the time of the return from the Babylonian CAPTIVITY; prime builder of the Second Temple.

Zerubbabel is a shadowy figure who emerges as the political and spiritual head of the tribe of Judah at the time of the Babylonian captivity. Zerubbabel led the first group of captives back to Jerusalem and set about rebuilding the Temple on the old site. For some 20 years he was closely associated with prophets, priests, and kings until the new Temple was dedicated and the Jewish sacrificial system was reestablished.

As a child of the Captivity, Zerubbabel's name literally means "begotten in Babylon." He was the son of Shealtiel or Salathiel (Ezra 3:2, 8; Hag. 1:1; Matt. 1:12) and the grandson of Jehoiachin, the captive king of Judah (1 Chr. 3:17). Zerubbabel was probably Shealtiel's adopted or levirate son (1 Chr. 3:19). Whatever his blood relationship to king Jehoiachin, Zerubbabel was Jehoiachin's legal successor and heir.

A descendant of David, Zerubbabel was in the direct line of the ancestry of Jesus (Luke 3:27; Matt. 1:12). Zerubbabel apparently attained considerable status with his captors while living in Babylon. During the early reign of Darius, he was recognized as a "prince of Judah" (Ezra 1:8). Zerubbabel was probably in the king's service since he had been given an Aramaic name (Sheshbazzar) and was appointed by Cyrus as governor of Judea (Hag. 1:1).

With the blessings of Cyrus (Ezra 1:1–2), Zerubbabel and Jeshua the high priest led the first band of captives back to Jerusalem (Ezra 2:2). They also returned the gold and silver vessels which NEBUCHADNEZZAR had removed from the ill-fated Temple (Ezra 1:11). Almost immediately they set up an altar for burnt offerings, kept the Feast of the Tabernacles, and took steps to rebuild the Temple (Ezra 3:2–3, 8).

After rebuilding the Temple foundation the first two years, construction came to a standstill for 17 years. This delay came principally because of opposition from settlers in Samaria who wanted to help with the building (Ezra 4:1–2). When the offer was refused because of the Samaritans' association with heathen worship, the Samaritans disrupted the building project (Ezra 4:4). Counselors were hired who misrepresented the captives in court (Ezra 4:5), causing the Persian king to withdraw his support (Ezra 4:21). The delay in building also was due to the preoccupation of Zerubbabel and other captives with building houses for themselves (Hag. 1:2–4).

Urged by the prophets Haggai and Zechariah (Ezra 5:1–2), Zerubbabel diligently resumed work on the Temple in the second year of the reign of Darius Hystaspes in Persia (Hag. 1:14). This renewed effort to build the Temple was a model of cooperation involving the captives, the prophets, and Persian kings (Ezra 6:14). Zerubbabel received considerable grants of money and materials from Persia (Ezra 6:5) and continuing encouragement from the prophets HAGGAI and ZECHARIAH (Ezra 5:2).

The Temple was finished in four years (516 B.C.) and dedicated with great pomp and rejoicing (Ezra 6:16). The celebration was climaxed with the observance of the Passover (Ezra 6:19). If there was a discordant note, it likely came from older Jews who had earlier wept because the new Temple lacked the splendor of Solomon's Temple (Ezra 3:12).

For some mysterious reason, Zerubbabel is not mentioned in connection with the Temple dedication. Neither is he mentioned after this time. Perhaps he died or retired from public life upon completion of the Temple. His influence was so great, however, that historians designate the Second Temple as "Zerubbabel's Temple."

God was apparently pleased with Zerubbabel's role in bringing the captives home and reestablishing Temple worship (Ezra 3:10). On God's instructions, Haggai promised Zerubbabel a special blessing: "I will take you, Zerubbabel My servant, the son of Shealtiel, says the Lord, and will make you as a signet ring; for I have chosen you" (Hag. 2:23).

ZERUIAH [zeh roo EYE ah] (*balm* or *perfume*) — a sister, or perhaps half sister of David (1 Chr. 2:16). Her three sons—Abishai, Joab, and Asahel—were commanders in David's army. One of her sons, ASAHEL, was killed by Abner (2 Sam. 2:17–23). Most of the references to Zeruiah, therefore, are as the mother of JOAB (2 Sam. 2:13, 8:16) and ABISHAI (1 Sam. 26:6; 2 Sam. 16:9).

ZETHAM [ZEE tham] (*olive tree*) — a Gershonite Levite, a descendant of Laadan (1 Chr. 23:8; 26:22).

ZETHAN [ZEE than] (*olive tree*) — a descendant of Bilthan, of the tribe of Benjamin (1 Chr. 7:10).

ZETHAR [ZEE thar] (*conqueror*) — one of the seven eunuchs, or household servants, who had charge of the harem of King Ahasuerus (Xerxes) of Persia (Esth. 1:10).

ZEUS [zoose] (*bright sky of day*) — the principal god of the ancient Greeks, considered ruler of the heavens and father of other gods. The Romans equated Zeus with their own supreme god, Jupiter. Barnabas was called Zeus by the people after the apostle Paul performed a miraculous healing at Lystra (Acts 14:12–13; 19:35; Jupiter, KJV). The temple of Zeus at Athens was the largest in Greece. His statue at Olympia was one of the seven wonders of the ancient world. Also see GODS, PAGAN.

ZIA [ZIE ah] (*trembling*) — a Gadite who lived in Bashan (1 Chr. 5:13).

ZIBA [ZIE bah] (*post, statue*) — a servant of King Saul (2 Sam. 9:2–4, 9–12; 16:1–4; 19:17, 29). When Saul and Jonathan were killed by the Philistines at Mount Gilboa, David wished to remember his promise to Jonathan and asked if any descendants of Saul still lived. Ziba answered that a son of Jonathan, Mephibosheth, lived in the house of Machir in Lo Debar (2 Sam. 9:3–6). David brought Mephibosheth to Jerusalem and decreed that he should eat bread at the king's table (vv. 10–11). He also commanded Ziba to work the land for Mephibosheth.

Years later, when Absalom revolted against David, Ziba met David with much-needed provisions. David rewarded Ziba for his faithfulness by giving him part of Mephibosheth's land (2 Sam. 19:24–30).

ZIBEON [ZIHB eh uhn] (*hyena*) — the name of two men in the Old Testament:

1. A Hivite, grandfather of Aholibamah, one of Esau's wives (Gen. 36:2).

2. One of the sons of Seir the Horite (Gen. 36:20, 24, 29; 1 Chr. 1:38, 40). Zibeon was the father of two sons: Ajah and Anah (Gen. 36:24; 1 Chr. 1:40). This Zibeon may be the same person as Zibeon No. 1.

ZIBIA [ZIB ih ah] (*gazelle*) — one of the seven sons of Shaharaim and his wife Hodesh (1 Chr. 8:9).

ZIBIAH [ZIB ih ah] (*gazelle*) — a woman of Beersheba who became the wife of AHAZIAH and the mother of JEHOASH or Joash—both kings of Judah (2 Kin. 12:1; 2 Chr. 24:1).

ZICHRI [ZICK rih] (*remembered*) — the name of 12 men in the Old Testament:

1. One of the three sons of Izhar (Ex. 6:21).

2. The son of Shimei (1 Chr. 8:19).

3. The son of Shashak (1 Chr. 8:23).

4. The son of Jeroham (1 Chr. 8:27).

5. A Levite who lived in Jerusalem after the Captivity (1 Chr. 9:15). Zichri is believed to be the same person as Zabdi (Neh. 11:17) and Zaccur (1 Chr. 25:2).

6. A Levite descended from Moses' son, Eliezer (1 Chr. 26:25). Zichri and his kinsmen were responsible for the treasuries in David's time (v. 26).

7. The father of Eliezer (1 Chr. 27:16). Eliezer was the officer over the Reubenites during the days of David.

The restored bottom stories of a ziggurat at ancient Ur. Built about 2100 B.C., all but the foundation of the structure had eroded away by the time it was uncovered by archaeologists.

8. A man of the tribe of Judah and father of Amasiah (2 Chr. 17:16). Amasiah was a captain in the army of King Jehoshaphat.

9. The father of Elishaphat (2 Chr. 23:1).

10. A "mighty man of Ephraim" who killed Maaseiah the king's son during the reign of Ahaz, king of Judah (2 Chr. 28:7).

11. The father of Joel (Neh. 11:9). Joel was overseer of the Benjamites in Jerusalem after the Captivity.

12. A priest in the family of Abijah in the days of Nehemiah (Neh. 12:17).

ZIDDIM [ZIHD deem] (*flanks*) — a fortified city of Naphtali (Josh. 19:35), location unknown.

ZIDKIJAH [zid KIE jah] — a form of ZEDEKIAH.

ZIDON [ZIE dun] — a form of SIDON.

ZIGGURAT [ZIG guh rat] (*pinnacle* or *summit*) — an ancient Mesopotamian temple tower consisting of a lofty pyramid–like structure built in successive stages with outside staircases and a shrine at the top.

The ziggurat was an architectural form common to the Sumerians, Babylonians, and Assyrians from about 2000 to 600 B.C. The ancient ziggurat at UR is typical of others built in this part of the world. It is a massive, solid structure with a mud–brick core and fired–brick shell. This tower originally stood to a height of about 21 meters (70 feet) above the plain, although only about 15 meters (50 feet) of the lowest platform now remains. At the summit was a shrine of Nannar, the moon god.

The ziggurat was thought to symbolize a mountain, with the temple on top bridging the gap that separates humanity from the gods. The Tower of Babel (Gen. 11:1–9) is thought by many scholars to be the model of this ancient Babylonian shrine.

Also see BABEL, TOWER OF.

ZIHA [ZIE hah] (*sunniness*) — the name of two men in the Old Testament:

1. The founder or head of a family of NETHINIM (Temple servants) who returned with Zerubbabel from Babylon to Palestine (Ezra 2:43; Neh. 7:46).

2. An overseer of the Nethinim in Jerusalem (Neh. 11:21).

ZIKLAG [ZIKK lag] (meaning unknown) — a city in the NEGEV (see Map 4, A–4), or southern Judah (Josh. 15:1, 31), assigned to the tribe of Simeon (Josh. 19:5; 1 Chr. 4:30). When David was pursued by Saul, he and his 600 men fled to the land of the Philistines and found sanctuary with Achish, king of Gath. Achish gave the city of Ziklag to David and his men, and it became David's military base for raids against the nomadic tribes of the Negev (1 Sam. 27:1–12). Many of Saul's followers defected to David and joined David at Ziklag (1 Chr. 12:1–22).

The identification of Ziklag is not certain. It is probably Tell es–Khuweilfeh, about 16 kilometers (10 miles) northeast of Beersheba and about 8 kilometers (5 miles) southwest of Tell Beit Mirsim (Debir).

ZILLAH [ZIHL lah] (*shadow*) — the second wife of Lamech (Gen. 4:19, 22–23). She bore a son, Tubal-Cain, who was the originator of metalworking. Zillah also bore a daughter, Naamah.

ZILLETHAI [ZIHL eh thigh] (*God is a shadow*) — the name of two men in the Old Testament:

1. A son of Shimei listed in the family tree of King Saul (1 Chr. 8:20; Zilthai, KJV).

2. A captain of the tribe of Manasseh who defected to David at Ziklag (1 Chr. 12:20; Zilthai, KJV).

ZILPAH [ZILL pah] (meaning unknown) — the mother of Gad and Asher (Gen. 30:9–13; 35:26).

Zilpah was one of the female slaves of Laban, the father of Leah and Rachel. When Leah married Jacob, Laban gave her Zilpah to serve as her maid (Gen. 29:24; 46:18). Later, Leah gave Zilpah to Jacob as a Concubine (Gen. 30:9).

ZILTHAI [ZILL thigh] — a form of Zillethai.

ZIMMAH [ZIMM ah] (*counsel*) — the name of two men in the Old Testament:
1. A descendant of Jahath (1 Chr. 6:20) and a tabernacle musician in David's time.
2. A Gershonite Levite, the father of Joah (2 Chr. 29:12).

ZIMRAN [ZIMM ran] (meaning unknown) — the first son of Abraham by Keturah (Gen. 25:2; 1 Chr. 1:32), his female slave, or Concubine.

ZIMRI [ZIMM rye] (*my protection*) — the name of four men and a tribe or district in the Old Testament:
1. A son of Salu, a Simeonite prince (Num. 25:14). In an outrageous move, Zimri brought a Midianite woman, Cozbi, into the camp while Israel was repenting for having worshiped Baal. When Phinehas, the son of Eleazar, saw Zimri take her to his tent, he was enraged, took a javelin in his hand, went into Zimri's tent, and thrust both of them through.
2. The fifth king of Israel (1 Kin. 16:8–20). Before he became king, Zimri was a servant of King Elah and commander of half of his chariots. One day, Zimri killed the drunken Elah and proclaimed himself king. When Omri, the commander of Elah's army, heard about the assassination, he abandoned the siege of Gibbethon and besieged Tirzah, the capital city. When Zimri saw that the city was taken, he "burned the king's house down upon himself" (1 Kin. 16:18). Zimri's reign lasted only seven days (1 Kin. 16:15).
3. The oldest of the five sons of Zerah (1 Chr. 2:6).
4. A Benjamite, son of Jehoaddah (1 Chr. 8:36) or Jarah (1 Chr. 9:42). Zimri was a descendant of King Saul and of King Saul's son, Jonathan.
5. An unknown place or people (Jer. 25:25).

ZIN [zihn] (meaning unknown) — a wilderness (see Map 2, C–1) through which the Israelites passed on their journey to Canaan (Num. 13:21; 20:1). The Wilderness of Zin stretched along the extreme southern limits of the Promised Land (Num. 13:21).

ZINA [ZIE nah] (*abundant, fruitful*) — the second son of Shimei, a Gershonite Levite (1 Chr. 23:10; Ziza, NEB, NIV). He is also called Zizah (1 Chr. 23:11).

ZION [ZIE un] (*fortification*) — the city of David and the city of God. The meaning of the word Zion underwent a distinct progression in its usage throughout the Bible.
The first mention of Zion in the Bible is in 2 Samuel 5:7: "David took the stronghold of Zion

(that is, the City of David)." Zion, therefore, was the name of the ancient Jebusite fortress situated on the southeast hill of Jerusalem at the junction of the Kidron Valley and the Tyropoeon Valley. The name came to stand not only for the fortress but also for the hill on which the fortress stood. After David captured "the stronghold of Zion" by defeating the Jebusites, he called Zion "the City of David" (1 Kin. 8:1; 1 Chr. 11:5; 2 Chr. 5:2).
When Solomon built the Temple on Mount Moriah (a hill distinct and separate from Mount Zion), and moved the ark of the covenant there, the word Zion expanded in meaning to include also the Temple and the Temple area (Ps. 2:6; 48:2, 11–12; 132:13). It was only a short step until Zion was used as a name for the city of Jerusalem, the land of Judah, and the people of Israel as a whole (Is. 40:9; Jer. 31:12). The prophet Zechariah spoke of the sons of Zion (Zech. 9:13). By this time the word Zion had come to mean the entire nation of Israel.
The most important use of the word Zion is in a religious or theological sense. Zion is used figuratively of Israel as the people of God (Is. 60:14). The spiritual meaning of Zion is continued in the New Testament, where it is given the Christian meaning of God's spiritual kingdom, the church of God, the heavenly Jerusalem (Heb. 12:22; Rev. 14:1; Sion, KJV).
Also see David, City of.

ZIOR [ZIE or] (*smallness*) — a city in the hill country of Judah, near Hebron (Josh. 15:54).

ZIPH [ziff] (*refining place*) — the name of two cities and two men in the Old Testament:
1. A city in the Negev of Judah, "toward the border of Edom in the south" (Josh. 15:24). It has been identified as present–day Khirbet ez–Zeifeh, about 40 to 48 kilometers (25 to 30 miles) southwest of the Dead Sea.
2. A city in the Maon district of Judah (Josh. 15:55). It is Tell Zif, about six kilometers (four miles) southeast of Hebron. David hid from Saul in the Wilderness of Ziph, the barren desert region surrounding this city (1 Sam. 23:14–24; 26:2). Psalm 54 has traditionally been associated with this time in David's life.
3. A son of Mesha of the family of Caleb, tribe of Judah (1 Chr. 2:42).
4. The oldest of the four sons of Jahaleleel (1 Chr. 4:16).

ZIPHAH [ZIE fah] (*lent*) — a son of Jahaleleel, of the tribe of Judah (1 Chr. 4:16).

ZIPHIM [ZIFF ihm] — the inhabitants of Ziph No. 2 (Ps. 54, title, KJV). Also see Ziphites.

ZIPHION [ZIFF ih on] (*dark, wintry*) — a son of Gad (Gen. 46:16), also called Zephon (Num. 26:15).

ZIPHITES [ZIFF ights] — the inhabitants of Ziph No. 2 (1 Sam. 23:19; 26:1; Ps. 54, title).

ZIPHRON [ZIFF run] (*a stench or odor*) — the

northern boundary of the Promised Land, near Hazar Enan (Num. 34:9). The exact location is unknown.

ZIPPOR [ZIP or] (*bird, sparrow*) — the father of Balak (Num. 22:2; Josh. 24:9). Balak was the king of Moab who hired BALAAM the soothsayer (Josh. 13:22) to curse Israel.

ZIPPORAH [zip POE rah] (*little bird*) — a daughter of Jethro, priest of Midian, and wife of Moses (Ex. 2:21-22; 4:25; 18:2-4). Their sons were Gershom and Eliezer. When the Lord sought to kill Moses because Eliezer had not been circumcised, Zipporah grabbed a sharp stone and immediately circumcised the child. She and the two sons must have returned to Jethro rather than continuing on to Egypt with Moses, because she is not mentioned again until after the EXODUS. Along with Jethro, she and her two sons visited Moses in the wilderness after the Hebrew people left Egypt (Ex. 18:1-5).

ZITHER (see MUSICAL INSTRUMENTS).

ZITHRI [ZITH rye] (*Jehovah conceals*) — a son of Uzziel, a descendant of Levi through Kohath (Ex. 6:22; Sithri, RSV, NIV, NEB, NASB). Zithri was a cousin of Moses.

ZIV [zihv] (*brightness*) — the eighth month of the civil year and the second month of the sacred year in the Hebrew CALENDAR (1 Kin. 6:1, 37; Zif, KJV).

ZIZ, ASCENT OF [zihz] (*flower*) — a steep ascent in a pass that runs from the western shore of the Dead Sea, at a point slightly north of En Gedi, into the Wilderness of Judah, toward Tekoa. Through the ascent of Ziz (2 Chr. 20:16) the allied forces of Ammon, Moab, and Mount Seir made their journey from En Gedi to attack the army of Jehoshaphat, king of Judah.

ZIZA [ZIE zah] (*shining*) — the name of three men in the Old Testament:
1. A son of Shiphi (1 Chr. 4:37). Ziza was one of the leaders who participated in the expansion of the tribe of Simeon toward Gedor during the reign of Hezekiah, king of Judah.
2. A son of Rehoboam, king of Judah (2 Chr. 11:20).
3. A Gershonite Levite, second son of Shimei (1 Chr. 23:10-11, NEB, NIV).

ZIZAH [ZIE zah] (*abundant*) — a Gershonite Levite, the second son of Shimei (1 Chr. 23:11; Ziza, NEB, NIV). He is also called Zina (1 Chr. 23:10).

ZOAN [zone] — an ancient city in Egypt that dates back to the time of Abraham. Built seven years after Hebron (Num. 13:22), Zoan has often been identified with one of the royal cities in northern Egypt. The Greek translation of the Old Testament identified Zoan with TANIS, a city which is sometimes associated with the ancient capital of Egypt, RAMSES (Ex. 1:11). Now many scholars identify Ramses with Qantir.

ZOAR [ZOE er] (*little*) — an ancient city (see Map 2, C-1) apparently situated near the southeast corner of the Dead Sea (Gen. 13:10), and also known as Bela (Gen. 14:2, 8). It was one of five city-states in the area, each with its own king.

Zoar figures prominently in the story of Lot and the destruction of the wicked "cities of the plain" (Gen. 13:12; 19:29). Warned to flee to the mountains, Lot sought further mercy by asking to go instead to Zoar. His reasoning was that Zoar is only a "little" city (hence its name). His request was granted and Zoar was spared, while the four other cities (Sodom, Gomorrah, Admah, and Zeboiim) were destroyed (Gen. 19:22-23, 30).

Many scholars believe the site of Zoar to be es-Safi, at the foot of the mountains of Moab, about seven kilometers (4.5 miles) up the River Zered from where it empties into the Dead Sea. Tradition has placed Zoar at the southeastern end of the Dead Sea. The original site may now be covered with water.

ZOBAH, ZOBA [ZOE bah] (*bronze, copper*) — an Aramean kingdom situated in Syria, south of Hamath, northeast of Damascus, and east of Byblos in the Biqa Valley between the Lebanon and Anti-Lebanon Mountains (see Map 4, C-1). Generally speaking, Zobah was the land between the Orontes River and the Euphrates River.

Saul fought successfully against the kings of Zobah (1 Sam. 14:47). David clashed with Hadadezer, king of Zobah (2 Sam. 8:3; 1 Chr. 18:3). When the Syrians of Damascus tried to aid Hadadezer, David slaughtered them (2 Sam. 8:5; 1 Chr. 18:5).

David took much bronze as booty from Berothai, Betah (or Tibhath), and Chun, cities of Zobah (2 Sam. 8:8; 1 Chr. 18:8). When Israel battled the Ammonites, the Ammonites hired mercenaries from Zoba (2 Sam. 10:6). Israel was caught between the Ammonites and the Syrians (2 Sam. 10:8). Israel overcame the fighting on two fronts (2 Sam. 10:9-14). The Syrians of Zobah rallied their forces under Hadadezer's commander, Shobach, but were defeated (2 Sam. 10:15-19).

The historical background of Psalm 60 is David's struggle against Zobah (see the superscription of Psalm 60).

Later, God used Rezon, "who had fled from his lord, Hadadezer king of Zobah" (1 Kin. 11:23), to chastise Solomon (vv. 24-25).

ZOBEBAH [zoe BEE bah] (*affable*) — a son of Koz, of the tribe of Judah (1 Chr. 4:8).

ZOHAR [ZOE har] (meaning unknown) — the name of three men in the Old Testament:
1. The father of Ephron (Gen. 23:8; 25:9), a Hittite prince from whom Abraham purchased the cave of Machpelah.
2. A son of Simeon and grandson of Jacob (Gen. 46:10). He is also called Zerah (Num. 26:13).
3. A son of Helah, of the tribe of Judah (1 Chr. 4:7; Jezoar, KJV, NEB; Izhar, RSV, NASB).

ZOHELETH, STONE OF [ZOE heh leth] (*creeping one*) — apparently a sacred stone near EN ROGEL in Jerusalem (1 Kin. 1:9; Serpent's Stone, RSV), a fountain situated south of Jerusalem, just below the junction of the Kidron Valley and the Valley of Hinnom. By this Zoheleth, Adonijah, the son of David, prepared a great celebration in anticipation of being proclaimed king to succeed his father. Adonijah's ambition failed, because David named Solomon king instead.

ZOHETH [ZOE heth] (*strong, proud*) — a son of Ishi (1 Chr. 4:20) and head of a family in the tribe of Judah.

ZOPHAH [ZOE fah] (*bellied jug*) — a son of Helem, of the tribe of Asher (1 Chr. 7:35-36).

ZOPHAI [ZOE fie] (*watcher*) — a son of Elkanah, a Kohathite Levite (1 Chr. 6:26). Also see ZUPH.

ZOPHAR [ZOE fer] (*twittering bird*) — the third of the "friends" of Job to speak. He is called a NAAMATHITE (Job 2:11; 11:1; 20:1; 42:9), indicating he was from Naamah, in northern Arabia. Zophar's two discourses are found in Job 11:1-20 and 20:1-29. He accused Job of wickedness and hypocrisy, urged Job to turn from his rebellion, and charged that God was punishing Job far less than his sins deserved (Job 11:6). Also see BILDAD; ELIHU; ELIPHAZ.

ZOPHIM [ZOE fihm] (*watchers*) — a HIGH PLACE in Moab near the northeastern end of the Dead Sea. Balak brought Balaam the soothsayer to Zophim so he could view the Israelites and curse them (Num. 23:14).

ZORAH [ZOE rah] (*place of hornets*) — a city in the Shephelah, or lowland, of Judah (Josh. 15:33; Zoreah, KJV), allotted to the tribe of Dan (Josh. 19:41). Zorah was the home of Manoah, the father of Samson (Judg. 13:2). In the time of the judges five Danites from Zorah and Eshtaol were sent to spy out Laish, a city later captured by the Danites and renamed Dan (Judges 18). Later Rehoboam strengthened the walls of Zorah (2 Chr. 11:5-12).

ZORATHITES [ZOE rath ites] — natives or inhabitants of ZORATH, a Danite city in the territory of Judah near Eshtaol (1 Chr. 2:53; Zareathites, KJV, NEB; 1 Chr. 4:2).

ZOREAH [ZOE reh ah] — a form of ZORAH.

ZORITES [ZORE ites] — descendants of Salma, of the tribe of Judah (1 Chr. 2:54). They were either the same as ZORATHITES (1 Chr. 2:53; 4:2) or inhabitants of some unknown place.

ZOROASTRIANISM [zoe roh ASS tree un ism] — the religious system founded in Persia by the prophet Zoroaster, or Zarathustra (sixth century B.C.) and set forth in the Avesta, or Zend-Avesta, but with many additions. Zoroastrianism is characterized by worship of Ahura Mazda (also known as

Ormazd or Ormuzd), the Supreme Being represented as a spirit of light, truth, and goodness.

Ahura Mazda is opposed by an archrival, Ahriman (or Angra Mainyu), a spirit of darkness, falsehood, and evil. Thus man's soul becomes a seat of war between the dualistic forces of good and evil. Ahura Mazda requires men's good deeds for help in this cosmic struggle against Ahriman. The struggle is desperate and bitter—the sons of light against the sons of darkness. Zoroaster taught, however, that eventually Ahura Mazda will defeat Ahriman and good will triumph over evil.

Zoroastrianism has barely survived in its homeland. Fewer than 10,000 persons in Iran (ancient Persia) practice the religion today. A larger group has survived in India under the name Parseeism. The present-day Parsees of India are descendants of Persians who moved there from Persia several centuries before the birth of Christ.

ZUAR [ZOU er] (*little*) — the father of Nethaneel (Num. 1:8). Nethaneel was leader of the tribe of Issachar at the time of the Exodus.

ZUPH [zuff] (*honeycomb*) — the name of a man and a district in the Old Testament:
1. An Ephraimite, an ancestor of the prophet Samuel (1 Sam. 1:1).
2. A land or district northwest of Jerusalem where Saul searched for his father's lost donkeys (1 Sam. 9:5). The exact location of the land of Zuph is not known, but scholars believe this district was in the territory of EPHRAIM. The land of Zuph probably received its name from the family of Zuph No. 1 who settled in this area.

ZUR [zuhr] (*rock*) — the name of two men in the Old Testament:
1. A Midianite leader, the father of Cozbi (Num. 25:15). Zur was one of the five kings of Midian killed in a battle against the Hebrew people under Moses (Num. 31:8; Josh. 13:21).
2. A Benjamite, the brother of Kish, King Saul's father (1 Chr. 8:30; 9:36).

ZURIEL [ZOU rih ehl] (*my rock is God*) — a son of Abihail (Num. 3:35). A Levite, Zuriel was chief of the house of Merari at the time of the Exodus.

ZURISHADDAI [zou rih SHAD die] (*the Almighty is a rock*) — the father of Shelumiah (Num. 1:6; 2:12; 7:36, 41; 10:19). Shelumiah was the leader of the tribe of Simeon at the time of the Exodus.

ZUZIM, ZUZIMS [ZOU zim] (*powerful ones*) — a primitive tribe who lived in HAM, a place east of the Jordan River between Bashan and Moab. The Zuzim were conquered by the Elamite king CHEDORLAOMER (Gen. 14:5; Zuzims, KJV). Some scholars identify the Zuzim with the Zamzummim (Deut. 2:20), a tribe of the REPHAIM living in the region later occupied by the Ammonites, but this is uncertain.

Index to Maps

The following index is divided into two parts—one for Map 5, Jerusalem, and the other for all the other maps. Place names are usually given as shown on the maps; sometimes they are followed by alternate names and spellings, which are set in parentheses. If a place name is not given as shown on the map, it is followed, in parentheses, by the alternate name or spelling that does appear on the map (example: *Melita; Malta* on map). Where a place name refers to a large area, the index gives the location of the name. Where a name refers to a river, the index gives the source and mouth of the river.

In the index to Maps 1 through 4 and 6 through 9, major political divisions, such as countries and regions, are shown in capital letters (examples: EGYPT, PALESTINE). Cities are shown in upper and lower case as usual (example: Hebron). Geographical features are shown in italics (example: *Jordan River*).

Map 1: The Nations of Genesis 10
Map 2: The Exodus from Egypt
Map 3: The Conquest of Canaan
Map 4: The Kingdom Years

Map 6: Palestine in Christ's Time
Map 7: Paul's First and Second Journeys
Map 8: Paul's Third and Fourth Journeys
Map 9: The Holy Land in Modern Times

INDEX TO MAPS

Map 5: Jerusalem—From David to Christ

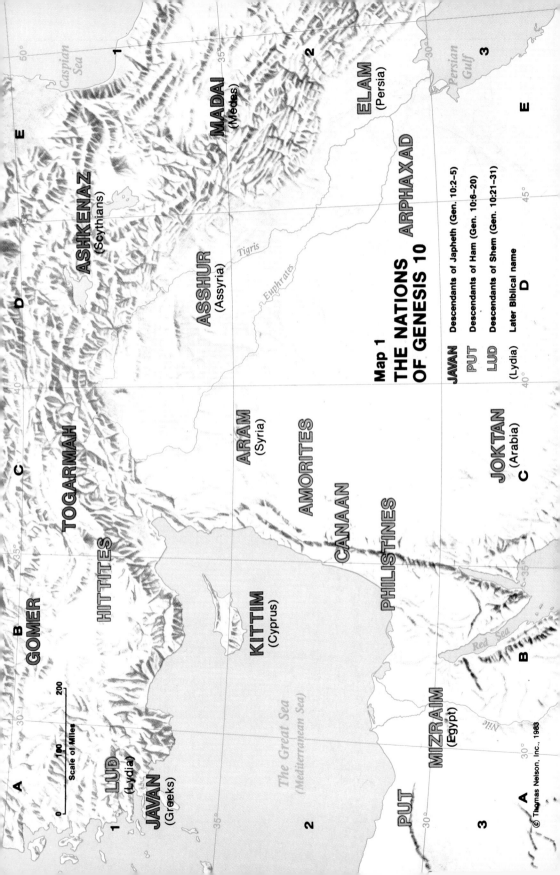

Map 1

THE NATIONS OF GENESIS 10

JAVAN — Descendants of Japheth (Gen. 10:2–5)
PUT — Descendants of Ham (Gen. 10:6–20)
LUD — Descendants of Shem (Gen. 10:21–31)
(Lydia) — Later Biblical name

GOMER
TOGARMAH
HITTITES
ASHKENAZ
(Scythians)
MADAI
(Medes)
ASSHUR
(Assyria)
ELAM
(Persia)
ARPHAXAD
ARAM
(Syria)
KITTIM
(Cyprus)
AMORITES
CANAAN
PHILISTINES
JOKTAN
(Arabia)
MIZRAIM
(Egypt)
PUT
LUD
(Lydia)
JAVAN
(Greeks)

Caspian Sea
Tigris
Euphrates
The Great Sea
(Mediterranean Sea)
Red Sea
Nile
Persian Gulf

Scale of Miles
0   100   200

© Thomas Nelson, Inc., 1983

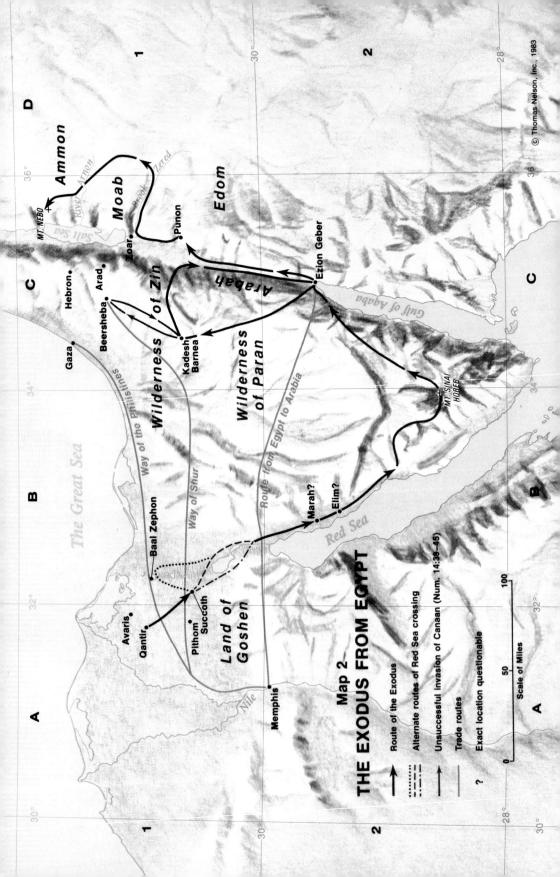

Map 2
THE EXODUS FROM EGYPT

→ Route of the Exodus
┊┊┊ Alternate routes of Red Sea crossing
➤ Unsuccessful invasion of Canaan (Num. 14:39–45)
— Trade routes
? Exact location questionable

Scale of Miles
0   50   100

The Great Sea

Gaza
Hebron
Arad
Beersheba
Zoar
Punon

Way of the Philistines
Way of Shur

Wilderness of Zin
Wilderness of Paran

Kadesh Barnea

Baal Zephon

Avaris
Qantir
Pithom
Succoth

Land of Goshen

Memphis

Nile

Marah?
Elim?

Red Sea

Route from Egypt to Arabia

MT. SINAI
HOREB

Gulf of Aqaba

Ezion Geber

Arabah

Edom
Moab
Ammon

MT. NEBO
Salt Sea

River Arnon
Brook Zered

© Thomas Nelson, Inc., 1983

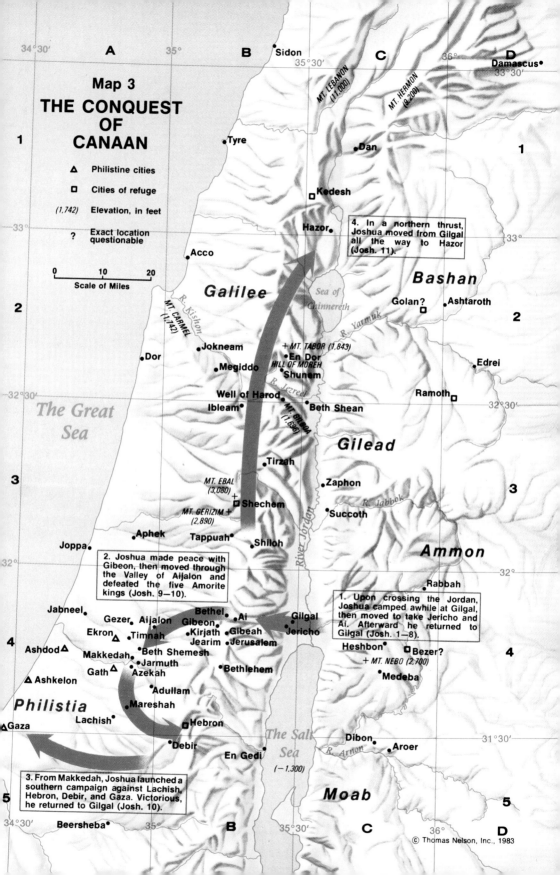

Map 3
THE CONQUEST OF CANAAN

△   Philistine cities

□   Cities of refuge

(1,742)   Elevation, in feet

?   Exact location questionable

0   10   20
Scale of Miles

34°30'   A   35°   B   35°30'   C   36°   D

Sidon

Damascus

MT. LEBANON (11,000)

MT. HERMON (9,200)

Tyre

Dan

1

Kedesh

Hazor

4. In a northern thrust, Joshua moved from Gilgal all the way to Hazor (Josh. 11).

Bashan

Acco

Galilee

Sea of Chinnereth

Golan?

Ashtaroth

2

MT. CARMEL (1,742)

R. Kishon

Jokneam

Dor

Megiddo

MT. TABOR (1,843)

En Dor

HILL OF MOREH

Shunem

R. Yarmuk

Edrei

Well of Harod

Ibleam

R. Jezreel

MT. GILBOA (1,696)

Beth Shean

Gilead

Ramoth

The Great Sea

Tirzah

Zaphon

MT. EBAL (3,080)

Shechem

R. Jabbok

3

MT. GERIZIM (2,890)

Succoth

Aphek

Tappuah

Shiloh

Joppa

River Jordan

Ammon

2. Joshua made peace with Gibeon, then moved through the Valley of Aijalon and defeated the five Amorite kings (Josh. 9—10).

Rabbah

Jabneel

Gezer   Aijalon   Bethel   Ai   Gilgal

Gibeon

Ekron   Timnah   Kirjath   Gibeah   Jericho

Jearim   Jerusalem

1. Upon crossing the Jordan, Joshua camped awhile at Gilgal, then moved to take Jericho and Ai. Afterward he returned to Gilgal (Josh. 1—8).

Ashdod

Makkedah

Beth Shemesh

Heshbon

Bezer?

Gath   Jarmuth

4

Azekah

Bethlehem

MT. NEBO (2,700)

Ashkelon

Adullam

Medeba

Philistia

Mareshah

Lachish

Hebron

Gaza

Debir

The Salt Sea (-1,300)

Dibon

Aroer

En Gedi

R. Arnon

3. From Makkedah, Joshua launched a southern campaign against Lachish, Hebron, Debir, and Gaza. Victorious, he returned to Gilgal (Josh. 10).

Moab

5

34°30'   Beersheba   35°   B   35°30'   C   36°   D

© Thomas Nelson, Inc., 1983

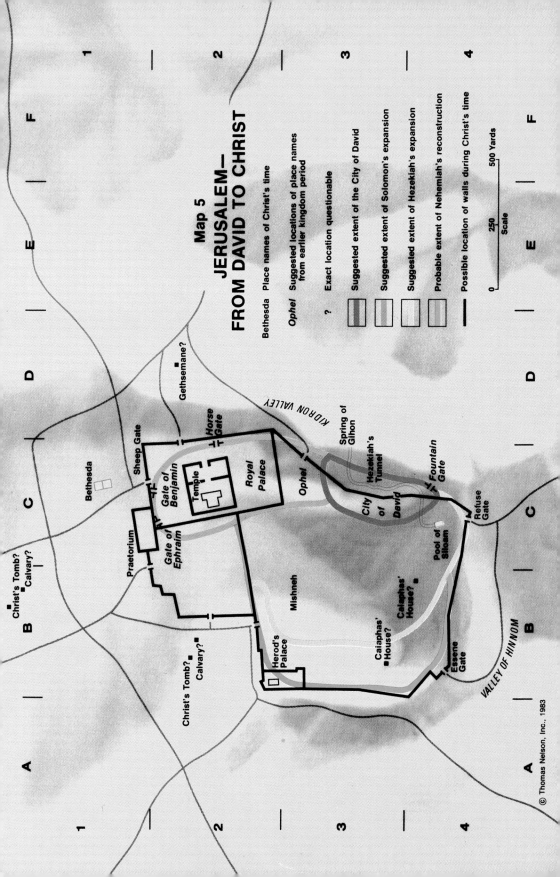

Map 5

JERUSALEM—
FROM DAVID TO CHRIST

Bethesda   Place names of Christ's time

Ophel   Suggested locations of place names
          from earlier kingdom period

?   Exact location questionable

   Suggested extent of the City of David

   Suggested extent of Solomon's expansion

   Suggested extent of Hezekiah's expansion

   Probable extent of Nehemiah's reconstruction

   Possible location of walls during Christ's time

Scale

0   250   500 Yards

Christ's Tomb?
■ Calvary?

Bethesda

Sheep Gate

Gethsemane?

Horse Gate

Praetorium

Gate of Benjamin

Temple

Gate of Ephraim

Royal Palace

KIDRON VALLEY

Christ's Tomb? ■
Calvary? ■

Herod's Palace

Mishneh

Ophel

Spring of Gihon

City of David

Hezekiah's Tunnel

Caiaphas' House? ■

Caiaphas' House? ■

Pool of Siloam

Fountain Gate

Refuse Gate

Essene Gate

VALLEY OF HINNOM

© Thomas Nelson, Inc., 1983

Map 6
PALESTINE
IN
CHRIST'S TIME

(1,742)   Elevation, in feet

?   Exact location
    questionable

0   10   20
Scale of Miles

A · 35° · B · Sidon · C · 36° · D
Damascus·

Phoenicia
MT. LEBANON (11,000)
MT. HERMON (9,200)

Zarephath·

Iturea

·Tyre
Panias·
(Caesarea Philippi)

Trachonitis

33°
·Ptolemais
Galilee

Chorazin
Capernaum·   Bethsaida?·
Magdala·   Gergesa·
Cana·   Tiberias·
Sea
of
Galilee

R. Kishon
MT. CARMEL (1,742)

R. Yarmuk

·MT. TABOR (1,843)
Nazareth·   Gadara?·
Nain·

Esdraelon·

32°30'
·Caesarea   Scythopolis·
MT. GILBOA (1,696)

The Great
Sea

Decapolis

Samaria
Samaria·   ·Gerasa
Sychar·

MT. GERIZIM + (2,890)

R. Jabbok

Antipatris·
Joppa·

Perea

·Arimathea   Ephraim·   Gadara?·
Lydda·   Philadelphia·

Emmaus·   Jericho·
Kirjath Jearim·   Jerusalem·   Bethabara·
Azotus·   Beth Haccerem·   Bethany·   Qumran·
Bethlehem·   Medeba·
Herodium·

·Ashkelon

Judea
Machaerus·
·Hebron

The Salt
Sea
(−1,300)
R. Arnon

·Gaza

Idumea   Masada·

Beersheba·

A · 35° · B · 35°30' · C · 36° · D

© Thomas Nelson, Inc., 1983

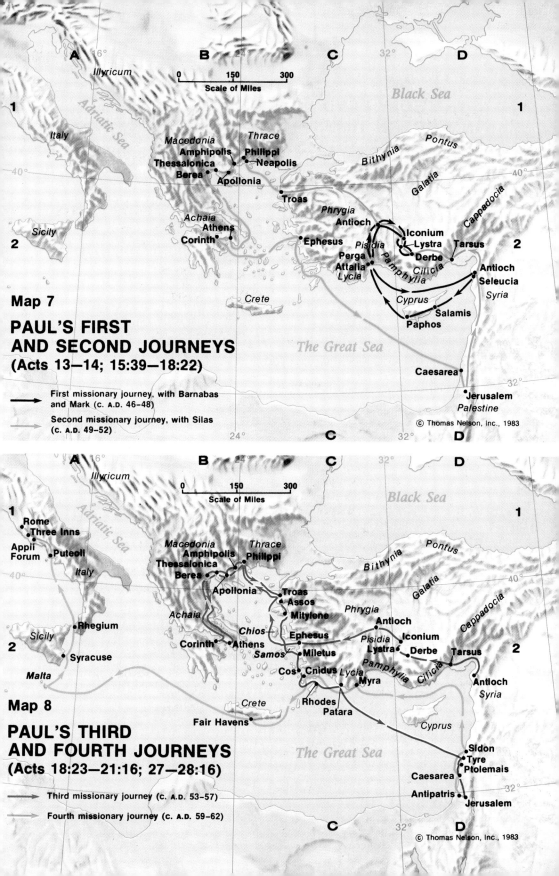

Map 7

**PAUL'S FIRST
AND SECOND JOURNEYS**
(Acts 13—14; 15:39—18:22)

First missionary journey, with Barnabas and Mark (c. A.D. 46-48)

Second missionary journey, with Silas (c. A.D. 49-52)

© Thomas Nelson, Inc., 1983

Map 8

**PAUL'S THIRD
AND FOURTH JOURNEYS**
(Acts 18:23—21:16; 27—28:16)

Third missionary journey (c. A.D. 53-57)

Fourth missionary journey (c. A.D. 59-62)

© Thomas Nelson, Inc., 1983

Map 9

THE HOLY LAND
IN MODERN TIMES

Area occupied by Israel
since June, 1967

0   25   50
Scale of Miles

LEBANON

Tripoli

BEKAA VALLEY

Beirut

LEBANON MTS.   *ANTI-LEBANON MTS.*

Sidon

Damascus

Tyre

Dan

U.N. Buffer Zone
1973 Line

Qiryat
Shemona

Quneitra
1967 Cease-Fire Line

SYRIA

Nahariyya

Safad

*Golan
Heights*

Akko

*Sea of
Galilee*

Haifa

Tiberias

Dera

Nazareth

Ramtha

Mediterranean Sea

Afula

Beth Shean

Hadera

Jarash

Netanya

Tulkarm

Herzliyya

Nablus

*West
Bank*

Jordan River

Tel Aviv

Yafo

Petah
Tiqwa

Rishon le Zion

Amman

Ramla

Lod

Ramalah

Ashdod

Jericho

Ashqelon

Jerusalem
Bethlehem

Madaba

Qiryat
Gat

Gaza

Hebron

Dhiban

En Gedi

*Dead
Sea*

Al-Arish

Beersheba

Karak

JORDAN

ISRAEL

EGYPT

Negev

Arabah

Sinai

Elat
Aqaba

© Thomas Nelson, Inc., 1983